The Porter Sargent Handbook Series

THE HANDBOOK OF
PRIVATE SCHOOLS

PUBLISHER'S STATEMENT

Esteemed educational and social critic Porter Sargent established *The Handbook of Private Schools* in 1914, with the aim "to present a comprehensive and composite view of the private school situation as it is today. No attempt has been made at completeness. The effort on the contrary has been to include only the best, drawing the line somewhat above the average."

Today, **The Porter Sargent Handbook Series** continues its founder's mission: to serve parents, educators and others concerned with the independent and critical evaluation of primary and secondary educational options, leading to a suitable choice for each student.

The Handbook of Private Schools, Guide to Summer Camps and Summer Schools (1924) and *Schools Abroad of Interest to Americans* (1959) provide the tools for objective comparison of programs in their respective fields. *The Directory for Exceptional Children,* first published in 1954, broadens that mission and service to parents and professionals seeking the optimal educational, therapeutic or clinical environment for special-needs children.

dbook of Private Schools

Copyright © 2005 by the Estate of J. Kathryn Sargent
Previous editions copyrighted 1915-2004

PRINTED IN CANADA

LIBRARY OF CONGRESS CATALOG CARD NUMBER 15-12869

ISBN-10 0-87558-154-4
ISBN-13 978-0-87558-154-5
ISSN 0072-9884

All information as reported o Porter Sargent Publishers, Inc., as of May 28, 2005. Schools and or iizations should be contacted for updated information.

All rights reserved. No part of this book may be reproduced or transmitted in any form or by any means, electronic or mechanical, including photocopying, recording, or by any information storage and retrieval system, without permission in writing from the publisher.

Cost: US$99.00 + $7.00 shipping and handling in the USA. Additional copies are available from booksellers, or from the Publisher's customer service center: 400 Bedford St., Ste. 322, Manchester, NH 03101. Tel: 800-342-7470. Fax: 603-669-7945. orders@portersargent.com. www.portersargent.com.

TABLE OF CONTENTS

A GUIDE TO THE *HANDBOOK*

PREFACE 11
EDITORIAL POLICY 12
HOW TO READ THE SCHOOL DESCRIPTIONS 14
GLOSSARY 19
KEY TO ABBREVIATIONS 23
KEY TO ADMISSION TESTS 27
KEY TO ACCREDITING ASSOCIATIONS 29

SCHOOL FEATURE INDEXES

INDEX (by State and City, with Enrollment, Grade Ranges and Other Features) 32

SCHOOLS WITH A SPECIAL FOCUS

ARTS 111
BILINGUAL PROGRAMS 111
BUSINESS 112
INTERNATIONAL BACCALAUREATE
 AND FRENCH BACCALAUREATE 112
LEARNING DISABILITIES AND
 UNDERACHIEVEMENT 113
MILITARY 115
SPORTS 116
VOCATIONAL 117

INDEXES OF SPECIAL INTEREST

SCHOOLS WITH COORDINATE
 SINGLE-GENDER PROGRAMS 118
SCHOOLS WITH ELEMENTARY BOARDING 119
SCHOOLS WITH AT LEAST 25% INTERNATIONAL
 STUDENTS 122
COEDUCATIONAL SCHOOLS WITH GIRLS-ONLY
 MATH OR SCIENCE PROGRAMS 123
SCHOOLS WITH 25% OR MORE
 NONWHITE FACULTY 124
SCHOOLS WITH 50% OR MORE
 NONWHITE STUDENTS 126

LEADING PRIVATE SCHOOLS

These schools are presented together in the belief that they are of first interest to the readers of the Handbook. *They may be included because of their international and historical renown, because they command general respect of parents and educators, and also because our information discloses unique or significant aspects of their programs that are deserving of the reader's attention.*

1. NEW ENGLAND STATES
    - Connecticut 131
    - Maine 178
    - Massachusetts 187
    - New Hampshire 255
    - Rhode Island 268
    - Vermont 276

2. MIDDLE ATLANTIC STATES
    - Delaware 283
    - District of Columbia 288
    - Maryland 295
    - New Jersey 323
    - New York 350
    - Pennsylvania 419

3. SOUTHERN STATES
    - Alabama 461
    - Florida 466
    - Georgia 491
    - Kentucky 505
    - North Carolina 510
    - South Carolina 524
    - Tennessee 531
    - Virginia 543
    - West Virginia 569

4. GREAT LAKES STATES
    - Illinois 571
    - Indiana 582
    - Michigan 591
    - Ohio 600
    - Wisconsin 616

5. PLAINS STATES
- Iowa 623
- Kansas 625
- Minnesota 627
- Missouri 635
- Nebraska 645

6. SOUTH CENTRAL STATES
- Arkansas 647
- Louisiana 649
- Mississippi 655
- Oklahoma 657
- Texas 661

7. MOUNTAIN STATES
- Colorado 677
- Idaho 684

8. SOUTHWEST STATES
- Arizona 685
- New Mexico 692
- Utah 696

9. PACIFIC STATES
- California 697
- Hawaii 748
- Oregon 754
- Washington 756

CONCISE SCHOOL LISTINGS

These are, in part, schools similar to those found in the Leading Private Schools section about which sufficient information is not currently available to allow inclusion there. Also included here are schools whose enrollment is more strictly limited to a local area or with specialized objectives and programs.

- New England States *(CT, ME, MA, NH, RI, VT)* 763
- Middle Atlantic States *(DE, DC, MD, NJ, NY, PA)* 793
- Southern States *(AL, FL, GA, KY, NC, SC, TN, VA, WV)* 865
- Great Lakes States *(IL, IN, MI, OH, WI)* 939
- Plains States *(IA, KS, MN, MO, NE, SD)* 979
- South Central States *(AR, LA, MS, OK, TX)* 997
- Mountain States *(CO, ID, MT)* 1025
- Southwest States *(AZ, NV, NM, UT)* 1035
- Pacific States *(AK, CA, HI, OR, WA)* 1047

TERM PROGRAMS

This section describes secondary-level academic term programs (usually operating on a semester system) that combine credit-bearing course work with experiential learning. Programs may have an environmental focus and typically employ the local environs as a significant teaching tool. Curricula are designed to promote academic continuity between the student's home school and the term program.

Maine	1095
Vermont	1095
New York	1096
North Carolina	1096
Colorado	1097
California	1097

PRIVATE SCHOOLS ILLUSTRATED

This section is provided as a supplement to the basic descriptions. More than 200 schools have paid for this space to portray, in their own words and pictures, their programs, objectives and ideals. These announcements are separated into groups as shown below. Summer programs, schools for exceptional children and foreign schools are included that are not elsewhere described in the Handbook.

INDEX TO SCHOOL ANNOUNCEMENTS	1103
INDEXES TO SUMMER PROGRAMS	1109
INDEX TO SCHOOLS FOR EXCEPTIONAL CHILDREN	1110
INDEX TO SCHOOLS ABROAD	1111
COEDUCATIONAL SCHOOLS	1114
GIRLS' SCHOOLS	1289
BOYS' SCHOOLS	1325
THE UNDERACHIEVER	1353
SCHOOLS FOR EXCEPTIONAL CHILDREN	1381
SCHOOLS ABROAD	1387
SUMMER PROGRAMS	1399

ASSOCIATIONS AND ORGANIZATIONS

ACCREDITING ASSOCIATIONS	1403
ADVOCACY ORGANIZATIONS	1404
PROFESSIONAL ORGANIZATIONS	1406
SCHOOL MEMBERSHIP ASSOCIATIONS	1410
TESTING ORGANIZATIONS	1417
ASSOCIATION DISPLAY ANNOUNCEMENTS	1418

CLASSIFIED DIRECTORIES OF FIRMS AND AGENCIES

- INDEX TO FIRMS AND AGENCIES 1421
- EDUCATIONAL CONSULTANTS 1423
- FUNDRAISING AND
  PUBLIC RELATIONS COUNSEL 1425
- INSURANCE 1426
- TUITION REFUND INSURANCE..1426

INDEX OF SCHOOLS 1429

CLASSIFIED DISPLAY ANNOUNCEMENTS 1472

THE HANDBOOK OF PRIVATE SCHOOLS

Senior Editor	Daniel P. McKeever
Production Manager	Leslie A. Weston
Editor	Adam G. Reich
Editorial Assistant	James S. Martinho

PORTER SARGENT PUBLISHERS, INC.

Publisher	Cornelia E. Sargent
President	John P. Yonce
Director	Keith L. Hughes

Publishers

1914-1950	Porter E. Sargent
1951-1975	F. Porter Sargent
1976-1999	J. Kathryn Sargent

PREFACE

The original guide to nonpublic elementary and secondary schools in the United States, *The Handbook of Private Schools* was first published by eminent social critic Porter Sargent in 1915. The annual *Handbook* soon became a trusted resource for parents, educational advisors and others concerned with private education and interested in placing children in suitable private school settings.

Now in its 86th edition, the *Handbook* remains the one truly objective resource on nonpublic education in the United States. Unlike other available school guides, this book does not require listed schools to subscribe for space. Programs are selected on the basis of their merits, as evaluated by our editorial staff.

The aim of the *Handbook* is not to briefly list every operating nonpublic elementary and secondary program. Rather, we seek to provide in-depth information on schools that satisfy our criteria. We have established strict guidelines for acceptance into the *Handbook*. Prior to consideration, schools must complete at least five academic years of operation. Other criteria weighed by our editors during the evaluative process include accreditation earned by the school, appeal to readers beyond the immediate vicinity of the school, institutions attended by school graduates, and the overall depth and breadth of the curriculum.

New to the 86th edition is a special section of secondary-level academic term programs that combine credit-bearing course work with experiential learning. Students enroll for a term, then return to their home schools. Such programs have become increasingly popular in recent years.

Two editorial listing features debut in this edition. Coordinate programs (schools with separately operating boys' and girls' divisions) are now described as such—and cross-referenced in the School Features Indexes. Second, honors classes are no longer listed, as we have found that Advanced Placement courses are often a more reliable and objective measure of a high school curriculum's rigor. Thus, we now list only AP offerings.

Of course, we cannot list schools—however well they may fit our criteria—unless the schools complete our annual *Handbook* questionnaire. For this reason, some eligible programs do not appear in this volume; however, the roster of listed schools is both impressive and varied and will appeal to readers with a broad range of interests.

In closing, we wish to express our gratitude to the many school administrators who have devoted the necessary time and effort to update their school listings for this edition. Without their kind assistance, this book would not be possible.

EDITORIAL POLICY

We offer the following remarks to clarify the aim of the *Handbook* and the lines of editorial policy that necessarily follow. They are intended to assist readers in understanding our reporting methods and school administrators who feel that their requests for editorial change are overlooked. The following should be read in conjunction with the section How to Read the School Descriptions.

In the Leading Private Schools section, we present—at no cost or obligation to the schools—the information parents and advisors want and ought to know. The statistics are printed as supplied by the schools, whose thorough response to our annual questionnaire enables yearly revisions to be computerized readily and smoothly. Inadequately completed questionnaires jeopardize comprehensive updating of statistics, or even retention in the Leading Private Schools section.

A long-standing purpose of the paragraph descriptions has been to provide a historical summary of each school and, consequently, of independent education. Growth is organic, even among institutions, and the recounting of previous trends often helps to convey the tenor of a school. Consistent support has served to strengthen this intent. Our annual invitation to schools to supply new and interesting material has continued to elicit many useful suggestions—as well as a significant number of protestations. From an aggregate of information we select those aspects that seem to most effectively characterize a school in the limited space available.

In revising the paragraphs, all suggestions are carefully reviewed, but our editorial staff reserves the right to determine which changes are pertinent and significant in keeping with our long tradition of impartial reporting of facts. Suggested revisions often cite a school's stimulating atmosphere, emphasis on basic skills, small classes and concern for the individual. While such statements may be undeniably valid, their reiteration for school after school is out of place in a compendium serving persons who seek reliable, specific information. Moreover, many of these generalizations are evidenced in a more focused way by the statistics reported above the paragraphs.

We often receive the broad remark that a particular item, or even whole entry, is obsolete, superseded or misleading, but without a specific reason or supporting evidence. Or a school may submit a totally new fact without indicating how it relates to a whole series of other facts long included in the write-up, thus resulting in more questions than answers. When error or new information is clearly identified and substantiated, we endeavor to respond quickly and appropriately.

The technique of vanity publishing—where length of listing is determined by purchase of advertising space—has never been part of the policy in publishing the *Handbook*. No school pays for a listing in the book, and space is allotted solely on the basis of our judgment of a school's interest to our audience. Nor does a school's purchase of space in the autonomous Private Schools Illustrated section affect the length or content of its free listing.

The 86th edition of the *Handbook* comprises free listings of 1584 schools. In addition, more than 200 schools elect to reserve space in the Private Schools Illustrated section. Through these Illustrated Announcements, schools are able to stress features they consider most significant in describing their programs and aims. All those concerned with independent education welcome the opportunity to read these distinctive statements, and a sponsoring school thereby furthers not only recruitment, but also public relations in general.

The most complete and meaningful presentation of a school is achieved through the editor's independent report in conjunction with the school's own statement of purpose in an Illustrated Announcement. The one is objective reporting of facts; the other is an individualized account of each school's philosophy, policy and spirit. These two views provide a perspective that cannot be achieved by either alone.

HOW TO READ THE SCHOOL DESCRIPTIONS

The Leading Private Schools are arranged geographically by region, progressing from east to west across the country, then alphabetically by state and alphabetically by city or town within each state. Each city or town is briefly described prior to listings for that city. Refer also to the US map on the front end leaf. For information on additional schools, consult the Concise Listing of Schools section or refer to the Index of Schools.

1.   **PORTER SARGENT ACADEMY**

                Bdg — Boys Gr 9-PG; Day — Coed K-PG

2. Boston, MA 02108. 11 Beacon St, Ste 1400. Tel: 617-523-1670. Fax: 617-523-1021. www.portersargent.com E-mail: info@portersargent.com

3. Herbert Paul Brooks, Head. BA, Univ of Minnesota-Twin Cities, MEd, EdD, Cornell Univ. **Bryan Ferry, Adm.**

4. Col Prep. IB Diploma. AP—Eng Calc US_Hist. **Feat**—Fr Span Lat Ger Russ Stats Computers Ethics Music Art_Hist Journ. **Supp**—Tut Rev Dev_Read Rem_Math Rem_Read Makeup ESL.

5. Adm (Bdg Gr 9-11; Day Gr K-10): 100/yr. Bdg 30. Day 70. Appl due: Feb. Accepted: 64%. Yield: 51%. **Tests** IQ SSAT.

6. Enr 480. B 95/180. G 205. Elem 196. Sec 270. PG 14. Wh 88%. Hisp 4%. Blk 3%. Am Ind 1%. Asian 4%. Avg class size: 18. Uniforms. **Fac 75.** M 50/3. F 22. Wh 90%. Hisp 5%. Blk 5%. Adv deg: 31%. In Dorms 27.

7. Grad '04—90. Col—85. (Boston U 4, Brown 3, Yale 3, Stanford 2, Trinity Col-CT 2, Marist 1). Avg SAT: 1230. Avg ACT: 26. Alum 5500.

8. Tui '04-'05: Bdg $26,650 (+$1000). **Day $13,000-18,750** (+$600-850). **Aid:** Merit 23 ($32,500). Need 360 ($1,050,000). Work prgm 2 ($2000).

9. Summer: Acad Enrich. Tui Bdg $1900. Tui Day $195/crse. 6 wks.

10. Endow $13,750,000. Plant val $22,000,000. Bldgs 20. Dorms 2. Dorm rms 76. Class rms 32. 2 Libs 22,650 vols. Sci labs 4. Lang labs 1. Comp labs 2. Music studios 3. Art studios 2. Gyms 2. Fields 4. Courts 12. Pools 1.

11. Est 1914. Nonprofit. Religious Society of Friends. Tri (Sept-June). **Assoc** CLS NEASC.

12. Founded by Robert Gordon Orr, long a leader in progressive education, PSA continues to maintain a reputation for sound college preparation. Originally a boys' boarding school, it began accepting day boys and girls in 1960.

The experiential lower school curriculum includes French from grade 2, and Latin and Spanish from grade 6. The upper school offers a broad curriculum with liberal arts electives, Advanced Placement courses and a strong foreign language department. Qualified seniors may participate in on- or off-campus independent study or may spend a trimester at an affiliated secondary school in Paris, France. Most graduates enter New England colleges, although an increasing number are attending schools in other parts of the country.

Supplementing the full interscholastic athletic program are Outward Bound activities and lifetime sports. Drama, vocal and dance groups, publications, interest clubs and a compulsory community service program provide further enrichment.

13.   **See Also Page 0000**

1. SCHOOL NAME and TYPE. Sex and grade range of students are provided here. Age spans replace grade ranges for ungraded programs. If the school conducts both boys' and girls' single-gender programs, the term "Coordinate" appears prior to the grade range to distinguish the school from coeducational institutions. Consult the Glossary for more information about coordinate programs.

2. CITY or TOWN, STATE, ZIP CODE, STREET ADDRESS, TELEPHONE and FAX NUMBERS, and WEB SITE and E-MAIL ADDRESSES. If a school has divisions at more than one location, separate addresses may be found in the paragraph description at the end of the free listing.

3. ACADEMIC HEAD OF SCHOOL. An active president or superintendent may be listed for larger schools, followed in many cases by the head of school or principal. Whenever possible, degrees and granting institutions are also given. The director of admissions (or the administrator who fills this role) immediately follows, unless the academic head serves in this capacity.

4. ACADEMIC ORIENTATION and CURRICULUM. The basic curriculum is described as college preparatory, pre-preparatory, general academic or, in some cases, vocational or business.

Availability of one or more of the curricula designed by the International Baccalaureate Organization is indicated next. The Primary Years Programme (PYP) serves children ages 3-12, the Middle Years Programme (MYP) runs from age 11 through age 16, and the Diploma Programme is offered to pupils ages 16-19. Schools that prepare students for the French Baccalaureate are so designated. Consult the Glossary for further details about these international programs.

Bilingual programs are then noted. Additional information about bilingual instruction is provided in the school's paragraph description. Schools that primarily serve underachievers or students with learning disabilities are indicated as such, as are institutions with specialized programs for athletes or aspiring artists. For a full listing of specific course offerings, consult the school's catalogue.

"AP" indicates regularly offered Advanced Placement courses. In the model, AP course work is offered in English, Calculus and US History. Available in the upper high school grades, courses listed here follow the curriculum formulated by the College Board and prepare students for standardized Advanced Placement examinations.

"Feat" denotes courses of interest that the school does not offer at the Advanced Placement level. Disciplines commonly addressed in this section include foreign language, computer and the arts.

Supplemental areas of instruction appear after the notation "Supp" and comprise limited learning disabilities programs, tutoring, review, remedial and developmental reading, remedial math, makeup and English as a Second Language.

5. NEW ADMISSIONS. "Adm" refers to the total number of new students enrolled during the previous year. A parenthetical grade range is present for schools that do not accept new pupils at all grade levels. When available, the number of new boarding and day pupils is listed. The annual application due month (or "Rolling" if applications are considered year-round), the percentage of applicants accepted and the percentage of accepted students who enroll (yield) follow. Reported next are the abbreviations of tests used (although not necessarily required) for admission purposes by the school. Consult the Key to Admission Tests for details.

6. ENROLLMENT and FACULTY. The total number of students enrolled during the current academic year is reported with the following breakdown: number of boys boarding/day; number of girls boarding/day; and enumeration of students in elementary, secondary and postgraduate divisions. Information about the student body's racial makeup appears in many listings. "Uniforms" indicates that the school requires its students to wear uniforms.

How to Read the School Descriptions 17

Faculty figures are detailed as follows: total faculty; number of males full-time/part-time; females full-time/part-time. If simply one figure follows a slash, only part-time faculty are employed; if there are no part-time teachers, slashes are omitted. When provided by the school, racial composition of the teaching staff is indicated next.

The percentage of teaching faculty members who have earned advanced degrees follows. At boarding schools, faculty members may reside on campus. "In Dorms" reports the number of resident teaching faculty dwelling in dormitories. (This figure does not include instructors who live elsewhere on campus.) The student-teacher ratio can be deduced from a comparison of teaching faculty and enrollment figures.

7. GRADUATE RECORD. These figures specify the total number of students in the previous academic year's graduating class and the number who matriculated at nonpublic preparatory schools or two- or four-year colleges. As many as six schools entered by the largest number of class members are cited. Secondary school listings may include average ACT assessment results, in addition to average combined math and critical reading Scholastic Aptitude Test (SAT) scores. Some elementary schools report average scores for students taking the Secondary School Admission Test (SSAT). The number of active alumni(-ae) appears at the end of this section.

8. TUITION and AID. When both boarding and day departments are maintained, both tuitions are given. Grouped tuition figures (e.g., $13,000-18,750) typically show the fee span from the lowest to the highest grade. Tuition figures for young children who do not attend for a full school day are omitted. The school's estimate of extra expenses incurred by the average student follows in parentheses. Note: Reference school year for listed tuition figure(s) precedes this data.

The number of students receiving merit scholarships is reported with the school's total scholarship allotment. Financial aid figures follow, with total dollar amount provided again listed after number of recipients. Finally, the number of students participating in remunerative work programs, with corresponding dollar values, is cited where applicable. Children of faculty members are excluded from all aid categories.

9. SUMMER SESSION. The type, orientation, fees and duration are specified for schools with summer programs.

10. PLANT EVALUATION and ENDOWMENT. Following the dollar values of the endowment and the physical plant is a brief listing of the school's facilities.

11. ESTABLISHMENT and CALENDAR. The establishment date, the organizational nature (if the school is incorporated or incorporated

nonprofit) and the religious or other affiliation are cited. Division of the academic year and months of operation follow.

Accreditation by the seven associations listed under "Accrediting Associations" in the Associations and Organizations section is recorded based upon lists provided by these associations. Advocacy, testing, school membership and professional organizations are also part of the Associations and Organizations compilation.

12. PARAGRAPH DESCRIPTION. These comments often begin with highlights of the school's founding and early development. Significant aspects of the academic and extracurricular programs are then summarized.

    Descriptions adhere to the publisher's Editorial Policy and are based upon annual questionnaires and supplementary literature submitted by school officials. Material is not presented when it does not serve to objectively define a school. All revisions suggested by the schools must be accompanied by substantiating reports or catalogues for consideration.

13. PAGE CROSS-REFERENCE TO ILLUSTRATED ANNOUNCEMENT. Many schools supply their own appraisals of ideals and objectives in the Private Schools Illustrated section; page cross-references are appended to the paragraph descriptions of participating schools.

GLOSSARY

ACT assessment: Composed of a multiple-choice section that addresses English, math, reading and science, as well as an optional writing section that measures skill in planning and writing a short essay, this college entrance exam assesses high school students' general educational development and evaluates their ability to complete college-level work.

advanced degree: Regarding teaching faculty members, this figure designates the percentage of teachers who hold any degree more advanced than a bachelor's degree.

alumni: Totals that appear in the free listings refer to alumni still in contact with the school, not the cumulative number of school graduates.

Advanced Placement: "AP" courses, which comprise advanced material and follow the syllabi set forth by the College Board in Princeton, NJ, are listed after the AP designation in the statistical portion of the editorial listing. Upon completing each AP course, students may sit for the standardized Advanced Placement examination. Favorable scores in these examinations may lead to advanced standing at the college level.

coordinate: Used to describe schools that share some key administrators and admit both boys and girls, yet operate separate boys' and girls' divisions. Classes at such schools are not typically coeducational, although there are exceptions. Some schools operate coeducationally at certain grade levels and coordinately at others.

country day school: This concept became popular in the 1930s, when day schools (with boarding school aspirations in terms of academic rigor) flourished in rustic settings and placed importance on physical education as a complement to academics. The term lives on in many school names, although it now has no concrete meaning.

developmental reading: Instruction that focuses upon fundamental reading skills.

endowment: Funds or property donated to a school as a source of income.

enrichment: Supplemental instruction (such as a field trip) intended to amplify or extend classroom learning.

elementary: When used in the statistical portion of the editorial listing, "Elem" refers to grades preschool through eight.

French Baccalaureate: The completion of the French high school curriculum leads to this diploma. Taught entirely in French and found primarily in the US at French-American schools, it follows curricular guidelines established by the French Ministry of Education. Students must complete grade 12 and pass externally assessed examinations to earn the French Baccalaureate.

honors: Many high schools designate certain advanced courses with this label. Unlike Advanced Placement courses, however, honors courses meet no specific curricular requirements and thus gain the honors distinction at the discretion of the school.

independent school: An institution of this type does not rely upon local or federal government funding, but instead operates on the basis of tuition fees, donations and, in many instances, the investment yield gained from the school's endowment.

interim program: Commonly referred to as "winterim" when it operates in the winter, this program enables students to explore topics of interest or participate in internships on an intensive, short-term basis. The program typically lasts a week or two and runs between two school terms.

International Baccalaureate: The International Baccalaureate Organization (IBO) is a nonprofit, international foundation that works with more than 1500 schools (in 120 countries) to oversee three distinct programs. The Primary Years Programme (PYP), for students ages 3-12, is a comprehensive international curriculum that comprises learning guidelines, a teaching methodology and assessment strategies. The Middle Years Programme (MYP) is a five-year program for students ages 11-16 that is flexible enough to encompass other subjects not determined by the IBO but required by local authorities. The Diploma Programme, the most commonly utilized IB program in the United States, is a two-year, precollege course of study that leads to standardized examinations. It is designed for highly motivated students ages 16-19. While these programs form a continuous sequence, each may be offered independently.

learning disabilities: Comprising such conditions as dyslexia, dysgraphia and dyscalculia, learning disabilities are a group of neurological disorders that affect the brain's ability to receive, process, store and respond to information and stimuli.

makeup: An opportunity for the student to retake a course in which mastery was not previously displayed.

merit scholarship: Tuition assistance granted in recognition of noteworthy academic achievement or a special talent. It is often provided to students with accompanying financial need.

Montessori: Developed in the early 1900s by Maria Montessori, Italy's first female physician, the Montessori method of education incorporates manipulative materials with which children essentially teach themselves. Multi-age groupings are commonly found in Montessori settings, and the Montessori approach is usually employed during the elementary years.

need-based aid: Tuition assistance granted to families in recognition of financial need.

nonprofit: Refers to schools that are legally categorized as Section 501(c)(3) organizations, and thus not designed to be profit-making businesses.

plant: The physical facilities and land owned by the school.

postgraduate: Typically a year in duration, "PG" offers course work to high school graduates who wish to bolster their academic credentials, improve their readiness for college, or both.

preschool: For reasons of standardization, "PS" in the statistical portion of the editorial listings refers to any schooling prior to five-year-old kindergarten (for example, nursery, transitional kindergarten or pre-kindergarten), regardless of how the school itself refers to such grade level(s).

remedial: Intended to remedy a deficit, often in the areas of math or reading.

review: Reinforcement of previously covered material.

secondary: When used in the statistical portion of the editorial listing, "Sec" refers to grades nine through 12.

tutoring: One-on-one or small-group instruction for students requiring extra assistance in a subject.

underachiever: Underachieving students, who are typically of average or above-average intelligence, have failed to learn to potential due to motivational, emotional, behavioral or learning problems.

Waldorf: Developed by Austrian intellectual Rudolf Steiner in 1919, Waldorf education typically incorporates play and toys as important learning tools for children. Instructors follow a developmental approach that seeks to address the changing needs of the child as he grows and matures.

work program: Opportunities for students to perform chores or other duties that aid in the maintenance of the school. Only programs resulting in tuition reimbursement are referenced in the statistical portion of the editorial listing, although nonpaying work programs are frequently noted in the paragraph descriptions.

yield: The percentage of accepted students who matriculate at the school.

KEY TO ABBREVIATIONS

For further clarification, refer to How to Read the School Descriptions

Acad	Academic, Academy
Achieve	Achievement
ACT	American College Test
Actg	Acting
Adm	Admissions, Director of Admission(s)
Admin	Administration, Administrator
Alum	Alumnae, Alumni
Am, Amer	American
Anat	Anatomy
Anthro	Anthropology
AP	Advanced Placement
Appl	Applications
Archaeol	Archaeology
Architect	Architectural, Architecture
ASL	American Sign Language
Assoc	Associate, Association
Astron	Astronomy
Aud	Auditorium
Avg	Average
B	Boys
Bac	Baccalaureate
Bdg	Boarding
Bio	Biology
Bldg	Building
Blk	Black
Bus	Business
Calc	Calculus
CC	Community College
Chem	Chemistry
Chin	Chinese
Chrm	Chairman
Co Day	Country Day
Coed	Coeducational
Col	College

Comp	Comparative, Computer
Coord	Coordinate
Crse	Course
Deg	Degrees
Dev	Development, Developmental
Dir	Director
Dorm	Dormitory
Ec, Econ	Economics
Ecol	Ecology
Ed, Educ	Education
Elem	Elementary (Preschool–Grade 8)
Endow	Endowment
Eng	English
Enr	Enrollment
Enrich	Enrichment
Environ	Environmental
ESL	English as a Second Language
Est	Established
Eur	European
Exec	Executive
F	Females
Fac	Faculty
Feat	Featured Courses
Fr	French
G	Girls
Gen	General
Geog	Geography
Geol	Geology
Ger	German
Govt	Government
Gr	Grade(s)
Grad	Graduates
Head	Headmaster, Headmistress, Head of School
Hist	History
Hisp	Hispanic
HS	High School
IB	International Baccalaureate

Key to Abbreviations

Ind	Indian
Indus	Industrial
Int	Interim
Intl	International
Ital	Italian
Japan	Japanese
JC	Junior College
Journ	Journalism
JROTC	Junior Reserve Officers Training Corps
K	Kindergarten
Lab	Laboratory
Lang	Language(s)
Lat	Latin
LD	Learning Disabilities
Lib	Library
Lit	Literature
M	Males
Man	Manual
Mech	Mechanical
Med	Medicine
Milit	Military
Mo	Month
Mod	Modern
MYP	Middle Years Programme
Oceanog	Oceanography
PG	Postgraduate
Philos	Philosophy
Photog	Photography
Physiol	Physiology
Pol	Political, Politics
Prep	Preparation, Preparatory
Pres	President
Prgm	Program
Prin	Principal
PS	Preschool
Psych	Psychology
PYP	Primary Years Programme

Quar	Quarter
Read	Reading
Rec	Recreational
Relig	Religion
Rem	Remedial
Res	Residential
Rev	Review
Rm	Room
Russ	Russian
SAT	Scholastic Aptitude Test
Sch	School
Sci	Science
Sculpt	Sculpture
Sec	Secondary (Grades 9–12)
Sem	Semester
Ses	Session
Soc	Social
Sociol	Sociology
Span	Spanish
Speak	Speaking
SSAT	Secondary School Admission Test
Stats	Statistics
Stud	Studies
Supp	Supplementary
Supt	Superintendent
Tech	Technical, Technology
Theol	Theology
Tri	Trimester
Trng	Training
Tui	Tuition
Tut	Tutorial, Tutoring
U, Univ	University
Val	Value
Voc	Vocational
Vols	Volumes
Wh	White
Wk	Week
Yr	Year

KEY TO ADMISSION TESTS

Standardized tests of ability, aptitude and achievement are frequently requisites for admission to independent schools. These tests may be administered by the school, an agency or a testing service. Listed below are major tests utilized by schools in the Handbook.

CEEB COLLEGE ENTRANCE EXAMINATION BOARD tests include the PSAT/NMSQT (Preliminary SAT/National Merit Scholarship Qualifying Test), the SAT I and the SAT II. The PSAT prepares high school juniors for the SAT I, which is designed to measure a student's ability to perform in college. Both the PSAT and the SAT I comprise critical reading and mathematical sections, while the SAT II measures knowledge in specific subjects. Changes effected to the SAT in March 2005 were the addition of an essay writing section and modifications to the critical reading and mathematics sections.

CTP 4 COMPREHENSIVE TESTING PROGRAM measures achievement in grades 1-12, as well as verbal and quantitative ability in grades 3-12.

DAT DIFFERENTIAL APTITUDE TESTS measure aptitudes of adolescents in grades 7-12 and adults.

HSPT HIGH SCHOOL PLACEMENT TEST, developed by Scholastic Testing Service (STS) but administered by the schools themselves, is utilized for the evaluation of middle school students by many Roman Catholic high schools. The test consists of five multiple-choice sections: verbal, reading, qualitative, math and language.

IQ INTELLIGENCE QUOTIENT—Intelligence tests, designed to evaluate an individual's academic aptitude, are many, with varying purposes, scales and results. The most common are the Stanford-Binet, WISC and Otis-Lennon.

ISEE INDEPENDENT SCHOOL ENTRANCE EXAMINATION comprises tests for verbal and quantitative ability, reading comprehension and mathematics achievement, in addition to an essay.

MAT METROPOLITAN ACHIEVEMENT TESTS, for grades K-12, measure student achievement in reading, mathematics, language, science and social studies.

MRT METROPOLITAN READINESS TESTS assess literacy and mathematics development in prekindergarten to grade 1.

SSAT SECONDARY SCHOOL ADMISSION TEST assesses scholastic ability of students applying for admission to independent secondary schools. Five sections include quantitative, verbal and reading categories.

Stanford STANFORD ACHIEVEMENT TEST, for grades K-12, measures student achievement in reading, mathematics, language, spelling, study skills, science, social science and listening.

TACHS TEST FOR ADMISSION INTO CATHOLIC HIGH SCHOOLS is a Roman Catholic high school entrance test, similar in structure to the HSPT, that is employed predominantly in the Archdiocese of New York.

TOEFL TEST OF ENGLISH AS A FOREIGN LANGUAGE, which evaluates the English proficiency of individuals whose native language is not English, consists of three sections: listening comprehension, structure and written expression, and reading comprehension.

KEY TO ACCREDITING ASSOCIATIONS

Association accreditation and membership data are supplied by the following associations and recorded in each school listing.

Listed below are the six regional accrediting associations serving the United States and its territories at the elementary, secondary and college levels.

MSA	Middle States Association of Colleges and Schools
NAAS	Northwest Association of Accredited Schools
NCA	North Central Association
	Commission on Accreditation and School Improvement
NEASC	New England Association of Schools and Colleges
SACS	Southern Association of Colleges and Schools
	Council on Accreditation and School Improvement
WASC	Western Association of Schools and Colleges

The association listed below accredits secondary schools from throughout the United States.

CLS   Cum Laude Society

For more information about the above associations—as well as other organizations that serve independent schools, parents and educational professionals—refer to the list of Associations and Organizations beginning on page 1403.

SCHOOL FEATURE INDEXES

INDEX (by State and City, with Enrollment,
   Grade Ranges* and Other Features)..............................32
   * "C" denotes a Coordinate Single-Gender Program

SCHOOLS WITH A SPECIAL FOCUS
   Arts 111
   Bilingual Programs 111
   Business 112
   International Baccalaureate
      and French Baccalaureate 112
   Learning Disabilities and Underachievement 113
   Military 115
   Sports 116
   Vocational 117

INDEXES OF SPECIAL INTEREST
   Schools with Coordinate
      Single-Gender Programs 118
   Schools with Elementary Boarding 119
   Schools with at Least 25% International
      Students 122
   Coeducational Schools with Girls-Only
      Math or Science Programs 123
   Schools with 25% or More
      Nonwhite Faculty 124
   Schools with 50% or More
      Nonwhite Students 126

School Feature Indexes

School	Town	Girls' Grade Range Bdg	Girls' Grade Range Day	Boys' Grade Range Bdg	Boys' Grade Range Day	Enr	Learning Disabilities	ESL	Relig Affil	Page
ALABAMA										
DONOHO	Anniston		PS-12		PS-12	358				461
HIGHLANDS-AL	Birmingham		PS-8		PS-8	258				865
LYMAN WARD	Camp Hill			6-12		200				865
BAYSIDE	Daphne		PS-12		PS-12	700	Prgm			865
HOUSTON ACAD	Dothan		PS-12		PS-12	632				462
MARS HILL	Florence		PS-12		PS-12	558			Nondenom Christian	866
RANDOLPH SCH	Huntsville		K-12		K-12	757		•		463
INDIAN SPRINGS	Indian Springs	9-PG	8-12	9-PG	8-12	268				461
MADISON	Madison		PS-12		PS-12	849				866
MARION	Marion	9-12	9-12	9-12	9-12	115		•		867
MCGILL-TOOLEN	Mobile		9-12		9-12	1024	Prgm		Roman Catholic	867
ST LUKE'S EPIS-AL	Mobile		PS-8		PS-8	400			Episcopal	868
ST PAUL'S EPIS-AL	Mobile		PS-12		PS-12	1580	Prgm		Episcopal	464
AL CHRISTIAN	Montgomery		K-12		K-12	923			Un. Ch. of Christ	868
MONTGOMERY ACAD	Montgomery		K-12		K-12	846				465
ST JAMES SCH-AL	Montgomery		PS-12		PS-12	1175				868
TUSCALOOSA ACAD	Tuscaloosa		PS-12		PS-12	450		•		869
ALASKA										
GRACE CHRISTIAN	Anchorage		K-12		K-12	683			Grace Brethren	1047

Index by State and City

PACIFIC NORTHERN	Anchorage		PS-12		PS-12		1047
				ARIZONA			
ORME	Mayer	7-PG	7-PG	7-PG	7-PG	•	685
CAMELBACK DESERT	Paradise Valley		PS-8		PS-8		1035
PHOENIX CO DAY	Paradise Valley		PS-12		PS-12		687
ALL SAINTS' EPIS-AZ	Phoenix		K-8		K-8	Episcopal	686
BROPHY	Phoenix			9-12	1200	Roman Catholic	686
PARADISE VALLEY PREP	Phoenix		PS-8		PS-8	Nondenom Christian	1035
PHOENIX CHRISTIAN	Phoenix		7-12		7-12	Nondenom Christian	1035
ST MARY'S HS-AZ	Phoenix		9-12		9-12	Roman Catholic	1036
ST PAUL'S PREP	Phoenix			9-12	9-12	Episcopal	1036
SS SIMON & JUDE	Phoenix		K-8		K-8	Roman Catholic	1037
SCOTTSDALE CHRISTIAN	Phoenix		PS-12		PS-12	Prgm Nondenom Christian	1037
SOUTHWESTERN-AZ	Rimrock		9-12	9-12	9-12	•	688
VERDE VALLEY	Sedona	9-PG	9-PG	9-PG	9-PG	•	689
FENSTER	Tucson		9-12	9-12	9-12	•	690
GREEN FIELDS	Tucson		K-12		K-12		690
IMMACULATE HEART	Tucson		9-12		9-12	• Roman Catholic	691
SALPOINTE	Tucson		9-12		9-12	Roman Catholic	1038
ST GREGORY COL PREP	Tuscon		6-12		6-12		1038
OAK CREEK	West Sedona	6-12		6-12		•	1038
				ARKANSAS			

School Feature Indexes

	School	Town	Girls' Grade Range Bdg	Girls' Grade Range Day	Boys' Grade Range Bdg	Boys' Grade Range Day	Enr	Learning Disabilities	ESL	Relig Affil	Page
AR	MT ST MARY-AR	Little Rock		9-12			600			Roman Catholic	997
	PULASKI	Little Rock		PS-12		PS-12	1270				647
	CENTRAL AR CHRISTIAN	North Little Rock		PS-12		PS-12	1037			Nondenom Christian	997
	SUBIACO	Subiaco			9-12	9-12	179		•	Roman Catholic	648
			CALIFORNIA								
	RAMONA	Alhambra		7-12			560			Roman Catholic	1048
	PASADENA WALDORF	Altadena		K-8		K-8	244				1048
	CORNELIA CONNELLY	Anaheim		9-12			232			Roman Catholic	1048
	FAIRMONT	Anaheim		PS-12		PS-12	2250				1049
	ST CATHERINE'S MILIT	Anaheim			K-8	K-8	180		•	Roman Catholic	697
	SERVITE	Anaheim				9-12	785			Roman Catholic	1049
	MENLO	Atherton		6-12		6-12	757				698
	NOTRE DAME-BELMONT	Belmont		9-12			720	Prgm		Roman Catholic	1050
	ARROWSMITH	Berkeley		9-12		9-12	120		•		1050
	E BAY FR-AMER	Berkeley		PS-8		PS-8	503		•		1050
	PROVIDENCE HS	Burbank		9-12		9-12	556			Roman Catholic	1051
	VIEWPOINT	Calabasas		K-12		K-12	1158				716
	ARMY & NAVY	Carlsbad		7-12	7-12	7-12	333		•		699
	ALL SAINTS' EPIS-CA	Carmel		PS-8		PS-8	210			Episcopal	1051
	JESUIT HS-CA	Carmichael				9-12	1025			Roman Catholic	1052

Index by State and City

ST MICHAEL'S EPIS	Carmichael		PS-8		PS-8	Episcopal	1052
CATE	Carpinteria	9-12	9-12	9-12	266		744
SIERRA CANYON	Chatsworth		PS-8		700		1052
FOOTHILL CO DAY	Claremont		PS-8	PS-8	180		699
WEBB SCHS-CA	Claremont	9-12	9-12	9-12	355		700
HARBOR DAY	Corona del Mar		K-8	K-8	406		701
MARIN CO DAY	Corte Madera		K-8	K-8	541	Prgm	702
TURNING POINT	Culver City		PS-8	PS-8	338		715
PROSPECT SIERRA	El Cerrito		K-8	K-8	487		1053
WINDRUSH	El Cerrito		K-8	K-8	250		1053
E BAY WALDORF	El Sobrante		K-12	K-12	297	Prgm	1053
SACRAMENTO WALDORF	Fair Oaks		PS-12	PS-12	423		729
NAWA	French Gulch	7-12		7-12	45	Focus	1054
FRESNO ADVENTIST	Fresno		K-12	K-12	300	Adventist	1054
ROSARY	Fullerton		9-12		709	Roman Catholic	1055
ST LUCY'S	Glendora		9-12		870	Roman Catholic	1055
MOREAU	Hayward		9-12	9-12	1040	Roman Catholic	1055
CRYSTAL SPGS UPLANDS	Hillsborough		6-12	6-12	350		702
HEBREW ACAD	Huntington Beach		PS-12	PS-12	360	Jewish	1056
PEGASUS	Huntington Beach		PS-8	PS-8	565		703
IDYLLWILD	Idyllwild	8-PG	9-PG	9-PG	255		704
BISHOP'S	La Jolla		7-12	7-12	685	Episcopal	705

School Feature Indexes

School	Town	Girls' Grade Range Bdg	Girls' Grade Range Day	Boys' Grade Range Bdg	Boys' Grade Range Day	Enr	Learning Disabilities	ESL	Relig Affil	Page
CA GILLISPIE	La Jolla		PS-6		PS-6	283				1056
LA JOLLA CO DAY	La Jolla		PS-12		PS-12	1006				706
LUTHERAN HS-CA	La Verne		9-12		9-12	135		•	Lutheran-Missouri	1056
MARIN MIDDLE	Larkspur		PS-8		PS-8	353				1057
WESTERLY	Long Beach		K-8		K-8	170				1057
ARCHER	Los Angeles		6-12			450				1058
BERKELEY HALL	Los Angeles		PS-8		PS-8	240				1058
CURTIS	Los Angeles		K-8		K-8	520				709
JOHN THOMAS DYE	Los Angeles		K-6		K-6	331				710
LYCEE FRANCAIS-LA	Los Angeles		PS-12		PS-12	900		•		711
LOYOLA HS-CA	Los Angeles				9-12	1200			Roman Catholic	1059
MARLBOROUGH	Los Angeles		7-12			530				711
MARYMOUNT HS	Los Angeles		9-12			398			Roman Catholic	712
MIRMAN	Los Angeles		1-9		1-9	349				713
PAGE	Los Angeles		PS-8		PS-8	300				1059
PILGRIM	Los Angeles		PS-12		PS-12	370		•	Congregational	714
PLAY MTN	Los Angeles		PS-5		PS-5	100				1059
SACRED HEART HS-CA	Los Angeles		9-12			334			Roman Catholic	1060
WINDWARD-CA	Los Angeles		7-12		7-12	474				1060
HILLBROOK	Los Gatos		PS-8		PS-8	315				716

Index by State and City

DUNN	Los Olivos	9-12	6-12	9-12	6-12	172	Prgm		717
MIDLAND	Los Olivos	9-12		9-12		76			718
PHILLIPS BROOKS	Menlo Park		PS-5		PS-5	260			1060
MT TAMALPAIS	Mill Valley		K-8		K-8	240			1061
CENTRAL CATHOLIC-CA	Modesto		9-12		9-12	441		Roman Catholic	1061
SANTA CATALINA	Monterey	9-12	PS-12		PS-8	566		Roman Catholic	719
YORK SCH	Monterey		8-12		8-12	226		Episcopal	1062
SAKLAN	Moraga		PS-8		PS-8	146			1062
JUSTIN-SIENA	Napa		9-12		9-12	661	Prgm	Roman Catholic	1062
SUGAR BOWL	Norden	8-PG	6-PG	8-PG	6-PG	45			1063
CAMPBELL HALL	North Hollywood		K-12		K-12	1061		Episcopal	707
HARVARD-WESTLAKE	North Hollywood		7-12		7-12	1550		Episcopal	709
OAKWOOD SCH-CA	North Hollywood		K-12		K-12	756			713
BENTLEY	Oakland		K-12		K-12	602			1063
BISHOP O'DOWD	Oakland		9-12		9-12	1140		Roman Catholic	1064
COLLEGE PREP	Oakland		9-12		9-12	329			719
HEAD-ROYCE	Oakland		K-12		K-12	750			720
HOLY NAMES HS	Oakland		9-12			277		Roman Catholic	1064
ST ELIZABETH	Oakland		9-12		9-12	276	Prgm	Roman Catholic	1065
ST PAUL'S EPIS-CA	Oakland		K-8		K-8	338		Episcopal	1065
HAPPY VALLEY	Ojai	9-12	9-12	9-12	9-12	86		•	721
OAK GROVE SCH	Ojai	9-12	PS-12	9-12	PS-12	200		•	1065

School Feature Indexes

	School	Town	Girls' Grade Range Bdg	Girls' Grade Range Day	Boys' Grade Range Bdg	Boys' Grade Range Day	Enr	Learning Disabilities	ESL	Relig Affil	Page
CA	OJAI VALLEY	Ojai	3-12	PS-12	3-12	PS-12	370		•		721
	THACHER	Ojai	9-12	9-12	9-12	9-12	241				722
	ELDORADO-EMERSON	Orange		PS-12		PS-12	171		•		723
	ST MATTHEW'S	Pacific Palisades		PS-8		PS-8	325			Episcopal	1066
	INTL SCH PENINSULA	Palo Alto		PS-8		PS-8	485		•		724
	ROLLING HILLS PREP	Palos Verdes Estates		6-12		6-12	260		•		1066
	CHADWICK	Palos Verdes Peninsula		K-12		K-12	795				708
	MARANATHA HS	Pasadena		9-12		9-12	450	Prgm		Nondenom Christian	1067
	MAYFIELD JR	Pasadena		K-8		K-8	460			Roman Catholic	1067
	MAYFIELD SR	Pasadena		9-12			305			Roman Catholic	1067
	PASADENA TOWNE	Pasadena		PS-8		PS-8	300				1068
	WALDEN	Pasadena		PS-6		PS-6	240				1068
	WESTRIDGE	Pasadena		4-12			510				725
	ROB L STEVENSON-CA	Pebble Beach	9-12	K-12	9-12	K-12	753				726
	WOODSIDE PRIORY	Portola Valley	9-12	6-12	9-12	6-12	340			Roman Catholic	725
	ST JOHN'S EPIS-CA	Rancho Santa Margarita		PS-8		PS-8	870			Episcopal	1069
	MERCY HS-RED BLUFF	Red Bluff		9-12			155			Roman Catholic	1069
	VALLEY PREP	Redlands		PS-8		PS-8	243				727
	PENINSULA HERITAGE	Rolling Hills Estates		PS-5		PS-5	197				1069
	ROLLING HILLS CO DAY	Rolling Hills Estates		K-8		K-8	363				1070

Index by State and City

BRANSON	Ross		9-12	320		728
BROOKFIELD SCH	Sacramento		K-8	150		1070
SACRAMENTO CO DAY	Sacramento		PS-12	551		728
SAN DOMENICO	San Anselmo	9-12	PS-12	562	• Roman Catholic	730
ACAD OUR LADY PEACE	San Diego		9-12	760	Roman Catholic	1070
ST AUGUSTINE HS	San Diego		9-12	699	Roman Catholic	1071
WARREN-WALKER	San Diego		PS-8	383		1071
BRIDGEMONT	San Francisco		6-12	92	Nondenom Christian	1072
CATHEDRAL SCH BOYS	San Francisco		K-8	244	Episcopal	731
CHIN AMER INTL	San Francisco		PS-8	361	•	1072
DREW	San Francisco		9-12	250	•	731
FR-AMER INTL	San Francisco		PS-12	888	Prgm •	732
HAMLIN	San Francisco		K-8	402		733
HILLWOOD	San Francisco		K-8	56		733
IMMACULATE CONCEPT	San Francisco		9-12	262	Roman Catholic	1072
KATHERINE D BURKE	San Francisco		K-8	394		734
LICK-WILMERDING	San Francisco		9-12	407		735
LIVE OAK	San Francisco		K-8	229		1073
MERCY-SAN FRANCISCO	San Francisco		9-12	580	Roman Catholic	1073
PRESIDIO HILL	San Francisco		K-8	180		735
SAN FRANCISCO DAY	San Francisco		K-8	395		736
SAN FRANCISCO SCH	San Francisco		PS-8	276		737

School Feature Indexes

School	Town	Girls' Grade Range Bdg	Girls' Grade Range Day	Boys' Grade Range Bdg	Boys' Grade Range Day	Enr	Learning Disabilities	ESL	Relig Affil	Page
CA										
SAN FRANCISCO U HS	San Francisco		9-12		9-12	391				737
SCHS-SACRED HEART	San Francisco		K-12C		K-12C	1032			Roman Catholic	738
TOWN SCH FOR BOYS	San Francisco				K-8	400				739
URBAN	San Francisco		9-12		9-12	257				740
CLAIRBOURN	San Gabriel		PS-8		PS-8	420			Christian Science	1074
HARKER	San Jose		K-12		K-12	1594				740
PRESENTATION	San Jose		9-12			750			Roman Catholic	1074
ST MARGARET'S EPIS	San Juan Capistrano		PS-12		PS-12	1208			Episcopal	741
SOUTHWESTERN-CA	San Marino	6-PG	6-PG	6-PG	6-PG	122				742
ALPHA BEACON	San Mateo		PS-12		PS-12	225			Nondenom Christian	1074
JUNIPERO SERRA	San Mateo				9-12	985			Roman Catholic	1075
MARIN ACAD	San Rafael		9-12		9-12	404				743
ST MARK'S SCH-CA	San Rafael		K-8		K-8	380				1075
MATER DEI HS	Santa Ana		9-12		9-12	2200	Prgm		Roman Catholic	1076
CRANE	Santa Barbara		K-8		K-8	230				1076
LAGUNA BLANCA	Santa Barbara		K-12		K-12	376				745
MARYMOUNT SANTA BARB	Santa Barbara		K-8		K-8	232			Roman Catholic	1076
ST LAWRENCE	Santa Clara		9-12		9-12	347	Prgm		Roman Catholic	1077
CROSSROADS-CA	Santa Monica		K-12		K-12	1140				746
P S #1	Santa Monica		K-6		K-6	176				1077

SONOMA CO DAY	Santa Rosa		K-8	287		1077
BAYMONTE	Scotts Valley		PS-8	518		1078
BUCKLEY SCH-CA	Sherman Oaks		K-12	750		706
NOTRE DAME-SHER OAKS	Sherman Oaks		9-12	1148	Roman Catholic	1078
ST MICHAEL'S PREP	Silverado	9-12		70	Roman Catholic	1078
WOODCREST	Tarzana		K-5	250		1079
LAURENCE	Valley Glen		K-6	226		1079
DORRIS-EATON	Walnut Creek		PS-8	450		1080
SEVEN HILLS-CA	Walnut Creek		PS-8	374		1080
MONTE VISTA	Watsonville	9-12	6-12	970	• Evangelical	747

COLORADO

ASPEN CO DAY	Aspen		PS-8	165		677
REGIS JESUIT	Aurora		9-12C	1143	Roman Catholic	1025
SHINING MTN	Boulder		PS-12	320		1025
HOLY FAMILY HS	Broomfield		9-12	525	Roman Catholic	1026
CO ROCKY MTN	Carbondale	9-12	9-12	165	•	680
FOUNTAIN VALLEY	Colorado Springs	9-12	9-12	225	•	678
ST MARY'S HS-CO	Colorado Springs		9-12	360	Roman Catholic	1026
BEACON	Denver		PS-8	150		1026
CO ACAD	Denver		PS-12	828		679
DENVER ACAD	Denver		1-12	441	Focus	1027
DENVER JEWISH EDUC	Denver		K-12	363	• Jewish	1027

School Feature Indexes

School	Town	Girls' Grade Range Bdg	Girls' Grade Range Day	Boys' Grade Range Bdg	Boys' Grade Range Day	Enr	Learning Disabilities	ESL	Relig Affil	Page
CO DENVER INTL	Denver		PS-8		PS-8	230		•		1028
DENVER LUTHERAN	Denver		9-12		9-12	220			Lutheran-Missouri	1028
GRALAND	Denver		K-9		K-9	620				680
LOGAN	Denver		K-8		K-8	213				1028
MONTCLAIR ACAD	Denver		PS-8		PS-8	250				1029
ST ANNE'S EPISCOPAL	Denver		PS-8		PS-8	428				1029
U OF DENVER HS	Denver		9-12		9-12	120				1030
CO TIMBERLINE	Durango	9-PG	9-PG	9-PG	9-PG	25		•		1030
ALEXANDER DAWSON	Lafayette		K-12		K-12	420				681
CAMPION	Loveland	9-12	9-12	9-12	9-12	202			Adventist	1030
LOWELL WHITEMAN	Steamboat Springs	9-12	9-12	9-12	9-12	98				682
VAIL MTN	Vail		K-12		K-12	263				683
FOOTHILLS ACAD	Wheat Ridge		PS-12		PS-12	229				1031
CONNECTICUT										
AVON	Avon		9-PG	9-PG	9-PG	369				131
ACAD HOLY FAMILY	Baltic	9-12	9-12			56		•	Roman Catholic	763
WOODHALL	Bethlehem			9-PG	9-PG	40	Focus	•		132
BESS & PAUL SIGEL	Bloomfield		PS-8		PS-8	145		•	Jewish	763
WIGHTWOOD	Branford		PS-8		PS-8	88				133
CHESHIRE	Cheshire	9-PG	6-PG	9-PG	6-PG	333		•		133

Index by State and City

IMMACULATE HS	Danbury		9-12		438		Roman Catholic	764
WOOSTER	Danbury		K-12		417		Episcopal •	134
ENFIELD MONTESSORI	Enfield		PS-6		115		Roman Catholic	764
FAIRFIELD COL PREP	Fairfield		9-12		890		Roman Catholic	135
FAIRFIELD CO DAY	Fairfield		K-9		272			136
UNQUOWA	Fairfield		PS-8		171			136
MISS PORTER'S	Farmington	9-12	9-12		314		•	137
GREENS FARMS	Greens Farms		K-12		580			174
BRUNSWICK	Greenwich		PS-12		877			138
CONVENT SAC HEART-CT	Greenwich		PS-12		685		Roman Catholic	138
EAGLE HILL-GREENWICH	Greenwich		Ungraded	Ungraded	210	Focus		764
GREENWICH ACAD	Greenwich		PS-12		776			139
GREENWICH CO DAY	Greenwich		PS-9	PS-9	839			140
STANWICH	Greenwich		K-9	K-9	346			765
WHITBY	Greenwich		PS-8	PS-8	305			141
HAMDEN HALL	Hamden		PS-12	PS-12	566			154
SACRED HEART ACAD-CT	Hamden		9-12		486		Roman Catholic	765
WATKINSON	Hartford		6-PG	6-PG	277			143
MOORELAND HILL	Kensington		5-9	5-9	45			144
KENT SCH-CT	Kent	9-PG	9-12	9-12	565		Episcopal •	145
MARVELWOOD	Kent	9-12	9-12	9-12	150		•	146
HOTCHKISS	Lakeville	9-PG	9-PG	9-PG	556			147

	School	Town	Girls' Grade Range Bdg	Girls' Grade Range Day	Boys' Grade Range Bdg	Boys' Grade Range Day	Enr	Learning Disabilities	ESL	Relig Affil	Page
CT	INDIAN MTN	Lakeville	6-9	PS-9	6-9	PS-9	261		•		148
	FORMAN	Litchfield	9-12	9-12	9-12	9-12	170	Focus	•		148
	COUNTRY SCH-CT	Madison		PS-8		PS-8	300				765
	GROVE SCH	Madison	6-PG	6-PG	6-PG	6-PG	105	Focus	•		766
	E CATHOLIC	Manchester		9-12		9-12	667			Roman Catholic	766
	WESTOVER	Middlebury	9-12	9-12			201		•		149
	INDEPENDENT DAY-CT	Middlefield		PS-8		PS-8	202				150
	MERCY HS-CT	Middletown		9-12			674			Roman Catholic	767
	XAVIER-CT	Middletown				9-12	849			Roman Catholic	767
	ACAD OUR LADY MERCY	Milford		9-12			440			Roman Catholic	767
	NEW CANAAN COUNTRY	New Canaan		PS-9		PS-9	608				151
	ST LUKE'S SCH-CT	New Canaan		5-12		5-12	460				152
	COLD SPRING	New Haven		PS-6		PS-6	104				153
	FOOTE	New Haven		K-9		K-9	470				153
	HOPKINS	New Haven		7-12		7-12	650				154
	ST THOMAS'S DAY	New Haven		PS-6		PS-6	157			Episcopal	156
	WILLIAMS-CT	New London		7-12		7-12	331				156
	CANTERBURY-CT	New Milford	9-PG	9-PG	9-PG	9-PG	366		•	Roman Catholic	157
	WASH MONTESSORI	New Preston		PS-8		PS-8	272				768
	ST THOMAS MORE-CT	Oakdale			8-PG		211	Focus	•	Roman Catholic	158

NEW HAVEN HEBREW	Orange		PS-8		PS-8	155		•	Jewish	768
POMFRET	Pomfret	9-PG	9-PG	9-PG	9-PG	359			Episcopal	159
RECTORY	Pomfret		5-9	5-9	5-9	168	Prgm	•	Episcopal	160
RIDGEFIELD	Ridgefield		PS-8		PS-8	290				769
SALISBURY-CT	Salisbury			9-PG	9-PG	285			Episcopal	160
ETHEL WALKER	Simsbury	9-PG	6-PG			184				161
WESTMINSTER SCH-CT	Simsbury	9-PG	9-PG	9-PG	9-PG	368				163
SOUTH KENT	South Kent			9-PG	9-PG	125	Prgm	•	Episcopal	164
EAGLE HILL-SOUTHPORT	Southport	Ungraded		Ungraded		107	Focus			769
BI-CULTURAL DAY	Stamford		K-8		K-8	431	Prgm		Jewish	769
KING/LOW-HEY THOMAS	Stamford		PS-12		PS-12	650				165
LONG RIDGE	Stamford		PS-5		PS-5	146				165
MEAD SCH	Stamford		PS-8		PS-8	173				770
TRINITY CATHOLIC	Stamford		9-12		9-12	425			Roman Catholic	770
PINE PT	Stonington		PS-9		PS-9	263				166
SUFFIELD	Suffield	9-PG	9-12	9-PG	9-12	402		•		167
MARIANAPOLIS	Thompson	9-PG	9-PG	9-PG	9-PG	250		•	Roman Catholic	168
CHRISTIAN HERITAGE	Trumbull		K-12		K-12	535			Nondenom Christian	770
CHOATE	Wallingford	9-PG	9-PG	9-PG	9-PG	870				168
GLENHOLME	Washington	3-12	3-12	3-12	3-12	100	Focus	•		771
GUNNERY	Washington	9-PG	9-PG	9-PG	9-PG	276		•		170
RUMSEY	Washington Depot	5-9	K-9	5-9	K-9	315		•		170

School Feature Indexes

School	Town	Girls' Grade Range Bdg	Girls' Grade Range Day	Boys' Grade Range Bdg	Boys' Grade Range Day	Enr	Learning Disabilities	ESL	Relig Affil	Page
CT CHASE	Waterbury		PS-12		PS-12	438				171
TAFT	Watertown	9-PG	9-PG	9-PG	9-PG	563				172
HARTFORD CHRISTIAN	West Hartford		K-12		K-12	105			Baptist	771
HEBREW HS	West Hartford		9-12		9-12	65			Jewish	772
KINGSWOOD-OXFORD	West Hartford		6-PG		6-PG	580				142
NORTHWEST CATHOLIC	West Hartford		9-12		9-12	653			Roman Catholic	772
RENBROOK	West Hartford		PS-9		PS-9	555				143
NOTRE DAME HS-CT	West Haven				9-12	704	Prgm		Roman Catholic	772
MASTER'S SCH-CT	West Simsbury		PS-12		PS-12	426			Nondenom Christian	162
OXFORD ACAD	Westbrook			9-PG		48	Prgm	•		173
LOOMIS CHAFFEE	Windsor	9-PG	9-PG	9-PG	9-PG	723				175
EZRA	Woodbridge		K-8		K-8	225		•	Jewish	773
HYDE SCH-WOODSTOCK	Woodstock	9-12	9-12	9-12	9-12	200				176
DELAWARE										
ARCHMERE	Claymont		9-12		9-12	480			Roman Catholic	284
SANFORD	Hockessin		PS-12		PS-12	702				284
ST ANDREW'S SCH-DE	Middletown	9-12		9-12		270			Episcopal	283
INDEPENDENCE	Newark		PS-8		PS-8	846				793
PILOT	Wilmington		K-8		K-8	163	Focus			793
ST EDMOND'S	Wilmington				4-8	266			Roman Catholic	793

Index by State and City

SALESIANUM	Wilmington		9-12	1010	Roman Catholic	794
TATNALL SCH	Wilmington	PS-12	PS-12	730		285
TOWER HILL	Wilmington	PS-12	PS-12	755		286
URSULINE ACAD-DE	Wilmington	PS-12	PS-3	705	Roman Catholic	794
WILMINGTON FRIENDS	Wilmington	PS-12	PS-12	801	Friends	286

DISTRICT OF COLUMBIA

CAPITOL HILL DAY	Washington	PS-8	PS-8	224		795
EMERSON	Washington	9-12	9-12	75	•	288
FIELD	Washington	7-12	7-12	280		795
GEORGETOWN DAY	Washington	PS-12	PS-12	1025		288
GONZAGA COL HS	Washington		9-12	893	Roman Catholic	795
LAB SCH	Washington	K-12	K-12	328	Focus	796
MARET	Washington	K-12	K-12	600		289
NATL CATHEDRAL	Washington	4-12		572	Episcopal	290
NATL PRESBYTERIAN	Washington	PS-6	PS-6	235	Presbyterian	796
PARKMONT	Washington	6-12	6-12	55		797
ROCK CREEK	Washington	PS-8	PS-8	240	•	797
ST ALBANS	Washington		4-12 9-12	565	Episcopal	291
ST JOHN'S COL HS	Washington	9-12	9-12	1078	Prgm Roman Catholic	797
ST PATRICK'S EPIS	Washington	PS-8	PS-8	487	Episcopal	798
SHERIDAN	Washington	K-8	K-8	212		291
SIDWELL FRIENDS	Washington	PS-12	PS-12	1091	Friends	292

School Feature Indexes

School	Town	Girls' Grade Range Bdg	Girls' Grade Range Day	Boys' Grade Range Bdg	Boys' Grade Range Day	Enr	Learning Disabilities	ESL	Relig Affil	Page
DC WASH INTL	Washington		PS-12		PS-12	830		•	Nondenom Christian	293
FLORIDA										
BOCA RATON CHRISTIAN	Boca Raton		PS-12		PS-12	580				869
DONNA KLEIN	Boca Raton		K-12		K-12	650			Jewish	870
GRANDVIEW	Boca Raton		PS-12		PS-12	268				870
ST ANDREW'S SCH-FL	Boca Raton	9-12	K-12	9-12	K-12	1073		•	Episcopal	466
BRADENTON CHRISTIAN	Bradenton		PS-12		PS-12	626				870
ST STEPHEN'S EPIS-FL	Bradenton		PS-12		PS-12	801			Episcopal	467
BRANDON ACAD	Brandon		K-8		K-8	235	Prgm			871
ST PAUL'S SCH-FL	Clearwater		PS-8		PS-8	504			Episcopal	871
NORTH BROWARD PREP	Coconut Creek		PS-12		PS-12	2035	Focus			872
ST PHILIP'S	Coral Gables		PS-6		PS-6	180			Episcopal	872
ST THOMAS EPISCOPAL	Coral Gables		PS-6		PS-6	436			Episcopal	872
ZION LUTHERAN	Deerfield Beach		PS-12		PS-12	691			Lutheran	873
FT LAUDERDALE PREP	Fort Lauderdale		PS-12		PS-12	180	Prgm	•		873
PINE CREST	Fort Lauderdale		PS-12		PS-12	1656				468
ST MARK'S EPIS SCH	Fort Lauderdale		PS-8		PS-8	574			Episcopal	874
U SCH OF NOVA	Fort Lauderdale		PS-12		PS-12	1619				468
WESTMINSTER ACAD	Fort Lauderdale		PS-12		PS-12	1112			Presbyterian	874
CANTERBURY-FT MYERS	Fort Myers		PS-12		PS-12	660				469

Index by State and City

OAK HALL	Gainesville		PS-12		PS-12		874
GULF STREAM	Gulf Stream		PS-8		PS-8	236	470
CHAMINADE-MADONNA	Hollywood		9-12		9-12	870	Roman Catholic 875
BOLLES	Jacksonville	7-PG	PS-12	7-PG	PS-12	1711	• 471
EPISCOPAL HS-FL	Jacksonville		6-12		6-12	895	Episcopal 472
HENDRICKS	Jacksonville		PS-8		PS-8	347	875
JACKSONVILLE CO DAY	Jacksonville		PS-6		PS-6	529	472
RIVERSIDE	Jacksonville		PS-6		PS-6	484	Presbyterian 473
ST MARK'S EPIS DAY	Jacksonville		PS-6		PS-6	515	Episcopal 876
BEACHES EPISCOPAL	Jacksonville Beach		PS-6		PS-6	280	Episcopal 876
VANGUARD	Lake Wales	5-PG	5-PG	5-PG	5-PG	134	Focus 474
LAKELAND CHRISTIAN	Lakeland		K-12		K-12	920	Prgm Nondenom Christian 876
PACE-BRANTLEY HALL	Longwood		1-12		1-12	130	Focus 877
SWEETWATER EPISCOPAL	Longwood		PS-5		PS-5	253	Episcopal 877
FL AIR	Melbourne	6-12	6-12	6-12	6-12	356	• 475
HOLY TRINITY ACAD	Melbourne		PS-12		PS-12	911	Episcopal 878
ATLANTIS	Miami		K-12		K-12	190	Focus • 878
CARROLLTON SCH	Miami		PS-12		PS-12	655	Roman Catholic 878
CUSHMAN	Miami		PS-8		PS-8	466	Prgm 879
DADE CHRISTIAN	Miami		PS-12		PS-12	1294	Baptist 879
LA SALLE HS	Miami		9-12		9-12	630	Roman Catholic 477
MIAMI CO DAY	Miami		PS-12		PS-12	1000	• 477

	School	Town	Girls' Grade Range Bdg	Girls' Grade Range Day	Boys' Grade Range Bdg	Boys' Grade Range Day	Enr	Learning Disabilities	ESL	Relig Affil	Page
FL	PALMER TRINITY	Miami		6-12		6-12	600		•	Episcopal	478
	RANSOM EVERGLADES	Miami		6-12		6-12	981				479
	WESTMINSTER-MIAMI	Miami		PS-12		PS-12	1100	Prgm		Nondenom Christian	880
	MONTVERDE	Montverde	7-12	PS-12	7-12	PS-12	377		•		880
	COMMUNITY SCH-FL	Naples		PS-12		PS-12	756				479
	BENJAMIN	North Palm Beach		PS-12		PS-12	1164				881
	ST JOHNS CO DAY	Orange Park		PS-12		PS-12	705				480
	BISHOP MOORE	Orlando		9-12		9-12	1091			Roman Catholic	881
	LAKE HIGHLAND	Orlando		PS-12		PS-12	1890				882
	NEW SCH OF ORLANDO	Orlando		K-8		K-8	140				882
	PALM BEACH DAY	Palm Beach		K-9		K-9	392				481
	GULLIVER	Pinecrest		PS-12		PS-12	2062				476
	AM HERITAGE	Plantation		PS-12		PS-12	2388	Prgm	•		882
	CARDINAL MOONEY-FL	Sarasota		9-12		9-12	540			Roman Catholic	884
	JULIE ROHR	Sarasota		PS-8		PS-8	271		•		884
	OUT-OF-DOOR	Sarasota		PS-12		PS-12	599				484
	ADMIRAL FARRAGUT	St Petersburg	6-12	K-12	6-12	K-12	475		•		482
	CANTERBURY SCH OF FL	St Petersburg		PS-12		PS-12	410			Episcopal	483
	KESWICK	St Petersburg		PS-12		PS-12	622			Nondenom Christian	883
	SHORECREST	St Petersburg		PS-12		PS-12	987				484

Index by State and City

School	City		Grades	Enrollment		Affiliation	Page
WELLINGTON-FL	St Petersburg		PS-8	385			883
ST MICHAEL'S INDEP	Stuart		PS-8	430			485
MACLAY	Tallahassee		PS-12	1001			486
ACAD HOLY NAMES	Tampa		PS-12	884		Roman Catholic	884
BAYSHORE	Tampa		PS-12	397		United Methodist	885
BERKELEY PREP	Tampa		PS-12	1172		Episcopal	487
CAMBRIDGE SCH-FL	Tampa		PS-12	664		Nondenom Christian	885
JESUIT HS-FL	Tampa		9-12	650		Roman Catholic	886
ST JOHNS EPIS PARISH	Tampa		PS-8	460		Episcopal	886
ST MARY'S EPIS DAY	Tampa		PS-8	435		Episcopal	487
TAMPA BAPTIST	Tampa		PS-12	420	Prgm	Southern Baptist	886
TAMPA PREP	Tampa		6-12	640			488
ST EDWARD'S SCH	Vero Beach		PS-12	900		Episcopal	489
CARDINAL NEWMAN	West Palm Beach		9-12	830		Roman Catholic	887
TRINITY PREP	Winter Park		6-12	802		Episcopal	489

GEORGIA

School	City		Grades	Enrollment		Affiliation	Page
DEERFIELD-WINDSOR	Albany		PS-12	730			887
ATHENS ACAD	Athens		PS-12	806			888
ATLANTA INTL	Atlanta		PS-12	878		•	491
BRANDON HALL	Atlanta	7-PG	4-PG	114	Focus	•	491
GALLOWAY	Atlanta		PS-12	744			888
HEISKELL	Atlanta		PS-8	360		Nondenom Christian	492

School Feature Indexes

School	Town	Girls' Grade Range Bdg	Girls' Grade Range Day	Boys' Grade Range Bdg	Boys' Grade Range Day	Enr	Learning Disabilities	ESL	Relig Affil	Page
GA HORIZONS	Atlanta	8-12	K-12	8-12	K-12	125		•		889
LOVETT	Atlanta		K-12		K-12	1555				493
MARIST	Atlanta		7-12		7-12	1034			Roman Catholic	493
MT VERNON	Atlanta		PS-10		PS-10	703			Presbyterian	889
PACE ACAD	Atlanta		K-12		K-12	916				494
PAIDEIA	Atlanta		PS-12		PS-12	882				495
ST MARTIN'S-GA	Atlanta		PS-8		PS-8	565			Episcopal	889
ST PIUS-GA	Atlanta		9-12		9-12	1012			Roman Catholic	890
TRINITY SCH-GA	Atlanta		PS-6		PS-6	520				890
WESTMINSTER SCHS-GA	Atlanta		K-12		K-12	1751				496
AQUINAS HS	Augusta		9-12		9-12	320	Prgm		Roman Catholic	891
EPISCOPAL DAY	Augusta		PS-8		PS-8	453			Episcopal	891
WESTMINSTER-AUGUSTA	Augusta		PS-12		PS-12	544			Nondenom Christian	891
OAK MTN	Carrollton		K-12		K-12	238			Nondenom Christian	892
WOODWARD	College Park		PS-12		PS-12	2860				496
BROOKSTONE	Columbus		PS-12		PS-12	826				498
PACELLI	Columbus		9-12		9-12	200			Roman Catholic	892
LANDMARK CHRISTIAN	Fairburn		PS-12		PS-12	605			Nondenom Christian	892
BRENAU	Gainesville	9-PG	9-PG			80	Prgm			498
RIVERSIDE MILIT	Gainesville			7-12	7-12	513		•		499

Index by State and City

N COBB	Kennesaw		PS-12		PS-12	895	Nondenom Christian	893
LAGRANGE	LaGrange		K-12		K-12	220		893
WHITEFIELD	Mableton		K-12		K-12	416	Nondenom Christian	894
FIRST PRESBYTERIAN	Macon		PS-12		PS-12	945	Prgm Presbyterian	894
MT DE SALES	Macon		6-12		6-12	660	Roman Catholic	894
STRATFORD ACAD	Macon		PS-12		PS-12	925	•	895
TATTNALL SQ	Macon		PS-12		PS-12	850	Nondenom Christian	895
WALKER	Marietta		PS-12		PS-12	1072		896
AUGUSTA PREP	Martinez		PS-12		PS-12	520		497
HERITAGE	Newnan		PS-12		PS-12	363		500
GREATER ATLANTA CHR	Norcross		PS-12		PS-12	1831	•	896
WESLEYAN	Norcross		K-12		K-12	1068	• Nondenom Christian	500
RABUN GAP-NACOOCHEE	Rabun Gap	7-12	6-12		6-12	283	• Presbyterian	501
DARLINGTON	Rome	9-PG	PS-12	9-PG	PS-12	909	•	502
HIGH MEADOWS	Roswell		PS-8		PS-8	341		896
ST FRANCIS SCH-GA	Roswell		K-12		K-12	876		897
ST ANDREW'S SCH-GA	Savannah		PS-12		PS-12	425		898
ST VINCENT'S	Savannah		9-12			350	Roman Catholic	898
SAVANNAH CO DAY	Savannah		PS-12		PS-12	972		503
FREDERICA	St Simons Island		PS-12		PS-12	350		897
BULLOCH	Statesboro		PS-12		PS-12	515		898
GA CHRISTIAN	Valdosta		PS-12		PS-12	230		899

School	Town	Girls' Grade Range Bdg	Girls' Grade Range Day	Boys' Grade Range Bdg	Boys' Grade Range Day	Enr	Learning Disabilities	ESL	Relig Affil	Page
GA VALWOOD	Valdosta		PS-12		PS-12	394				899
HAWAII										
HANAHAUOLI	Honolulu		PS-6		PS-6	205				748
HOLY NATIVITY	Honolulu		PS-6			180			Episcopal	1080
IOLANI	Honolulu		K-12		K-12	1830		•	Episcopal	749
MARYKNOLL	Honolulu		PS-12		PS-12	1395			Roman Catholic	1081
MID-PACIFIC	Honolulu		PS-12		PS-12	1130		•		749
PUNAHOU	Honolulu		K-12		K-12	3774				750
SACRED HRTS ACAD-HI	Honolulu		PS-12			1156		•	Roman Catholic	1081
ST ANDREW'S PRIORY	Honolulu		K-12			500		•	Episcopal	751
ST FRANCIS SCH-HI	Honolulu		6-12			374		•	Roman Catholic	1082
LE JARDIN	Kailua		PS-12		PS-12	600				752
HI PREP	Kamuela	6-12	K-12	6-12	K-12	589		•		752
ISLAND SCH	Lihue		PS-12		PS-12	277				1082
LANAKILA	Waipahu		K-12		K-12	250			Baptist	1082
IDAHO										
BISHOP KELLY	Boise		9-12		9-12	652			Roman Catholic	1031
GEM ST ADVENTIST	Caldwell	9-12	9-12	9-12	9-12	157			Adventist	1032
COMMUNITY SCH-ID	Sun Valley		PS-12		PS-12	315				684
ILLINOIS										

Index by State and City

School	City	Grades	Grades	Enroll	Prgm	Affiliation	Page
DRISCOLL CATHOLIC	Addison		9-12	465		Roman Catholic	939
ST VIATOR	Arlington Heights		9-12	1040		Roman Catholic	939
QUEEN OF PEACE	Burbank		9-12	825		Roman Catholic	939
BREHM	Carbondale	6-PG	6-PG	86	Focus		940
CARBONDALE NEW SCH	Carbondale		PS-8	61			940
CHICAGO ACAD ARTS	Chicago		9-12	160			571
CHICAGO CITY DAY	Chicago		PS-8	280	Prgm		941
DE LA SALLE INST	Chicago		9-12C	1280		Roman Catholic	941
FRANCIS W PARKER	Chicago		PS-12	901			571
HOLY TRINITY HS	Chicago		9-12	400		• Roman Catholic	942
LATIN	Chicago		PS-12	1083			572
LUTHER HS N	Chicago		9-12	260	Prgm	Lutheran-Missouri	942
LUTHER HS S	Chicago		9-12	230		Lutheran	942
MORGAN PARK	Chicago		PS-12	550			573
N SHORE SCH	Chicago		PS-8	100			943
SACRED HEART SCHS-IL	Chicago		K-8C	556	Prgm	Roman Catholic	573
ST IGNATIUS	Chicago		9-12	1321		Roman Catholic	943
ST PATRICK HS	Chicago		9-12	1035		• Roman Catholic	944
ST SCHOLASTICA	Chicago		9-12	290		Roman Catholic	944
U CHICAGO LAB SCHS	Chicago		PS-12	1716			574
MARIAN CATHOLIC	Chicago Heights		9-12	1658		Roman Catholic	575
WILLOWS	Des Plaines		6-12	218		Roman Catholic	944

School Feature Indexes

School	Town	Girls' Grade Range Bdg	Girls' Grade Range Day	Boys' Grade Range Bdg	Boys' Grade Range Day	Enr	Learning Disabilities	ESL	Relig Affil	Page
IL										
AVERY COONLEY	Downers Grove		PS-8		PS-8	362				576
ELGIN	Elgin		PS-12		PS-12	409				577
FOX RIVER CO DAY	Elgin	6-8	PS-8	6-8	PS-8	200		•		577
FOX VALLEY	Elgin		9-12		9-12	34			Lutheran	945
ROYCEMORE	Evanston		PS-12		PS-12	252				578
JOLIET CATHOLIC	Joliet		9-12		9-12	949	Prgm		Roman Catholic	945
LAKE FOREST ACAD	Lake Forest	9-12	9-12	9-12	9-12	321				579
LAKE FOREST CO DAY	Lake Forest		PS-8		PS-8	430				579
ILLIANA CHRISTIAN	Lansing		9-12		9-12	675	Prgm		Nondenom Christian	946
MT ASSISI	Lemont		9-12			311			Roman Catholic	946
BENET	Lisle		9-12		9-12	1290			Roman Catholic	946
MONTINI	Lombard		9-12		9-12	665			Roman Catholic	947
CHRIST HERITAGE ACAD	Northfield		PS-8		PS-8	394			Evangelical	947
FENWICK	Oak Park		9-12		9-12	1152			Roman Catholic	948
CHICAGO CHRISTIAN	Palos Heights		9-12		9-12	478			Nondenom Christian	948
QUINCY NOTRE DAME	Quincy		9-12		9-12	501			Roman Catholic	948
TRINITY HS-IL	River Forest		9-12			480			Roman Catholic	949
KEITH	Rockford		PS-12		PS-12	298				580
WHEATON	West Chicago		9-12		9-12	556	Prgm		Evangelical	949
ST FRANCIS HS-IL	Wheaton		9-12		9-12	731			Roman Catholic	950

Index by State and City

LOYOLA ACAD	Wilmette		9-12		Roman Catholic	950
N SHORE CO DAY	Winnetka		PS-12	9-12		581

INDIANA

CULVER	Culver	9-PG	9-PG	9-PG		582
EVANSVILLE DAY	Evansville		PS-12	PS-12		583
BISHOP DWENGER	Fort Wayne		9-12	9-12	Roman Catholic	951
BISHOP LUERS	Fort Wayne		9-12	9-12	Prgm Roman Catholic	951
CANTERBURY-IN	Fort Wayne		PS-12	PS-12		584
CONCORDIA LUTH-IN	Fort Wayne		9-12	9-12	Lutheran	951
KEYSTONE-IN	Fort Wayne		PS-12	PS-12	Nondenom Christian	952
HOWE	Howe	5-12		5-12	Episcopal	585
BREBEUF	Indianapolis		9-12	9-12	Roman Catholic	952
LUTHERAN HS-IN	Indianapolis		9-12	9-12	Lutheran	953
ORCHARD	Indianapolis		PS-8	PS-8		586
PARK TUDOR	Indianapolis		PS-12	PS-12		586
ST RICHARD'S	Indianapolis		PS-8	PS-8	Episcopal	587
SYCAMORE	Indianapolis		PS-8	PS-8		588
LA LUMIERE	La Porte	9-PG	9-PG	9-PG	Roman Catholic	589
FOREST RIDGE ACAD	Schererville		PS-8	PS-8		953
STANLEY CLARK	South Bend		PS-8	PS-8		589

IOWA

RIVERMONT COLLEGIATE	Bettendorf		PS-12	PS-12		623

School Feature Indexes

School	Town	Girls' Grade Range Bdg	Girls' Grade Range Day	Boys' Grade Range Bdg	Boys' Grade Range Day	Enr	Learning Disabilities	ESL	Relig Affil	Page
IA MAHARISHI	Fairfield	9-12	PS-12	9-12	PS-12	280				979
DOWLING	West Des Moines		9-12		9-12	1150			Roman Catholic	979
KANSAS										
THOMAS MORE PREP	Hays	9-12	9-12	9-12	9-12	260		•	Roman Catholic	980
HYMAN BRAND	Overland Park		K-12		K-12	297			Jewish	980
ST JOHN'S MILIT	Salina			6-12		156		•	Episcopal	625
TOPEKA COLLEGIATE	Topeka		PS-8		PS-8	275				980
INDEPENDENT SCH	Wichita		PS-12		PS-12	750				981
WICHITA COLLEGIATE	Wichita		PS-12		PS-12	967	Prgm			626
KENTUCKY										
ST HENRY	Erlanger		9-12		9-12	525			Roman Catholic	900
ST FRANCIS SCH-KY	Goshen		PS-8		PS-8	492			Episcopal	505
LEXINGTON SCH	Lexington		PS-8		PS-8	505				505
SAYRE	Lexington		PS-12		PS-12	650				506
ASSUMPTION	Louisville		9-12			975	Prgm		Roman Catholic	900
HAYFIELD	Louisville		PS-3		PS-3	100				900
KY CO DAY	Louisville		PS-12		PS-12	811				507
LOUISVILLE COLLEGIAT	Louisville		K-12		K-12	665				507
ST FRANCIS HS-KY	Louisville		9-12		9-12	125			Episcopal	508
ST XAVIER	Louisville				9-12	1440			Roman Catholic	901

TRINITY HS	Louisville			9-12	1445		Roman Catholic	901
ONEIDA	Oneida	6-12	6-12	6-12	278		• Southern Baptist	902
COVINGTON CATHOLIC	Park Hills			9-12	470		Roman Catholic	902
NOTRE DAME ACAD-KY	Park Hills		9-12		596	Prgm	Roman Catholic	902
VILLA MADONNA	Villa Hills		1-12	1-12	400		Roman Catholic	903

LOUISIANA

CATHOLIC HS-LA	Baton Rouge			8-12	915		Roman Catholic	998
DUNHAM	Baton Rouge		PS-12	PS-12	608	Prgm		998
EPISCOPAL HS-LA	Baton Rouge		K-12	K-12	1064		Episcopal	649
EPISCOPAL ACADIANA	Cade		PS-12	PS-12	458		Episcopal	998
ACAD SAC HRT-GR COT	Grand Coteau	8-12	PS-12		357		• Roman Catholic	999
ARCHBISHOP SHAW	Marrero			8-12	550		Roman Catholic	999
CRESCENT CITY BAPT	Metairie		PS-12	PS-12	520		• Baptist	1000
METAIRIE PARK CO DAY	Metairie		K-12	K-12	717			649
RIDGEWOOD PREP	Metairie		PS-12	PS-12	510			650
ST MARTIN'S-LA	Metairie		PS-12	PS-12	775		Episcopal	651
ACAD SAC HRT-NEW ORL	New Orleans		PS-12		819		Roman Catholic	651
HOLY CROSS SCH-LA	New Orleans			5-12	940		Roman Catholic	1000
ISIDORE NEWMAN	New Orleans		PS-12	PS-12	1154			652
JESUIT HS-LA	New Orleans			8-12	1459		Roman Catholic	1000
LOUISE S MCGEHEE	New Orleans		PS-12	PS-PS	475			653
MT CARMEL	New Orleans		8-12		1164		Roman Catholic	1001

School Feature Indexes

	School	Town	Girls' Grade Range Bdg	Girls' Grade Range Day	Boys' Grade Range Bdg	Boys' Grade Range Day	Enr	Learning Disabilities	ESL	Relig Affil	Page
LA	REDEEMER-SETON	New Orleans		9-12		9-12	361			Roman Catholic	1001
	ST ANDREW'S EPIS-LA	New Orleans		PS-6		PS-6	160			Episcopal	1002
	ST MARY'S DOMINICAN	New Orleans		8-12			1068			Roman Catholic	1002
	TRINITY EPIS-LA	New Orleans		PS-8		PS-8	399			Episcopal	1002
	WSTMNSTR CHRISTN-LA	Opelousas		PS-12		PS-12	929	Prgm		Nondenom Christian	1003
	LOYOLA COL PREP	Shreveport		9-12		9-12	400			Roman Catholic	1003
	SOUTHFIELD-LA	Shreveport		PS-8		PS-8	436				654
				MAINE							
	JOHN BAPST	Bangor		9-12		9-12	501				773
	HYDE SCH-BATH	Bath	9-12	9-12	9-12	9-12	202				178
	GOULD	Bethel	9-PG	9-PG	9-PG	9-PG	221				179
	GEO STEVENS	Blue Hill		9-12		9-12	341	Prgm	•		774
	LIBERTY	Blue Hill		9-12		9-12	55				774
	WASH ACAD	East Machias	9-12	9-12	9-12	9-12	344		•		774
	DECK HOUSE	Edgecomb			9-12		11				775
	FRYEBURG	Fryeburg	9-12	9-12	9-12	9-12	690	Prgm	•		181
	RILEY	Glen Cove		PS-9		PS-9	60				775
	HEBRON	Hebron	9-PG	6-PG	9-PG	6-PG	237	Prgm	•		182
	KENTS HILL	Kents Hill	9-PG	9-PG	9-PG	9-PG	215		•		183
	BRIDGTON	North Bridgton			PG-PG	PG-PG	190	Prgm			180

ME CENTRAL	Pittsfield						503	Prgm	•	184
BREAKWATER	Portland		PS-5			PS-5	171			775
CATHERINE MCAULEY	Portland		9-12				276		Roman Catholic	776
CHEVERUS	Portland		9-12			9-12	503	Prgm	Roman Catholic	776
WAYNFLETE	Portland		PS-12			PS-12	544		•	185
BERWICK	South Berwick		K-PG			K-PG	573			179
CHOP POINT	Woolwich	3-12	PS-12	3-12		PS-12	104		• Nondenom Christian	777
N YARMOUTH	Yarmouth		6-12			6-12	302			186

MARYLAND

ALEPH BET	Annapolis		K-5			K-5	61		Jewish	798
KEY	Annapolis		PS-12			PS-12	720			295
ST ANNE'S DAY	Annapolis		PS-8			PS-8	348		Episcopal	799
CHESAPEAKE-MD	Arnold		PS-5			PS-5	309			799
BALTIMORE HEBREW	Baltimore		K-8			K-8	240		Jewish	799
BOY'S LATIN	Baltimore					K-12	634			296
BRYN MAWR	Baltimore		PS-12			PS-PS	918			297
CALVERT HALL	Baltimore					9-12	1149	Prgm	Roman Catholic	298
CALVERT SCH	Baltimore		PS-8			PS-8	478			298
CATHOLIC BALTIMORE	Baltimore		9-12				300		Roman Catholic	800
FRIENDS SCH-MD	Baltimore		PS-12			PS-12	1005		Friends	299
GILMAN	Baltimore					K-12	983			299
MERCY HS-MD	Baltimore		9-12			9-12	515	Prgm	Roman Catholic	800

School Feature Indexes

	School	Town	Girls' Grade Range Bdg	Girls' Grade Range Day	Boys' Grade Range Bdg	Boys' Grade Range Day	Enr	Learning Disabilities	ESL	Relig Affil	Page
MD	MT ST JOSEPH HS	Baltimore				9-12	1100			Roman Catholic	801
	ROLAND PARK	Baltimore		K-12			710				300
	SETON KEOUGH	Baltimore		9-12			502	Prgm		Roman Catholic	801
	BARNESVILLE	Barnesville		PS-8		PS-8	250				801
	HARFORD DAY	Bel Air		PS-8		PS-8	352				301
	JOHN CARROLL	Bel Air		9-12		9-12	815			Roman Catholic	802
	WORCESTER PREP	Berlin		PS-12		PS-12	525				802
	FR INTL	Bethesda		PS-12		PS-12	1102		•		803
	HARBOR SCH	Bethesda		PS-2		PS-2	120				803
	HOLTON-ARMS	Bethesda		3-12			660				302
	LANDON	Bethesda				3-12	660				303
	NORWOOD	Bethesda		K-8		K-8	524				803
	PRIMARY DAY	Bethesda		PS-2		PS-2	138				804
	STONE RIDGE	Bethesda		PS-12		PS-K	792			Roman Catholic	303
	WASH EPISCOPAL	Bethesda		PS-8		PS-8	310			Episcopal	804
	WOODS	Bethesda		PS-8		PS-8	263			Roman Catholic	804
	ELIZABETH SETON	Bladensburg		9-12			553			Roman Catholic	805
	MARYVALE	Brooklandville		6-12			361			Roman Catholic	805
	PARK SCH-MD	Brooklandville		PS-PG		PS-PG	890				304
	ST PAUL'S SCH-MD	Brooklandville		K-4		K-12	864			Episcopal	305

Index by State and City

ST PAUL'S SCH SCH GIRLS	Brooklandville		5-12		463		Episcopal	306
KENT SCH-MD	Chestertown		PS-8		PS-8		191		806
MT AVIAT	Childs		PS-8		PS-8		265		Roman Catholic	806
W NOTTINGHAM	Colora	9-PG	6-PG	9-PG	6-PG	200	Prgm	•	307
COUNTRY SCH-MD	Easton		K-8		K-8	301			308
TRINITY SCH-MD	Ellicott City		K-8		K-8	375		Roman Catholic	806
ST JOHN'S LITERARY	Frederick		9-12		9-12	328		Roman Catholic	807
OLDFIELDS	Glencoe	8-PG	8-PG		187			308
GLENELG COUNTRY	Glenelg		PS-12		PS-12	764			309
HOLY TRINITY DAY	Glenn Dale		PS-8		PS-8	614		Episcopal	807
CALVERTON	Huntingtown		PS-12		PS-12	420			807
DEMATHA	Hyattsville			9-12	969		Roman Catholic	808
GRACE EPISCOPAL	Kensington		PS-6		PS-6	270		Episcopal	808
LEONARD HALL	Leonardtown		6-12		6-12	110			809
TOME	North East		K-12		K-12	355			809
ST JOHN'S EPIS-MD	Olney		K-8		K-8	321		Episcopal	310
GARRISON FOREST	Owings Mills	8-12	PS-12		PS-K	640		•	311
MCDONOGH	Owings Mills	9-12	K-12	9-12	K-12	1260			312
RUXTON	Owings Mills		K-8		K-8	225			809
GIBSON ISLAND	Pasadena		PS-5		PS-5	95			312
BULLIS	Potomac		3-12		3-12	624			313
CONNELLY HOLY CHILD	Potomac		6-12			440		Roman Catholic	314

School Feature Indexes

	School	Town	Girls' Grade Range Bdg	Girls' Grade Range Day	Boys' Grade Range Bdg	Boys' Grade Range Day	Enr	Learning Disabilities	ESL	Relig Affil	Page
MD	GERMAN SCH	Potomac		PS-PG		PS-PG	587				810
	MCLEAN	Potomac		K-12		K-12	495				315
	ST ANDREW'S EPIS-MD	Potomac		6-12		6-12	454			Episcopal	315
	ST FRANCIS EPIS-MD	Potomac		PS-5		PS-5	236			Episcopal	810
	CHARLES E SMITH	Rockville		K-12		K-12	1514		•	Jewish	810
	GREEN ACRES	Rockville		PS-8		PS-8	310				316
	MELVIN J BERMAN	Rockville		PS-12		PS-12	730	Prgm		Jewish	811
	SALISBURY-MD	Salisbury		PS-12		PS-12	400	Prgm			811
	SANDY SPRING FRIENDS	Sandy Spring	9-12	PS-12	9-12	PS-12	514		•	Friends	318
	ARCHBISHOP SPALDING	Severn		9-12		9-12	1049	Prgm		Roman Catholic	811
	BARRIE	Silver Spring		PS-12		PS-12	364				319
	CHELSEA	Silver Spring		5-12		5-12	100	Focus			812
	NEWPORT	Silver Spring		PS-12		PS-12	105				319
	THORNTON FRIENDS	Silver Spring		6-12		6-12	116			Friends	812
	ST JAMES SCH-MD	St James	8-12	8-12	8-12	8-12	223		•	Episcopal	317
	ST TIMOTHY'S	Stevenson	9-PG	9-PG			88		•	Episcopal	320
	LOYOLA BLAKEFIELD	Towson				6-12	970			Roman Catholic	812
	NOTRE DAME PREP-MD	Towson		6-12			736			Roman Catholic	813
	QUEEN ANNE	Upper Marlboro		6-12		6-12	279			Episcopal	321

MASSACHUSETTS

Index by State and City

PHILLIPS ACAD	Andover	9-PG	9-PG	9-PG	9-PG	1083		187
PIKE	Andover		PS-9	PS-9	PS-9	428		188
CUSHING	Ashburnham	9-PG	9-PG	9-PG	9-PG	425	•	189
TRINITY CHRISTIAN-MA	Barnstable		PS-10	PS-10	PS-10	94	Nondenom Christian	190
BELMONT DAY	Belmont		PS-8		PS-8	265		191
BELMONT HILL	Belmont			9-12	7-12	425		191
SHORE	Beverly		K-9		K-9	439		193
GLEN URQUHART	Beverly Farms		K-8		K-8	226		777
BOSTON U ACAD	Boston		8-12		8-12	156		194
COMMONWEALTH	Boston		9-12		9-12	145		194
KINGSLEY	Boston		PS-6		PS-6	141		195
LEARNING PROJECT	Boston		1-6		1-6	96		196
NEWMAN	Boston		9-PG		9-PG	230	•	777
WINSOR	Boston		5-12			420		197
THAYER	Braintree		6-12		6-12	663		198
DEXTER	Brookline				PS-11	353		201
PARK SCH-MA	Brookline		PS-9		PS-9	519		201
SOUTHFIELD-MA	Brookline		PS-10			336		202
GOV DUMMER	Byfield	9-12	9-12	9-12	9-12	376	•	203
BUCKINGHAM BROWNE	Cambridge		PS-12		PS-12	961		204
CAMBRIDGE FRIENDS	Cambridge		PS-8		PS-8	265	Friends	205
CAMBRIDGE MONTESSORI	Cambridge		PS-6		PS-6	200		778

School Feature Indexes

	School	Town	Girls' Grade Range Bdg	Girls' Grade Range Day	Boys' Grade Range Bdg	Boys' Grade Range Day	Enr	Learning Disabilities	ESL	Relig Affil	Page
MA	FAYERWEATHER	Cambridge		PS-8		PS-8	195				205
	SHADY HILL	Cambridge		PS-8		PS-8	500				206
	BEAVER CO DAY	Chestnut Hill		6-12		6-12	408				199
	BRIMMER & MAY	Chestnut Hill		PS-12		PS-12	390		•		199
	CHESTNUT HILL SCH	Chestnut Hill		PS-6		PS-6	242				200
	CONCORD ACAD	Concord	9-12	9-12	9-12	9-12	355				207
	FENN	Concord				4-9	308				208
	MIDDLESEX	Concord	9-12	9-12	9-12	9-12	341				209
	NASHOBA BROOKS	Concord		PS-8			300				210
	CLARK	Danvers		K-8		K-8	61				778
	ST JOHN'S PREP-MA	Danvers				9-12	1200			Roman Catholic	210
	DEDHAM CO DAY	Dedham		PS-8		PS-8	242				212
	NOBLE & GREENOUGH	Dedham	9-12	7-12	9-12	7-12	546				212
	URSULINE ACAD-MA	Dedham		7-12			395			Roman Catholic	779
	BEMENT	Deerfield	3-9	K-9	3-9	K-9	245		•		213
	DEERFIELD ACAD	Deerfield	9-PG	9-PG	9-PG	9-PG	603				214
	EAGLEBROOK	Deerfield			6-9	6-9	268		•		215
	BOSTON COL HS	Dorchester				9-12	1300		•	Roman Catholic	779
	EPIPHANY-MA	Dorchester		5-8		5-8	82	Prgm		Episcopal	779
	CHARLES RIVER	Dover		PS-8		PS-8	206				216

Index by State and City 67

RIVERVIEW	East Sandwich	6-PG	7-PG	6-PG	7-PG	182	Focus		238
WILLISTON NORTHAMPT	Easthampton	9-PG	9-12	9-PG	9-12	540		•	217
POPE JOHN XXIII	Everett		9-12		9-12	461		Roman Catholic	780
ANTIOCH	Fall River		PS-8		PS-8	87			780
FALMOUTH	Falmouth		7-12		7-12	210			218
APPLEWILD	Fitchburg		K-9		K-9	320			218
SAGE	Foxboro		PS-8		PS-8	160			780
SUDBURY VALLEY	Framingham	Ungraded		Ungraded		200			219
STONELEIGH-BURNHAM	Greenfield	8-PG	7-PG			157		•	220
GROTON	Groton	8-12	8-12	8-12	8-12	355		Episcopal	221
LAWRENCE ACAD	Groton	9-12	9-12	9-12	9-12	394		•	222
EAGLE HILL-MA	Hardwick	8-12	8-12	8-12	8-12	148	Focus		223
DERBY	Hingham		PS-9		PS-9	304			224
SACRED HEART HS-MA	Kingston		7-12		7-12	583		Roman Catholic	781
BERKSHIRE CO DAY	Lenox		PS-12		PS-12	353			224
LEXINGTON CHRISTIAN	Lexington		6-12		6-12	350	Prgm	• Nondenom Christian	225
LEXINGTON MONTESSORI	Lexington		PS-6		PS-6	231			781
CARROLL	Lincoln		2-8		2-8	233	Focus		226
MALDEN CATHOLIC	Malden		9-12		9-12	764		Roman Catholic	782
BROOKWOOD	Manchester		PS-8		PS-8	395			227
TOWER SCH	Marblehead		PS-9		PS-9	303			228
TABOR	Marion	9-12	9-12	9-12	9-12	492		•	228

School Feature Indexes

	School	Town	Girls' Grade Range Bdg	Girls' Grade Range Day	Boys' Grade Range Bdg	Boys' Grade Range Day	Enr	Learning Disabilities	ESL	Relig Affil	Page
MA	HILLSIDE	Marlborough			5-9	5-9	120	Prgm	•		229
	DELPHI	Milton		PS-8		PS-8	130				782
	MILTON ACAD	Milton	9-12	K-12	9-12	K-12	991				230
	MONTROSE	Natick		6-12			129				782
	WALNUT HILL	Natick	9-12	9-12	9-12	9-12	280		•		231
	ST SEBASTIAN'S	Needham				7-12	342			Roman Catholic	232
	NEWTON CO DAY	Newton		5-12			365			Roman Catholic	234
	MONTESSORI EDUCARE	Newton Centre		PS-6		PS-6	260				783
	BROOKS	North Andover	9-12	9-12	9-12	9-12	354			Episcopal	187
	BISHOP STANG	North Dartmouth		9-12		9-12	754			Roman Catholic	783
	FRIENDS ACAD-MA	North Dartmouth		PS-8		PS-8	277				211
	SMITH COL CAMPUS SCH	Northampton		K-6		K-6	263				234
	LINDEN HILL	Northfield			Ungraded		25	Focus	•		235
	NORTHFIELD MT HERMON	Northfield	9-PG	9-PG	9-PG	9-PG	886		•		236
	CAPE COD ACAD	Osterville		K-12		K-12	400				237
	MISS HALL'S	Pittsfield	9-12	9-12			171		•		237
	LANDMARK SCH	Prides Crossing	8-12	2-12	8-12	2-12	424	Focus			192
	BERKSHIRE SCH	Sheffield	9-PG	9-PG	9-PG	9-PG	385		•		239
	ST JOHN'S HS-MA	Shrewsbury				9-12	1058			Roman Catholic	252
	FAY	Southborough	6-9	1-9	6-9	1-9	385		•		240

Index by State and City

ST MARK'S SCH-MA	Southborough	9-12	9-12	9-12	9-12	329		Episcopal	241
MACDUFFIE	Springfield	9-12	6-12	9-12	6-12	215		•	242
PIONEER VALLEY	Springfield		PS-12		PS-12	320	Prgm		784
CORWIN-RUSSELL	Sudbury		6-PG		6-PG	51	Focus		784
WILLOW HILL	Sudbury		6-12		6-12	57	Focus		243
ACAD OF NOTRE DAME	Tyngsboro		K-12		K-8	750		Roman Catholic	784
BARTLETT	Waltham		PS-6		PS-6	140			243
CHAPEL HILL-CHAUNCY	Waltham	9-PG	9-PG	9-PG	9-PG	160	Prgm	•	244
DANA HALL	Wellesley	9-12	6-12			453			245
TENACRE	Wellesley		PS-6		PS-6	191			246
FESSENDEN	West Newton			5-9	K-9	476		•	233
CATHOLIC MEMORIAL	West Roxbury				7-12	850		Roman Catholic	785
ROXBURY LATIN	West Roxbury				7-12	295			196
WHITE OAK	Westfield		4-12		4-12	101	Focus		785
CAMBRIDGE SCH-MA	Weston	9-PG	9-PG	9-PG	9-PG	310		•	246
MEADOWBROOK-MA	Weston		PS-8		PS-8	278			247
RIVERS	Weston		6-12		6-12	410			248
XAVERIAN BROS	Westwood				9-12	1045		Roman Catholic	786
BUXTON	Williamstown	9-12	9-12	9-12	9-12	90		•	249
PINE COBBLE	Williamstown		PS-9		PS-9	145			250
WINCHENDON	Winchendon	8-PG	8-PG	8-PG	8-PG	219	Prgm	•	250
CHILDREN'S OWN	Winchester		PS-K		PS-K	80			786

School Feature Indexes

	School	Town	Girls' Grade Range Bdg	Girls' Grade Range Day	Boys' Grade Range Bdg	Boys' Grade Range Day	Enr	Learning Disabilities	ESL	Relig Affil	Page
MA	BANCROFT	Worcester		K-12		K-12	600				251
	HOLY NAME	Worcester		7-12		7-12	900			Roman Catholic	786
	NOTRE DAME-WORCESTER	Worcester		9-12			310			Roman Catholic	252
	WORCESTER ACAD	Worcester	9-PG	6-PG	9-PG	6-PG	643		•		253

MICHIGAN

	School	Town	Girls' Grade Range Bdg	Girls' Grade Range Day	Boys' Grade Range Bdg	Boys' Grade Range Day	Enr	Learning Disabilities	ESL	Relig Affil	Page
	GREENHILLS-MI	Ann Arbor		6-12		6-12	496				591
	SUMMERS-KNOLL	Ann Arbor		PS-8		PS-8	70				953
	DETROIT CO DAY	Beverly Hills	8-12	PS-12	8-12	PS-12	1536				594
	KENSINGTON	Beverly Hills		PS-8		PS-8	191			Roman Catholic	954
	OUR LADY QN MARTYRS	Beverly Hills		PS-8		PS-8	486			Roman Catholic	954
	ETON	Birmingham		1-12		1-12	190	Focus			954
	ACAD SACRED HEART-MI	Bloomfield Hills		PS-12[C]		PS-8[C]	520			Roman Catholic	592
	BR RICE	Bloomfield Hills				9-12	695			Roman Catholic	955
	CRANBROOK	Bloomfield Hills	9-12	PS-12[C]	9-12	PS-12[C]	1608		•		592
	ROEPER	Bloomfield Hills		PS-12		PS-12	627				594
	DETROIT WALDORF	Detroit		PS-8		PS-8	178				955
	MERCY HS-MI	Farmington Hills		9-12			843			Roman Catholic	956
	VALLEY SCH-MI	Flint		PS-12		PS-12	137				956
	LEELANAU	Glen Arbor	9-12	9-12	9-12	9-12	60	Focus	•		597
	GRAND RAPIDS BAPTIST	Grand Rapids		PS-12		PS-12	712	Prgm		Baptist	956

Index by State and City

School	City		Grades	Enrollment		Religion	Page
GRAND RAPIDS CHRIST	Grand Rapids		PS-12	2933			957
GROSSE POINTE	Grosse Pointe Farms		PS-8	365		•	595
U LIGGETT	Grosse Pointe Woods		PS-12	659			596
HILLSDALE	Hillsdale		K-12	154			957
INTERLOCHEN	Interlochen	9-PG	9-PG	455		•	597
MONSIGNOR JR HACKETT	Kalamazoo		9-12	480	Prgm	Roman Catholic	958
LANSING CATHOLIC	Lansing		9-12	510		Roman Catholic	958
LADYWOOD	Livonia		9-12	500		Roman Catholic	958
ST MARY CATHOLIC	Monroe		9-12	442		Roman Catholic	959
ST MARY'S PREP	Orchard Lake	9-12	9-12	500		Roman Catholic •	959
SPRING VALE	Owosso	9-12	9-12	27		Church of God	960
KINGSBURY SCH	Oxford		PS-8	132			598
NOTRE DAME PREP-MI	Pontiac		9-12	803		Roman Catholic	960
KALAMAZOO	Portage		PS-8	179	Prgm		960
BISHOP BORGESS	Redford		9-12	220	Prgm	Roman Catholic	961
GIBSON SCH	Redford		PS-8	100			961
SHRINE	Royal Oak		9-12	286		Roman Catholic	961
MI LUTHERAN	Saginaw	9-12	9-12	274		Lutheran •	962
DE LA SALLE	Warren		9-12	705		Roman Catholic	962

MINNESOTA

School	City		Grades	Enrollment		Religion	Page
MARANATHA CHRISTIAN	Brooklyn Park		PS-12	720		Nondenom Christian	981
ST JOHN'S PREP-MN	Collegeville	9-PG	7-PG	320		Roman Catholic •	627

School Feature Indexes

	School	Town	Girls' Grade Range Bdg	Girls' Grade Range Day	Boys' Grade Range Bdg	Boys' Grade Range Day	Enr	Learning Disabilities	ESL	Relig Affil	Page
MN	MARSHALL	Duluth		5-12		5-12	554				982
	INTL SCH OF MN	Eden Prairie		PS-12		PS-12	528		•		628
	BETHLEHEM	Faribault		7-12		7-12	235			Roman Catholic	982
	SHATTUCK-ST MARY'S	Faribault	6-PG	6-PG	6-PG	6-PG	294	Prgm	•	Episcopal	628
	HILLCREST	Fergus Falls	10-12	7-12	10-12	7-12	196		•	Lutheran	982
	BLAKE	Hopkins		PS-12		PS-12	1316				629
	MAYER LUTHERAN	Mayer		9-PG		9-PG	265			Lutheran-Missouri	983
	CONVENT VISITATION	Mendota Heights		PS-12		PS-6	578			Roman Catholic	632
	ST THOMAS ACAD	Mendota Heights				7-12	659			Roman Catholic	633
	BRECK	Minneapolis		PS-12		PS-12	1196			Episcopal	630
	DE LA SALLE HS-MN	Minneapolis		9-12		9-12	630			Roman Catholic	983
	MINNEHAHA	Minneapolis		PS-12		PS-12	1230			Evangelical Covenant	631
	MARTIN LUTHER-MN	Northrop		9-12		9-12	66			Lutheran-Missouri	984
	GROVES ACAD	St Louis Park		1-12		1-12	170	Focus			984
	FRIENDS SCH OF MN	St Paul		K-8		K-8	140			Friends	984
	ST AGNES SCH	St Paul		K-12		K-12	475			Roman Catholic	985
	ST PAUL ACAD/SUMMIT	St Paul		K-12		K-12	924				632
	COTTER	Winona	9-12	7-12	9-12	7-12	398		•	Roman Catholic	985

MISSISSIPPI

	School	Town	Bdg	Day	Bdg	Day	Enr		ESL	Relig Affil	Page
	ST STANISLAUS	Bay St Louis			6-12	6-12	550		•	Roman Catholic	1004

Index by State and City 73

MERCY CROSS	Biloxi		7-12	365	Roman Catholic	1004
JACKSON ACAD	Jackson		PS-12	1514	Prgm	1005
JACKSON PREP	Jackson		7-12	810	Prgm	1005
CATHEDRAL SCH-MS	Natchez		PS-12	660	Prgm Roman Catholic	1005
OXFORD U SCH	Oxford		PS-6	122		1006
ST ANDREW'S EPIS-MS	Ridgeland		PS-12	1161	Episcopal	655
ALL SAINTS' EPIS-MS	Vicksburg	7-12	7-12	112	• Episcopal	655

MISSOURI

CHESTERFIELD DAY	Chesterfield		PS-12	501		986
WILSON SCH-MO	Clayton		PS-6	181		643
OAKHILL DAY	Gladstone		PS-7	280		986
ARCHBISHOP O'HARA	Kansas City		9-12	507	Roman Catholic	986
BARSTOW	Kansas City		PS-12	623		635
LUTHERAN HS-MO	Kansas City		9-12	66	Lutheran-Missouri	987
PEMBROKE HILL	Kansas City		PS-12	1192		635
ROCKHURST	Kansas City		9-12	1032	Roman Catholic	987
ST PAUL'S EPIS DAY	Kansas City		PS-8	475	Episcopal	987
WENTWORTH	Lexington	10-PG	8-PG	217	•	636
MO MILIT	Mexico	6-PG		255	•	637
BISHOP DUBOURG	St Louis		9-12	669	Prgm Roman Catholic	988
CHAMINADE COL PREP	St Louis	6-12	6-12	948	Roman Catholic	638
COMMUNITY SCH-MO	St Louis		PS-6	335		639

School Feature Indexes

School	Town	Girls' Grade Range Bdg	Girls' Grade Range Day	Boys' Grade Range Bdg	Boys' Grade Range Day	Enr	Learning Disabilities	ESL	Relig Affil	Page
MO COR JESU	St Louis		9-12			569			Roman Catholic	988
CROSSROADS-MO	St Louis		7-12		7-12	205				989
DE SMET	St Louis				9-12	1260			Roman Catholic	989
FORSYTH SCH	St Louis		PS-6		PS-6	360				639
INCARNATE WORD-MO	St Louis		9-12			550			Roman Catholic	989
JOHN BURROUGHS	St Louis		7-12		7-12	590				640
LOGOS	St Louis		7-12		7-12	133	Focus			990
MARY INST ST LOUIS	St Louis		PS-12		PS-12	1227				640
METROPOLITAN	St Louis		5-12		5-12	63	Focus			990
NEW CITY	St Louis		PS-6		PS-6	360				990
NOTRE DAME HS-MO	St Louis		9-12			450			Roman Catholic	991
ROHAN WOODS	St Louis		PS-6		PS-6	150				991
ROSATI-KAIN	St Louis		9-12			401			Roman Catholic	992
ST JOSEPH'S ACAD	St Louis		9-12			629			Roman Catholic	992
ST LOUIS PRIORY	St Louis				7-12	390			Roman Catholic	641
THOMAS JEFFERSON	St Louis	7-12	7-12	7-12	7-12	81		•		642
VIANNEY	St Louis				9-12	720			Roman Catholic	992
VISITATION	St Louis		PS-12		PS-PS	690			Roman Catholic	993
WESTMINSTER CHRIST	St Louis		7-12		7-12	825			Nondenom Christian	993
WHITFIELD	St Louis		6-12		6-12	474				994

Index by State and City

NERINX HALL	Webster Groves	9-12		605		Roman Catholic	994
MONTANA							
HEADWATERS	Bozeman		6-12	6-9			1032
LUSTRE	Frazer	9-12	9-12	24		Nondenom Christian	1032
LOYOLA SACRED HEART	Missoula	9-12	9-12	34		Roman Catholic	1033
NEBRASKA							
MT MICHAEL	Elkhorn		9-12	208		Roman Catholic	645
MESSIAH LUTHERAN-NE	Lincoln	PS-6	9-12	165		Lutheran	995
BROWNELL-TALBOT	Omaha	PS-12	PS-6	327			645
			PS-12	475			
NEVADA							
BISHOP GORMAN	Las Vegas	9-12	9-12	857		Roman Catholic	1039
FAITH LUTHERAN	Las Vegas	6-12	6-12	1115		Lutheran	1039
MEADOWS	Las Vegas	PS-12	PS-12	870			1040
SAGE RIDGE	Reno	5-12	5-12	158			1040
NEW HAMPSHIRE							
PROCTOR	Andover	9-12	9-12	336	Prgm		255
WHITE MTN	Bethlehem	9-PG	9-PG	100	Prgm	Episcopal	256
CARDIGAN MTN	Canaan		6-9	192			257
ST PAUL'S SCH-NH	Concord	9-12	9-12	525		Episcopal	257
ST THOMAS AQUINAS HS	Dover		9-12	703		Roman Catholic	787
DUBLIN	Dublin	9-PG	9-PG	132	Focus		258
PHILLIPS EXETER	Exeter	9-PG	9-PG	1052			259

School Feature Indexes

School	Town	Girls' Grade Range Bdg	Girls' Grade Range Day	Boys' Grade Range Bdg	Boys' Grade Range Day	Enr	Learning Disabilities	ESL	Relig Affil	Page
NH DERRYFIELD	Manchester		6-12		6-12	378				261
KIMBALL UNION	Meriden	9-PG	9-PG	9-PG	9-PG	311				261
NEW HAMPTON	New Hampton	9-PG	9-PG	9-PG	9-PG	340		•		262
RUNNEMEDE	Plainfield		K-12		K-12	93				787
HOLDERNESS	Plymouth	9-PG	9-PG	9-PG	9-PG	280			Episcopal	263
HAMPSHIRE COUNTRY	Rindge			3-12		22	Focus			264
MEETING SCH	Rindge	8-PG	8-PG	8-PG	8-PG	30		•	Friends	265
TILTON	Tilton	9-PG	9-PG	9-PG	9-PG	231	Prgm	•	Methodist	266
WATERVILLE VALLEY	Waterville Valley	6-12	6-12	6-12	6-12	85				787
BREWSTER	Wolfeboro	9-PG	9-PG	9-PG	9-PG	367		•		267
NEW JERSEY										
BLAIR	Blairstown	9-PG	9-PG	9-PG	9-PG	434			Presbyterian	323
WOODLAND CO DAY	Bridgeton		PS-8		PS-8	155				324
ST MARY'S HALL-NJ	Burlington		PS-12		PS-12	187			Episcopal	324
ACAD OF ST ELIZABETH	Convent Station		9-12			242			Roman Catholic	335
HOLY CROSS HS-NJ	Delran		9-12		9-12	812			Roman Catholic	813
ACAD HOLY ANGELS	Demarest		9-12			546			Roman Catholic	814
WARDLAW-HARTRIDGE	Edison		PS-12		PS-12	420		•		325
BENEDICTINE ACAD	Elizabeth		9-12			190			Roman Catholic	814
DWIGHT-ENGLEWOOD	Englewood		PS-12		PS-12	1007				326

ELISABETH MORROW	Englewood		PS-8		PS-8	447	•		327
VILLA VICTORIA	Ewing		PS-12			280		Roman Catholic	815
FAR HILLS	Far Hills		PS-8		PS-8	415			327
GILL ST BERNARD'S	Gladstone		PS-12		PS-12	600			328
BAPTIST HS	Haddon Heights		9-12		9-12	223	Prgm	Baptist	815
HADDONFIELD FRIENDS	Haddonfield		PS-8		PS-8	146		Friends	815
NEWGRANGE	Hamilton		Ungraded		Ungraded	97	Focus		816
PEDDIE	Hightstown	9-PG	9-PG	9-PG	9-PG	520	•		329
HUDSON SCH	Hoboken		5-12		5-12	207	•		816
ST DOMINIC ACAD	Jersey City		9-12			485		Roman Catholic	816
ST PETER'S PREP	Jersey City				9-12	931		Roman Catholic	330
LAWRENCEVILLE	Lawrenceville	9-PG	9-PG	9-PG	9-PG	807			331
NOTRE DAME HS-NJ	Lawrenceville		9-12		9-12	1270		Roman Catholic	817
CHRISTIAN BROS-NJ	Lincroft				9-12	919		Roman Catholic	817
PINGRY	Martinsville		K-12		K-12	1016			332
ST JOSEPH HS-NJ	Metuchen				9-12	844		Roman Catholic	818
MONTCLAIR COOP	Montclair		PS-6		PS-6	160			818
MONTCLAIR KIMBERLEY	Montclair		PS-12		PS-12	1025			333
MOORESTOWN FRIENDS	Moorestown		PS-12		PS-12	717		Friends	334
DELBARTON	Morristown				7-12	542		Roman Catholic	336
MORRISTOWN-BEARD	Morristown		6-12		6-12	480			336
PECK	Morristown		K-8		K-8	306			337

Index by State and City   77

NJ

School	Town	Girls' Grade Range Bdg	Girls' Grade Range Day	Boys' Grade Range Bdg	Boys' Grade Range Day	Enr	Learning Disabilities	ESL	Relig Affil	Page
VILLA WALSH	Morristown		7-12			235			Roman Catholic	819
WILSON SCH-NJ	Mountain Lakes		PS-8		PS-8	75				338
FRIENDS MULLICA HILL	Mullica Hill		PS-8		PS-8	283			Friends	338
YAVNEH	Paramus		PS-8		PS-8	751	Prgm		Orthodox Jewish	819
COLLEGIATE-NJ	Passaic Park		PS-12		PS-12	170				339
PENNINGTON	Pennington	7-12	6-12	7-12	6-12	443	Prgm	•	Methodist	339
TIMOTHY CHRISTIAN-NJ	Piscataway		K-12		K-12	649	Prgm			819
PURNELL	Pottersville	9-12	9-12			106	Prgm	•		340
AM BOYCHOIR	Princeton			5-8	5-8	53				341
HUN	Princeton	9-PG	6-PG	9-PG	6-PG	587	Prgm	•		342
PRINCETON ACAD	Princeton				PS-8	210			Roman Catholic	820
PRINCETON DAY	Princeton		PS-12		PS-12	890				343
PRINCETON FRIENDS	Princeton		PS-8		PS-8	125			Friends	820
STUART CO DAY	Princeton		PS-12		PS-PS	552			Roman Catholic	344
RUMSON	Rumson		PS-8		PS-8	450				344
SADDLE RIVER	Saddle River		K-12		K-12	327				345
FAR BROOK	Short Hills		PS-8		PS-8	218				346
HILLTOP	Sparta		PS-8		PS-8	230				821
KENT PLACE	Summit		PS-12		PS-PS	632				347
OAK KNOLL	Summit		K-12		K-6	549			Roman Catholic	347

Index by State and City

COMMUNITY SCH-NJ	Teaneck						821
RANNEY	Tinton Falls	PS-12	PS-12	170	Focus		348
ELLISON	Vineland	PS-8	PS-8	124		•	821
SOLOMON SCHECHTER-NJ	West Orange	PS-12	PS-12	860		•	Jewish	822

NEW MEXICO

ALBUQUERQUE ACAD	Albuquerque	6-12	6-12	1064		692
BOSQUE	Albuquerque	6-12	6-12	408		1041
MANZANO	Albuquerque	PS-5	PS-5	435		692
MENAUL	Albuquerque	6-12	6-12	213	Presbyterian	1041
ST PIUS-NM	Albuquerque	9-12	9-12	1052	Roman Catholic	1042
SANDIA PREP	Albuquerque	6-12	6-12	645		693
MCCURDY	Espanola	PS-12	PS-12	405	United Methodist	1042
ARMAND HAMMER	Montezuma	11-12		200		•	694
REHOBOTH	Rehoboth	K-12	K-12	414	Nondenom Christian	1042
NM MILIT	Roswell	9-12		989		1043
RIO GRANDE	Santa Fe	K-6	K-6	122		1043
SANTA FE PREP	Santa Fe	7-12	7-12	333		695

NEW YORK

ALBANY ACAD	Albany	PS-PS	8-12	PS-PG	365		350
ALBANY ACAD GIRLS	Albany	PS-12	PS-12	332		350
CHRIST BROS-ALBANY	Albany		6-12	539	Roman Catholic	822
DOANE STUART	Albany	PS-12	PS-12	265		351

	School	Town	Girls' Grade Range Bdg	Girls' Grade Range Day	Boys' Grade Range Bdg	Boys' Grade Range Day	Enr	Learning Disabilities	ESL	Relig Affil	Page
NY	KILDONAN	Amenia	6-PG	2-PG	6-PG	2-PG	142	Focus			352
	MAPLEBROOK	Amenia	6-PG	6-PG	6-PG	6-PG	116	Focus			823
	RIPPOWAM CISQUA	Bedford		PS-9		PS-9	571				353
	SUSQUEHANNA	Binghamton		PS-10		PS-10	56				823
	MELROSE	Brewster		PS-8		PS-8	184			Episcopal	823
	ACAD OF MT ST URSULA	Bronx		9-12			450			Roman Catholic	824
	FORDHAM PREP	Bronx				9-12	905			Roman Catholic	354
	BERKELEY CARROLL	Brooklyn		PS-12		PS-12	785				357
	BISH KEARN-BROOKLYN	Brooklyn		9-12			1060	Prgm		Roman Catholic	824
	BISHOP LOUGHLIN	Brooklyn		9-12		9-12	880			Roman Catholic	825
	BROOKLYN HTS MONT	Brooklyn		PS-8		PS-8	238	Prgm			825
	PACKER	Brooklyn		PS-12		PS-12	935				358
	LONG ISLAND LUTHERAN	Brookville		6-12		6-12	604			Lutheran	825
	BUFFALO SEMINARY	Buffalo		9-12			173				359
	CANISIUS	Buffalo				9-12	800			Roman Catholic	826
	ELMWOOD FRANKLIN	Buffalo		PS-8		PS-8	369				359
	MT ST JOSEPH ACAD-NY	Buffalo		PS-8		PS-8	186			Roman Catholic	826
	NARDIN	Buffalo		PS-12		PS-8	973			Roman Catholic	827
	NICHOLS	Buffalo		5-12		5-12	590				360
	PARK SCH-NY	Buffalo		PS-12		PS-12	264		•		361

ST JOSEPH'S COLLEG	Buffalo		9-12	852		Roman Catholic	827
GREEN MEADOW	Chestnut Ridge	PS-12	PS-12	400	•		827
ST AGNES HS	College Point	9-12	9-12	500	•	Roman Catholic	828
ROCKLAND CO DAY	Congers	PS-12	PS-12	170			400
BROOKWOOD-NY	Cooperstown	PS-6	PS-6	75			828
NY MILIT	Cornwall-on-Hudson	7-12	7-12	389	•		361
STORM KING	Cornwall-on-Hudson	9-PG	7-PG	123	Prgm		362
MANLIUS PEBBLE HILL	DeWitt		PS-PG	587	•		413
MASTERS SCH-NY	Dobbs Ferry	9-12	5-12^C	504	•		363
LAUREL HILL	East Setauket		PS-8	450			829
CATHEDRAL PREP	Elmhurst		9-12	181		Roman Catholic	829
WINDSOR	Flushing	6-PG	6-PG	125	•		405
KEW-FOREST	Forest Hills	K-12	K-12	385			404
ST FRANCIS PREP	Fresh Meadows	9-12	9-12	2728		Roman Catholic	829
WALDORF SCH-GARDEN	Garden City	PS-12	PS-12	368			830
HAWTHORNE VALLEY	Ghent	PS-12	PS-12	315			830
GREEN VALE	Glen Head	PS-9	PS-9	475			831
HOOSIC	Hoosick	8-PG	8-PG	123	•	Episcopal	364
HOUGHTON	Houghton	9-PG	7-12	214	•	Wesleyan	831
LONG ISLAND SCH	Huntington Station	K-9	K-9	287			831
MARY LOUIS	Jamaica Estates	9-12		1037		Roman Catholic	832
HARVEY	Katonah	7-12	6-12	290			365

Index by State and City — 81

School	Town	Girls' Grade Range Bdg	Girls' Grade Range Day	Boys' Grade Range Bdg	Boys' Grade Range Day	Enr	Learning Disabilities	ESL	Relig Affil	Page
NY NATL SPORTS ACAD	Lake Placid	8-PG	8-PG	8-PG	8-PG	86	Prgm			832
N COUNTRY	Lake Placid	4-9	4-9	4-9	4-9	77		•		366
NORTHWOOD	Lake Placid	9-PG	9-PG	9-PG	9-PG	160		•		367
FR-AMER SCH	Larchmont		PS-10		PS-10	599		•		833
FRIENDS ACAD-NY	Locust Valley		PS-12		PS-12	748			Friends	367
PORTLEDGE	Locust Valley		PS-12		PS-12	408				368
ST GREGORY'S SCH	Loudonville		PS-K		PS-8	200			Roman Catholic	833
MARTIN LUTHER	Maspeth		9-12		9-12	419			Lutheran	833
GRACE DAY	Massapequa		PS-8		PS-8	400			Episcopal	834
DUTCHESS	Millbrook		K-8		K-8	160				369
MILLBROOK	Millbrook	9-12	9-12	9-12	9-12	238		•		369
CHAMINADE HS	Mineola				9-12	1600			Roman Catholic	834
SOUNDVIEW	Mount Kisco		6-12		6-12	80				834
DARROW	New Lebanon	9-PG	9-PG	9-PG	9-PG	125		•		371
IONA PREP	New Rochelle				9-12	775			Roman Catholic	835
URSULINE SCH	New Rochelle		6-12			811			Roman Catholic	835
ABRAHAM JOSHUA HESCH	New York		PS-12		PS-12	615		•	Jewish	836
ALEXANDER ROBERTSON	New York		K-5		K-5	68			Presbyterian	836
ALLEN-STEVENSON	New York				K-9	384				372
BEEKMAN	New York		9-PG		9-PG	80		•		372

82 School Feature Indexes

Index by State and City

BIRCH WATHEN LENOX	New York	K-12	K-12	450		373
BREARLEY	New York	K-12		676		374
BROWNING	New York		K-12	370		374
BUCKLEY SCH-NY	New York		K-9	351		375
CAEDMON	New York	PS-5	PS-5	200		836
CALHOUN	New York	PS-12	PS-12	669		376
CATHEDRAL SCH-NY	New York	K-8	K-8	241	Episcopal	376
CHAPIN-NY	New York	K-12	K-12	658		377
CHILDREN'S STOREFRNT	New York	PS-8	PS-8	176		837
CITY & COUNTRY	New York	PS-8	PS-8	268		378
COLLEGIATE-NY	New York		K-12	623		378
COLUMBIA GRAMMAR	New York	PS-12	PS-12	1022	Prgm •	379
CONVENT SAC HEART-NY	New York	PS-12		649	Roman Catholic	380
CORLEARS	New York	PS-4	PS-4	123		837
DALTON	New York	K-12	K-12	1316		381
DOMINICAN ACAD	New York	9-12	9-12	233	Roman Catholic	837
DWIGHT SCH	New York	PS-12	PS-12	431	Prgm •	382
GRACE CHURCH	New York	PS-8	PS-8	392	Episcopal	383
HEWITT	New York	K-12		461		383
LA SCUOLA D'ITALIA	New York	PS-12	PS-12	190	•	384
LITTLE RED/EL IRWIN	New York	PS-12	PS-12	550		385
LOYOLA SCH	New York	9-12	9-12	205	Roman Catholic	385

School	Town	Girls' Grade Range Bdg	Girls' Grade Range Day	Boys' Grade Range Bdg	Boys' Grade Range Day	Enr	Learning Disabilities	ESL	Relig Affil	Page
NY LYCEE FRANCAIS-NYC	New York		PS-12		PS-12	1200		•		386
LYCEUM KENNEDY	New York		PS-12		PS-12	145		•		386
MANHATTAN COUNTRY	New York		PS-8		PS-8	181				387
MANHATTAN DAY	New York		PS-8		PS-8	420	Prgm		Jewish	838
MARYMOUNT SCH	New York		PS-12		PS-PS	531			Roman Catholic	388
METROPOLITAN MONT	New York		PS-6		PS-6	193				838
NIGHTINGALE-BAMFORD	New York		K-12			533				388
PROFESSIONAL CHILD	New York		4-12		4-12	195		•		389
REGIS HS	New York				9-12	527			Roman Catholic	390
ROBT L STEVENSON-NY	New York		7-12		7-12	74	Focus			391
RODEPH SHOLOM	New York		PS-8		PS-8	650			Jewish	838
RUDOLF STEINER	New York		PS-12		PS-12	340				391
ST BERNARD'S	New York				K-9	367				392
ST DAVID'S-NY	New York				PS-8	375			Roman Catholic	392
ST LUKE'S SCH-NY	New York		PS-8		PS-8	195			Episcopal	393
ST THOMAS CHOIR	New York			4-8		33			Episcopal	394
ST VINCENT FERRER	New York		9-12			490			Roman Catholic	839
SOLOMON SCHECHTER-NY	New York		K-8		K-8	138			Jewish	839
SPENCE	New York		K-12			591				395
STEPHEN GAYNOR	New York		Ungraded		Ungraded	118	Focus			840

Index by State and City

TOWN SCH-NY	New York		PS-8	382		396
TREVOR	New York		PS-12	784		396
TRINITY SCH-NY	New York		K-12	959		Episcopal	397
UN INTL	New York		K-12	1460	•		398
WINSTON PREP	New York		6-12	140	Focus		840
XAVIER-NY	New York		9-12	926		Roman Catholic	840
YORK PREP	New York		6-12	310	Prgm		399
HOLY CHILD ACAD-NY	Old Westbury		PS-8	172		Roman Catholic	841
E WOODS	Oyster Bay		PS-9	250			400
TRINITY-PAWLING	Pawling		9-PG	7-PG	315	Prgm	• Episcopal	401
SETON CATHOLIC	Plattsburgh	7-12	7-12	350		• Roman Catholic	841
VINCENT SMITH	Port Washington		5-12	81	Focus		402
OAKWOOD FRIENDS	Poughkeepsie	9-12	6-12	158	Prgm	• Friends	403
POUGHKEEPSIE DAY	Poughkeepsie		PS-12	345			403
FIELDSTON	Riverdale		PS-12	1611	Prgm		353
HORACE MANN	Riverdale		PS-12	1740			355
RIVERDALE	Riverdale		PS-12	1059			356
ALLENDALE COLUMBIA	Rochester		PS-12	491			405
AQUINAS INST	Rochester		9-12	818		Roman Catholic	841
BISH KEARN-ROCHESTER	Rochester		9-12	477		Roman Catholic	842
HARLEY	Rochester		PS-12	490			406
MCQUAID	Rochester		7-12	886		Roman Catholic	842

School Feature Indexes

School	Town	Girls' Grade Range Bdg	Girls' Grade Range Day	Boys' Grade Range Bdg	Boys' Grade Range Day	Enr	Learning Disabilities	ESL	Relig Affil	Page
NY										
BUCKLEY CO DAY	Roslyn		PS-8		PS-8	303				407
RYE CO DAY	Rye		PS-12		PS-12	841				408
SCH OF HOLY CHILD	Rye		5-12			309			Roman Catholic	408
JFK CATHOLIC-NY	Somers		9-12		9-12	575			Roman Catholic	843
ST ANTHONY'S	South Huntington		9-12		9-12	2250			Roman Catholic	843
GOW	South Wales			7-PG		143	Focus			410
HARBOR CO DAY	St James		PS-8		PS-8	189				409
KNOX	St James	7-12	6-12	7-12	6-12	114		•		410
STATEN ISLAND ACAD	Staten Island		PS-12		PS-12	410		•		411
STONY BROOK	Stony Brook	7-12	7-12	7-12	7-12	375		•	Nondenom Christian	412
CHRIST BROS-SYRACUSE	Syracuse		7-12		7-12	730	Prgm		Roman Catholic	843
FAITH HERITAGE	Syracuse		PS-12		PS-12	500				844
HACKLEY	Tarrytown	9-12	K-12	9-12	K-12	794				414
EMMA WILLARD	Troy	9-PG	9-PG			312		•		415
LA SALLE INST	Troy				6-12	650			Roman Catholic	844
REDEMPTION CHRISTIAN	Troy	7-PG	PS-PG	7-PG	PS-PG	80	Prgm	•	Nondenom Christian	845
TUXEDO PARK	Tuxedo Park		PS-9		PS-9	195				416
WESTBURY FRIENDS	Westbury		PS-6		PS-6	173			Friends	845
ARCHBISHOP STEPINAC	White Plains				9-12	685			Roman Catholic	845
WINDWARD-NY	White Plains		1-9		1-9	470	Focus			417

LAWRENCE WOODMERE	Woodmere		PS-12		385		417
WOODSTOCK DAY	Woodstock		PS-10		192	•	846
STEIN YESHIVA	Yonkers		PS-8		109	Jewish	846
OUR MONTESSORI	Yorktown Heights		PS-6		320		846

NORTH CAROLINA

CHRIST SCH	Arden	8-12	8-12		192	• Episcopal	510
CAROLINA DAY	Asheville		PS-12		639	Prgm	511
BURLINGTON DAY	Burlington		PS-8		225		903
ARTHUR MORGAN	Burnsville	7-9	7-9		25		511
CHARLOTTE CATHOLIC	Charlotte		9-12		1140	Roman Catholic	904
CHARLOTTE CHRISTIAN	Charlotte		PS-12		984	Nondenom Christian	904
CHARLOTTE CO DAY	Charlotte		PS-12		1598	•	512
CHARLOTTE LATIN	Charlotte		K-12		1360		513
NORTHSIDE CHRISTIAN	Charlotte		PS-12		873	Baptist	904
PROVIDENCE DAY	Charlotte		PS-12		1478		514
CANNON	Concord		PS-12		803		905
CAROLINA FRIENDS	Durham		PS-12		481	Friends	515
DURHAM ACAD	Durham		PS-12		1128	Prgm	515
FAYETTEVILLE	Fayetteville		PS-12		372		905
GASTON DAY	Gastonia		PS-12		400	Prgm	906
WAYNE	Goldsboro		PS-12		242		906
CANTERBURY-NC	Greensboro		K-8		360	Episcopal	906

School Feature Indexes

School	Town	Girls' Grade Range Bdg	Girls' Grade Range Day	Boys' Grade Range Bdg	Boys' Grade Range Day	Enr	Learning Disabilities	ESL	Relig Affil	Page
NC GREENSBORO DAY	Greensboro		K-12		K-12	880				516
GREENSBORO MONTESS	Greensboro		PS-8		PS-8	365				907
NEW GARDEN FRIENDS	Greensboro		PS-8		PS-8	214			Friends	907
HARRELLS CHRISTIAN	Harrells		K-12		K-12	445				908
KERR-VANCE	Henderson		PS-12		PS-12	474				908
HICKORY	Hickory		K-8		K-8	90				908
WESTCHESTER ACAD	High Point		K-12		K-12	440				517
HOBGOOD	Hobgood		K-12		K-12	278				909
FORSYTH CO DAY	Lewisville		PS-12		PS-12	977	Prgm			518
OAK RIDGE	Oak Ridge	7-PG	7-PG	7-PG	7-PG	274		•		519
PATTERSON	Patterson	7-PG	7-PG	7-PG	7-PG	40	Prgm	•		909
N RALEIGH CO DAY	Raleigh		PS-5		PS-5	120				910
RAVENSCROFT	Raleigh		PS-12		PS-12	1095				519
ST DAVID'S-NC	Raleigh		K-12		K-12	479			Episcopal	910
ST MARY'S SCH	Raleigh	9-12	9-12			275			Episcopal	520
ROCKY MT	Rocky Mount		PS-12		PS-12	435				910
O'NEAL	Southern Pines		PS-12		PS-12	436	Prgm			911
CAPE FEAR	Wilmington		PS-12		PS-12	536				521
FRIENDS-WILMINGTON	Wilmington		PS-8		PS-8	172			Friends	911
SALEM	Winston-Salem	9-12	9-12			194		•	Moravian	522

Index by State and City

SUMMIT SCH	Winston-Salem		PS-9	PS-9	602		522

OHIO

JEROME LIPPMAN	Akron		K-8	K-8	100		Jewish	963
OLNEY FRIENDS	Barnesville	9-12	9-12	9-12	66	Prgm	Friends •	963
OLD TRAIL	Bath		PS-8	PS-8	539			600
AGNON	Beachwood		PS-8	PS-8	325		Jewish •	964
LAWRENCE SCH	Broadview Heights		1-12	1-12	217	Focus		964
CANTON CO DAY	Canton		PS-8	PS-8	281			600
NOTRE DAME-CATHEDRAL	Chardon		9-12	9-12	775		Roman Catholic	964
CINCINNATI CO DAY	Cincinnati		PS-12	PS-12	875			602
CINCINNATI HILLS	Cincinnati		K-12	K-12	1418	Prgm	Nondenom Christian	965
ELDER	Cincinnati		9-12	9-12	1060	Prgm	Roman Catholic	965
ST URSULA	Cincinnati		9-12	9-12	672	Prgm	Roman Catholic	603
SCHILLING	Cincinnati		K-12	K-12	34			966
SEVEN HILLS-OH	Cincinnati		PS-12	PS-12	1070			603
SUMMIT CO DAY	Cincinnati		PS-12	PS-12	1050		Roman Catholic	604
URSULINE ACAD-OH	Cincinnati		9-12	9-12	650		Roman Catholic	966
BENEDICTINE HS-OH	Cleveland			9-12	425		Roman Catholic	967
BEAUMONT	Cleveland Heights		9-12	9-12	453		Roman Catholic	967
BISHOP WATTERSON	Columbus		9-12	9-12	1159		Roman Catholic	967
COLUMBUS SCH GIRLS	Columbus		PS-12	PS-12	657			607
MARBURN	Columbus		1-10	1-10	103	Focus		968

School Feature Indexes

School	Town	Girls' Grade Range Bdg	Girls' Grade Range Day	Boys' Grade Range Bdg	Boys' Grade Range Day	Enr	Learning Disabilities	ESL	Relig Affil	Page
OH CUYAHOGA VALLEY CHR	Cuyahoga Falls		7-12		7-12	837			Nondenom Christian	968
WALSH	Cuyahoga Falls		9-12		9-12	890			Roman Catholic	969
MIAMI VALLEY	Dayton		PS-12		PS-12	481				608
COLUMBUS ACAD	Gahanna		PS-12		PS-12	1001				607
HAWKEN	Gates Mills		PS-12		PS-12	954				609
BETHANY	Glendale		K-8		K-8	254			Episcopal	601
STEPHEN T BADIN	Hamilton		9-12		9-12	660			Roman Catholic	969
WESTERN RESERVE	Hudson	9-PG	9-PG	9-PG	9-PG	400				610
U SCH-OH	Hunting Valley				K-12	871				613
LIMA CENT CATHOLIC	Lima		9-12		9-12	416			Roman Catholic	969
TUSCARAWAS CATHOLIC	New Philadelphia		9-12		9-12	176			Roman Catholic	970
LAKE RIDGE	North Ridgeville		K-12		K-12	408				611
PHILLIPS-OSBORNE	Painesville		PS-8		PS-8	226				970
PADUA	Parma		9-12		9-12	1010	Prgm		Roman Catholic	970
LUTHERAN HS W	Rocky River		9-12		9-12	414			Lutheran	971
MAGNIFICAT	Rocky River		9-12			856			Roman Catholic	971
HATHAWAY BROWN	Shaker Heights		PS-12		PS-12	830				612
LAUREL SCH	Shaker Heights		PS-12		PS-PS	681				612
REGINA	South Euclid		9-12			280			Roman Catholic	972
MAUMEE VALLEY	Toledo		PS-12		PS-12	469				614

ST FRANCIS DE SALES	Toledo		9-12	670	Roman Catholic	972
ANDREWS	Willoughby	6-12		170	•	606
CARDINAL MOONEY-OH	Youngstown		9-12	586	Roman Catholic	972

OKLAHOMA

CASADY	Oklahoma City		PS-12	866	Episcopal	657
HERITAGE HALL	Oklahoma City		PS-12	854		658
ST JOHN'S EPIS-OK	Oklahoma City		PS-8	205	Episcopal	1006
WESTMINSTER SCH-OK	Oklahoma City		PS-8	517		1007
BISHOP KELLEY	Tulsa		9-12	900	• Roman Catholic	1007
CASCIA HALL	Tulsa		6-12	580	Roman Catholic	1007
HOLLAND HALL	Tulsa		PS-12	1036	Episcopal	659
MONTE CASSINO	Tulsa		PS-8	997	Roman Catholic	1008
U SCH-OK	Tulsa		PS-8	190		1008

OREGON

VALLEY CATHOLIC	Beaverton		7-12	470	• Roman Catholic	1083
MILO ADVENTIST	Days Creek	9-12	9-12	162	Adventist	1083
OAK HILL SCH-OR	Eugene		K-12	104		1083
NESKOWIN VALLEY	Neskowin		PS-8	56		1084
INTL SCH-OR	Portland		PS-5	293		1084
JESUIT HS-OR	Portland		9-12	1130	Roman Catholic	1085
OR EPISCOPAL	Portland	9-12	PS-12	778	• Episcopal	754
PORTLAND LUTHERAN	Portland	8-12	PS-12	304	• Lutheran	755

School Feature Indexes

School	Town	Girls' Bdg	Girls' Day	Boys' Bdg	Boys' Day	Enr	Learning Disabilities	ESL	Relig Affil	Page
OR ST MARY'S ACAD	Portland		9-12			565			Roman Catholic	1085
BLANCHET	Salem		7-12		7-12	318			Roman Catholic	1085
W MENNONITE	Salem	9-12	6-12	9-12	6-12	199		•	Mennonite	1086
DELPHIAN	Sheridan	3-12	K-12	3-12	K-12	244		•		1086

PENNSYLVANIA

School	Town	Girls' Bdg	Girls' Day	Boys' Bdg	Boys' Day	Enr	Learning Disabilities	ESL	Relig Affil	Page
SWAIN	Allentown		PS-8		PS-8	330				419
BISHOP GUILFOYLE	Altoona		9-12		9-12	396			Roman Catholic	847
QUIGLEY	Baden		9-12		9-12	171			Roman Catholic	847
BEAVER COUNTY CHRIST	Beaver Falls		K-12		K-12	340				847
HOLY GHOST PREP	Bensalem				9-12	508			Roman Catholic	848
MORAVIAN	Bethlehem		PS-12		PS-12	802			Moravian	419
OAK LN	Blue Bell		PS-6		PS-6	111				420
BALDWIN	Bryn Mawr		PS-12			635				421
CO DAY SACRED HEART	Bryn Mawr		PS-12			380			Roman Catholic	422
ST ALOYSIUS	Bryn Mawr				K-8	270			Roman Catholic	848
SHIPLEY	Bryn Mawr		PS-12		PS-12	838				422
MONTGOMERY SCH	Chester Springs		PS-8		PS-8	342				423
OUR LADY OF LOURDES	Coal Township		9-12		9-12	194			Roman Catholic	849
DEVON PREP	Devon				6-12	278			Roman Catholic	849
HOLY CHILD ACAD-PA	Drexel Hill		PS-8		PS-8	220			Roman Catholic	849

Index by State and City

ERIE DAY	Erie		PS-8	180		850
PEN RYN	Fairless Hills		PS-8	285		Episcopal	424
MT ST JOSEPH ACAD-PA	Flourtown	9-12		561		Roman Catholic	850
GERMANTOWN ACAD	Fort Washington		PS-12	1136			442
MMI	Freeland		6-12	190			425
AQUINAS ACAD	Gibsonia		K-12	205		Roman Catholic	851
GLADWYNE	Gladwyne		PS-6	310			851
UPATTINAS	Glenmoore		K-12	112	•		851
GWYNEDD-MERCY	Gwynedd Valley	9-12		419		Roman Catholic	852
FRIENDS HAVERFORD	Haverford		PS-6	202		Friends	426
HAVERFORD	Haverford		PS-12	939			427
STRATFORD FRIENDS	Haverford		K-6	68	Focus	Friends	852
MILTON HERSHEY	Hershey	PS-12	PS-12	1274			852
JOHNSTOWN CHRISTIAN	Hollsopple		PS-12	265	Prgm	Nondenom Christian	853
ABINGTON FRIENDS	Jenkintown		PS-12	787		Friends	428
WYOMING SEMINARY	Kingston	9-PG	PS-12	813		Methodist •	457
BUCKINGHAM FRIENDS	Lahaska		K-8	176		Friends	429
LANCASTER CO DAY	Lancaster		PS-12	488			429
CHRISTOPHER DOCK	Lansdale	9-12	9-12	435		Mennonite	853
VALLEY SCH	Ligonier	K-9	K-9	200			430
LINDEN HALL	Lititz	6-PG		130	•		431
MALVERN PREP	Malvern		6-12	595		Roman Catholic	854

School Feature Indexes

School	Town	Girls' Grade Range Bdg	Girls' Grade Range Day	Boys' Grade Range Bdg	Boys' Grade Range Day	Enr	Learning Disabilities	ESL	Relig Affil	Page
PA PHELPS	Malvern			7-PG	7-PG	140	Focus	•		854
MEADOWBROOK-PA	Meadowbrook	PS-6			PS-6	204				432
BENCHMARK	Media		1-8		1-8	204	Focus			855
MEDIA-PROVIDENCE	Media		PS-8		PS-8	150			Friends	855
MERCERSBURG	Mercersburg	9-PG	9-PG	9-PG	9-PG	443				433
EPISCOPAL ACAD	Merion		PS-12		PS-12	1130			Episcopal	440
MERION	Merion Station		9-12			460			Roman Catholic	855
WALDRON MERCY	Merion Station		PS-8		PS-8	599			Roman Catholic	856
ST GREGORY'S ACAD	Moscow			9-12		61			Roman Catholic	856
CARSON LONG	New Bloomfield			6-12		190		•		434
SOLEBURY	New Hope	9-PG	7-PG	9-PG	7-PG	220	Prgm	•		435
GEORGE SCH	Newtown	9-12	9-12	9-12	9-12	537		•	Friends	436
NEWTOWN FRIENDS	Newtown		PS-8		PS-8	310			Friends	437
DE COUNTY CHRISTIAN	Newtown Square		PS-12		PS-12	963	Prgm	•	Nondenom Christian	857
CHURCH FARM	Paoli			7-12	7-12	188			Episcopal	438
CROSSROADS-PA	Paoli		K-8		K-8	96	Focus			857
DE VALLEY FRIENDS	Paoli		7-12		7-12	166	Focus		Friends	857
PERKIOMEN	Pennsburg	7-PG	5-PG	7-PG	5-PG	255	Prgm	•	Schwenkfelder	439
ARCHBISHOP RYAN	Philadelphia		9-12		9-12	2564	Prgm		Roman Catholic	858
CREFELD	Philadelphia		7-12		7-12	100	Focus			440

Index by State and City

School	City					Affiliation	Page
FR JUDGE	Philadelphia				9-12	1293	Roman Catholic	858
FRIENDS SELECT	Philadelphia			PS-12	482	Friends •	441
GERMANTOWN FRIENDS	Philadelphia			K-12	901	Friends	443
GIRARD	Philadelphia	1-12			678		859
GREENE ST FRIENDS	Philadelphia			PS-8	247	Friends	444
JOHN W HALLAHAN	Philadelphia			9-12	650	Roman Catholic	859
NAZARETH	Philadelphia			9-12	466	Roman Catholic	859
PHILADELPHIA SCH	Philadelphia			PS-8	364		860
ST PETER'S SCH	Philadelphia			PS-8	181		445
NEUMANN-GORETTI	Philadelphia			9-12	1173	Roman Catholic	860
SPRINGSIDE	Philadelphia			PS-12	628		446
W PHILADELPHIA CATH	Philadelphia			9-12	714	Roman Catholic	861
WM PENN CHARTER	Philadelphia			K-12	886	Friends	446
ELLIS	Pittsburgh			K-12	496		447
FALK	Pittsburgh			K-8	275		448
FOX CHAPEL	Pittsburgh			PS-5	131	Prgm Episcopal	861
ST EDMUND'S	Pittsburgh			PS-8	245	Episcopal	448
SHADY SIDE	Pittsburgh	9-12	K-12	9-12	946		449
WINCHESTER THURSTON	Pittsburgh			PS-12	589	•	450
PORTERSVILLE CHRIST	Portersville			K-12	253	Evangelical	861
HILL SCH-PA	Pottstown	9-PG	9-PG	9-PG	498		451
WYNDCROFT	Pottstown			PS-8	252		452

School Feature Indexes

	School	Town	Girls' Grade Range Bdg	Girls' Grade Range Day	Boys' Grade Range Bdg	Boys' Grade Range Day	Enr	Learning Disabilities	ESL	Relig Affil	Page
PA	UNITED FRIENDS	Quakertown		PS-8		PS-8	155			Friends	862
	SCH IN ROSE VALLEY	Rose Valley		PS-6		PS-6	123				432
	HILL TOP PREP	Rosemont		6-12		6-12	86	Focus			862
	ROSEMONT	Rosemont		PS-8		PS-8	303			Roman Catholic	863
	KISKI	Saltsburg			9-PG	9-PG	215		•		452
	SEWICKLEY	Sewickley		PS-12		PS-12	796				453
	WOODLYNDE	Strafford		K-12		K-12	339				863
	GRIER	Tyrone	7-PG				184	Prgm	•		454
	VALLEY FORGE	Wayne			7-PG		524		•		455
	WEST CHESTER FRIENDS	West Chester		PS-5		PS-5	131			Friends	863
	WESTTOWN	Westtown	9-12	PS-10	9-12	PS-10	782		•	Friends	455
	HARRISBURG	Wormleysburg		PS-12		PS-12	481				426
	LA SALLE COL HS	Wyndmoor				9-12	1050			Roman Catholic	444
	FRIENDS' CENTRAL	Wynnewood		PS-12		PS-12	992		•	Friends	458
	CHRISTIAN SCH YORK	York		PS-12		PS-12	459	Prgm		Nondenom Christian	864
	YORK CO DAY	York		PS-12		PS-12	207				459
	RHODE ISLAND										
	ST ANDREW'S SCH-RI	Barrington	9-12	6-12	9-12	6-12	194	Prgm	•	Episcopal	268
	MERCYMOUNT	Cumberland		PS-8		PS-8	368	Prgm		Roman Catholic	788
	ROCKY HILL	East Greenwich		PS-12		PS-12	330		•		268

Index by State and City

GORDON SCH	East Providence		PS-8		PS-8	392		272
PROVIDENCE CO DAY	East Providence		5-12		5-12	293	Prgm	274
ST GEORGE'S SCH-RI	Middletown	9-12	9-12		9-12	340		Episcopal	270
ST MICHAEL'S CO DAY	Newport		PS-8		PS-8	231		271
PENNFIELD	Portsmouth		PS-8		PS-8	204		788
PORTSMOUTH	Portsmouth	9-12	9-12		9-12	343		Roman Catholic	269
COMMUNITY PREP	Providence		3-8		3-8	158		789
LINCOLN	Providence		PS-12		PS-PS	439		Friends	272
MOSES BROWN	Providence		PS-12		PS-12	788		Friends	273
WHEELER	Providence		PS-12		PS-12	811	Prgm	274
PROUT	Wakefield		9-12		9-12	532		Roman Catholic	789
MT ST CHARLES	Woonsocket		7-12		7-12	1000		Roman Catholic	789

SOUTH CAROLINA

AIKEN PREP	Aiken		PS-12		PS-12	169	•	524
MEAD HALL	Aiken		PS-8		PS-8	149		912
BEAUFORT	Beaufort		PS-12		PS-12	350		525
CAMDEN MILIT	Camden		7-PG			292		525
ASHLEY HALL	Charleston		PS-12		PS-K	613		526
CHARLESTON DAY	Charleston		1-8		1-8	169		527
MASON	Charleston		1-8		1-8	350		912
PORTER-GAUD	Charleston		K-12		K-12	940		Episcopal	527
BEN LIPPEN	Columbia	6-12	PS-12	6-12	PS-12	873	Prgm	•	Nondenom Christian	912

School Feature Indexes

	School	Town	Girls' Grade Range Bdg	Girls' Grade Range Day	Boys' Grade Range Bdg	Boys' Grade Range Day	Enr	Learning Disabilities	ESL	Relig Affil	Page
SC	HAMMOND	Columbia		PS-12		PS-12	936				913
	HEATHWOOD	Columbia		PS-12		PS-12	760			Episcopal	528
	BYRNES	Florence		PS-12		PS-12	284				913
	BOB JONES	Greenville	9-12	9-12	9-12	9-12	554			Nondenom Christian	914
	CHRIST CHURCH EPIS	Greenville		K-12		K-12	953		•	Episcopal	529
	ST JOSEPH'S CATHOLIC	Greenville		6-12		6-12	370	Prgm		Roman Catholic	914
	SHANNON FOREST	Greenville		PS-12		PS-12	500	Prgm		Nondenom Christian	914
	HILTON HEAD PREP	Hilton Head Island		1-12		1-12	400	Prgm			915
	TRIDENT	Mt Pleasant		K-PG		K-PG	147	Focus			915
	LOWCOUNTRY	Pawleys Island		PS-12		PS-12	185		•		916
	SPARTANBURG DAY	Spartanburg		PS-12		PS-12	469	Prgm			530
	PINEWOOD PREP	Summerville		PS-12		PS-12	650				916
	WILSON HALL	Sumter		PS-12		PS-12	766				916
SOUTH DAKOTA											
	ST THOMAS MORE HS	Rapid City		9-12		9-12	190			Roman Catholic	995
	SIOUX FALLS CHRISTN	Sioux Falls		PS-12		PS-12	615			Nondenom Christian	995
TENNESSEE											
	WEBB SCH-BELL BUCKLE	Bell Buckle	7-PG	6-12	7-PG	6-12	280		•		531
	BRENTWOOD ACAD	Brentwood		6-12		6-12	735				917
	CURREY INGRAM	Brentwood		K-12		K-12	260	Focus			917

Index by State and City

BOYD-BUCHANAN	Chattanooga	PS-12		PS-12	999	Nondenom Christian	918
BRIGHT SCH	Chattanooga	PS-5		PS-5	357		532
CHATTANOOGA CHRIST	Chattanooga	K-12		K-12	1068	Nondenom Christian	918
GIRLS PREP	Chattanooga	6-12		6-12	738		532
MCCALLIE	Chattanooga		9-12	6-12	890		533
NOTRE DAME HS-TN	Chattanooga	9-12		9-12	565	Prgm Roman Catholic	919
COLUMBIA ACAD	Columbia	PS-12		PS-12	788		919
EVANGELICAL CHRIST	Cordova	K-12		K-12	1382	Evangelical	919
BATTLE GROUND	Franklin	K-12		K-12	925		920
SUMNER	Gallatin	PS-8		PS-8	232		920
ST GEORGE'S SCHS-TN	Germantown	PS-12		PS-12	839		534
U SCH OF JACKSON	Jackson	PS-12		PS-12	1310	•	535
EPISCOPAL KNOXVILLE	Knoxville	K-8		K-8	213	Episcopal	921
WEBB SCH KNOXVILLE	Knoxville	K-12		K-12	1049		535
FRIENDSHIP CHRISTIAN	Lebanon	PS-12		PS-12	513	Nondenom Christian	921
GRACE-ST LUKE'S	Memphis	PS-8		PS-8	484	Episcopal	536
HARDING-MEMPHIS	Memphis	PS-12		PS-12	1735	Nondenom Christian	921
HUTCHISON	Memphis	PS-12		PS-12	826		537
LAUSANNE	Memphis	PS-12		PS-12	725		537
MEMPHIS U SCH	Memphis		7-12	7-12	649		538
PRESBYTERIAN DAY	Memphis			PS-6	564	Presbyterian	539
ST MARY'S EPIS SCH	Memphis	PS-12		PS-12	824	Episcopal	539

	School	Town	Girls' Grade Range Bdg	Girls' Grade Range Day	Boys' Grade Range Bdg	Boys' Grade Range Day	Enr	Learning Disabilities	ESL	Relig Affil	Page
TN	WOODLAND PRESBY	Memphis		PS-8		PS-8	400			Presbyterian	922
	DAVID LIPSCOMB	Nashville		PS-12		PS-12	1457			Nondenom Christian	922
	FR RYAN	Nashville		9-12		9-12	940			Roman Catholic	540
	FRANKLIN RD	Nashville		PS-12		PS-12	905				922
	HARDING-NASHVILLE	Nashville		K-8		K-8	462				923
	HARPETH HALL	Nashville		5-12			588				541
	MONTGOMERY BELL	Nashville				7-12	663				542
	OAK HILL SCH-TN	Nashville		PS-6		PS-6	446	Prgm		Presbyterian	923
	ST CECILIA	Nashville		9-12			263			Roman Catholic	924
	PLEASANT VIEW CHRIST	Pleasant View		PS-12		PS-12	351			Baptist	924
	KING'S ACAD	Seymour	6-12	K-12	6-12	K-12	365		•	Southern Baptist	924
TEXAS											
	ST JOHN'S EP-ABILENE	Abilene		PS-5		PS-5	164			Episcopal	1009
	GREENHILL-TX	Addison		PS-12		PS-12	1248				663
	OAKRIDGE	Arlington		PS-12		PS-12	760				661
	HYDE PARK	Austin		K-12		K-12	754			Baptist	1009
	ST STEPHEN'S EPIS-TX	Austin	8-12	6-12	8-12	6-12	638		•	Episcopal	662
	ALL SAINTS-BEAUMONT	Beaumont		PS-8		PS-8	400		•	Episcopal	1009
	EPISCOPAL HS-TX	Bellaire		9-12		9-12	611			Episcopal	1010
	ALLEN	Bryan		PS-12	9-12	PS-12	309		•		662

Index by State and City

School	City	Grades	Enrollment		Affiliation	Page
CARROLLTON CHRISTIAN	Carrollton	K-12	530		Nondenom Christian	1010
INCARNATE WORD-TX	Corpus Christi	PS-12	745		Roman Catholic	1011
ST JAMES EPISCOPAL	Corpus Christi	PS-8	310		Episcopal	1011
EPISCOPAL SCH DALLAS	Dallas	PS-12	1118		Episcopal	1011
JESUIT COL PREP	Dallas	9-12	1010		Roman Catholic	664
LAKEHILL	Dallas	K-12	390			1012
LAMPLIGHTER	Dallas	PS-4	434			665
ST MARK'S SCH OF TX	Dallas	1-12	816			666
ST THERESE ACAD	Dallas	9-12	10		Roman Catholic	1012
ST THOMAS AQUINAS	Dallas	PS-8	754	Prgm	Roman Catholic	1013
SHELTON	Dallas	PS-12	812	Focus		1013
SOLOMON SCHECHTER-TX	Dallas	PS-8	475	•	Jewish	1014
URSULINE ACAD DALLAS	Dallas	9-12	800		Roman Catholic	1014
WINSTON SCH-TX	Dallas	1-12	217	Focus		1015
SELWYN	Denton	PS-10	294			666
CANTERBURY EPISCOPAL	DeSoto	K-12	245		Episcopal	1015
ST CLEMENT'S	El Paso	PS-8	390		Episcopal	1015
PARISH EPISCOPAL	Farmers Branch	PS-11	820		Episcopal	1012
FT WORTH ACAD	Fort Worth	K-8	231			1016
FT WORTH CO DAY	Fort Worth	K-12	1098			667
HOLY FAMILY SCH	Fort Worth	PS-8	210		Roman Catholic	1016
NOLAN	Fort Worth	7-12	1059		Roman Catholic	1017

School	Town	Girls' Grade Range Bdg	Girls' Grade Range Day	Boys' Grade Range Bdg	Boys' Grade Range Day	Enr	Learning Disabilities	ESL	Relig Affil	Page
TX ST RITA	Fort Worth		PS-8		PS-8	224			Roman Catholic	1017
TRINITY VALLEY	Fort Worth		K-12		K-12	950				668
TRINITY EPIS SCH-TX	Galveston		PS-8		PS-8	260			Episcopal	1017
MARINE MILIT	Harlingen			8-PG		406		•		669
ALEXANDER-SMITH	Houston		9-12		9-12	70				1018
AWTY	Houston		PS-12		PS-12	1135		•		669
DUCHESNE	Houston		PS-12			665			Roman Catholic	1018
HOLY SPIRIT	Houston		PS-8		PS-8	327			Episcopal	1019
KINKAID	Houston		PS-12		PS-12	1344				671
PRESBYTERIAN SCH	Houston		PS-8		PS-8	456			Presbyterian	1019
RIVER OAKS BAPTIST	Houston		PS-8		PS-8	779			Baptist	1019
ST AGNES ACAD	Houston		9-12			784			Roman Catholic	1020
ST FRANCIS EPISCOPAL	Houston		PS-8		PS-8	782			Episcopal	1020
ST PIUS-TX	Houston		9-12		9-12	670			Roman Catholic	1021
ST THOMAS HS	Houston				9-12	645			Roman Catholic	672
STRAKE JESUIT	Houston				9-12	868			Roman Catholic	1021
VILLAGE	Houston		PS-8		PS-8	700				1021
CISTERCIAN	Irving				5-12	346			Roman Catholic	672
ALL SAINTS-LUBBOCK	Lubbock		PS-9		PS-9	296			Episcopal	1022
TRINITY SCH-TX	Midland		PS-12		PS-12	453			Episcopal	1022

Index by State and City

SACRED HEART SCH-TX	Muenster		PS-12		PS-12	239		Roman Catholic	1023
ALEXANDER SCH-TX	Richardson		8-12		8-12	60			1023
KEYSTONE-TX	San Antonio		K-12		K-12	388			673
ST LUKE'S EPIS-TX	San Antonio		PS-8		PS-8	399		Episcopal	1023
ST MARY'S HALL-TX	San Antonio		PS-12		PS-12	890			674
SAN ANTONIO ACAD	San Antonio				PS-8	326			1024
TX MILIT	San Antonio	9-12	6-12		6-12	320		Episcopal	675
SAN MARCOS BAPTIST	San Marcos	8-12	6-12	6-12	6-12	215	•	Baptist	675
JOHN COOPER	The Woodlands		K-12		K-12	880			670

UTAH

WASATCH	Mt Pleasant	9-PG	9-PG	9-PG	9-PG	130	Prgm	Presbyterian	1044
PROVO CANYON	Orem	7-12		7-12		242	Prgm		1044
REID	Salt Lake City		PS-9		PS-9	209			1045
ROWLAND-ST MARK'S	Salt Lake City		PS-12		PS-12	971		Episcopal	696
WATERFORD	Sandy		PS-12		PS-12	994			1045

VERMONT

ROCK PT	Burlington	9-12	9-12	9-12	9-12	42		Episcopal	276
LONG TRAIL	Dorset	9-12	6-12	9-12	6-12	135	Prgm	•	276
LYNDON	Lyndon Center	9-12	9-12	9-12	9-12	617			790
BURR & BURTON	Manchester	9-12	9-12	9-12	9-12	597	Prgm	•	790
GRAMMAR	Putney		PS-8		PS-8	114			277
GREENWOOD	Putney	Ungraded	Ungraded	Ungraded	Ungraded	40	Focus		278

School Feature Indexes

School	Town	Girls' Grade Range Bdg	Girls' Grade Range Day	Boys' Grade Range Bdg	Boys' Grade Range Day	Enr	Learning Disabilities	ESL	Relig Affil	Page
VT PUTNEY	Putney	9-12	9-12	9-12	9-12	225		•		278
MT ST JOSEPH ACAD-VT	Rutland		9-12		9-12	170		•	Roman Catholic	791
VT ACAD	Saxtons River	9-PG	9-PG	9-PG	9-PG	255	Prgm	•		280
RICE	South Burlington		9-12		9-12	463			Roman Catholic	791
ST JOHNSBURY	St Johnsbury	9-PG	9-12	9-PG	9-12	976	Prgm	•		279
STRATTON MTN	Stratton Mountain	7-PG	7-PG	7-PG	7-PG	113		•		791
KING GEORGE	Sutton	9-12	9-12	9-12	7-PG	30				792
				VIRGINIA						
ALEXANDRIA CO DAY	Alexandria		K-8		K-8	237				925
BISHOP IRETON	Alexandria		9-12		9-12	818			Roman Catholic	925
BROWNE ACAD	Alexandria		PS-8		PS-8	293				926
BURGUNDY FARM	Alexandria		PS-8		PS-8	282				543
EPISCOPAL HS-VA	Alexandria	9-12		9-12		420			Episcopal	543
ST STEPHEN'S & AGNES	Alexandria		PS-12		PS-12	1155			Episcopal	544
OAKWOOD SCH-VA	Annandale		1-8		1-8	112	Focus			926
POWHATAN	Boyce		K-8		K-8	243				926
LINTON HALL	Bristow		PS-8		PS-8	214			Roman Catholic	927
COVENANT	Charlottesville		PS-12		PS-12	635			Nondenom Christian	927
ST ANNE'S-BELFIELD	Charlottesville	9-12	PS-12	9-12	PS-12	839		•		545
TANDEM	Charlottesville		5-12		5-12	223			Friends	928

CHATHAM HALL	Chatham	9-12	9-12		126		•	Episcopal	546
HARGRAVE	Chatham		7-PG	7-PG	7-PG	375		•	Baptist	547
WOODLAWN	Chatham		PS-8		PS-8	180				928
CHRISTCHURCH SCH	Christchurch		8-PG	8-PG	8-PG	216	Prgm	•	Episcopal	547
SOUTHAMPTON	Courtland			PS-12	PS-12	407				928
BROADWATER	Exmore		PS-12	PS-12	PS-12	460				929
CONGRESSIONAL SCHS	Falls Church		PS-8	PS-8	PS-8	386				929
FUQUA	Farmville		PS-12	PS-12	PS-12	523				929
FORK UNION	Fork Union			6-PG	6-PG	550			Baptist	549
RANDOLPH-MACON	Front Royal	6-PG	6-PG	6-PG	6-PG	404		•	Methodist	550
WARE	Gloucester		PS-8		PS-8	160				930
NYSMITH	Herndon		PS-8		PS-8	674				930
CHESAPEAKE-VA	Irvington		PS-8		PS-8	172				931
LITTLE KESWICK	Keswick			Ungraded		30	Focus			931
OAKLAND	Keswick	2-9	2-9	2-9	2-9	80	Focus			932
LOUDOUN CO DAY	Leesburg		PS-8	PS-8	PS-8	260				932
JAMES RIVER DAY	Lynchburg		K-8		K-8	260				932
VA EPISCOPAL	Lynchburg	9-12	9-12	9-12	9-12	268			Episcopal	551
CARLISLE	Martinsville		PS-12	PS-12	PS-12	428	Prgm			933
LANGLEY	McLean		PS-8		PS-8	466				551
MADEIRA	McLean	9-12	9-12			302		•		552
POTOMAC	McLean		K-12	K-12	K-12	875				553

School Feature Indexes

	School	Town	Girls' Grade Range Bdg	Girls' Grade Range Day	Boys' Grade Range Bdg	Boys' Grade Range Day	Enr	Learning Disabilities	ESL	Relig Affil	Page
VA	FOXCROFT	Middleburg	9-12				185				554
	HILL SCH-VA	Middleburg		K-8		K-8	236				555
	NOTRE DAME ACAD-VA	Middleburg		9-12		9-12	293	Prgm		Roman Catholic	933
	AYLETT	Millers Tavern		PS-8		PS-8	170				934
	OAK HILL ACAD-VA	Mouth of Wilson	8-12	8-12	8-12	8-12	104			Baptist	555
	HAMPTON RDS	Newport News		6-12		6-12	500				556
	ST ANDREW'S EPIS-VA	Newport News		K-5		K-5	223			Episcopal	934
	NORFOLK ACAD	Norfolk		1-12		1-12	1216				557
	FLINT HILL	Oakton		PS-12		PS-12	972	Prgm			934
	GRYMES	Orange		PS-8		PS-8	158				557
	BLESSED SACRAMENT	Powhatan		PS-12		PS-12	538			Roman Catholic	935
	COLLEGIATE-VA	Richmond		K-12^C		K-12^C	1528				558
	NEW COMMUNITY	Richmond		6-12		6-12	96	Focus			935
	ST CATHERINE'S SCH	Richmond	9-12	PS-12			818			Episcopal	559
	ST CHRISTOPHER'S	Richmond				PS-12	935			Episcopal	560
	STEWARD	Richmond		K-12		K-12	575		•		560
	ACHIEVEMENT CTR	Roanoke		K-9		K-9	60	Focus			935
	N CROSS	Roanoke		PS-12		PS-12	515				561
	BLUE RIDGE	St George			9-12		165		•	Episcopal	548
	STUART HALL-VA	Staunton	8-12	5-12		5-12	137		•	Episcopal	562

ST MARGARET'S SCH	Tappahannock	8-12	8-12			• Episcopal	563
HUNTER MCGUIRE	Verona		K-5	K-5	100		936
GREEN HEDGES	Vienna		PS-8	PS-8	191		936
CAPE HENRY	Virginia Beach		PS-12	PS-12	1020	•	564
TIDEWATER	Wakefield		PS-12	PS-12	227		937
HIGHLAND-VA	Warrenton		PS-12	PS-12	520	•	565
FISHBURNE	Waynesboro		8-12	8-12	200		566
WALSINGHAM	Williamsburg		PS-12	PS-12	705	Roman Catholic	937
WILLIAMSBURG CHRIST	Williamsburg		PS-12	PS-12	265	Prgm Nondenom Christian	937
WOODBERRY FOREST	Woodberry Forest		9-12		381		566
MASSANUTTEN	Woodstock	6-PG	6-PG	6-PG	169	•	567

WASHINGTON

COLUMBIA ADVENTIST	Battleground		9-12	9-12	95	Adventist	1087
LITTLE SCH	Bellevue		PS-6	PS-6	145		1087
ST THOMAS SCH	Medina		PS-6	PS-6	184		1087
BEAR CREEK	Redmond		K-12	K-12	610	• Nondenom Christian	1088
OVERLAKE	Redmond		5-12	5-12	482		756
BERTSCHI	Seattle		PS-5	PS-5	218	Prgm	1088
EPIPHANY-WA	Seattle		PS-5	PS-5	133		1088
HOLY NAMES ACAD	Seattle		9-12		610	Roman Catholic	1089
JFK MEMORIAL	Seattle		9-12	9-12	866	Prgm • Roman Catholic	1089
LAKESIDE SCH	Seattle		5-12	5-12	757		756

School Feature Indexes

School	Town	Girls' Grade Range Bdg	Girls' Grade Range Day	Boys' Grade Range Bdg	Boys' Grade Range Day	Enr	Learning Disabilities	ESL	Relig Affil	Page
WA NORTHWEST SCH	Seattle	9-12	6-12		6-12	434		•		757
SEATTLE CO DAY	Seattle		K-8		K-8	303				1090
SEATTLE WALDORF	Seattle		K-8		K-8	240	Prgm			1090
U PREP	Seattle		6-12		6-12	457				758
EVERGREEN	Shoreline		PS-8		PS-8	347				1090
GONZAGA	Spokane		9-12		9-12	900			Roman Catholic	1091
ST GEORGE'S SCH-WA	Spokane		K-12		K-12	370				759
ANNIE WRIGHT	Tacoma	9-12	K-12		K-8	406		•	Episcopal	759
CHARLES WRIGHT	Tacoma		PS-12		PS-12	682				760
WEST VIRGINIA
NOTRE DAME HS-WV	Clarksburg		7-12		7-12	149			Roman Catholic	938
COUNTRY DAY	Kearneysville		PS-8		PS-8	135				938
LINSLY	Wheeling	7-12	5-12	7-12	5-12	448				569
MT DE CHANTAL	Wheeling	9-12	PS-12		PS-6	217	Prgm	•	Roman Catholic	569
WISCONSIN
WAYLAND	Beaver Dam	9-12	9-12	9-12	9-12	180	Prgm	•		616
BROOKFIELD ACAD	Brookfield		PS-12		PS-12	724				617
ST JOHN'S NORTHWEST	Delafield			7-12	7-8	306		•	Episcopal	618
IMMANUEL LUTHERAN	Eau Claire	9-12	9-12	9-12	9-12	134			Lutheran Conf.	973
NOTRE DAME BAIE	Green Bay		9-12		9-12	741			Roman Catholic	973

U LAKE	Hartland	PS-12	PS-12	339		619
ARMITAGE	Kenosha	K-8	K-8	113		974
LAKESIDE LUTHERAN	Lake Mills	9-12		405	Lutheran	974
EDGEWOOD	Madison	9-12	9-12	600	Prgm Roman Catholic	974
MARQUETTE HIGH	Milwaukee		9-12	1056	Roman Catholic	975
MILWAUKEE LUTHERAN	Milwaukee	9-12	9-12	725	Prgm Lutheran-Missouri	975
PIUS	Milwaukee	9-12	9-12	1390	• Roman Catholic	976
U SCH OF MILWAUKEE	Milwaukee	PS-12	PS-12	1066		619
PRAIRIE HILL	Pewaukee	PS-8	PS-8	184		976
PRAIRIE SCH	Racine	PS-12	PS-12	669	•	620
DOMINICAN HS-WI	Whitefish Bay	9-12	9-12	342	Roman Catholic	976

SCHOOLS WITH A SPECIAL FOCUS

ARTS

Idyllwild .... Idyllwild, CA 704
  (Perform_Arts Visual_Arts Creative_Writing)
Chicago Acad Arts .... Chicago, IL 571
  (Perform_Arts Visual_Arts)
Walnut Hill .... Natick, MA 231
  (Perform_Arts Visual_Arts)
Interlochen .... Interlochen, MI 597
  (Perform_Arts Visual_Arts)
Am Boychoir .... Princeton, NJ 341
  (Perform_Arts)
Professional Child .... New York, NY 389
  (Perform_Arts Visual_Arts)
St Thomas Choir .... New York, NY 394
  (Perform_Arts)

BILINGUAL

E Bay Fr-Amer *(Fr)* .... Berkeley, CA 1050
Lycee Francais-LA *(Fr)* .... Los Angeles, CA 711
Intl Sch Peninsula *(Fr, Mandarin)* .... Palo Alto, CA 724
Chin Amer Intl *(Chin)* .... San Francisco, CA 1072
Fr-Amer Intl *(Fr)* .... San Francisco, CA 732
Denver Intl *(Fr, Mandarin, Span)* .... Denver, CO 1028
Rock Creek *(Fr, Span, Arabic)* .... Washington, DC 797
Wash Intl *(Fr, Span, Dutch)* .... Washington, DC 293
Atlanta Intl *(Fr, Ger, Span)* .... Atlanta, GA 491
Fr Intl *(Fr)* .... Bethesda, MD 803
German Sch *(Ger)* .... Potomac, MD 810
Fr-Amer Sch *(Fr)* .... Larchmont, NY 833
La Scuola d'Italia *(Ital)* .... New York, NY 384
Lycee Francais-NYC *(Fr)* .... New York, NY 386
Lyceum Kennedy *(Fr)* .... New York, NY 386
Solomon Schechter-NY *(Hebrew)* .... New York, NY 839
Agnon *(Hebrew)* .... Beachwood, OH 964
Intl Sch-OR *(Chin, Japan, Span)* .... Portland, OR 1084
Awty *(Arab, Fr, Ger, Ital, Span)* .... Houston, TX 669

BUSINESS

Illiana Christian	Lansing, IL	946
Lutheran HS-IN	Indianapolis, IN	953
St Henry	Erlanger, KY	900
Oneida	Oneida, KY	902
Wentworth	Lexington, MO	636
Cardinal Mooney-OH	Youngstown, OH	972
Nazareth	Philadelphia, PA	859
Neumann-Goretti	Philadelphia, PA	860
Lyndon	Lyndon Center, VT	790
Mt St Joseph Acad-VT	Rutland, VT	791
St Johnsbury	St Johnsbury, VT	279
Notre Dame HS-WV	Clarksburg, WV	938
Milwaukee Lutheran	Milwaukee, WI	975

INTERNATIONAL (IB) OR FRENCH (FB) BACCALAUREATE

Mt St Mary-AR *(IB)*	Little Rock, AR	997
Fairmont *(IB)*	Anaheim, CA	1049
Lycee Francais-LA *(FB)*	Los Angeles, CA	711
Fr-Amer Intl *(IB & FB)*	San Francisco, CA	732
Wilmington Friends *(IB)*	Wilmington, DE	286
Wash Intl *(IB)*	Washington, DC	293
Gulliver *(IB)*	Pinecrest, FL	476
Cardinal Newman *(IB)*	West Palm Beach, FL	887
Atlanta Intl *(IB)*	Atlanta, GA	491
Mid-Pacific *(IB)*	Honolulu, HI	749
St Scholastica *(IB)*	Chicago, IL	944
Trinity HS-IL *(IB)*	River Forest, IL	949
Fr Intl *(FB)*	Bethesda, MD	803
Detroit Co Day *(IB)*	Beverly Hills, MI	594
Armand Hammer *(IB)*	Montezuma, NM	694
Dwight Sch *(IB)*	New York, NY	382
Lycee Francais-NYC *(FB)*	New York, NY	386
Lyceum Kennedy *(FB)*	New York, NY	386
UN Intl *(IB)*	New York, NY	398
Charlotte Co Day *(IB)*	Charlotte, NC	512
George Sch *(IB)*	Newtown, PA	436
Prout *(IB)*	Wakefield, RI	789
Christ Church Epis *(IB)*	Greenville, SC	529
Allen *(IB)*	Bryan, TX	662
Awty *(IB & FB)*	Houston, TX	669
Carlisle *(IB)*	Martinsville, VA	933

LEARNING DISABILITIES & UNDERACHIEVEMENT

St Paul's Prep *(Underachiever)* .... Phoenix, AZ 1036
Southwestern-AZ *(Underachiever)* .... Rimrock, AZ 688
Fenster *(Underachiever)* .... Tucson, AZ 690
Oak Creek *(Underachiever)* .... West Sedona, AZ 1038
NAWA *(LD)* .... French Gulch, CA 1054
Southwestern-CA *(Underachiever)* .... San Marino, CA 742
Denver Acad *(LD & Underachiever)* .... Denver, CO 1027
Woodhall *(LD & Underachiever)* .... Bethlehem, CT 132
Eagle Hill-Greenwich *(LD)* .... Greenwich, CT 764
Marvelwood *(Underachiever)* .... Kent, CT 146
Forman *(LD)* .... Litchfield, CT 148
Grove Sch *(LD & Underachiever)* .... Madison, CT 766
St Thomas More-CT *(LD & Underachiever)* .... Oakdale, CT 158
Eagle Hill-Southport *(LD)* .... Southport, CT 769
Glenholme *(LD & Underachiever)* .... Washington, CT 771
Oxford Acad *(Underachiever)* .... Westbrook, CT 173
Pilot *(LD)* .... Wilmington, DE 793
Lab Sch *(LD)* .... Washington, DC 796
North Broward Prep *(LD)* .... Coconut Creek, FL 872
Vanguard *(LD)* .... Lake Wales, FL 474
PACE-Brantley Hall *(LD)* .... Longwood, FL 877
Atlantis *(LD)* .... Miami, FL 878
Brandon Hall *(LD & Underachiever)* .... Atlanta, GA 491
Brehm *(LD)* .... Carbondale, IL 940
Chelsea *(LD)* .... Silver Spring, MD 812
Thornton Friends *(Underachiever)* .... Silver Spring, MD 812
Landmark Sch *(LD)* .... Prides Crossing, MA 192
Eagle Hill-MA *(LD)* .... Hardwick, MA 223
Carroll *(LD)* .... Lincoln, MA 226
Hillside *(Underachiever)* .... Marlborough, MA 229
Linden Hill *(LD)* .... Northfield, MA 235
Riverview *(LD)* .... East Sandwich, MA 238
Corwin-Russell *(LD & Underachiever)* .... Sudbury, MA 784
Willow Hill *(LD & Underachiever)* .... Sudbury, MA 243
White Oak *(LD)* .... Westfield, MA 785
Eton *(LD)* .... Birmingham, MI 954
Leelanau *(LD & Underachiever)* .... Glen Arbor, MI 597
Groves Acad *(LD)* .... St Louis Park, MN 984
Logos *(LD & Underachiever)* .... St Louis, MO 990
Metropolitan *(LD)* .... St Louis, MO 990

LEARNING DISABILITIES & UNDERACHIEVEMENT CONT.

Dublin *(LD & Underachiever)* ....Dublin, NH..........258
Hampshire Country *(LD & Underachiever)*..........Rindge, NH..........264
Newgrange *(LD)* ....Hamilton, NJ..........816
Community Sch-NJ *(LD & Underachiever)* ....Teaneck, NJ..........821
Kildonan *(LD)*.. Amenia, NY..........352
Maplebrook *(LD & Underachiever)*...................... Amenia, NY..........823
Robt L Stevenson-NY *(LD & Underachiever)* New York, NY..........391
Stephen Gaynor *(LD)*... New York, NY..........840
Winston Prep *(LD)*... New York, NY..........840
Vincent Smith *(LD & Underachiever)* ...Port Washington, NY..........402
Gow *(LD)*...South Wales, NY..........410
Windward-NY *(LD)*..................................... White Plains, NY..........417
Lawrence Sch *(LD)*............................Broadview Heights, OH..........964
Marburn *(LD)*.. Columbus, OH..........968
Stratford Friends *(LD)* .... Havertown, PA..........852
Phelps *(LD & Underachiever)*............................... Malvern, PA..........854
Benchmark *(LD & Underachiever)*...........................Media, PA..........855
Crossroads-PA *(LD)*..Paoli, PA..........857
DE Valley Friends *(LD)*..Paoli, PA..........857
Crefeld *(LD & Underachiever)* ....Philadelphia, PA..........440
Hill Top Prep *(LD)*..Rosemont, PA..........862
Trident *(LD)* .... Mt Pleasant, SC..........915
Currey Ingram *(LD)*.. Brentwood, TN..........917
Shelton *(LD)* ....Dallas, TX........1013
Winston Sch-TX *(LD)* ....Dallas, TX........1015
Provo Canyon *(Underachiever)*................................. Orem, UT........1044
Greenwood *(LD)*... Putney, VT..........278
Oakwood Sch-VA *(LD)* .... Annandale, VA..........926
Little Keswick *(LD)*.. Keswick, VA..........931
Oakland *(LD)* .... Keswick, VA..........932
Oak Hill Acad-VA *(Underachiever)* ....Mouth of Wilson, VA..........555
New Community *(LD)*..Richmond, VA..........935
Achievement Ctr *(LD)* .... Roanoke, VA..........935

MILITARY

Lyman Ward	Camp Hill, AL	865
St Catherine's Milit	Anaheim, CA	697
Army & Navy	Carlsbad, CA	699
FL Air	Melbourne, FL	475
Admiral Farragut	St Petersburg, FL	482
Riverside Milit	Gainesville, GA	499
Culver	Culver, IN	582
Howe	Howe, IN	585
St John's Milit	Salina, KS	625
Leonard Hall	Leonardtown, MD	809
St Thomas Acad	Mendota Heights, MN	633
Wentworth	Lexington, MO	636
MO Milit	Mexico, MO	637
NM Milit	Roswell, NM	1043
Christ Bros-Albany	Albany, NY	822
NY Milit	Cornwall-on-Hudson, NY	361
La Salle Inst	Troy, NY	844
Oak Ridge	Oak Ridge, NC	519
Carson Long	New Bloomfield, PA	434
Valley Forge	Wayne, PA	455
Camden Milit	Camden, SC	525
Marine Milit	Harlingen, TX	669
TX Milit	San Antonio, TX	675
San Marcos Baptist	San Marcos, TX	675
Hargrave	Chatham, VA	547
Fork Union	Fork Union, VA	549
Randolph-Macon	Front Royal, VA	550
Fishburne	Waynesboro, VA	566
Massanutten	Woodstock, VA	567
St John's Northwest	Delafield, WI	618

SPORTS

NAWA *(Winter)*	French Gulch, CA	1054
Sugar Bowl *(Winter)*	Norden, CA	1063
Lowell Whiteman *(Winter)*	Steamboat Springs, CO	682
Waterville Valley *(Winter)*	Waterville Valley, NH	787
Natl Sports Acad *(Canoe/Kayak & Winter)*	Lake Placid, NY	832
Professional Child *(General)*	New York, NY	389
Rowland-St Mark's *(Winter)*	Salt Lake City, UT	696
Stratton Mtn *(Winter)*	Stratton Mountain, VT	791

VOCATIONAL

Denver Acad	Denver, CO	1027
GA Christian	Valdosta, GA	899
St Henry	Erlanger, KY	900
Oneida	Oneida, KY	902
Maranatha Christian	Brooklyn Park, MN	981
Maplebrook	Amenia, NY	823
Stephen T Badin	Hamilton, OH	969
Milton Hershey	Hershey, PA	852
Christopher Dock	Lansdale, PA	853
Lyndon	Lyndon Center, VT	790
Burr & Burton	Manchester, VT	790
St Johnsbury	St Johnsbury, VT	279
Pius	Milwaukee, WI	976

SCHOOLS WITH COORDINATE SINGLE-GENDER PROGRAMS

Webb Schs-CA .... Claremont, CA 700
Coord — Day Gr 9-10 (Bdg & Day — Coed 9-12)

Schs-Sacred Heart .... San Francisco, CA 738
Coord — Day Gr K-12 (Day — Coed K-12)

Regis Jesuit .... Aurora, CO 1025
Coord — Day Gr 9-12 (Day — Coed 9-12)

De La Salle Inst .... Chicago, IL 941
Coord — Day Gr 9-12 (Day — Coed 9-12)

Sacred Heart Schs-IL .... Chicago, IL 573
Coord — Day Gr 1-8 (Day — Coed K-8)

Dexter .... Brookline, MA 201
Coord — Day Gr PS-10 (Day — Boys PS-11)

Southfield-MA .... Brookline, MA 202
Coord — Day Gr PS-10 (Day — Girls PS-10)

Acad Sacred Heart-MI .... Bloomfield Hills, MI 592
Coord — Day Gr 5-8 (Day — Boys PS-8, Girls PS-12)

Cranbrook .... Bloomfield Hills, MI 592
Coord — Day Gr 6-8 (Bdg — Coed 9-12; Day — Coed PS-12)

Albany Acad .... Albany, NY 350
Coord — Day Gr K-12 (Bdg — Boys 8-12; Day — Boys PS-PG)

Albany Acad Girls .... Albany, NY 350
Coord — Day Gr K-12 (Day — Girls PS-12)

Masters Sch-NY .... Dobbs Ferry, NY 363
Coord — Day Gr 5-8 (Bdg — Coed 9-12; Day — Coed 5-12)

Collegiate-VA .... Richmond, VA 558
Coord — Day Gr 5-8 (Day — Coed K-12)

SCHOOLS WITH ELEMENTARY BOARDING

Lyman Ward..Camp Hill, AL..........865
(Bdg Boys Gr 6-12)

Oak Creek ....West Sedona, AZ........1038
(Bdg Coed Gr 6-12)

St Catherine's Milit.. Anaheim, CA..........697
(Bdg and Day — Boys Gr K-8)

Ojai Valley .... Ojai, CA..........721
(Bdg — Coed Gr 3-12; Day — Coed PS-12)

Southwestern-CA.. San Marino, CA..........742
(Bdg and Day — Coed Gr 6-PG)

Indian Mtn... Lakeville, CT..........148
(Bdg — Coed Gr 6-9; Day — Coed PS-9)

Grove Sch .... Madison, CT..........766
(Bdg & Day Coed Gr 6-PG)

Rectory... Pomfret, CT..........160
(Bdg — Boys Gr 5-9; Day — Coed 5-9)

Glenholme... Washington, CT..........771
(Bdg & Day Coed Gr 3-12)

Rumsey .... Washington Depot, CT..........170
(Bdg — Coed Gr 5-9; Day — Coed K-9)

Vanguard .... Lake Wales, FL..........474
(Bdg and Day — Coed Gr 5-PG)

FL Air... Melbourne, FL..........475
(Bdg and Day — Coed Gr 6-12)

Admiral Farragut... St Petersburg, FL..........482
(Bdg — Coed Gr 6-12; Day — Coed K-12)

HI Prep...Kamuela, HI..........752
(Bdg — Coed Gr 6-12; Day — Coed K-12)

Brehm.. Carbondale, IL..........940
(Bdg & Day Coed Gr 6-PG)

Fox River Co Day.. Elgin, IL..........577
(Bdg — Coed Gr 6-8; Day — Coed PS-8)

Howe...Howe, IN..........585
(Bdg — Coed Gr 5-12)

St John's Milit.. Salina, KS..........625
(Bdg — Boys Gr 6-12)

SCHOOLS WITH ELEMENTARY BOARDING CONT.

Oneida .... Oneida, KY 902
(Bdg & Day Coed Gr 6-12)

Chop Point .... Woolwich, ME 777
(Bdg Coed Gr 3-12; Day Coed PS-12)

Bement .... Deerfield, MA 213
(Bdg — Coed Gr 3-9; Day — Coed K-9)

Eaglebrook .... Deerfield, MA 215
(Bdg and Day — Boys Gr 6-9)

Hillside .... Marlborough, MA 229
(Bdg and Day — Boys Gr 5-9)

Fessenden .... West Newton, MA 233
(Bdg — Boys Gr 5-9; Day — Boys K-9)

Riverview .... East Sandwich, MA 238
(Bdg — Coed Gr 6-PG)

Fay .... Southborough, MA 240
(Bdg — Coed Gr 6-9; Day — Coed 1-9)

Shattuck-St Mary's .... Faribault, MN 628
(Bdg and Day — Coed Gr 6-PG)

St Stanislaus .... Bay St Louis, MS 1004
(Bdg & Day Boys Gr 6-12)

MO Milit .... Mexico, MO 637
(Bdg — Boys Gr 6-PG)

Chaminade Col Prep .... St Louis, MO 638
(Bdg and Day — Boys Gr 6-12)

Cardigan Mtn .... Canaan, NH 257
(Bdg and Day — Boys Gr 6-9)

Hampshire Country .... Rindge, NH 264
(Bdg — Boys Gr 3-12)

Waterville Valley .... Waterville Valley, NH 787
(Bdg & Day Coed Gr 6-12)

Am Boychoir .... Princeton, NJ 341
(Bdg and Day — Boys Gr 5-8)

Kildonan .... Amenia, NY 352
(Bdg — Coed Gr 6-PG; Day — Coed 2-PG)

Maplebrook .... Amenia, NY 823
(Bdg & Day Coed Gr 6-PG)

N Country .... Lake Placid, NY 366
(Bdg and Day — Coed Gr 4-9)

Indexes of Special Interest

St Thomas Choir .... New York, NY 394
(Bdg — Boys Gr 4-8)

Andrews .... Willoughby, OH 606
(Bdg and Day — Girls Gr 6-12)

Delphian .... Sheridan, OR 1086
(Bdg Coed Gr 3-12; Day Coed K-12)

Milton Hershey .... Hershey, PA 852
(Bdg Coed Gr PS-12)

Linden Hall .... Lititz, PA 431
(Bdg and Day — Girls Gr 6-PG)

Carson Long .... New Bloomfield, PA 434
(Bdg — Boys Gr 6-12)

Girard .... Philadelphia, PA 859
(Bdg Coed Gr 1-12)

Ben Lippen .... Columbia, SC 912
(Bdg Coed Gr 6-12; Day Coed PS-12)

King's Acad .... Seymour, TN 924
(Bdg Coed Gr 6-12; Day Coed K-12)

San Marcos Baptist .... San Marcos, TX 675
(Bdg — Boys Gr 6-12, Girls 8-12; Day — Coed 6-12)

Fork Union .... Fork Union, VA 549
(Bdg and Day — Boys Gr 6-PG)

Randolph-Macon .... Front Royal, VA 550
(Bdg and Day — Coed Gr 6-PG)

Oakland .... Keswick, VA 932
(Bdg & Day Coed Gr 2-9)

Massanutten .... Woodstock, VA 567
(Bdg and Day — Coed Gr 6-PG)

SCHOOLS WITH AT LEAST 25 PERCENT INTERNATIONAL STUDENTS

Southwestern-AZ *(60%)*	Rimrock, AZ	688
Idyllwild *(35%)*	Idyllwild, CA	704
Eldorado-Emerson *(30%)*	Orange, CA	723
Southwestern-CA *(51%)*	San Marino, CA	742
Marianapolis *(40%)*	Thompson, CT	168
Oxford Acad *(25%)*	Westbrook, CT	173
Vanguard *(35%)*	Lake Wales, FL	474
Palmer Trinity *(26%)*	Miami, FL	478
Montverde *(57%)*	Montverde, FL	880
Atlanta Intl *(50%)*	Atlanta, GA	491
Brandon Hall *(25%)*	Atlanta, GA	491
Horizons *(28%)*	Atlanta, GA	889
Avery Coonley *(29%)*	Downers Grove, IL	576
Oneida *(8%)*	Oneida, KY	902
Fr Intl *(85%)*	Bethesda, MD	803
German Sch *(80%)*	Potomac, MD	810
Cushing *(25%)*	Ashburnham, MA	189
Walnut Hill *(25%)*	Natick, MA	231
Northfield Mt Hermon *(25%)*	Northfield, MA	236
Winchendon *(30%)*	Winchendon, MA	250
Intl Sch of MN *(30%)*	Eden Prairie, MN	628
Shattuck-St Mary's *(29%)*	Faribault, MN	628
MO Milit *(41%)*	Mexico, MO	637
Cardigan Mtn *(36%)*	Canaan, NH	257
Armand Hammer *(75%)*	Montezuma, NM	694
Storm King *(26%)*	Cornwall-on-Hudson, NY	362
Hoosac *(25%)*	Hoosick, NY	364
Houghton *(35%)*	Houghton, NY	831
Fr-Amer Sch *(90%)*	Larchmont, NY	833
Dwight Sch *(30%)*	New York, NY	382
La Scuola d'Italia *(70%)*	New York, NY	384
Lycee Francais-NYC *(66%)*	New York, NY	386
Lyceum Kennedy *(30%)*	New York, NY	386
UN Intl *(68%)*	New York, NY	398
Patterson *(37%)*	Patterson, NC	909
Olney Friends *(33%)*	Barnesville, OH	963
Linden Hall *(26%)*	Lititz, PA	431
Kiski *(30%)*	Saltsburg, PA	452
Grier *(50%)*	Tyrone, PA	454
Awty *(54%)*	Houston, TX	669
Holy Spirit *(33%)*	Houston, TX	1019
Wasatch *(27%)*	Mt Pleasant, UT	1044
Annie Wright *(25%)*	Tacoma, WA	759

COEDUCATIONAL SCHOOLS OFFERING GIRLS-ONLY MATH OR SCIENCE

Webb Schs-CA *(Math & Sci)* .... Claremont, CA 700
NAWA *(Math & Sci)* .... French Gulch, CA 1054
Hebrew Acad *(Math & Sci)* .... Huntington Beach, CA 1056
Campbell Hall *(Math)* .... North Hollywood, CA 707
Rolling Hills Prep *(Math & Sci)* .... Palos Verdes Estates, CA 1066
San Francisco Sch *(Math)* .... San Francisco, CA 737
Schs-Sacred Heart *(Math & Sci)* .... San Francisco, CA 738
Regis Jesuit *(Math & Sci)* .... Aurora, CO 1025
St Anne's Episcopal *(Sci)* .... Denver, CO 1029
Cheshire *(Sci)* .... Cheshire, CT 133
Gunnery *(Math)* .... Washington, CT 170
Maret *(Math)* .... Washington, DC 289
Montverde *(Math & Sci)* .... Montverde, FL 880
St Michael's Indep *(Sci)* .... Stuart, FL 485
St Martin's-GA *(Math)* .... Atlanta, GA 889
Trinity Sch-GA *(Math & Sci)* .... Atlanta, GA 890
Walker *(Math & Sci)* .... Marietta, GA 896
Heritage *(Math & Sci)* .... Newnan, GA 500
De La Salle Inst *(Math & Sci)* .... Chicago, IL 941
Sacred Heart Schs-IL *(Math & Sci)* .... Chicago, IL 573
Keith *(Sci)* .... Rockford, IL 580
Maharishi *(Math & Sci)* .... Fairfield, IA 979
Lexington Sch *(Math & Sci)* .... Lexington, KY 505
Liberty *(Math)* .... Blue Hill, ME 774
Calvert Sch *(Sci)* .... Baltimore, MD 298
Groton *(Math & Sci)* .... Groton, MA 221
Cranbrook *(Sci)* .... Bloomfield Hills, MI 592
Blake *(Math & Sci)* .... Hopkins, MN 629
Mary Inst St Louis *(Math & Sci)* .... St Louis, MO 640
Manzano *(Math & Sci)* .... Albuquerque, NM 692
Rippowam Cisqua *(Math)* .... Bedford, NY 353
Carolina Day *(Math & Sci)* .... Asheville, NC 511
Charlotte Co Day *(Math)* .... Charlotte, NC 512
Charlotte Latin *(Math & Sci)* .... Charlotte, NC 513
Community Prep *(Math)* .... Providence, RI 789
Wheeler *(Math)* .... Providence, RI 274
St Joseph's Catholic *(Math & Sci)* .... Greenville, SC 914
Parish Episcopal *(Math)* .... Farmers Branch, TX 1012
Provo Canyon *(Math & Sci)* .... Orem, UT 1044
St Stephen's & Agnes *(Math & Sci)* .... Alexandria, VA 544

SCHOOLS WITH 25% OR MORE NONWHITE FACULTY

Pasadena Waldorf *(25%)*	Altadena, CA	1048
Arrowsmith *(40%)*	Berkeley, CA	1050
Providence HS *(33%)*	Burbank, CA	1051
Windrush *(25%)*	El Cerrito, CA	1053
Fresno Adventist *(43%)*	Fresno, CA	1054
St Lucy's *(34%)*	Glendora, CA	1055
Moreau *(28%)*	Hayward, CA	1055
Lutheran HS-CA *(25%)*	La Verne, CA	1056
Westerly *(30%)*	Long Beach, CA	1057
Pilgrim *(42%)*	Los Angeles, CA	714
Sacred Heart HS-CA *(35%)*	Los Angeles, CA	1060
Bishop O'Dowd *(26%)*	Oakland, CA	1064
Head-Royce *(28%)*	Oakland, CA	720
St Elizabeth *(31%)*	Oakland, CA	1065
St Paul's Epis-CA *(27%)*	Oakland, CA	1065
Eldorado-Emerson *(28%)*	Orange, CA	723
Mayfield Jr *(32%)*	Pasadena, CA	1067
Walden *(40%)*	Pasadena, CA	1068
Chin Amer Intl *(60%)*	San Francisco, CA	1072
Lick-Wilmerding *(26%)*	San Francisco, CA	735
San Francisco Sch *(27%)*	San Francisco, CA	737
Alpha Beacon *(57%)*	San Mateo, CA	1074
Denver Intl *(40%)*	Denver, CO	1028
Georgetown Day *(30%)*	Washington, DC	288
Rock Creek *(42%)*	Washington, DC	797
St Philip's *(27%)*	Coral Gables, FL	872
St Thomas Episcopal *(31%)*	Coral Gables, FL	872
Ft Lauderdale Prep *(30%)*	Fort Lauderdale, FL	873
Chaminade-Madonna *(30%)*	Hollywood, FL	875
Atlantis *(60%)*	Miami, FL	878
Dade Christian *(86%)*	Miami, FL	879
Gulliver *(34%)*	Pinecrest, FL	476
La Salle HS *(60%)*	Miami, FL	477
Palmer Trinity *(40%)*	Miami, FL	478
Westminster-Miami *(25%)*	Miami, FL	880
Tampa Baptist *(25%)*	Tampa, FL	886
Horizons *(38%)*	Atlanta, GA	889
Holy Nativity *(41%)*	Honolulu, HI	1080
Sacred Hrts Acad-HI *(80%)*	Honolulu, HI	1081
St Andrew's Priory *(46%)*	Honolulu, HI	751

Indexes of Special Interest

Le Jardin *(25%)*	Kailua, HI	752
Luther HS S *(53%)*	Chicago, IL	942
Archbishop Shaw *(35%)*	Marrero, LA	999
Newport *(30%)*	Silver Spring, MD	319
Cambridge Montessori *(30%)*	Cambridge, MA	778
Fayerweather *(27%)*	Cambridge, MA	205
Epiphany-MA *(50%)*	Dorchester, MA	779
Lexington Montessori *(30%)*	Lexington, MA	781
Montessori Educare *(40%)*	Newton Centre, MA	783
All Saints' Epis-MS *(30%)*	Vicksburg, MS	655
Benedictine Acad *(30%)*	Elizabeth, NJ	814
St Dominic Acad *(26%)*	Jersey City, NJ	816
Am Boychoir *(40%)*	Princeton, NJ	341
Menaul *(29%)*	Albuquerque, NM	1041
McCurdy *(28%)*	Espanola, NM	1042
Brooklyn Hts Mont *(31%)*	Brooklyn, NY	825
Martin Luther *(30%)*	Maspeth, NY	833
Beekman *(25%)*	New York, NY	372
Calhoun *(35%)*	New York, NY	376
Children's Storefrnt *(55%)*	New York, NY	837
Corlears *(25%)*	New York, NY	837
Dominican Acad *(28%)*	New York, NY	837
Manhattan Country *(54%)*	New York, NY	387
UN Intl *(39%)*	New York, NY	398
Redemption Christian *(85%)*	Troy, NY	845
Greene St Friends *(34%)*	Philadelphia, PA	444
Community Prep *(56%)*	Providence, RI	789
St Clement's *(25%)*	El Paso, TX	1015
Awty *(25%)*	Houston, TX	669
Strake Jesuit *(30%)*	Houston, TX	1021
Alexander Sch-TX *(43%)*	Richardson, TX	1023
Cape Henry *(28%)*	Virginia Beach, VA	564

SCHOOLS WITH 50% OR MORE NONWHITE STUDENTS

School	City	Page
St Mary's HS-AZ *(56%)*	Phoenix, AZ	1036
Southwestern-AZ *(56%)*	Rimrock, AZ	688
Ramona *(88%)*	Alhambra, CA	1048
St Catherine's Milit *(56%)*	Anaheim, CA	697
Providence HS *(83%)*	Burbank, CA	1051
Army & Navy *(54%)*	Carlsbad, CA	699
Moreau *(74%)*	Hayward, CA	1055
Pilgrim *(71%)*	Los Angeles, CA	714
Sacred Heart HS-CA *(97%)*	Los Angeles, CA	1060
Holy Names HS *(69%)*	Oakland, CA	1064
St Elizabeth *(95%)*	Oakland, CA	1065
St Paul's Epis-CA *(53%)*	Oakland, CA	1065
Pasadena Towne *(57%)*	Pasadena, CA	1068
Bridgemont *(64%)*	San Francisco, CA	1072
Chin Amer Intl *(85%)*	San Francisco, CA	1072
Hillwood *(73%)*	San Francisco, CA	733
Immaculate Concept *(86%)*	San Francisco, CA	1072
Mercy-San Francisco *(73%)*	San Francisco, CA	1073
Harker *(70%)*	San Jose, CA	740
Southwestern-CA *(73%)*	San Marino, CA	742
Mater Dei HS *(55%)*	Santa Ana, CA	1076
Ft Lauderdale Prep *(51%)*	Fort Lauderdale, FL	873
Atlantis *(59%)*	Miami, FL	878
Carrollton Sch *(66%)*	Miami, FL	878
La Salle HS *(98%)*	Miami, FL	477
Palmer Trinity *(60%)*	Miami, FL	478
Montverde *(61%)*	Montverde, FL	880
Tampa Baptist *(52%)*	Tampa, FL	886
Horizons *(65%)*	Atlanta, GA	889
Riverside Milit *(55%)*	Gainesville, GA	499
Hanahauoli *(69%)*	Honolulu, HI	748
Holy Nativity *(56%)*	Honolulu, HI	1080
Iolani *(82%)*	Honolulu, HI	749
Maryknoll *(69%)*	Honolulu, HI	1081
Sacred Hrts Acad-HI *(90%)*	Honolulu, HI	1081
St Andrew's Priory *(93%)*	Honolulu, HI	751
St Francis Sch-HI *(75%)*	Honolulu, HI	1082
De La Salle Inst *(67%)*	Chicago, IL	941
Holy Trinity HS *(90%)*	Chicago, IL	942
Luther HS S *(99%)*	Chicago, IL	942

St Scholastica *(65%)*	Chicago, IL	944
Elizabeth Seton *(65%)*	Bladensburg, MD	805
Holy Trinity Day *(56%)*	Glenn Dale, MD	807
McDonogh *(75%)*	Owings Mills, MD	312
Queen Anne *(60%)*	Upper Marlboro, MD	321
Epiphany-MA *(96%)*	Dorchester, MA	779
Delphi *(54%)*	Milton, MA	782
Detroit Waldorf *(61%)*	Detroit, MI	955
Bishop Borgess *(98%)*	Redford, MI	961
Wardlaw-Hartridge *(53%)*	Edison, NJ	325
Benedictine Acad *(80%)*	Elizabeth, NJ	814
St Dominic Acad *(60%)*	Jersey City, NJ	816
Menaul *(61%)*	Albuquerque, NM	1041
St Pius-NM *(64%)*	Albuquerque, NM	1042
McCurdy *(87%)*	Espanola, NM	1042
Armand Hammer *(51%)*	Montezuma, NM	694
Rehoboth *(78%)*	Rehoboth, NM	1042
Acad of Mt St Ursula *(89%)*	Bronx, NY	824
Bishop Loughlin *(99%)*	Brooklyn, NY	825
Mary Louis *(60%)*	Jamaica Estates, NY	832
Lyceum Kennedy *(69%)*	New York, NY	386
Manhattan Country *(53%)*	New York, NY	387
Windsor *(79%)*	Flushing, NY	405
Westbury Friends *(51%)*	Westbury, NY	845
Heritage Hall *(56%)*	Oklahoma City, OK	658
Milton Hershey *(53%)*	Hershey, PA	852
Church Farm *(54%)*	Paoli, PA	438
Girard *(98%)*	Philadelphia, PA	859
Greene St Friends *(54%)*	Philadelphia, PA	444
W Philadelphia Cath *(82%)*	Philadelphia, PA	861
Community Prep *(87%)*	Providence, RI	789
St Rita *(63%)*	Fort Worth, TX	1017
Awty *(63%)*	Houston, TX	669

LEADING PRIVATE SCHOOLS

The following schools are arranged geographically by state, progressing from east to west across the country. Within each state, schools are listed alphabetically by city or town.

These schools are presented together in the belief that they are of first interest to the readers of the *Handbook*. They may be included because of their international and historical renown, because they command general respect of parents and educators, and also because our information discloses unique or significant aspects of their programs that are deserving of the reader's attention.

New England States

CONNECTICUT

AVON, CT. (8 mi. WNW of Hartford, CT; 98 mi. NE of New York, NY) Suburban. Pop: 15,832. Alt: 201 ft.

AVON OLD FARMS SCHOOL
Bdg and Day — Boys Gr 9-PG

Avon, CT 06001. 500 Old Farms Rd. Tel: 860-673-3244. Fax: 860-675-6051.
www.avonoldfarms.com   E-mail: admissions@avonoldfarms.com
Kenneth H. LaRocque, Head. AB, MEd, Harvard Univ. **Brendon Welker, Adm.**

- **Col Prep. AP**—Eng Fr Span Calc Stats Comp_Sci Bio Physics US_Hist Econ US_Govt & Pol Studio_Art. **Feat**—Lat Geol African-Amer_Hist Philos Architect Digital_Photog Music Jazz_Ensemble Journ. **Supp**—Tut.
- **Adm:** 147/yr. Bdg 112. Day 35. Appl due: Feb. Accepted: 73%. **Tests** CEEB IQ ISEE SSAT TOEFL.
- **Enr 369.** B 272/97. Wh 92%. Hisp 3%. Blk 3%. Other 2%. Avg class size: 12. **Fac 51.** M 39/2. F 7/3. Wh 92%. Hisp 2%. Blk 4%. Asian 2%. Adv deg: 45%. In dorms 21.
- **Grad '04—117. Col—117.** (SMU, U of CT, U of VT, Holy Cross, U of WI-Madison, US Naval Acad). Avg SAT: 1088. Alum 3700.
- **Tui '05-'06: Bdg $34,650** (+$2300). **Day $24,800** (+$1300). **Aid:** Merit 17 ($61,000). Need 103 ($1,767,761).
- Endow $26,700,000. Plant val $100,000,000. Bldgs 35. Dorms 7. Dorm rms 193. Class rms 42. Lib 24,000 vols. Sci labs 6. Lang labs 1. Comp labs 3. Dark rms 1. Theaters 1. Art studios 1. Music studios 1. Wood shops 1. Gyms 1. Fields 11. Courts 16. Pools 1. Rinks 1. Weight rms 1.
- **Est 1927.** Nonprofit. Sem (Sept-May). **Assoc** CLS NEASC.

Theodate Pope Riddle designed and founded this architecturally unique school. Its location within 850 acres of forested land provides for a number of outdoor activities, including fishing, hiking, camping, biking and cross-country skiing.

The curriculum focuses on the development of writing, reading and mathematical skills. The academic courses are college preparatory, with electives provided in music, drama and the arts. Advanced Placement courses are available in every discipline, including computer science. Computer technology is an important aspect of school life. Graduates enter a wide range of colleges.

An enrichment hour each weekday evening provides opportunities for extra help. The day student program is unusual in that boys are strongly encouraged to take part in many boarding activities, including evening functions. In addition, the school assigns each pupil a campus job.

Every student participates in a sport or an alternate activity of his choice each season. The interscholastic athletics program comprises soccer, basketball, swimming, wrestling, ice hockey, riflery, track, skiing, baseball, football, lacrosse, tennis, squash, cross-country and golf.

BETHLEHEM, CT. (28 mi. WSW of Hartford, CT; 77 mi. NNE of New York, NY) Rural. Pop: 3422. Alt: 880 ft.

WOODHALL SCHOOL
Bdg and Day — Boys Gr 9-PG

Bethlehem, CT 06751. 58 Harrison Ln, PO Box 550. Tel: 203-266-7788.
  Fax: 203-266-5896.
  www.woodhallschool.org   E-mail: woodhallschool@lycos.com
Sally Campbell Woodhall, Head. MA, Fordham Univ.
  Col Prep. LD. Underachiever. AP—Eng Lat Calc Bio Chem US_Hist. **Feat**—Fr Greek Span. **Supp**—Dev_Read ESL Makeup Tut.
  Adm (Bdg Gr 9-11): 16/yr. Appl due: Rolling. Accepted: 50%. Yield: 48%.
  Enr 40. B 40. Sec 39. PG 1. Wh 90%. Hisp 7%. Asian 3%. Avg class size: 4. **Fac 15.** M 12. F 3. Wh 80%. Hisp 7%. Asian 13%. Adv deg: 53%. In dorms 10.
  Grad '04—12. Col—9. (U of MA-Amherst, San Diego St, Beloit, Hartwick, Lynn, Thiel). Avg SAT: 1076. Alum 152.
  Tui '04-'05: Bdg $45,000 (+$1000). **Day $33,800** (+$600).
  Endow $100,000. Plant val $5,500,000. Bldgs 7. Dorms 2. Dorm rms 22. Class rms 15. Lib 2000 vols. Sci labs 2. Auds 1. Art studios 1. Gyms 1. Fields 1. Courts 2.
  Est 1982. Nonprofit. Tri (Sept-June). **Assoc** NEASC.

Located on a 30-acre campus, the school enrolls boys who have not succeeded in traditional school environments. Woodhall accepts students of average to superior intellectual ability who have no serious emotional or behavioral problems and no chemical dependencies. Applicants may display one or more of the following characteristics: lack of motivation and low achievement; a mild learning disability; difficulty with reading, writing or math; poor concentration and attention; lack of self-confidence or poor self-esteem; long school absences due to illness; or school changes due to family mobility.

Staff design an individualized program for each student. The school provides small classes within a core college preparatory or general secondary-level curriculum in English, math, social studies, science and foreign languages; remedial programs in language arts, reading, writing and math; and English as a Second Language instruction. The intensive academic program is integrated with proctored study periods, small study groups and an evening study hall.

Communications groups help students develop skills of self-expression, and a daily athletic program promotes physical fitness, sportsmanship and teamwork. Interscholastic teams are available, and the school encourages pupils to take part in volunteer service programs. Woodhall conducts social and recreational activities and clubs on campus and in cooperation with nearby prep schools. Theater, concerts, and educational field trips to New Haven, Hartford and New York City complete the program. **See Also Page 1378**

BRANFORD, CT. (34 mi. SSW of Hartford, CT; 72 mi. NE of New York, NY) Urban. Pop: 28,683. Alt: 49 ft.

WIGHTWOOD SCHOOL
Day — Coed Gr PS-8

Branford, CT 06405. 56 Stony Creek Rd. Tel: 203-481-0363. Fax: 203-488-3985.
www.wightwoodschool.org   E-mail: ewaldman@wightwoodschool.org
Shelley Sprague, Head.
  Pre-Prep. Feat—Lib_Skills Span Studio_Art Music. **Supp**—Rev Tut.
  Adm: 21/yr. Appl due: Rolling. Accepted: 90%.
   Enr 88. B 46. G 42. Elem 88. Wh 80%. Hisp 5%. Blk 5%. Asian 10%. Avg class size: 12.
      Fac 13. M 3. F 7/3. Wh 92%. Hisp 8%. Adv deg: 46%.
   Grad '04—3. Prep—2. (Hamden Hall). Alum 59.
   Tui '04-'05: Day $9990-13,090 (+$50-100). **Aid:** Need 26 ($158,428).
   Summer: Enrich Rec. Tui Day $300/2-wk ses. 6 wks.
   Endow $47,000. Plant val $800,000. Bldgs 2. Class rms 10. Lib 4000 vols. Sci labs 1. Comp labs 1. Fields 2.
   Est 1972. Nonprofit. (Sept-June).

Founded by Jeanne S. Wight, this school was modeled after the British Integrated Day concept. Throughout the program, the core curriculum in math, language arts, social studies and science follows a thematic approach; students explore a single topic appropriate to the grade level through the use of all academic disciplines. Art, music, Spanish, library, physical education and multicultural studies instructors provide additional enrichment at all age levels. Small class size aids in the learning process.

Reading, arithmetic and writing, including creative writing, are stressed. Mathematics is taught with an emphasis on manipulative materials such as Dienes blocks and Cuisenaire rods, and computer instruction begins in grade 2. An enrichment art program serves children of all ages.

Field trips to libraries, museums and parks are part of the overall program. Wightwood also offers an extended-day enrichment program, a flexible prekindergarten program and an annual summer session.

CHESHIRE, CT. (21 mi. SSW of Hartford, CT; 79 mi. NE of New York, NY) Suburban. Pop: 28,543. Alt: 161 ft.

CHESHIRE ACADEMY
Bdg — Coed Gr 9-PG; Day — Coed 6-PG

Cheshire, CT 06410. 10 Main St. Tel: 203-272-5396. Fax: 203-250-7209.
www.cheshireacademy.org   E-mail: admissions@cheshireacademy.org
Ralph Van Inwagen, Head. Michael D. McCleery, Adm.
  Col Prep. Gen Acad. AP—Eng Fr Span Calc Bio Chem Physics Eur_Hist US_Hist US_Govt & Pol Studio_Art Music_Theory. **Feat**—Computers. **Supp**—ESL Tut.
  Adm: 116/yr. Bdg 72. Day 44. Appl due: Feb. **Tests** ISEE SSAT TOEFL.

Enr 333. B 106/104. G 56/67. Elem 49. Sec 272. PG 12. Wh 75%. Hisp 2%. Blk 3%. Am Ind 1%. Asian 19%. Avg class size: 12. **Fac 62.** M 29. F 33. Wh 95%. Blk 5%. Adv deg: 58%. In dorms 27.

Grad '04—74. Col—74. (Franklin & Marshall, Hartwick, Mt Ida, Roger Williams, U of New Haven, Northeastern U). Avg SAT: 1200. Avg SSAT: 65%. Alum 6000.

Tui '04-'05: Bdg $33,060 (+$1500). **Day $20,390-22,430** (+$800-1000). **Aid:** Merit 6 ($80,800). Need 90 ($1,104,746).

Summer: Acad Rec. Arts. ESL. Tui Bdg $4500. Tui Day $2400. 5 wks.

Endow $7,405,000. Plant val $30,000,000. Bldgs 20. Dorms 5. Dorm rms 90. Class rms 43. Lib 17,000 vols. Comp labs 2. Comp ctrs 1. Auds 1. Theaters 1. Art studios 2. Music studios 1. Gyms 2. Fields 6. Tennis courts 10. Pools 1.

Est 1794. Nonprofit. Sem (Sept-June). **Assoc** NEASC.

Founded as a coeducational community school, Cheshire Academy was established as the Episcopal Academy. In the mid-1800s, it became a boys' boarding school and, during the Civil War, adopted a military program. In the early 1900s, it gave up its military program and religious affiliation; renamed the Roxbury School, it then served as a preparatory school for Yale. In 1937, the school assumed its present name. It returned to coeducation in 1969, and in 1975 female boarders were first admitted.

The school offers small classes and supervision of each student's progress, supplemented by one-on-one instruction where advisable. The traditional upper school curriculum includes Advanced Placement and honors courses, as well as programs in the fine arts, technology, study skills and SAT preparation. Programs for independent study can be arranged by department heads in grades 9-PG, and semester-long study abroad opportunities are also available to qualified pupils. Cheshire's afternoon program comprises interscholastic athletics, performing arts options, community service, school publications and interest groups.

The middle school program (grades 6-8) is notable for its developmental approach and flexible scheduling. Music, foreign language, athletics, technology and the performing arts are components of the program. Field trips relevant to subject matter complement in-class learning.

DANBURY, CT. (48 mi. WSW of Hartford, CT; 56 mi. NNE of New York, NY) Suburban. Pop: 74,848. Alt: 378 ft.

WOOSTER SCHOOL
Day — Coed Gr K-12

Danbury, CT 06810. 91 Miry Brook Rd. Tel: 203-830-3900. Fax: 203-790-7147.
www.woosterschool.org   E-mail: samuel.gaudet@woostersch.org

George N. King, Jr., Head. BA, Murray State Univ, MS, New England Conservatory of Music. **Samuel L. Gaudet, Adm.**

Col Prep. Gen Acad. **AP**—Eng Fr Span Calc Stats Bio Chem Physics Eur_Hist US_Hist Econ Studio_Art Music_Theory. **Feat**—Japan Russ Engineering Computers Comp_ Graphics Pol_Sci Ethics Relig Ceramics Photog Sculpt Chorus Music Study_Skills. **Supp**—ESL.

Adm: 84/yr. Appl due: Feb. Accepted: 50%. **Tests** ISEE SSAT.

Enr 417. B 202. G 215. Elem 273. Sec 144. Wh 81%. Hisp 6%. Blk 4%. Asian 3%. Other

6%. Avg class size: 12. **Fac 78.** M 16/13. F 30/19. Wh 88%. Hisp 2%. Blk 2%. Asian 2%. Other 6%. Adv deg: 33%.

Grad '04—33. Col—33. (Cornell, Columbia, Boston Col, Dartmouth, NYU, Skidmore). Avg SAT: 1164. Alum 1800.

Tui '03-'04: Day $12,550-19,900 (+$125-1300). **Aid:** Need 102 ($1,217,645).

Summer: Gr PS-9. Enrich Rec. Sports. Tui Day $500/2-wk ses. 4 wks.

Endow $4,700,000. Plant val $24,000,000. Bldgs 15. Libs 2. Sci labs 3. Comp labs 2. Theaters 1. Art studios 5. Music studios 3. Drama studios 1. Gyms 3. Fields 5. Courts 2. Pools 1.

Est 1926. Nonprofit. Episcopal. Sem (Sept-June). **Assoc** CLS NEASC.

Since its founding, Wooster has sought academic excellence and a diverse student body, while emphasizing community responsibility and spiritual growth. The college preparatory curriculum provides a grounding in the basics of liberal education, while offering enough flexibility for individual interests. Special programs include Advanced Placement, a year abroad in France or Spain, independent study for seniors, individualized college guidance, and extensive fine arts and music offerings.

Students may participate in such extracurricular activities as team sports, drama, music, art, chess, newspaper, literary magazine and yearbook. All pupils, under the direction of the senior class, are accountable for the daily maintenance of the campus. **See Also Pages 1280-1**

FAIRFIELD, CT. (48 mi. NE of New York, NY; 53 mi. SW of Hartford, CT) Suburban. Pop: 57,340. Alt: 25 ft.

FAIRFIELD COLLEGE PREPARATORY SCHOOL
Day — Boys Gr 9-12

Fairfield, CT 06824. 1073 N Benson Rd. Tel: 203-254-4200. Fax: 203-254-4108.
 www.prep.fairfield.edu E-mail: gmarshall@mail.fairfield.edu

Rev. Michael G. Boughton, SJ, Pres. BA, MA, Boston College, MDiv, Weston School of Theology. **Gregory H. Marshall, Adm.**

Col Prep. AP—Eng Fr Lat Span Calc Eur_Hist US_Hist US_Govt & Pol. **Feat**—Environ_Sci Computers Theol Drawing Studio_Art Acting Drama Band Drafting. **Supp**—Tut.

Adm: 252/yr. Appl due: Dec.

Enr 890. B 890. Sec 890. Wh 92%. Hisp 3%. Blk 3%. Asian 3%. Avg class size: 22. **Fac 60.** M 39/2. F 19. Adv deg: 66%.

Grad '04—170. Col—165. (Fordham, U of CT, St Joseph's U, Fairfield, Loyola Col, Holy Cross). Avg SAT: 1199. Alum 11,000.

Tui '04-'05: Day $11,110 (+$335). **Aid:** Need 215 ($1,160,000).

Endow $5,000,000. Bldgs 2. Sci labs 4. Comp labs 2. Auds 1. Art studios 3. Music studios 1. Gyms 1. Fields 5. Courts 7. Pools 1.

Est 1942. Nonprofit. Roman Catholic. Sem (Aug-June). **Assoc** NEASC.

Situated on a 200-acre campus, this Jesuit-directed school offers a college preparatory program. Freshmen must complete a computer literacy course, and all students take part in a four-year developmental service program, working within the church and the community.

Extracurricular activities include school publications, debating, tutoring, a social service program, and language, camera and film clubs. Football, skiing, soccer, rugby, hockey, wrestling, golf, basketball, baseball, tennis, swimming, lacrosse, track, bowling and cross-country are included in the sports program.

FAIRFIELD COUNTRY DAY SCHOOL
Day — Boys Gr K-9

Fairfield, CT 06824. 2970 Bronson Rd. Tel: 203-259-2723. Fax: 203-259-3249.
www.fairfieldcountryday.org   E-mail: admissions@fcds.pvt.k12.ct.us
Robert D. Vitalo, Head. BS, New York Univ, MA, Columbia Univ. **Richard E. McGrath, Adm.**
  Pre-Prep. Feat—Fr Lat Span Computers. **Supp**—Tut.
  Adm: 40/yr. Appl due: Rolling. Accepted: 35%. **Tests** ISEE SSAT.
  Enr 272. B 272. Elem 260. Sec 12. Wh 90%. Hisp 3%. Blk 3%. Asian 4%. Avg class size: 13. **Fac 44.** M 16. F 25/3. Adv deg: 52%.
  Grad '04—10. Prep—9. (Taft, Hotchkiss, Peddie, Deerfield Acad, Phillips Exeter, Choate). Alum 1100.
  Tui '04-'05: Day $20,700-22,300. Aid: Need 23 ($203,000).
  Summer: Coed. Enrich Rec. Tui Day $275-325/wk. 7 wks.
  Endow $2,500,000. Plant val $10,000,000. Bldgs 4. Class rms 20. Lib 10,200 vols. Sci labs 2. Lang labs 1. Gyms 1. Fields 5. Tennis courts 1. Rinks 1.
  Est 1936. Nonprofit. Tri (Sept-June).

FCDS' academic program, conducted in small classes, includes conversational French classes beginning in kindergarten and accelerated math courses in grades 6-9. Computer instruction is also an integral part of the program. Such extracurricular activities as art, chorus, drama, community service, student council, publications and a broad-based athletic program complement class work.

THE UNQUOWA SCHOOL
Day — Coed Gr PS-8

Fairfield, CT 06825. 981 Stratfield Rd. Tel: 203-336-3801. Fax: 203-336-3479.
www.unquowa.com   E-mail: shansen@unquowa.com
Sharon Lauer, Head. BS, Millersville Univ of Pennsylvania. **Suellen Hansen, Adm.**
  Pre-Prep. Gen Acad. Feat—Span Computers Studio_Art Drama Music.
  Adm: 55/yr. Appl due: Rolling. Accepted: 61%. **Tests** ISEE.
  Enr 171. B 77. G 94. Elem 171. Wh 94%. Hisp 2%. Blk 3%. Asian 1%. Avg class size: 12. Uniform. **Fac 26.** M 3/1. F 19/3. Wh 96%. Hisp 4%. Adv deg: 50%.
  Grad '04—10. Prep—6. (Fairfield Col Prep, Greens Farms, St Luke's Sch-CT). Alum 7025.
  Tui '04-'05: Day $16,500-19,500. Aid: Merit 3 ($59,000). Need 17 ($165,650).
  Endow $153,000. Plant val $3,500,000. Bldgs 1. Class rms 20. Lib 5000 vols. Sci labs 1. Comp ctrs 1. Art studios 1. Music studios 1. Gyms 1.
  Est 1917. Nonprofit. Tri (Sept-June).

Situated on four acres along the Rooster River, Unquowa emphasizes the basic skills at all grade levels. Academic offerings center around a problem solving approach within the traditional disciplines. The early grades stress reading readiness, phonics, decoding and number skills. Spanish instruction begins in prekindergarten. Other areas of study include math, science, social studies, drama, art and music.

Physical education is conducted daily, and children may also take part in an after-school sports program.

FARMINGTON, CT. (8 mi. WSW of Hartford, CT; 93 mi. NE of New York, NY) Suburban. Pop: 23,641. Alt: 245 ft.

MISS PORTER'S SCHOOL
Bdg and Day — Girls Gr 9-12

Farmington, CT 06032. 60 Main St. Tel: 860-409-3530. Fax: 860-409-3531.
  www.missporters.org   E-mail: admissions@missporters.org
M. Burch Tracy Ford, Head. BA, Boston Univ, MSW, Simmons College, EdM, Harvard Univ.
Deborah Haskins, Adm.
  Col Prep. AP—Fr Lat Span Calc Stats Comp_Sci Bio Chem Physics Eur_Hist US_Hist Art_Hist Studio_Art. **Feat**—Creative_Writing Chin Greek Comp_Design Animation Middle_East_Hist African_Hist Lat-Amer_Hist Econ Intl_Relations Ethics World_Relig Photog Drama Music Journ. **Supp**—ESL Tut.
  Adm: 89/yr. Bdg 56. Day 33. Appl due: Jan. Accepted: 35%. Yield: 51%. **Tests** ISEE SSAT TOEFL.
  Enr 314. G 211/103. Sec 314. Wh 72%. Hisp 9%. Blk 9%. Am Ind 1%. Asian 9%. Avg class size: 11. **Fac 39.** M 14/2. F 21/2. Adv deg: 84%. In dorms 2.
  Grad '04—81. Col—81. (Boston U, Cornell, Georgetown, Yale, Wheaton-MA, Vassar). Avg SAT: 1198. Avg SSAT: 67%. Alum 5473.
  Tui '04-'05: Bdg $33,200 (+$1800). **Day $25,000** (+$1000). **Aid:** Merit 6 ($69,500). Need 30 ($600,000).
  Summer: Gr 7-9. Enrich. Arts. Leadership. Tui Bdg $500-3600. ½-4 wks.
  Endow $60,000,000. Plant val $28,112,000. Bldgs 50. Dorms 8. Dorm rms 106. Class rms 37. Lib 22,000 vols. Sci labs 1. Lang labs 1. Comp labs 3. Auds 1. Theaters 1. Art studios 2. Music studios 4. Dance studios 1. Gyms 2. Fields 4. Courts 6.
  Est 1843. Nonprofit. Sem (Sept-May). **Assoc** CLS NEASC.

Sarah Porter, sister of onetime Yale president Noah Porter, founded this school that bears her name. Using educational techniques ahead of her time, she made MPS preeminent in the field of education for young women. After her death in 1900, Elizabeth Dow, her close friend and colleague, conducted the school. In 1903, Elizabeth Vashti Hale Keep took responsibility for the school, which had continued to offer higher education in an era when few girls advanced beyond grammar school. From 1917 to 1943, Mrs. Keep's son and daughter-in-law presided over a rigorous curriculum that increasingly emphasized college preparation.

In the centenary year, the school was turned over to a nonprofit corporation. Today, the school's unified liberal arts curriculum provides sequential instruction in reading, writing, speaking, computing and symbolic reasoning. Honors and Advanced Placement courses are offered in all departments, and many electives are also available. Campus art studios provide girls with opportunities in photography, painting, sculpture, printmaking and jewelry making, and pupils may develop graphic design skills in the computer lab. Computer technology is an important component of school life.

Athletics, dramatics, orchestra, a cappella choir, interest clubs, school publications, school trips, art, dance, student government, community service and Model UN are among the student activities. Juniors may participate in such special programs as Maine Coast Semester, School Year Abroad, Rocky Mountain Semester and CITYterm.

GREENWICH, CT. (30 mi. NNE of New York, NY) Urban. Pop: 61,010. Alt: 28 ft.

BRUNSWICK SCHOOL
Day — Boys Gr PS-12

Greenwich, CT 06830. 100 Maher Ave. Tel: 203-625-5800. Fax: 203-625-5889.
www.brunswickschool.org   E-mail: jeffry_harris@brunswickschool.org
Thomas W. Philip, Head. BA, Bucknell Univ, MA, Wesleyan Univ. **Jeffry C. Harris, Adm.**

- **Col Prep. AP**—Fr Lat Span Calc Stats Comp_Sci Bio Chem Physics Eur_Hist US_Hist Econ Psych US_Govt & Pol Art_Hist Studio_Art. **Feat**—Chin Greek Oceanog Computers Photog Music. **Supp**—Dev_Read Rem_Math Rem_Read Rev.
- **Adm:** 136/yr. Appl due: Dec. Accepted: 25%. Yield: 90%. **Tests** CEEB CTP_4 IQ ISEE SSAT.
- **Enr 877.** B 877. Elem 561. Sec 316. Wh 88%. Hisp 3%. Blk 4%. Asian 2%. Other 3%. Avg class size: 15. **Fac 156.** M 74/3. F 65/14. Wh 93%. Hisp 3%. Blk 1%. Asian 1%. Other 2%. Adv deg: 55%.
- **Grad '04—76. Col—76.** (Columbia 5, U of PA 5, Duke 4, Yale 4, Boston Col 4, Middlebury 3). Avg SAT: 1360. Alum 2500.
- **Tui '04-'05: Day $18,200-23,400** (+$750). **Aid:** Need 66 ($1,208,300).
- **Summer:** Enrich Rev. Sports. 4-7 wks.
- Endow $65,000,000. Plant val $76,000,000. Bldgs 10. Class rms 35. 3 Libs 19,000 vols. Sci labs 8. Lang labs 2. Comp labs 4. Auds 3. Art studios 3. Music studios 2. Shops 1. Gyms 4. Fields 4. Rinks 1.
- **Est 1902.** Nonprofit. Sem (Sept-June). **Assoc** CLS NEASC.

Founded and directed for 30 years by George E. Carmichael, this school is divided into lower, middle and upper divisions. In the upper school, the majority of classes are conducted on a coordinate basis with Greenwich Academy, a neighboring girls' school. The rigorous college preparatory program provides honors and Advanced Placement courses in every subject and a comprehensive arts curriculum.

All students take part in the athletic program, through either intramural or interscholastic competition, and participate in a wide range of activities that includes various clubs, yearbook, literary magazine, school newspaper, dramatic productions and music groups. Every boy in grades 9-12 also gives some portion of his time in service to the school or the community.

CONVENT OF THE SACRED HEART
Day — Girls Gr PS-12

Greenwich, CT 06831. 1177 King St. Tel: 203-531-6500. Fax: 203-531-5206.
www.cshgreenwich.org   E-mail: admission@cshgreenwich.org

Sr. Joan Magnetti, RSCJ, Head. BA, Manhattanville College, MA, Union Theological Seminary. **Pamela R. McKenna, Adm.**
- **Col Prep. AP**—Eng Fr Span Calc Stats Bio Chem Physics US_Hist Comp_Govt & Pol. **Feat**—Shakespeare African-Amer_Lit Lat-Amer_Lit Lat Astron Comp_Sci Web_Design Psych Ethics Theol World_Relig Photog Studio_Art Drama Music Journ. **Supp**—Rev Tut.
- **Adm (Gr PS-10):** 114/yr. Appl due: Feb. Accepted: 40%. Yield: 80%. **Tests** CTP_4 ISEE.
- **Enr 685.** G 685. Elem 452. Sec 233. Wh 83%. Hisp 6%. Blk 9%. Asian 2%. Avg class size: 14. Uniform. **Fac 110.** M 15/1. F 90/4. Adv deg: 78%.
- **Grad '04—59. Col—59.** (Notre Dame 4, Holy Cross 3, NYU 3, Harvard 2, Cornell 2, Boston Col 2). Avg SAT: 1250. Alum 1600.
- **Tui '04-'05: Day $19,000-23,000** (+$1000-3000). **Aid:** Merit 6 ($60,000). Need 92 ($1,400,000).
- **Summer:** Enrich Rec. 5 wks.
- Endow $15,000,000. Plant val $4,200,000. Bldgs 5. Class rms 27. Libs 2. Chapels 1. Sci labs 6. Comp labs 2. Observatories 1. Auds 1. Art studios 2. Music studios 1. Dance studios 1. Photog studios 1. Art galleries 1. Gyms 1. Fields 4. Courts 6. Pools 1. Fitness rms 1. Student ctrs 1.
- **Est 1848.** Nonprofit. Roman Catholic. Tri (Sept-June). **Assoc** CLS NEASC.

Founded in New York City, the school moved to its 110-acre Greenwich campus in 1945, where renovations have since been made to the original mansion.

Sacred Heart integrates a rigorous academic program, the foundation of a strong faith, and the development of social responsibility. The curriculum emphasizes advanced course work and independent study; honors and AP courses are offered. Religious education begins in the lower school and includes prayer services, liturgies, retreats and other campus ministry programs. Community service begins informally in the earliest grades, and each student in the upper school fulfills an annual commitment. Students are evaluated for their work with various community, health, education, recreational and welfare agencies.

An exchange program for girls in grades 9-12 is conducted with other Sacred Heart schools in the United States and abroad. Various academic, community and social activities involving local boys' high schools, such as dances, community service projects, sports and dramatic arts, complement the extracurricular program. All girls participate in at least one extracurricular activity, with options including student government and committees; Model UN; yearbook; English, French and Spanish newspapers; chorus; a handbell choir; and dramatic and musical productions. Students also compete in an interscholastic athletic program.

See Also Pages 1292-3

GREENWICH ACADEMY

Day — Girls Gr PS-12

Greenwich, CT 06830. 200 N Maple Ave. Tel: 203-625-8900. Fax: 203-625-8991.
www.greenwichacademy.org   E-mail: admission_office@greenwichacademy.org
Molly H. King, Head. BA, Bowdoin College, EdM, Harvard Univ. **Nancy E. Hoffmann & Gloria Fernandez-Tearte, Adms.**
- **Col Prep. AP**—Fr Lat Span Calc Stats Comp_Sci Bio Chem Human_Geog Physics Eur_Hist US_Hist World_Hist Econ Psych US_Govt & Pol Art_Hist Studio_Art. **Feat**—Creative_Writing Chin Greek Ital Astron Geol Oceanog Comp_Graphics Film Theater Chorus Music Music_Theory Dance.

Adm (Gr PS-11): 114/yr. Appl due: Dec. Accepted: 25%. Yield: 84%. **Tests** CTP_4 ISEE SSAT.

Enr 776. G 776. Elem 479. Sec 297. Wh 82%. Hisp 3%. Blk 4%. Asian 5%. Other 6%. Avg class size: 14. Uniform. **Fac 108.** M 15/1. F 74/18. Wh 90%. Hisp 5%. Blk 5%. Adv deg: 65%.

Grad '04—70. Col—70. (U of PA, Stanford, Boston Col, Georgetown, Harvard, Princeton). Avg SAT: 1346. Alum 2679.

Tui '05-'06: Day $21,950-25,000 (+$500-2000). **Aid:** Need 73 ($1,432,950).

Summer: Enrich Rec. 3-10 wks.

Endow $67,308,000. Plant val $64,376,000. Bldgs 12. Class rms 46. Lib 29,000 vols. Sci labs 9. Lang labs 1. Comp labs 2. Auds 2. Theaters 2. Art studios 6. Music studios 4. Dance studios 2. Perf arts ctrs 1. Art galleries 1. Gyms 2. Fields 4. Tennis courts 6. Squash courts 5.

Est 1827. Nonprofit. Quar (Sept-June). **Assoc** CLS NEASC.

Located on a 38-acre campus, Greenwich Academy is a traditional girls' school with a structured liberal arts curriculum. Clearly defined requirements in English, mathematics, history, language arts and science are supplemented by a wide range of electives offered both at the academy and through coordination with neighboring Brunswick School for boys. Honors and Advanced Placement courses are available in most disciplines; in addition, the use of laptop computers is required in grades 7-12. Classes and projects in the arts are central to the curriculum, with choices in the performing and visual arts.

Interscholastic athletic competition begins in grade 7; basketball, crew, cross-country, field hockey, golf, ice hockey, lacrosse, sailing, soccer, softball, swimming, squash, tennis, track and volleyball are the available sports. Students produce a literary magazine, several newspapers and a yearbook. All students are expected to perform community service.

GA's coordinated program with Brunswick provides not only coeducational classes, but also many joint music, drama, art and community service projects.

See Also Page 1296

GREENWICH COUNTRY DAY SCHOOL

Day — Coed Gr PS-9

Greenwich, CT 06830. Old Church Rd, PO Box 623. Tel: 203-863-5600.
Fax: 203-622-6046.
www.gcds.net E-mail: admission@gcds.net

Adam C. Rohdie, Head. BA, Wesleyan Univ. MA, Stanford Univ. **Kirby Williams, Adm.**

Pre-Prep. Gen Acad. Feat—Fr Lat Span Computers Band Chorus. **Supp—**Dev_Read Rem_Read Tut.

Adm (Gr PS-8): 101/yr. Appl due: Dec. Accepted: 26%. Yield: 85%. **Tests** CEEB CTP_4 ISEE.

Enr 839. B 425. G 414. Elem 784. Sec 55. Wh 89%. Hisp 2%. Blk 5%. Asian 3%. Other 1%. Avg class size: 18. **Fac 135.** M 40. F 95.

Grad '04—58. Prep—56. (Greenwich Acad 12, Brunswick 7, Deerfield Acad 6, Choate 3, Millbrook 3, Peddie 3). Alum 3223.

Tui '04-'05: Day $13,000-22,400. Aid: Need 120 ($1,500,000).

Summer: Enrich Rec. Tui Day $1500-1800. 5 wks.

Endow $25,839,000. Bldgs 27. Class rms 60. Lib 20,000 vols. Labs 6. Music studios 7. Gyms 4. Fields 8. Tennis courts 4. Pools 2. Rinks 1.

Est 1926. Nonprofit. Tri (Sept-June).

GCDS emphasizes academic preparation while maintaining a varied extracurricular and artistic program. English, math, science and social studies are required at all grade levels, with a conversational Spanish language program and computer education both beginning in kindergarten. Art and choral music are offered, and the school has two full bands, piano, drama, and print and wood shops. The regular program also includes two- to five-day trips for students in grades 5-9 to such places as Mystic; Washington, DC; and outdoor education centers in New Jersey and New York State.

Athletics are required, combining physical education with interscholastic competition in the upper school. Dance, ice hockey and physical fitness balance a standard competitive program. Community service is stressed, and students serve both on campus and in community agencies and institutions.

WHITBY SCHOOL
Day — Coed Gr PS-8

Greenwich, CT 06831. 969 Lake Ave. Tel: 203-869-8464. Fax: 203-869-2215.
 www.whitbyschool.org   E-mail: info@whitbyschool.org
Michele Monson, Head. MEd, Lesley College, EdD, Harvard Univ. **Deborah B. Smith, Adm.**

Pre-Prep. Gen Acad. Feat—Fr Span Computers Studio_Art Drama Band Music. **Supp**—Dev_Read Rem_Math Rem_Read Rev Tut.

Adm: 81/yr. Appl due: Dec. Accepted: 40%. **Tests** CTP_4 ISEE.

Enr 305. B 161. G 144. Elem 305. Wh 84%. Hisp 3%. Blk 3%. Asian 6%. Other 4%. Avg class size: 21. Uniform. **Fac** 63. M 8. F 46/9. Adv deg: 33%.

Grad '04—8.

Tui '04-'05: Day $11,400-21,000 (+$135-1000). **Aid:** Need 25 ($362,700).

Endow $421,000. Plant val $11,140,000. Bldgs 4. Class rms 20. Lib 4000 vols. Labs 2. Art studios 1. Music studios 1. Gyms 1. Fields 3. Courts 2.

Est 1958. Nonprofit. Sem (Sept-June).

The oldest school in the country that adheres to the Montessori approach, Whitby brings forth natural growth of mind and body through a program designed to aid the child in becoming an independent learner. The school's multi-age approach allows students to stay with the same teacher for two to three years, thus enabling the instructor to follow each child's progress through an entire developmental cycle. The curriculum, while traditional in content, imposes no ceiling on learning.

The sharing of values and the development of a sense of community are integral parts of school life. The 24-acre campus, located in the backcountry of Greenwich, has its own pond, woods and playing fields. Students enroll from Fairfield and Westchester counties.

HARTFORD, CT. (65 mi. W of Providence, RI; 100 mi. NE of New York, NY) Urban. Pop: 121,578. Alt: 38 ft. Area also includes West Hartford.

KINGSWOOD-OXFORD SCHOOL

Day — Coed Gr 6-PG

West Hartford, CT 06119. 170 Kingswood Rd. Tel: 860-233-9631. Fax: 860-236-3651.
www.kingswood-oxford.org E-mail: fins.c@k-o.org

Lee M. Levison, Head. BA, Amherst College, MEd, EdD, Harvard Univ. **Jane Daly Seaberg, Adm.**

- Col Prep. AP—Eng Fr Lat Span Stats Comp_Sci Bio Chem Physics US_Hist Econ US_Govt & Pol Art_Hist. **Feat**—African-Amer_Lit Anat & Physiol Philos Relig Photog Acting. **Supp**—Tut.
- Adm: 128/yr. Appl due: Feb. Accepted: 71%. Yield: 51%. **Tests** IQ SSAT.
- **Enr 580.** B 301. G 279. Elem 198. Sec 381. PG 1. Wh 85%. Hisp 3%. Blk 7%. Asian 5%. Avg class size: 13. **Fac 89.** M 43/1. F 40/5. Wh 94%. Hisp 2%. Blk 1%. Asian 3%. Adv deg: 64%.
- **Grad '04—104. Col—104.** (U of CT 10, Skidmore 6, Trinity Col-CT 4, Geo Wash 4, Fordham 4, Northeastern U 4). Avg SAT: 1222. Alum 6300.
- **Tui '04-'05: Day $23,845** (+$650). **Aid:** Need 178 ($2,144,850).
- Endow $18,641,000. Plant val $17,778,000. Bldgs 9. Class rms 41. 2 Libs 35,000 vols. Sci labs 11. Comp labs 4. Comp ctrs 1. Auds 1. Theaters 1. Art studios 5. Music studios 5. Dance studios 1. Gyms 3. Athletic ctrs 1. Fields 8. Courts 7. Squash courts 4. Rinks 1.
- **Est 1909.** Nonprofit. Sem (Sept-June). **Assoc** CLS NEASC.

K-O is the result of the 1969 merger of Kingswood School for boys and Oxford School for girls. In fall 2003, the middle school (grades 6-8) moved from the former Oxford campus to the main, 30-acre former Kingswood campus, where the upper school (grades 9-12) has long been located. The student body represents a cross section of central Connecticut residents in their religious, social and economic backgrounds.

Offering a college preparatory program, the school maintains small classes and close contact between students and faculty. The well-rounded curriculum, which includes course work in English, history, math, science, foreign language, computer science, and the performing and visual arts, culminates in a wide selection of Advanced Placement classes. Independent study is encouraged. Seniors compose a required thesis during the third quarter of the academic year, and they may also pursue an on- or off-campus project during the last quarter. Upper school students may engage in foreign exchange programs for either a semester or a full school year.

Sports include cross-country, football, soccer, basketball, ice hockey, skiing, squash, swimming and diving, baseball, golf, lacrosse, tennis, track and field, weight training and conditioning, and dance for boys, and cross-country, field hockey, soccer, volleyball, basketball, gymnastics, ice hockey, skiing, squash, swimming and diving, golf, lacrosse, softball, tennis, track and field, weight training and conditioning, and dance for girls. Among K-O's extracurricular activities are publications, music, drama, clubs and community service.

RENBROOK SCHOOL
Day — Coed Gr PS-9

West Hartford, CT 06117. 2865 Albany Ave. Tel: 860-236-1661. Fax: 860-231-8206.
www.renbrook.org   E-mail: admission@renbrook.org
Jane C. Shipp, Head. BA, Rhodes College, MA, Brown Univ. **Katherine O. Nixon, Adm.**
  Pre-Prep. Feat—Lib_Skills Fr Lat Span Studio_Art Drama Music Study_Skills.
  Adm: 117/yr. Appl due: Feb. Accepted: 72%. Yield: 52%.
  Enr 555. B 279. G 276. Elem 529. Sec 26. Wh 80%. Hisp 1%. Blk 9%. Asian 5%. Other 5%. Avg class size: 14. **Fac 90.** M 18/3. F 56/13. Wh 92%. Hisp 2%. Blk 4%. Asian 2%. Adv deg: 57%.
  Grad '04—34. Prep—34. (Loomis Chaffee, Westminster Acad, Suffield, Miss Porter's, Kingswood-Oxford, Choate). Alum 2400.
  Tui '04-'05: Day $9400-21,945 (+$100-700). **Aid:** Need 75 ($1,134,934).
  Summer: Enrich Rec. Tui Day $1025. 3 wks.
  Endow $5,557,000. Plant val $20,327,000. Bldgs 10. Class rms 56. Lib 33,000 vols. Sci labs 5. Comp labs 4. Auds 2. Theaters 2. Art studios 4. Music studios 6. Gyms 2. Fields 4. Courts 3. Pools 3. Ropes crses 2. Playgrounds 4. Ponds 1.
  Est 1935. Nonprofit. Tri (Sept-June).

Located on the 75-acre Rentschler estate overlooking the city, Renbrook conducts preschool, elementary and middle school programs.

The 12-year academic program places emphasis on the development of sound study skills at all grade levels. Children of all ages receive instruction in language and listening skills, science, math, library studies, music, art and physical education. Renbrook's curriculum includes 10 years of French and Spanish, social studies, technology, learning strategies, drama and lab science, as well as four years of Latin. Honors courses, independent study opportunities, community service options and leadership classes complete the curriculum.

The physical education program (in which all students participate) comprises physical fitness and a variety of interscholastic sports, among them football, soccer, basketball, ice hockey, baseball, tennis, lacrosse, gymnastics, field hockey, softball and volleyball. Pupils in grades 4-9 participate in Project Adventure, a high and low ropes course. Extended-day services, an after-school program, vacation care and a summer day camp are also available.

WATKINSON SCHOOL
Day — Coed Gr 6-PG

Hartford, CT 06105. 180 Bloomfield Ave. Tel: 860-236-5618. Fax: 860-233-8295.
www.watkinson.org   E-mail: info@watkinson.org
John W. Bracker, Head. BA, Haverford College, MEd, Harvard Univ. **John J. Crosson, Adm.**
  Col Prep. Feat—ASL Fr Span Anat & Physiol Asian_Hist Ceramics Photog Sculpt Studio_Art Music. **Supp**—Dev_Read Rem_Read Tut.
  Adm: 85/yr. Appl due: Feb. Accepted: 66%. Yield: 72%. **Tests** ISEE SSAT Stanford.
  Enr 277. B 148. G 129. Elem 90. Sec 185. PG 2. Wh 79%. Hisp 4%. Blk 8%. Asian 3%. Other 6%. Avg class size: 13. **Fac 59.** M 15/3. F 29/12. Wh 90%. Hisp 2%. Blk 8%. Adv deg: 57%.
  Grad '04—48. Col—46. (U of CT 3, Clark U 2, Geo Wash 2, Harvey Mudd 2, NYU 2, U of Hartford 2). Avg SAT: 1133. Alum 1691.
  Tui '04-'05: Day $22,440 (+$1500). **Aid:** Need 72 ($1,004,610). Work prgm 19

($14,000).
Summer: Acad Enrich Rev Rem. 4 wks.
Endow $2,190,000. Plant val $8,532,000. Bldgs 5. Class rms 26. Lib 8000 vols. Labs 2. Sci labs 4. Comp labs 3. Auds 1. Theaters 1. Art studios 2. Music studios 1. Dance studios 1. Gyms 1. Fields 2. Courts 4.
Est 1881. Nonprofit. Tri (Sept-June). **Assoc** NEASC.

The school, established through the liberal bequest of David Watkinson, occupies 40 rural Hartford acres, just ten minutes from downtown and the state capitol. The campus includes a performing arts and athletic center that houses an indoor Greek theater where daily school meetings are held. The core college preparatory curriculum is enhanced by programs in writing, learning skills, computers and community service. A creative arts program offers a special diploma to preprofessional students in conjunction with Dance Connecticut and the Hartt School of Music.

Closely affiliated with the neighboring University of Hartford, with which it shares many cooperative programs, Watkinson provides access to the resources of a large university, as well as the opportunity for seniors to graduate with college credits. In addition, the Transition to College program bridges secondary school and college for 13th-year students.

KENSINGTON, CT. (10 mi. SSW of Hartford, CT; 90 mi. NE of New York, NY) Suburban. Pop: 8541. Alt: 64 ft.

MOORELAND HILL SCHOOL
Day — Coed Gr 5-9

Kensington, CT 06037. 166 Lincoln St. Tel: 860-223-6428. Fax: 860-223-3318.
  www.mooreland.org   E-mail: ccarlson@mooreland.org
Michael L. Waller, Head. BA, Univ of California-Irvine, MEd, Univ of San Francisco. **Cheryl C. Carlson, Adm.**
  Pre-Prep. Feat—Fr Lat Span Computers Studio_Art Drama Music.
  Adm: 12/yr. Appl due: Feb. **Tests** ISEE.
  Enr 45. Elem 43. Sec 2. Wh 82%. Hisp 9%. Blk 4%. Asian 7%. Other 3%. Avg class size: 12. **Fac 11.** M 3. F 5/3. Wh 100%. Adv deg: 45%.
  Grad '04—13. Prep—12. (Miss Porter's 6, Avon 3, Loomis Chaffee 3). Alum 965.
  Tui '04-'05: Day $15,930. Aid: Need 16 ($111,480).
  Endow $250,000. Plant val $4,500,000. Bldgs 5. Class rms 10. Libs 1. Sci labs 1. Comp labs 1. Photog labs 1. Auds 1. Art studios 1. Gyms 1. Fields 2. Courts 1. Basketball courts 1.
  Est 1930. Nonprofit. Sem (Aug-June).

Founded as the Shuttle Meadow School by New Britain industrialist families, the school became Mooreland Hill in 1937, in gratitude for property donated by E. Allen Moore. Today, the school enrolls students from more than two dozen central Connecticut towns. The curriculum is traditional, with emphasis placed on English, literature, history, math and science. Complementing the basics are offerings in French, Latin, computer, art, music, and human growth and development. Mooreland Hill maintains small average class sizes, and the curriculum includes advanced-level courses in all major disciplines.

A full complement of interscholastic athletics is offered for boys and girls, as are such noncompetitive options as hiking and life sports. Students may also participate in such extracurricular activities as chorus, drama, instrumental ensemble, school publications and interest clubs. Each pupil completes daily chores. Children in all grades participate in off-campus learning experiences, such as history and science trips to nearby cities; visits to local art museums, concerts and plays; and out-of-state class trips.

KENT, CT. (41 mi. W of Hartford, CT; 77 mi. NNE of New York, NY) Suburban. Pop: 2858. Alt: 395 ft.

KENT SCHOOL
Bdg — Coed Gr 9-PG; Day — Coed 9-12

Kent, CT 06757. Rte 341, PO Box 2006. Tel: 860-927-6111. Fax: 860-927-6109. www.kent-school.edu E-mail: admissions@kent-school.edu

Rev. Richardson W. Schell, Head. AB, Harvard Univ, MDiv, Yale Univ. **Marc L. Cloutier, Adm.**

Col Prep. AP—Eng Fr Ger Lat Span Calc Stats Comp_Sci Bio Chem Physics Eur_Hist US_Hist Econ Art_Hist. **Feat**—Chin Greek Astron Ecol Genetics Biotech Meteorology Asian_Stud Law Philos Theol World_Relig Ceramics Sculpt Music Music_Theory. **Supp**—ESL.

Adm (Bdg Gr 9-PG; Day 9-10): 219/yr. Bdg 197. Day 22. Appl due: Jan. Accepted: 48%. Yield: 50%. **Tests** CEEB SSAT TOEFL.

Enr 565. B 287/29. G 229/20. Sec 540. PG 25. Wh 78%. Hisp 4%. Blk 4%. Asian 13%. Other 1%. Avg class size: 11. **Fac 81.** M 46/3. F 30/2. Wh 96%. Hisp 1%. Blk 1%. Asian 1%. Other 1%. Adv deg: 58%. In dorms 30.

Grad '04—144. **Col**—144. (Boston U 9, Colby 6, Geo Wash 4, Hobart/Wm Smith 4, US Naval Acad 4, Princeton 3). Avg SAT: 1240. Alum 7650.

Tui '05-'06: Bdg $35,500 (+$3000). **Day $28,000** (+$2700). **Aid:** Merit 7 ($223,900). Need 152 ($3,215,300).

Summer: Acad Enrich Rec. Tui Bdg $2375. Tui Day $1875. 3 wks.

Endow $63,000,000. Plant val $78,000,000. Bldgs 15. Dorms 6. Dorm rms 147. Class rms 46. Lib 57,000 vols. Sci labs 14. Lang labs 1. Comp labs 1. Sci ctrs 1. Observatories 1. Auds 1. Art studios 3. Music studios 9. Dance studios 1. Gyms 2. Fields 18. Courts 15. Squash courts 3. Field houses 1. Pools 1. Rinks 1. Riding rings 6. Stables 1. Weight rms 1. Rowing ctrs 1.

Est 1906. Nonprofit. Episcopal. Tri (Sept-June). **Assoc** CLS NEASC.

One of the nation's most renowned schools, Kent has been characterized since its founding by simplicity, self-reliance and directness of purpose. Rev. Frederick H. Sill, a man of extraordinary genius and vigor, started the school in a small farm building. He developed the Kent plan of self-help, still in practice today, whereby students contribute to the school's maintenance.

Kent became coeducational in 1960, when it opened a campus for girls near its boys' campus. After operating for more than 30 years on two campuses, Kent consolidated its operations on one campus in 1992. The school facilities include St. Joseph's Chapel, a fine Norman chapel—complete with bell tower and cloister—at the center of the campus.

The school has a rigorous liberal arts program with Advanced Placement courses in every discipline—including computer science, environmental science and economics—and provides a course in study skills for all freshmen. Kent has an extracurricular program in the arts, drama and music, as well as in athletics. Sports open to both girls and boys are crew, soccer, cross-country running, basketball, swimming, ice hockey, squash, tennis, lacrosse, modern dance, mountain biking, golf and horseback riding. Boys participate in football and baseball; girls play field hockey and softball.

Graduates enter leading schools throughout the US, in Canada and abroad.

See Also Pages 1178-9

THE MARVELWOOD SCHOOL
Bdg and Day — Coed Gr 9-12

Kent, CT 06757. 476 Skiff Mountain Rd, PO Box 3001. Tel: 860-927-0047.
  Fax: 860-927-0021.
  www.themarvelwoodschool.com
  E-mail: marvelwoodadmissions@charterinternet.com
Scott Pottbecker, Head. BA, Univ of Connecticut. **Todd Holt, Adm.**

  Col Prep. Underachiever. AP—Stats. **Feat**—Creative_Writing Fr Span Anat & Physiol Ecol Environ_Sci Comp_Sci Psych Women's_Stud Ceramics Filmmaking Photog Studio_Art Drama Music. **Supp**—ESL Rev Tut.

  Adm: 72/yr. Bdg 70. Day 2. Appl due: Rolling. Accepted: 47%. **Tests** SSAT TOEFL.

  Enr 150. B 95/3. G 48/4. Sec 150. Wh 68%. Hisp 4%. Blk 9%. Asian 19%. Avg class size: 10. **Fac 42.** M 18. F 22/2. Adv deg: 40%. In dorms 16.

  Grad '04—40. Col—40. (Dean, Bryant, Clark Atlanta, Syracuse, NYU, Purdue). Alum 1300.

  Tui '05-'06: Bdg $34,500. Day $20,700. Aid: Need 16 ($540,200).

  Summer: Acad. Tui Bdg $5500. 5 wks.

  Endow $1,000,000. Plant val $10,000,000. Bldgs 17. Dorms 4. Dorm rms 92. Class rms 25. Lib 9000 vols. Labs 3. Theaters 1. Art studios 2. Music studios 1. Wood shops 1. Fields 5. Courts 6.

  Est 1956. Nonprofit. Tri (Sept-June). **Assoc** NEASC.

Marvelwood was founded by Robert A. Bodkin especially to help youngsters of average to above-average intelligence who have not lived up to academic potential in traditional school settings.

The college preparatory curriculum is sensitive to the individual who needs a structured program in order to fully realize his or her potential. One-quarter of the student body participates in a tutorial program designed to improve reading, writing, organizational and study skills. An extensive interscholastic sports program and many outdoor activities are offered. Graduates attend many different colleges.

In addition to a full range of competitive team sports, Marvelwood offers a year-round Wilderness Ways program that provides experiences in hiking, cross-country skiing, canoeing and mountain biking. All students participate in a weekly community service program. **See Also Pages 1200-1**

LAKEVILLE, CT. (41 mi. WNW of Hartford, CT; 93 mi. NNE of New York, NY) Rural. Pop: 1800. Alt: 800 ft.

THE HOTCHKISS SCHOOL
Bdg and Day — Coed Gr 9-PG

Lakeville, CT 06039. PO Box 800. Tel: 860-435-3102. Fax: 860-435-0042.
www.hotchkiss.org E-mail: admission@hotchkiss.org

Robert H. Mattoon, Jr., Head. AB, Dartmouth College, MA, Tulane Univ, PhD, Yale Univ.
William Leahy, Adm.

- **Col Prep. AP**—Eng Fr Lat Span Calc Stats Comp_Sci Bio Chem Human_Geog Physics Eur_Hist US_Hist Comp_Govt & Pol Econ Art_Hist Studio_Art Music_Theory. **Feat**—Creative_Writing Humanities Chin Ger Astron Bioethics Ecol Geol Biotechnology Limnology Forensic_Sci Web_Design Lat-Amer_Hist Govt Comp_Relig Ethics Architect Ceramics Printmaking Acting Hist_of_Jazz Dance. **Supp**—Rev Tut.
- **Adm:** 182/yr. Bdg 164. Day 18. Appl due: Jan. Accepted: 23%. **Tests** CEEB ISEE SSAT TOEFL.
- **Enr 556.** B 270/17. G 238/31. Sec 545. PG 11. Avg class size: 13. **Fac 110.** Adv deg: 72%. In dorms 46.
- **Grad '04**—168. **Col**—168. (U of VT, Bowdoin, Duke, Davidson, Harvard). Avg SAT: 1313. Alum 8949.
- **Tui '04-'05: Bdg $31,425** (+$500). **Day $26,725** (+$350). **Aid:** Need 193 ($4,332,644).
- **Summer:** Enrich. Tui Bdg $3200. 3 wks.
- Endow $311,648,000. Plant val $150,000,000. Bldgs 86. Dorms 10. Dorm rms 461. Class rms 37. Lib 74,000 vols. Sci labs 10. Lang labs 1. Comp labs 2. Photog labs 1. Dark rms 5. Comp ctrs 1. Auds 1. Theaters 2. Art studios 7. Music studios 16. Dance studios 1. Arts ctrs 1. Art galleries 2. Fields 14. Tennis courts 23. Squash courts 8. Field houses 1. Pools 1. Rinks 2. Tracks 1. Fitness ctrs 1.
- **Est 1891.** Nonprofit. Sem (Sept-June). **Assoc** CLS NEASC.

At the urging of Yale president Timothy Dwight, the school was founded by Maria Harrison Bissell Hotchkiss, who provided the land, the original buildings and the money for additional buildings. In 1974, Hotchkiss became a coeducational school.

The curriculum includes both required and elective courses in English, mathematics, history, modern and classical languages, science and the arts, and additional elective courses in such fields as computer, philosophy and religion. Students may receive instruction in Greek, German, Mandarin Chinese, a wide range of musical instruments, photography, filmmaking, dance, architecture and ceramics. Most departments offer Advanced Placement courses and independent study options for seniors. Affiliation with the English-Speaking Union and the School Year Abroad program encourages foreign study experiences.

Athletics include football, soccer, field hockey, golf, tennis, volleyball, basketball, ice hockey, cross-country, swimming, water polo, wrestling, baseball, lacrosse and track. Music, drama, dance, photography, publications, and various interest clubs and social services are among Hotchkiss' extracurricular activities. Lectures, concerts and exhibits enrich the program. **See Also Pages 1168-9**

INDIAN MOUNTAIN SCHOOL

Bdg — Coed Gr 6-9; Day — Coed PS-9

Lakeville, CT 06039. 211 Indian Mountain Rd. Tel: 860-435-0871. Fax: 860-435-0641.
www.indianmountain.org E-mail: admissions@indianmountain.org

C. **Dary Dunham, Head.** BA, Univ of Pennsylvania, MEd, Boston Univ. **Mark E. Knapp, Adm.**

Pre-Prep. Feat—Humanities Fr Lat Span Computers Studio_Art Drama Music. **Supp**—Dev_Read ESL Tut.

Adm: 100/yr. Bdg 38. Day 62. Appl due: Rolling. Accepted: 48%. Yield: 73%. **Tests** IQ.

Enr 261. B 51/101. G 20/89. Elem 222. Sec 39. Wh 87%. Hisp 6%. Blk 3%. Asian 2%. Other 2%. Avg class size: 11. **Fac 60.** M 23/4. F 21/12. Wh 100%. Adv deg: 40%. In dorms 9.

Grad '04—40. Prep—40. (Hotchkiss 8, Millbrook 6, Berkshire Sch 5, Choate 4, Salisbury-CT 4, St Paul's Sch-NH 2). Alum 2110.

Tui '04-'05: Bdg $31,395 (+$2500). **Day $16,880** (+$1500). **Aid:** Need 48 ($477,335).

Endow $4,500,000. Plant val $7,500,000. Bldgs 12. Dorms 3. Dorm rms 36. Class rms 33. Lib 10,000 vols. Sci labs 3. Comp labs 2. Sci/art ctrs 1. Comp ctrs 2. Auds 1. Theaters 1. Art studios 4. Music studios 5. Gyms 2. Fields 9. Tennis courts 3. Ropes crses 1. Skiing facilities yes.

Est 1922. Nonprofit. Tri (Sept-June).

Founded as a boarding school for boys by Francis Behn Riggs, a Groton graduate and friend of Dr. Endicott Peabody, Indian Mountain has maintained high academic standards over the years. Girls, long admitted as day students, were first accepted into the boarding program in 1991. In 2003, IMS effected a merger with the Town Hill School, a nearby elementary school that dates back to 1938, thereby expanding the day program from prekindergarten through grade 9. The program for children in grades pre-K-4 operates at the ten-acre Town Hill campus (204 Interlaken Rd.).

The curriculum is traditional, with strong emphasis placed on verbal and written skills and disciplined study habits. Curricular offerings include earth science and biology, a two-year American history course for seventh and eighth graders, and weekly computer instruction for pupils in grades 7-9. Special-help classes are held four times a week to reinforce classroom work. Students' effort and attitude are evaluated every two weeks and are discussed with their faculty advisors. IMS also operates a learning skills center that provides supportive, remedial and English as a Second Language tutoring.

The school's 600-acre main campus, which includes ponds, marshes and woodland, provides opportunities for exploration and outdoor education. The outdoor program features a ropes course.

LITCHFIELD, CT. (26 mi. W of Hartford, CT; 84 mi. NNE of New York, NY) Suburban. Pop: 8316. Alt: 956 ft.

FORMAN SCHOOL

Bdg and Day — Coed Gr 9-12

Litchfield, CT 06759. 12 Norfolk Rd, PO Box 80. Tel: 860-567-1802. Fax: 860-567-3501.
www.formanschool.org E-mail: admissions@formanschool.org

Mark B. Perkins, Head. BA, Hobart College, MA, Dartmouth College. **Beth A. Rainey, Adm.**
  Col Prep. LD. Feat—Fr Span Graphic_Arts Photog Studio_Art. **Supp**—Dev_Read ESL Rem_Math Rem_Read Tut.
  Adm: 79/yr. Bdg 70. Day 9. Appl due: Rolling. Accepted: 52%. Yield: 74%.
  Enr 170. B 110/12. G 43/5. Sec 170. Wh 90%. Hisp 1%. Blk 7%. Asian 2%. Avg class size: 12. **Fac 65.** M 29. F 36. Adv deg: 53%. In dorms 25.
  Grad '04—43. Col—41. (U of AZ, U of Denver, U of Dayton, Lynn, New England Col, Marshall). Avg SAT: 850. Alum 1900.
  Tui '04-'05: Bdg $43,000. Day $35,000. Aid: Need 39 ($707,000).
  Endow $3,500,000. Plant val $20,200,000. Bldgs 25. Dorms 12. Class rms 25. Lib 6000 vols. Sci labs 2. Comp labs 1. Lang ctrs 1. Video labs 1. Auds 1. Art studios 1. Music studios 1. Arts ctrs 1. Art galleries 1. Gyms 1. Fields 4. Courts 6.
  Est 1930. Nonprofit. Tri (Sept-June). **Assoc** NEASC.

The school was founded by John N. Forman as a school for young boys who would benefit from close personal attention. An upper school was added in 1935, and a girls' school was incorporated in 1942 under the direction of Mrs. Forman.

Serving pupils with learning differences, the school offers a college preparatory curriculum with a wide variety of courses. Language and math training programs are specifically designed to help students with learning differences.

The athletic program, which provides competition on both varsity and junior varsity levels, includes football, ice hockey, soccer and outdoor pursuits. Interest clubs, student government, debate, theater arts, publications, outdoor leadership opportunities and a community service program are among Forman's extracurricular activities.

MIDDLEBURY, CT. (28 mi. SW of Hartford, CT; 73 mi. NE of New York, NY) Suburban. Pop: 6451.

WESTOVER SCHOOL
Bdg and Day — Girls Gr 9-12

Middlebury, CT 06762. 1237 Whittemore Rd, PO Box 847. Tel: 203-758-2423.
  Fax: 203-577-4588.
  www.westoverschool.org E-mail: admission@westoverschool.org
Ann S. Pollina, Head. BA, Fordham Univ, MA, New York Univ. **Sara Lynn Leavenworth Renda, Adm.**
  Col Prep. AP—Eng Fr Lat Span Calc Comp_Sci Bio Chem Physics Eur_Hist US_Hist Art_Hist Studio_Art Music_Theory. **Feat**—Astron Environ_Sci Genetics Geol Programming Robotics Drawing Photog Drama Dance Journ. **Supp**—ESL Tut.
  Adm (Bdg Gr 9-11; Day 9-10): 59/yr. Bdg 41. Day 18. Appl due: Feb. Accepted: 56%. Yield: 51%. **Tests** ISEE SSAT TOEFL.
  Enr 201. G 125/76. Sec 201. Wh 83%. Hisp 2%. Blk 9%. Asian 4%. Other 2%. Avg class size: 11. **Fac 44.** M 10/2. F 22/10. Wh 86%. Blk 7%. Other 7%. Adv deg: 45%. In dorms 8.
  Grad '04—53. Col—53. (Emerson 2, Davidson 2, U of CT 2, U of Richmond 2, Fordham 2). Avg SAT: 1213. Avg ACT: 25. Alum 1819.
  Tui '04-'05: Bdg $32,200 (+$1000). **Day $22,200** (+$700). **Aid:** Merit 6 ($177,100). Need 101 ($1,797,050).

Summer: Enrich Rec. 1-2 wks.
Endow $36,000,000. Plant val $31,000,000. Bldgs 11. Dorms 1. Dorm rms 71. Class rms 30. Lib 18,000 vols. Sci labs 3. Lang labs 1. Comp labs 2. Auds 1. Theaters 1. Art studios 3. Music studios 5. Dance studios 1. Gyms 2. Fields 2. Courts 21.
Est 1909. Nonprofit. Tri (Sept-June). **Assoc** NEASC.

Established by Mary Robbins Hillard, formerly a principal at a local day school, with the assistance of her friend Theodate Pope Riddle, Connecticut's first female architect, Westover offers a college preparatory curriculum with a wide selection of electives and Advanced Placement courses. Visiting speakers complement the academic program. Graduates enter a variety of leading colleges.

A special cocurricular program, Women in Science and Engineering (WISE), is conducted in conjunction with Rensselaer Polytechnic Institute in Troy, NY. Girls who display an aptitude for and an interest in science and math may participate in this program. WISE combines the traditional Westover curriculum with additional math and science courses that meet primarily on Saturdays. Students design independent projects, often conducted with nearby corporations or universities. Successful completion of WISE ensures the student's acceptance into Rensselaer.

Two separate programs allow girls of outstanding ability in music or dance to complete a traditional Westover program and, on Saturdays, to attend either the Manhattan School of Music in New York City or the Brass City Ballet in Waterbury.

Competitive athletics comprise both intramurals and interscholastics. Team sports include tennis, squash, paddle tennis, basketball, dance, volleyball, soccer, softball, lacrosse, field hockey and cross-country, and an outdoor program consists of overnight camping, mountain climbing and canoeing.

Extracurricular activities include drama, art, language clubs, publications, student leadership and community service. Weekend social activities involve nearby boys' schools. Westover conducts exchanges with the All Saints School in Australia, St. Cyprian's School for Girls in South Africa and the Truro School for Girls in England. **See Also Page 1321**

MIDDLEFIELD, CT. (17 mi. S of Hartford, CT; 87 mi. NE of New York, NY) Suburban. Pop: 4203. Alt: 236 ft.

THE INDEPENDENT DAY SCHOOL
Day — Coed Gr PS-8

Middlefield, CT 06455. 115 Laurel Brook Rd, PO Box 451. Tel: 860-347-7235.
Fax: 860-347-8852.
www.idsmiddlefield.org   E-mail: ids@idsmiddlefield.org
Robert L. Fricker, **Head.** BA, Baldwin-Wallace College, MTS, Boston Univ. **Mary Lou Stewart, Adm.**
Pre-Prep. Gen Acad. **Feat**—Fr Span Computers Fine_Arts Performing_Arts Music. **Supp**—Dev_Read Rem_Math Rem_Read Rev.
Adm (Gr PS-7): 30/yr. Appl due: Rolling. Accepted: 52%. Yield: 81%. **Tests** IQ.
Enr 202. B 95. G 107. Elem 202. Wh 80%. Hisp 3%. Blk 4%. Asian 4%. Other 9%. Avg class size: 14. **Fac 33.** M 2/1. F 27/3. Wh 100%. Adv deg: 36%.

Grad '04—28. Prep—25. (Kingswood-Oxford 5, Choate 4, Loomis Chaffee 3, Williams-CT 1, Hotchkiss 1, Miss Porter's 1). Alum 561.
Tui '04-'05: Day $13,625-16,025 (+$300-425). **Aid:** Need 35 ($211,921).
Summer: Acad Enrich Rec. Arts. Tui Day $270/wk. 6 wks.
Endow $141,000. Plant val $3,500,000. Bldgs 2. Class rms 26. Lib 7000 vols. Sci labs 2. Comp labs 1. Theaters 1. Art studios 2. Music studios 2. Gyms 1. Fields 1. Basketball courts 1.
Est 1961. Nonprofit. Tri (Sept-June).

IDS provides preparation for college preparatory secondary schools. Classes for three-year-olds and older children through grade 5 are self-contained and reflect high standards of scholarship and citizenship. During these years, children develop a sound foundation in the essential subjects. In preparation for the departmentalization they will encounter in grades 6-8, fifth graders change teachers for reading, math and social studies instruction. The curriculum includes humanities, computers, French and Spanish, field trips, and a particular emphasis on reading, writing, organizational and study skills, and the fine and performing arts.

In addition to thrice weekly physical education, boys and girls in grades 5-8 may participate in interscholastic sports. **See Also Page 1166**

NEW CANAAN, CT.
(40 mi. NE of New York, NY) Suburban. Pop: 19,395. Alt: 550 ft.

NEW CANAAN COUNTRY SCHOOL
Day — Coed Gr PS-9

New Canaan, CT 06840. 545 Ponus Rdg, PO Box 997. Tel: 203-972-0771.
Fax: 203-966-5924.
www.countryschool.net   E-mail: poakes@countryschool.net
Timothy R. Bazemore, Head. BA, Middlebury College, MA, Univ of Pennsylvania. **Patricia F. Oakes, Adm.**
Pre-Prep. Feat—Fr Lat Span Studio_Art Drama Music Indus_Arts. **Supp**—Rem_Read Tut.
Adm (Gr PS-8): 93/yr. Accepted: 25%. Yield: 80%. **Tests** ISEE.
Enr 608. B 298. G 310. Elem 563. Sec 45. Wh 85%. Hisp 3%. Blk 6%. Asian 2%. Other 4%. Avg class size: 15. **Fac 104.** M 25/5. F 64/10. Wh 91%. Hisp 2%. Blk 5%. Asian 2%. Adv deg: 45%.
Grad '04—46. Prep—39. (Choate 4, Taft 3, Greenwich Acad 3, Greens Farms 3, Hotchkiss 2, Deerfield Acad 2). Alum 2508.
Tui '04-'05: Day $15,770-21,370 (+$25-2550). **Aid:** Need 81 ($1,350,000).
Endow $21,500,000. Plant val $50,000,000. Bldgs 8. Class rms 59. 2 Libs 23,774 vols. Sci labs 4. Comp labs 2. Auds 1. Art studios 3. Music studios 3. Dance studios 1. Wood shops 1. Gyms 2. Fields 7. Rinks 1.
Est 1916. Nonprofit. Sem (Sept-June).

NCCS was founded as The Community School by Edith Dudley and Effie Dunton, coprincipals from the founding date to 1933. Due to the growth of its student body, the school moved in 1936 to Grace Hill, where the institution assumed its present name. The campus has since undergone significant expansion and improvement.

The academic program features the basic disciplines of English, math, social studies, science and foreign language. Latin, Spanish and French constitute the foreign language program, and computer instruction begins in the lower school. All pupils are involved in a broad and varied creative arts program that makes music, art, wood shop, creative dance and drama an integral part of each student's education.

Field trips, guest speakers, films and community resources are used extensively to enrich the curriculum. Pupils in grades 6-9 embark on excursions of up to seven days to such destinations as Washington, DC; Quebec City, Canada; Nantucket, MA; Atlanta, GA, and Memphis, TN; Gettysburg, PA; and outdoor education centers in Connecticut and Rhode Island. Boys and girls perform community service projects on and off campus, and all upper schoolers take part in interscholastic athletics.

ST. LUKE'S SCHOOL
Day — Coed Gr 5-12

New Canaan, CT 06840. 377 N Wilton Rd, PO Box 1148. Tel: 203-966-5612.
Fax: 203-972-3450.
www.stlukesct.org   E-mail: williamsont@stlukesct.org
Mark C. Davis, Head. MA, Yale Univ, MALS, Wesleyan Univ. **David M. Suter, Adm.**

Col Prep. **AP**—Eng Fr Span Calc Comp_Sci Bio Chem Physics Eur_Hist US_Hist US_Govt & Pol Studio_Art Music_Theory. **Feat**—Shakespeare Astron Forensic_Sci Programming Psych Public_Speak.

Adm: 98/yr. Appl due: Feb. Accepted: 33%. **Tests** ISEE SSAT.

Enr 460. B 230. G 230. Elem 235. Sec 225. Wh 90%. Hisp 2%. Blk 6%. Asian 2%. Avg class size: 11. Uniform. **Fac 72.** Wh 95%. Hisp 2%. Blk 3%. Adv deg: 90%.

Grad '04—43. Col—43. (Cornell, Middlebury, Williams, Duke, St Lawrence, Boston Col). Avg SAT: 1240. Avg ACT: 26. Alum 3000.

Tui '04-'05: Day $21,810-23,075 (+$1500). **Aid:** Merit 4 ($90,000). Need 60 ($896,805). Endow $5,000,000. Plant val $18,000,000. Bldgs 5. Class rms 55. Lib 16,000 vols. Sci labs 6. Lang labs 2. Comp labs 4. Art studios 4. Music studios 4. Photog studios 1. Gyms 2. Fields 6. Courts 5.

Est 1928. Nonprofit. Sem (Sept-June). **Assoc** NEASC.

St. Luke's developmentally tailored middle school program, which places emphasis on skill acquisition and seeks to instill in boys and girls an appreciation of learning, prepares students for rigorous secondary school course work. The upper school curriculum integrates science and technology and stresses critical thinking skills and the development of aesthetic sensibilities. Honors and Advanced Placement courses are available in every discipline. The school draws its enrollment primarily from New Canaan, Stamford, Darien, Norwalk, Ridgefield and Westchester County, NY. Graduates enter highly competitive colleges throughout the nation.

Boys' sports are football, soccer, basketball, tennis, cross-country, lacrosse and squash; girls' offerings are field hockey, volleyball, basketball, softball, soccer, tennis, cross-country, lacrosse and squash. A coeducational crew team also competes interscholastically. Other activities include drama, publications, debate, environmental club and student council. Each upper school student fulfills a community service requirement.

NEW HAVEN, CT. (34 mi. SSW of Hartford, CT; 69 mi. NE of New York, NY) Urban. Pop: 123,626. Alt: 10 ft. Area also includes Hamden.

COLD SPRING SCHOOL
Day — Coed Gr PS-6

New Haven, CT 06513. 263 Chapel St. Tel: 203-787-1584. Fax: 203-787-9444.
 www.coldspringschool.org E-mail: pcoyne@coldspringschool.org
Jeff Jonathan, Dir. BA, Middlebury College, MA, Columbia Univ. **Paula Coyne, Adm.**
 Pre-Prep. Feat—Span Computers Studio_Art Music. **Supp**—Tut.
 Adm: 23/yr. Appl due: Feb. Accepted: 58%. Yield: 71%.
 Enr 104. B 57. G 47. Elem 104. Wh 70%. Hisp 9%. Blk 5%. Asian 10%. Other 6%. Avg class size: 18. **Fac 16.** M 1/1. F 11/3. Wh 94%. Hisp 6%. Adv deg: 31%.
 Grad '04—14. Prep—13. (Hamden Hall 6, Cheshire 4, Hopkins 3). Alum 123.
 Tui '04-'05: Day $14,140. Aid: Need 24 ($167,900).
 Endow $115,000. Plant val $3,100,000. Class rms 7. Lib 15,000 vols. Art studios 1. Music studios 1. Dance studios 1. Gyms 1. Fields 1. Playgrounds 2.
 Est 1982. Nonprofit. Sem (Sept-June).

Founded by a small group of local parents, Cold Spring enrolls boys and girls from 16 towns in Greater Hartford. The school follows a thematic approach that integrates the study of the traditional disciplines and incorporates creative projects (such as an art gallery and a garden), field trips, experiments and collaboration as learning tools. Under the direction of both a master teacher and an associate teacher, classes consist of mixed-age groups with two grades per classroom. CSS places considerable emphasis on technology, with computer availability and use increasing as children progress. Spanish instruction begins in kindergarten and continues through grade 6.

Extended-day programming and seasonal after-school activities are daily options.

FOOTE SCHOOL
Day — Coed Gr K-9

New Haven, CT 06511. 50 Loomis Pl. Tel: 203-777-3464. Fax: 203-777-2809.
 www.footeschool.org E-mail: laltshul@footeschool.org
David H. Feldman, Head. BS, Univ of Wisconsin-Madison, JD, John Marshall Law School.
 Laura O. Altshul, Adm.
 Pre-Prep. Feat—Fr Lat Span Computers Studio_Art Drama Music.
 Adm: 74/yr. Appl due: Feb. Accepted: 50%.
 Enr 470. B 236. G 234. Wh 72%. Hisp 2%. Blk 7%. Asian 5%. Other 14%. Avg class size: 17. **Fac 85.** M 10/1. F 72/2. Adv deg: 60%.
 Grad '04—20. Prep—13. (Choate, Hopkins, Hamden Hall, Taft, Westminster Sch-CT, Deerfield Acad). Alum 1500.
 Tui '04-'05: Day $14,550-16,780. Aid: Need 96 ($960,000).
 Summer: Ages 3-18. Enrich Rec. Tui Day $150-1000/wk. 7 wks.
 Endow $5,391,000. Plant val $14,500,000. Bldgs 10. Class rms 41. Lib 45,000 vols. Sci labs 2. Theaters 1. Art studios 2. Music studios 3. Gyms 1. Fields 3.
 Est 1916. Nonprofit. (Sept-June).

Founded by Martha Babcock Foote, the school occupies a nine-acre, wooded site near Yale University. The strong academic program, which is complemented by art, music, drama and computer, includes a required six-subject course schedule in the upper grades. Foote's summer program provides many options for enrichment and recreation for boys and girls ages 3-18. An after-school program is available daily to children in grades K-6, and alternative programs operate during certain school vacations and holidays.

HAMDEN HALL COUNTRY DAY SCHOOL
Day — Coed Gr PS-12

Hamden, CT 06517. 1108 Whitney Ave. Tel: 203-865-6158. Fax: 203-776-5852.
www.hamdenhall.org E-mail: admissionsoffice@hamdenhall.org

Steven L. Hahn, Head. AB, Princeton Univ, EdM, Harvard Univ. **Janet B. Izzo, Upper & Middle Sch Adm; Katharine Harris, Lower Sch Adm.**

Col Prep. AP—Eng Fr Lat Span Calc US_Hist Econ. **Feat**—Computers Ethics Studio_Art Music Outdoor_Ed.

Adm (Gr PS-11): 117/yr. Appl due: Feb. Yield: 54%. **Tests** ISEE SSAT.

Enr 566. B 315. G 251. Elem 312. Sec 254. Avg class size: 15. **Fac 79.** M 27/4. F 45/3. Adv deg: 69%.

Grad '04—51. Col—51. (Geo Wash 4, Yale 2, Brandeis 2, Brown 1, Wesleyan U 1, Williams 1). Avg SAT: 1200. Alum 2000.

Tui '04-'05: Day $11,340-20,300 (+$400). **Aid:** Need 169.

Summer: Acad Enrich Rev Rem Rec. Tui Day $250-1800. 6 wks.

Endow $3,000,000. Plant val $16,000,000. Bldgs 8. Class rms 46. Lib 25,000 vols. Sci labs 6. Lang labs 3. Comp labs 2. Theaters 1. Art studios 3. Music studios 3. Gyms 1. Fields 6.

Est 1912. Nonprofit. Sem (Sept-June). **Assoc** CLS NEASC.

One of the earlier country day schools, Hamden Hall has developed from a boys' elementary school to the present completely coed preparatory program. In the upper grades, students take at least five major academic subjects and have a variety of required courses, electives and independent study opportunities to choose from. Advanced Placement and honors courses are offered in all academic disciplines, and the curriculum prepares graduates for a variety of selective colleges.

Activities include theater, publications, debate, and peer leadership and community service projects. The school fields varsity, junior varsity and middle school teams in approximately 20 sports and offers a variety of noncompetitive options, including an outdoors program and a running club.

HOPKINS SCHOOL
Day — Coed Gr 7-12

New Haven, CT 06515. 986 Forest Rd. Tel: 203-397-1001. Fax: 203-389-2249.
www.hopkins.edu E-mail: admissions@hopkins.edu

Barbara M. Riley, Head. BA, MA, MPhil, Yale Univ. **Dana Blanchard, Adm.**

Col Prep. AP—Fr Lat Span Calc Stats Comp_Sci Bio Chem Human_Geog Physics Psych. **Feat**—Creative_Writing Russ_Lit Chin Greek Ital Astron Ecol Engineering Holocaust Civil_War African-Amer_Hist Asian_Stud Architect Video_Production Acting Drama Music Music_Theory Orchestra Jazz-Rock_Ensemble Journ Public_

Speak Outdoor_Ed. **Supp**—Dev_Read Tut.
Adm: 151/yr. Appl due: Feb. Accepted: 48%. **Tests** ISEE SSAT.
Enr 650. B 334. G 316. Wh 73%. Hisp 4%. Blk 11%. Asian 12%. Avg class size: 14. **Fac 104.** M 48/3. F 51/2. Wh 83%. Hisp 10%. Blk 5%. Asian 2%. Adv deg: 76%.
Grad '04—128. Col—127. (Yale 8, U of PA 7, Boston Col 6, Brown 6, Georgetown 5, U of CT 5). Avg SAT: 1385. Alum 6000.
Tui '04-'05: Day $22,825 (+$350). **Aid:** Need 136 ($1,836,100). Work prgm 136 ($193,600).
Summer: Acad Enrich Rev Rem Rec. Sports. 6 wks.
Endow $35,000,000. Plant val $30,000,000. Bldgs 9. Class rms 56. Lib 22,000 vols. Sci labs 10. Comp labs 2. Auds 1. Theaters 1. Art studios 3. Music studios 3. Gyms 2. Fields 9. Courts 11. Pools 1.
Est 1660. Nonprofit. Sem (Sept-June). **Assoc** CLS NEASC.

Edward Hopkins, seven-time governor of Connecticut Colony, bequeathed a portion of his estate to the American colonies to found schools dedicated to "the breeding up of hopeful youths . . . for the public service of the country in future times." With a portion of that bequest, Hopkins Grammar School was founded in the 17th century in a one-room building on the New Haven Green and settled in its present location on a hill overlooking the city in 1925. Two prominent girls' schools, the Day School (founded in 1907) and the Prospect Hill School (founded in 1930), consolidated in 1960 to form a strong center for the education of the area's young women. Cooperative ventures between Hopkins Grammar and Day Prospect Hill led to the 1972 merger that formed the present-day school.

The six grades are organized into three divisions—a junior school, a middle school and a senior school—each with its own academic schedule and curriculum, athletic teams and activities. The curriculum emphasizes a grounding in the basic skills, exposure to varied subject matter and rigorous preparation for advanced study. Many students are involved with college-level subjects by their senior year. After taking compulsory Latin courses in grades 7 and 8, pupils fulfill Hopkins' language requirement by studying French, Spanish, Greek, Latin, Chinese or Italian in the higher grades. Junior school students receive introductory instruction in the arts, and, in grades 9-12, all students complete at least one year of art study.

Every student participates in athletics throughout the year, selecting either interscholastics or an informal sport in each of the three seasons, although seniors may opt to take off one season. An independent athletics program enables boys and girls to pursue activities not offered at Hopkins, among them ballet and horseback riding. The school encourages students to become involved in extracurricular activities, with offerings such as student council, math team, debate team, newspaper, literary magazine, yearbook, singing groups, drama and tour guides. Service to others—in school, community and country—as envisioned by founder Edward Hopkins, remains an important element of student life.

The school's proximity to Yale University and New Haven provides students access to museums; historical sites; theatrical, orchestral and dance performances; and professional sporting events.

ST. THOMAS'S DAY SCHOOL

Day — Coed Gr PS-6

New Haven, CT 06511. 830 Whitney Ave. Tel: 203-776-2123. Fax: 203-776-3467.
www.stthomasday.org   E-mail: info@stthomasday.org

Fred Acquavita, Head. BS, Kansas State College of Pittsburg, MS, Southern Connecticut State College, MS, Bank Street College of Education. **Roxanne Turekian, Adm.**

Pre-Prep. Feat—Span Computers Relig Studio_Art Music.

Adm: 30/yr. Appl due: Feb. Accepted: 56%. Yield: 81%.

Enr 157. B 77. G 80. Elem 157. Wh 72%. Hisp 3%. Blk 13%. Asian 4%. Other 8%. Avg class size: 20. Uniform. **Fac 26.** M 5. F 11/10. Wh 85%. Hisp 7%. Blk 8%. Adv deg: 34%.

Grad '04—18. Prep—14. (Hopkins 9, Hamden Hall 3, St Margaret's-McTernan 1). Alum 561.

Tui '04-'05: Day $13,550 (+$150). **Aid:** Need 28 ($243,210).

Endow $574,000. Plant val $2,094,000. Bldgs 2. Libs 1. Sci labs 1. Comp ctrs 1. Art studios 1. Gyms 1. Playgrounds 2.

Est 1956. Nonprofit. Episcopal. Sem (Sept-June).

St. Thomas's is an independent Episcopal school serving children from diverse faiths and backgrounds. Small classes encourage students to work at an appropriate level. The reading program is based on a linguistic approach, and playwriting and drama are integral parts of the curriculum. The music program emphasizes choral work and music appreciation at all levels. Religion, Spanish, science, art, music, library and physical education are also included in the academic program.

An extended-day program includes such activities as computer, drama, sports, cooking and art.

NEW LONDON, CT. (43 mi. SE of Hartford, CT; 89 mi. SW of Boston, MA) Urban. Pop: 25,671. Alt: 45 ft.

THE WILLIAMS SCHOOL

Day — Coed Gr 7-12

New London, CT 06320. 182 Mohegan Ave. Tel: 860-443-5333. Fax: 860-439-2796.
www.williamsschool.org   E-mail: admissions@williamsschool.org

Charlotte L. Rea, Head. BA, Lake Erie College, MA, New York Univ, MEd, Columbia Univ. **Gayle A. Holt, Adm.**

Col Prep. AP—Fr Lat Span Calc Bio Chem Physics US_Hist Music_Theory. **Feat**—Comp_Sci Ger_Hist Econ Govt Studio_Art Acting Drama Theater Music Dance. **Supp**—Rev Tut.

Adm: 98/yr. Appl due: Feb. Accepted: 62%. **Tests** SSAT.

Enr 331. B 167. G 164. Elem 92. Sec 239. Wh 86%. Hisp 4%. Blk 3%. Am Ind 2%. Asian 1%. Other 4%. Avg class size: 12. **Fac 42.** M 15/2. F 18/7. Wh 98%. Hisp 2%. Adv deg: 78%.

Grad '04—73. Col—73. (U of CT 4, Brown 3, Boston U 3, U of VT 3, Vassar 2, Wellesley 2). Avg SAT: 1214. Alum 3428.

Tui '05-'06: Day $19,000 (+$450). **Aid:** Need 62 ($790,000).

Endow $2,700,000. Plant val $8,500,000. Bldgs 1. Class rms 18. Lib 8500 vols. Sci labs 5. Comp labs 2. Auds 1. Art studios 2. Music studios 1. Dance studios 1. Gyms 2. Fields 3.

Est 1891. Nonprofit. Quar (Aug-June). **Assoc** CLS NEASC.

Williams' college preparatory program emphasizes critical thinking and research skills, as well as student and teacher collaboration during the learning process. Pupils follow a seven-day rotating schedule—with major subjects meeting six of the seven days—that allows for variety, flexibility, and time for work on individual or group projects. The curriculum balances traditional humanities offerings with those in math and science. A particularly strong arts program commences with theater, music and dance courses in grades 7 and 8, and juniors and seniors may enroll in a digital film course. Technology education begins during the middle school years. Honors and Advanced Placement courses and independent study opportunities provide additional challenge for qualified older students.

Interscholastic sports, in which most students participate, include field hockey, soccer, baseball, golf, tennis, cross-country, basketball, sailing, swimming, softball and lacrosse. All students take part in an advisor program that enables boys and girls to receive assistance with their academic, social and personal needs.

See Also Page 1279

NEW MILFORD, CT. (39 mi. WSW of Hartford, CT; 69 mi. NNE of New York, NY) Suburban. Pop: 25,343. Alt: 480 ft.

CANTERBURY SCHOOL
Bdg and Day — Coed Gr 9-PG

New Milford, CT 06776. 160 Aspetuck Ave, Caller Box 5000. Tel: 860-210-3800.
Fax: 860-350-4425.
www.cbury.org   E-mail: admissions@cbury.org
Thomas J. Sheehy III, Head. BA, Bowdoin College, MA, Pennsylvania State Univ. **Keith R. Holton, Adm.**
Col Prep. **AP**—Eng Fr Span Calc Stats Eur_Hist World_Hist Studio_Art Music_Theory. **Feat**—Race_in_Amer_Lit Lat Anat & Physiol Geol Computers Programming Vietnam_War Anthro Psych Asian_Stud Theol World_Relig Art_Hist Film. **Supp**—ESL Rev Tut.
Adm (Gr 9-11): 140/yr. Bdg 100. Day 40. Appl due: Jan. Accepted: 49%. Yield: 45%. **Tests** SSAT TOEFL.
Enr 366. B 150/72. G 70/74. Sec 349. PG 17. Wh 91%. Hisp 1%. Blk 3%. Asian 5%. Avg class size: 12. **Fac 70.** M 39. F 31. Wh 96%. Hisp 3%. Blk 1%. Adv deg: 50%. In dorms 40.
Grad '04—105. **Col**—105. (Boston Col, Roger Williams, Providence, Salve Regina, St Michael's, U of PA). Avg SAT: 1100. Alum 3867.
Tui '04-'05: Bdg $33,300 (+$2000). **Day $24,400** (+$1000). **Aid:** Merit 2 ($5000). Need 146 ($2,400,000).
Endow $14,000,000. Plant val $20,000,000. Bldgs 26. Dorms 7. Dorm rms 220. Class rms 37. Lib 13,000 vols. Sci labs 4. Comp labs 2. Auds 1. Theaters 1. Art studios 3. Music studios 2. Gyms 2. Fields 9. Courts 4. Field houses 1. Pools 1. Rinks 1.
Est 1915. Nonprofit. Roman Catholic. Sem (Sept-June). **Assoc** NEASC.

Long holding a leadership position among Catholic boarding schools and appealing to families not only in New England but throughout the world, Canterbury is conducted by Catholic laity. The work accomplished by the first headmaster, Dr.

Nelson Hume, was recognized by Pope Pius XI, who appointed him to the Order of the Knights of St. Gregory in 1938.

Canterbury offers a college preparatory curriculum, with graduates attending both Catholic and nonsectarian colleges around the country. A wide range of elective courses, including ethics, political philosophy, oceanography, literature of women, and studio art, supplements required academics.

Participation in extracurricular activities is an integral element of Canterbury life. Among these activities are music, art, debating, dramatics, student publications and various community services. Sports for boys are football, baseball, soccer, ice hockey, cross-country, swimming, water polo, wrestling, basketball, lacrosse, tennis, golf and track; girls' options are soccer, field and ice hockey, cross-country, tennis, basketball, swimming, squash, water polo, volleyball, lacrosse, softball and riding. Sixth formers may take weightlifting for one season. **See Also Page 1128**

OAKDALE, CT. (34 mi. SE of Hartford, CT; 84 mi. SW of Boston, MA) Rural. Pop: 400.

SAINT THOMAS MORE SCHOOL
Bdg — Boys Gr 8-PG

Oakdale, CT 06370. 45 Cottage Rd. Tel: 860-823-3861. Fax: 860-823-3863.
www.stthomasmoreschool.com E-mail: stmadmit@stthomasmoreschool.com
James Fox Hanrahan, Jr., Head. BS, Fairfield Univ, MEd, Boston College. **Tim Riordan, Adm.**

Col Prep. LD. Underachiever. Feat—Mythology Span Environ_Sci Programming Comp_Relig Theol Fine_Arts Studio_Art. Supp—ESL Rev Tut.

Adm: 115/yr. Appl due: Rolling. **Tests** CEEB IQ SSAT TOEFL.

Enr 211. B 211. Elem 16. Sec 169. PG 26. Wh 52%. Hisp 4%. Blk 18%. Am Ind 4%. Asian 20%. Other 2%. Avg class size: 12. Uniform. **Fac 27.** M 22. F 5. Adv deg: 48%. In dorms 10.

Grad '04—38. Col—38. (Fordham, Quinnipiac, U of CT, Syracuse, St Anselm, U of MA-Amherst). Avg SAT: 1010. Alum 1810.

Tui '04-'05: Bdg $27,325-30,325 (+$1000). **Aid:** Merit ($54,900). Need 78 ($662,550).

Summer: Acad Enrich Rev Rem Rec. Tui Day $5495-5995. 5 wks.

Endow $8,500,000. Plant val $10,500,000. Bldgs 14. Dorms 3. Dorm rms 121. Class rms 18. Lib 6500 vols. Chapels 1. Sci labs 2. Lang labs 1. Comp labs 2. Auds 1. Art studios 1. Gyms 1. Fields 5. Courts 6. Pools 1.

Est 1962. Nonprofit. Roman Catholic. (Sept-May). **Assoc** NEASC.

Saint Thomas More prepares boys for college entrance by emphasizing study and organizational skills, which are incorporated into the regular curriculum. The school typically enrolls underachieving students of average to above-average intelligence who have no chronic social, emotional or behavioral problems. Classes are small and highly structured.

The school maintains a postgraduate program offering separate English and math courses to prepare students for college-level work. Special emphasis is given to preparation for the SAT exam. International pupils take part in an intensive English as a Second Language program that provides preparation for the TOEFL.

In addition to interscholastic sports, extracurricular activities include chess club, art, music, and skiing and photography groups. **See Also Pages 1374-6**

POMFRET, CT. (29 mi. W of Providence, RI; 57 mi. WSW of Boston, MA) Suburban. Pop: 3798. Alt: 389 ft.

POMFRET SCHOOL
Bdg and Day — Coed Gr 9-PG

Pomfret, CT 06258. 398 Pomfret St, PO Box 128. Tel: 860-963-6100. Fax: 860-963-2042.
www.pomfretschool.org   E-mail: admission@pomfretschool.org
Bradford Hastings, Head. BS, Union College, MEd, Harvard Univ. **Erik Bertelsen, Adm.**
  Col Prep. **AP**—Eng Fr Lat Span Calc Bio Chem Physics Eur_Hist US_Hist Econ Studio_Art Music_Theory. **Feat**—British_Lit Creative_Writing Shakespeare Stats Anat & Physiol Astron Geol Oceanog Programming Robotics Civil_War Vietnam_War World_Relig Art_Hist Ceramics Sculpt Drama Dance. **Supp**—Tut.
  Adm: 126/yr. Appl due: Feb. Accepted: 65%. **Tests** CEEB SSAT TOEFL.
  Enr 359. Sec 349. PG 10. Wh 87%. Hisp 3%. Blk 7%. Am Ind 1%. Asian 2%. Avg class size: 12. **Fac 60.** M 29/5. F 11/15. Wh 93%. Hisp 5%. Am Ind 1%. Asian 1%. Adv deg: 55%. In dorms 18.
  Grad '04—91. Col—90. (Bates, Hamilton, Hobart/Wm Smith, Wesleyan U, Trinity Col-CT, Colby). Alum 3507.
  Tui '04-'05: Bdg $34,550 (+$1750). **Day $22,300** (+$950). **Aid:** Need 74 ($1,418,450).
  Endow $30,000,000. Plant val $35,000,000. Bldgs 23. Dorms 9. Dorm rms 150. Class rms 31. Lib 17,000 vols. Labs 5. Observatories 1. Auds 1. Theaters 1. Art studios 2. Music studios 6. Dance studios 1. Gyms 1. Fields 10. Courts 8. Field houses 1. Rinks 1. Weight rms 1.
  Est 1894. Nonprofit. Episcopal. Tri (Sept-May). **Assoc** CLS NEASC.

William E. Peck, the former principal of St. Mark's School, established Pomfret as a preparatory school for boys. The school instituted coeducation in 1968, however, and now enrolls a varied student body that represents roughly 30 states and a dozen foreign countries.

Pomfret offers a varied curriculum with a wide range of electives to supplement a mandatory core of traditional courses. The school's curriculum comprises both year-long classes and term courses that last for one or two trimesters. Students typically take six courses per term. Honors and Advanced Placement sections are available in all academic disciplines. Academics are complemented by athletics and the arts, and students must fulfill requirements in both.

A cocurricular structure allows students to devote part of the day to athletics and the arts. Each pupil enrolls in arts courses the equivalent of two trimesters per year; classes, which convene during the week and every other Saturday, combine theory and instruction with hands-on work in the studio. All students are also involved in the athletic program, with options for both interscholastic and intramural participation. Other activities include a selection of clubs and organizations.

RECTORY SCHOOL

Bdg — Boys Gr 5-9; Day — Coed 5-9

Pomfret, CT 06258. 528 Pomfret St, PO Box 68. Tel: 860-928-1328. Fax: 860-928-4961.
www.rectoryschool.org E-mail: admissions@rectoryschool.org
Thomas F. Army, Jr., Head. BA, MALS, Wesleyan Univ. **Stephen A. DiPaolo, Adm.**

> **Pre-Prep. Feat**—Fr Lat Span Computers Studio_Art Music. **Supp**—Dev_Read ESL LD Makeup Tut.
>
> **Adm (Bdg Gr 5-9; Day 5-7):** 61/yr. Bdg 43. Day 18. Appl due: Rolling. Accepted: 82%. Yield: 64%. **Tests** IQ SSAT Stanford.
>
> **Enr** 168. B 107/36. G 25. Elem 125. Sec 43. Wh 66%. Hisp 7%. Blk 5%. Am Ind 2%. Asian 20%. Avg class size: 12. **Fac** 59. M 23. F 36. Wh 96%. Hisp 2%. Blk 2%. Adv deg: 38%. In dorms 16.
>
> **Grad '04—37. Prep—31.** (Pomfret 5, Suffield 4, Winchendon 4, Salisbury-CT 3, St Mark's Sch-MA 2, Tabor 2). Alum 2447.
>
> **Tui '04-'05: Bdg $31,000** (+$8000). **Day $15,300** (+$6500). **Aid:** Need 31 ($473,400).
>
> **Summer:** Acad Enrich Rev Rem Rec. Tui Bdg $6600. Tui Day $3750. 5 wks.
>
> Endow $8,625,000. Plant val $21,046,000. Bldgs 20. Dorms 7. Dorm rms 113. Class rms 42. Lib 6500 vols. Sci labs 3. Comp labs 3. Auds 1. Art studios 3. Music studios 2. Gyms 1. Fields 5. Courts 6. Pools 1.
>
> **Est 1920.** Nonprofit. Episcopal. Tri (Sept-June).

Rev. Frank H. Bigelow and his wife, Mabel, began this school as a small tutoring group in their home. Their pervasive kindness and untiring energy immediately attracted students.

Students are thoroughly grounded in the fundamentals and are prepared for many secondary boarding schools. All grades are divided homogeneously, and there are accelerated programs in various subject areas. Individual instruction is available five days a week, and a low student-teacher ratio is maintained. In addition to languages, math, science, social studies and a coordinated computer program, the curriculum includes courses in the arts, crafts and music.

Publications, photography, radio, fishing, drama, skiing, snowboarding, hiking and horseback riding are among Rectory's extracurriculars. Team sports are football, soccer, hockey, track, tennis, wrestling, cross-country, baseball, lacrosse, golf and basketball.

See Also Pages 1342-3

SALISBURY, CT. (41 mi. WNW of Hartford, CT; 95 mi. NNE of New York, NY) Suburban. Pop: 3977. Alt: 685 ft.

SALISBURY SCHOOL

Bdg and Day — Boys Gr 9-PG

Salisbury, CT 06068. 251 Canaan Rd. Tel: 860-435-5700. Fax: 860-435-5750.
www.salisburyschool.org E-mail: admissions@salisburyschool.org
Chisholm S. Chandler, Head. BA, Brown Univ, MEd, Harvard Univ. **Peter B. Gilbert, Adm.**

> **Col Prep. AP**—Eng Fr Calc Bio Eur_Hist US_Hist. **Feat**—Lat Span Anat Geol Forestry Freshwater_Ecol Computers Civil_War African_Hist Econ Bible Ethics Photog Studio_Art Music. **Supp**—Tut.
>
> **Adm:** 115/yr. Bdg 110. Day 5. Appl due: Feb. Accepted: 46%. Yield: 58%. **Tests** CEEB IQ ISEE SSAT TOEFL.

Enr 285. B 265/20. Sec 273. PG 12. Wh 80%. Hisp 2%. Blk 6%. Am Ind 1%. Asian 7%. Other 4%. Avg class size: 12. **Fac 65.** M 50. F 15. Adv deg: 43%.

Grad '04—83. Col—83. (Trinity Col-CT 4, Union Col-NY 4, U of Denver 4, U of VT 3, Hobart/Wm Smith 2, U of Richmond 2). Avg SAT: 1180. Alum 2420.

Tui '04-'05: Bdg $33,500 (+$2500). **Day $24,500** (+$1600). **Aid:** Merit 2 ($10,000). Need 89 ($1,900,000).

Summer: Coed. Acad Enrich Rem Rec. Tui Bdg $7200. 5 wks.

Endow $34,000,000. Plant val $44,000,000. Bldgs 25. Dorms 10. Dorm rms 170. Class rms 26. Lib 23,000 vols. Chapels 1. Sci labs 4. Lang labs 1. Dark rms 1. Sci ctrs 1. Reading ctrs 1. Theaters 1. Art studios 3. Music studios 3. Ceramics studios 1. Gyms 2. Fields 6. Basketball courts 2. Tennis courts 10. Volleyball courts 1. Squash courts 2. Rinks 1. Weight rms 1. Boathouses 1.

Est 1901. Nonprofit. Episcopal. Tri (Sept-May). **Assoc** CLS NEASC.

Founded by Rev. Dr. George Emerson Quaile on a hilltop campus that now spans 725 acres, Salisbury School offers a traditional curriculum that successfully prepares students for competitive colleges. Electives and Advanced Placement courses are available to juniors and seniors. A learning center offers support to students in need of additional help.

Sports include Alpine skiing, baseball, basketball, crew, cross-country, cycling, football, golf, ice hockey, kayaking, lacrosse, platform tennis, soccer, squash, tennis and wrestling. Among extracurricular activities are drama, publications, choral music, debating club and outing club. Students are encouraged to become involved in one of a number of community service projects. An active student entertainment committee plans gatherings with nearby girls' schools throughout the year.

SIMSBURY, CT. (10 mi. NW of Hartford, CT; 97 mi. WSW of Boston, MA) Suburban. Pop: 23,234. Alt: 164 ft. Area also includes West Simsbury.

ETHEL WALKER SCHOOL
Bdg — Girls Gr 9-PG; Day — Girls 6-PG

Simsbury, CT 06070. 230 Bushy Hill Rd. Tel: 860-408-4200. Fax: 860-408-4201. www.ethelwalker.org E-mail: admission_office@ethelwalker.org

Susanna A. Jones, Head. AB, Princeton Univ, MA, MPhil, Columbia Univ. **Anne Rodriguez Frame, Adm.**

Col Prep. **AP**—Eng Fr Span Calc Comp_Sci Bio Physics Eur_Hist US_Hist Psych Studio_Art. **Feat**—Lat-Amer_Stud Asian_Stud Ethics Art_Hist Ceramics Photog Drama Music Music_Theory Dance. **Supp**—Rev Tut.

Adm: 70/yr. Bdg 40. Day 30. Appl due: Feb. Accepted: 52%. **Tests** SSAT TOEFL.

Enr 184. G 97/87. Elem 27. Sec 157. Wh 81%. Hisp 5%. Blk 8%. Asian 6%. Avg class size: 10. **Fac 32.** M 11. F 21. Wh 98%. Blk 1%. Asian 1%. Adv deg: 75%. In dorms 4.

Grad '04—43. Col—42. (Trinity Col-CT, SMU, Boston U, Bates, U of CT). Alum 3100.

Tui '04-'05: Bdg $33,900 (+$650). **Day $21,850-24,200** (+$600). **Aid:** Need 68 ($1,200,000).

Endow $10,200,000. Plant val $8,437,000. Bldgs 30. Dorms 2. Dorm rms 79. Class rms 25. Lib 24,000 vols. Chapels 1. Sci labs 5. Lang labs 1. Comp labs 5. Auds 1. Theaters 2. Art studios 4. Music studios 9. Dance studios 1. Perf arts ctrs 1. Art galleries 1. Media ctrs 1. Gyms 1. Fields 4. Riding rings 4. Stables 1.

Est 1911. Nonprofit. Sem (Sept-June). **Assoc** CLS NEASC.

Ethel Walker opened this school in Lakewood, NJ, moving it to its present site in 1917. The founder, who retired as resident head but kept in close touch with operations, designed the program to give her students a sound college preparatory curriculum. From 1938 to 1944, Mrs. Elliott Speer did much to develop in the girls a sense of responsibility and self-discipline, allowing them an increased amount of freedom as they demonstrated the ability to use it wisely. Ahead of its time, the school was distinguished by its purpose: to prepare young women for college. In 1990, Ethel Walker opened a middle school division that now serves pupils in grades 6-8.

The long-maintained standards of college preparation continue, and the curriculum provides a complete program in mathematics, science, languages, literature, history, religion and the arts, with Advanced Placement and honors courses offered in every discipline. Computer instruction is an important element of the program. Elective courses offered in all departments produce an extensive and varied preparatory curriculum, and independent study is encouraged. The classroom experience offers opportunities for hands-on, project-based learning, and a senior project allows students to participate in an on- or off-campus internship to explore an academic or career interest. Graduates enter leading colleges throughout the country.

Athletic, social and leadership opportunities balance academics. Outdoor life is emphasized, and sports include cross-country, crew, judo, paddle tennis, field hockey, tennis, soccer, softball, volleyball, basketball, dance, lacrosse, riding and a faculty-led outdoor adventure program. The school has a strong student government, and all girls participate in a student-managed program of extracurricular activities that includes publications, debate, art, music clubs, photography, community service and drama. Walker's special-events schedule includes musical and dance performances, lectures, career panels and weekend social activities.

See Also Page 1298

THE MASTER'S SCHOOL

Day — Coed Gr PS-12

West Simsbury, CT 06092. Westledge Rd. Tel: 860-651-9361. Fax: 860-651-9363.
www.masterschool.org E-mail: masters.admissions@snet.net

Bruce Libonn, **Int Head.** BA, College of William and Mary, MA, Adelphi University. **Barbara Van Essendelft, Adm.**

Col Prep. AP—Bio. **Feat**—Fr Lat Span Computers Sociol Bible Music. **Supp**—Tut.

Adm: 132/yr. Appl due: Rolling. Accepted: 60%. **Tests** Stanford.

Enr 426. B 223. G 203. Elem 287. Sec 139. Wh 83%. Hisp 6%. Blk 10%. Asian 1%. Avg class size: 14. **Fac 55.** M 11/1. F 33/10. Wh 100%. Adv deg: 43%.

Grad '04—40. Col—37. (Gordon 4, Central CT St 3, U of CT 2, Taylor-Upland 2). Avg SAT: 1136. Alum 663.

Tui '04-'05: Day $6500-11,900 (+$500-950). **Aid:** Merit ($9600). Need ($656,000).

Summer: Rem. Tui Day $900. 6 wks.

Endow $25,000. Bldgs 10. Class rms 20. Lib 8000 vols. Comp labs 1. Art studios 5. Music studios 2. Photog studios 1. Gyms 2. Fields 3. Courts 2.

Est 1970. Nonprofit. Nondenom Christian. Sem (Sept-June). **Assoc** NEASC.

This nondenominational Christian school conducts four divisions: the early childhood center, the lower school, and the middle and upper schools. Reading and math are stressed in the lower school, with computers, French, music and art offered from grade 1. Strong emphasis is placed on academics in all programs.

Students in the middle and upper schools may follow an "aggressive" or a "standard" college preparatory program, depending on the level of math, science and language courses they elect. Curricular features include Advanced Placement classes, a senior seminar, computer and Bible. Electives are offered in computer science, art, music and chorus. Athletics, interest clubs and dramatics supplement academics.

WESTMINSTER SCHOOL
Bdg and Day — Coed Gr 9-PG

Simsbury, CT 06070. 995 Hopmeadow St, PO Box 337. Tel: 860-408-3060. Fax: 860-408-3042.
www.westminster-school.org   E-mail: admit@westminster-school.org

W. Graham Cole, Jr., Head. BA, Williams College, MA, Columbia Univ. **Jon C. Deveaux, Adm.**

Col Prep. AP—Eng Fr Lat Span Calc Stats Comp_Sci Bio Chem Physics Eur_Hist US_Hist Comp_Govt & Pol Econ Studio_Art Music_Theory. **Feat**—Engineering & Design Ethics Architect Theater_Arts. **Supp**—Tut.

Adm: 121/yr. Bdg 91. Day 30. Appl due: Jan. Accepted: 39%. Yield: 41%. **Tests** CEEB SSAT TOEFL.

Enr 368. B 138/65. G 107/58. Sec 358. PG 10. Wh 83%. Hisp 3%. Blk 8%. Asian 3%. Other 3%. Avg class size: 12. **Fac 54.** M 35. F 19. Wh 82%. Hisp 8%. Blk 6%. Asian 4%. Adv deg: 94%. In dorms 26.

Grad '04—104. Col—104. (Colby 3, Skidmore 3, U of Richmond 3, Middlebury 3, Duke 2, Holy Cross 2). Avg SAT: 1220. Avg SSAT: 71%. Alum 3545.

Tui '04-'05: Bdg $33,560 (+$1600). **Day $24,380** (+$1200). **Aid:** Need 107 ($2,341,000).

Endow $65,000,000. Plant val $77,500,000. Bldgs 38. Dorms 6. Dorm rms 148. Class rms 32. Lib 26,000 vols. Chapels 1. Sci labs 6. Lang labs 1. Comp labs 2. Dark rms 3. Observatories 1. Auds 1. Theaters 1. Art studios 4. Music studios 6. Dance studios 1. Arts ctrs 1. Perf arts ctrs 1. Architect studios 1. Gyms 2. Fields 10. Tennis courts 14. Squash courts 12. Paddleball courts 2. Pools 1. Rinks 1. Greenhouses 1. Student ctrs 1.

Est 1888. Nonprofit. Tri (Sept-June). **Assoc** NEASC.

Founded by William Lee Cushing as a boys' school, Westminster was inspired by the ancient Uppingham School, established in 1584 in Rutland, England. The school first admitted girls as day students in 1971. Then, in 1977, the school began enrolling girl boarders.

Today, Westminster students enjoy an unusual amount of contact with both headmaster and faculty. The student council, an advisory group, meets regularly with the headmaster, seeking ways of improving the functioning of the school. A cooperative work program of assigned tasks is the responsibility of all students. Art studios and a performing arts center house a comprehensive creative arts program in which all students take part. Social and educational relationships are maintained with nearby schools, and students are actively involved in community service programs. College preparatory work is of a high standard, and graduates enter a variety of competitive colleges.

Facilities for publications, art, music, discussion groups and hobby clubs, as well as those for athletics, are extensive. Sports include football, soccer, field hockey, basketball, ice hockey, dance, swimming, diving, squash, tennis, track, golf, cross-country, baseball, paddle tennis, softball and lacrosse. **See Also Pages 1270-1**

SOUTH KENT, CT. (41 mi. W of Hartford, CT; 74 mi. NNE of New York, NY) Rural. Pop: 108. Alt: 395 ft.

SOUTH KENT SCHOOL
Bdg and Day — Boys Gr 9-PG

South Kent, CT 06785. 40 Bull's Bridge Rd. Tel: 860-927-3539. Fax: 860-927-1161.
www.southkentschool.net   E-mail: admissions@southkentschool.net
Andrew Vadnais, Head. BA, Williams College, MA, Univ of Delaware. **William A. Darrin III, Adm.**

Col Prep. Feat—Creative_Writing Anat & Physiol Environ_Sci African-Amer_Hist Psych Art_Hist Photog Theater Music Public_Speak. **Supp**—ESL LD Tut.

Adm: 58/yr. Bdg 51. Day 7. Appl due: Mar. Accepted: 35%. **Tests** IQ SSAT TOEFL.

Enr 125. B 110/15. Sec 119. PG 6. Wh 57%. Hisp 5%. Blk 15%. Asian 10%. Other 13%. Avg class size: 8. Uniform. **Fac 35.** M 20/2. F 10/3. Wh 78%. Hisp 10%. Blk 4%. Other 8%. Adv deg: 57%. In dorms 11.

Grad '04—31. Col—30. (Endicott, Dickinson, Trinity Col-CT, Lafayette, U of MA-Amherst, Wash & Jefferson). Avg SAT: 1047. Alum 1650.

Tui '04-'05: Bdg $29,900 (+$2000). **Day $19,900** (+$1500). **Aid:** Merit 2 ($24,500). Need 55 ($841,050).

Endow $3,400,000. Plant val $23,000,000. Bldgs 32. Dorms 7. Dorm rms 120. Class rms 31. Lib 24,000 vols. Chapels 1. Sci labs 4. Lang labs 1. Comp labs 3. Auds 1. Theaters 1. Art studios 3. Music studios 1. Dance studios 1. Gyms 1. Fields 3. Courts 10. Pools 1. Rinks 1. Boating facilities yes. Student ctrs 1.

Est 1923. Nonprofit. Episcopal. Tri (Sept-May). **Assoc** CLS NEASC.

South Kent was founded by Samuel S. Bartlett and Richard M. Cuyler with the help of Rev. Frederick H. Sill, founder and headmaster of Kent School. Mr. Bartlett and Mr. Cuyler, graduates of Kent, adopted the Kent ideal of the self-help system.

The school's structured college preparatory curriculum places equal emphasis on essential academic skills and course content. Strong humanities, science and math programs are available, and Advanced Placement classes are open to qualified students. The school provides a full range of support services for those with different learning styles.

Founded as an Episcopal school, South Kent maintains an active chapel program that meets the needs of students of all faiths. An extensive activities schedule includes dances and other social events with various girls' and coed schools. The athletic program, which includes interscholastic football, soccer, cross-country, lacrosse, hockey, crew, basketball, tennis, golf and baseball teams, accommodates boys of all ability levels. **See Also Page 1347**

STAMFORD, CT. (36 mi. NE of New York, NY) Urban. Pop: 117,083. Alt: 34 ft.

KING & LOW-HEYWOOD THOMAS SCHOOL
Day — Coed Gr PS-12

Stamford, CT 06905. 1450 Newfield Ave. Tel: 203-322-3496. Fax: 203-461-9988.
www.klht.org E-mail: admission@klht.org

Thomas B. Main, **Head.** BA, Bates College, MA, Wesleyan Univ. **Catherine J. Seton, Adm.**

Col Prep. AP—Eng Fr Span Calc Stats Comp_Sci Bio Chem Physics Eur_Hist US_Hist Econ Studio_Art. **Feat**—Anat & Physiol Genetics Holocaust Japan_Hist Anthro Ethics Philos Printmaking Drama Theater_Arts Music. **Supp**—Dev_Read Rem_Math Rem_Read Rev Tut.

Adm: 121/yr. Appl due: Jan. Accepted: 35%. **Tests** ISEE.

Enr 650. B 335. G 315. Elem 400. Sec 250. Wh 84%. Hisp 3%. Blk 8%. Asian 5%. Avg class size: 15. **Fac 100.** M 41. F 58/1. Adv deg: 67%.

Grad '04—55. Col—55. (Bucknell 4, CT Col 3, NYU 3, Boston Col 2, Georgetown 2, U of CT 2). Avg SAT: 1215. Alum 2800.

Tui '04-'05: Day $15,500-23,000 (+$150-1000). **Aid:** Merit 10 ($68,430). Need 45 ($642,975).

Summer: Acad Enrich Rem Rec. 3-6 wks.

Endow $5,400,000. Plant val $11,250,000. Bldgs 9. Class rms 50. Lib 35,000 vols. Sci labs 7. Lang labs 2. Comp labs 3. Auds 1. Theaters 1. Art studios 3. Music studios 3. Gyms 2. Fields 7. Courts 2. Pools 1.

Est 1865. Nonprofit. Sem (Sept-June). **Assoc** CLS NEASC.

In 1988, the Low-Heywood Thomas School for girls (founded in 1865) and the King School for boys (founded in 1875) consolidated. The two schools had been located on adjacent campuses, and the resulting coeducational school continues to occupy the combined 40-acre area in North Stamford.

The school's curriculum emphasizes the liberal arts and sciences, including English, foreign languages, mathematics, history, biology, chemistry, physics and computer science, with Advanced Placement courses in all major subjects. In addition, KLHT conducts academic enrichment classes in the lower, middle and upper schools. Small classes and individual attention prepare graduates for entrance to leading colleges.

Intramural and interscholastic sports include field hockey, softball, tennis, basketball, football, soccer, baseball, ice hockey, lacrosse, gymnastics and volleyball. Students participate in numerous extracurricular activities. **See Also Pages 1182-3**

THE LONG RIDGE SCHOOL
Day — Coed Gr PS-5

Stamford, CT 06903. 478 Erskine Rd. Tel: 203-322-7693. Fax: 203-322-0406.
www.longridgeschool.org E-mail: mail@longridgeschool.org

Crystal Klein Bria, **Head.** BA, Carnegie-Mellon Univ, MA, Columbia Univ, MEd, Bank Street College of Education.

Gen Acad. Feat—Span Computers Studio_Art Drama Music Movement. **Supp**—Rem_Read Rev Tut.

Adm: 43/yr. Appl due: Rolling. Accepted: 80%.

Enr 146. B 78. G 68. Elem 146. Wh 89%. Hisp 3%. Blk 7%. Asian 1%. **Fac 18.** M 1. F 16/1. Adv deg: 66%.
Grad '04—11. Prep—4. (King & Low-Heywood Thomas, New Canaan Country, St Luke's Sch-CT, Harvey). Alum 500.
Tui '04-'05: Day $16,515-17,335 (+$475).
Summer: Rec. Tui Day $1325-2275/4-wk ses. 8 wks.
Bldgs 2. Class rms 15. Lib 6000 vols. Sci labs 1. Lang labs 1. Art studios 1. Music studios 1. Fields 2. Courts 1. Pools 3.
Est 1938. Nonprofit. Sem (Sept-June).

Founded as a nursery school in the home of educator Harriet Rowland, Long Ridge has gradually added elementary grades over the years. The school, which occupies ten and a half wooded acres in the Long Ridge section of the city, serves students from southern Connecticut and Westchester County, NY.

At all grade levels, Long Ridge follows a hands-on, multisensory approach. Academic groupings are small and are adjusted to the needs and capabilities of students. Whenever possible, classes are integrated around a core theme and involve projects to maintain high levels of interest. Instructors employ developmentally appropriate methods and materials to promote successful learning experiences for every child. Strong emphasis is placed on the arts, science, computers and the environment. Spanish instruction begins in kindergarten.

STONINGTON, CT. (42 mi. SW of Providence, RI; 83 mi. SW of Boston, MA) Suburban. Pop: 16,953. Alt: 7 ft.

PINE POINT SCHOOL
Day — Coed Gr PS-9

Stonington, CT 06378. 89 Barnes Rd. Tel: 860-535-0606. Fax: 860-535-8033.
www.pinepoint.org E-mail: admission@pinepoint.org
Paul G. Geise, Head. BA, Colgate Univ, MEd, Harvard Univ. **Julie W. Abbiati, Adm.**
Pre-Prep. Feat—Humanities Fr Lat Span Computers Studio_Art Music Dance. **Supp**—Dev_Read Makeup Tut.
Adm: 55/yr. Appl due: Mar. Accepted: 74%. **Tests** IQ SSAT.
Enr 263. B 129. G 134. Elem 256. Sec 7. Wh 77%. Hisp 3%. Blk 4%. Am Ind 9%. Asian 5%. Other 2%. Avg class size: 24. **Fac 38.** M 8/3. F 24/3. Adv deg: 55%.
Grad '04—21. Prep—13. (Williams-CT, Miss Porter's, Tabor, Middlesex, Williston Northampton). Alum 1043.
Tui '03-'04: Day $3990-14,180 (+$150). **Aid:** Need 22 ($198,800).
Summer: Enrich Rec. Tui Day $150/wk. 8 wks.
Endow $200,000. Plant val $3,932,000. Bldgs 3. Class rms 15. Lib 9000 vols. Labs 2. Auds 1. Art studios 2. Music studios 1. Dance studios 1. Gyms 1. Fields 3. Courts 1.
Est 1948. Nonprofit. Tri (Sept-June).

Pine Point offers a highly integrated, developmental program at the primary level that emphasizes problem solving and the basic skills. Creative writing/publishing, computer, art, music, dance and community service are available to all students. The middle school program (grades 6-9) features three foreign languages, advanced mathematics and English, an international studies program for ninth graders, environmental and oceanographic sciences, interscholastic athletics, and visits to such regional locations as Mystic Aquarium, Mystic Seaport, the Palmer House Museum and Martha's Vineyard, MA. Graduates enter leading preparatory schools.

SUFFIELD, CT. (15 mi. N of Hartford, CT; 87 mi. WSW of Boston, MA) Suburban. Pop: 13,552. Alt: 124 ft.

SUFFIELD ACADEMY
Bdg — Coed Gr 9-PG; Day — Coed 9-12

Suffield, CT 06078. 185 N Main St, PO Box 999. Tel: 860-386-4440. Fax: 860-668-2966.
www.suffieldacademy.org   E-mail: saadmit@suffieldacademy.org
Charles Cahn, Head. BA, Univ of Michigan, MALS, Wesleyan Univ. **Terry Breault, Adm.**
  Col Prep. AP—Bio Chem Physics Econ Art_Hist. **Feat**—Relig Studio_Art Music Outdoor_Ed. **Supp**—ESL.
  Adm: 134/yr. Bdg 90. Day 44. Appl due: Feb. Accepted: 40%. **Tests** SSAT TOEFL.
  Enr 402. B 141/78. G 91/92. Sec 394. PG 8. Wh 79%. Hisp 2%. Blk 6%. Asian 13%. Avg class size: 11. **Fac 78.** M 34/6. F 32/6. Adv deg: 57%. In dorms 24.
  Grad '04—101. Col—101. (U of CO-Boulder, Hobart/Wm Smith, Boston U, Suffolk, Hamilton, U of WI-Madison). Avg SAT: 1151. Avg SSAT: 54%. Alum 4671.
  Tui '04-'05: Bdg $33,650 (+$1250). **Day $23,700** (+$1250). **Aid:** Merit 21 ($147,000). Need 136 ($1,617,240).
  Summer: Acad Enrich Rev. ESL. Tui Bdg $4700 (+$500). Tui Day $2450 (+$100). 5 wks.
  Endow $14,600,000. Plant val $39,000,000. Bldgs 50. Dorms 12. Dorm rms 219. Class rms 47. Lib 20,000 vols. Labs 4. Comp ctrs 1. Theaters 1. Art studios 3. Music studios 2. Perf arts ctrs 1. Gyms 1. Fields 14. Courts 9. Pools 1. Tracks 1. Weight rms 1. Rifle ranges 1.
  Est 1833. Nonprofit. Tri (Sept-June). **Assoc** CLS NEASC.

Known at first as the Connecticut Literary Institution, the school initially prepared young men for the ministry. In 1843, Suffield Academy became coeducational; after World War II, however, it emerged as an independent, all-male, nondenominational boarding and day school. Suffield returned to coeducation in 1974.

The traditional liberal arts curriculum of more than 100 courses, including Advanced Placement work and term electives, prepares graduates for leading colleges throughout the country. All students participate in a leadership program.

Extensive extracurricular activities and interscholastic athletics supplement academics. The 350-acre campus is located in a small New England town, and students take advantage of athletic and cultural events in the nearby cities of Hartford and Springfield, MA. **See Also Page 1257**

THOMPSON, CT. (25 mi. WNW of Providence, RI; 51 mi. WSW of Boston, MA) Suburban. Pop: 8878. Alt: 540 ft.

MARIANAPOLIS PREPARATORY SCHOOL
Bdg and Day — Coed Gr 9-PG

Thompson, CT 06277. 26 Chase Rd, PO Box 304. Tel: 860-923-9565. Fax: 860-923-3730.
  www.marianapolis.org   E-mail: admissions@marianapolis.org
Marilyn Ebbitt, Head. BA, Marquette Univ, MS, Georgetown Univ. **Daniel M. Harrop, Adm.**
  Col Prep. AP—Eng Calc Physics Eur_Hist US_Hist. **Feat**—Lat-Amer_Lit Fr Span Stats Anat & Physiol Astron Bioethics Ecol Microbiol Comp_Sci Web_Design Psych Theol World_Relig Photog Studio_Art Debate Journ Woodworking. **Supp**—ESL Makeup Tut.
  Adm: 92/yr. Appl due: Rolling. Accepted: 70%. **Tests** SSAT TOEFL.
  Enr 250. B 65/60. G 35/90. Sec 245. PG 5. Wh 50%. Hisp 15%. Blk 5%. Asian 20%. Other 10%. Avg class size: 15. **Fac 26.** M 11/1. F 12/2. Wh 99%. Hisp 1%. Adv deg: 50%. In dorms 10.
  Grad '04—46. Col—46. (U of CT, U of MA-Amherst, Holy Cross, Johns Hopkins, Notre Dame, Wash & Lee). Avg SAT: 1140. Alum 1650.
  Tui '04-'05: Bdg $25,740 (+$1500). **Day $8540** (+$500). **Aid:** Merit 2 ($16,012).
  Summer: Acad Enrich Rev. ESL. Tui Bdg $6000. Tui Day $2000/crse. 6 wks.
  Plant val $7,000,000. Bldgs 6. Dorms 3. Class rms 18. Lib 10,000 vols. Labs 4. Gyms 1. Fields 6. Courts 4.
  Est 1926. Nonprofit. Roman Catholic. Quar (Sept-June). **Assoc** NEASC.

Originally for boys, Marianapolis was established by the Congregation of Marians of the Immaculate Conception. It moved to its present, 300-acre site, on an arboretum in the heart of the 440-acre Thompson Hill Historic District, in 1931. The coeducational day program was instituted in 1974, and in 1989 girls were admitted to the boarding program.

The school offers a college preparatory program that includes honors as well as standard sections in most academic subjects. College credit is granted by the University of Connecticut for courses in modern European history, and Advanced Placement classes are offered in several subjects. In addition, there are seven levels of English taught to students for whom it is a second language. The sports program includes both interscholastic competition and intramural play.

See Also Page 1202

WALLINGFORD, CT. (23 mi. SSW of Hartford, CT; 80 mi. NE of New York, NY) Urban. Pop: 43,026. Alt: 100 ft.

CHOATE ROSEMARY HALL
Bdg and Day — Coed Gr 9-PG

Wallingford, CT 06492. 333 Christian St. Tel: 203-697-2239. Fax: 203-697-2629.
  www.choate.edu   E-mail: admissions@choate.edu
Edward J. Shanahan, Head. BA, St Joseph's College, MA, Fordham Univ, PhD, Univ of Wisconsin-Madison. **Ray Diffley III, Adm.**

Col Prep. AP—Eng Fr Lat Span Calc Stats Comp_Sci Chem Physics Eur_Hist US_Hist Econ Psych. **Feat**—Etymology Irish_Lit Ger Ital Japan Russ Ecol Marine_Biol/Sci Govt Logic Relig Photog Dance. **Supp**—Rev.

Adm: 274/yr. Bdg 201. Day 73. Appl due: Jan. Accepted: 28%. Yield: 60%. **Tests** CEEB ISEE SSAT TOEFL.

Enr 870. Sec 850. PG 20. Wh 72%. Hisp 4%. Blk 7%. Am Ind 1%. Asian 16%. Avg class size: 12. **Fac 113.** Wh 86%. Hisp 3%. Blk 5%. Asian 6%. Adv deg: 72%. In dorms 55.

Grad '04—239. Col—239. (Brown 7, USC 7, Harvard 6, Yale 6, Cornell 6, U of PA 6). Avg SAT: 1332. Alum 15,780.

Tui '04-'05: Bdg $33,440 (+$415). **Day $24,280** (+$415). **Aid:** Need 27 ($5,700,000).

Summer: Acad Enrich. 1-5 wks.

Endow $198,000,000. Plant val $66,500,000. Bldgs 110. Dorms 30. Dorm rms 376. Class rms 90. Lib 60,000 vols. Lang labs 1. Comp labs 4. Sci ctrs 1. Auds 2. Theaters 3. Art studios 5. Music studios 20. Dance studios 2. Arts ctrs 1. Gyms 2. Fields 13. Tennis courts 23. Squash courts 8. Pools 1. Rinks 1. Fitness ctrs 1. Boathouses 1.

Est 1890. Nonprofit. Tri (Sept-June). **Assoc** CLS NEASC.

In 1890, Mary Atwater Choate, a descendent of one of Wallingford's first settlers, invited Caroline Ruutz-Rees, a young scholar from England, to establish a school for girls, Rosemary Hall. Six years after Rosemary Hall's founding, William Choate, Mary Atwater Choate's husband, established The Choate School for boys. Choate and Rosemary Hall announced the coordination of the two schools in 1968, and Rosemary Hall relocated from Greenwich to Wallingford in 1971. The schools officially merged and assumed the current name in 1974.

Located on 400 acres of open fields, rolling hills and woods, the school occupies a campus that reflects a melding of the old with the new. The older school buildings are mostly Georgian in style, and the campus also features two modern I. M. Pei-designed buildings: an arts center and a science center.

The sense of community at the school is strengthened by diverse residences where six to 70 students, who come from approximately 35 states and 35 foreign countries, live closely with faculty and their families.

Choate's rigorous curriculum includes core requirements in six academic departments: English; math and computer science; science; history, psychology, religion and social sciences; languages; and arts. In addition to traditional course offerings, students choose from a wide array of electives, may pursue honors and Advanced Placement course work, and may undertake directed studies. Two other special offerings are an arts concentration program and a science research program. The arts program provides opportunities in and out of the classroom for studio art, theater, music, dance and photography, and many performances, recitals and exhibits occur throughout the year.

Term abroad programs operate in Spain, Italy and China. Other cross-cultural pursuits include a summer program conducted with the Navajo Nation in Arizona and summer studies at schools in Japan, China, France and Spain.

Students choose from numerous interscholastic sports (most at three distinct levels) and intramural sports. Interest clubs and organizations, multiple student publications and a community service program round out the school's extracurriculars. **See Also Pages 1134-5**

WASHINGTON, CT. (34 mi. WSW of Hartford, CT; 74 mi. NNE of New York, NY) Suburban. Pop: 3596. Alt: 740 ft. Area also includes Washington Depot.

THE GUNNERY
Bdg and Day — Coed Gr 9-PG

Washington, CT 06793. 99 Green Hill Rd. Tel: 860-868-7334. Fax: 860-868-1614.
www.gunnery.org   E-mail: admissions@gunnery.org
Susan G. Graham, Head. BS, Kent State Univ, MS, Fordham Univ. **Thomas W. Adams, Adm.**
Col Prep. AP—Eng Span Calc Bio Physics Eur_Hist US_Hist. **Feat**—Creative_Writing Stats Marine_Biol/Sci Ethics Public_Speak. **Supp**—ESL Tut.
Adm: 108/yr. Bdg 68. Day 40. Appl due: Jan. **Tests** SSAT.
Enr 276. B 131/44. G 70/31. Sec 264. PG 12. Wh 82%. Hisp 2%. Blk 6%. Asian 8%. Other 2%. Avg class size: 14. **Fac 50.** M 28. F 22. Wh 100%. Adv deg: 52%. In dorms 17.
Grad '04—78. Col—78. (Boston U, CT Col, Dartmouth, Lehigh, US Naval Acad, U of CO-Boulder). Avg SAT: 1090. Alum 2700.
Tui '03-'04: Bdg $31,500 (+$1500). **Day $22,900** (+$1500).
Endow $17,500,000. Plant val $17,000,000. Bldgs 25. Dorms 10. Dorm rms 105. Class rms 22. Lib 14,000 vols. Sci labs 4. Comp labs 2. Auds 1. Theaters 1. Art studios 2. Music studios 2. Perf arts ctrs 1. Gyms 2. Fields 4. Courts 8. Rinks 1.
Est 1850. Nonprofit. Tri (Sept-June). **Assoc** CLS NEASC.

This historic school was established by abolitionist and teacher Frederick W. Gunn and his wife, Abigail Brinsmade. The school provides a rigorous, traditional education in readying its students for college. An independent study program and seminars are available for seniors, and The Gunnery emphasizes the development of writing and speaking skills at all grade levels. Preparation for Advanced Placement tests is available in every major discipline.

Extracurricular activities include publications, art, music, drama, current affairs and community service organizations. Sports include football, soccer, cross-country, ice hockey, basketball, softball, baseball, wrestling, lacrosse, crew, golf, field hockey, volleyball and tennis.

RUMSEY HALL SCHOOL
Bdg — Coed Gr 5-9; Day — Coed K-9

Washington Depot, CT 06794. 201 Romford Rd. Tel: 860-868-0535. Fax: 860-868-7907.
www.rumseyhall.org   E-mail: admiss@rumseyhall.org
Thomas W. Farmen, Head. BA, New England College, MSA, Western Connecticut State Univ. **Matthew S. Hoeniger, Adm.**
Pre-Prep. **Feat**—Lat Computers Studio_Art Music. **Supp**—Dev_Read ESL Rem_Read Tut.
Adm: 110/yr. Bdg 55. Day 55. Appl due: Rolling. Accepted: 45%. **Tests** IQ.
Enr 315. Elem 253. Sec 62. Wh 80%. Hisp 1%. Blk 3%. Asian 7%. Other 9%. Avg class size: 12. **Fac 53.** M 18. F 26/9. Adv deg: 47%. In dorms 30.
Grad '04—50. Prep—47. (Canterbury-CT, Suffield, Salisbury-CT, Taft, Kent Sch-CT, Choate). Alum 3043.
Tui '04-'05: Bdg $30,600 (+$2000). **Day $14,665** (+$1000). **Aid:** Merit 4 ($3600). Need

57 ($576,100).
Summer: Acad Enrich Rev Rem Rec. Tui Bdg $4600. Tui Day $1500. 5 wks.
Endow $2,500,000. Plant val $10,003,000. Bldgs 27. Dorms 7. Dorm rms 60. Class rms 25. Lib 5000 vols. Sci labs 4. Comp labs 2. Art studios 1. Music studios 1. Gyms 1. Fields 9. Courts 4.
Est 1900. Nonprofit. Tri (Sept-June).

Lillias Rumsey Sanford founded Rumsey Hall in Seneca Falls, NY, with the idea that children need a structured environment with an emphasis on effort. The school moved to larger quarters in Cornwall in 1907 and to the present campus, situated in the foothills of the Berkshires, in 1949. Effort continues to be a focus and earns students various privileges.

The traditional structure of the school provides a family atmosphere, and full sports and extracurricular programs complement the academic curriculum. All students take art and music classes and participate in afternoon athletics. An outdoor adventure program is available for those who wish a less competitive program.

Throughout the year, students may also become involved in activities such as fishing, computer, singing, bicycling, golf, newspaper, yearbook, art, chess, backgammon, swimming, hiking and backpacking, overnight camping trips, intramural sports, and dramatic and musical productions. Rumsey Hall schedules off-campus trips and various activities on weekends for boarders. **See Also Page 1238**

WATERBURY, CT. (23 mi. SW of Hartford, CT; 77 mi. NE of New York, NY) Urban. Pop: 107,271. Alt: 260 ft.

CHASE COLLEGIATE SCHOOL
Day — Coed Gr PS-12

Waterbury, CT 06708. 565 Chase Pky. Tel: 203-236-9500. Fax: 203-236-9503.
www.smmct.org   E-mail: admissions@smmct.org
John D. Fixx, Head. BA, Wesleyan Univ, MBA, Univ of Connecticut. **Margy Foulk, Adm.**
  Col Prep. AP—Eng Fr Lat Span Calc Stats Bio Chem Physics US_Hist World_Hist. **Feat**—Playwriting Greek Astron Ecol Geol Oceanog Comp_Animation Archaeol Intl_Relations Crime & Punishment Adolescent_Psych Ethics Film Fine_Arts Theater Directing Music_Theory Journ Woodworking. **Supp**—Rev Tut.
  Adm (Gr PS-11): 86/yr. Appl due: Jan. Accepted: 80%. Yield: 64%. **Tests** SSAT.
  Enr 438. B 220. G 218. Elem 295. Sec 143. Wh 86%. Blk 4%. Asian 4%. Other 5%. Avg class size: 13. **Fac 57.** M 21. F 30/6. Wh 100%. Adv deg: 64%.
  Grad '04—37. Col—37. (Am U 3, Johns Hopkins 1, NYU 1, Wm & Mary 1, Lehigh 1, Babson 1). Avg SAT: 1192. Avg SSAT: 64%. Avg ACT: 25. Alum 3500.
  Tui '04-'05: Day $12,250-21,210 (+$800). **Aid:** Merit 9 ($69,665). Need 116 ($1,277,584).
  Summer: Acad Enrich Rec. Tui Day $350/wk. 4 wks.
  Endow $5,649,000. Plant val $14,930,000. Bldgs 10. Class rms 62. Lib 22,000 vols. Sci labs 6. Lang labs 1. Comp labs 4. Dark rms 1. Auds 1. Theaters 1. Art studios 3. Music studios 6. Wood shops 1. Gyms 2. Fields 4. Courts 12.
  Est 1865. Nonprofit. Tri (Sept-June).

Formerly called St. Margaret's-McTernan School, the school resulted from the 1972 merger of St. Margaret's School (founded in 1865), a girls' boarding school, and the McTernan School (established in 1912), a boys' day school. Chase Collegiate now occupies a 47-acre, wooded campus on a hill overlooking the city. Separate buildings house the lower, middle and upper schools. The school assumed its current name in July 2005.

A rigorous traditional curriculum in English, history, mathematics, science and foreign languages is complemented by numerous electives in art, music, drama and computer technology. Many students take advantage of the array of honors and Advanced Placement courses. Field trips in each grade are planned throughout the academic year, with the focus on extending and enriching the classroom experience; the school sponsors European trips during March break. Drama internships are available through Waterbury's Seven Angels Theatre.

Team interscholastic sports begin in grade 6; other extracurricular offerings include publications, performing arts activities, digital photography, language clubs, student government, Model United Nations and Public Affairs Seminar. Community service projects are an important part of Chase Collegiate's extracurricular program at all grade levels. **See Also Page 1132**

WATERTOWN, CT. (25 mi. WSW of Hartford, CT; 78 mi. NNE of New York, NY) Urban. Pop: 21,661. Alt: 484 ft.

TAFT SCHOOL
Bdg and Day — Coed Gr 9-PG

Watertown, CT 06795. 110 Woodbury Rd. Tel: 860-945-7777. Fax: 860-945-7808.
  www.taftschool.org   E-mail: admissions@taftschool.org
William R. MacMullen, Head. BA, Yale Univ, MA, Middlebury College. **Frederick H. Wandelt III, Adm.**

Col Prep. AP—Eng Fr Lat Span Calc Stats Comp_Sci Bio Chem Physics Eur_Hist US_Hist Econ US_Govt & Pol Art_Hist Studio_Art Music_Theory. **Feat**—Humanities Chin Japan Anat & Physiol Philos Ceramics Drawing Photog Acting Music Jazz. **Supp**—Rev Tut.

Adm: 180/yr. Bdg 152. Day 28. Appl due: Jan. Accepted: 22%. Yield: 53%. **Tests** SSAT.

Enr 563. B 238/50. G 222/53. Sec 549. PG 14. Wh 77%. Hisp 2%. Blk 6%. Asian 11%. Other 4%. Avg class size: 11. **Fac 81.** M 42/9. F 22/8. Wh 91%. Hisp 2%. Blk 2%. Asian 5%. Adv deg: 71%. In dorms 35.

Grad '04—156. Col—154. (Harvard 7, Cornell 6, Middlebury 6, Boston U 5, Colby 5, Yale 5). Avg SAT: 1305. Avg SSAT: 80%. Alum 7000.

Tui '04-'05: Bdg $32,900 (+$1800). **Day $24,500** (+$1500). **Aid:** Need 174 ($3,772,800).

Summer: Acad Enrich. ESL. Computers. Arts. Tui Bdg $5150. Tui Day $3100. 5 wks.

Endow $147,000,000. Plant val $150,000,000. Bldgs 20. Dorms 8. Dorm rms 278. Class rms 40. Lib 56,000 vols. Lang labs 1. Comp labs 3. Dark rms 2. Math/sci ctrs 1. Learning ctrs 1. Auds 2. Theaters 2. Art studios 2. Music studios 3. Dance studios 1. Arts ctrs 1. Woodworking studios 2. Galleries 1. Gyms 2. Fields 16. Basketball courts 4. Tennis courts 16. Volleyball courts 2. Squash courts 8. Rinks 2. Tracks 2. Weight rms 1. Climbing walls 1. Golf crses 1.

Est 1890. Nonprofit. Sem (Sept-June). **Assoc** CLS NEASC.

Horace Dutton Taft, brother of the president, devoted 46 years to the creation and the development of this school. He began as a lawyer, but a love of teaching drew him first (in 1887) to Yale, where he tutored Latin, and then to establish his own school. He was a great headmaster and tremendous worker, and he inspired his boys to work, stamping his personality upon the school. Under him the only salvation was through hard work, but he won confidence with his geniality and large-heartedness, and his comradeship in the classroom and on the playground. In 1927, he placed the school under the control of a board of trustees, and in 1936 Mr. Taft ended his 46-year tenure as headmaster.

The school became fully coeducational in 1971, with girls being admitted into all grades as boarding and day students. In the ensuing years, Taft made major campus improvements, greatly elevated its endowment, expanded the scholarship program and further diversified its student body.

Due to a rigorous admissions policy and the expansion and revision of academic offerings within the curriculum, most seniors take Advanced Placement courses, for which they are prepared by stringent basic and honors courses in the lower classes. An independent learning program enables selected upper school students to pursue individual creative work of a high caliber. The school also supports lecture and concert series, in addition to a program of art and historical exhibits.

Taft's Center for Teacher Education attracts public, private and parochial school teachers and administrators from all parts of the country. These summer workshops are devoted to developing specific curricula and teaching techniques for Advanced Placement, science and values courses.

Patronage is national and international, and the scholarship program aids many students who otherwise might not be able to attend Taft. Graduates enter leading colleges.

Numerous athletic facilities occupy Taft's 220-acre campus, and the athletic program, which is both intramural and interscholastic, provides competition in most sports. In addition to the school's traditional sports offerings, there are opportunities to rock climb, learn wilderness survival techniques and practice modern dance. More than 40 extracurricular activities include arts and drama, publications, and vocal and instrumental music. Student-faculty policymaking committees and a student-run job program offer practical experience in organizational leadership.

See Also Page 1260

WESTBROOK, CT. (36 mi. SSE of Hartford, CT; 89 mi. ENE of New York, NY) Suburban. Pop: 6292. Alt: 34 ft.

OXFORD ACADEMY
Bdg — Boys Gr 9-PG

Westbrook, CT 06498. 1393 Boston Post Rd. Tel: 860-399-6247. Fax: 860-399-6805.
www.oxfordacademy.net   E-mail: admissions@oxfordacademy.net
Philip Hewes Davis, Head. BA, Middlebury College, MALS, Wesleyan Univ. **Michele M. Deane, Adm.**
    Col Prep. Gen Acad. Underachiever. AP—Eng Calc Eur_Hist. **Feat**—Fr Ger Lat Span

Stats Astron Environ_Sci Marine_Biol/Sci Microbiol Holocaust Civil_War Econ Pol_Sci Study_Skills. **Supp**—Dev_Read ESL LD Makeup Tut.

Adm: 17/yr. Appl due: Rolling. Accepted: 75%. Yield: 90%. **Tests** SSAT TOEFL.

Enr 48. B 48. Sec 46. PG 2. Wh 70%. Hisp 6%. Blk 3%. Asian 21%. Avg class size: 1. **Fac 24.** M 16/1. F 6/1. Wh 95%. Hisp 5%. Adv deg: 37%. In dorms 6.

Grad '04—18. Col—18. (SMU, Loyola U-LA, VA Milit, Bryant, Hartwick, Sch of the Museum of Fine Arts). Avg SAT: 1000. Alum 900.

Tui '04-'05: Bdg $44,370 (+$2000).

Summer: Acad Enrich Rev Rem. Tui Bdg $6175. 5 wks.

Endow $200,000. Plant val $3,700,000. Bldgs 10. Dorms 2. Dorm rms 26. Class rms 20. Lib 3100 vols. Sci labs 2. Lang labs 1. Comp labs 1. Art studios 1. Gyms 1. Fields 2. Courts 3.

Est 1906. Nonprofit. 5 terms (Sept-June). **Assoc** NEASC.

Founded in Pleasantville, NJ, by Joseph M. Weidberg, this school moved to Westbrook in 1973, after a fire had destroyed the main building. The academy, which draws its enrollment from throughout the country and the world, has successfully developed and pursued a program of totally individualized instruction that prepares all of its students for college or further secondary preparation.

The school serves young men who have experienced learning difficulties in a traditional school setting. The Socratic method of teaching is used, and a full curriculum extends from basic courses through Advanced Placement. Each class consists of one student and one teacher. An English as a Second Language program helps students from other countries to improve their English and prepare for entrance to American colleges.

Extracurricular activities include trips to concerts, museums, movies, deep-sea fishing sites and nearby points of interest. The athletic program offers interscholastic competition in soccer, basketball and tennis. **See Also Page 1369**

WESTPORT, CT. (44 mi. NE of New York, NY; 56 mi. SW of Hartford, CT) Suburban. Pop: 25,749. Alt: 26 ft. Area also includes Greens Farms.

GREENS FARMS ACADEMY

Day — Coed Gr K-12

Greens Farms, CT 06838. 35 Beachside Ave, PO Box 998. Tel: 203-256-7514. Fax: 203-256-7501.

www.gfacademy.org   E-mail: admissions@gfacademy.org

Janet M. Hartwell, Head. BA, University of Leeds (England), MA, Columbia Univ. **Stephanie Whitney, Adm.**

Col Prep. Feat—Comp_Design Animation Econ Visual_Arts Drama.

Adm: 78/yr. Appl due: Jan. Accepted: 24%. **Tests** ISEE SSAT.

Enr 580. B 291. G 289. Elem 336. Sec 244. Wh 89%. Hisp 2%. Blk 3%. Asian 2%. Other 4%. Avg class size: 12. **Fac 90.** M 31/3. F 51/5. Wh 92%. Hisp 3%. Blk 3%. Asian 2%. Adv deg: 55%.

Grad '04—58. Col—57. (Columbia, Colgate, Boston U, Hamilton, Duke, Brown). Avg SAT: 1260. Alum 1550.

Tui '03-'04: Day $21,350-23,350 (+$500). **Aid:** Need 57 ($1,084,575).

Summer: Acad Enrich Rev Rem Rec. 2-6 wks.

Endow $15,600,000. Plant val $14,542,000. Bldgs 4. Class rms 81. Lib 15,000 vols. Sci labs 5. Lang labs 1. Comp labs 1. Art studios 4. Music studios 4. Gyms 3. Fields 4. Courts 4.
Est 1925. Nonprofit. Tri (Sept-June). **Assoc** CLS NEASC.

The traditional college preparatory curriculum emphasizes study skills, the basics of the major disciplines, ample opportunities in the arts and, for upper school students, a wide array of Advanced Placement offerings. Students may choose to broaden their program further through independent study, study abroad or off-campus projects.

A full range of extracurricular activities, including student government, the arts and interscholastic sports, is available, and all students participate in the community service program. The school sends its graduates on to competitive colleges.

WINDSOR, CT. (6 mi. NNE of Hartford, CT; 90 mi. WSW of Boston, MA) Suburban. Pop: 28,237. Alt: 61 ft.

LOOMIS CHAFFEE SCHOOL
Bdg and Day — Coed Gr 9-PG

Windsor, CT 06095. 4 Batchelder Rd. Tel: 860-687-6000. Fax: 860-298-8756.
www.loomis.org   E-mail: admission@loomis.org

Russell H. Weigel, Head. BA, Bowdoin College, MA, George Washington Univ, PhD, Univ of Colorado-Boulder. **Thomas D. Southworth, Adm.**

Col Prep. AP—Eng Fr Lat Span Calc Stats Comp_Sci Chem Physics US_Hist Econ Studio_Art. **Feat**—Chin Ger Anat & Physiol Astron Genetics Geol Programming Web_Design Russ_Hist Lat-Amer_Stud Philos Relig Drama Music.

Adm: 246/yr. Bdg 146. Day 100. Appl due: Jan. Accepted: 44%. **Tests** CEEB ISEE SSAT TOEFL.

Enr 723. B 201/173. G 181/168. Wh 84%. Hisp 2%. Blk 6%. Asian 8%. Avg class size: 14.
Fac 158. M 66/8. F 58/26. Adv deg: 63%. In dorms 31.

Grad '04—200. Col—197. (Vanderbilt 6, Fordham 6, Geo Wash 6, Trinity Col-CT 5, Franklin & Marshall 5, Yale 4). Avg SAT: 1261. Alum 9000.

Tui '04-'05: Bdg $33,000 (+$600). **Day $24,700** (+$600). **Aid:** Need 200 ($4,200,000).

Endow $110,000,000. Plant val $150,000,000. Bldgs 66. Dorms 10. Dorm rms 271. Class rms 51. Lib 60,000 vols. Sci labs 9. Lang labs 1. Comp ctrs 1. Planetariums 1. Theaters 1. Art studios 2. Music studios 10. Dance studios 1. Arts ctrs 1. Gyms 3. Fields 13. Tennis courts 19. Squash courts 8. Pools 1. Rinks 1. TV stations 1. Radio stations 1.

Est 1914. Nonprofit. Tri (Sept-June). **Assoc** CLS NEASC.

In 1874, five members of the Loomis family, bereft of heirs, dedicated their resources and drew up a charter for a school on what had been (since 1639) the Loomis homestead, "for the free and gratuitous education of all persons of the age of 12 years and upwards to 20 years in all the departments of learning which are now taught or hereafter may be taught in the various grades of schools in this country . . . so far as the funds of the institute will permit." While members of the Loomis family and residents of Windsor were given preference under the charter, the school rapidly developed a wide geographical distribution of patronage.

Originally conceived as a coeducational institution, the Loomis Institute was divided in its early years into Loomis, a boys' boarding school, and Chaffee, a girls' day school. This separation came to an end in 1970 when Chaffee, returning from the far side of the Farmington River, moved into a spacious new building on the Loomis campus. In the spring of 1972, the operating name of the Loomis Institute became the Loomis Chaffee School.

The curriculum, constantly reviewed, offers an unusual variety of courses. Students choose from traditional subjects, as well as technological and globally inclusive ones. Course work and school life incorporate current world issues and social concerns. Electives are available in all departments, as are independent study programs. Loomis Chaffee's fully equipped art center supports a strong visual arts program. Pupils investigate an annual school-wide theme with the assistance of visiting speakers, debates, art exhibitions, classes and small-group discussions.

The School Year Abroad program offers opportunities to study in France, Spain and Beijing, China. German language students have the opportunity to spend the winter term of senior year at a German boarding school. Athletics are both interscholastic and intramural. Sports include cross-country, football, soccer, basketball, hockey, riflery, golf, swimming, wrestling, baseball, lacrosse, tennis, track and water polo for boys, and field hockey, soccer, cross-country, volleyball, ice hockey, swimming, softball, track, basketball, tennis, lacrosse, water polo, squash and modern dance for girls. Other activities include cycling, aerobics, cross-country skiing, jogging and Outward Bound activities.

All students and faculty participate in a work program that involves the daily maintenance of buildings, the efficient functioning of the dining facility, and assistance in many areas of school life. Student points of view are presented to the faculty by the elected student council. Among extracurricular activities are several publications, numerous clubs, dramatics, music and hobbies. Community service projects include a hospital medical aides group and tutoring of the underprivileged in depressed areas of Hartford. **See Also Pages 1192-3**

WOODSTOCK, CT. (30 mi. WNW of Providence, RI; 56 mi. WSW of Boston, MA) Rural. Pop: 7221. Alt: 592 ft.

HYDE SCHOOL AT WOODSTOCK
Bdg and Day — Coed Gr 9-12

Woodstock, CT 06281. 150 Rte 169, PO Box 237. Tel: 860-963-9096. Fax: 860-928-0612.
www.hyde.edu   E-mail: woodstock.admissions@hyde.edu
Malcolm W. Gauld, Pres. BA, Bowdoin College, MA, Harvard Univ. **Duncan F. McCrann, Head.** BA, Harvard Univ. **Michael V. Dawes, Adm.**

Col Prep. AP—Eng Calc Stats US_Hist US_Govt & Pol. **Feat**—Fr Span 20th-Century_ Hist Philos World_Relig Studio_Art Drama. **Supp**—Rem_Math Rev Tut.

Adm: 31/yr. Bdg 30. Day 1. Appl due: Rolling. Accepted: 60%.

Enr 200. B 132/3. G 64/1. Sec 200. Wh 80%. Hisp 3%. Blk 10%. Am Ind 2%. Asian 5%. Avg class size: 12. **Fac 38.** M 21. F 15/2. Wh 99%. Hisp 1%. In dorms 16.

Grad '04—44. Col—40. (Roger Williams 4, OH Wesleyan 3, U of VT 2, U of DE 2, U of MD-Col Park 1, Colgate 1). Avg SAT: 1100. Alum 500.

Tui '04-'05: Bdg $33,000 (+$3250). **Day $19,950** (+$1500). **Aid:** Need 42 ($550,000).

Summer: Rec. Leadership. Tui Bdg $6000. 5 wks.

Endow $4,900,000. Bldgs 6. Dorms 2. Dorm rms 133. Class rms 24. Lib 5400 vols. Sci labs 2. Lang labs 2. Comp labs 1. Theaters 1. Art studios 1. Music studios 1. Dance studios 1. Gyms 1. Fields 4. Courts 1.
Est 1996. Nonprofit. Tri (Sept-May).

An outgrowth of Hyde School at Bath (see separate listing), this school was founded in response to a growing demand for Hyde's character-based curriculum. The rural campus occupies a 120-acre site that once served as the location of a Catholic women's college.

Hyde's program focuses upon three elements: character development, college preparation and family involvement. All students fulfill requirements in athletics, the performing arts and community service. In addition to traditional grading, faculty and peer evaluations are stressed. An unusual amount of responsibility is given to each student in the overall decision-making and operation of the school. Parents must participate in the Family Education Program, which consists of a three-day, on-campus seminar; regional monthly meetings; twice-annual family weekends; and yearly regional retreats.

Acceptance to Hyde is based on a family interview conducted on campus, in conjunction with papers composed after the interview by both the prospective student and his or her parents. Admission to the school is year-round.

See Also Pages 1176-7

MAINE

BATH, ME. (26 mi. NE of Portland, ME; 126 mi. NNE of Boston, MA) Suburban. Pop: 9266. Alt: 79 ft.

HYDE SCHOOL AT BATH
Bdg and Day — Coed Gr 9-12

Bath, ME 04530. 616 High St. Tel: 207-443-5584. Fax: 207-442-9346.
  www.hyde.edu E-mail: bath.admissions@hyde.edu
Malcolm W. Gauld, Pres. BA, Bowdoin College, MA, Harvard Univ. **Laurie G. Hurd, Head.** BA, Bowdoin College. **Rich Truluck, Adm.**
  Col Prep. AP—Eng Calc Stats US_Hist US_Govt & Pol. **Feat**—Comp_Sci Performing_Arts. **Supp**—Rem_Math Rem_Read Tut.
  Adm (Day Gr 9-11): 93/yr. Bdg 90. Day 3. Appl due: Rolling.
  Enr 202. B 132/7. G 62/1. Sec 202. Wh 92%. Hisp 4%. Blk 3%. Asian 1%. Avg class size: 12. **Fac 26.** M 17. F 9. Wh 94%. Blk 6%. Adv deg: 30%. In dorms 20.
  Grad '04—60. Col—55. (U of CA-Berkeley 4, U of SC 3, Temple 3, U of CO-Boulder 3, Franklin & Marshall 2, Hobart/Wm Smith 2). Avg SAT: 1039. Alum 1500.
  Tui '04-'05: Bdg $33,000 (+$3250). **Day $19,950** (+$1450). **Aid:** Need ($464,550).
  Summer: Acad Rem Rec. Leadership. Tui Bdg $6000. 5 wks.
  Endow $7,200,000. Plant val $19,000,000. Bldgs 24. Dorms 8. Dorm rms 90. Class rms 20. Lib 6000 vols. Sci labs 2. Comp labs 1. Auds 1. Art studios 1. Music studios 1. Gyms 1. Fields 3. Tennis courts 4. Pools 1. Tracks 1.
  Est 1966. Nonprofit. Tri (Sept-May). **Assoc** NEASC.

After several years of planning and with the handsome estate of shipbuilder John S. Hyde for a campus, this school was opened by Joseph Gauld in 1966. The school became coeducational in 1971.

Hyde's college preparatory program is character based and promotes an interdisciplinary curriculum encompassing traditional secondary academics, athletics, the performing arts and community service. In addition to traditional grading, faculty and peer evaluations are stressed. An unusual amount of responsibility is given to each student in the overall decision-making and operation of the school. The Family Education Center, founded in 1977, assists parents in understanding Hyde's program and helps with a network of regional parent groups. Acceptance to Hyde is based on a family interview conducted on campus, in conjunction with papers composed after the interview by both the prospective student and his or her parents. Admission to the school is year-round.

Since July 1996, Hyde has operated a second campus in Woodstock, CT (see separate listing). **See Also Pages 1176-7**

BERWICK, ME. (43 mi. SW of Portland, ME; 65 mi. N of Boston, MA) Suburban. Pop: 6353. Alt: 102 ft. Area also includes South Berwick.

BERWICK ACADEMY
Day — Coed Gr K-PG

South Berwick, ME 03908. 31 Academy St. Tel: 207-384-2164. Fax: 207-384-3332.
www.berwickacademy.org   E-mail: dfield@berwickacademy.org
Richard W. Ridgway, Head. AB, Dartmouth College, MA, Columbia Univ. **Diane M. Field, Adm.**
  Col Prep. AP—Fr Lat Span Calc Comp_Sci Bio Chem Physics Studio_Art. **Feat**—Stats Anat & Physiol Astron Environ_Sci Programming Women's_Stud Photog Chorus Music Music_Theory. **Supp**—Tut.
  Adm: 106/yr. Appl due: Dec. Accepted: 52%. **Tests** CTP_4 SSAT.
  Enr 573. B 252. G 321. Elem 324. Sec 249. Wh 99%. Asian 1%. Avg class size: 14. **Fac 88.** M 25/7. F 45/11. Wh 100%. Adv deg: 45%.
  Grad '04—64. Col—63. (NYU 3, USC 2, Worcester Polytech 2, Boston U 2, Franklin & Marshall 1, Cornell 1). Avg SAT: 1230. Alum 2700.
  Tui '04-'05: Day $18,500 (+$1500). **Aid:** Need 120 ($1,150,000).
  Summer: Acad Enrich. Study Skills. Tui Day $130/wk. 2 wks.
  Endow $12,000,000. Plant val $3,500,000. Bldgs 14. Class rms 31. Lib 11,000 vols. Labs 4. Sci ctrs 1. Art studios 4. Music studios 4. Gyms 1. Athletic ctrs 1. Fields 4. Courts 6.
  Est 1791. Nonprofit. Quar (Sept-June). **Assoc** CLS NEASC.

The oldest school in Maine, BA holds a charter as an institution of higher learning, signed by Gov. John Hancock when Maine was a possession of Massachusetts. Albert L. Kerr, who assumed direction in 1957, established a college preparatory program that now offers a competitively rigorous curriculum, with training in fundamental academic skills, as well as honors and Advanced Placement courses. After 17 years as a combined boarding and day school, the academy reverted to country day status in 1976 and now enrolls students from three states.

Graduates favor New England schools, but many enter competitive colleges elsewhere in the country. Activities include competitive and noncompetitive sports, chorus, orchestra, drama, art exhibits, dance, newspaper and yearbook.

BETHEL, ME. (59 mi. NNW of Portland, ME; 143 mi. N of Boston, MA) Suburban. Pop: 2411. Alt: 643 ft.

GOULD ACADEMY
Bdg and Day — Coed Gr 9-PG

Bethel, ME 04217. Church St, PO Box 860. Tel: 207-824-7777. Fax: 207-824-2926.
www.gouldacademy.org   E-mail: contact@gouldacademy.org
Daniel A. Kunkle, Head. AB, Brown Univ, MEd, Harvard Univ. **John Kerney, Adm.**
  Col Prep. AP—Eng Calc Bio Chem US_Govt & Pol. **Feat**—S_African_Lit Fr Lat Span Stats Environ_Sci Celestial_Navigation Programming Robotics Middle_Eastern_Hist Anthro Econ Ethics Drawing Photog Sculpt Studio_Art Theater Chorus Design Black-

smithing Silversmithing Study_Skills. **Supp**—ESL.
Adm: 79/yr. Bdg 67. Day 12. Appl due: Feb. **Tests** CEEB IQ SSAT.
Enr 221. B 110/31. G 63/17. Sec 217. PG 4. Wh 90%. Blk 2%. Asian 8%. **Fac 37.** M 19/3. F 13/2. Adv deg: 59%. In dorms 14.
Grad '04—58. Col—50. (Bowdoin, Mt Holyoke, Plymouth St, U of CO-Boulder, Yale). Alum 4300.
Tui '04-'05: Bdg $33,700 (+$1000). **Day $20,000** (+$1000). **Aid:** Need 97 ($1,200,000).
Summer: Gr 10-PG. Acad Enrich Rec. Tui Bdg $4150. Tui Day $2500. 6 wks. Gr 7-9. Young Scholars Prgm. Acad Enrich Rec. Tui Bdg $2800. Tui Day $1900. 4 wks.
Endow $8,000,000. Plant val $17,000,000. Bldgs 30. Dorms 5. Class rms 35. Lib 15,000 vols. Sci labs 5. Comp labs 3. Gyms 2. Fields 4. Courts 8.
Est 1836. Nonprofit. Tri (Sept-May). **Assoc** NEASC.

Coeducational from its founding, Gould is situated adjacent to the White Mountain National Forest. Students enroll from many states and foreign countries.

The college preparatory program combines traditional curricular elements with forward-looking electives. Honors and Advanced Placement courses in most disciplines are available for talented students, and qualified pupils may pursue independent studies in fields of interest to them. Ninety-minute class blocks facilitate in-depth inquiry in humanities, social science and laboratory science courses.

Special offerings include experiential education programs; exchange programs with schools in Germany, France, Spain and Hungary; a university-level computer network; and noteworthy programs in the visual arts, science and technology. The school's setting allows for an extensive outdoor program and a varied ski program.

BRIDGTON, ME. (38 mi. NW of Portland, ME; 120 mi. N of Boston, MA) Suburban. Pop: 4883. Alt: 405 ft. Area also includes North Bridgton.

BRIDGTON ACADEMY
Bdg and Day — Boys Gr PG

North Bridgton, ME 04057. Rte 37, PO Box 292. Tel: 207-647-3322. Fax: 207-647-8513.
www.bridgtonacademy.org   E-mail: admit@bridgtonacademy.org
David N. Hursty, Head. BS, Salem State College, MA, Georgetown Univ. **Lisa M. Antell, Adm.**
Col Prep. Feat—Stats Anat & Physiol Environ_Sci Oceanog Civil_War Govt Psych. **Supp**—LD.
Adm: 190/yr. Bdg 184. Day 6. Appl due: Rolling. Accepted: 95%. **Tests** CEEB.
Enr 190. B 184/6. PG 190. Wh 84%. Hisp 2%. Blk 14%. Avg class size: 15. **Fac 20.** M 19. F 1. Wh 99%. Blk 1%. Adv deg: 25%. In dorms 8.
Grad '04—160. Col—160. (US Naval Acad 6, Merrimack 5, St Michael's 5, Plymouth St 4, Sacred Heart 3, OH Wesleyan 2). Avg SAT: 890. Alum 5534.
Tui '05-'06: Bdg $30,400 (+$1500). **Day $15,000** (+$1500). **Aid:** Need 89 ($1,135,200).
Endow $3,861,000. Plant val $3,470,000. Bldgs 22. Dorms 8. Dorm rms 84. Class rms 11. Lib 7000 vols. Chapels 1. Sci labs 4. Comp labs 1. Writing labs 1. Auds 1. Art studios 1. Museums 1. Gyms 1. Fields 5. Courts 4. Rinks 1. Weight rms 1.
Est 1808. Nonprofit. Sem (Sept-May). **Assoc** NEASC.

Bridgton was established by the Massachusetts legislature at a time when Maine was part of Massachusetts. The impetus for founding came from 37 local residents who furnished financial support to provide secondary schooling for boys and girls. In 1964, the academy adopted a new academic plan that resulted in the discontinuance of coeducation and the elimination of the lower grades: Bridgton became a one-year college preparatory school offering specific programs for older boys in grade 12 and for postgraduates. The present-day school serves postgraduate students who attend for one year only.

All aspects of school life address the needs of the boy capable of college-level work who stands to benefit from an additional year of study and growth prior to college entrance. The curriculum emphasizes writing, computation and critical reading, in addition to electives. Qualified students may take college courses for transferable college credit through partnerships with the University of Southern Maine, the University of New England and Plymouth State College. A separate program provides academic support for pupils who have been diagnosed with mild learning disabilities.

Students are encouraged to participate in interscholastic sports or in skiing, intramurals or the outing club. Most teams compete against college junior varsity squads, as well as against traditional prep school rivals. Clubs and organizations, which vary from year to year depending upon pupil interest, include student government, school newspaper and yearbook. Bridgton also schedules guest lectures and performances.

FRYEBURG, ME. (45 mi. WNW of Portland, ME; 116 mi. N of Boston, MA) Rural. Pop: 1549. Alt: 420 ft.

FRYEBURG ACADEMY

Bdg and Day — Coed Gr 9-12

Fryeburg, ME 04037. 745 Main St. Tel: 207-935-2013. Fax: 207-935-4292.
 www.fryeburgacademy.org   E-mail: admissions@fryeburgacademy.org
Daniel G. Lee, Jr., Head. BA, Yale Univ, MA, Wesleyan Univ. **Stephanie Morin, Adm.**
  Col Prep. Gen Acad. AP—Eng Fr Calc Stats Bio Chem Eur_Hist US_Hist Music_Theory.
    Feat—Lat Span Computers Indus_Arts. **Supp**—Dev_Read ESL LD Rem_Math Rem_Read Tut.
  Adm: 220/yr. Bdg 76. Day 144. Appl due: Rolling. Accepted: 95%. Yield: 55%.
    Enr 690. B 71/297. G 35/287. Sec 690. Wh 86%. Hisp 3%. Blk 4%. Asian 7%. Avg class size: 15. **Fac 63.** M 33. F 30. Wh 100%. Adv deg: 33%. In dorms 8.
  Grad '04—152. Col—132. (U of ME-Orono, Northeastern U, Boston U, Colby, Geo Wash, Middlebury). Avg SAT: 1040. Alum 7200.
  Tui '04-'05: Bdg $29,700 (+$1200). **Day $14,850** (+$500). **Aid:** Need 45 ($840,000).
    Endow $5,000,000. Plant val $9,800,000. Bldgs 14. Dorms 4. Dorm rms 120. Class rms 60. Lib 13,000 vols. Sci labs 6. Lang labs 1. Comp labs 2. Art studios 1. Music studios 1. Gyms 1. Fields 6. Courts 1.
  Est 1792. Nonprofit. Sem (Sept-June). **Assoc** NEASC.

Started and since maintained as a coeducational school, Fryeburg enjoyed as its first headmaster Paul Langdon, the Bernard Langdon of Oliver Wendell Holmes' novel *Elsie Venner.* His most eminent successor was Daniel Webster, who here made his first and only attempt at teaching school.

Serving the community through its day program, the academy also offers boarding enrollment to its students, who pursue either a college preparatory or a general course of study. Vocational programs, AP courses, tutorials and learning-disability services complement the academic program, and English as a Second Language courses are available for an additional fee. The school maintains a traditional selection of athletics and extracurricular activities, including particularly strong drama and music programs. **See Also Pages 1152-3**

HEBRON, ME. (38 mi. NNW of Portland, ME; 132 mi. NNE of Boston, MA) Rural. Pop: 1053. Alt: 600 ft.

HEBRON ACADEMY

Bdg — Coed Gr 9-PG; Day — Coed 6-PG

Hebron, ME 04238. Rte 119, PO Box 309. Tel: 207-966-2100. Fax: 207-966-1111. www.hebronacademy.org   E-mail: admissions@hebronacademy.org
John J. King, Head. BA, Williams College. Joseph M. Hemmings, Adm.

    Col Prep. AP—Eng Calc Bio Chem Physics US_Hist Studio_Art. Feat—Fr Lat Span Anat & Physiol Computers Econ Intl_Relations Psych Environ_Ethics World_Relig Photog Music. Supp—ESL LD.

    Adm: 89/yr. Bdg 67. Day 22. Appl due: Feb. Accepted: 70%. Tests SSAT TOEFL.

    Enr 237. Elem 42. Sec 182. PG 13. Wh 82%. Hisp 1%. Blk 6%. Am Ind 1%. Asian 10%. Avg class size: 7. Fac 40. M 21. F 19. Wh 100%. Adv deg: 35%. In dorms 12.

    Grad '04—67. Col—63. (Mt Allison-Canada, Elmira, U of VT, Assumption, St Lawrence, Hartwick). Avg SAT: 1100. Alum 5171.

    Tui '04-'05: Bdg $33,000 (+$600). Day $18,500 (+$400). Aid: Merit 2 ($10,000). Need 127 ($1,500,000).

    Endow $6,400,000. Plant val $8,000,000. Bldgs 9. Dorms 3. Dorm rms 107. Class rms 19. Lib 16,500 vols. Labs 5. Comp ctrs 1. Theaters 2. Art studios 2. Gyms 1. Courts 8. Rinks 1.

    Est 1804. Nonprofit. Tri (Sept-June). Assoc CLS NEASC.

The school, which was founded by Revolutionary War veterans as a coeducational academy, ended a long affiliation with Colby College in 1956. It became a boys' boarding school in the early 20th century before once again admitting girls and day students in 1972. A middle school program for students in grades 6-8 was added in 1991. Hebron occupies a 1500-acre campus, distinguished by the work of architect John Calvin Stevens at the turn of the century, in the foothills of western Maine.

The curriculum prepares students for higher education and includes a full range of Advanced Placement and honors-level courses, as well as a program for students with minor learning differences and English as a Second Language instruction. The interdisciplinary nature studies program consists of academic study and outdoor skills instruction. Classroom course work involves specialized, trimester-long English, math, science and history classes. In addition, students choose from extensive course offerings in art and music and a full complement of activities and interscholastic sports.

A variety of environmental and outdoor education experiences, including kayaking, canoeing, rock climbing, hiking, camping, skiing and snowboarding, is offered. The cultural resources of nearby Lewiston/Auburn and Portland provide theater, sporting and concert opportunities for students and faculty. **See Also Page 1164**

KENTS HILL, ME. (52 mi. NNE of Portland, ME; 152 mi. NNE of Boston, MA) Rural. Pop: 90.

KENTS HILL SCHOOL
Bdg and Day — Coed Gr 9-PG

Kents Hill, ME 04349. Rte 17, PO Box 257. Tel: 207-685-4914. Fax: 207-685-9529.
www.kentshill.org   E-mail: info@kentshill.org
Rist Bonnefond, Head. BA, Cornell Univ. **Loren B. Mitchell, Adm.**

Col Prep. AP—Eng Calc Bio Chem Physics Eur_Hist US_Hist Studio_Art. **Feat**—Dickens Fr Span Stats Astron Ecol Geol Computers Econ Govt Psych Art_Hist Ceramics Woodworking Study_Skills. **Supp**—ESL Rev Tut.

Adm: 98/yr. Bdg 76. Day 22. Appl due: Feb. Accepted: 80%. **Tests** SSAT TOEFL.

Enr 215. B 104/35. G 47/29. Sec 205. PG 10. Wh 75%. Hisp 3%. Blk 6%. Am Ind 1%. Asian 15%. Avg class size: 10. **Fac 40.** M 21. F 19. Wh 98%. Asian 2%. Adv deg: 62%.

Grad '04—83. Col—79. (St Michael's, Roger Williams, U of MA-Amherst, Boston U, U of VT, U of CO-Boulder). Avg SAT: 1032. Alum 4500.

Tui '04-'05: Bdg $33,900 (+$800). **Day $19,500** (+$800). **Aid:** Need 100 ($1,662,390).

Endow $4,500,000. Plant val $28,705,000. Bldgs 22. Dorms 4. Dorm rms 102. Class rms 32. Lib 10,000 vols. Labs 4. Photog labs 1. Comp ctrs 2. Theaters 1. Art studios 3. Music studios 1. Gyms 2. Athletic ctrs 1. Fields 7. Courts 8. Basketball courts 2. Rinks 1. Riding rings 1. Stables 1. Weight rms 1. Fitness ctrs 1. Equestrian ctrs 1.

Est 1824. Nonprofit. Tri (Sept-June). **Assoc** CLS NEASC.

One of the oldest coeducational boarding schools in the country, Kents Hill was established by Luther D. Sampson to offer "an educational program calculated to inspire intellectual growth and develop character."

The curriculum includes a wide variety of courses, ranging from the traditional to the progressive. Numerous electives supplement required courses. The school's learning center provides students with one-on-one instruction, and SAT preparation is available on a weekly basis.

Extracurricular activities comprise the arts (studio art, ceramics, music, dramatics and woodworking), publications, clubs and a full complement of sports. The school owns and operates its own on-campus ski and snowboard slope and complex of cross-country trails, thereby providing for a strong emphasis on winter sports. Nearby Lovejoy Pond is available for environmental research, as well as for canoeing, fishing and swimming. The school also plans hiking, rock climbing and biking trips in the area. Kents Hill's proximity to Portland and to Colby, Bates and Bowdoin colleges enables students to attend lectures, concerts, dances, athletic contests and other events.   **See Also Pages 1180-1**

PITTSFIELD, ME. (87 mi. NNE of Portland, ME; 187 mi. NNE of Boston, MA) Rural. Pop: 4214. Alt: 223 ft.

MAINE CENTRAL INSTITUTE
Bdg and Day — Coed Gr 9-PG

Pittsfield, ME 04967. 125 S Main St. Tel: 207-487-3355. Fax: 207-487-3512.
www.mci-school.org   E-mail: cwilliams@mci-school.org

Joanne Szadkowski, Head. BA, Lake Erie College, MA, Kent State Univ. **Clint Williams, Adm.**

Col Prep. Gen Acad. AP—Eng Calc Physics Studio_Art. **Feat**—Humanities Fr Span Anat & Physiol Astron Botany Environ_Sci Oceanog Computers Asian_Stud Architect_Drawing Video_Production Music_Hist Ballet Debate. **Supp**—ESL LD Tut.

Adm: Appl due: Rolling. Accepted: 68%. Yield: 55%. **Tests** CEEB SSAT TOEFL.

Enr 503. B 67/213. G 28/195. Sec 490. PG 13. Wh 84%. Hisp 1%. Blk 5%. Asian 10%. Avg class size: 15. **Fac 57.** M 28. F 29. Wh 98%. Blk 2%. Adv deg: 28%. In dorms 9.

Grad '04—106. Col—65. (U of ME-Orono 13, Hofstra 3, Boston U 2, MI St 2, U of S ME 2, U of ME-Augusta 2). Avg SAT: 950. Alum 6500.

Tui '04-'05: Bdg $29,000 (+$1500). **Day $9000. Aid:** Merit 3 ($32,000). Need 64 ($869,166).

Summer: Acad Rec. ESL. Tui Bdg $3500. 4 wks.

Endow $2,971,000. Plant val $9,996,000. Bldgs 11. Dorms 3. Dorm rms 53. Class rms 43. Libs 1. Sci labs 3. Comp labs 4. Art studios 1. Music studios 1. Dance studios 1. Gyms 2. Fields 6. Courts 8.

Est 1866. Nonprofit. Sem (Aug-June). **Assoc** NEASC.

Established by Rev. Oren Cheney, who had founded Bates College six years prior, MCI conducts a rigorous educational program for students of varying ability levels and interests. The school requires four years of math and science study, and its humanities curriculum integrates history, literature, art and music. Pupils may take Advanced Placement courses in humanities English, physics, art and calculus in grades 11 and 12, and honors classes are also part of the curriculum.

The senior project, a graduation requirement, encourages students to explore areas of interest in detail prior to delivering formal presentations. MCI's English as a Second Language program serves the university-bound international student, while the Personalized Learning Program offers content tutoring and yearlong instructional support for those with strong cognitive abilities and diagnosed learning differences.

The Bossov Ballet, headed by dancer Andrei Bossov, formerly of Russia's Kirov Ballet, is in residence at the school. Boys and girls may also take part in highly regarded vocal and instrumental jazz ensembles; approximately one-third of MCI's students participate in music, while many others are involved in drama and the visual arts. Among roughly two dozen varsity and junior varsity sports, the postgraduate basketball program and an increasingly popular fencing team are especially noteworthy. MCI's annual, three-day winter carnival is an enduring tradition.   **See Also Page 1199**

PORTLAND, ME. (101 mi. NNE of Boston, MA) Urban. Pop: 64,249. Alt: 26 ft.

WAYNFLETE SCHOOL
Day — Coed Gr PS-12

Portland, ME 04102. 360 Spring St. Tel: 207-774-5721. Fax: 207-772-4782.
  www.waynflete.org   E-mail: admissions@waynflete.org
Mark W. Segar, Head. AB, Harvard Univ, EdD, Univ of Massachusetts-Amherst. **Lynne Breen, Adm.**
  Col Prep. Feat—British_Lit Russ_Lit Fr Lat Span Stats Astron Bioethics Environ_Sci Vietnam_War Psych Philos Ceramics Acting Music_Theory. **Supp**—Dev_Read ESL Rem_Math Rem_Read Tut.
  Adm (Gr PS-11): 95/yr. Appl due: Feb. Accepted: 53%. Yield: 76%.
  Enr 544. B 254. G 290. Elem 300. Sec 244. Wh 82%. Hisp 4%. Blk 4%. Asian 5%. Other 5%. Avg class size: 12. **Fac 78.** M 22/7. F 34/15. Wh 97%. Blk 2%. Asian 1%. Adv deg: 51%.
  Grad '04—53. Col—52. (St Lawrence 3, Tufts 2, Bowdoin 2, Carleton 2, Oberlin 2, Boston U 2). Avg SAT: 1258. Alum 1650.
  Tui '04-'05: Day $11,190-17,510. Aid: Need 79 ($890,572).
  Summer: Enrich Rec. Tui Day $345-395/2-wk ses. 6 wks.
  Endow $6,900,000. Plant val $13,766,000. Bldgs 10. Class rms 42. Lib 17,615 vols. Sci labs 6. Comp labs 2. Auds 1. Art studios 3. Music studios 2. Dance studios 1. Gyms 1. Fields 6. Courts 3.
  Est 1897. Nonprofit. Sem (Sept-June). **Assoc** CLS NEASC.

Founders Agnes Lowell and Caroline Crisfield, who came to Portland from the Ogontz School in Philadelphia, PA, and served Waynflete until 1924, named the school after 15th-century statesman and educator William Waynflete. Rapid early growth prompted Lowell and Crisfield to relocate the campus to the former Horace Dudley estate, situated in the city's residential West End. In addition to its urban campus, Waynflete maintains a 35-acre site along the Fore River. Students enroll from more than 45 Greater Portland communities.

The lower school comprises four multi-age groups: early childhood (ages 3 and 4), kindergarten and grade 1, grades 2 and 3, and grades 4 and 5. As the program progresses, children assume additional responsibility and gain more independence. During the middle school years (grades 6-8), students build upon the skills they began developing in the lower school. Special programs provide enrichment, and competitive athletics and cocurricular activities supplement academics.

In the upper school, the rigorous college preparatory curriculum combines instruction in the traditional subject areas with electives, survey courses, interdisciplinary courses and seminar. Visual and performing arts offerings are noteworthy, and an applied arts program incorporates the artistic resources of Greater Portland.

Community service is an integral part of the program beginning in the middle school, and upper school students perform approximately 24 hours of volunteer work in the community. Upper schoolers participate in a fall outdoor experience through wilderness areas in northern New England, and juniors may pursue off-campus study opportunities through the Chewonki Foundation's Maine Coast Semester or the CITYterm program.

YARMOUTH, ME. (9 mi. N of Portland, ME; 109 mi. NNE of Boston, MA) Suburban. Pop: 8360. Alt: 87 ft.

NORTH YARMOUTH ACADEMY
Day — Coed Gr 6-12

Yarmouth, ME 04096. 148 Main St. Tel: 207-846-9051. Fax: 207-846-8829.
  www.nya.org   E-mail: admission@nya.org
Peter W. Mertz, Head. BA, Williams College, MBA, Barry Univ. **Joseph P. Silvestri, Adm.**
  Col Prep. **AP**—Eng Lat Calc Bio Eur_Hist US_Hist Art_Hist Studio_Art Music_Theory.
    Feat—Fr Span Marine_Biol/Sci Oceanog Computers Comp_Design Comp_Graphics Photog Drama Music Jazz_Band Dance Yoga. **Supp**—Tut.
  Adm: 70/yr. Appl due: Feb. Accepted: 69%. Yield: 76%. **Tests** SSAT.
  Enr 302. B 158. G 144. Elem 132. Sec 170. Wh 92%. Hisp 3%. Blk 2%. Am Ind 1%. Asian 2%. Avg class size: 14. **Fac 43.** M 19/1. F 19/4. Wh 100%. Adv deg: 41%.
  Grad '04—42. Col—41. (Bowdoin 3, Col of Wooster 3, Goucher 3, U of ME-Orono 3, Colby 2, Mt Holyoke 2). Avg SAT: 1222. Alum 1200.
  Tui '04-'05: Day $17,280 (+$500). **Aid:** Need 81 ($855,146).
  Summer: Acad Enrich Rec. Sports. 8 wks.
  Endow $3,000,000. Plant val $7,793,000. Bldgs 11. Class rms 20. Lib 9000 vols. Sci labs 3. Dark rms 1. Auds 1. Theaters 1. Art studios 2. Music studios 2. Dance studios 1. Perf arts ctrs 1. Pottery studios 1. Gyms 1. Fields 3. Tennis courts 3. Rinks 1. Greenhouses 1.
  Est 1814. Nonprofit. Tri (Sept-June). **Assoc** CLS NEASC.

Located on a 25-acre campus in the center of the village of Yarmouth, the academy serves approximately 35 communities. NYA offers students a structured academic program with strong faculty and parental support for academic, social and athletic development. An advisor system, small classes, opportunities for extra help and tutoring, and Advanced Placement course work in several major disciplines are integral to the academy's liberal arts curriculum. Pupils also choose from a variety of fine arts courses.

All students participate in either the afternoon arts program or an athletics program comprising soccer, track, field hockey, cross-country, boys' and girls' ice hockey, basketball, softball, lacrosse, volleyball, golf and tennis. In addition, boys and girls may engage in wilderness trips, publications, school government and various activities. Social service is also emphasized at NYA, with each student completing a two-week service project prior to graduation.

MASSACHUSETTS

ANDOVER, MA. (23 mi. NNW of Boston, MA) Suburban. Pop: 29,063. Alt: 85 ft. Area also includes North Andover.

BROOKS SCHOOL
Bdg and Day — Coed Gr 9-12

North Andover, MA 01845. 1160 Great Pond Rd. Tel: 978-725-6272. Fax: 978-725-6298. www.brooksschool.org E-mail: admissions@brooksschool.org
Lawrence W. Becker, Head. BA, Amherst College, MAT, Harvard Univ. **Judith S. Beams, Adm.**

Col Prep. AP—Eng Fr Lat Span Calc Comp_Sci Bio Chem Physics Eur_Hist US_Govt & Pol Art_Hist. **Feat**—Greek Ital Robotics Philos Theol Studio_Art Drama Music. **Supp**—Rev Tut.

Adm (Gr 9-11): 114/yr. Bdg 84. Day 30. Appl due: Feb. Accepted: 36%. **Tests** CEEB SSAT TOEFL.

Enr 354. B 140/50. G 101/63. Sec 354. Wh 83%. Hisp 7%. Blk 5%. Asian 5%. Avg class size: 12. **Fac 73.** M 38. F 29/6. Wh 93%. Hisp 1%. Blk 5%. Asian 1%. Adv deg: 78%. In dorms 39.

Grad '04—93. Col—91. (CT Col 6, U of PA 4, Tufts 4, Colby 4, Brown 3, Geo Wash 3). Avg SAT: 1210. Alum 3289.

Tui '05-'06: Bdg $34,440 (+$2280). **Day $25,400** (+$1880). **Aid:** Need ($1,600,000).

Summer: Acad Enrich Rec. Computers. Soccer. 8 wks.

Endow $63,100,000. Bldgs 48. Dorms 10. Class rms 25. Lib 26,000 vols. Labs 4. Auds 1. Art studios 3. Music studios 5. Fields 13. Courts 9. Rinks 1. Student ctrs 1.

Est 1926. Nonprofit. Episcopal. Sem (Sept-June). **Assoc** CLS NEASC.

Brooks was founded by Rev. Endicott Peabody, founder and onetime headmaster of Groton School. Named in honor of Phillips Brooks, former bishop of Massachusetts and native of North Andover, the school was given its land and original buildings by the Russell family. Girls were first admitted in 1979.

Students follow a flexible liberal arts curriculum and readily enter leading colleges. The school offers Advanced Placement courses in the major disciplines. Each student may choose his or her own faculty advisor; faculty and students share in many aspects of school governance and committee work.

A full complement of extracurricular activities, including athletics, the arts, publications, dramatics, music and civic projects, occupies the student's time out of class. Exchange programs with schools in Kenya, Scotland, South Africa and Hungary are available. Football, soccer, field hockey, basketball, ice hockey, squash, wrestling, lacrosse, baseball, softball, crew, cross-country, sailing, track and tennis are the available sports.

PHILLIPS ACADEMY
Bdg and Day — Coed Gr 9-PG

Andover, MA 01810. 180 Main St. Tel: 978-749-4000. Fax: 978-749-4068.

www.andover.edu   E-mail: admissions@andover.edu

Barbara Landis Chase, Head. AB, Brown Univ, MLA, Johns Hopkins Univ. **Jane F. Fried, Adm.**

Col Prep. AP—Fr Ger Lat Span Calc Stats Comp_Sci Bio Chem Physics Art_Hist Studio_Art. **Feat**—Chin Greek Japan Russ Anat & Physiol Astron Ecol Geol Computers Theater Music Dance Study_Skills. **Supp**—Tut.

Adm: 332/yr. Appl due: Feb. Accepted: 21%. Yield: 73%. **Tests** CEEB ISEE SSAT.

Enr 1083. B 381/154. G 403/145. Wh 66%. Hisp 5%. Blk 7%. Asian 16%. Other 6%. Avg class size: 13. **Fac 217.** M 96/17. F 60/44. Wh 82%. Hisp 4%. Blk 9%. Asian 5%. Adv deg: 71%. In dorms 90.

Grad '04—298. Col—280. (Harvard 17, Brown 15, Columbia 10, Yale 10, Cornell 9, Johns Hopkins 9). Avg SAT: 1363. Alum 18,293.

Tui '04-'05: Bdg $31,160 (+$2000). **Day $24,220** (+$2000). **Aid:** Need 422 ($10,225,000).

Summer: Acad Enrich. Tui Bdg $5200. Tui Day $3650. 5 wks.

Endow $569,000,000. Plant val $556,753,000. Bldgs 151. Dorms 43. Dorm rms 589. Class rms 95. 2 Libs 120,000 vols. Chapels 1. Sci labs 10. Lang labs 1. Comp labs 3. Sci ctrs 1. Auds 2. Theaters 2. Art studios 5. Music studios 15. Dance studios 2. Music ctrs 1. Gyms 3. Fields 18. Basketball courts 2. Tennis courts 18. Squash courts 8. Pools 2. Rinks 2. Observatories 1. Radio stations 1. Video ctrs 1.

Est 1778. Nonprofit. Tri (Sept-May). **Assoc** CLS NEASC.

Often referred to as Andover, PA was founded by Samuel Phillips, Jr., during the American Revolution. Paul Revere designed the school's seal, and John Hancock signed its Act of Incorporation. Andover seeks students from diverse ethnic, racial, socioeconomic and geographic backgrounds, drawing students from nearly every state and roughly 30 foreign countries and providing financial aid for both needy and middle-class families.

With some 300 course offerings in 18 academic departments, the curriculum comprises a required core of studies fundamental to a liberal education and includes elective courses designed to address individual interests. Advanced Placement and accelerated courses are available in virtually every department. Among several complementary programs are an exchange with a school in China, as well as School Year Abroad, which offers juniors and seniors a full academic year of study in China, France, Spain or Italy.

The athletic department features sport, dance and exercise options at every level of instruction. Recreational athletes have various intramural and instructional options, while interscholastic athletes prepare for competition with other prep schools and with Boston-area colleges. Outdoor adventure opportunities, including rock climbing, winter camping, and white-water canoeing and kayaking, are also available.

Pupils choose from many interest clubs and organizations, and more than half of the student body fulfill the mandate of the school's motto, *Non Sibi* ("Not for Self"), by volunteering in an extensive community service program. In addition, each student takes part in a school-wide work-duty program by engaging in such tasks as dorm cleaning, school office assistance and dining hall duties.

PIKE SCHOOL

Day — Coed Gr PS-9

Andover, MA 01810. Sunset Rock Rd. Tel: 978-475-1197. Fax: 978-475-3014.

www.pikeschool.org   E-mail: info@pikeschool.org
John M. Waters, Head. BA, Middlebury College, MA, Trinity College (CT). **Elizabeth Watson, Adm.**
- Pre-Prep. **Feat**—Fr Lat Span Studio_Art Drama Music. **Supp**—Dev_Read Tut.
- **Adm:** 72/yr. Appl due: Jan. **Tests** ISEE SSAT.
- **Enr 428.** B 214. G 214. Elem 421. Sec 7. Wh 76%. Hisp 7%. Blk 3%. Asian 14%. **Fac 56.** M 10. F 46. Wh 97%. Hisp 1%. Blk 1%. Asian 1%. Adv deg: 69%.
- Grad '04—56. Prep—52. (Phillips Acad, Brooks, Gov Dummer, Pingree, St John's HS-MA, Lawrence Acad). Alum 2700.
- **Tui '04-'05: Day $10,500-18,400** (+$300-1750). **Aid:** Need ($364,000).
- **Summer:** Enrich Rec. 1-6 wks.
- Endow $4,772,000. Plant val $9,992,000. Bldgs 5. Class rms 47. Lib 16,000 vols. Sci labs 6. Art studios 2. Music studios 2. Gyms 1. Fields 4. Courts 1. Media/tech ctrs 1.
- **Est 1926.** Nonprofit. Tri (Sept-June).

Founded by Mrs. Walter E. Pike, this school serves Andover and the communities of the Merrimack Valley. The school's five major buildings and athletic fields are located on a 36-acre tract of former farmland. The lower school (grades PS-2), the middle school (grades 3-5) and the upper school (grades 6-9) offer a coordinated academic program that emphasizes fundamental skills in the basic disciplines.

Outdoor education, which stresses environmental issues, begins in grade 5, while foreign language instruction commences in grade 6. Physical education and visual and performing arts offerings are integral to the program at all grade levels. Pike graduates are prepared to attend a variety of secondary schools, including leading independent schools.

ASHBURNHAM, MA. (50 mi. WNW of Boston, MA) Suburban. Pop: 5546. Alt: 1100 ft.

CUSHING ACADEMY
Bdg and Day — Coed Gr 9-PG

Ashburnham, MA 01430. 39 School St, PO Box 8000. Tel: 978-827-7300.
Fax: 978-827-6253.
www.cushing.org   E-mail: admission@cushing.org
M. Willard Lampe II, Head. BA, Muskingum College, MA, Univ of Vermont. **Melanie J. Glines, Adm.**
- Col Prep. **AP**—Eng Lat Span Calc Stats Bio Chem Physics US_Hist US_Govt & Pol Music_Theory. **Feat**—Fr Ecol Computers Econ Fine_Arts Stained_Glass Drama Dance Silversmithing. **Supp**—Dev_Read ESL Rem_Math Rem_Read Rev.
- **Adm (Gr 9):** 173/yr. Bdg 154. Day 19. Appl due: Feb. Accepted: 65%. Yield: 44%. **Tests** SSAT TOEFL.
- **Enr 425.** B 230/30. G 137/28. Sec 405. PG 20. Wh 60%. Hisp 2%. Blk 5%. Am Ind 1%. Asian 18%. Other 14%. Avg class size: 12. **Fac 66.** M 39. F 26/1. Wh 97%. Hisp 1%. Blk 1%. Asian 1%. Adv deg: 54%. In dorms 32.
- Grad '04—128. Col—125. (Suffolk 9, Boston U 5, Bentley 4, Northeastern U 4, U of CO-Boulder 4, Brown 2). Alum 5700.
- **Tui '04-'05: Bdg $34,415** (+$500). **Day $24,040** (+$500). **Aid:** Merit 12 ($60,000). Need 78 ($1,600,000).
- **Summer:** Acad Enrich. Tui Bdg $5450. Tui Day $2600. ESL. Tui Bdg $3800-4000. 6 wks.

Endow $12,300,000. Plant val $33,000,000. Bldgs 19. Dorms 11. Dorm rms 167. Class rms 23. Lib 25,000 vols. Sci labs 3. Lang labs 1. Comp labs 3. Auds 1. Art studios 5. Music studios 2. Gyms 1. Fields 8. Courts 6. Rinks 1.
Est 1865. Nonprofit. Tri (Sept-June). **Assoc** CLS NEASC.

Founded by a benefaction from Thomas Parkman Cushing, a native of Ashburnham, and enriched by several bequests, this academy owes its early growth chiefly to Dr. Hervey S. Cowell, beloved by his students and in office for nearly 40 years. Over the years, the school has seen an improvement of facilities and physical plant, with steady increases in enrollment and faculty, as well as heightened academic standards.

Cushing's college preparatory program features Advanced Placement courses, well-developed fine arts and computer curricula, opportunities for independent study, language development courses, ESL classes and trimester-length seminars. Extracurricular activities include publications, various interest clubs, and interscholastic and recreational sports.

Many faculty members reside on campus, and each pupil has a faculty advisor. The school draws its enrollment from many states and foreign countries.

BARNSTABLE, MA. (57 mi. SE of Boston, MA; 58 mi. E of Providence, RI) Suburban. Pop: 47,821. Alt: 37 ft.

TRINITY CHRISTIAN ACADEMY
Day — Coed Gr PS-10

Barnstable, MA 02630. 979 Mary Dunn Rd. Tel: 508-790-0114. Fax: 508-790-1293.
www.trinitycapecod.org E-mail: info@trinitycapecod.org
Frederick Caldwell, Head.
  Gen Acad. Feat—Fr Bible Art_Hist Music.
  Adm: 27/yr. Appl due: Rolling. Accepted: 90%.
  Enr 94. Elem 90. Sec 4. Wh 94%. Hisp 1%. Blk 5%. Avg class size: 8. Uniform. **Fac 18.** M /1. F 9/8. Wh 100%. Adv deg: 22%.
  Grad '04—11. Alum 95.
  Tui '03-'04: Day $4750-5850 (+$200).
  Summer: Rec. 6 wks.
  Bldgs 1. Class rms 10. Lib 2000 vols. Sci labs 1. Comp labs 1.
  Est 1967. Nonprofit. Nondenom Christian. Quar (Sept-June).

Characterized by a favorable student-faculty ratio, this Cape Cod school stresses reading instruction (with emphasis placed on the developmental approach) while offering strong programs in math and science. Staff also direct attention to the spiritual life of each child within a traditional Christian framework. Pupils attend Bible classes each day and a chapel service each week.

Trinity schedules experiential trips to local museums and theaters, as well as annual excursions to the Cape Cod National Seashore NEEDS Program and to Washington, DC.

BELMONT, MA. (9 mi. WNW of Boston, MA) Suburban. Pop: 24,194. Alt: 39 ft.

BELMONT DAY SCHOOL
Day — Coed Gr PS-8

Belmont, MA 02478. 55 Day School Ln. Tel: 617-484-3078. Fax: 617-489-1942.
www.belmontday.org E-mail: info@belmontday.org

Lenesa L. Leana, Head. AB, Oberlin College, MA, Univ of Missouri-Columbia. **Deborah Brissenden, Adm.**

Pre-Prep. Gen Acad. Feat—Fr Span Computers Studio_Art Drama Music Woodworking. **Supp**—Dev_Read.

Adm: 46/yr. Appl due: Jan. Accepted: 21%. Yield: 72%. **Tests** ISEE SSAT.

Enr 265. B 129. G 136. Elem 265. Wh 76%. Hisp 2%. Blk 4%. Asian 6%. Other 12%. Avg class size: 14. **Fac 43.** M 7/3. F 31/2. Wh 91%. Hisp 2%. Blk 5%. Asian 2%. Adv deg: 65%.

Grad '04—30. **Prep**—24. (Middlesex 3, Milton Acad 3, Rivers 3, Boston U Acad 2). Alum 800.

Tui '04-'05: Day $13,160-21,290. Aid: Need 53 ($703,464).

Summer: Enrich Rec. Tui Day $885/2-wk ses. 10 wks.

Endow $2,167,000. Plant val $16,000,000. Bldgs 1. Class rms 23. Lib 10,000 vols. Sci labs 1. Lang labs 1. Comp labs 2. Auds 1. Theaters 1. Art studios 2. Music studios 1. Gyms 1. Fields 2. Courts 1. Pools 1.

Est 1927. Nonprofit. Sem (Sept-June).

Founded by parents, this elementary and middle school prepares students for independent secondary schools in and around Boston. Children are taught in small learning groups that allow for individual attention in a supportive family atmosphere. The developmentally structured program combines academics with social competency skills instruction.

Belmont Day's core curriculum of language arts, math, social studies and science is enhanced by course work in studio art, music, orchestra, drama, technology, French, Spanish and physical education. Extended-day, after-school enrichment, and vacation and summer programs complement the regular academic sessions.

See Also Page 1116

BELMONT HILL SCHOOL
5-Day Bdg — Boys Gr 9-12; Day — Boys 7-12

Belmont, MA 02478. 350 Prospect St. Tel: 617-484-4410. Fax: 617-484-4688.
www.belmont-hill.org E-mail: admissions@belmont-hill.org

Richard I. Melvoin, Head. AB, Harvard Univ, MA, PhD, Univ of Michigan. **Michael R. Grant, Adm.**

Col Prep. AP—Fr Lat Span Calc Stats Bio Physics US_Hist Studio_Art. **Feat**—British_Lit Creative_Writing Shakespeare Greek Mandarin Astron Environ_Sci Geol Comp_Sci Econ Psych Art_Hist Photog Sculpt Music. **Supp**—Tut.

Adm (Bdg Gr 9-11; Day 7-11): 92/yr. Bdg 4. Day 88. Appl due: Feb. Accepted: 40%. **Tests** ISEE SSAT.

Enr 425. B 25/400. Elem 119. Sec 306. Wh 85%. Hisp 2%. Blk 8%. Asian 5%. Avg class size: 12. **Fac 56.** M 44. F 12. In dorms 4.

Grad '04—80. Col—80. (Harvard, Boston Col, Georgetown, Middlebury, Dartmouth, Tufts). Avg SAT: 1280. Avg SSAT: 70%. Alum 3400.
Tui '04-'05: 5-Day Bdg $30,070 (+$720). Day $25,020 (+$720). Aid: Need 94 ($1,600,000).
Summer: Acad Enrich Rem. Tui Day $700. 6 wks.
Endow $52,000,000. Bldgs 16. Dorms 2. Dorm rms 22. Class rms 32. Lib 18,000 vols. Chapels 1. Labs 4. Art studios 2. Music studios 1. Gyms 2. Fields 6. Courts 11. Rinks 1.
Est 1923. Nonprofit. Sem (Sept-May). Assoc CLS NEASC.

Belmont Hill provides a strong college preparatory program that combines a traditional curriculum with many elective opportunities. Expansion of opportunities in both curricular and extracurricular activities has been made possible by loyal alumni and parental support. The sectioning of classes allows for Advanced Placement in languages, mathematics, science, computer science and history. Qualified students may engage in independent study.

Exchange study programs to France, Spain and China are conducted during junior year. Extracurricular activities—often coordinated with the Winsor School for girls in Boston—emphasize dramatics, music, publications, student council and hobbies. The school fields intramural or interscholastic teams or both in football, soccer, basketball, hockey, wrestling, skiing, squash, baseball, rowing, golf, sailing, lacrosse, cross-country, track and tennis.

BEVERLY, MA. (18 mi. NNE of Boston, MA) Urban. Pop: 39,862. Alt: 26 ft. Area also includes Prides Crossing.

LANDMARK SCHOOL
Bdg — Coed Gr 8-12; Day — Coed 2-12

Prides Crossing, MA 01965. 429 Hale St, PO Box 227. Tel: 978-236-3000.
Fax: 978-927-7268.
www.landmarkschool.org   E-mail: jbloom@landmarkschool.org
Robert J. Broudo, Head. BA, Bates College, MEd, Boston Univ. Carolyn Orsini-Nelson, Adm.
Col Prep. LD. Feat—Anat & Physiol Environ_Sci Marine_Biol/Sci Anthro Psych Sociol Studio_Art Acting Drama Chorus Dance Woodworking Study_Skills. Supp—Dev_ Read Rem_Math Rem_Read Rev Tut.
Adm: 100/yr. Bdg 40. Day 60. Appl due: Rolling. Accepted: 45%. Yield: 80%. Tests IQ.
Enr 424. B 110/175. G 55/84. Elem 137. Sec 287. Wh 90%. Hisp 4%. Blk 1%. Asian 1%. Other 4%. Avg class size: 7. Fac 213. M 83/4. F 113/13. Adv deg: 51%. In dorms 35.
Grad '04—76. Col—70. (Suffolk 6, Curry 5, Lynn 5, U of New England 3, Johnson & Wales 3, Lesley 2). Alum 1800.
Tui '04-'05: Bdg $38,000-45,000 (+$1600). Day $27,600-34,600 (+$100).
Summer: Rev Rem Rec. Tui Bdg $7200-7600. Tui Day $3600-5500. 6 wks.
Endow $10,000,000. Plant val $23,000,000. Bldgs 26. Dorms 7. Dorm rms 89. Class rms 81. Libs 2. Sci labs 3. Comp labs 5. Art studios 2. Music studios 1. Dance studios 1. Gyms 2. Fields 4.
Est 1971. Nonprofit. Quar (Sept-June). Assoc NEASC.

A division of the Landmark Foundation, this school is designed to help those intellectually capable and emotionally healthy students who are not able to achieve in school because of language-based learning disabilities. Landmark is not capable of addressing the needs of boys and girls with more pervasive learning disabilities such as nonverbal learning disabilities, Asperger's syndrome, pervasive developmental disorder, bipolar disorder and developmental delay.

An intensive program of diagnostic prescriptive teaching based on one-on-one tutorials is provided. The school offers remedial, expressive language and college preparatory programs on two campuses along Boston's North Shore.

See Also Pages 1366-7

SHORE COUNTRY DAY SCHOOL

Day — Coed Gr K-9

Beverly, MA 01915. 545 Cabot St. Tel: 978-927-1700. Fax: 978-927-1822.
www.shoreschool.org   E-mail: lcarey@shoreschool.org

Lawrence A. Griffin, Head. BA, Florida Atlantic Univ, MALS, Dartmouth College. **Lilia N. Carey, Adm.**

Pre-Prep. Feat—Fr Lat Span Studio_Art Theater Music. **Supp**—Dev_Read.

Adm: 64/yr. Appl due: Jan. Accepted: 30%.

Enr 439. B 218. G 221. Elem 413. Sec 26. Wh 90%. Hisp 3%. Blk 3%. Asian 4%. Avg class size: 14. **Fac 51.** Wh 98%. Blk 2%. Adv deg: 58%.

Grad '04—45. Prep—40. (Pingree, Gov Dummer, Phillips Acad, St George's Sch-RI, Holderness, Phillips Exeter). Avg SSAT: 70%. Alum 1746.

Tui '04-'05: Day $15,190-21,690. Aid: Need 30 ($306,000).

Summer: Acad Enrich Rec. Tui Day $330/2-wk ses. 6 wks.

Endow $6,500,000. Plant val $16,000,000. Bldgs 4. Class rms 47. Lib 18,000 vols. Sci labs 5. Comp labs 2. Theaters 1. Art studios 2. Music studios 2. Gyms 2. Fields 6.

Est 1936. Nonprofit. (Sept-June).

With its roots in the Shore School and the North Shore Country Day School, the present school was incorporated in 1936. Courses in computer, science, art, music, health and physical education enhance the traditional curriculum at all grade levels. Drama instruction is introduced in grade 5, with modern languages in grade 7 and Latin in grade 8. The school's program was expanded in 1982 to include a readiness year for children of school age who are not developmentally prepared for kindergarten. The academic program culminates in a grade 9 curriculum that includes language, history, science and major course arts electives, leadership and service opportunities, independent studies, camping and interdisciplinary trips.

Extracurricular activities include chorus, a cappella chorus, theater, publications, math team, service opportunities, and interscholastic and intramural offerings in field hockey, basketball, ice hockey, soccer, lacrosse and baseball. Graduates enter leading preparatory boarding and day school programs at both ninth- and tenth-grade levels.

BOSTON, MA. Urban. Pop: 589,141. Alt: to 169 ft. Area also includes West Roxbury.

BOSTON UNIVERSITY ACADEMY
Day — Coed Gr 8-12

Boston, MA 02215. 1 University Rd. Tel: 617-353-9000. Fax: 617-353-8999.
  www.buacademy.org   E-mail: admissions@buacademy.org
James Tracy, Head. BA, Univ of Massachusetts-Boston, PhD, Stanford Univ, MBA, Boston Univ. **Sarah Morse, Adm.**
  Col Prep. Feat—Chin Fr Ger Greek Hebrew Ital Japan Lat Russ Span Portuguese Korean Hindi Arabic African_Lang Comp_Sci Drawing Graphic_Arts Painting Sculpt Drama Chorus Music.
  Adm (Gr 8-11): 42/yr. Appl due: Jan. Accepted: 45%. Yield: 59%. **Tests** SSAT.
  Enr 156. B 88. G 68. Elem 15. Sec 141. Wh 84%. Hisp 1%. Blk 2%. Am Ind 1%. Asian 5%. Other 7%. Avg class size: 14. **Fac 21.** M 8/4. F 8/1. Adv deg: 85%.
  Grad '04—33. Col—33. (U of Chicago 4, Wesleyan U 2, Boston Col 2, Hamilton 2, Brown 1, Columbia 1). Avg SAT: 1420. Alum 186.
  Tui '04-'05: Day $21,150 (+$500). **Aid:** Merit 32 ($132,586). Need 34 ($410,798).
  Bldgs 1. Class rms 19. Lib 3,000,000 vols. Sci labs 5. Lang labs 1. Comp labs 2. Auds 3. Theaters 1. Art studios 3. Music studios 1. Dance studios 1. Gyms 3. Fields 3. Courts 3. Pools 1. Rinks 1.
  Est 1993. Nonprofit. Sem (Sept-June). **Assoc** NEASC.

Utilizing the resources of Boston University, the academy provides students with an integrated program that seeks to explore the ethical and historical dimensions of knowledge, in addition to requiring basic skill mastery and the learning of facts.

The curriculum's accelerated pace enables pupils to begin taking college-credit courses during junior year: two classes in grade 11, four each semester in grade 12. All 12th graders enroll in a yearlong, two-unit senior thesis research project. After working on the thesis throughout the year, each senior submits a final draft of the paper following March break; boys and girls who elect to defend their theses before faculty members are eligible for a grade of high honors. Students graduate with as many as 48 college credits, allowing successful applicants to Boston University to enter as sophomores; entrants into other colleges typically receive applicable credit.

BUA fields interscholastic teams in soccer, basketball, sailing, tennis, fencing, golf and crew, and students may take part in such intramural and recreational options as European handball, figure skating, martial arts, dance and softball. Among other extracurricular activities are interest clubs, literary magazine, student council, model UN, newspaper and yearbook. All pupils in grades 8-10 fulfill a 20-hour community service requirement.

COMMONWEALTH SCHOOL
Day — Coed Gr 9-12

Boston, MA 02116. 151 Commonwealth Ave. Tel: 617-266-7525. Fax: 617-266-5769.
  www.commschool.org   E-mail: admissions@commschool.org
William D. Wharton, Head. AB, MA, Brown Univ. **Helene T. Carter, Adm.**

Col Prep. AP—Eng Fr Lat Span Calc Bio Chem Physics Eur_Hist US_Hist Music_Theory. **Feat**—Creative_Writing Urban_Fiction Greek Programming Japan_Hist African-Amer_Hist Lang & Ethics Bible Philos Ceramics Film Photog Studio_Art Acting Drama. **Supp**—Tut.
Adm (Gr 9-11): 44/yr. Appl due: Feb. Accepted: 42%. **Tests** ISEE SSAT.
Enr 145. B 70. G 75. Sec 145. Wh 78%. Hisp 3%. Blk 8%. Asian 10%. Other 1%. Avg class size: 10. **Fac 33.** M 12/4. F 11/6. Wh 82%. Blk 9%. Asian 3%. Other 6%. Adv deg: 63%.
Grad '04—31. Col—31. (Bryn Mawr 3, Wesleyan U 3, Cornell 2, Stanford 2, Smith 2, Yale 2). Avg SAT: 1420. Alum 1100.
Tui '04-'05: Day $23,460 (+$1495). **Aid:** Need 40 ($665,800).
Endow $9,200,000. Plant val $2,000,000. Bldgs 1. Class rms 12. Lib 6000 vols. Sci labs 2. Comp labs 1. Art studios 2.
Est 1957. Nonprofit. Sem (Sept-May). **Assoc** NEASC.

Charles Merrill founded Commonwealth with an eye toward taking advantage of its location in the heart of the city. A distinguished faculty and students of ability contribute to the school's spirited intellectual climate. The broadly based curriculum stresses critical writing, historical inquiry, social and cultural heritage, science, the studio and performing arts, mathematics and language study.

Soccer, basketball, sailing, baseball, fencing, squash and dance are offered in the varied athletic program. In addition, students participate in community service activities, dramatic productions, concerts and art shows. Commonwealth also conducts exchanges with schools in France and Spain.

KINGSLEY MONTESSORI SCHOOL
Day — Coed Gr PS-6

Boston, MA 02116. 30 Fairfield St. Tel: 617-536-5984. Fax: 617-536-7507.
  www.kingsley.org   E-mail: info@kingsley.org
Renee DuChainey-Farkes, Head. BS, MEd. **Jeni Schmitt,** Adm.
Pre-Prep. Feat—Span Computers. **Supp**—Dev_Read Rem_Read Tut.
Adm: 36/yr. Appl due: Jan. Accepted: 40%.
Enr 141. Elem 141. Wh 74%. Hisp 5%. Blk 8%. Asian 13%. Avg class size: 18. **Fac 31.** M 5/1. F 23/2. Wh 97%. Asian 3%.
Grad '04—6. Prep—3. Alum 750.
Tui '04-'05: Day $12,300-13,050 (+$150-250). **Aid:** Need 15 ($30,000).
Summer: Enrich Rec. 9 wks.
Plant val $1,500,000. Bldgs 1. Class rms 8. Lib 2000 vols. Sci labs 1. Art studios 1. Music studios 1. Dance studios 1. Fields 1. Courts 1. Courtyards 1.
Est 1938. Nonprofit. Tri (Sept-June).

Located in Boston's Back Bay in the historic Saltonstall homestead, this school began as a Montessori preschool and later added an elementary curriculum that extends through grade 6. The school offers a Montessori program in multi-age groupings of three- to six-year-olds, six- to nine-year-olds and nine- to 12-year-olds.

Kingsley Montessori utilizes Boston's resources to enhance the academic program. After-school and summer programs serve children ages 3-12.

THE LEARNING PROJECT ELEMENTARY SCHOOL
Day — Coed Gr 1-6

Boston, MA 02116. 107 Marlborough St. Tel: 617-266-8427. Fax: 617-266-3543.
www.learningproject.org   E-mail: admissions@learningproject.org
Michael McCord, Head. BA, Wesleyan Univ. **Pauline Hargreaves, Adm.**

Pre-Prep. Gen Acad. **Feat**—Span Computers Studio_Art Music. **Supp**—Dev_Read Rem_Math Rem_Read Rev.

Adm: 21/yr. Appl due: Jan. Accepted: 26%.

Enr 96. B 49. G 47. Elem 96. Wh 78%. Hisp 5%. Blk 12%. Asian 5%. Avg class size: 16. **Fac 17.** M 1/1. F 15. Adv deg: 52%.

Grad '04—17. **Prep**—10. (Beaver Co Day, Roxbury Latin, Milton Acad). Alum 435.

Tui '04-'05: Day $13,850-14,350. **Aid:** Need 24 ($206,220).

Endow $1,200,000. Plant val $2,265,000. Bldgs 1. Class rms 8. Sci labs 1. Art studios 1.

Est 1973. Nonprofit. Tri (Sept-June).

Located in an original schoolhouse in the Back Bay, the school maintains a small size and an average class size of 16 to permit children of different ages to teach and learn from each other. Program emphasis is on the study of basic skills, and the school takes an integrated approach to its curriculum. Social studies, science, language arts, Spanish, computers, physical education, art, problem solving, music and math form the core of each child's weekly schedule.

Children in grades 3-6 undertake a major independent study project in the spring, and field trips include a week in Washington, DC, for sixth graders. Students also stage three major musical performances annually. Two extended-day programs, serving children in grades 1-3 and 4-6, are available for an additional fee.

ROXBURY LATIN SCHOOL
Day — Boys Gr 7-12

West Roxbury, MA 02132. 101 St Theresa Ave. Tel: 617-325-4920. Fax: 617-325-3585.
www.roxburylatin.org   E-mail: admission@roxburylatin.org
Kerry P. Brennan, Head. BA, Amherst College, MA, Columbia Univ. **Michael C. Obel-Omia, Adm.**

Col Prep. AP—Calc Stats Comp_Sci. **Feat**—Fr Greek Lat Econ Photog Studio_Art Drama Music Music_Theory.

Adm (Gr 7-9): 61/yr. Appl due: Jan. Accepted: 16%. Yield: 94%. **Tests** ISEE SSAT.

Enr 295. B 295. Elem 90. Sec 205. Wh 76%. Hisp 5%. Blk 13%. Asian 6%. Avg class size: 14. **Fac 34.** M 30. F 3/1. Adv deg: 64%.

Grad '04—57. **Col**—51. (Harvard, Bowdoin, Princeton, Williams, Boston Col, Brown). Alum 2433.

Tui '04-'05: Day $16,000 (+$500). **Aid:** Need 97 ($1,152,375). Work prgm 6 ($2600).

Endow $100,000,000. Plant val $19,000,000. Bldgs 5. Class rms 27. Lib 13,000 vols. Labs 4. Tech ctrs 2. Sci ctrs 1. Arts ctrs 1. Gyms 2. Fields 8. Courts 7.

Est 1645. Nonprofit. 5 terms (Aug-June). **Assoc** CLS NEASC.

This oldest endowed secondary school in the nation was established during the reign of King Charles I. Originally "the Free Schoole in Roxburie" for Roxbury boys, it was modeled after the English grammar schools. John Eliot, "Apostle to the Indians," when minister of the First Church of Roxbury, signed a statement with others of the town that they, "in consideration of their religious care of posterity, have taken into consideration how necessary the education of their children in literature will be, to fit them for public service, both in Church and Commonwealth, in succeeding ages. They, therefore, unanimously have consented and agreed to erect a free school in the said Town of Roxbury." In 1671, Thomas Bell, formerly of Roxbury, died in London, England, willing 150 acres of Roxbury lands to the school and naming Rev. John Eliot and two other officers of the First Church as trustees of the endowment.

William C. Collar, headmaster from 1867 to 1907, attained a national eminence in the educational world. Under his direction, the school pioneered the teaching of laboratory science and expanded its curriculum beyond the confines of the English grammar school tradition. In 1928, the school moved to its present campus of fields and wooded slopes in West Roxbury.

The academic program for younger boys emphasizes the development of basic skills in the arts, English, history, classical and modern languages, computer science, math and science. As they mature, students gain increasing flexibility in scheduling through elective options and independent study opportunities. In addition, many academic electives are offered, and there are full athletic and activity programs. All boys participate in on- and off-campus service projects.

WINSOR SCHOOL
Day — Girls Gr 5-12

Boston, MA 02215. Pilgrim Rd. Tel: 617-735-9500. Fax: 617-912-1381.
  www.winsor.edu   E-mail: admissions@winsor.edu
Rachel Friis Stettler, Dir. AB, Princeton Univ, MA, New School for Social Research. **Pamela Parks McLaurin, Adm.**

Col Prep. AP—Fr Lat Span Bio Chem Physics. **Feat**—Russ_Lit Greek Comp_Sci Philos Photog Studio_Art Drama Music. **Supp**—Dev_Read.

Adm (Gr 5-10): 62/yr. Appl due: Jan. Accepted: 20%. Yield: 70%. **Tests** ISEE SSAT.

Enr 420. G 420. Elem 188. Sec 232. Wh 78%. Hisp 1%. Blk 9%. Asian 12%. Avg class size: 14. **Fac 72.** M 14. F 53/5. Wh 83%. Hisp 2%. Blk 4%. Asian 5%. Other 6%. Adv deg: 75%.

Grad '04—50. Col—50. (Harvard, Yale, Dartmouth, Brown, Princeton, U of PA). Alum 4700.

Tui '04-'05: Day $25,200 (+$500). **Aid:** Need 91 ($1,600,000).

Endow $32,810,000. Plant val $14,000,000. Bldgs 2. Class rms 37. Lib 27,000 vols. Sci labs 8. Lang labs 1. Comp labs 3. Photog labs 1. Sci ctrs 1. Comp ctrs 1. Auds 1. Art studios 3. Music studios 5. Gyms 1. Fields 2. Tennis courts 6.

Est 1886. Nonprofit. Sem (Sept-June). **Assoc** NEASC.

The curriculum at Winsor reflects a sound balance between courses that stress fundamentals and those that allow students to pursue their own interests. Studies in math and science are extensive: Most students elect to study four years of science in the upper school. Advanced Placement courses are available in several disciplines. Offerings in the arts and a program of physical education complement academics.

Coordinate activities with Belmont Hill School and Roxbury Latin School include drama programs and the joint publication of a school newspaper. Winsor is also a member of the Mountain School Program of Milton Academy, which gives 11th graders an opportunity to participate for a semester in a coeducational residential experience in Vershire, VT. The school's urban location makes it accessible by public transportation.

BRAINTREE, MA. (9 mi. S of Boston, MA) Urban. Pop: 33,828. Alt: 94 ft.

THAYER ACADEMY
Day — Coed Gr 6-12

Braintree, MA 02184. 745 Washington St. Tel: 781-843-3580. Fax: 781-380-8785.
www.thayer.org   E-mail: admissions@thayer.org
W. Theodore Koskores, Head. BA, Boston Univ, MALS, Columbia Univ. **Jonathan R. White, Adm.**

- **Col Prep. AP**—Eng Fr Span Calc Comp_Sci Bio Chem Physics US_Hist. **Feat**—Fiction_Writing Lat Astron Meteorology African_Hist Lat-Amer_Hist Vietnam_War Econ Psych Sociol Photog Studio_Art Architect_Design Acting Drama Directing Music. **Supp**—Dev_Read Rev Tut.
- **Adm (Gr 6-11):** 136/yr. Appl due: Feb. Accepted: 41%. **Tests** ISEE SSAT.
- **Enr 663.** B 331. G 332. Elem 216. Sec 447. Wh 89%. Hisp 1%. Blk 6%. Asian 4%. Avg class size: 15. **Fac 94.** M 47/3. F 40/4. Wh 94%. Blk 3%. Am Ind 1%. Asian 2%. Adv deg: 54%.
- **Grad '04—100. Col—99.** (Boston U 8, Boston Col 5, Trinity Col-CT 5, CT Col 4, U of MA-Amherst 4, Lehigh 3). Alum 5300.
- **Tui '05-'06: Day $25,500. Aid:** Need 183 ($2,751,000).
- **Summer:** Acad Rec. 1-8 wks.
- Endow $36,000,000. Plant val $21,686,000. Bldgs 10. Class rms 50. Lib 21,000 vols. Comp labs 11. Observatories 1. Auds 2. Theaters 2. Art studios 2. Music studios 2. Dance studios 1. Gyms 3. Athletic ctrs 1. Fields 11. Courts 6. Pools 2.
- **Est 1877.** Nonprofit. Tri (Sept-June). **Assoc** CLS NEASC.

Thayer Academy was founded in 1877 by the will of Gen. Sylvanus Thayer, native of Braintree, "Father of West Point," and now honored in the Hall of Fame for Great Americans as the "Father of Technological Education in the United States."

The curricula of the middle and upper schools form one continuous program of college preparation. Middle school teachers emphasize the development of sound study and organizational skills, which provide a foundation for achievement at the upper school level. Public speaking is integral to the middle school program, with each student first memorizing a piece of published literature, then making a presentation in English class.

The upper school course of studies features honors and Advanced Placement options in every subject area. Boys and girls take one course each term from at least four of the five major disciplines (English, math, science, history and foreign language). Most pupils also take an arts elective; more than two dozen electives are available in studio art, music and theater. At all grade levels, Thayer offers classes at two levels: accelerated/advanced placement and college preparatory. Technology is an important learning tool, and the school maintains several hundred computers for student use.

Nearly every boy and girl participates in the school's community service program. Other extracurricular offerings include student government, athletics and interest clubs.

See Also Pages 1258-9

BROOKLINE, MA. (6 mi. W of Boston, MA) Suburban. Pop: 57,107. Alt: 43 ft. Area also includes Chestnut Hill.

BEAVER COUNTRY DAY SCHOOL
Day — Coed Gr 6-12

Chestnut Hill, MA 02467. 791 Hammond St. Tel: 617-738-2700. Fax: 617-738-2701.
www.bcdschool.org   E-mail: admission@bcdschool.org

Peter R. Hutton, Head. BA, St Lawrence Univ, MA, Wesleyan Univ. **Aline Gery, Adm.**

Col Prep. AP—Calc Bio Chem Physics. **Feat**—Lat-Amer_Poetry Playwriting Stats Bioethics Biotech Programming Studio_Art Drama Music Study_Skills. **Supp**—Tut.

Adm (Gr 6-11): 105/yr. Appl due: Feb. Accepted: 47%. Yield: 51%. **Tests** ISEE SSAT.

Enr 408. B 209. G 199. Elem 125. Sec 283. Wh 73%. Hisp 5%. Blk 15%. Asian 7%. Avg class size: 15. **Fac 64.** M 21/3. F 36/4. Wh 78%. Hisp 7%. Blk 12%. Asian 3%. Adv deg: 71%.

Grad '04—63. Col—63. (Colby 4, Brandeis 3, Bowdoin 2, Harvard 2, Columbia 2, Wesleyan U 2). Alum 4003.

Tui '04-'05: Day $25,080 (+$400). **Aid:** Need 102 ($1,980,000).

Summer: Ages 3-12. Rec. Tui Day $700-900/2-wk ses. 8 wks.

Endow $4,000,000. Plant val $12,000,000. Bldgs 3. Class rms 38. Lib 16,500 vols. Sci labs 5. Comp labs 2. Auds 1. Theaters 2. Art studios 7. Music studios 6. Dance studios 1. Gyms 2. Fields 4. Courts 4. Pools 3.

Est 1921. Nonprofit. Tri (Sept-June). **Assoc** CLS NEASC.

Shortly after World War I, a group of liberal-minded parents, desirous of bringing to the city more progressive educational methods than were then available, asked Eugene Randolph Smith, who had successfully developed the Park School of Baltimore, MD, to organize a similar school in Boston. He was extraordinarily successful in his 22 years as headmaster, adding constantly to the activities and the plant of the school, which became nationally noted as a leader in progressive education.

Beaver's rigorous academic program is unusually rich in the sciences, the humanities, and the performing and visual arts. Upper school students select from a variety of honors and Advanced Placement courses, and independent study is also available. Computers are used across many disciplines in all grades, as technology instruction is integrated into the general curriculum.

Extracurricular activities emphasize interscholastic sports, drama, music, the visual arts, community service and publications. All students take part in the school's afternoon program.

BRIMMER AND MAY SCHOOL
Day — Coed Gr PS-12

Chestnut Hill, MA 02467. 69 Middlesex Rd. Tel: 617-566-7462. Fax: 617-734-5147.
www.brimmerandmay.org   E-mail: admissions@brimmer.org

Anne C. Reenstierna, Head. BA, Wheaton College (MA), MEd, Lesley College. **Barbara P. Shoolman, Adm.**

Col Prep. AP—Eng Fr Span Calc Bio Econ Studio_Art. **Feat**—Environ_Sci Computers Comp_Graphics Law Psych Ceramics Drawing Photog Drama Theater_Arts Music Journ. **Supp**—ESL Tut.

Adm: 91/yr. Appl due: Jan. Accepted: 36%. **Tests** ISEE SSAT TOEFL.

Enr 390. B 179. G 211. Elem 270. Sec 120. Wh 76%. Hisp 5%. Blk 9%. Asian 6%. Other 4%. Avg class size: 14. **Fac 65.** M 16/2. F 45/2. Adv deg: 58%.
Grad '04—22. Col—22. (Bowdoin, Hamilton, CT Col, Wheaton-MA, Trinity Col-CT, Worcester Polytech).
Tui '04-'05: Day $15,900-25,500 (+$750). **Aid:** Need 79 ($1,300,000).
Summer: Rec. 1-8 wks.
Endow $800,000. Plant val $11,500,000. Bldgs 6. Class rms 39. Lib 12,000 vols. Sci labs 2. Writing ctrs 1. Theaters 1. Art studios 2. Music studios 2. Dance studios 1. Art/sci ctrs 1. Gyms 2. Fields 2. Courts 1. Pools 1.
Est 1880. Nonprofit. Sem (Sept-June). **Assoc** NEASC.

Brimmer and May School grew out of two schools originally founded on Boston's Beacon Hill: Miss Folsom's in 1880 and Miss Brown's Classical in 1887. Miss Folsom's School came to be known as the May School in 1902, while under the leadership of Mary May. The Classical School for Girls became the Brimmer School in 1914, offering a coeducational lower school and college preparatory girls' middle and upper schools. In 1939, the two schools merged and, in 1954, moved to Chestnut Hill. Brimmer and May became fully coeducational in 1994.

In the lower school, basic skills and programs in the creative arts and physical education are emphasized. Middle and upper school students take a program of academic subjects that is enriched by experiential learning programs, as well as community service, creative arts and athletic offerings. Brimmer and May's curriculum emphasizes problem solving, critical thinking, and analytical reading and writing.

Located three miles west of Boston, the school utilizes the cultural and educational resources of the city to further enrich the classroom experience.

See Also Page 1125

THE CHESTNUT HILL SCHOOL

Day — Coed Gr PS-6

Chestnut Hill, MA 02467. 428 Hammond St. Tel: 617-566-4394. Fax: 617-738-6602.
   www.tchs.org   E-mail: admissions@tchs.org
Gregory B. Blackburn, Head. BS, Hendrix College, MEd, Univ of Arkansas, PhD, Univ of Mississippi. **Wendy W. Borosavage, Adm.**
   Pre-Prep. Feat—Lib_Skills Span Computers Robotics Studio_Art Music Violin Woodworking. **Supp**—Tut.
   Adm (Gr PS-5): 51/yr. Appl due: Jan. Accepted: 28%. Yield: 82%.
   Enr 242. B 110. G 132. Elem 242. Wh 72%. Hisp 2%. Blk 15%. Asian 5%. Other 6%. Avg class size: 15. **Fac 35.** M 7/1. F 26/1. Wh 79%. Hisp 3%. Blk 14%. Asian 3%. Other 1%. Adv deg: 65%.
   Grad '04—16. Prep—13. (Buckingham Browne & Nichols 5, Rivers 2, Noble & Greenough 1, Belmont Hill 1, Milton Acad 1, Roxbury Latin 1). Alum 958.
   Tui '04-'05: Day $14,850-21,000. Aid: Need 48 ($700,000).
   Summer: Creative Arts. Sports. Tui Day $800-2800. 2-8 wks.
   Endow $2,500,000. Plant val $13,500,000. Bldgs 2. Class rms 24. Lib 7000 vols. Sci labs 1. Lang labs 2. Comp labs 2. Theaters 1. Art studios 2. Music studios 2. Wood shops 1. Gyms 1. Fields 2. Pools 2.
   Est 1860. Nonprofit. Sem (Sept-June).

One of the rooms in CHS' original building, modeled on the design of the Old Ship Church in Hingham, was the first church in Chestnut Hill and now serves as a library. The building has been steadily enlarged and remodeled to meet the growing needs of the school.

While maintaining a graded structure, the school conducts small classes that facilitate individual academic, social and emotional growth. The nursery program accommodates children ages 3 and 4. An extended-day program and an afternoon discovery program are offered, as is a creative arts and sports summer camp. Visits to the area's museums and historic locations are integral to the curriculum.

DEXTER SCHOOL

Day — Boys Gr PS-11

Brookline, MA 02445. 20 Newton St. Tel: 617-522-5544. Fax: 617-522-8166.
www.dexter.org   E-mail: administration@dexter.org
William F. Phinney, Head. AB, Harvard Univ. **Endicott P. Saltonstall, Jr., Adm.**
   Pre-Prep. AP—Eng Fr Lat Span Calc Stats Comp_Sci Bio Chem Physics Eur_Hist US_Hist Music_Theory. **Feat**—Greek Astron Marine_Biol/Sci Ethics Art_Hist Studio_Art Music Indus_Arts. **Supp**—Tut.
   Adm (Gr PS-10): 60/yr. Appl due: Rolling. **Tests** ISEE SSAT.
   Enr 353. B 353. Elem 334. Sec 19. Avg class size: 14. **Fac 67.** M 37. F 26/4. Adv deg: 55%.
   Grad '04—36. Prep—34. (Belmont Hill 3, Groton 2, St George's Sch-RI 2, St Mark's Sch-MA 2, Boston Col HS 2). Alum 3171.
   Tui '04-'05: Day $16,075-25,645 (+$1770). **Aid:** Need 66 ($1,110,770).
   Summer: Acad Enrich. Tui Day $960/2-wk ses. 6 wks. Rec. Tui Day $455/wk. 8 wks. Hockey. Tui Day $955/2-wk ses. 8 wks. Sci & Tech. Tui Day $980/2-wk ses. 6 wks. Marine Sci. Tui Bdg $685/wk. 8 wks. Sailing. Tui Bdg $685/wk. 8 wks.
   Endow $22,292,000. Plant val $45,748,000. Bldgs 11. Class rms 40. Lib 18,900 vols. Sci labs 3. Comp labs 4. Observatories 1. Auds 2. Art studios 2. Music studios 1. Arts ctrs 1. Shops 1. Gyms 1. Fields 5. Pools 1. Rinks 2.
   Est 1926. Nonprofit. Tri (Sept-June).

Located on a 36-acre estate opposite Larz-Anderson Park, Dexter was founded as a successor to the lower school of Noble and Greenough. With a firm emphasis upon academic fundamentals, the curriculum prepares boys from Greater Boston for leading colleges. The comprehensive intramural and interscholastic athletic programs are directed by a faculty coaching staff. Students attend a chapel assembly each week. Over the summer, the school operates enrichment, recreational, ice hockey, science and technology, marine science and sailing camps. Dexter founded its sister school, Southfield (separately listed), in 1992 on the same campus.

After originally serving pupils in grades PS-8, in fall 2003 Dexter began extending its program through high school with the addition of one grade per year.

See Also Page 1331

PARK SCHOOL

Day — Coed Gr PS-9

Brookline, MA 02445. 171 Goddard Ave. Tel: 617-277-2456. Fax: 617-232-1261.
www.parkschool.org   E-mail: admissions@parkschool.org
Jerrold I. Katz, Head. AB, Univ of Michigan, MEd, Boston Univ, EdD, Harvard Univ. **Cynthia Harmon, Adm.**

Pre-Prep. Feat—Fr Lat Span Computers Drama Music. **Supp**—Dev_Read Tut.
Adm: 75/yr. Accepted: 21%. **Tests** ISEE SSAT.
Enr 519. B 271. G 248. Elem 491. Sec 28. Wh 78%. Hisp 2%. Blk 12%. Asian 8%. **Fac 74.** M 18/4. F 35/17. Wh 88%. Hisp 9%. Am Ind 3%. Adv deg: 97%.
Grad '04—25. Prep—23. (Milton Acad, Noble & Greenough, Dana Hall, Concord Acad, Winsor). Alum 2500.
Tui '02-'03: Day $11,510-19,425. Aid: Need 75 ($708,210).
Summer: Ages 4-8. Enrich Rec. Ages 8-15. Creative Arts. Ages 4-15. Sports. 1-8 wks.
Endow $17,550,000. Plant val $15,000,000. Bldgs 2. Class rms 36. Lib 30,000 vols. Sci labs 5. Comp labs 3. Theaters 1. Art studios 3. Music studios 3. Gyms 2. Fields 6. Tennis courts 1. Pools 1. Playgrounds 3. Greenhouses 1.
Est 1888. Nonprofit. Tri (Sept-June).

Founded by Caroline A. Pierce as a small neighborhood school, Park now provides a diverse student body from the Greater Boston area with a strong coeducational program. In 1970, the school moved to a 25-acre site across from Larz Anderson Park, where the long tradition of small classes, rigorous academics and close contact with parents continues to be fostered.

The curriculum is designed to build basic skills and instill self-confidence. Music, art, drama and athletics are regular parts of the program. Extracurricular activities include community service, drama and interscholastic sports. Two-week work-study opportunities and language-study trips to France, Spain and Italy are integral to the grade 9 curriculum.

An after-school program offers both structured activities and free play time for the younger children in a relaxed atmosphere. During the summer, Park also conducts several day camp and special activity programs for children ages 4-15, the largest of which is a creative arts program.

SOUTHFIELD SCHOOL
Day — Girls Gr PS-10

Brookline, MA 02445. 10 Newton St. Tel: 617-522-6980. Fax: 617-522-8166.
www.southfield.org E-mail: administration@southfield.org
William F. Phinney, Head. AB, Harvard Univ. **Jacalyn M. Wright, Adm.**
Pre-Prep. Feat—Fr Greek Lat Span Astron Marine_Biol/Sci Comp_Sci Ethics Art_Hist Studio_Art Music Music_Theory Woodworking. **Supp**—Rem_Math Tut.
Adm (Gr PS-9): 42/yr. Appl due: Rolling. **Tests** ISEE SSAT.
Enr 336. G 336. Elem 324. Sec 12. Avg class size: 14. Uniform. **Fac 72.** M 26/1. F 43/2. Adv deg: 56%.
Grad '04—29. Prep—27. (St George's Sch-RI 3, Dana Hall 2, Middlesex 2, Milton Acad 1, Winsor 1). Alum 294.
Tui '04-'05: Day $15,300-23,875 (+$1770). **Aid:** Need 54 ($947,010).
Summer: Acad Enrich. Tui Day $960/2-wk ses. 6 wks. Rec. Tui Day $455/wk. 8 wks. Sci & Tech. Tui Day $980. 2 wks. Marine Sci. Tui Bdg $685/wk. 8 wks. Ice Hockey. Tui Day $955. 2 wks. Sailing. Tui Bdg $685/wk. 8 wks.
Endow $6,601,000. Plant val $45,748,000. Bldgs 9. Class rms 18. Lib 18,900 vols. Sci labs 3. Comp labs 4. Observatories 1. Auds 2. Art studios 2. Music studios 1. Shops 1. Gyms 1. Fields 5. Pools 1. Rinks 2.
Est 1992. Nonprofit. Tri (Sept-June).

Established by Dexter School for boys as a separate sister school and located on the 36-acre Dexter campus, Southfield has the use of all Dexter facilities, including a field station on Cape Cod for the study of marine science and a science and technology center. Southfield and Dexter share a head of school and other key administrators, and faculties of both schools meet together to plan a curriculum that assures similar expectations of all students. Occasional coordinate assemblies, musical productions and field trips are part of the program. In addition, a chapel assembly is held weekly.

Southfield's curriculum emphasizes the fundamentals of reading, writing and arithmetic, as well as such subjects as history, social studies, geography and science. Girls begin to study Latin in grade 6 and elect a modern language in grade 8. Additional courses include offerings in art, woodworking, music, health and computer science. Students in grades 3-6 participate in intramural sports; interscholastic athletics begin in grade 7 and provide competition in soccer, field hockey, basketball, ice hockey, swimming, softball, crew, cross-country, golf, tennis, squash and lacrosse.

After originally serving pupils in grades PS-8, Southfield began extending its program through high school with the addition of grade 9 in September 2004.

See Also Page 1318

BYFIELD, MA. (29 mi. N of Boston, MA) Rural. Pop: 1200. Alt: 66 ft.

GOVERNOR DUMMER ACADEMY
Bdg and Day — Coed Gr 9-12

Byfield, MA 01922. 1 Elm St. Tel: 978-465-1763. Fax: 978-462-1278.
www.gda.org   E-mail: admissions@gda.org

John M. Doggett, Jr., Head. BA, Williams College, MA, New York Univ. **Peter T. Bidstrup, Adm.**

Col Prep. AP—Eng Fr Ger Lat Span Calc Stats Bio Physics Eur_Hist US_Hist Studio_Art. **Feat**—Comp_Sci Middle_Eastern_Hist Amer_Stud Econ Pol_Sci Psych African_Stud Comp_Relig Ceramics Photog Drama Theater_Arts Music. **Supp**—ESL.

Adm (Gr 9-11): 118/yr. Bdg 79. Day 39. Appl due: Jan. Accepted: 33%. Yield: 50%. **Tests** ISEE SSAT TOEFL.

Enr 376. B 135/64. G 92/85. Sec 376. Wh 88%. Hisp 5%. Blk 5%. Asian 2%. Avg class size: 13. **Fac 59.** M 32/4. F 14/9. Wh 95%. Hisp 3%. Blk 2%. Adv deg: 64%. In dorms 18.

Grad '04—98. Col—98. (Boston U, Tufts, Geo Wash, USC, Dartmouth, Williams). Avg SAT: 1252. Alum 4650.

Tui '05-'06: Bdg $35,350 (+$2000). **Day** $27,950 (+$1500). **Aid:** Need 94 ($2,000,000).

Summer: Enrich Rec. Dance. 8 wks.

Endow $68,000,000. Plant val $61,000,000. Bldgs 42. Dorms 10. Dorm rms 227. Class rms 40. Lib 35,000 vols. Sci labs 8. Lang labs 1. Comp labs 2. Sci ctrs 1. Auds 1. Theaters 2. Art studios 4. Music studios 8. Dance studios 1. Perf arts ctrs 1. Gyms 1. Fields 10. Courts 10. Field houses 1. Rinks 1. Tracks 1. Golf crses 1. Machine shops 1.

Est 1763. Nonprofit. Sem (Sept-June). **Assoc** CLS NEASC.

The oldest boarding school in continuous operation in the country, the academy was founded by Lt. Gov. William Dummer of the Massachusetts Bay Colony, who bequeathed his beautiful Byfield home and 600-acre farm for that purpose. Under the celebrated Samuel Moody, who made it a grammar school of the earlier type, so many boys were prepared for "the College" that, between 1768 and 1790, one-fourth of Harvard's graduates were from the academy. Originally a boys' school, GDA first accepted girls as day students in 1971, then as boarders in 1973.

The academy's curriculum stresses in-depth exploration of critical academic skills and abilities. Longer class sessions (lasting 60 or 90 minutes), an emphasis on discussion and debate, and the use of a variety of methods and materials are characteristics of the curriculum. Hands-on lab and field experiments, oral presentations, group research, exhibits and technology-assisted presentations supplement traditional assessments (exams and papers). In addition, the academy maintains such structures as extra-help sessions, an advisory system and a supervised evening study program to assist boys and girls with time-management and study skills.

An afternoon program provides opportunities in athletics, drama and community service. In addition, GDA offers a full visual and performing arts program, student government, the usual publications, and numerous clubs and activities. Students are encouraged to develop self-discipline, individual responsibility, and respect for and an ability to work with others. **See Also Page 1155**

CAMBRIDGE, MA. (6 mi. WNW of Boston, MA) Urban. Pop: 101,355. Alt: 40 ft.

BUCKINGHAM BROWNE & NICHOLS SCHOOL
Day — Coed Gr PS-12

Cambridge, MA 02138. 80 Gerry's Landing Rd. Tel: 617-800-2136. Fax: 617-547-7696.
www.bbns.org   E-mail: admissions@bbns.org

Rebecca T. Upham, Head. BA, Middlebury College, MA, Columbia Univ. **Neville Lake, Upper Sch Adm; Martha Newport, Middle Sch Adm; Ann L. Niles, Lower Sch Adm.**

Col Prep. AP—Fr Lat Span Stats Comp_Sci Art_Hist. Feat—Mandarin Russ Anthro Econ Govt Pol_Sci Psych Relig Ceramics Film Photog Studio_Art Drama Chorus Music Orchestra. **Supp**—Tut.

Adm (Gr PS-11): 175/yr. Appl due: Feb. Accepted: 27%. Tests ISEE SSAT.

Enr 961. B 467. G 494. Elem 495. Sec 466. Wh 78%. Hisp 3%. Blk 8%. Asian 11%. Avg class size: 14. **Fac 132.** M 45/8. F 61/18. Wh 84%. Hisp 4%. Blk 5%. Asian 3%. Other 4%. Adv deg: 76%.

Grad '04—114. Col—112. (Boston Col, Harvard, NYU, Brown, Dartmouth, Cornell). Avg SAT: 1341. Avg SSAT: 74%. Alum 5042.

Tui '04-'05: Day $14,000-26,250 (+$500). **Aid:** Need 175 ($2,821,570).

Summer: Rec. Tui Day $270/wk. 8 wks.

Endow $29,840,000. Plant val $30,969,000. Bldgs 25. Class rms 64. Lib 20,000 vols. Theaters 2. Studios 5. Wood shops 1. Gyms 2. Fields 6. Courts 4. Rinks 1. Boathouses 1.

Est 1883. Nonprofit. Sem (Sept-May). **Assoc** CLS NEASC.

BB&N resulted from the January 1974 merger of two distinguished Cambridge independent schools, the Buckingham School and the Browne & Nichols School, both of which date from the 19th century. Offering a coordinated program, the school maintains three geographically separate campuses: lower, middle and upper.

Students are drawn from many parts of Greater Boston by the broad and challenging curriculum, which is enriched by many extracurricular activities. The school provides a program that meets the individual student's needs. Simple schedules within the lower school emphasize basic instruction in a relaxed atmosphere, while the middle school incorporates participatory activities into student instruction. Team sports are required in grades 7-9, and a social service requirement must be met in the upper school. Graduates enter a variety of selective colleges.

Activities include clubs for photography, debating, literature, Russian and Latin, among others, and a variety of sports, on both an interscholastic and an intramural basis. There are extensive programs in instrumental and vocal music and in the visual arts. The school maintains an outdoor education facility in Harrisville, NH.

CAMBRIDGE FRIENDS SCHOOL
Day — Coed Gr PS-8

Cambridge, MA 02140. 5 Cadbury Rd. Tel: 617-354-3880. Fax: 617-876-1815.
www.cambridgefriendsschool.org
E-mail: admissions@cambridgefriendsschool.org

Mary Newmann, Head. BA, Mount Holyoke College, MA, New York Univ, MEd, Bank Street College of Education. **Merle Jacobs, Adm.**

Pre-Prep. Feat—Span Studio_Art Drama Music. **Supp**—Dev_Read Tut.

Adm: 56/yr. Appl due: Jan. Accepted: 30%. **Tests** ISEE.

Enr 265. B 130. G 135. Elem 265. Wh 63%. Hisp 6%. Blk 16%. Am Ind 1%. Asian 14%. Avg class size: 16. **Fac 46.** M 7. F 36/3. Wh 78%. Hisp 1%. Blk 17%. Asian 3%. Other 1%. Adv deg: 73%.

Grad '04—27. **Prep**—12. (Commonwealth, Concord Acad, Phillips Acad, Dana Hall, Beaver Co Day, Brimmer & May). Alum 860.

Tui '04-'05: Day $13,500-16,200. Aid: Need 70 ($880,000).

Endow $5,000,000. Plant val $7,300,000. Bldgs 1. Class rms 19. Lib 11,000 vols. Labs 1. Theaters 1. Art studios 2. Music studios 1. Dance studios 1. Gyms 1. Fields 1.

Est 1961. Nonprofit. Religious Society of Friends. Sem (Sept-June).

The school's integrated curriculum, which emphasizes problem solving, reasoning and analysis, is particularly strong in language arts and social studies. Classroom teachers and specialists work together to integrate these subjects with course work in science, mathematics and the arts. Beginning in kindergarten, children utilize computers as a tool for developing their research, writing and math skills, and CFS introduces Spanish instruction in grade 4. Physical education classes, which are taught at all grade levels, focus upon both individual fitness and cooperative play. Learning specialists and a counselor work with students, parents and teachers to address pupils' needs.

CFS continues to emphasize Quaker principles and practices.

FAYERWEATHER STREET SCHOOL
Day — Coed Gr PS-8

Cambridge, MA 02138. 765 Concord Ave. Tel: 617-876-4746. Fax: 617-520-6700.
www.fayerweather.org E-mail: info@fayerweather.org

Susan E. Kluver, Head. BA, Simmons College, EdM, EdD, Harvard Univ. **Lisette Zinner,**

Adm.
Pre-Prep. Gen Acad. Feat—Lib_Skills Span Film Studio_Art Music Woodworking. **Supp**—Dev_Read Rev Tut.
Adm (Gr PS-7): 41/yr. Appl due: Jan. Accepted: 34%.
Enr 195. B 102. G 93. Elem 195. Wh 75%. Hisp 4%. Blk 7%. Am Ind 1%. Asian 11%. Other 2%. Avg class size: 21. **Fac 33.** M 4. F 18/11. Wh 73%. Hisp 6%. Blk 12%. Asian 9%. Adv deg: 75%.
Grad '04—13. Prep—12. (Dana Hall 2, Beaver Co Day 1, Commonwealth 1, Concord Acad 1, Northfield Mt Hermon 1). Alum 1000.
Tui '04-'05: Day $11,475-17,800. Aid: Need 54 ($503,000).
Summer: Enrich Rec. Environ Sci. Arts. Tui Day $630. 2 wks.
Endow $180,000. Plant val $3,000,000. Bldgs 1. Class rms 11. Lib 15,000 vols. Sci labs 1. Lang labs 1. Comp labs 1. Art studios 2. Music studios 1. Gyms 1. Fields 1. Courts 1.
Est 1967. Nonprofit. Sem (Sept-June).

Started by a group of Cambridge parents and educators, this school stresses competence in literacy, communication and computation; problem defining, research and problem solving; physical coordination; and interpersonal relations. Beginning in prekindergarten, children are presented with choices and learn to assess their results.

After kindergarten, in grades 1-8, learning occurs in mixed-age groups. Individualized folder work supplements choice times, literature and math groups, art, science and social studies activities, and daily times for writing and reading. Children work with specialist teachers in Spanish, wood shop, music, library and sports. Eighth graders perform in-school and community service as part of their program.

An after-school program that includes a variety of focused activities is available at all grade levels. The school's location allows for field trips that utilize the rich educational and cultural resources of the Boston/Cambridge community.

SHADY HILL SCHOOL

Day — Coed Gr PS-8

Cambridge, MA 02138. 178 Coolidge Hill. Tel: 617-868-1260. Fax: 617-520-9387. www.shs.org
Bruce A. Shaw, Dir. BA, Macalester College, MAT, Antioch College. **Becca Hunsicker, Adm.**
Pre-Prep. Feat—Fr Span Computers Studio_Art Music Indus_Arts. **Supp**—Tut.
Adm (Gr PS-7): 83/yr. Appl due: Jan. Accepted: 15%. **Tests** ISEE.
Enr 500. B 239. G 261. Elem 500. Wh 67%. Hisp 4%. Blk 15%. Asian 12%. Other 2%. Avg class size: 17. **Fac 66.** M 15. F 41/10. Wh 87%. Hisp 2%. Blk 8%. Asian 3%. Adv deg: 72%.
Grad '04—65. Prep—52. (Concord Acad, Buckingham Browne & Nichols, Beaver Co Day, Cambridge Sch-MA, Milton Acad, Noble & Greenough). Alum 3076.
Tui '05-'06: Day $13,480-21,590. Aid: Need 87 ($1,251,020).
Summer: Rec. 2-8 wks.
Endow $28,176,000. Plant val $25,000,000. Bldgs 18. Class rms 37. Lib 20,000 vols. Sci labs 4. Comp labs 2. Art studios 4. Music studios 2. Gyms 1. Fields 3. Courts 2.
Est 1915. Nonprofit. Quar (Sept-June).

Bearing the name of the estate of Charles Eliot Norton, Shady Hill was founded by Professor and Mrs. William Ernest Hocking on the porch of their Cambridge home. The school grew out of the desire of a group of local parents to build on the ideas of Frances Parker, John Dewey and Alfred Whitehead, and its program continues to strike a balance between innovation and continuity.

From kindergarten through grade 8, the curriculum is built around Central Subject, the year-long study of a people via their history, literature, geography, and arts and sciences. This approach to learning stresses the interrelationships of many disciplines and the use of original sources rather than textbooks. Foreign language study begins in grade 7, and all students participate in the visual and performing arts, as well as in shop. The sports program stresses movement education in the lower grades and the acquisition of team sports skills at the later levels.

CONCORD, MA. (19 mi. WNW of Boston, MA) Suburban. Pop: 16,993. Alt: 121 ft.

CONCORD ACADEMY
Bdg and Day — Coed Gr 9-12

Concord, MA 01742. 166 Main St. Tel: 978-402-2250. Fax: 978-287-4302.
www.concordacademy.org   E-mail: admissions@concordacademy.org
Jacob A. Dresden, Head. BA, MA, Univ of Pennsylvania. **Pamela J. Safford, Adm.**
  Col Prep. AP—Eng Fr Ger Span Calc Stats Comp_Sci Bio Chem Physics US_Hist.
    Feat—Lat Russ_Hist Econ Psych Comp_Relig Art_Hist Photog Media & Film Theater Music_Hist. **Supp**—Rev Tut.
  Adm (Gr 9-11): 116/yr. Bdg 46. Day 70. Appl due: Jan. Accepted: 50%. Yield: 49%. **Tests** CTP_4 ISEE SSAT TOEFL.
  Enr 355. B 76/95. G 82/102. Sec 355. Wh 73%. Hisp 3%. Blk 3%. Asian 7%. Other 14%. Avg class size: 12. **Fac 62.** M 14/14. F 12/22. Adv deg: 85%. In dorms 10.
  Grad '04—91. **Col**—91. (Brown 5, Bowdoin 4, CO Col 3, CT Col 3, Kenyon 3, NYU 3). Avg SAT: 1360. Alum 3710.
  Tui '04-'05: Bdg $33,900 (+$500-700). **Day $27,410** (+$500-700). **Aid:** Need 64 ($1,700,000).
  Endow $33,000,000. Plant val $26,247,000. Bldgs 16. Dorms 6. Dorm rms 75. Class rms 75. Lib 15,000 vols. Sci labs 6. Comp labs 3. Auds 1. Theaters 1. Art studios 3. Music studios 8. Arts ctrs 1. Film/TV studios 3. Gyms 1. Fields 4. Tennis courts 6. Squash courts 4. Pools 1. Student ctrs 1.
  Est 1922. Nonprofit. Sem (Sept-June). **Assoc** NEASC.

CA was incorporated as a result of the combined efforts of a group of local parents. The campus lies along the Sudbury River, a block and a half from the center of Concord. Residential campus buildings consist of 11 historic homes that once housed such luminaries as Ralph Waldo Emerson, Henry David Thoreau, Ulysses S. Grant, Sarah Orne Jewett and Daniel Chester French.

The traditional academic curriculum combines electives in every discipline with required courses. Visual arts electives include drawing, painting, ceramics, photography, filmmaking, textiles and sculpture. The performing arts department offers musical electives such as music theory, music history, improvisation, vocal and instrumental instruction, chorus, orchestra and jazz ensemble. In addition, dance (both ballet and modern) is taught at five levels. Qualified upperclassmen may engage in independent study in many disciplines.

Interscholastic sports offered are cross-country running, downhill skiing, field hockey, golf, soccer, wrestling, basketball, squash, volleyball, baseball, softball, tennis, lacrosse and ultimate Frisbee. The academy also conducts wide-ranging courses in skills and in fitness. Other activities include student publications, community service, outing clubs, affinity organizations and language clubs. CA's student center offers a program of events and activities designed to enrich the weekend life of boarders and day students by combining athletics and fitness, the performing arts and student life.

Students may attend school abroad for one year through programs connected with the Wooster School and Phillips Andover, or they may participate in a biennial summer exchange with a school in Ahrensburg, Germany. In addition, juniors may take part in the Mountain School, a semester-long academic and environmental program in Vermont; CITYterm, a one-semester academic and urban studies program in New York City; or the Rocky Mountain Semester, which emphasizes experiential education.

FENN SCHOOL
Day — Boys Gr 4-9

Concord, MA 01742. 516 Monument St. Tel: 978-369-5800. Fax: 978-371-7520. www.fenn.org E-mail: lkugler@fenn.org
Gerard J. G. Ward, Head. BA, Boston Univ, MEd, Harvard Univ. **Lori T. Kugler, Adm.**
   Pre-Prep. Feat—Lat Span Computers Studio_Art Drama Music Woodworking. **Supp**—Dev_Read Rem_Math Rem_Read Rev Tut.
   Adm: 66/yr. Appl due: Feb. Accepted: 44%. **Tests** IQ ISEE SSAT.
   Enr 308. B 308. Elem 273. Sec 35. Wh 87%. Hisp 4%. Blk 2%. Asian 7%. Avg class size: 14. **Fac 61.** M 24/3. F 22/12. Adv deg: 52%.
   Grad '04—54. Prep—33. (Concord Acad 5, Lawrence Acad 4, St Mark's Sch-MA 3, Groton 2, Middlesex 2, Northfield Mt Hermon 2). Alum 2300.
   Tui '04-'05: Day $20,550-24,050 (+$500). **Aid:** Need 26 ($484,000).
   Summer: Rec. 1-8 wks.
   Endow $12,000,000. Plant val $19,000,000. Bldgs 13. Class rms 34. Lib 14,000 vols. Sci labs 4. Comp labs 1. Dark rms 1. Auds 1. Theaters 1. Art studios 5. Music studios 2. Shops 1. Gyms 2. Fields 4. Pools 1. Climbing walls 1.
   Est 1929. Nonprofit. Tri (Sept-June).

Founded and headed until 1960 by Roger C. Fenn, this school sends its graduates largely to New England college preparatory schools. The academic curriculum emphasizes study habits and fundamentals. The use of flexible sectioning and a departmentalized faculty allows the school to respond to the student's individual needs. Woodworking, art, drama and music are integral parts of each boy's program, as is regular use of the school's computers.

The athletic program includes cross-country, ice hockey, football, soccer, baseball, lacrosse, track and field, wrestling, basketball and tennis. Fenn's marching band is a well-known attraction in the Concord area, and its chorus has performed abroad.

MIDDLESEX SCHOOL

Bdg and Day — Coed Gr 9-12

Concord, MA 01742. 1400 Lowell Rd, PO Box 9122. Tel: 978-369-2550. Fax: 978-402-1400.
www.middlesex.edu E-mail: admissions@middlesex.edu
Kathleen C. Giles, Head. AB, JD, MEd, Harvard Univ. **Sibyl F. Cohane, Adm.**

Col Prep. AP—Eng Fr Lat Span Calc Stats Comp_Sci Bio Chem Physics Eur_Hist US_Hist Econ US_Govt & Pol Art_Hist Studio_Art Music_Theory. **Feat**—Chin Greek Astron Bioethics Environ_Sci Relig Drama Music. **Supp**—Tut.

Adm (Gr 9-11): 107/yr. Bdg 74. Day 33. Appl due: Jan. Accepted: 26%. Yield: 44%. **Tests** ISEE SSAT TOEFL.

Enr 341. B 121/52. G 124/44. Sec 341. Wh 82%. Hisp 2%. Blk 7%. Asian 9%. Avg class size: 11. **Fac 60.** M 33/3. F 23/1. Wh 87%. Hisp 5%. Blk 5%. Asian 3%. Adv deg: 63%. In dorms 24.

Grad '04—85. Col—84. (Brown 8, Harvard 6, Cornell 5, Colby 4, Geo Wash 4, Tufts 4). Avg SAT: 1310. Alum 3084.

Tui '04-'05: Bdg $34,750 (+$1200). **Day $27,800** (+$1200). **Aid:** Need 86 ($2,215,050).

Summer: Enrich. Arts. Tui Day $1300. 5 wks.

Endow $75,000,000. Plant val $110,000,000. Bldgs 35. Dorms 9. Dorm rms 237. Class rms 37. Lib 37,000 vols. Sci labs 7. Lang labs 1. Comp labs 2. Sci ctrs 1. Auds 1. Theaters 1. Art studios 5. Music studios 3. Dance studios 1. Gyms 1. Fields 6. Squash courts 8. Rinks 1. Rowing crses 1. Boathouses 1. Ponds 1.

Est 1901. Nonprofit. (Sept-June). **Assoc** NEASC.

Frederick Winsor, with the aid of his brother and a group of Harvard colleagues, established Middlesex, where he combined elements of the house system with some of the features of the church schools in England. In the mid-1930s, to aid in recruiting pupils from a distance, he introduced his plan of competitive prize scholarships for boys from all parts of the country. In 1974, the school became coeducational.

From the start, the school has maintained a college preparatory curriculum. Many graduates enter Ivy League schools, while others attend leading colleges throughout the country. Each academic department is organized into the humanities, arts, social sciences or natural sciences division, with distributive requirements established by each division.

In the junior and senior years, students may choose from the unusually rich elective offerings, which include Advanced Placement courses in some two dozen subject areas. Courses beyond the AP level are available in math, English, history and the sciences. The school conducts small classes and maintains a low student-teacher ratio.

Located on 350 acres, the well-equipped campus allows for a wide variety of team and individual sports. Students participate in interscholastic team sports such as football, field hockey, soccer, cross-country, Alpine skiing, basketball, ice hockey, squash, wrestling, dance, lacrosse, crew, tennis, baseball, softball and golf. Facilities are provided for drama, figure drawing, oil painting, watercolor, ceramics, woodworking and photography.

Other extracurricular activities include student government, chorus, Model UN, community service and three school publications. Students produce three major theater productions annually, and Middlesex schedules various on-campus social and cultural activities throughout the year. The school's proximity to Boston and Cambridge offers further opportunities for enrichment.

MA *Leading Private Schools* 210

NASHOBA BROOKS SCHOOL
Day — Boys Gr PS-3, Girls PS-8

Concord, MA 01742. 200 Strawberry Hill Rd. Tel: 978-369-4591. Fax: 978-287-6038.
www.nbsc.org E-mail: admission@nbsc.org

E. Kay Cowan, Head. BA, Univ of Denver, MA, Manhattanville College. **Huyen Truong, Adm.**

Pre-Prep. **Feat**—Fr Lat Studio_Art Drama Music. **Supp**—Dev_Read.

Adm (Gr PS-8): 60/yr. Appl due: Jan. **Tests** ISEE.

Enr 300. B 74. G 226. Elem 300. Wh 84%. Blk 1%. Asian 8%. Other 7%. Avg class size: 15. **Fac 53.** M 2. F 51. Wh 96%. Asian 4%. Adv deg: 94%.

Grad '04—28. Prep—24. (Concord Acad, Lawrence Acad, Middlesex, Dana Hall, Phillips Acad, Milton Acad). Alum 1228.

Tui '04-'05: Day $17,120-22,352 (+$100-425). **Aid:** Need 26 ($299,012).

Endow $3,656,000. Plant val $11,000,000. Bldgs 3. Class rms 32. Libs 1. Sci labs 3. Comp labs 2. Auds 1. Art studios 2. Music studios 2. Gyms 2. Fields 2.

Est 1980. Nonprofit. Tri (Sept-June).

Situated on a 20-acre campus, Nashoba Brooks is the result of a merger between the Brooks School of Concord (founded in 1928) and Nashoba Country Day School (founded in 1958). Coeducational classes in the early years (age 3 through grade 3) lead into girls-only classes in grades 4-8. The educational program stresses a thorough grounding in fundamental skills and study habits and includes art, music, foreign languages and athletics. Computer specialists, who assist students of all ages, work with faculty to facilitate the integration of technology into the curriculum.

All children and faculty become involved in age-appropriate community service projects. Service consists of both direct assistance and indirect help (such as fundraising).

DANVERS, MA. (17 mi. NNE of Boston, MA) Suburban. Pop: 25,212. Alt: 50 ft.

ST. JOHN'S PREPARATORY SCHOOL
Day — Boys Gr 9-12

Danvers, MA 01923. 72 Spring St. Tel: 978-774-1050. Fax: 978-774-5069.
www.stjohnsprep.org E-mail: bflatley@stjohnsprep.org

Albert J. Shannon, Head. BA, PhD, Marquette Univ, MEd, Boston Univ. **Brian J. Flatley, Adm.**

Col Prep. **AP**—Eng Fr Ger Lat Span Calc Stats Comp_Sci Bio Chem Physics US_Hist Econ US_Govt & Pol. **Feat**—Anat & Physiol Environ_Sci Microbiol Zoology Neurosci Programming Holocaust Law World_Relig Studio_Art Acting Drama Directing Music Music_Theory Jazz_Ensemble Accounting. **Supp**—Tut.

Adm (Gr 9-11): 360/yr. Appl due: Dec. **Tests** HSPT SSAT.

Enr 1200. B 1200. Sec 1200. Wh 95%. Hisp 1%. Asian 4%. Avg class size: 20. **Fac 99.** Adv deg: 70%.

Grad '04—245. Col—243. (Boston Col 13, Boston U 10, U of VT 9, Providence 8, Northeastern U 7, U of MA-Amherst 7). Avg SAT: 1219. Alum 12,250.

Tui '05-'06: Day $13,800. Aid: Merit 89 ($340,100). Need 307 ($1,474,795).

Endow $5,200,000. Plant val $28,000,000. Bldgs 9. Class rms 51. Lib 21,500 vols. Cha-

pels 1. Labs 6. Arts ctrs 1. Fields 5. Courts 5.
Est 1907. Nonprofit. Roman Catholic. Quar (Sept-June). **Assoc** NEASC.

Sponsored by the Xaverian Brothers, St. John's occupies a 175-acre campus two miles from the center of town. Classes are offered at five ability levels in a curriculum that features many Advanced Placement and elective classes. Boys take compulsory religious studies classes during all four years, and students are expected to take at least one fine arts course before graduation. International exchange programs are available for both French and Spanish pupils. Graduates matriculate at leading colleges.

Students are encouraged to take part in St. John's wide range of extracurricular activities, which includes dramatics, publications, debate, art and language clubs, and a variety of other interest clubs. Athletic offerings include both intramurals and interscholastic competition in football, soccer, cross-country, water polo, fencing, sailing, volleyball, basketball, hockey, track, skiing, wrestling, swimming, baseball, golf, lacrosse, tennis and rugby. An active campus ministry program provides retreats at all grade levels, student-centered liturgies, and ample opportunities for service locally, in other parts of the country and internationally.

See Also Page 1344

DARTMOUTH, MA. (26 mi. ESE of Providence, RI; 48 mi. S of Boston, MA) Suburban. Pop: 30,666. Alt: 153 ft. Area also includes North Dartmouth.

FRIENDS ACADEMY
Day — Coed Gr PS-8

North Dartmouth, MA 02747. 1088 Tucker Rd. Tel: 508-999-1356. Fax: 508-997-0117.
www.friendsacademy-ma.org E-mail: generalinfo@friendsacademy-ma.org
Claudia McClure Daggett, Head. BS, Univ of Wisconsin-Madison, MSEd, National College of Education. **Cheryl Deane, Adm.**
   Pre-Prep. Feat—Lat Span Computers Studio_Art Drama Music Outdoor_Ed. **Supp**—Tut.
   Adm: 50/yr. Appl due: Jan. Accepted: 64%. Yield: 77%. **Tests** CTP_4.
   Enr 277. B 141. G 136. Elem 277. Wh 85%. Hisp 3%. Blk 2%. Am Ind 1%. Asian 4%. Other 5%. Avg class size: 14. **Fac 42.** M 10. F 30/2. Wh 98%. Hisp 1%. Blk 1%. Adv deg: 42%.
   Grad '04—32. Prep—24. (Tabor, Bishop Stang, Wheeler, Phillips Exeter, St George's Sch-RI, Moses Brown). Alum 1200.
   Tui '04-'05: Day $6550-16,300. Aid: Need 63 ($528,055).
   Summer: Enrich Rec. Tui Day $200/wk. 5 wks.
   Endow $1,400,000. Plant val $10,000,000. Bldgs 3. Class rms 20. Lib 13,000 vols. Labs 3. Auds 1. Art studios 2. Music studios 2. Perf arts ctrs 1. Gyms 1. Fields 4.
   Est 1810. Nonprofit. Tri (Sept-June).

Founded by a group of New Bedford Quakers, the academy became nondenominational in 1855. In 1949, it moved from New Bedford to its present, 68-acre estate, which overlooks rolling countryside.

The curriculum stresses the fundamentals of reading, writing, computing, speaking and listening, and it is enriched by offerings in human growth and development, library, art, music, drama, computer and physical education. The diverse student body comes from various Massachusetts and Rhode Island communities. Graduates enter leading preparatory schools.

DEDHAM, MA. (10 mi. SW of Boston, MA) Suburban. Pop: 23,464. Alt: 119 ft.

DEDHAM COUNTRY DAY SCHOOL
Day — Coed Gr PS-8

Dedham, MA 02026. 90 Sandy Valley Rd. Tel: 781-329-0850. Fax: 781-329-0551.
www.dedhamcountryday.org E-mail: etretter@dedhamcountryday.org
Sonia L. Valentine, Head. BS, Bicol Univ (Philippines), MA, Fordham Univ. **Ellen Tretter, Adm.**
  Pre-Prep. **Feat**—Lat Span Computers Studio_Art Drama Music Public_Speak Indus_Arts. **Supp**—Rem_Read Tut.
  Adm: 40/yr. Appl due: Jan. Accepted: 23%. **Tests** ISEE SSAT.
  Enr 242. B 120. G 122. Elem 242. Wh 84%. Hisp 5%. Blk 5%. Asian 6%. Avg class size: 15.
  Fac 45. M 10/1. F 28/6. Wh 94%. Blk 4%. Asian 2%. Adv deg: 60%.
  Grad '04—20. Prep—16. (Tabor, Thayer, St Sebastian's, Boston Col HS, Noble & Greenough). Alum 1222.
  Tui '04-'05: Day $14,655-22,350. **Aid:** Need 21 ($250,753).
  Summer: Rec. Tui Day $345/wk. 8 wks.
  Endow $2,400,000. Plant val $6,000,000. Bldgs 5. Class rms 18. Lib 13,600 vols. Sci labs 2. Comp labs 2. Auds 1. Theaters 1. Art studios 1. Music studios 4. Dance studios 1. Shops 1. Gyms 2. Fields 4. Pools 2.
  Est 1904. Nonprofit. Tri (Sept-June).

A traditional school with strong family involvement, DCD attracts students from 30 communities in and around Boston. The strong academic program emphasizes preparation in the basic disciplines, with Spanish offered in grades 4-8 and Latin in grades 6-8. Art, music, drama and shop are integral parts of the curriculum, as are athletics and physical education. In addition to regular one-day field trips, Dedham Country Day schedules an excursion of several days' duration for each upper school grade.

NOBLE AND GREENOUGH SCHOOL
5-Day Bdg — Coed Gr 9-12; Day — Coed 7-12

Dedham, MA 02026. 10 Campus Dr. Tel: 781-326-3700. Fax: 781-320-1329.
www.nobles.edu E-mail: admissions@nobles.edu
Robert P. Henderson, Jr., Head. AB, AM, Dartmouth College. **Jennifer Hines, Adm.**
  Col Prep. **AP**—Fr Lat Span Calc Stats Comp_Sci Bio Chem Physics Eur_Hist Art_Hist Studio_Art. **Feat**—Creative_Writing Shakespeare Japan Environ_Sci Marine_Biol/Sci Comp_Design Programming Econ Ethics Painting Photog Drama Theater Chorus Music Music_Theory Journ Public_Speak. **Supp**—Tut.

Adm (Bdg Gr 9-11; Day 7-11): 118/yr. Bdg 9. Day 109. Appl due: Feb. Accepted: 21%. Yield: 66%. **Tests** ISEE SSAT.

Enr 546. B 24/250. G 23/249. Elem 110. Sec 436. Wh 81%. Hisp 4%. Blk 6%. Asian 3%. Other 6%. Avg class size: 12. **Fac 85.** M 36/13. F 24/12. Wh 81%. Hisp 2%. Blk 9%. Am Ind 1%. Asian 3%. Other 4%. Adv deg: 63%. In dorms 6.

Grad '04—108. Col—108. (Duke 6, Harvard 6, Boston Col 5, Princeton 5, Bowdoin 4, Brown 4). Avg SAT: 1355. Alum 3589.

Tui '04-'05: 5-Day Bdg $29,800 (+$1000). **Day $25,700** (+$1000). **Aid:** Need 84 ($1,793,300).

Summer: Rec. Tui Day $445/2-wk ses. 8 wks.

Endow $47,826,000. Plant val $39,714,000. Bldgs 28. Dorms 1. Dorm rms 24. Class rms 60. Lib 35,000 vols. Labs 9. Auds 1. Theaters 1. Art studios 7. Music studios 4. Gyms 4. Athletic ctrs 1. Fields 11. Tennis courts 12. Squash courts 6. Pools 3. Rinks 1. Rowing facilities yes.

Est 1866. Nonprofit. Sem (Sept-June). **Assoc** CLS NEASC.

Established on Beacon Hill by George W. C. Noble, who was joined after a quarter of a century by James J. Greenough, this school originally tutored students for entrance to Harvard. Although some continue to enter Harvard, others attend such institutions as Dartmouth, Princeton, Middlebury and Williams. In 1892, the school changed its name to Noble and Greenough. After absorbing the Volkmann School in 1917, the school relocated to Dedham in 1922.

The college preparatory academic program is balanced by an afternoon program comprising athletics, community service, theater, outdoor education and independent projects. Sports include football, soccer, cross-country, basketball, ice hockey, wrestling, baseball, tennis, skiing, crew, field hockey, squash, dance, softball, golf and lacrosse. Students may participate in study-abroad programs in Spain, France, Chile, Ghana and Japan, or in the Maine Coast Semester program or School Year Abroad. Language clubs, student-sponsored clubs, publications, singing and dramatic groups, and debate are among the school's many extracurriculars.

See Also Page 1216

DEERFIELD, MA. (54 mi. N of Hartford, CT; 82 mi. W of Boston, MA) Suburban. Pop: 4750. Alt: 152 ft.

BEMENT SCHOOL
Bdg — Coed Gr 3-9; Day — Coed K-9

Deerfield, MA 01342. Main St. Tel: 413-774-7061. Fax: 413-774-7863.
www.bement.org E-mail: admit@bement.org

Shelley Borror Jackson, Head. BA, Wheaton College (MA), MA, Ohio State Univ. **Matthew T. Evans, Adm.**

Pre-Prep. Feat—Fr Lat Span Studio_Art Drama Music. **Supp**—ESL Rev Tut.

Adm (Bdg Gr 3-9; Day K-8): 58/yr. Bdg 10. Day 48. Appl due: Feb. Accepted: 60%. Yield: 75%. **Tests** SSAT.

Enr 245. B 14/101. G 17/113. Elem 225. Sec 20. Wh 86%. Hisp 1%. Blk 3%. Asian 8%. Other 2%. Avg class size: 12. **Fac 45.** M 19. F 25/1. Wh 90%. Hisp 2%. Blk 8%. Adv deg: 53%. In dorms 8.

Grad '04—21. Prep—18. (Northfield Mt Hermon, Suffield, Deerfield Acad, Williston

Northampton, Pomfret). Alum 1860.
Tui '04-'05: Bdg $32,350 (+$2000). **5-Day Bdg $26,780** (+$500). **Day $9975-14,680** (+$500). **Aid:** Need 67 ($301,000).
Summer: Girls. ESL. Tui Bdg $3800. 4 wks.
Endow $3,100,000. Plant val $4,000,000. Bldgs 10. Dorms 4. Dorm rms 18. Class rms 28. Libs 1. Sci labs 2. Comp labs 3. Art studios 3. Music studios 2. Fields 3.
Est 1925. Nonprofit. Tri (Sept-June).

Developed from an informal group that Grace Bement taught in her own home, this school for younger children has grown into a thriving boarding and day establishment housed in restored colonial buildings.

Art, music, drama and athletics are a daily part of the pre-preparatory curriculum. Between Thanksgiving and Christmas, Bement schedules a three-week mini-term that combines special courses, electives and speakers. Competitive and noncompetitive sports, including soccer, ice hockey, skiing, lacrosse, golf, cross-country, track, dance, field hockey, swimming, squash, basketball, baseball and softball, are available to students in grades 6-9. Among other activities are drama, band, concert choir and an intergenerational community service program.

Social and academic programs are conducted in cooperation with Deerfield Academy and Eaglebrook, Stoneleigh-Burnham and Northfield Mount Hermon schools. Field trips are taken to points of interest in New England and the Middle Atlantic States. Graduates attend well-regarded secondary schools.

See Also Page 1117

DEERFIELD ACADEMY
Bdg and Day — Coed Gr 9-PG

Deerfield, MA 01342. 7 Boyden Ln. Tel: 413-774-1400. Fax: 413-772-1100.
  www.deerfield.edu E-mail: admission@deerfield.edu
Eric Widmer, Head. BA, Williams College, PhD, Harvard Univ. **Patricia L. Gimbel, Adm.**
  Col Prep. **AP**—Eng Fr Lat Span Calc Stats Comp_Sci Bio Chem Physics Eur_Hist US_Hist Econ Art_Hist Studio_Art. **Feat**—Creative_Writing Humanities Shakespeare Arabic_Fiction Chin Greek Arabic Anat & Physiol Astron Geol Programming Asian_Hist Civil_Rights_Era Ethics Philos Relig World_Relig Ceramics Photog Acting Band Chorus Music Dance Health Study_Skills.
  Adm: 211/yr. Bdg 183. Day 28. Appl due: Jan. Accepted: 24%. Yield: 54%. **Tests** CEEB ISEE SSAT TOEFL.
  Enr 603. B 268/43. G 250/42. Sec 581. PG 22. Wh 75%. Hisp 5%. Blk 6%. Asian 13%. Other 1%. Avg class size: 12. **Fac 119.** M 62/5. F 47/5. Wh 91%. Hisp 2%. Blk 3%. Asian 4%. Adv deg: 65%. In dorms 49.
  Grad '04—190. Col—190. (Brown 9, Cornell 9, Yale 9, Harvard 8, Middlebury 8, Columbia 7). Avg SAT: 1330. Alum 11,200.
  Tui '04-'05: Bdg $32,100 (+$1000). **Day $24,600** (+$800). **Aid:** Need 190 ($4,503,050).
  Endow $270,000,000. Plant val $84,000,000. Bldgs 81. Dorms 17. Dorm rms 491. Class rms 57. Lib 85,000 vols. Sci labs 10. Lang labs 1. Comp labs 3. Planetariums 1. Auds 2. Theaters 2. Art studios 7. Music studios 2. Dance studios 2. Gyms 3. Fields 20. Tennis courts 23. Squash courts 9. Pools 1. Rinks 1. Tracks 1. Boathouses 1.
  Est 1797. Nonprofit. Tri (Sept-June). **Assoc** CLS NEASC.

On March 1, 1797, Gov. Samuel Adams signed a bill granting a charter for the founding of this academy in Deerfield, which now occupies a 280-acre campus in the historic village. After operating as a boys' school for nearly two centuries, the school became coeducational in the fall of 1989.

The Deerfield curriculum offers accelerated course sequences in all academic departments. A spring-term elective program and independent study opportunities give teachers and students a chance to work in areas of special interest or expertise. Faculty teach a number of interdisciplinary subjects as well. Seniors are encouraged to participate in the alternate study program, which may include a congressional internship, volunteer work in a hospital or a unique program designed by the student. Deerfield participates in off-campus and exchange programs located in Europe, Africa, Asia, Australia, and rural and coastal New England.

Participation in athletics, theater, or some significant activity or program each term is required of all students. The athletic program includes interscholastic competition and recreational and intramural sports. Among the academy's musical opportunities are chamber music, jazz ensembles and various singing groups. In addition, a range of student organizations, social activities and cultural programs, as well as the opportunity to take part in community service projects, is available.

EAGLEBROOK SCHOOL
Bdg and Day — Boys Gr 6-9

Deerfield, MA 01342. Pine Nook Rd. Tel: 413-774-9111. Fax: 413-774-9119.
www.eaglebrook.org E-mail: admissions@eaglebrook.org
Andrew C. Chase, Head. BA, Williams College. **Theodore J. Low, Adm.**
  Pre-Prep. Feat—Creative_Writing Fr Lat Span Anat Comp_Design Anthro Govt Ethics Ceramics Photog Sculpt Studio_Art Architect_Design Drama Band Chorus Music Public_Speak Woodworking Print_Shop. **Supp**—ESL Rev Tut.
  Adm: 117/yr. Bdg 90. Day 27. Appl due: Rolling. **Tests** IQ SSAT.
  Enr 268. B 198/70. Elem 177. Sec 91. Wh 78%. Hisp 9%. Blk 3%. Asian 10%. Avg class size: 10. **Fac 62.** Adv deg: 50%. In dorms 33.
  Grad '04—85. Prep—78. (Deerfield Acad, Phillips Exeter, Choate, Northfield Mt Hermon, Westminster Sch-CT, Hotchkiss). Alum 5000.
  Tui '04-'05: Bdg $33,350 (+$3000). **Day $20,850** (+$600). **Aid:** Need ($1,105,000).
  Summer: Coed. Acad Enrich Rec. Tui Bdg $4500. 4 wks.
  Endow $35,000,000. Plant val $55,000,000. Bldgs 15. Dorms 5. Dorm rms 120. Class rms 38. Lib 13,000 vols. Sci labs 3. Comp labs 2. Auds 1. Theaters 1. Art studios 7. Music studios 6. Photog studios 1. Shops 1. Gyms 1. Fields 7. Courts 10. Field houses 1. Pools 1. Rinks 1. Tracks 1. Rifle ranges 1. Skiing facilities yes.
  Est 1922. Nonprofit. Tri (Sept-May).

Under the skillful direction of Dr. C. Thurston Chase, associate of the founder, Howard B. Gibbs, and headmaster from 1928 to 1966, Eaglebrook became one of the leading boarding schools for younger boys. Parents and alumni help endow and expand the plant, which now covers more than 750 acres. The former classroom building, now used primarily for the arts, includes facilities for woodworking, stained glass, architectural design, computer-aided design, ceramics and photography, as well as acting and music rehearsal rooms.

Eaglebrook boys go on to secondary school having already had wide opportunities for responsibility and leadership in student government and in committees that direct many aspects of school life. Accelerated sections, as well as remedial classes, and the flexible program offer boys challenges at all levels. The curriculum is enriched by many electives, with particular emphasis placed on music and the arts. Programs of cultural value are held bimonthly. There are numerous correlative extracurricular activities, including student publications, printing, band, chorus and drama.

Each student participates every season in one of the many interscholastic and individual sports. Options are golf, football, ice hockey, skiing and snowboarding, swimming and diving, water polo, cycling, soccer, cross-country, wrestling, track and field, tennis, baseball, basketball, squash, lacrosse, ultimate Frisbee, mountain biking and hiking. Eaglebrook also encourages boys to take advantage of community service opportunities.

The fall Country Fair, the Winter Carnival and Grandparents' Day are special occasions that bring parents and alumni to the school. In addition, International Day and Cultural and Racial Awareness Day promote social and cultural maturity.

See Also Pages 1332-3

DOVER, MA. (15 mi. WSW of Boston, MA) Suburban. Pop: 5558. Alt: 156 ft.

CHARLES RIVER SCHOOL
Day — Coed Gr PS-8

Dover, MA 02030. 56 Centre St, PO Box 339. Tel: 508-785-0068. Fax: 508-785-8290.
    www.charlesriverschool.org   E-mail: info@charlesriverschool.org
Catherine H. Gately, Head. BA, MEd, Boston Univ. **Marion L. Earley, Adm.**
   Pre-Prep. Feat—Fr Span Computers Studio_Art Drama Music. **Supp**—Tut.
   Adm (Gr PS-7): 43/yr. Appl due: Jan. Accepted: 43%. Yield: 79%.
   Enr 206. B 92. G 114. Elem 206. Wh 87%. Hisp 2%. Blk 4%. Asian 7%. Avg class size: 21.
       Fac 35. M 6/3. F 22/4. Wh 88%. Hisp 2%. Blk 5%. Asian 5%. Adv deg: 65%.
   Grad '04—24. Prep—20. (Dana Hall, Milton Acad, Noble & Greenough, Middlesex, St Mark's Sch-MA, Rivers). Alum 1195.
   Tui '04-'05: Day $14,500-21,500 (+$300). **Aid:** Need 21 ($295,000).
   Summer: Enrich Rec. Creative Arts. Tui Day $1500/4-wk ses. 8 wks.
   Endow $5,300,000. Plant val $8,500,000. Bldgs 5. Class rms 16. Lib 8000 vols. Sci labs 2. Lang labs 1. Comp labs 2. Dark rms 1. Amphitheaters 1. Theaters 1. Art studios 1. Music studios 2. Gyms 1. Fields 3. Courts 2. Pools 1. Climbing walls 1.
   Est 1911. Nonprofit. Sem (Sept-June).

CRS provides forward-looking preparation for secondary schools for children from the Greater Boston area. Parents and faculty play an active role in the direction of the school.

The interdisciplinary curriculum emphasizes critical-thinking, reading, writing and math skills, as well as science, social studies, computer, and health and wellness. The arts are integral to the program. In all grades, consideration is given to each student's developmental level and learning style. French and Spanish are offered in grades 6-8, and global awareness and community service are important aspects of school life.

The sports program consists of soccer, field hockey, baseball, tennis, basketball, and boys' and girls' lacrosse. An extended-day option is available to all pupils.

EASTHAMPTON, MA. (35 mi. N of Hartford, CT; 85 mi. W of Boston, MA) Suburban. Pop: 15,994. Alt: 169 ft.

WILLISTON NORTHAMPTON SCHOOL
Bdg — Coed Gr 9-PG; Day — Coed 7-PG

Easthampton, MA 01027. 19 Payson Ave. Tel: 413-529-3000. Fax: 413-527-9494.
www.williston.com   E-mail: admission@williston.com

Brian R. Wright, Head. BA, Occidental College, MA, MPA, PhD, Princeton Univ. **Ann C. Pickrell, Adm.**

Col Prep. AP—Eng Fr Lat Span Calc Stats Comp_Sci Bio Chem Physics. **Feat**—Marine_Biol/Sci Animal_Behavior Soviet_Hist Econ Psych Philos Relig Fine_Arts Photog Drama Music Dance. **Supp**—ESL Tut.

Adm: 191/yr. Bdg 127. Day 64. Appl due: Feb. Accepted: 68%. **Tests** CEEB ISEE SSAT TOEFL.

Enr 540. B 138/129. G 132/141. Elem 90. Sec 432. PG 18. Wh 85%. Hisp 2%. Blk 5%. Asian 8%. Avg class size: 12. **Fac** 78. M 42/2. F 32/2. Adv deg: 69%. In dorms 30.

Grad '04—129. Col—126. (Hamilton, Middlebury, Boston U, Cornell, Tufts, Boston Col). Alum 9000.

Tui '04-'05: Bdg $32,500 (+$1400). **Day $20,600-23,100** (+$1000). **Aid:** Need 229 ($3,404,620).

Summer: Enrich Rec. Theater. Sports. Tui Bdg $2125. Tui Day $1250. 6 wks.

Endow $31,000,000. Plant val $46,000,000. Bldgs 56. Dorms 11. Dorm rms 188. Class rms 60. Lib 40,000 vols. Labs 6. Comp ctrs 1. Theaters 1. Art studios 6. Music studios 5. Dance studios 1. Gyms 1. Athletic ctrs 1. Fields 10. Basketball courts 2. Tennis courts 15. Squash courts 5. Pools 1. Rinks 1. Tracks 1.

Est 1841. Nonprofit. Sem (Sept-June). **Assoc** CLS NEASC.

Founded by local manufacturer Samuel Williston to provide the education of which he was deprived, Williston Seminary offered English, science and mathematics on an equal plane with the classics, a radical but realistic policy for that time. In the fall of 1971, Williston Academy merged with the Northampton School for Girls, founded in 1924 by Sarah B. Whitaker and Dorothy Bement. Today, the school maintains a traditional college preparatory curriculum and places its graduates in selective colleges throughout the country.

The academic program is broad based, with electives offered in many areas. Course work places particular emphasis on the development of critical thinking and writing skills. Juniors may participate in the School Year Abroad program in France or Spain, while seniors in good academic standing may undertake an internship or pursue independent study on or off campus.

Extracurricular activities include drama, singing, instrumental music, photography and publications. Competitive sports include football, soccer, cross-country, ice and field hockey, basketball, skiing, squash, swimming, wrestling, water polo, baseball, softball, track, tennis, volleyball, golf and lacrosse. Other available sports are judo, horseback riding, fitness training, aerobics and modern dance.

See Also Pages 1276-7

MA   *Leading Private Schools*   218

FALMOUTH, MA. (46 mi. ESE of Providence, RI; 58 mi. SSE of Boston, MA) Suburban. Pop: 29,030. Alt: 45 ft.

FALMOUTH ACADEMY
Day — Coed Gr 7-12

Falmouth, MA 02540. 7 Highfield Dr. Tel: 508-457-9696. Fax: 508-457-4112.
www.falmouthacademy.org

David C. Faus, Head. BA, Kenyon College, MSEd, Univ of Pennsylvania. **Michael J. Earley, Adm.**

Col Prep. Feat—Fr Ger Comp_Sci Studio_Art Music. **Supp**—Tut.

Adm: 50/yr. Appl due: Mar. Accepted: 70%. Yield: 76%. **Tests** SSAT.

Enr 210. B 100. G 110. Elem 80. Sec 130. Avg class size: 13. **Fac 35.** M 12. F 23. Adv deg: 71%.

Grad '04—35. Col—35. (Mt Holyoke 3, Williams 2, Denison 2). Avg SAT: 1277. Alum 1000.

Tui '04-'05: Day $15,515 (+$350). **Aid:** Merit 3 ($3000). Need 81 ($510,000).

Endow $1,500,000. Plant val $6,000,000. Bldgs 3. Class rms 16. Lib 8000 vols. Sci labs 4. Comp labs 1. Dark rms 1. Auds 1. Theaters 1. Art studios 1. Music studios 1. Gyms 1. Fields 2. Field houses 1.

Est 1977. Nonprofit. Tri (Sept-June). **Assoc** NEASC.

On a 34-acre campus located next to Beebe Woods conservation area and overlooking Martha's Vineyard, FA draws students from Cape Cod, the Vineyard and southeastern Massachusetts. Within the traditional college preparatory curriculum, students are required each year to study English, math, foreign languages, science and history, with an emphasis placed on writing. More than three dozen electives are offered in the fine and performing arts, publications, and other curricular areas.

Playing fields and a field house support interscholastic teams in soccer, basketball and lacrosse. The academy conducts exchanges with Holderlin Gymnasium in Heidelberg, Germany, and the College Marie de France in Montreal, Canada. The math and science programs take advantage of the academy's proximity to the Woods Hole scientific community, and field trips are common. Students attend an all-school daily meeting.

FITCHBURG, MA. (44 mi. WNW of Boston, MA) Urban. Pop: 39,102. Alt: 438 ft.

APPLEWILD SCHOOL
Day — Coed Gr K-9

Fitchburg, MA 01420. 120 Prospect St. Tel: 978-342-6053. Fax: 978-345-5059.
www.applewild.org   E-mail: ppelletier@applewild.org

William C. Marshall, Int Head. Donald James Hager III, Adm.

Pre-Prep. Feat—Fr Lat Span Computers Studio_Art Visual_Arts Drama Music Indus_Arts. **Supp**—Tut.

Adm (Gr K-8): 79/yr. Appl due: Feb. Accepted: 75%. **Tests** ISEE.

Enr 320. B 160. G 160. Elem 302. Sec 18. Wh 89%. Hisp 1%. Blk 4%. Asian 6%. Avg class

size: 15. **Fac 44.** M 14. F 30. Adv deg: 52%.
Grad '04—9. Prep—9. (Lawrence Acad, Middlesex, Deerfield Acad, Groton, Concord Acad, Phillips Acad). Alum 1030.
Tui '04-'05: Day $8645-16,190. **Aid:** Need 63 ($404,375).
Summer: Enrich Rec. 6 wks.
Endow $7,100,000. Plant val $5,286,000. Bldgs 6. Class rms 30. 2 Libs 15,000 vols. Sci labs 4. Comp labs 3. Photog labs 1. Theaters 2. Art studios 2. Music studios 2. Gyms 2. Fields 3. Pools 1.
Est 1957. Inc. (Sept-June).

Located on the former estate of Mr. and Mrs. Charles T. Crocker, Applewild serves students from dozens of communities in north-central Massachusetts and southern New Hampshire. The 50-acre campus is situated on a hill overlooking Fitchburg.

Applewild's traditional academic program stresses the application of basic skills and ideas, and the school groups students according to achievement and ability in certain disciplines at appropriate age levels. Departmentalization begins in grade 7. The school's visual arts program consists of drawing, printmaking, sculpture, 3-D construction, photography and collage, while the industrial arts program allows participants to progress from simple woodworking in the lower school to advanced furniture making in the upper school.

Athletics are a mandatory part of the curriculum, and Applewild sponsors interscholastic sports teams for pupils in grades 7-9. The school's mentor program allows upper schoolers to instruct younger children in areas where interest and expertise have been demonstrated. The community service program allows pupils to volunteer at area agencies, such as the local hospital and a residential medical center for the elderly. Upper school students may participate in either community service or the mentor program in lieu of athletics.

FRAMINGHAM, MA. (22 mi. W of Boston, MA) Urban. Pop: 66,910. Alt: 189 ft.

SUDBURY VALLEY SCHOOL
Day — Coed Ages 4-19

Framingham, MA 01701. 2 Winch St. Tel: 508-877-3030. Fax: 508-788-0674.
www.sudval.org   E-mail: office@sudval.org
Michael Sadofsky, Pres. Hanna Greenberg, Adm.
  Col Prep. Gen Acad. Supp—Tut.
  Adm: 35/yr. Accepted: 99%.
  Enr 200. B 110. G 90. **Fac 10.** M 5. F 4/1. Adv deg: 30%.
  Grad '04—20. Col—15. Alum 600.
  Tui '04-'05: Day $5400.
  Plant val $2,000,000. Bldgs 2. Lib 20,000 vols.
  Est 1968. Nonprofit. Sem (Sept-June).

Sudbury Valley offers alternative education stressing self-motivation and self-direction. The ungraded program encourages students to learn at their own rates in an informal and personal atmosphere. While addressing individual needs, the school's major emphasis is on promoting a sense of responsibility.

The school's location on the 10-acre former estate of Nathaniel Bowditch, adjoining the conservation lands of the Sudbury Valley, allows for a variety of outdoor activities. Opportunities for ice skating and fishing at the nearby millpond are accompanied by seasonal field trips. Informal athletic activities include baseball, basketball, football, hockey, skiing and hiking.

GREENFIELD, MA. (57 mi. N of Hartford, CT; 83 mi. WNW of Boston, MA) Suburban. Pop: 13,716. Alt: 240 ft.

STONELEIGH-BURNHAM SCHOOL
Bdg — Girls Gr 8-PG; Day — Girls 7-PG

Greenfield, MA 01301. 574 Bernardston Rd. Tel: 413-774-2711. Fax: 413-772-2602.
www.sbschool.org   E-mail: admissions@sbschool.org

Martha W. Shepardson-Killam, Head. BA, Ohio Wesleyan Univ, MA, Middlebury College. Sharon Pleasant, Adm.

  Col Prep. AP—Eng Fr Span Calc Eur_Hist US_Hist Studio_Art. Feat—Creative_Writing Poetry Chin Anat & Physiol Astron Ecol Sports_Med Computers Pol_Sci Psych Architect Weaving Acting Drama Music Music_Theory Dance Study_Skills Nutrition. Supp—ESL Tut.

  Adm (Bdg Gr 8-12; Day 7-10): 68/yr. Bdg 42. Day 26. Appl due: Feb. Accepted: 82%. Yield: 52%. Tests CEEB SSAT TOEFL.

  Enr 157. G 94/63. Elem 10. Sec 143. PG 4. Wh 79%. Hisp 7%. Blk 7%. Am Ind 1%. Asian 3%. Other 2%. Avg class size: 10. Fac 43. M 10/2. F 21/10. Wh 95%. Other 5%. Adv deg: 53%. In dorms 15.

  Grad '04—49. Col—49. (Smith 2, VA Commonwealth 2, Mt Holyoke 2, HI Pacific 2, Middlebury 1, Tufts 1). Alum 3875.

  Tui '04-'05: Bdg $32,100 (+$1100). Day $20,300 (+$900). Aid: Need 62 ($881,823).

  Summer: Enrich Rec. Debate. Dance. Riding. Sports. Tui Bdg $325-2000. 1-2 wks.

  Endow $2,000,000. Plant val $16,500,000. Bldgs 11. Dorms 2. Dorm rms 100. Class rms 20. Lib 10,000 vols. Labs 2. Sci labs 5. Comp labs 5. Photog labs 1. Theaters 1. Art studios 4. Music studios 7. Dance studios 1. Gyms 1. Fields 4. Pools 1. Riding rings 4. Stables 2.

  Est 1869. Nonprofit. Tri (Sept-June). Assoc NEASC.

Stoneleigh-Burnham School grew out of the 1968 merger of two old New England preparatory schools: Mary A. Burnham School, which was located in Northampton for over 90 years, and Stoneleigh-Prospect Hill School, which occupied the present 100-acre, wooded campus in residential Greenfield in the Pioneer Valley. After operating for many years solely as a high school, SBS opened a middle school division in the fall of 2004.

The college preparatory curriculum, designed for students of varying levels of ability, stresses the basics of language, mathematics, science and history. Broad course offerings include electives, a strong skills program, Advanced Placement classes in all disciplines, and English as a Second Language. These curricular features are enhanced by opportunities in the visual, performing and communicative arts.

Athletic facilities are provided for field hockey, soccer, volleyball, basketball, skiing, tennis, lacrosse, softball, dance and riding. Athletic competition is available in all major sports. The school maintains its own equestrian facilities. Competition includes jumping, equitation, dressage and showing. **See Also Page 1319**

GROTON, MA. (34 mi. WNW of Boston, MA) Suburban. Pop: 8083. Alt: 300 ft.

GROTON SCHOOL
Bdg and Day — Coed Gr 8-12

Groton, MA 01450. Farmers Row, PO Box 991. Tel: 978-448-7510. Fax: 978-448-9623.
www.groton.org   E-mail: admission_office@groton.org
Richard B. Commons, Head. BA, Univ of Virginia, MA, Stanford Univ, MA, Middlebury College. **John M. Niles, Adm.**
- **Col Prep. AP**—Fr Span Calc Stats Bio Chem Physics World_Hist Music_Theory. **Feat**—Shakespeare Ger Greek Lat Astron Ecol Archaeol Intl_Relations Bible Ethics Art_Hist Music Dance Woodworking. **Supp**—Tut.
- **Adm (Gr 8-11):** 102/yr. Bdg 89. Day 13. Appl due: Jan. Accepted: 25%. Yield: 60%. **Tests** SSAT TOEFL.
- **Enr 355.** B 140/36. G 162/17. Elem 25. Sec 330. Wh 69%. Hisp 3%. Blk 7%. Asian 11%. Other 10%. Avg class size: 13. **Fac 66.** M 33/5. F 25/3. Wh 91%. Blk 6%. Asian 3%. Adv deg: 71%. In dorms 17.
- **Grad '04—90. Col—90.** (U of VA 7, Harvard 5, Cornell 5, Princeton 4, Yale 4, Oxford-England 3). Avg SAT: 1410. Alum 3042.
- **Tui '04-'05: Bdg $35,800** (+$1400). **Day $26,850** (+$900). **Aid:** Need 101 ($2,660,000).
- Endow $193,000,000. Plant val $177,000,000. Bldgs 16. Dorm rms 184. Class rms 39. Lib 50,000 vols. Chapels 1. Sci labs 4. Comp labs 4. Auds 1. Art studios 4. Music studios 7. Dance studios 1. Arts ctrs 1. Perf arts ctrs 2. Athletic ctrs 1. Fields 10. Basketball courts 3. Squash courts 12. Pools 2. Rinks 2. Tracks 1. Boathouses 1. Fitness ctrs 1.
- **Est 1884.** Nonprofit. Episcopal. Tri (Sept-June). **Assoc** NEASC.

Rev. Endicott Peabody founded Groton in order to provide a thorough education not only for college but also for the "active work of life." Established with close links to the Episcopal Church, the school draws its present student body and faculty from many different religious backgrounds. It was Mr. Peabody's hope that many of the graduates would engage in public service, and a significant number have entered the professions of government, education, medicine and religion. Originally a six-year boarding school, Groton now offers grades 8-12 (forms II-VI) to boarding and day boys and girls. Nearly all the main school buildings on the 340-acre campus are grouped around a central green.

Open-minded in introducing innovations in advance of his peers, Mr. Peabody expanded the curriculum to include printing, woodworking, academic science in all its forms, music and studio art. His plan to have faculty and students live together to foster the students' maturity and participation in social and academic affairs continues today, with a faculty resident living in each dormitory. Additionally, every student has a faculty advisor, and sports are coached almost entirely by the teachers, thus further encouraging faculty-student relationships.

In all forms, the rigorous academic program is conducted in small classes, with emphasis on student participation and group discussion. In the upper forms, students choose from a variety of electives; seniors may pursue independent study projects and tutorials. Advanced Placement courses are part of the curriculum in most subject areas.

Boys' interscholastic competition is available in football, soccer, ice hockey, squash, basketball, cross-country, crew, lacrosse, tennis and baseball. The girls' interscholastic program offers field hockey, ice hockey, soccer, squash, cross-country, basketball, tennis, crew and lacrosse. Groton students still play fives, an English handball game introduced by Mr. Peabody. Extracurricular activities include choir, madrigals, publications, dramatics, debating, chess, an outing club, community service programs and several student associations.

LAWRENCE ACADEMY

Bdg and Day — Coed Gr 9-12

Groton, MA 01450. Powderhouse Rd, PO Box 992. Tel: 978-448-6535.
  Fax: 978-448-9208.
  www.lacademy.edu   E-mail: admiss@lacademy.edu
D. Scott Wiggins, Head. BA, Boston Univ, JD, Arizona State Univ. **Andi O'Hearn, Adm.**
  Col Prep. AP—Eng Fr Lat Span Calc Comp_Sci Music_Theory. **Feat**—Astron Ecol Irish_Hist Japan_Hist Civil_War Econ Psych Ceramics Photog Sculpt. **Supp**—ESL Rev Tut.
  Adm: 121/yr. Appl due: Feb. Accepted: 43%. Yield: 50%. **Tests** ISEE SSAT TOEFL.
  Enr 394. B 107/101. G 83/103. Sec 394. Wh 83%. Hisp 2%. Blk 4%. Asian 11%. Avg class size: 14. **Fac 55.** M 30. F 25. Adv deg: 67%. In dorms 17.
  Grad '04—92. Col—92. (Boston Col, Geo Wash, Bates, Carnegie Mellon, Tufts, Babson). Alum 4400.
  Tui '05-'06: Bdg $36,900 (+$300). **Day $28,100** (+$300). **Aid:** Need 108 ($2,100,000). Endow $14,100,000. Plant val $27,000,000. Bldgs 19. Dorms 10. Dorm rms 100. Class rms 22. Lib 20,000 vols. Sci labs 7. Lang labs 1. Theaters 1. Art studios 7. Music studios 4. Dance studios 1. Arts ctrs 1. Art galleries 1. Gyms 1. Athletic ctrs 1. Fields 8. Courts 14. Rinks 1. Student ctrs 1. Math/sci complexes 1. Radio stations 1.
  Est 1793. Nonprofit. Tri (Sept-June). **Assoc** CLS NEASC.

Founded as the coeducational Groton Academy and renamed in 1846 in honor of Amos and William Lawrence, who endowed it, this college preparatory school enrolled only boys from 1898 to 1971, when it again became coeducational. Although one of the older schools in the country, its charter having been signed by Gov. John Hancock, Lawrence is modern in method and facilities.

The school's academic program allows students to select from a wide variety of courses, including honors and Advanced Placement classes and interdisciplinary offerings. The arts, namely dance, drama, music and the visual arts, are an integral part of the learning experience. Other program features include independent study options; LA II, which allows select students to build a course of study around an area of strong interest, such as music composition, journalism, astronomy or genetics; and Winterim, which offers each student the opportunity to learn from a hands-on experience that may involve travel, on-campus activities or community service. Every pupil meets daily with his or her faculty advisor.

Athletics include football, soccer, ice and field hockey, volleyball, wrestling, skiing, baseball, basketball, cross-country, softball, lacrosse, dance, golf and tennis.
See Also Page 1190

HARDWICK, MA. (61 mi. W of Boston, MA) Rural. Pop: 2622. Alt: 880 ft.

EAGLE HILL SCHOOL
Bdg and Day — Coed Gr 8-12

Hardwick, MA 01037. 242 Old Petersham Rd, PO Box 116. Tel: 413-477-6000.
  Fax: 413-477-6837.
  www.ehs1.org   E-mail: admission@ehs1.org
Peter John McDonald, Head. BS, Purdue Univ, MEd, Cambridge College, EdD, Univ of Massachusetts-Amherst. **Dana M. Harbert, Adm.**
  Col Prep. LD. Feat—British_Lit Chin Lat Russ Polish Environ_Sci Computers Psych Philos Film Graphic_Arts Studio_Art Journ. **Supp**—Dev_Read Makeup Tut.
  Adm (Bdg Gr Gr 8-11; Day 8-10): 49/yr. Bdg 46. Day 3. Appl due: Rolling. Accepted: 52%. **Tests** IQ.
  Enr 148. B 85/8. G 52/3. Elem 6. Sec 142. Wh 95%. Blk 1%. Asian 1%. Other 3%. Avg class size: 5. **Fac 41.** M 15/2. F 23/1. Wh 97%. Hisp 1%. Am Ind 1%. Other 1%. Adv deg: 39%. In dorms 8.
  Grad '04—**24. Col**—23. (Johnson & Wales 2, Mitchell 2, Worcester Polytech 2, Northeastern U 1, Providence 1, Ithaca 1). Avg ACT: 20. Alum 1150.
  Tui '04-'05: Bdg $42,530 (+$3000). **Day $30,100** (+$500).
  Summer: Acad Enrich Rev Rem Rec. Tui Bdg $5950 (+$500). 6 wks.
  Endow $1,100,000. Plant val $12,500,000. Bldgs 15. Dorms 3. Dorm rms 141. Class rms 38. Lib 5000 vols. Sci labs 4. Comp labs 3. Dark rms 1. Art studios 3. Wood shops 1. Gyms 1. Athletic ctrs 1. Fields 1. Tennis courts 3. Pools 1. Ropes crses 1.
  Est 1967. Nonprofit. Sem (Sept-June).

One of the few independent schools designed for the adolescent who has been diagnosed with a specific learning disability, attention deficit disorder or both, Eagle Hill accepts only students of average or above-average intelligence who are free of primary emotional and behavioral difficulties. The college preparatory program allows faculty to take advantage of the pupil's strengths while also providing remediation of learning deficits. An important aspect of the curriculum is the Pragmatics Program, which assists students with their verbal and nonverbal communicational skills. Specialized training in perceptual speech and language development is also available. In addition, the residential program facilitates the development of organizational, time management and social skills.

Activities include interscholastic team sports, intramural athletics, skiing, computers, student council, newspaper, literary magazine, ecology club, a campus radio station and community service.   **See Also Pages 1358-9**

HINGHAM, MA. (10 mi. SE of Boston, MA) Suburban. Pop: 19,882. Alt: 21 ft.

DERBY ACADEMY
Day — Coed Gr PS-9

Hingham, MA 02043. 56 Burditt Ave. Tel: 781-749-0746. Fax: 781-740-2542.
www.derbyacademy.org   E-mail: admissions@derbyacademy.org

Edward R. Foley, Head. BA, St Michael's College, MEd, Univ of Vermont. **Jay K. Sadlon, Adm.**
   Pre-Prep. Feat—Fr Lat Span Computers Studio_Art Drama Music Indus_Arts Sewing. **Supp**—Rem_Read Tut.
   Adm (Gr PS-8): 60/yr. Appl due: Jan. Accepted: 32%. Yield: 71%. **Tests** ISEE.
   Enr 304. B 157. G 147. Elem 298. Sec 6. Wh 87%. Hisp 2%. Blk 3%. Am Ind 1%. Asian 7%. Avg class size: 14. **Fac 54.** M 14/1. F 33/6. Wh 100%. Adv deg: 46%.
   Grad '04—46. Prep—35. (Thayer 9, Notre Dame Acad-MA 5, Milton Acad 3, Middlesex 3, Tabor 3, Noble & Greenough 3). Alum 2149.
   Tui '04-'05: Day $12,900-20,950 (+$400). **Aid:** Need 24 ($265,099).
   Summer: Acad Enrich Rev Rem Rec. Arts. Sports. Tui Day $1950. 5 wks.
   Endow $4,500,000. Plant val $9,084,000. Bldgs 14. Class rms 27. Lib 15,000 vols. Sci labs 2. Comp labs 3. Auds 1. Theaters 1. Art studios 2. Music studios 2. Arts ctrs 1. Gyms 2. Fields 4. Basketball courts 3.
   Est 1784. Nonprofit. Sem (Sept-June).

Founded by Madame Sarah Derby and in continuous operation since 1791, Derby Academy is the oldest independent, coeducational day school in New England. The school, situated on a 27-acre campus, moved from its original site in 1965, when the trustees deeded the old academy building to the Hingham Historical Society.

The nondenominational program emphasizes a well-balanced education with challenging academics, enriching arts, physical education and competitive team sports. In addition to traditional courses, the curriculum includes studio art, pottery, woodworking, music, sewing, dramatics and computer instruction. Derby's three divisions—lower school (grades pre-K-3), middle school (grades 4-6) and upper school (grades 7-9)—provide age-appropriate settings for its student body.

Summer Arts at Derby and the summer school utilize the campus in July and August, enrolling students interested in exploring fine arts and recreational offerings taught by area professionals and providing individualized instruction in a variety of academic disciplines. Most of the school's graduates continue their secondary education at independent schools, both boarding and day, in New England.

LENOX, MA. (34 mi. SE of Albany, NY; 116 mi. W of Boston, MA) Suburban. Pop: 5077. Alt: 1210 ft.

BERKSHIRE COUNTRY DAY SCHOOL
Day — Coed Gr PS-12

Lenox, MA 01240. PO Box 867. Tel: 413-637-0755. Fax: 413-637-8927.

www.berkshirecountryday.org   E-mail: info@berkshirecountryday.org
Robert R. Peterson, Head. BA, Williams College, MEd, Fairfield Univ. **William Pinakiewicz, Adm.**
  Col Prep. AP—Eng Fr Calc Bio Physics US_Hist. **Feat**—Classics Shakespeare Greek Ital Lat Span Comp_Sci Studio_Art Theater Theater_Arts Band Chorus Music Indus_Arts. **Supp**—Dev_Read Rem_Math Rem_Read Rev Tut.
  Adm: 70/yr. Appl due: Feb. Accepted: 85%. **Tests** CTP_4 ISEE SSAT.
  Enr 353. B 177. G 176. Elem 287. Sec 66. Wh 94%. Hisp 1%. Blk 4%. Asian 1%. Avg class size: 12. **Fac 63.** M 12/4. F 34/13. Adv deg: 39%.
  Alum 800.
  Tui '02-'03: Day $7925-15,125 (+$50-2000). **Aid:** Merit 1 ($15,125). Need 83 ($802,106).
  Endow $615,000. Plant val $4,800,000. Bldgs 8. Class rms 37. Lib 5800 vols. Sci labs 4. Comp labs 2. Theaters 1. Art studios 3. Music studios 2. Wood shops 1.
  Est 1946. Nonprofit. Tri (Sept-June). **Assoc** NEASC.

Located on 79 acres neighboring Tanglewood, BCD is housed in the attractive remodeled farm buildings of the former Anson Phelps Stokes and Winthrop estates. In the early grades (grades PS-3), classes are staffed by two homeroom teachers and specialists in science, French, art, music, chorus, library, computer and physical education. Students in grades 4-8 have three homeroom teachers and subject teachers. Pupils in grades 9-12 attend classes at the Winthrop campus, a mile and a half from the main site. Honors courses are available in all disciplines.

Interscholastic and intramural soccer, lacrosse, basketball, skiing, fencing, crew, golf and swimming constitute the sports program. BCD offers elective modules in Alpine and Nordic skiing, computer programming, drama, chorus and shop, as well as internships. Travel opportunities include domestic travel options and trips to France, Italy and Spain. All students perform community service.

LEXINGTON, MA. (13 mi. NW of Boston, MA) Suburban. Pop: 30,355. Alt: 200 ft.

LEXINGTON CHRISTIAN ACADEMY
Day — Coed Gr 6-12

Lexington, MA 02420. 48 Bartlett Ave. Tel: 781-862-7850. Fax: 781-863-8503.
  www.lexchristian.org   E-mail: admissions@lexchristian.org
J. Barry Koops, Head. AB, Calvin College, MA, PhD, Univ of Michigan. **Jill C. Schuhmacher, Adm.**
  Col Prep. AP—Eng Fr Span Calc Bio US_Hist. **Feat**—Lat Russ Computers Relig Studio_Art Drama Journ. **Supp**—ESL LD Tut.
  Adm: 95/yr. Appl due: Feb. **Tests** SSAT.
  Enr 350. B 178. G 172. Elem 114. Sec 236. Wh 76%. Hisp 2%. Blk 14%. Asian 8%. Avg class size: 17. **Fac 43.** M 18/4. F 19/2. Adv deg: 65%.
  Grad '04—54. **Col**—54. (Gordon, Boston U, Tufts, Emerson, Pepperdine, Grove City). Avg SAT: 1223. Alum 1712.
  Tui '04-'05: Day $13,500-15,250 (+$400).
  Summer: Rec. 1-7 wks.
  Endow $2,100,000. Plant val $2,800,000. Bldgs 1. Class rms 16. Lib 10,000 vols. Labs 4. Art studios 2. Music studios 2. Gyms 1. Fields 3. Courts 2. Pools 1.

MA   *Leading Private Schools*   226

Est 1946. Nonprofit. Nondenom Christian. Sem (Sept-June). **Assoc** NEASC.

Originally located in Boston and known as Boston Christian High School, the school moved to Cambridge in 1949 as the Christian High School. Since 1965, it has been located on a 30-acre campus in historic Lexington and, in 1970, the school changed its name to Lexington Christian Academy.

The evangelical Christian faith and religion courses are integral parts of LCA's college preparatory curriculum, which also features the fine arts, music, drama and computer science. Honors and Advanced Placement courses are available at the upper school level (grades 9-12), and various electives during these years address student interests and talents. A tutorial program serves highly motivated middle and upper school pupils who have mild learning disabilities.

An annual arts festival is among LCA's broad extracurricular programs. The interscholastic sports program comprises softball, basketball, baseball, wrestling, soccer, lacrosse, cross-country, golf, field hockey and cheerleading.

See Also Page 1194

LINCOLN, MA. (16 mi. WNW of Boston, MA) Suburban. Pop: 8056. Alt: 258 ft.

THE CARROLL SCHOOL
Day — Coed Gr 2-8

Lincoln, MA 01773. 25 Baker Bridge Rd. Tel: 781-259-8342. Fax: 781-259-8852.
www.carrollschool.org   E-mail: admissions@carrollschool.org
Steve Wilkins, Head. BA, Colgate Univ, MEd, Harvard Univ, PhD, Johns Hopkins Univ.
Veronica Kenney, Adm.

LD. Feat—Computers Studio_Art Drama Music Woodworking. **Supp**—Rem_Math Rem_Read Tut.
Adm (Gr 2-6): 72/yr. Appl due: Rolling. **Tests** IQ.
Enr 233. B 135. G 98. Elem 233. Wh 93%. Hisp 4%. Blk 3%. Avg class size: 7. Uniform.
Fac 72. M 9. F 51/12. Adv deg: 43%.
Grad '04—34. Alum 1000.
Tui '04-'05: Day $29,500. Aid: Need ($200,000).
Summer: Acad Rem Rec. Tui Day $3750. 5 wks.
Endow $2,800,000. Plant val $5,000,000. Bldgs 4. Comp labs 3. Auds 1. Art studios 1. Gyms 1. Fields 2.
Est 1968. Nonprofit. Quar (Sept-June). **Assoc** NEASC.

Carroll specializes in the education and the remediation of children of average to superior intelligence who have been diagnosed with dyslexia or a specific language disability. The program helps the language-disabled child grow to the point where he or she can successfully return to a regular public or private school setting. Children are grouped according to language competency and age, as well as physical and emotional maturity. In all subjects, teachers use a multisensory approach to learning and place emphasis on improving reading, writing and organizational skills.

A full academic program includes language, math, science, social studies, drama, art, woodworking and an Outward Bound-type program. Sports and physical education are offered at all levels, with interscholastic competition available in soccer, basketball and track. After-school electives are numerous and entail additional fees. Computers are employed in math and language classes: Younger students learn LOGO, while junior high pupils develop word processing skills.

The day camp complements the academic summer school. The academic summer program includes one-on-one tutoring and small-group instruction in language and math, in addition to a choice of electives. It offers a full range of activities aimed at building self-confidence.

MANCHESTER, MA. (21 mi. NE of Boston, MA) Suburban. Pop: 5228. Alt: 30 ft.

BROOKWOOD SCHOOL
Day — Coed Gr PS-8

Manchester, MA 01944. 1 Brookwood Rd, PO Box 1429. Tel: 978-526-4500.
Fax: 978-526-9303.
www.brookwood.edu E-mail: info@brookwood.edu
John C. Peterman, Head. BA, Wittenberg Univ, MEd, Loyola Univ of Chicago. **Barbara W. DiGuiseppe, Adm.**
  Pre-Prep. Feat—Fr Span Studio_Art Drama Music. **Supp**—Dev_Read Rem_Read Tut.
  Adm: 56/yr. Appl due: Feb. Tests IQ.
  Enr 395. Elem 395. Wh 94%. Blk 4%. Asian 2%. Avg class size: 18. **Fac 51.**
  Grad '04—53. Prep—50. (Pingree, Gov Dummer, Phillips Exeter, Groton, Brooks, St Paul's Sch-NH). Alum 1259.
  Tui '03-'04: Day $9800-16,500 (+$1500). Aid: Need 30 ($355,000).
  Summer: Rec. Tui Day $260/2-wk ses. 8 wks.
  Endow $1,600,000. Plant val $5,386,000. Bldgs 3. Class rms 40. Lib 9300 vols. Sci labs 3. Comp labs 1. Art studios 1. Music studios 1. Photog studios 1. Gyms 2. Fields 4. Greenhouses 1. Ponds 1.
  Est 1956. Nonprofit. Tri (Sept-June).

Founded by Philip Cutler, formerly at St. George's School in Newport, RI, this well-equipped elementary school advanced from the early grades to encompass grade 8 in 1963. Located on a 26-acre campus on the North Shore, the school's plant includes playing fields, a pond, and facilities for the performing and visual arts.

The broad academic curriculum emphasizes reading, mathematics and critical-thinking skills. A homeroom program in grades 4-8 encourages interaction among peers and younger children, while giving older students the opportunity to meet with homeroom teachers to hold discussions, view films, hear guest speakers and participate in other nonacademic activities. Interscholastic sports in grades 7 and 8, community service, student government, publications, field trips and a multicultural assembly program supplement academics. Before- and after-school programs are also available.

MARBLEHEAD, MA. (14 mi. NE of Boston, MA) Suburban. Pop: 20,377. Alt: 65 ft.

TOWER SCHOOL
Day — Coed Gr PS-9

Marblehead, MA 01945. 75 W Shore Dr. Tel: 781-631-5800. Fax: 781-631-2292.
www.towerschool.org   E-mail: admissions@towerschool.org
Peter S. Philip, Head. BA, Yale Univ, MALS, Wesleyan Univ. **Elizabeth D. Parker, Adm.**
  Pre-Prep. **Feat**—Lat Span Environ_Sci Computers Studio_Art Woodworking. **Supp**—Tut.
  Adm: 48/yr. Appl due: Feb.
  Enr 303. B 145. G 158. Wh 95%. Blk 3%. Asian 1%. Other 1%. Avg class size: 17. **Fac 42.** M 9/2. F 26/5. Wh 100%. Adv deg: 45%.
  Grad '04—35. Prep—23. (St John's Prep-MA 4, Brewster 2, Middlesex 2, Phillips Acad 2, St George's Sch-RI 2, Deerfield Acad 2). Alum 1025.
  Tui '04-'05: Day $9800-18,400. Aid: Need 39 ($442,755).
  Summer: Rec. Tui Day $595-930. 2-3 wks.
  Endow $1,300,000. Plant val $6,300,000. Bldgs 1. Class rms 25. Lib 10,000 vols. Sci labs 2. Comp labs 2. Theaters 1. Art studios 2. Music studios 2. Gyms 1. Fields 1. Pools 1.
  Est 1912. Nonprofit. Quar (Sept-June).

Established by Adeline Lane Tower in Salem and moved to Marblehead in 1941, the school emphasizes a strong program with offerings in reading, math, science, history, geography, global studies, Spanish, Latin, art, woodworking, music and physical education. Interscholastic sports include soccer, basketball, squash, tennis, wrestling and lacrosse. The school encourages all students to participate in service projects. Pupils enroll from a wide area of the North Shore, and the majority go on to New England preparatory schools.

MARION, MA. (35 mi. ESE of Providence, RI; 46 mi. SSE of Boston, MA) Suburban. Pop: 5123. Alt: 38 ft.

TABOR ACADEMY
Bdg and Day — Coed Gr 9-12

Marion, MA 02738. Front St. Tel: 508-748-2000. Fax: 508-748-0353.
www.taboracademy.org   E-mail: admissions@taboracademy.org
Jay S. Stroud, Head. BA, Carleton College, MA, Dartmouth College, EdM, Columbia Univ. **Andrew L. McCain, Adm.**
  Col Prep. AP—Eng Fr Ger Lat Span Stats Chem Physics Eur_Hist US_Hist World_Hist Econ. **Feat**—Creative_Writing Greek Astron Ecol Oceanog Meteorology Japan_Hist Vietnam_War Milit_Hist Govt World_Relig Ceramics Studio_Art Music Seamanship. **Supp**—ESL.
  Adm: 153/yr. Bdg 110. Day 43. Appl due: Jan. Accepted: 62%. **Tests** ISEE SSAT TOEFL.
  Enr 492. B 193/80. G 156/63. Sec 492. Wh 85%. Hisp 4%. Blk 4%. Asian 7%. Avg class size: 12. **Fac 77.** M 50/1. F 23/3. Adv deg: 54%. In dorms 50.
  Grad '04—115. Col—113. (U of VT 8, Boston U 6, Boston Col 4, Brown 3, NYU 3, CT Col 3). Avg SAT: 1230. Avg SSAT: 62%. Alum 6038.

Tui '04-'05: Bdg $33,300 (+$500). **Day $23,500** (+$350). **Aid:** Need 162 ($2,600,000).
Summer: Enrich Rec. Tui Bdg $4800-5800. 4-6 wks. Tui Day $530-2500. 2-6 wks.
Endow $33,000,000. Plant val $50,000,000. Bldgs 43. Dorms 19. Class rms 72. Libs 1. Comp labs 3. Auds 4. Theaters 3. Art studios 2. Music studios 10. Dance studios 1. Gyms 1. Fields 9. Tennis courts 11. Squash courts 9. Field houses 1. Rinks 1. Tracks 1.
Est 1876. Nonprofit. Sem (Sept-June). **Assoc** CLS NEASC.

Endowed and named by a wealthy whaling family, Tabor occupies a waterfront location near Cape Cod on Buzzards Bay. The school's curriculum, size and facilities have been increased over the years. Girls were readmitted as day students in 1979, and a boarding section was added in 1982.

The curriculum includes Advanced Placement courses and honors sections in all major disciplines. In addition to the basic subjects, pupils may study ecology, oceanography, creative writing, ceramics, law, government, acting and music. Opportunities for celestial navigation, piloting and seamanship are available aboard the school's 92-foot schooner, *Tabor Boy,* which cruises the waters of southern New England during the fall and the spring. Tabor is a nationally recognized Naval Honor School, allowing the school to nominate students to the US service academies.

Extracurricular activities include sailing, crew, football, soccer, field hockey, squash, ice hockey, basketball, tennis, wrestling, track, lacrosse, baseball, softball and cross-country. There is also a school radio station, a speech and debate program, theater, jazz band, music ensembles, orchestra, chorus, madrigal singers and community service opportunities. Tabor also publishes a literary magazine and a school newspaper.

MARLBOROUGH, MA. (27 mi. W of Boston, MA) Suburban. Pop: 36,255. Alt: 700 ft.

HILLSIDE SCHOOL

Bdg and Day — Boys Gr 5-9

Marlborough, MA 01752. 404 Robin Hill Rd. Tel: 508-485-2824. Fax: 508-485-4420.
www.hillsideschool.net   E-mail: admissions@hillsideschool.net
David Z. Beecher, Head. BA, Lake Forest College. **Thomas O'Dell, Adm.**
  Pre-Prep. Gen Acad. Underachiever. Feat—Fr Span Computers Studio_Art Woodworking Study_Skills. **Supp—**Dev_Read ESL LD Rem_Math Rem_Read Rev Tut.
  Adm: 41/yr. Appl due: Rolling. Accepted: 81%. **Tests** IQ SSAT TOEFL.
  Enr 120. B 75/45. Elem 73. Sec 27. Wh 70%. Hisp 2%. Blk 13%. Asian 10%. Other 5%. Avg class size: 10. **Fac 26.** M 18. F 8. Wh 90%. Hisp 2%. Blk 8%. Adv deg: 34%. In dorms 12.
  Grad '04—18. Prep—18. (Dublin 3, Brewster 2, Wilbraham & Monson 2, Pomfret 1, Concord Acad 1, Bancroft 1). Avg SSAT: 30%. Alum 400.
  Tui '04-'05: Bdg $38,500 (+$750). **5-Day Bdg $34,600** (+$750). **Day $21,700** (+$300). **Aid:** Need 36 ($700,000).
  Summer: Acad Enrich Rec. ESL. Soccer. Tui Bdg $3000. Tui Day $1500. 4 wks.
  Endow $6,000,000. Plant val $20,000,000. Bldgs 15. Dorms 5. Dorm rms 15. Class rms 13. Lib 5000 vols. Sci labs 2. Lang labs 1. Comp labs 1. Auds 1. Art studios 1. Music studios 1. Gyms 1. Fields 4. Courts 2. Pools 1.

Est 1901. Nonprofit. Tri (Sept-June).

Hillside School was founded as a farm school by Miss Charlotte Drinkwater and her sister, Mrs. Mary Drinkwater Warren, on a farm near the western boundary of Greenwich. When the original site was flooded in 1927 to create the Quabbin Reservoir, the school relocated to its current location on 200 acres of fields, ponds and forestland.

Hillside provides a structured and supportive environment for boys of average to above-average intelligence who have been underachieving in other school settings. In grades 7-9, the academic program includes English, history, science, math, studio art, wood shop, and French or Spanish; children in grades 5 and 6 receive instruction in math, language arts, social studies, reading, art and science. The curriculum is supplemented with a tutorial program that provides individualized support for boys who require extra attention in the areas of social skills, language remediation and organization. Programs for boys with minor learning disabilities and those with attentional disorders, as well as regular evaluations of each pupil's social and academic behavior, are other important elements of school life.

All students must participate in a sport or an athletic activity each trimester. Track and field, soccer, ice hockey, lacrosse, basketball, baseball, wrestling and cross-country constitute the competitive team sports program, while downhill skiing, hiking, eco team, intramurals and drama are the recreational options. Selected boys who are interested in assisting with the farm program live on the farm and are responsible for getting up early each morning to feed and water the animals.

MILTON, MA. (7 mi. SSW of Boston, MA) Suburban. Pop: 26,062. Alt: 24 ft.

MILTON ACADEMY

Bdg — Coed Gr 9-12; Day — Coed K-12

Milton, MA 02186. 170 Centre St. Tel: 617-898-2227. Fax: 617-898-1701.
www.milton.edu E-mail: admissions@milton.edu
Robin A. Robertson, Head. BA, Univ of Pennsylvania, PhD, Harvard Univ. Paul Rebuck, Adm.

Col Prep. AP—Fr Lat Span Calc Stats Comp_Sci Comp_Govt & Pol Econ Psych US_Govt & Pol Art_Hist Studio_Art. **Feat**—Creative_Writing Poetry Chin Greek Anat & Physiol Astron Ecol Environ_Sci Genetics Geol Marine_Biol/Sci Programming Middle_Eastern_Hist Asian_Hist African-Amer_Hist Anthro Philos Drama Music_Hist Music_Theory Dance. **Supp**—Rev Tut.

Adm (Bdg Gr 9-11; Day K-9): 213/yr. Bdg 114. Day 99. Appl due: Jan. Accepted: 21%. Yield: 70%. **Tests** ISEE SSAT.

Enr 991. Elem 300. Sec 691. Wh 68%. Hisp 3%. Blk 9%. Asian 13%. Other 7%. Avg class size: 14. **Fac 135.** Adv deg: 100%. In dorms 37.

Grad '04—179. Col—179. (Harvard 12, NYU 9, Tufts 9, Cornell 8, Boston Col 7, Brown 6). Avg SAT: 1360. Alum 8070.

Tui '04-'05: Bdg $32,725 (+$1250). **Day $25,675** (+$900).

Summer: Rec. Computers. Sports. **Supp**—Rev Tut.

Endow $140,000,000. Plant val $38,000,000. Bldgs 62. Dorms 8. Lib 50,000 vols. Labs 8. Lang labs 1. Photog labs 1. Art studios 6. Music studios 5. Perf arts ctrs 1. Art galleries

1. Gyms 4. Athletic ctrs 1. Fields 12. Tennis courts 13. Squash courts 7. Rinks 1. **Est 1798.** Nonprofit. Sem (Sept-June). **Assoc** CLS NEASC.

In 1798, Milton was chartered to provide education for the families then living in the small colonial village and on farms scattered through the forested Blue Hills area. Though Milton was originally coeducational, the academy was divided into separate schools in 1901, reacting to a marked increase in the interest in separate education for young women. For many years, the Milton Academy boys' school and girls' school maintained separate faculties, facilities and student bodies; in 1973, the academy returned to coeducation. Boarders enroll from numerous states and foreign countries, and day students, who commute from many communities of Metropolitan Boston, are invited to participate in the full schedule of on-campus weekend activities. Although the school is bordered to the south by 6000 acres of preservation land, it is located ten miles south of Boston, which is accessible by subway.

The academy occupies a 125-acre campus. The upper (grades 9-12) and middle (grades 6-8) schools share facilities, while the lower school (grades K-5) is housed in separate buildings on the same campus.

The academic program combines demanding training with innovative approaches. Students are placed at course levels and in sections according to interest and ability, rather than grade, sex or age. The curriculum is varied, with many electives offered in all areas of study. The required one-year arts program offers creative writing, dance, drama, speech, improvisational music, studio art and photography. Students may apply for an independent study project under faculty guidance. Seniors may design five-week spring term projects with faculty approval and supervision.

Activities and organizations are fully coeducational. The chamber singers have traveled to Romania, Kenya, Germany, the Czech Republic and Hawaii, and student publications, orchestra, speech team, the visual and graphic arts, and drama are prominent in school life. Milton has its own six-week exchange program for foreign study in England, France, Spain or China, and the academy is also an affiliate of School Year Abroad. In 1983, Milton purchased the Mountain School in Vershire Center, VT, to create a semester-long program for juniors from Milton and other member schools (see separate listing).

Sports and physical education constitute a vital school program. The usual interscholastic and intramural sports are offered, as are outdoor education, running club and sailing. Some students undertake special projects one season a year in lieu of a sports commitment.

NATICK, MA. (17 mi. WSW of Boston, MA) Suburban. Pop: 32,170. Alt: 158 ft.

WALNUT HILL SCHOOL
Bdg and Day — Coed Gr 9-12

Natick, MA 01760. 12 Highland St. **Tel: 508-650-5020. Fax: 508-655-3726.**
www.walnuthillarts.org E-mail: admissions@walnuthillarts.org
Stephanie B. Perrin, Head. AB, Boston Univ, MAT, Harvard Univ. **Matthew A. Derr, Adm.**
Col Prep. Perform_Arts Visual_Arts. Feat—Creative_Writing Fr Span Stats Comp_Sci

Art_Hist Studio_Art Visual_Arts Theater Music_Hist Music_Theory Ballet Dance. **Supp**—ESL Tut.
Adm: 113/yr. Bdg 87. Day 26. Appl due: Feb. Accepted: 46%. **Tests** SSAT TOEFL.
Enr 280. Sec 280. Avg class size: 14. **Fac 41.** M 18/2. F 18/3. Adv deg: 70%. In dorms 7.
Grad '04—82. **Col**—80. (Juilliard, NYU, New England Conservatory of Music, Boston U, Boston Conservatory, Sch of the Art Inst of Chicago). Alum 4500.
Tui '04-'05: Bdg $33,200 (+$1650-4000). **Day** $26,700 (+$1650-4000). **Aid:** Need 125 ($1,898,675).
Summer: Dance. Tui Bdg $4150. 4 wks. Theater. Tui Bdg $4400. 5 wks.
Endow $6,135,000. Plant val $20,000,000. Dorm rms 145. Class rms 25. Lib 7500 vols. Labs 3. Lang labs 1. Writing ctrs 1. Theaters 2. Art studios 6. Music studios 6. Dance studios 5. Arts ctrs 1. Practice rms 20. Fields 1. Courts 4. Pools 1.
Est 1893. Nonprofit. Sem (Sept-June). **Assoc** CLS NEASC.

Walnut Hill was founded as a college preparatory school for Wellesley College. In 1971, the trustees voted to form a coeducational cocurricular program, fully integrating the academic program with training in the fine and performing arts.

The curriculum provides a broad range of both college preparatory and performing and visual arts courses, with requirements in English, mathematics, science, foreign language and social science. Each student must also be accepted into one of the arts departments and must major in music, ballet, theater, visual arts or creative writing. The school program is enhanced by an affiliation with the New England Conservatory of Music. This combination of arts study and academics provides students with the preparation necessary for entrance into universities, conservatories, art colleges and professional dance companies.

NEEDHAM, MA. (12 mi. WSW of Boston, MA) Suburban. Pop: 28,911. Alt: 169 ft.

ST. SEBASTIAN'S SCHOOL
Day — Boys Gr 7-12

Needham, MA 02492. 1191 Greendale Ave. Tel: 781-449-5200. Fax: 781-449-5630.
www.stsebs.org   E-mail: admissions@stsebs.org
William L. Burke III, Head. BA, Middlebury College, MA, Boston College. David M. Emond, **Adm.**
Col Prep. AP—Eng Lat Span Calc Bio Chem Physics Eur_Hist US_Hist Studio_Art Music_Theory. **Feat**—Writing Greek Stats Govt Ethics Ceramics. **Supp**—Rev Tut.
Adm: 67/yr. Appl due: Feb. Accepted: 36%. Yield: 61%. **Tests** ISEE SSAT.
Enr 342. B 342. Elem 98. Sec 244. Wh 88%. Hisp 2%. Blk 6%. Asian 4%. Avg class size: 11. **Fac 56.** M 47. F 9. Wh 96%. Blk 2%. Asian 2%. Adv deg: 62%.
Grad '04—55. **Col**—55. (Boston Col 13, Holy Cross 3, Loyola U-LA 3, Harvard 3, Georgetown 3, Providence 3). Avg SAT: 1290. Alum 1938.
Tui '04-'05: Day $24,000 (+$750). **Aid:** Need 79 ($1,367,000).
Endow $8,800,000. Plant val $22,802,000. Bldgs 5. Class rms 32. Lib 10,000 vols. Sci labs 5. Comp labs 2. Auds 1. Theaters 1. Art studios 2. Music studios 1. Gyms 2. Fields 5. Courts 6. Rinks 1.
Est 1941. Roman Catholic. Quar (Sept-June). **Assoc** NEASC.

Established by Cardinal O'Connell, this college preparatory school combines the traditions of the New England independent school with Catholic education. The col-

MA New England States

lege preparatory curriculum is highly structured, with required courses in English, foreign language, social science, mathematics and laboratory science. Opportunities exist for honors and Advanced Placement work. Interscholastic athletics and an active extracurricular program complement academics.

NEWTON, MA. (10 mi. W of Boston, MA) Suburban. Pop: 83,829. Alt: 33 ft. Area also includes West Newton.

FESSENDEN SCHOOL

Bdg — Boys Gr 5-9; Day — Boys K-9

West Newton, MA 02465. 250 Waltham St. Tel: 617-630-2300. Fax: 617-630-2303.
www.fessenden.org E-mail: admissions@fessenden.org

Andrew W. Berry, Head. BA, Univ of Pennsylvania, MEd, Harvard Univ. **Caleb W. Thomson, Adm.**

Pre-Prep. Feat—Fr Lat Span Computers Ceramics Photog Studio_Art Video_Production Drama Music. **Supp**—ESL Tut.

Adm (Bdg Gr 5-9; Day K-7): 117/yr. Bdg 52. Day 65. **Tests** IQ ISEE SSAT.

Enr 476. B 103/373. Elem 423. Sec 53. Wh 91%. Blk 6%. Asian 3%. Avg class size: 11. **Fac 94.** M 32/6. F 32/24. Adv deg: 60%. In dorms 43.

Grad '04—56. Prep—54. (Middlesex, Milton Acad, Suffield, St George's Sch-RI, St Mark's Sch-MA, Phillips Exeter). Alum 3763.

Tui '04-'05: Bdg $35,700-36,700 (+$1000). **5-Day Bdg** $30,200 (+$1000). **Day** $17,500-23,700 (+$300). **Aid:** Need 42 ($660,000).

Summer: Coed. Ages 10-16. Acad. ESL. Tui Bdg $5225. 5 wks.

Endow $13,000,000. Plant val $40,000,000. Bldgs 25. Dorms 7. Dorm rms 105. Class rms 39. Lib 17,000 vols. Sci labs 4. Comp labs 4. Art studios 5. Music studios 3. Arts ctrs 1. Gyms 3. Athletic ctrs 1. Fields 7. Courts 13. Pools 2. Rinks 1.

Est 1903. Nonprofit. Tri (Sept-June).

Founded by Frederick J. Fessenden, the school balances a traditional curriculum with instruction in the visual and performing arts and training in athletics. Honors, regular and moderately paced sections accommodate individual needs in many subject areas. The lower school program emphasizes the basic skills of reading, oral and written language, and mathematics, enriched by courses in social studies, science and geography. In addition, Fessenden begins instruction in Spanish at the kindergarten level.

Team sports begin in grade 5, and boys choose one athletic offering every season from a varied list of competitive team, intramural and recreational sports. Ninth-grade students are required to complete ten hours of community service. The school's nonacademic programs (NAP) provide trips and activities for recreation and relaxation every weekend. Among the numerous options, which take advantage of the resources of Boston and New England, are seasonal outdoor activities, cultural and sporting events, school dances, sightseeing trips and movie nights.

NEWTON COUNTRY DAY SCHOOL OF THE SACRED HEART
Day — Girls Gr 5-12

Newton, MA 02458. 785 Centre St. Tel: 617-244-4246. Fax: 617-965-5313.
 www.newtoncountryday.org   E-mail: admissions@newtoncountryday.org
Sr. Barbara Rogers, RSCJ, Head. BA, Manhattanville College, MBA, Yale Univ. **Mary E. Delaney, Adm.**
  Col Prep. AP—Eng Fr Lat Span Calc Stats Bio Chem Physics Eur_Hist US_Hist Comp_Govt & Pol US_Govt & Pol Studio_Art. **Feat**—Creative_Writing Anat & Physiol Computers Psych Relig World_Relig Art_Hist Photog Visual_Arts Drama Music Music_Theory Dance Journ. **Supp**—Rev Tut.
  Adm (Gr 5-11): 80/yr. Appl due: Feb. Accepted: 36%. Yield: 58%. **Tests** ISEE SSAT.
  Enr 365. G 365. Elem 149. Sec 216. Wh 82%. Hisp 5%. Blk 7%. Asian 3%. Other 3%. Avg class size: 16. **Fac 67.** M 19/2. F 38/8. Wh 87%. Hisp 5%. Blk 3%. Asian 5%. Adv deg: 74%.
  Grad '04—51. Col—51. (Boston Col 10, Holy Cross 2, Bowdoin 1, U of CA-Berkeley 1, Yale 1, Columbia 1). Avg SAT: 1280. Alum 1881.
  Tui '04-'05: Day $24,950 (+$500). **Aid:** Need 87 ($1,395,000).
  Endow $8,100,000. Plant val $21,700,000. Bldgs 5. Class rms 37. Libs 1. Sci labs 6. Comp labs 1. Theaters 1. Art studios 3. Music studios 2. Dance studios 1. Gyms 1. Fields 2. Courts 4.
  Est 1880. Nonprofit. Roman Catholic. Quar (Sept-June). **Assoc** NEASC.

A member of the international Network of Sacred Heart Schools, NCDS provides a college preparatory curriculum for highly motivated girls from over 65 communities in the Greater Boston area. At all grade levels, the program is designed to be developmentally appropriate. The middle school curriculum (grades 5-8) emphasizes the development of writing, reading and math skills, while the upper school program (grades 9-12) culminates in Advanced Placement classes in the major disciplines during the junior and senior years. Qualified pupils may earn college credit for courses taken at nearby Boston College.

Students participate in a wide range of activities, including student government, Amnesty International, Model UN, debate, yearbook, drama, chorus, dance and interest clubs. The sports program offers interscholastic competition in soccer, field hockey, cross-country, basketball, ice hockey, volleyball, tennis, lacrosse, squash, golf, softball and sailing.

NORTHAMPTON, MA. (39 mi. N of Hartford, CT; 85 mi. W of Boston, MA) Suburban. Pop: 28,978. Alt: 124 ft.

SMITH COLLEGE CAMPUS SCHOOL
Day — Coed Gr K-6

Northampton, MA 01063. Gill Hall, Prospect St. Tel: 413-585-3270. Fax: 413-585-3285.
 www.smith.edu/sccs   E-mail: mlitwin@smith.edu
Cathy Hofer Reid, Prin. BA, Hamline Univ, MS, Utah State Univ, PhD, Univ of Connecticut. **Maureen Litwin, Adm.**
  Pre-Prep. Gen Acad. Feat—Span Computers Studio_Art Music. **Supp**—Tut.
  Adm: 25/yr. Appl due: Mar. Accepted: 44%.

Enr 263. B 135. G 128. Elem 263. Wh 83%. Hisp 5%. Blk 4%. Am Ind 1%. Asian 5%. Other 2%. Avg class size: 20. **Fac 22.** M 5/1. F 11/5. Wh 96%. Blk 4%. Adv deg: 100%.
Grad '04—41. Prep—24. (Williston Northampton, Eaglebrook, Pioneer Valley, Wilbraham & Monson, MacDuffie).
Tui '03-'04: Day $7225 (+$100-275). **Aid:** Need 68 ($218,500).
Plant val $2,000,000. Bldgs 2. Class rms 20. Lib 9000 vols. Labs 1. Art studios 1. Music studios 1. Gyms 1. Fields 2.
Est 1926. Nonprofit. Sem (Sept-May).

Under the auspices of the Smith College department of education and child study, the Campus School enrolls children of Northampton and surrounding towns in the Connecticut River Valley. The curriculum, which emphasizes concept mastery and skill development in the core subjects, includes programs in art, music, Spanish, computers and physical education.

NORTHFIELD, MA. (66 mi. N of Hartford, CT; 77 mi. WNW of Boston, MA) Suburban. Pop: 1141. Alt: 300 ft.

LINDEN HILL SCHOOL
Bdg — Boys Ages 9-16

Northfield, MA 01360. 154 S Mountain Rd. Tel: 413-498-2906. Fax: 413-498-2908.
www.lindenhs.org   E-mail: office@lindenhs.org
James A. McDaniel, Head. BA, Hamilton College, MA, Columbia Univ.
  Pre-Prep. LD. Feat—Computers Studio_Art Drama Music. **Supp**—Dev_Read ESL Rem_Math Rem_Read Tut.
Adm: 8/yr. Appl due: Rolling. Accepted: 90%. **Tests** IQ.
Enr 25. B 25. Wh 95%. Hisp 5%. Avg class size: 3. **Fac 13.** M 10. F 3. Adv deg: 30%. In dorms 4.
Grad '04—4. Prep—4. (Gow, Eagle Hill-MA, Winchendon, Gunnery). Alum 525.
Tui '04-'05: Bdg $38,800 (+$1000). **Aid:** Need 5 ($86,000).
Summer: Acad Rev Rem Rec. Tui Bdg $4750. 4½ wks.
Plant val $4,000,000. Bldgs 10. Dorms 4. Dorm rms 26. Class rms 17. Lib 3000 vols. Sci labs 2. Lang labs 4. Comp labs 1. Art studios 1. Wood shops 1. Gyms 1. Fields 1. Rinks 1. Stables 1.
Est 1961. Nonprofit. Tri (Sept-May). **Assoc** NEASC.

Linden Hill utilizes the Orton-Gillingham approach in remediating dyslexia and language-based learning differences. The multisensory approach to teaching and learning in all classes is geared to overcoming language deficiency and developing confidence. Residence of two to three years is typical, and boys are prepared to enter many leading preparatory schools.

Frequent trips to historic and interesting sites, recreation and outdoor activities make use of the attractive South Mountain campus and environs. Sports include skiing, soccer, tennis, biking, swimming and skating. The attractive campus occupies 130 acres. **See Also Page 1368**

NORTHFIELD MOUNT HERMON SCHOOL
Bdg and Day — Coed Gr 9-PG

Northfield, MA 01360. 206 Main St. Tel: 413-498-3227. Fax: 413-498-3152.
www.nmhschool.org   E-mail: admission@nmhschool.org
Thomas W. Sturtevant, Head. BA, Tufts Univ, MA, Stanford Univ. **Deborah J. Wright, Adm.**

> **Col Prep. AP**—Eng Fr Lat Span Calc Comp_Sci Bio Chem Physics Eur_Hist US_Hist Econ Psych Studio_Art Music_Theory. **Feat**—Creative_Writing Shakespeare Chin Russ Astron Bioethics Botany Ecol Geol Anthro Foreign_Policy Bible Ethics Philos Relig Theater Dance Outdoor_Ed. **Supp**—ESL Rev Tut.
>
> **Adm:** 263/yr. Bdg 209. Day 54. Accepted: 56%. Yield: 47%. **Tests** CEEB ISEE SSAT TOEFL.
>
> **Enr 886.** B 374/99. G 313/100. Sec 830. PG 56. Avg class size: 13. **Fac 180.** Adv deg: 68%.
>
> **Grad '04—331. Col—317.** (Boston U 19, Geo Wash 11, U of IL-Urbana 10, U of VT 10, Wesleyan U 9, Cornell 6). Avg SAT: 1194. Avg ACT: 24. Alum 26,000.
>
> **Tui '04-'05: Bdg $33,000** (+$1450-2050). **Day $24,400** (+$1525). **Aid:** Need 381 ($6,569,255).
>
> **Summer:** Acad Enrich. Tui Bdg $4800. Tui Day $2700. 5 wks.
>
> Endow $100,000,000. Plant val $163,396,000. Bldgs 183. Dorms 20. Dorm rms 515. Class rms 92. Lib 100,000 vols. Chapels 2. Sci labs 15. Lang labs 2. Comp labs 2. Auds 1. Theaters 2. Art studios 12. Music studios 23. Gyms 3. Fields 27. Tennis courts 20. Pools 2. Rinks 1.
>
> **Est 1879.** Nonprofit. Tri (Sept-June). **Assoc** CLS NEASC.

In 1879, Dwight L. Moody founded the Northfield Seminary for young ladies. Two years later, he founded Mount Hermon School for boys. Located on opposite banks of the Connecticut River, the schools were associated from the beginning in a variety of social, artistic and religious endeavors. In 1971, the schools joined to form a single coeducational institution on two campuses. Then, in the fall of 2005, NMH consolidated school operations onto the Mount Hermon campus.

The college preparatory program contains curricular teams in the following areas: the humanities, mathematics, world languages, the fine and performing arts, physical education and library media. Certain subject areas include as many as four levels of instruction, and a number of electives are also provided. The school also participates in an international studies program that permits juniors and seniors to live in New Zealand, Egypt, South Africa, Costa Rica, Australia, Italy, Ireland, Greece, France, Germany, the Dominican Republic or China; summer study options include an intensive language program in Spain. Students who develop appropriate apprenticeship placement also earn credit.

All students participate in a work program and contribute to the operation of the school community through a variety of jobs. The outreach volunteer program, offered on an extracurricular basis, allows students to work at elementary schools, nursing homes, soup kitchens, animal shelters and other area service organizations.

Extracurricular activities include publications, a radio station, choir, band, orchestras, dance and theatrical productions, interest clubs, and athletics ranging from interscholastic teams to intramurals to recreational programs.

OSTERVILLE, MA. (55 mi. ESE of Providence, RI; 59 mi. SSE of Boston, MA) Suburban. Pop: 2911. Alt: 70 ft.

CAPE COD ACADEMY
Day — Coed Gr K-12

Osterville, MA 02655. 50 Osterville-W Barnstable Rd, PO Box 469. Tel: 508-428-5400.
Fax: 508-428-0701.
www.capecodacademy.org   E-mail: admissions@capecodacademy.org
Thomas M. Evans, Head. AB, Dartmouth College. Warner James, Adm.
- Col Prep. Feat—Fr Lat Span Comp_Sci Studio_Art Music. Supp—Tut.
- Adm: 75/yr. Appl due: Feb. Accepted: 40%. Tests ISEE SSAT.
- Enr 400. Elem 228. Sec 172. Wh 96%. Hisp 2%. Blk 1%. Asian 1%. Avg class size: 14.
- Fac 65. Adv deg: 75%.
- Grad '04—40. Col—40. (Brown, Colby, Boston U, US Coast Guard Acad, Col of Charleston, St Lawrence). Avg SAT: 1224. Alum 250.
- Tui '04-'05: Day $13,500-16,500 (+$210-510). Aid: Need 91 ($470,945).
- Summer: Enrich Rec. 2-3 wks.
- Endow $2,500,000. Plant val $12,500,000. Bldgs 1. Class rms 32. 2 Libs 8000 vols. Sci labs 2. Comp labs 2. Art studios 3. Gyms 2. Fields 2. Courts 8. Basketball courts 2.
- Est 1976. Nonprofit. Tri (Sept-June). Assoc NEASC.

Situated on a 47-acre campus and drawing students from all of southeastern Massachusetts, the school has experienced rapid growth since its establishment. Students participate in a rigorous scholastic program while enrolling in five or six academic courses per year in grades 7-12. All pupils take Latin in grades 7 and 8, and those in grades 9-12 take at least three years of Spanish or French. Older students choose among Advanced Placement courses in most disciplines.

Extracurricular activities include interscholastic athletics, publications, drama, an outing club and student council.

PITTSFIELD, MA. (31 mi. ESE of Albany, NY; 115 mi. W of Boston, MA) Urban. Pop: 45,793. Alt: 1013 ft.

MISS HALL'S SCHOOL
Bdg and Day — Girls Gr 9-12

Pittsfield, MA 01201. 492 Holmes Rd. Tel: 413-499-1300. Fax: 413-448-2994.
www.misshalls.org   E-mail: info@misshalls.org
Jean K. Norris, Head. BMEd, Pittsburg State Univ, MM, Temple Univ. Kimberly Boland, Adm.
- Col Prep. AP—Eng Fr Lat Span Calc Bio Chem Eur_Hist US_Hist. Feat—Anat & Physiol Botany Environ_Sci Geol Forensic_Sci Econ Pol_Sci Psych Philos Relig Art_Hist Ceramics Photog Drama Music Music_Hist Mod_Dance Debate. Supp—ESL Rev Tut.
- Adm (Gr 9-11): 58/yr. Bdg 40. Day 18. Appl due: Feb. Accepted: 69%. Yield: 62%. Tests SSAT TOEFL.
- Enr 171. G 123/48. Sec 171. Wh 68%. Hisp 7%. Blk 7%. Asian 18%. Avg class size: 10.

Fac 35. M 7. F 23/5. Wh 91%. Hisp 3%. Blk 6%. Adv deg: 71%. In dorms 12.
Grad '04—29. Col—29. (Barnard, Carnegie Mellon, Georgetown, Geo Wash, Syracuse, Macalester). Alum 3029.
Tui '04-'05: Bdg $33,800 (+$900). **Day $19,800** (+$900). **Aid:** Merit 2 ($14,000). Need 80 ($1,521,100).
Endow $6,200,000. Plant val $20,000,000. Bldgs 17. Dorms 2. Dorm rms 90. Class rms 24. Lib 14,500 vols. Sci labs 3. Comp labs 2. Photog labs 1. Auds 2. Theaters 1. Art studios 1. Music studios 4. Dance studios 1. Gyms 1. Fields 4. Courts 8. Ski chalets 1.
Est 1898. Nonprofit. Sem (Sept-June). **Assoc** CLS NEASC.

The school was established by Mira Hinsdale Hall as a successor institution to the first girls' boarding school founded in Massachusetts in 1800. Upon her aunt's death in 1937, Margaret Hall assumed direction of the school, continuing the family tradition, conservative tone and standards of scholarship.

Miss Hall's offers both an honors tier and Advanced Placement courses, in addition to various electives. An established expressive arts program features photography, studio art, modern dance, theater and music. Internships with area businesses and science, cultural and community service organizations add breadth to the traditional college preparatory program. The athletic program includes skiing, soccer, softball, lacrosse, field hockey, basketball, volleyball, riding, tennis and a wilderness program. Emphasis is placed on attracting a geographically diverse student body and maintaining a family-style atmosphere. **See Also Page 1305**

SANDWICH, MA. (48 mi. SE of Boston, MA; 48 mi. E of Providence, RI) Suburban. Pop: 17,119. Alt: 20 ft. Area also includes East Sandwich.

RIVERVIEW SCHOOL
Bdg — Coed Gr 6-PG

East Sandwich, MA 02537. 551 Rte 6A. **Tel: 508-888-0489. Fax: 508-888-1315.**
www.riverviewschool.org   E-mail: admissions@riverviewschool.org
Maureen D. Brenner, Head. BA, University College Dublin (Ireland), MEd, Bridgewater State College. **Jeanne M. Pacheco, Adm.**
   LD. Feat—Computers Photog Studio_Art Speech Indus_Arts. **Supp**—Dev_Read Rem_Math Rem_Read.
   Adm: 39/yr. Appl due: Rolling. Accepted: 47%. Yield: 46%. **Tests** IQ.
   Enr 182. B 90. G 92. Elem 13. Sec 101. PG 68. Wh 96%. Hisp 1%. Blk 2%. Asian 1%. Avg class size: 8. **Fac 32.** M 9. F 23. Wh 100%. Adv deg: 62%.
   Grad '04—28. Col—25. (Cape Cod CC 20, NY Inst of Tech 3, Lesley 2). Alum 812.
   Tui '04-'05: Bdg $48,500-57,600 (+$1250). **Aid:** Need 11 ($99,500).
   Summer: Ages 14-22. Acad Rev Rem Rec. Computers. Sports. Tui Bdg $5800. 5 wks.
   Endow $2,400,000. Plant val $17,000,000. Bldgs 20. Dorms 10. Dorm rms 62. Class rms 29. Libs 1. Sci labs 1. Comp labs 2. Dark rms 1. Auds 1. Art studios 1. Music studios 1. Gyms 1. Fields 1. Courts 1. Greenhouses 1.
   Est 1957. Nonprofit. Quar (Sept-June). **Assoc** NEASC.

Riverview was established to serve the adolescent who has a primary diagnosis of a learning disability or a language disorder. Pupils, who have an IQ between 70 and 100, typically have experienced lifelong difficulties in academics and in making friends. The thematic, integrated program features academic, remedial and computer course work, while also addressing life skills and social skills development.

The program includes small, individualized academic classes, as well as reading, speech and language therapies. Structured evening and weekend programs provide support and are an important element of Riverview's predictable learning environment. **See Also Page 1371**

SHEFFIELD, MA. (42 mi. NW of Hartford, CT; 104 mi. NNE of New York, NY) Suburban. Pop: 3335. Alt: 679 ft.

BERKSHIRE SCHOOL
Bdg and Day — Coed Gr 9-PG

Sheffield, MA 01257. 245 N Undermountain Rd. Tel: 413-229-1003. Fax: 413-229-1016. www.berkshireschool.org E-mail: enrollment@berkshireschool.org
Michael J. Maher, Head. BA, Univ of Vermont, MA, Wesleyan Univ. **Lori Carpentier, Adm.**
  Col Prep. AP—Eng Fr Span Calc Stats Bio Chem Physics Eur_Hist US_Hist Comp_Govt & Pol Econ US_Govt & Pol Art_Hist Studio_Art. **Feat**—Creative_Writing Chin Lat Anat & Physiol Astron Geol Comp_Sci Ethics Philos Visual_Arts Theater Chorus Music Dance. **Supp**—ESL.
  Adm: 149/yr. Bdg 136. Day 13. Appl due: Feb. Accepted: 55%. **Tests** CEEB SSAT TOEFL.
  Enr 385. B 199/20. G 132/34. Sec 367. PG 18. Avg class size: 12. **Fac** 57. M 34. F 23. Wh 90%. Hisp 2%. Blk 6%. Asian 2%. Adv deg: 64%. In dorms 32.
  Grad '04—117. **Col**—113. (St Lawrence 10, Northeastern U 6, U of Hartford 6, U of WI-Madison 5, Boston U 5, Carnegie Mellon 4). Avg SAT: 1100. Alum 4400.
  Tui '04-'05: Bdg $33,450 (+$1000). **Day** $23,925 (+$800). **Aid:** Merit 9 ($75,500). Need 112 ($2,287,723).
  Endow $44,000,000. Plant val $90,000,000. Bldgs 33. Dorms 10. Dorm rms 185. Class rms 45. Lib 40,500 vols. Labs 5. Comp ctrs 2. Observatories 1. Theaters 2. Art studios 5. Music studios 4. Dance studios 1. Art galleries 1. Gyms 1. Fields 9. Courts 13. Rinks 1. Fitness ctrs 1. Student ctrs 1. Radio stations 1.
  Est 1907. Nonprofit. Sem (Sept-May). **Assoc** CLS NEASC.

In the fall of 1907, Mr. and Mrs. Seaver B. Buck rented the buildings of the Glenny farm at the foot of Mt. Everett and founded Berkshire School. For 35 years, the Bucks devoted themselves to educating young men about the values of academic pursuit and high personal standards. In 1969, this dedication to excellence was extended to girls, as the school became coeducational.

Berkshire provides a traditional curriculum, with honors and accelerated classes leading to a variety of Advanced Placement courses. Emphasis is placed on the acquisition of sound research skills, the integration of knowledge and an awareness of global issues. The school allows qualified students to explore specialized interests through independent study. Pupils are encouraged to develop their leadership skills and to take an active role in the governance of the school; seniors return a week prior to the start of school for intensive leadership training seminars.

Located on 500 acres in the hills of western Massachusetts, the school provides competition in many interscholastic sports, with recreational offerings available in skiing and mountain climbing. Extracurricular activities include theatrical productions, work at the 250-watt FM radio station, photography, computer animation, vocal and jazz ensembles, and publications. Berkshire schedules frequent lectures, concerts and art exhibits. **See Also Pages 1118-9**

SOUTHBOROUGH, MA. (26 mi. W of Boston, MA) Suburban. Pop: 8781. Alt: 314 ft.

FAY SCHOOL
Bdg — Coed Gr 6-9; Day — Coed 1-9

Southborough, MA 01772. 48 Main St, PO Box 9106. Tel: 508-485-0100.
Fax: 508-481-7872.
www.fayschool.org   E-mail: fayadmit@fayschool.org
Stephen C. White, Head. BA, Hartwick College. Suzanne Walker Buck, Adm.
  Pre-Prep. Feat—Fr Lat Span Computers Econ Govt Law Studio_Art Music. **Supp**—ESL Tut.
  Adm: 108/yr. Bdg 52. Day 56. Appl due: Rolling. Accepted: 46%. **Tests** IQ.
  Enr 385. B 68/149. G 43/125. Elem 316. Sec 69. Wh 75%. Hisp 1%. Blk 6%. Asian 18%. Avg class size: 12. **Fac 67.** Wh 97%. Hisp 1%. Asian 2%. Adv deg: 50%. In dorms 17.
  Grad '04—65. Prep—64. (St Mark's Sch-MA, Suffield, Brooks, Middlesex, Concord Acad, St Paul's Sch-NH). Alum 3800.
  Tui '05-'06: Bdg $36,500-37,320 (+$1500). **Day** $15,950-21,840 (+$500). **Aid:** Need 27 ($540,000).
  Summer: Acad Enrich Rec. ESL. Tui Bdg $7150. 6 wks. Rec. Tui Day $800. 1½ wks.
  Endow $23,000,000. Plant val $20,000,000. Bldgs 16. Dorms 4. Lib 13,000 vols. Sci labs 5. Comp labs 3. Dark rms 1. Theaters 1. Art studios 2. Music studios 3. Dance studios 1. Gyms 2. Arts ctrs 1. Fields 9. Basketball courts 6. Tennis courts 8. Pools 1.
  Est 1866. Nonprofit. Tri (Sept-June).

The oldest elementary boarding school in America, Fay School was founded by Harriet Burnett and Eliza Burnett Fay. Waldo B. Fay was headmaster from 1896 to 1918; his son, Edward Winchester Fay, served from 1918 to 1942. The school became coeducational in 1972, with the acceptance of girls. Boarding students enroll from various states and foreign countries, thus creating a diverse student body.

The traditional elementary curriculum in the lower school is enriched by arts, French, music instruction and age-appropriate physical education. In the upper school, which prepares students for leading secondary schools, the curriculum encompasses course work for the academically advanced and for students who require tutorial support work. French is introduced in grade 1, Spanish in grade 6 and Latin in grade 8. English courses within the upper school emphasize writing, novels, poetry, grammar and public speaking. A strong laboratory-oriented science curriculum includes biology and conceptual physics. Technology is an integral aspect of the curriculum. Fay conducts academic field trips and weekend enrichment excursions in Boston and throughout the surrounding area.

Students choose from many competitive and individual sports, as well as a wide selection of clubs and organizations, music, dramatics, photography, publications and student government.

SAINT MARK'S SCHOOL

Bdg and Day — Coed Gr 9-12

Southborough, MA 01772. 25 Marlborough Rd, PO Box 9105. Tel: 508-786-6000. Fax: 508-786-6120.

www.stmarksschool.org   E-mail: admission@stmarksschool.org

Antony J. deV. Hill, Co-Head. BA, Univ of Sydney (Australia), MEd, Boston Univ. **Elsa N. Hill, Co-Head.** AB, Smith College, MAT, Harvard Univ, LLB, Univ of New South Wales (Australia). **Anne E. Behnke, Adm.**

- **Col Prep. AP**—Eng Fr Lat Span Calc Stats Bio Chem Physics Eur_Hist US_Hist Psych Art_Hist Studio_Art Music_Theory. **Feat**—Ger Greek Astron Russ_Hist Civil_War Ethics Relig Ceramics Film Photog Sculpt Drama Theater Music_Hist. **Supp**—Tut.
- **Adm (Gr 9-11):** 103/yr. Bdg 80. Day 23. Appl due: Jan. Accepted: 47%. Yield: 39%. **Tests** SSAT TOEFL.
- **Enr 329.** B 127/39. G 125/38. Sec 329. Wh 74%. Hisp 3%. Blk 6%. Am Ind 1%. Asian 13%. Other 3%. Avg class size: 10. **Fac 65.** Wh 93%. Hisp 2%. Blk 3%. Asian 2%. Adv deg: 60%. In dorms 25.
- **Grad '04—79. Col—79.** (Union Col-NY 4, Middlebury 4, Georgetown 3, Colby 3, Geo Wash 3, Boston Col 3). Avg SAT: 1261. Alum 3600.
- **Tui '04-'05: Bdg $33,500** (+$1000). **Day $25,950** (+$500). **Aid:** Merit 1 ($12,500). Need 95 ($2,237,550).
- Endow $95,000,000. Plant val $70,000,000. Bldgs 24. Dorms 13. Dorm rms 175. Class rms 37. Lib 30,000 vols. Sci labs 8. Lang labs 1. Comp labs 3. Auds 1. Theaters 2. Art studios 3. Music studios 4. Dance studios 1. Mech drawing studios 1. Gyms 2. Fields 9. Basketball courts 2. Tennis courts 10. Squash courts 7. Pools 1. Rinks 1. Weight rms 1. Golf crses 1.
- **Est 1865.** Nonprofit. Episcopal. Sem (Sept-June). **Assoc** CLS NEASC.

Founded by Joseph Burnett as an Episcopal school, Saint Mark's remains grounded in its Judeo-Christian heritage. The school meets as a group five times per week in either the chapel or the student center. The 250-acre campus is centered around the main building, a large Tudor structure built in 1890.

The liberal arts curriculum includes requirements in English, mathematics, foreign language, history, science, religion and the arts. All departments except religion offer Advanced Placement courses, and students with demonstrated interest in a particular subject may pursue independent study under the guidance of a faculty advisor. Opportunities for study abroad and student exchanges complement Saint Mark's varied foreign language program.

Each student takes part in the school's athletic program. Third- and fourth-form students participate on interscholastic teams each season; fifth and sixth formers may instead pursue recreational athletics or, with faculty approval, independent study in the arts for one season each year. Cocurricular offerings at Saint Mark's include student publications, language clubs, drama, debate, community service, multicultural groups and an outing club. The school's proximity to Boston allows students to attend numerous cultural and sporting events.

SPRINGFIELD, MA. (25 mi. NNE of Hartford, CT; 80 mi. W of Boston, MA) Urban. Pop: 152,082. Alt: 119 ft.

THE MacDUFFIE SCHOOL
Bdg — Coed Gr 9-12; Day — Coed 6-12

Springfield, MA 01105. 1 Ames Hill Dr. Tel: 413-734-4971. Fax: 413-734-6693.
www.macduffie.com E-mail: headsoffice@macduffie.com
Kathryn P. Gibson, Head. BA, Vassar College, MA, Columbia Univ. **Linda Keating**, Adm.

Col Prep. AP—Eng Fr Span Calc Eur_Hist US_Hist. **Feat**—Creative_Writing Lat Astron Environ_Sci Computers Web_Design African-Amer_Hist Psych Studio_Art Visual_Arts Drama Theater Music Dance Journ Study_Skills. **Supp**—ESL Tut.

Adm: 68/yr. Bdg 17. Day 51. Appl due: Rolling. Accepted: 78%. Yield: 68%. **Tests** SSAT TOEFL.

Enr 215. B 12/76. G 23/104. Elem 61. Sec 154. Wh 67%. Hisp 7%. Blk 11%. Asian 15%. Avg class size: 12. **Fac 36.** M 15. F 20/1. Wh 100%. Adv deg: 58%. In dorms 1.

Grad '04—34. Col—34. (Brown 2, U of IL-Urbana 2, Emmanuel 2, Wheaton-MA 2, Assumption 2, U of MA-Amherst 1). Avg SAT: 1159. Alum 3600.

Tui '04-'05: Bdg $28,550 (+$1500-2000). **Day** $15,975-16,800 (+$500-800). **Aid:** Need 76 ($597,965).

Summer: Ages 5-13. Enrich Rec. Theater. ESL. Sports. 2-6 wks.

Endow $36,000. Plant val $10,800,000. Bldgs 15. Dorms 5. Dorm rms 20. Class rms 25. Lib 8000 vols. Sci labs 4. Comp labs 2. Auds 1. Theaters 1. Art studios 1. Music studios 1. Dance studios 1. Gyms 1. Fields 1. Courts 3.

Est 1890. Nonprofit. Sem (Sept-May). **Assoc** CLS NEASC.

The school was founded as a college preparatory school for girls by Dr. John MacDuffie, a Harvard alumnus, and his wife, Abby, a member of Radcliffe's first graduating class. The MacDuffie family directed the school until 1941. Over the years, the school expanded from a small cluster of buildings to its present configuration in the historic Maple Hill district of the city.

The course of studies at MacDuffie features an integrated curriculum at all levels. Teams of teachers work together in both the middle school and the upper school to create an interrelated program that includes the arts and the core subjects of English, mathematics, history, foreign languages and science. Advanced Placement and honors courses are offered in all subject areas. The school also conducts after-school extra-help sessions on a regular basis.

MacDuffie's extracurricular program features a variety of sports and interest clubs. Field hockey, soccer, basketball, volleyball, tennis, lacrosse, baseball and softball provide interscholastic competition. The school offers such clubs and activities as drama, dance, music, student council, publications, debate, math, chess and community service. Students take advantage of Springfield's cultural opportunities by attending events at the civic center, theaters, museums and the many local colleges of the western Massachusetts area.   **See Also Page 1198**

SUDBURY, MA. (21 mi. W of Boston, MA) Suburban. Pop: 16,841. Alt: 201 ft.

WILLOW HILL SCHOOL
Day — Coed Gr 6-12

Sudbury, MA 01776. 98 Haynes Rd. Tel: 978-443-2581. Fax: 978-443-7560.
www.willowhillschool.org   E-mail: info@willowhillschool.org

Judith Vaillancourt, Head. BA, Boston College, MA, San Francisco State Univ. **Nancy S. Brody, Adm.**
   Col Prep. LD. Underachiever. **Feat**—Span Computers Studio_Art Drama Wilderness_Ed. **Supp**—Dev_Read Makeup Tut.
   Adm (Gr 6-11): 18/yr. Appl due: Rolling. Accepted: 24%. **Tests** IQ.
   Enr 57. B 39. G 18. Elem 24. Sec 33. Avg class size: 8. **Fac 17.** M 5. F 12.
   Grad '04—9. Col—3. (Art Inst of Boston, U of Hartford). Alum 240.
   Tui '04-'05: Day $41,475.
   Endow $511,000. Plant val $4,518,000. Bldgs 3. Class rms 13. Libs 1. Comp labs 1. Art studios 1. Arts ctrs 1. Gyms 1.
   Est 1970. Nonprofit. Quar (Aug-June). **Assoc** NEASC.

The school offers a personalized education for students of average to high intelligence who are underachievers or who have dyslexia, learning-style differences or attentional difficulties. The college preparatory curriculum features small classes and courses in art, drama and computer science. Willow Hill also provides highly individualized one-on-one and small-group tutorials, sports, a wilderness exploration program and extracurricular activities.

Additional opportunities include language training, developmental reading and SAT preparation. All students participate in community service, as well as in college and career exploration.   **See Also Page 1377**

WALTHAM, MA. (12 mi. WNW of Boston, MA) Urban. Pop: 59,226. Alt: 51 ft.

BARTLETT SCHOOL
Day — Coed Gr PS-6

Waltham, MA 02451. 1841 Trapelo Rd. Tel: 781-890-1865. Fax: 781-890-5566.
www.bartlett.org   E-mail: bartlett@webcom.com

Molly Mattson-DiCecca, Head. MEd, Tufts Univ, MA, EdD, Columbia Univ. **Sarah Wilsterman, Adm.**
   Pre-Prep. **Feat**—Fr Lat Span Computers Studio_Art Music. **Supp**—Rev Tut.
   Adm: 20/yr. Appl due: Feb. Accepted: 50%.
   Enr 140. B 79. G 61. Elem 140. Wh 93%. Blk 3%. Asian 4%. Avg class size: 16. Uniform. **Fac 27.** M 3/1. F 20/3. Wh 97%. Hisp 2%. Blk 1%. Adv deg: 29%.
   Grad '04—14. Prep—9. (Lexington Christian, Winsor, Noble & Greenough, Belmont Hill, Rivers, Brimmer & May). Alum 5000.
   Tui '04-'05: Day $9475-13,830 (+$300). **Aid:** Need 5 ($30,000).
   Summer: Enrich Rec. 2-8 wks.

Bldgs 1. Class rms 12. Libs 1. Sci labs 1. Lang labs 4. Comp labs 1. Art studios 1. Music studios 1. Gyms 2. Fields 2. Pools 1.
Est 1933. Nonprofit. Quar (Sept-June).

Founded in Arlington by Norine D. Casey, Bartlett began as a class of 12 first graders. The school gradually expanded its facilities and staff to instruct children through grade 6 and to accommodate library, science, arts and physical education activities. After moving to leased quarters in Belmont in 1978, Bartlett assumed its current location in Waltham during the summer of 2003.

Emphasis is placed on basic studies. Class work includes computer studies, music, art, science, French or Spanish, and physical education at all levels and, beginning in grade 5, Latin. After entering grade 2, children are assigned homework as a means of reviewing and reinforcing class work. After-school activities include athletics, drama, science, computer, art and cooking. Children participate in at least two field trips each year.

CHAPEL HILL-CHAUNCY HALL SCHOOL
Bdg and Day — Coed Gr 9-PG

Waltham, MA 02452. 785 Beaver St. Tel: 781-894-2644. **Fax:** 781-894-5205.
www.chch.org   E-mail: admissions@chch.org

Siri Akal Khalsa, Head. BA, MS, City Univ of New York, MFA, Brandeis Univ, MA, EdD, Columbia Univ. **Lisa Zannella, Adm.**

Col Prep. AP—Eng Calc Studio_Art. **Feat**—Fr Span Stats Astron Programming Econ Adolescent_Psych Art_Hist Ceramics Chorus Music_Theory Journ. **Supp**—ESL LD Tut.

Adm: 40/yr. Appl due: Feb. Accepted: 55%. **Tests** IQ SSAT TOEFL.

Enr 160. B 38/58. G 25/39. Sec 158. PG 2. Wh 70%. Hisp 3%. Blk 11%. Asian 13%. Other 3%. Avg class size: 10. **Fac 40.** M 16/2. F 22. Adv deg: 60%. In dorms 13.

Grad '04—51. Col—50. (New England Col, Curry, Northeastern U, Fairfield, Sarah Lawrence, Geo Wash). Alum 3700.

Tui '05-'06: Bdg $35,800. Day $26,500. Aid: Need 25 ($513,189).

Endow $1,100,000. Plant val $8,000,000. Bldgs 16. Dorms 3. Dorm rms 52. Class rms 25. Lib 13,000 vols. Sci labs 3. Comp labs 6. Auds 1. Theaters 1. Art studios 1. Music studios 1. Dance studios 1. Photog studios 1. Ceramics studios 1. Wood shops 1. Gyms 1. Fields 2. Pools 1.

Est 1828. Nonprofit. Tri (Sept-June). **Assoc** NEASC.

Chapel Hill School for girls, a boarding school founded by New Church members in 1860, merged with the Chauncy Hall School for boys (established in 1828), a day school, on the Chapel Hill campus in 1971.

Enrolling students from throughout the country and the world, CH-CH stresses personal growth and independence while providing a structured, supportive environment that is flexible enough to address the varied needs and talents of its diverse student body. Within the traditional college preparatory curriculum, the school offers a learning center and a ninth-grade program specifically designed to support first-year students. Pupils partake of many cultural events in and around Boston.

WELLESLEY, MA. (14 mi. W of Boston, MA) Suburban. Pop: 26,613. Alt: 140 ft.

DANA HALL SCHOOL
Bdg — Girls Gr 9-12; Day — Girls 6-12

Wellesley, MA 02482. 45 Dana Rd, PO Box 9010. Tel: 781-235-3010. Fax: 781-235-0577. www.danahall.org E-mail: admission@danahall.org

Blair Jenkins, Head. BA, Wells College, MA, Vanderbilt Univ. **Heather Cameron, Adm.**

Col Prep. AP—Eng Fr Lat Span Calc Stats Comp_Sci Bio Chem Eur_Hist Studio_Art. **Feat**—Ecol Marine_Biol/Sci Web_Design Far_Eastern_Hist Econ Pol_Sci Russ_Stud African_Stud Lat-Amer_Stud Philos Architect Ceramics Drawing Photog Acting Drama Chorus Music Dance Journ Public_Speak.

Adm: 128/yr. Appl due: Feb. Accepted: 51%. **Tests** ISEE SSAT TOEFL.

Enr 453. G 136/317. Elem 127. Sec 326. Avg class size: 13. **Fac 59.** M 16/1. F 35/7. Adv deg: 61%. In dorms 1.

Grad '04—86. Col—86. (Geo Wash 3, Vanderbilt 3, Hamilton 3, Smith 3, Boston Col 2, U of PA 2). Avg SAT: 1236. Alum 5000.

Tui '04-'05: Bdg $34,425 (+$1845). **Day** $26,075 (+$1305). **Aid:** Need 86 ($2,196,980). Endow $20,669,000. Bldgs 37. Dorms 6. Dorm rms 81. Class rms 51. Lib 22,500 vols. Labs 6. Auds 1. Theaters 1. Art studios 1. Music studios 10. Dance studios 1. Fields 4. Courts 5. Riding rings 3. Stables 1.

Est 1881. Nonprofit. Tri (Sept-June). **Assoc** CLS NEASC.

In 1881, Wellesley College president Henry F. Durant encouraged the sisters Sarah and Julia Eastman to leave their teaching positions at Wellesley to establish a new college preparatory school a short distance from the college campus, on land donated by Charles B. Dana.

From the beginning, Dana Hall stressed that overall personal development was as important as "strict mental training." Under the leadership of Helen Temple Cooke from 1899 to 1951, the school achieved national prominence.

Numerous states and foreign countries are represented in the student body. All girls prepare for college and choose from many cocurricular activities. The curriculum includes Advanced Placement courses in all major disciplines. In addition, Dana Hall maintains a writing and math center that assists pupils with the review of material, essays, papers and college applications. The students make good use of the cultural advantages of Boston. Qualified students may enroll in credit courses at Wellesley College. Dana Hall provides foreign study and travel opportunities in France, Spain and Australia, and pupils may also take part in the Rocky Mountain Institute in Colorado.

The school's interscholastic sports program comprises field hockey, soccer, basketball, cross-country, volleyball, fencing, golf, ice hockey, tennis, lacrosse and softball. Extracurricular activities include drama, dance, student government, newspaper, literary magazine, music groups, and off-campus activities in Boston and Cambridge and at nearby universities. Girls may also choose from a variety of short- and long-term community service projects.

Dana Hall's middle school occupies its own on-campus building, although middle schoolers utilize upper school science, library and dining facilities. The middle school enrolls day students from the surrounding area.

See Also Pages 1294-5

TENACRE COUNTRY DAY SCHOOL

Day — Coed Gr PS-6

Wellesley, MA 02482. 78 Benvenue St. Tel: 781-235-2282. Fax: 781-237-7057.
www.tenacrecds.org   E-mail: sam_reece@tenacrecds.org
Christian B. Elliot, Head. AB, Princeton Univ. **Sam Reece, Adm.**

Pre-Prep. Feat—Span Computers Studio_Art Music. **Supp**—Dev_Read Rem_Math Rem_Read.

Adm: 37/yr. Appl due: Jan. Accepted: 30%. Yield: 86%.

Enr 191. B 91. G 100. Elem 191. Wh 77%. Hisp 4%. Blk 6%. Asian 8%. Other 5%. Avg class size: 24. **Fac 34.** M 5. F 21/8. Wh 94%. Blk 3%. Asian 3%. Adv deg: 70%.

Grad '04—24. Prep—22. (Noble & Greenough 5, Dana Hall 3, Roxbury Latin 3, Belmont Hill 2, Brimmer & May 2, Fay 2). Alum 1300.

Tui '04-'05: Day $13,950-19,600. Aid: Need 16 ($222,365).

Summer: Rec. 8 wks.

Endow $4,200,000. Plant val $6,750,000. Bldgs 4. Class rms 11. Lib 8000 vols. Sci labs 1. Comp labs 1. Auds 1. Theaters 1. Art studios 1. Music studios 1. Gyms 1. Fields 2. Courts 2.

Est 1910. Nonprofit. Sem (Sept-June).

Originally the elementary division of Dana Hall School, Tenacre formed its own corporation and board of trustees in 1972. The school has been coeducational since 1942, and was reorganized on its present campus as an elementary day school in 1952. Today, students enroll from more than 20 nearby communities.

In addition to an emphasis on fundamental learning skills in language arts and mathematics, the comprehensive program devotes a large amount of instructional time to social studies, science, art, music, computer, Spanish and physical education. The school maintains small classes and employs team teaching, assigning two teachers to each homeroom. Parental involvement is encouraged.

WESTON, MA. (15 mi. W of Boston, MA) Suburban. Pop: 11,469. Alt: 161 ft.

THE CAMBRIDGE SCHOOL OF WESTON

Bdg and Day — Coed Gr 9-PG

Weston, MA 02493. Georgian Rd. Tel: 781-642-8650. Fax: 781-398-8344.
www.csw.org   E-mail: admissions@csw.org
Jane Moulding, Head. BA, Univ of Warwick (England), AM, Harvard Univ. **Trish Saunders, Adm.**

Col Prep. AP—Calc. **Feat**—Creative_Writing ASL Fr Lat Span Stats Botany Ecol Environ_Sci Geol Marine_Biol/Sci Zoology Web_Design Econ Child_Dev Ethics Art_Hist Film Photog Drama Theater Music Dance Journ. **Supp**—ESL.

Adm: 100/yr. Bdg 29. Day 71. Appl due: Feb. Accepted: 50%. Yield: 55%. **Tests** ISEE SSAT TOEFL.

Enr 310. B 40/115. G 40/115. Sec 305. PG 5. Wh 84%. Hisp 3%. Blk 5%. Asian 5%. Other 3%. Avg class size: 12. **Fac 50.** M 20/5. F 20/5. Wh 84%. Hisp 4%. Blk 8%. Asian 4%. Adv deg: 76%. In dorms 15.

Grad '04—76. Col—76. (Brown, Columbia, RI Sch of Design, Oberlin, Smith). Avg SAT: 1200. Alum 3000.

Tui '04-'05: Bdg $34,230 (+$1000). **Day $25,515** (+$700). **Aid:** Need 65 ($1,200,000).

Summer: Acad Enrich Rec. Tui Day $2500. 5 wks.
Endow $5,000,000. Plant val $20,000,000. Bldgs 24. Dorms 4. Dorm rms 50. Class rms 30. Lib 15,000 vols. Sci labs 5. Lang labs 1. Comp labs 2. Auds 1. Theaters 2. Art studios 6. Music studios 10. Dance studios 2. Gyms 1. Fields 3. Courts 1. Pools 3. Fitness ctrs 1.
Est 1886. Nonprofit. 7 terms (Sept-June). **Assoc** NEASC.

The school was founded by Arthur Gilman to prepare young women for Radcliffe College, which he had established in 1879. In 1931, the school moved from Cambridge to its present wooded, 65-acre campus in suburban Weston; at that time, it became coeducational and instituted boarding.

In 1973, CSW devised the Module Plan, in which the academic year is divided into seven five-week terms, or "modules." The school day consists of three academic blocks, each 90 minutes long, allowing intensive learning in two or three subjects at a time; a fourth block is set aside at the end of the day for interscholastic and recreational sports and other activities. More than 300 courses—ranging from molecular biology to film animation—are available, including requirements in English, mathematics, history, science, foreign language and computer; integrated studies (team-taught, interdisciplinary courses); and, to address personal interests, electives. The visual and performing arts are an integral part of the curriculum, and by graduation students must complete a variety of arts courses, including art history.

In addition, CSW provides two distinct programs for postgraduates: liberal arts, for students who wish to add an extra year of study to their high school record, and visual arts, designed for students who need an extra year to prepare portfolios for art school applications, as well as for those wishing to explore their artistic potential.

Each year, students must earn athletic credits through participation in competitive interscholastics or in a combination of recreational sports, major theatrical productions, wilderness experiences and dance courses. The wilderness program offers day and weekend trips for hiking, rock climbing, bicycling, rafting, cross-country skiing, canoeing, mountain biking and survival camping. One block each year, students perform school service as daycare interns, office workers or admissions guides, and in other positions at such places as the dining hall, the CSW preschool and the campus store. CSW students also do off-campus volunteer work through a community service program. Other activities include publications and Amnesty International. Students and faculty serve together on many committees, and students participate in the school's decision-making process, from all-school town meetings (where students and faculty meet regularly to discuss campus issues and make recommendations to the head of school) to the board of trustees.

MEADOWBROOK SCHOOL
Day — Coed Gr PS-8

Weston, MA 02493. 10 Farm Rd. Tel: 781-894-1193. Fax: 781-894-0557.
www.meadowbrook-ma.org   E-mail: admissions@meadowbrook-ma.org
Stephen T. Hinds, Head. BSEd, Miami Univ (OH), MEd, Boston Univ. **Barbara T. Vincent, Adm.**
Pre-Prep. Feat—Fr Lat Span Studio_Art Pottery Music. **Supp**—Dev_Read Rem_Math Tut.
Adm: 61/yr. Appl due: Feb. Accepted: 15%. **Tests** ISEE SSAT.

Enr 278. B 140. G 138. Elem 278. Wh 84%. Hisp 3%. Blk 3%. Asian 10%. Avg class size: 24. **Fac 48.** M 12. F 27/9. Wh 88%. Hisp 4%. Blk 4%. Asian 4%. Adv deg: 56%.
Grad '04—28. Prep—20. (Phillips Exeter 2, Milton Acad 2, Belmont Hill 2, Boston U Acad 2, Middlesex 2, Noble & Greenough 2). Alum 988.
Tui '04-'05: Day $15,080-21,880. Aid: Need 24 ($400,895).
Summer: Gr K-6. Rec. Tui Day $1890-3400. 4-8 wks.
Endow $9,283,000. Plant val $16,446,000. Bldgs 7. Class rms 26. Lib 15,000 vols. Sci labs 2. Lang labs 2. Comp labs 2. Art studios 2. Music studios 2. Dance studios 1. Woodworking studios 1. Gyms 2. Fields 3. Pools 2.
Est 1923. Nonprofit. Sem (Sept-June).

Situated on a 26-acre campus, Meadowbrook maintains a low student-teacher ratio as it offers the opportunity for individual attention in a setting that emphasizes the basic skills. Boys and girls learn from two teachers in each homeroom in junior kindergarten through grade 5. Art, music, ceramics and computer studies are offered at all levels. French is available to students in grades 3-8, Spanish and Latin to pupils in grades 6-8. A modified Outward Bound program, field trips, drama, glee club, class projects and a strong athletic program are among the activities.

The school also conducts an after-school program and a recreational summer camp. Graduates matriculate at leading New England secondary schools.

THE RIVERS SCHOOL

Day — Coed Gr 6-12

Weston, MA 02493. 333 Winter St. Tel: 781-235-9300. Fax: 781-239-3614.
www.rivers.org   E-mail: g.lloyd@rivers.org
Thomas P. Olverson, Head. AB, Duke Univ, MEd, College of William and Mary. **Gillian M. Lloyd,** Adm.
Col Prep. AP—Eng Fr Lat Span Calc Stats Comp_Sci Bio Physics Eur_Hist US_Hist. **Feat**—Holocaust_Lit Scandinavian_Lit Greek Ecol Comp_Graphics Pol_Sci Art_Hist Filmmaking Sculpt Drama Theater Music Jazz_Band Jazz_Choir Public_Speak. **Supp**—Tut.
Adm (Gr 6-11): 110/yr. Appl due: Feb. Accepted: 36%. Yield: 47%. **Tests** ISEE SSAT.
Enr 410. Elem 96. Sec 314. Wh 90%. Hisp 1%. Blk 4%. Asian 3%. Other 2%. Avg class size: 12. **Fac 63.** M 28/5. F 25/5. Adv deg: 73%.
Grad '04—71. Col—71. (Trinity Col-CT 5, NYU 4, Boston U 3, Emory 3, Johns Hopkins 3, Skidmore 3). Avg SAT: 1280. Alum 2545.
Tui '05-'06: Day $27,250 (+$500). **Aid:** Need 73 ($1,441,240).
Summer: Ages 4-14. Rec. Tui Day $495/wk. 8 wks.
Endow $12,750,000. Plant val $38,000,000. Bldgs 12. Class rms 38. Lib 14,500 vols. Labs 6. Theaters 2. Art studios 6. Music studios 24. Theater/auds 1. Gyms 2. Fields 6. Courts 6. Field houses 1. Rinks 1.
Est 1915. Nonprofit. Tri (Sept-June). **Assoc** CLS NEASC.

At the suggestion of a group of prominent Boston physicians, Robert W. Rivers created an open-air school for boys in Brookline; it was widely believed that the open-air concept, popular in England, promoted good health in an environment conducive to scholarship and learning. Twenty-six years and one new campus later, the Country Day School for Boys of Boston merged with Rivers. The school moved its location twice more before settling on the Loker Farm acreage, surrounded by conservation wetlands and a pond, in 1960. Rivers became coeducational in 1989.

Rivers provides a traditional liberal arts curriculum supplemented by electives and cocurricular activities. The broad scope of the arts department is enhanced by The Rivers Music School, a community conservatory located on campus. Athletics at Rivers include interscholastic and intramural competition, individualized activities and fitness programs for the recreational athlete. Students are required to take part in athletics each year; those not participating during a given term must undertake other afternoon activities. Also offered are various outdoor and community service programs, organized trips abroad and a ropes course. **See Also Page 1236**

WILLIAMSTOWN, MA. (31 mi. E of Albany, NY; 114 mi. WNW of Boston, MA) Suburban. Pop: 4754. Alt: 604 ft.

BUXTON SCHOOL
Bdg and Day — Coed Gr 9-12

Williamstown, MA 01267. 291 South St. Tel: 413-458-3919. Fax: 413-458-9427.
www.buxtonschool.org   E-mail: admissions@buxtonschool.org
C. William Bennett, Dir. BA, Williams College. Franny Shuker-Haines, Adm.
   Col Prep. Feat—Creative_Writing Shakespeare Fr Span Geol Marine_Biol/Sci Vietnam_ War Middle_East_Hist Psych Philos Ceramics Photog Studio_Art Film_Hist Drama Chorus Music Dance. **Supp**—ESL.
   Adm (Gr 9-11): 33/yr. Bdg 32. Day 1. Appl due: Feb. **Tests** SSAT.
   Enr 90. B 44/1. G 45. Sec 90. Wh 69%. Hisp 11%. Blk 10%. Asian 10%. Avg class size: 12.
      Fac 20. M 10. F 10. Wh 90%. Hisp 5%. Asian 5%. Adv deg: 30%. In dorms 13.
   Grad '04—22. Col—22. (Hampshire 4, Smith 2, Guilford 2, Goucher 2, U of Chicago 1, Cornell 1). Alum 1000.
   Tui '04-'05: Bdg $32,500 (+$1200). **Day $19,700** (+$1200). **Aid:** Need 36 ($970,000).
   Endow $1,200,000. Plant val $6,000,000. Bldgs 17. Dorms 3. Dorm rms 34. Class rms 12. Lib 7000 vols. Sci labs 2. Comp labs 1. Theaters 1. Art studios 2. Music studios 4. Dance studios 1. Photog studios 1. Fields 2. Basketball courts 1. Skiing facilities yes. Ponds 3.
   Est 1928. Nonprofit. Sem (Sept-June). **Assoc** NEASC.

Buxton School, established in Williamstown in 1947, grew out of the Buxton Country Day School, which was founded in New Jersey in 1928 by Ellen Geer Sangster. She retired in 1963.

The traditional college preparatory curriculum also includes courses and activities in art, music, drama and dance. Courses of study are tailored to individual needs, with ample opportunities for advanced study. An essential element of the school is the ongoing attention given to community life. A work program and the annual all-school trip to a major North American city are of central importance; trip destinations have included Atlanta, GA; Chicago, IL; Toronto, Canada; Havana, Cuba; Washington, DC; Puerto Rico; and Mexico City, Mexico. Sports and a wide variety of activities are available.

MA   *Leading Private Schools*   250

PINE COBBLE SCHOOL
Day — Coed Gr PS-9

Williamstown, MA 01267. 163 Gale Rd. Tel: 413-458-4680. Fax: 413-458-8174.
  www.pinecobble.org   E-mail: pineinfo@pinecobble.org
Nicholas M. Edgerton, Head. AB, Brown Univ, MA, Columbia Univ. **Jay Merselis, Adm.**
    Pre-Prep. Feat—Fr Lat Span Computers Photog Studio_Art Drama Music. **Supp**—Dev_ Read Makeup Tut.
    Adm: 37/yr. Appl due: Rolling. **Tests** IQ Stanford.
    Enr 145. B 74. G 71. Elem 140. Sec 5. Wh 90%. Hisp 1%. Blk 4%. Asian 5%. Avg class size: 10. **Fac 32.** M 9. F 18/5. Adv deg: 43%.
    Grad '04—12. Prep—7. (Taft, Hotchkiss, Putney, Emma Willard, Miss Hall's, Hoosac). Alum 1800.
    Tui '04-'05: Day $8700-12,500 (+$275). **Aid:** Need 40 ($250,000).
    Summer: Acad Enrich Rec. Tui Day $120-400. 1-2 wks.
    Endow $200,000. Plant val $3,600,000. Bldgs 5. Class rms 15. Lib 5000 vols. Sci labs 2. Comp labs 2. Dark rms 1. Comp ctrs 1. Art studios 1. Music studios 2. Dance studios 1. Shops 1. Fields 2. Basketball courts 1. Tennis courts 2. Pools 1.
    Est 1937. Nonprofit. Sem (Sept-June).

Founded by Dr. and Mrs. Edgar W. Flinton, with the cooperation of a group of parents, Pine Cobble serves northern Berkshire County and adjacent communities in eastern New York State and southern Vermont. Within a traditional country day school environment, the program develops basic academic skills and offers a broad cocurricular program that features art, music, drama and athletics. French begins in kindergarten, while Latin and Spanish are available from grade 7. Cross-grade grouping in the upper school (grades 6-9) allows the program to address individual needs and provide opportunities for accelerated study.

In 1993, the school purchased a second campus in the hills just south of Williamstown. The main building, formerly the estate of George Alfred Cluett, and four classroom buildings occupy 20 acres. Field trips and outdoor experiences are numerous, and the entire school participates in an annual mountain climb and hike. A winter athletic program offers instruction in both cross-country and downhill skiing to children in grade 1 and above.

WINCHENDON, MA. (58 mi. WNW of Boston, MA) Suburban. Pop: 4246. Alt: 1180 ft.

THE WINCHENDON SCHOOL
Bdg and Day — Coed Gr 8-PG

Winchendon, MA 01475. 172 Ash St. Tel: 978-297-1223. Fax: 978-297-0911.
  www.winchendon.org   E-mail: admissions@winchendon.org
J. William LaBelle, Head. BS, MS, Univ of Massachusetts-Amherst, MEd, Bridgewater State College. **Richard John Plank, Adm.**
    Col Prep. AP—Eng Calc Bio Physics US_Hist. **Feat**—Fr Lat Span Programming Econ Pol_Sci Psych Art_Hist Graphic_Arts Photog Music. **Supp**—Dev_Read ESL LD Makeup Tut.
    Adm: 110/yr. Bdg 100. Day 10. Appl due: Rolling. Accepted: 90%. Yield: 90%. **Tests** IQ.
    Enr 219. B 145/18. G 42/14. Elem 5. Sec 194. PG 20. Wh 67%. Hisp 3%. Blk 10%. Asian

20%. Avg class size: 6. **Fac 33.** M 25/1. F 6/1. Wh 99%. Blk 1%. Adv deg: 27%. In dorms 20.
Grad '04—70. Col—70. (Boston U, U of MA-Amherst, UNH, Bentley, Curry, Northeastern U). Avg SAT: 1100. Alum 3500.
Tui '04-'05: Bdg $32,250 (+$2500). **Day $20,250** (+$1250). **Aid:** Need 60 ($1,500,000).
Summer: Acad Enrich Rev Rem. Tui Bdg $5600. 6 wks.
Endow $13,000,000. Plant val $12,000,000. Bldgs 35. Dorms 5. Dorm rms 162. Class rms 27. Lib 15,000 vols. Sci labs 4. Comp labs 1. Art studios 2. Music studios 1. Dance studios 1. Gyms 1. Athletic ctrs 1. Fields 4. Courts 2. Pools 1. Golf crses 1.
Est 1926. Nonprofit. Sem (Sept-June). **Assoc** NEASC.

Formerly the Hatch School of Newport, RI, this school adopted its present name in 1961 upon moving to Winchendon, where it occupies 350 wooded acres. Through personal attention to the academic capabilities of each student, the school has been able to aid those who have not previously developed sound study habits. The curriculum is college preparatory, with an emphasis on small, student-centered classes. In 1973, a remedial program for students with minor learning disabilities was added, and in 1974 the first female boarders were enrolled. Daily tutoring periods are offered.

The sports program includes cross-country running, soccer, Alpine and cross-country skiing, fall and spring tennis, ice hockey, basketball, volleyball, lacrosse, baseball, cycling and golf.

WORCESTER, MA.
(41 mi. W of Boston, MA) Urban. Pop: 172,648. Alt: 482 ft. Area also includes Shrewsbury.

BANCROFT SCHOOL
Day — Coed Gr K-12

Worcester, MA 01605. 110 Shore Dr. Tel: 508-853-2640. Fax: 508-853-7824.
www.bancroftschool.org E-mail: admission@bancroftschool.org
Scott R. Reisinger, Head. BA, MA, Univ of Rochester, MPhil, Columbia Univ. **Iris R. Bonet, Adm.**
Col Prep. AP—Eng Fr Lat Span Calc Bio Chem Eur_Hist US_Hist Art_Hist Studio_Art. **Feat**—Creative_Writing Marine_Biol/Sci Biotech Computers Programming Comp_Graphics Anthro Govt Psych Philos Relig Photog Drama Music. **Supp**—Rev.
Adm: 94/yr. Appl due: Feb. Accepted: 38%. **Tests** CEEB CTP_4 IQ SSAT.
Enr 600. B 268. G 332. Elem 361. Sec 239. Wh 88%. Hisp 2%. Blk 4%. Asian 6%. Avg class size: 16. **Fac 81.** M 20/1. F 54/6. Wh 97%. Hisp 1%. Blk 1%. Other 1%. Adv deg: 66%.
Grad '04—54. Col—54. (Worcester Polytech 5, Boston U 3, Tufts 3, Brown 2, Bowdoin 2, Colgate 2). Avg SAT: 1255. Avg ACT: 26. Alum 3101.
Tui '04-'05: Day $14,700-18,800. Aid: Merit 8 ($4000). Need 75 ($774,570).
Summer: Acad Enrich Rev. Tui Day $170-230. 2-3 wks.
Endow $8,759,000. Plant val $14,560,000. Bldgs 4. Class rms 40. 2 Libs 22,571 vols. Sci labs 3. Lang labs 2. Comp labs 2. Sci ctrs 1. Theaters 1. Art studios 2. Music studios 2. Arts ctrs 1. Gyms 1. Fields 3. Courts 3.
Est 1900. Nonprofit. (Sept-June). **Assoc** CLS NEASC.

The oldest coeducational independent day school in central Massachusetts, the school was named for George Bancroft, a diplomat, secretary of the Navy and historian who was born in Worcester in 1800. After outgrowing the original school buildings on Elm Street, Bancroft moved to more spacious quarters on Sever Street in 1922; in 1958, the school first occupied its current, 30-acre campus.

Bancroft's college preparatory curriculum features Advanced Placement courses in the major disciplines, including all three available foreign languages. Academics are enhanced by interscholastic and intramural sports, clubs and activities, drama, art and music. Each student completes 30 hours of community service.

NOTRE DAME ACADEMY
Day — Girls Gr 9-12

Worcester, MA 01609. 425 Salisbury St. Tel: 508-757-6200. Fax: 508-757-7200. www.nda.mec.edu
Sr. Ann E. Morrison, SND, Prin. BA, Emmanuel College, MA, St Louis Univ. **Mary F. Riordan, Adm.**
   Col Prep. AP—Calc Music_Theory. **Feat**—Shakespeare Fr Lat Span Anat & Physiol Computers Econ Psych Sociol Relig World_Relig Visual_Arts Drama Music.
   Adm: 81/yr. Appl due: Dec.
   Enr 310. G 310. Sec 310. Wh 93%. Hisp 1%. Blk 1%. Asian 5%. Avg class size: 18. **Fac 42.** M 3. F 36/3. Wh 100%. Adv deg: 59%.
   Grad '04—72. Col—72. (Holy Cross, U of MA-Amherst, Wellesley, Boston Col, Fairfield, MIT). Avg SAT: 1150. Alum 3100.
   Tui '04-'05: Day $7900 (+$600).
   Summer: Field Hockey. 2 wks.
   Plant val $1,678,000. Bldgs 3. Class rms 25. Lib 15,000 vols. Sci labs 2. Comp labs 2. Theaters 1. Art studios 1. Music studios 1. Gyms 1. Fields 1. Courts 1.
   Est 1951. Nonprofit. Roman Catholic. Quar (Sept-June). **Assoc** NEASC.

Founded by the Sisters of Notre Dame de Namur, this school occupies a 13-acre campus in a residential area. Religious studies are integrated into NDA's college preparatory program, which also emphasizes community involvement. Qualified students may enroll in advanced courses in a number of subjects. Various music, theater and arts classes and cocurricular activities enrich the program.

Field hockey, basketball, softball, cross-country, track, tennis, golf, skiing and swimming are among the academy's varsity sports.   **See Also Page 1307**

SAINT JOHN'S HIGH SCHOOL
Day — Boys Gr 9-12

Shrewsbury, MA 01545. 378 Main St. Tel: 508-842-8934. Fax: 508-842-3670. www.stjohnshigh.org   E-mail: slowe@stjohnshigh.org
Michael W. Welch, Head. BA, Marquette Univ, MA, Boston College. **Stephen D. Gregory, Prin. John Morse, Adm.**
   Col Prep. AP—Eng Fr Calc Stats Bio Chem Physics Eur_Hist US_Hist Comp_Govt & Pol Econ US_Govt & Pol Art_Hist. **Feat**—Span Anat & Physiol Computers Comp_Design Russian_Hist Relig Studio_Art Theater Directing Music.
   Adm (Gr 9-11): 288/yr. Appl due: Nov. Accepted: 75%. Yield: 75%. **Tests** HSPT.
   Enr 1058. B 1058. Sec 1058. Wh 94%. Hisp 1%. Blk 2%. Asian 3%. Avg class size: 26. **Fac**

69. M 55/1. F 12/1. Wh 96%. Hisp 1%. Blk 1%. Asian 1%. Other 1%. Adv deg: 82%.
Grad '04—245. Col—235. (U of MA-Amherst 16, U of CT 13, Providence 11, Boston Col 10, Worcester Polytech 9, Bryant 7). Avg SAT: 1184. Alum 10,000.
Tui '04-'05: Day $7350 (+$725). **Aid:** Merit 82 ($44,500). Need 237 ($426,000).
Summer: Acad Rev. Tui Day $350. 4 wks.
Bldgs 3. Class rms 41. Lib 10,000 vols. Sci labs 5. Comp labs 3. Auds 1. Theaters 1. Art studios 1. Music studios 1. Gyms 1. Fields 4. Courts 2. Pools 1.
Est 1894. Nonprofit. Roman Catholic. Quar (Aug-June). **Assoc** NEASC.

Founded in Worcester by the Xaverian Brothers and moved to its present location in 1961, Saint John's is staffed by both religious and lay faculty. The liberal arts curriculum features an extensive selection of Advanced Placement courses.

Varsity sports and a strong intramural program are available, and the campus ministry office coordinates many service projects. Various clubs round out the range of extracurricular options.

WORCESTER ACADEMY
Bdg — Coed Gr 9-PG; Day — Coed 6-PG

Worcester, MA 01604. 81 Providence St. Tel: 508-754-5302. Fax: 508-752-2382.
  www.worcesteracademy.org E-mail: admission@worcesteracademy.org
Dexter Morse, Head. AB, Bowdoin College, MEd, Univ of Vermont. **Jonathan G. Baker, Adm.**
  Col Prep. AP—Eng Fr Span Calc Comp_Sci Bio Chem Physics US_Hist World_Hist US_ Govt & Pol Studio_Art Music_Theory. **Feat**—Lat Web_Design Drama Theater_Arts Directing Music. **Supp**—ESL Tut.
  Adm (Bdg Gr 9-PG; Day Gr 6-11): 186/yr. Bdg 75. Day 111. Appl due: Feb. Accepted: 56%. Yield: 58%. **Tests** CEEB SSAT TOEFL.
  Enr 643. B 93/268. G 47/235. Elem 162. Sec 454. PG 27. Wh 79%. Hisp 1%. Blk 5%. Asian 15%. Avg class size: 13. **Fac 86.** M 40/9. F 28/9. Wh 99%. Hisp 1%. Adv deg: 54%. In dorms 27.
  Grad '04—130. Col—130. (Boston Col 7, Brandeis 3, Bowdoin 2, Brown 2, Carnegie Mellon 2, Tufts 2). Avg SAT: 1250. Alum 8000.
  Tui '04-'05: Bdg $33,200 (+$1200). **5-Day Bdg $29,650** (+$1200). **Day $17,300-18,500** (+$800). **Aid:** Merit 25 ($75,400). Need 165 ($1,750,000). Work prgm 46 ($25,000).
  Summer: Ages 8-14. Arts. Tui Day $425/2-wk ses. 4 wks.
  Endow $30,000,000. Plant val $44,000,000. Bldgs 4. Dorms 4. Dorm rms 142. Class rms 52. Lib 14,000 vols. Sci labs 6. Lang labs 1. Comp labs 3. Theaters 2. Art studios 2. Music studios 2. Gyms 2. Fields 8. Courts 4. Pools 1. Tracks 3.
  Est 1834. Nonprofit. Sem (Sept-June). **Assoc** CLS NEASC.

First organized as the Worcester County Manual Labor High School by a group of the leading men of Worcester, the school was renamed in 1844. Later reorganized as a boys' school, the academy again admitted girls into the student body in 1974. The campus includes six buildings listed in the National Register of Historic Places.

The academy's successful preparatory program combines academics, athletics and the arts. The curriculum includes clear requirements in the major disciplines and, through a full array of Advanced Placement courses, enables students to enroll in course sections appropriate to their abilities. Instruction in studio art, various aspects of drama, chorus and instrumental ensemble are part of the regular curriculum, and there is a strong emphasis on performance. WA fields interscholastic teams at both the varsity and the subvarsity levels, as well as at the middle school level.

Particular attention is given to student guidance and college placement by faculty members especially qualified to do this work. Students matriculate at colleges nationwide, with a strong orientation toward the most competitive colleges of the Northeast. The academy's urban location enables its students to take full advantage of the collegiate, university and cultural facilities of the city of Worcester.

See Also Page 1284

NEW HAMPSHIRE

ANDOVER, NH. (86 mi. NNW of Boston, MA) Rural. Pop: 2109. Alt: 620 ft.

PROCTOR ACADEMY
Bdg and Day — Coed Gr 9-12

Andover, NH 03216. 204 Main St, PO Box 500. Tel: 603-735-6212. Fax: 603-735-6284. www.proctoracademy.org E-mail: admission@proctornet.com
Stephen M. Wilkins, Head. BA, Colgate Univ, EdM, Harvard Univ. **Christopher Bartlett, Adm.**

- **Col Prep. AP**—Eng Fr Span Comp_Sci Bio Physics US_Hist US_Govt & Pol. **Feat**—British_Lit Poetry Playwriting Stats Anat & Physiol Zoology Wildlife_Sci Vietnam_War Econ Psych Sociol Bible & Koran Ceramics Photog Studio_Art Music_Theory Indus_Arts Mech_Drawing Woodworking. **Supp**—LD.
- **Adm:** 116/yr. Appl due: Feb. Accepted: 46%. **Tests** SSAT TOEFL.
- **Enr 336.** Sec 336. Wh 86%. Hisp 3%. Blk 6%. Am Ind 2%. Asian 3%. Avg class size: 12.
- **Fac 79.** M 26/11. F 23/19. Wh 97%. Blk 3%. Adv deg: 54%. In dorms 45.
- **Grad '04—88. Col—83.** (Geo Wash, CO Col, UNH, Bates, Wm & Mary, St Lawrence). Avg SAT: 1070. Avg SSAT: 50%. Alum 3350.
- **Tui '04-'05:** Bdg $34,300 (+$1650). **Day** $20,900 (+$1450). **Aid:** Need 90 ($1,610,000).
- Endow $22,000,000. Plant val $36,000,000. Bldgs 39. Dorms 21. Dorm rms 125. Class rms 32. Lib 23,000 vols. Sci labs 6. Comp labs 4. Auds 2. Theaters 1. Art studios 2. Music studios 2. Dance studios 1. Shops 4. Gyms 1. Fields 8. Courts 10. Field houses 1. Rinks 1. Riding rings 1. Stables 1.
- **Est 1848.** Nonprofit. Tri (Sept-June). **Assoc** NEASC.

This school, originally the coeducational Andover Academy, was renamed in 1879 in honor of a local benefactor and has long been affiliated with the Unitarian Church, although it has remained nondenominational in practice. In 1971, girls were admitted as boarding students and a coeducational day program was established. Over the years, the academy's campus has grown to encompass 2300 acres and now includes the central village of Andover and extensive woodland in Ragged Mountain.

Proctor's college preparatory program serves a cross section of college-bound students. Qualified pupils choose from a selection of honors and Advanced Placement courses, and the school also maintains a support system featuring structured extra-help and tutorial sessions.

The curriculum is enhanced by an extensive arts program and an Outward Bound-inspired mountain classroom elective in the desert Southwest. Pupils studying Spanish or French may participate in a ten-week program at a Proctor campus in Segovia, Spain; Aix-en-Provence, France; or Tangier, Morocco. A sailing adventure option, offered each fall term, allows students to earn full academic credit while sailing from New England to the Caribbean.

Among boys' and girls' sports are football, soccer, cross-country, technical rock climbing, skiing, ice hockey, basketball, lacrosse, field hockey, tennis, kayaking and baseball.

BETHLEHEM, NH. (85 mi. WNW of Portland, ME; 138 mi. NNW of Boston, MA) Rural. Pop: 2199. Alt: 978 ft.

WHITE MOUNTAIN SCHOOL
Bdg and Day — Coed Gr 9-PG

Bethlehem, NH 03574. 371 W Farm Rd. Tel: 603-444-2928. Fax: 603-444-5568.
www.whitemountain.org E-mail: wmsadmissions@whitemountain.org

Alan T. Popp, Head. BA, Allegheny College, MEd, Antioch New England Graduate School.
Laurie C. Zeiser, Adm.

Col Prep. Feat—Environ_Lit Women's_Lit Fr Span Anat & Physiol Environ_Sci Comp_Sci Japan_Hist Amer_Stud African_Stud Ethics Relig Photog Studio_Art. **Supp**—ESL LD Tut.

Adm: 48/yr. Bdg 41. Day 7. Appl due: Feb. Accepted: 60%. Yield: 75%. **Tests** IQ TOEFL.

Enr 100. B 44/8. G 42/6. Sec 99. PG 1. Wh 88%. Hisp 1%. Blk 7%. Asian 2%. Other 2%. Avg class size: 8. **Fac 30.** M 13/2. F 14/1. Wh 96%. Am Ind 3%. Asian 1%. Adv deg: 56%. In dorms 10.

Grad '04—31. Col—29. (Am U, Mt Holyoke, Lewis & Clark, UNH, U of Puget Sound, St Olaf). Alum 1300.

Tui '04-'05: Bdg $33,900 (+$2000). **Day $14,630** (+$1000).

Endow $1,000,000. Plant val $11,600,000. Bldgs 12. Dorms 5. Dorm rms 70. Class rms 23. Lib 13,000 vols. Sci labs 4. Lang labs 1. Comp labs 3. Theaters 1. Art studios 4. Music studios 1. Dance studios 1. Gyms 1. Athletic ctrs 1. Fields 2. Courts 3.

Est 1886. Nonprofit. Episcopal. Sem (Sept-June). **Assoc** NEASC.

Founded as St. Mary's School for girls in Concord by the Episcopal Diocese of New Hampshire, this school moved to its current location in 1936, became coeducational in 1969 and assumed its present name in 1972.

Utilizing interdisciplinary learning and hands-on experiences, WMS encourages active learning through writing, independent study, small-group work, research and extended field trips. Although the school employs the traditional letter grading system, grades assess mastery of six areas: content knowledge, complex thinking, information processing, collaboration, communication and self-direction. Extensive studio arts courses and a residential curriculum round out the program. For those students needing additional help, an optional learning assistance program is provided, and English as a Second Language is offered to international students.

Throughout the year, wilderness skills classes are taught after school and on weekends, and all students and faculty participate four times a year in three-day outdoor learning expeditions. Soccer and lacrosse are available as competitive team sports. Afternoon activities include hiking, paddling, rock climbing, mountain biking, soccer, lacrosse, tennis, theater, dance, snowboarding and recreational skiing. A service learning program comprises local weekly projects and optional Community Odysseys, which have taken place as far afield as Haiti, Honduras and Nicaragua. In addition, all students are involved in the upkeep of the school.

See Also Pages 1274-5

CANAAN, NH. (104 mi. NNW of Boston, MA) Rural. Pop: 3319. Alt: 942 ft.

CARDIGAN MOUNTAIN SCHOOL
Bdg and Day — Boys Gr 6-9

Canaan, NH 03741. 62 Alumni Dr. Tel: 603-523-3548. Fax: 603-523-3565.
www.cardigan.org   E-mail: rryerson@cardigan.org
Jamie H. Funnell, Int Head. Rich Ryerson, Adm.

Pre-Prep. Feat—Fr Lat Span Relig Music Indus_Arts Study_Skills. **Supp**—Dev_Read ESL Rem_Math Rem_Read Rev Tut.

Adm: 93/yr. Bdg 89. Day 4. Appl due: Rolling. Accepted: 79%. **Tests** IQ SSAT Stanford.

Enr 192. B 176/16. Elem 111. Sec 81. Wh 60%. Hisp 19%. Blk 4%. Asian 17%. Avg class size: 14. **Fac 52.** M 37/3. F 6/6. Wh 98%. Hisp 2%. Adv deg: 44%. In dorms 31.

Grad '04—52. Prep—41. (Northfield Mt Hermon 3, Avon 2, Lawrenceville 2, Westminster Sch-CT 2, Holderness 2, Lawrence Acad 2). Alum 3320.

Tui '04-'05: Bdg $33,250 (+$2750). **Day $19,000** (+$1000). **Aid:** Need 46 ($726,250).

Summer: Coed. Gr 4-8. Acad Enrich Rev Rem Rec. ESL. Tui Bdg $6700. Tui Day $3550. 6 wks.

Endow $13,500,000. Plant val $30,000,000. Bldgs 30. Dorms 13. Dorm rms 110. Class rms 37. Lib 13,000 vols. Labs 4. Lang labs 1. Auds 1. Theaters 1. Art studios 3. Music studios 3. Wood shops 1. Gyms 1. Fields 6. Courts 18. Rinks 1. Rifle/trap shooting ranges 1.

Est 1945. Nonprofit. Tri (Sept-June). **Assoc** NEASC.

Located in the foothills of the White Mountains and on the shores of Canaan Street Lake, Cardigan Mountain was established with the support of a group of industrialists and educators, including Ernest Hopkins, former president of nearby Dartmouth College.

The school's academic program incorporates a multitrack approach that caters to a broad spectrum of students. Parallel scheduling allows boys to work to potential in each discipline. Tutorials in math and reading and writing skills are available for a limited number of students. Daily conferences provide time for extra assistance.

Cardigan Mountain's extensive athletic facilities allow pupils to engage in an array of sports, as well as such outdoor pursuits as downhill and cross-country skiing. A diversified club program supplements various interscholastic and intramural activities. The school's graduates enter many different preparatory schools, predominantly ones in the Northeast.

CONCORD, NH. (68 mi. NNW of Boston, MA) Urban. Pop: 40,687. Alt: 244 ft.

ST. PAUL'S SCHOOL
Bdg — Coed Gr 9-12

Concord, NH 03301. 325 Pleasant St. Tel: 603-229-4700. Fax: 603-229-4771.
www.sps.edu   E-mail: admissions@sps.edu
William Matthews, Acting Rector. Michael G. Hirschfeld, Adm.

Col Prep. AP—Eng Fr Ger Lat Span Calc Stats Bio Chem Physics Studio_Art. **Feat**—Humanities Chin Greek Japan Astron Ecol Programming Robotics Philos Relig Architect Fine_Arts Photog Music Dance. **Supp**—ESL.

Adm (Gr 9-11): 147/yr. Appl due: Jan. Accepted: 23%. Yield: 66%. **Tests** SSAT TOEFL.

Enr 525. B 260. G 265. Sec 525. Wh 70%. Hisp 4%. Blk 7%. Asian 14%. Other 5%. Avg class size: 12. **Fac 71.** M 38/1. F 28/4. Wh 96%. Hisp 2%. Asian 2%. Adv deg: 77%. In dorms 42.

Grad '04—134. Col—131. (Brown 10, Harvard 7, U of VA 7, U of PA 7, Yale 5, Georgetown 5). Avg SAT: 1344. Alum 7987.

Tui '04-'05: Bdg $32,675 (+$2800). **Aid:** Merit 25 ($540,750). Need 172 ($4,500,000). Endow $311,000,000. Plant val $85,000,000. Bldgs 116. Dorms 18. Dorm rms 250. Class rms 47. Lib 70,000 vols. Chapels 2. Labs 8. Theaters 3. Art studios 3. Music studios 1. Dance studios 1. Drama studios 1. Observatories 3. Gyms 1. Fields 11. Courts 15. Pools 1. Rinks 2. Tracks 1.

Est 1856. Nonprofit. Episcopal. Tri (Sept-June). **Assoc** CLS NEASC.

Founded the previous year by Dr. George Cheyne Shattuck of Boston, who gave his country home in Concord for the school's use, St. Paul's opened on April 3, 1856, with an enrollment of three boys. As a church school, St. Paul's has had a long-time association with the Episcopal Church. Faculty and students continue to gather in the chapel four mornings each week.

The curriculum offers a solid foundation in the liberal arts. Course offerings in regular and advanced sections cover the subjects of the arts, the classics, computer science, the humanities, mathematics, modern languages, religion and science. Each student must complete courses in the humanities, math, science, the arts and languages. The arts offer students the opportunity to pursue music, dance, drama and the visual arts at a preprofessional level or as enriching cocurricular activities, while studies in the humanities integrate the disciplines of English, history and religion.

St. Paul's cosponsors School Year Abroad programs in France, China, Italy and Spain for students in the fifth and sixth forms. The school also has an association with Seikei School and the Toin School in Tokyo, Japan, in addition to conducting exchange programs with schools in England, France, Sweden, Denmark and Eastern Europe. An independent study program offers sixth form students the opportunity to learn from study and experience outside the classroom; student projects may be academic, vocational, social service oriented or experiential.

Athletics and extracurricular activities include interscholastic teams, intramurals, and instructional and recreational sports, as well as clubs and societies.

See Also Pages 1246-7

DUBLIN, NH. (66 mi. NW of Boston, MA) Rural. Pop: 1476. Alt: 1493 ft.

DUBLIN SCHOOL

Bdg and Day — Coed Gr 9-PG

Dublin, NH 03444. 18 Lehmann Way, PO Box 522. Tel: 603-563-8584. Fax: 603-563-7121.
www.dublinschool.org   E-mail: admission@dublinschool.org

Christopher R. Horgan, Head. BA, Bridgewater State College, MEd, Plymouth State College.
Marylou T. Marcus, Adm.
  Col Prep. LD. Underachiever. AP—Eng Fr Calc Bio US_Hist. **Feat**—Lat Span Geol Marine_Biol/Sci Computers Existentialism World_Relig Ceramics Sculpt Women_in_ Film Drama Music Debate Woodworking. **Supp**—ESL Rev Tut.
  Adm (Bdg Gr 9-PG; Day 9-10): 54/yr. Bdg 45. Day 9. Appl due: Jan. Accepted: 82%. Yield: 62%. **Tests** CTP_4 IQ SSAT TOEFL.
  Enr 132. B 61/20. G 37/14. Sec 130. PG 2. Avg class size: 12. **Fac 36.** M 21. F 15. Wh 100%. Adv deg: 41%. In dorms 10.
  Grad '04—41. Col—34. (UNH 4, Colby 2, U of VT 2, Sarah Lawrence 2, Rochester Inst of Tech 2, Smith 1). Avg SAT: 1121. Alum 1400.
  Tui '04-'05: Bdg $34,400 (+$1000). **Day $21,500** (+$1000). **Aid:** Merit 1 ($21,500). Need 41 ($716,800).
  Endow $1,900,000. Plant val $12,100,000. Bldgs 21. Dorms 7. Dorm rms 47. Class rms 17. Lib 12,000 vols. Sci labs 3. Lang labs 1. Comp labs 2. Sci ctrs 1. Auds 1. Theaters 1. Art studios 1. Music studios 2. Dance studios 1. Arts ctrs 1. Wood shops 1. Recording studios 1. Gyms 1. Fields 2. Tennis courts 6. Squash courts 2. Rinks 1. Weight rms 1. Skiing facilities yes. Boating facilities yes. Student ctrs 1. Lakes 1.
  Est 1935. Nonprofit. Tri (Sept-June). **Assoc** NEASC.

Paul Lehmann founded this successful school with his wife, Nancy. Girls were admitted on a day basis in 1969, and the girls' boarding division (opened in 1970) has firmly established coeducation for the school. The traditional college preparatory curriculum seeks to develop academic skills, artistic talents and athletic abilities. Faculty and students work together in small classes that facilitate individualized instruction. The curriculum comprises a distributed core of required courses, as well as electives in the disciplines of English, foreign language, math, science, art and history. Advanced Placement courses and independent study options enrich the program, and qualified pupils may pursue an honors-level diploma.

Dublin also conducts individualized learning skills and evening study programs for students who are intellectually capable but whose academic achievement has not yet matched their ability level. These programs may include boys and girls with diagnosed learning differences or those in need of organizational assistance. Each program represents a structured support system for the mainstream Dublin curriculum, not an alternative curriculum.

All students participate in the athletic program, which includes soccer, skiing, snowboarding, cross-country running, lacrosse, sailing, tennis, basketball and recreational sports. Participation in community service and a campus-wide jobs program is also compulsory. Extracurricular activities include theater, publications, singing and musical groups, school government, and on- and off-campus weekend events.

See Also Pages 1144-5

EXETER, NH. (44 mi. N of Boston, MA) Suburban. Pop: 9759. Alt: 58 ft.

PHILLIPS EXETER ACADEMY
Bdg and Day — Coed Gr 9-PG
Exeter, NH 03833. 20 Main St. Tel: 603-777-3437. Fax: 603-777-4399.

www.exeter.edu E-mail: admit@exeter.edu
Tyler C. Tingley, Prin. AB, MEd, EdD, Harvard Univ. **Michael Gary, Adm.**
- **Col Prep. AP**—Lat Comp_Sci. **Feat**—Humanities Chin Fr Ger Greek Ital Japan Russ Span Oceanog Nuclear_Physics Astronomy Asian_Hist Anthro Econ.
- **Adm:** 353/yr. Bdg 292. Day 61. Appl due: Jan. Accepted: 27%. Yield: 65%. **Tests** SSAT TOEFL.
- **Enr 1052.** B 449/93. G 401/109. Sec 1014. PG 38. Wh 62%. Hisp 5%. Blk 7%. Am Ind 1%. Asian 20%. Other 5%. Avg class size: 12. **Fac 171.** M 99. F 72. Wh 89%. Hisp 4%. Blk 2%. Asian 4%. Other 1%. Adv deg: 84%. In dorms 61.
- **Grad '04—322. Col—322.** (U of PA 15, Princeton 13, Harvard 13, Columbia 12, Georgetown 10, NYU 9). Avg SAT: 1390. Avg SSAT: 86%. Alum 20,000.
- **Tui '04-'05: Bdg $31,600** (+$1000). **Day $24,400** (+$500). **Aid:** Need 350 ($8,180,356).
- **Summer:** Acad Enrich. Tui Bdg $5595. Tui Day $995/crse. 5 wks.
- Endow $639,000,000. Bldgs 126. Dorms 29. Dorm rms 675. Class rms 119. Lib 148,000 vols. Sci labs 22. Lang labs 1. Comp labs 3. Sci ctrs 1. Observatories 1. Theaters 1. Art studios 4. Music studios 8. Dance studios 1. Galleries 1. Gyms 2. Fields 15. Tennis courts 23. Squash courts 14. Pools 2. Rinks 2. Stadiums 1.
- **Est 1781.** Nonprofit. Tri (Sept-June). **Assoc** CLS NEASC.

Established by John Phillips, whose nephew Samuel Phillips, Jr., had founded Phillips Academy at Andover, MA, three years earlier, Exeter is known for its outstanding faculty, diverse student body, and excellent academic and athletic facilities. The academy has been coeducational since 1970, when girls were first admitted as day students. The boarding program became coed the following fall. The present-day school enrolls a diverse student body from nearly every state, as well as various foreign countries.

Exeter's curriculum exhibits noteworthy breadth in diploma requirements. Broadly distributed requirements in science, history and the humanities form the main thrust of a curriculum that stresses knowledge acquisition in a liberal arts framework. Advanced Placement courses are offered in all disciplines, and most subjects go beyond the AP level.

At the center of an Exeter education is the Harkness Plan, made possible in the early 1930s by gifts from Edward S. Harkness, benefactor to many schools and colleges. A teacher and 12 students sit around a table forming and expressing ideas—a classroom in the seminar mode, where maximum participation is encouraged.

Students are assigned at the outset, especially in mathematics and foreign languages, to courses and sections according to demonstrated ability. Help in cultivating effective learning, speaking and thinking habits establishes a sound foundation. Through close daily association of students with the faculty in all areas of school life, Exeter seeks also to blend goodness of character with the growth in intellectual skills fostered by the Harkness Plan.

Exeter's comprehensive music program provides opportunities for study and performance. An orchestra and a chorus are the largest activities, while a number of other musical groups are available. Both varsity athletes and nonathletic students are involved in a daily physical education program. A dance program is also available at elementary through advanced levels.

Off-campus programs include a term spent in Washington, DC, as a congressional intern and a half year at the Milton Mountain School in Vershire, VT. Through School Year Abroad, students may study in France, Italy or Spain, or may spend a fall term in Beijing, China. Exchanges are also arranged with secondary schools in Germany, Mexico and Russia, and one-term programs are offered in Stratford, England, and Grenoble, France.

MANCHESTER, NH. (50 mi. NNW of Boston, MA) Urban. Pop: 107,006. Alt: 225 ft.

THE DERRYFIELD SCHOOL
Day — Coed Gr 6-12

Manchester, NH 03104. 2108 River Rd. Tel: 603-669-4524. Fax: 603-641-9521.
  www.derryfield.org   E-mail: admission@derryfield.org
Randle B. Richardson, Head. BA, Hamilton College, MALS, Wesleyan Univ. **Kathleen Rutty-Fey, Adm.**
  Col Prep. AP—Eng Fr Lat Span Calc Stats US_Hist. **Feat**—Creative_Writing Anat & Physiol Computers Psych Philos Art_Hist Film Drama Music String_Band Study_Skills. **Supp**—Tut.
  Adm: 92/yr. Appl due: Feb. Accepted: 79%. **Tests** SSAT.
  Enr 378. B 168. G 210. Elem 138. Sec 240. Wh 92%. Hisp 2%. Blk 2%. Asian 3%. Other 1%. Avg class size: 14. **Fac 54.** M 28/2. F 24. Wh 96%. Hisp 4%. Adv deg: 57%.
  Grad '04—57. Col—56. (Bates, Dartmouth, Trinity Col-CT, Emory, UNH, U of PA). Avg SAT: 1287. Avg SSAT: 75%. Avg ACT: 25. Alum 1440.
  Tui '04-'05: Day $18,550 (+$600). **Aid:** Need 51 ($478,214).
  Endow $3,300,000. Plant val $10,700,000. Bldgs 5. Class rms 32. Lib 16,477 vols. Sci labs 5. Comp labs 1. Auds 1. Theaters 1. Art studios 2. Music studios 1. Perf arts ctrs 1. Gyms 1. Fields 4. Courts 6.
  Est 1964. Nonprofit. Tri (Sept-June). **Assoc** NEASC.

The school serves more than 40 southern New Hampshire communities. It provides a traditional preparatory curriculum in combination with extensive sports, fine arts, extracurricular and community service programs. Derryfield also conducts Summerbridge Manchester, a tuition-free summer program for academically talented public school students; high school and college pupils interested in teaching serve as instructors for the six-week program.   **See Also Page 1133**

MERIDEN, NH. (104 mi. NW of Boston, MA) Rural. Pop: 500. Alt: 1000 ft.

KIMBALL UNION ACADEMY
Bdg and Day — Coed Gr 9-PG

Meriden, NH 03770. Main St, PO Box 188. Tel: 603-469-2100. Fax: 603-469-2041.
  www.kua.org   E-mail: admissions@kua.org
Michael J. Schafer, Head. BA, Colby College, MEd, Harvard Univ. **Joe Williams, Adm.**
  Col Prep. AP—Eng Fr Lat Span Calc Stats Comp_Sci Bio Chem Physics Eur_Hist US_Hist Art_Hist Studio_Art. **Feat**—Humanities Geol Marine_Biol/Sci Forestry Law Architect Drama Music Music_Production Dance Public_Speak Study_Skills. **Supp**—Tut.

NH *Leading Private Schools* 262

   Adm: 123/yr. Bdg 89. Day 34. Appl due: Feb. Accepted: 60%. **Tests** SSAT TOEFL.
   Enr 311. B 119/59. G 77/56. Sec 301. PG 10. Wh 86%. Hisp 2%. Blk 4%. Asian 8%. Avg class size: 12. **Fac 52.** M 31/1. F 16/4. Wh 100%. Adv deg: 61%. In dorms 35.
   Grad '04—79. Col—76. (Geo Wash 3, St Lawrence 3, Lynn 3, U of Denver 3, Bates 2, Boston Col 2). Avg SAT: 1180. Alum 3800.
   Tui '04-'05: Bdg $33,500 (+$1500). **Day $21,500** (+$750). **Aid:** Need 118 ($1,500,000). Endow $11,500,000. Plant val $30,000,000. Bldgs 35. Dorms 9. Dorm rms 145. Class rms 26. Lib 20,000 vols. Sci labs 6. Lang labs 1. Comp labs 2. Theaters 1. Art studios 3. Music studios 2. Dance studios 1. Arts ctrs 1. Gyms 2. Fields 7. Courts 8. Pools 1. Rinks 1. Fitness ctrs 2.
   Est 1813. Nonprofit. Tri (Sept-May). **Assoc** CLS NEASC.

Founded as a coeducational school, Kimball Union followed educational trends in 1935 and became a boys' school, which it remained until coeducation was reintroduced in 1974. The present-day institution, located 13 miles south of Dartmouth College, attracts a diverse student body from throughout the world.

The challenging liberal arts curriculum features small classes, supervised study halls for underclassmen, and Advanced Placement courses in every discipline. Graduation requirements include two years of foreign languages, arts, computer and health courses. An extensive environmental studies program makes use of Snow Mountain, the school's 750-acre wilderness area. Dartmouth College courses are arranged for those qualified to study a subject beyond the range of Kimball Union's curriculum.

All students participate in two seasons of a group activity each year and can spend the third in an activity such as recreational skiing, or in an arts program such as visual arts or photography. Arts programs involving larger groups—such as chorus, jazz and rock bands, dance and theater—have an exclusively allotted period around the dinner hour. Additional extracurriculars are publications, community service and student government, in addition to a number of other clubs and committees; pupils may also join the local volunteer fire department.

Students contribute to the running of the school through their participation in a work program, and KUA offers many leadership opportunities. The entire school community gathers for a morning meeting twice weekly. **See Also Page 1185**

NEW HAMPTON, NH. (93 mi. NNW of Boston, MA) Rural. Pop: 1950. Alt: 574 ft.

NEW HAMPTON SCHOOL
Bdg and Day — Coed Gr 9-PG

New Hampton, NH 03256. 70 Main St, PO Box 579. Tel: 603-677-3401.
   Fax: 603-677-3481.
   www.newhampton.org   E-mail: admissions@newhampton.org
Alan B. Crocker, Actg Head. Andrew H. Churchill, Adm.
   Col Prep. AP—Eng Calc Physics US_Hist Studio_Art. **Feat**—Fr Lat Span Anat & Physiol Ecol Environ_Sci Programming Econ Psych Ceramics Photog Acting Drama Music Dance Journ Speech. **Supp**—ESL Tut.
   Adm: 150/yr. Bdg 120. Day 30. Appl due: Feb. Accepted: 60%. **Tests** CEEB SSAT.
   Enr 340. B 140/55. G 90/55. Sec 320. PG 20. Wh 75%. Hisp 3%. Blk 6%. Asian 12%. Other

4%. Avg class size: 12. **Fac 72.** M 34. F 38.
Grad '04—120. **Col**—120. (UNH, St Lawrence, U of VT, Tulane, Geo Mason, MIT). Avg SAT: 1010. Alum 5000.
Tui '04-'05: Bdg $32,600 (+$1000). **Day $19,400** (+$500). **Aid:** Need 100 ($1,500,000). Endow $8,000,000. Plant val $15,000,000. Bldgs 27. Dorms 13. Dorm rms 150. Class rms 50. Lib 25,000 vols. Sci labs 5. Lang labs 1. Comp labs 3. Photog labs 1. Auds 1. Theaters 1. Art studios 1. Music studios 4. Dance studios 1. Gyms 2. Fields 5. Courts 9. Rinks 1. Radio stations 1.
Est 1821. Nonprofit. Tri (Sept-May). **Assoc** CLS NEASC.

New Hampton offers a well-regarded program that adheres to a national model for experience-based education. Recognizing that students learn in different ways and come from varying academic backgrounds, the school designs its classes to provide different learning experiences and to accommodate boys and girls with a range of academic skills. Honors, Advanced Placement and standard college preparatory offerings are available in each discipline, as are fine and performing arts courses, academic support services and English as a Second Language instruction.

Participation in an after-school program is compulsory during each of the three terms. Choices include Alpine ski racing, snowboarding, golf, lacrosse, tennis, rock climbing, weight training, volleyball, field hockey, softball, football, baseball, soccer, cross-country, basketball, equestrianship, outdoor adventure, kayaking, mountain biking, newspaper, yearbook, literary magazine, theater, ceramics, film, dance, music and photography.

Several Saturday mornings throughout the fall and spring terms are devoted to school-wide community service efforts. Another program, Alongside Saturdays, enables students to conduct workshops for their peers and teachers. Various other service opportunities are also available during the winter term.

See Also Pages 1212-3

PLYMOUTH, NH. (103 mi. NNW of Boston, MA) Rural. Pop: 5892. Alt: 514 ft.

HOLDERNESS SCHOOL
Bdg and Day — Coed Gr 9-PG

Plymouth, NH 03264. Chapel Ln, PO Box 1879. Tel: 603-536-1257. Fax: 603-536-1267.
www.holderness.org   E-mail: admissions@holderness.org
Phillip Peck, Head. BA, Dartmouth College, MA, EdD, Columbia Univ. **Peter B. Barnum, Adm.**
Col Prep. AP—Eng Fr Span Calc Bio Eur_Hist US_Hist Music_Theory. **Feat**—Lat Environ_Sci Computers Russ_Hist Cold_War & Vietnam Bible Theol Ceramics Photog Studio_Art Theater Music. **Supp**—Tut.
Adm (Gr 9-12): 103/yr. Bdg 85. Day 18. Appl due: Feb. Accepted: 50%. **Tests** IQ ISEE SSAT TOEFL.
Enr 280. B 144/30. G 75/31. Sec 276. PG 4. Wh 89%. Blk 4%. Am Ind 1%. Asian 5%. Other 1%. Avg class size: 13. **Fac 44.** M 27. F 15/2. Wh 95%. Blk 3%. Asian 2%. Adv deg: 65%. In dorms 28.
Grad '04—78. **Col**—78. (U of VT, Middlebury, Bates, St Lawrence, Brown, Georgetown). Avg SAT: 1145. Alum 2853.

Tui '02-'03: Bdg $29,800 (+$1000). **Day $17,700** (+$150). **Aid:** Need 60 ($1,341,775). Endow $25,140,000. Plant val $19,741,000. Bldgs 23. Dorms 14. Dorm rms 110. Class rms 30. Libs 1. Sci labs 6. Comp labs 3. Auds 1. Theaters 1. Art studios 4. Music studios 2. Gyms 1. Fields 3. Courts 6. Rinks 1.
Est 1879. Nonprofit. Episcopal. Sem (Sept-May). **Assoc** CLS NEASC.

The Holderness curriculum emphasizes the acquisition of those skills that prepare students for college entrance; in particular, course work addresses reading comprehension and clarity in writing. Focus in math and the physical science classes (as well as in the social sciences and languages) remains on critical thinking and application of the principals of logic. Art, music and drama, in addition to a daily job program and student government, complement standard course offerings.

During the month of March, pupils engage in grade-specific special programs. Freshmen and returning sophomores participate in Artward Bound, a creative collaboration with artists-in-residence that ends with an art exhibition, while returning sophomores take part in Habitat for Humanity community service projects. Juniors partake of an outdoor education experience in the White Mountains that calls upon both individual and team survival techniques. Seniors choose from either an intensive, college-style course taught by school faculty and visiting professors on a topic in the humanities, or an independent project that begins with two to three weeks of research and culminates in the composition of a ten-page paper and the delivery of an oral presentation to other students.

Holderness offers a wide selection of competitive athletics at the varsity, junior varsity and, in some cases, "prep" levels. The school's proximity to mountains also enables boys and girls to join Alpine ski teams or engage in recreational skiing or snowboarding.

RINDGE, NH. (58 mi. WNW of Boston, MA) Suburban. Pop: 5451. Alt: 1400 ft.

HAMPSHIRE COUNTRY SCHOOL
Bdg — Boys Gr 3-12

Rindge, NH 03461. 122 Hampshire Rd. Tel: 603-899-3325. Fax: 603-899-6521.
www.hampshirecountryschool.com   E-mail: hampshirecountry@monad.net
William Dickerman, Head. BA, Oberlin College, MA, PhD, Univ of Wisconsin-Madison.
  Col Prep. Gen Acad. LD. Underachiever. Feat—Ger. Supp—Rev Tut.
  Adm (Gr 3-9): 8/yr. Appl due: Rolling. Accepted: 50%.
  Enr 22. B 22. Elem 13. Sec 9. Wh 95%. Blk 5%. Avg class size: 5. **Fac 14.** M 8. F 4/2. Wh 100%. Adv deg: 7%. In dorms 6.
  Grad '04—1. Col—1. (New England Col).
  Tui '04-'05: Bdg $38,000 (+$1000).
  Plant val $1,000,000. Bldgs 7. Dorms 4. Dorm rms 20. Class rms 6. Lib 3000 vols. Labs 1. Theaters 1. Wood shops 1. Fields 1. Tennis courts 1. Riding rings 1. Stables 1.
  Est 1948. Nonprofit. Tri (Sept-June). **Assoc** NEASC.

Within the framework of a traditional educational program, HCS educates students of above-average ability who have been unable to succeed in other settings. Pupils typically enroll at middle school age and remain at the school for three or four years, although some complete their high school studies at HCS. The school can accommodate such special needs as hyperactivity, difficulty in dealing with peers or adults, unusually timid or fearful behavior, and school phobia. A low student-teacher ratio meets the needs of students who require extra structure and attention.

Located on 1700 acres of farm and woodland, the school offers an activities program that includes horseback riding, skating, sledding, soccer, canoeing, swimming, tennis and hiking. **See Also Page 1363**

THE MEETING SCHOOL
Bdg and Day — Coed Gr 8-PG

Rindge, NH 03461. 120 Thomas Rd. Tel: 603-899-3366. Fax: 603-899-6216.
  www.meetingschool.org   E-mail: office@meetingschool.org
Jacqueline Stillwell, Head. BA, Friends World College, MS, Antioch New England Graduate School. **Frederick Martin, Adm.**
  Col Prep. Gen Acad. Feat—Chin Span Peace_Stud Asian_Stud Culture & Agriculture. **Supp**—ESL Rem_Math Rem_Read Tut.
  Adm: 14/yr. Appl due: Rolling. Accepted: 95%.
  Enr 30. B 16/1. G 12/1. Avg class size: 6. **Fac 12.** M 6. F 6. Wh 95%. Blk 5%. Adv deg: 50%. In dorms 12.
  Grad '04—11. Col—6. (Warren Wilson, Friends World, Augsburg, Sterling). Alum 450.
  Tui '04-'05: Bdg $32,000 (+$600). **Day $17,500** (+$600). **Aid:** Need 23.
  Plant val $500,000. Bldgs 11. Dorms 5. Dorm rms 21. Class rms 6. Libs 1. Labs 2. Art studios 1. Music studios 1. Photog studios 1. Shops 1. Fields 1. Barns 1.
  Est 1957. Nonprofit. Religious Society of Friends. Tri (Sept-May). **Assoc** NEASC.

Established by members of the Religious Society of Friends (the Quakers), this small school in rural New England expects each person to accept responsibility for his or her own personal growth while participating fully in community life. Students live on campus in faculty homes. Meals, housecleaning, maintenance, farm work and gardening are part of a required work-study program. The entire community meets weekly to conduct school business, with decisions being made by consensus.

In addition to the traditional subjects, the curriculum includes courses in such areas as creative writing, peace studies, Asian studies, theater, ethics, African literature, culture and agriculture, pottery, weaving and conflict resolution. The academic program allows students and faculty to work together in areas of mutual interest. A four-week intersession program between winter and spring terms provides outside experience by developing independent projects off campus. Each student participates in a faculty-approved project of his or her design. Pupils are admitted throughout the school year.

TILTON, NH. (82 mi. NNW of Boston, MA) Suburban. Pop: 3477. Alt: 453 ft.

TILTON SCHOOL
Bdg and Day — Coed Gr 9-PG

Tilton, NH 03276. 30 School St. Tel: 603-286-1733. Fax: 603-286-1705.
  www.tiltonschool.org   E-mail: admissions@tiltonschool.org
James R. Clements, Head. BA, Univ of New Hampshire, MBA, Plymouth State College.
  Katherine E. Saunders, Adm.
  Col Prep. AP—Eng Fr Span Calc Bio Chem Physics Eur_Hist US_Hist Studio_Art. **Feat**—Creative_Writing Irish_Lit Stats Anat & Physiol Forensic_Sci Econ Pol_Sci Psych Sociol Criminal_Justice Ceramics Film Photog Chorus Music_Theory. **Supp**—ESL LD Rev Tut.
  Adm (Bdg Gr 9-12; Day 9-11): 93/yr. Appl due: Feb. Accepted: 57%. Yield: 43%. **Tests** CEEB IQ ISEE SSAT TOEFL.
  Enr 231. Sec 213. PG 18. Avg class size: 10. **Fac 39.** M 20/5. F 10/4. Wh 96%. Blk 2%. Asian 2%. Adv deg: 43%. In dorms 17.
  Grad '04—60. Col—59. (Plymouth St 5, Loyola U-LA 2, Bentley 2, U of VT 2, St Anselm 2, UNH 2). Avg SAT: 1006. Avg ACT: 20. Alum 4009.
  Tui '04-'05: Bdg $33,125 (+$1000). **Day $19,175** (+$500). **Aid:** Merit ($26,000). Need ($946,225).
  Endow $9,500,000. Plant val $25,600,000. Bldgs 28. Dorms 5. Dorm rms 122. Class rms 22. Lib 17,500 vols. Chapels 1. Sci labs 4. Comp labs 2. Auds 1. Theaters 1. Art studios 1. Music studios 1. Dance studios 1. Gyms 1. Fields 8. Tennis courts 3. Squash courts 2. Pools 1. Rinks 1. Fitness ctrs 1.
  Est 1845. Nonprofit. Methodist. Sem (Sept-May). **Assoc** CLS NEASC.

Founded as a secondary school for boarding and day boys and girls, the school was founded in Northfield, across the Winnipesaukee River from the present campus. A fire in the 1860s led the school to move to its current location. Over the years, Tilton has fulfilled different functions, according to community need: It has been as a coeducational boarding school, a boys' boarding school, a public school, a female college, a junior college, and a secondary school with both college and general courses. In 1939, the school stopped serving as the local high school and became a strictly independent boys' boarding and day school. General diploma courses were dropped in 1958, as the school focused solely on college preparation. Tilton reinstituted its girls' division in 1970.

The college preparatory curriculum, which qualifies graduates for many competitive colleges, includes Advanced Placement and honors courses. A learning center provides academic support, and the school schedules weekly extra-help periods and small-group advisor meetings. The +5 program requires participation beyond the school day in arts and culture, team athletics, outdoor experiences, community service and leadership activities.

Located on a 146-acre tract in New Hampshire's White Mountains and Lakes Region, the school's campus includes fields, trails, woodland, streams and ponds. Several ski areas are a short distance away. **See Also Page 1268**

WOLFEBORO, NH. (51 mi. W of Portland, ME; 87 mi. N of Boston, MA) Suburban. Pop: 2979. Alt: 508 ft.

BREWSTER ACADEMY
Bdg and Day — Coed Gr 9-PG

Wolfeboro, NH 03894. 80 Academy Dr. Tel: 603-569-7200. Fax: 603-569-7272.
www.brewsteracademy.org E-mail: admissions@brewsteracademy.org
Michael E. Cooper, Head. BA, State Univ of New York-Albany, MEd, St Lawrence Univ, PhD, Syracuse Univ. **Lynne M. Palmer, Adm.**

Col Prep. AP—Eng Calc Bio Physics Eur_Hist US_Hist. **Feat**—Fr Span Comp_Sci Comp_Graphics Ceramics Photog Theater Jazz_Band Dance Journ Yoga. **Supp**—ESL Tut.

Adm: 158/yr. Bdg 133. Day 25. Appl due: Feb. Accepted: 55%. Yield: 60%. **Tests** IQ SSAT TOEFL.

Enr 367. B 182/52. G 101/32. Sec 351. PG 16. Wh 79%. Hisp 1%. Blk 4%. Asian 13%. Other 3%. Avg class size: 11. **Fac 61.** M 30. F 31. Adv deg: 49%. In dorms 31.

Grad '04—101. Col—101. (St Michael's 5, Boston U 3, Emory 3, U of VA 3, UNH 3, Am U 2). Avg SAT: 1072. Avg ACT: 22. Alum 4350.

Tui '04-'05: Bdg $32,995 (+$2000). **Day $19,545** (+$600). **Aid:** Need 90 ($1,800,000).

Summer: Acad Enrich Rev Rec. Outdoor Ed. Tui Bdg $5995-6195. Tui Day $3595. 6 wks. Endow $12,300,000. Plant val $37,000,000. Bldgs 35. Dorms 20. Dorm rms 278. Class rms 40. Lib 45,000 vols. Labs 4. Sci labs 3. Comp labs 1. Theaters 1. Art studios 4. Music studios 5. Gyms 1. Fields 7. Courts 3. Tracks 1. Boathouses 1. Student ctrs 1.

Est 1820. Nonprofit. Tri (Sept-June). **Assoc** NEASC.

This small college preparatory school's concern for personal growth and development attracts students from dozens of states and foreign countries. The traditional college preparatory curriculum stresses an individualized approach to learning, facilitated by a 6:1 student-teacher ratio. In addition to its core classes, Brewster offers a variety of electives, among them visual and performing arts, computer graphics and journalism. Qualified pupils may also pursue honors and Advanced Placement courses. An academic support department includes writing and math centers and an English as a Second Language program.

Located in a resort village, the 80-acre campus on the shores of Lake Winnipesaukee provides the setting for a year-round sports program that includes outdoor skills, girls' and boys' ice hockey, sailing, crew, Alpine and Nordic skiing, snowboarding, field hockey, soccer, cross-country, golf, strength training and conditioning, tennis, basketball, horseback riding, tennis, lacrosse, baseball, softball and yoga. **See Also Pages 1122-3**

RHODE ISLAND

BARRINGTON, RI. (8 mi. SE of Providence, RI; 44 mi. SSW of Boston, MA) Suburban. Pop: 16,819. Alt: 24 ft.

ST. ANDREW'S SCHOOL
Bdg — Coed Gr 9-12; Day — Coed 6-12

Barrington, RI 02806. 63 Federal Rd. Tel: 401-246-1230. Fax: 401-246-0510.
www.standrews-ri.org   E-mail: inquiry@standrews-ri.org
John D. Martin, Head. BA, Tufts Univ, MEd, American International College, MDiv, Yale Univ.
R. Scott Telford, Adm.
   Col Prep. AP—Calc. **Feat**—Span Environ_Sci Computers Comp_Design Global_Issues Photog Studio_Art Theater_Arts Music. **Supp**—ESL LD Rem_Read Tut.
   Adm (Bdg Gr 9-11; Day 6-11): 64/yr. Bdg 14. Day 50. Appl due: Feb. Accepted: 48%. Yield: 35%. **Tests** ISEE SSAT.
   Enr 194. B 32/110. G 11/41. Elem 40. Sec 154. Wh 65%. Hisp 3%. Blk 22%. Am Ind 1%. Asian 8%. Other 1%. Avg class size: 10. **Fac 46.** M 15/2. F 25/4. Wh 78%. Hisp 1%. Blk 21%. Adv deg: 41%. In dorms 8.
   Grad '04—36. Col—34. (CC of RI 6, Savannah Col of Art & Design 2, Providence 2, New England Col 2, Bristol CC 2, Pratt 1). Avg SAT: 868. Alum 720.
   Tui '04-'05: Bdg $31,950 (+$2000). **Day $19,750** (+$300). **Aid:** Need 87 ($1,169,045). Endow $14,000,000. Plant val $25,000,000. Bldgs 24. Dorms 4. Dorm rms 45. Class rms 42. Lib 8200 vols. Sci labs 4. Lang labs 2. Comp labs 3. Auds 1. Theaters 1. Art studios 2. Music studios 1. Gyms 2. Fields 4. Tennis courts 4. Ropes crses 1.
   Est 1893. Nonprofit. Episcopal. Quar (Sept-June). **Assoc** NEASC.

Founded by Rev. William M. Chapin, St. Andrew's provides a traditional college preparatory curriculum within a structured, supportive environment. The curriculum is designed to help students develop sound academic skills and study habits, to provide college preparation, and to expose students to a variety of cocurricular activities. Small classes and a daily advisory system ensure individualized attention. The Resource and Focus programs, both of which are available for an additional fee, offer extra support to pupils with mild language-based learning disabilities or attentional concerns.

The school, which occupies an 83-acre site, offers a full range of athletic and extracurricular offerings. **See Also Pages 1240-1**

EAST GREENWICH, RI. (11 mi. S of Providence, RI; 52 mi. SSW of Boston, MA) Suburban. Pop: 12,948. Alt: 31 ft.

ROCKY HILL SCHOOL
Day — Coed Gr PS-12

East Greenwich, RI 02818. 530 Ives Rd. Tel: 401-884-9070. Fax: 401-885-4985.
www.rockyhill.org   E-mail: cwashburn@rockyhill.org

James J. Young III, Head. BS, Univ of Rhode Island, MEd, Harvard Univ. **Catherine T. Washburn, Adm.**
- **Col Prep. AP**—Eng Fr Lat Span Calc Bio US_Hist. **Feat**—Creative_Writing Marine_Biol/Sci Comp_Sci Anthro Psych Ceramics Studio_Art Music. **Supp**—ESL Rev Tut.
- **Adm:** 65/yr. Appl due: Feb. Accepted: 80%. Yield: 81%. **Tests** ISEE SSAT TOEFL.
- **Enr 330.** B 188. G 142. Elem 170. Sec 160. Wh 88%. Hisp 3%. Blk 5%. Am Ind 1%. Asian 3%. Avg class size: 12. **Fac 58.** M 21. F 35/2. Wh 98%. Hisp 1%. Blk 1%. Adv deg: 46%.
- **Grad '04**—41. **Col**—41. (Wheaton-MA 3, Brown 2, Geo Wash 2, Bucknell 1, Bates 1, Carnegie Mellon 1). Avg SAT: 1180. Avg SSAT: 67%. Alum 800.
- **Tui '04-'05: Day $17,000-19,500** (+$300-2600). **Aid:** Need 54 ($550,000).
- **Summer:** Enrich Rec. Arts. Sports. 1-6 wks.
- Endow $1,000,000. Plant val $8,000,000. Bldgs 13. Class rms 52. 2 Libs 13,000 vols. Sci labs 8. Comp labs 2. Auds 1. Art studios 3. Music studios 3. Wood shops 1. Gyms 1. Fields 3. Courts 4. Sailing facilities yes.
- **Est 1934.** Nonprofit. Sem (Sept-June). **Assoc** NEASC.

Located on a historic, 100-acre estate that borders Narragansett Bay, Rocky Hill makes use of its waterfront facilities for various activities and conducts marine and environmental programs at all grade levels. Students in grades 9-12 utilize Harkness tables and must have a laptop computer. Elective courses, independent study, Advanced Placement classes, an SAT preparation course and a senior project program are available in the upper school, with both AP biology and AP environmental science enriched by the school's natural setting.

Arts are emphasized, with specialized offerings provided in instrumental music, band, chorus, drama, drawing, painting, ceramics and sculpture. An expansive interscholastic athletic program includes soccer, basketball, field hockey, tennis, lacrosse and sailing.

NEWPORT, RI. (25 mi. SSE of Providence, RI; 61 mi. SSW of Boston, MA) Suburban. Pop: 26,475. Alt: 6 ft. Area also includes Middletown and Portsmouth.

PORTSMOUTH ABBEY SCHOOL
Bdg and Day — Coed Gr 9-12

Portsmouth, RI 02871. 285 Cory's Ln. Tel: 401-683-2000. Fax: 401-683-5888.
www.portsmouthabbey.org   E-mail: admissions@portsmouthabbey.org

James M. De Vecchi, Head. BA, St Francis College, MS, PhD, Univ of New Hampshire. **Geri Zilian, Adm.**
- **Col Prep. AP**—Eng Fr Lat Span Calc Stats Comp_Sci Bio Chem Physics Eur_Hist US_Hist Art_Hist Music_Theory. **Feat**—Humanities Greek Environ_Sci Econ Intl_Relations Pol_Sci Constitutional_Law Relig Studio_Art Drama Music. **Supp**—Tut.
- **Adm (Bdg Gr 9-11; Day 9-10):** 104/yr. Bdg 84. Day 20. Appl due: Jan. Accepted: 69%. Yield: 50%. **Tests** CEEB SSAT.
- **Enr 343.** B 123/65. G 80/75. Sec 343. Wh 89%. Hisp 2%. Blk 3%. Asian 6%. Avg class size: 14. **Fac 48.** M 26/8. F 8/6. Wh 98%. Hisp 1%. Blk 1%. Adv deg: 72%. In dorms 21.
- **Grad '04**—78. **Col**—78. (URI, NYU, Dickinson, Haverford, Catholic U, McGill-Canada). Avg SAT: 1197. Alum 3300.
- **Tui '05-'06: Bdg $33,450** (+$1000). **Day $23,325** (+$750). **Aid:** Merit 25 ($154,800).

Need 96 ($1,631,340).
Summer: Acad Enrich. Tui Bdg $4400. Tui Day $2300. 5 wks.
Endow $32,000,000. Plant val $25,000,000. Bldgs 24. Dorms 7. Dorm rms 133. Class rms 25. 2 Libs 30,000 vols. Labs 3. Auds 1. Art studios 1. Music studios 10. Gyms 2. Athletic ctrs 1. Fields 7. Courts 8. Rinks 1. Riding rings 1. Stables 1. Tracks 1. Golf crses 1. Boating facilities yes. FM radio stations 1.
Est 1926. Nonprofit. Roman Catholic. Tri (Sept-May). **Assoc** CLS NEASC.

Known as the Portsmouth Priory School until 1969, when the monastery of the English Benedictine Congregation that conducts the school was raised to the status of an abbey, Portsmouth has attained rank among the foremost New England preparatory schools. Both abbey and school are American in personnel. The faculty contains both monastic and lay members.

Founded by Rev. Dom John Hugh Diman, Portsmouth Abbey continues its goal of instilling in students "a genuine appreciation of scholarship, excellence in academic work and a belief in a broad and liberal education." The school is situated on a 500-acre site on Narragansett Bay and has been noted for the architectural design of its buildings.

The traditional college preparatory curriculum, which emphasizes English, math, humanities and languages, is augmented by Advanced Placement courses and interscholastic sports. Publications, music, drama, an FM radio station and a debating club are among the varied activities. In addition, Portsmouth Abbey schedules cultural expeditions to Boston, MA, and Providence. **See Also Pages 1226-8**

ST. GEORGE'S SCHOOL
Bdg and Day — Coed Gr 9-12

Middletown, RI 02842. 372 Purgatory Rd. Tel: 401-847-7565. Fax: 401-842-6696.
   www.stgeorges.edu   E-mail: admissions_office@stgeorges.edu
Charles A. Hamblet, Head. BS, Baldwin-Wallace College, MEd, Rutgers Univ, MAT, Brown Univ. **James A. Hamilton, Adm.**
Col Prep. AP—Eng Fr Lat Span Calc Stats Comp_Sci Bio Chem Physics Eur_Hist US_Hist World_Hist Econ US_Govt & Pol. **Feat**—Creative_Writing Mandarin Astron Environ_Sci Marine_Biol/Sci Preveterinary_Sci Programming Civil_War Psych World_Relig Art_Hist Painting Photog Acting Journ. **Supp**—Tut.
Adm: 119/yr. Bdg 107. Day 12. Appl due: Feb. Accepted: 32%. **Tests** ISEE SSAT TOEFL.
Enr 340. B 147/23. G 146/24. Sec 340. **Fac 72.**
Grad '04—86. Col—85. (Rollins, Carnegie Mellon, CT Col, Fordham, Harvard, U of TX-Austin). Alum 3430.
Tui '04-'05: Bdg $32,000 (+$1000). **Day $21,500** (+$700). **Aid:** Need ($2,100,000).
Summer: Acad. ESL. Tui Bdg $4500 (+$400). Tui Day $2000 (+$250). 5 wks.
Endow $84,000,000. Plant val $63,000,000. Bldgs 46. Dorms 21. Dorm rms 195. Class rms 48. Lib 25,000 vols. Sci labs 5. Comp labs 5. Photog labs 1. Auds 1. Theaters 1. Art studios 10. Music studios 5. Dance studios 1. Gyms 4. Fields 12. Courts 14. Squash courts 1. Field houses 1. Pools 1. Rinks 2.
Est 1896. Nonprofit. Episcopal. Sem (Sept-May). **Assoc** CLS NEASC.

St. George's was founded by Rev. John B. Diman, who later established Portsmouth Abbey, and in 1901 moved to its present, 200-acre campus overlooking the Atlantic Ocean and the city of Newport.

St. George's offers a traditional college preparatory curriculum with opportunities for numerous electives and advanced work. Art offerings—drawing, painting, printmaking, architecture, photography and art history—religious studies, and computer applications and programming are important curricular features. The music program offers diploma credit for private instruction in voice and instrumental music. Students attend from many states and foreign countries, and graduates enter leading colleges.

St. George's conducts work and study internships, as well as year-round research cruises for full academic credit that allow students to live and study for six weeks aboard the school research vessel, *Geronimo*. Marine biology and field research concentrate on the study of sharks and sea turtles, while oceanography, including meteorology and navigation, and English are taught by the on-board staff; pupils take other courses by correspondence with their teachers at the school.

Extracurricular activities include service groups, clubs and publications. Interscholastic sports include sailing, soccer, football, basketball, tennis, baseball, cross-country, track, lacrosse, ice and field hockey, swimming, squash and softball.

ST. MICHAEL'S COUNTRY DAY SCHOOL
Day — Coed Gr PS-8

Newport, RI 02840. 180 Rhode Island Ave. Tel: 401-849-5970. Fax: 401-849-7890.
 www.stmichaelscountryday.org E-mail: lrowe@smcds.org
Whitney C. Slade, Head. BA, Tufts Univ, MEd, Harvard Univ. **Charles Laurent, Adm.**
 Pre-Prep. Feat—Fr Span Computers Studio_Art Drama Music. **Supp**—Tut.
 Adm: 47/yr. Appl due: Jan. Accepted: 80%. **Tests** SSAT.
 Enr 231. Elem 231. Wh 94%. Hisp 1%. Blk 3%. Asian 2%. Avg class size: 12. **Fac 34.** M 4. F 29/1. Adv deg: 47%.
 Grad '04—36. Prep—30. (Portsmouth, St George's Sch-RI, Tabor, Wheeler, Middlesex, Hotchkiss). Alum 350.
 Tui '05-'06: Day $13,090-15,190 (+$215-495). **Aid:** Need 36 ($240,000).
 Summer: Ages 3-9. Enrich Rec. Theater. Tui Day $340-760. 2-8 wks.
 Endow $158,000. Plant val $2,163,000. Bldgs 4. Class rms 28. 2 Libs 8500 vols. Sci labs 2. Comp labs 1. Art studios 2. Music studios 2. Arts ctrs 1. Gyms 1. Fields 3. Playgrounds 3.
 Est 1938. Nonprofit. Sem (Sept-June).

Founded by Rt. Rev. James DeWolf Perry, onetime bishop of Rhode Island, St. Michael's moved to its current location in 1943 and served as the parish day school of Trinity Church for many years. In 1976, the school was reincorporated as a nondenominational independent school with a self-perpetuating board of trustees.

Situated on a seven-acre tract in a historic residential section of Newport, St. Michael's provides an interdisciplinary curriculum at all grade levels. French, computer, library, art, music, drama and physical education classes enrich the program throughout. Field trips and special activities complement class work. The school also sponsors the Publishing House, a volunteer-run program in which children in grades K-4 write, illustrate and bind their own books.

Extracurricular opportunities include drama, choral and instrumental music, graphic design and studio art. The interscholastic sports program consists of tennis, soccer, basketball and lacrosse. An extended-day option is available.

PROVIDENCE, RI. (41 mi. SSW of Boston, MA) Urban. Pop: 173,618. Alt: 12 ft. Area also includes East Providence.

GORDON SCHOOL
Day — Coed Gr PS-8

East Providence, RI 02914. 45 Maxfield Ave. Tel: 401-434-3833. Fax: 401-431-0320.
www.gordonschool.org E-mail: admission@gordonschool.org
Ralph L. Wales, Head. AB, MEd, Harvard Univ. **Emily C. Anderson & Julie Cucchi**, Adms.
  Pre-Prep. Gen Acad. Feat—Fr Span Computers Photog Studio_Art Music Jazz_Band. Supp—Dev_Read Tut.
  Adm: 70/yr. Appl due: Feb. Accepted: 40%. Yield: 63%.
  Enr 392. B 190. G 202. Elem 392. Wh 75%. Hisp 2%. Blk 5%. Asian 5%. Other 13%. Avg class size: 13. **Fac 56.** M 7. F 42/7. Wh 84%. Hisp 2%. Blk 7%. Am Ind 2%. Asian 5%. Adv deg: 51%.
  Grad '04—28. Prep—27. (Wheeler 11, Moses Brown 6, Providence Co Day 4, St Mark's Sch-MA 2, Portsmouth 1). Alum 1500.
  Tui '04-'05: Day $14,820-17,800 (+$330-435). **Aid:** Need 63 ($688,319).
  Endow $4,000,000. Plant val $9,000,000. Bldgs 5. Class rms 29. Lib 18,000 vols. Sci labs 3. Comp labs 2. Art studios 2. Music studios 1. Gyms 2. Fields 2.
  Est 1910. Nonprofit. Sem (Sept-June).

Dr. Helen West Cooke, one of the few practicing female pediatricians in the area at the time, founded this school for her son Gordon. The oldest independent, coeducational elementary school in the state, the school encourages cooperation and independence. A rigorous, integrated and multicultural curriculum forms the basis for a challenging academic program. The middle school (grades 5-8) provides an integrated math/science and humanities curriculum, as well as an individualized advisory program, leadership opportunities and community service.

Team sports commence in grade 5, and extended-day programs are available to all pupils.

LINCOLN SCHOOL
Day — Boys Gr PS, Girls PS-12

Providence, RI 02906. 301 Butler Ave. Tel: 401-331-9696. Fax: 401-751-6670.
www.lincolnschool.org E-mail: info@lincolnschool.org
Joan Cannady Countryman, Head. BA, Sarah Lawrence College, MUS, Yale Univ. **Jennifer Devine**, Actg Adm.
  Col Prep. AP—Eng Fr Lat Span Calc Stats Bio Chem Physics US_Hist Art_Hist. Feat—Ethics Studio_Art Theater Chorus Music. Supp—Tut.
  Adm (Gr PS-12): 82/yr. **Tests** ISEE SSAT.
  Enr 439. B 11. G 428. Wh 90%. Hisp 2%. Blk 4%. Asian 4%. Avg class size: 13. Uniform. **Fac 74.** M 11/2. F 44/17. Adv deg: 56%.
  Grad '04—43. Col—42. (CT Col, Brown, Colby, MIT, Suffolk, U of VT). Alum 2600.
  Tui '02-'03: Day $16,700 (+$500-1000). **Aid:** Need ($722,050).
  Summer: Rec. Sports. Tui Day $150/wk. 2 wks.
  Endow $4,800,000. Plant val $14,800,000. Bldgs 6. Class rms 36. 3 Libs 12,000 vols. Labs 8. Art studios 4. Music studios 2. Gyms 2. Fields 3. Tennis courts 8.
  Est 1884. Nonprofit. Religious Society of Friends. **Assoc** CLS NEASC.

This school, enrolling students from Rhode Island and nearby Massachusetts, has long been noted for its strong academic program and commitment to Quaker values. Emphasis is on basic academics in preparation for college, with Advanced Placement courses available in most disciplines.

Lincoln has a 32-acre farm with full athletic facilities and opportunities for indoor and outdoor learning projects. Expanded facilities, a computer arts studio, and a middle school guided-study program complement the basic curriculum. Athletics, science, public speaking, music, health, theater, computer and art programs commence in the earliest grades, encouraging students with special interests in these fields.

MOSES BROWN SCHOOL
Day — Coed Gr PS-12

Providence, RI 02906. 250 Lloyd Ave. Tel: 401-831-7350. **Fax:** 401-455-0084.
www.mosesbrown.org   E-mail: administration@mosesbrown.org
Joanne P. Hoffman, Head. BA, Marymount College, MA, Trinity College (CT). **Claude E. Anderson, Adm.**

Col Prep. AP—Eng Fr Lat Span Calc Stats Bio Chem Physics. **Feat**—African-Amer_Lit Japan Astron Environ_Sci Meteorology Computers Econ Psych World_Relig Music Indus_Arts. **Supp**—Tut.

Adm (Gr PS-11): 110/yr. Appl due: Feb. Accepted: 27%. Yield: 79%. **Tests** ISEE SSAT.

Enr 788. B 385. G 403. Elem 390. Sec 398. Wh 84%. Hisp 4%. Blk 3%. Am Ind 1%. Asian 5%. Other 3%. Avg class size: 15. **Fac 100.** M 33/4. F 50/13. Wh 87%. Hisp 5%. Blk 3%. Asian 3%. Other 2%. Adv deg: 69%.

Grad '04—88. Col—88. (Brown 4, Loyola U-LA 4, Skidmore 4, U of PA 3, Harvard 2, NYU 2). Avg SAT: 1378. Avg ACT: 27. Alum 4170.

Tui '04-'05: Day $17,420-18,980 (+$175-875). **Aid:** Need 114 ($1,376,243).

Summer: Rec. 1-6 wks.

Endow $14,000,000. Plant val $25,000,000. Bldgs 16. Class rms 90. 2 Libs 30,000 vols. Sci labs 8. Lang labs 2. Art studios 5. Music studios 2. Dance studios 1. Music rms 5. Wood shops 1. Gyms 3. Fields 8. Courts 9.

Est 1784. Nonprofit. Religious Society of Friends. Sem (Sept-June). **Assoc** CLS NEASC.

Opened as Friends School in Portsmouth, this institution was reestablished in Providence in 1819 through the energy and generosity of Moses Brown, an influential Quaker whose family established Brown University. It was further endowed by his son, Obadiah, and the present name was adopted in 1904. The school remained coeducational until 1926, when the girls' department ceased operation. In 1976, girls were readmitted and the school reinstituted coeducation.

The school has upper, middle and lower divisions. All students must meet basic requirements, but there is a wealth of electives and extracurricular activities available as well. Offerings include Advanced Placement courses in English, world languages, science and mathematics. A feature of the school's Quaker heritage is the requirement that every student participate in a community service project prior to graduation. When appropriate, students in the upper school may also pursue independent projects.   **See Also Pages 1210-1**

RI   *Leading Private Schools*   274

PROVIDENCE COUNTRY DAY SCHOOL
Day — Coed Gr 5-12

East Providence, RI 02914. 660 Waterman Ave. Tel: 401-438-5170. Fax: 401-435-4514.
www.providencecountryday.org   E-mail: bailey@providencecountryday.org
Susan M. Haberlandt, Head. BA, MA, Trinity College (CT). Suzanne L. Bailey, Adm.

    Col Prep. AP—Eng Lat Calc Bio US_Hist Studio_Art. Feat—Fr Span Environ_Sci Computers Photog Music. Supp—Dev_Read LD Rev Tut.

    Adm: 84/yr. Appl due: Feb. Accepted: 50%. Tests ISEE SSAT.

    Enr 293. B 191. G 102. Elem 99. Sec 194. Wh 90%. Hisp 2%. Blk 6%. Asian 2%. Avg class size: 12. Fac 47. M 16/2. F 21/8. Adv deg: 59%.

    Grad '04—38. Col—38. (U of VT, Hobart/Wm Smith, Hartwick, Trinity Col-CT, McGill-Canada, Bowdoin). Avg SAT: 1100. Alum 2400.

    Tui '03-'04: Day $17,700 (+$1000). Aid: Need 80 ($800,000).

    Summer: Ages 4-14. Theater. 2-3 wks.

    Endow $1,200,000. Plant val $10,000,000. Bldgs 5. Class rms 24. Lib 15,000 vols. Sci labs 5. Comp labs 2. Auds 1. Art studios 2. Music studios 1. Gyms 1. Fields 4. Courts 6. Field houses 1.

    Est 1923. Nonprofit. Quar (Sept-June). Assoc CLS NEASC.

The school was founded by a group of business leaders, educators and parents who were interested in establishing a college preparatory school in a rural setting. Originally a boys' school, PCD first enrolled girls in the fall of 1991. In 1997, an extensive consolidation and building project culminated in the movement and subsequent renovation of two historic buildings (both erected in 1927) to the east side of campus. Several other plant improvements accompanied this building project.

Personal but structured in atmosphere, the school provides sound college preparation, with graduates entering a wide array of colleges. An extensive selection of electives is offered in grades 11 and 12. All students participate in athletics and the arts.

Middle school students take a variety of off-campus trips to northern New England, the Alton Jones campus of the University of Rhode Island, and Nantucket Island. All twelfth graders take part in senior projects for four weeks in the spring. The school council and the judicial board, both consisting of students and faculty, concern themselves actively with the school's operating policies. PCD encourages pupils to perform community service both on campus and off.

WHEELER SCHOOL
Day — Coed Gr PS-12

Providence, RI 02906. 216 Hope St. Tel: 401-421-8100. Fax: 401-751-7674.
www.wheelerschool.org   E-mail: admissions@wheelerschool.org
Dan Miller, Head. BA, Amherst College, MA, PhD, Harvard Univ. Jeanette Epstein, Adm.

    Col Prep. AP—Fr Span Bio US_Hist. Feat—Chin Anat & Physiol Engineering Psych Performing_Arts Drama Music Handbells Dance. Supp—Dev_Read LD Tut.

    Adm: 155/yr. Appl due: Jan. Accepted: 50%. Yield: 63%. Tests ISEE SSAT.

    Enr 811. B 440. G 371. Elem 492. Sec 319. Wh 85%. Hisp 2%. Blk 3%. Asian 3%. Other 7%. Avg class size: 15. Fac 106. M 32/1. F 67/6. Wh 91%. Hisp 3%. Asian 4%. Other 2%. Adv deg: 50%.

    Grad '04—80. Col—80. (NYU 7, Brown 4, Boston U 3, Bates 2, Boston Col 2, Georgetown 2). Avg SAT: 1230. Alum 3000.

    Tui '04-'05: Day $17,515-18,890 (+$150-400). Aid: Need 121 ($1,429,080).

Summer: Acad Enrich Rec. 1-3 wks.
Endow $6,844,000. Plant val $15,782,000. Bldgs 12. Class rms 85. 2 Libs 31,236 vols. Sci labs 8. Comp labs 4. Auds 1. Art studios 9. Music studios 6. Gyms 2. Fields 7. Courts 9. Pools 1.
Est 1889. Nonprofit. (Sept-June). **Assoc** CLS NEASC.

The school bears the name of its founder, Mary Colman Wheeler, a leader in art and education in the early 1900s. The college preparatory program, which includes Advanced Placement courses in most academic areas, is further enriched by classes in music, art and theater and prepares graduates for success in college. The school strives to develop the individual talents of each student in a supportive educational atmosphere. The traditional curriculum is supplemented at all levels by a variety of elective courses, special-interest activities and enrichment experiences. The school's computer center promotes the acquisition of computer skills at all levels of the instructional program. A substantial enrichment program features specially designed activities, games and studies several times per week. Qualifying juniors may elect to spend a semester in Vershire, VT, at the Mountain School.

The Hamilton School at Wheeler, established in 1988, serves high-potential language-disabled students in grades 1-8. The curriculum is based on a structured, multisensory approach applied to reading, spelling, grammar and writing skills.

The school owns a 120-acre farm a few miles east of Providence. Athletics include interscholastic competition in such team sports as field hockey, soccer, lacrosse, basketball, baseball, tennis, swimming, squash, golf, cross-country and track.

VERMONT

BURLINGTON, VT. (186 mi. NW of Boston, MA) Urban. Pop: 38,889. Alt: 113 ft.

ROCK POINT SCHOOL
Bdg and Day — Coed Gr 9-12

Burlington, VT 05401. 1 Rock Point Rd. Tel: 802-863-1104. Fax: 802-863-6628.
  www.rockpoint.org   E-mail: ledson@rockpoint.org
John Rouleau, Head. BS, MEd, Univ of Vermont. **Hillary Kramer, Adm.**
  Col Prep. Gen Acad. **Feat**—Studio_Art. **Supp**—Dev_Read Makeup Tut.
  Adm: 14/yr. Bdg 12. Day 2. Appl due: Rolling. Accepted: 70%.
  Enr 42. B 18/3. G 18/3. Sec 42. Wh 93%. Hisp 1%. Blk 1%. Asian 5%. Avg class size: 10.
    Fac 6. Adv deg: 50%.
  Grad '04—11. Col—10. (Curry, Fisher, Smith). Alum 350.
  Tui '04-'05: Bdg $36,200 (+$500). **Day $19,950. Aid:** Need 9 ($150,000).
  Endow $1,600,000. Plant val $5,300,000. Bldgs 2. Dorms 2. Dorm rms 29. Class rms 6.
    Lib 3000 vols. Comp labs 1. Art studios 2. Fields 1. Courts 1.
  Est 1928. Nonprofit. Episcopal. Quar (Sept-June). **Assoc** NEASC.

Rock Point conducts a high school program for pupils of average to above-average intelligence who stand to benefit from the structure and personal contact available in a small-school environment. The school places particular emphasis on the arts and community service. A senior seminar assists students with college placement and applications.

The 150-acre campus is situated on a peninsula in Lake Champlain, about one mile from the center of the city. Rock Point stresses accountability and work within the school community: Students attend frequently scheduled school meetings and meet with an advisor for 40 minutes once a week. Prominent evening and weekend offerings include trips to Montreal, Canada, New York City and Boston, MA, as well as a lively off-campus outdoor program that features hiking, camping, cross-country skiing and snowboarding.

DORSET, VT. (54 mi. NE of Albany, NY; 123 mi. WNW of Boston, MA) Rural. Pop: 2036. Alt: 899 ft.

LONG TRAIL SCHOOL
Bdg — Coed Gr 9-12; Day — Coed 6-12

Dorset, VT 05251. 1045 Kirby Hollow Rd. Tel: 802-867-5717. Fax: 802-867-0147.
  www.longtrailschool.org   E-mail: lts@longtrailschool.org
David D. Wilson, Head. BS, Indiana Univ of Pennsylvania, MA, Antioch College. **Courtney M. Callo, Adm.**
  Col Prep. AP—Eng Fr Span Calc Stats Comp_Sci US_Hist Psych Studio_Art. **Feat—**

Environ_Sci Web_Design Govt Law Sociol Photog Music. **Supp**—Dev_Read ESL LD Makeup Tut.

Adm: 48/yr. Appl due: Rolling. Accepted: 91%.

Enr 135. B 2/65. G 1/67. Elem 67. Sec 68. Wh 93%. Hisp 3%. Blk 1%. Asian 3%. Avg class size: 11. **Fac 32.** M 7/6. F 13/6. Adv deg: 50%.

Grad '04—16. Col—13. (Clarkson, Colgate, Davidson, Middlebury, Rochester Inst of Tech, Williams). Avg SAT: 1175. Alum 424.

Tui '04-'05: Bdg $21,000 (+$4000). **Day $16,900** (+$500). **Aid:** Need 70 ($572,239).

Summer: Gr PS-8. Acad Rec. Arts. Drama. Adventure. 1-6 wks.

Endow $5,000,000. Plant val $10,000,000. Bldgs 1. Class rms 21. Lib 8000 vols. Sci labs 3. Comp labs 2. Theaters 1. Art studios 3. Music studios 2. Dance studios 1. Gyms 1. Fields 2.

Est 1975. Nonprofit. Sem (Aug-June). **Assoc** NEASC.

LTS features small-group instruction and maintains a family-like environment. Each student completes a common core of subjects in the disciplines of English, math, science, social studies and world languages during each year of attendance. Requirements also include participation in Arts Core, a two-year overview of the dramatic, musical and visual arts, and Connections, a multidisciplinary course that focuses on critical thinking and knowledge acquisition. A wide selection of Advanced Placement classes provides additional challenge. All boys and girls fulfill an annual community service requirement, and seniors take part in a weeklong internship.

Athletic options include four soccer teams, softball, golf, tennis, sailing, downhill and cross-country skiing, snowboarding and more than two dozen physical development activities.

The LTS community convenes for a morning meeting four days a week, and for three or four days each fall the entire student body and faculty participate in a team-building experience off campus that emphasizes cooperation, teamwork, trust and self-confidence. A limited number of learning-disabled students enroll each year. International students live with families in private homes.

PUTNEY, VT. (68 mi. ENE of Albany, NY; 88 mi. WNW of Boston, MA) Rural. Pop: 2634. Alt: 251 ft.

THE GRAMMAR SCHOOL
Day — Coed Gr PS-8

Putney, VT 05346. 69 Hickory Ridge Rd S. Tel: 802-387-5364. Fax: 802-387-4744.
  www.tgs-putney.org   E-mail: tgs@sover.net

Chris Osgood, Head. AB, Dartmouth College, MS, Univ of Massachusetts-Amherst. **Marcia Leader, Adm.**

Pre-Prep. Feat—Fr Computers Studio_Art Drama Music. **Supp**—Tut.

Adm (Gr PS-7): 24/yr. Appl due: Mar. Accepted: 78%. Yield: 98%.

Enr 114. Elem 114. Wh 96%. Blk 2%. Asian 2%. Avg class size: 10. **Fac 21.** M 4. F 11/6. Adv deg: 42%.

Grad '04—15. Prep—10. (Putney, Northfield Mt Hermon, VT Acad, Stratton Mtn, Deerfield Acad). Alum 300.

Tui '04-'05: Day $5200-11,350 (+$200). **Aid:** Merit 33 ($96,000).

VT   *Leading Private Schools*   278

Summer: Enrich. Arts. 3 wks.
Endow $119,000. Plant val $683,000. Bldgs 3. Class rms 9. Lib 8000 vols. Comp labs 1. Art studios 1. Music studios 1. Fields 2.
Est 1960. Nonprofit. Tri (Sept-June). **Assoc** NEASC.

The curriculum prepares students for secondary school by emphasizing language arts; history; geography; the physical, environmental and life sciences; and mathematics. The visual and performing arts, computer literacy and physical skills development are also incorporated. In addition, French is taught in grades K-8.

TGS utilizes the rural and recreational assets of southern Vermont extensively.

GREENWOOD SCHOOL
Bdg — Boys Ages 9-15

Putney, VT 05346. 14 Greenwood Ln. Tel: 802-387-4545. Fax: 802-387-5396.
   www.greenwood.org   E-mail: info@greenwood.org
John Alexander, Head. MEd, Harvard Univ. **Stewart Miller, Adm.**
   Pre-Prep. LD. Feat—Computers Studio_Art Speech. **Supp**—Rem_Math Rem_Read Tut.
   Adm: 17/yr. Appl due: Rolling. Accepted: 75%. **Tests** IQ.
   Enr 40. B 40. Avg class size: 5. **Fac 20.** M 13. F 7. Adv deg: 30%. In dorms 3.
   Grad '04—17. Prep—17. (Kildonan, Cushing, Eagle Hill-MA, Forman, Gow, Pine Ridge). Alum 345.
   Tui '04-'05: Bdg $45,135 (+$1000). **Aid:** Need 4 ($45,000).
   Endow $6000. Plant val $1,500,000. Bldgs 9. Dorms 1. Dorm rms 18. Class rms 10. Lib 5500 vols. Art studios 1. Music studios 1. Gyms 1. Fields 1.
   Est 1978. Nonprofit. Tri (Sept-June). **Assoc** NEASC.

Greenwood's program is designed to help boys overcome dyslexia and related language disabilities. Faculty members are trained in the Orton-Gillingham method. A 60-minute period of language training is conducted daily in classes of two students. Class size ranges from two to ten pupils. One-on-one tutoring is provided when necessary, and an optional speech/language therapy program is available for an additional fee.

The school's 100-acre campus allows for athletic opportunities in soccer, downhill and cross-country skiing, rock climbing, basketball, cricket and mountain biking. Activities in art, drama, construction, and metal and wood crafts are available as well. Greenwood's graduates enter preparatory schools throughout the country.

THE PUTNEY SCHOOL
Bdg and Day — Coed Gr 9-12

Putney, VT 05346. Elm Lea Farm, 418 Houghton Brook Rd. Tel: 802-387-6219.
   Fax: 802-387-6278.
   www.putneyschool.org   E-mail: admission@putneyschool.org
Brian G. Morgan, Dir. BA, MA, Cambridge Univ (England). **Richard H. Cowan, Adm.**
   Col Prep. Feat—Creative_Writing Shakespeare Fr Russ Span Stats Anat & Physiol Astron Ecol Environ_Sci Computers Lat-Amer_Hist Comp_Relig Philos Painting Photog Sculpt Printmaking Drama Music. **Supp**—ESL Rev Tut.
   Adm (Gr 9-11): 75/yr. Bdg 59. Day 16. Appl due: Jan. Accepted: 85%. **Tests** SSAT TOEFL.

Enr 225. Sec 225. Wh 86%. Hisp 5%. Blk 5%. Am Ind 1%. Asian 3%. Avg class size: 12. **Fac 42.** M 18/2. F 11/11. Wh 90%. Hisp 5%. Blk 2%. Asian 3%. Adv deg: 69%. In dorms 17.

Grad '04—65. Col—62. (Hampshire, Beloit, Cornell, Earlham, Macalester, Sch of the Museum of Fine Arts). Avg SAT: 1190. Avg ACT: 25. Alum 3500.

Tui '04-'05: Bdg $32,200 (+$500-1500). **Day $20,100** (+$500-1500). **Aid:** Need 82 ($1,205,820).

Summer: Enrich Rec. Writing. Arts. Tui Bdg $2500/3-wk ses. Tui Day $950/3-wk ses. ESL. Tui Bdg $2700/3-wk ses. 6 wks.

Endow $11,000,000. Plant val $18,000,000. Bldgs 37. Dorms 9. Dorm rms 95. Class rms 17. Lib 27,000 vols. Sci labs 3. Comp labs 1. Auds 1. Theaters 1. Art studios 7. Music studios 14. Dance studios 1. Fields 3. Courts 3. Riding rings 2. Stables 1. Greenhouses 2. Sugarhouses 1. Barns 2.

Est 1935. Nonprofit. Sem (Sept-June). **Assoc** NEASC.

"To make school life a more real, less sheltered, less self-centered venture; to educate the individual in the light of what he can later do toward solving the problems of society" was Carmelita Hinton's vision in opening this preparatory school. Vigorous, dynamic, broad-visioned, unsparing of her energy, Mrs. Hinton selected her faculty, including many specialists in the arts, from outstanding progressive and conservative schools and colleges in this country and in Europe.

Through small, seminar-style classes, Putney offers students opportunities for acceleration and for independence in academic pursuits. The curriculum is complemented by a Vermont farm experience, an outdoor program with competitive and noncompetitive sports, and opportunities in the arts. The wide range of student activities includes an evening activity period two times a week during which students learn about such subjects as jewelry making, blacksmithing, jazz, chamber music, African drumming, photography, pottery, weaving and woodworking.

Every student participates in the work program, rotating through jobs in the kitchen, the barns, the dairy, the forest, the gardens and other sites on campus. The school community is, in many ways, self-sustaining, producing much of its own food, firewood and lumber.

ST. JOHNSBURY, VT. (153 mi. NNW of Boston, MA) Rural. Pop: 6319. Alt: 711 ft.

ST. JOHNSBURY ACADEMY
Bdg — Coed Gr 9-PG; Day — Coed 9-12

St Johnsbury, VT 05819. 1000 Main St, PO Box 906. Tel: 802-751-2130.
  Fax: 802-748-5463.
  www.stjohnsburyacademy.org   E-mail: admissions@stjohnsburyacademy.org
Thomas W. Lovett, Head. BS, Providence College, AM, Brown Univ. **John J. Cummings,** Adm.
  Col Prep. Gen Acad. Voc. Bus. AP—Eng Fr Span Calc Stats Comp_Sci Bio Chem Physics Eur_Hist US_Hist Psych US_Govt & Pol Studio_Art. **Feat—**Creative_Writing Japan Lat Mandarin Anat & Physiol Sports_Med Web_Design Photog Acting Theater Music_Theory Dance Accounting Journ Culinary_Arts. **Supp—**ESL LD.
  Adm: 297/yr. Bdg 85. Day 212. Appl due: Rolling. Accepted: 91%. Yield: 80%. **Tests** SSAT

TOEFL.
Enr 976. B 108/414. G 64/390. Sec 971. PG 5. Wh 91%. Hisp 2%. Blk 2%. Asian 5%. Avg class size: 15. **Fac 102.** M 59. F 43. Wh 98%. Hisp 1%. Asian 1%. Adv deg: 99%. In dorms 20.
Grad '04—246. Col—206. (Lyndon St 20, U of VT 12, VT Tech 5, U of MI 4, Am U 3, Dartmouth 2). Avg SAT: 1050.
Tui '05-'06: Bdg $29,920. Day $10,520. Aid: Need 30 ($327,065).
Summer: ESL. Tui Bdg $5000. 6 wks.
Endow $16,500,000. Plant val $48,800,000. Bldgs 26. Dorms 9. Lib 20,000 vols. Lang labs 2. Comp labs 3. Auds 1. Theaters 2. Music studios 2. Dance studios 1. Gyms 1. Fields 5. Courts 5. Field houses 1. Pools 1.
Est 1842. Nonprofit. Sem (Aug-June). **Assoc** NEASC.

This old New England academy was founded by Erastus, Joseph and Thaddeus (inventor of the platform scale) Fairbanks to provide intellectual, moral and religious training for their own children and those of the community. Since then, the academy has provided a secondary education to youth of the northeastern Vermont area through its day school and to students from all over the world through its boarding program. It presently occupies a campus of 142 acres.

A comprehensive high school, the academy offers courses for students of all levels of ability, including remedial education and Advanced Placement work. In all academic courses, students are grouped according to ability. Graduates go on to attend colleges throughout the US and Canada.

The academy also maintains a technical education department that offers courses in electricity/electronics, construction trades, drafting, forestry and culinary arts, each in a two-year sequence. All of these programs incorporate hands-on experiences in real-world projects; the construction trades class annually builds a house.

A full program of sports and extracurricular activities, including dramatics, student publications, music, and language and science clubs, is offered throughout the year.

SAXTONS RIVER, VT. (73 mi. ENE of Albany, NY; 94 mi. NW of Boston, MA) Rural. Pop: 519. Alt: 528 ft.

VERMONT ACADEMY
Bdg and Day — Coed Gr 9-PG

Saxtons River, VT 05154. 20 Pleasant St, PO Box 500. Tel: 802-869-6229.
Fax: 802-869-6242.
www.vermontacademy.org E-mail: admissions@vermontacademy.org
James C. Mooney, Head. BA, Yale Univ, MA, Stanford Univ. **William J. Newman, Adm.**
Col Prep. AP—Calc Stats. **Feat—**Fr Ital Russ Span Astron Bioethics Environ_Sci Kinesiology Programming Russ_History Pacific_Rim_Hist Econ Psych Women's_Stud Holocaust Conflict_Resolution Art_Hist Graphic_Arts Study_Skills. **Supp—**ESL LD Rev Tut.
Adm: 118/yr. Appl due: Feb. Accepted: 70%. Yield: 46%. **Tests** CEEB CTP_4 IQ ISEE SSAT TOEFL.
Enr 255. B 123/45. G 49/38. Wh 93%. Hisp 1%. Blk 3%. Am Ind 2%. Asian 1%. Avg class size: 11. **Fac 48.** M 23/1. F 22/2. Wh 98%. Hisp 2%. Adv deg: 33%. In dorms 18.

Grad '04—60. Col—59. (U of VT, Skidmore, Simmons, US Naval Acad, Brown, Williams). Avg SAT: 1090. Alum 3700.

Tui '04-'05: Bdg $33,560 (+$1000-1500). **Day $19,840** (+$700-1200). **Aid:** Need 68 ($748,728).

Endow $5,000,000. Plant val $12,500,000. Bldgs 21. Dorms 10. Dorm rms 155. Class rms 32. Lib 14,000 vols. Sci labs 3. Comp labs 1. Auds 1. Art studios 4. Music studios 6. Gyms 1. Fields 7. Courts 6. Rinks 1. Skiing facilities yes. Ropes crses 1.

Est 1876. Nonprofit. Sem (Sept-May). **Assoc** CLS NEASC.

Located on a 515-acre campus, this nationally known college preparatory institution serves primarily as a boarding school. High-achieving pupils may enroll in VA's honors courses, while students who need extra help may, for an additional fee, take part in a learning skills program that emphasizes study skills. The academy maintains small classes and a low student-teacher ratio. A small number of international students attend the school each year.

A full complement of activities and athletics serves pupils at all levels of ability. The sports program consists of cross-country, horseback riding, field hockey, football, soccer, basketball, dance, ice hockey, skiing, snowboarding, baseball, golf, lacrosse, softball, tennis, and track and field. During one season per year, students may instead participate in an activity such as photography, drama, community service, rock climbing, mountain biking, silversmithing or outdoor challenge.

See Also Pages 1262-3

Middle Atlantic States

DELAWARE

MIDDLETOWN, DE. (22 mi. SSW of Wilmington, DE; 49 mi. SW of Philadelphia, PA) Suburban. Pop: 6161. Alt: 67 ft.

ST. ANDREW'S SCHOOL
Bdg — Coed Gr 9-12

Middletown, DE 19709. 350 Noxontown Rd. Tel: 302-285-4231. Fax: 302-378-7120. www.standrews-de.org   E-mail: lzendt@standrews-de.org

Daniel T. Roach, Head. AB, Williams College, MA, Middlebury College. **Louisa H. Zendt, Adm.**

- **Col Prep. AP**—Fr Stats. **Feat**—Creative_Writing Chin Span Comp_Sci Amer_Stud Philos World_Relig Film Photog Studio_Art Drama Music Music_Theory.
- **Adm (Gr 9-11):** 75/yr. Appl due: Jan. Accepted: 32%. Yield: 65%. **Tests** CEEB SSAT TOEFL.
- **Enr 270.** B 145. G 125. Sec 270. Wh 80%. Hisp 2%. Blk 12%. Am Ind 1%. Asian 5%. Avg class size: 10. **Fac 55.** M 35. F 18/2. Wh 80%. Hisp 4%. Blk 9%. Asian 6%. Other 1%. Adv deg: 78%. In dorms 22.
- **Grad '04—78. Col—78.** (Williams 12, Davidson 11, Dartmouth 9, Duke 7, Middlebury 7, U of VA 7). Avg SAT: 1340. Alum 2770.
- **Tui '04-'05: Bdg $31,000** (+$1000). **Aid:** Need 118 ($2,853,700).
- Endow $163,000,000. Plant val $63,000,000. Bldgs 12. Dorms 6. Dorm rms 144. Class rms 28. Lib 36,000 vols. Chapels 3. Sci labs 3. Lang labs 1. Comp labs 4. Theaters 1. Music studios 6. Arts ctrs 1. Performance halls 1. Gyms 2. Fields 10. Tennis courts 9. Squash courts 5. Pools 1. Boathouses 1.
- **Est 1930.** Nonprofit. Episcopal. Sem (Sept-May). **Assoc** MSA.

Founded and endowed by Alexis Felix Du Pont, this Episcopal school is situated on 2200 acres of wetlands, farmland and forestland. Rev. Walden Pell, a St. Mark's graduate, headmaster from the founding, developed sound scholarship and a loyal following during his administration.

St. Andrew's offers its students a rigorous and varied college preparatory program that sends graduates to leading colleges. The traditional curriculum includes theater, studio art, music and advanced electives in the life sciences, history, computer science and mathematics.

Extracurricular activities range from theatrical productions, choir, band, woodworking and school publications to clubs for the pursuit of a variety of interests, including yachting, photography, foreign languages, astronomy, studio arts and community services. Athletics include field hockey, football, soccer, volleyball, cross-country, basketball, squash, wrestling, swimming, baseball, crew, tennis, lacrosse, aerobics, yoga and dance. **See Also Page 1239**

WILMINGTON, DE. (28 mi. SW of Philadelphia, PA) Urban. Pop: 72,664. Alt: 134 ft. Area also includes Claymont and Hockessin.

ARCHMERE ACADEMY
Day — Coed Gr 9-12

Claymont, DE 19703. 3600 Philadelphia Pike, PO Box 130. Tel: 302-798-6632.
 Fax: 302-798-7290.
 www.archmereacademy.com E-mail: dhickey@archmereacademy.com
Rev. John C. Zagarella, OPraem, Head. Daniel Hickey, Adm.
  Col Prep. AP—Eng Fr Ger Span Calc Stats Comp_Sci Bio Chem Physics Eur_Hist US_Hist World_Hist. **Feat**—Econ Relig Ceramics Drawing Photog Chorus Music Speech Driver_Ed. **Supp**—Tut.
  Adm (Gr 9-11): 130/yr. Appl due: Dec.
  Enr 480. B 250. G 230. Sec 480. Wh 90%. Hisp 2%. Blk 2%. Asian 6%. Avg class size: 16. Uniform. **Fac 60.** M 33. F 27. Adv deg: 80%.
  Grad '04—110. Col—110. (U of DE, St Joseph's U, Villanova, PA St, Johns Hopkins, U of PA). Avg SAT: 1250. Alum 3500.
  Tui '04-'05: Day $14,675 (+$450-600). **Aid:** Merit 30 ($30,000). Need ($550,000).
  Endow $5,250,000. Plant val $4,500,000. Bldgs 4. Class rms 34. Lib 13,000 vols. Sci labs 5. Lang labs 1. Comp labs 3. Auds 1. Theaters 1. Art studios 9. Music studios 4. Gyms 2. Fields 4. Basketball courts 2. Tennis courts 4. Weight rms 1.
  Est 1932. Nonprofit. Roman Catholic. Sem (Sept-June). **Assoc** MSA.

Founded by the Norbertine Fathers, Archmere is situated on a 39-acre campus. Students choose from a number of electives, including band, chorus, drawing, computer science, environmental science and driver education. Pupils fulfill graduation requirements in foreign language, religion, speech and electives, and Advanced Placement courses are available. Student activities, clubs, athletics and services complement the curriculum.

SANFORD SCHOOL
Day — Coed Gr PS-12

Hockessin, DE 19707. 6900 Lancaster Pike, PO Box 888. Tel: 302-239-5263.
 Fax: 302-239-5389.
 www.sanfordschool.org E-mail: admissions@sanfordschool.org
Douglas W. MacKelcan, Jr., Head. BA, Hobart College, MALS, Wesleyan Univ. Andrew Walpole, Adm.
  Col Prep. AP—Eng Fr Ger Span Calc Stats Bio Chem Physics US_Hist World_Hist. **Feat**—Creative_Writing Lat Anat & Physiol Ecol Environ_Sci Programming Web_Design Econ Law Psych Photog Studio_Art Music.
  Adm: 135/yr. Appl due: Rolling. Accepted: 50%. **Tests** CTP_4 SSAT.
  Enr 702. B 362. G 340. Elem 465. Sec 237. Wh 81%. Hisp 2%. Blk 9%. Asian 6%. Other 2%. Avg class size: 15. **Fac 83.** M 25. F 58. Wh 95%. Hisp 3%. Blk 2%. Adv deg: 72%.

Grad '04—54. Col—54. (U of DE 10, Dickinson 2, Harvard 2, Yale 1, Georgetown 1, U of VA 1). Avg SAT: 1197. Alum 1700.
Tui '04-'05: Day $10,420-16,460 (+$300-600). **Aid:** Need 121 ($900,000).
Summer: Acad Enrich Rev. 5 wks.
Endow $5,950,000. Plant val $20,000,000. Bldgs 15. Class rms 58. 3 Libs 30,000 vols. Sci labs 6. Comp labs 7. Art studios 7. Music studios 3. Gyms 2. Fields 6. Courts 9. Pools 1.
Est 1930. Nonprofit. Tri (Sept-June). **Assoc** CLS MSA.

Founded as a boarding school by Ellen Q. Sawin, Sanford is located on a 100-acre campus. The liberal arts college preparatory curriculum features a formal world language program in grades 4-12, humanities, studio and performing arts, an individualized reading program in the lower school, history, mathematics, sciences, computer science and Advanced Placement courses.

The school conducts a variety of extracurricular programs. The extensive athletic program includes soccer, field hockey, volleyball, basketball, baseball, cross-country, tennis, wrestling, lacrosse, golf and swimming.

TATNALL SCHOOL
Day — Coed Gr PS-12

Wilmington, DE 19807. 1501 Barley Mill Rd. Tel: 302-998-2292. Fax: 302-998-7051.
www.tatnall.org   E-mail: admissions@tatnall.org
Eric G. Ruoss, Head. BA, Ursinus College, MDiv, Union Theological Seminary, MSEd, Iona College, PhD, Univ of Virginia. **Jeffrey Eckerson, Adm.**
Col Prep. AP—Eng Fr Lat Span Calc Stats Bio Physics Eur_Hist US_Hist Psych Studio_Art. **Feat**—Humanities Shakespeare Astron Botany Electronics Comp_Sci Vietnam_War Govt Drama Theater_Arts Chorus Music. **Supp**—Rev Tut.
Adm (Gr PS-10): 119/yr. Appl due: Jan. Accepted: 50%. Yield: 65%. **Tests** CTP_4 ISEE.
Enr 730. B 370. G 360. Elem 467. Sec 263. Wh 88%. Hisp 1%. Blk 6%. Asian 5%. Avg class size: 13. **Fac 107.** M 31. F 69/7. Wh 96%. Blk 3%. Asian 1%. Adv deg: 57%.
Grad '04—57. Col—57. (U of DE 12, Duke 4, Geo Wash 3, Emory 3, Boston U 2, Hobart/Wm Smith 2). Avg SAT: 1240. Alum 1800.
Tui '04-'05: Day $16,800 (+$100-300). **Aid:** Need 115 ($875,000).
Summer: Rec. 2-6 wks.
Endow $19,000,000. Plant val $26,000,000. Bldgs 4. Class rms 60. 3 Libs 38,000 vols. Sci labs 8. Comp labs 5. Theaters 1. Art studios 5. Music studios 4. Gyms 3. Fields 12. Courts 8. Pools 4.
Est 1930. Nonprofit. Tri (Sept-June). **Assoc** CLS MSA.

The school, founded by Frances D. S. Tatnall in her home, moved in 1952 to its present 110-acre, wooded campus. The broad liberal arts curriculum is college preparatory and is enriched by public speaking, computer science, foreign languages, community service and athletics. Honors and Advanced Placement courses are available in many subjects. Tatnall places particular emphasis on the arts, with students of all ages taking part in a program that combines exposure, instruction and participation. Upper schoolers take a service learning course, then complete a compulsory, 40-hour community service project prior to graduation.

Boys and girls of all ability levels choose from a wide selection of interscholastic sports. Among other extracurricular options are student council, clubs and organizations. The school operates a year-round extended-day program and also conducts a summer program that provides opportunities for enrichment and recreation.

TOWER HILL SCHOOL
Day — Coed Gr PS-12

Wilmington, DE 19806. 2813 W 17th St. Tel: 302-575-0550. Fax: 302-657-8373.
  www.towerhill.org   E-mail: thsadmit@towerhill.org
Christopher D. Wheeler, Head. BA, Univ of the Arts, MA, PhD, State Univ of New York-Stony Brook. Nancy H. Guare, Int Adm.
  Col Prep. AP—Fr Lat Span Calc Stats Bio Physics Eur_Hist Studio_Art Music_Theory. Feat—Creative_Writing Shakespeare Anat Comp_Sci Web_Design Psych Art_Hist Ceramics Drawing Film Photog Sculpt Theater_Arts Speech Indus_Arts Driver_Ed.
  Adm: 98/yr. Tests CTP_4 IQ SSAT.
  Enr 755. Elem 525. Sec 230. Wh 87%. Hisp 1%. Blk 6%. Asian 6%. Avg class size: 17. Fac 88. M 31/3. F 46/8. Wh 96%. Hisp 2%. Blk 2%. Adv deg: 48%.
  Grad '04—52. Col—52. (U of DE 7, U of Richmond 3, U of PA 3, Vanderbilt 3, Princeton 2, Georgetown 2). Avg SAT: 1311. Alum 3535.
  Tui '04-'05: Day $12,190-17,020 (+$245-1430). Aid: Need 102 ($971,940).
  Endow $26,001,000. Plant val $24,932,000. Bldgs 4. Class rms 30. 2 Libs 24,000 vols. Sci labs 7. Lang labs 1. Comp labs 4. Auds 1. Theaters 1. Art studios 6. Music studios 3. Dance studios 1. Arts ctrs 1. Gyms 2. Fields 6. Courts 8. Field houses 1. Tracks 2.
  Est 1919. Nonprofit. (Sept-June). Assoc CLS MSA.

Tower Hill's strong college preparatory program includes Advanced Placement and accelerated courses, various of electives and a technology component. In addition to academic work, all upper schoolers complete a community service project. Tower Hill's well-developed arts program culminates in the spring with an all-school evening of exhibits and performances. Student publications and musical activities supplement the school's varied dramatic and visual arts offerings.

In the upper school, all students participate in the athletic program, although juniors and seniors may elect not to take part in one season each year. Tower Hill provides interscholastic competition in field hockey, football, soccer, cross-country, volleyball, basketball, wrestling, swimming, baseball, lacrosse, tennis and track.

WILMINGTON FRIENDS SCHOOL
Day — Coed Gr PS-12

Wilmington, DE 19803. 101 School Rd. Tel: 302-576-2900. Fax: 302-576-2939.
  www.wilmingtonfriends.org   E-mail: admissions@wilmingtonfriends.org
Kathleen Hopkins, Adm.
  Col Prep. IB Diploma. AP—Calc Stats Art_Hist. Feat—Japan Geol Computers Peace_Stud Relig Film_Production Drama Theater Music World_Music Jazz Journ.
  Adm: 120/yr. Appl due: Rolling. Accepted: 52%. Yield: 69%. Tests CTP_4 SSAT.
  Enr 801. B 396. G 405. Elem 564. Sec 237. Wh 81%. Hisp 1%. Blk 11%. Asian 2%. Other 5%. Avg class size: 17. Fac 101. M 29/2. F 58/12. Wh 82%. Hisp 2%. Blk 10%. Asian 6%. Adv deg: 47%.
  Grad '04—59. Col—59. (U of DE 14, Gettysburg 4, U of PA 2, U of CO-Boulder 2, U of Richmond 2). Avg SAT: 1231. Alum 3027.
  Tui '04-'05: Day $11,225-15,825 (+$200). Aid: Need 165 ($1,507,634).
  Summer: Enrich. Tui Day $850. 3 wks.
  Endow $14,252,000. Plant val $16,324,000. Bldgs 4. Class rms 54. 2 Libs 30,000 vols. Sci labs 8. Comp labs 3. Auds 1. Art studios 3. Music studios 3. Gyms 5. Fields 6. Courts 6. Fitness ctrs 1.
  Est 1748. Nonprofit. Religious Society of Friends. Sem (Sept-June).

Founded by area Quakers to educate children of diverse backgrounds, Wilmington Friends is one of the oldest independent preparatory schools in the country and the oldest in Delaware. Although enrollment is interdenominational, the religious ideals of the Society of Friends are stressed at all grade levels.

The curriculum is entirely college preparatory. Wilmington Friends conducts the two-year International Baccalaureate degree program, while also offering individual IB courses. Independent study options, advanced work and other specialized options provide qualified students with research and study opportunities in various areas of interest. Community service is a programmatic component from prekindergarten on, and each upper schooler completes a major individual service project prior to graduation. Athletics, cultural arts, school publications, and an array of committees and clubs are among the school's extracurricular activities.

DISTRICT OF COLUMBIA

WASHINGTON, DC. Urban. Pop: 572,059. Alt: 50 ft.

EMERSON PREPARATORY SCHOOL
Day — Coed Gr 9-12

Washington, DC 20036. 1324 18th St NW. Tel: 202-785-2877. Fax: 202-785-2228.
www.emersonprep.net E-mail: info@emersonprep.net
Margot Ann Walsh, Dir. BS, Wilson College.
> **Col Prep. Gen Acad. Feat**—Humanities Chin Fr Ger Ital Japan Lat Russ Span Astron Environ_Sci Anthro Econ Law Comp_Relig Philos. **Supp**—Dev_Read ESL Tut.
> **Adm:** 50/yr. Appl due: Rolling. Accepted: 95%. **Tests** IQ.
> **Enr 75.** B 40. G 35. Sec 75. Wh 67%. Hisp 3%. Blk 19%. Am Ind 3%. Asian 8%. Avg class size: 10. **Fac 17.** M 2/6. F 3/6. Adv deg: 70%.
> **Grad '04—50. Col—49.** (U of CO-Boulder, Am U, Manhattanville, Geo Mason). Avg SAT: 1200. Alum 10,000.
> **Tui '04-'05: Day $18,000** (+$500). **Aid:** Need 4 ($30,000).
> **Summer:** Acad Enrich Rev. Tui Day $1800. 6 wks.
> Plant val $4,000,000. Bldgs 2. Class rms 11. Libs 1. Sci labs 1. Comp labs 1.
> **Est 1852.** Nonprofit. Sem (Sept-June).

The intensive program at this school, which evolved from the Emerson Institute, allows for the completion of a full year of high school academic work in one four-and-a-half-month term. An SAT preparation course provides instruction in verbal and math skills. Summer session offerings include math, science, history, government, English composition and literature, as well as an English workshop for foreign students.

GEORGETOWN DAY SCHOOL
Day — Coed Gr PS-12

Washington, DC 20016. 4200 Davenport St NW. Tel: 202-274-3210. Fax: 202-274-3211.
www.gds.org E-mail: info@gds.org
Peter M. Branch, Head. BA, Williams College, MA, Indiana Univ. **Wes Gibson, Adm.**
> **Col Prep. AP**—Fr Lat Span Calc Stats Comp_Sci Bio Chem Physics US_Hist Comp_Govt & Pol Psych US_Govt & Pol Studio_Art Music_Theory. **Feat**—Creative_Writing Film Photog Sculpt Theater Chorus Music.
> **Adm:** 144/yr. Appl due: Jan. Accepted: 20%. **Tests** IQ ISEE SSAT.
> **Enr 1025.** B 515. G 510. Elem 575. Sec 450. Wh 70%. Hisp 4%. Blk 20%. Asian 6%. Avg class size: 14. **Fac 160.** M 48/3. F 99/10. Wh 70%. Hisp 5%. Blk 20%. Asian 4%. Other 1%. Adv deg: 55%.
> **Grad '04—115. Col—113.** (Oberlin, U of PA, Cornell, Harvard, Yale, Princeton). Avg SAT: 1343. Alum 2500.
> **Tui '04-'05: Day $19,922-22,975** (+$500). **Aid:** Need 157 ($1,900,000).
> **Summer:** Acad Rec. 2-4 wks.
> Endow $6,240,000. Plant val $22,000,000. Bldgs 2. Class rms 80. Lib 22,000 vols. Labs 20. Sci labs 10. Theaters 2. Art studios 6. Music studios 4. Gyms 2.

Est 1945. Nonprofit. Sem (Sept-June). **Assoc** MSA.

The first racially integrated school in the city, this parent-owned school now enrolls a student body with one-third pupils of color. The curriculum combines college preparation with an emphasis on the humanities and the arts and sciences. Features of the lower school program (grades pre-K-5) are the commencement of regular science study in prekindergarten and foreign language instruction beginning in grade 3. During the middle school years (grades 6-8), academic demands increase and pupils take part in such projects as the consumer science fair, on-site studies of Chesapeake Bay, and a two-month study of constitutional issues that includes personal interviews with national experts. GDS' varied high school curriculum (grades 9-12) incorporates block scheduling, as well as honors and Advanced Placement classes in most disciplines, and students have increased flexibility in course selection.

Student government, intramural and interscholastic sports, theatrical productions and debate team are among the school's extracurricular opportunities. In addition, high schoolers fulfill a 60-hour community service requirement through involvement with local, national and international service organizations. The lower and middle schools are conducted at 4530 MacArthur Blvd. NW, 20007.

MARET SCHOOL
Day — Coed Gr K-12

**Washington, DC 20008. 3000 Cathedral Ave NW. Tel: 202-939-8814. Fax: 202-939-8884.
www.maret.org   E-mail: admissions@maret.org
Marjo Talbott, Head.** BA, Williams College, MEd, Harvard Univ. **Annie Farquhar, Adm.**

Col Prep. **AP**—Calc. **Feat**—British_Lit Classics Creative_Writing Humanities African-Amer_Lit Southern_Lit Latino_Lit World_Lit Stats Anat & Physiol Ecol Geol Islamic_Hist 20th-Century_Europe 20th-Century_Africa Hist_of_War Econ Lat_Amer_Stud Comp_Relig Art_Hist Ceramics Film Photog Sculpt Studio_Art Film_Hist Drama Music. **Supp**—Tut.

Adm (Gr K-11): 84/yr. Appl due: Jan. Accepted: 11%. **Tests** IQ ISEE SSAT.

Enr 600. B 298. G 302. Elem 309. Sec 291. Wh 75%. Hisp 3%. Blk 13%. Asian 5%. Other 4%. Avg class size: 14. **Fac 93.** M 33/1. F 51/8. Wh 77%. Hisp 3%. Blk 16%. Asian 4%. Adv deg: 68%.

Grad '04—69. Col—69. (Brown, Cornell, Trinity Col-CT, Haverford, Wm & Mary, Yale). Avg SAT: 1349. Alum 1642.

Tui '04-'05: Day $18,925-22,460 (+$300-500). **Aid:** Need 73 ($1,066,082).

Summer: Acad Enrich Rev. Tui Day $450-1175. Travel Abroad. Tui Bdg $4300-5000. 3-6 wks.

Endow $5,072,000. Plant val $24,000,000. Bldgs 6. Class rms 62. 2 Libs 12,000 vols. Sci labs 6. Comp labs 3. Auds 1. Art studios 4. Music studios 3. Dance studios 1. Gyms 2. Fields 1.

Est 1911. Nonprofit. Sem (Sept-June). **Assoc** CLS.

Since its founding by Louise Maret, a teacher born in Switzerland and educated in the US, the school has undergone several evolutions. Originally a girls' boarding school for French nationals preparing for the Baccalaureate exams, it expanded to include boys in 1937, added a traditional American college preparatory program in the 1940s, and finally abandoned the Baccalaureate program in 1969. In 1952, the school moved to its present location on the former Woodley Oaks Estate, a site that was considered for the Capitol by George Washington and, in the 19th century, became the summer residence of two presidents.

In addition to course requirements in mathematics and the humanities, each student takes French or Spanish, science, computers, art and music from kindergarten through the high school years. Summer study in France, Costa Rica and Florida is conducted under the direction of the Maret faculty.

A full sports program includes baseball, football, soccer, basketball, Pilates, track, cross-country, wrestling, lacrosse, softball, volleyball, modern dance, weight training, golf, tennis and ultimate Frisbee. Extracurricular activities offer opportunities to participate in dramatic productions, musical performances, student council, and clubs such as Amnesty International, Model UN and the engineering team. Students may also elect involvement in the school's newspapers, yearbook and literary arts magazines.

NATIONAL CATHEDRAL SCHOOL
Day — Girls Gr 4-12

Washington, DC 20016. Mt St Alban. Tel: 202-537-6374. Fax: 202-537-2382.
www.ncs.cathedral.org

Kathleen O'Neil Jamieson, Head. BA, Univ of Maryland-College Park, MA, Columbia Univ.
Denise C. Buchanan, Adm.

Col Prep. AP—Eng Fr Lat Span Calc Stats Bio Chem Human_Geog Physics US_Hist Econ US_Govt & Pol Art_Hist. **Feat**—African-Amer_Lit Chin Greek Japan Russ Environ_Sci Pol_Sci Studio_Art Drama Music. **Supp**—Rev Tut.

Adm (Gr 4-11): 85/yr. Appl due: Feb. Accepted: 39%. Yield: 72%. **Tests** CTP_4 IQ ISEE SSAT.

Enr 572. G 572. Elem 274. Sec 298. Wh 76%. Hisp 4%. Blk 13%. Asian 6%. Other 1%. Avg class size: 15. **Fac 101.** M 20/5. F 61/15. Wh 90%. Hisp 1%. Blk 9%. Adv deg: 69%.

Grad '04—77. Col—77. (Columbia 5, Harvard 4, Princeton 4, U of VA 4, U of Chicago 3, Cornell 3). Avg SAT: 1395. Alum 3967.

Tui '04-'05: Day $23,270 (+$300-500). **Aid:** Need 89 ($1,361,000).

Summer: Enrich Rec. 4 wks.

Endow $15,300,000. Plant val $24,247,000. Bldgs 7. Class rms 44. 2 Libs 60,000 vols. Sci labs 7. Lang labs 1. Comp labs 4. Auds 3. Theaters 2. Art studios 4. Music studios 3. Dance studios 2. Gyms 3. Fields 2. Courts 3.

Est 1899. Nonprofit. Episcopal. Quar (Sept-May). **Assoc** CLS MSA.

After seven years of planning by Henry Yates Satterlee, the first Episcopal bishop of Washington, and local philanthropist and educator Phoebe Apperson Hearst, this girls' school opened with an enrollment of 16 day students and 32 boarders. The school's early years were closely linked with the beginning of the Diocese of Washington and the 1907 construction of the Cathedral of St. Peter and St. Paul. Today, NCS shares the 59-acre Cathedral Close with two related schools: Beauvoir, a coeducational primary school, and St. Albans, a boys' school consisting of grades 4-12. Since the 1970s, National Cathedral has conducted a program of coordinate classes and activities with St. Albans.

NCS is essentially a college preparatory school. Opportunities in publications, art, music, drama and sports are numerous, and there are many special programs reflecting student interests, including an environmental awareness group and government, literary and photography clubs. Girls participate in school government and volunteer for community service projects.

ST. ALBANS SCHOOL
Bdg — Boys Gr 9-12; Day — Boys 4-12

Washington, DC 20016. Mt St Alban. Tel: 202-537-6435. Fax: 202-537-2225.
www.sta.cathedral.org   E-mail: sta_admission@cathedral.org
Vance Wilson, Head. BA, Yale Univ, MA, Univ of Virginia. **Mason Lecky, Adm.**
- **Col Prep. AP**—Fr Lat Span Calc Stats Comp_Sci Bio Chem Human_Geog Physics Eur_Hist US_Govt & Pol. **Feat**—British_Lit Creative_Writing Shakespeare Chin Ger Greek Japan Russ Anat & Physiol Forensic_Sci Govt Relig Art_Hist Ceramics Photog Studio_Art Drama Music. **Supp**—Tut.
- **Adm:** 93/yr. Bdg 11. Day 82. Appl due: Jan. Accepted: 20%. **Tests** ISEE SSAT.
- **Enr 565.** B 30/535. Elem 255. Sec 310. Wh 74%. Hisp 2%. Blk 12%. Asian 6%. Other 6%. Avg class size: 16. **Fac 76.** M 53. F 23. Adv deg: 59%. In dorms 5.
- **Grad '04—79. Col—75.** (Yale 5, U of VA 5, Bowdoin 3, Dartmouth 3, Harvard 3, Princeton 3). Alum 3781.
- **Tui '04-'05: Bdg $32,897** (+$400-700). **Day $23,256** (+$400-700). **Aid:** Need 105 ($1,248,010).
- **Summer:** Acad Enrich Rev Rem Rec. Sports. Tui Day $400-1000. 6 wks.
- Endow $33,000,000. Plant val $14,879,000. Bldgs 7. Dorms 1. Class rms 30. Lib 17,000 vols. Labs 6. Theaters 1. Art studios 3. Music studios 3. Gyms 2. Fields 2. Courts 14. Pools 1.
- **Est 1909.** Nonprofit. Episcopal. Sem (Sept-May). **Assoc** CLS.

Founded as the National Cathedral School for Boys by the bequest of Harriet Lane Johnston, St. Albans has use of the 59-acre Close of Washington Cathedral. Well-equipped for both academic and extracurricular programs, with unusual opportunities for music at the cathedral, the school provides honors courses in history, math, science and languages. Reflecting the worldwide importance of Washington, the school enrolls students from many countries, with graduates entering leading colleges.

St. Albans provides many of the advantages of coeducation while retaining the strengths of separate education, for its sister school, the National Cathedral School, is also located in the Cathedral Close. Approximately 30 coordinate courses are open to students. The two schools come together for such extracurricular activities as glee club, dramatics and social events. St. Albans offers a vigorous sports program and provides opportunities for students to engage in social service activities in the Greater Washington area. The boarding department allows the school to attract students from other states and around the world.

SHERIDAN SCHOOL
Day — Coed Gr K-8

Washington, DC 20008. 4400 36th St NW. Tel: 202-362-7900. Fax: 202-244-4098.
www.sheridanschool.org   E-mail: admission@sheridanschool.org
C. Randall Plummer, Head. BS, Univ of Missouri, MEd, Boston Univ. **Julie C. Lewis, Adm.**
- **Pre-Prep. Feat**—Fr Span Computers Studio_Art Music. **Supp**—Rev Tut.
- **Adm:** 41/yr. Appl due: Jan. Accepted: 59%. Yield: 56%. **Tests** IQ SSAT.

Enr 212. B 111. G 101. Elem 212. Wh 79%. Hisp 4%. Blk 11%. Asian 1%. Other 5%. Avg class size: 23. **Fac 32.** M 8. F 21/3. Adv deg: 53%.
Grad '04—21. Prep—17. (Georgetown Day 3, Madeira 2, Maret 2, Natl Cathedral 2, Field 1). Avg SSAT: 82%. Alum 760.
Tui '04-'05: Day $18,689-20,752 (+$100-150). **Aid:** Need 32 ($294,567).
Summer: Enrich Rec. Sports. Arts. Tui Day $746-994. 3-7 wks.
Endow $1,700,000. Plant val $5,000,000. Bldgs 1. Class rms 10. Lib 8689 vols. Sci labs 2. Lang labs 2. Comp labs 1. Auds 1. Theaters 1. Art studios 1. Music studios 1. Gyms 1.
Est 1927. Nonprofit. Tri (Sept-June). **Assoc** MSA.

In 1927, Mrs. Frank Cummings Cook took over Miss Tomlin's School, a small, coed primary school, and renamed it Mrs. Cook's School. When she retired in 1952, the school was renamed "Sheridan" because of its location at Sheridan Circle on Massachusetts Avenue, NW. In 1962, it was incorporated by a group of parents as a nonprofit organization and expanded through grade 8. The school moved to its present location in 1964.

A small family school offering a strong academic program and a central-subject approach, Sheridan provides a progression in the basic skills. The Writing Process is introduced in the primary grades and continues through grade 8. Computer courses and French and Spanish instruction commence in kindergarten. Music and art are integral parts of the program, and trips are taken to local cultural and historical points of interest. A 130-acre campus in the Shenandoah Valley offers outdoor educational experiences for children at all grade levels, including trips during the school year, optional weekend backpacking excursions, and longer winter and summer educational sojourns. An after-school program, vacation camps and summer programs are open to all students.

SIDWELL FRIENDS SCHOOL
Day — Coed Gr PS-12

Washington, DC 20016. 3825 Wisconsin Ave NW. Tel: 202-537-8100. Fax: 202-537-8138. www.sidwell.edu   E-mail: admissions@sidwell.edu
Bruce B. Stewart, Head. AB, Guilford College, MEd, Univ of North Carolina-Chapel Hill.
Joshua P. Wolman, Adm.
Col Prep. AP—Fr Lat Span. **Feat**—Shakespeare Russ_Lit Chin Stats Bioethics Environ_Sci Programming African_Hist Amer_Stud Pol_Sci Comp_Relig Philos Studio_Art Acting Drama Theater_Arts Music Dance. **Supp**—Tut.
Adm: 155/yr. Appl due: Jan. Accepted: 19%. Yield: 75%. **Tests** IQ ISEE SSAT.
Enr 1091. B 563. G 528. Elem 625. Sec 466. Wh 62%. Hisp 4%. Blk 15%. Asian 9%. Other 10%. Avg class size: 17. **Fac 148.** M 49. F 99. Wh 76%. Hisp 6%. Blk 14%. Asian 4%. Adv deg: 50%.
Grad '04—120. Col—120. (Yale, U of PA, U of MI, Harvard, Columbia, Wash U). Avg SAT: 1400. Alum 4950.
Tui '04-'05: Day $21,415-22,415 (+$300-600). **Aid:** Need 217 ($3,155,040).
Summer: Acad Enrich Rev Rem Rec. Tui Bdg $625-2975. Tui Day $525-1600. 1-6 wks.
Endow $29,866,000. Plant val $31,001,000. Bldgs 11. Class rms 217. 3 Libs 39,242 vols. Sci labs 7. Lang labs 1. Comp labs 4. Auds 1. Art studios 6. Music studios 3. Dance studios 1. Arts ctrs 1. Gyms 3. Fields 6. Courts 8. Tracks 1.
Est 1883. Nonprofit. Religious Society of Friends. Sem (Sept-June). **Assoc** MSA.

Thomas W. Sidwell established and then conducted this school for 53 years according to Quaker concepts of education, emphasizing simplicity, friendliness, democratic group processes, and personal and community responsibility. The school began with 11 students in a Friends meetinghouse in downtown Washington, moving to its present, 15-acre location in 1922. Under five successive headmasters, the school developed this site and added a five-acre Bethesda, MD, campus in 1963 to house the lower school (grades PS-4).

The competitive academic program has strong departments of sciences, mathematics, languages, social studies and the arts being supplemented by extensive athletics. Graduation requirements include a significant community service program and a compulsory work program for students in grades 9-12. Both are central to the life of the school, as is a weekly Meeting for Worship. Students of diverse racial, economic and cultural backgrounds enter leading colleges throughout the country.

Taking advantage of its location in the nation's capital, the school offers many learning environments and teaching approaches. Upper school students have further opportunities for specialized study through the School Year Abroad program in France, Spain, China and Italy.

WASHINGTON INTERNATIONAL SCHOOL
Day — Coed Gr PS-12

Washington, DC 20008. 3100 Macomb St NW. Tel: 202-243-1800. Fax: 202-243-1807.
www.wis.edu E-mail: admissions@wis.edu
Richard P. Hall, Head. Dorrie Fuchs, Adm.

    Col Prep. IB Diploma. Bilingual. Feat—Chin Ital Japan Dutch Environ_Sci Computers Econ Studio_Art Drama Music Journ. **Supp**—ESL Tut.
    Adm (Gr PS-11): 154/yr. Appl due: Jan. Accepted: 30%.
    Enr 830. Elem 573. Sec 257. Wh 66%. Hisp 10%. Blk 14%. Asian 10%. Avg class size: 15. **Fac 112.** M 22/7. F 70/13.
    Grad '04—53. Col—52. (U of VA, U of Toronto-Canada, Geo Wash, King's Col London-England, London Sch of Econ-England, Oberlin). Alum 860.
    Tui '04-'05: Day $15,500-20,850 (+$420-750). **Aid:** Need 80 ($1,000,000).
    Summer: Acad Rev Rec. 2-3 wks.
    Endow $35,000. Plant val $6,500,000. Bldgs 8. Class rms 56. Libs 3. Labs 7. Comp labs 3. Auds 1. Art studios 3. Music studios 2. Gyms 2. Fields 2.
    Est 1966. Nonprofit. Tri (Sept-June). **Assoc** MSA.

WIS provides an international education for both American and international students, offering the cultural richness of an international staff and a curriculum drawn from many countries and educational traditions.

The primary school program includes language immersion classes in the prekindergarten and kindergarten, and children in grades 1-5 follow a bilingual curriculum with half the instruction in English and the remainder in French, Spanish or, for native speakers, Dutch. Intensive courses in these two languages are available for new pupils in grade 3 and above. History and geography are taught in French and Spanish through grade 8, although English-language sections are also available for newly enrolled students.

The curriculum enables youngsters to transfer readily to schools overseas. WIS offers both the Primary Years Program and the Middle Years Program of the International Baccalaureate. In their last two years, all students follow the IB Diploma

Program, a rigorous, comprehensive course of studies recognized by many colleges around the world. Extracurricular electives and sports supplement academic offerings.

The school is housed at two locations: Grades pre-K-5 are located on the primary school campus at Reservoir Road and 36th Street NW, while middle and upper school classes and activities take place at Tregaron, a 20-acre former residential estate in northwest Washington.

MARYLAND

ANNAPOLIS, MD. (23 mi. SSE of Baltimore, MD; 28 mi. E of Washington, DC) Suburban. Pop: 35,838. Alt: 40 ft.

KEY SCHOOL
Day — Coed Gr PS-12

Annapolis, MD 21403. 534 Hillsmere Dr. Tel: 410-263-9231. Fax: 410-280-5516.
  www.keyschool.org   E-mail: jdunleavy@keyschool.org
Marcella Yedid, Head. BS, Indiana Univ, MA, Brown Univ. **Jessie D. Dunleavy, Adm.**
  Col Prep. AP—Eng Fr Lat Span Calc Stats Bio Chem Physics US_Hist Studio_Art.
  Feat—Women's_Lit Computers Anthro Russ_Stud Playwriting Music Music_Theory Dance Outdoor_Ed. **Supp**—Tut.
  Adm: 118/yr. Appl due: Rolling. Accepted: 53%. **Tests** ISEE.
  Enr 720. B 303. G 417. Elem 514. Sec 206. Wh 84%. Hisp 2%. Blk 9%. Asian 3%. Other 2%. Avg class size: 17. **Fac 110.** M 26/1. F 70/13. Wh 90%. Blk 5%. Asian 2%. Other 3%. Adv deg: 45%.
  Grad '04—36. Col—36. (St Mary's Col of MD, U of MD-Col Park, Embry-Riddle, Bryn Mawr, Boston Col, Dartmouth). Alum 935.
  Tui '03-'04: Day $8600-17,150 (+$230-800). **Aid:** Need 98 ($867,500).
  Summer: Acad Enrich Rev Rec. 6 wks.
  Endow $781,000. Plant val $9,000,000. Bldgs 16. Class rms 60. Libs 3. Sci labs 6. Comp labs 2. Auds 1. Theaters 1. Art studios 3. Music studios 3. Gyms 2. Fields 3.
  Est 1958. Nonprofit. (Sept-June).

Founded by several tutors from nearby St. John's College who were determined to bring strong teachers and able students together, the school soon established a program combining experiential learning with a rigorous, essentially classical curriculum. Originally serving 18 pupils in grades 1-3, Key added one grade in each ensuing year until the 1970s, when the program ran from prekindergarten through grade 12 and enrollment had grown to 360 students. Ongoing plant renovations and new construction in the 1980s and 1990s enabled the school to meet the needs of a larger student body and an expanding educational program.

Boys and girls in the middle school (grades 5-8) take part in various multidisciplinary experiences and hands-on activities. Key's Orff Schulwerk music program, which begins in preschool and continues through middle school, is particularly strong. All boys and girls in the program engage in the daily study of speech, rhythm, instruments, singing, creative movement and dance, drama and improvisation. Students also learn to read music while gaining an understanding of basic theoretical concepts.

Electives such as non-Western literature, statistics, Women's literature, estuarine biology, dance and music theory supplement a standard upper school curriculum (grades 9-12) that features extensive modern and classical language and fine and performing arts programs. Emphasis is placed on writing, critical reading and thinking, and the curriculum incorporates interdisciplinary learning techniques and experiential education. College preparation is a primary goal, and Advanced Placement courses are available in the major subject areas.

For sport, students may participate in an intramural program or on interscholastic teams. Other activities include theater, chorus, instrumental ensemble, literary magazine and Model Congress. Extensive field trips (such as outdoor education camping excursions) are integral to school life.

BALTIMORE, MD. Urban. Pop: 651,154. Alt: to 445 ft.

BOYS' LATIN SCHOOL
Day — Boys Gr K-12

Baltimore, MD 21210. 822 W Lake Ave. Tel: 410-377-5192. Fax: 410-377-4312.
www.boyslatinmd.com   E-mail: lheubeck@boyslatinmd.com

Scott K. Gibson III, Head. BS, The Citadel, MS, Troy State Univ, MA, Georgetown Univ, MMAS, US Army Command and General Staff College. **James W. Currie, Jr., Upper & Middle Sch Adm; Kathleen M. Berger, Lower Sch Adm.**

- **Col Prep. AP**—Eng Calc Bio Chem. **Feat**—Fr Lat Span Stats Anat Ecol Genetics Geol Marine_Biol/Sci Comp_Sci African-Amer_Hist Govt Greek_Culture Studio_Art Music Journ. **Supp**—Tut.
- **Adm:** 121/yr. Appl due: Rolling. Accepted: 58%. Yield: 60%. **Tests** CTP_4 IQ ISEE MRT Stanford.
- **Enr 634.** B 634. Elem 373. Sec 261. Wh 87%. Blk 11%. Asian 2%. Avg class size: 15. **Fac 86.** M 34/3. F 45/4. Wh 95%. Blk 5%. Adv deg: 55%.
- **Grad '04—64. Col**—64. (U of MD-Col Park 5, Loyola Col 5, Col of Charleston 3, U of Miami 2, Randolph-Macon 2, Gettysburg 2). Avg SAT: 1167. Alum 1900.
- **Tui '04-'05: Day $13,500-16,400. Aid:** Need 118 ($978,600).
- Endow $19,206,000. Plant val $35,700,000. Bldgs 8. Class rms 64. 2 Libs 15,000 vols. Sci labs 6. Lang labs 1. Comp labs 3. Photog labs 1. Auds 1. Theaters 1. Art studios 2. Music studios 2. Gyms 2. Fields 5. Courts 6.
- **Est 1844.** Nonprofit. Sem (Sept-June). **Assoc** MSA.

Founded by Evert M. Topping, a Princeton professor, Boys' Latin serves the needs of young men in the Baltimore area. In 1960, the school moved from its downtown location to a 16-acre campus in Roland Park. Over the years, separate lower, middle and upper school plants and campuses have enlarged, with the school now occupying 41 acres.

The lower school emphasizes language arts and mathematics, while the middle school stresses the five traditional subjects. In the upper school, qualified juniors and seniors may choose from a variety of electives and Advanced Placement courses beyond the traditional disciplines. Technology is an important aspect of school life, and all boys are expected to develop computer literacy.

Student activities include publications, drama, debating, music, interest clubs and cooperative ventures with students from neighboring independent schools. Athletics offered are football, soccer, cross-country, wrestling, basketball, ice hockey, lacrosse, baseball, golf, tennis, volleyball and squash.

BRYN MAWR SCHOOL
Day — Boys Gr PS, Girls PS-12

Baltimore, MD 21210. 109 W Melrose Ave. Tel: 410-323-8800. Fax: 410-435-4678.
www.brynmawrschool.org E-mail: admissions@brynmawrschool.org

Maureen Walsh Heffernan, **Head.** BA, Wesleyan Univ, MA, Columbia Univ. **Patricia M. Nothstein, Adm.**

Col Prep. AP—Eng Fr Span Calc Stats Comp_Sci Bio Physics US_Hist Art_Hist. **Feat**—Creative_Writing Shakespeare Chin Ger Greek Russ Anat & Physiol Astron Genetics Forensic_Sci Web_Design Econ Holocaust Urban_Stud Ethics Film Fine_Arts Photog Drama Music Music_Theory Dance Finance Journ Engineering. **Supp**—Tut.

Adm (Gr PS-12): 179/yr. Accepted: 49%. Yield: 55%. **Tests** ISEE Stanford.

Enr 918. Elem 599. Sec 319. Wh 77%. Blk 11%. Asian 7%. Other 5%. Avg class size: 15. Uniform. **Fac 108.** M 16/1. F 80/11. Wh 92%. Hisp 6%. Blk 6%. Adv deg: 56%.

Grad '04—82. Col—82. (U of PA 4, Johns Hopkins 4, Vanderbilt 3, Harvard 3, Boston Col 3, Georgetown 3). Avg SAT: 1280. Alum 3264.

Tui '04-'05: Day $17,350-18,200 (+$100-450). **Aid:** Need 129 ($1,331,576).

Summer: Acad Enrich Rev Rec. 10 wks.

Endow $19,000,000. Plant val $19,300,000. Bldgs 21. Class rms 41. 2 Libs 27,000 vols. Labs 5. Comp labs 2. Sci ctrs 1. Auds 1. Theaters 1. Art studios 3. Music studios 4. Dance studios 1. Gyms 2. Fields 4. Tennis courts 6.

Est 1885. Nonprofit. Sem (Sept-June). **Assoc** CLS MSA.

Bryn Mawr School, one of the nation's first college preparatory schools for girls, is located on a 26-acre, wooded campus within the city limits. The school was originally established to prepare graduates for Bryn Mawr College. Among the five young Baltimore women who founded Bryn Mawr was M. Carey Thomas, the first dean and second president of Bryn Mawr College and a pioneer in women's education, and Mary Garrett, a Baltimore philanthropist who later made possible the founding of Johns Hopkins Medical School by donating a sum of money contingent upon the admission of women. Edith Hamilton, author of *The Greek Way*, was the first headmistress.

The rigorous college preparatory curriculum includes drama, art, physical education, music, values education and computer studies. These areas are complemented in the upper school by requirements in public speaking and community service. Bryn Mawr's coordinate program with neighboring Gilman School for boys and Roland Park Country School for girls allows for expanded course offerings. French instruction begins in kindergarten and is joined by Latin and Spanish in the middle school and by German, Greek, Russian and Chinese in the upper school.

The school offers a strong athletic program that includes dance, lacrosse, soccer, tennis, crew, field hockey, badminton, volleyball, cross-country, squash, softball, riding, aerobics and basketball. Among the extracurricular activities are choral groups, plays and concerts, instrumental ensembles, a newspaper, a literary magazine and a wide assortment of clubs. Foreign exchange programs are also available.

Bryn Mawr's preschool daycare program enrolls two- to five-year-old boys and girls; the division includes an infant/toddler center for children ages 2mos-2½.

CALVERT HALL COLLEGE HIGH SCHOOL
Day — Boys Gr 9-12

Baltimore, MD 21286. 8102 La Salle Rd. Tel: 410-825-4266. Fax: 410-825-6826.
www.calverthall.com E-mail: chc@calverthall.com
Br. **Kevin Stanton, Pres.** BA, La Salle Univ, MS, Univ of Notre Dame. **Louis E. Heidrick, Prin. Chris Bengel, Adm.**
- **Col Prep. AP**—Eng Fr Lat Span Calc Comp_Sci Bio Chem Physics Eur_Hist US_Hist World_Hist Comp_Govt & Pol Econ US_Govt & Pol Studio_Art Music_Theory. **Feat**—Humanities Ger Russ Web_Design Psych World_Relig Fine_Arts. **Supp**—LD Tut.
- **Adm:** 313/yr. Appl due: Dec. Accepted: 65%. **Tests** HSPT.
- **Enr 1149.** B 1149. Sec 1149. Wh 88%. Hisp 2%. Blk 6%. Asian 4%. Avg class size: 21. **Fac 92.** M 68. F 24. Wh 92%. Hisp 1%. Blk 2%. Asian 4%. Other 1%. Adv deg: 59%.
- **Grad '04—279. Col—273.** (Towson, U of MD-Col Park, Salisbury, Loyola Col, U of MD-Baltimore County, Villa Julie). Avg SAT: 1096. Alum 15,500.
- **Tui '04-'05: Day $8500 (+$150). Aid:** Merit 100 ($350,000). Need 400 ($1,000,000).
- **Summer:** Enrich Rev. 5 wks.
- Endow $4,000,000. Plant val $25,000,000. Bldgs 4. Class rms 80. Lib 23,000 vols. Labs 5. Auds 1. Theaters 1. Art studios 1. Music studios 1. Perf arts ctrs 1. Gyms 2. Fields 3. Pools 1. Stadiums 1.
- **Est 1845.** Nonprofit. Roman Catholic. Sem (Sept-June). **Assoc** MSA.

Founded by the Brothers of the Christian Schools, Calvert Hall has occupied its present, 33-acre campus since 1960. The curriculum is college preparatory, offering a variety of programs. A four-year scholars program includes courses designed for intellectually gifted students, incorporating accelerated content, in-depth study, small-group discussions, interdisciplinary approaches and experiential learning. The writing program includes a staffed writing center. The school also offers a program for students with identified language-learning difficulties. Students in this program are fully integrated into the academic environment and receive additional instruction from a language specialist.

A full athletic program includes football, soccer, cross-country, volleyball, water polo, basketball, indoor and outdoor track, wrestling, swimming, hockey, baseball, lacrosse, golf and tennis. Among other pursuits are musical groups, publications, forensics and more than 40 other student organizations and activities.

CALVERT SCHOOL
Day — Coed Gr PS-8

Baltimore, MD 21210. 105 Tuscany Rd. Tel: 410-243-6054. Fax: 410-243-0384.
www.calvertschool.org E-mail: admissions@calvertschool.org
Andrew A. Martire, Head. AB, Princeton Univ, MLA, Johns Hopkins Univ. **Deborah D. Frey, Adm.**
- **Pre-Prep. Feat**—Mythology Fr Lat Span Art_Hist Studio_Art Music.
- **Adm:** 84/yr. Appl due: Feb. Accepted: 28%. Yield: 93%. **Tests** CTP_4 IQ ISEE.
- **Enr 478.** B 238. G 240. Elem 478. Wh 87%. Blk 8%. Asian 4%. Other 1%. Avg class size: 15. Uniform. **Fac 59.** M 15. F 44. Wh 92%. Blk 8%. Adv deg: 66%.
- **Grad '04—45. Prep—45.** (Gilman, Roland Park, Bryn Mawr, St Paul's Sch-MD, McDonogh, Friends Sch-MD). Alum 2200.
- **Tui '04-'05: Day $7950-15,900. Aid:** Need 80 ($750,000).
- Endow $40,000,000. Plant val $30,000,000. Bldgs 2. Class rms 52. 2 Libs 15,000 vols. Sci labs 3. Comp labs 2. Auds 1. Theaters 1. Art studios 2. Music studios 2. Dance studios

1. Planetariums 1. Gyms 3. Fields 3.
Est 1897. Nonprofit. Sem (Sept-June). **Assoc** MSA.

The school, located in Roland Park, features a curriculum of science, geography, composition, foreign language, art history, music and art, in addition to the basic subjects. The library, science and computer labs and a planetarium provide a solid resource base for the student, and the athletic program fosters physical development and sportsmanship.

A home instruction program (grades K-8), developed and tested in the day school, helps parents to teach children at home. It is specially designed for parents without previous teaching experience or training. Many parents use these courses for supplementary or enrichment purposes.

FRIENDS SCHOOL
Day — Coed Gr PS-12

Baltimore, MD 21210. 5114 N Charles St. Tel: 410-649-3200. Fax: 410-649-3202.
www.friendsbalt.org   E-mail: admissions@mail.friendsbalt.org
Lila B. Lohr, Head. BA, Vassar College, MEd, Goucher College. **Grant L. Jacks III, Adm.**
  Col Prep. Feat—Fr Lat Russ Span Stats Ecol Environ_Sci Computers Econ Govt Photog Studio_Art Theater Music Journ. **Supp**—Rem_Math Rem_Read Tut.
  Adm: 139/yr. Appl due: Dec. Accepted: 39%. **Tests** IQ ISEE Stanford.
  Enr 1005. B 515. G 490. Elem 654. Sec 351. Wh 80%. Hisp 4%. Blk 10%. Asian 6%. Avg class size: 17. **Fac 115.** M 32/7. F 54/22. Wh 87%. Hisp 2%. Blk 10%. Asian 1%. Adv deg: 64%.
  Grad '04—79. Col—77. (Wesleyan U, Col of Charleston, Boston U, Am U, Duke, Harvard). Avg SAT: 1260. Alum 3600.
  Tui '04-'05: Day $14,475-16,610 (+$175-500). **Aid:** Need 216 ($1,743,566).
  Endow $12,000,000. Plant val $18,000,000. Bldgs 9. Class rms 65. 3 Libs 30,000 vols. Labs 8. Auds 1. Art studios 5. Music studios 6. Dance studios 1. Gyms 3. Fields 5. Courts 10.
  Est 1784. Nonprofit. Religious Society of Friends. (Sept-June). **Assoc** CLS MSA.

Providing a program from preprimary through high school, Friends carries forward the Quaker tradition from the school's 18th-century founding. Occupying a 33-acre site in northern Baltimore, the school's plant includes eight major educational buildings.

Quaker ideals serve as the cornerstone of the school's extensive social service program. Students in grades 9-12 must complete a community service requirement before graduation. The school offers a country day program providing a broad liberal education that prepares its graduates for many colleges.

Among student activities are publications, drama and music. Sports include football, soccer, cross-country, basketball, lacrosse, wrestling, tennis, field hockey, badminton, dance volleyball, weight training, flag football, softball, baseball and golf.

GILMAN SCHOOL
Day — Boys Gr K-12

Baltimore, MD 21210. 5407 Roland Ave. Tel: 410-323-3800. Fax: 410-532-6513.
  www.gilman.edu

Jon C. McGill, Head. BA, MA, Univ of Waterloo (Canada), MEd, Univ of London (England). **Robert J. Demeule, Adm.**

Col Prep. AP—Fr Lat Span Calc Stats Comp_Sci Bio Chem Physics Eur_Hist Psych Studio_Art. **Feat**—Chin Ger Greek Russ Anat & Physiol Astron Web_Design African-Amer_Hist Holocaust Architect Acting Music_Hist Music_Theory Speech Indus_Arts Study_Skills.

Adm: 130/yr. Appl due: Jan. Accepted: 34%. Yield: 79%. **Tests** ISEE.

Enr 983. B 983. Elem 543. Sec 440. Wh 76%. Hisp 1%. Blk 12%. Asian 9%. Other 2%. Avg class size: 16. **Fac 145.** M 90/4. F 45/6. Wh 89%. Hisp 1%. Blk 8%. Asian 2%. Adv deg: 72%.

Grad '04—105. Col—104. (Princeton 6, U of MD-Col Park 5, Georgetown 4, Johns Hopkins 4, Wash U 4, U of the South 4). Avg SAT: 1324. Alum 4420.

Tui '04-'05: Day $15,975-16,945 (+$350). **Aid:** Need ($2,500,000).

Summer: Acad Enrich Rev Rem. Tui Day $450/crse. 6 wks.

Endow $59,400,000. Bldgs 14. 3 Libs 40,000 vols. Labs 15. Sci labs 4. Comp labs 4. Auds 1. Art studios 3. Music studios 3. Gyms 2. Fields 8. Courts 11. Pools 1.

Est 1897. Nonprofit. Sem (Sept-June). **Assoc** CLS.

Founded as The Country School for Boys of Baltimore City by Anne Galbraith Carey, a mother seeking a strong school for her sons, Gilman was established as the nation's first country day school. In addition to enrolling students from all parts of the city, the school accepts boys of varying religious, cultural and socioeconomic backgrounds.

Gilman provides a solid preparatory curriculum supplemented by many electives. During the lower school years (grades pre-1-5), the program combines a focus on the fundamental skills of reading, writing and math with projects in such areas as science, music, art and woodworking. The middle school (grades 6-8) supplements content learning with instruction in study skills and organization, note taking, problem solving and communication. Boys in the upper school (grades 9-12) have increased scheduling flexibility to pursue interests and determine academic strengths.

The school extends its reach to the broader Baltimore community through community service programs and coordinate classes with two nearby girls' schools, Bryn Mawr School and Roland Park Country School. Many opportunities are available in publications, debating, dramatics, and hobby and interest clubs, and athletic participation is compulsory at the upper school level.

ROLAND PARK COUNTRY SCHOOL
Day — Girls Gr K-12

Baltimore, MD 21210. 5204 Roland Ave. Tel: 410-323-5500. Fax: 410-323-2164.
www.rpcs.org   E-mail: info@rpcs.org

Jean Waller Brune, Head. BA, Middlebury College, MLA, Johns Hopkins Univ. **Peggy K. Wolf, Adm.**

Col Prep. AP—Eng Fr Span Calc Stats Comp_Sci Bio Chem Physics Eur_Hist US_Hist Econ Psych US_Govt & Pol Art_Hist Studio_Art. **Feat**—Chin Ger Greek Japan Russ Photog Drama Music_Hist Dance.

Adm: 100/yr. Appl due: Jan. Accepted: 36%. **Tests** CTP_4 ISEE.

Enr 710. G 710. Wh 79%. Hisp 3%. Blk 12%. Asian 6%. Avg class size: 15. Uniform. **Fac 109.** Adv deg: 62%.

Grad '04—70. Col—70. (Johns Hopkins, Georgetown, U of MD-Col Park, Duke, U of PA,

Wash & Lee). Alum 2500.
Tui '04-'05: Day $16,950 (+$300-500). **Aid:** Need 140 ($936,550).
Endow $22,000,000. Plant val $8,000,000. Bldgs 1. Class rms 75. Lib 20,382 vols. Sci labs 7. Comp labs 2. Theaters 1. Music studios 5. Arts ctrs 1. Gyms 3. Fields 2. Courts 6.
Est 1901. Nonprofit. Sem (Sept-June). **Assoc** CLS.

Located on a 21-acre estate originally owned by Jerome Bonaparte, RPCS combines modern facilities with the original 19th-century mansion. The school offers a strong academic program that is complemented by more than 50 electives, extracurricular activities, community service opportunities, and interscholastic and intramural sports. Academic standards are high, and there are opportunities for students to take Advanced Placement courses in all disciplines, as well as for foreign travel and study in France, Spain, Japan and Russia.

Various activities include art, music, drama, dance, athletics, school government, international relations, publications, honor societies, and student clubs and organizations. There is the opportunity for career exploration through a senior internship, and a coordinate program with the neighboring Gilman School for boys provides possibilities for additional electives in a coed setting. After-school care is available for lower school girls.

BEL AIR, MD. (21 mi. NE of Baltimore, MD) Suburban. Pop: 10,080. Alt: 380 ft.

HARFORD DAY SCHOOL
Day — Coed Gr PS-8

Bel Air, MD 21014. 715 Moores Mill Rd. Tel: 410-838-4848. Fax: 410-836-5918.
 www.harfordday.org E-mail: donnadecker@harfordday.org
Susan G. Harris, Head. BS, Bucknell Univ. **Donna Decker, Int Adm.**
 Pre-Prep. Feat—Fr Lat Span Computers Studio_Art Drama Music. **Supp**—Dev_Read Rem_Math Rem_Read Tut.
 Adm: 149/yr. Appl due: Feb. Accepted: 37%. **Tests** ISEE MRT Stanford.
 Enr 352. **Elem** 352. Wh 92%. Hisp 3%. Blk 2%. Asian 2%. Other 1%. Avg class size: 18.
 Fac 41. M 8. F 27/6. Wh 97%. Blk 3%. Adv deg: 39%.
 Grad '04—37. Prep—36. (John Carroll, St Paul's Sch-MD, McDonogh, Loyola Blakefield, New Hampton, St Paul's Sch for Girls). Alum 700.
 Tui '04-'05: Day $10,500 (+$75). **Aid:** Need 61 ($261,450).
 Summer: Enrich Rec. 1-4 wks.
 Endow $1,000,000. Plant val $6,000,000. Bldgs 3. Class rms 34. Lib 9200 vols. Sci labs 1. Comp labs 5. Art studios 1. Music studios 1. Gyms 1. Fields 3. Field houses 1.
 Est 1957. Nonprofit. Quar (Sept-June).

Located 20 miles northeast of Baltimore, this school offers a comprehensive curriculum that includes Spanish, which is taught from prekindergarten. French instruction begins in grade 4, and Latin is taught in grade 8. Reading, writing, language arts and math skills, as well as reasoning and independent thinking, are emphasized. Each grade receives computer instruction, and students participate in art, music and dramatics. Frequent field trips to Baltimore, Washington, DC, and

Philadelphia, PA, enrich classroom learning, and small classes permit faculty members to address individual student needs.

The physical education program stresses fundamental athletic skills in the early grades. Middle school students may participate in such sports as lacrosse, tennis, soccer, field hockey and basketball. There is also an optional extended-day program.

BETHESDA, MD. (8 mi. NW of Washington, DC) Urban. Pop: 55,277. Alt: 340 ft. Area also includes North Bethesda.

HOLTON-ARMS SCHOOL
Day — Girls Gr 3-12

Bethesda, MD 20817. 7303 River Rd. Tel: 301-365-5300. Fax: 301-365-6071.
   www.holton-arms.edu   E-mail: admit@holton-arms.edu
Diana Coulton Beebe, Head. BA, College of Wooster, MA, Univ of Tulsa. **Sharron K. Rodgers, Adm.**
   Col Prep. AP—Fr Lat Span Calc Stats Comp_Sci Bio Physics Eur_Hist US_Hist Econ Art_Hist. **Feat**—Women's_Stud African-Amer_Stud Existentialism Philos Music Dance. **Supp**—Dev_Read Rev Tut.
   Adm: 108/yr. Appl due: Jan. **Tests** ISEE SSAT.
   Enr 660. G 660. Elem 346. Sec 314. Avg class size: 15. Uniform. **Fac 88.** Adv deg: 70%.
   Grad '04—75. Col—75. (U of PA 4, U of VA 4, Amherst 3, Dartmouth 3, Duke 3, Princeton 3). Alum 6000.
   Tui '04-'05: Day $21,750 (+$500). **Aid:** Need 97 ($1,553,053).
   Summer: Enrich Rec. Fine Arts. 6 wks.
   Endow $43,000,000. Plant val $37,000,000. Bldgs 8. Class rms 52. 2 Libs 25,000 vols. Sci labs 9. Lang labs 1. Comp labs 2. Theaters 2. Art studios 3. Music studios 4. Dance studios 3. Gyms 1. Fields 3. Courts 7. Pools 1. Tracks 1.
   Est 1901. Nonprofit. Sem (Sept-June). **Assoc** CLS MSA.

Founded in Washington, DC, as a small girls' school by Jessie Moon Holton and Carolyn Hough Arms, this school has been at its present, suburban campus since 1963. Faculty utilize a variety of teaching methods while emphasizing the processes of inquiry, critical thinking and reading, and problem solving.

The sequential college preparatory curriculum features strong arts and athletic programs, honors and Advanced Placement courses, and a number of electives, particularly in the social sciences. Juniors and seniors may complete an independent study course and may register for one or two classes at the nearby Landon School for boys. In May, all seniors take part in either a senior project or a structured seminar.

Interscholastic and club athletic teams, community service opportunities, publications and interest clubs are among Holton's extracurriculars.

LANDON SCHOOL
Day — Boys Gr 3-12

Bethesda, MD 20817. 6101 Wilson Ln. Tel: 301-320-3200. Fax: 301-320-2787.
www.landon.net
David M. Armstrong, Head. BA, Princeton Univ, JD, Univ of Denver. **Russell L. Gagarin, Adm.**
    Col Prep. AP—Fr Lat Span Calc Stats Bio Chem Physics Eur_Hist US_Hist Econ US_Govt & Pol Art_Hist Studio_Art. **Feat**—Mandarin Music. **Supp**—Dev_Read Rem_Math Rev Tut.
    Adm (Gr 3-9): 104/yr. Appl due: Jan. Accepted: 25%. **Tests** ISEE.
    Enr 660. B 660. Elem 335. Sec 325. Wh 74%. Hisp 5%. Blk 10%. Asian 11%. Avg class size: 15. **Fac 95.** M 68/5. F 20/2. Adv deg: 60%.
    Grad '04—76. Col—76. (Vanderbilt, Davidson, U of VA, Princeton, Johns Hopkins). Avg SAT: 1326. Alum 2450.
    Tui '05-'06: Day $22,450-24,500 (+$500). **Aid:** Need 111 ($1,500,000).
    Summer: Acad Enrich Rev Rem Rec. Arts. Music. Sports. Travel. 6 wks.
    Endow $14,000,000. Plant val $39,000,000. Bldgs 13. Class rms 44. 3 Libs 25,000 vols. Labs 9. Auds 1. Theaters 2. Art studios 7. Music studios 15. Media ctrs 3. Gyms 2. Fields 9. Courts 12. Pools 1. Rifle ranges 1.
    Est 1929. Nonprofit. Quar (Sept-June). **Assoc** CLS MSA.

Paul Landon Banfield, a graduate of St. John's College who had taught and coached at Emerson Institute and Dewitt Preparatory School, founded this school for boys with his wife, Mary Lee. The school relocated in 1934 from its original location on Massachusetts Avenue in Washington, DC, to a campus on Bradley and Wilson lanes in Bethesda. Two years later, the school moved to its present, 75-acre location.

Landon's structured college preparatory program emphasizes a solid grounding in fundamental academic skills while seeking to promote intellectual curiosity, artistic impression and social awareness. In grades 3 and 4, the school provides a self-contained, traditional classroom setting. Departmentalization begins in grade 5. During the middle school years (grades 6-8), the rigorous academic program focuses on the development of critical-thinking skills.

Upon reaching the upper school (grades 9-12), boys encounter a less structured program that allows for independent study and a greater degree of personal responsibility. Required courses and activities are replaced by increased elective choices, and pupils select from a broad range of advanced classes. In addition to a well-developed athletic and arts programs, Landon conducts an extensive extracurricular program at the upper school level that includes community service opportunities.

See Also Page 1328

STONE RIDGE SCHOOL OF THE SACRED HEART
Day — Boys PS-K, Girls Gr PS-12

Bethesda, MD 20814. 9101 Rockville Pike. Tel: 301-657-4322. Fax: 301-657-4393.
www.stoneridge.org   E-mail: admissions@stoneridge.org
Sr. Anne Dyer, RSCJ, Head. BA, Wheaton College (MA), MA, Manhattanville College, MSA, Univ of Notre Dame. **Michelle McPherson, Adm.**
    Col Prep. AP—Eng Fr Lat Span Calc Stats Comp_Sci Bio Physics Eur_Hist US_Hist US_Govt & Pol Art_Hist Studio_Art. **Feat**—Relig Ceramics Fine_Arts.

Adm (Gr PS-12): 122/yr. Appl due: Jan. Accepted: 60%. **Tests** CTP_4 HSPT IQ ISEE SSAT.
Enr 792. B 6. G 786. Elem 455. Sec 337. Wh 74%. Hisp 5%. Blk 10%. Asian 7%. Other 4%. Avg class size: 15. Uniform. **Fac 86.** M 12/3. F 55/16. Wh 91%. Hisp 3%. Blk 4%. Am Ind 2%. Adv deg: 55%.
Grad '04—83. Col—83. (Duke, Vanderbilt, Georgetown, Trinity Col-CT, Princeton, Northwestern). Alum 2025.
Tui '03-'04: Day $8880-16,650 (+$300-500).
Summer: Enrich Rec. 4 wks.
Endow $12,000,000. Plant val $11,081,000. Bldgs 12. Class rms 38. Libs 3. Labs 5. Studios 3. Music studios 1. Gyms 3. Fields 3. Courts 4. Pools 1.
Est 1923. Nonprofit. Roman Catholic. Sem (Aug-June). **Assoc** MSA.

Stone Ridge offers accelerated and advanced courses in English, history, foreign language, chemistry, physics, biology and calculus, in addition to independent study. Students may study for one semester at a Sacred Heart school in another state or in a foreign country, and those advanced in science may work and receive credit for research done at the nearby Bethesda Naval Hospital or the National Institutes of Health.

Extracurricular activities include a variety of clubs, publications, forensics, drama, chorus, art and music, as well as inter-league participation in field hockey, tennis, soccer, softball, lacrosse, track, basketball, volleyball and cross-country. Swimming and diving competitions are held off campus.

BROOKLANDVILLE, MD. (9 mi. NNW of Baltimore, MD) Rural. Pop: 800. Alt: 300 ft.

PARK SCHOOL
Day — Coed Gr PS-PG

Brooklandville, MD 21022. 2425 Old Court Rd, PO Box 8200. Tel: 410-339-7070.
Fax: 410-339-4125.
www.parkschool.net   E-mail: admission@parkschool.net
David E. Jackson, Head. BA, Williams College, EdD, Columbia Univ. **Marcia Holden, Adm.**
Col Prep. Gen Acad. AP—Fr Span Calc Stats Comp_Sci Eur_Hist US_Hist Studio_Art Music_Theory. **Feat**—Shakespeare Anat & Physiol Astron Computers Art_Hist Film Photog Acting Drama Outdoor_Ed. **Supp**—Tut.
Adm (Gr PS-11): 121/yr. Appl due: Jan. Accepted: 49%. Yield: 57%. **Tests** IQ ISEE Stanford.
Enr 890. B 459. G 431. Elem 562. Sec 328. Wh 82%. Hisp 1%. Blk 9%. Asian 3%. Other 5%. Avg class size: 16. **Fac 120.** M 37/8. F 68/7. Wh 85%. Hisp 4%. Blk 8%. Asian 2%. Other 1%. Adv deg: 60%.
Grad '04—79. Col—79. (Oberlin 4, U of PA 3, Wash U 3, Skidmore 3, St Mary's Col of MD 3, IN U 3). Avg SAT: 1245. Alum 3000.
Tui '04-'05: Day $16,330-17,900 (+$400-1000). **Aid:** Need 151 ($1,721,520).
Summer: Rec. Challenge Prgm. 6 wks.
Endow $21,447,000. Plant val $25,651,000. Bldgs 4. Class rms 60. 2 Libs 45,000 vols. Sci labs 7. Comp labs 3. Sci/math/tech ctrs 1. Auds 1. Theaters 1. Art studios 4. Music studios 2. Dance studios 1. Gyms 3. Fields 9. Courts 5. Pools 1. Riding rings 1. Stables 1. Tracks 1.

Est 1912. Nonprofit. Sem (Sept-June).

One of the nation's first progressive institutions, Park was the laboratory school at which Eugene Randolph Smith developed his nationally known methods. Since 1959, the school has occupied a 100-acre, wooded campus.

Within a broad liberal arts curriculum, the program emphasizes inquiry, analysis, problem solving, independent thinking and fundamental skills. In the early years, Park's integrated curriculum is characterized by an experiential approach that provides room for individualization. At upper grade levels, a broad range of electives complements required course work. Advanced classes are available in all disciplines, and the school's senior term features a required six-week, off-campus project. Park conducts student exchanges with schools in Central America and France.

ST. PAUL'S SCHOOL
Day — Boys Gr K-12, Girls K-4

Brooklandville, MD 21022. 11152 Falls Rd, PO Box 8100. Tel: 410-825-4400.
Fax: 410-427-0390.
www.stpaulsschool.org E-mail: admissions@stpaulsschool.org
Thomas J. Reid, Head. BA, Univ of Pennsylvania, MEd, Univ of Connecticut. **Catherine L. Andrzejewski, Adm.**
Col Prep. AP—Eng Fr Span Calc Stats Bio Physics Eur_Hist US_Hist Psych. **Feat**—Ger Japan Anat & Physiol Oceanog Sports_Med Forensic_Sci Cold_War Econ Geog Ethics Philos Relig Studio_Art Drama Music Dance.
Adm: 134/yr. Day 139. Appl due: Jan. Accepted: 39%. **Tests** ISEE.
Enr 864. B 738. G 126. Elem 546. Sec 318. Avg class size: 17. **Fac 107.** M 52/3. F 48/4. Wh 90%. Hisp 3%. Blk 3%. Am Ind 1%. Asian 3%. Adv deg: 64%.
Grad '04—72. Col—72. (Dickinson 6, Johns Hopkins 3, U of MD-Col Park 3, Wake Forest 3, U of VT 2, Columbia 2). Alum 2174.
Tui '04-'05: Day $16,450 (+$400). **Aid:** Need 163 ($1,429,300).
Summer: Acad Enrich Rev Rem Rec. 6 wks.
Endow $23,000,000. Plant val $27,900,000. Bldgs 27. 3 Libs 30,600 vols. Sci labs 6. Lang labs 1. Comp labs 3. Theaters 1. Art studios 4. Music studios 8. Gyms 4. Fields 8. Tennis courts 14. Ropes crses 1.
Est 1849. Nonprofit. Episcopal. Sem (Sept-June). **Assoc** CLS.

Affiliated with the Episcopal Church, St. Paul's was founded in a Sunday school room of St. Paul's Parish in downtown Baltimore. In 1952, the school moved to its current, 95-acre campus, which includes Brooklandwood, a mansion built in 1793 by Charles Carroll, a signer of the Declaration of Independence. St. Paul's is coordinated with the adjacent St. Paul's School for Girls, and a common center for the arts joins the two campuses. St. Paul's lower school is coeducational through grade 4, and most of the girls proceed to St. Paul's School for Girls. During the middle and upper school years, boys and girls of the two schools share many activities, projects and classes, including all electives and most language courses.

The school places an emphasis on the arts, beginning in the lower school, when children take such courses as visual arts, music and dance, and movement. Middle school pupils gain exposure to various artistic media, while upper schoolers may pursue the arts through group classes, private lessons, and performances and shows. Among the graduation requirements are electives, study of world religions, one year of art and community service.

A three-week program at the end of May enables seniors to gain career insights through internships with community businesses and organizations, and the Mountain School program of Milton Academy provides juniors and seniors the opportunity to study for a semester in a rural setting in Vermont. St. Paul's also encourages foreign exchange and travel programs and is involved in study programs in Spain, Germany and France. Other student programs and organizations provide opportunities in peer leadership, musical groups, student council and various publications. Middle school students take part in an outdoor education program, and upper school students must participate in ten of 12 athletic seasons.

ST. PAUL'S SCHOOL FOR GIRLS
Day — Girls Gr 5-12

Brooklandville, MD 21022. 11232 Falls Rd, PO Box 8000. Tel: 410-823-6323.
Fax: 410-828-7238.
www.spsfg.org   E-mail: info@spsfg.org
Nancy Laufe Eisenberg, Head. BA, Wellesley College, MEd, Univ of Houston. **Charlotte D. Douglas, Adm.**
Col Prep. **AP**—Eng Fr Span Calc Bio Chem Physics US_Hist Econ Psych Studio_Art. **Feat**—Ger Japan Stats Ethics World_Relig Art_Hist Fine_Arts Performing_Arts. **Supp**—Dev_Read Tut.
Adm (Gr 5-11): 67/yr. Appl due: Jan. Accepted: 50%. **Tests** CEEB ISEE.
Enr 463. G 463. Elem 193. Sec 270. Wh 87%. Hisp 1%. Blk 8%. Asian 4%. Avg class size: 16. Uniform. **Fac 64.** M 10. F 54. Wh 89%. Hisp 2%. Blk 8%. Asian 1%. Adv deg: 54%.
Grad '04—51. Col—51. (Vanderbilt, Johns Hopkins, U of PA, Franklin & Marshall, Wake Forest, UNH). Avg SAT: 1165. Avg ACT: 24. Alum 1145.
Tui '04-'05: Day $17,485 (+$350). **Aid:** Merit 4 ($66,120). Need 85 ($744,073).
Summer: Acad Enrich Rev Rec. Tui Day $175. 1 wk.
Endow $5,960,000. Plant val $17,500,000. Bldgs 3. Class rms 43. Lib 10,191 vols. Sci labs 8. Comp labs 2. Theaters 1. Art studios 2. Music studios 2. Dance studios 1. Gyms 2. Fields 3. Courts 4.
Est 1959. Nonprofit. Episcopal. (Sept-June). **Assoc** CLS.

Affiliated with the boys' school, St. Paul's School for Girls has separate facilities and administration. Children in the middle school follow a developmentally appropriate, interdisciplinary curriculum, while students in the upper school pursue a college preparatory program of traditional liberal arts subjects. Advanced Placement courses are offered in all subjects.

Faculty and students alternately conduct daily assemblies and weekly chapel services, with the assistance of outside speakers. Activities include art club, choir, modern dance, sports, publications, Model UN, and other organizations and interest clubs.

COLORA, MD. (37 mi. NE of Baltimore, MD) Rural. Pop: 160. Alt: 450 ft.

WEST NOTTINGHAM ACADEMY
Bdg — Coed Gr 9-PG; Day — Coed 6-PG

Colora, MD 21917. 1079 Firetower Rd. Tel: 410-658-5556. Fax: 410-658-9264.
www.wna.org E-mail: admissions@wna.org

D. John Watson, Head. BME, Northern Michigan Univ, MA, PhD, Univ of Minnesota-Twin Cities. **Heidi K. L. Sprinkle,** Adm.

Col Prep. AP—Eng Fr Span Calc Bio Eur_Hist US_Hist Studio_Art. **Feat**—Lat Anat & Physiol Sports_Med Computers African-Amer_Hist E_Asian_Hist Psych Aesthetics Relig Acting Music_Theory Journ. **Supp**—ESL LD Rem_Read Tut.

Adm: 73/yr. Appl due: Rolling. Accepted: 74%. **Tests** IQ ISEE SSAT TOEFL.

Enr 200. Elem 35. Sec 164. PG 1. Wh 73%. Hisp 3%. Blk 11%. Am Ind 2%. Asian 10%. Other 1%. Avg class size: 10. **Fac 33.** M 18. F 15. Adv deg: 75%. In dorms 16.

Grad '04—38. Col—37. (U of MD-Col Park, PA St, Am U, St Mary's Col of MD, U of DE, Wash Col). Avg SAT: 1100. Alum 1500.

Tui '04-'05: Bdg $30,200 (+$2000). **Day $15,540** (+$1000). **Aid:** Need 43 ($340,000).

Endow $3,200,000. Plant val $7,000,000. Bldgs 16. Dorms 4. Dorm rms 65. Class rms 25. Lib 8500 vols. Sci labs 3. Comp labs 1. Comp ctrs 1. Auds 1. Art studios 1. Music studios 1. Dance studios 1. Gyms 1. Fields 6. Courts 3. Field houses 1. Pools 1.

Est 1744. Nonprofit. Tri (Sept-June). **Assoc** MSA.

Noted graduates of this school, founded by Rev. Samuel Finley, include colonial leaders Benjamin Rush and Richard Stockton, both signers of the Declaration of Independence. The campus is located on 120 acres of northeastern Maryland countryside.

West Nottingham offers a college preparatory curriculum and supports students through its advisor program and individual academic support. A strong sense of community exists in campus life. As a complement to the academic program, the academy offers athletic and community service programs and makes use of the recreational and cultural resources of the Baltimore/Philadelphia, PA, area.

In addition to its traditional program, WNA offers the Chesapeake Learning Center curriculum (available for an additional fee), a regular high school course of studies adapted for students with learning differences who are of average to above-average intelligence. The multisensory CLC Program features smaller classes, a structured study hall and ongoing tutorial assistance.

As a third program option, West Nottingham provides a well-developed English as a Second Language curriculum that prepares international students for US colleges. The program, which features beginning, intermediate and advanced levels, also includes instruction in mathematics, science, history and the arts. Participants incur an additional fee.

EASTON, MD. (47 mi. SE of Baltimore, MD) Urban. Pop: 11,708. Alt: 38 ft.

COUNTRY SCHOOL
Day — Coed Gr K-8

Easton, MD 21601. 716 Goldsborough St. Tel: 410-822-1935. Fax: 410-822-1971.
www.countryschool.org E-mail: info@countryschool.org
Neil Mufson, Head. AB, Brown Univ, MEd, Tufts Univ. **Kim Balderson, Adm.**
- **Pre-Prep. Gen Acad. Feat**—Fr Lat Span Ecol Computers Music. **Supp**—Tut.
- **Adm:** 48/yr. Appl due: Rolling. **Tests** CTP_4.
- **Enr 301.** Elem 301. Wh 87%. Blk 1%. Asian 6%. Other 6%. Avg class size: 17. Uniform. **Fac 38.** M 7. F 23/8. Wh 97%. Blk 3%. Adv deg: 44%.
- **Grad '04—35. Prep—19.** (St Andrew's Episcopal-MD 2, Blair 1, McDonogh 1, St James Sch-MD 1). Alum 981.
- **Tui '04-'05: Day $9950. Aid:** Need 49 ($220,205).
- **Summer:** Enrich Rec. Art. 1 wk.
- Endow $6,399,000. Plant val $6,109,000. Bldgs 3. Class rms 28. Lib 16,000 vols. Sci labs 2. Comp labs 2. Auds 1. Gyms 1. Fields 2.
- **Est 1934.** Nonprofit. (Sept-June).

The school provides a traditional and structured yet child-centered curriculum that features small classes and individual attention in a family setting. Varied non-academic activities, including the fine and performing arts, instrumental music, community service, physical education and life skills, are offered. Interscholastic sports are available in grades 6-8; students may participate in soccer, field hockey, basketball and lacrosse.

GLENCOE, MD. (17 mi. N of Baltimore, MD) Rural. Pop: 215. Alt: 600 ft.

OLDFIELDS SCHOOL
Bdg and Day — Girls Gr 8-PG

Glencoe, MD 21152. 1500 Glencoe Rd, PO Box 697. Tel: 410-472-4800.
Fax: 410-472-6839.
www.oldfieldsschool.org E-mail: admissions@oldfieldsschool.org
George S. Swope, Jr., Head. BA, Lawrence Univ, MA, MBA, Northwestern Univ. **Kimberly C. Loughlin, Adm.**
- **Col Prep. AP**—Eng Fr Span Calc Bio US_Hist Studio_Art. **Feat**—British_Lit Lat Marine_Biol/Sci Computers Sociol Ceramics Photog Drama Dance. **Supp**—Tut.
- **Adm (Day Gr 8-11):** 75/yr. Bdg 52. Day 23. Appl due: Feb. Accepted: 87%. Yield: 50%. **Tests** IQ ISEE SSAT TOEFL.
- **Enr 187.** Elem 12. Sec 174. PG 1. Wh 69%. Hisp 2%. Blk 17%. Asian 5%. Other 7%. Avg class size: 10. **Fac 42.** M 10/2. F 30. Wh 92%. Hisp 2%. Blk 4%. Am Ind 2%. Adv deg: 59%. In dorms 16.
- **Grad '04—39. Col—39.** (Sweet Briar 2, Hobart/Wm Smith 1, Col of Charleston 1, Smith 1, VA Polytech 1, Goucher 1). Alum 1899.

Tui '04-'05: Bdg $33,700 (+$600). **Day $21,400** (+$400). **Aid:** Need 54 ($1,209,934). Endow $10,000,000. Plant val $29,872,000. Bldgs 22. Dorms 7. Dorm rms 76. Class rms 23. Lib 10,000 vols. Sci labs 5. Comp labs 2. Theaters 1. Art studios 4. Music studios 2. Dance studios 1. Gyms 1. Fields 4. Courts 5. Pools 1. Riding rings 3. Stables 1. Barns 1.
Est 1867. Nonprofit. Sem (Aug-June). **Assoc** MSA.

Mrs. John Sears McCulloch founded Oldfields to provide instruction to her own and neighboring girls. Mrs. McCulloch fostered high standards among her girls and at the same time always retained the family-like atmosphere of the school. Under the leadership of Mrs. McCulloch and succeeding members of her family, Oldfields was among the first schools to offer girls complete programs in chemistry, athletics, the fine and performing arts, riding and student government. The McCulloch family directed the school through 1960, when the last McCulloch retired. Oldfields is operated as a nonsectarian school under a board of trustees composed of parents, past parents and alumnae.

School life is informal, but structured. From its beginnings, the school has helped each girl select a course of study appropriate to her needs, and, since early this century, Oldfields has offered a personalized curriculum. Flexible scheduling enables college preparatory course work to accommodate both the motivated student of average ability and the gifted pupil. Each student and faculty member has a laptop computer, as technology is integral to the curriculum. Extensive extracurricular opportunities, field trips, outings and weekend activities enrich the academic experience and routinely take students to places of interest in the four-state area. Each spring, Oldfields offers two-week, self-contained programs in a variety of academic and social disciplines for all students; options include faculty-supervised language and cultural immersion experiences in France, Spain, Peru and Belize, as well as on-campus programs and internship opportunities for seniors.

The athletic program includes field hockey, soccer, basketball, tennis, lacrosse, softball, volleyball, indoor soccer, yoga, badminton, dance and aerobics. The school maintains extensive riding facilities, including an indoor riding arena, two outdoor show rings, an extensive cross-country course and trails along the Gunpowder River.

See Also Pages 1308-9

GLENELG, MD.
(21 mi. W of Baltimore, MD) Rural. Pop: 40. Alt: 580 ft.

GLENELG COUNTRY SCHOOL
Day — Coed Gr PS-12

Glenelg, MD 21737. 12793 Folly Quarter Rd, PO Box 190. Tel: 410-531-7347. Fax: 410-531-7363.
www.glenelg.org   E-mail: wootton@glenelg.org
Ryland O. Chapman III, Head. BA, Randolph-Macon College, MLA, Johns Hopkins Univ, MEd, Loyola College. **Karen Wootton, Adm.**
Col Prep. AP—Eng Fr Lat Span Calc Stats Comp_Sci Eur_Hist US_Hist Art_Hist Music_ Theory. **Feat**—British_Lit Creative_Writing World_Lit Anat & Physiol Astron Anthro Psych Asian_Stud Islamic_Stud Photog Studio_Art Drama Chorus. **Supp**—Rev Tut.

Adm: 140/yr. Appl due: Feb. **Tests** CTP_4 ISEE Stanford.
Enr 764. B 390. G 374. Elem 532. Sec 232. Wh 75%. Hisp 1%. Blk 6%. Asian 8%. Other 10%. Avg class size: 16. **Fac 105.** M 30. F 75. Wh 86%. Hisp 2%. Blk 5%. Other 7%. Adv deg: 38%.
Grad '04—40. Col—40. (VA Polytech, Lehigh, Franklin & Marshall, Rochester Inst of Tech, Johns Hopkins, Geo Wash). Avg SAT: 1200. Alum 1240.
Tui '04-'05: Day $14,600-16,835 (+$1000). **Aid:** Need 130 ($680,000).
Summer: Acad Enrich Rev Rec. Drama. Adventure. Sports. 3-6 wks.
Plant val $29,000,000. Bldgs 6. Class rms 55. 4 Libs 18,000 vols. Sci labs 6. Comp labs 4. Auds 1. Theaters 1. Art studios 4. Music studios 3. Dance studios 1. Gyms 1. Fields 4. Courts 1. Pools 1.
Est 1954. Nonprofit. Quar (Sept-June). **Assoc** MSA.

Located in historic Glenelg Manor (dating from 1740) on 87 acres of fields and woodland, GCS was established for students in Howard County and the surrounding area. Emphasis is placed on academics, with creative arts, athletics and community service included. French and Spanish are offered from prekindergarten, Latin from grade 6. Each year of high school features a compulsory interdisciplinary course: freshmen take a humanities class that combines the origins of human society, history, anthropology and sociology with English literature; sophomores take a course combining Western literature with arts and ideas; juniors study American literature and expository writing in conjunction with a US history course; and seniors take part in an integrative seminar that reflects upon the "product and process of learning" across the curriculum. Advanced Placement courses, internships and independent study opportunities broaden the academic program.

Soccer, field hockey, lacrosse, basketball, baseball, tennis, cross-country, track, golf and ice hockey are the school's available sports. Field trips to Baltimore and Washington, DC, allow students to take advantage of cultural amenities such as art galleries, museums, the theater and historical sites.

OLNEY, MD. (17 mi. NNW of Washington, DC) Suburban. Pop: 31,438. Alt: 544 ft.

ST. JOHN'S EPISCOPAL SCHOOL
Day — Coed Gr K-8

Olney, MD 20832. 3427 Olney-Laytonsville Rd. Tel: 301-774-6804. Fax: 301-774-2375.
www.stjes.com   E-mail: wes.wehunt@stjes.com
John H. Zurn, Head. BA, Williams College, MSEd, Univ of Pennsylvania. **Wes Wehunt, Adm.**
Pre-Prep. Feat—Fr Lat Span Computers Robotics Relig Studio_Art Music. **Supp**—Dev_Read Rem_Math Rem_Read Tut.
Adm: 51/yr. Appl due: Feb.
Enr 321. B 165. G 156. Elem 321. Wh 91%. Hisp 4%. Blk 2%. Asian 3%. Avg class size: 18. Uniform. **Fac 37.** Adv deg: 40%.
Grad '04—36. Prep—29. Alum 333.
Tui '04-'05: Day $10,342 (+$295-570). **Aid:** Need 43 ($147,000).
Endow $285,000. Plant val $4,800,000. Bldgs 2. Lib 10,000 vols. Sci labs 2. Comp labs 2. Music studios 2. Gyms 1. Fields 1.

Est 1961. Nonprofit. Episcopal. Tri (Sept-June).

Serving the Montgomery County area, this Episcopal school offers a well-balanced curriculum and small classes, giving students a solid grounding in the fundamentals. The school strives to develop students' study, organizational and test-taking skills through its standard pre-preparatory curriculum. Emphasis on reading and writing begins with an introduction to phonics in kindergarten and culminates with the preparation of research papers in the upper grades. Math classes are tracked beginning in grade 6, allowing qualified students to take algebra in grade 8. Field trips to local historical sites and science and nature facilities supplement social studies and science instruction. Spanish study begins in kindergarten, while Latin starts in grade 7.

Weekly chapel, social outreach participation and family involvement are integral aspects of school life. Extracurricular offerings include chorus, dramatics, yearbook, newspaper and a variety of team sports.

OWINGS MILLS, MD. (12 mi. NW of Baltimore, MD) Rural. Pop: 9474. Alt: 496 ft.

GARRISON FOREST SCHOOL
Bdg — Girls Gr 8-12; Day — Boys PS-K, Girls PS-12

Owings Mills, MD 21117. 300 Garrison Forest Rd. Tel: 410-363-1500. Fax: 410-363-8441. www.gfs.org   E-mail: gfs_info@gfs.org

G. Peter O'Neill, Jr., Head. BA, St Michael's College, MA, Trinity College (CT). **Mrs. A. Randol Benedict, Adm.**

Col Prep. AP—Eng Fr Lat Span Calc Bio Chem US_Hist Art_Hist. **Feat**—Creative_Writing Anat & Physiol Ecol Animal_Behavior Comp_Sci Econ Child_Dev Ethics World_Relig Drawing Photog Studio_Art Drama Theater_Arts Music Dance. **Supp**—ESL.

Adm: 123/yr. Bdg 21. Day 102. Appl due: Jan. Accepted: 45%. Yield: 61%. **Tests** ISEE SSAT.

Enr 640. Elem 419. Sec 221. Wh 78%. Hisp 3%. Blk 14%. Asian 3%. Other 2%. Avg class size: 14. Uniform. **Fac 100.** M 9/3. F 82/6. Wh 93%. Hisp 3%. Blk 3%. Asian 1%. Adv deg: 59%. In dorms 5.

Grad '04—50. Col—50. (Geo Wash 3, U of PA 2, Brown 2, Georgetown 2, NYU 2, U of DE 2). Avg SAT: 1259. Avg SSAT: 50%. Avg ACT: 27. Alum 3500.

Tui '04-'05: Bdg $32,500 (+$2500). **Day $8900-18,400** (+$200-1000). **Aid:** Need 126 ($1,361,795).

Summer: Acad Rec. Tui Day $200-1590. 1-6 wks.

Endow $29,000,000. Plant val $31,000,000. Bldgs 17. Dorms 3. Dorm rms 50. Class rms 50. Lib 16,000 vols. Chapels 1. Labs 6. Comp ctrs 3. Theaters 1. Art studios 5. Music studios 6. Dance studios 1. Arts ctrs 1. Gyms 2. Athletic ctrs 1. Fields 4. Tennis courts 7. Riding rings 4. Stables 2. Weight rms 1. Student ctrs 1.

Est 1910. Nonprofit. (Sept-June). **Assoc** CLS MSA.

Established by Mary M. Livingston, Garrison Forest has always been characterized by high academic standards and a close association between faculty and students. The curriculum, with an emphasis on academic fundamentals, prepares students for leading colleges. In addition to the core courses of English, history, math, science, modern languages and Latin, girls choose among electives in the humanities, science and the arts. Advanced Placement courses are available in every discipline.

Student government, service league, theater, the arts, publications, language clubs, dance and music, as well as a full schedule of team sports that includes riding and polo, are popular activities.

Boys may enroll in the preschool and kindergarten programs only.

See Also Page 1300

McDONOGH SCHOOL
5-Day Bdg — Coed Gr 9-12; Day — Coed K-12

Owings Mills, MD 21117. 8600 McDonogh Rd. Tel: 410-363-0600. Fax: 410-581-4777.
  www.mcdonogh.org E-mail: admissions@mcdonogh.org
W. Boulton Dixon, Head. AB, Princeton Univ, MEd, Temple Univ. **Anita Hilson, Adm.**
  Col Prep. Feat—Marine_Biol/Sci Environ_Design African_Hist Eastern_Philos Music Jazz_Band.
  Adm: 140/yr. Bdg 8. Day 132. Appl due: Jan. **Tests** ISEE.
  Enr 1260. Wh 25%. Hisp 25%. Blk 25%. Asian 25%. Avg class size: 15. **Fac 143.** M 65. F 78. Adv deg: 88%. In dorms 5.
  Grad '04—131. Col—131. (U of MD-Col Park, U of PA, Geo Wash, Johns Hopkins, Princeton, U of VA). Alum 5702.
  Tui '04-'05: 5-Day Bdg $23,960. **Day** $15,440-17,800. **Aid:** Need 164 ($2,090,590).
  Summer: Acad Rec. 2 wks.
  Endow $56,400,000. Plant val $80,000,000. Bldgs 44. Dorms 2. Class rms 58. Lib 30,000 vols. Labs 10. Comp labs 5. Theaters 1. Art studios 6. Music studios 12. Gyms 2. Fields 19. Courts 21. Pools 1. Riding rings 4. Stables yes.
  Est 1873. Nonprofit. Tri (Sept-June). **Assoc** CLS.

Established by the endowment of John McDonogh as a school for scholarship students, this institution began accepting paying students in 1922. In 1975, coeducation was instituted in the day department. The boarding department became coeducational in 1983.

Music, dramatics and various clubs are among the extracurricular activities. Athletic participation is required of all students. The school has competitive teams in all major sports, plus golf, tennis, riding and swimming. The riding program features 80 horses and extensive professional facilities on the school's 800-acre campus. Graduates have entered Brown, Princeton, Johns Hopkins, Duke, Harvard, Yale, Stanford and many other schools.

PASADENA, MD. (13 mi. SSE of Baltimore, MD) Urban. Pop: 12,093. Alt: 80 ft.

GIBSON ISLAND COUNTRY SCHOOL
Day — Coed Gr PS-5

Pasadena, MD 21122. 5191 Mountain Rd. Tel: 410-255-5370. Fax: 410-255-0416.
  www.gics.org E-mail: admissions@gics.org

Cameron V. Noble, Head. BA, St Lawrence Univ, MS, Johns Hopkins Univ. **Gretchen Snow, Adm.**
Pre-Prep. Gen Acad. Feat—Fr Computers Studio_Art Music. **Supp**—Rev Tut.
Adm: 25/yr. Appl due: Jan. Accepted: 80%.
Enr 95. Elem 95. Avg class size: 14. Uniform. **Fac 15.** F 11/4. Adv deg: 6%.
Grad '04—15. Prep—13. (Severn, St Paul's Sch-MD, Gilman, Glenelg Country, McDonogh). Alum 400.
Tui '04-'05: Day $8300-9700 (+$225). **Aid:** Need ($75,000).
Endow $2,250,000. Plant val $2,000,000. Bldgs 3. Class rms 13. Lib 4000 vols. Sci labs 1. Lang labs 1. Comp labs 1. Auds 1. Art studios 1. Music studios 1. Gyms 1. Fields 1.
Est 1947. Nonprofit. Tri (Sept-June).

Established to serve the expanding needs of the area, this school has grown from its initial enrollment of 43 and now serves 13 communities in Anne Arundel County. Classes are small, allowing teachers to work individually with students. Instructors emphasize a strong academic foundation, and the program integrates French, music, art, library, computer, physical education and waterfront studies.

Field trips and leadership opportunities complement academics. Extracurricular activities include student government and community service. Graduates attend leading Maryland preparatory schools.

POTOMAC, MD. (13 mi. NW of Washington, DC) Suburban. Pop: 44,822. Alt: 360 ft.

THE BULLIS SCHOOL
Day — Coed Gr 3-12

Potomac, MD 20854. 10601 Falls Rd. Tel: 301-299-8500. Fax: 301-634-3659.
www.bullis.org E-mail: info@bullis.org
Thomas B. Farquhar, Head. BA, Earlham College, MEd, Univ of Pennsylvania. **Nancy L. Spencer, Adm.**
Col Prep. AP—Eng Fr Lat Span Calc Stats Comp_Sci Bio Chem Physics US_Hist World_Hist Psych Art_Hist Studio_Art Music_Theory. **Feat**—Econ Fine_Arts.
Adm (Gr 3-11): 141/yr. Appl due: Feb. Accepted: 50%. **Tests** CTP_4 IQ ISEE SSAT.
Enr 624. B 343. G 281. Elem 268. Sec 356. Wh 73%. Hisp 4%. Blk 12%. Asian 6%. Other 5%. Avg class size: 15. Uniform. **Fac 96.** M 38. F 53/5. Wh 90%. Hisp 3%. Blk 5%. Asian 1%. Other 1%. Adv deg: 62%.
Grad '04—79. Col—79. (Boston U 3, Brigham Young 3, Geo Wash 3, Miami U-OH 3, U of CO-Boulder 3). Avg SAT: 1200. Avg SSAT: 60%. Alum 4500.
Tui '04-'05: Day $20,275-22,690 (+$1000-1200). **Aid:** Need 87 ($1,326,600).
Summer: Acad Enrich Rev Rec. Tui Day $700/3-wk ses. 6 wks.
Endow $10,534,000. Plant val $60,000,000. Bldgs 12. Class rms 70. Libs 1. Sci labs 6. Comp labs 5. Photog labs 1. Art studios 6. Dance studios 1. Theater/auds 1. Gyms 2. Fields 6. Courts 11.
Est 1930. Nonprofit. Tri (Sept-June). **Assoc** MSA.

Founded in Washington, DC, as a one-year preparatory school for the US service academies, the school moved to Silver Spring four years later. At that time, Bullis began to offer a four-year program. In 1963, the school's present, 80-acre tract in

Potomac was purchased. The school's program subsequently grew to encompass grades 3-12.

In the lower and middle schools, students develop research and study skills in preparation for future academic work. The upper school's curriculum enables pupils to choose from various Advanced Placement courses, as well as a number of social studies, visual and performing arts, computer science and foreign language electives. Community service, cocurricular activities, the arts, and intramural and interscholastic athletics are integral elements of the program. Graduates attend leading colleges.

CONNELLY SCHOOL OF THE HOLY CHILD
Day — Girls Gr 6-12

Potomac, MD 20854. 9029 Bradley Blvd. Tel: 301-365-0955. Fax: 301-365-0981.
 www.holychild.org   E-mail: admissions@holychild.org
Maureen K. Appel, Head. BA, Rosemont College, MS, Long Island Univ. **Sheri M. Mural, Adm.**

Col Prep. AP—Eng Fr Span Calc Stats Bio Chem US_Hist. **Feat**—Humanities Anat & Physiol Bioethics Environ_Sci Genetics Forensic_Sci Relig Photog Studio_Art Drama Theater_Arts Music.

Adm: 112/yr. **Tests** HSPT ISEE SSAT.

Enr 440. G 440. Elem 128. Sec 312. Avg class size: 16. Uniform. **Fac 60.** M 8/2. F 36/14. Adv deg: 66%.

Grad '04—77. Col—77. (U of MD-Col Park 4, Elon 3, St Joseph's U 3, PA St 3, U of Richmond 3, Villanova 3). Alum 2000.

Tui '04-'05: Day $15,750-16,850.

Bldgs 4. Class rms 26. Lib 13,000 vols. Sci labs 4. Comp labs 2. Art studios 2. Music studios 2. Dance studios 1. Gyms 1. Fields 2.

Est 1961. Nonprofit. Roman Catholic. (Sept-June). **Assoc** MSA.

Founded by the Society of the Holy Child Jesus, the school offers a college preparatory curriculum in a supportive Christian environment. Drawing its enrollment from the Greater Washington, DC, area, the school takes advantage of the resources of the nation's capital. Campus ministry and service programs reinforce Christian values.

Courses in religion, English, math, science, social studies, foreign languages and fine arts, as well as physical education, are required of all students. Honors and Advanced Placement courses are available in most disciplines, and seminars in economics, media analysis and the history of segregation and civil rights in America are offered jointly with other area independent schools. Holy Child conducts tours abroad each spring.

Interscholastic sports include field hockey, lacrosse, basketball, softball, tennis, soccer, volleyball, swimming, track, cross-country, diving, dance team and equestrian team. Drama, chorus, school publications and interest clubs complete the cocurricular program.

McLEAN SCHOOL OF MARYLAND
Day — Coed Gr K-12

Potomac, MD 20854. 8224 Lochinver Ln. Tel: 301-299-8277. Fax: 301-299-1639.
www.mcleanschool.org   E-mail: admission@mcleanschool.org
Darlene B. Pierro, Head. AB, Sweet Briar College, MEd, Univ of Maryland-College Park.
Catherine A. Biern, Adm.

Col Prep. AP—Eng Calc Bio US_Hist US_Govt & Pol. Feat—Lat Span Computers Anthro Film Studio_Art Drama Jazz_Ensemble Debate. Supp—Tut.

Adm (Gr K-11): 93/yr. Appl due: Feb. Accepted: 33%. Tests IQ SSAT.

Enr 495. B 294. G 201. Elem 368. Sec 127. Wh 83%. Hisp 2%. Blk 6%. Asian 4%. Other 5%. Avg class size: 14. Uniform. Fac 76. M 16. F 56/4. Wh 87%. Hisp 4%. Blk 6%. Asian 3%. Adv deg: 63%.

Grad '04—19. Col—19. (Dean 2, Guilford 1, Rollins 1, Elon 1, FL Atlantic 1, Tulane 1). Avg SAT: 1045. Avg ACT: 23. Alum 500.

Tui '04-'05: Day $18,200-23,300 (+$700-1200). Aid: Need 39 ($523,000).

Summer: Acad Rec. Sports. 2-5 wks.

Endow $1,500,000. Plant val $15,000,000. Bldgs 1. Class rms 41. Lib 18,000 vols. Sci labs 7. Lang labs 2. Comp labs 3. Art studios 3. Music studios 3. Gyms 2. Fields 2.

Est 1954. Nonprofit. Quar (Sept-June).

Founded by local businesspersons and parents Delbert and Lenore Foster, McLean conducts a flexible academic program that addresses the needs of a broad range of learners. After many years of serving children in grades K-9, the school extended its program through the high school years by adding grade 10 in 2000, grade 11 in 2001 and grade 12 in 2002.

The lower school (grades K-4) and the middle school (grades 5-8) curricula emphasize language arts and math and include art, music, computer and daily physical education classes. Upper school classes are departmentalized, with both English and literature studies provided. Drama, art, music and computer are among the requirements.

Interscholastic sports are field hockey, lacrosse, soccer, basketball, volleyball, cross-country, wrestling, and track and field. **See Also Page 1206**

ST. ANDREW'S EPISCOPAL SCHOOL
Day — Coed Gr 6-12

Potomac, MD 20854. 8804 Postoak Rd. Tel: 301-983-5200. Fax: 301-983-4620.
www.saes.org   E-mail: admission@saes.org
Robert F. Kosasky, Head. BA, Yale Univ, MA, Columbia Univ. Julie Jameson, Adm.

Col Prep. AP—Eng Fr Span Calc Bio US_Hist Econ Studio_Art. Feat—Lat Stats Robotics Relig Photojourn Journ.

Adm (Gr 6-11): 95/yr. Appl due: Feb. Tests SSAT.

Enr 454. B 236. G 218. Elem 140. Sec 314. Wh 82%. Hisp 4%. Blk 4%. Am Ind 1%. Asian 4%. Other 5%. Avg class size: 15. Fac 66. M 31. F 35. Wh 88%. Hisp 3%. Blk 9%. Adv deg: 92%.

Grad '04—71. Col—69. (Syracuse 4, Bucknell 4, U of Miami 3, Gettysburg 3, Boston Col 2, Duke 2). Alum 1128.

Tui '04-'05: Day $22,150-23,385 (+$400-700). Aid: Need 48 ($733,840).

Summer: Acad Rec. 8 wks.

Endow $1,047,000. Plant val $17,138,000. Bldgs 5. Class rms 45. Lib 14,000 vols. Sci labs 3. Lang labs 1. Comp labs 2. Theater/auds 1. Art studios 3. Music studios 3. Dance

studios 2. Gyms 1. Fields 3. Courts 1.
Est 1978. Nonprofit. Episcopal. Tri (Sept-June). **Assoc** CLS MSA.

St. Andrew's offers a thorough college preparatory program from a Christian perspective. The basic core curriculum is integrated with regular community worship, and it includes courses in English, history, the sciences, languages and mathematics. Studies in religion include ethics and morals, theology, the Old and New Testaments, and comparative world religions.

Some of the extracurricular activities offered are drama, newspaper, yearbook, art, dance, intramural and interscholastic athletics, driver education and outing clubs.

ROCKVILLE, MD. (14 mi. NNW of Washington, DC) Urban. Pop: 47,388. Alt: 451 ft.

GREEN ACRES SCHOOL
Day — Coed Gr PS-8

Rockville, MD 20852. 11701 Danville Dr. Tel: 301-881-4100. Fax: 301-881-3319.
  www.greenacres.org   E-mail: info@greenacres.org
Louis M. Silvano, Head. BMus, Univ of London (England), MA, Marymount College (NY).
  Marge Dimond, Adm.
  Pre-Prep. Feat—Humanities Span Computers Ceramics Photog Studio_Art Drama Chorus Music Handbells Creative_Movement Outdoor_Ed. **Supp**—Tut.
  Adm: 67/yr. Appl due: Jan. Accepted: 68%.
  Enr 310. B 161. G 149. Elem 310. Wh 73%. Hisp 4%. Blk 8%. Am Ind 1%. Asian 4%. Other 10%. Avg class size: 11. **Fac 65.** M 11/13. F 30/11. Wh 79%. Hisp 2%. Blk 9%. Asian 6%. Other 4%. Adv deg: 64%.
  Grad '04—31. Prep—24. (Georgetown Day, St Andrew's Sch-DE, Sidwell Friends, Sandy Spring Friends, George Sch, Bullis). Alum 1000.
  Tui '05-'06: Day $21,515 (+$45-795). **Aid:** Need 53 ($580,000).
  Summer: Rec. Tui Day $925-1750. 4-6 wks.
  Endow $2,800,000. Plant val $4,960,000. Bldgs 7. Class rms 32. Lib 20,000 vols. Sci labs 3. Comp labs 3. Photog labs 1. Auds 2. Theaters 1. Art studios 2. Music studios 1. Dance studios 1. Perf arts ctrs 1. Amphitheaters 1. Gyms 1. Fields 2. Courts 2. Pools 1. Playgrounds 3.
  Est 1934. Nonprofit. (Sept-June). **Assoc** MSA.

Green Acres has its roots in the traditions of progressive education. The school's board of trustees is composed of parents, teachers and two local educators. An active parents' association provides parents with many opportunities for involvement in the school community.

Green Acres' integrated, multicultural programs and curricula are developmentally oriented and consider the needs and interests of the students. Small classes allow teachers to work with children individually and in small groups, and Green Acres also encourages cooperation among students. Emphasis is placed on pupils involving themselves in their own learning through touch, exploration, experimentation, reading, discussion, research and practice. Boys and girls in grades 5-8 may participate in intramural soccer, basketball, softball and lacrosse.

The school's 15-acre campus in suburban Washington, DC, provides opportunities for pupils to study animal and plant life in woods and streams. Environmental concerns are integral to the curriculum.

ST. JAMES, MD. (60 mi. NW of Washington, DC) Rural. Pop: 100. Alt: 464 ft.

SAINT JAMES SCHOOL
Bdg and Day — Coed Gr 8-12

St James, MD 21781. 17641 College Rd. Tel: 301-733-9330. Fax: 301-739-1310.
   www.stjames.edu   E-mail: admissions@stjames.edu
Rev. **D. Stuart Dunnan, Head.** AB, AM, Harvard Univ, MA, DPhil, Oxford Univ (England). **William W. Ellis, Jr., Adm.**

- **Col Prep. AP**—Eng Fr Lat Span Calc Bio Chem Physics Eur_Hist US_Hist Studio_Art. **Feat**—British_Lit Stats Environ_Sci Computers Econ Theol World_Relig Art_Hist Music Music_Hist. **Supp**—ESL Tut.
- **Adm (Bdg Gr 8-11; Day 8-10):** 66/yr. Bdg 45. Day 21. Appl due: Jan. Accepted: 67%. Yield: 62%. **Tests** SSAT TOEFL.
- **Enr 223.** B 94/43. G 63/23. Elem 26. Sec 197. Wh 78%. Hisp 2%. Blk 8%. Asian 7%. Other 5%. Avg class size: 13. **Fac 32.** M 17/1. F 12/2. Wh 94%. Hisp 3%. Blk 3%. Adv deg: 65%. In dorms 17.
- **Grad '04—41. Col—41.** (U of VA 3, U of MD-Col Park 2, Geo Wash 2, Hampden-Sydney 2, Col of Santa Fe 2, Amherst 1). Avg SAT: 1260. Alum 1529.
- **Tui '04-'05: Bdg $27,000** (+$1000). **Day $18,000** (+$500). **Aid:** Merit 4 ($20,000). Need 54 ($699,080).
- Endow $12,115,000. Plant val $37,641,000. Bldgs 31. Dorms 5. Dorm rms 101. Class rms 25. Lib 20,000 vols. Chapels 1. Sci labs 4. Comp labs 2. Auds 1. Theaters 1. Art studios 1. Music studios 1. Dance studios 2. Gyms 1. Fields 7. Courts 12. Field houses 1.
- **Est 1842.** Nonprofit. Episcopal. Tri (Aug-June). **Assoc** CLS MSA.

Saint James is the oldest Episcopal boarding school in America, modeled on the English "public school" plan. Originally a boys' preparatory school and college, Saint James dropped the college division when it reopened after the Civil War. Girls were admitted as day students during the 1970s, and the school became fully coeducational with the addition of female boarders in 1991.

The school's traditional core curriculum is designed to provide pupils with a firm foundation in the major disciplines while preparing them for college attendance. Advanced and Advanced Placement courses are available for able students who wish to pursue subjects in greater depth. In addition, upper school electives provide enrichment and allow students to explore areas of individual interest. Students are required to attend chapel and also to fulfill a community service requirement.

Music, drama, a historical society, publications and various clubs are among the available extracurricular activities. Sports include football, basketball, wrestling, soccer, field hockey, cross-country, baseball, tennis, golf, lacrosse, volleyball and softball.   **See Also Page 1245**

SANDY SPRING, MD. (25 mi. WSW of Baltimore, MD) Rural. Pop: 1200. Alt: 484 ft.

SANDY SPRING FRIENDS SCHOOL
Bdg — Coed Gr 9-12; Day — Coed PS-12

Sandy Spring, MD 20860. 16923 Norwood Rd. Tel: 301-774-7455. Fax: 301-924-1115.
www.ssfs.org   E-mail: admissions@ssfs.org
Kenneth W. Smith, Head. BS, Trinity Univ, MDiv, ThM, Princeton Theological Seminary, DMin, Southern Methodist Univ. **Mecha Inman, Adm.**

Col Prep. Gen Acad. AP—Eng Fr Span Calc Stats Chem Physics US_Hist Music_Theory. **Feat**—British_Lit Russ_Lit Ceramics Photog Studio_Art Video_Production Weaving Drama Music Handbells Dance Woodworking Yoga. **Supp**—ESL Tut.

Adm (Bdg Gr 9-11; Day PS-11): 110/yr. Bdg 18. Day 92. Appl due: Jan. Accepted: 59%. Yield: 66%. **Tests** IQ SSAT TOEFL.

Enr 514. B 18/231. G 21/244. Elem 295. Sec 219. Wh 66%. Hisp 1%. Blk 13%. Asian 5%. Other 15%. Avg class size: 15. **Fac 67.** M 16/3. F 42/6. Wh 88%. Hisp 6%. Blk 4%. Asian 1%. Other 1%. Adv deg: 53%. In dorms 3.

Grad '04—52. Col—52. (Bowdoin, Dickinson, U of MD-Col Park, Earlham, VA Polytech, Dartmouth). Avg SAT: 1200. Alum 1901.

Tui '04-'05: Bdg $32,150-32,650 (+$2000). **5-Day Bdg $26,750-27,250** (+$1700). **Day $13,750-19,500** (+$500). **Aid:** Need 80 ($682,046).

Summer: Rec. Tui Day $250/2-wk ses. 10 wks.

Endow $584,000. Plant val $40,000,000. Bldgs 13. Dorms 1. Dorm rms 28. Class rms 33. Lib 25,000 vols. Sci labs 5. Comp labs 3. Theaters 1. Art studios 4. Music studios 3. Perf arts ctrs 1. Print shops 1. Gyms 3. Fields 4. Courts 4.

Est 1961. Nonprofit. Religious Society of Friends. Sem (Sept-June).

Established as a result of community effort by the Sandy Spring Monthly Meeting, this school provides a college preparatory program within the framework of the Quaker philosophy. The school operated as a boarding and day high school until 1982, when it added a middle school division (grades 6-8). The lower school was added in 1993, when Sandy Spring Friends effected a merger with Friends Elementary School.

Curricular features include a foreign language program that enables students to take Spanish from age 5 through graduation, a sequential math program that allows acceleration beginning in the middle school, and integrated English and history offerings. The ninth-grade curriculum emphasizes both academic and organizational skills development and an awareness of social and community issues. An extensive selection of courses, including Advanced Placement offerings in the core subjects, is available in the upper school. The school's spring intersession allows pupils to engage in a one- to two-week project pertaining to community service, intensive arts study, a rigorous physical activity or travel.

Excursions to Washington, DC, and Baltimore, dances, camping trips and service-oriented projects are among the extracurricular and weekend activities. The athletic program comprises basketball, soccer, softball, baseball, golf, track and field, tennis, cross-country, lacrosse and volleyball.   **See Also Page 1253**

SILVER SPRING, MD. (8 mi. N of Washington, DC) Suburban. Pop: 76,540. Alt: 340 ft.

THE BARRIE SCHOOL
Day — Coed Gr PS-12

Silver Spring, MD 20906. 13500 Layhill Rd. Tel: 301-576-2800. Fax: 301-576-2803.
www.barrie.org   E-mail: dsommer@barrie.org
Timothy L. Trautman, Head. BA, Univ of Pennsylvania, MA, Gonzaga Univ. **Doris L. Sommer,** Adm.
  Col Prep. **AP**—Eng Fr Span Calc Stats Bio Chem Physics US_Hist. **Feat**—Humanities Shakespeare Mythology Anat Ecol Comp_Sci African_Hist Anthro Econ Psych Women's_Stud Relig Ceramics Film Photog Studio_Art Drama Music Journ TV_Production. **Supp**—Tut.
  Adm (Gr PS-11): 82/yr. Appl due: Jan. Accepted: 60%. Yield: 50%. **Tests** IQ SSAT.
  Enr 364. B 191. G 173. Elem 271. Sec 93. Wh 65%. Hisp 3%. Blk 19%. Asian 6%. Other 7%. **Fac 48.** M 12/1. F 32/3. Wh 80%. Hisp 4%. Blk 6%. Asian 2%. Other 8%. Adv deg: 62%.
  Grad '04—20. **Col**—20. (Elon 2, U of MD-Col Park 2, Oberlin 1, Skidmore 1, Vassar 1). Avg SAT: 1292. Alum 268.
  Tui '05-'06: Day $14,490-20,890 (+$600). **Aid:** Need 49 ($340,600).
  Endow $1,033,000. Plant val $10,412,000. Bldgs 25. Class rms 50. 3 Libs 20,000 vols. Sci labs 2. Comp labs 4. Theaters 1. Art studios 3. Music studios 2. Gyms 2. Fields 3. Pools 1. Riding rings 1. Stables 1.
  Est 1932. Nonprofit. Quar (Aug-June). **Assoc** MSA.

The school is located on a wooded, 45-acre campus just north of Washington, DC. At all grade levels, the experiential program provides opportunities to explore individual interests. Barrie's lower school (grades pre-K-5) employs a Montessori approach that emphasizes the development of fundamental academic skills and problem-solving strategies.

In addition to course requirements in humanities, math, science, foreign language, art and physical education, the middle school program (grades 6-8) includes community service, an extended study week, special on- and off-campus study opportunities, and athletics. Among electives for seventh and eighth graders are creative writing, criminal justice, oceanography, stage production, astronomy and photography. Barrie's curriculum continues to broaden during the high school years (grades 9-12), during which students choose from such electives as art and design, television production, philosophy and wildlife biology. Advanced Placement courses are available to juniors and seniors.

NEWPORT SCHOOL
Day — Coed Gr PS-12

Silver Spring, MD 20902. 10914 Georgia Ave. Tel: 301-942-4550. Fax: 301-949-2654.
www.newportschool.org   E-mail: admission@newportschool.org
Ronald W. Stephens, Head. MA, Univ of Windsor (Canada). **Marilyn N. Grossblatt,** Adm.
  Col Prep. **AP**—Psych. **Feat**—Span Computers Studio_Art Drama Music.
  Adm: 35/yr. Appl due: Rolling. Accepted: 70%. Yield: 55%.

Enr 105. B 55. G 50. Elem 88. Sec 17. Wh 55%. Hisp 5%. Blk 25%. Asian 15%. Avg class size: 7. Uniform. **Fac 25.** M 7/3. F 13/2. Wh 70%. Hisp 20%. Blk 5%. Asian 5%. Adv deg: 24%.
Grad '04—2. Col—2. (U of MD-Baltimore County, Am U). Avg SAT: 1027. Alum 200.
Tui '04-'05: Day $8950-17,395. Aid: Need 7 ($32,000).
Endow $86,500. Bldgs 1. Class rms 20. Lib 10,000 vols. Sci labs 1. Comp labs 2. Art studios 3. Music studios 1.
Est 1930. Nonprofit. (Sept-June). **Assoc** MSA.

Newport traces its origins to the Town and Country Day School, an elementary school founded in the early 1900s. An affiliated upper school opened in 1981 under the name of Newport Preparatory School and, in the fall of 1995, the two institutions joined together and assumed the current school name.

In addition to fundamental skills instruction, the school provides many opportunities for creative work and problem solving. Science, Spanish, computer, art and music are taught from nursery through high school, with French also offered in grades 7-12. The curriculum also features photography, drama and fine arts offerings.

STEVENSON, MD. (9 mi. NW of Baltimore, MD) Rural. Pop: 600. Alt: 320 ft.

ST. TIMOTHY'S SCHOOL
Bdg and Day — Girls Gr 9-PG

Stevenson, MD 21153. 8400 Greenspring Ave. Tel: 410-486-7400. Fax: 410-486-1167. www.sttimothysschool.com   E-mail: info@sttims-school.org
Randy S. Stevens, Head. BA, Univ of South Carolina, MPA, Cornell Univ. **Patrick Finn, Adm.**
Col Prep. Feat—Computers Relig Drama Music Dance. **Supp**—ESL Tut.
Adm: 32/yr. Bdg 16. Day 16. Appl due: Feb. Accepted: 70%. **Tests** ISEE SSAT TOEFL.
Enr 88. G 49/39. Sec 87. PG 1. Wh 63%. Hisp 2%. Blk 20%. Asian 14%. Other 1%. Avg class size: 9. Uniform. **Fac 25.** M 5/5. F 14/1. Wh 96%. Blk 4%. Adv deg: 60%. In dorms 5.
Grad '04—27. Col—27. (St Mary's Seminary & U, Columbia, Tufts, Wesleyan U, Vanderbilt, Wash & Lee). Avg SAT: 1190. Alum 2525.
Tui '02-'03: Bdg $29,400 (+$1500). **Day $17,750** (+$1500). **Aid:** Merit 1 ($10,000). Need 36 ($600,000).
Endow $11,700,000. Plant val $7,000,000. Bldgs 22. Dorms 2. Dorm rms 45. Class rms 18. Lib 22,000 vols. Sci labs 3. Comp labs 3. Auds 1. Theaters 1. Art studios 2. Music studios 7. Dance studios 1. Perf arts ctrs 1. Gyms 1. Fields 2. Courts 9. Platform tennis courts 2. Pools 1. Riding rings 2. Stables 1.
Est 1882. Nonprofit. Episcopal. Sem (Sept-June). **Assoc** MSA.

The school, founded in Catonsville by the Misses Sally and Polly Carter, moved to its present, rural site in the Green Spring Valley in 1951. In 1974, St. Tim's merged with the Hannah More Academy, which, founded in 1832, was the oldest Episcopal girls' school in the country. Named after the Englishwoman who had pioneered for girls' education, Hannah More Academy had served as the diocesan school since 1873. Effective with the merger was the transfer of all school activities to the St. Tim's campus.

St. Timothy's academic curriculum features honors and Advanced Placement courses and electives, along with visual and performing arts offerings. The Cross Curricular Connections program operates in conjunction with all academic courses and technology to provide students with practice in research and public speaking. Seniors may undertake independent study during the final three weeks of the spring term. For her independent study project, the pupil may work in a corporate setting, conduct scientific research with a medical professional or engage in an internship in the arts. Each participant in this program makes a presentation to the student body at the conclusion of her project.

All girls participate in athletics; choices are tennis, cross-country, field hockey, soccer, basketball, softball, lacrosse, dance and riding. The equestrian program accommodates both competitive and noncompetitive riders. Students take part in various school organizations, including a social services club that provides opportunities for volunteerism. Extensive cultural and social options, among them concerts, mixers and outdoor activities, round out the program.

UPPER MARLBORO, MD. (15 mi. ESE of Washington, DC) Rural. Pop: 648. Alt: 39 ft.

QUEEN ANNE SCHOOL
Day — Coed Gr 6-12

Upper Marlboro, MD 20774. 14111 Oak Grove Rd. Tel: 301-249-5000. Fax: 301-249-3838. www.queenanne.org E-mail: bwalker@queenanne.org

J. Temple Blackwood, Head. BA, Univ of Hartford, MA, Washington College. **Brenda B. Walker, Adm.**

Col Prep. **AP**—Eng Fr Span Calc Bio Chem Physics US_Hist Econ Psych US_Govt & Pol. **Feat**—Lat Sociol Philos Relig Ceramics Film Photog Drama Chorus Music Dance. **Supp**—Rev Tut.

Adm: 79/yr. Appl due: Rolling. Accepted: 85%. **Tests** ISEE.

Enr 279. B 132. G 147. Elem 123. Sec 156. Wh 40%. Hisp 1%. Blk 54%. Am Ind 2%. Asian 3%. Avg class size: 17. **Fac 39.** M 12/5. F 20/2. Wh 84%. Hisp 2%. Blk 13%. Asian 1%. Adv deg: 35%.

Grad '04—28. Col—28. (U of MD-Col Park, Vanderbilt, Cornell, Salisbury, Johns Hopkins, Wash U). Avg SAT: 1162. Alum 772.

Tui '03-'04: Day $13,200-14,700 (+$200-300). **Aid:** Need 80 ($562,000).

Summer: Enrich. Tui Day $75-140. 1-2 wks.

Endow $865,000. Plant val $9,000,000. Bldgs 8. Class rms 16. Lib 11,000 vols. Sci labs 4. Comp labs 1. Sci ctrs 1. Auds 1. Theaters 1. Art studios 3. Music studios 1. Gyms 1. Fields 3. Courts 2. Tennis courts 2.

Est 1964. Nonprofit. Episcopal. Quar (Aug-June). **Assoc** CLS MSA.

This traditional country day school was established by the vestry of Queen Anne Parish. The college preparatory curriculum, which is centered on study for competence in English, mathematics, science, social studies, and the modern and classical languages, also features course work in the fine arts. Among the campus buildings is historic St. Barnabas' Church. A program of interscholastic sports competition serves both boys and girls.

NEW JERSEY

BLAIRSTOWN, NJ. (68 mi. N of Philadelphia, PA) Suburban. Pop: 5747. Alt: 351 ft.

BLAIR ACADEMY
Bdg and Day — Coed Gr 9-PG

Blairstown, NJ 07825. 2 Park St, PO Box 600. Tel: 908-362-2024. Fax: 908-362-7975.
www.blair.edu   E-mail: admissions@blair.edu
T. Chandler Hardwick III, Head. BA, Univ of North Carolina-Chapel Hill, MA, Middlebury College. **Barbara H. Haase, Adm.**

Col Prep. AP—Eng Fr Lat Span Calc Stats Comp_Sci Bio Chem Physics Eur_Hist US_Hist Econ US_Govt & Pol Art_Hist Studio_Art. **Feat**—Chin Asian_Hist Filmmaking Video_Production Architect_Design Theater Music Mech_Drawing. **Supp**—Tut.

Adm (Bdg Gr 9-PG; Day 9): 150/yr. Bdg 125. Day 25. Appl due: Feb. Accepted: 58%. Yield: 50%. **Tests** SSAT TOEFL.

Enr 434. B 193/51. G 144/46. Sec 417. PG 17. Wh 83%. Hisp 2%. Blk 6%. Asian 9%. Avg class size: 12. **Fac 70.** M 42/3. F 19/6. Wh 92%. Hisp 2%. Blk 5%. Asian 1%. Adv deg: 58%. In dorms 28.

Grad '04—121. Col—120. (Cornell 4, U of PA 4, Geo Wash 4, Colgate 3, Vanderbilt 3, UNC-Chapel Hill 3). Avg SAT: 1206. Alum 5000.

Tui '04-'05: Bdg $33,100. Day $24,300. Aid: Need 123 ($2,265,000).

Endow $50,000,000. Plant val $70,000,000. Bldgs 38. Dorms 10. Dorm rms 215. Class rms 35. Lib 22,000 vols. Sci labs 5. Lang labs 1. Comp labs 7. Auds 1. Theaters 2. Art studios 5. Music studios 7. Dance studios 1. Arts ctrs 1. Gyms 3. Fields 7. Tennis courts 11. Squash courts 3. Pools 1. Golf crses 1.

Est 1848. Nonprofit. Presbyterian. Sem (Sept-May). **Assoc** CLS MSA.

Opening with a coeducational enrollment, then, in 1915, serving boys only, the school once again became completely coeducational in 1970, and it now draws students from many states and from other countries to its competitive program. Though Presbyterian-affiliated, with an appropriate chapel service, the school selects a multidenominational enrollment.

With a guidance program based on modern education and an emphasis on academic fundamentals, Blair has sent graduates to more than 200 different colleges. Advanced Placement courses and electives are open to juniors and seniors, and seniors also participate in independent study projects. Performing and visual arts offerings, which include architectural design course work, are emphasized at the academy.

Sports include football, soccer, basketball, hockey, field hockey, crew, softball, skiing, squash, swimming, wrestling, baseball, cross-country, track, golf, tennis and lacrosse. An outdoor skills program provides opportunities for hiking, rock climbing, and canoeing and kayaking on the Delaware River. Dramatics, chorus, dance, publications, aviation science and interest clubs are among Blair's other activities.

See Also Page 1121

BRIDGETON, NJ. (40 mi. S of Philadelphia, PA) Urban. Pop: 22,771. Alt: 30 ft.

WOODLAND COUNTRY DAY SCHOOL
Day — Coed Gr PS-8

Bridgeton, NJ 08302. 1216 Roadstown Rd. Tel: 856-453-8499. Fax: 856-453-1648.
www.woodlandcountrydayschool.org
E-mail: school@woodlandcountrydayschool.org
Cosmo F. Terrigno, Head. BA, Rowan Univ, MA, Villanova Univ. **Heidi Reilley, Adm.**
  Pre-Prep. Feat—Fr Lat Span Computers Studio_Art Music Study_Skills. **Supp**—Rem_ Math Rem_Read.
  Adm: 41/yr. Appl due: Rolling. **Tests** ISEE.
  Enr 155. Elem 155. Avg class size: 13. **Fac 21.** M 5/1. F 11/4. Adv deg: 23%.
  Grad '04—12. Prep—5. (Archmere, Wilmington Friends). Alum 490.
  Tui '04-'05: Day $6100-8100 (+$300). **Aid:** Need ($100,000).
  Summer: Enrich. Tui Day $150/2-wk ses. 8 wks.
  Endow $800,000. Plant val $1,200,000. Bldgs 7. Class rms 24. Lib 10,000 vols. Sci labs 1. Comp labs 1. Art studios 1. Music studios 1. Gyms 2. Fields 3.
  Est 1959. Nonprofit. Sem (Sept-June). **Assoc** MSA.

Founded as St. John's Day School by a group of families from Salem and Cumberland counties, Woodland serves students within a 30-mile radius. The school moved from its quarters in the parish hall of St. John's Episcopal Church in Salem to the historic Wood Mansion in Jericho. Computer, science lab, music and art supplement the traditional curriculum. Woodland offers French and Spanish from prekindergarten, Latin in grades 7 and 8.

The extracurricular program includes a student union, dramatics, chorus, student work squad, and interscholastic and intramural sports. The school schedules field trips to nearby cultural and educational centers.

BURLINGTON, NJ. (16 mi. ENE of Philadelphia, PA) Urban. Pop: 9736. Alt: 14 ft.

ST. MARY'S HALL/DOANE ACADEMY
Day — Coed Gr PS-12

Burlington, NJ 08016. 350 Riverbank. Tel: 609-386-3500. Fax: 609-386-5878.
www.thehall.org   E-mail: nnaftulin@thehall.org
John F. McGee, Head. BA, MA, Univ of Notre Dame. **Nancy Naftulin, Adm.**
  Col Prep. AP—Eng Fr Lat Span Calc Comp_Sci Bio Eur_Hist US_Hist Studio_Art. **Feat**—Creative_Writing Lib_Skills Poetry Shakespeare Civil_War African-Amer_Hist Ethics Music. **Supp**—Tut.
  Adm: 41/yr. Appl due: Rolling. Accepted: 80%. Yield: 67%. **Tests** CTP_4 ISEE MAT SSAT Stanford TOEFL.
  Enr 187. B 91. G 96. Elem 113. Sec 74. Wh 64%. Hisp 5%. Blk 25%. Am Ind 1%. Asian 5%. Avg class size: 13. Uniform. **Fac 29.** M 7/2. F 17/3. Wh 97%. Hisp 3%. Adv deg: 41%.
  Grad '04—17. Col—16. (Drexel, Temple, Geo Wash, Susquehanna, Albright, Arcadia).

Avg SAT: 1100. Alum 1200.
Tui '04-'05: Day $7675-9890 (+$600). **Aid:** Need 55 ($116,000).
Endow $250,000. Plant val $3,000,000. Bldgs 7. Class rms 32. Lib 12,000 vols. Sci labs 4. Comp labs 2. Art studios 2. Music studios 1. Gyms 1. Fields 1.
Est 1837. Nonprofit. Episcopal. Sem (Sept-June). **Assoc** CLS MSA.

Founded as a girls' boarding school by Rt. Rev. George Washington Doane, second Episcopal bishop of New Jersey, St. Mary's Hall became a day school in 1953, accepting boys in the elementary grades. Classes became coed in 1974, when the school merged with Doane Academy, founded in 1965 as a coordinate boys' school for students in grades 6-12. SMH-DA is now fully coeducational.

The school's college preparatory curriculum prepares graduates for many leading colleges. Reading instruction, which takes a phonics- and literature-based approach, enables children to read age-appropriate novels beginning in grade 2; writing skills are also a focus of the early grades.

A varied activity program, featuring art, music and dramatics, provides students with the opportunity to learn beyond the curriculum. Athletics include cross-country, soccer, baseball, softball, basketball and crew.

EDISON, NJ. (24 mi. WSW of New York, NY) Suburban. Pop: 97,687.

WARDLAW-HARTRIDGE SCHOOL
Day — Coed Gr PS-12

Edison, NJ 08820. 1295 Inman Ave. Tel: 908-754-1882. Fax: 908-754-9678.
  www.whschool.org E-mail: admission@whschool.org
Andrew Webster, Head. AB, Brown Univ, MA, Univ of Virginia. **Kerry Mercurio Cox, Int Adm.**
Col Prep. AP—Eng Fr Lat Span Calc Comp_Sci Bio Chem Physics Eur_Hist US_Hist US_Govt & Pol Art_Hist Studio_Art Music_Theory. **Feat**—Astron Ecol Environ_Sci Marine_Biol/Sci Drama Journ Driver_Ed. **Supp**—ESL Tut.
Adm (Gr PS-11): 87/yr. Appl due: Feb. Accepted: 69%. Yield: 61%. **Tests** CTP_4 ISEE SSAT.
Enr 420. B 230. G 190. Elem 273. Sec 147. Wh 47%. Hisp 5%. Blk 14%. Asian 27%. Other 7%. Avg class size: 13. **Fac 61.** M 15/2. F 36/8. Wh 90%. Hisp 3%. Asian 7%. Adv deg: 55%.
Grad '04—35. Col—35. (Rutgers 2, Mt Holyoke 2, Villanova 2, Drexel 2, U of Hartford 2). Avg SAT: 1235. Alum 1800.
Tui '04-'05: Day $14,250-19,500 (+$200-600). **Aid:** Merit 11 ($37,000). Need 113 ($1,064,000).
Summer: Acad Enrich Rev Rem Rec. ESL. Tui Day $695-1030. 6 wks.
Endow $1,552,000. Plant val $18,100,000. Bldgs 1. Class rms 54. Lib 28,000 vols. Sci labs 6. Lang labs 1. Comp labs 4. Sci/tech ctrs 1. Art studios 3. Music studios 3. Gyms 2. Fields 6. Courts 9. Pools 1. Weight rms 1.
Est 1882. Nonprofit. Sem (Sept-June). **Assoc** CLS.

The school was reconfigured in 1976 when the Wardlaw Country Day School, founded in 1882, merged with the Hartridge School, founded in 1884. Situated on a 36-acre tract, the school now occupies a single campus. All high school students utilize laptop computers in a variety of required and elective subjects. Honors and

Advanced Placement courses are available, and pupils are encouraged to select enrichment courses in the areas of art, music and computers. Twelfth graders deliver a compulsory senior speech and present a senior public policy thesis on an issue of contemporary concern.

A weeklong trip is integrated into the curriculum in each middle school year (grades 6-8). In grades 7 and 8, all boys and girls participate in interscholastic competition; those in grades 9-12 may elect to play on athletic teams. Wardlaw-Hartridge offers a variety of extracurricular activities, such as newspaper and yearbook, student council and many interest clubs.

ENGLEWOOD, NJ. (15 mi. N of New York, NY) Suburban. Pop: 26,203. Alt: 24 ft.

DWIGHT-ENGLEWOOD SCHOOL
Day — Coed Gr PS-12

Englewood, NJ 07631. 315 E Palisade Ave, PO Box 489. Tel: 201-569-9500.
Fax: 201-568-9451.
www.d-e.org E-mail: admissions@d-e.org
Ralph E. Sloan, Head. AB, AM, EdD, Harvard Univ. **Sherronda L. Oliver, Upper Sch Adm; Whitney A. Brusman, Middle Sch Adm; Joni Hartsough, Lower Sch Adm.**

    Col Prep. AP—Eng Fr Lat Span Calc Stats Comp_Sci Bio Chem Physics US_Hist US_Govt & Pol Studio_Art. **Feat**—Bioethics Law Ethics Ceramics Graphic_Arts Photog Drama Music. **Supp**—Dev_Read Makeup Tut.

    Adm: 182/yr. **Tests** ISEE.

    Enr 1007. B 508. G 499. Wh 70%. Hisp 4%. Blk 5%. Asian 21%. Avg class size: 18. **Fac** 130. Adv deg: 63%.

    Grad '04—109. **Col**—109. (Columbia, Boston U, Brown, NYU, Geo Wash, Johns Hopkins). Alum 7500.

    Tui '05-'06: Day $13,545-22,735 (+$150-525). **Aid:** Need 101 ($989,000).

    Summer: Acad Enrich Rec. Sports. 6 wks.

    Endow $4,550,000. Plant val $26,000,000. Bldgs 10. Class rms 78. 2 Libs 20,000 vols. Sci labs 10. Lang labs 1. Comp labs 4. Auds 1. Theaters 1. Art studios 2. Music studios 2. Arts ctrs 1. Gyms 3. Fields 4. Courts 5.

    Est 1889. Nonprofit. Sem (Sept-June). **Assoc** CLS MSA.

Dwight-Englewood School resulted from the merger of Dwight School, a girls' school founded in 1889, and Englewood School for Boys, founded in 1928. After a decade of increasingly coordinated campuses and classes, the two schools were completely merged in 1974. In 1992, Dwight-Englewood expanded its upper and middle school curriculum to include the lower grades when it incorporated Bede School, an elementary school that opened in 1963.

Enrolling students from northern New Jersey, Rockland County and the New York City metropolitan area, the school offers a preschool and kindergarten program. In the lower and middle grades, emphasis is on building a strong foundation in the core disciplines and in problem-solving skills. The upper school program, which includes honors and Advanced Placement courses and a fully integrated math/science/technology program, prepares graduates for admission to selective colleges. The study of ethics and the fulfillment of a community service requirement are included in the program. Participation in a wide range of artistic, athletic and community activities is encouraged.

ELISABETH MORROW SCHOOL
Day — Coed Gr PS-8

Englewood, NJ 07631. 435 Lydecker St. Tel: 201-568-5566. Fax: 201-816-9416.
www.elisabethmorrow.org E-mail: mail@elisabethmorrow.org

David M. Lowry, Head. BA, Haverford College, MS, PhD, Columbia Univ. **Laurel Zimmermann, Adm.**

Pre-Prep. **Feat**—Writing Fr Lat Span Computers Studio_Art Music. **Supp**—Dev_Read ESL Tut.

Adm: 89/yr. Accepted: 70%. **Tests** CTP_4 IQ ISEE.

Enr 447. B 217. G 230. Elem 447. Wh 59%. Hisp 2%. Blk 7%. Asian 20%. Other 12%. Avg class size: 16. **Fac 78.** M 5/1. F 59/13. Wh 95%. Hisp 2%. Asian 2%. Other 1%. Adv deg: 61%.

Grad '04—58. Prep—50. (Dwight-Englewood, Horace Mann, Saddle River, Fieldston). Alum 1631.

Tui '03-'04: Day $8750-18,000 (+$100). **Aid:** Need 47 ($358,500).

Summer: Acad Enrich Rev Rem Rec. Tui Day $950-1425/3-wk ses. 6 wks.

Endow $2,150,000. Plant val $15,500,000. Bldgs 4. Class rms 43. 3 Libs 23,000 vols. Sci labs 3. Lang labs 2. Comp labs 2. Art studios 2. Music studios 2. Gyms 2. Fields 1. Playgrounds 3.

Est 1930. Nonprofit. Sem (Sept-June). **Assoc** MSA.

Originally the Little School, the school was renamed in 1948 for its cofounder, a daughter of Dwight Morrow. Located on a 14-acre, wooded campus in a residential area ten miles from New York City, the school draws students from more than 50 surrounding communities.

The curriculum stresses a thematic approach to learning developmentally appropriate skills. Literature-based reading and writing and problem solving in mathematics form the core of the program. Extracurricular activities include orchestra, choir, drama, computers, intramural sports and chess. After-school, summer and childcare programs are available.

FAR HILLS, NJ. (36 mi. W of New York, NY) Rural. Pop: 859. Alt: 200 ft.

FAR HILLS COUNTRY DAY SCHOOL
Day — Coed Gr PS-8

Far Hills, NJ 07931. Rte 202, PO Box 8. Tel: 908-766-0622. Fax: 908-766-6705.
www.fhcds.org E-mail: admissions@fhcds.org

Jayne Geiger, Head. BA, MEd, Rutgers Univ, MS, Bank Street College of Education. **Charlotte N. L. Davis, Adm.**

Pre-Prep. **Feat**—Fr Lat Span Computers Studio_Art Music. **Supp**—Tut.

Adm (Gr PS-7): 70/yr. Appl due: Feb. **Tests** CTP_4 SSAT Stanford.

NJ　　　　　　　　　*Leading Private Schools*　　　　　　　　　*328*

Enr 415. B 208. G 207. Elem 415. Wh 89%. Hisp 2%. Blk 1%. Asian 7%. Other 1%. Avg class size: 15. **Fac 61.** M 10. F 51. Adv deg: 57%.
Grad '04—30. Prep—29. (Peddie, Pingry, Delbarton, Lawrenceville, Morristown-Beard, Rutgers Prep). Alum 1208.
Tui '04-'05: Day $15,150-20,575.
Summer: Rec. Tui Day $170-280/wk. 6 wks.
Endow $4,000,000. Bldgs 5. Class rms 28. Lib 12,000 vols. Comp ctrs 1. Theaters 1. Art studios 2. Music studios 2. Gyms 2. Fields 3. Ropes crses 1.
Est 1929. Nonprofit. Tri (Sept-June). **Assoc** MSA.

Founded in Morristown as the Mount Kemble School, FHCDS moved to its present site and assumed its current name in 1944. The rural, 54-acre campus in Somerset County is accessible to both New York City and Princeton.

In the primary and intermediate schools (grades pre-K-5), children take part in self-contained classes in most academic areas, while specialists provide instruction in art, music, library, computer, science, Spanish and physical education. The fully departmentalized upper school (grades 6-8) features such supplemental offerings as forensics, concert choir, bell choir, band and drama. In addition, all pupils take Latin in grades 7 and 8.

A full sports program includes soccer, volleyball, fitness, field hockey, tennis, cross-country, basketball, ice hockey, track and field, and lacrosse. The school's adventure program consists of experiential learning and adventure trips from grade 5.

GLADSTONE, NJ. (38 mi. W of New York, NY) Rural. Pop: 2111. Alt: 300 ft.

GILL ST. BERNARD'S SCHOOL
Day — Coed Gr PS-12

Gladstone, NJ 07934. St Bernard's Rd, PO Box 604. **Tel: 908-234-1611.**
Fax: 908-234-1715.
www.gsbschool.org   E-mail: admission@gsbschool.org
S. A. Rowell, Head. BA, MA, Trinity College (CT). **Joyce E. Miller, Adm.**
Col Prep. AP—Eng Fr Span Calc Comp_Sci Bio US_Hist US_Govt & Pol. **Feat**—Creative_Writing Lat Stats Astron Oceanog Psych Philos Film Photog Studio_Art. **Supp**—Tut.
Adm (Gr PS-11): 104/yr. Appl due: Feb. **Tests** CTP_4 ISEE SSAT.
Enr 600. B 300. G 300. Elem 436. Sec 164. Wh 87%. Hisp 1%. Blk 3%. Asian 7%. Other 2%. Avg class size: 13. **Fac 78.** M 23. F 55. Wh 97%. Blk 1%. Asian 2%. Adv deg: 44%.
Grad '04—38. Col—38. (Bucknell 2, Centenary-NJ 2, Northeastern U 2, U of PA 2). Alum 1840.
Tui '04-'05: Day $20,995 (+$200-500).
Summer: Rec. 6 wks.
Endow $1,800,000. Plant val $15,000,000. Bldgs 22. Class rms 53. 2 Libs 20,000 vols. Sci labs 4. Comp labs 2. Theaters 1. Art studios 2. Music studios 1. Art galleries 1. Gyms 2. Fields 7. Courts 5. Tracks 1. Fitness rms 1.
Est 1900. Nonprofit. Sem (Aug-June). **Assoc** MSA.

The school resulted from the 1972 merger of the Gill School in Bernardsville, which was founded by Elizabeth Gill in 1934, and St. Bernard's School in Gladstone, founded by Rev. Thomas Conover as an Episcopal boarding school in 1900.

The lower school offers a curriculum that includes language arts, computer, foreign languages, mathematics, social studies, science, art and music at all levels. In addition to regular classes, the upper school provides a two-week unit at the end of the school year during which students enroll in one course that meets four and a half hours per day. Intensive college preparatory study is supported by community service and experiential learning. Older students take advantage of travel-study opportunities in foreign countries.

Extracurricular activities in drama, music and student government are available. Sports include soccer, baseball, wrestling, basketball, track, cross-country and tennis.

HIGHTSTOWN, NJ. (37 mi. ENE of Philadelphia, PA) Suburban. Pop: 5216. Alt: 97 ft.

PEDDIE SCHOOL
Bdg and Day — Coed Gr 9-PG

Hightstown, NJ 08520. S Main St, PO Box A. Tel: 609-490-7501. Fax: 609-944-7901.
www.peddie.org   E-mail: edevillafranca@peddie.org

John F. Green, Head. BA, Wesleyan Univ, MEd, Harvard Univ. **Edward A. de Villafranca, Adm.**

Col Prep. AP—Fr Lat Span Calc Stats Bio Chem Eur_Hist US_Hist Psych Art_Hist Music_Theory. **Feat**—Poetry Shakespeare Fiction_Writing Playwriting Chin Astron Ecol Environ_Sci Marine_Biol/Sci Programming Film Acting Drama Music Opera. **Supp**—Dev_Read ESL Tut.

Adm: 158/yr. Bdg 116. Day 42. Appl due: Jan. Accepted: 23%. Yield: 69%. **Tests** CEEB SSAT TOEFL.

Enr 520. B 184/99. G 144/93. Elem 24. Sec 480. PG 16. Wh 79%. Hisp 6%. Blk 8%. Asian 7%. Avg class size: 12. **Fac 85.** M 50. F 35. Adv deg: 78%. In dorms 32.

Grad '04—128. Col—128. (U of PA, Carnegie Mellon, Columbia, Georgetown, Cornell, Boston Col). Alum 8000.

Tui '04-'05: Bdg $32,100 (+$700). **Day $23,800** (+$350). **Aid:** Need 218 ($4,300,000).

Summer: Acad Enrich. Tui Day $525/crse. 6 wks.

Endow $214,000,000. Plant val $95,000,000. Bldgs 23. Dorms 14. Dorm rms 322. Class rms 47. Lib 30,000 vols. Chapels 1. Sci labs 11. Comp labs 2. Theaters 1. Art studios 4. Music studios 2. Gyms 1. Athletic ctrs 1. Fields 9. Courts 14. Pools 2. Golf crses 1. Student ctrs 1.

Est 1864. Nonprofit. Tri (Sept-May). **Assoc** CLS MSA.

Peddie offers a demanding academic program that attracts able students from many states and foreign countries. The broad college preparatory curriculum includes core courses and a wide variety of electives (available in one-, two- and three-term sequences) in the performing and visual arts, music, science, math, computer and information technology, and history. Honors and Advanced Placement sections are available in the major disciplines. Technology is an important aspect of Peddie's program, as the campus is predominantly wireless. Each pupil receives a laptop computer upon enrollment. The school's library maintains a direct link with Princeton University, and all boys and girls have Internet access.

All students take part in a physical education program that includes both interscholastic and intramural sports. The 230-acre campus provides the setting for football, baseball, swimming, track, basketball, lacrosse, soccer, volleyball, golf, wrestling, field hockey, cross-country, softball, crew and tennis. Students are also required to participate in community service and work programs. Other activities include extensive drama, art and music programs; publications; and various student-run clubs. Study abroad opportunities are also available.

JERSEY CITY, NJ. (7 mi. WNW of New York, NY) Urban. Pop: 240,055. Alt: 83 ft.

ST. PETER'S PREPARATORY SCHOOL
Day — Boys Gr 9-12

Jersey City, NJ 07302. 144 Grand St. Tel: 201-434-4400. Fax: 201-547-6421.
www.stpetersprep.org   E-mail: admissions@stpetersprep.org

Rev. James F. Keenan, SJ, **Pres.** BA, MA, Fordham Univ. **Kevin P. Cuddihy, Prin.** BA, Connecticut College, MS, Fordham Univ. **John Irvine, Adm.**

Col Prep. AP—Eng Span Calc Stats Comp_Sci Bio Chem US_Hist. **Feat**—African-Amer_Lit Ger Greek Bioethics Holocaust Relig Ceramics Sculpt Studio_Art Video_Production Music Journ. **Supp**—Rev.

Adm: 278/yr. Appl due: Nov. Accepted: 50%. **Tests** SSAT.

Enr 931. B 931. Sec 931. Wh 63%. Hisp 14%. Blk 4%. Asian 14%. Other 5%. Avg class size: 22. Uniform. **Fac 74.** M 48/2. F 24. Wh 95%. Hisp 3%. Blk 1%. Asian 1%. Adv deg: 77%.

Grad '04—166. Col—164. (Rutgers, St Peter's, Seton Hall, NJ Inst of Tech, St Joseph's U, Fairfield). Avg SAT: 1130. Alum 12,500.

Tui '04-'05: Day $6300 (+$675). **Aid:** Merit 147 ($180,000). Need 250 ($770,000).

Summer: Acad. Tui Day $225/crse. 5 wks.

Endow $9,000,000. Plant val $8,800,000. Bldgs 3. Libs 2. Sci labs 5. Comp labs 2. Gyms 1. Fields 1.

Est 1872. Nonprofit. Roman Catholic. Sem (Sept-June). **Assoc** MSA.

Located in the Paulus Hook section of the city, this Jesuit school offers a college preparatory curriculum enriched by Advanced Placement, honors and religion courses. All boys fulfill a two-year Latin requirement, and Prep maintains a strong fine arts department featuring courses that combine theory and practice. Technology forms an integral component of academic life at the school: Computers are employed extensively in science classes, and workstations in the computer center are available to students at lunchtime and after school (as well as in computer science courses).

As part of the foreign language program, St. Peter's plans noncredit exchanges for students of German, French and Italian. In addition to its formal exchange programs, Prep regularly conducts summer tours to such countries as France, Spain and Mexico.

The school encourages boys to participate in at least one sport. Hockey, baseball, football, basketball, cross-country, track, lacrosse, wrestling, soccer, tennis, swimming, golf, volleyball and bowling are available at the varsity level, with many sports also having subvarsity teams. Among other extracurricular activities are debate, student government, publications and interest clubs.

LAWRENCEVILLE, NJ. (30 mi. NE of Philadelphia, PA) Suburban. Pop: 4081. Alt: 123 ft.

LAWRENCEVILLE SCHOOL
Bdg and Day — Coed Gr 9-PG

Lawrenceville, NJ 08648. 2500 Main St. Tel: 609-896-0400. Fax: 609-895-2217.
www.lawrenceville.org   E-mail: admissions@lawrenceville.org

Elizabeth A. Duffy, Head. AB, Princeton Univ, MBA, AM, Stanford Univ. **Gregg W. M. Maloberti, Adm.**

Col Prep. AP—Fr Span Calc Stats Comp_Sci Bio Chem Physics Eur_Hist US_Hist Comp_Govt & Pol Econ US_Govt & Pol Art_Hist Studio_Art Music_Theory. **Feat**—Humanities Poetry African-Amer_Lit Chin Greek Japan Astron Ecol Environ_Sci Amer_Stud Bible Ethics Philos Relig Architect Visual_Arts Theater Music Dance Journ.

Adm (Bdg Gr 9-PG; Day 9-12): 253/yr. Bdg 186. Day 67. Appl due: Jan. Accepted: 29%. Yield: 65%. **Tests** ISEE SSAT TOEFL.

Enr 807. B 315/124. G 226/142. Sec 786. PG 21. Wh 68%. Hisp 5%. Blk 7%. Asian 15%. Other 5%. Avg class size: 11. **Fac 107.** M 64/3. F 38/2. Adv deg: 76%. In dorms 37.

Grad '04—220. Col—217. (U of PA 11, Duke 10, Princeton 10, NYU 8, Harvard 7, Columbia 6). Avg SAT: 1360. Alum 11,074.

Tui '04-'05: Bdg $32,460 (+$800). **Day $26,460** (+$500). **Aid:** Merit 9 ($165,780). Need 232 ($5,447,845).

Endow $201,202,000. Plant val $110,790,000. Bldgs 36. Dorms 17. Dorm rms 430. Class rms 105. Lib 40,000 vols. Sci labs 14. Lang labs 1. Comp labs 2. Sci ctrs 1. Theaters 1. Art studios 4. Music studios 6. Dance studios 1. Arts ctrs 1. Music ctrs 1. Gyms 1. Fields 17. Courts 19. Squash courts 10. Field houses 1. Pools 1. Rinks 1. Weight rms 2. Golf crses 1. Ropes crses 1. Boathouses 1.

Est 1810. Nonprofit. Tri (Sept-June). **Assoc** CLS MSA.

The school was founded when Isaac Van Arsdale Brown, a Presbyterian minister, began to teach lessons to nine local boys in his front parlor. Initially known as the Academy of Maidenhead, for the town's original name, and run under such names as Lawrenceville High School and the Lawrenceville Classical and Commercial High School for some 70 years thereafter, it was not until 1883 that it became the Lawrenceville School. The center of the 700-acre campus is the Circle, which was landscaped and designed by Frederick Law Olmsted and has been designated a national historic landmark.

Two noteworthy features are the house system and the conference plan. The first is a dormitory system that follows the example of such English public schools as Rugby and Eton. House identity is maintained through separate dining rooms in the dining center and athletic teams that compete intramurally. Each house has its own student government and traditions and, as students move through different levels, they assume increased responsibility for management of themselves and their house. The conference style of teaching allows for approximately a dozen students, along with the instructor, to sit around an oval Harkness table, thus challenging students to be well prepared and to participate in the discussion.

Based on a traditional approach to education, Lawrenceville's program exposes its students to courses in many disciplines through electives and departmental requirements. The comprehensive curriculum prepares students to take AP examinations and is complemented by an array of opportunities in the visual and performing arts. Other options include off-campus projects, independent study and Island School, a semester-long, intensive marine science program open to sophomores and juniors that utilizes the resources of the marine environment in Eleuthera, Bahamas. In addition, pupils who have completed their second year of Spanish or French may spend a term at an affiliated institution in either Alicante, Spain or Angouleme, France.

Students must participate in an approved athletic activity at least four times a week until the senior year, when they are required to take part three times a week. Among the choices are interscholastics, a comprehensive intramural program and instruction in any of a number of lifetime sports (such as aerobics, cricket, golf, karate, kayaking, riding and tennis). Extracurricular clubs and organizations cover a range of interests that includes writing, acting, debating, music, art, history, religion, science, photography, woodworking and scuba diving. A ropes course and a modern dance program are also available. All students satisfy a community service requirement. **See Also Page 1191**

MARTINSVILLE, NJ. (33 mi. W of New York, NY) Rural. Pop: 900. Alt: 306 ft.

THE PINGRY SCHOOL
Day — Coed Gr K-12

Martinsville, NJ 08836. Martinsville Rd, PO Box 366. Tel: 908-647-5555.
  Fax: 908-647-3703.
  www.pingry.org E-mail: info@pingry.org
Nathaniel E. Conard, Head. BS, Yale Univ, MBA, Dartmouth College. **Sara Boisvert, Adm.**
  Col Prep. **AP**—Fr Ger Lat Span Calc Comp_Sci Bio Chem Physics Eur_Hist US_Hist Econ Psych US_Govt & Pol Art_Hist Studio_Art Music_Theory. **Feat**—British_Lit Creative_Writing World_Lit Anat & Physiol Philos Filmmaking Photog Sculpt Drama.
  Adm (Gr K-11): 171/yr. Appl due: Jan. Accepted: 34%. Yield: 79%. **Tests** CTP_4 ISEE SSAT.
  Enr 1016. B 531. G 485. Elem 503. Sec 513. Wh 79%. Hisp 2%. Blk 4%. Asian 9%. Other 6%. Avg class size: 16. **Fac 134.** M 49/6. F 70/9. Wh 90%. Hisp 4%. Blk 2%. Asian 4%. Adv deg: 56%.
  Grad '04—120. Col—120. (Georgetown 6, U of PA 6, U of Richmond 6, Yale 4, Harvard 4, NYU 4). Alum 4960.
  Tui '04-'05: Day $17,430-22,290 (+$2000). **Aid:** Need 77 ($1,246,000).
  Summer: Enrich. 6 wks.
  Endow $48,000,000. Plant val $34,000,000. Bldgs 2. Class rms 70. Lib 37,500 vols. Labs 9. Theaters 3. Art studios 6. Music studios 8. Gyms 3. Fields 8. Courts 12. Pools 1.

Tracks 1.
Est 1861. Nonprofit. Sem (Sept-June). **Assoc** CLS MSA.

Dr. John F. Pingry founded the school in Elizabeth to provide boys with moral education and scholastic training in the classical tradition. The school remained at its original site until 1953, at which time it moved a short distance to Hillside. In the early 1970s, Pingry first enrolled girls and also effected a merger with Short Hills Country Day School, thereby expanding the program to kindergarten through grade 12 and increasing the size of the student body. In 1983, the school moved from Hillside to Martinsville; this campus now serves pupils in grades 7-12. The Short Hills campus (Country Day Dr., 07078), located about 25 minutes away, accommodates children in grades K-6.

The school draws its students from 95 central and northern New Jersey communities. The curriculum features small classes and a varied selection of Advanced Placement and honors courses. The honor code, one of Pingry's traditions, dates from 1925 and remains an important component of school life.

More than two dozen varsity teams compete annually, and most sports field a junior varsity squad. Boys and girls also choose from an array of clubs, organizations, and dramatic, artistic and musical activities.

MONTCLAIR, NJ. (18 mi. NW of New York, NY) Suburban. Pop: 38,977. Alt: 41 ft.

MONTCLAIR KIMBERLEY ACADEMY
Day — Coed Gr PS-12

Montclair, NJ 07042. 201 Valley Rd. Tel: 973-746-9800. Fax: 973-509-4526.
www.montclairkimberley.org E-mail: admissions@montclairkimberley.org
Thomas W. Nammack, Head. AB, Brown Univ, MEd, Univ of Pennsylvania. **John D. Zurcher, Adm.**
  Col Prep. AP—Fr Lat Span Comp_Sci Chem Physics Studio_Art. **Feat**—Poetry Shakespeare Writing Astron Oceanog Web_Design Econ Ethics Visual_Arts Drama Music Dance. **Supp**—Tut.
  Adm: 140/yr. Appl due: Jan. Accepted: 71%. **Tests** ISEE SSAT.
  Enr 1025. B 522. G 503. Elem 599. Sec 426. Wh 81%. Hisp 3%. Blk 10%. Asian 5%. Other 1%. Avg class size: 13. **Fac 153.** M 51/2. F 96/4. Adv deg: 64%.
  Grad '04—100. **Col**—100. (U of PA 5, NYU 4, Princeton 3, Geo Wash 3, Rutgers 3, Boston U 3). Avg SAT: 1250. Alum 4870.
  Tui '04-'05: Day $16,500-21,900 (+$1000). **Aid:** Need 85 ($1,213,200).
  Summer: Acad Enrich Rev Rec. Tui Day $300-700/crse. 2-6 wks.
  Endow $12,000,000. Plant val $23,000,000. Bldgs 11. Class rms 90. 3 Libs 32,000 vols. Sci labs 11. Comp labs 5. Drama labs 2. Auds 3. Theaters 1. Art studios 5. Music studios 2. Dance studios 1. Gyms 4. Fields 4. Courts 6. Pools 2.
  Est 1887. Nonprofit. (Sept-June). **Assoc** CLS MSA.

In 1974, Montclair Academy for boys (founded in 1887) merged with The Kimberley School for girls (founded in 1906). The academy's three campuses, located in residential northern New Jersey, enroll a diverse student population from Montclair and over 70 neighboring communities.

The college preparatory upper school curriculum features various electives and Advanced Placement courses, as well as a selection of honors courses. Typical semester- and year-long offerings include literature electives, creative writing seminars, economics, political theory, astronomy, ethics, jazz dance, band, studio art and biopsychology. MKA's Core Works program enables pupils at all grade levels to undertake in-depth study of notable works of literature and art from both Western and non-Western traditions. Outdoor education, field trips at all grade levels, and community and school service activities afford students opportunities to learn outside the classroom. The fine and performing arts are integrated into the school's curriculum, and pupils on all three campuses participate in musical and dramatic productions.

Intramural sports are available in grades K-5. The interscholastic athletic program begins in grade 6 and features competition in soccer, football, cross-country, ice and field hockey, swimming, baseball, basketball, volleyball, lacrosse, golf, tennis, wrestling and fencing.

MOORESTOWN, NJ. (11 mi. ESE of Philadelphia, PA) Suburban. Pop: 19,017. Alt: 71 ft.

MOORESTOWN FRIENDS SCHOOL
Day — Coed Gr PS-12

Moorestown, NJ 08057. 110 E Main St. Tel: 856-235-2900. Fax: 856-235-6684.
www.mfriends.org E-mail: admiss@mfriends.org

Laurence R. Van Meter, Head. BA, Hamilton College, MBA, Dartmouth College. **Karin B. Miller, Adm.**

Col Prep. **AP**—Fr Span Calc Physics. **Feat**—Anat & Physiol Environ_Sci Comp_Sci Holocaust Constitutional_Law Relig Ceramics Photog Studio_Art Music Music_Theory. **Supp**—Rem_Read Rev Tut.

Adm (Gr PS-11): 135/yr. Appl due: Rolling. Accepted: 52%. Yield: 82%. **Tests** CTP_4 Stanford.

Enr 717. B 341. G 376. Elem 446. Sec 271. Wh 73%. Hisp 2%. Blk 9%. Asian 8%. Other 8%. Avg class size: 18. **Fac 89.** M 22/6. F 54/7. Wh 89%. Hisp 4%. Blk 6%. Asian 1%. Adv deg: 44%.

Grad '04—54. Col—54. (Cornell 3, Boston U 3, Haverford 2, U of PA 1, Georgetown 1, Emory 1). Avg SAT: 1258. Alum 2448.

Tui '04-'05: Day $11,000-14,550 (+$400). **Aid:** Need 103 ($747,169).

Endow $8,415,000. Plant val $11,295,000. Bldgs 9. Class rms 50. Lib 30,000 vols. Sci labs 4. Comp labs 3. Auds 1. Art studios 2. Music studios 4. Gyms 4. Fields 6. Courts 5.

Est 1785. Nonprofit. Religious Society of Friends. Tri (Sept-June). **Assoc** CLS MSA.

Moorestown Friends, operated under the care of the Moorestown Monthly Meeting, originated when the Quakers opened a school on the present, 40-acre site. All students, faculty and staff attend weekly meetings for worship. The school draws students of all backgrounds from South Jersey communities.

The college preparatory program in the middle and upper schools is varied, with attention given to the arts and learning experiences that provide off-campus opportunities each year. Students choose from a variety of extracurricular activities, including athletic competition in field hockey, soccer, tennis, basketball, lacrosse, baseball, cross-country and fencing.

In the lower school, children are grouped in traditional grade levels. The developmental curriculum incorporates thematic and experiential learning. Three- and four-year-old students learn in a separate house on campus; the program emphasizes socialization and developmentally appropriate early childhood experiences.

MORRISTOWN, NJ. (29 mi. WNW of New York, NY) Suburban. Pop: 18,544. Alt: 350 ft. Area also includes Convent Station.

ACADEMY OF SAINT ELIZABETH
Day — Girls Gr 9-12

Convent Station, NJ 07961. PO Box 297. Tel: 973-290-5200. Fax: 973-290-5232.
www.academyofsaintelizabeth.org
Sr. Patricia Costello, OP, Prin. BA, MA. **Kathy Thomas, Adm.**
   Col Prep. AP—Eng Lat Calc Chem US_Hist. **Feat**—British_Lit Fr Span Ecol Environ_Sci Web_Design Psych Relig Art_Hist Studio_Art Theater Chorus Dance Journ Driver_Ed. **Supp**—Tut.
   Adm: 75/yr. Appl due: Rolling. Accepted: 85%.
   Enr 242. G 242. Sec 242. Wh 82%. Hisp 8%. Blk 3%. Asian 7%. Avg class size: 15. Uniform. **Fac 27.** M 5/1. F 18/3. Adv deg: 37%.
   Grad '04—60. Col—60. Alum 1700.
   Tui '04-'05: Day $11,000 (+$700).
   Bldgs 2. Class rms 20. Libs 1. Chapels 1. Sci labs 3. Comp labs 1. Auds 1. Theaters 1. Art studios 1. Music studios 1. Dance studios 1. Gyms 1. Fields 4. Courts 1. Pools 1.
   Est 1860. Nonprofit. Roman Catholic. Quar (Sept-June). **Assoc** MSA.

In 1859, Mother Mary Xavier, a young Sister of Charity from New York, was commissioned by Bishop James Roosevelt Bayley to establish this school for young women; it is the oldest girls' high school in the state. The academy offers Advanced Placement programs in calculus, chemistry, English, US history and foreign languages, and honors classes in each major academic discipline. The academy offers a career-oriented program to seniors during the last two weeks before graduation in which each student chooses an area of interest and selects a mentor in that field. Internship participants follow up with reports submitted to the entire student body at an assembly.

The academy fields a full complement of varsity teams, and intramural programs are offered in riding and skiing. Cocurricular activities include student council, peer tutoring, newspaper, literary magazine, yearbook, forensics, mock trial, environmental club, service clubs, math, and clubs for all the foreign languages offered in the curriculum. Students also plan and participate in liturgical celebrations, lead the school in daily prayer and volunteer for service projects. Annual retreats are conducted off campus for each class. The school's foreign travel program sponsors an annual two-week trip.

DELBARTON SCHOOL

Day — Boys Gr 7-12

Morristown, NJ 07960. 230 Mendham Rd. Tel: 973-538-3231. Fax: 973-538-8836.
www.delbarton.org   E-mail: admissions@delbarton.org
Rev. Luke L. Travers, OSB, Head. BA, Columbia Univ, MA, Catholic Univ of America, EdM, Harvard Univ. **David Donovan, Adm.**
- **Col Prep. AP**—Eng Fr Ger Lat Span Calc Stats Comp_Sci Bio Chem Physics US_Hist Econ Psych Art_Hist Studio_Art Music_Theory. **Feat**—Creative_Writing Russ Philos Film.
- **Adm (Gr 7-11):** 114/yr. Appl due: Jan. Accepted: 33%. Yield: 93%. **Tests** IQ Stanford.
- **Enr 542.** B 542. Elem 81. Sec 461. Wh 92%. Hisp 1%. Blk 2%. Asian 5%. Avg class size: 14. **Fac 79.** M 66. F 13. Adv deg: 54%.
- **Grad '04—101. Col—101.** (Columbia 7, Boston Col 7, Duke 6, Villanova 6, Princeton 5, Georgetown 5). Avg SAT: 1380. Alum 3360.
- **Tui '04-'05: Day $20,776** (+$1800). **Aid:** Need 60 ($820,000).
- **Summer:** Acad. Tui Day $1050. Enrich. Tui Day $525. 5 wks.
- Endow $16,563,000. Plant val $16,600,000. Bldgs 5. Class rms 40. Lib 20,000 vols. Sci labs 6. Lang labs 1. Comp labs 5. Art studios 2. Music studios 3. Gyms 2. Fields 6. Courts 6. Pools 1. Greenhouses 1.
- **Est 1939.** Nonprofit. Roman Catholic. Tri (Sept-June). **Assoc** MSA.

Founded on the Delbarton estate of Luther Kountze by Benedictine monks, this preparatory school offers a strict academic curriculum integrated with religious study in the Benedictine tradition. The campus, which includes spacious playing fields, ponds and woodland, is adjacent to Jockey Hollow National Park.

In addition to traditional liberal arts classes, the curriculum offers Advanced Placement courses in all disciplines and such electives as economics and film study. Delbarton provides one-on-one music lessons in many instruments.

Varsity and intramural sports offered are football, soccer, squash, cross-country, wrestling, basketball, lacrosse, ice hockey, swimming, skiing, baseball, track and field, tennis, bowling and golf. The activities program includes student council, school publications and a variety of interest clubs.

MORRISTOWN-BEARD SCHOOL

Day — Coed Gr 6-12

Morristown, NJ 07960. 70 Whippany Rd. Tel: 973-539-3032. Fax: 973-539-1590.
www.mobeard.org   E-mail: admissions@mobeard.org
Alex D. Curtis, Head. BA, Swarthmore College, PhD, Princeton Univ. **Alison Cady, Adm.**
- **Col Prep. AP**—Fr Lat Span Calc Stats Bio Chem Eur_Hist US_Hist Studio_Art. **Feat**—Ecol Genetics Comp_Sci African_Stud Constitutional_Law Philos.
- **Adm (Gr 6-11):** 125/yr. Appl due: Rolling. Accepted: 60%. Yield: 70%. **Tests** CTP_4 ISEE SSAT.
- **Enr 480.** B 240. G 240. Elem 120. Sec 360. Wh 88%. Hisp 2%. Blk 7%. Asian 1%. Other 2%. Avg class size: 12. **Fac 75.** M 23/5. F 39/8. Wh 92%. Hisp 1%. Blk 3%. Asian 4%. Adv deg: 66%.
- **Grad '04—76. Col—74.** (St Lawrence 3, Dickinson 3, Quinnipiac 3, Bucknell 2, Lehigh 2, Rutgers 2). Avg SAT: 1100. Alum 3300.
- **Tui '05-'06: Day $21,765** (+$3000). **Aid:** Merit 3 ($14,000). Need 52 ($850,000).
- **Summer:** Acad Enrich Rec. Arts. Tui Day $1700. 8 wks.
- Endow $8,000,000. Plant val $50,000,000. Bldgs 12. Class rms 51. Lib 14,000 vols. Sci

labs 8. Comp labs 5. Theaters 1. Art studios 3. Music studios 2. Gyms 2. Fields 4. Courts 4. Pools 1.
Est 1891. Nonprofit. Sem (Sept-June). **Assoc** CLS MSA.

Morristown-Beard was formed in 1971 by a merger of the Morristown School for boys and the Beard School for girls. Morristown, which was founded in 1891 by three Harvard graduates—Thomas Q. Browne, Arthur P. Butler and Francis C. Woodman—was long considered a preparatory school for Harvard. Beard was established the same year in Orange by Lucie C. Beard.

The school is located on a 22-acre campus that is bordered on two sides by a county park arboretum. The college preparatory curriculum features Advanced Placement, honors, independent study and developmental programs. Electives in creative writing, speech, ceramics, film studies, photography, journalism and printmaking complement required courses. The math center allows students access to a system of microcomputers. Community service and the completion of a senior project are graduation requirements.

Extracurricular activities include field trips, dramatic and musical productions, publications and several interest clubs. Football, baseball, volleyball, field and ice hockey, golf, tennis, soccer, track, swimming, lacrosse, softball, basketball and cross-country are among the school's athletics. **See Also Page 1214**

THE PECK SCHOOL
Day — Coed Gr K-8

Morristown, NJ 07960. 247 South St. Tel: 973-539-8660. Fax: 973-539-6894.
  www.peckschool.org   E-mail: pdodge@peckschool.org
John J. Kowalik, Head. BA, Williams College, MA, Columbia Univ. **Patricia E. Dodge, Adm.**
  Pre-Prep. **Feat**—Fr Lat Span Computers Studio_Art Music Woodworking.
  Adm: 57/yr. Appl due: Rolling. Accepted: 31%. **Tests** CTP_4 IQ SSAT.
  Enr 306. B 155. G 151. Elem 306. Wh 89%. Blk 4%. Asian 5%. Other 2%. Avg class size: 17. Uniform. **Fac 43.** M 10/1. F 27/5. Wh 96%. Blk 2%. Asian 2%. Adv deg: 46%.
  Grad '04—36. Prep—36. (Newark Acad, Pingry, Lawrenceville, Phillips Exeter, Delbarton, Hotchkiss). Alum 2100.
Tui '05-'06: Day $18,900-22,100. **Aid:** Need 12 ($191,050).
  Endow $9,000,000. Plant val $12,000,000. Bldgs 5. Class rms 30. Lib 7000 vols. Sci labs 2. Comp labs 2. Auds 1. Art studios 1. Music studios 1. Woodworking studios 1. Gyms 2. Fields 3.
  Est 1893. Nonprofit. Tri (Sept-June). **Assoc** MSA.

Founded and for many years conducted by Lorraine T. Peck, the school, upon his retirement in 1944, was incorporated by a group of parents, and the activities and the curriculum broadened.

The school, located on a wooded, 12-acre campus, emphasizes a traditional academic program. The acquisition of skills in English and mathematics, with enrichment in social studies, French, Latin, science, and the fine and performing arts, is stressed. Technology is fully integrated into the curriculum. Physical education and athletics are part of the regular program.

MOUNTAIN LAKES, NJ. (30 mi. WNW of New York, NY) Suburban. Pop: 4256. Alt: 513 ft.

THE WILSON SCHOOL
Day — Coed Gr PS-8

Mountain Lakes, NJ 07046. 271 Boulevard. Tel: 973-334-0181. Fax: 973-334-1852.
www.the-wilson-school.org   E-mail: info@the-wilson-school.org
Carolyn K. Borlo, Head. BA, Lake Erie College, MAT, Colgate Univ, MAEd, New York Univ.
Liz Kovacs, Adm.
Pre-Prep. Feat—Fr Span Computers Studio_Art Music. Supp—Tut.
Adm: 19/yr. Appl due: Rolling. Accepted: 50%.
Enr 75. B 40. G 35. Elem 75. Wh 57%. Hisp 10%. Blk 13%. Asian 20%. Avg class size: 9. Uniform. Fac 22. M 1/1. F 20. Wh 95%. Asian 5%. Adv deg: 27%.
Grad '04—4. Prep—4. (Morristown-Beard, Morris Catholic). Alum 400.
Tui '04-'05: Day $12,400-16,000. Aid: Merit 2 ($5,000). Need 10 ($62,000).
Endow $160,000. Plant val $3,700,000. Bldgs 2. Class rms 43. Lib 2000 vols. Sci labs 1. Comp labs 1. Theaters 1. Art studios 1. Gyms 1. Pools 1.
Est 1909. Nonprofit. Tri (Sept-June). Assoc MSA.

Formerly St. John's School and continuing to be nonsectarian in practice, this school was renamed in 1965 after its founder, Rev. Henry B. Wilson. Consisting of a lower school (grades pre-K-4) and a middle school (grades 5-8), Wilson seeks to meet the specific needs of its students. Teacher teams assigned to each grade meet regularly to review children's progress and determine future class themes.

The sports program features intramural sports and interscholastic competition with nearby schools in volleyball and swimming. Extracurricular activities include drama, publications, skiing, chorus, chime choir and instrumental music. An extended-day program is also available.

MULLICA HILL, NJ. (19 mi. SSW of Philadelphia, PA) Rural. Pop: 1658. Alt: 97 ft.

FRIENDS SCHOOL MULLICA HILL
Day — Coed Gr PS-8

Mullica Hill, NJ 08062. 15 High St. Tel: 856-478-2908. Fax: 856-478-0263.
www.friendsmh.org   E-mail: info@friendsmh.org
Drew Smith, Head. BA, Earlham College. Adrienne Samuel, Adm.
Pre-Prep. Gen Acad. Feat—Fr Span Computers. Supp—Rem_Math Rem_Read.
Adm: 58/yr. Appl due: Rolling. Accepted: 95%. Tests ISEE.
Enr 283. B 144. G 139. Elem 283. Wh 87%. Hisp 2%. Blk 9%. Asian 2%. Avg class size: 16. Fac 40. M 10. F 24/6. Adv deg: 25%.
Grad '04—27. Prep—25. Alum 447.
Tui '03-'04: Day $8750-9740. Aid: Need 50 ($19,000).
Endow $130,000. Plant val $1,320,000. Bldgs 6. Class rms 23. Lib 5000 vols. Sci labs 2. Comp labs 1. Art studios 1. Music studios 1. Gyms 1.
Est 1969. Nonprofit. Religious Society of Friends. Quar (Sept-June). Assoc MSA.

The Friends School provides an academic program based on the traditional concepts of a Quaker education. The curriculum in the lower school is rounded out by classes in art, music, physical education and Spanish. Both Spanish and French are offered in the middle school, and all students receive computer instruction. Interscholastic sports begin in grade 6.

PASSAIC, NJ. (16 mi. NW of New York, NY) Urban. Pop: 67,861. Alt: 57 ft. Area also includes Passiac Park.

COLLEGIATE SCHOOL
Day — Coed Gr PS-12

Passaic Park, NJ 07055. 22 Kent Ct. Tel: 973-777-1714. Fax: 973-777-3255.
  www.collegiatenj.org   E-mail: businessoffice@collegiatenj.org
Angela C. Gibson, Head. BA, Barnard College, MA, Columbia Univ.
  Col Prep. Feat—Mythology Fr Span Stats Anat Comp_Sci Econ Pol_Sci Studio_Art Music. **Supp**—Rev Tut.
  Adm: 45/yr. **Tests** CEEB IQ.
  Enr 170. B 84. G 86. Elem 125. Sec 45. Avg class size: 13. **Fac 19.** M 6. F 13. Adv deg: 42%.
  Grad '04—8. Col—8. (Rutgers, Montclair St, St Thomas Aquinas). Avg SAT: 1150.
  Tui '04-'05: Day $6500-7525 (+$100-200). **Aid:** Need 56 ($238,000).
  Plant val $3,000,000. Bldgs 1. Class rms 28. Lib 5000 vols. Sci labs 1. Lang labs 2. Comp labs 1. Auds 1. Art studios 1. Music studios 1. Gyms 1. Fields 1.
  Est 1895. Nonprofit. Sem (Sept-June). **Assoc** MSA.

This traditional school provides preparation for both secondary schools and colleges. Spanish and French classes commence in prekindergarten. Science, math, English and history are stressed in the intermediate and higher grades. Computer science is offered from grade 1. Collegiate provides both before- and after-school care.

PENNINGTON, NJ. (29 mi. NE of Philadelphia, PA) Suburban. Pop: 2699. Alt: 189 ft.

THE PENNINGTON SCHOOL
Bdg — Coed Gr 7-12; Day — Coed 6-12

Pennington, NJ 08534. 112 W Delaware Ave. Tel: 609-737-6128. Fax: 609-730-1405.
  www.pennington.org   E-mail: admiss@pennington.org
Lyle D. Rigg, Head. BA, Miami Univ (OH), MA, West Texas State Univ, EdM, Harvard Univ.
Diane P. Monteleone, Adm.
  Col Prep. AP—Eng Fr Lat Span Calc Bio Chem Physics Eur_Hist US_Hist Econ US_Govt & Pol Studio_Art Music_Theory. **Feat**—Ger Marine_Biol/Sci Computers Robotics Relig Drama Chorus. **Supp**—ESL LD.
  Adm (Bdg Gr 7-11; Day 6-9): 96/yr. Bdg 33. Day 63. Appl due: Feb. Accepted: 35%.

Tests SSAT.
Enr 443. Elem 90. **Sec** 353. Wh 80%. Hisp 2%. Blk 8%. Asian 10%. Avg class size: 13. **Fac 86.** M 32/6. F 37/11. Wh 96%. Blk 3%. Asian 1%. Adv deg: 46%. In dorms 22.
Grad '04—85. Col—85. (Ithaca 4, Boston U 3, St Joseph's U 3, Lafayette 3, Carnegie Mellon 2, Johns Hopkins 2). Avg SAT: 1150. Alum 3300.
Tui '04-'05: Bdg $32,500 (+$800). **Day $21,900** (+$600). **Aid:** Merit 6 ($132,000). Need 98 ($1,000,000).
Endow $19,000,000. Plant val $11,000,000. Bldgs 18. Dorms 3. Dorm rms 130. Class rms 65. Lib 17,000 vols. Sci labs 4. Comp labs 3. Theaters 2. Art studios 4. Music studios 4. Gyms 2. Fields 5. Tennis courts 5. Pools 1. Tracks 1.
Est 1838. Nonprofit. Methodist. Quar (Sept-June). **Assoc** MSA.

Founded by the Methodist Church, Pennington offers a college preparatory curriculum distinguished by small classes, individual attention, and honors and Advanced Placement courses in all disciplines. An athletic program and extensive extracurricular opportunities for both boys and girls help students develop skills and interests outside the classroom.

In addition to its regular academic program, Pennington maintains a small learning center that prepares students with language-based learning differences for college study. The school's international pupils develop fluency in English through ESL course work. **See Also Page 1224**

POTTERSVILLE, NJ. (41 mi. W of New York, NY) Rural. Pop: 400. Alt: 228 ft.

PURNELL SCHOOL
Bdg and Day — Girls Gr 9-12

Pottersville, NJ 07979. 51 Pottersville Rd, PO Box 500. **Tel:** 908-439-2154.
Fax: 908-439-2090.
www.purnell.org E-mail: info@purnell.org
Jenifer Fox, Head. BA, Univ of Wisconsin-Madison, MA, Middlebury College, MEd, Harvard Univ. **Darlene Snell, Adm.**
Col Prep. Feat—Fr Span Photog Studio_Art Drama Music Dance. **Supp**—ESL LD Tut.
Adm: 58/yr. Bdg 54. Day 4. Appl due: Rolling. Accepted: 95%. Yield: 67%. **Tests** IQ SSAT TOEFL.
Enr 106. G 86/20. **Sec** 106. Wh 73%. Hisp 2%. Blk 11%. Asian 13%. Other 1%. Avg class size: 9. Uniform. **Fac 18.** M 4/1. F 13. Adv deg: 94%. In dorms 6.
Grad '04—20. Col—19. (Savannah Col of Art & Design 2, Am U 1, Guilford 1, Ithaca 1, PA St 1, Temple 1). Alum 959.
Tui '04-'05: Bdg $33,975 (+$1000). **5-Day Bdg $28,500** (+$1000). **Day $23,800** (+$1000). **Aid:** Need 30 ($444,113). Work prgm 10 ($2000).
Endow $5,500,000. Plant val $7,500,000. Bldgs 23. Dorms 3. Dorm rms 59. Class rms 12. Lib 7000 vols. Labs 1. Theaters 1. Art studios 1. Music studios 4. Dance studios 1. Athletic ctrs 1. Fields 3. Courts 5.
Est 1963. Nonprofit. Tri (Sept-June). **Assoc** MSA.

Situated on an 83-acre former farm/estate, Purnell conducts a noncompetitive academic program that incorporates cooperative, experiential learning opportunities and places a particular emphasis on the studio and performing arts. The curriculum is interdisciplinary and highly structured in grades 9 and 10; older students choose electives from among the subjects of English, history/social studies, foreign language, math, science, performing arts and studio arts. The school accepts girls with mild learning disabilities, in addition to those who excel academically. A learning center provides support for all students.

In midwinter, students participate in Project Exploration, a hands-on, project-oriented mini-term during which they work intensely on a project in a field of interest; time is built in for field trips as well. Juniors and seniors have the opportunity to travel for two weeks in a French- or Spanish-speaking country, at which time they take French or Spanish language courses and engage in cultural immersion. Each senior takes part in a compulsory internship, as well as in a public speaking course that culminates in a speech delivered to the student body about her high school experience. Every girl meets with her faculty advisor weekly; advisors then confer weekly to assess student progress.

Each trimester, students choose sports from Purnell's competitive (soccer, tennis, basketball, volleyball, softball, lacrosse and dance) and noncompetitive offerings, of which horseback riding, yoga and kickboxing are options. Leadership opportunities, performing groups and general activities are available, while students also complete required community service projects. **See Also Pages 1310-1**

PRINCETON, NJ. (35 mi. NE of Philadelphia, PA) Suburban. Pop: 14,203. Alt: 290 ft.

AMERICAN BOYCHOIR SCHOOL
Bdg and Day — Boys Gr 5-8

Princeton, NJ 08540. 19 Lambert Dr. Tel: 609-924-5858. Fax: 609-924-5812.
  www.americanboychoir.org   E-mail: shoule@americanboychoir.org
Karl Leopold Reiss, Head. BS, Nazareth College, EdD, Univ of Houston. **Susan Houle, Adm.**
Pre-Prep. Perform_Arts. Feat—Span Chorus Music_Theory. **Supp—**Dev_Read Rev Tut.
Adm (Gr 5-7): 18/yr. Bdg 12. Day 6. Appl due: Rolling. Accepted: 40%. Yield: 50%.
Enr 53. B 35/18. Elem 53. Wh 79%. Hisp 7%. Blk 5%. Am Ind 1%. Asian 8%. Avg class size: 12. Uniform. **Fac 10.** M 2/1. F 5/2. Wh 60%. Hisp 20%. Blk 10%. Asian 10%. Adv deg: 60%. In dorms 1.
Grad '04—20. Prep—16. (Lawrenceville, Woodberry Forest, Blair, Peddie, Walnut Hill, Avon). Alum 1617.
Tui '04-'05: Bdg $19,100-21,995 (+$2000). **Day $15,750-17,185** (+$600). **Aid:** Need 30 ($262,811).
Summer: Enrich Rec. Vocal & Instrumental Music. Tui Bdg $965/2-wk ses. Tui Day $755/2-wk ses. 6 wks.
Endow $6,700,000. Plant val $3,500,000. Bldgs 5. Dorms 2. Dorm rms 21. Class rms 7. Lib 1800 vols. Sci labs 1. Comp labs 1. Music studios 6. Fields 2. Courts 2. Pools 1.
Est 1937. Nonprofit. Tri (Sept-June). **Assoc** MSA.

Founded by Herbert Huffman as Columbus Boychoir School in Columbus, OH, this school moved to Princeton in 1950 and became the American Boychoir School in 1980. The school's program includes professional concert tours with renowned orchestras, conducted domestically and abroad, as well as classroom instruction, physical education and music study. International tours have included trips to Japan, Latvia, Sweden and Denmark.

Boys are admitted on the basis of musical potential, as demonstrated by an audition, and scholastic aptitude. Instruction covers all areas of academics, vocal performance and music theory. Class size is small and academic study is closely supervised, with required evening study and extra help. A special curriculum is designed for those occasions when the choir is on tour, an opportunity that affords many educational and cultural opportunities.

THE HUN SCHOOL OF PRINCETON
Bdg — Coed Gr 9-PG; Day — Coed 6-PG

Princeton, NJ 08540. 176 Edgerstoune Rd. Tel: 609-921-7600. Fax: 609-279-9398.
www.hunschool.org   E-mail: admiss@hunschool.org

James M. Byer, Head. BA, Marietta College, MA, Rider College, EdS, EdD, Nova Univ. **P. Terence Beach, Adm.**

- **Col Prep. AP**—Eng Fr Span Calc Stats Comp_Sci Bio Chem Physics Eur_Hist US_Hist Art_Hist Studio_Art. **Feat**—Lat Anat & Physiol Environ_Sci Marine_Biol/Sci Amer_Stud Econ Govt Ethics Architect Photog Video_Production Music Public_Speak Woodworking. **Supp**—ESL LD Tut.
- **Adm:** 165/yr. Bdg 64. Day 101. Appl due: Jan. Accepted: 35%. **Tests** SSAT TOEFL.
- **Enr 587.** B 87/235. G 60/205. Elem 100. Sec 475. PG 12. Wh 85%. Hisp 2%. Blk 5%. Asian 8%. Avg class size: 13. **Fac 79.** M 37/3. F 30/3. Wh 91%. Hisp 2%. Blk 3%. Asian 2%. Other 2%. Adv deg: 50%. In dorms 14.
- **Grad '04—131. Col—131.** (Gettysburg 5, Georgetown 4, Northwestern 4, Princeton 4, Geo Wash 4, Wash U 3). Avg SAT: 1200. Alum 4700.
- **Tui '04-'05: Bdg $33,145** (+$500). **Day $22,765** (+$500). **Aid:** Merit 3 ($69,000). Need 101 ($2,000,000).
- **Summer:** Acad Enrich Rev. Tui Bdg $4785. Tui Day $1120-1900. Theater. Tui Day $800. ESL. Tui Bdg $5870. Tui Day $2650. 5 wks.
- Endow $6,500,000. Plant val $27,000,000. Bldgs 9. Dorms 3. Dorm rms 96. Class rms 54. Lib 50,000 vols. Sci labs 3. Comp labs 3. Photog labs 2. Aquariums 1. Theaters 1. Art studios 1. Music studios 1. Ceramics & sculpture studios 1. Wood shops 1. Gyms 2. Fields 5. Courts 8. Boathouses 1. Ponds 1.
- **Est 1914.** Nonprofit. Sem (Sept-June). **Assoc** CLS MSA.

The school was established as the Princeton Math School by John Gale Hun, an assistant professor of mathematics at Princeton University, and it originally met in a few small rooms near the university campus. The program's founding goal was to tutor Princeton University undergraduates. By 1925, when the school assumed its present name, it had evolved into a college preparatory institution with boarding facilities. Hun moved to its present location, a 45-acre campus just west of the university, in 1942. Girls were first enrolled as day students in 1971 and as boarders in 1975. The middle school was established in 1973, and grade 6 was added in 1977.

The traditional curriculum includes foreign language and fine arts requirements, electives and interdisciplinary courses. Advanced Placement and honors courses are provided in all disciplines. The fine and performing arts are an integral part of a Hun education; in addition to completing course work in the arts, all students attend arts assemblies during the year. The athletic program includes interscholastic teams, intramural sports, fitness training and a running club. A wide variety of extracurricular organizations and clubs includes drama productions, instrumental and choral music groups, publications, environmental club and math club. Beginning in grade 9, students perform compulsory community service each year.

A program for students of above-average ability having specific, diagnosed learning differences is also available. **See Also Pages 1174-5**

PRINCETON DAY SCHOOL
Day — Coed Gr PS-12

Princeton, NJ 08542. The Great Rd, PO Box 75. Tel: 609-924-6700. Fax: 609-924-8944. www.pds.org E-mail: admissions@pds.org

Judith R. Fox, Head. BS, Cornell Univ, MS, City Univ of New York, EdD, Columbia Univ. **Kelly Dun, Adm.**

    Col Prep. AP—Fr Span Calc Stats Bio Chem Physics US_Hist Comp_Govt & Pol Art_Hist. **Feat**—Creative_Writing Lat Astron Environ_Sci Computers Programming Comp_Relig Philos Architect Ceramics Photog Studio_Art Drama Music Music_Theory Woodworking. **Supp**—Tut.

    Adm (Gr PS-11): 143/yr. Appl due: Jan. **Tests** SSAT.

    Enr 890. B 456. G 434. Elem 517. Sec 373. Wh 80%. Hisp 3%. Blk 7%. Asian 10%. Avg class size: 13. **Fac 130.** M 45/6. F 62/17. Adv deg: 61%.

    Grad '04—94. Col—94. (Lehigh 7, U of PA 5, U of Miami 5, Middlebury 4, Princeton 4, Cornell 3). Avg SAT: 1310. Alum 3450.

    Tui '04-'05: Day $18,300-22,500 (+$400-600). **Aid:** Need 156 ($1,934,100).

    Summer: Acad Enrich Rec. Tui Day $180-850. 1-4 wks.

    Endow $25,000,000. Plant val $50,000,000. Libs 3. Sci labs 8. Lang labs 1. Comp labs 3. Photog labs 1. Sci ctrs 1. Auds 2. Theaters 1. Art studios 3. Music studios 4. Art galleries 1. Planetariums 1. Gyms 3. Fields 10. Courts 8. Rinks 1. Greenhouses 1.

    Est 1899. Nonprofit. Tri (Sept-June). **Assoc** CLS MSA.

PDS traces its origins to the late 1800s, when May Margaret Fine founded a school in Princeton to prepare girls for college. Miss Fine's School was very unusual for its time, as women were not then expected to attend college, and only a small percentage of girls even went to elementary and secondary school. In 1927, a small group of area parents established an elementary school for boys, locating it next to Miss Fine's School. Although this school, Princeton Country Day School and Miss Fine's School fared quite well over the years, the two institutions decided in 1965 to merge and form a coeducational school.

The college preparatory program at PDS, which places particular emphasis on verbal and quantitative reasoning and creative self-expression, includes a variety of courses in literature, languages, history, math, computer and the sciences. Instructors encourage boys and girls to apply their learning skills to problem solving in the traditional subject areas. Notable curricular features are fine arts, music, drama, architecture and religion classes.

Interscholastic sports for boys include football, basketball, ice hockey, soccer, tennis, lacrosse and baseball; among the girls' teams are field and ice hockey, softball, lacrosse, tennis, soccer, volleyball and basketball. The school also maintains coed golf, squash, cross-country, figure skating and fencing squads.

See Also Pages 1230-1

STUART COUNTRY DAY SCHOOL
OF THE SACRED HEART
Day — Boys Gr PS, Girls PS-12

Princeton, NJ 08540. 1200 Stuart Rd. Tel: 609-921-2330. Fax: 609-497-0784.
  www.stuartschool.org E-mail: admissions@stuartschool.org
Sr. Frances de la Chapelle, RSCJ, Head. BA, Maryville College, MA, Catholic Univ of America, MSA, Univ of Notre Dame. **Stephanie Lupero, Adm.**
  Col Prep. AP—Eng Fr Lat Span Calc Comp_Sci Physics Eur_Hist US_Hist Studio_Art. **Feat**—Stats Astron Marine_Biol/Sci Oceanog Intl_Relations Ethics Relig World_Relig Film Photog Visual_Arts Drama Music Music_Hist Debate.
  Adm (Gr PS-11): 87/yr. Appl due: Jan. Accepted: 71%. Yield: 65%. **Tests** SSAT.
  Enr 552. B 22. G 530. Elem 400. Sec 152. Wh 80%. Hisp 2%. Blk 5%. Asian 2%. Other 11%. Avg class size: 15. **Fac 94.** M 5. F 89. Wh 98%. Other 2%. Adv deg: 55%.
  Grad '04—22. Col—21. (U of PA 2, Cornell 1, Harvard 1, Yale 1, Princeton 1, Stanford 1). Avg SAT: 1273. Avg ACT: 27. Alum 954.
  Tui '04-'05: Day $17,500-21,500 (+$100-600). **Aid:** Merit 9 ($59,121). Need 76 ($904,994).
  Endow $5,900,000. Plant val $40,000,000. Bldgs 2. Class rms 50. 2 Libs 24,800 vols. Chapels 1. Sci labs 6. Comp labs 2. Auds 1. Theaters 1. Art studios 5. Music studios 2. Gyms 2. Fields 2. Tennis courts 5.
  Est 1963. Nonprofit. Roman Catholic. Tri (Sept-June). **Assoc** MSA.

Founded as an independent girls' school, Stuart is part of the Network of Sacred Heart schools. The school seeks to integrate a strong academic foundation with an awareness and an appreciation of the religious dimensions of life. Students represent many different faiths.

In the lower school (grades PS-5), emphasis is placed on the acquisition of basic skills. Foreign language study begins in grade 1. The upper school (grades 9-12) includes an increased choice of electives, an international and national exchange program, and Advanced Placement courses. Students participate in community service and cocurricular activities.

Physical education is offered at every level, and middle and upper school teams compete with other schools in tennis, field and ice hockey, basketball, lacrosse, track and field, cross-country and squash. **See Also Page 1320**

RUMSON, NJ. (21 mi. S of New York, NY) Suburban. Pop: 7137. Alt: 15 ft.

RUMSON COUNTRY DAY SCHOOL
Day — Coed Gr PS-8

Rumson, NJ 07760. 35 Bellevue Ave. Tel: 732-842-0527. Fax: 732-758-6528.
  www.rcds.com E-mail: spost@rcds.com
Chad Browning Small, Head. BA, Ohio Wesleyan Univ, MEd, Univ of Virginia, EdD, Seton Hall Univ. **Suzanne R. Post, Adm.**
  Pre-Prep. Feat—Fr Lat Span Computers Filmmaking Music Woodworking. **Supp**—Tut.
  Adm: 71/yr. Appl due: Rolling. Accepted: 48%. Yield: 71%. **Tests** CTP_4.
  Enr 450. B 236. G 214. Elem 450. Wh 91%. Hisp 1%. Blk 2%. Asian 4%. Other 2%. Avg class size: 15. Uniform. **Fac 61.** M 10/1. F 46/4. Wh 98%. Asian 2%. Adv deg: 34%.

Grad '04—46. Prep—24. (Christian Bros-NJ 6, Peddie 3, Hill Sch-PA 3, Ranney 3, Lawrenceville 1, Dalton 1). Alum 1800.
Tui '04-'05: Day $10,700-14,900 (+$100-200). Aid: Need 29 ($205,500).
Endow $5,500,000. Plant val $7,700,000. Bldgs 3. Class rms 42. 3 Libs 14,000 vols. Sci labs 3. Comp labs 1. Observatories 1. Auds 1. Art studios 2. Music studios 2. Shops 1. Gyms 2. Fields 4.
Est 1926. Nonprofit. Tri (Sept-June). Assoc MSA.

Rumson enrolls students from more than 30 communities in the semirural shore area. The school is divided into two administrative departments: the lower school (grades PS-4) is organized by heterogeneous homerooms; the upper school (grades 5-8) is departmentalized, with honors courses available beginning in grade 6. In addition to offering a traditional academic program, Rumson provides instruction in computer literacy, music, drama, art, crafts, woodworking and keyboarding. French language instruction begins in kindergarten, with a choice of French or Spanish in grades 5-8, and a required Latin course in grades 7 and 8.

The school also offers nonacademic minicourses that meet weekly, an interscholastic athletic program for children in grades 5-8, a strong community service program and after-school care for all students.

SADDLE RIVER, NJ. (26 mi. NNW of New York, NY) Suburban. Pop: 3201. Alt: 175 ft.

SADDLE RIVER DAY SCHOOL
Day — Coed Gr K-12

Saddle River, NJ 07458. 147 Chestnut Ridge Rd. Tel: 201-327-4050. Fax: 201-327-6161.
  www.saddleriverday.org   E-mail: dtreue@saddleriverday.org
Donald G. Treue, Adm.
Col Prep. AP—Eng Fr Lat Span Calc Bio Chem Physics Eur_Hist US_Hist Studio_Art. Feat—World_Lit Econ Pol_Sci Psych Sociol World_Affairs Philos Drama Theater_Arts Band Chorus Public_Speak Finance. Supp—Dev_Read Rev Tut.
Adm (Gr K-11): 73/yr. Appl due: Rolling. Accepted: 67%. Tests IQ ISEE SSAT.
Enr 327. B 147. G 180. Elem 178. Sec 149. Wh 82%. Hisp 4%. Blk 6%. Asian 7%. Other 1%. Avg class size: 12. Fac 49. M 21. F 28. Wh 86%. Hisp 6%. Blk 2%. Asian 4%. Other 2%. Adv deg: 67%.
Grad '04—42. Col—42. (Cornell, Haverford, Muhlenberg, Geo Wash, NYU, Wash U). Avg SAT: 1215. Avg ACT: 29. Alum 1483.
Tui '04-'05: Day $14,500-19,884 (+$320). Aid: Merit 14 ($198,911). Need 13 ($98,750).
Summer: Acad Enrich Rec. Tui Day $950. 6 wks.
Endow $2,600,000. Plant val $12,000,000. Bldgs 3. Class rms 32. 2 Libs 30,000 vols. Sci labs 6. Lang labs 1. Comp ctrs 2. Theaters 1. Art studios 2. Music studios 1. Arts ctrs 1. Amphitheaters 1. Gyms 2. Fields 2. Tennis courts 1. Fitness ctrs 1.
Est 1957. Nonprofit. Sem (Sept-June). Assoc CLS MSA.

Serving able, college-bound students from roughly 60 communities in New Jersey and New York State, this coeducational day school offers concentrated work in five major academic areas. Foreign language instruction consists of French and Spanish in grades K-12, and Latin in grades K-6. Handbell choir and concert choir complement course work in the standard subjects. Honors and Advanced Placement courses are offered, and eligible seniors may participate in an independent project in the final term of the year. Small class size and a low student-teacher ratio are maintained.

The extracurricular program includes field trips in the Metropolitan New York City area. In addition, there are publications and recreational and interest clubs. Sports include baseball, soccer, softball, volleyball, basketball, skiing, cross-country, track, fencing, golf and tennis. The school is actively involved in the North Jersey Cultural Council programs, the Academic Decathlon, the New Jersey Math League and the Cum Laude Society. The foreign language department sponsors a cultural trip abroad in the spring and conducts an exchange program with a French school.

SHORT HILLS, NJ. (21 mi. WNW of New York, NY) Suburban. Pop: 19,500. Alt: 600 ft.

FAR BROOK SCHOOL
Day — Coed Gr PS-8

Short Hills, NJ 07078. 52 Great Hills Rd. Tel: 973-379-3442. Fax: 973-379-6740.
  E-mail: ileonard@farbrook.org
Mary Wearn Wiener, Dir. BA, Agnes Scott College. **Iris D. Leonard, Adm.**
  Pre-Prep. **Feat**—Fr Computers Studio_Art Drama Music Creative_Movement Woodworking. **Supp**—Rem_Math Rem_Read Tut.
  Adm (Gr PS-7): 37/yr. Appl due: Rolling. Accepted: 33%. **Tests** CTP_4 ISEE SSAT.
  Enr 218. B 109. G 109. Elem 218. Wh 76%. Hisp 3%. Blk 8%. Asian 13%. Avg class size: 18. **Fac 37.** M 5. F 23/9. Wh 92%. Blk 5%. Asian 3%. Adv deg: 37%.
  Grad '04—19. Prep—12. (Newark Acad, Pingry, Lawrenceville, Phillips Exeter, Hotchkiss, Morristown-Beard). Alum 700.
  Tui '05-'06: Day $15,570-20,000 (+$100-150). **Aid:** Merit 2 ($4000). Need 13 ($191,815).
  Summer: Rec. 7 wks.
  Endow $2,012,000. Plant val $6,859,000. Bldgs 11. Class rms 19. Lib 11,000 vols. Sci labs 2. Lang labs 1. Comp labs 2. Art studios 1. Music studios 4. Woodworking & jewelry studios 1. Gyms 1. Fields 1.
  Est 1948. Nonprofit. (Sept-June). **Assoc** MSA.

A group of parents, led by former director Winifred Moore, subsidized its own independent school in 1948. The curriculum at Far Brook is based on the discipline of great subject matter, humanized and sustained by the arts, with an emphasis placed on choral music and drama.

The lower school program stresses the development of sound basic skills and problem-solving processes. The middle school and junior high programs focus on the history of man, with courses on Ancient Egypt, Greece, Rome, the Middle Ages, the Renaissance and American history. Each grade studies a civilization or historical period extensively, learning about its architecture, music, art, literature, science, agriculture, clothing and everyday life. Science offers a strong foundation of basic concepts and techniques through observation and active participation in experiments. Students also conduct studies utilizing the seven acres of woodland, meadow and swamp on which the school is located.

Every fall, the junior high takes a five-day wilderness trip with faculty to northern New York State. Each June, a Shakespearean play is performed by graduating students. Traditional events at Far Brook include daily morning meetings, Pergolesi's *Stabat Mater,* the Thanksgiving Processional and the Christmas Masque.

See Also Pages 1148-9

SUMMIT, NJ. (22 mi. W of New York, NY) Suburban. Pop: 21,131. Alt: 540 ft.

KENT PLACE SCHOOL
Day — Boys Gr PS, Girls PS-12

Summit, NJ 07902. 42 Norwood Ave. Tel: 908-273-0900. Fax: 908-273-9390.
www.kentplace.org   E-mail: admission@kentplace.org
Susan C. Bosland, Head. BA, Denison Univ, MA, Columbia Univ. **Nancy J. Humick, Adm.**
  Col Prep. AP—Eng Fr Lat Span Calc Stats Comp_Sci Bio Chem Physics Eur_Hist US_Hist Econ Art_Hist Studio_Art. **Feat**—British_Lit Creative_Writing Russ_Lit Anat & Physiol Programming Web_Design Women's_Stud Drama Music_Hist Music_Theory Dance.
  Adm (Gr PS-11): 107/yr. Appl due: Feb. **Tests** ISEE SSAT.
  Enr 632. B 20. G 612. Elem 380. Sec 252. Wh 78%. Hisp 3%. Blk 11%. Asian 8%. **Fac 85.** M 6/1. F 63/15. Wh 91%. Hisp 4%. Blk 2%. Asian 1%. Other 2%. Adv deg: 70%.
  Grad '04—48. Col—48. (Brown 6, Boston Col 6, Columbia 6, Geo Wash 6, U of PA 6, Yale 5). Avg SAT: 1283. Alum 3000.
  Tui '04-'05: Day $7568-22,808 (+$350-500).
  Endow $15,000,000. Plant val $14,000,000. Bldgs 6. Class rms 48. Lib 17,000 vols. Labs 6. Auds 1. Theaters 1. Art studios 2. Music studios 2. Dance studios 1. Fields 2. Courts 5. Field houses 1.
  Est 1894. Nonprofit. Tri (Sept-June). **Assoc** CLS MSA.

This college preparatory school is located on a suburban, 26-acre campus, with many playing fields, embracing both half-timbered Old English and modern buildings. Students select from a broad range of academic offerings, with opportunities in more than a dozen areas affording qualified girls Advanced Placement credit. Activities emphasize publications, art, dramatics, music, language clubs, service work and a student-faculty senate.

Athletics include field hockey, lacrosse, volleyball, basketball, track, swimming, softball, soccer and tennis. Modern dance is also available. The school's location enables pupils to take advantage of the museums, theaters and other cultural facilities of nearby New York City.

OAK KNOLL SCHOOL OF THE HOLY CHILD
Day — Boys Gr K-6, Girls K-12

Summit, NJ 07901. 44 Blackburn Rd. Tel: 908-522-8100. Fax: 908-277-1838.

www.oakknoll.org   E-mail: admissions@oakknoll.org
Timothy J. Saburn, Head. BA, St Lawrence Univ, EdM, Harvard Univ. **Suzanne Kimm Lewis, Adm.**
Col Prep. Feat—Writing Fr Span Comp_Sci Studio_Art Drama Music Dance.
Adm (Gr K-12): 102/yr. Appl due: Jan. **Tests** CTP_4 ISEE SSAT.
Enr 549. B 121. G 428. Elem 314. Sec 235. Wh 87%. Hisp 3%. Blk 5%. Asian 4%. Other 1%. Avg class size: 15. Uniform. **Fac 68.** Adv deg: 44%.
Grad '04—60. Col—60. (Georgetown 4, Villanova 4, Geo Wash 4, Boston Col 3, Colgate 3, NYU 3). Alum 2000.
Tui '04-'05: Day $16,960-20,990. Aid: Need ($913,000).
Summer: Ages 3-14. Rec. 2-8 wks.
Endow $7,500,000. Plant val $11,370,000. Bldgs 4.
Est 1924. Nonprofit. Roman Catholic. Tri (Sept-June). **Assoc** CLS MSA.

Oak Knoll is a network of schools operated by the Sisters of the Holy Child Jesus, an order founded by Cornelia Connelly in 1846. The lower school (grades K-6) is coeducational, while the upper school (grades 7-12) enrolls girls only.

The lower school features an innovative teaching program based on small groups and learning centers, with an enrichment program that includes computers, music, art, drama, dance and Afterschool Adventures. The upper school's curriculum, which focuses on the liberal arts in a value-centered environment, provides a rigorous college preparatory program.

Student government, clubs and competitive sports constitute the extracurricular activities. The campus ministry program offers a volunteer service program.

TINTON FALLS, NJ. (28 mi. SSW of New York, NY) Suburban. Pop: 15,053. Alt: 45 ft.

RANNEY SCHOOL
Day — Coed Gr PS-12

Tinton Falls, NJ 07724. 235 Hope Rd. Tel: 732-542-4777. Fax: 732-460-1078.
www.ranneyschool.org   E-mail: hrudisi@ranneyschool.com
Lawrence S. Sykoff, Head. BBA, City Univ of New York, MEd, EdD, Univ of San Diego. **Heather Rudisi, Adm.**
Col Prep. AP—Eng Fr Span Calc Comp_Sci Bio Chem Physics Eur_Hist Econ Art_Hist Studio_Art. **Feat**—Lat Stats Environ_Sci Web_Design British_Hist Lat-Amer_Hist Psych Govt & Pol Ceramics Music.
Adm: 135/yr. Appl due: Rolling.
Enr 740. B 386. G 354. Elem 524. Sec 216. Wh 67%. Hisp 2%. Blk 3%. Asian 28%. Avg class size: 15. **Fac 85.** Adv deg: 40%.
Grad '04—44. Col—44. (Geo Wash, Barnard, Duke, U of PA, NYU, Cornell). Avg SAT: 1289. Alum 1200.
Tui '04-'05: Day $9900-19,550 (+$100-850).
Summer: Enrich. ESL. 6 wks. Rec. 4-8 wks.
Plant val $18,000,000. Bldgs 11. Class rms 96. 2 Libs 21,500 vols. Sci labs 5. Lang labs 1. Comp labs 3. Theaters 1. Art studios 3. Music studios 2. Gyms 2. Fields 6. Tennis courts 5. Pools 1. Weight rms 1. Playgrounds 1.
Est 1960. Nonprofit. (Sept-June). **Assoc** CLS MSA.

With a strong preparatory course, Ranney places particular emphasis upon the development of reading, composition and effective study skills. The 60-acre campus, situated on a former country estate, has ample facilities for a full sports program. Regular preparatory work, starting as early as grade 7, has produced notable test results on College Board examinations and the National Merit Scholarship Test.

Publications, forensics, drama and chess are among the extracurricular activities. An optional after-school program of athletic and cultural activities is available to students beginning in grade 3. **See Also Page 1234**

NEW YORK

ALBANY, NY. (84 mi. NW of Hartford, CT; 138 mi. N of New York, NY) Urban. Pop: 95,658. Alt: to 30 ft.

THE ALBANY ACADEMY
Bdg — Boys Gr 8-12; Day — Boys PS-PG, Girls PS

Albany, NY 12208. 135 Academy Rd. Tel: 518-465-1461. Fax: 518-465-0989.
  www.albany-academy.org   E-mail: admissions@albany-academy.org
Caroline B. Mason, Head. BA, Denison Univ, MA, Case Western Reserve Univ. **Christine Amitrano, Adm.**
  Col Prep. AP—Eng Fr Lat Span Calc Bio Chem Physics Eur_Hist US_Hist US_Govt & Pol Studio_Art. **Feat**—Anat & Physiol Astron Computers Civil_War Econ Psych Philos Ceramics Drawing Photog Theater Music Music_Theory Dance. **Supp**—Rem_Math Rem_Read Tut.
  Adm: 86/yr. Appl due: Rolling. Accepted: 73%. Yield: 83%. **Tests** ISEE.
  Enr 365. Elem 167. Sec 191. PG 7. Avg class size: 12. Uniform. **Fac 44.** M 20/1. F 21/2. Adv deg: 52%. In dorms 1.
  Grad '04—64. Col—64. (Rensselaer Polytech, Syracuse, Middlebury, U of MA-Amherst, U of Richmond, Bentley). Avg SAT: 1211. Alum 3200.
  Tui '04-'05: Bdg $21,500-23,500. Day $10,000-16,500 (+$900). **Aid:** Need 106 ($549,337). Work prgm 7 ($3500).
  Summer: Rec. 12 wks.
  Endow $5,000,000. Plant val $7,500,000. Bldgs 3. Class rms 35. 2 Libs 17,000 vols. Sci labs 3. Lang labs 1. Comp labs 2. Auds 1. Theaters 1. Art studios 2. Music studios 2. Dance studios 1. Gyms 2. Fields 5. Courts 4. Pools 1. Rinks 1. Weight rms 1.
  Est 1813. Nonprofit. Tri (Sept-June). **Assoc** CLS.

This country day school's curriculum provides a full complement of Advanced Placement courses and electives. A coordinate program with the Albany Academy for Girls, which is located across the street, allows upper school students (grades 9-12) at both schools to take courses on either campus, thus providing a broader range of academic offerings and the opportunity to experience coeducational education. All students in grades 9-12 participate in a leadership program. Extracurricular activities such as athletics, drama, publications and student government are available.

A small boarding program at the academy can accommodate up to 12 older boys who come from outside the Capital District.

ALBANY ACADEMY FOR GIRLS
Day — Girls Gr PS-12

Albany, NY 12208. 140 Academy Rd. Tel: 518-463-2201. Fax: 518-463-5096.
  www.albanyacademyforgirls.org   E-mail: carterl@albanyacademyforgirls.org
Caroline B. Mason, Head. BA, Denison Univ, MA, Case Western Reserve Univ. **Lauren B. Carter, Adm.**
  Col Prep. AP—Eng Fr Lat Span Calc Comp_Sci Bio Chem Physics Eur_Hist US_Hist

US_Govt & Pol Studio_Art. **Feat**—Astrophysics Drama Music Dance. **Supp**—Rev Tut.
Adm: 68/yr. Appl due: Rolling. Accepted: 68%. **Tests** CEEB CTP_4 ISEE SSAT.
Enr 332. G 332. Elem 186. Sec 146. Avg class size: 15. Uniform. **Fac 54.** M 7/2. F 40/5. Adv deg: 79%.
Grad '04—36. Col—36. (Boston Col, Barnard, Boston U, Carnegie Mellon, Cornell, Stanford). Alum 1600.
Tui '04-'05: Day $10,000-16,500. Aid: Merit 3 ($9000). Need 80 ($360,000).
Summer: Acad Enrich. 10 wks.
Endow $5,500,000. Plant val $7,000,000. Bldgs 1. Class rms 31. Lib 14,000 vols. Sci labs 5. Comp labs 3. Art studios 2. Music studios 1. Dance studios 2. Media ctrs 1. Gyms 2. Fields 3. Squash courts 2. Tracks 1.
Est 1814. Nonprofit. Tri (Sept-June). **Assoc** CLS.

Founded as Albany Female Academy, AAG, the oldest continuously operating girls' school in the country, sends graduates to leading colleges. In 1959, the school moved to its present location, where a multipurpose, contemporary building and 22 wooded acres provide full facilities for the college preparatory program. Renovations and new construction have since augmented the plant.

The lower school curriculum is enriched by a special science program and offerings in music, art, drama, dance, computer, library, physical education, Spanish and French. The middle school emphasizes experiential learning and the development of skills necessary for success in the upper school's college preparatory program. The traditional upper school program features Advanced Placement in the major disciplines, with a variety of electives and opportunities for internships and independent study also provided. There is extensive cross enrollment with the nearby Albany Academy. Many extracurricular activities are available, and interscholastic sports include soccer, field hockey, volleyball, basketball, softball, tennis, lacrosse, track and swimming.

DOANE STUART SCHOOL
Day — Coed Gr PS-12

Albany, NY 12202. 799 S Pearl St. Tel: 518-465-5222. Fax: 518-465-5230.
www.doanestuart.org   E-mail: contact@doanestuart.org
Richard D. Enemark, Head. BA, Colgate Univ, MA, Univ of Vermont, MPhil, PhD, Columbia Univ. **Tonya Drewniak, Adm.**
Col Prep. **AP**—Eng Fr Span Bio US_Hist Econ US_Govt & Pol Studio_Art. **Feat**—Ger_Lit Dickens Austen Tolstoy African-Amer_Hist Women's_Hist Psych Sociol Ethics Relig Buddhism Art_Hist Fine_Arts. **Supp**—Rev.
Adm: 63/yr. Appl due: Rolling. Accepted: 74%. Yield: 72%. **Tests** CTP_4 DAT ISEE SSAT.
Enr 265. B 134. G 131. Elem 165. Sec 100. Wh 87%. Hisp 1%. Blk 9%. Asian 2%. Other 1%. Avg class size: 14. Uniform. **Fac 41.** M 14/3. F 20/4. Wh 99%. Hisp 1%. Adv deg: 53%.
Grad '04—12. Col—12. (Brown, U of Chicago, Hamilton, Kenyon, CT Col, USC). Avg SAT: 1274. Alum 2192.
Tui '04-'05: Day $10,000-16,000 (+$350). **Aid:** Need 98 ($622,491).
Summer: Gr PS-6. Rec. Tui Day $200/wk. 7 wks.
Endow $1,000,000. Bldgs 3. Class rms 24. 2 Libs 24,000 vols. Sci labs 3. Comp labs 3. Photog labs 2. Auds 1. Theaters 1. Art studios 1. Music studios 2. Gyms 2. Fields 3. Courts 4.
Est 1852. Nonprofit. (Sept-June). **Assoc** CLS.

Doane Stuart was established upon the 1975 merger of Kenwood Academy, founded in 1852 by the Religious of the Sacred Heart, and Saint Agnes School, founded in 1870 by the Episcopal diocese of Albany. The resulting institution represents the only successful merger between Catholic and Protestant private schools. Today, the school enrolls pupils of all faiths and backgrounds. The 80-acre campus overlooks the Hudson River at the southern edge of Albany.

The curriculum is college preparatory, with a broad range of electives. There are opportunities in grades 11 and 12 for participation in classes at the University at Albany (State University of New York) and in an exchange program through the Network of Sacred Heart Schools in other states and countries. Students may also pursue independent study and internship or research options. A variety of team and individual sports is available at both intramural and interscholastic levels.

AMENIA, NY. (45 mi. W of Hartford, CT; 84 mi. NNE of New York, NY) Suburban. Pop: 5195. Alt: 573 ft.

THE KILDONAN SCHOOL
Bdg — Coed Gr 6-PG; Day — Coed 2-PG

Amenia, NY 12501. 425 Morse Hill Rd. Tel: 845-373-8111. Fax: 845-373-9793.
www.kildonan.org   E-mail: admissions@kildonan.org

Ronald A. Wilson, Head. BS, State Univ of New York-Brockport, MS, Western Connecticut State Univ. **Bonnie A. Wilson, Adm.**

LD. Feat—Computers Studio_Art. **Supp**—Tut.

Adm: 54/yr. Appl due: Rolling.

Enr 142. Elem 65. Sec 77. Wh 96%. Hisp 2%. Blk 2%. Avg class size: 7. **Fac 59.** M 23. F 35/1. Wh 98%. Blk 2%. Adv deg: 20%. In dorms 24.

Grad '04—16. **Col**—15. (Mitchell, Dean, Davis & Elkins, Syracuse). Alum 1037.

Tui '04-'05: Bdg $40,800 (+$1500). **5-Day Bdg $38,800** (+$1500). **Day $23,000-28,000** (+$500). **Aid:** Need 24 ($117,500).

Summer: Ages 8-16. Acad Rec. Tui Bdg $7300. Tui Day $3725-5725. 6 wks.

Endow $636,000. Plant val $1,500,000. Bldgs 18. Dorms 3. Dorm rms 93. Class rms 21. Lib 14,975 vols. Sci labs 1. Comp labs 1. Art studios 2. Fields 4. Courts 3. Riding rings 1. Stables 1.

Est 1969. Nonprofit. Tri (Sept-June).

The school primarily serves students of normal intelligence who have learning difficulties arising from dyslexia. Although enrollment was limited to boys after the first year of operation, Kildonan began admitting girls as day students in 1985, then became fully coeducational in 1991. The teaching program, which is highly individualized, provides intensive remedial work pertaining to basic English and mathematical skills. The Orton-Gillingham approach is used. Typing and word processing are part of the school's program.

Located on a 450-acre estate, the school offers interscholastic sports, work projects, art, woodworking, riding, skiing and other outdoor activities. Dunnabeck, a remedial and recreational summer program, operates on the Kildonan campus.

See Also Pages 1364-5

BEDFORD, NY. (40 mi. NNE of New York, NY) Suburban. Pop: 16,906. Alt: 200 ft.

RIPPOWAM CISQUA SCHOOL
Day — Coed Gr PS-9

Bedford, NY 10506. 439 Cantitoe Rd, PO Box 488. Tel: 914-234-3674. Fax: 914-234-6751.
www.rcsny.org   E-mail: beth_skudder@rcsny.org

Eileen F. Lambert, Head. BA, Bowdoin College, MA, Univ of Cincinnati. **Elizabeth Skudder & Ashley Harrington, Adms.**

Pre-Prep. Feat—Fr Lat Span Computers Studio_Art Drama Music. Supp—Dev_Read Makeup Tut.

Adm: 85/yr. Appl due: Jan. Tests ISEE.

Enr 571. B 284. G 287. Elem 548. Sec 23. Wh 93%. Hisp 1%. Blk 3%. Asian 3%. Avg class size: 16. Uniform. Fac 98. M 24/1. F 64/9. Adv deg: 54%.

Grad '04—21. Prep—17. (Hackley, Masters Sch-NY, Hotchkiss, Taft, Westminster Sch-CT, Greenwich Acad). Alum 2000.

Tui '04-'05: Day $20,300-23,950. Aid: Need 74 ($1,200,000).

Summer: Rec. Tui Day $800/2-wk ses. 6 wks.

Endow $7,900,000. Plant val $3,800,000. Bldgs 4. Class rms 39. 2 Libs 25,200 vols. Sci labs 5. Comp labs 3. Theaters 2. Art studios 4. Music studios 4. Gyms 3. Fields 8.

Est 1917. Nonprofit. Tri (Sept-June).

Resulting from a 1973 merger of the Bedford-Rippowam School and the Cisqua School, this country day school prepares graduates for secondary boarding, day and public schools.

The curriculum incorporates both traditional and hands-on educational programs. RCS offers allied arts and computer science programs in grades K-9, a Spanish curriculum that begins in kindergarten, a cross-cultural approach to humanities, social studies and foreign language beginning in the middle school years, and a portfolio and thesis project in grade 9. Community service and parental involvement are important aspects of the program. The Cisqua campus (325 W. Patent Rd., Mount Kisco 10549) accommodates children in grades PS-4, while grades 5-9 are located on the Rippowam campus in Bedford.

BRONX, NY. Urban. Pop: 1,332,650. Alt: 70 ft. Area also includes Riverdale.

ETHICAL CULTURE FIELDSTON SCHOOL
Day — Coed Gr PS-12

Riverdale, NY 10471. Fieldston Rd. Tel: 718-329-7300. Fax: 718-329-7305.
www.ecfs.org   E-mail: admissions_fieldston@ecfs.org

Joseph P. Healey, Head. PhL, PhB, Pontifical Gregorian Univ (Italy), STB, MA, Catholic Univ of America, PhD, Harvard Univ. **Taisha M. Thompson, Rita McRedmond & Soraya Barth, Adms.**

Col Prep. Feat—British_Lit Poetry Shakespeare African-Amer_Lit Fr Greek Lat Span Computers Chin_Hist NYC_Hist African_Stud Ethics Art_Hist Studio_Art Drama

Music Dance Journ. **Supp**—Dev_Read LD Makeup Tut.
Adm: 187/yr. Appl due: Nov. Accepted: 17%. **Tests** ISEE SSAT.
Enr 1611. B 810. G 801. Elem 1093. Sec 518. Wh 80%. Hisp 5%. Blk 10%. Asian 5%. Avg class size: 18. **Fac 231.** M 59/16. F 117/39. Adv deg: 63%.
Grad '04—128. Col—119. (Wesleyan U, U of WI-Madison, Yale, Cornell, U of PA, Wash U). Avg SAT: 1364. Alum 6500.
Tui '03-'04: Day $22,600-25,300 (+$600). **Aid:** Need 340 ($4,556,136).
Summer: Enrich Rec. Gr PS-8. Tui Day $360-750. 1-2 wks. Outdoor Ed. Ages 5-12. Tui Day $2900. 6 wks. Sports. Tui Day $340. 2 wks.
Endow $45,000,000. Lib 60,000 vols. Theaters 2. Art studios 5. Music studios 5. Dance studios 1. Photog studios 1. Gyms 5. Fields 3. Tennis courts 4. Pools 1.
Est 1878. Nonprofit. Sem (Sept-June).

Since its establishment by Felix Adler, this school has provided an ethnically diverse student body with an enriched curriculum that integrates academics, the arts and sciences, and ethical values.

Fieldston (grades 7-12), located in the Riverdale section of the Bronx, offers many courses in the visual and performing arts to supplement academic college preparation. Community service is required for graduation. Extracurricular activities include league sports, the performing arts and student publications. Graduates enter leading colleges throughout the country.

Both elementary facilities, Fieldston Lower, which shares the 18-acre, wooded grounds in Riverdale, and Ethical Culture, located at 33 Central Park West in midtown Manhattan, offer students in grades pre-K-6 a program that focuses on building basic skills within a modified core curriculum. Specialists augment the program with laboratory science, computer, ethics, art, music, library, social studies workshop, wood shop and drama.

FORDHAM PREPARATORY SCHOOL
Day — Boys Gr 9-12

Bronx, NY 10458. E Fordham Rd. Tel: 718-367-7500. Fax: 718-367-7598.
www.fordhamprep.org   E-mail: admissions@fordhamprep.org
Rev. Kenneth J. Boller, SJ, Pres. BA, Fordham Univ, MA, New York Univ, MDiv, Woodstock College. **Robert J. Gomprecht, Prin.** BA, MA, Fordham Univ. **Christopher D. Lauber, Adm.**
Col Prep. AP—Eng Lat Span Calc Stats Bio Chem Physics Eur_Hist US_Hist Econ US_Govt & Pol Art_Hist Studio_Art. **Feat**—Ger Greek Ital Programming Relig Music Debate.
Adm (Gr 9-11): 237/yr. Appl due: Dec. Accepted: 50%. **Tests** HSPT ISEE SSAT TACHS.
Enr 905. B 905. Sec 905. Wh 71%. Hisp 14%. Blk 6%. Asian 5%. Other 4%. Avg class size: 24. **Fac 97.** M 74/7. F 16. Adv deg: 72%.
Grad '04—211. Col—208. (Fordham 17, Manhattan Col 10, NYU 9, Boston U 7, Loyola Col 7, SUNY-Binghamton 6). Avg SAT: 1165. Alum 9000.
Tui '04-'05: Day $9730 (+$300). **Aid:** Merit 131 ($300,000). Need 258 ($850,000).
Endow $10,000,000. Plant val $12,000,000. Bldgs 2. Class rms 35. Lib 10,000 vols. Sci labs 5. Lang labs 1. Comp ctrs 1. Theater/auds 1. Fields 3. Courts 9. Pools 1.
Est 1841. Nonprofit. Roman Catholic. Quar (Sept-May). **Assoc** MSA.

This Jesuit preparatory school, located on a five-acre portion of the Fordham University campus, uses some of the university's facilities.

The academic program consists of a flexible system of scheduling that allows boys to work at different rates. Beginning in grade 9, Fordham Prep conducts honors and Advanced Placement courses, and all freshmen take Latin and biology. A well-equipped computer center supports the technology program. The school offers a full complement of activities and athletics, in addition to a four-year service program.   **See Also Page 1335**

HORACE MANN SCHOOL

Day — Coed Gr PS-12

Riverdale, NY 10471. 231 W 246th St. Tel: 718-432-4100. Fax: 718-432-3610.
 www.horacemann.org   E-mail: admissions@horacemann.org
Dr. Thomas M. Kelly, Head. BA, Fairfield Univ, MEd, MA, MPhil, PhD, Columbia Univ. **Lisa J. Moreira, Adm.**
- **Col Prep. AP**—Eng Fr Ger Lat Span Calc Bio Chem Physics Eur_Hist US_Hist World_Hist Music_Theory. **Feat**—Greek Ital Japan Russ Astron Govt Drama Dance. **Supp**—Rev Tut.
- **Adm:** 220/yr. Appl due: Dec. **Tests** ISEE SSAT.
- **Enr 1740.** Elem 1035. Sec 705. Wh 77%. Hisp 3%. Blk 6%. Asian 7%. Other 7%. Avg class size: 19. **Fac 245.** M 87. F 158.
- **Grad '04—166. Col—166.** (Columbia, Harvard, Cornell, Yale, Princeton, U of PA). Alum 7000.
- **Tui '03-'04:** Day $17,500-24,500 (+$50-450). **Aid:** Need 326 ($4,950,000).
- **Summer:** Acad Enrich Rev Rem Rec. Tui Day $2300. 6 wks.
- Endow $67,000,000. Plant val $88,700,000. Bldgs 23. Class rms 95. Lib 45,000 vols. Sci labs 7. Lang labs 1. Comp labs 4. Auds 1. Theaters 1. Art studios 8. Music studios 4. Dance studios 1. Gyms 3. Fields 4. Courts 8. Pools 1.
- **Est 1887.** Nonprofit. Tri (Sept-May). **Assoc** CLS MSA.

Horace Mann School was established by Nicholas Murray Butler as an experimental and demonstration unit of Teachers College, Columbia University. The coeducational school included all grades from kindergarten through high school until 1914, at which time Horace Mann School for Boys was established in its present location in suburban Riverdale; it was among the first country day schools in the United States. The kindergarten, elementary and girls' school continued at Teachers College until 1946 and, in that same year, the boys' school received its own charter from the state board of regents and became an independent institution. In 1969, Horace Mann again became a coeducational school beginning with the youngest level. The 18-acre middle (grades 6-8) and upper (grades 9-12) division campus overlooks Van Cortlandt Park. Across the street, at 4440 Tibbett Ave., the lower school houses grades K-5, and the nursery school (nursery, prekindergarten and kindergarten) occupies a historic building at 55 E. 90th St., New York 10128.

Horace Mann's program is strongly rooted in the liberal arts tradition, with AP courses, a wide variety of electives, interdisciplinary offerings, and options such as independent study and study abroad. Foreign language instruction begins in grade 1 with French and Spanish, and upper division students choose from eight languages, among them Japanese and Russian. Middle and upper division course requirements include classes in the visual and performing arts, computer science and community service; children in the nursery and lower division also participate in activities in these areas. As they progress, pupils have an increasing degree of choice in their course options, including the chance to undertake an independent research seminar. Students design these research projects, which address subjects not included in the curriculum or provide further study of a topic covered in a previous course.

Frequent outings and field trips are arranged for the youngest students. Their older counterparts participate in clubs relating to such subjects as skiing, Amnesty International, Model UN and Shakespeare. HM's students also have access to minority organizations; service groups; a weekly newspaper; and several magazines, journals and reviews. Opportunities for musical and artistic expression include numerous performance bands, glee club and orchestra, four major theatrical productions annually, private instrumental music instruction, and a full schedule of visual arts festivals and exhibits. Starting in grade 7, boys and girls may participate in sports competition on interscholastic teams. Beginning in grade 2, students partake of a variety of conservation, science and outdoor living experiences at the 96-acre John Dorr Nature Laboratory in Washington, CT.

RIVERDALE COUNTRY SCHOOL
Day — Coed Gr PS-12

Riverdale, NY 10471. 5250 Fieldston Rd. Tel: 718-549-8810. Fax: 718-519-2795. www.riverdale.edu

John R. Johnson, Head. AB, MA, PhD, Univ of California-Los Angeles. **Ridie Markenson, Upper & Middle Sch Adm; Sarah M. Lafferty, Lower Sch Adm.**

    Col Prep. AP—Eng Fr Lat Span Calc Stats Bio Chem Physics Eur_Hist Comp_Govt & Pol Psych US_Govt & Pol Art_Hist Music_Theory. **Feat**—Shakespeare African-Amer_Lit Japan Anat & Physiol Biophysics Comp_Sci Film Photog Theater.

    Adm (Gr PS-11): 162/yr. Appl due: Dec. Accepted: 21%. **Tests** ISEE SSAT.

    Enr 1059. B 545. G 514. Elem 591. Sec 468. Avg class size: 16. **Fac 139.** M 55. F 84. Adv deg: 71%.

    Grad '04—107. Col—107. (Yale 6, Brown 5, Columbia 4, Wash U 4, Williams 4). Alum 4995.

    Tui '04-'05: Day $22,470-27,175 (+$2000). **Aid:** Need 209 ($3,757,000).

    Endow $24,328,000. Plant val $37,229,000. Bldgs 13. Class rms 76. 2 Libs 35,000 vols. Sci labs 8. Lang labs 1. Comp labs 6. Observatories 1. Auds 2. Theaters 2. Art studios 8. Music studios 9. Arts ctrs 1. Gyms 2. Fields 4. Courts 8. Pools 1.

    Est 1907. Nonprofit. Sem (Sept-June). **Assoc** CLS.

Established by Dr. Frank S. Hackett, this was among the earliest country day schools to be located near a metropolitan center. Through his vision and drive, the school quickly gained an enviable reputation. In 1972, the school became coeducational when the boys' and girls' divisions merged. In 1985, the school was significantly reorganized with the consolidation of the lower, middle and upper schools into two divisions—lower (grades pre-K-6) and upper (grades 7-12)—on separate campuses. The school was restructured in fall 2005 into three divisions, with the lower school (grades pre-K-5) on one campus and the middle school (grades 6-8) and upper school (grades 9-12) on another.

Riverdale's traditional college preparatory curriculum is characterized by unusual breadth in Advanced Placement courses, languages, the arts and interdisciplinary studies. A summer day camp operates during July and August. The school also sponsors Summerbridge at Riverdale, a year-round academic program at which college and high school students work with sixth and seventh graders from public and parochial schools.

The full extracurricular program includes art, drama, debate, several school publications, an orchestra and community service opportunities. The sports program is both intramural and interscholastic, with competition provided in football, soccer, basketball, volleyball, wrestling, fencing, swimming, track, tennis, gymnastics, field hockey, lacrosse, cross-country, baseball, softball and golf.

BROOKLYN, NY. Urban. Pop: 2,465,326. Alt: to 109 ft.

BERKELEY CARROLL SCHOOL
Day — Coed Gr PS-12

Brooklyn, NY 11217. 181 Lincoln Pl. Tel: 718-789-6060. Fax: 718-398-3640.
www.berkeleycarroll.org   E-mail: bcs@berkeleycarroll.org

Richard F. Barter, Head. BA, Univ of Maine-Orono, MAT, PhD, Johns Hopkins Univ. **Christopher Weeks, Upper & Middle Sch Adm; Pamela Cunningham, Lower Sch Adm.**

Col Prep. AP—Eng Fr Span Calc Stats Bio Chem Physics Eur_Hist US_Hist Econ Art_Hist Studio_Art. Feat—Lib_Skills Lat Computers Drama Music Dance.

Adm: 110/yr. Appl due: Dec. Tests ISEE.

Enr 785. Wh 77%. Hisp 5%. Blk 13%. Asian 5%. Avg class size: 16. **Fac 110.** M 38/2. F 66/4. Adv deg: 82%.

Grad '04—49. Col—49. (NYU 3, Brown 2, Barnard 2, Brandeis 2, Wesleyan U 2, Syracuse 2). Alum 1100.

Tui '04-'05: Day $11,000-22,950 (+$100-890).

Summer: Enrich Rec. Arts. Tui Day $2000. 5 wks.

Endow $2,000,000. Plant val $9,000,000. Bldgs 5. Class rms 45. 3 Libs 35,000 vols. Sci labs 2. Comp labs 3. Auds 1. Theaters 1. Art studios 3. Music studios 3. Dance studios 2. Gyms 3. Courts 3. Pools 1.

Est 1982. Nonprofit. Sem (Sept-June). **Assoc** CLS MSA.

The school resulted from a merger between the Carroll Street School (founded in 1966) and the Berkeley Institute (founded in 1886). Located in Brooklyn's historic Park Slope section, Berkeley Carroll's campus consists of two building complexes housing its lower school (grades PS-4) at 701 Carroll St., 11215, and its middle and upper schools (grades 5-12) at 181 Lincoln Pl. The school also operates a childcare center at 515 6th St., 11215.

The comprehensive curriculum includes a full program of Advanced Placement courses, independent study and internships, as well as electives in creative writing, studio art and computer science. There are direct cultural and academic exchanges with secondary schools in France and Spain. Computer proficiency and a senior internship are required for graduation. Athletics, community service, interest clubs, theater, chorus, government and school publications complement academic offerings. **See Also Page 1120**

PACKER COLLEGIATE INSTITUTE
Day — Coed Gr PS-12

Brooklyn, NY 11201. 170 Joralemon St. Tel: 718-875-6644. Fax: 718-875-1363.
www.packer.edu   E-mail: mnespole@packer.edu
Bruce Dennis, Head. BA, MA, City Univ of New York. **Kristy Foster, Upper & Middle Sch Adm; Kati Crowley, Lower Sch & PS Adm.**

Col Prep. AP—Eng Fr Lat Span Calc Stats Comp_Sci Bio Physics Eur_Hist US_Hist US_Govt & Pol Art_Hist Studio_Art. **Feat**—Mandarin Anat & Physiol Astron Drama Band Chorus Music Orchestra Dance.

Adm: 134/yr. Appl due: Dec. Accepted: 24%. **Tests** CTP_4 ISEE SSAT.

Enr 935. B 418. G 517. Elem 635. Sec 300. Wh 74%. Hisp 7%. Blk 12%. Asian 7%. Avg class size: 16. **Fac 138.**

Grad '04—73. Col—73. (Brown, Williams, Wesleyan U, Skidmore, Cornell, Amherst). Avg SAT: 1380. Alum 4875.

Tui '04-'05: Day $16,585-20,600 (+$600-1000).

Summer: Enrich Rec. 6 wks.

Endow $13,900,000. Plant val $63,000,000. Bldgs 8. Class rms 77. 2 Libs 18,000 vols. Sci labs 10. Lang labs 4. Comp labs 2. Dark rms 1. Auds 1. Theaters 1. Art studios 1. Music studios 6. Dance studios 1. Gyms 2. Weight rms 1. Garden/play areas 1.

Est 1845. Nonprofit. Sem (Sept-June). **Assoc** CLS.

Founded as the Brooklyn Female Academy, the school took its current name in honor of William S. Packer, whose widow donated money to rebuild the original structure, which had burned in 1853. Coeducational since 1972, Packer Collegiate is located in the Brooklyn Heights historical district.

Packer comprises a preschool and lower school (grades pre-K-4), a middle school (grades 5-8) and an upper school (grades 9-12). In the upper school, freshmen and sophomores have a structured curriculum, while the schedules for juniors and seniors are more flexible. Students fulfill course and elective requirements in English, a foreign language, mathematics, humanities and American history, science and the arts. Advanced Placement classes and upper-level electives are available across the academic departments. Independent study is recommended, and senior projects allow those interested to pursue a self-designed course of study throughout the second semester. A science department program also provides opportunities for independent research.

Travel abroad opportunities are offered and, each semester, a few juniors may enroll in Maine Coast Semester or the Rocky Mountain Institute.

Beginning in the middle school, students are encouraged to participate in an array of extracurriculars. Student activities include clubs and organizations, artistic programs and athletics. Students are required to complete service to the school community and to the community at large, and all students in grades 5-12 attend a nonsectarian chapel at least once a week.

BUFFALO, NY. (174 mi. NE of Cleveland, OH) Urban. Pop: 292,648. Alt: 600 ft.

BUFFALO SEMINARY
Day — Girls Gr 9-12

Buffalo, NY 14222. 205 Bidwell Pky. Tel: 716-885-6780. Fax: 716-885-6785.
www.buffaloseminary.org E-mail: cstark@buffaloseminary.org

Sandra P. Gilmor, Head. BA, Univ of British Columbia (Canada), MA, Long Island Univ. Cynthia B. Stark, Adm.

Col Prep. AP—Eng Fr Span Calc Stats Bio Physics Eur_Hist US_Hist Comp_Govt & Pol US_Govt & Pol Art_Hist. Feat—Lat Astron Computers Performing_Arts Studio_Art Music. Supp—Rev Tut.

Adm (Gr 9-11): 57/yr. Appl due: Nov. Accepted: 80%. Yield: 55%. Tests DAT IQ.

Enr 173. G 173. Sec 173. Wh 81%. Hisp 3%. Blk 10%. Asian 3%. Other 3%. Avg class size: 13. Fac 30. M 3/2. F 15/10. Wh 91%. Hisp 3%. Blk 6%. Adv deg: 56%.

Grad '04—36. Col—36. (St Lawrence, St Michael's, Loyola U-LA, Syracuse, SUNY-Buffalo). Avg SAT: 1173. Alum 3150.

Tui '04-'05: Day $11,500 (+$1000). Aid: Merit 5 ($8000). Need 80 ($400,000).

Summer: Acad Enrich Rec. 1-6 wks.

Endow $1,775,000. Plant val $5,846,000. Bldgs 2. Class rms 17. Lib 9850 vols. Sci labs 3. Comp labs 1. Auds 1. Theaters 1. Art studios 1. Music studios 1. Dance studios 1. Gyms 1. Fields 1.

Est 1851. Nonprofit. Quar (Sept-June). Assoc CLS MSA.

Established as one of the earlier nondenominational girls' academies, the school has a curriculum that includes instruction in mathematics, the sciences, English, history and cultures, languages, computers, and the visual and performing arts. Extracurricular activities enable students to pursue interests in government, social responsibility, cultural diversity, music, drama, art and athletics.

ELMWOOD FRANKLIN SCHOOL
Day — Coed Gr PS-8

Buffalo, NY 14216. 104 New Amsterdam Ave. Tel: 716-877-5035. Fax: 716-877-9680.
www.elmwoodfranklin.org E-mail: eacker@elmwoodfranklin.org

Keith Weller Frome, Head. BA, Univ of Hartford, MA, Univ of Connecticut, MTS, Harvard Univ, EdD, Columbia Univ. Elaine Zehr Acker, Adm.

Pre-Prep. Gen Acad. Feat—Computers Studio_Art Drama Music Outdoor_Ed. Supp—Dev_Read Rem_Math Rem_Read Rev Tut.

Adm: 59/yr. Appl due: Mar. Accepted: 34%. Tests IQ MAT.

Enr 369. B 188. G 181. Elem 369. Wh 84%. Hisp 1%. Blk 8%. Am Ind 1%. Asian 5%. Other 1%. Avg class size: 18. Fac 47. M 5/1. F 35/6. Wh 96%. Hisp 2%. Blk 2%. Adv deg: 61%.

Grad '04—30. Prep—26. (Nichols, Canisius, Buffalo Seminary, St Joseph's Collegiate, Park Sch-NY). Alum 1527.

Tui '03-'04: Day $10,415-12,030. Aid: Need 63 ($327,273).

Summer: Acad Enrich Rec. Tui Day $120/2-wk ses. 6 wks.

Endow $5,903,000. Plant val $5,757,000. Bldgs 1. Class rms 38. Lib 12,000 vols. Sci labs 3. Lang labs 2. Comp labs 3. Auds 1. Art studios 1. Music studios 1. Gyms 1. Fields 2.

Est 1895. Nonprofit. Quar (Sept-June).

The oldest preschool through grade 8 independent school in western New York State, EFS conducts a varied program that emphasizes basic learning skills and traditional subject matter. During the early years, four-, five- and six-year-olds take part in a well-developed reading program that incorporates storytelling, art, discussion, writing and dramatization throughout the school day. The lower school curriculum augments the standard subjects with music, art, foreign language, drama and daily physical education classes. Small skill-based groupings allow for individualization, and reading and math labs complement classroom instruction.

Departmentalization begins in the upper school. Interdisciplinary themes integrate music, art, literature, history, science, math and foreign language. Elmwood Franklin's outdoor education program combines group problem solving with environmental and science studies. Special classes enable pupils to explore arts, computers, sports, science and nature, while extended winter options include skiing, tennis and extensive computer study. Two annual musical productions, as well as interscholastic and intramural teams, are integral to the program.

NICHOLS SCHOOL
Day — Coed Gr 5-12

Buffalo, NY 14216. 1250 Amherst St. Tel: 716-875-8212. Fax: 716-875-2169.
www.nicholsschool.org E-mail: jmitchell@nicholsschool.org
Richard C. Bryan, Jr., Head. BA, Trinity College, MA, Univ of North Carolina-Charlotte. **John Mitchell, Adm.**

Col Prep. AP—Fr Lat Span Calc Bio Chem Physics Comp_Govt & Pol US_Govt & Pol Art_Hist. **Feat**—British_Lit Creative_Writing Anat & Physiol Environ_Sci Computers Medieval_Stud Psych Urban_Stud Philos Relig Photog Visual_Arts Drama Theater Band Chorus Music Ballet Dance. **Supp**—Dev_Read Rem_Read Tut.

Adm: 122/yr. Appl due: Rolling. Accepted: 70%. **Tests** CTP_4 IQ Stanford.

Enr 590. B 314. G 276. Elem 190. Sec 400. Wh 77%. Hisp 2%. Blk 3%. Am Ind 1%. Asian 17%. Avg class size: 14. **Fac 80.** M 37/2. F 41. Adv deg: 65%.

Grad '04—92. **Col**—92. (St Lawrence, SUNY-Buffalo, Johns Hopkins, Brown, Ithaca, Cornell). Avg SAT: 1240. Alum 5000.

Tui '03-'04: Day $13,000-14,800 (+$500). **Aid:** Need 147 ($940,000).

Summer: Acad Enrich. 6 wks.

Endow $14,000,000. Plant val $22,000,000. Bldgs 8. Class rms 38. 2 Libs 20,000 vols. Sci labs 7. Comp labs 5. Auds 1. Theaters 1. Art studios 4. Music studios 2. Dance studios 1. Perf arts ctrs 1. Gyms 2. Fields 5. Courts 7. Squash courts 2. Rinks 2.

Est 1892. Nonprofit. Quar (Sept-May). **Assoc** CLS.

Established by William Nichols of Boston, then under the vigorous leadership of Dr. Joseph Dana Allen beginning in 1909, Nichols has always been characterized by efficient college preparation. In January 1972, the school became coeducational, with girls being admitted into all grades.

In addition to the traditional courses offered as part of a college preparatory program, an extensive arts program (including photography, dance, painting, computer graphics, chorus and orchestra) is available. Nichols provides a full athletic program that includes hockey, baseball, soccer, cross-country, lacrosse, tennis, track, basketball, wrestling, squash, volleyball, softball, golf, crew and field hockey. Extracurricular activities are conducted in music, art, theater, drama, ballet and publications. Nichols encourages all upper schoolers to perform community service.

For years, the middle school (grades 5-8) was located on the Nottingham campus, one mile from the upper school (grades 9-12). In August 2001, however, Nichols consolidated campuses by adding a middle school building at its Amherst Street location.

THE PARK SCHOOL
Day — Coed Gr PS-12

Buffalo, NY 14226. 4625 Harlem Rd. Tel: 716-839-1242. Fax: 716-839-2014.
www.theparkschool.org   E-mail: jgoodfellow@theparkschool.org
Donald H. Grace, Head. BA, MAT, Harvard Univ. **Janice M. Goodfellow, Adm.**

Col Prep. AP—Eng Fr Span Calc Comp_Sci US_Hist US_Govt & Pol. **Feat**—Botany Microbiol Studio_Art Drama Music Outdoor_Ed. **Supp**—ESL Rev Tut.

Adm: 54/yr. Appl due: Rolling. Accepted: 93%. Yield: 53%. **Tests** CTP_4 IQ ISEE.

Enr 264. B 134. G 130. Elem 161. Sec 103. Wh 72%. Blk 10%. Am Ind 4%. Asian 7%. Other 7%. Avg class size: 15. **Fac 40.** M 12/1. F 19/8. Wh 95%. Hisp 3%. Blk 2%. Adv deg: 47%.

Grad '04—32. Col—32. (Berklee Col of Music 2, St Lawrence 2, SUNY-Buffalo 2, U of MI 2, Swarthmore 1, Tufts 1). Avg SAT: 1183. Avg ACT: 25. Alum 2367.

Tui '04-'05: Day $8900-14,000 (+$300). **Aid:** Merit 17 ($54,337). Need 68 ($550,077).

Summer: Rec. 1-6 wks.

Endow $1,500,000. Plant val $3,500,000. Bldgs 15. Class rms 32. 2 Libs 18,500 vols. Sci labs 4. Comp labs 2. Theaters 1. Art studios 5. Music studios 2. Gyms 2. Fields 3. Courts 4. Pools 1.

Est 1912. Nonprofit. Sem (Sept-June).

First of the Park Schools headed by Mary H. Lewis, this one, founded by a group of parents, has remained markedly holistic and child centered throughout its history. The college preparatory curriculum incorporates art, music and drama, and it features a sequence in outdoor education at all grade levels. Qualified students may take advanced courses at area colleges and have opportunities to undertake independent projects.

The 34-acre school plant permits firsthand investigation of many natural phenomena. Rolling admissions make it possible to enroll students throughout the school year, provided an appropriate space is available.

Extracurricular activities include publications, drama, an active student government program in both middle and upper schools, mock trial and Model UN. Sports include soccer, basketball, baseball, track, golf, lacrosse, softball and tennis.

CORNWALL-ON-HUDSON, NY. (53 mi. N of New York, NY) Suburban. Pop: 3058. Alt: 282 ft.

NEW YORK MILITARY ACADEMY
Bdg and Day — Coed Gr 7-12

Cornwall-on-Hudson, NY 12520. 78 Academy Ave. Tel: 845-534-3710.
Fax: 845-534-7699.

www.nyma.org   E-mail: admissions@nyma.ouboces.org
Maj. Gen. James M. Lyle, USA (Ret), Supt. BA, College of William and Mary, MA, Lehigh Univ. **Maureen T. Kelly, Adm.**

Col Prep. Milit. AP—Eng Human_Geog Eur_Hist US_Hist. **Feat**—Creative_Writing Fr Lat Span Environ_Sci Computers Govt/Econ Criminology Bus_Law Fine_Arts Studio_Art Band Music Journ JROTC Aviation Equitation. **Supp**—ESL Tut.

Adm: 128/yr. Appl due: Rolling. Accepted: 42%. **Tests** CEEB IQ SSAT Stanford TOEFL.

Enr 389. B 307/20. G 57/5. Wh 63%. Hisp 7%. Blk 16%. Asian 11%. Other 3%. Avg class size: 15. Uniform. **Fac 41.** M 20/1. F 19/1. Wh 97%. Hisp 2%. Blk 1%. Adv deg: 48%.

Grad '04—54. Col—52. (SUNY-Stony Brook, Norwich, Rutgers, St John's U-NY, Purdue, VA Milit). Avg SAT: 953. Alum 4599.

Tui '04-'05: Bdg $19,700 (+$6755). **Day $9000** (+$5000). **Aid:** Need 42 ($140,000).

Summer: Acad Enrich Rev. JROTC. Tui Bdg $4000. ESL. Tui Bdg $5200. 5 wks.

Endow $2,500,000. Plant val $20,000,000. Bldgs 13. Dorms 4. Dorm rms 170. Class rms 47. Lib 16,000 vols. Sci labs 3. Comp labs 1. Comp ctrs 2. Auds 1. Art studios 1. Music studios 1. Gyms 1. Fields 6. Courts 10. Pools 3. Riding rings 1. Stables 1. Weight rms 1. Rifle ranges 1.

Est 1889. Nonprofit. Sem (Sept-June). **Assoc** MSA.

Drawing its enrollment from many states and foreign countries, this well-known academy was founded by Col. Charles J. Wright. The school became coeducational in 1976, and today girls play an important role in all school activities.

The academic program is college preparatory, with special emphasis placed on science, mathematics, modern languages and composition. Science and the humanities are supplemented by numerous electives. Part of NYMA's technology program, a campus-wide network enables all boarding cadets to have computer connections in their dorm rooms. A compulsory athletic program includes interscholastic sports and fitness training. The guidance department counsels early on college choices and career development. Graduates matriculate at many competitive colleges, including the nation's five service academies.

Among the available extracurricular activities are weightlifting, drill team and riding. NYMA maintains teams in the following sports: football, soccer, basketball, swimming, wrestling, riflery, track, baseball, tennis, cross-country, lacrosse, golf and volleyball.   **See Also Page 1215**

THE STORM KING SCHOOL
Bdg — Coed Gr 9-PG; Day — Coed 7-PG

Cornwall-on-Hudson, NY 12520. 314 Mountain Rd. Tel: 845-534-9860.
Fax: 845-534-4128.
www.sks.org   E-mail: admissions@sks.org
Helen Stevens Chinitz, Head. BA, Bennington College, MA, New York Univ. **Stephen T. Lifrak, Adm.**

Col Prep. AP—Calc Studio_Art. **Feat**—ASL Span Environ_Sci Econ Govt Psych Photog Theater_Arts Music Dance Outdoor_Ed. **Supp**—Dev_Read ESL LD Rem_Math Rev Tut.

Adm: 52/yr. Bdg 36. Day 16. Appl due: Rolling. Accepted: 56%. **Tests** IQ ISEE SSAT Stanford TOEFL.

Enr 123. B 63/23. G 23/14. Avg class size: 8. Uniform. **Fac 32.** M 17/5. F 7/3. Wh 88%. Hisp 6%. Blk 6%. Adv deg: 46%. In dorms 9.

Grad '04—43. Col—43. (Manhattan Col, Marist, Mt St Mary-NY, Pratt, SUNY-Stony Brook, St John's U-NY). Avg SAT: 1014. Alum 1681.

Tui '03-'04: Bdg $29,300-33,110. **Day** $15,800. **Aid:** Merit 7 ($26,000). Need 3 ($57,000).
Endow $1,500,000. Plant val $5,500,000. Bldgs 22. Dorms 5. Dorm rms 73. Class rms 22. Lib 10,000 vols. Sci labs 10. Lang labs 1. Comp labs 1. Observatories 1. Auds 1. Theaters 1. Art studios 1. Music studios 1. Dance studios 1. Gyms 1. Fields 3. Courts 5.
Est 1867. Nonprofit. Tri (Sept-June). **Assoc** CLS MSA.

Storm King, which was founded by Rev. Louis P. Ledoux, provides a flexible and individualized academic curriculum with AP classes, in addition to electives. An enrichment center offers support to students with specific educational needs or mild learning differences. Performing and visual arts programs include studio art, sculpture, photography and printmaking, as well as theatrical productions and a variety of music and dance options.

All students are expected to participate in a daily afternoon activity—either athletic or extracurricular—each sport season; one interscholastic sport per year and another athletic offering are required. Recreational alternatives include karate, skiing, intramurals, yoga, weightlifting, hiking and tennis. Among the school's extracurricular choices are theater, dance, publications, and on- and off-campus community service.

DOBBS FERRY, NY. (24 mi. N of New York, NY) Suburban. Pop: 10,662. Alt: 12 ft.

THE MASTERS SCHOOL

Bdg — Coed Gr 9-12; Day — Coed 5-12
(Coord — Day 5-8)

Dobbs Ferry, NY 10522. 49 Clinton Ave. Tel: 914-479-6420. Fax: 914-693-7295.
www.themastersschool.com E-mail: admission@themastersschool.com
Maureen Fonseca, Head. BA, Vassar College, MA, PhD, Fordham Univ. **Susan D. Hendricks & David B. Stettler, Adms.**
Col Prep. **AP**—Eng Fr Lat Span Calc Stats Bio Chem Physics Eur_Hist US_Hist Studio_Art Music_Theory. **Feat**—Greek Amer_Stud Econ Pol_Sci Ethics World_Relig Film Drama Dance. **Supp**—ESL.
Adm (Bdg Gr 9-11; Day 5-11): 144/yr. Bdg 52. Day 92. Appl due: Jan. Accepted: 49%. Yield: 60%. **Tests** ISEE SSAT TOEFL.
Enr 504. B 65/164. G 80/195. Elem 126. Sec 378. Avg class size: 12. **Fac 79.** M 34/1. F 41/3. Wh 88%. Hisp 4%. Blk 5%. Asian 3%. Adv deg: 62%. In dorms 26.
Grad '04—75. Col—74. (NYU 5, Cornell 3, Franklin & Marshall 3, Middlebury 2, Lafayette 2, Barnard 2). Avg SAT: 1235. Alum 4893.
Tui '04-'05: Bdg $32,300 (+$1500). **Day** $22,800-23,400 (+$1500). **Aid:** Need 120 ($2,232,100).
Endow $20,000,000. Plant val $20,280,000. Bldgs 12. Dorms 6. Dorm rms 120. Class rms 55. Lib 28,000 vols. Sci labs 4. Lang labs 1. Photog labs 2. Auds 1. Theaters 1. Art studios 2. Music studios 6. Dance studios 1. Gyms 1. Fields 5. Tennis courts 9.
Est 1877. Nonprofit. Tri (Sept-June). **Assoc** CLS MSA.

Established as a school for girls by Eliza B. Masters and her sister, Sarah, the Masters School became coeducational in 1995, offering parallel middle schools (grades 5-8): one for girls and one for boys. The upper school (grades 9-12) presents a coeducational framework, following the Harkness method of teaching, which features an oval table in each classroom around which students and teacher actively engage in learning.

Masters offers a college preparatory curriculum that includes more than a dozen Advanced Placement courses. Seniors may design independent projects either on or off campus. The visual and performing arts program has extensive facilities and is an integral part of the school. Teachers use the cultural resources of Westchester County and New York City to augment their courses. Some students are selected to participate in CITYterm, a semester-long, interdisciplinary urban studies program that draws upon the resources of New York City for its academic and experiential curriculum (see separate listing).

The school provides ESL instruction at intermediate and advanced levels. Students may take part in international exchanges in such countries as England, Australia, Russia and South Africa.

The interscholastic athletic program features tennis, basketball, ice hockey, volleyball, fencing, field hockey, soccer, softball, lacrosse, cross-country and baseball teams. **See Also Pages 1204-5**

HOOSICK, NY. (28 mi. ENE of Albany, NY; 155 mi. NNE of New York, NY) Suburban. Pop: 6759. Alt: 458 ft.

HOOSAC SCHOOL
Bdg and Day — Coed Gr 8-PG

Hoosick, NY 12089. Pine Valley Rd, PO Box 9. Tel: 518-686-7331. Fax: 518-686-3370. www.hoosac.com E-mail: info@hoosac.com

Richard J. Lomuscio, Head. BA, MA, New York Univ. **Dean S. Foster, Adm.**

  Col Prep. AP—Eng Calc US_Hist. **Feat**—Fr Astron Computers Psych Ethics Theol Film Photog Studio_Art Drama Music Dance Marketing. **Supp**—ESL Rev Tut.

  Adm (Bdg Gr 8-11; Day 8-9): 58/yr. Bdg 54. Day 4. Appl due: Rolling. Accepted: 100%. Yield: 99%.

  Enr 123. B 86/8. G 26/3. Elem 5. Sec 114. PG 4. Wh 77%. Blk 8%. Asian 15%. Avg class size: 8. **Fac 20.** M 10/1. F 6/3. Adv deg: 30%. In dorms 11.

  Grad '04—36. Col—35. (Northwestern, Boston U, IN U, Assumption, Old Dominion, Lake Forest). Avg SAT: 1000. Alum 1200.

  Tui '04-'05: Bdg $25,200 (+$1050). **Day $13,500** (+$200). **Aid:** Need 34 ($519,345).

  Endow $1,093,000. Plant val $11,500,000. Bldgs 16. Dorms 9. Dorm rms 65. Class rms 15. Lib 10,000 vols. Sci labs 2. Comp labs 2. Dark rms 1. Observatories 1. Auds 1. Art studios 1. Arts ctrs 1. Gyms 1. Athletic ctrs 1. Fields 7. Courts 3. Pools 1. Skiing facilities yes. Ponds 1.

  Est 1889. Nonprofit. Episcopal. Tri (Sept-June). **Assoc** MSA.

Founded by Dr. Edward D. Tibbits, Hoosac was perhaps the first American boarding school to develop a work program where students play a role in maintaining their environment.

The curriculum encompasses a wide range of academic skills and includes advanced work, independent projects and tutorials, in addition to formal and remedial classes. Hoosac utilizes a mastery education approach whereby the student may retake an exam until he or she exhibits sufficient mastery of the subject matter. An advisor system and a low student-teacher ratio are important aspects of the school's program.

Varsity teams compete in soccer, basketball, ice hockey, softball, tennis, volleyball and lacrosse. Students may also participate in the skiing and snowboarding program and, informally, in swimming and cross-country.

KATONAH, NY. (43 mi. NNE of New York, NY) Rural. Pop: 2340. Alt: 320 ft.

THE HARVEY SCHOOL
5-Day Bdg — Coed Gr 7-12; Day — Coed 6-12

Katonah, NY 10536. 260 Jay St. Tel: 914-232-3161. Fax: 914-232-6034.
www.harveyschool.org   E-mail: romanowicz@harveyschool.org
Barry W. Fenstermacher, Head. BA, Drew Univ. **Ronald Romanowicz, Adm.**

- **Col Prep. AP**—Eng Calc Bio Chem Physics Eur_Hist US_Hist. **Feat**—Fr Greek Japan Lat Span Comp_Sci Studio_Art Theater Music. **Supp**—Makeup Tut.
- **Adm:** 91/yr. Bdg 9. Day 82. Appl due: Rolling. Accepted: 50%.
- **Enr 290.** B 12/155. G 13/110. Avg class size: 12. **Fac 72.** M 42/3. F 21/6. Adv deg: 33%. In dorms 8.
- **Grad '04—50. Col—47.** (PA St, Cornell, Drew, Colgate, Syracuse, Brown). Alum 1700.
- **Tui '04-'05: 5-Day Bdg $28,700** (+$600). **Day $21,600-22,100** (+$600). **Aid:** Merit 10 ($10,000). Need 60 ($450,000).
- Endow $900,000. Plant val $6,000,000. Bldgs 12. Dorms 2. Dorm rms 30. Class rms 20. Lib 20,000 vols. Labs 4. Art studios 3. Music studios 1. Gyms 1. Fields 6. Rinks 1.
- **Est 1916.** Nonprofit. Tri (Sept-June).

The school was founded by Dr. Herbert Carter, a physician from New York City. Originally located at Dr. Carter's farm in Hawthorne, Harvey provided the traditional education of an English prep school for boys in grades 4-8. In 1959, construction on the Taconic Parkway forced the school to relocate to the 100-acre Sylvan Weil estate, where it started to draw a population of day students. Harvey began the transition to its current structure with a middle and an upper school in 1969 and subsequently, in 1971, enrolled the first female day students. In 1987, the boarding program was converted to a five-day option and girls were given the option to board.

Harvey offers a traditional college preparatory curriculum, with classes ranging from basic levels to Advanced Placement and honors courses. Pupils attend small classes while fulfilling requirements in English, math, science, history and the arts. The Krasne Project provides for the integration of computer technology into most subjects and allows students to work at two Internet-accessible computer labs. Strong art, music, drama and creative writing programs enrich the curriculum.

Extracurriculars are mandatory for all except junior and senior day students. Most compete in Harvey's interscholastic athletic program, which comprises football, field hockey, ice hockey, cross-country, soccer, basketball, lacrosse, rugby, softball and baseball. A range of clubs and other activities is also available, and pupils may specially arrange off-campus participation in such activities as gymnastics, martial arts, skiing and swimming. **See Also Page 1163**

LAKE PLACID, NY. (112 mi. N of Albany, NY) Rural. Pop: 2638. Alt: 1742 ft.

NORTH COUNTRY SCHOOL
Bdg and Day — Coed Gr 4-9

Lake Placid, NY 12946. Cascade Rd, PO Box 187. Tel: 518-523-9329. Fax: 518-523-4858. www.nct.org   E-mail: admissions@nct.org

David Hochschartner, Dir. BA, Union College, MEd, Columbia Univ. **Christine LeFevre, Adm.**

    Pre-Prep. Gen Acad. Feat—Span Computers Studio_Art Music Dance Mountaineering. **Supp**—Dev_Read ESL Rem_Math Rem_Read Tut.

    Adm: 33/yr. Appl due: Rolling. Accepted: 89%.

    Enr 77. B 42. G 35. Elem 65. Sec 12. Wh 88%. Blk 12%. Avg class size: 13. **Fac 26.** M 8/2. F 13/3. Wh 84%. Hisp 4%. Blk 12%. Adv deg: 23%. In dorms 11.

    Grad '04—15. Prep—7. (Masters Sch-NY, Williston Northampton, Cushing, Suffield, Buxton, Darrow). Alum 1400.

    Tui '05-'06: Bdg $38,300 (+$200). **5-Day Bdg $24,950** (+$200). **Day $14,200** (+$200). **Aid:** Need 25 ($412,900).

    Summer: Rec. ESL. Tui Bdg $5700. 7 wks.

    Endow $7,000,000. Plant val $3,000,000. Bldgs 11. Dorms 6. Dorm rms 40. Class rms 15. Lib 8000 vols. Sci labs 2. Lang labs 1. Comp labs 1. Auds 1. Art studios 4. Music studios 3. Dance studios 1. Gyms 1. Fields 2. Courts 1. Basketball courts 2. Riding rings 1. Skiing facilities yes. Barns 1.

    Est 1938. Nonprofit. Tri (Sept-June).

NCS is located on a 200-acre working farm in the Adirondack Forest Preserve, a wilderness area of mountains, lakes and forests. Children, who live in house groups of eight to ten under the supervision of a teaching-staff couple, participate in all phases of housework and farm work. The school grows many of its own vegetables organically. Along with formal school work, each child has some daily responsibility.

A solid curriculum in the basic subjects prepares graduates for leading preparatory schools and is reinforced through field trips to points of environmental, cultural and social significance. Facilities for music study in orchestral instruments, piano and voice are offered. The arts program offers creative work in painting, drawing, sculpture, weaving, ceramics, woodwork, batik and photography. Practical shop work is gained through routine repairs and construction around the premises.

Physical exercise balances useful, productive work with recreation and sport. Soccer, touch football, horseback riding, softball and tennis are available in the fall and the spring. Skating, skiing on the school's rope-tow-equipped hill, cross-country skiing and snowshoeing are winter pursuits. Mountaineering and hiking opportunities exist year-round, and Lake Placid's 1980 Winter Olympics facilities are only seven miles away. **See Also Page 1217**

NORTHWOOD SCHOOL
Bdg and Day — Coed Gr 9-PG

Lake Placid, NY 12946. Northwood Rd, PO Box 1070. Tel: 518-523-3357.
Fax: 518-523-3405.
www.northwoodschool.com   E-mail: admissions@northwoodschool.com
Edward M. Good, Head. AB, Bowdoin College, MAT, Brown Univ. **Timothy Weaver, Adm.**
   Col Prep. AP—Eng Calc Stats Bio US_Hist. **Feat**—Fr Span Environ_Sci Geol Psych Sociol Ceramics Drawing Photog Sculpt Studio_Art Music Journ Study_Skills. **Supp**—ESL Tut.
   Adm: 70/yr. Appl due: Rolling. Accepted: 80%. **Tests** ISEE SSAT TOEFL.
   Enr 160. B 80/20. G 35/25. Sec 155. PG 5. Wh 91%. Blk 1%. Asian 8%. Avg class size: 8.
      Fac 30. M 17. F 11/2. Adv deg: 43%. In dorms 17.
   Grad '04—52. **Col**—52. (Clarkson, Hamilton, Bates, St Lawrence, Wellesley, Holy Cross). Avg SAT: 1130. Alum 2000.
   Tui '04-'05: Bdg $30,500 (+$1500). **Day $15,925** (+$1500). **Aid:** Need 80 ($800,000). Endow $10,000,000. Plant val $6,000,000. Bldgs 9. Dorms 4. Dorm rms 105. Class rms 18. Lib 20,000 vols. Sci labs 4. Lang labs 1. Comp labs 1. Auds 1. Art studios 4. Music studios 5. Dance studios 1. Gyms 1. Fields 4. Courts 7.
   Est 1905. Nonprofit. Sem (Sept-June). **Assoc** CLS.

Northwood's rigorous academic program emphasizes college preparation in a structured, small-class setting. Advanced Placement and honors courses, as well as a varied choice of electives, supplement the standard curricular offerings. The school also maintains a particularly strong arts program.

Students gain opportunities for initiative and responsibility through a broadly based student government program. The school enables pupils to engage in many different kinds of community service projects. Need-based scholarship funds for students of promise are provided by the school, and a strong board of trustees has aided the growth of the school, which attracts able students from a wide area.

A full program of athletics includes soccer, skiing, hockey and crew. In addition, local woodland and mountain areas and the nearby Olympic Arena provide numerous opportunities for winter sports participation. **See Also Page 1220**

LOCUST VALLEY, NY. (24 mi. NE of New York, NY) Suburban. Pop: 3521. Alt: 121 ft.

FRIENDS ACADEMY
Day — Coed Gr PS-12

Locust Valley, NY 11560. Duck Pond Rd. Tel: 516-676-0393. Fax: 516-465-1718.
   www.fa.org   E-mail: info@fa.org
William G. Morris, Jr., Head. BA, Bucknell Univ, MA, Univ of Connecticut, MA, Columbia Univ. **Patty Ziplow, Adm.**
   Col Prep. Feat—Greek Ital Psych Relig Photog Theater_Arts Music.
   Adm: 134/yr. Appl due: Jan. Accepted: 56%. **Tests** CEEB SSAT.
   Enr 748. B 383. G 365. Elem 392. Sec 356. Wh 80%. Hisp 3%. Blk 8%. Asian 9%. Avg class size: 15. **Fac 78.** M 43. F 35. Wh 83%. Hisp 1%. Blk 12%. Asian 4%. Adv deg: 80%.
   Grad '04—88. **Col**—88. (Cornell, NYU, Columbia, Brown, Georgetown, McGill-Canada).

Avg SAT: 1240. Alum 3500.
Tui '03-'04: Day $15,000-20,600 (+$500). **Aid:** Need 105 ($1,442,600).
Summer: Enrich Rec. Tui Day $3500/4-wk ses. 8 wks.
Endow $12,000,000. Plant val $65,000,000. Bldgs 10. Class rms 50. 2 Libs 35,000 vols. Sci labs 5. Lang labs 2. Comp labs 5. Photog labs 1. Comp ctrs 1. Auds 1. Theaters 1. Art studios 5. Music studios 5. Dance studios 3. Gyms 2. Fields 6. Courts 7. Field houses 1. Pools 2.
Est 1877. Nonprofit. Religious Society of Friends. Sem (Sept-June). **Assoc** CLS.

Founded by local businessman Gideon Frost for "the children of Friends and those similarly sentimented," the academy continues to reflect Quaker educational principles. The college preparatory curriculum features Advanced Placement courses and an array of electives. Technology is an important aspect of the program. For three weeks each spring, seniors pursue off-campus independent service projects that are related to their special interests.

There is a wide range of activities, including dramatics, music, community service and outdoor education. Among sports in the interscholastic athletic program are football, soccer, basketball, lacrosse, field hockey, tennis, baseball, cross-country, wrestling, crew, cheerleading and track. Students assist in decision making through the student-faculty board.

PORTLEDGE SCHOOL
Day — Coed Gr PS-12

Locust Valley, NY 11560. 355 Duck Pond Rd. Tel: 516-750-3100. Fax: 516-671-2039.
www.portledge.org   E-mail: emooney@portledge.org
Huson R. Gregory, Head. AB, Dartmouth College, MEd, Rutgers Univ. **Elisabeth D. Mooney, Adm.**
Col Prep. AP—Eng Fr Comp_Sci Chem Physics Eur_Hist Music_Theory. **Feat**—Span Programming Russ_Hist Psych Architect Photog Sculpt Studio_Art Drama Music Public_Speak.
Adm (Gr PS-11): 89/yr. Appl due: Rolling. Accepted: 66%. **Tests** SSAT.
Enr 408. B 216. G 192. Elem 276. Sec 132. Wh 67%. Hisp 1%. Blk 12%. Asian 5%. Other 15%. Avg class size: 12. **Fac 72.** M 20/3. F 42/7. Wh 88%. Hisp 2%. Blk 8%. Asian 2%. Adv deg: 56%.
Grad '04—32. **Col**—30. (Stanford, Brown, Colgate, Harvard, Tufts, Wesleyan U). Avg SAT: 1220. Alum 667.
Tui '04-'05: Day $5500-21,200 (+$300). **Aid:** Need 65 ($841,100).
Summer: Acad Enrich Rev. Environ Sci. Music. Drama. 1-6 wks.
Endow $1,400,000. Plant val $8,500,000. Bldgs 5. Class rms 56. 2 Libs 17,000 vols. Sci labs 6. Comp labs 2. Dark rms 1. Auds 1. Art studios 2. Music studios 4. Wood shops 1. Gyms 2. Fields 4. Courts 5.
Est 1933. Nonprofit. Sem (Sept-June). **Assoc** CLS.

Serving Nassau and Suffolk counties, Portledge is located in the North Shore community of Locust Valley. The outgrowth of Miss Stoddart's elementary school, Portledge moved to its 62-acre campus in 1965 and began adding a grade each year. The school graduated its first senior class in 1976.

Portledge provides a traditional college preparatory program. French and computer instruction begin in kindergarten, lab science in grade 3, and ability grouping for academically advanced students in grade 5. Advanced Placement courses are available in all major disciplines, and the school also conducts a strong music program. Student government shares the responsibility for the implementation of rules and for participation in the community service program.

An extensive activities program is offered. Athletics are conducted on intramural and interscholastic levels and include soccer, field and ice hockey, basketball, fencing, lacrosse, golf and tennis. The school's picturesque campus is adjacent to a 75-acre sanctuary.

MILLBROOK, NY. (52 mi. W of Hartford, CT; 78 mi. N of New York, NY) Rural. Pop: 1429. Alt: 567 ft.

DUTCHESS DAY SCHOOL
Day — Coed Gr K-8

Millbrook, NY 12545. 415 Rte 343. Tel: 845-677-5014. Fax: 845-677-6722.
  www.dutchessday.org   E-mail: ddsadmis@dutchessday.org
Andrea Archer, Head. MA, MEd, Oxford Univ (England). **Ellen Potter, Adm.**
  Pre-Prep. Feat—Fr Lat Computers Studio_Art Music Health Study_Skills. **Supp**—Tut.
  Adm: 30/yr. Accepted: 60%.
  Enr 160. B 74. G 86. Elem 160. Wh 87%. Hisp 4%. Blk 1%. Asian 8%. Avg class size: 17.
    Fac 30. M 2/1. F 23/4. Adv deg: 56%.
  Grad '04—19. Prep—15. (Millbrook 6, Hotchkiss 1, St Paul's Sch-NH 1, Miss Porter's 1, St George's Sch-RI 1). Alum 350.
  Tui '04-'05: Day $13,500-15,700 (+$300). **Aid:** Need ($176,748).
  Summer: Acad Enrich Rev. 1 wk.
  Bldgs 3. Class rms 17. Lib 6300 vols. Labs 2. Art studios 1. Music studios 1. Gyms 2. Fields 3.
  Est 1955. Nonprofit. Quar (Sept-June).

Founded by a group of local parents, DDS offers a traditional curriculum designed to prepare students for secondary school. The academic program emphasizes the development of fundamental skills, and small classes allow students to pursue individual projects and interests. Offerings in computer, foreign language and the arts enrich the curriculum. Students in grades 5-8 may take part in interscholastic athletics.

MILLBROOK SCHOOL
Bdg and Day — Coed Gr 9-12

Millbrook, NY 12545. School Rd. Tel: 845-677-8261. Fax: 845-677-8598.
  www.millbrook.org   E-mail: admissions@millbrook.org
Drew J. Casertano, Head. BA, Amherst College, EdM, Harvard Univ. **Cynthia S. McWilliams, Adm.**
  Col Prep. AP—Eng Fr Span Calc. **Feat**—Astron Ecol Zoology Psych Philos Drawing Photog Drama Band Chorus Music Music_Theory Dance. **Supp**—ESL.
  Adm: 80/yr. Bdg 62. Day 18. Appl due: Jan. Accepted: 48%. **Tests** ISEE SSAT TOEFL.
  Enr 238. B 104/24. G 82/28. Sec 238. Wh 87%. Hisp 3%. Blk 5%. Am Ind 1%. Asian 4%. Avg class size: 10. **Fac 58.** M 24/4. F 29/1. Wh 96%. Hisp 1%. Blk 3%. Adv deg: 44%. In dorms 20.

Grad '04—60. Col—58. (Union Col, St Lawrence, Bates, Colby, Middlebury, Yale). Avg SAT: 1100. Avg SSAT: 60%. Alum 2586.

Tui '04-'05: Bdg $32,725 (+$1100-1400). **Day $23,810** (+$1100-1400). **Aid:** Need 55 ($1,159,380).

Endow $12,000,000. Plant val $50,200,000. Bldgs 69. Dorms 7. Dorm rms 112. Class rms 24. Lib 18,000 vols. Sci labs 4. Dark rms 3. Comp ctrs 1. Observatories 1. Art studios 4. Music studios 5. Dance studios 1. Arts ctrs 1. Gyms 1. Athletic ctrs 1. Fields 6. Basketball courts 1. Tennis courts 7. Squash courts 8. Rinks 1. Stables 4.

Est 1931. Nonprofit. Tri (Sept-May). **Assoc** CLS.

Founded in 1931 by Edward Pulling, Millbrook first admitted girls as day students in 1971, and as boarding students in 1975. The academic program offers a rigorous, traditional college preparatory curriculum featuring a variety of AP courses, independent studies and electives supplemented by arts and scientific field trips, forums with guest speakers, student news and literary publications, and an intersession. Unique features of the 643-acre campus include mature oak-maple-beech forests, the Highley Wetlands Sanctuary and boardwalk, extensive fields and meadows, bird-banding sites, nature trails, an experimental forest canopy walkway, and the six-acre, nationally accredited Trevor Zoo. Other physical resources are the Howard Observatory, a weather station, a herbarium, egg vaults with over 15,000 specimens, fossils and minerals, and hundreds of taxidermy mounts and study slides.

Each student plays an active role in the functioning of the school and is required to choose one activity in the community service program. Students may, for example, work with the animals at the zoo, distribute and maintain athletic supplies and equipment, recycle and compost campus wide, run the school's weather station, or serve food at the snack bar. Science classes take advantage of the surroundings and directly involve students in Millbrook's wild and managed resources. Term electives include conservation biology, zoo science, animal behavior, astronomy, ornithology and independent study. Additionally, students can work with local research institutions through projects, seminars and tours. Science-related community service includes the zoo, bird banding, the weather station, the observatory and a laboratory assistance program.

Students must play team sports during at least two of the three athletic seasons. While many choose competitive athletics all three terms, electives such as a zoo squad, a forestland improvement project, dance, and horseback riding and other recreational sports may be selected as alternatives. The school encourages its students to participate in summer activities that reinforce their studies the rest of the year. Options may include international travel and language study, including home-study programs; community service programs; outdoor adventures; scientific study; visual and performing arts programs; and sports-related programs.

NEW LEBANON, NY.

(25 mi. SE of Albany, NY; 127 mi. NNE of New York, NY) Rural. Pop: 2454. Alt: 699 ft.

DARROW SCHOOL
Bdg and Day — Coed Gr 9-PG

New Lebanon, NY 12125. 110 Darrow Rd. Tel: 518-794-6000. Fax: 518-794-7065.
www.darrowschool.org E-mail: admissions@darrowschool.org
Nancy Maslack Wolf, Head. MEd, Loyola College. Sean Fagan, Adm.

Col Prep. Feat—Fr Russ Span Anat & Physiol Environ_Sci Computers Econ Psych Ethics Ceramics Drawing Graphic_Arts Painting Studio_Art Woodworking. **Supp**—Dev_Read ESL Rev Tut.

Adm: 62/yr. Appl due: Rolling. Accepted: 56%. **Tests** CEEB CTP_4 ISEE SSAT Stanford TOEFL.

Enr 125. B 55/7. G 56/7. Sec 124. PG 1. Avg class size: 9. **Fac 34.** M 15/2. F 15/2. Adv deg: 35%. In dorms 15.

Grad '04—34. Col—34. (Boston U, Earlham, Guilford, NYU, RI Sch of Design, U of Hartford). Avg SAT: 1025. Alum 2000.

Tui '05–'06: Bdg $35,750 (+$4000). **Day $20,400** (+$4000). **Aid:** Need 39 ($760,000).
Endow $1,400,000. Plant val $4,500,000. Bldgs 24. Dorms 6. Dorm rms 50. Class rms 15. Lib 15,000 vols. Sci labs 4. Comp labs 2. Theaters 1. Art studios 1. Arts ctrs 1. Gyms 1. Fields 4. Courts 2. Skiing facilities yes.

Est 1932. Nonprofit. Sem (Sept-June). **Assoc** MSA.

Darrow occupies the 360-acre site and buildings of the first and largest organized Shaker village in America, established in 1787. Originally the Lebanon School for Boys, which opened its doors under the direction of Charles H. Jones, the school was later renamed after George Darrow, the farmer who had originally donated the land to the Shakers, and became coeducational in 1970.

The school offers a college preparatory curriculum within a structured, supportive environment. Small classes, individual advisors, supervised study and an intensive tutorial program provide individual attention for each student.

Darrow recognizes different learning styles and serves students with a variety of abilities; most enrolled have struggled in other learning environments. The school is unable, however, to work with severe learning or behavioral problems. The tutorial program allows participants to work individually two or four times a week with a teacher toward improving study habits and learning skills. Those who wish to pursue a more challenging curriculum may use this support to pursue advanced study or to work with a tutor on an independent project, supplementing regular courses in such areas as literature or history.

The comprehensive curriculum offers a range of courses in English, history, languages, mathematics and science, as well as art, music and drama. A number of electives are also available. An important aspect of the academic program is its environmental focus: An environmental center features a working wastewater treatment process situated in an 1800-square-foot greenhouse. Hands-on assistance with the center's operation familiarizes pupils with new technologies, and students develop public-speaking skills by conducting tours of the facility.

Darrow fields interscholastic teams in soccer, basketball, baseball, softball, lacrosse and tennis. Other extracurricular activities include skiing, rock climbing, fitness, theater and the arts, horseback riding and community service.

NY *Leading Private Schools*

As an outgrowth of the Shaker motto "Hands to Work, Hearts to God," the school sets aside Wednesday mornings to foster the dignity of labor and cooperative effort. All members of the community—administrators, teachers and students—participate in such projects and tasks as chopping wood, making apple cider and maple syrup, landscaping and woodworking. **See Also Pages 1140-1**

NEW YORK, NY. Urban. Pop: 7,428,162. Alt: 54 ft.

ALLEN-STEVENSON SCHOOL
Day — Boys Gr K-9

New York, NY 10021. 132 E 78th St. Tel: 212-288-6710. Fax: 212-288-6802.
www.allen-stevenson.org E-mail: info@allen-stevenson.org
David R. Trower, Head. AB, Brown Univ, MDiv, Union Theological Seminary. **Ronnie R. Jankoff, Adm.**
Pre-Prep. Feat—Fr Span Computers Music. Supp—Dev_Read Rem_Read Rev Tut.
Adm: 64/yr. Appl due: Nov. Accepted: 19%. Yield: 66%. **Tests** ISEE.
Enr 384. B 384. Elem 371. Sec 13. Wh 84%. Hisp 4%. Blk 6%. Asian 3%. Other 3%. Avg class size: 20. Uniform. Fac 78. Wh 90%. Hisp 6%. Blk 3%. Asian 1%. Adv deg: 61%.
Grad '04—44. Prep—44. (Horace Mann, Riverdale, Trinity Sch-NY, Collegiate-NY, Friends Seminary). Alum 1940.
Tui '04-'05: Day $24,300-25,550. **Aid:** Need 52 ($950,000).
Summer: Rec. Tui Day $800/2-wk ses. 6 wks.
Endow $18,000,000. Plant val $18,000,000. Bldgs 4. Class rms 28. Lib 11,800 vols. Sci labs 2. Comp labs 1. Theaters 1. Art studios 1. Music studios 2. Shops 1. Gyms 2.
Est 1883. Nonprofit. Sem (Sept-June).

Founded by Francis B. Allen, the school merged in 1904 with the one started by Robert A. Stevenson. Allen-Stevenson's traditional curriculum prepares students for entrance to secondary schools. In addition to the basic subjects, the curriculum includes foreign language, computers, shop, music, art and physical education.

Extracurricular activities such as orchestra, student council, publications, arts and drama groups are also offered. The sports program includes hockey, football, lacrosse, soccer, basketball, baseball, skating, swimming, wrestling and track.

BEEKMAN SCHOOL
Day — Coed Gr 9-PG

New York, NY 10022. 220 E 50th St. Tel: 212-755-6666. Fax: 212-888-6085.
www.beekmanschool.org
George Higgins, Head. BA, Salisbury Univ, MA, New York Univ.
Col Prep. Gen Acad. AP—Calc. Feat—Creative_Writing Fr Lat Span Astron Bioethics Computers Web_Design Comp_Animation Econ Govt Psych Philos Film Photog Studio_Art. Supp—Dev_Read ESL Makeup Tut.
Adm (Gr 9-12): 25/yr. Appl due: Rolling.
Enr 80. B 42. G 38. Sec 79. PG 1. Wh 71%. Hisp 5%. Blk 9%. Asian 15%. Avg class size: 8. Fac 20. M 6/3. F 7/4. Wh 75%. Hisp 10%. Asian 15%. Adv deg: 90%.
Grad '04—25. Col—22. (Marymount Col-NY, NYU, Columbia, Boston U, Fordham,

Ithaca). Avg SAT: 1050. Alum 3100.
Tui '05-'06: Day $22,500 (+$500).
Summer: Acad Enrich Rev Rem. Tui Day $1500. 6 wks.
Plant val $2,500,000. Bldgs 1. Class rms 8. Libs 1. Sci labs 1. Comp labs 1. Art studios 1. Gyms 1. Pools 1. Gardens 1.
Est 1925. Inc. Quar (Sept-June).

Founded by George Matthew as the Tutoring School of New York, this small preparatory school is located in an East Side Manhattan townhouse. In the highly individualized program, the school does not place boys and girls in grades according to age, but rather by ability level. Beekman maintains a maximum class size of ten students, and schedules are arranged according to the pupil's needs and abilities. Students requiring extra help in a given subject receive daily small-group instruction as a supplement to regular course work. A full complement of electives is available. **See Also Pages 1114-5**

BIRCH WATHEN LENOX SCHOOL
Day — Coed Gr K-12

New York, NY 10021. 210 E 77th St. Tel: 212-861-0404. Fax: 212-879-3388.
 www.bwl.org   E-mail: admissions@bwl.org
Frank J. Carnabuci, Head. BA, Drew Univ, MA, Columbia Univ, EdM, Harvard Univ. **Julianne Kaplan, Adm.**
 Col Prep. Feat—Shakespeare Fr Japan Span Astron Computers Philos Ceramics Film Photog Sculpt Studio_Art Music.
 Adm: 88/yr. Accepted: 10%. Yield: 40%. **Tests** ISEE.
 Enr 450. Wh 82%. Hisp 6%. Blk 6%. Asian 6%. Avg class size: 12. **Fac 79.** Adv deg: 49%.
 Grad '04—42. Col—42. (Tulane 4, U of PA 2, Columbia 2, U of Chicago 2, Haverford 1, CT Col 1). Avg SAT: 1240. Alum 4100.
Tui '04-'05: Day $21,174-24,258 (+$1500).
 Endow $5,200,000. Plant val $30,000,000. Bldgs 1. Class rms 40. Lib 15,000 vols. Labs 5. Auds 1. Art studios 5. Music studios 3. Gyms 1.
 Est 1916. Nonprofit. (Sept-June). **Assoc** CLS.

Formed by the 1991 consolidation of the Birch Wathen School (founded in 1921) and the Lenox School (founded in 1916), Birch Wathen Lenox provides a challenging academic curriculum with a commitment to maintaining a balance among traditional education, innovation, student achievement and social development. This is achieved through small classes, individual attention and a favorable student-teacher ratio.

The curriculum includes a program in English, composition, math, science, history, foreign languages beginning in grade 4, computer science at all grade levels, art, instrumental and vocal music, word processing and woodworking. Advanced courses are available in all major curricular areas. In addition, students in grades 8-12 may take part in an overseas program that enables them to study the humanities and the social sciences under the supervision and the guidance of BWL faculty.

Activities such as school newspaper, literary journal, theater, community service, foreign language clubs, student council, business club, yearbook, student-faculty judiciary committee, photography club and Model UN complement academics. A comprehensive physical education program and a full interscholastic athletic sports program include soccer, basketball, softball, volleyball, swimming, tennis, team handball, modern dance and fitness.

BREARLEY SCHOOL
Day — Girls Gr K-12

New York, NY 10028. 610 E 83rd St. Tel: 212-744-8582. Fax: 212-472-8020.
www.brearley.org E-mail: admissions@brearley.org
Stephanie J. Hull, Head. PhD, Harvard Univ. Joan Kaplan, Actg Upper & Middle Sch Adm; Winifred M. Mabley, Actg Lower Sch Adm.
Col Prep. Feat—Chin Fr Greek Lat Span Programming Studio_Art Drama Music. Supp—Dev_Read Rem_Read Rev Tut.
Adm: 96/yr. Appl due: Dec. Accepted: 21%. Yield: 61%. Tests ISEE.
Enr 676. G 676. Elem 474. Sec 202. Wh 72%. Hisp 2%. Blk 9%. Asian 17%. Avg class size: 12. Fac 159. M 30/2. F 101/26. Wh 83%. Hisp 4%. Blk 5%. Asian 8%. Adv deg: 66%.
Grad '04—50. Col—50. (Harvard 6, Cornell 4, U of Chicago 4, U of PA 4, Princeton 3, Yale 3). Avg SAT: 1432. Alum 4000.
Tui '04-'05: Day $26,200-26,700. Aid: Need 138 ($2,657,000).
Summer: Rec. Tui Day $625. 2 wks.
Endow $71,000,000. Plant val $32,500,000. Bldgs 2. Class rms 60. Lib 25,000 vols. Sci labs 6. Comp labs 2. Auds 1. Art studios 5. Music studios 5. Dance studios 1. Gyms 3. Fields 1. Field houses 1.
Est 1884. Nonprofit. Sem (Sept-June).

Established by Samuel Brearley to provide a more substantial college preparatory program than most girls' schools of the time offered, Brearley has continuously maintained scholastic standards in the forefront among preparatory schools.

With a substantial scholarship program, the school seeks racial, religious and economic diversity in its student body. Since 1929 in a building overlooking the East River, the school offers a curriculum integrating many of the academic subjects and affording strong work in music and the arts. Although Brearley offers no honors or Advanced Placement courses, the school's regular classes prepare girls for the AP exams. Computers are utilized for instruction across the curriculum.

The school offers a wide variety of extracurricular activities, and it participates in a coordinated interscholastic academic and afternoon program with seven other New York City schools. Graduates enter leading colleges throughout the country.

THE BROWNING SCHOOL
Day — Boys Gr K-12

New York, NY 10021. 52 E 62nd St. Tel: 212-838-6280. Fax: 212-355-5602.
www.browning.edu E-mail: khenderson@browning.edu
Stephen M. Clement III, Head. BA, Yale Univ, MDiv, Union Theological Seminary, MEd, EdD, Harvard Univ. Jacqueline A. Casey, Adm.
Col Prep. Gen Acad. AP—Calc. Feat—Fr Lat Span Stats Anat & Physiol Computers Pol_Sci Psych Philos Ceramics Drawing Painting Visual_Arts Drama Chorus Music.
Adm: 64/yr. Appl due: Rolling. Tests ISEE SSAT.
Enr 370. B 370. Elem 264. Sec 106. Wh 79%. Hisp 5%. Blk 4%. Asian 2%. Other 10%. Avg class size: 15. Fac 49. M 19/3. F 25/2. Wh 94%. Hisp 2%. Blk 4%. Adv deg: 89%.
Grad '04—28. Col—28. (U of DE 4, Geo Wash 3, Vanderbilt 2, U of VA 2, Union Col-NY

2, Brown 1). Alum 1453.
Tui '04-'05: Day $25,598-25,698. Aid: Need 57 ($1,050,000).
Summer: Rec. 1-3 wks.
Endow $9,000,000. Plant val $5,338,000. Bldgs 3. Class rms 21. Lib 12,353 vols. Sci labs 4. Art studios 2. Music studios 1. Gyms 2. Fields 2.
Est 1888. Nonprofit. Tri (Sept-May).

Since its founding by John A. Browning, the school has offered a solid college preparatory program to students of varied interests and strong academic backgrounds. The curriculum offers elective courses in every department, and a wide variety of advanced courses and extracurricular activities is available. Browning participates in a cooperative program with seven other New York City schools that offers opportunities for academic sharing and extracurricular participation throughout the year. Older students may also take coordinate courses at girls' schools such as Marymount School and Hewitt School.

The athletic program includes intramural offerings, in addition to interscholastic soccer, basketball, baseball, tennis and cross-country teams.

THE BUCKLEY SCHOOL
Day — Boys Gr K-9

New York, NY 10021. 113 E 73rd St. **Tel:** 212-535-8787. **Fax:** 212-535-4622.
www.buckleyschoolnyc.org **E-mail:** admission@buckleyschoolnyc.org
Gregory J. O'Melia, Head. AB, EdM, Harvard Univ. **Jo Ann E. Lynch, Adm.**
   Pre-Prep. Feat—Fr Lat Span Computers Studio_Art Music Woodworking. **Supp**—Tut.
   Adm: 44/yr. Appl due: Rolling. Accepted: 16%. **Tests** IQ ISEE.
   Enr 351. B 351. Elem 336. Sec 15. Avg class size: 18. Uniform. **Fac 55.** M 17. F 38. Adv deg: 61%.
   Grad '04—37. Prep—37. (Trinity Sch-NY, Hotchkiss, Phillips Acad, Riverdale, Deerfield Acad, Taft). Alum 2006.
   Tui '02-'03: Day $17,800-20,000 (+$2300). **Aid:** Need 25 ($466,000).
   Endow $14,000,000. Plant val $18,000,000. Bldgs 3. Class rms 29. 2 Libs 18,000 vols. Sci labs 3. Comp labs 1. Math labs 1. Auds 1. Theaters 1. Art studios 2. Music studios 2. Wood shops 1. Gyms 4. Fields 4. Courts 1.
   Est 1913. Nonprofit. Tri (Sept-June).

This school was founded by B. Lord Buckley, a professional educator and innovator. Originally located above a milliner's shop on Madison Avenue, the school moved to larger quarters on 74th Street in 1917. After experiencing significant plant and educational improvements in response to changing times and a growing enrollment in the 1930s and 1940s, Buckley was fully remodeled in 1963. It then expanded and connected to an addition on 73rd Street. This expansion resulted in a broadening of the teaching program and the eventual addition of grade 9. Other plant improvements have followed, particularly after the 1996 acquisition of adjacent property on 73rd Street.

The balanced curriculum emphasizes mastery of academic fundamentals. During the lower school years, boys develop basic skills in the areas of reading, writing and math. Understanding of concepts and successful application of new skills take precedence over the rate of knowledge acquisition. Lower schoolers do not receive letter grades; instead, faculty submit to parents twice-yearly written comments concerning each area of the student's progress. In the transitional middle school years, boys gain an increased level of independence while improving their academic skills and study habits. The upper school program continues to stress the fundamentals and boys may undertake more independent research projects, assume greater responsibility for class participation and develop their abstract thinking skills. The arts are integral to the program, beginning in the early years. A skills and remediation specialist provides small-group instruction at all grade levels.

All boys participate in the athletic program. Soccer, football, basketball, baseball and lacrosse are later supplemented by cross-country, track and field, wrestling and gymnastics. After playing sports intramurally in the lower and middle school, all students engage in interscholastic competition at the junior varsity or varsity level.

CALHOUN SCHOOL
Day — Coed Gr PS-12

New York, NY 10024. 433 W End Ave. Tel: 212-497-6510. Fax: 212-497-6531.
www.calhoun.org   E-mail: admissions@calhoun.org
Steven J. Nelson, Head. BA, Case Western Reserve Univ. **Nancy Sherman, Upper & Middle Sch Adm; Robin Otton, Lower Sch Adm.**

- **Col Prep. Feat**—Fr Span Stats Comp_Sci Web_Design Law Psych African_Art Labor & Film Drama.
- **Adm:** 127/yr. Accepted: 37%. Yield: 31%. **Tests** CTP_4 ISEE.
- **Enr 669.** B 324. G 345. Elem 492. Sec 177. Wh 77%. Hisp 9%. Blk 6%. Am Ind 1%. Asian 7%. Avg class size: 14. **Fac 118.** M 44/3. F 68/3. Wh 65%. Hisp 10%. Blk 16%. Asian 9%. Adv deg: 55%.
- **Grad '04—43. Col—43.** (NYU, Sarah Lawrence, Bard, Wesleyan U, Skidmore, Colgate). Avg SAT: 1200. Alum 1717.
- **Tui '04-'05: Day $21,700-25,600** (+$100-400). **Aid:** Need 136 ($2,237,200).
- Endow $1,604,000. Plant val $20,609,000. Bldgs 2. Class rms 69. 2 Libs 20,000 vols. Sci labs 5. Lang labs 4. Comp labs 3. Auds 1. Theaters 2. Art studios 3. Music studios 4. Dance studios 1. Gyms 2.
- **Est 1896.** Nonprofit. Sem (Sept-June). **Assoc** CLS.

Founded by Laura Jacobi as the Jacobi School for Girls, the school assumed its present name in 1924, while under the leadership of Mary E. Calhoun. The school became coeducational in 1971. From its beginnings, it has been a college preparatory institution located on Manhattan's Upper West Side. A second West Side campus hosts three-year-old through first grade programs.

The curriculum reflects a progressive, interdisciplinary approach and allows for individualization through independent study projects and enrichment activities. A strong advisory system supports students in all areas of school life. Other distinctive features include active studio art and theater programs; computer literacy and community service requirements; a student exchange program; leadership and peer tutoring programs; and an extensive extracurricular program that includes varsity sports, dramatic productions, student publications and many interest clubs.

THE CATHEDRAL SCHOOL
Day — Coed Gr K-8

New York, NY 10025. 1047 Amsterdam Ave. Tel: 212-316-7500. Fax: 212-316-7558.

NY Middle Atlantic States 377

www.cathedralnyc.org   E-mail: admission@cathedralnyc.org
Marsha K. Nelson, Head. BS, Univ of Texas-Austin, BME, Baylor Univ, MA, Columbia Univ.
Linda D. Mathews, Adm.
  Pre-Prep. Feat—Fr Lat Span Computers Studio_Art Music. **Supp**—Dev_Read.
  Adm (Gr K-7): 47/yr. Appl due: Dec. Accepted: 45%. Yield: 27%. **Tests** CTP_4 ISEE.
  Enr 241. B 127. G 114. Elem 241. Wh 73%. Hisp 5%. Blk 16%. Asian 5%. Other 1%. Avg
    class size: 14. Uniform. **Fac 42.** M 9/1. F 24/8. Wh 76%. Hisp 5%. Blk 10%. Asian 9%.
    Adv deg: 54%.
  Grad '04—30. Prep—23. (Dalton 4, Friends Seminary 2, Marymount Sch 2, Trinity Sch-NY 1, Riverdale 1). Alum 750.
  Tui '04-'05: Day $20,950-21,650 (+$800-1050). **Aid:** Need 85 ($874,970).
  Endow $3,600,000. Plant val $3,600,000. Bldgs 1. Class rms 16. Lib 7000 vols. Sci labs 2.
    Comp labs 1. Art studios 2. Music studios 1. Gyms 2.
  Est 1901. Nonprofit. Episcopal. Tri (Sept-June).

The school was founded by Rt. Rev. Henry Codman Potter, the Episcopal bishop of New York City, as a boys' boarding school to provide the choir for the Cathedral of St. John the Divine. In 1964, Cathedral began enrolling male day students of all faiths. Girls were first admitted in 1974.

Located in a building on the 13-acre Cathedral Close, the school offers a solid foundation in the basic elementary school subjects that integrates the arts, athletics and leadership opportunities. French and Spanish instruction begins in kindergarten. Older pupils take French or Spanish in grades 4-8, while also enrolling in Latin courses in grades 7 and 8. Every student attends two chapel services weekly, and community service is part of the curriculum. On the basis of auditions, 25 to 28 boys and girls in grades 4-8 have the option of serving as choristers of the affiliated Cathedral of St. John the Divine; in exchange, they receive a partial scholarship.

Extracurricular activities include student council, yearbook and sports.

THE CHAPIN SCHOOL
Day — Girls Gr K-12

New York, NY 10028. 100 E End Ave. Tel: 212-744-2335. Fax: 212-535-8138.
  www.chapin.edu   E-mail: admissions@chapin.edu
Patricia T. Hayot, Head. BA, MA, PhD, Univ of Michigan. **Tina I. Herman, Adm.**
  Col Prep. AP—Eng Fr Lat Span Calc Stats Bio Physics Eur_Hist US_Hist Art_Hist
    Studio_Art. **Feat**—Shakespeare Russ_Lit Chin Greek Astron Programming Women's_Hist Asian_Hist Terrorism African-Amer_Experience Comp_Relig Philos Drama
    Music Ballet Dance Gymnastics. **Supp**—Rev Tut.
  Adm: 72/yr. Appl due: Dec. Accepted: 24%. **Tests** IQ ISEE.
  Enr 658. G 658. Elem 468. Sec 190. Wh 75%. Hisp 3%. Blk 7%. Asian 6%. Other 9%. Avg
    class size: 16. Uniform. **Fac 117.** M 12/3. F 98/4. Wh 85%. Hisp 5%. Blk 4%. Asian
    6%. Adv deg: 64%.
  Grad '04—39. Col—39. (Colgate 3, Harvard 2, Brown 2, Columbia 2, Middlebury 2, Williams 2). Alum 4000.
  Tui '04-'05: Day $23,700 (+$800-2000). **Aid:** Need 102 ($2,123,000).
  Endow $51,000,000. Plant val $29,600,000. Bldgs 1. Class rms 62. Lib 32,000 vols. Sci
    labs 6. Lang labs 1. Comp labs 2. Theaters 1. Art studios 4. Music studios 2. Dance
    studios 2. Gyms 4. Greenhouses 1.
  Est 1901. Nonprofit. (Sept-June).

Founded as a primary school by Maria Bowen Chapin under the name of Miss Chapin's School for Girls, this school was incorporated as an elementary and secondary school in 1925. In 1928, it moved from two brownstone houses on East 57th Street to its own building on East End Avenue at 84th Street. The school assumed its current name in 1934.

The course of study emphasizes the liberal arts, the sciences and technology. Elective courses provide opportunities for study at an advanced level. Girls participate in a diverse extracurricular program that includes art, dance, drama, gymnastics, literary magazine, music, newspaper, photography, science and sports. School offerings are enriched by an individual study program in the senior year, special off-campus term programs, volunteer community service, and an academic and extracurricular exchange through the eight-school New York City consortium.

CITY & COUNTRY SCHOOL
Day — Coed Gr PS-8

New York, NY 10011. 146 W 13th St. Tel: 212-242-7802. Fax: 212-242-7996.
www.cityandcountry.org   E-mail: lisah@cityandcountry.org
Kate Turley, Prin. BA, State Univ of New York-Oswego, MA, New York Univ. **Lisa Horner, Adm.**

Pre-Prep. Feat—Lib_Skills Span Computers Studio_Art Drama Music Orchestra Carpentry. **Supp**—Dev_Read.

Adm (Gr PS-7): 60/yr. Appl due: Dec. Accepted: 25%. **Tests** CTP_4.

Enr 268. B 130. G 138. Elem 268. Wh 86%. Hisp 5%. Blk 4%. Asian 4%. Other 1%. Avg class size: 15. **Fac 51.** M 6. F 42/3. Wh 99%. Blk 1%.

Grad '04—14. Prep—11. (Trevor 2, Packer 2, Dalton 1, Loyola Sch 1). Alum 1572.

Tui '04-'05: Day $10,700-20,900 (+$1425). **Aid:** Need 36 ($260,400).

Summer: Enrich Rec. Tui Day $145-245/wk. 6 wks.

Plant val $2,000,000. Bldgs 5. Lib 8000 vols. Labs 1. Auds 1. Art studios 2. Music studios 2. Shops 1. Gyms 1.

Est 1914. Nonprofit. Sem (Sept-June).

Founded by Caroline Pratt, City & Country conducts a curriculum designed to help students explore firsthand experiences, play and responsible work, and to develop social and academic skills in an atmosphere of trust. For children ages 8-13, a strong history and social studies curriculum is built around a job program in which each class runs a school service (supplies, mail service, print shop and so on). The program includes opportunities for individualized work and research at each age, as well as a natural daily impetus for perfecting reading, writing, mathematical and creative skills.

Art, woodworking, science, music, computer and rhythms are integral to the program. The library, specially developed over the years as a source for the social studies program, is notable for its collection of primary source material.

COLLEGIATE SCHOOL
Day — Boys Gr K-12

New York, NY 10024. 260 W 78th St. Tel: 212-812-8500. Fax: 212-812-8514.
www.collegiateschool.org   E-mail: admissions@collegiateschool.org

W. Lee Pierson, Int Head. BA, Princeton Univ, MA, Univ of Pennsylvania, EdD, Harvard Univ.
Joanne P. Heyman, Adm.
- Col Prep. **Feat**—Shakespeare Russ & Chin_Lit Chin Fr Greek Lat Span Stats Anat & Physiol Astron Computers Japan & Chin_Hist Relig Art_Hist Ceramics Film Studio_Art Drama.
- **Adm (Gr K-11):** 68/yr. Appl due: Dec. Accepted: 12%. Yield: 81%. **Tests** ISEE SSAT.
- **Enr 623.** B 623. Elem 417. Sec 206. Wh 73%. Hisp 5%. Blk 9%. Asian 13%. Avg class size: 16. **Fac 102.** M 45/4. F 46/7. Wh 79%. Hisp 4%. Blk 6%. Asian 7%. Other 4%. Adv deg: 68%.
- **Grad '04—49. Col—49.** (U of PA, Princeton, Harvard, Hamilton, Yale, Columbia). Avg SAT: 1460. Alum 2800.
- **Tui '04-'05: Day $23,900-24,300. Aid:** Need 115 ($2,400,000).
- Endow $52,000,000. Plant val $25,000,000. Bldgs 3. Class rms 60. Lib 40,000 vols. Sci labs 3. Comp labs 3. Theaters 2. Art studios 2. Music studios 6. Gyms 3. Courts 2.
- **Est 1628.** Nonprofit. Sem (Sept-June). **Assoc** CLS.

The oldest school in the country, Collegiate traces its history back to the early settlement of Manhattan by the Dutch; it operated as a parish day school for two and a half centuries, interrupted only when the city was occupied by British troops during the Revolution. In 1887, it became a grammar school, in 1891 preparatory, and after 1894 for boys only. Incorporated in 1940 as a nonprofit institution, the school is governed by a board, one-fifth of which represents the consistory of the Collegiate Dutch Reformed Church. In 1978, Collegiate purchased the 12-story West End Plaza Hotel, which is adjacent to the school campus on 78th Street. Six floors of the building have been converted to school use. In the late 1990s, the school erected a new building and completed renovations to existing space, thereby increasing the physical plant by one-fourth.

The rigorous academic program affords thorough grounding for leading colleges. There are many electives, especially in English and history. Both advanced courses and independent study opportunities are also part of the curriculum. Interscholastic competition is provided in cross-country, soccer, basketball, tennis, baseball, track and wrestling. Extracurricular activities include drama, music, debate, publications and interest clubs.

COLUMBIA GRAMMAR AND PREPARATORY SCHOOL
Day — Coed Gr PS-12

New York, NY 10025. 5 W 93rd St. Tel: 212-749-6200. Fax: 212-865-4278.
www.cgps.org   E-mail: info@cgps.org
Richard J. Soghoian, Head. BA, Univ of Virginia, PhD, Columbia Univ. **Simone Hristidis, Adm.**
- Col Prep. **AP**—Bio Chem Physics Eur_Hist US_Hist Psych US_Govt & Pol. **Feat**—Creative_Writing NY_Lit Chin Fr Japan Lat Span Anat & Physiol Ecol Genetics Geol Microbiol Meteorology Computers Econ Pol_Sci Lat-Amer_Stud Philos World_Relig Ceramics Film Photog Drama Band Chorus Music_Theory Orchestra. **Supp**—Dev_Read ESL LD Makeup Tut.
- **Adm (Gr PS-9):** 155/yr. Appl due: Dec. Accepted: 23%. Yield: 45%. **Tests** ISEE.
- **Enr 1022.** B 517. G 505. Elem 659. Sec 363. Wh 87%. Hisp 5%. Blk 4%. Asian 4%. Avg class size: 13. **Fac 161.** M 41/7. F 92/21. Wh 92%. Hisp 2%. Blk 2%. Asian 4%. Adv deg: 65%.
- **Grad '04—85. Col—85.** (NYU 6, U of PA 5, Skidmore 4, Boston U 4, Columbia 3, U of MI 3). Avg SAT: 1280. Alum 3800.

Tui '04-'05: Day $22,750-25,700. **Aid:** Need 219 ($2,560,550).
Endow $12,500,000. Plant val $50,000,000. Bldgs 9. Class rms 75. Lib 27,500 vols. Sci labs 11. Comp labs 4. Dark rms 1. Theaters 2. Art studios 6. Music studios 7. Gyms 3. Pools 1.
Est 1764. Nonprofit. Sem (Sept-June).

Founded as a preparatory school for Columbia College and under the direction of the university for 100 years, this school rose to high prominence in the mid-19th century under Dr. Charles Anthon, America's earliest classical scholar. Today, the school is an independent institution with a board of trustees.

The curriculum prepares graduates for leading colleges throughout the country. Elective courses are offered in English, social sciences, science, math, art, film, drama and music, and Advanced Placement courses many disciplines. Juniors and seniors may complete independent work through study tutorials.

Publications, drama, chorus and orchestra, studio art, filmmaking, photography, student government and various other activities complement academics. CGPS provides intramural and interscholastic athletic competition in soccer, basketball, swimming, baseball, tennis, softball, golf, volleyball, track and cross-country.

CONVENT OF THE SACRED HEART
Day — Girls Gr PS-12

New York, NY 10128. 1 E 91st St. Tel: 212-722-4745. Fax: 212-996-1784.
www.cshnyc.org   E-mail: info@cshnyc.org
Mary Blake, Head. BS, St John's Univ (NY), MA, New School for Social Research, MA, Antioch College, EdD, Nova Southeastern Univ. **Barbara S. Root, Adm.**
   Col Prep. AP—Eng Fr Lat Span Calc Stats Bio Chem Physics US_Hist Studio_Art Music_Theory. **Feat—**Shakespeare Robotics Ceramics Film Photog Drama Chorus Dance Debate.
Adm: 91/yr. Appl due: Dec. Accepted: 18%. **Tests** ISEE.
Enr 649. G 649. Elem 453. Sec 196. Wh 75%. Hisp 10%. Blk 5%. Asian 8%. Other 2%. Avg class size: 16. Uniform. **Fac 109.** M 16. F 93. Adv deg: 74%.
Grad '04—47. Col—47. (Cornell, NYU, Fordham, U of PA, Boston Col). Alum 3500.
Tui '04-'05: Day $23,875 (+$800). **Aid:** Need 110 ($1,700,000).
Summer: Ages 6-15. Rec. Creative Arts. Tui Day $1400. 4 wks.
Endow $18,200,000. Plant val $40,000,000. Bldgs 2. Class rms 36. 3 Libs 35,000 vols. Chapels 1. Sci labs 3. Comp labs 3. Theaters 1. Art studios 3. Music studios 3. Gyms 2.
Est 1881. Nonprofit. Roman Catholic. Sem (Sept-June).

The oldest private girls' school in Manhattan, Sacred Heart offers a solid college preparatory program with an emphasis on small-class instruction, a diversity of backgrounds among faculty and students, and community service in the urban environment. Features of the curriculum include independent study, Advanced Placement courses, and a broad selection of electives that includes creative writing, studio art, pottery, photography, computer graphics and the theater arts. Opportunity for exchange study is available within the worldwide Network of Sacred Heart Schools. Over the years, students have attended Sacred Heart schools in France, Spain and Belgium for a semester, as well as some of the schools in the US; their counterparts have come here. Religion courses are required of all students.

Cocurricular activities include choir, a drama workshop, publications, an active student council, clubs, dance and various sports. Located on Fifth Avenue opposite Central Park, the school's two buildings have been designated as city landmarks for their architectural styles. The principal structure is the former Otto Kahn residence, a copy of an Italian Renaissance palace; the adjoining rococo-style mansion had belonged to James Burden.

DALTON SCHOOL
Day — Coed Gr K-12

New York, NY 10128. 108 E 89th St. Tel: 212-423-5200. Fax: 212-423-5259.
 www.dalton.org E-mail: admissions@dalton.org
Ellen C. Stein, Head. BA, Univ of Pennsylvania, MBA, Columbia Univ. **Eva Rado & Elisabeth Krents,** Adms.

- **Col Prep. Feat**—Creative_Writing Poetry Shakespeare Russ_Lit African-Amer_Lit Fr Greek Lat Mandarin Span Stats Comp_Sci Web_Design Psych Govt & Pol Philos Art_Hist Sculpt Acting Drama Music Music_Hist Music_Theory Dance Journ. **Supp**—Rem_Math Rem_Read Tut.
- **Adm (Gr K-11):** 160/yr. Appl due: Dec. Accepted: 16%. **Tests** ISEE SSAT.
- **Enr 1316.** B 644. G 672. Wh 72%. Hisp 3%. Blk 9%. Asian 8%. Other 8%. Avg class size: 15. **Fac 198.** M 50/8. F 119/21. Wh 82%. Hisp 5%. Blk 5%. Asian 3%. Other 3%. Adv deg: 71%.
- **Grad '04—112. Col**—112. (Yale, Harvard, U of PA, Brown, Wesleyan U, U of WI-Madison). Avg SAT: 1420. Alum 5000.
- **Tui '04-'05: Day $27,600. Aid:** Need 261 ($4,600,000). Endow $30,000,000. Plant val $35,000,000. Bldgs 5. Class rms 96. Lib 65,000 vols. Labs 4. Theaters 2. Art studios 4. Music studios 4. Gyms 4.
- **Est 1919.** Nonprofit. Sem (Sept-June).

Founded by Helen Parkhurst, the school applies the theories of her widely known Dalton Plan. The plan utilizes "the House, the Assignment and the Laboratory" to assist each student in accepting increasing responsibility for his or her education.

The present building opened in the autumn of 1929. Eleanor Roosevelt, who admired Miss Parkhurst's work, played an important role in expanding the school by promoting a merger between the Todhunter School and Dalton in 1939. Today, Miss Parkhurst's basic techniques have been broadened and modernized from the First Program (grades K-3) through high school.

Approximately 140 full-time and semester courses are offered. High school students plan their own laboratory time and choose their courses with the help of an advisor. Computer science is required for graduation. Seniors may pursue independent projects during second semester, and qualified students may enroll in inter-school courses at seven other New York City independent schools. Dalton also offers internships and study projects in hospitals and business firms and funds a lectureship at the Metropolitan Museum of Art and the American Museum of Natural History, enabling students to take full advantage of its facilities and resources.

Varsity and junior varsity athletic programs include football, soccer, wrestling, volleyball, baseball, basketball and tennis. Among extracurricular activities is a wide variety of interest clubs.

THE DWIGHT SCHOOL
Day — Coed Gr PS-12

New York, NY 10024. 291 Central Park W. Tel: 212-724-2146. Fax: 212-724-2539.
www.dwight.edu   E-mail: admissions@dwight.edu

Stephen H. Spahn, Chancellor. AB, Dartmouth College, MA, Oxford Univ (England). **Marina Bernstein,** Gr 7-12 Adm; **Emily Lyons,** Gr K-6 Adm.

Col Prep. IB Diploma. IB PYP. IB MYP. **Feat**—Chin Ger Hebrew Ital Japan Mandarin Russ Dutch Arabic Hindi Philos Art_Hist Film Theater_Arts Music. **Supp**—ESL LD Rem_Math Rem_Read Tut.

Adm (Gr PS-11): 108/yr. Appl due: Dec. **Tests** CTP_4 ISEE SSAT.

Enr 431. B 244. G 187. Elem 188. Sec 243. Wh 70%. Hisp 5%. Blk 5%. Asian 10%. Other 10%. Avg class size: 15. Uniform. **Fac 80.** Adv deg: 73%.

Grad '04—67. Col—67. (Cornell, Dartmouth, NYU, Trinity Col-CT, Georgetown, Northwestern). Alum 2000.

Tui '04-'05: Day $23,400-25,100 (+$1500). **Aid:** Need 72 ($9,500,000).

Summer: Acad Enrich Rev. ESL. 2 wks.

Endow $5,000,000. Plant val $20,000,000. Bldgs 3. Class rms 34. 2 Libs 15,000 vols. Sci labs 3. Lang labs 1. Comp labs 1. Dark rms 1. Comp ctrs 2. Auds 1. Theaters 2. Art studios 2. Music studios 1. Dance studios 1. Gyms 2.

Est 1880. Inc. Tri (Sept-June). **Assoc** MSA.

The school was founded as an academy of classical studies. Most of its students at that time went on to Yale University. In 1888, Timothy Dwight, president of Yale, became active in school affairs, and the school was renamed in his honor. Dwight became the first independent day school in the US to establish a permanent international campus when it founded its London, England campus, the Woodside Park School, in 1972. In 1993, Dwight combined with the Anglo-American International School.

The school comprises a preschool and four houses: Timothy House (grades K-4), Bentley House (grades 5-8), Franklin House (grades 9 and 10) and Anglo House (grades 11 and 12). Students follow the International Baccalaureate curriculum at all grade levels. The IB Primary Years Program addresses the child's social, physical, emotional and cultural needs, in addition to his or her academic welfare. The IB Middle Years Program provides a comprehensive, developmentally appropriate framework of academics and life skills instruction. The curriculum concludes with the IB Diploma Program, a rigorous pre-university course of studies that leads to examinations suitable for motivated high schoolers. Graduates attend competitive US colleges, as well as such foreign universities as Oxford, Cambridge, the Sorbonne, and the universities of Edinburgh, Rome and Milan.

French and Chinese courses begin in kindergarten, while Spanish is added to the curriculum in grade 5. The high school program includes French, Spanish and Latin, as well as certain languages on a tutorial basis: Italian, Japanese, German, Dutch and Hindi, among others.

Extracurricular activities include various athletics, music and drama programs, student government, Model UN and neighborhood outreach programs. All high school students must be involved in some form of community service. Numerous publications are produced at all grade levels, and the school sponsors trips each year to such places as France, England and Costa Rica. The QUEST program provides individualized instruction for pupils with mild learning differences.

GRACE CHURCH SCHOOL
Day — Coed Gr PS-8

New York, NY 10003. 86 4th Ave. Tel: 212-475-5609. Fax: 212-475-5015.
www.gcschool.org E-mail: mhirschman@gcschool.org
George P. Davison, Head. BA, Yale Univ, MA, Columbia Univ. **Martha J. Hirschman, Adm.**

Pre-Prep. Feat—Fr Lat Span Computers Ethics Relig Studio_Art Drama Music. **Supp**—Rem_Math Rem_Read Tut.

Adm: 60/yr. Appl due: Dec. Accepted: 24%. **Tests** IQ ISEE.

Enr 392. B 176. G 216. Elem 392. Wh 77%. Hisp 4%. Blk 8%. Asian 9%. Other 2%. Avg class size: 22. Uniform. **Fac 64.** M 19/1. F 40/4. Adv deg: 43%.

Grad '04—41. Prep—36. (Trinity Sch-NY 4, Spence 4, Chapin 3, Brearley 2, Dalton 2, Lawrenceville 2). Alum 1520.

Tui '04-'05: Day $20,650-23,150 (+$50-400). **Aid:** Need 73 ($1,070,425).

Endow $8,000,000. Plant val $17,000,000. Bldgs 5. Class rms 22. Lib 10,000 vols. Sci labs 3. Comp labs 3. Art studios 3. Music studios 1. Dance studios 1. Shops 1. Gyms 1. Greenhouses 1.

Est 1894. Nonprofit. Episcopal. Sem (Sept-June).

Established as a choir school for boys and still an integral part of Grace Church, GCS has evolved into a coeducational pre-preparatory school. Ethical and scholastic development and Judeo-Christian beliefs are emphasized, and upper school students perform regular community service. Preparing students for leading secondary schools, the curriculum features enrichment opportunities in computer, music, art and drama, as well as various electives in the upper grades.

All children in the interracial and interdenominational student body attend chapel and take courses in the Bible, world religions and ethics. The after-school program serves as an extension of the academic day and also includes the arts and sports.

HEWITT SCHOOL
Day — Girls Gr K-12

New York, NY 10021. 45 E 75th St. Tel: 212-288-1919. Fax: 212-472-7531.
www.hewittschool.org E-mail: admissions@hewittschool.org
Linda MacMurray Gibbs, Head. MALS, Wesleyan Univ. **Anita Edwards, Adm.**

Col Prep. AP—Eng Fr Lat Span Calc Bio Art_Hist. **Feat**—Stats Anat & Physiol Astron Ecol Computers Econ Psych Comp_Relig Relig Film Photog Studio_Art Drama Chorus Music Dance Public_Speak.

Adm (Gr K-10): 81/yr. Appl due: Dec. Accepted: 46%. Yield: 41%. **Tests** ISEE.

Enr 461. G 461. Elem 347. Sec 114. Wh 86%. Hisp 5%. Blk 4%. Asian 3%. Other 2%. Avg class size: 16. **Fac 70.** M 16. F 54. Wh 93%. Hisp 1%. Blk 2%. Am Ind 1%. Asian 1%. Other 2%. Adv deg: 80%.

Grad '04—23. Col—23. (Geo Wash 2, NYU 2, CT Col 2, Duke 1, Brown 1, Georgetown 1). Avg SAT: 1210. Alum 2000.

Tui '04-'05: Day $24,050-26,175. Aid: Need 61 ($1,044,161).

Summer: Rec. Tui Day $550. 2 wks.

Endow $4,000,000. Plant val $38,000,000. Bldgs 3. Class rms 40. 2 Libs 12,000 vols. Sci labs 3. Comp labs 2. Dark rms 1. Auds 2. Theaters 1. Art studios 3. Music studios 3. Dance studios 1. Gyms 1.

Est 1920. Nonprofit. Sem (Sept-June).

The college preparatory curriculum at this small school provides students with a firm grounding in the liberal arts, with emphasis placed upon the humanities, the sciences and the arts. In the lower school (grades K-3), children develop basic academic skills through an interdisciplinary program that enables them to engage in problem solving and creative thinking. Foreign language study and the integrated use of technology both begin in kindergarten.

During the middle school years (grades 4-7), girls continue to build their analytical thinking and study skills through a content-rich curriculum that also prepares them for advanced work in the traditional disciplines. Upper schoolers (grades 8-12), who choose from a range of Advanced Placement offerings, take four or five academic courses per year, as well as one or two arts classes. Technology is integral to the program at all levels, as evidenced by a laptop program that commences in grade 8.

Hewitt's Upper East Side location permits students and faculty to make extensive use of the city's museums, parks, galleries and theaters; in addition, this location enables girls to volunteer for a variety of community service projects. Extracurricular activities at the school include publications, student council, drama, interest clubs and interscholastic athletics.

LA SCUOLA D'ITALIA
Day — Coed Gr PS-12

New York, NY 10128. 12 E 96th St. Tel: 212-369-3290. Fax: 212-369-1164.
www.lascuoladitalia.org   E-mail: admin@lascuoladitalia.org
Bianca Maria Padolecchia Goodrich, Head. Pia Pedicini, Adm.

Col Prep. Bilingual. Feat—Fr Ital Lat Anat & Physiol Ecol Geol Comp_Sci Geog Sociol Philos Studio_Art Drama Music Indus_Arts. **Supp**—ESL Rem_Math Tut.

Adm: 50/yr. Appl due: Rolling. **Tests** CTP_4.

Enr 190. B 96. G 94. Elem 177. Sec 13. Wh 92%. Hisp 6%. Blk 1%. Asian 1%. Avg class size: 15. **Fac 31.** M 5/3. F 18/5. Wh 98%. Hisp 1%. Blk 1%. Adv deg: 54%.

Grad '04—2. Col—2. (Bocconi-Italy, Fordham, Normale-Italy, U of Bologna-Italy). Avg SAT: 1200. Alum 100.

Tui '05-'06: Day $14,500-17,000 (+$1000-1100).

Plant val $5,500,000. Bldgs 2. Class rms 15. Lib 3000 vols. Sci labs 1. Comp labs 2. Auds 1. Gyms 1.

Est 1977. Nonprofit. Sem (Sept-June).

La Scuola d'Italia Guglielmo Marconi integrates educational features of Italian and American schools. Students become bilingual and bicultural through the use of English and Italian as languages of instruction from preschool through 12th grade. The main curriculum spans a wide range of studies in mathematics and computer science, the natural and physical sciences, the humanities, the social sciences and the arts. French is mandatory in grades 7-9, and, in the upper school, students follow a compulsory program of studies that includes a four-year Latin requirement.

Upon adding a second location at 406 E. 67th St. in September 2000, La Scuola launched a new curriculum at the middle school level (grades 6-8) that employs English as the language of instruction. This program combines a firm grounding in math, science and the liberal arts with rigorous language instruction that provides a strong foundation for advanced study at the high school and college levels. Participating students also develop a deeper appreciation of the Italian and European cultures.

LITTLE RED SCHOOL HOUSE AND ELISABETH IRWIN HIGH SCHOOL

Day — Coed Gr PS-12

New York, NY 10014. 272 6th Ave. Tel: 212-477-5316. Fax: 212-677-9159.
www.lrei.org   E-mail: admissions@lrei.org
Philip Kassen, Dir. Samantha Kirby Caruth, Adm.
  Col Prep. Feat—Writing Fr Span Environ_Sci Engineering Comp_Design Robotics Econ Urban_Stud Film Photog Studio_Art Video Drama Music Dance Indus_Arts.
  Adm: 115/yr. Appl due: Dec. **Tests** ISEE.
  Enr 550. Elem 399. Sec 151. Wh 74%. Hisp 7%. Blk 12%. Asian 7%. Avg class size: 20. **Fac 90.** Adv deg: 43%.
  Grad '04—30. Col—30. (NYU 2, Bard 2, Northeastern U 2, Drexel 2, Yale 1, Columbia 1). Alum 1750.
  Tui '04-'05: Day $21,410-24,555 (+$400).
  Plant val $5,000,000. Bldgs 2. Class rms 30. 2 Libs 15,000 vols. Sci labs 3. Comp labs 2. Dark rms 1. Auds 1. Theaters 1. Art studios 3. Music studios 2. Wood shops 1. Gyms 2.
  Est 1921. Nonprofit. (Sept-June).

LREI is a college preparatory day school. The student body comes from all parts of New York City, reflecting the city's economic, ethnic and cultural diversity. The school began as an experiment in the New York City public schools, but it has been independent since 1932.

The curriculum throughout the school revolves around core themes, integrating language arts/English and social studies/history, as well as a required arts program. Writing is emphasized in all curricular areas. In the lower school (grades pre-K-4), understanding and skills in reading, mathematics and science are stressed. The middle school (grades 5-8) was established as a formal entity in 1986. Its program, which is based on a strong humanities curriculum, stresses theme studies and skills development.

The high school (grades 9-12), established in 1941, offers an academically demanding course of study with a wide range of electives. Advanced courses for upperclassmen prepare boys and girls for the AP exams. Graduates attend competitive colleges.

LOYOLA SCHOOL

Day — Coed Gr 9-12

New York, NY 10028. 980 Park Ave. Tel: 212-288-3522. Fax: 212-861-1021.
www.loyola-nyc.org   E-mail: admissions@loyola-nyc.org
Rev. Stephen Katsouros, SJ, Pres. BA, Univ of Maryland-College Park, MS, Fordham Univ, MA, Loyola Univ of Chicago, MDiv, Weston Jesuit School of Theology, EdM, Harvard Univ, EdD, Columbia Univ. **James Lyness, Head.** BA, MST, Boston College, MS, Manhattan College. **Lillian Diaz-Imbelli, Adm.**
  Col Prep. AP—Eng Fr Lat Span Stats Bio Chem Physics Eur_Hist US_Hist. **Feat**—Creative_Writing Ital Comp_Sci Econ Govt Psych Theol World_Relig Graphic_Arts Chorus Music Orchestra.
  Adm (Gr 9-11): 60/yr. Appl due: Dec. **Tests** Stanford.
  Enr 205. B 115. G 90. Sec 205. Wh 78%. Hisp 12%. Blk 5%. Asian 5%. Avg class size: 15. Uniform. **Fac 23.** M 14. F 9. Adv deg: 95%.
  Grad '04—57. Col—57. (Holy Cross, Fordham, Harvard, NYU, Georgetown, Boston Col).

Avg SAT: 1240. Alum 1600.
Tui '04-'05: Day $19,025 (+$650).
Endow $3,000,000. Bldgs 2. Class rms 13. Lib 10,500 vols. Sci labs 2. Comp labs 1. Theaters 1. Art studios 1. Music studios 1. Gyms 1.
Est 1900. Nonprofit. Roman Catholic. Quar (Sept-May). **Assoc** MSA.

Advantageously located in close proximity to many of Manhattan's museums, libraries and theaters, this well-known Jesuit school offers a solid college preparatory program. The flexible curriculum includes Advanced Placement courses and electives. All students fulfill a theology requirement.

The performing and visual arts, instrumental and choral groups, community service programs and interest clubs complement academics. Students may compete interscholastically on the soccer, basketball, volleyball, baseball, softball, track and cross-country teams, or they may participate in the intramural program.

LYCEE FRANCAIS DE NEW YORK
Day — Coed Gr PS-12

New York, NY 10021. 505 E 75th St. Tel: 212-369-1400. Fax: 212-439-4210.
 www.lfny.org E-mail: admissions@lfny.org
Yves Theze, Head. Martine Lala, Adm.
   Col Prep. Fr Bac. Bilingual. Feat—Ger Greek Ital Span Comp_Sci Philos. **Supp**—ESL Rem_Read Rev Tut.
   Adm: 270/yr. Appl due: Rolling.
   Enr 1200. Wh 82%. Hisp 4%. Blk 13%. Asian 1%. Avg class size: 20. **Fac 121.** M 32. F 85/4. Adv deg: 66%.
   Grad '04—35. Col—35. (McGill-Canada, Tufts, Fordham, Georgetown, Barnard, NYU). Alum 3000.
   Tui '04-'05: Day $14,000-19,000 (+$750). **Aid:** Need 200 ($225,000).
Bldgs 1. Class rms 62. 2 Libs 18,000 vols. Sci labs 6. Comp labs 2. Theaters 1. Art studios 2. Music studios 3. Dance studios 1. Gyms 2.
Est 1935. Nonprofit. Tri (Sept-June).

A preparatory program offers bilingual instruction leading to the high school diploma and the French Baccalaureate at the LFNY. Knowledge of French is required for admission from kindergarten on. Graduates attend a variety of competitive American and European colleges, at which they may attain advanced standing.

See Also Pages 1196-7

LYCEUM KENNEDY
Day — Coed Gr PS-12

New York, NY 10017. 225 E 43rd St. Tel: 212-681-1877. Fax: 212-681-1922.
 www.lyceumkennedy.com E-mail: info1@lyceumkennedy.com
Yves Rivaud, Head.
   Col Prep. Gen Acad. Fr Bac. Bilingual. AP—Fr Span. **Feat**—Govt Studio_Art Music. **Supp**—ESL Rem_Read Tut.
   Adm: 30/yr. Appl due: Mar.
   Enr 145. Wh 31%. Blk 69%. Avg class size: 10. Uniform. **Fac 30.**
   Grad '04—3. Col—3. (SUNY-Stony Brook).
   Tui '04-'05: Day $13,000-16,000 (+$800-1000).

Bldgs 1. Class rms 14. Lib 7000 vols. Sci labs 1. Comp labs 1. Auds 1. Theaters 1. Art studios 1. Music studios 1. Dance studios 1. Gyms 1. Courts 1.
Est 1964. Inc. Tri (Sept-June).

This French international bilingual school was founded for the education of French-speaking and American children and formerly used the same methods of teaching as the French school system. A new administration in 1986 resulted in a more international student body, and today the school provides a multilingual education that emphasizes a cross-cultural exchange of ideas. Lyceum Kennedy is accredited by both the French Government and the State of New York.

Subjects are taught in English and French, thereby enabling students to achieve fluency in both languages; even the youngest children are immersed in the French language and tradition. Two-thirds of the curriculum is conducted in French, while the remaining third is in English. Some basics of Latin are taught in grade 7, and pupils are introduced to Latin and Spanish literature beginning in grade 8. SAT preparation, as well as American history and government, is required in the senior high school, and older students work toward Advanced Placement tests. Graduates earn a high school diploma, and students may prepare for the French Baccalaureate.

MANHATTAN COUNTRY SCHOOL
Day — Coed Gr PS-8

New York, NY 10128. 7 E 96th St. Tel: 212-348-0952. Fax: 212-348-1621.
 www.manhattancountryschool.org
 E-mail: admissions@manhattancountryschool.org
Michele Sola, Dir. BA, Cornell Univ, MAT, Indiana Univ, EdD, Boston Univ. **Elizabeth Jarvis, Adm.**
 Pre-Prep. Feat—Lib_Skills Span Computers Studio_Art Music Dance Indus_Arts.
 Adm (Gr PS-7): 35/yr. Appl due: Dec. Accepted: 30%. Yield: 47%. **Tests** ISEE.
 Enr 181. B 90. G 91. Elem 181. Wh 47%. Hisp 18%. Blk 27%. Asian 8%. Avg class size: 18.
 Fac 33. M 3/4. F 20/6. Wh 46%. Hisp 18%. Blk 28%. Asian 8%. Adv deg: 69%.
 Grad '04—20. Prep—12. (Little Red & Elisabeth Irwin 3, Fieldston 2, Riverdale 1, Packer 1, Friends Seminary 1, Phillips Acad 1). Alum 630.
 Tui '04-'05: Day $18,000-22,000 (+$100). **Aid:** Need 140 ($1,466,379).
 Summer: Rec. Farm Prgm. Tui Bdg $3000. 3 wks.
  Endow $8,000,000. Plant val $3,500,000. Bldgs 2. Class rms 10. Lib 6500 vols. Sci labs 1. Comp labs 1. Art studios 2. Music studios 1. Shops 1. Farms 1.
 Est 1966. Nonprofit. Sem (Sept-June).

Founded to carry out the ideas of Martin Luther King, Jr., by teaching and practicing democracy in the classroom, MCS enrolls a racially and economically diverse student body. Combining the progressive principles of John Dewey with a multicultural approach to its curriculum, the school's program includes both individualized instruction and group learning experiences within a defined structure.

The school owns a 185-acre farm in the Catskill Mountains to which all students above age 7 make regular, extended trips. Its program emphasizes farm work, food production, cooking and nutrition, textiles from the farm's wool, nature studies and the responsibilities of an interdependent community.

MARYMOUNT SCHOOL

Day — Boys Gr PS, Girls PS-12

New York, NY 10028. 1026 5th Ave. Tel: 212-744-4486. Fax: 212-744-0163.
www.marymount.k12.ny.us   E-mail: admissions@marymount.k12.ny.us

Concepcion R. Alvar, Head. BA, Maryknoll College (Philippines), MA, Columbia Univ. **Lillian Issa, Adm.**

Col Prep. AP—Eng Fr Lat Span Calc Stats Bio Chem Physics Eur_Hist US_Hist Art_Hist Studio_Art. **Feat**—Greek Astron Meteorology Econ African_Stud Relig Drama Music Speech.

Adm: 94/yr. Appl due: Dec. Accepted: 34%. Yield: 52%. **Tests** ISEE.

Enr 531. B 4. G 527. Elem 343. Sec 188. Avg class size: 16. Uniform. **Fac 86.** M 8. F 75/3. Adv deg: 76%.

Grad '04—42. Col—42. (Davidson 3, NYU 2, Wesleyan U 2, U of PA 2, Skidmore 2, Columbia 2). Avg SAT: 1200. Avg ACT: 24. Alum 1500.

Tui '04-'05: Day $24,100 (+$800). **Aid:** Merit 98 ($1,210,325).

Summer: Acad Rec. Sci. Drama. Tui Day $1500-3150. 2-5 wks.

Endow $4,100,000. Plant val $50,000,000. Bldgs 4. Class rms 37. 3 Libs 16,504 vols. Chapels 1. Sci labs 5. Lang labs 1. Comp labs 3. Auds 1. Art studios 4. Music studios 1. Gyms 1.

Est 1926. Nonprofit. Roman Catholic. Sem (Sept-June).

Mother Joseph Butler of the Religious of the Sacred Heart of Mary founded this school. Located directly opposite the Metropolitan Museum of Art and Central Park, Marymount occupies four turn-of-the-20th-century Beaux Arts mansions that are designated landmarks of the Metropolitan Museum Historic District.

At all grade levels, Marymount's curriculum makes extensive use of computer technology. The lower school (grades PS-3) aims to develop the child's language, reading, mathematical and science skills within a structured environment. Only boys with a sibling at the school may enroll in the coeducational preschool program. Marymount schedules weekly visits to science laboratories beginning at the nursery level, and children attend lab three times per week by grade 3. Art, music, dance and physical education form an integral part of the curriculum.

The middle school (grades 4-7) utilizes modified and gradually increasing departmentalization in the major subject areas. The foreign language program commences with French in grade 4; Latin is added in grade 5. Within the program, girls have various opportunities to achieve and to display independence and leadership.

The upper school curriculum (grades 8-12) features honors classes in all disciplines, a full Advanced Placement program, and various electives. Emphasizing the classic disciplines and scientific inquiry, the curriculum prepares students for competitive colleges. A strong extracurricular program; a five-week, off-campus internship for seniors; and community service at all levels complement academics. Girls may take part in international exchange programs, including a year abroad in London, England, or Rome, Italy.

NIGHTINGALE-BAMFORD SCHOOL

Day — Girls Gr K-12

New York, NY 10128. 20 E 92nd St. Tel: 212-289-5020. Fax: 212-876-1045.
www.nightingale.org   E-mail: info@nightingale.org

Dorothy A. Hutcheson, Head. AB, Duke Univ, MSEd, Duquesne Univ. **Barbara H. Scott,**

Adm.
Col Prep. AP—Lat Chem Physics. **Feat**—Computers Studio_Art Drama Music Public_ Speak.
Adm: 81/yr. Appl due: Dec. Accepted: 13%. **Tests** IQ ISEE SSAT.
Enr 533. G 533. Elem 372. Sec 161. Wh 72%. Hisp 5%. Blk 9%. Am Ind 1%. Asian 8%. Other 5%. Avg class size: 11. Uniform. **Fac 76.** M 17. F 47/12. Wh 82%. Hisp 4%. Blk 8%. Asian 6%. Adv deg: 67%.
Grad '04—42. Col—42. (Cornell, Georgetown, Harvard, Brown, Princeton, Yale). Avg SAT: 1380. Alum 2954.
Tui '03-'04: Day $21,400-22,765 (+$1080). **Aid:** Need 186 ($1,800,000).
Summer: Gr K-4. Rec. Tui Day $300/wk. 4 wks.
Endow $42,700,000. Plant val $35,000,000. Bldgs 1. Lib 65,000 vols. Sci labs 4. Lang labs 1. Comp labs 3. Auds 1. Theaters 1. Art studios 4. Music studios 2. Dance studios 1. Gyms 1.
Est 1920. Nonprofit. Sem (Sept-June). **Assoc** CLS.

Founded by Frances N. Nightingale and Maya Stevens Bamford, the school offers a rigorous college preparatory program. The arts curriculum includes photography, drama, dance, music and studio art. Physical education and more than one dozen team sports are offered, among them swimming, tennis, lacrosse and fitness training.

Field trips are regularly scheduled for all classes. Upper school students participate in academic travel programs and student exchanges to New England, Europe, Japan and Australia. Extracurricular activities include a coed after-school program for children in grades K-4, student government, student publications and clubs. The school is a member of the inter-school consortium of eight schools, which offers academic courses and other cooperative activities. All students participate in service activities within the school and the community.

PROFESSIONAL CHILDREN'S SCHOOL

Day — Coed Gr 4-12

New York, NY 10023. 132 W 60th St. Tel: 212-582-3116. Fax: 212-307-6542.
www.pcs-nyc.org   E-mail: pcs@pcs-nyc.org
James Dawson, Head. BS, PhD, State Univ of New York-Albany. **Sherrie A. Hinkle, Adm.**
Col Prep. Gen Acad. Perform_Arts Visual_Arts. Sports (General). Feat—Fr Span African-Amer_Hist Govt Law Studio_Art Drama Music Music_Theory. **Supp**—Dev_Read ESL Rem_Math Tut.
Adm: 67/yr. Appl due: Rolling. Accepted: 80%. Yield: 70%. **Tests** CTP_4 ISEE SSAT.
Enr 195. B 63. G 132. Elem 45. Sec 150. Wh 53%. Hisp 6%. Blk 8%. Am Ind 6%. Asian 27%. Avg class size: 13. **Fac 25.** M 10. F 14/1. Wh 88%. Hisp 4%. Blk 8%. Adv deg: 84%.
Grad '04—50. Col—42. (Juilliard 5, Duke 2, Columbia 2, Brown 2, Harvard 1, MIT 1). Alum 3000.
Tui '04-'05: Day $21,000-24,000 (+$500-2500). **Aid:** Need 41 ($350,000).
Endow $2,500,000. Plant val $1,000,000. Bldgs 1. Class rms 19. Lib 15,000 vols. Sci labs 2. Comp labs 1. Theaters 1. Art studios 1. Music studios 1. Gyms 1.
Est 1914. Nonprofit. Sem (Sept-June).

Located opposite Lincoln Center for the Performing Arts, this unique school offers a college preparatory education to professional, preprofessional and nonprofessional students. PCS conducts its program in an atmosphere that is respectful of the arts. Scheduling and guided-study assignments are arranged so that students may meet both their academic and their professional commitments without conflict.

Among PCS' alumni are doctors, lawyers and teachers, as well as well-known performing artists and competitive athletes. **See Also Page 1229**

REGIS HIGH SCHOOL
Day — Boys Gr 9-12

New York, NY 10028. 55 E 84th St. Tel: 212-288-1100. Fax: 212-794-1221.
www.regis-nyc.org

Rev. J. Philip G. Judge, SJ, Pres. BA, MA, Fordham Univ, MA, Univ of California-Berkeley, MDiv, STM, Jesuit School of Theology at Berkeley. **Rev. Vincent L. Biagi, SJ, Prin.** AB, Fordham Univ, MA, New York Univ, MDiv, Weston Jesuit School of Theology. **Eric P. DiMichele, Adm.**

Col Prep. Feat—Creative_Writing Shakespeare Russian_Lit Fr Ger Greek Ital Lat Mandarin Span Programming Psych Theol Architect Art_Hist Film Graphic_Arts Studio_Art Theater Band Music.

Adm (Gr 9): 145/yr. Appl due: Oct. Accepted: 17%. Yield: 95%. **Tests** HSPT.

Enr 527. B 527. Sec 527. Wh 72%. Hisp 15%. Blk 4%. Asian 9%. Avg class size: 12. **Fac** 57. M 35/1. F 19/2. Wh 94%. Hisp 2%. Blk 3%. Asian 1%. Adv deg: 89%.

Grad '04—128. Col—128. (Loyola Col 11, Holy Cross 9, Harvard 7, Georgetown 7, Fordham 7, NYU 6). Avg SAT: 1414. Alum 6320.

Tui '04-'05: Day $0 (+$385).

Endow $42,000,000. Sci labs 5. Art studios 1. Gyms 2.

Est 1914. Nonprofit. Roman Catholic. Tri (Sept-June). **Assoc** MSA.

Named for St. John Francis Regis, a French Jesuit who performed missionary work among southern France's poor in the early 17th century, the school began when a wealthy Catholic widow's looking to anonymously donate her fortune to charity met up with a parish pastor on Manhattan's Upper East Side. The widow agreed to help the pastor realize his dream of founding a tuition-free school for the education of Catholic boys. Virtually from Regis' inception, competition for admission has been extremely intense; to best select worthy new students, the school formulated an admissions process that initially involved a rigorous entrance examination and later incorporated interviews. The present-day school, which continues to charge no tuition, serves a socioeconomically diverse group of students who commute an average of one hour each way. As transfer pupils are not accepted, only eighth-grade boys may apply.

In accordance with the educational tradition of the Society of Jesus, the curriculum originally placed particular emphasis on the classical languages and the liberal arts. Over the years, developments in both education in general and the Jesuit educational tradition in particular have led to an increased curricular prominence of science, math, foreign languages and the fine arts. Course work, which is largely standard for all students during the first three years, is intensive and accelerated, with unusual latitude built into the schedule in the areas of independent study, individualized instruction and unscheduled time. Seniors fulfill requirements in English, physics (if not taken in grade 11) and theology, then select their remaining classes from electives in any discipline. Each senior devotes Tuesday mornings to Christian service; during his final trimester, the student may either work full-time on his service project or undertake a full-time career internship with an area business.

Activities at Regis include student government, debate, drama, band, chorus, several school publications, and academic and interest clubs. Soccer, basketball, track, baseball, volleyball and tennis are the interscholastic sports, and a few intramural offerings are also available.

ROBERT LOUIS STEVENSON SCHOOL
Day — Coed Gr 7-12

New York, NY 10023. 24 W 74th St. Tel: 212-787-6400. Fax: 212-873-1872.
  www.stevenson-school.org   E-mail: dherron@stevenson-school.org
B. H. Henrichsen, Head.
  Col Prep. LD. Underachiever. Feat—Ecol Comp_Sci Econ Psych Sociol Philos Film Studio_Art. **Supp**—Rem_Math Rem_Read.
  Adm: 34/yr. Appl due: Rolling. Accepted: 50%. Yield: 80%. **Tests** IQ.
  Enr 74. B 52. G 22. Elem 9. Sec 65. Wh 63%. Hisp 16%. Blk 12%. Asian 9%. Avg class size: 10. **Fac 12.** M 6. F 6. Adv deg: 50%.
  Grad '04—16. Col—14. (SUNY-Purchase, Stevens Inst of Tech, SUNY-Stony Brook, CUNY, Brandeis).
  Tui '05-'06: Day $34,500. Aid: Need 2 ($8000).
  Summer: Acad Enrich Rev Rem. Tui Day $1100/crse. 4 wks.
  Bldgs 1. Class rms 11.
  Est 1908. Nonprofit. Quar (Sept-June).

Derived from the merger of the Scoville School (established in 1882) and the Robert Louis Stevenson School (established in 1908), this school has been located at its present site since 1960.

The Stevenson School accepts only bright underachievers, preparing them for high school graduation and college entrance and seeking to develop their organizational and study skills. The educational environment is designed to strengthen self-motivation, encouraging the fulfillment of each student's academic potential. Parental involvement is modified, and students are expected to complete homework assignments under school supervision and on their own initiative.

Athletics and physical education balance academic life through interscholastic sports and a fitness program. Students are encouraged to participate in student government, clubs, yearbook and computers. The school takes full advantage of the cultural opportunities of New York City through curricular and extracurricular activities.   **See Also Pages 1372-3**

RUDOLF STEINER SCHOOL
Day — Coed Gr PS-12

New York, NY 10021. 15 E 79th St. Tel: 212-327-1457. Fax: 212-774-4457.
  www.steiner.edu   E-mail: crogutsky@steiner.edu
Lucy Schneider, Fac Chrm. BA, Vassar College. **Miranda Litt, Upper Sch Adm; Irene Mantel, Lower Sch Adm.**
  Col Prep. Feat—British_Lit Poetry Shakespeare Russ_Lit Romantic_Poetry Ecol Environ_Sci Zoology Programming Philos Architect Studio_Art Music Music_Theory.
  Adm: Appl due: Jan. Accepted: 25%. **Tests** ISEE.
  Enr 340. Avg class size: 21. **Fac 52.** M 8/6. F 32/6.
  Grad '04—12. Col—12. (Smith, Amherst, Swarthmore, Lafayette, Sarah Lawrence).

Alum 752.
Tui '05-'06: Day $22,400-24,600.
Endow $350,000. Plant val $25,000,000. Bldgs 2. Class rms 21. Libs 2. Sci labs 1. Comp labs 1. Auds 1. Art studios 3.
Est 1928. Nonprofit. Sem (Sept-June).

Instruction at this school is based on the educational principles of Rudolf Steiner, who founded the first Waldorf school in 1919 in Stuttgart, Germany. Literature, history, modern languages, the sciences and mathematics form the core academic curriculum. Intensive academic seminars, skills courses that run throughout the year, and workshops for studio art, drama and practical arts enhance different learning tasks. Student exchanges may be arranged with Waldorf schools in other countries.

The upper school is located nearby at 15 E. 78th St.

ST. BERNARD'S SCHOOL
Day — Boys Gr K-9

New York, NY 10029. 4 E 98th St. Tel: 212-289-2878. Fax: 212-410-6628.
 www.stbernards.org E-mail: d_kripal@stbernards.org
Stuart H. Johnson III, Head. BA, Yale Univ. **Anne S. Nordeman & Heidi R. Gore, Adms.**
 Pre-Prep. Feat—Fr Lat Span Computers Studio_Art Music. **Supp**—Rev Tut.
 Adm: 49/yr. Appl due: Dec. **Tests** IQ ISEE.
 Enr 367. B 367. Elem 356. Sec 11. Wh 77%. Hisp 6%. Blk 7%. Asian 10%. Avg class size: 20. **Fac 64.** M 36. F 27/1. Adv deg: 59%.
 Grad '04—40. Prep—40. (Trinity Sch-NY, Phillips Acad, Hotchkiss, Lawrenceville, Phillips Exeter, Horace Mann). Alum 2450.
 Tui '05-'06: Day $23,115 (+$2275).
 Endow $38,000,000. Plant val $40,000,000. Bldgs 1. Class rms 38. Lib 15,000 vols. Comp labs 1. Theaters 1. Art studios 1. Music studios 1. Gyms 3.
 Est 1904. Nonprofit. Tri (Sept-June).

St. Bernard's prepares boys for their secondary years by providing a strong, traditional academic program. The curriculum emphasizes composition, literature, mathematics and science, and it includes music, dramatics, art, computer studies, carpentry and physical education.

SAINT DAVID'S SCHOOL
Day — Boys Gr PS-8

New York, NY 10128. 12 E 89th St. Tel: 212-369-0058. Fax: 212-369-5788.
 www.saintdavids.org E-mail: admissions@saintdavids.org
P. David O'Halloran, Head. BA, Brisbane College of Theology (Australia), MA, Bank Street College of Education, PhD, Fordham Univ. **Janet H. Sughrue & Julie B. Sykes, Adms.**
 Pre-Prep. Feat—Fr Lat Span Anat & Physiol Computers Art_Hist Studio_Art Drama Music Indus_Arts. **Supp**—Dev_Read Tut.
 Adm (Gr PS-7): 54/yr. Appl due: Dec. Accepted: 18%. Yield: 82%. **Tests** CTP_4 IQ ISEE.
 Enr 375. B 375. Elem 375. Wh 84%. Hisp 6%. Blk 5%. Asian 5%. Avg class size: 18. **Fac 46.** M 17. F 29. Adv deg: 69%.
 Grad '04—39. Prep—34. (Suffield 6, Riverdale 4, Loyola Sch 4, Trinity Sch-NY 3, Hotchkiss 2). Alum 1700.
 Tui '04-'05: Day $16,275-24,500. Aid: Need 26 ($448,400).

Summer: Rec. Tui Day $250/wk. 2 wks.
Endow $14,600,000. Plant val $18,300,000. Bldgs 5. Class rms 25. 2 Libs 17,000 vols. Sci labs 3. Comp labs 1. Art studios 3. Music studios 1. Gyms 5.
Est 1951. Nonprofit. Roman Catholic. Tri (Sept-June).

Founded as an independent school by nine Catholic families, Saint David's enrolls boys of all religious and ethnic backgrounds. During the pre-primary years (prekindergarten and kindergarten), children learn to work and play together as they begin to pursue their own interests. Developmentally appropriate language arts and math programs, which begin in grade 1, promote mastery of carefully sequenced concepts and skills. Small-group reading instruction emphasizes phonics and comprehension, and writing is integral to the language arts program. Weekly science, social studies, art, pottery and woodworking classes augment the core curriculum, and formal computer instruction commences in grade 3.

In grades 4-8 (the upper school), students further develop their reading, writing and reasoning abilities. Faculty stress study and note taking skills and the use of reference materials, and the curriculum synthesizes the study of literature, history and science. Ability grouping is utilized in the math department, allowing more able boys to progress rapidly to new material. Latin study is compulsory in grade 5, after which time it is available as an elective. Boys fulfill their foreign language requirement in grades 6-8 with either French or Spanish. A well-developed computer program allows students to progress from basic keyboarding skills to word processing, spreadsheets and databases. As in the lower school, parental involvement is an important element of the program.

Community service opportunities, which further enrich the curriculum, begin in the lower school. After-school activities, available for an additional fee to boys in grades K-8, include art, chess, computers, drama, pottery, basketball and tennis.

ST. LUKE'S SCHOOL
Day — Coed Gr PS-8

New York, NY 10014. 487 Hudson St. Tel: 212-924-5960. Fax: 212-924-1352.
www.stlukeschool.org E-mail: jhoyt@stlukeschool.org
Ann Mellow, **Head.** BA, Middlebury College, MEd, Harvard Univ. **Susan Parker, Adm.**
  Pre-Prep. **Feat**—Lib_Skills Fr Span Computers Comp_Relig World_Relig Studio_Art Drama Music Outdoor_Ed. **Supp**—Rem_Read.
  Adm (Gr PS-7): 32/yr. Appl due: Dec. Accepted: 27%. Yield: 64%. **Tests** ISEE.
  Enr 195. B 85. G 110. Elem 195. Wh 77%. Blk 10%. Asian 8%. Other 5%. Avg class size: 21. **Fac 30.** M 9/1. F 20. Wh 85%. Hisp 3%. Blk 6%. Asian 6%. Adv deg: 56%.
  Grad '04—19. Prep—16. (Nightingale-Bamford 1, Trinity Sch-NY 1, Friends Seminary 1, Packer 1, Westover 1). Alum 900.
  Tui '04-'05: Day $20,000-20,975 (+$510-785). **Aid:** Need 39 ($547,325).
  Endow $625,000. Plant val $5,000,000. Bldgs 3. Class rms 15. Lib 22,000 vols. Chapels 1. Sci labs 1. Comp labs 1. Auds 1. Theaters 1. Art studios 1. Music studios 1. Gyms 1. Playgrounds 3.
  Est 1945. Nonprofit. Episcopal. (Sept-June).

Established by the Church of Saint Luke in the Fields, the school prepares boys and girls of all faiths for independent secondary schools and specialized public high schools. Located in a historic residential neighborhood in the West Village, the school sits on a two-acre enclosed block with tree-shaded gardens and playgrounds.

The program at St. Luke's emphasizes the development of creativity and critical-thinking and academic skills using a variety of educational approaches and techniques. In addition to academics, students participate in a range of extracurricular activities, including yearbook, drama, chorus, musicals, student council and canteen. Chapel, comparative religion classes and service learning are important aspects of school life, as is outdoor education. SLS also conducts an after-school program and a physical education program that features varsity and junior varsity sports.

ST. THOMAS CHOIR SCHOOL
Bdg — Boys Gr 4-8

New York, NY 10019. 202 W 58th St. Tel: 212-247-3311. Fax: 212-247-3393.
www.choirschool.org   E-mail: info@choirschool.org
Rev. Charles Wallace, Head. Ruth S. Cobb, Adm.
- **Pre-Prep. Gen Acad. Perform_Arts. Feat**—Greek Lat Computers Theol Studio_Art Music Music_Theory. **Supp**—Dev_Read Rem_Math Rem_Read Rev Tut.
- **Adm (Gr 4-5):** 7/yr. Appl due: Rolling. Accepted: 25%. Yield: 100%. **Tests** Stanford.
- **Enr 33.** B 33. Elem 33. Wh 70%. Blk 12%. Asian 18%. Avg class size: 6. Uniform. **Fac 23.** M 7/9. F 2/5. Wh 95%. Blk 5%. Adv deg: 26%. In dorms 10.
- **Grad '04—6. Prep—4.** (St Mark's Sch-MA, Hun). Alum 520.
- **Tui '04-'05: Bdg** $9500 (+$300). **Aid:** Need 28 ($175,000).
- Endow $18,000,000. Plant val $20,000,000. Bldgs 1. Dorms 1. Dorm rms 17. Class rms 7. Lib 7300 vols. Labs 1. Art studios 1. Gyms 1.
- **Est 1919.** Nonprofit. Episcopal. Quar (Sept-June).

Founded by the British composer and organist Dr. T. Tertius Noble, who was accustomed to directing the traditional English cathedral choir at Ely and York Minster, and modeled on English choir schools, St. Thomas today combines the English choir tradition with an American independent school academic and sports program.

The academic program of this church-affiliated school features English, mathematics, history, science, art, computer technology, foreign languages (including Greek), theology, music theory and instrumental study. Graduates of the Choir School enter leading secondary schools or return to their local schools.

The choir rehearses daily and prepares more than 400 pieces of sacred music each year for six weekly services at St. Thomas Church on Fifth Avenue. In addition, the choir presents a concert series, tours domestically and abroad, and makes recordings. Candidates for admission must demonstrate musical aptitude, but need not have prior musical training.

All students participate in interscholastic sports, some of which are played on fields in nearby Central Park. Field trips to museums and exhibitions in Manhattan round out the school's program. **See Also Page 1346**

THE SPENCE SCHOOL
Day — Girls Gr K-12

New York, NY 10128. 22 E 91st St. Tel: 212-289-5940. Fax: 212-996-5689.
www.spenceschool.org E-mail: admissions@spenceschool.org
Arlene Joy Gibson, Head. BA, Bryn Mawr College, MA, Georgetown Univ. **Alice Shedlin, Adm.**
Col Prep. AP—Fr Studio_Art. **Feat**—Stats Web_Design Ceramics Drawing Photog Sculpt Drama.
Adm (Gr K-9): 66/yr. **Tests** ISEE.
Enr 591. G 591. Elem 409. Sec 182. Wh 78%. Hisp 4%. Blk 8%. Asian 8%. Other 2%. Avg class size: 14. Uniform. **Fac 94.** M 20/7. F 67. Adv deg: 65%.
Grad '04—39. Col—39. (Cornell, Yale, Princeton, U of PA, Harvard, Duke). Avg SAT: 1342. Alum 2525.
Tui '02-'03: Day $19,650-20,700 (+$1345-1995). **Aid:** Need 95.
Endow $52,500,000. Bldgs 1. Class rms 35. Lib 24,013 vols. Sci labs 4. Comp labs 2. Auds 1. Art studios 5. Music studios 4. Dance studios 1. Gyms 2.
Est 1892. Nonprofit. Tri (Sept-June).

Founded by Clara B. Spence, this school for girls was originally located in midtown Manhattan, where it enrolled both boarding and day students. Spence's early growth necessitated two relocations to larger quarters, the second of which established the school at its present location in 1929. Boarding was discontinued in 1952.

Drawing its enrollment from Manhattan, Brooklyn, Queens and the Bronx, as well as from nearby suburbs, Spence serves a student body that reflects the multiracial and international character of the city. The school's varied curriculum emphasizes skill development while encouraging creative thinking and clear expression.

In the lower school (grades K-5), the developmental approach to reading and writing emphasizes the connection between the two. Computer classes in the computer lab are part of the curriculum, and girls take either French or Spanish beginning in grade 3. During the middle school years (grades 6-8), students gain more independence while also receiving the necessary support and structure. Departmentalization begins in grade 6, when girls begin to follow a more complex daily schedule. Middle school faculty also typically teach upper school courses, thus enabling instructors to prepare middle schoolers for the upper grades.

The upper school curriculum (grades 9-12) balances requirements and electives, giving pupils the chance to explore areas of interest. In addition to Advanced Placement courses, upper-level classes in English, history and science ready students for the AP exams. Extracurricular activities and a well-developed athletic program provide leadership opportunities.

Spence capitalizes on its East Side location by scheduling cultural field trips to museums, theaters and other local points of interest. Study abroad and student exchange programs are available, as is an after-school program for lower schoolers.

Primarily to meet the needs of children in grades 1-4, Spence opened new lower school facilities in autumn 2003 at 56 E. 93rd St.

THE TOWN SCHOOL
Day — Coed Gr PS-8

New York, NY 10021. 540 E 76th St. Tel: 212-288-4383. Fax: 212-988-5846.
www.thetownschool.org   E-mail: admissions@townschool.org
Christopher Marblo, Head. BA, College of Saint Rose, MA, New York Univ. **Natasha Sahadi, Adm.**

Pre-Prep. Feat—Fr Lat Span Computers Studio_Art Drama Music Dance.
Adm: 59/yr. **Tests** ISEE.
Enr 382. B 190. G 192. Elem 382. Avg class size: 18. **Fac 83.** M 18. F 65. Wh 90%. Hisp 6%. Blk 3%. Asian 1%. Adv deg: 63%.
Grad '04—37. Prep—21. (Trinity Sch-NY, Columbia Grammar & Prep, Horace Mann, Dalton, Riverdale). Alum 796.
Tui '03-'04: Day $11,400-22,500.
Summer: Acad Enrich Rec. 6 wks.
Endow $17,000,000. Plant val $9,000,000. Bldgs 1. Class rms 37. Lib 13,000 vols. Sci labs 2. Lang labs 2. Comp labs 1. Theaters 1. Art studios 2. Music studios 2. Dance studios 1. Gyms 1.
Est 1913. Nonprofit. Tri (Sept-June).

Founded by Hazel Hyde as a small nursery school, the Town School expanded to a full elementary program and assumed its present location near the East River in 1961. Town prepares its graduates for independent day and boarding schools, as well as for the competitive city high schools.

The curriculum emphasizes the acquisition of basic skills in the humanities, the sciences and the creative arts. The program stresses reading, writing, speaking, and mathematical and scientific reasoning skills. Spanish instruction commences in kindergarten, French begins in grade 5, and Latin is required in grades 7 and 8. The school's extensive physical education program includes interscholastic competition in volleyball, soccer, softball and basketball.

TREVOR DAY SCHOOL
Day — Coed Gr PS-12

New York, NY 10024. 1 W 88th St. Tel: 212-426-3360. Fax: 212-873-8520.
www.trevor.org
Thomas E. Tinker, Actg Head. BA, Columbia Univ, MA, Brown Univ. **Marcia Roesch, Upper Sch Adm; Deborah Ashe, Lower Sch Adm.**

Col Prep. AP—Fr Span Calc Comp_Sci US_Hist. **Feat**—Russ_Lit Ital Environ_Sci Genetics Web_Design Ceramics Film Photog Stained_Glass Theater Chorus Music Dance. **Supp**—Tut.
Adm (Gr PS-11): 124/yr. Appl due: Jan. **Tests** ISEE SSAT.
Enr 784. B 396. G 388. Elem 545. Sec 239. Wh 83%. Hisp 8%. Blk 7%. Asian 2%. Avg class size: 16. **Fac 134.** M 37/5. F 81/11. Adv deg: 67%.
Grad '04—57. Col—57. (Wash U 3, Columbia 1, Georgetown 1, Wesleyan U 1, Haverford 1, Northwestern 1). Alum 1142.
Tui '04-'05: Day $16,200-26,800 (+$2000). **Aid:** Need 135 ($2,305,279).
Endow $7,000,000. Plant val $30,000,000. Bldgs 3. Class rms 48. 3 Libs 55,000 vols. Sci labs 5. Dark rms 2. Auds 2. Theaters 2. Art studios 5. Music studios 4. Dance studios 1. Gyms 2. Fields 1.
Est 1930. Nonprofit. Tri (Sept-June).

Founded as a nursery school called The Day School, the institution expanded its program through grade 8 in the 1960s, and a high school division was added in 1991. The school assumed its present name in 1997.

Trevor maintains a low student-teacher ratio, allowing instructors to conduct courses seminar style. The program emphasizes critical thinking, time management and collaborative work skills. Ample opportunities in the arts and other areas include dance, dramatics, choral music, instrumental music and ensembles, filmmaking, photography, student government, publications and a full sports program.

Each student fulfills an 80-hour community service requirement during the high school years, and seniors may elect to undertake an independent project. An after-school program for younger children is available, and an outdoor education program serves pupils in grades 2-12. All students in grades 5-12 utilize laptop computers.

Grades PS-5 are housed in the joined facilities at 11 E. 89th St. and 4 E. 90th St.

TRINITY SCHOOL

Day — Coed Gr K-12

New York, NY 10024. 139 W 91st St. Tel: 212-873-1650. Fax: 212-932-6812.
www.trinityschoolnyc.org   E-mail: sandy.oshea@trinity.nyc.ny.us

Henry C. Moses, Head. AB, Princeton Univ, PhD, Cornell Univ. **Jan S. Burton, Upper & Middle Sch Adm; June Hilton, Lower Sch Adm.**

Col Prep. AP—Fr Lat Span. **Feat**—Greek Computers Relig Art_Hist Ceramics Photog Studio_Art Theater Music Speech.

Adm (Gr K-11): 130/yr. Appl due: Jan. Accepted: 14%. **Tests** ISEE SSAT.

Enr 959. B 473. G 486. Elem 532. Sec 427. Wh 76%. Hisp 4%. Blk 8%. Asian 12%. Avg class size: 15. **Fac 148.** M 53/15. F 65/15. Adv deg: 69%.

Grad '04—83. Col—83. (U of PA, Brown, Harvard, Princeton, Columbia, Yale). Alum 3500.

Tui '05-'06: Day $22,160-26,470 (+$1135-1785).

Endow $30,000,000. Plant val $10,000,000. Bldgs 3. Class rms 75. 2 Libs 36,000 vols. Chapels 2. Sci labs 8. Comp labs 2. Auds 1. Theaters 2. Art studios 4. Music studios 7. Gyms 3. Fields 1. Courts 2. Pools 2.

Est 1709. Nonprofit. Episcopal. Sem (Sept-June). **Assoc** CLS.

Founded by royal charter, this school was housed at Trinity Church for its first 100 years and was formally affiliated with the parish until 1970. Although Trinity is no longer an Episcopal school, religion remains an important part of school life. An Episcopal chaplain leads weekly chapel services, students in grades 5 and 6 take introductory religion courses, and upper school students fulfill a religion requirement.

In the middle school, the fifth- and sixth-grade curriculum includes English, French or Spanish, mathematics, history, science, religion, music, art, computer and physical education. Latin begins in grade 6. Seventh- and eighth-grade studies in the traditional disciplines are complemented by an elective program in the arts. In the upper school, advanced classes, AP courses or both are available in every discipline, and the arts department offers instruction in studio art, drama, photography, music and art history. All ninth graders spend a night before the start of school at Frost Valley in the Catskills with 12th graders and faculty; seniors act as group advisors and bunk counselors.

The athletic program begins swimming instruction in kindergarten and tennis in grade 3, while interscholastic sports commence in grade 7. Activities addressing interests such as Model UN, debating, international and global issues, and a variety of publications are among the numerous clubs and organizations. A student volunteer service organization oversees the work of several groups; every student in the upper school is expected to perform community service.

The student body comes primarily from Manhattan, but three other New York City boroughs—in addition to New Jersey—are represented.

UNITED NATIONS INTERNATIONAL SCHOOL
Day — Coed Gr K-12

New York, NY 10010. 24-50 FDR Dr. Tel: 212-584-3071. Fax: 212-685-5023.
www.unis.org   E-mail: admissions@unis.org

Kenneth J. Wrye, Dir. MS, California State Univ, EdD, Univ of San Francisco. **Anne Lowenstein, Adm.**

Col Prep. IB Diploma. Feat—Chin Ger Ital Japan Russ Arabic Comp_Sci Intl_Relations Film Photog Studio_Art Video_Production Drama Theater_Arts Chorus Journ. **Supp**—ESL Rev.

Adm: 238/yr. Appl due: Nov. Accepted: 54%. Yield: 64%. **Tests** CTP_4 ISEE SSAT.

Enr 1460. B 693. G 767. Elem 1031. Sec 429. Wh 60%. Hisp 8%. Blk 12%. Asian 20%. Avg class size: 20. **Fac 207.** M 57/16. F 122/12. Wh 61%. Hisp 19%. Blk 8%. Asian 12%. Adv deg: 71%.

Grad '04—106. Col—104. (Boston U 5, U of VA 4, Wellesley 3, Barnard 3, Duke 3, McGill-Canada 3). Avg SAT: 1216. Alum 2147.

Tui '04-'05: Day $17,200-19,100 (+$530). **Aid:** Need 152 ($762,573).

Summer: Rec. ESL. Tui Day $440/wk. 5 wks.

Endow $14,633,000. Plant val $15,936,000. Bldgs 2. Class rms 97. 3 Libs 63,000 vols. Sci labs 10. Lang labs 2. Comp labs 4. Theaters 1. Art studios 6. Music studios 15. Dance studios 1. Gyms 5. Courts 2.

Est 1947. Nonprofit. Sem (Sept-June).

Providing for the education of local children, as well as those from the United Nations and international communities, this school prepares its students through the International Baccalaureate and US examinations for entrance to universities here and, to a lesser degree, abroad. Over the years, IB students have been granted advanced standing of up to one year at many US colleges. In addition to following a rigorous program of study in the liberal arts and sciences, students may specialize in music or art.

The school has over 100 nationalities represented in its enrollment, and more than 70 nationalities among its faculty and staff. English is the principal language of instruction, but students may enter without previous knowledge of the language. In addition to the Manhattan campus, which overlooks the East River, the school maintains a second campus for children in grades K-8 in Jamaica Estates, a residential section of Queens.

Extracurricular activities include orchestra, ensemble groups, chorus, dance, arts and crafts, drama, photography, chess, clubs, yearbook, newspaper and literary magazines. Among athletic activities are soccer, softball, skiing, rhythmic gymnastics, tennis, baseball, track and volleyball. Instruction is also available in judo,

YORK PREPARATORY SCHOOL
Day — Coed Gr 6-12

New York, NY 10023. 40 W 68th St. Tel: 212-362-0400. Fax: 212-362-7106.
  www.yorkprep.org E-mail: admissions@yorkprep.org
Ronald P. Stewart, Head. BA, BCL, MA, Oxford Univ (England). **Christopher Durnford, Prin.** BSc, Western Ontario Univ (Canada). **Lisa Smith, Adm.**

Col Prep. AP—Fr Span Calc. **Feat**—ASL Ital Japan Anat & Physiol Environ_Sci Zoology Comp_Sci Law Pol_Sci Psych Ethics Graphic_Arts Studio_Art Film_Hist. **Supp**—Dev_Read LD Rem_Math Rem_Read Tut.

Adm: 90/yr. Appl due: Jan. Accepted: 25%. **Tests** ISEE.

Enr 310. B 189. G 121. Elem 97. Sec 213. Wh 66%. Hisp 2%. Blk 23%. Asian 9%. Avg class size: 14. Uniform. **Fac 50.** M 18. F 32. Adv deg: 72%.

Grad '04—59. Col—59. (Syracuse, U of VT, Bennington, Fordham, NYU, Tulane). Alum 2500.

Tui '05-'06: Day $25,900-26,400 (+$1500). **Aid:** Merit ($490,000).

Summer: Acad Rem. 6 wks.

Plant val $10,000,000. Bldgs 1. Class rms 25. Lib 10,000 vols. Sci labs 2. Comp labs 2. Auds 1. Art studios 1. Music studios 1. Gyms 1.

Est 1969. Inc. Quar (Sept-June). **Assoc** MSA.

The school was originally chartered in 1896 as a branch of the New York Preparatory, but was not established until 1969, where it opened at 116 E. 85th St.; it relocated to its present site in 1997. Mr. Stewart, an Oxford-educated Englishman, has been the school's only headmaster.

Enrolling pupils from throughout the Metropolitan New York City area, York Prep offers a traditional academic program that emphasizes college preparation. The school's tracking system places every student in one of several ability groups maintained in each discipline, thus enabling pupils to learn with others of similar skill and ability levels.

The curriculum features electives in most fields, as well as several Advanced Placement courses. With the headmaster's recommendation, seniors and advanced juniors may take courses at Columbia University, New York University or Hunter College. The school also allows qualified pupils to participate in independent study. Faculty utilize York's Upper West Side location by incorporating available cultural and recreational opportunities into their curricula.

Publications, drama, crafts and clubs are among the extracurricular activities. Varsity and junior varsity athletics include soccer, volleyball, basketball, tennis, track, softball, cross-country, golf and fencing.   **See Also Page 1285**

NYACK, NY. (29 mi. N of New York, NY) Suburban. Pop: 6737. Alt: 68 ft. Area also includes Congers.

THE ROCKLAND COUNTRY DAY SCHOOL
Day — Coed Gr PS-12

Congers, NY 10920. 34 Kings Hwy. Tel: 845-268-6802. Fax: 845-268-4644.
  www.rocklandcds.org   E-mail: jfyfe@rocklandcds.org
James P. Handlin, Head. BA, Iona College, MA, Fordham Univ, MS, Bank Street College of Education, MEd, EdD, Columbia Univ. **Jim Fyfe, Adm.**
  Col Prep. AP—Calc Bio Physics Eur_Hist US_Hist. **Feat**—Humanities ASL Fr Lat Span Stats Psych Sociol Philos Art_Hist Ceramics Photog Studio_Art Video Music. **Supp**—Rev.
  Adm (Gr PS-10): 41/yr. Appl due: Apr. Accepted: 63%. **Tests** CTP_4 ISEE SSAT.
  Enr 170. B 79. G 91. Wh 76%. Hisp 7%. Blk 8%. Asian 9%. Avg class size: 12. **Fac 30.** M 8/1. F 20/1. Wh 87%. Hisp 10%. Blk 3%. Adv deg: 36%.
  Grad '04—14. Col—14. (IN U, WV U, Green Mtn, Manhattanville, James Madison, Stetson). Avg SAT: 1110. Alum 300.
  Tui '04-'05: Day $11,984-19,887 (+$90-700). **Aid**: Merit ($15,838). Need ($201,348).
  Summer: Enrich. 4 wks.
  Plant val $2,000,000. Bldgs 5. Class rms 21. Lib 16,256 vols. Sci labs 2. Comp labs 4. Art studios 1. Music studios 2. Gyms 1. Fields 3.
  Est 1959. Nonprofit. Sem (Sept-June).

Founded in Nyack by a group of community leaders, RCDS moved to its present, 20-acre campus in 1962. The curriculum provides preparation for college and beyond, with an emphasis placed on critical reading and clear writing skills. Honors and Advanced Placement courses are offered. French and Spanish begin in kindergarten, while Latin instruction commences in grade 5. Performing and visual arts courses are part of the core curriculum. All students fulfill a community service requirement.

Off-campus outdoor programs conducted during the fall seek to develop self-reliance and class cohesiveness.

OYSTER BAY, NY. (26 mi. ENE of New York, NY) Suburban. Pop: 6687. Alt: 8 ft.

EAST WOODS SCHOOL
Day — Coed Gr PS-9

Oyster Bay, NY 11771. 31 Yellow Cote Rd. Tel: 516-922-4400. Fax: 516-922-2589.
  www.eastwoods.org   E-mail: admissions@eastwoods.org
Nathaniel W. Peirce, Head. BS, Northeastern Univ, EdM, Harvard Univ, EdD, Columbia Univ. **Carol Rogers, Adm.**
  Pre-Prep. **Feat**—Fr Lat Span Photog Studio_Art Drama Music. **Supp**—Rem_Math Rem_Read Rev Tut.
  Adm: 47/yr.
  Enr 250. B 131. G 119. Elem 250. Wh 90%. Hisp 3%. Blk 4%. Asian 3%. Avg class size:

20. Uniform. **Fac 55.** M 7. F 48. Wh 99%. Hisp 1%. Adv deg: 20%.
Grad '04—14. Prep—12. (Friends Acad-NY, Hill Sch-PA, St Paul's Sch-NH, Phillips Exeter, St Andrew's Sch-RI, Choate). Alum 1300.
Tui '04-'05: Day $7900-17,900 (+$1500). **Aid:** Merit 8 ($93,500). Need 18 ($158,600).
Summer: Enrich Rec. Tui Day $1450-2000. 3-6 wks.
Endow $3,200,000. Plant val $6,000,000. Bldgs 6. Class rms 30. Lib 19,000 vols. Sci labs 1. Comp labs 2. Art studios 2. Music studios 2. Shops 1. Gyms 2. Fields 4. Pools 2.
Est 1946. Nonprofit. Tri (Sept-June).

Founded by a group of interested parents in Cold Spring Harbor, this school moved to its present, 42-acre campus in 1948. The school draws students from 15 school districts in Nassau and Suffolk counties.

The child-centered curriculum is characterized by academic rigor in all subject areas. Foreign language instruction, which commences in kindergarten with Spanish, includes French in grades 5-9 and compulsory Latin in grades 7 and 8. Advanced programs in science, math and technology complement standard course offerings, and writing and research projects are integral to the program.

A strong performing and creative arts program includes shop, dramatics, music, photography and dance-drama. The physical education program includes movement education for preschool and elementary children and interscholastic athletics for older pupils. Soccer, basketball, ice hockey, baseball, softball and lacrosse are among the team sports available.

PAWLING, NY. (49 mi. WSW of Hartford, CT; 64 mi. NNE of New York, NY) Rural. Pop: 7521. Alt: 465 ft.

TRINITY-PAWLING SCHOOL
Bdg — Boys Gr 9-PG; Day — Boys 7-PG

Pawling, NY 12564. 700 Rte 22. Tel: 845-855-3100. Fax: 845-855-3816.
www.trinitypawling.org E-mail: kdefonce@trinitypawling.org
Archibald A. Smith III, Head. BS, Trinity College (CT), MALS, Wesleyan Univ. **MacGregor Robinson, Adm.**
Col Prep. **AP**—Eng Fr Lat Span Calc Stats Comp_Sci Bio Chem Physics Eur_Hist US_Hist Econ. **Feat**—Astron Oceanog Pol_Sci Psych Bible Comp_Relig Philos Relig Art_Hist Photog Studio_Art Drama Theater_Arts Music Public_Speak Mech_Drawing. **Supp**—Dev_Read ESL LD Rem_Read.
Adm (Bdg Gr 9-PG; Day 7-12): 126/yr. Bdg 106. Day 20. Appl due: Feb. Accepted: 67%. Yield: 54%. **Tests** SSAT TOEFL.
Enr 315. B 230/85. Elem 23. Sec 282. PG 10. Wh 85%. Hisp 2%. Blk 6%. Asian 7%. Avg class size: 12. **Fac 56.** M 42/3. F 8/3. Wh 98%. Hisp 2%. Adv deg: 53%. In dorms 42.
Grad '04—86. Col—86. (Gettysburg 4, Rochester Inst of Tech 4, Siena Col 3, Col of Charleston 3, Bentley 2, Syracuse 2). Avg SAT: 1150. Alum 4000.
Tui '04-'05: Bdg $33,000 (+$1500). **Day $16,000-22,500** (+$750). **Aid:** Need 108 ($1,400,000).
Endow $20,000,000. Plant val $50,000,000. Bldgs 20. Dorms 8. Dorm rms 135. Class rms 37. Lib 25,000 vols. Labs 5. Theaters 1. Art studios 1. Music studios 1. Arts ctrs 1. Shops 1. Gyms 1. Fields 10. Courts 12. Rinks 1.
Est 1907. Nonprofit. Episcopal. Tri (Sept-May). **Assoc** CLS.

Established and conducted by Frederick L. Gamage, this school merged with Trinity of New York City when the latter took over the property in 1946, and a year later the school transferred its small boarding department here. In 1978, a board of trustees for Trinity-Pawling School was established, an absolute charter was granted by the board of regents of New York State, and Trinity-Pawling became separate from and independent of Trinity School.

The school offers more than 100 courses, including Advanced Placement classes. A language program for bright students who have been diagnosed with a mild language-based learning disability is offered to a limited number of students.

Activities include publications, choir, drama and interest clubs. Athletics are football, soccer, cross-country, basketball, ice hockey, wrestling, squash, skiing, baseball, golf, tennis, track, cycling and lacrosse. **See Also Page 1348**

PORT WASHINGTON, NY. (18 mi. NE of New York, NY) Suburban. Pop: 15,215.

VINCENT SMITH SCHOOL
Day — Coed Gr 5-12

Port Washington, NY 11050. 322 Port Washington Blvd. Tel: 516-365-4900.
 Fax: 516-627-5648.
  www.vincentsmithschool.org   E-mail: awishnew@vincentsmithschool.org
Arlene Wishnew, Head. BA, MS, Long Island Univ. **Robert Klein, Prin.**
 Col Prep. Gen Acad. LD. Underachiever. Feat—Span Comp_Sci Studio_Art Music. **Supp**—Dev_Read Rem_Math Rem_Read Rev Tut.
 Adm: 23/yr. Appl due: Rolling. Accepted: 70%. **Tests** IQ MAT.
 Enr 81. B 61. G 20. Elem 30. Sec 51. Wh 78%. Hisp 4%. Blk 15%. Asian 3%. Avg class size: 10. Uniform. **Fac 16.** M 2/1. F 12/1. Wh 94%. Hisp 6%. Adv deg: 37%.
 Grad '04—13. Col—10. (Nassau CC, Adelphi, U of AZ, Curry, Long Island, Dowling). Alum 4176.
 Tui '04-'05: Day $17,950 (+$550).
 Plant val $8,000,000. Bldgs 3. Class rms 20. Lib 5000 vols. Sci labs 1. Comp labs 1. Auds 1. Art studios 1. Music studios 1. Gyms 1. Fields 1.
 Est 1924. Nonprofit. Quar (Sept-June).

Vincent Smith's highly structured program, known for its individualized program for reluctant learners and students with learning disabilities, emphasizes the development of reading, organizational and study skills. The school maintains a low student-teacher ratio, and tutoring, remedial reading services and writing skills classes are important parts of the curriculum. In addition to traditional courses, pupils take compulsory classes in computers, art, music, health and physical education.

Extracurricular activities include student council; newspaper; yearbook; chorus; and math, drama and art clubs. Interscholastic sports, available to secondary students, are soccer, basketball and softball.

POUGHKEEPSIE, NY. (64 mi. W of Hartford, CT; 71 mi. N of New York, NY) Urban. Pop: 29,871. Alt: 156 ft.

OAKWOOD FRIENDS SCHOOL
Bdg — Coed Gr 9-12; Day — Coed 6-12

Poughkeepsie, NY 12603. 22 Spackenkill Rd. Tel: 845-462-4200. Fax: 845-462-4251.
  www.oakwoodfriends.org E-mail: admissions@oakwoodfriends.org
Peter F. Baily, Head. BA, Earlham College, ME, Husson College, MA, Bryn Mawr. **Robert J. Suphan, Adm.**
  Col Prep. AP—Eng Fr Span Calc Bio Chem US_Hist. **Feat**—Playwriting Ecol Ethics Philos Quakerism Art_Hist Drama Music_Theory Journ. **Supp**—ESL LD.
  Adm (Bdg Gr 9-11; Day 6-11): 38/yr. Bdg 14. Day 24. Appl due: Rolling. Accepted: 62%. Yield: 50%. **Tests** TOEFL.
  Enr 158. B 18/67. G 22/51. Elem 36. Sec 122. Wh 72%. Hisp 8%. Blk 6%. Asian 13%. Other 1%. Avg class size: 12. **Fac 33.** M 11/4. F 10/8. Wh 85%. Hisp 6%. Blk 9%. Adv deg: 45%. In dorms 4.
  Grad '04—32. Col—32. (Manhattanville 3, Goucher 2, Sch of Visual Arts 2, Carnegie Mellon 1, Sarah Lawrence 1, Swarthmore 1). Avg SAT: 1100. Alum 2242.
  Tui '04-'05: Bdg $30,500 (+$400). **5-Day Bdg $26,500** (+$400). **Day $15,200-17,600** (+$350). **Aid:** Need 69 ($480,000).
  Endow $3,000,000. Plant val $15,700,000. Bldgs 21. Dorms 4. Dorm rms 76. Class rms 20. Lib 12,000 vols. Sci labs 3. Comp labs 1. Theaters 1. Art studios 1. Music studios 1. Dance studios 1. Media ctrs 1. Fields 5. Courts 4.
  Est 1876. Nonprofit. Religious Society of Friends. Tri (Sept-June).

A Quaker school, Oakwood enrolls a diverse student body that comes from overseas and from all sections of the US. In a simple, friendly atmosphere that promotes close relations between students and faculty, Oakwood maintains high academic standards and sends its graduates to leading colleges throughout the country.

In addition to providing a strong base in traditional subjects, Oakwood has developed a unified senior program that includes intensive interdisciplinary and Advanced Placement courses, as well as various off-campus community service opportunities.

Students help operate the school through a work-job program and participation in student government. A substantial drama program, with both on-stage and technical theater instruction, complements art and music offerings. Sports include interscholastic soccer, softball, cross-country running, basketball, baseball, swimming, volleyball and tennis. **See Also Page 1221**

POUGHKEEPSIE DAY SCHOOL
Day — Coed Gr PS-12

Poughkeepsie, NY 12603. 260 Boardman Rd. Tel: 845-462-7600. Fax: 845-462-7602.
  www.poughkeepsieday.org E-mail: pdsadmissions@poughkeepsieday.org
Mary Jane Yurchak, Dir. BA, Vassar College, MEd, EdD, Harvard Univ. **Jill Lundquist, Adm.**
  Col Prep. AP—Eng Fr Calc. **Feat**—Span Comp_Sci Studio_Art Drama Music. **Supp**—Dev_Read Rem_Math Tut.
  Adm: 68/yr. Appl due: Jan. Accepted: 62%. Yield: 84%.

NY   *Leading Private Schools*   *404*

Enr 345. B 165. G 180. Elem 226. Sec 119. Wh 83%. Hisp 5%. Blk 4%. Asian 6%. Other 2%. Avg class size: 12. **Fac 54.** M 15/4. F 27/8. Wh 90%. Hisp 4%. Blk 2%. Asian 2%. Other 2%. Adv deg: 55%.

Grad '04—18. Col—18. (Vassar 2, Amherst 1, Swarthmore 1, Cooper Union 1, CT Col 1, Skidmore 1). Avg SAT: 1206. Alum 1650.

Tui '04-'05: Day $13,350-16,875 (+$125). **Aid:** Need 68 ($340,300).

Summer: Enrich Rec. Theater. Tui Day $110-220/wk. 6 wks.

Endow $2,840,000. Plant val $10,000,000. Bldgs 3. Class rms 40. 2 Libs 18,000 vols. Sci labs 3. Comp labs 2. Auds 1. Theaters 1. Art studios 2. Music studios 2. Drama studios 1. Gyms 1. Fields 1. Basketball courts 1. Playgrounds 1.

Est 1934. Nonprofit. Quar (Sept-June).

PDS was founded by Vassar College faculty and local families with the purpose of "advancing the cause of liberal and progressive education." The school's 35-acre campus overlooking the Catskill Mountains includes historic Kenyon House, a Mediterranean-style mansion. Influenced by the theories of John Dewey and Jean Piaget, the student-centered program utilizes an interdisciplinary, problem-solving approach to academic and creative study.

The school utilizes mixed-age groupings throughout; each year, middle and upper schoolers follow a modular block schedule that consists of 90-minute academic classes. PDS requires community service participation, either on campus or in the larger Poughkeepsie area, of all middle and upper school students. In addition, all diploma candidates must complete a month-long, off-campus senior internship.

QUEENS, NY. Urban. Pop: 2,229,379. Alt: 75 ft. Area also includes Flushing and Forest Hills.

THE KEW-FOREST SCHOOL
Day — Coed Gr K-12

Forest Hills, NY 11375. 119-17 Union Tpke. Tel: 718-268-4667. Fax: 718-268-9121.
   www.kewforest.org   E-mail: ndumaresq@kewforest.org

Peter S. Lewis, Head. BA, Middlebury College, MA, PhD, Stanford Univ. **Katherine Garcia, Adm.**

Col Prep. AP—Eng Fr Lat Span Calc Stats Bio Chem Physics Eur_Hist US_Hist. **Feat**—Geol Marine_Biol/Sci Comp_Sci Intl_Relations Ethics Philos Art_Hist Film Studio_Art Music Music_Hist Music_Theory Journ.

Adm: 82/yr. Appl due: Jan. Accepted: 85%. Yield: 90%. **Tests** ISEE.

Enr 385. B 195. G 190. Elem 210. Sec 175. Wh 65%. Hisp 10%. Blk 10%. Asian 15%. Avg class size: 18. Uniform. **Fac 45.** M 20/3. F 17/5. Wh 90%. Hisp 6%. Blk 4%. Adv deg: 46%.

Grad '04—40. Col—40. (NYU 5, Cornell 1, Barnard 1, Columbia 1, Wesleyan U 1, Lafayette 1). Avg SAT: 1129. Alum 1800.

Tui '04-'05: Day $12,650-13,650 (+$1790-2810). **Aid:** Need 43 ($280,000).

Summer: Gr 7-12. Acad Enrich. Tui Day $900/2-wk ses. Gr K-6. Rec. Tui Day $1000/4-wk ses. 8 wks.

Endow $1,500,000. Plant val $12,000,000. Class rms 25. 2 Libs 6000 vols. Sci labs 2. Tech ctrs 2. Auds 1. Art studios 2. Music studios 2. Gyms 1.

Est 1918. Nonprofit. Tri (Sept-June). **Assoc** MSA.

Kew-Forest was founded by Louis D. Marriott and Guy H. Catlin. In 1941, upon the retirement of Mr. Marriott, the school was incorporated by the parents.

Attracting students from throughout Queens County and Long Island, the school stresses college preparation and sends graduates to leading colleges. Activities include mock trial, Model UN, drama, vocal and instrumental music, student publications, community service and student government, as well as a competitive athletic program for boys and girls in the middle and upper schools. An outdoor education program is incorporated into the middle school, and an active field trip program serves students in the lower and upper schools. Kew-Forest takes juniors and seniors on college visits.

WINDSOR SCHOOL
Day — Coed Gr 6-PG

Flushing, NY 11355. 41-60 Kissena Blvd. Tel: 718-359-8300. Fax: 718-359-1876.
www.windsorschool.com   E-mail: admin@thewindsorschool.com
Martin Cohen, Head. BS, MA, City Univ of New York, PhD, Kensington Univ. **Philip A. Stewart, Adm.**

    Col Prep. AP—Calc Chem. Feat—Fr Span Programming Econ Govt Intl_Relations Law Psych Sociol Studio_Art Music Bus Marketing. **Supp**—Dev_Read ESL Makeup Tut.

    Adm: 48/yr. Accepted: 90%.

    Enr 125. B 72. G 53. Elem 17. Sec 108. Wh 21%. Hisp 8%. Blk 14%. Asian 57%. Avg class size: 12. **Fac 14.** M 9/1. F 3/1. Adv deg: 85%.

    Grad '04—26. Col—24. (SUNY 7, St John's U-NY 6, U of AZ 1, NY Inst of Tech 1, Cooper Union 1, Oberlin 1). Alum 1535.

    Tui '04-'05: Day $12,800-14,900 (+$375).

    Summer: Acad Enrich Rev Rem. Tui Day $430/crse. 6½ wks.

    Plant val $3,250,000. Bldgs 3. Class rms 18. Libs 1. Sci labs 2. Comp labs 1. Art studios 2. Gyms 1. Fields 1.

    Est 1968. Inc. Tri (Sept-June). **Assoc** MSA.

This coeducational day school prepares its graduates for leading colleges throughout the country while emphasizing individual development and progress by means of a strong guidance program. A tutorial/extracurricular period is part of the regular school day. Those who already have a high school diploma may enroll in the postgraduate program. Foreign students are accepted and, if necessary, receive intensive English as a Second Language instruction.   **See Also Page 1282**

ROCHESTER, NY. (66 mi. ENE of Buffalo, NY) Urban. Pop: 219,773. Alt: 513 ft.

ALLENDALE COLUMBIA SCHOOL
Day — Coed Gr PS-12

Rochester, NY 14618. 519 Allens Creek Rd. Tel: 585-381-4560. Fax: 585-383-1191.
www.allendalecolumbia.org   E-mail: kcegelski@allendalecolumbia.org
Charles F. Hertrick, Head. AB, Lafayette College, MA, Carnegie Mellon Univ, MEd, Harvard

Univ. **Karen M. Cegelski, Adm.**
Col Prep. AP—Eng Fr Lat Span Calc Comp_Sci Chem Physics Eur_Hist US_Hist Studio_Art. **Feat**—Creative_Writing Stats Anat Astron Anthro Econ Constitutional_Law Ceramics Drawing Photog Music.

Adm: 86/yr. Appl due: Rolling. Accepted: 47%. Yield: 72%. **Tests** CTP_4.

Enr 491. B 230. G 261. Elem 328. Sec 163. Wh 81%. Hisp 3%. Blk 8%. Am Ind 1%. Asian 5%. Other 2%. Avg class size: 14. **Fac 57.** M 19. F 31/7. Wh 88%. Hisp 4%. Blk 2%. Asian 6%. Adv deg: 61%.

Grad '04—38. Col—38. (Oberlin 3, Denison 2, Syracuse 2, U of Rochester 2, Cornell 2, Rochester Inst of Tech 2). Avg SAT: 1247. Alum 2400.

Tui '04-'05: Day $6350-14,900. Aid: Merit 4 ($13,775). Need 165 ($1,563,790).

Summer: Rec. 1-8 wks.

Endow $13,918,000. Plant val $16,000,000. Bldgs 5. Class rms 42. Lib 16,000 vols. Labs 6. Lang labs 1. Theaters 1. Art studios 2. Music studios 3. Gyms 2. Fields 6. Courts 4.

Est 1890. Nonprofit. Sem (Sept-June). **Assoc** CLS.

The Columbia School for girls, established in 1890, and the Allendale School for boys, established in 1926, merged in 1971 to form the current coeducational school. Students enroll from the urban, suburban and rural areas of Rochester. The school has four main divisions: preprimary (PS-K), lower school (grades 1-5), middle school (grades 6-8) and upper school (grades 9-12).

Conducted in a small-class setting, Allendale Columbia's liberal arts curriculum emphasizes college preparation. Beginning in the lower school, students receive instruction from specialists in foreign language and science. In addition to the traditional subjects, the school offers art, music, library and computer classes. A majority of seniors take at least one Advanced Placement course (AP classes are available in every major discipline), and qualified seniors design, pursue and receive credit for community- or career-oriented off-campus internships in the last month of school.

Extracurricular and athletic opportunities include community service, drama, music, interscholastic team and individual sports, and a variety of committees and clubs. All students in grades 9 and 10 elect at least one competitive sport per year.

HARLEY SCHOOL

Day — Coed Gr PS-12

Rochester, NY 14618. 1981 Clover St. Tel: 585-442-1770. Fax: 585-442-5758.
 www.harleyschool.org E-mail: admissions@harleyschool.org

Paul Schiffman, Head. BS, State Univ of New York-Albany, MS, State Univ of New York-Brockport. **Kimberley C. Moore, Adm.**

Col Prep. AP—Eng Fr Span Calc Bio Chem Physics Eur_Hist US_Hist Econ Psych US_Govt & Pol Studio_Art. **Feat**—Creative_Writing Shakespeare Lat Comp_Graphics Vietnam_War Ceramics Film Filmmaking Photog Sculpt Finance Speech. **Supp**—Tut.

Adm (Gr PS-11): 77/yr. Appl due: Rolling. Accepted: 80%. Yield: 71%. **Tests** CTP_4 IQ.

Enr 490. B 241. G 249. Elem 333. Sec 157. Wh 86%. Hisp 2%. Blk 7%. Asian 5%. Avg class size: 12. **Fac 80.** M 21/4. F 46/9. Wh 96%. Hisp 2%. Blk 2%. Adv deg: 70%.

Grad '04—38. Col—38. (SUNY-Geneseo 2, U of Rochester 2, Nazareth 2, Brown 1, Cornell 1, Vassar 1). Avg SAT: 1236. Alum 2025.

Tui '04-'05: Day $12,025-14,250 (+$200). **Aid:** Need 151 ($782,765).

Summer: Enrich Rem Rec. Computers. Drama. Tui Day $200/wk. 8 wks.

Endow $6,800,000. Plant val $19,500,000. Bldgs 4. Class rms 47. 2 Libs 21,000 vols. Sci

labs 5. Comp labs 2. Theaters 1. Art studios 3. Music studios 3. Dance studios 1. Gyms 2. Fields 2. Courts 7. Pools 1.
Est 1917. Nonprofit. Tri (Sept-June).

The college preparatory program at Harley emphasizes individualized instruction, with a low student-teacher ratio maintained. Students satisfy broad distribution requirements for graduation, and academic flexibility is achieved through electives and opportunities for independent and off-campus study. Music and art are offered at all levels, and Advanced Placement courses are available.

Student government, sports, community service and publications are among the school's extracurricular activities. The summer program provides recreation and reinforces academic skills.

ROSLYN, NY. (18 mi. ENE of New York, NY) Rural. Pop: 2570. Alt: 37 ft.

BUCKLEY COUNTRY DAY SCHOOL
Day — Coed Gr PS-8

Roslyn, NY 11576. I U Willets Rd. Tel: 516-627-1910. Fax: 516-627-8627.
  www.buckleycountryday.org E-mail: aduffy@buckleycountryday.com
Jean-Marc Juhel, Head. BA, MA, Univ of Paris (France), MA, Columbia Univ, PhD, Michel de Montaigne Univ (France). **Ann V. Duffy, Adm.**
  Pre-Prep. **Feat**—Fr Lat Span Computers Studio_Art Band Music Indus_Arts.
  Adm (Gr PS-7): 59/yr. Appl due: Rolling. Accepted: 67%. Yield: 72%.
  Enr 303. B 161. G 142. Elem 303. Wh 69%. Hisp 2%. Blk 5%. Asian 11%. Other 13%. Avg class size: 14. Uniform. **Fac 50.** M 8. F 32/10. Adv deg: 57%.
  Grad '04—20. Prep—18. (Friends Acad-NY 7, Westover 2, Spence 1, Hackley 1, Kent Sch-CT 1). Alum 2000.
Tui '04-'05: Day $12,355-17,765. Aid: Merit 3 ($9000). Need 28 ($309,295).
Summer: Enrich Rec. Tui Day $3500-5400. 4-8 wks.
Endow $1,828,000. Plant val $8,935,000. Bldgs 1. Class rms 30. Lib 15,620 vols. Sci labs 2. Lang labs 3. Comp labs 1. Art studios 1. Music studios 1. Shops 1. Gyms 3. Fields 4. Courts 4. Pools 4. Roller rinks 1.
Est 1923. Nonprofit. Quar (Sept-June).

This school, one of the suburban schools founded by B. Lord Buckley and known until 1938 as Great Neck Preparatory, moved in 1955 from Great Neck to its present location with double the former acreage, as well as a new plant and facilities.

Pupils develop basic skills in reading, mathematics and writing. French and Spanish are introduced in kindergarten, Latin in grade 7. Intensive science study and lab work begins in grade 1. Buckley schedules regular periods for art, music, physical education, library and computer. Many cocurricular activities and athletics, among them baseball, softball, badminton, basketball, volleyball, tennis, soccer and lacrosse, supplement the academic program.

RYE, NY. (24 mi. NE of New York, NY) Suburban. Pop: 14,955. Alt: 49 ft.

RYE COUNTRY DAY SCHOOL
Day — Coed Gr PS-12

Rye, NY 10580. Cedar St. Tel: 914-967-1417. Fax: 914-967-1418.
www.rcds.rye.ny.us   E-mail: rcds_admin@rcds.rye.ny.us
Scott Alan Nelson, Head. AB, Brown Univ, MS, Fordham Univ. **Gregory Schneider, Adm.**

- **Col Prep. AP**—Eng Fr Lat Span Calc Stats Comp_Sci Bio Chem Physics Eur_Hist US_Hist Psych US_Govt & Pol Art_Hist Studio_Art Music_Theory. **Feat**—Creative_Writing African-Amer_Lit Greek Astron Geol Comp_Design Econ Film Photog Drama Music Public_Speak.
- **Adm:** 136/yr. Appl due: Jan. Accepted: 30%. Yield: 77%. **Tests** CTP_4 ISEE SSAT.
- **Enr 841.** B 436. G 405. Elem 473. Sec 368. Wh 82%. Hisp 2%. Blk 6%. Asian 5%. Other 5%. Avg class size: 13. **Fac 115.** M 35. F 75/5. Wh 88%. Hisp 4%. Blk 5%. Asian 3%. Adv deg: 63%.
- **Grad '04—82. Col—80.** (Wake Forest 5, Cornell 4, Vanderbilt 4, NYU 4, Trinity Col-CT 4, U of PA 3). Avg SAT: 1321. Alum 3000.
- **Tui '04-'05: Day $14,880-23,450** (+$225-2400). **Aid:** Need 94 ($1,795,775).
- **Summer:** Acad Enrich Rev Rem. Driver Ed. Tui Day $475-700. 6 wks.
- Endow $13,200,000. Plant val $43,650,000. Bldgs 6. Class rms 40. 2 Libs 30,000 vols. Sci labs 9. Comp labs 4. Theaters 1. Art studios 3. Music studios 8. Dance studios 1. Perf arts ctrs 1. Photog studios 2. Gyms 2. Fields 5. Tennis courts 4. Squash courts 4. Field houses 1. Rinks 1. Fitness ctrs 1.
- **Est 1869.** Nonprofit. Sem (Sept-June). **Assoc** MSA.

This college preparatory school offers a comprehensive program and enrolls primarily students from Westchester and Fairfield counties. A required laptop computer program in grades 7-12, independent study, community service and the creative arts are features of the school's curriculum. Elective courses in English, science, languages, the arts and history are available to juniors and seniors. A full physical education program offers interscholastic sports in grades 7-12.

Apart from the regular schedule, the school provides an academic summer session for motivated students of color, in addition to its regular summer school. RCDS conducts annual exchanges with schools in France and Costa Rica.

SCHOOL OF THE HOLY CHILD
Day — Girls Gr 5-12

Rye, NY 10580. 2225 Westchester Ave. Tel: 914-967-5622. Fax: 914-967-6476.
www.holychildrye.org   E-mail: admissions@holychildrye.org
Ann F. Sullivan, Head. BA, Good Counsel College, MA, New York Univ. **Andrea Fletcher, Adm.**

- **Col Prep. AP**—Eng Fr Lat Span Calc Bio Eur_Hist US_Hist US_Govt & Pol Art_Hist Studio_Art Music_Theory. **Feat**—Stats Anat Programming Anthro Econ Psych Theol World_Relig Chorus Music. **Supp**—Rev Tut.
- **Adm (Gr 5-11):** 62/yr. Appl due: Jan. Accepted: 43%. Yield: 45%. **Tests** ISEE SSAT TACHS.
- **Enr 309.** G 309. Elem 102. Sec 207. Wh 83%. Hisp 4%. Blk 9%. Am Ind 1%. Asian 3%.

Avg class size: 17. Uniform. **Fac 40.** M 2/1. F 29/8. Wh 97%. Hisp 2%. Blk 1%. Adv deg: 72%.
Grad '04—44. Col—33. (Boston Col 4, NYU 3, Loyola Col 3, Fordham 3, U of MI 2, Fairfield 2). Avg SAT: 1197. Alum 2000.
Tui '04-'05: Day $17,340-17,740. Aid: Merit 33 ($97,740). Need 67 ($554,200).
Bldgs 2. Lib 9000 vols. Lang labs 1. Art studios 1. Music studios 1. Gyms 1. Fields 2.
Est 1904. Nonprofit. Roman Catholic. Tri (Sept-June). **Assoc** MSA.

Holy Child offers girls college preparation while stressing Christian values in a small-class environment. Advanced Placement courses are available in all major disciplines, and theology is required at all grade levels. Pupils in grades 7-12 take part in the school's laptop program, and students may pursue independent study in selected advanced courses.

Among extracurricular activities are cultural field trips to New York City, spiritual retreats, and a variety of organizations, clubs and interscholastic sports.

See Also Page 1317

ST. JAMES, NY. (44 mi. ENE of New York, NY) Rural. Pop: 13,268. Alt: 163 ft.

HARBOR COUNTRY DAY SCHOOL
Day — Coed Gr PS-8

St James, NY 11780. 17 Three Sisters Rd. **Tel: 631-584-5555. Fax: 631-862-7664.**
www.harborcountrydayschool.org   E-mail: info@harborcountrydayschool.org
Arthur L. Strawbridge, Head. BA, Hobart College, MA, Villanova Univ.
  Pre-Prep. Feat—Fr Span Computers Studio_Art Music.
  Adm: 74/yr. Appl due: Rolling.
  Enr 189. Elem 189. Wh 82%. Hisp 4%. Blk 7%. Asian 7%. Avg class size: 11. Uniform. **Fac 26.** M 2/1. F 21/2. Adv deg: 80%.
  Grad '04—12. Prep—5. (Stony Brook 2). Alum 400.
  Tui '04-'05: Day $2750-8695 (+$180-380). **Aid:** Merit 6 ($39,128). Need 4 ($17,390).
  Summer: Acad Enrich Rev Rem Rec. Art. Tui Day $95-425/wk. 7 wks.
  Plant val $2,750,000. Bldgs 1. Class rms 17. Lib 8925 vols. Sci labs 1. Comp labs 1. Art studios 1. Music studios 1. Gyms 1. Fields 3. Pools 1.
  Est 1958. Nonprofit. Quar (Sept-June).

This traditional school, founded by a group of local parents, serves western Suffolk County. The curriculum focuses on the basic academic disciplines of language arts, mathematics, science and social studies. Studio art, music, computer, French, Spanish, musical productions and athletics are important elements of the coordinated program. The school seeks to develop proper study habits at all grade levels.

Students participate in various community service projects during the course of the year. Graduates enter leading area preparatory schools.

KNOX SCHOOL

Bdg — Coed Gr 7-12; Day — Coed 6-12

St James, NY 11780. 541 Long Beach Rd. Tel: 631-584-6562. Fax: 631-584-6566.
www.knoxschool.org E-mail: mbrown@knoxschool.org
David B. Stephens, Head. BS, Hobart College, MS, Syracuse Univ. **Mary H. Brown, Actg Adm.**

Col Prep. AP—Calc Chem Physics. **Feat**—Creative_Writing Fr Span Environ_Sci Computers Govt Art_Hist Photog Studio_Art Music_Hist Dance. **Supp**—Dev_Read ESL Tut.

Adm: 42/yr. Appl due: Rolling. **Tests** IQ ISEE SSAT Stanford TOEFL.

Enr 114. B 28/35. G 21/30. Elem 39. Sec 75. Wh 63%. Hisp 3%. Blk 12%. Am Ind 2%. Asian 20%. Avg class size: 8. Uniform. **Fac 33.** M 12/2. F 16/3. Wh 92%. Hisp 8%. Adv deg: 54%. In dorms 12.

Grad '04—25. Col—25. (Geo Wash, NYU, Lynn, Sarah Lawrence, U of MI, Chapman). Alum 2550.

Tui '04-'05: Bdg $29,750 (+$3100-8100). **Day $14,200-15,125** (+$2000-8000). **Aid:** Merit 6. Need 15.

Endow $1,000,000. Plant val $6,500,000. Bldgs 12. Dorms 5. Dorm rms 54. Class rms 24. Lib 25,000 vols. Sci labs 2. Comp labs 2. Photog labs 1. Art studios 1. Music studios 3. Dance studios 1. Gyms 1. Fields 6. Courts 4. Riding rings 2. Stables 1.

Est 1904. Nonprofit. Tri (Sept-May). **Assoc** MSA.

Established as a girls' school in Briarcliff Manor by Mary Alice Knox, the school has always been located in New York State. It occupied quarters in Tarrytown and Cooperstown before settling at its present campus, a 68-acre estate on Long Island's North Shore, in 1954. Knox first enrolled boys in 1973.

The school's structured college preparatory program, which is rooted in the liberal arts, features small classes, flexible scheduling and a varied curriculum. Course work in the visual and performing arts is integral to the program. Knox offers a full range of opportunities in athletics, including an extensive equestrian program. Its proximity to New York City enables the school to schedule frequent weekend activities there. **See Also Page 1188**

SOUTH WALES, NY. (19 mi. SE of Buffalo, NY; 181 mi. ENE of Cleveland, OH) Rural. Pop: 450. Alt: 900 ft.

THE GOW SCHOOL

Bdg — Boys Gr 7-PG

South Wales, NY 14139. 2491 Emery Rd, PO Box 85. Tel: 716-652-3450. Fax: 716-687-2003.
www.gow.org E-mail: admissions@gow.org
M. Bradley Rogers, Jr., Head. BA, Univ of Dayton, MA, Johns Hopkins Univ. **Robert Garcia, Adm.**

Col Prep. LD. Feat—Computers Fine_Arts Drama Music. **Supp**—Dev_Read Makeup Tut.

Adm (Gr 7-12): 43/yr. Appl due: Rolling. Accepted: 90%. Yield: 68%. **Tests** IQ Stanford TOEFL.

Enr 143. B 143. Elem 17. Sec 126. Wh 83%. Hisp 5%. Blk 3%. Am Ind 1%. Asian 5%. Other

3%. Avg class size: 4. Uniform. **Fac 38.** M 27/3. F 6/2. Adv deg: 50%. In dorms 19.
Grad '04—22. Col—22. (Lynn 3, Manhattanville 2, U of Cincinnati 2, Minneapolis Col of Art & Design 1, Lyndon St 1, ME Maritime 1). Avg SAT: 886. Alum 2167.
Tui '04-'05: Bdg $39,500 (+$1600). **Aid:** Need 36 ($490,000).
Summer: Coed. Rem. Tui Bdg $5975. Tui Day $3900. 5 wks.
Endow $4,200,000. Plant val $15,142,000. Bldgs 21. Dorms 6. Dorm rms 75. Class rms 32. Lib 10,000 vols. Labs 3. Comp labs 1. Comp ctrs 1. Auds 1. Theaters 1. Art studios 1. Music studios 1. Gyms 1. Fields 1. Courts 5.
Est 1926. Nonprofit. Sem (Sept-May).

The school was established by Peter Gow as a college preparatory institution for those with dyslexia or similar language learning differences. All programs are individually planned, and nearly all graduates enter college.

The school enrolls students of average to above-average intelligence who have specific language difficulties. Classes are small, averaging four to six pupils each. The core of the program at Gow is "reconstructive language" and multisensory mathematics, both of which are designed to improve and extend the student's academic ability within a college preparatory setting.

The athletic program features soccer, cross-country, basketball, skiing, lacrosse, boxing, crew, squash and tennis. An Outward Bound-type outdoors program and various clubs and student publications are among other school activities.

See Also Pages 1360-1

STATEN ISLAND, NY. Urban. Pop: 443,728. Alt: 9 ft.

STATEN ISLAND ACADEMY
Day — Coed Gr PS-12

Staten Island, NY 10304. 715 Todt Hill Rd. Tel: 718-987-8100. Fax: 718-979-7641.
  www.statenislandacademy.org   E-mail: mmcshane@statenislandacademy.org
Diane J. Hulse, Head. BA, Beloit College, MA, New York Univ. **Linda Shuffman, Adm.**
  Col Prep. AP—Eng Fr Lat Span Calc Comp_Sci Bio Chem Eur_Hist US_Hist Econ Psych US_Govt & Pol Music_Theory. **Feat—** Film Photog Music Music_Hist Public_Speak. **Supp—**Dev_Read ESL Rev Tut.
  Adm: 86/yr. Appl due: Jan. Accepted: 60%. **Tests** IQ ISEE Stanford.
  Enr 410. Elem 280. Sec 130. Wh 85%. Hisp 2%. Blk 3%. Am Ind 2%. Asian 8%. Avg class size: 17. **Fac 68.** M 19. F 46/3. Adv deg: 61%.
  Grad '04—37. Col—37. (Wagner 3, NYU 2, Drew 2, St John's U-NY 2, Brown 1, Amherst 1). Avg SAT: 1158. Alum 1186.
  Tui '04-'05: Day $15,900-18,999 (+$850). **Aid:** Need ($1,000,000).
  Summer: Enrich Rec. Sports. Tui Day $450-478/wk. 9 wks.
  Endow $4,500,000. Plant val $5,900,000. Bldgs 7. Lib 18,000 vols. Sci labs 3. Lang labs 1. Comp ctrs 2. Auds 1. Theaters 1. Art studios 2. Music studios 2. Gyms 1. Fields 4. Courts 3. Pools 2. Fitness ctrs 1.
  Est 1884. Nonprofit. (Sept-June). **Assoc** MSA.

The academy, which traces its origins back to the 19th century, is the only independent school on Staten Island. Expansion began in earnest in the 1930s, when the school combined with several other private schools before eventually merging with the Dongan Hall-Arden School. By 1963, SIA had moved all operations from its original location to a 12-acre site in Todt Hill that formerly served as the Dongan Hall-Arden campus.

Academic standards are rigorous and the curriculum is comprehensive in all three divisions. The lower school curriculum (grades pre-K-4) includes accelerated programs in English and math, as well as an enrichment program in science. Middle school pupils (grades 5-8) follow a developmentally appropriate program of studies. The upper school course of studies (grades 9-12) offers Advanced Placement courses in every discipline, an independent study program, electives, an advanced science track and an accelerated math curriculum.

Student government, athletics, arts options, community service opportunities, publications and interest clubs complement academics.

STONY BROOK, NY. (46 mi. ENE of New York, NY) Suburban. Pop: 13,726. Alt: 108 ft.

STONY BROOK SCHOOL
Bdg and Day — Coed Gr 7-12

Stony Brook, NY 11790. 1 Chapman Pky. Tel: 631-751-1800. Fax: 631-751-4211.
www.stonybrookschool.org E-mail: admissions@stonybrookschool.org
Robert E. Gustafson, Jr., Head. BA, Univ of Virginia, MDiv, Gordon-Conwell Theological Seminary, MA, Columbia Univ. **Jane A. Taylor, Adm.**
Col Prep. AP—Eng Fr Lat Span Calc Bio Chem Physics Eur_Hist US_Hist Psych US_Govt & Pol. **Feat**—Stats Marine_Biol/Sci Computers Econ Bible Photog. **Supp**—ESL.
Adm: 120/yr. Appl due: Rolling. Accepted: 42%. **Tests** SSAT.
Enr 375. B 88/126. G 73/88. Elem 74. Sec 301. Wh 64%. Hisp 3%. Blk 8%. Asian 18%. Other 7%. Avg class size: 18. **Fac 46.** M 21/5. F 16/4. Adv deg: 54%. In dorms 14.
Grad '04—71. Col—71. (Carnegie Mellon, Davidson, Emory, Northwestern, Wheaton-IL). Avg SAT: 1215. Alum 3595.
Tui '04-'05: Bdg $28,000 (+$200). **5-Day Bdg $22,000** (+$200). **Day $11,000-16,900** (+$200). **Aid:** Need 110.
Endow $7,661,000. Plant val $25,000,000. Bldgs 14. Dorms 8. Dorm rms 107. Class rms 32. Lib 18,000 vols. Labs 7. Art studios 1. Gyms 2. Fields 2. Tennis courts 6. Pools 1.
Est 1922. Nonprofit. Nondenom Christian. Sem (Aug-May). **Assoc** CLS MSA.

Stony Brook's founding headmaster, Frank E. Gaebelein, was determined to establish a school where an educational program of rigorous college preparation would be conducted within the context of the Christian faith and basic values, at a time when many were moving toward secular approaches to education. The school preserves the classic tradition, which Dr. Gaebelein articulated, of integrating faith and learning.

Academics stress the development of abstract thinking, intensive reading and careful research from within a traditional liberal arts curriculum. The humanities are emphasized, with Advanced Placement courses offered in many subjects, and an independent learning program is available. The school hosts the Staley Lecture Series, held annually to foster intellectual curiosity and critical thinking.

Cocurricular activities include the theatrical arts, choir and various interest clubs. Upper-class honor students participate in a program of tutoring. Student exchange

NY   *Middle A.*

opportunities include a year of postgraduate stuc͟ͅ
abroad. Boys' interscholastic competition is offereu
try, basketball, swimming, wrestling, baseball, lacros͟.
track, and tennis; girls compete in soccer, cross-counu
softball, tennis, sailing, volleyball, and winter and spring tr͟.

SYRACUSE, NY.

(122 mi. WNW of Albany, NY) Urban. P͟
Alt: 400 ft. Area also includes DeWitt.

MANLIUS PEBBLE HILL SCHOOL
Day — Coed Gr PS-PG

DeWitt, NY 13214. 5300 Jamesville Rd. Tel: 315-446-2452. Fax: 315-446-2620.
   www.mph.net   E-mail: mphinfo@mph.net

Baxter F. Ball, Head. BA, Kenyon College, MA, Bowling Green State Univ. **Lynne Allard, Adm.**

Col Prep. AP—Eng Fr Lat Span Calc Stats Comp_Sci Bio Chem Physics Eur_Hist US_Hist Studio_Art. **Feat**—Acting Theater Chorus Music Dance. **Supp**—ESL Tut.

Adm: 105/yr. Appl due: Rolling. Accepted: 67%. **Tests** CTP_4.

Enr 587. B 304. G 283. Elem 323. Sec 263. PG 1. Wh 82%. Hisp 1%. Blk 5%. Am Ind 3%. Asian 4%. Other 5%. Avg class size: 16. **Fac 96.** M 28/11. F 46/11. Wh 94%. Hisp 2%. Blk 3%. Asian 1%. Adv deg: 52%.

Grad '04—71. Col—70. (Cornell, Rochester Inst of Tech, Brown, Union Col-NY, Tufts, Swarthmore). Avg SAT: 1343. Alum 3200.

Tui '03-'04: Day $10,050-13,600 (+$1475). **Aid:** Merit 58 ($390,409). Need 168 ($711,112).

Summer: Acad Enrich Rev Rec. Tui Day $330/2-wk ses. 6 wks.

Endow $2,000,000. Plant val $6,000,000. Bldgs 9. Class rms 24. Lib 12,500 vols. Sci labs 4. Lang labs 4. Comp labs 3. Theaters 1. Art studios 4. Music studios 3. Dance studios 1. Gyms 1. Fields 4. Courts 4.

Est 1869. Nonprofit. Quar (Sept-June). **Assoc** MSA.

Manlius Pebble Hill School was formed in 1970 by a merger of the Manlius School (a boys' military boarding school founded in 1869) and Pebble Hill School (a coeducational day school begun in 1927). With the merger, the military program was dropped and the school assumed its present status.

The lower school offers individualized instruction with an emphasis on skills in reading and mathematics, as well as full curricula in science and social studies. Foreign language conversation and culture are also introduced. All-day prekindergarten and kindergarten programs are available. Middle and upper school classes follow a college preparatory curriculum. MPH offers Advanced Placement courses in all disciplines, and the school also provides opportunities for independent study, community service and travel abroad. Fine and performing arts programs and physical education serve pupils at all grade levels. Both boys and girls participate in interscholastic sports.

A limited boarding program enables students in grades 9-PG to live with host families chosen from parents, faculty members and administrators.

— Coed K-12

642. Fax: 914-366-2636.
:hool.org
iiv of Pennsylvania, MA, Columbia

_Sci Bio Chem Physics Art_Hist
Ger Greek Ital Russ Ecol Genet-
ion Anthro Econ Architect Photog

8. Appl due: Dec. Accepted: 39%.

Elem 417. Sec 377. Wh 70%. Hisp 11%. Blk 8%. Asian 11%. Avg class size: 15. **Fac 115.** M 41. F 74. Wh 89%. Hisp 3%. Blk 4%. Asian 4%. Adv deg: 74%. In dorms 6.

Grad '04—92. Col—92. (Columbia, Cornell, Hamilton, Harvard, NYU, U of PA). Alum 3390.

Tui '04-'05: 5-Day Bdg $32,200 (+$1000). **Day** $21,100-24,600 (+$1000). **Aid:** Need 119.

Endow $20,000,000. Plant val $50,000,000. Bldgs 19. Dorms 2. Dorm rms 46. Class rms 55. Lib 32,000 vols. Labs 7. Art studios 3. Music studios 3. Perf arts ctrs 1. Gyms 1. Athletic ctrs 1. Fields 6. Tennis courts 6. Squash courts 4. Pools 1.

Est 1899. Nonprofit. Sem (Sept-June). **Assoc** CLS.

Established as a liberal arts boarding school for boys, Hackley now offers a rigorous academic program for both boys and girls. The lower school stresses both art and music, in addition to the traditional disciplines. Projects, field trips and hands-on activities supplement daily instruction, and interdisciplinary projects are common. Community service, environmental awareness, international studies and geography are integral aspects of the curriculum at this level. The study of foreign languages begins in the lower school, while field trips, assemblies, extracurricular activities, sports and social events complement the middle school schedule.

Students in the upper school choose from a wider array of courses, sports and activities. In many disciplines, the program offers AP classes, as well as tutorials and seminars that provide extensive choice to the students through a wide range of electives. Graduation requirements include foreign language, anthropology, and performing or visual arts course work.

The athletic program for grades 7 and 8 stresses team sports at the interscholastic level; in the upper school, those who do not participate in interscholastic sports must choose a noncompetitive activity each season for after-school recreation. Such fitness electives include dance, squash and open gym. Among the extracurricular activities are newspaper and literary magazine, a yearly delegation to Model Congress and Model UN, debate team, a wide variety of social service projects, and a performing arts program that includes concerts, recitals, serious drama and musicals.

See Also Pages 1160-1

TROY, NY. (8 mi. NE of Albany, NY; 143 mi. N of New York, NY) Urban. Pop: 49,170. Alt: 35 ft.

EMMA WILLARD SCHOOL
Bdg and Day — Girls Gr 9-PG

Troy, NY 12180. 285 Pawling Ave. Tel: 518-833-1320. Fax: 518-833-1805.
www.emmawillard.org   E-mail: admissions@emmawillard.org

Trudy E. Hall, Head. BS, St Lawrence Univ, MEd, Harvard Univ, MALS, Duke Univ. Kent H. Jones, Adm.

Col Prep. AP—Eng Fr Lat Span Calc Stats Comp_Sci Bio Chem Physics Eur_Hist US_Hist US_Govt & Pol Art_Hist. **Feat**—Russ Bioethics Neurosci Econ Philos Ceramics Drawing Film Photog Theater Chorus Music Orchestra Ballet Dance. **Supp**—ESL.

Adm (Gr 9-11): 113/yr. Bdg 68. Day 45. Appl due: Feb. Accepted: 65%. Yield: 61%. **Tests** CEEB ISEE SSAT TOEFL.

Enr 312. G 187/125. Sec 312. Wh 87%. Hisp 4%. Blk 6%. Asian 2%. Other 1%. Avg class size: 11. **Fac 66.** M 16/1. F 39/10. Wh 94%. Hisp 2%. Blk 2%. Asian 2%. Adv deg: 78%. In dorms 7.

Grad '04—81. Col—81. (Colgate, Hobart/Wm Smith, U of Rochester, NYU, Wellesley, Yale). Avg SAT: 1270. Alum 7271.

Tui '04-'05: **Bdg** $32,750 (+$850-900). **Day** $20,400 (+$650-700). **Aid:** Merit 15 ($48,500). Need 112 ($1,888,900).

Summer: Enrich Rec. Tui Bdg $2500/2-wk ses. 6 wks.

Endow $71,735,000. Plant val $142,000,000. Bldgs 31. Dorms 3. Dorm rms 144. Class rms 28. Lib 28,861 vols. Labs 8. Lang labs 1. Auds 2. Theaters 1. Art studios 5. Music studios 11. Gyms 1. Fields 3. Courts 9. Pools 1. Tracks 1.

Est 1814. Nonprofit. Sem (Sept-June). **Assoc** CLS.

Emma Willard School maintains a tradition of scholastic excellence, enrolling girls from families of varying backgrounds from throughout the nation and the world. Founded in Middlebury, VT, by Emma Willard, pioneer in the education of women, in 1821 it came upon invitation to Troy as Troy Female Seminary, and was reorganized under its present name in 1892. Among educationally influential alumnae was Mrs. Russell Sage, who provided the site that the school has occupied since 1910.

All students have a core of required courses and are expected to develop a strong foundation of academic skills. The program encourages flexibility within the structure so that students take courses in all major areas. The program consists of divisions in the following areas: the arts, computer science, English, history, languages, math, physical education and health, and science. The foreign language curriculum includes tutorial Italian classes, while dance, drama, music and visual arts classes are among the arts division offerings.

The well-supervised independent study program may include part-time projects in the Troy/Albany/Schenectady area. Projects have included internships with a veterinary clinic, the New York State Supreme Court and the New York State Assembly. Emma Willard also operates a speaker series that brings prominent individuals to the school for 24-hour residencies.

Extracurricular activities include school government, school publications, singing and drama groups, orchestra, dance, an outing club, community service organizations, and environmental awareness and cultural clubs. The athletic program emphasizes both competitive and lifetime sports, offering varsity competition in crew, field hockey, soccer, cross-country, volleyball, basketball, tennis, lacrosse, swimming, track, water polo and softball, as well as a variety of physical education classes. **See Also Page 1297**

TUXEDO PARK, NY. (39 mi. NNW of New York, NY) Rural. Pop: 731. Alt: 620 ft.

TUXEDO PARK SCHOOL
Day — Coed Gr PS-9

Tuxedo Park, NY 10987. Mountain Farm Rd. Tel: 845-351-4737. Fax: 845-351-4219.
www.tuxedoparkschool.com   E-mail: bheissenbuttel@tuxedoparkschool.com
James T. Burger, Head. BA, Hamilton College, JD, Case Western Reserve Univ. **Beverly J. Heissenbuttel, Adm.**

Pre-Prep. Feat—Fr Lat Span Computers Studio_Art Drama Music Dance. **Supp**—Dev_Read Rem_Read Rev Tut.

Adm: 35/yr. Appl due: Rolling. Accepted: 44%. **Tests** CTP_4.

Enr 195. B 95. G 100. Elem 185. Sec 10. Wh 88%. Hisp 1%. Blk 4%. Asian 3%. Other 4%. Avg class size: 16. Uniform. **Fac 32.** M 7/1. F 24. Adv deg: 59%.

Grad '04—13. Prep—13. (Phillips Exeter, Salisbury-CT, Tabor, Nightingale-Bamford, Montclair Kimberley, Avon). Alum 2500.

Tui '04-'05: Day $10,000-20,100. Aid: Need ($360,000).

Endow $10,000,000. Plant val $13,000,000. Bldgs 3. Class rms 20. Lib 12,000 vols. Sci labs 3. Learning labs 2. Theaters 2. Art studios 1. Music studios 1. Gyms 2. Fields 2.

Est 1900. Nonprofit. Tri (Sept-June).

Located just north of the New Jersey border, Tuxedo Park serves students from New York State and New Jersey who live within a 35-mile radius. A traditional academic approach—with particular emphasis placed on reading, writing and mathematics—is combined with innovative programs in science, computer, and the fine and performing arts. TPS features interdisciplinary learning projects at all grade levels.

Students in grades 7-9 choose from a variety of electives that includes photography, yearbook, literary magazine, choral performances, drama and set design. French study begins in kindergarten, and all pupils also take Latin in grades 7-9. The sports program includes soccer, skiing, basketball, lacrosse and field hockey, with interscholastics offered in grades 7-9.

WHITE PLAINS, NY. (26 mi. NNE of New York, NY) Suburban. Pop: 53,077. Alt: 201 ft.

WINDWARD SCHOOL
Day — Coed Gr 1-9

White Plains, NY 10605. 13 Windward Ave. Tel: 914-949-6968. Fax: 914-949-8220.
  www.windward-school.org   E-mail: tmonte@windwardny.org
James E. Van Amburg, Head. AB, Dartmouth College, MA, Columbia Univ, EdD, Stanford Univ. **Maureen A. Sweeney, Adm.**
  LD. Supp—Dev_Read Rem_Math Rem_Read.
  Adm: 120/yr. Appl due: Rolling. Accepted: 27%. **Tests** IQ.
  Enr 470. B 300. G 170. Wh 90%. Hisp 4%. Blk 5%. Asian 1%. **Fac 115.** M 20/1. F 90/4. Adv deg: 63%.
  Grad '04—10.
  Tui '04-'05: Day $31,000 (+$100). **Aid:** Need ($950,000).
  Endow $1,000,000. Plant val $10,500,000. Bldgs 5. Class rms 40. Lib 14,000 vols. Labs 4. Art studios 4. Gyms 2. Fields 3.
  Est 1926. Nonprofit. (Sept-June).

Windward's language-based curriculum serves students of average to superior intelligence who have learning disabilities. Small-group basic skills remediation is supplemented by physical education, art, computer and library skills. Math, science and social studies are taught daily. The goal is to academically prepare the student for a return to the independent or public school of his or her choice.

The upper and middle school campus is located at 40 Red Oak Ln., 10604, while the lower school operates at the Windward Avenue address.   **See Also Page 1368**

WOODMERE, NY. (12 mi. E of New York, NY) Suburban. Pop: 16,447. Alt: 30 ft.

LAWRENCE WOODMERE ACADEMY
Day — Coed Gr PS-12

Woodmere, NY 11598. 336 Woodmere Blvd. Tel: 516-374-9000. Fax: 516-374-4707.
  www.lawrencewoodmere.org   E-mail: inquire@lawrencewoodmere.org
Alan Bernstein, Head. MusB, Boston University, MEd, City Univ of New York. **Susan Lettieri, Adm.**
  Col Prep. AP—Eng Fr Span Calc Comp_Sci Bio Chem Physics US_Hist World_Hist Studio_Art. **Feat**—Genetics Ethics Drama Band Chorus Music Bus Journ. **Supp**—ESL.
  Adm: 100/yr.
  Enr 385. Elem 220. Sec 165. Wh 56%. Hisp 3%. Blk 21%. Asian 20%. Avg class size: 13. **Fac 75.** Adv deg: 82%.
  Grad '04—51. Col—51. (Princeton, Wesleyan U, NYU, Cornell, Northwestern, Williams). Alum 3000.
  Tui '03-'04: Day $8200-20,400 (+$500).
  Summer: Rev Rec. 8 wks.

Plant val $4,000,000. Bldgs 1. Class rms 22. Lib 32,000 vols. Labs 3. Comp ctrs 3. Theaters 1. Art studios 1. Music studios 2. Gyms 1. Fields 3. Courts 3. Pools 2.
Est 1990. Inc. (Sept-June). **Assoc** CLS.

The school was formed by the 1990 consolidation of Lawrence Country Day School (founded in 1891) and Woodmere Academy (founded in 1912). Writing skills are emphasized in all course work, while the traditional curriculum is enriched by honors and Advanced Placement courses in a variety of disciplines. Instruction follows an individualized approach at all grade levels.

Computer science, athletics, student publications, concert band, community service, Model UN, visual arts and drama are all part of the program.

PENNSYLVANIA

ALLENTOWN, PA. (45 mi. NNW of Philadelphia, PA) Urban. Pop: 106,632. Alt: 304 ft.

SWAIN SCHOOL
Day — Coed Gr PS-8

Allentown, PA 18103. 1100 S 24th St. Tel: 610-433-4542. Fax: 610-433-8280.
  www.swain.org   E-mail: info@swain.org
Lynald E. Silsbee, Head. BS, MEd, Bloomsburg State College, PhD, Univ of Maryland-College Park. **Claire Plunkett, Adm.**
  Pre-Prep. Feat—Lib_Skills Lat Span Computers Studio_Art Drama Music. **Supp**—Dev_Read Rem_Read Tut.
  Adm: 67/yr. Appl due: Rolling. Accepted: 90%.
  Enr 330. Elem 330. Wh 89%. Blk 2%. Asian 8%. Other 1%. Avg class size: 12. Uniform.
  Fac 40. M 2/5. F 31/2. Adv deg: 45%.
  Grad '04—20. Prep—13. (Hill Sch-PA, Wyoming Seminary, Bullis, Moravian, Mercersburg). Alum 3400.
  Tui '03-'04: Day $10,640-12,250 (+$200). **Aid:** Merit 4 ($14,000). Need 70 ($450,800).
  Summer: Acad Enrich Rev. 4 wks.
  Endow $208,000. Plant val $5,300,000. Bldgs 2. Lib 9800 vols. Sci labs 1. Comp labs 1. Comp ctrs 1. Theaters 1. Art studios 1. Music studios 2. Gyms 1. Fields 3.
  Est 1929. Nonprofit. Quar (Sept-June). **Assoc** MSA.

Located on an 22-acre campus five minutes from downtown Allentown, Swain has grown considerably since being established by Dr. D. Esther Swain as a single kindergarten class.

At all grade levels, classroom faculty work closely with specialists in art, music, technology and library science. The lower school, comprising grades PS-5, occupies its own building. Conversational Spanish is introduced in kindergarten, while Latin instruction begins in grade 6.

The middle school stresses the basic disciplines, and emphasis is also placed on study, library and research skills. Swain offers such extracurricular activities as creative writing courses, drama, language clubs, honor societies, chorus and musical theater. Field hockey, soccer, basketball and lacrosse are available in grades 5-8.

BETHLEHEM, PA. (45 mi. NNW of Philadelphia, PA) Urban. Pop: 71,329. Alt: 235 ft.

MORAVIAN ACADEMY
Day — Coed Gr PS-12

Bethlehem, PA 18020. 4313 Green Pond Rd. Tel: 610-691-1600. Fax: 610-691-3354.
  www.moravian.k12.pa.us   E-mail: landerson@moravian.k12.pa.us

Barnaby J. Roberts, Head. BA, MA, Cambridge Univ (England), DipEd, Oxford Univ (England). **Suzanne H. Mason, Upper Sch Adm; Christine L. Murphy, Middle Sch Adm; Karen M. Jacob, Lower Sch Adm.**

Col Prep. AP—Eng Fr Span Calc Chem US_Hist US_Govt & Pol. **Feat**—Japan Lat Stats Anat & Physiol Computers Econ Law Ethics World_Relig Studio_Art Music Health. **Supp**—Rev.

Adm (Gr PS-11): 124/yr. Appl due: Rolling. Accepted: 76%. Yield: 78%. **Tests** CTP_4 IQ.

Enr 802. B 401. G 401. Elem 518. Sec 284. Wh 72%. Hisp 2%. Blk 3%. Asian 12%. Other 11%. Avg class size: 15. **Fac 95.** M 27/1. F 51/16. Adv deg: 55%.

Grad '04—65. Col—65. (U of Pittsburgh 6, Franklin & Marshall 5, Lehigh 5, Carnegie Mellon 3, NYU 3, Geo Wash 3). Avg SAT: 1280. Alum 2500.

Tui '04-'05: Day $6770-15,700 (+$560-900). **Aid:** Need 105 ($844,835).

Summer: Acad Enrich Rev. 1 wk. Rec. Gr PS-7. Tui Day $110-220. 1-2 wks.

Endow $9,800,000. Plant val $23,700,000. Bldgs 15. Class rms 69. Lib 23,000 vols. Sci labs 5. Auds 3. Art studios 4. Music studios 4. Gyms 3. Fields 6. Courts 6. Pools 1.

Est 1742. Nonprofit. Moravian. (Aug-June). **Assoc** CLS MSA.

The school is the result of a 1971 merger between Moravian Seminary for Girls, the oldest American girls' boarding school, and Moravian Preparatory School, both founded in 1742. The lower (422 Heckwelder Pl., 18018) and middle (11 W. Market St., 18018) schools occupy the old Preparatory campus in the midst of the historic colonial section of Bethlehem.

The seminary was founded by the Countess Benigna, daughter of Count Zinzendorf of Saxony. Eleanor Lee, grandniece of Washington, was among its pupils, as were Chancellor Livingston's daughter, Cornelia, wife of Robert Fulton; two daughters of Nathaniel Greene; and others representing the old colonial families of Dutch, German, Quaker, French and English heritage. Some of the original buildings of the academy are now part of Moravian College. The upper school occupies a beautiful, 120-acre country estate with modern buildings, an alumna gift of one of the last pieces of property held by the heirs of William Penn in direct grant from the English crown.

In addition to classes in the standard disciplines, Moravian's college preparatory curriculum includes religion, fine arts and foreign language course work. MA's Scholars Program allows a limited number of qualified seniors to take college-level classes at nearby colleges. Independent study programs may be arranged, and some pupils may participate in a study abroad program. All students perform community service during the academic year.

Sports include soccer, cross-country, lacrosse, field hockey, tennis, softball, golf and basketball. Among other activities are publications, music, drama, service, studio art, ceramics and interest clubs. **See Also Page 1209**

BLUE BELL, PA. (12 mi. NW of Philadelphia, PA) Rural. Pop: 6395. Alt: 360 ft.

OAK LANE DAY SCHOOL
Day — Coed Gr PS-6

Blue Bell, PA 19422. 137 Stenton Ave. Tel: 610-825-1055. Fax: 610-825-9288.

www.oaklanedayschool.org   E-mail: admissions@oaklanedayschool.org
Karl A. Welsh, Head. BA, Wake Forest Univ, MS, Univ of Pennsylvania. **Sharon Fichthorn, Adm.**
  Pre-Prep. Feat—Environ_Sci Studio_Art Music.
  Adm: 16/yr. Appl due: Rolling. Yield: 85%.
  Enr 111. B 59. G 52. Elem 111. Wh 74%. Hisp 3%. Blk 9%. Asian 5%. Other 9%. Avg class size: 12. **Fac 21.** M 2. F 16/3. Wh 100%. Adv deg: 38%.
  Grad '04—8. Prep—7. (Abington Friends 5, DE Valley Friends 2, Germantown Friends 1). Alum 1500.
  Tui '04-'05: Day $10,000-13,315. Aid: Merit 3 ($19,972). Need 11 ($62,312).
  Summer: Enrich Rec. Tui Day $2470. 8 wks.
  Endow $65,000. Plant val $3,000,000. Bldgs 3. Class rms 16. Lib 6000 vols. Labs 2. Art studios 1. Music studios 1. Gyms 1. Fields 3. Pools 2.
  Est 1916. Nonprofit. Tri (Sept-June).

The school, founded by a group of Philadelphia intellectuals motivated by the innovations of progressive education, served as the demonstration school for Temple University until 1960. Located on the grounds of a 30-acre country estate, the campus includes a variety of classroom and studio facilities, as well as extensive natural areas for environmental studies.

The pre-preparatory curriculum features physical science, environmental science, art, music and physical education at all grade levels. Dance, drama, private instrumental instruction and athletic programs are also available.

BRYN MAWR, PA. (10 mi. W of Philadelphia, PA) Suburban. Pop: 4382. Alt: 413 ft.

THE BALDWIN SCHOOL
Day — Girls Gr PS-12

Bryn Mawr, PA 19010. 701 W Montgomery Ave. Tel: 610-525-2700. Fax: 610-581-7231.
  www.baldwinschool.org   E-mail: admissions@baldwinschool.org
Blair D. Stambaugh, Head. BA, Wheaton College (MA). **Sarah J. Goebel, Adm.**
  Col Prep. AP—Fr Lat Span. **Feat**—Creative_Writing Greek Programming Comp_Relig Ethics Logic Art_Hist Ceramics Photog Sculpt Studio_Art Architect_Design Theater Music Music_Theory Speech.
  Adm: 90/yr. Appl due: Jan. Accepted: 74%. **Tests** CTP_4 IQ ISEE SSAT.
  Enr 635. G 635. Elem 443. Sec 192. Wh 78%. Hisp 1%. Blk 9%. Asian 8%. Other 4%. Avg class size: 16. Uniform. **Fac 90.** M 8. F 82. Wh 88%. Hisp 2%. Blk 5%. Asian 4%. Other 1%. Adv deg: 71%.
  Grad '04—51. Col—51. (U of PA 4, Boston Col 3, Princeton 2, Brown 2, U of MI 2, Geo Wash 2). Avg SAT: 1343. Alum 4000.
  Tui '04-'05: Day $12,500-19,865 (+$300-1000). **Aid:** Need 96 ($1,091,213).
  Endow $5,300,000. Plant val $22,500,000. Bldgs 9. Class rms 71. 3 Libs 28,000 vols. Sci labs 5. Lang labs 1. Comp labs 3. Theaters 1. Art studios 8. Music studios 4. Gyms 2. Fields 3. Courts 3. Pools 3.
  Est 1888. Nonprofit. Sem (Sept-June). **Assoc** MSA.

The school was founded by Florence Baldwin to prepare students for Bryn Mawr College. Baldwin offers a complete academic program in which computer study is required beginning in the lower school. The college preparatory curriculum prepares students for the nation's leading colleges.

Baldwin has strong art, music and drama programs, as well as a full athletic schedule. The Service League stresses personal contributions to the school and the community. The school's location enables girls to partake of Philadelphia's cultural and educational institutions, and to take advantage of programs at Bryn Mawr and Haverford. Academic and social activities are conducted regularly with nearby boys' and coed schools.

COUNTRY DAY SCHOOL OF THE SACRED HEART
Day — Girls Gr PS-12

Bryn Mawr, PA 19010. 480 Bryn Mawr Ave. Tel: 610-527-3915. Fax: 610-527-0942.
   www.cdssh.org   E-mail: lnowlan@cdssh.org
Sr. Matthew Anita MacDonald, SSJ, Head. AB, Chestnut Hill College, MA, PhD, Univ of Pennsylvania. **Laurie Nowlan, Adm.**
   Col Prep. AP—Eng Fr Eur_Hist US_Hist. **Feat**—Humanities Lat Span Environ_Sci Econ Relig Art_Hist Film Studio_Art Music Music_Theory.
   Adm (Gr PS-11): 80/yr. Appl due: Rolling. Accepted: 50%. **Tests** CTP_4 IQ Stanford.
   Enr 380. G 380. Elem 181. Sec 199. Wh 95%. Blk 4%. Asian 1%. Avg class size: 16. Uniform. **Fac 35.** Adv deg: 60%.
   Grad '04—45. Col—45. (St Joseph's U, Villanova, Fordham, Catholic U, PA St, Holy Cross). Avg SAT: 1180. Alum 2014.
   Tui '04-'05: Day $6950-11,750 (+$350). **Aid:** Merit 23 ($70,000). Need 32 ($100,000).
   Summer: Enrich. 1-4 wks.
   Endow $1,528,000. Plant val $3,288,000. Bldgs 3. Class rms 28. Lib 10,000 vols. Sci labs 2. Comp labs 2. Art studios 1. Music studios 1. Gyms 1. Fields 2.
   Est 1865. Nonprofit. Roman Catholic. Quar (Sept-June). **Assoc** MSA.

Originally established in Philadelphia by the Religious of the Sacred Heart, the school was located in suburban Overbrook for many years before relocating to Bryn Mawr in 1978. The college preparatory curriculum features college-level courses in French, English, history, biology and math. Students fulfill course requirements in religion and art history, and CDSSH integrates a particularly strong humanities program into its curriculum.

Athletics, music and community service projects augment the traditional academics. The school offers exchange opportunities with 20 other Sacred Heart institutions throughout the US.

THE SHIPLEY SCHOOL
Day — Coed Gr PS-12

Bryn Mawr, PA 19010. 814 Yarrow St. Tel: 610-525-4300. Fax: 610-525-5082.
   www.shipleyschool.org   E-mail: admit@shipleyschool.org
Steven S. Piltch, Head. BA, Williams College, MEd, EdD, Harvard Univ. **Gregory W. Coleman, Adm.**
   Col Prep. AP—Eng Fr Lat Span Calc Stats Comp_Sci Bio Chem Physics Eur_Hist US_Hist Art_Hist Studio_Art Music_Theory. **Feat**—Humanities Programming Chin & Japan_Hist Amer_Stud Econ Philos Hist_of_Relig. **Supp**—Tut.
   Adm: 135/yr. Day 125. Appl due: Jan. Accepted: 48%. Yield: 54%. **Tests** IQ ISEE SSAT.

Enr 838. B 424. G 414. Elem 511. Sec 327. Wh 89%. Hisp 1%. Blk 6%. Asian 3%. Other 1%. Avg class size: 16. **Fac 112.** M 30/8. F 58/16. Wh 91%. Hisp 1%. Blk 4%. Asian 4%. Adv deg: 53%.
Grad '04—78. Col—78. (U of PA 3, Columbia 3, Wesleyan U 3, Stanford 2, MD Inst-Col of Art 2, Brown 2). Avg SAT: 1280. Alum 4425.
Tui '04-'05: Day $14,200-20,200 (+$900). **Aid:** Merit 122 ($1,532,125).
Summer: Acad Enrich Rev Rem Rec. Tui Day $625. 6 wks.
Endow $14,000,000. Plant val $60,400,000. Bldgs 14. Class rms 65. 2 Libs 25,000 vols. Sci labs 8. Comp labs 3. Dark rms 1. Auds 1. Theaters 1. Art studios 5. Music studios 4. Pottery rms 1. Gyms 3. Fields 7. Courts 6.
Est 1894. Nonprofit. Quar (Sept-June). **Assoc** MSA.

This nonsectarian school was founded by three Quaker sisters, the Misses Hannah, Elizabeth and Katherine Shipley, who in 1911 turned it over to their niece, Alice G. Howland, and her associate, Eleanor O. Brownell, who directed the school until their retirement in 1942. Established to prepare girls for Bryn Mawr College, Shipley became coeducational in 1972, and the school now enrolls roughly the same number of boys and girls.

The sound college preparatory program—which includes electives and a full complement of AP courses—and the friendly atmosphere have long appealed both to families in Philadelphia's Main Line suburbs and to families in the city. Use is made of the cultural advantages of Philadelphia and of nearby Bryn Mawr College, and to a lesser extent those of New York City and Washington, DC. Tutoring and community service opportunities help to broaden the basic curriculum, and students participate in conferences on national and international affairs. In addition, all boys and girls perform community service. Sophomores, juniors and seniors may take academic trips during spring vacation or over the summer. Graduates attend an array of competitive colleges in the US and abroad.

Athletics include soccer, field hockey, squash, crew, basketball, tennis, lacrosse, volleyball, cross-country, baseball, softball and golf. Dramatics, publications, computer club, student council, photography and Model UN are among Shipley's other activities. **See Also Page 1256**

CHESTER SPRINGS, PA. (25 mi. WNW of Wilmington, DE; 26 mi. WNW of Philadelphia, PA) Suburban. Pop: 4413. Alt: 260 ft.

MONTGOMERY SCHOOL
Day — Coed Gr PS-8

Chester Springs, PA 19425. 1141 Rte 113. Tel: 610-827-7222. Fax: 610-827-7639.
    www.montgomeryschool.org   E-mail: mfrank@montgomeryschool.org
Kevin R. Conklin, Head. BA, Lake Forest College, MA, Columbia Univ. **Susan M. Marotta, Adm.**
   Pre-Prep. Feat—Fr Span Computers Studio_Art Public_Speak. **Supp—**Rev Tut.
   Adm: 67/yr. Appl due: Feb. Accepted: 71%. Yield: 72%. **Tests** IQ ISEE.
   Enr 342. B 152. G 190. Elem 342. Wh 92%. Hisp 2%. Blk 3%. Asian 2%. Other 1%. Avg class size: 16. Uniform. **Fac 40.** M 5. F 35. Wh 90%. Hisp 2%. Blk 5%. Asian 3%. Adv deg: 47%.
   Grad '04—32. Prep—26. (Hill Sch-PA 8, Westtown 3, Shipley 3, Bishop Shanahan 2, St

Andrew's Sch-DE 1). Alum 800.
Tui '04-'05: Day $13,300-15,500 (+$400). **Aid:** Merit 6 ($32,750). Need 32 ($230,103).
Bldgs 6. Class rms 24. Lib 9000 vols. Sci labs 2. Comp labs 1. Amphitheaters 1. Art studios 2. Music studios 2. Gyms 1. Fields 5.
Est 1915. Nonprofit. (Sept-June).

Founded as a boys' preparatory school in Wynnewood by Rev. Gibson Bell, this school graduated its last senior class in 1938. In 1943, the school was reorganized as a coeducational elementary and middle school. A decline in middle-school-aged children in the 1980s resulted in Montgomery's relocation to Chester Springs in the summer of 1988.

The school's varied curriculum prepares students for competitive area independent and public high schools. An early childhood center provides problem-solving, communicational and life skills training beginning at age 3. Later in the lower school grades, Montgomery supplements course work in the traditional elementary subjects with computer education and an introduction to foreign languages. The lower school music curriculum includes enriching field trips, special assembly programs and study, and children learn more about the visual arts through excursions to local museums and art shows.

In the middle school (grades 6-8), instruction in all subject areas becomes more in-depth to help students prepare for advanced high school courses. The arts programs at this level emphasize appreciation and participation in music, art and drama.

The athletic program consists of soccer, field hockey, basketball, baseball, lacrosse, swimming and cross-country teams. All middle schoolers take part in at least one of the three annual athletic seasons.

FAIRLESS HILLS, PA. (19 mi. NE of Philadelphia, PA) Urban. Pop: 8365. Alt: 100 ft.

PEN RYN SCHOOL
Day — Coed Gr PS-8

Fairless Hills, PA 19030. 235 S Olds Blvd. Tel: 215-547-1800. Fax: 215-946-2877.
www.penryn.org   E-mail: kbruno@penryn.org
Kathy Cristoph, Head. BS, MS, Indiana Univ. **Kathy Bruno, Adm.**
Pre-Prep. Feat—Lib_Skills Span Computers Studio_Art Music. **Supp**—Rem_Math Rem_Read Tut.
Adm: 61/yr. Appl due: Mar. **Tests** IQ.
Enr 285. Elem 285. Wh 88%. Blk 3%. Asian 2%. Other 7%. Avg class size: 18. **Fac 35.** M 3. F 22/10. Wh 100%. Adv deg: 8%.
Grad '04—28. **Prep**—28. (Nazareth 4, Archbishop Ryan 2, Wm Penn Charter 1, Christopher Dock 1). Alum 800.
Tui '04-'05: Day $6055-7160 (+$175-210). **Aid:** Need 9 ($12,800).
Endow $250,000. Plant val $5,000,000. Bldgs 1. Class rms 21. Lib 5000 vols. Sci labs 1. Comp labs 1. Auds 1. Art studios 1. Music studios 1. Gyms 1. Fields 2. Courts 1.
Est 1946. Nonprofit. Episcopal. Quar (Sept-June). **Assoc** MSA.

Located on a 15-acre campus, Pen Ryn emphasizes basic skills in a nurturing environment with personalized attention and small classes. The curriculum provides a continuous foundation in the core subjects, and course work emphasizes reading, writing and study skills. Computer technology, art, music, library and Spanish complement the traditional subjects.

The extracurricular program offers enrichment classes and student leadership opportunities for boys and girls in all grades, and athletics begin in grade 5. Students enroll from northeast Philadelphia and Bucks County.

FREELAND, PA. (81 mi. NNW of Philadelphia, PA) Suburban. Pop: 3643. Alt: 1836 ft.

MMI PREPARATORY SCHOOL
Day — Coed Gr 6-12

Freeland, PA 18224. 154 Centre St. Tel: 570-636-1108. Fax: 570-636-0742.
 www.mmiprep.org E-mail: mmi@mmiprep.org
William A. Shergalis, Pres. BS, MS, PhD. Julie M. Lenio, Adm.

Col Prep. AP—Eng Calc Chem Physics Eur_Hist US_Hist Studio_Art. **Feat**—Ger Lat Span. **Supp**—Rem_Math Tut.

Adm: 40/yr. Appl due: Aug. Accepted: 88%. **Tests** IQ ISEE.

Enr 190. B 104. G 86. Elem 69. Sec 121. Wh 85%. Hisp 3%. Asian 12%. Avg class size: 33. **Fac 22.** M 5/5. F 7/5. Wh 100%. Adv deg: 68%.

Grad '04—36. Col—36. (PA St, Drexel, Lehigh, Muhlenberg, Johns Hopkins, Wm & Mary). Avg SAT: 1261. Alum 1602.

Tui '02-'03: Day $9200 (+$275). **Aid:** Merit 46 ($34,500). Need 77 ($208,600). Work prgm 63 ($99,925).

Summer: Acad Enrich Rem. Tui Day $175/crse. 6 wks.

Endow $8,900,000. Plant val $7,000,000. Bldgs 1. Class rms 18. Lib 12,000 vols. Sci labs 2. Comp labs 1. Gyms 1. Fields 1.

Est 1879. Nonprofit. Sem (Aug-May). **Assoc** MSA.

Founded by Eckley B. Coxe as the Mining and Mechanical Institute, an evening school for miners, the school became a college preparatory day school in 1902. In 1970, the school became coeducational and the present name was adopted. In 1977, a middle school was added as the result of an expressed community need, and the school first offered grade 6 in 1999.

Today, MMI offers a traditional education to students who live within a 40-mile radius of the school. Utilizing a developmental approach, the school provides a sequence of classes that proceeds from a general review of topics to highly specialized offerings during the junior and senior years. Specific minor courses designed to enrich the college preparatory program complement major academic classes. Athletics and a varied selection of interest clubs round out the program.

HARRISBURG, PA. (81 mi. WNW of Wilmington, DE; 94 mi. WNW of Philadelphia, PA) Urban. Pop: 48,950. Alt: 374 ft. Area also includes Wormleysburg.

HARRISBURG ACADEMY
Day — Coed Gr PS-12

Wormleysburg, PA 17043. 10 Erford Rd. Tel: 717-763-7811. Fax: 717-975-0894.
  www.harrisburgacademy.org   E-mail: rboyer@harrisburgacademy.org
James Newman, Head. Jessica A. Warren, Adm.
  Col Prep. AP—Eng Calc Stats Comp_Sci Bio Chem Physics US_Hist Psych Studio_Art.
    Feat—Japan Computers Geog Philos Relig Drama Music Speech.
  Adm: 92/yr.
  Enr 481. B 239. G 242. Elem 351. Sec 130. Wh 84%. Hisp 3%. Blk 6%. Asian 7%. **Fac 56.** M 14/2. F 34/6.
  Grad '04—29. Col—28. (U of Chicago, Boston U, CT Col, U of Pittsburgh, Franklin & Marshall). Alum 1252.
  Tui '02-'03: Day $7308-11,962. Aid: Need 81 ($391,600).
  Summer: Ages 3-11. Enrich Rec. Tui Day $200/2-wk ses. 6 wks.
  Endow $3,130,000. Plant val $4,500,000. Bldgs 1. Class rms 41. 2 Libs 15,000 vols. Sci labs 4. Comp labs 2. Auds 1. Art studios 2. Music studios 2. Gyms 1. Fields 2. Courts 4.
  Est 1784. Nonprofit. Quar (Sept-June). **Assoc** MSA.

The academy was a boarding and day school for boys until merging with Seiler School and becoming coeducational in 1947. The academy is located in East Pennsboro, across the Susquehanna River from Harrisburg.

The academy's program features foreign language and drama in all grades. Varied electives in the upper school broaden the traditional curriculum. Weekly guidance periods and a Great Books program in the middle school, process writing in all divisions, and school-wide community service activities enrich the program.

Extracurricular activities include student government, publications, academic teams, drama, music, mock trial and outing club. The interscholastic sports program, which begins in the middle school, offers soccer, basketball, lacrosse and tennis for boys, field hockey, basketball, softball, tennis and lacrosse for girls.

The summer session, in operation since 1969, consists of special-interest and sports camps, as well as study skills and enrichment courses for older students.

HAVERFORD, PA. (9 mi. W of Philadelphia, PA) Suburban. Pop: 48,498. Alt: 383 ft.

FRIENDS SCHOOL HAVERFORD
Day — Coed Gr PS-6

Haverford, PA 19041. 851 Buck Ln. Tel: 610-642-2334. Fax: 610-642-0870.
  www.friendshaverford.org   E-mail: fsh@friendshaverford.org
Martha B. Bryans, Head. BA, Bryn Mawr College, MA, EdD, Univ of Pennsylvania. **Elizabeth**

Krick, Adm.
Pre-Prep. Feat—Lib_Skills Span Computers Studio_Art Music. **Supp**—Dev_Read Rev Tut.
Adm: 43/yr. Appl due: Rolling. Accepted: 85%. Yield: 58%. **Tests** IQ Stanford.
Enr 202. B 105. G 97. Elem 202. Wh 76%. Hisp 4%. Blk 12%. Am Ind 1%. Asian 7%. Avg class size: 15. **Fac 34.** M 6. F 23/5. Wh 96%. Hisp 2%. Blk 2%. Adv deg: 50%.
Grad '04—18. Prep—11. (Friends' Central 4, Shipley 2, DE Valley Friends 2, Wm Penn Charter 1, Germantown Friends 1, Church Farm 1). Alum 1200.
Tui '04-'05: Day $11,520-13,655 (+$215). **Aid:** Need 50 ($386,155).
Endow $1,170,000. Plant val $2,500,000. Bldgs 3. Class rms 17. Lib 9000 vols. Sci labs 1. Comp labs 1. Auds 1. Art studios 1. Music studios 1. Gyms 1. Fields 3.
Est 1885. Nonprofit. Religious Society of Friends. Sem (Sept-June).

Governed by its school committee under the care of the Haverford Monthly Meeting, FSH offers an academic curriculum in an environment based on Quaker values. Reading, writing, mathematics, science, social studies, computers, music, art, Spanish, library and physical education are interwoven in all grades to form a program appropriate to the developmental level of the student.

Central to the life of the school is the weekly Meeting for Worship, at which children and adults gather for a brief time of quiet reflection. The physical education program offers soccer, field hockey, basketball and volleyball. The school schedules regular field trips to cultural and historical sites in the Philadelphia area.

HAVERFORD SCHOOL
Day — Boys Gr PS-12

Haverford, PA 19041. 450 Lancaster Ave. Tel: 610-642-3020. Fax: 610-642-8724.
www.haverford.org   E-mail: stassoni@haverford.org
Joseph T. Cox, Head. BA, Lafayette College, MA, PhD, Univ of North Carolina-Chapel Hill.
Kevin P. Seits, Adm.
Col Prep. AP—Ger Lat Comp_Sci Chem Physics US_Hist Music_Theory. **Feat**—Chin Greek Anat & Physiol Astron Psych Ceramics Theater Woodworking.
Adm: 135/yr. Appl due: Rolling. Accepted: 36%. **Tests** IQ ISEE SSAT.
Enr 939. B 939. Elem 611. Sec 328. Wh 85%. Hisp 1%. Blk 6%. Asian 4%. Other 4%. Avg class size: 15. Uniform. **Fac 140.** M 76/1. F 61/2. Wh 86%. Hisp 1%. Blk 10%. Asian 3%. Adv deg: 46%.
Grad '04—78. Col—74. (U of PA, Franklin & Marshall, Hamilton, U of VA, Harvard, Princeton). Avg SAT: 1259. Alum 3750.
Tui '04-'05: Day $15,500-20,500 (+$300-800). **Aid:** Need 142 ($1,427,500).
Summer: Coed. Age 2-12. Acad Enrich Rev. Tui Day $800-1495. 3-6 wks.
Endow $25,000,000. Plant val $24,000,000. Bldgs 10. Class rms 80. 2 Libs 40,000 vols. Sci labs 11. Comp labs 5. Auds 3. Theaters 2. Art studios 6. Music studios 9. Gyms 3. Fields 4. Courts 4. Pools 1. Tracks 1.
Est 1884. Nonprofit. (Sept-June). **Assoc** CLS MSA.

Haverford has served boys since its founding. Established at the request of railroad executive Alexander Cassatt and his wife, Lois, under the guidance of Haverford College, the school began as the Haverford College Grammar School. It became independent of the college when it moved to its current location in 1903 and adopted its present name and nonsectarian orientation.

The curriculum, with close individual guidance, prepares boys for a variety of leading colleges. Distinctive offerings include school-wide programs in computer education, music and the visual arts. German, Chinese and molecular biology highlight curricular options. In addition to broad opportunities in the arts, the school provides a comprehensive athletic program.

JENKINTOWN, PA. (6 mi. N of Philadelphia, PA) Suburban. Pop: 4263. Alt: 211 ft.

ABINGTON FRIENDS SCHOOL
Day — Coed Gr PS-12

Jenkintown, PA 19046. 575 Washington Ln. Tel: 215-886-4350. Fax: 215-886-9143.
www.abingtonfriends.net   E-mail: mchristian@abingtonfriends.net

Thomas W. Price, Head. BA, Lake Forest College, MA, Columbia Univ. **Marnie Christian, Adm.**

Col Prep. AP—Eng Fr Lat Span Calc Comp_Sci US_Hist. **Feat**—Greek Ecol Quakerism Studio_Art Theater Music Study_Skills.

Adm: 165/yr. Appl due: Feb. Accepted: 56%. **Tests** IQ ISEE SSAT.

Enr 787. Elem 527. Sec 260. Avg class size: 18. **Fac 83.** M 31. F 52. Adv deg: 56%.

Grad '04—54. Col—54. (U of Pittsburgh, Rollins, Geo Wash, Muhlenberg, Wesleyan U, U of PA). Avg SAT: 1230. Alum 1675.

Tui '02-'03: Day $10,200-15,900 (+$250-300). **Aid:** Need 209 ($1,477,000).

Summer: Enrich Rec. Tui Day $2100. 7 wks.

Endow $12,000,000. Plant val $12,000,000. Bldgs 8. Class rms 42. Lib 20,000 vols. Sci labs 5. Comp labs 4. Auds 1. Theaters 1. Art studios 3. Music studios 3. Dance studios 1. Gyms 3. Fields 4. Courts 6. Pools 2.

Est 1697. Nonprofit. Religious Society of Friends. Sem (Sept-June). **Assoc** CLS MSA.

Abington Friends is the third-oldest Quaker school in the country. Founded by the Religious Society of Friends, it is the only 17th-century school still occupying its original site. The academic program, which emphasizes college preparation, includes Advanced Placement courses in most subjects, as well as an independent study option for qualified students. Emphasis is placed on character development and physical fitness.

Soccer, basketball, wrestling, lacrosse, tennis, baseball, softball, golf and cross-country teams compete interscholastically. Other activities include yearbook, choir, musical ensemble, theater, newspaper and community service. Foreign travel and frequent excursions to the cultural and historical sites of Philadelphia are offered. Each student attends Meeting for Worship, a central dimension of the school's program, once a week.

LAHASKA, PA. (24 mi. NNE of Philadelphia, PA) Rural. Pop: 200. Alt: 290 ft.

BUCKINGHAM FRIENDS SCHOOL
Day — Coed Gr K-8

Lahaska, PA 18931. 5684 York Rd, PO Box 159. Tel: 215-794-7491. Fax: 215-794-7955.
www.bfs.org E-mail: postmaster@bfs.org
Peter S. Pearson, Prin. BA, Ursinus College, BA, Immaculata College, MEd, College of New Jersey.
  Pre-Prep. Feat—Fr Span Relig Fine_Arts Music Woodworking.
  Enr 176. Elem 176. Wh 99%. Blk 1%. Avg class size: 20. **Fac 25.**
  Grad '04—20. Prep—16. (George Sch, Solebury, Lawrenceville). Alum 800.
  Tui '04-'05: Day $12,361. Aid: Need 37.
  Summer: Rec. Arts. 6 wks.
  Endow $1,300,000. Plant val $4,000,000. Bldgs 4. Class rms 12. Lib 10,000 vols. Labs 1. Auds 1. Theaters 1. Gyms 1. Fields 2.
  Est 1794. Nonprofit. Religious Society of Friends. Sem (Sept-June).

Founded by Buckingham Friends Meeting, BFS conducts a traditional curriculum and emphasizes the development of fundamental skills. Buckingham offers French, wood shop, art and music at all grade levels. Some remedial reading and math are provided for students who need extra help.

A variety of activities is available, and BFS encourages students to engage in outreach projects and community service.

LANCASTER, PA. (46 mi. WNW of Wilmington, DE; 62 mi. W of Philadelphia, PA) Urban. Pop: 56,348. Alt: 357 ft.

LANCASTER COUNTRY DAY SCHOOL
Day — Coed Gr PS-12

Lancaster, PA 17603. 725 Hamilton Rd. Tel: 717-392-2916. Fax: 717-392-0425.
  www.e-lcds.org E-mail: admiss@e-lcds.org
Michael J. Mersky, Head. BS, Lock Haven Univ, MS, St Joseph's Univ. **Vicki R. Daniel, Adm.**
  Col Prep. AP—Eng Fr Span Calc Stats Comp_Sci Bio Chem US_Hist. **Feat**—Creative_Writing Humanities Lat Oceanog Econ Govt Psych Sociol Film Graphic_Arts Photog Studio_Art Drama Theater Chorus Music Music_Hist Dance Study_Skills. **Supp**—Tut.
  Adm (Gr PS-11): 73/yr. Accepted: 68%. Yield: 87%. **Tests** CTP_4.
  Enr 488. B 225. G 263. Elem 310. Sec 178. Wh 89%. Hisp 4%. Blk 3%. Asian 3%. Other 1%. Avg class size: 14. **Fac 74.** M 20/1. F 47/6. Wh 98%. Hisp 1%. Blk 1%. Adv deg: 48%.
  Grad '04—51. Col—51. (Rochester Inst of Tech 4, U of DE 3, Dartmouth 2, Bryn Mawr 2, U of Denver 2, Loyola Col 2). Avg SAT: 1200. Alum 1446.
  Tui '04-'05: Day $12,000-14,500 (+$250-350). **Aid:** Need 86 ($687,450).
  Summer: Enrich Rec. 6 wks.

Endow $13,000,000. Plant val $8,000,000. Bldgs 1. Class rms 60. Lib 27,000 vols. Sci labs 5. Comp labs 4. Comp ctrs 4. Theaters 1. Art studios 5. Music studios 2. Gyms 2. Fields 5. Tennis courts 6. Gardens 1.

Est 1908. Nonprofit. Tri (Aug-June).

The Shippen School for Girls (founded in 1908) and the Franklin and Marshall Academy for boys (established in 1787) came together in 1943 to form LCDS. In 1949, the doors opened at the current 26-acre, suburban campus.

Country Day provides a college preparatory curriculum based in the liberal arts tradition, with AP subjects, opportunities for independent study, and arts requirements. Competitive athletics begin in the middle school (grades 6-8). Independent, off-campus senior projects include participation in the International Model UN in The Hague, The Netherlands.

Annual outdoor expeditions, athletics, clubs, student government, theater, music and field trips supplement the curriculum. LCDS constructed a Habitat for Humanities house as part of its service program.

LIGONIER, PA. (41 mi. ESE of Pittsburgh, PA) Rural. Pop: 6973. Alt: 1290 ft.

VALLEY SCHOOL OF LIGONIER
Day — Coed Gr K-9

Ligonier, PA 15658. PO Box 616. Tel: 724-238-6652. Fax: 724-238-6838.
www.valleyschoolofligonier.org   E-mail: jderose@valleyschoolofligonier.org
Michael J. Kennedy, Head. BA, La Salle College, MA, Univ of Virginia. **Johnette DeRose, Adm.**

Pre-Prep. Feat—Fr Lat Span Computers Studio_Art Music. **Supp**—Dev_Read.

Adm (Gr K-8): 30/yr. Appl due: Rolling. Accepted: 89%. Yield: 88%. **Tests** CTP_4.

Enr 200. B 88. G 112. Elem 183. Sec 17. Wh 94%. Hisp 1%. Asian 5%. Avg class size: 13. Uniform. **Fac 26.** M 9. F 17. Adv deg: 42%.

Grad '04—18. Prep—10. (St Andrew's Sch-DE 3, Shady Side 3, Blair 1, Episcopal Acad 1, Mercersburg 1). Alum 841.

Tui '04-'05: Day $8500 (+$300). **Aid:** Merit 13 ($17,500). Need 48 ($254,600).

Summer: Rec. Tui Day $120/wk. 5 wks.

Endow $22,146,000. Plant val $12,834,000. Bldgs 3. Class rms 16. Lib 13,000 vols. Sci labs 3. Lang labs 3. Comp labs 2. Comp ctrs 1. Auds 1. Art studios 1. Music studios 3. Gyms 2. Fields 4.

Est 1946. Nonprofit. Tri (Sept-June).

Established by Gen. and Mrs. Richard King Mellon, the school was under the direction of Peter C. Messer from the founding date until his retirement in 1978.

Originally housed in the former residence of William C. Carnegie, the school has renovated and expanded its facilities over the years to better serve its student body. The curriculum is traditional, with an emphasis on the development of basic skills. Art, music, computers, physical education and science are included in the curriculum at all grade levels, and computers are located in all classrooms. French instruction begins in grade 1, Spanish in grade 5 and Latin in grade 6.

LITITZ, PA. (50 mi. NW of Wilmington, DE; 63 mi. W of Philadelphia, PA) Suburban. Pop: 9029. Alt: 360 ft.

LINDEN HALL SCHOOL FOR GIRLS
Bdg and Day — Girls Gr 6-PG

Lititz, PA 17543. 212 E Main St. Tel: 717-626-8512. Fax: 717-627-1384.
  www.lindenhall.org   E-mail: admissions@lindenhall.org
Thomas W. Needham, Head. BA, Eastern Connecticut State Univ, MEd, Lesley College. **Madelyn P. Nix, Adm.**

- **Col Prep. AP**—Eng Calc Stats Physics US_Hist. **Feat**—Writing Fr Lat Span Environ_Sci Marine_Biol/Sci Computers Ethics Photog Studio_Art Music Dance Study_Skills Equestrian_Stud. **Supp**—ESL Rev Tut.
- **Adm (Gr 6-12):** 44/yr. Bdg 31. Day 13. Appl due: Rolling. Accepted: 65%. Yield: 57%. **Tests** IQ ISEE SSAT Stanford TOEFL.
- **Enr 130.** G 80/50. Elem 34. Sec 95. PG 1. Wh 53%. Hisp 13%. Blk 15%. Asian 14%. Other 5%. Avg class size: 8. Uniform. **Fac 41.** Wh 98%. Blk 2%. Adv deg: 41%. In dorms 14.
- **Grad '04—12. Col—12.** (Sarah Lawrence, PA St, Bard, Goucher, Hollins, MD Inst-Col of Art). Avg SAT: 1104. Alum 1710.
- **Tui '04-'05: Bdg $32,450** (+$2000). **5-Day Bdg $30,560** (+$2000). **Day $14,520** (+$1000). **Aid:** Need 39 ($380,800).
- **Summer:** Ages 6-12. Acad Enrich Rec. Tui Day $395/3-wk ses. 9 wks.
- Endow $2,042,000. Plant val $16,534,000. Bldgs 5. Dorms 5. Dorm rms 60. Class rms 20. Lib 12,500 vols. Sci labs 2. Comp labs 2. Dark rms 1. Theaters 1. Art studios 4. Music studios 2. Dance studios 1. Arts ctrs 1. Perf arts ctrs 1. Art galleries 1. Gyms 1. Athletic ctrs 1. Fields 2. Courts 6. Pools 1. Riding rings 2. Stables 1.
- **Est 1746.** Nonprofit. Tri (Sept-May). **Assoc** MSA.

Established by members of the Moravian Church, Linden Hall is the oldest continuously operating girls' boarding school in the country. Now nonsectarian in nature, the school's program prepares students for college, with special emphasis placed on the development of academic skills and sound study habits. The school specializes in helping each student achieve her optimal level of scholarship by providing an honors program and Advanced Placement courses for qualified pupils, as well as allotting time daily for extra help. Academics are enhanced by opportunities in the fine and performing arts, and Linden Hall maintains affiliations with the Pennsylvania Academy of Music and local colleges. A strong equestrian program and interscholastic competition in riding, basketball, volleyball, tennis and soccer are also part of the regular program.

The school's 47-acre campus, which combines both modern and traditional structures, contains the full range of facilities. Girls enroll from foreign countries and locations throughout the US, and English as a Second Language is available during the academic year for international students desiring to improve their command of written and spoken English. Most graduates matriculate at competitive four-year colleges. **See Also Page 1304**

MEADOWBROOK, PA. (8 mi. NNE of Philadelphia, PA) Rural. Pop: 150. Alt: 411 ft.

MEADOWBROOK SCHOOL
Day — Coed Gr PS-6

Meadowbrook, PA 19046. 1641 Hampton Rd. Tel: 215-884-3238. Fax: 215-884-9143.
www.themeadowbrookschool.org
E-mail: kmosteller@themeadowbrookschool.org
Robert Sarkisian, Head. BA, Colgate Univ, MEd, Beaver College. **Kelly A. Mosteller, Adm.**
Pre-Prep. Gen Acad. **Feat**—Fr Computers Studio_Art Music. **Supp**—Tut.
Adm: 45/yr. Appl due: Rolling. Accepted: 73%. **Tests** IQ.
Enr 204. B 102. G 102. Elem 204. Wh 71%. Hisp 1%. Blk 22%. Asian 4%. Other 2%. Avg class size: 14. Uniform. **Fac 32.** M 3. F 21/8. Wh 99%. Blk 1%. Adv deg: 31%.
Grad '04—26. Prep—21. (Wm Penn Charter 11, Chestnut Hill Acad 2, Springside 2, Germantown Friends 2, Abington Friends 2, Germantown Acad 1). Alum 1056.
Tui '04-'05: Day $10,800-14,100 (+$1400-1500). **Aid:** Need 73 ($649,600).
Summer: Rec. Sci. Art. Field Hockey. 1-3 wks.
Endow $852,000. Plant val $4,000,000. Bldgs 6. Class rms 16. Lib 12,000 vols. Sci labs 1. Lang labs 1. Comp labs 1. Sci ctrs 1. Auds 1. Art studios 1. Music studios 1. Dance studios 1. Gyms 1. Fields 2. Tennis courts 3.
Est 1919. Nonprofit. Tri (Sept-June).

Located on a 20-acre, wooded campus, this school features a family atmosphere and small classes. A structured curriculum emphasizes the development of strong basic skills, and a number of special enrichment programs supplement the traditional academics. French, science, music, art, physical education, computer and library specialists complement the work of the regular classroom teachers.

Additional activities—such as choir, recorder, gymnastics, ice skating, interscholastic sports, clubs, yearbook, and a dining hall waiter program in which fifth and sixth graders serve hot lunches to younger children—complete the student's experiences.

MEDIA, PA. (15 mi. WSW of Philadelphia, PA; 15 mi. NNE of Wilmington, DE) Suburban. Pop: 5533. Alt: 330 ft. Area also includes Rose Valley.

THE SCHOOL IN ROSE VALLEY
Day — Coed Gr PS-6

Rose Valley, PA 19063. 20 School Ln. Tel: 610-566-1088. Fax: 610-566-4640.
www.theschoolinrosevalley.org E-mail: admissions@theschoolinrosevalley.org

Carlye Nelson-Major, Prin. BA, Univ of Vermont, MEd, Cabrini College. **Dana Marcus, Adm.**
  Gen Acad. Feat—Lib_Skills Environ_Sci Computers Studio_Art Music Woodworking. **Supp**—Rev Tut.
  Adm (Gr PS-5): 30/yr. Appl due: Mar. Accepted: 60%. Yield: 90%.
  Enr 123. B 64. G 59. Elem 123. Wh 79%. Hisp 1%. Blk 4%. Asian 6%. Other 10%. Avg class size: 13. **Fac 17.** M 2. F 11/4. Wh 87%. Blk 1%. Asian 12%. Adv deg: 47%.
  Grad '04—7. Prep—4. (Media-Providence Friends 2, Westtown 1, DE Valley Friends 1). Alum 600.
  Tui '04-'05: Day $11,235-12,460 (+$240). **Aid:** Need 229 ($110,000).
  Summer: Rec. Tui Day $250/wk. 8 wks.
  Endow $1,000,000. Plant val $2,000,000. Bldgs 6. Class rms 11. Lib 10,000 vols. Sci labs 1. Comp labs 3. Auds 2. Theaters 2. Art studios 1. Music studios 1. Gyms 1. Fields 1. Pools 2.
  Est 1929. Nonprofit. Sem (Sept-June).

A group of parents organized this progressive school in cooperation with the department of education at Swarthmore College. Parents helped construct the buildings and continue to maintain a strong partnership with the staff and administration, helping to shape school philosophy and support the school's management. The developmentally appropriate curriculum, based on concrete experiences whenever possible, emphasizes shop, art, music, environmental science, computers and noncompetitive sports, in addition to language arts, math and social studies.

MERCERSBURG, PA. (118 mi. ESE of Pittsburgh, PA) Rural. Pop: 1540. Alt: 595 ft.

MERCERSBURG ACADEMY
Bdg and Day — Coed Gr 9-PG

Mercersburg, PA 17236. 300 E Seminary St. Tel: 717-328-6173. Fax: 717-328-6319.
  www.mercersburg.edu   E-mail: admission@mercersburg.edu
Douglas Hale, Head. BA, Univ of Tennessee, MA, Middlebury College. **Christopher R. Tompkins, Adm.**
  Col Prep. AP—Eng Fr Ger Lat Span Calc Stats Comp_Sci Bio Chem Physics Eur_Hist US_Hist US_Govt & Pol Art_Hist. **Feat**—Chin Women's_Hist Theater.
  Adm (Bdg Gr 9-12; Day 9-11): 158/yr. Bdg 130. Day 28. Appl due: Feb. Accepted: 40%. Yield: 64%. **Tests** ISEE SSAT TOEFL.
  Enr 443. B 203/34. G 167/39. Sec 431. PG 12. Wh 84%. Hisp 3%. Blk 5%. Asian 4%. Other 4%. Avg class size: 12. **Fac 94.** M 57/3. F 34. Wh 91%. Hisp 1%. Blk 2%. Asian 3%. Other 3%. Adv deg: 68%. In dorms 90.
  Grad '04—110. Col—106. (US Naval Acad 5, OH Wesleyan 5, Geo Wash 4, CT Col 3, U of VA 2, Smith 2). Avg SAT: 1233. Alum 9000.
  Tui '04-'05: Bdg $32,750 (+$1000). **Day $24,700** (+$1000). **Aid:** Merit 40 ($262,000). Need 150 ($2,559,992).
  Summer: Enrich Rec. ESL. 1-5 wks.
  Endow $140,000,000. Plant val $110,000,000. Bldgs 19. Dorms 7. Dorm rms 182. Class rms 37. Lib 55,000 vols. Chapels 1. Sci labs 7. Lang labs 1. Comp labs 3. Comp ctrs 3. Astronomy ctrs 1. Auds 1. Theaters 1. Art studios 4. Music studios 3. Dance studios 1. Gyms 4. Fields 9. Tennis courts 14. Volleyball courts 1. Squash courts 10. Pools 1.
  Est 1893. Nonprofit. Tri (Sept-June). **Assoc** CLS MSA.

The history of Mercersburg goes back to 1836, when Marshall College was founded here. In 1853, Marshall College moved to Lancaster, where it joined with Franklin College to become Franklin and Marshall College, but the preparatory department of the college continued on its original site under private direction until 1865, when it was chartered as Mercersburg College. In 1893, the board of regents of the college elected William Mann Irvine to lead the institution. Within months, Dr. Irvine changed the college's name to Mercersburg Academy and began his work as the founder and first headmaster of the present-day school. He opened the school that same year with an enrollment of 40 boys. The academy became coeducational in 1969.

The curriculum provides a rigorous college preparatory course of study. Admitting students of above-average ability who have been achieving well, the school maintains small classes. The major disciplines are English, foreign language, mathematics, science and history, with requirements in religion and the fine arts. Advanced Placement work is available in all academic areas. Foreign study opportunities are provided for a limited number of students through Mercerburg's affiliation with the School Year Abroad program and the English-Speaking Union.

Interscholastic team sports include football, cross-country, basketball, skiing, golf, swimming, diving, tennis, indoor track, wrestling, lacrosse, squash, field hockey, soccer, volleyball, baseball, softball, and track and field. Mercersburg maintains an extensive fine and performing arts department that features instrumental and voice opportunities; theater productions; ballet, modern dance and hip-hop; and musical theater. More than 30 extracurricular clubs and organizations—including publications, photography and an outdoor education program—reflect a wide array of student and faculty interests. **See Also Page 1208**

NEW BLOOMFIELD, PA. (100 mi. WNW of Wilmington, DE; 112 mi. WNW of Philadelphia, PA) Rural. Pop: 1092. Alt: 800 ft.

CARSON LONG MILITARY INSTITUTE

Bdg — Boys Gr 6-12

New Bloomfield, PA 17068. 200 N Carlisle St, PO Box 98. Tel: 717-582-2121.
Fax: 717-582-8763.
www.carsonlong.org E-mail: carson6@pa.net
Col. Carson E. R. Holman, USAR (Ret), Pres. BS, US Military Academy, MA, Bucknell Univ.
Lt. Col. David M. Comolli, Adm.
Col Prep. Gen Acad. Milit. Feat—Fr Span Computers Econ Speech JROTC. Supp—ESL Makeup Tut.
Adm: 115/yr. Appl due: Rolling. Accepted: 88%. Tests DAT.
Enr 190. B 190. Elem 46. Sec 144. Avg class size: 15. Uniform. Fac 21. M 15/3. F /3. Wh 100%. Adv deg: 52%. In dorms 13.
Grad '04—30. Col—26. (SUNY, Hofstra, U of MA-Amherst, Syracuse, Alvernia, U of CA-Berkeley). Avg SAT: 1300. Alum 1370.
Tui '05-'06: Bdg $14,900 (+$1000). Aid: Need 9 ($15,000).
Endow $1,500,000. Plant val $3,000,000. Bldgs 11. Dorms 6. Dorm rms 77. Class rms 18. Lib 6758 vols. Chapels 1. Sci labs 3. Lang labs 2. Comp labs 2. Auds 1. Art studios 1.

Music studios 1. Gyms 1. Fields 1. Courts 5.
  Est 1837. Nonprofit. Sem (Sept-June). **Assoc** MSA.

The school was founded by Theodore K. Long in the plant of the local academy. The basic curriculum combines college preparation with honors courses, English as a Second Language, Junior ROTC and vocational guidance. The structured and controlled environment offers small classes and supervised study. Great emphasis is placed on public speaking for all students.

Among Carson Long's extracurricular activities are student government, declamation, and debating, ski and glee clubs, as well as a drill team and a drum and bugle corps. Sports include interscholastic football, baseball, basketball, tennis, soccer, riflery, track and cross-country, in addition to intramurals.

See Also Page 1325

NEW HOPE, PA. (26 mi. NNE of Philadelphia, PA) Rural. Pop: 2252. Alt: 86 ft.

SOLEBURY SCHOOL
Bdg — Coed Gr 9-PG; Day — Coed 7-PG

New Hope, PA 18938. 6820 Phillips Mill Rd, PO Box 429. Tel: 215-862-5261.
  Fax: 215-862-3366.
    www.solebury.org   E-mail: admissions@solebury.com
John D. Brown, Head. BA, Beloit College, MS, Bank Street College of Education. **Denise DiFiglia, Adm.**
  Col Prep. AP—Eng Fr Span Calc Stats. **Feat**—Shakespeare Lat-Amer_Lit Anat & Physiol Comp_Design Programming Modern_Ireland Modern_Middle_East Psych Art_Hist Ceramics Photog Sculpt Studio_Art Theater Chorus Music_Theory Debate. **Supp**—ESL LD Tut.
  Adm: 70/yr. Bdg 20. Day 50. Appl due: Jan. Accepted: 68%. **Tests** SSAT TOEFL.
  Enr 220. Elem 29. Sec 189. PG 2. Wh 72%. Hisp 2%. Blk 8%. Asian 10%. Other 8%. Avg class size: 13. **Fac 46.** M 18/2. F 22/4. Wh 85%. Hisp 2%. Blk 7%. Asian 2%. Other 4%. Adv deg: 41%. In dorms 5.
  Grad '04—37. Col—34. (Boston Col, Albright, Duke, Rochester Inst of Tech, Franklin & Marshall, U of PA). Avg SAT: 1090. Alum 2256.
  Tui '05-'06: Bdg $31,200 (+$600). **Day $19,300-20,700** (+$600). **Aid:** Merit 7 ($44,100). Need 68 ($889,200).
  Summer: Acad. ESL. Tui Bdg $6000. 6 wks.
  Endow $2,000,000. Plant val $14,500,000. Bldgs 22. Dorms 2. Dorm rms 64. Lib 12,000 vols. Sci labs 4. Comp labs 3. Sci ctrs 1. Theaters 1. Art studios 3. Music studios 1. Gyms 1. Fields 4. Courts 4. Pools 1.
  Est 1925. Nonprofit. Tri (Sept-June). **Assoc** MSA.

Situated on a 90-acre campus midway between Philadelphia and New York City, this school conducts a varied college preparatory program. Solebury's curriculum includes AP classes, honors courses in all disciplines, and opportunities for independent study. A number of electives and course work in computers and the arts are among the school's graduation requirements. Advanced middle school students may take some high school courses for credit. In mid-May, another element of the curriculum allows seniors in good standing to leave campus for three weeks to work as an apprentice or a volunteer, to conduct independent research, or to pursue a creative project.

Each year, an academic theme promoting interdisciplinary learning is highlighted for which both faculty and students participate in summer reading, workshops, special films and assemblies, department presentations, weekend activities, play productions and art shows. In addition, Solebury offers a learning skills program for bright pupils with learning differences and, for international students, spring, summer and full-year programs in English as a Second Language.

The interscholastic sports program consists of soccer, basketball, baseball, field hockey, lacrosse, softball, tennis, cross-country and track, and other athletic pursuits include rock climbing, horseback riding, golf and biking. Among the school's extra-curricular activities are yearbook, literary magazine, theater, music, interest clubs and student council. Solebury schedules trips to such areas as France and Mexico, in addition to a dog-sledding excursion in Maine. Solebury also conducts student exchanges and a community service program in Brazil.

NEWTOWN, PA. (19 mi. NE of Philadelphia, PA) Suburban. Pop: 2523. Alt: 180 ft.

GEORGE SCHOOL

Bdg and Day — Coed Gr 9-12

Newtown, PA 18940. Rte 413, PO Box 4000. Tel: 215-579-6547. Fax: 215-579-6549.
www.georgeschool.org   E-mail: admissions@georgeschool.org

Nancy Starmer, Head. BA, College of Wooster, MEd, Boston Univ. **Karen Suplee Hallowell, Adm.**

Col Prep. IB Diploma. **AP**—Fr Lat Span Calc Stats Bio Physics US_Hist Studio_Art. **Feat**—Astron Oceanog Comp_Sci Robotics African_Hist Lat-Amer_Hist Middle_Eastern_Hist Asian_Hist Econ Ceramics Photog Video_Production Theater Design Woodworking Horticulture. **Supp**—ESL.

Adm: 146/yr. Bdg 80. Day 66. **Tests** SSAT.

Enr 537. B 154/116. G 142/125. Sec 537. Wh 77%. Hisp 5%. Blk 9%. Am Ind 1%. Asian 7%. Other 1%. Avg class size: 14. **Fac 87.** M 33/2. F 42/10. Wh 81%. Hisp 3%. Blk 6%. Asian 6%. Other 4%. Adv deg: 68%. In dorms 30.

Grad '04—129. Col—129. (PA St 7, Boston U 5, Carnegie Mellon 3, Haverford 3, U of PA 3, U of Chicago 3). Alum 8600.

Tui '05-'06: Bdg $33,800 (+$1000). **Day $24,700** (+$1000). **Aid:** Merit 14 ($140,000). Need 226 ($4,600,000).

Endow $65,000,000. Plant val $42,900,000. Bldgs 14. Dorms 8. Dorm rms 160. Class rms 40. Lib 25,000 vols. Sci labs 6. Lang labs 1. Meetinghouses 1. Art studios 7. Music studios 6. Gyms 2. Fields 8. Courts 18. Pools 1. Riding rings 1. Stables 1.

Est 1893. Nonprofit. Religious Society of Friends. Tri (Sept-June). **Assoc** MSA.

This Friends' school owes its name to its founder, John M. George, whose will provided for the education of the children of Friends and others. The campus is located on 265 acres of wooded countryside in Bucks County, within easy access of the cultural centers of Philadelphia, Princeton, NJ, and New York City. The spirit of the school is in the Friends tradition, and students of every religious, racial and economic background attend from many states and foreign countries.

George School's curriculum includes traditional college preparatory courses and a variety of special term electives. Accommodating students with differing learning styles and abilities, the curriculum's four-level system enables students to study with appropriate degrees of intensity in each discipline. GS is one of the only boarding schools in the country that offers the two-year International Baccalaureate curriculum, a rigorous course of study (taken in grades 11 and 12) that often results in a full year of credit earned for US colleges or opportunities for university study abroad. Advanced Placement classes are also available to qualified pupils. An English as a Second Language program serves international students.

Complementing its academic offerings, the school provides a wide selection of extracurricular activities in the following areas: athletics, the performing and visual arts, and community service. Each year, students must participate in team or intramural sports, take a yearlong arts course and participate in the school's cooperative work program. Service projects to coastal Georgia and Arizona's Navajo Nation, as well as international work camps conducted in Cuba, France, South Korea, Israel/Palestine, Vietnam, Nicaragua and South Africa, are part of GS's prominent community service program.

NEWTOWN FRIENDS SCHOOL
Day — Coed Gr PS-8

Newtown, PA 18940. 1450 Newtown-Langhorne Rd, PO Box 978. Tel: 215-968-2225. Fax: 215-968-9346.

www.newtownfriends.org   E-mail: info@newtownfriends.org

Steven R. Nierenberg, Head. BA, Earlham College, MSEd, Temple Univ. **Betsy N. Rendall, Adm.**

Pre-Prep. Feat—Lib_Skills Lat Span Computers Studio_Art Music. **Supp**—Dev_Read.

Adm: 60/yr. Appl due: Rolling. Accepted: 75%. **Tests** SSAT.

Enr 310. B 156. G 154. Elem 310. Wh 85%. Hisp 2%. Blk 5%. Asian 3%. Other 5%. Avg class size: 18. **Fac 37.** M 5/1. F 20/11. Wh 94%. Blk 5%. Asian 1%. Adv deg: 43%.

Grad '04—34. Prep—31. (George Sch 16, Pennington 4, Princeton Day 3, Abington Friends 3, Lawrenceville 3, Solebury 2). Alum 1165.

Tui '04-'05: Day $11,650-12,450. **Aid:** Need 54 ($284,000).

Summer: Rec. 1-6 wks.

Endow $1,100,000. Plant val $6,000,000. Bldgs 1. Class rms 21. Lib 10,000 vols. Sci labs 2. Comp labs 1. Auds 1. Art studios 1. Music studios 1. Gyms 1. Fields 2.

Est 1948. Nonprofit. Religious Society of Friends. Tri (Sept-June).

Occupying a seven-acre site in Bucks County, Newtown Friends was founded by area Quakers and parents. The curriculum comprises course work in language arts, math, science, foreign language (Spanish and Latin), social studies, music and drama, art, computer and physical education. In grades K-8, the school divides each grade into two sections of roughly 16 to 18 pupils; in the prekindergarten, there is one class of approximately 15 children. Instruction at all levels combines hands-on experiences, group and individual projects, interdisciplinary approaches and traditional methods.

An important aspect of school life is an intergenerational program that provides students with opportunities for interaction with individuals at Pennswood Village, a

Friends' continuing care retirement community that occupies quarters next to Newtown Friends. In addition, the school's curriculum includes a community service program in grades 6-8.

PAOLI, PA. (19 mi. W of Philadelphia, PA; 21 mi. N of Wilmington, DE) Urban. Pop: 5425. Alt: 541 ft.

CFS
THE SCHOOL AT CHURCH FARM
Bdg and Day — Boys Gr 7-12

Paoli, PA 19301. PO Box 2000. Tel: 610-363-5347. Fax: 610-280-6746.
   www.gocfs.net   E-mail: rlunardi@gocfs.net

Charles W. Shreiner III, Head. BS, Nichols College, MA, Villanova Univ. **Richard Lunardi, Adm.**

   Col Prep. AP—Eng Calc US_Hist. Feat—Fr Span Computers Fine_Arts Music. **Supp**—Rev Tut.

   Adm (Bdg Gr 7-11; Day 7-10): 56/yr. Bdg 48. Day 8. Appl due: May. Accepted: 54%. Yield: 84%. **Tests** SSAT.

   Enr 188. B 155/33. Elem 49. Sec 139. Wh 46%. Hisp 10%. Blk 29%. Asian 14%. Other 1%. Avg class size: 10. **Fac 33.** M 21/7. F 3/2. Wh 91%. Hisp 6%. Blk 3%. Adv deg: 54%. In dorms 1.

   Grad '04—35. Col—35. (Drexel 4, Ursinus 2, CUNY 2, Columbia 1, U of Chicago 1, U of MI 1). Avg SAT: 1093. Alum 1012.

   Tui '04-'05: Bdg $4000-18,000 (+$750). **Day** $4000-12,500 (+$500). **Aid:** Need 188 ($5,695,750).

   Endow $160,000,000. Plant val $50,000,000. Bldgs 19. Dorms 10. Dorm rms 180. Class rms 26. Lib 28,000 vols. Sci labs 4. Comp labs 1. Auds 1. Art studios 1. Music studios 1. Gyms 2. Fields 4. Courts 6. Pools 1.

   Est 1918. Nonprofit. Episcopal. Sem (Sept-June). **Assoc** MSA.

Founded by Rev. Dr. Charles W. Shreiner, Sr., CFS has traditionally offered a college preparatory program in a Christian environment for boys from single-parent settings. In 1988, the school began admitting a number of academically qualified and financially deserving boys from homes with both parents present. Originally operating exclusively as a boarding school, CFS established an increasingly prominent day division in 1995. Tuition for all students is determined along a sliding scale.

The curriculum includes required and elective course work in the major content areas, as well as foreign language, religion, the fine arts, technology education, health and computer studies. Students may pursue Advanced Placement or honors courses in all major academic departments. Mandatory work and community service programs provide valuable nonclassroom experiences both on and off campus.

Pupils choose from such extracurricular activities as student vestry, school newspaper, yearbook and student council. As sports are an important component of school life, all boys participate in some kind of interscholastic or intramural athletic activity.   **See Also Pages 1326-7**

PENNSBURG, PA. (33 mi. NW of Philadelphia, PA) Rural. Pop: 2732. Alt: 425 ft.

PERKIOMEN SCHOOL
Bdg — Coed Gr 7-PG; Day — Coed 5-PG

Pennsburg, PA 18073. 200 Seminary Ave, PO Box 130. Tel: 215-679-9511. Fax: 215-679-1146.

www.perkiomen.org   E-mail: cdougherty@perkiomen.org

George K. Allison, Head. AB, Union College, MA, Trinity College (CT). **Carol S. Dougherty, Adm.**

Col Prep. AP—Eng Fr Span Calc Stats Comp_Sci Bio Chem Physics Eur_Hist US_Hist. **Feat**—Lat Environ_Sci Archaeol Econ Law Pol_Sci Psych Relig Art_Hist Drama Music Music_Hist Music_Theory. **Supp**—ESL LD Tut.

Adm (Bdg Gr 7-10; Day 5-9): 75/yr. Bdg 46. Day 29. Appl due: Rolling. Accepted: 66%. Yield: 78%. **Tests** SSAT.

Enr 255. B 93/53. G 50/59. Elem 50. Sec 200. PG 5. Wh 69%. Hisp 3%. Blk 8%. Asian 20%. Avg class size: 12. **Fac 49.** M 28. F 19/2. Wh 97%. Hisp 1%. Blk 1%. Asian 1%. Adv deg: 59%. In dorms 22.

Grad '04—48. Col—48. (Northwestern 2, Purdue 2, Emory 2, U of IL-Urbana 2, U of MI 2, U of Chicago 1). Avg SAT: 1080. Alum 4436.

Tui '04-'05: Bdg $31,200 (+$1500). **Day $18,300** (+$800). **Aid:** Merit 33 ($87,000). Need 73 ($877,150).

Endow $3,800,000. Plant val $42,000,000. Bldgs 18. Dorms 5. Dorm rms 160. Class rms 33. Lib 17,000 vols. Labs 4. Comp labs 3. Auds 1. Theaters 1. Art studios 4. Music studios 5. Dance studios 2. Gyms 1. Fields 8. Courts 5. Pools 1.

Est 1875. Nonprofit. Schwenkfelder. Tri (Sept-May). **Assoc** MSA.

Founded by Dr. C. S. Wieand, the descendant of a Schwenkfelder immigrant, Perkiomen provides a traditional college preparatory program within a structured environment. The upper school curriculum includes traditional course requirements and electives, such as language, history, science, math and the arts, in each grade. All departments offer Advanced Placement and honors classes. Two special programs supplement the traditional academic courses: A highly individualized developmental language program aids above-average students with mild learning disabilities or gaps in learning skills, while an extensive ESL program provides individual support for international students until they are proficient in speaking and writing. Religious studies consist of course offerings in the upper school and a chapel program that convenes at least once a month.

The fine arts program includes both curricular and extracurricular options. During the academic day, course offerings encompass instrumental and voice instruction, studio art, theater and private lessons. Students in the middle school take fine art classes five times a week, while those in grades 9-12 participate in a variety of electives, such as art history, studio art, photography, drawing, digital art, ceramics, stage makeup and play writing. After class, individualized programs in studio art, dance, voice and instrumental music are available to advanced students.

Also among the extracurricular activities are student publications and other campus organizations that appeal to the varied interests and hobbies of the student body. These include computer club; drama club; student senate; French, Spanish and international clubs; and a forensic league. The athletic program offers middle school, junior varsity and varsity teams, as well as such noncompetitive sports as tae kwon do. **See Also Page 1225**

PHILADELPHIA, PA. Urban. Pop: 1,517,550. Alt: to 440 ft. Area also includes Fort Washington, Merion and Wyndmoor.

CREFELD SCHOOL
Day — Coed Gr 7-12

Philadelphia, PA 19118. 8836 Crefeld St. Tel: 215-242-5545. Fax: 215-242-8869.
   www.crefeld.org   E-mail: info@crefeld.org
Mark Piechota, Head. BA, Williams College, MEd, EdD, Harvard Univ. **Stacey Cunitz, Adm.**
   Col Prep. LD. Underachiever. Feat—Span Computers Sculpt Glass_Blowing Acting Dance. **Supp**—Tut.
   Adm (Gr 7-11): 28/yr. Appl due: Rolling. Accepted: 70%. Yield: 90%.
   Enr 100. B 61. G 39. Elem 23. Sec 77. Wh 80%. Hisp 5%. Blk 7%. Other 8%. Avg class size: 11. **Fac 23.** M 10/4. F 7/2. Wh 91%. Hisp 9%. Adv deg: 43%.
   Grad '04—15. Col—12. (Alfred, Drexel, Franklin & Marshall, Harcum JC, Skidmore, IN U of PA). Avg SAT: 1180. Alum 775.
   Tui '04-'05: Day $17,550-18,950 (+$300). **Aid:** Need 25 ($168,000).
   Summer: Enrich. Arts. Tui Day $800/4-wk ses. 8 wks.
   Plant val $2,000,000. Bldgs 2. Class rms 21. Libs 1. Sci labs 1. Lang labs 1. Comp labs 2. Auds 1. Theaters 1. Art studios 3. Music studios 1. Dance studios 1. Gyms 1. Fields 1. Basketball courts 1.
   Est 1970. Nonprofit. Sem (Sept-June).

Located in a Victorian mansion on a four-acre site in the Chestnut Hill section of Philadelphia, Crefeld, formerly Miquon Upper School, serves students who have not prospered in traditional classroom settings. The school's approach accommodates learning style differences by tailoring each program to individual strengths and weaknesses. Staff work closely with parents and outside professionals to coordinate programming and plan teaching strategies.

Various electives, with an emphasis on the arts, complement the academic program. Students fulfill a weekly community service requirement.

EPISCOPAL ACADEMY
Day — Coed Gr PS-12

Merion, PA 19066. 376 N Latches Ln. Tel: 610-667-9612. Fax: 610-667-8629.
   www.ea1785.org   E-mail: admission@ea1785.org
L. Hamilton Clark, Head. BA, Trinity College (CT), MEd, Harvard Univ. **Ellen M. Hay, Adm.**
   Col Prep. AP—Eng Fr Lat Span Calc Stats Comp_Sci Bio Chem Physics US_Hist World_Hist Art_Hist Music_Theory. Feat—Greek Econ Psych Philos Relig Drama Music. **Supp**—Dev_Read Tut.
   Adm: 180/yr. Appl due: Jan. Accepted: 46%. Yield: 67%. **Tests** IQ ISEE SSAT.
   Enr 1130. B 582. G 548. Elem 684. Sec 446. Wh 84%. Hisp 2%. Blk 7%. Asian 3%. Other 4%. Avg class size: 17. **Fac 177.** M 68/2. F 96/11. Wh 85%. Hisp 3%. Blk 7%. Asian 5%. Adv deg: 63%.

Grad '04—99. Col—99. (U of PA 9, Princeton 5, Geo Wash 5, Georgetown 5, Cornell 5, Dickinson 5). Avg SAT: 1310. Alum 3980.
Tui '04-'05: Day $13,870-19,900 (+$200-600). **Aid:** Need 111 ($1,539,196).
Summer: Acad Enrich Rem Rec. Tui Day $300-800. 3-6 wks.
Endow $16,500,000. Plant val $60,000,000. Bldgs 28. Class rms 69. 3 Libs 53,100 vols. Chapels 2. Sci labs 13. Lang labs 2. Comp labs 6. Auds 2. Theaters 2. Art studios 3. Music studios 3. Dance studios 1. Gyms 3. Fields 10. Courts 8. Pools 1.
Est 1785. Nonprofit. Episcopal. Tri (Sept-June). **Assoc** CLS MSA.

One of the country's largest Episcopal day schools, Episcopal Academy was founded as a school for boys under the auspices of Rev. William White (who became the first bishop of Pennsylvania), Robert Morris, Francis Hopkinson and others. In 1787, the state legislature granted the school a charter and 10,000 acres of land. Dr. Greville Haslam, headmaster for a 36-year period during which the school made tremendous strides in enrollment, plant and curriculum, retired in 1957 and was succeeded by Dr. James H. McK. Quinn, who had been a member of the faculty since 1943 and assistant headmaster since 1953. Under his leadership, further curricular revisions were made, including the addition of Advanced Placement programs and independent study. Salaries were increased, a new chapel, a gymnasium and a swimming pool were constructed, and an additional classroom building was purchased. Dr. Quinn retired in 1975 and was succeeded by Mr. Crawford, an alumnus of the academy. The school has since become coeducational, has developed a second campus for grades PS-5 at 905 S. Waterloo Rd., Devon 19333 (a western suburb of Philadelphia), and has increased its enrollment. In addition, EA has added full programs in vocal and instrumental music and theater during his tenure.

The student body represents all denominations. The college preparatory curriculum, with individualized student scheduling, prepares graduates for many selective colleges. There are additional opportunities in art, music, and foreign travel and study trips. The plant includes excellent facilities for clubs, programs in the arts, publications, and an extensive program of varsity athletics for boys and girls. All students assist in community service on and off campus.

FRIENDS SELECT SCHOOL
Day — Coed Gr PS-12

Philadelphia, PA 19103. 17th St & Benjamin Franklin Pky. Tel: 215-561-5900.
   Fax: 215-864-2979.
   www.friends-select.org
Rose Hagan, Head. BA, Temple Univ, MA, Southern Illinois Univ. **Sherry Claypool, Gr 7-12 Adm; Stuart Land, Gr PS-6 Adm.**
   Col Prep. Feat—Lat Marine_Biol/Sci Computers Law Ethics Film Drama Music Journ. **Supp**—Dev_Read ESL.
   Adm: 93/yr. Appl due: Jan. Accepted: 58%. **Tests** ISEE SSAT.
   Enr 482. B 226. G 256. Elem 276. Sec 206. Wh 66%. Hisp 4%. Blk 16%. Am Ind 1%. Asian 7%. Other 6%. Avg class size: 16. **Fac 68.** M 17/4. F 43/4. Wh 81%. Hisp 1%. Blk 15%. Asian 3%. Adv deg: 69%.
   Grad '04—39. Col—39. (U of PA, Temple, U of Pittsburgh, Geo Wash, Mt Holyoke, Columbia). Alum 2820.
   Tui '02-'03: Day $8625-15,965 (+$125). **Aid:** Need 165 ($1,100,000).
   Summer: Acad Enrich Rev. Tui Day $500. 6 wks.
   Endow $9,500,000. Plant val $8,500,000. Bldgs 1. Class rms 30. 2 Libs 17,000 vols. Sci

labs 4. Comp labs 2. Auds 1. Theaters 1. Art studios 4. Music studios 2. Dance studios 1. Gyms 2. Fields 2. Courts 7. Pools 1.

Est 1689. Nonprofit. Religious Society of Friends. Sem (Sept-June). **Assoc** CLS.

Located in the cultural, corporate and business center of Philadelphia, Friends Select traces its Quaker beginnings to 1689. Coeducational since 1886, the school is still under the direct management of Friends, and religious course work is provided.

The school's college preparatory curriculum, rooted in Quaker values, encourages the development of conceptual understanding and creative thought while emphasizing the ability to serve the community. Small classes and individual attention are program characteristics at all grade levels.

Physical education is required at all levels. Interscholastic sports begin in grade 6: Boys choose from soccer, basketball, wrestling, baseball, tennis and swimming, while girls may participate in soccer, field hockey, basketball, swimming, softball and tennis; cross-country is available for both boys and girls. The school also offers after-school and vacation care, as well as summer programs for young children.

GERMANTOWN ACADEMY
Day — Coed Gr PS-12

Fort Washington, PA 19034. 340 Morris Rd, PO Box 287. Tel: 215-646-3300. Fax: 215-646-1216.

www.germantownacademy.org   E-mail: admission@germantownacademy.org

James W. Connor, Head. BA, Eckerd College, MA, Univ of Pennsylvania. **Barbara H. Serrill, Adm.**

Col Prep. AP—Eng Fr Span Calc Stats Bio Chem Physics Eur_Hist US_Hist World_Hist Music_Theory. **Feat**—Lat Russ Environ_Sci Marine_Biol/Sci Biotech Civil_War Econ Film Theater_Arts. **Supp**—Dev_Read.

Adm (Gr PS-11): 157/yr. Appl due: Rolling. Accepted: 43%. Yield: 83%. **Tests** IQ ISEE SSAT.

Enr 1136. B 580. G 556. Elem 650. Sec 486. Wh 89%. Hisp 1%. Blk 5%. Asian 4%. Other 1%. **Fac 148.** M 58/3. F 78/9. Wh 90%. Hisp 2%. Blk 3%. Asian 2%. Other 3%. Adv deg: 65%.

Grad '04—120. Col—120. (Drexel 5, Geo Wash 4, Villanova 4, U of DE 4, U of PA 3, Cornell 3). Avg SAT: 1275. Alum 4272.

Tui '04-'05: Day $12,460-18,245 (+$250). **Aid:** Merit 8 ($8000). Need 175 ($1,605,000). **Summer:** Acad Enrich Rev Rem Rec. Tui Day $200-475/wk. 6 wks.

Endow $36,000,000. Plant val $25,000,000. Bldgs 8. Class rms 106. Lib 18,000 vols. Sci labs 6. Lang labs 12. Comp labs 2. Sci ctrs 1. Auds 1. Theaters 1. Art studios 2. Music studios 2. Arts ctrs 1. Photog studios 1. Design studios 1. Gyms 2. Field houses 1. Pools 1.

Est 1759. Nonprofit. Sem (Sept-June). **Assoc** CLS MSA.

The oldest nonsectarian independent day school in the country, GA was founded as Germantown Union School. The academy served both boys and girls on its original campus in the Germantown section of Philadelphia until 1836, when, by virtue of demand for space, the enrollment was limited to boys. A generous land gift in 1959 facilitated the school's move to its present, 110-acre campus in Fort Washington in 1961; the same year, GA reinstated coeducation.

The curriculum includes course requirements in English, history, mathematics, science, foreign language, the visual and performing arts, and physical education.

Qualified students may complete Advanced Placement work in computer science and the major disciplines. Technology is an important aspect of the program: in addition to classroom computers, the academy maintains computer labs and provides extensive Internet access. All middle and upper school pupils have E-mail addresses.

Among other opportunities are an independent, off-campus study project at the end of senior year; elective summer internship programs; the Academy Scholars program for sophomores and juniors; and foreign exchange programs in France, Spain and Latin America. The school hosts international students through the English-Speaking Union, the Community of Bosnia Foundation and Rotary International.

GA provides numerous opportunities for pupils to satisfy middle and upper school extracurricular requirements. A full complement of varsity athletic teams allows students to compete in more than 20 sports, beginning at the middle school level. Other activities include school government, publications, on- and off-campus community service, and competitions such as Model UN and Mock Trial. Choral and orchestral groups travel and perform abroad and throughout the US on an annual basis.

GERMANTOWN FRIENDS SCHOOL
Day — Coed Gr K-12

Philadelphia, PA 19144. 31 W Coulter St. Tel: 215-951-2300. Fax: 215-951-2312.
  www.germantownfriends.org   E-mail: nancyb@gfsnet.org
Richard L. Wade, Head. BA, College of William and Mary, MA, Northwestern Univ. **Eleanor M. Elkinton, Adm.**

  Col Prep. Feat—Fr Greek Lat Span Stats Programming Lat_Hist Philos Art_Hist Photog Drama Theater_Arts Chorus Music_Theory. **Supp**—Tut.

  Adm: 126/yr. Appl due: Dec. Accepted: 45%. Yield: 68%. **Tests** IQ ISEE SSAT.

  Enr 901. B 444. G 457. Elem 549. Sec 352. Wh 71%. Hisp 3%. Blk 18%. Asian 6%. Other 2%. Avg class size: 18. **Fac 134.** M 32/13. F 59/30. Wh 83%. Hisp 1%. Blk 12%. Asian 4%. Adv deg: 59%.

  Grad '04—94. Col—93. (U of PA 10, Cornell 5, Temple 5, Columbia 4, Tufts 4, U of Chicago 4). Avg SAT: 1312. Alum 4716.

  Tui '04-'05: Day $11,965-17,665 (+$50-500). **Aid:** Need 176 ($1,505,197).

  Endow $26,600,000. Plant val $36,420,000. Bldgs 20. Class rms 78. Lib 60,000 vols. Sci labs 7. Lang labs 5. Comp labs 3. Theaters 3. Art studios 7. Music studios 7. Gyms 5. Fields 7. Courts 13.

  Est 1845. Nonprofit. Religious Society of Friends. (Sept-June). **Assoc** MSA.

The importance and the influence of this Friends school developed during the time of Stanley R. Yarnall, with the school from 1898, and principal from 1906 until his retirement in 1941. The present-day school serves a multicultural student body and combines Quaker principles with a strong academic program.

GFS' thematic lower school curriculum progresses to a team-taught middle school and a college preparatory upper school program. Students may pursue advanced courses in science, mathematics, English, history, and classical and modern languages. Strong programs in art, music and theater are integrated with academics. Also noteworthy is a double-credit Latin history course that combines intermediate Latin language instruction with study of the origins of civilization in the Near East and its development in the Bronze Age and classical Greece. With faculty approval, students in grades 10-12 may engage in directed independent study for credit at a standard or accelerated level.

Pupils take part in numerous athletic and other extracurricular activities, as well as local service projects. International travel and exchange programs are available, particularly through the modern language department's exchanges with schools in France and Mexico, advanced language, choir and athletic trips, and Germantown Friends' membership in the National Network of Complementary Schools.

Sports include soccer, track, wrestling, basketball, squash, baseball, softball, cross-country, tennis, field hockey and lacrosse.

GREENE STREET FRIENDS SCHOOL
Day — Coed Gr PS-8

Philadelphia, PA 19144. 5511 Greene St. Tel: 215-438-7545. Fax: 215-438-1121.
www.greenestreetfriends.org   E-mail: mblackman@greenestreetfriends.org
Edward Marshall, Head. BA, Temple Univ, PhD, Univ of Pennsylvania. **Leanne G. Clancy, Adm.**

Pre-Prep. Feat—Span Computers Econ Studio_Art Drama Music. **Supp**—Rem_Read Tut.

Adm: 74/yr. Appl due: Jan. Accepted: 30%. **Tests** CTP_4 ISEE.

Enr 247. B 129. G 118. Sec 247. Wh 46%. Hisp 5%. Blk 47%. Asian 2%. Avg class size: 18. **Fac 36.** M 5. F 20/11. Wh 66%. Hisp 6%. Blk 28%. Adv deg: 38%.

Grad '04—20. Prep—8. (Germantown Friends, Friends Select, Abington Friends, Friends' Central, Wm Penn Charter, George Sch).

Tui '05-'06: Day $8950-10,350 (+$200). **Aid:** Need 50 ($175,000).

Summer: Rec. 2-6 wks.

Endow $150,000. Plant val $10,000,000. Bldgs 5. Class rms 20. Lib 5000 vols. Sci labs 1. Comp labs 1. Auds 1. Theaters 1. Art studios 1. Music studios 1. Gyms 1.

Est 1855. Nonprofit. Religious Society of Friends. Tri (Sept-June).

First opened for children of the Green Street Monthly Meeting and others in the Germantown community, this Friends school continues to provide a caring environment for learning. The program includes music, art, computer instruction, foreign language and physical education, as well as training in the basic academic skills. In the middle school, students choose from such electives as sign language, nature study, newspaper, yearbook, theater arts, and the practical and fine arts. After-school sports and an extended-day program are available.

LA SALLE COLLEGE HIGH SCHOOL
Day — Boys Gr 9-12

Wyndmoor, PA 19038. 8605 Cheltenham Ave. Tel: 215-233-2911. Fax: 215-233-1418.
www.lschs.org   E-mail: explorer@lschs.org
Br. Richard Kestler, FSC, Pres. MA, La Salle Univ, MA, Villanova Univ, MA, St John's Univ (NY). **Br. James F. Rieck, FSC, Adm.**

Col Prep. AP—Eng Fr Ger Span Calc Stats Bio Chem Physics Eur_Hist US_Hist Econ US_Govt & Pol. **Feat**—Relig Studio_Art Chorus Music. **Supp**—Rev Tut.

Adm: 292/yr. Appl due: Dec. **Tests** HSPT.

Enr 1050. B 1050. Sec 1050. Wh 92%. Hisp 1%. Blk 4%. Asian 3%. Avg class size: 21. **Fac**

92. M 70/2. F 18/2. Wh 95%. Hisp 2%. Blk 1%. Asian 2%. Adv deg: 77%.
Grad '04—238. Col—236. (PA St, St Joseph's U, Drexel, La Salle, Temple, Villanova). Avg SAT: 1173. Alum 10,500.
Tui '05-'06: Day $11,700 (+$400). **Aid:** Merit 70 ($280,000). Need 275 ($825,000). Work prgm 2 ($3000).
Summer: Acad Enrich Rev. Tui Day $725. 5 wks.
Endow $10,400,000. Plant val $29,000,000. Bldgs 10. Class rms 40. Lib 13,000 vols. Sci labs 6. Lang labs 1. Comp labs 7. Auds 2. Art studios 2. Music studios 3. Gyms 3. Fields 5. Tennis courts 5. Pools 2. Arboretums 1.
Est 1858. Nonprofit. Roman Catholic. Sem (Sept-June). **Assoc** MSA.

Founded in Philadelphia and relocated to its present, 50-acre campus in 1960, this school is conducted by the De La Salle Christian Brothers. Advanced Placement classes are available; electives in psychology, economics, computer programming and networking, music, studio art and other subjects are also provided. The curriculum includes a full four-year program of religious studies, an extensive community service program and a campus ministry program that organizes yearly retreats.

La Salle features strong student participation in athletics, offering intramurals and more than a dozen interscholastic teams. Jazz band, string and choral programs; a competing band; and a wide selection of clubs are notable components of the extracurricular program.

ST. PETER'S SCHOOL
Day — Coed Gr PS-8

Philadelphia, PA 19147. 319 Lombard St. Tel: 215-925-3963. Fax: 215-925-3351.
  www.stpetersonline.org   E-mail: tkyle@stpetersonline.org
David J. Costello, **Head.** AB, Bowdoin College, MALS, Wesleyan Univ. **Trish Kyle, Adm.**
Pre-Prep. Feat—Poetry Fr Computers Studio_Art Music.
Adm: 47/yr. Appl due: Rolling. Accepted: 56%. Yield: 80%. **Tests** IQ.
Enr 181. B 81. G 100. Elem 181. Wh 66%. Blk 14%. Asian 6%. Other 14%. Avg class size: 12. **Fac 25.** M 4/3. F 14/4. Wh 92%. Hisp 4%. Asian 4%. Adv deg: 60%.
Grad '04—19. Prep—16. (Shipley 3, Wm Penn Charter 2, Friends Select 2, Episcopal Acad 2, Haverford 1, Friends' Central 1). Alum 560.
Tui '05-'06: Day $12,715-17,160 (+$525). **Aid:** Need 54 ($621,065).
Summer: Enrich. Tui Day $250/wk. 6 wks.
Endow $1,000,000. Bldgs 1. Class rms 18. Lib 4000 vols. Comp labs 1. Theaters 1. Art studios 2. Music studios 1. Gyms 1. Fields 1.
Est 1834. Nonprofit. Tri (Sept-June).

This school was established as a parish school for the girls of St. Peter's Church by Bishop William White, bishop to the Continental Congress during the Revolutionary War. In the following years it became coeducational, and from 1904 to 1964 it was a renowned boys' choir school for St. Peter's Episcopal Church. St. Peter's incorporated independently of the church in 1969 and grew from a student body of 89 to its present size.

The school continues to draw students of all economic backgrounds, races and religions from the Metropolitan Philadelphia area. The traditional academic program emphasizes literature, mathematics, history and science, and St. Peter's requires students to take part in music, art, physical education and technology courses. The school takes full advantage of surrounding cultural and historic institutions, while offering field trips to the New Jersey Shore and the Pennsylvania mountains.

Competitive sports include soccer, basketball and softball. An after-school enrichment program consists of modern dance, book club, art, photography, needlework and athletics.   **See Also Page 1244**

SPRINGSIDE SCHOOL
Day — Girls Gr PS-12

Philadelphia, PA 19118. 8000 Cherokee St. Tel: 215-247-7007. Fax: 215-247-7308.
  www.springside.org   E-mail: admissions@springside.org
Priscilla Sands, Head. BFA, Univ of Rhode Island, MA, Villanova Univ. **Jann Douple, Upper & Middle Sch Adm; Margaret Klein Mandell, Lower Sch Adm.**
  Col Prep. AP—Eng Fr Lat Span Calc Comp_Sci Bio Physics Eur_Hist US_Govt & Pol. **Feat**—Web_Design Digital_Art Jazz Dance.
  Adm (Gr PS-11): 102/yr. Appl due: Jan. Accepted: 59%. **Tests** IQ ISEE SSAT.
  Enr 628. G 628. Elem 453. Sec 175. Wh 76%. Hisp 2%. Blk 14%. Asian 3%. Other 5%. Avg class size: 18. Uniform. **Fac 104.** M 21. F 83. Wh 91%. Hisp 5%. Blk 3%. Asian 1%. Adv deg: 58%.
  Grad '04—38. Col—38. (U of PA, Bryn Mawr, U of the Arts, Princeton, Brown, Columbia). Avg SAT: 1260. Alum 3000.
  Tui '05-'06: Day $13,000-19,850. Aid: Need 122 ($1,062,650).
  Endow $17,000,000. Plant val $19,000,000. Bldgs 1. Class rms 40. 2 Libs 30,000 vols. Sci labs 9. Lang labs 3. Comp labs 6. Auds 2. Art studios 6. Music studios 4. Dance studios 1. Gyms 2. Fields 5. Tennis courts 4. Squash courts 6.
  Est 1879. Nonprofit. Quar (Sept-June). **Assoc** CLS.

Springside conducts a coordinate program with Chestnut Hill Academy, an adjacent boys' school comprising grades K-12. Music, art and languages are coed in grades 9 and 10, while all academics are coed for juniors and seniors.

During the summers preceding their junior and senior years, students may participate in a cultural exchange program in France or Costa Rica. Qualified juniors and seniors may select options of independent study or courses at area colleges. More than half of the school's graduates enter college with Advanced Placement credits.

Athletics include field hockey, tennis, basketball, softball, volleyball, squash, lacrosse, crew, soccer and track. Student government, dramatics and publications are major activities. An extended-day program is available.

WILLIAM PENN CHARTER SCHOOL
Day — Coed Gr K-12

Philadelphia, PA 19144. 3000 W School House Ln. Tel: 215-844-3460. Fax: 215-844-5537.
  www.penncharter.com
Earl J. Ball III, Head. BA, Middlebury College, MAT, Johns Hopkins Univ, EdD, Univ of Pennsylvania. **Stephen A. Bonnie, Adm.**
  Col Prep. AP—Fr Lat Span Calc Stats Bio Chem Physics Eur_Hist US_Hist US_Govt & Pol Art_Hist. **Feat**—Comp_Sci Econ Relig Filmmaking Studio_Art Music.
  Adm (Gr K-11): 156/yr. Appl due: Rolling. Accepted: 43%. Yield: 57%. **Tests** ISEE SSAT.
  Enr 886. B 498. G 388. Elem 461. Sec 425. Wh 79%. Hisp 2%. Blk 14%. Asian 5%. Avg

class size: 15. **Fac 107.** M 48/6. F 52/1. Wh 82%. Hisp 5%. Blk 8%. Asian 4%. Other 1%. Adv deg: 86%.
Grad '04—86. Col—84. (U of PA 5, Boston U 4, Bucknell 4, Drexel 4, Geo Wash 3, Pomona 3). Alum 4469.
Tui '04-'05: Day $12,090-18,410 (+$1000-2500). **Aid:** Need 221 ($2,091,610).
Summer: Rec. Tui Day $855. 3 wks.
Endow $35,097,000. Plant val $50,200,000. Bldgs 9. Class rms 62. 2 Libs 26,563 vols. Sci labs 7. Comp labs 3. Auds 3. Theaters 1. Art studios 3. Music studios 3. Dance studios 1. Art galleries 1. Gyms 5. Fields 9. Courts 7. Field houses 1. Pools 1.
Est 1689. Nonprofit. Religious Society of Friends. Tri (Sept-June). **Assoc** CLS MSA.

In 1701, a dozen years after the school's founding, William Penn granted the first of three charters that were to define the school's operation. It is still conducted under his final charter of 1711. Richard Mott Jones, who served as headmaster from 1874 to 1916, brought the school a national reputation, largely due to his further development of the arts and athletic programs. Increasing enrollment resulted in Penn Charter's 1925 move from 8 S. 12th St. to its present Germantown location. In 1980, the overseers voted to admit girls into all grades for the first time.

The cosmopolitan student body emphasizes self-government and community participation. The curriculum, with its rotating schedule, trimester system and wide scope of elective courses for upper school students, permits not only sound preparation for college, but also admission with advanced standing and opportunities for major units in art. Math and writing centers enhance the academic program. A comprehensive senior project is part of the academic program.

Publications, dramatics, athletics, and various societies and clubs are among the available activities. Graduates matriculate at leading colleges.

PITTSBURGH, PA. Urban. Pop: 334,563. Alt: 715-1240 ft.

ELLIS SCHOOL
Day — Girls Gr K-12

Pittsburgh, PA 15206. 6425 5th Ave. Tel: 412-661-5992. Fax: 412-661-3979.
www.theellisschool.org   E-mail: admissions@theellisschool.org
Mary H. Grant, Head. AB, Smith College, EdD, George Washington Univ. **Holly Hatcher-Frazier, Adm.**
Col Prep. Feat—British_Lit Fr Lat Span Programming Anthro Pol_Sci Art_Hist Studio_Art. **Supp**—Rev Tut.
Adm: 89/yr. Appl due: Rolling. Accepted: 56%. Yield: 35%. **Tests** ISEE.
Enr 496. G 496. Elem 318. Sec 178. Wh 73%. Hisp 1%. Blk 15%. Am Ind 1%. Asian 9%. Other 1%. Avg class size: 12. Uniform. **Fac 77.** M 14. F 50/13. Wh 90%. Hisp 4%. Blk 2%. Asian 2%. Other 2%. Adv deg: 68%.
Grad '04—41. Col—41. (Barnard, Carnegie Mellon, Case Western Reserve, Drexel, U of MD-Col Park, Yale). Avg SAT: 1250. Alum 2530.
Tui '04-'05: Day $12,500-17,150. Aid: Need 103 ($1,020,400).
Summer: Rec. Tui Day $150/wk. 2 wks.
Endow $23,918,000. Plant val $12,940,000. Bldgs 9. Class rms 44. 2 Libs 45,248 vols. Sci labs 7. Comp labs 6. Photog labs 1. AV rms 1. Auds 1. Art studios 4. Music studios 4. Gyms 4. Fields 1.
Est 1916. Nonprofit. (Sept-June). **Assoc** CLS MSA.

Founded by Sara Frazer Ellis to prepare students for Eastern women's colleges, Ellis has grown from its initial enrollment of 40 and faculty of six to meet the increasing demands of the community. The school has occupied its present, seven-acre campus since 1959, and it has expanded facilities on several occasions over the years.

The rigorous traditional curriculum is sufficiently flexible to meet the needs of individual students. In addition to a three-week minicourse program each spring, a full range of electives featuring art, drama and music is available. An athletic program encourages broad participation. The resources of the city are utilized in field trips, senior projects, independent study and volunteer work. Graduates attend leading colleges.

FALK SCHOOL
Day — Coed Gr K-8

Pittsburgh, PA 15261. Allequippa St. Tel: 412-624-8020. Fax: 412-624-1303.
 www.pitt.edu/~fls   E-mail: fls@pitt.edu

William E. McDonald, Dir. BA, St Bonaventure Univ, MEd, PhD, Univ of Pittsburgh. **Marian Vollmer, Adm.**

Gen Acad. Feat—Lib_Skills Japan Span Studio_Art Music. **Supp**—Rem_Math Rem_Read Tut.

Adm: 30/yr. Accepted: 30%.

Enr 275. B 137. G 138. Elem 275. Wh 82%. Hisp 2%. Blk 7%. Asian 9%. Avg class size: 22. **Fac 27.** M 4. F 23. Wh 96%. Am Ind 4%. Adv deg: 100%.

Grad '04—36.

Tui '03-'04: Day $6700 (+$200). **Aid:** Need 13 ($21,000).

Plant val $850,000. Bldgs 2. Class rms 18. Lib 12,000 vols. Labs 1. Art studios 1. Music studios 1. Gyms 1. Fields 1.

Est 1931. Nonprofit. (Sept-June).

Now a campus school, Falk grew out of the Community School, established in 1922, and was presented to the University of Pittsburgh by Leon Falk, Jr. in 1931. It assists in the training of elementary and secondary school teachers. The nongraded curriculum provides advanced work for those who exhibit the ability.

ST. EDMUND'S ACADEMY
Day — Coed Gr PS-8

Pittsburgh, PA 15217. 5705 Darlington Rd. Tel: 412-521-1907. Fax: 412-521-1260.
 www.stedmunds.net   E-mail: saraimbriglia@stedmunds.net

Anthony W. Sherer, Head. BA, Vassar College, MFA, Yale Univ, MA, Columbia Univ. **Sara Imbriglia, Adm.**

Pre-Prep. Feat—Fr Lat Span Computers Bible Theol Studio_Art Music Study_Skills. **Supp**—Rev Tut.

Adm: 34/yr. Appl due: Rolling. **Tests** CTP_4.

Enr 245. B 153. G 92. Elem 245. Wh 82%. Hisp 1%. Blk 10%. Asian 3%. Other 4%. Avg class size: 15. Uniform. **Fac 37.** M 9/2. F 21/5. Wh 95%. Blk 5%. Adv deg: 56%.

Grad '04—24. Prep—13. (Ellis, Western Reserve, Shady Side, Sewickley). Alum 846.

Tui '04-'05: Day $8450-13,500. Aid: Merit 1 ($2000). Need 57 ($346,441).

Summer: Gr PS-3. Rec. Tui Day $190/wk. 5 wks.

Endow $3,262,000. Plant val $8,007,000. Bldgs 5. Class rms 29. Lib 10,000 vols. Sci labs 2. Comp labs 4. Auds 1. Art studios 2. Music studios 2. Gyms 1. Fields 2.
Est 1947. Nonprofit. Episcopal. Tri (Sept-June). **Assoc** MSA.

Founded as Ascension Academy, a boys' Episcopal school, St. Edmund's became coeducational in 1983 and now serves a multidenominational student body. The school's present name was adopted in 1952 and, after moving several times in its early years, St. Edmund's assumed its current location in the city's Squirrel Hill section in 1955.

The school's traditional pre-preparatory curriculum stresses learning skills development and process writing. French and Spanish begin in grade 5, while compulsory Latin courses start in grade 7. Computer instruction commences in prekindergarten.

Sports include interscholastic and intramural soccer, field hockey, basketball and lacrosse. Extracurricular activities offer participation in school publications, musical and dramatic productions, and various interest clubs.

SHADY SIDE ACADEMY
5-Day Bdg — Coed Gr 9-12; Day — Coed K-12

Pittsburgh, PA 15238. 423 Fox Chapel Rd. Tel: 412-968-3000. Fax: 412-968-3213.
www.shadysideacademy.org   E-mail: kmihm@shadysideacademy.org
Thomas N. Southard, Pres. BA, Univ of South Carolina, MA, Univ of South Florida. **Katherine H. Mihm, Adm.**
  Col Prep. AP—Fr Ger Lat Span Comp_Sci. Feat—Poetry Chin Stats Environ_Sci Programming Web_Design Econ Ethics Philos Architect Art_Hist Photog Studio_Art Theater Music Music_Theory. Supp—Dev_Read Rev Tut.
  Adm (Bdg Gr 9-11; Day K-11): 155/yr. Bdg 7. Day 148. Appl due: Feb. Accepted: 63%. Yield: 60%. **Tests** ISEE SSAT TOEFL.
  Enr 946. B 32/506. G 8/400. Elem 443. Sec 503. Avg class size: 13. **Fac** 114. M 49/2. F 53/10. Wh 94%. Hisp 1%. Blk 4%. Asian 1%. Adv deg: 63%. In dorms 4.
  Grad '04—121. Col—121. (Carnegie Mellon 4, Kenyon 4, U of PA 4, Columbia 3, Emory 3, Geo Wash 3). Avg SAT: 1275. Alum 5000.
  Tui '04-'05: 5-Day Bdg $27,100 (+$400-600). **Day** $14,000-18,850 (+$400-600). **Aid:** Merit 27 ($80,170). Need 136 ($1,723,302).
  Summer: Acad Enrich Rev Rem Rec. Tui Day $730-1325. 3-6 wks.
  Endow $40,500,000. Plant val $75,000,000. Bldgs 26. Dorms 2. Dorm rms 45. Class rms 80. 3 Libs 47,000 vols. Sci labs 4. Lang labs 1. Comp labs 4. Auds 3. Art studios 3. Music studios 4. Arts ctrs 1. Gyms 4. Fields 8. Courts 10. Pools 1. Rinks 1.
  Est 1883. Nonprofit. Tri (Sept-June). **Assoc** CLS MSA.

Founded in Pittsburgh's East End by W. R. Crabbe as a college preparatory school for boys, Shady Side Academy now occupies three campuses and enrolls both boys and girls. The senior school moved from the Shadyside area of Pittsburgh to suburban Fox Chapel (on Fox Chapel Road) in 1922. At that time, a gift of land from the estate of trustee Wallace H. Rowe enabled Shady Side to establish a combination country day and boarding school on a 125-acre campus; five-day boarding still remains an option. The middle school (500 Squaw Run Rd. E) was established in 1958 with the acquisition of a 60-acre campus, in the same Fox Chapel area as the senior school. The junior school (400 S. Braddock Ave., 15221) is located on a seven-acre campus in the East End that served as the site of the Arnold School, which merged with the academy in 1940.

Enrolling students from western Pennsylvania, the school conducts a rigorous college preparatory curriculum that is rooted in the liberal arts tradition. The structured, integrated junior school curriculum (grades K-5) addresses broad themes designed to help boys and girls make connections between subjects as they acquire basic skills and learn new concepts. At the middle school level (grades 6-8), the curriculum becomes more diverse and faculty prepare students for high school academics. Critical and creative thinking are points of emphasis in the senior school program (grades 9-12), through which pupils gain a deeper understanding of the humanities, math and science, and the arts.

Extracurricular activities include interest clubs, a strong community service program, and various visual and performing arts options. All students are encouraged to participate in athletics. Middle and senior school students compete interscholastically in football, soccer, cross-country, basketball, wrestling, swimming, squash, field hockey, ice hockey, tennis, softball, baseball and lacrosse. The senior school program also includes golf.

WINCHESTER THURSTON SCHOOL
Day — Coed Gr PS-12

Pittsburgh, PA 15213. 555 Morewood Ave. Tel: 412-578-7500. **Fax:** 412-578-7504. www.winchesterthurston.org   **E-mail:** admissions@winchesterthurston.org
Gary J. Niels, Head. MEd, Columbia Univ. **Rebecca King, Adm.**

Col Prep. AP—Eng Fr Lat Span Calc Stats Comp_Sci Bio Chem Physics Eur_Hist US_Hist Art_Hist. **Feat**—Anat Women's_Hist Comparative_Govt Architect Fine_Arts Visual_Arts Music Dance Journ Public_Speak. **Supp**—ESL Tut.

Adm (Gr PS-11): 110/yr. Appl due: Dec. Accepted: 65%. Yield: 60%. **Tests** ISEE SSAT.

Enr 589. B 315. G 274. Elem 413. Sec 176. Wh 81%. Hisp 1%. Blk 9%. Asian 9%. Avg class size: 15. **Fac 86.** M 18/1. F 54/13. Wh 94%. Hisp 2%. Blk 4%. Adv deg: 50%.

Grad '04—38. Col—38. (U of Pittsburgh 4, Boston U 3, U of MD-Col Park 2, Carnegie Mellon 1, Oberlin 1, U of CO-Boulder 1). Avg SAT: 1210. Alum 2100.

Tui '04-'05: Day $10,950-17,950 (+$525-1650). **Aid:** Need 131 ($1,250,000).

Summer: Gr PS-8. Enrich Rec. 1-3 wks.

Endow $6,700,000. Plant val $16,900,000. Bldgs 4. Class rms 51. 3 Libs 25,000 vols. Sci labs 4. Comp labs 3. Auds 1. Art studios 3. Music studios 4. Dance studios 1. Drama studios 1. Gyms 2. Fields 1.

Est 1887. Nonprofit. Tri (Sept-June). **Assoc** MSA.

Winchester Thurston School derives from schools begun by Alice Thurston and Elizabeth and Mary Mitchell. The college preparatory curriculum emphasizes experiential learning and includes process writing, a hands-on science program, a literature-based reading and English program, applied and conceptual mathematics, and global awareness. Advanced Placement courses are offered, as is a bridge and tutoring program that provides one-on-one tutoring for students with learning differences. A wide selection of extracurricular activities and a large array of visual and performing arts classes complement the academic program.

Located in the Oakland section of Pittsburgh, the school's main campus, serving students in kindergarten readiness through grade 12, utilizes the many cultural, technological and educational resources of the area. In 1988, the school established a second campus for children in grades K-5 in the North Hills (4225 Middle Rd., Allison Park 15101). Both campuses utilize the same curriculum and faculty, and students have access to the opportunities and resources of each location. An extended-day program is available each day before and after school.

POTTSTOWN, PA. (32 mi. WNW of Philadelphia, PA; 36 mi. N of Wilmington, DE) Urban. Pop: 21,859. Alt: 250 ft.

THE HILL SCHOOL
Bdg and Day — Coed Gr 9-PG

Pottstown, PA 19464. 717 E High St. Tel: 610-326-1000. Fax: 610-705-1753.
www.thehill.org   E-mail: admission@thehill.org

David R. Dougherty, Head. BA, Washington and Lee Univ, MA, Georgetown Univ, MLitt, Middlebury College. Sally Keidel, Adm.

    Col Prep. AP—Eng Fr Ger Lat Span Calc Stats Comp_Sci Bio Chem Physics Eur_Hist US_Hist Econ Psych Art_Hist Studio_Art. **Feat**—Humanities Chin Greek Amer_Stud Archaeol Music. **Supp**—Rev Tut.

    Adm (Bdg Gr 9-PG; Day 9-11): 177/yr. Bdg 124. Day 53. Appl due: Feb. Accepted: 50%. Yield: 51%. **Tests** ISEE SSAT.

    Enr 498. B 238/60. G 145/55. Sec 478. PG 20. Avg class size: 13. **Fac 83.** M 46/11. F 22/4. Adv deg: 60%. In dorms 30.

    Grad '04—137. **Col**—133. (U of DE 7, PA St 6, U of the South 4, U of PA 3, U of Richmond 3, US Naval Acad 3). Avg SAT: 1250. Avg ACT: 26. Alum 8135.

    Tui '04-'05: Bdg $32,500 (+$1000-2800). **Day $21,900** (+$1000-2800). **Aid:** Need 188 ($3,256,300).

    Endow $100,000,000. Plant val $130,800,000. Bldgs 60. Dorms 12. Dorm rms 190. Class rms 66. Libs 1. Sci labs 9. Lang labs 1. Comp labs 1. Auds 1. Theaters 2. Art studios 1. Music studios 8. Gyms 3. Fields 13. Courts 23. Pools 1. Rinks 1. Golf crses 1. Trap & skeet ranges 1. Greenhouses 1.

    Est 1851. Nonprofit. Tri (Sept-May). **Assoc** CLS MSA.

Rev. Matthew Meigs, a Presbyterian minister, founded The Hill as a "family boarding school." In 1920, ownership of the school was transferred from the Meigs family to Hill alumni. After more than a century of educating only boys, the school became coeducational in the fall of 1998.

The curriculum includes both required and elective courses in English, mathematics, history, modern and classical languages, science, the arts and theology. The humanities program includes special courses, a concert series, art exhibits and other opportunities. Honors and Advanced Placement courses are available, and qualified seniors may pursue independent study under the guidance of a faculty member. The school provides extensive computer instruction for all students.

Interscholastic sports include field hockey, football, soccer, ice hockey, basketball, golf, tennis, lacrosse, swimming, cross-country, water polo, track, baseball, softball, squash and wrestling. All students must participate in athletics at some level. Extracurricular activities include instrumental and vocal music, journalistic organizations, dramatics, debate, honor council and student government.

See Also Page 1165

THE WYNDCROFT SCHOOL
Day — Coed Gr PS-8

Pottstown, PA 19464. 1395 Wilson St. Tel: 610-326-0544. Fax: 610-326-9931.
   www.wyndcroft.org   E-mail: mschmidt@wyndcroft.org
Kathleen E. Wunner, Head. PhD, Univ of Pennsylvania. **Maureen K. Schmidt, Adm.**
   Pre-Prep. **Feat**—Fr Lat Computers Fine_Arts Music.
   Adm: 40/yr. Accepted: 68%. **Tests** IQ.
   Enr 252. B 121. G 131. Elem 252. Wh 95%. Hisp 1%. Blk 2%. Asian 2%. Avg class size: 12. **Fac 30.** M 2. F 27/1. Wh 100%. Adv deg: 30%.
   Grad '04—11. Prep—9. (Hill Sch-PA, Shipley, St Andrew's Episcopal-MD). Alum 500.
   Tui '03-'04: Day $10,000-11,500 (+$135). **Aid:** Need 25 ($135,725).
   Plant val $3,200,000. Bldgs 1. Sci labs 1. Comp labs 1. Gyms 1.
   Est 1918. Nonprofit. Quar (Sept-June).

The school was founded on the Hill School campus by the wives of Hill School faculty who wanted to provide a sound elementary education for their young children. Although Wyndcroft has been independent since 1920, it continues to maintain a close relationship with Hill. The academic program provides a sound foundation in English, math, science, social studies and the arts. French instruction begins in the early childhood program and continues through grade 8, while Latin is introduced in grade 4.

Team sports (in grades 6-8) include field hockey, soccer, basketball and lacrosse. Music, art groups and field trips are among the extracurricular activities.

SALTSBURG, PA. (28 mi. E of Pittsburgh, PA) Rural. Pop: 955. Alt: 852 ft.

KISKI SCHOOL
Bdg and Day — Boys Gr 9-PG

Saltsburg, PA 15681. 1888 Brett Ln. Tel: 724-639-3586. Fax: 724-639-8596.
   www.kiski.org   E-mail: admissions@kiski.org
Christopher A. Brueningsen, Head. BS, Muhlenberg College, MEd, Indiana Univ of Pennsylvania. **Lawrence J. Jensen, Adm.**
   Col Prep. AP—Eng Calc Stats Bio Chem Eur_Hist US_Hist Psych. **Feat**—Fr Span Comp_Sci Econ Studio_Art Theater Music Music_Theory. **Supp**—ESL Rev.
   Adm (Bdg Gr 9-PG; Day 9-11): 110/yr. Bdg 95. Day 15. Appl due: Rolling. Accepted: 75%. Yield: 80%. **Tests** ISEE SSAT TOEFL.
   Enr 215. B 200/15. Sec 205. PG 10. Wh 85%. Hisp 3%. Blk 4%. Asian 8%. Avg class size: 9. Uniform. **Fac 38.** Wh 91%. Hisp 3%. Blk 3%. Asian 3%. Adv deg: 57%. In dorms 20.
   Grad '04—53. Col—53. (US Naval Acad 7, Carnegie Mellon 4, U of Pittsburgh 4, Emory 3, PA St 3, Johns Hopkins 2). Avg SAT: 1140. Avg ACT: 21. Alum 3850.
   Tui '05-'06: Bdg $29,500 (+$750). **Day $15,500** (+$500). **Aid:** Merit 10 ($10,000). Need 60 ($1,090,000).
   Summer: Gr 5-8. Enrich Rec. Tui Bdg $2400. Tui Day $2000. 4 wks.
   Endow $25,000,000. Plant val $50,000,000. Bldgs 44. Dorms 9. Dorm rms 138. Class rms 28. Lib 23,000 vols. Labs 3. Music studios 1. Gyms 3. Fields 9. Courts 7. Pools 2. Stadiums 2. Golf crses 1. Skiing facilities yes. Radio stations 1.

Est 1888. Nonprofit. Tri (Sept-May).

Founded by Dr. Andrew W. Wilson, director until 1933, Kiski prepares its students for college with a rigorous academic program. The curriculum consists of five main subject areas—English, history, math, science and foreign languages—and is supplemented by requirements in art and music and a senior research paper. Supervised study periods for underclassmen are held in dorm rooms each evening. Students have the opportunity to receive individual instruction during evening hours with resident faculty members. Honors and Advanced Placement courses are offered in the main subject areas. Technology is an important aspect of the curriculum: Every boy utilizes a laptop computer in class.

Kiski's diversified athletic program includes various individual and team-based interscholastic sports. Each student must participate in three sports during the year; competition is offered in baseball, basketball, football, track and field, golf, swimming, soccer, cross-country, tennis, wrestling, lacrosse and hockey. An extensive extracurricular activities program features participation in a national forensic competition, a political and literary forum, publications, interest clubs and off-campus cultural events.
See Also Pages 1336-7

SEWICKLEY, PA. (13 mi. WNW of Pittsburgh, PA) Suburban. Pop: 3902. Alt: 732 ft.

SEWICKLEY ACADEMY
Day — Coed Gr PS-12

Sewickley, PA 15143. 315 Academy Ave. Tel: 412-741-2230. Fax: 412-741-1411.
  www.sewickley.org   E-mail: dgoodman@sewickley.org
Kolia O'Connor, Head. BA, Boston Univ, MA, Columbia Univ, MA, Univ of Avignon (France).
  Douglas J. Goodman, Adm.
  Col Prep. AP—Fr Ger Span Calc Stats Comp_Sci Bio Chem Physics Eur_Hist US_Hist Studio_Art. **Feat**—Ital Drama Music.
  Adm (Gr PS-11): 131/yr. Appl due: Feb. Accepted: 39%. **Tests** CTP_4 ISEE.
  Enr 796. B 423. G 373. Elem 497. Sec 299. Wh 83%. Hisp 1%. Blk 8%. Asian 8%. Avg class size: 15. **Fac** 91. M 26/5. F 56/4. Wh 93%. Blk 3%. Asian 2%. Other 2%. Adv deg: 65%.
  Grad '04—79. **Col**—79. (Carnegie Mellon 4, Northwestern 3, U of PA 3, PA St 3, Elon 3, Allegheny 3). Avg SAT: 1298. Alum 2900.
  Tui '04-'05: Day $10,525-16,750 (+$300). **Aid:** Need ($911,150).
  Summer: Acad Enrich Rev Rem Rec. Sports. Tui Day $100-350. 1-4 wks.
  Endow $18,800,000. Plant val $30,000,000. Bldgs 11. Class rms 84. 2 Libs 29,400 vols. Sci labs 7. Lang labs 1. Comp labs 3. Auds 1. Theaters 1. Art studios 4. Music studios 3. Dance studios 1. Gyms 2. Fields 4. Courts 6.
  Est 1838. Nonprofit. Sem (Sept-June). **Assoc** CLS.

The academy began as a classical elementary school for boys, then became coeducational 30 years later. It has occupied the present plant since 1929. Enrollment steadily increased in the years that followed, and a secondary school was added in 1963. The campus has since undergone further building and renovation, resulting in extensive physical improvements to each school division.

The comprehensive curriculum offers a full college prep program and an extensive use of technology across the disciplines. Extracurricular activities include a newspaper, a literary magazine, performing arts, forensics, cultural clubs, a computer club, quiz teams, foreign student exchanges, exchange programs with schools in Australia, Spain, France, Germany and China, and a full array of interscholastic sports.

TYRONE, PA. (93 mi. E of Pittsburgh, PA) Suburban. Pop: 5528. Alt: 868 ft.

GRIER SCHOOL
Bdg — Girls Gr 7-PG

Tyrone, PA 16686. Rte 453, PO Box 308. Tel: 814-684-3000. Fax: 814-684-2177.
www.grier.org   E-mail: admissions@grier.org
Andrea Hollnagel, Head. MS, Mankato State Univ. **Andrew M. Wilson, Adm.**
　Col Prep. Gen Acad. AP—Calc Bio Art_Hist Studio_Art. **Feat**—Fr Span Fine_Arts Photog Music Dance. **Supp**—Dev_Read ESL LD Makeup Tut.
　Adm: 100/yr. Accepted: 80%. **Tests** IQ SSAT.
　Enr 184. G 184. Elem 30. Sec 151. PG 3. Wh 57%. Hisp 14%. Blk 5%. Asian 24%. Avg class size: 9. **Fac 32.** M 10. F 20/2. Wh 95%. Asian 5%. Adv deg: 25%.
　Grad '04—41. Col—41. (S AR, Drexel, Whittier, John Carroll, Lynn, Sch of the Art Inst of Chicago). Avg SAT: 1050. Alum 1330.
　Tui '05-'06: Bdg $33,900 (+$2500). **Aid:** Need 64 ($697,870). Work prgm 22 ($62,660).
　Summer: Acad Rec. Tui Bdg $950/wk. 6 wks.
　Endow $2,000,000. Plant val $6,250,000. Bldgs 15. Dorms 4. Dorm rms 81. Class rms 16. Lib 10,000 vols. Lang labs 1. Comp labs 2. Comp ctrs 1. Art studios 3. Music studios 2. Dance studios 1. Arts ctrs 1. Gyms 1. Fields 2. Tennis courts 5. Pools 2. Riding rings 3. Stables 1.
　Est 1853. Nonprofit. Sem (Sept-June). **Assoc** MSA.

Incorporated in 1853 by a group of local citizens, and in 1857 purchased by Dr. Lemuel G. Grier, the school has since been under the guidance of four generations of the Grier family. Alvin R. Grier succeeded his father in 1887. In 1932, the school came into the capable hands of his son, Thomas C. Grier, who served for 33 years. Mrs. Grier, cohead with her husband for 26 years, carried on his administration until 1969, when their son Douglas became headmaster. Raymond A. Kelly was appointed headmaster when Douglas Grier became director in 1981, Angelica A. Wutz was named head in 1990, and Mrs. Hollnagel assumed the post in 1997.

The school conducts a two-track academic curriculum. The upper track offers honors courses. The second track is designed for students who require extra structure and intensive learning skills development. Crossover is permitted between the tracks, according to ability. Grier also provides a comprehensive English as a Second Language program for international students.

Students may compete in basketball, soccer, softball, tennis and riding. The creative arts program, which includes modern dance, jazz and ballet, complements the academic curriculum. While retaining a mellow charm, all older buildings have been modernized over the years. **See Also Pages 1302-3**

WAYNE, PA. (14 mi. W of Philadelphia, PA) Suburban. Pop: 39,944. Alt: 404 ft.

VALLEY FORGE MILITARY ACADEMY
Bdg — Boys Gr 7-PG

Wayne, PA 19087. 1001 Eagle Rd. Tel: 610-989-1300. Fax: 610-688-1545.
www.vfmac.edu   E-mail: admissions@vfmac.edu

Rear Adm. Peter A. C. Long, USN (Ret), Pres. BS, US Naval Academy, PhD, Nova Southeastern Univ. **Lt. Col. Kelly M. DeShane, Adm.**

Col Prep. Milit. Feat—Lib_Skills Lat JROTC Aviation_Tech. Supp—Dev_Read ESL Rem_Read Tut.

Adm: 279/yr. Appl due: Rolling. Accepted: 57%. **Tests** CEEB IQ SSAT.

Enr 524. B 524. Elem 54. Sec 453. PG 17. Wh 66%. Hisp 14%. Blk 10%. Asian 10%. Avg class size: 13. Uniform. **Fac 62.** M 44/10. F 7/1. Adv deg: 51%.

Grad '04—157. **Col**—153. (Valley Forge Milit, US Milit Acad, Lynn, PA St, Purdue, Hofstra). Alum 9200.

Tui '04-'05: Bdg $26,600 (+$725). **Aid:** Merit 102 ($250,000). Need 76 ($105,000). Work prgm 54 ($20,000).

Summer: Acad Enrich Rec. Tui Bdg $3100-3200. 4 wks. ESL. Tui Bdg $3300. 5 wks. Band. Tui Bdg $2900. Tui Day $1900. 4 wks.

Endow $9,000,000. Plant val $50,000,000. Bldgs 84. Dorms 6. Dorm rms 404. Class rms 65. Lib 70,000 vols. Labs 8. Music studios 1. Gyms 2. Fields 9. Courts 5. Pools 2. Riding rings 1. Stables 1. Rifle ranges 1.

Est 1928. Nonprofit. Sem (Sept-May). **Assoc** MSA.

Founded by Lt. Gen. Milton G. Baker, this well-known academy has an enrollment recruited from many states and foreign countries. The academy grew from a modest beginning to a campus of 84 buildings occupying over 119 acres. Students are prepared not only for its own college but also for other colleges throughout the country. A strong emphasis on leadership and character development is evident at all grade levels.

Many activities and special programs complement academic work. Options include the Boy Scouts, JROTC drill and raider challenge teams, ski club and other outdoor activity clubs, marksmanship, community service, flight training, instrumental and vocal music, and equitation. The sports program consists of football, baseball, basketball, soccer, lacrosse, wrestling, cross-country, track, swimming, polo, tennis, golf, riflery and intramurals.

WESTTOWN, PA. (14 mi. N of Wilmington, DE; 23 mi. WSW of Philadelphia, PA) Suburban. Pop: 9937. Alt: 265 ft.

WESTTOWN SCHOOL
Bdg — Coed Gr 9-12; Day — Coed PS-10

Westtown, PA 19395. Westtown Rd, PO Box 1799. Tel: 610-399-7900. Fax: 610-399-7909.
www.westtown.edu   E-mail: admissions@westtown.edu

John W. Baird, Head. AB, Princeton Univ, MA, Providence College. **Kate Holz, Adm.**
- **Col Prep. AP**—Fr Ger Lat Span Calc Stats Bio Chem Physics US_Hist. **Feat**—Amer_Indian_Lit Ecol Environ_Sci Astrophysics Vietnam_War Lat-Amer_Hist Relig World_Relig Quakerism Art_Hist Photog Sculpt Acting Theater Directing Band Music_Theory Orchestra Woodworking. **Supp**—Dev_Read ESL Rem_Math Rem_Read Tut.
- **Adm:** 153/yr. Bdg 53. Day 100. Accepted: 54%. Yield: 62%. **Tests** ISEE SSAT TOEFL.
- **Enr 782.** B 151/230. G 149/252. Elem 378. Sec 404. Wh 82%. Hisp 4%. Blk 8%. Asian 3%. Other 3%. Avg class size: 15. **Fac 114.** M 45/7. F 54/8. Wh 91%. Hisp 2%. Blk 6%. Asian 1%. Adv deg: 40%. In dorms 27.
- **Grad '04—95. Col—95.** (Sarah Lawrence 4, Guilford 4, Brown 3, Temple 3, U of MI 2, Bates 2). Alum 7500.
- **Tui '04-'05: Bdg** $30,730 (+$500). **Day** $13,125-18,950 (+$500). **Aid:** Need 186 ($2,877,360).
- Endow $52,000,000. Plant val $60,000,000. Bldgs 12. Dorms 4. Dorm rms 159. Class rms 61. 2 Libs 45,700 vols. Sci labs 6. Comp labs 5. Dark rms 1. Observatories 1. Theaters 1. Art studios 4. Music studios 9. Dance studios 1. Art galleries 1. Gyms 4. Fields 9. Tennis courts 14. Field houses 1. Pools 1. Weight rms 1. Greenhouses 1. Lakes 1.
- **Est 1799.** Nonprofit. Religious Society of Friends. Tri (Sept-June). **Assoc** MSA.

Philadelphia Quakers established Westtown as a coeducational boarding school emphasizing high academic standards and such Quaker values as peace, integrity, equality, personal responsibility and service. A diverse student body comprises pupils from many states and foreign countries.

Westtown's college preparatory curriculum combines strong academics with the flexibility to address individual talents and interests. Course work during grades 9 and 10 revolves around a core curriculum that provides a firm liberal arts foundation for future study. The program in grades 11 and 12 allows students to choose electives and pursue areas of interest in greater depth, and more than a dozen advanced courses are available. All seniors complete an independent project during the first two weeks of March. Boarding is an important aspect of school life: Roughly half of all freshmen and sophomores and all juniors and seniors live on campus.

The school's 620-acre campus, which includes woods, meadows, a lake, an arboretum and a working farm, provides many opportunities for the study of nature and the environment. Drama classes frequently attend theatrical productions, while art classes visit museums and galleries on a regular basis. In addition, Westtown schedules field trips to Philadelphia; Wilmington, DE; Washington, DC; and New York City as a means of enriching various subjects.

Sports for girls include varsity and intramural field hockey, soccer, cross-country, volleyball, swimming, diving, basketball, lacrosse, track and field, tennis, dance, softball and golf. Sports for boys are soccer, cross-country, basketball, wrestling, swimming, diving, baseball, track and field, lacrosse, tennis, dance and golf. Among noncompetitive activities are aerobics, weight training, swimming, jogging, indoor soccer and yoga.

WILKES-BARRE, PA. (94 mi. NNW of Philadelphia, PA) Urban. Pop: 43,123. Alt: 642 ft. Area also includes Kingston.

WYOMING SEMINARY
Bdg — Coed Gr 9-PG; Day — Coed PS-12

Kingston, PA 18704. 201 N Sprague Ave. Tel: 570-270-2160. Fax: 570-270-2191.
www.wyomingseminary.org E-mail: admission@wyomingseminary.org
H. Jeremy Packard, Pres. BA, Williams College, MA, Columbia Univ. **Randolph I. Granger, Adm.**
- **Col Prep. AP**—Eng Fr Lat Span Calc Stats Comp_Sci Bio Chem Physics Eur_Hist US_Hist Econ Psych US_Govt & Pol Art_Hist Studio_Art Music_Theory. **Feat**—Russ Marine_Biol/Sci Forensic_Sci Fine_Arts Drama Chorus Dance Speech. **Supp**—ESL Rev Tut.
- **Adm:** 140/yr. Bdg 45. Day 95. Appl due: Rolling. Accepted: 62%. Yield: 63%. **Tests** CEEB ISEE SSAT TOEFL.
- **Enr 813.** Elem 341. Sec 457. PG 15. Wh 86%. Hisp 2%. Blk 4%. Am Ind 1%. Asian 5%. Other 2%. Avg class size: 13. **Fac 104.** M 33/11. F 54/6. Wh 95%. Blk 3%. Asian 2%. Adv deg: 68%. In dorms 22.
- **Grad '04—120. Col—118.** (Syracuse 6, US Naval Acad 4, Lafayette 3, Cornell 3, Denison 2, Geo Wash 2). Alum 8050.
- **Tui '04-'05: Bdg $32,100** (+$450). **Day $9450-16,450** (+$650-1050). **Aid:** Merit 26 ($106,175). Need 193 ($2,229,025).
- **Summer:** Acad Enrich Rev Rec. Performing Arts. ESL. Tui Bdg $3200-7000. Tui Day $550-1650. 3-9 wks.
- Endow $42,100,000. Plant val $15,500,000. Bldgs 11. Dorms 4. Dorm rms 125. Class rms 56. Lib 19,750 vols. Sci labs 5. Comp labs 2. Music labs 1. Auds 1. Art studios 4. Music studios 4. Dance studios 1. Gyms 2. Fields 5. Courts 4. Pools 1.
- **Est 1844.** Nonprofit. Methodist. Tri (Aug-May). **Assoc** CLS MSA.

Wyoming Seminary's College Preparatory School offers a varied program that readies graduates for competitive colleges. There is a large choice of electives (including Advanced Placement courses) in history, the fine arts, mathematics, computer, science and English. College planning workshops, enrichment opportunities, sports camps, ESL programs and an elite performing arts institute are among the summer offerings.

Extracurricular activities include publications, music, studio art, dance, science research projects, photography, drama, intramural sports, community service and interest clubs. Interscholastic competition for boys is available in football, golf, ice hockey, basketball, baseball, wrestling, swimming, lacrosse, cross-country, tennis and soccer, and for girls in field hockey, basketball, tennis, soccer, softball, cross-country, swimming, ice hockey and lacrosse.

The Wyoming Seminary Lower School is separately located three miles away at 1560 Wyoming Ave., Forty Fort 18704. Academics include accelerated courses, and computer science, art, music, health and physical education are integral parts of the program. Instruction in French and Spanish begins in grade 3, while Latin commences in grade 7.

WYNNEWOOD, PA. (7 mi. W of Philadelphia, PA) Suburban. Pop: 7700. Alt: 316 ft.

FRIENDS' CENTRAL SCHOOL
Day — Coed Gr PS-12

Wynnewood, PA 19096. 1101 City Ave. Tel: 610-649-7440. Fax: 610-649-5669.
www.friendscentral.org

David M. Felsen, Head. BA, Haverford College, MA, Univ of Pennsylvania. **Barbara Behar, Adm.**

- **Col Prep. AP**—Fr Lat Span Calc Stats Comp_Sci Bio Chem Physics. **Feat**—Intl_Relations Psych Philos Relig Architect Photog Studio_Art Drama Music Music_Hist Music_Theory Woodworking. **Supp**—Dev_Read ESL Rem_Read.
- **Adm (Gr PS-11):** 139/yr. Appl due: Jan. Accepted: 48%. Yield: 58%. **Tests** IQ ISEE SSAT.
- **Enr 992.** B 510. G 482. Elem 605. Sec 387. Wh 78%. Hisp 2%. Blk 15%. Asian 4%. Other 1%. Avg class size: 16. **Fac 119.** M 44/1. F 64/10. Wh 89%. Hisp 2%. Blk 8%. Asian 1%. Adv deg: 59%.
- **Grad '04—91. Col—91.** (U of PA 9, Franklin & Marshall 4, Princeton 4, Brown 3, Haverford 3, Yale 3). Avg SAT: 1298. Alum 3300.
- **Tui '04-'05: Day $11,350-18,995** (+$400). **Aid:** Need 193 ($2,309,809).
- **Summer:** Acad Enrich. Tui Day $325-600. 6 wks.
- Endow $10,600,000. Plant val $50,058,000. Bldgs 16. Class rms 86. 2 Libs 30,000 vols. Sci labs 7. Comp labs 7. Auds 2. Art studios 7. Music studios 3. Dance studios 1. Gyms 4. Fields 9. Courts 9. Pools 2.
- **Est 1845.** Nonprofit. Religious Society of Friends. Tri (Sept-June). **Assoc** CLS.

Friends' Central has conducted a comprehensive day program since 1925, when this Quaker school moved to its present middle and upper school site of 23 acres on the edge of the city. The lower school (grades pre-K-4) operates at an 18-acre second campus at 228 Old Gulph Rd.

Over the years, Friends' Central has enjoyed the direction of a number of notable educators. The integrated course of study begins with an individualized curriculum in the lower school that precedes an increasingly rigorous college preparatory program as students progress through the upper grades. Course work includes excellent opportunities in the arts and a number of departmental electives. Seniors also have the option of independent study during the final spring term.

Boys participate in soccer, tennis, wrestling, cross-country, basketball, baseball and track. Girls' sports include field hockey, soccer, softball, tennis, basketball, cross-country and lacrosse. Dramatics, community service projects, dance, orchestra, chorus, international relations club and publications are some of the other school activities.

YORK, PA. (66 mi. WNW of Wilmington, DE; 85 mi. W of Philadelphia, PA) Urban. Pop: 40,862. Alt: 370 ft.

YORK COUNTRY DAY SCHOOL
Day — Coed Gr PS-12

York, PA 17403. 1071 Regents' Glen Blvd. Tel: 717-843-9805. Fax: 717-848-4726.
www.ycds.org   E-mail: wdiskin@ycds.org
Robert W. Shanner, Head. William D. Diskin, Adm.

   Col Prep. **AP**—Eng Fr Span Calc Bio Chem US_Hist World_Hist Studio_Art. **Feat**—Lat Computers. **Supp**—Dev_Read Rev Tut.

   Adm: 62/yr. **Tests** IQ ISEE Stanford.

   Enr 207. Wh 91%. Hisp 3%. Blk 4%. Asian 2%. Avg class size: 13. **Fac 50.** Adv deg: 32%.

   Grad '04—22. Col—22. (Lehigh, Dickinson, Franklin & Marshall, Tufts, Elizabethtown, Middlebury). Avg SAT: 1260. Alum 725.

   Tui '04-'05: Day $1810-11,335 (+$500).

   Summer: Acad Enrich Rec. Tui Day $150/wk. 8 wks.

   Endow $135,000. Plant val $2,750,000. Bldgs 1. Class rms 25. Lib 5000 vols. Sci labs 2. Art studios 1. Music studios 1. Gyms 1. Fields 4. Courts 1.

   Est 1953. Inc. Spons: York College of Pennsylvania. Sem (Sept-June). **Assoc** MSA.

Founded by a group of parents seeking a demanding academic program for the children of York County, the school prospered and grew under the leadership of its first headmaster, J. Kenneth Snyder, and his wife, Elizabeth. Beginning in a converted home in York City, Mr. Snyder built a new school in 1956 on a 17-acre plot in the suburbs southwest of York. In 1975, the school became affiliated with York College of Pennsylvania, and the academic program was enriched by the inclusion of courses at the college for qualified students.

The liberal arts curriculum balances a combination of requirements and electives. Proficiency in the use of a computer is required, as are two semesters in the arts. Students in grade 9 are required to take a semester-long course in public speaking. Elective courses are available in each department. Scheduled activity periods each week allow students to pursue extracurricular interests, and York Country Day fields a selection of interscholastic teams.

Southern States

ALABAMA

ANNISTON, AL. (58 mi. E of Birmingham, AL; 80 mi. W of Atlanta, GA) Suburban. Pop: 24,276. Alt: 710 ft.

THE DONOHO SCHOOL
Day — Coed Gr PS-12

Anniston, AL 36207. 2501 Henry Rd. Tel: 256-237-5477. Fax: 256-237-6474.
www.donohoschool.com   E-mail: donoho@donohoschool.com
Janice D. Hurd, Pres. EdS, Jacksonville State Univ. **Laura Phillips, Adm.**
- **Col Prep. AP**—Eng Fr Span Calc US_Hist. **Feat**—Lat Environ_Sci Govt Psych Sociol Fine_Arts Studio_Art Drama Band Music Speech.
- **Adm:** 56/yr. Appl due: Rolling.
- **Enr 358.** B 199. G 159. Elem 247. Sec 111. Wh 90%. Hisp 1%. Blk 4%. Asian 5%. Avg class size: 15. **Fac 38.** M 6/2. F 26/4. Wh 95%. Hisp 4%. Blk 1%. Adv deg: 65%.
- **Grad '04—27. Col—27.** (U of AL-Tuscaloosa, Auburn, U of AL-Birmingham, U of GA, Birmingham-Southern). Avg SAT: 1199. Avg ACT: 25. Alum 1199.
- **Tui '04-'05: Day $4700-6350** (+$400). **Aid:** Need 22 ($37,787).
- **Summer:** Enrich Rec. 1-6 wks.
- Endow $3,750,000. Plant val $7,050,000. Bldgs 6. Class rms 40. Lib 12,770 vols. Labs 4. Art studios 1. Fields 2. Courts 2.
- **Est 1963.** Nonprofit. Sem (Aug-June). **Assoc** SACS.

Established to satisfy the need for a sound college preparatory program in the Anniston area, the school, since its inception, has maintained its original purpose, with all of its graduates accepted by colleges. The comprehensive academic program is complemented by a wide variety of clubs, publications and athletics. An intersession program provides students with the opportunity to work in various fields of career interest and to pursue independent study projects.

BIRMINGHAM, AL. (138 mi. W of Atlanta, GA) Urban. Pop: 242,820. Alt: 620 ft. Area also includes Indian Springs.

INDIAN SPRINGS SCHOOL
Bdg — Coed Gr 9-PG; Day — Coed 8-12

Indian Springs, AL 35124. 190 Woodward Dr. Tel: 205-988-3350. Fax: 205-988-3797.

www.indiansprings.org   E-mail: admissions@indiansprings.org
Melville G. MacKay III, Dir. AB, Harvard Univ, MAT, Univ of North Carolina-Chapel Hill. **E. T. Brown, Adm.**
- **Col Prep. AP**—Eng Fr Lat Span Calc Stats Bio Chem Physics Eur_Hist US_Hist Econ US_Govt & Pol Music_Theory. **Feat**—Computers Web_Design Russ_Hist Philos World_Relig Film Photog Studio_Art Jazz Pottery Video_Programming Theater_Arts Woodworking. **Supp**—Tut.
- **Adm (Bdg Gr 9-11; Day 8-11):** 77/yr. Bdg 20. Day 57. Appl due: Rolling. Accepted: 61%. Yield: 81%. **Tests** SSAT TOEFL.
- **Enr 268.** B 38/106. G 31/93. Elem 35. Sec 233. Wh 81%. Blk 7%. Asian 12%. Avg class size: 15. **Fac 37.** M 17/3. F 15/2. Wh 88%. Hisp 6%. Other 6%. Adv deg: 70%. In dorms 3.
- **Grad '04—58. Col—58.** (Birmingham-Southern 7, U of AL-Birmingham 5, U of AL-Tuscaloosa 4, Brown 3, Boston U 2, Duke 2). Avg SAT: 1281. Alum 2600.
- **Tui '04-'05: Bdg $23,365** (+$1000). **5-Day Bdg $21,625** (+$1000). **Day $12,925** (+$1000). **Aid:** Merit 10 ($47,850). Need 58 ($544,527). Work prgm 27 ($20,000).
- Endow $19,000,000. Plant val $16,000,000. Bldgs 11. Dorm rms 58. Class rms 12. Lib 17,000 vols. Labs 3. Auds 1. Theaters 1. Art studios 1. Music studios 4. Gyms 1. Fields 3. Courts 4.
- **Est 1952.** Nonprofit. Sem (Aug-May). **Assoc** SACS.

Established through the bequest of Birmingham industrialist Harvey G. Woodward, ISS was conceived as a boys' school. Dr. Louis E. Armstrong, former chairman of the curriculum department of George Peabody College, served as the first director. Today, the school is coeducational, with a socially and culturally diverse student body.

Open only to students of above-average intelligence, the school offers a heavily academic curriculum and prepares its graduates for leading colleges. A favorable student-teacher ratio facilitates learning. Students govern themselves by "town meeting" and elected officials. Photography, publications, computer programming, dramatics and glee club are among the extracurricular offerings. Interscholastic teams include soccer, basketball, tennis, golf, cross-country, girls' volleyball, softball, baseball, scholars bowl and debate.

The spacious, landscaped campus is part of a 350-acre, school-owned tract, partly forested and cultivated, abutting Oak Mountain State Park.

DOTHAN, AL. (93 mi. SE of Montgomery, AL; 183 mi. SSW of Atlanta, GA) Urban. Pop: 57,737. Alt: 326 ft.

HOUSTON ACADEMY
Day — Coed Gr PS-12

Dothan, AL 36303. 901 Buena Vista Dr. Tel: 334-794-4106. Fax: 334-793-4053.
www.houstonacademy.com
John P. O'Connell, Jr., Head. BA, MA, Loyola Univ of Chicago.
- **Col Prep. AP**—Eng Fr Lat Span Calc Comp_Sci Eur_Hist US_Hist. **Feat**—Anat & Physiol Econ Psych Studio_Art Band Chorus Journ. **Supp**—Tut.
- **Adm:** 84/yr. Accepted: 80%. **Tests** IQ Stanford.
- **Enr 632.** B 344. G 288. Elem 348. Sec 284. Wh 95%. Hisp 1%. Blk 1%. Asian 3%. Avg class size: 20. **Fac 54.** M 7. F 47. Wh 98%. Hisp 2%. Adv deg: 48%.

Grad '04—48. Col—48. (Auburn 12, U of AL-Tuscaloosa 10, Birmingham-Southern 5, Furman 2, Notre Dame 1, Wash & Lee 1). Avg SAT: 1230. Avg ACT: 26. Alum 954.
Tui '04-'05: Day $7650-7700 (+$300). **Aid:** Merit 8 ($61,600). Need 90 ($345,290). Endow $80,000. Plant val $2,047,000. Bldgs 5. Class rms 44. Lib 10,500 vols. Labs 3. Art studios 1. Music studios 1. Gyms 2. Fields 2.
Est 1970. Nonprofit. Sem (Aug-May). **Assoc** SACS.

Founded by local civic and business leaders, the school offers a full college preparatory program. The preschool curriculum incorporates a multisensory approach to learning, and social studies and science units are taught. In the intermediate school, children have the opportunity to move above their assigned grade levels in language arts and mathematics. The curricula for the middle and upper schools provide honors and college placement courses in English, foreign language, history, mathematics and science. Students may also choose from a variety of electives, including art, computer, chorus and journalism.

Among extracurricular activities are interest clubs, drama and music. An extensive athletic program includes football, volleyball, basketball, cross-country, baseball, tennis, softball and track.

HUNTSVILLE, AL. (142 mi. WNW of Atlanta, GA) Urban. Pop: 158,216. Alt: 635 ft.

RANDOLPH SCHOOL
Day — Coed Gr K-12

Huntsville, AL 35802. 1005 Drake Ave SE. Tel: 256-881-1701. Fax: 256-881-1784. www.randolphschool.net   E-mail: nhodges@randolphschool.net
M. Edward Krenson, Pres. BA, Univ of the South, MS, Purdue Univ. **Nancy S. Hodges, Adm.**
Col Prep. AP—Eng Fr Span Calc Bio Chem Physics Eur_Hist US_Hist Comp_Govt & Pol US_Govt & Pol. **Feat**—Southern_Lit Stats Anat & Physiol Environ_Sci Marine_Biol/Sci Econ Psych Sociol Foreign_Policy Film Drama Music Journ. **Supp**—ESL Tut.
Adm: 120/yr. Appl due: Mar. Accepted: 76%. **Tests** ISEE Stanford.
Enr 757. B 369. G 388. Wh 86%. Hisp 1%. Blk 1%. Asian 10%. Other 2%. Avg class size: 16. **Fac 80.** M 14. F 65/1. Wh 89%. Hisp 6%. Blk 1%. Asian 4%. Adv deg: 61%.
Grad '04—60. Col—60. (Auburn, Birmingham-Southern, U of AL-Tuscaloosa, Vanderbilt, RI Sch of Design, U of AL-Birmingham). Avg SAT: 1240. Avg ACT: 26. Alum 1613.
Tui '05-'06: Day $8830-10,900 (+$375-625). **Aid:** Merit 5 ($3322). Need 20 ($82,000). Endow $1,924,000. Plant val $8,368,000. Bldgs 7. Class rms 52. 2 Libs 29,000 vols. Sci labs 5. Comp labs 3. Auds 1. Theaters 1. Art studios 3. Music studios 1. Gyms 1. Fields 4. Courts 4.
Est 1959. Nonprofit. Sem (Aug-May). **Assoc** CLS SACS.

Founded by a group of Huntsville parents, Randolph provides a balanced program for college-bound students in the northern part of the state. The curriculum is based on individual guidance, with students grouped according to ability, not chronological age. Art, music, drama and various electives are integrated with the traditional disciplines. Laptop computers and a wireless computer network enhance the curriculum. A one-week interim enables middle and upper school students to pursue learning experiences outside of the regular program. Qualified juniors and seniors choose from a wide array of Advanced Placement courses.

Complementing academics are sports, clubs, art, music, choral groups, publications, drama, speech, forensics, field trips, electives, films and lectures.

MOBILE, AL. (118 mi. ENE of New Orleans, LA) Urban. Pop: 198,915. Alt: 7 ft.

ST. PAUL'S EPISCOPAL SCHOOL
Day — Coed Gr PS-12

Mobile, AL 36608. 161 Dogwood Ln. Tel: 251-342-6700. Fax: 251-342-1844.
  www.stpaulsmobile.net   E-mail: jtaylor@stpaulsmobile.net
Robert H. Rutledge, Head. BS, Millsaps College, MA, Florida State Univ. Julie L. Taylor, Adm.
  Col Prep. AP—Eng Calc Bio Chem Physics Eur_Hist US_Hist Econ US_Govt & Pol Studio_Art. Feat—Fr Lat Span Computers Photog Drama Journ. Supp—Dev_Read LD Tut.
  Adm: 191/yr. Appl due: Rolling. Accepted: 75%. Yield: 72%. Tests CTP_4 IQ.
  Enr 1580. B 832. G 748. Elem 984. Sec 596. Wh 95%. Blk 3%. Asian 2%. Avg class size: 21. Uniform. Fac 160. M 26/12. F 118/4. Wh 99%. Blk 1%. Adv deg: 73%.
  Grad '04—142. Col—142. (Auburn, U of AL-Tuscaloosa, Birmingham-Southern, U of S AL, LA St-Baton Rouge, U of MS). Alum 2700.
  Tui '04-'05: Day $4136-6920 (+$93). Aid: Merit 10 ($8000). Need 89 ($290,000).
  Summer: Acad Enrich Rec. 7 wks.
  Endow $1,000,000. Plant val $10,000,000. Bldgs 14. Class rms 95. 3 Libs 13,000 vols. Sci labs 3. Comp labs 4. Photog labs 1. Art studios 4. Music studios 5. Dance studios 1. Theater/auds 1. Gyms 2. Fields 5. Pools 1. Tracks 1.
  Est 1947. Nonprofit. Episcopal. Quar (Aug-May). Assoc SACS.

St. Paul's Episcopal School was founded as a nursery school and became an independent school with a board of trustees in 1969. In 1974, the first high school class graduated.

Teachers are available for tutoring after school, and extensive individual tutoring may be scheduled. The college preparatory high school curriculum includes such courses as journalism, computer science, chemistry and physics, as well as various honors and Advanced Placement offerings. Interested students may enroll in special laptop computer-based classes in disciplines across the curriculum.

Among student activities are publications and numerous academic and interest clubs. Boys' teams participate in football, tennis, golf, baseball, track, cross-country, wrestling, swimming, basketball and soccer. Girls compete in swimming, volleyball, golf, tennis, track, soccer, cross-country, softball and basketball.

MONTGOMERY, AL. (145 mi. SW of Atlanta, GA) Urban. Pop: 201,568. Alt: 190 ft.

THE MONTGOMERY ACADEMY

Day — Coed Gr K-12

Montgomery, AL 36106. 3240 Vaughn Rd. Tel: 334-272-8210. Fax: 334-277-3240.
www.montgomeryacademy.org   E-mail: cleveland.s@montgomeryacademy.org
Archibald Douglas, Head. BA, Yale Univ, MEd, Harvard Univ. **Susannah Cleveland, Adm.**
  Col Prep. AP—Eng Fr Lat Span Calc Bio Chem Physics Eur_Hist US_Hist Comp_Govt & Pol Econ Art_Hist Studio_Art Music_Theory. **Feat**—Comp_Sci Photog Drama Chorus Debate.
  Adm: 129/yr. Appl due: Rolling. Accepted: 81%. **Tests** CTP_4 IQ ISEE Stanford.
  Enr 846. B 433. G 413. Elem 579. Sec 267. Wh 93%. Blk 4%. Asian 3%. Avg class size: 16. Uniform. **Fac 78.** M 18. F 54/6. Adv deg: 64%.
  Grad '04—57. Col—57. (U of AL-Tuscaloosa 18, Auburn 6, Birmingham-Southern 3, Col of Charleston 2, U of GA 2, Samford 2). Avg SAT: 1210. Avg ACT: 26. Alum 1500.
  Tui '05-'06: Day $5100-9600 (+$100-500). **Aid:** Need 64 ($311,145).
  Endow $2,800,000. Plant val $24,598,000. Bldgs 8. Class rms 70. 2 Libs 35,000 vols. Sci labs 4. Lang labs 1. Comp labs 5. Art studios 7. Music studios 2. Gyms 3. Fields 5. Courts 5.
  Est 1959. Nonprofit. Sem (Aug-May). **Assoc** CLS SACS.

The academy offers a comprehensive college preparatory curriculum with a wide choice of elective courses. Honors and Advanced Placement courses provide opportunities for acceleration. Graduates attend competitive four-year colleges.

Student government, publications, forensics team, and French, Spanish and Latin clubs, as well as interscholastic athletics, supplement the academic program. In addition, the academy offers a variety of visual and performing arts offerings.

FLORIDA

BOCA RATON, FL. (42 mi. N of Miami, FL) Urban. Pop: 74,764. Alt: 16 ft.

SAINT ANDREW'S SCHOOL
Bdg — Coed Gr 9-12; Day — Coed K-12

Boca Raton, FL 33434. 3900 Jog Rd. Tel: 561-210-2020. Fax: 561-210-2027.
www.saintandrewsschool.net E-mail: admission@saintandrewsschool.net

Rev. George E. Andrews II, Head. BA, Trinity College (CT), MDiv, Virginia Theological Seminary. **Kilian J. Forgus, Adm.**

Col Prep. AP—Eng Calc Stats Bio Chem Physics Eur_Hist US_Hist Econ Art_Hist. **Feat**—Theol Journ. **Supp**—ESL Tut.

Adm: 446/yr. Bdg 40. Day 406. **Tests** SSAT.

Enr 1073. B 45/501. G 47/480. Elem 520. Sec 553. Wh 86%. Hisp 10%. Blk 2%. Asian 2%. Avg class size: 15. **Fac 140.** M 55. F 85. Adv deg: 63%. In dorms 10.

Grad '04—131. Col—131. (U of FL, FL Intl, Emory, Brown, Boston Col, Tulane). Alum 3000.

Tui '05-'06: Bdg $33,500. Day $14,300-17,500.

Summer: Acad Enrich Rev. ESL. Tui Bdg $5000/4-wk ses. Tui Day $950/4-wk ses. 6 wks.

Endow $5,000,000. Plant val $37,500,000. Bldgs 38. Dorms 2. Dorm rms 63. Class rms 78. Lib 18,000 vols. Sci labs 9. Lang labs 1. Comp labs 7. Auds 1. Theaters 1. Art studios 7. Music studios 2. Gyms 1. Fields 6. Courts 10. Pools 1.

Est 1961. Nonprofit. Episcopal. Sem (Aug-June). **Assoc** CLS.

Originally a boys' boarding school, Saint Andrew's became coeducational in 1971. Situated on an 80-acre site, the school admits day students at all grade levels and boarding students in the high school grades. The broad curriculum, which includes Advanced Placement and honors courses, affords rigorous preparation for colleges throughout the nation. Requirements in English, foreign language, math, science and history form the core of the academic program. Other graduation requirements include courses in the arts, theology and computer; students also perform compulsory community service.

Interscholastic sports include football, soccer, tennis, volleyball, swimming, golf, cross-country, baseball, lacrosse and basketball. There is also a cheerleading squad. Students are involved in numerous activities, including student government, publications and clubs.   **See Also Page 1242**

BRADENTON, FL. (33 mi. S of Tampa, FL) Urban. Pop: 49,504. Alt: 25 ft.

SAINT STEPHEN'S EPISCOPAL SCHOOL
Day — Coed Gr PS-12

Bradenton, FL 34209. 315 41st St W. Tel: 941-746-2121. Fax: 941-746-5699.
www.saintstephens.org   E-mail: jsoutherland@saintstephens.org

Janet S. Pullen, Head. BS, Florida State Univ, MEd, National-Louis Univ. **Judith C. Southerland, Adm.**

Col Prep. AP—Eng Fr Lat Span Calc Comp_Sci Bio Chem Physics Eur_Hist US_Hist World_Hist Art_Hist Studio_Art. **Feat**—Marine_Biol/Sci Econ Govt Ceramics Film Photog Drama Band Music Journ Broadcasting.

Adm: 168/yr. Appl due: Rolling. Accepted: 78%. Yield: 77%. **Tests** CTP_4 IQ.

Enr 801. B 402. G 399. Elem 501. Sec 300. Wh 88%. Hisp 3%. Blk 2%. Asian 7%. Avg class size: 15. **Fac 89.** M 21/4. F 54/10. Wh 88%. Hisp 8%. Blk 2%. Asian 2%. Adv deg: 52%.

Grad '04—68. Col—68. (U of FL 5, Stetson 5, FL St 3, Northeastern U 3, Wake Forest 2, Princeton 1). Avg SAT: 1234. Avg ACT: 25. Alum 853.

Tui '05-'06: Day $7800-11,650 (+$900). **Aid:** Merit 3 ($34,950). Need 72 ($393,107).

Summer: Acad Enrich Rec. Tui Day $120-180/wk. 6 wks.

Endow $433,000. Plant val $22,000,000. Bldgs 10. Class rms 35. 2 Libs 15,000 vols. Sci labs 7. Lang labs 1. Comp labs 3. Art studios 3. Music studios 1. Drama studios 1. Gyms 1. Fields 3.

Est 1970. Nonprofit. Episcopal. Sem (Aug-June). **Assoc** CLS.

Founded by a group of community leaders from Sarasota and Manatee counties, Saint Stephen's provides traditional college preparation. In the upper school, Advanced Placement classes are available in all departments. The fine arts department features courses in the visual arts, music and drama. A religious studies program, from which a compulsory component of community service is derived, is also available. In addition, all students have access to computers and the Internet.

The school's Interim Quest program, conducted during the final weeks of each academic year and required for students at all grade levels, allows upper school students to participate in specialized studies on campus, internships in the business community, or domestic or foreign travel programs. Interscholastic sports competition begins in grade 7, and a variety of extracurricular programs includes clubs and societies, student government and publications. Some out-of-town students reside at the IMG Sports Academies in Bradenton while pursuing their academic work at the school. **See Also Page 1251**

FORT LAUDERDALE, FL. (26 mi. N of Miami, FL) Urban. Pop: 152,397. Alt: 10 ft.

PINE CREST SCHOOL
Day — Coed Gr PS-12

Fort Lauderdale, FL 33334. 1501 NE 62nd St. Tel: 954-492-4103. Fax: 954-492-4188.
www.pinecrest.edu   E-mail: pcadmit@pinecrest.edu

Lourdes M. Cowgill, Pres. BA, Barry Univ, MEd, Florida Atlantic Univ, MA, PhD, Bryn Mawr College. **Robert Goldberg, Head.** BA, Temple Univ, MAT, Rutgers Univ. **Elena Del Alamo, Adm.**

Col Prep. AP—Eng Fr Ger Span Calc Stats Comp_Sci Bio Chem Human_Geog Physics Eur_Hist US_Hist Comp_Govt & Pol Econ Psych Art_Hist Studio_Art Music_Theory. **Feat**—Marine_Biol/Sci Sociol Comp_Relig Ethics Film Graphic_Arts Photog Drama Band Orchestra Dance Debate. **Supp**—Dev_Read Tut.

Adm: 211/yr. Appl due: Rolling. **Tests** CTP_4 IQ SSAT.
Enr 1656. B 794. G 862. Elem 900. Sec 756. Wh 75%. Hisp 11%. Blk 5%. Asian 3%. Other 6%. Avg class size: 17. Uniform. **Fac 124.** M 40. F 81/3. Adv deg: 70%.
Grad '04—199. **Col**—199. (U of FL, U of Miami, Boston U, FL St, U of PA, Columbia). Avg SAT: 1294. Alum 5990.
Tui '04-'05: Day $13,100-16,100. Aid: Need 164 ($1,658,252).
Summer: Acad Enrich Rev Rec. 6 wks.
Endow $25,000,000. Plant val $30,000,000. Bldgs 27. Class rms 93. 2 Libs 59,000 vols. Sci labs 6. Lang labs 1. Comp labs 3. Auds 4. Theaters 2. Art studios 4. Music studios 15. Dance studios 2. Gyms 2. Fields 6. Courts 6. Pools 3.
Est 1934. Nonprofit. Tri (Aug-June). **Assoc** CLS SACS.

Founded by Mae McMillan, Pine Crest has grown from a tutoring school for winter visitors to a large college preparatory program on a 49-acre campus. In 1987, Pine Crest merged with Boca Raton Academy, forming a second campus in Boca Raton (2700 St. Andrews Blvd., 33434) that serves students through grade 8. Its graduates are invited to complete their preparatory school education on the Fort Lauderdale campus.

Honors sections and Advanced Placement courses offer able students opportunities for more intensive studies. Activities include forensics, drama, dance, student government, publications, photography, service clubs, several chorus groups, and active band and orchestra programs. Available sports are football, swimming and diving, tennis, wrestling, lacrosse, track, crew, soccer, volleyball, golf, baseball, cross-country and basketball for boys, and volleyball, basketball, crew, lacrosse, swimming and diving, tennis, cross-country, soccer, softball, track and golf for girls. Graduates enter colleges throughout the US and Canada.

The school also conducts a variety of summer programs on both campuses.

UNIVERSITY SCHOOL
OF NOVA SOUTHEASTERN UNIVERSITY
Day — Coed Gr PS-12

Fort Lauderdale, FL 33314. 3301 College Ave, Sonken Bldg. Tel: 954-262-4400. Fax: 954-262-3971.
www.uschool.nova.edu   E-mail: usadmin@nsu.nova.edu

Jerome S. Chermak, Head. BA, MAT, State Univ of New York-Binghamton, EdD, Boston Univ.
Kiki Kelrick, Upper & Middle Sch Adm; Lynne Fazzio, Lower Sch Adm.
  Col Prep. AP—Eng Fr Span Calc Stats Comp_Sci Bio Chem Human_Geog Physics US_Hist World_Hist Psych US_Govt & Pol Studio_Art Music_Theory. **Feat**—Creative_Writing Lat Marine_Biol/Sci Global_Stud Film. **Supp**—Rem_Math Rem_Read.
  Adm: 290/yr. Appl due: Rolling. Accepted: 72%. **Tests** MAT.
  Enr 1619. B 818. G 801. Elem 1145. Sec 474. Wh 80%. Hisp 10%. Blk 3%. Am Ind 1%. Asian 4%. Other 2%. Avg class size: 20. Uniform. **Fac 134.** M 35. F 99. Wh 85%. Hisp 9%. Blk 3%. Asian 3%. Adv deg: 82%.
  Grad '04—126. Col—126. (U of FL 24, U of Central FL 13, U of Miami 8, FL St 7, Geo Wash 4). Avg SAT: 1229. Avg ACT: 25. Alum 1392.
  Tui '04-'05: Day $9560-12,500 (+$100-600). **Aid:** Need 163 ($422,000).
  Summer: Enrich Rec. Tui Day $850/4-wk ses. 8 wks.
  Endow $800,000. Plant val $19,300,000. Bldgs 4. 3 Libs 34,067 vols. Sci labs 9. Lang labs 1. Comp labs 5. Theaters 1. Art studios 3. Music studios 3. Dance studios 1. Gyms 2. Fields 3. Courts 7. Pools 3.
  Est 1971. Nonprofit. Sem (Aug-June). **Assoc** SACS.

Offering group instruction and individualized learning activities, this school occupies 25 acres of the central Nova Southeastern University campus.

Programming for both average and academically advanced children begins in kindergarten; other special programs include cultural arts offerings, internships and independent study. A community service commitment is required of students in grades 9-12. Qualified upper school students may enroll in Advanced Placement and college courses held at the school.

Activities include yearbook; newspaper; chorus; chess, forensics, debate, language and math clubs; and dramatic productions. Students may participate in intramural and interscholastic sports, among them baseball, basketball, cheerleading, cross-country, golf, ice and roller hockey, soccer, softball, swimming, tennis, track and field, volleyball and wrestling.

FORT MYERS, FL. (99 mi. SSE of Tampa, FL) Urban. Pop: 48,028. Alt: 10 ft.

CANTERBURY SCHOOL
Day — Coed Gr PS-12

Fort Myers, FL 33919. 8141 College Pky. Tel: 239-481-4323. Fax: 239-481-8339.
www.canterburyfortmyers.org   E-mail: jpeters@canterburyfortmyers.org
R. Mason Goss, Head. BA, Rollins College, MS, Georgia State Univ, EdD, Nova Southeastern Univ. **Julie A. Peters, Adm.**
  Col Prep. AP—Eng Fr Span Calc Stats Bio Chem Human_Geog Physics Eur_Hist US_Hist Econ US_Govt & Pol. **Feat**—British_Lit Creative_Writing Lat Anat & Physiol Marine_Biol/Sci Law Psych Sociol Ceramics Drawing Film Theater_Arts. **Supp**—Rev.
  Adm: 124/yr. Appl due: Rolling. Accepted: 64%. **Tests** CTP_4 SSAT.
  Enr 660. B 313. G 347. Elem 452. Sec 208. Wh 89%. Hisp 4%. Blk 3%. Asian 3%. Other 1%. Avg class size: 17. **Fac 81.** M 31. F 47/3. Wh 91%. Hisp 5%. Blk 2%. Asian 2%. Adv deg: 54%.
  Grad '04—56. Col—56. (U of Richmond 4, U of FL 4, Rollins 3, Rice 3, GA Inst of Tech 2, Dartmouth 2). Avg SAT: 1230. Alum 750.

Tui '04-'05: Day $9775-13,850 (+$1200). **Aid:** Merit 23 ($127,000). Need 136 ($870,000).
Summer: Enrich Rec. Tui Day $300/2-wk ses. 4 wks.
Endow $800,000. Plant val $16,000,000. Bldgs 12. Class rms 41. 2 Libs 8500 vols. Sci labs 5. Lang labs 1. Comp labs 3. Auds 1. Art studios 1. Music studios 1. Perf arts ctrs 1. Gyms 2. Fields 2. Courts 2.
Est 1964. Nonprofit. Sem (Aug-June). **Assoc** SACS.

Canterbury's college preparatory curriculum is marked by high academic standards and rigorous academic requirements. The full-day kindergarten programs, for four- and five-year-olds, prepare pupils in reading and math skills while stimulating social, physical and creative development. In the lower and middle schools, academic development is augmented by the introduction of scientific techniques, independent reading and writing projects, and library research methods. Opportunities for curriculum-related field trips and culture study are available.

The upper school emphasizes traditional academic subjects while promoting writing, research and discussion skills. Advanced Placement courses are offered to qualified students, and additional electives are offered in the arts, computer science and speech. A high degree of involvement is encouraged in such activities as service clubs, student council, yearbook, newspaper, chorus, drama, forensics, cheerleading and interscholastic team sports. **See Also Page 1129**

GULF STREAM, FL. (50 mi. N of Miami, FL) Rural. Pop: 716. Alt: 7 ft.

GULF STREAM SCHOOL
Day — Coed Gr PS-8

Gulf Stream, FL 33483. 3600 Gulf Stream Rd. Tel: 561-276-5225. Fax: 561-276-7115.
www.gulfstreamschool.org E-mail: admissions@gulfstreamschool.org
Joseph J. Zaluski, Head. BS, MS, Univ of Dayton. **Helen C. Burns, Adm.**
Pre-Prep. Feat—Fr Lat Span Computers Studio_Art Music. **Supp**—Dev_Read Tut.
Adm: 46/yr. Appl due: Feb. Accepted: 53%. Yield: 72%. **Tests** IQ.
Enr 236. B 122. G 114. Elem 236. Wh 95%. Hisp 1%. Blk 3%. Asian 1%. Avg class size: 18. Uniform. **Fac 36.** M 9/1. F 22/4. Adv deg: 38%.
Grad '04—17. Prep—15. (St Andrew's Sch-FL, Culver, Deerfield Acad, Taft, Loomis Chaffee, Pine Crest). Avg SSAT: 71%. Alum 969.
Tui '04-'05: Day $8700-13,700 (+$1100-3400).
Summer: Ages 3-5. Enrich Rem Rec. Tui Day $150-175/wk. 4 wks.
Endow $2,200,000. Plant val $3,500,000. Bldgs 9. Class rms 26. Lib 13,500 vols. Chapels 1. Sci labs 2. Comp ctrs 2. Auds 1. Music studios 1. Arts ctrs 2. Fields 1. Field houses 1.
Est 1938. Nonprofit. Sem (Aug-June).

In addition to the school's regular primary curriculum, Gulf Stream also conducts a seasonal tutorial program between January and March for pupils spending the winter with their families in south Florida. Generally traditional in approach and tone, the school features innovative fine arts, early childhood language study and computer programs; laptop computers are integrated into the curriculum in grades 6-8. Gulf Stream maintains a close faculty-student relationship and small classes.

Community service projects, publications, dramatic and choral groups, and intramural volleyball, flag football, golf, tennis, basketball, lacrosse and soccer round out the program.

JACKSONVILLE, FL. (127 mi. N of Orlando, FL) Urban. Pop: 695,877. Alt: 43 ft.

THE BOLLES SCHOOL
Bdg — Coed Gr 7-PG; Day — Coed PS-12

Jacksonville, FL 32217. 7400 San Jose Blvd. Tel: 904-733-9292. Fax: 904-733-0606.
www.bolles.org E-mail: admissions@bolles.org

John E. Trainer, Jr., Pres. BS, Muhlenberg College, MA, Wake Forest Univ, PhD, Univ of Oklahoma. **Bradford L. Reed, Adm.**

Col Prep. AP—Eng Fr Lat Span Calc Stats Comp_Sci Bio Chem Physics Eur_Hist US_Hist US_Govt & Pol Art_Hist Studio_Art. **Feat**—Humanities Chin Japan Environ_Sci Marine_Biol/Sci Music Music_Hist Dance. **Supp**—ESL Tut.

Adm (Bdg Gr 7-12; Day PS-12): 297/yr. Bdg 51. Day 246. Appl due: Rolling. Accepted: 33%. Yield: 75%. **Tests** CEEB ISEE SSAT.

Enr 1711. B 68/814. G 40/789. Elem 944. Sec 765. PG 2. Wh 87%. Hisp 2%. Blk 2%. Asian 6%. Other 3%. Avg class size: 17. **Fac 156.** M 47. F 106/3. Wh 97%. Hisp 1%. Asian 1%. Other 1%. Adv deg: 52%. In dorms 12.

Grad '04—190. Col—190. (U of FL 32, FL St 17, U of GA 8, Geo Wash 5, Emory 4, SMU 4). Avg SAT: 1217. Avg ACT: 25. Alum 7835.

Tui '05-'06: Bdg $30,750 (+$2500). **Day $14,500** (+$500-750). **Aid:** Need 103 ($899,315).

Summer: Acad Enrich Rev Rem Rec. 6 wks.

Endow $9,000,000. Plant val $12,500,000. Bldgs 18. Dorms 4. Dorm rms 40. Class rms 57. 2 Libs 16,500 vols. Sci labs 6. Lang labs 1. Comp labs 4. Auds 2. Art studios 4. Music studios 1. Dance studios 1. Perf arts ctrs 1. Art galleries 1. Gyms 2. Fields 6. Basketball courts 2. Volleyball courts 1. Pools 3. Weight rms 1.

Est 1933. Nonprofit. Quar (Aug-May). **Assoc** SACS.

Established as a military school for boys in grades 7-12, Bolles dropped its military affiliation in 1962 and became coeducational in 1971. The school's balanced college preparatory program combines academics, offerings in the fine and performing arts, approximately three dozen athletic teams, leadership and service opportunities, and a nationally known guidance program. The boarding program, in which boys and girls reside on different campuses, complements the coeducational learning environment. After-school activities on each campus include many coeducational pursuits.

An ongoing development program has enabled the school to make substantial improvements to its physical plant over the years. In 1991, the school acquired the Bartram campus at 2264 Bartram Rd., which allowed for the addition of a separate middle school facility and a girls' boarding section. In addition, Bolles opened a campus in Ponte Vedra Beach in 1999 to serve students from the Beaches area in grades pre-K-5.

Continuing to stress efficient college preparation, with extensive work in languages, science and mathematics, Bolles sends graduates to many competitive

FL   *Leading Private Schools*   *472*

colleges. Publications, musical organizations, debate, drama and clubs are available as extracurricular activities. Physical education is required and sports are offered at both intramural and interscholastic levels. Athletics include football, basketball, baseball, swimming, soccer, track, wrestling, tennis, cross-country, crew, volleyball, softball and golf. Morning tutorials are provided for students requiring additional academic assistance.

EPISCOPAL HIGH SCHOOL
Day — Coed Gr 6-12

Jacksonville, FL 32207. 4455 Atlantic Blvd. Tel: 904-396-5751. Fax: 904-396-7209. www.episcopalhigh.org   E-mail: admissions@episcopalhigh.org
Charles F. Zimmer, Head. AB, Duke Univ, MAT, Univ of Notre Dame. **Peggy P. Fox, Adm.**

- **Col Prep. AP**—Eng Fr Ger Lat Span Calc Stats Comp_Sci Bio Chem Physics Eur_Hist US_Hist US_Govt & Pol Art_Hist Studio_Art Music_Theory. **Feat**—Creative_Writing Shakespeare Environ_Sci Marine_Biol/Sci Holocaust African-Amer_Hist Econ Relig Photog Theater Journ Public_Speak. **Supp**—Tut.
- **Adm:** 185/yr. Appl due: Jan. Accepted: 63%. **Tests** CTP_4 ISEE.
- **Enr 895.** B 473. G 422. Wh 89%. Hisp 2%. Blk 6%. Asian 2%. Other 2%. Avg class size: 17. **Fac 88.** Wh 97%. Hisp 2%. Blk 1%. Adv deg: 51%.
- **Grad '04—129. Col—128.** (U of FL, FL St, Auburn, Stetson, U of GA, U of N FL). Avg SAT: 1239. Avg ACT: 25. Alum 3053.
- **Tui '04-'05:** Day **$12,070-12,900** (+$750). **Aid:** Merit 4 ($21,610). Need 121 ($771,505).
- **Summer:** Acad Enrich Rev Rec. Arts. Theater. 1-6 wks.
- Endow $5,373,000. Plant val $16,541,000. Bldgs 26. Class rms 40. Lib 19,122 vols. Sci labs 8. Lang labs 1. Theaters 2. Studios 6. Gyms 2. Fields 4. Courts 6. Pools 1.
- **Est 1966.** Nonprofit. Episcopal. Sem (Aug-May). **Assoc** SACS.

Founded on a 58-acre campus on the south bank of the St. Johns River, Episcopal High School is five miles from downtown Jacksonville. The establishment of the school was made possible by a broadly based community effort, augmented by Mrs. Alfred I. DuPont.

Religion, the arts and classical languages are distinctive features of the solid college preparatory curriculum, which is offered in a Christian environment. While the majority of graduates attend Southern colleges, the school is well represented at leading universities throughout the country.

Varsity and intramural sports, service and interest clubs, as well as student government, are available to the active student.

JACKSONVILLE COUNTRY DAY SCHOOL
Day — Coed Gr PS-6

Jacksonville, FL 32256. 10063 Baymeadows Rd. Tel: 904-641-6644. Fax: 904-641-1494. www.jcds.com   E-mail: admiss@jcds.com
S. Terry Bartow, Head. BS, Univ of Massachusetts-Amherst, MS, Cornell Univ. **Pat Walker, Adm.**

- **Pre-Prep. Feat**—Lib_Skills Span Computers Studio_Art Music. **Supp**—Rev Tut.
- **Adm:** 110/yr. Appl due: Jan. **Tests** IQ Stanford.
- **Enr 529.** B 245. G 284. Elem 529. Wh 79%. Hisp 5%. Blk 4%. Asian 5%. Other 7%. Avg class size: 21. Uniform. **Fac 55.** M 3. F 45/7. Wh 99%. Other 1%. Adv deg: 27%.

Grad '04—61. Prep—53. (Episcopal HS-FL, Bolles, St Johns Co Day). Avg SAT: 91. Alum 1075.
Tui '04-'05: Day $6700-7950 (+$245-525). **Aid:** Merit 1 ($7400). Need ($11,900).
Summer: Acad Enrich Rec. Tui Day $230/2-wk ses. 8 wks.
Endow $500,000. Plant val $6,400,000. Bldgs 6. Class rms 27. Lib 10,000 vols. Sci labs 1. Comp labs 1. Auds 1. Art studios 1. Music studios 1. Arts ctrs 1. Amphitheaters 1. Gyms 1. Fields 4. Courts 3. Pools 2.
Est 1960. Nonprofit. Tri (Aug-May). **Assoc** SACS.

Founded as Southside Country Day School, JCDS assumed its current name in 1975. The program is designed primarily for those who are planning to attend a college preparatory secondary school. The school moved in 1964 to its present spacious and modern campus, located on a 17-acre site in the center of Jacksonville.

Cocurricular offerings include art, music, Spanish, library skills and laboratory science. The school incorporates the use of technology and computers into every aspect of its curriculum and emphasizes parental participation at all grade levels. In addition to the comprehensive physical education program, JCDS conducts an after-school intramural sports program that includes soccer, softball, volleyball and basketball; also available after school are such activities as band, art, karate, jazz and ballet, computer and music lessons. Morning and afternoon extended care is available.

RIVERSIDE PRESBYTERIAN DAY SCHOOL
Day — Coed Gr PS-6

Jacksonville, FL 32204. 830 Oak St. Tel: 904-353-5511. Fax: 904-358-3837.
www.rpds.com E-mail: ssteedley@rpds.com
Robert W. Littell, Head. BA, Colorado College, MS, Johns Hopkins Univ. **Shirley Francis, Adm.**
Pre-Prep. Gen Acad. Feat—Creative_Writing Span Computers Relig Studio_Art Music.
  Supp—Dev_Read Rem_Math Rem_Read Tut.
Adm: 92/yr. Appl due: Rolling. Accepted: 73%. **Tests** CTP_4 IQ ISEE Stanford.
Enr 484. B 251. G 233. Elem 484. Wh 92%. Hisp 1%. Blk 5%. Asian 1%. Other 1%. Avg class size: 18. **Fac 39.** M 5. F 32/2. Wh 97%. Hisp 1%. Blk 2%. Adv deg: 51%.
Grad '04—56. Prep—50. (Episcopal HS-FL 24, Bolles 18, St Johns Co Day 5, Hendricks 3). Alum 1574.
Tui '04-'05: Day $4810-7755 (+$100). **Aid:** Need 40 ($143,000).
Summer: Enrich Rev Rec. Tui Day $125/wk. 8 wks.
Endow $2,900,000. Plant val $10,000,000. Bldgs 6. Class rms 27. Libs 1. Sci labs 1. Comp labs 1. Auds 1. Art studios 2. Music studios 1. Fields 2. Courts 1.
Est 1948. Nonprofit. Presbyterian. Tri (Aug-June). **Assoc** SACS.

RPDS comprises three divisions: a developmental prekindergarten and kindergarten that follows a half-day schedule; primary grades 1-3; and upper elementary grades 4-6 (with departmentalization beginning in grade 5). At all grade levels, the reading program is enriched by various materials and resources, while the language arts curriculum places increasing emphasis on writing skills as children progress. Math instruction incorporates manipulatives to facilitate mastery of computation and a firm grasp of concepts. In addition to the basic subjects, children study art, music, Bible, computer, Spanish and library skills.

Other noteworthy elements of the curriculum include creative writing, chorus, dance, drama, study trips and outdoor educational experiences. Student council and service organizations are available to older pupils. **See Also Page 1235**

LAKE WALES, FL. (44 mi. SSW of Orlando, FL; 55 mi. E of Tampa, FL) Suburban. Pop: 10,194. Alt: 147 ft.

VANGUARD SCHOOL

Bdg and Day — Coed Gr 5-PG

Lake Wales, FL 33859. 22000 US Hwy 27. Tel: 863-676-6091. Fax: 863-676-8297.
www.vanguardschool.org E-mail: vanadmin@vanguardschool.org

James R. Moon, Pres. BA, Washington and Jefferson College, MBA, Nova Southeastern Univ, MS, PhD, Virginia Polytechnic Institute. **Melanie Anderson, Adm.**

Col Prep. Gen Acad. LD. Feat—Creative_Writing Span Computers Econ Govt Law Performing_Arts Studio_Art Accounting Journ Drafting Woodworking Home_Ec. **Supp**—Dev_Read Rem_Math Rem_Read Tut.

Adm: 39/yr. Bdg 34. Day 5. Appl due: Rolling. Accepted: 45%. **Tests** IQ.

Enr 134. B 66/9. G 55/4. Elem 29. Sec 105. Wh 80%. Hisp 5%. Blk 12%. Asian 1%. Other 2%. Avg class size: 10. **Fac 28.** M 5. F 23. Wh 95%. Hisp 2%. Blk 1%. Asian 2%. Adv deg: 50%.

Grad '04—21. Col—19. (Johnson & Wales, Barry, Savannah Col of Art & Design, U of N TX, Mary Baldwin, Vincennes). Alum 500.

Tui '04-'05: Bdg $34,750 (+$1000). **Day $19,150. Aid:** Merit 1 ($5000). Need 23 ($179,900).

Endow $3,000,000. Plant val $8,000,000. Bldgs 13. Dorms 3. Dorm rms 72. Class rms 20. Lib 6300 vols. Sci labs 1. Lang labs 3. Comp labs 2. Dark rms 1. Gyms 1. Athletic ctrs 1. Fields 3. Courts 2. Pools 1.

Est 1966. Nonprofit. Sem (Sept-June). **Assoc** SACS.

Vanguard provides an individualized program for students with dyslexia, attention deficit disorder and other learning disabilities through a combination of classroom instruction and individual tutorial sessions. Structured classes emphasize organizational skills, study habits and the acquisition of fundamental academic skills. The core subjects of reading, language arts and mathematics, complemented by science and social studies, form the basic curriculum. Electives in art, computer skills, home economics, wood shop, small engines, drafting, performing arts, law studies and Spanish complete the program. Two diploma programs are available in the upper school: one geared toward college-oriented academics, the other focusing on career-oriented practical studies.

Athletics include physical education classes and interscholastic teams in volleyball, soccer, basketball, golf, track and field, cross-country, tennis, bowling, weightlifting and cheerleading. Students may take part in supervised programs in a range of activities, among them swimming, tennis, fishing, weightlifting, canoeing and other seasonal sports.

MELBOURNE, FL. (52 mi. ESE of Orlando, FL) Urban. Pop: 69,779. Alt: 21 ft.

FLORIDA AIR ACADEMY
Bdg and Day — Coed Gr 6-12

Melbourne, FL 32901. 1950 S Academy Dr. Tel: 321-723-3211. Fax: 321-676-0422.
  www.flair.com   E-mail: admissions@flair.com

Col. James Dwight, Pres. BA, Middlebury College, MA, Columbia Univ, MS, Florida Institute of Technology. **Michael Finnegan, Adm.**

  Col Prep. Milit. AP—Eng Span Calc Physics US_Hist. Feat—Astron Environ_Sci Oceanog Comp_Sci Econ Govt Music Public_Speak JROTC. Supp—Dev_Read ESL Makeup Tut.

  Adm: 166/yr. Appl due: Rolling. Accepted: 85%.

  Enr 356. Elem 76. Sec 280. Wh 58%. Hisp 17%. Blk 17%. Am Ind 1%. Asian 3%. Other 4%. Avg class size: 15. Uniform. **Fac 35.** M 12/2. F 19/2. Adv deg: 45%.

  Grad '04—64. Col—63. (Embry-Riddle, U of S FL, FL Intl, U of FL, St Leo, FL Inst of Tech). Alum 2340.

  Tui '05-'06: Bdg $23,000 (+$1500). **Day $7000** (+$500). **Aid:** Need 64 ($450,000).

  Summer: Acad Enrich Rev Rec. Flight Trng. Driver Ed. Scuba. Tae Kwon Do. ESL. Tui Bdg $4200 (+$800). Tui Day $1700 (+$500). 6 wks.

  Plant val $5,000,000. Bldgs 12. Dorms 1. Dorm rms 72. Class rms 33. Lib 4500 vols. Sci labs 1. Lang labs 1. Comp labs 3. Art studios 1. Music studios 1. Gyms 1. Fields 1. Courts 2. Pools 1.

  Est 1961. Inc. Sem (Aug-May). **Assoc** SACS.

Founded by Col. Jonathan Dwight, Florida Air provides a combined program of academic study and leadership training. After enrolling only boys for more than 40 years, the school opened both its boarding and its day divisions to girls in the fall of 2005. The college preparatory curriculum, which is grounded in the core subjects, includes honors and Advanced Placement courses in the major disciplines. Structured classroom instruction and compulsory study periods are characteristics of the program. An intensive English as a Second Language program serves international students.

Operating as an official US Air Force Junior ROTC Unit, the school offers aerospace science and military instruction. Flight training for academic credit, including simulator instruction and aircraft experience, provides the groundwork needed to qualify for a private pilot certificate.

Cadets are encouraged to participate in the academy's extracurricular program. Activities include interscholastic athletics, scuba diving, martial arts, drum and bugle corps, Boy Scouts, Civil Air Patrol, Web design team and social events. Leadership opportunities exist for all pupils.   **See Also Pages 1150-1**

MIAMI, FL. Urban. Pop: 362,470. Alt: 10 ft. Area also includes Pinecrest.

GULLIVER SCHOOLS
Day — Coed Gr PS-12

Pinecrest, FL 33156. 6575 N Kendall Dr. Tel: 305-666-7937. Fax: 305-665-3791.
www.gulliverschools.org E-mail: info@gulliverschools.org

Marian Krutulis, Dir. BA, Univ of Miami, MA, Univ of Chicago. **Carol A. Bowen, Gr 9-12 Adm; Bobbye Shearer, Gr PS-8 Adm.**

- Col Prep. IB Diploma. **AP**—Fr Span. **Feat**—ASL Ger Ital Lat Stats Engineering Comp_Sci Econ Govt Law Psych Ethics Art_Hist Studio_Art Video_Production Architect_Design Drama Music Music_Theory Dance Debate TV_Production. **Supp**—Dev_Read Rem_Math Rem_Read Tut.
- **Adm:** Appl due: Mar. Accepted: 62%. Yield: 88%. **Tests** IQ SSAT.
- **Enr 2062.** B 1134. G 928. Elem 1171. Sec 891. Wh 57%. Hisp 31%. Blk 2%. Asian 2%. Other 8%. Avg class size: 16. Uniform. **Fac 255.** Wh 66%. Hisp 29%. Blk 4%. Asian 1%. Adv deg: 42%.
- **Grad '04—216. Col—216.** (U of Miami 23, FL St 17, FL Intl 16, U of FL 13, Boston U 8, Cornell 4). Avg SAT: 1222. Avg ACT: 26. Alum 3765.
- **Tui '04-'05: Day $6600-21,000** (+$500).
- **Summer:** Acad Enrich Rev Rem Rec. Tui Day $500-900. 6 wks.
- Plant val $28,000,000. Bldgs 35. Class rms 225. Lib 39,000 vols. Sci labs 16. Comp labs 7. Auds 1. Theaters 2. Art studios 6. Music studios 4. Dance studios 2. Gyms 1. Fields 7. Courts 6. Pools 2.
- **Est 1926.** Nonprofit. Sem (Aug-June). **Assoc** SACS.

Gulliver Schools, with campuses in Coral Gables, South Miami and the Village of Pinecrest, traces it roots to Gulliver Academy, which was founded in Miami by Mr. and Mrs. Arthur Gulliver. Mrs. Krutulis purchased the school in 1952 and moved it 15 years later to the Coral Gables site (12595 Red Rd., Coral Gables 33156). The first high school class graduated in 1977, a year before the high school was established on a separate campus. Today, the school occupies five locations within a two-mile radius: Gulliver Academy (pre-K-8) is situated in a residential area of Coral Gables five miles south of Miami, while the South Miami campus (grades K-4) is at 8530 S.W. 57th Ave., Miami 33143, also in a residential section; the Pinecrest Middle campus serves children in grades 5-8 at 7500 S.W. 120th St.; Gulliver Preparatory School (grades 9-12) is situated on North Kendall Drive; and Pinecrest Prep (grades 9-12) is situated at 8000 S.W. 56th St., Miami 33155.

The primary school encompasses grades pre-K-1. Conversational Spanish is offered in the lower school (grades 2-4), while an independent study program is available in grades 3-8. In the middle school (grades 5-8), French, Spanish and Latin are electives in grades 7 and 8, and the study of Latin is particularly encouraged as a basis for the study of other languages. Many students also enroll in the Talent Identification Program at Duke University. Qualified boys and girls participate in a project-oriented independent study program. Band, chorus and drama are electives.

Gulliver Preparatory School offers the International Baccalaureate diploma and a college-credit program with the University of Miami, as well as dual-credit courses through Florida International University and Miami-Dade Community College.

A variety of organized activities accommodates student interests. Athletic teams provide competition at the high school level; boys and girls in the academy play both interscholastic and intramural sports. **See Also Pages 1158-9**

LA SALLE HIGH SCHOOL
Day — Coed Gr 9-12

Miami, FL 33133. 3601 S Miami Ave. Tel: 305-854-2334. Fax: 305-858-5971.
www.lasallehighschool.com E-mail: aroca@lasallehighschool.com
Sr. Patricia Roche, FMA, Prin. BA, MEd, Seton Hall Univ, MS, Manhattan College. **Ana Laura Garciga-Rodriguez, Adm.**

Col Prep. AP—Eng Span Calc Comp_Sci Physics Eur_Hist US_Hist US_Govt & Pol. **Feat**—Humanities Fr Ital Anat & Physiol Psych Sociol Theol Fine_Arts Drama Music Journ.

Adm: 230/yr. Appl due: Apr. Accepted: 75%.

Enr 630. B 250. G 380. Sec 630. Wh 2%. Hisp 97%. Asian 1%. Avg class size: 30. Uniform. **Fac 41.** M 18. F 22/1. Wh 40%. Hisp 60%. Adv deg: 51%.

Grad '04—152. Col—152. (FL Intl, Miami-Dade CC, U of Miami, Barry, St Thomas U-FL, Boston Col). Avg ACT: 20.

Tui '03-'04: Day $4600 (+$1625). **Aid:** Need 27 ($20,000).

Summer: Acad Enrich. Tui Day $300/crse. 4 wks.

Plant val $12,000,000. Bldgs 7. Class rms 35. Lib 40,000 vols. Sci labs 3. Lang labs 1. Comp labs 3. Auds 1. Theaters 1. Art studios 1. Dance studios 1. Gyms 1. Fields 1. Courts 1.

Est 1959. Nonprofit. Roman Catholic. Sem (Aug-June). **Assoc** SACS.

La Salle is administered by the Salesian Sisters of Saint John Bosco and is staffed by lay teachers. The school's 13-acre campus is located on Biscayne Bay, and its curriculum features a selection of Advanced Placement classes, including one in computer programming. An integral component of school life, the youth ministry program encourages students to participate in youth encounters and retreats and serve as liturgical ministers. Participants in all competitive sports may take part in a structured, supervised weightlifting and body-conditioning program.

MIAMI COUNTRY DAY SCHOOL
Day — Coed Gr PS-12

Miami, FL 33161. 601 NE 107th St. Tel: 305-779-7230. Fax: 305-758-5107.
www.miamicountryday.org E-mail: admissions@miamicountryday.org
John Davies, Head. BS, Merrimack College, MA, Texas A&M Univ, EdD, Florida International Univ. **J. Victor McGlone, Adm.**

Col Prep. AP—Fr Span Calc Stats Bio Chem Physics US_Hist World_Hist US_Govt & Pol. **Feat**—Animal_Behav Web_Design Psych Relig Drawing Film Photog Drama Directing Orchestra Dance Journ. **Supp**—ESL.

Adm: 182/yr. Appl due: Feb. Accepted: 76%. **Tests** CTP_4 ISEE SSAT.

Enr 1000. B 577. G 423. Elem 649. Sec 351. Wh 71%. Hisp 21%. Blk 3%. Other 5%. Avg class size: 20. Uniform. **Fac 126.** M 42/4. F 77/3. Wh 79%. Hisp 18%. Blk 2%. Asian 1%.

Grad '04—68. Col—68. (U of FL, FL Intl, Wellesley, FL St, U of Miami, Vassar). Avg SAT: 1240. Alum 2000.

Tui '03-'04: Day $11,550-20,000 (+$750-1250). **Aid:** Need 121 ($737,675).

Summer: Acad Enrich Rev Rec. Tui Day $540-1800. 3-6 wks.
Endow $1,300,000. Plant val $13,800,000. Bldgs 12. Class rms 77. 2 Libs 26,000 vols. Sci labs 7. Comp labs 3. Auds 1. Art studios 3. Music studios 2. Dance studios 1. Gyms 1. Fields 2. Courts 3. Pools 1.
Est 1938. Nonprofit. Quar (Aug-June). **Assoc** SACS.

MCDS' college preparatory curriculum features small classes and emphasizes the mastery of academic fundamentals. The lower, middle and upper divisions of the school stress both scholastic achievement and student involvement in a full range of activities. International pupils, who enroll from approximately 30 countries, benefit from an academically rigorous support program.

Intramural and interscholastic sports are an integral part of school life, as are publications, student government and activities in music, art and drama.

PALMER TRINITY SCHOOL
Day — Coed Gr 6-12

Miami, FL 33157. 7900 SW 176th St. Tel: 305-251-2230. Fax: 305-251-0607.
www.palmertrinity.org   E-mail: kwhite@palmertrinity.org
Sean Murphy, Head. BA, Dartmouth College, MA, St John's College. **Danny E. Reynolds, Adm.**
Col Prep. AP—Eng Fr Span Calc Bio Chem Physics Eur_Hist US_Hist US_Govt & Pol. **Feat**—Creative_Writing Psych Ethics Philos Relig Film Drama Music Journ. **Supp**—ESL.
Adm: 160/yr. Appl due: Feb. Accepted: 42%. **Tests** ISEE.
Enr 600. B 306. G 294. Elem 240. Sec 360. Wh 40%. Hisp 40%. Blk 5%. Am Ind 1%. Asian 5%. Other 9%. Avg class size: 16. Uniform. **Fac 60.** M 27. F 33. Wh 60%. Hisp 35%. Blk 2%. Asian 2%. Other 1%. Adv deg: 71%.
Grad '04—75. Col—75. (U of Miami, U of PA, Boston U, Wake Forest, IN U, RI Sch of Design). Avg SAT: 1180. Avg ACT: 26. Alum 1390.
Tui '04-'05: Day $15,400-16,000 (+$2350). **Aid:** Merit 4 ($20,000). Need 93 ($800,000).
Summer: Acad Enrich Rec. Tui Day $1000. 6 wks.
Endow $250,000. Plant val $10,000,000. Bldgs 7. Class rms 60. Lib 16,000 vols. Labs 9. Auds 1. Theaters 1. Art studios 3. Music ctrs 1. Gyms 1. Fields 4. Courts 4.
Est 1973. Nonprofit. Episcopal. Tri (Aug-June). **Assoc** SACS.

The result of a 1991 merger between Palmer School (founded in 1973) and Trinity Episcopal School (established in 1983), Palmer Trinity is situated on a 22-acre campus near Biscayne Bay in the southeastern section of the city. Students build a firm foundation in the basic subjects of English, math, science, history and foreign languages, and they have the opportunity for independent study. Honors and Advanced Placement courses are offered in all major subjects, an intensive English as a Second Language instruction is available, and pupils in all grades participate in a wireless laptop program. The educational program prepares students for colleges throughout the country.

Elective offerings, student activities and sports enrich the program. Students may participate in no-cut interscholastic athletics, and a comprehensive extracurricular program includes student government, publications, interest clubs, community service and opportunities in the arts.

RANSOM EVERGLADES SCHOOL
Day — Coed Gr 6-12

Miami, FL 33133. 3575 Main Hwy. Tel: 305-460-8800. Fax: 305-854-1846.
www.ransomeverglades.org E-mail: admission@ransomeverglades.org
Ellen Y. Moceri, Head. BA, MA, Washington Univ. **Elaine J. Mijalis-Kahn, Adm.**

- **Col Prep. AP**—Eng Fr Lat Span Calc Stats Comp_Sci Bio Chem Physics Eur_Hist US_Hist World_Hist Comp_Govt & Pol Econ Psych US_Govt & Pol Art_Hist Music_Theory. **Feat**—Ethics Fine_Arts Outdoor_Ed.
- **Adm:** 219/yr. Appl due: Feb. Accepted: 44%. Yield: 77%. **Tests** SSAT.
- **Enr 981.** B 488. G 493. Elem 427. Sec 554. Wh 53%. Hisp 35%. Blk 4%. Asian 5%. Other 3%. Avg class size: 14. **Fac 97.** M 39/1. F 51/6. Wh 84%. Hisp 12%. Blk 3%. Other 1%. Adv deg: 67%.
- **Grad '04—145. Col—145.** (U of PA 11, Duke 10, U of FL 8, Boston Col 7, Geo Wash 6, Brown 5). Avg SAT: 1313. Alum 4000.
- **Tui '04-'05: Day $18,900** (+$450). **Aid:** Need 98 ($1,320,980).
- **Summer:** Acad. 6 wks.
- Endow $10,114,000. Plant val $26,627,000. Bldgs 22. Class rms 54. 2 Libs 33,000 vols. Sci labs 11. Comp labs 4. Auds 2. Theaters 2. Art studios 6. Music studios 3. Gyms 1. Fields 2. Courts 6. Pools 1.
- **Est 1903.** Nonprofit. Quar (Aug-June). **Assoc** CLS SACS.

Ransom Everglades was founded in 1974 upon the merger of two established secondary schools in the Coconut Grove area of Miami: the Ransom School for Boys, opened under the direction of Paul C. Ransom in 1903 and originally known as the Adirondack Florida School, and the Everglades School for Girls, established in 1955. Now completely coeducational in all operations, the school occupies two campuses, with the middle school located at 2045 S. Bayshore Dr.

Ransom Everglades provides college preparation in a small-class setting. Academic offerings in the upper school include numerous Advanced Placement courses. A variety of computer-based programs, such as a writing workshop that utilizes the computer in the development of student writing skills, enriches the upper school curriculum. In addition to the basic academic program, a number of experiences in the visual and performing arts are also offered.

Extracurricular activities include publications, dramatics, service groups, and clubs in the areas of languages, math, science, sailing, the environment and politics. The interscholastic athletic program offers competition in volleyball, football, baseball, wrestling, soccer, tennis, softball, lacrosse, crew, swimming, water polo, cross-country, track, basketball and golf.

NAPLES, FL. (102 mi. WNW of Miami, FL) Urban. Pop: 20,976. Alt: 9 ft.

THE COMMUNITY SCHOOL OF NAPLES
Day — Coed Gr PS-12

Naples, FL 34109. 13275 Livingston Rd. Tel: 239-597-7575. Fax: 239-598-2973.
www.communityschoolnaples.org
E-mail: khammer@communityschoolnaples.org

John E. Zeller, Jr., Head. BA, Miami Univ (OH). **Amy Clemons, Adm.**
  Col Prep. AP—Eng Fr Lat Span Calc Stats Comp_Sci Bio Chem Physics Eur_Hist US_Hist World_Hist Comp_Govt & Pol US_Govt & Pol. **Feat**—Creative_Writing Humanities Ger Ital Anat & Physiol Marine_Biol/Sci Robotics Ethics Film Photog Music_Theory. **Supp**—Rev Tut.
  Adm: 117/yr. Appl due: Rolling. Accepted: 82%. Yield: 79%. **Tests** ISEE.
  Enr 756. B 365. G 391. Elem 504. Sec 252. Wh 94%. Hisp 2%. Blk 1%. Asian 2%. Other 1%. Avg class size: 16. **Fac 100.** M 27/8. F 57/8. Wh 100%. Adv deg: 50%.
  Grad '04—51. Col—50. (Georgetown, U of Central FL, U of FL, U of PA, Wash U). Avg SAT: 1227. Alum 330.
  Tui '04-'05: Day $14,357-17,700 (+$200-300). **Aid:** Need 42 ($442,887).
  Summer: Enrich. 2 wks.
  Endow $4,500,000. Plant val $62,000,000. Bldgs 17. Class rms 88. Lib 26,000 vols. Sci labs 11. Lang labs 3. Comp labs 8. Theaters 1. Art studios 5. Music studios 3. Dance studios 1. Gyms 2. Fields 3. Pools 1.
  Est 1982. Nonprofit. Sem (Aug-June).

Founded by a group of area parents seeking to address a community need, CSN began as a school serving fewer than 50 children in grades K-8. An increasing enrollment and an expanding campus over the years led the school to add a high school division in 1993; the first senior class graduated in 1996.

Community School provides a comprehensive curriculum that places emphasis on the development of basic skills and an appreciation of music and the arts. Maintaining a low student-teacher ratio, the school provides instruction at every level—beginning in prekindergarten—in French, computers, library skills, photography, drama, music and physical education. College preparation is an integral aspect of the program, with most middle and upper school classes taught at the honors level, and Advanced Placement courses available at various grade levels in all major disciplines. Graduates matriculate at competitive colleges throughout the country.

A wide selection of cocurricular activities complements academics. Popular choices are academic and interest clubs, Model UN, mock trial, Model Congress, journalism, and musical and dramatic activities. Softball, baseball, soccer, basketball, volleyball, tennis, golf, swimming, crew and lacrosse are among the CSN's athletics. Community service is a graduation requirement; options include Habitat for Humanity and Head Start, among others.

ORANGE PARK, FL. (12 mi. SSW of Jacksonville, FL; 116 mi. N of Orlando, FL) Suburban. Pop: 9081. Alt: 24 ft.

ST. JOHNS COUNTRY DAY SCHOOL
Day — Coed Gr PS-12

Orange Park, FL 32073. 3100 Doctors Lake Dr. Tel: 904-264-9572. Fax: 904-264-0375.
  www.stjohnscds.com   E-mail: admissionsinfo@stjohnscds.com
Stephen F. Russey, Head. AB, Bowdoin College, MA, Univ of Rhode Island. **Amy Weaver, Adm.**
  Col Prep. AP—Fr Lat Span Calc Bio. **Feat**—Stats Astron Sports_Med Comp_Sci Econ Govt Psych Art_Hist Studio_Art Music_Theory Journ. **Supp**—Rem_Math Tut.
  Adm: 120/yr. Appl due: Rolling. Accepted: 75%. **Tests** IQ Stanford.

Enr 705. B 348. G 357. Elem 489. Sec 216. Wh 85%. Hisp 2%. Blk 3%. Asian 10%. Avg class size: 18. **Fac 86.** M 18/1. F 62/5. Wh 98%. Hisp 1%. Am Ind 1%. Adv deg: 37%.
Grad '04—47. Col—47. (U of FL, FL St, U of N FL, U of Miami, Stetson, Duke). Avg SAT: 1230. Avg ACT: 26. Alum 1304.
Tui '04-'05: Day $4745-9990 (+$110-185). **Aid:** Need 81 ($266,986).
Summer: Acad Enrich Rev Rem. Tui Day $775. 6 wks.
Endow $2,417,000. Plant val $7,167,000. Bldgs 14. Class rms 50. Lib 15,000 vols. Sci labs 6. Lang labs 1. Comp labs 2. Theaters 1. Art studios 3. Music studios 1. Gyms 1. Fields 4. Courts 4. Pools 1. Tracks 1.
Est 1953. Nonprofit. Quar (Aug-June). **Assoc** CLS SACS.

Located just south of Jacksonville, this country day school offers a strong college preparatory program for able students at all grade levels. A diverse curriculum with honors and Advanced Placement courses, laboratory sciences, foreign language instruction beginning in kindergarten, and a fine arts program prepares students for selective colleges throughout the country.

The academic program is balanced by diverse physical education and athletic programs, with interscholastic competition in 17 sports. In addition, there are extracurricular opportunities in student government, dramatics, publications, interest clubs and intramural athletics. Cultural exchange visits are ongoing with schools in England, France, Germany and Costa Rica. An academic program and a day camp with adventure components provide summertime opportunities on the St. Johns campus.

PALM BEACH, FL. (64 mi. N of Miami, FL) Suburban. Pop: 9646. Alt: 15 ft.

PALM BEACH DAY SCHOOL

Day — Coed Gr K-9

Palm Beach, FL 33480. 241 Seaview Ave. Tel: 561-655-1188. Fax: 561-655-5794.
www.pbds.org   E-mail: jthompson@pbds.org
John L. Thompson, Head. BA, MA, Trinity College. **Andrew L. Scheffer, Adm.**
Pre-Prep. **Feat**—Computers Art_Hist Studio_Art Drama Music. **Supp**—Dev_Read Rem_Math Rem_Read Rev Tut.
Adm: 86/yr. Appl due: Rolling. Accepted: 84%. **Tests** CTP_4 SSAT Stanford.
Enr 392. B 199. G 193. Elem 374. Sec 18. Wh 92%. Hisp 4%. Blk 2%. Asian 2%. Avg class size: 12. Uniform. **Fac 54.** M 14. F 40. Wh 91%. Hisp 7%. Blk 2%. Adv deg: 50%.
Grad '04—18. Prep—18. (Lawrenceville, Benjamin, St George's Sch-RI, Hotchkiss, St Andrew's Sch-FL, Loomis Chaffee). Avg SSAT: 70%. Alum 1770.
Tui '02-'03: Day $10,200-14,500 (+$1200). **Aid:** Need 24 ($35,000).
Endow $3,000,000. Plant val $17,500,000. Bldgs 4. Class rms 27. 2 Libs 11,000 vols. Sci labs 1. Lang labs 1. Comp labs 3. Auds 2. Theaters 1. Art studios 2. Music studios 1. Gyms 1. Fields 2.
Est 1921. Nonprofit. Sem (Sept-June).

PBDS provides a traditional curriculum with an emphasis on basic skills, enhanced by extensive extracurricular programs. Learning styles programs in the lower, middle and upper schools address special student needs. Students are offered a full athletic program. Activities include music, art, ceramics, dramatics, student council and publications.

Early study of Spanish and computer in the lower grades, combined with departmentalized instruction in all subjects from grade 6, provide for entrance at the secondary level.

ST. PETERSBURG, FL. (17 mi. SW of Tampa, FL) Urban. Pop: 248,232. Alt: 44 ft.

ADMIRAL FARRAGUT ACADEMY
Bdg — Coed Gr 6-12; Day — Coed K-12

St Petersburg, FL 33710. 501 Park St N. Tel: 727-384-5500. Fax: 727-347-5160.
 www.farragut.org   E-mail: admissions@farragut.org

Capt. Robert J. Fine, Head. BA, Carroll College, MEd, National-Louis Univ. **Cmdr. David Graham, Adm.**

Col Prep. Milit. AP—Eng Fr Span Calc Chem US_Hist. Feat—Creative_Writing ASL Ger Stats Anat & Physiol Environ_Sci Marine_Biol/Sci Aerodynamics Meteorology Comp_Sci Law Psych Ethics Pottery Drama Music_Hist Journ JROTC SAT_Prep Aviation Naval_Sci. **Supp**—ESL Tut.

Adm (Bdg Gr 6-11; Day K-11): 153/yr. Bdg 83. Day 70. Appl due: Rolling. Accepted: 85%. **Tests** CTP_4 ISEE SSAT Stanford.

Enr 475. B 102/219. G 23/131. Elem 191. Sec 284. Wh 76%. Hisp 12%. Blk 7%. Am Ind 1%. Asian 4%.Uniform. **Fac 46.** M 23. F 22/1. Wh 92%. Hisp 4%. Blk 2%. Asian 2%. Adv deg: 50%. In dorms 16.

Grad '04—55. Col—55. (U of FL 5, FL St 5, U of the South 4, U of Tampa 4, U of Central FL 3, U of Air Force Acad 2/1. Avg SAT: 1120. Avg ACT: 22. Alum 6300.

Tui '05-'06: Bdg $27,240-27,720 (+$4000). **5-Day Bdg** $22,000 (+$4000). **Day** $7590-12,960 (+$300-2600). **Aid:** Need 65 ($359,000).

Summer: Rec. Leadership Trng. 1-2 wks.

Endow $2,500,000. Plant val $9,500,000. Bldgs 11. Dorms 1. Dorm rms 80. Class rms 26. Lib 12,000 vols. Labs 3. Comp labs 2. Art studios 1. Music studios 1. Gyms 1. Fields 4. Courts 5. Pools 1.

Est 1933. Nonprofit. Sem (Aug-May). **Assoc** SACS.

Admiral Farragut Academy was founded as a boys' school at Pine Beach, NJ, under the leadership of Adm. S. S. Robison, USN (Ret), a former superintendent of the US Naval Academy, and Brig. Gen. Cyrus S. Radford, USMC (Ret). In 1945, when the school reached maximum enrollment, the Florida campus was established. (The New Jersey campus closed in 1994.) AFA became coeducational in January of 1990. The lower division (grades K-4), which began accepting students in 1999, provides a nonmilitary program.

This naval preparatory school offers college preparatory work on a 55-acre campus on the state's Gulf Coast that permits outdoor activities throughout the school year. The highly structured academic program stresses math and science, while strong English and history departments emphasize reading and writing skills. Individual college advisement and SAT preparation, as well as a full English for Speakers of Other Languages program, give all possible assurance of each student's success.

All students in grades 9-12 enroll in the Naval JROTC program, which includes drill team, color guard, rifle team and summer cruises aboard naval vessels. In addition, boys and girls must earn a sailing certification prior to graduation.

Athletics include tennis, baseball, track and field, cross-country, wrestling, swimming, volleyball, softball, football, soccer, riflery, golf, basketball and cheerleading. Among other activities are academic clubs, sailing, scuba, debate, forensics, marching and jazz bands, and National Honor Society.

THE CANTERBURY SCHOOL OF FLORIDA
Day — Coed Gr PS-12

St Petersburg, FL 33703. 901 58th Ave NE. Tel: 727-525-1419. Fax: 727-525-2545.
www.canterbury-fl.org   E-mail: ddeberry@canterbury-fl.org
Ellen Welsh, Head. BA, Michigan State Univ, MEd, Univ of Pittsburgh. **J. Russell Ball, Upper Sch Adm; Jan E. Herzik, Lower Sch Adm.**

Col Prep. AP—Eng Fr Span Calc Comp_Sci Bio Chem US_Hist Psych US_Govt & Pol Art_Hist. **Feat—**British_Lit World_Lit Lat Marine_Biol/Sci Relig Studio_Art Drama Music. **Supp—**Tut.

Adm: 71/yr. Appl due: Rolling. Accepted: 80%. Yield: 95%. **Tests** CEEB CTP_4 IQ.

Enr 410. Elem 323. Sec 87. Wh 87%. Hisp 4%. Blk 3%. Am Ind 1%. Asian 4%. Other 1%. Avg class size: 14. **Fac 53.** M 12/3. F 36/2. Wh 98%. Hisp 1%. Other 1%. Adv deg: 41%.

Grad '04—21. Col—19. (U of FL 2, FL St 2, FL Inst of Tech 2, U of S FL 2, Davidson 1, Eckerd 1). Alum 506.

Tui '04-'05: Day $7600-9950 (+$240-675). **Aid:** Need 37 ($267,300).

Summer: Acad Enrich Rev Rec. 3 wks.

Endow $50,000. Plant val $6,000,000. Bldgs 6. Class rms 27. 2 Libs 16,415 vols. Sci labs 5. Lang labs 1. Comp labs 2. Auds 1. Theaters 1. Art studios 3. Music studios 3. Galleries 1. Gyms 1. Fields 4. Courts 1.

Est 1968. Nonprofit. Episcopal. Quar (Aug-June).

Although affiliated with the Episcopal Church, Canterbury enrolls students of all faiths. The curriculum provides honors and Advanced Placement courses, in addition to an array of extracurricular activities that ranges from interscholastic athletics to offerings in the fine and performing arts.

Fall and spring mini-terms give all upper school students a chance to gain extensive exposure to subjects or activities beyond the scope of the regular curriculum. Offerings have included career shadowing, broadcasting, trips abroad, ecology trips to the Florida Keys, SAT review, technical theater and community service, among others. Juniors and seniors may use mini-term as a chance to embark on college visits.

Varsity and junior varsity teams compete in soccer, cross-country, volleyball, basketball, baseball, softball, golf and tennis. Other activities include study skills, leadership opportunities, trips by grade level in the middle and upper schools, interest clubs, honor societies, student council, yearbook, student government and cheerleading. All seniors complete a compulsory senior seminar and fulfill a community service requirement.

Canterbury operates two campuses. The lower school (grades pre-K-4) conducts classes at the Hough Campus at 1200 Snell Isle Blvd. NE, 33704, while the middle

FL *Leading Private Schools* 484

school (grades 5-8) and the upper school (grades 9-12) occupy the Knowlton campus on 58th Avenue Northeast.

SHORECREST PREPARATORY SCHOOL
Day — Coed Gr PS-12

St Petersburg, FL 33703. 5101 1st St NE. Tel: 727-522-2111. Fax: 727-527-4191.
  www.shorecrest.org   E-mail: admissions@shorecrest.org
Mary H. Booker, Head. BS, Univ of Georgia, MEd, Nova Univ. **Diana N. Craig, Adm.**
  Col Prep. AP—Eng Fr Span Calc Comp_Sci Bio Chem Physics Eur_Hist US_Hist World_Hist Econ Psych Art_Hist Studio_Art Music_Theory. **Feat**—Humanities Playwriting Marine_Biol/Sci Web_Design Pol_Sci Fine_Arts Photog Video Drama Journ. **Supp**—Tut.
  Adm: 146/yr. Appl due: Rolling. Accepted: 68%. Yield: 72%. **Tests** CEEB CTP_4 ISEE SSAT.
  Enr 987. B 498. G 489. Elem 755. Sec 232. Wh 88%. Hisp 4%. Blk 3%. Asian 5%. Avg class size: 15. **Fac 104.** M 26/4. F 64/10. Adv deg: 44%.
  Grad '04—51. Col—47. (U of Central FL 5, U of FL 4, Vanderbilt 4, FL St 2, U of PA 2, Yale 1). Avg SAT: 1237. Avg ACT: 26. Alum 1581.
  Tui '04-'05: Day $8800-13,200 (+$500). **Aid:** Need 75 ($400,000).
  Summer: Rec. Tui Day $300-1000. 2-6 wks.
  Endow $600,000. Plant val $20,000,000. Bldgs 40. Class rms 73. Lib 20,000 vols. Sci labs 4. Lang labs 3. Comp labs 8. Theaters 2. Art studios 2. Music studios 2. Dance studios 1. Gyms 1. Fields 4. Courts 3.
  Est 1923. Nonprofit. Sem (Aug-May). **Assoc** CLS SACS.

The oldest independent school in the Tampa Bay area, the school occupies a 28-acre campus in northeast St. Petersburg. Shorecrest conducts a college preparatory program with a broad range of honors and Advanced Placement courses.

A strong athletic program offers a full complement of sports for boys and girls. Fine arts enrichment at the school introduces students to various musical forms and theatrical performances. Students are encouraged to participate in extracurricular activities, which include student government, sports and a variety of service organizations, publications and clubs.

SARASOTA, FL. (43 mi. S of Tampa, FL) Urban. Pop: 52,715. Alt: 27 ft.

OUT-OF-DOOR ACADEMY
Day — Coed Gr PS-12

Sarasota, FL 34240. 5950 Deer Dr. Tel: 941-349-3223. Fax: 941-970-1251.
  www.oda.edu   E-mail: admissions@oda.edu
David Mahler, Head. BA, Wesleyan Univ, MEd, Univ of Virginia. **Scott Hinckley, Adm.**
  Col Prep. AP—Eng Fr Span Calc Comp_Sci Bio Chem Physics Eur_Hist US_Hist Studio_Art. **Feat**—Lat Marine_Biol/Sci Econ Govt Drama Music. **Supp**—Dev_Read Rem_Math Rem_Read Rev Tut.
  Adm: 120/yr. Appl due: Feb. Accepted: 80%. **Tests** CTP_4 SSAT.
  Enr 599. B 308. G 291. Elem 408. Sec 191. Wh 95%. Hisp 2%. Blk 1%. Asian 2%. Avg

class size: 16. **Fac 64.** Wh 98%. Hisp 1%. Blk 1%. Adv deg: 45%.
Grad '04—33. Col—33. (FL St, Col of Charleston, U of Central FL, U of FL, U of Miami, Vanderbilt). Avg SAT: 1177. Avg ACT: 26. Alum 2080.
Tui '04-'05: Day $9650-13,350 (+$180-500). **Aid:** Need 69 ($452,000).
Endow $780,000. Plant val $12,000,000. Bldgs 16. Class rms 61. 2 Libs 20,000 vols. Comp labs 5. Auds 1. Theaters 1. Art studios 4. Music studios 2. Gyms 1. Fields 2.
Est 1924. Nonprofit. (Aug-June).

Founded as an elementary school on Siesta Key by Fanneal Harrison, ODA was purchased by a parent group and was incorporated as a not-for-profit corporation in 1977. The school opened a high school division in 1996 and now offers a full pre-K-12 program to students in Manatee, Sarasota and Charlotte counties.

The academy provides college preparatory instruction in the traditional disciplines, as well as a broad selection of enrichment classes. Small class size throughout the school results in individual attention. The lower school curriculum (grades pre-K-6) emphasizes the fundamentals of reading, language arts, mathematics, science and social studies. Children also receive instruction in marine science, computers, library skills, art, music and physical education. While continuing to stress the traditional subject areas, the upper school program (grades 7-12) also includes honors and Advanced Placement course work. The use of technology is an important part of the curriculum at all grade levels. Both lower and upper school students may participate in after-school athletics, as well as in student government, drama and various enrichment clubs.

The lower school occupies the original campus, on Siesta Key (444 Reid St., 34242), while the upper school is situated on the mainland at Lakewood Ranch on Deer Drive.

STUART, FL. (98 mi. N of Miami, FL) Suburban. Pop: 14,633. Alt: 14 ft.

SAINT MICHAEL'S INDEPENDENT SCHOOL
Day — Coed Gr PS-8

Stuart, FL 34996. 1300 E 10th St. Tel: 772-283-1222. Fax: 772-220-9149.
www.stmikesschool.org   E-mail: stmikes@stmikesschool.org
James Cantwell, Head. BA, Univ of Vermont, MAT, Antioch College, MEd, EdD, Columbia Univ. **Judith Chamberlin, Adm.**
Pre-Prep. Feat—Robotics Computers Studio_Art Music Dance. **Supp**—Tut.
Adm: 94/yr. Appl due: Rolling. Accepted: 95%.
Enr 430. B 222. G 208. Elem 430. Wh 94%. Hisp 1%. Blk 2%. Asian 3%. Avg class size: 16. Uniform. **Fac 45.** M 5. F 40. Wh 99%. Hisp 1%. Adv deg: 28%.
Grad '04—18. Prep—5. (St Edward's Sch, Benjamin). Alum 427.
Tui '05-'06: Day $7000-12,500 (+$1000). **Aid:** Need 30 ($200,000).
Summer: Acad Enrich Rec. Tui $180/wk. 5 wks.
Endow $850,000. Plant val $4,000,000. Bldgs 9. Class rms 26. Lib 14,000 vols. Sci labs 2. Lang labs 1. Comp labs 1. Auds 1. Art studios 1. Music studios 1. Gyms 1. Fields 3. Courts 2.
Est 1969. Nonprofit. Quar (Aug-May).

Founded as the Pine School, Saint Michael's is situated on an 11-acre campus in the heart of Stuart and serves Martin, Palm Beach and St. Lucie counties. The traditional curriculum is reinforced by individualized instruction and small classes. Early learning through grade 5 classes are self-contained, while grades 6-8—which are conducted at a separate, adjacent facility—are departmentalized. Specialists in Spanish, art, music, computers and physical education meet with students several times a week.

Community service is an important element of the program. Competitive athletic offerings include lacrosse, soccer, cross-country, basketball and volleyball.

TALLAHASSEE, FL. (157 mi. W of Jacksonville, FL) Urban. Pop: 150,624. Alt: 190 ft.

MACLAY SCHOOL
Day — Coed Gr PS-12

Tallahassee, FL 32312. 3737 N Meridian Rd. Tel: 850-893-2138. Fax: 850-893-7434.
www.maclay.org   E-mail: mhoppe@maclay.org
William W. Jablon, Head. BA, Boston College, MA, Florida State Univ. **Michael Obrecht, Adm.**

- **Col Prep. AP**—Fr Span Calc Stats Bio Chem Eur_Hist US_Hist. **Feat**—Humanities Lat Anat Marine_Biol/Sci Comp_Sci Econ Psych Sociol Fine_Arts.
- **Adm:** 127/yr. Appl due: Rolling.
- **Enr 1001.** B 495. G 506. Elem 673. Sec 328. Wh 85%. Hisp 2%. Blk 4%. Am Ind 1%. Asian 2%. Other 6%. Avg class size: 20. **Fac 90.** M 19/2. F 63/6. Wh 95%. Hisp 2%. Blk 3%. Adv deg: 52%.
- **Grad '04—79. Col—79.** (FL St 18, U of FL 10, Tallahassee CC 7, U of the South 3, U of Central FL 3, U of GA 2). Avg SAT: 1240. Avg ACT: 27. Alum 2346.
- **Tui '04-'05: Day $7800-8200** (+$250). **Aid:** Need 65 ($276,685).
- **Summer:** Acad Rem. Tui Day $350. 6 wks.
- Endow $1,500,000. Plant val $16,000,000. Bldgs 12. Class rms 72. Lib 30,402 vols. Sci labs 7. Comp labs 3. Theaters 1. Art studios 3. Music studios 2. Gyms 2. Fields 5. Courts 12. Pools 1. Tracks 1.
- **Est 1968.** Nonprofit. Sem (Aug-May). **Assoc** CLS SACS.

Located on a 100-acre, wooded campus, Maclay offers a college preparatory curriculum that includes accelerated programs for students seeking early admission to college.

The lower school's basic academic curriculum is supplemented by courses in dictionary skills, computer-assisted instruction and library skills. Special features include a half-day prekindergarten program, after-school classes in computer programming, concentrated study of Spanish language and culture, and a summer reading program. The middle school's transitional curriculum is supplemented by intramural sports, a science fair, essay-writing contests and an annual field trip to Washington, DC.

At the upper school level, students may pursue directed individual studies in areas of their choosing, and nonacademic electives are offered on a pass-fail basis. Varsity and junior varsity interscholastic teams compete in volleyball, soccer, basketball, baseball, softball, track, swimming, golf and tennis. A full range of activities is offered.

TAMPA, FL. Urban. Pop: 303,447. Alt: 57 ft.

BERKELEY PREPARATORY SCHOOL
Day — Coed Gr PS-12

Tampa, FL 33615. 4811 Kelly Rd. Tel: 813-885-1673. Fax: 813-886-6933.
 www.berkeleyprep.org   E-mail: thomamar@berkeleyprep.org
Joseph A. Merluzzi, Head. BS, Western Connecticut State College, MA, Fairfield Univ. **Mary Will Thomas, Adm.**

- **Col Prep. AP**—Eng Fr Lat Span Calc Stats Comp_Sci Bio Chem Physics Eur_Hist US_Hist Econ Psych. **Feat**—Mandarin Anat & Physiol Astron Genetics Microbio African_Hist World_Relig Studio_Art Drama Orchestra Dance Speech. **Supp**—Tut.
- **Adm:** 184/yr. Appl due: Jan. Accepted: 45%. **Tests** IQ SSAT.
- **Enr 1172.** Elem 697. Sec 475. Avg class size: 20. **Fac 145.** Adv deg: 50%.
- **Grad '04—101. Col—101.** (U of FL, GA Inst of Tech, Vanderbilt, Emory, U of Miami, U of Central FL). Avg SAT: 1302. Avg ACT: 26. Alum 2432.
- **Tui '04-'05:** Day $11,450-14,550.
- **Summer:** Acad Enrich Rev Rem Rec. Arts. Sports. 10 wks.
- Endow $2,500,000. Plant val $23,000,000. Bldgs 12. Class rms 80. 2 Libs 19,000 vols. Sci labs 5. Lang labs 1. Auds 1. Theaters 1. Art studios 2. Music studios 2. Dance studios 1. Gyms 2. Fields 3. Courts 3. Pools 1. Tracks 1. Student ctrs 1.
- **Est 1960.** Nonprofit. Episcopal. Quar (Aug-June). **Assoc** CLS.

Located on a 64-acre, suburban site that includes separate lower, middle and upper division administrative and teaching facilities, Berkeley serves the Tampa Bay area. The school immerses all students in the core subjects of math, English, science, history and foreign language. Pupils begin taking Spanish, athletics, drama, music and visual arts in prekindergarten, while sixth graders participate in double sessions of English. The flexible program in grades 9-12 allows qualified students to begin Advanced Placement course work as early as sophomore year, and Berkeley also offers a selection of honors courses and advanced topics.

ST. MARY'S EPISCOPAL DAY SCHOOL
Day — Coed Gr PS-8

Tampa, FL 33629. 2101 S Hubert Ave. Tel: 813-258-5508. Fax: 813-258-5603.
 www.smeds.org   E-mail: kathleen.lopez@smeds.org
Scott D. Laird, Head. BS, West Chester Univ of Pennsylvania, MEd, MA, Florida Atlantic Univ. **Kathleen Lopez, Adm.**

- **Pre-Prep. Feat**—Lat Span Computers Fine_Arts Video_Production Drama Public_Speak Study_Skills. **Supp**—Dev_Read Rev Tut.
- **Adm:** 56/yr. Appl due: Rolling. Accepted: 42%. Yield: 85%.
- **Enr 435.** B 203. G 232. Elem 435. Wh 92%. Hisp 4%. Blk 2%. Asian 1%. Other 1%. Avg class size: 22. Uniform. **Fac 48.** M 5/1. F 40/2. Wh 96%. Hisp 2%. Blk 2%. Adv deg: 39%.
- **Grad '04—43. Prep—27.** (Jesuit HS-FL 17, Acad of the Holy Names 4, Tampa Prep 2).

Alum 1200.
Tui '04-'05: Day $7950 (+$1000).
Endow $250,000. Plant val $5,000,000. Bldgs 2. Class rms 30. Lib 16,000 vols. Sci labs 2. Comp labs 2. Auds 1. Art studios 1. Music studios 1. Gyms 1. Fields 1. Courts 2.
Est 1953. Nonprofit. Episcopal. (Aug-May).

Located on an eight-acre campus, St. Mary's was founded by a group of parents who recognized the need for a church-affiliated school with a strong academic environment in the South Tampa area. Children are assigned to homerooms with consideration to the mix of personalities, but are placed in academic sections for mathematics and foreign language according to ability and achievement. Parents may choose a half- or full-day prekindergarten program. The basic core curriculum is supplemented by a wide range of cocurricular activities, including public speaking, student council, drama, chorus, band, an acolyte program and yearbook. Computer programming is offered to all.

The school fields interscholastic teams in soccer, volleyball, cheerleading, basketball, softball, baseball, track, cross-country and tennis.

TAMPA PREPARATORY SCHOOL

Day — Coed Gr 6-12

Tampa, FL 33606. 727 W Cass St. Tel: 813-251-8481. Fax: 813-254-2106.
  www.tampaprep.org   E-mail: admissions@tampaprep.org
D. Gordon MacLeod, Head. BA, Univ of York (England), ScM, Brown Univ. **W. Dennis Facciolo, Adm.**
  Col Prep. AP—Eng Fr Lat Span Calc Stats Bio Chem Physics Psych US_Govt & Pol. **Feat**—Creative_Writing Japan Astron Bioethics Genetics Marine_Biol/Sci Comp_Graphics WWII Anthro Fine_Arts Photog Drama Dance.
  Adm: 165/yr. Appl due: Feb. Accepted: 85%. **Tests** ISEE SSAT.
  Enr 640. B 308. G 332. Elem 200. Sec 440. Wh 82%. Hisp 6%. Blk 7%. Asian 5%. Avg class size: 16. **Fac 53.** M 19. F 31/3. Wh 86%. Hisp 6%. Blk 6%. Asian 2%. Adv deg: 52%.
  Grad '04—98. Col—98. (FL St 16, U of FL 12, Davidson 7, U of Miami 2, Wake Forest 2, Yale 2). Avg SAT: 1200. Alum 1421.
  Tui '05-'06: Day $13,270-13,875 (+$1200). **Aid:** Merit 7 ($90,610). Need 92 ($753,102).
  Summer: Acad Enrich Rec. Sports. 1-6 wks.
  Endow $1,849,000. Plant val $23,000,000. Bldgs 4. Class rms 37. Lib 9000 vols. Sci labs 6. Comp labs 3. Theaters 1. Art studios 3. Music studios 2. Dance studios 1. Gyms 1. Fields 2. Field houses 1. Pools 1.
  Est 1974. Nonprofit. Sem (Aug-June). **Assoc** CLS SACS.

Located in downtown Tampa, this school offers a college preparatory curriculum. In grades 6-10, emphasis is placed on establishing fundamental skills and concepts in the various disciplines. The program in grades 11 and 12 allows for more choice of electives on the part of the student.

Courses include computer programming, literature, creative writing and ancient history. Seventeen Advanced Placement courses are offered, and independent study for credit is also available.

After-school athletics include swimming, soccer, tennis, cross-country, volleyball, basketball, baseball, softball, wrestling, golf, crew, and track and field. A performing arts program and a variety of organizations and clubs supplement academics.

VERO BEACH, FL. (84 mi. SE of Orlando, FL) Suburban. Pop: 17,705. Alt: 20 ft.

SAINT EDWARD'S SCHOOL
Day — Coed Gr PS-12

Vero Beach, FL 32963. 1895 Saint Edward's Dr. Tel: 772-231-4136. Fax: 772-231-2427.
www.steds.org E-mail: info@steds.org

Charles Clark, Head. BA, MEd, St Lawrence Univ, EdD, Univ of Delaware. **Thomas Eccleston, Adm.**
- **Col Prep. AP**—Eng Fr Span Calc Stats Comp_Sci Bio Chem Human_Geog Physics Eur_Hist US_Hist World_Hist Econ US_Govt & Pol. **Feat**—Chin Environ_Sci Marine_Biol/Sci Programming Psych Sociol Comp_Relig Ethics Art_Hist Studio_Art Theater_Arts Chorus Music Journ. **Supp**—Tut.
- **Adm:** 176/yr. Appl due: Feb. Accepted: 95%. Yield: 72%. **Tests** SSAT.
- **Enr 900.** Elem 568. Sec 332. Wh 92%. Hisp 2%. Blk 2%. Asian 4%. Avg class size: 17. **Fac 85.** M 23. F 62. Wh 94%. Hisp 2%. Blk 2%. Other 2%. Adv deg: 51%.
- **Grad '04—72. Col—72.** (U of FL 6, Denison 4, Elon 3, SMU 3, U of Miami 2, Villanova 2). Avg SAT: 1226. Avg ACT: 25. Alum 1300.
- **Tui '04-'05: Day $5100-15,000** (+$1325). **Aid:** Need 98 ($901,960).
- **Summer:** Enrich Rec. Tui Day $650/wk. 6 wks.
- Endow $2,000,000. Plant val $30,000,000. Bldgs 17. Class rms 65. 2 Libs 26,000 vols. Sci labs 7. Comp labs 5. Theaters 1. Art studios 4. Music studios 4. Gyms 2. Fields 6. Courts 2. Pools 1.
- **Est** 1965. Nonprofit. Episcopal. Sem (Aug-June). **Assoc** CLS.

This traditional school was founded to fill a community need for sound college preparation. The college preparatory curriculum emphasizes core subjects, and considerable interest is shown in athletics, dramatics, art, music and student government. The lower school campus (grades pre-K-5) is located at 2225 Club Dr., three miles from the middle and upper school campus. **See Also Page 1244**

WINTER PARK, FL. (7 mi. NNE of Orlando, FL) Suburban. Pop: 24,090. Alt: 94 ft.

TRINITY PREPARATORY SCHOOL
Day — Coed Gr 6-12

Winter Park, FL 32792. 5700 Trinity Prep Ln. Tel: 407-671-4140. Fax: 407-671-6935.
www.trinityprep.org E-mail: inquire@trinityprep.org

Craig S. Maughan, Head. BA, Washington Univ, MSPH, Univ of North Carolina-Chapel Hill, MBA, Univ of Kansas. **Sherryn Hay, Adm.**
- **Col Prep. AP**—Eng Fr Lat Span Calc Stats Comp_Sci Bio Chem Physics US_Hist World_Hist Econ Psych US_Govt & Pol Studio_Art Music_Theory. **Feat**—Creative_Writing Humanities Playwriting Anat & Physiol Bible Comp_Relig Ethics Photog Christianity & Film Music Journ Speech. **Supp**—Tut.
- **Adm:** 155/yr. Appl due: Feb. Accepted: 60%. Yield: 65%. **Tests** CTP_4 ISEE SSAT TOEFL.
- **Enr 802.** B 406. G 396. Elem 331. Sec 471. Wh 80%. Hisp 7%. Blk 5%. Asian 8%. Avg

class size: 15. **Fac 77.** M 33. F 44. Wh 91%. Hisp 9%. Adv deg: 64%.
Grad '04—124. Col—124. (U of FL 24, FL St 15, U of Central FL 8, NYU 5, Duke 3, Vanderbilt 3). Avg SAT: 1272. Avg ACT: 27. Alum 1998.
Tui '04-'05: Day $12,200 (+$500). **Aid:** Need 97 ($716,000).
Summer: Enrich Rem Rec. 6 wks.
Endow $2,465,000. Plant val $12,478,000. Bldgs 12. Class rms 54. Lib 10,000 vols. Sci labs 7. Comp labs 3. Auds 1. Theaters 1. Art studios 2. Music studios 2. Gyms 2. Fields 5. Tennis courts 7. Pools 1.
Est 1966. Nonprofit. Episcopal. Sem (Aug-June). **Assoc** CLS.

Trinity is an independent Episcopal school that was founded by a group of central Florida community leaders. The traditional liberal arts curriculum includes Advanced Placement and honors courses. Special-help sessions four days per week after school allow teachers to aid those students who need extra guidance or explanation in a particular discipline.

Additional opportunities for enrichment are offered through participation in academic, service and recreational activities. The athletic program fields teams for students in grades 6-12. The school occupies a 100-acre campus bordered by lakes and woods.

GEORGIA

ATLANTA, GA. Urban. Pop: 416,474. Alt: 1032 ft. Area also includes College Park.

ATLANTA INTERNATIONAL SCHOOL
Day — Coed Gr PS-12

Atlanta, GA 30305. 2890 N Fulton Dr. Tel: 404-841-3840. Fax: 404-841-3873.
 www.aischool.org   E-mail: info@aischool.org
David B. Hawley, **Head.** BA, Framingham State College, MEd, EdD, Harvard Univ. **Aileen Williams, Adm.**
 Col Prep. IB Diploma. IB PYP. Bilingual. Feat—Fr Ger Lat Mandarin Span Comp_Sci Studio_Art Visual_Arts Theater_Arts Music. **Supp**—ESL Tut.
 Adm: 165/yr. Appl due: Feb. **Tests** SSAT.
 Enr 878. B 404. G 474. Elem 611. Sec 267. Avg class size: 15. **Fac 108.** Adv deg: 61%.
 Grad '04—59. Col—59. (U of GA 5, Emory 5, GA Inst of Tech 5, Brown 2, U of Miami 2, Geo Wash 2). Avg SAT: 1302. Alum 458.
 Tui '04-'05: Day $12,875-15,375 (+$3000). **Aid:** Need ($730,000).
 Summer: Acad Enrich Rev Rec. Tui Day $625-1200. 2-4 wks.
 Endow $5,640,000. Plant val $6,454,000. Bldgs 4. Class rms 78. Lib 20,000 vols. Sci labs 6. Lang labs 1. Comp labs 3. Auds 1. Theaters 1. Art studios 3. Music studios 7. Dance studios 1. Gyms 1. Fields 1.
 Est 1985. Nonprofit. Sem (Aug-June). **Assoc** SACS.

Founded by a group of international educators and members of the business community, AIS offers multicultural education to children of American and international families in the Atlanta area. Both students and faculty represent numerous nationalities, and 50 percent of the students are US citizens.

Children in the primary division (through grade 5) participate in a program in which they spend half their time taking all subjects in English and the other half taking all subjects in another language (French, German or Spanish). In grades 6-10, students pursue a curriculum designed to prepare them for the rigorous International Baccalaureate program, which they follow as juniors and seniors. Those students who successfully complete the entire program, including exams, receive both the IB diploma and the AIS diploma.

After-school activities include sports teams, Model UN, chess, yearbook, music, band, choir and drama.

BRANDON HALL SCHOOL
Bdg — Boys Gr 7-PG; Day — Coed 4-PG

Atlanta, GA 30350. 1701 Brandon Hall Dr. Tel: 770-394-8177. Fax: 770-804-8821.
 www.brandonhall.org   E-mail: admissions@brandonhall.org
Paul R. Stockhammer, **Pres.** BA, MEd, Mercer Univ. **Marcia Shearer, Adm.**
 Col Prep. Gen Acad. LD. Underachiever. Feat—Fr Span Comp_Sci Fine_Arts. **Supp**—Dev_Read ESL Makeup Tut.
 Adm: 40/yr. Appl due: Rolling. Accepted: 85%.

Enr 114. B 47/50. G 17. Elem 30. Sec 83. PG 1. Wh 70%. Blk 10%. Asian 15%. Other 5%. Avg class size: 4. Uniform. **Fac 34.** M 22/1. F 9/2. Wh 81%. Hisp 3%. Blk 10%. Am Ind 3%. Other 3%. Adv deg: 73%. In dorms 4.

Grad '04—37. Col—35. (GA Col 5, GA Perimeter 4, Gainesville 4, Piedmont Col 3, State U of W GA 3, GA Southern 3). Avg SAT: 904. Alum 1500.

Tui '04-'05: Bdg $40,800 (+$4000). **5-Day Bdg $38,700** (+$2500). **Day $24,850** (+$1200). **Aid:** Need 10 ($120,000).

Summer: Acad Enrich Rev. 2-6 wks.

Endow $250,000. Plant val $9,500,000. Bldgs 10. Dorms 1. Dorm rms 36. Class rms 20. Lib 5000 vols. Sci labs 3. Lang labs 1. Comp labs 2. Auds 1. Theaters 1. Gyms 1. Fields 1. Courts 2.

Est 1959. Nonprofit. Sem (Aug-May).

Brandon Hall stresses college preparatory skills, independent study habits and personal self-discipline for the underachiever and for other bright students with different learning styles. Reconstruction of basic skills, accelerated course work and Advanced Placement courses are also available. All seniors receive SAT preparation. Class size varies from one-on-one instruction (offered in all courses) to small groups of four to eight. Sports and clubs supplement the curriculum. A tutorial program is conducted over the summer. **See Also Page 1353**

THE HEISKELL SCHOOL

Day — Coed Gr PS-8

Atlanta, GA 30305. 3260 Northside Dr. Tel: 404-262-2233. Fax: 404-262-2575.
www.heiskell.net E-mail: writeus@heiskell.net

Cyndie Heiskell, Dir. BA, College of William and Mary, MA, Georgia State Univ. **Virginia G. Peebles, Adm.**

Pre-Prep. Feat—Fr Lat Computers Bible Studio_Art Music Ballet.

Adm: 100/yr. Appl due: Feb. **Tests** IQ SSAT Stanford.

Enr 360. Elem 360. Wh 80%. Blk 18%. Other 2%. Avg class size: 15. Uniform. **Fac 30.**

Grad '04—12. Col—12.

Tui '04-'05: Day $9555 (+$125-700). **Aid:** Need 40 ($150,000).

Plant val $1,750,000. Bldgs 2. Class rms 34. 2 Libs 12,000 vols. Sci labs 1. Comp labs 1. Media labs 1. Art studios 1. Gyms 1. Fields 1. Tennis courts 1. Tracks 1.

Est 1949. Inc. Nondenom Christian. Quar (Aug-June). **Assoc** SACS.

Founded as a nursery school and kindergarten by Mrs. James M. Heiskell, this nondenominational Christian school added an elementary division in 1970. Heiskell, located in the Buckhead section of northwest Atlanta, stresses the development of reading, mathematical and motor skills. A strong emphasis is placed on phonetics in the preschool.

Heiskell comprises three sections: preschool (age 2 through kindergarten), elementary (grades 1-5) and junior high (grades 6-8). Students take courses in art, music, computer and Bible, in addition to the basic disciplines. Pupils join in worship services each week and participate in community service programs throughout the year.

A variety of athletics includes softball, track and field, and basketball. There are also frequent field trips to local places of interest. Over the years, the school has enrolled qualified international students from around the world.

THE LOVETT SCHOOL

Day — Coed Gr K-12

Atlanta, GA 30327. 4075 Paces Ferry Rd NW. Tel: 404-262-3032. Fax: 404-261-1967.
www.lovett.org   E-mail: admissions@lovett.org
William S. Peebles IV, Head. AB, Princeton Univ, MBA, Univ of Virginia. **Debbie Lange, Adm.**

- **Col Prep. AP**—Eng Fr Ger Lat Span Calc Stats Comp_Sci Bio Chem Physics Eur_Hist US_Govt & Pol Music_Theory. **Feat**—Chin Genetics Zoology Relig Photog Studio_Art Drama Music Journ. **Supp**—Rev Tut.
- **Adm:** 232/yr. Appl due: Feb. Accepted: 22%. Yield: 74%. **Tests** IQ SSAT.
- **Enr 1555.** Elem 943. Sec 612. Wh 87%. Hisp 1%. Blk 7%. Asian 3%. Other 2%. Avg class size: 16. Uniform. **Fac 140.** M 41/1. F 92/6. Wh 93%. Hisp 3%. Blk 2%. Asian 1%. Other 1%. Adv deg: 63%.
- **Grad '04—144. Col—144.** (U of GA, U of MS, SMU, Auburn, GA Inst of Tech, U of AL-Tuscaloosa). Alum 4500.
- **Tui '04-'05: Day $13,000-15,530** (+$500). **Aid:** Need 140 ($1,000,280).
- **Summer:** Acad Enrich Rev Rem Rec. Tui Day $650/crse. 3 wks.
- Endow $31,100,000. Plant val $29,931,000. Bldgs 18. Class rms 91. 2 Libs 56,000 vols. Sci labs 9. Comp labs 8. Theaters 2. Art studios 2. Music studios 3. Drama studios 1. Gyms 3. Fields 6. Courts 10. Pools 1.
- **Est 1926.** Nonprofit. Sem (Aug-May). **Assoc** CLS SACS.

Mrs. Eva Edwards Lovett founded this school and remained head until 1954. During the next eight years, the school expanded to include a kindergarten and 12 grades. Since 1963, Lovett has been an independent school governed by a board of trustees.

Bordered by the Chattahoochee River, this college preparatory school is located on 100 wooded acres in northwest Atlanta. In addition to a selection of honors and Advanced Placement courses, Lovett's curriculum includes a varied fine arts program. Students in need of additional help receive one-on-one or small-group remedial instruction through the learning lab. The school is concerned with the development of all aspects of the child and seeks to assist students in developing positive self-concepts.

Extracurricular activities include chorus, orchestra, band, publications, and interest and service clubs, as well as interscholastic and intramural sports.

See Also Page 1195

MARIST SCHOOL

Day — Coed Gr 7-12

Atlanta, GA 30319. 3790 Ashford-Dunwoody Rd NE. Tel: 770-457-7201.
Fax: 770-457-8402.
www.marist.com   E-mail: info@marist.com
Rev. Richmond J. Egan, SM, Pres. BA, MA, Catholic Univ of America, MA, American Univ, ThM, Princeton Theological Seminary, JD, Hamline Univ. **Rev. Joel M. Konzen, SM, Prin.** BA, St Meinrad College, MDiv, Univ of Notre Dame, MA, MAEd, Catholic Univ of America. **James G. Byrne, Adm.**

- **Col Prep. AP**—Eng Fr Lat Span Calc Stats Comp_Sci Bio Chem Physics Eur_Hist US_Hist Econ US_Govt & Pol Art_Hist Studio_Art Music_Theory. **Feat**—Greek Relig Fine_Arts. **Supp**—Tut.
- **Adm:** 221/yr. Appl due: Feb. Accepted: 50%. **Tests** SSAT.

GA   *Leading Private Schools*   *494*

Enr 1034. B 515. G 519. Elem 261. Sec 773. Wh 88%. Hisp 4%. Blk 5%. Am Ind 1%. Asian 2%. Avg class size: 19. Uniform. **Fac 105.** M 58. F 47. Adv deg: 79%.

Grad '04—193. Col—193. (U of GA, GA Inst of Tech, Vanderbilt, Boston Col, Furman, Notre Dame). Avg SAT: 1219. Alum 6400.

Tui '05-'06: Day $13,200 (+$700). **Aid:** Need 122 ($866,000).

Endow $8,600,000. Plant val $35,000,000. Bldgs 18. Class rms 42. Lib 20,000 vols. Chapels 1. Sci labs 8. Comp labs 3. Auds 1. Theaters 1. Art studios 1. Music studios 2. Dance studios 1. Gyms 3. Fields 6. Tennis courts 4. Pools 1. Tracks 1. Stadiums 1.

Est 1901. Nonprofit. Roman Catholic. Tri (Aug-June). **Assoc** SACS.

Marist School was founded by Rev. John E. Gunn, a member of the Society of Mary (the Marists). Known as Marist College until 1962, the school moved from downtown Atlanta to its present, 57-acre campus in northeast Atlanta to accommodate a growing enrollment.

The college preparatory curriculum offers year-long courses in most major disciplines and a large variety of term courses, including drama, creative writing, statistics, geology, political science, accounting and driver education. A wide selection of Advanced Placement courses are also available. Graduation requirements include religion, computer literacy and community service.

Extracurricular activities offered are student council, retreats, key club, band, math and science club, drama club, debate team, photography, newspaper and literary magazine. Varsity team sports include wrestling, golf, tennis, volleyball, softball, soccer, swimming, track, football, basketball and baseball.

PACE ACADEMY

Day — Coed Gr K-12

Atlanta, GA 30327. 966 W Paces Ferry Rd NW. Tel: 404-262-1345. Fax: 404-264-9376.
   www.paceacademy.org   **E-mail: cstrowd@paceacademy.org**

Frederick G. Assaf, Head. BA, Johns Hopkins Univ, MEd, Univ of Virginia. **George K. Mengert, Upper Sch Adm; Susan Gruber, Lower Sch Adm.**

Col Prep. AP—Eng Fr Lat Span Calc Stats Bio Chem Physics Eur_Hist US_Hist Comp_Govt & Pol US_Govt & Pol Art_Hist Studio_Art Music_Theory. **Feat—**Ecol Comp_Sci Architect_Drawing Ceramics Drawing Photog Sculpt Theater_Arts Music Debate Public_Speak. **Supp—**Tut.

Adm: 190/yr. Appl due: Feb. Accepted: 32%. Yield: 70%. **Tests** SSAT.

Enr 916. B 464. G 452. Elem 541. Sec 375. Wh 87%. Hisp 2%. Blk 6%. Asian 4%. Other 1%. Avg class size: 15. **Fac 100.** M 35. F 65. Wh 89%. Hisp 3%. Blk 5%. Asian 3%. Adv deg: 71%.

Grad '04—88. Col—88. (Vanderbilt 4, Tulane 4, U of GA 4, U of CO-Boulder 4, U of VA 3, Duke 3). Avg SAT: 1313. Alum 1700.

Tui '04-'05: Day $12,075-15,840 (+$500). **Aid:** Need 62 ($698,235).

Summer: Acad Enrich Rev Rec. Theater. Debate. 1-3 wks.

Endow $20,000,000. Plant val $35,000,000. Bldgs 8. Class rms 60. 2 Libs 20,000 vols. Sci labs 7. Lang labs 2. Comp labs 7. Auds 1. Theaters 1. Art studios 6. Music studios 3. Gyms 2. Fields 3. Courts 4. Pools 1.

Est 1958. Nonprofit. Sem (Aug-June). **Assoc** CLS SACS.

Located on a 25-acre tract (with five acres of woodland) in a residential section of northern Atlanta, Pace offers a curriculum with the flexibility to address students' varying needs, abilities and learning styles. Balancing challenge and support, the program features single-gender math groups in grade 3, accelerated classes in grade 4, in-depth writing workshops in grade 5, honors courses in grade 8, and both honors and Advanced Placement classes for upper schoolers. Computer use commences in the early grades and becomes increasingly prominent as the pupil progresses. After-school extra-help sessions provide daily opportunities for individual assistance. Interested students may participate in exchange programs with schools in England, Japan and Korea.

The creative and performing arts play an important role in school life. Among Pace's course options in this area are painting, sculpture, drawing, photography, ceramics and printmaking, and students also choose from three singing groups and three instrumental music groups. In addition, the academy conducts a well-regarded drama program.

As community involvement is stressed, all pupils fulfill a 40-hour service requirement prior to graduation. A range of sports and athletic opportunities that includes intramural games and interscholastic teams accommodates boys and girls of varying skill levels. **See Also Page 1223**

THE PAIDEIA SCHOOL
Day — Coed Gr PS-12

Atlanta, GA 30307. 1509 Ponce de Leon Ave. Tel: 404-377-3491. Fax: 404-377-0032. www.paideiaschool.org E-mail: admissions@paideiaschool.org
Paul F. Bianchi, Head. AB, MAT, Harvard Univ. **Caroline Quillian Stubbs, Adm.**

Col Prep. AP—Calc Bio Chem Physics Eur_Hist Psych. **Feat**—Computers Anthro Relig Ceramics Photog Studio_Art Drama Chorus Music Orchestra Journ. **Supp**—Tut.

Adm: 122/yr. Appl due: Feb. Accepted: 23%.

Enr 882. B 408. G 474. Elem 496. Sec 386. Wh 77%. Hisp 3%. Blk 16%. Asian 4%. Avg class size: 14. **Fac 121.** M 45/4. F 62/10. Wh 85%. Hisp 4%. Blk 11%. Adv deg: 68%.

Grad '04—89. Col—89. (U of GA, Emory, Yale, Columbia, Morehouse, Oberlin). Alum 1298.

Tui '04-'05: Day $12,786-14,505 (+$100-300). **Aid:** Need 103 ($859,334).

Summer: Rec. Tui Day $400/3-wk ses. 6 wks.

Endow $10,400,000. Plant val $17,984,000. Bldgs 14. Class rms 60. 2 Libs 18,800 vols. Sci labs 4. Comp labs 4. Auds 1. Theaters 1. Art studios 5. Music studios 4. Gyms 1. Fields 3.

Est 1971. Nonprofit. (Aug-June). **Assoc** SACS.

Paideia encompasses a half-day program (morning and afternoon sessions) for three- to five-year-olds and a full-day program for those in grades K-12. The academic curriculum is characterized by individualized instruction and achievement at a pace in keeping with the student's development. The college preparatory high school program includes classes, seminars, independent study and community service.

In addition to academics, there is a wide range of activities in the areas of athletics, the performing and visual arts, publications, interest clubs and music. Paideia's performing arts and sports facilities, as well as significant faculty and parental involvement, support strong programs and school-wide participation.

THE WESTMINSTER SCHOOLS
Day — Coed Gr K-12

Atlanta, GA 30327. 1424 W Paces Ferry Rd NW. Tel: 404-355-8673. Fax: 404-355-6606.
www.westminster.net   E-mail: mainoffice@westminster.net
William Clarkson IV, Pres. BA, Duke Univ, MDiv, General Theological Seminary, DMin, Southern Methodist Univ. **Marjorie Mitchell, Adm.**

Col Prep. AP—Eng Fr Ger Lat Span Calc Stats Comp_Sci Bio Chem Physics Eur_Hist US_Hist Art_Hist Studio_Art Music_Theory. **Feat**—Anat & Physiol Astron Geol Amer_Stud Econ Psych Bible World_Relig. **Supp**—Dev_Read Rev Tut.

Adm (Gr K-11): 218/yr. Appl due: Feb. Accepted: 20%. Yield: 95%. **Tests** IQ SSAT.

Enr 1751. B 897. G 854. Elem 970. Sec 781. Wh 82%. Hisp 2%. Blk 8%. Asian 6%. Other 2%. Avg class size: 14. **Fac 234.** M 82/2. F 127/23. Wh 91%. Hisp 3%. Blk 3%. Asian 2%. Other 1%. Adv deg: 84%.

Grad '04—188. Col—188. (U of GA 26, U of VA 12, Wake Forest 9, Emory 9, Duke 9, Stanford 7). Avg SAT: 1349. Avg ACT: 29. Alum 8410.

Tui '04-'05: Day $12,846-15,112 (+$500-600). **Aid:** Need 135 ($1,240,077).

Summer: Acad Enrich Rev. Tui Day $460-1450/3-wk ses. 6 wks.

Endow $184,000,000. Plant val $81,000,000. Bldgs 31. Class rms 147. 3 Libs 81,000 vols. Sci labs 21. Lang labs 1. Comp labs 9. Photog labs 1. Auds 2. Theaters 1. Art studios 6. Music studios 5. Gyms 3. Fields 7. Courts 16. Pools 2.

Est 1951. Nonprofit. Sem (Aug-June). **Assoc** CLS SACS.

Originally the North Avenue Presbyterian School (established in 1909), the institution assumed its present name and became nondenominational in 1951. Shortly thereafter, the school relocated to the northwest section of the city. Westminster later merged with Washington Seminary, founded in 1878.

Located on 176 acres, Westminster maintains a strong academic program that features a wide range of Advanced Placement courses, as well as extensive offerings in art, debate, drama and music. Extracurricular activities include service projects, clubs, school publications and athletics.   **See Also Page 1278**

WOODWARD ACADEMY
Day — Coed Gr PS-12

College Park, GA 30337. 1662 Rugby Ave. Tel: 404-765-4001. Fax: 404-765-4009.
www.woodward.edu   E-mail: admissions@woodward.edu
Harry C. Payne, Pres. BA, MA, PhD, Yale Univ. **Russell L. Slider, Adm.**

Col Prep. AP—Eng Fr Ger Span Calc Stats Comp_Sci Bio Chem Physics Eur_Hist US_Hist Econ US_Govt & Pol Music_Theory. **Feat**—Japan Lat Studio_Art Music. **Supp**—Tut.

Adm (Gr PS-11): 400/yr. Appl due: Mar. Accepted: 35%. **Tests** SSAT.

Enr 2860. Wh 84%. Hisp 2%. Blk 11%. Asian 3%. Avg class size: 17. Uniform. **Fac 340.** Adv deg: 78%.

Grad '04—256. Col—256. (U of GA 27, Auburn 14, GA Inst of Tech 14, U of AL-Tuscaloosa 7, U of MI 7, Vanderbilt 7). Avg SAT: 1240. Avg ACT: 27. Alum 6000.

Tui '04-'05: Day $10,000-15,300 (+$500-700).

Endow $60,000,000. Plant val $70,000,000. Bldgs 55. Class rms 155. Lib 40,000 vols. Sci labs 10. Lang labs 1. Art studios 12. Music studios 6. TV studios 1. Gyms 6. Fields 6. Courts 8.

Est 1900. Nonprofit. Sem (Aug-May). **Assoc** SACS.

Known from its founding date until 1966 as Georgia Military Academy, this large school offers a strenuous program for college preparation. There is also a student transition education program for bright students with minor learning disabilities. Computer literacy and advanced programming courses are offered at each grade level. Woodward conducts a European travel program for juniors and seniors.

Located on an 80-acre site, Woodward offers the following athletics: football, cross-country, soccer, softball, wrestling, volleyball, basketball, baseball, golf, lacrosse, tennis, track, riflery, weightlifting, swimming and diving, and cheerleading. **See Also Page 1283**

AUGUSTA, GA. (75 mi. WSW of Columbia, SC; 142 mi. E of Atlanta, GA) Urban. Pop: 195,182. Alt: 143 ft. Area also includes Martinez.

AUGUSTA PREPARATORY DAY SCHOOL
Day — Coed Gr PS-12

Martinez, GA 30907. 285 Flowing Wells Rd. Tel: 706-863-1906. Fax: 706-863-6198. www.augustaprep.org   E-mail: admissions@augustaprep.org

Jack R. Hall, Head. BA, Davidson College, MS, Georgia State Univ, MA, Columbia Univ.
Rosie Herrmann, Adm.

  Col Prep. AP—Eng Fr Lat Span Calc Stats Bio Chem Physics Eur_Hist US_Hist Studio_Art. Feat—Anat Bioethics Ecol Geog Psych Govt/Econ Civil_Rights World_Relig Theater. Supp—Tut.

  Adm: 98/yr. Appl due: Rolling. Accepted: 90%. Tests CTP_4 MRT.

  Enr 520. Elem 339. Sec 181. Wh 87%. Hisp 3%. Blk 4%. Asian 6%. Avg class size: 14. Fac 63. M 16. F 44/3. Wh 95%. Hisp 1%. Blk 3%. Asian 1%. Adv deg: 34%.

  Grad '04—34. Col—34. (U of GA, U of SC, Augusta St, Furman, Wash & Lee, Auburn). Avg SAT: 1207. Avg ACT: 24. Alum 1122.

  Tui '05-'06: Day $4347-10,095 (+$250-750). Aid: Merit 2. Need 71 ($194,754).

  Endow $2,193,000. Plant val $4,500,000. Bldgs 5. Class rms 43. 2 Libs 20,000 vols. Sci labs 4. Comp labs 3. Sci ctrs 1. Gyms 1. Fields 3. Courts 4.

  Est 1960. Nonprofit. Sem (Aug-June). Assoc CLS SACS.

Located on a 50-acre campus, this school resulted from a 1988 merger between Augusta Preparatory School (established in 1960) and Augusta Country Day School (founded in 1972). A traditional college preparatory program, with an integrated curriculum in the lower, middle and upper schools, is complemented by honors and Advanced Placement courses in the upper school. The program is characterized by an emphasis on fine arts, athletics and character development.

A variety of extracurricular activities is offered. Sports include soccer, volleyball, golf, basketball, baseball, cheerleading, cross-country, tennis and track.

GA   *Leading Private Schools*   *498*

COLUMBUS, GA. (83 mi. E of Montgomery, AL; 90 mi. SSW of Atlanta, GA) Urban. Pop: 185,781. Alt: 265 ft.

BROOKSTONE SCHOOL

Day — Coed Gr PS-12

Columbus, GA 31904. 440 Bradley Park Dr. Tel: 706-324-1392. Fax: 706-571-0178. www.brookstoneschool.org   E-mail: admissions@brookstoneschool.org

Scott A. Wilson, Head. BA, Univ of Georgia, MEd, Univ of South Carolina. **Mary S. Snyder, Adm.**

Col Prep. AP—Eng Fr Lat Span Calc Stats Comp_Sci Bio Chem Physics Eur_Hist US_Hist Comp_Govt & Pol US_Govt & Pol. **Feat**—Humanities Anat & Physiol Astron Ecol Geol Zoology Ornithology Civil_War Econ Psych Comp_Relig Philos Art_Hist Studio_Art Drama Music Communications. **Supp**—Dev_Read Rev Tut.

Adm (Gr PS-11): 113/yr. Appl due: Rolling. Accepted: 93%. Yield: 81%. **Tests** Stanford.

Enr 826. B 406. G 420. Elem 560. Sec 266. Wh 91%. Blk 3%. Asian 5%. Other 1%. Avg class size: 17. **Fac 70.** M 18/2. F 46/4. Wh 98%. Blk 2%. Adv deg: 67%.

Grad '04—61. Col—61. (U of GA 10, Auburn 5, Columbus St 4, U of MS 4, Furman 3, Wake Forest 2). Avg SAT: 1213. Alum 1550.

Tui '04-'05: Day $5540-9830 (+$80-375). **Aid:** Merit 35 ($227,965). Need 79 ($565,730).

Summer: Enrich Rec. 1-6 wks.

Endow $18,941,000. Plant val $20,297,000. Bldgs 14. Class rms 57. 2 Libs 20,120 vols. Sci labs 3. Lang labs 1. Comp labs 3. Auds 1. Art studios 2. Music studios 5. Arts ctrs 1. Gyms 2. Fields 4. Tennis courts 6.

Est 1951. Nonprofit. Sem (Aug-May). **Assoc** CLS SACS.

Founded as Trinity School, Brookstone has occupied its present, 112-acre campus since 1969. The curriculum, designed for the college-bound student, offers Advanced Placement courses and a variety of electives. The school's interscholastic sports program consists of football, softball, soccer, wrestling, baseball, basketball, track, tennis, cross-country, golf, competitive cheerleading and volleyball. Pupils may also take part in such activities as debate, one-act plays and literary events.

GAINESVILLE, GA. (50 mi. NE of Atlanta, GA) Suburban. Pop: 25,578. Alt: 1200 ft.

BRENAU ACADEMY

Bdg and Day — Girls Gr 9-PG

Gainesville, GA 30501. 1 Centennial Cir. Tel: 770-534-6140. Fax: 770-534-6298. www.brenauacademy.org   E-mail: enroll@lib.brenau.edu

Frank M. Booth, Head. BA, Hampden-Sydney College, MA, Marshall Univ, MEd, EdD, Univ of Georgia. **Leslie N. Miller, Adm.**

Col Prep. Gen Acad. Feat—British_Lit Fr Span Computers Govt/Econ Studio_Art Drama Chorus Music Dance. **Supp**—LD Rev Tut.

Adm (Gr 9-12): 25/yr. Bdg 22. Day 3. Appl due: Rolling.

Enr 80. G 73/7. Sec 80. Wh 82%. Blk 7%. Am Ind 4%. Asian 7%. Avg class size: 12. **Fac 12.** M 2/1. F 6/3. Adv deg: 75%.

Grad '04—13. Col—13. (U of GA, Brenau, Mercer, Geo Wash, Auburn, Ringling Sch of

Art & Design). Alum 2000.
Tui '04-'05: Bdg $20,500 (+$400). **Day $8900** (+$400).
Endow $50,000,000. Plant val $28,000,000. Bldgs 64. Dorms 3. Class rms 12. Lib 150,000 vols. Sci labs 1. Lang labs 1. Comp labs 2. Auds 2. Theaters 3. Art studios 1. Music studios 2. Dance studios 1. Arts ctrs 1. Gyms 1. Fields 1. Courts 9. Pools 1.
Est 1928. Nonprofit. Sem (Aug-May). **Assoc** SACS.

Founded by Dr. H. S. Pearce on the campus of Brenau University Women's College, the academy is separately housed and independently organized. Elective courses are available in music, drama, dance and visual arts. The school offers a strong program in the fine arts, a program for girls with learning differences, and a dual-enrollment option with Brenau University Women's College.

Extracurricular activities include interscholastic sports, with competitive teams fielded in tennis and volleyball. Other opportunities feature cultural field trips, clubs and interest groups, community activities, supervised weekend outings, and domestic and international travel opportunities. **See Also Pages 1290-1**

RIVERSIDE MILITARY ACADEMY

Bdg and Day — Boys Gr 7-12

Gainesville, GA 30501. 2001 Riverside Dr. Tel: 770-532-6251. Fax: 678-291-3364. www.cadet.com E-mail: admissions@cadet.com
Col. H. Michael Hughes, Supt. BS, US Military Academy, MEd, Univ of North Carolina-Chapel Hill, PhD, Univ of Virginia. **Donna Davis, Adm.**
 Col Prep. Milit. AP—Eng Calc Bio Physics US_Hist World_Hist. **Feat**—British_Lit Fr Ger Lat Span Stats Computers Govt & Econ Ethics Art_Hist Photog Studio_Art Music Journ Speech JROTC. **Supp**—Dev_Read ESL Tut.
Adm: 129/yr. Appl due: Rolling. Accepted: 30%. **Tests** IQ TOEFL.
Enr 513. B 500/13. Elem 58. Sec 455. Wh 45%. Hisp 15%. Blk 15%. Asian 20%. Other 5%. Avg class size: 10. Uniform. **Fac** 65. M 38. F 27. Wh 80%. Hisp 10%. Blk 10%. Adv deg: 70%.
Grad '04—85. Col—85. (Citadel, GA St, U of GA, Wofford, NYU, Boston Col).
Tui '05-'06: Bdg $23,950. Day $15,000.
Summer: Acad Enrich Rev Rem Rec. Tui Bdg $3685. 5 wks.
Bldgs 9. Dorms 1. Dorm rms 270. Libs 1. Sci labs 3. Lang labs 3. Comp labs 3. Theaters 1. Art studios 3. Music studios 3. Arts ctrs 1. Gyms 1. Fields 5. Courts 6. Pools 1.
Est 1907. Nonprofit. Sem (Aug-May).

RMA offers a structured program for college-bound boys that emphasizes problem-solving and critical-thinking skills and features Advanced Placement and honors courses. Small classes, evening tutorial opportunities and weekly grade reports are programmatic elements designed to increase the student's likelihood for success. Instructors teach organizational and time-management skills, and cadets also learn how to take notes and study in a manner that accounts for their styles of processing information. All boys in grades 9-12 take part in Riverside's Junior ROTC program, which focuses upon citizenship, leadership and responsibility.

Athletics are an integral aspect of school life. Each cadet spends two hours per day engaging in a sport at the varsity, junior varsity or intramural level; certain options are also available as seventh and eighth grade prep sports. Among RMA's other extracurricular activities are environmental club, literary society, drill team, mock trial, academic bowl and school publications.

NEWNAN, GA. (34 mi. SW of Atlanta, GA) Urban. Pop: 16,242. Alt: 1001 ft.

THE HERITAGE SCHOOL
Day — Coed Gr PS-12

Newnan, GA 30263. 2093 Hwy 29 N. Tel: 770-253-9898. Fax: 770-253-4850.
www.heritagehawks.org E-mail: jbowdoin@heritagehawks.org
Judith Griffith, Head. BA, MEd, State Univ of West Georgia. **Julie Bowdoin, Adm.**
- Col Prep. **AP**—Eng Fr Span Calc Chem Physics Eur_Hist US_Hist Psych. **Feat**—Computers Art_Hist Graphic_Design Video Drama Chorus Music. **Supp**—Tut.
- **Adm:** 90/yr. Appl due: Mar. Accepted: 81%. **Tests** IQ.
- **Enr 363.** B 180. G 183. Elem 278. Sec 85. Wh 90%. Hisp 3%. Blk 3%. Asian 1%. Other 3%. Avg class size: 15. **Fac 49.** M 9/2. F 29/9. Wh 98%. Hisp 2%. Adv deg: 28%.
- **Grad '04—14. Col—13.** (GA Inst of Tech, U of AL-Tuscaloosa, Wesleyan Col, GA Southern, State U of W GA, Stetson). Avg SAT: 1102. Alum 313.
- **Tui '04-'05: Day $5275-9990** (+$300). **Aid:** Need 59 ($277,397).
- Endow $1,575,000. Plant val $4,900,000. Bldgs 12. Class rms 35. Lib 12,699 vols. Labs 1. Sci labs 2. Lang labs 4. Comp labs 2. Auds 1. Theaters 1. Art studios 2. Music studios 3. Gyms 2. Fields 2. Courts 5.
- **Est 1970.** Nonprofit. Quar (Aug-May). **Assoc** SACS.

Situated on a 63-acre campus in the midst of an active pecan grove, the school serves students from Coweta, Fayette, South Fulton and surrounding counties. The lower school curriculum features introductory language study, and the middle and upper schools stress the liberal arts while preparing students for college entrance. Computer, foreign language, music and art classes begin in kindergarten and continue through grade 12. A one-week, off-campus interim program allows students to learn more about potential careers.

Activities include yearbook, chorus, drama, student government, honor council and community service. The school's interscholastic sports program consists of soccer, basketball, tennis, golf, softball, baseball, track and cross-country squads.

NORCROSS, GA. (17 mi. NE of Atlanta, GA) Suburban. Pop: 8410. Alt: 1057 ft.

WESLEYAN SCHOOL
Day — Coed Gr K-12

Norcross, GA 30092. 5405 Spalding Dr. Tel: 770-448-7640. Fax: 770-448-3699.
www.wesleyanschool.org
Zach Young, Head. BA, Univ of Virginia, MEd, Harvard Univ. **Bobbie Lencke, Adm.**
- Col Prep. **AP**—Eng Fr Lat Span Calc Comp_Sci Bio Chem Eur_Hist US_Hist Studio_Art. **Feat**—British_Lit Stats Environ_Sci Econ Psych Bible Film Theater_Arts Music Public_Speak. **Supp**—ESL.
- **Adm:** 152/yr. Appl due: Feb. Accepted: 30%. **Tests** CEEB IQ SSAT.
- **Enr 1068.** B 551. G 517. Elem 659. Sec 409. Wh 94%. Blk 3%. Asian 2%. Other 1%. Avg class size: 20. Uniform. **Fac 131.** M 47. F 82/2. Wh 98%. Blk 2%. Adv deg: 56%.

GA   *Southern States*   501

> **Grad '04—105. Col—104.** (U of GA 15, Auburn 9, U of AL-Tuscaloosa 6, GA Inst of Tech 5, Vanderbilt 5, Clemson 4). Avg SAT: 1200.
> **Tui '04-'05: Day $10,970-13,670** (+$500). **Aid:** Need 27 ($176,910).
> **Summer:** Enrich Rec. Tui Day $100/wk. 8 wks.
> Endow $1,800,000. Plant val $49,000,000. Bldgs 8. Class rms 83. 2 Libs 12,000 vols. Chapels 2. Sci labs 6. Lang labs 1. Comp labs 6. Auds 1. Theaters 1. Art studios 3. Music studios 4. Drama studios 1. Gyms 3. Fields 7. Basketball courts 5. Tennis courts 5. Pools 1. Tracks 1. Stadiums 1.
> **Est 1963.** Nonprofit. Nondenom Christian. Sem (Aug-May). **Assoc** SACS.

This Christian school was established as a preschool by Sandy Springs United Methodist Church. Soon thereafter, Wesleyan expanded to include elementary and middle school divisions. Following the school's divestiture from the founding church and the addition of a high school program, Wesleyan relocated in summer 1996 to its current, 70-acre site.

The school conducts a varied curriculum at all grade levels. In the lower school (grades K-4), children develop a foundation in the fundamentals as they follow a core curriculum that includes Bible, foreign language, computer science, music and art classes. Wesleyan's middle school program (grades 5-8) serves as a bridge between the lower and high schools and helps students form sound study habits, assume a higher degree of responsibility for their learning and learn to budget time effectively. During the high school years (grades 9-12), the college preparatory curriculum provides opportunities for acceleration while also encouraging pupils to take part in a variety of activities within the arts, athletics and fellowship groups.

A strict honor code, uniform requirements and regular chapel programs are integral aspects of school life.

RABUN GAP, GA. (102 mi. NE of Atlanta, GA) Rural. Pop: 200. Alt: 2000 ft.

RABUN GAP-NACOOCHEE SCHOOL
Bdg — Coed Gr 7-12; Day — Coed 6-12

Rabun Gap, GA 30568. 339 Nacoochee Dr. Tel: 706-746-7467. Fax: 706-746-2594.
   www.rabungap.org   E-mail: admission@rabungap.org
John D. Marshall, Head. Adele Yermack, Adm.
> **Col Prep. AP**—Eng Fr Lat Span Calc Bio Chem Eur_Hist US_Hist World_Hist US_Govt & Pol. **Feat**—Botany Comp_Sci Econ Studio_Art Music Journ Mech_Drawing Outdoor_Ed. **Supp**—ESL Rev Tut.
> **Adm:** 93/yr. Bdg 61. Day 32. Appl due: Rolling. Accepted: 73%. Yield: 45%. **Tests** CEEB ISEE SSAT TOEFL.
> **Enr 283.** B 64/80. G 62/77. Elem 73. Sec 210. Avg class size: 14. Uniform. **Fac 49.** M 20/6. F 17/6. Wh 92%. Hisp 8%. Adv deg: 48%.
> **Grad '04—47. Col—47.** (Agnes Scott 3, GA Inst of Tech 3, U of GA 2, GA Perimeter 2, Vanderbilt 1, Furman 1). Avg SAT: 1140. Alum 2500.
> **Tui '04-'05: Bdg $22,600** (+$2000-3000). **Day $10,300** (+$1200). **Aid:** Merit 32 ($413,545). Need 163 ($1,342,030).
> **Summer:** Enrich. Fine Arts. 2-4 wks.
> Endow $78,000,000. Plant val $75,000,000. Bldgs 22. Dorms 7. Dorm rms 126. Class rms

32. Lib 13,000 vols. Sci labs 5. Lang labs 1. Comp labs 8. Observatories 1. Auds 1. Theaters 2. Art studios 2. Music studios 2. Dance studios 1. Arts ctrs 1. Museums 1. Galleries 3. Gyms 2. Fields 4. Courts 4. Pools 1. Tracks 3. Weight rms 1. Lakes 2.
Est 1903. Nonprofit. Presbyterian. Sem (Aug-June). **Assoc** SACS.

Formed by the 1927 merger of Rabun Gap School and Nacoochee Institute, this school was established by Harvard graduate Andrew J. Ritchie to provide educational opportunities for children from the surrounding mountains. Rabun Gap now enrolls students from approximately ten states and more than a dozen foreign countries.

The academic program includes honors courses at all grade levels, as well as several Advanced Placement courses. Latin, French and Spanish instruction begins in grade 6. Seniors complete a compulsory research paper under the supervision of a faculty mentor. All students work on campus, usually after school each afternoon.

Extracurricular activities include a comprehensive outdoor program, visual and performing arts opportunities, interest clubs and a farm program. Soccer, basketball, baseball, swimming, volleyball, tennis, track, skiing, golf, cross-country and softball provide interscholastic competition. Skiing is available at Georgia's only ski resort, located six miles from campus. **See Also Page 1233**

ROME, GA. (56 mi. NW of Atlanta, GA) Urban. Pop: 34,980. Alt: 610 ft.

DARLINGTON SCHOOL
Bdg — Coed Gr 9-PG; Day — Coed PS-12

Rome, GA 30161. 1014 Cave Spring Rd. Tel: 706-235-6051. Fax: 706-232-3600.
www.darlingtonschool.org   E-mail: admission@darlingtonschool.org
Thomas Whitworth III, Pres. BA, Univ of North Carolina-Chapel Hill, MEd, The Citadel. **David Rhodes, Head.** BS, Wake Forest Univ, MEd, West Georgia College. **Casey Zimmer, Adm.**

Col Prep. AP—Eng Fr Span Calc Stats Comp_Sci Bio Chem Physics Eur_Hist US_Hist US_Govt & Pol Studio_Art. **Feat**—Creative_Writing Environ_Sci Film Graphic_Arts Video_Production Drama Theater Chorus Music. **Supp**—ESL Tut.

Adm (Bdg Gr 9-12; Day PS-11): 165/yr. Bdg 82. Day 83. Appl due: Rolling. **Tests** CEEB IQ SSAT TOEFL.

Enr 909. B 97/375. G 78/359. Elem 424. Sec 485. Avg class size: 14. **Fac 83.** M 37. F 46. Wh 95%. Hisp 1%. Blk 1%. Other 3%. Adv deg: 75%. In dorms 19.

Grad '04—123. Col—123. (U of GA 14, Mercer 11, U of MS 6, IN U 3, U of the South 3, UNC-Chapel Hill 2). Avg SAT: 1157. Alum 6438.

Tui '05-'06: Bdg $28,600 (+$2000). **Day $9700-12,150** (+$1000). **Aid:** Merit 16 ($298,200). Need 123 ($922,710).

Summer: Rec. 1-7 wks.

Endow $33,400,000. Plant val $49,600,000. Bldgs 17. Dorms 6. Dorm rms 104. Class rms 47. Lib 19,224 vols. Chapels 1. Sci labs 3. Comp labs 6. Theaters 1. Art studios 1. Music studios 2. Dance studios 1. Gyms 4. Athletic ctrs 1. Fields 9. Courts 9. Pools 1.
Est 1905. Nonprofit. Tri (Aug-May). **Assoc** CLS SACS.

The school was founded as an independent day school by John Paul and Alice Allgood Cooper and was named for Joseph James Darlington, who had been Mr.

Cooper's teacher at a private school in Rome. The boarding department opened in 1923, as did a lower school in 1973. That same year, Darlington established coeducation through a merger with the Thornwood School for girls, founded in 1958.

Students follow a required core curriculum including foreign language and the fine arts, and they may pursue special interests through a wide range of electives. Honors courses are available in most subject areas, and Advanced Placement courses are also offered in many disciplines.

Both boys and girls may participate in varsity athletics, and intramural offerings include traditional sports and such activities as aerobics and lacrosse. Among Darlington's other extracurriculars are community service, drama, chess, bridge, woodworking, choral and instrumental music, scholar bowl and student publications. On-campus weekend activities are scheduled, as are frequent excursions to Atlanta and Chattanooga, TN. An outdoor adventure program features backpacking, canoeing, kayaking, mountain biking, rock climbing and spelunking.

A faculty advisor assists each resident student with academic and extracurricular matters. In addition, the school matches each boarder with a local family—usually headed by parents of a current day student—in an effort to provide further support.

See Also Pages 1138-9

SAVANNAH, GA. (85 mi. SW of Charleston, SC) Urban. Pop: 131,510. Alt: 42 ft.

SAVANNAH COUNTRY DAY SCHOOL

Day — Coed Gr PS-12

Savannah, GA 31419. 824 Stillwood Dr. Tel: 912-925-8800. Fax: 912-920-7800.
 www.savcds.org E-mail: admissions@savcds.org
Thomas C. Bonnell, Head. BA, Duke Univ, MA, Univ of Texas-Austin. **Terri S. Barfield, Adm.**

Col Prep. AP—Eng Fr Lat Span Calc Stats Comp_Sci Bio Chem Physics Eur_Hist US_Hist World_Hist US_Govt & Pol Studio_Art. **Feat**—British_Lit Anat & Physiol Engineering Russ_Hist Photog Theater Music Dance Public_Speak Speech Study_Skills. **Supp**—Dev_Read Rem_Math Rem_Read Tut.

Adm (Gr PS-11): 128/yr. Appl due: Jan. Accepted: 63%. Yield: 85%. **Tests** CTP_4 IQ Stanford.

Enr 972. B 484. G 488. Elem 670. Sec 302. Wh 92%. Hisp 1%. Blk 3%. Asian 4%. Avg class size: 16. **Fac 95.** M 32/1. F 52/10. Wh 97%. Hisp 1%. Blk 1%. Asian 1%. Adv deg: 64%.

Grad '04—75. **Col**—75. (U of GA 10, U of MS 3, U of VA 2, NYU 2, Elon 2, U of CO-Boulder 2). Avg SAT: 1277. Alum 3100.

Tui '04-'05: Day $5850-12,430 (+$500). **Aid:** Need 70 ($331,580).

Summer: Acad Enrich Rev Rem Rec. 10 wks.

Endow $4,517,000. Plant val $11,272,000. Bldgs 19. Class rms 58. 2 Libs 36,408 vols. Sci labs 5. Lang labs 1. Comp labs 4. Auds 1. Theaters 1. Art studios 4. Music studios 3. Gyms 3. Fields 6. Courts 6. Tracks 1. Weight rms 1. Stadiums 1.

Est 1955. Nonprofit. Quar (Aug-May). **Assoc** CLS SACS.

A college preparatory school whose graduates attend mostly Southern and Eastern colleges, Savannah Country Day emphasizes academic work and an honor system. The upper school offers Advanced Placement courses, in addition to honors work in every subject.

The school also offers art, band, a jazz ensemble, strings instruction, drama and modern dance. There are many extracurricular activities, including a well-developed community service program. Athletics include football, cross-country, soccer, girls' softball, baseball, basketball, track, golf, tennis, volleyball and crew.

KENTUCKY

GOSHEN, KY. (15 mi. NNE of Louisville, KY) Rural. Pop: 907. Alt: 700 ft.

ST. FRANCIS SCHOOL
Day — Coed Gr PS-8

Goshen, KY 40026. 11000 US Hwy 42. Tel: 502-228-1197. Fax: 502-228-6723.
www.stfrancisschool.org E-mail: sfs@stfrancisschool.org
Michael G. Schuler, Head. BA, Washington and Lee Univ, MAT, College of Notre Dame of Maryland. **Krista N. Wilson, Adm.**
  Pre-Prep. Feat—Humanities Fr Studio_Art Music. **Supp**—Dev_Read Rem_Math Rem_Read Rev Tut.
  Adm: 50/yr. Accepted: 73%.
  Enr 492. B 242. G 250. Elem 492. Wh 91%. Hisp 3%. Blk 2%. Other 4%. **Fac 78.** M 9. F 63/6. Wh 99%. Other 1%. Adv deg: 39%.
  Grad '04—42. Prep—33. (Trinity HS-KY, St Xavier). Alum 1000.
  Tui '03-'04: Day $7900-12,240 (+$300). **Aid:** Need 19 ($114,000).
  Summer: Acad Enrich Rec. Tui Day $200/wk. 9 wks.
  Endow $1,081,000. Plant val $4,675,000. Bldgs 2. Class rms 35. Lib 15,000 vols. Sci labs 2. Comp labs 2. Theaters 1. Art studios 2. Music studios 2. Dance studios 1. Gyms 1. Fields 4. Tracks 1.
  Est 1965. Nonprofit. Episcopal. Tri (Aug-June).

St. Francis was started by a group of young Episcopal parents who hired Rev. Frank Q. Cayce as headmaster and gave him the task of creating an alternative to the existing schools in the Louisville area. In 1970, the school moved its facilities to a strikingly contemporary building on 90 acres of land.

The developmentally designed curriculum provides individualized programs in basic skills, life skills and foreign language instruction in grades K-8, and an outdoor environmental science lab. In addition to the standard subjects, St. Francis emphasizes drama, music, the fine arts and physical education. Enrichment is provided through many field trips, as well as visits by artists, musicians and craftsmen.

LEXINGTON, KY. (71 mi. ESE of Louisville, KY) Urban. Pop: 260,512. Alt: 946 ft.

THE LEXINGTON SCHOOL
Day — Coed Gr PS-8

Lexington, KY 40504. 1050 Lane Allen Rd. Tel: 859-278-0501. Fax: 859-278-8604.
www.thelexingtonschool.org E-mail: admissions@thelexingtonschool.org
Charles Baldecchi, Head. BA, Denison Univ, MA, St John's College (MD). **Beth Pride, Adm.**

Pre-Prep. Feat—Fr Span Geol Computers Govt Studio_Art Music. **Supp**—Tut.
Adm: 94/yr. **Tests** CTP_4 IQ.
Enr 505. B 250. G 255. Elem 505. Wh 93%. Hisp 2%. Blk 2%. Asian 3%. Avg class size: 15. **Fac 72.** M 11/1. F 56/4. Adv deg: 56%.
Grad '04—11. Prep—8. (Lexington Sch, St George's Sch-RI, Phillips Acad, Lawrenceville, VA Episcopal, Sayre). Alum 1182.
Tui '04-'05: Day $11,100-12,500. Aid: Need 67.
Summer: Acad Rec. 2 wks.
Endow $7,000,000. Plant val $3,800,000. Bldgs 1. Class rms 52. Lib 15,000 vols. Labs 7. Comp labs 3. Theaters 1. Art studios 3. Music studios 3. Gyms 2. Fields 4.
Est 1959. Nonprofit. Tri (Aug-June).

Located on a 25-acre campus four miles from the heart of the business district, this school opened with the primary grades and later added grades 7 and 8. A Montessori preschool class and a full-day kindergarten program are available. Basic skills form the core of the curriculum in grades 1-3.

Foreign language study is introduced in the preschool and departmentalized instruction commences in grade 4. The academic program is enriched by the visual and performing arts, as well as by instrumental and choral music. Electives include newspaper, speech, drama and yearbook. Athletics feature interscholastic competition in basketball, soccer and tennis.

SAYRE SCHOOL
Day — Coed Gr PS-12

Lexington, KY 40507. 194 N Limestone St. Tel: 859-254-1361. **Fax:** 859-254-5627.
   www.sayreschool.org   **E-mail:** bparsons@sayreschool.org
Clayton G. Chambliss, Head. BA, Emory Univ, MAT, Jacksonville Univ. **Barbara N. Parsons, Adm.**
Col Prep. AP—Eng Fr Span Calc Stats Comp_Sci Bio Chem Physics Eur_Hist US_Hist Studio_Art Music_Theory. **Supp**—Tut.
Adm (Gr PS-11): 100/yr. Appl due: Rolling. Accepted: 85%. Yield: 87%. **Tests** Stanford.
Enr 650. B 323. G 327. Elem 417. Sec 233. Wh 92%. Hisp 1%. Blk 2%. Asian 4%. Other 1%. Avg class size: 15. **Fac 80.** M 24. F 56. Wh 99%. Blk 1%. Adv deg: 68%.
Grad '04—43. Col—43. (U of KY 5, Davidson 2, Wake Forest 2, Centre 2, U of the South 2, Auburn 2). Avg SAT: 1189. Avg ACT: 26. Alum 1666.
Tui '04-'05: Day $5700-13,000 (+$500). **Aid:** Merit 12 ($9000). Need 65.
Summer: Enrich. Tui Day $300/2-wk ses. 6 wks.
Endow $6,000,000. Plant val $25,000,000. Bldgs 11. Class rms 75. Lib 18,500 vols. Sci labs 7. Lang labs 4. Comp labs 4. Art studios 4. Music studios 3. Gyms 1. Fields 1.
Est 1854. Nonprofit. Sem (Aug-May).

Established as the Sayre Female Institute by David A. Sayre, this school was the first in the region to offer college-level work for women. At the turn of the 20th century, boys were admitted to the primary department. In the 1960s, when it was revitalized as Sayre School, the school became coeducational and now serves pupils from age 3 through high school.

The liberal arts curriculum includes a strong language arts program with an emphasis on writing skills. Modern language instruction begins in the lower grades, while fine arts classes are available at all grade levels. Advanced Placement courses are available in all major disciplines.

Extracurricular activities include student government, newspaper, yearbook, National Honor Society and a full interscholastic athletic program. Community service is an important aspect of school life in each division. Both Montessori and traditional curricula are provided for children ages 3-5, and an extended-day program is available for students in grades pre-K-5.

LOUISVILLE, KY. (92 mi. SW of Cincinnati, OH) Urban. Pop: 256,231. Alt: 462 ft.

KENTUCKY COUNTRY DAY SCHOOL
Day — Coed Gr PS-12

Louisville, KY 40241. 4100 Springdale Rd. Tel: 502-423-0440. Fax: 502-423-0445.
  www.kcd.org   E-mail: admissions@kcd.org
Bradley E. Lyman, Head. BA, Hanover College, MA, Armstrong Atlantic State Univ. **Marche Harris, Adm.**
  Col Prep. AP—Eng Fr Lat Span Calc Comp_Sci Bio Chem Physics Eur_Hist US_Hist Psych Studio_Art. **Feat**—Drama Music Music_Theory. **Supp**—Tut.
  Adm (Gr PS-11): 146/yr. Appl due: Jan. Accepted: 81%. Yield: 73%. **Tests** CTP_4 Stanford.
  Enr 811. B 421. G 390. Elem 592. Sec 219. Wh 87%. Hisp 1%. Blk 5%. Asian 1%. Other 6%. Avg class size: 16. **Fac 92.** M 22/3. F 59/8. Wh 99%. Blk 1%. Adv deg: 75%.
  Grad '04—51. Col—51. (IN U 6, Centre 5, U of KY 4, Miami U-OH 3, Furman 2, U of VA 2). Avg SAT: 1227. Alum 2670.
  Tui '05-'06: Day $9300-13,380 (+$350). **Aid:** Need 73 ($652,393).
  Summer: Acad Enrich Rec. 7 wks.
  Endow $7,000,000. Plant val $20,000,000. Bldgs 3. Class rms 89. Lib 30,000 vols. Sci labs 6. Lang labs 2. Comp labs 3. Art studios 3. Music studios 3. Gyms 2. Fields 10. Courts 8. Pools 1. Tracks 1.
  Est 1972. Nonprofit. Tri (Aug-June). **Assoc** CLS.

In 1972, the Kentucky Home for Girls (founded in 1863) merged with the Louisville Country Day School (founded in 1948), which had previously consolidated with Aquinas Preparatory School and Kentucky Military Institute, to become Kentucky Country Day School. KCD moved to its present, 85-acre campus in 1978.

The school offers Advanced Placement courses, in addition to a selection of electives. Among student activities are instrumental music, chorus, debate, drama, publications and a variety of clubs. Sports include football, basketball, soccer, swimming, track, baseball, field hockey, cross-country, volleyball, wrestling, gymnastics, tennis and golf.

LOUISVILLE COLLEGIATE SCHOOL
Day — Coed Gr K-12

Louisville, KY 40204. 2427 Glenmary Ave. Tel: 502-479-0340. Fax: 502-454-8549.
  www.loucol.com   E-mail: info@loucol.com
Barbara Burnett Groves, Head. AB, Oberlin College, MST, Portland State Univ. **Evelyn Gordinier, Adm.**

Col Prep. AP—Calc Bio Chem Physics Eur_Hist US_Hist Comp_Govt & Pol. **Feat**—Marine_Biol/Sci Studio_Art Drama Music.
Adm: 93/yr. Appl due: Dec. **Tests** CTP_4 IQ Stanford.
Enr 665. Elem 500. Sec 165. Wh 89%. Hisp 1%. Blk 4%. Asian 2%. Other 4%. Uniform. **Fac 85.** M 23/1. F 51/10. Adv deg: 54%.
Grad '04—51. Col—50. (U of Louisville, Wake Forest, Northwestern, U of Richmond, Georgetown, U of MI). Avg SAT: 1227. Avg ACT: 26. Alum 1500.
Tui '05-'06: Day $10,700-14,500. Aid: Need 101 ($650,365).
Summer: Acad Enrich Rev Rec. Tui Day $58-230. 2-6 wks.
Endow $4,405,000. Plant val $12,000,000. Bldgs 8. Class rms 61. Lib 21,000 vols. Labs 5. Art studios 3. Music studios 2. Gyms 2. Fields 2.
Est 1915. Nonprofit. Tri (Aug-June). **Assoc** CLS.

This school emphasizes a liberal arts curriculum at all levels, with specialized instruction in areas such as art, music and laboratory science. A strong advisory program complements academic and extracurricular life at the school. All subjects are departmentalized in grade 5. Foreign languages are introduced in grade 1 and can be continued through grade 12. A sequentially structured program emphasizing reading, writing, speaking and listening is used to develop communicational skills. Other aspects of the curriculum are an emphasis on sophisticated technology and a late-winter interim program.

To prepare students for independent study projects in the upper school, the middle school emphasizes methods of inquiry: gathering information, analyzing concepts and organizing ideas. Upper school students may choose electives according to their talents and interests. Students also participate in an exchange program with a Swiss school, summer travel to Europe and Mexico, athletics and extracurricular activities.

ST. FRANCIS HIGH SCHOOL
Day — Coed Gr 9-12

Louisville, KY 40202. 233 W Broadway. Tel: 502-736-1000. Fax: 502-736-1049.
www.stfrancishighschool.com E-mail: gorman@stfrancishighschool.com
Alexandra S. Thurstone, Head. AB, Harvard Univ, MBA, Univ of Chicago. **Suzanne Gorman, Adm.**
Col Prep. AP—Eng Fr Span Calc Bio Chem Physics US_Hist. **Feat**—Computers Relig Photog Video Drama Journ. **Supp**—Rev Tut.
Adm: 35/yr. Appl due: Jan. Accepted: 90%.
Enr 125. B 60. G 65. Sec 125. Wh 86%. Hisp 3%. Blk 9%. Asian 2%. Avg class size: 11. **Fac 19.** M 7/5. F 5/2. Wh 84%. Other 16%. Adv deg: 52%.
Grad '04—30. Col—30. (DePaul, U of PA, Bowdoin, Rice, Carleton, Pomona). Alum 800.
Tui '04-'05: Day $13,125 (+$650). **Aid:** Merit 11 ($59,750). Need 33 ($360,500).
Summer: Acad Enrich Rev. Tui Day $350. 1 wk.
Endow $1,600,000. Plant val $1,600,000. Bldgs 1. Class rms 13. Libs 1. Sci labs 3. Lang labs 4. Comp labs 1. Dark rms 1. Studios 1. Theater/auds 1.
Est 1976. Nonprofit. Episcopal. Quar (Aug-June).

St. Francis offers a progressive college preparatory program that utilizes the diverse resources of downtown Louisville. Advanced Placement and college-level courses, drama, photography and studio art courses are among the academic offerings. Biweekly community service is required of all students and faculty members each year. An interdisciplinary senior project is a graduation requirement.

Approximately two-thirds of St. Francis' students compete on interscholastic athletic or academic teams. Boys and girls also take part in a variety of other extracurricular activities, and the school encourages pupils to propose and develop new programs.

NORTH CAROLINA

ARDEN, NC. (88 mi. ESE of Knoxville, TN; 97 mi. WNW of Charlotte, NC) Rural. Pop: 800. Alt: 2228 ft.

CHRIST SCHOOL
Bdg and Day — Boys Gr 8-12

Arden, NC 28704. 500 Christ School Rd. Tel: 828-684-6232. Fax: 828-684-4869.
www.christschool.org   E-mail: admission@christschool.org
Paul Krieger, Head. BA, Gettysburg College, MA, Immaculata Univ. **Denis Stokes, Adm.**

- **Col Prep. AP**—Eng Bio Music_Theory. **Feat**—Fr Lat Span Astron Environ_Sci Geol Marine_Biol/Sci Computers Econ Govt Relig Studio_Art Drama Music Journ. **Supp**—ESL Tut.
- **Adm:** 98/yr. Accepted: 80%. Yield: 69%. **Tests** IQ SSAT TOEFL.
- **Enr 192.** B 160/32. Elem 12. Sec 180. Wh 89%. Blk 5%. Asian 6%. Avg class size: 12. **Fac 41.** M 22/7. F 9/3. Wh 100%. Adv deg: 56%. In dorms 12.
- **Grad '04—47. Col—47.** (Duke, GA Inst of Tech, UNC-Chapel Hill, Emory, VA Polytech, Denison). Alum 2150.
- **Tui '04-'05: Bdg $29,885** (+$1000). **5-Day Bdg $28,910** (+$1000). **Day $14,985** (+$700). **Aid:** Merit 18 ($165,000). Need 52 ($640,000).
- Endow $6,800,000. Plant val $22,000,000. Bldgs 16. Dorms 6. Dorm rms 97. Class rms 29. Lib 16,000 vols. Sci labs 3. Comp labs 1. Auds 1. Art studios 1. Music studios 1. Gyms 1. Fields 5. Courts 8. Student ctrs 1.
- **Est 1900.** Nonprofit. Episcopal. Sem (Aug-May).

Established by Rev. and Mrs. Thomas Wetmore for children in the Asheville area, this school offers a college preparatory curriculum to boys from approximately a dozen states and roughly ten foreign countries. Founded as a coeducational day school, the school became an all-male boarding institution in the late 1920s.

Christ School emphasizes preparation for leading colleges throughout the country. Although affiliated with the Episcopal Church, the school enrolls students of many religious faiths. A work program instituted at the school's founding includes each boy in the supervision and the maintenance of the 500-acre campus.

Interscholastic competition in football, cross-country, soccer, wrestling, basketball, swimming, baseball, track and field, lacrosse, golf and tennis is available. The school provides extracurricular activities in the areas of SAT preparation, debate, choir, music, photography, journalism, publications, skiing and outdoor education. In addition, a particularly active outdoor program enables boys to engage in various pursuits in the surrounding Blue Ridge and Smoky Mountain areas.

See Also Page 1328

ASHEVILLE, NC. (83 mi. ESE of Knoxville, TN; 100 mi. WNW of Charlotte, NC) Suburban. Pop: 68,889. Alt: 2200 ft.

CAROLINA DAY SCHOOL
Day — Coed Gr PS-12

Asheville, NC 28803. 1345 Hendersonville Rd. Tel: 828-274-0757. Fax: 828-274-0756.
www.cdschool.org   E-mail: admissions@cdschool.org
Beverly H. Sgro, Head. PhD, Virginia Polytechnic Institute. **Genevieve H. Fortuna, Adm.**
  Col Prep. AP—Eng Fr Span Calc Stats Comp_Sci Bio Chem Physics Eur_Hist US_Hist Psych US_Govt & Pol Art_Hist Studio_Art. **Feat**—Genetics Disease & Immunology Film Drama Music. **Supp**—LD Tut.
  Adm: 117/yr. Appl due: Rolling. Accepted: 70%. Yield: 65%. **Tests** CEEB ISEE SSAT.
  Enr 639. B 337. G 302. Elem 444. Sec 195. Wh 94%. Hisp 1%. Blk 2%. Asian 2%. Other 1%. Avg class size: 18. **Fac 102.** M 26/6. F 45/25. Wh 98%. Hisp 1%. Asian 1%. Adv deg: 40%.
  Grad '04—49. Col—49. (UNC-Chapel Hill, Appalachian St, UNC-Asheville, Davidson, Bryn Mawr, Elon). Avg SAT: 1290. Alum 3075.
  Tui '04-'05: Day $7430-14,210 (+$500). **Aid:** Need 59 ($478,736).
  Summer: Enrich Rec. Tui Day $110-300. 1-2 wks.
  Endow $2,480,000. Plant val $10,030,000. Bldgs 10. Class rms 63. 2 Libs 8521 vols. Sci labs 4. Comp labs 4. Art studios 3. Music studios 3. Gyms 2. Fields 2.
  Est 1987. Nonprofit. Sem (Aug-May). **Assoc** SACS.

Founded upon the merger of Asheville Country Day School (established in 1936) and St. Genevieve/Gibbons Hall School (established in 1908), Carolina Day School enrolls students from seven counties of western North Carolina into its college preparatory program. Computer science, the fine arts, Advanced Placement courses, outdoor education, sports and community service projects are integrated into the curriculum. Children in grades 1-8 with language-based learning differences may enroll in a special program that features language tutorial classes, a 3:1 student-teacher ratio and an emphasis on skill development.

The school's Summer Quest program offers enrichment in the arts, the sciences and athletics.

BURNSVILLE, NC. (93 mi. E of Knoxville, TN; 96 mi. WNW of Charlotte, NC) Rural. Pop: 1623. Alt: 2814 ft.

ARTHUR MORGAN SCHOOL
Bdg and Day — Coed Gr 7-9

Burnsville, NC 28714. 60 AMS Cir. Tel: 828-675-4262. Fax: 828-675-0003.
www.arthurmorganschool.org   E-mail: info@arthurmorganschool.org
Sherrill Senseney, Co-Clerk. BA, Columbia College (Illinois), MCE, Emory Univ. **Kate Paxton, Co-Clerk.** BA, Williams College, MEd, Univ of Vermont. **Amelia Stevens, Adm.**
  Pre-Prep. Gen Acad. Feat—Fr Span Ceramics Drawing Studio_Art Drama Music Metal_Shop Woodworking Jewelry_Making Printmaking Blacksmithing Outdoor_Ed. **Supp**—Rem_Math Rem_Read Tut.

Adm: 7/yr. Bdg 6. Day 1. Appl due: Rolling. Accepted: 65%.
Enr 25. B 10/6. G 9. Wh 80%. Hisp 8%. Blk 12%. Avg class size: 8. **Fac 14.** M 6/1. F 6/1. Adv deg: 28%. In dorms 8.
Grad '04—11. Prep—3. (Scattergood Friends). Alum 300.
Tui '03-'04: Bdg $16,750 (+$250). **Day $8750** (+$150). **Aid:** Need 11 ($55,000).
Endow $1,000,000. Plant val $700,000. Bldgs 9. Dorm rms 4. Class rms 5. Lib 1000 vols. Sci labs 1. Comp labs 1. Art studios 1. Music studios 1. Dance studios 1. Fields 1. Courts 1. Ponds 1.
Est 1962. Nonprofit. Tri (Sept-May).

Elizabeth Morgan founded this school in accordance with the principles of Montessori, Pestalozzi, Grundtvig, Gandhi and Arthur Morgan, as well as her own Quaker values. The program continues to address the needs and interests of early adolescents. The school occupies a 100-acre campus in the Black Mountains.

The program integrates academic and practical skills, relating them to community life. Students participate in a daily work program and an outdoor hiking program. Academics feature small classes, and electives include offerings in the performing and visual arts. Eighteen-day field trips in late February allow pupils to explore the wilderness areas of the South and to take part in community service projects.

CHARLOTTE, NC. (80 mi. N of Columbia, SC) Urban. Pop: 540,828. Alt: 721 ft.

CHARLOTTE COUNTRY DAY SCHOOL
Day — Coed Gr PS-12

Charlotte, NC 28226. 1440 Carmel Rd. Tel: 704-943-4500. Fax: 704-943-4536.
 www.charlottecountryday.org E-mail: riggins@ccds.charlotte.nc.us
Margaret E. Gragg, Head. AB, Duke Univ, MAT, Univ of North Carolina-Chapel Hill. **Nancy R. Ehringhaus, Adm.**
Col Prep. IB Diploma. AP—Eng Fr Ger Lat Span Calc Stats Comp_Sci Bio Chem Physics Eur_Hist US_Hist Psych US_Govt & Pol Art_Hist Studio_Art Music_Theory. **Feat**—Chin Anat & Physiol Ecol Biotech Web_Design Econ Bioethics Drama Chorus Dance. **Supp**—ESL Tut.
Adm: 174/yr. Accepted: 55%. Yield: 67%. **Tests** CTP_4 IQ ISEE.
Enr 1598. B 776. G 822. Elem 1149. Sec 449. Wh 92%. Hisp 1%. Blk 5%. Asian 2%. Avg class size: 15. **Fac 197.** M 49/1. F 140/7. Wh 92%. Hisp 3%. Blk 3%. Asian 1%. Other 1%. Adv deg: 41%.
Grad '04—121. Col—121. (UNC-Chapel Hill, NC St, Duke, U of the South, Wake Forest, Davidson). Avg SAT: 1261. Alum 3500.
Tui '04-'05: Day $10,400-15,550 (+$100). **Aid:** Need 95 ($954,969).
Summer: Acad Enrich Rem. 1-6 wks.
Endow $13,900,000. Plant val $50,000,000. Bldgs 24. Class rms 105. 3 Libs 43,000 vols. Sci labs 6. Lang labs 1. Comp labs 6. Theaters 1. Art studios 10. Music studios 7. Dance studios 2. Gyms 1. Fields 5. Courts 8.
Est 1941. Nonprofit. Sem (Aug-June). **Assoc** CLS SACS.

Founded by Dr. Thomas Burton, Country Day is the oldest and largest independent school in the Charlotte area. The school moved to its permanent campus in the southeastern part of the city in 1960, and a 1979 merger with Carmel Academy gave CCDS two campuses. The upper and lower schools share the 60-acre Cannon campus on Carmel Road, while the middle school is situated four miles south on the 40-acre Bissell campus at 5936 Green Rea Rd.

College preparation is the main focus of the rigorous curriculum. The lower school (junior kindergarten through grade 4), which emphasizes early foreign language work, science, computer instruction and the arts, includes after-school and coordinate programs. The middle school (grades 5-8) enhances its academic program with a range of activities designed specifically for emerging adolescents. The upper school features Advanced Placement courses, an International Baccalaureate diploma program, and language instruction in French, Latin, Spanish, German and Chinese. Well-established guidance and advisory programs aid pupils in all three divisions.

The academic program is enriched by strong visual and performing arts programs, computer technology, library facilities and SCOLA satellite capabilities. Athletic offerings include a wide range of boys' and girls' sports teams and opportunities, including trainer-supervised weight and wellness conditioning.

The student population includes international students from many countries, and English as a Second Language is offered. The school cooperates with Andover in School Year Abroad programs to France, China and Spain, the Maine Coast Experience, teacher and student exchanges with King Edward VI School in Britain, other trips and exchanges in every division, and numerous summer travel opportunities.

See Also Page 1131

CHARLOTTE LATIN SCHOOL
Day — Coed Gr K-12

Charlotte, NC 28277. 9502 Providence Rd. Tel: 704-846-1100. Fax: 704-846-6990.
  www.charlottelatin.org   E-mail: admissions@charlottelatin.org
Arch N. McIntosh, Jr., Head. BA, Marshall Univ, MEd, Univ of South Alabama. **Kathryn B. Booe, Adm.**
  Col Prep. **AP**—Eng Fr Ger Lat Span Calc Stats Comp_Sci Bio Chem Physics US_Hist US_Govt & Pol. **Feat**—Greek Environ_Sci Sports_Med Econ Fine_Arts Visual_Arts Theater Debate Engineering. **Supp**—Dev_Read Rev Tut.
  Adm: 168/yr. Appl due: Feb. Accepted: 40%. Yield: 33%. **Tests** CTP_4 ISEE.
  Enr 1360. B 706. G 654. Elem 896. Sec 464. Avg class size: 18. **Fac 165.** M 51/4. F 87/23. Wh 94%. Hisp 2%. Blk 3%. Asian 1%. Adv deg: 43%.
  Grad '04—104. Col—104. (UNC-Chapel Hill 18, VA Polytech 6, NC St 5, Duke 4, Clemson 4, Wofford 4). Avg SAT: 1272. Alum 2400.
  Tui '04-'05: Day **$11,400-14,300** (+$500). **Aid:** Merit 9 ($88,400). Need 71 ($712,000).
  Summer: Acad Enrich Rev Rec. Sports. 8 wks.
  Endow $11,957,000. Plant val $35,000,000. Bldgs 14. Class rms 96. Lib 47,000 vols. Sci labs 10. Comp labs 12. Auds 1. Theaters 1. Art studios 5. Music studios 5. Dance studios 1. Gyms 3. Fields 7. Courts 6. Pools 1.
  Est 1970. Nonprofit. Sem (Aug-June). **Assoc** CLS SACS.

Occupying a 122-acre campus, Latin offers a complete elementary and secondary program. Language arts, phonics and mathematics are emphasized in the lower school. The college preparatory courses and extracurricular activities in the middle and upper grades afford cultural exposure and promote a sense of community involvement.

The middle and upper schools (grades 6-12) operate on a semester system. Students are expected to acquire independent study habits and to make use of both the school media center and outside sources of reference. Computer training is a curricular feature in grades K-12, with optional courses available to upper school students. All disciplines offer advanced-level courses.

Extracurricular features include student government, honor council, service clubs, a variety of productions by the drama department, art competitions, and the publication of a student newspaper and a yearbook in both the middle and upper school divisions. Latin fields competitive teams in baseball, basketball, cross-country, field hockey, football, golf, lacrosse, soccer, softball, swimming, tennis, track, ultimate Frisbee, volleyball and wrestling.

PROVIDENCE DAY SCHOOL
Day — Coed Gr PS-12

Charlotte, NC 28270. 5800 Sardis Rd. Tel: 704-887-7041. Fax: 704-887-7520.
www.providenceday.org E-mail: susan.beattie@providenceday.org

Eugene A. Bratek, Head. BA, Univ of Virginia, MAT, Trenton State College, MEd, Rutgers Univ. **Susan A. Beattie, Adm.**

Col Prep. AP—Eng Fr Ger Lat Span Calc Stats Comp_Sci Bio Chem Physics Eur_Hist US_Hist World_Hist Psych US_Govt & Pol Art_Hist Studio_Art Music_Theory. **Feat**—Chin Anat & Physiol Astron Bioethics Sports_Med Meteorology Civil_War African-Amer_Hist Econ Intl_Relations Photog Theater Dance Accounting Public_Speak. **Supp**—Tut.

Adm: 195/yr. Appl due: Feb. Accepted: 51%. Yield: 72%. **Tests** CEEB CTP_4 IQ ISEE.

Enr 1478. B 734. G 744. Elem 1009. Sec 469. Wh 90%. Hisp 1%. Blk 5%. Asian 1%. Other 3%. Avg class size: 17. **Fac 125.** M 42/5. F 75/3. Wh 94%. Hisp 1%. Blk 3%. Asian 2%. Adv deg: 39%.

Grad '04—104. **Col**—104. (UNC-Chapel Hill 16, Wake Forest 9, NC St 8, VA Polytech 5, GA Inst of Tech 4, Elon 4). Avg SAT: 1260. Avg SSAT: 26%. Alum 1850.

Tui '04-'05: Day $10,000-14,672 (+$500). **Aid:** Need 95 ($921,561).

Summer: Acad Enrich Rec. 10 wks.

Endow $2,241,000. Plant val $30,377,000. Bldgs 17. Class rms 81. 3 Libs 40,729 vols. Sci labs 7. Comp labs 6. Sci & tech ctrs 1. Theaters 1. Art studios 3. Music studios 4. Gyms 2. Fields 5. Courts 10. Field houses 1. Playgrounds 1.

Est 1970. Nonprofit. Sem (Aug-June). **Assoc** CLS SACS.

Since opening with an enrollment of 150, Providence Day has experienced outstanding growth and expansion in curriculum, enrollment and plant. The 48-acre campus has athletic facilities with fields for football, soccer, baseball, lacrosse, field hockey and softball, areas for physical education classes, a playground and tennis courts.

Language arts is emphasized in the lower-middle school, as are math, science, computers, health, social studies, art, music, theater and physical education. The upper school curriculum includes college preparatory material, as well as enrichment electives. Advanced Placement courses are offered in every major discipline. Each senior is involved in a two-week community project that provides the opportunity to sample various professions and in a senior venture program that stresses group dependency and leadership skills.

Providence Day's interscholastic sports program consists of baseball, basketball, football, golf, soccer, field hockey, softball, swimming, wrestling, tennis, volleyball, track and field, cross-country and lacrosse. **See Also Page 1232**

DURHAM, NC. (18 mi. NW of Raleigh, NC) Urban. Pop: 179,212. Alt: 406 ft.

CAROLINA FRIENDS SCHOOL
Day — Coed Gr PS-12

Durham, NC 27705. 4809 Friends School Rd. Tel: 919-383-6602. Fax: 919-383-6009.
  www.cfsnc.org   E-mail: admissions@cfsnc.org
Mike Hanas, Prin. BA, College of the Holy Cross, MEd, Harvard Univ. **Kathleen Davidson March, Adm.**
  Col Prep. Gen Acad. Feat—Span Comp_Sci Studio_Art Drama Dance.
  Adm (Gr PS-11): 83/yr. Appl due: Feb. Accepted: 39%. Yield: 29%.
  Enr 481. B 230. G 251. Elem 329. Sec 152. Wh 79%. Hisp 3%. Blk 8%. Asian 5%. Other 5%. Avg class size: 12. **Fac 61.** M 20/7. F 29/7. Wh 95%. Hisp 2%. Blk 3%. Adv deg: 34%.
  Grad '04—37. Col—33. (UNC-Wilmington, UNC-Chapel Hill, UNC-Asheville, UNC-Greensboro, Bennett, Warren Wilson).
  Tui '04-'05: Day $9610-11,360 (+$50-400). **Aid:** Need 80 ($423,600).
  Summer: Enrich Rec. Tui Day $99-240/wk. 10 wks.
  Endow $3,700,000. Plant val $5,320,000. Bldgs 16. Libs 2. Sci labs 2. Comp labs 2. Art studios 2. Music studios 3. Dance studios 1. Gyms 1. Fields 6.
  Est 1962. Nonprofit. Religious Society of Friends. Tri (Aug-June).

Founded by local Quakers and still affiliated with the Society of Friends, this nonsectarian school encourages students to progress at their own rates in a challenging and cooperative environment. The wooded, 67-acre campus is accessible to Hillsborough, Durham and Chapel Hill.

The early curriculum emphasizes the development of basic skills through an integrated program involving thematic studies, field trips and cooperative learning in small, mixed-age groups. In addition to required course work, middle and upper school pupils engage in electives in language arts, math, science, social studies, the visual and dramatic arts, music, dance, woodworking, physical education and community service. Mini-sessions between terms and at year's end encourage community involvement, experiential learning and self-reliance.

Extracurricular activities include sports, publications, trips and retreats.

DURHAM ACADEMY
Day — Coed Gr PS-12

Durham, NC 27705. 3501 Ridge Rd. Tel: 919-493-5787. Fax: 919-489-4893.
  www.da.org   E-mail: admissions@da.org
Edward R. Costello, Head. BA, Syracuse Univ, MA, Wesleyan Univ. **Jessica U. Carothers, Adm.**
  Col Prep. AP—Eng Fr Ger Lat Span Calc Stats Comp_Sci Bio Chem Physics Eur_Hist

US_Hist Studio_Art. **Feat**—Bioethics Vietnam_War Econ Relig Film Photog Drama Music_Theory Dance. **Supp**—LD.
Adm: 158/yr. Appl due: Jan. Accepted: 38%. **Tests** CTP_4 ISEE SSAT.
Enr 1128. B 542. G 586. Elem 742. Sec 386. Wh 80%. Hisp 3%. Blk 7%. Am Ind 1%. Asian 4%. Other 5%. Avg class size: 18. **Fac 148.** M 40/5. F 79/24. Wh 87%. Hisp 1%. Blk 9%. Asian 2%. Other 1%. Adv deg: 61%.
Grad '04—93. Col—93. (UNC-Chapel Hill 16, Duke 12, NC St 4, Vanderbilt 3, Brown 2, Stanford 2). Avg SAT: 1318. Alum 3040.
Tui '04-'05: Day $9950-15,300 (+$250-650). **Aid:** Need 103 ($993,451).
Summer: Acad Enrich Rec. Tui Day $145-585. 1-6 wks.
Endow $6,653,000. Plant val $26,683,000. Bldgs 28. Class rms 89. 3 Libs 45,000 vols. Sci labs 15. Comp labs 8. Auds 3. Art studios 6. Music studios 2. Dance studios 2. Arts ctrs 2. Gyms 3. Fields 8. Courts 6.
Est 1933. Nonprofit. Sem (Aug-June). **Assoc** CLS SACS.

Founded and known as the Calvert Method School for its first 25 years, DA occupies two campuses in the southwestern section of Durham, near Duke University and the University of North Carolina at Chapel Hill. In 1959, the academy assumed its current name and began expanding beyond the elementary school years, culminating in the establishment of the upper school (grades 9-12) in 1972. The academy dedicated its second campus, on Academy Road, to the middle school in August 2002; the preschool, lower school and upper school occupy the Ridge Road campus.

The college preparatory curriculum includes AP courses in all major subjects, as well as term- and year-long electives and opportunities for advanced study. Students fulfill requirements in English, a foreign language, math, lab science, the fine arts, computer and physical education. The academy stresses community service through clubs and an advisory system, and the athletic program enables boys and girls to participate in various varsity sports.

The Hill Center, an affiliate of the academy, serves students with specific learning disabilities who do not have primary emotional or behavioral problems.

GREENSBORO, NC. (68 mi. WNW of Raleigh, NC) Urban. Pop: 223,891. Alt: 843 ft.

GREENSBORO DAY SCHOOL
Day — Coed Gr K-12

Greensboro, NC 27455. 5401 Lawndale Dr. Tel: 336-288-8590. Fax: 336-282-2905.
www.greensboroday.org E-mail: dmorton@greensboroday.org
D. Ralph Davison, Jr., **Head.** AB, Hamilton College, MA, Middlebury College, PhD, Univ of Virginia. **Danette L. Morton, Adm.**
Col Prep. AP—Eng. **Feat**—Creative_Writing Marine_Biol/Sci Sports_Med Psych Ceramics Photog Video_Production Drama Chorus Journ. **Supp**—ESL.
Adm: 139/yr. Appl due: Rolling. Accepted: 73%. **Tests** CEEB CTP_4 SSAT TOEFL.
Enr 880. B 448. G 432. Elem 560. Sec 320. Wh 91%. Hisp 1%. Blk 4%. Asian 2%. Other 2%. Avg class size: 14. **Fac 95.** M 28/5. F 52/10. Wh 94%. Hisp 4%. Blk 2%. Adv deg: 61%.
Grad '04—83. Col—83. (UNC-Chapel Hill 14, NC St 8, Duke 5, Appalachian St 4). Avg

SAT: 1240. Alum 1620.
Tui '04-'05: Day $6075-13,995 (+$886-1950). **Aid:** Need 86 ($786,200).
Summer: Acad Enrich Rev Rem Rec. 7 wks.
Endow $6,654,000. Plant val $11,156,000. Bldgs 9. Class rms 61. 2 Libs 34,000 vols. Sci labs 9. Lang labs 1. Comp labs 2. Theaters 2. Art studios 5. Music studios 5. Gyms 3. Fields 7. Courts 10. Tracks 1.
Est 1970. Nonprofit. Sem (Aug-June). **Assoc** CLS SACS.

Situated on a 57-acre campus a few miles north of Greensboro, this college preparatory school emphasizes the basic disciplines. Course offerings in art, music, physical education and experiential/outdoor education are also fundamental to the program.

The lower school stresses the child's development of specific abilities, attitudes and work habits. Art, music, foreign language, science laboratory, computers and physical education, as well as language and mathematical skills, are the curriculum's foundation. All boys and girls participate in a laptop computer program beginning in grade 6. An environmental awareness and outdoor education program is an integral part of the curriculum at all grade levels. Seniors pursue independent projects or internships for credit, and honors and Advanced Placement courses are available in all major subjects.

Competitive sports, introduced at the middle school level, are basketball, baseball, softball, lacrosse, soccer, tennis, cross-country, volleyball, swimming and track. A number of interest clubs, publications, volunteer service opportunities and dramatic productions constitute the extracurricular activities.

HIGH POINT, NC.
(72 mi. NE of Charlotte, NC; 76 mi. W of Raleigh, NC) Urban. Pop: 85,839. Alt: 939 ft.

WESTCHESTER ACADEMY
Day — Coed Gr K-12

High Point, NC 27265. 204 Pine Tree Ln. Tel: 336-869-2128. Fax: 336-869-9298.
www.westchesteracademy.com   E-mail: admissions@westchesteracademy.com
Thomas P. Hudgins, Jr., Head. BA, Washington and Lee Univ, MS, Old Dominion Univ.
Donna P. Meyerhoeffer, Adm.
Col Prep. AP—Eng Fr Span Calc Bio Chem Physics Eur_Hist US_Hist Art_Hist Studio_Art. **Feat**—Comp_Sci Pol_Sci Film Drama Music. **Supp**—Rem_Math Rem_Read Rev Tut.
Adm: 62/yr. Appl due: Rolling. Accepted: 97%. Yield: 70%. **Tests** CTP_4 IQ ISEE SSAT.
Enr 440. B 211. G 229. Elem 284. Sec 156. Wh 92%. Hisp 1%. Blk 2%. Asian 5%. Avg class size: 15. **Fac 44.** M 16. F 25/3. Wh 94%. Hisp 5%. Blk 1%. Adv deg: 63%.
Grad '04—45. Col—45. (UNC-Chapel Hill 14, NC St 13, Elon 7, Duke 6, Appalachian St 3, UNC-Greensboro 2). Avg SAT: 1260. Avg ACT: 27. Alum 140.
Tui '04-'05: Day $6425-10,055 (+$625). **Aid:** Merit 16 ($54,000). Need 45 ($132,000).
Summer: Rec. Tui Day $100/2-wk ses. 4 wks.
Endow $2,100,000. Plant val $7,500,000. Bldgs 6. Class rms 35. Lib 9000 vols. Sci labs 4. Comp labs 2. Auds 1. Art studios 2. Gyms 2. Fields 3.
Est 1967. Nonprofit. Sem (Aug-May). **Assoc** SACS.

This college preparatory school serves High Point, Greensboro, Winston-Salem (the Triad) and neighboring communities. Located in a country setting, the school's 52-acre campus is accessible to the varied educational opportunities and facilities of the Triad.

The program at Westchester follows the classical liberal arts tradition of academics, athletics and the arts. A low student-teacher ratio and a family-like atmosphere enhance the learning process. Advanced Placement courses are available, and interscholastic sports, drama and debate are among the activities offered. In addition, a community service project is required during senior year.

LEWISVILLE, NC. (66 mi. NNE of Charlotte, NC) Urban. Pop: 8826. Alt: 973 ft.

FORSYTH COUNTRY DAY SCHOOL
Day — Coed Gr PS-12

Lewisville, NC 27023. 5501 Shallowford Rd, PO Box 549. Tel: 336-945-3151.
Fax: 336-945-2907.
www.fcds.org   E-mail: luannewood@fcds.org
Henry M. Battle, Jr., Head. BA, Univ of North Carolina-Greensboro, MA, Union Theological Seminary. **LuAnne C. Wood, Adm.**
  Col Prep. AP—Eng Fr Span Calc Stats Bio Chem Eur_Hist US_Hist US_Govt & Pol. Feat—Lat Comp_Sci Studio_Art Music. Supp—LD Tut.
  Adm: 176/yr. Appl due: Rolling. Accepted: 73%. Yield: 95%. **Tests** CTP_4.
  Enr 977. B 551. G 426. Elem 604. Sec 373. Wh 97%. Blk 2%. Asian 1%. Avg class size: 18. **Fac** 175. M 40. F 135. Adv deg: 30%.
  Grad '04—92. Col—92. (UNC-Chapel Hill, NC St, Furman, Wake Forest, Duke, U of TN-Knoxville). Avg SAT: 1230. Alum 986.
  Tui '04-'05: Day $11,050-13,275 (+$100).
  Summer: Acad Enrich Rec. Tui Day $160-250. Basketball. Tui Day $90-130. 1 wk.
  Endow $2,500,000. Plant val $6,000,000. Bldgs 9. Class rms 60. 2 Libs 26,000 vols. Labs 44. Comp ctrs 1. Art studios 3. Music studios 2. Gyms 2. Fields 4.
  Est 1970. Nonprofit. Quar (Aug-June). **Assoc** CLS SACS.

Located on a 60-acre campus slightly west of Winston-Salem, Forsyth offers a traditional college preparatory education through its lower (grades PS-4), middle (grades 5-8) and upper (grades 9-12) schools. The upper school's academic offerings include courses in economics, microcomputers and psychology. Advanced Placement classes in all major disciplines are also available.

Boys' athletic teams are fielded in baseball, football, basketball, wrestling, golf, soccer, lacrosse and tennis. Girls' teams include basketball, softball, tennis, soccer, volleyball and field hockey squads. Activities in cross-country, swimming and track are coeducational.

OAK RIDGE, NC. (73 mi. S of Roanoke, VA; 78 mi. WNW of Raleigh, NC) Rural. Pop: 950. Alt: 1040 ft.

OAK RIDGE MILITARY ACADEMY
Bdg and Day — Coed Gr 7-PG

Oak Ridge, NC 27310. 2317 Oak Ridge Rd, PO Box 498. Tel: 336-643-4131.
 Fax: 336-643-1797.
 www.oakridgemilitary.com E-mail: admissions@oakridgemilitary.com
Col. William K. Orris, Pres. Sgt. Maj. Dan Carpinetti, USA (Ret), Adm.
 Col Prep. Milit. AP—Fr Ger Span. **Feat**—Mythology Computers Psych Sociol JROTC SAT_Prep. **Supp**—ESL Makeup Tut.
 Adm: 174/yr. Appl due: Rolling.
 Enr 274. Wh 81%. Hisp 5%. Blk 8%. Asian 6%. Avg class size: 11. Uniform. **Fac 30.** M 14/1. F 14/1. Adv deg: 56%. In dorms 7.
 Grad '04—38. Col—38. (UNC-Chapel Hill, UNC-Greensboro, Appalachian St, Citadel, VA Milit, Duke). Avg SAT: 1100. Alum 7000.
 Tui '04-'05: Bdg $19,990 (+$1850). **Day** $11,325 (+$1850). **Aid:** Need 100 ($154,822).
 Summer: Acad Enrich Rem Rec. Leadership Trng. Tui Bdg $2200-2500. 3 wks.
 Endow $3,500,000. Plant val $8,000,000. Bldgs 18. Dorms 4. Class rms 25. Lib 20,000 vols. Sci labs 3. Lang labs 1. Comp labs 1. Music studios 1. Gyms 2. Fields 4. Courts 6. Pools 1. Rifle ranges 2.
 Est 1852. Nonprofit. Sem (Aug-May). **Assoc** SACS.

Oak Ridge was a private institution from its founding date until 1965, when it became the property of Oak Ridge Foundation, a nonprofit body dedicated to the preservation of the school's tradition. The country's first coeducational military academy, ORMA maintains a favorable student-teacher ratio, as well as faculty-supervised study halls and extra-help classes.

Athletics include soccer, baseball, basketball, golf, wrestling, volleyball, softball, cross-country, tennis and track, while band, chorus, drama and scouting are among the academy's other activities.

RALEIGH, NC. (130 mi. ENE of Charlotte, NC) Urban. Pop: 276,093. Alt: 316 ft.

RAVENSCROFT SCHOOL
Day — Coed Gr PS-12

Raleigh, NC 27615. 7409 Falls of the Neuse Rd. Tel: 919-847-0900. Fax: 919-846-2371.
 www.ravenscroft.org E-mail: pjamison@ravenscroft.org
Doreen C. Kelly, Head. BA, MS, Univ of Pennsylvania. Pamela J. Jamison, Adm.
 Col Prep. AP—Eng Fr Lat Span Calc Stats Comp_Sci Bio Chem Physics Eur_Hist US_Hist Comp_Govt & Pol Econ US_Govt & Pol Art_Hist Studio_Art. **Feat**—Greek Anat & Physiol Vietnam_War Civil_War Intl_Relations Photog Drama Music Music_Theory Dance. **Supp**—Rev Tut.
 Adm: 187/yr. Appl due: Dec. Accepted: 77%. Yield: 53%. **Tests** CTP_4.
 Enr 1095. B 572. G 523. Wh 88%. Blk 7%. Asian 3%. Other 2%. Avg class size: 17. **Fac**

160. M 43/4. F 90/23. Wh 96%. Blk 4%. Adv deg: 50%.
Grad '04—89. Col—89. (UNC-Chapel Hill, NC St, Appalachian St, E Carolina, Col of Charleston, UNC-Wilmington). Avg SAT: 1264. Alum 2000.
Tui '04-'05: Day $7800-12,950 (+$500). **Aid:** Merit 20 ($41,060). Need 108 ($739,052).
Summer: Acad Enrich Rev Rec. 2-8 wks.
Endow $13,000,000. Plant val $30,000,000. Bldgs 9. Class rms 135. 3 Libs 32,004 vols. Labs 20. Theaters 1. Art studios 4. Music studios 8. Dance studios 1. Gyms 4. Fields 7. Courts 8. Pools 1. Tracks 1.
Est 1862. Nonprofit. Sem (Aug-June). **Assoc** SACS.

Ravenscroft was operated by Christ Episcopal Church from its founding until 1968, when it was turned over to an independent board of trustees. The school is named for Rt. Rev. John Stark Ravenscroft, the first Episcopal bishop of North Carolina. In 1970, the school moved to its present, 127-acre campus on the northern edge of Raleigh and expanded to include an upper school. Ravenscroft graduated its first senior class in 1973.

The college preparatory program features foreign languages, the fine and performing arts, and a broad array of off-campus experiential education programs. Various Advanced Placement courses are offered in the upper school. Interscholastic athletics are football, soccer, lacrosse, wrestling, volleyball, cross-country, track, basketball, softball, tennis, swimming and golf. Graduates attend competitive colleges in the Southeast and elsewhere in the country.

SAINT MARY'S SCHOOL

Bdg and Day — Girls Gr 9-12

Raleigh, NC 27603. 900 Hillsborough St. Tel: 919-424-4100. Fax: 919-424-4122.
  www.saint-marys.edu   E-mail: admiss@saint-marys.edu
Theo W. Coonrod, Pres. BA, MA, Univ of Texas-Austin. **Matthew R. Crane, Adm.**
  Col Prep. AP—Eng Calc Bio Chem Physics US_Hist Psych US_Govt & Pol Studio_Art.
    Feat—Fr Lat Span Philos Relig Drama Music.
  Adm (Gr 9-11): 118/yr. Bdg 58. Day 60. Appl due: Jan. Accepted: 88%. Yield: 63%. **Tests** SSAT TOEFL.
  Enr 275. G 117/158. Sec 275. Wh 97%. Blk 1%. Asian 1%. Other 1%. Avg class size: 13.
    Fac 45. M 9/3. F 23/10. Wh 98%. Hisp 1%. Blk 1%. Adv deg: 44%. In dorms 7.
  Grad '04—57. Col—57. (E Carolina, NC St, UNC-Chapel Hill, Appalachian St, Meredith, UNC-Wilmington). Avg SAT: 1110. Alum 8600.
  Tui '04-'05: Bdg $29,915 (+$500). **Day $15,865** (+$500). **Aid:** Merit 59 ($864,800). Need 45 ($381,950).
  Endow $23,771,000. Plant val $24,541,000. Bldgs 27. Dorms 2. Dorm rms 70. Class rms 34. Lib 40,000 vols. Labs 3. Lang labs 1. Auds 1. Art studios 1. Music studios 4. Dance studios 3. Gyms 1. Fields 1. Courts 6. Pools 1.
  Est 1842. Nonprofit. Episcopal. Sem (Aug-May). **Assoc** SACS.

Situated on a 23-acre, wooded campus that is listed on the National Register of Historic Places, this Episcopal school became affiliated with the Church in the two Carolinas in 1897. Founder and for 36 years director was Rev. Dr. Aldert Smedes.

Saint Mary's provides a liberal arts curriculum that includes a selection of honors and Advanced Placement classes and is supplemented by a chapel program. A particularly strong arts program include a wide selection of courses and instrumental music lessons. There are many extracurricular activities, most notably music, dance, dramatics, religious organizations, publications and service clubs. Girls may also participate in the following sports: swimming, field hockey, volleyball, golf, basketball, cross-country, softball, tennis, soccer, and track and field.

WILMINGTON, NC. (119 mi. SSE of Raleigh, NC) Urban. Pop: 75,838. Alt: 35 ft.

CAPE FEAR ACADEMY
Day — Coed Gr PS-12

Wilmington, NC 28412. 3900 S College Rd. Tel: 910-791-0287. Fax: 910-791-0290.
www.capefearacademy.org   E-mail: info@capefearacademy.org
John B. Meehl, Head. BA, Pomona College, MA, Stanford Univ. **Susan M. Harrell, Adm.**
- **Col Prep. AP**—Eng Span Calc Stats Bio Physics Eur_Hist US_Hist Comp_Govt & Pol US_Govt & Pol Music_Theory. **Feat**—Creative_Writing Marine_Biol/Sci Comp_Sci Ceramics Studio_Art Video_Production Drama Music Journ Public_Speak. **Supp**—Rev Tut.
- **Adm:** 101/yr. Appl due: Rolling. Accepted: 64%. Yield: 76%. **Tests** CEEB CTP_4 ISEE SSAT.
- **Enr 536.** B 276. G 260. Elem 365. Sec 171. Wh 92%. Hisp 3%. Blk 2%. Asian 3%. Avg class size: 20. Uniform. **Fac 58.** M 13/1. F 26/18. Wh 98%. Blk 2%. Adv deg: 41%.
- **Grad '04—36. Col—36.** (UNC-Chapel Hill 7, UNC-Wilmington 5, NC St 3, Duke 3, Wake Forest 2, E Carolina 2). Avg SAT: 1210. Alum 736.
- **Tui '04-'05: Day $11,000** (+$500). **Aid:** Merit 41 ($82,370). Need ($322,000).
- **Summer:** Acad Enrich Rec. 1-8 wks.
- Endow $50,000. Plant val $12,000,000. Bldgs 5. Class rms 49. 2 Libs 6500 vols. Sci labs 5. Comp labs 2. Art studios 2. Music studios 3. Gyms 1. Fields 3. Tennis courts 4. Playgrounds 1.
- **Est 1967.** Nonprofit. Tri (Aug-June). **Assoc** SACS.

The school originated along the Lower Cape Fear River in 1867, operating for 50 years as a school for boys. In 1967, a group of Wilmington citizens established the current coeducational school on a suburban site. Located on a 27-acre campus, the academy's physical plant features five buildings, including a student center.

The academy's preschool, kindergarten and lower school prepare pupils in the fundamentals. Specialists in art, music, science, computers, physical education, foreign language and library science supplement the lower school's basic curriculum. Children participate in outdoor play, arts and crafts, cooking, dramatics, stories, games, music and field trips.

The middle school (grades 6-8) offers an interdisciplinary academic program that emphasizes central curricular themes and is enhanced by an outdoor education program. Students in the upper school prepare for college entrance with a selection of honors and Advanced Placement courses and electives supplementing the required curriculum. Final-term seniors choose an individual community service project.

Students enjoy a variety of intramural sports, as well as middle school, junior varsity and varsity basketball, volleyball, cheerleading, field hockey, lacrosse, swimming, cross-country, softball, soccer, tennis and golf squads. A full range of extracurricular activities, including extensive drama offerings, is also provided.

WINSTON-SALEM, NC. (70 mi. NNE of Charlotte, NC) Urban. Pop: 168,086. Alt: 1000 ft.

SALEM ACADEMY

Bdg and Day — Girls Gr 9-12

Winston-Salem, NC 27101. 500 E Salem Ave. Tel: 336-721-2643. Fax: 336-917-5340.
www.salemacademy.com   E-mail: academy@salem.edu

Wayne Burkette, Head. BA, Univ of North Carolina-Chapel Hill, MDiv, Moravian Theological Seminary, DMin, Union Theological Seminary. **Lucia Uldrick, Adm.**

    Col Prep. AP—Eng Fr Lat Span Calc Bio Chem Physics US_Hist Psych. **Feat**—Computers Relig Studio_Art Drama Music. **Supp**—ESL Tut.

    Adm (Gr 9-11): 70/yr. Bdg 38. Day 32. Appl due: Rolling. Accepted: 70%. Yield: 66%. **Tests** SSAT TOEFL.

    Enr 194. G 97/97. Sec 194. Avg class size: 13. **Fac 25.** F 21/4. Adv deg: 88%.

    Grad '04—48. Col—48. (UNC-Chapel Hill 6, NC St 6, Campbell 2, Davidson 2, UNC-Greensboro 2, UNC-Wilmington 2). Avg SAT: 1203. Alum 2550.

    Tui '04-'05: Bdg $25,830 (+$500). **Day $14,494** (+$500). **Aid:** Merit 18 ($52,630). Need 68 ($1,055,280).

    Endow $3,000,000. Plant val $6,500,000. Dorms 7. Dorm rms 60. Class rms 24. Lib 8000 vols. Sci labs 3. Lang labs 2. Comp labs 2. Auds 1. Theaters 1. Art studios 1. Music studios 2. Dance studios 1. Gyms 2. Fields 3. Courts 12. Pools 1. Student ctrs 1.

    Est 1772. Nonprofit. Moravian. Sem (Aug-May). **Assoc** SACS.

Located near the restored 18th-century Moravian village of Old Salem, Salem Academy offers a January term program in which students may either travel abroad or undertake an off-campus internship.

Girls are given sound preparation for prestigious colleges throughout the country. The curriculum is complemented by Salem College's lectures, concerts, facilities and classes, and advanced pupils may take courses at Salem College. The athletic program provides for interscholastic teams and competitive sports in tennis, swimming, volleyball, softball, field hockey, soccer, cross-country, track and basketball. Music and theater are major interests, and the glee club performs locally, nationally and internationally. In addition to participation in extracurricular activities, the academy encourages students to seek leadership positions.

See Also Pages 1314-5

SUMMIT SCHOOL

Day — Coed Gr PS-9

Winston-Salem, NC 27106. 2100 Reynolda Rd. Tel: 336-722-2777. Fax: 336-724-0099.
www.summitschool.com   E-mail: kmemory@summitschool.com

Sandra P. Adams, Head. BA, MA, Wake Forest Univ, EdD, Univ of North Carolina-Greensboro. **Katherine Memory, Adm.**

    Pre-Prep. Gen Acad. Feat—Fr Lat Span Computers Robotics. **Supp**—Dev_Read Rem_Read Tut.

    Adm: 87/yr. Appl due: Rolling. Accepted: 50%. Yield: 98%. **Tests** CTP_4.

    Enr 602. B 315. G 287. Elem 577. Sec 25. Wh 80%. Hisp 3%. Blk 10%. Am Ind 1%. Asian 6%. Avg class size: 20. **Fac 94.** M 14/1. F 64/15. Wh 88%. Hisp 1%. Blk 8%. Am Ind 1%. Asian 1%. Other 1%. Adv deg: 47%.

Grad '04—40. Prep—18. (Forsyth Co Day, Salem, Episcopal HS-VA, Woodberry Forest, McCallie). Alum 3519.
Tui '04-'05: Day $9045-13,890 (+$130). **Aid:** Need 73 ($621,195).
Summer: Enrich Rec. Tui Day $150/wk. 6 wks.
Endow $13,000,000. Plant val $21,000,000. Bldgs 9. Class rms 45. 2 Libs 30,000 vols. Labs 3. Comp ctrs 5. Theaters 1. Art studios 3. Music studios 2. Gyms 3. Fields 3.
Est 1933. Nonprofit. Tri (Aug-June). **Assoc** SACS.

Housed in a modern, functional plant specially designed for young children, Summit combines recent methods of teaching with sound academic standards, while also making special provisions for acceleration. A teaching/learning center contains science labs for grades K-6, a computer center, a counseling center, a language arts and communication lab, and a photography darkroom.

Approximately 70 percent of fifth graders participate in student-exchange visits with schools in the US or Canada. The arts are an integral part of the curriculum at all grade levels. Photography, art, cooking, pottery, robotics, community service and various sports are among the activities.

SOUTH CAROLINA

AIKEN, SC. (59 mi. SW of Columbia, SC; 156 mi. E of Atlanta, GA) Urban. Pop: 25,337. Alt: 490 ft.

AIKEN PREPARATORY SCHOOL

Day — Coed Gr PS-12

Aiken, SC 29801. 619 Barnwell Ave NW. Tel: 803-648-3223. Fax: 803-648-6482.
www.aikenprep.org   E-mail: admissions@aikenprep.org
Deborah Taussig-Boehner, Admin. BS, MA, Syracuse Univ. **Susan B. Player, Adm.**

Col Prep. Feat—Fr Span Comp_Sci Web_Design Studio_Art Theater Music Public_Speak. **Supp**—ESL Rev Tut.

Adm (Gr PS-10): 37/yr. Appl due: Rolling. Accepted: 99%. Yield: 100%. **Tests** IQ Stanford.

Enr 169. B 92. G 77. Elem 130. Sec 39. Wh 87%. Hisp 2%. Blk 3%. Asian 3%. Other 5%. Avg class size: 12. Uniform. **Fac 45.** M 4/5. F 12/24. Wh 99%. Hisp 1%. Adv deg: 15%.

Grad '04—6. Col—6. (U of SC-Aiken). Avg SAT: 1165. Avg ACT: 26. Alum 1300.

Tui '05-'06: Day $4300-8500 (+$800-1250). **Aid:** Need 17 ($53,000).

Summer: Acad Enrich Rec. 8 wks.

Endow $1,000,000. Plant val $1,352,000. Bldgs 9. Class rms 23. Lib 5000 vols. Sci labs 2. Comp labs 1. Auds 1. Theaters 1. Art studios 1. Music studios 1. Gyms 1. Fields 3. Courts 3. Pools 1. Rifle ranges 1.

Est 1916. Nonprofit. (Aug-May).

Aiken Prep was established by Louise Eustis Hitchcock and F.A.M. Tabor as a junior boarding school for boys. In 1989, APS merged with Aiken Day School, adding a coeducational day program while expanding the lower school grades. The school discontinued its boarding division in August 2000, while also adding grades 10-12.

Offerings in foreign language, art, computer and music complement the students' foundation in the core academic subject areas. Honors classes in all core subjects are part of the high school curriculum. A tutorial program is available for those in need of additional academic support.

Students in grades 6-9 participate in a daily after-school athletic program. Boys and girls may choose to play on interscholastic teams in such sports as basketball, volleyball, soccer, tennis, baseball and golf. In addition, APS offers students the option of a nontraditional physical education program. Horseback riding is also available in the nearby, 2000-acre Hitchcock Woods.

BEAUFORT, SC. (48 mi. WSW of Charleston, SC) Suburban. Pop: 12,950. Alt: 15 ft.

BEAUFORT ACADEMY
Day — Coed Gr PS-12

Beaufort, SC 29907. 240 Sams Point Rd. Tel: 843-524-3393. Fax: 843-524-1171.
www.beaufortacademy.org   E-mail: msuber@beaufortacademy.org
Timothy D. Johnston, Head. Bethany Biaett, Adm.
  Col Prep. **Feat**—Lat Computers Econ Philos Relig Studio_Art Journ. **Supp**—Tut.
  Adm: 85/yr. Accepted: 75%. **Tests** CTP_4 IQ.
  Enr 350. Wh 93%. Hisp 1%. Blk 2%. Asian 4%. Avg class size: 15. **Fac 50.** Adv deg: 50%.
  Grad '04—20. Col—11. (U of SC, Col of Charleston, Presbyterian, Clemson, Randolph-Macon, UNC-Chapel Hill). Avg SAT: 1124. Avg ACT: 24. Alum 880.
  Tui '05-'06: Day $5800-8495 (+$350). **Aid:** Need 70.
  Summer: Enrich. Computers. 4 wks.
  Endow $500,000. Plant val $4,000,000. Bldgs 8. Class rms 32. Lib 16,500 vols. Sci labs 2. Comp labs 2. Art studios 1. Music studios 1. Gyms 1. Fields 3. Courts 2. Tracks 1.
  Est 1965. Nonprofit. Sem (Aug-May). **Assoc** SACS.

Founded in St. Helena's Episcopal Church, Beaufort Academy is now located on Lady's Island in the Carolina low country. Boys and girls follow a core curriculum in all grades and have the opportunity for intensive and advanced study during the final two years. Foreign language study begins in kindergarten, and Latin is offered in the middle school. Computer science is taught at all grade levels, as are the fine arts. BA maintains strong programs in the humanities, the fine arts, the sciences and student government.

Students participate in a full interscholastic sports program offering at least two boys' and two girls' sports at the varsity, junior varsity and middle school levels each season.

CAMDEN, SC. (22 mi. NE of Columbia, SC) Suburban. Pop: 6682. Alt: 222 ft.

CAMDEN MILITARY ACADEMY
Bdg — Boys Gr 7-PG

Camden, SC 29020. 520 US Hwy 1 N. Tel: 803-432-6001. Fax: 803-425-1020.
www.camdenmilitary.com   E-mail: admissions@camdenmilitary.com
Col. Eric Boland, Head. R. Casey Robinson, Adm.
  Col Prep. Milit. AP—Calc. **Feat**—Fr Lat Span Computers Music. **Supp**—Dev_Read Rem_Math Tut.
  Adm: 151/yr. Appl due: Rolling. Accepted: 80%.
  Enr 292. B 292. Elem 90. Sec 200. PG 2. Wh 86%. Hisp 2%. Blk 11%. Asian 1%. Avg class size: 15. Uniform. **Fac 33.** M 23/8. F 1/1. Wh 79%. Hisp 15%. Asian 6%. Adv deg: 51%.
  Grad '04—74. Col—67. (Auburn, Appalachian St, Col of Charleston, Clemson, U of SC,

Citadel). Alum 4688.
Tui '04-'05: Bdg $14,995 (+$1375).
Summer: Acad Rec. Tui Bdg $1995. 6 wks.
Endow $1,000,000. Plant val $6,500,000. Bldgs 11. Dorms 4. Dorm rms 146. Class rms 17. Lib 9000 vols. Labs 4. Gyms 1. Fields 3. Tennis courts 3. Pools 1. Rifle ranges 1.
Est 1950. Nonprofit. Sem. **Assoc** SACS.

Originally founded as Camden Academy by a group of citizens, the academy began operating under the present administration in 1958, at which time the school assumed its present name.

In addition to the preparatory curriculum, the discipline of drill ceremonies and two classes in military educational training per week are required. Students may participate in a full program of athletics, band, debate and publications, among other extracurricular activities.

CHARLESTON, SC. (101 mi. SSE of Columbia, SC) Urban. Pop: 95,650. Alt: 10 ft.

ASHLEY HALL
Day — Boys PS-K, Girls Gr PS-12

Charleston, SC 29403. 172 Rutledge Ave. Tel: 843-722-4088. Fax: 843-720-2868.
www.ashleyhall.org   E-mail: enrollment@ashleyhall.org
Jill Swisher Muti, **Head.** BMus, DePauw Univ, MA, Duke Univ. **Elizabeth H. Peters, Adm.**
  Col Prep. AP—Eng Fr Lat Span Calc Stats Bio Chem Physics Eur_Hist US_Hist Econ US_Govt & Pol Art_Hist Studio_Art. **Feat**—Greek Hebrew Marine_Biol/Sci Programming Web_Design Psych Ceramics Photog Drama Music. **Supp**—Tut.
  Adm (Gr PS-12): 117/yr. Appl due: Jan. Accepted: 67%. Yield: 72%. **Tests** CTP_4 IQ.
  Enr 613. B 23. G 590. Elem 441. Sec 172. Wh 92%. Hisp 1%. Blk 5%. Asian 2%. Avg class size: 15. **Fac 72.** Wh 96%. Blk 3%. Asian 1%. Adv deg: 65%.
  Grad '04—43. Col—43. (U of SC, Clemson, Davidson, Col of Charleston, U of FL, Duke). Avg SAT: 1175. Alum 2500.
  Tui '04-'05: Day $8452-13,527 (+$475). **Aid:** Merit 37 ($85,523). Need 49 ($230,615). Work prgm 20 ($12,260).
  Summer: Enrich Rec. Tui Day $125/wk. 8 wks.
  Endow $1,260,000. Plant val $10,000,000. Bldgs 8. Class rms 45. 2 Libs 15,000 vols. Sci labs 4. Comp labs 3. Photog labs 1. Dark rms 1. Auds 2. Art studios 2. Music studios 4. Dance studios 1. Recital halls 1. Gyms 1. Fields 1. Pools 1.
  Est 1909. Nonprofit. Sem (Aug-May). **Assoc** SACS.

Founded by Mary Vardrine McBee, a graduate of Smith College, the school gained prominence through the breadth of educational ideals that she brought to bear and maintained for 40 years. Upon her retirement, the school was continued under the Ashley Hall Foundation.

The school's early education center, created in 1990, offers a coeducational preschool and kindergarten program. Computer and foreign language courses begin in prekindergarten and continue throughout. The upper school program includes Advanced Placement offerings, as well as various electives. Art, music and drama are offered.

Extracurricular activities include dramatics, music, publications, student council and interest clubs. Volunteerism and community service are encouraged. Physical education is required of all students, and sports include tennis, volleyball, basketball, soccer, track, softball and sailing. Graduates matriculate at colleges throughout the country.   **See Also Page 1289**

CHARLESTON DAY SCHOOL
Day — Coed Gr 1-8

Charleston, SC 29401. 15 Archdale St. Tel: 843-722-7791. Fax: 843-720-2143.
www.charlestondayschool.org   E-mail: barnessb@charlestondayschool.org
Brendan J. O'Shea, Head. BS, MEd, Univ of Virginia. **Sallie B. Barnes, Adm.**
  Pre-Prep. Feat—Fr Span Computers Ethics Studio_Art Music.
  Adm (Gr 1-6): 27/yr. Appl due: Jan. Accepted: 75%. Yield: 26%. **Tests** CTP_4.
  Enr 169. B 92. G 77. Elem 169. Wh 100%. Avg class size: 20. **Fac 23.** M 3. F 16/4. Wh 100%. Adv deg: 47%.
  Grad '04—22. Prep—21. (Woodberry Forest 5, Ashley Hall 4, Porter-Gaud 2, Hotchkiss 2, Episcopal HS-VA 1). Alum 1200.
  Tui '04-'05: Day $10,400. Aid: Merit 1 ($5000).
  Endow $1,100,000. Plant val $3,000,000. Bldgs 5. Class rms 14. Lib 10,000 vols. Sci labs 1. Comp labs 1. Art studios 1. Music studios 1. Arts ctrs 1. Amphitheaters 1. Gyms 1.
  Est 1937. Nonprofit. Sem (Aug-May).

Founded by Emily E. Tenney and Mary Stuart, who directed the school until 1971, CDS provides a varied elementary program for children in Greater Charleston. The school has relocated three times to accommodate growth and now occupies quarters in the city's historic district.

While Charleston Day places particular emphasis on its core curriculum (math, reading, language arts and science), pupils at all grade levels also take French, computer, art, music and physical education courses. Students in grades 7 and 8 may take Spanish and advanced math classes (including honors algebra). Special academic programs, team sports, community service and fine arts productions provide enrichment.

PORTER-GAUD SCHOOL
Day — Coed Gr K-12

Charleston, SC 29407. 300 Albemarle Rd. Tel: 843-556-3620. Fax: 843-769-9926.
www.portergaud.edu   E-mail: cherie.cabe@portergaud.edu
Cherie Cabe, Adm.
  Col Prep. AP—Eng Calc Stats Comp_Sci Bio Chem Physics Eur_Hist US_Hist US_Govt & Pol. **Feat**—Fr Ger Lat Span Econ Ethics Philos Relig Art_Hist Music Music_Theory.
  Adm: 183/yr. Appl due: Rolling. Accepted: 60%. **Tests** CTP_4 IQ.
  Enr 940. B 566. G 374. Elem 614. Sec 326. Wh 92%. Hisp 1%. Blk 4%. Asian 2%. Other 1%. Avg class size: 18. **Fac 85.** M 33. F 52. Wh 97%. Hisp 1%. Blk 2%. Adv deg: 74%.
  Grad '04—81. Col—71. (Clemson, Col of Charleston, Duke, Wofford, U of GA, U of SC). Avg SAT: 1271. Avg ACT: 27. Alum 2560.
  Tui '04-'05: Day $10,750-13,320 (+$375-1390). **Aid:** Need 65 ($553,722).

Summer: Rem Rec. 10 wks.
Endow $4,019,000. Plant val $30,000,000. Bldgs 14. Class rms 55. 2 Libs 25,200 vols. Sci labs 10. Comp labs 3. Sci/tech ctrs 1. Auds 1. Art studios 3. Music studios 4. Dance studios 1. Gyms 2. Athletic ctrs 1. Fields 5. Courts 6.
Est 1867. Nonprofit. Episcopal. Tri (Aug-May). **Assoc** CLS SACS.

In 1964, Gaud School for Boys (founded in 1908) merged with Porter-Military Academy (founded in 1867) to form the larger Porter-Gaud School, now located on a 70-acre campus overlooking the Ashley River. The school discontinued its military program at that time, and girls were first admitted in 1972.

Porter-Gaud combines a traditional college preparatory program with a variety of extracurricular opportunities. Elective courses are offered in music, art, art history, computer and public speaking. There is widespread participation among upper school students in community outreach programs, which may involve, for example, tutoring at an inner-city school, working on a food or toy drive, or providing peer counseling.

Activities include publications, drama, music, choral groups, handbells, debate and interest clubs. Available sports are football, soccer, basketball, track, tennis, cross-country, golf, baseball, softball, volleyball and swimming.

COLUMBIA, SC. (80 mi. S of Charlotte, NC) Urban. Pop: 116,278. Alt: 332 ft.

HEATHWOOD HALL EPISCOPAL SCHOOL
Day — Coed Gr PS-12

Columbia, SC 29201. 3000 S Beltline Blvd. Tel: 803-765-2309. Fax: 803-343-0437.
www.heathwood.org   E-mail: hhes2@heathwood.org
Stephen D. Hickman, Head. BSS, Loyola Univ (LA), MS, Johns Hopkins Univ, JD, George Mason Univ. **Lindsey F. Smith, Jr., Adm.**
Col Prep. **AP**—Eng Fr Span Calc Stats US_Hist World_Hist. **Feat**—Women_Writers Anthro Econ Ethics Philos Relig Drama Music Outdoor_Ed. **Supp**—Dev_Read Rem_Math Rem_Read Rev Tut.
Adm: 126/yr. Appl due: Rolling. Accepted: 84%. **Tests** CTP_4.
Enr 760. Wh 91%. Blk 7%. Asian 2%. Avg class size: 15. **Fac 99.** M 19/13. F 54/13. Adv deg: 100%.
Grad '04—45. Col—45. (U of SC, Clemson, Wofford, Col of Auburn, Furman). Avg SAT: 1204. Alum 1300.
Tui '03-'04: Day $9330-11,070 (+$400-600).
Summer: Acad Enrich Rev Rem Rec. 1-6 wks.
Endow $4,500,000. Plant val $20,000,000. Bldgs 24. Class rms 91. Lib 26,000 vols. Labs 5. Art studios 4. Music studios 3. Arts & sci ctrs 2. Gyms 2. Fields 5. Tracks 1.
Est 1951. Nonprofit. Episcopal. Sem (Aug-May). **Assoc** SACS.

Heathwood Hall, founded by a group of parents in cooperation with the Episcopal Diocese of upper South Carolina, is the oldest independent school in Columbia. The school moved in 1974 to its present, 133-acre campus near the downtown area. The high school division, which opened in 1973, graduated its first class in 1977.

The curriculum is college preparatory, and admission is by examination. Instruction is highly personalized, with a low student-teacher ratio, special tutoring programs and customized curricular packages to meet pupils' needs. The interdenominational student body pursues intensive and rigorous academic and athletic programs designed to promote educational, spiritual and physical growth. An after-school child development program operates throughout the school year for children through grade 8. Graduates enter competitive colleges across the nation.

GREENVILLE, SC. (91 mi. WSW of Charlotte, NC; 139 mi. ENE of Atlanta, GA) Urban. Pop: 56,002. Alt: 1040 ft.

CHRIST CHURCH EPISCOPAL SCHOOL
Day — Coed Gr K-12

Greenville, SC 29607. 245 Cavalier Dr. Tel: 864-299-1522. Fax: 864-299-8861.
www.cces.org   E-mail: info@cces.org
Leland H. Cox, Jr., Head. BA, Wake Forest Univ, MA, PhD, Univ of South Carolina. **Pam Matthews, Adm.**
  Col Prep. IB Diploma. AP—Eng Lat Span Calc Stats Bio Chem Physics Eur_Hist US_Hist. **Feat**—Computers Comp_Design Anthro Econ Psych. **Supp**—ESL.
  Adm: 151/yr. Appl due: Rolling. Accepted: 78%. **Tests** CTP_4.
  Enr 953. Elem 665. Sec 288. Wh 97%. Blk 1%. Asian 1%. Other 1%. Avg class size: 18. **Fac 94.** M 17/1. F 72/4. Adv deg: 51%.
  Grad '04—71. Col—70. (Clemson, Col of Charleston, U of GA, U of SC, U of the South, Wofford). Avg SAT: 1250. Alum 1700.
  Tui '03-'04: Day $9975-11,950 (+$750-1000). **Aid:** Need ($587,601).
  Summer: Acad Enrich Rev Rem Rec. Tui Day $199/wk. 6 wks.
  Endow $5,300,000. Plant val $18,300,000. Bldgs 5. Class rms 85. 3 Libs 21,000 vols. Sci labs 6. Lang labs 2. Comp labs 5. Auds 1. Theaters 1. Art studios 5. Music studios 5. Gyms 1. Fields 5. Courts 5. Tracks 1.
  Est 1959. Nonprofit. Episcopal. Tri (Aug-June). **Assoc** CLS SACS.

Established as an elementary school offering grades K-6, Christ Church expanded to grade 9 upon completion of the Parish House of Christ Church. In 1969, the vestry decided to add grades 9-12 and acquired the 68-acre campus that now houses all three school divisions.

CCES offers a broad college preparatory curriculum that features an International Baccalaureate program, a full complement of Advanced Placement courses, and a strong fine and performing arts department. Christian education at the lower school and religious studies in formal classes are required for graduation, and all students attend chapel (although the school serves pupils of all faiths).

Extracurricular activities include interest clubs, musical productions, publications, trips, overnight camp outs and retreats, dances and parties, interscholastic athletics and community service projects. The student body displays a significant international presence, with pupils enrolling from more than 20 countries.

SPARTANBURG, SC. (64 mi. WSW of Charlotte, NC; 164 mi. ENE of Atlanta, GA) Urban. Pop: 39,673. Alt: 680-875 ft.

SPARTANBURG DAY SCHOOL

Day — Coed Gr PS-12

Spartanburg, SC 29307. 1701 Skylyn Dr. Tel: 864-582-7539. Fax: 864-948-0026.
www.sdsgriffin.org   E-mail: robbie.richards@sdsgriffin.org
Christopher A. Dorrance, Head. BA, Amherst College, MAT, Reed College. **Robbie Richards, Adm.**

- **Col Prep. Gen Acad. IB PYP. AP**—Eng Fr Ger Lat Span Calc Stats Comp_Sci Bio Chem Physics Eur_Hist US_Hist Art_Hist Studio_Art Music_Theory. **Feat**—Native_Amer_Stud. **Supp**—Dev_Read LD Rem_Math Rem_Read Rev Tut.
- **Adm (Gr PS-11):** 93/yr. Appl due: Rolling. Accepted: 70%. Yield: 90%. **Tests** IQ Stanford.
- **Enr 469.** B 216. G 253. Elem 340. Sec 129. Wh 91%. Hisp 1%. Blk 3%. Asian 2%. Other 3%. Avg class size: 18. **Fac 65.** M 13. F 40/12. Wh 100%. Adv deg: 66%.
- **Grad '04—40. Col—40.** (Clemson 4, Col of Charleston 2, Coastal Carolina U 2, Emory 2, U of Tampa 2, U of SC 2). Avg SAT: 1212. Alum 1049.
- **Tui '04-'05: Day $4500-10,100** (+$300-500). **Aid:** Need 31 ($265,000).
- **Summer:** Acad Enrich Rem Rec. 1-9 wks.
- Endow $2,000,000. Plant val $9,137,000. Bldgs 9. Class rms 52. 3 Libs 18,631 vols. Sci labs 4. Comp labs 3. Art studios 4. Music studios 3. Arts ctrs 1. Aud/gyms 1. Gyms 1. Fields 4. Courts 9.
- **Est 1957.** Nonprofit. Sem (Aug-May). **Assoc** CLS SACS.

With an emphasis on small classes, this school offers a classical college preparatory curriculum that stresses English and mathematical skills. Mathematics, English, art, music, history and science are departmentalized in grades 5-12. The foreign language program allows pupils to begin Spanish study in prekindergarten, Latin in grade 7, and French and German in grade 8.

The International Baccalaureate Primary Programme (serving children through grade 6) and a learning laboratory for boys and girls with learning differences are noteworthy curricular features. Art is required through grade 8 and available through grade 12. Graduates enter competitive colleges throughout the country.

TENNESSEE

BELL BUCKLE, TN. (46 mi. SSE of Nashville, TN) Rural. Pop: 391. Alt: 846 ft.

WEBB SCHOOL
Bdg — Coed Gr 7-PG; Day — Coed 6-12

Bell Buckle, TN 37020. Sawney Webb Memorial Hwy, PO Box 488. Tel: 931-389-6003. Fax: 931-389-6657.
www.thewebbschool.com   E-mail: admissions@webbschool.com

A. Jon Frere, Head. BA, Franklin and Marshall College, MA, Middlebury College. **Chad C. Sartini, Adm.**

Col Prep. AP—Eng Fr Ger Span Calc Stats Chem Physics Eur_Hist US_Hist. **Feat**—Lat Forestry Computers Econ Psych Ethics Acting Speech Wilderness_Ed. **Supp**—ESL Tut.

Adm: 79/yr. Bdg 35. Day 44. Appl due: Rolling. Accepted: 60%. **Tests** ISEE SSAT TOEFL.

Enr 280. Elem 80. Sec 200. Wh 85%. Hisp 1%. Blk 6%. Asian 8%. Avg class size: 11. **Fac 36.** M 15/2. F 17/2. Wh 100%. Adv deg: 66%. In dorms 8.

Grad '04—40. Col—40. (Vanderbilt 12, Harvard 3, U of the South 3, Wash U 3, Wake Forest 2, UNC-Chapel Hill 2). Avg SAT: 1230. Alum 2650.

Tui '04-'05: Bdg $28,000 (+$3300). **Day $11,500** (+$2065). **Aid:** Need 117 ($900,000).

Summer: Acad Enrich. ESL. Tui Bdg $3500. Tui Day $1500. 6 wks.

Endow $17,000,000. Plant val $17,000,000. Bldgs 24. Dorms 4. Dorm rms 60. Class rms 24. Lib 22,000 vols. Sci labs 7. Lang labs 5. Comp labs 2. Dark rms 1. Auds 1. Theaters 1. Art studios 3. Music studios 3. Gyms 5. Courts 4. Pools 1.

Est 1870. Nonprofit. Sem (Aug-May). **Assoc** CLS SACS.

The school was founded in Culleoka by William R. Webb, active in educational, religious, political, social and community affairs and affectionately known as "Old Sawney." His brother, John M. Webb, joined the school in 1874 and served as coprincipal from that time until his death in 1916. Through the united efforts of the two brothers, the school soon attracted boys from all over the South and became a center of influence in the region. In 1886, the school was moved from Culleoka to its present location at Bell Buckle. William R. Webb, Jr., son of Old Sawney, joined the faculty in 1897, became a principal along with his father and his uncle in 1908, and took over as sole principal in 1926, upon the death of his father. During the years of his service, the school began to develop its present dormitory system. Webb is situated on 150 acres in a rural setting, and school facilities have been improved and enlarged over the years.

Academically, the college preparatory program is structured. Numerous sports, dramatics, public speaking, publications and an outdoor education program are among activities. A six-week summer program combining academic work with outdoor adventure is also offered. An extensive college counseling program begins early in each student's career at Webb. There is a large body of loyal alumni.

See Also Page 1272

CHATTANOOGA, TN. (83 mi. ENE of Huntsville, AL) Urban. Pop: 155,554. Alt: 674 ft.

THE BRIGHT SCHOOL

Day — Coed Gr PS-5

Chattanooga, TN 37405. 1950 Hixson Pike. Tel: 423-267-8546. Fax: 423-265-0025.
  www.brightschool.com   E-mail: penloe@brightschool.com
O. J. Morgan, Head. BA, Colby College, MAT, Northwestern Univ, MTh, Harvard Univ. **Peggy E. Enloe, Adm.**
  Pre-Prep. Feat—Writing Span Computers Studio_Art Music Indus_Arts. **Supp**—Rem_Math Rem_Read Tut.
  Adm: 65/yr. **Tests** CTP_4 ISEE Stanford.
  Enr 357. B 180. G 177. Elem 357. Wh 89%. Blk 3%. Asian 8%. Avg class size: 18. Uniform.
  Fac 42. M 2/5. F 32/3. Wh 100%. Adv deg: 33%.
  Grad '04—52. Prep—50. (Girls Prep, Baylor, McCallie). Alum 2827.
  Tui '03-'04: Day $5800-8800 (+$40). **Aid:** Need 34 ($93,900).
  Summer: Enrich Rec. Tui Day $125/wk. 10 wks.
  Endow $2,754,000. Plant val $4,997,000. Bldgs 1. Class rms 23. Lib 16,960 vols. Sci labs 1. Comp labs 1. Auds 1. Art studios 1. Music studios 1. Man arts studios 1. Gyms 1. Fields 2.
  Est 1913. Nonprofit. Sem (Aug-May). **Assoc** SACS.

Founded by Mary Gardner Bright and was under her direction for 48 years, this is the oldest independent elementary school in the state. The curriculum, which prepares students for local independent secondary schools, is enriched by specialized areas that include music, art, manual arts, computer, Spanish and physical education.

Beyond the academic offerings, an extended-care program offers intramural athletics, music and art lessons, ballet and computer instruction. Situated on a 55-acre campus, the school's facilities include modern computer and science labs, as well as a computerized library.

GIRLS PREPARATORY SCHOOL

Day — Girls Gr 6-12

Chattanooga, TN 37405. 205 Island Ave, PO Box 4736. Tel: 423-634-7600.
  Fax: 423-634-7643.
  www.gps.edu   E-mail: dmoore@gps.edu
Stanley R. Tucker, Jr., Head. BA, Jacksonville Univ, MEd, Univ of North Florida. **Diane C. Moore, Adm.**
  Col Prep. AP—Eng Fr Lat Span Calc Comp_Sci Bio Chem Physics Eur_Hist US_Hist. **Feat**—Astron Environ_Sci Forensic_Sci E_Asian_Hist Econ Govt Constitutional_Law Graphic_Arts Drama Music Dance. **Supp**—Rev Tut.
  Adm (Gr 6-11): 112/yr. Appl due: Rolling. Accepted: 83%. Yield: 54%. **Tests** ISEE.
  Enr 738. G 738. Elem 299. Sec 439. Wh 92%. Blk 4%. Asian 4%. Avg class size: 15. Uniform. **Fac 89.** M 19. F 63/7. Wh 97%. Hisp 1%. Blk 2%. Adv deg: 57%.
  Grad '04—106. Col—106. (U of TN-Knoxville 15, U of GA 7, Auburn 7, Berry 3, Emory 3, Wash U 3). Avg SAT: 1220. Avg ACT: 26. Alum 4511.
  Tui '04-'05: Day $14,980 (+$500-2000). **Aid:** Merit 2 ($29,960). Need 156 ($1,297,966).
  Summer: Acad Enrich Rec. Sports. Tui Day $220-975. 1-6 wks.

Endow $24,452,000. Plant val $52,000,000. Bldgs 11. Class rms 90. Lib 26,823 vols. Sci labs 9. Lang labs 1. Comp labs 2. Dark rms 1. Auds 1. Theaters 2. Art studios 3. Music studios 2. Dance studios 2. Gyms 2. Fields 4. Courts 16. Pools 1. Tracks 1. Weight rms 1.
Est 1906. Nonprofit. Sem (Aug-May). **Assoc** CLS SACS.

Founded by Grace McCallie, Tommie Duffy and Eula Jarnagin, Girls Preparatory School offers a college preparatory curriculum with honors and Advanced Placement courses in all disciplines. A coordinate program with the McCallie School combines GPS' single-sex school with coeducational extracurricular and social activities in such areas as the performing arts; pupils choose from coed evening classes offered on both campuses. Students participate in community service projects throughout the year.

Athletics include cross-country, track and field, diving and swimming, basketball, softball, soccer, crew, tennis, cheerleading, volleyball and golf.

See Also Page 1301

McCALLIE SCHOOL

Bdg — Boys Gr 9-12; Day — Boys 6-12

Chattanooga, TN 37404. 500 Dodds Ave. Tel: 423-624-8300. Fax: 423-493-5426. www.mccallie.org E-mail: admission@mccallie.org

Kirk Walker, Head. BA, Univ of North Carolina-Chapel Hill, MS, PhD, Vanderbilt Univ. **Randy Roach, Adm.**

Col Prep. AP—Eng Fr Lat Span Calc Comp_Sci Bio Chem Physics Eur_Hist US_Hist Econ Studio_Art. **Feat**—Ger Greek Japan Bioethics Environ_Sci Oceanog Hist_of_the_South Bible Music_Theory Journ Speech. **Supp**—Tut.

Adm (Bdg Gr 9-11; Day 6-11): 204/yr. Bdg 80. Day 124. Appl due: Jan. Accepted: 78%. Yield: 77%. **Tests** ISEE SSAT.

Enr 890. B 231/659. Elem 259. Sec 631. Wh 90%. Hisp 1%. Blk 5%. Asian 2%. Other 2%. Avg class size: 13. **Fac 104.** M 70/9. F 15/10. Wh 94%. Blk 5%. Asian 1%. Adv deg: 48%. In dorms 20.

Grad '04—157. Col—156. (U of TN-Knoxville 19, Auburn 7, U of TN-Chattanooga 7, U of GA 7, U of KY 6, U of MS 5). Alum 10,200.

Tui '05-'06: Bdg $31,500 (+$500). **Day $16,410** (+$500). **Aid:** Merit 52 ($600,000). Need 161 ($1,800,000).

Summer: Enrich Rec. Sports. Tui Bdg $1650. 2 wks.

Endow $42,000,000. Plant val $60,000,000. Bldgs 32. Dorms 5. Dorm rms 114. Class rms 41. Lib 32,000 vols. Labs 5. Black-box theaters 1. Art studios 4. Music studios 2. Gyms 6. Fields 7. Courts 14. Pools 2.

Est 1905. Nonprofit. Sem (Aug-May). **Assoc** CLS SACS.

The McCallie brothers, Prof. Spencer J. McCallie and Dr. J. Park McCallie, conducted the school they founded from 1905 to 1949. With a consistently demanding faculty, they developed superior academic standards and athletic facilities comparable to those of Northern schools. Graduates go on to competitive colleges in the South and around the country. Through a year of Bible study, activities such as Young Life, FCA and Big Brothers, and the honor system, emphasis is put on the development of Christian character. A coordinate program with Girls Preparatory School provides a limited number of coed courses and joint theater productions, a cheerleading squad, activities and social events. Extracurricular activities are varied and include student government, religious groups, music, dramatics, and numerous interest and hobby clubs.

A weekend activities program and an extensive academic counseling program provide additional stimuli. Faculty members conduct one-on-one tutorials four times per week for those students requiring extra help. In addition to interscholastic sports such as football, lacrosse, crew, cross-country, basketball, soccer, swimming, wrestling, track, tennis, golf, baseball and rock climbing, McCallie maintains a comprehensive physical fitness program in which all participate.

See Also Pages 1338-9

GERMANTOWN, TN. (12 mi. E of Memphis, TN) Urban. Pop: 37,348. Alt: 379 ft.

ST. GEORGE'S INDEPENDENT SCHOOLS
Day — Coed Gr PS-12

Germantown, TN 38138. 8250 Poplar Ave. Tel: 901-261-2300. Fax: 901-261-2311.
www.stgeorgesschools.org E-mail: info@stgeorgesschools.org

Richard H. Ferguson, Pres. BA, Southern Methodist Univ, MEd, North Texas State Univ. **Jay Philpott, Jennifer Taylor & Ginny Henderson, Adms.**

Col Prep. Feat—Fr Lat Span Computers Relig Studio_Art Music. Supp—Dev_Read Makeup Tut.

Adm: 172/yr. Appl due: Rolling. **Tests** CTP_4 ISEE Stanford.

Enr 839. B 424. G 415. Elem 709. Sec 130. Avg class size: 20. **Fac 94.** M 21. F 70/3. Wh 95%. Blk 4%. Other 1%. Adv deg: 48%.

Alum 1000.

Tui '05-'06: Day $10,600-11,580 (+$300).

Summer: Acad Enrich Rev Rec. Tui Day $200/wk. 5 wks.

Endow $1,200,000. Plant val $44,000,000. Bldgs 15. Class rms 50. Lib 14,000 vols. Sci labs 2. Comp labs 2. Auds 2. Theaters 2. Art studios 2. Music studios 2. Gyms 3. Fields 8. Pools 1.

Est 1959. Nonprofit. Tri (Aug-May).

St. George's conducts elementary and secondary curricula that place strong emphasis on language arts, mathematics and science. Beginning in the middle school grades, classes are conducted by separate math, reading, science and social studies departments, while instruction in the lower grades is in self-contained homerooms with the involvement of specialty teachers.

The development of Judeo-Christian values is a recognized part of the educational process. Pupils study art, religion, foreign language, music, computer, physical education and library skills at all levels.

As part of a multi-phase expansion of the program, St. George's opened a second elementary campus in August 2001 at 3749 Kimball Ave., Memphis 38111, then started a high school division (grades 6-12) in fall 2002 at 1880 Wolf River Blvd., Collierville 38017.

JACKSON, TN. (76 mi. ENE of Memphis, TN) Urban. Pop: 59,643. Alt: 450 ft.

UNIVERSITY SCHOOL OF JACKSON
Day — Coed Gr PS-12

Jackson, TN 38305. 232 McClellan Rd. Tel: 731-664-0812. Fax: 731-664-5046.
  www.usj.tn.org   E-mail: admin@usj.tn.org
Steve Maloan, Head. BS, Univ of Tennessee-Martin, MEd, Middle Tennessee State Univ. **Kay Shearin, Adm.**
  Col Prep. AP—Eng Calc Bio Chem Physics Eur_Hist US_Hist Studio_Art Music_Theory. **Feat**—Fr Span Anat & Physiol Comp_Sci Psych Govt/Econ World_Relig Music Journ. **Supp**—ESL Tut.
  Adm: 186/yr. Appl due: Rolling. Accepted: 87%. Yield: 92%. **Tests** IQ.
  Enr 1310. B 702. G 608. Elem 946. Sec 364. Wh 91%. Blk 2%. Asian 5%. Other 2%. Avg class size: 20. Uniform. **Fac 91.** M 17. F 73/1. Adv deg: 31%.
  Grad '04—76. **Col**—76. (U of TN-Knoxville 13, Middle TN St 8, U of AL-Tuscaloosa 6, MS St 5, U of MS 5, Union U 4). Avg SAT: 1110. Avg ACT: 25. Alum 1476.
  Tui '04-'05: Day $4310-5730 (+$75-125). **Aid:** Need 44 ($100,000).
  Summer: Acad Enrich Rec. 1-6 wks.
  Endow $75,000. Plant val $1,400,000. Bldgs 3. Class rms 50. 3 Libs 17,000 vols. Sci labs 4. Comp labs 5. Theaters 1. Art studios 4. Music studios 4. Gyms 4. Fields 5. Courts 6.
  Est 1970. Nonprofit. Quar (Aug-May). **Assoc** SACS.

Situated on a 140-acre campus, this school offers a college preparatory curriculum for average and above-average students. Advanced Placement and honors classes are available in the major disciplines. Spanish classes begin in kindergarten, and French and Spanish are available in grades 6-12. The fine arts department includes chorus, music, band, show choir, plays, musicals and speech. Pupils may also participate in a comprehensive sports program. USJ organizes both regional and international student trips.

KNOXVILLE, TN. (97 mi. NE of Chattanooga, TN) Urban. Pop: 173,890. Alt: 889 ft.

WEBB SCHOOL OF KNOXVILLE
Day — Coed Gr K-12

Knoxville, TN 37923. 9800 Webb School Dr. Tel: 865-693-0011. Fax: 865-691-8057.
  www.webbschool.org   E-mail: terrie_balak@webbschool.org
Scott L. Hutchinson, Pres. BA, Duke Univ, MEd, College of William and Mary. **Terrie Balak, Upper & Middle Sch Adm; Angie Crabtree, Lower Sch Adm.**
  Col Prep. AP—Eng Fr Ger Lat Span Calc Bio Chem Physics Eur_Hist World_Hist Econ Psych Art_Hist Studio_Art Music_Theory. **Feat**—Comp_Sci Vietnam_War E_TN_Hist Relig Photog Theater_Arts. **Supp**—Rem_Math Rem_Read Tut.
  Adm: 153/yr. Appl due: Jan. Accepted: 73%. Yield: 82%. **Tests** SSAT.
  Enr 1049. B 559. G 490. Elem 589. Sec 460. Wh 93%. Blk 3%. Am Ind 1%. Asian 3%. Avg class size: 17. Uniform. **Fac 101.** M 35. F 59/7. Wh 95%. Hisp 3%. Asian 2%. Adv

deg: 67%.
Grad '04—93. Col—93. (U of TN-Knoxville 14, U of MS 4, Middle TN St 4, E TN St 3, U of AL-Tuscaloosa 3, Vanderbilt 3). Avg SAT: 1200. Avg ACT: 26. Alum 3400.
Tui '04-'05: Day $11,346-12,898 (+$200-480). **Aid:** Need 9 ($16,700).
Summer: Ages 12-17. Rem. Tui Day $450/3-wk ses. Ages 5-12. Rec. Tui Day $180/wk. Ages 15-17. Driver Ed. Tui Day $300/3-wk ses. 9 wks.
Endow $5,000,000. Plant val $31,000,000. Bldgs 7. Class rms 80. 2 Libs 39,800 vols. Sci labs 7. Lang labs 3. Comp labs 3. Writing ctrs 1. Auds 1. Art studios 5. Music studios 5. Gyms 3. Fields 5. Courts 8. Pools 1.
Est 1955. Nonprofit. (Aug-May). **Assoc** CLS SACS.

Serving Greater Knoxville, Webb offers a traditional college preparatory curriculum that includes Advanced Placement courses in all major disciplines. All students perform 25 hours of community service annually. Dramatics, publications, musical groups, clubs and student government are among the upper school activities.

Interscholastic athletic competition for boys includes basketball, lacrosse, sailing, baseball, track, football, soccer, swimming, bowling, cross-country, wrestling, golf and tennis. Girls may compete in tennis, track, golf, sailing, soccer, cross-country, basketball, bowling, volleyball, softball, field hockey and swimming.

MEMPHIS, TN. (136 mi. ENE of Little Rock, AR) Urban. Pop: 650,100. Alt: 273 ft.

GRACE-ST. LUKE'S EPISCOPAL SCHOOL
Day — Coed Gr PS-8

Memphis, TN 38104. 246 S Belvedere Blvd. Tel: 901-278-0200. Fax: 901-272-7119.
www.gslschool.org   E-mail: ntaylor@gslschool.org
Thomas A. Beazley, Head. BS, Denison Univ, MS, Univ of Pennsylvania. **Nancy G. Taylor, Adm.**
Pre-Prep. Feat—Lat Span Computers Relig Studio_Art Drama Music.
Adm (Gr PS-7): 73/yr. Appl due: May. Accepted: 80%. Yield: 90%. **Tests** ISEE.
Enr 484. B 254. G 230. Elem 484. Wh 92%. Blk 3%. Asian 3%. Other 2%. Avg class size: 16. Uniform. **Fac 57.** M 4/1. F 49/3. Wh 99%. Blk 1%. Adv deg: 47%.
Grad '04—29. Prep—26. (Memphis U Sch 11, Lausanne 2, St Mary's Episcopal Sch 1). Alum 600.
Tui '04-'05: Day $5125-8780 (+$100). **Aid:** Need 39 ($120,140).
Summer: Acad Enrich Rev Rec. Tui Day $200/wk. 8 wks.
Endow $899,000. Plant val $4,700,000. Bldgs 5. Class rms 40. Lib 15,000 vols. Sci labs 2. Comp labs 2. Theaters 1. Art studios 2. Music studios 1. Gyms 1. Fields 1.
Est 1947. Nonprofit. Episcopal. Tri (Aug-May). **Assoc** SACS.

Begun as a kindergarten, the school now draws students from eastern Arkansas and northern Mississippi, in addition to those from its home state. The college preparatory curriculum is academically advanced and provides a complete fine arts program. Supplementary after-school activities include a program for children through grade 5; a middle school study hall; enrichment in gymnastics, dance, music, drama and sports; and church-sponsored sports, choirs and scouting.

Interscholastic competitions are held in football, baseball, softball, basketball, volleyball, tennis and track. Organizations include student council, honor council, literary magazine, yearbook and newspaper. Students attend and participate in chapel services regularly.

HUTCHISON SCHOOL
Day — Girls Gr PS-12

Memphis, TN 38119. 1740 Ridgeway Rd. Tel: 901-761-2220. Fax: 901-683-3510.
 www.hutchisonschool.org E-mail: ccovington@hutchisonschool.org
Annette C. Smith, Head. EdD, Univ of Mississippi. **Candy Covington, Adm.**
  Col Prep. AP—Eng Fr Lat Span Calc Bio Chem Physics US_Hist World_Hist US_Govt & Pol Art_Hist Studio_Art. **Feat**—Creative_Writing Mandarin Anat Genetics Computers Econ Govt Psych Relig Film Drama Theater Music Dance. **Supp**—Rev.
  Adm: 98/yr. Appl due: Rolling. Accepted: 55%. **Tests** CTP_4 IQ ISEE MRT.
  Enr 826. G 826. Elem 570. Sec 256. Wh 88%. Hisp 1%. Blk 7%. Asian 2%. Other 2%. Avg class size: 18. **Fac 114.** M 13. F 89/12. Wh 98%. Blk 2%. Adv deg: 62%.
  Grad '04—55. Col—55. (U of TN-Knoxville, Vanderbilt, Auburn, Boston U, U of AL-Tuscaloosa). Avg SAT: 1240. Avg ACT: 28. Alum 3400.
  Tui '03-'04: Day $12,400 (+$300). **Aid:** Need 73 ($625,000).
  Summer: Acad Enrich Rec. 10 wks.
  Endow $10,000,000. Plant val $29,250,000. Bldgs 6. Class rms 56. 2 Libs 21,100 vols. Sci labs 5. Comp labs 4. Auds 1. Theaters 1. Art studios 3. Music studios 2. Dance studios 1. Gyms 2. Fields 2. Courts 12. Pools 1.
  Est 1902. Nonprofit. Quar (Aug-May). **Assoc** CLS SACS.

The school, founded by Mary Grimes Hutchison, is located on a 50-acre campus in residential east Memphis. The upper school curriculum instructs each student in the traditional liberal arts disciplines, emphasizing the study of literature, languages, mathematics, history, science and the arts. Both honors and AP courses are available. In the upper school, a coordinate program with the adjacent Memphis University School for boys involves students in courses and extracurricular activities.

Activities include dramatic and musical presentations, concert choir, publications, various organizations, competitive sports, community service and opportunities for study abroad.

LAUSANNE COLLEGIATE SCHOOL
Day — Coed Gr PS-12

Memphis, TN 38120. 1381 W Massey Rd. Tel: 901-474-1000. Fax: 901-682-1696.
 www.lausanneschool.com E-mail: mcook@lausanneschool.com
Stuart McCathie, Head. BEd, Lancaster Univ (England), MEd, Univ of North Carolina-Wilmington. **Molly B. Cook, Adm.**
  Col Prep. Gen Acad. AP—Eng Fr Lat Span Calc Stats Bio Chem Physics US_Hist Comp_Govt & Pol Studio_Art. **Feat**—British_Lit Creative_Writing Humanities Satire & Comedy Environ_Sci Biotech Programming World_War_II Theater_Arts Chorus Music_Theory. **Supp**—Dev_Read Rev Tut.
  Adm: 134/yr. Appl due: Jan. Accepted: 54%. Yield: 41%. **Tests** CTP_4 IQ ISEE SSAT.
  Enr 725. B 341. G 384. Elem 509. Sec 216. Wh 77%. Hisp 1%. Blk 10%. Asian 12%. Avg class size: 18. **Fac 93.** M 23. F 65/5. Wh 91%. Hisp 2%. Blk 5%. Asian 1%. Other 1%. Adv deg: 49%.
  Grad '04—49. Col—49. (U of MS 5, U of Memphis 5, Middle TN St 3, Emory 2, Rhodes

2, Savannah Col of Art & Design 2). Alum 1250.

Tui '05-'06: Day $8300-10,975 (+$500-3175). **Aid:** Merit 12 ($62,563). Need 52 ($236,908).

Summer: Acad Enrich Rev Rec. Tui Day $600-800. 5 wks.

Endow $872,000. Plant val $7,700,000. Bldgs 10. Class rms 50. Lib 21,000 vols. Sci labs 6. Lang labs 1. Comp labs 1. Theaters 2. Art studios 4. Music studios 3. Dance studios 1. Gyms 1. Fields 2. Courts 4. Ropes crses 2. Climbing walls 1.

Est 1926. Nonprofit. Quar (Aug-May).

One of the oldest continuously operating schools in the region, Lausanne was founded by Emma DeSaussure Jett and Bessie Satler as a girls-only institution on a rustic, 28-acre campus that is bordered by woodlands and Blue Heron Lake. After operating for more than 50 years as a single-gender program, the school became coeducational in 1977.

In the early years, three- to five-year-olds engage in a play-based curriculum that introduces them to pre-reading, music, art, math, social studies, science and Spanish. The lower school (junior kindergarten through grade 4) emphasizes mastery of the fundamental academic skills in a developmentally appropriate setting that incorporates cocurricular offerings in the fine arts, computer technology, Spanish and physical education. The transitional middle school (grades 5-8) demands increasing levels of student responsibility and provides opportunities for advancement in math, literature composition, foreign language, history and science. Art, music and drama classes are also available during these years, and each grade level embarks on an annual class trip.

College preparation is the primary focus of the rigorous upper school program (grades 9-12). The curriculum progresses from skill building in foundation subjects and exposure to various disciplines in grades 9 and 10 to a choice of Advanced Placement courses and a greater number of electives in grades 11 and 12. The arts are integral to the upper school course of studies, and a strong athletic program includes both individual and team sports. Class-, club- and school-sponsored service projects encourage boys and girls to engage themselves in the Memphis community.

MEMPHIS UNIVERSITY SCHOOL

Day — Boys Gr 7-12

Memphis, TN 38119. 6191 Park Ave. Tel: 901-260-1300. Fax: 901-260-1355. www.musowls.org E-mail: sheila.bohannon@musowls.org

Ellis L. Haguewood, Head. BA, Harding College, MA, Memphis State Univ. **William L. Askew III, Adm.**

Col Prep. AP—Eng Fr Lat Span Calc Stats Bio Physics US_Hist Econ US_Govt & Pol Art_Hist. **Feat**—Humanities Ger Theater Music_Theory. **Supp**—Rev Tut.

Adm (Gr 7-11): 142/yr. Accepted: 85%. Yield: 91%. **Tests** ISEE.

Enr 649. B 649. Elem 212. Sec 437. Wh 90%. Hisp 1%. Blk 2%. Asian 7%. Avg class size: 16. **Fac 66.** M 50. F 10/6. Adv deg: 81%.

Grad '04—83. Col—83. (U of TN-Knoxville, U of MS, Vanderbilt, SMU, U of GA, Auburn). Avg SAT: 1290. Avg ACT: 28. Alum 2760.

Tui '04-'05: Day $11,975 (+$600). **Aid:** Need 115 ($821,000).

Summer: Enrich Rev Rec. 4 wks.

Endow $14,000,000. Plant val $37,000,000. Bldgs 7. Class rms 35. Lib 25,000 vols. Sci labs 6. Lang labs 3. Comp labs 2. Auds 2. Art studios 1. Vocal & instrumental music

rms 2. Gyms 2. Fields 6. Courts 8.
Est 1893. Nonprofit. Sem (Aug-May). **Assoc** CLS SACS.

Founded as the Werts and Rhea School, the school is the result of a 1954 reorganization and incorporation. Conducted on a 94-acre campus, the strong academic program emphasizes college preparation and features Advanced Placement courses in the major disciplines. MUS maintains a coordinate program with the Hutchison School, a girls' school whose adjacent campus allows for joint academic, athletic, civic service and leadership programs. An honor code plays a major role in school life. All students perform community service, with many opportunities available through local churches and synagogues.

Extracurricular activities include student government, honor groups, publications, theater, music and interest clubs. The athletic program includes physical education four times weekly, as well as interscholastic competition in football, baseball, lacrosse, track, basketball, cross-country, soccer, tennis, wrestling, golf and swimming.

PRESBYTERIAN DAY SCHOOL
Day — Boys Gr PS-6

Memphis, TN 38111. 4025 Poplar Ave. Tel: 901-842-4600. Fax: 901-327-7564.
   www.pdsmemphis.org   E-mail: jconder@pdsmemphis.org
A. Lee Burns III, Head. AB, Dartmouth College, MEd, Harvard Univ. **Jan Conder, Adm.**
   Pre-Prep. Feat—Span Computers Bible Studio_Art Music.
   Adm: 103/yr. Appl due: Jan. Accepted: 84%. **Tests** CTP_4 IQ ISEE.
   Enr 564. B 564. Elem 564. Wh 93%. Blk 3%. Asian 2%. Other 2%. Avg class size: 16. **Fac 62.** M 6. F 53/3. Wh 99%. Blk 1%. Adv deg: 41%.
   Grad '04—58. Prep—53. (Memphis U Sch, Schs of St George's, Woodland Presbyterian, Evangelical Christian). Alum 3040.
   Tui '04-'05: Day $7025-9825 (+$500).
   Summer: Acad Enrich Rev Rem Rec. Musical Theater. Sports. Tui Day $100-600. 2-4 wks.
   Endow $6,000,000. Plant val $2,400,000. Bldgs 2. Class rms 36. Lib 17,000 vols. Sci labs 1. Comp labs 1. Art studios 1. Music studios 2. Gyms 1. Fields 1.
   Est 1949. Nonprofit. Presbyterian. Quar (Aug-May). **Assoc** SACS.

Developed from a kindergarten when the Pentecost-Garrison School for Boys was closed, PDS now offers junior kindergarten through grade 6. Although the school is affiliated with the Second Presbyterian Church of Memphis, boys of many other faiths enroll. Academic standards are high, and the extracurricular activities include athletics, publications, computer, art, music and clubs. Many graduates enter Memphis University School, which was reactivated in 1955 as a direct outgrowth of Presbyterian Day School.

ST. MARY'S EPISCOPAL SCHOOL
Day — Girls Gr PS-12

Memphis, TN 38117. 60 N Perkins Rd. Tel: 901-537-1405. Fax: 901-685-1098.
   www.stmarysschool.org   E-mail: admission@stmarysschool.org
Marlene Rutledge Shaw, Head. BS, Louisiana State Univ-Baton Rouge, ME, Univ of New

Orleans. **Mandy Yandell, Adm.**
- **Col Prep. AP**—Eng Fr Lat Span Calc Bio Chem Physics Eur_Hist US_Hist Art_Hist Studio_Art Music_Theory. **Feat**—Humanities Computers Psych Global_Issues Drama. **Supp**—Tut.
- **Adm (Gr PS-11):** 101/yr. Appl due: Rolling. Accepted: 77%. Yield: 72%. **Tests** CTP_4 IQ ISEE.
- **Enr 824.** G 824. Elem 585. Sec 239. Wh 85%. Hisp 1%. Blk 5%. Asian 8%. Other 1%. Avg class size: 15. **Fac 104.** M 6. F 88/10. Wh 98%. Hisp 1%. Blk 1%. Adv deg: 54%.
- **Grad '04—62. Col—62.** (U of Richmond 3, Furman 3, Vanderbilt 3, Princeton 2, Northwestern 2, Duke 2). Avg SAT: 1270. Avg ACT: 27. Alum 1725.
- **Tui '04-'05: Day $9300-12,100** (+$125-700). **Aid:** Need 93 ($450,633).
- **Summer:** Acad Enrich Rev Rec. 9 wks.
- Endow $7,720,000. Plant val $12,608,000. Bldgs 10. Class rms 63. 3 Libs 33,000 vols. Sci labs 6. Lang labs 1. Comp labs 5. Theaters 1. Art studios 5. Music studios 3. Dance studios 1. Gyms 2. Fields 2. Tennis courts 2.
- **Est 1847.** Nonprofit. Episcopal. Sem (Aug-May). **Assoc** CLS SACS.

The school's program places significant emphasis on college preparation, with honors and Advanced Placement courses available in many disciplines. Extracurricular activities include athletics, drama, art, music, interest clubs, publications, academically enriching programs such as mock trial and Model UN, and various opportunities for community service. Graduates of St. Mary's attend competitive colleges throughout the country.

NASHVILLE, TN. (101 mi. N of Huntsville, AL) Urban. Pop: 545,524. Alt: 450 ft.

FATHER RYAN HIGH SCHOOL
Day — Coed Gr 9-12

Nashville, TN 37204. 700 Norwood Dr. Tel: 615-383-4200. Fax: 615-383-9056.
www.fatherryan.org E-mail: postmaster@fatherryan.org

James A. McIntyre, Prin. BA, Univ of North Texas, MEd, Texas A&M Univ-Commerce. **Connie Hansom, Adm.**
- **Col Prep. AP**—Eng Fr Lat Span Calc Stats Bio Chem Physics Eur_Hist US_Hist Psych US_Govt & Pol Studio_Art Music_Theory. **Feat**—Comp_Sci Theol Chorus Music. **Supp**—Tut.
- **Adm:** 280/yr. Appl due: Dec. Accepted: 98%. Yield: 84%. **Tests** HSPT.
- **Enr 940.** B 499. G 441. Sec 940. Wh 91%. Hisp 2%. Blk 5%. Asian 1%. Other 1%. Avg class size: 19. Uniform. **Fac 78.** M 41. F 37. Wh 95%. Hisp 3%. Blk 2%. Adv deg: 55%.
- **Grad '04—228. Col—215.** (U of TN-Knoxville 41, Middle TN St 31, TN Tech 12, U of TN-Martin 9, St Louis U 8, W KY 8). Avg SAT: 1085. Avg ACT: 22. Alum 9400.
- **Tui '04-'05: Day $10,400** (+$310). Catholic $6500 (+$310)**Aid:** Merit 5 ($11,840). Need 124 ($298,800).
- **Summer:** Acad Enrich Rev. Tui Day $200. 4 wks.
- Endow $5,000,000. Plant val $20,000,000. Bldgs 5. Class rms 57. Lib 22,000 vols. Sci labs 2. Comp labs 3. Theaters 1. Art studios 2. Music studios 1. Dance studios 1. Gyms 1. Fields 4.
- **Est 1925.** Nonprofit. Roman Catholic. Sem (Aug-May). **Assoc** CLS SACS.

Father Ryan was founded as Nashville Catholic High School for Boys by Bishop Alphonse Smith. Upon moving to Elliston Place (near Vanderbilt University) in 1928, the school assumed its current name in honor of 19th-century Southern priest and poet Rev. Abram J. Ryan. Girls were first enrolled in 1970, and Father Ryan relocated to its present, 40-acre campus in Oak Hill in 1991.

The curriculum includes honors and advanced courses at all grade levels and in every major subject. In addition, AP courses are available to juniors and seniors. Clubs relating to special groups and subject interests—such as drama, newspaper and yearbook journalism, band and student government—and athletics are among the extracurricular options. Daily prayer and opportunities for community service round out the program.

HARPETH HALL SCHOOL

Day — Girls Gr 5-12

Nashville, TN 37215. 3801 Hobbs Rd. Tel: 615-297-9543. Fax: 615-297-0480.
www.harpethhall.org   E-mail: wild@harpethhall.org
Ann M. Teaff, Head. BA, Fontbonne College, MAT, Vanderbilt Univ. **Dianne B. Wild, Adm.**

Col Prep. AP—Eng Fr Lat Span Calc Bio Chem Physics Eur_Hist US_Hist Art_Hist Studio_Art. **Feat**—Environ_Sci Psych World_Relig Videography Media Nutrition. **Supp**—Rev Tut.

Adm: 129/yr. Appl due: Jan. Accepted: 85%. Yield: 75%. **Tests** ISEE.

Enr 588. G 588. Elem 218. Sec 370. Wh 90%. Hisp 1%. Blk 5%. Asian 2%. Other 2%. Avg class size: 16. Uniform. **Fac 72.** M 17. F 44/11. Wh 95%. Hisp 1%. Asian 4%. Adv deg: 79%.

Grad '04—77. **Col**—77. (U of GA 9, U of TN-Knoxville 9, Auburn 6, U of MS 6, U of VA 5, Wake Forest 3). Alum 6600.

Tui '04-'05: Day $13,950-14,175 (+$3000). **Aid:** Merit 1 ($2500). Need 70 ($570,800).

Summer: Acad Enrich Rec. Tui Day $150-400. 1-3 wks.

Endow $21,000,000. Bldgs 7. Libs 1. Sci labs 9. Comp labs 3. Theaters 1. Art studios 3. Music studios 1. Dance studios 2. Gyms 2. Fields 3. Courts 8. Tracks 1.

Est 1951. Nonprofit. Sem (Aug-May). **Assoc** CLS SACS.

Founded as a successor to The Ward-Belmont School, Harpeth Hall conducts a rigorous liberal arts curriculum complemented by more than a dozen AP courses, independent study, academic travel, work-study and community service. The school employs an interdisciplinary team-teaching approach in which teams are organized horizontally by grade and vertically by subject.

A winterim program provides opportunities for students to learn and achieve outside the classroom and in nontraditional areas. The fine arts program features visual and performing arts ranging from photography and art to dance and theater. All pupils in grades 7-12 own and use laptop computers.

Students participate in academic clubs, honorary societies, civic organizations, interest clubs, outdoor programs, science and environmental clubs, and a comprehensive athletic program. Harpeth Hall also encourages girls to engage in community service.

MONTGOMERY BELL ACADEMY

Day — Boys Gr 7-12

Nashville, TN 37205. 4001 Harding Rd. Tel: 615-298-5514. Fax: 615-297-0271.
www.montgomerybell.com   E-mail: admission@montgomerybell.com

Bradford Gioia, Head. BA, Univ of the South, MA, Middlebury College. **Robert Black, Adm.**

Col Prep. AP—Eng Fr Ger Lat Span Calc Stats Comp_Sci Bio Chem Physics Eur_Hist US_Hist World_Hist Art_Hist Studio_Art Music_Theory. **Feat**—Greek Astron Econ Theater_Arts Speech. **Supp**—Rev Tut.

Adm: 137/yr. Appl due: Feb. Accepted: 71%. **Tests** ISEE.

Enr 663. B 663. Elem 188. Sec 475. Wh 93%. Blk 4%. Am Ind 1%. Asian 2%. Avg class size: 13. **Fac 85.**

Grad '04—112. Col—112. (Vanderbilt 7, U of VA 5, U of GA 5, Auburn 5, Wake Forest 4, U of FL 4). Avg SAT: 1310. Avg ACT: 28. Alum 3000.

Tui '04-'05: Day $14,575 (+$200). **Aid:** Need 100 ($530,921).

Endow $43,888,000. Plant val $30,592,000. Bldgs 8. Libs 1. Auds 1. Theaters 1. Art studios 1. Music studios 1. Gyms 2. Fields 4. Courts 4.

Est 1867. Nonprofit. Sem (Sept-May). **Assoc** CLS SACS.

Located on 37 acres in West Nashville, MBA began as a two-room school serving 26 grammar school and high school boys. (During its early years, MBA also included a two-year junior college program.) The school was named for Pennsylvanian Montgomery Bell, who came to Dickson County around 1800 and achieved financial success as owner of an iron company. A monetary gift that Mr. Bell left to the University of Tennessee upon his death in 1855 was later used by John Berrien Lindsley to open the academy. The current-day school draws students from nine counties in Middle Tennessee.

The academic program includes honors sections at all grade levels, in addition to an unusually broad selection of Advanced Placement courses. The school strongly encourages boys to take part in the community service program, and each high school student is required to participate in the after-school athletic program in two of the three seasons. Other activities include a forensics program, music, student publications and a wide range of interest clubs.

VIRGINIA

ALEXANDRIA, VA. (7 mi. SSW of Washington, DC) Urban. Pop: 128,283. Alt: 32 ft.

BURGUNDY FARM COUNTRY DAY SCHOOL
Day — Coed Gr PS-8

Alexandria, VA 22303. 3700 Burgundy Rd. Tel: 703-960-3431. Fax: 703-960-5056.
www.burgundyfarm.org   E-mail: info@burgundyfarm.org

Natalie Hall, Int Co-Head. BA, Univ of Iowa, MA, Univ of Illinois, EdD, Nova Southeastern Univ. **Nancy Kaplan, Int Co-Head.** BA, Barnard College, MA, Columbia Univ. **Dia Harris, Adm.**

Pre-Prep. Feat—Fr Span Computers Studio_Art Drama Music. **Supp**—Dev_Read Tut.

Adm: 53/yr. Appl due: Feb. Accepted: 28%. **Tests** IQ.

Enr 282. B 135. G 147. Elem 282. Wh 67%. Hisp 3%. Blk 20%. Asian 8%. Other 2%. Avg class size: 12. **Fac 41.** M 6/1. F 24/10. Wh 81%. Hisp 5%. Blk 12%. Asian 2%. Adv deg: 34%.

Grad '04—33. Prep—15. (Georgetown Day, Bishop Ireton, Maret, Sidwell Friends, Field). Alum 2000.

Tui '04-'05: Day $16,780-17,610 (+$500). **Aid:** Need 41 ($434,576).

Summer: Enrich Rec. Tui Day $290/wk. 8 wks.

Endow $300,000. Plant val $5,400,000. Bldgs 13. Class rms 23. Lib 17,000 vols. Sci labs 2. Comp labs 1. Photog labs 1. Theaters 1. Art studios 2. Music studios 1. Gyms 1. Fields 1. Pools 1. Barns 1.

Est 1946. Nonprofit. Quar (Sept-June).

A cooperative since its founding, Burgundy provides opportunities for parents to take part in many aspects of school life. The curriculum features language arts, math, foreign languages, science and social studies. Physical education, annual plays, music and an art program that includes painting, pottery and photography are integral parts of the school's program. Study in the natural sciences is supplemented by a mountain campus in West Virginia. An extended-day enrichment and recreational program is offered.

EPISCOPAL HIGH SCHOOL
Bdg — Coed Gr 9-12

Alexandria, VA 22302. 1200 N Quaker Ln. Tel: 703-933-4062. Fax: 703-933-3016.
www.episcopalhighschool.org   E-mail: admissions@episcopalhighschool.org

F. Robertson Hershey, Head. BA, Williams College, MEd, Univ of Virginia. **Douglas C. Price, Adm.**

Col Prep. Gen Acad. AP—Eng Fr Lat Span Calc Stats Bio Chem Human_Geog Physics Eur_Hist Econ. **Feat**—Creative_Writing Shakespeare Ger Greek Anat & Physiol Astron Ecol Genetics Programming Psych Comp_Relig Ethics Ceramics Photog Music Orchestra Dance. **Supp**—Rev Tut.

Adm (Gr 9-11): 135/yr. Appl due: Jan. Accepted: 40%. Yield: 60%. **Tests** CEEB ISEE SSAT.

Enr 420. B 235. G 185. Sec 420. Wh 80%. Hisp 3%. Blk 8%. Asian 7%. Other 2%. Avg class size: 12. **Fac 64.** M 42/1. F 19/2. Wh 93%. Hisp 3%. Blk 4%. Adv deg: 75%. In dorms 22.

Grad '04—102. Col—101. (U of VA, UNC-Chapel Hill, NC St, Wash & Lee, Duke, U of the South). Avg SAT: 1260. Avg SSAT: 75%. Alum 4600.

Tui '04-'05: Bdg $31,500 (+$2000). **Aid:** Merit 21 ($115,000). Need 109 ($2,133,100). Endow $105,000,000. Plant val $125,000,000. Bldgs 25. Dorms 9. Dorm rms 230. Class rms 44. Libs 2. Labs 4. Auds 2. Theaters 3. Art studios 1. Music studios 2. Gyms 4. Fields 7. Courts 25. Pools 1.

Est 1839. Nonprofit. Episcopal. Sem (Sept-June). **Assoc** CLS SACS.

This renowned boarding school enrolls students from approximately 30 states and roughly a dozen foreign countries. Located 10 minutes from Washington, DC, the suburban campus occupies 135 acres.

EHS' college preparatory curriculum, which is based on a liberal arts approach, emphasizes analytical, reasoning and independent thinking skills. More than 40 Advanced Placement and honors courses are available, and the school maintains strong programs in the arts and community service. Integrated technology enhances classroom study—all students have laptop computers and classrooms are fully wired for individual network access—and the school's Washington Program (conducted each Wednesday) enables pupils to engage in discussions with professionals in fields that relate to course work. Seniors may pursue a month-long internship in which they work on Capitol Hill or with a local organization of personal interest.

Summer trips to France, Spain and Italy enhance the foreign language program. EHS also conduct an exchange with a school in Scotland, and students may take advantage of additional overseas study opportunities through School Year Abroad and the English-Speaking Union.

Extensive arts opportunities, extracurriculars and activities supplement academics. Among the varied arts options are offerings in music, drama, the visual arts and dance. The school's athletic program combines interscholastic sports with noncompetitive options such as aerobics, an outdoor program and weight training. Weekends include social events, dorm activities, and excursions to museums and cultural events in Washington, DC. **See Also Page 1147**

ST. STEPHEN'S AND ST. AGNES SCHOOL
Day — Coed Gr PS-12

Alexandria, VA 22304. 1000 St Stephen's Rd. Tel: 703-751-2700. Fax: 703-838-0032. www.sssas.org E-mail: info@sssas.org

Joan G. Ogilvy Holden, Head. BA, Tufts Univ, EdM, Harvard Univ. **Diane Dunning, Adm.**

Col Prep. AP—Eng Fr Lat Span Calc Stats Bio Chem Physics Eur_Hist US_Hist Comp_ Govt & Pol US_Govt & Pol Art_Hist Studio_Art Music_Theory. **Feat**—Creative_Writing Playwriting Programming Robotics Ethics Relig Sculpt Drama Directing Music Jazz_Ensemble.

Adm (Gr PS-11): 177/yr. Appl due: Jan. **Tests** IQ ISEE SSAT.

Enr 1155. B 580. G 575. Elem 710. Sec 445. Avg class size: 15. **Fac 158.** M 47/3. F 92/16. Wh 90%. Hisp 3%. Blk 6%. Asian 1%. Adv deg: 56%.

Grad '04—104. Col—104. (Wm & Mary 7, U of VA 5, VA Polytech 4, James Madison 4, Howard 3, Brown 3). Avg SAT: 1276. Alum 4705.

Tui '04-'05: Day $16,550-20,780 (+$1000-2500). **Aid:** Need 203 ($2,554,699).

Summer: Acad Enrich Rec. Econ. 6-7 wks.

Endow $14,596,000. Plant val $72,600,000. Bldgs 14. Class rms 77. 3 Libs 43,500 vols.

Chapels 1. Sci labs 10. Lang labs 1. Comp labs 5. Art studios 9. Music studios 6. Perf arts ctrs 1. Gyms 4. Fields 7. Courts 6.
Est 1924. Nonprofit. Episcopal. Quar (Sept-June). **Assoc** CLS.

St. Stephen's and St. Agnes School, a church school in the Episcopal diocese of Virginia, was created by the 1991 merger of St. Stephen's School (founded in 1944) and St. Agnes School (founded in 1924). The strong academic program includes single-gender science and math classes in grades 6-8, an interdisciplinary history program in grades 9-12, and many honors and Advanced Placement courses. The school emphasizes participation in community service, athletics and the arts. Graduates enter leading colleges across the country.

Seminars and field trips to historical, cultural and political points of interest in Washington, DC, augment the academic program. Cocurricular programs offer opportunities to study and travel abroad. The lower school (junior kindergarten through grade 5) is located at 400 Fontaine St., 22302, while the middle school (grades 6-8) operates at 4401 W. Braddock Rd.

Baseball, football, golf, track, wrestling, field hockey, ice hockey, basketball, swimming, cross-country, lacrosse, soccer, softball, tennis and volleyball are offered at the varsity level. Other activities include student government, service committee, publications, drama, chorus and band, as well as language, science, art, computer, debate, multicultural, outing and other interest clubs. Students participate in community service programs at all grade levels. An extended-day program is available for children through grade 8.

CHARLOTTESVILLE, VA. (65 mi. WNW of Richmond, VA; 100 mi. SW of Washington, DC) Urban. Pop: 45,049. Alt: 480 ft.

ST. ANNE'S-BELFIELD SCHOOL
Bdg — Coed Gr 9-12; Day — Coed PS-12

Charlottesville, VA 22903. 2132 Ivy Rd. Tel: 434-296-5106. Fax: 434-979-1486.
www.stab.org E-mail: admission@stab.org
Rev. George E. Conway, Head. BA, Wilkes College, MDiv, Princeton Theological Seminary, DMin, Boston Univ. **Jean W. Craig, Adm.**
Col Prep. AP—Eng Fr Lat Span Calc Stats Bio Chem Physics Eur_Hist US_Hist. **Feat**—Humanities Shakespeare Greek Civil_War Econ Govt & Pol Lat-Amer_Stud Relig Ceramics Photog Sculpt Studio_Art Drama Music Music_Theory. **Supp**—ESL.
Adm: 143/yr. Appl due: Rolling. Accepted: 65%. Yield: 75%. **Tests** SSAT TOEFL.
Enr 839. Elem 539. Sec 300. Wh 87%. Hisp 1%. Blk 5%. Asian 2%. Other 5%. Avg class size: 12. **Fac 105.** Adv deg: 82%. In dorms 1.
Grad '04—89. Col—89. (U of VA 20, Wm & Mary 8, Mary Wash 8, Geo Mason 4, Hamilton 3, Duke 2). Avg SAT: 1239. Alum 2580.
Tui '04-'05: Bdg $37,550 (+$750). **5-Day Bdg $28,550** (+$600). **Day $7500-15,800** (+$300). **Aid:** Need 268 ($2,600,000).
Summer: Acad Enrich Rev Rem Rec. Music. 1-8 wks.
Endow $2,100,000. Plant val $17,300,000. Bldgs 10. Dorms 1. Dorm rms 27. Class rms 84. 2 Libs 21,000 vols. Sci labs 7. Comp labs 2. Theaters 1. Art studios 3. Music studios 2. Gyms 2. Fields 7. Courts 6. Field houses 1.
Est 1910. Nonprofit. Sem (Aug-May). **Assoc** CLS.

St. Anne's-Belfield was formed in 1970 by the merger of Belfield Elementary School (founded in 1955) and Saint Anne's School, a girls' residential secondary school (established in 1910). The school occupies two campuses totaling approximately 50 acres.

The academic program, which includes a variety of Advanced Placement courses, provides a solid background in the major disciplines, and all students are required to supplement their curricula with courses in art, music, drama and computer study. A comprehensive athletic program includes football, lacrosse, basketball, volleyball, tennis, field hockey, cross-country, soccer, wrestling, golf, baseball, softball, weight training and fitness. International students may take part in a seven-day-boarding English as a Second Language program. **See Also Page 1243**

CHATHAM, VA. (44 mi. SE of Roanoke, VA; 194 mi. SW of Washington, DC) Rural. Pop: 1338. Alt: 828 ft.

CHATHAM HALL

Bdg and Day — Girls Gr 9-12

Chatham, VA 24531. 800 Chatham Hall Cir. Tel: 434-432-2941. Fax: 434-432-2405. www.chathamhall.org E-mail: admission@chathamhall.org

Gary J. Fountain, Rector. AB, Brown Univ, MAR, Yale Univ, PhD, Boston Univ. **S. Victoria Muradi, Adm.**

Col Prep. **AP**—Eng Fr Lat Span Calc Bio Chem Human_Geog Eur_Hist US_Hist Studio_Art Music_Theory. **Feat**—DNA_Sci Comp_Sci Ethics Relig Drama Music Dance. **Supp**—ESL Rev Tut.

Adm (Gr 9-11): 35/yr. Bdg 30. Day 5. Appl due: Feb. Accepted: 65%. **Tests** CTP_4 ISEE SSAT TOEFL.

Enr 126. G 105/21. Sec 126. Wh 90%. Hisp 3%. Blk 5%. Asian 1%. Other 1%. Avg class size: 8. **Fac 37.** M 9. F 27/1. Wh 95%. Other 5%. Adv deg: 51%. In dorms 5.

Grad '04—33. Col—33. (Dartmouth, U of VA, Cornell, UNC-Chapel Hill, Georgetown, Vassar). Alum 3000.

Tui '04-'05: Bdg $32,500 (+$1500). **Day** $11,700 (+$600). **Aid:** Need 44 ($893,950).

Summer: Acad Enrich Rec. 2 wks.

Endow $14,900,000. Plant val $25,000,000. Bldgs 10. Dorms 3. Dorm rms 87. Class rms 20. Lib 30,000 vols. Sci labs 3. Lang labs 1. Theaters 1. Art studios 1. Music studios 5. Dance studios 1. Gyms 1. Fields 3. Courts 8. Riding rings 3. Stables 2.

Est 1894. Nonprofit. Episcopal. Tri (Sept-June). **Assoc** CLS SACS.

Founded by Rev. C. Orlando Pruden, this school was called Chatham Episcopal Institute until 1924. The college preparatory program emphasizes spoken and written expression, in addition to analytical and computational skills. Math and science courses make extensive use of computer technology. Many students take honors and Advanced Placement classes, and the school conducts well-developed dance, fine arts and riding programs.

An honor code governs all aspects of school life. Chatham Hall offers school-based study abroad programs and also participates in the English-Speaking Union. Internships, extensive weekend activities and an endowed speaker series provide enrichment opportunities.

HARGRAVE MILITARY ACADEMY
Bdg — Boys Gr 7-PG; Day — Coed 7-PG

Chatham, VA 24531. 200 Military Dr. Tel: 434-432-2481. Fax: 434-432-3129.
www.hargrave.edu   E-mail: admissions@hargrave.edu

Col. Wheeler Baker, USMC (Ret), Pres. BS, Univ of Tampa, MS, Salve Regina Univ, MS, Catholic Univ of America, PhD, Univ of New Mexico. **Frank L. Martin III, Adm.**

Col Prep. Gen Acad. Milit. **AP**—Span. **Feat**—Fr Environ_Sci Computers Econ Govt Psych Sociol Bible Ethics Art_Hist Fine_Arts Debate Journ Study_Skills. **Supp**—Dev_Read ESL Rem_Math Rem_Read Rev Tut.

Adm: 200/yr. Appl due: Aug. Accepted: 92%.

Enr 375. B 324/40. G 11. Wh 83%. Hisp 3%. Blk 12%. Asian 1%. Other 1%. Avg class size: 14. Uniform. **Fac 48.** M 24. F 24. Adv deg: 64%.

Grad '04—98. Col—98. (US Naval Acad, VA Milit, Citadel, Wm & Mary, VA Polytech). Avg SAT: 1052. Alum 5000.

Tui '04-'05: Bdg $22,500 (+$750). **Day $10,650** (+$1250). **Aid:** Need 106 ($251,000).

Summer: Acad Enrich Rev Rem Rec. Sports. Tui Bdg $3500. Tui Day $800. 5 wks.

Endow $3,500,000. Plant val $7,700,000. Bldgs 10. Dorms 10. Dorm rms 240. Class rms 49. Lib 16,000 vols. Sci labs 3. Lang labs 1. Comp labs 4. Photog labs 2. Auds 1. Theaters 1. Art studios 1. Music studios 2. Gyms 2. Fields 4. Courts 6. Pools 1. Weight rms 1. Rifle ranges 1. Airstrips 1.

Est 1909. Nonprofit. Baptist. Sem (Aug-May). **Assoc** SACS.

When a Baptist minister with six sons convinced a local entrepreneur of the need for boys in the area to obtain a Christian education, the two men combined resources to establish a school. Rev. T. Ryland Sanford served as Chatham Training School's first president, and his benefactor, J. Hunt Hargrave, served as chairman of the board of trustees. In 1925, the school's name was changed to honor the man who had given form to Rev. Sanford's vision.

Hargrave offers a sound college preparatory curriculum, with the majority of graduates matriculating at competitive colleges. The cadet corps organization, based on an infantry battalion, provides opportunities for leadership development and the assumption of responsibility. Extracurricular activities include Boy Scouts, music, skeet, photography, drill team and various student clubs. Athletic teams compete in football, soccer, marksmanship, cross-country, basketball, baseball, wrestling, tennis, swimming, volleyball, golf and lacrosse. In addition, postgraduate squads play football and basketball. **See Also Page 1162**

CHRISTCHURCH, VA.
(52 mi. E of Richmond, VA; 93 mi. SSE of Washington, DC) Rural. Pop: 100. Alt: 89 ft.

CHRISTCHURCH SCHOOL
Bdg — Boys Gr 8-PG; Day — Coed 8-PG

Christchurch, VA 23031. 49 Seahorse Ln. Tel: 804-758-2306. Fax: 804-758-0721.
www.christchurchschool.org   E-mail: admission@christchurchschool.org

John E. Byers, Head. BA, Washington and Lee Univ, MA, Virginia Commonwealth Univ. **Nancy M. Nolan, Adm.**

Col Prep. **AP**—Eng Fr Span Calc Bio Chem US_Hist World_Hist US_Govt & Pol. **Feat**—Marine_Biol/Sci Studio_Art. **Supp**—ESL LD.

Adm (Gr 8-11): 75/yr. Bdg 50. Day 25. Appl due: Feb. Accepted: 65%. Yield: 60%. **Tests** SSAT TOEFL.

Enr 216. B 124/51. G 41. Elem 8. Sec 207. PG 1. Wh 89%. Other 11%. Avg class size: 12. **Fac 39.** M 22/2. F 13/2. Wh 94%. Hisp 3%. Blk 3%. Adv deg: 53%. In dorms 9.

Grad '04—51. Col—51. (Randolph-Macon, VA Commonwealth, U of VA, VA Polytech, Hampden-Sydney, James Madison). Avg SAT: 1100. Alum 1500.

Tui '05-'06: Bdg $33,600 (+$2400). **5-Day Bdg $30,450** (+$2400). **Day $14,700** (+$1200). **Aid:** Need 63 ($585,400).

Summer: Acad Enrich Rev Rem Rec. Tui Bdg $3800. Tui Day $490/wk. 4 wks.

Endow $1,800,000. Plant val $14,000,000. Bldgs 12. Dorms 3. Dorm rms 100. Class rms 17. Lib 9500 vols. Labs 5. Theaters 1. Art studios 1. Gyms 2. Fields 6. Tennis courts 6. Pools 1.

Est 1921. Nonprofit. Episcopal. Sem (Sept-June).

Christchurch provides a supportive and challenging environment for students of varying abilities. Within a caring community, the school emphasizes the development of self-esteem and life skills through a flexible curriculum and an extensive athletic program.

The traditional, structured college preparatory curriculum features Advanced Placement courses in all content areas, in addition to marine science and learning skills programs. All students participate in athletics each season; options include football, soccer, basketball, baseball, tennis, golf, lacrosse, indoor soccer, field hockey, wrestling, cross-country, weight training, sailing and crew. Christchurch's student body comprises pupils from approximately 20 states and roughly a dozen foreign countries. **See Also Page 1329**

DYKE, VA. (77 mi. NW of Richmond, VA; 94 mi. WSW of Washington, DC) Rural. Pop: 25. Area also includes St. George.

THE BLUE RIDGE SCHOOL
Bdg — Boys Gr 9-12

St George, VA 22935. Hwy 627, Bacon Hollow Rd. Tel: 434-985-2811. Fax: 434-985-7215. www.blueridgeschool.com   E-mail: info@blueridgeschool.com

David A. Bouton, Head. BBA, Univ of Notre Dame, PhD, Virginia Commonwealth Univ. **David E. Hodgson, Adm.**

Col Prep. Feat—Fr Lat Span Anat Astron Ecol Computers Studio_Art Drama Outdoor_Ed. **Supp**—ESL Tut.

Adm: 68/yr. Appl due: Rolling. Accepted: 65%. Yield: 63%.

Enr 165. B 165. Sec 165. Avg class size: 8. **Fac 34.** M 27. F 6/1. Wh 91%. Hisp 6%. Blk 3%. Adv deg: 52%. In dorms 9.

Grad '04—40. Col—40. (Hampden-Sydney, Roanoke Col, Lynchburg, James Madison, U of MS, Brown). Avg SAT: 1120. Alum 1800.

Tui '04-'05: Bdg $29,358 (+$2000). **Aid:** Need 39 ($566,300).

Summer: Rec. Tui Bdg $400-900. ½-1 wk.

Endow $9,000,000. Plant val $17,445,000. Bldgs 11. Dorms 2. Dorm rms 103. Class rms 21. Lib 11,000 vols. Sci labs 1. Comp labs 2. Auds 1. Theaters 1. Art studios 1. Music studios 1. Gyms 2. Fields 8. Courts 4. Pools 1. Driving ranges 1. Ropes crses 1. Climbing towers 1.

Est 1909. Nonprofit. Episcopal. Tri (Sept-May). **Assoc** SACS.

Founded as an Episcopal mission school, Blue Ridge reorganized as an independent boarding school and adopted its current focus in 1962. The school provides a college preparatory education for capable boys who are suited to a program that incorporates small classes, a faculty advisor program, and a predictable daily schedule designed to help students develop sound study habits and time management skills. Sufficient flexibility is built into the program to allow instructors to work with the student's strengths and needs. A learning center provides additional academic support as needed.

Occupying 800 acres on the eastern slope of the Blue Ridge Mountains, the school's campus is accessible to Charlottesville, Richmond and Washington, DC. Blue Ridge's outdoor program provides opportunities for hiking, camping, mountain biking, canoeing, fishing and ropes work. The athletic program, in which participation is mandatory, accommodates all ability levels. Each student attends chapel services two mornings a week and on Sundays.

FORK UNION, VA. (46 mi. WNW of Richmond, VA; 104 mi. SW of Washington, DC) Suburban. Pop: 2500. Alt: 900 ft.

FORK UNION MILITARY ACADEMY
Bdg and Day — Boys Gr 6-PG

Fork Union, VA 23055. 4744 James Madison Hwy, PO Box 278. Tel: 434-842-3212.
 Fax: 434-842-4300.
 www.forkunion.com   E-mail: akersj@fuma.org
 Lt. Gen. John E. Jackson, Jr., USAF (Ret), Pres. BA, Alderson-Broaddus College, MA, Central Michigan Univ. **Lt. Col. Jim Akers, Adm.**

    Col Prep. Milit. AP—Eng Bio US_Hist US_Govt & Pol. **Feat**—Humanities Writing Fr Ger Span Astron Computers Asian_Stud Econ Pol_Sci Sociol Relig Journ. **Supp**—Dev_ Read Rev Tut.

    Adm: 280/yr. Bdg 270. Day 10. Appl due: Rolling. Accepted: 67%. **Tests** CEEB Stanford.

    Enr 550. B 530/20. Elem 100. Sec 410. PG 40. Wh 77%. Hisp 4%. Blk 18%. Asian 1%. Avg class size: 12. Uniform. **Fac 47.** M 39. F 8. Wh 98%. Hisp 1%. Blk 1%. Adv deg: 61%. In dorms 4.

    Grad '04—140. Col—139. (VA Polytech, VA Milit, U of VA, U of TN-Knoxville, Hampden-Sydney, Citadel). Avg SAT: 1050. Avg ACT: 22. Alum 6500.

    Tui '04-'05: Bdg $19,990 (+$1250-2990). **Day $13,655** (+$1345). **Aid:** Need ($340,000).

    Summer: Gr 7-12. Acad Enrich Rev Rem. Tui Bdg $3300 (+$60). 4 wks.

    Endow $13,300,000. Plant val $34,000,000. Bldgs 11. Dorms 4. Dorm rms 303. Class rms 58. Lib 19,000 vols. Labs 7. Sci labs 5. Lang labs 2. Comp labs 5. Auds 1. Music studios 1. Gyms 3. Fields 6. Courts 14. Pools 1. Tracks 2.

    Est 1898. Nonprofit. Baptist. (Sept-May).

This military school has received wide acclaim, particularly for its One-Subject Plan, which has been in use since 1950 in the upper school. Students focus intensively on single subjects for seven-week periods throughout the school year. Honors, Advanced Placement and college-credit courses provide opportunities for acceleration. The middle school (grades 6-8), which operates in separate facilities, features a small-class learning environment. Students represent a variety of denominations and enroll from many states and several foreign countries. Graduates enter leading colleges.

The extensive athletic facilities support intramural and interscholastic competition in approximately a dozen sports. **See Also Page 1340**

FRONT ROYAL, VA. (70 mi. W of Washington, DC) Suburban. Pop: 13,589. Alt: 492 ft.

RANDOLPH-MACON ACADEMY
Bdg and Day — Coed Gr 6-PG

Front Royal, VA 22630. 200 Academy Dr. Tel: 540-636-5200. Fax: 540-636-5419.
www.rma.edu   E-mail: admissions@rma.edu
Maj. Gen. Henry M. Hobgood, USAF (Ret), Pres. BA, North Carolina State Univ, MS, Troy State Univ. **Pia G. Crandell, Adm.**

Col Prep. Milit. AP—Eng Ger Calc US_Hist US_Govt & Pol. **Feat**—Shakespeare Fr Lat Span Bible Band Chorus Finance Driver_Ed JROTC Flight_Trng. **Supp**—ESL Tut.

Adm (Gr 6-12): 175/yr. Bdg 153. Day 22. Appl due: Apr. Accepted: 90%. Yield: 72%. **Tests** TOEFL.

Enr 404. B 253/49. G 73/29. Elem 75. Sec 327. PG 2. Avg class size: 16. Uniform. **Fac 53.** M 29/3. F 18/3. Wh 96%. Blk 4%. Adv deg: 37%. In dorms 3.

Grad '04—68. Col—67. (VA Polytech, VA Commonwealth, Towson, Shenandoah, Catholic U). Avg SAT: 1100. Alum 4000.

Tui '04-'05: Bdg $19,140 (+$3500). **Day $8825** (+$1800). **Aid:** Merit 7 ($15,175). Need 42 ($114,353). Work prgm 16 ($27,670).

Summer: Acad Enrich Rev Rem Rec. ESL. Tui Bdg $2300 (+$700). Tui Day $800. 4 wks. Endow $3,100,000. Plant val $27,013,000. Bldgs 11. Dorms 3. Dorm rms 225. Class rms 53. 2 Libs 9000 vols. Sci labs 9. Comp labs 3. Theaters 1. Gyms 1. Fields 8. Courts 5. Pools 1. Rifle ranges 1.

Est 1892. Nonprofit. Methodist. Quar (Sept-June). **Assoc** SACS.

This United Methodist-affiliated preparatory academy became coeducational in 1974. Students enroll from many states and foreign countries. Graduates enter a wide variety of the nation's colleges, including the service academies. Air Force Junior ROTC is an integral part of the upper school curriculum, as is optional flight training in academy-owned aircraft.

Varsity teams compete in football, basketball, baseball, lacrosse, swimming, track, wrestling, golf, soccer, riflery, volleyball, cross-country and tennis. Other student activities include marching band, handbells, choir, journalistic organizations, a precision drill team, debate team, calisthenics, weightlifting, chess team and horseback riding. Randolph-Macon's 135-acre campus is situated 70 miles west of Washington, DC.

A cooperative program with a local university provides more than 40 hours of college credit in English, science, math and social science for qualified seniors and postgraduate students.

LYNCHBURG, VA. (43 mi. ENE of Roanoke, VA) Urban. Pop: 65,269. Alt: 517 ft.

VIRGINIA EPISCOPAL SCHOOL
Bdg and Day — Coed Gr 9-12

Lynchburg, VA 24505. 400 Virginia Episcopal School Rd, PO Box 408.
  Tel: 434-385-3607. Fax: 434-385-3603.
  www.ves.org   E-mail: admissions@ves.org
Phillip Lance Hadley, Head. BS, MA, Ohio Univ, PhD, Univ of Texas. Pamela D. Barile, Adm.
  Col Prep. AP—Eng Fr Lat Span Calc Stats Comp_Sci Bio Chem Eur_Hist US_Hist Studio_Art Music_Theory. Feat—Environ_Sci Sports_Med Russ_Civilization Econ World_Relig Art_Hist Fine_Arts Graphic_Arts Video_Production Drama Music_Hist Public_Speak. Supp—Tut.
  Adm (Gr 9-11): 116/yr. Bdg 79. Day 37. Appl due: Feb. Accepted: 80%. Yield: 69%. Tests SSAT.
  Enr 268. B 104/58. G 61/45. Sec 268. Wh 87%. Hisp 2%. Blk 5%. Asian 6%. Avg class size: 12. Uniform. Fac 44. M 27/3. F 14. Wh 100%. Adv deg: 61%. In dorms 11.
  Grad '04—66. Col—61. (UNC-Chapel Hill 2, U of VA 2, U of GA 2, Carnegie Mellon 1, Rice 1, Smith 1). Avg SAT: 1150. Alum 4066.
  Tui '04-'05: Bdg $28,600 (+$2525). 5-Day Bdg $20,950 (+$2210). Day $13,950 (+$1450). Aid: Merit 10 ($65,800). Need 53 ($784,730).
  Endow $14,000,000. Plant val $15,740,000. Bldgs 10. Dorms 6. Dorm rms 89. Class rms 25. Lib 16,000 vols. Sci labs 4. Comp labs 1. Art studios 1. Gyms 4. Fields 7. Courts 8. Pools 1. Riding rings 1.
  Est 1916. Nonprofit. Episcopal. Tri (Sept-May). Assoc CLS.

This church-related school was founded by the first bishop of the Diocese of Southwestern Virginia, Rev. Dr. Robert Carter Jett. The college preparatory curriculum is presented in an environment that emphasizes the student's academic, social and athletic development.

Lynchburg offers many cultural opportunities for supplementing the school program. Graduates of the traditional, thorough curriculum enter many colleges, predominantly institutions in the South. Among the extracurricular activities are choir, glee club, dramatics, art, publications and hobby clubs. Athletics include football, cross-country, soccer, basketball, tennis, baseball, track, golf, wrestling, volleyball and lacrosse.   **See Also Page 1269**

McLEAN, VA. (9 mi. WNW of Washington, DC) Suburban. Pop: 38,929. Alt: 300 ft.

THE LANGLEY SCHOOL
Day — Coed Gr PS-8

McLean, VA 22101. 1411 Balls Hill Rd. Tel: 703-356-1920. Fax: 703-790-9712.
  www.langley.edu.net   E-mail: admission@langley.edu.net
Doris E. Cottam, Head. BA, MEd, Brigham Young Univ. Kerry Moody & Mark Saunders,

Adm.
Pre-Prep. Feat—Fr Span Computers Photog Studio_Art Drama Music. **Supp**—Dev_ Read.
Adm: 96/yr. Appl due: Jan. Accepted: 33%. Yield: 57%. **Tests** CTP_4 IQ ISEE SSAT.
Enr 466. B 231. G 235. Elem 466. Wh 72%. Hisp 6%. Blk 6%. Asian 10%. Other 6%. Avg class size: 18. **Fac 69.** M 14/1. F 49/5. Wh 77%. Hisp 6%. Blk 7%. Am Ind 2%. Asian 7%. Other 1%. Adv deg: 47%.
Grad '04—40. Prep—38. (Madeira, Potomac, St Stephen's & St Agnes, Georgetown Prep, Gonzaga, Landon). Alum 1500.
Tui '04-'05: Day $19,300-20,500 (+$200). **Aid:** Need 30 ($395,000).
Summer: Acad Rev Rec. Tui Day $350/3-wk ses. 8 wks.
Endow $2,380,000. Plant val $10,000,000. Bldgs 9. Class rms 30. Lib 20,000 vols. Sci labs 3. Lang labs 2. Comp labs 4. Art studios 2. Music studios 2. Gyms 1. Fields 1.
Est 1942. Nonprofit. (Sept-June). **Assoc** SACS.

The varied curriculum at this school prepares students for leading area preparatory schools. Modern language instruction begins in kindergarten, and fine arts courses are integral to the program at all grade levels. Science classes utilize a hands-on approach and feature research projects, speakers and field trips, while technology is integrated across the curriculum. Middle school language arts courses include daily writing assignments and informal oral presentations.

Such extracurricular activities as drama productions, band performances and interscholastic sports round out the program. **See Also Page 1189**

MADEIRA SCHOOL
Bdg and Day — Girls Gr 9-12

McLean, VA 22102. 8328 Georgetown Pike. Tel: 703-556-8200. Fax: 703-821-2845.
www.madeira.org E-mail: admissions@madeira.org
Elisabeth Griffith, Head. BA, Wellesley College, MA, Johns Hopkins Univ, PhD, American Univ. **Cheryl Plummer, Adm.**
Col Prep. AP—Eng Fr Lat Span Calc Bio Chem Physics US_Hist Comp_Govt & Pol US_Govt & Pol Studio_Art. **Feat**—Irish_Lit Public_Affairs Ethics Photog Drama Music Dance Public_Speak. **Supp**—ESL Rev Tut.
Adm: 88/yr. Bdg 49. Day 39. Appl due: Jan. Accepted: 65%. **Tests** SSAT TOEFL.
Enr 302. G 158/144. Sec 302. Wh 73%. Hisp 3%. Blk 8%. Am Ind 1%. Asian 12%. Other 3%. Avg class size: 12. **Fac 52.** M 9. F 43. In dorms 4.
Grad '04—81. Col—81. (Wm & Mary, U of VA, Geo Wash, Tufts, Williams, Georgetown). Avg SAT: 1250. Alum 4700.
Tui '04-'05: Bdg $34,780 (+$1000). **Day $24,280** (+$700). **Aid:** Merit 4 ($25,000). Need 53 ($1,064,152).
Summer: Day. Sports. 6 wks.
Endow $34,000,000. Plant val $20,000,000. Bldgs 34. Dorms 6. Dorm rms 116. Class rms 35. Lib 20,000 vols. Chapels 1. Labs 4. Dark rms 1. Auds 1. Theaters 1. Art studios 1. Music studios 1. Dance studios 1. Perf arts ctrs 1. Photog studios 1. Gyms 1. Fields 3. Courts 8. Pools 1. Riding rings 1. Stables 1.
Est 1906. Nonprofit. (Sept-June).

Lucy Madeira established her school in Washington, DC, after teaching at Sidwell Friends School and serving as headmistress of Potomac School. The school moved 12 miles west of Washington, DC, to a 376-acre campus overlooking the Potomac River, in 1931.

The scholastic standards of the school have always been high. Students come from many states and foreign countries, and graduates go on to leading colleges. The curriculum includes more than 100 courses, and Advanced Placement courses are offered in all academic departments. Courses as diverse as calculus, Irish literature and American studies are offered, and facilities are available for the studio and performing arts and athletics. Madeira also provides English as a Second Language instruction.

A Wednesday cocurricular program is an integral part of the academic program. Freshmen attend on-campus seminars that focus on leadership and skill development, and participate in Outdoor Adventure. Sophomores volunteer for off-campus community service organizations, while juniors spend Wednesdays as congressional interns. Seniors explore various career interests.

All girls belong to the student government association, through which they participate in forming and enforcing school rules, as well as developing programs. All students also play on junior varsity or varsity athletic teams or engage in such individual pursuits as dance, riding and fitness. The school plans events with nearby schools and takes advantage of the cultural and recreational activities of Washington, DC.

POTOMAC SCHOOL
Day — Coed Gr K-12

McLean, VA 22101. 1301 Potomac School Rd, PO Box 430. Tel: 703-749-6313.
Fax: 703-356-1764.
www.potomacschool.org
Geoffrey A. Jones, Head. BS, MS, Indiana State Univ. **Charlotte Nelsen, Adm.**
  Col Prep. AP—Eng Fr Lat Span Calc Stats Comp_Sci Bio Chem Physics US_Hist Studio_Art Music_Theory. **Feat**—Creative_Writing Japan Anat & Physiol Bioethics Environ_Sci Robotics African-Amer_Hist Govt Comp_Relig Photog Theater Music.
  Adm: 116/yr. Appl due: Jan. **Tests** IQ ISEE SSAT.
  Enr 875. B 433. G 442. Elem 566. Sec 309. Wh 71%. Hisp 2%. Blk 9%. Asian 6%. Other 12%. Avg class size: 16. **Fac 133.** M 42/4. F 68/19. Wh 86%. Hisp 2%. Blk 7%. Asian 3%. Other 2%. Adv deg: 69%.
  Grad '04—83. Col—83. (U of VA, U of PA, Duke, Harvard, Princeton, Yale). Avg SAT: 1350. Alum 3200.
  Tui '04-'05: Day $18,615-21,385 (+$520-1600). **Aid:** Need 103 ($1,586,759).
  Summer: Enrich Rec. Tui Day $895/3-wk ses. 8 wks.
  Endow $20,000,000. Plant val $35,000,000. Bldgs 14. Class rms 90. 3 Libs 39,500 vols. Sci labs 10. Comp labs 6. Theaters 2. Art studios 5. Music studios 8. Gyms 2. Fields 5. Basketball courts 2. Tennis courts 4. Pools 1.
  Est 1904. Nonprofit. Sem (Sept-June).

Potomac was established as a girls' school in Washington, DC, by parents, with Lucy Madeira Wing as its first principal. The school completed its transition to a coeducational student body in 1964. In 1951, Potomac moved to its present location, where the cultural and educational resources of the city remain within easy reach of a quiet and spacious campus. Over the years, additions to the property enlarged it to 83 acres of hills, playing fields and nature trails.

The academic program is college preparatory in design. It provides a grounding in the liberal arts through its core curriculum and offers a variety of electives and Advanced Placement courses. Science, art and music begin in kindergarten, and foreign languages are introduced in grade 7. Interscholastic teams compete in grades 7-12, and various extracurricular offerings are present at all levels. The school conducts is a school-wide community service program. Students enroll from the Washington, DC, metropolitan area.

MIDDLEBURG, VA. (39 mi. W of Washington, DC) Rural. Pop: 637. Alt: 492 ft. Area also includes The Plains.

FOXCROFT SCHOOL
Bdg and Day — Girls Gr 9-12

Middleburg, VA 20118. PO Box 5555. Tel: 540-687-5555. Fax: 540-687-3627.
  www.foxcroft.org   E-mail: admissions@foxcroft.org
Mary Louise Leipheimer, Head. BS, Indiana Univ of Pennsylvania. **Rebecca B. Gilmore, Adm.**

- **Col Prep. AP**—Eng Fr Span Calc Stats Bio Chem Physics US_Hist Econ. **Feat**—Lat Anat Astron Pharmacology Forensic_Sci Civil_War Intl_Relations Constitutional_Law Graphic_Arts Photog Studio_Art Drama Music Music_Theory. **Supp**—Rev Tut.
- **Adm (Gr 9-11):** 53/yr. Bdg 43. Day 10. Appl due: Feb. Accepted: 74%. Yield: 48%. **Tests** SSAT TOEFL.
- **Enr 185.** G 135/50. Sec 185. Wh 77%. Hisp 3%. Blk 8%. Asian 10%. Other 2%. Avg class size: 10. **Fac 30.** M 10. F 20. Wh 87%. Blk 10%. Am Ind 3%. Adv deg: 66%. In dorms 11.
- **Grad '04—43. Col—43.** (U of CO-Boulder 3, U of the Arts 2, Bryn Mawr 2, Stanford 2, Mt Holyoke 2, Wake Forest 1). Avg SAT: 1134. Avg ACT: 23. Alum 2238.
- **Tui '05-'06: Bdg $34,680** (+$1000). **Day $24,255** (+$1000). **Aid:** Merit 8 ($73,694). Need 37 ($715,953).
- Endow $23,160,000. Plant val $37,000,000. Bldgs 52. Dorms 5. Dorm rms 55. Class rms 14. Lib 50,000 vols. Sci labs 3. Lang labs 1. Comp labs 3. Observatories 1. Auds 1. Theaters 1. Art studios 2. Music studios 2. Dance studios 1. Gyms 1. Fields 4. Courts 8. Pools 1. Riding rings 4. Stables 1.
- **Est 1914.** Nonprofit. Sem (Sept-June). **Assoc** CLS.

Foxcroft, founded by Charlotte H. Noland, was given to the alumnae and reorganized as a nonprofit institution in 1937. The school is situated on 500 acres between the Blue Ridge and Bull Run mountains, one hour west of Washington, DC.

The school's structured college preparatory curriculum features a variety of electives, as well as Advanced Placement courses in all disciplines. Other features include a March interim program that focuses on global awareness and other current topics; career internships; independent study opportunities; a fellowship program that brings renowned figures to campus for classes and discussions; an annual, two-day poetry festival; and trips abroad. Graduates attend leading institutions throughout the country.

The athletic program, which consists of both intramural and interscholastic offerings, includes field hockey, basketball, softball, volleyball, soccer, riding, tennis and lacrosse. Art, drama, dance, instrumental and vocal music, publications and interest clubs round out the activities. Washington, DC, is used extensively for field trips to historical and cultural sites. Foxcroft's enrollment comprises students from a wide range of states and foreign countries. **See Also Page 1299**

HILL SCHOOL
Day — Coed Gr K-8

Middleburg, VA 20118. 130 S Madison St, PO Box 65. Tel: 540-687-5897.
  Fax: 540-687-3132.
  www.thehillschool.org   E-mail: tlord@thehillschool.org
Thomas A. Northrup, Head. BA, MSEd, Univ of Pennsylvania.
  Pre-Prep. Feat—Lat Studio_Art Drama Music. **Supp**—Dev_Read Makeup Tut.
  Adm: 37/yr.
  Enr 236. B 120. G 116. Elem 236. Wh 96%. Blk 3%. Asian 1%. **Fac 45.** M 13/1. F 25/6. Adv deg: 51%.
  Grad '04—30. Prep—24. (Highland-VA 9, Notre Dame Acad-VA 5, Foxcroft 4, Episcopal HS-VA 2, Mercersburg 2, Randolph-Macon 2). Alum 1076.
  Tui '04-'05: Day $11,700-15,500 (+$250).
  Summer: Enrich Rec. Tui Day $100-250/wk. 6 wks.
  Class rms 25. Lib 8000 vols. Labs 1. Art studios 1. Music studios 1. Perf arts ctrs 1. Athletic ctrs 1. Fields 4.
  Est 1926. Nonprofit. Tri (Sept-June).

The program at this elementary school stresses the teaching of basic skills, with art, music and drama balanced in the curriculum. Computers are utilized in all classes. Physical education is emphasized, with interscholastic competition in soccer, field hockey, track and basketball. The intramural program includes gymnastics, skiing, hiking and lacrosse. Field trips to Washington, DC, 40 miles away, are frequently scheduled.

MOUTH OF WILSON, VA. (90 mi. WSW of Roanoke, VA) Rural. Pop: 100. Alt: 2500 ft.

OAK HILL ACADEMY
Bdg and Day — Coed Gr 8-12

Mouth of Wilson, VA 24363. 2635 Oak Hill Rd. Tel: 276-579-2619. Fax: 276-579-4722.
  www.oak-hill.net   E-mail: info@oak-hill.net
Michael D. Groves, Pres. BA, Marshall Univ, MDiv, PhD, Southern Baptist Theological Seminary.
  Col Prep. Gen Acad. Underachiever. AP—US_Govt & Pol. **Feat**—Creative_Writing Span Comp_Sci Psych Relig World_Relig Photog Theater Accounting Bus Public_Speak Study_Skills. **Supp**—Dev_Read Rem_Math Rem_Read Tut.
  Adm (Gr 8-11): 46/yr. Bdg 45. Day 1. Appl due: Rolling. Accepted: 97%. Yield: 94%.
  Enr 104. B 63/1. G 37/3. Elem 2. Sec 102. Avg class size: 10. Uniform. **Fac 18.** M 12/1. F 3/2. Wh 94%. Am Ind 6%. Adv deg: 38%. In dorms 1.
  Grad '04—39. Col—36. (Ferrum, Bluefield, Appalachian St, UNC-Chapel Hill, U of MD-Col Park, U of SC). Avg SAT: 970. Alum 1597.
  Tui '04-'05: Bdg $17,500 (+$3500). **Day $5000** (+$1250). **Aid:** Need ($300,000).
  Summer: Acad Rec. Tui Bdg $3500. Tui Day $500. 5 wks.

Endow $696,000. Plant val $10,000,000. Bldgs 22. Dorms 5. Dorm rms 104. Class rms 21. Lib 5250 vols. Sci labs 2. Lang labs 1. Comp labs 2. Auds 1. Art studios 1. Music studios 2. Gyms 1. Fields 2. Courts 5. Riding rings 1. Stables 1. Parks 1. Lakes 1.
Est 1878. Nonprofit. Baptist. Sem (Sept-May).

Designed to provide a suitable environment for boys and girls who have experienced difficulties at previous schools, Oak Hill conducts a structured, nonmilitary program that can meet the needs of underachievers and unmotivated pupils. The school offers general academic and college preparatory curricula in a Christian setting. Students may participate in the advanced studies honors program, and those who need extra assistance may seek help in the school's learning labs.

Students attend compulsory weekly services at the local church. For recreation, pupils may take part in clubs or school publications and may also participate in extracurricular activities and interscholastic sports. The nearby New River and Grayson Highlands State Park provide opportunities for hiking, canoeing and picnicking. **See Also Pages 1218-9**

NEWPORT NEWS, VA. (18 mi. NW of Norfolk, VA) Urban. Pop: 180,150. Alt: 20 ft.

HAMPTON ROADS ACADEMY
Day — Coed Gr 6-12

Newport News, VA 23602. 739 Academy Ln. Tel: 757-884-9100. Fax: 757-884-9137. www.hra.org   E-mail: admissions@hra.org

Thomas D. Harvey, Head. AB, Saint Peter's College, MALS, Wesleyan Univ, MBA, Rockhurst College. **Mary S. Stevens, Adm.**

Col Prep. **AP**—Eng Fr Ger Lat Span Calc Stats Bio Chem Physics Eur_Hist US_Hist US_Govt & Pol Art_Hist Studio_Art. **Feat**—Marine_Biol/Sci Computers Programming Ceramics Photog Drama Band Strings Journ. **Supp**—Rev Tut.

Adm: 110/yr. Appl due: Mar. **Tests** CTP_4.

Enr 500. B 262. G 238. Elem 192. Sec 308. Avg class size: 16. **Fac** 65. Adv deg: 49%.

Grad '04—74. Col—74. (U of VA 11, Wm & Mary 8, James Madison 8, VA Polytech 6, VA Commonwealth 6, Hampden-Sydney 4). Avg SAT: 1278. Alum 1713.

Tui '04-'05: Day $9300-10,500 (+$850).

Summer: Acad Enrich Rev. 4 wks.

Plant val $10,000,000. Bldgs 3. Class rms 50. Lib 14,500 vols. Labs 3. Comp ctrs 2. Auds 1. Art studios 2. Drama studios 1. Gyms 3. Fields 6. Courts 6. Weight rms 1.

Est 1959. Nonprofit. Sem (Aug-June). **Assoc** CLS.

Founded by a group of parents, HRA occupies a 52-acre tract of land. Middle and upper school divisions prepare students for college entrance. Advanced Placement courses are available in many subjects, and the school maintains strong visual arts, music and drama programs.

Athletics, interest clubs and organizations, and compulsory community service supplement the academic program.

NORFOLK, VA. (80 mi. ESE of Richmond, VA) Urban. Pop: 234,403. Alt: 12 ft.

NORFOLK ACADEMY
Day — Coed Gr 1-12

Norfolk, VA 23502. 1585 Wesleyan Dr. Tel: 757-461-6236. Fax: 757-455-3199.
 www.norfolkacademy.org   E-mail: fholcombe@norfolkacademy.org
Dennis G. Manning, Head. BA, MA, Wake Forest Univ. **Frances C. Holcombe, Adm.**
 Col Prep. **Feat**—Fr Ger Ital Lat Span Stats Econ Govt Film Studio_Art Theater Music_ Hist Music_Theory Speech.
 Adm (Gr 1-11): 143/yr. Appl due: Feb. Accepted: 41%. Yield: 88%. **Tests** CTP_4 IQ Stanford.
 Enr 1216. B 613. G 603. Elem 744. Sec 472. Wh 84%. Blk 7%. Asian 4%. Other 5%. Avg class size: 20. **Fac 125.** M 45. F 80. Wh 92%. Hisp 2%. Blk 6%. Adv deg: 78%.
 Grad '04—107. Col—107. (U of VA 19, Wm & Mary 13, James Madison 8, Hampden-Sydney 6, Duke 3, VA Polytech 3). Avg SAT: 1277. Alum 4190.
 Tui '04-'05: Day $11,200-12,700 (+$300). **Aid:** Need 192 ($1,387,400).
 Summer: Acad Enrich Rec. Tui Day $250/wk. 6 wks.
 Endow $30,000,000. Plant val $45,000,000. Bldgs 10. Class rms 54. 2 Libs 48,000 vols. Sci labs 10. Comp labs 6. Auds 1. Art studios 3. Music studios 3. Dance studios 2. Gyms 2. Fields 14. Tennis courts 8. Pools 1.
 Est 1728. Nonprofit. Sem (Aug-June). **Assoc** CLS SACS.

The academy has been in operation since before the American Revolution. The solid college preparatory curriculum, enriched by study of contemporary affairs and public speaking, as well as athletic, fine arts and community service programs, prepares students for competitive institutions throughout the country. Exchange programs with schools in France, Germany, Spain and South Africa are available.

In 1966, the academy consummated a long-planned merger with Country Day School, located in Virginia Beach. The school occupies facilities on a 64-acre campus between Norfolk and Virginia Beach.

ORANGE, VA. (60 mi. NW of Richmond, VA; 75 mi. SW of Washington, DC) Suburban. Pop: 4123. Alt: 521 ft.

GRYMES MEMORIAL SCHOOL
Day — Coed Gr PS-8

Orange, VA 22960. 13775 Spicer's Mill Rd, PO Box 1160. Tel: 540-672-1010. Fax: 540-672-9167.
 www.grymesschool.org   E-mail: lberry@grymesschool.org
Thomas E. Short, Head. BA, Roanoke College. **Lee D. Berry, Adm.**
 Pre-Prep. **Feat**—Span Studio_Art Drama Music. **Supp**—Rev Tut.
 Adm (Gr PS-7): 36/yr. Appl due: Rolling. Accepted: 81%. Yield: 69%. **Tests** CTP_4 IQ.
 Enr 158. B 88. G 70. Elem 158. Wh 90%. Blk 8%. Other 2%. Avg class size: 16. **Fac 27.** M 2/1. F 21/3. Wh 100%. Adv deg: 37%.
 Grad '04—11. Prep—8. (Woodberry Forest 3, Episcopal HS-VA 1, Covenant 1). Alum

743.
Tui '04-'05: Day $5985-8700 (+$200). **Aid:** Need 49 ($140,000).
Endow $2,100,000. Bldgs 2. Lib 10,000 vols. Sci labs 1. Lang labs 1. Comp labs 1. Art studios 1. Music studios 1. Gyms 1. Fields 4.
Est 1947. Nonprofit. Sem (Sept-June).

Tracing its origins back to a program Emily Grymes began in her home, this school experienced rapid early growth before moving to its current site near the Blue Ridge Mountains in the 1950s. Grymes now provides a balanced elementary curriculum for pupils from Fredericksburg and the counties of Orange, Madison, Spotsylvania, Louisa, Culpeper and Greene.

Students receive a thorough background in the fundamentals as the majority prepare for entrance to independent high schools. Spanish instruction begins in prekindergarten and runs through grade 8. The arts constitute an integral part of the program, with art, music and drama carefully woven into the curriculum. Athletic competition and various leadership opportunities round out the program.

RICHMOND, VA. (98 mi. SSW of Washington, DC) Urban. Pop: 197,790. Alt: 20 ft.

COLLEGIATE SCHOOL
Day — Coed Gr K-12
(Coord — Day 5-8)

Richmond, VA 23229. N Mooreland Rd. Tel: 804-740-7077. Fax: 804-741-9797.
www.collegiate-va.org   E-mail: admissions@collegiate-va.org
Keith A. Evans, Head. BA, Davidson College, EdM, Harvard Univ, MS, Univ of Tennessee.
Amanda L. Surgner, Adm.
  Col Prep. AP—Fr Lat Span Calc Stats Bio Chem US_Hist Econ. **Feat**—Computers Ethics Relig Photog Studio_Art Chorus Journ. **Supp**—Rev Tut.
  Adm (Gr K-11): 181/yr. Appl due: Rolling. Accepted: 41%. Yield: 70%. **Tests** CTP_4 IQ SSAT.
  Enr 1528. B 735. G 793. Elem 1047. Sec 481. Wh 92%. Blk 5%. Asian 3%. Avg class size: 15. **Fac 179.** M 41/7. F 91/40. Adv deg: 73%.
  Grad '04—118. Col—118. (U of VA, James Madison, U of GA, VA Polytech, Duke, U of Richmond). Avg SAT: 1280. Alum 4619.
  Tui '04-'05: Day $12,320-14,830 (+$500-750). **Aid:** Need 114 ($1,066,441).
  Summer: Acad Enrich Rev Rem Rec. Sports. 8 wks.
  Endow $31,800,000. Plant val $52,000,000. Bldgs 27. Class rms 120. 2 Libs 39,000 vols. Sci labs 12. Lang labs 2. Comp labs 7. Auds 3. Theaters 2. Art studios 5. Music studios 4. Dance studios 1. Gyms 3. Athletic ctrs 1. Fields 17. Courts 8.
  Est 1915. Nonprofit. Sem (Aug-May). **Assoc** CLS SACS.

Collegiate was founded downtown as a girls' school. The coeducational Collegiate Country Day School was established in 1953 as a separate division on a campus 10 miles from the original Collegiate Town School. In 1960, the schools consolidated and now occupy a 55-acre campus. At one time divided into girls' and boys' schools, Collegiate reorganized in 1986 to form a coeducational lower school (grades K-4) and coordinate upper levels (grades 5-12), with boys' and girls' divisions operating on the same campus. A 1986 restructuring resulted in full coeducation. Classes in the lower and upper schools are coed, while boys and girls in the middle school (grades 5-8) attend same-sex academic classes.

Math, science, foreign languages, art, music, physical education, computer literacy and economics are required elements of the curriculum. Collegiate offers a global economics course in conjunction with the University of Richmond; in addition, a summer economics institute involving work at companies in the community is available.

Extracurricular activities, along with a strong athletic program for boys and girls in grades 7-12, are provided.

ST. CATHERINE'S SCHOOL
Bdg — Girls Gr 9-12; Day — Girls PS-12

Richmond, VA 23226. 6001 Grove Ave. Tel: 804-288-2804. Fax: 804-285-8169.
www.st.catherines.org   E-mail: admissions@st.catherines.org
Auguste Johns Bannard, Head. AB, Princeton Univ. **Katherine S. Wallmeyer, Adm.**
  Col Prep. AP—Eng Fr Lat Span Calc Stats Comp_Sci Bio Chem Physics Eur_Hist US_Hist Comp_Govt & Pol Econ US_Govt & Pol Art_Hist Music_Theory. **Feat**—Mandarin Relig Studio_Art Hist_of_Architect Dance. **Supp**—Dev_Read Rev Tut.
  Adm: 104/yr. Bdg 19. Day 85. Appl due: Rolling. **Tests** SSAT TOEFL.
  Enr 818. G 52/766. Elem 514. Sec 304. Wh 89%. Blk 5%. Asian 2%. Other 4%. Avg class size: 17. **Fac 117.** M 14/8. F 62/33. Adv deg: 34%. In dorms 6.
  Grad '04—85. Col—85. (James Madison 9, Wm & Mary 6, U of VA 6, VA Polytech 5, U of GA 5, Wash & Lee 2). Alum 5640.
  Tui '04-'05: Bdg **$29,750** (+$200-800). **Day $11,560-14,720** (+$200-800). **Aid:** Need 78 ($1,534,235).
  Summer: Enrich Rec. Arts. Sports. Tui Day $290-1045. 3-6 wks.
  Endow $47,000,000. Bldgs 28. Dorms 4. Dorm rms 59. Class rms 50. Lib 19,000 vols. Sci labs 6. Lang labs 1. Comp labs 4. Theaters 1. Art studios 3. Music studios 9. Dance studios 1. Gyms 3. Fields 6. Courts 4. Pools 1. Fitness ctrs 1.
  Est 1890. Nonprofit. Episcopal. Tri (Sept-June). **Assoc** CLS.

St. Catherine's, which was founded by Virginia Randolph Ellett to prepare girls for colleges requiring entrance exams, was acquired by the Episcopal Church in the Diocese of Virginia in 1920.

In addition to traditional course selections, St. Catherine's offers special opportunities in art, drama and modern dance; day or evening electives in creative writing, critical thinking and ceramics; and a two-week, late-winter mini-mester of short courses comprising academic enrichment, cultural experiences overseas and in the US, career exploration and individual community service projects. Mandarin Chinese is a four-year language offering. Through coordination with nearby St. Christopher's for boys, a substantial number of upper school classes and extracurriculars are coeducational.

Extracurricular activities include mixers, ski trips, canoeing, climbing and backpacking, chorale, dramatic arts, dance and team sports. Graduates enter a variety of competitive colleges. **See Also Page 1316**

ST. CHRISTOPHER'S SCHOOL

Day — Boys Gr PS-12

Richmond, VA 23226. 711 St Christopher's Rd. Tel: 804-282-3185. Fax: 804-673-6632.
www.stchristophers.com   E-mail: admissions@stcva.org
Charles M. Stillwell, Head. AB, Princeton Univ, MA, Brown Univ. **Anne D. Booker, Adm.**

- **Col Prep. AP**—Eng Fr Span Calc Stats Comp_Sci Bio Chem Physics US_Hist Econ US_Govt & Pol Art_Hist Music_Theory. **Feat**—Humanities Geol Chinese_Hist Vietnam_War Law Comp_Relig Ethics Photog Studio_Art Theater Music Music_Hist Guitar. **Supp**—Dev_Read Rem_Math Rem_Read Rev Tut.
- **Adm:** 137/yr. Appl due: Rolling. Accepted: 50%. Yield: 70%. **Tests** IQ Stanford.
- **Enr 935.** B 935. Elem 638. Sec 297. Wh 91%. Hisp 1%. Blk 6%. Asian 1%. Other 1%. Avg class size: 16. **Fac 148.** M 49/7. F 75/17. Wh 95%. Hisp 3%. Blk 1%. Asian 1%. Adv deg: 53%.
- **Grad '04—70. Col—70.** (U of VA 10, Wash & Lee 4, UNC-Chapel Hill 3, Wake Forest 3, James Madison 3, Hampton 3). Alum 4400.
- **Tui '04-'05:** Day $11,475-14,925 (+$465-1075). **Aid:** Need 129 ($1,303,225).
- **Summer:** Enrich Rem Rec. Sports. Tui Day $130-870. 1-6 wks.
- Endow $46,000,000. Plant val $27,880,000. Bldgs 23. Class rms 100. Lib 16,400 vols. Sci labs 8. Lang labs 1. Comp labs 5. Auds 2. Theaters 1. Art studios 3. Music studios 6. Dance studios 1. Gyms 4. Fields 6. Courts 9. Pools 1.
- **Est 1911.** Nonprofit. Episcopal. Tri (Sept-June).

St. Christopher's offers a complete college preparatory program and provides a liberal arts education with an emphasis on Christian ideals. At the lower school level (junior kindergarten through grade 5), teachers take into account boys' varying developmental needs and learning styles, while also emphasizing the development of independent and critical thinking and problem solving skills. The middle school (grades 6-8) continues to address differing intellectual needs as it emphasizes skill development in preparation for higher learning. Instruction moves from predominantly concrete intellectual exercises in grade 6 to more abstract forms of reasoning by grade 8.

In the upper school (grades 9-12), pupils follow a rigorous academic program that includes honors or Advanced Placement courses in all subject areas. A coordinate program with nearby St. Catherine's School during these years permits a broader curriculum and a wider choice of electives and AP courses in a coeducational context. Seniors have a two-week period of independent study in the spring.

Student council, honor council and publications are among the available extracurricular activities. Sports include football, baseball, basketball, soccer, wrestling, track, golf, cross-country, sailing, swimming, lacrosse and tennis. The coeducational Halsey Waterman Program involves upperclassmen in canoeing and rock climbing; ninth graders may enroll if space permits.

THE STEWARD SCHOOL

Day — Coed Gr K-12

Richmond, VA 23238. 11600 Gayton Rd. Tel: 804-740-3394. Fax: 804-740-1464.
www.stewardschool.org   E-mail: smoncure@stewardschool.org
Kenneth H. Seward, Head. BA, Middlebury College, MA, Case Western Reserve Univ. **A. Scott Moncure, Adm.**

- **Col Prep. AP**—Eng Fr Lat Span Calc Stats Bio Chem US_Hist US_Govt & Pol Studio_Art.

Feat—Creative_Writing Anat & Physiol Environ_Sci Programming Econ Psych Sociol Comp_Relig Graphic_Arts Photog Drama Music Journ Public_Speak Woodworking. **Supp**—ESL Tut.

Adm: 126/yr. Appl due: Rolling. **Tests** IQ.

Enr 575. B 252. G 323. Elem 398. Sec 177. Wh 92%. Hisp 2%. Blk 4%. Asian 2%. Avg class size: 15. **Fac 57.** M 15. F 42. Adv deg: 35%.

Grad '04—36. Col—36. (James Madison, VA Polytech, Christopher Newport, Clemson, VA Commonwealth, Longwood). Avg SAT: 1100. Alum 475.

Tui '04-'05: Day $12,500-14,000 (+$900). **Aid:** Need 59.

Summer: Acad Enrich Rev Rem Rec. 2-6 wks.

Endow $5,000,000. Plant val $1,778,000. Bldgs 7. Class rms 50. Lib 20,000 vols. Sci labs 3. Comp labs 5. Auds 1. Theaters 2. Art studios 4. Music studios 2. Gyms 2. Fields 3. Courts 6.

Est 1972. Nonprofit. Sem (Sept-June).

Steward's college preparatory program provides opportunities for pupils to receive one-on-one tutoring. Environmental studies is an integral part of the lower and upper school programs, and the fine arts are promoted throughout the curriculum. Students fulfill graduation requirements in public speaking, economics and computer.

The school fields boys' interscholastic teams in soccer, basketball, tennis, golf and lacrosse, as well as girls' squads in field hockey, basketball, tennis and golf; other activities are publications, interest clubs, community service and various trips. Steward conducts a student exchange with a sister school in the United Kingdom.

See Also Page 1252

ROANOKE, VA. (138 mi. W of Richmond, VA) Urban. Pop: 94,911. Alt: 904 ft.

NORTH CROSS SCHOOL
Day — Coed Gr PS-12

Roanoke, VA 24018. 4254 Colonial Ave. Tel: 540-989-6641. Fax: 540-989-7299.
www.northcross.org   E-mail: ebrown@northcross.org

Paul J. Stellato, Head. BA, Hamilton College, MFA, Columbia Univ. **Emily Brown, Adm.**

Col Prep. AP—Eng Fr Lat Span Calc Comp_Sci US_Hist. **Feat**—Stats Ecol Women's_Hist Vietnam_War Anthro Drawing Painting Photog Drama Chorus. **Supp**—Tut.

Adm: 95/yr.

Enr 515. B 278. G 237. Elem 349. Sec 166. Wh 78%. Hisp 2%. Blk 8%. Asian 12%. Avg class size: 13. **Fac 68.** M 32. F 32/4. Wh 90%. Blk 1%. Asian 4%. Other 5%. Adv deg: 72%.

Grad '04—32. Col—32. (U of VA 11, Wm & Mary 4, VA Polytech 4, Wash & Lee 2, Duke 2). Avg SAT: 1210. Avg ACT: 29. Alum 1800.

Tui '04-'05: Day $5400-9700. Aid: Merit 6 ($21,000). Need 48 ($303,000).

Summer: Rec. 4-8 wks.

Endow $8,000,000. Plant val $24,000,000. Bldgs 6. Class rms 45. Lib 12,000 vols. Sci labs 5. Comp labs 3. Theaters 1. Art studios 5. Music studios 2. Dance studios 1. Gyms 1. Fields 5. Courts 12. Pools 1.

Est 1960. Nonprofit. Tri (Sept-June). **Assoc** CLS.

Located on a 77-acre campus, North Cross was founded to provide college preparation for its students through a comprehensive program. A traditional core curriculum is the academic focus throughout the school and is supported by enrichment classes, electives, and a wide selection of cocurricular activities and athletic programs.

The phonics-based lower school program (junior kindergarten through grade 5) includes an introduction to foreign languages in junior kindergarten, in addition to course work in music, art, computer and library skills. The middle school (grades 6-8) continues to provide boys and girls with a grounding in the fundamentals and features choral and instrumental music. The upper school curriculum includes electives in every discipline and a full complement of Advanced Placement courses.

North Cross' interscholastic sports program consists of football, basketball, wrestling, soccer, volleyball, tennis, golf, baseball, field hockey, swimming, cross-country and lacrosse. As part of its service program, the school devotes three school days per year to community work that involves much of the student body, faculty advisors, select staff members and parents.

STAUNTON, VA. (78 mi. NE of Roanoke, VA) Suburban. Pop: 23,853. Alt: 1379 ft.

STUART HALL

Bdg — Girls Gr 8-12; Day — Coed 5-12

Staunton, VA 24401. 235 W Frederick St. Tel: 540-885-0356. Fax: 540-886-2275.
www.stuart-hall.org   E-mail: admissions@stuart-hall.org
Mark H. Eastham, Head. Jessica Hyde, Actg Adm.

Col Prep. AP—Eng Fr Calc Bio US_Hist World_Hist US_Govt & Pol. **Feat**—Creative_ Writing Computers Relig Studio_Art Drama Theater Chorus Music. **Supp**—ESL Tut.

Adm: 35/yr. Bdg 13. Day 22. Appl due: Rolling. Accepted: 90%. **Tests** SSAT Stanford TOEFL.

Enr 137. B 30. G 47/60. Elem 52. Sec 85. Wh 86%. Hisp 1%. Blk 3%. Asian 10%. Avg class size: 7. Uniform. **Fac 23.** M 7/1. F 12/3. Wh 92%. Blk 4%. Other 4%. Adv deg: 56%. In dorms 4.

Grad '04—15. Col—15. (VA Commonwealth, James Madison, U of VA, Brown, Sweet Briar, NYU). Avg SAT: 1150. Alum 2200.

Tui '05-'06: Bdg $32,000 (+$1000). **5-Day Bdg $29,000** (+$1000). **Day $10,500** (+$250). **Aid:** Merit 17 ($79,825). Need 36 ($276,200).

Endow $2,634,000. Plant val $4,973,000. Bldgs 2. Dorms 8. Dorm rms 68. Class rms 25. Lib 12,000 vols. Sci labs 4. Comp labs 2. Auds 1. Theaters 1. Art studios 2. Music studios 1. Gyms 1. Fields 1. Courts 3.

Est 1844. Nonprofit. Episcopal. Sem (Sept-May).

The oldest girls' boarding school in Virginia, Stuart Hall was founded as Virginia Female Institute and was renamed in honor of Mrs. J.E.B. Stuart, who was principal for 19 years. Since its founding, the school has been affiliated with the Episcopal Diocese of Virginia. Boys first enrolled as day students in grades 6-8 in 1992, and in grades 9-12 in 1999.

Within a Christian setting, the school offers a curriculum that includes an honors program beginning in grade 9 and a selection of AP courses. The school's well-developed visual and performing arts program comprises four elements: dance, drama, art and music. Pupils requiring academic support or assistance with their organizational or study skills may meet with Stuart Hall's learning resource specialist.

TAPPAHANNOCK, VA. (43 mi. NE of Richmond, VA) Rural. Pop: 2068. Alt: 22 ft.

ST. MARGARET'S SCHOOL
Bdg and Day — Girls Gr 8-12

Tappahannock, VA 22560. 444 Water Ln, PO Box 158. Tel: 804-443-3357. Fax: 804-443-6781.
www.sms.org   E-mail: admit@sms.org
Margaret R. Broad, Head. BA, Denison Univ, MA, Univ of Virginia. **Kimberly A. McDowell, Adm.**
- **Col Prep. AP**—Eng Calc Eur_Hist US_Hist. **Feat**—Fr Lat Span Anat & Physiol Ecol Environ_Sci Marine_Biol/Sci Computers Relig Studio_Art Music. **Supp**—ESL Rem_Math Rev Tut.
- **Adm (Day Gr 8-11):** 48/yr. Bdg 42. Day 6. Appl due: Rolling. Accepted: 82%. Yield: 59%. **Tests** SSAT.
- **Enr 146.** G 115/31. Elem 8. Sec 138. Avg class size: 12. Uniform. **Fac 35.** M 6. F 28/1. Adv deg: 71%. In dorms 8.
- **Grad '04—36. Col—32.** (VA Polytech 3, Roanoke Col 3, VA Commonwealth 2, Auburn 2, James Madison 2, Carnegie Mellon 1). Alum 2000.
- **Tui '05-'06: Bdg** $32,800 (+$1500). **Day** $12,400 (+$800). **Aid:** Need 45 ($675,800).
- Endow $4,800,000. Plant val $15,000,000. Bldgs 18. Dorms 3. Dorm rms 58. Class rms 24. Lib 10,000 vols. Sci labs 2. Comp labs 2. Tech ctrs 1. Theaters 1. Art studios 1. Music studios 1. Dance studios 1. Gyms 1. Fields 1. Courts 3. Pools 1.
- **Est 1921.** Nonprofit. Episcopal. Tri (Sept-June). **Assoc** SACS.

One of the church schools in the Episcopal Diocese of Virginia, St. Margaret's takes advantage of its small-town setting in the historic Virginia Tidewater. Girls learn in a Christian, homelike atmosphere in which they are held to high academic standards. The curriculum, emphasizing individual attention and college preparation, encompasses a variety of courses, ranging from world civilizations and physics to piano and studio art. All seniors complete a two-week career exploration internship in the spring. St. Margaret's participates in an exchange program with other members of the Queen Margaret of Scotland Girls' Schools Association.

Among activities are clubs, publications, the visual and performing arts, community service and honor committees. Sports include field hockey, soccer, softball, basketball, volleyball, tennis, cross-country, swimming and crew.

See Also Pages 1312-3

VIRGINIA BEACH, VA. (17 mi. SE of Norfolk, VA) Suburban. Pop: 425,257. Alt: 18 ft.

CAPE HENRY COLLEGIATE SCHOOL
Day — Coed Gr PS-12

Virginia Beach, VA 23454. 1320 Mill Dam Rd. Tel: 757-481-2446. Fax: 757-481-9194. www.capehenry.org E-mail: admissionschcs@capehenry.org

John P. Lewis, Head. BS, MA, Saint Peter's College, EdD, Seton Hall Univ. **Kay Temme, Upper & Middle Sch Adm; Julie Levine, Lower Sch Adm.**

- **Col Prep. AP**—Eng Fr Lat Span Calc Comp_Sci Bio Chem Physics Eur_Hist US_Hist US_Govt & Pol Studio_Art. **Feat**—Creative_Writing Ger Japan Stats Anat & Physiol Ecol Marine_Biol/Sci Paleontology Web_Design Econ Sociol Ethics Photog Drama Music Music_Hist Music_Theory Ballet Dance Journ. **Supp**—ESL Tut.
- **Adm:** 184/yr. Appl due: Rolling. Accepted: 50%. Yield: 50%. **Tests** CTP_4 ISEE.
- **Enr 1020.** B 538. G 482. Elem 664. Sec 356. Wh 84%. Hisp 1%. Blk 6%. Am Ind 1%. Asian 4%. Other 4%. Avg class size: 18. **Fac 135.** M 25/17. F 70/23. Wh 72%. Hisp 3%. Blk 13%. Am Ind 2%. Asian 5%. Other 5%. Adv deg: 41%.
- **Grad '04—69. Col—69.** (U of VA, James Madison, Wm & Mary, Old Dominion, VA Polytech). Alum 1040.
- **Tui '04-'05: Day $10,545-12,235** (+$135-165). **Aid:** Need 144 ($920,745).
- **Summer:** Acad Enrich Rec. 3-6 wks.
- Endow $3,100,000. Plant val $15,200,000. Bldgs 7. Class rms 79. Libs 1. Sci labs 4. Lang labs 1. Comp labs 6. Photog labs 1. Auds 1. Theaters 1. Art studios 3. Music studios 4. Dance studios 1. Gyms 2. Fields 4.
- **Est 1924.** Nonprofit. Tri (Aug-June).

Formerly the Everett School, Cape Henry Collegiate is Virginia Beach's oldest independent school. Students are encouraged to balance academics, athletics, the arts and community involvement.

The curriculum is college preparatory, emphasizing English, math, foreign languages, social studies and science. The developmental lower school program offers an extended-day program for children in grades pre-K-5. The middle school (grades 6-8) provides an interdisciplinary curriculum and an enrichment program that includes electives in literary magazine, newspaper, music, drama and art. Emphasis upon computer literacy in core subjects begins in the lower school and continues through the upper school. The upper school curriculum emphasizes writing, critical thinking and research skills. Advanced Placement and honors courses in all disciplines, as well as a variety of activities, public speaking and community service requirements, are featured.

Boys' interscholastic teams compete in soccer, lacrosse, basketball, volleyball, baseball, tennis, wrestling, swimming, cross-country, track, crew and golf; girls choose from field hockey, soccer, basketball, lacrosse, volleyball, tennis, swimming, cheerleading, softball, cross-country, golf, crew and track. Students enroll from Virginia Beach, Norfolk, Portsmouth and Chesapeake, and several foreign countries are represented.

WARRENTON, VA. (44 mi. WSW of Washington, DC) Suburban. Pop: 6670. Alt: 700 ft.

HIGHLAND SCHOOL
Day — Coed Gr PS-12

Warrenton, VA 20186. 597 Broadview Ave. Tel: 540-347-1221. Fax: 540-341-7164.
www.highlandschool.org   E-mail: admissions@highlandschool.org

David P. Plank, Head. BSc, Univ of Sheffield (England), MEd, Univ of Manitoba (Canada).
James M. Slay, Jr., Adm.

Col Prep. AP—Eng Fr Lat Span Calc Stats Comp_Sci Bio Physics Eur_Hist US_Hist Studio_Art. **Feat**—Women's_Lit Greek Marine_Biol/Sci African-Amer_Hist Econ Law Psych International_Relations Drama Band Chorus Music Debate Journ SAT_Prep. **Supp**—ESL Tut.

Adm: 93/yr. Appl due: Rolling. Accepted: 60%. Yield: 98%. **Tests** CEEB CTP_4 ISEE SSAT Stanford TOEFL.

Enr 520. B 260. G 260. Elem 330. Sec 190. Wh 97%. Hisp 1%. Blk 1%. Asian 1%. Avg class size: 14. **Fac 77.** M 22. F 55. Wh 91%. Hisp 4%. Blk 4%. Asian 1%. Adv deg: 55%.

Grad '04—40. Col—40. (U of VA, VA Polytech, US Milit Acad, U of PA, U of Richmond, Wm & Mary). Avg SAT: 1175. Alum 500.

Tui '05-'06: Day $7035-14,410 (+$100). **Aid:** Merit 7 ($81,200). Need 35 ($169,900).

Summer: Rec. 1-8 wks.

Endow $1,238,000. Plant val $15,400,000. Bldgs 3. Class rms 45. Lib 8000 vols. Sci labs 5. Comp labs 2. Art studios 5. Music studios 3. Gyms 2. Fields 8. Courts 4.

Est 1928. Nonprofit. Sem (Sept-June).

Founded as the Warrenton branch of the Calvert School of Baltimore, MD, this school initially utilized the Calvert curriculum. Founders Lavinia Hamilton and Dorothy Montgomery moved the school on a couple of occasions to accommodate growth; the institution assumed its present location in 1957. That same year, an independent program replaced the Calvert system, and the name was changed to Highland School. A group of community leaders acquired the school in 1961.

Developmental in nature, the prekindergarten through fifth grade program emphasizes skill development in language arts, mathematics, social studies, science, computer science, foreign language, music, art and physical education. Specialist teachers conduct science, computer, foreign language, music, art and physical education classes during these years. Children in grades 6-8 take six courses per semester in the standard disciplines, including Latin, as well as an elective from among art, drama, band, community service, forensics and chorus. Pupils in grades 4-8 participate in interscholastic athletics.

Highland's comprehensive college preparatory curriculum in grades 9-12 includes honors and Advanced Placement courses and selections in science, the humanities, and the fine and performing arts. The upper school provides both honors and standard college preparatory levels; pupils need not take classes at exclusively one level or the other, however. All Highland upper schoolers take a music course and an art class, while also fulfilling an annual community service requirement.

Cocurricular activities include opportunities for participation in student government, honor council, Key Club, journalism, the fine and performing arts, yearbook, and field trips in the arts and sciences. Interscholastic competition is held in soccer, basketball, lacrosse, cross-country, golf, swimming, volleyball, tennis, field hockey, cheerleading and dance.

WAYNESBORO, VA. (80 mi. NE of Roanoke, VA; 87 mi. WNW of Richmond, VA) Urban. Pop: 19,520. Alt: 1407 ft.

FISHBURNE MILITARY SCHOOL
Bdg and Day — Boys Gr 8-12

Waynesboro, VA 22980. 225 S Wayne Ave, PO Box 988. Tel: 540-946-7700.
  Fax: 540-946-7738.
  www.fishburne.org   E-mail: lambert@fishburne.org
Col. William W. Alexander, Jr., Supt. BA, East Tennessee State Univ, MA, Univ of Kansas.
  Col. William W. Sedr, Jr., Head. BA, Virginia Military Institute, MA, Virginia Polytechnic Institute. **Capt. Carl V. Lambert, Adm.**
  Col Prep. Milit. Feat—Fr Span Anat & Physiol Computers Econ Law Sociol Studio_Art Public_Speak JROTC. **Supp**—Makeup Tut.
  Adm: 100/yr. Bdg 89. Day 11. Appl due: Rolling.
  Enr 200. B 178/22. Elem 17. Sec 183. Wh 79%. Hisp 6%. Blk 10%. Asian 5%. Uniform. **Fac 30.** M 27. F 3. Adv deg: 36%.
  Grad '04—24. **Col**—23. (U of MD-Col Park 2). Alum 3200.
  Tui '04-'05: Bdg $21,900 (+$1500). **Day $10,500** (+$1000).
  Summer: Acad. Tui Bdg $2950. Tui Day $950. 4 wks.
  Endow $6,500,000. Plant val $8,000,000. Bldgs 4. Dorms 1. Dorm rms 81. Class rms 20. Lib 10,000 vols. Labs 2. Comp ctrs 1. Auds 1. Gyms 1. Fields 1. Basketball courts 2. Tennis courts 5. Weight rms 1. Rifle ranges 1.
  Est 1879. Nonprofit. Quar (Aug-May). **Assoc** SACS.

James Fishburne, a student and close friend of Robert E. Lee's, established this school at age 29 with the aim of preparing boys "for the duties and responsibilities of life." The school's college preparatory curriculum is complemented by a full athletic program, military organizations such as rifle and drill teams, and activities that include publications, band, drama, debating, clubs and scouting. Most graduates go on to attend Eastern colleges.   **See Also Page 1334**

WOODBERRY FOREST, VA. (64 mi. NW of Richmond, VA; 76 mi. SW of Washington, DC) Rural. Pop: 450.

WOODBERRY FOREST SCHOOL
Bdg — Boys Gr 9-12

Woodberry Forest, VA 22989. 898 Woodberry Forest Rd. Tel: 540-672-6023.
  Fax: 540-672-6471.
    www.woodberry.org   E-mail: wfs_admissions@woodberry.org
Dennis M. Campbell, Head. AB, PhD, Duke Univ, BD, Yale Univ. **Joseph G. Coleman, Adm.**
  Col Prep. AP—Fr Ger Lat Span Calc Stats Comp_Sci Bio Chem Physics Econ Psych

US_Govt & Pol Art_Hist Studio_Art Music_Theory. **Feat**—Chin Relig Photog Drama Mech_Drawing.
Adm (Gr 9-11): 128/yr. Appl due: Feb. Accepted: 39%. **Tests** SSAT.
Enr 381. B 381. Sec 381. Wh 80%. Hisp 8%. Blk 12%. Avg class size: 12. **Fac 77.** M 67. F 10. Adv deg: 74%. In dorms 14.
Grad '04—110. Col—110. (U of VA, UNC-Chapel Hill, Vanderbilt, Wash & Lee, U of the South, NC St). Avg SAT: 1270. Alum 7800.
Tui '04-'05: Bdg $30,200 (+$500-700). **Aid:** Need 99 ($1,600,000).
Endow $180,000,000. Plant val $100,000,000. Bldgs 77. Dorms 9. Dorm rms 205. Lib 55,000 vols. Sci labs 4. Lang labs 1. Comp labs 4. Theaters 1. Art studios 5. Music studios 10. Gyms 2. Fields 11. Courts 17. Pools 2. Tracks 1. Golf crses 1.
Est 1889. Nonprofit. Tri (Sept-May). **Assoc** CLS SACS.

Woodberry Forest was established by Capt. Robert S. Walker and was carried on under family ownership and control until 1926 by three of his six sons.

The school's college preparatory curriculum features honors and Advanced Placement courses in many disciplines. Students choose among electives in math, English, the humanities, computer science and general subjects. Extracurricular activities include drama, choir, orchestra, Outward Bound, photography, journalism and debate.

Participation in athletics is required; sports such as football, basketball, golf, tennis, soccer, lacrosse, track, wrestling, baseball, swimming, squash and cross-country are available. Also offered are summer study programs in France, Spain, Japan, England, Australia, Scotland and Israel. Graduates attend competitive four-year colleges. **See Also Page 1349**

WOODSTOCK, VA. (81 mi. W of Washington, DC) Suburban. Pop: 3952. Alt: 820 ft.

MASSANUTTEN MILITARY ACADEMY
Bdg and Day — Coed Gr 6-PG

Woodstock, VA 22664. 614 S Main St. Tel: 540-459-2167. Fax: 540-459-5421.
  www.militaryschool.com   E-mail: admissions@militaryschool.com
Col. Roy F. Zinser, Pres. BS, MBA, The Citadel, MS, Salve Regina College, MS, Naval War College. **Matt Gifford, Adm.**
Col Prep. Gen Acad. Milit. AP—US_Govt & Pol. **Feat**—Fr Span Econ Criminal_Justice Ceramics Photog Journ JROTC SAT_Prep. **Supp**—Dev_Read ESL Makeup Tut.
Adm: 91/yr. Bdg 91. Day 0. Appl due: Rolling. Accepted: 95%. Yield: 70%.
Enr 169. B 123/2. G 42/2. Wh 68%. Hisp 5%. Blk 15%. Asian 9%. Other 3%. Avg class size: 9. Uniform. **Fac 27.** M 12/6. F 7/2. Wh 92%. Blk 4%. Asian 2%. Other 2%. Adv deg: 29%. In dorms 3.
Grad '04—36. Col—34. (Geo Mason 2, VA Polytech 2, Radford 2, Mary Baldwin 2, Citadel 2, U of GA 1). Avg SAT: 914. Avg ACT: 19. Alum 2567.
Tui '04-'05: Bdg $19,750 (+$300). **Day $12,100** (+$300). **Aid:** Need 38 ($110,000).
Summer: Acad Enrich Rev Rem Rec. JROTC. Tui Bdg $2750. Tui Day $1325. 5 wks.
Endow $11,000,000. Plant val $12,000,000. Bldgs 19. Dorms 4. Dorm rms 116. Class rms 23. Lib 6000 vols. Sci labs 3. Comp labs 3. Auds 2. Art studios 1. Music studios 1. Gyms 1. Fields 2. Tennis courts 3. Pools 1. Rifle ranges 1.
Est 1899. Nonprofit. Quar (Aug-June). **Assoc** SACS.

The school was founded by the Virginia Classis of the Reformed Church to prepare the children of the Shenandoah Valley for college. For 50 years, with the assistance of a board of trustees representing several religious denominations, Howard J. Benchoff devoted his energies to its development. In 1917, the academy adopted a military program whose structured environment remains an integral part of school life. Robert J. Benchoff succeeded his father in 1955 and continued to expand the enrollment and the plant facilities until his death in 1968.

Within a small-class environment, MMA emphasizes its core curriculum of English, math, science, social studies and foreign language. Noteworthy aspects of the program include reading comprehension courses, dual-enrollment college-credit courses in math and American history, and various fine and performing arts offerings. A daily academic assistance period, an evening study period, a homework assistance program and an academic advisor program provide academic support.

The academy's rural location on 40 acres in the middle of the Shenandoah Valley allows for a variety of activities. Every cadet has the opportunity to participate in MMA's interscholastic athletic program. Scheduled trips are made to cultural and athletic events in Washington, DC, and Baltimore, MD. Other pursuits include hiking and skiing in the nearby Massanutten Range of the Blue Ridge Mountains and in the George Washington National Forest.

WEST VIRGINIA

WHEELING, WV. (46 mi. WSW of Pittsburgh, PA) Urban. Pop: 31,419. Alt: 642 ft.

LINSLY SCHOOL
Bdg — Coed Gr 7-12; Day — Coed 5-12

Wheeling, WV 26003. 60 Knox Ln. Tel: 304-233-1436. Fax: 304-234-4614.
  www.linsly.org   E-mail: admit@linsly.org
Reno F. DiOrio, Head. BA, Dickinson College, MEd, Univ of Dayton. **Chad Barnett, Adm.**
  Col Prep. AP—Eng Fr Ger Calc Comp_Sci Bio Chem Physics US_Hist Psych. **Feat**—Humanities Lat Studio_Art Theater_Arts Music_Theory. **Supp**—Tut.
  Adm: 107/yr. Appl due: Rolling. Tests IQ TOEFL.
  Enr 448. B 38/228. G 28/154. Wh 86%. Blk 6%. Asian 8%. Avg class size: 15. Uniform. **Fac 45.** M 23. F 21/1. Adv deg: 60%. In dorms 9.
  Grad '04—56. Col—56. (WV U, OH St, Miami U-OH, Case Western Reserve, Marshall, Duquesne). Alum 2660.
  Tui '05-'06: Bdg $21,950. Day $10,820. Aid: Need 95 ($725,000).
  Summer: Acad Enrich Rev Rem. Tui Day $380. 5 wks.
  Endow $10,700,000. Plant val $9,000,000. Bldgs 20. Dorms 4. Dorm rms 75. Class rms 37. Lib 7000 vols. Sci labs 5. Lang labs 1. Comp labs 2. Art studios 4. Music studios 1. Gyms 3. Fields 3. Courts 3. Pools 1.
  Est 1814. Nonprofit. Sem (Aug-May). **Assoc** NCA.

Founded by Noah Linsly as the Wheeling Lancastrian Academy, Linsly, renamed for its benefactor, is the oldest independent preparatory school west of the Allegheny Mountains. The traditional college preparatory curriculum includes Advanced Placement classes in all the major disciplines, as well as a contemporary approach to the utilization of technology in the classroom. The program also features compulsory art and music appreciation courses.

Interscholastic athletic competition is offered from grade 5 through the varsity level. All students spend time each year at the Linsly Outdoor Center, an experiential and environmental training facility located on 300 acres of parkland.

MOUNT DE CHANTAL VISITATION ACADEMY
Bdg — Girls Gr 9-12; Day — Boys PS-6, Girls PS-12

Wheeling, WV 26003. 410 Washington Ave. Tel: 304-233-3771. Fax: 304-233-8598.
  www.mountdechantal.org   E-mail: admissions@mountdechantal.org
Sandra L. Clerici, Pres. BA, Chatham College, MA, Rensselaer Polytechnic Institute. **John M. Rowan, Adm.**
  Col Prep. AP—Eur_Hist Art_Hist. **Feat**—Fr Ger Ital Japan Span Anat & Physiol Comp_Sci Comp_Relig Studio_Art Music_Hist Music_Theory. **Supp**—ESL LD Tut.
  Adm (Bdg Gr 9-12; Day PS-11): 48/yr. Bdg 9. Day 39. Appl due: Rolling. Accepted: 94%. Yield: 82%. Tests IQ TOEFL.
  Enr 217. B 20. G 17/180. Wh 98%. Blk 2%. Avg class size: 12. Uniform. **Fac 37.** M 4/1. F 30/2. Wh 100%. Adv deg: 48%.

Grad '04—17. Col—17. (OH St 2, Carnegie Mellon 1, U of Pittsburgh 1, MIT 1, Duquesne 1, Marshall 1). Avg SAT: 1390. Alum 1400.

Tui '04-'05: Bdg $16,950 (+$500). **Day $8450** (+$500). **Aid:** Merit 13 ($44,000). Need 71 ($450,000). Work prgm 28 ($14,000).

Summer: Acad Enrich Rev. 4 wks.

Endow $3,000,000. Plant val $14,000,000. Bldgs 4. Dorms 1. Dorm rms 5. Class rms 21. Lib 18,000 vols. Sci labs 2. Lang labs 1. Comp labs 2. Auds 1. Art studios 1. Music studios 1. Dance studios 1. Gyms 1. Fields 1. Tennis courts 3.

Est 1848. Nonprofit. Roman Catholic. Sem (Aug-May). **Assoc** NCA.

Offering a comprehensive elementary and secondary program, the academy prepares its graduates for competitive colleges. The Mount's boarding division, reinstated in 2000, allows high school girls to reside in either a traditional dormitory or a fully renovated home a block from campus. A Montessori program for boys and girls ages 2½-6 is offered, and grades 1-6 are also coeducational. The school conducts a limited learning disabilities curriculum.

Modular scheduling is in effect, and Advanced Placement and independent study options are available for qualified students. In addition, select pupils may take courses at adjoining Wheeling Jesuit College. The school, a National Historic Landmark located on a 30-acre campus, maintains a strong ecumenical orientation.

Great Lakes States

ILLINOIS

CHICAGO, IL. Urban. Pop: 2,896,016. Alt: 593 ft.

CHICAGO ACADEMY FOR THE ARTS
Day — Coed Gr 9-12

Chicago, IL 60622. 1010 W Chicago Ave. Tel: 312-421-0202. Fax: 312-421-3816.
www.chicagoacademyforthearts.org
E-mail: generalinfo@chicagoacademyforthearts.org
Pamela Jordan, Head. Mark Taylor, Adm.

Col Prep. Perform_Arts Visual_Arts. **AP**—Eng Fr Span Calc Eur_Hist Art_Hist. **Feat**—Ital Anat & Physiol World_Relig Visual_Arts Acting Theater Musical_Theater Music Dance Media_Arts. **Supp**—Tut.

Adm: 79/yr. Appl due: Rolling. **Tests** ISEE.

Enr 160. B 71. G 89. Sec 160. Wh 63%. Hisp 4%. Blk 29%. Asian 1%. Other 3%. **Fac 31.** M 6/14. F 6/5. Adv deg: 45%.

Grad '04—43. **Col**—40. (Milwaukee Inst of Art & Design, Columbia Col-IL, NYU, SUNY-Purchase, RI Sch of Design). Alum 676.

Tui '04-'05: Day $12,900 (+$300-450). **Aid:** Merit 49 ($54,400). Need 44 ($67,500).

Summer: Ages 12-17. Arts. Tui Day $500. 4 wks.

Endow $407,000. Bldgs 1. Libs 1. Sci labs 2. Comp labs 1. Theaters 1. Art studios 4. Music studios 4. Dance studios 3. Drama studios 1.

Est 1981. Nonprofit. Quar (Sept-May). **Assoc** NCA.

The academy focuses on the integration of arts and academics. Every day, students spend five hours in college preparatory academic classes, followed by four hours of instruction in each student's major: visual arts, music, theater, dance, musical theater or communications/writing arts. The academy offers more than 50 arts courses, among them ballet, jazz and modern dance, vocal and instrumental lessons, acting, directing, stagecraft, drawing, painting, sculpting, design, printmaking, film studies, video production, speech, poetry and prose fiction, and publishing.

The majority of graduates matriculate at colleges or conservatories, while others immediately begin professional arts careers.

FRANCIS W. PARKER SCHOOL
Day — Coed Gr PS-12

Chicago, IL 60614. 330 W Webster Ave. Tel: 773-353-3000. Fax: 773-549-4669.

www.fwparker.org   E-mail: admissions@fwparker.org
Daniel B. Frank, Prin. BA, Amherst College, MA, PhD, Univ of Chicago. **Kate Pivinski & Cokey Evans, Adms.**
  Col Prep. **Feat**—Fr Lat Span Computers Econ Studio_Art Drama Music Dance Journ. **Supp**—Dev_Read Rem_Math Rem_Read Rev Tut.
  Adm: 116/yr. Appl due: Dec. Accepted: 20%. **Tests** ISEE.
  Enr 901. B 434. G 467. Elem 589. Sec 312. Avg class size: 18. **Fac 102.** M 32/6. F 60/4.
  Grad '04—75. Col—75. (U of MI, Brown, Kenyon, U of WI-Madison, CO Col, U of PA). Alum 5500.
  Tui '04-'05: Day $14,037-17,985. Aid: Need 133 ($1,930,000).
  Summer: Ages 4-13. Enrich Rec. 1-4 wks. Ages 10-18. Basketball. Tui Day $140. 1 wk.
  Endow $10,900,000. Plant val $45,000,000. Bldgs 2. Class rms 56. Lib 46,000 vols. Sci labs 8. Lang labs 1. Comp labs 5. Auds 1. Art studios 7. Music studios 2. Dance studios 1. Gyms 3. Fields 1.
  Est 1901. Nonprofit. Sem (Sept-June). **Assoc** NCA.

Flora J. Cooke founded this school to carry out the ideas of one of the world's great educators, Col. Francis Wayland Parker. She served as principal for 33 years.

Although the curriculum is a rigorous one, every effort is made to adapt academics to each child's needs. A wide range of work is provided in music, art, dramatics and shop. Emphasis is placed on the development of student responsibility and its attendant activities. Graduates enter leading colleges across the country.

Sports include a balanced program of soccer, basketball, baseball, golf and tennis for boys, and field hockey, volleyball, basketball, softball and tennis for girls.

LATIN SCHOOL OF CHICAGO
Day — Coed Gr PS-12

Chicago, IL 60610. 59 W North Blvd. Tel: 312-582-6000. Fax: 312-582-6011.
  www.latinschool.org   E-mail: info@latinschool.org
Shelley Greenwood, Head. BS, New York Univ, MEd, Univ of Wisconsin-Madison. **Anne Frame, Adm.**
  Col Prep. **AP**—Fr Lat Span Calc Stats Bio Chem Physics Eur_Hist US_Hist Art_Hist Studio_Art. **Feat**—Humanities Shakespeare African-Amer_Lit Chin Anat & Physiol Astron Amer_Stud Anthro Econ Human_Sexuality World_Relig Photog Acting Dance.
  Adm: 154/yr. Accepted: 35%. **Tests** ISEE.
  Enr 1083. B 519. G 564. Elem 659. Sec 424. Wh 82%. Hisp 5%. Blk 6%. Asian 4%. Other 3%. Avg class size: 15. **Fac 142.** M 49/2. F 89/2. Adv deg: 69%.
  Grad '04—110. Col—108. (Northwestern 6, Geo Wash 5, U of WI-Madison 5, U of IL-Urbana 4, Colby 3, Yale 2). Alum 3150.
  Tui '04-'05: Day $14,635-19,550 (+$1000-1500). **Aid:** Need 113 ($1,787,813).
  Summer: Acad Enrich Rec. Tui Day $295-940. 2-6 wks.
  Plant val $18,000,000. Bldgs 2. Class rms 55. 2 Libs 41,200 vols. Labs 6. Dark rms 1. Comp ctrs 1. Theaters 1. Art studios 4. Music studios 2. Gyms 4. Fields 3. Pools 1.
  Est 1888. Nonprofit. Quar (Aug-June). **Assoc** CLS NCA.

Latin offers a traditional college preparatory curriculum supplemented by the performing and applied arts, clubs, athletics and student-run publications. The middle school curriculum includes computer programming, a writing lab, and an arts cycle that consists of art, drama, music and dance. A featured course for ninth graders is an interdisciplinary humanities class that examines Western culture through the perspectives of history, art, literature and science.

The upper school curriculum features four foreign languages; an extensive selection of electives in history, English, science; and AP courses in many subjects. Latin's life skills program, running from the middle school through the upper school, allows pupils to explore issues pertaining to values, relationships and ethics. An annual project week provides nontraditional learning opportunities for those in grades 6-12 in an on- or off-campus setting.

Latin conducts an extensive interscholastic sports program; the vast majority of middle and upper school students participate in at least one sport annually.

MORGAN PARK ACADEMY
Day — Coed Gr PS-12

Chicago, IL 60643. 2153 W 111th St. Tel: 773-881-6700. Fax: 773-881-8409.
www.morganparkacademy.org

J. William Adams, Head. AB, Harvard Univ, MEd, Boston Univ. **Melissa Harmening, Adm.**

Col Prep. AP—Eng Fr Span Calc Stats Bio Chem US_Hist. **Feat**—Creative_Writing Computers Pol_Sci Studio_Art Drama Music Journ.

Adm: 104/yr. Appl due: Rolling. Accepted: 33%. **Tests** Stanford.

Enr 550. B 280. G 270. Elem 368. Sec 182. Wh 59%. Hisp 2%. Blk 28%. Asian 11%. Avg class size: 14. **Fac 62.** M 16. F 46. Adv deg: 54%.

Grad '04—42. Col—42. (U of IL-Urbana, U of Chicago, Northwestern, DePaul, Stanford, Butler). Alum 292.

Tui '02-'03: Day $5300-12,300 (+$800). **Aid:** Merit 15 ($165,000).

Summer: Acad Enrich Rev Rem Rec. Tui Day $1020/2-wk ses. 6 wks.

Endow $1,200,000. Plant val $16,500,000. Bldgs 6. Class rms 43. Lib 26,000 vols. Labs 5. Music studios 2. Arts ctrs 1. Gyms 1. Fields 2. Tennis courts 4.

Est 1873. Nonprofit. (Sept-June). **Assoc** CLS NCA.

The academy is located 15 miles southwest of downtown Chicago in a residential community. Morgan Park served as the preparatory department of the University of Chicago from 1892 to 1907, then existed as a military academy until 1958. The program places special emphasis on English, foreign languages, history, science and mathematics.

Continuing emphasis is placed on small classes and the development of a competitive and selective academic school of exacting standards. Foreign language instruction begins in preschool, and throughout the school emphasis is placed on the development of reading and writing skills. Honors and Advanced Placement courses are available in all major disciplines in the upper school. Course offerings in the areas of art, computer science, drama, music and physical education are provided at all levels.

The athletic program includes interscholastic competition in basketball, baseball, softball, track, tennis, volleyball and soccer. A wide range of extracurricular activities is available.

SACRED HEART SCHOOLS
Day — Coed Gr K-8
(Coord — Day 1-8)

Chicago, IL 60660. 6250 N Sheridan Rd. Tel: 773-262-4446. Fax: 773-262-6178.

www.shschicago.org E-mail: admissions@shschicago.org
Sr. Susan Maxwell, RSCJ, Dir. BA, MA, Manhattanville College, MA, Northwestern Univ. **Judith Corrin, Adm.**
  Pre-Prep. Feat—Fr Span Computers Relig Studio_Art Music Health. **Supp**—LD Tut.
  Adm: 111/yr. Appl due: Jan. Accepted: 61%. Yield: 72%.
  Enr 556. B 253. G 303. Elem 556. Wh 81%. Hisp 3%. Blk 3%. Asian 4%. Other 9%. Avg class size: 18. Uniform. **Fac 63.** M 8. F 55. Wh 83%. Hisp 7%. Blk 4%. Am Ind 2%. Asian 4%. Adv deg: 50%.
  Grad '04—49. Prep—33. (Loyola Acad 14, St Ignatius 8, Latin 5, Francis W Parker 2). Alum 2600.
  Tui '04-'05: Day $11,500-11,885 (+$750). **Aid:** Need 113 ($735,000).
  Summer: Acad Enrich Rec. Tui Day $125/300/wk. 6 wks.
  Endow $7,086,000. Plant val $12,870,000. Bldgs 5. Class rms 48. Lib 12,000 vols. Sci labs 2. Comp labs 2. Auds 1. Art studios 2. Music studios 2. Stages 1. Gyms 1. Courts 2. Playgrounds 3.
  Est 1876. Nonprofit. Roman Catholic. Sem (Sept-June). **Assoc** NCA.

Part of the Network of Sacred Heart Schools in the US, this school consists of a coeducational kindergarten and two distinct elementary programs for children in grades 1-8: the Academy of the Sacred Heart for girls and Hardey Preparatory School for boys. The academy, which was founded on Dearborn Street in 1876 as one of Chicago's first independent schools, moved to its current location overlooking Lake Michigan on Sheridan Road in 1929. Hardey Prep was added to the school complex in 1935.

Developmental readiness is at the core of the kindergarten program. In addition to language arts, math, social studies and science, children gain an exposure to music, art, physical education and religion. During the lower school years (grades 1-5), boys and girls learn in single-sex classrooms in the core subjects. Students follow similar curricula and thematic study units while also sharing many school activities. Departmentalization begins in the middle school (grades 6-8). Among special subjects at this level are foreign language, music, art, computer, health and religion.

Beginning in kindergarten, all boys and girls engage in community service projects that revolve around an age-appropriate theme. Extracurricular options include the following: performance opportunities in the arts; entrance in national scholastic competitions; after-school workshops in studio arts; and intramural and interscholastic basketball, volleyball, soccer, baseball, softball and track. In addition, Sacred Heart schedules frequent field trips at all grade levels.

THE UNIVERSITY OF CHICAGO LABORATORY SCHOOLS
Day — Coed Gr PS-12

Chicago, IL 60637. 1362 E 59th St. Tel: 773-702-9450. Fax: 773-702-7455.
www.ucls.uchicago.edu E-mail: lab@ucls.uchicago.edu
David Magill, Dir. BS, Ohio State Univ, EdM, EdD, Temple Univ. **D. Michael Veitch, Adm.**
  Col Prep. AP—Fr Ger Span Calc Stats Comp_Sci Bio Chem Physics Eur_Hist US_Hist World_Hist Econ Music_Theory. **Feat**—Lat Web_Design African-Amer_Hist Holocaust Art_Hist Photog Studio_Art Drama Music Journ. **Supp**—Dev_Read Rem_Read.
  Adm: 222/yr. Appl due: Dec. Accepted: 43%. Yield: 79%. **Tests** ISEE.
  Enr 1716. B 816. G 900. Elem 1232. Sec 484. Wh 63%. Hisp 3%. Blk 11%. Asian 13%.

Other 10%. Avg class size: 22. **Fac 209.** M 40/5. F 149/15. Wh 82%. Hisp 4%. Blk 7%. Asian 5%. Other 2%. Adv deg: 73%.

Grad '04—101. Col—100. (U of Chicago 8, NYU 6, Boston U 5, U of IL-Urbana 4, U of MI 4, Northwestern 3). Avg SAT: 1307. Avg ACT: 28. Alum 6500.

Tui '04-'05: Day $12,699-17,103 (+$15-600). **Aid:** Need 152 ($730,000).

Summer: Acad Enrich Rec. Tui Day $300-1900. 2-6 wks.

Endow $8,191,000. Plant val $10,000,000. Bldgs 4. Class rms 54. 2 Libs 80,000 vols. Sci labs 9. Lang labs 1. Comp labs 4. Auds 1. Theaters 2. Art studios 7. Music studios 8. Dance studios 1. Gyms 4. Fields 3. Courts 5. Pools 1. Playgrounds 5.

Est 1896. Nonprofit. Quar (Sept-June). **Assoc** NCA.

The Laboratory Schools, established by John Dewey as a laboratory for curricular development and teacher training, are part of the University of Chicago. Approximately half of the pupils are children of university faculty and staff members, while the rest of the student body come from all parts of the Chicago metropolitan area. Graduates continue study at the college level, but beyond academic preparation for college, the program encourages autonomy in intellectual development and endeavors to provide an environment for healthy personal and social growth. An Advanced Placement program is offered.

Students have the opportunity to participate in a wide variety of activities, clubs, interest groups and service organizations. Community service projects are encouraged at all grade levels. Popular extracurricular pursuits include student government, drama, music, Model UN, math team, art and literary magazines, filmmaking, and video and photography clubs, as well as interscholastic and intramural sports.

CHICAGO HEIGHTS, IL. (23 mi. S of Chicago, IL) Urban. Pop: 32,776. Alt: 689 ft.

MARIAN CATHOLIC HIGH SCHOOL
Day — Coed Gr 9-12

Chicago Heights, IL 60411. 700 Ashland Ave. Tel: 708-755-7565. Fax: 708-755-0042.
www.marianchs.com   E-mail: mchsinfo@marianchs.com

Sr. Mary Paul McCaughey, OP, Pres. BS, Quincy College, MA, St Louis Univ, MBA, Univ of Notre Dame. **Sr. Dorothy Marie Solak, OP, Adm.**

Col Prep. AP—Eng Lat Span Calc Stats Comp_Sci Bio Chem Physics Eur_Hist US_Hist World_Hist Econ Psych. **Feat**—Creative_Writing Fr Anat & Physiol Govt Relig Studio_Art Drama Band Chorus Music Bus Journ. **Supp**—Rev Tut.

Adm: 451/yr. Appl due: Mar. Accepted: 50%. **Tests** HSPT IQ.

Enr 1658. B 787. G 871. Sec 1658. Wh 79%. Hisp 5%. Blk 14%. Asian 2%. Avg class size: 28. **Fac 100.** M 52. F 48. Wh 88%. Hisp 4%. Blk 6%. Asian 2%. Adv deg: 94%.

Grad '04—396. Col—392. (U of IL-Urbana 30, IL St 24, DePaul 22, N IL 18, Loyola U of Chicago 13, U of IA 12). Avg SAT: 1148. Avg ACT: 23. Alum 12,000.

Tui '04-'05: Day $6200 (+$300). **Aid:** Need ($350,000). Work prgm 8 ($6000).

Summer: Acad Enrich Rev. Tui Day $400/3-wk ses. 6 wks.

Endow $4,000,000. Plant val $12,800,000. Bldgs 1. Class rms 56. Lib 25,000 vols. Sci labs 6. Comp labs 3. Theaters 1. Art studios 1. Music studios 4. Gyms 2. Fields 6. Courts 8.

Est 1958. Nonprofit. Roman Catholic. Sem (Aug-June). **Assoc** NCA.

Owned and operated by the Dominican Sisters of Springfield, Marian Catholic is one of the largest coeducational Catholic college preparatory schools in Illinois. Students enroll from more than 50 nearby communities, covering a radius of over 400 miles. Located on a 72-acre campus, the plant has undergone four expansion projects since the school's establishment.

The curriculum concentrates on traditional college preparatory courses, and Marian Catholic requires daily religious instruction of all students. In addition, honors and Advanced Placement classes are provided in all of the major fields. Electives include speech, music, art, drama, business and computer courses.

The school maintains a strong athletic program. For boys, football, basketball, cross-country, wrestling, soccer, track, baseball, golf, hockey, lacrosse and tennis are provided; girls may participate in volleyball, swimming, basketball, gymnastics, softball, track, tennis, cross-country and golf. Extracurricular activities include campus ministry, yearbook, newspaper, cheerleading, volunteer services, marching band and a variety of clubs.

DOWNERS GROVE, IL. (17 mi. W of Chicago, IL) Suburban. Pop: 48,724. Alt: 718 ft.

AVERY COONLEY SCHOOL
Day — Coed Gr PS-8

Downers Grove, IL 60515. 1400 Maple Ave. Tel: 630-969-0800. Fax: 630-969-0131.
 www.averycoonley.org   E-mail: whitann@averycoonley.org
Thomas A. Kracht, Head. Ann Whitney, Adm.
  Pre-Prep. **Feat**—Fr Computers Studio_Art Drama Music.
  Adm: 52/yr. Appl due: Rolling. **Tests** IQ.
  Enr 362. B 179. G 183. Elem 362. Wh 73%. Hisp 4%. Blk 1%. Asian 17%. Other 5%. Avg class size: 16. **Fac 33.** Wh 100%. Adv deg: 54%.
  Grad '04—32. Prep—18. (Benet, U of Chicago Lab Schs, St Ignatius, Groton, Morgan Park). Alum 1000.
  Tui '04-'05: Day $12,900 (+$50-1300). **Aid:** Need 15 ($90,250).
  Summer: Acad Enrich Rec. 2-6 wks.
  Endow $743,000. Plant val $8,000,000. Bldgs 2. Class rms 28. Lib 18,000 vols. Sci labs 2. Comp labs 2. Auds 1. Art studios 1. Music studios 1. Gyms 1. Fields 1. Pools 1.
  Est 1906. Nonprofit. Tri (Aug-June). **Assoc** NCA.

Founded in Riverside by Mrs. Queene Ferry Coonley and Lucia Burton Morse and moved to its present location in 1929, ACS has gained more than local prominence over the years. Drawing students from roughly 40 suburban communities, Avery Coonley emphasizes fundamental skills and the creative arts.

Various accelerated and enriched programs serve a student body that consists of bright and academically gifted children. Courses in art, computer science, French, music and physical education begin in kindergarten and continue through grade 8. Academic and enrichment classes are available in the summer program.

IL   *Great Lakes States*

ELGIN, IL. (34 mi. WNW of Chicago, IL) Urban. Pop: 94,487. Alt: 715 ft.

ELGIN ACADEMY
Day — Coed Gr PS-12

Elgin, IL 60120. 350 Park St. Tel: 847-695-0300. Fax: 847-695-5017.
www.elginacademy.org   E-mail: info@elginacademy.org
John W. Cooper, Head. BA, MA, Florida State Univ, PhD, Syracuse Univ. **Erik C. Calhoun, Adm.**
Col Prep. AP—Eng Calc Bio Chem Physics Eur_Hist US_Hist Psych Studio_Art. **Feat**—Fine_Arts Performing_Arts. **Supp**—Tut.
Adm: 130/yr. Appl due: Rolling. Accepted: 84%.
Enr 409. B 221. G 188. Elem 292. Sec 117. Wh 83%. Hisp 1%. Blk 5%. Asian 11%. **Fac 47.** M 12/2. F 29/4. Wh 94%. Blk 4%. Asian 2%. Adv deg: 61%.
Grad '04—30. Col—30. (Wash U, Millikin, Bowdoin, Macalester, Wellesley, U of Denver). Alum 1500.
Tui '05–'06: Day $8250-14,600 (+$500-1350). **Aid:** Need 60 ($533,400).
Endow $500,000. Plant val $2,500,000. Bldgs 7. Class rms 30. Lib 18,000 vols. Sci labs 3. Comp labs 2. Theaters 1. Art studios 2. Music studios 2. Gyms 1. Fields 3. Courts 4.
Est 1839. Nonprofit. Sem (Aug-June). **Assoc** CLS NCA.

The oldest independent preparatory school west of the Allegheny Mountains, the academy was founded by James Gifford, who four years earlier had founded the city of Elgin. On a 18-acre campus, the plant has been expanded and remodeled over the years.

The liberal arts curriculum emphasizes college preparation. The fine arts, athletics and extracurricular activities are integral to the program. Special features include a comprehensive lower and middle school foreign language program, as well as a month-long immersion program that allows lower school pupils to learn about another country.   **See Also Page 1133**

FOX RIVER COUNTRY DAY SCHOOL
Bdg — Coed Gr 6-8; Day — Coed PS-8

Elgin, IL 60120. 1600 Dundee Ave. Tel: 847-888-7910. Fax: 847-888-7947.
www.frcds.org   E-mail: admissions@frcds.org
John Friborg, Head. **Charles R. Harvuot, Adm.**
Pre-Prep. Gen Acad. **Feat**—Lib_Skills Span Environ_Sci Computers Studio_Art Music. **Supp**—Dev_Read ESL Tut.
Adm: 76/yr. Appl due: Feb. **Tests** Stanford TOEFL.
Enr 200. B 12/84. G 6/98. Elem 200. Avg class size: 12. **Fac 26.** M 5. F 16/5. Adv deg: 11%.
Grad '04—6. Prep—6. (Wayland 2, Hun 1, George Sch 1, Marianapolis 1). Alum 1030.
Tui '04–'05: Bdg $26,950-27,490. 5-Day Bdg $22,845. Day $9050-11,450 (+$840).
Bldgs 10. Dorms 1. Dorm rms 12. Class rms 9. Lib 8000 vols. Sci labs 1. Comp labs 1. Art studios 1. Music studios 1. Gyms 1. Fields 1. Pools 1.
Est 1913. Nonprofit. Tri (Sept-June). **Assoc** NCA.

Founded as Chicago Junior School, FRCDS assumed its current name in 2003. Located on a 53-acre campus, the school provides an academic program that readies students for a college preparatory high school curriculum. Music, drama, sports, and particularly strong environmental education and arts programs provide enrichment at all grade levels. Computer lab and Spanish are available beginning in kindergarten, and a reading specialist aids children who require additional assistance. As a complement to academics, FRCDS emphasizes character development through a curriculum that addresses moral and ethical issues.

EVANSTON, IL. (14 mi. N of Chicago, IL) Suburban. Pop: 74,239. Alt: 603 ft.

ROYCEMORE SCHOOL
Day — Coed Gr PS-12

Evanston, IL 60201. 640 Lincoln St. Tel: 847-866-6055. Fax: 847-866-6545.
www.roycemoreschool.org E-mail: bturnbull@roycemoreschool.org
Joseph A. Becker, Head. BA, Northwestern Univ. **Barbara B. Turnbull, Adm.**

Col Prep. AP—Fr Span Eur_Hist US_Hist. **Feat**—Drawing Sculpt Music_Theory Public_Speak.

Adm: 69/yr. Appl due: Rolling. Accepted: 67%.

Enr 252. B 140. G 112. Elem 176. Sec 76. Wh 70%. Hisp 2%. Blk 14%. Asian 6%. Other 8%. Avg class size: 17. **Fac 37.** M 8. F 25/4. Wh 89%. Hisp 3%. Blk 5%. Asian 3%. Adv deg: 54%.

Grad '04—18. Col—17. (U of Chicago, Northwestern, Bryn Mawr, NYU, Miami U-OH, DePaul). Avg SAT: 1090. Avg ACT: 24. Alum 1300.

Tui '03-'04: Day $4750-15,810 (+$770-1760). **Aid:** Merit 5 ($79,600). Need 127 ($1,207,000).

Summer: Enrich Rec. Tui Day $113-250/wk. 9 wks.

Endow $1,000,000. Plant val $3,000,000. Bldgs 1. Class rms 16. Lib 8500 vols. Sci labs 2. Comp labs 1. Art studios 2. Music studios 1. Gyms 1. Fields 1.

Est 1915. Nonprofit. Sem (Aug-June). **Assoc** NCA.

This independent, nondenominational school, influential in Chicago, Evanston and the North Shore, prepares students for competitive colleges throughout the country. Art, music, dramatics, computer literacy and physical education complement traditional academic subjects. The upper school has a January short term for special projects, and foreign language study begins in kindergarten. Advanced students may take courses at Northwestern University for credit at no additional charge. Roycemore also conducts a summer program for gifted pupils.

Publications, photography and dramatics are among the extracurricular activities. Interscholastic sports include soccer, volleyball and basketball. The physical education program offers basketball, gymnastics, softball, dance, weight training and volleyball.

LAKE FOREST, IL. (29 mi. NNW of Chicago, IL) Suburban. Pop: 20,059. Alt: 704 ft.

LAKE FOREST ACADEMY
Bdg and Day — Coed Gr 9-12

Lake Forest, IL 60045. 1500 W Kennedy Rd. Tel: 847-234-3210. Fax: 847-615-3202.
www.lfanet.org E-mail: info@lfanet.org

John Strudwick, Head. BSc, London School of Economics (England), MA, Queens Univ (Canada), PhD, Univ of Toronto (Canada). **Chris Wheeler, Adm.**
  Col Prep. AP—Eng Calc Stats Bio Chem Physics Eur_Hist US_Hist. **Feat**—Astron Ecol Environ_Sci Electronics Psych Philos Film Filmmaking Photog. **Supp**—Rev Tut.
  Adm: 123/yr. Bdg 52. Day 71. Appl due: Mar. Accepted: 60%. **Tests** SSAT TOEFL.
  Enr 321. B 84/93. G 62/82. Sec 321. Wh 68%. Hisp 5%. Blk 9%. Asian 18%. Avg class size: 12. **Fac 43.** M 24/1. F 17/1. Wh 93%. Blk 7%. Adv deg: 67%. In dorms 16.
  Grad '04—78. Col—76. (IN U, Holy Cross-IN, IL Wesleyan, U of MI, Denison, U of CO-Boulder). Avg SAT: 1170. Avg ACT: 25. Alum 6000.
  Tui '02-'03: Bdg $25,500 (+$500). **Day** $17,850 (+$500). **Aid:** Merit 26 ($109,500). Need 99 ($1,607,360).
  Endow $13,200,000. Plant val $26,500,000. Bldgs 9. Dorms 4. Dorm rms 100. Class rms 25. Lib 27,000 vols. Labs 5. Sci labs 3. Lang labs 1. Comp labs 1. Comp ctrs 1. Auds 1. Theaters 1. Art studios 3. Music studios 1. Dance studios 1. Perf arts ctrs 1. Gyms 1. Fields 6. Courts 3. Pools 1. Rinks 1. Tracks 1.
  Est 1857. Nonprofit. Sem (Aug-May). **Assoc** CLS NCA.

One of the leading Midwestern schools, LFA resulted from the 1974 merger of two institutions known for their college preparatory programs: Lake Forest Academy for boys (established in 1857) and Ferry Hall School for girls (founded in 1869). Before the consolidation, the two schools had operated for four years as coordinated academic programs. The academy has occupied its present, 160-acre campus in this suburb on Chicago's North Shore since 1948.

College preparation guides LFA's program. The traditional curriculum, which includes Advanced Placement courses in all departments, also includes electives in many disciplines. Among extracurricular activities are several publications, music, dramatics, interscholastic academic competitions, community service opportunities, various clubs, and outside programs designed to take advantage of Chicago's cultural offerings. All students participate in interscholastic sports, which include football, soccer, cross-country, volleyball, baseball, track, golf, tennis, field and ice hockey, basketball, swimming, softball and wrestling.

LAKE FOREST COUNTRY DAY SCHOOL
Day — Coed Gr PS-8

Lake Forest, IL 60045. 145 S Green Bay Rd. Tel: 847-234-2350. Fax: 847-234-8725.
www.lfcds.org E-mail: nicoletc@lfcds.org

Kristi A. Kerins, Head. BA, Skidmore College, MEd, Virgina Commonwealth Univ. **Christine R. Nicoletta, Adm.**
  Pre-Prep. Feat—Fr Span Computers Studio_Art Drama Music Outdoor_Ed. **Supp**—Tut.
  Adm: 70/yr. Appl due: Rolling. Accepted: 60%. **Tests** CTP_4 IQ.
  Enr 430. B 217. G 213. Elem 430. Wh 88%. Hisp 2%. Blk 3%. Asian 7%. Avg class size:

10. Fac 49. M 12. F 32/5. Wh 100%. Adv deg: 48%.
Grad '04—51. Prep—18. (Lake Forest Acad, Deerfield Acad, Lawrenceville, Kent Sch-CT, Phillips Exeter). Alum 3000.
Tui '04-'05: Day $13,475-16,975 (+$300-400). **Aid:** Need 26 ($240,000).
Summer: Enrich Rec. 8 wks.
Endow $15,000,000. Plant val $14,000,000. Bldgs 1. Class rms 51. Lib 22,000 vols. Sci labs 3. Comp labs 1. Auds 1. Art studios 2. Music studios 2. Perf arts ctrs 1. Gyms 2. Fields 3.
Est 1888. Nonprofit. Tri (Sept-June). **Assoc** NCA.

Lake Forest Country Day School was established in 1958 as the result of a merger of the Bell School, founded in 1888, and the Lake Forest Day School, founded in 1927.

The school's early childhood program (ages 3-6) seeks to develop decision-making and critical-thinking skills through an experiential learning approach. In the elementary and middle schools, strong emphasis is placed upon the acquisition of organizational skills and sound study habits. The curriculum features a literature-based language arts program, a skills-oriented math sequence, and a hands-on method in science classes. French and Spanish foreign language classes begin in senior kindergarten and continue through grade 8. The traditional core curriculum in grades 5-8 utilizes an interdisciplinary approach.

A wide variety of activities, including choral music, band, drama, studio art and publications, is offered. Field trips and use of the computer center and the library are integral parts of the curriculum. Athletics are required, and interscholastic competition is available in grades 6-8.

ROCKFORD, IL. (77 mi. WNW of Chicago, IL; 78 mi. SW of Milwaukee, WI) Urban. Pop: 150,115. Alt: 730 ft.

KEITH SCHOOL

Day — Coed Gr PS-12

Rockford, IL 61107. 1 Jacoby Pl. Tel: 815-399-8823. Fax: 815-399-2470.
  www.keithschool.com E-mail: admissions@keithschool.com
Jon S. Esler, Head. BA, Univ of Colorado-Boulder, MA, Univ of Denver. **Marcia Aramovich, Adm.**
  Col Prep. AP—Eng Bio Chem Eur_Hist US_Hist Music_Theory. **Feat**—Fr Greek Lat Span Stats Environ_Sci Computers Govt World_Relig Ceramics Photog Studio_Art Drama Music Music_Hist Speech. **Supp**—Dev_Read Tut.
Adm: 65/yr. Appl due: Rolling. Accepted: 84%. Yield: 66%. **Tests** CTP_4 ISEE.
Enr 298. B 149. G 149. Elem 204. Sec 94. Avg class size: 18. **Fac 42.** M 9/2. F 27/4. Wh 98%. Hisp 1%. Asian 1%. Adv deg: 59%.
Grad '04—29. Col—29. (DePaul 2, Loyola U of Chicago 2, U of Chicago 1, Emory 1, Northwestern 1, Wash U 1). Avg SAT: 1275. Avg ACT: 26. Alum 2000.
Tui '04-'05: Day $4900-11,230 (+$125-400). **Aid:** Merit 30 ($160,550). Need 83 ($375,238).
Summer: Gr 6-12. Rec. 1-2 wks.
Endow $513,000. Plant val $2,227,000. Bldgs 3. Class rms 38. Libs 1. Labs 3. Art studios 2. Music studios 2. Gyms 2. Fields 2.
Est 1916. Nonprofit. Sem (Aug-June). **Assoc** NCA.

Founded by artist Belle Emerson Keith, this school occupies a 15-acre campus overlooking the Rock River. Serving students from northern Illinois and southern Wisconsin, Keith introduces both Spanish and French in preschool and teaches the languages to all students through grade 5; Latin is added in grade 6. In the upper school, requirements include fine arts, computers, foreign language, speech, and research and reference, and Advanced Placement courses are offered. In addition, all pupils and faculty in grades 6-12 utilize laptop computers. A senior project is compulsory.

A student volunteer program requires each student to perform 90 hours of community service during the four high school years, and all are encouraged to participate in team sports, the fine arts and other after-school activities.

WINNETKA, IL. (19 mi. N of Chicago, IL) Suburban. Pop: 12,419. Alt: 655 ft.

NORTH SHORE COUNTRY DAY SCHOOL
Day — Coed Gr PS-12

Winnetka, IL 60093. 310 Green Bay Rd. Tel: 847-446-0674. Fax: 847-446-0675.
www.nscds.org

W. Thomas Doar III, Head. BA, Univ of Minnesota-Twin Cities, MA, Univ of St Thomas (MN), EdM, Columbia Univ. **Dale L. Wentz, Adm.**

Col Prep. AP—Eng Fr Span Comp_Sci US_Hist. **Feat**—Mandarin Asian_Stud Studio_Art Theater Music. **Supp**—Tut.

Adm: 100/yr. **Tests** CTP_4 ISEE SSAT.

Enr 460. Avg class size: 12. **Fac** 76. M 27. F 49. Adv deg: 47%.

Grad '04—45. **Col**—45. (Notre Dame, SMU, DePaul, Williams, U of MI, Stanford). Alum 3000.

Tui '03-'04: Day $14,955-17,175 (+$630). **Aid:** Need ($600,000).

Summer: Acad Rec. 8 wks.

Endow $16,500,000. Plant val $7,200,000. Bldgs 9. Class rms 36. 2 Libs 23,000 vols. Sci labs 6. Comp labs 3. Auds 1. Theaters 1. Art studios 3. Music studios 5. Shops 1. Gyms 2. Fields 2. Tennis courts 3. Pools 1. Playgrounds 1. Greenhouses 1.

Est 1919. Nonprofit. Tri (Aug-June). **Assoc** NCA.

North Shore offers a strong academic program that includes electives in many areas, including drama, computer science and Asian studies. Technology is an integral part of the program at all grade levels. Language instruction includes Spanish from junior kindergarten, French beginning in grade 6 and Mandarin Chinese commencing in grade 9. Advanced Placement is offered in the major disciplines for qualified students.

The athletic program features interscholastic options for both boys and girls. Independent study is emphasized at the junior and senior levels. An interim week for pupils in grades 9-12 provides in-depth experiences off campus and frequently includes travel abroad.

INDIANA

CULVER, IN. (33 mi. SSW of South Bend, IN; 78 mi. ESE of Chicago, IL) Rural. Pop: 1539. Alt: 743 ft.

THE CULVER ACADEMIES
Bdg and Day — Coed Gr 9-PG

Culver, IN 46511. 1300 Academy Rd, Box 157. Tel: 574-842-7100. Fax: 574-842-8066.
www.culver.org   E-mail: admissions@culver.org
John Buxton, Head. AB, Brown Univ. **Mike Turnbull, Adm.**

    Col Prep. Milit. AP—Eng Fr Ger Lat Span Calc Stats Comp_Sci Bio Chem Physics Eur_Hist US_Hist Econ US_Govt & Pol Music_Theory. **Feat**—Creative_Writing Humanities Shakespeare Chin Anat & Physiol Astron Vietnam_War Russ_Hist Psych Comp_Relig Art_Hist Film Photog Studio_Art Drama Music Dance Aviation Horsemanship. **Supp**—ESL Tut.

    Adm: 262/yr. Bdg 240. Day 22. Appl due: Apr. Accepted: 87%. Yield: 61%. **Tests** CEEB ISEE SSAT TOEFL.

    Enr 760. B 394/35. G 291/40. Sec 758. PG 2. Wh 73%. Hisp 9%. Blk 6%. Asian 9%. Other 3%. Avg class size: 15. Uniform. **Fac 91.** M 60/1. F 25/5. Wh 96%. Hisp 2%. Blk 1%. Asian 1%. Adv deg: 86%. In dorms 4.

    Grad '04—181. **Col**—179. (Purdue 20, IN U 7, Miami U-OH 6, U of MI 5, Butler 4, U of IL-Urbana 3). Avg SAT: 1169. Avg ACT: 24. Alum 11,000.

    Tui '05-'06: Bdg $28,900 (+$3000-4500). **Day** $21,000 (+$1750). **Aid:** Merit 53 ($1,172,600). Need 347 ($5,613,650).

    Summer: Ages 9-17. Acad Rev Rec. Naval. Woodcraft. Aviation. Horsemanship. Tui Bdg $800-3575. 2-6 wks.

    Endow $135,000,000. Plant val $150,000,000. Bldgs 39. Dorms 7. Dorm rms 366. Class rms 59. Lib 50,000 vols. Sci labs 9. Lang labs 2. Comp labs 6. Auds 1. Theaters 1. Art studios 4. Music studios 12. Dance studios 1. Gyms 2. Fields 17. Courts 15. Pools 1. Rinks 2. Riding rings 1. Stables yes. Golf crses 1. Student ctrs 1. Airports 1.

    Est 1894. Nonprofit. Quar (Aug-June). **Assoc** CLS NCA.

The large and well-known Culver Military Academy was founded by Henry Harrison Culver of St. Louis, MO, as a selective military academy for boys. His stated purpose at that time was that of "thoroughly preparing young men for the best colleges, scientific schools, and businesses of America," and he believed that a system of military discipline would best accomplish his objective.

In 1896, a fire at Missouri Military Academy resulted in its consolidation with Culver. Col. Alexander F. Fleet, Missouri Military's headmaster at that time, assumed command of the newly formed school and led a period of significant progress at Culver. By 1939, under the leadership of Gen. Leigh Gignilliat, the school had achieved national and international prominence. Girls first enrolled at the school in 1971, when Culver Girls Academy was founded on the same campus; unlike the boys' division, the girls' academy is organized in a prefect system of leadership. Classes at the school are coeducational.

Graduates in recent years have attended more than 200 colleges throughout the country. The extensive curriculum provides Advanced Placement courses, as well as independent study options and a variety of elective courses. In addition to academic preparation for college, the academies stress self-discipline and leadership skills for all pupils.

Culver's 1800-acre campus provides many athletic and extracurricular opportunities. Both boys and girls choose from a wide selection of varsity sports, and intramural athletics are provided for those not involved in interscholastic competition. There are also numerous religious, athletic, hobby and student groups.

During the summer, Culver offers extensive programs in sailing, horsemanship, aviation, aquatics and athletics for girls and boys ages 9-17.

EVANSVILLE, IN. (100 mi. W of Louisville, KY; 154 mi. ESE of St. Louis, MO) Urban. Pop: 121,582. Alt: 394 ft.

EVANSVILLE DAY SCHOOL
Day — Coed Gr PS-12

Evansville, IN 47715. 3400 N Green River Rd. Tel: 812-476-3039. Fax: 812-476-4061.
www.evansvilledayschool.org   E-mail: admission@evansvilledayschool.org
Benjamin Hebebrand, **Head.** BA, Warren Wilson College, MA, Georgia State Univ. **Gerri A. Rice, Adm.**

- **Col Prep. AP**—Eng Fr Span Calc Bio Chem Physics US_Hist US_Govt & Pol. **Feat**—Creative_Writing Zoology Comp_Sci Econ Sociol Asian_Stud World_Relig Art_Hist Music Journ. **Supp**—Rev Tut.
- **Adm:** 53/yr. Appl due: Rolling. Accepted: 95%. **Tests** CTP_4.
- **Enr 312.** B 160. G 152. Elem 239. Sec 73. Wh 84%. Hisp 1%. Blk 6%. Asian 1%. Other 8%. Avg class size: 20. **Fac 42.** M 10/2. F 26/4. Wh 98%. Hisp 1%. Asian 1%. Adv deg: 42%.
- **Grad '04—4. Col—4.** (Samford, Berea, U of Evansville, DePauw). Avg SAT: 1134. Avg ACT: 24.
- **Tui '04-'05: Day $18,180** (+$100-2000). **Aid:** Need 52 ($280,000).
- **Summer:** Acad. 1-4 wks.
- Endow $380,000. Plant val $1,700,000. Bldgs 1. Class rms 40. Lib 8000 vols. Sci labs 4. Comp labs 3. Auds 1. Art studios 1. Music studios 1. Gyms 1. Fields 3.
- **Est 1946.** Nonprofit. Quar (Aug-May). **Assoc** NCA.

Established as an outgrowth of the Evansville Pre-School, under the direction of J. B. Davis, the Evansville Day School expanded rapidly. New facilities in 1961 permitted the addition of secondary grades, and the school has since offered a full college preparatory program. In 1968, the school moved to its current, 57-acre campus.

The program in grades 8-12 features 90-minute classes, and the curriculum is supplemented by specialized short-term courses in photography, ecology and ceramics, French films and theater appreciation. Intersession opportunities and senior projects provide students with off-campus curricular options.

Extracurricular activities include dramatics, clubs, student leadership, sports and cultural experiences. Tennis, soccer, basketball and golf are offered in the athletic program.

FORT WAYNE, IN. (72 mi. SE of South Bend, IN; 142 mi. ESE of Chicago, IL) Urban. Pop: 205,727. Alt: 790 ft.

CANTERBURY SCHOOL
Day — Coed Gr PS-12

Fort Wayne, IN 46804. 3210 Smith Rd. Tel: 260-436-0746. Fax: 260-436-5137.
www.canterburyschool.org   E-mail: canterbury@canterburyschool.org

Jonathan Hancock, Head. BA, MA, Oxford Univ (England), EdM, Harvard Univ. Susan Johnson, HS Adm; Krista Lohmar, Middle & Lower Sch Adm; Paula Pritchard, PS Adm.

Col Prep. AP—Eng Fr Lat Span Calc Stats Comp_Sci Bio Chem Physics Eur_Hist US_Hist. Feat—British_Lit Creative_Writing Shakespeare Japan Astron Marine_Biol/Sci Meteorology Programming Japan_Hist Psych World_Relig Photog Studio_Art Theater Music.

Adm: 111/yr. Appl due: Rolling. Accepted: 55%. Yield: 75%. Tests ISEE.

Enr 895. Elem 620. Sec 275. Wh 84%. Blk 3%. Asian 8%. Other 5%. Avg class size: 17. Fac 84. M 21/2. F 45/16. Wh 96%. Asian 2%. Other 2%. Adv deg: 53%.

Grad '04—64. Col—64. (IN U 8, Purdue 4, U of St Francis 4, Princeton 3, Vanderbilt 3, Furman 2). Avg SAT: 1250. Avg ACT: 27. Alum 700.

Tui '04-'05: Day $10,125-10,325 (+$780-945). Aid: Merit 10 ($10,000). Need 161 ($749,740).

Endow $6,987,000. Plant val $6,204,000. Bldgs 2. 3 Libs 18,000 vols. Sci labs 2. Comp labs 4. Dark rms 1. Auds 2. Art studios 3. Gyms 2. Fields 3. Courts 2. Tennis courts 5.

Est 1977. Nonprofit. Quar (Aug-June). Assoc CLS NCA.

First opened in the educational wing of Trinity Episcopal Church to students in grades K-6, this school now enrolls students in an early childhood through high school program. Canterbury occupies two campuses: lower and middle school classes (early childhood through grade 8) are held at 5601 Covington Rd., while the high school program (grades 9-12) is conducted at the Smith Road address. The curriculum, which emphasizes academic achievement, features a required fine arts course of study and a competitive athletics program.

Instruction in French, Spanish, computers and the fine arts begins in the primary grades, where small classes provide for individual attention and development. An accelerated middle school program in all major disciplines includes a four-year science program and mathematics through algebra II. Pupils choose either Spanish or French for four years of study in grades 5-8, and they may add Latin or Japanese as an additional language in grades 7 and 8. High school course work focuses upon accelerated college preparation. An Advanced Placement program offers college-level studies in many disciplines.

Students choose from extracurricular activities in such areas as athletics, the fine arts, speech, debate and publications.

HOWE, IN. (44 mi. E of South Bend, IN; 117 mi. E of Chicago, IL) Rural. Pop: 550. Alt: 882 ft.

HOWE MILITARY SCHOOL
Bdg — Coed Gr 5-12

Howe, IN 46746. PO Box 240. Tel: 260-562-2131. Fax: 260-562-3678.
  www.howemilitary.com   E-mail: admissions@howemilitary.com
Duane VanOrden, Supt. BA, Univ of South Florida, MBA, Nova Univ, MA, Ball State Univ, PhD, Nova Univ. **Brent E. Smith, Adm.**
  Col Prep. Milit. AP—Eng Calc. Feat—Creative_Writing Fr Ger Span Environ_Sci Computers Econ Geog Govt Sociol Ethics World_Relig Music Bus Journ Indus_Arts. **Supp**—Makeup Tut.
  Adm: 58/yr. Accepted: 90%. Yield: 50%. **Tests** IQ.
  Enr 186. B 154. G 32. Elem 50. Sec 136. Wh 79%. Hisp 3%. Blk 11%. Am Ind 1%. Asian 4%. Other 2%. Avg class size: 10. Uniform. **Fac 24.** Wh 100%. Adv deg: 70%.
  Grad '04—23. Col—22. (MI St, Loyola U of Chicago, N MI, Defiance, Purdue, Morehouse). Alum 3700.
  Tui '04-'05: Bdg $18,900 (+$3000).
  Summer: Acad Rev Rec. Milit Trng. Tui Bdg $1800-3200. 3-6 wks.
  Endow $24,000,000. Plant val $5,000,000. Bldgs 19. Dorms 5. Class rms 26. Lib 15,000 vols. Labs 4. Auds 1. Music studios 2. Gyms 2. Fields 4. Courts 5. Pools 1. Rifle ranges 1.
  Est 1884. Nonprofit. Episcopal. Sem (Aug-June). **Assoc** CLS NCA.

This school was made possible by a bequest of John Badlam Howe, who provided in his will for the foundation of a school to train young men for the Episcopal priesthood. The military program was instituted in 1895 and, since 1920, Howe has had a high school ROTC unit sponsored by the Department of the Army. Female students were admitted beginning in the fall of 1988.

Howe emphasizes spiritual, intellectual and physical education in a structured environment. The campus houses two separate schools: a junior high school (grades 5-8) and a senior high school (grades 9-12). The junior high provides a standard curriculum consisting of English, reading, mathematics, science and social studies; eighth graders may enroll in an elective class for high school credit. The college preparatory high school course of study includes units from the fields of English, mathematics, science, social studies, foreign language, physical education, health and computer education, supplemented by electives in the fine arts, the industrial arts and business. The mandatory JROTC program provides classroom instruction, physical training, and practice in conducting parades and ceremonies. The military department also sponsors a drill team, a rifle team and an adventure group. Cadets must participate in sports, either organized or intramural, and attendance and participation at worship is a required part of the school program.

See Also Pages 1170-1

INDIANAPOLIS, IN. (109 mi. NNW of Louisville, KY) Urban. Pop: 781,870. Alt: 708 ft.

THE ORCHARD SCHOOL
Day — Coed Gr PS-8

Indianapolis, IN 46260. 615 W 64th St. Tel: 317-251-9253. Fax: 317-254-8454.
  www.orchard.org   E-mail: khein@orchard.org
Joseph P. Marshall, Head. BA, Franklin and Marshall College, MEd, Hofstra Univ. **Kristen J. Hein, Adm.**
  Pre-Prep. Feat—Span Computers Studio_Art Drama Band Chorus Dance Outdoor_Ed. **Supp**—Dev_Read Rem_Math Rem_Read Tut.
  Adm (Gr PS-7): 95/yr. Appl due: Feb. Accepted: 46%. Yield: 32%.
  Enr 614. B 294. G 320. Elem 614. Wh 75%. Hisp 1%. Blk 12%. Asian 4%. Other 8%. Avg class size: 19. **Fac 85.** M 15. F 70. Wh 87%. Blk 7%. Am Ind 2%. Asian 2%. Other 2%. Adv deg: 47%.
  Grad '04—56. Prep—46. (Brebeuf 15, Park Tudor 14, Phillips Exeter 1). Alum 2010.
  Tui '04-'05: Day $11,025-12,320 (+$675-1234). **Aid:** Need 147 ($1,038,095).
  Summer: Acad Enrich Rec. Travel. Tui Day $100-200/wk. 8 wks.
  Endow $46,036,000. Plant val $18,218,000. Bldgs 2. Class rms 51. Lib 18,000 vols. Sci labs 3. Comp labs 2. Dark rms 1. Aquariums 2. Weather stations 1. Theaters 1. Art studios 2. Music studios 3. Dance studios 1. Gyms 2. Fields 4. Tracks 1. Ropes crses 1. Ponds 1.
  Est 1922. Nonprofit. Quar (Aug-May). **Assoc** NCA.

Nine local women established Orchard as a progressive school for 20 children in a frame house located at 5050 N. Meridian St. The present-day school occupies a 45-acre, wooded campus and serves a student body some 30 times larger.

The comprehensive curriculum integrates language arts, social studies, math, music, art, drama, science, foreign language and physical education, as well as technology and outdoor education. Classroom instruction incorporates multiple perspectives and approaches while emphasizing problem solving and critical thinking. Student government, community service and field trips are features of the program. Learning support, speech-language therapy, assessment and evaluation, and school counseling are available.

Orchard conducts an intramural sports program in grades 1-4, in addition to an interscholastic program in the later grades. The school offers extended-day activities both before and after school, in addition to a summer camp.   **See Also Page 1222**

PARK TUDOR SCHOOL
Day — Coed Gr PS-12

Indianapolis, IN 46240. 7200 N College Ave, PO Box 40488. Tel: 317-415-2700. Fax: 317-254-2714.
  www.parktudor.org   E-mail: info@parktudor.org
Douglas S. Jennings, Head. BA, Lafayette College, MA, Montclair State College, MA, Columbia Univ. **David A. Amstutz, Adm.**
  Col Prep. AP—Eng Fr Ger Span Calc Bio Chem US_Hist Art_Hist Music_Theory. **Feat**—Greek Stats Sociol Drama Music_Hist Speech. **Supp**—Dev_Read Tut.
  Adm: 142/yr. Accepted: 55%. **Tests** CTP_4.

Enr 975. B 496. G 479. Elem 572. Sec 403. Wh 83%. Hisp 2%. Blk 7%. Asian 5%. Other 3%. Avg class size: 14. **Fac 128.** M 34/5. F 72/17. Wh 94%. Blk 4%. Asian 1%. Other 1%. Adv deg: 50%.
Grad '04—98. Col—97. (IN U, Duke, Vanderbilt, Purdue, Emory, Wash U). Avg SAT: 1284. Alum 3600.
Tui '04-'05: Day $13,695-14,805 (+$1000). **Aid:** Merit 55 ($386,136). Need 110 ($955,208).
Summer: Acad Enrich Rev Rem Rec. Tui Day $60-600. 1-3 wks.
Endow $78,700,000. Plant val $30,000,000. Bldgs 9. Class rms 57. 4 Libs 38,000 vols. Sci labs 7. Comp labs 9. Sci ctrs 1. Auds 1. Theaters 1. Art studios 2. Music studios 6. Dance studios 1. Gyms 3. Fields 6. Courts 12.
Est 1970. Nonprofit. Quar (Aug-May). **Assoc** CLS NCA.

Park Tudor was established in 1970 from the merger of two long-standing private schools: Tudor Hall School for Girls, founded in 1902, and Park School for Boys, founded in 1914. The present-day school continues the tradition established by its predecessors by offering a liberal arts curriculum, small class size, a support staff of counselors and learning specialists, and fully equipped facilities.

Located on a 52-acre campus, Park Tudor offers a sequential curriculum that provides children with age-appropriate learning experiences grounded in the basics and aimed at college preparation. Advanced courses in English, history, math, foreign languages and the sciences make use of the school's resources, as well as the cultural opportunities of Indianapolis.

The fine arts program offers curricular and extracurricular experiences in drama, vocal and instrumental music, the visual arts and dance. Community service clubs, Model UN, foreign language clubs, competitive academic teams, speech team and publications are among more than 20 other extracurricular options.

The athletic program features physical education and team sports. Park Tudor offers both interscholastic and intramural competition in football, soccer, lacrosse, basketball, baseball, swimming, softball, volleyball, cross-country, tennis, wrestling, track, crew, golf and hockey.

ST. RICHARD'S SCHOOL

Day — Coed Gr PS-8

Indianapolis, IN 46205. 33 E 33rd St. Tel: 317-926-0425. Fax: 317-921-3367.
www.strichardsschool.org   E-mail: kmorris@strichardsschool.org
Stephen B. Harrison, Head. BA, MDiv. **Kim Morris, Adm.**
  Pre-Prep. Feat—Fr Lat Span Computers Relig Studio_Art Music. **Supp—**Tut.
  Adm: 83/yr. Appl due: Dec. Accepted: 60%. **Tests** IQ.
  Enr 369. B 192. G 177. Elem 369. Wh 77%. Hisp 1%. Blk 15%. Asian 5%. Other 2%. Avg class size: 20. **Fac 41.** M 5. F 35/1. Wh 90%. Blk 5%. Other 5%. Adv deg: 39%.
  Grad '04—35. Prep—27. (Brebeuf, Park Tudor). Alum 700.
  Tui '05-'06: Day $11,000-11,500 (+$400).
  Summer: Enrich Rec. Tui Day $150/wk. 9 wks.
  Endow $2,021,000. Plant val $11,300,000. Bldgs 3. Class rms 20. Lib 3500 vols. Sci labs 1. Comp labs 1. Auds 1. Art studios 1. Music studios 2. Gyms 1. Fields 1.
  Est 1960. Nonprofit. Episcopal. Tri (Sept-June). **Assoc** NCA.

Affiliated with Trinity Episcopal Church and founded by Rev. G. Ernest Lynch in honor of St. Richard of Chichester, an English saint and scholar, this school patterned itself after Great Britain's parish day schools. St. Richard's first teachers, who were brought to the US from Britain specifically to teach at the school, imparted a British flavor that remains manifest today.

Technology is an important element of the curriculum: all pupils have access to computers and to one on-site computer lab. French is required from transitional kindergarten through grade 5, while both French and Latin are foreign language options in the later grades. Chapel services are conducted daily. Interscholastic sports are available to students in grade 5 and above; intramural programs begin in grade 1. In the middle school, student government and community service, along with such activities as interest clubs and publications, complement the academic curriculum. Students in grades 6 and 7 attend overnight retreats, and the eighth grade takes an annual graduation trip to Washington, DC, Monticello (VA) and Williamsburg, VA.

SYCAMORE SCHOOL
Day — Coed Gr PS-8

Indianapolis, IN 46260. 1750 W 64th St. Tel: 317-253-5288. Fax: 317-479-3359.
www.sycamoreschool.org   E-mail: skarpicke@sycamoreschool.org

Nyle Kardatzke, Head. BS, Anderson Univ, MA, PhD, Univ of California-Los Angeles. **Susan Karpicke, Adm.**

Pre-Prep. Feat—Humanities Span Computers Studio_Art Music.

Adm: 63/yr. Appl due: Feb. Accepted: 40%. Yield: 30%. **Tests** IQ.

Enr 412. B 200. G 212. Elem 412. Wh 83%. Blk 4%. Asian 6%. Other 7%. Avg class size: 20. **Fac 61.** M 3. F 46/12. Wh 100%. Adv deg: 34%.

Grad '04—37. Prep—19. (Brebeuf 10, Park Tudor 7, Kent Sch-CT 1, Interlochen 1). Alum 411.

Tui '04-'05: Day $10,500 (+$95-790). **Aid:** Need 23 ($128,809).

Summer: Enrich Rec. 1-3 wks.

Endow $284,000. Plant val $6,000,000. Bldgs 1. Class rms 24. Lib 12,000 vols. Sci labs 3. Comp labs 2. Auds 1. Art studios 2. Music studios 2. Gyms 1. Fields 2.

Est 1984. Nonprofit. Tri (Aug-May). **Assoc** NCA.

Founded by area parents and educators to address a community need, Sycamore provides acceleration and enrichment for academically gifted students. The curriculum exhibits greater complexity and depth and maintains a faster learning pace than do programs found in traditional elementary schools. In addition to the core academic subjects, students receive instruction from specialists in art, music, computer science, Spanish and physical education. Children learn through various means, and Sycamore enriches its program with guest speakers and field trips.

Various extracurricular options supplement academics. Lower school children may take part in intramural team sports, while upper school pupils may play on interscholastic teams. The school adheres to a no-cut athletic policy, and students incur a participation fee.

LA PORTE, IN. (24 mi. W of South Bend, IN; 53 mi. ESE of Chicago, IL) Urban. Pop: 21,621. Alt: 812 ft.

LA LUMIERE SCHOOL
Bdg and Day — Coed Gr 9-PG

La Porte, IN 46350. 6801 N Wilhelm Rd. Tel: 219-326-7450. **Fax: 219-325-3185.**
www.lalumiere.org   E-mail: admissions@lalumiere.org
Michael Kennedy, Head. BA, Boston College, MS, Univ of Notre Dame. **Melissa Machaj, Adm.**

Col Prep. AP—Eng Fr Span Calc Physics US_Hist. **Feat**—Computers Theol Studio_Art. **Supp**—ESL Rev Tut.

Adm (Gr 9-12): 57/yr. Bdg 32. Day 25. Appl due: Mar. Accepted: 70%. Yield: 69%. **Tests** CEEB SSAT TOEFL.

Enr 119. B 31/35. G 26/27. Sec 119. Wh 69%. Hisp 3%. Blk 5%. Asian 13%. Other 10%. Avg class size: 12. Uniform. **Fac 16.** M 9. F 7. Wh 93%. Blk 7%. Adv deg: 31%. In dorms 6.

Grad '04—27. Col—27. (IN U 2, U of S IN 2, Ball St 2, DePauw 1, DePaul 1, Hope 1). Avg SAT: 1135. Avg ACT: 24. Alum 950.

Tui '04-'05: Bdg $20,550 (+$500). **Day $6608** (+$500). **Aid:** Merit 9 ($5000). Need 21 ($119,440).

Endow $1,000,000. Plant val $5,000,000. Bldgs 12. Dorms 5. Class rms 16. Lib 9000 vols. Sci labs 2. Lang labs 2. Comp labs 1. Theaters 1. Art studios 1. Music studios 1. Gyms 2. Fields 3. Courts 2. Ropes crses 1. Lakes 1.

Est 1963. Nonprofit. Roman Catholic. Sem (Aug-May). **Assoc** NCA.

Founded by Catholic families, La Lumiere provides a rigorous college preparatory education for students from a rich diversity of backgrounds who enroll from various states and foreign countries. The wooded, 155-acre campus lies 60 miles southeast of Chicago, IL, thus enabling pupils to make use of that city's scholastic and cultural facilities.

Course work emphasizes critical thinking and the mastery of verbal and writing skills. Foreign language, art, ethics, computer science and theology classes, as well as a range of electives, supplement the core curriculum. Advanced Placement courses are also available. All students participate in three athletic seasons; options include soccer, volleyball, football, basketball, tennis, baseball and track.

SOUTH BEND, IN. (74 mi. E of Chicago, IL) Urban. Pop: 107,789. Alt: 726 ft.

STANLEY CLARK SCHOOL
Day — Coed Gr PS-8

South Bend, IN 46614. 3123 Miami St. Tel: 574-291-4200. Fax: 574-299-4170.
www.stanleyclark.org   E-mail: rdouglass@stanleyclark.org
Robert G. Douglass, Head. BA, MA, Univ of Bridgeport. **Barbara T. Beach, Adm.**

Pre-Prep. Feat—Mythology Fr Lat Span Computers Studio_Art Drama Music. **Supp**—Dev_Read Rem_Math Rem_Read Rev Tut.

Adm: 67/yr. Appl due: Rolling. Accepted: 69%. **Tests** IQ.
Enr 424. B 209. G 215. Elem 424. Wh 83%. Hisp 2%. Blk 3%. Asian 6%. Other 6%. Avg class size: 20. **Fac 45.** M 9. F 30/6. Wh 100%. Adv deg: 46%.
Grad '04—39. Prep—13. (Marian Catholic, Culver). Alum 1451.
Tui '03-'04: Day $6560-9690 (+$50-350). **Aid:** Merit 10 ($1500). Need 71 ($359,925).
Summer: Enrich Rec. Tui Day $130-250. 6 wks.
Endow $2,394,000. Plant val $3,964,000. Bldgs 3. Class rms 35. Lib 10,000 vols. Sci labs 2. Comp labs 4. Art studios 2. Music studios 2. Dance studios 1. Gyms 3. Fields 2.
Est 1958. Nonprofit. Tri (Aug-June). **Assoc** NCA.

This school for boys and girls of above-average to superior intelligence strives to provide each student with the solid foundation necessary for educational achievement. A program in computer science is available, and foreign languages are offered beginning in kindergarten. The fine arts, physical education and an enrichment center supplement academic offerings.

MICHIGAN

ANN ARBOR, MI. (36 mi. WSW of Detroit, MI) Urban. Pop: 114,024. Alt: 840 ft.

GREENHILLS SCHOOL
Day — Coed Gr 6-12

Ann Arbor, MI 48105. 850 Greenhills Dr. Tel: 734-769-4010. Fax: 734-769-5029.
  www.greenhillsschool.org   E-mail: admission@greenhillsschool.org
Peter B. Fayroian, Head. BA, Univ of Vermont, MA, Middlebury College. **Melvin Rhoden, Adm.**

Col Prep. AP—Eng Fr Lat Span Calc Stats Bio Chem Physics Eur_Hist US_Hist Econ US_Govt & Pol. **Feat**—Creative_Writing World_Lit Astron Computers African-Amer_Hist Middle_Eastern_Stud Chin_Stud Ceramics Fine_Arts Photog Studio_Art Theater Chorus Orchestra Jazz_Band.

Adm: 113/yr. Appl due: Rolling. **Tests** SSAT.

Enr 496. B 231. G 265. Elem 209. Sec 287. Wh 82%. Hisp 1%. Blk 5%. Asian 7%. Other 5%. Avg class size: 15. **Fac 68.** M 19/13. F 23/13. Wh 92%. Hisp 1%. Blk 6%. Asian 1%. Adv deg: 70%.

Grad '04—74. Col—71. (U of MI, Wesleyan U, Cornell, Brown, Wash U, Northwestern). Avg SAT: 1297. Avg ACT: 28. Alum 1552.

Tui '04-'05: Day $14,670 (+$450). **Aid:** Need 76 ($674,311).

Summer: Acad Enrich Rec. Tui Day $200. 1 wk.

Endow $4,650,000. Plant val $17,000,000. Bldgs 1. Class rms 51. Lib 15,901 vols. Sci labs 4. Comp labs 2. Theaters 1. Art studios 1. Music studios 2. Dance studios 1. Gyms 2. Fields 4. Courts 8. Tracks 1.

Est 1968. Nonprofit. Sem (Sept-June). **Assoc** CLS NCA.

Located on a wooded, 30-acre campus, Greenhills offers a traditional liberal arts program designed to prepare students for college. Emphasis is on the development of critical thinking and communicational skills, as well as creative expression. The program accommodates a broad range of students and includes advanced courses and off-campus field trips.

Cocurricular programs and social, cultural and athletic activities are also available. The athletic program includes varsity sports for boys and girls. School publications, photography, debate and dramatics are among the other activities. Graduates enter competitive colleges throughout the country.

MI   *Leading Private Schools*   592

BLOOMFIELD HILLS, MI. (15 mi. NNW of Detroit, MI) Suburban.
Pop: 3940. Alt: 850 ft.

ACADEMY OF THE SACRED HEART
Day — Boys Gr PS-8, Girls PS-12
(Coord — Day 5-8)

Bloomfield Hills, MI 48304. 1250 Kensington Rd. Tel: 248-646-8900. Fax: 248-646-4143.
www.ashmi.org   E-mail: admissions@ashmi.org

Sr. **Bridget Bearss, RSCJ, Head.** BA, Maryville College, MA, Washington Univ. **Barbara Lopiccolo, Adm.**

Col Prep. AP—Eng Calc Eur_Hist US_Hist Studio_Art. **Feat**—World_Lit Fr Lat Span Comp_Sci Theol Drama Music. **Supp**—Rev Tut.

Adm (Gr PS-11): 95/yr. Appl due: Rolling. Accepted: 90%. Yield: 65%. **Tests** HSPT Stanford.

Enr 520. B 130. G 390. Elem 388. Sec 132. Wh 82%. Hisp 1%. Blk 10%. Asian 3%. Other 4%. Avg class size: 12. Uniform. **Fac** 69. M 6/3. F 48/12. Wh 94%. Hisp 1%. Blk 2%. Asian 3%. Adv deg: 43%.

Grad '04—23. **Col**—23. (U of MI, MI St, Syracuse, Fordham, Hope, Oakland U). Avg SAT: 1160. Avg ACT: 24. Alum 1423.

Tui '04-'05: Day $14,000-15,990 (+$400-500). **Aid:** Merit 5 ($6000). Need 80 ($705,520).

Summer: Acad Enrich Rec. Tui Day $185/wk. 6 wks.

Endow $3,296,000. Plant val $12,841,000. Bldgs 1. Class rms 60. 2 Libs 16,200 vols. Sci labs 4. Lang labs 1. Comp labs 3. Reading labs 1. Auds 1. Theaters 1. Art studios 5. Music studios 1. Dance studios 1. Photog studios 1. Gyms 2. Fields 3. Courts 8.

Est 1851. Nonprofit. Roman Catholic. Quar (Aug-June). **Assoc** NCA.

The school moved to its present, 44-acre campus in 1958, over a century after the founding date. The curriculum, which is highly individualized in the coeducational early grades (grades PS-4), emphasizes college preparation throughout. Boys and girls learn in single-gender settings during the middle school years (grades 5-8). Girls in the upper school (grades 9-12) choose from independent study and Advanced Placement options in a variety of subjects.

A range of sports and activities, including community service, is available. As part of an international network of schools, Sacred Heart provides students with the opportunity to participate in exchanges abroad or within the United States.

CRANBROOK SCHOOLS
Bdg — Coed Gr 9-12; Day — Coed PS-12
(Coord — Day 6-8)

Bloomfield Hills, MI 48303. PO Box 801. Tel: 248-645-3610. Fax: 248-645-3025.
www.schools.cranbrook.edu   E-mail: admission@cranbrook.edu

Arlyce M. Seibert, Dir. AB, Univ of Detroit, MAT, Oakland Univ. **Drew Miller, Adm.**

Col Prep. Feat—Humanities Ger Lat Stats Astron Botany Genetics Comp_Design Comp_Sci Econ Geog Philos Relig Photog Studio_Art Ceramics Weaving Drama Theater_Arts Music Dance Public_Speak Metal_Shop Wilderness_Ed. **Supp**—ESL Tut.

Adm (Bdg Gr 9-11; Day PS-11): 286/yr. Bdg 96. Day 190. Appl due: Feb. Accepted: 31%. **Tests** CTP_4 IQ SSAT TOEFL.

Enr 1608. Elem 838. Sec 770. Wh 69%. Hisp 1%. Blk 6%. Asian 6%. Other 18%. Avg class size: 16. **Fac 220.** M 109. F 111. In dorms 15.
Grad '04—180. Col—178. (U of MI, MI St, Yale, Northwestern, Emory, Miami U-OH). Avg SAT: 1270. Avg ACT: 27. Alum 9620.
Tui '04-'05: Bdg $29,290 (+$1200). **Day $20,940** (+$600). **Aid:** Merit 7 ($162,000). Need 335 ($4,000,000).
Endow $150,000,000. Plant val $150,000,000. Bldgs 21. Dorms 5. Dorm rms 214. Class rms 120. 7 Libs 100,000 vols. Sci labs 12. Lang labs 2. Theaters 2. Art studios 8. Music studios 13. Gyms 4. Fields 17. Courts 15. Pools 1. Rinks 1. Lakes 1.
Est 1922. Nonprofit. Sem (Sept-June). **Assoc** CLS NCA.

Founded by Mr. and Mrs. George G. Booth as part of the Cranbrook Educational Community, the Cranbrook and Kingswood campuses were designed by the Finnish architect Eliel Saarinen. Within walking distance of one another, the campuses are a part of a 325-acre estate of woods, lakes and rolling hills.

Cranbrook School for boys and Kingswood School for girls were united to form one school in 1984, although coordinated classes had been conducted since 1971. The school consists of one coeducational upper school (grades 9-12), a middle school with separate programs for boys and girls (grades 6-8) and Brookside School, the coeducational elementary division (grades pre-K-5).

From its opening, Cranbrook Schools has enrolled students from throughout the US and from other countries. Affiliation with Cranbrook Institute of Science and Cranbrook Academy of Art and Museum enriches the academic and cultural life of the school. Freshmen may combine their English, history and religion classes through an interdisciplinary program. Other distinctive features are the Tennessee Wilderness Expedition for sophomores, Senior May during the spring term, and Advanced Placement preparation in 15 test areas. In addition, juniors may study in England for a semester. Elective courses are available in all departments.

Activities include dramatics, music, film, dance, and many interest clubs and publications, as well as social, special academic and student affairs events. Among intramural and interscholastic athletics are football, field hockey, soccer, cross-country, basketball, ice hockey, volleyball, skiing, swimming, baseball, softball, tennis, lacrosse, track, crew and fencing.

Brookside enrolls students in grades pre-K-5. The traditional academic curriculum is augmented by a strong emphasis on the arts and physical education, as well as by enrichment programs not generally offered in other schools. Included are the science, library, visual studies and drama programs; reading enrichment; and Orff-Schulwerk, instrumental and strings music programs. Computer studies are integrated into the classroom curriculum. Authors, illustrators and performing groups visit the school throughout the year. Students are encouraged in personal growth and individual expression, sound study habits and a respect for learning.

Small class size, a nurturing environment and a talented, dedicated faculty are the cornerstones of the school. Most students progress to the Cranbrook Kingswood Middle School, where the gender-specific academic program continues the traditional academic curriculum with special emphasis on the basics of writing and mathematics. **See Also Pages 1136-7**

THE ROEPER SCHOOL
Day — Coed Gr PS-12

Bloomfield Hills, MI 48303. 41190 Woodward Ave, PO Box 329. Tel: 248-203-7300. Fax: 248-203-7310.
www.roeper.org   E-mail: admissions@roeper.org

Randall Dunn, Head. BA, Brown Univ, MA, Harvard Univ. **Lori Zinser, Adm.**

Col Prep. AP—Eng Fr Lat Span Calc Stats Bio Physics Eur_Hist Comp_Govt & Pol Art_Hist Music_Theory. **Feat**—Shakespeare Satire African-Amer_Lit Greek Bioethics Comp_Sci Web_Design Civil_War Econ Comp_Relig Philos Drawing Studio_Art Theater Dance Journ.

Adm: 113/yr. Appl due: Rolling. Accepted: 52%. **Tests** IQ.

Enr 627. B 346. G 281. Elem 440. Sec 187. Wh 75%. Hisp 1%. Blk 11%. Asian 3%. Other 10%. Avg class size: 11. **Fac 90.** M 10/3. F 58/19. Adv deg: 40%.

Grad '04—42. Col—37. (U of MI, MI St, Oakland U, Albion, Northwestern, Kalamazoo). Avg SAT: 1250. Avg ACT: 26. Alum 1083.

Tui '04-'05: Day $12,700-17,300. Aid: Need 132 ($1,012,700).

Summer: Enrich Rec. Tui Day $460/2-wk ses. 8 wks. Theater. Tui Day $665/3-wk ses. 6 wks.

Endow $3,176,000. Plant val $1,800,000. Bldgs 11. Class rms 43. Lib 10,000 vols. Sci labs 6. Comp labs 3. Art studios 2. Music studios 3. Fields 2. Pools 1.

Est 1941. Nonprofit. Sem (Sept-June). **Assoc** NCA.

The school was founded by Annemarie and George Roeper, noted German educators who immigrated to the US during World War II, and in 1956 it became a pioneer by structuring its programs for gifted children. The open classroom approach is utilized in the lower school, and stress is placed on a humanistic education at all grade levels. The expansion to a complete high school program was completed in 1969. George A. Roeper retired as headmaster of the upper school in 1979, and Annemarie Roeper retired as head of the lower school the following year.

Roeper admits students with outstanding ability and seeks enrollment from a wide variety of geographical, social and economic backgrounds. An extensive selection of course offerings and electives meets the diverse needs of gifted students. Admission is based on tests, interviews and teacher evaluations. Students in the middle school (grades 6-8) and the upper school (grades 9-12) attend Roeper's campus in Birmingham (1051 Oakland Ave., 48009). **See Also Page 1237**

DETROIT, MI. Urban. Pop: 951,270. Alt: 579 ft. Area also includes Beverly Hills, Grosse Point Farms and Grosse Point Woods.

DETROIT COUNTRY DAY SCHOOL
Bdg — Coed Gr 8-12; Day — Coed PS-12

Beverly Hills, MI 48025. 22305 W 13 Mile Rd. Tel: 248-646-7717. Fax: 248-203-2184.
www.dcds.edu   E-mail: jprosperi@dcds.edu

Gerald T. Hansen, Head. BA, Northern Michigan Univ, MA, Rutgers Univ. **Jorge Dante Hernandez Prosperi, Adm.**

Col Prep. IB Diploma. AP—Calc Stats Bio Chem Physics Eur_Hist US_Govt & Pol Studio_Art. **Feat**—Humanities Fr Japan Lat Span Anat & Physiol Astron Ecol Genetics Oceanog Programming Civil_War Econ African-Amer_Stud Photog Sculpt Music.

Supp—Tut.
Adm: 215/yr. Appl due: Rolling. **Tests** IQ ISEE Stanford.
Enr 1536. B 3/809. G 3/721. Avg class size: 15. Uniform. **Fac 181.** M 53. F 128. Adv deg: 61%.
Grad '04—134. Col—134. (U of MI, MI St, Princeton, Johns Hopkins, Columbia, Harvard). Avg SAT: 1308. Avg ACT: 27. Alum 3000.
Tui '04-'05: Bdg $29,250. Day $14,470-20,690. Aid: Need 123 ($2,600,000).
Summer: Acad Enrich Rev Rec. 1-5 wks.
Endow $9,000,000. Plant val $30,377,000. Bldgs 9. Class rms 115. 4 Libs 25,000 vols. Sci labs 14. Lang labs 2. Comp labs 5. Art studios 8. Music studios 6. Perf arts ctrs 1. Gyms 4. Fields 8. Courts 10.
Est 1914. Nonprofit. Tri (Sept-June). **Assoc** CLS NCA.

Since its establishment, DCDS has emphasized sound scholarship, a natural, caring atmosphere, and a program comfortably filled with activities. Detroit Country Day opened its Maple Road campus in 1986.

The school maintains four campuses: the lower school (grades pre-K-2), the junior school (grades 3-5), the middle school (grades 6-8), and the upper school (grades 9-12). A limited cottage boarding program allows a few students in grades 8-12 to reside on campus with faculty families. Country Day's computer-based learning program requires all middle and upper school pupils to employ laptops for class exercises, homework, tests and research. Qualified students may enter the two-year International Baccalaureate program beginning in grade 11. A cultural enrichment program is also available.

Extracurricular activities are an integral aspect of school life. In all school divisions, students may participate in musical organizations, enrichment and interest clubs, and athletics. Sports include football, soccer, baseball, basketball, cross-country, track, field hockey, ice hockey, lacrosse, tennis, softball, swimming and wrestling. **See Also Pages 1142-3**

GROSSE POINTE ACADEMY
Day — Coed Gr PS-8

Grosse Pointe Farms, MI 48236. 171 Lake Shore Rd. Tel: 313-886-1221.
Fax: 313-886-2904.
www.gpacademy.org E-mail: mmcdermott@gpacademy.org
Phil Demartini, Jr., Head. BA, Columbia Univ, MEd, Fordham Univ. **Molly McDermott, Adm.**
Pre-Prep. Feat—Fr Span Environ_Sci Relig Studio_Art Music.
Adm: 76/yr. **Tests** CTP_4.
Enr 365. Elem 365. Wh 86%. Blk 14%. Avg class size: 15. Uniform. **Fac 48.** M 5/1. F 33/9. Adv deg: 22%.
Grad '04—31. Prep—31. (U Liggett). Alum 1459.
Tui '04-'05: Day $11,800-14,400 (+$500).
Summer: Enrich. Sports. 8 wks.
Endow $7,500,000. Plant val $10,000,000. Bldgs 7. Class rms 33. Lib 7200 vols. Sci labs 2. Comp labs 1. Auds 1. Art studios 2. Music studios 1. Gyms 1. Fields 3. Courts 4. Field houses 1.
Est 1885. Nonprofit. Sem (Sept-June). **Assoc** NCA.

Founded as the Academy of the Sacred Heart and originally operated by the Society of the Sacred Heart, GPA assumed its present name and nondenominational status in 1969. A Montessori early school program, the oldest of its kind in Michigan, serves children ages 2½-5. The school's pre-preparatory curriculum stresses basic skills development and features French and Spanish, art, environmental science, music and religion courses. Various electives are also available.

Located on a 20-acre campus overlooking Lake St. Clair, the academy supplements in-class instruction with museum visits, a day-long on-site biology class, and a multi-day trip to Washington, DC. Eighth graders complete a research project in art, literature, journalism or science. **See Also Page 1156**

UNIVERSITY LIGGETT SCHOOL
Day — Coed Gr PS-12

Grosse Pointe Woods, MI 48236. 1045 Cook Rd. Tel: 313-884-4444. Fax: 313-884-1775. www.uls.org   E-mail: mbarnes@uls.org

Matthew H. Hanly, Head. AB, Bowdoin College, MEd, Harvard Univ. Patrick Roberts, Adm.
  Col Prep. AP—Eng Fr Lat Calc Bio Chem Physics US_Hist World_Hist Studio_Art Music_Theory. Feat—British_Lit Greek Stats Environ_Sci Ceramics Drawing Photog Drama Band Chorus. Supp—Tut.

Adm: 92/yr. Appl due: Rolling. Accepted: 60%. Yield: 91%. Tests CTP_4 SSAT.

Enr 659. B 325. G 334. Elem 422. Sec 237. Wh 76%. Hisp 2%. Blk 11%. Asian 5%. Other 6%. Avg class size: 14. Fac 90. M 31. F 59. Wh 95%. Hisp 3%. Blk 2%. Adv deg: 70%.

Grad '04—61. Col—61. (MI St 9, U of MI 7, Wayne St 5, Albion 3, Kalamazoo 3, Loyola U of Chicago 3). Avg SAT: 1197. Alum 4000.

Tui '04-'05: Day $10,600-17,000 (+$300). Aid: Merit 60 ($123,500). Need 137 ($989,540).

Summer: Acad Enrich Rev. 6 wks.

Endow $32,000,000. Plant val $30,000,000. Bldgs 5. Class rms 87. 3 Libs 24,000 vols. Sci labs 8. Comp labs 4. Auds 3. Art studios 4. Music studios 4. Dance studios 1. Gyms 3. Fields 9. Courts 11. Pools 2. Rinks 1.

Est 1878. Nonprofit. (Sept-June). Assoc CLS NCA.

ULS came into being when the Liggett School and Grosse Pointe University School merged in 1969. The Liggett School, founded by Rev. James D. Liggett in 1878, was the oldest independent school in Michigan. The Grosse Pointe University School was the result of a 1954 consolidation of the Detroit University School and the Grosse Pointe Country Day School.

The present school occupies two campuses: The primary (prekindergarten and kindergarten), lower (grades 1-5) and upper (grades 9-12) schools are situated on a 40-acre site on Cook Road, while the middle school (grades 6-8) is located on a 15-acre campus at 850 Briarcliff Dr. While most pupils are from the Grosse Pointes, a significant number come from Detroit, elsewhere in southeastern Michigan, or Canada.

The curriculum provides honors and Advanced Placement courses in all fields and also meets the needs of the average student. Participation in athletics and the creative and performing arts is required. Electives encompass the history of the Vietnam War, geology, computer science, and a wide range of music, art and sports offerings. A semester in Switzerland is available to sophomores. Graduates enter leading colleges throughout the country.

GLEN ARBOR, MI. (135 mi. N of Grand Rapids, MI; 161 mi. NE of Milwaukee, WI) Rural. Pop: 788. Alt: 591 ft.

LEELANAU SCHOOL
Bdg and Day — Coed Gr 9-12

Glen Arbor, MI 49636. 1 Old Homestead Rd. Tel: 231-334-5800. Fax: 231-334-5898.
www.leelanau.org   E-mail: admissions@leelanau.org
Richard F. Odell, Pres. BMus, Heidelberg College, MA, Bowling Green State Univ. **Heather M. Sack,** Adm.
  Col Prep. LD. Underachiever. Feat—Fr Ger Span Astron Ecol Drawing Studio_Art Drama Music Bus Journ. Supp—Dev_Read ESL Tut.
  Adm: 20/yr. Bdg 19. Day 1. Appl due: Rolling. Accepted: 80%. **Tests** SSAT TOEFL.
  Enr 60. B 38/3. G 18/1. Sec 60. Wh 71%. Blk 9%. Asian 20%. Avg class size: 8. Fac 16. M 7/2. F 6/1. Wh 100%. Adv deg: 43%. In dorms 5.
  Grad '04—16. Col—16. (U of Tampa 3, U of MI 2, U of IL-Urbana 1, MI St 1, Sch of the Art Inst of Chicago 1, U of Tulsa 1). Alum 1650.
  Tui '04-'05: Bdg **$27,575** (+$1500). **5-Day Bdg $20,680** (+$1500). **Day $14,615** (+$500). Aid: Merit 2 ($1000). Need 24 ($289,679).
  Summer: Acad Enrich. Tui Bdg $4895. Tui Day $2825. 5 wks. Writing. Tui Bdg $1650. 2 wks.
  Endow $400,000. Plant val $5,000,000. Bldgs 13. Dorms 5. Dorm rms 48. Class rms 13. Lib 10,000 vols. Labs 2. Observatories 1. Auds 1. Art studios 3. Music studios 1. Gyms 1. Fields 3. Courts 4. Weight rms 1. Greenhouses 1.
  Est 1929. Nonprofit. Sem (Aug-May). **Assoc** NCA.

The school is located on the Crystal River, within the 72,000-acre Sleeping Bear Dunes National Park on the western shore of Lake Michigan. Leelanau is an experientially based college preparatory school that serves students with learning differences. Parents may track their children's progress through updates that are available every 72 hours.

Leelanau's multisensory approach utilizes an integrated curriculum. Within the humanities department, for example, instructors place emphasis on the historical timelines and events that correlate with the literature of the time; in a similar fashion, math and science course work enables boys and girls to study the relationship between mathematical models and scientific principals.

Recreational and competitive sports, opportunities in the arts and community service options complement the curriculum.

INTERLOCHEN, MI. (116 mi. N of Grand Rapids, MI; 155 mi. NE of Milwaukee, WI) Rural. Pop: 150. Alt: 849 ft.

INTERLOCHEN ARTS ACADEMY
Bdg and Day — Coed Gr 9-PG

Interlochen, MI 49643. PO Box 199. Tel: 231-276-7472. Fax: 231-276-7464.
www.interlochen.org   E-mail: admissions@interlochen.org
Jeffrey S. Kimpton, Pres. BA, MA Univ of Illinois. **Amy N. Packard,** Adm.

Col Prep. Perform_Arts Visual_Arts. AP—Calc Stats Physics. **Feat**—Creative_Writing Fr Ger Span Anat Ecol Geol Computers Pol_Sci Music. **Supp**—Dev_Read ESL Makeup Tut.

Adm: 251/yr. Appl due: Feb. Accepted: 58%.

Enr 455. B 162/15. G 259/19. Sec 438. PG 17. Wh 78%. Hisp 1%. Blk 4%. Asian 17%. Avg class size: 12. Uniform. **Fac 77.** M 47. F 30. Adv deg: 77%.

Grad '04—186. Col—164. (U of MI, U of Rochester, Oberlin, Juilliard, Manhattan Sch of Music, Johns Hopkins). Avg SAT: 1179. Avg ACT: 24.

Tui '03-'04: Bdg $28,900-30,100 (+$1100-5000). **Day $17,700-18,900** (+$1100-5000). **Aid:** Need 319 ($4,600,000).

Summer: Ages 8-18. Rec. Visual Arts. Music. Theater. Creative Writing. Dance. Tui Bdg $3328-4998. 4-8 wks.

Endow $22,000,000. Plant val $26,200,000. Bldgs 25. Dorms 5. Dorm rms 246. Class rms 55. 2 Libs 21,000 vols. Labs 12. Lang labs 1. Theaters 4. Art studios 5. Music studios 29. Fields 1. Courts 2.

Est 1961. Nonprofit. Sem (Sept-May). **Assoc** NCA.

Interlochen was founded by Dr. Joseph E. Maddy as an outgrowth of the National Music Camp, now known as Interlochen Arts Camp. The 1200-acre, wooded campus hugs the shores of two northern Michigan glacial lakes, and encompasses both rivers and fields. The academy provides preprofessional arts training together with a rigorous college preparatory education.

Students major in creative writing, dance, music, theater arts or visual arts. A variety of offerings in English and literature, English as a Second Language, world languages, history and political science, science, mathematics, and physical and health education is available. Students are regularly exposed to a wide range of talent in their fields, as visiting artist-instructors hold master classes at the academy. Off-campus performance tours in the different arts divisions are an integral part of the curriculum.

Movies, theatrical performances, coffeehouses, dances, art exhibits, orchestra, band and small-ensemble concerts, readings, recitals and jam sessions are some of the regularly scheduled on-campus activities. In addition, each weekday evening, the academy provides organized physical recreation. Boarding students fulfill several hours weekly of community service on campus; work responsibilities may include food service, residence hall desk duty, tech crew, recycling crew, mail delivery or academic tutoring.

Graduates are admitted to the most selective colleges and conservatories in the nation and, while many continue studying in their arts specialty, others pursue varied careers unrelated to the arts.

OXFORD, MI. (31 mi. NNW of Detroit, MI) Suburban. Pop: 3540. Alt: 1062 ft.

KINGSBURY SCHOOL

Day — Coed Gr PS-8

Oxford, MI 48370. 5000 Hosner Rd. Tel: 248-628-2571. Fax: 248-628-3612.
  www.kingsburyschool.org   E-mail: adibble@kingsburyschool.org
Gil Webb, Head. BS, Pennsylvania State Univ, MA, EdM, Columbia Univ. **Audrey Smith-**

Dibble, Adm.
Pre-Prep. Feat—Span Environ_Sci Computers Studio_Art Drama Music.
Adm: 35/yr. Appl due: Mar.
Enr 132. B 67. G 65. Elem 132. Wh 93%. Asian 2%. Other 5%. Avg class size: 14. **Fac 18.** M 3. F 15. Wh 95%. Asian 5%. Adv deg: 16%.
Grad '04—17. Prep—14. (Notre Dame Prep-MI, Br Rice, Roeper, Cranbrook). Alum 447.
Tui '05-'06: Day $9500-11,000. Aid: Merit 1 ($4975). Need 8 ($30,350).
Summer: Enrich Rec. Tui Day $180/wk. 3 wks.
Endow $1,200,000. Plant val $5,000,000. Bldgs 3. Class rms 16. Lib 6400 vols. Sci labs 1. Lang labs 1. Comp labs 1. Art studios 1. Music studios 1. Gyms 1. Fields 2.
Est 1953. Nonprofit. Quar (Sept-June). **Assoc** NCA.

In the early grades, Kingsbury's developmentally oriented curriculum emphasizes basic academic skills. The middle school program (grades 6-8) provides broader curricular choices in the form of electives. At all grade levels, pupils utilize computers in the classroom and the computer lab. The athletic program features an all-school skiing program, as well as interscholastic and intramural sports for older students.

The school's 125-acre, rural campus serves as a natural setting of woods, fields, ponds, wetlands and trails for the environmental studies program.

OHIO

AKRON, OH. (29 mi. SSE of Cleveland, OH) Urban. Pop: 217,074. Alt: 873 ft. Area also includes Bath.

OLD TRAIL SCHOOL
Day — Coed Gr PS-8

Bath, OH 44210. 2315 Ira Rd, PO Box 827. Tel: 330-666-1118. Fax: 330-666-2187.
www.oldtrail.org   E-mail: jbrookhart@oldtrail.org

John S. Farber, Head. BA, Trinity Univ, MA, Antioch Univ. **Judy Brookhart, Adm.**

  Pre-Prep. Gen Acad. Feat—Fr Lat Span Computers Studio_Art Theater_Arts Music. Supp—Dev_Read Rem_Math Rem_Read Rev Tut.

  Adm: 81/yr. Appl due: Rolling. Accepted: 62%. Yield: 75%. **Tests** ISEE MRT.

  Enr 539. B 245. G 294. Elem 539. Wh 84%. Blk 5%. Asian 6%. Other 5%. Avg class size: 18. **Fac 64.** M 7/4. F 49/4. Wh 100%. Adv deg: 73%.

  Grad '04—55. Prep—48. (Western Reserve, Walsh, U Sch-OH, Laurel, Archbishop Hoban, Hathaway Brown). Alum 1550.

  Tui '04-'05: Day $9000-12,750. Aid: Need 80 ($450,000).

  Summer: Acad Enrich Rev Rec. Tui Day $110/wk. 7 wks.

  Endow $1,600,000. Plant val $9,000,000. Bldgs 5. Class rms 42. Lib 11,500 vols. Sci labs 2. Comp labs 2. Auds 1. Art studios 4. Music studios 2. Gyms 1. Fields 3. Courts 3. Pools 1.

  Est 1920. Nonprofit. Quar (Aug-June). **Assoc** NCA.

From a girls' community primary school has grown this modern, coeducational country day school. The school moved to its present, 60-acre campus in 1967 and is now within the environs of the Cuyahoga Valley National Park. French language instruction begins in the preschool, while both Spanish and Latin are available in grades 7 and 8. The school serves Akron and Cleveland suburbs.

CANTON, OH. (49 mi. SSE of Cleveland, OH) Urban. Pop: 80,806. Alt: 1052 ft.

CANTON COUNTRY DAY SCHOOL
Day — Coed Gr PS-8

Canton, OH 44718. 3000 Demington Ave NW. Tel: 330-453-8279. Fax: 330-453-6038.
www.ccd-school.org   E-mail: office@ccd-school.org

Pamela Shaw, Head. BA, Providence College, MEd, Boston Univ. **R. Paul Monks, Adm.**

  Pre-Prep. Feat—Fr Computers Econ Govt Studio_Art Music Dance Movement. Supp—Tut.

  Adm: 54/yr. Appl due: Rolling. Accepted: 80%. **Tests** IQ ISEE.

  Enr 281. Elem 281. Wh 87%. Blk 8%. Asian 4%. Other 1%. Avg class size: 14. **Fac 29.** M 4/1. F 19/5. Adv deg: 37%.

  Grad '04—17. Prep—7. (Western Reserve, Rectory, Hathaway Brown). Alum 456.

Tui '03-'04: Day $8200-9720. **Aid:** Need ($400,000).
Summer: Enrich. 1-2 wks.
Endow $3,500,000. Plant val $7,500,000. Bldgs 1. Class rms 27. Libs 1. Sci labs 2. Comp labs 2. Art studios 2. Music studios 2. Gyms 1. Fields 2.
Est 1964. Nonprofit. Tri (Aug-June). **Assoc** NCA.

As part of the school's elementary curriculum, CCDS students develop a solid foundation in the fine arts, and children at all grade levels study French. In addition to a variety of local and regional field trips, the program features educational trips in the middle school (grades 5-8) that include visits to Williamsburg, VA, and Washington, DC, and an outdoor experience at Nature's Classroom. Boys and girls in grades 7 and 8 have the opportunity to participate in interscholastic sports, as well as in student government and a student-produced yearbook. Community service programs are also available.

CINCINNATI, OH. (92 mi. NE of Louisville, KY; 98 mi. ESE of Indianapolis, IN) Urban. Pop: 331,285. Alt: 490 ft. Area also includes Glendale.

BETHANY SCHOOL

Day — Coed Gr K-8

Glendale, OH 45246. 495 Albion Ave. Tel: 513-771-7462. Fax: 513-771-2292.
www.bethanyschool.org   E-mail: pez@bethanyschool.org
Cheryl L. Pez, Head. BS, MEd, Miami Univ (OH). Jean Macejko, Adm.
   Pre-Prep. Feat—Span Environ_Sci Computers Relig Drawing Photog Studio_Art Dance Yoga. **Supp**—Dev_Read Rem_Read Tut.
   Adm: $50/yr. Appl due: Rolling. **Tests** IQ Stanford.
   Enr 254. B 125. G 129. Elem 254. Wh 60%. Hisp 1%. Blk 28%. Asian 11%. Avg class size: 15. Uniform. **Fac 34.** M 5/1. F 21/7. Wh 89%. Hisp 8%. Asian 3%. Adv deg: 38%.
   Grad '04—30. Prep—28. (Ursuline Acad-OH, Summit Co Day, Cincinnati Hills Christian).
   Tui '04-'05: Day $6950 (+$390-470). **Aid:** Need 26 ($130,200).
   Summer: Acad Enrich. Tui Day $200. 1 wk.
   Bldgs 7. Class rms 23. Libs 1. Comp labs 2. Auds 1. Art studios 1. Music studios 1. Gyms 1. Fields 1.
   Est 1898. Nonprofit. Episcopal. Quar (Aug-June).

Located on 15 wooded acres in the suburban village of Glendale, Bethany provides a challenging academic program for boys and girls from Cincinnati who plan on attending college. The school was established by the Episcopal Society of the Transfiguration; however, the diverse student body represents various religious backgrounds.

Bethany's curriculum places strong emphasis on the development of sound reading and math skills. A reading lab for children in grades 1-6 and a multi-text approach complement the regular programs. Computer education is an important part of the overall program for all boys and girls, and a problem-solving lab enriches the program in grades K-3. Field trips, excursions and overnights are other integral instructional tools.

Extracurricular activities include student council, yearbook, handbell and chapel choirs, strings and interscholastic sports. Students may also participate in interscholastic academic competitions in such areas as mathematics, writing, computer use and general knowledge.

CINCINNATI COUNTRY DAY SCHOOL
Day — Coed Gr PS-12

Cincinnati, OH 45243. 6905 Given Rd. Tel: 513-979-0220. Fax: 513-527-7614.
 www.countryday.net   E-mail: admission@countryday.net

Robert Macrae, Head. BA, Wesleyan Univ, MA, Stanford Univ, MA, EdD, Columbia Univ. **Aaron B. Kellenberger, Adm.**

Col Prep. AP—Fr Span Calc Comp_Sci Bio Chem US_Hist Studio_Art. **Feat**—Lat Fine_Arts Performing_Arts Drama Music. **Supp**—Rev Tut.

Adm: 140/yr. Appl due: Mar. Accepted: 75%. Yield: 68%. **Tests** CEEB CTP_4 IQ ISEE SSAT Stanford.

Enr 875. B 466. G 409. Elem 564. Sec 311. Wh 83%. Hisp 1%. Blk 9%. Asian 5%. Other 2%. Avg class size: 18. **Fac 123.** M 40. F 60/23. Wh 91%. Hisp 1%. Blk 6%. Asian 2%. Adv deg: 54%.

Grad '04—77. Col—77. (Miami U-OH, Stanford, U of Cincinnati, U of CO-Boulder, Harvard, Rochester Inst of Tech). Avg SAT: 1276. Alum 2200.

Tui '04-'05: Day $16,735 (+$2800). **Aid:** Need 100 ($773,000).

Summer: Acad Enrich Rev Rec. 10 wks.

Bldgs 8. Class rms 78. 2 Libs 15,000 vols. Labs 10. Comp ctrs 1. Observatories 1. Auds 3. Theaters 1. Art studios 3. Music studios 3. Media ctrs 1. Gyms 2. Fields 8. Courts 7. Pools 1. Tracks 1. Greenhouses 1.

Est 1926. Nonprofit. Sem (Aug-June). **Assoc** CLS NCA.

Located on 62 wooded acres in suburban Indian Hill, CCDS provides thorough college preparation for students from Cincinnati and neighboring Indiana and Kentucky. The school has a tradition of academic excellence and sends its graduates to leading colleges throughout the country. Computer technology is incorporated into all aspects of the curriculum, with all pupils having Internet and E-mail access, and each student in grades 5-12 being equipped with a laptop computer. Children gain exposure to physical education and the arts in the early childhood program, and foreign language instruction commences in kindergarten.

The lower school (grades PS-2) provides developmentally appropriate instruction designed to stimulate an interest in learning. Increased levels of independence and collaboration, as well as more advanced reasoning skills, are in evidence during the elementary school years (grades 3-5). Middle school programming (grades 6-8) particularly addresses the varying learning and social needs of young adolescents. The upper school curriculum (grades 9-12) readies students for college through an emphasis on critical thinking, problem solving and the application of knowledge to new situations.

Class work is complemented by various extracurricular activities, among them student government, academic teams, drama and music, community service opportunities and interscholastic athletics.

ST. URSULA ACADEMY
Day — Girls Gr 9-12

Cincinnati, OH 45206. 1339 E McMillan St. Tel: 513-961-3410. Fax: 513-961-3856.
www.saintursula.org   E-mail: cpriest@saintursula.org
Judith A. Wimberg, Pres. BA, Edgecliff College, MA, Xavier Univ (OH). **Jill A. Loch, Adm.**
- **Col Prep. AP**—Eng Fr Lat Span Calc Bio Chem Physics Eur_Hist US_Hist US_Govt & Pol Art_Hist. **Feat**—British_Lit Creative_Writing Shakespeare Stats Anat & Physiol Programming Econ Psych Relig World_Relig Drawing Sculpt Acting Theater_Arts Music_Hist Music_Theory. **Supp**—LD Tut.
- **Adm:** 183/yr. Appl due: Dec. Accepted: 81%. **Tests** HSPT.
- **Enr 672.** G 672. Sec 672. Wh 93%. Blk 6%. Asian 1%. Avg class size: 20. Uniform. **Fac 56.** M 6. F 43/7. Wh 98%. Blk 1%. Asian 1%. Adv deg: 55%.
- **Grad '04**—187. **Col**—187. (Miami U-OH 24, U of Dayton 18, U of Cincinnati 16, OH St 13, Xavier-OH 7, IN U 7). Avg SAT: 1208. Avg ACT: 25. Alum 4300.
- **Tui '04-'05: Day $7560** (+$350). **Aid:** Merit 15 ($47,560). Need 105 ($255,180). Work prgm 21 ($31,340).
- Endow $900,000. Plant val $24,425,000. Bldgs 6. Class rms 48. Lib 12,287 vols. Sci labs 8. Lang labs 1. Comp labs 3. Theaters 1. Art studios 4. Music studios 7. Gyms 1. Fields 1.
- **Est 1910.** Nonprofit. Roman Catholic. Quar (Aug-June).

Sponsored by the Ursulines of Cincinnati, this Walnut Hills secondary school draws students from approximately 20 school districts in the Greater Cincinnati area. The academy conducts a rigorous college preparatory program in the fields of English, math, science, social studies, foreign language and religion. With the permission of the academic dean, qualified girls may pursue Advanced Placement course work during the junior or senior year.

St. Ursula maintains a program for college-bound girls of above-average ability who have either dyslexia or another learning disability. Students enrolled in this program are completely mainstreamed within the regular curriculum, but certain modifications and services are in place to address their special learning needs. Program participants incur some additional costs.

A selection of interest and scholastic clubs complements academics. In addition, the following sports are available: volleyball, tennis, soccer, golf, field hockey, cross-country, crew, basketball, swimming and diving, bowling, track and field, softball and lacrosse.

THE SEVEN HILLS SCHOOL
Day — Coed Gr PS-12

Cincinnati, OH 45227. 5400 Red Bank Rd. Tel: 513-271-9027. Fax: 513-271-2471.
www.7hills.org   E-mail: admissions@7hills.org
Sandra J. Theunick, Head. BA, Newton College of the Sacred Heart, MDiv, Washington Theological Union. **Peter Egan, Adm.**
- **Col Prep. AP**—Eng Fr Lat Span Calc Comp_Sci Bio Chem Physics Eur_Hist US_Hist US_Govt & Pol Art_Hist. **Feat**—Creative_Writing Anat & Physiol Environ_Sci Women's_Hist Middle_East_Hist Econ Psych African-Amer_Stud Comp_Relig Studio_Art Drama Music Journ Speech. **Supp**—Tut.
- **Adm:** 150/yr. Appl due: Dec. Accepted: 60%. **Tests** ISEE Stanford.
- **Enr 1070.** B 515. G 555. Elem 750. Sec 320. Wh 85%. Hisp 1%. Blk 7%. Asian 5%. Other 2%. Avg class size: 15. **Fac 137.** Wh 90%. Hisp 3%. Blk 4%. Asian 3%. Adv deg:

48%.
Grad '04—66. Col—66. (Denison 5, Emory 3, Harvard 2, U of MI 2, Tufts 2, Vanderbilt 2). Avg SAT: 1310. Alum 4000.
Tui '04-'05: Day $7250-15,000 (+$300). **Aid:** Merit 10 ($8000). Need 136 ($1,000,000).
Summer: Enrich Rev Rec. 8 wks.
Endow $12,000,000. Plant val $44,000,000. Bldgs 21. Class rms 108. Libs 3. Comp labs 4. Art studios 5. Music studios 3. Gyms 4.
Est 1974. Nonprofit. Sem (Aug-June). **Assoc** CLS NCA.

Seven Hills traces its roots in the community back to 1906, when the College Preparatory School was founded in East Walnut Hills by Mary Harlan Doherty; to 1916, when Helen G. Lotspeich began the Clifton Open-Air School in her home; and to 1927, when community leaders founded Hillsdale School to provide an area alternative in private education. Today, the school is housed on two campuses located six miles apart: Doherty School for grades pre-K-5 occupies the Doherty campus at 2726 Johnstone Pl., 45206 in East Walnut Hills, while Lotspeich School, also pre-K-5, shares the 25-acre Hillsdale campus in Madisonville with the middle and upper schools.

In the lower school, every child works with specialists in art, music, French or Spanish, drama, library and physical education starting in kindergarten. The computer curriculum begins in prekindergarten, and work with a science specialist begins in first grade.

The middle school curriculum addresses the particular academic and interpersonal needs of young adolescents. Study skills are emphasized during these years. Foreign language offerings (French, Spanish and Latin), accelerated math groupings, art, music, drama, extracurricular activities and athletics accommodate individual abilities and interests.

In the upper school, every student must complete a traditional college preparatory program, pass writing and computer competency examinations, fulfill a community services requirement and complete a personal project of his or her own design. The fine and performing arts are integral to the curriculum, and honors and Advanced Placement courses are offered in all major disciplines. Students choose from a wide selection of electives and take advantage of a highly developed computer curriculum.

Other opportunities include interscholastic sports and various extracurricular activities. Sophomores may participate in the Swiss Semester program in Zermatt, Switzerland.

In addition, an outdoor program is conducted for students in grades 4-12. Trips, led by teachers experienced in outdoor education, vary from weekends spent cycling, hiking, climbing, caving and canoeing in nearby locations to longer excursions during school vacations. After-school enrichment (grades 1-5), extended-day and holiday care (grades pre-K-5), and summer programs (age 2 through grade 12) are also available.

SUMMIT COUNTRY DAY SCHOOL

Day — Coed Gr PS-12

Cincinnati, OH 45208. 2161 Grandin Rd. Tel: 513-871-4700. Fax: 513-533-5373.
www.summitcds.org E-mail: schiess_k@summitcds.org

Joseph T. Devlin, Head. BA, Univ of Scranton, MA, Villanova Univ. **Kelley K. Schiess, Adm.**
- **Col Prep. AP**—Fr Lat Span Calc Stats Comp_Sci Bio Chem Physics Eur_Hist US_Hist Psych US_Govt & Pol Music_Theory. **Feat**—Anat & Physiol Marine_Biol/Sci Holocaust Philos World_Relig Drama Speech.
- **Adm:** 133/yr. Appl due: Rolling. **Tests** CTP_4 ISEE Stanford.
- **Enr** 1050. B 501. G 549. Elem 733. Sec 317. Wh 85%. Hisp 4%. Blk 6%. Asian 2%. Other 3%. Avg class size: 15. Uniform. **Fac 124.** M 33. F 81/10. Wh 95%. Hisp 3%. Blk 1%. Asian 1%. Adv deg: 63%.
- **Grad '04—74. Col—74.** (Boston U, OH St, Wm & Mary, St Louis U, Clemson, DePauw). Avg SAT: 1280. Avg ACT: 28. Alum 3400.
- **Tui '04-'05: Day $10,480-12,645** (+$275-675).
- **Summer:** Acad Enrich Rev Rem Rec. Astronomy. 12 wks.
- Endow $4,500,000. Plant val $24,000,000. Bldgs 10. Class rms 90. 4 Libs 15,000 vols. Sci labs 11. Lang labs 1. Comp labs 7. Auds 2. Theaters 1. Art studios 4. Music studios 13. Gyms 4. Athletic ctrs 2. Fields 5. Courts 4.
- **Est 1890.** Nonprofit. Roman Catholic. Sem (Aug-June). **Assoc** NCA.

Founded by the Sisters of Notre Dame de Namur and now independently owned and governed by a board of trustees, Summit occupies a 23-acre site in Hyde Park. Three contiguous school divisions share the campus: a lower school comprising a Montessori prekindergarten and kindergarten and grades 1-4, a middle school (grades 5-8) and an upper school (grades 9-12). Developmentally appropriate instruction characterizes each division.

Throughout, the curriculum places emphasis on technology: Keyboarding classes begin in grade 1, and middle and upper school pupils benefit from wireless mobile laptop labs and hardware and software resources through classroom computers, as well as Internet-based resources for home access. Programs in art, foreign language and religion are important aspects of the curriculum, and students also receive instruction in drama, music, health and library skills.

During the primary school years, students have a homeroom teacher who is responsible for instruction in the core subjects; specialists teach French or Spanish, technology, library, art, music and physical education classes. The middle school employs a team-teaching approach with specialized teachers in each subject area and accelerated curricular offerings, including upper-school-level French, Spanish and Latin classes, as well as algebra I for qualified seventh graders. Study skills and leadership development are integral to the middle school program.

In the upper school, Advanced Placement and other advanced courses in many areas complement an array of electives. The college preparatory program stresses writing and incorporates the fine arts. Prior to graduation, pupils complete a senior project and fulfill a 48-hour community service requirement. Various extracurricular and athletic activities round out the program. An important aspect of school life is the Educating for Character Program, which focuses upon the qualities of respect, responsibility and honesty.

CLEVELAND, OH. Urban. Pop: 478,403. Alt: 690 ft. Area also includes Willoughby.

ANDREWS SCHOOL
Bdg and Day — Girls Gr 6-12

Willoughby, OH 44094. 38588 Mentor Ave. Tel: 440-942-3606. Fax: 440-954-5020.
www.andrews-school.org   E-mail: admissions@andrews-school.org
David Norris Rath, Head. BA, Kenyon College, EdD, George Washington Univ. **Sylke Castellarin, Actg Adm.**
- **Col Prep. AP**—Eng Calc Bio Chem US_Hist. **Feat**—Fr Span Stats Astron Environ_Sci Computers Econ Govt Women's_Stud Ethics Ceramics Film Studio_Art Dance. **Supp**—ESL Rev Tut.
- **Adm:** 57/yr. Bdg 26. Day 31. Appl due: Rolling. **Tests** ISEE SSAT TOEFL.
- **Enr 170.** G 55/115. Wh 78%. Blk 20%. Asian 1%. Other 1%. Avg class size: 12. Uniform.
- **Fac 35.** M 12. F 21/2. Wh 89%. Blk 11%. Adv deg: 51%. In dorms 12.
- **Grad '04—29. Col—29.** (OH Wesleyan, OH St, Am U, Pepperdine, Heidelberg, Savannah Col of Art & Design).
- **Tui '04-'05: Bdg $26,215** (+$2000). **5-Day Bdg $21,360** (+$2000). **Day $14,280-15,590** (+$600). **Aid:** Need 90 ($738,522).
- **Summer:** Equestrian. Girls Ages 9-15. Tui Bdg $600/wk. Coed Ages 8-14. Tui Day $225/wk. 8 wks.
- Plant val $7,700,000. Bldgs 19. Dorms 4. Class rms 30. Lib 13,100 vols. Sci labs 5. Lang labs 5. Comp labs 7. Auds 1. Theaters 1. Art studios 2. Music studios 1. Dance studios 1. Gyms 2. Fields 4. Courts 4. Field houses 1. Riding rings 7. Stables 80.
- **Est 1910.** Nonprofit. Sem (Aug-June). **Assoc** NCA.

This nonsectarian school was established in accordance with the will of area businessman Wallace Corydon Andrews and his wife, Margaret St. John Andrews.

In a small-class setting, the academic program encourages individual growth and prepares girls for college. Andrews' middle school curriculum (grades 6-8) integrates various projects and group activities, as well as enrichment field trips. Outdoor education is an important aspect of middle school life, as girls develop riding skills in the equestrian center and also engage in such activities as rock climbing, canoeing, backpacking and work on Andrews' ropes course.

The liberal arts program during the upper school years (grades 9-12) features honors, Advanced Placement and independent study courses, as well as a senior research project. A wide selection of electives accommodates varying student interests. Also available is an English as a Second Language program for international students.

All girls engage in both on- and off-campus community service. Other extracurricular activities include interest clubs, class trips, fine arts options and student council. Equestrianism, field hockey, tennis, soccer, volleyball, basketball, swimming, fast- and slow-pitch softball, and lacrosse constitute Andrews' interscholastic athletic program.

COLUMBUS, OH. (100 mi. NE of Cincinnati, OH; 124 mi. SW of Cleveland, OH) Urban. Pop: 711,470. Alt: 744 ft. Area also includes Gahanna.

THE COLUMBUS ACADEMY
Day — Coed Gr PS-12

Gahanna, OH 43230. 4300 Cherry Bottom Rd, PO Box 30745. Tel: 614-337-4309. Fax: 614-475-0396.
www.columbusacademy.org E-mail: lou_schultz@columbusacademy.org
John M. Mackenzie, Head. AB, Bowdoin College, MA, Columbia Univ. **Louis A. Schultz, Adm.**
- **Col Prep. AP**—Eng Fr Lat Span Calc Comp_Sci Bio Chem Physics Eur_Hist US_Hist Econ. **Feat**—British_Lit Chin Russ_Hist Milit_Hist Govt & Pol Ceramics Drawing Photog Sculpt Studio_Art Band Chorus Music_Theory.
- **Adm:** 172/yr. Appl due: Feb. Accepted: 56%. Yield: 77%. **Tests** ISEE SSAT.
- **Enr 1001.** B 526. G 475. Elem 676. Sec 325. Wh 82%. Hisp 1%. Blk 8%. Asian 9%. Avg class size: 15. **Fac 126.** M 40/2. F 74/10. Wh 93%. Hisp 4%. Blk 1%. Asian 2%. Adv deg: 59%.
- **Grad '04—78. Col—78.** (Miami U-OH 9, OH St 6, Vanderbilt 4, Rice 2, Notre Dame 2, Stanford 2). Avg SAT: 1303. Avg ACT: 27. Alum 2352.
- **Tui '04-'05: Day $13,425-15,550** (+$300-400). **Aid:** Need 123 ($1,014,548).
- **Summer:** Acad Enrich Rev Rec. Arts. Theater. Tui Day $800-900/3-wk ses. 9 wks.
- Endow $17,500,000. Plant val $40,000,000. Bldgs 16. Class rms 83. 3 Libs 30,000 vols. Sci labs 12. Lang labs 1. Comp labs 5. Comp ctrs 2. Theaters 1. Art studios 6. Music studios 4. Gyms 3. Fields 8. Courts 8. Pools 1.
- **Est 1911.** Nonprofit. Sem (Aug-June). **Assoc** CLS NCA.

Founded by Frank P. R. Van Syckel and conducted by him for 30 years, this was one of the earliest country day schools in the United States. Graduates of the traditional, thorough curriculum enter leading colleges in Ohio and throughout the country. In September 1968, the school moved to a new 230-acre, suburban campus. Originally enrolling boys only, the academy instituted coeducation in 1990.

The academy offers a broad educational program that incorporates a variety of electives in the upper grades, including course work in both the performing and the visual arts. Numerous extracurricular activities are available, including student government and various interest clubs and organizations. Upper school students are required to participate in community service. Available interscholastic sports are soccer, football, field hockey, tennis, basketball, volleyball, wrestling, swimming, cross-country, track, baseball, lacrosse and golf.

COLUMBUS SCHOOL FOR GIRLS
Day — Girls Gr PS-12

Columbus, OH 43209. 56 S Columbia Ave. Tel: 614-252-0781. Fax: 614-252-0571.
www.columbusschoolforgirls.org
E-mail: admissions@columbusschoolforgirls.org
Diane B. Cooper, Head. BA, St Joseph's College, MA, Univ of North Texas, EdD, Univ of San Francisco. **Donna Lindberg & Ann Boston Timm, Adms.**
- **Col Prep. AP**—Eng Fr Ger Lat Span Calc Comp_Sci Bio Chem Physics Comp_Govt

& Pol Psych US_Govt & Pol Studio_Art. **Feat**—Fine_Arts Performing_Arts. **Supp**—Dev_Read Rem_Read Rev Tut.

Adm: 109/yr. Appl due: Feb. Accepted: 51%. Yield: 77%. **Tests** CTP_4 ISEE.

Enr 657. G 657. Elem 413. Sec 244. Wh 80%. Hisp 1%. Blk 10%. Asian 7%. Other 2%.Uniform. **Fac 105.** M 14. F 79/12. Wh 94%. Hisp 3%. Blk 1%. Asian 2%. Adv deg: 51%.

Grad '04—56. Col—56. (Miami U-OH 5, Boston Col 2, U of KY 2, OH St 2, Villanova 2). Avg SAT: 1251. Avg ACT: 26. Alum 2800.

Tui '05-'06: Day $14,620-16,520 (+$200). **Aid:** Need 95 ($720,900).

Summer: Acad Enrich Rec. 3-6 wks.

Endow $23,149,000. Plant val $21,000,000. Bldgs 8. Class rms 64. 2 Libs 37,000 vols. Sci labs 4. Lang labs 1. Comp labs 5. Theaters 1. Art studios 3. Music studios 3. Gyms 2. Athletic ctrs 1. Fields 5. Tennis courts 8. Pools 1.

Est 1898. Nonprofit. Sem (Sept-June). **Assoc** CLS NCA.

Founded to offer girls a college preparatory education, CSG sends its graduates to leading colleges throughout the country. A strong academic program is complemented by an active school life that includes student government, team sports, journalism, fine arts, theater, music and voluntary community service.

The college preparatory curriculum features Advanced Placement courses, a modern and classical language program that begins in grade 4, and various sports. A month-long off-campus experience for seniors takes place each May.

See Also Page 1296

DAYTON, OH. (47 mi. NNE of Cincinnati, OH; 177 mi. SW of Cleveland, OH) Urban. Pop: 166,179. Alt: 740 ft.

MIAMI VALLEY SCHOOL
Day — Coed Gr PS-12

Dayton, OH 45429. 5151 Denise Dr. Tel: 937-434-4444. Fax: 937-434-1415.
www.mvschool.com   E-mail: chend@mvschool.com

Thomas G. Brereton, Head. BA, Cornell Univ, MAT, Colgate Univ. **Denise Chenoweth, Adm.**

Col Prep. AP—Calc Stats Bio Chem Eur_Hist US_Hist. **Feat**—Creative_Writing Fr Lat Span Anat & Physiol Psych Ethics World_Relig Art_Hist Ceramics Drawing Music_Theory Bus Journ Speech.

Adm: 75/yr. Appl due: Rolling. Accepted: 51%. **Tests** IQ.

Enr 481. B 222. G 259. Elem 305. Sec 176. Avg class size: 16. **Fac 65.** M 15/1. F 42/7. Wh 95%. Hisp 2%. Blk 2%. Asian 1%. Adv deg: 66%.

Grad '04—52. Col—52. (Georgetown, Princeton, Pomona, U of MI, OH St, Sarah Lawrence). Avg SAT: 1230. Avg ACT: 26. Alum 900.

Tui '04-'05: Day $13,041 (+$500). **Aid:** Merit 15 ($72,000). Need 77 ($450,000).

Endow $1,500,000. Plant val $5,000,000. Bldgs 3. Class rms 46. Lib 16,500 vols. Labs 6. Art studios 2. Music studios 4. Gyms 2. Fields 3. Courts 6.

Est 1957. Nonprofit. Tri (Aug-June). **Assoc** NCA.

Dayton's only independent college preparatory school, Miami Valley strikes a careful balance among academic fundamentals, creative activities and extracurricular opportunities. The elementary program emphasizes the measurement of educational needs through individualized and group instruction in self-contained classrooms. Specific contacts in the community enable older pupils to enroll in college-level courses or take part in internships relating to business, government, industry or the arts. Independent study is available to eligible juniors and seniors, and March is reserved for in-depth seminars on selected subjects for those in grades 10-12. During the same time period, freshmen participate in a month of special academic and nonacademic pursuits. Opportunities in sports, publications and the arts round out the upper school program.

Local companies, foundations and parents support the school's scholarship program. Miami Valley has occupied a 24-acre site in Washington Township since 1966.

GATES MILLS, OH. (14 mi. ENE of Cleveland, OH) Suburban. Pop: 2493. Alt: 750 ft.

HAWKEN SCHOOL
Day — Coed Gr PS-12

Gates Mills, OH 44040. 12465 County Line Rd, PO Box 8002. Tel: 440-423-4446.
Fax: 440-423-2960.
www.hawken.edu   E-mail: adm@hawken.edu
James S. Berkman, Head. BA, JD, Harvard Univ, MPhil, Oxford Univ (England). **Frank P. Brandt, Adm.**
Col Prep. AP—Eng Fr Lat Span Calc Stats Bio Chem Physics US_Hist Studio_Art. **Feat**—Humanities Japan_Lit Ecol Animal_Physiol African-Amer_Stud Graphic_Arts Music. **Supp**—Rev Tut.
Adm: 145/yr. Appl due: Mar. Accepted: 50%. Yield: 65%. **Tests** ISEE.
Enr 954. B 495. G 459. Elem 526. Sec 428. Wh 83%. Hisp 1%. Blk 9%. Asian 4%. Other 3%. Avg class size: 15. **Fac 113.** M 44/15. F 38/16. Wh 95%. Hisp 1%. Blk 3%. Asian 1%. Adv deg: 57%.
Grad '04—109. Col—109. (Miami U-OH 10, OH U 8, U of Rochester 5, U of Dayton 4, Kenyon 3, OH St 3). Avg SAT: 1290. Avg ACT: 27. Alum 3653.
Tui '04-'05: Day $12,900-18,050 (+$1900-2400). **Aid:** Need 138 ($1,802,242).
Summer: Acad Enrich Rev. Tui Day $280-1000. 6 wks.
Endow $40,919,000. Plant val $36,336,000. Bldgs 23. Class rms 60. 2 Libs 21,000 vols. Sci labs 8. Comp labs 4. Auds 1. Theaters 1. Art studios 4. Music studios 4. Dance studios 1. Gyms 5. Athletic ctrs 1. Fields 17. Courts 11. Pools 2.
Est 1915. Nonprofit. Sem (Aug-June). **Assoc** CLS NCA.

Established by James A. Hawken and a group of local parents, this school was founded as a boys' program serving children from Greater Cleveland in grades K-8. The school operated in Lyndhurst (5000 Clubside Rd., 44124) as an elementary school until 1961, when it added a second campus in Gates Mills to house an upper school. The school instituted coeducation in 1973 and opened its preschool in 1993.

The college preparatory program includes honors and Advanced Placement courses, and the school features a variety of electives, sports and extracurricular activities. Hawken offers upper school students over 125 courses and considerable opportunities in the fine and performing arts, and computer literacy is emphasized at all grade levels. The athletic program features extensive interscholastic competition. Hawken's outdoor leadership program teaches wilderness survival skills to upper schoolers while utilizing the substantial woodland on its 325-acre Gates Mills campus. Students may participate in the School Year Abroad program; recent participants have studied in Spain, France and Israel.

Approximately one-third of recent seniors have received National Merit recognition, and graduates go on to leading colleges. The school maintains a well-funded financial aid program that permits enrollment of academically qualified students from various backgrounds.

HUDSON, OH. (20 mi. SE of Cleveland, OH) Suburban. Pop: 22,439. Alt: 1055 ft.

WESTERN RESERVE ACADEMY
Bdg and Day — Coed Gr 9-PG

Hudson, OH 44236. 115 College St. Tel: 330-650-9717. Fax: 330-650-5858.
  www.wra.net E-mail: admission@wra.net
Henry E. Flanagan, Jr., **Head.** BA, Rutgers Univ, MEd, Harvard Univ, PhD, Univ of Michigan.
  Barbara M. Flanagan, **Adm.**
  Col Prep. AP—Eng Fr Ger Lat Span Calc Stats Comp_Sci Bio Chem Physics Eur_Hist US_Hist Music_Theory. **Feat**—Mandarin Astron Environ_Sci Zoology Studio_Art Drama Music Dance. **Supp**—Tut.
  Adm: 108/yr. Bdg 78. Day 30. Appl due: Feb. Accepted: 60%. **Tests** ISEE SSAT.
  Enr 400. B 151/79. G 109/61. Sec 400. Wh 78%. Blk 6%. Asian 16%. Avg class size: 12. Uniform. **Fac 70.** M 40. F 30. Wh 93%. Blk 4%. Other 3%. Adv deg: 61%. In dorms 19.
  Grad '04—107. **Col**—107. (Geo Wash 6, Case Western Reserve 5, Denison 4, Colgate 3, Duke 2, U of PA 2). Avg SAT: 1220. Alum 5300.
  Tui '05-'06: Bdg $32,000 (+$500). **Day $23,000** (+$500). **Aid:** Need ($3,000,000).
  Endow $80,000,000. Plant val $30,000,000. Bldgs 49. Dorms 10. Dorm rms 128. Class rms 49. Lib 50,000 vols. Sci labs 5. Lang labs 1. Comp labs 3. Observatories 2. Auds 1. Theaters 1. Art studios 2. Music studios 5. Dance studios 1. Gyms 3. Fields 17. Courts 14. Field houses 1. Pools 1. Tracks 2.
  Est 1826. Nonprofit. Quar (Sept-May). **Assoc** CLS NCA.

Established as the preparatory school of Western Reserve College, the academy took over the plant when the college moved to Cleveland in 1882. The affiliation between the two institutions continued until 1903, when the academy closed for lack of funds. Endowed in 1910 by James W. Ellsworth and reopened in 1916, the school came to more vigorous life in 1926 when it was reorganized on the Ellsworth Foundation with a trust fund of four million dollars.

During the past 70 years, Reserve has always placed its major emphasis on college preparation. The academy offers a number of Advanced Placement courses, and its drama and music programs send some students on to advanced professional study. Courses for college credit at Kenyon College, independent study options and a variety of exchange programs are also available.

Extracurricular activities include a radio station, publications, music and dramatic productions, SADD, Student Environmental Action League, Student Intercultural Club, Green Key (student center), Opus (theater), and chess and culinary clubs. Students must participate in athletics at some level each season of the school year. Interscholastic sports are football, cross-country, soccer, ice hockey, basketball, wrestling, swimming, track, golf, baseball, softball, riflery, fencing, lacrosse, field hockey, volleyball and tennis. Intramural athletics include cross-country skiing, squash, racquetball, soccer, running, aerobics, dance, weightlifting and kickboxing. **See Also Page 1273**

NORTH RIDGEVILLE, OH. (19 mi. WSW of Cleveland, OH) Suburban. Pop: 22,338. Alt: 700 ft.

LAKE RIDGE ACADEMY
Day — Coed Gr K-12

North Ridgeville, OH 44039. 37501 Center Ridge Rd. Tel: 440-777-9434.
 Fax: 440-327-3641.
 www.lakeridgeacademy.org   E-mail: admission@lakeridgeacademy.org
Deborah M. Cook, Head. Terry Finefrock, Adm.
 Col Prep. AP—Eng Bio Chem Physics US_Hist World_Hist. Feat—Span Stats Ecol Computers Anthro Econ Psych Philos Ceramics Photog Studio_Art Drama Music. Supp—Tut.
 Adm: 85/yr. Appl due: Rolling. Accepted: 74%. Tests IQ Stanford.
 Enr 408. B 207. G 201. Elem 272. Sec 136. Wh 78%. Hisp 4%. Blk 5%. Asian 8%. Other 5%. Avg class size: 14. Fac 60. M 15. F 44/1. Wh 93%. Hisp 2%. Blk 3%. Asian 2%. Adv deg: 56%.
 Grad '04—36. Col—36. (Kenyon, Harvard, Columbia, Brown, U of PA, Amherst). Avg SAT: 1326. Alum 874.
 Tui '02-'03: Day $12,600-19,200 (+$1000). Aid: Need 122 ($1,469,000).
 Summer: Acad Enrich Rev Rec. Tui Day $195/crse. 3 wks.
 Endow $4,100,000. Plant val $12,000,000. Bldgs 11. Class rms 56. 2 Libs 35,000 vols. Sci labs 7. Lang labs 1. Comp labs 3. Auds 1. Theaters 2. Art studios 4. Music studios 3. Gyms 1. Fields 5. Courts 6.
 Est 1963. Nonprofit. Sem (Aug-June). Assoc NCA.

LRA is located on the eastern edge of Lorain County. The school draws students from Cuyahoga, Lorain and contiguous counties.

The curriculum emphasizes college preparation. Art, music, foreign language, technology, and physical and outdoor education are incorporated into the lower school curriculum. Major emphasis is placed on literacy and math skills in the lower grades. The upper school curriculum consists of course work in the five basic disciplines, as well as technology. Students may enhance their studies with accelerated classes in math, Advanced Placement courses and independent study.

Activities include interscholastic sports such as soccer, field hockey, basketball, tennis, golf and track. Drama, music and arts are also available. Upper school students participate in various programs that allow them to pursue interests beyond the classroom by means of internships, community service, student exchanges, and two-week travel and study trips.

SHAKER HEIGHTS, OH. (7 mi. E of Cleveland, OH) Suburban. Pop: 29,405. Alt: 978 ft. Area also includes Hunting Valley.

HATHAWAY BROWN SCHOOL
Day — Boys Gr PS, Girls PS-12

Shaker Heights, OH 44122. 19600 N Park Blvd. Tel: 216-932-4214. Fax: 216-371-1501.
www.hb.edu   E-mail: admissions@hb.edu

William Christ, Head. BA, Washington and Lee Univ, MA, Univ of Pennsylvania. **Sarah Liotta Johnston, Adm.**

Col Prep. AP—Eng Fr Lat Span Calc Stats Comp_Sci Bio Chem Physics US_Hist Studio_Art. **Feat**—Writing Chin Pol_Sci Art_Hist Dance. **Supp**—Tut.

Adm (Gr PS-12): 138/yr. Appl due: Rolling. **Tests** IQ ISEE Stanford.

Enr 830. B 34. G 796. Elem 538. Sec 292. Wh 82%. Hisp 1%. Blk 10%. Asian 4%. Other 3%. Avg class size: 15. **Fac 114.** M 15. F 89/10. Wh 90%. Hisp 3%. Blk 4%. Asian 3%. Adv deg: 62%.

Grad '04—68. Col—68. (Harvard 3, Cornell 3, MIT 2, U of PA 2, Brown 2, Georgetown 2). Avg SAT: 1315. Alum 3278.

Tui '04-'05: Day $13,250-18,560 (+$1700). **Aid:** Need 149 ($1,643,500).

Summer: Acad Enrich Rev Rec. Tui Day $360-900/crse. 5 wks.

Endow $23,600,000. Plant val $46,000,000. Bldgs 3. Class rms 60. Lib 14,000 vols. Sci labs 10. Lang labs 1. Theaters 2. Art studios 3. Music studios 2. Dance studios 2. Gyms 2. Fields 6. Courts 6.

Est 1876. Nonprofit. Sem (Sept-June). **Assoc** CLS NCA.

Hathaway Brown traces its origins to the establishment of an afternoon program for girls at Brook School, a church school for boys. In 1886, Anne Hathaway Brown purchased the school and changed its name from Home and Day School to Miss Anne H. Hathaway Brown's School for Girls. HB has occupied its current, 16-acre campus in Shaker Heights since 1927.

Hathaway Brown's coeducational preschool consists of an early childhood program serving children ages 3-5; grades K-12 admit girls only. Qualified students may participate in individual projects beyond the basic curriculum. The adventure learning program, which features a ropes course, is a required element of the middle school curriculum. The traditional college preparatory upper school program is supplemented by honors and Advanced Placement classes in most disciplines, as well as by fellowships in creativity. Special offerings include art, drama, music, photography, computer studies and Broad Horizons summer enrichment for academically and creatively gifted girls.

Extracurricular involvement in art, drama and music is encouraged. The school also features a strong interscholastic athletic program and an active student government.

LAUREL SCHOOL
Day — Boys Gr PS, Girls PS-12

Shaker Heights, OH 44122. 1 Lyman Cir. Tel: 216-464-1441. Fax: 216-464-8996.
www.laurelschool.com   E-mail: admission@laurelschool.com

Ann V. Klotz, Head. BA, Yale Univ, MA, New York Univ. **Thomas G. Wilschutz, Adm.**

Col Prep. AP—Eng Fr Lat Span Calc Bio Chem Physics US_Hist. **Feat**—Engineering Computers Philos Drama Music Speech. **Supp**—Dev_Read Rem_Math Rem_Read Rev Tut.

Adm (Gr PS-12): 135/yr. Appl due: Rolling. Accepted: 67%. **Tests** ISEE.

Enr 681. B 43. G 638. Elem 461. Sec 220. Avg class size: 15. Uniform. **Fac 106.** Adv deg: 39%.

Grad '04—56. Col—56. (Col of Wooster, Am U, Case Western Reserve, Boston U, Mary Wash, Boston Col). Avg SAT: 1251. Avg ACT: 27. Alum 3300.

Tui '03-'04: Day $6750-17,500 (+$1133-1828). **Aid:** Need 155 ($1,424,121).

Summer: Rec. Theater. Tui Day $475-1000. 6 wks.

Endow $28,669,000. Plant val $29,000,000. Bldgs 2. Class rms 57. 2 Libs 15,000 vols. Sci labs 6. Lang labs 1. Comp labs 3. Theaters 1. Art studios 2. Music studios 2. Dance studios 1. Gyms 2. Fields 9. Courts 12.

Est 1896. Nonprofit. Sem (Aug-June). **Assoc** CLS NCA.

One of the leading schools in the area, Laurel was first located in Cleveland, when Jennie Prentiss opened a private school for girls in her own home. The school moved in 1928 to its present location in suburban Shaker Heights, where it has undergone subsequent expansion, including the 2002 addition of a 140-acre outdoor education and athletic facility 20 minutes east of the main campus.

Laurel accepts both boys and girls into its early childhood center, which utilizes a hands-on, experiential approach. The theme-based primary school emphasizes fundamental academic skills, while the middle school offers an integrated approach to the sciences and the humanities and commences formal foreign language instruction. The upper school curriculum allows qualified girls to take Advanced Placement classes or to enroll in college-level courses through a program coordinated with Kenyon College. The school also maintains a program with the Cleveland Institute of Music. Cross-registration with a nearby boys' school is available.

Among the school's extracurricular activities are publications, art, Model UN, dance, drama, music and interest clubs. Laurel fields varsity and junior varsity teams in field hockey, tennis, soccer, basketball, volleyball, lacrosse, softball, golf, track and swimming.

UNIVERSITY SCHOOL

Day — Boys Gr K-12

Hunting Valley, OH 44022. 2785 SOM Center Rd. Tel: 216-831-2200. Fax: 216-292-7808.
www.us.edu E-mail: admissions@us.edu

Stephen S. Murray, **Head.** BA, Williams College, AM, MEd, Harvard Univ. **David Stewart & Christopher S. Barton, Adms.**

Col Prep. Feat—Fr Greek Lat Span Ecol Comp_Sci Econ Psych Art_Hist Film Music. **Supp**—Dev_Read.

Adm (Gr K-11): 134/yr. Accepted: 63%. Yield: 81%. **Tests** ISEE.

Enr 871. B 871. Elem 473. Sec 398. Wh 85%. Blk 10%. Asian 5%. Avg class size: 15. Uniform. **Fac 137.** Adv deg: 82%.

Grad '04—100. Col—100. (OH U 8, Miami U-OH 6, Elon 5, Cornell 3, Boston Col 3). Avg SAT: 1275. Alum 4600.

Tui '04-'05: Day $12,980-18,475 (+$600-995). **Aid:** Need 136 ($1,860,000).

Summer: Acad Enrich Rev Rec. 4-6 wks.

Endow $52,000,000. Plant val $53,726,000. Bldgs 6. Class rms 69. Lib 16,000 vols. Labs 14. Auds 1. Theaters 2. Gyms 3. Fields 11. Courts 22. Pools 2.

Est 1890. Nonprofit. Tri (Aug-June). **Assoc** CLS NCA.

From its inception, this school has conducted a country day school program that features a strong college preparatory curriculum. The Shaker Heights campus, located at 20701 Brantley Rd., 44122, has been occupied since 1926 and now enrolls children in grades K-8. US added the Hunting Valley upper school campus (grades 9-12) in 1970.

The elementary school curriculum, which evolved out of an intensive study of the developmental patterns of very young boys, develops and coordinates skills in individual and group research projects. Older boys may take college-level work in every academic subject and are offered special courses in subjects such as ecology, theater production, computer science, business economics and philosophy.

More than half of the school's graduates attend Eastern colleges, including Ivy League institutions. A major development program has allowed for enlargement of the faculty and broadening of the curriculum, resulting in increased emphasis on advanced studies. Athletic, visual and performing arts, community service and independent study programs are also offered.

TOLEDO, OH. (55 mi. SSW of Detroit, MI) Urban. Pop: 313,619. Alt: 587 ft.

MAUMEE VALLEY COUNTRY DAY SCHOOL
Day — Coed Gr PS-12

Toledo, OH 43614. 1715 S Reynolds Rd. Tel: 419-381-1313. Fax: 419-381-9941.
www.mvcds.org   E-mail: vkoelsch@mvcds.net

Phineas Anderson, Head. BA, Trinity College (CT), MEd, Harvard Univ. **Vicki Koelsch, Adm.**

Col Prep. AP—Span Calc Stats Bio. Feat—Fr Comp_Sci Human_Growth & Dev Filmmaking Studio_Art Drama Music. Supp—Dev_Read Tut.

Adm: 99/yr. Appl due: Rolling. Accepted: 80%. Yield: 69%. Tests CTP_4 IQ.

Enr 469. B 254. G 215. Elem 294. Sec 175. Wh 67%. Hisp 2%. Blk 8%. Asian 12%. Other 11%. Avg class size: 15. Fac 55. M 21. F 34. Wh 94%. Blk 4%. Asian 2%. Adv deg: 63%.

Grad '04—41. Col—41. (Miami U-OH 6, OH St 5, Bowling Green St 3, Denison 2, NYU 1, U of PA 1). Avg SAT: 1290. Alum 850.

Tui '04-'05: Day $8450-12,450 (+$150). Aid: Merit 24 ($96,000). Need 103 ($600,000).

Summer: Acad Enrich Rec. Tui Day $135/wk. 8 wks.

Endow $4,414,000. Plant val $14,700,000. Bldgs 6. Class rms 46. 2 Libs 27,000 vols. Sci labs 3. Comp labs 2. Comp ctrs 1. Auds 1. Theaters 1. Art studios 3. Music studios 2. Dance studios 1. Arts ctrs 1. Art galleries 1. Gyms 3. Fields 3. Courts 4. Riding rings 1. Tracks 1.

Est 1884. Nonprofit. Sem (Aug-June). **Assoc** CLS NCA.

As the only nonsectarian independent day school in Toledo, Maumee Valley has deep roots in the community that it serves. Originally the Smead School for Girls, the school moved in 1934 to its present, 72-acre campus, ten miles from downtown Toledo.

Maumee Valley's college preparatory curriculum includes a wide variety of electives and places a strong emphasis on the fine arts. Qualified students are able to earn college credit for work done in English, French, history and art. Each year, students engage in three weeks of intensive study during the school's winterim program. Options include electives, internships, independent study opportunities, language and cultural travel, work in the research laboratories of the Medical College of Ohio, and school exchanges. The school encourages participation in such interscholastic sports as soccer, track, basketball, baseball, cross-country, lacrosse, field hockey, tennis and golf.

There are separate units for the preschool, the lower school, the middle school and the upper school, with all sharing common dining facilities.

WISCONSIN

BEAVER DAM, WI. (52 mi. WNW of Milwaukee, WI) Urban. Pop: 15,169. Alt: 872 ft.

WAYLAND ACADEMY
Bdg and Day — Coed Gr 9-12

Beaver Dam, WI 53916. 101 N University Ave. Tel: 920-885-3373. Fax: 920-887-3373.
www.wayland.org   E-mail: admissions@wayland.org
Robert L. Esten, Pres. AB, Stanford Univ. **Eric S. Peters, Adm.**

- **Col Prep. AP**—Eng Ger Lat Span Calc Stats Bio Chem Physics Eur_Hist US_Hist. **Feat**—Ecol Govt Studio_Art Drama Music. **Supp**—Dev_Read ESL LD Tut.
- **Adm (Bdg Gr 9-12; Day 9-10):** 84/yr. Bdg 63. Day 21. Appl due: Rolling. Accepted: 82%. **Tests** CEEB CTP_4 SSAT Stanford.
- **Enr 180.** B 73/23. G 60/24. Sec 180. Wh 83%. Hisp 6%. Blk 5%. Asian 6%. Avg class size: 11. **Fac 31.** M 18. F 12/1. Wh 100%. Adv deg: 87%. In dorms 11.
- **Grad '04—36. Col—36.** (St Norbert 6, Notre Dame 1, Northwestern 1, U of CA-Berkeley 1, U of MI 1, Macalester 1). Avg SAT: 1141. Avg ACT: 24. Alum 3750.
- **Tui '04-'05: Bdg $27,820** (+$500). **Day $13,700** (+$500). **Aid:** Merit 71 ($305,540). Need 82 ($1,107,652).
- Endow $8,000,000. Plant val $35,000,000. Bldgs 25. Dorms 4. Dorm rms 210. Class rms 25. Lib 21,500 vols. Sci labs 5. Lang labs 1. Comp labs 1. Dark rms 2. Observatories 1. Auds 1. Theaters 1. Art studios 1. Music studios 12. Dance studios 1. Gyms 2. Fields 5. Courts 11. Pools 1.
- **Est 1855.** Nonprofit. Sem (Aug-May). **Assoc** CLS NCA.

Initially called Wayland University, this school was named in honor of Dr. Francis Wayland, an educational reformer and onetime president of Brown University. The academy is the oldest continuously coeducational secondary boarding school in the country.

The curriculum offers college preparatory, honors and Advanced Placement levels of course work, with requirements in English, the fine arts, foreign language, mathematics, science, and social studies and history, in addition to compulsory academic electives, health education and athletics. An educational support program provides instruction in reading and study skills, as well as a coordinated tutorial program that enrolls a limited number of students in grades 9-11 who have identified special learning needs.

Students compete in a wide range of interscholastics and, as an alternative to organized athletics, sophomores, juniors and seniors may choose to participate in a variety of extracurricular activities through the Alternate Activities Program. AAP combines nonathletic and creative pursuits, such as yearbook, art, community service and photography, with lifetime sports, including cycling, aerobics and weight training. Weekly chapel services are offered, and at least four weekends are set aside each school year for trips that feature enrichment activities throughout the Midwest.

BROOKFIELD, WI. (8 mi. W of Milwaukee, WI) Suburban. Pop: 6390. Alt: 835 ft.

BROOKFIELD ACADEMY
Day — Coed Gr PS-12

Brookfield, WI 53045. 3460 N Brookfield Rd. Tel: 262-783-3200. Fax: 262-783-3213.
www.brookfieldacademy.org   E-mail: sharon.koenings@brookfieldacademy.org

Robert E. Solsrud, Head. BS, Univ of Wisconsin-Eau Claire, MEd, EdD, Marquette Univ. **Sharon Koenings, Adm.**

Col Prep. AP—Eng Fr Ger Lat Span Calc Stats Comp_Sci Bio Chem Physics US_Hist Econ Studio_Art. **Feat**—Classics Creative_Writing Shakespeare Programming Asian_Hist Middle_East_Hist Govt Art_Hist Drama Music. **Supp**—Tut.

Adm: 121/yr. Appl due: Rolling. Accepted: 99%. **Tests** ISEE.

Enr 724. B 352. G 372. Elem 507. Sec 217. Wh 77%. Hisp 2%. Blk 6%. Asian 15%. **Fac 87.** M 30/2. F 52/3. Wh 99%. Hisp 1%. Adv deg: 42%.

Grad '04—47. **Col**—47. (U of WI-Madison 5, Marquette 4, U of WI-Milwaukee 3, St Norbert 3, Milwaukee Sch of Engineering 2, Yale 1). Avg SAT: 1217. Avg ACT: 27. Alum 908.

Tui '04-'05: Day $11,150-11,750 (+$75-500). **Aid:** Merit 28 ($109,825). Need 61 ($377,269).

Summer: Acad Enrich Rev Rec. Tui Day $400. 2 wks.

Endow $2,196,000. Plant val $13,525,000. Bldgs 6. Class rms 48. Libs 3. Sci labs 6. Comp labs 3. Theaters 1. Art studios 4. Music studios 2. Gyms 2. Fields 11. Courts 8.

Est 1962. Nonprofit. Sem (Sept-June).

BA was founded in 1962 as the Academy of Basic Education. Located on 116 acres, the school combines a rigorous college preparatory curriculum with traditional values.

The lower school (grades pre-K-5) focuses on establishing and strengthening the basic skills of reading, writing and mathematics. Reading is taught through a phonics approach. Students are also exposed to music, art, physical education, history, geography, computers, science and English grammar.

The middle school curriculum (grades 6-8) emphasizes reading, composition, classics, Latin, math, science, history and geography. French and Spanish are offered in grades 7 and 8. Students also have classes in music, art, computers, speech and drama.

The upper school prepares students for a wide variety of competitive colleges. Students are required to take four years of English, four of math, three of science, three of history (including one year of economics) and four of a foreign language. Advanced Placement courses are available in the major disciplines.

Extracurriculars include athletics, drama, travel, yearbook staff, service club, mock trial and academic decathlon. **See Also Page 1126**

DELAFIELD, WI. (22 mi. W of Milwaukee, WI) Rural. Pop: 6472. Alt: 1242 ft.

ST. JOHN'S NORTHWESTERN MILITARY ACADEMY
Bdg — Boys Gr 7-12; Day — Boys 7-8

Delafield, WI 53018. 1101 N Genesee St. Tel: 262-646-7199. Fax: 262-646-7128.
www.sjnma.org   E-mail: admissions@sjnma.org

Jack H. Albert, Jr., **Pres.** BA, Glenville State College, MEd, James Madison Univ. **Maj. Charles E. Moore, Adm.**

Col Prep. Milit. Feat—Ger Span Stats Environ_Sci Computers Geog Psych Sociol Studio_Art Drama Band Chorus Journ JROTC SAT_Prep Aviation_Sci. **Supp**—ESL Tut.

Adm (Bdg Gr 7-11; Day 7-8): 125/yr. Bdg 123. Day 2. Appl due: Rolling. Accepted: 55%. **Tests** SSAT TOEFL.

Enr 306. B 299/7. Elem 40. Sec 266. Wh 68%. Hisp 18%. Blk 5%. Am Ind 2%. Asian 2%. Other 5%. Avg class size: 12. Uniform. **Fac 38.** M 31/3. F 4. Wh 98%. Hisp 2%. Adv deg: 36%. In dorms 2.

Grad '04—71. Col—71. (U of IL-Chicago 4, Milwaukee Sch of Engineering 4, DePaul 2, U of WI-Madison 2, Norwich 2, Purdue 1). Avg ACT: 22. Alum 5000.

Tui '04-'05: Bdg $26,500 (+$4000). **Day $11,000** (+$2000). **Aid:** Merit 62 ($120,000). Need 61 ($520,711).

Summer: Acad Rec. Adventure. ESL. Tui Bdg $800-3000. Tui Day $400-800. 1-3 wks.

Endow $4,000,000. Plant val $23,000,000. Bldgs 20. Dorms 3. Dorm rms 197. Class rms 42. Lib 14,000 vols. Sci labs 6. Comp labs 2. Art studios 1. Music studios 1. Gyms 1. Fields 7. Courts 9. Pools 1. Golf crses 1. Rifle ranges 2.

Est 1884. Nonprofit. Episcopal. Sem (Sept-June). **Assoc** NCA.

SJNMA was formed by the 1995 merger of St. John's Military Academy, which was established in 1884, and Northwestern Military and Naval Academy, founded in 1888. A number of required courses are supplemented by electives in each discipline. The supervised two-hour study period each evening is an integral part of the academic day, and daily tutorials are available for individual help. The military program, which promotes a structured cadet lifestyle, requires JROTC leadership training each year for all high school students.

Sports include football, basketball, soccer, track and field, golf, wrestling, cross-country, skiing, hockey, swimming, tennis, riflery, rugby and tae kwon do. Among the extracurricular activities are weightlifting, lifeguard training, scuba, rappelling, drama, choir, band, chess and Boy Scouts. A course in aviation science is available; in addition, those students who earn a private pilot's license during junior year may take an advanced course leading to an instrument rating. Cadets attend nondenominational chapel services twice a week.

HARTLAND, WI. (19 mi. W of Milwaukee, WI) Suburban. Pop: 7905. Alt: 930 ft.

UNIVERSITY LAKE SCHOOL
Day — Coed Gr PS-12

Hartland, WI 53029. 4024 Nagawicka Rd, PO Box 290. Tel: 262-367-6011.
Fax: 262-367-3146.
www.universitylake.org   E-mail: kbaty@universitylake.org
Bradley F. Ashley, Head. AB, Dartmouth College, MAT, Univ of New Hampshire. **Kristin M. Baty, Adm.**
Col Prep. Feat—Computers Drama Music. **Supp**—Dev_Read Rev Tut.
Adm: 65/yr. Appl due: Rolling.
Enr 339. B 171. G 168. Elem 247. Sec 92. Wh 93%. Hisp 1%. Blk 1%. Asian 1%. Other 4%. Avg class size: 13. **Fac 38.** M 9/1. F 23/5. Adv deg: 78%.
Grad '04—13. Col—13. (N MI, Winona St, Dartmouth, U of VT, Butler, Clark U). Avg SAT: 1089. Avg ACT: 23. Alum 850.
Tui '05-'06: Day $9160-12,670 (+$750). **Aid:** Merit 61 ($86,750). Need 42 ($190,129).
Summer: Acad Enrich Rev Rem Rec. 1-6 wks.
Endow $12,162,000. Plant val $10,409,000. Bldgs 5. Class rms 30. 3 Libs 14,000 vols. Labs 3. Art studios 2. Music studios 2. Gyms 3. Fields 5. Courts 3.
Est 1956. Nonprofit. Sem (Sept-June). **Assoc** CLS NCA.

University Lake maintains a strong college preparatory program. The 180-acre, wooded campus, located in the lake country of northwestern Waukesha County, provides a rural setting.

The lower school emphasizes academics (reading, math, writing, history, science and Spanish) the arts—with offerings provided in music and movement—and athletics. This program continues in the middle school with the addition of dramatics, team sports and student government. Computer science is available in all grades, and the upper school curriculum includes Advanced Placement and honors courses in most subject areas.

High school sports are field hockey, soccer, basketball, tennis and golf. Most high school students are involved in drama, chorus or student government.

MILWAUKEE, WI. Urban. Pop: 596,974. Alt: 750 ft.

UNIVERSITY SCHOOL OF MILWAUKEE
Day — Coed Gr PS-12

Milwaukee, WI 53217. 2100 W Fairy Chasm Rd. Tel: 414-352-6000. Fax: 414-352-8076.
www.usm.k12.wi.us   E-mail: admissions@usm.k12.wi.us
Ward J. Ghory, Head. BA, Yale Univ, MEd, EdD, Univ of Massachusetts-Amherst. **Kathleen Friedman, Adm.**
Col Prep. AP—Eng Fr Span Calc Stats Comp_Sci Bio Chem Physics Eur_Hist US_Hist Econ US_Govt & Pol. **Feat**—Lat Programming Film Studio_Art Acting Drama Music. **Supp**—Tut.
Adm: 170/yr. Appl due: Rolling. Accepted: 82%. Yield: 78%. **Tests** CTP_4 Stanford.

Enr 1066. B 546. G 520. Elem 718. Sec 348. Wh 80%. Hisp 2%. Blk 6%. Am Ind 1%. Asian 3%. Other 8%. Avg class size: 17. **Fac 105.** M 38/1. F 54/12. Wh 98%. Blk 2%. Adv deg: 62%.

Grad '04—72. Col—71. (U of WI-Madison 4, Middlebury 4, Harvard 3, OH Wesleyan 3, Geo Wash 2, Boston Col 2). Avg SAT: 1288. Avg ACT: 28. Alum 5600.

Tui '04-'05: Day $10,552-14,832 (+$100-1000). **Aid:** Need 123 ($1,009,414).

Summer: Acad Enrich Rev Rem Rec. Art. Sports. 10 wks.

Endow $41,000,000. Plant val $32,000,000. Bldgs 2. Class rms 111. 3 Libs 34,000 vols. Sci labs 8. Lang labs 2. Comp labs 3. Theaters 1. Art studios 4. Music studios 3. Dance studios 1. Gyms 3. Fields 7. Courts 8. Rinks 1.

Est 1851. Nonprofit. Tri (Aug-June). **Assoc** CLS NCA.

USM resulted from a 1964 merger of Milwaukee Country Day School, Milwaukee Downer Seminary and Milwaukee University School. The school occupies a 127-acre campus in suburban River Hills.

The lower school program (grades pre-K-4) integrates the core subjects—language arts, mathematics, social studies, science and foreign language—with the visual arts, music, dance, technology and daily physical education. Writing across the curriculum, the development of study skills, and the continuation of foreign language and technology offerings are features of the middle school curriculum (grades 5-8). Academics in the upper school (grades 9-12) are college preparatory, and students at this level may enroll in Advanced Placement courses in all major disciplines and choose from a wide selection of arts classes.

Student activities include music, theater arts, interest clubs and publications. The sports program provides interscholastic competition at varsity and junior varsity levels for both boys and girls, and it includes ice hockey on the school's indoor rink. Travel abroad programs are available both during the school year and over the summer.

RACINE, WI. (25 mi. SSE of Milwaukee, WI) Urban. Pop: 81,855. Alt: 626 ft.

THE PRAIRIE SCHOOL
Day — Coed Gr PS-12

Racine, WI 53402. 4050 Lighthouse Dr. Tel: 262-260-3845. Fax: 262-260-3790.
www.prairieschool.com   E-mail: msweetman@prairieschool.com

William Mark H. Murphy, Head. BA, Norwich Univ, MA, State Univ of New York-Buffalo. **Molly Lofquist, Adm.**

Col Prep. AP—Eng Fr Span Calc Bio Chem Physics Eur_Hist US_Hist Music_Theory. **Feat**—Computers Studio_Art Glass_Blowing Communications. **Supp**—Dev_Read ESL Makeup Tut.

Adm: 92/yr. Appl due: Rolling. Accepted: 75%.

Enr 669. B 319. G 350. Elem 443. Sec 226. Wh 74%. Hisp 3%. Blk 2%. Asian 8%. Other 13%. Avg class size: 20. **Fac 65.** M 21. F 41/3. Wh 94%. Hisp 3%. Blk 2%. Other 1%. Adv deg: 52%.

Grad '04—42. Col—42. (U of WI-Madison 6, U of MN-Twin Cities 4, Vanderbilt 2, U of WI-Oshkosh 2, Marquette 1, U of WI-La Crosse 1). Avg SAT: 1230. Avg ACT: 25. Alum 1100.

Tui '04-'05: Day $8550-10,550 (+$300-800). **Aid:** Merit 16 ($112,000). Need ($900,000).
Summer: Acad Enrich Rem Rec. Sports. 10 wks.
Endow $33,000,000. Plant val $30,000,000. Bldgs 2. Class rms 35. Lib 24,000 vols. Labs 5. Photog labs 1. Art studios 7. Music studios 5. Perf arts ctrs 1. Gyms 2. Fields 5. Courts 6. Field houses 1.
Est 1965. Nonprofit. Tri (Aug-June). **Assoc** CLS NCA.

Prairie was established by area mothers Imogene Johnson and Willie Hilpert to fill a need for an independent college preparatory school in southeastern Wisconsin. Its name derives from the style of its buildings, which were designed by associates of Frank Lloyd Wright.

In the primary and middle schools, academics and the fine arts are blended with opportunities for individually guided work. Leadership and team-building programs are part of the curriculum beginning in the primary grades. The upper school curriculum is accented by Advanced Placement courses and opportunities in the fine, creative and performing arts. Juniors and seniors may take part in an interim program that features on-campus seminars and projects throughout the country and abroad.

Cocurricular activities include varsity and junior varsity sports, yearbook, literary magazine, student government, musical and dramatic productions, and a variety of clubs.

Plains States

IOWA

DAVENPORT, IA. (62 mi. ESE of Cedar Rapids, IA) Urban. Pop: 98,359. Alt: 559 ft. Area also includes Bettendorf.

RIVERMONT COLLEGIATE
Day — Coed Gr PS-12

Bettendorf, IA 52722. 1821 Sunset Dr. Tel: 563-359-1366. Fax: 563-359-7576.
www.rvmt.org   E-mail: admission@rvmt.org

Richard E. St. Laurent, Head. BA, MS, Indiana Univ-Purdue Fort Wayne. **Heidi J. Herman, Adm.**

Col Prep. AP—Eng Fr Span Calc Stats Bio US_Hist World_Hist. **Feat**—Humanities Lat Computers Studio_Art Drama Music. **Supp**—Tut.

Adm (Gr PS-11): 52/yr. Appl due: Rolling. Accepted: 70%.

Enr 235. B 105. G 130. Elem 195. Sec 40. Wh 73%. Hisp 1%. Blk 6%. Asian 19%. Other 1%. Avg class size: 16. **Fac 33.** M 3/2. F 23/5. Wh 100%. Adv deg: 33%.

Grad '04—9. Col—9. (U of IA 3, Rutgers 1, USC 1, U of OK 1, U of MO-Columbia 1, St Ambrose 1). Avg SAT: 1210. Avg ACT: 28. Alum 625.

Tui '04-'05: Day $8550-9240 (+$600). **Aid:** Merit 5 ($12,815). Need 49 ($250,000).

Summer: PS. Acad Enrich Rec. Tui Day $100/wk. 6 wks.

Endow $2,142,000. Plant val $1,700,000. Bldgs 5. Class rms 23. Libs 1. Comp labs 2. Art studios 1. Gyms 1. Fields 1. Courts 1.

Est 1884. Nonprofit. Quar (Aug-June). **Assoc** NCA.

Established as an Episcopal boarding school for girls by the Episcopal bishop of Iowa and the trustees of Griswold College through a legacy from the estate of Sarah Burr, and for 41 years conducted by the Episcopal Sisters of Saint Mary, the school came under the control of the diocese of Iowa in 1943, and has since operated as a nondenominational institution and has also become coeducational. Enrolling students from eastern Iowa and western Illinois, Rivermont Collegiate occupies quarters on a bluff overlooking the Mississippi River.

The college preparatory curriculum features independent study, interdisciplinary electives and Advanced Placement courses for qualified students. Rivermont's program stresses writing, inquiry and reasoning at all levels, and students can accelerate as early as grade 1. French, Spanish and study skills classes begin in kindergarten.

Annual school events include an autumn trip, winter skiing excursions and spring outings. A full complement of activities includes student council, community service, annual dramatic and musical productions, choir, band, yearbook, French club, academic fair, and athletics such as golf, soccer, volleyball and basketball.

KANSAS

SALINA, KS. (105 mi. W of Topeka, KS) Urban. Pop: 45,679. Alt: 1200 ft.

ST. JOHN'S MILITARY SCHOOL
Bdg — Boys Gr 6-12

Salina, KS 67402. N End Santa Fe Ave, PO Box 827. Tel: 785-823-7231.
  Fax: 785-823-7236.
  www.sjms.org   E-mail: duaner@sjms.org
Col. Jack R. Fox, USA (Ret), Pres. BA, New Mexico State Univ, MEd, Georgia State Univ.
  Duane Rutherford, Adm.
  Col Prep. Gen Acad. Milit. **Feat**—Span Computers Econ Relig Studio_Art Drama Band Music Speech JROTC Study_Skills. **Supp**—Dev_Read ESL Tut.
  Adm: 64/yr. Appl due: Rolling. Accepted: 97%.
  Enr 156. B 156. Wh 87%. Hisp 5%. Blk 5%. Asian 3%. Avg class size: 12. Uniform. **Fac 27.** M 18. F 9. Wh 100%. Adv deg: 59%. In dorms 2.
  Grad '04—30. Col—16. (Ft Lewis, Johnson County CC, Hutchinson CC, IA St, San Jose St, Norwich). Avg SAT: 950. Avg ACT: 22. Alum 1200.
  Tui '05-'06: Bdg $21,663 (+$3000). **Aid:** Need 15 ($60,000).
  Summer: Acad Enrich Rev Rem. Leadership. Tui Bdg $3150. 5 wks.
  Endow $9,000,000. Plant val $10,000,000. Bldgs 18. Dorms 3. Dorm rms 110. Class rms 22. Lib 8000 vols. Labs 3. Art studios 1. Music studios 1. Gyms 1. Fields 3. Courts 2. Fitness ctrs 1. Rifle ranges 1.
  Est 1887. Nonprofit. Episcopal. Sem (Sept-May). **Assoc** NCA.

St. John's was founded by Rt. Rev. Elisha Smith Thomas and a group of concerned Salina businessmen. Students must complete either the standard or the college preparatory curriculum, in addition to JROTC and religion. Both require units in language arts, math, science, social science, computer science, physical education and health, plus electives; the latter includes a mandatory foreign language. Elective courses are offered in such subjects as art, band, philosophy and industrial careers, among others.

St. John's is represented by varsity teams in football, baseball, basketball, wrestling, track, tennis, golf and riflery. A more limited range of sports is available for boys in grades 6-8, and a physical training program is provided for cadets who do not compete in varsity athletics. Extracurricular activities include a number of clubs and organizations. Each student attends religious services three times per week.

WICHITA, KS. (129 mi. SW of Topeka, KS) Urban. Pop: 344,284. Alt: 1325 ft.

WICHITA COLLEGIATE SCHOOL
Day — Coed Gr PS-12

Wichita, KS 67206. 9115 E 13th St. Tel: 316-634-0433. Fax: 316-634-0598.
www.wcsks.com   E-mail: ssteed@wcsks.com
Tom Davis, Head. BS, Rice Univ, MBA, Wichita State Univ. **Susie Steed, Adm.**

- **Col Prep. AP**—Eng Fr Lat Span Calc Stats Comp_Sci Bio Chem Physics US_Hist Econ US_Govt & Pol. **Feat**—Humanities Studio_Art Videography Music. **Supp**—LD Rev Tut.
- **Adm:** 139/yr. Appl due: Rolling. Accepted: 91%. Yield: 73%. **Tests** IQ Stanford.
- **Enr 967.** B 512. G 455. Elem 666. Sec 301. Wh 80%. Hisp 3%. Blk 3%. Am Ind 1%. Asian 5%. Other 8%. Avg class size: 15. **Fac 97.** M 22/2. F 62/11. Wh 96%. Hisp 1%. Blk 1%. Asian 1%. Other 1%. Adv deg: 35%.
- **Grad '04—65. Col—63.** (U of KS 11, Wichita St 6, KS St 5, Trinity U 5, Creighton 3, NYU 2). Avg SAT: 1239. Avg ACT: 26. Alum 1150.
- **Tui '04-'05: Day $7050-10,450** (+$100-600). **Aid:** Need 152 ($620,000).
- **Summer:** Acad Enrich Rev. Tui Day $75-500/crse. 11 wks.
- Endow $1,200,000. Plant val $16,000,000. Bldgs 7. Class rms 80. Lib 16,000 vols. Sci labs 5. Comp labs 2. Art studios 1. Music studios 2. Dance studios 1. Gyms 2. Fields 2. Courts 6.
- **Est 1963.** Nonprofit. Sem (Aug-May). **Assoc** CLS.

Founded by parents seeking an alternative to public education and commencing as an elementary program, this school gradually expanded to provide complete college preparation, adding grade 12 in 1966. Students follow a common prescribed curriculum that emphasizes traditional discipline. Pupils must take part in the AP program, and all have opportunities in the arts and interscholastic athletics. Boys and girls may participate in community service and mentor programs.

MINNESOTA

COLLEGEVILLE, MN. (69 mi. NW of Minneapolis, MN) Rural. Pop: 100. Alt: 1094 ft.

SAINT JOHN'S PREPARATORY SCHOOL
Bdg — Coed Gr 9-PG; Day — Coed 7-PG

Collegeville, MN 56321. 1857 Watertower Rd, PO Box 4000. Tel: 320-363-3321.
Fax: 320-363-3513.
www.sjprep.net   E-mail: admitprep@csbsju.edu
Rev. Gordon Tavis, OSB, Pres. BA, St John's Univ (MN), MMgt, Massachusetts Institute of Technology. **Bryan Backes, Adm.**
- **Col Prep. Feat**—Stats Computers Econ Law Theol Ceramics Drawing Photog Sculpt Studio_Art Theater Music. **Supp**—ESL Tut.
- **Adm:** 120/yr. Bdg 34. Day 86. Appl due: Rolling. Accepted: 91%. **Tests** DAT.
- **Enr 320.** Elem 60. Sec 260. Wh 77%. Hisp 3%. Blk 1%. Am Ind 1%. Asian 2%. Other 16%. Avg class size: 16. **Fac 33.** M 15/6. F 6/6. Wh 97%. Blk 3%. Adv deg: 54%.
- **Grad '04—62. Col—60.** (St John's U-MN, Col of St Benedict, U of WI-Madison, Lewis & Clark, U of St Thomas-MN, CO Col). Avg SAT: 1266. Avg ACT: 26. Alum 760.
- **Tui '04-'05: Bdg $23,407. 5-Day Bdg $20,829. Day $5025-10,207. Aid:** Merit 39 ($30,036). Need 94 ($352,288). Work prgm 71 ($44,700).
- **Summer:** Rec. Tui Bdg $295-320/wk. Tui Day $210/wk. 7 wks.
- Endow $4,128,000. Plant val $4,125,000. Bldgs 12. Dorms 2. Dorm rms 117. Class rms 18. Lib 6000 vols. Sci labs 4. Comp labs 2. Auds 1. Theaters 1. Art studios 3. Music studios 2. Arts ctrs 1. Fields 6. Courts 9. Pools 2.
- **Est 1857.** Nonprofit. Roman Catholic. Sem (Aug-May). **Assoc** NCA.

Saint John's Preparatory School's modern facilities are located on 2600 acres of woodland 14 miles west of St. Cloud. The school moved to its present site on the east side of Saint John's Abbey in 1962.

A traditional college preparatory course of study is supplemented by offerings in the fine arts, social studies and theology. Each department provides the opportunity for qualified students to participate in an independent study program. Advanced courses are available and some carry college credit. In addition, pupils may take college courses at Saint John's University, a liberal arts college for men that shares Prep's campus. A number of university facilities are open to Prep students, and the school's computer system is linked directly to the university's. Prep students also have access to the programs and facilities of the College of Saint Benedict, a nearby liberal arts college for women that operates in conjunction with the university. The residential program for girls, started in 1992, is conducted in cooperation with the college, located four miles away in St. Joseph. Girls live a building on the college campus that is staffed by Prep professionals; the school provides free transportation between the two campuses.

The Melk Program is a nine-month course of study and travel at the Benedictine Abbey School of Melk, Austria, that is open to members of the junior and senior classes. A variety of extracurricular activities supplements academics.

EDEN PRAIRIE, MN. (12 mi. SW of Minneapolis, MN) Urban. Pop: 54,901. Alt: 875 ft.

THE INTERNATIONAL SCHOOL OF MINNESOTA
Day — Coed Gr PS-12

Eden Prairie, MN 55344. 6385 Beach Rd. Tel: 952-918-1800. Fax: 952-918-1801.
  www.ism-sabis.net   E-mail: admissions@ism-sabis.net
Susan Berg, Dir. Kelley Kosmides, Adm.
  Col Prep. AP—Eng Fr Span Calc Stats Comp_Sci Bio Chem Physics Eur_Hist Econ US_Govt & Pol Art_Hist Music_Theory. Feat—British_Lit Govt Studio_Art. Supp—ESL Rev Tut.
  Adm: 98/yr. Appl due: Rolling. Accepted: 50%. Yield: 84%. Tests CTP_4 IQ.
  Enr 528. B 261. G 267. Elem 426. Sec 102. Wh 55%. Hisp 8%. Blk 3%. Am Ind 5%. Asian 21%. Other 8%. Avg class size: 18. Uniform. Fac 56. M 11/1. F 44. Wh 87%. Hisp 11%. Asian 2%. Adv deg: 46%.
  Grad '04—22. Col—22. (Northwestern 2, U of St Thomas-MN 2, Gustavus Adolphus 2, U of MN-Twin Cities 2, Wellesley 1, Drexel 1). Avg SAT: 1223. Avg ACT: 26. Alum 133.
  Tui '04-'05: Day $11,300-11,600 (+$600). Aid: Need ($160,000).
  Summer: Rec. Tui Day $225/wk. 8 wks.
  Lib 18,000 vols. Sci labs 1. Comp labs 2. Auds 1. Art studios 1. Music studios 3. Gyms 1. Fields 2. Courts 8. Pools 1.
  Est 1985. Inc. Tri (Aug-June). Assoc NCA.

ISM is one of 27 schools of the worldwide SABIS network, which was established in Lebanon in 1886. Offered in a multicultural setting, the curriculum features various Advanced Placement courses and places an emphasis on English, world languages, math, science and the humanities. In accordance with ISM's global approach, pupils begin participating in the daily world language program at the preschool level.

The school's fine arts program is particularly strong, and varsity and junior varsity athletics, publications and clubs round out the educational experience. Students at the school, which occupies a 55-acre campus, enroll from more than 40 nations.

FARIBAULT, MN. (46 mi. S of Minneapolis, MN) Urban. Pop: 19,214. Alt: 981 ft.

SHATTUCK-ST. MARY'S SCHOOL
Bdg and Day — Coed Gr 6-PG

Faribault, MN 55021. 1000 Shumway Ave, PO Box 218. Tel: 507-333-1618.
  Fax: 507-333-1661.
  www.s-sm.org   E-mail: admissions@s-sm.org
Nick J. B. Stoneman, Head. BA, Bowdoin College, MEd, Columbia Univ. Amy Wolf, Adm.
  Col Prep. AP—Eng Fr Lat Span Calc Bio Chem Physics Eur_Hist US_Hist Studio_Art. Feat—British_Lit Mandarin Comp_Design Robotics Govt & Pol Ethics Relig Photog Drama Chorus Speech. Supp—ESL LD Rev Tut.

Adm (Gr 6-12): 108/yr. Bdg 81. Day 27. Appl due: Rolling. Accepted: 57%. Yield: 64%. **Tests** CEEB ISEE SSAT TOEFL.

Enr 294. B 134/58. G 70/32. Elem 57. Sec 237. Wh 78%. Hisp 2%. Blk 2%. Am Ind 1%. Asian 16%. Other 1%. Avg class size: 14. **Fac 45.** M 22/8. F 11/4. Wh 96%. Blk 2%. Other 2%. Adv deg: 37%. In dorms 15.

Grad '04—61. Col—56. (U of MN-Twin Cities, U of WI-Madison, Northwestern, Johns Hopkins, MIT, Carnegie Mellon). Avg SAT: 1140. Avg ACT: 24. Alum 6000.

Tui '04-'05: Bdg $29,300 (+$1500). **Day $19,600** (+$1500). **Aid:** Merit 27 ($163,600). Need 109 ($1,100,000).

Summer: Acad Enrich Rec. Tui Bdg $3000. 4 wks.

Endow $10,000,000. Plant val $35,000,000. Bldgs 12. Dorms 5. Dorm rms 110. Class rms 30. Lib 25,000 vols. Sci labs 4. Comp labs 3. Comp ctrs 1. Auds 1. Theaters 1. Art studios 2. Music studios 3. Dance studios 1. Gyms 2. Fields 6. Courts 8. Rinks 2. Tracks 1. Golf crses 1.

Est 1858. Nonprofit. Episcopal. Tri (Sept-May). **Assoc** CLS NCA.

One of the oldest boarding schools in the Midwest, Shattuck-St. Mary's was founded by Rev. James L. Breck as an Episcopal mission. Separate schools were established for boys and girls in the 1860s and merged in 1972. Today, the school is located on 250 acres on a wooded hilltop, 45 miles south of Minneapolis.

The curriculum is college preparatory, with honors, accelerated and Advanced Placement courses offered in all major disciplines. The fine and performing arts curriculum is noteworthy for its scope, and courses in religion, ethics and values are available. Cultural, social and recreational opportunities include a full athletic program in interscholastic and intramural sports (featuring a particularly strong ice hockey program), in addition to a diverse selection of on-campus organizations and activities.

The middle school has separate faculty, facilities and programs.

MINNEAPOLIS, MN. Urban. Pop: 382,618. Alt: 812 ft. Area also includes Hopkins.

THE BLAKE SCHOOL
Day — Coed Gr PS-12

Hopkins, MN 55343. 110 Blake Rd S. Tel: 952-988-3420. Fax: 952-988-3455.
www.blakeschool.org   E-mail: communications@blakeschool.org

John C. Gulla, Head. BA, Amherst College, MA, Columbia Univ. **Adaline Shinkle, Adm.**

Col Prep. AP—Eng Fr Ger Span Calc Stats Bio Chem Eur_Hist Studio_Art. **Feat**—Computers Drama Theater_Arts Music Public_Speak. **Supp**—Rev.

Adm: 187/yr. Appl due: Jan. Accepted: 50%. **Tests** CEEB CTP_4 IQ.

Enr 1316. Elem 829. Sec 487. Wh 82%. Hisp 1%. Blk 6%. Am Ind 1%. Asian 6%. Other 4%. Avg class size: 16. **Fac 138.** M 56. F 82. Wh 94%. Hisp 2%. Blk 3%. Other 1%. Adv deg: 81%.

Grad '04—107. Col—107. (Northwestern, Williams, U of Puget Sound, Yale, DePauw, U of WI-Madison). Avg SAT: 1310. Avg ACT: 29. Alum 8000.

Tui '05-'06: Day $10,600-18,100 (+$980). **Aid:** Need 184 ($2,760,762).

Summer: Acad Enrich Rec. Art. Sports. Driver Ed. 7-8 wks.

Endow $36,000,000. Plant val $60,000,000. Bldgs 5. Class rms 150. Libs 4. Chapels 1. Sci

labs 9. Lang labs 1. Comp labs 5. Auds 2. Art studios 7. Music studios 7. Drama studios 3. Gyms 4. Fields 6. Courts 10. Pools 1. Rinks 1.
Est 1900. Nonprofit. Sem (Sept-June). **Assoc** CLS NCA.

One of the largest independent day schools in Greater Minneapolis/St. Paul, this coeducational school resulted from the 1972 merger of Blake School for boys, Northrop Collegiate School for girls and the Highcroft Country Day School. The school is located on three campuses, with the upper school (grades 9-12) on the Northrop campus in Minneapolis (511 Kenwood Pky., 55403) and the middle school (grades 6-8) and administrative offices on the Blake campus in Hopkins. The lower school operates at two locations: the Blake campus (grades pre-K-5) and the Highcroft campus (grades K-5) in Wayzata (301 Peavey Ln., 55391).

Blake's rigorous college preparatory course of studies features an integrated program of academic, artistic and athletic activities, and the school also offers a wide range of electives, approximately a dozen Advanced Placement courses and independent study options for seniors. Students gain exposure to foreign languages in each division. Computer technology is integrated into the curriculum at all grade levels: Students work with online resources, software and multimedia processes to access information and develop presentations. The arts program is particularly strong, with such courses as ceramics, printmaking, photography, drama, chorus and instrumental music.

School publications, student government and interest clubs supplement academics. All pupils either take part in physical education or join an athletic team. The school offers interscholastic sports at several levels for girls and boys.

BRECK SCHOOL
Day — Coed Gr PS-12

Minneapolis, MN 55422. 123 Ottawa Ave N. Tel: 763-381-8100. Fax: 763-381-8288.
www.breckschool.org   E-mail: info@breckschool.org
Samuel A. Salas, Head. BA, Univ of Chile, MA, Univ of Michigan. **Michael J. Weiszel, Adm.**
  Col Prep. **AP**—Eng Fr Span Calc Bio Chem Physics US_Hist Studio_Art. **Feat**—Shakespeare Chin Econ Relig Fine_Arts Performing_Arts Music_Theory. **Supp**—Rem_Math Rem_Read Tut.
  Adm: 141/yr. Appl due: Feb. Accepted: 19%. **Tests** CTP_4.
  Enr 1196. Elem 801. Sec 395. Wh 78%. Hisp 4%. Blk 10%. Am Ind 2%. Asian 6%. Avg class size: 18. **Fac 134.** Adv deg: 38%.
  Grad '04—96. Col—96. (Skidmore 5, St Olaf 5, Geo Wash 4, Miami U-OH 4, Boston Col 3, U of Chicago 3). Avg SAT: 1220. Alum 3000.
  Tui '04-'05: Day $15,885 (+$1305-2785). **Aid:** Need 173 ($2,185,408).
  Endow $37,200,000. Plant val $9,729,000. Bldgs 1. Class rms 73. 3 Libs 51,700 vols. Sci labs 8. Comp labs 6. Art studios 4. Music studios 5. Dance studios 1. Drama studios 1. Gyms 3. Fields 5. Courts 7. Basketball courts 4. Field houses 1. Pools 1. Rinks 1. Tracks 2. Weight rms 1.
  Est 1886. Nonprofit. Episcopal. Sem (Aug-June). **Assoc** CLS NCA.

Breck was established as an Episcopal school in Wilder by the same Bishop Whipple who founded the Faribault Schools. Named in honor of Rev. James Lloyd Breck, it relocated first (in 1917) to St. Paul and then, in 1956, to West River Parkway. In 1981, it moved to its present, 50-acre campus minutes west of downtown Minneapolis.

The curriculum features Spanish and Chinese instruction in grades K-12. All upper school students perform weekly community service and participate in the May Program, the two-week, in-depth study of an approved topic. Frequent field trips are made to Minneapolis and St. Paul theaters, museums, orchestra halls and zoological gardens, and annual trips are taken to China, France and other countries.

The athletic program includes baseball, football, ice hockey and skiing for boys, and gymnastics, softball, volleyball, ice hockey and skiing for girls. Basketball, soccer, tennis, cross-country running, swimming, golf, track and lacrosse are open to both boys and girls. Breck conducts two chapel services per week for each division, as well as a monthly all-school service. **See Also Page 1124**

MINNEHAHA ACADEMY
Day — Coed Gr PS-12

Minneapolis, MN 55406. 3100 W River Pky. Tel: 612-728-7756. Fax: 612-728-7757.
www.minnehahaacademy.net   E-mail: admissions@minnehahaacademy.net
John B. Engstrom, Pres. BS, Wheaton College (IL), MS, MA, State Univ of New York-Stony Brook, EdD, Columbia Univ. **Paul A. Norby, Adm.**

Col Prep. AP—Eng Lat Calc Stats Comp_Sci Bio Chem Physics Eur_Hist US_Hist World_Hist Econ US_Govt & Pol Studio_Art. **Feat**—Bible Music Indus_Arts Study_Skills. **Supp**—Rev Tut.

Adm: 215/yr. Appl due: Rolling. Accepted: 47%. **Tests** IQ.

Enr 1230. B 618. G 612. Elem 716. Sec 514. Avg class size: 18. **Fac 102.** M 35/5. F 55/7. Wh 97%. Blk 2%. Asian 1%. Adv deg: 52%.

Grad '04—124. Col—122. (U of MN-Twin Cities, N Park, Bethel, St Olaf, U of WI-Madison, Luther). Avg SAT: 1164. Avg ACT: 24. Alum 9300.

Tui '04-'05: Day $9970-11,125 (+$300-390). **Aid:** Need 170 ($670,000).

Summer: Enrich Rev Rec. 10 wks.

Endow $3,200,000. Plant val $20,000,000. Bldgs 4. Class rms 46. Lib 22,000 vols. Labs 3. Lang labs 1. Auds 1. Theaters 1. Art studios 3. Music studios 6. Gyms 3. Courts 1. Rinks 1.

Est 1913. Nonprofit. Evangelical Covenant. (Sept-June). **Assoc** NCA.

This Christian school, large and well equipped, draws most of its enrollment from the region. In addition to basic academics, Bible is taught at all grade levels. A full complement of honors and Advanced Placement courses provides additional challenge for qualified pupils. Extracurricular activities include musical groups, athletics and dramatics. Graduates matriculate predominantly at Midwestern colleges.

The main lower and middle school campus (grades PS-8) occupies a separate site at 4200 W. River Pky., while a third campus serving children in grades K-5 is located ten miles south, at 10150 Xerxes Ave. S, Bloomington 55431.

MN   *Leading Private Schools*   632

ST. PAUL, MN. (8 mi. E of Minneapolis, MN) Urban. Pop: 287,151. Alt: 703 ft. Area also includes Mendota Heights.

CONVENT OF THE VISITATION SCHOOL
Day — Boys Gr PS-6, Girls PS-12

Mendota Heights, MN 55120. 2455 Visitation Dr. Tel: 651-683-1700. Fax: 651-454-7144. www.visitation.net E-mail: vischool@vischool.org

Dawn Nichols, Head. BA, Ursuline College, MA, Western Illinois Univ, EdD, Nova Southeastern Univ. **Patty Healy, Adm.**

Col Prep. AP—Eng Fr Span Calc Stats Bio Eur_Hist US_Hist US_Govt & Pol. **Feat**—Creative_Writing Lat Computers Psych Sociol Relig Ceramics Drawing Graphic_Arts Ballet. **Supp**—Rem_Math Rem_Read Tut.

Adm (Gr PS-11): 117/yr. Appl due: Rolling. Accepted: 75%. Yield: 65%. **Tests** CTP_4 IQ Stanford.

Enr 578. B 89. G 489. Elem 290. Sec 288. Wh 92%. Hisp 3%. Blk 1%. Asian 3%. Other 1%. Avg class size: 19. Uniform. **Fac 61.** M 7/3. F 36/15. Wh 98%. Hisp 2%. Adv deg: 54%.

Grad '04—75. Col—75. (Northwestern 16, U of St Thomas-MN 10, Creighton 6, Providence 4, St Olaf 3, U of WI-Madison 1). Avg SAT: 1206. Avg ACT: 27. Alum 2400.

Tui '04-'05: Day $5164-12,948 (+$850). **Aid:** Need 89 ($565,000).

Summer: Acad Enrich Rev Rem. Tui Day $150-450. 6 wks.

Endow $5,811,000. Plant val $18,274,000. Bldgs 7. Class rms 42. 2 Libs 16,000 vols. Sci labs 4. Comp labs 2. Auds 1. Theaters 1. Art studios 2. Music studios 2. Dance studios 1. Gyms 2. Fields 3. Basketball courts 4. Tennis courts 8. Volleyball courts 4.

Est 1873. Nonprofit. Roman Catholic. Sem (Aug-June). **Assoc** NCA.

This Catholic school was founded when six nuns from the Order of the Visitation, at the request of Bishop Thomas Grace, boarded a steamboat in St. Louis, MO, and traveled north to establish a school for young women in the St. Paul area. Over the years, the school has occupied four different campuses.

Today, Visitation comprises an early learning center, a Montessori preschool, a coeducational lower school, a middle school for boys and girls through grade 6—as well as for girls in grades 7 and 8—and an upper school for girls only. Visitation's upper school serves as the only all-girls secondary program in the state. Throughout, emphasis is placed on the fine arts, and a family-like atmosphere and a low student-teacher ratio provide individual attention. An extended-day program serves children in grades K-6.

The school's athletic program allows pupils to take part in team sports beginning in grade 5. At the upper school level, students may play on freshman, junior varsity or varsity squads in approximately a dozen sports. Community service is another important aspect of school life.

ST. PAUL ACADEMY AND SUMMIT SCHOOL
Day — Coed Gr K-12

St Paul, MN 55105. 1712 Randolph Ave. Tel: 651-698-2451. Fax: 651-698-6787. www.spa.edu E-mail: sfoster@admin.spa.edu

Pamela J. Clarke, Head. BA, Vassar College, MA, Yale Univ, MEd, Harvard Univ. **Sally D.**

Foster, Adm.
Col Prep. Feat—Marine_Biol/Sci Econ Law Psych Philos Ceramics Drawing Photog Drama Debate Journ Speech.
Adm: 134/yr. Appl due: Feb. Accepted: 59%. **Tests** CTP_4.
Enr 924. B 476. G 448. Elem 534. Sec 390. Wh 80%. Hisp 2%. Blk 6%. Am Ind 1%. Asian 11%. Avg class size: 15. **Fac 104.** M 44. F 60. Adv deg: 66%.
Grad '04—101. **Col**—100. (U of WI-Madison, CO Col, Carleton, Wash U, NYU, Tulane). Avg SAT: 1297. Avg ACT: 29. Alum 4050.
Tui '03-'04: Day $17,860-19,400 (+$200). **Aid:** Need 117 ($1,350,865).
Summer: Acad Enrich Rec. Tui Day $550-950. 3-6 wks.
Endow $26,589,000. Plant val $39,542,000. Bldgs 3. Class rms 110. Lib 22,000 vols. Sci labs 9. Comp labs 3. Auds 1. Theaters 1. Art studios 5. Music studios 3. Gyms 3. Fields 9. Courts 12. Rinks 1. Playgrounds 2. Gardens 1.
Est 1969. Nonprofit. Sem (Aug-June). **Assoc** CLS NCA.

SPA was formed in 1969 from the merger of St. Paul Academy for boys, founded in 1900, and Summit School for girls, founded in 1917. The upper school, for students in grades 9-12, shares the Randolph Avenue campus in Highland Park with the middle school (grades 6-8); the lower school (grades K-5) is located at 1150 Goodrich Ave. in St. Paul's Crocus Hill neighborhood.

Graduation requirements include foreign language study and a course in word processing. Electives are available beginning in grade 9, and work that prepares students to take AP examinations is offered in all academic disciplines. There is a strong emphasis on the fine arts; most students pursue drama, visual arts and music beyond the requirements. Musical instrument training is offered on both campuses.

A senior speech before the student body is mandatory, and an optional senior project during the month of May incorporates self-designed study, community service and career exploration, culminating in an oral presentation to the review committee. Independent study provides students in grades 9-12 with an opportunity to study something that is not offered in the regular program or to learn it in a different way. Projects involve a variety of experiences, such as research, fieldwork, creative writing, courses at other institutions, training in music or art, correspondence study and community involvement.

Other learning opportunities include a course for students in grades 10-12 in which participants receive three weeks of training in preparation for a nine-day wilderness expedition and the option to study off campus for a full year, a semester or a quarter through a number of organizations. The upper school offers a full range of girls' and boys' varsity sports, and extracurricular activities include intercultural club, debate, language clubs, math team, community service groups, drama and publications. Students are encouraged to participate in a variety of community service opportunities.

SAINT THOMAS ACADEMY
Day — Boys Gr 7-12

Mendota Heights, MN 55120. 949 Mendota Heights Rd. Tel: 651-454-4570.
Fax: 651-454-4574.
www.cadets.com   E-mail: sta@cadets.com
Thomas B. Mich, Head. PhD. **John Kenney, Adm.**
Col Prep. Milit. AP—Eng Fr Span Calc Stats Comp_Sci Bio US_Hist Econ US_Govt &

Pol. **Feat**—Lat Relig JROTC. **Supp**—Tut.
Adm: 149/yr. Appl due: Jan. Accepted: 95%. Yield: 95%.
Enr 659. B 659. Elem 151. Sec 508. Wh 90%. Hisp 4%. Blk 2%. Asian 3%. Other 1%. Avg class size: 18. Uniform. **Fac 61.** M 39/1. F 20/1. Wh 94%. Hisp 3%. Blk 3%. Adv deg: 78%.
Grad '04—115. Col—115. (U of St Thomas-MN 19, Creighton 8, U of WI-Madison 7, U of MN-Twin Cities 6, St John's U-MN 5, U of MN-Duluth 5). Avg SAT: 1181. Avg ACT: 25. Alum 6600.
Tui '04-'05: Day $12,500 (+$1000). **Aid:** Merit 38 ($43,000). Need 195 ($1,240,000).
Summer: Acad Enrich. Study Skills. 1-6 wks.
Endow $15,300,000. Plant val $29,500,000. Bldgs 3. Class rms 35. Lib 12,000 vols. Sci labs 5. Lang labs 4. Comp labs 3. Auds 1. Theaters 1. Art studios 2. Music studios 1. Gyms 2. Fields 7. Courts 6. Pools 1. Rinks 1. Stadiums 1. Rifle ranges 1.
Est 1865. Nonprofit. Roman Catholic. Sem (Aug-June). **Assoc** NCA.

Founded by Archbishop John Ireland, STA has offered a military program since 1890. It serves as the only Catholic, military high school for boys in the state. Academic instruction focuses on college preparation, with an emphasis on the development of strong study skills and on the core courses of English, literature, history, foreign languages, math and the physical sciences. Boys choose from approximately one dozen Advanced Placement classes.

Activities include a full program of cocurriculars, athletics, music and art.

MISSOURI

KANSAS CITY, MO. Urban. Pop: 441,545. Alt: 750 ft.

BARSTOW SCHOOL
Day — Coed Gr PS-12

Kansas City, MO 64114. 11511 State Line Rd. Tel: 816-942-3255. Fax: 816-942-3227.
www.barstowschool.org   E-mail: llinn@barstowschool.org

Art Atkinson, Head. BA, Univ of Arkansas-Fayetteville, MA, Univ of Alabama-Birmingham. Laura Lyddon Linn, Adm.

Col Prep. AP—Eng Fr Calc Stats Comp_Sci Bio Chem Physics Eur_Hist US_Hist US_Govt & Pol. Feat—Chin Japan Ceramics Studio_Art Music Debate. Supp—Tut.

Adm (Gr PS-11): 119/yr. Appl due: Feb. Accepted: 77%. Yield: 73%. Tests CTP_4 IQ.

Enr 623. B 327. G 296. Elem 439. Sec 184. Wh 86%. Hisp 1%. Blk 5%. Asian 1%. Other 7%. Avg class size: 15. Fac 66. M 16/2. F 42/6. Wh 95%. Hisp 3%. Blk 1%. Asian 1%. Adv deg: 81%.

Grad '04—32. Col—32. (U of PA 4). Avg SAT: 1240. Avg ACT: 29. Alum 2041.

Tui '04-'05: Day $8845-13,660 (+$1000). Aid: Merit 8 ($36,500). Need 73 ($583,187).

Summer: Acad Enrich Rec. Tui Day $80/wk. 8 wks.

Endow $4,000,000. Plant val $19,000,000. Bldgs 5. Class rms 64. 2 Libs 16,200 vols. Sci labs 4. Comp labs 3. Auds 1. Art studios 3. Music studios 2. Gyms 2. Fields 3. Courts 4.

Est 1884. Nonprofit. Sem (Aug-May). Assoc CLS NCA.

Founded by Wellesley graduates Mary L. C. Barstow and Ada Brann at the request of several prominent Kansas City families, the school currently offers a holistic liberal arts program that emphasizes college preparation. Barstow draws its diverse student body from Greater Kansas City and Johnson County, KS.

A strong core of required courses is supplemented by electives in such areas as foreign languages, forensics, the social sciences and the arts. Pupils also benefit from a well-developed technology program. Community service, an integral part of both the middle and the upper school programs, is required for graduation. Student government, many sports, publications, dramatics and clubs are among the activities offered. After-school enrichment activities, a comprehensive summer program and year-round extended care are available.

PEMBROKE HILL SCHOOL
Day — Coed Gr PS-12

Kansas City, MO 64112. 400 W 51st St. Tel: 816-936-1200. Fax: 816-936-1218.
www.pembrokehill.org   E-mail: phs@pembrokehill.org

Richard D. Hibschman, Head. BS, Ball State Univ, MS, Northern Illinois Univ, EdD, Harvard Univ. Carolyn Sullivan, Adm.

Col Prep. AP—Fr Lat Span Calc Stats Bio Chem Physics Econ Psych US_Govt & Pol Studio_Art. Feat—Drama Music. Supp—Dev_Read Rem_Math Rem_Read.

Adm: 170/yr. Accepted: 40%. Tests IQ.

Enr 1192. B 607. G 585. Elem 784. Sec 408. Wh 83%. Hisp 1%. Blk 5%. Asian 5%. Other

6%. **Fac 112.** M 35/2. F 61/14. Wh 95%. Blk 5%. Adv deg: 63%.

Grad '04—94. Col—94. (U of KS, SMU, Emory, U of PA, Dartmouth, St Louis U). Avg SAT: 1265. Avg ACT: 27. Alum 4500.

Tui '05-'06: Day $12,325-14,105 (+$40-1815). **Aid:** Merit 13 ($24,000). Need 147 ($945,500).

Summer: Acad Enrich Rev Rec. 1-3 wks.

Endow $35,000,000. Plant val $50,000,000. Bldgs 14. Class rms 87. Lib 43,000 vols. Sci labs 8. Lang labs 1. Comp labs 4. Auds 2. Theaters 2. Art studios 7. Music studios 4. Gyms 3. Fields 6. Field houses 2. Tracks 1.

Est 1910. Nonprofit. Sem (Aug-May). **Assoc** CLS NCA.

Pembroke Hill was created in 1984 as the result of a merger of the Sunset Hill School for girls and the Pembroke-Country Day School for boys. Both predecessor schools were founded by Vassie Ward Hill and a group of progressive-minded parents.

The school maintains a low student-teacher ratio and provides a variety of course options in all disciplines, including languages, science, math, computer, history, English, and the visual and performing arts. Independent study projects and Advanced Placement courses are also available. The school offers interscholastic sports for both girls and boys. A wide variety of extracurricular activities encompasses publications, performing arts, social service, and interest clubs and organizations. An extended-day program is available.

The school is located on two campuses less than a mile apart: the Wornall campus (400 W. 51st St.) for children in grades PS-5 and the Ward Parkway campus (5121 State Line Rd.) for students in grades 6-12.

LEXINGTON, MO. (37 mi. E of Kansas City, MO) Suburban. Pop: 4453. Alt: 806 ft.

WENTWORTH MILITARY ACADEMY
Bdg — Boys Gr 8-PG, Girls 10-PG

Lexington, MO 64067. 1880 Washington Ave. Tel: 660-259-2221. Fax: 660-259-2677.
  www.wma.edu   E-mail: admissions@wma1880.org

Maj. Gen. John H. Little, Supt. Maj. Todd L. Kitchen, Sr., Adm.

Col Prep. Gen Acad. Bus. Milit. Feat—Ger Russ Span Computers Econ Govt Psych Sociol Studio_Art Chorus JROTC. **Supp**—ESL Rem_Math Rev Tut.

Adm: 108/yr. Appl due: Rolling. Accepted: 60%. Yield: 40%.

Enr 217. Elem 14. Sec 108. PG 95. Wh 80%. Hisp 17%. Blk 2%. Asian 1%. Avg class size: 12. Uniform. **Fac 16.** M 11/2. F 2/1. Wh 100%. Adv deg: 50%. In dorms 2.

Grad '04—19. Col—15. (Wentworth Milit JC, U of IA, OK St, IA St, U of MO-Columbia, U of KS). Avg ACT: 20. Alum 21,350.

Tui '04-'05: Bdg $15,800 (+$6195). **Aid:** Need 70 ($464,000).

Summer: Acad Rev Rem Rec. Tui Bdg $4800. 3 wks. Adventure. Tui Bdg $695/wk. 6 wks.

Endow $1,400,000. Plant val $2,880,000. Bldgs 9. Dorms 4. Dorm rms 260. Class rms 30. Lib 20,000 vols. Labs 5. Music studios 1. Fields 4. Courts 10. Field houses 1. Pools 1. Golf crses 1. Rifle ranges 1.

Est 1880. Nonprofit. (Aug-May). **Assoc** NCA.

This college preparatory school, situated on a modern, 137-acre campus, stresses a military program designed to develop self-discipline and confidence. Small classes, a strong English program supplemented by separately scheduled writing periods, a computer science program, and student participation in such extracurricular activities as marching band, chorus, drill team, flying, journalism, scouting, ranger platoon and clubs highlight the program. Wentworth faculty supervise a mandatory evening study program, and qualified seniors may take college courses.

In 1993, Wentworth began accepting females into its affiliated junior college division; shortly thereafter, the academy started admitting girls into grades 10-12. Due to the school's relationship with its junior college, students may earn dual-enrollment credits. Graduates of Wentworth Junior College enrolled in the Military Contract Program qualify for commission as second lieutenants in the Army, the Army Reserve and the Army National Guard.

A summer school session and a full athletic program are available.

MEXICO, MO. (95 mi. WNW of St. Louis, MO) Suburban. Pop: 11,320. Alt: 806 ft.

MISSOURI MILITARY ACADEMY
Bdg — Boys Gr 6-PG

Mexico, MO 65265. 204 Grand Ave. Tel: 573-581-1776. Fax: 573-581-0081.
 www.mma-cadet.org   E-mail: info@mma.mexico.mo.us
Col. Ronald J. Kelly, Pres. BA, California State Univ-Fresno. **Maj. Dennis Diederich, Adm.**
 Col Prep. Gen Acad. Milit. **Feat**—Humanities Mythology Comp_Sci Govt/Econ Studio_Art Drama Journ. **Supp**—Dev_Read ESL Rem_Math.
 Adm (Gr 6-12): 116/yr. Appl due: Rolling. Accepted: 98%.
 Enr 255. B 255. Elem 54. Sec 201. Wh 61%. Hisp 32%. Blk 1%. Asian 6%. Avg class size: 11. Uniform. **Fac 37.** M 30. F 6/1. Wh 95%. Asian 5%. Adv deg: 56%. In dorms 6.
 Grad '04—54. Col—54. (Instituto Tecnologico de Monterrey-Mexico, IL St, U of MO-Kansas City, KS St, U of TX-Austin, U of CO-Boulder). Avg SAT: 1000. Avg ACT: 20. Alum 6000.
 Tui '04-'05: Bdg $18,933 (+$7000). **Aid:** Need 53 ($341,481).
 Summer: Ages 8-16. Rec. Tui Bdg $835-1515. 1-2 wks.
 Endow $25,000,000. Plant val $20,000,000. Bldgs 19. Dorms 4. Dorm rms 172. Class rms 28. Lib 8000 vols. Sci labs 1. Lang labs 1. Comp labs 3. Auds 1. Art studios 1. Music studios 10. Gyms 1. Fields 6. Courts 8. Field houses 1. Pools 1. Stables 1. Tracks 1. Rifle ranges 1.
 Est 1889. Nonprofit. Tri (Sept-May). **Assoc** NCA.

This military school was founded by Col. A. F. Fleet; Gov. Charles H. Hardin of Missouri served as MMA's first superintendent. After its original campus was destroyed by fire in 1896, the academy was reestablished in 1900 at its present location on the eastern outskirts of the city. The 70-acre main campus lies adjacent to a 218-acre wilderness area that features a lake, a lodge, a stream, and woodlands with riding and hiking trails.

MMA comprises a high school (grades 9-PG) and a separate junior school (grades 6-8). Learning resource centers operate at both schools. Instructors at these centers track and assist students in need of additional assistance with their academic work. Required extra-help sessions and supervised evening study are important elements of the program. Qualified students may take dual-enrollment courses, conducted in cooperation with a local college, that meet high school graduation requirements and lead to college credit.

The academy has been rated as an Honor School with Distinction by the Army JROTC for more than four decades. The student body is organized as a battalion, and student government is vested in a cadet council.

Extracurricular activities include private instrumental and voice lessons, drama, marching and stage bands, a drum and bugle corps, aviation, art, journalism, yearbook, drill team and equitation. Football, soccer, cross-country, basketball, swimming, wrestling, marksmanship, track, tennis, golf and weightlifting are among the available athletics. **See Also Page 1341**

ST. LOUIS, MO.
Urban. Pop: 348,189. Alt: 455 ft. Area also includes Clayton.

CHAMINADE COLLEGE PREPARATORY SCHOOL
Bdg and Day — Boys Gr 6-12

St Louis, MO 63131. 425 S Lindbergh Blvd. Tel: 314-993-4400. Fax: 314-993-5732.
www.chaminademo.com   E-mail: rhill@chaminade-stl.com

Rev. Ralph A. Siefert, SM, Pres. BA, St Mary's Univ of San Antonio, MA, Northwestern Univ, MA, St Louis Univ, DMin, Andover Newton Theological School. **Roger L. Hill, Adm.**

Col Prep. AP—Eng Calc Bio Chem Eur_Hist US_Hist World_Hist. **Feat**—Japan Sociol Architect Drama Music Accounting Speech. **Supp**—Tut.

Adm (Gr 6-11): 197/yr. Appl due: Jan. Accepted: 69%. **Tests** ISEE.

Enr 948. B 58/890. Elem 350. Sec 598. Wh 89%. Hisp 1%. Blk 3%. Am Ind 1%. Asian 5%. Other 1%. Avg class size: 22. **Fac 89.** M 64/4. F 18/3. Wh 88%. Hisp 6%. Blk 3%. Asian 3%. Adv deg: 61%. In dorms 4.

Grad '04—148. Col—147. (U of MO-Columbia, St Louis U, DePaul, U of Dayton, Webster, Loyola U of Chicago). Alum 6350.

Tui '05-'06: Bdg $22,650 (+$3955). **5-Day Bdg** $21,650 (+$3955). **Day** $10,900 (+$2005). **Aid:** Merit 53 ($60,000). Need 220 ($844,000).

Endow $3,000,000. Plant val $21,500,000. Bldgs 12. Dorms 1. Dorm rms 54. Class rms 56. Lib 15,000 vols. Sci labs 7. Comp labs 3. Theaters 1. Art studios 1. Music studios 2. Gyms 2. Fields 5. Tennis courts 12. Volleyball courts 2. Pools 1.

Est 1910. Nonprofit. Roman Catholic. Sem (Aug-May). **Assoc** NCA.

Sponsored by the Society of Mary, Chaminade offers honors and AP courses, as well as electives, and places a strong emphasis on the arts. Additional classes, taught by school faculty in affiliation with St. Louis University, allow students to receive college credit through the university. Chaminade also coordinates international exchange programs with schools in France, Spain, Mexico and Japan.

Various activities and athletics, along with retreats, a campus ministry and liturgical celebrations, complement academics. Seniors perform compulsory off-campus community service.

COMMUNITY SCHOOL

Day — Coed Gr PS-6

St Louis, MO 63124. 900 Lay Rd. Tel: 314-991-0005. Fax: 314-991-1512.
www.communityschool.com E-mail: mail@communityschool.com

Matthew A. Gould, Head. BA, Earlham College, PhD, Univ of Chicago. **Dana Scott Saulsberry**, Adm.

Pre-Prep. Feat—Fr Computers Studio_Art Drama Music Indus_Arts Outdoor_Ed. **Supp**—Dev_Read Tut.

Adm: 59/yr. Appl due: Jan. **Tests** CTP_4.

Enr 335. Elem 335. Wh 82%. Blk 11%. Asian 1%. Other 6%. **Fac** 50. Adv deg: 36%.

Grad '04—40. Prep—36. (John Burroughs, Mary Inst & St Louis Co Day, Whitfield). Alum 2148.

Tui '04-'05: Day $12,155.

Summer: Rec. 2-6 wks.

Endow $8,443,000. Plant val $4,946,000. Bldgs 3. Class rms 17. Lib 50,000 vols. Comp labs 1. Art studios 1. Music studios 1. Man arts studios 1. Gyms 1. Fields 3.

Est 1914. Nonprofit. Sem (Sept-June). **Assoc** NCA.

Founded in 1914 by a group of concerned parents, Community School, located on a 16-acre, wooded campus in Ladue, continues to encourage parental involvement in the life of the school. Community provides a full-day program for children from age 3 through grade 6. The integrated curriculum emphasizes reading at all grade levels. Nursery and kindergarten programs utilize a developmental approach, while the curriculum in grades 1-4 stresses the acquisition of basic skills. French instruction begins at age 3. Grades 5 and 6 are semidepartmentalized.

Students have physical education every day, and art, music and shop each week. Nature and outdoor activities form an integral part of the program.

FORSYTH SCHOOL

Day — Coed Gr PS-6

St Louis, MO 63105. 6235 Wydown Blvd. Tel: 314-726-4542. Fax: 314-726-0112.
www.forsythonline.com E-mail: admission@forsythonline.com

Rebecca Glenn, Head. AB, PhD, Washington Univ. **Ann F. Babington**, Adm.

Pre-Prep. Gen Acad. Feat—Lib_Skills Fr Lat Span Computers Performing_Arts Studio_Art Drama Band Music Creative_Movement Outdoor_Ed. **Supp**—Tut.

Adm: 75/yr. Appl due: Feb. Accepted: 40%. **Tests** ISEE.

Enr 360. B 182. G 178. Elem 360. Wh 78%. Hisp 1%. Blk 6%. Asian 7%. Other 8%. Avg class size: 22. **Fac** 47. M 13. F 34. Wh 90%. Hisp 1%. Blk 9%. Adv deg: 57%.

Grad '04—39. Prep—35. (Mary Inst & St Louis Co Day 13, John Burroughs 12, Whitfield 4, St Louis Priory 2, Crossroads-MO 1). Alum 1236.

Tui '04-'05: Day $11,995. **Aid:** Need 28 ($123,800).

Summer: Acad Enrich Rec. Tui Day $350-400/2-wk ses. 10 wks.

Endow $740,000. Plant val $4,359,000. Bldgs 7. Class rms 20. 2 Libs 11,000 vols. Sci labs 2. Comp labs 1. Art studios 1. Music studios 1. Perf arts ctrs 1. Gyms 1. Fields 1. Courts 1. Tracks 1.

Est 1961. Nonprofit. Sem (Aug-June). **Assoc** NCA.

Forsyth, located across the street from Washington University, stresses individual attention by maintaining a low student-faculty ratio and team teaching in each classroom. Classes meet in historic homes with contemporary classrooms, art and music studios, a library, science labs and an athletic/performing arts center. The curriculum is enriched by full-time specialist teachers, a director of studies and a learning specialist.

In addition to year-round programming, Forsyth offers such before- and after-school activities as enrichment classes, outdoor education, soccer, baseball or softball, concert band, instrumental lessons, scouting and community service.

JOHN BURROUGHS SCHOOL
Day — Coed Gr 7-12

St Louis, MO 63124. 755 S Price Rd. Tel: 314-993-4040. Fax: 314-993-6458.
www.jburroughs.org   E-mail: admiss@jburroughs.org

Keith E. Shahan, Head. BA, Amherst College, MAT, EdD, Harvard Univ. **Caroline G. LaVigne, Adm.**

Col Prep. AP—Fr Ger Lat Span Calc Comp_Sci Bio Chem Physics US_Hist Art_Hist Music_Theory. **Feat**—Greek Russ Ecol Robotics Architect_Drawing Film Video_Production Orchestra Jazz_Band Outdoor_Ed.

Adm (Gr 7-11): 108/yr. Appl due: Jan. Accepted: 51%. Yield: 88%. **Tests** ISEE.

Enr 590. B 298. G 292. Elem 187. Sec 403. Wh 78%. Hisp 1%. Blk 10%. Asian 7%. Other 4%. Avg class size: 14. **Fac 97.** M 37/6. F 31/23. Wh 90%. Hisp 4%. Blk 6%. Adv deg: 77%.

Grad '04—98. Col—97. (Wash U 17, Cornell 5, U of Miami 4, Duke 3, Tufts 3, U of MO-Columbia 3). Avg SAT: 1390. Alum 6014.

Tui '04-'05: Day $16,250 (+$1000). **Aid:** Need 96 ($898,485).

Endow $37,100,000. Plant val $35,500,000. Bldgs 7. Class rms 50. Lib 30,000 vols. Sci labs 5. Lang labs 1. Comp labs 3. Auds 1. Art studios 2. Music studios 5. Gyms 3. Fields 8. Courts 10. Pools 2.

Est 1923. Nonprofit. Tri (Sept-May). **Assoc** NCA.

Located on a 47½-acre campus in the residential community of Ladue, Burroughs, which was established by a group of local men and women, is committed to providing an educational experience that strikes a balance among academics, the arts, athletics and activities. The college preparatory curriculum provides a firm foundation in the five basic disciplines: English, science, math, social studies/history and foreign languages. An outdoor, year-round laboratory in the Ozarks enhances the school's outdoor education projects and special programs that stress individual development.

The vast majority of students take part in Burroughs' voluntary community service program. Opportunities include a jointly conducted faculty-pupil program that provides volunteer options for students, a summer camp for underprivileged children, a summer school program for at-risk children and an annual eighth grade community service project. Each class contributes between 9000 and 10,000 cumulative hours of service while at the school.

MARY INSTITUTE AND SAINT LOUIS COUNTRY DAY SCHOOL
Day — Coed Gr PS-12

St Louis, MO 63124. 101 N Warson Rd. Tel: 314-993-5100. Fax: 314-995-7470.
www.micds.org   E-mail: admissions@micds.org

Matthew E. Gossage, Head. BA, MAT, Vanderbilt Univ, MEd, Harvard Univ. **Peggy B. Laramie, Adm.**

  Col Prep. AP—Eng Fr Ger Lat Span Calc Stats Bio Chem Physics Eur_Hist US_Hist Comp_Govt & Pol Econ US_Govt & Pol Art_Hist Studio_Art Music_Theory. **Feat**—Creative_Writing Shakespeare Anat & Physiol Astron Environ_Sci Forensic_Sci Robotics Web_Design Psych Photog Drama Music Speech. **Supp**—Tut.

  Adm: 176/yr. Appl due: Jan. Accepted: 50%. Yield: 66%. **Tests** ISEE SSAT.

  Enr 1227. B 606. G 621. Elem 645. Sec 582. Wh 80%. Hisp 1%. Blk 9%. Asian 7%. Other 3%. Avg class size: 16. **Fac 138.** M 58/2. F 68/10. Wh 95%. Hisp 2%. Blk 2%. Other 1%. Adv deg: 56%.

  Grad '04—141. Col—141. (Wash U 13, U of MO-Columbia 7, SMU 6, Emory 4, IN U 4, Northwestern 4). Avg SAT: 1286. Avg ACT: 28. Alum 9258.

  Tui '04-'05: Day $13,510-16,345 (+$300-500).

  Summer: Rec. Tui Day $300-800/2-wk ses. 6 wks.

  Endow $65,614,000. Plant val $60,640,000. Bldgs 9. Class rms 122. 3 Libs 55,000 vols. Sci labs 16. Lang labs 2. Comp labs 8. Photog labs 1. Observatories 1. Auds 2. Theaters 3. Art studios 7. Music studios 5. Dance studios 1. AV rms 1. Gyms 3. Fields 12. Courts 15. Pools 1. Playgrounds 1.

  Est 1859. Nonprofit. (Aug-June). **Assoc** CLS NCA.

Located on a 100-acre campus, Mary Institute and Saint Louis Country Day School comprises a lower school for children in grades pre-K-4, a middle school for those in grades 5-8, and an upper school serving grades 9-12. The entire school is coed, with single-sex academic classes in the core subjects conducted in the middle school.

Founded in the mid-19th century, Mary Institute and Smith Academy were departments of Washington University. In 1917, Saint Louis Country Day School became the successor to Smith Academy. Both schools were independent of the university by 1949. In 1992, the two schools joined together and began to function as one.

The lower school offers a literature-based reading program and an integrated core curriculum with specialists in science, Spanish, computer, art, music, drama and physical education. Middle schoolers take part in a departmentalized curriculum that features interdisciplinary units. The upper school's traditional college preparatory curriculum includes English, history, mathematics, science, foreign language, the arts and physical education. Advanced Placement courses are available in all disciplines, and most students take at least one AP class before graduating. Upper school students select from a variety of activities, including athletics. Summer school and camp opportunities are open to various age groups.

See Also Page 1203

SAINT LOUIS PRIORY SCHOOL

Day — Boys Gr 7-12

St Louis, MO 63141. 500 S Mason Rd. Tel: 314-434-3690. Fax: 314-576-7088.
  www.priory.org   E-mail: admissions@priory.org

Rev. Gregory Mohrman, OSB, Head. BA, Univ of Pennsylvania, MA, MDiv, St John's Univ (MN), MA, Middlebury College. **Dennis P. Guilliams, Adm.**

  Col Prep. AP—Lat Span Calc Stats Comp_Sci Bio Chem Physics Eur_Hist US_Hist US_Govt & Pol Studio_Art Music_Theory. **Feat**—Creative_Writing Shakespeare Writing Fr Greek Comp_Relig Filmmaking Photog Visual_Arts Acting Theater Theater_Arts.

Adm: 75/yr. Appl due: Jan. Accepted: 46%. **Tests** ISEE.
Enr 390. B 390. Elem 138. Sec 252. Wh 87%. Hisp 4%. Blk 2%. Asian 7%. Avg class size: 17. **Fac 51.** Wh 96%. Hisp 4%. Adv deg: 74%.
Grad '04—58. Col—58. (U of MO-Columbia, U of Miami, UNC-Chapel Hill, Notre Dame, Stanford, Georgetown). Avg SAT: 1329. Avg ACT: 29. Alum 1305.
Tui '03-'04: Day $12,100 (+$1000). **Aid:** Need 97 ($600,000).
Summer: Acad Enrich Rev Rec. 6 wks.
Endow $17,000,000. Plant val $18,500,000. Bldgs 18. Lib 65,000 vols. Gyms 2. Courts 9. Weight rms 1.
Est 1956. Nonprofit. Roman Catholic. Tri (Aug-May). **Assoc** NCA.

This college preparatory day school for boys is operated by Saint Louis Abbey, a Benedictine monastery founded by Ampleforth Abbey in England. Saint Louis Abbey and its school became independent of the founding Abbey in 1973. The 150-acre, wooded campus is situated on rolling hills in west St. Louis County.

The course of studies imparts a solid, traditional liberal arts education through the disciplines of religion, English, classical and modern foreign languages, mathematics, the natural sciences, history and computer science. Priory offers AP courses in most subjects, and independent study is an option for exceptional students in their junior and senior years. A special feature of the senior year is a thesis or exhibition; each student must submit a research thesis, a work of creative writing, or a project in the visual or performing arts. Service to the community is also required for graduation; juniors and seniors render service to the sick, the elderly, the young and many others in need. Once each week, the school community comes together to pray and to celebrate the liturgy.

Participation in athletics is required, and both interscholastic competition and noncompetitive physical activities are offered. Students in the high school are expected to take part in an interscholastic sport at least two trimesters each year. School newspaper, Amnesty International, mock trial, debate, scholar team, yearbook, political review, calligraphy guild, theater and environmental club are among Priory's extracurricular activities.

THOMAS JEFFERSON SCHOOL
Bdg and Day — Coed Gr 7-12

St Louis, MO 63127. 4100 S Lindbergh Blvd. Tel: 314-843-4151. Fax: 314-843-3527.
www.tjs.org   E-mail: admissions@tjs.org
William C. Rowe, Head. BA, Wesleyan Univ, MA, Washington Univ. **Marie De Jesus, Adm.**
  Col Prep. AP—Eng Fr Calc Bio Chem Physics Eur_Hist US_Hist US_Govt & Pol. **Feat—**Greek Ital Lat Studio_Art Music. **Supp—**ESL.
  Adm (Bdg Gr 7-11; Day 7-10): 30/yr. Bdg 16. Day 14. Appl due: Feb. Accepted: 74%. Yield: 73%. **Tests** ISEE SSAT TOEFL.
  Enr 81. B 19/28. G 14/20. Elem 26. Sec 55. Wh 76%. Hisp 2%. Blk 7%. Asian 15%. Avg class size: 12. **Fac 18.** M 6/5. F 6/1. Wh 89%. Blk 5%. Asian 5%. Other 1%. Adv deg: 33%. In dorms 7.
  Grad '04—11. Col—11. (Vanderbilt, Swarthmore, Rochester Inst of Tech, Wesleyan U, PA St, Loyola U of Chicago). Avg SAT: 1370. Alum 473.
  Tui '04-'05: Bdg $27,800 (+$1300). **5-Day Bdg $26,100** (+$1300). **Day $17,100** (+$1100). **Aid:** Need 31 ($469,000).
  Summer: Enrich. European Travel. Tui Bdg $3500. 3 wks.
  Endow $800,000. Plant val $1,400,000. Bldgs 9. Dorms 7. Dorm rms 25. Class rms 8. Lib

3000 vols. Sci labs 2. Art studios 1. Gyms 1. Fields 1. Courts 5.
Est 1946. Nonprofit. Sem (Sept-May). **Assoc** NCA.

Thomas Jefferson was established as a boys' school by Robin McCoy, Charles Merrill, Jr., and Graham Spring, three Harvard alumni. Mr. McCoy was headmaster for 34 years, until his retirement in 1980, while Mr. Merrill taught for ten years and eventually moved to Boston, MA, and started the Commonwealth School. The 20-acre campus is located on a former private estate in the residential neighborhood of Sunset Hills; its main building occupies the estate's original home. The school became coeducational in 1971.

English and mathematics form the foundation of the curriculum, along with science, social studies, and both classical and modern foreign languages. By the senior year, a typical student's program is entirely at the Advanced Placement level. All classes are held in the morning; part of the afternoon is spent engaged in study—the youngest pupils begin with a supervised study hall and advance to independent study at faculty discretion—while the rest is structured with labs, athletics and extracurricular meetings. A mandatory fine arts class meets one afternoon a week; typical options include choir, appreciation courses in art and music, and studio courses in drawing and painting, ceramics and photography.

Participation in athletics is required several days a week; students choose one sport or activity per season from among both interscholastic and intramural options. Extracurriculars include student council, newspaper, yearbook, assisting the admission office in guiding visiting applicants on campus tours, drama and a variety of volunteer opportunities. Student involvement in off-campus activities is encouraged, and all pupils fulfill a community service requirement between grade 9 and graduation. In addition, TJS schedules optional weekend activities such as concerts and sporting events.

The entire student body attends productions at the St. Louis Repertory Theater, and individual classes take field trips to the symphony, the art museum, and other exhibits and events. In addition, the headmaster leads a trip to Europe approximately every other summer. These trips, which focus on Florence, Italy, and London, England, with side excursions made to other cities, pay particular attention to art, architecture, theater and historical sites. **See Also Page 1261**

THE WILSON SCHOOL
Day — Coed Gr PS-6

Clayton, MO 63105. 400 DeMun Ave. Tel: 314-725-4999. Fax: 314-725-5242.
  www.wilsonschool.com   E-mail: info@wilsonschool.com
Eugene D. Ruth, Jr., Head. AB, Kenyon College, MA, EdD, Columbia Univ. **Laura C. Hartung, Adm.**
  Pre-Prep. Gen Acad. Feat—Lib_Skills Fr Lat Computers Studio_Art Music.
  Adm: 42/yr. Appl due: Jan. **Tests** CTP_4 ISEE.
  Enr 181. B 94. G 87. Elem 181. Wh 76%. Hisp 2%. Blk 13%. Am Ind 1%. Asian 3%. Other 5%. Avg class size: 20. **Fac 27.** M 4. F 20/3. Wh 83%. Hisp 11%. Blk 3%. Am Ind 3%. Adv deg: 29%.
  Grad '04—11. Prep—11. (Crossroads-MO, John Burroughs, St Louis Priory, Visitation, Whitfield, Mary Inst & St Louis Co Day).
  Tui '04-'05: Day $10,950 (+$140-2310). **Aid:** Need 35 ($121,978).
  Summer: Enrich Rec. Tui Day $145/wk. 9 wks.

Plant val $1,600,000. Bldgs 1. Class rms 16. Lib 27,000 vols. Sci labs 1. Lang labs 1. Comp labs 1. Auds 1. Art studios 1. Music studios 1. Gyms 1. Fields 2.
Est 1913. Nonprofit. Sem (Aug-June). **Assoc** NCA.

Named for its original director, Mabel Wilson, this school was founded as St. Louis' first independent preschool by a group of Central West End parents. Language arts, math, science, social studies, foreign language, art, music, physical education, library skills and technology form the core of the integrated curriculum at all grade levels. At all grade levels, the program emphasizes time management, writing and study skills.

The hands-on preschool program (pre-K and K), which enrolls children beginning at age 3, gears work and play toward developing a foundation in the basic skills; an emphasis on reading and an early exposure to computer technology are characteristics of the preschool. During the lower school years (grades 1-3), students further develop their reading and math skills, with classes becoming more challenging and daily homework beginning. Study of the environment, ecology and life science is part of the lower school science curriculum.

In the upper school (grades 4-6), course work in all departments allows for more depth. A substantial library book collection enriches the literature-based reading program. Technology is a strong component of the curriculum: Classrooms include computer workstations, and Internet access is available through the technology lab. Specialists teach classes in French, Latin, art, music, science, technology, library resource and physical education.

As a complement to traditional course work, all boys and girls participate in community service and character education programs. Wilson's proximity to Washington University, Forest Park, museums and concert halls provides opportunities for cultural enrichment.

NEBRASKA

ELKHORN, NE. (12 mi. W of Omaha, NE) Rural. Pop: 6062. Alt: 1200 ft.

MOUNT MICHAEL BENEDICTINE HIGH SCHOOL
5-Day Bdg and Day — Boys Gr 9-12

Elkhorn, NE 68022. 22520 Mt Michael Rd. Tel: 402-289-2541. Fax: 402-289-4539.
www.mountmichaelhs.com   E-mail: information@mountmichael.org
Rev. Raphael Walsh, OSB, Pres. Tom Ridder, Prin. BS, MS, EdS, Univ of Nebraska-Lincoln. **Jim Clements, Adm.**

- **Col Prep. AP**—Eng Calc Comp_Sci Bio Physics Eur_Hist US_Hist. **Feat**—Fr Span Econ Govt Relig Studio_Art Band Chorus Accounting Bus Debate Journ Speech. **Supp**—Rem_Read Tut.
- **Adm (Gr 9-11):** 36/yr. Appl due: Rolling. Accepted: 75%.
- **Enr 165.** B 152/13. Sec 165. Avg class size: 17. **Fac 25.** M 13/4. F 5/3. Wh 95%. Hisp 5%. Adv deg: 80%. In dorms 1.
- **Grad '04—28. Col—28.** (St Louis U, U of NE-Lincoln, Benedictine Col, IA St). Avg SAT: 1290. Alum 1225.
- **Tui '04-'05: 5-Day Bdg $11,200** (+$400). **Day $6800** (+$400). **Aid:** Need 120 ($100,000). Work prgm 50 ($100,000).
- Endow $2,000,000. Plant val $3,000,000. Bldgs 2. Dorms 1. Dorm rms 40. Class rms 10. Lib 33,000 vols. Chapels 1. Labs 3. Art studios 3. Music studios 4. Gyms 2. Fields 3. Courts 2.
- **Est 1956.** Nonprofit. Roman Catholic. Sem (Aug-May). **Assoc** NCA.

A Benedictine school, Mount Michael emphasizes close student-teacher relationships and community living for highly motivated students. The Catholic, intellectual and physical aspects of education are combined to prepare boys for college. Interscholastic and intramural sports are provided, and family activities are planned throughout the year. Students enroll from cities and towns within a 100-mile radius.

OMAHA, NE. (126 mi. W of Des Moines, IA) Urban. Pop: 390,007. Alt: 1034 ft.

BROWNELL-TALBOT SCHOOL
Day — Coed Gr PS-12

Omaha, NE 68132. 400 N Happy Hollow Blvd. Tel: 402-556-3772. Fax: 402-553-2994.
www.brownell.edu   E-mail: info@brownell.edu
Dianne K. Desler, Head. BS, MS, EdS, Univ of Nebraska-Omaha. **Melissa Gathje, Adm.**

- **Col Prep. AP**—Eng Fr Lat Span Calc Comp_Sci Bio Chem Eur_Hist US_Hist. **Feat**—Comp_Design Studio_Art Drama Music Yoga.

Adm: 75/yr. Appl due: Rolling. **Tests** CTP_4 IQ.
Enr 475. Elem 330. Sec 145. Avg class size: 16. Uniform. **Fac 45.**
Grad '04—29. Col—29. (U of Chicago, Creighton). Alum 2016.
Tui '04-'05: Day $9000-11,900 (+$450-600).
Endow $3,300,000. Plant val $6,000,000. Bldgs 4. Class rms 40. Lib 9000 vols. Labs 5. Auds 1. Art studios 2. Music studios 2. Dance studios 1. Arts ctrs 1. Gyms 2. Fields 2. Field houses 1. Pools 1.
Est 1863. Nonprofit. Sem (Sept-June). **Assoc** NCA.

Founded in 1863 by Episcopal bishop Joseph Talbot to educate children of Nebraska's early pioneers, Brownell-Talbot is now a nonsectarian school that emphasizes college preparation. Located on a 17-acre, wooded campus, the school offers a program supplemented by Advanced Placement courses.

Forensics, plays, musical productions, intramural and interscholastic athletics, and publications are among the extracurricular activities.

South Central States

ARKANSAS

LITTLE ROCK, AR. (136 mi. W of Memphis, TN) Urban. Pop: 183,133. Alt: 300 ft.

PULASKI ACADEMY
Day — Coed Gr PS-12

Little Rock, AR 72212. 12701 Hinson Rd. Tel: 501-604-1923. Fax: 501-225-1974.
www.pulaskiacademy.org   E-mail: ledbetter.gregg@pulaskiacademy.org

W. Ellis Arnold III, Pres. BA, Hendrix College, JD, Univ of Arkansas-Little Rock. **Gregg R. Ledbetter, Sr., Adm.**

Col Prep. AP—Eng Fr Span Calc Stats Comp_Sci Bio Chem Human_Geog Physics World_Hist Comp_Govt & Pol Econ US_Govt & Pol Art_Hist Studio_Art. **Feat**—British_Lit Anat & Physiol Ecol Web_Design Drama Music Communications Journ. **Supp**—Tut.

Adm: 200/yr. Appl due: Rolling. Accepted: 81%. **Tests** IQ Stanford.

Enr 1270. B 670. G 600. Elem 865. Sec 405. Wh 93%. Hisp 1%. Blk 2%. Am Ind 1%. Asian 3%. Avg class size: 15. Uniform. **Fac 100.** Wh 98%. Hisp 1%. Blk 1%. Adv deg: 65%.

Grad '04—106. Col—106. (U of AR-Fayetteville, Baylor, Vanderbilt, U of MS, Davidson, Harvard). Avg SAT: 1250. Avg ACT: 27. Alum 1625.

Tui '04-'05: Day $7300 (+$800). **Aid:** Need 120 ($420,000).

Summer: Acad Enrich Rec. Sports. 1-6 wks.

Endow $500,000. Plant val $4,000,000. Bldgs 4. Class rms 75. 2 Libs 12,000 vols. Sci labs 4. Comp labs 1. Auds 1. Art studios 2. Music studios 2. Arts ctrs 1. Gyms 1. Fields 1. Courts 1.

Est 1971. Nonprofit. Sem (Aug-June). **Assoc** CLS NCA.

Located on a 15-acre campus in West Little Rock, Pulaski Academy was founded by a group of local citizens. The early childhood division (ages 3 and 4) provides a program that guides children through prescriptive activities in the areas of reading and math readiness, in addition to language, social and motor development. The kindergarten program stresses reading and math skills, with increasing emphasis placed on social skills, computer usage, scientific processes and thought development. In the lower school (grades 1-4), pupils take part in an interactive, developmentally appropriate curriculum. Basic skills are enriched by programs in physical education, art, music, drama and computer instruction.

The middle school (grades 5-8) provides an academic program with a strong core curriculum that emphasizes multidisciplinary units, study skills, and creative and critical thinking. The college preparatory upper school encourages the development of academic and critical-thinking skills. Advanced Placement courses are an integral part of the program. Special activities and programs include field trips, guest lecturers and performers, dramatic productions and interscholastic sports. All upper schoolers perform community service.

SUBIACO, AR. (83 mi. WNW of Little Rock, AR) Rural. Pop: 439. Alt: 510 ft.

SUBIACO ACADEMY
Bdg and Day — Boys Gr 9-12

Subiaco, AR 72865. 405 N Subiaco Ave. Tel: 479-934-1000. Fax: 479-934-1033.
www.subi.org   E-mail: subiaco@centurytel.net
Rev. Aaron Pirrera, OSB, Head. Jason Gaskell, Adm.
  Col Prep. AP—Eng Calc Stats Bio Chem Eur_Hist US_Hist. **Feat**—Fr Lat Span Computers Civics Econ Relig World_Relig Studio_Art Drama Music. **Supp**—ESL Tut.
  Adm: 73/yr. Bdg 56. Day 17. Accepted: 67%. **Tests** HSPT.
  Enr 179. B 132/47. Sec 179. Avg class size: 14. Uniform. **Fac 33.** M 22/6. F 4/1. Wh 94%. Hisp 6%. Adv deg: 54%. In dorms 6.
  Grad '04—54. Col—54. (U of AR-Fayetteville, TX Tech, US Naval Acad, US Air Force Acad, Vanderbilt, Savannah Col of Art & Design). Avg SAT: 1084. Avg ACT: 24. Alum 2300.
  Tui '05-'06: Bdg $14,500 (+$825-1175). **Day $4450** (+$625-975).
  Endow $1,200,000. Plant val $12,500,000. Bldgs 10. Dorms 4. Dorm rms 55. Class rms 24. Libs 1. Sci labs 2. Comp labs 1. Auds 1. Theaters 1. Art studios 1. Arts ctrs 1. Gyms 1. Fields 3. Courts 4. Pools 1.
  Est 1887. Nonprofit. Roman Catholic. Quar (Aug-May). **Assoc** NCA.

Benedictine monks from Switzerland founded Subiaco, which is located in the foothills of the Ozarks some 110 miles northwest of Little Rock. Courses in Christian doctrine are required of all students and are an integral part of the college preparatory program. The academy offers a selection of honors and Advanced Placement courses, and pupils complete compulsory course work in the arts.

Boys compete interscholastically in football, basketball, baseball, track, tennis, golf and soccer. All students participate either in athletics or in journalism, drama, music or community service. The academy provides private instruction in piano, organ and other instruments.

LOUISIANA

BATON ROUGE, LA. (76 mi. WNW of New Orleans, LA) Urban. Pop: 227,818. Alt: 58 Ft.

EPISCOPAL HIGH SCHOOL
Day — Coed Gr K-12

Baton Rouge, LA 70816. 3200 Woodland Ridge Blvd. Tel: 225-753-3180.
   Fax: 225-756-0926.
      www.ehsbr.org   E-mail: info@ehsbr.org
Henry P. Briggs, Int Head. AB, MAT, Harvard Univ. **Ruth D. Hill, Adm.**
   Col Prep. AP—Eng Fr Lat Span Calc Stats Comp_Sci Studio_Art. **Feat**—Japan Naval_ Sci Relig Drawing Sculpt Drama Band Music Dance. **Supp**—Dev_Read Tut.
   Adm: 171/yr. Appl due: Rolling. Accepted: 75%. **Tests** CTP_4.
   Enr 1064. B 515. G 549. Elem 659. Sec 405. Wh 88%. Hisp 1%. Blk 7%. Asian 4%. Avg class size: 16. Uniform. **Fac 106.** M 30. F 76. Wh 98%. Hisp 1%. Blk 1%. Adv deg: 53%.
   Grad '04—102. Col—101. (LA St-Baton Rouge, Tulane, U of GA, U of SC, U of Richmond, Vanderbilt). Avg SAT: 1150. Avg ACT: 26. Alum 1900.
   Tui '04-'05: Day $8000-10,500 (+$1600). **Aid:** Need 105 ($1,300,000).
   Endow $8,575,000. Plant val $17,573,000. Bldgs 15. Class rms 62. 2 Libs 32,000 vols. Sci labs 9. Comp labs 7. Theaters 1. Art studios 3. Music studios 2. Dance studios 1. Gyms 2. Fields 6. Courts 1. Pools 1.
   Est 1965. Nonprofit. Episcopal. Sem (Aug-May).

The school offers an extensive Advanced Placement program that features courses in English, French, Spanish, Latin, calculus, physics, biology, chemistry, American and modern European history, American government, studio art and computer science. Interscholastic sports, publications, chorus, drama, band, community service and interest clubs are also available.

METAIRIE, LA. (15 mi. WSW of New Orleans, LA) Suburban. Pop: 146,136. Alt: 5 ft.

METAIRIE PARK COUNTRY DAY SCHOOL
Day — Coed Gr K-12

Metairie, LA 70005. 300 Park Rd. Tel: 504-837-5204. Fax: 504-837-0015.
   www.mpcds.com   E-mail: admissions@mpcds.com
David Drinkwater, Head. BA, PhD, Oxford Univ (England). **Amy White, Adm.**
   Col Prep. AP—Eng Fr Span Calc Bio Chem Physics Eur_Hist US_Hist US_Govt & Pol. **Feat**—Creative_Writing Computers Psych Film Painting Photog Sculpt Studio_Art Acting Drama Music Dance.
   Adm: 101/yr. Appl due: Rolling. Accepted: 48%. **Tests** IQ SSAT Stanford.
   Enr 717. B 368. G 349. Elem 481. Sec 236. Wh 81%. Hisp 4%. Blk 11%. Asian 3%. Other

1%. Avg class size: 15. **Fac 101.** M 25/2. F 65/9. Wh 89%. Hisp 3%. Blk 5%. Other 3%. Adv deg: 57%.
Grad '04—58. Col—58. (U of AL-Tuscaloosa 6, Geo Wash 4, Tulane 4, SMU 4, TX Christian 3, U of VA 2). Alum 2771.
Tui '04-'05: Day $10,930-13,515 (+$1500). **Aid:** Need 112 ($854,515).
Summer: Enrich. Creative Arts. 5 wks.
Endow $6,523,000. Plant val $31,000,000. Bldgs 24. Class rms 50. 2 Libs 56,000 vols. Labs 9. Theater/auds 1. Art studios 7. Music studios 3. Dance studios 1. Gyms 1. Fields 1.
Est 1929. Nonprofit. Quar (Aug-May). **Assoc** CLS.

The first country day school in the region, MPCDS is of interest for its varied curriculum, which focuses on the individual and society. The college preparatory program emphasizes academics, and the fine arts program is an integral part of the humanistic education. Traditional subjects are taught as faculty promote writing and the expression of ideas in the classroom. Advanced Placement courses and a variety of electives in all subject areas are offered to qualified students. Summer study in France and Spain is also available.

The school occupies 14 acres, two of which provide open land for athletic playing fields. Beginning in grade 7, Country Day offers interscholastic competition in nine boys' and eight girls' sports.

RIDGEWOOD PREPARATORY SCHOOL
Day — Coed Gr PS-12

Metairie, LA 70001. 201 Pasadena Ave. Tel: 504-835-2545. Fax: 504-837-1864.
   www.ridgewoodprep.com   E-mail: rps@ridgewoodprep.com
M. J. Montgomery, Jr., Head. BS, MEd, Loyola Univ (LA). **Marlena Templet, Adm.**
   Col Prep. Gen Acad. Feat—Lib_Skills Fr Span Comp_Sci Econ Studio_Art Debate Journ.
   Adm: 90/yr. Appl due: Feb. Accepted: 45%. **Tests** Stanford.
   Enr 510. B 250. G 260. Wh 78%. Hisp 10%. Blk 9%. Asian 3%. Avg class size: 22. **Fac 38.** M 12/2. F 23/1. Wh 96%. Hisp 2%. Asian 2%. Adv deg: 65%.
   Grad '04—58. Col—58. (U of New Orleans, LA St-Baton Rouge, Southeastern LA, U of LA-Lafayette, Tulane, Nicholls St). Avg SAT: 1150. Avg ACT: 24. Alum 2771.
   Tui '03-'04: Day $4830 (+$600).
   Endow $50,000. Plant val $4,500,000. Bldgs 6. Class rms 28. Lib 15,500 vols. Sci labs 1. Comp labs 1. Art studios 1. Music studios 1. Gyms 1. Fields 1.
   Est 1948. Nonprofit. 6 terms (Aug-June). **Assoc** SACS.

Founded as a college preparatory school for boys, Ridgewood became coeducational in 1952. The school is organized as a primary school, a middle school and a high school, with a selection of honors courses available in the upper grades. Computer science and fine arts units are required for graduation, and elective choices include French, Spanish, journalism, speech, art and library science.

High school students have access to a wide variety of extracurricular and cocurricular activities, in addition to diverse athletic opportunities.

ST. MARTIN'S EPISCOPAL SCHOOL
Day — Coed Gr PS-12

Metairie, LA 70003. 5309 Airline Dr. Tel: 504-733-0353. Fax: 504-736-8801.
www.stmsaints.com   E-mail: charles.maumus@stmsaints.com
Barbara Ryan, Int Head. BS, Univ of New Orleans. **Charles Maumus, Adm.**

Col Prep. AP—Eng Fr Lat Span Calc Stats Bio Chem US_Hist Econ Studio_Art. **Feat**—Creative_Writing Environ_Sci Comp_Sci Civics Law Psych Sociol Relig Film Drama Music_Theory Journ Speech. **Supp**—Dev_Read Rem_Math Rev.

Adm: 124/yr. Appl due: Rolling. Accepted: 76%. Yield: 61%. **Tests** CEEB CTP_4 IQ ISEE.

Enr 775. B 457. G 318. Elem 498. Sec 277. Wh 77%. Hisp 4%. Blk 3%. Asian 16%. Avg class size: 20. **Fac 85.** M 22/1. F 58/4. Wh 90%. Hisp 5%. Blk 1%. Asian 3%. Other 1%. Adv deg: 72%.

Grad '04—62. Col—62. (LA St-Baton Rouge 13, Tulane 4, U of MS 3, Loyola U-LA 3, Rhodes 3, Vanderbilt 2). Alum 660.

Tui '04-'05: Day $7900-13,150 (+$350). **Aid:** Merit 19 ($124,025). Need 128 ($677,775).

Summer: Acad Enrich Rev Rem Rec. 2-8 wks.

Endow $3,240,000. Plant val $23,000,000. Bldgs 22. Class rms 51. 2 Libs 35,000 vols. Chapels 1. Sci labs 6. Lang labs 1. Comp ctrs 4. Theaters 1. Art studios 4. Music studios 2. Gyms 2. Fields 2. Pools 1. Tracks 1. Weight rms 1.

Est 1947. Nonprofit. Episcopal. Sem (Aug-June). **Assoc** CLS.

Founded under the auspices of the Episcopal Church, this independent school provides a rigorous academic curriculum with Advanced Placement and honors programs in most upper school disciplines. Graduation requirements include courses in foreign language, computer science, the fine arts and religion, in addition to a number of electives. A two-week senior internship project exposes each student to work placements before graduation in the areas of government, business, medicine, law, the arts and nonprofit organizations. St. Martin's allows concurrent enrollment with Tulane University and the University of New Orleans for academically qualified upperclassmen.

Middle and upper school students take life skills courses that explore issues from substance abuse and stress management to decision making and self-esteem; in the upper school, a component teaches practical skills. Religion is taught at all levels, while service projects begin in the lower school and culminate in a graduation requirement of 50 hours of direct, hands-on volunteering.

Interscholastic sports teams are available in cross-country, swimming, basketball, soccer, tennis, track and field, volleyball, softball, baseball, golf, wrestling and football. Other extracurriculars include a speech and debate team, honor societies, student government, performing arts, quiz bowl, publications, and clubs for those with interests in science, math and other specific fields.

NEW ORLEANS, LA. Urban. Pop: 484,674. Alt: 5 ft.

ACADEMY OF THE SACRED HEART
Day — Girls Gr PS-12

New Orleans, LA 70115. 4521 St Charles Ave. Tel: 504-891-1943. Fax: 504-891-9939.

www.ashrosary.org E-mail: ash@ashrosary.org

Timothy M. Burns, Head. BA, John Carroll Univ, MA, Georgetown Univ, PhD, Ohio State Univ. **Diane Killeen, Adm.**

Col Prep. AP—Eng Fr Span Calc Bio Chem US_Hist World_Hist US_Govt & Pol. **Feat**—African-Amer_Lit Southern_Lit African_Lit Anat & Physiol Ecol Computers Psych Relig Ceramics Film Sculpt Music.

Adm: 102/yr. Appl due: Rolling. Accepted: 71%. **Tests** HSPT IQ SSAT Stanford.

Enr 819. G 819. Elem 553. Sec 266. Wh 91%. Hisp 2%. Blk 5%. Asian 1%. Other 1%. Avg class size: 18. Uniform. **Fac 97.** M 17. F 59/21. Wh 95%. Hisp 3%. Blk 1%. Asian 1%. Adv deg: 53%.

Grad '04—72. **Col**—72. (LA St-Baton Rouge, U of GA, U of VA, Savannah Col of Art & Design, Col of Charleston, U of New Orleans). Avg SAT: 1147. Avg ACT: 25. Alum 2550.

Tui '03-'04: Day $7550-9150 (+$100-195). **Aid:** Need 102 ($359,390). Work prgm 2 ($700).

Endow $4,400,000. Plant val $16,200,000. Bldgs 5. Class rms 78. 2 Libs 41,586 vols. Sci labs 6. Comp labs 3. Auds 2. Art studios 2. Music studios 1. Gyms 1. Fields 1.

Est 1887. Nonprofit. Roman Catholic. Sem (Aug-June).

Part of an international network of educational institutions directed by the Society of the Sacred Heart, the school comprises four developmentally focused divisions: preschool (nursery and kindergarten), lower school (grades 1-4), middle school (grades 5-8) and high school (grades 9-12).

Serving three- and four-year-olds, the nursery and prekindergarten programs introduce basic concepts with the aid of manipulative materials and games. A thematic structure is in use, and the prekindergarten gradually integrates language arts, math, science and social studies. Kindergarten programming combines structured and unstructured activities, and teachers employ various modalities. The lower school emphasizes effective communication and seeks to develop age-appropriate study and organizational skills. Middle school girls engage in a broader curriculum that includes electives and an exposure to Latin and either French or Spanish. In addition to honors and AP courses, the high school program features independent study options and the opportunity to take classes at nearby colleges. Each high schooler must purchase a laptop computer for classroom use.

The academy's strong athletic program commences in the preschool with general activities that focus on fitness. Interscholastic competition begins at the middle school level; league contests are held in volleyball, basketball, softball and soccer. Options increase in high school, when swimming, tennis, cross-country, golf and cheerleading become available.

ISIDORE NEWMAN SCHOOL

Day — Coed Gr PS-12

New Orleans, LA 70115. 1903 Jefferson Ave. Tel: 504-899-5641. Fax: 504-896-8597.
www.newmanschool.org E-mail: admission@newmanschool.org

Scott McLeod, Head. BA, Wesleyan Univ, MAT, Harvard Univ, EdD, Univ of Massachusetts-Amherst. **Merry Sorrells, Adm.**

Col Prep. AP—Comp_Sci US_Govt & Pol. **Feat**—Humanities Fr Hebrew Lat Span Anat & Physiol Astron Genetics Econ Architect Art_Hist Studio_Art Drama Music Debate Speech Photojourn.

Adm: 183/yr. Appl due: Rolling. Accepted: 45%. **Tests** CTP_4 IQ ISEE.

Enr 1154. B 631. G 523. Elem 715. Sec 439. Wh 82%. Hisp 3%. Blk 8%. Asian 7%. Avg class size: 18. **Fac 182.** M 47. F 135. Wh 90%. Hisp 4%. Blk 5%. Asian 1%. Adv deg: 48%.
Grad '04—120. Col—120. (U of GA 6, NYU 6, Tulane 6, LA St-Baton Rouge 5, IN U 4, Princeton 3). Alum 4540.
Tui '04-'05: Day $10,500-13,760 (+$260-1280). **Aid:** Need 202 ($1,420,000).
Summer: Acad Enrich Rem Rec. 2-8 wks.
Endow $26,000,000. Plant val $18,100,000. Bldgs 14. Class rms 65. Lib 69,000 vols. Sci labs 10. Lang labs 1. Comp labs 4. Sci ctrs 1. Auds 1. Theaters 1. Art studios 4. Music studios 3. Perf arts ctrs 2. Drama studios 2. Gyms 2. Fields 1. Pools 1. Tracks 1.
Est 1903. Nonprofit. Sem (Aug-June). **Assoc** CLS SACS.

Founded by Isidore Newman, a noted financier and philanthropist, Isidore Newman Manual Training School opened in 1903. Over the years, the emphasis in curriculum gradually shifted from manual training to college preparation, and the name of the institution changed to Isidore Newman School.

Located on an 11-acre campus, Newman offers a challenging sequential curriculum addressing the humanities, the sciences and the fine arts. Advanced Placement courses and independent study opportunities are available across the curriculum, and an interdisciplinary humanities project is required of seniors. Computer instruction begins in kindergarten.

Interest clubs, debate, student government and school publications are among Newman's extracurriculars. Interscholastic athletic competition commences in grade 7.

LOUISE S. McGEHEE SCHOOL
Day — Boys Gr PS, Girls PS-12

New Orleans, LA 70130. 2343 Prytania St. Tel: 504-561-1224. Fax: 504-525-7910.
www.mcgehee.k12.la.us   E-mail: gate@mcgehee.k12.la.us
Eileen Friel Powers, Head. BS, Marymount Manhattan College, MAT, Univ of Massachusetts-Amherst. **Sarah Caskey Smith, Adm.**
Col Prep. AP—Fr Span Calc Eur_Hist. **Feat—**Comp_Sci Women's_Hist Anthro Psych Sociol Art_Hist Photog Studio_Art Music. **Supp—**Dev_Read Rem_Read Rev Tut.
Adm: 72/yr. Appl due: Rolling. **Tests** CTP_4 IQ Stanford.
Enr 475. Elem 337. Sec 138. Wh 81%. Hisp 5%. Blk 10%. Asian 4%. Avg class size: 18. Uniform. **Fac 73.** M 12. F 61. Adv deg: 73%.
Grad '04—29. Col—29. (U of GA, LA St-Baton Rouge, Geo Wash, Wesleyan Col, Tulane, U of AL-Tuscaloosa). Alum 2100.
Tui '04-'05: Day $8400-12,400 (+$400-1000).
Endow $5,000,000. Plant val $6,000,000. Bldgs 11. Class rms 40. Lib 20,000 vols. Sci labs 4. Lang labs 1. Comp labs 2. Auds 1. Art studios 1. Music studios 1. Photog studios 1. Ceramics studios 1. Gyms 1.
Est 1912. Nonprofit. Sem (Aug-June).

Louise S. McGehee founded this school to insure the opportunity for young women to have an education equal to that offered men. Located in a historic residential area of New Orleans, McGehee conducts a college preparatory curriculum that includes independent study and Advanced Placement courses.

Among the school's extracurricular activities are dramatics, choral music, team sports and interest clubs. Art facilities consist of a photography lab, potter's wheels and large areas for painting. Seniors participate in a two-week internship program that is required for graduation. McGehee offers an afternoon care program and after-school enrichment classes during the academic year, in addition to a coeducational early childhood program for two- and three-year-olds.

SHREVEPORT, LA. (176 mi. SSW of Little Rock, AR) Urban. Pop: 200,145. Alt: 210 ft.

SOUTHFIELD SCHOOL
Day — Coed Gr PS-8

Shreveport, LA 71106. 1100 Southfield Rd. Tel: 318-868-5375. Fax: 318-869-0890.
www.southfield-school.org   E-mail: ccoburn@southfield-school.org

Jeffrey W. Stokes, Head. BA, State Univ of New York-Albany, MAT, Univ of North Carolina-Chapel Hill. **Clare Coburn, Adm.**

Pre-Prep. Feat—Fr Span Computers Ethics Studio_Art Drama Music Journ.

Adm: 97/yr. Appl due: Rolling. Accepted: 90%. Yield: 90%. **Tests** Stanford.

Enr 436. B 219. G 217. Elem 436. Wh 86%. Hisp 1%. Blk 5%. Am Ind 1%. Asian 5%. Other 2%. Avg class size: 17. **Fac 40.** M 5. F 28/7. Wh 94%. Blk 3%. Am Ind 3%. Adv deg: 30%.

Grad '04—32. Prep—7. (Loyola Col Prep 7). Alum 2400.

Tui '04-'05: Day $4170-7530 (+$225-340). **Aid:** Merit 3 ($13,000). Need 67 ($252,000).

Summer: Enrich Rec. Tui Day $200/2-wk ses. 6 wks.

Endow $1,400,000. Plant val $7,750,000. Bldgs 10. Class rms 27. Lib 14,000 vols. Sci labs 2. Comp labs 2. Theaters 3. Art studios 1. Music studios 1. Gyms 1. Fields 1. Courts 1.

Est 1934. Nonprofit. Quar (Aug-May).

Opened by a group of parents, Southfield is located on an eight-acre campus and has become an institution with wide influence throughout the state. The curriculum of the lower school stresses the acquisition of basic academic skills, and the middle school emphasizes study skills and the fundamentals in the major disciplines.

Southfield's extended campus provides a program of travel and on-site learning. Middle school students take a four-day Louisiana history excursion and a geology trip to Texas. An afternoon enrichment program is available to children in all grades. A wide range of athletics is offered to students, and the fine arts are an integral part of the overall program. The school also stresses community and school service.

MISSISSIPPI

JACKSON, MS. (140 mi. NNE of Baton Rouge, LA; 156 mi. N of New Orleans, LA) Urban. Pop: 184,256. Alt: 296 ft. Area also includes Ridgeland.

ST. ANDREW'S EPISCOPAL SCHOOL
Day — Coed Gr PS-12

Ridgeland, MS 39157. 370 Old Agency Rd. Tel: 601-853-6000. Fax: 601-853-6005.
www.gosaints.org   E-mail: sa@gosaints.org
Stephen R. Blanchard, Head. BA, Oklahoma City Univ, MEd, North Texas State Univ. **Ellen M. Ford, Adm.**
- **Col Prep. AP**—Eng Fr Lat Span Calc Stats Bio Physics Eur_Hist US_Hist Comp_Govt & Pol US_Govt & Pol Art_Hist Studio_Art Music_Theory. **Feat**—Southern_Writers Greek Comp_Sci Web_Design African-Amer_Hist Psych World_Relig Film Drama Theater_Arts. **Supp**—Rev Tut.
- **Adm:** 182/yr. Appl due: Rolling. Accepted: 73%. Yield: 73%. **Tests** CTP_4 MAT Stanford.
- **Enr 1161.** B 565. G 596. Elem 868. Sec 293. Wh 84%. Hisp 1%. Blk 8%. Asian 6%. Other 1%. **Fac 117.** M 26. F 86/5. Wh 96%. Hisp 1%. Blk 3%. Adv deg: 29%.
- **Grad '04—68. Col—67.** (MS St 6, U of MS 5, Loyola U-LA 4, U of the South 3, U of MT 3, U of S MS 3). Avg SAT: 1285. Avg ACT: 28. Alum 1450.
- **Tui '04-'05: Day $6950-8700** (+$400). **Aid:** Need 89 ($350,006).
- **Summer:** Acad Enrich Rec. Tui Day $150-400. 1-3 wks.
- Endow $1,089,000. Plant val $15,038,000. Bldgs 13. Class rms 61. 3 Libs 30,000 vols. Chapels 2. Sci labs 9. Lang labs 1. Comp labs 2. Observatories 1. Auds 2. Theaters 1. Art studios 6. Music studios 5. Dance studios 2. Gyms 2. Fields 4. Field houses 1.
- **Est 1947.** Nonprofit. Episcopal. Quar (Aug-May). **Assoc** CLS SACS.

St. Andrew's, which is operated by an independent board of trustees, offers a college preparatory curriculum that stresses the study of classical literature and the mastery of scientific and mathematical methods. Community service projects, a fine and performing arts program that is built into the curriculum, a varied athletic program, and a number of student-sponsored religious celebrations and activities supplement the regular program. Students may also participate in an exchange program with St. Andrew's School for boys in Osaka, Japan.

Student life is governed by a student-written and -enforced honor code.

VICKSBURG, MS. (130 mi. N of Baton Rouge, LA; 166 mi. NNW of New Orleans, LA) Urban. Pop: 26,047. Alt: 196 ft.

ALL SAINTS' EPISCOPAL SCHOOL
Bdg and Day — Coed Gr 7-12

Vicksburg, MS 39180. 2717 Confederate Ave. Tel: 601-636-5266. Fax: 601-636-8987.
www.allsaintsweb.com   E-mail: allsaint@vicksburg.com

Rev. William V. Martin, Head. AB, Princeton Univ, MBA, Southern Methodist Univ, MDiv, Seabury-Western Theological Seminary. **Carole W. Martin, Adm.**
    Col Prep. Feat—Poetry Screenwriting Fr Span Anat & Physiol Botany Computers Hist_of_the_Old_South Psych Sociol Govt/Econ Bible Logic Film Studio_Art Drama Music. **Supp**—ESL Rev.
    Adm: 39/yr. **Tests** TOEFL.
    Enr 112. B 30/7. G 42/33. Elem 30. Sec 82. Wh 70%. Blk 10%. Other 20%. **Fac 24.** M 8. F 14/2. Wh 70%. Blk 10%. Other 20%. Adv deg: 66%.
    Grad '04—24. Col—24. (MS St, U of MS, LA St-Baton Rouge, U of AR-Fayetteville, U of TX-Austin, U of S MS). Avg SAT: 1029. Avg ACT: 23.
    Tui '04-'05: Bdg $22,497 (+$2200). **Day $5997** (+$1535). **Aid:** Need 17 ($90,400).
    Endow $3,287,000. Plant val $5,000,000. Bldgs 14. Dorms 6. Dorm rms 93. Class rms 18. Lib 20,000 vols. Sci labs 3. Comp labs 1. Art studios 1. Music studios 2. Gyms 1. Fields 4. Courts 6. Pools 1.
    Est 1908. Nonprofit. Episcopal. Sem (Aug-May). **Assoc** SACS.

All Saints' traces its origins back to 1860, when Rt. Rev. William Mercer Green, the state's first bishop, saw the need for a diocesan school for girls in the area. Although the Civil War prevented this school from becoming a reality, Bishop Theodore Dubose Bratton established All Saints' Episcopal College as a girls' college in 1908. In 1971, All Saints' first admitted boys and became a coeducational boarding school. The school is now owned by the Episcopal dioceses of Arkansas, Louisiana, Mississippi and western Louisiana, and the school's head and representatives from these dioceses constitute the board of trustees.

The school's comprehensive college preparatory curriculum features a low student-teacher ratio and accommodates pupils of average to above-average intelligence. Course work requires mastery of basic skills in the humanities, the sciences and the arts. Students choose from a varied array of electives, and honors courses are also available. The curriculum displays a strong emphasis on the arts.

All Saints' Academic Support Program (ASP) helps pupils become more successful, responsible and independent learners. Teachers offer daily individualized instruction for one to four students per class period. Instructors monitor academic assignments, grades and overall scholastic performance by consulting with other teachers and administrators. Typical areas of emphasis include time management, organization, reading and writing skills, and note- and test-taking strategies.

International boys and girls with varying levels of English proficiency may participate in a well-developed English as a Second Language program in place of a regular English class. Instruction addresses grammar, pronunciation, and written and oral expression. The school charges an additional tuition fee for both the ASP and the ESL programs.

Opportunities for religious involvement, community service, and a selection of traditional and nontraditional sports complete the program.

OKLAHOMA

OKLAHOMA CITY, OK. (189 mi. NNW of Dallas, TX) Urban. Pop: 506,132. Alt: 1214 ft.

CASADY SCHOOL
Day — Coed Gr PS-12

Oklahoma City, OK 73156. 9500 N Pennsylvania Ave, PO Box 20390. Tel: 405-749-3100. Fax: 405-749-3214.
www.casady.org   E-mail: admissions@casady.org
Charles W. Britton, Head. BA, Lake Forest College, MA, Middlebury College. **Lesa Wilson, Adm.**

Col Prep. AP—Physics. **Feat**—Creative_Writing Fr Ger Lat Span Stats Geol Govt Art_Hist Studio_Art Drama Music Orchestra Speech. **Supp**—Tut.

Adm: 107/yr. Appl due: Rolling. Accepted: 79%. Yield: 69%.

Enr 866. B 434. G 432. Elem 533. Sec 333. Wh 82%. Hisp 2%. Blk 4%. Am Ind 2%. Asian 10%. Avg class size: 15. **Fac 116.** M 45/8. F 58/5. Adv deg: 61%.

Grad '04—80. Col—80. (U of OK 17, SMU 4, Duke 3, Harvard 2, Princeton 1, Brown 1). Avg SAT: 1259. Alum 3200.

Tui '04-'05: Day $5700-13,320 (+$500). **Aid:** Need 120 ($690,000).

Summer: Acad Enrich Rev Rem Rec. Tui Day $50-320. 1-6 wks.

Endow $11,800,000. Plant val $24,000,000. Bldgs 29. Class rms 67. 2 Libs 30,000 vols. Chapels 1. Sci labs 6. Lang labs 2. Comp labs 5. Auds 3. Theaters 1. Art studios 4. Music studios 4. Dance studios 1. Arts ctrs 1. Gyms 2. Fields 7. Courts 12.

Est 1947. Nonprofit. Episcopal. Tri (Aug-June). **Assoc** CLS.

Situated on an 80-acre campus around a six-acre lake, this school was established by Rt. Rev. Thomas Casady, then Episcopal bishop of Oklahoma, and by members of the laity. Bible instruction is given in grades 1-8; kindergartners go to chapel service once a week, while students in grades 1-12 attend daily.

The upper division offers a rigorous college preparatory education enhanced by strong arts and sports programs and an extensive activities program. Students complete courses in English, mathematics, modern or classical languages, history, laboratory sciences, computer science and the fine arts. In addition, students are encouraged to choose from a large selection of electives, including Advanced Placement courses in every discipline and independent studies. Conversational French is introduced in grade 1, and students have a choice of French or Spanish in grade 6; Latin is required in grades 7 and 8.

Activities and sports are an essential part of the school day. Activities include student council, foreign language clubs, drama club, orchestra, choir, art club, outing club, publications, peer tutoring and a service-learning component. Competitive sports begin in grade 7, and a comprehensive program of recreation, exercise and interscholastic sports is provided in grades 7-12.

HERITAGE HALL SCHOOL
Day — Coed Gr PS-12

Oklahoma City, OK 73120. 1800 NW 122nd St. Tel: 405-749-3000. Fax: 405-751-7372.
www.heritagehall.com   E-mail: admissions@heritagehall.com
Guy A. Bramble, Head. BA, Amherst College, EdM, Harvard Univ. **Debbie Bolding, Adm.**

Col Prep. AP—Eng Fr Span Calc Bio Chem Physics Eur_Hist US_Hist Studio_Art. **Feat**—Creative_Writing Humanities Lat Stats Neurosci Programming Web_Design Econ Intl_Relations Psych Philos Art_Hist Ceramics Photog Theater_Arts Music Debate.

Adm (Gr PS-9): 112/yr. Appl due: Mar. Accepted: 75%. **Tests** CTP_4 IQ ISEE.

Enr 854. B 427. G 427. Elem 530. Sec 324. Wh 44%. Blk 5%. Am Ind 3%. Asian 3%. Other 45%. **Fac** 112. M 27/6. F 75/4. Wh 94%. Hisp 1%. Blk 2%. Am Ind 1%. Asian 2%. Adv deg: 41%.

Grad '04—64. Col—64. (U of OK 15, U of Central OK 5, OK St 4, TX Christian 3, U of KS 3, DePauw 2). Avg SAT: 1345. Avg ACT: 29.

Tui '04-'05: Day $10,960. Aid: Merit 4 ($16,000). Need 105 ($614,000).

Summer: Acad Enrich Rev Rem Rec. Tui Day $125/wk. 8 wks.

Bldgs 8. Libs 2. Sci labs 6. Lang labs 3. Comp labs 3. Auds 1. Art studios 4. Music studios 3. Dance studios 1. Gyms 3. Fields 5. Tennis courts 8. Ponds 2.

Est 1969. Nonprofit. Quar (Aug-May).

Located on a 92-acre campus in the northwestern part of the city, Heritage Hall offers a college preparatory curriculum that combines foundational core subjects with an array of enrichment courses. The lower school (grades PS-4), which commences with a three-year-old preschool, places emphasis on the acquisition of basic learning, critical thinking, problem solving, technology and communicational skills. Instructors employ various teaching methods in a setting that can accommodate children with differing learning rates and styles. Visual arts and music course work is particularly strong.

During the middle school years (grades 5-8), programming provides a foundation for the upper school by focusing on language arts, math, science and social studies, and students also gain an exposure to foreign language. Annual standardized testing diagnoses areas in need of reinforcement and assists teachers with appropriate placement and course selection. Heritage Hall's upper school (grades 9-12) continues to stress the traditional disciplines. Freshmen and sophomores may enroll in advanced math and science courses, while able upperclassmen choose from honors and Advanced Placement offerings in the major subject areas.

Particularly strong cocurricular activities include speech and debate, choral music and art programs. Other popular options are student government, interest clubs and, in grades 7-12, community service projects at area nonprofit agencies. The athletic program includes both interscholastic teams and instruction in lifetime sports.

TULSA, OK. (101 mi. ENE of Oklahoma City, OK) Urban. Pop: 393,049. Alt: 800 ft.

HOLLAND HALL SCHOOL
Day — Coed Gr PS-12

Tulsa, OK 74137. 5666 E 81st St. Tel: 918-481-1111. Fax: 918-481-1145.
www.hollandhall.org E-mail: ladams@hollandhall.org

Mark D. Desjardins, Head. BA, Bates College, MEd, PhD, Univ of Virginia. **Lori Adams, Adm.**

- **Col Prep. AP**—Eng Fr Lat Span Calc Stats Comp_Sci Bio Chem Physics Eur_Hist US_Hist US_Govt & Pol Music_Theory. **Feat**—Chin Relig Ceramics Photog Studio_Art Theater_Arts Stagecraft Jazz_Band Debate Speech. **Supp**—Rev Tut.
- **Adm (Gr PS-11):** 156/yr. Appl due: Rolling. Accepted: 55%. Yield: 67%. **Tests** CTP_4 ISEE.
- **Enr 1036.** B 550. G 486. Elem 675. Sec 361. Wh 87%. Hisp 1%. Blk 2%. Am Ind 1%. Asian 3%. Other 6%. Avg class size: 16. Uniform. **Fac 116.** M 39. F 77. Wh 78%. Hisp 4%. Blk 3%. Am Ind 2%. Asian 2%. Other 11%. Adv deg: 50%.
- **Grad '04—77. Col—76.** (U of Tulsa 9, U of OK 8, Wash U 3, NYU 3, U of TX-Austin 3, OK St 3). Avg SAT: 1253. Avg ACT: 27. Alum 2556.
- **Tui '04-'05:** Day **$8700-12,400** (+$870-1300). **Aid:** Merit 29 ($143,600). Need 90 ($763,050).
- **Summer:** Enrich Rev Rec. Arts. Leadership. Tui Day $210-300/2-wk ses. 8 wks.
- Endow $68,000,000. Plant val $34,300,000. Bldgs 9. Class rms 89. 3 Libs 70,000 vols. Chapels 1. Sci labs 9. Lang labs 1. Comp labs 4. Photog labs 1. Theaters 1. Art studios 6. Music studios 6. Dance studios 1. Arts ctrs 1. Art galleries 1. Recording studios 1. Gyms 3. Fields 10. Courts 12. Tracks 1. Weight rms 1.
- **Est 1922.** Nonprofit. Episcopal. Sem (Aug-May). **Assoc** CLS.

The city's first independent school, Holland Hall opened at a site near downtown Tulsa, before later moving to Birmingham Place. Realizing in the late 1960s that developments in technology, math and foreign language would soon demand additional space and technical support, the board of trustees decided to relocate the school to a 162-acre campus in a wooded area of south Tulsa in the fall of 1970.

The humanities, the sciences, the arts and technology form the core of the academic program at all grade levels. The primary school (grades PS-3) employs an open classroom approach that takes into account the child's particular learning needs. Learning centers, self-directed technology projects, hands-on science experiments, art and music experiences, Spanish, creative writing and religious studies are important aspects of the primary curriculum.

During the middle school years (grades 4-8), the interdisciplinary program balances a solid curriculum with developmental, exploratory experiences; pupils gain increasing levels of independence as they progress through grades 7 and 8. Spanish is part of the program in the earlier middle school grades, while Latin and French are both added in grade 6. Art and music classes, competitive athletics (starting in grade 7), community service projects, student-faculty plays, mini-mester courses, ecology outings and field trips are other notable aspects of middle school life.

Students in the upper school (grades 9-12) follow a flexible modular schedule that adheres to liberal arts principles. In addition to Advanced Placement and honors courses, the curriculum provides opportunities for research and experimentation in various fields, foreign language study, math competitions, technology projects and community service. An intern program allows seniors to work for one month at an area business or organization. Weekly chapel programs, arts and athletic opportunities, interest clubs and student publications supplement academics.

TEXAS

ARLINGTON, TX. (22 mi. WSW of Dallas, TX) Urban. Pop: 332,969. Alt: 616 ft.

THE OAKRIDGE SCHOOL
Day — Coed Gr PS-12

Arlington, TX 76013. 5900 W Pioneer Pky. Tel: 817-451-4994. Fax: 817-457-6681.
www.theoakridgeschool.org   E-mail: lhbroadus@esc11.net

Andy J. Broadus, Head. BS, Jacksonville Univ, MEd, Univ of North Florida. **Linda Broadus, Adm.**

    Col Prep. **AP**—Eng Calc Bio Chem Physics Eur_Hist US_Hist US_Govt & Pol. **Feat**—Anthro.

    Adm: 118/yr. Appl due: Rolling. Accepted: 65%. **Tests** CTP_4 IQ ISEE Stanford.

    Enr 760. B 373. G 387. Elem 532. Sec 228. Wh 75%. Hisp 4%. Blk 8%. Asian 7%. Other 6%. Avg class size: 15. Uniform. **Fac 98.** M 24. F 70/4. Wh 95%. Hisp 2%. Blk 2%. Asian 1%. Adv deg: 48%.

    Grad '04—56. Col—56. (TX Christian, U of TX-Austin, TX Tech, Baylor, Trinity U, Vanderbilt). Avg SAT: 1206. Avg ACT: 26. Alum 524.

    Tui '04-'05: Day $9230-11,370 (+$50-600). **Aid:** Merit 73 ($379,790). Need 103 ($492,259).

    Summer: Acad Enrich Rev Rec. Tui Day $250-800. 2-4 wks.

    Endow $220,000. Plant val $9,000,000. Bldgs 9. Class rms 59. Lib 18,000 vols. Sci labs 6. Lang labs 1. Comp labs 4. Auds 1. Art studios 4. Music studios 2. Dance studios 1. Gyms 2. Fields 4.

    Est 1979. Nonprofit. Sem (Aug-May).

Situated on a 35-acre campus east of Fort Worth, this school maintains a well-rounded college preparatory curriculum. The three-, four- and five-year-old kindergarten programs provide children with an introduction to math, language arts, science, social studies, Spanish, music, art and physical education. The lower school (grades 1-4) stresses the development of basic skills and conducts a strong enrichment program, while the middle school (grades 5-8) features the addition of French, geography, club activities and class trips. Various Advanced Placement courses and electives supplement standard course selections in the upper school (grades 9-12). Course work in all academic areas and grades incorporates computer technology.

Extracurricular offerings include honor societies, student government, and drama and foreign language clubs. Beginning in grade 7, boys may participate in interscholastic baseball, basketball, football, golf, soccer, tennis, track and cross-country; girls' sports include basketball, soccer, track, tennis, golf, volleyball, softball, cross-country and field hockey.

AUSTIN, TX. (181 mi. SSW of Dallas, TX) Urban. Pop: 656,562. Alt: 600 ft.

ST. STEPHEN'S EPISCOPAL SCHOOL
Bdg — Coed Gr 8-12; Day — Coed 6-12

Austin, TX 78746. 2900 Bunny Run. Tel: 512-327-1213. Fax: 512-327-6771.
www.sstx.org   E-mail: admission@ststephens-texas.com

Rev. Roger Bowen, Head. BA, The Citadel, MDiv, Virginia Theological Seminary. **Lawrence Sampleton, Adm.**

Col Prep. AP—Fr Span Calc Stats Eur_Hist US_Hist Art_Hist Studio_Art Music_Theory. **Feat**—Chin Mandarin Astrophysics Ethics Theol Photog Drama. **Supp**—ESL Tut.

Adm: 175/yr. Bdg 73. Day 102. Appl due: Feb. Accepted: 60%. **Tests** ISEE.

Enr 638. B 87/238. G 73/240. Elem 204. Sec 434. Wh 72%. Hisp 4%. Blk 3%. Asian 7%. Other 14%. Avg class size: 16. **Fac 105.** Adv deg: 63%. In dorms 50.

Grad '04—99. Col—99. (U of TX-Austin, SMU, Rhodes, U of CO-Boulder, Brown, Boston U). Avg SAT: 1282. Alum 4004.

Tui '02-'03: Bdg $25,300 (+$3500). **Day $15,500** (+$1500). **Aid:** Need ($1,119,212).

Summer: Acad Enrich. 4 wks.

Endow $5,507,000. Plant val $25,000,000. Bldgs 40. Dorms 10. Dorm rms 94. Class rms 37. Lib 17,000 vols. Chapels 1. Sci labs 6. Comp labs 5. Dark rms 1. Theaters 2. Art studios 2. Music studios 2. Arts ctrs 1. Gyms 2. Fields 7. Courts 14. Field houses 1. Pools 1.

Est 1950. Nonprofit. Episcopal. Tri (Aug-May). **Assoc** CLS.

This school was founded by the Diocese of Texas under the leadership of Rt. Rev. John Hines. Rev. William Brewster, formerly of St. Mark's School in Southborough, MA, was headmaster of St. Stephen's from its founding until his death in 1953.

The college preparatory curriculum stresses a thorough understanding of English, social studies, math, science and foreign language while featuring the fine arts. A course in theology is required for graduation, and independent study is available for advanced students. College counseling begins in grade 11. Private lessons in voice, instrumental music, acting, art, pottery and photography are offered. Opportunities to study abroad in Spain, China, Greece, France, Great Britain and Italy constitute the Summer Adventures Program.

Extracurricular activities include choir, volunteer activities, student government, publications, interest clubs, drama productions and interscholastic sports. Students also take advantage of the cultural offerings of nearby cities.

BRYAN, TX. (85 mi. NW of Houston, TX; 86 mi. ENE of Austin, TX) Suburban. Pop: 65,660. Alt: 914 ft.

ALLEN ACADEMY
Bdg — Boys Gr 9-12; Day — Coed PS-12

Bryan, TX 77802. 3201 Boonville Rd. Tel: 979-776-0731. Fax: 979-774-7769.
www.allenacademy.org

Robert Meyer, Head. BA, Dominican College of San Rafael, MA, California State Univ.

Camilla Viator, Adm.
Col Prep. IB Diploma. AP—Eng Fr Span Bio Chem Physics Eur_Hist US_Govt & Pol Art_Hist. **Feat**—Computers Drama Chorus Music Journ Speech. **Supp**—ESL Tut.
Adm (Bdg Gr 9-11; Day PS-11): 67/yr. Bdg 7. Day 60. Appl due: Rolling. Accepted: 60%. Yield: 98%.
Enr 309. B 15/152. G 142. Elem 230. Sec 79. Wh 85%. Hisp 3%. Blk 3%. Asian 7%. Other 2%. Avg class size: 18. Uniform. **Fac 43.** M 8. F 31/4. Wh 94%. Hisp 4%. Am Ind 1%. Other 1%. Adv deg: 16%. In dorms 3.
Grad '04—22. Col—22. (TX A&M 6, Sam Houston St 2, U of TX-Austin 2, Southwestern U 1, Emory 1, TX Christian 1). Avg SAT: 1160. Alum 3500.
Tui '04-'05: Bdg $20,000 (+$1670). **Day $5175-7080** (+$830). **Aid:** Merit 3 ($15,000). Need 20 ($85,000).
Summer: Acad Enrich. ESL. Tui Bdg $3000. Tui Day $500/credit. 4 wks.
Endow $200,000. Plant val $4,000,000. Dorms 1. Dorm rms 10. Class rms 35. Lib 10,000 vols. Sci labs 3. Comp labs 2. Art studios 1. Music studios 2. Gyms 1. Fields 3.
Est 1886. Nonprofit. Sem (Aug-May). **Assoc** SACS.

Founded in Madisonville as Madison Academy by Mississippi educator John Hodges Allen, the school assumed its current name in 1896. After approximately 100 years of enrollment and curricular growth, the academy relocated to its 40-acre campus in Bryan in 1988. Allen changed over the years from a boys' boarding institution to one that combines a coeducational day program with a limited boys' boarding division.

The school's college preparatory program emphasizes the liberal arts. Computer technology, foreign languages, and mini-session excursions abroad and throughout the United States enrich the curriculum. An honor's diploma is available to pupils interested in pursuing a more intensive course of studies. Allen's seven-period daily schedule enables qualified juniors and seniors to attend college classes for credit at Texas A&M University or Blinn College.

Students participate in student government, drama, music and interest clubs. In addition, select boys and girls in grades 10-12 may attend national conferences and workshops in government and politics. Allen's strong interscholastic athletic program comprises football, volleyball, basketball, soccer, golf, tennis, baseball, softball and track.

Boarders must remain on campus at least one weekend per month. International students may take English as a Second Language courses both during the school year and over the summer.

DALLAS, TX. Urban. Pop: 1,188,580. Alt: 475 ft. Area also includes Addison.

GREENHILL SCHOOL
Day — Coed Gr PS-12

Addison, TX 75001. 4141 Spring Valley Rd. Tel: 972-628-5400. Fax: 972-404-8217.
www.greenhill.org   E-mail: admission@greenhill.org
Scott A. Griggs, Head. BS, Centre College, MA, Ohio State Univ. **Lynn Switzer Bozalis, Adm.**
Col Prep. AP—Eng Fr Lat Span Calc Stats Bio Chem Physics US_Govt & Pol Studio_Art.

Feat—Poetry Shakespeare Chaucer Chin Astron Robotics Web_Design Sociol World_Relig Photog Video_Production Acting Theater_Arts Debate.
Adm: 175/yr. Accepted: 25%. Yield: 79%. **Tests** CTP_4 ISEE MRT.
Enr 1248. B 605. G 643. Elem 822. Sec 426. Wh 76%. Hisp 5%. Blk 7%. Asian 12%. Avg class size: 16. **Fac 136.** M 47/3. F 81/5. Wh 88%. Hisp 4%. Blk 6%. Asian 2%. Adv deg: 45%.
Grad '04—105. Col—105. (U of TX-Austin 6, SMU 5, Occidental 5, Tufts 4, U of SC 3). Avg SAT: 1282. Alum 2600.
Tui '04-'05: Day $13,950-17,150 (+$675-750). **Aid:** Need 148 ($1,423,000).
Summer: Acad Enrich Rec. Tui Day $110-1500. 1-7 wks.
Endow $13,500,000. Plant val $36,000,000. Bldgs 14. Class rms 75. Lib 50,000 vols. Lang labs 2. Comp labs 4. Comp ctrs 1. Theaters 1. Art studios 3. Music studios 5. Dance studios 2. Gyms 2. Fields 8. Tennis courts 8. Field houses 1. Pools 1.
Est 1950. Nonprofit. Tri (Aug-May).

Founded by Bernard Fulton and a group of Dallas citizens, this school opened with 60 students and a faculty of ten. In 1959, Greenhill moved to its present, 78-acre site in Addison.

Greenhill combines a creative academic program with comprehensive arts and athletics. The curriculum is sequential in grades K-12. Integrated course materials, in addition to interdisciplinary and team-teaching techniques, are utilized in support of the college preparatory program. Honors and Advanced Placement courses are available in the upper school. Competitive sports, physical education and the fine arts form part of the curriculum at all levels, and a variety of clubs and student publications is available.

JESUIT COLLEGE PREPARATORY SCHOOL OF DALLAS

Day — Boys Gr 9-12

Dallas, TX 75244. 12345 Inwood Rd. Tel: 972-387-8700. Fax: 972-661-9349.
www.jesuitcp.org   E-mail: thost@jesuitcp.org
Rev. Philip Postell, SJ, Pres. Michael Earsing, Prin. BS, State Univ of New York-Fredonia, MEd, Univ of North Texas. **Tim Host, Adm.**
Col Prep. AP—Eng Fr Span Calc Stats Comp_Sci Bio Chem Physics US_Hist World_Hist Comp_Govt & Pol Econ US_Govt & Pol. **Feat**—Lat Astron Web_Design Psych Theol Ceramics Studio_Art Theater_Arts Journ Public_Speak.
Adm (Gr 9-10): 270/yr. Appl due: Mar. Accepted: 60%. Yield: 60%. **Tests** ISEE.
Enr 1010. B 1010. Sec 1010. Wh 79%. Hisp 10%. Blk 3%. Asian 5%. Other 3%. Avg class size: 17. Uniform. **Fac 100.** M 68. F 32. Wh 95%. Hisp 3%. Blk 2%. Adv deg: 56%.
Grad '04—237. Col—237. (St Edward's 19, U of TX-Dallas 13, St Louis U 11, SMU 10, U of TX-Austin 14, Boston Col 10). Avg SAT: 1220. Alum 7500.
Tui '04-'05: Day $9700 (+$500). **Aid:** Merit 30 ($30,000). Need 202 ($1,127,000).
Summer: Acad Enrich Rem. Tui Day $400/crse. 4 wks.
Endow $21,000,000. Plant val $30,000,000. Bldgs 2. Libs 1. Sci labs 3. Comp labs 5. Auds 2. Theaters 1. Art studios 3. Music studios 3. Gyms 2. Fields 3. Courts 6.
Est 1942. Nonprofit. Roman Catholic. Sem (Aug-May).

Originally named Jesuit High School, the school was established shortly after Rev. Joseph P. Lynch, bishop of Dallas, commissioned the Society of Jesus to found a school in Dallas based on the principles of Jesuit secondary education. In 1969,

Jesuit assumed its present name to reflect the school's new emphasis on college preparation.

The rigorous curriculum features honors or Advanced Placement courses (or both) in English, foreign language, social studies, math, science and computer science. Religion and community service are integral aspects of school life. The entire Jesuit community gathers each Friday morning for a prayer service, and schoolwide liturgies are held at least once a month. Seniors fulfill a 100-hour community service requirement during the school year while engaging in a placement at one of 75 local sites.

Outside the classroom, boys participate in such pursuits as student council, newspaper, debate, math and language clubs, Big Brothers, environmental club and interest clubs. Students may compete interscholastically with private and public schools at the freshman, junior varsity and varsity levels in the following sports: cross-country, swimming, basketball, crew, diving, football, lacrosse, tennis, baseball, wrestling, fencing, golf, hockey, rugby, soccer, track and field, and cheerleading.

THE LAMPLIGHTER SCHOOL
Day — Coed Gr PS-4

Dallas, TX 75229. 11611 Inwood Rd. Tel: 214-369-9201. Fax: 214-369-5540.
  www.thelamplighterschool.org E-mail: tls@thelamplighterschool.org
Arnold S. Cohen, Head. BA, Dickinson College, MA, PhD, Ohio State Univ. **Matthew S. Brenner, Adm.**
Pre-Prep. Feat—Span Environ_Sci Computers Studio_Art Drama Music Horticulture.
Adm: 119/yr. Appl due: Oct. Accepted: 33%. Yield: 90%.
Enr 434. B 212. G 222. Elem 434. Wh 91%. Hisp 3%. Blk 1%. Asian 2%. Other 3%. Avg class size: 13. **Fac 47.** M 3. F 44. Wh 89%. Hisp 1%. Blk 5%. Am Ind 1%. Asian 3%. Other 1%. Adv deg: 46%.
Grad '04—55. Prep—53. (Hockaday 9, St Mark's Sch of TX 9, Episcopal Sch of Dallas 8, Parish Episcopal 7, Greenhill-TX 3). Alum 545.
Tui '04-'05: Day $6995-12,675. Aid: Need 18 ($130,000).
Summer: Enrich Rec. Tui Day $425/2-wk ses. 6 wks.
Endow $3,560,000. Plant val $10,000,000. Bldgs 2. Class rms 35. Lib 30,000 vols. Auds 1. Arts ctrs 1. Gyms 2. Greenhouses 1. Barns 1.
Est 1953. Nonprofit. Tri (Aug-May).

Lamplighter originated with a kindergarten and a first grade housed in an old farmhouse, complete with a barn and animals that soon became an integral part of the school's program. Today's curriculum recognizes the individual differences, needs and capacities of each student and encourages intellectual curiosity, critical thinking and creativity. Pupil progress is reported by direct parental observation through one-way windows and by several parent-teacher conferences yearly. The school operates on a modified open-classroom plan, allowing for team teaching. A nature trail leading to woods and a creek enhance Lamplighter's learning environment, and the outdoor environmental science classroom includes gardens in which pupils study native plants and trees; a greenhouse and a barn also provide enrichment opportunities for students.

Peer tutoring plays an important role at Lamplighter, as it encourages leadership skills and social-emotional development. As part of the fine arts curriculum, a study of opera begins in grade 3 and culminates in grade 4, when pupils stage an original opera production at the end of the school year. **See Also Pages 1186-7**

ST. MARK'S SCHOOL OF TEXAS
Day — Boys Gr 1-12

Dallas, TX 75230. 10600 Preston Rd. Tel: 214-346-8000. Fax: 214-346-8002.
www.smtexas.org   E-mail: admission@smtexas.org

Arnold E. Holtberg, Head. AB, Princeton Univ, MA, Lutheran Theological Seminary. **David Baker, Adm.**

Col Prep. **AP**—Eng Ger Lat Span Calc Stats Bio Chem Physics Eur_Hist US_Hist Econ. **Feat**—Creative_Writing Humanities Shakespeare Japan Astron Comp_Sci Holocaust Cold_War Philos Art_Hist Film Fine_Arts. **Supp**—Rev Tut.

Adm (Gr 1-11): 118/yr. Accepted: 29%. Yield: 84%. **Tests** CTP_4 IQ ISEE Stanford.

Enr 816. B 816. Elem 462. Sec 354. Wh 74%. Hisp 5%. Blk 6%. Asian 10%. Other 5%. Avg class size: 15. Uniform. **Fac 111.** M 62/1. F 45/3. Wh 85%. Hisp 6%. Blk 4%. Asian 4%. Other 1%. Adv deg: 70%.

Grad '04—82. Col—81. (Yale 6, Harvard 5, U of TX-Austin 4, Dartmouth 3, U of PA 3, U of CO-Boulder 3). Avg SAT: 1410. Alum 3200.

Tui '04-'05: Day $14,784-18,911. **Aid:** Need 149 ($1,437,001).

Summer: Acad Enrich Rec. Sports. 2-6 wks.

Endow $93,000,000. Plant val $20,000,000. Bldgs 14. Class rms 80. 2 Libs 45,000 vols. Chapels 1. Sci labs 14. Comp labs 4. Sci ctrs 1. Observatories 1. Planetariums 1. Auds 1. Theaters 2. Art studios 3. Music studios 3. Gyms 2. Athletic ctrs 1. Fields 5. Courts 9. Pools 1. Fitness ctrs 1. Greenhouses 1.

Est 1906. Nonprofit. Tri (Sept-May). **Assoc** CLS.

Texas Country Day School (founded in 1933) and Cathedral School for Boys (established in 1946), formerly the Terrill School (opened in 1906), were consolidated in 1950 to form St. Mark's School. Though the school itself is nondenominational, chapel affiliation is with the Episcopal Church. After decades of serving residential students, the school closed its boarding division in 1959, thereby permitting a larger day enrollment. St. Mark's has traditionally maintained an impressive plant, particularly for a day school.

The academic curriculum provides studies in the arts, the sciences and the humanities, and offers a wide variety of extracurricular activities. The program is complemented by interscholastic sports, a debate squad, a student-operated radio station, electives in chorus and drama, and wilderness and camping experiences. Six-week summer study/travel programs to France, Spain and Mexico are available.

DENTON, TX. (36 mi. NW of Dallas, TX) Urban. Pop: 80,537. Alt: 602 ft.

SELWYN SCHOOL
Day — Coed Gr PS-10

Denton, TX 76207. 3333 W University Dr. Tel: 940-382-6771. Fax: 940-383-0704.

www.selwynschool.com E-mail: maribeller@charter.net
Robert Estes, Head. BS, MS, Univ of North Texas. **Maribelle Robbins, Adm.**
  Pre-Prep. Gen Acad. Feat—Computers Studio_Art Drama Music.
  Adm: 97/yr. Appl due: Rolling. Accepted: 83%. **Tests** IQ.
  Enr 294. Elem 284. Sec 10. Wh 80%. Hisp 5%. Blk 4%. Asian 11%. Avg class size: 12. Uniform. **Fac 26.** M 5/4. F 13/4. Wh 97%. Hisp 1%. Blk 1%. Asian 1%. Adv deg: 19%.
  Grad '04—13. Alum 787.
  Tui '03-'04: Day $2250-8700 (+$100-250). **Aid:** Need 16 ($65,000).
  Summer: Acad Enrich. Tui Day $390-470/3-wk ses. 12 wks.
  Plant val $2,500,000. Bldgs 9. Class rms 24. Lib 12,000 vols. Sci labs 1. Comp labs 1. Dark rms 1. Comp ctrs 1. Amphitheaters 1. Theaters 1. Art studios 1. Music studios 2. Gyms 1. Fields 2. Tennis courts 1. Pools 1. Stables 1. Lakes 1.
  Est 1957. Nonprofit. Sem (Aug-May).

Occupying a 90-acre campus on the northern end of town, Selwyn enrolls students from over two dozen north Texas communities. The preschool utilizes a developmental approach, while Selwyn's elementary program features a Montessori curriculum for children age 3 through grade 3, as well as an academically enriched traditional approach in grades K-5. During the middle school years (grades 6-8), students refine their academic skills in preparation for high school. College preparation is of paramount importance beginning in grade 9.

A well-developed enrichment program supports academics. Students take part in the Perspectives Program, an educational travel adventure that consists of outdoor, academic and artistic experiences. Other enrichment opportunities are foreign language, music, art, computers, photography, rock climbing and community service projects. A competitive athletic program is available in grades 4-10; options include soccer, volleyball, basketball, tennis, track, softball and swimming. Student council, music lessons and horseback riding round out the extracurricular offerings.

FORT WORTH, TX. (33 mi. W of Dallas, TX) Urban. Pop: 534,694. Alt: 670 ft.

FORT WORTH COUNTRY DAY SCHOOL
Day — Coed Gr K-12

Fort Worth, TX 76109. 4200 Country Day Ln. Tel: 817-732-7718. Fax: 817-377-3425.
  www.fwcds.org E-mail: info@fwcds.org
Evan D. Peterson, Head. BS, West Virginia Wesleyan College, MA, Kean College. **Barbara Waldron Jiongo, Adm.**
  Col Prep. AP—Eng Fr Span Calc Stats Comp_Sci Bio Chem Physics Eur_Hist US_Hist US_Govt & Pol Art_Hist Studio_Art. **Feat**—Econ World_Relig Music. **Supp**—Rev Tut.
  Adm: 142/yr. Appl due: Feb. Accepted: 51%. Yield: 88%. **Tests** IQ ISEE.
  Enr 1098. B 579. G 519. Wh 88%. Hisp 1%. Blk 3%. Am Ind 3%. Asian 1%. Other 4%. Avg class size: 18. Uniform. **Fac 109.** M 37. F 68/4. Wh 92%. Hisp 4%. Blk 3%. Other 1%. Adv deg: 55%.
  Grad '04—91. Col—91. (U of TX-Austin 6, U of Tulsa 5, SMU 4, TX A&M 4, U of OK 4, Vanderbilt 4). Avg SAT: 1310. Alum 2300.
  Tui '04-'05: Day $11,770-12,660 (+$205-1070). **Aid:** Merit 1 ($1000). Need 102 ($807,430).
  Summer: Acad Enrich Rev Rec. 1-4 wks.

Endow $20,000,000. Plant val $17,000,000. Bldgs 15. Class rms 91. Lib 39,241 vols. Sci labs 12. Comp labs 5. Theaters 1. Art studios 5. Music studios 6. Dance studios 1. Arts ctrs 1. Gyms 2. Fields 10. Tennis courts 6. Tracks 1. Stadiums 1.
Est 1962. Nonprofit. Sem (Aug-May). **Assoc** CLS.

Modeled after Northeastern independent schools, Country Day was established by Fort Worth families to meet a local need. The program in the lower school (grades K-4) facilitates the mastery of basic language and mathematical skills. Children begin studying a foreign language in kindergarten. Reading and effective writing skills are stressed at every level, and computer studies are offered to all students. The middle school program (grades 5-8) includes accelerated math and language courses, in addition to compulsory fine arts course work.

The college preparatory upper school program (grades 9-12) offers a wide selection of courses, with an emphasis on research methods, study skills and SAT preparation. Electives supplement required courses, and students choose from Advanced Placement selections in most academic departments. All middle and upper school pupils participate in both athletics and the arts. The extensive program in the visual and performing arts includes theater, dance, orchestra, band, chorus, painting, photography and ceramics. Football, soccer, track, basketball, cross-country, girls' swimming, tennis, wrestling, field hockey, baseball, golf, volleyball and softball constitute the interscholastic sports program.

TRINITY VALLEY SCHOOL
Day — Coed Gr K-12

Fort Worth, TX 76132. 7500 Dutch Branch Rd. Tel: 817-321-0100. Fax: 817-321-0105. www.trinityvalleyschool.org E-mail: tvs@trinityvalleyschool.org
Judith S. Kinser, Adm.

Col Prep. AP—Eng Fr Lat Span Calc Bio Chem Physics US_Hist Econ. Feat—Creative_Writing Asian_Hist British_Hist Psych Comp_Relig Ceramics Photog Video_Production Chorus Music Speech. Supp—Tut.

Adm: 125/yr. Accepted: 55%. **Tests** CTP_4 ISEE Stanford.

Enr 950. B 500. G 450. Elem 631. Sec 319. Wh 83%. Hisp 2%. Blk 3%. Asian 6%. Other 6%. Avg class size: 17. Uniform. **Fac 89.** M 30. F 59. Wh 92%. Hisp 6%. Blk 2%. Adv deg: 60%.

Grad '04—71. Col—71. (TX A&M, TX Christian, U of TX-Austin, Southwestern U, Tulane, Wash & Lee). Avg SAT: 1230. Alum 1734.

Tui '04-'05: Day $11,675-12,320 (+$400). **Aid:** Need 117 ($747,130).

Summer: Enrich Rec. 1-2 wks.

Endow $15,000,000. Plant val $33,700,000. Bldgs 7. Class rms 47. 2 Libs 28,000 vols. Sci labs 7. Lang labs 3. Comp labs 3. Auds 1. Theaters 1. Art studios 4. Music studios 2. Gyms 2. Fields 8. Tennis courts 8.

Est 1959. Nonprofit. Sem (Aug-May).

Trinity Valley is a traditional college preparatory school that requires pupils to take at least five major courses per year. Upper school students generally take four years of math, English and history, three years of science and a foreign language, fine arts and economics. Lower school students acquire basic skills in all subject areas.

Elective courses are available in calculus, physics, Asian history, British history, creative writing, computer science, journalism and drama, among others. Competitive sports include football, soccer, tennis, golf, field hockey, basketball, baseball, softball, volleyball, cross-country and track. Extracurricular activities include theater and numerous interest clubs.

HARLINGEN, TX. (107 mi. SSW of Corpus Christi, TX) Suburban. Pop: 57,564. Alt: 40 ft.

MARINE MILITARY ACADEMY
Bdg — Boys Gr 8-PG

Harlingen, TX 78550. 320 Iwo Jima Blvd. Tel: 956-423-6006. Fax: 956-412-3848.
   www.mma-tx.org   E-mail: admissions@mma-tx.org
Maj. Gen. W. E. Rollings, USMC (Ret), Pres. Col. Tom A. Hobbs, USMC (Ret), Adm.
   Col Prep. Milit. AP—Eng Calc Stats Chem Physics. **Feat**—Marine_Biol/Sci Computers Econ JROTC Aerospace_Sci. **Supp**—ESL Tut.
   Adm: 222/yr. Appl due: Rolling. Accepted: 68%. **Tests** HSPT.
   Enr 406. B 406. Elem 53. Sec 353. Wh 65%. Hisp 24%. Blk 3%. Am Ind 1%. Asian 7%. Avg class size: 11. Uniform. **Fac 46.** M 23/3. F 20. Adv deg: 39%.
   Grad '04—62. Col—62. (TX A&M, U of TX-Austin, US Naval Acad, VA Milit, TX Tech, Citadel). Avg SAT: 1062. Alum 2533.
   Tui '03-'04: Bdg $21,950. Aid: Need 46 ($452,280).
   Summer: Rec. Milit Trng. Tui Bdg $3000. 4 wks.
   Endow $18,000,000. Plant val $28,556,000. Bldgs 43. Dorms 7. Dorm rms 200. Class rms 35. Lib 16,000 vols. Sci labs 4. Lang labs 1. Comp labs 3. Auds 1. Theaters 1. Music studios 1. Movie theaters 1. Gyms 3. Fields 5. Courts 6. Tennis courts 6. Pools 1. Rifle ranges 2.
   Est 1965. Nonprofit. Sem (Aug-May). **Assoc** SACS.

Founded by a group of former Marine officers on the site of the former Air Force Navigation School, MMA offers a full academic program, especially in the sciences and math, while stressing competitive sports and military discipline. An English composition course is required for sophomores. The program is based on Marine Corps concepts of leadership.

The aerospace program features a full flight operation that utilizes flight schools adjacent to the campus, and a private pilot's license may be earned. Enrollment is geographically diverse, with students coming from more than 30 states and roughly half a dozen foreign countries.

HOUSTON, TX. Urban. Pop: 1,845,967. Alt: 38 ft. Area also includes The Woodlands.

AWTY INTERNATIONAL SCHOOL
Day — Coed Gr PS-12

Houston, TX 77055. 7455 Awty School Ln. Tel: 713-686-4850. Fax: 713-686-4956.
   www.awty.org   E-mail: bbrowning@awty.org

David Watson, Head. BA, MS, Univ of Bristol (England), PhD, Univ of Zagreb (Croatia). **Beth Anne Browning, Adm.**
- Col Prep. IB Diploma. Fr Bac. Bilingual. **Feat**—Creative_Writing Fr Ger Ital Span Arabic Dutch Norwegian Computers Fine_Arts. **Supp**—ESL Tut.
- **Adm:** 261/yr. Appl due: Dec. Accepted: 55%. **Tests** CEEB CTP_4 ISEE.
- **Enr 1135.** B 563. G 572. Elem 813. Sec 322. Wh 37%. Hisp 3%. Blk 2%. Asian 1%. Other 57%. Avg class size: 19. Uniform. **Fac 127.** M 36. F 78/13. Wh 75%. Hisp 20%. Blk 5%. Adv deg: 41%.
- **Grad '04—61. Col—61.** (U of TX-Austin, Rice, McGill-Canada, Wellesley, Emory, U of Warwick-England). Avg SAT: 1300. Alum 550.
- **Tui '04-'05: Day $9825-13,465** (+$1500). **Aid:** Need 43 ($256,074).
- Endow $435,000. Plant val $16,986,000. Bldgs 9. Class rms 100. 3 Libs 44,141 vols. Sci labs 6. Lang labs 2. Comp labs 6. Art studios 2. Music studios 3. Gyms 3. Fields 2.
- **Est 1956.** Nonprofit. Tri (Aug-June).

This international school's early childhood curriculum (three-year-old prekindergarten through kindergarten) consists of completely bilingual French/English or Spanish/English instruction. Beginning in grade 1, Awty conducts parallel but separate English- and French-speaking programs. Students work toward an American high school diploma and either the International Baccalaureate or the French Baccalaureate. Well-qualified students may earn both French and American credentials.

The curriculum provides a sound foundation in English, mathematics, science, history, the fine arts and foreign languages. Community service is required, and advanced courses, physical education and electives, including extensive computer offerings, are available. Travel groups are organized during school vacations, and students may also choose to participate in exchange programs.

Students come from around the world to create a multicultural environment. An intensive English as a Second Language program is conducted, and instruction in French, Spanish, German, Arabic and Italian is available at the native-language level.

THE JOHN COOPER SCHOOL

Day — Coed Gr K-12

The Woodlands, TX 77381. 1 John Cooper Dr. Tel: 281-367-0900. Fax: 281-298-5715.
www.johncooper.org   E-mail: admissions@johncooper.org

Michael F. Maher, Head. BS, MA, Catholic Univ of America. **Craig Meredith, Adm.**
- Col Prep. **AP**—Eng Fr Span Calc Comp_Sci Bio Chem Physics Eur_Hist US_Hist Studio_Art. **Feat**—Creative_Writing Southern_Lit Lat Stats Holocaust Econ Pol_Sci Psych World_Relig Film Photog Sculpt Printmaking Theater_Arts Band Chorus Speech.
- **Adm:** 147/yr. Appl due: Jan. Accepted: 63%. Yield: 87%. **Tests** CEEB CTP_4 IQ ISEE.
- **Enr 880.** B 418. G 462. Elem 577. Sec 303. Wh 74%. Hisp 7%. Blk 2%. Asian 13%. Other 4%. Avg class size: 18. **Fac 85.** M 19/3. F 51/12. Wh 93%. Hisp 6%. Other 1%. Adv deg: 54%.
- **Grad '04—64. Col—64.** (SMU 4, U of TX-Austin 4, TX Tech 4, Rice 3, Vanderbilt 3, Tulane 2). Avg SAT: 1280. Avg ACT: 28. Alum 519.
- **Tui '04-'05: Day $11,670-13,050** (+$500-900). **Aid:** Need 45 ($268,950).
- **Summer:** Acad Enrich Rev Rec. Sports. Tui Day $290-480. 2-4 wks.
- Endow $515,000. Plant val $15,300,000. Bldgs 6. Class rms 86. 2 Libs 18,700 vols. Comp labs 3. Auds 2. Art studios 3. Music studios 2. Dance studios 1. Gyms 4. Fields 2. Courts 4.

Est 1988. Nonprofit. Quar (Aug-May). **Assoc** CLS.

Located on a 43-acre campus 27 miles northwest of Houston, this college preparatory school provides a varied elementary and secondary program. An intensive foreign language program begins Spanish instruction at the kindergarten level and introduces French and Latin in the middle school. Upper schoolers choose from a full complement of Advanced Placement courses, as well as such electives as drama, yearbook, band, choir, painting and drawing, sculpture, photography and literary magazine. Lower and middle school children receive application-specific and curriculum-integrated computer instruction, while upper school pupils choose from applications and programming courses.

An extensive array of clubs, service organizations and leadership opportunities supplements academics. In addition, Cooper fields interscholastic athletic teams in approximately a dozen sports beginning in the middle school.

See Also Page 1184

KINKAID SCHOOL

Day — Coed Gr PS-12

Houston, TX 77024. 201 Kinkaid School Dr. Tel: 713-782-1640. Fax: 713-782-3543.
www.kinkaid.org   E-mail: admissions@kinkaid.org

Donald C. North, Head. BA, Vanderbilt Univ, MA, Middlebury College. **Bettie Hankamer, Adm.**

Col Prep. AP—Eng Fr Lat Span Calc Stats Comp_Sci Bio Chem Physics Eur_Hist US_Hist Studio_Art Music_Theory. **Feat**—Creative_Writing Astron Environ_Sci Econ Govt Psych Philos World_Relig Architect Photog Drama Dance Debate Journ Speech.

Adm: 186/yr. Appl due: Dec. Accepted: 26%. Yield: 79%. **Tests** IQ ISEE.

Enr 1344. B 669. G 675. Elem 823. Sec 521. Wh 84%. Hisp 3%. Blk 4%. Asian 5%. Other 4%. Avg class size: 18. **Fac 159.** M 44/9. F 94/12. Wh 87%. Hisp 4%. Blk 5%. Asian 2%. Other 2%. Adv deg: 49%.

Grad '04—114. Col—113. (Tulane 11, TX Christian 11, U of TX-Austin 11, SMU 6, LA St-Baton Rouge 5, Vanderbilt 5). Avg SAT: 1321. Avg ACT: 27. Alum 3946.

Tui '04-'05: Day $10,090-13,790 (+$150-550). **Aid:** Merit 5 ($56,160). Need 77 ($836,640).

Summer: Acad Enrich Rev Rem Rec. Arts. ESL. Tui Day $300-800. 1-5 wks.

Endow $74,800,000. Plant val $47,539,000. Bldgs 10. Class rms 126. 3 Libs 79,668 vols. Sci labs 12. Comp labs 7. Auds 4. Theaters 1. Art studios 4. Music studios 5. Dance studios 1. Gyms 3. Fields 5. Courts 7. Tracks 1.

Est 1906. Nonprofit. Sem (Aug-June). **Assoc** CLS.

The oldest coeducational independent school in the city, Kinkaid was founded by Margaret Hunter Kinkaid, who originally operated the school out of her home. In 1957, the school assumed its present, 40-acre location in Piney Point Village. From its early days, the school has placed emphasis upon both academic attainment and character development.

Kinkaid combines rigorous academics with well-developed programs in athletics and the fine and performing arts. Upper schoolers take part in a three-week interim program each January that consists of various enrichment courses, independent study opportunities, internships and travel options.

ST. THOMAS HIGH SCHOOL

Day — Boys Gr 9-12

Houston, TX 77007. 4500 Memorial Dr. Tel: 713-864-6348. Fax: 713-864-5750.
www.sths.org E-mail: alice.arbour@sths.org

Rev. Ronald G. Schwenzer, CSB, Prin. BA, St John Fisher College, STB, Univ of St Michael's College, MS, Purdue Univ. **Alice Arbour, Adm.**

Col Prep. AP—Eng Span Calc Bio Chem Physics US_Govt & Pol. **Feat**—Fr Lat Astron Geol Oceanog Comp_Sci Econ Theol Studio_Art Music Journ.

Adm: 250/yr. Appl due: Feb. Accepted: 75%. **Tests** Stanford.

Enr 645. B 645. Sec 645. Wh 70%. Hisp 20%. Blk 3%. Asian 5%. Other 2%. Avg class size: 20. **Fac 60.** M 40. F 20. Adv deg: 45%.

Grad '04—150. **Col**—153. (TX A&M, U of TX-Austin, U of St Thomas-TX, U of Houston, TX Tech, Rice). Avg SAT: 1168. Alum 9600.

Tui '04-'05: Day $8500 (+$600-700). **Aid:** Merit 40 ($36,000). Need 120 ($400,000).

Summer: Acad Rem. Tui Day $400. 3-7 wks.

Endow $2,500,000. Plant val $17,000,000. Bldgs 4. Lib 10,000 vols. Sci labs 3. Comp labs 3. Auds 1. Art studios 1. Music studios 1. Amphitheaters 1. Gyms 1. Fields 2. Tennis courts 1. Tracks 1. Stadiums 1.

Est 1900. Nonprofit. Roman Catholic. Sem (Aug-May).

St. Thomas, Houston's oldest boys' college preparatory school, was founded by three priests of the Congregation of St. Basil on the site of a former monastery, and it moved to its present, 17-acre location in 1940. The student body is drawn from Houston and the surrounding community.

Curriculum and activities are conducted with an emphasis on Catholic values and teachings. The normal course load is seven subjects, with requirements in English, math, science, history and theology. Students may qualify for honors courses that include advanced studies in most subject areas.

Cultural, social and service activities are considered an important complement to academics. Students participate in Spanish and French clubs, publications, student council, and bowling, karate, chess and science clubs. Boys assist the campus ministry by serving as lectors, Mass servers and Eucharistic ministers. Competitive team sports include football, baseball, basketball, track, soccer, tennis, swimming, cross-country, wrestling, roller hockey, tae kwon do, rugby and golf.

IRVING, TX. (13 mi. WNW of Dallas, TX) Urban. Pop: 191,615. Alt: 470 ft.

CISTERCIAN PREPARATORY SCHOOL

Day — Boys Gr 5-12

Irving, TX 75039. 3660 Cistercian Rd. Tel: 469-499-5400. Fax: 469-499-5440.
www.cistercian.org E-mail: admissions@cistercian.org

Rev. Peter Verhalen, OCist, Head. BA, MA, Univ of Dallas, MA, Univ of Texas-Arlington, MA, Univ of Washington. **Robert J. Haaser, Adm.**

Col Prep. AP—Physics. **Feat**—Creative_Writing Fr Lat Span Stats Anat Astron Comp_Sci Robotics Civil_War Econ Govt Psych Theol Photog Studio_Art Music. **Supp**—Rev.

Adm (Gr 5-11): 63/yr. Appl due: Jan. Accepted: 47%. Yield: 87%. **Tests** HSPT IQ.

Enr 346. B 346. Elem 170. Sec 176. Wh 79%. Hisp 6%. Blk 1%. Asian 5%. Other 9%. Avg

class size: 22. Uniform. **Fac 37.** M 27/2. F 7/1. Wh 97%. Hisp 3%. Adv deg: 78%.
Grad '04—42. Col—42. (U of TX-Austin 8, Austin 5, Stanford 3, Notre Dame 3, TX A&M 2, Wash & Lee 2). Avg SAT: 1399. Avg ACT: 30. Alum 917.
Tui '04-'05: Day $10,300-11,650 (+$500-700). **Aid:** Need 51 ($265,500).
Summer: Acad Enrich Rev Rem Rec. Tui Day $200-385. 2-4 wks.
Endow $4,300,000. Plant val $12,300,000. Bldgs 7. Class rms 22. Lib 23,000 vols. Labs 4. Auds 1. Theaters 1. Art studios 2. Music studios 1. Gyms 2. Fields 4. Courts 5.
Est 1962. Nonprofit. Roman Catholic. Quar (Aug-May). **Assoc** CLS.

Cistercian Fathers founded and conduct this college preparatory school, which accepts boys of all faiths and offers a varied curriculum. Students fulfill course requirements in English, foreign languages, math, science, social studies and theology. Seniors take dual-enrollment college courses in English, calculus, American government and sciences through the Dallas County community college system. Senior projects, under the direction of a faculty member, are conducted during the fourth quarter.

The athletic program offers football, cross-country, baseball, basketball, soccer, swimming, track and tennis. Extracurricular activities include drama, quiz bowl, camera and other interest clubs, newspaper, literary magazine, yearbook and student government. **See Also Page 1330**

SAN ANTONIO, TX. Urban. Pop: 1,144,646. Alt: 700 ft.

KEYSTONE SCHOOL
Day — Coed Gr K-12

San Antonio, TX 78212. 119 E Craig Pl. Tel: 210-735-4022. Fax: 210-734-5508.
www.keystoneschool.org E-mail: cobra@keystoneschool.org
Hugh McIntosh, Head. Robyn Good, Adm.
Col Prep. AP—Calc Eur_Hist. **Feat**—Fr Span Studio_Art.
Adm: 75/yr. Appl due: Aug. Accepted: 90%. **Tests** CEEB IQ Stanford.
Enr 388. B 206. G 182. Elem 276. Sec 112. Wh 60%. Hisp 10%. Blk 10%. Asian 10%. Other 10%. Avg class size: 14. **Fac 38.** M 7. F 30/1. Wh 90%. Hisp 10%. Adv deg: 31%.
Grad '04—28. Col—28. (Wash U, Trinity U, Carnegie Mellon, Rice, Harvard, Yale). Avg SAT: 1405.
Tui '03-'04: Day $11,350 (+$100). **Aid:** Merit 3 ($4000). Need 27 ($200,856).
Endow $250,000. Plant val $5,500,000. Bldgs 10. Class rms 35. Libs 2. Sci labs 3. Lang labs 1. Comp labs 2. Theaters 1. Art studios 1. Music studios 1. Dance studios 1. Perf arts ctrs 1. Gyms 1.
Est 1948. Nonprofit. Sem (Aug-May).

Serving students of above-average ability, Keystone conducts a college preparatory program that emphasizes knowledge acquisition, study skills and the mastery of fundamental skills. Lower and middle schoolers (grades K-8) engage in core course work in language arts, math, science and social studies; specialists teach Spanish, studio art, music, computer applications and physical education classes. The upper school (grades 9-12) is characterized by a strong technology component and a broad selection of honors and Advanced Placement offerings. Field trips, which provide enrichment at all grade levels, range from daylong trips to Austin and San Marcos to several-day hiking and camping excursions to the Yellowstone, Glacier and Rocky Mountain national parks.

Extracurricular options include language clubs, school publications, and active middle and upper school student councils. Through Keystone's interscholastic sports program, boys may compete in basketball, soccer and lacrosse, and girls in volleyball, basketball and softball.

SAINT MARY'S HALL
Day — Coed Gr PS-12

San Antonio, TX 78217. 9401 Starcrest Dr. Tel: 210-483-9234. Fax: 210-655-5211.
www.smhall.org E-mail: admissions@smhall.org
Bob Windham, Head. BS, Texas A&M Univ, MEd, Univ of Houston. **Elena D. Hicks, Adm.**

- **Col Prep. AP**—Eng Fr Lat Span Calc Stats Comp_Sci Bio Chem Physics Eur_Hist US_Hist US_Govt & Pol Art_Hist Studio_Art Music_Theory. **Feat**—Japan Psych Theol Music Dance Debate. **Supp**—Rev Tut.
- **Adm:** 183/yr. Appl due: Feb. Accepted: 63%. Yield: 71%. **Tests** ISEE.
- **Enr 890.** B 413. G 477. Elem 574. Sec 316. Avg class size: 15. Uniform. **Fac 134.** M 33/4. F 94/3. Adv deg: 49%.
- **Grad '04—83. Col—82.** (Carnegie Mellon, SMU, Stanford, Rice, U of VA, Harvard). Avg SAT: 1247. Alum 3244.
- **Tui '04-'05: Day $7975-14,975** (+$500). **Aid:** Merit 57 ($293,625). Need 95 ($715,200).
- **Summer:** Acad Enrich Rec. 4 wks.
- Endow $42,000,000. Plant val $22,000,000. Bldgs 25. Class rms 100. 2 Libs 23,000 vols. Sci labs 8. Lang labs 1. Comp labs 3. Photog labs 1. Theaters 1. Art studios 3. Music studios 8. Dance studios 3. Arts ctrs 1. Gyms 2. Fields 3. Courts 7. Pools 1.
- **Est 1879.** Nonprofit. Sem (Aug-May). **Assoc** CLS.

Saint Mary's Hall was founded by Bishop Robert W. B. Elliott, the first bishop of the Episcopal Diocese of West Texas. A school for boys and girls of all denominations, Saint Mary's Hall still has a historical affiliation with the Episcopal Church. Over the years, the school has grown by the admission of boys into all grades and the addition of primary grades, a Montessori preschool, a traditional kindergarten and a postgraduate program. In the fall of 1968, the school moved to its present site, a wooded, 60-acre campus that overlooks San Antonio.

The school conducts a traditional college preparatory curriculum that is complemented by various cocurricular options. Honors and Advanced Placement courses in many disciplines are available in the upper school. An extensive fine arts program provides opportunities in the visual and performing arts.

The cocurricular program stresses athletics, student government, honor organizations, interest clubs and community service. The lower school provides intramural opportunities in soccer, basketball and softball, while the middle and upper schools offer interscholastic competition in cross-country, field hockey, boys' and girls' volleyball, lacrosse, golf, track, baseball, softball, tennis, basketball, wrestling, soccer and swimming.

TEXAS MILITARY INSTITUTE

Bdg — Coed Gr 9-12; Day — Coed 6-12

San Antonio, TX 78257. 20955 W Tejas Trl. Tel: 210-698-7171. Fax: 210-698-0715.
www.tmi-sa.org   E-mail: admissions@tmi-sa.org
Ronald J. Tribo, Head. BA, Univ of California-Los Angeles, MBA, Inter-American Univ.
Megan Maturo, Adm.
  Col Prep. Milit. AP—Eng Lat Span Calc Stats Comp_Sci Bio Chem Physics Eur_Hist US_Hist Studio_Art. **Feat**—Greek Relig Fine_Arts JROTC.
  Adm: 80/yr. Bdg 8. Day 72. Appl due: Feb. **Tests** CTP_4 ISEE SSAT.
  Enr 320. B 14/167. G 6/133. Elem 100. Sec 220. Avg class size: 15. Uniform. **Fac 39.** M 20. F 19. Adv deg: 61%. In dorms 4.
  Grad '04—52. Col—52. (TX A&M 5, Westmont 5, Baylor 4, U of TX-Austin 4, Vanderbilt 2, TX Christian 2). Avg SAT: 1250. Alum 3500.
  Tui '04-'05: Bdg $27,845 (+$800-1800). **Day $13,370-14,320** (+$800-1800). **Aid:** Merit 33 ($232,820). Need 55 ($372,980).
  Summer: Acad Enrich Rev Rec. Sports. 6 wks.
  Endow $1,400,000. Plant val $14,200,000. Bldgs 12. Dorms 5. Dorm rms 30. Class rms 30. Lib 20,000 vols. Labs 3. Comp labs 3. Auds 1. Theaters 1. Art studios 1. Gyms 1. Fields 3. Courts 3. Pools 1. Rifle ranges 1.
  Est 1893. Inc. Episcopal. Sem (Aug-May).

The school was founded as a boys' military program by Rt. Rev. J. S. Johnston, bishop of the Diocese of West Texas of the Protestant Episcopal Church. In 1926, it merged with San Antonio Academy and the name was changed to Texas Military Institute. The Episcopal Church once again assumed ownership and direction in 1952. The school began admitting girls and expanded to include grades 6-8 in 1972. Two years later, the military program became optional.

The traditional college preparatory curriculum of the upper school consists of five core fields—English, mathematics, science, social studies and foreign language—supplemented by offerings in the fine arts, athletics, religion and an optional military science program. Honors and Advanced Placement courses provide an additional challenge for the exceptionally capable student. Electives are available in such areas as drama, vocal music, photography, yearbook publication and art.

Extracurricular options include student government and a range of clubs and athletic teams. Students are encouraged to participate in service programs, and JROTC is available to boys and girls beginning in grade 6. The curriculum includes required religion courses, and daily chapel involves both students and faculty.

SAN MARCOS, TX. (45 mi. NE of San Antonio, TX) Suburban. Pop: 34,733. Alt: 581 ft.

SAN MARCOS BAPTIST ACADEMY

Bdg — Boys Gr 6-12, Girls 8-12; Day — Coed 6-12

San Marcos, TX 78666. 2801 Ranch Rd 12. Tel: 512-753-8000. Fax: 512-753-8031.
  www.smba.org   E-mail: admissions@smba.org
Lt. Col. Victor H. Schmidt, Pres. Bobby Dupree, Adm.

Col Prep. Milit. Feat—Fr Span Astron Computers Bible JROTC. **Supp**—Dev_Read ESL Rev Tut.

Adm: 84/yr. **Tests** ISEE.

Enr 215. B 111/29. G 49/26. Wh 83%. Hisp 12%. Blk 1%. Asian 4%.Uniform. **Fac 36.** M 18. F 18. Adv deg: 58%. In dorms 3.

Grad '04—52. Col—48. (Baylor, Southwest TX St, TX Tech, SMU, TX A&M, U of TX-Austin). Alum 5200.

Tui '03-'04: Bdg $22,275 (+$2000). **Day $6787-7199** (+$1000). **Aid:** Need 84 ($464,000).

Endow $3,801,000. Plant val $17,662,000. Bldgs 7. Dorms 3. Dorm rms 180. Class rms 32. Lib 17,418 vols. Labs 4. Theaters 1. Art studios 1. Music studios 1. Courts 4. Pools 1. Stables 1. Rifle ranges 1.

Est 1907. Nonprofit. Baptist. Sem (Aug-May). **Assoc** SACS.

Situated on a 200-acre campus, San Marcos is one of a number of correlated schools of the Baptist General Convention of Texas. The curriculum emphasizes college preparation, and honors courses are available to qualified students. All upper school boys participate in the Junior ROTC program; it is optional for girls, who may instead take part in a leadership program.

The academy's honor program seeks the development of critical-thinking and independent research skills by means of small classes and technology-assisted learning. Course work in the fine arts, Christian studies, computer science and leadership supplements requirements in the traditional subjects. Upperclassmen may take Advanced Placement classes and may also earn college credits from nearby universities through enrollment in dual-credit courses.

Among student activities are athletic options and fine arts offerings, in addition to an equestrian program.

Mountain States

COLORADO

ASPEN, CO. (112 mi. WSW of Denver, CO) Suburban. Pop: 5914. Alt: 7908 ft.

ASPEN COUNTRY DAY SCHOOL
Day — Coed Gr PS-8

Aspen, CO 81611. 3 Music School Rd. Tel: 970-925-1909. Fax: 970-925-7074.
www.aspencds.org   E-mail: info@aspencds.org
John Suitor, Head. BA, MA, Univ of Vermont. **Gillian Baxter, Adm.**

Pre-Prep. Feat—Fr Lat Span Computers Studio_Art Drama Music Outdoor_Ed. **Supp**—Dev_Read Rem_Math Rem_Read Tut.

Adm: 45/yr. Appl due: May. Accepted: 74%. **Tests** SSAT Stanford.

Enr 165. B 80. G 85. Elem 165. Wh 97%. Hisp 1%. Am Ind 1%. Asian 1%. Avg class size: 15. **Fac 36.** M 12. F 20/4. Wh 100%. Adv deg: 30%.

Grad '04—18. Prep—12. (CO Rocky Mtn, Fountain Valley, Phillips Exeter, Holderness, Tabor, Middlesex). Avg SSAT: 82%. Alum 220.

Tui '03-'04: Day $10,700-17,850 (+$900). **Aid:** Merit 6 ($107,100). Need 34 ($450,000). Endow $850,000. Plant val $1,950,000. Bldgs 7. Class rms 18. Libs 1. Sci labs 1. Comp labs 1. Theaters 1. Art studios 1. Music studios 1. Gyms 1. Fields 1. Rinks 1.

Est 1969. Nonprofit. Sem (Sept-June).

Small classes provide individualized instruction throughout the school. The curriculum is ungraded in the lower school (grades PS-4), and French and Spanish are introduced at this stage. The middle school places particular emphasis on critical and creative writing skills.

An outdoor education program offers skiing, skating and sledding one afternoon a week to lower school students, while middle school students participate in three four-day wilderness trips each year. Activities include backpacking, desert trips, trail breaking, rock climbing, rappelling and snow shelter building, depending on the time of year. During ski season, a winter program in the upper grades involves a restructured academic day twice a week that enables students of all ability levels to receive afternoon ski instruction. A flexible academic schedule for skiers competing on the international or national level provides specially arranged tutorials and individual study opportunities.

Students compete interscholastically in soccer, skiing and basketball, and they may participate on community teams in ice hockey, volleyball, equestrian riding, figure skating, gymnastics and skiing.

COLORADO SPRINGS, CO. (63 mi. S of Denver, CO) Urban. Pop: 360,890. Alt: 5978 ft.

FOUNTAIN VALLEY SCHOOL
Bdg and Day — Coed Gr 9-12

Colorado Springs, CO 80911. 6155 Fountain Valley School Rd. Tel: 719-390-7035.
Fax: 719-390-7762.
www.fvs.edu   E-mail: admission@fvs.edu

John Edward Creeden, Head. BA, College of the Holy Cross, MA, PhD, Univ of Wisconsin-Madison. **Kelye S. Modarelli, Adm.**

Col Prep. AP—Eng Fr Span Calc Stats Bio Physics US_Hist World_Hist US_Govt & Pol Studio_Art. **Feat**—Genetics Geol Web_Design Film Filmmaking Theater Music Metal_Shop. **Supp**—ESL Rev Tut.

Adm (Bdg Gr 9-12; Day 9-11): 85/yr. Bdg 56. Day 29. Appl due: Feb. Accepted: 50%. Yield: 64%. **Tests** ISEE SSAT TOEFL.

Enr 225. B 59/41. G 73/52. Sec 225. Wh 76%. Hisp 4%. Blk 4%. Am Ind 4%. Asian 12%. Avg class size: 11. **Fac 45.** M 16/6. F 16/7. Wh 95%. Hisp 1%. Blk 2%. Asian 2%. Adv deg: 66%. In dorms 11.

Grad '04—43. Col—43. (U of CO-Boulder 5, U of Denver 2, Lewis & Clark 2, U of Puget Sound 2, Whitman 2, Willamette 2). Avg SAT: 1213. Avg ACT: 26. Alum 2600.

Tui '04-'05: Bdg $29,600 (+$840). **Day $16,825** (+$840). **Aid:** Merit 6 ($66,000). Need 69 ($1,100,000).

Endow $28,000,000. Plant val $30,000,000. Bldgs 36. Dorms 7. Dorm rms 85. Class rms 36. Lib 25,000 vols. Sci labs 6. Comp labs 3. Sci ctrs 1. Theaters 1. Art studios 6. Music studios 3. Dance studios 1. Art galleries 1. Gyms 1. Fields 5. Courts 9. Pools 1. Riding rings 2. Stables 2. Weight rms 1. Riding facilities yes. Student ctrs 1.

Est 1929. Nonprofit. Sem (Aug-May). **Assoc** CLS.

Located on an 1100-acre main campus, this school was founded to provide a Western alternative to the college preparatory boarding schools of the East. Originally a boys' school, Fountain Valley began operation with a board of trustees composed of prominent scientists, physicians, businesspeople and political figures from Boston, MA, Chicago, IL, Washington, DC, and Colorado Springs, as well as noted educator John Dewey. Day students were first admitted in 1951, and the school instituted full coeducation in 1975.

FVS' academic program features honors and Advanced Placement courses in the major disciplines. The program incorporates a science center and computer labs, and the school conducts a technology curriculum that culminates in advanced topics. Qualified seniors may design independent study projects during the spring term, and all 12th graders take part in a weeklong, off-campus seminar. Also available are an ESL program for international students and an interim program, involving all students, that has included trips to Baja for marine biology, the Southwest for the study of Native American archaeology, and France and Spain for language study.

Fountain Valley offers a traditional selection of extracurriculars (including varsity and junior varsity soccer, field hockey, tennis, basketball, volleyball and girls' swimming), and the school's performing and visual arts, outdoor education and riding programs are particularly strong. Skiing, rock climbing, hiking/backpacking and horse packing trips round out the program. The school maintains a separate,

CO   *Mountain States*

40-acre mountain campus for additional experiential and outdoor education opportunities.

DENVER, CO. Urban. Pop: 554,636. Alt: 5280 ft. Area also includes Englewood.

COLORADO ACADEMY
Day — Coed Gr PS-12

Denver, CO 80235. 3800 S Pierce St. Tel: 303-986-1501. Fax: 303-914-2589.
www.coloradoacademy.org   E-mail: info@mail.coloacad.org

Christopher Babbs, Head. BA, Stanford Univ, MA, Univ of Colorado-Boulder. **Catherine Laskey, Adm.**

Col Prep. AP—Eng Fr Span Calc Stats Comp_Sci Bio Chem Physics Eur_Hist US_Govt & Pol. **Feat**—Photog Studio_Art Drama Theater_Arts Music.

Adm: 144/yr. Appl due: Feb. **Tests** IQ ISEE SSAT.

Enr 828. B 401. G 427. Elem 534. Sec 294. Wh 84%. Hisp 3%. Blk 3%. Asian 4%. Other 6%. Avg class size: 17. **Fac 100.** Adv deg: 64%.

Grad '04—72. Col—72. (U of CO-Boulder, MIT, US Air Force Acad, NYU, Bowdoin, CO Col). Avg SAT: 1243. Alum 1520.

Tui '04-'05: Day $9500-15,425 (+$500). **Aid:** Need 99 ($1,114,000).

Summer: Acad Enrich Rec. Arts. Sports. Tui Day $220/wk. 8 wks.

Endow $10,000,000. Plant val $17,150,000. Bldgs 13. Class rms 65. 2 Libs 18,000 vols. Sci labs 7. Lang labs 1. Comp labs 5. Auds 1. Theaters 1. Art studios 4. Music studios 10. Gyms 1. Athletic ctrs 1. Fields 8. Courts 4. Pools 1.

Est 1906. Nonprofit. Tri (Aug-June).

Located on a 75-acre campus in southwest Denver, the academy maintains three divisions to meet the developmental and learning needs of its students: a lower school (grades pre-K-5), a middle school (grades 6-8) and an upper school (grades 9-12). Each division has its own curriculum, principal, faculty, classroom building, library, and science and computer laboratories. The entire school community meets for assembly on a regular basis.

The curriculum, which is integrated throughout the school and builds on each preceding grade, emphasizes group and individual study of the liberal arts. A favorable student-teacher ratio allows faculty to work with individual students. Pupils in the lower grades take physical education, while those in grades 7-12 choose from a variety of fall, winter and spring sports. Fine arts offerings in all three divisions include instrumental and choral music, drama and visual arts. Twelfth graders complete a two-week senior project that takes the form of either a community internship or an independent project.

A diverse student body enrolls from throughout the metropolitan and suburban areas. Graduates enter leading colleges nationwide.

GRALAND COUNTRY DAY SCHOOL
Day — Coed Gr K-9

Denver, CO 80220. 30 Birch St. Tel: 303-399-0390. Fax: 303-388-2803.
www.graland.org   E-mail: info@graland.org
Robert Stein, Head. BA, Middlebury College, MA, Stanford Univ, EdD, Harvard Univ. **Carolyn Craig, Adm.**

Pre-Prep. Gen Acad. Feat—Computers Studio_Art Visual_Arts Drama Music Indus_Arts. **Supp**—Dev_Read Rem_Read Rev Tut.

Adm (Gr K-8): 91/yr. Appl due: Jan. Accepted: 57%. **Tests** CTP_4 IQ ISEE SSAT.

Enr 620. B 306. G 314. Elem 577. Sec 43. Wh 80%. Hisp 3%. Blk 7%. Asian 4%. Other 6%. Avg class size: 18. **Fac 70.** M 22/1. F 46/1. Wh 91%. Hisp 4%. Blk 4%. Asian 1%. Adv deg: 47%.

Grad '04—44. Prep—22. (CO Acad, Kent Denver, Milton Acad, Taft, Kent Sch-CT). Alum 2600.

Tui '04-'05: Day $13,090-13,930 (+$400). **Aid:** Need 73 ($844,032).

Endow $18,500,000. Plant val $12,911,000. Bldgs 10. Class rms 60. Lib 27,000 vols. Sci labs 3. Lang labs 1. Comp labs 3. Theaters 2. Art studios 3. Music studios 2. Gyms 1. Fields 2.

Est 1924. Nonprofit. Sem (Aug-June).

Founded by a group of parents, Graland has met the community's need for an educational program that develops a child's individual abilities. The school continues to reflect the experience of Georgia Nelson, founding head, who had been at both Francis Parker School and Shady Hill School before she came to Graland. Diversity, multiculturalism, parental education and support, integrated learning and study skills development are important aspects of the program.

The school offers a broad curriculum of academic, artistic and athletic programs, with studies in lab science, computers and foreign languages. A comprehensive trip program complements the traditional curriculum. Upper schoolers participate in such interscholastic sports as soccer, field hockey, football, softball, baseball, basketball and lacrosse.

GLENWOOD SPRINGS, CO. (132 mi. W of Denver, CO) Suburban. Pop: 7736. Alt: 5747 ft. Area also includes Carbondale.

COLORADO ROCKY MOUNTAIN SCHOOL
Bdg and Day — Coed Gr 9-12

Carbondale, CO 81623. 1493 County Rd 106. Tel: 970-963-2562. Fax: 970-963-9865.
www.crms.org   E-mail: admission@crms.org
Andrew V. Menke, Head. BS, Towson State Univ. **Kate Wheaton, Adm.**

Col Prep. AP—Eng Stats Chem US_Hist. **Feat**—Fr Span Environ_Sci Computers Anthro Ceramics Photog Studio_Art Drama Woodworking Blacksmithing. **Supp**—ESL Rev Tut.

Adm: 67/yr. Bdg 43. Day 24. Appl due: Mar. **Tests** SSAT TOEFL.

Enr 165. B 52/37. G 44/32. Sec 165. Wh 88%. Hisp 1%. Am Ind 1%. Asian 8%. Other 2%. Avg class size: 10. **Fac 34.** M 19. F 14/1. Wh 100%. Adv deg: 67%. In dorms 11.

Grad '04—39. Col—38. (Ft Lewis, U of Puget Sound, U of CO-Boulder, U of MT, Lewis & Clark, CO Col). Avg SAT: 1136. Avg ACT: 22. Alum 2425.

Tui '04-'05: Bdg $29,500 (+$2000). **Day $17,950** (+$1500). **Aid:** Merit 2 ($7000). Need 62 ($633,250).

Endow $13,000,000. Plant val $17,000,000. Bldgs 23. Dorms 6. Dorm rms 72. Class rms 16. Lib 17,000 vols. Sci labs 1. Comp labs 3. Photog labs 1. Theaters 1. Art studios 5. Music studios 1. Blacksmithing studios 3. Gyms 1. Fields 2. Courts 2. Climbing walls 1. Student ctrs 1.

Est 1953. Nonprofit. Sem (Sept-May).

Inspired by the precept and example of Eastern coeducational schools and by a desire to integrate intellectual, manual, musical, athletic and artistic skills, Ann and John Holden established this school for college-bound students.

The curriculum is college preparatory, stressing the development of basic intellectual skills, including writing, logical reasoning and research, within the context of individual courses. The program emphasizes environmental studies, energy and resources, and organic gardening. Instruction in the performing and visual arts is offered in photography, ceramics, jewelry making, studio art, blacksmithing, sculpture, acting and music. A one-week interim in March allows students and faculty to undertake group projects. These have included filmmaking, poetry writing and the study of desert ecology on a Navajo reservation, as well as a home-stay language trip to Mexico.

Located on a 350-acre ranch, CRMS requires all students to participate in ranch, household and construction projects. Utilizing the area surrounding the campus, the school emphasizes mountain and river sports, in addition to snowboarding, tennis and soccer. Alpine and Nordic skiing, both competitive and recreational, are offered as winter sports. The wilderness session, offered to all new students prior to the start of the academic year, is an intensive ten days of conditioning, team building, map reading, climbing, camping and team building.

Among a varied selection of extracurricular activities, outdoor education is offered throughout the school year and includes fall and spring excursions.

LAFAYETTE, CO. (20 mi. NW of Denver, CO) Suburban. Pop: 23,197. Alt: 5236 ft.

ALEXANDER DAWSON SCHOOL
Day — Coed Gr K-12

Lafayette, CO 80026. 10455 Dawson Dr. Tel: 303-665-6679. Fax: 303-665-0757.
  www.dawsonschool.org   E-mail: sjensen@dawsonschool.org
Anthony S. Kandel, Actg Head. Jim Mitchell, Adm.
  Col Prep. AP—Eng Fr Span Calc Comp_Sci Bio Chem Physics US_Hist World_Hist Comp_Govt & Pol. **Feat**—Computers Photog Drama Music. **Supp**—Tut.
  Adm: 118/yr. **Tests** CTP_4 IQ.
  Enr 420. B 213. G 207. Wh 97%. Hisp 1%. Blk 1%. Asian 1%. Avg class size: 15. **Fac 58.** M 19/5. F 21/13. Adv deg: 48%.
  Grad '04—39. Col—39. (Amherst, Bates, Colby, Carleton, Emory, Smith). Alum 308.
  Tui '05-'06: Day $15,425 (+$300-500). **Aid:** Need 108 ($600,000).
  Summer: Rec. Sports. Tui Day $170-325/wk. 5 wks.
  Plant val $28,000,000. Bldgs 14. Class rms 43. 2 Libs 20,000 vols. Sci labs 5. Lang labs 1. Comp labs 6. Auds 1. Theaters 1. Art studios 4. Music studios 3. Dance studios 1.

Photog studios 1. Wood shops 1. Gyms 2. Fields 8. Tennis courts 6. Pools 1.
Est 1970. Nonprofit. Tri (Aug-June). **Assoc** NCA.

Located on an 89-acre campus near Boulder, Alexander Dawson provides opportunities for honors and advanced study. In addition to traditional academic subjects, students choose from a wide variety of electives in art, music, drama, dance, photography and woodworking. Community service projects are promoted, and cocurriculars include student government, as well as several clubs and organizations. Varsity sports are basketball, baseball, track, cross-country, soccer, skiing, tennis, volleyball, and canoeing and kayaking.

STEAMBOAT SPRINGS, CO. (114 mi. WNW of Denver, CO) Suburban. Pop: 9815. Alt: 6728 ft.

LOWELL WHITEMAN SCHOOL
Bdg and Day — Coed Gr 9-12

Steamboat Springs, CO 80487. 42605 Routt County Rd 36. **Tel:** 970-879-1350.
Fax: 970-879-0506.
www.whiteman.edu   E-mail: admissions@whiteman.edu

Walter H. Daub, Head. BA, Hamilton College, MA, Univ of Delaware. **Mike Whitacre, Adm.**
  Col Prep. Sports (Winter). **AP**—Eng Fr Span Calc. **Feat**—Comp_Sci Film Studio_Art. **Supp**—Tut.
  Adm (Gr 9): 41/yr. Bdg 21. Day 20. Appl due: July. Accepted: 45%. Yield: 85%. **Tests** CEEB Stanford.
  Enr 98. B 32/28. G 22/16. Sec 98. Wh 96%. Am Ind 1%. Asian 3%. Avg class size: 7. **Fac 22.** M 9/3. F 9/1. Wh 100%. Adv deg: 50%. In dorms 3.
  Grad '04—18. Col—17. (Cornell 2, U of Denver 1, CO Col 1, Mt Holyoke 1, U of Richmond 1, CA St U-Fresno 1). Avg SAT: 1070. Alum 670.
  Tui '04-'05: Bdg $29,245 (+$3000-4000). **Day $15,535** (+$3000). **Aid:** Need 26 ($222,533).
  Endow $750,000. Plant val $10,000,000. Bldgs 14. Dorms 3. Dorm rms 40. Class rms 14. Lib 4500 vols. Sci labs 2. Comp labs 2. Auds 1. Theaters 1. Art studios 1. Gyms 1. Fields 2. Riding rings 1. Stables 1.
  Est 1957. Nonprofit. Sem (Aug-May).

Founded by Lowell Whiteman, the school offers traditional academics and features small classes, required proctored evening study halls and a heavy emphasis on academic effort. Most graduates attend four-year colleges.

Located near a mountain resort community, the school utilizes its environment for academic and recreational purposes. In addition to a full range of college preparatory courses, further opportunities include skiing, snowboarding, ecological studies, mountaineering, horseback riding, white-water rafting and backpacking. Annual foreign travel is required of all students—except for high-ability competitive skiers and snowboarders. Extracurricular activities include video filming and editing, photography, music, ice skating, drama, community service, snowboarding, mountain biking, riding and rock climbing.

Whiteman provides a well-balanced academic/athletic program for high school snowboarders and Alpine, Nordic and freestyle ski competitors. A number of school graduates have participated in the Winter Olympics.

VAIL, CO. (80 mi. W of Denver, CO) Suburban. Pop: 4531. Alt: 8160.

VAIL MOUNTAIN SCHOOL
Day — Coed Gr K-12

Vail, CO 81657. 3000 Booth Falls Rd. Tel: 970-476-3850. Fax: 970-476-3860.
www.vms.edu   E-mail: info@vms.edu
Peter M. Abuisi, Head. Kate Blakslee, Adm.
  Col Prep. Feat—Fr Anat & Physiol Multimedia_Design Psych Ethics. **Supp**—Dev_Read Tut.
  Adm: 50/yr. Appl due: Mar. Accepted: 46%.
  Enr 263. B 133. G 130. Elem 185. Sec 78. Wh 98%. Hisp 2%. Avg class size: 18. **Fac 60.** M 38/1. F 19/2. Adv deg: 20%.
  Grad '04—21. Col—20. (U of CO-Boulder, Dartmouth, Lehigh, Colby, Santa Clara, Wellesley). Avg SAT: 1193. Avg ACT: 24. Alum 324.
  Tui '03-'04: Day $10,500-12,600 (+$300). **Aid:** Need 44 ($343,900).
  Endow $9,200,000. Plant val $5,000,000. Bldgs 3. Class rms 18. Lib 15,000 vols. Sci labs 2. Comp labs 1. Dark rms 1. Theaters 1. Art studios 2. Gyms 1. Fields 1.
  Est 1962. Nonprofit. Tri (Aug-May).

Founded as a boarding high school to meet the needs of early settlers of an emerging resort community, VMS changed location and mission several times in its early years. Significant alterations in the program commenced in 1978, when administrators decided to shift the academic focus to college preparation and discontinue boarding. The program gradually expanded to include middle school children and then younger students, with the first kindergarten class enrolled in 1984.

The school offers a broad college preparatory program with an emphasis on traditional educational skills, often utilizing individualized instruction. Community service plays an important role in school life, with VMS offering a variety of age-appropriate options for its pupils. As part of the school's tripping program, older boys and girls go on excursions to locations such as Mexico and New York City. In addition, all children in grades 5-8 participate in backcountry hut trips in which telemark skiing is the encouraged mode of travel. The athletic program, making wide use of the outdoor environment, stresses skiing and soccer.

IDAHO

SUN VALLEY, ID. (94 mi. E of Boise, ID) Rural. Pop: 1427. Alt: 5920 ft.

THE COMMUNITY SCHOOL
Day — Coed Gr PS-12

Sun Valley, ID 83353. 181 Dollar Rd, PO Box 2118. Tel: 208-622-3955. Fax: 208-622-3962. www.communityschool.org   E-mail: abaker@communityschool.org

Jon Maksik, Head. BA, Univ of Southern California, MA, California State Univ, PhD, Univ of California-Los Angeles. **Andrea Baker, Adm.**

Col Prep. Feat—Fr Span Computers Comp_Design Psych Debate Metal_Shop Outdoor_Ed Wilderness_Ed. **Supp**—Tut.

Adm: 53/yr. Appl due: Mar. Accepted: 59%. **Tests** SSAT.

Enr 315. B 162. G 153. Elem 200. Sec 115. Wh 92%. Hisp 1%. Other 7%. Avg class size: 15. **Fac 41.** M 16/3. F 17/5. Wh 100%. Adv deg: 48%.

Grad '04—31. Col—29. (Lewis & Clark, MT St-Billings, U of CO-Boulder, U of Denver, Dartmouth, Smith). Avg SAT: 1192. Alum 583.

Tui '04-'05: Day $15,975-17,985 (+$100-600). **Aid:** Merit 4 ($10,700). Need 66 ($645,450).

Summer: Acad Rec. 3-6 wks.

Endow $4,000,000. Plant val $4,000,000. Bldgs 6. Class rms 35. Lib 32,000 vols. Sci labs 1. Lang labs 1. Comp labs 2. Dark rms 1. Auds 1. Theaters 1. Art studios 2. Music studios 2. Gyms 1. Fields 3.

Est 1973. Nonprofit. Sem (Aug-June). **Assoc** NAAS.

Located between Ketchum and Sun Valley, the school lies in the Wood River Valley on Trail Creek. The core curriculum emphasizes mastery of fundamental academic skills, while enriching pupils' class schedules with electives designed to capitalize on individual interests. The school features multiple-subject primary enrichment, a college preparatory curriculum for students in grades 6-12, and an integrated outdoor education program. Seniors participate in a six-week, off-campus independent project.

Southwest States

ARIZONA

MAYER, AZ. (60 mi. N of Phoenix, AZ) Rural. Pop: 1408. Alt: 3800 ft.

ORME SCHOOL
Bdg and Day — Coed Gr 7-PG

Mayer, AZ 86333. 1000 Orme Rd, HC 63, Box 3040. Tel: 928-632-7601.
 Fax: 928-632-7605.
 www.ormeschool.org E-mail: admissions@ormeschool.org
Stephen Robinson, Head. BA, Bethany Nazarene College, MA, Southern Nazarene Univ, PhD, Oklahoma State Univ. **Alex Spence, Adm.**
 Col Prep. AP—Eng Fr Span Calc Physics US_Hist. Feat—Lat Astron Geol Computers Anthro Archaeol Econ Geog Photog Studio_Art. **Supp**—ESL Tut.
 Adm: 95/yr. Appl due: Feb. Accepted: 54%. **Tests** IQ SSAT TOEFL.
 Enr 165. Wh 75%. Hisp 2%. Blk 6%. Am Ind 2%. Asian 15%. Avg class size: 10. **Fac 24.** M 12/1. F 10/1. Adv deg: 58%. In dorms 1.
 Grad '04—41. Col—41. (U of AZ, AZ St, N AZ, Dartmouth, MI St). Avg SAT: 1150. Avg ACT: 24. Alum 6514.
 Tui '05-'06: Bdg $29,190 (+$1500). **Day $14,910** (+$1000).
 Summer: Horsemanship. Tui Bdg $1850-2690. 2-3 wks.
 Endow $7,000,000. Plant val $10,000,000. Dorm rms 122. Class rms 21. Lib 23,000 vols. Labs 4. Art studios 3. Fields 4. Courts 5. Pools 1. Riding facilities yes.
 Est 1929. Nonprofit. Quar (Aug-June). **Assoc** CLS NCA.

Mr. and Mrs. Charles H. Orme founded this school for local ranch children. Beginning as a one-room school, Orme has grown into a modern college preparatory institution on a 26,000-acre ranch. The academic curriculum includes honors and Advanced Placement courses in the major disciplines. Complementing the academic program are interscholastic athletics, horsemanship (both English and Western) and outdoor leadership opportunities. The arts program is supported by a weeklong midwinter festival, at which time students and faculty are joined by professional artists from all over the country. The visiting artists teach such media as ceramics, photography, dance, music, sculpture and filmmaking.

The academic program prepares students for a wide variety of colleges throughout the country. The Southwestern environment of the school is stressed through special courses, field trips, varied outdoor activities and an annual caravan.

AZ   *Leading Private Schools*   *686*

PHOENIX, AZ. Urban. Pop: 1,321,045. Alt: 1082 ft. Area also includes Paradise Valley.

ALL SAINTS' EPISCOPAL DAY SCHOOL
Day — Coed Gr K-8

Phoenix, AZ 85012. 6300 N Central Ave. Tel: 602-274-4866. Fax: 602-274-0365.
   www.allsaints.org   E-mail: dmoll@allsaints.org

Edward C. Young, Head. BA, Middlebury College, MLA, Southern Methodist Univ. **Nancy Winship, Adm.**
   Pre-Prep. Feat—Lib_Skills Relig Studio_Art Drama Music. **Supp**—Dev_Read Rev Tut.
   Adm: 101/yr. Appl due: Rolling. Accepted: 40%. **Tests** CTP_4.
   Enr 485. B 242. G 243. Elem 485. Wh 85%. Hisp 3%. Blk 2%. Asian 7%. Other 3%. Avg class size: 19. Uniform. **Fac 66.** M 5. F 60/1. Wh 97%. Blk 3%. Adv deg: 28%.
   Grad '04—61. Prep—50. (Brophy, Phoenix Co Day). Alum 750.
   Tui '02-'03: Day $9870 (+$200). **Aid:** Need 37 ($220,000).
   Summer: Enrich Rec. 2-6 wks.
   Endow $514,000. Plant val $10,000,000. Bldgs 12. Class rms 40. Lib 12,143 vols. Sci labs 3. Comp labs 2. Auds 1. Art studios 1. Music studios 1. Ampitheater 1. Gyms 1. Fields 1. Courts 2.
   Est 1963. Nonprofit. Episcopal. Sem (Sept-May).

All Saints' offers a comprehensive pre-preparatory program within a Christian environment. In grades K-3, classes are self-contained, with each grade-level teacher providing instruction in the fundamental subject areas. Beginning with grade 4, classes are departmentalized. Communication and critical-thinking skills development is stressed. Courses in computers, Spanish, religion, art, music and physical education are taught at all grade levels, and pupils in grades 5-8 go on interdisciplinary field trips to Arizona, Mexico and California. Weekly chapel attendance is required of all.

Students in grades 4-8 may serve on the student council. Among other activities are chorus, instrumental lessons, drama, community service, interest clubs, student publications, and boys' and girls' team sports.

BROPHY COLLEGE PREPARATORY SCHOOL
Day — Boys Gr 9-12

Phoenix, AZ 85012. 4701 N Central Ave. Tel: 602-264-5291. Fax: 602-234-1669.
   www.brophyprep.org   E-mail: admissions@brophyprep.org

Rev. Edward A. Reese, SJ, Pres. MA, STM, MDiv. **Edwin J. Hearn, Prin.** BS, Loyola Univ, MA, California State Univ-Los Angeles. **Michael Ward, Adm.**
   Col Prep. AP—Eng Lat Span Calc Comp_Sci Bio Chem Physics Eur_Hist US_Hist Econ Psych US_Govt & Pol Art_Hist Studio_Art Music_Theory. **Feat**—Humanities Fr Photog Black_Box_Theater. **Supp**—Tut.
   Adm (Gr 9-11): 354/yr. Appl due: Jan. Accepted: 72%. Yield: 91%. **Tests** CEEB.
   Enr 1200. B 1200. Sec 1200. Wh 76%. Hisp 12%. Blk 2%. Am Ind 2%. Asian 4%. Other 4%. Avg class size: 25. **Fac 80.** M 64. F 16. Wh 97%. Hisp 1%. Blk 1%. Other 1%. Adv deg: 57%.
   Grad '04—275. Col—274. (AZ St 85, U of AZ 61, Loyola Marymount 15, Santa Clara 12, USC 9, Gonzaga 4). Avg SAT: 1219. Avg ACT: 25. Alum 6910.

Tui '04-'05: Day $8700 (+$450). **Aid:** Need 224 ($1,204,010). Work prgm 220 ($252,320).
Summer: Acad. Tui Day $440. 6 wks. Enrich Rec. Tui Day $160/crse. 5 wks.
Endow $16,682,000. Plant val $18,550,000. Bldgs 7. Class rms 48. Lib 17,000 vols. Sci labs 4. Comp labs 1. Auds 1. Theaters 1. Art studios 3. Music studios 2. Gyms 1. Fields 4. Courts 5. Pools 2.
Est 1928. Nonprofit. Roman Catholic. Sem (Aug-May). **Assoc** NCA.

This Jesuit college preparatory high school was founded by Mrs. William Henry Brophy in memory of her late husband. While open only to male applicants, Brophy shares most activities and some courses with Xavier College Preparatory, a girls' school located on adjoining property.

Students follow an extensive college preparatory course of studies, including a number of Advanced Placement courses, and pursue a wide range of extracurricular activities, among them newspaper, yearbook, speech and debate, student government, Model UN, ski club, hiking and other creative clubs. Athletics include football, cross-country, basketball, baseball, track, swimming, golf, soccer, wrestling, weightlifting, tennis, volleyball, lacrosse and cricket.

PHOENIX COUNTRY DAY SCHOOL
Day — Coed Gr PS-12

Paradise Valley, AZ 85253. 3901 E Stanford Dr. Tel: 602-955-8200. Fax: 602-955-1286. www.pcds.org   E-mail: tsylvest@pcds.org
Galen Brewster, Head. BA, MEd, Harvard Univ. **Thomas O. Sylvester, Adm.**
Col Prep. AP—Eng Fr Lat Span Calc Stats Bio Chem Physics US_Hist Art_Hist. **Feat**—Shakespeare African-Amer_Lit Anat & Physiol Astron Programming Vietnam_War Holocaust Russian_Hist Econ Govt Comp_Relig Photog Drama Music Orchestra.
Adm (Gr PS-11): 125/yr. Appl due: Feb. Accepted: 47%. Yield: 82%. **Tests** CTP_4 IQ.
Enr 741. B 374. G 367. Elem 483. Sec 258. Wh 80%. Hisp 3%. Blk 1%. Am Ind 1%. Asian 13%. Other 2%. Avg class size: 15. **Fac 90.** Adv deg: 62%.
Grad '04—60. Col—60. (Dartmouth, U of AZ, Harvard, U of PA, USC, Northwestern). Avg SAT: 1380. Alum 1200.
Tui '04-'05: Day $17,700 (+$1000). **Aid:** Need 70 ($850,000).
Summer: Acad Enrich Rev Rec. Tui Day $225/wk. 6 wks.
Endow $14,000,000. Plant val $5,000,000. Bldgs 19. Class rms 75. 3 Libs 28,000 vols. Sci labs 7. Comp labs 3. Art studios 7. Music studios 4. Arts ctrs 1. Fields 4. Courts 8. Pools 2.
Est 1961. Nonprofit. (Aug-June). **Assoc** CLS.

Situated on a 44-acre campus, this school was founded to meet the needs of a rapidly growing city. PCDS consists of three distinct school divisions, each designed to address the developmental needs of the age group involved. Conversational Spanish instruction begins in preschool, and laboratory science and computer studies both commence in kindergarten.

Music, art and drama play an important role, and other activities include photography, sports and publications. The school's varied athletic program features swimming, baseball, tennis, golf, lacrosse, softball, basketball, volleyball and soccer teams.

AZ *Leading Private Schools* 688

RIMROCK, ARIZONA. (79 mi. NNE of Phoenix, AZ) Rural. Pop: 3203. Alt: 5400 ft.

SOUTHWESTERN ACADEMY
Bdg and Day — Coed Gr 9-12

Rimrock, AZ 86335. HC 64, Box 235. Tel: 928-567-4581. Fax: 928-567-5036.
www.southwesternacademy.edu   E-mail: admissions@southwesternacademy.edu
Marshall Whitmire, Head. BA, MA, EdD, Arizona State Univ. **Jane Whitmire, Adm.**

Col Prep. Gen Acad. Underachiever. AP—Eng Calc US_Hist. **Feat**—Span Environ_Sci Comp_Sci Anthro Econ Govt Pol_Sci Studio_Art Drama Music Speech Outdoor_Ed. **Supp**—Dev_Read ESL Rem_Math Rem_Read Rev Tut.

Adm: 12/yr. Bdg 11. Day 1. Appl due: Rolling. Accepted: 90%. Yield: 88%. **Tests** CEEB ISEE SSAT TOEFL.

Enr 23. B 11/1. G 11. Sec 23. Wh 44%. Hisp 4%. Blk 4%. Asian 48%. Avg class size: 7. **Fac 8.** M 3. F 5. Wh 100%. Adv deg: 50%.

Grad '04—7. Col—7. (N AZ 2, AZ St 2, Occidental 1, U of AZ 1, Purdue 1). Avg SAT: 1100.

Tui '05-'06: Bdg $29,500 (+$2000). **Day** $13,800 (+$1000). **Aid:** Need 11 ($196,450).

Summer: Acad Rec. Tui Bdg $1500-4800. Tui Day $750-2400. 2-8 wks.

Endow $9,273,000. Plant val $21,628,000. Bldgs 19. Dorms 5. Dorm rms 20. Class rms 6. Libs 1. Sci labs 1. Comp labs 1. Auds 1. Art studios 1. Gyms 1. Fields 1. Courts 2. Pools 1.

Est 1965. Nonprofit. Sem (Sept-June).

Established as a complement to the original Southwestern campus in San Marino, CA (see separate listing), the 180-acre Beaver Creek Ranch Campus follows an experiential approach to learning. The school admits students who require additional attention to realize their potential; it is not staffed to serve boys and girls with learning disabilities, behavioral problems, chemical dependencies or defiant attitudes. Small classes increase contact between teacher and pupil while also allowing students to pursue interests beyond the curriculum.

Environmental sustainability is a central theme of the academic program at this location. Delivered seminar style, the integrated course of studies comprises science, math, writing and critical-thinking components. The desert wilderness is integral to the teaching process: Hands-on, experiential and project/assignment-based field trips enrich classroom study and help boys and girls apply what they have learned. Outdoor education promotes environmental responsibility.

Students have the option of dividing time between the two Southwestern campuses.   **See Also Pages 1254-5**

SEDONA, AZ. (92 mi. N of Phoenix, AZ) Suburban. Pop: 10,192. Alt: 4000 ft.

VERDE VALLEY SCHOOL
Bdg and Day — Coed Gr 9-PG

Sedona, AZ 86351. 3511 Verde Valley School Rd. Tel: 928-284-2272. Fax: 928-284-0432. www.vvsaz.org   E-mail: admission@verdevalleyschool.org
Paul Domingue, Head. BA, Providence College, MFA, Univ of Massachusetts-Dartmouth. **Donald W. Smith, Adm.**
Col Prep. AP—Calc. **Feat**—Shakespeare Russ_Lit Chin/Japan_Lit Computers Comp_ Graphics Anthro Studio_Art Dance. **Supp**—ESL.
Adm: 53/yr. Bdg 45. Day 8. Appl due: Rolling. Accepted: 60%. **Tests** CEEB IQ SSAT.
Enr 110. B 49/5. G 47/5. Wh 62%. Hisp 7%. Blk 6%. Am Ind 12%. Asian 13%. Avg class size: 9. **Fac 20.** M 9/3. F 7/1. Wh 90%. Hisp 5%. Asian 5%. Adv deg: 55%. In dorms 5.
Grad '04—24. Col—24. (Clark U, Columbia, Stanford, U of CO-Boulder, Rochester Inst of Tech, Whittier). Avg SAT: 1142. Avg ACT: 24. Alum 1318.
Tui '03-'04: Bdg $29,500 (+$1500). **Day $15,600** (+$700). **Aid:** Need 47 ($704,355).
Summer: Acad Rec. Tui Bdg $2000-2500. 5 wks.
Endow $1,800,000. Plant val $7,000,000. Bldgs 48. Dorms 6. Dorm rms 102. Class rms 14. Lib 34,000 vols. Sci labs 2. Comp labs 1. Auds 1. Theaters 1. Art studios 2. Music studios 1. Dance studios 1. Amphitheaters 1. Photog studios 1. Fields 3. Courts 2. Volleyball courts 1. Pools 1. Riding rings 1. Stables 1. Climbing walls 3. Ropes crses 1.
Est 1948. Nonprofit. Sem (Aug-May).

This unique school, founded and developed by Hamilton and Barbara Warren with the advice of leading educators and anthropologists here and abroad, strives to promote intercultural and interracial understanding.

The academic program consists of college preparatory courses, including Advanced Placement work. Electives are offered in math, the sciences, history, foreign languages, studio arts, dance, drama and music. Complementing the core curriculum are three programs designed to expose students to a variety of disciplines: a selection of studio and performing arts offerings that ranges from ceramics, painting and drawing to piano, acting and dance; a ten-day project period during the second semester in which each student completes intensive work in a chosen field or undertakes an internship with an area professional; and a 16-day field trip in March that allows students to either live with a Mexican or Native American family, work at an inner-city social service agency, or travel to a wilderness area such as the Grand Canyon or the Baja Peninsula for camping, hiking and investigation of the natural environment. Another important aspect of school life is the work program, in which all students and faculty aid in school maintenance.

Rock climbing, mountain biking, martial arts and horseback riding are offered through the school's athletic program. Interscholastic competition is offered in baseball, soccer, volleyball, basketball and softball.

AZ   *Leading Private Schools*

TUCSON, AZ. (115 mi. SE of Phoenix, AZ) Urban. Pop: 486,699. Alt: 2376 ft.

FENSTER SCHOOL
Bdg and Day — Coed Gr 9-12

Tucson, AZ 85750. 8500 E Ocotillo Dr. Tel: 520-749-3340. Fax: 520-749-3349.
www.fenster-school.com   E-mail: bblehm@att.net

Don Saffer, Head. BA, Univ of California-Los Angeles, MA, Univ of Southern California. Michael J. Lyles, Adm.

    Col Prep. Underachiever. Feat—Span Computers Archaeol Studio_Art Study_Skills. Supp—Dev_Read ESL Rem_Math Rem_Read Rev Tut.

    Adm: 55/yr. Bdg 52. Day 3. Appl due: Rolling. Accepted: 70%.

    Enr 97. B 56/3. G 36/2. Sec 97. Wh 64%. Hisp 12%. Blk 10%. Asian 14%. Avg class size: 8. **Fac 17.** M 7. F 8/2. Wh 95%. Hisp 5%. Adv deg: 41%. In dorms 3.

    Grad '04—26. Col—25. (U of AZ, AZ St, OK St, Pima CC, U of TX-El Paso, N AZ). Avg SAT: 1050. Avg ACT: 22.

    Tui '05-'06: Bdg $26,900 (+$1600). **Day** $13,450 (+$2500).

    Summer: Acad Enrich Rev Rem. Tui Bdg $4500. Tui Day $500/crse. 6 wks.

    Plant val $2,000,000. Bldgs 24. Dorms 8. Class rms 22. Lib 5000 vols. Sci labs 2. Comp labs 1. Art studios 1. Fields 1. Courts 2. Pools 1. Riding rings 2. Stables 1.

    Est 1944. Nonprofit. Sem (Aug-May). **Assoc** NCA.

Fenster was founded by Mr. and Mrs. George Fenster as the first coeducational boarding school in southern Arizona. Located on a 150-acre site in the foothills of the Santa Catalina Mountains, the school offers a structured college preparatory curriculum for underachievers of average and above-average intelligence. Small classes provide for individualized instruction within the mainstream classroom setting. Excursions to local cultural sites, malls and theaters complement class work.

Extracurricular activities, including student council and recreational and interscholastic sports, are conducted. Outdoor activities include horseback riding, hiking, rock climbing and swimming.

GREEN FIELDS COUNTRY DAY SCHOOL
Day — Coed Gr K-12

Tucson, AZ 85741. 6000 N Camino de la Tierra. Tel: 520-297-2288. Fax: 520-297-2072.
www.greenfields.org   E-mail: admissions@greenfields.org

Rick Belding, Head. BSE, Princeton Univ. Carole C. Knapp, Adm.

    Col Prep. AP—Eng Fr Span Calc Bio Eur_Hist US_Hist Econ US_Govt & Pol Studio_Art. Feat—Web_Design Drama Music Journ. Supp—Tut.

    Adm: 50/yr. Appl due: Rolling. **Tests** CEEB CTP_4 IQ ISEE SSAT Stanford.

    Enr 184. B 91. G 93. Elem 97. Sec 87. Wh 74%. Hisp 8%. Blk 2%. Asian 1%. Other 15%. Avg class size: 13. **Fac 29.** M 10/2. F 10/7. Wh 78%. Hisp 18%. Asian 4%. Adv deg: 62%.

    Grad '04—24. Col—24. (U of AZ 4, Willamette 3, N AZ 3, Stanford 1, Occidental 1, Barnard 1). Avg SAT: 1185. Alum 700.

    Tui '04-'05: Day $7500-11,900 (+$500). **Aid:** Merit 1 ($2975). Need 49 ($374,238).

    Endow $960,000. Plant val $1,840,000. Bldgs 22. Class rms 23. Lib 7500 vols. Sci labs 2. Comp labs 3. Theaters 1. Art studios 1. Music studios 1. Gyms 1. Fields 4. Courts 4. Pools 1.

Est 1933. Nonprofit. Sem (Aug-May). **Assoc** NCA.

Established by Mr. and Mrs. George Howard Atchley as a ranch-style boarding school for boys, the school closed its boarding department in 1960 and became coeducational in 1966. The upper school curriculum includes Advanced Placement classes, along with varied academic and fine arts electives. Juniors and seniors may, with permission, enroll in courses at the University of Arizona. A one-week spring interim period includes on-campus projects, groups that divide time between campus and local sites, and longer trips to destinations in the Southwest and abroad.

Athletics include interscholastic competition in volleyball, basketball, softball, baseball and soccer. Student publications, performances in music and drama, and art shows are among the other activities. Community service is an integral part of education at Green Fields.

An all-day, all-school forum on a controversial topic is orchestrated entirely by members of the junior class, and the senior class plans and hosts an orientation at the start of each school year.

IMMACULATE HEART HIGH SCHOOL
Day — Coed Gr 9-12

Tucson, AZ 85704. 625 E Magee Rd. Tel: 520-297-2851. Fax: 520-797-7374.
www.ihprep.com E-mail: woodn@ihprep.com
Daniel Ethridge, Head.
  Col Prep. Feat—Fr Span Programming Fine_Arts Journ. **Supp**—ESL Tut.
  Adm: 14/yr. Appl due: Sept. Accepted: 100%. **Tests** HSPT Stanford.
  Enr 56. B 26. G 30. Sec 56. Wh 53%. Hisp 43%. Blk 1%. Asian 3%. Avg class size: 6. Uniform. **Fac 10.** M 4/2. F 3/1. Wh 99%. Hisp 1%. Adv deg: 50%.
  Grad '04—25. Col—24. (U of AZ, Pima CC, U of Tulsa). Avg SAT: 1002. Avg ACT: 25. Alum 3531.
  Tui '04-'05: Day $5000 (+$550). **Aid:** Need 12 ($40,000).
  Plant val $3,207,000. Bldgs 2. Class rms 18. Lib 6500 vols. Sci labs 2. Lang labs 1. Comp labs 1. Art studios 1. Music studios 1. Fields 2. Courts 1. Pools 1.
  Est 1931. Nonprofit. Roman Catholic. (Aug-May). **Assoc** NCA.

Conducted by the Sisters of the Immaculate Heart of Mary, this school serves both the Tucson area and the international community. Besides offerings in language arts, math, science and social studies, the curriculum also includes courses in foreign languages, the fine arts, journalism, computer programming, business computers and word processing. The school conducts intensive English as a Second Language in which foreign students take a full program of ESL classes, from beginning through advanced levels.

Interscholastic athletics provide competition in volleyball, soccer, basketball, baseball, softball and track; extracurricular activities include student council, yearbook and other school publications.

NEW MEXICO

ALBUQUERQUE, NM. (54 mi. SW of Santa Fe, NM) Urban. Pop: 448,607. Alt: 4930 ft.

ALBUQUERQUE ACADEMY
Day — Coed Gr 6-12

Albuquerque, NM 87109. 6400 Wyoming Blvd NE. Tel: 505-828-3200. Fax: 505-828-3128.
www.aa.edu   E-mail: info@aa.edu
Andrew T. Watson, Head. BS, Ohio State Univ, MS, Yale Univ. **Judy Hudenko, Adm.**

- **Col Prep. AP**—Fr Ger Span Calc Comp_Sci Bio Chem Physics Eur_Hist US_Hist Econ US_Govt & Pol Art_Hist. **Feat**—Creative_Writing Humanities Playwriting Mandarin Stats Anat & Physiol Astron Ecol Genetics Geol Robotics Native_Amer_Hist Anthro Intl_Relations Ethics Philos World_Relig Fine_Arts Photog Theater_Arts Music_Theory Public_Speak.
- **Adm:** 182/yr. Appl due: Feb. Accepted: 30%. Yield: 82%. **Tests** ISEE SSAT.
- **Enr 1064.** Wh 61%. Hisp 22%. Blk 3%. Am Ind 3%. Asian 9%. Other 2%. Avg class size: 15. **Fac 152.** M 79/6. F 63/4. Wh 84%. Hisp 10%. Blk 2%. Am Ind 1%. Asian 3%. Adv deg: 77%.
- **Grad '04—148. Col—148.** (U of NM 17, Trinity U 6, Baylor 4, Northwestern 4, Stanford 4, Wash U 4). Avg SAT: 1297. Avg ACT: 28. Alum 3500.
- **Tui '04-'05:** Day $12,950 (+$250-500). **Aid:** Need 286 ($2,595,884).
- **Summer:** Acad Enrich Rec. 6 wks.
- Endow $200,000,000. Plant val $55,000,000. Bldgs 16. Lib 96,492 vols. Sci labs 10. Lang labs 1. Comp labs 4. Dark rms 2. Comp ctrs 1. Auds 1. Theaters 1. Art studios 4. Music studios 4. Dance studios 1. Art galleries 1. Amphitheaters 1. Music ctrs 1. Gyms 2. Fields 5. Basketball courts 3. Tennis courts 10. Pools 2. Aquatic ctrs 1.
- **Est 1955.** Nonprofit. Sem (Aug-May). **Assoc** CLS.

This school offers a traditional college preparatory curriculum. In 1966, the school moved to a 312-acre campus, allowing for considerable expansion in plant and enrollment. The academy includes in its curriculum for grades 6-10 an outdoor experiential education requirement. Students backpack, ski, canoe and climb into wilderness areas of the Southwest to learn through direct experience about the natural world. In addition, juniors and seniors may take an elective course in outdoor leadership.

Seniors may participate in the Senior Project Program, which involves a six-week, off-campus internship under the sponsorship of a professional. Cocurricular activities include newspaper, literary magazine, speech and debate, science Olympiad, chess club, community service, student senate, language clubs, Model UN and dramatic productions.

MANZANO DAY SCHOOL
Day — Coed Gr PS-5

Albuquerque, NM 87104. 1801 Central Ave NW. Tel: 505-243-6659. Fax: 505-243-4711.
www.manzanodayschool.org   E-mail: mprokopiak@manzanodayschool.org

Neal Piltch, Head. Madonna Prokopiak, Adm.
>Pre-Prep. Feat—Span Computers Logic Studio_Art Music. **Supp**—Dev_Read Tut.
>**Adm:** 111/yr. Appl due: Rolling. Accepted: 95%.
>**Enr 435.** Elem 435. Wh 60%. Hisp 16%. Blk 1%. Am Ind 3%. Asian 4%. Other 16%. Avg class size: 18. **Fac 49.** M 4. F 43/2. Adv deg: 32%.
>**Grad '04—61. Prep—59.** (Bosque, Sandia Prep, Albuquerque Acad). Alum 1371.
>**Tui '05-'06: Day $8636-10,692. Aid:** Merit 5 ($27,405).
>**Summer:** Ages 4-8. Rec. Tui Day $920. 6 wks.
>Endow $382,000. Plant val $3,453,000. Bldgs 3. Class rms 34. Libs 1. Comp labs 1.
>**Est 1938.** Nonprofit. Sem (Aug-May).

Small classes and an advantageous student-teacher ratio permit individualized instruction at MDS. Spanish, music, art and physical education are taught from kindergarten, and a full technology program is offered. The campus includes a 300-year-old Spanish hacienda located in the Old Town section of Albuquerque. An environmental studies program at the school's Fenton Camp in the nearby Jemez Mountains is offered during both the school year and the summer session.

SANDIA PREPARATORY SCHOOL
Day — Coed Gr 6-12

Albuquerque, NM 87113. 532 Osuna Rd NE. Tel: 505-338-3000. Fax: 505-338-3099.
www.sandiaprep.org   E-mail: info@sandiaprep.org
>**Richard L. Heath, Head.** AB, Cornell Univ, MAT, Colgate Univ. **Ester Tomelloso, Adm.**
>Col Prep. **AP**—Fr Span. **Feat**—Creative_Writing Irish_Lit Astron Computers Econ Art_Hist Film Fine_Arts Visual_Arts Drama Music Dance Journ. **Supp**—Tut.
>**Adm:** 115/yr. Appl due: Feb. Accepted: 65%. **Tests** CTP_4.
>**Enr 645.** Wh 80%. Hisp 12%. Blk 1%. Am Ind 4%. Asian 3%. Avg class size: 15. **Fac 73.** Adv deg: 61%.
>**Grad '04—79. Col—79.** (U of NM 19, U of Denver 4, Knox 3, U of San Diego 2, USC 2, U of WA 2). Avg SAT: 1260. Avg ACT: 27. Alum 2000.
>**Tui '04-'05: Day $11,600** (+$400). **Aid:** Need 95 ($560,650).
>**Summer:** Acad Enrich Rev Rem Rec. Arts. Tui Day $300/3-wk ses. 6 wks.
>Endow $4,090,000. Plant val $12,400,000. Bldgs 15. Class rms 45. Lib 16,000 vols. Sci labs 7. Comp labs 2. Dark rms 1. Auds 3. Theaters 1. Art studios 3. Music studios 1. Gyms 2. Fields 5. Tennis courts 4. Field houses 1. Tracks 1.
>**Est 1966.** Nonprofit. Sem (Aug-June).

Sandia Prep originated as Sandia School, a private day and boarding school for girls that was founded by Ruth Hanna McCormick Simms in 1932. Circumstances during World War II forced the school to cease operations. Under the leadership of Mrs. Albert G. Simms II, the present school came into being in 1966. The school became coeducational in 1973.

Students are required to take courses in English, the fine arts or journalism, history, mathematics, modern languages and science. An extensive journalism program features newspaper and yearbook production, as well as photography and desktop publishing. Students pursue academic interests in-depth in elective courses in the various disciplines. Qualified seniors may enroll in one or more courses for credit at the University of New Mexico and may participate in an occupation or a profession that particularly interests them during the last month of the school year.

Sandia Prep encourages all students to participate in sports and fields a number of interscholastic teams for boys and girls. Many pupils choose to engage in community service.

LAS VEGAS, NM. (42 mi. E of Santa Fe, NM) Urban. Pop: 14,565. Alt: 6391 ft. Area also includes Montezuma.

ARMAND HAMMER UNITED WORLD COLLEGE
Bdg — Coed Gr 11-12

Montezuma, NM 87731. State Rd 65, PO Box 248. Tel: 505-454-4201. Fax: 505-454-4294. www.uwc-usa.org E-mail: admission@uwcaw.uwc.org

Lisa A. H. Darling, Pres. BA, George Fox College, MDiv, Princeton Theological Seminary, MLS, State Univ of New York. **Tim Smith, Adm.**

Col Prep. IB Diploma. Feat—Fr Ger Span Environ_Sci World_Relig Theater Music. **Supp**—ESL.

Adm: 100/yr. Appl due: Feb. Yield: 99%. **Tests** CEEB SSAT.

Enr 200. B 100. G 100. Sec 200. Wh 49%. Hisp 20%. Blk 15%. Am Ind 1%. Asian 15%. **Fac 28.** M 12/1. F 13/2. Adv deg: 60%. In dorms 6.

Grad '04—100. Col—90. (Johns Hopkins 5, Princeton 4, Harvard 4, Colby 4, Middlebury 3, Earlham 3). Alum 2000.

Tui '04-'05: Bdg $0.

Endow $84,000,000. Bldgs 30. Dorms 6. Dorm rms 104. Class rms 40. Lib 18,000 vols. Chapels 1. Sci labs 2. Lang labs 1. Comp labs 1. Tech ctrs 1. Auds 1. Art studios 1. Music studios 1. Dance studios 1. Gyms 1. Fields 2. Courts 3. Pools 1.

Est 1982. Nonprofit. Tri (Aug-May).

One of ten United World colleges, the school provides an international education emphasizing the two-year International Baccalaureate curriculum and community service. Cocurricular programs addressing conflict resolution and global issues are also integral to school life. Wilderness training and a ten-day project week in March allow students to pursue community and individual interests, and boys and girls also may participate in various cross-cultural experiences.

Traditional school activities include chorus, drama, photography, folk and modern dance, and sports. The student body is predominantly international, with roughly three-quarters of UWC's pupils enrolling from other countries. All American students receive full Davis Scholarships covering tuition, room and board, and two years of study.

SANTA FE, NM. (54 mi. NE of Albuquerque, NM) Urban. Pop: 62,203. Alt: 6950 ft.

SANTA FE PREPARATORY SCHOOL
Day — Coed Gr 7-12

Santa Fe, NM 87505. 1101 Camino de la Cruz Blanca. Tel: 505-982-1829.
Fax: 505-982-2897.
www.santafeprep.org   E-mail: admissions@sfprep.org

James W. Leonard, Head. BA, Williams College, MA, Middlebury College. **Marta M. Miskolczy, Adm.**

Col Prep. AP—Fr Span Calc. Feat—Web_Design Ceramics Photog Studio_Art Drama Music Journ.

Adm: 82/yr. Appl due: Mar. **Tests** CTP_4.

Enr 333. B 161. G 172. Elem 107. Sec 226. Wh 74%. Hisp 14%. Blk 2%. Am Ind 4%. Asian 4%. Other 2%. Avg class size: 14. **Fac 76.** M 35. F 41. Adv deg: 68%.

Grad '04—49. Col—48. (Boston U, U of CO-Boulder, U of NM, U of Denver, Georgetown, Dartmouth). Avg SAT: 1400. Avg ACT: 26. Alum 1000.

Tui '02-'03: Day $12,150 (+$800). **Aid:** Need 64 ($348,000).

Endow $2,066,000. Plant val $6,289,000. Bldgs 4. Class rms 22. Lib 11,000 vols. Sci labs 4. Comp labs 1. Auds 1. Theaters 1. Art studios 7. Music studios 1. Gyms 1. Fields 3.

Est 1961. Nonprofit. Sem (Aug-June). **Assoc** CLS.

Combining both creative and traditional approaches to education, this school provides a thorough foundation for college work. Primary emphasis is placed on the academic curriculum and the mastery of verbal and mathematical tools of expression. An interdisciplinary approach to learning is encouraged, and the program includes senior independent study. A full program in the fine and performing arts is part of the varied curriculum.

Athletics include soccer, basketball, track, field hockey, tennis, lacrosse, volleyball and cross-country, while additional activities are chorus, drama, student government, publications, Model UN, chess club, outdoor education and community service.

UTAH

SALT LAKE CITY, UT. Urban. Pop: 181,743. Alt: 4400 ft.

ROWLAND HALL-ST. MARK'S SCHOOL
Day — Coed Gr PS-12

Salt Lake City, UT 84102. 843 Lincoln St. Tel: 801-355-7494. Fax: 801-355-0474. www.rhsm.org E-mail: karenhyde@rhsm.org

Alan C. Sparrow, Head. AB, Brown Univ, MA, MS, Univ of Rochester. **Karen Hyde, Upper & Middle Sch Adm; Kathy Gundersen, Lower Sch Adm.**

> Col Prep. Sports (Winter). **AP**—Eng Fr Lat Span Calc Stats Bio Chem Physics Eur_Hist US_Hist Psych Studio_Art Music_Theory. **Feat**—Environ_Sci Geol Computers Pol_Sci Ceramics Photog Theater Music. **Supp**—Rev Tut.
>
> **Adm:** 163/yr. Appl due: Mar. Accepted: 65%. Yield: 82%. **Tests** CTP_4 ISEE SSAT TOEFL.
>
> **Enr 971.** B 491. G 480. Elem 677. Sec 294. Wh 85%. Hisp 3%. Blk 2%. Asian 8%. Other 2%. Avg class size: 14. **Fac 116.** M 25/2. F 72/17. Wh 98%. Other 2%. Adv deg: 38%.
>
> **Grad '04—67. Col—65.** (U of UT 6, Stanford 3, Boston Col 3, Bates 2, Pomona 2, U of WA 2). Avg SAT: 1245. Avg ACT: 27. Alum 1160.
>
> **Tui '04-'05: Day $10,910-13,180** (+$300-1000). **Aid:** Merit 6 ($51,600). Need 120 ($901,135).
>
> **Summer:** Acad. Tui Day $175/crse. 3-6 wks.
>
> Endow $4,000,000. Plant val $30,000,000. Bldgs 6. Class rms 69. 2 Libs 20,000 vols. Chapels 1. Sci labs 8. Comp labs 4. Auds 1. Art studios 3. Music studios 2. Dance studios 1. Gyms 2. Fields 4.
>
> **Est 1880.** Nonprofit. Episcopal. Tri (Aug-June). **Assoc** NAAS.

The merger of Rowland Hall and St. Mark's School in 1964 created this single school offering a coeducational program. Established in 1867, St. Mark's School suspended operations about the turn of the century, reopening in 1956 as a college preparatory school for boys. Rowland Hall was founded for girls in 1880 by Rt. Rev. Daniel S. Tuttle, first missionary Episcopal bishop of Utah, with funds provided by Benjamin Rowland of Philadelphia, PA.

RHSM offers a broad liberal arts curriculum with course work in the traditional subject areas. Advanced Placement classes are available in many disciplines, and both the arts and athletics are integral to the program. Small classes and a low student-teacher ratio are other characteristics of the school, which sends its graduates to colleges throughout the country. Rowmark Ski Academy, an adjunct of the school, offers an intense ski-racing program. Through the Family Live-In Program, pupils from outside Salt Lake City attend the school while living with a family within the school community.

Lower school children (age 2 through grade 5) attend classes on the McCarthy campus at 720 Guardsman Way, 84108.

Pacific States

CALIFORNIA

ANAHEIM, CA. (36 mi. ESE of Los Angeles, CA) Urban. Pop: 328,014. Alt: 165 ft.

ST. CATHERINE'S MILITARY SCHOOL
Bdg and Day — Boys Gr K-8

Anaheim, CA 92805. 215 N Harbor Blvd. Tel: 714-772-1363. Fax: 714-772-3004.
www.stcatherinesmilitary.com

Sr. Mary Menegatti, OP, Prin. Lori Gutierrez, Adm.

Pre-Prep. Milit. Feat—Computers. **Supp**—Dev_Read ESL Rem_Math Rem_Read Tut.

Adm: 67/yr. Bdg 28. Day 39. Appl due: Rolling. Accepted: 33%.

Enr 180. B 70/110. Elem 180. Wh 44%. Hisp 27%. Blk 5%. Asian 24%. Avg class size: 16. Uniform. **Fac 15.** M 4/1. F 8/2. Adv deg: 33%.

Grad '04—40. Prep—32. (Servite, Mater Dei HS, NM Milit, Army & Navy). Alum 2400.

Tui '04-'05: Bdg $27,930 (+$2500). **5-Day Bdg $21,930** (+$2000). **Day $8280** (+$1000). **Aid:** Need 30 ($80,000).

Summer: Acad Enrich Rec. ESL. Tui Bdg 2100-3100. Tui Day $1150. 4 wks.

Endow $30,000. Plant val $25,000,000. Bldgs 10. Dorms 4. Class rms 10. Libs 1. Comp labs 1. Music studios 2. Gyms 1. Fields 1. Courts 1. Pools 1.

Est 1889. Nonprofit. Roman Catholic. Sem (Sept-June). **Assoc** WASC.

Conducted by the Dominican Sisters, St. Catherine's offers a pre-preparatory curriculum stressing academic skills. Math is a particularly strong subject at the school, and English as a Second Language is available.

The military program, which begins in grade 2, provides training in military courtesy, discipline and leadership skills. School activities include intramural and interscholastic sports, supervised weekend field trips for boarding students, speech and debate team, and a music program that features both band and piano.

Christian-oriented activities include sacramental preparation, weekly Mass and family-life education. The student body represents a variety of religious backgrounds, and graduates attend both college preparatory schools and secondary military academies.

ATHERTON, CA. (22 mi. WNW of San Jose, CA; 30 mi. SE of San Francisco, CA) Rural. Pop: 7194. Alt: 52 ft.

MENLO SCHOOL

Day — Coed Gr 6-12

Atherton, CA 94027. 50 Valparaiso Ave. Tel: 650-330-2000. Fax: 650-330-2012.
www.menloschool.org   E-mail: info@menloschool.org

Norman M. Colb, Head. BA, Brandeis Univ, MAT, Harvard Univ. **Dectora Coe Jeffers, Upper Sch Adm; Lisa Schiavenza, Middle Sch Adm.**

  Col Prep. AP—Eng Fr Lat Span Stats Comp_Sci Chem Physics Eur_Hist US_Hist Econ US_Govt & Pol Studio_Art Music_Theory. **Feat**—British_Lit Shakespeare Japan Anat & Physiol Astron Environ_Sci Biotech_Research Asian_Stud Art_Hist Film Photog Digital_Multimedia Journ. **Supp**—Tut.

  Adm: 153/yr. Appl due: Jan. Accepted: 33%. Yield: 60%. **Tests** ISEE SSAT.

  Enr 757. B 375. G 382. Elem 217. Sec 540. Wh 82%. Hisp 3%. Blk 3%. Asian 8%. Other 4%. Avg class size: 16. **Fac 87.** M 30/4. F 45/8. Wh 89%. Hisp 3%. Blk 6%. Asian 2%. Adv deg: 83%.

  Grad '04—129. Col—129. (Stanford 15, USC 9, UCLA 6, U of CO-Boulder 6, Princeton 4, U of CA-San Diego 4). Avg SAT: 1295. Alum 3336.

  Tui '04-'05: Day $24,800 (+$2000). **Aid:** Need 106 ($1,827,031). Work prgm 7 ($7000). Endow $9,074,000. Plant val $39,555,000. Bldgs 23. Class rms 76. Lib 20,000 vols. Sci labs 9. Comp labs 3. Multimedia labs 1. Theaters 1. Art studios 1. Music studios 3. Dance studios 1. Gyms 1. Fields 3. Courts 12. Pools 1. Weight rms 1.

  Est 1915. Nonprofit. Sem (Aug-June). **Assoc** WASC.

Located on a 35-acre campus that includes separate facilities for middle and upper school students, Menlo conducts a college preparatory curriculum designed to address the specific needs of each age group.

At the middle school level (grades 6-8), the program incorporates small classes, an integrated, interdisciplinary curriculum, and a varied selection of age-appropriate athletic and extracurricular activities. Most classes meet for 95 minutes, allowing time for hands-on exercises and classroom discussions, and pupils frequently work together on projects. Art, music and drama are integral to the program.

During the upper school years (grades 9-12), students further develop their critical thinking and independent learning skills. In addition to Advanced Placement courses, Menlo offers opportunities for independent study in such areas as biotechnology research, multimedia technology and history research. Particularly strong visual arts, choral and instrumental music, and dramatic programs are available at this level, as are peer leadership and student government programs. The school encourages all to participate in clubs and athletics. **See Also Page 1207**

CA   Pacific States   699

CARLSBAD, CA.
(23 mi. NNW of San Diego, CA) Suburban. Pop: 78,247. Alt: 42 ft.

ARMY AND NAVY ACADEMY
Bdg and Day — Boys Gr 7-12

Carlsbad, CA 92018. 2605 Carlsbad Blvd, PO Box 3000. Tel: 760-729-2385.
  Fax: 760-434-5948.
  www.armyandnavyacademy.org   E-mail: admissions@armyandnavyacademy.org
Brig. Gen. Stephen Bliss, Pres. BA, US Military Academy, MS, Univ of Missouri-Columbia, MBA, Univ of Texas-Dallas. **Elizabeth A. Kalivas, Adm.**
  Col Prep. Gen Acad. Milit. AP—Eng Span Calc Bio Chem Physics Eur_Hist US_Hist Studio_Art. **Feat**—Creative_Writing Fr Astron Environ_Sci Computers Psych Comp_Relig Art_Hist Photog Drama Band Music Journ JROTC. **Supp**—ESL Tut.
  Adm: 137/yr. Bdg 128. Day 9. Appl due: Rolling. Accepted: 80%. **Tests** ISEE SSAT Stanford TOEFL.
  Enr 333. B 308/25. Elem 46. Sec 287. Wh 46%. Hisp 11%. Blk 5%. Am Ind 1%. Asian 19%. Other 18%. Avg class size: 15. Uniform. **Fac 36.** M 13/11. F 5/7. Wh 81%. Hisp 1%. Blk 11%. Am Ind 1%. Asian 1%. Other 5%. Adv deg: 36%.
  Grad '04—46. Col—43. (U of CA-Davis, U of CA-Irvine, U of AZ, U of San Diego, San Diego St, U of CA-Riverside). Avg SAT: 1100. Alum 2000.
  Tui '04-'05: Bdg $25,990 (+$2500). **Day $15,950** (+$2200). **Aid:** Need 12 (+$105,490).
  Summer: Acad. Tui Bdg $4500 (+$400). Tui Day $600/crse (+$200). 5 wks.
  Endow $6,000,000. Plant val $10,000,000. Bldgs 30. Dorms 14. Dorm rms 150. Class rms 32. Lib 3000 vols. Sci labs 4. Comp labs 1. Auds 1. Art studios 1. Music studios 1. Dance studios 1. Gyms 1. Fields 1. Courts 3. Pools 1. Rifle ranges 1.
  Est 1910. Nonprofit. Sem (Sept-June). **Assoc** WASC.

Established at Pacific Beach in 1910 and relocated to Carlsbad in 1936, this military school prepares its students for both competitive colleges nationwide and the US service academies. Honors and Advanced Placement courses in the major disciplines provide qualified cadets with opportunities for acceleration. A well-developed computer program, a learning strategies program, and a fine and performing arts department that enables pupils to take part in dramatic productions, art exhibitions, concerts and marching band are other features of the academy's program.

ANA's 16-acre, oceanfront location allows for various interscholastic sports, as well as an intramural program that includes surfing, volleyball and weightlifting, among other options. In addition, the school schedules monthly dances with neighboring schools and other weekend activities.

CLAREMONT, CA.
(40 mi. E of Los Angeles, CA) Suburban. Pop: 33,998. Alt: 1144 ft. See also Los Angeles.

FOOTHILL COUNTRY DAY SCHOOL
Day — Coed Gr PS-8

Claremont, CA 91711. 1035 W Harrison Ave. Tel: 909-626-5681. Fax: 909-625-4251.
  www.foothillcds.org   E-mail: dzondervan@foothillcds.org
Mark W. Lauria, Head. BA, Claremont McKenna College, MEd, PhD, Claremont Graduate School. **Denise Zondervan, Adm.**

Pre-Prep. Feat—Lib_Skills Lat Span Computers Studio_Art Drama Music Dance. **Supp**—Tut.
Adm: 27/yr. Appl due: Mar. Accepted: 40%. Yield: 100%. **Tests** CTP_4.
Enr 180. B 93. G 87. Elem 180. Wh 61%. Hisp 18%. Blk 1%. Asian 20%. Avg class size: 20. **Fac 22.** M 3/2. F 11/6. Wh 99%. Blk 1%. Adv deg: 50%.
Grad '04—20. Prep—13. (Webb Schs-CA, St Lucy's, Polytech Sch). Alum 857.
Tui '04-'05: Day $11,500-12,445. Aid: Merit 15 ($34,800).
Summer: Acad Enrich. Tui Day $650. 5 wks.
Endow $1,805,000. Plant val $2,500,000. Bldgs 7. Class rms 16. Lib 20,000 vols. Sci labs 2. Comp labs 2. Auds 1. Theaters 1. Art studios 1. Music studios 1. Dance studios 1. Gyms 1. Fields 2. Courts 3. Pools 1.
Est 1954. Nonprofit. Quar (Sept-June). **Assoc** WASC.

Founded by Howell and Betty Webb, FCDS provides a structured program that emphasizes a mastery of skills in reading and literature, writing, math, science, social studies, Spanish (in grades K-8) and Latin (in grades 6 and 7). Enrichment courses include computer technology, library skills, drama, music, art and physical education. Each grade produces an annual play, and pupils take active roles in the daily chapel program. In addition, students participate in several community service projects. The school conducts field trips for children at all grade levels, and after-school programs are available.

Foothill also maintains a preschool division, The Seedling School, for children ages 3-5. This program balances developmentally appropriate instruction with creative play in a structured environment.

WEBB SCHOOLS

Bdg and Day — Coed Gr 9-12
(Coord — Day 9-10)

Claremont, CA 91711. 1175 W Baseline Rd. Tel: 909-626-3587. Fax: 909-621-4582. www.webb.org   E-mail: admissions@webb.org
Susan A. Nelson, Head. BA, Wagner College, MA, New York Univ. **Leo G. Marshall,** Adm.
Col Prep. AP—Eng Fr Span Calc Stats Bio Chem Physics Eur_Hist US_Hist World_Hist Econ Psych Art_Hist Studio_Art Music_Theory. **Feat**—Geol Paleontology Neurosci Computers Drama Music. **Supp**—Rev Tut.
Adm: 96/yr. Bdg 66. Day 30. Appl due: Jan. Accepted: 65%. **Tests** ISEE SSAT.
Enr 355. B 127/68. G 96/64. Sec 355. Wh 61%. Hisp 5%. Blk 4%. Asian 30%. Avg class size: 15. **Fac 49.** M 28/1. F 19/1. Adv deg: 83%. In dorms 8.
Grad '04—80. Col—80. (USC, Stanford, Boston U, Wellesley, U of PA, U of CA-Berkeley). Avg SAT: 1300. Alum 3000.
Tui '04-'05: Bdg $35,135 (+$1020). **Day $24,945** (+$1020). **Aid:** Merit 2 ($20,000). Need 62 ($1,047,000).
Summer: Acad Enrich. 5 wks.
Endow $14,000,000. Plant val $55,000,000. Bldgs 55. Dorms 10. Dorm rms 186. Class rms 22. Lib 26,000 vols. Sci labs 4. Lang labs 5. Comp labs 2. Observatories 1. Auds 1. Art studios 1. Music studios 1. Museums 1. Gyms 1. Fields 4. Tennis courts 6. Pools 1. Tracks 1. Student ctrs 1.
Est 1922. Nonprofit. Sem (Sept-June). **Assoc** CLS WASC.

The school comprises Webb School of California for boys and Vivian Webb School for girls. The former was started in 1922, when Dr. Thompson and Vivian Webb moved west from Bell Buckle, TN, to Claremont to found a boys' school in the foothills of the San Gabriel Mountains. Thompson Webb was part of a school-making tradition that had been started by his father, Sawney Webb, in Tennessee. Sawney Webb founded Webb School of Bell Buckle after the Civil War and helped it earn a national reputation based on its academic excellence and student honor code. Thompson took his father's principles to California when he founded the Webb School of California. In 1981, Vivian Webb School, a separate day school for girls, opened on the 70-acre campus and, four years later, began accepting boarding students.

Under the coordinate program, the Webb Schools share faculty and facilities, while maintaining their own student governments, school traditions and graduation ceremonies. Students in grades 9 and 10 take single-gender courses in math, science, history and English, while juniors and seniors attend coeducational classes. The two schools come together for meals, social and recreational activities, fine arts productions and other campus-wide events. Advanced Placement and honors courses are offered in all major disciplines, and upperclassmen with faculty approval may attend classes at one of the nearby Claremont colleges. Graduates enter leading colleges throughout the country.

Extracurricular activities include student publications, a radio station, orchestral and choral groups, the studio arts, backpacking, camping, fossil-gathering excursions, community service programs, and such interest clubs as Amnesty International and Junior Statesmen of America. Each year, the two schools collaborate on three dramatic productions and three dance productions. All students participate in interscholastic athletics at least one season per year; the school organizes teams in baseball, basketball, cross-country, football, soccer, softball, tennis, track, volleyball, swimming and diving, water polo and wrestling.

CORONA DEL MAR, CA. (47 mi. SE of Los Angeles, CA) Rural. Pop: 2757. Alt: 80 ft.

HARBOR DAY SCHOOL

Day — Coed Gr K-8

Corona del Mar, CA 92625. 3443 Pacific View Dr. Tel: 949-640-1410. Fax: 949-640-0908. www.harborday.org E-mail: sdupont@harborday.org

Sidney I. DuPont, Head. BS, MS, Central Connecticut State Univ, PhD, Univ of Connecticut. Kristin Rowe, Adm.

Pre-Prep. Feat—Fr Lat Span Computers Studio_Art Music.

Adm: 62/yr. Appl due: Mar. Accepted: 30%. **Tests** CTP_4 ISEE.

Enr 406. B 194. G 212. Elem 406. Wh 95%. Hisp 2%. Asian 3%. Avg class size: 22. Uniform. **Fac 34.** M 6. F 26/2. Wh 100%. Adv deg: 55%.

Grad '04—42. Prep—10. (St Margaret's Episcopal, Cate, Thacher, Santa Catalina, Choate, Phillips Acad). Alum 1450.

Tui '05-'06: Day $12,975 (+$200). **Aid:** Need 2 ($20,000).

Summer: Rev. Oceanography. Tui Day $125/wk. 8 wks.

Endow $9,000,000. Plant val $9,500,000. Bldgs 5. Class rms 30. Lib 12,000 vols. Sci labs 2. Comp labs 3. Auds 1. Art studios 3. Music studios 1. Wood shops 1. Gyms 2. Fields 2. Courts 5.

Est 1952. Nonprofit. Tri (Sept-June). **Assoc** WASC.

Serving Orange Coast communities, Harbor Day moved to a six-acre campus overlooking the Pacific in 1973. The traditional curriculum features an integrated sequence of courses in math and the English language, and it includes frequent field trips and the study of foreign languages and computer technology. The sports program comprises volleyball, soccer, basketball, gymnastics and softball.

CORTE MADERA, CA. (9 mi. NNE of San Francisco, CA) Suburban. Pop: 9100. Alt: 27 ft.

MARIN COUNTRY DAY SCHOOL

Day — Coed Gr K-8

Corte Madera, CA 94925. 5221 Paradise Dr. Tel: 415-927-5900. Fax: 415-924-2224.
www.mcds.org   E-mail: admission@mcds.org

Lucinda Lee Katz, Head. BA, MA, San Francisco State Univ, PhD, Univ of Illinois-Urbana. **Jeffrey Escabar & Ann Borden, Adms.**

Pre-Prep. Feat—Span Computers Studio_Art Drama Music Outdoor_Ed. **Supp**—Dev_ Read LD Tut.

Adm: 80/yr. Appl due: Jan. Accepted: 22%. Yield: 93%. **Tests** CTP_4 ISEE.

Enr 541. B 258. G 283. Elem 541. Wh 74%. Hisp 3%. Blk 5%. Asian 9%. Other 9%. Avg class size: 18. **Fac 83.** M 19/4. F 30/30. Wh 87%. Hisp 5%. Blk 2%. Asian 2%. Other 4%. Adv deg: 42%.

Grad '04—68. Prep—58. (Marin Acad 13, San Francisco U HS 11, Branson 9, St Ignatius 4, Urban 4, Lick-Wilmerding 2). Alum 1929.

Tui '04-'05: Day $17,925-20,770. Aid: Need 107 ($1,309,940).

Summer: Acad Enrich Rem Rec. Computers. Tui Day $330/wk. 5 wks.

Endow $10,300,000. Plant val $4,970,000. Bldgs 20. Class rms 34. Lib 23,000 vols. Sci labs 3. Comp labs 1. Auds 1. Art studios 2. Music studios 2. Gyms 1. Fields 2.

Est 1956. Nonprofit. Sem (Sept-June). **Assoc** WASC.

Founded by a group of parents as the only country day school in the San Francisco Bay Area, MCDS provides a broad and balanced program. Located on a 35-acre, waterfront campus, the school enrolls students from San Francisco and Marin counties.

Students work in self-contained classroom groups in grades K-5 and in a homeroom/departmentalized arrangement in grades 6-8. The program emphasizes inquiry and experiential learning at all grade levels. MCDS is characterized by a focus on interdisciplinary teaching, the arts and the sciences.

HILLSBOROUGH, CA. (20 mi. SE of San Francisco, CA) Suburban. Pop: 10,825. Alt: 32 ft.

CRYSTAL SPRINGS UPLANDS SCHOOL

Day — Coed Gr 6-12

Hillsborough, CA 94010. 400 Uplands Dr. Tel: 650-342-4175. Fax: 650-342-7611.
www.csus.com   E-mail: admission@csus.com

Amy C. Richards, Head. BA, MA, Univ of New Hampshire. **Abby H. Wilder, Adm.**

Col Prep. AP—Eng Fr Span Calc Bio Physics Eur_Hist US_Hist Comp_Govt & Pol US_Govt & Pol. **Feat**—Shakespeare Lat Astron Photog Drama.

Adm: 103/yr. Appl due: Jan. Accepted: 32%. **Tests** ISEE SSAT.
Enr 350. B 170. G 180. Elem 100. Sec 250. Wh 67%. Hisp 3%. Blk 4%. Asian 18%. Other 8%. Avg class size: 14. **Fac 53.** M 25/4. F 20/4. Wh 83%. Hisp 3%. Asian 14%. Adv deg: 50%.
Grad '04—62. Col—62. (USC, Stanford, U of CA-Berkeley, U of Puget Sound, UCLA, Brown). Avg SAT: 1333. Alum 2000.
Tui '04-'05: Day $23,280 (+$1100). **Aid:** Need 53 ($821,144).
Summer: Enrich. Tui Day $1600. 5 wks.
Endow $8,800,000. Plant val $23,000,000. Bldgs 4. Class rms 32. Lib 10,000 vols. Labs 3. Sci labs 5. Lang labs 1. Comp labs 2. Theaters 1. Art studios 2. Music studios 1. Dance studios 1. Gyms 1. Fields 2. Courts 3.
Est 1952. Nonprofit. Sem (Aug-June). **Assoc** CLS WASC.

Crystal Springs opened as an independent school for girls. In 1956, it moved to Uplands, the former Templeton Crocker estate in Hillsborough. The school now occupies the Renaissance-style mansion, its surrounding ten acres and an academic building, a fine arts building and a gymnasium. Boys were first admitted to the school in 1977, and today the program is fully coeducational.

The school augments its rigorous college preparatory curriculum with a strong extracurricular program. Students may participate in school government, publications, fine arts activities, community service, travel and outdoor education. Interscholastic sports for boys and girls—which include soccer, cross-country, tennis, volleyball, baseball, basketball, badminton, swimming and golf—are also available.

HUNTINGTON BEACH, CA. (37 mi. SE of Los Angeles, CA) Suburban. Pop: 189,594. Alt: 28 ft.

THE PEGASUS SCHOOL
Day — Coed Gr PS-8

Huntington Beach, CA 92646. 19692 Lexington Ln. Tel: 714-964-1224. Fax: 714-962-6047.
www.pegasus-school.net   E-mail: nconklin@pegasus-school.net
Laura S. Hathaway, Head. BA, City Univ of New York, MA, California State Univ-Long Beach, EdD, Univ of Southern California. **Nancy Conklin, Adm.**
Pre-Prep. Feat—Span Computers Photog Studio_Art Animation Drama Music Woodworking Outdoor_Ed. **Supp—**Dev_Read Tut.
Adm: 99/yr. Appl due: Jan. Accepted: 33%. **Tests** CTP_4 ISEE.
Enr 565. B 282. G 283. Elem 565. Wh 80%. Hisp 2%. Blk 1%. Am Ind 1%. Asian 10%. Other 6%. Avg class size: 19. **Fac 44.** M 12. F 32. Wh 90%. Hisp 10%. Adv deg: 36%.
Grad '04—54. Prep—32. (Mater Dei HS, Cate, Thacher, HI Prep, St Margaret's Episcopal, Santa Catalina). Alum 245.
Tui '05-'06: Day $11,880-11,980 (+$500). **Aid:** Need 42 ($160,000).
Summer: Acad Enrich Rec. Tui Day $500/2-wk ses. 6 wks.
Plant val $14,000,000. Bldgs 10. Class rms 37. Lib 18,000 vols. Sci labs 3. Comp labs 2. Auds 1. Theaters 1. Art studios 1. Music studios 1. Gyms 1. Fields 2. Courts 4.
Est 1984. Nonprofit. Tri (Sept-June).

The school traces its origins to 1979, when a summer program entitled Pegasus Programs first operated. Its success led founder Laura S. Hathaway to open The

Pegasus School in 1984. After serving 40 preschoolers in its first year, the school gradually expanded through grade 8.

During the lower school years (grades PS-5), the curriculum combines basic skills instruction with open-ended opportunities for children to pursue areas of interest. In addition to the core subjects, pupils take specialist-taught classes in Spanish (beginning in grade 3), science, technology, art, music and physical education. Field trips, visiting guests and performers, and annual special events enrich the lower school program.

Course work at the middle school level (grades 6-8) is suitable for gifted learners. A strong science program addresses topics within the physical, life and earth sciences. The outdoor education program features weeklong expeditions designed to enhance students' understanding of the environment, demonstrate the practical applications of science and history, and illustrate the importance of teamwork.

Middle school students participate in an after-school sports program that includes flag football, volleyball, basketball and soccer. Pegasus also offers an extended-day program and after-school activities for boys and girls at all grade levels.

See Also Page 1207

IDYLLWILD, CA. (68 mi. NNE of San Diego, CA) Rural. Pop: 3504. Alt: 5400 ft.

IDYLLWILD ARTS ACADEMY

Bdg — Coed Gr 8-PG; Day — Coed 9-PG

Idyllwild, CA 92549. 52500 Temecula Rd, PO Box 38. Tel: 909-659-2171.
  Fax: 909-659-2058.
  www.idyllwildarts.org   E-mail: admission@idyllwildarts.org
William M. Lowman, Head. BA, Univ of Redlands. **Karen Porter, Adm.**
  Col Prep. Perform_Arts Visual_Arts Creative_Writing. AP—Fr Span Calc. **Feat**—Environ_Sci Computers Econ Govt. **Supp**—ESL Rev Tut.
  Adm: 102/yr. Bdg 74. Day 28. **Tests** SSAT.
  Enr 255. Elem 10. Sec 244. PG 1. Avg class size: 10. **Fac 62.** In dorms 14.
  Grad '04—64. Col—61. (Boston U, USC, Sch of the Art Inst of Chicago, Juilliard, NYU, Yale). Alum 350.
  Tui '05-'06: Bdg $37,950 (+$1500). **Day $20,775** (+$700). **Aid:** Need 123 ($1,885,000). Work prgm 5 ($5000).
  Summer: Arts. Tui Bdg $1950/2-wk ses. 7 wks.
  Endow $302,000. Plant val $9,708,000. Bldgs 40. Dorms 5. Class rms 15. Lib 3000 vols. Sci labs 3. Comp labs 1. Theaters 1. Art studios 6. Music studios 14. Dance studios 2. Fields 1. Pools 1.
  Est 1986. Nonprofit. Sem (Sept-June). **Assoc** WASC.

Trees and meadows dominate this 205-acre campus, which is set in the pine forests of the San Jacinto Mountains. The academy's location offers students recreational opportunities such as hiking, rock climbing and cross-country skiing. Roads and trails in and around the campus encourage running and cycling.

Students receive demanding preprofessional training in the arts and a strong college preparatory education. Academic courses are scheduled in the mornings, balanced by arts courses that meet in the afternoons; both range from introductory to honors levels. Each student's course of study is composed of a combination of the required arts courses for each major and the academic courses necessary to meet graduation requirements in English, history/social studies, foreign language, mathematics, science, physical education and computer literacy.

Major areas of arts study include music, dance, theater, visual arts, moving pictures and creative writing; an individualized arts major is designed for those who have demonstrated high academic achievement and have a strong interest in two or more arts major areas. Performances, publications and exhibition center openings supplement the arts program, while the academic curriculum utilizes hands-on activities, experiments, field trips, cooperative learning and group problem solving. Arts Academy graduates are accepted into both colleges and conservatories.

LA JOLLA, CA. (8 mi. WNW of San Diego, CA) Suburban. Pop: 28,800. Alt: 110 ft.

THE BISHOP'S SCHOOL
Day — Coed Gr 7-12

La Jolla, CA 92037. 7607 La Jolla Blvd. Tel: 858-459-4021. Fax: 858-459-3914.
www.bishops.com E-mail: admissions@bishops.com
Michael W. Teitelman, Head. AB, Albright College, MAT, Brown Univ. **Josie Alvarez, Adm.**
  Col Prep. AP—Eng Fr Lat Span Stats Bio Chem Physics Eur_Hist US_Hist Comp_Govt & Pol Econ US_Govt & Pol Art_Hist Studio_Art. **Feat**—Creative_Writing Humanities Mandarin Anat & Physiol Ecol Genetics Oceanog Comp_Sci Women's_Hist Philos Relig Photog Drama Music Dance Journ. **Supp**—Rev Tut.
  Adm: 162/yr. Appl due: Feb. Accepted: 45%. **Tests** IQ ISEE.
  Enr 685. B 337. G 348. Elem 221. Sec 464. Wh 77%. Hisp 9%. Blk 4%. Asian 10%. Avg class size: 14. Uniform. **Fac 85.** M 29. F 56. Wh 93%. Hisp 5%. Blk 2%. Adv deg: 64%.
  Grad '04—108. **Col**—107. (USC 6, Stanford 4, Georgetown 4, Santa Clara 4, Yale 3, Harvard 3). Avg SAT: 1328. Alum 5200.
  Tui '04-'05: Day $19,500 (+$1500). **Aid:** Need 134 ($1,500,000).
  Summer: Acad Enrich Rev. Tui Day $220-1350. 3-6 wks.
  Endow $16,000,000. Plant val $12,000,000. Bldgs 5. Class rms 62. Lib 12,000 vols. Sci labs 6. Lang labs 1. Comp labs 4. Theaters 1. Art studios 3. Music studios 1. Dance studios 1. Gyms 1. Athletic ctrs 1. Fields 2. Courts 5. Pools 1.
  Est 1909. Nonprofit. Episcopal. Sem (Aug-June). **Assoc** CLS WASC.

The school was established by the bishop of the Los Angeles Episcopal Diocese through benefactions of land and money from Ellen and Virginia Scripps. Founded as a girls' boarding school, Bishop's became coeducational in 1971, when it merged with the San Miguel School for Boys. The boarding department closed in 1983, creating a completely coeducational day school.

Bishop's 11-acre campus is a block from the ocean. The college preparatory program offers a balance between required courses and electives; Advanced Placement courses and independent study provide opportunities for acceleration. Attendance at weekly chapel services is required, and a six-year format of community service involves all students.

The interscholastic athletic program allows boys and girls to compete on freshman, junior varsity and varsity teams in a number of sports. Activities include academic league, student council, academic and enrichment clubs, religious organizations, and publications and yearbook.

LA JOLLA COUNTRY DAY SCHOOL
Day — Coed Gr PS-12

La Jolla, CA 92037. 9490 Genesee Ave. Tel: 858-453-3440. Fax: 858-453-8210.
  www.ljcds.org   E-mail: info@ljcds.org
Judith R. Glickman, Head. AB, MA, Univ of California-Berkeley, PhD, Univ of Southern California. **Lisa Okelberry, Adm.**
  Col Prep. AP—Eng Fr Span Calc Stats Comp_Sci Bio Chem Physics Eur_Hist US_Hist Psych US_Govt & Pol Art_Hist Studio_Art Music_Theory. **Feat**—Astron Marine_Biol/Sci Econ Outdoor_Ed. **Supp**—Tut.
  Adm: 169/yr. Appl due: Feb. Accepted: 55%. Yield: 76%. **Tests** CTP_4 ISEE.
  Enr 1006. B 485. G 521. Elem 643. Sec 363. Avg class size: 18. **Fac 120.** M 30/1. F 81/8. Wh 92%. Hisp 3%. Blk 2%. Asian 3%. Adv deg: 46%.
  Grad '04—90. Col—86. (USC 5, Boston U 3, Loyola Marymount 3, Stanford 3, UCLA 3, U of CA-Santa Barbara 3). Avg SAT: 1279. Alum 1750.
  Tui '04-'05: Day $15,000-17,900 (+$345-2000). **Aid:** Need 139 ($1,343,158).
  Summer: Acad Enrich Rev Rec. Tui Day $180-1000. 1-6 wks.
  Endow $931,000. Plant val $31,500,000. Bldgs 20. Class rms 75. Lib 27,000 vols. Sci labs 9. Comp labs 3. Photog labs 1. Observatories 1. Theaters 2. Art studios 3. Music studios 3. Amphitheaters 1. Photog studios 1. AV rms 1. Gyms 1. Fields 4. Tennis courts 6.
  Est 1926. Nonprofit. Sem (Aug-June). **Assoc** CLS WASC.

Country Day traces its origins to the Balmer School, a primary school founded by Louise C. Balmer in 1926. In 1955, seeing the need for a local independent day school with a full nursery through grade 12 curriculum, Mrs. Balmer and a group of interested parents helped bring about the formation of the current program. The school moved to its present, 24-acre campus in 1961.

In the early grades, individualized techniques dominate the teaching philosophy. Reading and phonics are stressed in all grades, and creative writing, foreign language, art, music and physical education enhance the curriculum. The middle school is designed to meet the specific needs of students in that age group.

Emphasis in the upper school program is on college preparation in the basic subject areas, with college credit available in all departments through Advanced Placement. Computer science instruction begins in kindergarten and runs through grade 12. Programs in the fine and performing arts and interscholastic and intramural athletics are also offered. All upper school students perform community service.

LOS ANGELES, CA. Urban. Pop: 3,694,820. Alt: 338 ft. Area also includes Calabasas, Culver City, North Hollywood, Palos Verdes Peninsula and Sherman Oaks.

BUCKLEY SCHOOL
Day — Coed Gr K-12

Sherman Oaks, CA 91423. 3900 Stansbury Ave. Tel: 818-783-1610. Fax: 818-461-6714.

www.buckleyla.org E-mail: admissions@buckleyla.org
Paul S. Horovitz, Head. BA, Lake Forest College, JD, Boston Univ. **Carinne M. Barker, Adm.**

   Col Prep. AP—Eng Fr Lat Span Calc Comp_Sci Bio Chem Physics US_Hist US_Govt & Pol Studio_Art Music_Theory. **Feat**—British_Lit Astron Programming Japan_Hist Ceramics Photog Sculpt Theater Dance Journ. **Supp**—Rem_Math Rev Tut.

   Adm (Gr K-11): 93/yr. Accepted: 38%. Yield: 49%. **Tests** ISEE.

   Enr 750. B 372. G 378. Elem 440. Sec 310. Wh 73%. Hisp 3%. Blk 2%. Am Ind 1%. Asian 6%. Other 15%. Avg class size: 15. Uniform. **Fac 105.** M 41/3. F 57/4. Wh 88%. Hisp 3%. Blk 3%. Am Ind 1%. Asian 2%. Other 3%. Adv deg: 45%.

   Grad '04—57. Col—56. (U of CA-Berkeley 6, USC 6, Loyola Marymount 4, U of CO-Boulder 3, Columbia 2, RI Sch of Design 2). Avg SAT: 1230. Alum 1523.

   Tui '04-'05: Day $19,250-21,900 (+$1000-1650). **Aid:** Need 60 ($934,550).

   Summer: Acad. Tui Day $1600. 6 wks.

   Endow $2,657,000. Plant val $11,095,000. Bldgs 14. Class rms 63. 2 Libs 32,000 vols. Sci labs 4. Lang labs 2. Comp labs 3. Auds 1. Art studios 3. Music studios 3. Dance studios 2. Gyms 1. Fields 1. Pools 1.

   Est 1933. Nonprofit. Sem (Aug-June). **Assoc** WASC.

Founded by Isabelle Buckley, the author of *A Guide to a Child's World* and *College Begins at Two*, this school subscribes to a philosophy of "self-expression through self-discipline." Dr. Buckley's ideas, influenced by the observation of educational systems while living abroad, call for a balance between the academic demands of prewar French schools and the athletic programs of the British system.

Situated on a 19-acre campus, Buckley adheres to the beliefs of its founder in placing equal emphasis on academic training, creative self-expression, physical education and moral education. The school conducts a rigorous liberal arts program that features Advanced Placement courses in most disciplines. A particularly strong arts curriculum, which commences with integrated art across the curriculum in the lower school, incorporates artist visits at all grade levels. Upper school students participate in an international exchange program, outdoor education and volunteer community service. The sports program includes basketball, soccer, track, baseball, swimming and tennis, among others.

CAMPBELL HALL SCHOOL
Day — Coed Gr K-12

North Hollywood, CA 91607. 4533 Laurel Canyon Blvd. Tel: 818-980-7280. Fax: 818-505-5319.

   www.campbell.pvt.k12.ca.us E-mail: flemina@campbellhall.org

Rev. Julian P. Bull, Head. BA, Dartmouth College, MA, Boston College. **Alice Fleming, Adm.**

   Col Prep. Gen Acad. AP—Eng Fr Span Calc Stats Comp_Sci Bio Chem Human_Geog Physics Eur_Hist US_Hist Psych US_Govt & Pol Art_Hist. **Feat**—Creative_Writing Japan Environ_Sci Marine_Biol/Sci Programming Robotics Amer_Stud Sociol Comp_ Relig Ethics Philos Ceramics Photog Drama Theater Music_Hist Music_Theory Dance. **Supp**—Makeup Tut.

   Adm (Gr K-11): 165/yr. Appl due: Feb. Accepted: 36%. **Tests** CTP_4 ISEE.

   Enr 1061. B 535. G 526. Elem 571. Sec 491. Wh 77%. Hisp 5%. Blk 6%. Asian 7%. Other 5%.Uniform. **Fac 121.** M 45/4. F 65/7. Wh 81%. Hisp 6%. Blk 7%. Asian 6%. Adv deg: 47%.

   Grad '04—107. Col—107. (UCLA, USC, U of CA-Santa Barbara, Boston U, Emory). Alum 1500.

Tui '04-'05: Day $14,260-19,320 (+$1000-1200). **Aid:** Need 127 ($1,493,990).
Summer: Acad Enrich Rec. Creative Arts. Tui Day $400/wk. Rec. Tui Day $400-1050/wk. 6 wks.
Endow $2,000,000. Plant val $12,000,000. Bldgs 22. Class rms 60. Libs 1. Labs 5. Theaters 1. Art studios 3. Music studios 2. Dance studios 1. Gyms 2. Fields 2. Courts 7.
Est 1944. Nonprofit. Episcopal. Sem (Sept-June). **Assoc** CLS WASC.

Founded by Rev. Alexander K. Campbell, the school provides sound preparatory training within the Judeo-Christian tradition. With its structured, enriched college preparatory curriculum, Campbell Hall prepares students for an array of colleges. Chapel is held five times a week for the elementary school and twice a week for the secondary school; however, religion is not a required course. Varied arts and music programs are part of the course of studies.

Physical education classes are required and, because of widespread interest at all levels, both varsity and junior varsity competition exists in most sports. Other activities include drama, chanters' chorus and interest clubs. **See Also Page 1127**

CHADWICK SCHOOL
Day — Coed Gr K-12

Palos Verdes Peninsula, CA 90274. 26800 S Academy Dr. Tel: 310-377-1543.
Fax: 310-377-0380.
www.chadwickschool.org   E-mail: admissions@chadwickschool.org
Frederick T. Hill, Head. BA, Univ of North Carolina-Chapel Hill, MA, Middlebury College, MEd, Harvard Univ. **Judith Shaw Wolstan, Adm.**
Col Prep. AP—Eng Fr Span Bio US_Hist Art_Hist Studio_Art. **Feat**—Comp_Sci Photog Drama Music Dance Outdoor_Ed.
Adm (Gr K-11): 127/yr. Appl due: Jan. Accepted: 25%. **Tests** CTP_4 ISEE Stanford.
Enr 795. B 377. G 418. Elem 462. Sec 333. Wh 64%. Hisp 3%. Blk 8%. Asian 22%. Other 3%. Avg class size: 18. **Fac 92.** M 30/4. F 53/5. Wh 86%. Hisp 4%. Blk 6%. Am Ind 1%. Asian 3%. Adv deg: 52%.
Grad '04—76. Col—76. (USC 6, U of CO-Boulder 5, U of CA-Berkeley 3, U of CA-Santa Cruz 3, Yale 2, Wash U 2). Avg SAT: 1346. Alum 2500.
Tui '04-'05: Day $15,274-18,958 (+$400-600). **Aid:** Need 96 ($1,103,108).
Summer: Acad Enrich Rec. Arts. Tui Day $400-1600. 1-5 wks.
Endow $20,000,000. Bldgs 18. 2 Libs 28,000 vols. Sci labs 7. Comp labs 5. Auds 1. Theaters 1. Art studios 5. Music studios 3. Dance studios 1. Amphitheaters 1. Gyms 1. Fields 2. Pools 1.
Est 1935. Nonprofit. Sem (Sept-June). **Assoc** CLS WASC.

Drawing students from Long Beach, the South Bay and West Los Angeles, Chadwick conducts a college preparatory curriculum that enables boys and girls to develop talents in art, music and drama. In grades K-6, course work emphasizes fundamental learning skills, sound study habits and an appreciation for the arts. Foreign language instruction commences with Spanish in kindergarten, and pupils may switch to French in grade 6.

Technology is integrated into the curriculum in every grade. Qualified upper school students may enroll in Advanced Placement courses in the major disciplines. Outdoor education, which is an integral part of the program, features exploration of the diverse Southwestern landscape through a wilderness leadership program.

Various community service opportunities and academic and interest clubs are offered. Upper schoolers (grades 9-12) may compete interscholastically in football, water polo, cross-country, volleyball, tennis, golf, basketball, soccer, baseball, swimming and diving, track, lacrosse and softball. **See Also Page 1130**

CURTIS SCHOOL
Day — Coed Gr K-8

Los Angeles, CA 90049. 15871 Mulholland Dr. Tel: 310-476-1251. Fax: 310-476-1542. www.curtisschool.org

Stephen E. Switzer, Head. BA, Hanover College, MA, Oberlin College. **Mimi W. Petrie, Adm.**

Pre-Prep. Feat—Computers Studio_Art Drama Music. **Supp**—Rem_Math Rem_Read Tut.

Adm: 99/yr. Appl due: Nov. Accepted: 31%. **Tests** ISEE.

Enr 520. B 262. G 258. Elem 520. Avg class size: 22. Uniform. **Fac 48.** M 12/1. F 32/3. Wh 94%. Hisp 2%. Blk 2%. Asian 2%. Adv deg: 37%.

Grad '04—85. Prep—78. (Harvard-Westlake, Windward-CA, Crossroads-CA, Marlborough). Alum 3000.

Tui '04-'05: Day $15,850-18,680 (+$1500). **Aid:** Need 18 ($200,559).

Summer: Acad Enrich Rem Rec. Tui Day $1750/3-wk ses. 6 wks.

Endow $6,000,000. Plant val $20,000,000. Bldgs 8. Class rms 26. Lib 14,000 vols. Sci labs 3. Comp labs 2. Auds 1. Art studios 2. Music studios 2. Gyms 1. Fields 3. Basketball courts 3. Tennis courts 1. Volleyball courts 1. Pools 1.

Est 1925. Nonprofit. Tri (Sept-June).

Situated on a 27-acre tract at the summit of the Santa Monica Mountains, Curtis maintains a traditional elementary program for children with varying learning styles. In the lower school years (grades K-3), the curriculum focuses on the child's natural curiosity while providing an academic foundation for future learning. Pupils become increasingly independent in the self-contained middle school (grades 4-8). Grades 7 and 8 provide students with a structured small-class environment that prepares them for competitive area secondary schools. Study skills and work habits receive particular emphasis in the later years.

The arts are integral to school life, with regularly scheduled dramatic performances, poetry recitals, readings and other artistic activities complementing classroom studies. The school's well-developed athletic program includes interscholastic competition for both boys and girls in grades 4-8.

HARVARD-WESTLAKE SCHOOL
Day — Coed Gr 7-12

North Hollywood, CA 91604. 3700 Coldwater Canyon Ave. Tel: 818-980-6692. Fax: 818-487-6631.

www.harvardwestlake.com   E-mail: admissions@hw.com

Thomas C. Hudnut, Head. AB, Princeton Univ, MA, Tufts Univ. **Elizabeth B. Gregory, Adm.**

Col Prep. AP—Eng Fr Lat Span Calc Stats Bio Chem Human_Geog Physics US_Hist World_Hist Comp_Govt & Pol US_Govt & Pol Art_Hist Studio_Art. **Feat**—Chin Japan Anat & Physiol Astron Genetics Geol Oceanog Psych Film Drama Debate Journ Speech.

Adm (Gr 7-11): 295/yr. Appl due: Jan. **Tests** ISEE SSAT.

Enr 1550. B 790. G 760. Elem 460. Sec 1090. Wh 70%. Hisp 5%. Blk 7%. Asian 18%. Avg class size: 16. **Fac 218.** M 100/3. F 110/5. Adv deg: 66%.

Grad '04—267. Col—267. (USC 20, U of PA 15, Columbia 13, Stanford 11, U of MI 11,

NYU 10). Avg SAT: 1392. Alum 7000.
Tui '04-'05: Day $21,400 (+$2000). **Aid:** Need 213 ($2,088,100).
Summer: Acad Enrich Rec. Tui Day $90-1500. 1-4 wks.
Endow $26,000,000. Plant val $52,000,000. Bldgs 19. Class rms 131. Lib 20,000 vols. Sci labs 7. Lang labs 1. Comp labs 2. Photog labs 2. Auds 1. Art studios 4. Music studios 3. Dance studios 2. Arts ctrs 2. Gyms 2. Fields 2. Courts 4. Pools 2.
Est 1900. Nonprofit. Episcopal. Sem (Sept-June). **Assoc** CLS WASC.

Harvard-Westlake School was formed from the 1989 merger of Harvard School for boys, founded in 1900, and the Westlake School for girls, established in 1904. The school occupies both former campuses, with grades 7-9 located at the Westlake campus (700 N. Faring Rd., Los Angeles 90077) and grades 10-12 conducted on the Harvard campus on Coldwater Canyon Avenue.

The college preparatory curriculum features individualized work and instruction, and it is supplemented by a variety of elective courses. A more tightly structured program is offered in the lower grades, with increased independent responsibility introduced as the student progresses.

Seniors may develop their own independent study programs. Students may participate in School Year Abroad or Mountain School, and student exchange programs with sister schools in Tokyo, Japan, and Russia are also available. Boys and girls fulfill community service requirements in all grades.

Extracurricular activities include student government, publications, debate, drama, music and clubs. Harvard-Westlake's interscholastic sports program features a wide range of teams for both boys and girls.

JOHN THOMAS DYE SCHOOL

Day — Coed Gr K-6

Los Angeles, CA 90049. 11414 Chalon Rd. Tel: 310-476-2811. Fax: 310-476-9176.
  www.jtdschool.com   E-mail: jhirsch@jtdschool.com
Raymond R. Michaud, Jr., Head. BA, Univ of San Francisco, MA, California Lutheran College. **Judy Hirsch, Adm.**
  Pre-Prep. Feat—Computers Studio_Art Music. **Supp**—Rev Tut.
  Adm: 53/yr. Appl due: Rolling. **Tests** CTP_4.
  Enr 331. B 156. G 175. Elem 331. Wh 77%. Hisp 5%. Blk 6%. Asian 10%. Other 2%. Avg class size: 20. Uniform. **Fac 43.** M 6. F 37. Wh 97%. Hisp 1%. Asian 2%. Adv deg: 25%.
  Grad '04—47. Prep—47. (Harvard-Westlake, Marlborough, Campbell Hall, Windward-CA). Alum 1200.
  Tui '03-'04: Day $15,950 (+$1500). **Aid:** Need 24 ($234,800).
  Summer: Acad Rec. Tui Day $375-750. 2-3 wks.
  Endow $14,000,000. Plant val $12,000,000. Bldgs 5. Class rms 18. Lib 12,000 vols. Sci labs 1. Comp labs 1. Art studios 1. Music studios 1. Gyms 1. Fields 1.
  Est 1929. Nonprofit. Sem (Sept-June). **Assoc** WASC.

In the hills overlooking the Pacific, JTD, formerly called Bel Air Town and Country School, is an outgrowth of Brentwood Town and Country School and is the oldest private elementary school in the city. The curriculum provides a rigorous academic program, along with a full program of arts, music, computer science and physical education. Community service is an integral part of school life.

After-school sports, including flag football, soccer, volleyball, baseball, basketball and track, begin in grade 4. John Dye prepares its students for secondary schools throughout the Los Angeles area.

LE LYCEE FRANCAIS DE LOS ANGELES
Day — Coed Gr PS-12

Los Angeles, CA 90034. 3261 Overland Ave. Tel: 310-836-3464. Fax: 310-558-8069.
www.mindspring.com/~lfla   E-mail: lfla@mindspring.com
Alain Anselme, Dir. Laurence Lagorce, Adm.
  Col Prep. Fr Bac. Bilingual. **Feat**—Fr Ger Greek Lat Span Film. **Supp**—ESL Rem_Read Tut.
  Adm: 494/yr. Appl due: Feb. Accepted: 20%. **Tests** SSAT.
  Enr 900. B 420. G 480. Elem 500. Sec 400. Wh 65%. Hisp 6%. Blk 18%. Am Ind 1%. Asian 10%. Avg class size: 20. Uniform. **Fac 125.** M 57. F 68. Adv deg: 56%.
  Grad '04—30. Col—30. (UCLA, U of Paris-France, USC, Princeton, Stanford, U of CA-Berkeley). Alum 838.
  Tui '01-'02: Day $8000-12,000 (+$1000). **Aid:** Need 120 ($200,000).
  Summer: Acad Enrich Rev Rem Rec. Tui Day $1500. 6 wks.
  Plant val $39,000,000. Bldgs 11. Class rms 72. 2 Libs 30,000 vols. Sci labs 2. Comp labs 5. Auds 1. Theaters 1. Art studios 2. Music studios 2. Dance studios 2. Courts 4. Pools 1.
  Est 1964. Nonprofit. Sem (Sept-June). **Assoc** WASC.

Le Lycee is an international, bicultural and bilingual institution. The curriculum is philosophically oriented to the academies of ancient Greece and adapted to the French national educational system. Students may prepare for the French Baccalaureate examination. Various athletics and extracurricular activities complement academics.

All first graders, along with most kindergartners, attend school at the Century City campus (10361 W. Pico Blvd., 90064). In addition, the school conducts preschool and kindergarten programs at 3055 Overland Ave. and at its Pacific Palisades campus (16720 Marquez Ave., Pacific Palisades 90272).

MARLBOROUGH SCHOOL
Day — Girls Gr 7-12

Los Angeles, CA 90004. 250 S Rossmore Ave. Tel: 323-935-1147. Fax: 323-933-0542.
www.marlboroughschool.org
Barbara E. Wagner, Head. BM, Michigan State Univ, MME, Univ of Colorado-Boulder. **Jeanette Woo Chitjian, Adm.**
  Col Prep. AP—Eng Fr Lat Span Calc Bio Chem Eur_Hist US_Hist World_Hist. **Feat**—Astron Genetics Geol Microbiol Fine_Arts Drama Dance Yoga.
  Adm: 159/yr. Appl due: Jan. Accepted: 44%. Yield: 63%. **Tests** ISEE.
  Enr 530. G 530. Elem 178. Sec 352. Wh 57%. Hisp 3%. Blk 10%. Asian 13%. Other 17%. Avg class size: 13. Uniform. **Fac 61.** M 17/4. F 31/9. Wh 91%. Hisp 3%. Asian 3%. Other 3%. Adv deg: 81%.
  Grad '04—76. Col—76. (USC 7, Stanford 6, Yale 4, Boston U 3, NYU 3, Tufts 3). Avg SAT: 1333. Alum 800.
  Tui '04-'05: Day $22,400 (+$1000-3000). **Aid:** Need 69 ($1,182,720).
  Summer: Enrich Rec. 6 wks.
  Endow $31,300,000. Plant val $50,000,000. Bldgs 4. Class rms 23. Lib 22,000 vols. Labs

5. Lang labs 1. Comp ctrs 1. Auds 1. Theaters 1. Art studios 2. Music studios 1. Dance studios 2. Perf arts ctrs 1. Media ctrs 1. Gyms 1. Fields 1. Courts 3. Pools 1.
Est 1889. Nonprofit. Sem (Sept-June). **Assoc** CLS WASC.

Established when Maine's Mary S. Caswell took two decades of work experience in Eastern schools to the West Coast, Marlborough is the oldest independent school for girls in southern California. The school now draws students from more than 100 area public and private elementary schools. Originally located in downtown Los Angeles, it moved to its present, four-acre site in Hancock Park in 1916.

At all grade levels, the curriculum incorporates discussion-based lessons, teamwork among students and hands-on learning. Marlborough maintains high academic standards, with the traditional academic program supplemented by a variety of electives, off-campus internships and community service opportunities. The school also maintains strong fine arts and performing arts programs. Through the integrated technology curriculum, girls are taught to use computers efficiently and to employ them as a learning aid.

Student council, publications, student government, interest clubs, debate, photography and community service projects are popular activities. Girls may compete interscholastically in tennis, swimming, volleyball, softball, soccer, basketball, track, cross-country and badminton.

MARYMOUNT HIGH SCHOOL

Day — Girls Gr 9-12

Los Angeles, CA 90077. 10643 Sunset Blvd. Tel: 310-472-1205. Fax: 310-476-0910.
www.mhs-la.org   E-mail: shelin@mhs-la.org
Mary Ellen Gozdecki, Head. BA, Marymount College, MA, PhD, Univ of Southern California. **Sharon Stephens, Adm.**

Col Prep. AP—Eng Fr Span Calc Bio Physics Eur_Hist US_Hist US_Govt & Pol Art_Hist. **Feat**—Humanities Irish_Lit Anat & Physiol Oceanog Engineering & Robotics Computers Econ Psych World_Relig Studio_Art Music.

Adm (Gr 9-11): 109/yr. Appl due: Jan. Accepted: 65%. **Tests** ISEE.

Enr 398. G 398. Sec 398. Wh 84%. Hisp 4%. Blk 5%. Am Ind 1%. Asian 6%. Avg class size: 15. Uniform. **Fac 57.** Adv deg: 63%.

Grad '04—101. Col—101. (U of CA-Berkeley, UCLA, Loyola Marymount, SMU, USC, Santa Clara). Avg SAT: 1207. Avg ACT: 25. Alum 2960.

Tui '04-'05: Day $18,600 (+$675-850). **Aid:** Merit 16 ($16,000). Need 59 ($527,524).

Summer: Acad Enrich Rec. Tui Day $500/crse. 5 wks.

Endow $3,332,000. Bldgs 6. Class rms 32. Lib 15,000 vols. Sci labs 5. Lang labs 1. Comp labs 2. Photog labs 1. Auds 1. Theaters 1. Art studios 1. Music studios 1. Gyms 1. Fields 1. Tennis courts 2. Pools 1.

Est 1923. Nonprofit. Roman Catholic. Sem (Aug-June). **Assoc** WASC.

Founded by the Religious of the Sacred Heart of Mary, Marymount emphasizes critical thinking and writing at all grade levels. The curriculum includes honors or Advanced Placement courses or both in all subject areas, and qualified girls may also engage in independent study projects. An extensive elective program allows students to pursue interests in such areas as oceanography, engineering and robotics, journalism and photography.

Drama productions, musicals, stage crew, talent shows, chorus, dance, instrumental music, handbell choir, photography, studio art and publications are among the cocurricular options, and girls may also take part in coeducational social activities. In addition, Marymount fields more than 20 varsity and junior varsity athletic teams. An active campus ministry program features class retreats and a community service requirement of 30 hours.

THE MIRMAN SCHOOL

Day — Coed Gr 1-9

Los Angeles, CA 90049. 16180 Mulholland Dr. Tel: 310-476-2868. Fax: 310-471-1532.
www.mirman.org
John Thomas West III, Head. Leslie Mirman Geffen, Adm.
   Pre-Prep. **Feat**—Creative_Writing Shakespeare Mythology Lat Span Computers Studio_Art Drama Chorus Music Orchestra Speech.
   Adm: 50/yr. Appl due: Mar. Accepted: 55%. **Tests** IQ.
   Enr 349. B 166. G 183. Elem 349. Wh 76%. Hisp 2%. Blk 5%. Asian 6%. Other 11%. Avg class size: 23. Uniform. **Fac 35.** M 11/1. F 21/2. Wh 86%. Hisp 8%. Blk 3%. Asian 3%. Adv deg: 37%.
   Grad '04—14. Prep—10. (Harvard-Westlake, Flintridge, Marymount HS, Campbell Hall, Buckley Sch-CA). Alum 338.
   Tui '04-'05: Day $15,250-16,300 (+$250-500). **Aid:** Need 49 ($327,564).
   Summer: Enrich. Travel. 1-5 wks.
   Endow $1,000,000. Plant val $3,000,000. Bldgs 4. Class rms 25. Lib 9330 vols. Sci labs 2. Comp labs 2. Auds 1. Art studios 1. Music studios 1. Fields 1. Courts 2.
   Est 1962. Nonprofit. Quar (Sept-June). **Assoc** WASC.

Founded by Beverly and Norman Mirman, the school provides an educational setting where academically gifted children may maximize their mental, physical, social and emotional potential. Mirman School admits only highly gifted children with IQs of 145 or above and allows students to proceed at an accelerated pace.

As the student population is gifted, the curriculum stresses depth, complexity, novelty and critical thinking at all grade levels. The well-rounded educational program encompasses the arts, computer science, foreign language and sports. Emphasis is placed on community service and the values of personal integrity, respect and caring. After-school enrichment classes and extracurricular activities are offered by both parents and teachers at various times during the school year.

OAKWOOD SCHOOL

Day — Coed Gr K-12

North Hollywood, CA 91601. 11600 Magnolia Blvd. Tel: 818-752-4400.
Fax: 818-766-1285.
   www.oakwoodschool.org   E-mail: mllinas@oakwoodschool.org
James Alan Astman, Head. BA, Univ of Rochester, MA, Colgate Rochester Divinity School, PhD, Claremont Graduate School. **Julia Coley,** Gr 7-12 Adm; **Nancy Goldberg,** Gr K-6 Adm.
   Col Prep. **AP**—Eng Fr Span Calc Stats Comp_Sci Bio Chem Physics US_Hist Comp_Govt & Pol Psych Art_Hist Music_Theory. **Feat**—Creative_Writing Shakespeare Fiction_Writing Japan Lat Number_Theory Astron Geol Econ Bible Philos Relig Ceramics Film Photog Sculpt African-Amer_Music Theater_Arts Music Ballet. **Supp**—Tut.
   Adm: 102/yr. Appl due: Feb. Accepted: 25%. **Tests** ISEE.
   Enr 756. B 365. G 391. Elem 442. Sec 314. Wh 80%. Hisp 6%. Blk 6%. Asian 7%. Other 1%. Avg class size: 20. **Fac 81.** Wh 85%. Hisp 2%. Blk 5%. Asian 8%. Adv deg: 56%.
   Grad '04—80. Col—79. (NYU 5, USC 5, UCLA 4, U of CA-Berkeley 4, U of MI 4, Yale 2).

Avg SAT: 1300. Avg ACT: 26. Alum 1380.
Tui '04-'05: Day $17,610-20,610 (+$975-1975). **Aid:** Need 97 ($1,388,720).
Summer: Enrich. 4 wks.
Endow $4,800,000. Plant val $17,774,000. Bldgs 22. Class rms 49. Libs 2. Sci labs 6. Comp labs 2. Auds 1. Theaters 1. Art studios 7. Music studios 3. Dance studios 1. Gyms 1. Weight rms 1.
Est 1951. Nonprofit. Sem (Sept-June). **Assoc** WASC.

Oakwood's location in North Hollywood offers students convenient access to the cultural, intellectual and recreational advantages of the Los Angeles metropolitan area. The curriculum combines a rigorous academic program with a broad exposure to the fine and performing arts.

Opportunities beyond the traditional college preparatory curriculum are offered through electives, special studies, field trips and extracurricular activities. Electives include African-American music in society, film in society, modern American literature, number theory and cryptology, philosophy of mathematics, psychological theory and social philosophy. Students may develop their own areas of interest for special study.

As a complement to classroom learning, Oakwood students in grades 6-11 spend a week away from school participating in an organized experiential program. Settings include Washington, DC; the mountains surrounding Big Bear Lake; the Catalina Island Marine Institute; Joshua Tree National Park; Sequoia National Park; and the Sonoran Desert, where 11th graders canoe down the Colorado River.

Among Oakwood's extracurricular activities are student government, publications, a variety of interscholastic and intramural team and individual sports, and dramatic productions. Students may also participate in mathematics competitions, county and national science fairs, and the school's annual arts festival.

The school's two campuses occupy nearly four acres. Each location has a nearby park to use for a variety of athletic activities. The elementary school occupies quarters at 11230 Moorpark St., 91602.

PILGRIM SCHOOL

Day — Coed Gr PS-12

Los Angeles, CA 90020. 540 S Commonwealth Ave. Tel: 213-385-7351.
Fax: 213-386-7264.
www.pilgrim-school.org   E-mail: info@pilgrim-school.org
Valerie Pearson, Int Head. BA, California State Univ-Los Angeles. **Becky Riley Fisher, Adm.**
Col Prep. AP—Eng Span Calc Bio Chem US_Hist Art_Hist. **Feat**—Japan Ethics World_Relig Photog Studio_Art Dance Journ. **Supp**—Dev_Read ESL Makeup Tut.
Adm: 63/yr. Appl due: Mar. **Tests** CEEB CTP_4 ISEE.
Enr 370. B 198. G 172. Wh 29%. Hisp 9%. Blk 34%. Asian 28%. Avg class size: 14. Uniform. **Fac** 52. M 18/3. F 29/2. Wh 58%. Hisp 14%. Blk 13%. Am Ind 9%. Other 6%. Adv deg: 38%.
Grad '04—18. Col—18. (USC, UCLA, Stanford, CA Col of Arts & Crafts, Pitzer, San Diego St). Avg SAT: 1130. Alum 1760.
Tui '04-'05: Day $9700-14,500 (+$350-750). **Aid:** Need 72 ($205,200).
Summer: Acad Rem Rec. 2-6 wks.
Plant val $5,000,000. Bldgs 2. Class rms 43. Lib 11,000 vols. Labs 3. Art studios 1.
Est 1958. Nonprofit. Congregational. Sem (Sept-June). **Assoc** WASC.

A division of the First Congregational Church of Los Angeles, Pilgrim School offers a college preparatory program that emphasizes the mastery of fundamental skills. Preschoolers, who may enroll prior to age 3, meet weekly with specialists in the areas of music, storytelling, athletics and library usage. Kindergartners and first graders receive instruction in reading, arithmetic, phonics and penmanship. The program in grades 2-6 includes English grammar, history, geography, social science and math. Foreign language study begins in kindergarten and features Spanish and Japanese. Art, music, computers and values education are conducted at all grade levels.

The secondary school (grades 7-12) provides a traditional college preparatory program that includes AP classes. Among elective courses are dance, drama, journalism, music, choir and psychology. Physical education offerings include group and individual sports, eight-man football, basketball, baseball and volleyball.

TURNING POINT SCHOOL

Day — Coed Gr PS-8

Culver City, CA 90232. 8780 National Blvd. Tel: 310-841-2505. Fax: 310-841-5420.
www.turningpointschool.org   E-mail: info@turningpointschool.org

Deborah Richman, Head. BSE, Stephen F Austin State Univ, MEd, Univ of Houston. **Maggi Wright, Adm.**

Pre-Prep. Feat—Lat Span Environ_Sci Studio_Art Music. **Supp**—Dev_Read Tut.

Adm (Gr PS-7): 75/yr. Appl due: Jan. Accepted: 59%. Yield: 57%. **Tests** ISEE.

Enr 338. B 170. G 168. Elem 338. Wh 74%. Hisp 2%. Blk 7%. Asian 4%. Other 13%. Avg class size: 17. **Fac 53.** M 10/2. F 40/1. Adv deg: 28%.

Grad '04—17. Prep—13. (Buckley Sch-CA 2, Campbell Hall 2, Archer 2, Crossroads-CA 1, Harvard-Westlake 1, Marymount HS 1). Alum 560.

Tui '04-'05: Day $15,360-17,410 (+$1000). **Aid:** Need 29 ($210,405).

Summer: Enrich Rec. Tui Day $300-1300. 1-6 wks.

Endow $421,000. Plant val $12,000,000. Bldgs 1. Class rms 20. Lib 10,000 vols. Sci labs 2. Lang labs 1. Comp labs 1. Auds 1. Art studios 1. Music studios 1. Dance studios 1. Gyms 1. Fields 1. Courts 1.

Est 1970. Nonprofit. (Sept-June). **Assoc** WASC.

Founded as Montessori of Los Angeles by a group of local educators and business professionals who adhered to the teachings of Maria Montessori, the school assumed its present name in October 1989. The Montessori-based primary division leads to an elementary division (grades K-5) that provides a traditional curriculum and includes specialist-taught classes in art, music, Spanish, science and athletics. Turning Point's middle school (grades 6-8) seeks to further develop students' interests while preparing them for secondary education.

Beginning in the elementary school, study tours augment classroom instruction. These tours may include field trips to museums, cultural centers, regions of geographical interest and other educational destinations. Activities frequently incorporate current events and relevant social issues. Athletics and opportunities in the fine arts complete the program.

VIEWPOINT SCHOOL

Day — Coed Gr K-12

Calabasas, CA 91302. 23620 Mulholland Hwy. Tel: 818-340-2901. Fax: 818-591-0834.
www.viewpoint.org   E-mail: info@viewpoint.org

Robert J. Dworkoski, Head. BA, George Washington Univ, MA, New York Univ, MA, PhD, Columbia Univ. **Laurel Baker Tew, Adm.**

Col Prep. AP—Eng Fr Span Calc Comp_Sci Robotics Bio Chem Physics Eur_Hist US_Hist World_Hist Comp_Govt & Pol Psych Studio_Art Music_Theory. **Feat**—Creative_Writing Humanities Poetry Lat Mandarin Stats Ecol Environ_Sci Oceanog Neurosci Asian_Hist African_Hist Middle_Eastern_Hist Econ Intl_Relations Pol_Sci Art_Hist Ceramics Film Photog Sculpt Drama Band Chorus Orchestra Dance Speech Outdoor_Ed. **Supp**—Tut.

Adm: 177/yr. Appl due: Jan. Accepted: 56%. Yield: 72%. **Tests** ISEE.

Enr 1158. B 581. G 577. Elem 731. Sec 427. Wh 77%. Hisp 4%. Blk 3%. Am Ind 1%. Asian 9%. Other 6%. Avg class size: 18. **Fac 107.** M 42. F 65. Wh 86%. Hisp 4%. Blk 2%. Asian 4%. Other 4%. Adv deg: 39%.

Grad '04—82. Col—82. (U of CA 20, USC 7, U of San Diego 6, U of CO-Boulder 4, Yale 3, Stanford 3). Avg SAT: 1285. Alum 1167.

Tui '04-'05: Day $15,750-17,800 (+$475-1000). **Aid:** Need 92.

Summer: Acad Enrich Rev Rem. Tui Day $1890. 6 wks.

Endow $4,401,000. Plant val $14,410,000. Bldgs 23. Class rms 78. 3 Libs 20,000 vols. Sci labs 8. Comp labs 6. Theaters 1. Art studios 5. Music studios 5. Gyms 1. Fields 3. Courts 4. Pools 3. Weight rms 1.

Est 1961. Nonprofit. Sem (Sept-June). **Assoc** CLS WASC.

Viewpoint provides an enriched, traditional program for children in the elementary grades, and a comprehensive, college preparatory curriculum for students in grades 6-12 that includes an array of honors and Advanced Placement courses. In addition to increasing factual knowledge, the school's academic program further develops pupils' critical-thinking skills. Viewpoint's small-class setting enables teachers to work closely with each student.

Various creative, athletic and extracurricular options complement academics. Extracurricular activities include foreign exchanges, publications, dramatic productions, chorus, orchestra, student government, mock trial, a science fair, rocketry competitions and an array of interest clubs. **See Also Pages 1264-5**

LOS GATOS, CA. (8 mi. SW of San Jose, CA; 51 mi. SE of San Francisco, CA) Suburban. Pop: 28,592. Alt: 428 ft.

HILLBROOK SCHOOL

Day — Coed Gr PS-8

Los Gatos, CA 95032. 300 Marchmont Dr. Tel: 408-356-6116. Fax: 408-358-1286.
www.hillbrook.org   E-mail: hillbrook@hillbrook.org

Sarah Bayne, Head. BA, Sarah Lawrence College, MA, Columbia Univ. **Ann Morrissey, Adm.**

Pre-Prep. Gen Acad. Feat—Span Computers Ceramics Studio_Art Music Woodworking.

Adm (Gr PS-6): 53/yr. Appl due: Jan.

Enr 315. B 145. G 170. Elem 315. Wh 70%. Hisp 2%. Blk 3%. Am Ind 1%. Asian 14%. Other 10%. Uniform. **Fac 38.** M 6/1. F 26/5. Adv deg: 36%.

Grad '04—35. Prep—19. (Castilleja, Milton Acad). Alum 1000.
Tui '04-'05: Day $16,150.
Bldgs 14. Class rms 21.
Est 1936. Nonprofit. Tri (Sept-June).

Located on a 14-acre campus in the foothills of the Santa Cruz Mountains, Hillbrook offers a balanced program that combines academic rigor with active and experiential elements. In addition to the core subjects, the curriculum includes art, music, drama, Spanish, physical education, and wood shop and ceramics beginning in grade 1. Swimming, football, volleyball, softball and basketball are part of the physical education program.

LOS OLIVOS, CA.
(28 mi. NW of Santa Barbara, CA; 105 mi. WNW of Los Angeles, CA) Rural. Pop: 800. Alt: 1000 ft.

DUNN SCHOOL
Bdg — Coed Gr 9-12; Day — Coed 6-12

Los Olivos, CA 93441. 2555 Hwy 154, PO Box 98. Tel: 805-688-6471. Fax: 805-686-2078.
www.dunnschool.org E-mail: admissions@dunnschool.org

James L. Munger, Head. BA, Goddard College, MEd, Sierra Univ. **Ann Greenough-Coats, Adm.**

Col Prep. AP—Eng Fr Span Calc Stats Bio Chem Physics US_Hist. **Feat**—Computers Comp_Design Econ Human_Dev Ceramics Photog Drama Music Outdoor_Ed. **Supp**—LD.

Adm: 54/yr. Appl due: Feb. Accepted: 38%. **Tests** ISEE SSAT TOEFL.

Enr 172. B 66/35. G 38/33. Wh 85%. Hisp 5%. Blk 4%. Asian 3%. Other 3%. Avg class size: 12. **Fac 32.** M 14/2. F 15/1. Wh 91%. Hisp 9%. Adv deg: 46%. In dorms 7.

Grad '04—33. Col—33. (U of CA-Riverside, U of CA-Santa Barbara, Menlo, U of AZ, Lewis & Clark, CA St Polytech). Avg SAT: 1200. Alum 934.

Tui '04-'05: Bdg $32,200. Day $12,400-14,800. Aid: Need 44 ($347,050).

Summer: Acad Enrich Rec. Tui Bdg $5000. Tui Day $450/crse. 6 wks.

Endow $3,000,000. Plant val $5,400,000. Bldgs 15. Dorms 4. Dorm rms 66. Class rms 18. Lib 10,000 vols. Sci labs 3. Comp labs 1. Art studios 2. Music studios 1. Ceramics studios 1. Gyms 1. Fields 1. Courts 4. Pools 1.

Est 1957. Nonprofit. Sem (Sept-June). **Assoc** WASC.

The English-born and -educated Anthony B. Dunn established this preparatory school as a boys' program providing a rigorous academic program in a family atmosphere. Girls were admitted as day students in 1971, and, in 1990, Dunn opened its boarding facilities to girls for the first time.

Located in the Santa Ynez Valley, the school borders on the Los Padres National Forest. The approach is traditional and the curriculum college preparatory. The school also operates an well-developed outdoor education program. Class sizes average ten to 12 students.

Dunn offers a learning skills program at an additional cost for high-ability students with learning disabilities. Limited to 34 pupils, this program allows students to participate in the regular curriculum and also receive daily, one-on-one remediation with specialists in language skills.

Pupils may engage in such activities as camping, kayaking and ceramics. Athletics include soccer, lacrosse, basketball, cross-country, volleyball, baseball, swimming, track and field, and tennis. Students assist in maintaining the school through a daily jobs program.

MIDLAND SCHOOL

Bdg — Coed Gr 9-12

Los Olivos, CA 93441. 5100 Figueroa Mountain Rd, PO Box 8. Tel: 805-688-5114. Fax: 805-686-2470.

www.midland-school.org   E-mail: dsvennungsen@midland-school.org

David S. Lourie, Head. BA, Yale Univ. **Derek Svennungsen, Adm.**

Col Prep. Feat—Creative_Writing Geol Holocaust Anthro Ceramics Music_Theory Metal_Shop. **Supp**—Tut.

Adm (Gr 9-11): 41/yr. Appl due: Rolling. Accepted: 40%. **Tests** ISEE SSAT Stanford.

Enr 76. B 48. G 28. Sec 76. Wh 65%. Hisp 20%. Blk 3%. Asian 12%. Avg class size: 11.
Fac 15. M 6/4. F 4/1. Wh 85%. Hisp 15%. Adv deg: 20%. In dorms 15.

Grad '04—22. Col—20. (U of CA-Davis, Wellesley, NYU, Bryn Mawr, Lewis & Clark, Reed).

Tui '04-'05: Bdg $27,500 (+$500). **Aid:** Need 32 ($535,000).

Endow $3,000,000. Plant val $30,000,000. Libs 1. Sci labs 2. Lang labs 1. Comp labs 1. Art studios 1. Music studios 1. Gyms 1. Fields 2. Riding rings 1. Gardens 1.

Est 1932. Nonprofit. Sem (Sept-June). **Assoc** WASC.

With an outdoor ranch life that utilizes opportunities provided by the school's setting, Midland retains the rugged simplicity that has characterized the school since its inception. Influential in the region, this successful college preparatory school was the creation of Paul and Louise Squibb, its founders and heads for 20 years.

Midland's curriculum provides a solid liberal arts grounding in the basic disciplines and allows qualified pupils to participate in independent study and Advanced Placement programs. Academic classes meet Monday through Saturday, with each specific course generally assembling on five of the six days; students attend four or five classes per day. Elective choice varies annually depending upon student interest.

All pupils live on campus in wood cabins. As the school is a working ranch, students grow and harvest their own food in a 12-acre organic garden. Boys and girls also share various other chores on the ranch. Seniors oversee the work program with the supervision of faculty, thereby developing leadership skills.

In addition to the integrated communal projects, students take part in such activities as cultural excursions and interscholastic and intramural athletics. Interscholastic offerings include volleyball, baseball, soccer, lacrosse and cross-country, and a popular equestrian program consists of horse husbandry and both English and Western riding. Situated on a 2860-acre tract in the Santa Ynez Valley, the school also provides students with many opportunities for camping and hiking.

MONTEREY, CA. (48 mi. S of San Jose, CA; 90 mi. SSE of San Francisco, CA) Urban. Pop: 29,674. Alt: 40 ft.

SANTA CATALINA SCHOOL
Bdg — Girls Gr 9-12; Day — Boys PS-8, Girls PS-12

Monterey, CA 93940. 1500 Mark Thomas Dr. Tel: 831-655-9356. Fax: 831-655-7535. www.santacatalina.org   E-mail: admissions@santacatalina.org

Sr. Claire Barone, Head. BA, Univ of San Francisco. **Marian Donovan Corrigan, Adm.**

    Col Prep. AP—Eng Fr Span Calc Bio Chem US_Hist Studio_Art. **Feat**—Creative_Writing Humanities Lat Stats Marine_Biol/Sci Computers African-Amer_Hist Econ World_Relig Photog Drama. **Supp**—Tut.

    Adm (Bdg Gr 9-11; Day PS-11): 104/yr. Bdg 59. Day 45. Appl due: Feb. **Tests** SSAT.

    Enr 566. B 102. G 155/309. Elem 266. Sec 300. Wh 84%. Hisp 3%. Blk 1%. Asian 8%. Other 4%. Avg class size: 14. Uniform. **Fac 41.** M 19. F 22. Adv deg: 78%. In dorms 37.

    Grad '04—69. Col—69. (Boston U 3, U of CA-Davis 3, Loyola Marymount 3, CT Col 2, NYU 2, Stanford 2). Avg SAT: 1250. Alum 2700.

    Tui '04-'05: Bdg $33,000 (+$1000). **Day $20,400** (+$675). **Aid:** Merit 7 ($7900). Need 58 ($1,282,100).

    Summer: Gr 3-9. Enrich Rec. Tui Bdg $2200-4000. 2½-5 wks.

    Endow $23,000,000. Bldgs 21. Dorms 3. Dorm rms 92. Class rms 26. Lib 33,000 vols. Sci labs 4. Lang labs 3. Comp labs 3. Theaters 1. Art studios 2. Music studios 6. Dance studios 1. Recital halls 1. Gyms 1. Fields 1. Courts 6. Pools 1.

    Est 1950. Nonprofit. Roman Catholic. Sem (Aug-June). **Assoc** CLS WASC.

The academic curriculum concentrates in all the traditional college preparatory areas, with particular emphasis placed on the arts and sciences. The coeducational lower school (grades pre-K-8) stresses a firm foundation in the basic academic skills; limited class size and individual attention help to develop self-reliance and good citizenship. Computer technology is an important aspect of the program.

The location of the school on the Monterey Peninsula and the 36-acre campus afford many opportunities for outdoor activities. Among the team and individual sports are tennis, swimming and diving, field hockey, softball, soccer, lacrosse, volleyball, basketball, track, cross-country, golf, water polo and horseback riding.

OAKLAND, CA. (18 mi. E of San Francisco, CA) Urban. Pop: 399,484. Alt: 155 ft.

THE COLLEGE PREPARATORY SCHOOL
Day — Coed Gr 9-12

Oakland, CA 94618. 6100 Broadway. Tel: 510-652-0111. Fax: 510-652-7467. www.college-prep.org   E-mail: nettie_anthony-harris@college-prep.org

Murray Cohen, Head. BA, MA, PhD, Johns Hopkins Univ. **Nettie Anthony-Harris, Adm.**

    Col Prep. AP—Fr Lat Span Calc Stats Bio Chem Studio_Art Music_Theory. **Feat**—Japan Astron Genetics Computers Psych Animal_Behavior Philos Health. **Supp**—Tut.

    Adm (Gr 9-11): 85/yr. Appl due: Jan. Accepted: 43%. Yield: 63%. **Tests** ISEE.

    Enr 329. B 163. G 166. Sec 329. Avg class size: 14. **Fac 46.** M 17/2. F 24/3. Wh 83%. Hisp 4%. Blk 4%. Asian 9%. Adv deg: 76%.

Grad '04—78. Col—77. (Stanford 7, U of CA-Berkeley 7, UCLA 4, U of CA-San Diego 4, Harvard 3, Columbia 3). Avg SAT: 1395. Alum 2086.

Tui '04-'05: Day $21,550 (+$1000). **Aid:** Need 70 ($1,053,100).

Endow $7,360,000. Plant val $6,356,000. Bldgs 14. Class rms 15. Lib 14,000 vols. Sci labs 5. Lang labs 1. Comp labs 3. Dark rms 1. Theater/auds 1. Art studios 2. Music studios 1. Dance studios 1. Gyms 1. Fields 1.

Est 1960. Nonprofit. Sem (Sept-June). **Assoc** CLS WASC.

Founded by Mary H. Jenks and Ruth M. Willis, this day school with a strong academic emphasis prepares students in small classes for colleges throughout the country. The program stresses the development of both communicational skills and historical perspective, and it includes offerings in art, drama, dance, photography, music and debate. Advanced Placement courses in most subjects are available to qualified juniors and seniors.

Debate, class retreats, an intra-term program and community service are integral school features. Soccer, volleyball, basketball, tennis, swimming, baseball, softball, cross-country, track, golf and lacrosse are among the interscholastic sports offered.

HEAD-ROYCE SCHOOL

Day — Coed Gr K-12

Oakland, CA 94602. 4315 Lincoln Ave. Tel: 510-531-1300. Fax: 510-530-8329.
www.headroyce.org   E-mail: lkoven@headroyce.org

Paul D. Chapman, Head. BA, Yale Univ, MA, PhD, Stanford Univ. **Catherine Epstein, Adm.**

Col Prep. AP—Eng Fr Lat Span Calc Stats Comp_Sci Bio Physics Eur_Hist US_Hist Art_Hist Studio_Art Music_Theory. **Feat**—Shakespeare Astron Marine_Biol/Sci Psych Film Theater Music.

Adm (Gr K-11): 122/yr. Appl due: Jan. Accepted: 25%. **Tests** ISEE.

Enr 750. B 370. G 380. Elem 430. Sec 320. Wh 60%. Hisp 4%. Blk 10%. Asian 16%. Other 10%. Avg class size: 15. **Fac 96.** M 36. F 60. Wh 72%. Hisp 5%. Blk 8%. Asian 14%. Other 1%. Adv deg: 53%.

Grad '04—81. Col—81. (U of CA-Berkeley, UCLA, USC, Stanford, Harvard, U of PA). Avg SAT: 1358. Alum 2500.

Tui '04-'05: Day $15,620-21,685 (+$2000). **Aid:** Need 119 ($1,250,000). Work prgm 68 ($15,000).

Summer: Gr K-8. Acad Enrich Rev Rec. 6 wks.

Endow $10,000,000. Plant val $20,000,000. Bldgs 5. Class rms 38. Libs 2. Sci labs 2. Lang labs 1. Comp labs 3. Auds 1. Theaters 1. Art studios 6. Music studios 2. Gyms 1. Fields 2. Courts 1. Pools 1.

Est 1887. Nonprofit. (Aug-June). **Assoc** CLS WASC.

Founded in Berkeley as the Anna Head School for Girls, this school relocated in 1964 to its present campus. The Josiah Royce School for Boys opened at an adjacent site in 1971 as a coordinate school. Since 1978, Head-Royce has been fully coeducational.

Head-Royce's college preparatory curriculum allows graduates to gain admittance to leading colleges. The cocurricular program is stressed, and there are many interest clubs, publications, and drama, art and music offerings. Students may also participate in and earn credits for an academic year abroad program or a student exchange program. The school offers intramural and interscholastic competition in field sports, tennis, swimming and basketball.

CA Pacific States 721

OJAI, CA. (27 mi. E of Santa Barbara, CA; 53 mi. WNW of Los Angeles, CA) Suburban. Pop: 7862. Alt: 750 ft.

HAPPY VALLEY SCHOOL
Bdg and Day — Coed Gr 9-12

Ojai, CA 93024. 8585 Ojai-Santa Paula Rd, PO Box 850. Tel: 805-646-4343.
 Fax: 805-646-4371.
 www.hvs.org E-mail: admin@hvs.org
David Anderson, Dir. Adrian Sweet, Adm.

> **Col Prep. AP**—Eng Physics. **Feat**—Fr Span Environ_Sci Comp_Sci 20th-Century_Hist Anthro Psych Comp_Relig Ethics Ceramics Photog Studio_Art Digital_Arts Drama Music_Theory. **Supp**—ESL Tut.
> **Adm (Bdg Gr 9-10; Day 9):** 47/yr. Bdg 36. Day 11. Appl due: Rolling. Accepted: 78%. **Tests** SSAT.
> **Enr 86.** B 35/10. G 26/15. Sec 86. Wh 55%. Hisp 2%. Blk 1%. Am Ind 1%. Asian 40%. Avg class size: 11. **Fac 17.** M 4/5. F 4/4. Wh 94%. Hisp 5%. Blk 1%. In dorms 4.
> **Grad '04—24. Col—24.** (U of CA-Santa Cruz 2, Evergreen St 2, San Francisco St 2, HI Pacific 2, CA St Polytech 1, Sarah Lawrence 1). Avg SAT: 1200. Alum 735.
> **Tui '04-'05: Bdg $33,800** (+$1500). **Day $17,900** (+$1500). **Aid:** Need 1 ($17,000).
> Plant val $4,000,000. Bldgs 9. Dorms 2. Class rms 17. Lib 10,000 vols. Labs 2. Theaters 1. Art studios 3. Music studios 2. Perf arts ctrs 1. Fields 1. Courts 2.
> **Est** 1946. Nonprofit. Sem (Sept-June). **Assoc** WASC.

A project of the Happy Valley Foundation, a cultural organization established by Dr. Annie Besant for educational purposes, this school occupies a rural campus on a 450-acre tract.

The varied program provides sound academic preparation, and Happy Valley maintains a community setting that stresses responsibility and mutual consideration. An active fine arts program supplements course work in the core subjects and constitutes an integral part of the school curriculum. HVS has been successful in preparing students for college, while also promoting the development of wide intellectual and artistic interests and an international outlook.

OJAI VALLEY SCHOOL
Bdg — Coed Gr 3-12; Day — Coed PS-12

Ojai, CA 93023. 723 El Paseo Rd. Tel: 805-646-1423. Fax: 805-646-0362.
 www.ovs.org E-mail: admission@ovs.org
Michael D. Hermes, Pres. John H. Williamson, Adm.

> **Col Prep. Gen Acad. AP**—Eng Fr Span Calc Bio Chem Studio_Art. **Feat**—Humanities Poetry Lat Stats Geol Computers Econ Psych Philos Film Photog Drama Music Equitation. **Supp**—ESL Rem_Math Rem_Read Tut.
> **Adm (Bdg Gr 3-11; Day PS-11):** 75/yr. Bdg 48. Day 27. Appl due: Rolling. Accepted: 70%. **Tests** ISEE SSAT Stanford TOEFL.
> **Enr 370.** B 86/95. G 84/105. Elem 236. Sec 134. Wh 81%. Hisp 1%. Blk 2%. Am Ind 1%. Asian 15%. Avg class size: 12. **Fac 59.** M 21/2. F 35/1. Wh 99%. Other 1%. Adv deg: 30%. In dorms 7.
> **Grad '04—23. Col—23.** (UCLA, U of CA-Riverside, U of CA-Santa Barbara, U of CO-Boulder, St Lawrence, Mt Holyoke). Avg SAT: 1144. Alum 3047.
> **Tui '04-'05: Bdg $34,070** (+$1520). **5-Day Bdg $27,300** (+$570). **Day $8690-15,500** (+$570-1125). **Aid:** Need 38 ($200,000).

Summer: Acad Enrich Rev Rem Rec. ESL. Riding. Soccer. Tui Bdg $2175-5930. Tui Day $1175-3200. 2-6 wks.

Endow $1,000,000. Plant val $7,300,000. Bldgs 26. Dorms 4. Dorm rms 173. Class rms 26. Lib 12,000 vols. Sci labs 3. Lang labs 1. Comp ctrs 2. Art studios 2. Music studios 1. Amphitheaters 1. Shops 1. Fields 5. Courts 7. Pools 2. Riding rings 2. Stables 2. Ropes crses 1.

Est 1911. Nonprofit. Sem (Sept-June). **Assoc** WASC.

Ojai Valley was founded by Mr. and Mrs. Walter Bristol as the Bristol School, which conducted tutorials for elementary students. Edward Yeomans, a businessman interested in education, purchased the school in 1922. Under his direction, the school was renamed Ojai Valley and its program was expanded using Mr. Yeomans' progressive philosophy of "learning by doing." During the tenure of headmaster Wallace Burr (1943 to 1970), the school changed in character from a small country day program to a predominantly boarding school. Mr. Burr also built an upper school campus in the East End of Ojai Valley, and today the school encompasses 200 acres bordering national forest property. The upper school is six miles from the lower school.

Academic work and life experiences are integrated at Ojai, and emphasis is placed on the development of leadership and decision-making skills. Motivated students benefit from the college preparatory curriculum, which includes Advanced Placement classes. Opportunities offered beyond the small classes are student government, community service, an extensive equestrian program, camping and outdoor skills, interscholastic sports, music and the arts. Weekend excursions throughout southern California provide students with entertainment options, as well as cultural and recreational activities.

THE THACHER SCHOOL

Bdg and Day — Coed Gr 9-12

Ojai, CA 93023. 5025 Thacher Rd. Tel: 805-646-4377. Fax: 805-646-9490.
www.thacher.org   E-mail: admission@thacher.org

Michael K. Mulligan, **Head.** BA, MA, Middlebury College, EdM, Harvard Univ. **William P. McMahon, Adm.**

Col Prep. AP—Eng Fr Span Calc Stats Bio Chem Physics US_Hist Art_Hist Studio_Art Music_Theory. **Feat**—Chin Anat & Physiol Astron Ecol Geol Marine_Biol/Sci Civil_ War Econ Govt Philos Public_Speak. **Supp**—Rev Tut.

Adm (Gr 9-11): 75/yr. Bdg 67. Day 8. Appl due: Feb. Accepted: 27%. Yield: 89%. **Tests** ISEE SSAT.

Enr 241. B 110/10. G 112/9. Sec 241. Wh 71%. Hisp 6%. Blk 8%. Am Ind 2%. Asian 12%. Other 1%. Avg class size: 12. **Fac 45.** M 17/5. F 17/6. Wh 88%. Hisp 6%. Blk 2%. Am Ind 2%. Asian 2%. Adv deg: 82%. In dorms 12.

Grad '04—62. Col—62. (Stanford, USC, Brown, CO Col, U of CA-Berkeley, Northwestern). Avg SAT: 1340. Alum 2193.

Tui '04-'05: Bdg $32,750 (+$400). **Day** $21,850 (+$200). **Aid:** Need 70.

Endow $60,000,000. Plant val $35,000,000. Bldgs 85. Dorms 9. Dorm rms 167. Class rms 31. Lib 29,000 vols. Chapels 2. Sci labs 3. Lang labs 1. Comp labs 2. Observatories 1. Auds 1. Theaters 1. Art studios 3. Music studios 2. Gyms 1. Fields 4. Courts 10. Pools 1. Riding facilities yes. Rifle ranges 1.

Est 1889. Nonprofit. Sem (Sept-May). **Assoc** CLS WASC.

The school was founded by Sherman Thacher, who combined the New England boarding school tradition with Western character, emphasizing the value of the outdoors. Thacher is situated on the old Casa de Piedra Ranch: 400 acres nestled at the east end of the Ojai Valley at the foot of the Los Padres National Forest.

The academic program includes a core curriculum of requirements in English, mathematics, foreign language, the sciences, history and the fine arts. Students expand beyond this core through a rich array of electives and Advanced Placement courses, independent study and senior exhibitions (interdisciplinary research and demonstration projects). Several exchange programs provide learning opportunities beyond the school.

Competitive athletics include tennis, soccer, track, volleyball, baseball, cross-country, lacrosse and basketball, all of which are offered at two or more levels. Dance and general fitness/weightlifting are also available. All students take part each season in either a team sport, the horse program or the outdoor program, which features such activities as rock and ice climbing, telemarking, downhill and cross-country skiing, winter camping, sea and river kayaking, and snowshoeing. While ninth graders may participate in athletics, their primary afternoon focus is on the horse program, a century-long tradition that requires each student to ride and care for one of Thacher's horses. The first-year experience culminates in the Big Gymkhana—games and races participants take part in while on horseback.

The fine arts program includes musical, studio art, dance and dramatic instruction. Other activities at Thacher include publications, a radio station, interest clubs, student government and a wide range of community service options.

ORANGE, CA. (40 mi. ESE of Los Angeles, CA) Urban. Pop: 128,821. Alt: 176 ft.

ELDORADO-EMERSON SCHOOL
Day — Coed Gr PS-12

Orange, CA 92869. 4100 E Walnut St. Tel: 714-633-4774. Fax: 714-744-3304.
www.eldorado-emerson.org   E-mail: majelix@socal.rr.com
Glory B. Ludwick, Dir. AB, Univ of California-Berkeley, MD, Univ of California-San Francisco. **Jeanne Weller, Adm.**

- **Col Prep. AP**—Eng Span Calc Bio. **Feat**—Fr Ger Greek Hebrew Mandarin Arabic Drama Chorus Music Orchestra Fitness & Nutrition. **Supp**—Dev_Read ESL Rem_Math Rem_Read Tut.
- **Adm:** 30/yr. Appl due: Rolling. Accepted: 80%. **Tests** Stanford TOEFL.
- **Enr 171.** B 99. G 72. Elem 121. Sec 50. Wh 68%. Hisp 3%. Blk 4%. Am Ind 1%. Asian 23%. Other 1%. Avg class size: 15. **Fac 25.** M 6/2. F 14/3. Wh 72%. Hisp 12%. Asian 12%. Other 4%. Adv deg: 24%.
- **Grad '04—22. Col—22.** (U of CA, CA St U, Chapman, USC). Avg SAT: 1300. Alum 400.
- **Tui '03-'04: Day $8230** (+$800). **Aid:** Merit 2 ($16,000). Need 15 ($80,000).
- **Summer:** Acad Enrich Rev Rem Rec. Tui Day $850. 6 wks.
- Plant val $4,000,000. Bldgs 10. Class rms 24. Lib 20,000 vols. Sci labs 1. Lang labs 2. Comp labs 1. Theater/auds 1. Art studios 2. Music studios 2. Dance studios 1. Art galleries 3. Gyms 1. Fields 1. Courts 2. Pools 2.
- **Est 1959.** Nonprofit. Sem (Sept-July). **Assoc** WASC.

Eldorado-Emerson provides instruction for elementary students in ungraded achievement groups. The curriculum comprises English, math, computer, foreign languages, science, social studies, physical education, music and art. High school students choose from a variety of honors and Advanced Placement courses, and they may earn college credit in several disciplines. The music program includes orchestral and choral instruction.

An after-school program addresses the needs of children at risk of developing dyslexia. Drama, kung fu and strength training are among the extracurricular options.

PALO ALTO, CA. (17 mi. WNW of San Jose, CA; 35 mi. SE of San Francisco, CA) Urban. Pop: 58,598. Alt: 63 ft. Area also includes Portola Valley.

INTERNATIONAL SCHOOL OF THE PENINSULA

Day — Coed Gr PS-8

Palo Alto, CA 94303. 151 Laura Ln. Tel: 650-251-8500. Fax: 650-251-8501.
   www.istp.org   E-mail: istp@istp.org
Philippe Dietz, Head. James Pao, Adm.
   Gen Acad. IB MYP. Bilingual. Feat—Humanities Fr Mandarin Span Computers Studio_ Art Music. **Supp**—ESL Rem_Math Rem_Read Rev Tut.
   Adm: 146/yr. Appl due: Rolling. Accepted: 75%.
   Enr 485. Elem 485. Wh 80%. Hisp 1%. Blk 2%. Asian 17%. Avg class size: 15. **Fac 72.** Wh 87%. Asian 13%. Adv deg: 72%.
   Grad '04—18.
   Tui '05-'06: Day $13,610-16,500 (+$500-750). **Aid:** Need ($300,000).
   Summer: Enrich Rec. Fr. Mandarin. Tui Day $400/2-wk ses. 8 wks.
   Endow $90,000. Plant val $8,000,000. Bldgs 2. Class rms 30. 3 Libs 12,000 vols. Sci labs 1. Comp labs 1. Studios 1. Gyms 1. Fields 1. Courts 2.
   Est 1979. Nonprofit. Sem (Sept-June). **Assoc** WASC.

ISTP opened its doors as the Peninsula French-American School and, in 1996, became the International School of the Peninsula, adding a Chinese-American section, a middle school and a second campus. Providing immersion-based bilingual and multicultural education, the school maintains an additional location at 3233 Cowper St., 94306. The lower campus on Cowper Street serves children in prekindergarten and kindergarten, while the main campus on Laura Lane offers instruction for pupils in grades 1-8.

The French-American section, which prepares students to continue their studies at French, American or international high schools, admits only French-speaking students after kindergarten. A full program of computer science, nature study, athletics, music and art complements the academic curriculum.

A second curriculum, provided for those in prekindergarten through grade 4, devotes equal time to Mandarin Chinese and English and prepares children to enter American secondary schools.

The international middle school program is based upon the International Baccalaureate Middle Years curriculum. Students of this program attain proficiency in at least two languages from the following group: English, French, Mandarin Chinese and Spanish. Academic course work addresses all major subject areas and emphasizes critical thinking.

WOODSIDE PRIORY SCHOOL

Bdg — Coed Gr 9-12; Day — Coed 6-12

Portola Valley, CA 94028. 302 Portola Rd. Tel: 650-851-8221. Fax: 650-851-2839.
www.woodsidepriory.com   E-mail: azappelli@woodsidepriory.com

Timothy Molak, Head. BA, Christian Brothers Univ, MA, St Mary's Univ, MAEd, St Thomas Univ. **Al D. Zappelli, Adm.**

Col Prep. AP—Eng Calc Bio US_Hist Econ Studio_Art. **Feat**—Fr Span Stats Astron Comp_Sci Anthro Psych Theol Architect Ceramics Film Photog Drama Speech. **Supp**—Tut.

Adm (Bdg Gr 9-11; Day 6-11): 82/yr. Bdg 12. Day 70. Appl due: Jan. Accepted: 36%. **Tests** CTP_4 HSPT ISEE SSAT TOEFL.

Enr 340. B 32/158. G 8/142. Avg class size: 18. **Fac 70.** Wh 92%. Hisp 5%. Am Ind 3%. Adv deg: 61%. In dorms 8.

Grad '04—50. Col—50. (Stanford 5, UCLA 3, U of CA-Santa Barbara 3, USC 3, Harvard 1, Princeton 1). Avg SAT: 1250. Alum 1000.

Tui '04-'05: Bdg $35,015 (+$750). **Day $23,830** (+$750). **Aid:** Merit 1 ($10,000). Need 60 ($832,000).

Endow $1,000,000. Bldgs 12. Dorms 2. 2 Libs 20,000 vols. Chapels 1. Sci labs 5. Lang labs 3. Comp labs 2. Auds 1. Theaters 1. Art studios 1. Music studios 1. Gyms 1. Fields 4. Courts 4. Tennis courts 4. Pools 1.

Est 1957. Nonprofit. Roman Catholic. Sem (Aug-June). **Assoc** WASC.

Begun by a group of Benedictine monks, Woodside Priory operated as a boys' boarding and day school until 1991, when girls were first admitted as day students. In fall 2003, the school expanded its boarding program to include girls. The school currently employs a monastic and lay faculty that directs a rigorous academic program supplemented with athletics, the fine arts, community service and a strong program of cocurricular activities.

Students receive a solid academic grounding in English, science, math, social studies, the fine arts and foreign language. A broad range of elective, honors and Advanced Placement classes supplements the curriculum. Approved students may pursue directed individual study, and specially gifted students may arrange to take college-level courses. Among the graduation requirements are foreign language, computer science, theology, the fine and performing arts, and electives; community service is also mandatory in the high school.

Activities include publications, a variety of interest clubs, student government and Amnesty International. Woodside Priory fields teams in soccer, volleyball, basketball, tennis, cross-country and track, baseball, swimming and softball.

PASADENA, CA. (16 mi. ENE of Los Angeles, CA) Urban. Pop: 133,936. Alt: 829 ft. See also Los Angeles.

WESTRIDGE SCHOOL

Day — Girls Gr 4-12

Pasadena, CA 91105. 324 Madeline Dr. Tel: 626-799-1153. Fax: 626-799-9236.
www.westridge.org

Fran Norris Scoble, Head. BA, Baylor Univ, MAT, Vanderbilt Univ. **Helen Varlas Hopper, Adm.**

Col Prep. AP—Eng Fr Lat Span Calc Stats Comp_Sci Bio Chem Physics Eur_Hist US_

Hist Art_Hist Studio_Art. **Feat**—Creative_Writing Shakespeare Psych Asian_Stud Comp_Relig Photog Theater Music Music_Hist Music_Theory Dance. **Supp**—Tut.
Adm: 75/yr. Appl due: Feb. Accepted: 33%. **Tests** CTP_4 ISEE.

Enr 510. G 510. Elem 247. Sec 263. Wh 63%. Hisp 6%. Blk 4%. Asian 21%. Other 6%. Avg class size: 19. Uniform. **Fac 54.** M 36/1. F 12/5. Wh 83%. Hisp 3%. Blk 3%. Asian 9%. Other 2%. Adv deg: 68%.

Grad '04—61. Col—60. (Boston U, USC, UCLA, U of CA-Santa Cruz, U of Chicago, Wash U).

Tui '04-'05: Day $18,000-19,300 (+$725). **Aid:** Need 72 ($654,495).

Summer: Acad Enrich Rec. Tui Day $150-385. 1-4 wks.

Endow $10,700,000. Plant val $11,986,000. Bldgs 15. Class rms 41. Lib 21,289 vols. Sci labs 3. Comp labs 4. Auds 2. Theaters 2. Art studios 4. Music studios 4. Dance studios 1. Gyms 1. Fields 1.

Est 1913. Nonprofit. Sem (Aug-June). **Assoc** CLS WASC.

Westridge was founded when two mothers concerned that there was no school for their daughters on Pasadena's west side convinced noted area architect Mary Lowther Ranney to open a girls' school in her home. From the start, enrollment exceeded expectations, leading Miss Ranney to purchase a larger home on Madeline Drive and move the school to the Tudor building that now serves as the campus centerpiece. Upon Miss Ranney's retirement in 1936, a group of parents purchased the school and chartered it as a nonprofit institution with a board of trustees.

The structured lower school curriculum (grades 4-6) emphasizes independent learning and the development of sound study skills. Westridge's middle school (grades 7-8) provides a transitional program that readies girls for more intensive course work in the higher grades. Students choose from an array of honors and Advanced Placement courses in the upper school (grades 9-12), while also taking part in performing arts activities, athletics and experiential education. Field trips to various points of interest provide enrichment.

Extracurricular activities include music, drama, publications, Junior Classical League, student government and community service. All girls take part in the athletic program; interscholastic and intramural competition is available in tennis, volleyball, basketball, swimming and diving, soccer, softball, and track and field.

PEBBLE BEACH, CA. (57 mi. S of San Jose, CA; 101 mi. SSE of San Francisco, CA) Suburban. Pop: 4700.

ROBERT LOUIS STEVENSON SCHOOL

Bdg — Coed Gr 9-12; Day — Coed K-12

Pebble Beach, CA 93953. 3152 Forest Lake Rd. Tel: 831-625-8300. Fax: 831-625-5208. www.rlstevenson.org   E-mail: info@rlstevenson.org

Joseph E. Wandke, Pres. BA, St Olaf College, MA, Stanford Univ. **Thomas W. Sheppard, Adm.**

Col Prep. AP—Eng Fr Lat Span Calc Bio Chem Physics Eur_Hist US_Hist Econ Studio_Art. **Feat**—Ital Japan Marine_Biol/Sci Comp_Sci Psych Film Photog Drama.

Adm (Bdg Gr 9-11; Day K-11): 209/yr. Bdg 112. Day 97. Appl due: Feb. Accepted: 41%. Yield: 60%. **Tests** SSAT TOEFL.

Enr 753. B 135/241. G 133/244. Elem 209. Sec 544. Wh 68%. Hisp 2%. Blk 2%. Am Ind 1%. Asian 16%. Other 11%. Avg class size: 14. **Fac 74.** M 39/1. F 29/5. Wh 95%. Hisp

1%. Blk 2%. Asian 2%. Adv deg: 52%. In dorms 20.
Grad '04—121. Col—121. (USC 12, U of CA-Berkeley 5, UCLA 4, Stanford 3, Boston U 3, Cornell 2). Avg SAT: 1279. Alum 4700.
Tui '04-'05: Bdg $33,600 (+$2000). **Day $20,050** (+$2000). **Aid:** Need 84 ($1,200,000).
Summer: Enrich Rec. Tui Bdg $4100. Tui Day $2200. 5 wks.
Endow $13,000,000. Plant val $55,000,000. Bldgs 37. Dorms 6. Dorm rms 171. Class rms 41. Lib 17,000 vols. Labs 7. Theaters 1. Art studios 2. Dance studios 2. Gyms 1. Fields 3. Courts 8. Pools 1. Student ctrs 1.
Est 1952. Nonprofit. Tri (Sept-May). **Assoc** WASC.

Stevenson offers a rigorous liberal arts preparatory program for leading colleges. The traditional curriculum emphasizes trust and self-reliance. Basic skills courses are supplemented by opportunities for exploring special interests in depth. Beginning and advanced courses are offered in all of the fine arts. Subjects such as studio art, ceramics, photography, stagecraft, acting and voice are available.

A broad range of athletic programs and several student exchange programs complement academics. The school is located in the Del Monte Forest and shares in the climatic and scenic advantages of the Monterey Peninsula. The lower and middle school campus is situated in nearby Carmel (24800 Dolores St., 93923).

REDLANDS, CA. (71 mi. E of Los Angeles, CA) Urban. Pop: 63,591. Alt: 1351 ft.

VALLEY PREPARATORY SCHOOL
Day — Coed Gr PS-8

Redlands, CA 92373. 1605 Ford St. Tel: 909-793-3063. Fax: 909-798-5963.
www.valleypredlands.org   E-mail: info@valleypredlands.org
Jerald E. Klocek, Head. BA, Baldwin-Wallace College, MA, Univ of California-Riverside.
Pre-Prep. Feat—Lib_Skills Fr Span Computers Studio_Art Drama Music. **Supp**—Tut.
Adm: 45/yr. Appl due: Rolling. Accepted: 90%. **Tests** ISEE.
Enr 243. Elem 243. Wh 67%. Hisp 7%. Blk 3%. Am Ind 3%. Asian 20%. Avg class size: 18. Uniform. **Fac 24.** M 5. F 17/2. Wh 87%. Hisp 7%. Blk 3%. Asian 3%. Adv deg: 29%.
Grad '04—20. Prep—5.
Tui '04-'05: Day $5824-8189. Aid: Merit 4 ($2000). Need 35 ($72,373).
Summer: Enrich Rev Rec. Tui Day $75/crse. 2-6 wks.
Endow $100,000. Plant val $2,000,000. Bldgs 7. Class rms 25. Libs 1. Sci labs 1. Comp labs 1. Art studios 1. Music studios 1. Fields 1.
Est 1957. Nonprofit. (Sept-June). **Assoc** WASC.

Founded by a group of parents, Valley provides a traditional elementary program for average and above-average students living in Redlands and the surrounding areas. An extended-day program features cooking, crafts, physical education and study hall. Foreign languages are taught beginning in prekindergarten.

A full athletic program, as well as computers, music, and visual and performing arts offerings, is also offered.

ROSS, CA. (12 mi. N of San Francisco, CA) Rural. Pop: 2329. Alt: 23 ft.

BRANSON SCHOOL
Day — Coed Gr 9-12

Ross, CA 94957. 39 Fernhill Ave, PO Box 887. Tel: 415-454-3612. Fax: 415-454-4669. www.branson.org E-mail: bridget_anderson@branson.org

Paul Druzinsky, Head. BA, Claremont McKenna College, EdM, Harvard Univ. **Bridget N. Anderson, Adm.**

    Col Prep. AP—Eng Fr Lat Span Calc Stats Bio Chem Physics US_Hist World_Hist Art_Hist. **Feat**—Ital Japan Marine_Biol/Sci Comp_Design Programming Cold_War Econ Psych Comp_Relig Philos Architect Ceramics Photog Acting Music Music_Theory Study_Skills.

    Adm: 87/yr. Appl due: Jan. Accepted: 22%. **Tests** SSAT.

    Enr 320. B 155. G 165. Sec 320. Wh 83%. Hisp 1%. Blk 8%. Am Ind 1%. Asian 7%. **Fac 40.**

    Grad '04—80. Col—80. (Stanford, U of CA-Berkeley, U of MI, Brown, Duke). Avg SAT: 1301. Avg SSAT: 90%. Alum 2650.

    Tui '03-'04: Day $23,400 (+$500-1000). **Aid:** Need 52 ($525,000).

    Summer: Acad Rec. 6 wks.

    Endow $1,500,000. Plant val $4,100,000. Bldgs 15. Class rms 26. Lib 12,000 vols. Sci labs 5. Lang labs 1. Photog labs 1. Comp ctrs 1. Auds 1. Theaters 3. Art studios 7. Music studios 2. Amphitheaters 1. Drama studios 1. Gyms 1. Fields 1. Basketball courts 2. Pools 1. Weight rms 1.

    Est 1920. Nonprofit. Tri (Sept-June). **Assoc** CLS WASC.

In 1920, Katharine F. Branson reorganized the San Rafael Girls' School, established in 1917. It was renamed the Katherine Branson School, and in 1922 it moved to Ross. Mount Tamalpais, the coordinate school founded by KBS for day boys, opened on the campus in 1972. The name was changed to the Branson School in 1985.

The campus is located on 18 wooded acres, 15 miles north of San Francisco. The college preparatory curriculum offers Advanced Placement courses in every discipline, a wide selection of electives, courses in the fine arts, independent study and a three-week work-study intern program for all seniors.

All students participate in the physical education program. Both team and individual sports are offered in such areas as hiking, crew, riding, fencing, track, swimming, field hockey, baseball, softball, soccer, tennis, cross-country, rock climbing, backpacking, badminton, basketball, cycling, dance, golf, lacrosse, skiing and volleyball.

SACRAMENTO, CA. (80 mi. NE of San Francisco, CA) Urban. Pop: 407,018. Alt: 30 ft. Area also includes Fair Oaks.

SACRAMENTO COUNTRY DAY SCHOOL
Day — Coed Gr PS-12

Sacramento, CA 95864. 2636 Latham Dr. Tel: 916-481-8811. Fax: 916-481-6016.

www.saccds.org   E-mail: lbloedau@saccds.org

Stephen T. Repsher, Head. BA, Union College (NY), MA, New York Univ. **Lonna Bloedau, Adm.**

Col Prep. AP—Eng Fr Lat Span Calc Bio Chem Physics Eur_Hist US_Hist Art_Hist. Feat—British_Lit Japan Environ_Sci World_War_II Fine_Arts. **Supp**—Tut.

Adm (Gr PS-11): 102/yr. Appl due: Rolling.

Enr 551. B 262. G 289. Wh 75%. Hisp 3%. Blk 2%. Asian 5%. Other 15%. Avg class size: 15. **Fac 67.** Adv deg: 47%.

Grad '04—40. Col—40. (U of CA-Santa Cruz 12, U of CA-Davis 10, St Mary's Col of CA 6, Occidental 5, Whittier 5, Whitman 5). Avg SAT: 1231. Alum 340.

Tui '04-'05: Day $9400-12,800 (+$25-1000).

Summer: Acad Enrich Rec. Sports. 10 wks.

Bldgs 20. Class rms 36. 2 Libs 15,000 vols. Labs 3. Art studios 1. Music studios 1. Gyms 1. Fields 4.

Est 1964. Nonprofit. Sem (Sept-June). **Assoc** CLS WASC.

Established by Herbert H. Matthews, SCDS has grown steadily since its founding. Students in grades 7-12 participate in an enrichment program that offers courses in art, drama, debate, journalism, computers, music, yearbook and poetry. Daily team sports and physical education are required of all students. Soccer, basketball, volleyball, and track and field are included in this program.

SACRAMENTO WALDORF SCHOOL

Day — Coed Gr PS-12

Fair Oaks, CA 95628. 3750 Bannister Rd. Tel: 916-961-3900. Fax: 916-961-3970.
www.sacwaldorf.org   E-mail: info@sacwaldorf.org

Elizabeth Beaven, Admin. BA, MA, Univ of Auckland (New Zealand). **Lisa Moore, Adm.**

Col Prep. Feat—Ger Greek Studio_Art Drama Music Dance Eurythmy Gardening. **Supp**—Makeup Tut.

Adm: 63/yr. Appl due: Jan. Accepted: 82%. **Tests** TOEFL.

Enr 423. Avg class size: 22. **Fac 56.** M 11/7. F 24/14. Wh 91%. Hisp 7%. Blk 2%. Adv deg: 23%.

Grad '04—29. Col—27. (U of CA-Santa Cruz, Chapman, Am River, Stanford, Vassar, US Air Force Acad). Avg SAT: 1204. Alum 540.

Tui '03-'04: Day $6500-10,250 (+$500). **Aid:** Need 91 ($166,500).

Summer: Rec. Tui Day $150/wk. 5 wks.

Endow $294,000. Plant val $4,000,000. Bldgs 16. Class rms 25. Lib 2500 vols. Labs 2. Auds 1. Theaters 1. Art studios 1. Music studios 2. Gyms 1. Fields 3.

Est 1959. Nonprofit. Sem (Sept-June). **Assoc** WASC.

Through its artistic approach to education, the basis of the Waldorf philosophy, the school provides a firm foundation in the arts, the humanities and the sciences. With main lessons studied in blocks for several weeks at a time, objective scientific subjects are alternated with the humanities to give variety and rhythm to the school year.

In grades 1-8, a teacher remains with his or her class as it advances each year, thereby giving each child security and confidence while deepening the teacher's responsibility for and knowledge of the pupil. Specialist teachers provide instruction in grades 9-12. Foreign language instruction commences in grade 1, when both German and Spanish are introduced.

Sacramento Waldorf schedules field trips to local points of interest, and students in grades 4-12 take camping trips and engage in community service.

SAN ANSELMO, CA. (13 mi. N of San Francisco, CA) Suburban. Pop: 12,378. Alt: 45 ft.

SAN DOMENICO SCHOOL

Bdg — Girls Gr 9-12; Day — Boys PS-8, Girls PS-12

San Anselmo, CA 94960. 1500 Butterfield Rd. Tel: 415-258-1905. Fax: 415-258-1906.
www.sandomenico.org   E-mail: admissions@sandomenico.org

Mathew Heersche, Head. BA, MA, California State Univ-Northridge, EdD, Univ of San Francisco. **Wendy Feltham, Adm.**

- Col Prep. Gen Acad. **AP**—Eng Fr Span Calc Stats Bio Chem Physics US_Hist Studio_Art. **Feat**—Creative_Writing Computers Amer_Stud Intl_Relations Ethics Relig Art_Hist Photog Drama Theater_Arts Music Music_Hist Dance. **Supp**—ESL Tut.
- **Adm (Bdg Gr 9-11; Day PS-11):** 116/yr. Bdg 15. Day 101. Appl due: Jan. Accepted: 55%. **Tests** HSPT ISEE SSAT TOEFL.
- **Enr 562.** Elem 402. Sec 160. Wh 84%. Hisp 2%. Blk 2%. Asian 12%. Avg class size: 12. Uniform. **Fac 88.** M 17/4. F 46/21. Wh 97%. Hisp 3%. Adv deg: 28%. In dorms 5.
- **Grad '04—36. Col—36.** (U of CA-Berkeley 6, UCLA 4, U of CA-Davis 2, Catholic U 2, U of CO-Boulder 2). Avg SAT: 1230. Avg SSAT: 80%. Alum 2700.
- **Tui '04-'05: Bdg $37,202** (+$1500). **Day $13,624-21,642** (+$1000). **Aid:** Merit 21 ($448,972). Need 71 ($813,875).
- **Summer:** Enrich Rec. 8 wks.
- Endow $5,000,000. Plant val $18,000,000. Bldgs 10. Dorms 3. Dorm rms 35. Class rms 55. Lib 21,000 vols. Sci labs 5. Comp labs 3. Auds 2. Theaters 1. Art studios 2. Dance studios 1. Conservatories 1. Gyms 1. Fields 2. Courts 6. Pools 1. Riding rings 3. Stables yes.
- **Est 1850.** Nonprofit. Roman Catholic. Sem (Aug-June). **Assoc** WASC.

The school was founded in Monterey by Sr. Mary Goemaere, a Dominican nun from Paris, France, and later relocated to Benicia. In 1889, the school moved again, this time to San Rafael, where, as Dominican Convent, it provided preparatory and elementary education for 76 years. Renamed San Domenico in 1965, when it shifted operations to its present, 515-acre campus, the school is the oldest independent school in California. The primary and middle schools enroll both girls and boys, while the upper school accepts girls only. Although the program is sponsored by the Dominican Sisters of San Rafael, approximately half of the students come from non-Catholic families.

San Domenico's primary and middle school curricula provide a firm grounding in the basic skills. In addition to the core courses of math, English, science, social studies and religion, young students receive instruction in foreign language, computer, physical education, music and art.

At the high school level, girls follow an integrated curriculum that features honors and Advanced Placement classes in all subject areas. San Domenico offers many opportunities for involvement in athletics, the performing arts and service learning. Particularly noteworthy is the school's music conservatory, which provides music and voice instruction for students of all ages, as well as preprofessional music training for high schoolers. A preprofessional theater program allows girls to act, direct and participate in all aspects of technical design.

SAN FRANCISCO, CA. Urban. Pop: 776,733. Alt: to 155 ft.

CATHEDRAL SCHOOL FOR BOYS
Day — Boys Gr K-8

San Francisco, CA 94108. 1275 Sacramento St. Tel: 415-771-6600. Fax: 415-771-2547.
www.cathedralschool.net   E-mail: postmaster@cathedralschool.net
Michael Ferreboeuf, Head. BA, Univ of California-Berkeley, MA, Univ of San Francisco. **Dorothy Sayward Wylie, Adm.**
- **Pre-Prep. Feat**—Fr Lat Mandarin Span Computers Ethics Drama Chorus Music Public_ Speak. **Supp**—Dev_Read.
- **Adm:** 42/yr. Appl due: Jan. Accepted: 34%. Yield: 66%.
- **Enr 244.** B 244. Elem 244. Wh 66%. Hisp 4%. Blk 5%. Asian 11%. Other 14%. Avg class size: 15. Uniform. **Fac 37.** M 12/1. F 16/8. Wh 97%. Hisp 1%. Blk 1%. Asian 1%. Adv deg: 51%.
- **Grad '04—34. Prep—34.** (Lick-Wilmerding 4, San Francisco U HS 2, Urban 2, Marin Acad 2). Alum 792.
- **Tui '04-'05: Day** $16,100. **Aid:** Merit 1 ($16,100). Need 47 ($463,100).
- **Summer:** Acad Enrich. 4-8 wks.
- Endow $9,000,000. Plant val $6,000,000. Bldgs 2. Class rms 17. Lib 12,000 vols. Sci labs 1. Comp labs 1. Auds 1. Theaters 1. Art studios 1. Music studios 2. Gyms 1. Courts 2.
- **Est 1957.** Nonprofit. Episcopal. Quar (Sept-June). **Assoc** WASC.

Cathedral provides a traditional pre-preparatory program. The literature-based language arts program features a reading specialist and a developmental approach to reading (with small reading groups across grade levels), while the math curriculum progresses from a manipulative approach to a more abstract one that emphasizes computational and thinking skills. Spanish and Mandarin courses begin in grade 5, while all boys study Latin in grades 7 and 8. CSB's curriculum also includes an English language structures class for fifth and sixth graders. A full science lab and a technology lab further enrich Cathedral's program.

Music and art programs are integral to school life. Some boys enter the Grace Cathedral choir in grade 4, although most take part in the regular music program, which includes a handbell choir and voice training. Band, string ensemble and instrumental music lessons are also available. A well-developed art program, taught in both classroom and studio settings, is integrated at all grade levels. Sports include soccer, basketball, baseball and cross-country.

Other notable aspects of the program are electives in grades 3-8, regular field trips, weeklong environmental excursions, community service opportunities and international travel during intersession and winter break. An extended-day program serving children in grades K-6 operates before and after school.

DREW COLLEGE PREPARATORY SCHOOL
Day — Coed Gr 9-12

San Francisco, CA 94115. 2901 California St. Tel: 415-409-3739. Fax: 415-346-0720.
www.drewschool.org   E-mail: todd@drewschool.org
Samuel M. Cuddeback III, Head. AB, MALS, Dartmouth College. **Tearon Joseph, Adm.**
- **Col Prep. AP**—Fr Span Calc Chem Physics US_Govt & Pol. **Feat**—Humanities Shakespeare Computers Anthro Econ Psych Sociol. **Supp**—ESL Rev Tut.
- **Adm:** 85/yr. Appl due: Jan. **Tests** SSAT.

Enr 250. Sec 250. Wh 67%. Hisp 1%. Blk 5%. Asian 27%. Avg class size: 14. **Fac 30.** M 10/1. F 17/2. Adv deg: 60%.
Grad '04—48. Col—46. (U of CA-Berkeley, U of CA-Santa Cruz, U of CO-Boulder, San Francisco St, Brandeis). Alum 750.
Tui '04-'05: Day $23,200. Aid: Need 65 ($800,000).
Summer: Acad Enrich Rem. Tui Day $600/4-wk ses. 8 wks.
Bldgs 1. Class rms 14. Lib 15,000 vols. Sci labs 2. Lang labs 1. Comp labs 1. Theaters 1. Art studios 1. Music studios 1. Dance studios 1.
Est 1908. Nonprofit. Sem (Aug-June). **Assoc** WASC.

Founded by John S. Drew, this school combines college preparation with a variety of electives, arts and athletics. The full preparatory curriculum includes Advanced Placement courses in the major disciplines, as well as French and Spanish language classes. Drama, music, drawing, photography, computer programming and literary magazine are among the school's nonacademic electives. All freshmen participate in a special class designed to ease the transition into high school.

As students from outside the US constitute roughly five percent of its enrollment, Drew provides intermediate and advanced English as a Second Language instruction. An outdoor education program organizes day hikes and overnight camping trips throughout the year. Students may compete on interscholastic teams in volleyball, soccer, basketball and baseball.

FRENCH-AMERICAN INTERNATIONAL SCHOOL

Day — Coed Gr PS-12

San Francisco, CA 94102. 150 Oak St. Tel: 415-558-2000. Fax: 415-558-2024.
www.fais-ihs.org   E-mail: fais@fais-ihs.org
Jane Camblin, Head. Betsy Brody & Edie Wexler, Adms.

Col Prep. IB Diploma. Fr Bac. Bilingual. Feat—Creative_Writing Ger Mandarin Span Computers Econ Philos Studio_Art Drama Music Debate Journ Speech. **Supp**—ESL LD.
Adm: 150/yr. Appl due: Jan. Accepted: 30%. **Tests** ISEE SSAT.
Enr 888. Elem 583. Sec 305. Wh 79%. Hisp 4%. Blk 8%. Asian 9%. Avg class size: 20. **Fac 100.** Adv deg: 54%.
Grad '04—65. Col—65. (UCLA, Oxford-England, Yale, Cornell, Columbia, Tufts).
Tui '05-'06: Day $23,790 (+$500). **Aid:** Need 222.
Summer: Rec. 3-9 wks.
Endow $1,030,000. Plant val $25,000,000. Bldgs 2. Lib 18,000 vols. Sci labs 5. Comp labs 4. Theaters 1. Art studios 2. Music studios 2. Gyms 1. Playgrounds 3.
Est 1962. Nonprofit. (Sept-June). **Assoc** WASC.

Founded as the French-American Bilingual School, FAIS changed its name in 1984 to reflect its growing international focus and established the International High School in 1976. In 1997, FAIS and IHS moved from rented facilities at the University of California Extension complex to their present location at the International Schools Campus in San Francisco's Civic Center. Approximately 70 percent of FAIS' students are American; the remaining 30 percent represent numerous countries and languages. No previous French language background is required to enter the lower school at the prekindergarten or kindergarten level or the ninth grade of IHS. English as a Second Language and French as a Second Language may be available.

French is the language of instruction 80 percent of the time throughout the early childhood immersion program, while, in grades 3-5, students are taught academic subjects half the time in French and half in English. A third language (Mandarin, German or Spanish) is introduced in sixth grade. Students at the International High School of FAIS choose between the French Baccalaureate and the International Baccalaureate programs; in addition, they may prepare for Advanced Placement exams. Graduates matriculate at universities throughout the world, and those enrolling at American universities may enter with up to a full year of college credit.

All high school students participate in a cocurricular program consisting of such "creative, action and service" activities as drama, art, theater, sports and various community service programs. Exchange trips allow participants to live and learn with students and families of the host country. Opportunities also exist for extended study abroad.

HAMLIN SCHOOL

Day — Girls Gr K-8

San Francisco, CA 94115. 2120 Broadway. Tel: 415-922-0300. Fax: 415-674-5409.
www.hamlin.org E-mail: newlin@hamlin.org
Coreen Ruiz Hester, Head. AB, MEd, Stanford Univ. **Lisa Lau Aquino, Adm.**

Pre-Prep. Feat—Computers Studio_Art Drama Dance.

Adm: 71/yr. Appl due: Dec. Accepted: 58%. Tests CTP_4 ISEE.

Enr 402. G 402. Elem 402. Wh 69%. Hisp 5%. Blk 4%. Asian 19%. Other 3%. Avg class size: 22. Uniform. Fac 48. M 6/0. F 37/5. Wh 88%. Blk 2%. Asian 8%. Other 2%. Adv deg: 39%.

Grad '04—44. Prep—42. (San Francisco U HS, Lick-Wilmerding, Drew, Urban, Marin Acad). Alum 1800.

Tui '04-'05: Day $18,350. Aid: Need 37 ($500,000).

Summer: Rec. Tui Day $900/3-wk ses. 9 wks.

Endow $3,460,000. Plant val $13,700,000. Bldgs 4. Class rms 25. Lib 14,000 vols. Sci labs 2. Comp ctrs 2. Auds 1. Art studios 2. Music studios 2. Gyms 1.

Est 1863. Nonprofit. Sem (Sept-June).

As the first nonsectarian school for girls in California, Hamlin continues to provide leadership in the education of young girls. Situated in Pacific Heights, overlooking San Francisco Bay and the Marin Headlands, Hamlin reflects the diversity and the traditions of San Francisco. Hamlin offers an academic program balanced by the fine arts, physical education and interscholastic sports, with electives in values, yearbook, public speaking and musical production.

Before- and after-school care and an extensive after-school activities program are available. Hamlin graduates attend leading secondary schools.

HILLWOOD ACADEMIC DAY SCHOOL

Day — Coed Gr K-8

San Francisco, CA 94115. 2521 Scott St. Tel: 415-931-0400. Fax: 415-921-2900.
www.hillwoodschool.com E-mail: ericgrantz@mindspring.com
Eric Grantz, Dir. MPA, Univ of San Francisco.

Gen Acad.

Adm: 11/yr. Appl due: Dec. Accepted: 60%. Tests SSAT Stanford.

Enr 56. Elem 56. Wh 27%. Asian 73%.Uniform. **Fac 7.** M 1/1. F 3/2. Adv deg: 57%.
Grad '04—5. Prep—5. (Sacred Heart HS-CA, Archbishop Riordan).
Tui '03-'04: Day $450/mo.
Summer: Rev Rec. Tui Day $400. 4 wks.
Plant val $1,500,000.
Est 1949. Sem (Sept-June).

Hillwood, located in the city's Pacific Heights section, offers a rich and varied program with special emphasis on the basic mathematical and language skills. Books, daily hot lunch and after-school supervision are included in the monthly tuition rate. The school offers special instruction for foreign students learning English. **See Also Page 1167**

KATHERINE DELMAR BURKE SCHOOL

Day — Girls Gr K-8

San Francisco, CA 94121. 7070 California St. Tel: 415-751-0177. Fax: 415-666-0535.
www.kdbs.org   E-mail: siobhan@kdbs.org

Jessie-Lea Abbott, Head. BS, Smith College, MS, State Univ of New York. **Siobhan O'Connell, Adm.**

Pre-Prep. Feat—Fr Mandarin Span Studio_Art Drama Music Outdoor_Ed. **Supp—**Dev_Read Tut.

Adm: 56/yr. Appl due: Dec. Accepted: 40%. **Tests** CTP_4 ISEE.

Enr 394. G 394. Elem 394. Wh 73%. Hisp 2%. Blk 3%. Am Ind 1%. Asian 21%. Avg class size: 20. Uniform. **Fac 64.** M 2/2. F 47/13. Wh 85%. Hisp 2%. Blk 8%. Asian 5%. Adv deg: 46%.

Grad '04—44. Prep—39. (San Francisco U HS, Drew, Urban, Convent of the Sacred Heart-CA). Alum 2550.

Tui '03-'04: Day $15,652-16,230 (+$225-780). **Aid:** Need 88 ($763,397).

Summer: Enrich. Tui Day $175/wk. 6 wks.

Endow $4,200,000. Plant val $10,437,000. Bldgs 9. Class rms 30. Lib 10,000 vols. Sci labs 2. Comp labs 2. Art studios 2. Gyms 1. Fields 1. Courts 2.

Est 1908. Nonprofit. Tri (Sept-June).

Founded by Katherine Delmar Burke, a native San Franciscan and gifted teacher, this school moved several times during the early years to increasingly large quarters in the city. Upon Miss Burke's death in 1929, the school passed to the direction of her young niece, Barbara Burke, under whose guidance it continued to grow until her retirement in 1960. During this period, the school expanded to the present campus in Sea Cliff, splitting the primary school into two distinct campuses. In 1975, Burke School terminated its high school program and moved its entire operation to the Sea Cliff campus, which today occupies three and a half acres.

The curriculum includes a demanding academic program; a rich variety of music, art and drama offerings; and a comprehensive athletic and sports program. Outdoor education is an integral part of the curriculum for grades 3-8. Beginning in grade 3, all students spend two or three nights each year at Mountain Mill House, the school's 203-acre outdoor education center located in Napa County. The site contains a variety of ecosystems: steep, wild, forested hillsides; an orchard; streams; a pond; and natural springs. Older students travel to such sites as Yosemite and Joshua Tree.

Upper school students participate in student government, and throughout there are both opportunities and requirements for service to the school community and others. All Burke students, faculty and staff participate in "family" groups, which consist of at least one adult and one student from each grade, that work and play together. After school, a study hall is offered for students in grades 5 and 6 and a sports program is available to those in grades 5-8.

LICK-WILMERDING HIGH SCHOOL
Day — Coed Gr 9-12

San Francisco, CA 94112. 755 Ocean Ave. Tel: 415-333-4021. Fax: 415-333-9443.
  www.lwhs.org E-mail: lwadmit@lwhs.org
Albert M. Adams II, Head. BA, Univ of Pennsylvania, MAT, Colorado College, EdD, Harvard Univ. **Jane W. Faller, Adm.**
  Col Prep. AP—Fr Span Calc Stats Bio Chem Physics World_Hist Music_Theory. **Feat**—Anat & Physiol Photog Studio_Art Acting Theater Chorus Music Dance Drafting.
  Adm (Gr 9): 111/yr. Appl due: Jan. Accepted: 10%. Yield: 75%. **Tests** ISEE SSAT.
  Enr 407. B 198. G 209. Sec 407. Wh 52%. Hisp 5%. Blk 4%. Asian 22%. Other 17%. Avg class size: 15. **Fac 53.** M 20/3. F 21/9. Wh 74%. Hisp 8%. Blk 2%. Asian 8%. Other 8%. Adv deg: 69%.
  Grad '04—91. Col—91. (Brown 5, Barnard 4, Vassar 4, Stanford 4, U of CA-Davis 4, U of PA 4). Avg SAT: 1340. Alum 2800.
  Tui '04-'05: Day $24,600. Aid: Need 172 ($2,485,000).
  Endow $37,000,000. Plant val $14,700,000. Bldgs 7. Class rms 28. Lib 13,500 vols. Sci labs 4. Comp labs 3. Theaters 1. Art studios 2. Music studios 1. Dance studios 1. Tech arts shops 4. Gyms 1.
  Est 1895. Nonprofit. Sem (Sept-June). **Assoc** WASC.

Founded by James Lick and Jellis Wilmerding, this school offers a curriculum that integrates the liberal, technical and performing arts. Students select from a variety of Advanced Placement courses, including French and Spanish language and literature classes. A variety of technical and fine arts offerings is also available, and course work in these disciplines is compulsory. L-W offers a flexible tuition program that allows families who would not expect to be eligible for financial aid to apply for reduced tuition, thus enabling pupils from varying economic backgrounds to attend.

The school runs a five-week summer outreach program that provides tuition-free academic enrichment for local middle school children from low-income households and allows Lick-Wilmerding students to serve as teaching assistants.

Extracurricular activities include drama, music and dance productions, a literary magazine, a school newspaper and dozens of interest clubs. Interscholastic teams are offered in soccer, basketball, volleyball, lacrosse, tennis, swimming, baseball, cross-country and track.

PRESIDIO HILL SCHOOL
Day — Coed Gr K-8

San Francisco, CA 94118. 3839 Washington St. Tel: 415-751-9318. Fax: 415-751-9334.
  www.presidiohill.org E-mail: info@presidiohill.org
Carey Davis, Dir. AB, Princeton Univ, EdM, Harvard Univ. **Sunan Lazarin, Adm.**
  Pre-Prep. Gen Acad. Feat—Span Studio_Art Drama Music. **Supp**—Dev_Read Tut.
  Adm: 37/yr. Appl due: Jan. Accepted: 42%.
  Enr 180. B 95. G 85. Elem 180. Avg class size: 16. **Fac 22.** M 4/2. F 15/1. Adv deg: 45%.

Grad '04—16. Prep—12. (Lick-Wilmerding, Urban, Convent of the Sacred Heart-CA, Drew, Fr-Amer Intl, Marin Acad).
Tui '04-'05: Day $14,520-15,680 (+$475). **Aid:** Need 36 ($290,000).
Summer: Rec. 2-8 wks.
Plant val $11,000,000. Bldgs 1. Class rms 13. Libs 1. Sci labs 2. Theaters 1. Music studios 1.
Est 1918. Nonprofit. Tri (Sept-June).

Established by a group of local parents as the Presidio Open Air School, this progressive program has an enrollment policy aimed at reflecting the cultural, economic and ethnic diversity of the city.

The project-based curriculum places an emphasis on writing across the disciplines. Music and the visual arts are considered fundamental. Spanish is introduced in kindergarten and continues through grade 8. Physical education includes intramural sports in the upper grades, as well as creative movement and games in the lower grades. Students participate in as many as three outdoor education experiences per year.

Parental involvement is encouraged and is considered essential. After-school care is available for an additional fee.

SAN FRANCISCO DAY SCHOOL

Day — Coed Gr K-8

San Francisco, CA 94118. 350 Masonic Ave. Tel: 415-931-2422. Fax: 415-931-1753.
www.sfds.net E-mail: mrhodes@sfds.net
John C. Lin, Head. BA, Carleton College, MA, Middlebury College, MPhil, Oxford Univ (England). **Margarita Rhodes, Adm.**

Pre-Prep. Gen Acad. Feat—Lat Span Computers Studio_Art Music. **Supp**—Dev_Read Rem_Read Tut.
Adm (Gr K-7): 59/yr. Appl due: Jan. Accepted: 5%. **Tests** CTP_4.
Enr 395. B 195. G 200. Elem 395. Wh 72%. Hisp 7%. Blk 6%. Asian 11%. Other 4%. Avg class size: 22. **Fac 55.** M 16. F 35/4.
Grad '04—41. Prep—41. (San Francisco U HS, Urban, Lick-Wilmerding, Drew, Schs of the Sacred Heart). Alum 531.
Tui '04-'05: Day $17,490. Aid: Need 77 ($820,000).
Summer: Rec. Drama. Tui Day $925. 4 wks.
Endow $6,771,000. Plant val $10,971,000. Bldgs 1. Lib 15,500 vols. Sci labs 2. Comp labs 1. Art studios 2. Music studios 2. Gyms 1.
Est 1981. Nonprofit. Sem (Sept-June).

Founded by a group of parents, this school originally opened for kindergartners through second graders, adding one grade each year until reaching its current grade range. Strong emphasis is placed on such basic skills as reading, writing, computation and problem solving. The school offers an outdoor education program to students in grades 3-8 that involves a weeklong, off-campus course of study each year.

An afternoon enrichment program, available to children at all grade levels, provides sports, art, music, drama and computer programs after school hours. At all grade levels, students may also select special instruction classes in such areas as typing, karate, orchestra, ceramics and computers. **See Also Page 1251**

THE SAN FRANCISCO SCHOOL
Day — Coed Gr PS-8

San Francisco, CA 94134. 300 Gaven St. Tel: 415-239-5065. Fax: 415-239-4833.
www.sfschool.org   E-mail: info@sfschool.org
Terry Edeli, Head. BS, MA, Stanford Univ. **Wendy Wilkinson, Adm.**
- Pre-Prep. Gen Acad. **Feat**—Span Environ_Sci Computers Studio_Art Music. **Supp**—Dev_Read Tut.
- **Adm:** 56/yr. Appl due: Jan. Accepted: 25%. Yield: 74%. **Tests** CTP_4 ISEE Stanford.
- **Enr 276.** B 137. G 139. Elem 276. Wh 59%. Hisp 14%. Blk 10%. Asian 15%. Other 2%. Avg class size: 19. **Fac 39.** M 7/2. F 27/3. Wh 73%. Hisp 9%. Blk 4%. Asian 14%. Adv deg: 23%.
- **Grad '04—32. Prep—27.** (Lick-Wilmerding 6, Urban 4, Drew 4). Alum 1150.
- **Tui '04-'05: Day $14,045-15,165 (+$200). Aid:** Need 73 ($528,000).
- **Summer:** Acad Enrich Rec. 2-6 wks.
- Endow $857,000. Plant val $3,482,000. Bldgs 3. Libs 1. Sci labs 1. Lang labs 2. Comp labs 1. Auds 1. Art studios 1. Music studios 1. Dance studios 1. Playgrounds 3.
- **Est 1966.** Nonprofit. Sem (Sept-June).

Interested in establishing a school based on the principles of Italian physicist and educator Maria Montessori, a small group of preschool teachers and parents formed the San Francisco Montessori School in a church basement in the city's Portola District. Its rapid growth led to the school's move to its present location and the addition of grade 1 in 1969. Organic growth continued through the 1970s, and the school consciously shifted from the Montessori method to a progressive approach that combined Montessori ideals with current teaching practices. In the 1980s, the school added a middle school program and assumed its current name.

SFS' increasingly demanding educational program is integrated and articulated across the grades, with specific goals and objectives set for each subject area. The preschool combines traditional Montessori teaching tools with blocks of various sizes and shapes, a playhouse, toys, board games and manipulative materials. In the elementary program (grades 1-5), children compile journals, assume classroom responsibilities, embark on field trips and overnight excursions, and engage in environmental studies.

Students in the middle school (grades 6-8) follow an integrated curriculum that emphasizes the development of study and organizational skills. Boys and girls choose from elective minicourses in such areas as painting, video production and book discussion. Seventh graders explore areas of vocational interest by undertaking a field experience that enables them to spend up to three days in the workplace.

In addition to the recreational after-school sports program, students may take part in interscholastic athletics or play in citywide sports leagues.   **See Also Page 1252**

SAN FRANCISCO UNIVERSITY HIGH SCHOOL
Day — Coed Gr 9-12

San Francisco, CA 94115. 3065 Jackson St. Tel: 415-447-3100. Fax: 415-447-5801.
www.sfuhs.org   E-mail: karen.hurtt@sfuhs.org
Michael Diamonti, Head. BA, Seton Hall Univ, MEd, Rutgers Univ, PhD, Boston College.
Karen N. Hurtt, Adm.
- Col Prep. **AP**—Fr Lat Span Calc Stats Comp_Sci Chem Physics Eur_Hist US_Hist Econ Art_Hist Studio_Art. **Feat**—Poetry Astron Genetics Marine_Biol/Sci Psych Asian_Stud Comp_Relig Photog Drama Music. **Supp**—Tut.

Adm: 123/yr. Appl due: Jan. Accepted: 30%. **Tests** SSAT.
Enr 391. Sec 391. Wh 68%. Hisp 6%. Blk 4%. Asian 22%. Avg class size: 14. **Fac 69.** M 27. F 42. Wh 83%. Hisp 5%. Blk 6%. Asian 6%. Adv deg: 63%.
Grad '04—93. Col—93. (U of CA-Berkeley, Columbia, NYU, Barnard, Princeton, Vassar). Avg SAT: 1348. Alum 1500.
Tui '04-'05: Day $23,750 (+$700). **Aid:** Need 80 ($1,300,000).
Summer: Acad Enrich Rev. 6 wks.
Endow $12,000,000. Plant val $11,000,000. Bldgs 2. Class rms 14. Sci labs 5. Lang labs 1. Comp labs 2. Auds 1. Theaters 1. Art studios 4. Music studios 3. AV studios 1. Gyms 1. Courts 1.
Est 1973. Nonprofit. Sem (Aug-June).

UHS' campus extends through two city blocks in the northern section of San Francisco. The majority of students come from the city, though some commute from East Bay cities, Marin County and the Peninsula. The college preparatory course of study combines a core of required courses with numerous electives aimed at meeting special needs and interests. Advanced Placement courses are available in the major disciplines. The arts program includes offerings in chamber music, jazz, ensemble singing, ceramics, sculpture, design, drawing, photography and theater. Among other elective subjects are classical literature, economics, contemporary world issues and computer programming. All students participate in community service each year.

The physical education program provides a climbing wall and such activities as tae kwon do, flag football and tennis, and the school fields numerous interscholastic teams. Students also participate in school publications and independent study projects. UHS schedules frequent field trips to areas of interest.

SCHOOLS OF THE SACRED HEART
Day — Coed Gr K-12
(Coord — Day K-12)

San Francisco, CA 94115. 2222 Broadway. Tel: 415-563-2900. Fax: 415-292-3183. www.sacredsf.org   E-mail: heart@sacredsf.org

Pamela Hayes, Dir. BA, Briarcliffe College, MAT, Manhattanville College. **Courtney Glenn & Michael Barclay, HS Adms; Pamela Thorp, Elem Sch Adm.**
  Col Prep. AP—Eng Fr Lat Span Calc Comp_Sci Bio Chem Human_Geog Physics Eur_Hist US_Hist US_Govt & Pol Art_Hist Music_Theory. **Feat**—Creative_Writing Japan Mandarin Relig Ceramics Film Fine_Arts Photog Drama Chorus Journ. **Supp**—Rev Tut.
Adm: 198/yr. Appl due: Jan. **Tests** CTP_4 HSPT SSAT.
Enr 1032. B 492. G 540. Elem 656. Sec 376. Avg class size: 17. Uniform. **Fac 155.** M 42/4. F 94/15. Adv deg: 54%.
Grad '04—81. Col—80. (UCLA 3, U of AZ 3, U of CO-Boulder 3, U of the Pacific 3, Goucher 2, U of CA-Berkeley 2). Alum 4126.
Tui '04-'05: Day $16,825-22,475 (+$300-900). **Aid:** Need 234 ($2,455,392).
Summer: Acad Enrich Rev Rec. Sci. Sports. Tui Day $450-470/3-wk ses. 6 wks.
Endow $7,000,000. Plant val $62,000,000. Bldgs 9. Class rms 72. 3 Libs 30,000 vols. Sci labs 8. Comp labs 4. Auds 2. Theaters 1. Art studios 5. Music studios 4. Gyms 2.
Est 1887. Nonprofit. Roman Catholic. Sem (Aug-June). **Assoc** WASC.

Founded by the Religious of the Sacred Heart, SSH comprises two girls' schools, Convent of the Sacred Heart High School (grades 9-12) and Convent of the Sacred Heart Elementary School (grades K-8), and two boys' schools, Stuart Hall for Boys (grades K-8) and Stuart Hall High School (grades 9-12). Among the oldest and largest independent schools in the city, Schools of the Sacred Heart employ a coordinate approach that enables boys and girls to learn in single-gender classes within a coeducational community. The rigorous academic program features a strong computer curriculum, art, ceramics, photography, chorus, music, drama and sports. Honors and Advanced Placement classes are available in most disciplines.

As a member of the Network of Sacred Heart Schools in the United States, SSH participates in a student exchange program that offers eligible high school students the opportunity to study at another Sacred Heart school.

Students in grades 7-12 serve the community in outreach programs. Boys and girls are encouraged to pursue leadership opportunities through student council, the classroom and student activities.

TOWN SCHOOL FOR BOYS

Day — Boys Gr K-8

San Francisco, CA 94115. 2750 Jackson St. Tel: 415-921-3747. Fax: 415-921-2968.
www.townschool.com E-mail: mckannay@townschool.com

W. Brewster Ely IV, Head. BA, Ithaca College, MA, Middlebury College. **Lynn McKannay, Adm.**

Pre-Prep. Feat—Fr Lat Span Computers Econ Studio_Art Music. **Supp**—Dev_Read Rem_Math Rem_Read Rev Tut.

Adm: 54/yr. Appl due: Jan. **Tests** CTP_4 Stanford.

Enr 400. B 400. Elem 400. Avg class size: 22. **Fac 60.** M 16/4. F 33/7. Adv deg: 33%.

Grad '04—46. Prep—39. (San Francisco U HS 13, Lick-Wilmerding 3, Marin Acad 3, Urban 3, Branson 3). Alum 1800.

Tui '04-'05: Day $17,000 (+$300). **Aid:** Need 78 ($733,000).

Summer: Coed. Acad Enrich Rev. Tui Day $325/2-wk ses. 6 wks.

Endow $10,200,000. Plant val $8,800,000. Bldgs 1. Class rms 28. Lib 17,500 vols. Sci labs 1. Comp labs 1. Sci ctrs 1. Theaters 1. Art studios 1. Music studios 2. Wood shops 1. Gyms 1. Fields 2. Courts 1.

Est 1939. Nonprofit. Sem (Sept-June). **Assoc** WASC.

The upper school curriculum includes study in literature, composition and creative writing; ancient and modern history; mathematics; social sciences; geography; economics; and the earth, life and physical sciences. Beginning in grade 5, students can choose either French or Spanish, and Latin is a required course in grade 6. A laptop learning program requires every boy in grades 5-8 to purchase a laptop computer for classroom use.

Complementing the core academic program are opportunities in art, music, community service, athletics, drama, journalism, student council, desktop publishing, digital photography and public speaking. Town School also offers students a broad range of hands-on projects, outdoor activities, school and grade-level assemblies and performances, after-school activities, and field trips around and beyond the Bay Area.

With sound elementary work, the school sends its graduates to the foremost secondary schools throughout the country. Fine arts offerings and athletics supplement an intensive academic program.

THE URBAN SCHOOL OF SAN FRANCISCO
Day — Coed Gr 9-12

San Francisco, CA 94117. 1563 Page St. Tel: 415-626-2919. Fax: 415-626-1125.
www.urbanschool.org   E-mail: admissions@urbanschool.org
Mark Salkind, Dir. BA, Yale Univ. **Angela N. Brown, Adm.**

Col Prep. AP—Fr Span Calc Chem. **Feat**—Botany Genetics Marine_Biol/Sci Ornithology Neurobio Computers Law Constitutional_Law Theater Music.

Adm: 77/yr. Appl due: Jan. Accepted: 18%. **Tests** SSAT.

Enr 257. B 116. G 141. Sec 257. Wh 74%. Hisp 1%. Blk 5%. Asian 5%. Other 15%. Avg class size: 14. **Fac 35.** M 10/7. F 11/7. Wh 83%. Blk 3%. Asian 3%. Other 11%. Adv deg: 62%.

Grad '04—70. Col—69. (U of CA, NYU, Vassar, Wesleyan U, Oberlin, Stanford). Avg SAT: 1280. Alum 1188.

Tui '04-'05: Day $24,000 (+$1350). **Aid:** Need 58 ($793,000).

Endow $530,000. Plant val $8,300,000. Bldgs 2. Class rms 18. Lib 13,000 vols. Sci labs 3. Comp labs 5. Theaters 1. Art studios 3. Gyms 1.

Est 1966. Nonprofit. 6 terms (Sept-June). **Assoc** WASC.

Urban's program is designed to develop individual responsibility, student initiative and cooperative work habits. The school's block system, which divides the school year into six six-week periods of intensive work, allows for the in-depth study of each subject through discussions, films, projects, research and fieldwork.

The variety of topics explored includes constitutional law, Latin American and African literature, the Civil War, Russian history, neurobiology, marine biology, painting, music composition and circus movement. Advanced work in the humanities, math, science and the arts is required for graduation. In addition, each student is expected to undertake a yearly project that combines a personal interest with service to the community.

Among activities, the school offers students the opportunity to serve on the board of trustees and on other committees, as well as to assist the faculty in planning new courses and special programs. Participation in physical activities, which range from rock climbing, backpacking and competitive athletic teams to nature hiking, jogging and tennis in Golden Gate Park, is encouraged. Urban organizes numerous outdoor activities and trips throughout the year, and it sponsors many extracurricular opportunities for students. The school also houses a tuition-free summer program for middle school students from low-income families.

SAN JOSE, CA. (51 mi. SE of San Francisco, CA) Urban. Pop: 894,943. Alt: 118 ft.

HARKER SCHOOL
Day — Coed Gr K-12

San Jose, CA 95129. 500 Saratoga Ave. Tel: 408-249-2510. Fax: 408-984-2325.
www.harker.org   E-mail: admissions@harker.org
Christopher Nikoloff, Head. BA, MAT, Boston Univ. **Nan Nielsen, Adm.**

Col Prep. AP—Eng Fr Lat Span Calc Stats Comp_Sci Bio Chem Physics Eur_Hist US_Hist Psych Art_Hist Music_Theory. **Feat**—Japan Anat & Physiol Astron Engineering Electronics Holocaust Architect Film Sculpt Studio_Art Drama Music. **Supp**—Rev

Tut.
Adm: 262/yr. Appl due: Jan. **Tests** CTP_4 IQ ISEE SSAT.
Enr 1594. B 803. G 791. Elem 1009. Sec 585. Wh 30%. Hisp 2%. Blk 1%. Asian 38%. Other 29%. Avg class size: 18. **Fac 168.** Adv deg: 55%.
Grad '04—133. Col—133. (U of CA-Berkeley 15, U of PA 11, USC 8, U of CA-San Diego 8, Carnegie Mellon 6, Stanford 5). Avg SAT: 1392. Alum 3600.
Tui '04-'05: Day $19,249-24,019 (+$500-800).
Summer: Acad Enrich Rec. Tui Day $4700. 8 wks.
Plant val $90,000,000. Bldgs 21. Class rms 105. 2 Libs 15,000 vols. Sci labs 10. Comp labs 8. Art studios 5. Music studios 3. Dance studios 3. Gyms 2. Fields 3. Courts 18. Pools 2. Archery ranges 1.
Est 1893. Nonprofit. Sem (Aug-June). **Assoc** WASC.

Manzanita Hall, established in 1893 as a boys' preparatory school for Stanford University, and the Harker School, founded in 1902 for girls, were merged under the same management in 1959. In 1972, the two schools began joint operations at the Saratoga Avenue location, which now serves pupils in grades 9-12; children in grades K-5 attend classes at a second campus at 4300 Bucknall Rd., 95130; and students in the middle school (grades 6-8) learn on a third site at 3800 Blackford Ave, 95129, that opened in the fall of 2005. An inter-campus shuttle serves the three locations, which are proximate to each other.

Situated in the heart of the Santa Clara Valley, Harker provides a traditional college preparatory program enriched with offerings in the fine arts, computer science and athletics. Technology, through wired and wireless networks, is an integral aspect of the program and is interwoven into many courses. A varied extracurricular program, serving students at all grade levels, includes age-appropriate activities in the arts, intramural and interscholastic athletics, community service, computers, dance, debate, drama, newspaper, student government and yearbook. Both daylong and extended field trips enhance the curriculum.

SAN JUAN CAPISTRANO, CA. (61 mi. SE of Los Angeles, CA)
Urban. Pop: 33,826. Alt: 120 ft.

ST. MARGARET'S EPISCOPAL SCHOOL
Day — Coed Gr PS-12

San Juan Capistrano, CA 92675. 31641 La Novia Ave. Tel: 949-661-0108.
Fax: 949-661-8637.
www.smes.org   E-mail: jhaiding@smes.org
Marcus Hurlbut, Head. BA, Union College (NY), MA, Dartmouth College. **Judy Haidinger, Adm.**
Col Prep. AP—Eng Fr Lat Span Calc Bio Chem Physics US_Hist World_Hist US_Govt & Pol Studio_Art Music_Theory. **Feat**—Creative_Writing Humanities Greek Japan Anat & Physiol Geol Oceanog Anthro Econ Philos Relig Drama Music Journ.
Adm: 206/yr. Appl due: Mar. Accepted: 49%. **Tests** ISEE.
Enr 1208. B 605. G 603. Elem 830. Sec 378. Wh 80%. Hisp 3%. Blk 2%. Am Ind 1%. Asian 7%. Other 7%. Avg class size: 17. Uniform. **Fac 101.** M 28/6. F 58/9. Wh 92%. Blk 4%. Asian 4%. Adv deg: 42%.
Grad '04—82. Col—81. (U of CA-Berkeley, USC, Georgetown, U of PA, Stanford, Duke). Avg SAT: 1250. Alum 770.
Tui '05-'06: Day $14,200-16,800 (+$600). **Aid:** Need 90 ($582,400).

Summer: Acad Enrich. Tui Day $400-1500. 4-6 wks.
Endow $50,000. Plant val $29,000,000. Bldgs 9. Class rms 81. Lib 35,000 vols. Chapels 1. Sci labs 7. Comp labs 4. Auds 1. Art studios 3. Music studios 2. Dance studios 1. Gyms 1. Fields 3.
Est 1979. Nonprofit. Episcopal. Sem (Sept-June). **Assoc** CLS WASC.

St. Margaret's Episcopal School, named for Scotland's patron of education, was founded through the efforts of Canon Ernest D. Sillers, an Episcopal priest who persuaded the bishop of the diocese to acquire land on which a church and a school could be built. Chapel has been a part of St. Margaret's since its founding, and worship services, religion classes and a service program provide the structure of the school community.

In the upper school, Advanced Placement courses are offered, and all students take an elective each semester. Graduation requirements include courses in foreign language, the fine arts, religion or philosophy, history and computer science, as well as a year of advanced history, mathematics, science or language and a community service project.

Interscholastic athletics are available in softball, football, soccer, basketball, baseball, lacrosse, volleyball, cross-country, golf and tennis; in addition, an equestrian team represents the school at competitive meets. Additional activities include student government, peer counseling, newspapers, and interest and service clubs.

SAN MARINO, CA. (17 mi. E of Los Angeles, CA) Suburban. Pop: 12,945. Alt: 557 ft. See also Los Angeles.

SOUTHWESTERN ACADEMY
Bdg and Day — Coed Gr 6-PG

San Marino, CA 91108. 2800 Monterey Rd. Tel: 626-799-5010. Fax: 626-799-0407.
www.southwesternacademy.edu   E-mail: admissions@southwesternacademy.edu
Kenneth R. Veronda, Head. BA, MA, Stanford Univ. **Jane Whitmire, Adm.**
Col Prep. Gen Acad. Underachiever. **AP**—Eng Calc Physics US_Hist. **Feat**—British_Lit Span Environ_Sci Comp_Sci Anthro Econ Govt Pol_Sci Psych Sociol Studio_Art Drama Music Speech Driver_Ed Outdoor_Ed. **Supp**—Dev_Read ESL Rem_Math Rem_Read Rev Tut.
Adm (Bdg Gr 6-PG; Day 6-12): 52/yr. Bdg 30. Day 22. Appl due: Rolling. Accepted: 54%. Yield: 80%. **Tests** CEEB SSAT TOEFL.
Enr 122. B 49/30. G 27/16. Wh 27%. Hisp 9%. Blk 7%. Asian 55%. Other 2%. Avg class size: 10. **Fac 17.** M 11. F 6. Wh 88%. Asian 12%. Adv deg: 52%. In dorms 2.
Grad '04—20. Col—20. (U of MN-Twin Cities 2, CA St U 2, U of CA-Berkeley 2, Pitzer 2). Avg SAT: 1100. Alum 3062.
Tui '05-'06: Bdg $28,500 (+$2000). **Day** $13,800 (+$1000). **Aid:** Need 34 ($711,150).
Summer: Acad Enrich Rev. Tui Bdg $1700-4800. 2-6 wks. ESL. Tui Bdg $15,900. Tui Day $7973. 14 wks.
Endow $9,273,000. Plant val $21,628,000. Bldgs 26. Dorm rms 71. Class rms 26. Lib 17,000 vols. Chapels 1. Sci labs 3. Lang labs 2. Comp labs 3. Auds 1. Theaters 2. Art studios 2. Music studios 2. Amphitheaters 1. Gyms 2. Fields 3. Basketball courts 2. Tennis courts 2. Volleyball courts 2. Pools 1. Greenhouses 1. Student ctrs 3.
Est 1924. Nonprofit. Sem (Sept-June). **Assoc** WASC.

Southwestern was founded by Maurice Veronda, who personally directed its growth until his death in 1961. Kenneth Veronda has been headmaster since his father's death. Southwestern occupies separate campuses in San Marino and Rimrock, AZ (see separate listing), each with a distinct learning environment. The school admits students who require additional attention to realize their potential; it is not staffed to serve boys and girls with learning disabilities, behavioral problems, chemical dependencies or defiant attitudes. Small classes increase contact between teacher and pupil while also allowing students to pursue interests beyond the curriculum.

The San Marino campus is located in an eight-acre, suburban setting. The program features achievement grouping, honors and Advanced Placement courses, and English as a Second Language instruction. Students in grades 9-12 may divide time between the two Southwestern campuses, both of which follow University of California curricular guidelines.

Southwestern offers a wide range of drama, music, journalism, photography and art activities. Student government, publications, and exchanges between campuses involve students of all ages. Frequent field trips enrich class work. Athletic programs include a variety of intramural and interscholastic teams, as well as individual sports.
See Also Pages 1254-5

SAN RAFAEL, CA. (13 mi. NNE of San Francisco, CA) Urban. Pop: 56,063. Alt: 7 ft.

MARIN ACADEMY
Day — Coed Gr 9-12

San Rafael, CA 94901. 1600 Mission Ave. Tel: 415-453-4550. Fax: 415-453-8538.
www.ma.org   E-mail: admissions@ma.org
Bodie Brizendine, Head. BA, Towson State Univ, MLA, Johns Hopkins Univ. **Dan Babior, Adm.**

Col Prep. AP—Fr Span Calc Stats Comp_Sci Bio Chem Physics Eur_Hist US_Hist US_Govt & Pol. **Feat**—British_Lit Poetry African-Amer_Lit Shakespeare Japan Anat & Physiol Astron Geol Oceanog Computers Russ_Hist Sociol Ceramics Photog Drama Chorus Music Dance Journ.

Adm: 119/yr. Appl due: Jan. Accepted: 31%. Yield: 57%. **Tests** CTP_4 ISEE SSAT Stanford.

Enr 404. B 194. G 210. Sec 404. Wh 78%. Hisp 3%. Blk 4%. Asian 2%. Other 13%. Avg class size: 15. **Fac 50.** M 22/2. F 20/6. Wh 80%. Blk 6%. Asian 10%. Other 4%. Adv deg: 74%.

Grad '04—109. Col—108. (Brown 5, Boston U 5, NYU 4, U of CA-Davis 4, USC 4, U of CA-Berkeley 4). Avg SAT: 1295. Alum 1600.

Tui '04-'05: Day $24,315 (+$600-900). **Aid:** Need 81 ($1,447,822).

Endow $1,945,000. Plant val $29,583,000. Bldgs 11. Class rms 30. Lib 14,000 vols. Sci labs 4. Lang labs 2. Comp labs 3. Sci bldgs 1. Auds 1. Theaters 2. Art studios 4. Music studios 3. Dance studios 1. Arts ctrs 1. Gyms 2. Fields 2. Courts 2. Pools 1. Student ctrs 1.

Est 1971. Nonprofit. Sem (Aug-June). **Assoc** CLS WASC.

Located on a 10-acre campus 12 miles north of San Francisco, MA draws students from all over the Bay Area. Its college preparatory curriculum features

Advanced Placement and honors courses in all disciplines, as well as numerous electives. The school maintains a favorable student-teacher ratio and a small average class size. Opportunities for independent study, senior projects, international studies and study abroad are available. Practicing artists teach in the performing arts and visual arts department. All students perform community service.

Team athletics are conducted at varsity and junior varsity levels in approximately a dozen sports. A wilderness education program offers weekend opportunities for individual sports, while cultivating an appreciation of the outdoors. Through this program, students may pursue backpacking, cross-country skiing, scuba diving and rock climbing.

SANTA BARBARA, CA. (78 mi. WNW of Los Angeles, CA) Urban. Pop: 92,325. Alt: 100 ft. Area also includes Carpinteria.

CATE SCHOOL
Bdg and Day — Coed Gr 9-12

Carpinteria, CA 93014. 1960 Cate Mesa Rd, PO Box 5005. Tel: 805-684-4127.
   Fax: 805-684-2279.
      www.cate.org   E-mail: admission@cate.org
Benjamin D. Williams IV, Head. BA, Williams College, MA, Brown Univ. **Peter J. Mack, Adm.**
   Col Prep. AP—Eng Fr Span Calc Stats Bio Chem Physics US_Hist US_Govt & Pol. **Feat**—Humanities Chin Japan Anat & Physiol Marine_Biol/Sci Intl_Relations Asian_Stud Drama Music.
   Adm: 88/yr. Appl due: Feb. Accepted: 30%. **Tests** SSAT TOEFL.
   Enr 266. B 107/19. G 107/33. Sec 266. Wh 67%. Hisp 7%. Blk 9%. Am Ind 1%. Asian 10%. Other 6%. Avg class size: 11. **Fac 50.** M 27. F 23. Adv deg: 72%. In dorms 20.
   Grad '04—66. Col—66. (Northwestern, Columbia, Princeton, Stanford, USC, NYU). Avg SAT: 1320. Avg SSAT: 81%. Alum 2516.
   Tui '04-'05: Bdg $33,075 (+$1000). **Day $24,475** (+$500). **Aid:** Need 71 ($1,400,000).
   Endow $45,000,000. Plant val $20,000,000. Bldgs 20. Dorms 8. Dorm rms 136. Class rms 17. Lib 24,000 vols. Labs 5. Comp ctrs 1. Theaters 1. Art studios 3. Music studios 4. Gyms 2. Fields 4. Courts 8. Pools 1.
   Est 1910. Nonprofit. Sem (Sept-June). **Assoc** CLS WASC.

Curtis Wolsey Cate was a graduate of Harvard who journeyed west to teach. In 1910, he founded the Miramar School in Santa Barbara's Mission Canyon. The following year, Mr. Cate moved the school to the foot of a rural mesa bounded by Lillingston and Gobernador canyons in the Carpinteria Valley. He changed its name to the Santa Barbara School. In 1929, he moved it again, this time to the top of "the Mesa," as the 150-acre campus has come to be known. In 1950, the school was formally renamed Cate School to honor its founder, who served as headmaster until that year. Originally, the school featured grades 6-12, but the younger classes were gradually phased out. Girls were admitted for the first time in 1981.

Lower school students (grades 9 and 10) are required to take a course in each of six academic departments—the arts, English, foreign language, history, mathematics and science—in addition to a human development curriculum. Those in the upper school (grades 11 and 12) choose electives in all disciplines, including honors and Advanced Placement sections, and may take noncredit enrichment classes. Directed studies permit students to pursue a particular interest by designing a course not offered in the regular curriculum; these may combine academic study with fieldwork. Seniors are allowed to spend the last marking period working on individually designed projects, either on or off campus.

Athletics are integral to the overall program at Cate. All students take part in after-school options during each of the three seasons. An extensive selection of interscholastics and intramurals is available; an outdoor program and recreational sports provide an alternative to competitive teams. Other extracurriculars include clubs, services, special events and publications. Public service is strongly encouraged through participation in local community projects and involvement outside the school, and all but seniors perform daily chores ranging from kitchen duty to dormitory and campus cleanup.

The entire school community convenes each week for convocations, and individual classes spend time together during an outing week in the early fall. Five-week summer language and culture programs based in Spain, Japan, China and Thailand enable participants to improve their foreign language skills by living, traveling and studying in a foreign country.

LAGUNA BLANCA SCHOOL
Day — Coed Gr K-12

Santa Barbara, CA 93110. 4125 Paloma Dr. Tel: 805-687-2461. Fax: 805-682-2553.
www.lagunablanca.org   E-mail: admissions@lagunablanca.org
Douglas W. Jessup, Head. BA, Amherst College, EdM, Harvard Univ. **Erin Guerra, Adm.**
  Col Prep. AP—Eng Fr Lat Span Calc Stats Bio Chem Physics US_Hist World_Hist US_Govt & Pol. **Feat**—Marine_Biol/Sci Intl_Relations Women's_Stud Film Drama Music Journ. **Supp**—Rev Tut.
  Adm: 85/yr. Appl due: Feb. Accepted: 83%. **Tests** CTP_4 ISEE Stanford.
  Enr 376. B 187. G 189. Elem 199. Sec 177. Wh 86%. Hisp 5%. Blk 1%. Asian 8%. Avg class size: 23. **Fac 61.** M 20/4. F 25/12. Wh 87%. Hisp 7%. Blk 2%. Asian 3%. Other 1%. Adv deg: 59%.
  Grad '04—33. Col—30. (U of Denver, USC, CA St Polytechn-San Luis Obispo, Cornell, Emerson, U of San Francisco). Avg SAT: 1207. Alum 1600.
  Tui '03-'04: Day $13,900-16,500 (+$300-800). **Aid:** Merit 9 ($28,500). Need 51 ($526,170).
  Summer: Rec. Arts. 1-4 wks.
  Endow $3,300,000. Plant val $11,444,000. Bldgs 31. Class rms 25. 2 Libs 15,000 vols. Sci labs 6. Comp labs 3. Auds 1. Theaters 1. Art studios 4. Music studios 2. Gyms 1. Fields 6. Courts 2.
  Est 1933. Nonprofit. (Sept-June). **Assoc** CLS WASC.

Offered in a small-class setting, Laguna Blanca's program combines college preparatory academics with ample opportunities in leadership, community service, the visual and performing arts, interscholastic athletics and student publications. One-on-one advising and college counseling are integral aspects of school life.

Off-campus study options enrich the curriculum. Students in grades 5-8 take weeklong trips that focus on natural science; ninth graders embark on a two-day southern California cultural excursion that incorporates visits to monuments and museums, as well as attendance at theatrical productions; and seniors participate in a required, three-week professional internship. Laguna Blanca also conducts an upper school exchange with a school in Trowbridge, England.

Grades K-4 convene at 260 San Ysidro Rd., Montecito 93108, while grades 5-12 are conducted in Hope Ranch Park at the Paloma Drive address.

SANTA MONICA, CA. (8 mi. SW of Los Angeles, CA) Urban. Pop: 84,084. Alt: 64 ft. See also Los Angeles.

CROSSROADS SCHOOL
Day — Coed Gr K-12

Santa Monica, CA 90404. 1714 21st St. Tel: 310-829-7391. Fax: 310-828-5636.
www.xrds.org

Roger H. Weaver, Head. BA, Univ of California-Santa Barbara, MEd, Univ of California-Los Angeles. **Gennifer Yoshimaru, Adm.**

Col Prep. Gen Acad. AP—Eng Calc Stats Bio Chem Physics World_Hist. **Feat**—Japan Computers Human_Dev Film Drama Chorus Dance Journ Outdoor_Ed. **Supp**—Tut.

Adm: 162/yr. Accepted: 31%. **Tests** ISEE.

Enr 1140. B 555. G 585. Elem 648. Sec 492. Wh 69%. Hisp 4%. Blk 6%. Asian 3%. Other 18%. Avg class size: 20. **Fac 140.** M 44/10. F 59/27. Wh 80%. Hisp 6%. Blk 6%. Asian 4%. Other 4%. Adv deg: 48%.

Grad '04—115. Col—112. (NYU, U of CA-Santa Cruz, U of CO-Boulder, USC, U of CA-Berkeley, Bard). Avg SAT: 1163. Alum 2426.

Tui '03-'04: Day $17,300-20,400 (+$350). **Aid:** Merit 5 ($56,000). Need 153 ($2,258,894).

Summer: Acad Enrich Rev Rem Rec. Tui Day $550/crse. 6 wks. Sports. 1 wk.

Endow $5,361,000. Plant val $26,500,000. Bldgs 22. Class rms 87. Libs 2. Sci labs 8. Lang labs 1. Comp labs 3. Theaters 1. Art studios 3. Music studios 2. Dance studios 2. Gyms 2. Fields 1. Pools 1.

Est 1971. Nonprofit. Sem (Sept-June). **Assoc** CLS WASC.

Located on the West Side of Los Angeles, Crossroads provides a college preparatory curriculum consisting of English, mathematics, science, foreign languages, history, classics and the arts. Physical education, human development and community service are required parts of each student's program.

The middle school stresses composition and reading skills in all areas. The upper school supplements the fundamentals with courses in the visual arts, classical music, film, journalism, chorus and dance. Required community service projects include gerontology studies and fieldwork, and government and community internships in grades 11 and 12. The athletic program comprises volleyball, cross-country, softball, tennis, golf, basketball, soccer, baseball, track and swimming. Crossroads also offers performing arts majors in art, music and drama, in addition to a classics program.

Crossroads' elementary school (1715 Olympic Blvd.) offers a curriculum for children in grades K-5. It features courses in science, computer studies, art, drama, music, dance and service learning.

WATSONVILLE, CA. (27 mi. S of San Jose, CA; 74 mi. SE of San Francisco, CA) Suburban. Pop: 44,265. Alt: 25 ft.

MONTE VISTA CHRISTIAN SCHOOL
Bdg — Coed Gr 9-12; Day — Coed 6-12

Watsonville, CA 95076. 2 School Way. Tel: 831-722-8178. Fax: 831-722-6003.
www.mvcs.org   E-mail: info@mvcs.org

Stephen J. Sharp, Supt. Susan S. Bernal, Adm.

Col Prep. Gen Acad. **AP**—Eng Span Calc Stats Comp_Sci Physics Eur_Hist US_Hist Psych US_Govt & Pol. **Feat**—Fr Japan Anat & Physiol Marine_Biol/Sci Web_Design Econ Bible Photog Drama Music Journ Culinary_Arts. **Supp**—ESL Rem_Math Rem_Read Tut.

Adm: 141/yr. Bdg 51. Day 90. Appl due: Rolling. Accepted: 90%. **Tests** SSAT TOEFL.

Enr 970. Elem 247. Sec 723. Wh 79%. Hisp 9%. Blk 1%. Asian 11%. Avg class size: 21. **Fac 62.** Adv deg: 25%.

Grad '04—189. Col—173. (U of CA-Berkeley, CA St U, Boston U, St Mary's Col of CA, Santa Clara, Rensselaer Polytech). Avg SAT: 1067. Alum 1345.

Tui '05-'06: Bdg $26,000-29,700 (+$1000). **Day $7007-7392** (+$250-500).

Summer: Acad. ESL. Tui Bdg $4900. Tui Day $425/crse. 6 wks.

Plant val $12,000,000. Bldgs 25. Dorms 2. Dorm rms 55. Class rms 26. Lib 10,000 vols. Sci labs 2. Lang labs 1. Comp labs 1. Art studios 1. Music studios 2. Gyms 2. Fields 2. Courts 1. Pools 1. Riding rings 2. Stables 1.

Est 1926. Nonprofit. Evangelical. Sem (Aug-June). **Assoc** WASC.

Monte Vista offers two types of academic programs: college preparatory, which includes AP and honors classes and general studies. A resource center is provided for a select number of students who are not achieving to potential, and international students enroll in ESL and college prep courses.

Interscholastic teams and intramural athletic activities are available, and students may receive English and Western instruction at the school's equestrian center. In addition, students may participate in the performing and visual arts in drama, concert choir, voice and marching band. Community service is required of all students in grades 9-12.

HAWAII

HONOLULU, HI. Urban. Pop: 371,657. Alt: 18 ft.

HANAHAUOLI SCHOOL
Day — Coed Gr PS-6

Honolulu, HI 96822. 1922 Makiki St. Tel: 808-949-6461. Fax: 808-941-2216.
www.hanahauoli.org E-mail: ckomo@hanahauoli.org

Robert G. Peters, Head. BA, MA, EdD, Univ of Massachusetts-Amherst. **Carol M. Komo, Adm.**

Pre-Prep. Feat—Lib_Skills Fr Computers Arts Music Indus_Arts. **Supp**—Dev_Read Tut.

Adm: 31/yr. Appl due: Dec. Accepted: 20%.

Enr 205. B 100. G 105. Elem 205. Wh 31%. Blk 1%. Asian 68%. Avg class size: 25. **Fac 23.** M 2/1. F 13/7. Adv deg: 43%.

Grad '04—25. Prep—25. (Punahou, La Pietra). Alum 1350.

Tui '04-'05: Day $11,850.

Summer: Acad Enrich Rec. Tui Day $500. 6 wks.

Endow $2,500,000. Bldgs 8. Class rms 8. Lib 14,000 vols. Sci labs 1. Lang labs 1. Tech labs 1. Art studios 1. Music studios 1. Shops 1.

Est 1918. Nonprofit. (Aug-June). **Assoc** WASC.

Established by George and Sophie Cooke to fill the need for a small school with a more informal program, Hanahauoli utilizes an experiential learning approach based on the ideas of John Dewey. The broad program encourages children to experiment and solve problems in a variety of integrated subject areas. A foundation in traditional academic subjects is offered, with basic skills balanced by an emphasis on concept development. Students receive in-depth instruction in art, music, woodworking, physical education, French, social studies, science, literature and computers.

Hanahauoli traditions are celebrated throughout the school year to bring students together and to enhance their sense of community. The "makahiki" is celebrated by the students at Thanksgiving in ancient Hawaiian fashion in honor of Lono, the god of agriculture. At the school's Olympic games and oratory, sixth graders retell Greek myths and compete in various track and field events. Stepping Stone Day commemorates each sixth grader's contribution to the school. Each graduating student's own stepping stone is unveiled before the school and remains on campus as a permanent symbol of the child.

Parental involvement plays an important role in the workings of the school. Parents drive students on field trips and contribute to classroom units as lecturers on their particular professions or cultural traditions. The parent organization sponsors numerous events during the year that serve to raise funds for the school and bring families together. Hanahauoli conducts an optional after-school care program and several enrichment programs at an additional cost.

IOLANI SCHOOL
Day — Coed Gr K-12

Honolulu, HI 96826. 563 Kamoku St. Tel: 808-949-5355. Fax: 808-943-2297.
www.iolani.org E-mail: admission@iolani.org

Val T. Iwashita, Head. BEd, MEd, Univ of Hawaii, EdD, Brigham Young Univ. **Patricia Novak Liu, Adm.**

Col Prep. AP—Eng Fr Lat Span Calc Stats Comp_Sci Bio Chem Physics Eur_Hist US_Hist Econ US_Govt & Pol Studio_Art. **Feat**—Creative_Writing Shakespeare Chin Japan Web_Design Asian_Stud Relig Theater Chorus Music Dance. **Supp**—ESL Tut.

Adm: 236/yr. Appl due: Dec. Accepted: 21%. Yield: 78%. **Tests** IQ SSAT.

Enr 1830. B 906. G 924. Elem 891. Sec 939. Wh 18%. Hisp 1%. Blk 1%. Asian 74%. Other 6%. Avg class size: 16. **Fac 165.** M 62/3. F 97/3. Adv deg: 59%.

Grad '04—238. Col—238. (U of HI-Manoa 32, USC 22, U of WA 8, Santa Clara 8, U of San Francisco 8, Creighton 3). Avg SAT: 1300. Avg ACT: 27. Alum 8000.

Tui '04-'05: Day $11,500 (+$500). **Aid:** Need 169 ($940,000).

Summer: Acad Enrich Rev Rec. Tui Day $140-575. 3-6 wks.

Endow $120,000,000. Bldgs 25. Class rms 101. Lib 25,000 vols. Labs 5. Art studios 4. Music studios 4. Dance studios 2. Gyms 2. Fields 3. Courts 6. Pools 1. Weight rms 1.

Est 1863. Nonprofit. Episcopal. Sem (Aug-June). **Assoc** CLS WASC.

Situated on 25 acres within one mile of Waikiki Beach, this school was founded by the first Anglican bishop of the islands during the reign of King Kamehameha IV. Iolani emphasizes Christian values and serves students of diverse religious and racial backgrounds.

Iolani's college-oriented academic program places a special emphasis on English, mathematics and science, with five foreign languages being offered in the upper school. An accelerated academic program has been established, with Advanced Placement offered in all major areas of study. An independent studies program is open to seniors, and qualified students may take courses at the nearby University of Hawaii.

Interest clubs supplement the strong academic curriculum. Art is introduced and developed in the lower grades, resulting in elective studio art courses in silk-screen, oil painting, sculpture, ceramics, metal sculpture and photography. The performing arts program consists of band, chorus, dance, orchestra, stage band and theater. Sports include football, basketball, baseball, bowling, soccer, swimming, water polo, tennis, golf, wrestling, softball, paddling, volleyball and track.

MID-PACIFIC INSTITUTE
Day — Coed Gr PS-12

Honolulu, HI 96822. 2445 Kaala St. Tel: 808-973-5000. Fax: 808-973-5099.
www.midpac.edu E-mail: admissions@midpac.edu

Joe C. Rice, Pres. BA, Univ of Washington, MA, Central Washington Univ. **John Williamson, Adm.**

Col Prep. IB Diploma. AP—Eng Calc Stats Bio Chem Physics US_Hist. **Feat**—Fr Japan Lat Span Computers Studio_Art Theater_Arts. **Supp**—ESL Tut.

Adm: 319/yr. Appl due: Jan. Accepted: 45%. **Tests** SSAT TOEFL.

Enr 1130. Avg class size: 20. **Fac 94.** Adv deg: 14%.

Grad '04—187. Col—185. (U of HI-Manoa, HI Pacific, Kapiolani CC, Honolulu CC, U of CA-Berkeley, U of WA). Alum 5800.

Tui '05-'06: Day $12,970.

Summer: Acad Enrich Rec. ESL. Tui Day $575/crse. 4-6 wks.

Endow $30,000,000. Plant val $120,000,000. Bldgs 26. Libs 1. Sci labs 8. Lang labs 2. Comp labs 6. Auds 1. Theaters 2. Art studios 4. Music studios 3. Dance studios 2. Fine arts ctrs 1. Gyms 1. Fields 2. Courts 2. Pools 1.
Est 1864. Nonprofit. Quar (Aug-May). **Assoc** WASC.

MPI dates back to 1908, when Kawaiaha'o Seminary for Girls (established in 1864) merged with Mills Institute for Boys (founded in 1892) and moved to Manoa from the schools' previous downtown locations. Although officially incorporated as a single entity, the two schools kept their separate names and programs for another 15 years. Today, Mid-Pacific serves a culturally diverse, international student body that includes boys and girls from Hawaii, Asia, Europe and the US Mainland.

The curriculum is particularly noteworthy for inclusion of the two-year International Baccalaureate program; MPI is the only school in the state to prepare students for the IB diploma. Another feature of the curriculum is the Mid-Pacific Institute School of the Arts (MPSA), a preprofessional arts training program that pupils may take part in as a complement to college preparatory academics. MPSA offers rigorous conservatory training in theater, musical theater, dance, hula and instrumental music, in addition to comprehensive programming in media and the visual arts. A well-developed technology center enables Mid-Pacific to enhance student learning with current computer technology.

Available for an additional annual fee, the school's ESL program provides intensive, broad-based instruction designed to facilitate the pupil's transition into the standard college preparatory curriculum.

MPI's varied interscholastic athletic program includes such sports as baseball, basketball, softball, golf, bowling, tennis, volleyball, soccer, canoe paddling, kayaking and swimming. Interest clubs, school publications, committees and other organized activities round out the extracurricular program.

PUNAHOU SCHOOL
Day — Coed Gr K-12

Honolulu, HI 96822. 1601 Punahou St. Tel: 808-944-5711. Fax: 808-944-5779. www.punahou.edu   E-mail: admission@punahou.edu

James K. Scott, Pres. AB, Stanford Univ, MA, Univ of San Francisco, MEd, EdD, Harvard Univ. **Betsy S. Hata, Adm.**

Col Prep. Gen Acad. AP—Eng Fr Span Calc Comp_Sci US_Hist. **Feat**—Japan Mandarin Hawaiian Marine_Biol/Sci Oceanog Asian_Hist Amer_Stud Sports_Psych Glass_Blowing TV_Journ Theater Band Chorus Music Orchestra JROTC. **Supp**—Rev Tut.

Adm: 517/yr. Appl due: Dec. Accepted: 23%. Yield: 78%. **Tests** IQ SSAT.

Enr 3774. B 1865. G 1909. Elem 2038. Sec 1736. Avg class size: 23. **Fac 320.** M 114/12. F 157/37. Adv deg: 58%.

Grad '04—416. Col—410. (U of HI-Manoa 45, USC 22, Santa Clara 21, U of WA 20, Loyola Marymount 16, U of CO-Boulder 9). Avg SAT: 1281. Alum 23,293.

Tui '04–'05: Day $12,885 (+$1250). **Aid:** Merit 13 ($167,505). Need 402 ($2,339,000).

Summer: Acad Enrich Rev Rec. Tui Day $64-730. 6 wks.

Endow $135,012,000. Plant val $154,000,000. Bldgs 36. Class rms 163. 3 Libs 96,000 vols. Labs 15. Comp labs 3. Auds 2. Theaters 1. Art studios 6. Music studios 16. Arts ctrs 1. Gyms 2. Fields 6. Courts 11. Pools 1.

Est 1841. Nonprofit. Sem (Aug-June). **Assoc** WASC.

Established by New England Congregational missionary families for their own children, Punahou was the first American college preparatory school west of the

Rocky Mountains. For over a century, the school served descendants of the early missionaries, as well as island children of various races and religions and later arrivals from the mainland. Today, Punahou serves as the largest independent, coeducational college preparatory school in the United States. The student body reflects Hawaii's ethnic, cultural and socioeconomic diversity. Located on a 76-acre campus, the well-developed school plant is noteworthy for its arts and athletic facilities.

The junior school (grades K-8) comprises four smaller, self-contained sections designed to meet the specific needs of children of different ages. Outdoor and camp experiences provide supplemental learning opportunities during these years. In the academy (grades 9-12), pupils fulfill requirements in English, science, social studies, math, foreign language, physical education, the performing arts and community service. Boys and girls participate in a modular system in which classes vary in length and size according to the needs of instruction, allowing for significant individualization in scheduling.

Punahou's athletic program, which emphasizes both competitive and lifetime sports, provides teams for boys and girls in grades 7-12. Students at all grade levels choose from a wide array of extracurricular activities.

ST. ANDREW'S PRIORY SCHOOL
Day — Girls Gr K-12

Honolulu, HI 96813. 224 Queen Emma Sq. Tel: 808-536-6102. Fax: 808-538-1035.
www.priory.net   E-mail: sawargo@priory.net
Marilyn A. Matsunaga, Head. BA, MBA, Univ of Denver. Sue Ann Wargo, Adm.
  Col Prep. AP—Eng Fr Span Calc Bio Chem Physics US_Hist. Feat—Japan Hawaiian Stats Astron Ecol Comp_Sci Psych Sociol Relig Studio_Art Music. Supp—ESL Tut.
  Adm: 130/yr. Appl due: Rolling. Tests SSAT.
  Enr 500. G 500. Elem 330. Sec 170. Wh 7%. Blk 1%. Asian 92%. Avg class size: 13. Uniform. Fac 65. M 12/3. F 48/2. Wh 54%. Hisp 3%. Am Ind 3%. Asian 32%. Other 8%. Adv deg: 50%.
  Grad '04—43. Col—43. (U of HI-Manoa 10, Seattle U 3, San Jose St 2, Smith 1, USC 1, Marquette 1). Alum 3500.
  Tui '04-'05: Day $9555-9885 (+$1200). Aid: Merit 7 ($119,628). Need 104 ($259,792).
  Summer: Acad Enrich Rev Rec. Sports. Tui Day $500/crse. 6-10 wks.
  Endow $3,120,000. Plant val $13,000,000. Bldgs 11. Class rms 44. 2 Libs 25,000 vols. Sci labs 5. Comp labs 1. Art studios 5. Music studios 6. Dance studios 2. Gyms 1. Courts 1.
  Est 1867. Nonprofit. Episcopal. Sem (Aug-June). Assoc WASC.

St. Andrew's Priory School, Hawaii's first school for girls, was founded by Anglican sisters and Queen Emma, wife of King Kamehameha IV. Curricular offerings include extensive visual and performing arts selections, computer, foreign languages and Advanced Placement preparation.

Located in downtown Honolulu, the Priory is easily accessible to all parts of Oahu. Students may participate in interscholastic sports, drama, science fair, and speech and math competitions. In addition to the regular day school program, the Priory offers educational opportunities to the larger community from preschool to adults through its self-supporting Queen Emma Center.

KAILUA, HI. (7 mi. NE of Honolulu, HI) Urban. Pop: 36,818. Alt: 10 ft.

LE JARDIN
WINDWARD OAHU ACADEMY
Day — Coed Gr PS-12

Kailua, HI 96734. 917 Kalanianaole Hwy. Tel: 808-261-0707. Fax: 808-262-9339.
www.lejardinacademy.com   E-mail: staylor@lejardinacademy.com
Adrian Allan, Head. MA, Univ of Alabama. **Susan Taylor, Adm.**
- Pre-Prep. Feat—Japan Span Computers Studio_Art Music. **Supp**—Rev Tut.
- **Adm:** 155/yr. Appl due: Jan. **Tests** MAT SSAT.
- **Enr 600.** B 300. G 300. Elem 500. Sec 100. Wh 63%. Blk 1%. Asian 36%. Avg class size: 21. **Fac 80.** M 6. F 69/5. Wh 75%. Other 25%. Adv deg: 20%.
- **Grad '04—40. Prep—40.** (Punahou, Iolani, La Pietra, Mid-Pacific). Alum 550.
- **Tui '04-'05:** Day $9905-10,055 (+$200). **Aid:** Merit 18. Need 65.
- **Summer:** Acad Enrich Rev Rem. Tui Day $350/crse. 5 wks.
- Endow $2,000,000. Plant val $3,000,000. Bldgs 8. Class rms 35. Libs 2. Sci labs 2. Comp labs 2. Auds 2. Theaters 1. Art studios 2. Music studios 2. Fields 2. Pools 1.
- **Est 1961.** Nonprofit. (Aug-June). **Assoc** WASC.

Founded by Henriette D. Neal, a native of France, the academy provides a strong academic base in all subjects and an enriching fine arts program. Basic communicational skills are taught using the Spalding method, a multisensory approach to the teaching of reading, writing and spelling. French is taught at all grade levels, including prekindergarten and junior kindergarten (ages 3 and 4), and Japanese instruction begins in grade 5. Computer, library, physical education, art and music round out the curriculum.

Field trips are planned during the school year at each grade level. Enrichment programs offer after-school activities in orchestra, band, ukulele choir, dance, choir, sports, art, yearbook, newspaper, drama and student council.

KAMUELA, HI. (42 mi. WNW of Hilo, HI) Rural. Pop: 5972. Alt: 2600 ft.

HAWAII PREPARATORY ACADEMY
Bdg — Coed Gr 6-12; Day — Coed K-12

Kamuela, HI 96743. 65-1692 Kohala Mountain Rd. Tel: 808-885-7321. Fax: 808-881-4003.
www.hpa.edu   E-mail: admissions@hpa.edu
Olaf Jorgenson, Head. BA, MA, Washington State Univ, EdD, Arizona State Univ. **Brian K. Chatterley, Adm.**
- Col Prep. AP—Eng Fr Span Calc Stats Comp_Sci Bio Chem Physics Eur_Hist US_Hist Econ Psych Art_Hist Studio_Art Music_Theory. **Feat**—Japan Lat Astron Marine_Biol/Sci Hawaiian_Hist Drama Music. **Supp**—ESL Tut.
- **Adm (Bdg Gr 6-12; Day K-11):** 124/yr. Bdg 83. Day 41. Appl due: Feb. Accepted: 56%. Yield: 41%. **Tests** ISEE SSAT.
- **Enr 589.** B 101/200. G 94/194. Elem 237. Sec 352. Avg class size: 15. **Fac 62.** M 19/6. F 32/5. Adv deg: 66%. In dorms 14.

Grad '04—76. Col—73. Avg SAT: 1121. Alum 2500.
Tui '04-'05: Bdg $29,000-31,000. 5-Day Bdg $26,000. Day $11,300-14,500. Aid: Need 117 ($800,000).
Summer: Acad Enrich Rec. Tui Bdg $3800. Tui Day $475-1325. 4 wks.
Endow $16,000,000. Plant val $33,000,000. Bldgs 38. Dorms 4. Dorm rms 116. Class rms 55. 2 Libs 17,000 vols. Sci labs 5. Comp labs 5. Art studios 2. Music studios 2. Dance studios 1. Gyms 1. Fields 7. Basketball courts 2. Tennis courts 4. Volleyball courts 1. Pools 1.
Est 1949. Nonprofit. Sem (Aug-May). **Assoc** CLS WASC.

HPA has two campuses in the town of Waimea on the island of Hawaii. The upper school is situated on 126 acres at the foot of the Kohala Mountains, in the heart of Hawaii's ranching country; the campus housing the lower and middle schools occupies six acres near the center of Waimea. Students come from the Hawaiian Islands, more than a dozen mainland states and territories, and a similar number of foreign countries.

Among the graduation requirements are modern language, fine arts and computer science courses, and electives. Advanced Placement classes are available in all disciplines. Students are required to participate in the cocurricular component of athletics and may choose interscholastic competition, intramurals or noncompetitive activities each weekday. Sports include baseball, basketball, cross-country, football, golf, soccer, swimming, tennis, track, volleyball, wrestling, canoe paddling and girls' water polo; in addition, equestrianship and scuba diving are offered. Students may also choose from such extracurriculars as debate, drama, scuba club, Amnesty International, yearbook, newspaper, environmental studies, robotics, service learning, tutoring and peer assistance, math league and an array of musical offerings.

Some of the weekend activities scheduled are camping trips, deep-sea fishing, scuba diving, shopping trips, excursions and hikes to points of interest on the island, surfing outings and regular Sunday trips to Hapuna Beach. HPA operates a compulsory work program that consists of two hours of on-campus chores each week.

OREGON

PORTLAND, OR. Urban. Pop: 529,121. Alt: 175 ft.

OREGON EPISCOPAL SCHOOL
Bdg — Coed Gr 9-12; Day — Coed PS-12

Portland, OR 97223. 6300 SW Nicol Rd. Tel: 503-246-7771. Fax: 503-768-3140.
www.oes.edu E-mail: admit@oes.edu

Dulany O. Bennett, Head. BA, Swarthmore College, MS, Univ of Pennsylvania, PhD, Pacific Univ. **Pam Dreisin, Adm.**

Col Prep. AP—Eng Fr Span US_Hist. **Feat**—Japan Computers Intl_Relations Global_Stud Philos Relig Drama Music Study_Skills. **Supp**—ESL.

Adm: 139/yr. Bdg 20. Day 119. Appl due: Jan. Accepted: 53%. Yield: 65%. **Tests** CTP_4 ISEE SSAT TOEFL.

Enr 778. B 29/363. G 23/363. Elem 516. Sec 262. Wh 72%. Hisp 1%. Blk 2%. Asian 18%. Other 7%. **Fac 108.** M 25/10. F 44/29. Wh 95%. Hisp 1%. Blk 1%. Asian 3%. Adv deg: 60%. In dorms 7.

Grad '04—54. Col—53. (Duke 4, OR St 3, U of WA 2, U of OR 2, Pepperdine 2, Pitzer 2). Avg SAT: 1270. Alum 1999.

Tui '04-'05: Bdg $31,550 (+$500-700). **Day $13,330-17,370** (+$400-500). **Aid:** Need 42 ($448,500).

Summer: Acad Enrich Rev Rec. Tui Day $220-465. 1½ wks.

Endow $11,978,000. Plant val $22,000,000. Bldgs 14. Dorms 2. Dorm rms 42. Class rms 89. 3 Libs 35,000 vols. Labs 5. Sci labs 5. Comp labs 6. Art studios 6. Music studios 3. Gyms 2. Fields 3. Courts 7. Tracks 1. Skiing facilities yes.

Est 1869. Nonprofit. Episcopal. Sem (Sept-June). **Assoc** CLS NAAS.

The school traces its origin to a pioneer institution founded by the Episcopal Church in 1861. In 1869, St. Helens Hall for girls was formally established by Bishop Benjamin Wistar Morris and Miss Mary Rodney. From 1903 to 1944, it was directed by the Episcopal Sisters of St. John Baptist. In 1965, after St. Helens Hall had relocated to its present, 59-acre campus, Bishop Dagwell Hall for boys was added as a coordinate institution. In 1968, the two schools merged as Oregon Episcopal School, becoming fully coeducational in 1972.

Educational objectives and admissions criteria are demanding, and students are prepared for college through a balanced curriculum in English, history, math, science, foreign languages and religion/philosophy. Global studies are emphasized, and English as a Second Language is offered to international students. All students participate in an age-appropriate service program. Art, music, drama and sports are an integral part of the overall program, with cocurricular activities offered in many areas. OES integrates an outdoor/experiential program into the curriculum, and an on-campus wetland area is used as a field biology lab. The school has a traditional student council and many community activities involving students, faculty and parents.

PORTLAND LUTHERAN SCHOOL

Bdg — Coed Gr 8-12; Day — Coed PS-12

Portland, OR 97233. 740 SE 182nd Ave. Tel: 503-667-3199. Fax: 503-667-4520.
www.portland-lutheran.org
Karl Birnstein, Exec Dir. BS, Concordia College (NE).

- **Col Prep. AP**—Eng. **Feat**—Fr Japan Span Computers Programming Econ Govt Pol_Sci Psych Relig Studio_Art Drama Music Sports_Marketing. **Supp**—ESL Tut.
- **Adm:** 76/yr. Bdg 19. Day 57. Appl due: Rolling. Accepted: 95%. Yield: 85%.
- **Enr 304.** B 20/136. G 13/135. Elem 189. Sec 115. Wh 80%. Hisp 2%. Blk 2%. Asian 16%. Avg class size: 22. **Fac 24.** M 6/3. F 10/5. Wh 100%. Adv deg: 37%.
- **Grad '04—21. Col**—15. (Mt Hood CC 3, Concordia U-OR 3, U of OR 2, U of Portland 2, Geo Fox 1, Pacific Lutheran 1). Avg SAT: 1140. Avg ACT: 27.
- **Tui '04-'05: Bdg $15,000** (+$500). **Day $4650-6300** (+$500). **Aid:** Merit 2 ($2000). Need 34 ($49,406).
- Endow $339,000. Plant val $7,500,000. Bldgs 6. Class rms 23. Lib 10,000 vols. Sci labs 2. Comp labs 2. Auds 1. Art studios 1. Music studios 2. Gyms 2. Fields 2.
- **Est 1905.** Nonprofit. Lutheran. Sem (Aug-June). **Assoc** NAAS.

Founded as Concordia Academy to prepare young men for the Lutheran ministry, PLS gradually evolved into a Christian, coeducational elementary and secondary school, culminating in the assumption of its present name in 1989. The school now offers a broad education in the humanities, math, science, language arts and the fine arts. As part of the college preparatory high school curriculum, qualified students in grades 10-12 may enroll in honors courses.

A comprehensive sports program serves boys and girls at all grade levels, while such activities as publications, jazz ensemble, drama and student leadership form a vital component of the high school program. Religious education is part of everyday school life.

PLS maintains a home-stay program for international students. Arranged with compatibility in mind, home stays are available throughout Portland, as well as in the outlying areas of Vancouver, WA, and Sandy. ESL instruction assists international pupils with English pronunciation, grammar, vocabulary development, conversational skills and skill application.

WASHINGTON

REDMOND, WA. (12 mi. ENE of Seattle, WA) Suburban. Pop: 45,256. Alt: 42 ft.

THE OVERLAKE SCHOOL
Day — Coed Gr 5-12

Redmond, WA 98053. 20301 NE 108th St. Tel: 425-868-1000. Fax: 425-868-6770.
www.overlake.org   E-mail: info@overlake.org

Francisco J. Grijalva, Head. BA, San Francisco State Univ, MA, Stanford Univ, EdD, Univ of San Francisco. **Lori Maughan, Adm.**
- **Col Prep. AP**—Eng Fr Lat Span Calc Comp_Sci Bio Chem Eur_Hist US_Hist Art_Hist. **Feat**—Japan Ornithology Econ Photog Studio_Art Drama Theater_Arts Chorus Music Outdoor_Ed. **Supp**—Rev Tut.
- **Adm:** 95/yr. Appl due: Jan. Accepted: 52%. Yield: 71%. **Tests** ISEE.
- **Enr 482.** B 242. G 240. Elem 215. Sec 267. Wh 69%. Hisp 1%. Blk 1%. Asian 13%. Other 16%. Avg class size: 13. **Fac 53.** Adv deg: 73%.
- **Grad '04—64. Col—62.** (U of WA 9, Santa Clara 8, USC 5, Stanford 4, U of Rochester 2). Alum 1229.
- **Tui '04-'05:** Day $18,500 (+$900-1200). **Aid:** Need 72 ($620,706).
- Endow $6,000,000. Plant val $32,000,000. Bldgs 17. Class rms 47. Lib 16,000 vols. Labs 6. Sci labs 1. Lang labs 1. Comp labs 1. Auds 1. Theaters 1. Art studios 4. Music studios 4. Arts ctrs 2. Gyms 2. Fields 1. Tennis courts 4.
- **Est 1967.** Nonprofit. Tri (Aug-June). **Assoc** NAAS.

Overlake, located on a rustic, 75-acre campus, offers a rigorous college preparatory curriculum. Sports, a strong arts program, and Advanced Placement and honors courses in all major disciplines complement traditional course offerings. College counseling services are available to upper school students.

Athletic options include track, lacrosse, soccer, cross-country, basketball, baseball, wrestling, volleyball, golf and tennis. Students may participate in such extracurricular activities as student government, theatrical productions, newspaper and various clubs. Overlake provides opportunities for travel abroad, and the school hosts foreign pupils each year.

SEATTLE, WA. Urban. Pop: 563,374. Alt: to 123 ft.

LAKESIDE SCHOOL
Day — Coed Gr 5-12

Seattle, WA 98125. 14050 1st Ave NE. Tel: 206-368-3600. Fax: 206-368-3638.
www.lakeside.org   E-mail: admissions@lakesideschool.org

Bernard Noe, Head. BA, Boston Univ, MA, Georgetown Univ, MPh, George Washington Univ. **Rachael N. Beare, Adm.**
- **Col Prep. Feat**—Asian-Amer_Lit Fr Lat Mandarin Span Anat & Physiol Astron Environ_Sci Marine_Biol/Sci Computers Holocaust Vietnam_War Amer_Stud Anthro Philos World_Relig Art_Hist Digital_Media Drama. **Supp**—Tut.

WA   Pacific States   757

Adm: 146/yr. Appl due: Jan. Accepted: 32%. Yield: 80%. **Tests** ISEE.
Enr 757. B 377. G 380. Elem 254. Sec 503. Wh 65%. Hisp 3%. Blk 9%. Am Ind 2%. Asian 18%. Other 3%. Avg class size: 16. **Fac 88.** M 39/2. F 36/11. Wh 77%. Hisp 4%. Blk 8%. Asian 8%. Other 3%. Adv deg: 64%.
Grad '04—112. Col—112. (U of WA 7, Stanford 5, U of PA 4, Middlebury 4, Whitman 4, Brown 3). Avg SAT: 1410. Alum 5500.
Tui '04-'05: Day $18,550-19,320 (+$250-3200). **Aid:** Need 155 ($1,857,000).
Summer: Acad Enrich Rec. Tui Day $0. 6 wks.
Endow $50,800,000. Plant val $47,341,000. Bldgs 22. Class rms 75. 2 Libs 40,000 vols. Sci labs 8. Comp labs 6. Comp ctrs 2. Auds 2. Theaters 2. Art studios 7. Music studios 2. Perf arts ctrs 2. AV ctrs 2. Gyms 2. Fields 4. Field houses 1.
Est 1919. Nonprofit. (Sept-June). **Assoc** NAAS.

Located at the northern edge of Seattle, the school draws its enrollment from the city's metropolitan area. Originally a boys' boarding and day school, Lakeside discontinued its boarding department in 1964. The school became coeducational in 1971 after effecting a merger with St. Nicholas School for girls. Lakeside's campus consists of the upper school (grades 9-12) and, a block away, the middle school (grades 5-8).

The school's academic program provides students with a strong foundation in the arts, the humanities and the sciences, while also allowing them to pursue individual interests through a wide variety of curricular offerings. Both school divisions have ample facilities to support course work in sciences and the visual and performing arts. Outdoor education, community service and physical education programs complement academics. All students in grades 7-12 utilize laptop computers.

In addition to fulfilling diploma requirements in the traditional subject areas, upper school pupils take an outdoor education trip and complete 80 hours of community service. Students have the opportunity to travel internationally to locations in Europe, South America and Asia through the Lakeside Intercultural Program, and the school also conducts long-standing student and faculty exchanges with institutions in Russia and Costa Rica.

Students have access to a variety of extracurricular activities, among them student government, chess club, literary magazine, newspaper and diversity committee. Baseball, basketball, crew, cross-country, football, golf, lacrosse, soccer, softball, swimming, tennis, track and field, and volleyball are the interscholastic sports.

THE NORTHWEST SCHOOL

Bdg — Coed Gr 9-12; Day — Coed 6-12

Seattle, WA 98122. 1415 Summit Ave. Tel: 206-682-7309. Fax: 206-467-7353.
www.northwestschool.org   E-mail: admissions@northwestschool.org
Ellen Taussig, Head. BA, Bennington College, MAT, Yale Univ. **Anne Smith, Adm.**
  Col Prep. Feat—Humanities Fr Span Stats Philos Arts. **Supp**—ESL Tut.
  Adm: 88/yr. Bdg 12. Day 76. Appl due: Jan. Accepted: 40%. Yield: 52%. **Tests** ISEE.
  Enr 434. B 26/196. G 12/200. Elem 116. Sec 318. Wh 70%. Hisp 2%. Blk 4%. Am Ind 1%. Asian 23%. Avg class size: 18. **Fac 69.** M 18/17. F 18/16. Adv deg: 66%.
  Grad '04—65. Col—63. (U of WA 5, Seattle U 5, Occidental 3, Bard 3, Macalester 2, Brown 2). Alum 1078.
  Tui '04-'05: Bdg $30,375. Day $18,775-20,165. **Aid:** Need 56 ($890,665).
  Summer: Acad Enrich Rev Rem Rec. Arts. ESL. Tui Bdg $1285/2-wk ses. Tui Day $650/2-wk ses. 6 wks.
  Endow $234,000. Plant val $9,555,000. Bldgs 3. Dorms 1. Dorm rms 30. Class rms 30.

Libs 1. Sci labs 4. Lang labs 3. Comp labs 1. Auds 1. Theaters 1. Art studios 3. Music studios 2. Dance studios 1. Courts 1.
Est 1978. Nonprofit. 5 terms (Sept-June). **Assoc** NAAS.

Northwest's sequential college preparatory curriculum comprises academic, arts, international and athletic programs. The academic studies program, which seeks to improve critical thinking, articulation and synthesizing skills, consists of math, science, language and humanities components. Pupils in all grades receive credit for both English and history through the core humanities program; students in grades 9-12 follow a chronological history of civilization sequence that progresses from 3000 BC to the present day. The arts program features required music, dance, theater and visual arts courses, all of which are taught by practicing artists. The boarding division serves international students only. The international program offers ESL courses and foreign exchange opportunities.

The athletic program provides interscholastic competition in soccer, basketball, crew, ultimate Frisbee, cross-country, volleyball and track. The school operates an environment program in which all students clean and maintain the campus, each grade level goes on at least one major camping trip per year, and frequent wilderness excursions are offered.

UNIVERSITY PREPARATORY ACADEMY
Day — Coed Gr 6-12

Seattle, WA 98115. 8000 25th Ave NE. Tel: 206-523-6407. Fax: 206-525-5320.
www.universityprep.org E-mail: rcibella@universityprep.org
Erica L. Hamlin, Head. BA, Smith College, MALS, Wesleyan Univ. **Roger D. Cibella, Adm.**
   Col Prep. Feat—Creative_Writing Fr Japan Span Stats Astron Japan_Hist Econ Govt Psych Philos Photog Music Music_Theory Orchestra Jazz_Ensemble Dance. **Supp**—Tut.
   Adm: 99/yr. Appl due: Jan. Accepted: 24%. **Tests** ISEE.
   Enr 457. B 223. G 234. Elem 204. Sec 253. Wh 78%. Hisp 1%. Blk 4%. Am Ind 1%. Asian 9%. Other 7%. Avg class size: 16. **Fac 57.** M 16/4. F 30/7. Adv deg: 63%.
   Grad '04—52. **Col**—52. (Geo Wash 3, U of San Francisco 3, Chapman 2, Emory 2, U of WA 2, Willamette 2). Alum 978.
   Tui '04-'05: Day $17,587-18,694 (+$1000). **Aid:** Merit 1 ($5000). Need 69 ($906,843). Endow $2,303,000. Plant val $22,550,000. Bldgs 3. Class rms 23. Libs 1. Sci labs 7. Lang labs 7. Comp labs 3. Art studios 3. Music studios 6. Gyms 2. Fields 1.
   Est 1976. Nonprofit. Sem (Sept-June). **Assoc** NAAS.

The college preparatory curriculum at University Prep emphasizes the liberal arts and sciences. Two-week winter interim workshops in areas not covered during the academic year—such as photography, videography, career exploration, animation, first aid, pottery, domestic and international travel, and self-defense—are available. Cocurricular activities include publications, interscholastic athletics, interest clubs and student government, and students participate in compulsory community service projects. A senior thesis incorporating independent research is required for graduation.

SPOKANE, WA. (230 mi. E of Seattle, WA) Urban. Pop: 195,629. Alt: 1943 ft.

SAINT GEORGE'S SCHOOL
Day — Coed Gr K-12

Spokane, WA 99208. 2929 W Waikiki Rd. Tel: 509-466-1636. Fax: 509-467-3258.
www.sgs.org   E-mail: debbie.duvoisin@sgs.org
Mo Copeland, Head. BA, Reed College.
  Col Prep. **AP**—Eng Fr Calc Bio Chem Physics Eur_Hist US_Hist Studio_Art. **Feat**—Span Comp_Sci Asian_Hist Russ_Hist Govt Music_Theory. **Supp**—Dev_Read Rev Tut.
  Adm: 65/yr. Appl due: Rolling. Accepted: 86%. Yield: 63%. **Tests** TOEFL.
  Enr 370. B 197. G 173. Elem 244. Sec 126. Wh 82%. Hisp 3%. Blk 3%. Am Ind 1%. Asian 7%. Other 4%. Avg class size: 15. **Fac 46.** M 16/4. F 18/8. Wh 87%. Hisp 11%. Asian 2%. Adv deg: 54%.
  Grad '04—26. Col—25. (Claremont McKenna 2, Master's 2, Gonzaga 1, U of WA 1, MIT 1, Rose-Hulman Inst of Tech 1). Avg SAT: 1264. Alum 951.
  Tui '04-'05: Day $11,040-12,840 (+$440-1020). **Aid:** Merit 12 ($41,000). Need 68 ($279,373).
  Endow $3,000,000. Plant val $2,000,000. Bldgs 10. Class rms 29. 2 Libs 10,000 vols. Labs 6. Theaters 1. Art studios 2. Music studios 2. Gyms 2. Fields 6. Courts 3.
  Est 1955. Nonprofit. Sem (Sept-June). **Assoc** CLS NAAS.

This rigorous school conducts a full elementary and secondary program while preparing its graduates for competitive colleges nationwide. The curriculum features Advanced Placement courses in the major disciplines, in addition to a full complement of electives.

Extracurricular activities include publications, drama, fine arts, photography, chorus, community service, outdoor experiential education and travel. Among the athletic offerings are basketball, baseball, volleyball, track, softball, tennis, soccer and rock climbing.

TACOMA, WA. (26 mi. SSW of Seattle, WA) Urban. Pop: 193,556. Alt: 75 ft.

ANNIE WRIGHT SCHOOL
Bdg — Girls Gr 9-12; Day — Boys K-8, Girls K-12

Tacoma, WA 98403. 827 N Tacoma Ave. Tel: 253-272-2216. Fax: 253-572-3616.
www.aw.org   E-mail: admission@aw.org
Dr. Jayasri Ghosh, Head. BA, Univ of Calcutta (India), MEd, PhD, Univ of Georgia. **Robert Booth, Adm.**
  Col Prep. **AP**—Econ. **Feat**—Japan Anat & Physiol Bioethics Genetics Marine_Biol/Sci Microbiol Computers African_Stud Asian_Stud Relig Studio_Art Drama Music. **Supp**—ESL Rev Tut.
  Adm (Day Gr K-12): 77/yr. Bdg 15. Day 62. **Tests** ISEE SSAT.
  Enr 406. B 110. G 39/257. Elem 313. Sec 93. Wh 66%. Hisp 3%. Blk 1%. Am Ind 2%. Asian 13%. Other 15%. Avg class size: 18. Uniform. **Fac 52.** M 17. F 35. Wh 92%. Blk 4%. Asian 4%. Adv deg: 42%. In dorms 6.
  Grad '04—24. Col—24. (U of WA, IN U, Smith, U of Chicago, Reed, Pepperdine). Avg

SAT: 1150. Avg ACT: 24. Alum 1500.
Tui '03-'04: Bdg $32,677 (+$800). **Day $13,324-16,438** (+$800). **Aid:** Merit 17 ($82,900). Need 57 ($372,523).
Endow $12,000,000. Plant val $22,000,000. Bldgs 2. Dorm rms 56. Class rms 45. Lib 19,000 vols. Chapels 1. Sci labs 4. Comp labs 2. Dark rms 1. Auds 1. Theaters 1. Art studios 3. Music studios 3. Dance studios 1. Gyms 2. Fields 1. Courts 3. Pools 1.
Est 1884. Nonprofit. Episcopal. Tri (Sept-June). **Assoc** NAAS.

The school was founded by Rt. Rev. John A. Paddock, first Episcopal bishop of the Washington Territory, and Charles B. Wright, with the aim that "not only the intellect, but the character, manners and morals of the pupil are subjects of earnest care and solicitude." Located in Tacoma's historic North End, Annie Wright offers a curriculum that combines a rigorous academic program with varied athletic and extracurricular offerings. English as a Second Language classes are available in grades 9-12. Emphasis is on college preparation, and graduates enter leading colleges.

Among the school's activities are student government, community service, literary magazine, choir and interest clubs.

CHARLES WRIGHT ACADEMY
Day — Coed Gr PS-12

Tacoma, WA 98467. 7723 Chambers Creek Rd W. Tel: 253-620-8300. Fax: 253-620-8431. www.charleswright.org E-mail: admissions@mail.charleswright.org
Robert A. Camner, Head. BA, Oberlin College, MS, Ohio State Univ. **Noel Blyler, Adm.**
  Col Prep. AP—Eng Fr Span Calc Stats Comp_Sci Chem Physics Eur_Hist US_Hist Econ. **Feat**—Japan Studio_Art Band Orchestra Outdoor_Ed. **Supp**—Dev_Read Tut.
  Adm: 121/yr. Appl due: Rolling. Accepted: 74%. Yield: 67%. **Tests** ISEE SSAT.
  Enr 682. B 378. G 304. Elem 404. Sec 278. Wh 75%. Hisp 1%. Blk 5%. Asian 12%. Other 7%. Avg class size: 16. **Fac 80.** M 40. F 36/4. Adv deg: 53%.
  Grad '04—72. Col—72. Alum 1500.
  Tui '04-'05: Day $9490-15,935 (+$100-400).
  Endow $12,000,000. Plant val $8,000,000. Bldgs 10. Class rms 50. Lib 40,000 vols. Sci labs 7. Lang labs 2. Comp labs 3. Art studios 8. Music studios 3. Gyms 3. Fields 4. Courts 6.
  Est 1957. Nonprofit. Sem (Aug-June). **Assoc** CLS NAAS.

Located on a suburban, 90-acre campus, CWA was founded by parents interested in providing a rigorous curriculum in the liberal arts for their sons. In 1970, the school became coeducational.

Elective courses in all disciplines, computer science, an Advanced Placement program and the opportunity for independent study complement the traditional college preparatory curriculum. The academy also offers complete arts, athletic and outdoor education programs.

CONCISE SCHOOL LISTINGS

The following schools complement those in the Leading Private Schools chapter. They are arranged geographically by state, progressing from east to west across the country. Within each state, schools are listed alphabetically by city or town.

These are, in part, schools similar to those found in the Leading Private Schools section about which sufficient information is not currently available to allow inclusion there. Also included here are schools whose enrollment is more strictly limited to a local area or with specialized objectives and programs.

For schools not included in the *Handbook,* consult our other publications: *The Directory for Exceptional Children, Guide to Summer Camps and Summer Schools* and *Schools Abroad of Interest to Americans.*

New England States

CONNECTICUT

ACADEMY OF THE HOLY FAMILY   **Girls Gr 9-12**
Baltic, CT 06330. 54 W Main St, PO Box 691.   **Bdg & Day**
Tel: 860-822-9272. Fax: 860-822-1318.
www.academyoftheholyfamily.org   E-mail: academy.holy.family@snet.net
    Sr. Mary Patrick Mulready, SCMC, Prin. MS, Eastern Connecticut State Univ, MS, Dayton Univ, MAT, Sacred Heart Univ.

    Col Prep. Gen Acad. Feat—Creative_Writing Fr Lat Span Environ_Sci Computers Psych Relig Music Speech Home_Ec. **Supp**—ESL Rem_Math. **Adm:** 22/yr. Bdg 6. Day 16. Appl due: Rolling. Accepted: 90%. **Enr 56.** G 8/48. Sec 56. Avg class size: 10. Uniform. **Fac 16.** F 11/5. Wh 94%. Blk 6%. Adv deg: 50%. In Dorms 2. **Grad '04**—12. Col—10. Alum 825. **Tui '03-'04:** Bdg $13,600 (+$1214). 5-Day Bdg $12,100 (+$1214). Day $3100 (+$780). **Est 1874.** Nonprofit. Roman Catholic. Quar (Aug-June). **Assoc** NEASC. Founded by the Sisters of Charity, the academy conducts its educational program from a traditional Catholic perspective. The program of studies includes history, languages, religion, math and science, in addition to art, family studies, business skills, computer science and physical education. School life is enriched by a number of activities and clubs, among them an a cappella choir, drama, student council and school newspaper. Sports include soccer in the fall, basketball in the winter and softball in the spring, as well as cheerleading.

BESS AND PAUL SIGEL HEBREW ACADEMY   **Day Coed Gr PS-8**
Bloomfield, CT 06002. 53 Gabb Rd.
Tel: 860-243-8333. Fax: 860-243-3986.
www.sigelacademy.org   E-mail: mloiterman@sigelacademy.org
    Rabbi Mordechai Loiterman, Prin. BA, Hebrew Theological College, MEd, Simon Fraser Univ (Canada). Ellen Hoehne, Adm.

    Pre-Prep. Feat—Hebrew Span Computers Judaic_Stud Studio_Art Music. **Supp**—Dev_Read ESL Rem_Math Rem_Read. **Adm:** 22/yr. Appl due: Rolling. Accepted: 100%. **Tests** CTP_4. **Enr 145.** B 82. G 63. Elem 145. Wh 100%. Avg class size: 12. **Fac 25.** M 3. F 5/17. Adv deg: 44%. **Grad '04**—15. Prep—14. **Tui '04-'05:** Day $8500 (+$2000). Aid: Merit 34 ($150,000). **Est 1940.** Nonprofit. Jewish. Tri (Sept-June). The academy offers a Judaic studies program integrated with a curriculum in the language arts, the social sciences, math and the physical sciences, and supplemented by music, art, physical education and computer literacy. The Judaic curriculum combines Bible study, Hebrew language, and Jewish history, beliefs and practices. Each seventh and eighth grader is required to complete an independent study project, as well as a number of supervised community service hours.

IMMACULATE HIGH SCHOOL
Day Coed Gr 9-12
Danbury, CT 06810. 73 Southern Blvd.
Tel: 203-744-1510. Fax: 203-744-1275.
www.immaculatehs.org   E-mail: ihsmailbox@immaculatehs.org

Richard T. Stoops, Prin. BS, Western Connecticut State Univ, MA, Fairfield Univ. Rev. Corey Piccinino, Adm.

Col Prep. AP—Studio_Art. **Feat**—Fr Lat Span Web_Design Govt Relig Drama Band Chorus Jazz Dance Journ Public_Speak. **Supp**—Rev Tut. **Adm:** 150/yr. Appl due: Rolling. Accepted: 70%. Yield: 50%. **Enr 438.** B 212. G 226. Sec 438. Wh 91%. Hisp 2%. Blk 3%. Am Ind 1%. Asian 3%. Avg class size: 23. Uniform. **Fac 41.** M 8/3. F 24/6. Wh 95%. Blk 5%. Adv deg: 68%. **Grad '04—86.** Col—82. Avg SAT: 1080. Alum 6200. **Tui '04-'05:** Day $6700 (+$300). Aid: Merit 40 ($81,000). Need 55 ($50,000). **Summer:** Acad Enrich. 4 wks. **Est 1962.** Nonprofit. Roman Catholic. Quar (Aug-June). **Assoc** NEASC. Advanced Placement and honors courses are available in the major disciplines. Activities include student council, various interest clubs, student publications, academic quiz bowl, musical offerings and intramural sports.

ENFIELD MONTESSORI SCHOOL
Day Coed Gr PS-6
Enfield, CT 06082. 1370 Enfield St.
Tel: 860-745-5847. Fax: 860-745-2010.
E-mail: montessori@snet.net

Sr. Mary Anastasia Holak, CSSF, Prin. BA, Regis College, MEd, Rivier College.

Pre-Prep. Feat—Fr. **Supp**—Rem_Math Rem_Read Tut. **Adm:** 20/yr. Appl due: Apr. Accepted: 50%. **Enr 115.** B 65. G 50. Elem 115. Wh 98%. Asian 2%. Avg class size: 23. Uniform. **Fac 6.** F 5/1. Wh 100%. Adv deg: 33%. Alum 760. **Tui '02-'03:** Day $2725 (+$75). Aid: Need 4 ($4500). **Est 1965.** Nonprofit. Roman Catholic. Quar (Sept-June). The school offers French instruction in the upper grades.

EAGLE HILL SCHOOL
5-Day Bdg Coed Ages 10-16
Day Coed Ages 6-16
Greenwich, CT 06831. 45 Glenville Rd.
Tel: 203-622-9240. Fax: 203-622-0914.
www.eaglehillschool.org   E-mail: r.griffin@eaglehill.org

Mark J. Griffin, Head. BA, Merrimack College, MA, Assumption College, MEd, Worcester State College, PhD, Fordham Univ. Rayma-Joan Griffin, Adm.

LD. Feat—Computers Study_Skills. **Supp**—Rem_Math Rem_Read Rev Tut. **Adm:** 65/yr. Bdg 15. Day 50. Appl due: Rolling. Accepted: 60%. Yield: 98%. **Tests** IQ. **Enr 210.** B 20/115. G 10/65. Elem 195. Sec 15. Wh 90%. Hisp 2%. Blk 8%. Avg class size: 6. **Fac 80.** M 30. F 45/5. Adv deg: 92%. In Dorms 7. **Grad '04—65.** Prep—48. Alum 1200. **Tui '04-'05:** 5-Day Bdg $52,100 (+$500). Day $40,750. Aid: Need 21 ($600,000). **Summer:** Ages 6-13. Acad Rev Rem. Tui Day $2200. 5½ wks. **Est 1975.** Nonprofit. Sem (Sept-June). The school offers boys and girls of average or high intelligence remediation for learning disabilities. Students have typically failed to reach potential in traditional educational environments. Graduates enter leading prep schools and local public and private schools.

See Also Pages 1356-7

THE STANWICH SCHOOL
Day Coed Gr K-9

Greenwich, CT 06830. 257 Stanwich Rd.
Tel: 203-869-4515. Fax: 203-869-4641.
www.stanwichschool.org   E-mail: info@stanwichschool.org

Patricia G. Young, Head. BA, Sweet Briar College, MA, Fairfield Univ. Mauri Clarke, Adm.

Pre-Prep. Feat—Fr Lat Span Computers Ethics Fine_Arts Drama Music. **Supp**—Dev_Read. **Adm:** 78/yr. Appl due: Dec. Accepted: 40%. Yield: 64%. **Tests** CTP_4 ISEE. **Enr 346.** B 176. G 170. Avg class size: 17. Uniform. **Fac 49.** M 8/4. F 34/3. Wh 96%. Hisp 2%. Blk 2%. Adv deg: 61%.**Tui '04-'05:** Day $18,800-20,500 (+$600-1300). Aid: Need 25 ($376,850). **Est 1998.** (Sept-June). In a small-class setting, Stanwich conducts a demanding curriculum while utilizing both traditional and contemporary teaching methods. Notable features of the program include accelerated math and language arts groupings; a foreign language program that begins with French in kindergarten; a fully integrated fine arts and performing arts program; individualized scheduling and assigned academic advisors starting in grade 7; a focus on technology that culminates in a laptop program; and a directed study hall. Field trips, clubs and after-school programs enrich the curriculum, and all boys and girls engage in community service throughout the school year.

SACRED HEART ACADEMY
Day Girls Gr 9-12

Hamden, CT 06514. 265 Benham St.
Tel: 203-288-2309. Fax: 203-230-9680.
www.sha-excelsior.org   E-mail: elamboley@sha-excelsior.org

Sr. Ritamary Schulz, Prin. BS, St Louis Univ, MS, Iona College, MS, Southern Connecticut State Univ. Elaine M. Lamboley, Adm.

Col Prep. AP—Eng Fr Lat Span Calc Comp_Sci Bio Chem US_Hist Psych US_Govt & Pol. **Feat**—British_Lit Stats Anat & Physiol Genetics Econ Law Relig Painting Studio_Art Music_Theory Accounting Finance. **Adm:** 130/yr. Appl due: Nov. Accepted: 60%. **Tests** HSPT. **Enr 486.** G 486. Sec 486. Wh 92%. Hisp 2%. Blk 2%. Am Ind 1%. Asian 2%. Other 1%. Avg class size: 20. Uniform. **Fac 46.** M 10. F 33/3. Wh 94%. Hisp 2%. Blk 2%. Asian 2%. Adv deg: 80%. **Grad '04—125.** Col—125. Avg SAT: 1123. **Tui '04-'05:** Day $7870 (+$800). Aid: Merit 4 ($8000). Need 50 ($90,000). **Est 1954.** Nonprofit. Roman Catholic. Sem (Sept-June). Sacred Heart's traditional college preparatory curriculum seeks to provide girls with a strong foundation in the humanities and the arts and sciences. All freshmen take a noncredit seminar course that addresses such topics as time management, decision making, substance abuse and stress. AP and honors classes are available to qualified girls, and electives enable pupils to further explore areas of interest. Community service opportunities, interest clubs, athletics and pursuits in the arts complete the program.

THE COUNTRY SCHOOL
Day Coed Gr PS-8

Madison, CT 06443. 341 Opening Hill Rd.
Tel: 203-421-3113. Fax: 203-421-4390.
www.thecountryschool.org   E-mail: jcrampton@thecountryschool.org

Mr. William Powers, Head. BA, Fairfield Univ, MA, Wesleyan Univ. Janice Crampton, Adm.

Pre-Prep. Feat—Creative_Writing Fr Lat Span Computers Studio_Art Drama Music Woodworking Outdoor_Ed. **Supp**—Dev_Read Rev Tut. **Adm:** 65/yr. Appl due: Feb. Accepted: 40%. **Tests** ISEE. **Enr 300.** Elem 300. Wh 89%. Hisp 2%. Blk 6%. Asian 3%. Avg class size: 16. **Fac 63.** Adv deg: 34%. **Grad '04—34.** Prep—31. Alum 514. **Tui '03-'04:** Day $9550-15,580 (+$275). **Est 1955.** Nonprofit. The school offers an elementary-level curriculum that is augmented by experiences in the creative arts. French begins in prekindergarten. Children take part in a life skills program in grades 5-8, and electives offered in grades 7 and 8 include computer graphics and music theater. Older students participate in a sports program that includes soccer, volleyball, basketball, lacrosse, baseball and outdoor education.

GROVE SCHOOL   **Coed Gr 6-PG**
Madison, CT 06443. 175 Copse Rd, PO Box 646.   **Bdg & Day**
Tel: 203-245-2778. Fax: 203-245-6098.
www.groveschool.org   E-mail: info@groveschool.org

Richard L. Chorney, Pres. BA, Bard College, MS, Southern Connecticut State Univ. Peter J. Chorney, Exec Dir. BA, Bucknell Univ, MS, Southern Connecticut State Univ. Kathy Kimmel, Adm.

Col Prep. Gen Acad. LD. Underachiever. Feat—Span Bus_Math Marine_Biol/Sci Comp_Networking Econ Psych Sociol Philos Filmmaking Graphic_Design. **Supp**—Dev_Read ESL Makeup Tut. **Adm:** 30/yr. Appl due: Rolling. Accepted: 60%. **Tests** IQ. **Enr 105.** B 57/5. G 43. Elem 20. Sec 79. PG 6. Wh 95%. Hisp 2%. Blk 3%. Avg class size: 6. **Fac 28.** M 16. F 12. Adv deg: 42%. In Dorms 28. **Grad '04—19.** Col—19. Avg SAT: 1000. **Tui '05-'06:** Bdg $76,800 (+$1500). Day $54,400 (+$500). **Est 1934.** Inc. Year-round. Students who have failed to make satisfactory adjustments at home, at school or in their social relationships are offered individual and group therapy and a supportive milieu in a creative, active environment. Pupils of normal to superior intelligence are individually guided through the use of extensive academic, therapeutic and recreational facilities.

See Also Page 1157

EAST CATHOLIC HIGH SCHOOL   **Day Coed Gr 9-12**
Manchester, CT 06040. 115 New State Rd.
Tel: 860-649-5336. Fax: 860-649-7191.
www.echs.com

Peg Siegmund, Prin. Jacqueline Gryphon, Adm.

Col Prep. AP—Eng Calc Bio Chem Eur_Hist US_Hist. **Feat**—Fr Lat Span Psych Graphic_Arts Sculpt Studio_Art Band Chorus Music Orchestra. **Supp**—Dev_Read Tut. **Adm:** 200/yr. **Tests** SSAT. **Enr 667.** B 341. G 326. Sec 667. Wh 93%. Hisp 3%. Blk 3%. Asian 1%. Uniform. **Fac 50.** M 21/1. F 26/2. Adv deg: 86%. **Grad '04—138.** Col—135. Avg SAT: 1063. Alum 7000. **Tui '04-'05:** Day $8275 (+$250). **Est 1960.** Nonprofit. Roman Catholic. Quar (Aug-June). **Assoc** NEASC. Students at ECHS take part in a traditional college preparatory curriculum. Activities include dramatics, a variety of clubs, photography and publications, and a wide range of interscholastic and intramural sports is conducted.

MERCY HIGH SCHOOL
Day Girls Gr 9-12

Middletown, CT 06457. 1740 Randolph Rd.
Tel: 860-346-6659. Fax: 860-344-9887.
www.mercyhigh.com   E-mail: info@mercyhigh.com

Sr. Mary A. McCarthy, RSM, Prin. MA, Trinity College (CT). Jo-Ellen Narstis, Adm.

Col Prep. AP—Eng Fr Lat Span Calc Stats Bio Chem Physics US_Hist. **Feat**—Govt Law Psych Sociol Ethics Relig Photog Studio_Art Theater_Arts Music Accounting Bus. **Supp**—Dev_Read Rem_Math. **Adm (Gr 9-11):** 196/yr. Accepted: 91%. Yield: 56%. **Tests** HSPT. **Enr 674.** G 674. Sec 674. Wh 92%. Hisp 3%. Blk 3%. Asian 2%. Avg class size: 21. Uniform. **Fac 54.** M 5/2. F 40/7. Wh 94%. Blk 4%. Asian 2%. Adv deg: 75%. **Grad '04—159.** Col—157. Avg SAT: 1064. Alum 6355. **Tui '04-'05:** Day $7050-7550 (+$800-1800). Aid: Merit 34 ($52,100). Need 160 ($191,300). **Est 1963.** Nonprofit. Roman Catholic. Quar (Sept-June). **Assoc** NEASC. Mercy High features the liberal arts, offering students honors, college preparatory and general academic programs and focusing on college and career preparation. Electives and AP classes are available, and students take a compulsory religion course each year. Field trips, retreats, Masses and other celebrations, and Christian service projects complement the curriculum. Extracurricular opportunities include interscholastic and intramural sports, interest clubs and activities with Xavier High School, a nearby boys' school.

XAVIER HIGH SCHOOL
Day Boys Gr 9-12

Middletown, CT 06457. 181 Randolph Rd.
Tel: 860-346-7735. Fax: 860-346-6859.
www.xavierhighschool.org   E-mail: lisak@xavierhighschool.org

Br. William Ciganek, CFX, Head. BS, Worcester State College, MAT, St Michael's College. Br. Thomas Fahey, CFX, Adm.

Col Prep. AP—Eng Bio Physics Econ US_Govt & Pol Studio_Art. **Feat**—Humanities Chin Fr Lat Span Anat & Physiol Ecol Genetics Computers Sociol Relig Music Bus Speech. **Supp**—Dev_Read Makeup Tut. **Adm:** 249/yr. Appl due: Dec. **Tests** HSPT. **Enr 849.** B 849. Sec 849. Wh 94%. Hisp 1%. Blk 3%. Asian 1%. Other 1%. Avg class size: 25. **Fac 58.** M 43. F 14/1. **Grad '04—169.** Col—166. Avg SAT: 1043. Alum 5579. **Tui '04-'05:** Day $7050-7350 (+$350). Aid: Merit 10 ($20,000). Need 371 ($425,000). **Summer:** Acad Enrich. Tui Day $250/crse. 3 wks. **Est 1963.** Nonprofit. Roman Catholic. Quar (Sept-June). **Assoc** NEASC. Xavier provides academic, religious, service, athletic and extracurricular programs. Three distinct curricula—college prep, accelerated and honors—are offered.

ACADEMY OF OUR LADY OF MERCY LAURALTON HALL
Day Girls Gr 9-12

Milford, CT 06460. 200 High St.
Tel: 203-877-2786. Fax: 203-876-9760.
www.lauraltonhall.org   E-mail: kshine@lauraltonhall.org

Barbara C. Griffin, Pres. BA, College of St Elizabeth, MA, Fairleigh Dickinson Univ, MEd, Rutgers Univ. Ann M. Pratson, Prin. BA, Univ of Connecticut, MAT, Sacred Heart Univ. Kathleen O. Shine, Adm.

Col Prep. AP—Eng Fr Lat Span Calc Bio Physics Eur_Hist US_Hist Econ. **Feat**—Oceanog Computers Relig World_Relig Art_Hist Graphic_Arts Studio_Art Music Bus. **Adm:** 130/yr. Accepted: 33%. **Tests** HSPT. **Enr 440.** G 440. Sec 440. Wh 88%. Hisp 4%. Blk 3%. Am Ind 1%. Asian 4%. Avg class size: 15. Uniform. **Fac** 53. M 2/2. F 48/1. Adv deg: 71%. **Grad '04—103.** Col—103. Alum 8000. **Tui '05-'06:** Day $10,600 (+$250). Aid: Need 70 ($295,000). **Est 1905.** Nonprofit. Roman Catholic. **Assoc** NEASC. The oldest girls' Catholic college preparatory school in the state, Lauralton Hall provides a varied liberal arts curriculum that includes Advanced Placement and honors courses. All students take religion classes and fulfill a community service requirement. Among school activities are a mentoring program, academic honor societies, four publications, quiz bowl, school government, fine arts and varsity athletics.

WASHINGTON MONTESSORI SCHOOL
Day Coed Gr PS-8

New Preston, CT 06777. 240 Litchfield Tpke.
Tel: 860-868-0551. Fax: 860-868-1362.
www.washingtonmontessori.org   E-mail: inquiries@washingtonmontessori.org
 Patricia D. Werner, Head. BA, Drew Univ, MS, Western Connecticut State Univ.

Pre-Prep. Feat—Lat Span Computers Studio_Art Music. **Adm:** 54/yr. Appl due: Rolling. **Enr 272.** Elem 272. Wh 95%. Hisp 2%. Blk 1%. Asian 2%. Avg class size: 24. **Fac** 55. M 5. F 46/4. **Grad '04—23.** Alum 300. **Tui '04-'05:** Day $6860-12,980 (+$65-550). Aid: Need 37 ($140,750). **Est 1965.** Nonprofit. (Sept-June). Washington Montessori provides an individualized and structured, academically oriented curriculum based on the Montessori principles of child-centered teaching. Children study in ungraded, mixed-age groups that span three years, enabling students of varying ages and developmental stages to learn from each other.

NEW HAVEN HEBREW DAY SCHOOL
Day Coed Gr PS-8

Orange, CT 06477. 261 Derby Ave.
Tel: 203-795-5261. Fax: 203-891-9719.
www.nhhds.org   E-mail: nhhds@nhhds.org
 Rabbi Sheya Hecht, Head. Jeanne S. Rice, Adm.

Gen Acad. Feat—Hebrew Span Computers Judaic_Stud Studio_Art. **Supp**—ESL Rem_Math Rem_Read Tut. **Adm:** 15/yr. Appl due: May. Accepted: 100%. Yield: 100%. **Tests** Stanford. **Enr 155.** Elem 155. Wh 90%. Other 10%. Avg class size: 15. Uniform. **Fac** 37. M 3/4. F 12/18. Wh 92%. Hisp 4%. Asian 2%. Other 2%. Adv deg: 70%.**Tui '04-'05:** Day $8000-9750 (+$1525). Aid: Need ($520,000). **Est 1946.** Nonprofit. Jewish. Tri (Sept-June). NHHDS combines a general academic program with a traditional Judaic studies curriculum. Language arts, science, math, world and American history, geography and social studies are core elements of the general studies program, and students take weekly classes in art and computers as well. The Judaic portion of the school day features study of the Torah and on Jewish history, laws and traditions. Instructors place strong emphasis on Hebrew language skills and Israel's history and culture.

RIDGEFIELD ACADEMY
Day Coed Gr PS-8

Ridgefield, CT 06877. 223A W Mountain Rd.
Tel: 203-894-1800. Fax: 203-894-1810.
www.ridgefieldacademy.com E-mail: lmacgregor@ridgefieldacademy.com

James P. Heus, Head. BA, Hobart College, MA, Columbia Univ. Libby B. Clippinger, Adm.

Col Prep. Feat—Writing Fr Lat Span Computers Studio_Art Music Study_Skills. **Adm:** 107/yr. Appl due: Rolling. **Tests** ISEE. **Enr 290.** B 130. G 160. Elem 290. Wh 91%. Hisp 2%. Asian 7%. Avg class size: 15. **Fac 46.** M 4/1. F 32/9. Wh 94%. Hisp 2%. Asian 2%. Other 2%. Adv deg: 36%. **Grad '04—21. Tui '03-'04:** Day $10,500-14,200. Aid: Need 18 ($125,720). **Summer:** Acad Enrich Rec. Tui Day $585/2-wk ses. 6 wks. **Est 1975.** Nonprofit. Tri (Sept-June). French, science, music and arts and crafts are integrated into Ridgefield's preschool program. An extensive fine and performing arts curriculum that consists of music, art, theater and dance complements academics. Sports, computers, chess and cooking are among the after-school activities.

EAGLE HILL-SOUTHPORT
Day Coed Ages 6-16

Southport, CT 06890. 214 Main St.
Tel: 203-254-2044. Fax: 203-255-4052.
www.eaglehillsouthport.org E-mail: info@eaglehillsouthport.org

Leonard Tavormina, Head. BA, Boston Univ, MA, Fairfield Univ. Carolyn Lavender, Adm.

LD. Feat—Studio_Art Speech. **Supp**—Rem_Math Rem_Read Rev Tut. **Adm:** 43/yr. Appl due: Rolling. Accepted: 63%. **Tests** IQ. **Enr 107.** B 90. G 17. Wh 92%. Hisp 3%. Blk 4%. Asian 1%. Avg class size: 4. Uniform. **Fac 29.** M 8/2. F 18/1. Wh 100%. Adv deg: 51%. **Grad '04—39.** Prep—21. Alum 547. **Tui '04-'05:** Day $32,400. Aid: Need 12 ($158,000). **Summer:** Acad Rem. Tui Day $2100. 5 wks. **Est 1985.** Nonprofit. Sem (Aug-June). Eagle Hill offers a linguistically based language arts curriculum for children of average or above-average intelligence with language/learning disabilities. Each child receives individual or small-group tutorial instruction and small skills classes in a structured yet flexible environment. Students generally attend for two or three years, as the school aims to place children in a more traditional setting. Art, athletics and other extracurricular activities are offered. **See Also Page 1353**

BI-CULTURAL DAY SCHOOL
Day Coed Gr K-8

Stamford, CT 06903. 2186 High Ridge Rd.
Tel: 203-329-2186. Fax: 203-329-0464.
www.bcds.org E-mail: bcds@optonline.net

Walter Shuchatowitz, Prin. BA, City Univ of New York, MA, Columbia Univ, MHL, Yeshiva Univ (NY).

Gen Acad. Feat—Hebrew Span Computers Judaic_Stud. **Supp**—LD Tut. **Adm:** 63/yr. Appl due: Rolling. Accepted: 85%. **Tests** IQ. **Enr 431.** B 214. G 217. Elem 431. Wh 99%. Asian 1%. Avg class size: 16. **Fac 82.** M 14/6. F 46/16. Wh 100%. Adv deg: 65%. **Grad '04—36.** Prep—18. Alum 824. **Tui '02-'03:** Day $8800-10,200 (+$85). Aid: Need 8 ($72,000). **Est 1956.** Nonprofit. Jewish. Sem

(Sept-June). The BCDS academic program represents a full curriculum of secular and Judaic subject matter, with instruction in small groups. Athletics include soccer, basketball, volleyball, softball and gymnastics. Students in grade 8 spend the month of March in Israel.

MEAD SCHOOL   Day Coed Gr PS-8
Stamford, CT 06903. 1095 Riverbank Rd.
Tel: 203-595-9500. Fax: 203-595-0735.
www.meadschool.org   E-mail: admissions@meadschool.org

Joe Ferber, Dir. BA, George Washington Univ, MS, American Univ. Brooke Wachtel, Adm.

Gen Acad. Feat—Span Computers Studio_Art Drama Music. **Supp**—Dev_Read Rev. **Adm:** 46/yr. Appl due: Mar. Accepted: 39%. Yield: 26%. **Enr 173.** B 93. G 80. Elem 173. Wh 83%. Hisp 2%. Blk 2%. Asian 1%. Other 12%. Avg class size: 6. **Fac 29.** M 5. F 22/2. Wh 90%. Hisp 3%. Blk 3%. Asian 4%. Adv deg: 31%. **Grad '04—13.** Col—6. Alum 300. **Tui '04-'05:** Day $6000-22,700 (+$175-800). Aid: Need 22 ($250,520). **Summer:** Gr 1-9. Enrich Rec. Creative Arts. Tui Day $1200. 5 wks. **Est 1969.** Nonprofit. Sem (Sept-June). Mead's two-teacher system features a traditional curriculum supplemented by expressive arts such as drama, music, art and dance. Interscholastic athletic competition is available. Negotiation and mediation skills and community service are emphasized.

TRINITY CATHOLIC HIGH SCHOOL   Day Coed Gr 9-12
Stamford, CT 06905. 926 Newfield Ave.
Tel: 203-322-3401. Fax: 203-322-5330.
www.trinitycatholic.org   E-mail: tchs1@juno.com

Kevin Burke, Pres. Robert D'Aquila, Prin. Connie McGoldrick, Adm.

Col Prep. AP—Eng Span Calc Chem Physics Eur_Hist US_Hist. **Feat**—Fr Ital Computers Econ Relig Fine_Arts Bus. **Supp**—Dev_Read Rem_Read Tut. **Adm:** 125/yr. Appl due: July. Accepted: 90%. **Tests** HSPT Stanford. **Enr 425.** B 216. G 209. Sec 425. Wh 86%. Hisp 6%. Blk 5%. Asian 3%. Avg class size: 19. Uniform. **Fac 35.** M 18. F 16/1. Wh 100%. Adv deg: 85%. **Grad '04—101.** Col—96. Avg SAT: 1049. Alum 9000. **Tui '04-'05:** Day $7600 (+$600). Aid: Merit 8 ($62,000). Need 40 ($120,000). **Summer:** Rem. Tui Day $550/crse. 6 wks. **Est 1957.** Nonprofit. Roman Catholic. Quar (Aug-June). **Assoc** NEASC. Situated on a 26-acre campus, this regional high school offers classes in numerous subjects, among them religion, fine arts and business. AP and honors courses are available, and student activities include clubs and organizations, as well as sports. All freshmen participate in the community service program.

CHRISTIAN HERITAGE SCHOOL   Day Coed Gr K-12
Trumbull, CT 06611. 575 White Plains Rd.
Tel: 203-261-6230. Fax: 203-452-1531.
www.kingsmen.org   E-mail: jthompson@kingsmen.org

Barry F. Giller, Head. BA, Wheaton College (IL), MS, Nova Southeastern Univ. Jennifer Thompson, Adm.

Col Prep. Gen Acad. AP—Eng Fr Span Calc Bio US_Hist US_Govt & Pol. **Feat**—Shakespeare Victorian_Lit Greek_Lit Stats Bible Philos Studio_Art Band Chorus Drafting. **Supp**—Rem_Read Tut. **Adm:** 104/yr. Appl due: Rolling. Accepted: 68%. **Tests** IQ Stanford. **Enr 535.** B 254. G 281. Elem 373. Sec 162. Wh 88%. Hisp 4%. Blk 7%. Asian 1%. Avg class size: 22. Uniform. **Fac 49.** M 12/5. F 24/8. Wh 100%. Adv deg: 51%. **Grad '04—46.** Col—45. Avg SAT: 1180. Alum 562. **Tui '04-'05:** Day $5865-9750 (+$500). **Est 1976.** Nonprofit. Nondenom Christian. Quar (Sept-June). **Assoc** NEASC. This college preparatory school emphasizes Christian values and requires each class to participate in one community service project during the year. Electives offered include art, band, chorus, painting, computer science, drafting and word processing. Soccer, cross-country, basketball, cheerleading, volleyball, softball, golf, tennis and track constitute the interscholastic athletic program.

THE GLENHOLME SCHOOL
Coed Gr 3-12
Washington, CT 06793. 81 Sabbaday Ln. **Bdg & Day**
Tel: 860-868-7377. Fax: 860-868-7413.
www.theglenholmeschool.org   E-mail: info@theglenholmeschool.org
Gary L. Fitzherbert, Exec Dir. MEd. Kathi Fitzherbert, Adm.

LD. Underachiever. Feat—Span. **Supp**—Dev_Read ESL Rem_Math Rem_Read Rev Tut. **Adm:** Appl due: Rolling. **Enr 100.** B 60/3. G 35/2. Elem 38. Sec 62. Avg class size: 10. Uniform. **Fac 25.** M 5/1. F 18/1. Adv deg: 28%. **Grad '04—46.** **Tui '04-'05:** Bdg $93,775. Day $35,475. **Est 1968.** Nonprofit. Spons: The Devereux Foundation. Year-round. **Assoc** NEASC. This therapeutic school conducts a highly structured, 12-month program for children and adolescents with a range of special needs, among them mildly disruptive behavioral disorders, attentional disorders, anxiety problems, mood disorders, obsessive-compulsive disorder, posttraumatic stress disorder, Tourette's syndrome, Asperger's syndrome and learning disabilities. Course work makes use of students' creativity through the integration of the arts into all academic classes. The supportive, small-class learning environment is designed to prepare graduates for higher education. **See Also Page 1362**

HARTFORD CHRISTIAN ACADEMY
Day Coed Gr K-12
West Hartford, CT 06107. 155 Mountain Rd.
Tel: 860-521-8380.
www.hartfordchristian.org
Gary Jones, Admin. BA, Bob Jones Univ, MA, Calvary Baptist Theological Seminary. Mark Cronemeyer, Prin.

Col Prep. Feat—Fr Computers Bible. **Supp**—Tut. **Adm:** 23/yr. Appl due: Aug. Accepted: 100%. **Tests** Stanford. **Enr 105.** B 61. G 44. Elem 75. Sec 30. Wh 83%. Hisp 4%. Blk 13%. Avg class size: 8. **Fac 16.** M 2/1. F 11/2. Wh 100%. Adv deg: 18%. **Grad '04—14.** Col—12. Alum 249. **Tui '05-'06:** Day $3100 (+$330-440). Aid: Merit 4 ($1500). **Est 1976.** Nonprofit. Baptist. Quar (Sept-June). A ministry of Farmington Avenue Baptist Church, this school utilizes the Bob Jones University Press Curriculum for Christian Schools in all grades. A wide range of subjects, centered around Bible study, is offered at varying levels. Reading instruction follows a phonetic approach, math a conceptual one.

HEBREW HIGH SCHOOL OF NEW ENGLAND
Day Coed Gr 9-12
West Hartford, CT 06117. 1244 N Main St.
Tel: 860-231-0317. Fax: 860-236-7623.
www.hhne.org

Rabbi Zvi Kahn, Prin. BA, Tulane Univ, MS, Yeshiva Univ (NY). Rabbi Shimmy Trencher, Adm.

Col Prep. AP—Eng Calc Bio Eur_Hist US_Hist. **Feat**—British_Lit Hebrew Israeli_Hist Govt Judaic_Stud Bible Talmud. **Supp**—Rem_Math Rem_Read Rev. **Adm (Gr 9-11):** 19/yr. Appl due: Mar. Accepted: 85%. **Tests** IQ SSAT. **Enr 65.** B 32. G 33. Sec 65. Wh 100%. Avg class size: 15. **Fac 22.** M 3/10. F 1/8. Wh 95%. Other 5%. **Grad '04**—**22.** Col—22. Avg SAT: 1240. Alum 30. **Tui '03-'04:** Day $10,500 (+$600). **Est 1996.** Nonprofit. Jewish. Quar (Sept-June). HHNE conducts a dual curriculum of college preparatory courses and Judaic studies. Following a daily community breakfast, students attend four Judaic studies courses. Boys and girls also enroll in five college preparatory, honors or AP courses chosen from the disciplines of English, math, science, history and world language. Each afternoon, pupils engage in an activity period in which they rotate among physical education, art and music electives, and community service.

NORTHWEST CATHOLIC HIGH SCHOOL
Day Coed Gr 9-12
West Hartford, CT 06117. 29 Wampanoag Dr.
Tel: 860-236-4221. Fax: 860-586-0911.
www.nwcath.org   E-mail: nbannon@nwcath.org

Michael S. Griffin, Pres. PhD, Univ of Connecticut. Margaret Williamson, Prin. Nancy Bannon, Adm.

Col Prep. AP—Eng Fr Span Calc Comp_Sci Bio Chem Physics US_Hist US_Govt & Pol Studio_Art Music_Theory. **Feat**—Creative_Writing Lat Oceanog Dance Outdoor_Ed. **Supp**—Tut. **Adm:** 211/yr. Appl due: May. **Tests** HSPT. **Enr 653.** B 309. G 344. Sec 653. Wh 72%. Hisp 5%. Blk 18%. Am Ind 1%. Asian 3%. Other 1%. Avg class size: 17. Uniform. **Fac 57.** M 25/2. F 24/6. Wh 98%. Blk 2%. Adv deg: 77%. **Grad '04**—**128.** Col—128. Avg SAT: 1073. Alum 6047. **Tui '04-'05:** Day $9495 (+$450). **Summer:** Enrich Rev. 2 wks. **Est 1961.** Nonprofit. Roman Catholic. Quar (Aug-June). **Assoc** NEASC. The school offers honors courses in math, English, history, languages and science, as well as classes in the arts and business. An AP program is also available. Student activities include Outward Bound, Model UN, drama, music, pep club, student government, TV club, sports, social action committee, student publications, poetry club and math team.

NOTRE DAME HIGH SCHOOL
Day Boys Gr 9-12
West Haven, CT 06516. 24 Ricardo St.
Tel: 203-933-1673. Fax: 203-933-2474.
www.notredamehs.com   E-mail: info@notredamehs.com

Br. James Branigan, CSC, Head. MS, St John's Univ (NY), MS, Fordham Univ. Benny Amarone, Adm.

Col Prep. Feat—Ital Lat Computers Programming Holocaust Relig. **Supp**—Dev_Read LD Rem_Math Rem_Read Rev Tut. **Adm:** 215/yr. Appl due: Rolling. Accepted: 87%. **Tests** HSPT. **Enr 704.** B 704. Sec 704. Wh 86%. Hisp 3%. Blk 6%.

Asian 2%. Other 3%. Avg class size: 22. **Fac 56.** M 36/2. F 17/1. Wh 97%. Hisp 3%. Adv deg: 71%. **Grad '04**—146. Col—144. **Tui '03-'04:** Day $6775 (+$350-400). Aid: Need 160 ($203,875). **Summer:** Acad Rev. Tui Day $185/crse. 4 wks. **Est 1946.** Nonprofit. Roman Catholic. Quar (Aug-June). **Assoc** NEASC. Sponsored by the Brothers of Holy Cross, the school offers a variety of Advanced Placement, honors and college preparatory courses. Community service and Christian retreats are important aspects of a well-developed campus ministry program. Interscholastic sports at Notre Dame are baseball, basketball, cross-country, football, golf, ice hockey, soccer, swimming, tennis, and indoor and outdoor track.

EZRA ACADEMY Day Coed Gr K-8
Woodbridge, CT 06525. 75 Rimmon Rd.
Tel: 203-389-5500. Fax: 203-387-5607.
www.ezraacademy.net E-mail: nkatz@ezraacademy.net
 Shelley G. Kreiger, Prin. BA, George Washington Univ, MA, Montclair State College. Nancy Katz, Adm.

 Pre-Prep. Gen Acad. Feat—Hebrew Span Bible Judaic_Stud. **Supp**—Dev_Read ESL Rem_Math Rem_Read Tut. **Adm:** 41/yr. Accepted: 95%. **Enr 225.** B 115. G 110. Elem 225. Wh 98%. Blk 1%. Asian 1%. Avg class size: 14. Uniform. **Fac 33.** M 3/1. F 29. Adv deg: 21%. **Grad '04**—18. Prep—9. **Tui '04-'05:** Day $11,100 (+$100). Aid: Need 60. **Est 1966.** Nonprofit. Jewish. Sem (Sept-June). A Solomon Schechter day school, Ezra integrates secular and Judaic studies within a community environment. The academy's secular studies curriculum includes language arts, literature, math, science and social studies; Spanish instruction commences in grade 7. Hebrew language study, Bible, prayer, Rabbinics and Jewish history constitute the Judaic studies program. Field trips, musical and dramatic performances, community service and student publications complement classroom learning.

MAINE

JOHN BAPST MEMORIAL HIGH SCHOOL Day Coed Gr 9-12
Bangor, ME 04401. 100 Broadway.
Tel: 207-947-0313. Fax: 207-941-2474.
www.johnbapst.org E-mail: bhusson@johnbapst.org
 Landis Green, Head. Colleen Grover, Adm.

 Col Prep. AP—Eng Lat Calc Stats Bio Chem Physics Eur_Hist US_Hist US_Govt & Pol Studio_Art. **Feat**—Fr Span Anat & Physiol Astron Ecol Web_Design Econ Theater_Arts Band Chorus Journ. **Supp**—Tut. **Adm:** 147/yr. Appl due: Feb. Accepted: 85%. Yield: 90%. **Enr 501.** B 214. G 287. Sec 501. Wh 96%. Hisp 1%. Blk 1%. Am Ind 1%. Asian 1%. Avg class size: 16. **Fac 39.** M 15/1. F 18/5. Adv deg: 61%. **Grad '04**—109. Col—107. Alum 4600. **Tui '04-'05:** Day $7500 (+$600). Aid: Need 23 ($80,000). **Est 1980.** Nonprofit. Sem (Aug-June). **Assoc** NEASC. With emphasis on both college preparation and skill development, John Bapst offers a varied curriculum comprising the humanities, the arts and sciences, and business. Extracurricular and cocurricular clubs, teams and organizations cater to a broad range of student interests. Athletics are particularly strong, with the school fielding more than two dozen teams.

GEORGE STEVENS ACADEMY Day Coed Gr 9-12
Blue Hill, ME 04614. 23 Union St.
Tel: 207-374-2808. Fax: 207-374-2982.
www.georgestevensacademy.org E-mail: bbrokaw@georgestevensacademy.org
Jo Ann Douglass, Head. BS, Bates College. Bayard Brokaw, Adm.

Col Prep. Gen Acad. AP—Eng Calc Stats US_Hist Studio_Art. **Feat**—Creative_Writing Fr Ger Lat Span Bus Indus_Arts Home_Ec. **Supp**—Dev_Read ESL LD Rem_Math Rem_Read. **Adm:** 76/yr. Appl due: Rolling. Accepted: 100%. **Enr 341.** B 168. G 173. Sec 341. Wh 99%. Other 1%. **Fac 31.** M 15/1. F 12/3. Wh 100%. Adv deg: 67%. **Grad '04—86.** Col—59. Avg SAT: 1025. Alum 2900. **Tui '04-'05:** Day $7290 (+$495). **Est 1803.** Nonprofit. Sem (Sept-June). **Assoc** NEASC. In addition to the regular college preparatory curriculum, this school provides honors courses and classes for students with dyslexia. Opportunities for independent study are available for pupils in grades 11 and 12.

LIBERTY SCHOOL Day Coed Gr 9-12
Blue Hill, ME 04614. South St, PO Box 857.
Tel: 207-374-2886. Fax: 207-374-5918.
www.liberty-school.org E-mail: nbarrett@liberty.pvt.k12.me.us
Arnold Greenberg, Dir. BS, MA, Temple Univ. Charlotte Martin-Berry, Adm.

Col Prep. Gen Acad. Feat—Lat-Amer_Lit Fr Lat Span Photog. **Supp**—Rem_Math Tut. **Adm:** 10/yr. Appl due: Rolling. Accepted: 100%. **Enr 55.** B 34. G 21. Sec 55. Wh 100%. Avg class size: 7. **Fac 12.** M 7/2. F /3. Wh 92%. Hisp 8%. Adv deg: 25%. **Grad '04—11.** Col—6. Alum 50. **Tui '03-'04:** Day $6966 (+$50). **Est 1997.** Nonprofit. Tri (Sept-June). Liberty's unusual program combines a solid academic curriculum with a secondary focus on artistic work and skill development. Students compose their own schedules in order to pursue individual academic and creative interests. The school's classical music program allows young musicians in private study to expand their music education and prepare for study at a conservatory or a music college.

WASHINGTON ACADEMY Coed Gr 9-12
East Machias, ME 04630. High St, PO Box 190. Bdg & Day
Tel: 207-255-8301. Fax: 207-255-8303.
www.washingtonacademy.org E-mail: admissions@washingtonacademy.org
Judson McBrine, Head. BS, MEd, Univ of Maine-Orono. Charlene D. Cates, Adm.

Col Prep. AP—Eng Span Calc Bio US_Hist. **Feat**—Fr Lat Environ_Sci Digital_Video Music Music_Hist. **Supp**—Dev_Read ESL Makeup Tut. **Adm:** Appl due: Rolling. **Enr 344.** B 19/152. G 15/158. Sec 344. Wh 88%. Hisp 1%. Blk 1%. Am Ind 1%. Asian 9%. Avg class size: 14. **Fac 30.** M 15. F 13/2. Wh 100%. Adv deg: 50%. **Grad '04—66.** Col—44. Avg SAT: 1000. **Tui '05-'06:** Bdg $22,400-24,600 (+$2500). Aid: Merit 22 ($132,000). Need 12 ($66,000). **Est 1792.** Nonprofit. Sem

(Aug-June). In addition to the traditional academic subjects, Washington Academy offers hands-on programs in boat building and environmental science. Electives such as video production, music appreciation, creative writing, computer programming and Web design are part of a curriculum that includes honors and Advanced Placement courses. Qualified juniors and seniors may take tuition-free classes at the nearby University of Maine-Machias.

DECK HOUSE SCHOOL   **Bdg Boys Gr 9-12**
Edgecomb, ME 04556. 124 Deck House Rd.
Tel: 207-882-7055. Fax: 207-882-8151.
www.deckhouseschool.org   E-mail: admissions@deckhouseschool.org
    Thomas D. Blackford, Head. BA, Bates College. Jeremiah Burrow, Adm.

    Col Prep. Feat—Creative_Writing Span Marine_Biol/Sci Govt Studio_Art Drama Study_Skills. **Supp**—Rem_Math Rem_Read Tut. **Adm:** 9/yr. Appl due: Rolling. Accepted: 75%. **Enr 11.** B 11. Sec 11. Wh 100%. **Fac 8.** M 4. F 3/1. Wh 87%. Hisp 13%. Adv deg: 12%. In Dorms 1. **Grad '04**—**3.** Col—3. Avg SAT: 1040. Alum 167. **Tui '04-'05:** Bdg $39,729 (+$900). **Est 1979.** Nonprofit. Tri (Sept-June). The school's program is designed for boys who have not had success in other school settings. Each student is involved in maintaining the 180-acre campus and its facilities. Deck House provides close personal and academic attention.

RILEY SCHOOL   **Day Coed Gr PS-9**
Glen Cove, ME 04846. Warrenton Rd, PO Box 300.
Tel: 207-596-6405. Fax: 207-596-0007.
www.rileyschool.org   E-mail: rileyschool@adelphia.net
    Glenna W. Plaisted, Dir. BA, Boston Univ.

    Pre-Prep. Gen Acad. Feat—Creative_Writing Humanities Lat Span Environ_Sci Philos Photog Studio_Art Theater Music Dance. **Supp**—Dev_Read Rev Tut. **Adm:** 12/yr. Appl due: Rolling. Accepted: 90%. **Enr 60.** B 29. G 31. Elem 60. Wh 97%. Hisp 3%. Avg class size: 6. **Fac 12.** M 1. F 6/5. Wh 99%. Hisp 1%. Adv deg: 25%. **Grad '04**—**6.** Prep—1. Avg SSAT: 90%. Alum 110. **Tui '04-'05:** Day $5173-7759 (+$500). Aid: Need 23 ($51,000). **Summer:** Ages 8-14. Arts. Sci. Tui Day $400-1600. 3-6 wks. **Est 1972.** Nonprofit. Sem (Sept-June). **Assoc** NEASC. The school's curriculum emphasizes the fundamentals in reading, language arts and writing, in addition to the basic principles of mathematics, foreign language and scientific inquiry. Creative activities are offered at all levels. Electives and extracurricular activities include pottery, photography, field trips, softball, swimming, skiing, skating, camping trips, music, soccer, sewing, a special-interest fair and art.

BREAKWATER SCHOOL   **Day Coed Gr PS-5**
Portland, ME 04102. 856 Brighton Ave.
Tel: 207-772-8689. Fax: 207-772-1327.
www.breakwaterschool.com   E-mail: info@breakwaterschool.com
    Cesca Galluccio-Steele, Head. Susan Fowler, Adm.

    Pre-Prep. Feat—Fr Studio_Art Music. **Supp**—Dev_Read. **Adm:** 44/yr. Appl due: Feb. Accepted: 80%. **Enr 171.** B 92. G 79. Elem 171. Wh 93%. Hisp 2%.

Blk 2%. Asian 3%. Avg class size: 14. **Fac 25.** M 5/2. F 11/7. Wh 100%. Adv deg: 48%. **Grad '04**—17. Prep—8. **Tui '04-'05:** Day $10,820-12,400. Aid: Need 26 ($74,550). **Summer:** Enrich Rec. Tui Day $195/wk. 6 wks. **Est 1956.** Nonprofit. Sem (Sept-June). Breakwater's program includes French, computers, art, music, field trips and community service opportunities. Children study literature and develop their writing skills through the school's language arts program. In grades 1-5, students improve their spelling and grammar by writing and editing original stories, then sharing them in a workshop setting.

CATHERINE McAULEY HIGH SCHOOL   Day Girls Gr 9-12
Portland, ME 04103. 631 Stevens Ave.
Tel: 207-797-3802. Fax: 207-797-3804.
www.mcauleyhs.org   E-mail: dlavoie@mcauleyhs.org

Sr. Mary Morey, RSM, Pres. BA, Saint Joseph's College of Maine, MA, St Michael's College. Sr. Edward Mary Kelleher, RSM, Prin. BA, Saint Joseph's College of Maine, MA, Boston College. Debra Lavoie, Adm.

Col Prep. AP—Eng Calc Bio US_Hist US_Govt & Pol. **Feat**—Creative_Writing Fr Lat Span Anat & Physiol Ecol Environ_Sci Comp_Sci Econ Psych Relig Studio_Art Chorus. **Adm:** 80/yr. Appl due: Feb. Accepted: 90%. Yield: 90%. **Tests** HSPT SSAT Stanford. **Enr 276.** G 276. Sec 276. Wh 97%. Hisp 1%. Blk 1%. Asian 1%. Avg class size: 18. Uniform. **Fac 28.** M 3/1. F 13/11. Wh 100%. Adv deg: 35%. **Grad '04**—72. Col—71. Avg SAT: 1052. Alum 3347. **Tui '04-'05:** Day $8000 (+$400). Aid: Merit 1 ($500). Need 67 ($192,900). **Summer:** Enrich. Study Skills. Tui Day $150. 4 wks. **Est 1881.** Nonprofit. Roman Catholic. Quar (Sept-June). **Assoc** NEASC. The college preparatory program at this girls' school integrates daily prayer, religion courses and retreat days. Social justice and ethical issues are taught from a Christian perspective. Each year, juniors take part in a weeklong career exploration program that exposes students to jobs in education, medicine, business and communication, among others. All girls fulfill a 20-hour annual community service requirement.

CHEVERUS HIGH SCHOOL   Day Coed Gr 9-12
Portland, ME 04103. 267 Ocean Ave.
Tel: 207-774-6238. Fax: 207-828-0207.
www.cheverus.org   E-mail: admissions@cheverus.org

Rev. John W. Keegan, SJ, Pres. BA, MA, Boston College. John H. R. Mullen, Prin. Jack Dawson, Adm.

Col Prep. AP—Eng Lat Span Calc Stats Bio US_Hist Econ. **Feat**—Fr Greek Comp_Design Programming Govt Relig Studio_Art Music_Theory. **Supp**—LD Tut. **Adm:** 165/yr. Appl due: Feb. Accepted: 81%. **Tests** HSPT. **Enr 503.** B 350. G 153. Sec 503. Wh 96%. Hisp 1%. Blk 3%. Avg class size: 18. **Fac 43.** M 24/2. F 12/5. Wh 97%. Hisp 3%. Adv deg: 60%. **Grad '04**—113. Col—108. Avg SAT: 1134. **Tui '04-'05:** Day $9200 (+$400). Aid: Merit 20 ($25,000). Need 220 ($436,000). Work prgm 220 ($110,000). **Est 1917.** Nonprofit. Roman Catholic. Sem (Sept-June). **Assoc** NEASC. Sponsored by the Society of Jesus, the school conducts a rigorous program that emphasizes college preparation. Gifted students choose from honors and Advanced Placement courses in most subjects, and Cheverus addresses study skill development for pupils who have a demonstrated need in this area. Up-to-date computer labs are an integral part of the school's strong technology program. Students fulfill a four-week community service requirement prior to graduation.

CHOP POINT SCHOOL   **Bdg Coed Gr 3-12**
Woolwich, ME 04579. 420 Chop Point Rd.   **Day Coed PS-12**
Tel: 207-443-5860. Fax: 207-443-6760.
www.choppoint.org   E-mail: info@choppoint.org
    Peter Willard, Dir. BA, Baylor Univ, MS, Univ of Wyoming. Franklin Hayward, Prin. BS, Univ of Maine-Orono, MS, Univ of Wyoming.

    Col Prep. Feat—Span Computers Archaeol Econ Psych Studio_Art Music. **Supp**—ESL Rem_Math Rev Tut. **Adm:** 39/yr. Appl due: Rolling. Accepted: 90%. **Enr 104.** B 1/56. G 1/46. Elem 79. Sec 25. Avg class size: 8. **Fac 22.** M 3/4. F 10/5. Wh 90%. Hisp 10%. Adv deg: 13%. **Grad '04—4.** Col—4. Avg SAT: 950. **Tui '02-'03:** Bdg $19,525. 5-Day Bdg $15,525. Day $4175-4700. Aid: Need 3 ($5000). **Summer:** Rec. Tui Bdg $1750/3-wk ses. 6 wks. **Est 1987.** Nonprofit. Nondenom Christian. Sem (Aug-May). This Christian school limits its classes to 12 students, thereby allowing staff to provide individual attention and to cover material at a faster pace. In the early years, Chop Point emphasizes reading and math skills, and children have several periods of Spanish, art, music and computer each week. The high school program features typical college preparatory course requirements and a choice of electives. A limited boarding program serves pupils from abroad.

MASSACHUSETTS

GLEN URQUHART SCHOOL   **Day Coed Gr K-8**
Beverly Farms, MA 01915. 74 Hart St.
Tel: 978-927-1064. Fax: 978-921-0060.
www.gus.org   E-mail: lmarchesseault@gus.org
    Raymond Nance, Head. BA, Texas Tech Univ, MTh, Southern Methodist Univ. Leslie Marchesseault, Adm.

    Pre-Prep. Feat—Lat Span Computers Drawing Visual_Arts Theater Chorus Music Orchestra. **Supp**—Tut. **Adm:** 41/yr. Appl due: Jan. Accepted: 15%. **Enr 226.** Elem 226. Wh 94%. Hisp 2%. Blk 2%. Asian 2%. Avg class size: 18. **Fac 36.** M 2/1. F 19/14. Wh 92%. Hisp 4%. Blk 4%. Adv deg: 52%. **Grad '04—32.** Prep—22. Alum 250. **Tui '02-'03:** Day $9950-14,900 (+$200). Aid: Need 38 ($336,320). **Summer:** Acad Enrich Rec. Tui Day $250/2-wk ses. 6 wks. **Est 1977.** Nonprofit. Tri (Sept-June). Glen Urquhart's thematic, interdisciplinary curriculum emphasizes problem solving and critical thinking. The school's program utilizes experiential and traditional learning modes, as well as the arts.

THE NEWMAN SCHOOL   **Day Coed Gr 9-PG**
Boston, MA 02116. 247 Marlborough St.
Tel: 617-267-4530. Fax: 617-267-7070.
www.newmanboston.org   E-mail: kbriggs@newmanboston.org

Harry Lynch, Head. BA, College of the Holy Cross, MBA, Northeastern Univ. Michael Dornisch, Adm.

Col Prep. Gen Acad. AP—Eng Calc Bio US_Hist US_Govt & Pol. **Feat**—Anthro Econ Psych Sociol Bus_Law Studio_Art Chorus Music. **Supp**—Dev_Read ESL Makeup Tut. **Adm (Gr 9-12):** 75/yr. Appl due: Rolling. Accepted: 60%. **Tests** HSPT SSAT. **Enr 230.** B 119. G 111. Sec 228. PG 2. Wh 68%. Hisp 5%. Blk 9%. Am Ind 1%. Asian 17%. Avg class size: 15. **Fac 20.** M 10/1. F 8/1. Adv deg: 30%. **Grad '04—51.** Col—48. **Tui '04-'05:** Day $9300-14,340. Aid: Merit 32 ($50,000). Need 40 ($100,000). **Summer:** Acad Enrich Rev. ESL. Tui Day $900/crse. 10 wks. **Est 1945.** Nonprofit. Sem (Sept-June). **Assoc** NEASC. Preparatory courses for colleges, nursing schools, and business and technical schools are offered at Newman. Students may take between four and seven courses per year, progressing as rapidly as capability dictates.

CAMBRIDGE MONTESSORI SCHOOL   Day Coed Gr PS-6
Cambridge, MA 02138. 161 Garden St.
Tel: 617-492-3410. Fax: 617-576-5154.
www.cambridgemontessori.net   E-mail: info@cambridgemontessori.net
David B. Harris, Head. BA, Univ of Pennsylvania. Tracy Kukkonen, Adm.

Pre-Prep. Feat—Span Computers Studio_Art Music. **Supp**—Dev_Read Rem_Math Rem_Read Rev. **Adm:** 46/yr. Appl due: Feb. Accepted: 43%. Yield: 75%. **Enr 200.** B 97. G 103. Elem 200. Avg class size: 17. **Fac 33.** M 2/1. F 20/10. Wh 70%. Hisp 12%. Blk 6%. Asian 12%. Adv deg: 30%. **Grad '04**—2. Prep—2. **Tui '05-'06:** Day $14,900-16,970. Aid: Need 24 ($155,850). **Summer:** Enrich Rec. Tui Day $400/wk. 7 wks. **Est 1963.** Nonprofit. Sem (Sept-June). CMS' curriculum offers learning experiences in the sciences, the arts, math and foreign language. Children may enter the hands-on toddler program at age 21 months. The primary program (ages 3-5) introduces boys and girls to music, art and computers, while the elementary program (grades 1-6) seeks to build strong foundations in the core subjects. The elementary building is located at 129 Sherman St., 02140.

THE CLARK SCHOOL   Day Coed Gr K-8
Danvers, MA 01923. 487 Locust St.
Tel: 978-777-4699. Fax: 978-774-3088.
www.clarkschool.com   E-mail: clarkschool@clarkschool.com
Sharon J. Clark, Head. BFA, California College of Arts and Crafts, MSEd, Wheelock College.

Pre-Prep. Gen Acad. Feat—Creative_Writing Shakespeare Span Computers Geog Studio_Art Drama Chorus Music. **Adm:** 18/yr. Appl due: Rolling. Accepted: 60%. **Tests** Stanford. **Enr 61.** B 35. G 26. Elem 61. Avg class size: 15. **Fac 14.** M 2/3. F 6/3. Adv deg: 57%. **Grad '04—5.** Prep—5. Alum 100. **Tui '04-'05:** Day $11,900-13,500 (+$500-800). Aid: Need 5 ($40,000). **Est 1978.** Nonprofit. Sem (Sept-June). Featuring multi-age grouping and stressing history and the arts, the school provides individual diagnostic assessments twice yearly. Computer use is integral to the writing program, while science courses deal with aspects of life science, physics and chemistry. Frequent field trips complement academic work.

URSULINE ACADEMY
Day Girls Gr 7-12

Dedham, MA 02026. 85 Lowder St.
Tel: 781-326-6161. Fax: 781-326-4898.
www.ursulineacademy.net   E-mail: ursuline@ursulineacademy.net
   Kathleen Levesque, Pres. Sr. Mercedes Videira, OSU, Prin. Ann Murphy, Adm.

   Col Prep. AP—Eng Calc Bio US_Hist. **Feat**—Fr Lat Span Anat & Physiol Environ_Sci Comp_Sci Govt Psych Relig Fine_Arts Public_Speak Driver_Ed Study_Skills. **Adm (Gr 7-10):** 69/yr. Appl due: Dec. Accepted: 43%. **Tests** HSPT. **Enr 395.** G 395. Elem 116. Sec 279. Wh 89%. Hisp 3%. Blk 2%. Am Ind 1%. Asian 5%. Avg class size: 16. Uniform. **Fac 40. Grad '04—66.** Col—66. Avg SAT: 1230. Alum 2500. **Tui '04-'05:** Day $8205 (+$75). Aid: Merit 16 ($80,000). Need 55 ($110,000). **Est** 1946. Nonprofit. Roman Catholic. Sem (Sept-June). **Assoc** NEASC. Ursuline complements a solid college preparatory curriculum with a varied athletic program and a selection of extracurricular activities. Each student fulfills a service requirement. Transportation to the school is available from neighboring communities.

BOSTON COLLEGE HIGH SCHOOL
Day Boys Gr 9-12

Dorchester, MA 02125. 150 Morrissey Blvd.
Tel: 617-436-3900. Fax: 617-474-5015.
www.bchigh.edu   E-mail: admissions@bchigh.edu
   William J. Kemeza, Pres. BA, Temple Univ, MA, Andover Newton Theological School. Stephen Hughes, Prin. Michael Brennan, Adm.

   Col Prep. AP—Lat. **Feat**—Creative_Writing Irish_Lit Anat & Physiol Astron Marine_Biol/Sci Programming Psych Ethics Relig World_Relig Art_Hist Studio_Art Drama Music. **Supp**—ESL Tut. **Adm (Gr 9-11):** 550/yr. Appl due: Dec. Accepted: 50%. **Tests** HSPT SSAT. **Enr 1300.** B 1300. Sec 1300. Wh 87%. Hisp 3%. Blk 4%. Asian 4%. Other 2%. Avg class size: 25. **Fac 108.** M 72. F 36. Adv deg: 90%. **Grad '04—310.** Col—303. Avg SAT: 1250. Alum 10,000. **Tui '05-'06:** Day $10,600 (+$400). Aid: Merit 87. Need 250 ($1,500,000). **Summer:** Acad Enrich Rev Rem. 5 wks. **Est** 1863. Nonprofit. Roman Catholic. Sem (Sept-June). **Assoc** NEASC. This college preparatory school, founded as a department of Boston College, became independent in 1913. Ample opportunities for Advanced Placement and honors work are part of the rigorous curriculum. Extracurricular activities include debate, publications, clubs, religious organizations and a strong athletic program. Jesuit traditions prevail.

EPIPHANY SCHOOL
Day Coed Gr 5-8

Dorchester, MA 02124. 154 Centre St.
Tel: 617-326-0425. Fax: 617-326-0424.
www.epiphanyschool.com   E-mail: info@epiphanyschool.com
   John H. Finley IV, Head. AB, Harvard Univ. Walker Coppedge, Adm.

   Pre-Prep. Gen Acad. Feat—Relig Studio_Art Music. **Supp**—Dev_Read LD Rem_Math Rem_Read Rev Tut. **Adm (Gr 5):** 22/yr. Appl due: Apr. Accepted: 50%. Yield: 95%. **Enr 82.** B 39. G 43. Elem 82. Wh 4%. Hisp 19%. Blk 66%. Asian 4%. Other 7%. Avg class size: 10. Uniform. **Fac 19.** M 8. F 11. Wh 50%. Hisp 5%. Blk 20%. Other 25%. Adv deg: 21%. **Grad '04—20.** Prep—15. **Tui '04-'05:** Day $0.

Summer: Acad Enrich Rev Rec. Tui Day $0. 4 wks. **Est 1997.** Nonprofit. Episcopal. Tri (Sept-June). This tuition-free middle school serves children of diverse religious and racial backgrounds who come from economically disadvantaged families. Conducted in a small-class environment, the individualized program makes use of an extended school day. All applicants must reside in one of Boston's neighborhoods and must qualify for free or reduced-cost school lunches from the State of Massachusetts.

POPE JOHN XXIII HIGH SCHOOL Day Coed Gr 9-12
Everett, MA 02149. 888 Broadway.
Tel: 617-389-0240. Fax: 617-389-2201.
www.popejohnhs.org   E-mail: kclark@popejohnhs.org
  Thomas P. Arria, Jr., Prin. BS, Boston State College, MEd, Univ of Massachusetts-Amherst. Joseph Cuticchia, Adm.

  Col Prep. AP—Eng Calc Bio US_Hist. **Feat**—Ital Span Comp_Sci Theol Fine_Arts. **Supp**—Tut. **Adm:** 149/yr. Appl due: Jan. Accepted: 80%. **Enr 461.** B 148. G 313. Sec 461. Wh 81%. Hisp 6%. Blk 8%. Am Ind 2%. Asian 3%. Avg class size: 22. Uniform. **Fac 32.** M 17/3. F 12. Wh 100%. Adv deg: 31%. **Grad '04—98.** Col—83. Alum 5000. **Tui '04-'05:** Day $6900. Aid: Need 400 ($375,000). **Summer:** Acad. Tui Day $200/crse. 3 wks. **Est 1966.** Nonprofit. Roman Catholic. Quar (Sept-June). Founded by Cardinal Richard Cushing to serve Everett and nearby cities and towns, this school provides college preparation in a Catholic setting. The basic program, which includes four years of theology, is combined with supplementary courses at each grade level, among them College Board math and English, fine arts and online classes. A full program of interscholastic sports is available.

ANTIOCH SCHOOL Day Coed Gr PS-8
Fall River, MA 02720. 618 Rock St.
Tel: 508-673-6767. Fax: 508-676-9597.
www.antioch-school.org   E-mail: office@antioch-school.org
  John M. Frost, Prin. BA, Univ of Lowell, BS, MS, MA, Salve Regina Univ.

  Pre-Prep. Gen Acad. Feat—Portuguese Studio_Art Music. **Supp**—Tut. **Adm:** 27/yr. Appl due: Mar. Accepted: 94%. Yield: 89%. **Enr 87.** B 50. G 37. Elem 87. Wh 94%. Hisp 2%. Blk 2%. Asian 2%. Avg class size: 9. **Fac 15.** M 1/2. F 8/4. Wh 93%. Blk 7%. Adv deg: 13%. **Grad '04—5.** Prep—4. **Tui '04-'05:** Day $4050-4350 (+$200). **Summer:** Enrich. Tui Day $125/wk. 9 wks. **Est 1978.** Nonprofit. Quar (Sept-June). A limited enrollment and a low student-teacher ratio enable this structured school to address the abilities, needs and interests of each child. In addition to instruction in the standard subjects, Antioch's program includes Portuguese, music, art and after-school enrichment. Guest speakers and performers, in addition to off-campus excursions to museums and other sites of interest, complement in-class study.

THE SAGE SCHOOL Day Coed Gr PS-8
Foxboro, MA 02035. 171 Mechanic St.
Tel: 508-543-9619. Fax: 508-543-1152.
www.sageschool.org   E-mail: sageschl@sageschool.org

Katherine G. Windsor, Head. BA, Univ of Rochester, MA, College of Notre Dame. Elizabeth Lussier, Adm.

Pre-Prep. Feat—Humanities Fr Lat Span Computers Studio_Art Music. **Adm:** Appl due: Feb. Accepted: 37%. **Tests** IQ. **Enr 160.** Elem 160. Avg class size: 15. **Fac 34.** M 3. F 28/3. Adv deg: 35%. **Grad '04—11.** Prep—9. Alum 21. **Tui '04-'05:** Day $14,200-16,700. Aid: Need 16 ($102,250). **Summer:** Enrich Rec. Tui Day $200/wk. 6 wks. **Est 1989.** Nonprofit. Tri (Sept-June). Specializing in the education of academically gifted children, the school serves high-ability boys and girls in the Greater Boston area. Rather than following traditional grade levels, Sage utilizes three school divisions: prime (ages 4-7), junior (ages 8-10) and middle (ages 11-14). Each division consists of multi-age classrooms, allowing staff to assess students regularly and group them with others from similar academic levels. The curriculum's flexibility provides depth and room for acceleration.

SACRED HEART HIGH SCHOOL Day Coed Gr 7-12
Kingston, MA 02364. 399 Bishops Hwy.
Tel: 781-585-7511. Fax: 781-585-7063.
www.sacredheart-hs.org   E-mail: info@sacredheart-hs.org

John F. Enos III, Prin. Maureen A. Fagan, Upper Sch Adm; Jane Enos, Intermediate Sch Adm.

Col Prep. AP—Eng Calc Bio. **Feat**—Mythology Fr Ger Lat Span Stats Astron Oceanog Paleobio Comp_Sci Psych Foreign_Policy Relig Film Sculpt Studio_Art Video_Production Theater Music Journ. **Adm: Gr 7-11. Tests** Stanford. **Enr 583.** Elem 202. Sec 381. Wh 96%. Hisp 1%. Blk 2%. Asian 1%. Avg class size: 20. Uniform. **Fac 44. Grad '04—85.** Col—85. Avg SAT: 1108. Alum 4500. **Tui '04-'05:** Day $8550 (+$500). **Summer:** Enrich. Math. Speech. 5 wks. **Est 1953.** Nonprofit. Roman Catholic. Quar (Aug-June). **Assoc** NEASC. Sacred Heart offers a wide range of advance courses and organizes annual trips abroad. Students are encouraged to participate in extracurricular activities such as performing arts, music, sports and student publications. The school schedules annual trips abroad.

LEXINGTON MONTESSORI SCHOOL Day Coed Gr PS-6
Lexington, MA 02421. 130 Pleasant St.
Tel: 781-862-8571. Fax: 781-674-0079.
www.lexmontessori.org   E-mail: admissions@lexmontessori.org

William Valentine, Head. Nancy S. Hartman, Adm.

Pre-Prep. Gen Acad. Feat—Span Studio_Art Music. **Supp**—Dev_Read Tut. **Adm:** 53/yr. Appl due: Jan. Accepted: 29%. **Enr 231.** Elem 231. Wh 74%. Hisp 8%. Blk 4%. Asian 14%. Avg class size: 22. **Fac 32.** M 5. F 25/2. Wh 70%. Hisp 10%. Blk 5%. Asian 10%. Other 5%. Adv deg: 18%. **Grad '04—15.** Prep—7. Alum 75. **Tui '04-'05:** Day $10,535-16,125. Aid: Need 44 ($403,500). **Summer:** Ages 2-15. Enrich Rec. Tui Day $250/wk. 8 wks. **Est 1963.** Nonprofit. (Sept-June). Pupils may enroll at Lexington Montessori as early as age 1½. The core Montessori curriculum utilizes varied learning materials and is supplemented by foreign language, art, music and physical education. Children in the toddler and preschool programs participate in sensorial learning, language arts and practical life exercises. Classes in the elementary school utilize multi-age groupings and cover a standard elementary curriculum, with an emphasis on reading, mathematics and writing.

MALDEN CATHOLIC HIGH SCHOOL   **Day Boys Gr 9-12**
Malden, MA 02148. 99 Crystal St.
Tel: 781-322-3098. Fax: 781-397-0573.
www.maldencatholic.org
    Thomas Arria, Jr., Head. BS, MEd, Boston State College. Br. Thomas Puccio, Prin. Richard D. Gill, Adm.

    Col Prep. AP—Eng Fr Span Calc Chem Physics US_Hist. **Feat**—Creative_Writing Humanities Marine_Biol/Sci Web_Design Amer_Stud Relig Theol. **Supp**—Rev Tut. **Adm:** 202/yr. Appl due: Jan. Accepted: 75%. **Tests** SSAT. **Enr 764.** B 764. Sec 764. Wh 90%. Hisp 2%. Blk 3%. Asian 5%. Avg class size: 23. **Fac 50.** M 33/1. F 15/1. Adv deg: 62%. **Grad '04—132.** Col—128. Avg SAT: 1032. Avg ACT: 22. Alum 7212. **Tui '04-'05:** Day $7585. Aid: Merit 81 ($172,000). Need 211 ($424,290). **Summer:** Acad Enrich Rev Rem. Tui Day $230/crse. 3 wks. **Est 1932.** Nonprofit. Roman Catholic. Sem (Sept-June). **Assoc** NEASC. Sponsored by the Xaverian Brothers, Malden Catholic requires participation in its religious program. Honors and Advanced Placement courses in all major disciplines are available to qualified students. Athletics include interscholastic and intramural sports teams.

DELPHI ACADEMY   **Day Coed Gr PS-8**
Milton, MA 02186. 564 Blue Hill Ave.
Tel: 617-333-9610. Fax: 617-333-9613.
www.delphiboston.org   E-mail: info@delphiboston.org
    Barbara Roy, Exec Dir. Jeff Rouelle, Adm.

    Pre-Prep. Gen Acad. Feat—Span Anat & Physiol Govt. **Adm:** 35/yr. Appl due: Feb. Accepted: 50%. **Enr 130.** B 68. G 62. Elem 130. Wh 46%. Hisp 2%. Blk 40%. Asian 12%. Avg class size: 15. **Fac 18.** M 1/2. F 14/1. Wh 92%. Blk 8%. **Grad '04—6.** Prep—4. **Tui '03-'04:** Day $10,000 (+$750). **Summer:** Acad Enrich Rec. Swimming. Tui Day $1270/4-wk ses. 7 wks. **Est 1979.** Nonprofit. Quar (Sept-June). Applying the principles of L. Ron Hubbard, Delphi conducts small, seminar-style classes designed to increase group interaction and communication. Teachers work with new students to formulate a suitable individual program based upon age, interests, and strengths and weaknesses. The school places particular emphasis on reading skills and requires pupils to read in great volume, with the average student reading some 150 books annually.

MONTROSE SCHOOL   **Day Girls Gr 6-12**
Natick, MA 01760. 45 E Central St.
Tel: 508-650-6925. Fax: 508-650-6926.
E-mail: admissions@montroseschool.org
    Karen E. Bohlin, Head. BA, Boston College, EdM, EdD, Boston Univ. Patricia M. Keefe, Adm.

    Col Prep. AP—Eng Calc. **Feat**—Fr Span Programming Theol Studio_Art Drama Music. **Supp**—Tut. **Adm:** 30/yr. Appl due: Feb. Accepted: 60%. **Tests** ISEE

SSAT. **Enr 129.** G 129. Elem 74. Sec 55. Wh 92%. Hisp 6%. Asian 2%. Uniform. **Fac 25.** Adv deg: 52%. **Grad '04**—13. Col—13. Avg SAT: 1310. Alum 245. **Tui '03-'04:** Day $9450 (+$700). Aid: Need 39. **Est 1979.** Nonprofit. Quar (Sept-June). Montrose supplements its traditional liberal arts curriculum with Catholic theology courses, choral music, art, drama and computer programming. The middle school (grades 6-8) prepares girls for high school by stressing study skills and the mastery of basic concepts, while the college preparatory high school (grades 9-12) emphasizes critical thinking, sound reasoning and clear expression.

MONTESSORI EDUCARE SCHOOL — Day Coed Gr PS-6
Newton Centre, MA 02459. 80 Crescent Ave.
Tel: 617-332-0581. Fax: 617-332-1190.
www.montessorieducare.org   E-mail: info@montessorieducare.org

Pheroza N. Madon, Head. BA, Rhode Island College, MA, Boston College. Jeanne van Dijk, Adm.

Pre-Prep. Feat—Lat Span Studio_Art Music. **Adm:** 77/yr. Appl due: Jan. Accepted: 57%. **Enr 260.** B 130. G 130. Elem 260. Wh 67%. Hisp 6%. Blk 8%. Asian 15%. Other 4%. Avg class size: 20. **Fac 60.** M 4/2. F 44/10. Wh 60%. Hisp 10%. Blk 5%. Asian 17%. Other 8%. Adv deg: 20%. **Grad '04—8. Tui '04-'05:** Day $11,600-13,000 (+$250). **Summer:** Rec. 8 wks. **Est 1972.** Nonprofit. Sem (Sept-June). The school offers Montessori programs for infants, toddlers, preschoolers, kindergartners and elementary-age children. At all levels, students work both individually and in small groups with hands-on, self-correcting materials that enable them to progress at an appropriate pace. The school employs multi-age groupings, with pupils assigned to four sections: Nido (ages three months to 3 years), primary (ages 3-6), lower elementary (ages 6-9) and upper elementary (ages 9-12). Extracurricular lessons in piano, martial arts, music and movement, yoga, French and chess complement required class work.

BISHOP STANG HIGH SCHOOL — Day Coed Gr 9-12
North Dartmouth, MA 02747. 500 Slocum Rd.
Tel: 508-996-5602. Fax: 508-994-6756.
www.bishopstang.com   E-mail: admits@bishopstang.com

Theresa E. Dougall, Pres. BS, Stonehill College, MEd, Bridgewater State College. Glenn Forgue, Adm.

Col Prep. AP—Eng Calc Bio Chem Physics Eur_Hist Psych. **Feat**—Fr Lat Span Portuguese Stats Bioethics Ecol Marine_Biol/Sci Web_Design Sociol Studio_Art Music Accounting Bus Mech_Drawing. **Supp**—Rem_Math Rem_Read Tut. **Adm:** 225/yr. Appl due: Rolling. Accepted: 65%. **Tests** HSPT. **Enr 754.** Sec 754. Wh 96%. Blk 2%. Am Ind 1%. Asian 1%. Avg class size: 25. Uniform. **Fac 57.** M 17/1. F 38/1. Wh 96%. Hisp 2%. Blk 2%. Adv deg: 40%. **Grad '04—167.** Col—155. Avg SAT: 1070. Alum 7500. **Tui '04-'05:** Day $6250 (+$300). Aid: Need ($290,000). **Est 1959.** Nonprofit. Roman Catholic. Sem (Sept-June). **Assoc** NEASC. Bishop Stang offers a wide variety of courses on four levels (AP, honors, college preparatory and standard); electives may be chosen from among the different disciplines. A campus ministry program and a Christian service program, in which juniors and seniors are required to participate, are available. Varsity, junior varsity and freshman interscholastic sports, in addition to a choice of cocurricular activities, balance academics.

PIONEER VALLEY CHRISTIAN SCHOOL — Day Coed Gr PS-12
Springfield, MA 01119. 965 Plumtree Rd.
Tel: 413-782-8031. Fax: 413-782-8033.
www.pvcs.org E-mail: info@pvcs.org

Timothy Duff, Head. BA, Univ of Maine-Orono, MRE, Grand Rapids Baptist Seminary. Denise Ridley, Adm.

Col Prep. AP—Eng Calc Bio Chem. **Feat**—Fr Span Computers Sociol Bible Graphic_Arts Drama Music Accounting Speech. **Supp**—Dev_Read LD Makeup Tut. **Adm:** 76/yr. Accepted: 90%. **Tests** IQ Stanford. **Enr 320.** B 175. G 145. Elem 133. Sec 187. Wh 79%. Hisp 5%. Blk 12%. Asian 4%. Avg class size: 17. **Fac 34.** M 7/2. F 20/5. Wh 100%. Adv deg: 41%. **Grad '04**—30. Col—28. Avg SAT: 1055. Alum 369. **Tui '03-'04:** Day $4600-6900 (+$160). Aid: Need ($288,000). **Est 1972.** Nonprofit. Sem (Aug-June). **Assoc** NEASC. Located on 25 acres, the school offers a college preparatory curriculum that incorporates Christian values and ethics. Advanced Placement English is available, as is a program for students with learning differences. Activities include art, chamber ensemble, choir, band, drama, various clubs and sports.

THE CORWIN-RUSSELL SCHOOL AT BROCCOLI HALL — Day Coed Gr 6-PG
Sudbury, MA 01776. 142 North Rd.
Tel: 978-369-1444. Fax: 978-369-1026.
www.corwin-russell.org E-mail: brochall@corwin-russell.org

Jane-Elisabeth Jakuc, Head. AB, Boston Univ, MEd, Framingham State College. Kristen Call, Adm.

Col Prep. LD. Underachiever. Feat—Fr Ger Japan Span Computers Studio_Art Drama Music SAT_Prep. **Supp**—Makeup Tut. **Adm:** 12/yr. Appl due: Rolling. Accepted: 20%. **Tests** IQ. **Enr 51.** B 38. G 13. Elem 15. Sec 36. Wh 87%. Hisp 4%. Blk 2%. Asian 7%. Avg class size: 10. **Fac 16.** M 4/1. F 8/3. Wh 100%. Adv deg: 43%. **Grad '04**—6. Col—5. Avg SAT: 1160. Alum 300. **Tui '04-'05:** Day $29,404 (+$300). **Est 1970.** Nonprofit. Sem (Sept-June). This small school serves college-bound students of average to superior intelligence who display a variety of learning styles. Multi-modal instruction is available in all traditional academic areas, and CRS also offers foreign language study, career education and social service opportunities. Students engage in visual and performing arts activities, technology, outdoor education and study partnerships with area cultural institutions and colleges. A tutorial program assists boys and girls with organizational needs and provides opportunities for course replacement, SAT preparation and skill advancement.

ACADEMY OF NOTRE DAME — Day Boys Gr K-8, Girls K-12
Tyngsboro, MA 01879. 180 Middlesex Rd.
Tel: 978-649-7611. Fax: 978-649-2909.
www.notredame.mec.edu E-mail: krourke@mec.edu

Sr. Kathryn Lawrence McGuiggan, SND, CEO. AB, Emmanuel College, MA, Boston College. Katie Rourke, Adm.

Col Prep. AP—Calc Chem. **Feat**—Computers Econ Govt Law Psych Sociol Relig Photog Accounting Marketing. **Supp**—Tut. **Adm (Gr K-12):** 172/yr. Appl due: Dec. **Tests** HSPT. **Enr 750.** B 168. G 582. Elem 490. Sec 260. Wh 86%. Hisp 4%. Blk 1%. Asian 9%. Avg class size: 20. Uniform. **Fac 55.** M 4. F 51. Adv deg: 49%. **Grad '04—62.** Col—62. **Tui '02-'03:** Day $7020. Aid: Merit 61 ($41,300). **Est 1854.** Nonprofit. Roman Catholic. Quar (Aug-June). **Assoc** NEASC. This school, originally established in Lowell, is under the direction of the Sisters of Notre Dame de Namur. A variety of honors and Advanced Placement courses is available. After-school activities (which vary according to student interest) and athletic teams supplement academics.

CATHOLIC MEMORIAL SCHOOL   Day Boys Gr 7-12
West Roxbury, MA 02132. 235 Baker St.
Tel: 617-469-8000. Fax: 617-325-0888.
www.catholicmemorial.org   E-mail: office@cath-mem.org

Br. James MacDonald, CFC, Pres. BA, Iona College, MEd, Boston College. Richard Chisholm, Prin. BS, MEd, Boston State College. John Mazza, Adm.

Col Prep. AP—Eng Fr Calc Comp_Sci Eur_Hist US_Hist US_Govt & Pol. **Feat**—Lat Span Jazz_Ensemble Journ. **Adm:** 220/yr. **Tests** HSPT. **Enr 850.** B 850. Elem 210. Sec 640. Wh 85%. Hisp 4%. Blk 7%. Asian 1%. Other 3%. Avg class size: 25. Uniform. **Fac 65.** Adv deg: 75%. **Grad '04—107.** Col—100. Alum 6300. **Tui '04-'05:** Day $8600 (+$250). **Summer:** Acad Enrich. Tui Day $350/crse. 4 wks. **Est 1957.** Nonprofit. Roman Catholic. Quar (Sept-June). **Assoc** NEASC. Founded by—and in part staffed by—the Congregation of Christian Brothers, CM offers Advanced Placement courses in English, social studies, mathematics, science and art. Extracurriculars include interscholastic and intramural sports, various clubs and organizations, and community action.

WHITE OAK SCHOOL   Day Coed Gr 4-12
Westfield, MA 01085. 533 North Rd.
Tel: 413-562-9500. Fax: 413-562-9010.
E-mail: admin@whiteoakschool.org

David R. Drake, Head. BA, Wesleyan Univ, MA, Univ of California-Los Angeles. Susan Edgerly, Adm.

Col Prep. Gen Acad. LD. Supp—Rem_Math Rem_Read Tut. **Adm:** 24/yr. Appl due: May. Accepted: 60%. **Tests** IQ. **Enr 101.** B 77. G 24. Elem 40. Sec 61. Wh 93%. Hisp 2%. Blk 2%. Asian 3%. Avg class size: 8. **Fac 35.** M 8/1. F 25/1. Adv deg: 57%. **Grad '04—20.** Col—18. Avg SAT: 920. Alum 150. **Tui '02-'03:** Day $$24,898. **Summer:** Enrich Rem. Tui Day $2025. 6 wks. **Est 1990.** Nonprofit. Sem (Sept-June). Serving students who have been referred to the school for language-based learning disabilities, White Oak provides an educational program consisting of daily, 50-minute one-to-one tutorials in literacy skills and small-class instruction in content areas. A computer is available for every pupil. The school seeks to develop the student's language literacy and study skills to the point where a successful return to a regular academic program is possible.

XAVERIAN BROTHERS HIGH SCHOOL
Day Boys Gr 9-12

Westwood, MA 02090. 800 Clapboardtree St.
Tel: 781-326-6392. Fax: 781-320-0458.
www.xbhs.com   E-mail: xaverian@xbhs.com

Br. Daniel Skala, CFX, Head. BA, MA, PhD, Boston College. Br. Raymond Hoyt, CFX, Adm.

Col Prep. AP—Eng Calc Bio Chem Physics Studio_Art. **Feat**—Fr Span Stats Anat & Physiol Marine_Biol/Sci Programming Web_Design Theol Film Theater Chorus Music Music_Theory Accounting. **Adm:** 270/yr. Appl due: Dec. **Tests** HSPT. **Enr 1045.** B 1045. Sec 1045. Avg class size: 24. **Fac 73.** M 58. F 15. Adv deg: 72%. **Grad '04—238.** Col—234. Alum 7112. **Tui '04-'05:** Day $9000 (+$300). **Est 1963.** Nonprofit. Roman Catholic. Quar (Sept-June). **Assoc** NEASC. Offering a traditional college preparatory program, the school groups students according to ability and features a strong foreign language department. Theology is a mandatory part of the program, and an active campus ministry conducts retreats and other activities.

CHILDREN'S OWN SCHOOL
Day Coed PS-K

Winchester, MA 01890. 86 Main St.
Tel: 781-729-2689. Fax: 781-729-4192.
E-mail: coswin@theworld.com

Rosina Orr Cullinane, Dir. MEd.

Gen Acad. Feat—Fr Studio_Art Music Creative_Movement. **Adm:** 24/yr. Appl due: Jan. **Enr 80.** B 31. G 49. Elem 80. Wh 80%. Asian 10%. Other 10%. Avg class size: 20. **Fac 11.** F 8/3. Adv deg: 18%. **Grad '04—24. Tui '04-'05:** Day $5765-7455. **Summer:** Acad Enrich Rec. Tui Day $280/2-wk ses. 6 wks. **Est 1942.** Nonprofit. Tri (Sept-June). Located on the former Russell Farm, Children's Own is the oldest Montessori school in New England. Within a noncompetitive environment, the school utilizes a multisensory approach to address varying learning needs.

HOLY NAME CENTRAL CATHOLIC JUNIOR/SENIOR HIGH SCHOOL
Day Coed Gr 7-12

Worcester, MA 01604. 144 Granite St.
Tel: 508-753-6371. Fax: 508-831-1287.
www.holyname.net

Mary Riordan, Head. BA, College of Our Lady of the Elms, MA, Anna Maria College, MEd, Framingham State College. Edward Reynolds, Prin. BA, Univ of Massachusetts-Amherst, MA, Worcester State College.

Col Prep. Gen Acad. AP—Eng Calc Physics US_Hist. **Feat**—Fr Span Anat & Physiol Comp_Sci Govt Psych Art_Hist Studio_Art Theater Band Chorus Bus. **Supp**—Rev Tut. **Adm:** 320/yr. **Enr 900.** Wh 93%. Hisp 3%. Blk 3%. Asian 1%. Avg class size: 25. Uniform. **Fac 55.** M 22. F 33. Wh 90%. Hisp 3%. Blk 4%. Asian 2%. Other 1%. Adv deg: 47%. **Grad '04—160.** Col—155. Alum 8290. **Tui '05-'06:** Day $5500 (+$700). Aid: Need ($250,000). **Summer:** Acad. Tui Day $100/crse. 3 wks. **Est 1942.** Nonprofit. Roman Catholic. Quar (Aug-June). **Assoc** NEASC. Founded by the Sisters of St. Anne, Holy Name stresses academics, the arts and athletics. The art program includes sculpture, ceramics, art history and graphic design. Students take part in service projects in Maine and Worcester.

NEW HAMPSHIRE

ST. THOMAS AQUINAS HIGH SCHOOL — Day Coed Gr 9-12
Dover, NH 03820. 197 Dover Point Rd.
Tel: 603-742-3206. Fax: 603-749-7822.
www.stalux.org   E-mail: sta@stalux.org
   Jeffrey A. Quinn, Prin. Patricia Krupsky, Adm.

   Col Prep. AP—Eng Calc Bio Chem Physics US_Hist US_Govt & Pol. **Feat**—Anat & Physiol Marine_Biol/Sci Computers Econ Psych Sociol Theol Music Accounting Bus. **Adm:** 185/yr. **Tests** HSPT. **Enr 703.** B 328. G 375. Sec 703. Wh 100%. Avg class size: 21. **Fac 50.** M 19. F 31. Wh 96%. Hisp 4%. Adv deg: 42%. **Grad '04—165.** Col—157. Avg SAT: 1138. Alum 4100. **Tui '02-'03:** Day $5800 (+$200). Aid: Need 36 ($115,000). **Est 1960.** Nonprofit. Roman Catholic. Quar (Aug-June). **Assoc** NEASC. St. Thomas Aquinas provides honors-level courses in most subject areas, and Advanced Placement classes are also available. All students enroll in a theology course each year. Between the first and second semesters, St. Thomas sponsors a weeklong academic program during which students and teachers concentrate on specialized and intensive courses. The campus ministry program offers a service program, leadership opportunities and worship experiences.

RUNNEMEDE SCHOOL — Day Coed Gr K-12
Plainfield, NH 03781. 1050 Rte 12A, PO Box 120.
Tel: 603-675-2933. Fax: 603-675-2040.
www.runnemedeschool.org   E-mail: info@runnemedeschool.org
   Auburn Cole, Int Head. Amy Bernhardt, Adm.

   Col Prep. AP—Fr. **Feat**—Shakespeare Span Astron Environ_Sci Marine_Biol/Sci Govt Studio_Art Drama Music Music_Hist. **Adm:** 19/yr. Appl due: Mar. Accepted: 20%. **Tests** SSAT. **Enr 93.** Elem 65. Sec 28. Wh 81%. Hisp 6%. Blk 4%. Am Ind 6%. Asian 3%. Avg class size: 12. **Fac 13.** M 6/1. F 6. Adv deg: 100%. **Grad '04—6.** Col—6. Avg SAT: 1300. **Tui '04-'05:** Day $6100-8250 (+$275-375). Aid: Need 16 ($62,000). **Summer:** Enrich Rec. Theater. Tui Day $400/2-wk ses. 6 wks. **Est 1997.** Nonprofit. Tri (Sept-June). Children enrolled in Runnemede's lower school (grades K-4) focus on the development of reading and math skills, while upper school students (grades 5-8) explore lab science, foreign language and topics in literature. The school maintains an extensive arts program that consists of theater, studio art, and choral and instrumental music. High school juniors and seniors may take courses at Dartmouth as part of their curriculum.

WATERVILLE VALLEY ACADEMY — Coed Gr 6-12 Bdg & Day
Waterville Valley, NH 03215. 95 Valley Rd, PO Box 270.
Tel: 603-236-4246. Fax: 603-236-9906.
www.wvbbts.org   E-mail: gbenedix@wvbbts.org

Gary W. Benedix, Head.

Sports (Winter). Feat—Fr Ger Span Comp_Sci Psych Sociol Studio_Art. **Supp**—Rem_Math Rem_Read Rev. **Adm:** Appl due: Rolling. **Enr 85.** Avg class size: 2. **Fac 40. Grad '04**—10. Col—10. **Tui '04-'05:** Bdg $16,500 (+$1000). Day $12,500 (+$1000). **Est 1972.** Nonprofit. (Nov-Mar). This five-month ski academy offers coaching in Alpine and freestyle skiing, as well as in snowboarding. The academic program operates as an individual teaching program that follows the syllabus sent by the home school.

RHODE ISLAND

MERCYMOUNT COUNTRY DAY SCHOOL   Day Coed Gr PS-8
Cumberland, RI 02864. Wrentham Rd.
Tel: 401-333-5919. Fax: 401-333-5150.
www.mercymount.org   E-mail: ride5179@ride.ri.net

Sr. Martha Mulligan, RSM, Prin. BA, Salve Regina Univ, MEd, Bridgewater State Univ.

Pre-Prep. Gen Acad. Feat—Span Computers Studio_Art Music. **Supp**—LD Rem_Math Rem_Read Rev Tut. **Adm:** 55/yr. Appl due: Feb. Yield: 90%. **Enr 368.** B 180. G 188. Elem 368. Wh 85%. Hisp 5%. Asian 10%. Avg class size: 22. Uniform. **Fac 27.** M 4. F 23. Wh 93%. Hisp 7%. Adv deg: 33%. **Grad '04**—21. Prep—18. **Tui '04-'05:** Day $5100 (+$400). Aid: Need 18 ($23,000). **Est 1948.** Nonprofit. Roman Catholic. Tri (Aug-June). Conducted by the Sisters of Mercy of the Americas, Mercymount offers a traditional Catholic elementary program. Computer classes begin in kindergarten, and the use of laptop computers is integrated into the curriculum in grades 5-8. Middle schoolers participate in a three-day trip as part of the environmental education curriculum. Older students also take part in outreach service activities.

PENNFIELD SCHOOL   Day Coed Gr PS-8
Portsmouth, RI 02871. 110 Sandy Point Ave.
Tel: 401-849-4646. Fax: 401-847-6720.
www.pennfield.org   E-mail: ride3395@ride.ri.net

Robert A. Kelley, Head. BA, MA, Tufts Univ. Polly Meadows, Adm.

Pre-Prep. Feat—Fr Span Computers Studio_Art Music. **Adm:** 54/yr. Appl due: Rolling. Accepted: 98%. Yield: 50%. **Tests** CTP_4 MAT. **Enr 204.** B 110. G 94. Elem 204. Wh 99%. Blk 1%. Avg class size: 17. **Fac 32.** M 3/3. F 20/6. Wh 97%. Blk 3%. Adv deg: 34%. **Grad '04**—19. Prep—19. **Tui '04-'05:** Day $5005-12,470 (+$500). **Summer:** Arts. Tui Day $130/wk. 3 wks. **Est 1971.** Nonprofit. Tri (Sept-June). Pennfield utilizes traditional and modern teaching methods to develop artistic, intellectual, spiritual and athletic potential in its students. Instruction in both French and Spanish begins in kindergarten. The school's curriculum places strong emphasis on the arts at all grade levels.

COMMUNITY PREPARATORY SCHOOL Day Coed Gr 3-8
Providence, RI 02907. 126 Somerset St.
Tel: 401-521-9696. Fax: 401-521-9715.
www.communityprep.org   E-mail: ride2992@ride.ri.net
  Daniel Corley, Head. AB, Brown Univ. Patricia McDonald Luca, Adm.

  Pre-Prep. Feat—Span Creative_Arts Public_Speak. **Supp**—Dev_Read Tut. **Adm:** 42/yr. Appl due: Feb. Accepted: 30%. **Tests** ISEE SSAT. **Enr 158.** B 68. G 90. Elem 158. Wh 13%. Hisp 22%. Blk 40%. Am Ind 1%. Asian 13%. Other 11%. Avg class size: 18. Uniform. **Fac 19.** M 6/2. F 7/4. Wh 44%. Hisp 11%. Blk 39%. Asian 4%. Other 2%. Adv deg: 26%. **Grad '04—35.** Prep—21. Alum 295. **Tui '05-'06:** Day $9000 (+$250). Aid: Need 135 ($1,000,000). **Summer:** Enrich Rec. Tui Day $150. 4 wks. **Est 1984.** Nonprofit. Tri (Sept-June). Community Prep provides promising students from diverse cultural and economic backgrounds with the preparation necessary for a college preparatory high school. After-school electives, including photography, computer science and languages, are available to those who qualify academically.

PROUT SCHOOL Day Coed Gr 9-12
Wakefield, RI 02879. 4640 Tower Hill Rd.
Tel: 401-789-9262. Fax: 401-782-2262.
www.theproutschool.org   E-mail: kneed@theproutschool.org
  Gary Delneo, Prin. BA, Fordham Univ, MA, Univ of Vermont. Kristen P. Need, Adm.

  Col Prep. IB_Diploma. Feat—Fr Ital Span Anat & Physiol Environ_Sci Oceanog Computers Econ Psych Relig Art_Hist Studio_Art Acting Drama. **Adm:** 147/yr. Appl due: Jan. Accepted: 50%. **Tests** HSPT. **Enr 532.** B 185. G 347. Sec 532. Wh 96%. Hisp 1%. Blk 1%. Am Ind 1%. Asian 1%. Avg class size: 22. Uniform. **Fac 50.** M 22. F 28. Wh 98%. Hisp 2%. Adv deg: 54%. **Grad '04—98.** Col—97. **Tui '05-'06:** Day $7950 (+$420-635). **Summer:** Rec. Tui Day $495/2-wk ses. 4 wks. **Est 1966.** Nonprofit. Roman Catholic. Quar (Aug-June). Within a college preparatory environment, Prout supplements its core courses with work in art, music, philosophy and economics. The curriculum is especially noteworthy for its inclusion of the rigorous International Baccalaureate Program, which often leads to college credit and which is recognized by universities throughout the world. Outside the classroom, pupils engage in honor societies, interest clubs, interscholastic sports, academic clubs and community service organizations.

MOUNT SAINT CHARLES ACADEMY Day Coed Gr 7-12
Woonsocket, RI 02895. 800 Logee St.
Tel: 401-769-0310. Fax: 401-762-2327.
www.mountsaintcharles.org   E-mail: mtstchrles@aol.com
  Herve Richer, Prin. BA, Assumption College, MEd, Providence College. Joseph J. O'Neill, Adm.

  Col Prep. AP—Eng Calc Bio Chem Eur_Hist US_Hist Psych US_Govt & Pol Studio_Art Music_Theory. **Feat**—Fr Span Anat & Physiol Environ_Sci Econ Relig Architect Film Drama Dance. **Supp**—Dev_Read. **Adm (Gr 7-10):** 215/yr. Appl due: Mar. Accepted: 40%. **Tests** HSPT. **Enr 1000.** B 490. G 510. Elem 320. Sec

680. Wh 97%. Blk 1%. Asian 2%. Avg class size: 25. Uniform. **Fac 60.** M 26/3. F 27/4. Adv deg: 65%. **Grad '04—151.** Col—145. Alum 6000. **Tui '04-'05:** Day $7250 (+$400). **Summer:** Enrich. Art. Soccer. Tui Day $250-300. 2 wks. **Est 1924.** Nonprofit. Roman Catholic. Sem (Aug-June). **Assoc** NEASC. Administered by the Brothers of the Sacred Heart, Mount Saint Charles offers honors and Advanced Placement courses, in addition to its regular high school curriculum. Extracurricular activities include foreign language clubs, student government, drama, art, music and journalism. The athletic department features a particularly strong hockey program.

VERMONT

LYNDON INSTITUTE   **Coed Gr 9-12**
Lyndon Center, VT 05850. College Rd, PO Box 127.   **Bdg & Day**
Tel: 802-626-5232. Fax: 802-626-9164.
www.lyndoninstitute.org   E-mail: admissions@lyndon.k12.vt.us
    Richard D. Hilton, Head. BS, Univ of Notre Dame, MEd, Villanova Univ. Mary B. Thomas, Adm.

    Col Prep. Gen Acad. Voc. Bus. Feat—Creative_Writing Fr Lat Span Environ_Sci Comp_Design VT_Hist Econ Law Photog Studio_Art Music Music_Theory Drafting Indus_Arts Metal_Shop. **Adm:** 168/yr. Appl due: Rolling. **Tests** CEEB SSAT TOEFL. **Enr 617.** Sec 617. Avg class size: 10. **Fac 70.** M 33/2. F 31/4. Adv deg: 37%. **Grad '04—145.** Col—84. Avg SAT: 973. Alum 6200. **Tui '03-'04:** Bdg $24,040 (+$300). Day $8885 (+$300). **Summer:** Arts. Tui Bdg $650-1600. Tui Day $500-1000. 1-2 wks. **Est 1867.** Nonprofit. Sem (Aug-June). **Assoc** NEASC. LI offers college preparatory, business and technical education courses. Extracurricular activities include band, chorus, drama and hobby clubs, and a full complement of athletic teams. Skiing is particularly notable, with Alpine and Nordic opportunities in the nearby areas.

BURR AND BURTON ACADEMY   **Coed Gr 9-12**
Manchester, VT 05254. Seminary Ave, PO Box 498.   **Bdg & Day**
Tel: 802-362-1775. Fax: 802-362-0574.
www.burrburton.org   E-mail: rurbanski@burrburton.org
    Charles W. Scranton, Head. BS, Wagner College, MEd, Rutgers Univ. Philip G. Anton, Adm.

    Col Prep. Gen Acad. Voc. AP—Eng Span Calc Bio US_Hist Psych. **Feat**—Creative_Writing Fr Ger Econ Govt Art_Hist Film Drama Music Dance Accounting Journ TV_Production Drafting Woodworking. **Supp**—Dev_Read ESL LD Makeup Tut. **Adm:** 190/yr. **Enr 597.** B 4/307. G 2/284. Sec 597. Wh 99%. Asian 1%. Avg class size: 19. **Fac 59.** M 31. F 27/1. Wh 100%. Adv deg: 62%. **Grad '04—109.** Col—83. Avg SAT: 1050. Alum 5500. **Tui '03-'04:** Bdg $22,000. Day $9000. **Summer:** Enrich Rec. Tui Day $325/2-wk ses. 4 wks. **Est 1829.** Nonprofit. Sem (Aug-June). **Assoc** NEASC. Burr and Burton operates under a block scheduling system of four classes per semester, with Advanced Placement courses available. All students also must complete 50 hours of community service during their four years at the academy. The small boarding program is made up of students who reside with families or in the one faculty-supervised house on campus.

MOUNT SAINT JOSEPH ACADEMY
Day Coed Gr 9-12
Rutland, VT 05701. 127 Convent Ave.
Tel: 802-775-0151. Fax: 802-775-0424.
www.msjvermont.org   E-mail: admissions@msjvermont.org
Sr. Kathryn Gallagher, SSJ, Prin. BA, MS. Ellie Chiccarelli, Adm.

Col Prep. Bus. AP—Eng Calc Bio Physics Studio_Art. **Feat**—Fr Span Web_Design Theol Chorus. **Supp**—ESL Rev Tut. **Adm:** 55/yr. Appl due: Mar. Accepted: 99%. **Enr 170.** B 95. G 75. Sec 170. Avg class size: 18. Uniform. **Fac 21.** M 10/2. F 7/2. Adv deg: 80%. **Grad '04—62.** Col—59. Avg SAT: 1051. Avg ACT: 25. Alum 6200. **Tui '04-'05:** Day $4000-5400 (+$425). Aid: Need 51. **Est 1882.** Nonprofit. Roman Catholic. Sem (Aug-June). In a Catholic setting, MSJ offers Advanced Placement courses in the major disciplines, as well as French and Spanish courses. Foreign students, who reside with host families, enroll at additional cost in both diploma and nondiploma programs that include English as a Second Language instruction. Drama, music, student government, community service and athletics are among the academy's activities.

RICE MEMORIAL HIGH SCHOOL
Day Coed Gr 9-12
South Burlington, VT 05403. 99 Proctor Ave.
Tel: 802-862-6521. Fax: 802-864-9931.
www.ricehs.org   E-mail: admissions@ricehs.org
Alan Crowley, Prin. Kevin Clark, Adm.

Col Prep. AP—Eng Fr Calc Stats Bio Eur_Hist US_Hist. **Feat**—Ger Lat Span Relig Ceramics Studio_Art Chorus Music_Theory Accounting. **Supp**—Tut. **Adm:** 103/yr. Appl due: Feb. Accepted: 97%. **Enr 463.** B 218. G 245. Sec 463. Wh 94%. Hisp 1%. Blk 1%. Asian 2%. Other 2%. Avg class size: 20. Uniform. **Fac 41.** M 15/2. F 22/2. Wh 94%. Hisp 2%. Blk 2%. Am Ind 2%. Adv deg: 68%. **Grad '04—107.** Col—97. Avg SAT: 1092. **Tui '05-'06:** Day $6972. Aid: Need 150 ($400,000). Work prgm 10 ($5000). **Est 1959.** Nonprofit. Roman Catholic. Quar (Aug-June). Boys and girls enroll at Rice High School from approximately 50 communities throughout northwest and central Vermont. The variety of courses offered in each discipline enables students to meet graduation and college-entrance requirements, while also allowing the school to serve pupils of differing ability levels. A well-established athletic program provides competition in such sports as indoor and outdoor track and field, soccer, softball, ice hockey, basketball and baseball.

STRATTON MOUNTAIN SCHOOL
Coed Gr 7-PG
Bdg & Day
Stratton Mountain, VT 05155. World Cup Cir.
Tel: 802-297-1886. Fax: 802-297-0020.
www.gosms.org   E-mail: sms@gosms.org
Christopher G. Kaltsas, Head. Todd Ormiston, Adm.

Col Prep. Sports (Winter). Feat—British_Lit Creative_Writing Fr Ger Lat Span Stats Environ_Sci Computers Econ Govt Art_Hist Studio_Art Journ. **Supp**—

ESL Tut. **Adm:** 40/yr. Bdg 26. Day 14. Appl due: Mar. Accepted: 70%. **Enr 113.** B 36/27. G 25/25. Elem 21. Sec 87. PG 5. Wh 95%. Hisp 2%. Asian 3%. Avg class size: 7. **Fac 18.** M 8/2. F 4/4. Wh 100%. Adv deg: 38%. In Dorms 4. **Grad '04—27.** Col—25. Alum 650. **Tui '03-'04:** Bdg $28,800 (+$5000). Day $19,800 (+$5000). Aid: Need 41 ($375,000). Work prgm 1 ($4000). **Summer:** Skiing. Tui Bdg $500-3000. 2-6 wks. **Est 1972.** Nonprofit. Quar (Sept-June). SMS offers a strong college preparatory curriculum to competitive winter sports athletes. The school year and daily schedules are designed to maximize training time and accommodate competition schedules. Residential students participate in weekly evening workshops and field trips.

KING GEORGE SCHOOL   **Bdg Coed Gr 9-12**
Sutton, VT 05867. 2684 King George Farm Rd.
Tel: 802-467-1200. Fax: 802-467-1041.
www.kinggeorgeschool.com   E-mail: mreinhardt.kgs@gmail.com
    Karen Fitzhugh, Head. BA, Univ of California-Los Angeles, MA, PhD, Univ of California-Riverside. Mary Reinhardt, Adm.

    Col Prep. Gen Acad. Feat—British_Lit Span Govt Studio_Art Jazz_Dance Theater_Arts Ballet Outdoor_Ed Tae_Kwon_Do. **Supp**—Dev_Read Makeup Tut. **Adm:** 20/yr. Appl due: Rolling. Accepted: 80%. **Enr 30.** B 17. G 13. Sec 30. Wh 92%. Hisp 4%. Other 4%. Avg class size: 8. Uniform. **Fac 19.** M 11. F 8. Wh 95%. Other 5%. Adv deg: 31%. **Grad '04—21.** Col—18. Avg SAT: 1020. **Tui '04-'05:** Bdg $47,700 (+$2000). Aid: Need 3 ($40,500). **Est 1998.** Inc. Quar (Sept-Aug). Students at King George devote each morning to community focus meetings and two academic courses. After two afternoon courses, boys and girls conclude the day with a combination of visual or performing arts classes, communicational skills training, exercise and directed study time. The 330-acre campus provides opportunities for such outdoor activities as mountain biking, hiking, cross-country skiing and snowshoeing.

Middle Atlantic States

DELAWARE

THE INDEPENDENCE SCHOOL Day Coed Gr PS-8
Newark, DE 19711. 1300 Paper Mill Rd.
Tel: 302-239-0330. Fax: 302-239-3696.
www.theindependenceschool.org
E-mail: michele.wingrave@theindependenceschool.org
  Christopher C. Pryor, Head. BA, Roanoke College, MA, Columbia Univ. Michele Wingrave, Adm.

  Pre-Prep. Gen Acad. Feat—Lib_Skills Fr Ger Lat Span Computers Art_Hist Instrumental_Music. **Supp**—Tut. **Adm:** 207/yr. Appl due: Rolling. Accepted: 51%. **Tests** IQ. **Enr 846.** B 433. G 413. Elem 846. Wh 82%. Hisp 2%. Blk 3%. Asian 13%. Avg class size: 18. **Fac 63.** M 7/1. F 47/8. Wh 94%. Hisp 6%. Adv deg: 30%. **Grad '04—65.** Prep—54. Alum 1165. **Tui '04-'05:** Day $8970. Aid: Merit 12 ($12,000). Need 53 ($174,600). **Summer:** Rec. Tui Day $150/wk. 10 wks. **Est 1978.** Nonprofit. Tri (Sept-June). **Assoc** MSA. The school's curriculum emphasizes the basics, with all pupils in grades 1-8 required to study a foreign language. Students participate in a variety of interscholastic sports.

THE PILOT SCHOOL Day Coed Gr K-8
Wilmington, DE 19803. 100 Garden of Eden Rd.
Tel: 302-478-1740. Fax: 302-478-1746.
www.pilotschool.org   E-mail: info@pilotschool.org
  Kathleen B. Craven, Dir. BS, McPherson College, MEd, Millersville Univ.

  LD. Feat—Lib_Skills Computers Studio_Art. **Supp**—Dev_Read Rem_Math Rem_Read Rev. **Adm:** 41/yr. Appl due: Rolling. **Tests** IQ. **Enr 163.** B 117. G 46. Elem 163. Wh 95%. Hisp 1%. Blk 3%. Asian 1%. Avg class size: 6. **Fac 43.** M 11. F 32. Wh 100%. Adv deg: 37%. **Grad '04—38.** Prep—22. Alum 1007. **Tui '03-'04:** Day $18,226. Aid: Need 39 ($264,100). **Est 1957.** Nonprofit. (Sept-June). **Assoc** MSA. Pilot, which maintains a favorable student-teacher ratio, offers intensive small-group and individual remedial-developmental instruction to students of average or above potential who have learning differences. Applicants must take a series of psychological, educational and language tests prior to acceptance.

SAINT EDMOND'S ACADEMY Day Boys Gr 4-8
Wilmington, DE 19810. 2120 Veale Rd.
Tel: 302-475-5370. Fax: 302-475-0913.
www.stedmondsacademy.org   E-mail: amarinelli@stedmondsacademy.org
  Michael A. Marinelli, Head. BS, Univ of Delaware, MA, Widener Univ, EdD, Wilmington College (DE). Angela Marinelli, Adm.

  Pre-Prep. Feat—Span Computers Relig Studio_Art Drama Music. **Supp**—Rem_Math Tut. **Adm:** 60/yr. Appl due: Rolling. Accepted: 80%. **Tests** CTP_4. **Enr**

266. B 266. Elem 266. Wh 92%. Hisp 2%. Blk 4%. Asian 2%. Avg class size: 17. Uniform. **Fac 26.** M 15/1. F 10. Wh 100%. Adv deg: 57%. **Grad '04—57.** Prep—48. Alum 1800. **Tui '04-'05:** Day $9390 (+$550). Aid: Merit 10 ($28,480). Need 24 ($73,000). **Summer:** Rec. Tui Day $150/wk. 3 wks. **Est 1959.** Nonprofit. Roman Catholic. Tri (Sept-June). **Assoc** MSA. This boys' school, which was founded in the educational tradition of the Holy Cross Brothers, places particular emphasis on the development of fundamental academic skills. A rotating six-day schedule incorporates academics, physical and social activities, music, art and spiritual pursuits. The academy's athletic program offers varsity, junior varsity intramural competition in soccer, cross-country, basketball, wrestling, track, baseball and lacrosse; student government, literary magazine, Model UN, yearbook and academic clubs are some of the other extracurriculars.

SALESIANUM SCHOOL
Day Boys Gr 9-12
Wilmington, DE 19802. 1801 N Broom St.
Tel: 302-654-2495. Fax: 302-654-7767.
www.salesianum.org E-mail: dharris@salesianum.org

Rev. John J. Fisher, OSFS, Prin. BA, Allentown College of St Francis de Sales, MA, Villanova Univ, MDiv, DeSales School of Theology, EdD, Wilmington College (DE). Dennis R. Harris, Jr., Adm.

Col Prep. AP—Eng Fr Lat Span Calc Stats Comp_Sci Bio Chem Physics Eur_Hist US_Hist World_Hist Psych. **Feat**—Ital Relig. **Adm:** 285/yr. **Tests** HSPT. **Enr 1010.** B 1010. Sec 1010. Avg class size: 26. **Fac 79.** Adv deg: 64%. **Grad '04—246.** Col—240. Avg SAT: 1110. **Tui '04-'05:** Day $7970 (+$350-450). **Est 1903.** Roman Catholic. Quar (Sept-June). **Assoc** MSA. At Salesianum, governed by the Oblates of St. Francis de Sales, boys follow a core program that includes four years of religious studies and two consecutive years of a foreign language. A fine arts program, student clubs, religious activities and a full range of athletics supplement academic work.

URSULINE ACADEMY
Day Boys Gr PS-3, Girls PS-12
Wilmington, DE 19806. 1106 Pennsylvania Ave.
Tel: 302-658-7158. Fax: 302-658-4297.
www.ursuline.org E-mail: jamiejones@ursuline.org

James Keegan, Int Pres. BS, Univ of Notre Dame. Jamie Jones, Adm.

Col Prep. AP—Calc Stats Bio Chem Physics. **Feat**—Lat Computers Relig Theol Music. **Adm (Gr PS-12):** 123/yr. Appl due: Rolling. Accepted: 70%. **Tests** CTP_4. **Enr 705.** B 60. G 645. Elem 478. Sec 227. Wh 91%. Hisp 3%. Blk 3%. Asian 3%. Avg class size: 17. Uniform. **Fac 81.** M 9/2. F 62/8. Wh 100%. Adv deg: 56%. **Grad '04—42.** Col—42. Avg SAT: 1155. Alum 2900. **Tui '05-'06:** Day $10,550-12,825 (+$45-3500). Aid: Merit 41 ($87,000). Need 68 ($327,530). **Summer:** Acad Enrich Rec. Tui Day $480/2-wk ses. 10 wks. **Est 1893.** Nonprofit. Roman Catholic. Quar (Sept-June). A Montessori program is conducted for children ages 3-5, with a traditional class structure employed beginning in grade 1. All students in grades 7-12 must have a laptop computer, and upper schoolers choose from a variety of honors and Advanced Placement courses. Compulsory religion course work, a fine arts curriculum and varied athletics round out the program.

DISTRICT OF COLUMBIA

CAPITOL HILL DAY SCHOOL   Day Coed Gr PS-8
Washington, DC 20003. 210 S Carolina Ave SE.
Tel: 202-547-2244. Fax: 202-543-4597.
www.chds.org   E-mail: admissions@chds.org
    Catherine M. Peterson, Head. BA, Smith College, MEd, Goucher College. Mary Beth Moore, Adm.

    Pre-Prep. Gen Acad. Feat—Poetry Fr Span Computers Studio_Art Drama Music. **Supp**—Dev_Read Rev Tut. **Adm:** 40/yr. Appl due: Jan. Accepted: 50%. **Tests** IQ. **Enr 224.** B 109. G 115. Elem 224. Wh 70%. Hisp 2%. Blk 22%. Asian 6%. Avg class size: 24. **Fac 40.** M 6/1. F 15/18. Wh 77%. Hisp 5%. Blk 13%. Asian 5%. Adv deg: 52%. **Grad '04—21.** Prep—18. Alum 1000. **Tui '05-'06:** Day $16,620-19,260. Aid: Need 36 ($309,174). **Summer:** Acad Rec. Tui Day $325-380/wk. 7 wks. **Est 1968.** Nonprofit. Quar (Sept-June). CHDS offers a strong academic curriculum in a supportive environment. The arts are integrated into mathematics, literature, science and social studies classes. French and Spanish instruction begins in prekindergarten. Drama, computer, team sports and community service programs are available in the upper grades. The school utilizes the resources of Greater Washington to augment classroom work.

THE FIELD SCHOOL   Day Coed Gr 7-12
Washington, DC 20007. 2301 Foxhall Rd NW.
Tel: 202-295-5800. Fax: 202-295-5858.
www.fieldschool.org   E-mail: admission@fieldschool.org
    Elizabeth C. Ely, Dir. BA, Duke Univ. Clay Kaufman, Adm.

    Col Prep. AP—Fr Span. **Feat**—Writing Lat Zoology Computers Art_Hist Studio_Art Journ. **Supp**—Rev Tut. **Adm:** 81/yr. Appl due: Jan. **Tests** SSAT. **Enr 280.** B 140. G 140. Elem 70. Sec 210. Wh 83%. Hisp 2%. Blk 12%. Asian 1%. Other 2%. Avg class size: 11. **Fac 50.** Adv deg: 36%. **Grad '04—40.** Col—40. Alum 565. **Tui '04-'05:** Day $23,250 (+$500). **Est 1972.** Nonprofit. Quar (Sept-June). **Assoc** MSA. In addition to an academic curriculum, this school emphasizes its extensive studio arts offerings, which include ceramics, drama, music, painting and drawing, photography, digital arts and video, and journalism. Students perform community service work as part of a two-week February internship program. In alternate years, the school sponsors a two-week trip to a Spanish- or French-speaking country.

GONZAGA COLLEGE HIGH SCHOOL   Day Boys Gr 9-12
Washington, DC 20001. 19 Eye St NW.
Tel: 202-336-7100. Fax: 202-454-1188.
www.gonzaga.org   E-mail: rmatting@gonzaga.org
    Rev. Allen Novothy, SJ, Pres. MS, MBA, Loyola College. Rev. Robert Mattingly, SJ, Adm.

    Col Prep. AP—Eng Fr Span Calc Comp_Sci Bio Chem Physics Eur_Hist US_Hist. **Feat**—British_Lit Creative_Writing Ger Greek Lat Programming Govt Psych

Ethics Philos Relig Film Fine_Arts Photog Band Chorus Music Music_Theory Communications. **Adm (Gr 9-11):** 225/yr. Appl due: Dec. Accepted: 40%. **Tests** HSPT. **Enr 893.** B 893. Sec 893. Wh 78%. Hisp 5%. Blk 14%. Asian 3%. Avg class size: 22. Uniform. **Fac 107.** M 78. F 29. **Grad '04—217.** Avg SAT: 1224. Alum 6500. **Tui '04-'05:** Day \$11,500. Aid: Merit 93 (\$76,500). Need 200 (\$1,300,000). **Summer:** Acad Enrich Rec. SAT Prep. Tui Day \$300-350. 8 wks. **Est 1821.** Nonprofit. Roman Catholic. Quar (Aug-June). Gonzaga offers advanced courses in the core academic subjects, as well as in the arts. Additional requirements for boys include religious studies, computer programming and community service participation. Student clubs and literary organizations, band, drama and radio are some of the extracurricular options.

THE LAB SCHOOL OF WASHINGTON
Day Coed Gr K-12

Washington, DC 20007. 4759 Reservoir Rd NW.
Tel: 202-965-6600. Fax: 202-965-5105.
www.labschool.org

Sally L. Smith, Dir. BA, Bennington College, MA, New York Univ. Susan F. Feeley, Adm.

Col Prep. Gen Acad. LD. Feat—Lat Span Film Studio_Art Drama Music Dance. **Supp**—Dev_Read Makeup Tut. **Adm:** 46/yr. Appl due: Feb. **Tests** IQ. **Enr 328.** B 213. G 115. Elem 191. Sec 137. Wh 77%. Hisp 6%. Blk 13%. Asian 3%. Other 1%. Avg class size: 12. **Fac 92.** M 27. F 62/3. Wh 91%. Blk 4%. Asian 1%. Other 4%. Adv deg: 81%. **Grad '04—25.** Col—24. **Tui '04-'05:** Day \$23,575-25,385. **Summer:** Acad Enrich Rev Rem Rec. Tui Day \$1800-2100. 5 wks. **Est 1967.** Nonprofit. Sem (Sept-June). **Assoc** MSA. The Lab School serves children of average to superior intelligence with moderate to severe learning disabilities. The arts are central to the curriculum, and the teaching methods are creative, individualized and multisensory. Most students enter college upon graduation.

NATIONAL PRESBYTERIAN SCHOOL
Day Coed Gr PS-6

Washington, DC 20016. 4121 Nebraska Ave NW.
Tel: 202-537-7500. Fax: 202-537-7568.
www.nps-dc.org   E-mail: school@nps-dc.org

Jay R. Roudebush, Head. BA, Occidental College, MAEd, American Univ. Anne Gutman, Adm.

Pre-Prep. Feat—Fr Span Computers Studio_Art Music. **Supp**—Dev_Read Tut. **Adm:** 48/yr. Appl due: Feb. Accepted: 52%. **Tests** IQ. **Enr 235.** B 118. G 117. Elem 235. Wh 84%. Hisp 1%. Blk 7%. Asian 3%. Other 5%. Avg class size: 12. **Fac 34.** M 3. F 31. Wh 90%. Blk 9%. Other 1%. Adv deg: 50%. **Grad '04—24.** Prep—23. Alum 230. **Tui '04-'05:** Day \$16,500 (+\$100). Aid: Need 27 (\$285,385). **Summer:** Enrich Rec. Tui Day \$465-735. 2 wks. **Est 1969.** Nonprofit. Presbyterian. Tri (Sept-June). **Assoc** MSA. Core courses at NPS typically feature two classroom teachers and roughly a dozen pupils. Students learn from specialist instructors in math, science, technology, reading, music, art and physical education. All children attend weekly chapel services that convene at the National Presbyterian Church. Before- and after-school classes supplement the NPS curriculum, and a flexible extended-day program is also available.

PARKMONT SCHOOL
Day Coed Gr 6-12

Washington, DC 20011. 4842 16th St NW.
Tel: 202-726-0740. Fax: 202-726-0748.
www.parkmont.org E-mail: gduffin@parkmont.org
Ron McClain, Dir. AB, Harvard Univ. Gina Duffin, Adm.

Col Prep. Feat—British_Lit Span Anat & Physiol Ecol Robotics Govt World_Relig Film Studio_Art. **Adm:** 18/yr. Appl due: Rolling. Accepted: 80%. **Enr 55.** B 31. G 24. Elem 16. Sec 39. Wh 57%. Hisp 17%. Blk 25%. Asian 1%. Avg class size: 9. **Fac 14.** M 5/1. F 4/4. Wh 79%. Blk 14%. Asian 7%. Adv deg: 14%. **Grad '04—5.** Col—5. Alum 200. **Tui '04-'05:** Day $19,475. Aid: Need 18 ($220,000). **Summer:** Acad. 5 wks. **Est 1972.** Nonprofit. 5 terms (Sept-June). Enrolling an ethnically diverse student body that is kept quite small, Parkmont employs a modular scheduling system consisting of five annual terms that reduces the pupil's academic load to three courses at a time and increases opportunities for teachers to incorporate experiential activities and field trips into the curriculum. Classes comprise multi-age groups of students with differing learning styles. At the high school level (grades 9-12), boys and girls devote 180 hours per year to internships that may involve one or two placements.

ROCK CREEK INTERNATIONAL SCHOOL
Day Coed Gr PS-8

Washington, DC 20007. 1550 Foxhall Rd NW.
Tel: 202-965-8700. Fax: 202-965-8973.
www.rcis.org E-mail: admission@rcis.org
J. Daniel Hollinger, Head. PhD, Univ of Virginia. Alejandra A. Maudet, Adm.

Pre-Prep. IB_PYP. IB_MYP. Bilingual. Feat—Fr Span Arabic Computers Studio_Art Drama Music. **Supp**—ESL Rem_Math Rem_Read Tut. **Adm:** 86/yr. Appl due: Feb. Accepted: 69%. Yield: 50%. **Enr 240.** B 111. G 129. Elem 240. Wh 50%. Hisp 12%. Blk 18%. Asian 6%. Other 14%. Avg class size: 8. **Fac 40.** Wh 58%. Hisp 18%. Blk 13%. Other 11%. Adv deg: 37%. **Grad '04—3.** Prep—3. **Tui '04-'05:** Day $17,975. Aid: Need 89 ($889,990). **Summer:** Acad Enrich Rec. Tui Day $750/3-wk ses. 9 wks. **Est 1988.** Nonprofit. Tri (Sept-June). **Assoc** MSA. This bilingual school, which follows the IB Primary and Middle Years Programmes, promotes fluency in two languages by conducting a curriculum taught in English on one day and either French, Spanish or Arabic the next. Taking an international perspective, RCIS' teaching methods emphasize inquiry-based learning and account for students' specific learning styles, knowledge and interests. After-school enrichment classes allow children to pursue special interests in the areas of sports, music, arts and crafts, information technology and languages not available during the school day.

ST. JOHN'S COLLEGE HIGH SCHOOL
Day Coed Gr 9-12

Washington, DC 20015. 2607 Military Rd NW.
Tel: 202-363-2316. Fax: 202-686-5162.
www.stjohns-chs.org E-mail: admissions@stjohns-chs.org
Br. Thomas Gerrow, FSC, Pres. BA, La Salle Univ, MS, Duquesne Univ. Jeffrey W. Mancabelli, Prin. BA, Univ of Scranton, MA, George Washington Univ. Christopher Themistos, Adm.

Col Prep. AP—Eng Fr Span Calc Comp_Sci Bio Chem Physics Eur_Hist US_Hist Psych US_Govt & Pol Art_Hist Studio_Art. **Feat**—British_Lit Creative_Writing Shakespeare Stats Anat & Physiol Astron Sports_Med Zoology Web_Design Econ Relig Chorus Music Dance Accounting Bus JROTC. **Supp**—LD Tut. **Adm:** 312/yr. Appl due: Dec. Accepted: 60%. **Tests** HSPT. **Enr 1078.** B 628. G 450. Sec 1078. Wh 57%. Hisp 9%. Blk 27%. Asian 5%. Other 2%. Avg class size: 23. Uniform. **Fac 81.** M 46. F 31/4. Adv deg: 59%. **Grad '04—245.** Col—238. Alum 7995. **Tui '04-'05:** Day $9960 (+$500). **Summer:** Acad Enrich Rev. 4 wks. **Est 1851.** Nonprofit. Roman Catholic. Quar (Aug-June). **Assoc** MSA. The second-oldest Christian Brothers school in the US, St. John's offers a comprehensive program of academics, arts and service opportunities. The school's elective Junior ROTC program seeks to develop teamwork and leadership skills through daily activities. Interdisciplinary science and technology studies are integral to the curriculum.

ST. PATRICK'S EPISCOPAL DAY SCHOOL   Day Coed Gr PS-8
Washington, DC 20007. 4700 Whitehaven Pky NW.
Tel: 202-342-2805. Fax: 202-342-7001.
www.stpatsdc.org   E-mail: admission@stpatsdc.org
    Peter A. Barrett, Head. BA, Trinity College, MAT, Northwestern Univ. Jennifer S. Danish, Adm.

Gen Acad. Feat—Humanities Span Computers Relig Studio_Art Music. **Supp**—Dev_Read Tut. **Adm:** 87/yr. Appl due: Jan. Accepted: 38%. **Tests** IQ SSAT. **Enr 487.** B 245. G 242. Sec 487. Wh 68%. Hisp 3%. Blk 15%. Am Ind 1%. Asian 4%. Other 9%. Avg class size: 17. **Fac 80.** M 9. F 58/13. Wh 86%. Hisp 3%. Blk 8%. Asian 2%. Other 1%. Adv deg: 61%. **Grad '04—53.** Prep—53. Alum 871. **Tui '04-'05:** Day $19,200-20,150 (+$100-800). Aid: Need 12 ($136,000). **Summer:** Acad Enrich Rec. Tui Day $910-1850. 3-8 wks. **Est 1956.** Nonprofit. Episcopal. Tri (Sept-June). **Assoc** MSA. The school's enriched curriculum includes computer, religion, music, art, video production and library skills. Community service opportunities, sports and after-school programs supplement academics.

MARYLAND

ALEPH BET JEWISH DAY SCHOOL   Day Coed Gr K-5
Annapolis, MD 21403. 1125 Spa Rd.
Tel: 410-263-9044. Fax: 410-263-5740.
www.alephbet.org   E-mail: info@alephbet.org
    Nan Jarashow, Head. BA, Carleton College, MAT, George Washington Univ.

Pre-Prep. Gen Acad. Feat—Hebrew Judaic_Stud Studio_Art Drama Music. **Adm (Gr K-4):** 18/yr. Appl due: Feb. Accepted: 96%. **Enr 61.** B 32. G 29. Elem 61. Wh 94%. Blk 3%. Asian 3%. Avg class size: 10. **Fac 10.** F 5/5. Wh 100%. Adv deg: 20%. **Grad '04—9.** Prep—4. **Tui '05-'06:** Day $7885 (+$400). Aid: Need 15 ($60,000). **Est 1989.** Nonprofit. Jewish. Tri (Aug-June). Aleph Bet's dual curriculum combines general academics with course work in Judaic studies. Hebrew language study and instruction in Jewish values, ethics and history are among the topics addressed in the Judaic studies curriculum. Enrichment classes in music, art and drama round out the program.

ST. ANNE'S DAY SCHOOL Day Coed Gr PS-8
Annapolis, MD 21403. 3112 Arundel on the Bay Rd.
Tel: 410-263-8650. Fax: 410-280-8720.
www.saintannes.org E-mail: admissions@saintannes.org
 Frances C. Lukens, Head. BA, Connecticut College, MEd, Goucher College. Caroline Cather Aras, Adm.

Pre-Prep. Feat—Fr Span Computers Relig Studio_Art Music. **Adm:** 76/yr. Appl due: Feb. Accepted: 79%. **Tests** ISEE Stanford. **Enr** 348. B 139. G 209. Elem 348. Wh 90%. Hisp 1%. Blk 5%. Asian 1%. Other 3%. Avg class size: 16. Uniform. **Fac 41.** M 4/1. F 34/2. Wh 96%. Hisp 1%. Blk 1%. Other 2%. Adv deg: 31%. **Grad '04—38.** Prep—27. **Tui '04-'05:** Day $5505-12,815 (+$250-375). Aid: Need 78 ($410,386). **Summer:** Acad Rec. 2-8 wks. **Est** 1992. Nonprofit. Episcopal. Tri (Sept-June). Lower schoolers (grades 1-4) take part in a lab-based science program at St. Anne's that focuses on experimentation and research skill development, and in a foreign language program that provides an introduction to French through twice-weekly classes. At the middle school level (grades 5-8), boys and girls participate in a hands-on program that emphasizes critical-thinking and problem-solving skills. The visual and performing arts play an important role in the middle school, with students taking music and art classes all four years. A competitive sports program commences in grade 6.

CHESAPEAKE ACADEMY Day Coed Gr PS-5
Arnold, MD 21012. 1185 Baltimore Annapolis Blvd.
Tel: 410-647-9612. Fax: 410-647-6088.
www.chesapeakeacademy.com E-mail: susanfu@chesapeakeacademy.com
 David Michelman, Head. BA, Hamilton College, JD, George Washington Univ. Susan Fu, Adm.

Pre-Prep. Feat—Span Computers Studio_Art Drama Music. **Supp**—Dev_Read Rev Tut. **Adm:** 54/yr. Appl due: Jan. Accepted: 64%. **Tests** IQ. **Enr** 309. B 173. G 136. Elem 309. Wh 91%. Hisp 1%. Blk 3%. Asian 5%. Avg class size: 16. Uniform. **Fac 37.** M 2. F 26/9. Wh 97%. Hisp 1%. Blk 1%. Asian 1%. Adv deg: 18%. **Grad '04—32.** Prep—28. Alum 281. **Tui '03-'04:** Day $9420-9810 (+$400-540). Aid: Need 28 ($126,643). **Summer:** Acad Rec. Sports. 2-6 wks. **Est** 1980. Nonprofit. Tri (Sept-June). This school offers an early childhood program, in addition to its pre-preparatory core curriculum. Activities include gymnastics, cultural arts, chorus and sports. Before- and after-school care is available.

BALTIMORE HEBREW CONGREGATION Day Coed Gr K-8
DAY SCHOOL
Baltimore, MD 21208. 7401 Park Heights Ave.
Tel: 410-764-1867. Fax: 410-764-8138.
www.bhcds.org E-mail: admissions@bhcong.org
 Nancy Epstein, Head. MEd. Karie Falck, Adm.

Pre-Prep. Gen Acad. Feat—Hebrew Span Judaic_Stud. Adm: 46/yr. Appl due: Rolling. Accepted: 61%. Enr 240. Elem 240. Avg class size: 16. Fac 56. M 3/3. F 45/5. Grad '04—28. Tui '03-'04: Day $7000-8800. Aid: Need 43 ($101,775). Est 1991. Nonprofit. Jewish. Tri (Aug-June). Students at BHCDS attend Judaic studies courses and receive Hebrew language instruction at all grade levels. Beginning in grade 6, boys and girls take lessons in Torah reading, chanting and Hebrew prayer book interpretation. The school's language arts program, which incorporates Jewish and historical theme-based literature, seeks to develop pupils' research and writing skills. Art, music, creative writing and choir are among the enrichment options.

THE CATHOLIC HIGH SCHOOL OF BALTIMORE
Day Girls Gr 9-12

Baltimore, MD 21213. 2800 Edison Hwy.
Tel: 410-732-6200. Fax: 410-732-7639.
http://tchsnt2.tchs.loyola.edu/tchs2001.htm   E-mail: chsb@tchs.loyola.edu

Barbara D. Nazelrod, Pres. BA, MEd, Loyola College, PhD, Univ of Maryland-College Park. Keith Harmeyer, Prin. BS, Towson Univ, MEd, McDaniel College. Sherri Barnwell, Adm.

Col Prep. AP—Fr Span Calc Comp_Sci US_Govt & Pol. Feat—Environ_Sci Geol Accounting. Supp—Dev_Read Rem_Math Rem_Read. Adm: 89/yr. Appl due: Dec. Accepted: 83%. Tests HSPT. Enr 300. G 300. Sec 300. Wh 80%. Hisp 2%. Blk 14%. Am Ind 1%. Asian 3%. Avg class size: 20. Uniform. Fac 29. M 7/2. F 18/2. Wh 97%. Hisp 3%. Adv deg: 65%. Grad '04—100. Col—95. Avg SAT: 1001. Avg ACT: 17. Alum 9108. Tui '05-'06: Day $8000 (+$250). Aid: Merit 40 ($42,300). Need 292 ($314,805). Summer: Enrich. 1-2 wks. Est 1939. Nonprofit. Roman Catholic. Sem (Aug-June). Assoc MSA. Four years of theology, as well as an honors program and Advanced Placement courses, enrich the curriculum. The school also conducts an integrated humanities and fine arts program. Extracurricular activities include sports, forensics, the performing arts, leadership and service organizations, publications and clubs. Catholic High offers annual mentorship opportunities, in addition to a winter interim program that allows seniors to earn college credit through local community colleges.

MERCY HIGH SCHOOL
Day Girls Gr 9-12

Baltimore, MD 21239. 1300 E Northern Pky.
Tel: 410-433-8880. Fax: 410-323-8816.
www.mercyhighschool.com   E-mail: info@mercyhighschool.com

Sr. Carol E. Wheeler, RSM, Prin. MA, Georgetown Univ, MA, Univ of Chicago. Jacqueline Stilling, Adm.

Col Prep. AP—Calc US_Hist Psych. Feat—Creative_Writing Women_Writers Fr Span Marine_Biol/Sci Zoology Computers Web_Design Ceramics Music_Theory. Supp—LD Rev Tut. Adm: 161/yr. Appl due: Jan. Tests HSPT. Enr 515. G 515. Sec 515. Wh 82%. Hisp 1%. Blk 14%. Asian 2%. Avg class size: 20. Uniform. Fac 43. M 3/1. F 34/5. Wh 89%. Hisp 9%. Asian 2%. Adv deg: 81%. Grad '04—101. Col—101. Alum 6181. Tui '03-'04: Day $7450 (+$500). Est 1960. Nonprofit. Roman Catholic. (Aug-June). Assoc MSA. Mercy's curriculum features independent studies in career fields, college-level writing workshops, a model college and career planning program, and a community service program. Elective courses include environmental science, philosophy and economics. Clubs, organizations and sports complement the curriculum. The school also organizes trips abroad.

MOUNT ST. JOSEPH HIGH SCHOOL   Day Boys Gr 9-12
Baltimore, MD 21229. 4403 Frederick Ave.
Tel: 410-644-3300. Fax: 410-646-6220.
www.msjnet.edu   E-mail: cclark@admin.msjnet.edu

Br. James M. Kelly, CFX, Pres. BA, Catholic Univ of America, MA, Wesleyan Univ, MA, St Joseph College. Barry J. Fitzpatrick, Prin. BA, Catholic Univ of America, MA, Loyola Univ, MEd, Harvard Univ. Craig S. Clark, Adm.

Col Prep. AP—Eng Fr Span Calc Eur_Hist US_Hist Econ Psych US_Govt & Pol. **Feat**—Lat Comp_Design Relig Studio_Art Drama Music. **Supp**—Dev_Read LD Rem_Math Rem_Read Tut. **Adm:** 350/yr. Appl due: Jan. Accepted: 78%. **Tests** HSPT. **Enr 1100.** B 1100. Sec 1100. Wh 79%. Hisp 2%. Blk 13%. Am Ind 4%. Asian 2%. Avg class size: 21. **Fac 78.** M 54/2. F 20/2. Adv deg: 60%. **Grad '04—241.** Col—220. Avg SAT: 1110. Alum 15,000. **Tui '04-'05:** Day $8200 (+$650). Aid: Merit 25 ($72,500). Need 370 ($777,000). **Summer:** Acad Enrich Rev Rem. Tui Day $300/crse. 6 wks. **Est 1876.** Nonprofit. Roman Catholic. Quar (Aug-June). **Assoc** MSA. This school functions under the sponsorship of the Brothers of St. Francis Xavier. The academic curriculum includes Advanced Placement and honors courses, and community service is required. Interscholastic sports are also available.

SETON KEOUGH HIGH SCHOOL   Day Girls Gr 9-12
Baltimore, MD 21227. 1201 Caton Ave.
Tel: 410-646-4444. Fax: 443-573-0107.
www.setonkeough.com   E-mail: info@setonkeough.com

Sr. Patricia Anne Bossle, DC, Pres. B. Curtis Turner, Prin. BS, Howard Univ, MEd, EdD, Univ of Massachusetts-Amherst. Miki Kulacki, Adm.

Col Prep. AP—Eng Calc US_Hist. **Feat**—Computers Orchestra. **Supp**—Dev_Read LD Rev Tut. **Adm (Gr 9-11):** 151/yr. Appl due: Jan. **Tests** HSPT. **Enr 502.** G 502. Sec 502. Wh 71%. Hisp 2%. Blk 23%. Am Ind 1%. Asian 3%. Avg class size: 18. Uniform. **Fac 47.** M 7. F 39/1. Wh 87%. Blk 6%. Am Ind 3%. Asian 2%. Other 2%. Adv deg: 91%. **Grad '04—114.** Col—112. Avg SAT: 1051. Alum 17,700. **Tui '03-'04:** Day $7300-9100. Aid: Merit 56 ($42,851). Need 87 ($84,610). **Summer:** Rem. Tut. Tui Day $100/crse. 4 wks. **Est 1988.** Nonprofit. Roman Catholic. Sem (Aug-June). **Assoc** MSA. The school resulted from the merger of Seton High School, established in 1926, and Archbishop Keough High School, established in 1965. A broad curriculum that comprises a wide range of required and elective courses is offered. In addition to an honors program leading to Advanced Placement courses in the junior and senior years, the school conducts a basic skills program and a special program for students with mild learning disabilities.

THE BARNESVILLE SCHOOL   Day Coed Gr PS-8
Barnesville, MD 20838. 21830 Peach Tree Rd, PO Box 404.
Tel: 301-972-0341. Fax: 301-972-4076.
www.barnesville-school.com   E-mail: info@barnesville-school.com

Jaralyn L. Hough, Head. BS, Boston Univ, MA, Hood College. Judy Marsh, Adm.

Pre-Prep. Feat—Span Studio_Art Chorus Music. **Adm:** 50/yr. Appl due: Jan. Accepted: 60%. **Tests** ISEE. **Enr 250.** B 120. G 130. Elem 250. Wh 90%. Hisp 3%. Blk 1%. Asian 6%. Avg class size: 14. **Fac 33.** M 5/1. F 22/5. Adv deg: 48%. **Grad '04—28.** Prep—19. **Tui '05-'06:** Day $11,010-11,780 (+$275-425). **Summer:** Rec. Tui Day $425/2-wk ses. 11 wks. **Est 1969.** Nonprofit. Tri (Sept-June). This country school offers a strong academic program in a flexible, supportive atmosphere that emphasizes hands-on activities. Particularly strong science and music programs enhance the basic curriculum. Courses feature small class size. Barnesville encourages parents to become involved in activities.

JOHN CARROLL SCHOOL   Day Coed Gr 9-12
Bel Air, MD 21014. 703 Churchville Rd.
Tel: 410-838-8333. Fax: 410-836-8514.
www.johncarroll.loyola.edu   E-mail: jcs@johncarroll.loyola.edu
Paul G. Barker, Prin. MLA, St John's College (MD), MEd, Ursuline College. Kim Brueggemann, Adm.

Col Prep. AP—Eng Calc Bio Chem Human_Geog Physics Eur_Hist US_Hist Psych. **Feat**—Ger Lat Russ Marine_Biol/Sci Computers Relig. **Supp**—Dev_Read Makeup Tut. **Adm:** 250/yr. Appl due: Jan. **Tests** HSPT. **Enr 815.** B 399. G 416. Sec 815. Wh 95%. Hisp 1%. Blk 1%. Asian 3%. Avg class size: 19. Uniform. **Fac 67.** M 30/3. F 33/1. Wh 99%. Blk 1%. Adv deg: 55%. **Grad '04—205.** Col—200. Alum 7000. **Tui '03-'04:** Day $9150 (+$500). Aid: Merit 50 ($104,000). Need 181 ($625,115). Work prgm 40 ($32,000). **Summer:** Acad Rev. Tui Day $180-300/crse. 2-6 wks. **Est 1964.** Nonprofit. Roman Catholic. Quar (Aug-June). **Assoc** MSA. Affiliated with the Archdiocese of Baltimore, this community-oriented day school features flexible modular scheduling, independent study and elective senior intern experiences. In addition, John Carroll conducts one-month exchange programs with schools in Spain, France, Germany and Russia.

WORCESTER PREPARATORY SCHOOL   Day Coed Gr PS-12
Berlin, MD 21811. 508 S Main St, PO Box 1006.
Tel: 410-641-3575. Fax: 410-641-3586.
www.worcesterprep.org   E-mail: lcook@worcesterprep.org
Barry W. Tull, Head. BS, MEd, Salisbury Univ, EdD, Univ of Maryland-College Park. Lisa Cook, Adm.

Col Prep. AP—Eng Calc Stats Bio Chem Physics US_Hist. **Feat**—Lat Engineering Paleontology Computers Photog Music. **Adm (Gr PS-11):** 72/yr. Appl due: Rolling. Accepted: 64%. **Tests** CEEB HSPT IQ SSAT Stanford. **Enr 525.** B 262. G 263. Elem 384. Sec 141. Wh 92%. Hisp 1%. Blk 2%. Other 5%. Avg class size: 14. Uniform. **Fac 59.** M 13/1. F 45. Wh 97%. Blk 3%. Adv deg: 74%. **Grad '04—13.** Col—13. Avg SAT: 1265. Alum 697. **Tui '02-'03:** Day $7800 (+$600). **Summer:** Acad Enrich. 1-2 wks. **Est 1970.** Nonprofit. Sem (Sept-June). **Assoc** MSA. The school's college preparatory curriculum includes language instruction in French, Spanish and Latin. Lab science and advanced mathematics courses are other noteworthy features of the program.

FRENCH INTERNATIONAL SCHOOL
Day Coed Gr PS-12

Bethesda, MD 20814. 9600 Forest Rd.
Tel: 301-530-8260. Fax: 301-564-5779.
www.rochambeau.org   E-mail: finucan@rochambeau.org
   Martine Quelen, Prin. Agnes Finucan, Adm.

   Col Prep. Gen Acad. Fr_Bac. Bilingual. Feat—Fr Ger Ital Span Philos. **Supp**—ESL. **Adm:** 300/yr. **Enr 1102.** Elem 807. Sec 295. Wh 74%. Hisp 2%. Blk 24%. Avg class size: 22. **Fac 92. Grad '04—58.** Col—58. Avg SAT: 1200. **Tui '04-'05:** Day $8472-10,983 (+$500). **Summer:** Fr. Rec. Tui Day $200/wk. 6 wks. **Est 1962.** Nonprofit. Tri (Sept-June). Located on 18 acres, the school follows the French system of instruction and enrolls students from approximately 50 countries. The French academic program, supplemented by English and American history classes, leads to both the French Baccalaureate and the US high school diploma. No prior knowledge of French is required for admission to the nursery school.

THE HARBOR SCHOOL
Day Coed Gr PS-2

Bethesda, MD 20817. 7701 Bradley Blvd.
Tel: 301-365-1100. Fax: 301-365-7491.
www.theharborschool.org   E-mail: harborsl72@aol.com
   Linda Perry, Head. BS, MA, Univ of North Carolina-Chapel Hill. Marti Jacobs, Adm.

   Pre-Prep. Gen Acad. Feat—Lib_Skills Studio_Art Music Dance. **Supp**—Dev_Read. **Adm:** 46/yr. Appl due: Feb. **Enr 120.** B 70. G 50. Elem 120. Wh 89%. Hisp 5%. Blk 1%. Asian 5%. Avg class size: 15. **Fac 25.** F 11/14. Adv deg: 12%. **Grad '04—11.** Prep—8. **Tui '04-'05:** Day $13,742 (+$450). Aid: Need 7 ($47,122). **Summer:** Rec. 2-6 wks. **Est 1972.** Nonprofit. Sem (Sept-June). The school's kindergarten program features art, reading, handwriting, math, science and social studies. Primary grades emphasize reading and math skill development while continuing the curriculum established in kindergarten. The nursery school also provides programming in creative movement.

NORWOOD SCHOOL
Day Coed Gr K-8

Bethesda, MD 20817. 8821 River Rd.
Tel: 301-365-2595. Fax: 301-365-7644.
www.norwoodschool.org   E-mail: info@norwoodschool.org
   Richard T. Ewing, Jr., Head. BA, Yale Univ, MEd, Univ of Virginia, EdD, Harvard Univ. Renee Johnson, Adm.

   Gen Acad. Feat—Fr Lat Span Computers Studio_Art Drama Music. **Supp**—Tut. **Adm (Gr K-7):** 91/yr. Appl due: Jan. Accepted: 33%. **Tests** IQ ISEE SSAT. **Enr 524.** B 267. G 257. Elem 524. Wh 79%. Hisp 3%. Blk 9%. Asian 8%. Other 1%. Avg class size: 19. **Fac 82.** M 19/2. F 55/6. Wh 77%. Hisp 4%. Blk 13%. Asian 3%. Other 3%. Adv deg: 47%. **Grad '04—52.** Prep—52. Alum 1800. **Tui '04-'05:** Day $19,075-21,175. Aid: Need 51 ($639,155). **Summer:** Rec. Adventure. Sports. Tui Day $375-1000. 2-3 wks. **Est 1952.** Nonprofit. Quar (Sept-June). Composed of a lower school (grades K-4) and a middle school (grades 5-8), Norwood supplements course work in the traditional disciplines with classes in art, drama, technology and physical education at all grade levels. In addition, French and Spanish are available in grades 2-8, Latin in grades 7 and 8, and instrumental or choral music in grades 5-8. At the middle school level, children choose from interscholastic soccer, lacrosse, field hockey, basketball, softball, baseball, cross-country and track.

THE PRIMARY DAY SCHOOL   Day Coed Gr PS-2
Bethesda, MD 20817. 7300 River Rd.
Tel: 301-365-4355. Fax: 301-469-8611.
www.theprimarydayschool.org   E-mail: j.mccaffery@theprimarydayschool.org
    Louise Plumb, Dir. BA, State Univ of New York-Oneonta. Julie McCaffery, Adm.

    Gen Acad. Feat—Creative_Writing Computers Studio_Art Music. **Supp**—Rem_Math Rem_Read Tut. **Adm (Gr PS-1):** 45/yr. Appl due: Jan. Accepted: 32%. **Enr 138.** B 64. G 74. Elem 138. Wh 81%. Hisp 1%. Blk 3%. Asian 15%. Avg class size: 17. **Fac 24.** M /1. F 20/3. Wh 99%. Asian 1%. Adv deg: 16%. **Grad '04—36.** Alum 2465. **Tui '05-'06:** Day $9600-13,300. **Est 1944.** Nonprofit. Sem (Sept-June). Primary Day's traditional curriculum emphasizes fundamental skills, sound work habits and an appreciation for the arts. Music, art, computer, creative writing, literature and physical education classes complement instruction in the core subjects. Students participate in weekly assemblies designed to develop poise and public-speaking skills.

WASHINGTON EPISCOPAL SCHOOL   Day Coed Gr PS-8
Bethesda, MD 20816. 5600 Little Falls Pky.
Tel: 301-652-7878. Fax: 301-652-7255.
www.w-e-s.org   E-mail: admissions@w-e-s.org
    Stuart Work, Head. AB, Bowdoin College. Kathleen Herman, Adm.

    Pre-Prep. Feat—Fr Lat Span Computers Studio_Art Drama Music. **Supp**—Tut. **Adm:** 69/yr. Appl due: Feb. Accepted: 30%. Yield: 75%. **Tests** CTP_4 IQ ISEE SSAT. **Enr 310.** B 160. G 150. Elem 310. Wh 90%. Hisp 2%. Blk 7%. Asian 1%. Avg class size: 16. **Fac 54.** M 10/1. F 30/13. Wh 97%. Hisp 1%. Adv deg: 38%. **Grad '04—26.** Prep—25. Alum 295. **Tui '04-'05:** Day $18,990 (+$350). Aid: Need 49 ($585,840). **Summer:** Acad Enrich Rev Rec. Tui Day $240-650. 1-3 wks. **Est 1986.** Nonprofit. Episcopal. Tri (Sept-June). **Assoc** MSA. The school features small classes and a rigorous academic program. French or Spanish study begins in prekindergarten, while Latin is first offered in grade 5. After-school enrichment classes and an extended-day program are also available. Seventh graders travel to Italy in the spring, while eighth graders may participate in a trip to France.

WOODS ACADEMY   Day Coed Gr PS-8
Bethesda, MD 20817. 6801 Greentree Rd.
Tel: 301-365-3080. Fax: 301-469-6439.
www.woodsacademy.org   E-mail: admissions@woodsacademy.org
    Mary C. Worch, Head. BA, MA, Trinity College (DC). Barbara B. Snyder, Adm.

    Pre-Prep. Feat—Fr Computers Studio_Art Drama Music. **Adm:** 84/yr. Appl due: Feb. Accepted: 48%. **Tests** ISEE Stanford. **Enr 263.** B 136. G 127. Elem 263.

Wh 86%. Hisp 5%. Blk 1%. Asian 8%. Avg class size: 20. **Fac 35.** M 3/2. F 26/4. **Grad '04—28.** Prep—26. **Tui '05-'06:** Day $13,000-14,195. **Est 1975.** Nonprofit. Roman Catholic. Quar (Sept-June). **Assoc** MSA. The academy has a Montessori preschool and kindergarten. French is taught at all grade levels, and an extended-day program is provided.

ELIZABETH SETON HIGH SCHOOL
Day Girls Gr 9-12

Bladensburg, MD 20710. 5715 Emerson St.
Tel: 301-864-4532. Fax: 301-864-8946.
www.setonhs.org E-mail: admin@setonhs.org

Sr. Virginia Ann Brooks, Pres. BS, St Joseph's College, MEd, Loyola College (MD), MA, Catholic Univ of America. Dawn Slone, Adm.

Col Prep. AP—Eng Span Calc Stats Bio Chem US_Hist Psych US_Govt & Pol Studio_Art. **Feat**—Fr Lat Comp_Sci Relig Ceramics Band Chorus. **Supp**—Tut. **Adm (Gr 9-11):** 152/yr. Appl due: Dec. Accepted: 75%. Yield: 70%. **Tests** HSPT Stanford. **Enr 553.** G 553. Sec 553. Wh 35%. Hisp 4%. Blk 52%. Am Ind 1%. Asian 2%. Other 6%. Avg class size: 19. Uniform. **Fac 49.** M 5/1. F 40/3. Wh 86%. Hisp 2%. Blk 4%. Asian 8%. Adv deg: 44%. **Grad '04—119.** Col—119. Avg SAT: 1055. Avg ACT: 24. Alum 4327. **Tui '04-'05:** Day $7200 (+$300). Aid: Merit 60 ($33,100). Need 214 ($242,020). Work prgm 20 ($11,886). **Summer:** Enrich Rev. Tui Day $150. 4 wks. SAT Prep. Tui Day $125. 5 wks. **Est 1959.** Nonprofit. Roman Catholic. Quar (Aug-June). **Assoc** MSA. Established by the Daughters of Charity, Elizabeth Seton provides a college preparatory program for students drawn largely from area Catholic elementary and middle schools. Small classes, honors and Advanced Placement offerings, and an emphasis on community service are noteworthy elements of the program. Many sports are available at the varsity level, and an array of clubs, musical groups, interest clubs and publications rounds out the school's extracurricular program.

MARYVALE PREPARATORY SCHOOL
Day Girls Gr 6-12

Brooklandville, MD 21022. 11300 Falls Rd.
Tel: 410-252-3366. Fax: 410-308-1497.
www.maryvale.com E-mail: info@maryvale.com

Sr. Shawn Marie Maguire, SND, Head. BS, Trinity College, MA, Temple Univ, MA, Loyola College. Monica C. Graham, Adm.

Col Prep. AP—Eng Fr Span Calc Bio US_Hist. **Feat**—Writing Lat Environ_Sci Programming Relig Studio_Art Drama Music Communications. **Adm (Gr 6-10):** 71/yr. Appl due: Jan. Accepted: 49%. Yield: 37%. **Tests** HSPT. **Enr 361.** G 361. Elem 103. Sec 258. Wh 91%. Hisp 2%. Blk 4%. Asian 2%. Other 1%. Avg class size: 9. Uniform. **Fac 39.** M 4/1. F 32/2. Wh 99%. Hisp 2%. Adv deg: 74%. **Grad '04—66.** Col—66. Avg SAT: 1169. Avg ACT: 23. Alum 1800. **Tui '04-'05:** Day $11,800 (+$450). Aid: Need 60 ($223,875). **Est 1945.** Inc. Roman Catholic. Quar (Sept-May). **Assoc** MSA. Owned by the Sisters of Notre Dame de Namur, the school occupies a 113-acre former estate. The college preparatory curriculum is conducted in small classes. Elective courses in drama, art, writing, computer programming, environmental science and mass media are offered. Extracurricular activities include chorus, drama, social service, newspaper, yearbook and literary magazine. Varsity, junior varsity and middle school teams play field hockey, volleyball, basketball, soccer, cross-country, indoor track and lacrosse.

KENT SCHOOL
Day Coed Gr PS-8
Chestertown, MD 21620. 6788 Wilkins Ln.
Tel: 410-778-4100. Fax: 410-778-7357.
www.kentschool.org   E-mail: admisks@friend.ly.net
P. Edmund Barnes, Head. MA, Univ of Pennsylvania. Beth Collins, Adm.

Pre-Prep. Feat—Span Environ_Sci. **Supp**—Dev_Read Rev. **Adm:** 46/yr. Appl due: Rolling. **Tests** SSAT. **Enr 191.** B 107. G 84. Elem 191. Wh 92%. Hisp 1%. Blk 1%. Asian 3%. Other 3%. Avg class size: 20. **Fac 24.** M 3. F 20/1. Adv deg: 29%. **Grad '04—20.** Prep—17. Alum 450. **Tui '04-'05:** Day $6385-9840 (+$125-385). Aid: Need 48. **Summer:** Rec. 2 wks. **Est 1967.** Nonprofit. (Sept-June). **Assoc** MSA. Kent places strong emphasis on language arts, mathematics, the arts and athletics. Many field trips are offered to area museums and the Smithsonian Institute, and the sports program includes interscholastic competition in soccer, field hockey, basketball and lacrosse.

MOUNT AVIAT ACADEMY
Day Coed Gr PS-8
Childs, MD 21916. 399 Childs Rd, PO Box 85.
Tel: 410-398-2206. Fax: 410-398-8063.
www.mountaviat.org   E-mail: school@mountaviat.org
Sr. John Elizabeth, OSFS, Prin. BS, Lincoln Univ, MEd, Loyola College.

Pre-Prep. Feat—Fr Computers Relig Studio_Art Drama Music Speech. **Supp**—Rem_Read Tut. **Adm:** 32/yr. Appl due: Rolling. Accepted: 20%. **Enr 265.** B 130. G 135. Elem 265. Wh 92%. Hisp 2%. Blk 1%. Asian 3%. Other 2%. Avg class size: 27. Uniform. **Fac 19.** M /3. F 11/5. Wh 97%. Blk 3%. Adv deg: 31%. **Grad '04—23.** Prep—22. **Tui '04-'05:** Day $3850 (+$300). Aid: Need 35 ($44,000). **Est 1969.** Nonprofit. Roman Catholic. Tri (Sept-June). **Assoc** MSA. Tutoring is available at this school, and French instruction begins in grade 1. Elective programs include musical and dramatic presentations, academic competitions, and health and speech courses in grades 5-8.

TRINITY SCHOOL
Day Coed Gr K-8
Ellicott City, MD 21041. 4985 Ilchester Rd, PO Box 299.
Tel: 410-744-1524. Fax: 410-744-3617.
www.trinitynews.org   E-mail: trinitymainoff@trinitynews.org
Sr. Catherine Phelps, SND, Pres. BS, Trinity College (DC), MS, Fordham Univ. Frangiska Lewis, Prin. Mary Joan Voshell, Adm.

Pre-Prep. Feat—Fr Lat Span Relig Studio_Art Drama Music. **Supp**—Dev_Read Rem_Read Tut. **Adm:** 42/yr. Appl due: Rolling. Accepted: 90%. Yield: 82%. **Enr 375.** B 185. G 190. Elem 375. Wh 84%. Hisp 1%. Blk 6%. Asian 5%. Other 4%. Avg class size: 20. Uniform. **Fac 29.** M 3. F 22/4. Wh 99%. Hisp 1%. Adv deg: 34%. **Grad '04—35.** Prep—28. **Tui '04-'05:** Day $8800. Aid: Need 46 ($165,155). **Summer:** Rec. Tui Day $185/wk. 8 wks. **Est 1941.** Nonprofit. Roman Catholic. Sem (Sept-June). The pre-preparatory elementary curriculum at Trinity places particular emphasis upon reading and writing. Students develop critical-thinking skills through problem solving techniques, avenues of creative expression and use of the scientific method. Foreign language classes begin in the middle school, while religion, art, music, drama and athletics are available at all grade levels. Computerized library facilities and science and computer laboratories enrich the program.

ST. JOHN'S LITERARY INSTITUTION   Day Coed Gr 9-12
AT PROSPECT HALL
Frederick, MD 21703. 889 Butterfly Ln.
Tel: 301-662-4210. Fax: 301-662-5166.
www.stjph.org   E-mail: jdoyle@stjph.org
    Richard E. Fairley, Head. Julie O. Doyle, Adm.

    Col Prep. AP—Eng Fr Lat Span Calc Bio Chem Physics US_Hist Comp_Govt & Pol Studio_Art. **Feat**—Computers Philos Theol Film. **Supp**—Tut. **Adm (Gr 9-11):** 109/yr. Appl due: Rolling. Accepted: 90%. Yield: 69%. **Tests** HSPT. **Enr 328.** Sec 328. Avg class size: 19. Uniform. **Fac 35.** M 13/4. F 17/1. Adv deg: 45%. **Grad '04—75.** Col—75. Avg SAT: 1130. Alum 1600. **Tui '04-'05:** Day $8825 (+$700). Aid: Need 50 ($116,500). **Est 1829.** Nonprofit. Roman Catholic. Quar (Aug-June). **Assoc** MSA. The traditional college preparatory program of St. John's at Prospect Hall features several honors and Advanced Placement courses. Graduates matriculate at four-year colleges.

HOLY TRINITY EPISCOPAL DAY SCHOOL   Day Coed Gr PS-8
Glenn Dale, MD 20769. 11902 Daisey Ln.
Tel: 301-464-3215. Fax: 301-449-9725.
www.htrinity.org   E-mail: sanderson@htrinity.org
    Margaret C. Reiber, Head. Suzanne Anderson, Adm.

    Pre-Prep. Feat—Fr Lat Span Computers Studio_Art Music. **Supp**—Tut. **Adm:** 125/yr. **Tests** IQ MAT. **Enr 614.** Elem 614. Wh 44%. Hisp 2%. Blk 46%. Asian 2%. Other 6%. Avg class size: 20. Uniform. **Fac 57.** M 4. F 50/3. Adv deg: 21%. **Grad '04—56.** Prep—50. Alum 659. **Tui '05-'06:** Day $6865-8320. Aid: Need 5 ($5000). **Summer:** Acad Enrich Rev Rec. Tui Day $115/wk. 9 wks. **Est 1963.** Nonprofit. Episcopal. Sem (Sept-June). **Assoc** MSA. Holy Trinity offers an integrated academic program complemented by an outdoor education program, French, Spanish, Latin (in grade 8), computer, music, art, library, chapel and team sports, as well as visits to area cultural and scientific centers. An extended-day program is available.

THE CALVERTON SCHOOL   Day Coed Gr PS-12
Huntingtown, MD 20639. 300 Calverton School Rd.
Tel: 410-535-0216. Fax: 410-535-6934.
www.calvertonschool.org   E-mail: ecasalino@calvertonschool.org
    Elizabeth Cataldi, Dir. BS, Indiana Univ of Pennsylvania, MEd, EdD, Univ of Pittsburgh. Erna A. Casalino, Adm.

    Col Prep. AP—Eng Fr Span Calc Bio Chem Physics US_Hist. **Feat**—Humanities Lat Environ_Sci Marine_Biol/Sci Computers Chin_Hist Law Art_Hist Film. **Supp**—Tut. **Adm:** 60/yr. Appl due: Rolling. Accepted: 46%. **Tests** IQ. **Enr 420.**

B 226. G 194. Elem 298. Sec 122. Wh 90%. Hisp 1%. Blk 2%. Asian 2%. Other 5%. Avg class size: 15. Uniform. **Fac 42.** M 9. F 32/1. Wh 99%. Other 1%. Adv deg: 42%. **Grad '04—19.** Col—19. Alum 310. **Tui '03-'04:** Day $11,220-14,076 (+$300). Aid: Need ($300,000). **Summer:** Ages 5-15. Acad Enrich Rec. Tui Day $80-90/wk. 6 wks. **Est 1967.** Nonprofit. (Sept-June). **Assoc** MSA. Calverton's academic program includes Advanced Placement classes in the major disciplines, as well as electives in Chesapeake Bay studies, computer and the arts. The school maintains an active interscholastic sports program and, at the middle and upper school levels, provides students with various opportunities in the visual and performing arts.

DeMATHA CATHOLIC HIGH SCHOOL   Day Boys Gr 9-12
Hyattsville, MD 20781. 4313 Madison St.
Tel: 301-864-3666. Fax: 301-864-0248.
www.dematha.org   E-mail: tponton@dematha.org

Rev. William J. Sullivan, OSST, Rector. Daniel J. McMahon, Prin. BA, Mount Saint Mary's College, MA, PhD, Univ of Maryland-College Park. Michael Jones, Adm.

Col Prep. Feat—Psych Theol Photog Studio_Art Chorus Music Bus Journ. **Supp**—Dev_Read Rev Tut. **Adm:** 289/yr. Appl due: Dec. Accepted: 50%. **Enr 969.** B 969. Sec 969. Wh 60%. Hisp 2%. Blk 34%. Asian 2%. Other 2%. Avg class size: 23. Uniform. **Fac 76.** M 59/2. F 11/4. Adv deg: 51%. **Grad '04—204.** Col—201. Avg SAT: 1076. Alum 4000. **Tui '04-'05:** Day $7500 (+$225-300). Aid: Merit 89 ($75,500). Work prgm 262 ($494,242). **Summer:** Acad Rev. Tui Day $250/crse. 5 wks. **Est 1946.** Nonprofit. Roman Catholic. (Aug-June). **Assoc** MSA. DeMatha's college preparatory curriculum includes computer studies, the fine arts, and instrumental and choral music. A compulsory religious studies program incorporates historical, ethical and psychological viewpoints.

GRACE EPISCOPAL DAY SCHOOL   Day Coed Gr PS-6
Kensington, MD 20895. 9411 Connecticut Ave.
Tel: 301-949-5860. Fax: 301-949-8398.
www.geds.org   E-mail: admissions@geds.org

Carol Franek, Head. BS, Millersville Univ of Pennsylvania, MEd, Pennsylvania State Univ. Michelle Siraj, Adm.

Gen Acad. Feat—Lib_Skills Lat Span Computers Studio_Art Music. **Supp**—Dev_Read Rem_Read. **Adm:** 70/yr. Appl due: Feb. Accepted: 50%. Yield: 70%. **Tests** IQ. **Enr 270.** B 130. G 140. Elem 270. Wh 63%. Hisp 7%. Blk 25%. Asian 5%. Avg class size: 16. **Fac 37.** M 5. F 24/8. Wh 84%. Hisp 8%. Blk 4%. Am Ind 4%. Adv deg: 21%. **Grad '04—25. Tui '04-'05:** Day $12,535-12,695 (+$165). Aid: Need 32 ($133,597). **Summer:** Acad Enrich Rec. Tui Day $1800. 6 wks. **Est 1960.** Nonprofit. Episcopal. Tri (Sept-June). All students at Grace attend weekly chapel services. The nursery, prekindergarten and kindergarten programs are conducted at 9115 Georgia Ave., Silver Spring 20910. Before- and after-school programs are available, as are after-school enrichment classes.

LEONARD HALL JUNIOR NAVAL ACADEMY Day Coed Gr 6-12
Leonardtown, MD 20650. 41740 Baldridge St, PO Box 507.
Tel: 301-475-8029. Fax: 301-475-8518.
E-mail: lhjna@yahoo.com
   Suzanne C. Youngson, Head.

Col Prep. Milit. Feat—Span Relig Milit_Sci Naval_Sci. **Supp**—Dev_Read Tut. **Adm:** 35/yr. Appl due: Rolling. Accepted: 95%. **Tests** IQ. **Enr 110.** B 75. G 35. Elem 65. Sec 45. Wh 94%. Blk 5%. Asian 1%. Avg class size: 15. Uniform. **Fac 10.** M 5. F 5. Wh 100%. Adv deg: 50%. **Grad '04—14.** Col—14. **Tui '02-'03:** Day $4200-4500. **Summer:** Acad Rev. Tui Day $20/hr. 8 wks. **Est 1909.** Nonprofit. Sem (Aug-June). A military high school (grades 9-12) and a junior naval academy (grades 6-8) provide military drill instruction and a full scholastic program that includes religious education. Interscholastic basketball and soccer teams are available.

THE TOME SCHOOL Day Coed Gr K-12
North East, MD 21901. 581 S Maryland Ave.
Tel: 410-287-2050. Fax: 410-287-8999.
www.dol.net/~tome E-mail: drdarcy.williams@verizon.net
   F. Darcy Williams, Head. BS, College of Saint Elizabeth, MS, PhD, Rutgers Univ.

Col Prep. Feat—Fr Lat Span Environ_Sci Computers Econ Geog Govt Studio_Art Music. **Adm:** 70/yr. **Tests** Stanford. **Enr 355.** B 170. G 185. Elem 271. Sec 84. Wh 91%. Hisp 3%. Blk 2%. Asian 4%. Avg class size: 20. Uniform. **Fac 29.** M 5/1. F 16/7. Adv deg: 27%. **Grad '04—13.** Col—12. Alum 1550. **Tui '03-'04:** Day $5000 (+$175). **Summer:** Acad Enrich Rev. Tui Day $300. 6 wks. **Est 1889.** Nonprofit. Sem (Aug-May). Founded by local philanthropist Jacob Tome, the school received its first students in 1894 and has been in continuous operation ever since. In the summer of 1971, the school moved to the 100-acre campus in North East. The curriculum is nonelective and college preparatory.

RUXTON COUNTRY SCHOOL Day Coed Gr K-8
Owings Mills, MD 21117. 11202 Garrison Forest Rd.
Tel: 443-544-3000. Fax: 443-544-3010.
www.ruxtoncountryschool.org E-mail: rgarfield@ruxtoncountryschool.org
   Stephen K. Barker, Head. AB, EdM, Harvard Univ. Roberta Garfield, Adm.

Pre-Prep. Gen Acad. Feat—Span Computers Studio_Art Drama Music Dance. **Supp**—Dev_Read Rem_Math Rem_Read Tut. **Adm:** 72/yr. Appl due: Rolling. Accepted: 80%. Yield: 60%. **Tests** IQ Stanford. **Enr 225.** B 125. G 100. Elem 225. Wh 70%. Hisp 30%. Avg class size: 12. Uniform. **Fac 52.** M 11. F 36/5. Wh 98%. Blk 2%. Adv deg: 57%. **Grad '04—28.** Prep—24. Alum 800. **Tui '04-'05:** Day $13,750-15,950 (+$350). Aid: Need 76. **Est 1913.** Nonprofit. Tri (Sept-June). In addition to traditional subjects, the school offers keyboarding and computers, foreign language, art, drama and dance. An after-school program includes interscholastic athletics and creative arts. Students also participate in a variety of community service projects. Small classes enable Ruxton to address varying learning styles.

GERMAN SCHOOL
Day Coed Gr PS-PG
Potomac, MD 20854. 8617 Chateau Dr.
Tel: 301-365-4400. Fax: 301-365-3905.
www.dswashington.org E-mail: mail@dswash.org
Klaus-Dieter Bloch, Prin. Klara A. Fabina, Adm.

Col Prep. Bilingual. Feat—Ger Lat Span Studio_Art Music. **Supp**—Tut. **Adm:** 150/yr. Appl due: Rolling. Accepted: 90%. **Enr 587.** B 293. G 294. Elem 425. Sec 144. PG 18. Wh 96%. Hisp 2%. Blk 1%. Asian 1%. Avg class size: 20. **Fac 65. Grad '04**—32. Col—16. Avg SAT: 1300. **Tui '02-'03:** Day $4210-8590 (+$800). Aid: Need 41. **Est 1961.** Sem (Aug-June). Serving an international student body, the school follows the curricular guidelines set by the German Ministry of Education, and the Maryland State Department of Education.

ST. FRANCIS EPISCOPAL DAY SCHOOL
Day Coed Gr PS-5
Potomac, MD 20854. 10033 River Rd.
Tel: 301-365-2642. Fax: 301-299-0412.
www.sfeds.org E-mail: ryans@sfeds.org
Walter T. McCoy, Head. BA, MA, Univ of New Orleans. Jo Anne Zinsmeister, Adm.

Pre-Prep. Feat—Lib_Skills Span Computers Studio_Art Music. **Enr 236.** Elem 236. Avg class size: 12. **Fac 34.** M 2. F 27/5.**Tui '05-'06:** Day $14,270 (+$900). Aid: Need 16 ($65,000). **Summer:** Ages 3-7. Enrich Rec. 2 wks. **Est 1988.** Nonprofit. Episcopal. Sem (Sept-June). St. Francis' curriculum serves as an introduction to the core academic subjects, as well as to computers, Spanish, library skills and music. The compulsory Christian studies program includes daily prayer, religious services and evening activities. An extensive after-school program, offering classes such as tae kwon do, cooking, arts and crafts, chess and drama, is available to children in grades pre-K-5.

CHARLES E. SMITH JEWISH DAY SCHOOL
Day Coed Gr K-12
Rockville, MD 20852. 11710 Hunters Ln.
Tel: 301-881-1400. Fax: 301-881-6453.
www.cesjds.org E-mail: cesjds@cesjds.org
Jonathan Cannon, Head. Robin Shapiro, Upper Sch Adm; Susan Cohen, Lower Sch Adm.

Col Prep. Feat—Creative_Writing Fr Hebrew Anat & Physiol Genetics Computers Psych Bible Comp_Relig Rabbinics Film Photog Studio_Art Music Journ. **Supp**—ESL. **Adm:** 187/yr. Appl due: Jan. Accepted: 90%. **Enr 1514.** Elem 1076. Sec 438. Wh 97%. Hisp 1%. Blk 1%. Asian 1%. Avg class size: 18. **Fac 134. Grad '04**—85. Col—85. Avg SAT: 1350. Alum 886. **Tui '04-'05:** Day $13,440-16,990 (+$65-385). **Summer:** Sports. 4 wks. **Est 1966.** Nonprofit. Jewish. (Sept-June). **Assoc** MSA. Drawing its students from the Metropolitan Washington, DC, area, this school offers a rigorous college preparatory curriculum featuring Hebrew instruction at all grade levels, as well as Judaic studies classes. The school observes Jewish religious practices. Pupils may participate in a five-month academic and travel program to Israel after graduation. The lower school occupies a separate campus at 1901 E. Jefferson St.

MELVIN J. BERMAN HEBREW ACADEMY   **Day Coed Gr PS-12**
Rockville, MD 20853. 13300 Arctic Ave.
Tel: 301-962-9400. Fax: 301-962-3991.
www.mjbha.org   E-mail: kaiserl@mjbha.org

    Rabbi William Altshul, Head. BA, MS, Yeshiva Univ (NY). Linda Kaiser, Adm.

    Col Prep. AP—Eng Calc Stats Comp_Sci Bio Chem Physics Eur_Hist. **Feat**—Span Hebrew Jewish_Hist. **Supp**—Dev_Read LD Makeup Tut. **Enr 730.** Elem 545. Sec 185. Wh 100%. Avg class size: 16. **Fac 115. Grad '04**—37. Col—37. Avg SAT: 1286. Alum 1042. **Tui '04-'05:** Day $6825-13,450 (+$700-1120). **Est 1944.** Nonprofit. Jewish. (Aug-June). This curriculum provides religious and secular education, including Hebrew for pupils in grades K-12 and a selection of Advanced Placement and accelerated courses. Independent study and off-campus study of accelerated courses are also available. Most students enter leading colleges upon graduation, while some defer college admission to spend a year in Israel.

SALISBURY SCHOOL   **Day Coed Gr PS-12**
Salisbury, MD 21802. 6279 Hobbs Rd, PO Box 2295.
Tel: 410-742-4464. Fax: 410-546-2310.
www.salisbury-school.org   E-mail: info@salisbury-school.org

    James G. Landi, Head. BA, Ohio Northern Univ, MA, Montclair State College. Margaret Long, Adm.

    Col Prep. AP—Eng Lat Span Calc Bio US_Hist. **Feat**—Photog Studio_Art Drama Band Chorus. **Supp**—LD Tut. **Adm:** 58/yr. Appl due: Rolling. Accepted: 88%. **Tests** CTP_4 ISEE SSAT. **Enr 400.** Elem 285. Sec 115. Wh 71%. Hisp 8%. Blk 5%. Asian 6%. Other 10%. Avg class size: 12. **Fac 56.** M 15/3. F 38. Wh 96%. Hisp 2%. Blk 1%. Asian 1%. Adv deg: 39%. **Grad '04**—16. Col—16. Avg SAT: 1210. Alum 270. **Tui '04-'05:** Day $5700-10,947 (+$500). Aid: Need 50 ($179,000). **Summer:** Rec. 10 wks. **Est 1970.** Nonprofit. Tri (Sept-June). Situated on 45 acres, Salisbury has a modified open-learning environment and traditional college preparatory academics. All upper school students use laptop computers.
                                                                                  See Also Pages 1248-9

ARCHBISHOP SPALDING HIGH SCHOOL   **Day Coed Gr 9-12**
Severn, MD 21144. 8080 New Cut Rd.
Tel: 410-969-9105. Fax: 410-969-1026.
www.archbishopspalding.org   E-mail: millert@archbishopspalding.org

    Michael E. Murphy, Pres. EdD, Univ of Sarasota. Kathleen K. Mahar, Prin. MA, George Washington Univ. Thomas E. Miller, Adm.

    Col Prep. AP—Eng Lat Span Calc Stats Comp_Sci Bio Chem Physics Eur_Hist US_Hist Comp_Govt & Pol US_Govt & Pol Studio_Art. **Feat**—Fr Ger Relig Drama Music. **Supp**—Dev_Read LD Rev Tut. **Adm:** 307/yr. Appl due: Jan. Accepted: 44%. Yield: 78%. **Tests** HSPT. **Enr 1049.** B 494. G 555. Sec 1049. Wh 90%. Hisp 1%. Blk 5%. Am Ind 1%. Asian 2%. Other 1%. Avg class size: 22. Uniform. **Fac 69.** M 23. F 46. Wh 99%. Hisp 1%. Adv deg: 46%. **Grad '04**—227. Col—223. Avg SAT: 1100. Avg ACT: 23. Alum 4466. **Tui '04-'05:** Day $8275 (+$500). Aid: Merit 75 ($100,000). Need 139 ($248,000). Work prgm 3 ($7000). **Est 1966.** Nonprofit. Roman Catholic. Quar (Aug-June). Spalding offers a broad selection of Advanced Placement, honors and college preparatory courses. Extensive music and fine arts options are part of the curriculum. The school's Aquinas Program serves college-bound students with varying information processing skills in the areas of reading and language.

CHELSEA SCHOOL Day Coed Gr 5-12
Silver Spring, MD 20910. 711 Pershing Dr.
Tel: 301-585-1430. Fax: 301-585-5865.
www.chelseaschool.edu E-mail: information@chelseaschool.edu
  Peter Smith, Int Head. Dale Frengel, Adm.

  Col Prep. LD. Feat—British_Lit 20th-Century_African-Amer_Lit Span Anat Govt Graphic_Arts Performing_Arts Studio_Art. **Supp**—Rem_Math Rem_Read Tut. **Adm:** 15/yr. Appl due: Rolling. Accepted: 30%. Yield: 50%. **Tests** IQ. **Enr 100.** Wh 50%. Hisp 4%. Blk 45%. Asian 1%. Avg class size: 6. **Fac 36.** M 8/1. F 26/1. Adv deg: 58%. **Grad '04—20.** Col—20. Alum 145. **Tui '04-'05:** Day $32,020. Aid: Need 3 ($30,000). **Summer:** Acad Enrich Rem Rec. 5 wks. **Est 1976.** Nonprofit. Quar (Sept-June). Learning strategies are integral to the education this school offers to students with learning disabilities. The curriculum focuses on academic preparation for college and career transition. Students incur additional hourly fees for counseling and therapy.

THORNTON FRIENDS SCHOOL Day Coed Gr 6-12
Silver Spring, MD 20904. 13925 New Hampshire Ave.
Tel: 301-384-6672. Fax: 301-879-8238.
www.thorntonfriends.org E-mail: admissions@thorntonfriends.org
  Michael DeHart, Head. BA, Univ of Maryland-College Park, MSW, Catholic Univ of America. Jeane Perszyk, Adm.

  Col Prep. Underachiever. Feat—Span. **Supp**—Rem_Math Rev Tut. **Adm:** 35/yr. Appl due: Rolling. Accepted: 85%. **Enr 116.** B 65. G 51. Elem 30. Sec 86. Wh 79%. Hisp 6%. Blk 9%. Asian 5%. Other 1%. Avg class size: 9. **Fac 24.** M 10. F 14. Wh 90%. Blk 10%. Adv deg: 50%. **Grad '04—22.** Col—13. Alum 563. **Tui '02-'03:** Day $14,095-14,995 (+$400-450). Aid: Need 28 ($207,511). **Summer:** Acad. 2 wks. **Est 1973.** Nonprofit. Religious Society of Friends. Tri (Sept-June). The school, which accepts bright underachievers, places a strong emphasis on writing, speaking and listening skills. Required community service is an important aspect of the curriculum. Outdoor education consists of rafting, skiing, camping, hiking and rock climbing in nearby mountains. The middle school is conducted at 11612 New Hampshire Ave. Thornton Friends operates a second high school campus (grades 9-12) at 3830 Seminary Rd., Alexandria, VA 22304.

LOYOLA BLAKEFIELD Day Boys Gr 6-12
Towson, MD 21204. 500 Chestnut Ave.
Tel: 443-841-3680. Fax: 443-841-3105.
www.blakefield.loyola.edu E-mail: mbreschi@blakefield.loyola.edu
  Rev. John M. Dennis, SJ, Pres. MEd. Michael R. Breschi, Adm.

  Col Prep. AP—Eng Fr Ger Lat Span Calc Stats Bio Chem Physics Eur_Hist

US_Hist US_Govt & Pol Studio_Art. **Feat**—Comp_Sci Relig Photog Drama Music Accounting. **Supp**—Rev Tut. **Adm (Gr 6-11):** 200/yr. Appl due: Dec. **Tests** HSPT ISEE. **Enr 970.** B 970. Elem 225. Sec 745. Wh 92%. Hisp 1%. Blk 4%. Asian 3%. Avg class size: 20. **Fac 102.** M 73. F 29. Wh 93%. Hisp 2%. Blk 5%. Adv deg: 67%. **Grad '04—168.** Col—168. Avg SAT: 1228. **Tui '04-'05:** Day $10,820 (+$650). Aid: Need 270 ($1,100,000). **Summer:** Acad Enrich. 5-6 wks. **Est 1852.** Nonprofit. Roman Catholic. (Sept-June). The traditional college preparatory curriculum at Blakefield offers honors and Advanced Placement courses, as well as electives for qualified juniors and seniors. All students must complete a program in social service, computer instruction, art, music appreciation and religious studies. Cocurricular activities include language clubs, forensics, instrumental music ensemble and chorus, interscholastic and intramural sports, student government, drama and publications. Student trips or exchanges with schools in Great Britain and Germany are also offered.

NOTRE DAME PREPARATORY SCHOOL Day Girls Gr 6-12
Towson, MD 21286. 815 Hampton Ln.
Tel: 410-825-6202. Fax: 410-825-0982.
www.notredameprep.com   E-mail: admissions@notredameprep.com
Sr. Patricia McCarron, SSND, Head. PhD, Catholic Univ of America. Katherine Goetz, Adm.

Col Prep. AP—Eng Fr Span Calc Stats Chem Physics Eur_Hist US_Hist Econ US_Govt & Pol. **Feat**—Creative_Writing Ital Japan Lat Anat & Physiol Environ_Sci Marine_Biol/Sci Relig Architect_Drawing Photog Studio_Art Music Journ. **Supp**—Tut. **Adm (Gr 6-9):** 173/yr. Appl due: Dec. Accepted: 58%. Yield: 85%. **Tests** CEEB HSPT ISEE Stanford. **Enr 736.** G 736. Elem 169. Sec 567. Wh 86%. Hisp 2%. Blk 4%. Asian 5%. Other 3%. Avg class size: 17. Uniform. **Fac 87.** M 13. F 67/7. Wh 93%. Hisp 3%. Blk 2%. Asian 1%. Other 1%. Adv deg: 64%. **Grad '04—132.** Col—132. Avg SAT: 1199. Alum 6000. **Tui '04-'05:** Day $11,900 (+$500). Aid: Need 143 ($844,400). **Est 1873.** Nonprofit. Roman Catholic. Sem (Sept-June). **Assoc** CLS MSA. The school utilizes a multi-phase approach in which the academic needs of all students are met. NDP, which is owned and operated by the School Sisters of Notre Dame, gears classes in each discipline toward college preparation by grade 9. All grades participate in appropriate social service activities, and several upper-grade courses combine classroom instruction with direct service within the Baltimore community.

NEW JERSEY

HOLY CROSS HIGH SCHOOL Day Coed Gr 9-12
Delran, NJ 08075. 5035 Rte 130 S.
Tel: 856-461-5400. Fax: 856-764-0806.
www.hclance.org   E-mail: kelly.roman@hclance.org
Joseph R. Lemme, Prin. Gerard McConnell, Adm.

Col Prep. AP—Calc US_Hist Comp_Govt & Pol Econ US_Govt & Pol. **Feat**—Ger Geol Law Psych Sociol. **Supp**—Dev_Read Tut. **Adm:** 175/yr. **Tests** HSPT.

Enr 812. Sec 812. Avg class size: 25. Uniform. **Fac 55.** M 32. F 23. Adv deg: 54%. **Grad '04**—231. Col—225. Alum 11,880. **Tui '03-'04:** Day $6430 (+$450). **Est 1957.** Nonprofit. Roman Catholic. Quar (Sept-June). **Assoc** MSA. Emphasizing Christian values, the school supplements its curriculum with art, music, marching and concert band, clubs and community work. An exchange program with a Spanish school is offered during the summer.

ACADEMY OF THE HOLY ANGELS   Day Girls Gr 9-12
Demarest, NJ 07627. 315 Hillside Ave.
Tel: 201-768-7822. Fax: 201-768-6933.
www.holyangels.org   E-mail: info@holyangels.org
    Mary Farrell Cherif, Pres. Jennifer Moran, Prin. Margaux E. Pena, Adm.

    Col Prep. AP—Eng Fr Lat Span Calc Stats Comp_Sci Bio Chem Physics US_Hist Art_Hist Studio_Art. **Feat**—Ger Ital Anat & Physiol Film Theater_Arts Journ. **Supp**—Tut. **Adm (Gr 9-11):** 168/yr. Appl due: Dec. Accepted: 52%. Yield: 82%. **Enr 546.** G 546. Sec 546. Wh 63%. Hisp 16%. Blk 7%. Asian 14%. Avg class size: 19. Uniform. **Fac 55.** M 9/1. F 43/2. Wh 100%. Adv deg: 72%. **Grad '04—148.** Col—148. Avg SAT: 1157. Alum 4800. **Tui '04-'05:** Day $8300 (+$500). Aid: Merit 42 ($30,000). Need 81 ($45,000). **Summer:** Acad Rec. Tui Day $100-300. 2-3 wks. **Est 1879.** Nonprofit. Roman Catholic. Quar (Sept-June). **Assoc** MSA. Located on a well-equipped, 22-acre campus, this school provides a college prep program including Advanced Placement and honors courses in most disciplines, extensive fine arts offerings, laptop and wireless computer programs, and enrichment day trips to nearby New York City. Extracurricular offerings include student clubs and interscholastic sports teams. Opportunities for European travel and study abroad are also available.

BENEDICTINE ACADEMY   Day Girls Gr 9-12
Elizabeth, NJ 07208. 840 N Broad St.
Tel: 908-352-0670. Fax: 908-352-9424.
www.benedictineacad.org   E-mail: admissions@benedictineacad.org
    Sr. Germaine Fritz, OSB, Prin. Barbara R. Millman, Adm.

    Col Prep. AP—Eng Span Calc Bio Chem Physics US_Hist. **Feat**—Fr Child_Psych Relig. **Supp**—Rem_Math Rem_Read Tut. **Adm (Gr 9-11):** 62/yr. Appl due: Rolling. Accepted: 50%. Yield: 75%. **Tests** CTP_4. **Enr 190.** G 190. Sec 190. Wh 20%. Hisp 25%. Blk 50%. Asian 5%. Avg class size: 14. Uniform. **Fac 20.** M 5. F 15. Wh 70%. Hisp 10%. Blk 10%. Asian 10%. Adv deg: 90%. **Grad '04—43.** Col—43. Avg SAT: 1190. Alum 575. **Tui '04-'05:** Day $5200 (+$500). Aid: Merit 30. Need 107 ($325,000). **Est 1915.** Nonprofit. Roman Catholic. Sem (Sept-June). **Assoc** MSA. Conducted in the Benedictine tradition, the academy places significant emphasis on Christian values. The diverse student population, which enrolls from Union and Essex counties, follows a college preparatory liberal arts program that includes Advanced Placement course work. Student council, academic clubs, drama, art and athletics are among Benedictine's extracurricular activities.

NJ Middle Atlantic States 815

VILLA VICTORIA ACADEMY Day Girls Gr PS-12
Ewing, NJ 08628. 376 W Upper Ferry Rd.
Tel: 609-882-1700. Fax: 609-882-8421.
www.villavictoria.org   E-mail: admissions@villavictoria.org
 Sr. Lillian Harrington, MPF, Pres. BS, Trenton State College, MS, Univ of Notre Dame. Marcie Sandleben, Adm.

 Col Prep. AP—Eng Fr Span Calc Chem US_Hist US_Govt & Pol Studio_Art. **Feat**—Creative_Writing Astron Computers Psych Relig Film Music. **Adm:** 58/yr. Appl due: Rolling. **Tests** SSAT. **Enr 280.** G 280. Elem 189. Sec 91. Wh 88%. Hisp 2%. Blk 8%. Asian 2%. Avg class size: 20. **Fac 41.** M 4/1. F 30/6. Wh 100%. Adv deg: 46%. **Grad '04—23.** Col—23. Avg SAT: 1290. Alum 1290. **Tui '04-'05:** Day $7600-8375 (+$400). **Summer:** Acad Enrich Rev Rem. Tui Day $260/wk. 4 wks. **Est 1933.** Nonprofit. Roman Catholic. Sem (Sept-June). **Assoc** MSA. Multimedia instruction; private music, dance, acting and art lessons; student government; and athletics supplement the traditional curriculum at Villa Victoria. The school offers Spanish instruction beginning in kindergarten; an extensive fine arts curriculum in grades 7-12; art, music and computer discovery classes in grade 9; and Advanced Placement courses for juniors and seniors.

BAPTIST HIGH SCHOOL Day Coed Gr 9-12
Haddon Heights, NJ 08035. 3rd & Station Aves.
Tel: 856-547-2996. Fax: 856-547-6584.
www.baptisthigh.com   E-mail: bhs@myzoe.org
 Lynn L. Conahan, Prin. BS, Cedarville College.

 Col Prep. Gen Acad. Feat—Computers Studio_Art Drama Music. **Supp**—LD Rem_Math Rem_Read Tut. **Adm:** 62/yr. Accepted: 100%. **Tests** Stanford. **Enr 223.** B 104. G 119. Sec 223. Wh 81%. Hisp 3%. Blk 12%. Asian 4%. Avg class size: 25. **Fac 20.** M 8. F 8/4. Wh 95%. Blk 5%. Adv deg: 25%. **Grad '04—36.** Col—31. Avg SAT: 1090. Avg ACT: 22. Alum 936. **Tui '03-'04:** Day $5000 (+$200). Aid: Need 23 ($27,000). **Est 1972.** Nonprofit. Baptist. Sem (Sept-June). Founded to assist parents in the religious teaching of their children, the school enrolls a large number of Baptist students, as well as Christians of other denominations. Advanced courses in math, science, English and foreign languages are complemented by business and general programs, and a learning center aids students with learning disabilities. Bible study is a yearly requirement. Extracurricular activities include clubs, music, drama, and boys' and girls' interscholastic athletics.

HADDONFIELD FRIENDS SCHOOL Day Coed Gr PS-8
Haddonfield, NJ 08033. 47 N Haddon Ave.
Tel: 856-429-6786. Fax: 856-429-6376.
www.haddonfieldfriends.org   E-mail: psacchetti@haddonfieldfriends.org
 Deborah Kost, Head. BA, Univ of Arizona. Sandy Trezza, Adm.

 Pre-Prep. Feat—Span Studio_Art Music. **Adm:** 41/yr. Appl due: Rolling. Accepted: 80%. **Enr 146.** B 73. G 73. Elem 146. Avg class size: 11. **Fac 26.** M /1. F 14/11. Wh 100%. Adv deg: 11%. **Grad '04—2. Tui '04-'05:** Day $9000 (+$150). Aid: Merit 11 ($30,316). Need 26 ($62,059). **Summer:** Rec. Tui Day $500/2-wk ses. 8 wks. **Est 1786.** Nonprofit. Religious Society of Friends. Tri (Sept-June).

Assoc MSA. This Quaker school provides instruction in language arts, math, science, social studies, art, music, Spanish and physical education. HFS organizes service projects for its student body throughout the year, some of which are sponsored and managed by individual classes, others of which are handled by a service committee. The extended day program, which includes activity clubs, offers student care before and after school for an additional fee.

NEWGRANGE SCHOOL Day Coed Ages 8-18
Hamilton, NJ 08629. 526 S Olden Ave.
Tel: 609-584-1800. Fax: 609-430-3030.
www.thenewgrange.org   E-mail: info@thenewgrange.org
  Gordon F. Sherman, Exec Dir. PhD. Sue Morris, Adm.

  Col Prep. Gen Acad. LD. Feat—Computers Studio_Art. **Supp**—Dev_Read Rem_Math Rem_Read. **Adm:** Appl due: Sept. **Enr 97.** B 71. G 26. **Fac 35.** M 5. F 30. Wh 99%. Blk 1%. Adv deg: 34%. **Grad '04—6. Tui '02-'03:** Day $31,850. **Summer:** Acad Rev Rem. Tui Day $375. 4 wks. **Est 1977.** Nonprofit. Sem (Sept-June). Newgrange offers an individualized, intensive and full-time academic program for students with learning difficulties. Basic skills and problem solving are stressed, and a full remedial and tutorial program is available. The average length of stay is three years; some students remain until graduation, while others move on to district or other schools.

THE HUDSON SCHOOL Day Coed Gr 5-12
Hoboken, NJ 07030. 601 Park Ave.
Tel: 201-659-8335. Fax: 201-222-3669.
www.thehudsonschool.org   E-mail: hudson@thehudsonschool.org
  Suellen F. Newman, Dir. BA, Oberlin College, MA, Univ of Chicago.

  Col Prep. AP—Fr Lat Span Calc Comp_Sci Chem Physics US_Hist Psych Music_Theory. **Feat**—Classics Creative_Writing Mythology Ger Greek Japan Lat-Amer_Hist Comp_Relig Philos Film Video_Production Drama Chorus Music. **Supp**—ESL Tut. **Adm:** 65/yr. Appl due: Apr. Accepted: 33%. **Tests** ISEE SSAT. **Enr 207.** B 100. G 107. Elem 117. Sec 90. Wh 56%. Hisp 14%. Blk 12%. Asian 18%. Avg class size: 18. **Fac 50.** M 10/10. F 12/18. Wh 92%. Hisp 4%. Blk 2%. Am Ind 1%. Asian 1%. Adv deg: 40%. **Grad '04**—20. Col—19. Avg SAT: 1150. **Tui '04-'05:** Day $10,340-11,540 (+$500). Aid: Need 60 ($300,000). **Summer:** Enrich Rec. Theater. Tui Day $650. 4 wks. **Est 1978.** Nonprofit. Quar (Sept-June). **Assoc** MSA. Hudson's rigorous program emphasizes the study of modern and classical languages, among them Greek, German and Japanese. Electives include acting, yoga, journalism, chess, video, creative writing, calligraphy, painting, chorus, sculpture, cooking and dance. Students are encouraged to spend one year studying abroad. All boys and girls perform community service. **See Also Page 1173**

SAINT DOMINIC ACADEMY Day Girls Gr 9-12
Jersey City, NJ 07304. 2572 Kennedy Blvd.
Tel: 201-434-5938. Fax: 201-434-2603.
www.stdominicacad.com   E-mail: stdominicacad@hotmail.com

Sr. Vivien Jennings, OP, Prin. BA, Caldwell College, MA, Catholic Univ of America, MS, Syracuse Univ, PhD, Fordham Univ. Sr. Danelle McCarthy, OP, Adm.

Col Prep. AP—Eng Fr Span Calc US_Hist Psych Art_Hist. **Feat**—Ital Programming Relig Studio_Art. **Supp**—Tut. **Adm:** 150/yr. Appl due: Nov. Accepted: 70%. **Enr 485.** G 485. Sec 485. Wh 40%. Hisp 18%. Blk 10%. Asian 32%. Avg class size: 22. Uniform. **Fac 42.** M 12. F 30. Wh 74%. Hisp 5%. Blk 5%. Asian 16%. Adv deg: 42%. **Grad '04—114.** Col—114. Avg SAT: 1010. Alum 6550. **Tui '04-'05:** Day $6400. Aid: Merit 12. Need 15. **Summer:** Acad Enrich Rem Rec. Tui Day $200. 5-6 wks. **Est 1878.** Nonprofit. Roman Catholic. Sem (Sept-June). **Assoc** MSA. A Catholic academy operated in the Dominican tradition, Saint Dominic includes honors (beginning freshman year) and Advanced Placement courses as part of its curriculum. In addition, qualified seniors may enroll in classes at nearby Saint Peter's College. During junior year, each girl completes a 25-hour Christian service project.

NOTRE DAME HIGH SCHOOL Day Coed Gr 9-12
Lawrenceville, NJ 08648. 601 Lawrence Rd.
Tel: 609-882-7900. Fax: 609-882-5723.
www.ndnj.org   E-mail: rileyb@ndnj.org

Mary Liz Ivins, Prin. BS, St Joseph's Univ, MA, Princeton Theological Seminary, MA, Rider Univ. Peggy Miller, Adm.

Col Prep. AP—Eng Fr Span Calc Bio Chem Physics Eur_Hist US_Hist Psych US_Govt & Pol. **Feat**—Creative_Writing Ger Lat Anat & Physiol Sports_Med Comp_Sci Econ Relig Ceramics Photog Acting Theater_Arts Accounting Journ Public_Speak. **Supp**—Rev Tut. **Adm (Gr 9-11):** 326/yr. Appl due: Nov. Accepted: 80%. Yield: 80%. **Tests** HSPT. **Enr 1270.** B 660. G 610. Sec 1270. Wh 80%. Hisp 4%. Blk 14%. Am Ind 1%. Asian 1%. Avg class size: 24. Uniform. **Fac 85.** M 35. F 50. Wh 97%. Hisp 2%. Blk 1%. Adv deg: 44%. **Grad '04—284.** Col—281. Avg SAT: 1106. Alum 9215. **Tui '04-'05:** Day $7400 (+$600). Aid: Need 120 ($175,000). **Summer:** Enrich Rec. Creative Writing. Art. Drama. 6 wks. **Est 1957.** Nonprofit. Roman Catholic. Sem (Sept-June). Affiliated with the Religious Sisters of Mercy, Notre Dame combines a solid college preparatory curriculum with service opportunities and cocurricular activities. Honors and Advanced Placement courses are available in most disciplines, and instructors employ various teaching strategies to address different learning styles. Boys and girls follow a block schedule, consisting of four 80-minute periods per day, that enables pupils to complete a yearlong course in one semester. An interdisciplinary project and a professional internship are notable aspects of the grade 12 curriculum.

CHRISTIAN BROTHERS ACADEMY Day Boys Gr 9-12
Lincroft, NJ 07738. 850 Newman Springs Rd.
Tel: 732-747-1959. Fax: 732-747-1643.
www.cbalincroftnj.org

Br. Ralph Montedoro, FSC, Prin. BA, MS, Monmouth College.

Col Prep. AP—Eng Fr Span Calc Stats Comp_Sci Bio Chem Physics US_Hist World_Hist Econ Psych Music_Theory. **Feat**—Creative_Writing Humanities Lat

Astron Marine_Biol/Sci Govt Relig Film Bus Journ. **Supp**—Tut. **Adm:** 251/yr. Accepted: 50%. **Enr 919.** B 919. Sec 919. Wh 93%. Hisp 2%. Blk 1%. Asian 4%. Avg class size: 18. **Fac 70.** M 51. F 19. Wh 99%. Hisp 1%. Adv deg: 57%. **Grad '04—207.** Col—206. Avg SAT: 1200. Alum 5920. **Tui '04-'05:** Day $9200 (+$500). Aid: Merit 17 ($34,000). Need 71 ($395,000). **Est 1959.** Nonprofit. Roman Catholic. Sem (Sept-June). **Assoc** MSA. The academy is conducted by the Brothers of the Christian Schools. Honors and Advanced Placement courses are available in the major disciplines, and French, Spanish and Latin constitute the foreign language offerings. A full extracurricular and interscholastic athletic program supplements academics.

ST. JOSEPH HIGH SCHOOL Day Boys Gr 9-12
Metuchen, NJ 08840. 145 Plainfield Ave.
Tel: 732-549-7600. Fax: 732-549-0664.
www.stjoes.org   E-mail: alumni@stjoes.org

Br. Dennis Wermert, SC, Pres. BS, Saint Peter's College, MS, Fordham Univ, MA, St Joseph's Seminary, DMin, Oxford Univ (England). Lawrence Walsh, Prin. David Gandy, Adm.

Col Prep. AP—Eng Calc Comp_Sci Bio Chem Physics Eur_Hist US_Hist. **Feat**—Fr Ger Span Astron Meteorology Civil_War Pol_Sci Relig Drawing Film Photog Journ. **Supp**—Tut. **Adm (Gr 9-11):** 235/yr. Appl due: Rolling. Accepted: 50%. Yield: 80%. **Tests** HSPT. **Enr 844.** B 844. Sec 844. Avg class size: 25. Uniform. **Fac 60.** M 37/2. F 20/1. Wh 92%. Hisp 8%. Adv deg: 65%. **Grad '04—199.** Col—197. Avg SAT: 1120. Alum 7837. **Tui '05-'06:** Day $8100 (+$325-625). Aid: Merit 10. Need 44 ($51,000). **Summer:** Enrich Rem. Tui Day $400. 4 wks. **Est 1961.** Nonprofit. Roman Catholic. Sem (Aug-June). **Assoc** MSA. Conducted by the Brothers of the Sacred Heart, St. Joseph provides a college preparatory curriculum that encourages critical and creative thinking. Students from more than 70 central New Jersey public, parochial and private elementary schools enroll in a varied program that features an array of accelerated and Advanced Placement courses. Extracurricular opportunities include an extensive athletic program, academic and interest clubs, music groups and school publications. **See Also Page 1345**

MONTCLAIR COOPERATIVE SCHOOL Day Coed Gr PS-6
Montclair, NJ 07042. 65 Chestnut St.
Tel: 973-783-4955. Fax: 973-783-1316.
www.montclaircoop.org   E-mail: info@montclaircoop.org

Bruce Kanze, Head. BA, Columbia College, MA, MS, Bank Street College of Education. Susan Ross, Adm.

Pre-Prep. Feat—Span Studio_Art Drama Music Dance. **Supp**—Dev_Read Rem_Math Rem_Read Tut. **Adm:** 36/yr. Appl due: Rollin. Accepted: 25%. **Enr 160.** B 92. G 68. Elem 160. Wh 85%. Hisp 1%. Blk 10%. Asian 3%. Other 1%. Avg class size: 17. **Fac 28.** M 2. F 19/7. Wh 90%. Blk 10%. Adv deg: 25%. **Grad '04—11.** Alum 320. **Tui '03-'04:** Day $10,900 (+$500). Aid: Need 24 ($110,000). **Summer:** Rec. Tui Day $660. 4 wks. **Est 1963.** Nonprofit. Sem (Sept-June). Utilizing the open classroom approach, the school emphasizes the integrated development of basic skills, creative ability and social interaction. Art, Spanish, music, ice

VILLA WALSH ACADEMY
Day Girls Gr 7-12

Morristown, NJ 07960. 455 Western Ave.
Tel: 973-538-3680. Fax: 973-538-6733.
www.villawalsh.org   E-mail: villawalsh@aol.com
   Sr. Doris Lavinthal, MPF, Dir. BS, MS. Sr. Patricia Pompa, MPF, Prin. BA, MA.
   Col Prep. AP—Eng Fr Span Calc Bio Chem Physics Eur_Hist US_Hist. **Feat**—Ital Comp_Sci Theol Fine_Arts Chorus. **Supp**—Rev Tut. **Adm:** 56/yr. Appl due: Feb. Accepted: 30%. **Tests** IQ. **Enr 235.** G 235. Elem 32. Sec 203. Wh 90%. Hisp 5%. Blk 2%. Asian 3%. Avg class size: 12. Uniform. **Fac 35.** M 5. F 25/5. Wh 91%. Hisp 2%. Blk 2%. Asian 5%. Adv deg: 68%. **Grad '04—48.** Col—48. Avg SAT: 1340. Alum 650. **Tui '04-'05:** Day $10,500 (+$500). Aid: Need 16 ($39,000). **Est 1967.** Nonprofit. Roman Catholic. Tri (Sept-June). **Assoc** MSA. Villa Walsh's curriculum features AP preparation, honors sections, independent study and an emphasis on the fine arts. Students fulfill course requirements in theology, modern foreign language and the fine arts. A full varsity sports program is available.

YAVNEH ACADEMY
Day Coed Gr PS-8

Paramus, NJ 07652. 155 N Farview Ave.
Tel: 201-262-8494. Fax: 201-262-0463.
www.yavnehacademy.org   E-mail: yavnehacademy@soinmail.com
   Joel Kirschner, Exec Dir. Rabbi Peretz Hochbaum, Dean.
   Pre-Prep. Gen Acad. Feat—Lib_Skills Hebrew Computers Holocaust Studio_Art Drama Music. **Supp**—Dev_Read LD Rem_Math Rem_Read Tut. **Adm:** 49/yr. **Enr 751.** Elem 751. Wh 100%. Avg class size: 22. **Fac 83.** M 10/1. F 57/15. **Grad '04—70.** **Tui '04-'05:** Day $9500-10,350 (+$750-2417). Aid: Need 100 ($490,000). **Est 1942.** Nonprofit. Orthodox Jewish. Quar (Sept-June). Students receive both Judaic and secular education. The language of instruction in Judaic studies is modern Hebrew. Athletics, drama and extracurricular activities augment the academic program.

TIMOTHY CHRISTIAN SCHOOLS
Day Coed Gr K-12

Piscataway, NJ 08854. 2008 Ethel Rd.
Tel: 732-985-0300. Fax: 732-985-8008.
www.timothychristian.org   E-mail: tcs@timothychristian.org
   Michael J. Keller, Admin. BS, Monmouth College.
   Col Prep. AP—Eng Calc Comp_Sci. **Feat**—Creative_Writing Fr Span Psych Bible Studio_Art Drama Band Chorus Music_Theory Accounting Debate Journ Woodworking Home_Ec. **Supp**—LD Tut. **Adm:** 117/yr. Appl due: Sept. Accepted: 93%. **Tests** IQ SSAT Stanford. **Enr 649.** Elem 389. Sec 260. Wh 62%. Hisp 6%. Blk 18%. Asian 8%. Other 6%. Avg class size: 21. Uniform. **Fac 45.** M 15. F 28/2. Wh 98%. Blk 2%. Adv deg: 57%. **Grad '04—50.** Col—45. Avg SAT: 1029. Alum 750. **Tui '05-'06:** Day $4490-7250 (+$250). Aid: Need 43 ($82,936). **Est 1949.**

Nonprofit. Sem (Sept-June). With a teaching staff consisting entirely of bornagain Christians, TCS bases its elementary and secondary programs on Biblical principles. Honors and AP course work is available in the upper grades, as are a full complement of electives. Interscholastic sports, student government, musical and dramatic productions, social events and educational trips round out the high school program.

PRINCETON ACADEMY   Day Boys Gr PS-8
OF THE SACRED HEART
Princeton, NJ 08540. 101 Drake's Corner Rd.
Tel: 609-921-6499. Fax: 609-921-9198.
www.princetonacademy.org   E-mail: tvonoehsen@princetonacademy.org
    Olen Kalkus, Head. BA, Colby College, MA, Salve Regina Univ, MEd, Columbia Univ. Tom von Oehsen, Adm.

    Pre-Prep. Feat—Span Relig Studio_Art Music. **Supp**—Dev_Read. **Adm (Gr PS-7):** 39/yr. Appl due: Jan. Accepted: 80%. Yield: 70%. **Tests** CTP_4 SSAT. **Enr 210.** B 210. Elem 210. Wh 86%. Hisp 3%. Blk 3%. Asian 2%. Other 6%. Avg class size: 12. Uniform. **Fac 27.** M 8. F 17/2. Wh 90%. Hisp 7%. Blk 3%. Adv deg: 44%. **Grad '04—11.** Prep—11. Alum 11. **Tui '04-'05:** Day $16,950-17,950 (+$300). Aid: Need 43 ($375,275). **Summer:** Rec. Tui Day $600/2-wk ses. 6 wks. **Est 1998.** Nonprofit. Roman Catholic. Tri (Sept-June). The curriculum at this boys' school, which emphasizes reading, writing and discussion, provides frequent opportunities for hands-on learning. Spanish instruction begins in junior kindergarten and becomes a daily part of the program in grade 1; music, drama and the visual arts are also integrated into the lower school curriculum. Experiential teaching and a focus on independent thought are characteristics of the upper school program. As social awareness is integral to school life, the academy encourages students to engage in age-appropriate community service.

PRINCETON FRIENDS SCHOOL   Day Coed Gr PS-8
Princeton, NJ 08540. 470 Quaker Rd.
Tel: 609-683-1194. Fax: 609-252-0686.
www.princetonfriendsschool.org   E-mail: friends@princetonfriendsschool.org
    Jane Fremon, Dir. AB, Princeton Univ, MEd, Bank Street College of Education. Bonnie Benbow, Adm.

    Pre-Prep. Feat—Mandarin Span Studio_Art Music. **Supp**—Tut. **Adm (Gr PS-7):** 22/yr. Appl due: Jan. Accepted: 62%. Yield: 63%. **Enr 125.** B 54. G 71. Elem 125. Wh 74%. Hisp 6%. Blk 9%. Asian 6%. Other 5%. Avg class size: 12. **Fac 20.** M 6/1. F 10/3. Wh 80%. Hisp 10%. Asian 10%. Adv deg: 75%. **Grad '04—15.** Prep—7. Alum 130. **Tui '04-'05:** Day $14,500 (+$60-330). Aid: Need 23 ($237,025). **Summer:** Rec. Tui Day $235/wk. 9 wks. **Est 1987.** Nonprofit. Religious Society of Friends. Sem (Sept-June). The school's integrated curriculum focuses upon a yearly central theme that students explore in multi-age groupings. Pupils receive weekly instruction in Spanish and Mandarin Chinese in grades preK-2, then choose one of these languages as a focus in grades 3-8. The curriculum also exposes students to art, music and dance. Community service is integral to the program in grades 1-8.

HILLTOP COUNTRY DAY SCHOOL
Day Coed Gr PS-8

Sparta, NJ 07871. 32 Lafayette Rd.
Tel: 973-729-5485. Fax: 973-729-9057.
www.hilltopcds.org
    Joseph Stefani, Head. Lisa Tsemberlis, Adm.

    Pre-Prep. Feat—Fr Span Computers Studio_Art Music. **Supp**—Dev_Read Rem_Read. **Adm:** Appl due: Rolling. **Enr 230.** B 119. G 111. Elem 230. Avg class size: 13. **Fac 34.** M 4/1. F 26/3. Adv deg: 29%. **Grad '04—13. Tui '05-'06:** Day $10,145-11,680 (+$250). **Summer:** Acad Enrich Rem Rec. 3-6 wks. **Est 1967.** Nonprofit. Quar (Sept-June). Hilltop's traditional preschool and elementary program places particular emphasis upon the arts, including both art and music appreciation. Foreign language instruction commences in kindergarten with the introduction of both French and Spanish. After-school enrichment offerings range from activities in the arts (painting, instrumental music, and arts and crafts) to athletics (tennis, karate and golf) to academics (computer enrichment and SSAT preparation).

COMMUNITY SCHOOL
Day Coed Gr 9-PG

Teaneck, NJ 07666. 1135 Teaneck Rd.
Tel: 201-862-1796. Fax: 201-862-1791.
www.communityschoolnj.org   E-mail: tbraunstein@communityhighschool.org
    Dennis Cohen, Prgm Dir. MA. Toby Braunstein, Educ Dir. MA.

    Col Prep. LD. Underachiever. Feat—Span Computers Studio_Art Drama Music. **Supp**—Rem_Math Rem_Read. **Adm:** 47/yr. Appl due: Rolling. **Enr 170.** B 136. G 34. Sec 170. Wh 74%. Hisp 8%. Blk 18%. **Fac 80.** M 15. F 65. **Grad '04—40.** Col—36. **Tui '04-'05:** Day $35,186. **Est 1967.** Nonprofit. Quar (Sept-June). This college preparatory curriculum is designed for students with learning and attentional difficulties. First-year college support services are also provided. An enriched elementary program, located at 11 W. Forest Ave., closely resembles that of the high school.   **See Also Page 1354**

THE ELLISON SCHOOL
Day Coed Gr PS-8

Vineland, NJ 08361. 1017 S Spring Rd.
Tel: 856-691-1734. Fax: 856-794-8361.
www.ellisonschool.org   E-mail: golin@ellisonschool.org
    Gerri Olin, Head. BA, Rider College.

    Pre-Prep. Feat—Lib_Skills Span Computers Studio_Art Music Study_Skills. **Supp**—ESL Rem_Math Rem_Read Tut. **Adm:** 27/yr. Accepted: 97%. Yield: 90%. **Enr 124.** B 62. G 62. Elem 124. Wh 85%. Hisp 5%. Blk 6%. Asian 4%. Avg class size: 11. **Fac 20.** M 3. F 14/3. Wh 90%. Hisp 5%. Blk 5%. Adv deg: 5%. **Grad '04—8.** Prep—2. Alum 165. **Tui '04-'05:** Day $6890-7815 (+$150). Aid: Need 20 ($52,600). **Summer:** Rec. Tui Day $250/2-wk ses. 10 wks. **Est 1959.** Nonprofit. Tri (Sept-June). **Assoc** MSA. This elementary school serves children from Vineland, Millville, Hammonton, Mays Landing, the shore area and surrounding communities. Ellison's curriculum, which is taught in small, individualized classes, features art, music, computer, physical education and Spanish instruction. Beginning in the lower grades, the school emphasizes sound study habits, the ability to work independently, personal responsibility, and organizational and critical-thinking skills. Departmentalization begins in grade 5.

SOLOMON SCHECHTER DAY SCHOOL Day Coed Gr PS-12
West Orange, NJ 07052. 1418 Pleasant Valley Way.
Tel: 973-325-7994. Fax: 973-669-5921.
www.ssdsofessexandunion.org
   Seth Linfield, Head. Mary Lou Allen, Adm.

   Col Prep. Feat—Fr Span Arabic Computers Bible Relig Hebrew Judaic_Studies Photog Studio_Art Music. **Supp**—ESL Tut. **Adm:** 123/yr. Appl due: Feb. Accepted: 75%. **Tests** ISEE Stanford. **Enr 860.** Elem 600. Sec 260. Wh 98%. Hisp 1%. Asian 1%. Avg class size: 14. **Fac 180. Grad '04—65.** Col—65. Avg SAT: 1299. Alum 800. **Tui '03-'04:** Day $6700-16,000. Aid: Need 344. **Est 1965.** Nonprofit. Jewish. Sem (Sept-June). **Assoc** MSA. Affiliated with the Conservative movement of Judaism, SSDS offers an integrated dual curriculum of general and Judaic studies. The latter is composed of courses in Bible, Hebrew language, Rabbinics, and Jewish history, literature and philosophy. AP and honors courses and creative individualized research are aspects of the general curriculum. The school maintains three campuses: a lower campus in West Orange (122 Gregory Ave.), a second lower campus in Cranford (721 Orange Ave., 07016), and the upper school location on Pleasant Valley Way, which serves middle and high school students.

NEW YORK

CHRISTIAN BROTHERS ACADEMY Day Boys Gr 6-12
Albany, NY 12205. 12 Airline Dr.
Tel: 518-452-9809. Fax: 518-452-9804.
www.cbaalbany.org   E-mail: oharem@cbaalbany.org
   David R. McGuire, Prin. BS, Le Moyne College, MA, State Univ of New York-Albany. Martin McGraw, Adm.

   Col Prep. Milit. AP—Eng Calc Bio Chem Eur_Hist US_Hist World_Hist. **Feat**—Fr Span Geol Comp_Sci Web_Design Econ Law Psych Sociol Criminal_Justice Philos Relig Studio_Art Music Accounting Bus Mech_Drawing JROTC. **Supp**—Rem_Math Rem_Read Rev Tut. **Adm (Gr 6-11):** 134/yr. Appl due: Rolling. Accepted: 98%. Yield: 98%. **Tests** IQ. **Enr 539.** B 539. Elem 138. Sec 401. Wh 91%. Hisp 1%. Blk 6%. Asian 1%. Other 1%. Avg class size: 22. Uniform. **Fac 43.** M 30/2. F 10/1. Wh 98%. Blk 2%. Adv deg: 48%. **Grad '04—82.** Col—81. Avg SAT: 1079. Alum 6000. **Tui '04-'05:** Day $8000-8500 (+$450). Aid: Merit 36 ($130,000). Need 160 ($380,000). Work prgm 2 ($1200). **Summer:** Acad Enrich Rec. Tui Day $185/wk. 4 wks. **Est 1859.** Nonprofit. Roman Catholic. Sem (Sept-June). **Assoc** MSA. CBA provides a junior high school and a senior military high school. Both AP and honors courses are available, and graduation requirements include art or music, religion, military science and electives. The school offers a well-rounded program of extracurricular activities and interscholastic sports.

MAPLEBROOK SCHOOL

Coed Gr 6-PG
Bdg & Day

Amenia, NY 12501. 5142 Rte 22.
Tel: 845-373-9511. Fax: 845-373-7029.
www.maplebrookschool.org   E-mail: mbsecho@aol.com

Roger A. Fazzone, Pres. MA, Pepperdine Univ, EdD, Nova Univ. Donna M. Konkolics, Head. MA, State Univ of New York-New Paltz. Jennifer L. Scully, Adm.

Gen Acad. Voc. LD. Underachiever. Feat—Span Computers Econ Govt Psych Performing_Arts Studio_Art Journ Home_Ec. **Supp**—Dev_Read Rem_Math Rem_Read Tut. **Adm (Gr 6-11):** 37/yr. Bdg 34. Day 3. Appl due: Rolling. **Tests** IQ Stanford. **Enr 116.** B 52/4. G 57/3. Sec 79. PG 37. Wh 87%. Hisp 4%. Blk 7%. Asian 2%. Avg class size: 8. **Fac 30.** M 10/1. F 17/2. Adv deg: 53%. In Dorms 10. **Grad '04—23.** Col—19. Alum 650. **Tui '05-'06:** Bdg $43,900 (+$400). 5-Day Bdg $39,400 (+$400). Day $27,900 (+$200). Aid: Need 12 ($116,425). Work prgm 3 ($3000). **Summer:** Acad Enrich Rev Rem Rec. Tui Bdg $7000. 6 wks. **Est 1945.** Nonprofit. Sem (Sept-June). **Assoc** MSA. Maplebrook offers academic and social programs to adolescents who are unable to thrive in traditional school settings or whose learning differences require more individual attention. The program emphasizes multisensory instruction and the development of social skills and self-esteem. CAPS (The Center for the Advancement of Post Secondary Studies), a postsecondary program providing either vocational or college programming, is available to students ages 18-21 for an additional fee.

THE SUSQUEHANNA SCHOOL

Day Coed Gr PS-10

Binghamton, NY 13903. 75 Pennsylvania Ave.
Tel: 607-723-5797. Fax: 607-723-5797.
www.thesusquehannaschool.org   E-mail: tss@stny.rr.com

Carol C. Matruski, Dir. BA, MSEd, State Univ of New York-Binghamton.

Gen Acad. Feat—Fr Span Fine_Arts. **Adm:** 13/yr. Appl due: Rolling. Accepted: 100%. **Enr 56.** B 28. G 28. Elem 49. Sec 7. Wh 81%. Hisp 2%. Blk 4%. Asian 13%. Avg class size: 14. **Fac 9.** M 1. F 4/4. Adv deg: 55%. **Grad '04—3.** Alum 300. **Tui '05-'06:** Day $8650 (+$600). Aid: Need (18). **Summer:** Enrich Rec. 8 wks. **Est 1970.** Nonprofit. (Sept-June). The school features multi-age/multi-grade classrooms, as well as small class size. After-school enrichment classes cover sign language, Japanese, Italian, French and Spanish.

THE MELROSE SCHOOL

Day Coed Gr PS-8

Brewster, NY 10509. 120 Federal Hill Rd.
Tel: 845-279-2406. Fax: 845-279-3878.
www.melrose.edu   E-mail: admissions@melrose.edu

William Sinfield, Head. BA, Wilfrid Laurier Univ (Canada), BEd, Brock Univ (Canada), MEd, Simon Fraser Univ (Canada). Kimberly Holliday, Adm.

Pre-Prep. Feat—Lib_Skills Fr Lat Computers Art_Hist Studio_Art Music Music_Theory. **Adm:** 44/yr. Appl due: Feb. **Tests** IQ. **Enr 184.** B 90. G 94. Elem 184. Wh 76%. Hisp 3%. Blk 3%. Am Ind 1%. Asian 8%. Other 9%. Avg class size: 16. **Fac 27.** M 4. F 23. Wh 98%. Hisp 1%. Blk 1%. Adv deg: 44%. **Grad '04—19.** Prep—14. **Tui '04-'05:** Day $11,250-13,250 (+$150). **Summer:** Acad Enrich. 3

wks. **Est 1963.** Nonprofit. Episcopal. Tri (Sept-June). **Assoc** MSA. Beginning in grade 6, Melrose's curriculum features honors English, as well as accelerated language arts, foreign language and math classes. The academic program incorporates computers, French and the fine arts at all grade levels, beginning with the full-day kindergarten. After-school extracurricular offerings include sports, theater, chess and academic clubs.

ACADEMY OF MOUNT ST. URSULA Day Girls Gr 9-12
Bronx, NY 10458. 330 Bedford Park Blvd.
Tel: 718-364-5353. Fax: 718-364-2354.
www.amsu.org   E-mail: bcalamari@amsu.org
  Sr. Mary Beth Read, OSU, Prin. BA, Catholic Univ of America, MS, Fordham Univ. Sr. Barbara Calamari, Adm.

  Col Prep. AP—Eng Span Calc Bio US_Hist. **Feat**—Fr Ital Lat Anat & Physiol Computers Anthro Sociol Bus_Law Studio_Art Music Accounting. **Supp**—Dev_Read Rev Tut. **Adm (Gr 9-11):** 135/yr. Appl due: Nov. Accepted: 57%. Yield: 30%. **Tests** TACHS. **Enr 450.** G 450. Sec 450. Wh 11%. Hisp 48%. Blk 32%. Asian 9%. Avg class size: 25. Uniform. **Fac 37.** M 8/1. F 22/6. Wh 87%. Hisp 5%. Blk 2%. Asian 6%. Adv deg: 62%. **Grad '04**—97. Col—95. Alum 10,000. **Tui '04-'05:** Day $4975 (+$450). Aid: Merit 110 ($252,400). Need 63 ($93,725). **Est 1855.** Nonprofit. Roman Catholic. Sem (Sept-June). **Assoc** MSA. The oldest continuously operated Catholic girls' school in New York State, MSU is conducted by the Ursuline Sisters of the Roman Union. Advanced Placement courses allow qualified juniors and seniors to earn college credit, and an internship program is also available. Interest clubs and athletic teams complement academics, and service activities are a school focus. Most graduates continue their studies at college or professional school.

BISHOP KEARNEY HIGH SCHOOL Day Girls Gr 9-12
Brooklyn, NY 11204. 2202 60th St.
Tel: 718-236-6363. Fax: 718-236-7784.
www.bishopkearneyhs.org   E-mail: info@bishopkearneyhs.org
  Sr. Thomasine Stagnitta, CSJ, Prin. BS, City Univ of New York, MA, Pace Univ. Diane Brereton, Adm.

  Col Prep. AP—Eng Calc Chem Physics Eur_Hist US_Hist Psych. **Feat**—Marine_Biol/Sci Computers Music. **Supp**—LD Rem_Math Rem_Read Rev Tut. **Adm (Gr 9-10):** 257/yr. Appl due: Mar. Accepted: 93%. **Tests** TACHS. **Enr 1060.** G 1060. Sec 1060. Wh 74%. Hisp 8%. Blk 10%. Asian 3%. Other 5%. Avg class size: 32. Uniform. **Fac 87.** M 16. F 71. Wh 98%. Blk 1%. Asian 1%. Adv deg: 82%. **Grad '04**—280. Col—270. Avg SAT: 985. Alum 9720. **Tui '03-'04:** Day $6600 (+$100-300). Aid: Merit 110 ($328,000). Need 174 ($217,740). **Summer:** Rec. Tui Day $200/wk. 2 wks. **Est 1961.** Nonprofit. Roman Catholic. Sem (Sept-June). Enrolling a diverse student body comprising girls from throughout Brooklyn and Queens, Kearney provides a college preparatory curriculum that has at its core religion courses, liturgical celebrations and retreat experiences. Qualified pupils may take Advanced Placement classes during the junior and senior years, and college-credit courses are available through St. Joseph's College and St. John's University.

BISHOP LOUGHLIN MEMORIAL HIGH SCHOOL

Day Coed Gr 9-12

Brooklyn, NY 11238. 357 Clermont Ave.
Tel: 718-857-2700. Fax: 718-398-4227.
www.bishoploughlin.org E-mail: admissions@blmhs.org

Br. Dennis Cronin, FSC, Prin. MEd. Br. John Guasconi, FSC, Adm.

Col Prep. Gen Acad. AP—Eng US_Hist US_Govt & Pol. **Feat**—Fr Span Web_Design Relig Painting Studio_Art Music. **Supp**—Dev_Read Makeup Tut. **Adm (Gr 9-11):** 275/yr. Appl due: Oct. Accepted: 95%. Yield: 93%. **Enr 880.** B 490. G 390. Sec 880. Wh 1%. Hisp 12%. Blk 86%. Asian 1%. Avg class size: 32. Uniform. **Fac 43.** M 22. F 21. Adv deg: 69%. **Grad '04—201.** Col—195. Alum 14,000. **Tui '04-'05:** Day $6000 (+$655). Aid: Merit 73 ($500,000). Need 270 ($280,000). **Summer:** Acad Rev. Tui Day $350. 6 wks. **Est 1851.** Nonprofit. Roman Catholic. Sem (Sept-June). **Assoc** MSA. Bishop Loughlin is staffed by De La Salle Christian Brothers, Dominican Sisters and Catholic lay teachers. Each pupil studies religion two quarters per year.

BROOKLYN HEIGHTS MONTESSORI SCHOOL

Day Coed Gr PS-8

Brooklyn, NY 11201. 185 Court St.
Tel: 718-858-5100. Fax: 718-858-0500.
www.bhmsny.org E-mail: info@bhmsny.org

Dane L. Peters, Head. BA, Central Connecticut State Univ, MEd, Pepperdine Univ. Molly Foran, Adm.

Pre-Prep. Gen Acad. Feat—Span Ceramics Photog Studio_Art Chorus Music Dance. **Supp**—LD. **Adm (Gr PS-7):** 57/yr. Appl due: Dec. Accepted: 56%. Yield: 62%. **Tests** ISEE. **Enr 238.** B 113. G 125. Elem 238. Avg class size: 16. **Fac 42.** M 6/2. F 28/6. Wh 69%. Hisp 10%. Blk 14%. Asian 7%. Adv deg: 38%. **Grad '04—6.** Prep—4. Alum 250. **Tui '04-'05:** Day $17,100-19,700 (+$250-500). Aid: Need 45 ($250,000). **Summer:** Rec. 8 wks. **Est 1965.** Nonprofit. (Sept-June). Children work in multi-age classes structured to develop practical skills and enhance learning. Preschool, kindergarten and lower elementary (grades 1-3) students build an academic foundation in the core courses, while upper elementary pupils (grades 4-6) explore concentrated topics in math, science, technology, Spanish, literature and the arts. In the middle school (grades 7 and 8), boys and girls further develop their skills in writing, language arts and the social sciences.

LONG ISLAND LUTHERAN MIDDLE AND HIGH SCHOOL

Day Coed Gr 6-12

Brookville, NY 11545. 131 Brookville Rd.
Tel: 516-626-1700. Fax: 516-622-7459.
www.luhi.org E-mail: info@luhi.org

David Hahn, Head. BA, Concordia Univ (IL), MEd, Towson State Univ, PhD, Univ of Minnesota-Twin Cities. Barbara Ward, Adm.

Col Prep. AP—Eng Fr Span Calc Comp_Sci US_Hist Econ US_Govt & Pol Music_Theory. **Feat**—Creative_Writing Anat Environ_Sci Law Psych Sociol Relig Studio_Art Bus Journ Marketing. **Supp**—Tut. **Adm (Gr 6-11):** 137/yr. Appl due: Rolling. Accepted: 65%. Yield: 90%. **Tests** IQ. **Enr 604.** B 295. G 309. Elem 206. Sec 398. Wh 70%. Hisp 1%. Blk 23%. Asian 3%. Other 3%. Avg class size: 18. Uniform. **Fac 49.** M 16. F 33. Adv deg: 81%. **Grad '04—94.** Col—94. Avg SAT: 1125. Avg SSAT: 23%. Alum 2300. **Tui '04-'05:** Day $5625-8375 (+$480). Aid: Merit 20 ($10,000). Need 120 ($170,000). **Summer:** Rec. Sports. 2-8 wks. **Est 1960.** Nonprofit. Lutheran. Sem (Sept-June). **Assoc** MSA. Situated on a 32-acre estate, this school operates in the Lutheran-Christian tradition. LuHi's strong academic curriculum features advanced studies, honors classes in most subjects, and college-credit courses. A state program provides students with vocational education opportunities. Outside the classroom, pupils take part in such activities as student council, academic clubs and publications, drama organizations (which put on annual plays and musicals), an assortment of singing and instrumental groups, and athletic teams for both boys and girls.

CANISIUS HIGH SCHOOL   Day Boys Gr 9-12
Buffalo, NY 14209. 1180 Delaware Ave.
Tel: 716-882-0466. Fax: 716-883-1870.
www.canisiushigh.org   E-mail: weislo@canisiushigh.org
    Rev. James P. Higgins, SJ, Pres. Frank D. Tudini, Prin. Thomas H. Weislo, Adm.

    Col Prep. AP—Eng Span Calc Comp_Sci Bio Chem Physics Eur_Hist US_Hist World_Hist Econ US_Govt & Pol. **Feat**—Fr Ger Greek Lat Relig Studio_Art Music. **Supp**—Tut. **Adm:** 235/yr. Appl due: Rolling. **Enr 800.** Sec 800. Wh 93%. Hisp 2%. Blk 4%. Asian 1%. Avg class size: 18. **Fac 62.** Adv deg: 66%. **Grad '04— 205.** Col—203. Alum 7000. **Tui '04-'05:** Day $7275. **Summer:** Enrich Rem. Tui Day $450. 5 wks. **Est 1870.** Nonprofit. Roman Catholic. Quar (Sept-June). **Assoc** MSA. Honors and accelerated courses are offered all four years; college-level and AP courses are available in virtually all subjects. Seniors participate in a Christian service program that requires them to spend time each week working in a voluntary service activity. Every student is encouraged to engage in at least one cocurricular activity annually; athletics and a variety of clubs are among the choices.

MOUNT ST. JOSEPH ACADEMY   Day Coed Gr PS-8
Buffalo, NY 14208. 2064 Main St.
Tel: 716-883-1515. Fax: 716-882-9053.
www.msja.org   E-mail: msjaprinc@adelphia.net
    John E. Kingston, Prin.

    Pre-Prep. Feat—Computers Relig Studio_Art Music. **Supp**—Dev_Read Rem_Read Tut. **Adm:** 45/yr. Appl due: Rolling. Accepted: 50%. **Tests** Stanford. **Enr 186.** B 100. G 86. Elem 186. Wh 75%. Hisp 2%. Blk 22%. Asian 1%. Avg class size: 15. Uniform. **Fac 24.** M 5. F 17/2. Wh 100%. Adv deg: 33%. **Grad '04—17.** Prep—15. Alum 6500. **Tui '03-'04:** Day $4800 (+$100). **Est 1891.** Nonprofit. Roman Catholic. Sem (Sept-June). **Assoc** MSA. French, Spanish and computer science are introduced to children at the kindergarten level at MSJA. An intramural and interscholastic sports program is available, and religion is an integral aspect of school life.

NARDIN ACADEMY
Day Boys Gr PS-8, Girls PS-12

Buffalo, NY 14222. 135 Cleveland Ave.
Tel: 716-881-6262. Fax: 716-881-4190.
www.nardin.org E-mail: info@nardin.org

Sr. Barbara Wentworth, DHM, Pres. BA, Maryville College, MA, Loyola Univ (LA). Donna Seymour, Adm.

Col Prep. AP—Eng Fr Lat Span Calc Bio Chem Eur_Hist US_Hist US_Govt & Pol Art_Hist. **Feat**—Creative_Writing Stats Environ_Sci Marine_Biol/Sci Comp_Sci Econ Relig Drawing Photog Theater Music_Theory Journ Public_Speak. **Supp**—Rem_Read Rev Tut. **Adm (Gr PS-12):** 199/yr. **Enr 973.** B 214. G 759. Elem 482. Sec 491. Wh 94%. Hisp 1%. Blk 2%. Asian 2%. Other 1%. **Fac 105.** M 8/3. F 76/18. Adv deg: 55%. **Grad '04—112.** Col—112. **Tui '04-'05:** Day $6420-6775 (+$35-300). Aid: Merit 61 ($87,000). Need 8 ($37,450). Work prgm 98 ($80,888). **Summer:** PS. Rec. 2 wks. **Est 1857.** Nonprofit. Roman Catholic. Quar (Sept-June). **Assoc** MSA. The academy comprises three divisions: a coed Montessori preschool (occupying a separate campus at 700 W. Ferry St., 14222), a coed elementary school (grades 1-8) and an all-girls high school. All pupils, regardless of religious orientation, take compulsory religious studies courses each year. The high school curriculum features AP courses, as well as both required and elective computer classes.

ST. JOSEPH'S COLLEGIATE INSTITUTE
Day Boys Gr 9-12

Buffalo, NY 14223. 845 Kenmore Ave.
Tel: 716-874-4024. Fax: 716-874-4956.
www.sjci.com E-mail: sjci@sjci.com

Br. William Batt, FSC, Pres. Robert T. Scott, Prin. BA, Marist College, MA, Canisius College. John Kenny, Adm.

Col Prep. AP—Eng Fr Ger Span Calc Bio Chem Eur_Hist US_Hist US_Govt & Pol Studio_Art. **Feat**—Programming Philos Relig Drama Music. **Supp**—Tut. **Adm:** 235/yr. Appl due: Rolling. **Enr 852.** B 852. Sec 852. Wh 96%. Hisp 1%. Blk 2%. Asian 1%. Avg class size: 26. **Fac 55.** M 47/3. F 4/1. **Grad '04—191.** Col—186. Alum 7000. **Tui '03-'04:** Day $6610 (+$290). **Est 1861.** Nonprofit. Roman Catholic. Sem (Sept-June). **Assoc** MSA. Sponsored by the De La Salle Christian Brothers, St. Joseph's offers four levels of courses: Advanced Placement, honors, New York State board of regents and basic. The academic program features several electives, such as creative arts, music, theater and environmental science. Intramural and competitive sports round out the school day, and extracurricular activities include publications, student council, and music and academic clubs.

GREEN MEADOW WALDORF SCHOOL
Day Coed Gr PS-12

Chestnut Ridge, NY 10977. 307 Hungry Hollow Rd.
Tel: 845-356-2514. Fax: 845-356-2921.
www.gmws.org E-mail: info@gmws.org

Kay Hoffman, Admin. Shirley Aigen, Adm.

Gen Acad. Feat—Fr Ger Span Computers Studio_Art Music. **Supp**—ESL. **Adm:** 30/yr. **Enr 400.** Elem 300. Sec 100. Wh 91%. Hisp 3%. Blk 1%. Asian 5%. Avg class size: 30. **Fac 50. Grad '04—21.** Col—20. Alum 139. **Tui '04-'05:** Day $9895-14,135. **Est 1950.** Nonprofit. Sem (Sept-June). The elementary program combines required handwork, woodworking, French, German, chorus and orchestra classes with humanities and science course work. The high school program features advanced electives in literature, math and science. All disciplines emphasize artistic elements. Many high school students perform community service during the school day.

ST. AGNES HIGH SCHOOL   Day Girls Gr 9-12
College Point, NY 11356. 13-20 124th St.
Tel: 718-353-6276. Fax: 718-353-6068.
www.stagneshs.org   E-mail: jmartin@stagneshs.org
Sr. Joan Martin, OP, Prin. BSEd, St John's Univ, MSEd, Fordham Univ.

Col Prep. Gen Acad. AP—Eng Span US_Hist. **Feat**—British_Lit Fr Ecol Computers Econ Law Psych Relig Drawing Studio_Art Chorus Music_Hist. **Supp**—Dev_Read ESL Rem_Math. **Adm:** 129/yr. Appl due: Feb. Accepted: 15%. **Tests** IQ SSAT. **Enr 500.** G 500. Sec 500. Wh 53%. Hisp 32%. Blk 9%. Asian 6%. Avg class size: 14. Uniform. **Fac 34.** M 6. F 28. Adv deg: 100%. **Grad '04—87.** Col—85. Alum 7100. **Tui '04-'05:** Day $6200. Aid: Merit 15 ($119,000). **Est 1908.** Nonprofit. Roman Catholic. Sem (Sept-June). Sponsored by the Sisters of St. Dominic, St. Agnes is a traditional girls' Catholic school that emphasizes college preparation. Computer technology is an integral aspect of the curriculum. In addition to honors classes, academically talented students may participate in the school's ACE Program, which provides the opportunity for enriched, advanced study in the major disciplines and leads to Advanced Placement and college-credit course work.

THE BROOKWOOD SCHOOL   Day Coed Gr PS-6
Cooperstown, NY 13326. 687 County Hwy 59.
Tel: 607-547-4060. Fax: 607-547-2835.
www.dmcom.net/brookwood   E-mail: brookwood@stny.rr.com
Amy Williams, Dir. BA, MA, State Univ of New York-Oneonta.

Gen Acad. Feat—Fr Computers Studio_Art Music. **Adm:** 36/yr. Appl due: May. Accepted: 95%. **Enr 75.** B 38. G 37 Elem 75. Wh 94%. Hisp 2%. Blk 2%. Asian 2%. Avg class size: 15. **Fac 7.** F 5/2. Wh 100%. Adv deg: 42%. **Grad '04—4.** **Tui '04-'05:** Day $3600 (+$100). Aid: Need 6 ($8500). **Summer:** Enrich Rec. Tui Day $110/wk. 11 wks. **Est 1981.** Nonprofit. Sem (Sept-June). Preschoolers and kindergartners at this Montessori school gain an introduction to children's literature and natural science. In grades 1 and 2, Brookwood focuses on reading, mathematics and basic concepts in physical science. Older pupils (grades 3-6) address such social studies topics as mythology, government and geography. Students may also explore bookmaking, origami and other art forms.

LAUREL HILL SCHOOL
Day Coed Gr PS-8
East Setauket, NY 11733. 201 Old Town Rd.
Tel: 631-751-1154. Fax: 631-751-2421.
www.laurelhillschool.org   E-mail: info@laurelhillschool.org

Robert H. Stark, Head. BA, New York Univ, MA, City Univ of New York. Rosemary Marturano, Adm.

Pre-Prep. Gen Acad. Feat—Lib_Skills Fr Lat Span Computers Drama Music. **Supp**—Rem_Math Rem_Read Tut. **Adm:** Appl due: Feb. **Enr 450.** B 218. G 232. Elem 450. Avg class size: 16. Uniform. **Fac 60.** M 3. F 34/23. **Grad '04—18.** Prep—12. **Tui '04-'05:** Day $8050-10,050. **Est 1973.** Inc. Tri (Sept-June). Laurel Hill's structured preschool (ages 2-4) and elementary program includes small classes and independent learning opportunities. The school assigns an educational assistant to each class, and specialists teach such subjects as computers, foreign language and physical education. LHS employs varying teaching methods to address different learning styles, with students encouraged to progress at an appropriate pace. The computer lab enables boys and girls to develop computer skills through multimedia projects and Web design workshops.

CATHEDRAL PREPARATORY SEMINARY
Day Boys Gr 9-12
Elmhurst, NY 11373. 56-25 92nd St.
Tel: 718-592-6800. Fax: 718-592-5574.
www.cathedralprepseminary.com

Rev. Joseph P. Calise, Prin. BA, Cathedral College of the Immaculate Conception, STB, Pontificia Universita Gregoriana (Italy). Daniel O'Keefe, Adm.

Col Prep. AP—Eng Bio US_Hist US_Govt & Pol. **Feat**—Creative_Writing Fr Lat Span Environ_Bio Comp_Sci Econ Relig Film Studio_Art Music. **Supp**—Rev Tut. **Adm:** 58/yr. Accepted: 62%. **Tests** TACHS. **Enr 181.** B 181. Sec 181. Wh 66%. Hisp 19%. Blk 4%. Am Ind 1%. Asian 8%. Other 2%. Avg class size: 20. **Fac 20.** M 16. F 4. Wh 85%. Hisp 15%. Adv deg: 45%. **Grad '04—36.** Col—34. Avg SAT: 1000. Alum 500. **Tui '04-'05:** Day $5500 (+$400-700). Aid: Merit 26 ($104,950). Need 4 ($10,375). **Summer:** Acad Enrich Rec. Tui Day $150. 4 wks. **Est 1914.** Nonprofit. Roman Catholic. Sem (Sept-June). Cathedral Prep provides a college preparatory curriculum, including Advanced Placement classes and senior electives, for those considering the priesthood. An extensive intramural program is offered after school, in addition to varsity and junior varsity sports teams and a range of organizations.

ST. FRANCIS PREPARATORY SCHOOL
Day Coed Gr 9-12
Fresh Meadows, NY 11365. 6100 Francis Lewis Blvd.
Tel: 718-423-8810. Fax: 718-224-2108.
www.stfrancisprep.org   E-mail: 21stcentury@stfrancisprep.org

Br. Leonard Conway, OSF, Prin. BS, St Francis College, MS, Pratt Institute. Theodore Jahn, Adm.

Col Prep. AP—Eng Span Calc Bio Chem Physics US_Hist Psych Art_Hist Studio_Art Music_Theory. **Feat**—Shakespeare Fr Ger Ital Stats Anat & Physiol Programming Robotics Econ Sociol Relig World_Relig Music Music_Hist Accounting Bus. **Supp**—Rev Tut. **Adm:** 752/yr. Appl due: Feb. Accepted: 50%. **Enr 2728.** B

1328. G 1400. Sec 2728. Wh 56%. Hisp 18%. Blk 12%. Asian 14%. Avg class size: 35. Uniform. **Fac 150.** M 73/2. F 74/1. Wh 96%. Hisp 2%. Blk 1%. Asian 1%. Adv deg: 86%. **Grad '04—640.** Col—635. Avg SAT: 1061. Alum 24,000. **Tui '04-'05:** Day $5700 (+$250). Aid: Merit 211 ($855,752). Need 120 ($85,850). **Summer:** Rem. Tui Day $260/crse. 6 wks. **Est 1858.** Nonprofit. Roman Catholic. Quar (Sept-June). **Assoc** MSA. Founded by the Franciscan Brothers, the school conducts a college preparatory program with a variety of electives. St. Francis provides honors and Advanced Placement courses in the major disciplines, and qualified pupils may pursue an advanced science track. A junior-year elective offering allows students to perform community service at local nursing homes, shelters and hospitals.

WALDORF SCHOOL OF GARDEN CITY — Day Coed Gr PS-12
Garden City, NY 11530. Cambridge Ave.
Tel: 516-742-3434. Fax: 516-742-3457.
www.waldorfgarden.org   E-mail: walshs@waldorfgarden.org
   Roxanne Murphy, Fac Co-Chair. Patricia Foster, Fac Co-Chair. Sara Walsh, Adm.

   Col Prep. Feat—Fr Ger Lat Studio_Art Drama Music. **Supp**—Tut. **Adm (Gr PS-11):** 68/yr. Appl due: Rolling. Accepted: 43%. Yield: 92%. **Tests** SSAT. **Enr 368.** B 164. G 204. Elem 272. Sec 96. Wh 66%. Hisp 4%. Blk 17%. Asian 12%. Other 1%. Avg class size: 29. **Fac 51.** M 6/6. F 25/14. Wh 95%. Hisp 2%. Blk 2%. Asian 1%. Adv deg: 33%. **Grad '04—25.** Col—24. Avg SAT: 1240. Alum 866. **Tui '04-'05:** Day $12,250-14,250 (+$200). Aid: Merit 9 ($52,051). Need 134 ($754,877). **Summer:** Gr PS-7. Enrich Rec. 6 wks. **Est 1947.** Nonprofit. Quar (Sept-June). Basing its program on the educational philosophy of Dr. Rudolf Steiner, the school integrates the fine and performing arts into its liberal arts curriculum. A varied foreign language program is part of the college preparatory program: French and German classes begin in grade 1 and continue through high school, while Latin is compulsory in grades 7 and 8. Enrollment is from many communities in Nassau and Queens counties.

HAWTHORNE VALLEY SCHOOL — Day Coed Gr PS-12
Ghent, NY 12075. 330 Rte 21C.
Tel: 518-672-7092. Fax: 518-672-0181.
www.hawthornevalleyschool.org   E-mail: hawthornevalley@taconic.net
   Candace Bachrach, Fac Chair. BA, Hollins Univ. Regine Shemroske, Adm.

   Col Prep. Gen Acad. Feat—Shakespeare Russ_Lit Fr Ger Span Botany Ecol Econ Drama. **Supp**—Rem_Math Rem_Read Tut. **Adm:** 40/yr. Appl due: Rolling. Accepted: 90%. **Enr 315.** Wh 95%. Hisp 3%. Blk 2%. Avg class size: 20. **Fac 29.** M 12. F 17. Wh 98%. Hisp 2%. Adv deg: 62%. **Grad '04—26.** Col—24. Avg SAT: 1000. Alum 430. **Tui '02-'03:** Day $8800 (+$500). Aid: Need 102 ($275,755). **Est 1973.** Nonprofit. Tri (Sept-June). This Waldorf school's early childhood program consists of three mixed-age kindergartens that focus on creative, free play. Boys and girls in the elementary school stay with the same class teacher from grade 1 through grade 8, with specialty instructors teaching supplementary courses. During the high school years (grades 9-12), academics revolve around the main lesson, a two-hour, concentrated period at the start of the school day in one of the core subjects. By special arrangement, students in grades 9-12 may board with a local family.

GREEN VALE SCHOOL

Day Coed Gr PS-9

Glen Head, NY 11545. 250 Valentine's Ln.
Tel: 516-621-2420. Fax: 516-621-1317.
www.greenvaleschool.org E-mail: info@greenvaleschool.org
  Stephen H. Watters, Head. BA, Denison Univ, MAT, Univ of Massachusetts-Amherst. Anne B. Watters, Adm.

  Pre-Prep. Feat—Fr Lat Span Computers Studio_Art Chorus Music Woodworking. **Supp**—Dev_Read Rem_Math Rem_Read Rev Tut. **Adm:** 72/yr. Appl due: Rolling. Accepted: 65%. **Enr 475.** Wh 91%. Hisp 1%. Blk 7%. Asian 1%. Avg class size: 14. **Fac 70.** M 15. F 55. Adv deg: 62%. **Grad '04**—30. Prep—30. Alum 2400. **Tui '04-'05:** Day $8000-17,000 (+$1000). **Est 1923.** Nonprofit. Tri (Sept-June). Green Vale, which provides a traditional liberal arts-based education, is divided into three divisions: the early childhood department (PS-K), the lower school (grades 1-5) and the upper school (grades 6-9). The arts and computer education are integral components of the school's curriculum, and students participate in interscholastic sports starting in grade 5.

HOUGHTON ACADEMY

Bdg Coed Gr 9-PG
Day Coed 7-12

Houghton, NY 14744. 9790 Thayer St.
Tel: 585-567-8115. Fax: 585-567-8048.
www.houghtonacademy.org E-mail: admissions@houghtonacademy.org
  Philip G. Stockin, Head. BA, Houghton College, MA, Grace Seminary. Ronald J. Bradbury, Adm.

  Col Prep. Feat—Fr Span Environ_Sci Econ Geog Govt Bible Studio_Art Band Chorus Music_Theory Accounting Driver_Ed Health. **Supp**—ESL Tut. **Adm:** 65/yr. Appl due: Rolling. Accepted: 70%. Yield: 90%. **Tests** CEEB SSAT TOEFL. **Enr 214.** Elem 140. Sec 70. PG 4. Wh 71%. Hisp 2%. Blk 3%. Asian 24%. Avg class size: 17. **Fac 24.** M 14. F 7/3. Wh 100%. Adv deg: 37%. In Dorms 5. **Grad '04**—48. Col—45. Avg SAT: 1150. Alum 1475. **Tui '04-'05:** Bdg $17,710. Day $5935. **Est 1883.** Nonprofit. Wesleyan. Sem (Sept-June). **Assoc** MSA. Each student at the academy has a daily work job, and dual-credit college courses are offered to upperclassmen at nearby Houghton College. Sports include soccer, basketball, golf, volleyball, baseball, softball and cross-country. Other activities include publications, music, art and interest clubs.

LONG ISLAND SCHOOL FOR THE GIFTED

Day Coed Gr K-9

Huntington Station, NY 11746. 165 Pidgeon Hill Rd.
Tel: 631-423-3557. Fax: 631-423-4368.
www.lisg.org E-mail: lisgifted@aol.com
  Roberta Tropper, Prin. Carol Yilmaz, Dir.

  Pre-Prep. Feat—Fr Span Computers Global_Stud Studio_Art Music Study_Skills. **Adm:** 43/yr. Appl due: Rolling. **Tests** IQ. **Enr 287.** B 145. G 142. Elem 268. Sec 19. Wh 68%. Hisp 4%. Blk 5%. Asian 23%. Avg class size: 16. **Fac 34.** M 3. F 29/2. Adv deg: 94%. **Grad '04**—18. Alum 52. **Tui '04-'05:** Day $8700-9800 (+$390). **Est 1980.** Nonprofit. Tri (Sept-June). LISG's curriculum is individualized for the gifted student, with emphasis on creative thinking, problem solving and acceleration. Candidates for admission should be working at least two years beyond grade level.

THE MARY LOUIS ACADEMY
Day Girls Gr 9-12
Jamaica Estates, NY 11432. 176-21 Wexford Ter.
Tel: 718-297-2120. Fax: 718-739-0037.
www.tmla.org   E-mail: admissions@tmla.org
Sr. Kathleen McKinney, CSJ, Prin. BA, St Joseph's College, MS, Adelphi Univ, EdD, St John's Univ. Sr. Filippa Luciano, CSJ, Adm.

Col Prep. AP—Eng Span Calc Bio Chem Physics Eur_Hist US_Hist Studio_Art. **Feat**—Fr Ital Lat Environ_Sci Computers Econ Psych Sociol World_Relig Music Music_Theory Driver_Ed. **Supp**—Rev Tut. **Adm (Gr 9-11):** 275/yr. Appl due: Dec. Accepted: 54%. Yield: 50%. **Tests** TACHS. **Enr 1037.** G 1037. Sec 1037. Wh 40%. Hisp 22%. Blk 15%. Asian 12%. Other 11%. Avg class size: 28. Uniform. **Fac 78.** M 15/1. F 61/1. Wh 92%. Hisp 4%. Asian 4%. Adv deg: 70%. **Grad '04—259.** Col—259. Avg SAT: 1062. Alum 11,000. **Tui '04-'05:** Day $5700 (+$800). Aid: Merit 148 ($332,726). Need 31 ($44,950). **Summer:** Enrich. Tui Day $125/crse. 2 wks. **Est 1936.** Nonprofit. Roman Catholic. Tri (Sept-June). **Assoc** MSA. Established by the Sisters of Saint Joseph, Brentwood, the academy enables seniors to earn college credit through an affiliation with St. John's University. Sequences are offered in art, languages, mathematics, music and science. Community service is a required element of the religious studies curriculum. Extracurricular activities include student government, athletics, orchestra, chorus, forensics, theater, publications and interest clubs.

NATIONAL SPORTS ACADEMY
Coed Gr 8-PG
Bdg & Day
Lake Placid, NY 12946. 12 Lake Placid Club Dr.
Tel: 518-523-3460. Fax: 518-523-3488.
www.nationalsportsacademy.com
E-mail: admissions@nationalsportsacademy.com
David Wenn, Head. BA, State Univ of New York-Cortland. Bill Ward, Adm.

Col Prep. Sports (Canoe/Kayak & Winter). AP—Eng Bio US_Hist. **Feat**—Fr Span Sociol. **Supp**—LD Tut. **Adm:** 32/yr. Appl due: Mar. Accepted: 70%. **Tests** SSAT. **Enr 86.** B 32/19. G 24/11. Sec 81. PG 5. Wh 93%. Hisp 2%. Blk 2%. Am Ind 2%. Asian 1%. Avg class size: 8. **Fac 16.** M 8. F 8. Adv deg: 43%. In Dorms 7. **Grad '04—42.** Col—40. Avg SAT: 1061. Alum 412. **Tui '03-'04:** Bdg $21,400 (+$1000-5750). Day $9975 (+$1000-5750). **Est 1979.** Nonprofit. Sem (Sept-June). NSA accepts student-athletes who are training and competing in such Olympic winter sports as Alpine, Nordic and freestyle skiing; ski jumping; snowboarding; biathlon; luge; figure and speed skating; and ice hockey. In addition, the academy also provides training in one Olympic summer sport: canoeing/kayaking. Seven- and nine-month programs are available.

FRENCH-AMERICAN SCHOOL OF NEW YORK
Day Coed Gr PS-10

Larchmont, NY 10538. 111 Larchmont Ave.
Tel: 914-834-3002. Fax: 914-698-8696.
www.fasny.org   E-mail: aagopian@fasny.org
   Robert M. Leonhardt, Head. Antoine Agopian, Adm.

   Gen Acad. Bilingual. Feat—Ger Lat Span Computers Econ Studio_Art Music Public_Speak. **Supp**—ESL Rev Tut. **Adm:** 136/yr. Appl due: Rolling. **Enr 599.** B 279. G 320. Elem 550. Sec 49. Wh 83%. Hisp 3%. Blk 5%. Asian 4%. Other 5%. Avg class size: 19. **Fac 80.** M 11. F 52/17. Wh 88%. Blk 10%. Asian 1%. Other 1%. Adv deg: 66%. **Grad '04—27. Tui '05-'06:** Day $14,770-19,750 (+$700). Aid: Need 41 ($312,000). **Est 1980.** Nonprofit. Tri (Sept-June). Offering bilingual instruction (French and English), FAS offers a dual curriculum that emphasizes critical-thinking skills and problem solving. The preschool, which focuses on verbal skills, books, art and music, is conducted in both languages. In the upper and lower schools (grades 1-10), math is taught in French, while science and social studies instruction is in English. Student clubs, musical and theatrical productions, interscholastic sports and school trips round out the program.

SAINT GREGORY'S SCHOOL
Day Boys Gr PS-8, Girls PS-K

Loudonville, NY 12211. 121 Old Niskayuna Rd.
Tel: 518-785-6621. Fax: 518-782-1364.
www.saintgregorysschool.org   E-mail: hcharbonneau@saintgregorysschool.org
   Francis X. Foley, Jr., Head. AB, John Carroll Univ, MA Fairfield Univ. Howard J. Charbonneau, Jr., Adm.

   Pre-Prep. Gen Acad. Feat—Eng Fr Lat Span Computers Relig Music. **Adm:** 32/yr. Appl due: Rolling. **Enr 200.** B 185/15. Elem 200. Wh 89%. Blk 6%. Asian 5%. Avg class size: 17. Uniform. **Fac 27.** Adv deg: 48%. **Grad '04—16.** Alum 609. **Tui '04-'05:** Day $5925-9425 (+$150-250). **Summer:** Rec. 2-6 wks. **Est 1962.** Nonprofit. Roman Catholic. Tri (Sept-June). Predominantly a boys' school, Saint Gregory's maintains a structured learning program that provides opportunities for acceleration. Well-developed computer, physical science and life science programs are integral to the curriculum. French instruction begins in prekindergarten, Spanish and Latin in grade 7. The French program culminates in a four-day learning experience in Quebec, Canada.

MARTIN LUTHER HIGH SCHOOL
Day Coed Gr 9-12

Maspeth, NY 11378. 60-02 Maspeth Ave, PO Box 780017.
Tel: 718-894-4000. Fax: 718-894-1469.
E-mail: mlutherhs@aol.com
   Ben Herbrich, Exec Dir. BS, Concordia Teachers College, MA, New York Univ. Elizabeth Crowe, Prin.

   Col Prep. Gen Acad. Feat—Fr Ger Span Computers Psych Child_Dev Adolescent_Dev Theol Photog Studio_Art Music Accounting Bus. **Supp**—Makeup Tut. **Adm:** 123/yr. Appl due: Rolling. Accepted: 53%. Yield: 53%. **Enr 419.** B 192. G 227. Sec 419. Wh 54%. Hisp 18%. Blk 20%. Asian 8%. Avg class size: 25. Uniform. **Fac 29.** M 11/2. F 13/3. Wh 70%. Hisp 10%. Blk 10%. Asian 10%. Adv deg: 34%.

NY   *Concise School Listings*   *834*

Grad '04—99. Col—88. Alum 3750. **Tui '04-'05:** Day $6000 (+$500). Aid: Merit 64 ($104,600). Need 108 ($81,000). **Summer:** Acad Rev Rem. Driver Ed. Tui Day $95-675. 6 wks. **Est 1960.** Nonprofit. Lutheran. Quar (Sept-June). **Assoc** MSA. In addition to college preparatory academics, students participate in such activities as publications, choir, drama, computer club and interest clubs. Sports include baseball, softball, basketball, soccer, track, cross-country, wrestling, tennis and volleyball. Under a special program with St. John's and Adelphi universities, seniors may take college-credit courses in English, history, science and math.

GRACE DAY SCHOOL   **Day Coed Gr PS-8**
Massapequa, NY 11758. 23 Cedar Shore Dr.
Tel: 516-798-1122. Fax: 516-799-0711.
www.gracedayschool.org   E-mail: info@gracedayschool.org
     Robert J. Montheard, Head. BA, MEd. Patricia Quinto, Adm.

     Pre-Prep. Feat—Fr Computers Relig. **Adm:** 84/yr. Appl due: Rolling. Accepted: 65%. **Enr 400.** B 200. G 200. Elem 400. Wh 94%. Hisp 1%. Blk 5%. Avg class size: 15. Uniform. **Fac 41.** M 2/2. F 15/22. Wh 100%. Adv deg: 36%. **Grad '04—18.** Alum 588. **Tui '04-'05:** Day $7475-7775. **Summer:** Rec. Tui Day $515/2-wk ses. 6 wks. **Est 1955.** Nonprofit. Episcopal. Tri (Sept-June). The school provides a Christian education for students who are at or above grade level. Basic skills are taught, and problem-solving activities and creative opportunities are part of the curriculum.

CHAMINADE HIGH SCHOOL   **Day Boys Gr 9-12**
Mineola, NY 11501. 340 Jackson Ave.
Tel: 516-742-5555. Fax: 516-742-1989.
www.chaminade-hs.org   E-mail: admissions@chaminade-hs.org
     Rev. James C. Williams, SM, Pres. BS, Manhattan College, MS, Adelphi Univ, MDiv, St Joseph's Seminary, STB, St Thomas Aquinas College. Br. Joseph D. Belizzi, SM, Prin. BA, St John's Univ, MA, New York Univ.

     Col Prep. Feat—Fr Ger Lat Span Computers Relig Studio_Art Music. **Adm (Gr 9):** 450/yr. Appl due: Dec. **Tests** TACHS. **Enr 1600.** B 1600. Sec 1600. Wh 93%. Hisp 3%. Blk 2%. Asian 2%. Uniform. **Fac 74.** M 65/3. F 6. Adv deg: 85%. **Grad '04—388.** Col—388. Alum 20,000. **Tui '04-'05:** Day $5615 (+$50). Aid: Merit 37 ($36,750). Need 39 ($91,025). Work prgm 75 ($40,000). **Est 1930.** Nonprofit. Roman Catholic. Tri (Sept-June). **Assoc** MSA. Conducted by Marianist priests and brothers, basic intellectual disciplines, as well as cocurricular and extracurricular programs, are offered. College courses are available to seniors through the C. W. Post Center of Long Island University.

SOUNDVIEW PREPARATORY SCHOOL   **Day Coed Gr 6-12**
Mount Kisco, NY 10549. 272 N Bedford Rd.
Tel: 914-242-9693. Fax: 914-242-9658.
www.soundviewprep.org   E-mail: info@soundviewprep.org
     W. Glyn Hearn, Head. BA, MA, Univ of Texas-Austin. Mary E. Ivanyi, Adm.

     Col Prep. AP—Eng Fr Span Calc US_Hist. **Feat**—British_Lit Ital Lat Environ_

Sci Econ Psych Philos Fine_Arts Photog Studio_Art Drama Music Debate Study_ Skills. **Adm (Gr 6-11):** 23/yr. Appl due: Rolling. Accepted: 40%. Yield: 95%. **Tests** ISEE. **Enr 80.** B 50. G 30. Elem 21. Sec 59. Wh 88%. Hisp 2%. Blk 10%. Avg class size: 8. **Fac 26.** M 6. F 20. Wh 92%. Hisp 8%. **Grad '04—10.** Col—10. Avg SAT: 1230. **Tui '04-'05:** Day $24,000 (+$1350). Aid: Need 13 ($218,000). **Summer:** Acad Enrich. Tui Day $900/crse. 6 wks. **Est 1989.** Nonprofit. Sem (Sept-June). Soundview's college preparatory curriculum includes both honors and Advanced Placement courses. A wide range of electives includes art, computer programming, debate, drama and psychology, among others. Students are required to earn one credit of community service each school year.

IONA PREPARATORY SCHOOL

Day Boys Gr 9-12

New Rochelle, NY 10804. 255 Wilmot Rd.
Tel: 914-632-0714. Fax: 914-632-9760.
www.ionaprep.org E-mail: admissions@ionapre.org

Br. Gerard Gaffney, Pres. Anthony Baxter, Head. BA, Villanova Univ, MS, Iona College. Ann Slocum, Adm.

Col Prep. AP—Eng Lat Span Calc Bio Chem Physics US_Hist Psych US_Govt & Pol. **Feat**—Fr Ital Astron Computers Relig Studio_Art Music. **Supp**—Tut. **Adm:** 217/yr. Appl due: Mar. Accepted: 60%. **Tests** HSPT ISEE SSAT. **Enr 775.** B 775. Sec 775. Wh 81%. Hisp 8%. Blk 6%. Am Ind 1%. Asian 4%. Avg class size: 26. Uniform. **Fac 60.** M 36/1. F 22/1. Wh 94%. Hisp 2%. Blk 2%. Asian 2%. Adv deg: 83%. **Grad '04—180.** Col—180. Avg SAT: 1200. Alum 9000. **Tui '02-'03:** Day $8775 (+$100). Aid: Merit 60 ($125,000). Need 100 ($250,000). **Est 1916.** Nonprofit. Roman Catholic. Sem (Sept-June). **Assoc** MSA. This independent Catholic school's college preparatory curriculum offers courses at four different levels: Regents, honors, accelerated and Advanced Placement. Students complete four-year course requirements in English, math, science, social studies; the core curriculum also includes foreign language, computer, fine arts and health classes. In addition, Iona Prep features a range of electives for seniors as a supplement to compulsory course work. Extracurriculars include a variety of clubs and activities, competitive athletics, intramural sports, and a speech and debate team.

URSULINE SCHOOL

Day Girls Gr 6-12

New Rochelle, NY 10804. 1354 North Ave.
Tel: 914-636-3950. Fax: 914-636-3949.
www.ursuline.pvt.k12.ny.us E-mail: admin@ursuline.pvt.k12.ny.us

Sr. Jean Baptiste Nicholson, OSU, Pres. BA, College of New Rochelle, MA, Catholic Univ of America.

Col Prep. AP—Eng Fr Lat Span Calc Bio Physics Eur_Hist US_Hist Studio_ Art. **Feat**—Greek Ital Stats Computers Relig Music Health Study_Skills. **Supp**— Dev_Read Rev Tut. **Adm:** 174/yr. Accepted: 70%. Yield: 40%. **Tests** HSPT ISEE TACHS. **Enr 811.** G 811. Elem 147. Sec 664. Wh 81%. Hisp 4%. Blk 10%. Asian 5%. Avg class size: 22. Uniform. **Fac 84.** M 8/2. F 70/4. Wh 98%. Blk 2%. Adv deg: 85%. **Grad '04—145.** Col—145. Avg SAT: 1175. Alum 4500. **Tui '04-'05:** Day $10,350 (+$500). Aid: Merit 157 ($430,225). Need 65 ($165,000). **Est 1897.** Nonprofit. Roman Catholic. Quar (Sept-June). **Assoc** MSA. Honors and Advanced Placement courses are available for talented students. Classes are small, and pupils use laptop computers throughout the curriculum. Various athletic and extracurricular activities round out the program.

ABRAHAM JOSHUA HESCHEL SCHOOL Day Coed Gr PS-12
New York, NY 10024. 270 W 89th St.
Tel: 212-595-7087. Fax: 212-595-7252.
www.heschel.org E-mail: info@heschel.org
Roanna Shorofsky, Head. BA, City Univ of New York. Marsha Feris, Adm.

Gen Acad. Feat—Fr Hebrew Lat Span Programming Bible Relig Theol Studio_Art Theater_Arts Music Music_Hist Journ. **Supp**—ESL Rem_Math Rem_Read. **Adm:** 102/yr. Appl due: Dec. **Tests** CTP_4 ISEE. **Enr 615.** B 279. G 336. Elem 615. Sec 471. PG 144. Wh 98%. Hisp 1%. Blk 1%. Avg class size: 23. **Fac 108.** M 16/4. F 75/13. **Tui '03-'04:** Day $14,200-22,200 (+$375-600). **Est 1983.** Nonprofit. Jewish. (Sept-June). Named for Rabbi Heschel, a prominent scholar, philosopher and theologian, the school integrates Jewish tradition and history into its secular curriculum. Students come from a variety of Jewish backgrounds. The middle school is located at 314 W. 91st St., while the high school division, which opened in 2002, operates at 20 W. End Ave., 10023.

ALEXANDER ROBERTSON SCHOOL Day Coed Gr K-5
New York, NY 10025. 3 W 95th St.
Tel: 212-663-6441. Fax: 212-663-1571.
www.alexanderrobertson.com E-mail: admissions@alexanderrobertson.com
Rev. Leslie Merlin, Head. BA, Wagner College, MDiv, Princeton Theological Seminary. Barbara P. Winn, Adm.

Gen Acad. Feat—Writing Fr Computers Studio_Art Music Music_Theory. **Supp**—Tut. **Adm:** 22/yr. Appl due: Dec. Accepted: 70%. **Tests** CTP_4. **Enr 68.** B 44. G 24. Elem 68. Avg class size: 11. Uniform. **Fac 12.** M /2. F 7/3. Wh 92%. Blk 4%. Am Ind 4%. Adv deg: 66%. **Grad '04—6. Tui '04-'05:** Day $13,500 (+$250). Aid: Need 43 ($160,000). **Est 1789.** Nonprofit. Presbyterian. Quar (Sept-June). This traditional and structured elementary school, which serves a diverse student body, includes course work in music, French, art, computer and physical education. Small classes enable children to receive individualized attention. An after-school program is available.

THE CAEDMON SCHOOL Day Coed Gr PS-5
New York, NY 10021. 416 E 80th St.
Tel: 212-879-2296. Fax: 212-879-0627.
www.caedmonschool.org E-mail: admissions@caedmonschool.org
Carol Gose De Vine, Head. BA, Albertus Magnus College, MA, EdM, Columbia Univ. Erica A. Lowenfels, Adm.

Pre-Prep. Feat—Lib_Skills Writing Span Computers Art_Hist Studio_Art Music Yoga. **Supp**—Rem_Math Rem_Read Rev Tut. **Adm:** 50/yr. Appl due: Nov. **Tests** CTP_4 IQ ISEE. **Enr 200.** B 100. G 100. Elem 200. Wh 69%. Hisp 9%. Blk 9%. Asian 13%. Avg class size: 17. **Fac 34.** M 3. F 28/3. Wh 88%. Hisp 3%. Blk 9%. Adv deg: 44%. **Grad '04—12.** Prep—12. Alum 2407. **Tui '04-'05:** Day

$15,950-19,500. Aid: Need 28 ($388,175). **Est 1962.** Nonprofit. Sem (Sept-June). Caedmon offers a Montessori-based curriculum in the early program (through age 4). Throughout the elementary program, the school combines elements of Montessori with a varied curriculum that features instruction by specialists in many areas. Field trips throughout the city, an instrumental music program, after-school classes and clubs, and school-wide theatrical productions provide further enrichment.

THE CHILDREN'S STOREFRONT SCHOOL   Day Coed Gr PS-8
New York, NY 10035. 70 E 129th St.
Tel: 212-427-7900. Fax: 212-348-2988.
www.thechildrensstorefront.org   E-mail: danielbrewer@thechildrensstorefront.org
    Kathy Egmont, Head. BA, Barrington College, MEd, Boston Univ.
    Pre-Prep. Feat—Computers Fine_Arts. **Adm:** 25/yr. Appl due: Rolling. Accepted: 2%. **Enr 176.** B 78. G 98. Elem 176. Hisp 5%. Blk 95%. Other 5%. Avg class size: 17. **Fac 25.** M 4/3. F 17/1. Wh 45%. Hisp 5%. Blk 45%. Other 5%. Adv deg: 28%. **Grad '04—15.** Prep—10. **Tui '04-'05:** Day $0. **Est 1966.** Nonprofit. (Sept-June). Providing tuition-free schooling for children from Harlem, Storefront offers a Montessori-based preschool that emphasizes language and vocabulary skills. In the lower school (grades 1-4), students focus on the basic skills of English and math and begin their study of history, science, social studies and the arts. Upper schoolers (grades 5-8) study more concentrated topics in science and literature, while also exploring computers and the fine arts.

CORLEARS SCHOOL   Day Coed Gr PS-4
New York, NY 10011. 324 W 15th St.
Tel: 212-741-2800. Fax: 212-807-1550.
www.corlearsschool.org   E-mail: office@corlearsschool.org
    Thya Merz, Head. BA, Norwich Univ, MS, Johns Hopkins Univ. Rorry Romeo, Adm.
    Pre-Prep. Feat—Span Studio_Art Music Movement. **Supp**—Dev_Read. **Adm:** 32/yr. Appl due: Dec. Accepted: 55%. Yield: 41%. **Enr 123.** B 70. G 53. Elem 123. Wh 71%. Hisp 7%. Blk 10%. Asian 1%. Other 11%. Avg class size: 17. **Fac 24.** M 2/3. F 13/6. Wh 75%. Hisp 8%. Blk 13%. Other 4%. Adv deg: 41%. **Grad '04—16.** Alum 232. **Tui '04-'05:** Day $17,564-19,886 (+$600). Aid: Need 39 ($478,694). **Est 1968.** Nonprofit. (Sept-June). Situated in two townhouses, Corlears offers special courses in science, art, movement, Spanish, music and physical education.

DOMINICAN ACADEMY   Day Girls Gr 9-12
New York, NY 10021. 44 E 68th St.
Tel: 212-744-0195. Fax: 212-744-0375.
www.dominicanacademy.org   E-mail: mkunesh@dominicanacademy.org
    Sr. Martha Kunesh, OP, Prin. BA, Ohio Dominican College, MAT, Purdue Univ, MS, Fordham Univ.
    Col Prep. AP—Eng Calc Bio Chem Physics Eur_Hist US_Hist Econ US_Govt & Pol. **Feat**—Creative_Writing Ital Astron Computers Psych Relig Debate.

Supp—Rev Tut. **Adm:** 58/yr. Appl due: Feb. **Enr 233.** G 233. Sec 233. Wh 50%. Hisp 34%. Blk 8%. Asian 8%. Avg class size: 21. Uniform. **Fac 29.** Wh 72%. Hisp 8%. Blk 8%. Asian 12%. Adv deg: 100%. **Grad '04—59.** Col—59. Avg SAT: 1195. Alum 2100. **Tui '03-'04:** Day $7650 (+$375). Aid: Merit 86 ($200,000). **Est 1897.** Nonprofit. Roman Catholic. Quar (Sept-June). Advanced Placement courses are available in all major disciplines at the academy. Christian values and social involvement are stressed, and a wide range of activities and clubs is offered. Dominican schedules at least one European trip annually, and a culture program makes use of nearby museums and cultural centers.

MANHATTAN DAY SCHOOL   Day Coed Gr PS-8
New York, NY 10023. 310 W 75th St.
Tel: 212-376-6800. Fax: 212-376-6389.
www.mds-yot.org   E-mail: mbesser@mdsweb.org
    Rabbi Mordechai Besser, Prin. BA, MA, Yeshiva Univ (NY), MS, Hofstra Univ.

    Gen Acad. Supp—Dev_Read LD Rem_Math Rem_Read Rev Tut. **Adm:** 40/yr. Appl due: Rolling. Accepted: 80%. **Enr 420.** B 200. G 220. Elem 420. Wh 98%. Hisp 1%. Blk 1%. Avg class size: 18. **Fac 73. Grad '04—38. Tui '03-'04:** Day $11,775-14,365. Aid: Need 150 ($600,000). **Est 1943.** Nonprofit. Jewish. Sem (Sept-June). Small classes and individualized instruction are characteristics of the school's curriculum. MDS maintains an enrichment program for all students, and a special-education program for children with learning disabilities is also available.

METROPOLITAN MONTESSORI SCHOOL   Day Coed Gr PS-6
New York, NY 10024. 325 W 85th St.
Tel: 212-579-5525. Fax: 212-579-5526.
www.mmsny.org
    Mary Gaines, Head. BA, Princeton Univ, MSW, Columbia Univ. Jeanette Mall, Adm.

    Pre-Prep. Feat—Fr Span Visual_Arts Music. **Supp**—Dev_Read Rem_Math Rem_Read Tut. **Adm:** 37/yr. Appl due: Dec. **Enr 193.** Elem 193. Wh 69%. Hisp 6%. Blk 8%. Asian 17%. Avg class size: 23. **Fac 27.** M 4. F 22/1. Wh 88%. Hisp 1%. Blk 1%. Asian 10%. Adv deg: 55%. **Grad '04—10.** Prep—9. **Tui '04-'05:** Day $18,800-20,300 (+$3000). Aid: Need 25. **Est 1964.** Nonprofit. Tri (Sept-June). In the school's primary program (ages 3-6), boys and girls gain an exposure to basic concepts in mathematics and language development. Social studies, science and foreign language course work commences in grade 1. Enrichment classes in music, visual arts and computers are integral to the program.

RODEPH SHOLOM SCHOOL   Day Coed Gr PS-8
New York, NY 10024. 10 W 84th St.
Tel: 212-362-8769. Fax: 212-874-0117.
www.rodephsholomschool.org
    Irwin Shlachter, Head. BA, MA, City Univ of New York. Alice Barzilay, Adm.

    Pre-Prep. Feat—Fr Hebrew Span Computers Judaic_Stud Studio_Art Music.

Supp—Dev_Read Rem_Math Rem_Read. **Adm:** 130/yr. Appl due: Dec. **Tests** ISEE. **Enr 650.** B 325. G 325. Elem 650. Wh 99%. Asian 1%. Avg class size: 16. **Fac 133.** M 21. F 112. Wh 99%. Blk 1%. Adv deg: 71%. **Grad '04—36.** Prep—36. Alum 311. **Tui '05-'06:** Day $8900-26,950. Aid: Need 50 ($500,000). **Est 1970.** Nonprofit. Jewish. Sem (Sept-June). A developmentally based curriculum emphasizes language arts, mathematics, science, computer, music, art, social studies, Judaic studies and Hebrew. The nursery division is located at 7 W. 83rd St., classes for children in prekindergarten, kindergarten and grade 1 convene on West 84th Street, and grades 2-8 are conducted at 168 W. 79th St.

SAINT VINCENT FERRER HIGH SCHOOL   Day Girls Gr 9-12
New York, NY 10021. 151 E 65th St.
Tel: 212-535-4680. Fax: 212-988-3455.
www.saintvincentferrer.com
   Sr. Gail Morgan, OP, Prin. Julie Ferenc, Adm.

   Col Prep. AP—Eng Calc Chem Eur_Hist US_Hist. **Feat**—Humanities Shakespeare Fr Span Computers Econ Law Psych Sociol Relig Studio_Art Theater Chorus Accounting. **Supp**—Rev Tut. **Adm:** 130/yr. Appl due: Feb. **Tests** TACHS. **Enr 490.** G 490. Sec 490. Avg class size: 20. Uniform. **Fac 30.** M 9. F 21. **Grad '04—103. Tui '04-'05:** Day $5500 (+$100-300). **Summer:** Enrich Rev Rem. 3-4 wks. **Est 1909.** Nonprofit. Roman Catholic. Sem (Sept-June). SVF's college preparatory curriculum features a number of AP courses, and classes in foreign language, religion and the fine arts are among the graduation requirements. Among the cocurricular activities are academic organizations, student government, athletics, publications and interest clubs. Girls may apply for the school's Scholars Program, which allows able students to receive a two-thirds scholarship for four years tuition.

SOLOMON SCHECHTER SCHOOL   Day Coed Gr K-8
OF MANHATTAN
New York, NY 10128. 50 E 87th St.
Tel: 212-427-9500. Fax: 212-427-5300.
www.sssm.org   E-mail: info@sssm.org
   Steven C. Lorch, Head. BA, Rutgers College, EdM, Harvard Univ, PhD, Columbia Univ. Daneet Brill, Adm.

   Gen Acad. Bilingual. Feat—Hebrew Span Studio_Art Music. **Adm:** 35/yr. Appl due: Dec. **Tests** ISEE. **Enr 138.** B 70. G 68. Elem 138. Wh 99%. Blk 1%. Avg class size: 14. Uniform. **Fac 25.** M 3/3. F 17/2. Wh 99%. Hisp 1%. Adv deg: 32%.**Tui '04-'05:** Day $20,400 (+$500-1000). Aid: Need 54. **Est 1996.** Nonprofit. Jewish. Sem (Sept-June). This Conservative Jewish school offers a thematic, interdisciplinary curriculum that features two bilingual teachers in each classroom. In addition to completing course work in the core disciplines, students develop fluency in Hebrew and an understanding of Jewish culture. Boys and girls choose topics of study based upon their interests, then explore these topics from a variety of perspectives. Both English and Hebrew are used on a daily basis, with the school's goal being for all children to be Hebrew speakers by the end of kindergarten and to be literate in the language by the end of grade 1.

NY   *Concise School Listings*   *840*

STEPHEN GAYNOR SCHOOL   Day Coed Ages 5-13
New York, NY 10023. 22 W 74th St.
Tel: 212-787-7070. Fax: 212-787-3312.
www.sgaynor.com   E-mail: info@sgaynor.com
   Scott Gaynor, Head. Lilli Friedman & Jackie Long, Adms.

    Gen Acad. LD. Feat—Writing Computers Studio_Art Music Speech. **Supp**— Rem_Math Rem_Read Tut. **Adm:** 24/yr. **Enr 118.** B 76. G 42. Wh 88%. Hisp 4%. Blk 5%. Am Ind 1%. Asian 2%. **Fac 37.** M 7. F 30. Adv deg: 2%. **Grad '04—30. Tui '03-'04:** Day $31,400. Aid: Need 14 ($57,500). **Est 1962.** Nonprofit. (Sept-June). The program addresses the needs of children of average to above-average intelligence with language-based learning differences. The curriculum, which emphasizes the mastery of basic subjects, employs a remedial approach that features multisensory teaching methods. Individual support supplements small-group instruction in ungraded classrooms. Teachers, speech and language therapists, reading and math specialists, and occupational therapists work together to return the student to a mainstream environment.

WINSTON PREPARATORY SCHOOL   Day Coed Gr 6-12
New York, NY 10011. 126 W 17th St.
Tel: 646-638-2705.
www.winstonprep.edu   E-mail: admissions@winstonprep.edu
   Scott Bezsylko, Head. BS, La Salle Univ, MA, Columbia Univ. Erinn Murray, Adm.

    Col Prep. Gen Acad. LD. Feat—Studio_Art. **Supp**—Dev_Read Rem_Math Rem_Read Rev Tut. **Adm:** 42/yr. Appl due: Rolling. **Tests** IQ. **Enr 140.** B 98. G 42. Elem 60. Sec 80. Wh 70%. Hisp 8%. Blk 18%. Am Ind 2%. Asian 2%. Avg class size: 11. **Fac 48.** M 15. F 33. **Grad '04—22.** Col—20. **Tui '03-'04:** Day $33,450 (+$40). **Est 1981.** Nonprofit. Sem (Sept-June). Winston Prep provides a language-based curriculum with a multisensory approach for students of average to above-average intelligence who have learning differences such as dyslexia, nonverbal learning disabilities and attentional disorders. The skills-based curriculum offers intensive instruction with a favorable student-teacher ratio in academics, organizational skills and study strategies. High schoolers who demonstrate sufficient levels of commitment and ability may participate in the school's honors program.

XAVIER HIGH SCHOOL   Day Boys Gr 9-12
New York, NY 10011. 30 W 16th St.
Tel: 212-924-7900. Fax: 212-924-0303.
www.xavierhs.org   E-mail: wierzbowskit@xavierhs.org
   Rev. Daniel J. Gatti, SJ, Pres. BA, MS, Fordham Univ, MDiv, Woodstock College. Thomas Wierzbowski, Adm.

    Col Prep. AP—Eng Span Calc Bio Physics Eur_Hist US_Hist World_Hist US_Govt & Pol Studio_Art. **Feat**—Fr Ital Lat Comp_Sci Robotics Band Chorus Music_Theory Accounting JROTC. **Adm:** 252/yr. Appl due: Dec. **Tests** TACHS. **Enr 926.** B 926. Sec 926. Wh 73%. Hisp 14%. Blk 5%. Am Ind 1%. Asian 7%. Avg class size: 25. Uniform. **Fac 63.** M 50. F 13. Adv deg: 77%. **Grad '04—206.** Col—203. Alum 9500. **Tui '04-'05:** Day $8200 (+$500). **Summer:** Acad Rem Rec. Tui Day $330/

crse. 6 wks. **Est 1847.** Nonprofit. Roman Catholic. Quar (Sept-June). **Assoc** MSA. A broad and varied curriculum with many electives is offered. Advanced Placement programs are available in the major disciplines. Extracurricular activities include forensics, dramatics, band, and clubs ranging from chess to cartooning. Available sports are track, football, basketball, swimming, precision drill squad, tennis, golf, baseball, rugby, wrestling, bowling, soccer and ice hockey.

HOLY CHILD ACADEMY   **Day Coed Gr PS-8**
Old Westbury, NY 11568. 25 Store Hill Rd.
Tel: 516-626-9300. Fax: 516-626-7914.
www.holychildacademy.org
    Michael O'Donoghue, Head. BS, MA, MS, Adelphi Univ.

    Pre-Prep. Gen Acad. Feat—Fr Lat Span Computers Relig Studio_Art. **Supp**—Dev_Read Rem_Math Rem_Read Rev Tut. **Adm:** Appl due: Rolling. **Enr 172.** B 84. G 88. Elem 172. Wh 80%. Hisp 2%. Blk 10%. Asian 4%. Other 4%. Avg class size: 15. Uniform. **Fac 37.** M 4. F 31/2. Adv deg: 94%. **Grad '04—12.** Alum 1200. **Tui '04-'05:** Day $11,250-15,600 (+$1000). Aid: Need 35 ($225,000). **Summer:** Acad Rec. 2-8 wks. **Est 1959.** Nonprofit. Roman Catholic. Tri (Sept-June). Holy Child is part of the international network of SHCJ schools. Foreign language instruction begins in prekindergarten with French; older students continue their studies in French or begin Spanish or Latin. The program combines rigorous academics with the arts, athletics and service to the community. Religious studies and liturgical celebrations are integral aspects of school life.

SETON CATHOLIC CENTRAL   **Coed Gr 7-12**
Plattsburgh, NY 12903. 206 New York Rd.   **Bdg & Day**
Tel: 518-561-4031. Fax: 518-563-1193.
www.setonchs.com   E-mail: gcote@setonchs.com
    Gwen Cote, Prin. MA, Manhattan College.

    Col Prep. AP—Eng Calc Chem US_Hist. **Feat**—Fr Span Ecol Computers Psych Sociol Relig Music Bus. **Supp**—ESL. **Adm:** 88/yr. **Enr 350.** Wh 83%. Hisp 4%. Asian 12%. Other 1%. Avg class size: 20. **Fac 28.** M 7. F 16/5. Wh 99%. Asian 1%. **Grad '04—65.** Avg SAT: 1097. Alum 317. **Tui '04-'05:** Bdg $15,000. 5-Day Bdg $10,000. Day $6000 (+$150). **Est 1989.** Nonprofit. Roman Catholic. Sem (Sept-June). The school offers a Catholic education with a college preparatory curriculum. Course offerings include business, music, French, Spanish and computers. Course work in religion is a graduation requirement. Boarding students reside in host homes.

AQUINAS INSTITUTE   **Day Coed Gr 9-12**
Rochester, NY 14613. 1127 Dewey Ave.
Tel: 585-254-2020. Fax: 585-254-7401.
www.aquinasinstitute.com   E-mail: jknapp@aquinasinstitute.com
    Rev. Joseph A. Grasso, CPPS, Prin. Joseph B. Knapp, Adm.

    Col Prep. AP—Eng Span Calc Stats Bio Physics Eur_Hist US_Hist Psych US_Govt & Pol. **Feat**—Fr Lat Econ Law Fine_Arts Accounting Bus. **Supp**—

Rem_Math Rev Tut. **Adm (Gr 9-11):** 232/yr. **Tests** HSPT. **Enr 818.** B 451. G 367. Sec 818. Wh 89%. Hisp 2%. Blk 7%. Asian 2%. Avg class size: 28. **Fac 62.** M 33/1. F 27/1. Adv deg: 67%. **Grad '04—220.** Col—214. Avg SAT: 1090. Avg ACT: 24. Alum 12,500. **Tui '04-'05:** Day $6250 (+$150). Aid: Merit 75 ($40,750). Need 294 ($444,937). **Est 1902.** Nonprofit. Roman Catholic. Sem (Sept-June). The school's curriculum allows pupils to major in art, business, language, music, mathematics and science. Students are required to have two majors. Advanced Placement courses are available, and activities include athletics, band, drama, debate, publications and student government.

BISHOP KEARNEY HIGH SCHOOL — Day Coed Gr 9-12
Rochester, NY 14617. 125 Kings Hwy S.
Tel: 585-342-4000. Fax: 585-342-4694.
www.bkhs.org E-mail: admissions@bkhs.org
Mark S. Peterson, Pres. Louis D'Angelo, Prin. Leslie Ball, Adm.

Col Prep. AP—Eng Span Calc Bio Chem Eur_Hist US_Hist Studio_Art. **Feat**—Fr Ital Holocaust Pol_Sci Drama Journ TV_Production. **Supp**—Rev Tut. **Adm:** 142/yr. Appl due: Rolling. Accepted: 90%. Yield: 90%. **Tests** TACHS. **Enr 477.** B 282. G 195. Sec 477. Wh 75%. Hisp 6%. Blk 16%. Asian 3%. Avg class size: 35. Uniform. **Fac 32.** M 12. F 20. Wh 94%. Other 6%. Adv deg: 100%. **Grad '04—109.** Col—106. Avg SAT: 1040. Alum 11,000. **Tui '04-'05:** Day $6325 (+$200). Aid: Need ($350,000). **Summer:** Acad Enrich Rec. 10 wks. **Est 1962.** Nonprofit. Roman Catholic. Quar (Sept-June). **Assoc** MSA. Established by the Congregation of Christian Brothers and School Sisters of Notre Dame, Bishop Kearney provides a Catholic education that emphasizes leadership development and community service. A college preparatory curriculum is supplemented by activities in art, music and sports. Students may receive college credits for courses taken at St. John Fisher College; in addition, BKHS graduates qualify for automatic acceptance to the college.

McQUAID JESUIT HIGH SCHOOL — Day Boys Gr 7-12
Rochester, NY 14618. 1800 S Clinton Ave.
Tel: 585-473-1130. Fax: 585-256-6171.
www.mcquaid.org E-mail: mcquaid@mcquaid.org
Rev. Philip G. Judge, SJ, Prin. MA, Fordham Univ, MA, Univ of California-Berkeley. Christopher Parks, Adm.

Col Prep. AP—Eng Span Calc Stats Comp_Sci Bio Chem Physics Eur_Hist US_Hist World_Hist Econ Psych Music_Theory. **Feat**—Fr Ger Ital Lat Biotech Govt Relig Art_Hist Studio_Art Drama Chorus. **Supp**—Tut. **Adm (Gr 7-11):** 199/yr. Appl due: Dec. **Tests** HSPT. **Enr 886.** B 886. Elem 199. Sec 687. Wh 89%. Hisp 3%. Blk 5%. Asian 3%. Avg class size: 24. **Fac 65.** M 41/9. F 14/1. Adv deg: 76%. **Grad '04—151.** Col—149. Alum 7262. **Tui '04-'05:** Day $7300 (+$75). **Est 1954.** Nonprofit. Roman Catholic. Sem (Sept-June). **Assoc** MSA. This Catholic school accepts students of all faiths. Electives in the academic program include Advanced Placement courses. A broad extracurricular program complements class work, and all pupils fulfill a community service requirement.

JOHN F. KENNEDY CATHOLIC HIGH SCHOOL
Day Coed Gr 9-12

Somers, NY 10589. 54 Rte 138.
Tel: 914-232-5061. Fax: 914-232-3416.
www.kennedycatholic.org E-mail: development@kennedycatholic.org
  Rev. Stephen P. Norton, Prin. MDiv, St Joseph's Seminary, MEd, Boston College. Sr. Barbara Heil, RDC, Adm.

  Col Prep. AP—Eng Calc Bio Eur_Hist US_Hist US_Govt & Pol Studio_Art. **Feat**—Creative_Writing Ital Lat Span Programming Econ Law Psych Relig Drawing Painting Band Chorus Music Dance Accounting Bus Driver_Ed Health Marketing. **Supp**—Rev Tut. **Adm (Gr 9-11):** 190/yr. Appl due: Aug. **Tests** TACHS. **Enr 575.** B 276. G 299. Sec 575. Wh 92%. Hisp 5%. Blk 2%. Asian 1%. Avg class size: 30. Uniform. **Fac 38.** M 15. F 20/3. Wh 98%. Hisp 1%. Other 1%. Adv deg: 81%. **Grad '04**—142. Col—142. Avg SAT: 1173. Alum 6100. **Tui '04-'05:** Day $5400 (+$200). Aid: Merit 50 ($50,000). Need 7 ($12,000). **Est 1966.** Nonprofit. Roman Catholic. Quar (Sept-June). JFK's curriculum includes both Advanced Placement and honors courses. Students are required to complete 120 hours of community service during their four-year stay at the school. Boys and girls enroll from New York's Westchester, Putnam and Dutchess counties, as well as from neighboring Connecticut.

SAINT ANTHONY'S HIGH SCHOOL
Day Coed Gr 9-12

South Huntington, NY 11747. 275 Wolf Hill Rd.
Tel: 631-271-2020. Fax: 631-351-1507.
www.stanthonyshs.org E-mail: brdonan@stanthonyshs.org
  Br. Gary Cregan, OSF, Prin. Br. Donan Conrad, OSF, Adm.

  Col Prep. AP—Span Calc Bio Chem Physics US_Hist. **Feat**—Ital Lat Computers Govt Relig Studio_Art Drama Music Accounting Public_Speak. **Adm:** 750/yr. Accepted: 60%. **Enr 2250.** B 1250. G 1000. Sec 2250. Wh 89%. Hisp 4%. Blk 3%. Asian 4%. Avg class size: 29. Uniform. **Fac 146.** M 66. F 80. Adv deg: 57%. **Grad '04**—496. Col—492. Avg SAT: 1120. Alum 11,700. **Tui '02-'03:** Day $5300 (+$200). **Summer:** Acad Rev Rem. Sports. 6 wks. **Est 1933.** Nonprofit. Roman Catholic. Quar (Sept-June). **Assoc** MSA. Curriculum features at Saint Anthony's include computer math, accounting, public speaking, music, art and drama. Students participate in activities such as academic honor societies, publications, clubs and organizations, and sports.

CHRISTIAN BROTHERS ACADEMY
Day Coed Gr 7-12

Syracuse, NY 13214. 6245 Randall Rd.
Tel: 315-446-5960. Fax: 315-446-3393.
www.cbasyracuse.org E-mail: info@cbasyracuse.org
  Br. Thomas Zoppo, FSC, Prin. BS, Villanova Univ, MS, Manhattan College. Holly Dowd, Adm.

  Col Prep. AP—Eng US_Hist. **Feat**—British_Lit Creative_Writing Fr Lat Span Anat & Physiol Environ_Sci Comp_Sci Econ Relig World_Relig Studio_Art Drama Music Public_Speak Drafting. **Supp**—LD Rev Tut. **Adm (Gr 7-10):** 168/yr. Appl due: Rolling. Accepted: 80%. **Tests** HSPT. **Enr 730.** B 438. G 292. Elem 240. Sec

490. Avg class size: 25. Uniform. **Fac 57.** M 23. F 34. Adv deg: 84%. **Grad '04—124.** Col—122. Alum 5000. **Tui '04-'05:** Day $6800-7100 (+$180). Aid: Merit 20 ($51,000). Need 200 ($465,000). **Est 1900.** Nonprofit. Roman Catholic. Sem (Sept-June). **Assoc** MSA. Operated by the De La Salle Christian Brothers and serving a largely Catholic student body, CBA enrolls qualified boys and girls of all faiths. Students pursue course work in the traditional disciplines, while also choosing from an array of electives and Advanced Placement offerings. Athletics (many of which are available at both junior high and high school levels), opportunities in the arts, publications, student government and interest clubs complement academics.

FAITH HERITAGE SCHOOL
Day Coed Gr PS-12

Syracuse, NY 13205. 3740 Midland Ave.
Tel: 315-469-7777. Fax: 315-492-7440.
www.faithheritageschool.org   E-mail: fhs@faithheritageschool.org

Dean Whiteway, Head. BA, Gordon College, MPA, Harvard Univ. Kenneth W. Fuller, Adm.

Col Prep. AP—Eng Span Calc US_Hist. **Feat**—Comp_Sci Bible Photog Studio_Art Music. **Supp**—Rem_Math Rem_Read. **Adm:** 100/yr. Appl due: Aug. Accepted: 90%. **Tests** Stanford. **Enr 500.** Elem 250. Sec 250. Wh 94%. Blk 4%. Asian 2%. Avg class size: 22. **Fac 45. Grad '04—48.** Col—48. Avg SAT: 1117. **Tui '02-'03:** Day $4452-5076 (+$360-468). Aid: Need 200 ($250,000). **Est 1972.** Nonprofit. Sem (Sept-June). Faith Heritage's Bible-based academic program is integrated with a Christian worldview. Academics at the elementary level include reading, spelling, handwriting, mathematics, social studies and science. High schoolers choose from college preparatory courses, Advanced Placement classes, and electives in technology and the fine arts.

LA SALLE INSTITUTE
Day Boys Gr 6-12

Troy, NY 12180. 174 Williams Rd.
Tel: 518-283-2500. Fax: 518-283-6265.
www.lasalleinstitute.org   E-mail: bcbelleman@lasalleinstitute.org

Br. Christopher J. Belleman, FSC, Prin. BA, Marygrove College, MA, State Univ of New York-Albany. Jane Fitzmaurice, Adm.

Col Prep. Milit. AP—Eng Span Calc Stats Physics Eur_Hist US_Hist. **Feat**—Relig Milit_Sci. **Supp**—Tut. **Adm:** 151/yr. Accepted: 89%. **Tests** HSPT. **Enr 650.** B 650. Elem 220. Sec 430. Wh 93%. Hisp 1%. Blk 4%. Asian 2%. Avg class size: 24. Uniform. **Fac 54.** M 37/5. F 12. Wh 98%. Blk 2%. Adv deg: 72%. **Grad '04—96.** Col—96. Avg SAT: 1153. Avg ACT: 26. Alum 10,000. **Tui '03-'04:** Day $7000-7800 (+$400). Aid: Merit 110 ($145,500). Need 150 ($305,000). **Summer:** Enrich Rev. Tui Day $200/wk. 2 wks. **Est 1850.** Nonprofit. Roman Catholic. 6 terms (Sept-June). **Assoc** MSA. Operated by the Brothers of the Christian Schools, La Salle accommodates students of varying learning styles. The school offers French and Spanish beginning in grade 7, as well as an accelerated mathematics sequence that commences in grade 7 and later allows eligible pupils to take advanced courses at Hudson Valley Community College. The traditional selection of extracurriculars includes an extensive community service program.

REDEMPTION CHRISTIAN ACADEMY

Bdg Coed Gr 7-PG
Day Coed PS-PG

Troy, NY 12181. 192 9th St, PO Box 753.
Tel: 518-272-6679. Fax: 518-270-8039.
www.rcastudents.com   E-mail: info@rcastudents.com
Elder John Massey, Jr., Prin. Frances Grimes, Adm.

Col Prep. Supp—Dev_Read ESL LD Rem_Math Rem_Read Tut. **Adm:** Appl due: Rolling. **Enr 80.** B 25/25. G 10/20. Elem 44. Sec 26. PG 10. Hisp 5%. Blk 95%. Avg class size: 15. Uniform. **Fac 12.** M 1. F 9/2. Wh 15%. Blk 85%. Adv deg: 16%. In Dorms 2. **Grad '04**—10. Col—9. **Tui '04-'05:** Bdg $15,000. 5-Day Bdg $10,000. Day $5000. **Summer:** Acad Enrich. Tui Bdg $1600. Tui Day $500. 4 wks. **Est 1979.** Nonprofit. Nondenom Christian. Sem (Sept-June). One of only four African-American boarding schools in the US, RCA offers a college preparatory program in a small-class setting. Both remedial and advanced courses are part of the technology-based curriculum. Boarders take part in various evening and weekend activities.

WESTBURY FRIENDS SCHOOL

Day Coed Gr PS-6

Westbury, NY 11590. 550 Post Ave.
Tel: 516-333-3178. Fax: 516-333-1353.
www.westburyfriends.org   E-mail: info@westburyfriends.org
Ida Edelman, Dir. BA, Univ of Rochester, EdS, Trenton State College.

Pre-Prep. Gen Acad. Feat—Fr Span Computers Studio_Art Music. **Supp**—Dev_Read Rem_Math Rem_Read Rev Tut. **Adm:** 40/yr. Accepted: 50%. **Tests** CTP_4. **Enr 173.** B 98. G 75. Elem 173. Wh 49%. Hisp 8%. Blk 34%. Asian 9%. Avg class size: 16. **Fac 19.** M 2. F 15/2. Wh 99%. Hisp 1%. Adv deg: 68%. **Grad '04**—7. Prep—5. **Tui '04-'05:** Day $5000-9500 (+$400). Aid: Need 25 ($84,000). **Est 1957.** Nonprofit. Religious Society of Friends. (Sept-June). Under the care of Westbury Friends Meeting, this school emphasizes a literature-based reading program, writing skills, problem solving, science, computers, social studies, art, music and physical education.

ARCHBISHOP STEPINAC HIGH SCHOOL

Day Boys Gr 9-12

White Plains, NY 10605. 950 Mamaroneck Ave.
Tel: 914-946-4800. Fax: 914-684-2591.
www.stepinac.org   E-mail: stepinac@stepinac.org
Msgr. Anthony Marchitelli, Pres. Paul Carty, Prin. Sr. Margaret Morrissey, RSHM, Adm.

Col Prep. AP—Eng Calc Comp_Sci Bio Eur_Hist US_Hist US_Govt & Pol. **Feat**—Ital Lat Span Marine_Biol/Sci Electronics Web_Design Bible Relig Studio_Art Band Chorus Music_Hist. **Supp**—Dev_Read Rem_Math Rev Tut. **Adm:** 236/yr. Appl due: May. Accepted: 85%. **Enr 685.** B 685. Sec 685. Wh 72%. Hisp 11%. Blk 11%. Asian 6%. Avg class size: 25. **Fac 44.** Adv deg: 77%. **Grad '04**—141. Col—139. Alum 10,000. **Tui '04-'05:** Day $6200 (+$400). **Est 1948.** Nonprofit. Roman Catholic. Quar (Sept-June). Curricular features at Stepinac include computer studies, religion, orchestra and drama. The school also offers a pre-engineering program.

WOODSTOCK DAY SCHOOL
Day Coed Gr PS-10

Woodstock, NY 12498. PO Box 1.
Tel: 845-246-3744. Fax: 845-246-0053.
www.woodstockdayschool.org   E-mail: info@woodstockdayschool.org

Dan Shornstein, Head. BS, State Univ of New York-Geneseo, MA, Bank Street College of Education. Cicily Wilson, Adm.

Gen Acad. Feat—Fr Lat Span Studio_Art Theater Music. **Supp**—Dev_Read Makeup Tut. **Adm:** 51/yr. Appl due: Mar. **Enr 192.** B 101. G 91. Elem 173. Sec 19. Wh 90%. Hisp 2%. Blk 6%. Asian 2%. Avg class size: 15. **Fac 28.** M 2/1. F 22/3. Wh 93%. Hisp 7%. Adv deg: 50%.**Tui '05-'06:** Day $12,950-14,300 (+$800). Aid: Need 57 ($274,122). **Summer:** Enrich Rec. 6-12 wks. **Est 1972.** Nonprofit. Tri (Sept-June). Enrichment classes in Spanish, science, music and art are scheduled throughout the week beginning in kindergarten. In grades 5-8, students enroll in a weekly two-hour elective in a topic such as sculpture, theater, dance and choreography, gardening or carpentry. All boys and girls take part in the school's library program beginning in grade 5. In addition to course work in the core subjects, high schoolers are encouraged to take classes in the arts each year.

STEIN YESHIVA OF LINCOLN PARK
Day Coed Gr PS-8

Yonkers, NY 10704. 287 Central Park Ave.
Tel: 914-965-7082. Fax: 914-965-1902.

Rabbi Joseph Cherns, Prin. MA. Sharon Pollock, Adm.

Pre-Prep. Gen Acad. Feat—Hebrew Computers Judaic_Stud. **Supp**—ESL Rem_Math Rem_Read Tut. **Adm:** 18/yr. Appl due: Rolling. Accepted: 85%. **Enr 109.** B 58. G 51. Elem 109. Wh 100%. Avg class size: 12. Uniform. **Fac 26.** M 5. F 14/7. Wh 100%. Adv deg: 61%. **Grad '04—14.** Prep—14. **Tui '04-'05:** Day $6500-7900 (+$360-860). Aid: Need 20 ($80,000). **Summer:** Rec. Tui Day $1150. 7 wks. **Est 1986.** Nonprofit. Jewish. Tri (Sept-June). Providing instruction in both general studies and Judaic studies, this school emphasizes Orthodox Jewish learning and Hebrew language. Computer instruction, trips, physical education, parent/child education and after-school programs are also provided.

OUR MONTESSORI SCHOOL
Day Coed Gr PS-6

Yorktown Heights, NY 10598. PO Box 72.
Tel: 914-962-9466. Fax: 914-962-9470.

Betty M. Hengst, Dir. BA, Univ of Florida, MEd, Long Island Univ. June Willis, Adm.

Pre-Prep. Feat—Fr Lat Computers Studio_Art Drama Music Dance. **Supp**—Dev_Read Rem_Math Rem_Read Rev Tut. **Adm:** 140/yr. Appl due: Rolling. Accepted: 90%. **Enr 320.** B 170. G 150. Elem 320. Wh 80%. Hisp 7%. Blk 6%. Asian 7%. Avg class size: 15. **Fac 50.** M 2. F 28/20. Wh 86%. Hisp 4%. Blk 4%. Asian 6%. Adv deg: 10%. **Grad '04—5.** Prep—3. Alum 2500. **Tui '04-'05:** Day $2650-11,650. **Summer:** Acad Enrich Rec. Tui Day $95-320/wk. 10 wks. **Est 1972.** Inc. (Sept-June). The school emphasizes individualized instruction and experiential learning. French is introduced in the nursery division, and the arts, field trips and visitors from outside the classroom are central to the program. The curriculum

PENNSYLVANIA

BISHOP GUILFOYLE HIGH SCHOOL Day Coed Gr 9-12
Altoona, PA 16602. 2400 Pleasant Valley Blvd.
Tel: 814-944-4014. Fax: 814-944-8695.
http://guilfoyle.daj.k12.pa.us
    Rev. Leo A. Lynch, Prin.

  Col Prep. Gen Acad. AP—Eng Calc Bio Eur_Hist. **Feat**—Fr Lat Span Computers Psych Sociol Relig Studio_Art Music Bus. **Adm:** 99/yr. Accepted: 100%. **Enr 396.** Sec 396. Wh 98%. Hisp 1%. Blk 1%. Uniform. **Fac 24.** M 9. F 15. Wh 100%. **Grad '04—66.** Col—50. Alum 8000. **Tui '01-'02:** Day $3875 (+$125). Aid: Need 340 ($457,253). **Est 1922.** Nonprofit. Roman Catholic. Quar (Aug-June). **Assoc** MSA. BG provides a varied secondary program that emphasizes critical-thinking skills and problem-solving strategies. Serving pupils from roughly two dozen area parishes, the faculty comprises a blend of clergy, religious and laypeople. In addition to interscholastic athletics, students may engage in such extracurricular pursuits as student council, chess team, fencing club, forensics, mock trial, and a competing marching band and guard.

QUIGLEY CATHOLIC HIGH SCHOOL
Day Coed Gr 9-12
Baden, PA 15005. 200 Quigley Dr.
Tel: 724-869-2188. Fax: 724-869-3091.
www.qchs.org E-mail: office@qchs.org
    Rev. David C. Menegay, Prin. BA, La Salle Univ, MA, Villanova Univ, MA, MDiv, Mount Saint Mary's College (MD), MEd, Duquesne Univ. Tara Colonna, Adm.

  Col Prep. AP—Eng Eur_Hist US_Hist. **Feat**—Fr Span Comp_Sci Relig Ceramics Studio_Art Chorus. **Supp**—Tut. **Adm:** 52/yr. Appl due: Rolling. Accepted: 98%. Yield: 75%. **Enr 171.** B 93. G 78. Sec 171. Wh 94%. Hisp 3%. Other 3%. Avg class size: 18. Uniform. **Fac 16.** M 8. F 8. Wh 100%. Adv deg: 87%. **Grad '04—55.** Col—53. Avg SAT: 1039. Alum 5000. **Tui '04-'05:** Day $7050. Catholic $6000. Aid: Merit 21 ($11,750). Need 88 ($228,750). Work prgm 37 ($14,800). **Est 1967.** Nonprofit. Roman Catholic. Quar (Aug-June). **Assoc** MSA. QCHS offers a college preparatory curriculum with accelerated and advanced courses in most disciplines. Christian values are emphasized, and students have the opportunity to participate in community service projects. Various sports and extracurricular activities are available.

BEAVER COUNTY CHRISTIAN SCHOOL Day Coed Gr K-12
Beaver Falls, PA 15010. 3601 Short St.
Tel: 724-843-8331. Fax: 724-891-3315.
www.thebccs.org E-mail: info@thebccs.org
    Jeffrey J. Miller, Supvg Prin. BA, Geneva College, MEd, Florida Atlantic Univ. Renee Squire, Adm.

Col Prep. Feat—Ger Span Environ_Sci Journ. **Supp**—Rem_Read. **Adm:** 83/yr. Accepted: 98%. **Tests** Stanford. **Enr 340.** B 154. G 186. Elem 230. Sec 110. Wh 98%. Blk 2%. Avg class size: 21. **Fac 29.** M 7/1. F 11/10. Adv deg: 20%. **Grad '04**—28. Col—12. Alum 250. **Tui '02-'03:** Day $3950. Aid: Need 49 ($57,000). **Est 1969.** Nonprofit. Sem (Aug-June). BCCS offers a full elementary and secondary program that reflects a Christian worldview. Students attend trips to points of historical and literary interest as part of their course of study. The athletic program includes soccer, basketball and volleyball. In addition, students in grades 9-12 may take independent study correspondence courses through Indiana University in Bloomington, IN, and seniors may earn college credits for courses taken at Geneva College.

HOLY GHOST PREPARATORY SCHOOL
Day Boys Gr 9-12
Bensalem, PA 19020. 2429 Bristol Pike.
Tel: 215-629-2102. Fax: 215-639-4225.
www.holyghostprep.org   E-mail: rabram01@holyghostprep.org

Rev. Jeffrey T. Duaime, CSSp, Pres. MDiv, Catholic Theological Union. Ryan T. Abramson, Adm.

Col Prep. AP—Eng Fr Lat Span Calc Comp_Sci Bio Chem Physics Eur_Hist US_Hist World_Hist US_Govt & Pol Studio_Art Music_Theory. **Feat**—Creative_Writing Stats Anat & Physiol Astron Genetics Web_Design Psych Philos World_Relig Drama Journ. **Adm (Gr 9-11):** 130/yr. Appl due: Nov. **Tests** HSPT. **Enr 508.** B 508. Sec 508. Avg class size: 17. **Fac 60.** M 31. F 29. Adv deg: 70%. **Grad '04**—114. Col—114. Avg SAT: 1250. **Tui '04-'05:** Day $11,075 (+$100). Aid: Merit 68 ($217,000). Need 92 ($220,000). **Summer:** Acad Enrich. Tui Day $735. 5 wks. **Est 1897.** Nonprofit. Roman Catholic. Sem (Aug-May). Founded by members of the Congregation of the Holy Ghost, this Catholic school offers a college preparatory curriculum that features Advanced Placement work in every major discipline. A comprehensive humanities program and an emphasis on technology are important aspects of academic life. Boys choose from more than two dozen interscholastic sports; other extracurriculars include drama, musical organizations, interest clubs and school publications. Freshmen and sophomores complete 10 hours of annual community service, while juniors and seniors fulfill a 20-hour commitment.

ST. ALOYSIUS ACADEMY
Day Boys Gr K-8
Bryn Mawr, PA 19010. 401 S Bryn Mawr Ave.
Tel: 610-525-1670. Fax: 610-525-5140.
www.staloysiusacademy.org   E-mail: soar@staloysiusacademy.org

Sr. Carolyn M. Dimick, IHM, Prin. BA, Immaculata College, MA, Santa Clara Univ, MEd, Villanova Univ. Sr. Joseph Patrice Considine, IHM, Adm.

Pre-Prep. Feat—Lat Span Computers Relig Studio_Art Band Chorus Music. **Supp**—Rem_Read Tut. **Adm:** 40/yr. Appl due: Jan. Accepted: 95%. **Tests** IQ. **Enr 270.** B 270. Elem 270. Wh 97%. Blk 2%. Asian 1%. Avg class size: 18. Uniform. **Fac 39.** M 3/3. F 31/2. Wh 98%. Hisp 1%. Asian 1%. Adv deg: 23%. **Grad '04**—28. Prep—21. Alum 800. **Tui '04-'05:** Day $7600 (+$600). Aid: Merit 17 ($39,070). Need 4 ($11,440). **Est 1895.** Nonprofit. Roman Catholic. Tri (Sept-June). **Assoc** MSA. St. Aloysius emphasizes basic skills in all areas; religion and moral development are also stressed. Children in grades K-5 study Spanish, while pupils in grades

6-8 study Latin. The sports program consists of football, soccer, basketball, track and baseball.

OUR LADY OF LOURDES REGIONAL HIGH SCHOOL
Day Coed Gr 9-12

Coal Township, PA 17866. 2001 Clinton Ave.
Tel: 570-644-0375. Fax: 570-644-7655.
www.lourdes.k12.pa.us   E-mail: lourdes@lourdes.k12.pa.us
  John A. McKay, Prin.

  Col Prep. Gen Acad. Feat—Fr Span Environ_Sci. **Supp**—Rem_Math Rem_Read. **Adm:** 52/yr. Accepted: 100%. **Enr 194.** B 94. G 100. Sec 194. Wh 98%. Blk 1%. Asian 1%. Avg class size: 15. Uniform. **Fac 27.** M 16. F 11. Wh 100%. Adv deg: 48%. **Grad '04—58.** Col—53. Avg SAT: 969. Alum 7100. **Tui '04-'05:** Day $5300 (+$100). Catholic $3000 (+$100). Aid: Need 82 ($64,000). Work prgm 42 ($12,500). **Est 1959.** Nonprofit. Roman Catholic. (Aug-June). **Assoc** MSA. Advanced courses are available at Lourdes in English, math, science and foreign languages. All students are encouraged to participate in community service, and seniors complete compulsory science projects.

DEVON PREPARATORY SCHOOL
Day Boys Gr 6-12

Devon, PA 19333. 363 Valley Forge Rd.
Tel: 610-688-7337. Fax: 610-688-2409.
www.devonprep.com   E-mail: info@devonprep.com
  Rev. James J. Shea, SchP, Head. BEE, Villanova Univ, MA, MDiv, Oblate College. Peter Crippen, Adm.

  Col Prep. AP—Eng Fr Ger Span Calc Comp_Sci Bio Chem Physics Eur_Hist US_Hist US_Govt & Pol. **Feat**—Ital Lat Anat & Physiol Civil_War Vietnam_War Econ Law Philos Relig Art_Hist Studio_Art Music Accounting. **Supp**—Dev_Read. **Adm (Gr 6-10):** 67/yr. Appl due: Rolling. Accepted: 55%. Yield: 70%. **Tests** CEEB HSPT. **Enr 278.** B 278. Elem 89. Sec 189. Wh 94%. Hisp 1%. Blk 1%. Am Ind 1%. Asian 3%. Avg class size: 15. **Fac 33.** M 19/4. F 8/2. Wh 100%. Adv deg: 45%. **Grad '04—53.** Col—53. Avg SAT: 1270. Alum 1600. **Tui '04-'05:** Day $12,400-12,800 (+$300). Aid: Merit 174 ($584,600). Need 46 ($161,850). **Est 1956.** Nonprofit. Roman Catholic. Quar (Sept-June). **Assoc** MSA. Founded by the Piarist Fathers, this school offers a college preparatory curriculum with Advanced Placement courses and opportunities for field study. A religion class is required each year. Extracurricular activities include math club, computer club, outdoor club, publications, student council, a Christian action program and varsity athletic teams.

HOLY CHILD ACADEMY
Day Coed Gr PS-8

Drexel Hill, PA 19026. 475 Shadeland Ave.
Tel: 610-259-2712. Fax: 610-259-1862.
www.holychildacademy.com   E-mail: admissions@holychildacademy.com
  Anita P. Coll, Head. BA, Rosemont College, MA, Villanova Univ. Kelly Hornak, Adm.

  Pre-Prep. Feat—Eng Fr Span Computers Relig Studio_Art Drama Music.

Supp—Dev_Read Rem_Math Rem_Read Rev Tut. **Adm (Gr PS-6):** 44/yr. Appl due: Rolling. Accepted: 71%. Yield: 83%. **Tests** IQ. **Enr 220.** B 93. G 127. Elem 220. Wh 84%. Hisp 4%. Blk 7%. Asian 5%. Avg class size: 14. Uniform. **Fac 31.** M 1/2. F 18/10. Wh 99%. Blk 1%. Adv deg: 48%. **Grad '04—28.** Prep—27. Alum 1150. **Tui '04-'05:** Day $8500 (+$1000). Aid: Need 39 ($80,000). **Summer:** Rec. Tui Day $440/2-wk ses. 8 wks. **Est 1927.** Nonprofit. Roman Catholic. Sem (Sept-June). Curriculum basics at Holy Child are complemented by computer, algebra, art, music, religion, service, French, Spanish, geography, physical education and field trips. Small-group instruction and close student-teacher rapport are emphasized. Extracurriculars include volleyball, basketball, soccer, track, softball, science clubs, student council, band, choir, brass and string ensembles, and drama.

ERIE DAY SCHOOL Day Coed Gr PS-8
Erie, PA 16505. 1372 W 6th St.
Tel: 814-452-4273. Fax: 814-455-5184.
www.eriedayschool.com
  William L. Kindler, Head. PhD.

Pre-Prep. Feat—Fr Span Computers Studio_Art Drama Music. **Supp**—Rem_Math Rem_Read. **Adm (Gr PS-7):** 44/yr. Appl due: July. Accepted: 80%. **Enr 180.** B 92. G 88. Elem 180. Wh 92%. Hisp 1%. Blk 2%. Asian 5%. Avg class size: 15. Uniform. **Fac 22.** M 2/1. F 15/4. Wh 90%. Hisp 10%. Adv deg: 27%. **Grad '04—22. Tui '05-'06:** Day $5560-10,235 (+$1000). Aid: Merit 18 ($120,915). Need 13 ($65,748). **Summer:** Enrich Rec. Tui Day $65/wk. 6 wks. **Est 1929.** Sem (Sept-June). EDS' curriculum combines course work in the standard subjects with instruction in music, art, drama, foreign language and physical education. Children receive technology and computer training beginning in early childhood. Students in the middle school (grades 6-8) take part in a noteworthy program that replaces traditional grade levels with a mixed-grade curriculum that consists of five core subjects and five special programs. In addition to working toward graduation requirements, middle schoolers also have the scheduling flexibility to pursue course areas of interest and strength.

MOUNT SAINT JOSEPH ACADEMY Day Girls Gr 9-12
Flourtown, PA 19031. 120 W Wissahickon Ave.
Tel: 215-233-3177. Fax: 215-233-4734.
www.msjacad.org   E-mail: admiss@msjacad.org
  Sr. Kathleen Brabson, SSJ, Pres. BA, Chestnut Hill College, MA, Villanova Univ. Sr. Karen Dietrich, SSJ, Prin. MS, Villanova Univ, PhD, Capella Univ. Carol Finney, Adm.

Col Prep. AP—Eng Fr Lat Span Calc Stats Bio Physics Eur_Hist US_Hist Psych US_Govt & Pol Music_Theory. **Feat**—British_Lit Comp_Sci Web_Design Relig Theater_Arts. **Adm (Gr 9-11):** 153/yr. Appl due: Oct. Accepted: 59%. Yield: 62%. **Tests** HSPT. **Enr 561.** G 561. Sec 561. Wh 93%. Hisp 1%. Blk 4%. Asian 1%. Other 1%. Avg class size: 19. Uniform. **Fac 56.** M 10/1. F 40/5. Adv deg: 89%. **Grad '04—138.** Col—138. Avg SAT: 1247. Alum 4800. **Tui '05-'06:** Day $10,000 (+$900). **Est 1858.** Nonprofit. Roman Catholic. Quar (Sept-June). **Assoc** MSA. MSJA's program provides opportunities for course work at area colleges, Advanced

Placement programs and independent study. Pupils also may participate in a diverse extracurricular program, as well as in a variety of varsity sports.

AQUINAS ACADEMY OF PITTSBURGH Day Coed Gr K-12
Gibsonia, PA 15044. 2308 W Hardies Rd.
Tel: 724-444-0722. Fax: 724-444-0750.
www.aquinasacademy-pittsburgh.org
E-mail: info@aquinasacademy-pittsburgh.org

Leslie M. Mitros, Head. BA, St Mary's College (IN), MEd, Univ of Pittsburgh. Juan Mata, Adm.

Col Prep. AP—Eng Lat Calc Physics US_Hist US_Govt & Pol. **Feat**—Humanities Span Comp_Sci Philos Relig Studio_Art Music. **Adm:** 45/yr. Appl due: Rolling. Accepted: 90%. **Enr 205.** Elem 165. Sec 40. Wh 96%. Hisp 2%. Blk 2%. Avg class size: 17. Uniform. **Fac 27.** M 6/2. F 8/11. Wh 95%. Hisp 5%. Adv deg: 7%. **Grad '04—10.** Col—10. Avg SAT: 1246. Alum 26. **Tui '04-'05:** Day $3900-6000. **Est 1996.** Nonprofit. Roman Catholic. Sem (Aug-June). Conducted in the Catholic educational tradition, the academy encourages the development of critical thinking and independent learning skills. Children build an academic foundation in the early years in phonics, reading, writing, spelling, math, history and science. Beginning in middle school, students take six major subjects (including foreign languages and religion) and four auxiliary courses (art, music, health and physical education, and computer). Advanced Placement course work is available, as are study skills courses and SAT and AP test preparation classes.

GLADWYNE MONTESSORI SCHOOL Day Coed Gr PS-6
Gladwyne, PA 19035. 920 Youngsford Rd.
Tel: 610-649-1761. Fax: 610-649-7978.
www.gladwyne.org   E-mail: mail@gladwyne.org

Usha Balamore, Head. MA, PhD, Bryn Mawr College. Robyn Stearne, Adm.

Pre-Prep. Feat—Fr Computers Studio_Art Music. **Adm:** 85/yr. Appl due: Rolling. **Enr 310.** Elem 310. Wh 76%. Hisp 12%. Blk 3%. Asian 9%. Avg class size: 20. **Fac 39.** M 3. F 17/19. Wh 97%. Blk 1%. Other 2%. Adv deg: 12%.**Tui '04-'05:** Day $11,289-12,362. **Summer:** Rec. Tui Day $750-1575. 7 wks. **Est 1962.** Nonprofit. (Sept-June). This Montessori school emphasizes individualized instruction and experiential learning. The arts, field trips, drama, ecology and community service are important parts of the program, and French instruction begins in the primary division (ages 3-6). In both the primary and the elementary units, children work with the same teacher and peer group in the same classroom for three years.

UPATTINAS SCHOOL Day Coed Gr K-12
Glenmoore, PA 19343. 429 Greenridge Rd.
Tel: 610-458-5138. Fax: 610-458-8688.
www.upattinas.org   E-mail: office@upattinas.org

Sandra M. Hurst, Dir. BME, Oberlin College. Kim Coffin, Adm.

Col Prep. Gen Acad. Feat—Fr Ital Japan Span Comp_Art Outdoor_Ed. **Supp**—ESL Makeup Tut. **Adm:** 15/yr. Appl due: Rolling. Accepted: 95%. **Enr**

112. B 60. G 52. Elem 44. Sec 68. Wh 88%. Hisp 3%. Blk 5%. Asian 4%. Avg class size: 6. **Fac 14.** M 4/2. F 5/3. Wh 79%. Blk 14%. Asian 7%. Adv deg: 14%. **Grad '04—34.** Col—24. Alum 30. **Tui '04-'05:** Day $9625 (+$500). Aid: Need 57 ($100,000). Work prgm 3 ($3000). **Summer:** Enrich Rec. Tui Day $250/2-wk ses. 6 wks. **Est 1971.** Nonprofit. Sem (Sept-June). This small community school features independent study, a travel program and an academic curriculum leading to a high school diploma. A resource center provides full- and part-time programs, as well as home education services. International students may reside with a host family for an additional fee.

GWYNEDD-MERCY ACADEMY   Day Girls Gr 9-12
Gwynedd Valley, PA 19437. 1345 Sumneytown Pike, PO Box 902.
Tel: 215-646-8815. Fax: 215-646-4361.
www.gmahs.org
    Sr. Kathleen Boyce, RSM, Prin. BA, Gwynedd-Mercy College, MA, Villanova Univ. Kimberly D. Scott, Adm.

    Col Prep. AP—Lat Span Calc Eur_Hist US_Hist. **Feat**—Fr Comp_Sci Econ Theol Studio_Art Accounting. **Adm:** 105/yr. Appl due: Nov. **Tests** HSPT. **Enr 419.** G 419. Sec 419. Wh 100%. Avg class size: 18. Uniform. **Fac 45.** M 6. F 39. Wh 100%. Adv deg: 55%. **Grad '04—86.** Col—86. Avg SAT: 1141. Avg ACT: 26. Alum 3600. **Tui '04-'05:** Day $9900 (+$300). Aid: Merit 39 ($110,000). Need 4 ($30,000). **Est 1861.** Nonprofit. Roman Catholic. Quar (Sept-June). **Assoc** MSA. In addition to required course work, GMA offers an extensive program of electives. Honors and Advanced Placement courses are available for qualified students.

STRATFORD FRIENDS SCHOOL   Day Coed Gr K-6
Havertown, PA 19083. 5 Llandillo Rd.
Tel: 610-446-3144. Fax: 610-446-6381.
www.stratfordfriends.org   E-mail: gvare@stratfordfriends.org
    Sandra Howze, Dir. BA, MSEd, Temple Univ. Nancy D'Angelo, Adm.

    Pre-Prep. LD. Feat—Studio_Art Music Woodworking. **Supp**—Dev_Read Rem_Math Rem_Read Rev Tut. **Adm:** 22/yr. Appl due: Rolling. **Tests** IQ. **Enr 68.** B 44. G 24. Elem 68. Wh 63%. Hisp 4%. Blk 27%. Am Ind 3%. Other 3%. Avg class size: 6. **Fac 17.** M 2. F 13/2. Wh 92%. Blk 8%. Adv deg: 47%. **Grad '04—14.** Prep—11. Alum 230. **Tui '04-'05:** Day $22,700 (+$50). Aid: Need 28 ($158,763). **Summer:** Acad Enrich Rev Rem Rec. Tui Day $1000. 4 wks. **Est 1976.** Nonprofit. Religious Society of Friends. Sem (Sept-June). Stratford enrolls children of average to gifted intelligence who have learning differences. The multisensory program includes speech, math and reading instruction. The reading program utilizes the Orton-Gillingham approach.

MILTON HERSHEY SCHOOL   Bdg Coed Gr PS-12
Hershey, PA 17033. 430 E Governor Rd, PO Box 830.
Tel: 717-520-2100. Fax: 717-520-2117.
www.mhs-pa.org   E-mail: mhs-admissions@mhs-pa.org
    John O'Brien, Pres. BA, Princeton Univ, MA, Johns Hopkins Univ. Mark Seymour, Adm.

Col Prep. Voc. **AP**—Eng Fr Ger Span Calc Bio US_Hist Music_Theory. **Feat**—Lat Arts. **Supp**—Dev_Read Makeup Tut. **Adm (Gr PS-10):** 235/yr. Appl due: Rolling. **Tests** IQ. **Enr 1274.** B 628. G 646. Elem 701. Sec 573. Wh 47%. Hisp 11%. Blk 32%. Asian 1%. Other 9%. Avg class size: 15. **Fac 161.** M 58/8. F 86/9. Wh 86%. Hisp 4%. Blk 7%. Asian 3%. Adv deg: 58%. **Grad '04—112.** Col—92. Avg SAT: 905. Alum 5823. **Tui '04-'05:** Bdg $0. **Summer:** Acad Enrich Rem Rec. Sports. Tui Bdg $0. 4-6 wks. **Est 1909.** Nonprofit. Quar (Aug-June). **Assoc** MSA. MHS was founded by chocolate magnate Milton S. Hershey and his wife, Catherine. To be considered for enrollment, students must come from families with limited income. Pupils are provided with an educational program, clothing, meals and lodging, and assistance with health care and dental expenses during their enrollment. Each student home on campus has a married couple in residence. The extensive counseling program includes both job placement and follow-up. Athletics include football, basketball, swimming, track, baseball, softball, field hockey, soccer and wrestling. All school services are provided at no charge.

JOHNSTOWN CHRISTIAN SCHOOL Day Coed Gr PS-12
Hollsopple, PA 15935. 125 Christian School Rd.
Tel: 814-288-2588. Fax: 814-288-1447.
www.bluejay.org E-mail: jcs@bluejay.org
  Linda R. Gundlach, Admin. BS, Taylor Univ, MRE, Grand Rapids Baptist Seminary.
  Col Prep. Feat—Span Drama Chorus Music. **Supp**—LD Rem_Math Rem_Read. **Adm:** 55/yr. Appl due: Aug. Accepted: 95%. **Enr 265.** Elem 168. Sec 97. Wh 98%. Blk 1%. Asian 1%. Avg class size: 19. **Fac 25.** M 4. F 16/5. Wh 100%. Adv deg: 20%. **Grad '04—17.** Col—11. Avg SAT: 1110. Avg ACT: 22. Alum 600. **Tui '04-'05:** Day $3540 (+$150). Aid: Need ($80,000). **Est 1944.** Nonprofit. Nondenom Christian. Sem (Aug-June). Founded by a group of Mennonite families, this Christian school conducts a college preparatory curriculum that emphasizes spiritual growth and development. Elementary students receive daily instruction in music, art, science and physical education, while older pupils attend eight rotating academic periods. JCS' music program enables younger boys and girls to develop fundamental musical skills, while providing concert and choral performance opportunities for high schoolers.

CHRISTOPHER DOCK MENNONITE Day Coed Gr 9-12
HIGH SCHOOL
Lansdale, PA 19446. 1000 Forty Foot Rd.
Tel: 215-362-2675. Fax: 215-362-2943.
www.christopherdock.org E-mail: cdock@christopherdock.org
  Elaine A. Moyer, Prin. BA, Bluffton College, MS, Marshall Univ. Lois Boaman, Adm.
  Col Prep. Gen Acad. Voc. AP—Span Calc. **Feat**—Creative_Writing Anat & Physiol Astron Ecol Environ_Sci Geol Programming Web_Design Govt Bible Art_Hist Photog Music Accounting Bus. **Supp**—Tut. **Adm:** 130/yr. Appl due: Rolling. Accepted: 85%. Yield: 95%. **Enr 435.** B 216. G 219. Sec 435. Wh 95%. Blk 4%. Asian 1%. Avg class size: 22. **Fac 32.** M 16. F 15/1. Wh 100%. Adv deg: 50%. **Grad '04—95.** Col—80. Avg SAT: 1052. Alum 3800. **Tui '04-'05:** Day $9850

(+$100). Aid: Need 112 ($270,518). **Est 1952.** Nonprofit. Mennonite. Quar (Aug-June). **Assoc** MSA. The school was named for an early Mennonite schoolmaster. Students choose from three curricula: academic, general and vocational/technical. Sports include soccer, cross-country, basketball, baseball, softball, field hockey, tennis, golf, track and volleyball.

MALVERN PREPARATORY SCHOOL   Day Boys Gr 6-12
Malvern, PA 19355. 418 S Warren Ave.
Tel: 484-595-1100. Fax: 484-595-1124.
www.malvernprep.com   E-mail: jstewart@malvernprep.org
    Rev. David J. Duffy, OSA, Pres. James H. Stewart, Head. BA, La Salle College, MA, Middlebury College, MA, Villanova Univ. William R. Gibson, Adm.

    Col Prep. AP—Eng Fr Span Calc Stats Bio Chem Physics US_Hist Econ. **Feat**—Astron Environ_Sci Sports_Med Law Comp_Relig Philos Theol Ceramics Fine_Arts Graphic_Arts Photog Sculpt Studio_Art Band Chorus Music. **Supp**—Rev Tut. **Adm (Gr 6-11):** 133/yr. Appl due: Rolling. Accepted: 30%. **Tests** HSPT ISEE SSAT. **Enr 595.** B 595. Elem 163. Sec 432. Wh 94%. Hisp 1%. Blk 3%. Asian 2%. Avg class size: 20. Uniform. **Fac 75.** M 60. F 15. Wh 97%. Blk 3%. Adv deg: 56%. **Grad '04—106.** Col—106. Avg SAT: 1234. Alum 3900. **Tui '04-'05:** Day $17,950-18,650 (+$100-565). Aid: Merit 41 ($203,100). Need 88 ($874,150). **Summer:** Acad Enrich Rem. 3-6 wks. **Est 1842.** Nonprofit. Roman Catholic. Sem (Sept-May). **Assoc** MSA. Located on the Villanova University campus, Malvern provides a rigorous curriculum that incorporates a full complement of Advanced Placement and honors courses. Beginning in grade 6, students acquire basic computer skills and choose from a variety of computer classes, including AP computer science. Art and music electives, as well as photography, printmaking and graphic design, represent some of the arts options. Juniors and seniors perform 40 hours of annual community service, while all seniors take part in a two-week internship program and embark on a retreat.

PHELPS SCHOOL   Boys Gr 7-PG
Malvern, PA 19355. 583 Sugartown Rd, PO Box 476.   **Bdg & Day**
Tel: 610-644-1754. Fax: 610-644-6679.
www.thephelpsschool.org   E-mail: admis@thephelpsschool.org
    Norman T. Phelps, Jr., Head. BA, Randolph-Macon College, MA, Villanova Univ. F. Christopher Chirieleison, Adm.

    Col Prep. LD. Underachiever. Feat—Span Astron Environ_Sci Geol Computers Web_Design Econ Govt Psych Sociol Ceramics Drawing Photog Sculpt. **Supp**—Dev_Read ESL Rem_Math Rem_Read Rev Tut. **Adm:** 76/yr. Bdg 67. Day 9. **Enr 140.** B 120/20. Elem 10. Sec 128. PG 2. Avg class size: 7. **Fac 28.** M 21. F 7. Adv deg: 46%. In Dorms 20. **Grad '04—46.** Col—45. Alum 1228. **Tui '04-'05:** Bdg $26,250 (+$1500). Day $15,500 (+$200). Aid: Need ($164,500). **Summer:** Acad Rev Rem. Tui Bdg $4000. Tui Day $3000. 5 wks. **Est 1946.** Nonprofit. Quar (Sept-May). **Assoc** MSA. The school offers a college preparatory program to boys who are underachieving or who have a specific learning disability such as dyslexia or attention deficit disorder. Phelps features small classes and individualized scheduling. All students participate in an afternoon activity program that includes such sports as soccer, baseball, basketball, golf, bowling, tennis, cross-country and lacrosse, as well as farm work, riding, arts and crafts, wood shop, photography, drama and computers.

BENCHMARK SCHOOL   **Day Coed Gr 1-8**
Media, PA 19063. 2107 N Providence Rd.
Tel: 610-565-3741. Fax: 610-565-3872.
www.benchmarkschool.org   E-mail: benchmarkinfo@benchmarkschool.org
    Irene W. Gaskins, Head. BS, Univ of Idaho, MS, EdD, Univ of Pennsylvania. Adam Lemisch, Adm.
    Pre-Prep. LD. Underachiever. Feat—Studio_Art Music. **Supp**—Dev_Read Rem_Math Rem_Read Tut. **Adm (Gr 1-5):** 40/yr. Appl due: June. Accepted: 51%. Yield: 100%. **Tests** IQ. **Enr 204.** B 131. G 73. Elem 204. Wh 91%. Hisp 1%. Blk 7%. Asian 1%. Avg class size: 13. Uniform. **Fac 61.** M 8. F 53. Wh 100%. Adv deg: 55%. **Grad '04—30.** Prep—25. Alum 912. **Tui '04-'05:** Day $18,800 (+$100). Aid: Need 25 ($196,500). **Summer:** Acad Rem Rec. Tui Day $2400. 5 wks. **Est 1970.** Nonprofit. Tri (Sept-June). Benchmark serves bright underachievers, providing a complete program of social studies, math, science, art, music, physical education and health, in addition to reading and language arts. Instruction in all subjects is individualized according to the student's needs. The program includes professional guidance in helping students to overcome social and emotional problems that may accompany academic underachievement. The successful return of each student to mainstream education is a school goal.

MEDIA-PROVIDENCE FRIENDS SCHOOL   **Day Coed Gr PS-8**
Media, PA 19063. 125 W 3rd St.
Tel: 610-565-1960. Fax: 610-565-9866.
www.mpfs.org   E-mail: minfantino@fox.mpfs.org
    Lynn W. Oberfield, Head. Francy Strathmann, Adm.
    Pre-Prep. Feat—Span Environ_Sci Computers Fine_Arts. **Adm:** 39/yr. Appl due: Rolling. **Enr 150.** B 72. G 78. Elem 150. Wh 62%. Hisp 2%. Blk 23%. Asian 1%. Other 12%. **Fac 23.** M 5/1. F 13/4. Wh 87%. Hisp 4%. Blk 9%. Adv deg: 26%. **Grad '04**—11. Prep—6. Alum 630. **Tui '04-'05:** Day $9260-13,980. Aid: Need 44 ($193,000). **Summer:** Rec. Tui Day $180/wk. 8 wks. **Est 1876.** Nonprofit. Religious Society of Friends. Tri (Sept-June). Spanish, art, music and athletics enrich the traditional academic program at MPFS. Quaker principles and processes are integral to school life, although the student body comprises pupils of various backgrounds.

MERION MERCY ACADEMY   **Day Girls Gr 9-12**
Merion Station, PA 19066. 511 Montgomery Ave.
Tel: 610-664-6655. Fax: 610-664-6322.
www.merion-mercy.com   E-mail: admissions@merion-mercy.com
    Sr. Regina Ward, Prin. BS, Gwynedd-Mercy College, MAEd, Beaver College. Eileen Daly Killeen, Adm.
    Col Prep. AP—Eng Calc Stats Bio Chem US_Hist Econ US_Govt & Pol. **Feat**—Fr Lat Span Psych Relig Studio_Art Drama Music. **Supp**—Rev Tut. **Adm:**

120/yr. Appl due: Nov. Accepted: 50%. **Tests** HSPT. **Enr 460.** G 460. Sec 460. Wh 91%. Hisp 3%. Blk 4%. Asian 1%. Other 1%. Avg class size: 17. Uniform. **Fac 44.** M 6. F 38. Wh 96%. Hisp 4%. Adv deg: 59%. **Grad '04—110.** Col—110. Avg SAT: 1210. Alum 2900. **Tui '04-'05:** Day $10,450 (+$500). Aid: Merit 74 ($125,000). Need 175 ($310,000). **Summer:** Acad Enrich Rec. Sports. 1-4 wks. **Est 1884.** Nonprofit. Roman Catholic. Quar (Sept-June). **Assoc** MSA. Advanced Placement and honors courses in the major disciplines are supplemented by electives in contemporary fiction, drama, journalism, speech, psychology and computer. Activities comprise various academic clubs, music and the arts, publications, service organizations, student council, honor societies and sports.

WALDRON MERCY ACADEMY   **Day Coed Gr PS-8**
Merion Station, PA 19066. 513 Montgomery Ave.
Tel: 610-664-9847. Fax: 610-664-6364.
www.waldronmercy.org   E-mail: wma@waldronmercy.org
Sr. Patricia Smith, Prin. BA, Gwynedd-Mercy College, MA, La Salle Univ. Susan Smith, Adm.

Pre-Prep. Gen Acad. Feat—Fr Lat Span Computers Relig Studio_Art Drama Music. **Supp**—Tut. **Adm:** 110/yr. Appl due: Rolling. Accepted: 91%. **Tests** IQ. **Enr 599.** B 290. G 309. Elem 599. Wh 76%. Hisp 1%. Blk 18%. Asian 3%. Other 2%. Avg class size: 19. Uniform. **Fac 55.** M 7. F 48. Adv deg: 29%. **Grad '04—59.** Prep—57. Alum 2300. **Tui '05-'06:** Day $8400 (+$150-300). Aid: Merit 1 ($1000). **Summer:** Acad Enrich Rev Rec. 2-8 wks. **Est 1923.** Nonprofit. Roman Catholic. Tri (Sept-June). **Assoc** MSA. WMA's focus on religious education features religion classes and community service projects. The academy provides instruction in computers and three foreign languages and conducts strong music, art and drama programs. Students publish their own works as part of the English program. Extracurricular activities and athletics supplement academics.

ST. GREGORY'S ACADEMY   **Bdg Boys Gr 9-12**
Moscow, PA 18444. Griffin Rd, RR 8, Box 8214.
Tel: 570-842-8112. Fax: 570-842-4513.
www.stgregorysacademy.org
Alan J. Hicks, Head. BA, MA, Univ of Kansas.

Col Prep. Feat—Humanities Lat Logic Relig Music Gregorian_Chant Rhetoric. **Adm:** 20/yr. **Enr 61.** B 61. Sec 61. Wh 93%. Hisp 2%. Blk 5%. Avg class size: 15. Uniform. **Fac 10.** M 7/2. F /1. Adv deg: 50%. In Dorms 5. **Grad '04—15.** Col—12. Avg SAT: 1105. **Tui '02-'03:** Bdg $8550 (+$500). **Est 1993.** Nonprofit. Roman Catholic. Quar (Sept-May). St. Gregory's maintains a liberal arts curriculum based upon the Latin liturgy and classical Western literature. The daily schedule comprises celebration of the Latin Mass, recitation of the rosary, rigorous course work and participation in athletics. While some graduates go on to the seminary, most matriculate at competitive colleges.

DELAWARE COUNTY CHRISTIAN SCHOOL   Day Coed Gr PS-12
Newtown Square, PA 19073. 462 Malin Rd.
Tel: 610-353-6522. Fax: 610-356-9684.
www.dccs.org   E-mail: dccs@dccs.org

Stephen P. Dill, Head. BA, Wheaton College (IL), MA, Villanova Univ, EdD, Temple Univ. Kenneth H. Tanis, Adm.

Col Prep. AP—Eng Ger Span Calc Physics Eur_Hist US_Hist. **Feat**—Psych Bible Film Theater_Arts Debate Journ. **Supp**—ESL LD Rem_Math Rem_Read Tut. **Adm:** 162/yr. Appl due: Rolling. **Enr 963.** Elem 569. Sec 394. Wh 87%. Hisp 1%. Blk 7%. Asian 4%. Other 1%. Avg class size: 21. Uniform. **Fac 108.** M 35/2. F 51/20. Adv deg: 61%. **Grad '04—92.** Col—91. Avg SAT: 1140. Alum 1800. **Tui '04-'05:** Day $5489-8745 (+$325-600). Aid: Need 257 ($500,000). **Summer:** Rec. 6 wks. **Est** 1950. Nonprofit. Nondenom Christian. Sem (Sept-June). **Assoc** MSA. DC integrates honors and Advanced Placement courses into a curriculum that also features, for an additional fee, individualized therapy and small-group resource rooms for students with learning differences. Pupils enroll from five Delaware Valley counties within a 25-mile radius of the school. The elementary division (grades pre-K-5) is located at a separate campus on Bishop Hollow Road.

CROSSROADS SCHOOL   Day Coed Gr K-8
Paoli, PA 19301. 1681 N Valley Rd, PO Box 730.
Tel: 610-296-6765. Fax: 610-296-6772.
www.thecrossroadsschool.net   E-mail: admissions@thecrossroadsschool.net

George B. Vosburgh, Head. BA, Univ of Colorado-Boulder, MA, Univ of Denver. Julia G. Sadtler, Adm.

Pre-Prep. LD. Feat—Study_Skills. **Supp**—Rem_Math Rem_Read. **Adm (Gr K-7):** 15/yr. Appl due: Rolling. Accepted: 46%. Yield: 77%. **Tests** IQ. **Enr 96.** B 66. G 30. Elem 96. Wh 95%. Hisp 2%. Blk 1%. Asian 1%. Other 1%. Avg class size: 12. Uniform. **Fac 37.** M 1. F 33/3. Adv deg: 67%. **Grad '04—11.** Prep—9. Alum 575. **Tui '04-'05:** Day $17,750-21,090 (+$805). Aid: Need 11 ($89,600). **Summer:** Acad Rem Rec. Tui Day $2195. 5 wks. **Est** 1977. Nonprofit. Tri (Sept-June). Crossroads employs a language-based and multisensory approach for intelligent students with learning differences. The program consists of a comprehensive elementary and middle school curriculum that emphasizes individualized instruction.

DELAWARE VALLEY FRIENDS SCHOOL   Day Coed Gr 7-12
Paoli, PA 19301. 19 E Central Ave.
Tel: 610-640-4150. Fax: 610-296-9970.
www.dvfs.org   E-mail: wynnk@fc.dvfs.org

Katherine Schantz, Head. BA, Kalamazoo College, MEd, Harvard Univ. Jeannie Bowman, Adm.

Col Prep. LD. Feat—Lat Span Asian_Stud Photog Studio_Art Music Outdoor_Ed. **Supp**—Dev_Read Rem_Math Rem_Read Tut. **Adm:** 43/yr. Appl due: Rolling. Accepted: 50%. **Tests** IQ. **Enr 166.** B 109. G 57. Elem 35. Sec 131. Wh 89%. Hisp 1%. Blk 7%. Asian 2%. Other 1%. Avg class size: 7. **Fac 37.** M 14/3. F 18/2. **Grad '04—22.** Col—19. Alum 234. **Tui '03-'04:** Day $24,250 (+$600). Aid: Merit 3 ($3000). Need 35 ($186,610). **Summer:** Acad Enrich Rem. Tui Day

$2750. 5 wks. **Est 1986.** Nonprofit. Religious Society of Friends. Tri (Sept-June). Enrolling intelligent students with learning disabilities, Delaware Friends features language arts learning skills laboratories that provide small-group remedial and developmental assistance. All students take part in a daily reading and writing lab, and the school conducts an adaptive Outward Bound-type program that includes courses in rock climbing, backpacking, bicycle touring, ropes and hiking. Seniors participate in a compulsory, off-campus work-study internship, and each pupil is required to perform community service.

ARCHBISHOP RYAN HIGH SCHOOL — Day Coed Gr 9-12
Philadelphia, PA 19154. 11201 Academy Rd.
Tel: 215-637-1800. Fax: 215-637-8833.
www.archbishopryan.com   E-mail: bropat@ryanalumni.com
  Mr. Michael J. McArdle, Pres. Michael O'Donnell, Adm.

  Col Prep. Gen Acad. AP—Eng Calc Bio Chem Physics Eur_Hist US_Hist US_Govt & Pol. **Feat**—Fr Ger Ital Lat Span Computers Econ Law Psych Band Chorus Music Communications Journ. **Supp**—Dev_Read LD Rem_Math Rem_Read Tut. **Adm:** 629/yr. **Enr 2564.** B 1133. G 1431. Sec 2564. Wh 97%. Hisp 1%. Blk 1%. Asian 1%. Avg class size: 21. Uniform. **Fac 130.** M 64. F 66. Adv deg: 62%. **Grad '04—620.** Col—527. Avg SAT: 1050. Alum 30,000. **Tui '04-'05:** Day $4760 (+$175). Catholic $3900 (+$175). Aid: Merit 250 ($250,000). Need 450 ($200,000). **Est 1966.** Nonprofit. Roman Catholic. Sem (Sept-June). **Assoc** MSA. Archbishop Ryan is a full-spectrum high school offering college preparatory courses, business education and opportunities for technical training. Honors courses are available in English and religion, while AP courses are provided in four areas. Top seniors are invited to take college classes for credit at area Catholic colleges.

FATHER JUDGE HIGH SCHOOL — Day Boys Gr 9-12
Philadelphia, PA 19136. 3301 Solly Ave.
Tel: 215-338-9494. Fax: 215-338-0250.
www.fatherjudge.com   E-mail: info@fatherjudge.com
  Rev. Joseph Campellone, OSFS, Pres. BA, DeSales School of Theology, MDiv, DeSales Univ. Joseph DeAngelis, Prin. James Greene, Adm.

  Col Prep. Gen Acad. AP—Eng Calc Bio Physics Eur_Hist US_Govt & Pol. **Feat**—Fr Lat Span Anat & Physiol Psych Theol Studio_Art Music Bus Drafting. **Supp**—Tut. **Adm (Gr 9-11):** 346/yr. Appl due: July. Accepted: 95%. **Enr 1293.** B 1293. Sec 1293. Wh 95%. Hisp 2%. Blk 1%. Asian 1%. Other 1%. Avg class size: 24. Uniform. **Fac 65.** M 50. F 15. Wh 99%. Blk 1%. Adv deg: 35%. **Grad '04—302.** Col—234. Alum 22,000. **Tui '04-'05:** Day $3900 (+$425). **Summer:** Acad Enrich Rem. Tui Day $200. 2 wks. **Est 1954.** Nonprofit. Roman Catholic. Quar (Sept-June). **Assoc** MSA. Subjects are provided at different levels of academic difficulty, ranging from advanced to remedial. AP courses are offered, and qualified seniors take courses at local Catholic colleges each semester for college credit. Various extracurricular activities and athletic programs are available.

GIRARD COLLEGE
Bdg Coed Gr 1-12
Philadelphia, PA 19121. 2101 S College Ave.
Tel: 215-787-2620. Fax: 215-787-4402.
www.girardcollege.com   E-mail: admissions@girardcollege.com
Dominic M. Cermele, Pres. Frances E. Smith, Head. Tamara Hoch, Adm.

Col Prep. Gen Acad. AP—Eng Calc. **Feat**—Fr Span Psych Philos Studio_Art Video_Production. **Supp**—Dev_Read Rem_Math Rem_Read Tut. **Adm (Gr 1-10):** 159/yr. Appl due: June. Accepted: 29%. Yield: 84%. **Tests** IQ Stanford. **Enr 678.** B 310. G 368. Elem 487. Sec 191. Wh 2%. Hisp 3%. Blk 82%. Asian 6%. Other 7%. Avg class size: 18. Uniform. **Fac 53.** M 22. F 31. Wh 82%. Hisp 2%. Blk 14%. Asian 2%. Adv deg: 52%. In Dorms 2. **Grad '04**—44. Col—41. Avg SAT: 990. Avg ACT: 19. Alum 4000. **Tui '04-'05:** Bdg $0. **Summer:** Rec. Tui Day $0. 1 wk. **Est 1848.** Nonprofit. Quar (Sept-June). **Assoc** MSA. Stephen Girard, an early American businessman, endowed this school to educate orphaned boys. Today, Girard College enrolls boys and girls from limited-income families without one or both parents; the school furnishes full scholarships for its students. In addition to providing a college preparatory curriculum, Girard conducts a special program that addresses five areas: study skills, behavior, appearance, care of property and community service. Students also participate in recreational and enrichment activities at local museums, parks, historical sites, theaters, universities and sporting facilities.

JOHN W. HALLAHAN CATHOLIC GIRLS' HIGH SCHOOL
Day Girls Gr 9-12
Philadelphia, PA 19103. 311 N 19th St.
Tel: 215-563-8930. Fax: 215-563-3809.
www.jwhallahan.org
Margaret Gallagher, Pres. BS, Pennsylvania State Univ. Sr. Susan Marie Kuk, IHM, Prin. BA, Randolph-Macon Woman's College, EdD, Nova Southeastern Univ.

Col Prep. Gen Acad. AP—Eng Calc Bio Chem US_Hist. **Feat**—Fr Span Anat & Physiol Environ_Sci Computers Govt/Econ Theol Studio_Art Music Accounting. **Supp**—Dev_Read Rem_Read. **Adm:** 210/yr. **Enr 650.** G 650. Sec 650. Wh 68%. Hisp 5%. Blk 24%. Asian 3%. Avg class size: 30. Uniform. **Fac 33.** M 5. F 28. Adv deg: 48%. **Grad '04**—175. Alum 10,000. **Tui '02-'03:** Day $3700 (+$300). **Est 1901.** Nonprofit. Roman Catholic. (Sept-June). **Assoc** MSA. At Hallahan, standard, honors and Advanced Placement classes provide students with both college and career preparation. The school emphasizes a strong foundation in theology, math, science and the humanities and offers electives such as foreign languages, environmental science and fine arts. In addition, a work experience program prepares students for the business world by introducing the latest technology and providing on-the-job training at Center City firms.

NAZARETH ACADEMY HIGH SCHOOL
Day Girls Gr 9-12
Philadelphia, PA 19114. 4001 Grant Ave.
Tel: 215-637-7676. Fax: 215-637-8523.
www.nazarethacademyhs.org   E-mail: info@nazarethacademyhs.org
Sr. Mary Joan Jacobs, CSFN, Prin. BA, Holy Family Univ, MA, Villanova Univ, EdD, St Joseph's Univ. Maryann Kendall, Adm.

Col Prep. Gen Acad. Bus. AP—Eng Lat Calc Stats Bio US_Hist US_Govt & Pol Studio_Art Music_Theory. **Feat**—ASL Fr Ger Ital Span Polish Anat & Physiol Comp_Design Programming Web_Design Law Psych Sociol Bus_Law Relig Theol Film Theater_Arts Music Accounting Bus Finance Public_Speak Study_Skills. **Supp**—Tut. **Adm (Gr 9-11):** 122/yr. Appl due: Oct. Accepted: 75%. Yield: 41%. **Tests** HSPT. **Enr 466.** G 466. Sec 466. Avg class size: 23. Uniform. **Fac 52.** M 9/4. F 27/12. Wh 98%. Hisp 1%. Blk 1%. Adv deg: 63%. **Grad '04—105.** Col—105. Avg SAT: 1084. Avg ACT: 24. Alum 4269. **Tui '04-'05:** Day $6500 (+$300). Aid: Merit 32 ($61,500). Need 10 ($11,000). **Summer:** Enrich. Tui Day $300. 4 wks. Gr 9. Basketball. Soccer. 1 wk. **Est 1928.** Nonprofit. Roman Catholic. Sem (Aug-June). **Assoc** MSA. NAHS' curriculum features Advanced Placement and honors courses, in addition to a variety of electives. In addition to requirements in the standard subjects, pupils complete four years of theology course work. Student activities include publications, various honor societies, service organizations, academic clubs, fine arts offerings and social awareness clubs. **See Also Page 1306**

THE PHILADELPHIA SCHOOL   **Day Coed Gr PS-8**
Philadelphia, PA 19146. 2501 Lombard St.
Tel: 215-545-5323. Fax: 215-546-1798.
www.thephiladelphiaschool.org

Sandra Dean, Prin. BS, Univ of Pennsylvania, MEd, Temple Univ. Abigail S. Levner, Adm.

Pre-Prep. Feat—Lat Span Studio_Art Drama Music. **Supp**—Dev_Read Rem_Math Rem_Read Rev Tut. **Adm (Gr PS-7):** 89/yr. Appl due: Rolling. Accepted: 50%. Yield: 82%. **Enr 364.** B 162. G 202. Elem 364. Wh 72%. Hisp 5%. Blk 7%. Asian 6%. Other 10%. **Fac 44.** M 6/1. F 34/3. Wh 84%. Hisp 5%. Blk 2%. Asian 9%. Adv deg: 54%. **Grad '04—37.** Prep—28. Alum 425. **Tui '04-'05:** Day $10,120-15,505. Aid: Need 69 ($602,124). **Summer:** Acad Enrich. Art. Music. Tui Day $500. 3 wks. **Est 1970.** Nonprofit. (Sept-June). TPS places strong emphasis on its academic program. The cultural resources of Philadelphia and a 125-acre rural site, where an environmental education program is implemented, supplement the curriculum. After-school daycare, sports and activities (including instrumental music lessons) are available.

SAINTS JOHN NEUMANN   **Day Coed Gr 9-12**
AND MARIA GORETTI CATHOLIC HIGH SCHOOL
Philadelphia, PA 19148. 1736 S 10th St.
Tel: 215-465-8437. Fax: 215-462-2410.
www.neumanngoretti.com

Rev. Michael S. Olivere, Pres. EdD. Patricia C. Sticco, Prin. Mary Catherine Alveario, Adm.

Col Prep. Gen Acad. Bus. AP—Eng Calc Bio US_Hist Studio_Art. **Feat**—British_Lit Creative_Writing Ital Span Environ_Sci Comp_Sci Psych Theol Theater Music Dance Nutrition. **Supp**—Dev_Read Rem_Math Rem_Read Tut. **Enr 1173.** B 529. G 644. Sec 1173. Wh 77%. Hisp 1%. Blk 15%. Asian 7%. Uniform. **Fac 64.** M 42. F 22. Wh 97%. Blk 3%. Adv deg: 40%.**Tui '04-'05:** Day $4760 (+$500). Catholic $3900 (+$500). **Est 1936.** Nonprofit. Roman Catholic. Quar (Sept-June). **Assoc** MSA. Tailoring its curriculum to students' specific needs, Neumann-Goretti offers five programs of study: Advanced Placement, honors, college placement, general and remedial support. The school's business and technology department allows pupils to take such courses as economics and business technology, business law and accounting. A strong computer program is part of the curriculum, and fine arts offerings include instrumental and vocal music, dance and art.

WEST PHILADELPHIA CATHOLIC HIGH SCHOOL
Day Coed Gr 9-12

Philadelphia, PA 19139. 4501 Chestnut St.
Tel: 215-386-2244. Fax: 215-222-1651.
www.westcatholic.org
Sr. Mary E. Bur, IHM, Prin. Sr. Mary Ignatius Kerrigan & Brian Fluck, Adms.

Col Prep. Gen Acad. AP—Eng Calc US_Hist US_Govt & Pol Studio_Art. **Feat**—Fr Ger Span Computers Econ Intl_Relations Psych Child_Dev Relig Music Bus Mech_Drawing Home_Ec. **Supp**—Dev_Read Rem_Math Rem_Read Rev Tut. **Adm:** 206/yr. Appl due: June. Accepted: 95%. **Tests** SSAT. **Enr 714.** B 374. G 340. Sec 714. Wh 18%. Hisp 2%. Blk 71%. Asian 9%. Avg class size: 34. Uniform. **Fac 41.** M 19/6. F 14/2. Wh 98%. Blk 2%. Adv deg: 78%. **Grad '04—170.** Col—164. Avg SAT: 800. Alum 33,000. **Tui '04-'05:** Day $5245. Aid: Merit 92 ($165,640). Need 480 ($719,101). **Summer:** Enrich. Tui Day $200. 4 wks. **Est 1916.** Nonprofit. Roman Catholic. Sem (Sept-June). The school's liberal arts curriculum comprises honors, college prep and remedial programs of study. West Catholic participates in a program that allows seniors to take classes at area Catholic colleges for college credit. Technology is integral to the program.

FOX CHAPEL COUNTRY DAY SCHOOL
Day Coed Gr PS-5

Pittsburgh, PA 15238. 620 Squaw Run Rd E.
Tel: 412-963-8644. Fax: 412-963-7123.
www.foxchapelcountryday.com   E-mail: fccdspa@city-net.com
Robert E. Kirkpatrick, Head. BA, Kenyon College, MAT, Colgate Univ.

Pre-Prep. Gen Acad. Feat—Span Studio_Art Drama Music. **Supp**—LD Tut. **Adm (Gr PS-3):** 26/yr. Accepted: 50%. Yield: 79%. **Enr 131.** B 76. G 55. Elem 131. Wh 100%. Asian 5%. Avg class size: 18. Uniform. **Fac 15.** M 1. F 12/2. Wh 100%. Adv deg: 40%. **Grad '04—14.** Alum 605. **Tui '04-'05:** Day $4800-8980. **Summer:** Gr K-3. Enrich. Sci. Gr 4-5. Art. Music. Tui Day $175/wk. 3 wks. **Est 1948.** Nonprofit. Episcopal. Tri (Sept-June). Beginning with its age 4 prekindergarten, Country Day places balanced emphasis on academics and the arts. The traditional elementary-level curriculum features small classes and ample flexibility to address pupils' varying needs. Although the program is nonsectarian, all children attend weekly chapel. Opportunities for outdoor play and exploration of the school's environs complement academics.

PORTERSVILLE CHRISTIAN SCHOOL
Day Coed Gr K-12

Portersville, PA 16051. 343 E Portersville Rd.
Tel: 724-368-8787. Fax: 724-368-3100.
E-mail: pcsschooloffice@zoominternet.net
Patricia Watters, Admin. BS, Geneva College, MA, Liberty Univ.

Col Prep. Feat—Fr Span Computers Econ Bible Chorus Music. **Adm:** 40/yr. Appl due: Rolling. Accepted: 75%. **Enr 253.** B 114. G 139. Elem 138. Sec 115. Wh 99%. Other 1%. Avg class size: 18. **Fac 28.** M 4/3. F 14/7. Wh 100%. Adv deg: 28%. **Grad '04—23.** Col—19. Avg SAT: 1100. Alum 25. **Tui '04-'05:** Day $3920-4020. Aid: Need 32 ($49,860). **Est 1963.** Nonprofit. Evangelical. Quar (Aug-June). **Assoc** MSA. From a Christian perspective, PCS offers honors courses in such areas as chemistry and calculus. Students choose from the following sports: volleyball and basketball for girls, and soccer and basketball for boys.

UNITED FRIENDS SCHOOL — Day Coed Gr PS-8
Quakertown, PA 18951. 1018 W Broad St.
Tel: 215-538-1733. Fax: 215-538-3140.
www.unitedfriendsschool.org E-mail: csellers@unitedfriendsschool.org

Craig N. Sellers, Head. AB, Franklin and Marshall College, JD, New York Law School, MA, Columbia Univ. Marie Knapp, Adm.

Gen Acad. Feat—Span Studio_Art Music. **Adm:** 48/yr. Appl due: Rolling. Accepted: 95%. **Enr 155.** B 62. G 93. Elem 155. Wh 94%. Hisp 3%. Asian 3%. Avg class size: 16. **Fac 19.** M 1/1. F 11/6. Wh 95%. Blk 5%. Adv deg: 15%. **Grad '04—13.** Prep—5. Alum 200. **Tui '03-'04:** Day $7510 (+$50). Aid: Need 37 ($56,305). **Summer:** Rec. Tui Day $135/wk. 8 wks. **Est 1983.** Nonprofit. Religious Society of Friends. Sem (Sept-June). Emphasis is on cooperative learning through open-ended, student-centered exploratory activities and an integrated curriculum. The UFS middle school program is enhanced by community mentoring opportunities and a more advanced approach to research, independent study, computer access and academic evaluation. Each year, students participate in many service projects, and the school community participates in weekly Meeting for Worship. The lower school occupies separate quarters at 20 S. 10th St.

HILL TOP PREPARATORY SCHOOL — Day Coed Gr 6-12
Rosemont, PA 19010. 737 S Ithan Ave.
Tel: 610-527-3230. Fax: 610-527-7683.
www.hilltopprep.org E-mail: thiggins@hilltopprep.org

Leslie McLean, Head. BA, Univ of the South, MS, Union College, EdD, Vanderbilt Univ. Tara L. Higgins, Adm.

Col Prep. LD. Feat—Photog Drama. **Supp**—Dev_Read Rem_Math Rem_Read. **Adm:** 38/yr. Day 28. Appl due: Rolling. Accepted: 25%. **Enr 86.** B 68. G 18. Elem 28. Sec 58. Wh 90%. Blk 9%. Asian 1%. Avg class size: 7. **Fac 31.** M 13. F 18. Wh 100%. Adv deg: 83%. **Grad '04—12.** Col—11. Alum 284. **Tui '04-'05:** Day $28,375. Aid: Need 13 ($89,000). **Summer:** Acad Enrich Rev Rem Rec. Tui Day $1950. 4 wks. **Est 1971.** Nonprofit. Quar (Sept-June). **Assoc** MSA. For students of average and above-average intelligence who have learning disabilities or attention deficit disorder, this specially designed program utilizes individualized instruction to prepare students for college and employment. Reality-oriented group counseling sessions are an integral part of the program.

ROSEMONT SCHOOL OF THE HOLY CHILD Day Coed Gr PS-8
Rosemont, PA 19010. 1344 Montgomery Ave.
Tel: 610-922-1000. Fax: 610-525-7128.
www.rosemontschool.org   E-mail: jmblair@rosemontschool.org
  Sr. Mary Broderick, SHCJ, Head. BA, Villanova Univ, MA, Marywood College. Jeanne Marie Blair, Adm.
  Pre-Prep. Gen Acad. Feat—Lat Span Computers Relig Studio_Art Drama Music. **Adm (Gr PS-7):** 54/yr. Appl due: Dec. Accepted: 95%. **Tests** IQ. **Enr 303.** B 155. G 148. Elem 303. Wh 92%. Hisp 1%. Blk 6%. Asian 1%. Avg class size: 15. Uniform. **Fac 41.** M 6. F 34/1. Wh 97%. Hisp 1%. Blk 1%. Other 1%. Adv deg: 60%. **Grad '04**—25. Prep—25. Alum 1000. **Tui '04-'05:** Day $5750-13,875 (+$500). Aid: Need 28 ($270,000). **Summer:** Enrich. Tui Day $150/wk. 4 wks. **Est 1949.** Nonprofit. Roman Catholic. Tri (Sept-June). A traditional curriculum and religious training are augmented by enrichment opportunities in art, music, computers and drama. Rosemont conducts a varied extracurricular activities program. Varsity athletics include track, basketball, football, field hockey and swimming, and intramural sports are also available.   **See Also Page 1237**

WOODLYNDE SCHOOL Day Coed Gr K-12
Strafford, PA 19087. 445 Upper Gulph Rd.
Tel: 610-687-9660. Fax: 610-687-4752.
www.woodlynde.org   E-mail: info@woodlynde.org
  Cinda L. Russell, Int Head. MA, Arizona State Univ, EdD, Univ of Arizona. Barbara Zbrzeznj, Upper & Middle Sch Adm; Nancy Dunlap, Lower Sch Adm.
  Col Prep. Feat—Fr Lat Span Pol_Sci Psych Sociol Photog Studio_Art Drama Music. **Supp**—Dev_Read Rem_Math Rem_Read Tut. **Adm:** 70/yr. Appl due: Rolling. Accepted: 30%. **Tests** IQ. **Enr 339.** B 187. G 152. Elem 210. Sec 129. Wh 90%. Hisp 1%. Blk 7%. Asian 1%. Other 1%. Avg class size: 12. **Fac 62.** M 14/1. F 46/1. Wh 100%. Adv deg: 40%. **Grad '04**—22. Col—22. Alum 435. **Tui '04-'05:** Day $18,500 (+$400-825). Aid: Need 52 ($422,910). **Summer:** Enrich Rev Rec. Tui Day $325-1300. 4 wks. **Est 1976.** Nonprofit. Tri (Sept-June). Woodlynde provides a standard college preparatory curriculum. Students are required to participate in one extracurricular activity; aside from the athletic program, school newspaper, drama, chorus, student council, yearbook, literary magazine, lab assistants and community service are among the choices. Seniors take a full-time unpaid position for two weeks as participants in a senior project program.

WEST CHESTER FRIENDS SCHOOL Day Coed Gr PS-5
West Chester, PA 19380. 415 N High St.
Tel: 610-696-2937. Fax: 610-431-1457.
www.wcfriends.org   E-mail: admissions@wcfriends.org
  Matthew Bradley, Head. BA, Univ of Notre Dame, MA, Columbia Univ. Barbara B. Rowe, Adm.
  Gen Acad. Feat—Lib_Skills Span Comp_Sci Quakerism Studio_Art Music. **Adm:** 31/yr. Appl due: Jan. **Enr 131.** Elem 131. Wh 85%. Blk 8%. Asian 2%. Other 5%. Avg class size: 11. **Fac 22.** M 2/3. F 14/3. Wh 99%. Hisp 1%. Adv deg: 45%. **Grad '04**—18. Alum 2134. **Tui '04-'05:** Day $12,500. **Est 1836.** Nonprofit. Reli-

gious Society of Friends. Tri (Sept-June). All boys and girls at this Quaker school study Spanish, computer and library science, in addition to the usual elementary courses. Community scholarships are open to all applicants. Before- and after-school care is available.

CHRISTIAN SCHOOL OF YORK Day Coed Gr PS-12
York, PA 17404. 907 Greenbriar Rd.
Tel: 717-767-6842. Fax: 717-767-4904.
www.csyonline.com   E-mail: info@csyonline.com
Michael R. Leaming, Supt. BA, MA, Pensacola Christian College, EdD, Nova Southeastern Univ. Kim Martin, Adm.

Col Prep. Gen Acad. AP—Eng. **Feat**—Creative_Writing Fr Span Environ_Sci Comp_Sci Bible Studio_Art Music Music_Theory Accounting. **Supp**—LD Rem_Math Rem_Read. **Adm:** 69/yr. Appl due: June. Accepted: 95%. Yield: 98%. **Tests** DAT Stanford. **Enr 459.** B 234. G 225. Elem 297. Sec 162. Wh 96%. Hisp 1%. Blk 1%. Asian 1%. Other 1%. Avg class size: 20. **Fac 47.** M 13. F 27/7. Wh 100%. Adv deg: 19%. **Grad '04—30.** Col—23. Avg SAT: 1139. Alum 1076. **Tui '04-'05:** Day $6265 (+$185). Aid: Need 164 ($300,000). **Est 1956.** Nonprofit. Nondenom Christian. Quar (Aug-June). Emphasis is placed on a Christian education at CSY. Christian service projects are incorporated into the curriculum. A supplemental learning disabilities program serves students in grades 1-12.

Southern States

ALABAMA

HIGHLANDS SCHOOL Day Coed Gr PS-8
Birmingham, AL 35213. 4901 Old Leeds Rd.
Tel: 205-956-9731. Fax: 205-951-8127.
www.highlandsschool.org   E-mail: ajohnston@highlandsschool.org
  Dale Hanson, Int Head. BS, Univ of Maine-Orono, MS, Univ of New Hampshire. Annette N. Johnston, Adm.

  Pre-Prep. Feat—Fr Span Studio_Art Drama Music Outdoor_Ed. **Supp**—Tut. **Adm:** 58/yr. Appl due: Rolling. Accepted: 63%. Yield: 79%. **Tests** CTP_4 IQ ISEE Stanford. **Enr 258.** B 135. G 123. Elem 258. Wh 89%. Blk 7%. Asian 3%. Other 1%. Avg class size: 16. **Fac 30.** M 6. F 21/3. Wh 100%. Adv deg: 56%. **Grad '04—3.** Prep—2. Alum 1300. **Tui '04-'05:** Day $6550-8315 (+$500). Aid: Merit 12 ($18,765). Need 10 ($34,833). **Summer:** Enrich Rec. Tui Day $150/wk. 12 wks. **Est 1958.** Nonprofit. Tri (Aug-June). **Assoc** SACS. The school places emphasis on advanced academic preparation, as well as on art and music. Instructors commonly provide individualized and small-group instruction. Soccer, basketball, instrumental music, and track and field are among extracurricular options, and extended-day programming is available.

LYMAN WARD MILITARY ACADEMY Bdg Boys Gr 6-12
Camp Hill, AL 36850. PO Drawer 550.
Tel: 256-896-4127. Fax: 256-896-4661.
www.lwma.org   E-mail: info@lwma.org
  Chester C. Carroll, Pres. Michael C. Burke, Adm.

  Col Prep. Milit. AP—Eng Calc Chem Econ US_Govt & Pol. **Feat**—Ger Span Computers. **Supp**—Dev_Read Rem_Math Rem_Read. **Adm:** 130/yr. Appl due: Rolling. Accepted: 80%. **Enr 200.** B 200. Elem 65. Sec 135. Wh 82%. Hisp 12%. Blk 5%. Asian 1%. Avg class size: 14. Uniform. **Fac 28.** Adv deg: 25%. In Dorms 4. **Grad '04—18.** Col—18. Alum 600. **Tui '03-'04:** Bdg $14,950 (+$2600). Aid: Need 37 ($40,000). **Summer:** Rec. Adventure. Tui Bdg $1150/2-wk ses. 4 wks. **Est 1898.** Nonprofit. Sem (Aug-May). **Assoc** SACS. Offering a college preparatory program within a military setting, this school also provides special help in reading and study skills. Graduates attend a variety of Southern colleges. The academic program is supplemented by a full sports program, in addition to rifle and drill teams.

BAYSIDE ACADEMY Day Coed Gr PS-12
Daphne, AL 36526. 303 Dryer Ave.
Tel: 251-626-2840. Fax: 251-626-2899.
www.baysideacademy.org   E-mail: afoster@baysideacademy.org
  Thomas Johnson, Head. BA, MEd, Valdosta State College. Alan M. Foster, Adm.

Col Prep. AP—Eng Fr Span Calc Bio Physics Eur_Hist US_Hist Studio_Art. **Feat**—Anat Environ_Sci Genetics Marine_Biol/Sci Programming Econ Psych Ceramics Film Sculpt. **Supp**—LD. **Adm:** 90/yr. Appl due: Rolling. Accepted: 60%. **Tests** Stanford. **Enr 700.** B 340. G 360. Elem 480. Sec 220. Wh 95%. Hisp 2%. Blk 1%. Asian 2%. Avg class size: 16. Uniform. **Fac 93.** M 17. F 76. Adv deg: 36%. **Grad '04—53.** Col—53. Alum 750. **Tui '04-'05:** Day $4000-6965 (+$600). Aid: Merit 25 ($100,000). Need 85 ($220,000). **Summer:** Enrich Rec. Tui Day $25-45/wk. 8 wks. **Est 1967.** Nonprofit. Sem (Aug-May). **Assoc** SACS. The academy's main campus is located on a 22-acre site on Mobile Bay; a second campus, Bayside East, serves grades PS-4 at 6900 Hwy. 59, Gulf Shores 36542. The lower school offers art, music, physical education, computer science and conversational Spanish. Drama, service clubs and a full athletic program are part of the total program for grades 1-12. A learning resource center assists students with attention deficits and mild learning disabilities.

MARS HILL BIBLE SCHOOL — Day Coed Gr PS-12
Florence, AL 35630. 698 Cox Creek Pky.
Tel: 256-767-1203. Fax: 256-767-6304.
www.mhbs.org

Kenny Barfield, Pres. EdD, Univ of Alabama-Tuscaloosa. David Willingham, Adm.

Col Prep. AP—Calc US_Hist Psych US_Govt & Pol. **Feat**—Span Anat & Physiol Ecol Marine_Biol/Sci Comp_Sci Econ Bible Drama Chorus Bus Debate. **Adm:** 94/yr. Appl due: Aug. Accepted: 95%. **Enr 558.** B 290. G 268. Elem 381. Sec 177. Wh 95%. Blk 3%. Asian 2%. Avg class size: 20. **Fac 44.** M 12/2. F 28/2. Wh 99%. Blk 1%. Adv deg: 63%. **Grad '04—50.** Col—50. Avg SAT: 1143. Avg ACT: 23. **Tui '04-'05:** Day $4056 (+$300). Aid: Need 99 ($125,000). **Est 1947.** Nonprofit. Nondenom Christian. Quar (Aug-May). As part of MHBS' curriculum, all students fulfill yearly Bible study requirements. Middle schoolers (grades 6-8) choose from various enrichment classes each quarter, while older high school pupils may take Advanced Placement and honors courses. Among extracurricular options are band, chorus, debate, drama and service clubs.

MADISON ACADEMY — Day Coed Gr PS-12
Madison, AL 35758. 325 Slaughter Rd.
Tel: 256-971-1619. Fax: 256-971-1436.
www.macademy.org   E-mail: msmith@macademy.org

Robert F. Burton, Pres. BS, David Lipscomb Univ, MEd, Alabama A&M Univ. Chris Berry, High Sch Adm; Carmelita Burton, Elem Sch Adm.

Col Prep. AP—Eng Calc. **Feat**—Fr Span Environ_Sci Comp_Sci Econ Govt Psych Bible Studio_Art Photojourn Drama Music_Theory. **Supp**—Dev_Read Rev Tut. **Adm:** 147/yr. **Tests** CEEB IQ Stanford. **Enr 849.** B 430. G 419. Elem 587. Sec 262. Wh 91%. Blk 6%. Asian 2%. Other 1%. Avg class size: 18. Uniform. **Fac 65.** M 16. F 44/5. Wh 100%. Adv deg: 43%. **Grad '04—64.** Col—49. Avg ACT: 24. Alum 1450. **Tui '04-'05:** Day $4500-4950 (+$500). Aid: Need 40 ($66,500). **Est 1955.** Nonprofit. Sem (Aug-May). **Assoc** SACS. The academy's college preparatory curriculum includes a dual-enrollment option for qualified juniors and seniors that enables them to earn college credit through one of three area colleges. Daily

Bible study and chapel attendance are required, and community service is a compulsory part of the Bible program. Extracurricular offerings include robotics team, scholars bowl, chess club, yearbook, historical field studies, band and choral trips, and student government, as well as such sports as football, basketball, volleyball, baseball, softball, soccer, golf and cheerleading.

MARION MILITARY INSTITUTE

Coed Gr 9-12
Bdg & Day

Marion, AL 36756. 1101 Washington St.
Tel: 334-683-2306. Fax: 334-683-2383.
www.marionmilitary.edu   E-mail: admissions@marionmilitary.edu

Col. James H. Benson, USMC (Ret), Pres. BA, Bridgewater College, MS, Univ of Tennessee-Knoxville, MPA, Pennsylvania State Univ. Dan Sumlin, Adm.

Col Prep. Feat—Fr Span Comp_Sci Econ Law Fine_Arts Public_Speak JROTC. **Supp**—ESL Makeup Tut. **Adm:** 50/yr. Bdg 42. Day 8. Appl due: Aug. Accepted: 90%. **Tests** CEEB IQ SSAT Stanford TOEFL. **Enr 115.** Sec 115. Wh 76%. Blk 20%. Asian 4%. Avg class size: 12. Uniform. **Fac 14.** M 11. F 3. Wh 93%. Blk 7%. Adv deg: 85%. **Grad '04**—29. Col—28. Avg SAT: 1170. Avg ACT: 24. Alum 12,000. **Tui '04-'05:** Bdg $14,066-15,066. Day $9981-10,981. **Est 1842.** Nonprofit. Sem (Aug-May). **Assoc** SACS.   MMI conducts this military preparatory school, as well as a junior college. In addition, a service academy preparation program readies cadets for the national service academies. All cadets participate in Army ROTC programs and in either physical education, intramural sports, recreational sports or physical conditioning.

McGILL-TOOLEN CATHOLIC HIGH SCHOOL

Day Coed Gr 9-12

Mobile, AL 36604. 1501 Old Shell Rd.
Tel: 251-432-0784. Fax: 251-433-8356.
www.mcgill-toolen.org   E-mail: merritw@mcgill.pvt.k12.al.us

Rev. W. Bry Shields, Jr., Pres. MDiv, Yale Univ, MEd, Univ of South Alabama. Michelle Haas, Prin. Wayne T. Merritt, Adm.

Col Prep. Gen Acad. AP—Eng Fr Span Calc Bio Chem Physics Studio_Art. **Feat**—British_Lit Lat Anat & Physiol Environ_Sci Marine_Biol/Sci Comp_Sci Psych Theol World_Relig Art_Hist Ceramics Band Chorus Music Music_Theory Speech. **Supp**—LD. **Enr 1024.** B 497. G 527. Sec 1024. Wh 88%. Hisp 1%. Blk 11%. Avg class size: 25. Uniform. **Fac 78.** M 29/3. F 46. Wh 97%. Blk 2%. Am Ind 1%. Adv deg: 67%. **Grad '04**—262. Col—252. Avg ACT: 22. **Tui '05-'06:** Day $5780. Catholic $4500. **Summer:** Rem. 4 wks. **Est 1896.** Nonprofit. Roman Catholic. Sem (Aug-June).   Serving Mobile and Baldwin counties and Jackson County, MS, this Catholic school requires students to take four years of religion or theology courses, in addition to work in the core disciplines. Pupils enroll in at least two electives from the following areas: the humanities, business and technology, the fine arts and foreign language. Interest clubs, band, theater and athletics are among McGill-Toolen's extracurricular offerings.

ST. LUKE'S EPISCOPAL SCHOOL Day Coed Gr PS-8
Mobile, AL 36693. 980 Azalea Rd.
Tel: 251-666-2991. Fax: 251-666-2996.
www.sles.cc   E-mail: jmacphee@sles.cc

Joyce Macphee, Head. BS, Elizabethtown College, MEd, Miami Univ (OH). Leigh Eblen, Adm.

Pre-Prep. Feat—Lib_Skills Span Computers Studio_Art Music. **Supp**—Makeup Tut. **Adm:** 87/yr. Appl due: Mar. Accepted: 90%. **Tests** Stanford. **Enr 400.** B 190. G 210. Elem 400. Wh 95%. Hisp 1%. Blk 2%. Asian 2%. Avg class size: 17. Uniform. **Fac 34.** M 2/1. F 28/3. Wh 100%. Adv deg: 35%. **Grad '04—29.** Prep—25. **Tui '04-'05:** Day $2250-4645 (+$350). Aid: Need 27 ($35,000). **Summer:** Rec. Tui Day $85/wk. 11 wks. **Est 1961.** Nonprofit. Episcopal. Quar (Aug-May). **Assoc** SACS. The core subjects of reading, English, math, science, social studies and physical education are supplemented by courses in art, music, Spanish, journalism and computer science. Extracurricular activities include a yearbook, musical productions, student council, honor society, service clubs and newspaper, as well as a variety of competitive and intramural sports.

ALABAMA CHRISTIAN ACADEMY Day Coed Gr K-12
Montgomery, AL 36109. 4700 Wares Ferry Rd.
Tel: 334-277-1985. Fax: 334-279-0604.
www.alabamachristian.com

Ronnie C. Sewell, Pres. BA, MA, Univ of Alabama-Birmingham. Milton Slauson, Prin. BA, MA, PhD, Univ of Alabama-Tuscaloosa. Abbie Huber, Adm.

Col Prep. AP—US_Hist. **Feat**—Span Computers Bible Studio_Art Drama Music. **Supp**—Tut. **Adm:** 98/yr. **Enr 923.** B 454. G 469. Wh 97%. Blk 3%. Avg class size: 22. **Fac 54.** M 14. F 38/2. Adv deg: 40%. **Grad '04—59.** Col—59. Avg ACT: 21. **Tui '04-'05:** Day $4289-4636 (+$190-600). Aid: Need 40 ($50,000). **Est 1942.** Nonprofit. United Church of Christ. Sem (Aug-May). **Assoc** SACS. ACA offers a college preparatory program, with Bible study being an integral part of the curriculum. Honors courses are offered in English, science and math, and electives are available in music, art, Spanish and computer. Extracurricular activities include drama, student publications and sports.

SAINT JAMES SCHOOL Day Coed Gr PS-12
Montgomery, AL 36116. 6010 Vaughn Rd.
Tel: 334-277-8033. Fax: 334-277-2542.
www.stjweb.org   E-mail: asteineker@stjweb.org

John H. Lindsell, Head. AB, Wheaton College (IL), MTS, Gordon-Conwell Theological Seminary, EdD, Harvard Univ. Aimee B. Steineker, Adm.

Col Prep. Feat—Fr Lat Russ Span Computers Fine_Arts Theater Debate Speech. **Supp**—Tut. **Adm:** 161/yr. Appl due: Rolling. Accepted: 80%. **Tests** IQ Stanford. **Enr 1175.** Wh 95%. Blk 2%. Asian 3%. Avg class size: 19. **Fac 88.** M 13. F 75. Wh 100%. Adv deg: 52%. **Grad '04—88.** Col—88. Avg ACT: 23. Alum 1400. **Tui '04-'05:** Day $4300-7260 (+$435). Aid: Need 40 ($123,900). **Est 1955.** Nonprofit. Sem (Aug-May). **Assoc** SACS. The city's oldest and largest nonsectarian independent school, Saint James provides a college preparatory curriculum that features honors courses in grades 7-9, as well as Advanced Placement offerings in grades 10-12. The school offers strong visual and performing arts programs, speech and debate teams, and competitive athletics for boys and girls grades 6-12.

TUSCALOOSA ACADEMY   **Day Coed Gr PS-12**
Tuscaloosa, AL 35406. 420 Rice Valley Rd N.
Tel: 205-758-4462. Fax: 205-758-4418.
www.tuscaloosaacademy.org   E-mail: taknights@tuscaloosaacademy.org
    George B. Elder, Head. Lane Parker, Adm.

    Col Prep. Gen Acad. AP—Fr Calc Comp_Sci Bio US_Hist. **Feat**—Lat Anat Art_Hist Music. **Supp**—Dev_Read ESL Rem_Math Rev Tut. **Adm:** 96/yr. Appl due: Rolling. Accepted: 98%. **Tests** CEEB. **Enr 450.** Elem 300. Sec 150. Wh 95%. Blk 2%. Asian 3%. Avg class size: 16. **Fac 45.** M 8/1. F 33/3. Wh 98%. Hisp 1%. Blk 1%. Adv deg: 55%. **Grad '04—38.** Col—38. Avg SAT: 1150. Avg ACT: 24. Alum 838. **Tui '03-'04:** Day $4745-6995. Aid: Merit 16 ($45,680). Need 18 ($71,570). **Summer:** Acad Enrich Rem Rec. 9 wks. **Est 1966.** Nonprofit. (Aug-May). **Assoc** SACS. The academy's college preparatory program places emphasis on reading and composition. Independent study is encouraged.

FLORIDA

BOCA RATON CHRISTIAN SCHOOL   **Day Coed Gr PS-12**
Boca Raton, FL 33432. 315 NW 4th St.
Tel: 561-391-2727. Fax: 561-367-6808.
www.bocachristian.org   E-mail: bocachristian@bocachristian.org
    Robert H. Tennies, Head. BS, Wheaton College (IL), MA, Univ of South Florida, EdS, EdD, Florida Atlantic Univ. Eileen Travasos, Adm.

    Col Prep. AP—Eng Calc Comp_Sci Psych Music_Theory. **Feat**—British_Lit World_Lit Fr Span Environ_Sci Web_Design Econ Govt Sociol Bible Philos Drama. **Supp**—Tut. **Adm:** 121/yr. Appl due: Rolling. Accepted: 85%. Yield: 80%. **Enr 580.** B 275. G 305. Elem 475. Sec 105. Wh 81%. Hisp 13%. Blk 3%. Asian 2%. Other 1%. Avg class size: 22. Uniform. **Fac 47.** M 11. F 25/11. Wh 98%. Other 2%. Adv deg: 34%. **Grad '04—23.** Col—20. Avg SAT: 1054. **Tui '04-'05:** Day $5960-6730 (+$200-1000). Aid: Need 92 ($206,745). **Summer:** Acad Enrich Rev Rem. Tui Day $425/crse. 2 wks. **Est 1973.** Nondenom Christian. (Aug-June). Located on BRCS' main campus in downtown Boca Raton, the elementary program emphasizes mastery and application of basic skills and includes enrichment and remedial activities. The high school, situated at a separate campus at 1551 W. Camino Real, 33486, offers three diplomas: standard, college and advanced. Students in the three diploma programs take varying amounts of math, science, social studies and foreign language. Advanced boys and girls may participate in dual-enrollment, credit-bearing courses at Florida Atlantic University or Palm Beach Community College.

DONNA KLEIN JEWISH ACADEMY
Day Coed Gr K-12

Boca Raton, FL 33428. 9701 Donna Klein Blvd.
Tel: 561-852-3300. Fax: 561-852-3327.
www.dkja.org   E-mail: info@dkja.org

Karen Feller, Head. BA, Newark State College, MA, Kean College of New Jersey. Lynda Levin, Adm.

Col Prep. AP—Eng Span Calc Bio Physics Eur_Hist US_Hist World_Hist Psych. **Feat**—Shakespeare Jewish_Lit Hebrew Stats Anat Astron Genetics Programming Latin-Amer_Hist Asian_Hist Israeli_Hist Econ Govt Bus_Law Judaic_Stud Architect Drama. **Adm:** 85/yr. Appl due: Rolling. Accepted: 50%. **Tests** CTP_4 SSAT. **Enr 650.** B 320. G 330. Elem 592. Sec 58. Wh 97%. Hisp 2%. Blk 1%. Avg class size: 20. **Fac 100. Grad '04**—14. Col—14. **Tui '05-'06:** Day $12,712-13,450. Aid: Need ($1,300,000). **Est 1979.** Nonprofit. Jewish. Sem (Aug-June). A community day school, DKJA conducts a rigorous elementary and secondary program that integrates the arts, science, math, Judaic studies and the humanities. Importance is placed on the Jewish religious heritage and an understanding of other cultures. Utilizing a hands-on method, the school seeks to develop problem-solving and independent and collaborative learning skills. Instructors employ a cross-disciplinary approach that allows students to gain a greater depth of knowledge by recognizing connections between different subjects.

GRANDVIEW PREPARATORY SCHOOL
Day Coed Gr PS-12

Boca Raton, FL 33431. 336 Spanish River Blvd NW.
Tel: 561-416-9737. Fax: 561-416-9739.
www.grandviewprep.net   E-mail: klambert@grandviewprep.net

Jacqueline R. Westerfield, Head. BA, Univ of Iowa, JD, Univ of Illinois-Urbana. Kimberly J. Lambert, Adm.

Col Prep. AP—Eng Span Bio US_Hist Studio_Art. **Feat**—Humanities Art_Hist Drama Chorus Music Music_Hist Dance. **Supp**—Tut. **Adm:** 60/yr. Appl due: Rolling. Accepted: 85%. Yield: 70%. **Tests** SSAT Stanford. **Enr 268.** B 154. G 114. Elem 184. Sec 84. Avg class size: 18. Uniform. **Fac 35.** M 12. F 23. Wh 94%. Hisp 5%. Blk 1%. Adv deg: 31%. **Grad '04**—**19.** Col—19. Avg SAT: 1010. **Tui '04-'05:** Day $9000-12,100 (+$1500). **Summer:** Rec. Arts. Sports. Tui Day $350/2-wk ses. 8 wks. **Est 1997.** Inc. Quar (Aug-June). Grandview's traditional liberal arts program places considerable emphasis on technology. Hands-on activities are prominent during the lower school years (grades K-5), while the middle school program (grades 6-8) prepares students for future academic work and integrates a critical-thinking skills sequence. Advanced Placement courses and dual-enrollment opportunities at nearby colleges are elements of the comprehensive upper school curriculum.

BRADENTON CHRISTIAN SCHOOL
Day Coed Gr PS-12

Bradenton, FL 34209. 3304 43rd St W.
Tel: 941-792-5454. Fax: 941-795-7190.
www.bcspanthers.org

Dan van der Kooy, Supt. Darlene King, Adm.

Col Prep. Gen Acad. AP—Calc Eur_Hist US_Hist Psych. **Feat**—Computers

Econ Bible Studio_Art Music Bus. **Supp**—Dev_Read Rem_Math Rem_Read Rev Tut. **Adm:** 100/yr. Accepted: 97%. **Tests** Stanford. **Enr 626.** Elem 462. Sec 164. Wh 90%. Hisp 3%. Blk 4%. Am Ind 1%. Asian 2%. Avg class size: 17. **Fac 57.** M 16. F 38/3. Wh 98%. Blk 2%. Adv deg: 52%. **Grad '04—31.** Col—28. Avg SAT: 1036. Alum 620. **Tui '03-'04:** Day $5374-7921 (+$300). Aid: Merit 1. Need 55. **Est 1960.** Nonprofit. Quar (Aug-June). **Assoc** SACS. Students are required to participate in community service and senior projects, while off-campus and independent study is also offered. Spanish instruction is available in grades K-12.

BRANDON ACADEMY
Day Coed Gr K-8

Brandon, FL 33510. 801 Limona Rd.
Tel: 813-689-1952. Fax: 813-651-4278.
www.brandon-academy.com   E-mail: cliggitt@brandon-academy.com
    Teresa Curry, Head. BA, MEd, Univ of South Florida. Kathy Bishop, Adm.

Pre-Prep. Gen Acad. Feat—Lib_Skills Span Computers Studio_Art Music Journ. **Supp**—LD Tut. **Adm:** 55/yr. Appl due: Rolling. Accepted: 98%. Yield: 88%. **Tests** IQ SSAT. **Enr 235.** B 129. G 106. Elem 235. Avg class size: 15. Uniform. **Fac 22.** M 4/1. F 16/1. Wh 97%. Hisp 1%. Other 2%. Adv deg: 13%. **Grad '04—25.** Prep—2. **Tui '04-'05:** Day $5800-6000 (+$500). **Summer:** Acad Enrich Rem. Tui Day $125/wk. 10 wks. **Est 1969.** Inc. Quar (Aug-May). At all grade levels, this elementary school balances its emphasis on reading, math and science with instruction in Spanish, computers, writing and physical education. The developmentally appropriate lower school provides a foundation for future learning, while the middle school serves average and above-average students who have mastered the fundamentals. All middle schoolers choose yearlong electives as a supplement to core courses. Interest clubs, intramural activities, after-school sports, off-campus field trips and guest speakers round out the middle school program.

SAINT PAUL'S SCHOOL
Day Coed Gr PS-8

Clearwater, FL 33764. 1600 St Paul's Dr.
Tel: 727-536-2756. Fax: 727-531-2276.
www.st.pauls.edu   E-mail: admissions@st.pauls.edu
    Douglas C. Eveleth, Head. BS, Olivet College, MEd, Arizona State Univ. Judy E. Evans, Adm.

Pre-Prep. Feat—Fr Span Study_Skills. **Supp**—Dev_Read Rem_Math Rem_ Read Rev Tut. **Adm:** 90/yr. Appl due: Feb. Accepted: 50%. **Tests** CTP_4 SSAT. **Enr 504.** B 242. G 262. Elem 504. Wh 86%. Hisp 3%. Blk 3%. Asian 1%. Other 7%. Avg class size: 18. Uniform. **Fac 67.** M 10. F 57. Wh 96%. Hisp 4%. Adv deg: 29%. **Grad '04—41.** Prep—14. Alum 50. **Tui '03-'04:** Day $6750-11,230 (+$150-500). Aid: Need 63 ($293,260). **Summer:** Acad Enrich Rem Rec. Tui Day $100-300. 1-6 wks. **Est 1968.** Nonprofit. Episcopal. Quar (Aug-May). Located on a ten-acre campus, this school enrolls students of above-average ability. The curriculum is supplemented by foreign languages, study skills, the fine arts, computers, various clubs and activities, and an interscholastic athletic program.

THE NORTH BROWARD   **Day Coed Gr PS-12**
PREPARATORY SCHOOLS
Coconut Creek, FL 33073. 7600 Lyons Rd.
Tel: 954-247-0011. Fax: 954-247-0012.
www.nbps.org   E-mail: trentacostes@nbps.org

Philip E. Morgaman, Pres. Michael A. Rossi, Head. BA, Belmont Abbey College, MA, EdD, George Washington Univ. Jacki Fagan, Adm.

Col Prep. LD. AP—Eng Calc Stats Comp_Sci Bio Chem Physics US_Hist US_Govt & Pol Art_Hist Studio_Art. **Feat**—Ger Lat Drama Theater Band Chorus. **Supp**—Dev_Read. **Adm:** 443/yr. Appl due: Mar. Accepted: 85%. **Tests** SSAT. **Enr 2035.** B 1131. G 904. Elem 1298. Sec 737. Wh 82%. Hisp 15%. Blk 2%. Asian 1%. Avg class size: 18. Uniform. **Fac 175.** M 42. F 133. Wh 82%. Hisp 15%. Blk 3%. **Grad '04—86.** Col—86. Avg SAT: 1150. **Tui '05-'06:** Day $11,800-24,700 (+$1500). Aid: Merit 80 ($800,000). Need 100 ($500,000). **Summer:** Acad Enrich. Tui Day $500. 6 wks. **Est 1957.** Inc. Tri (Sept-June). Serving Palm Beach and Broward counties, NBPS comprises two programs: the North Broward School, which provides a traditional independent school education, and Lighthouse Point Academy, which offers a similar education to pupils with mild learning disabilities. Qualified high schoolers may enter an academic honors scholarship program. The lower schools operate on separate campuses at 3701 N.E. 22nd Ave., Lighthouse Point 33064 (grades pre-K-5); 3251 NW 101 Ave., Coral Springs 33065 (grades pre-K-3); and 10044 NW 31st St., Coral Springs 33065 (grades 4 and 5).

ST. PHILIP'S EPISCOPAL SCHOOL   **Day Coed Gr PS-6**
Coral Gables, FL 33134. 1142 Coral Way.
Tel: 305-444-6366. Fax: 305-442-0236.
www.saintphilips.net   E-mail: spes@saintphilips.net

Rev. Eric Kahl, Rector. BS, Florida State Univ, MA, Church Divinity School of the Pacific. George F. Devin III, Head. Joy MacIntosh, Adm.

Pre-Prep. Feat—Fr Span Computers Relig Studio_Art Music. **Supp**—Dev_ Read Rem_Math Rem_Read Tut. **Adm:** 21/yr. Appl due: Rolling. **Tests** MRT Stanford. **Enr 180.** B 91. G 89. Elem 180. Wh 62%. Hisp 33%. Blk 3%. Asian 2%. Avg class size: 20. Uniform. **Fac 26.** M 2/3. F 13/8. Wh 73%. Hisp 23%. Asian 4%. Adv deg: 34%. **Grad '04—11.** Prep—11. Alum 190. **Tui '04-'05:** Day $7033-9996 (+$602-645). Aid: Need 16 ($94,000). **Summer:** Acad Enrich Rec. Tui Day $495 (+$100)/3-wk ses. 6 wks. **Est 1953.** Nonprofit. Episcopal. Tri (Aug-June). The school serves children of average and above-average ability. Features of the program are character education, chapel, foreign language instruction, physical education/tennis lessons, pre- and after-school care, a full range of enrichment courses and a summer camp.

ST. THOMAS EPISCOPAL PARISH SCHOOL   **Day Coed Gr PS-6**
Coral Gables, FL 33156. 5692 N Kendall Dr.
Tel: 305-665-4851. Fax: 305-669-9449.
www.stepsmia.org   E-mail: admission@stepsmia.org

Kris M. Charlton, Head. BA, Long Island Univ, MS, Southern Connecticut State Univ. Valerie C. Douberley, Adm.

Pre-Prep. Feat—Span Computers Studio_Art Music Dance. **Adm:** 73/yr. Appl due: Rolling. **Tests** Stanford. **Enr 436.** B 229. G 207. Elem 436. Wh 67%. Hisp 30%. Blk 3%. Avg class size: 18. Uniform. **Fac 53.** M 5. F 48. Wh 69%. Hisp 30%. Other 1%. Adv deg: 18%. **Grad '04—39.** Prep—37. Alum 80. **Tui '04-'05:** Day $7390-9840 (+$625-750). Aid: Need 9 ($88,560). **Summer:** Acad Enrich Rem Rec. Tui Day $400/2-wk ses. 6 wks. **Est 1953.** Nonprofit. Episcopal. Quar (Aug-June). Language arts, science and social studies form the core of the St. Thomas curriculum. In addition, students receive specialized instruction in Spanish, art, music, dance, physical education, library skills and computers. All fourth, fifth and sixth graders use laptop computers. An extensive after-school extracurricular program includes a comprehensive sports program and such offerings as computer club, dance, ceramics, gymnastics and chorus.

ZION LUTHERAN CHRISTIAN SCHOOL   Day Coed Gr PS-12
Deerfield Beach, FL 33441. 959 SE 6th Ave.
Tel: 954-421-3146. Fax: 954-421-5465.
www.zion-lutheran.org
  Robert Lofthouse, Head. Kathleen Maselli & Becki Coffy, Adms.

  Col Prep. AP—Eng US_Govt & Pol. **Feat**—Creative_Writing Fr Span Comp_Sci Econ Geog Psych Sociol Relig Architect Ceramics Drawing Film Studio_Art Drama Band Chorus Journ. **Supp**—Makeup Tut. **Adm:** 100/yr. Appl due: Feb. Accepted: 96%. Yield: 99%. **Tests** Stanford. **Enr 691.** Elem 565. Sec 126. Wh 78%. Hisp 14%. Blk 6%. Asian 2%. Avg class size: 20. Uniform. **Fac 48.** M 10/1. F 34/3. Wh 88%. Hisp 9%. Asian 2%. Other 1%. Adv deg: 20%. **Grad '04—25.** Col—18. Avg SAT: 1100. Avg ACT: 21. Alum 250. **Tui '04-'05:** Day $5180-6550 (+$425-500). Aid: Merit 3 ($10,000). Need 35 ($35,000). **Summer:** Acad Rem. Tui Day $350. 3 wks. **Est 1964.** Nonprofit. Lutheran. Quar (Aug-May). Zion Lutheran offers a college preparatory program with honors and Advanced Placement classes. Spanish instruction at the school begins in kindergarten. Qualified seniors may take courses at Florida Atlantic University for both high school and college credit. Extracurricular activities include athletic teams for both boys and girls, activity clubs, student council, vocal and band music groups, drama and National Honor Society.

FORT LAUDERDALE   Day Coed Gr PS-12
PREPARATORY SCHOOL
Fort Lauderdale, FL 33311. 3275 W Oakland Park Blvd.
Tel: 954-485-7500. Fax: 954-485-1732.
www.flps.org   E-mail: admissions@flps.org
  Anita Lonstein, Dir. BA, City Univ of New York. Lawrence Berkowitz, Head. Michelle Dykens, Adm.

  Col Prep. Feat—Fr Japan Span Computers Fine_Arts Speech. **Supp**—Dev_Read ESL LD Makeup Tut. **Adm:** 30/yr. Appl due: July. Accepted: 95%. **Tests** IQ Stanford. **Enr 180.** B 102. G 78. Elem 100. Sec 80. Wh 49%. Hisp 11%. Blk 27%. Am Ind 9%. Asian 4%. Avg class size: 15. Uniform. **Fac 23.** M 8. F 12/3. Wh 70%. Hisp 10%. Blk 15%. Other 5%. Adv deg: 78%. **Grad '04—22.** Col—22. Avg SAT: 1100. Alum 225. **Tui '02-'03:** Day $6625-8925 (+$750-1200). Aid: Merit 8 ($40,000). Need 35 ($125,000). **Summer:** Acad Enrich Rev Rem Rec. Tui Day $500/3-wk ses. 6 wks. **Est 1986.** Inc. Sem (Sept-June). This school features individualized academic programs within small classes and an integrated computer curriculum. Advanced Placement and honors programs are also part of the curriculum, and a remedial program for academic underachievers is provided for an additional fee.

ST. MARK'S EPISCOPAL SCHOOL Day Coed Gr PS-8
Fort Lauderdale, FL 33334. 1750 E Oakland Park Blvd.
Tel: 954-563-4508. Fax: 954-563-0504.
www.saintmarks.com   E-mail: info@saintmarks.com
   James R. Colee, Head. EdD, Nova Univ. Gale Losch, Adm.

   Pre-Prep. Feat—Lib_Skills Span Relig Studio_Art Band Chorus Music. **Supp**—Tut. **Adm:** 101/yr. Appl due: Rolling. Accepted: 70%. Yield: 52%. **Tests** ISEE MRT. **Enr 574.** B 288. G 286. Elem 574. Wh 92%. Hisp 5%. Blk 2%. Asian 1%. Avg class size: 18. Uniform. **Fac 56.** M 8. F 45/3. Wh 89%. Hisp 10%. Blk 1%. Adv deg: 28%. **Grad '04—65.** Prep—62. Alum 1053. **Tui '04-'05:** Day $7300-9900 (+$450). Aid: Need 28 ($90,975). **Summer:** Rec. Tui Day $395-430/2-wk ses. 6 wks. **Est 1959.** Nonprofit. Episcopal. Quar (Aug-June). **Assoc** SACS. St. Mark's offers an academic curriculum designed to prepare students for selective secondary schools. Field trips, cocurricular activities and a variety of athletics, together with music, art, Spanish, computers, yearbook and chapel services, supplement the academic program.

WESTMINSTER ACADEMY Day Coed Gr PS-12
Fort Lauderdale, FL 33308. 5601 N Federal Hwy.
Tel: 954-771-4600. Fax: 954-491-3021.
www.wacad.edu   E-mail: westminster@wacad.edu
   Rev. Gregory Beaupied, Int Head. BA, Univ of Florida, MDiv, Knox Theological Seminary. Guy Metzger, Adm.

   Col Prep. Gen Acad. AP—Eng Span Comp_Sci Bio Eur_Hist US_Hist US_Govt & Pol. **Feat**—Fr Lat Econ Bible Fine_Arts Orchestra Jazz_Band. **Adm:** 152/yr. Appl due: Mar. Accepted: 90%. Yield: 80%. **Enr 1112.** B 536. G 576. Elem 644. Sec 468. Wh 89%. Hisp 4%. Blk 4%. Asian 1%. Other 2%. Avg class size: 22. Uniform. **Fac 85.** M 22/1. F 57/5. Wh 99%. Other 1%. Adv deg: 48%. **Grad '04—120.** Col—118. Avg SAT: 1176. Avg ACT: 24. Alum 2244. **Tui '05-'06:** Day $4940-10,690 (+$450-1375). Aid: Need ($640,000). **Summer:** Ages 5-14. Acad Enrich Rem. Tui Day $350-700. 3-5 wks. **Est 1971.** Nonprofit. Presbyterian. Quar (Aug-June). **Assoc** SACS. The curriculum at Westminster, conducted within a Christian environment, features Advanced Placement and honors courses. Fine arts and athletic offerings are available.

OAK HALL SCHOOL Day Coed Gr PS-12
Gainesville, FL 32607. 8009 SW 14th Ave.
Tel: 352-332-3609. Fax: 352-332-4975.
www.oakhall.org

Richard H. Gehman, Head. AB, Princeton Univ, MEd, Univ of Massachusetts-Amherst. Alice Garwood, Upper & Middle Sch Adm; Donna Dover, Lower Sch Adm.

Col Prep. AP—Eng Bio Chem Physics US_Hist Studio_Art. **Feat**—Computers Ceramics Photog Sculpt Video_Production Acting Music. **Adm:** 100/yr. **Tests** Stanford TOEFL. **Enr 424.** Elem 175. Sec 249. Wh 90%. Hisp 7%. Blk 2%. Asian 1%. Avg class size: 18. **Fac 43.** Adv deg: 69%. **Grad '04—74.** Col—74. Alum 1000. **Tui '04-'05:** Day $6770-8585. Aid: Need 11 ($80,000). **Summer:** Enrich. Athletics. Tui Day $150/wk. 4 wks. **Est 1970.** Nonprofit. Sem (Aug-May). **Assoc** CLS. Oak Hall offers a traditional liberal arts program of study that includes English, history, science, mathematics, foreign language and the arts. Beyond the core curriculum, elective opportunities are available. Qualified upper school students are encouraged to enroll in honors and Advanced Placement courses, and may also earn college credit through dual enrollment at the University of Florida or Santa Fe Community College.

CHAMINADE-MADONNA COLLEGE PREPARATORY
Day Coed Gr 9-12

Hollywood, FL 33021. 500 Chaminade Dr.
Tel: 954-989-5150. Fax: 954-983-4663.
www.cmlions.org   E-mail: info@cmlions.org

Rev. John Thompson, SM, Pres. BA, State Univ of New York-Binghamton, MDiv, Franciscan School of Theology. M. Gloria Ramos, Prin. George Sayour, Adm.

Col Prep. Gen Acad. AP—Eng Calc Bio Physics US_Hist Econ US_Govt & Pol. **Feat**—Fr Span Comp_Design Programming Law Theol Studio_Art Video_Production Theater Band Accounting Bus. **Supp**—Dev_Read ESL Rem_Math Rem_Read Tut. **Adm:** 310/yr. Appl due: Rolling. Accepted: 80%. **Tests** SSAT. **Enr 870.** B 500. G 370. Sec 870. Wh 50%. Hisp 20%. Blk 20%. Other 10%. Avg class size: 25. Uniform. **Fac 60.** M 35. F 25. Wh 70%. Hisp 20%. Blk 5%. Other 5%. Adv deg: 50%. **Grad '04—200.** Col—200. Avg SAT: 1200. Alum 2700. **Tui '04-'05:** Day $5800-6800 (+$1200). Aid: Need 200 ($250,000). **Summer:** Acad Enrich Rem. 4 wks. **Est 1960.** Nonprofit. Roman Catholic. Sem (Aug-May). **Assoc** SACS. The result of a 1988 merger between Chaminade and its sister school, Madonna Academy, this school is operated by the Marianist Society of priests and brothers. Qualified seniors can dually enroll in St. Thomas University or Barry University, and pupils may earn college credit in English, calculus, physics and computer. Religious retreats and service groups complement the traditional selection of activities.

HENDRICKS METHODIST DAY SCHOOL
Day Coed Gr PS-8

Jacksonville, FL 32207. 4000 Spring Park Rd.
Tel: 904-737-6880. Fax: 904-737-5109.
www.hmds.net   E-mail: admissions@hmds.net

Sally D. Lott, Head. Linda Langham, Adm.

Pre-Prep. Gen Acad. Feat—Lat Span Computers Studio_Art Theater Music. **Adm:** 84/yr. Appl due: Feb. Accepted: 92%. Yield: 100%. **Enr 347.** B 191. G 156. Elem 347. Avg class size: 23. Uniform. **Fac 41.** M 3. F 38. **Grad '04—43.**

Prep—43. **Tui '04-'05:** Day $2950-6250. **Est 1970.** Tri (Aug-May). This progressive elementary school prepares its children for high school through an emphasis on critical-thinking and study skills development. HMDS utilizes various techniques to address differing learning styles. The enrichment program, which begins at age 5, allows students to gain an introduction to music, art, technology, health, theater and foreign language. Student council, honor society and math club are extracurricular options.

ST. MARK'S EPISCOPAL DAY SCHOOL   Day Coed Gr PS-6
Jacksonville, FL 32210. 4114 Oxford Ave.
Tel: 904-388-2632. Fax: 904-387-5647.
www.stmarksdayschool.org   E-mail: smeds@stmarksdayschool.org
  Ruth E. Jacobs, Head. MAEd, Washington Univ. Susan C. Kwartler, Adm.

  Pre-Prep. Feat—Lib_Skills Span Computers Relig Studio_Art Music. **Supp**—Dev_Read Rev Tut. **Adm:** 125/yr. Appl due: Rolling. Accepted: 100%. Yield: 84%. **Enr 515.** B 278. G 237. Elem 515. Avg class size: 18. Uniform. **Fac 40.** M 3. F 37. Wh 97%. Hisp 3%. Adv deg: 27%. **Grad '04—38.** Prep—36. Alum 800. **Tui '04-'05:** Day $7320-7840 (+$350-400). Aid: Need 17 ($65,810). **Summer:** Acad Rec. Tui Day $100/wk. 8 wks. **Est 1970.** Nonprofit. Episcopal. Tri (Aug-May). This parish school's curriculum, which emphasizes independent study skills, includes art, music, computers, Spanish, library and Christian education. Special events and after-school opportunities supplement class work, and extended-day and summer programs are available. An early learning program for one and two-year olds is also offered. Most graduates attend local independent secondary schools.

BEACHES EPISCOPAL SCHOOL   Day Coed Gr PS-6
Jacksonville Beach, FL 32250. 1150 5th St N.
Tel: 904-246-2466. Fax: 904-246-1626.
www.beachesepiscopalschool.org   E-mail: info@beachesepiscopalschool.org
  Jackie Busse, Head. BS, Western Illinois Univ, MEd, Univ of North Florida. Michelle Leemis, Adm.

  Gen Acad. Feat—Lib_Skills Span Computers Studio_Art Music. **Supp**—Dev_Read Rem_Math Rem_Read Rev Tut. **Adm:** 84/yr. Appl due: Rolling. Accepted: 95%. **Tests** Stanford. **Enr 280.** Elem 280. Wh 95%. Blk 3%. Asian 2%. Avg class size: 16. Uniform. **Fac 28.** M 1. F 27. Wh 93%. Hisp 3%. Blk 1%. Asian 3%. Adv deg: 10%. **Grad '04—39.** Prep—32. **Tui '05-'06:** Day $6500-7300 (+$700). Aid: Need 18 ($42,500). **Est 1952.** Nonprofit. Episcopal. Tri (Aug-May). The school provides a well-rounded curriculum of traditional academic subjects, religious education, the fine arts, Spanish, computer science, library and physical education in a Christian setting. Christian education consists of classroom instruction, chapel services and outreach. An extended-day program is available.

LAKELAND CHRISTIAN SCHOOL   Day Coed Gr K-12
Lakeland, FL 33803. 1111 Forest Park St.
Tel: 863-688-2771. Fax: 863-682-5637.
www.lcsonline.org   E-mail: info@lcsonline.org

Mike Sligh, Head. MEd, Univ of Florida, MEd, Univ of South Florida. Reva Thornton, Adm.

Col Prep. Gen Acad. AP—Eng Calc US_Hist. **Feat**—Greek Lat Span Marine_Biol/Sci Comp_Design Econ Govt Bible Accounting Mech_Drawing. **Supp**—LD Makeup Tut. **Adm:** 192/yr. Appl due: Feb. Accepted: 95%. Yield: 93%. **Tests** Stanford. **Enr 920.** B 436. G 484. Elem 645. Sec 275. Wh 95%. Hisp 1%. Blk 2%. Asian 2%. Avg class size: 25. **Fac 68.** M 11/1. F 50/6. Wh 98%. Hisp 1%. Blk 1%. Adv deg: 23%. **Grad '04—64.** Col—44. Avg SAT: 1045. Avg ACT: 23. Alum 1300. **Tui '04-'05:** Day $4750-5650 (+$500-1000). Aid: Need 151 ($278,740). **Est 1954.** Nonprofit. Nondenom Christian. Quar (Aug-May). LCS offers a traditional academic curriculum in which Bible study is compulsory. Extracurricular activities include athletic competition, academic contests, drama, and vocal and instrumental music.

PACE-BRANTLEY HALL SCHOOL Day Coed Gr 1-12
Longwood, FL 32779. 3221 Sand Lake Rd.
Tel: 407-869-8882. Fax: 407-869-8717.
www.pacebrantleyhall.org E-mail: pabhschool@yahoo.com

Kathleen Shattock, Prin. BSE, Saint John's College (MD), MEd, Xavier Univ. Barbara Winter, Adm.

Col Prep. Gen Acad. LD. Feat—Span Econ Studio_Art Speech. **Supp**—Dev_Read Makeup Tut. **Adm:** 28/yr. Appl due: Rolling. Accepted: 33%. **Tests** IQ Stanford. **Enr 130.** B 99. G 31. Elem 83. Sec 47. Wh 92%. Hisp 4%. Blk 1%. Asian 2%. Other 1%. Avg class size: 10. Uniform. **Fac 22.** M 2. F 20. Wh 91%. Blk 9%. Adv deg: 22%. **Grad '04—11.** Col—9. Avg SAT: 950. Avg ACT: 20. Alum 74. **Tui '04-'05:** Day $11,850-12,500 (+$1000). Aid: Need 10 ($13,000). **Summer:** Acad Enrich Rev Rem Rec. Tui Day $325-600/3-wk ses. 6 wks. **Est 1972.** Nonprofit. Sem (Aug-May). PACE provides reading, language arts and math programs for the learning-disabled child whose needs have not been met in traditional school settings. Teaching methods combine four distinct learning approaches: auditory, visual, tactile and whole body. Frequently scheduled field trips enhance classroom learning.

SWEETWATER EPISCOPAL ACADEMY Day Coed Gr PS-5
Longwood, FL 32779. 251 E Lake Brantley Dr.
Tel: 407-862-1882. Fax: 407-788-1714.
www.sweetwaterepiscopal.org E-mail: kbailey@sweetwaterepiscopal.org

Janet Stroup, Head. BA, Grove City College, MEd, Millersville Univ of Pennsylvania. Lynda Delius, Adm.

Pre-Prep. Feat—Lib_Skills Span Computers Relig Studio_Art Music. **Supp**—Tut. **Adm:** 69/yr. Appl due: Rolling. Accepted: 90%. **Enr 253.** B 125. G 128. Elem 253. Wh 83%. Hisp 1%. Blk 5%. Am Ind 1%. Asian 4%. Other 6%. Avg class size: 20. Uniform. **Fac 27.** M 4. F 23. Wh 87%. Hisp 11%. Blk 2%. Adv deg: 11%. **Grad '04—35. Tui '04-'05:** Day $7150-7650. Aid: Need 6 ($20,125). **Est 1974.** Nonprofit. Episcopal. Quar (Aug-May). Computer instruction begins in prekindergarten at this Christian school. Other enrichment classes include art, library, music, religion and Spanish. For an additional fee, students may take part in such after-school offerings as chess, art, music, science and sports.

HOLY TRINITY EPISCOPAL ACADEMY   **Day Coed Gr PS-12**
Melbourne, FL 32940. 5625 Holy Trinity Dr.
Tel: 321-723-8323. Fax: 321-308-9077.
www.htacademy.org   E-mail: pcraig@htes.org
    Catherine A. Ford, Head. BS, MS, Auburn Univ. Patricia Craig, Gr 7-12 Adm; Virginia Campbell, Gr PS-6 Adm.

    Col Prep. Gen Acad. AP—Eng Fr Lat Span Calc Stats Comp_Sci Bio Chem Physics Eur_Hist US_Hist US_Govt & Pol Studio_Art. **Feat**—British_Lit Creative_Writing Greek Anat & Physiol Ecol Web_Design Econ Theater Music Dance Journ. **Supp**—Tut. **Adm:** Appl due: Rolling. **Tests** Stanford. **Enr 911.** Elem 597. Sec 314. Wh 91%. Hisp 3%. Blk 2%. Asian 4%. Avg class size: 18. Uniform. **Fac 75. Tui '04-'05:** Day $3550-8350. **Est 1957.** Nonprofit. Episcopal. Sem (Aug-May). **Assoc** SACS. Holy Trinity complements its traditional curriculum with full extracurricular, physical education and interscholastic sports programs. Christian living and life management courses are important elements of the program. The lower school (grades PS-6) occupies a separate campus at 50 W. Strawbridge Ave., 32901.

ATLANTIS ACADEMY   **Day Coed Gr K-12**
Miami, FL 33176. 9600 SW 107th Ave.
Tel: 305-271-9771. Fax: 305-271-7078.
www.atlantisacademy.com   E-mail: pginer@atlantisacademy.com
    Carlos R. Aballi, Dir. BA, MS, Indiana State Univ, EdS, Indiana Univ. Patricia Giner, Adm.

    LD. Feat—Fr Span Computers Studio_Art. **Supp**—Dev_Read ESL Rem_Math Rem_Read. **Adm:** 35/yr. Appl due: Rolling. Accepted: 60%. **Tests** IQ. **Enr 190.** B 140. G 50. Elem 136. Sec 54. Wh 41%. Hisp 52%. Blk 6%. Asian 1%. Avg class size: 8. Uniform. **Fac 27.** M 4. F 23. Wh 40%. Hisp 45%. Blk 15%. Adv deg: 33%. **Grad '04—16.** Col—14. Alum 230. **Tui '04-'05:** Day $12,700-14,600 (+$550). Aid: Need 4 ($50,000). **Summer:** Rem Rec. 8 wks. **Est 1976.** Inc. Sem (Aug-June). **Assoc** SACS. Students with reading and learning difficulties receive individualized instruction in small classes and a clinical setting at Atlantis. All students have access to computers, and pupils in grade 3 and above receive formal instruction in computer usage and keyboarding on personal laptops.

CARROLLTON SCHOOL   **Day Girls Gr PS-12**
OF THE SACRED HEART
Miami, FL 33133. 3747 Main Hwy.
Tel: 305-446-5673. Fax: 305-446-4160.
www.carrollton.org   E-mail: admissions@carrollton.org
    Sr. Suzanne Cooke, RSCJ, Head. BA, Manhattanville College, MA, Univ of Chicago. Ana J. Luna, Adm.

    Col Prep. AP—Eng Calc Comp_Sci Bio Physics Studio_Art. **Feat**—Anat &

Physiol Relig Photog Drama Music Dance. **Supp**—Rev Tut. **Adm (Gr PS-11):** 99/yr. Appl due: Feb. Accepted: 40%. **Enr 655.** G 655. Elem 425. Sec 230. Wh 34%. Hisp 60%. Blk 5%. Asian 1%. Uniform. **Fac 74.** M 10. F 55/9. Adv deg: 47%. **Grad '04—51.** Col—51. Avg SAT: 1121. Alum 1088. **Tui '04-'05:** Day $11,900-17,425 (+$900). Aid: Need 100 ($792,000). **Summer:** Enrich. Tui Day $175/wk. 10 wks. **Est 1961.** Nonprofit. Roman Catholic. Quar (Aug-June). Carrollton's two campuses are on Biscayne Bay, within walking distance of each other. Community service is required of all high school students, and quarter-, semester- and yearlong exchanges are available with the other Sacred Heart schools. Advanced Placement and honors courses are offered, as is a Montessori preschool.

CUSHMAN SCHOOL   Day Coed Gr PS-8
Miami, FL 33137. 592 NE 60th St.
Tel: 305-757-1966. Fax: 305-757-1632.
www.cushmanschool.org   E-mail: admissions@cushmanschool.org
Joan D. Lutton, Head. BA, Rutgers Univ, MS, Barry College, EdD, Univ of Florida. Cheryl Rogers, Adm.

Pre-Prep. Gen Acad. Feat—Lat Span Ecol Computers Studio_Art Drama Music Public_Speak Speech. **Supp**—Dev_Read LD Rem_Math Rem_Read Tut. **Adm:** 88/yr. Appl due: Rolling. **Enr 466.** B 233. G 233. Elem 466. Wh 73%. Hisp 14%. Blk 10%. Asian 2%. Other 1%. Avg class size: 18. Uniform. **Fac 70.** M 7. F 63. Wh 81%. Hisp 11%. Blk 6%. Asian 1%. Other 1%. Adv deg: 50%. **Grad '04—25.** Alum 500. **Tui '04-'05:** Day $8925-17,850 (+$310-775). Aid: Need 17 ($126,037). Work prgm 49 ($384,468). **Summer:** Acad Enrich Rem. Tui Day $175-350/wk. 12 wks. **Est 1924.** Nonprofit. Sem (Aug-June). Cushman offers conversational Spanish throughout and uses computer instruction (featuring laptops in grades 5-8) to develop students' reading and reasoning skills. Activities include cultural field trips, instrumental music, chorus, dramatics, student council, school newspaper, literary magazine and sports.

DADE CHRISTIAN SCHOOL   Day Coed Gr PS-12
Miami, FL 33015. 6601 NW 167th St.
Tel: 305-822-7690. Fax: 305-826-4072.
www.dadechristian.org   E-mail: hhenning@dadechristian.org
Dino Pedrone, Pres. DMin. Michael L. Hiltibidal, Head. MS, Pensacola Christian College. Margie Rodriguez, Adm.

Col Prep. Gen Acad. AP—Eng Span Calc Bio US_Hist Psych US_Govt & Pol Studio_Art. **Feat**—Fr Stats Marine_Biol/Sci Programming Web_Design Civil_War Holocaust Econ Ethics World_Relig Ceramics Chorus. **Supp**—Makeup Tut. **Adm:** 226/yr. Appl due: Rolling. Accepted: 80%. Yield: 70%. **Enr 1294.** Elem 944. Sec 350. Avg class size: 23. Uniform. **Fac 115.** Wh 14%. Hisp 74%. Blk 10%. Asian 2%. Adv deg: 35%. **Grad '04—76.** Col—74. Avg SAT: 1022. Avg ACT: 22. **Tui '04-'05:** Day $8850 (+$600). **Summer:** Rem. Tui Day $250. 3 wks. **Est 1961.** Nonprofit. Baptist. Quar (Aug-May). Dade Christian's Christ-centered elementary curriculum (age 3 kindergarten through grade 6) emphasizes cooperative and experiential learning in the early years, and later stresses critical-thinking skills. Geared toward college preparation, the secondary school (grades 7-12) features honors and Advanced Placement courses, as well as a strong fine arts program. Technology is an important aspect of the curriculum, as computer science instruction begins in kindergarten and continues through grade 12. Student clubs, mission trips and a highly regarded interscholastic athletic program balance academics.

WESTMINSTER CHRISTIAN SCHOOL   Day Coed Gr PS-12
Miami, FL 33157. 6855 SW 152nd St.
Tel: 305-233-2030. Fax: 305-253-9623.
www.wcsmiami.org   E-mail: cstone@wcsmiami.org
    George J. W. Lawrence, Jr., Supt. BA, Covenant College, MEd, California State Univ-Fresno. Caroline H. Stone, Adm.
    Col Prep. AP—Eng Span Calc Stats Bio Chem US_Hist World_Hist Econ US_Govt & Pol Studio_Art. **Feat**—Creative_Writing Anat & Physiol Programming Web_Design Vietnam_War Psych Sociol Bible World_Relig Drama Debate. **Supp**—LD Rem_Math. **Adm (Gr PS-11):** 127/yr. Appl due: Feb. Accepted: 92%. Yield: 90%. **Enr 1100.** B 547. G 553. Elem 408. Sec 692. Wh 54%. Hisp 44%. Blk 1%. Asian 1%. Avg class size: 22. Uniform. **Fac 83.** M 21. F 60/2. Wh 75%. Hisp 25%. Adv deg: 38%. **Grad '04**—**104.** Col—104. Avg SAT: 1112. Avg ACT: 22. **Tui '05-'06:** Day $8450-11,900. Aid: Need 125 ($480,000). **Summer:** Acad. Tui Day $500-1000/crse. 3-6 wks. **Est 1961.** Nonprofit. Nondenom Christian. Sem (Aug-May). Taught from a Christian perspective, the thematic curriculum in Westminster's preschool and elementary school (grades K-5) integrates Bible, language arts, math, music, Spanish, social studies, art, computer and physical education. At the middle school level (grades 6-8), the school employs interdisciplinary units to facilitate the development of problem-solving, creativity, decision-making and critical-thinking skills. Honors and Advanced Placement offerings enrich the high school years (grades 9-12), as do strong fine arts and athletic programs. Support for students who are experiencing academic difficulties is available both during the school day and after school.

MONTVERDE ACADEMY   Bdg Coed Gr 7-12
Montverde, FL 34756. 17235 7th St.   Day Coed PS-12
Tel: 407-469-2561. Fax: 407-469-3711.
www.montverde.org   E-mail: admissions@montverde.org
    Kasey Kesselring, Head. BA, Dickinson College, MEd, Middle Tennessee State Univ. Alan Whittemore, Adm.
    Col Prep. AP—Eng Span Calc Bio Chem Eur_Hist US_Hist. **Feat**—Stats Anat & Physiol Comp_Sci Govt Ethics Photog Drama Music Woodworking. **Supp**—ESL Tut. **Adm:** 69/yr. Appl due: Rolling. Accepted: 73%. Yield: 90%. **Enr 377.** B 77/114. G 49/137. Elem 210. Sec 167. Wh 39%. Hisp 17%. Blk 8%. Am Ind 1%. Asian 28%. Other 7%. Avg class size: 20. Uniform. **Fac 42.** M 17/2. F 20/3. Wh 88%. Hisp 9%. Blk 3%. Adv deg: 30%. In Dorms 1. **Grad '04**—**42.** Col—40. Avg SAT: 866. Alum 3500. **Tui '05-'06:** Bdg $23,000 (+$1700). Day $6500-9125 (+$1700). Aid: Need 17. **Summer:** Acad Enrich. Tui Bdg $1525-3059. Tui Day $735-1470. 3-6 wks. **Est 1912.** Nonprofit. Sem (Sept-June). Offering a varied college preparatory curriculum that includes honors classes and Advanced Placement work in all major subject areas, Montverde enrolls a substantial percentage of international pupils. The academy schedules a tutorial period every Monday through Thursday at the end of the class day; extra help is also available after school. Students may take certain

noncredit courses on an extracurricular basis, among them SAT preparation, tae kwon do, photography and dance.

BENJAMIN SCHOOL   **Day Coed Gr PS-12**
North Palm Beach, FL 33408. 11000 Ellison Wilson Rd.
Tel: 561-626-3747. Fax: 561-691-8823.
www.benjaminschool.com   E-mail: kmclaughlin@benjaminschool.com
    Peter F. Graham, Head. BEd, Plymouth State Univ, MEd, Salem State College. Mary Lou Primm, Adm.

    Col Prep. AP—Eng Fr Span Calc Stats Comp_Sci Bio Chem Physics Eur_Hist US_Hist Econ US_Govt & Pol Studio_Art. **Feat**—Anat & Physiol Ecol Genetics Marine_Biol/Sci Programming Psych Drawing Photog Video_Production Drama Music Dance Debate. **Supp**—Dev_Read Makeup Tut. **Adm:** 200/yr. Appl due: Feb. Accepted: 55%. **Tests** ISEE SSAT. **Enr 1164.** B 573. G 591. Elem 814. Sec 350. Wh 94%. Hisp 3%. Blk 3%. Avg class size: 17. Uniform. **Fac 133.** Adv deg: 23%. **Grad '04**—**87.** Col—87. Alum 1361. **Tui '04-'05:** Day $11,900-15,900. **Summer:** Acad Enrich. 6 wks. **Est 1960.** Nonprofit. Sem (Aug-June). This school provides a college preparatory program with an English curriculum that emphasizes grammar/composition, literature, speech and expository writing. Advanced Placement courses are available in many areas, French is offered beginning in kindergarten and Spanish is available from grade 4. Electives include creative writing, art, music, dance, journalism and band. The school supplements its curriculum with a full sports program for boys and girls in grades 6-12.

BISHOP MOORE   **Day Coed Gr 9-12**
CATHOLIC HIGH SCHOOL
Orlando, FL 32804. 3901 Edgewater Dr.
Tel: 407-293-7561. Fax: 407-296-8135.
www.bishopmoore.org   E-mail: admissions@bishopmoore.org
    Maureen Kane, Prin. BA, Fontbonne College, MEd, EdS, Georgia State Univ. Philip Richart, Adm.

    Col Prep. Gen Acad. AP—Eng Fr Lat Span Calc Stats Bio Chem Human_Geog Physics US_Hist World_Hist Econ US_Govt & Pol Studio_Art. **Feat**—Anat Marine_Biol/Sci Law Psych Sociol Theol Fine_Arts Sculpt. **Supp**—Tut. **Adm:** 256/yr. **Enr 1091.** Sec 1091. Avg class size: 22. Uniform. **Fac 75.** M 27/1. F 47. Adv deg: 56%. **Grad '04**—**262.** Col—256. Alum 7500. **Tui '05-'06:** Day $9696 (+$450). Catholic $6948 (+$450). Aid: Need 147 ($189,352). **Summer:** Acad Enrich Rem. 6 wks. **Est 1954.** Nonprofit. Roman Catholic. Sem (Aug-May). **Assoc** SACS. Situated on 54 acres along Little Lake Fairview, BMHS combines academic studies with religious education. Advanced Placement and honors courses are available, as are electives in business and the fine arts. Extracurricular activities include athletics, chorus, marching band, student government, yearbook, academic clubs and sports.

LAKE HIGHLAND PREPARATORY SCHOOL Day Coed Gr PS-12
Orlando, FL 32803. 901 N Highland Ave.
Tel: 407-206-1900. Fax: 407-206-1933.
www.lhps.org E-mail: admissions@lhps.org
Warren Hudson, Pres. BA, Vanderbilt Univ, MEd, Tulane Univ, MPA, Harvard Univ. Susan Clayton, Adm.

Col Prep. AP—Eng Fr Lat Span Calc Comp_Sci Bio Chem Physics Eur_Hist US_Hist Psych US_Govt & Pol Studio_Art Music_Theory. **Feat**—Mandarin Bus_Law Debate. **Supp**—Tut. **Adm:** 282/yr. Appl due: Rolling. Accepted: 52%. Yield: 78%. **Tests** SSAT Stanford. **Enr 1890.** B 938. G 952. Elem 1255. Sec 635. Wh 81%. Hisp 4%. Blk 2%. Am Ind 1%. Asian 3%. Other 9%. Avg class size: 19. Uniform. **Fac 168.** M 41. F 127. Adv deg: 41%. **Grad '04—138.** Col—138. Alum 2133. **Tui '04-'05:** Day $8400-11,600 (+$2000). **Summer:** Acad Enrich Rec. Tui Day $110-420/crse. 1-3 wks. **Est 1970.** Nonprofit. Sem (Aug-May). **Assoc** CLS SACS. LHPS offers a diversified curriculum and small, seminar-style classes. In the lower school, a daily enrichment period provides art, drama, music, computers, Spanish and library skills. Students in the upper school may take honors courses beginning in grade 7, and Advanced Placement classes are available starting in freshman year. All pupils study composition, speech, the humanities and computers.

NEW SCHOOL OF ORLANDO Day Coed Gr K-8
Orlando, FL 32803. 130 E Marks St.
Tel: 407-246-0556. Fax: 407-246-0822.
www.newschoolorlando.org E-mail: director@newschoolorlando.org
Morris Sorin, Dir. BS, MA, Case Western Reserve Univ.

Pre-Prep. Feat—Span Studio_Art Theater Music Dance. **Adm:** Appl due: Rolling. **Enr 140.** Elem 140. Wh 82%. Hisp 16%. Blk 2%. Avg class size: 18. Uniform. **Fac 16.** M 3. F 12/1. Wh 82%. Hisp 16%. Blk 2%. Adv deg: 62%. **Grad '04—18.** Prep—15. **Tui '04-'05:** Day $7750 (+$450). **Est 1995.** Inc. Tri (Aug-May). NSO bases its educational approach on Multiple Intelligence Theory. The school's literature-based language arts program draws on varying genres, time periods and cultures, while a progressive math program incorporates measurement, data manipulation and graphing. Units on earth science, physical science, biology and astronomy are part of a science curriculum that stresses logic, conceptual thinking and problem solving. The social studies program culminates in grade 8 with the in-depth study of the events leading to World War II and the Holocaust.

AMERICAN HERITAGE SCHOOL Day Coed Gr PS-12
Plantation, FL 33325. 12200 W Broward Blvd.
Tel: 954-472-0022. Fax: 954-472-3088.
www.ahschool.com E-mail: admissions@ahschool.com
William R. Laurie, Pres. BA, Univ of the South, MEd, Univ of Florida.

Col Prep. AP—Eng Fr Span Calc Chem Physics Eur_Hist US_Hist World_Hist Econ Psych US_Govt & Pol Music_Theory. **Feat**—Sports_Med Computers World_Relig Architect. **Supp**—Dev_Read ESL LD Makeup Tut. **Adm:** 559/yr. Appl due: Rolling. Accepted: 92%. Yield: 88%. **Tests** IQ Stanford. **Enr 2388.** B 1337. G 1051. Elem 1366. Sec 1022. Wh 69%. Hisp 20%. Blk 6%. Asian 5%. Avg class size: 18.

Uniform. **Fac 176.** M 35. F 141. Wh 93%. Hisp 6%. Blk 1%. Adv deg: 49%. **Grad '04—167.** Col—162. Avg SAT: 1120. Avg ACT: 22. Alum 1577. **Tui '04-'05:** Day $11,341-14,274 (+$1000). Aid: Merit 158 ($1,267,004). Need 521 ($2,887,412). **Summer:** Acad Enrich Rev Rem Rec. Tui Day $620/3-wk ses. 9 wks. **Est 1969.** Inc. Quar (Aug-June). **Assoc** SACS. Located on a 40-acre campus, American Heritage begins Spanish instruction at age 4, while French is introduced in grade 7. Extensive fine arts offerings are available in the high school, as is a special track for students interested in pursuing a legal or health-related career. The school's American Academy program, available for an additional fee, serves pupils with moderate learning disabilities who are working below grade level. An athletic program includes varsity and junior varsity teams.

KESWICK CHRISTIAN SCHOOL Day Coed Gr PS-12
St Petersburg, FL 33708. 10101 54th Ave N.
Tel: 727-393-9100. Fax: 727-397-5378.
www.keswickchristian.org
    Steven G. Sinclair, Head. BA, Trinity College, MEd, Univ of South Florida. Nancy Watkins, Adm.

    Col Prep. AP—Eng Span Calc Bio US_Hist Studio_Art. **Feat—**Marine_Biol/Sci Computers Bible Debate. **Supp—**Dev_Read Rem_Read Tut. **Adm:** 131/yr. **Tests** Stanford. **Enr 622.** Wh 91%. Hisp 3%. Blk 3%. Asian 3%. Avg class size: 24. Uniform. **Fac 45.** M 12. F 33. Wh 100%. Adv deg: 28%. **Grad '04—31.** Col—31. Avg SAT: 1049. Avg ACT: 21. Alum 904. **Tui '04-'05:** Day $4625-6308 (+$150-200). Aid: Need 99 ($40,000). **Est 1953.** Nonprofit. Nondenom Christian. Quar (Aug-May). **Assoc** SACS. Keswick Christian offers a college preparatory curriculum that emphasizes Christian values. Academically advanced pupils may earn college credit through a dual-enrollment program, and Advanced Placement courses are part of the high school curriculum. Extracurricular activities include athletics, publications, band, chorus, drama and student government.

WELLINGTON SCHOOL Day Coed Gr PS-8
St Petersburg, FL 33714. 5175 45th St N.
Tel: 727-528-8717. Fax: 727-528-8915.
www.wellingtonschool.com   E-mail: kdeakley@wellingtonschool.com
    Cynthia Moon, Head. Karen Deakley, Adm.

    Pre-Prep. Gen Acad. Feat—Lat Span Computers Studio_Art Music. **Supp—**Tut. **Adm:** 85/yr. Appl due: Rolling. Accepted: 95%. Yield: 98%. **Enr 385.** B 185. G 200. Elem 385. Wh 89%. Hisp 2%. Blk 2%. Asian 2%. Other 5%. Avg class size: 16. Uniform. **Fac 41.** M 4. F 37. Wh 97%. Hisp 1%. Blk 1%. Asian 1%. Adv deg: 24%. **Grad '04—43.** Prep—10. **Tui '04-'05:** Day $6595 (+$850). Aid: Need 13 ($15,395). **Summer:** Rec. Tui Day $256-306/2-wk ses. 10 wks. **Est 1974.** Inc. Sem (Aug-May). From the early years, Wellington utilizes hands-on experiences as a learning tool. The art curriculum, which formally begins in grade 1, includes drawing, painting, printmaking, sculpture and field trips to local art museums. Children are introduced to typing in grade 3, and computer skills expand through keyboarding, Internet research and word processing composition. The early childhood and primary levels (grades junior K-3) operate on a separate campus at 8000 Starkey Rd., Seminole 33777 (727-397-4565).

CARDINAL MOONEY HIGH SCHOOL Day Coed Gr 9-12
Sarasota, FL 34232. 4171 Fruitville Rd.
Tel: 941-371-4917. Fax: 941-371-6924.
www.cmhs-sarasota.org E-mail: schristie@cmhs-sarasota.org

Sr. Mary Lucia Haas, SND, Pres. BS, Notre Dame College (OH), MTS, College of William and Mary. Stephen J. Christie, Prin. BS, Manhattan College, MS, Hofstra Univ.

Col Prep. AP—Eng Fr Span Calc Comp_Sci Bio Chem US_Hist US_Govt & Pol. **Feat**—Creative_Writing Anat & Physiol Environ_Sci Marine_Biol/Sci Web_Design Econ Govt Psych Sociol Relig Studio_Art Drama Music Dance Accounting Journ Speech. **Supp**—Rem_Math Rem_Read Tut. **Adm (Gr 9-11):** 180/yr. Appl due: Mar. Accepted: 99%. **Tests** HSPT. **Enr 540.** B 280. G 260. Sec 540. Wh 96%. Hisp 2%. Blk 1%. Asian 1%. Avg class size: 25. Uniform. **Fac 45.** M 19/1. F 24/1. Wh 98%. Hisp 2%. Adv deg: 60%. **Grad '04—121.** Col—120. Avg SAT: 1060. Avg ACT: 22. Alum 2700. **Tui '04-'05:** Day $8550 (+$500). Aid: Merit 3 ($3000). **Est 1958.** Nonprofit. Roman Catholic. Quar (Aug-June). **Assoc** SACS. As part of its college preparatory curriculum, Cardinal Mooney offers honors and Advanced Placement courses and a full complement of electives. The four-year religious studies curriculum is required of all students, who also complete at least 100 hours of community service prior to graduation. A learning strategies curriculum assists those who need special help.

JULIE ROHR ACADEMY Day Coed Gr PS-8
Sarasota, FL 34232. 4466 Fruitville Rd.
Tel: 941-371-4979. Fax: 941-379-5816.
www.julierohracademy.com E-mail: info@julierohracademy.com

Julie Rohr McHugh, Dir. BM, MM, Univ of Miami. Cecilia R. Blankenship, Adm.

Gen Acad. Feat—Span Performing_Arts Studio_Art Music. **Supp**—Dev_Read ESL Rem_Math Rem_Read Rev Tut. **Adm:** 51/yr. Appl due: Rolling. Accepted: 98%. **Enr 271.** B 133. G 138. Elem 271. Wh 91%. Hisp 1%. Blk 1%. Asian 1%. Other 6%. Avg class size: 15. **Fac 25.** M 3. F 21/1. Wh 96%. Hisp 4%. Adv deg: 16%. **Grad '04—7.** Prep—1. **Tui '04-'05:** Day $5895-6375 (+$500-650). Aid: Merit 4 ($24,760). **Summer:** Rec. Tui Day $1540. 10 wks. **Est 1974.** Inc. Sem (Aug-May). Children at this school are placed according to academic ability. Students take enrichment classes in Spanish, art, music and physical education. Developmental learning activities are used in nursery school through kindergarten, and a strong performing arts curriculum includes chorus for students at all grade levels. Interested boys and girls may take private or group music lessons after school.

ACADEMY OF THE HOLY NAMES Day Boys Gr PS-8, Girls PS-12
Tampa, FL 33629. 3319 Bayshore Blvd.
Tel: 813-839-5371. Fax: 813-839-1486.
www.holynamestpa.org E-mail: kamurphy@holynamestpa.org

Colleen K. Brady, Pres. BA, Carroll College, MS, Univ of Wisconsin. Lisa D. Quinones, Adm.

Col Prep. AP—Eng Lat Span Calc Bio Chem Physics US_Hist US_Govt & Pol

Art_Hist Studio_Art. **Feat**—Fr Anat & Physiol Marine_Biol/Sci Econ Law Ethics World_Relig Photog Theater Dance Accounting Journ Marketing. **Supp**—Dev_ Read Tut. **Adm (Gr PS-11):** 174/yr. Appl due: Jan. Accepted: 90%. Yield: 62%. **Tests** Stanford. **Enr 884.** B 202. G 682. Elem 525. Sec 359. Wh 67%. Hisp 27%. Blk 2%. Asian 4%. Avg class size: 15. Uniform. **Fac 67.** M 6. F 56/5. Adv deg: 47%. **Grad '04—77.** Col—77. Avg SAT: 1131. Avg ACT: 25. Alum 3500. **Tui '04-'05:** Day $8670-10,780 (+$700). Aid: Merit 30 ($46,560). Need 63 ($253,070). Work prgm 23 ($13,800). **Summer:** Enrich Rec. Tui Day $100/wk. 10 wks. **Est 1881.** Nonprofit. Roman Catholic. Sem (Aug-June). **Assoc** SACS. Courses in music, computer science, religion and speech are among the additional offerings at Academy of the Holy Names. Spanish instruction begins in prekindergarten.

BAYSHORE CHRISTIAN SCHOOL　　　　　　　　**Day Coed Gr PS-12**
Tampa, FL 33611. 3909 S MacDill Ave.
Tel: 813-839-4297. Fax: 813-835-1404.
www.bayshorechristian.com　　E-mail: bcs@iolfl.com
　　Donna C. Brooks, Head. BA, MA, Univ of South Florida, EdS, Nova Southeastern Univ. Pam Sander, Adm.

　　Col Prep. Feat—Span Comp_Design Programming Web_Design Performing_Arts Music. **Supp**—Makeup Tut. **Adm (Gr PS-11):** 84/yr. Appl due: Rolling. Accepted: 95%. Yield: 85%. **Tests** Stanford. **Enr 397.** B 189. G 208. Elem 303. Sec 94. Wh 74%. Hisp 10%. Blk 7%. Asian 1%. Other 8%. Avg class size: 14. Uniform. **Fac 43.** M 6/2. F 29/6. Wh 85%. Hisp 10%. Blk 5%. Adv deg: 9%. **Grad '04—24.** Col—22. Avg SAT: 1044. Avg ACT: 22. Alum 625. **Tui '04-'05:** Day $5000-6300 (+$600). Aid: Need 55 ($162,870). **Summer:** Gr PS-8. Enrich Rec. Tui Day $25/day. 11 wks. **Est 1971.** Nonprofit. United Methodist. Sem (Aug-May). Bayshore offers such enrichment courses as computer, library, art, music and physical education beginning in kindergarten, and daily Bible study is an integral part of the academic program at all grade levels. Honors and advanced courses begin in grade 7.

THE CAMBRIDGE SCHOOL　　　　　　　　　　**Day Coed Gr PS-12**
Tampa, FL 33614. 6101 N Habana Ave.
Tel: 813-872-6744. Fax: 813-202-8108.
www.tcslancers.com　　E-mail: slouer@tcslancers.com
　　Ron G. Whipple, Head. BA, MA, Stetson Univ. Sherry Louer, Adm.

　　Col Prep. AP—Eng Calc Stats Bio Chem Physics Eur_Hist US_Hist Psych. **Feat**—Fr Ger Lat Span Comp_Sci Bible Studio_Art Theater_Arts Chorus Music. **Supp**—Dev_Read Tut. **Adm:** 135/yr. Appl due: Rolling. Accepted: 82%. Yield: 81%. **Tests** CEEB SSAT. **Enr 664.** B 313. G 351. Elem 494. Sec 170. Wh 80%. Hisp 14%. Blk 4%. Am Ind 1%. Asian 1%. Avg class size: 18. Uniform. **Fac 66.** M 12/1. F 52/1. Wh 89%. Hisp 7%. Blk 1%. Asian 1%. Other 2%. Adv deg: 30%. **Grad '04—36.** Col—36. Avg SAT: 1105. Avg ACT: 21. Alum 397. **Tui '04-'05:** Day $7100-8975 (+$950-1200). Aid: Need 34 ($113,738). **Est 1964.** Nonprofit. Nondenom Christian. Sem (Aug-June). TCS integrates the classical model of education (logic and rhetoric) with traditional college preparatory academics. The core curriculum comprises English, science, mathematics, foreign language, social studies, fine arts and practical arts. Advanced Placement courses and an honors track in English and math are available for qualified students, and formal computer instruction begins in grade 1.

JESUIT HIGH SCHOOL   **Day Boys Gr 9-12**
Tampa, FL 33614. 4701 N Himes Ave.
Tel: 813-877-5344. Fax: 813-872-1853.
www.jesuittampa.org
    Rev. Joseph F. Doyle, SJ, Pres. BS, Fordham Univ, BA, Le College de l'Immaculee Conception (Canada), MDiv, MA, St Mary's Univ (Canada). Joseph Sabin, Prin. BA, MA, Univ of South Florida.
    Col Prep. AP—Eng Span Calc Chem US_Hist Studio_Art. **Feat**—Fr Lat Stats Anat & Physiol Marine_Biol/Sci Comp_Sci Psych Govt/Econ Theol Chorus Music Speech. **Adm (Gr 9-10):** 182/yr. Appl due: Dec. **Tests** HSPT. **Enr 650.** B 650. Sec 650. Wh 77%. Hisp 14%. Blk 2%. Asian 3%. Other 4%. Avg class size: 21. **Fac 51.** M 35. F 16. Wh 98%. Hisp 1%. Blk 1%. Adv deg: 68%. **Grad '04—139.** Col—139. Avg SAT: 1230. Avg ACT: 25. **Tui '04-'05:** Day $9200. **Summer:** Rem. 5 wks. **Est 1899.** Nonprofit. Roman Catholic. Sem (Aug-May). **Assoc** SACS. JHS' college preparatory curriculum includes honors and Advanced Placement courses in most academic departments. Students take four years of theology and participate in regularly scheduled religious functions such as chapel services and retreats. Intramural and interscholastic athletics, forensic league debates and campus literary organizations are among the extracurricular options. Each boy performs 150 hours of community service hours during his four years.

ST. JOHN'S EPISCOPAL   **Day Coed Gr PS-8**
PARISH DAY SCHOOL
Tampa, FL 33606. 906 S Orleans Ave.
Tel: 813-489-5200. Fax: 813-258-2548.
www.stjohnseagles.org   E-mail: jarmstrong@stjohnseagles.org
    David A. Frothingham, Head. Sharon S. Cox, Adm.
    Pre-Prep. Feat—Span Computers Relig Art_Hist Studio_Art Music Music_Theory. **Supp**—Dev_Read Rem_Math Rem_Read Tut. **Adm:** 85/yr. Accepted: 46%. **Tests** CTP_4 ISEE. **Enr 460.** B 242. G 218. Elem 460. Wh 92%. Hisp 2%. Blk 2%. Asian 4%. Avg class size: 20. Uniform. **Fac 41.** M 5. F 34/2. Wh 95%. Hisp 3%. Asian 2%. Adv deg: 7%. **Grad '04—41.** Alum 1350. **Tui '03-'04:** Day $5795 (+$900). Aid: Need 24 ($81,600). **Est 1951.** Nonprofit. Episcopal. Sem (Aug-May). St. John's conducts a rigorous elementary program that prepares graduates for private and public high schools in the Tampa area. At the middle school level, many pupils follow the honors curriculum, which enables them to earn high school credit in algebra, science, Latin and history. Competitive athletics and community outreach programs balance academics.

TAMPA BAPTIST ACADEMY   **Day Coed Gr PS-12**
Tampa, FL 33604. 300 E Sligh Ave.
Tel: 813-238-3229. Fax: 813-237-3426.
www.tba-rams.org   E-mail: projdir@tampabay.rr.com

Barbara A. Bode, Admin. BA, MA, PhD, Univ of South Florida.

Col Prep. Gen Acad. Feat—Span Anat & Physiol Computers Govt Psych Bible Studio_Art Music. **Supp**—LD Rem_Math Rem_Read Tut. **Adm:** 40/yr. Appl due: Rolling. Accepted: 99%. **Tests** Stanford. **Enr 420.** Elem 296. Sec 124. Wh 48%. Hisp 19%. Blk 22%. Asian 5%. Other 6%. Avg class size: 25. Uniform. **Fac 35.** M 8/3. F 22/2. Wh 75%. Hisp 11%. Blk 14%. Adv deg: 34%. **Grad '04—24.** Col—18. Avg SAT: 1001. Avg ACT: 21. Alum 180. **Tui '01-'02:** Day $3650-4950 (+$800). Aid: Merit 31 ($13,000). **Summer:** Acad Rem Rec. 11 wks. **Est 1957.** Nonprofit. Southern Baptist. (Aug-May). The academy combines academic studies and religious education, requiring students to attend Bible class and chapel programs. Electives and extracurricular activities include art, music, drama, computer, Spanish, clubs, field trips, retreats and sports.

CARDINAL NEWMAN HIGH SCHOOL   Day Coed Gr 9-12
West Palm Beach, FL 33409. 512 Spencer Dr.
Tel: 561-683-6266. Fax: 561-683-7307.
www.cardinalnewman.com   E-mail: cnhs@cardinalnewman.com

Rev. David W. Carr, Pres. BA, Univ of Notre Dame, MEd, Florida Atlantic Univ. John F. Clarke, Prin. Julie Carr & Jan Joy, Adms.

Col Prep. Gen Acad. IB_Diploma. AP—Eng Calc Bio US_Hist Econ. **Feat**—Creative_Writing Fr Lat Span Comp_Sci Relig Studio_Art Visual_Arts Band Chorus Music Speech. **Supp**—Dev_Read Makeup Tut. **Adm (Gr 9-11):** 260/yr. Appl due: Rolling. **Tests** HSPT SSAT. **Enr 830.** B 431. G 399. Sec 830. Wh 84%. Hisp 10%. Blk 4%. Asian 1%. Other 1%. Avg class size: 25. Uniform. **Fac 65.** M 27/2. F 35/1. Wh 97%. Hisp 1%. Blk 1%. Asian 1%. Adv deg: 69%. **Grad '04—193.** Col—185. Alum 7700. **Tui '04-'05:** Day $5850-6950 (+$850-900). **Summer:** Acad Rem. 3 wks. **Est 1961.** Nonprofit. Roman Catholic. Sem (Aug-June). **Assoc** SACS. Cardinal Newman offers a varied curriculum that features both college and career preparation. In addition to course work in the basic disciplines (English, foreign language, mathematics, science and social studies), all pupils take religion classes. Qualified juniors and seniors may enroll in the International Baccalaureate Diploma program. Students participate in a wide range of athletics, clubs and organizations.

GEORGIA

DEERFIELD-WINDSOR SCHOOL   Day Coed Gr PS-12
Albany, GA 31707. 2500 Nottingham Way.
Tel: 229-435-1301. Fax: 229-888-6085.
www.deerfieldwindsor.com   E-mail: wt.henry@deerfieldwindsor.com

W. T. Henry, Head. BS, Troy State Univ, MS, Florida State Univ. Sarah Orgel, Adm.

Col Prep. AP—Eng Span Calc Bio Physics US_Hist. **Feat**—Fr Lat Environ_Sci Comp_Sci Bible Ethics Fine_Arts Drama Theater Debate Journ Speech. **Supp**—Dev_Read Tut. **Adm:** 138/yr. Appl due: Mar. Accepted: 98%. Yield: 99%.

Tests CEEB IQ ISEE MAT. **Enr 730.** B 363. G 367. Elem 460. Sec 270. Wh 93%. Blk 4%. Asian 3%. Avg class size: 14. **Fac 69.** M 18/1. F 45/5. Wh 100%. Adv deg: 57%. **Grad '04—65.** Col—65. Avg SAT: 1169. Avg ACT: 24. Alum 1750. **Tui '04-'05:** Day $6856 (+$325). Aid: Merit 6 ($36,000). Need 50 ($140,000). **Est 1964.** Nonprofit. Sem (Aug-May). **Assoc** SACS. Deerfield-Windsor enrolls college-bound children of above-average intelligence. Emphasis is placed on math and language arts in the elementary division, while upper schoolers may enroll in honors and Advanced Placement courses. Drama productions, choral group, debate, academic teams and competitive athletics are among the elective options.

ATHENS ACADEMY
Day Coed Gr PS-12

Athens, GA 30606. 1281 Spartan Ln.
Tel: 706-549-9225. Fax: 706-354-3775.
www.athensacademy.org   E-mail: academy@athensacademy.org
  J. Robert Chambers, Jr., Head. BS, MEd, Univ of Georgia. Stuart Todd, Adm.

Col Prep. Feat—Fine_Arts. **Supp**—Rev Tut. **Adm:** 144/yr. **Tests** ISEE. **Enr 806.** B 414. G 392. Elem 497. Sec 309. Avg class size: 18. **Fac 73.** M 20. F 53. Adv deg: 63%. **Grad '04—85.** Col—85. Avg SAT: 1250. Alum 1200. **Tui '04-'05:** Day $5155-10,675 (+$1000). **Summer:** Enrich Rev Rem. Tui Day $80-300/2-wk ses. 8 wks. **Est 1966.** Nonprofit. Sem (Aug-May). **Assoc** CLS SACS. Middle school students may participate in instrumental lessons, performing arts groups or athletics. The upper school offers interest clubs, a full athletic program, and a wide variety of fine and performing arts options.

THE GALLOWAY SCHOOL
Day Coed Gr PS-12

Atlanta, GA 30342. 215 W Wieuca Rd NW.
Tel: 404-252-8389. Fax: 404-252-7770.
www.gallowayschool.org   E-mail: info@gallowayschool.org
  Linda Martinson, Head. BA, MA, Ohio State Univ, MS, PhD, Stanford Univ. Rosetta Gooden, Adm.

Col Prep. AP—Eng Calc Stats Comp_Sci Bio Chem Eur_Hist US_Hist Psych US_Govt & Pol. **Feat**—British_Lit Creative_Writing Fr Lat Span Anat & Physiol Ecol Genetics Robotics Econ Philos Journ Public_Speak. **Supp**—Rev Tut. **Adm:** 120/yr. Accepted: 38%. **Tests** SSAT. **Enr 744.** B 361. G 383. Elem 493. Sec 251. Wh 83%. Hisp 2%. Blk 7%. Asian 4%. Other 4%. Avg class size: 15. **Fac 96.** M 22/2. F 70/2. Wh 88%. Hisp 3%. Blk 9%. Adv deg: 60%. **Grad '04—53.** Col—53. Alum 1361. **Tui '04-'05:** Day $14,870. Aid: Need 47 ($358,000). **Summer:** Acad Enrich Rem. Tui Day $750/3-wk ses. 6 wks. **Est 1969.** Nonprofit. Sem (Aug-June). **Assoc** SACS. Galloway offers a college preparatory curriculum that features Advanced Placement courses in all disciplines. Academic emphasis is placed upon small-group instruction and close teacher-student interaction. Sports and extracurricular activities complement the curriculum.

HORIZONS SCHOOL
Bdg Coed Gr 8-12
Day Coed K-12
Atlanta, GA 30307. 1900 DeKalb Ave NE.
Tel: 404-378-2219. Fax: 404-378-8946.
www.horizonsschool.com   E-mail: horizonsschool@mindspring.com
Les Garber, Admin. BA, Emory Univ, MEd, Georgia State Univ.

Col Prep. AP—Eng Calc Psych. **Feat**—Fr Span Studio_Art Drama Music Bus. **Supp**—ESL Makeup Tut. **Adm:** 28/yr. Bdg 4. Day 24. Appl due: Rolling. Accepted: 70%. Yield: 95%. **Enr 125.** B 8/63. G 3/51. Elem 50. Sec 73. PG 2. Wh 35%. Hisp 5%. Blk 52%. Asian 8%. Avg class size: 14. **Fac 16.** M 2. F 11/3. Wh 62%. Hisp 38%. Adv deg: 25%. In Dorms 3. **Grad '04**—24. Col—22. Avg SAT: 1125. Alum 130. **Tui '04-'05:** Bdg $17,500 (+$450). Day $8800 (+$200). Aid: Need 30 ($90,000). Work prgm 38 ($30,400). **Est 1978.** Nonprofit. Sem (Aug-May). In Horizons' elementary division (grades K-5), teachers employ different approaches to suit individual learning styles. The transitional middle school program (grades 6 and 7) combines course work in the fundamentals with instruction in research, note-taking, communicational and study skills. Geared primarily toward college preparation, the high school (grades 8-12) encourages active participation and offers flexible scheduling and opportunities for special academic credit. A three-week short term in the fall provides a break from regular classes and enables students to engage in seminars pertaining to such subjects as finance, art and philosophy.

MOUNT VERNON PRESBYTERIAN SCHOOL
Day Coed Gr PS-10
Atlanta, GA 30328. 471 Mt Vernon Hwy NE.
Tel: 404-252-3448. Fax: 404-252-6777.
www.mvpschool.com   E-mail: s_simon@mvpschool.com
Jeff Jackson, Head. BS, Univ of Louisville, MA, Southern Baptist Theological Seminary, EdD, Tennessee State Univ. Martha Donnelly, Adm.

Pre-Prep. Feat—Fr Ger Span Ethics Studio_Art Drama Band Chorus. **Adm (Gr PS-9):** 174/yr. Appl due: Mar. Accepted: 75%. **Tests** IQ SSAT Stanford. **Enr 703.** B 344. G 359. Elem 689. Sec 14. Wh 70%. Hisp 10%. Blk 10%. Asian 10%. Avg class size: 16. Uniform. **Fac 76.** M 10/2. F 52/12. Wh 90%. Hisp 7%. Blk 3%. Adv deg: 43%. **Grad '04**—45. Prep—32. **Tui '04-'05:** Day $6475-11,850. Aid: Need ($245,000). **Est 1972.** Nonprofit. Presbyterian. Sem (Aug-May). Basic concepts in reading preparation, language arts and math are incorporated into Mount Vernon's preschool program. Beginning in grade 1, children study science, social studies and computers, and they may also elect to take Spanish or French. The middle school curriculum (grades 6-8) features courses in literature and lab science, while ninth and tenth graders fulfill religion/ethics requirements. Various student clubs and athletic options supplement academics.

ST. MARTIN'S EPISCOPAL SCHOOL
Day Coed Gr PS-8
Atlanta, GA 30319. 3110-A Ashford Dunwoody Rd NE.
Tel: 404-237-4260. Fax: 404-237-9311.
www.stmartinschool.org   E-mail: smes@stmartinschool.org
Rev. James E. Hamner, Head. BA, Washington and Lee Univ, MD, Univ of the South, MPhil, PhD, Oxford Univ (England). Jan Swoope, Adm.

Pre-Prep. Feat—Fr Span Computers Relig Studio_Art Music. **Supp**—Dev_ Read Rev Tut. **Adm:** 101/yr. Appl due: Feb. Accepted: 25%. **Tests** IQ MRT SSAT. **Enr 565.** B 289. G 276. Elem 565. Wh 95%. Hisp 1%. Blk 2%. Asian 2%. Avg class size: 16. Uniform. **Fac 70.** M 3/2. F 57/8. Wh 94%. Hisp 2%. Blk 4%. Adv deg: 41%. **Grad '04—36.** Prep—24. Alum 248. **Tui '03-'04:** Day $6826-10,627 (+$500). **Est 1959.** Nonprofit. Episcopal. Quar (Aug-June). **Assoc** SACS. St. Martin's supplements its core curriculum with computer, religion, art and music classes. In addition, French and Spanish are offered in the middle school. Advanced math grouping is available in grades 7 and 8.

ST. PIUS X CATHOLIC HIGH SCHOOL   Day Coed Gr 9-12
Atlanta, GA 30345. 2674 Johnson Rd NE.
Tel: 404-636-3023. Fax: 404-633-8387.
www.spx.org   E-mail: admissions@spx.org
Stephen W. Spellman, Prin. EdS, Univ of Georgia. Chuck Byrd, Adm.

Col Prep. AP—Eng Fr Span Calc Stats Comp_Sci Bio Chem Physics Eur_Hist US_Hist World_Hist Comp_Govt & Pol Econ Psych US_Govt & Pol Studio_Art. **Feat**—British_Lit Lat Anat & Physiol Marine_Biol/Sci Holocaust Sociol Bus_Law Comp_Relig Band Music_Theory Guitar Dance Accounting Journ. **Supp**—Dev_ Read Tut. **Adm:** 288/yr. Appl due: Feb. Accepted: 80%. **Tests** SSAT. **Enr 1012.** B 486. G 526. Sec 1012. Wh 79%. Hisp 6%. Blk 9%. Asian 2%. Other 4%. Avg class size: 17. Uniform. **Fac 87.** M 41/1. F 45. Wh 92%. Hisp 2%. Blk 5%. Other 1%. Adv deg: 70%. **Grad '04—235.** Col—235. Avg SAT: 1186. Alum 7000. **Tui '04-'05:** Day $8500 (+$350). Aid: Merit 36 ($45,650). Need 22 ($141,750). Work prgm 147 ($483,174). **Est 1958.** Nonprofit. Roman Catholic. Sem (Aug-June). Honors and Advanced Placement courses, as well as extensive offerings in the fine arts, computer, journalism and business, complement the core curriculum. St. Pius graduates attend a variety of colleges throughout the US.

TRINITY SCHOOL   Day Coed Gr PS-6
Atlanta, GA 30327. 4301 Northside Pky NW.
Tel: 404-231-8100. Fax: 404-231-8111.
www.trinityatl.org   E-mail: info@trinityatl.org
Stephen Kennedy, Head. MA, Univ of Tulsa. Adelaide Herrington, Adm.

Pre-Prep. Feat—Span Environ_Sci Music Outdoor_Ed. **Supp**—Dev_Read. **Adm:** 91/yr. Appl due: Jan. Accepted: 25%. Yield: 80%. **Tests** IQ SSAT. **Enr 520.** Elem 520. Wh 85%. Blk 9%. Asian 2%. Other 4%. Avg class size: 18. **Fac 88.** Wh 98%. Blk 2%. Adv deg: 44%. **Grad '04—36.** Prep—36. **Tui '04-'05:** Day $6130-13,200 (+$650). **Est 1951.** Nonprofit. Sem (Aug-June). **Assoc** SACS. Trinity's developmental academic program emphasizes reading, writing, math and science, and it is enhanced by a fine arts program. Spanish is taught to children age 4 and up.

AQUINAS HIGH SCHOOL
Day Coed Gr 9-12

Augusta, GA 30904. 1920 Highland Ave.
Tel: 706-736-5516. Fax: 706-736-2678.
www.aquinashigh.org   E-mail: aquinas@aquinashigh.org
   Robert Larcher, Prin. BA, MA, Seattle Univ, EdS, Univ of Toledo.

Col Prep. AP—Eng Calc Eur_Hist US_Hist Econ. **Feat**—Fr Lat Span Horticulture. **Supp**—LD Tut. **Adm:** 110/yr. Appl due: Rolling. Accepted: 95%. **Tests** HSPT. **Enr 320.** Sec 320. Wh 83%. Hisp 6%. Blk 7%. Am Ind 1%. Asian 3%. Avg class size: 19. **Fac 24.** M 9/2. F 11/2. Adv deg: 41%. **Grad '04—79.** Col—78. Alum 3500. **Tui '04-'05:** Day $6800 (+$475). Parishioners $5300 (+$475). Aid: Merit 2 ($3000). Need 80 ($100,000). **Est 1957.** Nonprofit. Roman Catholic. Sem (Aug-May). **Assoc** SACS. AHS' curriculum includes an honors program and Advanced Placement courses.

EPISCOPAL DAY SCHOOL
Day Coed Gr PS-8

Augusta, GA 30904. 2248 Walton Way.
Tel: 706-733-1192. Fax: 706-733-1388.
www.edsaugusta.com   E-mail: nmurray@edsaugusta.com
   Ned R. Murray, Head. BA, Univ of the South, MEd, Univ of Tennessee-Chattanooga. Karen B. Lilly, Adm.

Pre-Prep. Gen Acad. Feat—Span Computers Relig Studio_Art Music. **Supp**—Dev_Read Rem_Math Rem_Read Rev Tut. **Adm:** 89/yr. Appl due: Rolling. Accepted: 96%. **Tests** CEEB. **Enr 453.** Elem 453. Wh 92%. Hisp 2%. Blk 5%. Asian 1%. Avg class size: 16. Uniform. **Fac 62.** M 6. F 48/8. Wh 98%. Hisp 1%. Asian 1%. Adv deg: 20%. **Grad '04—41. Tui '04-'05:** Day $2375-7325 (+$250). Aid: Need 15 ($20,000). **Est 1944.** Nonprofit. Episcopal. Quar (Aug-May). **Assoc** SACS. Students at the school receive mathematics enrichment beginning in grade 1. Instruction in music, art, computer, religion and research skills is available at all grade levels. Pupils in grades 6-8 fulfill a community service requirement.

WESTMINSTER SCHOOLS OF AUGUSTA
Day Coed Gr PS-12

Augusta, GA 30909. 3067 Wheeler Rd.
Tel: 706-731-5260. Fax: 706-261-7786.
www.wsa.net   E-mail: crivers@wsa.net
   James A. Adare, Head. Alex McCallie, Adm.

Col Prep. Feat—Fr Greek Lat Span Comp_Sci Econ Govt Psych Bible Studio_Art Drama Music Debate. **Supp**—Rev Tut. **Adm (Gr PS-11):** 50/yr. Appl due: Rolling. Accepted: 82%. **Tests** CTP_4. **Enr 544.** B 272. G 272. Elem 381. Sec 163. Wh 95%. Blk 2%. Asian 3%. Avg class size: 18. **Fac 42.** M 11. F 27/4. Wh 100%. Adv deg: 52%. **Grad '04—43.** Col—43. Avg SAT: 1280. Alum 486. **Tui '04-'05:** Day $4202-8384 (+$375). Aid: Merit 5 ($3000). Need 60 ($175,000). **Est 1972.** Nonprofit. Nondenom Christian. Sem (Aug-June). **Assoc** SACS. WSA comprises Westminster Day School (grades pre-K-5), Westminster Middle School (grades 6-8) and Westminster Preparatory School (grades 9-12). The curriculum, which is based on a Christian worldview, includes Advanced Placement courses. Academics are supplemented by drama, music, publications and athletics.

OAK MOUNTAIN ACADEMY
Day Coed Gr K-12
Carrollton, GA 30116. 222 Cross Plains Rd.
Tel: 770-834-6651. Fax: 770-834-6785.
www.oak-mountain-academy.org   E-mail: chendrix@oak-mountain-academy.org
Rick Parmer, Head. Cindy Hendrix, Adm.

Col Prep. AP—Eng Calc Bio. **Feat**—Creative_Writing Fr Span Computers Econ Govt Bible Philos Studio_Art Drama Music. **Supp**—Tut. **Adm:** 42/yr. Appl due: Rolling. Accepted: 83%. **Tests** ISEE Stanford. **Enr 238.** B 113. G 125. Elem 163. Sec 75. Wh 91%. Blk 2%. Asian 7%. Avg class size: 14. **Fac 40.** M 6/1. F 31/2. Wh 98%. Blk 2%. Adv deg: 35%. **Grad '04**—13. Col—11. Avg SAT: 1220. Alum 226. **Tui '04-'05:** Day $5500-7300. Aid: Merit 3 ($6000). Need 41 ($100,000). **Est 1962.** Nonprofit. Nondenom Christian. Sem (Aug-June). This nondenominational Christian school offers a variety of AP courses and electives. OMA works with advanced students desiring college credits through a cooperative program with the State University of West Georgia. Extracurricular activities include interscholastic athletics, and participation in a community service program is required.

PACELLI HIGH SCHOOL
Day Coed Gr 9-12
Columbus, GA 31907. 3556 Trinity Dr.
Tel: 706-561-8243. Fax: 706-561-3243.
www.sasphs.net   E-mail: pacelli@sasphs.net
John R. Albert, Prin. BA, Saint Mary's Univ of Minnesota, MA, Univ of Notre Dame, MSEd, Univ of Wisconsin-River Falls, EdS, Univ of St Thomas (MN). Christina Vogler, Adm.

Col Prep. Gen Acad. AP—Eng Calc Bio US_Hist US_Govt & Pol. **Feat**—Creative_Writing Fr Lat Span Anat Sports_Med Comp_Sci Econ Psych Relig Studio_Art Drama Music. **Adm (Gr 9-11):** 88/yr. Appl due: Mar. Accepted: 98%. **Tests** IQ. **Enr 200.** B 111. G 89. Sec 200. Wh 68%. Hisp 4%. Blk 23%. Asian 4%. Other 1%. Avg class size: 20. Uniform. **Fac 17.** M 6/1. F 6/4. Adv deg: 88%. **Grad '04**—46. Col—45. Avg SAT: 1014. **Tui '04-'05:** Day $6500. Catholic $5400. **Est 1958.** Nonprofit. Roman Catholic. Sem (Aug-May). **Assoc** SACS. Essentially a college preparatory school, Pacelli also offers a general education curriculum. AP and honors courses are available, and a variety of activities and sports round out the program.

LANDMARK CHRISTIAN SCHOOL
Day Coed Gr PS-12
Fairburn, GA 30213. 50 E Broad St.
Tel: 770-306-0647. Fax: 770-969-6551.
www.landmarkchristianschool.org   E-mail: admissions@landmark-cs.org
Matthew H. Skinner, Head. BBA, Univ of Texas-Arlington, MEd, Covenant College. Tammy McCurry, Adm.

Col Prep. AP—Eng Calc Chem Physics US_Hist World_Hist US_Govt & Pol Studio_Art. **Feat**—Fr Span Computers Bible Fine_Arts. **Adm:** 121/yr. Appl due: Rolling. Accepted: 56%. Yield: 92%. **Enr 605.** Elem 366. Sec 239. Wh 75%. Hisp 1%. Blk 24%. Uniform. **Fac 63.** M 19. F 44. Wh 99%. Other 1%. **Grad '04**—82. Col—81. Avg SAT: 1130. **Tui '05-'06:** Day $4450-10,225. Aid: Need 96. **Est 1989.** Nonprofit. Nondenom Christian. Quar (Aug-May). A nondenominational school that operates according to a Christian worldview, Landmark provides a comprehensive elementary and secondary program for college-bound students. Boys and girls attend four 90-minute class blocks per day. Aside from Wednesdays, when all classes meet, specific subjects convene every other day. Younger children (through grade 5) may attend classes on a second campus in Peachtree City (777 Robinson Rd., 30269).

NORTH COBB CHRISTIAN SCHOOL Day Coed Gr PS-12
Kennesaw, GA 30144. 4500 Lakeview Dr.
Tel: 770-975-0252. Fax: 770-975-9051.
www.ncchristian.org E-mail: cborders@ncchristian.org
Gary Coker, Head. BA, Piedmont College, MA, Western Michigan Univ, PhD, Vanderbilt Univ. Cile Borders, Adm.

Col Prep. AP—Eng Calc Eur_Hist US_Hist. **Feat**—Fr Span Stats Environ_Sci Comp_Sci Web_Design Anthro Psych Bible Graphic_Arts Theater Band Chorus Orchestra Speech. **Supp**—Tut. **Adm:** 163/yr. Appl due: Rolling. Accepted: 85%. Yield: 87%. **Tests** Stanford. **Enr 895.** B 425. G 470. Elem 656. Sec 239. Wh 92%. Hisp 1%. Blk 5%. Asian 1%. Other 1%. Avg class size: 21. Uniform. **Fac 73.** M 18/1. F 47/7. Wh 96%. Hisp 1%. Blk 3%. Adv deg: 26%. **Grad '04—47.** Col—47. Avg SAT: 1103. Avg ACT: 22. Alum 140. **Tui '04-'05:** Day $5480-8025 (+$225-1010). Aid: Merit 7 ($29,238). Need 83 ($256,173). **Summer:** Enrich Rec. Tui Day $150/wk. 6 wks. **Est 1983.** Nonprofit. Nondenom Christian. Sem (Aug-May). Honors and Advanced Placement courses, Bible classes and an extensive fine arts department are noteworthy features of this Christian school's program. High school students follow a modified block schedule in which classes meet every other day for 90 minutes. In addition to meeting graduation requirements in various subject areas, pupils perform mandatory community service. Extracurricular options include band, chorus, theater, student government, athletics, clubs and honor societies.

LaGRANGE ACADEMY Day Coed Gr K-12
LaGrange, GA 30240. 1501 Vernon Rd.
Tel: 706-882-8097. Fax: 706-882-8640.
www.lagrangeacademy.org E-mail: admissions@la.lagrange.edu
Trigg Dalrymple, Head. BS, Piedmont College, MEd, EdS, Univ of Georgia. Gary Emmons, Adm.

Col Prep. Feat—Lat Span Computers Pol_Sci Drama Chorus. **Supp**—Rev Tut. **Adm:** 25/yr. Appl due: Rolling. Accepted: 75%. **Tests** IQ Stanford. **Enr 220.** B 108. G 112. Wh 95%. Hisp 1%. Blk 2%. Asian 2%. Avg class size: 16. **Fac 20.** M 6/1. F 12/1. Wh 94%. Hisp 3%. Blk 3%. Adv deg: 90%. **Grad '04—27.** Avg SAT: 1170. Alum 400. **Tui '04-'05:** Day $6990 (+$1500). Aid: Need 28 ($75,000). **Est 1970.** Nonprofit. Quar (Aug-June). **Assoc** SACS. The traditional academic curriculum is supplemented by Spanish, Latin, choir, drama, forensics and computer programming. Sports include baseball, basketball, tennis, golf, track, softball and soccer.

WHITEFIELD ACADEMY   Day Coed Gr K-12
Mableton, GA 30126. 1 Whitefield Dr.
Tel: 678-305-3000. Fax: 678-305-3010.
www.whitefieldacademy.com   E-mail: lindas@whitefieldacademy.com
    Timothy J. Hillen, Head. BS, Taylor Univ, MA, Eastern Michigan Univ. Linda Simpson, Adm.

    Col Prep. AP—Eng Span Calc Stats Comp_Sci Bio Chem Physics Eur_Hist US_Hist Studio_Art. **Feat**—Fine_Arts Theater Chorus Public_Speak. **Supp**—Tut. **Adm:** Appl due: Feb. Accepted: 76%. **Tests** SSAT. **Enr 416.** B 224. G 192. Elem 274. Sec 142. Wh 89%. Blk 11%. Avg class size: 17. Uniform. **Fac 55.** M 18/1. F 31/5. Wh 85%. Blk 15%. Adv deg: 29%. **Grad '04—19.** Col—19. Avg SAT: 1203. **Tui '05-'06:** Day $10,450-14,200 (+$800-900). Aid: Need 42 ($365,000). **Est 1996.** Nonprofit. Nondenom Christian. Sem (Aug-May). **Assoc** SACS. This Christ-centered preparatory school provides honors and AP courses, as well as classes in the visual arts, drama and music. Whitefield offers a full range of extracurricular activities and athletics for boys and girls.

FIRST PRESBYTERIAN DAY SCHOOL   Day Coed Gr PS-12
Macon, GA 31210. 5671 Calvin Dr.
Tel: 478-477-6505. Fax: 478-477-2804.
www.fpdmacon.org   E-mail: gthompson@fpdmacon.org
    Gregg Thompson, Head. Patricia C. Fountain, Adm.

    Col Prep. AP—Eng Calc Bio Eur_Hist US_Hist. **Feat**—British_Lit Fr Lat Span Environ_Sci Comp_Sci Web_Design Econ Govt Bible Comp_Relig Studio_Art Drama Band Chorus Dance Accounting Journ Public_Speak. **Supp**—LD Tut. **Adm:** 141/yr. Appl due: Jan. Accepted: 96%. **Tests** Stanford. **Enr 945.** B 464. G 481. Elem 626. Sec 319. Wh 97%. Hisp 1%. Blk 1%. Asian 1%. Avg class size: 20. **Fac 77.** M 23/3. F 45/6. Wh 100%. Adv deg: 59%. **Grad '04—76.** Col—76. Alum 1500. **Tui '05-'06:** Day $4870-8730. Aid: Merit 5 ($5500). Need 198 ($329,600). **Est 1970.** Inc. Presbyterian. Sem (Aug-May). In addition to fulfilling core academic requirements, elementary students at FPDS enroll in arts classes each semester. High school pupils select from a full complement of honors and Advanced Placement courses. Boys and girls with diagnosed learning disabilities may take part in the school's learning assistance program.

MOUNT DE SALES ACADEMY   Day Coed Gr 6-12
Macon, GA 31201. 851 Orange St.
Tel: 478-751-3240. Fax: 478-751-3241.
www.mds.macon.ga.us
    Kathleen R. Prebble, Pres. Linda Cardwell, Adm.

    Col Prep. AP—Eng Calc Comp_Sci Bio Eur_Hist US_Hist. **Feat**—Fr Span Econ Govt Psych Relig Fine_Arts Theater_Arts Chorus Music Debate Journ Speech. **Supp**—Tut. **Adm:** 164/yr. **Tests** Stanford. **Enr 660.** Elem 240. Sec 420. Wh 80%. Hisp 3%. Blk 16%. Asian 1%. Avg class size: 21. Uniform. **Fac 51.** M 19/2. F 26/4. Wh 96%. Hisp 2%. Blk 2%. Adv deg: 25%. **Grad '04—114.** Col—113. Alum 3513. **Tui '04-'05:** Day $7066. **Summer:** Rec. 2-8 wks. **Est 1876.** Nonprofit. Roman Catholic. Sem (Aug-May). **Assoc** SACS. This Catholic school is ecumenical in nature, enrolling students of other faiths and of diverse racial and economic backgrounds. A full program of cocurricular activities includes student council, publications, National Honor Society and an interscholastic literary competition. Athletic teams are fielded in baseball, basketball, football, golf, soccer, softball, tennis, track, cross-country, swimming and wrestling.

STRATFORD ACADEMY — Day Coed Gr PS-12
Macon, GA 31220. 6010 Peake Rd.
Tel: 478-477-8073. Fax: 478-477-0299.
www.stratford.org E-mail: admissions@stratford.org
David M. Wahl, Head. BA, Univ of Pittsburgh, MS, Carnegie Mellon Univ, MEd, Univ of Virginia. John Paul Gaddy, Adm.

Col Prep. AP—Eng Fr Lat Span Calc Bio Chem Eur_Hist US_Hist US_Govt & Pol Studio_Art. **Feat**—Creative_Writing Anat & Physiol Genetics Web_Design Holocaust Comp_Relig Drawing Photog Theater Music_Theory Debate Journ Public_Speak. **Supp**—Dev_Read ESL Rem_Math Rem_Read Rev Tut. **Adm:** 113/yr. Appl due: Rolling. Accepted: 74%. Yield: 91%. **Tests** CTP_4. **Enr 925.** B 460. G 465. Elem 643. Sec 282. Wh 92%. Hisp 1%. Blk 2%. Asian 4%. Other 1%. Avg class size: 17. **Fac 88.** M 26. F 55/7. Wh 99%. Blk 1%. Adv deg: 50%. **Grad '04—81.** Col—81. Alum 2900. **Tui '04-'05:** Day $5117-8987 (+$100). Aid: Need 70 ($200,000). **Summer:** Acad Enrich Rev Rec. Tui Day $60-120. 1 wk. **Est 1960.** Nonprofit. Sem (Aug-May). **Assoc** SACS. The curriculum includes Advanced Placement classes in chemistry, biology, history, math, art, Latin, Spanish, French and English, as well as courses in instrumental and choral music, drama, debate, public speaking and physical education. Interscholastic sports offered are football, basketball, baseball, softball, golf, soccer, tennis, track, cross-country and wrestling.

TATTNALL SQUARE ACADEMY — Day Coed Gr PS-12
Macon, GA 31210. 111 Trojan Trl.
Tel: 478-477-6760. Fax: 478-474-7887.
www.tattnall.org E-mail: tattnall@yahoo.com
Barney Hester, Head. BS, Georgia Southern Univ, MEd, Georgia College. Lynne Adams, Adm.

Col Prep. AP—Eng Calc US_Hist Studio_Art. **Feat**—Fr Lat Span Programming. **Supp**—ESL Tut. **Adm:** 144/yr. Accepted: 82%. **Enr 850.** B 450. G 400. Wh 98%. Blk 1%. Asian 1%. Avg class size: 15. **Fac 77.** M 11/7. F 53/6. Adv deg: 36%. **Grad '04—85.** Col—85. Alum 2000. **Tui '04-'05:** Day $6078-7080 (+$630). **Summer:** Rem. Tui Day $250. 6 wks. **Est 1968.** Nonprofit. Nondenom Christian. Quar (Aug-May). **Assoc** SACS. Tattnall provides a structured curriculum in a Christian atmosphere. In the elementary grades, emphasis is placed on acquiring proficiency in language and numerical skills. High school students are offered a traditional college preparatory program, as well as an AP program and courses in the fine arts and computer programming.

THE WALKER SCHOOL   **Day Coed Gr PS-12**
Marietta, GA 30062. 700 Cobb Pky N.
Tel: 770-427-2689. Fax: 770-514-8122.
www.thewalkerschool.org   E-mail: mozleyp@thewalkerschool.org
    Donald B. Robertson, Head. BS, College of William and Mary, MA, Rider Univ. Patricia H. Mozley, Adm.

    Col Prep. AP—Eng Fr Ger Lat Span Calc Stats Comp_Sci Bio Chem Physics Eur_Hist US_Hist World_Hist Econ Psych US_Govt & Pol Studio_Art. **Feat**—Lib_Skills Anat Astron Botany Zoology Philos Art_Hist Ceramics Painting Sculpt Drama Chorus Music Study_Skills. **Adm (Gr PS-11):** 171/yr. Appl due: Feb. Accepted: 20%. **Tests** IQ SSAT Stanford. **Enr 1072.** B 564. G 508. Elem 687. Sec 385. Wh 90%. Hisp 1%. Blk 3%. Asian 6%. Avg class size: 14. **Fac 139.** M 53. F 86. Wh 90%. Hisp 3%. Blk 7%. Adv deg: 94%. **Grad '04—85.** Col—85. Avg SAT: 1315. Alum 1150. **Tui '04-'05:** Day $10,425-12,880 (+$120-600). Aid: Need 75 ($250,000). **Est 1957.** Nonprofit. Sem (Aug-May). **Assoc** SACS. In Walker's four-year-old prekindergarten, children develop motor skills, visual perception and social skills while also working toward reading and math readiness. Foreign languages, drama, art, computer, library skills and music supplement basic academic subjects in the lower school (grades 1-5); middle school students (grades 6-8) take exploratory art, music, drama, computer and foreign language courses, in addition to work in the core subjects; and upper schoolers choose among Advanced Placement classes in all disciplines. Sports and other extracurricular activities are plentiful, and high schoolers must take part in several each year.

GREATER ATLANTA CHRISTIAN SCHOOL   **Day Coed Gr PS-12**
Norcross, GA 30093. 1575 Indian Trail Rd.
Tel: 770-243-2000. Fax: 770-243-2213.
www.greateratlantachristian.org   E-mail: lindacl@gacs.pvt.k12.ga.us
    David Fincher, Pres. BA, Harding Univ, MAT, Georgia State Univ, EdD, PhD, Univ of Georgia. Linda Clovis, Adm.

    Col Prep. AP—Eng Calc Stats Comp_Sci Bio Chem Physics Eur_Hist US_Hist World_Hist Psych US_Govt & Pol Studio_Art Music_Theory. **Feat**—British_Lit Fr Lat Span Anat & Physiol Econ Sociol Bible Comp_Relig Photog Drama Accounting Speech. **Supp**—ESL. **Adm:** 293/yr. Appl due: Mar. Accepted: 42%. **Enr 1831.** B 900. G 931. Elem 1223. Sec 608. Wh 81%. Hisp 2%. Blk 8%. Asian 8%. Other 1%. Avg class size: 17. Uniform. **Fac 128.** M 43. F 85. Wh 92%. Blk 6%. Am Ind 1%. Asian 1%. Adv deg: 56%. **Grad '04—143.** Col—143. Avg SAT: 1143. Alum 2796. **Tui '04-'05:** Day $8490-9815 (+$170-435). **Est 1961.** Nonprofit. Sem (Aug-June). **Assoc** SACS. Located on a 74-acre campus, GACS conducts daily Bible classes and offers such extracurricular activities as chorus, drama, band and athletics. Students may also participate in clubs, service activities and mission trips. Programming for gifted children begins in grade 2, while honors and Advanced Placement courses are available in the upper grades.

HIGH MEADOWS SCHOOL   **Day Coed Gr PS-8**
Roswell, GA 30075. 1055 Willeo Rd.
Tel: 770-993-2940. Fax: 770-993-8331.
www.highmeadows.org   E-mail: hcothrandrake@highmeadows.org

Liz Gembecki, Head. BA, St Joseph's College (NY), MS, City Univ of New York. Holly Cothran Drake, Adm.

Pre-Prep. Gen Acad. Feat—Span Environ_Sci Outdoor_Ed. **Supp**—Tut. **Adm:** 76/yr. Appl due: Rolling. Accepted: 70%. Yield: 49%. **Enr 341.** B 174. G 167. Elem 341. Avg class size: 20. **Fac 47.** M 6/2. F 29/10. Adv deg: 42%. **Grad '04—21.** Prep—4. **Tui '04-'05:** Day $8980-11,850 (+$475-1025). Aid: Need 5 ($27,620). **Summer:** Enrich Rec. 2-3 wks. **Est 1973.** Nonprofit. Tri (Aug-May). High Meadows utilizes thematic units in arts, language, math, science, technology and social science classes. As early as kindergarten, children begin working on projects that involve teamwork and technology and further develop presentational, organizational, problem solving and time management skills. The school conducts a highly regarded outdoor education program that features archery, ropes courses, stargazing, white-water rafting and hiking in the Appalachian Mountains.

ST. FRANCIS SCHOOL Day Coed Gr K-12
Roswell, GA 30075. 9375 Willeo Rd.
Tel: 770-641-8257. Fax: 770-641-0283.
www.stfranschool.com   E-mail: admissions@stfranschool.com

Drew Buccellato, Head. BS, MA, Fordham Univ, MS, Pace Univ. Ellen V. Brown, Adm.

Col Prep. AP—Eng US_Govt & Pol Studio_Art. **Feat**—Creative_Writing Fr Lat Span Environ_Sci Computers Civil_War Russ_Hist Psych Drawing Painting Drama Music Journ. **Supp**—Dev_Read Rem_Math Rem_Read Rev Tut. **Adm:** 170/yr. Appl due: Mar. **Enr 876.** Elem 560. Sec 316. Wh 95%. Hisp 2%. Blk 2%. Asian 1%. Avg class size: 12. Uniform. **Fac 130. Grad '04—75.** Col—75. **Tui '02-'03:** Day $12,900 (+$750). **Summer:** Gr 1-8. Acad Enrich Rev Rem Rec. Tui Day $600/2-wk ses. 4 wks. **Est 1976.** Nonprofit. Sem (Aug-June). St. Francis offers a comprehensive academic program that addresses the needs of students in need of a smaller teacher-pupil ratio than is available at most schools. Classes range in size from six to 16. In the high school (which occupies a separate campus at 13440 Cogburn Rd., Alpharetta 30004), students are encouraged to participate in a sport each term; in addition to athletics, extracurricular activities include yearbook, literary magazine, chorus, and spirit and community service clubs.

FREDERICA ACADEMY Day Coed Gr PS-12
St Simons Island, GA 31522. 200 Hamilton Rd.
Tel: 912-638-9981. Fax: 912-638-1442.
www.fredericaacademy.org   E-mail: rkelly@fredericaacademy.org

Ellen E. Fleming, Head. BA, George Washington Univ, MEd, Georgia State Univ.

Col Prep. AP—Eng Calc Bio US_Hist. **Feat**—British_Lit Lat Span Anat Ecol Comp_Sci Econ Govt Psych Sociol Photog Studio_Art Drama Chorus Debate. **Supp**—Tut. **Adm:** 68/yr. Appl due: Rolling. Accepted: 92%. **Tests** CEEB IQ SSAT Stanford. **Enr 350.** B 176. G 174. Elem 239. Sec 111. Wh 92%. Hisp 4%. Blk 2%. Asian 2%. Avg class size: 25. **Fac 36.** M 6/2. F 25/3. Wh 88%. Hisp 6%. Am Ind 3%. Asian 3%. Adv deg: 58%. **Grad '04—8.** Col—8. Avg SAT: 1213. Avg ACT: 25. Alum 495. **Tui '04-'05:** Day $4300-10,500 (+$500). Aid: Merit 11 ($66,800).

Need 73 ($387,842). **Summer:** Enrich Rev. Arts. Sports. Tui Day $45-200/wk. 5 wks. **Est 1970.** Nonprofit. Sem (Aug-May). **Assoc** SACS. Frederica provides a structured curriculum with attention to college preparation in the high school years. The school encourages all students to take part in service opportunities, the arts and athletics. Sports include soccer, basketball, golf, softball, baseball, tennis, cross-country and crew.

ST. ANDREW'S SCHOOL   **Day Coed Gr PS-12**
Savannah, GA 31410. 601 Penn Waller Rd, PO Box 30639.
Tel: 912-897-4941. Fax: 912-897-4943.
www.saintschool.com   E-mail: info@saintschool.com
    E. C. Hubbard, Head. MEd, Univ of South Carolina. Kelly Waldron, Adm.

    Col Prep. AP—Eng Span Calc Bio Chem. **Feat**—Creative_Writing Anat Ecol Microbiol Computers Anthro Psych Govt/Econ Philos Relig Ceramics Studio_Art Drama. **Supp**—Tut. **Adm:** 96/yr. Appl due: Rolling. Accepted: 80%. **Tests** SSAT TOEFL. **Enr 425.** B 225. G 200. Elem 285. Sec 140. Wh 90%. Blk 6%. Asian 4%. Avg class size: 15. **Fac 45.** Wh 100%. Adv deg: 33%. **Grad '04—21.** Col—21. Avg SAT: 1077. Alum 600. **Tui '05-'06:** Day $6250-8650 (+$300). **Summer:** Acad Enrich Rec. SAT Prep. 1-3 wks. **Est 1947.** Nonprofit. Sem (Aug-May). **Assoc** SACS. Located on Wilmington Island, St. Andrew's offers a college preparatory program. Honors and Advanced Placement courses are offered in every major discipline. Soccer, softball, tennis, basketball, baseball, volleyball, cross-country, football, track and golf are the interscholastic sports available.

ST. VINCENT'S ACADEMY   **Day Girls Gr 9-12**
Savannah, GA 31401. 207 E Liberty St.
Tel: 912-236-5508. Fax: 912-236-7877.
www.stvincentsacademy.com   E-mail: kgrayson@stvincentsacademy.com
    Sr. Helen Marie Buttimer, RSM, Prin. BA, Mount Saint Agnes College, MEd, Univ of Dayton. Sr. M. Jogues Smith, RSM, Adm.

    Col Prep. AP—Span Calc US_Hist. **Feat**—Fr Lat Anat Computers Holocaust Psych Relig Photog Music. **Supp**—Rev Tut. **Adm:** 91/yr. Appl due: Aug. Accepted: 100%. **Tests** HSPT. **Enr 350.** G 350. Sec 350. Wh 87%. Hisp 2%. Blk 11%. Avg class size: 12. Uniform. **Fac 25.** M 6/1. F 17/1. Wh 98%. Hisp 1%. Blk 1%. Adv deg: 40%. **Grad '04—89.** Col—81. Alum 4590. **Tui '04-'05:** Day $6100 (+$400). Catholic $5050 (+$400). Aid: Merit 3 ($3500). Need 80 ($83,120). **Est 1845.** Nonprofit. Roman Catholic. Sem (Aug-May). **Assoc** SACS. Founded by the Sisters of Mercy, St. Vincent's offers extracurricular clubs, activities and publications, in addition to interscholastic competition in basketball, tennis, softball, track, soccer, swimming, volleyball and riflery.

BULLOCH ACADEMY   **Day Coed Gr PS-12**
Statesboro, GA 30458. 873 Westside Rd.
Tel: 912-764-6297. Fax: 912-764-3165.
www.bullochacademy.com   E-mail: rhutcheson@bullochacademy.com

Barry Peterson, Head. BS, Moorhead State Univ, MEd, EdD, Univ of Alabama-Tuscaloosa.

Col Prep. AP—Eng US_Hist US_Govt & Pol. **Feat**—Creative_Writing Span Comp_Sci Ethics Fine_Arts Journ Speech. **Supp**—Makeup Tut. **Adm:** 40/yr. Appl due: Apr. Accepted: 95%. **Tests** CEEB. **Enr 515.** Elem 395. Sec 120. Wh 98%. Other 2%. Avg class size: 12. **Fac 56.** M 5. F 50/1. Wh 99%. Asian 1%. Adv deg: 17%. **Grad '04—24.** Col—24. Avg SAT: 1051. Alum 300. **Tui '05-'06:** Day $4013-4628 (+$1075). **Est 1971.** Nonprofit. Sem (Aug-May). **Assoc** SACS. Bulloch's curriculum stresses college preparation in the upper grades, and emphasis is placed on math, reading and writing skills, in addition to sound study habits. Varsity sports include football, basketball, soccer, track, tennis and golf, as well as girls' basketball, soccer and softball. A wide range of extracurricular activities is also available.

GEORGIA CHRISTIAN SCHOOL   Day Coed Gr PS-12
Valdosta, GA 31601. 4359 Dasher Rd.
Tel: 229-559-5131. Fax: 229-559-7401.
www.georgiachristian.org   E-mail: gcs@georgiachristian.org
Gale Koening, Prin. Gina Colson, Adm.

Col Prep. Voc. AP—Calc. **Feat**—Span Bible Studio_Art Chorus. **Adm:** 42/yr. **Enr 230.** Elem 165. Sec 65. Wh 96%. Hisp 2%. Blk 2%. Avg class size: 15. **Fac 28.** M 4/4. F 16/4. Adv deg: 10%. **Grad '04—17.** Col—15. Avg SAT: 1170. Alum 5000. **Tui '03-'04:** Day $2396-3475. **Est 1914.** Nonprofit. Sem (Aug-May). A Christian atmosphere pervades all activities at the school, including the curriculum. Athletics include track, basketball, baseball, softball, soccer, tennis and golf.

VALWOOD SCHOOL   Day Coed Gr PS-12
Valdosta, GA 31604. PO Box 4930.
Tel: 229-242-8491. Fax: 229-245-7894.
www.valwood.org   E-mail: dcrane@valwood.org
Cobb Atkinson, Head. BA, Emory Univ, BA, Middlebury College, MA, Harvard Univ. Dale H. Crane, Adm.

Col Prep. Feat—Computers Fine_Arts. **Adm:** 98/yr. Appl due: Rolling. Accepted: 85%. **Tests** CEEB IQ Stanford. **Enr 394.** B 207. G 187. Elem 280. Sec 114. Wh 95%. Hisp 1%. Blk 3%. Asian 1%. Avg class size: 18. **Fac 44.** M 9. F 27/8. Wh 93%. Hisp 2%. Other 5%. Adv deg: 34%. **Grad '04—18.** Col—18. Avg SAT: 1100. Avg ACT: 23. **Tui '03-'04:** Day $6500 (+$250). Aid: Need 34 ($121,152). **Est 1969.** Nonprofit. Sem (Aug-May). Valwood's curriculum focuses on the core academic skills necessary for college success. In addition to the academic program, which features an array of Advanced Placement and enrichment courses, the school provides students with opportunities in athletics and the arts. Many boys and girls engage in community service.

KENTUCKY

ST. HENRY DISTRICT HIGH SCHOOL Day Coed Gr 9-12
Erlanger, KY 41018. 3755 Scheben Dr.
Tel: 859-525-0255. Fax: 859-525-5855.
www.shdhs.org   E-mail: dmotte@shdhs.org
David M. Otte, Prin. BA, Thomas More College, MEd, Xavier Univ.

Col Prep. Gen Acad. Voc. Bus. Feat—Lat Span Psych Studio_Art. **Supp**—Dev_Read Rev Tut. **Adm:** 160/yr. Appl due: Aug. Accepted: 100%. **Enr 525.** B 269. G 256. Sec 525. Wh 97%. Hisp 1%. Blk 1%. Asian 1%. Avg class size: 22. Uniform. **Fac 40.** M 16/1. F 22/1. Wh 99%. Hisp 1%. Adv deg: 42%. **Grad '04—116.** Col—99. Avg SAT: 1069. Avg ACT: 22. Alum 1000. **Tui '04-'05:** Day $4700 (+$500). Aid: Merit 19 ($10,650). Need 30 ($35,000). Work prgm 5 ($8000). **Est 1933.** Nonprofit. Roman Catholic. Quar (Aug-May). Christian values and religious instruction receive priority at this college preparatory school. Students may pursue business, vocational or general studies as well.

ASSUMPTION HIGH SCHOOL Day Girls Gr 9-12
Louisville, KY 40205. 2170 Tyler Ln.
Tel: 502-458-9551. Fax: 502-454-8411.
www.ahsrockets.org   E-mail: susanna.patrick@ahsrockets.org
Mary Lee McCoy, Pres. BS, Univ of Georgia, MEd, Univ of Louisville. Mary Ann Steutermann, Prin. Martha Tedesco, Adm.

Col Prep. AP—Eng Fr Span Calc Stats Bio Chem Physics US_Hist Econ US_Govt & Pol Art_Hist Studio_Art Music_Theory. **Feat**—Forensic_Sci Holocaust Law Psych Bus_Law Theol Fine_Arts Graphic_Arts Journ Public_Speak. **Supp**—LD Rem_Math. **Adm (Gr 9-11):** 248/yr. Appl due: Mar. **Tests** HSPT. **Enr 975.** G 975. Sec 975. Wh 97%. Other 3%. Avg class size: 17. Uniform. **Fac 96.** M 16. F 77/3. Wh 98%. Hisp 2%. Adv deg: 81%. **Grad '04—240.** Col—236. Avg SAT: 1175. Avg ACT: 23. Alum 2000. **Tui '04-'05:** Day $7350 (+$100). Aid: Merit 6 ($5250). Need 142 ($264,000). **Est 1955.** Nonprofit. Roman Catholic. Sem (Aug-June). AHS' varied curriculum includes Advanced Placement, honors and college preparatory classes in a range of academic subjects, as well as college-credit course work for juniors and seniors through Bellarmine University. Individualized attention and special testing services are provided for pupils with diagnosed learning differences. Student clubs, interscholastic and intramural athletics, and community service round out the program.

HAYFIELD MONTESSORI SCHOOL Day Coed Gr PS-3
Louisville, KY 40205. 2000 Tyler Ln.
Tel: 502-454-7122. Fax: 502-479-8716.
www.hayfieldmontessori.com   E-mail: hayfield-montessori1@insightbb.com
Leo P. Denoncourt, Prin. MAT, Spalding Univ. Monique F. Denoncourt, Adm.

Gen Acad. Feat—Fr. **Supp**—Tut. **Adm (Gr PS-1):** 40/yr. Appl due: Rolling. Accepted: 95%. **Enr 100.** Elem 100. Wh 85%. Hisp 2%. Blk 3%. Asian 10%. Avg class size: 12. **Fac 11.** F 7/4. Wh 100%. Adv deg: 18%.**Tui '05-'06:** Day $5700

(+$10-200). **Est 1967.** Nonprofit. Sem (Aug-May). The school's program relies upon Montessori methods and tools of teaching. French is taught at all grade levels. The elementary section accepts new students into grade 1 only.

ST. XAVIER HIGH SCHOOL — Day Boys Gr 9-12
Louisville, KY 40217. 1609 Poplar Level Rd.
Tel: 502-637-4712. Fax: 502-634-2171.
www.saintx.com   E-mail: bobremski@saintx.com
  Perry E. Sangalli, Pres. BA, Bellarmine College, MAT, Univ of Louisville, EdD, Spalding Univ. Michael A. Glaser, Adm.
  Col Prep. AP—Eng Fr Ger Span Calc Stats Bio Chem Physics Eur_Hist US_Hist US_Govt & Pol Studio_Art. **Feat**—Chin Lat Web_Design. **Supp**—Dev_Read Rem_Math Rem_Read Tut. **Adm:** 385/yr. Appl due: Rolling. Accepted: 99%. **Tests** HSPT. **Enr 1440.** B 1440. Sec 1440. Wh 96%. Hisp 1%. Blk 2%. Asian 1%. Avg class size: 25. Uniform. **Fac 120.** M 90/2. F 27/1. Wh 99%. Hisp 1%. Adv deg: 79%. **Grad '04—399.** Col—390. Avg SAT: 1160. Avg ACT: 23. Alum 17,000. **Tui '05-'06:** Day $7875 (+$750). Aid: Merit 30 ($50,000). Need 280 ($830,000). Work prgm 10 ($20,000). **Est 1864.** Nonprofit. Roman Catholic. Sem (Aug-May). **Assoc** SACS. Sponsored by the Xaverian Brothers, St. X conducts three distinct programs of study to meet students' needs: honors, academic and traditional. Placement is determined by entrance test scores, previous grades and teacher recommendations. Full honors and Advanced Placement programs are available. A varied selection of athletics and other extracurricular activities supplements academics.

TRINITY HIGH SCHOOL — Day Boys Gr 9-12
Louisville, KY 40207. 4011 Shelbyville Rd.
Tel: 502-895-9427. Fax: 502-899-2052.
www.thsrock.net   E-mail: pricem@thsrock.net
  Robert J. Mullen, Pres. BS, Bellarmine Univ, EdD, Spalding Univ. Daniel Zoeller, Prin. BA, Eastern Kentucky Univ, MAT, Univ of Louisville. Mary Ann Hall, Adm.
  Col Prep. AP—Eng Fr Span Calc Bio Physics Eur_Hist Econ Psych. **Feat**—Ger Sociol Relig Journ. **Supp**—Dev_Read LD Rem_Math Rem_Read Tut. **Adm:** 400/yr. Appl due: Mar. Accepted: 95%. Yield: 95%. **Tests** HSPT. **Enr 1445.** B 1445. Sec 1445. Wh 91%. Hisp 3%. Blk 5%. Asian 1%. Avg class size: 21. Uniform. **Fac 110.** M 80/1. F 29. Wh 91%. Hisp 5%. Blk 3%. Am Ind 1%. Adv deg: 90%. **Grad '04—273.** Col—262. Avg SAT: 1230. Avg ACT: 22. Alum 11,500. **Tui '04-'05:** Day $7325 (+$100). Aid: Merit 92 ($55,825). Need 325 ($390,000). Work prgm 100 ($51,500). **Summer:** Acad Enrich Rem Rec. Tui Day $300. 7 wks. **Est 1953.** Nonprofit. Roman Catholic. Quar (Aug-June). **Assoc** SACS. The academic curriculum features advanced credit for college and independent study, and technology is an important learning and teaching tool at the school. A program is offered for students with learning differences. Athletics and a variety of extracurricular opportunities are also available.

ONEIDA BAPTIST INSTITUTE

Coed Gr 6-12
Bdg & Day

Oneida, KY 40972. PO Box 67.
Tel: 606-847-4111. Fax: 606-847-4496.
www.oneidaschool.org E-mail: admissions4obi@yahoo.com
W. F. Underwood, Pres. Billie Faye Hoover, Adm.

Col Prep. Gen Acad. Voc. Bus. AP—Eng US_Hist. **Feat**—Ger Span Fine_Arts Indus_Arts. **Supp**—Dev_Read ESL Makeup Tut. **Adm:** 63/yr. Appl due: Rolling. Accepted: 95%. Yield: 99%. **Enr 278.** B 145. G 133. Elem 67. Sec 211. Wh 67%. Hisp 4%. Blk 25%. Asian 4%. Avg class size: 13. **Fac 50.** M 23/1. F 24/2. Wh 100%. Adv deg: 12%. **Grad '04**—38. Col—30. Alum 300. **Tui '04-'05:** Bdg $4350-4950 (+$45-60/mo). Day $0. Aid: Need 175 ($324,228). **Summer:** Acad Rem. Tui Bdg $853-943. Tui Day $0. 6 wks. **Est 1899.** Nonprofit. Southern Baptist. Quar (Aug-May). OBI's Christian program features small classes, a tutoring lab, a nightly study hall and, for an additional fee, an ESL program. Advanced Placement courses meet the needs of the college-bound pupil, while vocational and fine arts classes enable boys and girls to pursue their talents and interests. An important aspect of school life is Oneida's work program, which requires students to work or engage in certain cocurricular activities one and a half hours each weekday and four hours on weekends. The school also operates a working farm and offers agricultural classes.

COVINGTON CATHOLIC HIGH SCHOOL

Day Boys Gr 9-12

Park Hills, KY 41011. 1600 Dixie Hwy.
Tel: 859-491-2247. Fax: 859-448-2242.
www.covcath.org
Michael Clines, Prin. BA, Northern Kentucky Univ, MEd, Univ of Cincinnati.

Col Prep. AP—Eng Span Calc Comp_Sci Physics Eur_Hist US_Hist. **Feat**—Ger Lat Stats Anat & Physiol Psych Sociol Film Studio_Art Music Accounting. **Supp**—Rev. **Adm:** 131/yr. Appl due: Rolling. Accepted: 100%. **Tests** HSPT. **Enr 470.** B 470. Sec 470. Wh 97%. Hisp 1%. Blk 1%. Asian 1%. Avg class size: 18. **Fac 33.** M 19/4. F 9/1. Wh 100%. Adv deg: 66%. **Grad '04**—113. Col—111. Avg SAT: 1149. Avg ACT: 22. Alum 6750. **Tui '04-'05:** Day $5240 (+$600). Aid: Merit 4 ($6000). Work prgm 20 ($80,000). **Summer:** Gr 9. Enrich. Tui Day $95. 2 wks. **Est 1925.** Nonprofit. Roman Catholic. Sem (Aug-May). The only boys' school in northern Kentucky, Covington Catholic offers a college preparatory curriculum that includes Advanced Placement courses in English, foreign language, math, science, history and computer science. Athletics and other extracurriculars round out the program.

NOTRE DAME ACADEMY

Day Girls Gr 9-12

Park Hills, KY 41011. 1699 Hilton Dr.
Tel: 859-261-4300. Fax: 859-292-7722.
www.nda-cvg.org E-mail: nda@nda-cvg.org
Sr. Elaine Marie Winter, SND, Prin. MEd.

Col Prep. AP—Eng Fr Lat Span Calc Bio Physics Eur_Hist US_Hist. **Feat**—British_Lit Ecol Marine_Biol/Sci Comp_Sci Psych Sociol World_Relig Studio_Art Visual_Arts Theater_Arts Music Accounting. **Supp**—Dev_Read LD Tut. **Adm:** 177/yr. Accepted: 100%. **Tests** Stanford. **Enr 596.** G 596. Sec 596. Wh 96%. Hisp

1%. Blk 1%. Am Ind 1%. Asian 1%. Avg class size: 25. Uniform. **Fac 48.** M 7. F 39/2. Wh 98%. Hisp 2%. Adv deg: 75%. **Grad '04—124.** Col—122. Avg ACT: 25. Alum 10,717. **Tui '04-'05:** Day $4850-6150. Aid: Merit 18 ($30,000). Need 62 ($60,000). Work prgm 45 ($129,000). **Est 1876.** Nonprofit. Roman Catholic. Sem (Aug-June). A strong religion program is integral to Notre Dame's Christian atmosphere. Modified scheduling allows for extended art and science labs and required, in addition to volunteer community service. The varied curriculum is enhanced by such extracurricular activities as chorus, art workshop, drama, athletics and language clubs. A learning differences program and student mentoring are also available.

VILLA MADONNA ACADEMY   **Day Coed Gr 1-12**
Villa Hills, KY 41017. 2500 Amsterdam Rd.
Tel: 859-331-6333. Fax: 859-331-8615.
www.villamadonna.net   E-mail: villamadonna@villamadonna.net
    Michael Whalen, Pres. BA, Thomas More College, MEd, Xavier Univ (OH). Pamela McQueen, Prin. BA, MA, Northern Kentucky Univ. Carole Lonneman, Upper Sch Adm; Donna Klus, Lower Sch Adm.
    Col Prep. AP—Fr Lat Span Calc Comp_Sci Bio Chem Physics Studio_Art. **Feat**—Programming. **Supp**—Rev Tut. **Adm:** 89/yr. Accepted: 90%. **Tests** HSPT. **Enr 400.** Elem 240. Sec 160. Avg class size: 20. Uniform. **Fac 40.** M 2. F 35/3. Wh 100%. Adv deg: 32%. **Grad '04—39.** Col—39. Avg SAT: 1220. Avg ACT: 23. Alum 2400. **Tui '04-'05:** Day $4910-5990 (+$600). **Est 1904.** Nonprofit. Roman Catholic. Sem (Aug-June). **Assoc** SACS. Overlooking the Ohio River, VMA offers Advanced Placement classes to qualified students. Music, art, speech, computer and foreign language courses are compulsory.

NORTH CAROLINA

BURLINGTON DAY SCHOOL   **Day Coed Gr PS-8**
Burlington, NC 27215. 1615 Greenwood Ter.
Tel: 336-228-0296. Fax: 336-226-6249.
www.burlingtondayschool.org   E-mail: admit@burlingtondayschool.org
    Alan Gibby, Head. MEd, Millersville Univ of Pennsylvania. Dex Davison, Adm.
    Pre-Prep. Feat—Fr Computers Drama Band. **Adm:** 31/yr. Appl due: Rolling. Accepted: 95%. **Tests** IQ Stanford. **Enr 225.** Elem 225. Wh 91%. Blk 4%. Asian 5%. Avg class size: 17. **Fac 20.** M 2/1. F 13/4. Wh 100%. Adv deg: 25%. **Grad '04—19.** Prep—11. Alum 1800. **Tui '02-'03:** Day $3896-6950 (+$300). Aid: Need 12 ($40,845). **Summer:** Acad Enrich Rec. Tui Day $100/wk. 2 wks. **Est 1954.** Nonprofit. Quar (Aug-May). **Assoc** SACS. The school offers an accelerated traditional curriculum supplemented by music, drama, technology, publications, athletics and various field trips.

CHARLOTTE CATHOLIC HIGH SCHOOL   Day Coed Gr 9-12
Charlotte, NC 28226. 7702 Pineville-Matthews Rd.
Tel: 704-543-1127. Fax: 704-543-1217.
www.gocougars.org   E-mail: bvacitelli@charlottecatholic.com

Gerald S. Healy, Prin. BA, Belmont Abbey College, MEd, Univ of North Carolina-Charlotte. Virginia Bond, Adm.

Col Prep. AP—Eng Fr Lat Span Calc Stats Bio Chem Physics US_Hist Econ US_Govt & Pol. **Feat**—Ger Relig Band Bus. **Supp**—Rev Tut. **Adm:** 350/yr. Appl due: Rolling. Accepted: 98%. **Tests** HSPT. **Enr 1140.** B 570. G 570. Sec 1140. Wh 90%. Hisp 2%. Blk 3%. Am Ind 1%. Asian 4%. Avg class size: 18. Uniform. **Fac 79.** M 27/3. F 43/6. Wh 92%. Hisp 3%. Blk 5%. Adv deg: 31%. **Grad '04—225.** Col—223. Avg SAT: 1260. Avg ACT: 23. Alum 5305. **Tui '04-'05:** Day $6137 (+$900). **Est 1887.** Nonprofit. Roman Catholic. (Aug-June). **Assoc** SACS. Daily religion classes are part of the school's curriculum. Extracurricular activities include honor societies in academic fields, service-oriented clubs, and interscholastic and intramural sports.

CHARLOTTE CHRISTIAN SCHOOL   Day Coed Gr PS-12
Charlotte, NC 28270. 7301 Sardis Rd.
Tel: 704-366-5657. Fax: 704-366-5678.
www.charlottechristian.com   E-mail: janet.aldridge@charchrist.com

Leo Orsino, Head. BS, New York Institute of Technology, MS, City Univ of New York, PhD, Ohio State Univ. Alicia Jesso, Adm.

Col Prep. AP—Eng Fr Lat Span Calc Stats Comp_Sci Bio Chem Physics Eur_Hist US_Hist US_Govt & Pol Art_Hist Studio_Art Music_Theory. **Feat**—British_Lit Ger Civil_War Bible Photog. **Supp**—Tut. **Adm:** 174/yr. Appl due: Rolling. Accepted: 50%. **Tests** CEEB IQ ISEE Stanford. **Enr 984.** B 525. G 459. Elem 648. Sec 336. Wh 93%. Blk 5%. Asian 1%. Other 1%. Avg class size: 20. **Fac 86.** M 24. F 58/4. Wh 97%. Hisp 2%. Blk 1%. Adv deg: 36%. **Grad '04—75.** Col—75. Avg SAT: 1111. Avg ACT: 23. **Tui '05-'06:** Day $9000-12,850 (+$500). Aid: Merit 31 ($89,500). Need 81 ($452,389). **Est 1950.** Nondenom Christian. Quar (Aug-June). This interdenominational school combines academics, service opportunities, athletics, the performing and fine arts, and computer technology. Foreign language study begins in junior kindergarten with Spanish and continues through the elementary grades; during the middle and upper school years, French, Latin and German are added. Boys and girls compete interscholastically at the varsity, junior varsity and middle school levels in various sports.

NORTHSIDE CHRISTIAN ACADEMY   Day Coed Gr PS-12
Charlotte, NC 28262. 333 Jeremiah Blvd.
Tel: 704-596-4074. Fax: 704-921-1384.
www.ncaknights.com   E-mail: nca@ncaknights.com

David Kilgore, Head. BA, Free Will Baptist Bible College, MEd, Trevecca Nazarene Univ. Pam Howell, Adm.

Col Prep. Gen Acad. AP—Eng Calc Bio US_Hist. **Feat**—Lat Span Anat & Physiol Computers Govt/Econ Bible Studio_Art Music Speech. **Supp**—Dev_Read Rem_Math Rem_Read Tut. **Adm:** 119/yr. Appl due: Rolling. Accepted: 96%. **Tests**

IQ Stanford. **Enr 873.** Wh 72%. Hisp 2%. Blk 19%. Asian 3%. Other 4%. Avg class size: 20. Uniform. **Fac 50.** M 13/1. F 34/2. Adv deg: 24%. **Grad '04—49.** Col—47. Avg SAT: 1034. Alum 890. **Tui '05-'06:** Day $2870-5760. Parishioners $2160-2870. Aid: Need 30 ($40,000). **Summer:** Rem. 6 wks. **Est 1961.** Nonprofit. Baptist. Sem (Aug-May). The academy's high school offers subject matter on three academic levels: advanced college preparatory, college preparatory and general studies. One unit of Bible is required each year of attendance, and students in grades 7-12 are involved in an annual community service project. NCA holds weekly chapel programs at which attendance is compulsory. Interscholastic sports and musical activities are also available.

CANNON SCHOOL Day Coed Gr PS-12
Concord, NC 28027. 5801 Poplar Tent Rd.
Tel: 704-786-8171. Fax: 704-788-7779.
www.cannonschool.org   E-mail: info@cannonschool.org
  Richard H. Snyder, Head. BA, MEd, Johns Hopkins Univ. Ann Blomquist, Adm.
  Col Prep. Gen Acad. AP—Eng Span Calc Stats Comp_Sci Bio Chem Physics US_Hist Psych US_Govt & Pol. **Feat**—Fr Studio_Art Drama Music Strings Dance. **Supp**—Tut. **Adm:** 153/yr. Appl due: Rolling. Accepted: 69%. Yield: 66%. **Tests** CTP_4 IQ MRT SSAT. **Enr 803.** B 390. G 413. Elem 590. Sec 213. Wh 87%. Hisp 1%. Blk 3%. Asian 2%. Other 7%. Avg class size: 16. **Fac 76.** M 19/1. F 54/2. Wh 90%. Hisp 2%. Blk 5%. Other 3%. Adv deg: 53%. **Grad '04—22.** Col—22. Avg SAT: 1239. Avg ACT: 25. Alum 250. **Tui '04-'05:** Day $6490-10,690 (+$1000). Aid: Merit 36 ($66,400). Need 71 ($433,995). **Est 1969.** Nonprofit. Quar (Aug-June). **Assoc** SACS. The school follows a traditional college preparatory curriculum. Instruction is offered in computers, foreign languages, lab science, physical education, art and music.

FAYETTEVILLE ACADEMY Day Coed Gr PS-12
Fayetteville, NC 28303. 3200 Cliffdale Rd.
Tel: 910-868-5131. Fax: 910-868-7351.
www.fayettevilleacademy.com   E-mail: email@fayettevilleacademy.com
  Virginia Satisky, Actg Head. Barbara E. Lambert, Adm.
  Col Prep. AP—Eng Span Calc Bio Eur_Hist US_Hist World_Hist Studio_Art. **Feat**—Fr Anat & Physiol Ecol Comp_Sci Psych Sociol Music. **Adm:** 74/yr. Appl due: Rolling. Accepted: 88%. Yield: 62%. **Tests** CTP_4 SSAT. **Enr 372.** B 201. G 171. Elem 238. Sec 134. Wh 77%. Hisp 1%. Blk 10%. Asian 10%. Other 2%. Avg class size: 15. **Fac 50.** M 5/7. F 31/7. Wh 94%. Blk 4%. Other 2%. Adv deg: 44%. **Grad '04—31.** Col—31. Avg SAT: 1205. Avg ACT: 26. Alum 1005. **Tui '04-'05:** Day $6364-9250 (+$350). Aid: Need 52 ($174,682). **Summer:** Enrich Rec. Tui Day $75/wk. 9 wks. **Est 1969.** Nonprofit. Sem (Aug-June). **Assoc** SACS. The academy's college preparatory curriculum includes Advanced Placement preparation in several subjects, as well as such enrichment courses as computer, art, band, chorus, communications and student newspaper. Among school activities are interscholastic sports, student government and interest clubs.

NC Concise School Listings 906

GASTON DAY SCHOOL   Day Coed Gr PS-12
Gastonia, NC 28056. 2001 Gaston Day School Rd.
Tel: 704-864-7744. Fax: 704-865-3813.
www.gastonday.org   E-mail: admissions@gastonday.org
    Richard Rankin, Head. BA, Univ of Virginia, PhD, Univ of North Carolina-Chapel Hill. Martha Jayne Ryhne, Adm.

    Col Prep. AP—Eng Calc Stats Bio Chem Physics US_Hist US_Govt & Pol Studio_Art. **Feat**—Fr Span Performing_Arts Visual_Arts Theater_Arts. **Supp**—LD Makeup Tut. **Adm:** 89/yr. Appl due: Rolling. Accepted: 80%. **Tests** CEEB. **Enr 400.** B 192. G 208. Elem 311. Sec 89. Wh 90%. Hisp 3%. Blk 5%. Asian 2%. Avg class size: 15. **Fac 42.** M 9. F 26/7. Wh 96%. Hisp 1%. Blk 2%. Other 1%. Adv deg: 47%. **Grad '04**—**28.** Col—28. Avg SAT: 1116. Alum 630. **Tui '04-'05:** Day $4545-10,630. Aid: Merit 44 ($140,562). Need 105 ($537,494). **Summer:** Rec. 1 wk. **Est 1967.** Nonprofit. Sem (Aug-June). **Assoc** SACS. Spanish, computer, art, music and physical education are offered from prekindergarten. A language acquisitions course is part of the grade 6 curriculum, while French and Spanish are the foreign language choices starting in grade 7. Academics also include honors and AP classes, as well as curriculum-based class trips. Volunteerism is integral to the program at all grade levels. Sports offered are volleyball, soccer, basketball, tennis, track and field, cross-country, baseball, softball, golf, wrestling and cheerleading.

WAYNE COUNTRY DAY SCHOOL   Day Coed Gr PS-12
Goldsboro, NC 27530. 480 Country Day Rd.
Tel: 919-736-1045. Fax: 919-583-9493.
www.waynecountryday.com   E-mail: wcds@waynecountryday.com
    Edward Radford, Head. Elidia Eason, Adm.

    Col Prep. Feat—Fr Lat Span Computers Studio_Art Drama Music. **Supp**—Dev_Read Tut. **Adm:** 71/yr. Accepted: 100%. **Tests** CTP_4 ISEE TOEFL. **Enr 242.** B 119. G 123. Elem 181. Sec 61. Wh 83%. Blk 8%. Asian 5%. Other 4%. Avg class size: 9. **Fac 41.** M 5. F 31/5. Wh 97%. Hisp 1%. Other 2%. Adv deg: 26%. **Grad '04**—**26.** Col—25. Avg SAT: 1067. Alum 600. **Tui '03-'04:** Day $4995-6224 (+$200). Aid: Need 14 ($36,117). **Summer:** Enrich Rec. Tui Day $120. 2 wks. **Est 1968.** Nonprofit. Sem (Aug-May). **Assoc** SACS. Wayne Country Day's primary purpose is to provide intensive college preparation. Excellent opportunities for involvement in the arts, athletics, clubs and student government are available, and all students perform community service.

CANTERBURY SCHOOL   Day Coed Gr K-8
Greensboro, NC 27455. 5400 Old Lake Jeanette Rd.
Tel: 336-288-2007. Fax: 336-288-1933.
www.canterburysch.org   E-mail: relost@canterburygso.org
    Rev. Lee H. Bristol III, Head. BA, Hamilton College, MDiv, Virginia Theological Seminary. Kathy Creekmuir, Adm.

    Pre-Prep. Gen Acad. Feat—Creative_Writing Lib_Skills Lat Span Computers Studio_Art Drama Music Health. **Supp**—Tut. **Adm (Gr K-7):** 56/yr. Appl due: Rolling. **Tests** CTP_4. **Enr 360.** B 166. G 194. Elem 360. Wh 89%. Hisp 1%. Blk 7%. Other 3%. Avg class size: 20. **Fac 50.** M 3/3. F 30/14. Wh 86%. Hisp 7%.

Blk 7%. Adv deg: 26%. **Grad '04**—37. Prep—16. Alum 180. **Tui '04-'05:** Day $9600. Aid: Need 65 ($391,436). **Summer:** Enrich Rec. Tui Day $105/wk. 3 wks. **Est 1992.** Nonprofit. Episcopal. Quar (Aug-June). During the lower school years (grades K-5), the school's broad-based approach to instruction emphasizes skill development in the fundamentals. In the middle school (grades 6-8), Latin and Spanish join the core curriculum and departmentalization begins. At all levels, Canterbury offers art, music, library, physical education and computer, and the extensive use of reference materials, audio-visual aids, computers, math manipulatives and current texts facilitates the learning process. Frequent chapel attendance is integral to school life.

GREENSBORO MONTESSORI SCHOOL   Day Coed Gr PS-8
Greensboro, NC 27410. 2856 Horse Pen Creek Rd.
Tel: 336-668-0119. Fax: 336-665-9531.
www.thegms.org   E-mail: gms@thegms.org

Frank W. Brainard, Head. BA, Central State Univ, MAT, Oklahoma City Univ, EdM, Harvard Univ. Andrea Bogan, Adm.

Pre-Prep. Feat—Span Computers Studio_Art Music. **Supp**—Dev_Read Rem_Math Rem_Read Tut. **Adm:** 90/yr. **Enr 365.** B 186. G 179. Elem 365. Wh 81%. Hisp 5%. Blk 5%. Asian 4%. Other 5%. Avg class size: 25. **Fac 41.** M 6/1. F 34. Wh 84%. Hisp 8%. Blk 5%. Asian 3%. Adv deg: 12%. **Grad '04**—11. Prep—3. **Tui '04-'05:** Day $8580-8880. Aid: Need 14 ($40,000). **Summer:** Acad Enrich Rev Rem Rec. Tui Day $80-175/wk. 4 wks. **Est 1974.** Nonprofit. Tri (Aug-June). **Assoc** SACS. In addition to the regular curriculum, students are offered Spanish, art, music, physical education and computer science. Team sports—provided for middle school students—are basketball, soccer and volleyball.

NEW GARDEN FRIENDS SCHOOL   Day Coed Gr PS-8
Greensboro, NC 27410. 1128 New Garden Rd.
Tel: 336-299-0964. Fax: 336-292-0347.
www.ngfs.org   E-mail: nfriendssc@aol.com

Martin Goldstein, Co-Head. BA, MEd, Univ of North Carolina-Greensboro. David R. Tomlin, Co-Head. BA, Guilford College.

Pre-Prep. Gen Acad. Feat—Span Computers Studio_Art Music. **Supp**—Dev_Read Rem_Math Rem_Read Tut. **Adm:** 25/yr. Appl due: Rolling. Accepted: 33%. **Enr 214.** B 106. G 108. Elem 214. Wh 83%. Hisp 4%. Blk 4%. Am Ind 2%. Asian 7%. Avg class size: 21. **Fac 24.** M 7. F 14/3. Wh 96%. Blk 4%. Adv deg: 45%. **Grad '04**—22. Prep—4. Alum 250. **Tui '04-'05:** Day $7800 (+$250-650). Aid: Need 51 ($164,500). **Summer:** Enrich Rec. Tui Day $160/wk. 8 wks. **Est 1971.** Nonprofit. Religious Society of Friends. Sem (Aug-June). NGFS maintains for a cooperative atmosphere and small classes with a strong sense of community. It is appropriate for students who wish to be actively involved in their own learning. Students work in multi-grade groups; interdisciplinary units, individualized and computer-aided instruction, field trips and community service are important segments of the curriculum.

HARRELLS CHRISTIAN ACADEMY
Day Coed Gr K-12

Harrells, NC 28444. 360 Tomahawk Hwy, PO Box 88.
Tel: 910-532-4575. Fax: 910-532-2958.
www.harrellschristianacademy.com   E-mail: hca2@intrstar.net
    Ronald L. Montgomery, Head. BS, EdD, Campbell Univ, MS, North Carolina Agricultural and Technical State Univ, EdS, Appalachian State Univ.
    Col Prep. AP—Eng Calc Chem Physics. **Feat**—Lat Span Comp_Sci Web_Design Bible Philos Relig Photog Studio_Art Drama Chorus Accounting Bus. **Adm:** 53/yr. Appl due: Rolling. Accepted: 99%. **Enr 445.** B 218. G 227. Elem 321. Sec 124. Wh 98%. Hisp 1%. Blk 1%. Avg class size: 20. **Fac 37.** M 5/1. F 29/2. Adv deg: 18%. **Grad '04—16.** Col—16. Avg SAT: 1010. Avg ACT: 18. **Tui '04-'05:** Day $4800-5280. Aid: Need 35 ($50,000). **Est 1969.** Nonprofit. Sem (Aug-June). **Assoc** SACS. Provisions for the total development of the student are made through a regular academic curriculum that is supplemented by religious studies, the fine arts, extracurricular activities and regular chapel services.

KERR-VANCE ACADEMY
Day Coed Gr PS-12

Henderson, NC 27537. 700 Vance Academy Rd.
Tel: 252-492-0018. Fax: 252-438-4652.
www.kerrvance.com   E-mail: kstewart@kerrvance.com
    Robert Byrd, Head. Kelly Stewart, Adm.
    Col Prep. AP—Eng Calc Bio US_Hist. **Feat**—Lat Span Comp_Sci Psych Studio_Art. **Supp**—Rev Tut. **Adm (Gr PS-11):** 54/yr. Appl due: Mar. **Tests** CEEB Stanford. **Enr 474.** B 245. G 229. Elem 353. Sec 121. Wh 96%. Blk 2%. Asian 1%. Other 1%. Avg class size: 15. **Fac 48.** M 8. F 40. Wh 100%. Adv deg: 27%. **Grad '04—38.** Col—38. Avg SAT: 1092. Alum 500. **Tui '04-'05:** Day $6080-6601. Aid: Need 18 ($63,950). **Summer:** Acad Enrich Rec. Tui Day $500. 4 wks. **Est 1968.** Nonprofit. Sem (Aug-May). **Assoc** SACS. This college preparatory school follows a liberal arts approach. Seniors work for one week in an area they are considering for a future career.

HICKORY DAY SCHOOL
Day Coed Gr K-8

Hickory, NC 28601. 2535 21st Ave NE.
Tel: 828-256-9492. Fax: 828-256-1475.
www.hickoryday.org   E-mail: hds@hickoryday.org
    William Valenta, Head. BA, MEd, State Univ of New York-New Paltz. Scott Owens, Adm.
    Pre-Prep. Feat—Lib_Skills Span Computers Studio_Art Music. **Supp**—Rem_Math Rem_Read Tut. **Adm:** 26/yr. Accepted: 70%. **Tests** CTP_4. **Enr 90.** Elem 90. Wh 90%. Hisp 2%. Asian 8%. Avg class size: 12. **Fac 19.** M 5. F 11/3. Wh 95%. Hisp 5%. Adv deg: 36%. **Grad '04—8.** Prep—3. Alum 36. **Tui '02-'03:** Day $7150 (+$300). Aid: Need 15 ($75,540). **Est 1993.** Nonprofit. Sem (Aug-May). HDS' developmentally appropriate lower school (grades pre-K-4) stresses basic skills development while gradually shifting the learning focus from the concrete to the abstract. During the middle school years (grades 5-8), children gain increasing levels of independence as they prepare for public and independent high schools.

Computers are present in all classrooms, in accordance with the school's emphasis on technology.

HOBGOOD ACADEMY
Day Coed Gr K-12

Hobgood, NC 27843. 201 Beech St.
Tel: 252-826-4116. Fax: 252-826-3400.
www.hobgoodacademy.com   E-mail: goraiders@coastalnet.com
 William H. Whitehurst, Head. BS, Atlantic Christian College.

Col Prep. Gen Acad. Feat—Span Environ_Sci Computers Psych Sociol Film Studio_Art Music Journ Woodworking Study_Skills. **Supp**—Rem_Math Rem_Read Tut. **Adm:** 30/yr. Appl due: Apr. Accepted: 98%. Yield: 100%. **Enr 278.** B 132. G 146. Elem 174. Sec 104. Wh 99%. Asian 1%. Avg class size: 21. **Fac 23.** M 6/1. F 15/1. Wh 100%. Adv deg: 8%. **Grad '04**—**25.** Col—24. Avg SAT: 1140. **Tui '04-'05:** Day $3335 (+$500). **Summer:** Enrich Rev Rem. 1-3 wks. **Est 1970.** Nonprofit. Sem (Aug-June). This traditional elementary and secondary school draws students from Edgecombe, Halifax, Martin, Nash and Pitt counties. In addition to classes in the core subjects, boys and girls may enroll in electives in such areas as horticulture, technology and the arts. An arrangement with Halifax Community College enables seniors to earn up to 12 hours of college credit through on-campus course work. Interscholastic athletic options are football, volleyball, basketball, golf, baseball, softball and soccer, while other extracurriculars include student government, quiz bowl, community service, drama and academic clubs.

See Also Page 1172

THE PATTERSON SCHOOL
Coed Gr 7-PG
Bdg & Day

Patterson, NC 28661. PO Box 500.
Tel: 828-758-2374. Fax: 828-758-9179.
www.pattersonschool.org   E-mail: info@pattersonschool.org
 John C. Cheska, Head. BA, Amherst College, MA, Univ of Massachusetts-Amherst.

Col Prep. AP—Eng Calc. **Feat**—British_Lit Creative_Writing Ger Span Ecol Comp_Sci Philos Relig Studio_Art Drama Music Journ. **Supp**—Dev_Read ESL LD Rem_Math Rem_Read Tut. **Adm:** Appl due: Rolling. **Tests** CEEB IQ Stanford TOEFL. **Enr 40.** B 12/7. G 19/2. Elem 4. Sec 32. PG 4. Wh 53%. Blk 25%. Asian 22%. Avg class size: 5. Uniform. **Fac 10.** M 5/1. F 2/2. Wh 80%. Asian 20%. Adv deg: 60%. In Dorms 4. **Grad '04**—**16.** Col—15. Avg SAT: 1100. Alum 2000. **Tui '04-'05:** Bdg $19,900. 5-Day Bdg $15,000. Day $8900. Aid: Need 12 ($130,000). Work prgm 6 ($67,000). **Summer:** Acad Enrich Rem. 6 wks. **Est 1909.** Nonprofit. Sem (Sept-May). On a 1400-acre campus, Patterson combines its college preparatory curriculum with work and service opportunities. Advanced Placement courses are part of the curriculum in the upper grades. The school's learning center serves pupils with dyslexia, ADD and ADHD; individualized educational plans are formulated for each participating student. Patterson's equestrian center serves both the student body and the community at large.

NORTH RALEIGH COUNTRY DAY SCHOOL Day Coed Gr PS-5
Raleigh, NC 27615. 10200 Strickland Rd.
Tel: 919-847-3120. Fax: 919-847-2120.
E-mail: robyn.cook@nlcinc.com
 Robyn Cook, Prin. Jennifer Coleman, Adm.

Gen Acad. Feat—Span Computers Studio_Art Music. **Supp**—Rev Tut. **Adm:** 60/yr. Appl due: Rolling. Accepted: 98%. Yield: 98%. **Enr 120.** B 60. G 60. Elem 120. Avg class size: 12. **Fac 20.** M /1. F 16/3. Wh 92%. Hisp 1%. Blk 7%. Adv deg: 10%. **Grad '04—4. Tui '04-'05:** Day $7100-7200 (+$300-1350). **Summer:** Enrich. Tui Day $700/4-wk ses. 9 wks. **Est 1985.** Inc. Spons: Nobel Learning Communities. Quar (Aug-May). Children in Country Day's kindergarten program gain an introduction to reading and language arts, in addition to basic mathematical and scientific concepts. First grade offers a chance for the student to acquire fundamental abilities through a skill-based curriculum. In grades 2-5, teachers emphasize problem solving and critical-thinking skills. The creative arts, foreign language, music, computer technology and physical education provide enrichment opportunities.

ST. DAVID'S SCHOOL Day Coed Gr K-12
Raleigh, NC 27609. 3400 White Oak Rd.
Tel: 919-782-3331. Fax: 919-571-3330.
www.sdsw.org E-mail: info@sdsw.org
 John A. Murray, Head. BA, Vanderbilt Univ, MALS, Dartmouth College. Paul Arceneaux, Adm.

Col Prep. AP—Eng Fr Lat Span Calc Stats Bio Chem Physics Eur_Hist US_Hist US_Govt & Pol Art_Hist Studio_Art. **Feat**—British_Lit Anat Geol Web_Design Philos Performing_Arts Chorus. **Supp**—Makeup Tut. **Adm:** 102/yr. Appl due: Feb. Accepted: 92%. Yield: 75%. **Tests** ISEE. **Enr 479.** B 248. G 231. Elem 282. Sec 197. Wh 94%. Blk 2%. Asian 2%. Other 2%. Avg class size: 13. **Fac 55.** M 20. F 34/1. Adv deg: 34%. **Grad '04—30.** Col—30. Avg SAT: 1214. Alum 700. **Tui '04-'05:** Day $9000-12,250 (+$250). Aid: Need 87 ($358,300). **Summer:** Acad Enrich Rec. Tui Day $100-200/wk. 10 wks. **Est 1972.** Nonprofit. Episcopal. Sem (Aug-May). **Assoc** SACS. A broad, accelerated curriculum is provided at this Christian school. Designed for the college-bound student of average to above-average ability, the upper school program features Advanced Placement courses in the major disciplines. Extracurricular activities such as art, music, drama, computer and competitive athletics supplement academics.

ROCKY MOUNT ACADEMY Day Coed Gr PS-12
Rocky Mount, NC 27803. 1313 Avondale Ave.
Tel: 252-443-4126. Fax: 252-937-7922.
www.rmacademy.com E-mail: headmaster@rmacademy.com
 Thomas R. Stevens, Head. BA, Yale Univ, MA, Columbia Univ. Millie H. Walker, Adm.

Col Prep. AP—Eng Calc Bio Chem Eur_Hist US_Hist Psych Studio_Art. **Feat**—Fr Lat Span Comp_Sci Music Public_Speak. **Supp**—Tut. **Adm:** 84/yr. Accepted: 94%. Yield: 99%. **Tests** IQ. **Enr 435.** B 227. G 208. Elem 285. Sec 150.

Wh 94%. Blk 2%. Asian 2%. Other 2%. Avg class size: 14. **Fac 47.** M 10/1. F 35/1. Wh 98%. Asian 2%. Adv deg: 34%. **Grad '04—13.** Col—13. Avg SAT: 1134. Alum 572. **Tui '04-'05:** Day $3065-8310 (+$200-400). Aid: Merit 25 ($80,448). Need 83 ($333,601). **Summer:** Acad Enrich Rev Rec. SAT Prep. Adventure. 1-10 wks. **Est 1968.** Nonprofit. Tri (Aug-June). **Assoc** SACS. RMA's college preparatory curriculum includes honors and Advanced Placement courses during the high school years, in addition to a well-established technology program. Community service is required in grades 10-12.

THE O'NEAL SCHOOL **Day Coed Gr PS-12**
Southern Pines, NC 28388. 3300 Airport Rd, PO Box 290.
Tel: 910-692-6920. Fax: 910-692-6930.
www.onealschool.org   E-mail: adroppers@onealschool.org
  John Neiswender, Head. BS, Furman Univ, MAT, Univ of South Carolina. Missy Quis, Adm.
  Col Prep. AP—Eng Calc Stats Bio Chem Physics Eur_Hist US_Hist. **Feat—**Creative_Writing Fr Lat Span Ceramics Film Photog Studio_Art Music. **Supp—**LD Rev Tut. **Adm:** 84/yr. Appl due: Rolling. Accepted: 90%. **Tests** IQ. **Enr 436.** B 216. G 220. Elem 279. Sec 157. Wh 92%. Hisp 1%. Blk 3%. Am Ind 1%. Asian 1%. Other 2%. Avg class size: 15. **Fac 47.** M 15/1. F 30/1. Wh 96%. Hisp 2%. Blk 2%. Adv deg: 36%. **Grad '04—31.** Col—31. Avg SAT: 1201. Alum 125. **Tui '04-'05:** Day $6890-10,980 (+$150). Aid: Merit 10 ($53,430). Need 94 ($514,532). **Summer:** Gr K-6. Acad Enrich Rec. Tui Day $150-375. 1-2 wks. **Est 1971.** Nonprofit. Sem (Aug-May). Serving students of average and above-average ability, O'Neal draws boys and girls from 20 towns within and outside of Moore County. The traditional, structured curriculum enables pupils to accelerate in grade 8 by enrolling in algebra and Latin classes, then to take Advanced Placement courses in the upper school. A special program serves students with learning differences such as dyslexia.

FRIENDS SCHOOL OF WILMINGTON **Day Coed Gr PS-8**
Wilmington, NC 28409. 350 Peiffer Ave.
Tel: 910-792-1811. Fax: 910-792-9274.
www.fsow.org   E-mail: fsw@isaac.net
  Ethan D. Williamson, Head. BS, Guilford College. Ann Souder & Amy Williamson, Adms.
  Gen Acad. Feat—Fr Span Computers Web_Design Quakerism Studio_Art Drama Music Study_Skills. **Supp—**Dev_Read. **Adm:** 36/yr. Appl due: Rolling. Accepted: 80%. **Enr 172.** B 89. G 83. Elem 172. Wh 92%. Blk 6%. Asian 2%. Avg class size: 18. **Fac 23.** M 4/3. F 9/7. Wh 100%. Adv deg: 21%. **Grad '04—24.** Alum 40. **Tui '05-'06:** Day $6800 (+$1000). Aid: Need 25 ($83,000). **Summer:** Rec. Tui Day $160-300/wk. 6 wks. **Est 1994.** Nonprofit. Religious Society of Friends. Quar (Aug-May). FSOW places significant emphasis on Quaker values and traditions, with students attending Meeting for Worship daily and engaging in an extended class period devoted to on- or off-campus community service projects each week; the curriculum also includes a Quakerism class. Whenever possible, instructors make connections across the academic disciplines in the basic subjects of language

SOUTH CAROLINA

MEAD HALL EPISCOPAL DAY SCHOOL Day Coed Gr PS-8
Aiken, SC 29801. 129 Pendleton St SW.
Tel: 803-644-1122. Fax: 803-644-1122.
www.meadhallschool.org   E-mail: meadhall@meadhallschool.org
Katherine B. Gordon, Head.

Gen Acad. Feat—Fr. **Supp**—Tut. **Adm:** 40/yr. Accepted: 90%. **Enr 149.** B 80. G 69. Elem 149. Wh 91%. Blk 8%. Asian 1%. Avg class size: 12. Uniform. **Fac 21.** F 11/10. Wh 100%. Adv deg: 19%.**Tui '04-'05:** Day $2000-5700 (+$150-180). **Est 1955.** Episcopal. Quar (Aug-May). Serving as the parish day school for St. Thaddeus Episcopal Church, Mead Hall offers French in grades K-8. Extracurricular options include dance, cross-country and soccer teams, robotics, violin and yearbook, and boys and girls engage in various service activities.

MASON PREPARATORY SCHOOL Day Coed Gr 1-8
Charleston, SC 29401. 56 Halsey Blvd.
Tel: 843-723-0664. Fax: 843-723-1104.
www.masonprep.org   E-mail: magliolaa@masonprep.org
James E. Mobley, Head. MEd, The Citadel. Anita Magliola, Adm.

Pre-Prep. Feat—Fr Lat Span Computers Ethics Studio_Art Drama Music Public_Speak. **Adm:** 66/yr. Appl due: Feb. **Enr 350.** Elem 350. Avg class size: 21. **Fac 43.** M 1. F 37/5. Adv deg: 23%. **Grad '04**—43. Prep—43. **Tui '04-'05:** Day $7045-7330 (+$650). **Est 1964.** Nonprofit. Quar (Aug-May). In grades 1-6, Mason Prep's curriculum emphasizes the core subjects of language arts, math, the natural sciences and social studies. Frequent field trips and guest speakers enrich the program during these years. Preparation for secondary school is of primary importance in grades 7 and 8, and advanced students may earn high school credit in algebra, French and Spanish.

BEN LIPPEN SCHOOL Bdg Coed Gr 6-12
Columbia, SC 29203. 7401 Monticello Rd. Day Coed PS-12
Tel: 803-786-7200. Fax: 803-744-1387.
www.benlippen.com   E-mail: blsadmissions@benlippen.com
Donald P. Kauffman, Head. BA, Eastern Nazarene College, MDiv, Nazarene Theological Seminary, MEd, Columbia International Univ. Bobby Young, Adm.

Col Prep. AP—Eng Calc Bio Chem Physics US_Hist Studio_Art. **Feat**—Humanities Lat Anat & Physiol Amer_Stud Sociol Bible Philos Music Accounting Driver_Ed. **Supp**—ESL LD Rem_Math Rem_Read. **Adm:** 141/yr. Appl due: Rolling. Accepted: 98%. **Tests** Stanford TOEFL. **Enr 873.** B 25/427. G 15/406. Elem 529. Sec 344. Avg class size: 20. **Fac 43.** Adv deg: 76%. In Dorms 2. **Grad**

'04—80. Col—78. Avg SAT: 1060. **Tui '05-'06:** Bdg $23,999 (+$1000). Day $5136-8748 (+$400-600). **Summer:** ESL. Tui Bdg $3200. 8 wks. **Est 1940.** Nonprofit. Nondenom Christian. Spons: Columbia International University. Sem (Aug-May). Ben Lippen's structured program combines academic and Bible curricula. Elementary students (grades PS-5) receive computer tutoring and attend art and music classes weekly. Middle and upper school pupils (grades 6-12) may enroll in honors and Advanced Placement courses. An ESL program serves international students, and an educational therapy program accommodates boys and girls with mild to moderate learning disabilities.

HAMMOND SCHOOL   Day Coed Gr PS-12
Columbia, SC 29209. 854 Galway Ln.
Tel: 803-776-0295. Fax: 803-776-0122.
www.hammondschool.org   E-mail: mail@hammondschool.org

Herbert B. Barks, Head. BA, Univ of Chattanooga, MDiv, Columbia Theological Seminary, DLitt, King's College. Julia S. Moore, Adm.

Col Prep. AP—Eng Fr Span Calc Stats Bio Chem Physics Eur_Hist US_Hist Studio_Art. **Feat**—British_Lit Creative_Writing Lat Arabic World_War_II Econ Govt Relig Theol Film Pottery Drama Chorus Journ Public_Speak. **Adm:** 146/yr. Appl due: Rolling. Accepted: 50%. Yield: 96%. **Tests** CEEB IQ SSAT. **Enr 936.** B 477. G 459. Wh 89%. Hisp 1%. Blk 9%. Asian 1%. Avg class size: 15. **Fac 110.** Wh 93%. Hisp 3%. Blk 3%. Asian 1%. **Grad '04—49.** Col—49. Avg SAT: 1230. **Tui '04-'05:** Day $8500-9905 (+$350-650). Aid: Need 78 ($369,198). **Est 1966.** Nonprofit. Sem (Aug-May). **Assoc** CLS SACS. With an educational approach that focuses on academic skills, Hammond places particular emphasis on reading and written expression, while also providing students with a grounding in math and science. In each division, the school's program allows pupils who have mastered the core curriculum to undertake accelerated or advanced work in every discipline, and college preparation and admission become primary objectives during the upper school years. Visits from speakers, writers, painters and poets from around the world enrich the fine arts program.

THE BYRNES SCHOOLS   Day Coed Gr PS-12
Florence, SC 29506. 1201 E Ashby Rd.
Tel: 843-662-0131. Fax: 843-669-2466.
www.byrnesschools.org   E-mail: info@byrnesschools.org

Jimmy H. Newsom, Head. BS, Appalachian State Univ, MA, EdS, East Tennessee State Univ.

Col Prep. AP—Eng Calc Bio Chem Physics Eur_Hist US_Hist. **Feat**—Span Environ_Sci Computers Econ Govt Psych Studio_Art Drama. **Adm:** 51/yr. Appl due: Rolling. **Tests** CEEB IQ Stanford. **Enr 284.** Elem 197. Sec 87. Wh 95%. Blk 3%. Asian 2%. Avg class size: 13. **Fac 30.** M 3. F 26/1. Wh 91%. Hisp 3%. Blk 6%. Adv deg: 46%. **Grad '04—25.** Col—25. Avg SAT: 1060. Alum 813. **Tui '04-'05:** Day $5295. **Summer:** Acad Enrich Rev Rem. 4 wks. **Est 1966.** Nonprofit. Sem (Aug-May). In addition to the standard course work, supplemental programs are available in computers, art and foreign languages beginning at the elementary level. Juniors and seniors may take honors courses in advanced subjects. Students are encouraged to participate in a variety of extracurricular activities, among them clubs, student government, publications and sports.

BOB JONES ACADEMY   **Coed Gr 9-12**
Greenville, SC 29614. 1700 Wade Hampton Blvd.   **Bdg & Day**
Tel: 864-242-5100. Fax: 864-271-7278.
www.bju.edu/bja   E-mail: admissions@bju.edu
   David A. Fisher, Prin. BS, MS, PhD, Bob Jones Univ. David Christ, Adm.

   Col Prep. Feat—Fr Ger Span Programming Econ Govt Bible Studio_Art Band Chorus Orchestra Bus Journ Public_Speak Speech Indus_Arts Driver_Ed. **Supp**—Rem_Math Tut. **Adm:** 186/yr. Bdg 10. Day 176. Appl due: Rolling. **Tests** Stanford TOEFL. **Enr 554.** B 24/240. G 29/261. Sec 554. Wh 88%. Hisp 2%. Asian 10%. **Fac 47.** M 14/8. F 13/12. Wh 100%. Adv deg: 55%. **Grad '04—138.** Col—133. Avg ACT: 23. Alum 6297. **Tui '04-'05:** Bdg $8340 (+$345). Day $3780 (+$345). **Summer:** Acad. Tui Bdg $1352. Tui Day $454. 6 wks. **Est 1927.** Inc. Nondenom Christian. Sem (Aug-May). Students at this Christian school are given frequent opportunities to perform community service. Debate and athletics are among the school's extracurricular options.

ST. JOSEPH'S CATHOLIC SCHOOL   **Day Coed Gr 6-12**
Greenville, SC 29607. 100 St Joseph's Dr.
Tel: 864-234-9009. Fax: 864-234-5516.
www.sjcatholicschool.org   E-mail: info@sjcatholicschool.org
   Keith F. Kiser, Head. BA, Grove City College, MEd, Duquesne Univ. Barbara McGrath, Adm.

   Col Prep. AP—Eng Lat Span Calc Stats Comp_Sci Bio Chem Physics Eur_Hist US_Hist Econ US_Govt & Pol. **Feat**—Fr Anat & Physiol Genetics Theol Fine_Arts Studio_Art Drama Dance Journ Speech. **Supp**—LD Tut. **Adm:** 133/yr. Appl due: Feb. Accepted: 95%. Yield: 80%. **Enr 370.** B 165. G 205. Elem 121. Sec 249. Wh 94%. Hisp 3%. Blk 3%. Avg class size: 17. Uniform. **Fac 33.** M 10/1. F 16/6. Adv deg: 45%. **Grad '04—40.** Col—49. Avg SAT: 1218. Avg ACT: 25. Alum 176. **Tui '04-'05:** Day $4625-6450 (+$1400-1700). Aid: Merit ($25,000). Need ($120,000). **Est 1992.** Nonprofit. Roman Catholic. Sem (Aug-May). St. Joseph's traditional liberal arts curriculum comprises the arts and sciences, the humanities and a complete Catholic theology program. In addition to an array of college preparatory, honors and Advanced Placement courses, high schoolers have access to a comprehensive college guidance program. The school conducts a program for college-bound boys and girls with mild language or learning disabilities. Academic clubs, enrichment activities, leadership and service organizations, performing arts opportunities and athletics balance academics.

SHANNON FOREST CHRISTIAN SCHOOL   **Day Coed Gr PS-12**
Greenville, SC 29615. 829 Garlington Rd.
Tel: 864-678-5107. Fax: 864-281-9372.
www.shannonforest.com   E-mail: esipe@shannonforest.com
   Brenda K. Millman, Head. BA, Taylor Univ, MA, Georgia Southern Univ.

Col Prep. AP—Eng Calc Comp_Sci Bio Eur_Hist US_Hist. **Feat**—Fr Span Econ Govt Law Psych Sociol E_Asian_Stud Bible Drama Journ SAT_Prep. **Supp**—LD Tut. **Adm:** 104/yr. Appl due: Rolling. Accepted: 95%. **Tests** CEEB. **Enr 500.** B 220. G 280. Elem 398. Sec 102. Wh 99%. Blk 1%. Avg class size: 17. **Fac 42.** M 9. F 32/1. Wh 100%. Adv deg: 47%. **Grad '04—9.** Col—9. Avg SAT: 1102. Alum 617. **Tui '05-'06:** Day $5032-7226 (+$175-375). Aid: Need 84 ($100,000). **Summer:** Gr 9-12. Enrich Rem Rec. Tui Day $25/hr. Gr PS-6. Rec. Tui Day $80/wk. 8 wks. **Est 1968.** Nonprofit. Nondenom Christian. Sem (Aug-May). **Assoc** SACS. Providing a Christian college preparatory education, Shannon Forest offers chapel services and Bible study. Honors and Advanced Placement courses are available, as is a program for students in grades 1-12 with learning differences.

HILTON HEAD PREPARATORY SCHOOL   Day Coed Gr 1-12
Hilton Head Island, SC 29928. 8 Fox Grape Rd.
Tel: 843-671-2286. Fax: 843-671-7624.
www.hhprep.org   E-mail: prepinfo@hhprep.org

Susan R. Groesbeck, Head. BA, Skidmore College, MA, EdD, Univ of Rochester. Lauren R. Marlis, Adm.

Col Prep. AP—Eng Fr Span Calc Stats Bio Chem Physics US_Hist. **Feat**—Lat Anat Ecol Marine_Biol/Sci Chorus Orchestra Journ. **Supp**—Dev_Read LD Tut. **Adm:** 70/yr. Appl due: Rolling. Accepted: 75%. Yield: 90%. **Tests** SSAT Stanford. **Enr 400.** Elem 255. Sec 145. Wh 88%. Hisp 4%. Blk 7%. Other 1%. Avg class size: 15. **Fac 49.** M 15. F 33/1. Wh 98%. Hisp 2%. Adv deg: 69%. **Grad '04—32.** Col—32. Avg SAT: 1093. Avg ACT: 22. Alum 1005. **Tui '04-'05:** Day $10,260-11,970 (+$500). Aid: Need 95. **Est 1965.** Nonprofit. Tri (Aug-May). **Assoc** SACS. Hilton Head Prep conducts an honors program in grades 6-12, as well as Advanced Placement courses in the upper school. Graduation requirements include community service, computer literacy and the delivery of a senior speech. A travel program and career internships are available. The school's learning center offers student and professional tutoring.

TRIDENT ACADEMY   Day Coed Gr K-PG
Mt Pleasant, SC 29464. 1455 Wakendaw Rd.
Tel: 843-884-3494. Fax: 843-884-1483.
www.tridentacademy.com   E-mail: admissions@tridentacademy.com

Myron C. Harrington, Jr., Head. BA, The Citadel, MPA, Shippensburg State College. Betsy A. Fanning, Adm.

Col Prep. Gen Acad. LD. Feat—Span. **Supp**—Dev_Read Rem_Math Rem_Read Rev Tut. **Adm:** 36/yr. Accepted: 99%. **Tests** IQ. **Enr 147.** B 4/106. G 1/36. Elem 95. Sec 52. Wh 99%. Blk 1%. Avg class size: 10. **Fac 39.** M 4/1. F 26/8. Adv deg: 53%. **Grad '04—6.** Col—5. Alum 236. **Tui '05-'06:** Day $13,840-18,840 (+$740-1030). Aid: Merit 2 ($2000). Need 20 ($66,250). **Summer:** Enrich Rem. Tui Day $800. 6 wks. **Est 1972.** Nonprofit. Sem (Aug-May). **Assoc** SACS. This college preparatory school serves children with learning disabilities who possess average to above-average intelligence. Diagnosis of a learning disability is required for admission. The academy utilizes a multisensory teaching approach within a structured, individualized environment. A limited number of students reside with local families.

SC *Concise School Listings* *916*

LOWCOUNTRY DAY SCHOOL Day Coed Gr PS-12
Pawleys Island, SC 29585. 300 Blue Stem Dr.
Tel: 843-237-4147. Fax: 843-237-4543.
www.ldspi.org E-mail: ldspi@sc.rr.com
  Martha Gates Lord, Head. BA, Johns Hopkins Univ, MS, Fairfield Univ. Emily K. Framptom, Adm.

  Col Prep. AP—Eng Calc Bio US_Govt & Pol. **Feat**—Fr Lat Span Computers Relig Studio_Art Drama Music. **Supp**—ESL. **Adm:** 33/yr. Appl due: Mar. Accepted: 80%. Yield: 95%. **Tests** IQ Stanford. **Enr 185.** Elem 166. Sec 19. Wh 89%. Blk 5%. Asian 1%. Other 5%. Avg class size: 12. **Fac 24.** M 5. F 19. Wh 99%. Asian 1%. Adv deg: 45%. **Grad '04**—10. Col—10. **Tui '04-'05:** Day $6400-7100. Aid: Need 29 ($125,000). **Summer:** Acad Enrich Rec. 1-6 wks. **Est 1995.** Nonprofit. Sem (Aug-May). In addition to core academics classes, students at LDS are encouraged to pursue course work in the arts. The lower school (grades PS-4) provides a solid foundation in the standard subjects. During the middle and upper school years (grades 5-12), pupils have enrichment options in the fields of music, drama, chorus, dance and computers. All middle and upper schoolers fulfill a community service requirement.

PINEWOOD PREPARATORY SCHOOL Day Coed Gr PS-12
Summerville, SC 29483. 1114 Orangeburg Rd.
Tel: 843-873-1643. Fax: 843-821-4257.
www.pinewoodprep.com E-mail: gcowlishaw@pinewoodprep.com
  Glyn Cowlishaw, Head. BEd, Univ of Reading (England), MEd, Univ of Leeds (England), EdD, South Carolina State Univ. Carolyn Baechtle, Adm.

  Col Prep. AP—Eng Fr Lat Calc Bio Chem Human_Geog Studio_Art. **Feat**—Ger. **Adm:** 111/yr. Appl due: Feb. Accepted: 50%. **Tests** IQ Stanford. **Enr 650.** Wh 97%. Hisp 1%. Blk 1%. Asian 1%. Avg class size: 15. **Fac 54.** M 13/2. F 36/3. Wh 98%. Hisp 2%. Adv deg: 37%. **Grad '04**—37. Col—37. Avg SAT: 1173. Alum 600. **Tui '05-'06:** Day $6000-7300 (+$350-500). Aid: Need 26 ($40,450). **Est 1952.** Nonprofit. Quar (Aug-June). **Assoc** SACS. Pinewood's college preparatory program features advanced-level instruction in math, English, science, history and foreign language. Art, music, study skills and physical education complement the core curriculum. Extracurricular activities include athletics, student government, publications, and service and academic organizations.

WILSON HALL Day Coed Gr PS-12
Sumter, SC 29150. 2801 S Wise Dr.
Tel: 803-469-3475. Fax: 803-469-3477.
www.wilsonhall.org E-mail: sean_hoskins@hotmail.com
  Frederick B. Moulton, Head. BS, MEd, Univ of South Carolina. Sean P. Hoskins, Adm.

  Col Prep. AP—Eng Calc Stats Comp_Sci Bio Chem Physics Eur_Hist US_Hist US_Govt & Pol Studio_Art. **Feat**—Fr Lat Span Philos Theol World_Relig Ceramics Photog Journ. **Supp**—Tut. **Adm:** 86/yr. Appl due: June. Accepted: 56%. Yield: 40%. **Tests** CEEB IQ Stanford. **Enr 766.** B 386. G 380. Elem 579. Sec 187. Wh 96%. Blk 2%. Other 2%. Avg class size: 13. **Fac 68.** M 13/2. F 43/10. Wh 98%.

Hisp 2%. Adv deg: 38%. **Grad '04—43.** Col—43. Avg SAT: 1193. Alum 1400. **Tui '04-'05:** Day $4200 (+$400). Aid: Need 12 ($7500). **Est 1966.** Nonprofit. Quar (Aug-June). **Assoc** SACS. Instruction at Wilson Hall is in small classes to provide each student with individual attention. The school offers all courses at the college preparatory level or higher. Community service is required each year.

TENNESSEE

BRENTWOOD ACADEMY   Day Coed Gr 6-12
Brentwood, TN 37027. 219 Granny White Pike.
Tel: 615-373-0611. Fax: 615-377-3709.
www.brentwoodacademy.com   E-mail: office@brentwoodacademy.com
    Curtis G. Masters, Head. BA, Wheaton College (IL), MS, Univ of Puget Sound, PhD, Univ of Miami. Susan Gering, Adm.

    Col Prep. AP—Eng Fr Lat Span Calc Chem Physics Eur_Hist US_Hist. **Feat—**Humanities Greek Anat & Physiol Marine_Biol/Sci Comp_Sci African-Amer_Hist Econ Relig Studio_Art Visual_Arts Music Journ Speech. **Supp—**Rev. **Adm:** 144/yr. Appl due: Rolling. Accepted: 79%. **Tests** Stanford. **Enr 735.** B 362. G 373. Elem 281. Sec 454. Wh 92%. Hisp 1%. Blk 6%. Other 1%. Avg class size: 18. **Fac 70.** M 24/7. F 36/3. Wh 95%. Blk 5%. Adv deg: 57%. **Grad '04—99.** Col—99. Avg SAT: 1120. Avg ACT: 25. Alum 1954. **Tui '04-'05:** Day $11,450 (+$500-1000). Aid: Need 95 ($653,600). **Summer:** Acad Enrich Rem. 1-3 wks. **Est 1969.** Nonprofit. Sem (Aug-May). **Assoc** SACS. This nondenominational school emphasizes traditional Christian values and ethics. Weekly Bible study and weekend retreats are popular features, although participation in religious activities is voluntary. The curriculum provides students with a solid background in traditional subjects and is supplemented by various sports and extracurriculars.

CURREY INGRAM ACADEMY   Day Coed Gr K-12
Brentwood, TN 37207. 6544 Murray Ln.
Tel: 615-507-3242. Fax: 615-507-3170.
www.curreyingram.org   E-mail: kathy.boles@curreyingram.org
    Kathleen G. Rayburn, Head. BS, Saint Mary-of-the-Woods College, MA, Butler Univ. Kathleen H. Boles, Adm.

    Col Prep. Gen Acad. LD. Feat—Span Govt Ethics Studio_Art Theater_Arts Music. **Supp—**Dev_Read Rem_Math Rem_Read Tut. **Adm (Gr K-11):** 42/yr. Appl due: Rolling. Accepted: 70%. Yield: 80%. **Tests** IQ. **Enr 260.** B 184. G 76. Elem 213. Sec 47. Wh 92%. Blk 5%. Asian 1%. Other 1%. Avg class size: 6. Uniform. **Fac 86.** M 21/2. F 53/10. Wh 98%. Hisp 2%. Adv deg: 58%.**Tui '04-'05:** Day $19,580-22,915. Aid: Need 53 ($518,039). **Summer:** Acad Enrich Rem Rec. Computer. Sports. Tui Day $1050/2-wk ses. 6 wks. **Est 1968.** Nonprofit. Quar (Aug-May). Currey Ingram provides an individualized elementary and secondary program for students of average to above-average intelligence who have learning differences. The school's college preparatory program assists pupils in developing effective learning strategies. In a setting that encourages active participation in the learning process, course work balances the acquisition of knowledge and skills with the meeting of individual and group needs.

BOYD-BUCHANAN SCHOOL
Day Coed Gr PS-12

Chattanooga, TN 37411. 4626 Bonnieway Dr.
Tel: 423-622-6177. Fax: 423-698-5844.
www.bbschool.org   E-mail: cwhite@bbschool.org

Robert Akins, Pres. BA, Harding Univ, MEd, Memphis State Univ. Charlotte White, Adm.

Col Prep. AP—Eng Fr Calc Chem US_Hist. **Feat**—Span Stats Comp_Sci Web_Design Econ Govt Psych Sociol Bible Drama Music_Theory Journ Speech. **Supp**—Rem_Math Rem_Read Tut. **Adm (Gr PS-11):** 150/yr. Appl due: Rolling. Accepted: 50%. Yield: 90%. **Enr 999.** B 534. G 465. Elem 647. Sec 352. Wh 95%. Blk 4%. Asian 1%. Avg class size: 15. Uniform. **Fac 66.** M 16. F 50. Wh 95%. Blk 5%. Adv deg: 22%. **Grad '04—65.** Col—65. Alum 1300. **Tui '04-'05:** Day $4643-6302 (+$200). Aid: Need 60 ($86,610). Work prgm 2 ($3000). **Est 1952.** Nonprofit. Nondenom Christian. Sem (Aug-May). **Assoc** SACS. In addition to core courses, Boyd-Buchanan offers exploratory classes in sign language, journalism, drama and other areas of interest. Music, art and drama are integral parts of the school's curriculum, and all students attend daily Bible classes. Extracurricular activities in band, chorus, drama, athletics, forensics and service clubs are available.

CHATTANOOGA CHRISTIAN SCHOOL
Day Coed Gr K-12

Chattanooga, TN 37409. 3354 Charger Dr.
Tel: 423-265-6411. Fax: 423-756-4044.
www.ccsk12.com   E-mail: holwerda@ccsk12.com

Donald J. Holwerda, Pres. BA, Calvin College, MSE, Drake Univ. Kathy Simmons, Adm.

Col Prep. AP—Eng Stats Bio Eur_Hist US_Hist Studio_Art. **Feat**—Fr Ger Lat Span Bible Music Jazz_Band Ballroom_Dancing Debate Indus_Arts. **Supp**—Tut. **Adm:** 156/yr. Appl due: Apr. Accepted: 60%. Yield: 90%. **Enr 1068.** B 533. G 535. Elem 665. Sec 403. Wh 84%. Hisp 2%. Blk 10%. Asian 4%. Avg class size: 18. **Fac 92.** M 32/3. F 54/3. Wh 94%. Hisp 2%. Blk 4%. Adv deg: 56%. **Grad '04—86.** Col—86. Avg SAT: 1150. Avg ACT: 25. Alum 1354. **Tui '04-'05:** Day $4525-6736 (+$180). Aid: Need 98 ($350,000). **Summer:** Acad Rem Rec. 6-12 wks. **Est 1970.** Nonprofit. Nondenom Christian. Sem (Aug-May). **Assoc** SACS. Serving children from Christian families, CCS teaches its educational program from a Biblical perspective. The high school provides strong fine arts, athletics and extracurricular activities, as well as an optional industrial arts program. The middle school offers its own program, sports teams, clubs, social events, classes and support, and regular and honors sections are available in several departments. Community service is a graduation requirement.

NOTRE DAME HIGH SCHOOL
Day Coed Gr 9-12
Chattanooga, TN 37404. 2701 Vermont Ave.
Tel: 423-624-4618. Fax: 423-624-4621.
www.myndhs.com E-mail: kfreno@myndhs.com
   Perry L. Storey, Prin. BS, MEd, Univ of Tennessee-Chattanooga. Sarah Provonsha, Adm.
   Col Prep. Gen Acad. AP—Eng Bio Chem Physics Eur_Hist US_Hist Studio_Art. **Feat**—Anat & Physiol Computers Govt Psych Sociol Relig Theater Music. **Supp**—Dev_Read LD Makeup Tut. **Adm:** 165/yr. **Enr 565.** B 280. G 285. Sec 565. Wh 86%. Hisp 2%. Blk 10%. Asian 2%. Avg class size: 18. Uniform. **Fac 52.** M 24. F 28. Wh 88%. Hisp 4%. Blk 8%. Adv deg: 59%. **Grad '04—139.** Col—139. Avg SAT: 1080. Avg ACT: 21. Alum 5000. **Tui '04-'05:** Day $9585. Catholic $7060. **Summer:** Acad Enrich Rev Rec. Fr. Computers. 8 wks. **Est 1876.** Nonprofit. Roman Catholic. Sem (Aug-May). **Assoc** SACS. Located on a 20-acre campus in the city's Glenwood section, the school provides a structured college preparatory program that features honors and Advanced Placement course work. In addition, dual-enrollment classes are offered in several disciplines in conjunction with Chattanooga State Technical Community College. As roughly ten percent of enrolled pupils have been diagnosed with a learning disability, Notre Dame conducts an individualized LD program. Approximately one-third of the students are non-Catholics.

COLUMBIA ACADEMY
Day Coed Gr PS-12
Columbia, TN 38401. 1101 W 7th St.
Tel: 931-388-5363. Fax: 931-380-8506.
www.columbia-academy.net E-mail: btwhite@colacademy.com
   Bill Thrasher, Pres. BA, MA, MSE, EdD. Benja White, Adm.
   Col Prep. Feat—Span Anat Environ_Sci Computers Econ Govt Bible Fine_Arts Band Chorus Music Journ Speech. **Supp**—Dev_Read Rem_Read. **Tests** IQ. **Enr 788.** Wh 98%. Blk 1%. Other 1%. Avg class size: 18. **Fac 50.** M 13. F 37. Wh 100%. Adv deg: 48%. **Grad '04—57.** Col—56. Avg ACT: 21. Alum 500. **Tui '05-'06:** Day $4650-4850. Aid: Need 15 ($25,000). Work prgm 15 ($15,000). **Summer:** Enrich. Tui Day $75/crse. 12 wks. **Est 1905.** Nonprofit. Sem (Aug-May). **Assoc** SACS. Formerly a military academy, this school emphasizes basic academics and Bible study. CA also conducts particularly strong fine arts and athletics programs.

EVANGELICAL CHRISTIAN SCHOOL
Day Coed Gr K-12
Cordova, TN 38088. 7600 Macon Rd, PO Box 1030.
Tel: 901-754-7217. Fax: 901-754-8123.
www.ecseagles.net E-mail: edickson@ecseagles.com
   J. Bryan Miller, Pres. BS, Millsaps College. Steve Collums, Head. Erin Dickson, Adm.
   Col Prep. AP—Eng Fr Lat Span Calc Bio Eur_Hist US_Hist US_Govt & Pol. **Feat**—Anat & Physiol Comp_Sci Bible Studio_Art Drama Finance Speech. **Supp**—Dev_Read Rem_Math Rem_Read Rev Tut. **Adm (Gr K-11):** 211/yr. Appl due: Rolling. Accepted: 78%. Yield: 96%. **Tests** IQ ISEE Stanford. **Enr 1382.** B 721. G 661. Elem 906. Sec 476. Wh 98%. Blk 2%. Avg class size: 14. **Fac 124.** M 26/2. F 66/30. Wh 99%. Asian 1%. Adv deg: 31%. **Grad '04—112.** Col—112. Avg

SAT: 1140. Avg ACT: 26. Alum 2884. **Tui '04-'05:** Day $3795-8500. Aid: Need 210 ($680,683). **Est 1964.** Nonprofit. Evangelical. Sem (Aug-May). **Assoc** SACS. During the lower school years (grades K-5) at this Bible-based school, children develop a foundation for future learning as they gain an introduction to Spanish and receive basic instruction in music and art. ECS' middle school program (grades 6-8) features an expanded curriculum and discussion-based classes. Upper schoolers choose from Advanced Placement and enrichment courses, in addition to standard offerings. The middle and upper schools operate on Macon Road, while ECS maintains lower school campuses at 735 Ridge Lake Blvd., Memphis 38120 and 1920 Forest Hill, Germantown 38139.

BATTLE GROUND ACADEMY   **Day Coed Gr K-12**
Franklin, TN 37065. PO Box 1889.
Tel: 615-794-3501. Fax: 615-595-7374.
www.battlegroundacademy.org
   Steven R. Lape, Adm.

Col Prep. AP—Eng Lat Calc Chem Eur_Hist US_Hist. **Feat**—Computers Econ Govt Fine_Arts. **Supp**—Makeup Tut. **Adm:** 157/yr. Appl due: Rolling. Accepted: 67%. **Tests** IQ ISEE Stanford. **Enr 925.** B 535. G 390. Wh 96%. Hisp 1%. Blk 1%. Asian 1%. Other 1%. Avg class size: 17. Uniform. **Fac 82.** M 31/2. F 44/5. Wh 96%. Hisp 1%. Blk 3%. Adv deg: 42%. **Grad '04—83.** Col—81. Avg SAT: 1210. Avg ACT: 26. Alum 2500. **Tui '02-'03:** Day $9485 (+$300). Aid: Need 68 ($375,554). Work prgm 16 ($14,973). **Summer:** Enrich Rev Rec. Tui Day $80-135/wk. 6 wks. **Est 1889.** Nonprofit. Sem (Aug-May). **Assoc** SACS. BGA's college preparatory program includes both honors and Advanced Placement courses. A comprehensive fine arts program and competitive athletics are also available. The academy operates on two campuses in proximity to one another: The lower school (grades K-4) occupies quarters at 150 Franklin Rd., 37064, while both the middle school (grades 5-8) and the upper school (grades 9-12) are located at 336 Ernest Rice Ln., 37069.

SUMNER ACADEMY   **Day Coed Gr PS-8**
Gallatin, TN 37066. 464 Nichols Ln.
Tel: 615-452-1914. Fax: 615-452-1923.
www.sumneracademy.org   E-mail: information@sumneracademy.org
   William E. Hovenden, Head. BA, Cornell College, MS, Indiana Univ, PhD, Florida State Univ. Becky E. Roy, Adm.

Pre-Prep. Gen Acad. Feat—Span Computers Studio_Art Music. **Supp**—Tut. **Adm:** 55/yr. Appl due: Rolling. Accepted: 90%. **Tests** IQ. **Enr 232.** B 123. G 109. Elem 232. Wh 95%. Blk 1%. Asian 4%. **Fac 28.** F 26/2. Wh 95%. Blk 1%. Asian 4%. Adv deg: 50%. **Grad '04—25.** Prep—24. Alum 50. **Tui '04-'05:** Day $7000. Aid: Need 44 ($125,000). **Summer:** Rec. Tui Day $450. 7 wks. **Est 1973.** Nonprofit. (Aug-May). **Assoc** SACS. In addition to a curriculum that offers advanced standing at every grade level, the academy provides special learning activities in music, art, computer, physical education and Spanish. Students are ability grouped for reading and math. The school schedule alternates nine weeks of classes with two weeks of vacation. Sumner schedules frequent guest lectures, concerts, films and field trips.

EPISCOPAL SCHOOL OF KNOXVILLE Day Coed Gr K-8
Knoxville, TN 37932. 950 Episcopal School Way.
Tel: 865-777-9032. Fax: 865-777-9034.
www.esknoxville.org E-mail: info@esknoxville.org
James J. Secor III, Head. BA, Virginia Wesleyan College, MEd, James Madison Univ.

Pre-Prep. Feat—Lib_Skills Fr Relig Studio_Art Music. **Supp**—Dev_Read. **Adm:** 44/yr. Appl due: Rolling. **Enr 213.** B 111. G 102. Elem 213. Wh 94%. Hisp 1%. Blk 2%. Asian 3%. Avg class size: 15. **Fac 34.** M 3. F 27/4. Wh 100%. Adv deg: 58%. **Grad '04**—22. Prep—10. **Tui '04-'05:** Day $8800-9400. Aid: Need 17 ($63,800). **Est 1998.** Nonprofit. Episcopal. Tri (Aug-May). Foreign language, art, music and religion classes are core components of each student's education. At the lower school level (grades K-5), programming focuses on the fundamentals of literature, math, science and social studies, while the middle school curriculum (grades 6-8) promotes critical thinking and study skills. Extracurricular activities include band and chorus, journalism and computer clubs, and interscholastic sports. Boys and girls attend daily chapel services and take part in community service projects.

FRIENDSHIP CHRISTIAN SCHOOL Day Coed Gr PS-12
Lebanon, TN 37087. 5400 Coles Ferry Pike.
Tel: 615-449-1573. Fax: 615-449-2769.
www.friendshipchristian.org E-mail: twilliams@friendshipchristian.org
Jon Shoulders, Pres. BBA, Freed-Hardeman Univ. Terresia Williams, Adm.

Col Prep. Feat—Fr Span Computers Bible. **Supp**—Tut. **Adm:** 86/yr. Appl due: Aug. Accepted: 98%. **Tests** IQ. **Enr 513.** Wh 95%. Blk 2%. Asian 3%. Avg class size: 15. **Fac 37.** Wh 99%. Blk 1%. Adv deg: 43%. **Grad '04**—50. Col—45. Avg ACT: 23. Alum 850. **Tui '03-'04:** Day $3600-5375 (+$250). Aid: Need 46. **Est 1973.** Nonprofit. Nondenom Christian. Sem (Aug-May). **Assoc** SACS. FCS' curriculum features extensive Bible instruction. Qualified students in the upper grades may take dual-enrollment courses through Cumberland University. A variety of interest clubs, publications and athletics complements the curriculum. Activities include the student council, the National Honor Society, interest clubs and band.

HARDING ACADEMY Day Coed Gr PS-12
Memphis, TN 38117. 1100 Cherry Rd.
Tel: 901-767-4494. Fax: 901-763-4949.
www.hardinglions.org E-mail: admissions@hardinglions.org
Tom Dickson, Head. BS, Univ of Oklahoma, MLA, Texas Christian Univ, MA, Naval War College. Betty Copeland, Adm.

Col Prep. AP—Eng Calc Bio US_Hist Studio_Art. **Feat**—Humanities Fr Span Comp_Sci Bible. **Supp**—Tut. **Adm:** 275/yr. Appl due: Rolling. Accepted: 79%. Yield: 71%. **Tests** IQ MAT Stanford. **Enr 1735.** B 843. G 892. Elem 1298. Sec 437. Wh 78%. Blk 17%. Asian 4%. Other 1%. Avg class size: 17. **Fac 116.** M 22/2. F 89/3. Wh 97%. Hisp 2%. Blk 1%. Adv deg: 37%. **Grad '04**—68. Col—68. Avg SAT: 1080. Avg ACT: 23. Alum 4681. **Tui '04-'05:** Day $5595-7795 (+$150). Aid: Merit 127 ($235,076). **Summer:** Acad Enrich Rev Rec. 10 wks. **Est 1952.** Nonprofit. Nondenom Christian. Quar (Aug-May). The school's five elementary campuses are located throughout Memphis. The junior/senior school shares its campus with Harding Graduate School of Religion. The college prep curriculum is augmented by extensive fine arts electives. Interscholastic sports are available in approximately a dozen areas. Daily Bible study is required.

WOODLAND PRESBYTERIAN SCHOOL Day Coed Gr PS-8
Memphis, TN 38119. 5217 Park Ave.
Tel: 901-685-0976. Fax: 901-761-2406.
www.woodlandschool.org   E-mail: info@woodlandschool.org
Donald P. Frazier, Pres. BA, St Andrew's Presbyterian College, MEd, Univ of Delaware, JD, Mercer Univ. Tim Tatum, Adm.

Pre-Prep. Gen Acad. Feat—Creative_Writing Fr Ger Lat Span Ecol. **Supp**—LD. **Adm:** 96/yr. Appl due: Rolling. Accepted: 70%. Yield: 91%. **Tests** IQ MRT Stanford. **Enr 400.** B 220. G 180. Elem 400. Wh 98%. Blk 1%. Asian 1%. Avg class size: 20. **Fac 39.** M 6. F 28/5. Wh 100%. Adv deg: 53%. **Grad '04**—35. Prep—32. Alum 1503. **Tui '04-'05:** Day $4250-7550 (+$200). Aid: Need 14 ($38,000). **Summer:** Rec. Tui Day $200/wk. 10 wks. **Est 1957.** Nonprofit. Presbyterian. Sem (Aug-May). **Assoc** SACS.   At all age levels, Woodland provides students with specialized instruction in both foreign languages and laboratory sciences. The school also features a gifted program designed around critical thinking. Remediation based upon contemporary research assists pupils of average or above-average ability who have mild learning difficulties.

DAVID LIPSCOMB CAMPUS SCHOOL Day Coed Gr PS-12
Nashville, TN 37204. 3901 Granny White Pike.
Tel: 615-269-1828. Fax: 615-386-7633.
www.dlcs.lipscomb.edu
Keith A. Nikolaus, Dir. BA, David Lipscomb College, MEd, EdD, Tennessee State Univ. Michael L. Roller, HS & Middle Sch Adm; Lisa Stinson, Elem Sch Adm.

Col Prep. AP—Span Calc Bio Chem. **Feat**—Fr Lat Econ Bible Accounting. **Supp**—Rev Tut. **Adm:** 200/yr. Appl due: Rolling. Accepted: 65%. **Tests** Stanford. **Enr 1457.** B 785. G 672. Elem 928. Sec 529. Wh 80%. Hisp 1%. Blk 1%. Other 18%. Avg class size: 22. **Fac 120.** M 27. F 73/20. Wh 99%. Blk 1%. Adv deg: 46%. **Grad '04**—123. Col—123. Avg SAT: 1040. Avg ACT: 25. Alum 500. **Tui '04-'05:** Day $6095-6495 (+$600). Aid: Need 42 ($70,000). **Est 1891.** Nonprofit. Nondenom Christian. Sem (Aug-May). **Assoc** SACS.   Operated by David Lipscomb University, the school bases its program on the principles of obedience to parents, government and God. Activities include forensics, band, athletics, chorus, drama and publications.

FRANKLIN ROAD ACADEMY Day Coed Gr PS-12
Nashville, TN 37220. 4700 Franklin Rd.
Tel: 615-832-8845. Fax: 615-834-4137.
www.frapanthers.com   E-mail: akinb@frapanthers.com

Margaret W. Wade, Head. BA, EdD, Vanderbilt Univ, MEd, Middle Tennessee State Univ. William B. Akin, Adm.

Col Prep. Feat—Computers Econ Bible Art_Hist Visual_Arts Drama Band Music_Hist. **Supp**—Rev Tut. **Adm:** 197/yr. Appl due: Nov. Accepted: 64%. **Tests** ISEE. **Enr 905.** Elem 604. Sec 301. Wh 97%. Blk 1%. Asian 2%. **Fac 85.** Wh 100%. Adv deg: 42%. **Grad '04**—64. Col—64. Avg SAT: 1150. Avg ACT: 25. Alum 1498. **Tui '02-'03:** Day $6945-9330 (+$400). Aid: Merit 6 ($6050). Need 13 ($50,100). **Summer:** Enrich Rec. 9 wks. **Est 1971.** Nonprofit. Sem (Aug-May). **Assoc** SACS. Following a Christian worldview, FRA offers honors and Advanced Placement courses in many traditional subjects as part of its college preparatory program. Considerable emphasis is placed on the fine and performing arts. Athletic teams are fielded in football, volleyball, basketball, soccer, track, wrestling, cross-country, tennis, golf, baseball, softball, bowling and swimming.

HARDING ACADEMY
Day Coed Gr K-8

Nashville, TN 37205. 170 Windsor Dr.
Tel: 615-356-5510. Fax: 615-356-0441.
www.hardingacademy.org   E-mail: admissions@hardingacademy.org

Donald S. Schwartz, Head. BS, Texas Christian Univ, MS, Tulane Univ. Becca Arnold, Adm.

Pre-Prep. Feat—Fr Lat Computers Studio_Art Drama Music. **Supp**—Tut. **Adm:** 76/yr. Appl due: Dec. **Tests** ISEE. **Enr 462.** B 218. G 244. Elem 462. Wh 99%. Blk 1%. Avg class size: 18. **Fac 54.** M 10. F 43/1. Wh 96%. Hisp 2%. Asian 2%. Adv deg: 59%. **Grad '04**—36. Prep—32. Alum 1736. **Tui '04-'05:** Day $10,450 (+$800 -1650). Aid: Need 13 ($85,605). **Summer:** Enrich Rec. 2-8 wks. **Est 1971.** Nonprofit. Sem (Aug-May). **Assoc** SACS. A traditional academic curriculum includes French in grades 5-8, computer studies from kindergarten, arts and physical education throughout, and athletics in the middle school.

OAK HILL SCHOOL
Day Coed Gr PS-6

Nashville, TN 37220. 4815 Franklin Rd.
Tel: 615-297-6544. Fax: 615-298-9555.
www.oakhillschool.org

Claire C. Wilkins, Head. BA, Baylor Univ, MEd, Houston Baptist Univ. Brenda Boon, Adm.

Pre-Prep. Feat—Lib_Skills Lat Span Computers Bible Studio_Art Drama Music. **Supp**—Dev_Read LD Rem_Math Rem_Read Tut. **Adm:** 68/yr. Appl due: Dec. Accepted: 35%. **Tests** ISEE. **Enr 446.** B 237. G 209. Elem 446. Wh 99%. Blk 1%. Avg class size: 16. **Fac 49.** M 2. F 47. Adv deg: 63%. **Grad '04**—62. Prep—62. Alum 1150. **Tui '04-'05:** Day $9025 (+$300). Aid: Need 8 ($22,309). **Summer:** Acad Enrich Rev Rem. 2 wks. **Est 1961.** Nonprofit. Presbyterian. Quar (Aug-May). The comprehensive course of studies at this Christian elementary school emphasizes the development of critical-thinking skills. Foreign language, drama, art, music/band and computer enrich the core curriculum. Oak Hill faculty take a hands-on, developmentally suitable approach at all grade levels, and children gradually gain more independence in learning. Sixth graders embark on a study trip to Williamsburg, VA, and Washington, DC, each year.

ST. CECILIA ACADEMY
Day Girls Gr 9-12
Nashville, TN 37205. 4210 Harding Rd.
Tel: 615-298-4525. Fax: 615-783-0561.
www.stcecilia.edu   E-mail: sheridanc@stcecilia.edu
Sr. Mary Sarah Galbraith, OP, Prin. Chad Sheridan, Adm.

Col Prep. AP—Eng Fr Ger Span Calc Bio Chem Eur_Hist US_Hist US_Govt & Pol Studio_Art. **Feat**—Humanities Lat Stats Ecol Comp_Sci Econ Relig Visual_Arts Drama Music Dance Journ. **Supp**—Tut. **Adm:** 65/yr. Appl due: Jan. **Tests** ISEE. **Enr 263.** G 263. Sec 263. Wh 93%. Hisp 1%. Blk 6%. Avg class size: 15. Uniform. **Fac 29.** M 3. F 23/3. Adv deg: 68%. **Grad '04—67.** Col—67. Avg SAT: 1102. Avg ACT: 23. Alum 1943. **Tui '04-'05:** Day $10,950 (+$680). Aid: Need 58 ($138,150). **Summer:** Enrich. Tui Day $100. 1 wk. **Est 1860.** Nonprofit. Roman Catholic. Quar (Aug-May). **Assoc** SACS. Established and operated by the Dominican Sisters, this college preparatory school offers Advanced Placement and honors courses, as well as a comprehensive arts program that offers both participatory and competitive opportunities in the visual arts, dance, drama, forensics and music. A one-week spring interim program provides such travel opportunities as Broadway theater and art tours, marine biology courses in Florida, wilderness studies in Utah and Arizona, and tours of Europe. St. Cecilia is affiliated with Overbrook School, an elementary school for boys and girls in grades PS-8.

PLEASANT VIEW CHRISTIAN SCHOOL
Day Coed Gr PS-12
Pleasant View, TN 37146. 160 Hicks Edgen Rd.
Tel: 615-746-8555. Fax: 615-746-2646.
www.pvchristian.org
Ken Riggs, Admin. BA, Free Will Baptist Bible College, MS, Old Dominion Univ, MEd, Middle Tennessee State Univ, PhD, Vanderbilt Univ.

Col Prep. Gen Acad. Feat—Fr Computers Bible Performing_Arts Music. **Supp**—Tut. **Tests** Stanford. **Enr 351.** Elem 271. Sec 80. Avg class size: 25. Uniform. **Fac 27.** M 4/3. F 18/2. Adv deg: 7%. **Grad '04—14.** Col—12. Alum 179. **Tui '04-'05:** Day $3200 (+$310). **Est 1978.** Nonprofit. Baptist. Sem (Aug-May). Reading instruction begins in kindergarten, and basic fundamentals are emphasized in the elementary school. A wide variety of music, sports and social activities supplements the academic curriculum during the high school years.

THE KING'S ACADEMY
Bdg Coed Gr 6-12
Day Coed K-12
Seymour, TN 37865. 202 Smothers Rd.
Tel: 865-573-8321. Fax: 865-573-8323.
www.thekingsacademy.net   E-mail: jmink@thekingsacademy.net
Walter Grubb, Pres. BA, California Baptist College, MS, California State Univ. Janice S. Mink, Adm.

Col Prep. AP—Eng Bio. **Feat**—Creative_Writing Lat Span Anat & Physiol Ecol Comp_Sci Econ Govt Psych Sociol Bible Studio_Art Chorus Music Bus Journ Health Outdoor_Ed. **Supp**—ESL Tut. **Adm (Bdg Gr 6-10):** 81/yr. Bdg 19. Day 62. Appl due: Rolling. Accepted: 95%. Yield: 95%. **Tests** IQ. **Enr 365.** B 30/159. G 18/158. Elem 237. Sec 128. Wh 82%. Blk 2%. Asian 13%. Other 3%. Avg class size: 20. Uniform. **Fac 33.** M 9/2. F 20/2. Wh 99%. Asian 1%. Adv deg: 42%. In Dorms

1. **Grad '04—17.** Col—15. Avg SAT: 1200. Avg ACT: 23. Alum 2968. **Tui '04-'05:** Bdg $13,919-14,729 (+$1200). 5-Day Bdg $10,445-11,255 (+$1200). Day $3880-5190 (+$100). Aid: Need 36 ($73,804). Work prgm 6 ($7000). **Summer:** Acad ESL. Tui Bdg $2600. Tui Day $1600. 5 wks. **Est 1880.** Nonprofit. Southern Baptist. Sem (Aug-May). **Assoc** SACS. Emphasizing a Christian education, the school is located 12 miles south of Knoxville. Athletics include football, basketball, baseball, softball, volleyball, golf, soccer, tennis, bowling, wrestling and cross-country.

VIRGINIA

ALEXANDRIA COUNTRY DAY SCHOOL — Day Coed Gr K-8
Alexandria, VA 22301. 2400 Russell Rd.
Tel: 703-548-4804. Fax: 703-549-9022.
www.acdsnet.org   E-mail: admissions@acdsnet.org
Alexander Harvey IV, Head. BS, Vanderbilt Univ, MEd, Loyola College. Julia M. Love, Adm.

Pre-Prep. Feat—Lib_Skills Span Computers Studio_Art Drama Music Outdoor_Ed. **Adm:** 45/yr. Appl due: Jan. Accepted: 56%. Yield: 50%. **Tests** IQ ISEE. **Enr 237.** B 111. G 126. Elem 237. Wh 86%. Hisp 4%. Blk 4%. Asian 3%. Other 3%. Avg class size: 13. Uniform. **Fac 37.** M 10/1. F 21/5. Wh 94%. Hisp 3%. Blk 3%. Adv deg: 45%. **Grad '04—28.** Prep—16. Alum 251. **Tui '04-'05:** Day $14,200-15,600. Aid: Need 28 ($197,926). **Summer:** Rec. Tui Day $200-400/wk. 7 wks. **Est 1983.** Nonprofit. Tri (Sept-June). Focusing on basic skills development, the primary division (grades K-2) offers specialist-taught enrichment classes in art, music, library, computer, Spanish and physical education. Enrichment courses continue in the elementary division (grades 3-5), when children may first participate in after-school activities. Computer use is integral to the interdisciplinary middle school (grades 6-8). Intensive computer, art and music classes enable middle schoolers to complete major projects in these areas. Community service begins in the primary division, and all students take part in an experiential outdoor learning program.

BISHOP IRETON HIGH SCHOOL — Day Coed Gr 9-12
Alexandria, VA 22314. 201 Cambridge Rd.
Tel: 703-751-7606. Fax: 703-212-8173.
www.bishopireton.org   E-mail: admissions@bishopireton.org
Rev. Matthew Hillyard, OSFS, Prin. BA, DeSales Univ, MDiv, Catholic Univ of America. Peter J. Hamer, Adm.

Col Prep. AP—Stats Human_Geog. **Feat**—Creative_Writing Shakespeare Fr Ger Lat Span Comp_Sci Govt Relig Film Studio_Art Music Public_Speak. **Supp**—Tut. **Adm:** 241/yr. Appl due: Jan. Accepted: 78%. Yield: 71%. **Tests** HSPT. **Enr 818.** B 372. G 446. Sec 818. Wh 79%. Hisp 6%. Blk 4%. Asian 11%. Avg class size: 24. Uniform. **Fac 61.** M 26/4. F 28/3. Adv deg: 72%. **Grad '04—193.** Col—191. Avg SAT: 1192. Alum 4000. **Tui '04-'05:** Day $8200-12,550 (+$850). Aid: Need 70 ($230,000). **Est 1964.** Nonprofit. Roman Catholic. Quar (Aug-June). **Assoc** SACS. Operated by the Oblates of St. Francis de Sales, Bishop Ireton offers honors, Advanced Placement and college prep courses. A symphonic wind ensemble, an academic enrichment program and a full sports program complement the curriculum. Juniors fulfill a community service requirement.

BROWNE ACADEMY Day Coed Gr PS-8
Alexandria, VA 22310. 5917 Telegraph Rd.
Tel: 703-960-3000. Fax: 703-960-7325.
www.browneacademyonline.org E-mail: kharris@browneacademy.org
 Mort Dukehart, Head. BA, Lafayette College, MAT, Univ of Georgia. Kerri Harris, Adm.

Pre-Prep. Feat—Fr Span Computers Studio_Art Music. **Supp**—Tut. **Adm:** 56/yr. Appl due: Feb. **Tests** IQ. **Enr 293.** B 149. G 144. Elem 293. Wh 64%. Hisp 4%. Blk 16%. Asian 4%. Other 12%. Avg class size: 15. **Fac 40.** M 8. F 32. Adv deg: 37%. **Grad '04—22. Tui '02-'03:** Day $6118-14,715 (+$900-1200). Aid: Need 43 ($250,000). **Summer:** Acad Enrich Rev Rem Rec. 8 wks. **Est 1941.** Nonprofit. Quar (Sept-June). At the academy, major subjects are introduced in preschool and are developed through grade 8. The school's individualized, interdisciplinary curriculum helps students develop their problem solving and critical-thinking skills. French begins in preschool, while Spanish commences in grade 3.

OAKWOOD SCHOOL Day Coed Gr 1-8
Annandale, VA 22003. 7210 Braddock Rd.
Tel: 703-941-5788. Fax: 703-941-4186.
www.oakwoodschool.com E-mail: mjedlicka@oakwoodschool.com
 Robert C. McIntyre, Head. BA, MA, Wheaton College (IL). Muriel A. Jedlicka, Adm.

LD. Feat—Computers Studio_Art. **Supp**—Dev_Read Rem_Math Rem_Read. **Adm:** 34/yr. Appl due: Rolling. **Tests** IQ. **Enr 112.** B 86. G 26. Elem 112. Wh 97%. Blk 2%. Other 1%. Avg class size: 10. **Fac 32.** M 5. F 27. Adv deg: 75%. **Grad '04—16. Tui '04-'05:** Day $22,700 (+$150-300). Aid: Need 6 ($40,000). **Est 1971.** Nonprofit. Sem (Sept-June). Serving pupils with mild to moderate learning differences, Oakwood conducts a program that includes adaptive physical education, individualized education planning, speech/language and occupational therapies, and psycho-educational evaluations.

POWHATAN SCHOOL Day Coed Gr K-8
Boyce, VA 22620. 49 Powhatan Ln.
Tel: 540-837-1009. Fax: 540-837-2558.
www.powhatan.pvt.k12.va.us E-mail: info@powhatan.pvt.k12.va.us
 John G. Lathrop, Head. BA, Univ of Pennsylvania, MEd, Harvard Univ. Clare M. Hamman, Adm.

Pre-Prep. Gen Acad. Feat—Writing Fr Span Computers Studio_Art Drama Music. **Supp**—Dev_Read Rem_Read Tut. **Adm:** 43/yr. Appl due: Rolling. Accepted: 70%. **Tests** CTP_4. **Enr 243.** B 121. G 122. Elem 243. Wh 92%. Hisp 1%. Blk 2%. Asian 3%. Other 2%. Avg class size: 15. **Fac 39.** M 9/1. F 23/6. Wh 95%. Blk 5%. Adv deg: 33%. **Grad '04—29.** Prep—9. Alum 685. **Tui '03-'04:** Day

$10,550-11,650 (+$450-550). Aid: Need 19 ($100,500). **Summer:** Enrich Rec. Tui Day $250-300. 1-2 wks. **Est 1948.** Nonprofit. Tri (Aug-June). Powhatan's elementary and middle school program—which serves pupils from Frederick, Clarke and Warren counties, as well as Winchester, Martinsburg and Charles Town—places particular emphasis on the development of sound study habits and oral and written communicational skills. Children study Spanish in grades K-4, French in grade 5, and either Spanish or French in grades 6-8. Extracurricular offerings include athletics, art, music, drama and computer.

LINTON HALL SCHOOL Day Coed Gr PS-8
Bristow, VA 20136. 9535 Linton Hall Rd.
Tel: 703-368-3157. Fax: 703-368-3036.
www.lintonhall.edu E-mail: lintonhall@aol.com
  Robert F. Manning, Prin.

  Gen Acad. Feat—Span Computers Relig Studio_Art Music Outdoor_Ed. **Supp**—Tut. **Adm:** 34/yr. **Enr 214.** B 103. G 111. Elem 214. Wh 89%. Hisp 4%. Blk 2%. Asian 4%. Other 1%. Avg class size: 22. Uniform. **Fac 21.** M 1/3. F 11/6. Adv deg: 38%. **Grad '04—16. Tui '04-'05:** Day $6840 (+$150). Aid: Need 10 ($27,000). **Est 1922.** Nonprofit. Roman Catholic. Quar (Aug-June). Linton Hall provides an independent Catholic program on a rural, 120-acre site located 35 miles southwest of Washington, DC. The school offers small classes, opportunities for advanced study and an accelerated reading program. The curriculum includes science, history, religion, computer science and language arts, and music, art, outdoor education and Spanish are also offered. Social activities, clubs and interscholastic athletics are among the extracurricular choices. An extended-day option is available.

THE COVENANT SCHOOL Day Coed Gr PS-12
Charlottesville, VA 22902. 175 Hickory St.
Tel: 434-220-7329. Fax: 434-220-7320.
www.covenantschool.org E-mail: dharris@covenantschool.org
  Ronald P. Sykes, Head. BA, MA, MEd, Univ of Memphis, EdD, Univ of Virginia. Donna B. Harris, Adm.

  Col Prep. AP—Eng Fr Lat Span Calc Bio Chem Eur_Hist US_Hist US_Govt & Pol Studio_Art. **Feat**—Bible Drama Journ Study_Skills. **Supp**—Rem_Read. **Adm:** 135/yr. Appl due: Rolling. Accepted: 95%. **Tests** SSAT. **Enr 635.** B 334. G 301. Elem 365. Sec 270. Wh 89%. Blk 3%. Asian 6%. Other 2%. Avg class size: 15. **Fac 62.** M 20. F 38/4. Wh 98%. Blk 2%. Adv deg: 45%. **Grad '04—67.** Col—63. Avg SAT: 1210. Alum 250. **Tui '04-'05:** Day $10,570 (+$500). Aid: Need 120 ($485,625). **Est 1985.** Nonprofit. Nondenom Christian. (Aug-May). Covenant's lower school (pre-K-6)—which occupies separate quarters at 1000 Birdwood Rd., 22903—offers course work in foreign language, language arts, math, science, the fine arts, history, Bible and physical education. An enrichment program assists children in grades K-4, while a resource teacher aids students in grades 1-6 who have reading or spelling difficulties. Honors and Advanced Placement courses are features of the upper school program.

TANDEM FRIENDS SCHOOL
Day Coed Gr 5-12

Charlottesville, VA 22902. 279 Tandem Ln.
Tel: 434-296-1303. Fax: 434-296-1886.
www.tandemfs.org   E-mail: jmcculloch@tandemfs.org
   Paul Perkinson, Head. BA, Earlham College, MA, Univ of Pennsylvania. Nica Waters, Adm.

   Col Prep. AP—Fr Span Calc Stats Bio Chem US_Hist. **Feat**—Lat Bioethics Govt Drama Band Music Jazz_Ensemble. **Supp**—Rem_Math Rem_Read Tut. **Adm:** 56/yr. Appl due: Mar. Accepted: 80%. **Enr 223.** B 107. G 116. Elem 99. Sec 124. Wh 90%. Hisp 1%. Blk 5%. Asian 2%. Other 2%. Avg class size: 15. **Fac 35.** M 13/6. F 13/3. Wh 91%. Hisp 3%. Blk 6%. Adv deg: 62%. **Grad '04—28.** Col—25. Avg SAT: 1268. Alum 440. **Tui '04-'05:** Day $11,375-12,760 (+$300-400). Aid: Need 62. **Summer:** Enrich Rec. Arts. Tui Day $360/2-wk ses. 4 wks. **Est 1970.** Nonprofit. Religious Society of Friends. Sem (Sept-June). Tandem Friends' curriculum integrates humanities studies and offers math, science, foreign language, and the performing and visual arts. Internships and classes at local colleges are also available to students. The entire community gathers for a Quaker Meeting once a week, and each afternoon students participate in the upkeep of the buildings and the grounds. Community service is integral to school life.

WOODLAWN ACADEMY
Day Coed Gr PS-8

Chatham, VA 24531. 956 Woodlawn Academy Rd.
Tel: 434-432-9244. Fax: 434-432-2010.
www.woodlawnacademy.net   E-mail: woodlawn@meckcom.net
   Stan T. Cocke, Head. MEd, EdD, Univ of Virginia.

   Gen Acad. Feat—Fr Computers Fine_Arts. **Supp**—Dev_Read Tut. **Adm:** 25/yr. Appl due: Apr. **Enr 180.** B 87. G 93. Elem 180. Wh 97%. Blk 3%. Avg class size: 23. **Fac 17.** M 1/1. F 11/4. Wh 100%. Adv deg: 5%. **Grad '04—4.** Alum 440. **Tui '04-'05:** Day $3288 (+$365). **Est 1969.** Nonprofit. Sem (Aug-May). In addition to the full elementary curriculum, students at Woodlawn may participate in dramatics, art programs, band and music. The academy schedules trips to points of historical and practical interest throughout the year.

SOUTHAMPTON ACADEMY
Day Coed Gr PS-12

Courtland, VA 23837. 26495 Old Plank Rd.
Tel: 757-653-2512. Fax: 757-653-0011.
www.southamptonacademy.org   E-mail: saraiders@hotmail.com
   Craig Jones, Head. Ellen Lee, Adm.

   Col Prep. AP—Eng Calc US_Hist US_Govt & Pol. **Feat**—British_Lit Lib_Skills Span Comp_Sci Psych Studio_Art Drama Band Chorus. **Supp**—Rev Tut. **Adm:** 51/yr. Appl due: Rolling. Accepted: 81%. **Tests** MAT Stanford. **Enr 407.** B 212. G 195. Elem 331. Sec 76. Wh 100%. Blk 1%. Asian 1%. Other 1%. Avg class size: 13. **Fac 38.** M 4. F 31/3. Wh 100%. Adv deg: 2%. **Grad '04—17.** Col—15. Avg SAT: 1042. Alum 666. **Tui '03-'04:** Day $4115-4867 (+$225-400). Aid: Need 59 ($82,014). **Summer:** Rem. Tui Day $250. 4 wks. **Est 1969.** Nonprofit. Sem (Aug-June). **Assoc** SACS. Located on a 30-acre tract in the state's largest peanut-producing county, the academy's demanding curriculum includes AP classes in the upper grades. Students may earn an honors diploma by completing additional science and foreign language course work. Activities at Southampton include interscholastic sports, publications, Beta club, scholastic bowl, chorus, forensics, honor council, student government and band.

BROADWATER ACADEMY   **Day Coed Gr PS-12**
Exmore, VA 23350. 3500 Broadwater Rd, PO Box 546.
Tel: 757-442-9041. Fax: 757-442-9615.
www.broadwateracademy.org   E-mail: bsharpley@broadwateracademy.org
    Kendell S. Berry, Head. BS, Lynchburg College, MA, Univ of Virginia. Beth D. Sharpley, Adm.

    Col Prep. Feat—Mythology Marine_Biol/Sci Oceanog Computers Architect Study_Skills. **Supp**—Tut. **Adm:** 58/yr. Appl due: Rolling. **Tests** IQ. **Enr 460.** Wh 98%. Blk 1%. Asian 1%. Avg class size: 18. **Fac 51.** M 6. F 43/2. **Grad '04—18.** Col—18. Avg SAT: 1144. Alum 900. **Tui '05-'06:** Day $5575-5825 (+$150). **Est 1966.** Nonprofit. Sem (Aug-June). The academy's liberal arts curriculum includes Advanced Placement courses, and computer instruction is available in every grade. Pupils in the upper school fulfill a community service requirement each year. Among Broadwater's activities are team sports for boys and girls, student government, drama, newspaper, yearbook and various interest clubs.

THE CONGRESSIONAL SCHOOLS   **Day Coed Gr PS-8**
OF VIRGINIA
Falls Church, VA 22042. 3229 Sleepy Hollow Rd.
Tel: 703-533-9711. Fax: 703-532-5467.
www.congressionalschools.org   E-mail: admissions@csov.org
    Shirley K. Fegan, Head. BS, Georgetown Univ. Starrette Galanis, Prin. Karen H. Weinberger, Adm.

    Pre-Prep. Feat—Fr Span Computers Studio_Art Music. **Supp**—Dev_Read Tut. **Adm:** 69/yr. Appl due: Rolling. Accepted: 41%. **Tests** IQ ISEE SSAT. **Enr 386.** B 206. G 180. Elem 386. Wh 60%. Hisp 8%. Blk 10%. Am Ind 2%. Asian 11%. Other 9%. Avg class size: 18. **Fac 44.** M 6. F 35/3. Adv deg: 54%. **Grad '04—41.** Prep—27. Alum 439. **Tui '04-'05:** Day $12,585-15,720 (+$1000). **Summer:** Enrich Rec. Tui Day $550-710/2-wk ses. 10 wks. **Est 1939.** Nonprofit. Quar (Sept-June). **Assoc** SACS. The strong core curriculum of English, social studies, math, science, foreign languages and technology is complemented by art, music, physical education, health, library and study skills. Extended hours, transportation and enrichment programs are available. The school's 40-acre, wooded campus is 15 minutes from Washington, DC.

FUQUA SCHOOL   **Day Coed Gr PS-12**
Farmville, VA 23901. 605 Fuqua Dr, PO Box 328.
Tel: 434-392-4131. Fax: 434-392-5062.
www.fuquaschool.com   E-mail: murphycm@fuquaschool.com
    Ruth S. Murphy, Pres. BA, Univ of North Carolina-Chapel Hill, MEd, Univ of North Carolina-Greensboro. Christy M. Murphy, Adm.

Col Prep. **AP**—Eng Calc Bio US_Govt & Pol. **Feat**—Lib_Skills Lat Span Environ_Sci Comp_Sci Ethics Art_Hist Studio_Art Theater Music Accounting Communications. **Supp**—Tut. **Adm (Gr PS-11):** 86/yr. Appl due: Apr. Accepted: 99%. Yield: 99%. **Tests** CEEB IQ Stanford. **Enr 523.** B 250. G 273. Elem 358. Sec 165. Wh 92%. Hisp 1%. Blk 2%. Am Ind 1%. Asian 2%. Other 2%. Avg class size: 16. Uniform. **Fac 43.** M 10/1. F 32. Wh 98%. Blk 2%. Adv deg: 20%. **Grad '04—29.** Col—29. Alum 1000. **Tui '04-'05:** Day $6320 (+$150). Aid: Merit 15 ($9000). Need 83 ($87,681). **Summer:** Enrich. Tui Day $100/wk. 8 wks. **Est 1959.** Nonprofit. Sem (Aug-June). Serving students from 13 counties within a 30-mile radius, the developmentally based program at Fuqua enables each pupil to advance at an appropriate rate of learning, as the school does not utilize traditional grade-level caps. The multi-age lower school (grades pre-K-5) enables boys and girls to remain with the same teacher for two years; specialists teach weekly art, music, media, computer and physical education classes. At the middle school level (grades 6-8), planning teams deliver instruction to monitor learning and allow for flexible scheduling. Semester block scheduling during the high school years (grades 9-12) enables students to complete a traditional yearlong course in one semester by taking four classes at a time instead of seven.

WARE ACADEMY — Day Coed Gr PS-8
Gloucester, VA 23061. 7936 John Clayton Memorial Hwy.
Tel: 804-693-3825. Fax: 804-694-0695.
www.wareacademy.org   E-mail: info@wareacademy.org
Thomas L. Thomas III, Head. BA, Univ of Richmond, MA, Virginia Polytechnic Institute. Nicolle Morgan, Adm.

Pre-Prep. Feat—Lib_Skills Span Fine_Arts Performing_Arts Music. **Supp**—Dev_Read Rem_Read Rev Tut. **Adm:** 28/yr. Appl due: Rolling. Accepted: 95%. Yield: 99%. **Tests** CTP_4. **Enr 160.** B 60. G 100. Elem 160. Wh 98%. Blk 2%. Avg class size: 14. Uniform. **Fac 24.** Wh 100%. Adv deg: 16%. **Grad '04—15.** Prep—5. Avg SSAT: 51%. Alum 53. **Tui '05-'06:** Day $5790. Aid: Merit 1 ($4800). Need 13 ($15,500). **Summer:** Acad Enrich Rec. 1-6 wks. **Est 1949.** Nonprofit. Sem (Sept-June). The academy's primary school (grades pre-K-2) introduces children to the fundamentals of reading, writing, speaking and listening. By second grade, boys and girls have gained exposure to creative writing and logically formed sentences, as well as computation and math problem solving. Pupils further develop language arts and math skills in the lower school (grades 3-5), with greater content depth evident in all subject areas. Ware's middle school curriculum, which prepares students for high school academics, includes such electives as forensics, art, journalism and drama.

NYSMITH SCHOOL FOR THE GIFTED — Day Coed Gr PS-8
Herndon, VA 20171. 13625 EDS Dr.
Tel: 703-713-3332. Fax: 703-713-3336.
www.nysmith.com   E-mail: mwhite@nysmith.com
Carole Nysmith, Co-Dir. Ken Nysmith, Co-Dir. Marian White, Adm.

Pre-Prep. Gen Acad. Feat—Fr Lat Span Computers Logic Studio_Art Music. **Adm:** 85/yr. Appl due: Jan. **Tests** IQ. **Enr 674.** B 337. G 337. Elem 674. Avg class size: 18. **Fac 135.** M 3/2. F 75/55. **Grad '04—44. Tui '05-'06:** Day $14,750-

21,620. **Summer:** Ages 3-12. Acad Rec. Tui Day $490-625/2-wk ses. 8 wks. **Est 1983.** Inc. Quar (Aug-June). This elementary program provides an individualized, accelerated curriculum for able students. As reading and math are considered the foundation of future learning, they are introduced at an early age. While children remain with their classmates, they progress at their own rates, with four to eight grade-level plans implemented in a typical classroom. The curriculum includes spelling, vocabulary, grammar, punctuation and math drills.

CHESAPEAKE ACADEMY — Day Coed Gr PS-8
Irvington, VA 22480. 107 Steamboat Rd, PO Box 8.
Tel: 804-438-5575. Fax: 804-438-6146.
www.chesapeakeacademy.org   E-mail: cbritton@chesapeakeacademy.org
   Seth W. Ahlborn, Head. BA, Univ of North Carolina-Chapel Hill, MS, Univ of Wisconsin-Madison. Charles E. Britton, Adm.
   Pre-Prep. Gen Acad. Feat—Lib_Skills Span Ethics Studio_Art Music. **Supp**—Tut. **Adm:** 43/yr. Appl due: Rolling. Accepted: 85%. Yield: 87%. **Tests** CTP_4 IQ. **Enr 172.** B 97. G 75. Elem 172. Wh 79%. Hisp 9%. Blk 5%. Asian 7%. Avg class size: 15. Uniform. **Fac 24.** M 3. F 21. Wh 100%. Adv deg: 16%. **Grad '04—14.** Prep—3. Alum 500. **Tui '05-'06:** Day $3150-6825. Aid: Need 36 ($105,284). **Summer:** Enrich Rec. Field Hockey. Lacrosse. Tui Day $175/wk. 4 wks. **Est 1889.** Nonprofit. Sem (Sept-June). Pupils at the academy follow a broad-based, sequential liberal arts curriculum that progresses from a hands-on early childhood division (preschool, prekindergarten and kindergarten) to a lower school featuring unit classrooms (grades 1-4) to a departmentalized middle school (grades 5-8). Chesapeake conducts a field study excursion to south Florida for eighth graders, and boys and girls in grades 5-8 take part in Inward Bound, an overnight trip to a local camp. Students enroll from Lancaster, Northumberland, Middlesex and Mathews counties.

LITTLE KESWICK SCHOOL — Bdg Boys Ages 10-17
Keswick, VA 22947. Rte 731, PO Box 24.
Tel: 434-295-0457. Fax: 434-977-1892.
www.avenue.org/lks   E-mail: columbuslks@aol.com
   Marc J. Columbus, Head. MEd, Univ of Virginia. Terry Columbus, Dir. MEd, Univ of Virginia.
   LD. Supp—Rem_Math Rem_Read Tut. **Adm:** 15/yr. Appl due: Rolling. **Tests** IQ. **Enr 30.** B 30. Avg class size: 7. **Fac 40.** M 20. F 20. **Grad '04—13.** Alum 340. **Tui '04-'05:** Bdg $55,175 (+$7340). **Summer:** Acad Enrich Rev Rem Rec. Tui Bdg $5585. 5 wks. **Est 1963.** Inc. Quar (Sept-June). This therapeutic, special-education boarding school serves boys of below-average to superior intelligence who have one or more of the following: learning problems, emotional disorders or behavioral disorders. While highly structured, the program operates in a small, open setting. LKS also offers specialized academics; an independent living program; individual and family counseling; and speech and language, occupational and art therapies.

OAKLAND SCHOOL
Coed Gr 2-9
Bdg & Day

Keswick, VA 22947. Boyd Tavern.
Tel: 434-293-9059. Fax: 434-296-8930.
www.oaklandschool.net   E-mail: oaklandschool@earthlink.net
  Carol Smieciuch, Dir. BA, MEd, Univ of Virginia.

LD. Feat—Study_Skills. **Supp**—Dev_Read Rem_Math Rem_Read Rev Tut. **Adm (Gr 2-8):** 20/yr. Bdg 15. Day 5. Appl due: Rolling. **Tests** IQ. **Enr 80.** B 26/16. G 22/16. Elem 70. Sec 10. Wh 90%. Hisp 2%. Blk 6%. Asian 2%. Avg class size: 5. **Fac 14.** M 4. F 10. Wh 100%. Adv deg: 35%. **Grad '04**—12. Prep—8. **Tui '04-'05:** Bdg $34,000 (+$500). Day $18,000 (+$100). **Est 1950.** Nonprofit. Year-round. Accepting children of average to above-average ability with dyslexia and other learning disabilities, Oakland provides a year-round academic curriculum stressing basic skills in one-on-one and small-class settings. The school specializes in the teaching of reading, math, written language and study skills. A full recreational program, team sports, daily physical education and horseback riding are also provided. Most students return to a traditional educational setting after two to four years.

LOUDOUN COUNTRY DAY SCHOOL
Day Coed Gr PS-8

Leesburg, VA 20176. 237 Fairview St NW.
Tel: 703-777-3841. Fax: 703-771-1346.
www.lcds.org   E-mail: info@lcds.org
  Randall Hollister, Head. BS, St Bonaventure Univ, MEd, Plymouth State College, EdM, PhD, State Univ of New York-Buffalo. Pam Larimer, Adm.

Pre-Prep. Feat—Fr Computers Studio_Art Chorus Music Orchestra. **Supp**—Rem_Math Rem_Read Tut. **Adm:** 51/yr. Appl due: Rolling. Accepted: 40%. **Tests** CTP_4 IQ. **Enr 260.** Elem 260. Wh 91%. Blk 1%. Asian 8%. Avg class size: 16. Uniform. **Fac 54.** M 2/1. F 47/4. Adv deg: 29%. **Grad '04**—19. Prep—12. Alum 466. **Tui '04-'05:** Day $7500-12,000 (+$100). **Summer:** Rec. 1-6 wks. **Est 1953.** Nonprofit. Tri (Sept-June). LCDS stresses proficiency in English and math skills, as well as science and technology. French is taught from prekindergarten. A diversified art program and music instruction, including chorus and orchestra, are part of the curriculum. Sports include soccer, field hockey, tennis, gymnastics, skiing, basketball, lacrosse, track, flag football and swimming.

JAMES RIVER DAY SCHOOL
Day Coed Gr K-8

Lynchburg, VA 24503. 5039 Boonsboro Rd.
Tel: 434-384-7385. Fax: 434-384-5937.
www.jamesriverdayschool.com   E-mail: email@jamesriverdayschool.com
  William S. Coursey III, Head. BA, MEd, Mercer Univ, EdS, Univ of Georgia. Katherine B. Manning, Adm.

Pre-Prep. Gen Acad. Feat—Fr Lat Span Studio_Art Chorus Music Study_Skills. **Supp**—Dev_Read Rem_Math Rem_Read. **Adm:** 47/yr. Appl due: Rolling. Accepted: 85%. **Tests** CTP_4 IQ. **Enr 260.** B 145. G 115. Elem 260. Wh 94%. Blk 2%. Asian 4%. Avg class size: 16. **Fac 30.** M 7. F 17/6. Wh 97%. Asian 3%. Adv deg: 30%. **Grad '04**—24. Prep—13. Alum 2000. **Tui '04-'05:** Day $5590-6090 (+$300-350). Aid: Merit 1 ($500). Need 20 ($23,100). **Summer:** Enrich Rec. Tui Day $100/wk. 8 wks. **Est 1971.** Nonprofit. Sem (Sept-June). James River's curriculum stresses basic academic skills and provides enrichment programs in computers, music, art and French. The program is designed for the child of average to above-average intelligence.

CARLISLE SCHOOL   **Day Coed Gr PS-12**
Martinsville, VA 24115. 300 Carlisle Rd, PO Box 5388.
Tel: 276-632-7288. Fax: 276-632-9545.
www.carlisleschool.org   E-mail: admissions@carlisleschool.org
    Simon Owen-Williams, Head. BA, Univ of Exeter (England), MA, Columbia Univ.

    Col Prep. IB_Diploma. IB_MYP. Feat—Span Econ Speech. **Supp**—LD Makeup Tut. **Adm (Gr PS-11):** 110/yr. Appl due: Rolling. Accepted: 82%. Yield: 86%. **Tests** Stanford. **Enr 428.** B 213. G 215. Elem 311. Sec 117. Wh 83%. Hisp 1%. Blk 11%. Am Ind 1%. Asian 2%. Other 2%. Avg class size: 12. **Fac 58.** M 7/1. F 43/7. Wh 89%. Hisp 1%. Blk 5%. Other 5%. Adv deg: 56%. **Grad '04—32.** Col—32. Avg SAT: 1155. Alum 447. **Tui '04-'05:** Day $4900-8400 (+$450). Aid: Need 42 ($164,945). **Summer:** Acad Enrich Rev Rec. 1-4 wks. **Est 1968.** Nonprofit. Sem (Aug-June). **Assoc** SACS. In addition to offering the International Baccalaureate diploma, Carlisle conducts a speech program that is required from grade 8 on. Facilities include a fine arts center, and the athletic program includes basketball, hockey, golf, tennis, cross-country, track and field, and soccer.

NOTRE DAME ACADEMY   **Day Coed Gr 9-12**
Middleburg, VA 20117. 35321 Notre Dame Ln.
Tel: 540-687-5581. Fax: 540-687-3103.
www.notredameva.org   E-mail: cstruder@notredameva.org
    Edward V. Hoffman, Int Head. BA, Mount Saint Mary's College (MD). Catherine Struder, Adm.

    Col Prep. AP—Eng Calc Chem US_Hist. **Feat**—Fr Lat Span Anat Energy_Mgmt Comp_Sci Anthro Econ Psych Sociol Ethics Philos Relig Architect Fine_Arts Debate SAT_Prep Martial_Arts. **Supp**—LD Makeup Tut. **Adm:** 111/yr. Appl due: Feb. **Tests** HSPT IQ ISEE SSAT. **Enr 293.** B 150. G 143. Sec 293. Avg class size: 14. Uniform. **Fac 35.** M 18. F 17. Adv deg: 48%. **Grad '04—66.** Col—66. Avg SAT: 1150. Alum 905. **Tui '04-'05:** Day $13,300 (+$600). **Summer:** Rec. Art. Sports. SAT Prep. 1-2 wks. **Est 1965.** Nonprofit. Roman Catholic. Quar (Sept-June). **Assoc** SACS. Conducted by the Sisters of Notre Dame, NDA offers a college preparatory curriculum with Advanced Placement courses, as well as a yearly school-wide retreat, tutorial services, off-campus independent study opportunities for qualified students, a career internship for seniors, and required community service. Sports consist of basketball, volleyball, tennis, soccer, cross-country, baseball, field hockey, golf, lacrosse and skiing. The music program provides instruction in voice, piano, guitar and orchestral instruments.

AYLETT COUNTRY DAY SCHOOL
Day Coed Gr PS-8

Millers Tavern, VA 23115. Rte 620, PO Box 70.
Tel: 804-443-3214. Fax: 804-443-3064.
www.acdspatriots.net   E-mail: info@acdspatriots.net
 John W. Colby, Jr., Head. BA, Univ of the South, MSS, Univ of Mississippi, MBA, Jacksonville Univ.

 Pre-Prep. Feat—Span Computers Studio_Art Music. **Adm:** 27/yr. **Enr 170.** B 73. G 97. Elem 170. Wh 96%. Blk 1%. Asian 3%. Avg class size: 15. **Fac 21.** M 1. F 11/9. Adv deg: 19%. **Grad '04—15.** Prep—13. **Tui '03-'04:** Day $5350-5600 (+$200). Aid: Need 30 ($38,600). **Est 1966.** Nonprofit. (Sept-June). ACDS provides a flexible learning structure and emphasizes the development of independence and self-reliance. Spanish is the school's foreign language option.

ST. ANDREW'S EPISCOPAL SCHOOL
Day Coed Gr K-5

Newport News, VA 23601. 45 Main St.
Tel: 757-596-6261. Fax: 757-596-7218.
www.standrewsschool.com   E-mail: standrews@standrewsschool.com
 Margaret D. Moore, Head.

 Gen Acad. Feat—Fr Computers Studio_Art Music. **Adm:** 52/yr. **Enr 223.** B 106. G 117. Elem 223. Wh 89%. Blk 8%. Asian 3%. Avg class size: 18. Uniform. **Fac 23.** M /1. F 15/7. Wh 100%. Adv deg: 17%. **Grad '04—35. Tui '03-'04:** Day $4099-4502 (+$500). Aid: Need 9 ($20,800). **Summer:** Acad Enrich. 2 wks. **Est 1946.** Nonprofit. Episcopal. Quar (Aug-June). St. Andrew's provides sound academic training within a Christian environment. Programs in French, art, music, physical education and computer provide enrichment. Small classes, field trips and the use of community resources are integral features of the program.

FLINT HILL SCHOOL
Day Coed Gr PS-12

Oakton, VA 22124. 3320 Jermantown Rd.
Tel: 703-584-2300. Fax: 703-584-2369.
www.flinthill.org   E-mail: jheard@flinthill.org
 John Thomas, Head. BA, Randolph-Macon College, MA, Towson State Univ. Pat Harden, Adm.

 Col Prep. AP—Eng Fr Lat Span Calc Stats Comp_Sci Bio Chem Physics Eur_Hist US_Hist Econ Psych US_Govt & Pol Music_Theory. **Feat**—Creative_Writing Satire Ecol Ornithology Civil_War World_Relig Ceramics Sculpt Theater. **Supp**—LD. **Adm:** 205/yr. Appl due: Feb. Accepted: 55%. Yield: 69%. **Tests** IQ SSAT. **Enr 972.** B 495. G 477. Elem 589. Sec 383. Uniform. **Fac 115.** M 40. F 75. Adv deg: 68%. **Grad '04—67.** Col—66. Avg SAT: 1291. Alum 1100. **Tui '04-'05:** Day $15,225-20,800. Aid: Need 104 ($1,267,825). **Summer:** Acad Enrich Rec. Tui Day $160-300. 1-3 wks. **Est 1956.** Nonprofit. Sem (Sept-June). Enrolling able students from Greater Washington, Flint Hill conducts a rigorous curriculum that prepares boys and girls for college through a combination of Advanced Placement courses and electives. Course work emphasizes learning skills development in the areas of critical thinking, problem solving and writing, and a learning center offers support for pupils with different learning styles. Varied arts offerings, an experiential education program and an athletic program that features competitive sports at the upper school level are important aspects of school life. The lower and middle schools (junior kindergarten through grade 8) occupy a separate campus at 10409 Academic Dr. **See Also Page 1154**

BLESSED SACRAMENT-HUGUENOT   Day Coed Gr PS-12

Powhatan, VA 23139. 2501 Academy Rd, PO Box 519.
Tel: 804-598-4211. Fax: 804-598-1053.
www.blessedsacramenthuguenot.com   E-mail: drhbsh@aol.com

Lou Ross Hopewell, Pres. DEd, College of William and Mary. Catherine L. Brown, Adm.

Col Prep. **Feat**—Lat Span Computers Studio_Art Music Debate. **Adm:** 60/yr. **Tests** IQ. **Enr 538.** Elem 384. Sec 154. Avg class size: 20. Uniform. **Fac 49.** M 12. F 36/1. Adv deg: 18%. **Grad '04—38.** Col—38. Alum 1500. **Tui '03-'04:** Day $2800-6850 (+$125). Aid: Need 34 ($61,000). **Est 1959.** Nonprofit. Roman Catholic. Tri (Aug-June). The school emphasizes individual attention in a family-like atmosphere. Students participate in such activities as honor council, forensics, quiz bowl and service projects. Interscholastic athletic competition begins in grade 6.

THE NEW COMMUNITY SCHOOL   Day Coed Gr 6-12

Richmond, VA 23227. 4211 Hermitage Rd.
Tel: 804-266-2494. Fax: 804-264-3281.
www.tncs.org   E-mail: info@tncs.org

Julia Ann Greenwood, Head. BA, College of William and Mary, MA, Marshall Univ. Gita Morris, Adm.

Col Prep. LD. **Supp**—Dev_Read Rem_Math Rem_Read. **Adm (Gr 6-11):** 30/yr. Appl due: Rolling. Accepted: 87%. Yield: 86%. **Tests** IQ Stanford. **Enr 96.** B 64. G 32. Elem 44. Sec 52. Wh 84%. Hisp 4%. Blk 8%. Asian 1%. Other 3%. Avg class size: 7. **Fac 31.** M 8/1. F 20/2. Wh 97%. Blk 3%. Adv deg: 48%. **Grad '04—10.** Col—8. Avg SAT: 964. Alum 440. **Tui '04-'05:** Day $17,600-18,600. Aid: Need 21 ($180,000). **Summer:** Acad Rem. Tui Day $200-800. 4 wks. **Est 1974.** Nonprofit. Sem (Sept-June). Providing college preparation for students with dyslexia, TNCS offers a highly structured, individualized educational environment that allows pupils to work at an appropriate intellectual level while developing language skills that help compensate for their learning difficulties. The curriculum includes both remediation of language skills and sufficient academic challenge for students of average to above-average intelligence. Once the pupil's reading, writing and spelling skills are commensurate with his or her intelligence level, the school may recommend transfer to a less-specialized setting.

THE ACHIEVEMENT CENTER   Day Coed Gr K-9

Roanoke, VA 24019. 312 Whitwell Dr.
Tel: 540-366-7399. Fax: 540-366-5523.
www.achievementcenter.org   E-mail: info@achievementcenter.org

Rebecca Clendenin, Dir.

LD. Feat—Computers Studio_Art Music. **Supp**—Dev_Read Rem_Math Rem_Read Tut. **Adm:** 9/yr. **Tests** IQ. **Enr 60.** B 43. G 17. Wh 78%. Blk 22%. Avg class size: 10. Uniform. **Fac 15.** M 1. F 13/1. Wh 95%. Blk 5%. Adv deg: 53%. **Tui '04-'05:** Day $9320 (+$140). Aid: Need 3 ($9772). **Summer:** Acad Enrich Rev Rem. Tui Day $675. 6 wks. **Est 1975.** Nonprofit. Sem (Aug-June). **Assoc** SACS. The center utilizes a multisensory approach for children with learning disabilities. The curriculum includes reading, language arts, mathematics, science, social studies, computer, art, music and physical education. In addition, professional services are provided in counseling and speech and language therapy.

HUNTER McGUIRE SCHOOL
Day Coed Gr K-5
Verona, VA 24482. 74 Quicks Mill Rd.
Tel: 540-248-2404. Fax: 540-248-5323.
www.huntermcguire.org   E-mail: admissions@huntermcguire.org

Barbara B. Cox, Head. BA, Univ of Richmond, MEd, Goucher College. Mia Kivlighan, Adm.

Pre-Prep. Feat—Lib_Skills Span Computers Studio_Art Music. **Supp**—Dev_Read. **Adm:** 21/yr. Appl due: Rolling. Accepted: 70%. **Enr 100.** B 44. G 56. Elem 100. Wh 96%. Blk 1%. Asian 1%. Other 2%. Avg class size: 16. **Fac 16.** M /1. F 7/8. Wh 94%. Hisp 6%. Adv deg: 25%. **Grad '04**—13. Prep—10. Alum 250. **Tui '03-'04:** Day $6990. Aid: Need 6 ($25,000). **Est 1986.** Nonprofit. (Aug-June). In addition to instruction in the core subjects, the curriculum at Hunter McGuire includes art, music, computer and science lab, Spanish, library and physical education. Course work emphasizes critical thinking and problem solving. Twice monthly, boys and girls from all grades convene to sing songs, act in skits and perform in other creative ways.

GREEN HEDGES SCHOOL
Day Coed Gr PS-8
Vienna, VA 22180. 415 Windover Ave NW.
Tel: 703-938-8323. Fax: 703-938-1485.
www.greenhedges.org   E-mail: ldixon@greenhedges.org

Frederick W. Williams, Head. BA, Boston Univ, MEd, Lesley Univ. Leslie Dixon, Adm.

Pre-Prep. Feat—Fr Lat Span Computers Studio_Art Drama Chorus Music Public_Speak. **Adm (Gr PS-7):** 39/yr. Appl due: Rolling. Yield: 65%. **Enr 191.** B 98. G 93. Elem 191. Wh 67%. Hisp 1%. Blk 3%. Asian 7%. Other 22%. Avg class size: 18. **Fac 33.** M 4/3. F 21/5. Wh 82%. Blk 9%. Asian 3%. Other 6%. Adv deg: 45%. **Grad '04**—12. Prep—6. **Tui '04-'05:** Day $15,975-16,240 (+$500). Aid: Need 24 ($196,222). **Summer:** Rec. Tui Day $700/3-wk ses. 6 wks. **Est 1942.** Nonprofit. Tri (Sept-June). A Montessori-based program in the early school (ages 3-5) transitions to a more traditional primary program in the elementary school (grades 1-5). All classes in the middle school (grades 6-8) are departmentalized. French instruction begins in the preschool, while Spanish and Latin are added in grades 5-8. Music, art, literature, drama and physical education are taught at all grade levels, and technology is integral to the program.

TIDEWATER ACADEMY
Day Coed Gr PS-12
Wakefield, VA 23888. 217 Church St, PO Box 536.
Tel: 757-899-5401. Fax: 757-899-2521.
www.tidewateracademy-pvt-va.us   E-mail: gfw@whro.net
  David Pitre, Head. BA, Univ of Louisiana-Lafayette, MA, Virginia Polytechnic Institute, PhD, Univ of South Carolina. Gail Ford-Westbrook, Adm.
  Col Prep. AP—Eng Calc US_Hist US_Govt & Pol. **Feat**—Shakespeare Southern_Lit Span Comp_Sci Photog Music Dance Bus. **Supp**—Tut. **Adm:** 36/yr. Appl due: Apr. Accepted: 75%. Yield: 100%. **Enr 227.** B 127. G 100. Elem 149. Sec 78. Wh 93%. Blk 6%. Asian 1%. Avg class size: 16. **Fac 29.** M 4/5. F 17/3. Wh 90%. Blk 10%. Adv deg: 13%. **Grad '04—15.** Col—14. Avg SAT: 1184. **Tui '04-'05:** Day $4900 (+$600). Aid: Need 39 ($92,990). **Est 1964.** Nonprofit. Quar (Aug-May).   The curriculum at this school includes college preparatory instruction and independent study opportunities. Lower schoolers (grades pre-K-6) attend classes at a second campus near Dendron. Tidewater assigns each student in grades 7-12 a faculty advisor who provides both academic and nonacademic mentoring. Extracurricular activities include student government and a variety of clubs and organizations.

WALSINGHAM ACADEMY
Day Coed Gr PS-12
Williamsburg, VA 23187. 1100 Jamestown Rd, PO Box 8702.
Tel: 757-229-6026. Fax: 757-259-1401.
www.walsingham.org   E-mail: doday@walsingham.org
  Sr. Mary Jeanne Oesterle, RSM, Pres. MEd, St Michael's College. Annie C. Chadwick, Lower Adm.
  Col Prep. AP—Eng Stats Bio Chem US_Hist Comp_Govt & Pol US_Govt & Pol. **Feat**—Programming. **Supp**—Tut. **Adm:** 50/yr. **Enr 705.** Elem 490. Sec 215. Wh 94%. Hisp 1%. Blk 1%. Am Ind 1%. Asian 3%. Avg class size: 16. Uniform. **Fac 67.** M 6. F 61. Wh 99%. Asian 1%. **Grad '04—55.** Col—53. Avg SAT: 1154. Alum 1778. **Tui '04-'05:** Day $6725-7910 (+$800). **Est 1947.** Nonprofit. Roman Catholic. Quar (Aug-June). **Assoc** SACS.   The college preparatory program at this school is conducted by the Sisters of Mercy. In the lower school, language instruction begins with Spanish in kindergarten.

WILLIAMSBURG CHRISTIAN ACADEMY
Day Coed Gr PS-12
Williamsburg, VA 23188. 101 Schoolhouse Ln.
Tel: 757-220-1978. Fax: 757-741-4009.
www.wcanet.org   E-mail: frontoffice@wcanet.org
  Gwen Martin, Prin. Zabrina Williams, Adm.
  Col Prep. AP—Eng Fr Span Calc Eur_Hist US_Hist. **Feat**—Lib_Skills Computers Econ Govt Bible Studio_Art Music. **Supp**—LD Tut. **Adm:** 58/yr. Appl due: Rolling. Accepted: 96%. Yield: 99%. **Enr 265.** B 130. G 135. Elem 200. Sec 65. Wh 90%. Hisp 1%. Blk 5%. Asian 3%. Other 1%. Avg class size: 15. Uniform. **Fac 38.** M 5/1. F 23/9. Wh 92%. Hisp 3%. Blk 3%. Asian 2%. Adv deg: 23%. **Grad '04—16.** Col—15. **Tui '04-'05:** Day $4000-5950. **Est 1978.** Nonprofit. Nondenom Christian. Quar (Aug-May).   The elementary school (grades PS-5) at WCA combines instruction in the basics with weekly Spanish, music, art, computer, library

skills and physical education classes. Focusing on study skills, middle school course work (grades 6-8) includes opportunities for advancement in all subject areas, as well as foreign language instruction in grade 8. High school students (grades 9-12) follow a college preparatory curriculum that includes both Advanced Placement courses and electives.

WEST VIRGINIA

NOTRE DAME HIGH SCHOOL   Day Coed Gr 7-12
Clarksburg, WV 26301. 127 E Pike St.
Tel: 304-623-1026. Fax: 304-623-1026.
www.notredamehighschool.net   E-mail: ndhs@iolinc.net
    Carroll K. Morrison, Prin. BA, Transylvania Univ, MA, EdD, West Virginia Univ.

    Col Prep. Bus. AP—Eng Calc Bio Chem US_Hist. **Feat**—Fr Ital Span Relig Music. **Supp**—Rem_Math Rem_Read Tut. **Adm:** 28/yr. **Enr 149.** B 52. G 97. Wh 95%. Blk 3%. Asian 2%. Avg class size: 20. Uniform. **Fac 15.** M 7. F 8. Wh 100%. Adv deg: 53%. **Grad '04**—**20.** Col—19. Alum 2500. **Tui '04-'05:** Day $2850-3950 (+$55-100). Catholic $2250-3750 (+$55-100). Aid: Need 44 ($47,320). Work prgm 6 ($9590). **Summer:** Acad. Tui Day $160/3-wk ses. 6 wks. **Est 1955.** Nonprofit. Roman Catholic. Sem (Aug-June). **Assoc** NCA. Notre Dame's curriculum includes Advanced Placement classes and such electives as speech, journalism and accounting. Course work in religion is compulsory. The affiliated St. Mary's Grade School (grades K-6) is located at 107 E. Pike St.

THE COUNTRY DAY SCHOOL   Day Coed Gr PS-8
Kearneysville, WV 25430. 449 Rose Hill Dr.
Tel: 304-725-1438. Fax: 304-728-8394.
www.thecountrydayschool.com   E-mail: headofschool@citynet.net
    Karen W. Stroup, Head. MA. Keith Biser, Adm.

    Pre-Prep. Feat—Creative_Writing Mythology Fr Span Computers Drama Music. **Supp**—Rev Tut. **Adm:** 40/yr. Appl due: Rolling. Accepted: 90%. **Tests** SSAT. **Enr 135.** B 61. G 74. Elem 135. Wh 83%. Hisp 2%. Blk 4%. Asian 11%. Avg class size: 10. Uniform. **Fac 31.** M 2/1. F 26/2. Wh 97%. Blk 1%. Am Ind 1%. Other 1%. Adv deg: 12%. **Grad '04**—**7.** Prep—6. Avg SSAT: 84%. Alum 50. **Tui '05-'06:** Day $5500-6300 (+$1000). Aid: Need 5. **Summer:** Acad Enrich Rev Rec. Tui Day $200/2-wk ses. 8 wks. **Est 1982.** Nonprofit. Quar (Sept-June). Located on a 30-acre campus, the school draws students from a wide tri-state area that includes Virginia, West Virginia and western Maryland. Field trips are planned throughout the year, for children at all grade levels, to such places as Washington, DC, and Williamsburg, VA. Sports, current events, art, music, drama and computer science complement the curriculum.

Great Lakes States

ILLINOIS

DRISCOLL CATHOLIC HIGH SCHOOL　　　　　　　Day Coed Gr 9-12
Addison, IL 60101. 555 N Lombard Rd.
Tel: 630-543-6310. Fax: 630-543-1638.
www.driscollcatholic.com　　E-mail: highlanders@driscollcatholic.com
Thomas Geraghty, Pres. Kim Hannigan, Adm.

Col Prep. AP—Eng Span Calc Bio US_Hist. **Feat**—Ital Computers Law Music. **Supp**—Dev_Read Rem_Math Rem_Read Tut. **Adm:** 135/yr. Appl due: Rolling. Accepted: 90%. **Enr 465.** B 260. G 205. Sec 465. Wh 91%. Hisp 3%. Blk 1%. Asian 5%. Avg class size: 23. **Fac 33.** M 14/2. F 15/2. Wh 91%. Hisp 3%. Asian 6%. Adv deg: 57%. **Grad '04—123.** Col—117. Alum 3700. **Tui '03-'04:** Day $6400 (+$150). Aid: Merit 25. Need 115 ($150,000). **Summer:** Rem. Tui Day $125/crse. 5 wks. **Est 1965.** Nonprofit. Roman Catholic. Sem (Aug-June). **Assoc** NCA. The college preparatory program offers Advanced Placement courses, English, languages, science and mathematics. Through the honors program, which is affiliated with the College of DuPage and St. Mary's University of Minnesota, seniors may earn college credit.

SAINT VIATOR HIGH SCHOOL　　　　　　　　　Day Coed Gr 9-12
Arlington Heights, IL 60004. 1213 E Oakton St.
Tel: 847-392-4050. Fax: 847-392-4329.
www.saintviator.com
Rev. Thomas von Behren, CSV, Pres. BA, Loyola Univ of Chicago, MEd, Univ of San Francisco.

Col Prep. AP—Eng Fr Ger Span Calc Bio Physics Eur_Hist US_Hist. **Feat**—Ital Computers Programming Relig Fine_Arts Photog Studio_Art Theater_Arts Band Music Dance Bus Study_Skills. **Supp**—Tut. **Adm:** 304/yr. **Enr 1040.** B 555. G 485. Sec 1040. Wh 94%. Hisp 3%. Blk 1%. Asian 2%. Avg class size: 25. **Fac 81.** M 26/3. F 47/5. Adv deg: 70%. **Grad '04—242.** Col—240. Avg SAT: 1174. Avg ACT: 25. Alum 11,000. **Tui '04-'05:** Day $8100 (+$300). Aid: Need 148 ($461,850). **Summer:** Acad. Tui Day $100. 3 wks. **Est 1961.** Nonprofit. Roman Catholic. Sem (Aug-June). **Assoc** NCA. Emphasizing religious education, Saint Viator supplements its college preparatory curriculum with school publications, the arts, clubs, organizations and other extracurricular activities. The athletic program consists of football, basketball, baseball, volleyball, cross-country, track, swimming, water polo, soccer, tennis, wrestling, golf and cheerleading.

QUEEN OF PEACE HIGH SCHOOL　　　　　　　Day Girls Gr 9-12
Burbank, IL 60459. 7659 S Linder Ave.
Tel: 708-458-7600. Fax: 708-458-5734.
www.queenofpeacehs.org　　E-mail: info@queenofpeacehs.org

Mary Klinefelter, Pres. BS, Northwestern Univ, MS, Univ of Wisconsin-Madison. Patricia Nolan-Fitzgerald, Prin. BA, Rosary College, MEd, Loyola Univ of Chicago. Susan Connelly, Adm.

Col Prep. AP—Eng Fr Span Calc Comp_Sci Bio Chem US_Hist World_Hist. **Feat**—Environ_Sci Amer_Stud Women's_Stud Relig Fine_Arts. **Supp**—Tut. **Adm:** 220/yr. Appl due: Rolling. **Tests** HSPT. **Enr 825.** G 825. Sec 825. Wh 60%. Hisp 25%. Blk 12%. Am Ind 1%. Asian 1%. Other 1%. Avg class size: 25. Uniform. **Fac 48.** M 4. F 40/4. Wh 89%. Hisp 7%. Am Ind 2%. Asian 2%. Adv deg: 79%. **Grad '04—248.** Col—237. Alum 12,200. **Tui '04-'05:** Day $6050. Aid: Merit 21 ($10,850). Need 286 ($320,146). **Summer:** Rem. Tui Day $75/crse. 3 wks. **Est 1962.** Nonprofit. Roman Catholic. Sem (Aug-June). **Assoc** NCA. Queen of Peace offers a complete college preparatory curriculum that includes Advanced Placement course work. An interdisciplinary studies curriculum provides team-taught classes in such areas as American studies, global culture, science and ethics, and women in psychology and literature. Qualified students may graduate with five years of high school credit in math and science.

BREHM PREPARATORY SCHOOL
Coed Gr 6-PG
Bdg & Day

Carbondale, IL 62901. 1245 E Grand Ave.
Tel: 618-457-0371. Fax: 618-529-1248.
www.brehm.org   E-mail: admissionsinfo@brehm.org

Richard G. Collins, Exec Dir. MA, PhD, St Louis Univ. Donna E. Collins, Adm.

Col Prep. LD. Supp—Dev_Read Rem_Read. **Adm:** 39/yr. Bdg 37. Day 2. Appl due: Rolling. Accepted: 90%. **Tests** IQ. **Enr 86.** B 56/6. G 24. Wh 90%. Hisp 5%. Blk 1%. Asian 3%. Other 1%. Avg class size: 8. **Fac 24.** M 6. F 18. Wh 100%. Adv deg: 58%. **Grad '04—15.** Col—7. Alum 350. **Tui '04-'05:** Bdg $45,900 (+$3000). Day $28,350 (+$1500). **Est 1982.** Nonprofit. Quar (Aug-June). Brehm provides a full range of services that addresses the academic, social and emotional needs of students with learning disabilities. Pupils with reading, spelling and written language deficits receive instruction using the Lindamood-Bell, Orton-Gillingham or Wilson Reading Program approach, depending upon the specific needs of the child. As the vast majority of students board, the school offers a well-developed residential program designed to improve the individual's social skills and problem-solving abilities.

CARBONDALE NEW SCHOOL
Day Coed Gr PS-8

Carbondale, IL 62902. 1302 E Pleasant Hill Rd.
Tel: 618-457-4765. Fax: 618-457-4765.
www.carbondalenewschool.com   E-mail: cnschool@msn.com

Linda M. Rohling, Dir.

Pre-Prep. Feat—Span. **Supp**—Dev_Read Rem_Read. **Adm:** 15/yr. Appl due: Aug. **Enr 61.** Elem 61. Wh 88%. Hisp 4%. Blk 8%. Avg class size: 15. **Fac 8.** F 8. Wh 100%. **Grad '04—2. Tui '03-'04:** Day $3700 (+$200). **Summer:** Rec. 6 wks. **Est 1974.** Nonprofit. Sem (Aug-June). Founded by area parents, the school provides a theme-based, integrated curriculum. Basic skills mastery, enrichment opportunities and parental participation are important features.

CHICAGO CITY DAY SCHOOL
Day Coed Gr PS-8

Chicago, IL 60657. 541 W Hawthorne Pl.
Tel: 773-327-0900. Fax: 773-327-6381.
www.chicagocitydayschool.org
   Galeta Kaar Clayton, Head. BA, Northwestern Univ, MEd, Loyola Univ of Chicago. Nicole Kelker, Adm.

Pre-Prep. Feat—Fr Span Computers Studio_Art Drama Music Indus_Arts. **Supp**—LD. **Adm (Gr PS-7):** 43/yr. Accepted: 50%. Yield: 75%. **Tests** Stanford. **Enr 280.** B 142. G 138. Elem 280. Wh 87%. Hisp 4%. Blk 3%. Asian 4%. Other 2%. **Fac 33.** M 5. F 24/4. Wh 82%. Hisp 12%. Blk 3%. Asian 3%. Adv deg: 103%. **Grad '04**—24. Prep—23. Alum 100. **Tui '04-'05:** Day $15,250-16,650 (+$900-1160). Aid: Need 21 ($300,000). **Summer:** Rec. 1 wk. **Est 1981.** Nonprofit. (Sept-June). City Day combines a strong grounding in the basic skills with enriched programs in science, foreign language, the fine arts and physical education. Teachers place particular emphasis on reading and math skill development, which the school considers essential to academic achievement. At all grade levels (including junior kindergarten), specialists provide instruction in science, foreign language, art, music, drama and physical education. The availability of at least two computers per classroom fosters computer literacy.

DE LA SALLE INSTITUTE
Day Coed Gr 9-12
(Coord 9-12)

Chicago, IL 60616. 3455 S Wabash Ave.
Tel: 312-842-7355. Fax: 312-842-5640.
www.dls.org   E-mail: kuhnc@dls.org
   James Krygier, Prin. BA, MA, Univ of Illinois-Urbana. Chuck Kuhn, Adm.

Col Prep. AP—Eng Fr Span Calc US_Hist US_Govt & Pol Studio_Art. **Feat**—Creative_Writing Anat & Physiol Environ_Sci Comp_Sci World_Relig Film Drama Chorus Woodworking. **Supp**—Dev_Read Rem_Math Rem_Read Rev Tut. **Adm (Gr 9-11):** 360/yr. Appl due: Rolling. Accepted: 58%. Yield: 90%. **Enr 1280.** B 900. G 380. Sec 1280. Wh 33%. Hisp 33%. Blk 32%. Asian 1%. Other 1%. Avg class size: 23. Uniform. **Fac 74.** M 46. F 28. Wh 83%. Hisp 7%. Blk 8%. Asian 1%. Other 1%. Adv deg: 77%. **Grad '04**—235. Col—205. Avg SAT: 1011. Avg ACT: 19. Alum 10,000. **Tui '04-'05:** Day $6300 (+$300). Aid: Merit 500 ($420,000). Need 350 ($240,000). Work prgm 35 ($52,498). **Summer:** Rev Rem. Tui Day $150/half-credit. 3 wks. **Est 1889.** Nonprofit. Roman Catholic. Sem. This Catholic high school offers coordinated single-gender programs at two distinct locations: the boys' campus at 3434 S. Michigan Ave., and the girls' campus at 1040 W. 32nd Pl., 60608. All pursuits aside from academics—activities, sporting events and Masses, for example—are conducted in a coeducational setting. The varied college preparatory curriculum enables qualified students to take both Advanced Placement courses and classes for college credit through St. Mary's University in Winona, MN. A well-established athletic program provides competition in approximately two dozen sports; other activities include school publications, arts clubs and service opportunities.

HOLY TRINITY HIGH SCHOOL
Day Coed Gr 9-12
Chicago, IL 60622. 1443 W Division St.
Tel: 773-278-4212. Fax: 773-278-0144.
www.holytrinity-hs.org   E-mail: mstratman@holytrinity-hs.org
Thomas V. Bednar, Pres. Melinda Stratman & Linda Bannon, Adms.

Col Prep. AP—Eng Span Calc. **Feat**—Astron Environ_Sci Comp_Sci Econ Govt Psych Relig Studio_Art Theater_Arts Music. **Supp**—Dev_Read ESL Rem_Math Rem_Read Rev Tut. **Adm:** 150/yr. Appl due: Jan. Accepted: 80%. **Enr 400.** Sec 400. Wh 10%. Hisp 50%. Blk 40%. Avg class size: 20. Uniform. **Fac 30.** M 16. F 14. Adv deg: 70%. **Grad '04**—95. Col—95. Alum 6000. **Tui '04-'05:** Day $5600 (+$300-400). Aid: Merit 50 ($112,100). Need 375 ($500,000). **Summer:** Acad Rev. Tui Day $85. 5 wks. **Est 1910.** Nonprofit. Roman Catholic. Quar (Aug-June). **Assoc** NCA. Conducted by the Brothers of Holy Cross, Holy Trinity offers a structured, rigorous college prep and general education curriculum. Among the courses required for graduation are religion, humanities, computers and consumer education. Beyond academics, students are required to participate in community service ministry within their local neighborhoods. Various student activities and competitive sports are also available.

LUTHER HIGH SCHOOL NORTH
Day Coed Gr 9-12
Chicago, IL 60634. 5700 W Berteau Ave.
Tel: 773-286-3600. Fax: 773-286-0304.
www.luthernorth.org   E-mail: jdaley@luthernorth.org
Jeffrey D. Daley, Prin. MA, Concordia Univ River Forest, PhD, Univ of Texas-Austin. Ronald Schaefer, Adm.

Col Prep. Gen Acad. AP—Eng Chem Psych US_Govt & Pol. **Feat**—Span Anat & Physiol Environ_Sci Comp_Sci Sociol Theol Fine_Arts Accounting Bus. **Supp**—Dev_Read LD Rem_Math Rem_Read Tut. **Adm:** 90/yr. Appl due: July. Accepted: 80%. Yield: 80%. **Tests** Stanford. **Enr 260.** B 151. G 109. Sec 260. Wh 71%. Hisp 17%. Blk 8%. Am Ind 1%. Asian 2%. Other 1%. Avg class size: 16. **Fac 24.** M 11/1. F 11/1. Wh 100%. Adv deg: 62%. **Grad '04**—78. Col—70. Avg ACT: 22. **Tui '04-'05:** Day $6400 (+$600). Aid: Merit 63. Need 60. **Summer:** Acad Enrich Rem Rec. 6-12 wks. **Est 1909.** Nonprofit. Lutheran-Missouri Synod. Sem (Aug-June). Luther North offers two diplomas, each with distinct graduation requirements: the standard high school diploma and the more rigorous college preparatory diploma. Boys and girls typically select their program of study in the spring of sophomore year. Band, chorus and drama are among the school's arts electives.

LUTHER HIGH SCHOOL SOUTH
Day Coed Gr 9-12
Chicago, IL 60652. 3130 W 87th St.
Tel: 773-737-1416. Fax: 773-737-2882.
www.luthersouth.org   E-mail: info@luthersouth.org
Anthony Rainey, Exec Dir. MEd.

Col Prep. AP—Eng Bio. **Feat**—British_Lit Fr Span Ecol Comp_Sci Psych Theol World_Relig Fine_Arts. **Supp**—Dev_Read Rem_Math Rem_Read Rev Tut. **Adm:** 84/yr. Appl due: Aug. **Enr 230.** B 124. G 106. Sec 230. Wh 1%. Blk 99%. Avg class size: 22. **Fac 21.** M 11. F 10. Wh 47%. Blk 52%. Other 1%. Adv deg:

52%. **Grad '04**—37. Col—35. Avg ACT: 18. **Tui '04-'05:** Day $5570 (+$650). **Summer:** Acad Rev Rem. 6 wks. **Est 1951.** Nonprofit. Lutheran. Sem (Aug-June). **Assoc** NCA. The curriculum at Luther South, which emphasizes college preparation, includes course work in theology, consumer education, the fine arts and computers. Students are encouraged to pursue special interests and choose from a number of activities, including band, poetry club, gospel choir, drama club, publications, interscholastic sports, academic clubs, student council and community service. An affiliated junior high division serves boys and girls in grades 7 and 8.

NORTH SHORE SCHOOL   Day Coed Gr PS-8
Chicago, IL 60626. 1217 W Chase Ave.
Tel: 773-274-5143. Fax: 773-274-5144.
www.northshoreschool.org   E-mail: info@northshoreschool.org
   Frances D. Wilkinson, Dir. BA, Northwestern Univ.

Pre-Prep. Feat—Great_Books Fr Computers Music. **Supp**—Tut. **Adm:** Appl due: Rolling. **Enr 100.** B 70. G 30. Elem 100. Wh 77%. Hisp 3%. Blk 15%. Asian 5%. Avg class size: 13. Uniform. **Fac 20.** M 3. F 15/2. Adv deg: 30%. **Grad '04—5. Tui '04-'05:** Day $5800-9000 (+$300). **Summer:** Rec. Tui Day $400/4-wk ses. 8 wks. **Est 1938.** Nonprofit. Sem (Sept-June). North Shore accepts average to gifted students and provides a structured enrichment curriculum. The faculty consists of special teachers for French, computer, science lab, physical education and music for each grade. The Junior Great Books program is included in grades 3-8. Drama club, camera club, chess, bowling, ice skating and team sports are part of the after-school program, and private piano and dance classes are available.

ST. IGNATIUS COLLEGE PREP   Day Coed Gr 9-12
Chicago, IL 60608. 1076 W Roosevelt Rd.
Tel: 312-421-5900. Fax: 312-421-7124.
www.ignatius.org   E-mail: staff@ignatius.org
   Rev. Brian G. Paulson, SJ, Pres. Catherine Karl, Prin. Claire Larmon, Adm.

Col Prep. AP—Eng Fr Lat Span Stats Comp_Sci Bio Chem Physics Eur_Hist US_Hist Comp_Govt & Pol Econ Studio_Art. **Feat**—British_Lit Creative_Writing Shakespeare Greek Anat & Physiol Astron Environ_Sci Genetics African-Amer_Hist World_Relig Film Photog Acting Chorus Music Dance Journ. **Supp**—Tut. **Adm:** 376/yr. Appl due: Mar. Accepted: 60%. **Enr 1321.** B 653. G 668. Sec 1321. Wh 74%. Hisp 10%. Blk 10%. Asian 6%. Avg class size: 25. **Fac 82.** M 43/3. F 31/5. Adv deg: 75%. **Grad '04**—312. Col—307. Avg SAT: 1200. Alum 17,500. **Tui '04-'05:** Day $8800 (+$400). Aid: Need 297 ($1,900,000). **Summer:** Acad Enrich Rem Rec. 6 wks. **Est 1870.** Nonprofit. Roman Catholic. Sem (Aug-June). **Assoc** NCA. St. Ignatius' curriculum reflects a liberal arts tradition in which mandatory foreign language and religious studies courses are supplemented by required classes in speech, the fine arts and computers. Juniors and seniors may take honors and AP courses. Students participate in a variety of community service projects.

SAINT PATRICK HIGH SCHOOL
Day Boys Gr 9-12

Chicago, IL 60634. 5900 W Belmont Ave.
Tel: 773-282-8844. Fax: 773-282-2361.
www.stpatrick.org   E-mail: info@stpatrick.org

Br. Konrad Diebold, FSC, Pres. BA, MEd, St Mary's College (MN). Joseph Schmidt, Prin. BA, MS, EdS, EdD, Northern Illinois Univ. Daniel Galante, Adm.

Col Prep. AP—Eng Fr Ger Span Calc US_Hist US_Govt & Pol. **Feat**—Computers Econ Relig Fine_Arts Video_Production Acting Theater_Arts Accounting. **Supp**—Dev_Read ESL. **Adm:** 346/yr. Appl due: Jan. Accepted: 99%. **Enr 1035.** B 1035. Sec 1035. Wh 69%. Hisp 20%. Blk 4%. Asian 6%. Other 1%. Avg class size: 26. **Fac 64.** M 47. F 16/1. Wh 92%. Hisp 4%. Asian 4%. Adv deg: 53%. **Grad '04**— 210. Col—198. Avg ACT: 22. Alum 16,225. **Tui '04-'05:** Day $6500 (+$300). Aid: Need 241 ($400,000). **Summer:** Acad Enrich Rem. Tui Day $225-300/crse. 3½ wks. **Est 1861.** Nonprofit. Roman Catholic. Sem (Aug-June). **Assoc** NCA. Course work at this boys' Catholic school emphasizes college preparation, and Advanced Placement examinations are given each year. A special, limited-enrollment program is available to students who are ill prepared for the college preparatory program or who are working below grade level, and a computer education facility integrates all curricula with computer applications and software. Students participate in an array of interscholastic sports and other extracurricular pursuits.

ST. SCHOLASTICA ACADEMY
Day Girls Gr 9-12

Chicago, IL 60645. 7416 N Ridge Blvd.
Tel: 773-764-5715. Fax: 773-764-0304.
www.scholastica.us   E-mail: jfurgason@scholastica.us

Sr. Suzanne Zuercher, OSB, Pres. BA, MA, Loyola Univ of Chicago. Anne Matz, Prin. Jamie Furgason , Adm.

Col Prep. IB_Diploma. AP—Eng Fr Calc Bio US_Hist. **Feat**—Creative_Writing Geol Computers Psych Theol Acting Music Speech. **Supp**—Tut. **Adm:** 90/yr. Appl due: Aug. Accepted: 96%. **Tests** HSPT. **Enr 290.** G 290. Sec 290. Wh 35%. Hisp 22%. Blk 28%. Am Ind 2%. Asian 13%. Avg class size: 16. Uniform. **Fac 31.** M 3/1. F 24/3. Wh 98%. Other 2%. Adv deg: 61%. **Grad '04**—69. Col—68. Avg ACT: 22. Alum 8600. **Tui '04-'05:** Day $6980 (+$400). Aid: Merit 12 ($28,000). Need 106 ($245,000). **Summer:** Acad Rev Rem. Tui Day $460. 6 wks. **Est 1863.** Nonprofit. Roman Catholic. Quar (Aug-June). **Assoc** NCA. Owned and operated by the Benedictine Sisters of Chicago, SSA features a strong liberal arts curriculum with honors offerings. Academic units in science, math, literature, social studies, modern language, theology, fine arts or business education, consumer economics and speech are among the requirements. In addition, the International Baccalaureate program is available to qualified juniors and seniors. During the junior year, all students participate in an on-site service placement that is chosen based on their particular social concerns and personal skills.

THE WILLOWS ACADEMY
Day Girls Gr 6-12

Des Plaines, IL 60016. 1012 Thacker St.
Tel: 847-824-6900. Fax: 847-824-7089.
www.willows.org   E-mail: info@willows.org

Tina Verhelst, Head. Dorothy Boland, Adm.

Col Prep. Gen Acad. AP—Eng Fr Span Calc Bio Eur_Hist US_Hist. **Feat**—Stats Computers Econ Pol_Sci Ethics Theol Studio_Art Chorus Speech. **Adm:** 55/yr. Appl due: Rolling. **Tests** CTP_4. **Enr 218.** G 218. Elem 102. Sec 116. Wh 91%. Hisp 2%. Blk 6%. Asian 1%. Avg class size: 18. Uniform. **Fac 26.** M /1. F 21/4. Adv deg: 57%. **Grad '04—21.** Col—21. Avg SAT: 1180. Avg ACT: 25. Alum 495. **Tui '05-'06:** Day $8250-9450 (+$675). **Est 1974.** Nonprofit. Roman Catholic. Quar (Aug-June). With its classic liberal arts orientation, Willows' college preparatory curriculum offers courses at the honors or AP level in most disciplines. A low student-teacher ratio characterizes the program at all grade levels. Extracurricular activities such as student government, sports, theater, clubs, organizations and service projects complement academics.

FOX VALLEY LUTHERAN ACADEMY Day Coed Gr 9-12
Elgin, IL 60120. 220 Division St.
Tel: 847-468-8207. Fax: 847-742-2930.
www.fvla.com   E-mail: fvla_jz@yahoo.com
Janet R. Zimdahl, Prin. MAEd, Concordia Univ (IL).

Col Prep. Gen Acad. Feat—British_Lit Span Computers Geog Govt Psych Sociol Relig Theol Studio_Art Music Bus Speech. **Adm:** 9/yr. Appl due: Rolling. Accepted: 80%. **Enr 34.** Sec 34. Wh 85%. Hisp 9%. Blk 6%. Avg class size: 10. **Fac 10.** M 1/2. F 4/3. Wh 100%. Adv deg: 60%. **Grad '04—9.** Col—9. Alum 900. **Tui '05-'06:** Day $5600 (+$400). **Est 1974.** Nonprofit. Lutheran. Sem (Aug-May). Four years of Spanish are offered at this small school. Among FVLA's extracurricular activities are choir, handbells, drama, student council and student aiding. Sports include basketball, volleyball, track and cross-country. The academy emphasizes service learning and leadership skills development.

JOLIET CATHOLIC ACADEMY Day Coed Gr 9-12
Joliet, IL 60435. 1200 N Larkin Ave.
Tel: 815-741-0500. Fax: 815-741-8825.
www.jca-online.org   E-mail: sbebar@jca-online.org
Sr. Faith Szambelanczyk, OSF, Pres. BS, College of St Francis, MS, St Mary's Univ of Minnesota. Michael Nadeau, Prin. Kris Horn, Adm.

Col Prep. AP—Eng Calc Bio Chem US_Hist US_Govt & Pol. **Feat**—Fr Lat Span Comp_Design Comp_Sci Relig Music Journ. **Supp**—LD Tut. **Adm:** 261/yr. Accepted: 90%. **Enr 949.** B 542. G 407. Sec 949. Wh 90%. Hisp 5%. Blk 3%. Am Ind 1%. Asian 1%. Avg class size: 23. **Fac 69.** M 34. F 35. Wh 98%. Hisp 2%. Adv deg: 47%. **Grad '04—198.** Col—194. Alum 18,000. **Tui '04-'05:** Day $6445 (+$300). Aid: Merit 3 ($70,000). Need 320 ($2,500,000). **Summer:** Acad Enrich Rec. Sports. 3 wks. **Est 1990.** Nonprofit. Roman Catholic. Sem (Aug-June). **Assoc** NCA. The school resulted from the 1990 merger of Joliet Catholic High School for boys (founded in 1918) and St. Francis Academy for girls (established in 1869). JCA offers a strong college preparatory program that includes a four-year honors program and Advanced Placement courses in the major disciplines.

ILLIANA CHRISTIAN HIGH SCHOOL
Day Coed Gr 9-12
Lansing, IL 60438. 2261 Indiana Ave.
Tel: 708-474-0515. Fax: 708-474-0581.
www.illianachristian.org   E-mail: peter.boonstra@illianachristian.org
Peter E. Boonstra, Prin.

Col Prep. Gen Acad. Bus. AP—Eng Ger Span Calc Chem US_Govt & Pol. **Feat**—Environ_Sci Computers Programming Econ Bible Accounting Bus. **Supp**—LD Tut. **Adm:** 215/yr. **Enr 675.** Sec 675. Wh 97%. Hisp 1%. Blk 1%. Asian 1%. Avg class size: 24. **Fac 45.** M 27. F 15/3. Adv deg: 64%. **Grad '04—170.** Col—122. Avg ACT: 24. Alum 6550. **Tui '04-'05:** Day $6125 (+$150). Aid: Need 12 ($12,600). **Est 1945.** Nonprofit. Nondenom Christian. Sem (Aug-June). **Assoc** NCA. Serving the local Reformed Christian community, this school emphasizes college preparation through a varied curriculum that features honors and AP courses in several disciplines. Although foreign language course work is not compulsory, Illiana Christian offers four years of both German and Spanish. Competitive boys' and girls' athletics are among the school's extracurriculars.

MOUNT ASSISI ACADEMY
Day Girls Gr 9-12
Lemont, IL 60439. 13860 Main St.
Tel: 630-257-7844. Fax: 630-257-6362.
www.mtassisiacademy.org   E-mail: maaprin@mtassisiacademy.org
Sr. M. Francine Hribar, OSF, Pres. BA, College of St Francis, MEd, DePaul Univ, MA, Marquette Univ. Sr. Mary Francis Werner, OSF, Prin.

Col Prep. Gen Acad. AP—Eng Fr Span Calc US_Hist. **Feat**—British_Lit Stats Anat & Physiol Environ_Sci Govt Psych Sociol Relig Studio_Art Music Journ. **Supp**—Rem_Math Rem_Read Rev Tut. **Adm:** 88/yr. Appl due: Aug. Accepted: 99%. **Enr 311.** G 311. Sec 311. Wh 94%. Hisp 4%. Other 2%. Avg class size: 22. Uniform. **Fac 28.** M 3. F 18/7. Wh 100%. Adv deg: 75%. **Grad '04—93.** Col—90. Avg ACT: 23. Alum 4345. **Tui '04-'05:** Day $5250 (+$400-500). Aid: Merit 3 ($1500). Need 6 ($5000). **Summer:** Acad Enrich Rec. Sports. 1-4 wks. **Est 1951.** Nonprofit. Roman Catholic. Sem (Aug-May). **Assoc** NCA. Established by the School Sisters of St. Francis of Christ the King, this girls' school continues to emphasize Franciscan ideals. Students pursue course work in three distinct programs: basic, academic and honors. Athletic offerings and extracurricular clubs and organizations supplement academics.

BENET ACADEMY
Day Coed Gr 9-12
Lisle, IL 60532. 2200 Maple Ave.
Tel: 630-969-6550. Fax: 630-719-0929.
www.benet.org   E-mail: jbrown@benet.org
Ernest Stark, Prin. BA, MEd, St Mary College, MA, Manhattan College. James Brown, Adm.

Col Prep. AP—Eng Calc Stats Bio US_Hist. **Feat**—Fr Ger Lat Span Computers Relig Band Chorus Bus. **Adm:** 356/yr. Appl due: Dec. Accepted: 58%. **Tests** HSPT. **Enr 1290.** B 653. G 637. Sec 1290. Wh 70%. Hisp 8%. Blk 1%. Asian 21%. Avg class size: 26. Uniform. **Fac 69.** M 40. F 29. Wh 100%. Adv deg: 82%. **Grad '04—309.** Col—309. Avg SAT: 1252. Avg ACT: 27. Alum 900. **Tui '03-'04:** Day $6000

(+$500). Aid: Need 27 ($41,000). **Est 1887.** Nonprofit. Roman Catholic. Sem (Aug-June). **Assoc** NCA. This Benedictine academy is closely affiliated with Benedictine University, which provides additional educational opportunities, advanced courses, increased library facilities and other collegiate advantages. Students may earn up to 24 college credits while still attending the academy by enrolling in courses at the university. All students take four years of religion.

MONTINI CATHOLIC HIGH SCHOOL Day Coed Gr 9-12
Lombard, IL 60148. 19 W 070 16th St.
Tel: 630-627-6930. Fax: 630-627-0537.
www.montini.org   E-mail: info@montini.org

James F. Segredo, Pres. BA, MEd, Univ of Illinois-Chicago. Maryann O'Neill, Prin. Michael Bukovsky, Adm.

Col Prep. AP—Eng Span Calc Bio Chem Eur_Hist US_Hist Econ US_Govt & Pol. **Feat**—Creative_Writing Fr Stats Environ_Sci Programming Web_Design Psych Sociol Theol Film Studio_Art Music. **Supp**—Dev_Read Rem_Math Rem_Read Rev Tut. **Adm (Gr 9-11):** 192/yr. Appl due: Rolling. Accepted: 92%. **Tests** HSPT. **Enr 665.** B 342. G 323. Sec 665. Wh 92%. Hisp 3%. Blk 1%. Asian 4%. Avg class size: 20. Uniform. **Fac 50.** M 25/1. F 22/2. Wh 97%. Hisp 3%. Adv deg: 74%. **Grad '04**—155. Col—153. Avg ACT: 23. Alum 5000. **Tui '04-'05:** Day $6900 (+$600). Aid: Need 80 ($95,000). Work prgm 20 ($20,000). **Summer:** Acad Enrich Rem Rec. Tui Day $200/crse. 6 wks. **Est 1966.** Nonprofit. Roman Catholic. Sem (Aug-June). **Assoc** NCA. This college preparatory school, named in honor of Pope Paul VI (whose family name was Montini), offers students a traditional curriculum supplemented by four years of religion. All juniors participate in a two-day retreat program consisting of prayer, community building, confession, Mass and recreation. Electives include applied design, band, typing and popular music. Athletic options are varied.

CHRISTIAN HERITAGE ACADEMY Day Coed Gr PS-8
Northfield, IL 60093. 315 Waukegan Rd.
Tel: 847-446-5252. Fax: 847-446-5267.
www.christian-heritage-academy.org
E-mail: admissions@christian-heritage-academy.org

Nancy A. Goodman, Admin. BS, Ashland Univ, MEd, National-Louis Univ. Laurie Peterson, Adm.

Gen Acad. Feat—Span Computers Geog Bible Fine_Arts Music Speech Study_Skills. **Supp**—Dev_Read Rem_Math Rem_Read Rev Tut. **Adm:** 86/yr. Appl due: Rolling. Accepted: 96%. **Enr 394.** B 215. G 179. Elem 394. Wh 80%. Hisp 1%. Blk 1%. Asian 17%. Other 1%. Avg class size: 16. **Fac 36.** M 3/2. F 23/8. Wh 99%. Asian 1%. Adv deg: 36%. **Grad '04**—58. Alum 325. **Tui '04-'05:** Day $7350-7450 (+$200-300). Aid: Need 68 ($211,305). **Summer:** Enrich Rec. 2-3 wks. **Est 1983.** Nonprofit. Evangelical. Quar (Aug-June). This nondenominational, parent-governed, evangelical Christian school integrates Bible instruction into all subject areas. Students attend weekly chapel services and convene once a month for all-school chapel. An annual sixth grade excursion to Eagle River, WI, focuses on outdoor science education, while a yearly eighth grade trip to Washington, DC, and Gettysburg, VA, enhances social studies and literature study.

FENWICK HIGH SCHOOL
Day Coed Gr 9-12
Oak Park, IL 60302. 505 W Washington Blvd.
Tel: 708-386-0127. Fax: 708-386-3052.
www.fenwickfriars.com   E-mail: admin@fenwickfriars.com
   Rev. Richard C. LaPata, OP, Pres. James J. Quaid, Prin. BA, Benedictine Univ, MA, Purdue Univ, MEd, PhD, Loyola Univ of Chicago. Patrick Van De Walle, Adm.

   Col Prep. AP—Eng Fr Span Calc Stats Comp_Sci Bio Chem Physics Eur_Hist US_Hist World_Hist Econ US_Govt & Pol Art_Hist. **Feat**—British_Lit Creative_Writing Ger Ital Lat Anat & Physiol Marine_Biol/Sci Theol Music_Hist. **Supp**—Tut. **Adm (Gr 9-11):** 310/yr. Appl due: Jan. Accepted: 65%. Yield: 83%. **Tests** HSPT. **Enr 1152.** B 649. G 503. Sec 1152. Avg class size: 17. Uniform. **Fac 79.** M 35/12. F 22/10. Wh 94%. Hisp 1%. Blk 3%. Am Ind 1%. Other 1%. Adv deg: 73%.Avg ACT: 26. Alum 10,000. **Tui '04-'05:** Day $8150. Aid: Need 288. **Summer:** Acad Enrich Rev Rem Rec. 5-6 wks. **Est 1929.** Nonprofit. Roman Catholic. Sem (Aug-June). Founded and still sponsored by the Dominican Friars, Fenwick provides students with a thorough grounding in English, math, computer science, foreign language, history and theology. Boys and girls take theology each year, and each junior fulfills a 40-hour Christian service requirement; half of this commitment may be completed during the summer prior to junior year. School publications, student council, drama club, choir, academic clubs, speech and debate teams, scholastic bowl, chess club and photography club are among the school's activities.

CHICAGO CHRISTIAN HIGH SCHOOL
Day Coed Gr 9-12
Palos Heights, IL 60463. 12001 S Oak Park Ave.
Tel: 708-388-7656. Fax: 708-388-0452.
www.swchristian.org   E-mail: cbrott@swchristian.org
   Robert Payne, Supt. Connie Brott, Adm.

   Col Prep. Gen Acad. AP—Eng Calc Bio US_Hist US_Govt & Pol. **Feat**—Fr Span Web_Design. **Supp**—Rev. **Adm:** 71/yr. Appl due: July. Accepted: 90%. Yield: 95%. **Tests** IQ. **Enr 478.** B 232. G 246. Sec 478. Wh 89%. Hisp 1%. Blk 9%. Asian 1%. Avg class size: 22. **Fac 34.** M 18. F 15/1. Wh 100%. Adv deg: 58%. **Grad '04—118.** Col—112. Avg ACT: 23. Alum 7200. **Tui '04-'05:** Day $6680. **Est 1901.** Nonprofit. Nondenom Christian. Quar (Aug-June). Serving a student body consisting entirely of practicing Christians from many different churches, CCHS offers a college preparatory program with a block scheduling approach that consists of four 85-minute classes daily. Bible is part of the daily curriculum, and all pupils attend chapel with staff once a week. Boys' sports are football, cross-country, tennis, golf, basketball, soccer, track and field, and baseball, while girls' offerings are volleyball, cross-country, tennis, basketball, soccer, softball, track and field, and cheerleading.

QUINCY NOTRE DAME HIGH SCHOOL
Day Coed Gr 9-12
Quincy, IL 62301. 1400 S 11th St.
Tel: 217-223-2479. Fax: 217-223-0023.
www.quincynotredame.org   E-mail: rheilmann@quincynotredame.org
   Raymond E. Heilmann, Prin. BA, MA, Northern Illinois Univ.

Col Prep. AP—Calc US_Hist. **Feat**—Ger Span Computers Psych Relig. **Supp**—Rem_Math Rem_Read Tut. **Adm:** 140/yr. Appl due: Aug. Accepted: 100%. **Enr 501.** B 264. G 237. Sec 501. Wh 98%. Other 2%. Avg class size: 23. **Fac 32.** M 15/4. F 12/1. Wh 99%. Other 1%. Adv deg: 46%. **Grad '04—128.** Col—114. Avg ACT: 22. **Tui '04-'05:** Day $3750 (+$300). Aid: Merit 1 ($3500). Need 117 ($91,000). Work prgm 6 ($6000). **Summer:** Rem. 6 wks. **Est 1959.** Nonprofit. Roman Catholic. Sem (Aug-May). **Assoc** NCA. Students at QND participate in a wide range of activities. Upper-level college preparatory offerings, as well as business, art and vocational courses, are available. Advanced Placement calculus and US history are offered. Extracurricular activities include student council and publications, as well as language, interest, service and career clubs.

TRINITY HIGH SCHOOL   Day Girls Gr 9-12
River Forest, IL 60305. 7574 W Division St.
Tel: 708-771-8383. Fax: 708-488-2014.
www.trinityhs.org   E-mail: trinity@trinityhs.org

Sr. Michelle Germanson, OP, Pres. BA, Edgewood College, MS, Loras College, MPS, Loyola Univ of Chicago. Michele Whitehead, Prin. MA, Loyola Univ of Chicago.

Col Prep. IB_Diploma. Feat—British_Lit Fr Ital Span Stats Econ Pol_Sci Psych Sociol Women's_Stud Theol World_Relig Ceramics Drawing Sculpt Drama Journ Speech. **Supp**—Tut. **Adm:** 120/yr. Appl due: Aug. Accepted: 95%. **Enr 480.** G 480. Sec 480. Wh 70%. Hisp 14%. Blk 10%. Asian 2%. Other 4%. Avg class size: 15. Uniform. **Fac 52.** M 5/1. F 36/10. Wh 96%. Hisp 4%. Adv deg: 76%. **Grad '04—133.** Col—132. Alum 9500. **Tui '04-'05:** Day $7500. Aid: Merit 24 ($21,700). Need 121 ($182,500). Work prgm 100 ($4000). **Est 1918.** Nonprofit. Roman Catholic. Quar (Aug-June). Drawing girls from Chicago and approximately 30 other communities, Trinity employs block scheduling, which allows students to meet for extended class periods while focusing on fewer classes at a time. Another noteworthy feature of the curriculum is the school's International Baccalaureate Program. Qualified juniors and seniors may take part in this program, which combines rigorous academics with a 150-hour community service requirement and often leads to advanced standing in college.

WHEATON ACADEMY   Day Coed Gr 9-12
West Chicago, IL 60185. 900 Prince Crossing Rd.
Tel: 630-562-7500. Fax: 630-231-0842.
www.wheatonacademy.org   E-mail: generalinfo@wheatonacademy.org

David L. Roth, Head. MA, EdD, Northern Illinois Univ. Jon Keith, Prin. David Underwood, Adm.

Col Prep. Gen Acad. AP—Eng Span Calc Bio. **Feat**—Humanities Fr Greek Comp_Sci Econ Relig Ceramics Drawing Studio_Art Music Music_Theory. **Supp**—LD Rev Tut. **Adm:** 167/yr. Appl due: Rolling. Accepted: 85%. Yield: 92%. **Enr 556.** B 249. G 307. Sec 556. Wh 92%. Hisp 2%. Blk 2%. Asian 2%. Other 2%. Avg class size: 20. **Fac 42.** M 15/4. F 17/6. Adv deg: 71%. **Grad '04—118.** Col—116. Avg ACT: 23. Alum 3636. **Tui '04-'05:** Day $9150 (+$515). Aid: Merit 18 ($27,000). Need 159 ($577,592). **Summer:** Acad Enrich. Tui Day $250. 3 wks. **Est 1853.** Nonprofit. Evangelical. Sem (Aug-June). **Assoc** NCA. This Christian school offers traditional academic and college preparatory curricula. Between semesters, a two-and-a-half-week interim period allows for concentrated and in-depth study, trips and internships. Six credits of Bible study are required, and all courses are interspersed with relevant Biblical themes. Weekly devotional chapels are compulsory. Students may participate in the full athletic program, drama productions, musical groups and tours, school organizations, and class activities and retreats.

ST. FRANCIS HIGH SCHOOL   **Day Coed Gr 9-12**
Wheaton, IL 60187. 2130 W Roosevelt Rd.
Tel: 630-668-5800. Fax: 630-668-5893.
www.sfhsnet.org   E-mail: tlynch@sfhsnet.org
    Raeann Huhn, Prin. BS, Eastern Illinois Univ, MS, Northern Illinois Univ. Meg Olsen, Adm.

    Col Prep. AP—Calc Stats Bio Chem Physics Psych US_Govt & Pol Music_ Theory. **Feat**—Fr Span Programming Econ Accounting. **Supp**—Tut. **Adm (Gr 9-11):** 191/yr. Appl due: Jan. **Tests** HSPT. **Enr 731.** B 360. G 371. Sec 731. Wh 94%. Hisp 2%. Blk 1%. Asian 2%. Other 1%. Uniform. **Fac 51.** M 19/5. F 21/6. Wh 99%. Hisp 1%. Adv deg: 54%. **Grad '04**—**150.** Avg SAT: 1172. Avg ACT: 24. Alum 6678. **Tui '04-'05:** Day $6300 (+$1000). Aid: Merit 8 ($12,000). Need 30 ($40,000). Work prgm 8 ($6000). **Est 1956.** Nonprofit. Roman Catholic. Sem (Aug-June). **Assoc** NCA. Operated by the Diocese of Joliet, St. Francis offers honors and Advanced Placement courses. The athletic program includes both interscholastic and intramural choices, while various class and social activities enable participation in clubs, publications, student government and theater, among others. An annual summer trip to Europe is taken alternately by French and Spanish classes.

LOYOLA ACADEMY   **Day Coed Gr 9-12**
Wilmette, IL 60091. 1100 N Laramie Ave.
Tel: 847-256-1100. Fax: 847-920-2552.
www.goramblers.org   E-mail: lseitzinger@loy.org
    Rev. Theodore G. Munz, SJ, Pres. STM, MBA, MDiv. Rev. Terrence Baum, SJ, Head. Les Seitzinger, Adm.

    Col Prep. AP—Eng Fr Lat Span Calc Stats Comp_Sci Bio Chem Physics Eur_Hist World_Hist Comp_Govt & Pol Art_Hist Studio_Art. **Feat**—British_Lit Shakespeare Ger Greek Anat & Physiol Genetics Ethics Theol Film Fine_Arts Theater Chorus Music Dance Communications. **Supp**—Tut. **Adm:** 500/yr. Appl due: Rolling. Accepted: 88%. **Enr 2000.** B 1050. G 950. Sec 2000. Wh 80%. Hisp 8%. Blk 3%. Asian 8%. Other 1%. **Fac 150.** Adv deg: 76%. **Grad '04**—**490.** Col—485. Alum 20,000. **Tui '05-'06:** Day $9650 (+$600). Aid: Need 350 ($800,000). **Summer:** Acad Enrich Rem Rec. 6 wks. **Est 1909.** Nonprofit. Roman Catholic. Quar (Aug-June). **Assoc** NCA. Founded by Rev. Henry J. Dumbach, SJ on the present campus of Loyola University of Chicago, and later moved to its 26-acre site in Wilmette, the academy offers an education in the classical liberal arts. Special features of its curriculum are the Dumbach Scholars Program, for gifted and talented students, and the O'Shaughnessy Program of developmental learning, for students who need a more integrated, structured and sequential learning program. Cocurricular clubs and activities are provided, and Loyola fields interscholastic teams in a variety of sports.

INDIANA

BISHOP DWENGER HIGH SCHOOL Day Coed Gr 9-12
Fort Wayne, IN 46825. 1300 E Washington Center Rd.
Tel: 260-496-4700. Fax: 260-496-4702.
www.bishopdwenger.com   E-mail: bdhs@bishopdwenger.com
   J. Fred Tone, Prin. BA, MEd, Indiana Univ.

   Col Prep. Gen Acad. AP—Eng Calc Stats Bio Chem. **Feat**—Fr Lat Span Anat & Physiol Genetics Econ Relig Theol Ceramics Fine_Arts Music. **Supp**—Dev_Read Rem_Math Rem_Read Rev Tut. **Adm:** 258/yr. Accepted: 100%. **Tests** TOEFL. **Enr 1026.** B 507. G 519. Sec 1026. Wh 95%. Hisp 2%. Blk 1%. Am Ind 1%. Asian 1%. Avg class size: 28. Uniform. **Fac 59.** M 22/3. F 31/3. Wh 98%. Hisp 1%. Other 1%. Adv deg: 49%. **Grad '04—245.** Col—218. Avg SAT: 1055. Avg ACT: 24. Alum 7500. **Tui '04-'05:** Day $4985 (+$940). Parishioners $3555 (+$940). Aid: Merit 10 ($5000). Need 240 ($285,000). **Summer:** Acad Rem. Tui Day $250/4-wk ses. 8 wks. **Est 1963.** Nonprofit. Roman Catholic. Sem (Aug-May). **Assoc** NCA. Bishop Dwenger's weighted curriculum offers remedial, honors and Advanced Placement courses. Advanced Placement is the areas of English, math and science. Cocurricular activities include athletic programs, academic teams, band, choir, drama, student government and school publications, in addition to language, interest and service clubs.

BISHOP LUERS HIGH SCHOOL Day Coed Gr 9-12
Fort Wayne, IN 46816. 333 E Paulding Rd.
Tel: 260-456-1261. Fax: 260-456-1262.
www.bishopluers.org   E-mail: tedgerton@bishopluers.org
   Mary Keefer, Prin. BA, MA, Indiana Univ–Purdue Univ Fort Wayne.

   Col Prep. AP—Eng Calc Bio Chem US_Govt & Pol. **Feat**—Creative_Writing Fr Lat Span Computers Psych Sociol Theol Studio_Art Theater Music Accounting Bus Design. **Supp**—LD Rem_Math Rev Tut. **Adm:** 150/yr. Appl due: Jan. Accepted: 95%. **Enr 569.** Sec 569. Wh 87%. Hisp 4%. Blk 6%. Asian 1%. Other 2%. Avg class size: 20. **Fac 44.** M 15/2. F 22/5. Adv deg: 56%. **Grad '04—106.** Col—100. Alum 6000. **Tui '04-'05:** Day $3425 (+$700). Aid: Merit 72 ($22,450). Work prgm 55 ($11,325). **Est 1958.** Nonprofit. Roman Catholic. Sem (Aug-May). **Assoc** NCA. BLHS offers courses at three levels: honors, academic and basic. The college preparatory curriculum includes advanced classes in math, science, social studies and English, and students take theology each semester. Vocational training is also available at Bishop Luers through a cooperative program with the Fort Wayne Community Schools' Anthis Career Center.

CONCORDIA LUTHERAN HIGH SCHOOL Day Coed Gr 9-12
Fort Wayne, IN 46805. 1601 St Joe River Dr.
Tel: 260-483-1102. Fax: 260-471-0180.
www.clhscadets.com
   David Widenhofer, Exec Dir. BA, Concordia Univ, MS, Univ of Wisconsin–Madison, MAR, Concordia Seminary. John Marks, Prin. David Koenig, Adm.

Col Prep. Gen Acad. AP—Eng Fr Ger Span Calc Stats Bio Chem Physics US_Hist US_Govt & Pol. **Feat**—Lat Comp_Sci Relig TV_Graphics & Animation TV_Production JROTC. **Supp**—Tut. **Adm:** 183/yr. Appl due: Rolling. Accepted: 95%. **Enr 702.** B 362. G 340. Sec 702. Wh 87%. Hisp 1%. Blk 8%. Asian 2%. Other 2%. Avg class size: 21. **Fac 47.** M 20/1. F 20/6. Wh 100%. Adv deg: 57%. **Grad '04—182.** Col—170. Avg SAT: 1094. Avg ACT: 24. Alum 8941. **Tui '04-'05:** Day $4700-6550 (+$300). Aid: Merit 20. Need 197. **Summer:** Acad. Tui Day $250/3-wk ses. 6 wks. **Est 1935.** Nonprofit. Lutheran. Sem (Aug-June). **Assoc** NCA. Concordia's curriculum includes JROTC, remedial courses and courses for the gifted, as well as honors classes in all academic areas. Extracurricular activities include varsity sports, choir, bands, orchestra, speech and drama.

KEYSTONE SCHOOLS Day Coed Gr PS-12
Fort Wayne, IN 46805. 1800 Laverne Ave.
Tel: 260-424-4523. Fax: 260-424-4525.
www.keystoneschools.org   E-mail: info@keystoneschools.org
Martin P. Gigler, Prin. BA, MS, City Univ of New York.

Col Prep. Feat—Creative_Writing Fr Span Computers Govt/Econ Bible Bus Journ. **Supp**—Tut. **Adm:** 48/yr. Appl due: Rolling. Accepted: 90%. **Enr 199.** Elem 144. Sec 55. Wh 83%. Blk 4%. Am Ind 1%. Other 12%. Avg class size: 13. **Fac 28.** M 4/1. F 17/6. Wh 93%. Blk 7%. Adv deg: 25%. **Grad '04—14.** Col—13. Alum 406. **Tui '04-'05:** Day $4275-4951 (+$100). Aid: Need 35 ($26,240). **Est 1967.** Nonprofit. Nondenom Christian. Sem (Aug-June). Located on two campuses, the school conducts a curriculum that includes Bible study, the fine arts and computer instruction. The main campus occupies quarters at the Laverne Avenue location, while the southwest campus (serving grades 1-4) is situated at 5421 Homestead Rd., 46814.

BREBEUF JESUIT PREPARATORY SCHOOL Day Coed Gr 9-12
Indianapolis, IN 46268. 2801 W 86th St.
Tel: 317-872-7050. Fax: 317-876-4728.
www.brebeuf.org   E-mail: admissions@brebeuf.org
Rev. Benjamin Hawley, SJ, Pres. Andrew Noga, Prin. Diantha Daniels, Adm.

Col Prep. AP—Eng Fr Span Calc Bio Chem Physics US_Hist Econ US_Govt & Pol Studio_Art. **Feat**—Ger Computers Relig Performing_Arts Speech. **Supp**—Rev Tut. **Adm:** 195/yr. Appl due: Dec. Accepted: 70%. **Tests** HSPT. **Enr 808.** B 412. G 396. Sec 808. Wh 85%. Hisp 3%. Blk 10%. Asian 2%. Avg class size: 24. **Fac 75.** M 27/1. F 43/4. Wh 93%. Hisp 3%. Blk 2%. Other 2%. Adv deg: 56%. **Grad '04—159.** Col—159. Avg SAT: 1210. Avg ACT: 26. Alum 5200. **Tui '05-'06:** Day $10,200 (+$250-600). Aid: Merit 3 ($20,685). Need 217 ($576,309). Work prgm 95 ($93,977). **Summer:** Acad. Tui Day $450/4-wk ses. 8 wks. **Est 1962.** Nonprofit. Roman Catholic. Sem (Aug-June). **Assoc** NCA. Qualified students at Brebeuf may earn college credits in English, languages, political science, US history, biology and chemistry through programs with St. Louis and Indiana universities.

LUTHERAN HIGH SCHOOL   **Day Coed Gr 9-12**
Indianapolis, IN 46237. 5555 S Arlington Ave.
Tel: 317-787-5474. Fax: 317-787-2794.
www.lhsi.org   E-mail: lhsi@lhsi.org

     David Beringer, Exec Dir. BA, Concordia Univ River Forest, MA, Concordia Univ Wisconsin.

     Col Prep. Gen Acad. Bus. AP—Calc Comp_Sci Bio Chem. **Feat**—British_Lit Humanities ASL Ger Japan Span Stats Anat & Physiol Environ_Sci Psych Sociol Relig Ceramics Sculpt Studio_Art Music_Theory Accounting. **Supp**—Makeup Tut. **Adm:** 92/yr. Appl due: Mar. Accepted: 100%. **Enr 293.** B 133. G 160. Sec 293. Wh 95%. Blk 1%. Asian 3%. Other 1%. Avg class size: 22. Uniform. **Fac 21.** M 12/1. F 7/1. Wh 95%. Asian 5%. Adv deg: 61%. **Grad '04—64.** Col—48. Avg SAT: 1047. Avg ACT: 23. **Tui '04-'05:** Day $6900 (+$300). Aid: Need 175 ($130,000). **Est 1976.** Nonprofit. Lutheran. Sem (Aug-May). Advanced Placement and honors courses are part of the school's college preparatory program. Drama, vocal and instrumental music, and such sports as cross-country, golf, soccer, tennis, volleyball, basketball, wrestling, baseball, softball, tennis and track are among Lutheran's extracurricular options.

FOREST RIDGE ACADEMY   **Day Coed Gr PS-8**
Schererville, IN 46375. 7300 Forest Ridge Dr.
Tel: 219-756-7300. Fax: 219-756-2365.
www.fra.edu   E-mail: mleitelt@netnitco.net

     Cindy Arnold, Head. BS, Ball State Univ. Diane Shultz, Adm.

     Pre-Prep. Gen Acad. Feat—Lib_Skills ASL Span Computers Studio_Art Chorus Music Orchestra Piano. **Supp**—Dev_Read Tut. **Adm:** 36/yr. Appl due: Apr. **Tests** IQ. **Enr 170.** B 96. G 74. Elem 170. Wh 67%. Hisp 2%. Blk 13%. Asian 18%. Avg class size: 14. Uniform. **Fac 25.** M 1. F 24. Adv deg: 52%. **Grad '04—10.** Prep—9. Alum 120. **Tui '04-'05:** Day $9530 (+$200). Aid: Need 16 ($70,000). **Summer:** Acad Enrich Rev Rem. Tui Day $500/4-wk ses. **Est 1982.** Nonprofit. Sem (Aug-June). **Assoc** NCA. FRA's academic program comprises a core curriculum of language arts, mathematics, social studies and science that is supplemented by Spanish, computer, physical education, art and music classes at all grade levels. Forest Ridge students participate in a number of field trips each year, and extracurricular activities are offered after school.

MICHIGAN

SUMMERS-KNOLL SCHOOL   **Day Coed Gr PS-8**
Ann Arbor, MI 48104. 2015 Manchester Rd.
Tel: 734-971-7991. Fax: 734-971-2018.
www.summers-knoll.org   E-mail: info@summers-knoll.org

     Will Purves, Head. Jody Fisher, Adm.

     Pre-Prep. Feat—Span Computers. **Supp**—Tut. **Adm:** 32/yr. Appl due: Rolling. Accepted: 70%. **Tests** IQ. **Enr 70.** B 40. G 30. Elem 70. Wh 78%. Hisp 2%. Blk 10%. Asian 10%. Avg class size: 12. **Fac 12.** M 1/1. F 5/5. Wh 92%. Blk 8%. Adv deg: 33%. **Grad '04**—2. Prep—2. Alum 20. **Tui '03-'04:** Day $7990-9990 (+$200). Aid: Need 5 ($21,000). **Summer:** Enrich Rec. Tui Day $52-198/wk. 10 wks. **Est 1994.** Nonprofit. Tri (Aug-June). The curriculum at Summers-Knoll, which is geared toward bright and creative children, incorporates thematic units and allows for acceleration. Themes addressed span content areas, grade levels and classrooms. Computers and the arts enrich the program for all students.

KENSINGTON ACADEMY   **Day Coed Gr PS-8**
Beverly Hills, MI 48025. 32605 Bellvine Trl.
Tel: 248-647-8060. Fax: 248-647-4239.
www.kensingtonacademy.org   E-mail: ka.williams@kensingtonacademy.org
    Thomas J. Herbst, Head. BS, St Joseph's College, MS, Michigan State Univ. Katherine E. Williams, Adm.

    Pre-Prep. Feat—Span Computers Studio_Art Music. **Supp**—Tut. **Adm:** 31/yr. Appl due: Feb. Accepted: 76%. Yield: 40%. **Enr 191.** B 95. G 96. Elem 191. Wh 82%. Hisp 3%. Blk 10%. Am Ind 2%. Asian 1%. Other 2%. Avg class size: 18. Uniform. **Fac 20.** M 1/1. F 16/2. Wh 99%. Hisp 1%. Adv deg: 25%. **Grad '04**—20. Prep—20. Alum 215. **Tui '04-'05:** Day $8500-12,050 (+$150). Aid: Need 20 ($60,000). **Est 1968.** Nonprofit. Roman Catholic. Quar (Aug-June). The youngest children at Kensington (age 3) engage in a Montessori program that focuses on the fundamentals, particularly reading and problem solving skills. The program in kindergarten and the lower school (grades 1-4) continues to address skill development, while also identifying strengths and weaknesses and working with individual learning styles. Programming in the middle school (grades 5-8) incorporates high school preparatory activities and a range of extracurricular activities.

OUR LADY QUEEN OF MARTYRS SCHOOL   **Day Coed Gr PS-8**
Beverly Hills, MI 48025. 32460 Pierce Rd.
Tel: 248-642-2616. Fax: 248-642-3671.
www.bbt.org/olqm.htm   E-mail: pferguson@olqm-parish.org
    Peter J. Ferguson, Prin. BA, Univ of Detroit, MSA, Univ of Notre Dame.

    Pre-Prep. Gen Acad. Feat—Fr Span Computers Relig Studio_Art Drama Chorus Music Journ Study_Skills. **Supp**—Rem_Read Tut. **Adm:** 70/yr. Appl due: May. Accepted: 75%. **Enr 486.** B 240. G 246. Elem 486. Wh 96%. Hisp 1%. Blk 2%. Asian 1%. Avg class size: 26. **Fac 31.** M 3. F 16/12. Adv deg: 29%. **Grad '04**—30. Prep—25. **Tui '03-'04:** Day $4275 (+$300). Parishioners $2985 (+$300). **Est 1954.** Nonprofit. Roman Catholic. Quar (Aug-June). Founded by the Sisters of Charity of Cincinnati, OH, the school conducts a Catholic-centered elementary curriculum. French language courses begin in grade 6, as does an electives program that includes computer, journalism, drama and study skills. Most graduates proceed to Catholic high schools.

ETON ACADEMY   **Day Coed Gr 1-12**
Birmingham, MI 48009. 1755 Melton Rd.
Tel: 248-642-1150. Fax: 248-642-3670.
www.etonacademy.org   E-mail: smorey@etonacademy.org
    Pete Pullen, Head. Sharon M. Morey, Adm.

Col Prep. LD. Feat—Span Studio_Art. **Supp**—Dev_Read Rem_Math Rem_Read. **Adm:** 58/yr. **Tests** IQ. **Enr 190.** B 125. G 65. Elem 140. Sec 50. Wh 91%. Hisp 1%. Blk 7%. Asian 1%. Avg class size: 8. **Fac 37.** M 10. F 27. Adv deg: 29%. **Grad '04**—11. Col—10. Alum 100. **Tui '03-'04:** Day $15,500-17,250. **Est 1980.** Nonprofit. Quar (Aug-June). **Assoc** NCA. The academy features an educational program for students of average and above-average academic potential who have dyslexia or other learning disabilities. Pupils receive computer-based instruction in a structured, supportive learning environment. The curriculum reflects a strong emphasis on reading, language arts and math, as well as on organizational and study skills.

BROTHER RICE HIGH SCHOOL

Day Boys Gr 9-12

Bloomfield Hills, MI 48301. 7101 Lahser Rd.
Tel: 248-647-2526. Fax: 248-647-2532.
www.brrice.edu   E-mail: sofran@brrice.edu

John Birney, Head. BA, MA, Univ of Michigan. David Sofran, Adm.

Col Prep. AP—Eng Fr Ger. **Feat**—Span Anat & Physiol Comp_Sci Govt Theol Speech. **Supp**—Rem_Math Rev Tut. **Adm:** 195/yr. Appl due: Aug. Accepted: 80%. **Tests** HSPT SSAT. **Enr 695.** B 695. Sec 695. Wh 83%. Hisp 1%. Blk 12%. Asian 3%. Other 1%. Avg class size: 20. Uniform. **Fac 45.** M 35. F 10. Adv deg: 46%. **Grad '04**—152. Col—152. Avg SAT: 1300. Alum 7700. **Tui '04-'05:** Day $7990 (+$500). Aid: Merit ($100,000). Need ($100,000). **Summer:** Rem. Tui Day $175/crse. 5 wks. **Est 1960.** Nonprofit. Roman Catholic. Sem (Aug-June). **Assoc** NCA. Brother Rice's college preparatory course of studies features a four-year theology program and a Christian service requirement. A core curriculum is supplemented by honors and AP courses; electives and credits in computer science, government, modern languages, speech, health and theology are required. Interscholastic teams and intramural sports are available, and a wide variety of extracurricular activities includes band, computer team, debate, drama, Model UN and newspaper.

DETROIT WALDORF SCHOOL

Day Coed Gr PS-8

Detroit, MI 48214. 2555 Burns Ave.
Tel: 313-822-0300. Fax: 313-822-4030.
www.detroitwaldorf.com   E-mail: detroitwaldorf@earthlink.net

Mary Leonhardi, Admin. BA, University of Minnesota-Twin Cities, MSW, Wayne State Univ. Bernice Eppes, Adm.

Pre-Prep. Gen Acad. Feat—Ger Span Studio_Art Music Woodworking. **Supp**—Dev_Read Makeup Tut. **Adm:** 30/yr. Appl due: Mar. Accepted: 75%. **Enr 178.** B 95. G 83. Elem 178. Wh 39%. Blk 48%. Other 13%. Avg class size: 17. **Fac 25.** M 5/1. F 16/3. Wh 76%. Hisp 4%. Blk 20%. Adv deg: 16%. **Grad '04**—17. Prep—8. **Tui '03-'04:** Day $4825-8175 (+$400). Aid: Need 49 ($128,853). **Summer:** Enrich Rec. Tui Day $140/wk. 8 wks. **Est 1965.** Nonprofit. Tri (Sept-June). One of the nation's oldest Waldorf schools, Detroit Waldorf offers a broad academic program that integrates music and the arts. Course work emphasizes creativity and critical-thinking skills. The foreign language curriculum begins with German and Spanish in grade 1, the same year that vocal and instrumental music classes also commence. Children requiring assistance with their language skills may take part in a supplementary language arts program.

MERCY HIGH SCHOOL
Day Girls Gr 9-12

Farmington Hills, MI 48336. 29300 11 Mile Rd.
Tel: 248-476-8020. Fax: 248-476-3691.
www.mercyhsmi.org   E-mail: mhs@mhsmi.org

Sr. Regina Marie Doelker, RSM, Pres. BA, Catholic Univ of America, MA, Univ of Detroit. Carolyn R. Witte, Prin. BS, Eastern Michigan Univ, MA, Michigan State Univ. Maureen P. Stirling, Adm.

Col Prep. AP—Calc Bio Chem Physics Eur_Hist US_Hist US_Govt & Pol. **Feat**—Fr Lat Span Comp_Sci Econ Relig Studio_Art Drama Theater_Arts Chorus Orchestra. **Supp**—Rem_Math Tut. **Adm:** 216/yr. Appl due: Apr. Accepted: 80%. Tests HSPT. **Enr 843.** G 843. Sec 843. Wh 75%. Hisp 1%. Blk 13%. Asian 2%. Other 9%. Avg class size: 25. Uniform. **Fac 59.** M 12. F 40/7. Wh 96%. Blk 1%. Asian 3%. Adv deg: 74%. **Grad '04**—**223.** Col—221. Avg SAT: 1135. Avg ACT: 23. Alum 12,000. **Tui '03-'04:** Day $7380 (+$300). **Summer:** Enrich Rem. Tui Day $190. 1-2 wks. **Est 1945.** Nonprofit. Roman Catholic. Sem (Aug-June). **Assoc** NCA. The college preparatory program encompasses the humanities, the sciences, religious studies and the fine arts. A semester of computer science study is required. Girls participate in various interscholastic sports and extracurricular activities.

THE VALLEY SCHOOL
Day Coed Gr PS-12

Flint, MI 48503. 1505 W Court St.
Tel: 810-767-4004. Fax: 810-767-0841.
www.valleyschool.org   E-mail: email@valleyschool.org

Charles Bryan, Head. BA, Univ of Michigan-Flint. Holly Lubowicki, Adm.

Col Prep. Feat—Fr Span Computers. **Adm:** 41/yr. Appl due: Rolling. Accepted: 95%. **Enr 137.** Elem 95. Sec 42. Wh 69%. Blk 9%. Other 21%. Avg class size: 14. **Fac 26.** M 4/1. F 12/9. Wh 92%. Blk 8%. Adv deg: 19%. **Grad '04**—**11.** Col—11. Avg SAT: 1049. Avg ACT: 24. Alum 50. **Tui '04-'05:** Day $7500 (+$400). Aid: Merit 12 ($7620). Need 41 ($182,416). **Est 1970.** Nonprofit. Quar (Sept-June). The school allows qualified juniors and seniors to dually enroll at the University of Michigan-Flint or Mott Community College. Valley offers an unusually broad arts curriculum, as professional artists from the community (many from the Flint Institute of the Arts) teach in their specialty areas on a part-time basis. The school schedules eight class periods per day, thus making it possible for boys and girls to take two courses from the same department in a given semester.

GRAND RAPIDS BAPTIST SCHOOLS
Day Coed Gr PS-12

Grand Rapids, MI 49525. 3101 Leonard St NE.
Tel: 616-942-0363. Fax: 616-942-6867.
www.grbs.org   E-mail: kooler@grbs.org

Richard S. Koole, Supt. BA, Cornerstone Univ, MA, EdD, Western Michigan Univ. Gary Childers, Adm.

Col Prep. Gen Acad. Feat—Fr Span Computers Bible. **Supp**—Dev_Read LD Rem_Math Rem_Read Tut. **Adm:** 144/yr. Appl due: July. Accepted: 93%. **Enr 712.** B 352. G 360. Elem 337. Sec 375. Wh 91%. Hisp 1%. Blk 5%. Asian 3%. Avg class size: 20. **Fac 46.** M 16/1. F 28/1. Wh 100%. Adv deg: 34%. **Grad '04**—**98.** Col—93. Avg ACT: 25. Alum 380. **Tui '03-'04:** Day $4410 (+$100-350). Aid: Need

98 ($100,000). **Est 1972.** Nonprofit. Baptist. Sem (Aug-June). GRBS's college preparatory program includes honors courses and a strong emphasis on religious instruction. Prayer is part of the school day, and pupils attend weekly chapel services. A full athletic program, leadership opportunities, and class trips and retreats supplement academic work.

GRAND RAPIDS CHRISTIAN SCHOOLS   Day Coed Gr PS-12
Grand Rapids, MI 49506. 1812 Sylvan Ave SE.
Tel: 616-574-6370. Fax: 616-245-6187.
www.grcs.org   E-mail: aorr@grcs.org
    David J. Koetje, Supt. BS, Grand Valley State Univ, MEd, DePaul Univ. Amy Orr, Adm.

    Col Prep. AP—Eng Calc Stats Chem. **Feat**—Creative_Writing Fr Ger Lat Span Astron Computers Econ Govt Psych Sociol Bible Relig Studio_Art Music Bus Debate Journ Speech Indus_Arts Home_Ec. **Supp**—Dev_Read ESL Makeup Tut. **Adm:** 355/yr. Appl due: Rolling. Accepted: 100%. **Enr 2933.** B 1463. G 1470. Wh 87%. Hisp 1%. Blk 6%. Asian 3%. Other 3%. Avg class size: 24. **Fac 179.** M 48/4. F 88/39. Adv deg: 56%. **Grad '04—274.** Col—255. Avg ACT: 24. Alum 18,000. **Tui '03-'04:** Day $3411-6218 (+$150). Aid: Need 348 ($788,670). **Est 1891.** Nonprofit. Sem (Aug-June). This private school system serves students from the Greater Grand Rapids area, operating a child development center, six elementary schools, four middle schools and one high school at eight locations throughout the city. The schools provide a comprehensive and rigorous curriculum that includes math, science, English, social science, foreign language, religion, art, music, computer and physical education. Various athletic, academic, artistic and social extracurricular activities are available.

HILLSDALE ACADEMY   Day Coed Gr K-12
Hillsdale, MI 49242. 1 Academy Ln.
Tel: 517-439-8644. Fax: 517-607-2794.
www.hillsdale.edu/academy   E-mail: pat.iszler@hillsdale.edu
    Kenneth Calvert, Head. MDiv, Gordon-Conwell Theological Seminary, ThM, Harvard Univ, PhD, Miami Univ (OH).

    Col Prep. Feat—Fr Lat Span Computers Econ Studio_Art Theater Music. **Adm (Gr K-11):** 23/yr. Appl due: Mar. Accepted: 72%. Yield: 100%. **Enr 154.** B 62. G 92. Elem 97. Sec 57. Wh 93%. Blk 3%. Other 4%. Avg class size: 10. Uniform. **Fac 23.** M 4/1. F 9/9. Wh 100%. Adv deg: 34%. **Grad '04—10.** Col—10. Avg SAT: 1173. Avg ACT: 25. **Tui '04-'05:** Day $2620-3990 (+$500). Aid: Need 20 ($21,000). **Est 1990.** Nonprofit. Tri (Aug-June). Founded as an elementary school, the academy added an upper school (grades 9-12) in 1998. As part of language study at the school, all students take French in grades 1-8 and Latin in grades 9-12; Spanish is also available during the upper school years. In addition to work in the standard subjects, course requirements in the college preparatory upper school include the following: two years of rhetoric; two or more years of electives in the areas of art, music, Spanish and physical education; and civics/economics in grade 12.   **See Also Page 1166**

MONSIGNOR JOHN R. HACKETT   Day Coed Gr 9-12
CATHOLIC CENTRAL HIGH SCHOOL
Kalamazoo, MI 49008. 1000 W Kilgore Rd.
Tel: 269-381-2646. Fax: 269-381-3919.
www.hackettcc.org   E-mail: hackett@hackettcc.org

Timothy Eastman, Prin. BA, Kalamazoo College, MA, Western Michigan Univ.

Col Prep. Gen Acad. AP—Calc Stats Bio. **Feat**—Creative_Writing Lat Computers Econ Govt Psych Sociol Relig Studio_Art Drama Band Music Accounting Bus Speech. **Supp**—Dev_Read LD Rem_Math Rem_Read Tut. **Adm:** 175/yr. Appl due: Rolling. Accepted: 95%. **Enr 480.** Sec 480. Wh 94%. Hisp 3%. Blk 2%. Asian 1%. Avg class size: 28. **Fac 27.** M 6/1. F 17/3. Wh 100%. Adv deg: 40%. **Grad '04—107.** Col—101. Avg ACT: 24. Alum 6500. **Tui '03-'04:** Day $1072-5350. Aid: Merit 5 ($1000). Need 80 ($125,000). **Est 1964.** Nonprofit. Roman Catholic. Sem (Aug-June). Three programs of study are available: general studies, college preparatory and honors. Requirements include courses in religion, government, economics, foreign language and fine arts. Athletics and a wide variety of extracurricular and cocurricular activities are offered. Catholic traditions and values are stressed through daily prayer, liturgies, service projects in the community, religious retreats and the campus ministry.

LANSING CATHOLIC CENTRAL   Day Coed Gr 9-12
HIGH SCHOOL
Lansing, MI 48912. 501 Marshall St.
Tel: 517-267-2100. Fax: 517-267-2135.
www.lcchs.org   E-mail: draminsk@lcchs.org

Thomas P. Maloney, Prin. BS, Alma College, MA, Michigan State Univ.

Col Prep. AP—Eng Calc Bio Physics US_Govt & Pol. **Feat**—Creative_Writing Fr Greek Lat Span Comp_Sci Econ Psych Sociol Philos Theol Fine_Arts Music Music_Theory Journ Speech. **Adm (Gr 9-11):** 129/yr. Appl due: Apr. Accepted: 99%. **Enr 510.** B 256. G 254. Sec 510. Wh 89%. Hisp 5%. Blk 3%. Asian 3%. Avg class size: 26. Uniform. **Fac 32.** M 8/2. F 20/2. Wh 97%. Hisp 3%. Adv deg: 56%. **Grad '04—121.** Col—119. Avg SAT: 1245. Avg ACT: 24. Alum 8324. **Tui '04-'05:** Day $5150 (+$250). Aid: Need 104 ($124,057). **Est 1970.** Nonprofit. Roman Catholic. Sem (Aug-June). LCCHS provides a comprehensive secondary program that emphasizes college preparation and enables students to earn college credits through honors and Advanced Placement course work. Service is an integral part of school life, and all pupils fulfill a service requirement in the community. Extracurricular activities include enrichment and travel opportunities, academic and language clubs, interscholastic and intramural athletics, student government and performing arts options.

LADYWOOD HIGH SCHOOL   Day Girls Gr 9-12
Livonia, MI 48154. 14680 Newburgh Rd.
Tel: 734-591-1545. Fax: 734-591-4214.
www.ladywood.org

Sr. Mary Ann Smith, CSSF, Prin. BA, Madonna College, MA, Wayne State Univ, MS, Univ of Dayton.

Col Prep. AP—Eng Calc Bio Studio_Art. **Feat**—Humanities Ital Computers Theol Film Bus Home_Ec. **Supp**—Tut. **Enr 500.** G 500. Sec 500. Wh 93%. Hisp 3%. Blk 1%. Asian 3%. Uniform. **Fac 43.** M 7/1. F 35. Adv deg: 18%. **Grad '04—132.** Col—132. Alum 5000. **Tui '02-'03:** Day $5000 (+$600). **Est 1950.** Nonprofit. Roman Catholic. Sem (Aug-June). **Assoc** NCA. Located on a 60-acre campus and owned and operated by the Felician Sisters, this school provides a full college preparatory program. Students are required to take four years of theology and to attend religious services and retreats. Extracurricular activities include interscholastic sports, Christian and community service programs, interest clubs and various social activities.

ST. MARY CATHOLIC CENTRAL HIGH SCHOOL
Day Coed Gr 9-12

Monroe, MI 48162. 108 W Elm Ave.
Tel: 734-241-0663. Fax: 734-241-9042.
www.smccmonroe.com   E-mail: bdusseau@smccmonroe.com
   Matthew J. Saxer, Pres. Beth Dusseau, Prin. BA, Marygrove College, MA, Univ of Toledo. Vicki White, Adm.

Col Prep. Gen Acad. AP—Eng Calc US_Hist US_Govt & Pol. **Feat**—Fr Span Computers Theol Studio_Art Music Bus. **Supp**—Tut. **Adm:** 107/yr. Appl due: Apr. Accepted: 100%. **Tests** HSPT. **Enr 442.** B 247. G 195. Sec 442. Wh 93%. Hisp 3%. Blk 1%. Am Ind 1%. Asian 2%. Avg class size: 20. Uniform. **Fac 29.** M 9/1. F 19. Wh 100%. Adv deg: 55%. **Grad '04—86.** Col—81. Avg SAT: 1150. Avg ACT: 23. Alum 9000. **Tui '04-'05:** Day $5400 (+$1000). Aid: Merit 63 ($157,500). Need 238 ($347,805). **Est 1986.** Nonprofit. Roman Catholic. Sem (Aug-June). **Assoc** NCA. St. Mary's comprehensive curriculum offers programs for all levels of academic ability and includes honors and Advanced Placement courses and four years of required theology classes. In the Christian tradition, daily prayer and monthly liturgies, as well as retreats for all grades, are available. Students also fulfill a community service requirement.

ST. MARY'S PREPARATORY SCHOOL
Boys Gr 9-12
Bdg & Day

Orchard Lake, MI 48324. 3535 Indian Trl.
Tel: 248-683-0532. Fax: 248-683-1740.
www.stmarysprep.com   E-mail: info@stmarysprep.com
   James M. Glowacki, Head. Kevin Kosco, Adm.

Col Prep. Feat—Creative_Writing Poetry Shakespeare Mythology Fr Ger Lat Span Polish Stats Anat Environ_Sci Programming Web_Design Econ Geog Govt Psych Theol World_Relig Fine_Arts Studio_Art Band Chorus Music_Theory Accounting Bus Debate Journ Speech Drafting. **Supp**—ESL Tut. **Adm:** 160/yr. Bdg 25. Day 135. Appl due: Feb. Accepted: 85%. **Enr 500.** B 80/420. Sec 500. Wh 70%. Hisp 5%. Blk 15%. Asian 10%. Avg class size: 17. Uniform. **Fac 57.** M 31. F 26. Wh 85%. Hisp 10%. Blk 5%. Adv deg: 45%. **Grad '04—115.** Col—115. Avg SAT: 1150. Avg ACT: 25. **Tui '04-'05:** Bdg $18,600 (+$328-753). 5-Day Bdg $15,535 (+$328-753). Day $7950 (+$328-753). **Est 1885.** Nonprofit. Roman Catholic. Sem (Aug-May). SMPS students supplement required course work with electives that reflect their interests. Seniors and selected juniors may enroll in classes for college credit at nearby St. Mary's College. Boys take four years of theology in the classroom and attend chapel services twice weekly. Extracurricular options include community service, class retreats, athletics and outdoor recreation.

SPRING VALE ACADEMY
Coed Gr 9-12
Bdg & Day
Owosso, MI 48867. 4150 S M-52.
Tel: 989-725-2391. Fax: 989-729-6408.
http://sva.cog7.org E-mail: offices@cog7.org
Jose Acosta, Dir. BS, Walla Walla College. Jonathan Albert, Adm.

Col Prep. Gen Acad. Feat—Creative_Writing Span Anat & Physiol Econ Govt Bible Drama Band Music Accounting Bus Journ Speech. **Supp**—Tut. **Adm (Bdg Gr 9-12; Day 9-10):** 14/yr. Bdg 13. Day 1. Appl due: July. Accepted: 95%. **Enr 27.** B 17/1. G 8/1. Sec 27. Wh 77%. Hisp 18%. Blk 5%. Avg class size: 8. **Fac 9.** M /5. F 2/2. Wh 100%. Adv deg: 11%. **Grad '04—18.** Col—8. Alum 802. **Tui '04-'05:** Bdg $10,000 (+$800). Day $3000 (+$500). Aid: Need 20 ($14,300). **Est 1948.** Nonprofit. Church of God (Seventh-Day). Sem (Aug-May). SVA's campus is located on 147 acres. Bible study, music, drama, writing and athletics are available. An on-campus work-study program is required of all students.

NOTRE DAME PREPARATORY SCHOOL
Day Coed Gr 9-12
Pontiac, MI 48340. 1300 Giddings Rd.
Tel: 248-373-5300. Fax: 248-373-8024.
www.ndprep.org
Rev. Leon Olszamowski, SM, Pres. PhD, Catholic Univ of America. Rev. Joseph C. Hindelang, SM, Prin. BA, Assumption College, MDiv, Weston School of Theology. Gregory Simon, Adm.

Col Prep. AP—Eng Fr Span Calc Comp_Sci Bio Chem Physics Eur_Hist US_Hist Econ Psych. **Feat**—Ger Stats Anat & Physiol Astron World_War_II Sociol Relig World_Relig Drawing Studio_Art Band Music Accounting. **Adm (Gr 9-11):** 230/yr. Appl due: Mar. Accepted: 75%. **Tests** HSPT. **Enr 803.** B 385. G 418. Sec 803. Wh 95%. Hisp 1%. Blk 1%. Asian 2%. Other 1%. Avg class size: 16. Uniform. **Fac 67.** M 26/5. F 34/2. Wh 93%. Hisp 3%. Blk 4%. Adv deg: 56%. **Grad '04—186.** Col—183. Avg SAT: 1198. Avg ACT: 25. **Tui '04-'05:** Day $7750 (+$500). Aid: Merit 86 ($82,650). Need 68 ($85,212). **Summer:** Enrich. Tui Day $300. 3 wks. **Est 1994.** Nonprofit. Roman Catholic. Sem (Aug-June). As nearly every graduate of Notre Dame Prep will attend college, the school offers two academic tracks: college preparatory and accelerated. Students choose from standard, honors and Advanced Placement courses offered through the English, modern language, math, religion, science, social science, business, art and music departments. The school encourages pupils to take part in athletics—which include both interscholastic and intramural opportunities for boys and girls—and performing arts activities.

KALAMAZOO ACADEMY
Day Coed Gr PS-8
Portage, MI 49002. 4221 E Milham Rd.
Tel: 269-329-0116. Fax: 269-329-1850.
www.kalamazooacademy.org E-mail: sbridenstine@kalamazooacademy.org
Sheila M. Bridenstine, Dir.

MI   *Great Lakes States*

Pre-Prep. Feat—Span Botany Computers Studio_Art Drama Band Music Dance. **Supp**—LD Rem_Math Rem_Read Tut. **Adm:** 58/yr. **Enr 179.** B 91. G 88. Elem 179. Wh 87%. Hisp 2%. Blk 3%. Asian 8%. Avg class size: 20. **Fac 22.** M 3. F 14/5. Wh 100%. Adv deg: 22%. **Grad '04—12.** Prep—6. Alum 157. **Tui '04-'05:** Day $7198 (+$50). Aid: Need 15 ($40,000). **Summer:** Acad Enrich Rec. Tui Day $125/wk. 6 wks. **Est 1979.** Nonprofit. Tri (Sept-June). **Assoc** NCA. In addition to addressing the basic skills, this school offers courses in music, studio art, band and computers. A special program for students with learning differences is also available. The Orton-Gillingham approach, as well as multisensory integrated learning, is used.

BISHOP BORGESS HIGH SCHOOL   Day Coed Gr 9-12
Redford, MI 48239. 11685 Appleton St.
Tel: 313-255-1100. Fax: 313-255-1102.
www.bishopborgess.com   E-mail: borgess@aol.com
    Sr. Joan Charnley, IHM, Prin. BA, Marygrove College, MA, Wayne State Univ.

Col Prep. Feat—Fr Span Psych. **Supp**—Dev_Read LD Makeup Tut. **Adm:** 50/yr. Appl due: Aug. Accepted: 95%. **Enr 220.** Elem 80. Sec 140. Wh 2%. Blk 98%. Avg class size: 15. Uniform. **Fac 18.** M 5. F 13. Adv deg: 50%. **Grad '04—50.** Col—45. Alum 8000. **Tui '04-'05:** Day $4595 (+$500). Aid: Need 50. **Summer:** Acad. Tui Day $150/crse. 8 wks. **Est 1966.** Nonprofit. Roman Catholic. Quar (Aug-June). Juniors and seniors at Bishop Borgess are eligible for concurrent enrollment at the University of Michigan. Advanced Placement courses are available in several subjects. A program for students with learning disabilities is also available.

GIBSON SCHOOL   Day Coed Gr PS-8
Redford, MI 48239. 12925 Fenton Rd.
Tel: 313-537-8688. Fax: 313-537-0233.
www.gibsonschool.org   E-mail: suzannemyoung@aol.com
    Suzanne M. Young, Head. MEd, Wayne State Univ. Jeanne Nance, Adm.

Pre-Prep. Feat—Lib_Skills Span Computers Studio_Art Music. **Supp**—Tut. **Adm:** 27/yr. Appl due: Rolling. **Tests** IQ. **Enr 100.** B 64. G 36. Elem 100. Wh 64%. Hisp 6%. Blk 25%. Asian 5%. Avg class size: 16. **Fac 15.** M 1/1. F 9/4. Wh 80%. Blk 13%. Asian 7%. Adv deg: 13%. **Grad '04—5.** Prep—2. Alum 300. **Tui '02-'03:** Day $8500. Aid: Need 17 ($27,819). **Summer:** Enrich Rec. Tui Day $320/2-wk ses. 10 wks. **Est 1972.** Nonprofit. Sem (Aug-June). **Assoc** NCA. Gibson instructs gifted students through multi-age groups. The school conducts a differentiated, experiential curriculum and maintains a favorable student-teacher ratio.

SHRINE CATHOLIC HIGH SCHOOL   Day Coed Gr 9-12
Royal Oak, MI 48073. 3500 W 13 Mile Rd.
Tel: 248-549-2925. Fax: 248-549-2953.
www.shrineschools.com   E-mail: info@shrineschools.com
    Thomas P. Kirkwood, Prin. BA, Sacred Heart Major Seminary, MA, Univ of Detroit. Catherine Padesky, Adm.

Col Prep. AP—Eng Fr Span Calc US_Hist US_Govt & Pol. **Feat**—Humanities

MI   *Concise School Listings*   962

Environ_Sci Comp_Sci Econ Relig Film Studio_Art Drama Music Music_Theory Public_Speak. **Supp**—Tut. **Adm (Gr 9-11):** 103/yr. Appl due: Apr. Accepted: 65%. **Tests** HSPT. **Enr 286.** B 132. G 154. Sec 286. Wh 79%. Hisp 3%. Blk 15%. Asian 1%. Other 2%. Avg class size: 20. Uniform. **Fac 26.** M 6/1. F 16/3. Wh 100%. Adv deg: 57%. **Grad '04—74.** Col—74. Avg SAT: 1110. Avg ACT: 23. Alum 8100. **Tui '04-'05:** Day $7650 (+$675-725). Parishioners $5600 (+$675-725). Aid: Merit 51 ($64,920). Need 24 ($41,300). **Est 1942.** Nonprofit. Roman Catholic. Sem (Aug-June). Drawing students from parochial and public schools from throughout the Metropolitan Detroit area, Shrine Catholic gears its program toward college preparation. Honors and Advanced Placement courses are available, and electives allow pupils to pursue areas of interest. An extensive arts program prepares many graduates for future careers in such areas as vocal and instrumental music, drama and graphic design. A well-established competitive athletics program serves both boys and girls.

MICHIGAN LUTHERAN SEMINARY   Coed Gr 9-12
Saginaw, MI 48602. 2777 Hardin St.   Bdg & Day
Tel: 989-793-1041. Fax: 989-793-4213.
www.mlsem.org   E-mail: info@mlsem.org

Paul T. Prange, Pres. BA, Northwestern College, MDiv, Wisconsin Lutheran Seminary. Karl M. Schmugge, Adm.

Col Prep. Feat—British_Lit Ger Lat Span Computers Govt Bible Music_Theory. **Supp**—ESL Tut. **Adm:** 80/yr. Bdg 53. Day 27. Appl due: Apr. Accepted: 80%. **Tests** Stanford. **Enr 274.** B 98/37. G 88/51. Sec 274. Wh 98%. Hisp 1%. Blk 1%. Avg class size: 21. **Fac 35.** M 22. F 8/5. Wh 100%. Adv deg: 42%. In Dorms 5. **Grad '04—87.** Col—85. Alum 3801. **Tui '05-'06:** Bdg $7400. Day $4760. Aid: Need ($380,000). **Est 1910.** Nonprofit. Lutheran. Sem (Aug-May). The school's enrollment is restricted to students preparing to work in the Wisconsin Evangelical Lutheran synod as pastors or teachers. MLS schedules late afternoon or early evening study halls for all dormitory pupils. Qualified students may complete summer study in Italy, Mexico or Germany.

DE LA SALLE COLLEGIATE HIGH SCHOOL   Day Boys Gr 9-12
Warren, MI 48088. 14600 Common Rd.
Tel: 586-778-2207. Fax: 586-778-5118.
www.delasallehs.com   E-mail: msaxer@delasallehs.com

Br. Robert Carnaghi, FSC, Pres. Terrence George, Prin. Richard Kopas, Adm.

Col Prep. AP—Eng Fr Span Calc Comp_Sci Bio Chem Physics Eur_Hist US_Hist US_Govt & Pol. **Feat**—Astron Ecol Law Psych Relig Studio_Art Band Chorus Accounting Journ Mech_Drawing. **Supp**—Tut. **Adm:** 202/yr. Appl due: Feb. Accepted: 85%. **Tests** HSPT. **Enr 705.** B 705. Sec 705. Wh 94%. Hisp 1%. Blk 2%. Asian 2%. Other 1%. Avg class size: 25. **Fac 60.** M 57/3. Adv deg: 65%. **Grad '04—201.** Col—200. Avg ACT: 24. Alum 9000. **Tui '05-'06:** Day $6950 (+$100-300). Aid: Merit 60 ($70,000). Need 140 ($130,000). **Summer:** Sports. 1-5 wks. **Est 1926.** Nonprofit. Roman Catholic. Sem (Aug-June). Conducted by the Christian Brothers, De La Salle offers an honors and a regular college prep curriculum, in addition to AP courses. Four years of religion classes are complemented by an active campus ministry program, and seniors must complete a service requirement

OHIO

JEROME LIPPMAN   Day Coed Gr K-8
JEWISH COMMUNITY DAY SCHOOL
Akron, OH 44320. 750 White Pond Dr.
Tel: 330-836-0419. Fax: 330-869-2514.
www.lippmandayschool.org   E-mail: admissions@jewishakron.org
    Joe Pryweller, Pres. Nehemia Ichilov, Head. Joan Sullivan, Adm.

    Gen Acad. Feat—Writing Hebrew Judaic_Stud. **Supp**—Tut. **Adm:** 19/yr. Appl due: June. Accepted: 100%. **Enr 100.** B 48. G 52. Elem 100. Wh 87%. Hisp 5%. Blk 8%. Avg class size: 11. **Fac 16.** M 2. F 12/2. Wh 94%. Blk 6%. Adv deg: 12%. **Grad '04—6.** Prep—1. **Tui '04-'05:** Day $4900 (+$50). Aid: Need 19. **Est 1965.** Nonprofit. Jewish. Quar (Aug-June). Lippman Day School conducts a dual curriculum of general and Judaic studies. Pupils study Hebrew as a foreign language and in the context of prayer and the Bible. The literature-based language arts program emphasizes phonics and enables children to publish books that they author. A strong performing arts program serves students at all grade levels, while computer labs and a computer presence in each classroom are aspects of the technology program.

OLNEY FRIENDS SCHOOL   Coed Gr 9-12
Barnesville, OH 43713. 61830 Sandy Ridge Rd.   **Bdg & Day**
Tel: 740-425-3655. Fax: 740-425-3202.
www.olneyfriends.org   E-mail: admissions@olneyfriends.org
    Richard F. Sidwell, Head. BA, Wilmington College (OH). Karen Hampton, Adm.

    Col Prep. AP—Eng Span Calc Physics. **Feat**—Humanities Environ_Sci Amer_Stud Relig Photog Studio_Art Chorus Music_Theory. **Supp**—ESL LD Rev Tut. **Adm (Gr 9-11):** 29/yr. Bdg 28. Day 1. Appl due: Rolling. Accepted: 88%. Yield: 75%. **Enr 66.** B 30/2. G 32/2. Sec 66. Wh 68%. Hisp 9%. Blk 8%. Asian 8%. Other 7%. Avg class size: 10. **Fac 16.** M 7/1. F 7/1. Wh 94%. Hisp 6%. Adv deg: 50%. In Dorms 6. **Grad '04—18.** Col—15. Avg SAT: 1210. Alum 1351. **Tui '04-'05:** Bdg $21,200 (+$500). Day $10,600 (+$200). Aid: Need 52 ($709,000). Work prgm 6 ($2000). **Est 1837.** Nonprofit. Religious Society of Friends. Quar (Aug-June). **Assoc** NCA. Emphasizing college preparation, this Quaker school accepts students of all denominations and enrolls a substantial number of international pupils. Course work at all levels emphasizes critical thinking skills, and Olney provides opportunities for acceleration through its AP program. The closely knit community life is supported by a low student-faculty ratio. Silent Meetings for Worship are held twice a week, and all students participate in the community service program.

AGNON SCHOOL
Day Coed Gr PS-8

Beachwood, OH 44122. 26500 Shaker Blvd.
Tel: 216-464-4055. Fax: 216-464-3229.
www.agnon.org   E-mail: agnon@agnon.org

Jerry Isaak-Shapiro, Head. MA, George Washington Univ. Nancy K. Kekst, Adm.

Pre-Prep. Gen Acad. Bilingual. Feat—Hebrew Computers Judaic_Stud Drama Chorus Music Israeli_Dance. **Supp**—Dev_Read ESL Rem_Math Rem_Read Rev Tut. **Adm:** 93/yr. Appl due: Feb. Accepted: 75%. **Enr 325.** B 170. G 155. Elem 325. Wh 97%. Hisp 2%. Blk 1%. Avg class size: 15. **Fac 55.** M 2/2. F 31/20. Wh 100%. Adv deg: 45%. **Grad '04—26.** Alum 273. **Tui '04-'05:** Day $3900-6500 (+$25-165). Aid: Need 88 ($357,465). **Summer:** PS. Rec. Tui Day $400-1200. 6 wks. **Est 1969.** Nonprofit. Jewish. (Aug-June). In the primary and elementary divisions, children at this Jewish school develop research and editing skills, learn problem-solving strategies, participate in a Hebrew curriculum that progresses from listening to speaking to reading and writing, and have access to computers in every classroom. Employing a thematic approach to learning, the middle school features daily access to science and computer labs; reading, writing and researching across the curriculum; a well-developed fine arts program; annual retreats and trips; and extracurricular activities.

LAWRENCE SCHOOL
Day Coed Gr 1-12

Broadview Heights, OH 44147. 1551 E Wallings Rd.
Tel: 440-526-0003. Fax: 440-526-0595.
www.lawrenceschool.org   E-mail: tbeam@lawrence.pvt.k12.oh.us

Mimi Mayer, Head. BA, Elmira College, MEd, Univ of Vermont. Douglas W. Hamilton, Adm.

Col Prep. LD. Feat—Span Computers Law Painting Studio_Art Music Journ Speech Graphic_Design. **Supp**—Rem_Math Rem_Read Tut. **Adm:** 55/yr. Appl due: Rolling. Accepted: 76%. Yield: 80%. **Tests** IQ. **Enr 217.** B 163. G 54. Elem 140. Sec 77. Wh 87%. Hisp 3%. Blk 9%. Asian 1%. Avg class size: 10. **Fac 40.** M 9. F 31. Wh 96%. Hisp 2%. Blk 2%. Adv deg: 12%. **Grad '04—34.** Col—21. Avg SAT: 977. Avg ACT: 20. **Tui '05-'06:** Day $12,940-13,750 (+$500). Aid: Need 48 ($195,100). **Summer:** Acad Rem Rec. Tui Day $800. Rec. Tui Day $600. 4 wks. **Est 1969.** Nonprofit. Quar (Aug-June). This state-chartered school provides remediation in the areas of academics and organizational and study skills for bright students with learning disabilities and attention deficits from approximately a dozen counties and 70 communities throughout Greater Cleveland and Akron. Lawrence employs ability grouping in a small-class setting to enable the student to progress at a suitable pace. The carefully sequenced curriculum places particular emphasis on language arts and mathematics, but also includes course work in social studies, science, art, music and physical education.

NOTRE DAME-CATHEDRAL LATIN SCHOOL
Day Coed Gr 9-12

Chardon, OH 44024. 13000 Auburn Rd.
Tel: 440-286-6226. Fax: 440-286-7199.
www.ndcl.org   E-mail: nd_corlew@lgca.org

Sr. Margaret Gorman, SND, Prin. BA, Notre Dame College (OH), MA, Univ of Minnesota-Twin Cities. Keith Corlew, Adm.

Col Prep. AP—Eng Calc Stats Comp_Sci Physics US_Hist. **Feat**—Fr Ger Span Web_Design Relig Bus. **Supp**—Rem_Math Rem_Read Rev Tut. **Adm:** 213/yr. Appl due: Jan. Accepted: 75%. **Tests** HSPT. **Enr 775.** B 372. G 403. Sec 775. Wh 98%. Blk 1%. Asian 1%. Avg class size: 22. Uniform. **Fac 68.** M 26. F 38/4. Wh 98%. Other 2%. Adv deg: 58%. **Grad '04—200.** Col—198. Avg SAT: 1100. Alum 18,500. **Tui '04-'05:** Day $7200 (+$400). Aid: Merit 56 ($68,950). Need 171 ($194,250). **Est 1878.** Nonprofit. Roman Catholic. Sem (Aug-June). Both general and college preparatory courses are offered, as are fine arts, home economics, computer, sports and a full extracurricular program. All students perform community service.

CINCINNATI HILLS CHRISTIAN ACADEMY   Day Coed Gr K-12
Cincinnati, OH 45249. 11525 Snider Rd.
Tel: 513-247-0900. Fax: 513-247-0950.
www.chca-oh.org   E-mail: admissions@chca-oh.org

T. Randall Brunk, Head. BS, Colorado State Univ, MEd, Regent Univ. Linda Wylie, Adm.

Col Prep. AP—Eng Span Calc Stats Bio Chem Eur_Hist US_Hist Studio_Art. **Feat**—Creative_Writing Ger Lat Hebrew Bible Journ Speech. **Supp**—LD. **Adm:** 242/yr. Appl due: Rolling. Accepted: 54%. **Tests** Stanford. **Enr 1418.** B 703. G 715. Elem 983. Sec 435. Wh 82%. Hisp 1%. Blk 13%. Am Ind 1%. Asian 2%. Other 1%. **Fac 154.** M 26/5. F 106/17. Wh 94%. Hisp 1%. Blk 4%. Asian 1%. Adv deg: 50%. **Grad '04—94.** Col—94. Avg SAT: 1124. Avg ACT: 25. Alum 500. **Tui '04-'05:** Day $7990-8410. Aid: Merit 27 ($57,000). Need 87 ($250,000). **Est 1989.** Nonprofit. Nondenom Christian. Sem (Aug-June). **Assoc** NCA. In a Christian setting, the school emphasizes development of the basic skills: reading, writing, comprehension, problem solving, study skills and critical thinking. In addition to work in the core subjects, the middle school curriculum includes several electives; various activities, including intramural and (in grades 7 and 8) interscholastic athletics, supplement academics. Small classes, AP offerings and mandatory community service are features of the high school curriculum.

ELDER HIGH SCHOOL   Day Boys Gr 9-12
Cincinnati, OH 45205. 3900 Vincent Ave.
Tel: 513-921-3744. Fax: 513-921-8123.
www.elderhs.org   E-mail: kelley.s@elderhs.org

Thomas R. Otten, Prin. BA, Thomas More College, MEd, Xavier Univ (OH). Thomas Bushman, Adm.

Col Prep. Gen Acad. AP—Eng Calc Comp_Sci Bio Chem Physics US_Hist Studio_Art. **Feat**—Fr Ger Lat Span Cincinnati_Hist Econ Relig Music Music_Theory Bus Graphic_Design. **Supp**—Dev_Read LD Rem_Math Rem_Read Tut. **Adm (Gr 9-11):** 301/yr. Appl due: May. Accepted: 99%. **Tests** CEEB HSPT. **Enr 1060.** B 1060. Sec 1060. Wh 94%. Hisp 1%. Blk 1%. Asian 3%. Other 1%. Avg class size: 18. **Fac 64.** M 55/3. F 4/2. Wh 94%. Hisp 1%. Blk 1%. Asian 3%. Other 1%. Adv deg: 37%. **Grad '04—239.** Col—215. Avg SAT: 1016. Avg ACT:

22. Alum 17,500. **Tui '05-'06:** Day $6550. Aid: Merit 100 ($300,000). Need 500 ($1,000,000). **Summer:** Enrich Rem. Tui Day $240/crse. 5-6 wks. **Est 1922.** Nonprofit. Roman Catholic. Quar (Aug-June). The school's curriculum, which incorporates Christian values, ranges from basic level to Advanced Placement courses, with a variety of electives. Independent study and community service are special features of the religion department. Participation in extracurricular activities, among them competitive sports, newspaper, yearbook and interest clubs, is encouraged.

THE SCHILLING SCHOOL FOR GIFTED CHILDREN
Day Coed Gr K-12

Cincinnati, OH 45240. 924 Halesworth Dr.
Tel: 513-851-1940. Fax: 513-851-1929.
www.schillingschool.org E-mail: schillingoffice@yahoo.com
   Sandra D. Kelly-Schilling, Head. BA, MPA, JD, Univ of Cincinnati.

Col Prep. Feat—Asian_Lit Chin Fr Japan Span Environ_Sci Econ Comp_Relig. **Adm:** 7/yr. Accepted: 95%. Yield: 100%. **Tests** IQ. **Enr 34.** B 26. G 8. Elem 14. Sec 20. Wh 88%. Blk 6%. Other 6%. **Fac 17.** M 1/7. F /9. Wh 82%. Am Ind 6%. Asian 12%. Adv deg: 35%. **Grad '04—4.** Col—4. Avg SAT: 1272. Avg ACT: 32. **Tui '04-'05:** Day $9500. Aid: Need 2 ($9500). **Est 1997.** Nonprofit. Quar. This small, unusual school serves only those students who have an IQ of 130 or higher. Academic programs are accelerated throughout, and Schilling considers all upper school classes to be at the honors level. Certain other courses, such as differential equations, discrete math, advanced Chinese and Asian literature, are taught at the college level. Foreign language instruction begins in kindergarten and involves four languages.

URSULINE ACADEMY
Day Girls Gr 9-12

Cincinnati, OH 45242. 5535 Pfeiffer Rd.
Tel: 513-791-5791. Fax: 513-791-5802.
www.ursulineacademy.org E-mail: cdehring@ursulineacademy.org
   Sharon L. Redmond, Prin. BA, Northern Kentucky Univ, MA, Xavier Univ (OH).

Col Prep. AP—Eng Fr Ger Lat Span Calc Bio Chem Physics Eur_Hist US_Hist US_Govt & Pol. **Feat**—Anat & Physiol Engineering Hist_of_Amer_Women Amer_Stud Econ Law Psych Relig Studio_Art Drama Music Accounting Journ Public_Speak. **Supp**—Tut. **Adm:** 180/yr. Appl due: Nov. Accepted: 33%. **Tests** HSPT ISEE. **Enr 650.** G 650. Sec 650. Wh 92%. Blk 5%. Asian 3%. Avg class size: 18. Uniform. **Fac 71.** M 8/4. F 41/18. Wh 98%. Hisp 1%. Blk 1%. Adv deg: 60%. **Grad '04—148.** Col—147. Avg SAT: 1227. Avg ACT: 28. Alum 6000. **Tui '04-'05:** Day $8450 (+$270). **Est 1896.** Nonprofit. Roman Catholic. Quar (Aug-June). **Assoc** NCA. Ursuline offers honors classes and Advanced Placement work for qualified girls. Cocurricular activities and sports complement the academic program. The academy conducts an extensive community service program.

BENEDICTINE HIGH SCHOOL
Day Boys Gr 9-12

Cleveland, OH 44104. 2900 Martin Luther King Jr Dr.
Tel: 216-421-2080. Fax: 216-421-1100.
www.cbhs.net E-mail: admissions@cbhs.net

Rev. Albert Marflak, OSB, Pres. MA. Rev. Gerard Gonda, OSB, Prin. MA. Kieran Patton, Adm.

Col Prep. AP—Eng Bio Eur_Hist US_Hist US_Govt & Pol. **Feat**—British_Lit Fr Ger Greek Lat Russ Span Programming African-Amer_Hist Psych Sociol Relig Studio_Art Chorus Music Journ. **Supp**—Dev_Read Tut. **Adm:** 120/yr. Appl due: Rolling. Accepted: 75%. **Tests** HSPT. **Enr** 425. B 425. Sec 425. Wh 70%. Blk 30%. Avg class size: 17. Uniform. **Fac 39.** M 36. F 3. Adv deg: 61%. **Grad '04—92.** Col—92. Avg SAT: 1047. Alum 8000. **Tui '04-'05:** Day $6775. Aid: Need 276. **Summer:** Rev Rem. 3 wks. **Est 1927.** Nonprofit. Roman Catholic. Sem (Aug-June). **Assoc** NCA. The curriculum stresses college preparatory courses in the arts, the sciences, languages and business administration. Athletics are intramural and interscholastic, and extracurricular activities include band and publications, as well as student government, drama, SADD, and language, science, chess, ski and debating clubs.

BEAUMONT SCHOOL
Day Girls Gr 9-12

Cleveland Heights, OH 44118. 3301 N Park Blvd.
Tel: 216-321-2954. Fax: 216-321-3947.
www.beaumontschool.org E-mail: info@beaumontschool.org

Sr. Ritamary Welsh, OSU, Pres. BSE, Saint John College of Cleveland, MEd, Univ of Akron. Margaret Supp Connell, Prin. MEd, John Carroll Univ, MEd, Ursuline College. Mary Reilly, Adm.

Col Prep. AP—Eng Fr Lat Span Chem US_Hist Psych US_Govt & Pol. **Feat**—British_Lit Comp_Sci Pol_Sci Women's_Stud Theol Art_Hist Fine_Arts. **Supp**—Rem_Math Rem_Read Tut. **Adm:** 126/yr. Appl due: Rolling. Accepted: 85%. **Tests** HSPT. **Enr** 453. G 453. Sec 453. Wh 83%. Hisp 1%. Blk 14%. Asian 1%. Other 1%. Avg class size: 21. Uniform. **Fac 48.** M 3/2. F 34/9. Wh 99%. Other 1%. Adv deg: 70%. **Grad '04—107.** Col—107. Avg SAT: 1083. Avg ACT: 23. Alum 5666. **Tui '04-'05:** Day $7590 (+$550). Aid: Merit 67 ($114,230). Need 141 ($128,955). Work prgm 59 ($19,765). **Summer:** Acad Enrich Rev. Tui Day $100-125/crse. 4-5 wks. Fine Arts. Tui Day $225/2-wk ses. 6 wks. **Est 1850.** Nonprofit. Roman Catholic. Quar (Aug-June). **Assoc** NCA. The oldest chartered school in Cleveland, Beaumont offers a rigorous liberal arts curriculum that features a strong technology component. Block scheduling enables students to take four 90-minute classes a day; one day per week, 45 minutes is built into each class for personal study time. Girls choose from a varied selection of interest clubs, school organizations and competitive athletics.

BISHOP WATTERSON HIGH SCHOOL
Day Coed Gr 9-12

Columbus, OH 43214. 99 E Cooke Rd.
Tel: 614-268-8671. Fax: 614-268-0551.
www.bishopwatterson.com E-mail: watterson@cd.pvt.k12.oh.us

Marian A. Hutson, Prin. BS, MS, Ohio State Univ. Chris Campbell, Adm.

Col Prep. AP—Eng Fr Lat Span Calc US_Hist US_Govt & Pol. Feat—Ital Anat & Physiol Comp_Sci Relig Music Bus. Supp—Tut. Enr 1159. B 526. G 633. Sec 1159. Wh 92%. Hisp 2%. Blk 2%. Am Ind 1%. Asian 2%. Other 1%. Uniform. Fac 71. M 25/11. F 29/6. Grad '04—244. Col—239. Avg SAT: 1124. Avg ACT: 25. Alum 10,800. Tui '04-'05: Day $5125. Est 1954. Nonprofit. Roman Catholic. Quar (Aug-June). The school's curriculum includes five years of French and Spanish, four years of Latin and Italian instruction, and an array of art and business courses. Each August, selected students attend the Shakespeare Festival in Stratford, Ontario (Canada). In addition to enrolling in on-site honors and Advanced Placement courses, Bishop Watterson pupils may take advanced classes at local colleges or may pursue dual-enrollment courses at a local university.

MARBURN ACADEMY
Day Coed Gr 1-10
Columbus, OH 43229. 1860 Walden Dr.
Tel: 614-433-0822. Fax: 614-433-0812.
www.marburnacademy.org   E-mail: marburnadmission@marburnacademy.org

Earl B. Oremus, Head. BA, Univ of Kentucky, MEd, Harvard Univ. Scott Burton, Adm.

LD. Feat—Study_Skills. Supp—Rem_Math Rem_Read Tut. Adm (Gr 1-9): 34/yr. Appl due: Rolling. Accepted: 20%. Tests IQ. Enr 103. B 68. G 35. Elem 92. Sec 11. Wh 92%. Blk 8%. Avg class size: 16. Uniform. Fac 17. M 1. F 16. Wh 94%. Blk 6%. Adv deg: 11%. Tui '04-'05: Day $15,900 (+$50). Aid: Need 60 ($190,950). Summer: Acad Enrich Rem. Tui Day $1500. 4 wks. Est 1981. Nonprofit. Quar (Aug-June). Assoc NCA. Enrolling learning-disabled pupils from approximately 30 central Ohio communities, Marburn provides a full primary and secondary program that seeks to remediate students with academic problems and return them successfully to their home schools. The academy's typical student possesses average to superior intelligence and has previously unremediated problems caused by dyslexia, ADHD or another specific learning disability. The program addresses academic skills, social interaction and problem solving.

CUYAHOGA VALLEY CHRISTIAN ACADEMY
Day Coed Gr 7-12
Cuyahoga Falls, OH 44224. 4687 Wyoga Lake Rd.
Tel: 330-929-0575. Fax: 330-929-0156.
www.cvcaroyals.org   E-mail: cvca@cvcaroyals.org

Roger Taylor, Pres. BA, Mount Vernon Nazarene College, MA, PhD, Kent State Univ. Jon F. Holley, Head. BA, Wheaton College (IL), MA, Middlebury College. Mindy Fullerton, Adm.

Col Prep. AP—Eng Calc Stats Bio Eur_Hist US_Hist Econ Music_Theory. Feat—Creative_Writing Poetry Fr Greek Lat Span Meteorology Computers Govt Psych Sociol Bible Band Chorus Handbells Strings Journ. Supp—Rem_Math Tut. Adm: 208/yr. Appl due: Aug. Accepted: 88%. Yield: 98%. Tests HSPT. Enr 837. B 437. G 400. Elem 304. Sec 533. Wh 81%. Hisp 1%. Blk 12%. Am Ind 1%. Asian 2%. Other 3%. Avg class size: 18. Uniform. Fac 71. M 28/4. F 32/7. Wh 97%. Blk 2%. Asian 1%. Adv deg: 49%. Grad '04—124. Col—122. Avg SAT: 1139. Avg ACT: 25. Alum 2350. Tui '04-'05: Day $6600 (+$175). Aid: Merit 23 ($28,825). Need 169 ($339,104). Summer: Acad Rec. 3-6 wks. Est 1968. Nonprofit. Nondenom Christian. Quar (Aug-June). As an evangelical, nondenominational school,

CVCA provides a curriculum centered in historical, Bible-based Christianity. All students are required to take Bible courses each semester, and pupils also must take several electives. Advanced Placement and honors courses provide qualified students with opportunities for acceleration. A strong cocurricular program in music, the performing arts and drama, in addition to a well-developed interscholastic sports program, supplements academics.

WALSH JESUIT HIGH SCHOOL Day Coed Gr 9-12
Cuyahoga Falls, OH 44224. 4550 Wyoga Lake Rd.
Tel: 330-929-4205. Fax: 330-929-9749.
www.walshjesuit.org   E-mail: reganm@walshjesuit.org
  Rev. James Prehn, SJ, Prin. BA, Oakland Univ, MA, Fordham Univ, EdD, Univ of San Francisco. Maureen Regan, Adm.
  Col Prep. AP—Eng Calc Bio Chem Physics Eur_Hist US_Hist Econ US_Govt & Pol. **Feat**—British_Lit Shakespeare Fr Ger Lat Span Stats Psych Sociol Theol Art_Hist Studio_Art Music_Theory Journ. **Supp**—Tut. **Adm:** 250/yr. Appl due: Jan. Accepted: 70%. **Tests** Stanford. **Enr 890.** B 445. G 445. Sec 890. Wh 93%. Hisp 1%. Blk 5%. Asian 1%. Avg class size: 25. Uniform. **Fac 78.** Adv deg: 75%. **Grad '04—207.** Col—207. Avg SAT: 1137. Avg ACT: 25. Alum 5000. **Tui '04-'05:** Day $7300 (+$300). Aid: Need 223 ($700,000). **Est 1964.** Nonprofit. Roman Catholic. Sem (Aug-June). **Assoc** NCA. College-level courses for credit, Advanced Placement work and numerous electives are offered at this Catholic high school. Walsh Jesuit also conducts a community service program.

STEPHEN T. BADIN HIGH SCHOOL Day Coed Gr 9-12
Hamilton, OH 45013. 571 New London Rd.
Tel: 513-863-3993. Fax: 513-785-2844.
www.badinhs.org   E-mail: fmargello@mail.badinhs.org
  Frank Margello, Prin. BA, MAEd, Xavier Univ.
  Col Prep. Gen Acad. Voc. AP—Eng Calc Bio US_Govt & Pol Studio_Art. **Feat**—Fr Lat Span Web_Design Relig Band Music Music_Theory. **Supp**—Dev_Read Makeup Tut. **Adm:** 150/yr. **Enr 660.** B 353. G 307. Sec 660. Wh 98%. Blk 1%. Asian 1%. Avg class size: 22. Uniform. **Fac 44.** M 20. F 24. Adv deg: 59%. **Grad '04—160.** Col—150. Alum 9700. **Tui '05-'06:** Day $5300-5500 (+$170). **Est 1966.** Nonprofit. Roman Catholic. Sem (Aug-June). **Assoc** NCA. The school takes its name from the first priest ordained in the US. Students may participate in academic school year abroad or student exchange programs.

LIMA CENTRAL CATHOLIC HIGH SCHOOL Day Coed Gr 9-12
Lima, OH 45805. 720 S Cable Rd.
Tel: 419-222-4276. Fax: 419-222-6933.
www.lcchs.edu   E-mail: cberger@lcc.noacsc.org
  Rev. Todd M. Dominique, Pres. Carl Berger, Adm.
  Col Prep. AP—Eng Fr Span Calc. **Feat**—Humanities Ger Anat & Physiol Computers Psych Sociol Relig Theol Studio_Art Band Music Bus. **Supp**—Rem_Math Rem_Read Tut. **Adm:** 150/yr. Appl due: Mar. Accepted: 85%. **Enr 416.** Sec 416.

Wh 92%. Hisp 2%. Blk 6%. Avg class size: 20. Uniform. **Fac 33.** M 15/3. F 10/5. Wh 95%. Blk 5%. Adv deg: 42%. **Grad '04—103.** Col—85. Alum 8565. **Tui '03-'04:** Day $3050 (+$225). Aid: Need 60 ($70,000). **Summer:** Acad Enrich. Tui Day $25. 1 wk. **Est 1956.** Nonprofit. Roman Catholic. Quar (Aug-June). **Assoc** NCA. Situated on a 73-acre campus, LCC provides programs in the traditional academic areas, as well as in music, art and computer science. All students take theology courses and participate in annual retreats and days of renewal. Interscholastic athletics and interest clubs supplement academics.

TUSCARAWAS CENTRAL CATHOLIC HIGH SCHOOL
Day Coed Gr 9-12

New Philadelphia, OH 44663. 777 3rd St NE.
Tel: 330-343-3302. Fax: 330-343-6388.
www.tccsaints.com   E-mail: ekorns@cdeducation.org
Dave DiDonato, Prin.

Col Prep. AP—Chem. **Feat—**Fr Span Anat Comp_Sci Web_Design Econ Govt Relig Studio_Art Music Journ. **Supp—**Tut. **Adm:** 44/yr. Accepted: 100%. **Tests** CEEB DAT. **Enr 176.** B 77. G 99. Sec 176. Wh 98%. Hisp 1%. Asian 1%. Avg class size: 24. Uniform. **Fac 13.** M 6. F 7. Wh 99%. Hisp 1%. Adv deg: 23%. **Grad '04—39.** Col—35. Avg ACT: 24. Alum 1513. **Tui '04-'05:** Day $3300 (+$62). **Est 1970.** Nonprofit. Roman Catholic. Quar (Aug-June). This Roman Catholic school offers a college preparatory education. Students perform volunteer work.

THE PHILLIPS-OSBORNE SCHOOL
Day Coed Gr PS-8

Painesville, OH 44077. 150 Gillette St.
Tel: 440-352-7574. Fax: 440-352-3083.
www.phillips-osborne.org   E-mail: pgwinn@phillips-osborne.org
Kevin M. Smith, Head. Rachelle Sundberg, Adm.

Pre-Prep. Feat—Fr Span Computers Econ Visual_Arts Drama Music Public_Speak. **Supp—**Tut. **Adm:** 71/yr. Appl due: Rolling. Accepted: 88%. **Enr 226.** B 109. G 117. Elem 226. Wh 92%. Hisp 1%. Blk 2%. Asian 4%. Other 1%. Avg class size: 13. **Fac 30.** M 3. F 23/4. Wh 99%. Hisp 1%. Adv deg: 26%. **Grad '04—26.** Prep—21. Alum 535. **Tui '04-'05:** Day $7850-9115 (+$100-575). **Est 1972.** Nonprofit. Tri (Aug-June). **Assoc** NCA. Enrolling children from age 3, Phillips-Osborne offers an accelerated, interdisciplinary elementary program. Notable curricular features include a technology lab and course work in algebra, chemistry, physics, Spanish and French. Public speaking is an important aspect of the curriculum at all grade levels.

PADUA FRANCISCAN HIGH SCHOOL
Day Coed Gr 9-12

Parma, OH 44134. 6740 State Rd.
Tel: 440-845-2444. Fax: 440-845-5710.
www.paduafranciscan.com   E-mail: padua@paduafranciscan.com
Rev. Ted Haag, OFM, Pres. BA, Quincy Univ, MDiv, Catholic Theological Union, MSSA, Case Western Reserve Univ. Christopher Keavy, Prin. BA, Assumption College, MA, Boston College. Lillian J. Gathers, Adm.

Col Prep. AP—Eng Calc Bio US_Hist Studio_Art. **Feat**—Fr Ger Ital Lat Span Comp_Sci Econ Govt Law Psych Sociol Child_Dev Theol Drama Music Accounting Bus. **Supp**—Dev_Read LD Rem_Math Rem_Read Rev Tut. **Adm:** 248/yr. Appl due: Jan. Accepted: 95%. **Tests** HSPT. **Enr 1010.** B 503. G 507. Sec 1010. Avg class size: 26. Uniform. **Fac 71.** M 28/5. F 35/3. Adv deg: 52%. **Grad '04—262.** Col—260. Avg SAT: 1060. Avg ACT: 23. Alum 9180. **Tui '04-'05:** Day $6550. Aid: Merit 403 ($201,500). Need 147 ($125,300). **Summer:** Enrich. Tui Day $100. 1 wk. **Est 1961.** Nonprofit. Roman Catholic. Sem (Aug-June). **Assoc** NCA. Padua's program of study offers selections in business, English, life skills, mathematics, science and social studies, with requirements in theology, foreign language, fine arts and computer science. Honors and AP classes and electives are provided. The athletic program comprises both interscholastic sports and intramural teams. Foreign exchange opportunities, community involvement, and a variety of student clubs and organizations supplement the curriculum.

LUTHERAN HIGH SCHOOL WEST
Day Coed Gr 9-12
Rocky River, OH 44116. 3850 Linden Rd.
Tel: 440-333-1660. Fax: 440-333-1729.
www.lutheranwest.com E-mail: admissions@lutheranwest.com
John Buetow, Prin. BA, Valparaiso Univ, MA, Univ of New Orleans.

Col Prep. Gen Acad. AP—Eng Calc Bio US_Hist US_Govt & Pol. **Feat**—Ger Span Stats Comp_Sci Web_Design Econ Sociol Photog Studio_Art Drama Music_Theory Journ Speech Woodworking. **Supp**—Tut. **Adm:** 135/yr. Appl due: Rolling. **Enr 414.** Sec 414. Wh 92%. Hisp 4%. Blk 2%. Asian 1%. Other 1%. Avg class size: 20. **Fac 35. Grad '04—93. Tui '04-'05:** Day $7000 (+$200). **Est 1948.** Nonprofit. Lutheran. Quar (Aug-June). **Assoc** NCA. Advanced Placement and honors classes are part of Lutheran West's curriculum, as is a specialized reading program. Participation in clubs, drama and music programs, student government and service organizations is encouraged. A sports program includes interscholastic competition for boys and girls, in addition to coed intramurals.

MAGNIFICAT HIGH SCHOOL
Day Girls Gr 9-12
Rocky River, OH 44116. 20770 Hilliard Blvd.
Tel: 440-331-1572. Fax: 440-331-7257.
www.magnificaths.org E-mail: smpcook@magnificaths.org
Sr. Carolyn Marshall, HM, Pres. BA, Notre Dame College (OH), MA, Westminster College. Sr. Mary Pat Cook, HM, Prin. BS, Notre Dame College (OH), MSEd, Indiana Univ. Terry Schabel Carney, Adm.

Col Prep. AP—Eng Fr Span Calc Stats Comp_Sci Bio Chem US_Hist Econ Art_Hist. **Feat**—Theol Photog Studio_Art Drama Theater_Arts Bus. **Supp**—Rem_Math Rem_Read Tut. **Adm (Gr 9-11):** 254/yr. Appl due: Jan. Accepted: 99%. **Tests** HSPT. **Enr 856.** G 856. Sec 856. Wh 93%. Hisp 1%. Blk 1%. Asian 5%. Avg class size: 22. Uniform. **Fac 77.** M 5/2. F 67/3. Wh 100%. Adv deg: 63%. **Grad '04—208.** Col—208. Avg SAT: 1224. Avg ACT: 28. Alum 9000. **Tui '04-'05:** Day $7750. Aid: Merit 180 ($100,000). Need 298 ($650,000). **Summer:** Acad Enrich Rec. Tui Day $75/wk. 5 wks. **Est 1955.** Nonprofit. Roman Catholic. Sem (Aug-June). **Assoc** NCA. Staffed by the Sisters of the Humility of Mary, this school conducts a college preparatory curriculum. Honors and Advanced Placement classes are offered in many subject areas. Magnificat maintains four-year programs in art, English, modern languages, math, science and theology, and computers are used extensively in all academic departments.

REGINA HIGH SCHOOL Day Girls Gr 9-12
South Euclid, OH 44121. 1857 S Green Rd.
Tel: 216-382-2110. Fax: 216-382-3555.
www.reginahigh.com E-mail: foxh@reginahigh.com
  Sr. Maureen Burke, SND, Prin. BA, Notre Dame College (OH), MA, Kent State Univ, MA, Baldwin-Wallace College. Hillary M. Fox, Adm.

  Col Prep. Feat—Fr Ger Span. **Supp**—Rem_Math Rem_Read Rev Tut. **Adm:** 80/yr. Appl due: Aug. Accepted: 80%. **Enr 280.** G 280. Sec 280. Wh 72%. Hisp 1%. Blk 26%. Asian 1%. Avg class size: 15. Uniform. **Fac 27.** M 6. F 19/2. Wh 99%. Other 1%. Adv deg: 62%. **Grad '04—68.** Col—67. Avg SAT: 1020. Alum 7000. **Tui '04-'05:** Day $6950 (+$100). **Est 1953.** Nonprofit. Roman Catholic. Sem (Aug-June). **Assoc** NCA. Students at Regina may accumulate college credit through courses at Notre Dame College or John Carroll University. European travel/study opportunities and a gifted and talented program are available. The school offers intramural and interscholastic athletics, student council, drama, choral and other extracurricular activities.

ST. FRANCIS DE SALES HIGH SCHOOL Day Boys Gr 9-12
Toledo, OH 43607. 2323 W Bancroft St.
Tel: 419-531-1618. Fax: 419-531-9740.
www.sfstoledo.org E-mail: sfs@sfstoldeo.org
  Andrew Hill, Prin. BA, MA, Univ of Toledo. Chris Steingass, Adm.

  Col Prep. AP—Eng Fr Ger Lat Span Calc Stats Comp_Sci Bio Chem Physics Eur_Hist US_Hist Econ Psych Art_Hist. **Feat**—Writing Greek Anat & Physiol Astron Geol Web_Design Govt Sociol Relig World_Relig Performing_Arts Chorus Public_Speak. **Supp**—Tut. **Adm:** 182/yr. Appl due: Aug. Accepted: 99%. Yield: 97%. **Tests** HSPT. **Enr 670.** B 670. Sec 670. Wh 90%. Hisp 4%. Blk 4%. Asian 1%. Other 1%. Avg class size: 27. **Fac 48.** M 31/5. F 10/2. Wh 100%. Adv deg: 56%. **Grad '04—145.** Col—141. Avg SAT: 1109. Avg ACT: 24. Alum 10,600. **Tui '04-'05:** Day $6200 (+$250). Aid: Merit 185 ($321,000). Need 200 ($341,690). Work prgm 200 ($72,074). **Summer:** Acad Enrich Rev Rem. Tui Day $75. 4 wks. **Est 1955.** Inc. Roman Catholic. Quar (Aug-June). Staffed by the Oblates of St. Francis de Sales, this school offers AP courses in every academic area and shares classes in some areas with a nearby girls' school. A retreat program is mandatory for all students, and after-school community service is required during the senior year.

CARDINAL MOONEY HIGH SCHOOL Day Coed Gr 9-12
Youngstown, OH 44507. 2545 Erie St.
Tel: 330-788-5007. Fax: 330-788-4511.
www.cardinalmooney.com E-mail: cardinalmooney@cboss.com
  Sr. Jane Marie Kudlacz, HM, Prin. BA, Notre Dame College (OH), MA, John Carroll Univ.

Col Prep. Gen Acad. Bus. AP—Eng Calc Bio Chem US_Hist. **Feat**—Creative_Writing Fr Ger Lat Span Stats Anat & Physiol Environ_Sci Genetics Programming Econ Govt Psych Sociol Theol World_Relig Photog Studio_Art Chorus Music Music_Theory Accounting Journ Indus_Arts. **Supp**—Dev_Read Rem_Math Rem_Read Tut. **Adm:** 161/yr. Accepted: 100%. **Enr 586.** B 293. G 293. Sec 586. Wh 88%. Hisp 1%. Blk 11%. Avg class size: 25. **Fac 49.** M 22/3. F 23/1. Wh 100%. Adv deg: 55%. **Grad '04—134.** Col—126. Avg SAT: 1076. Avg ACT: 22. Alum 11,617. **Tui '04-'05:** Day $4775. Aid: Need 300 ($250,000). Work prgm 35 ($12,000). **Est 1956.** Nonprofit. Roman Catholic. Sem (Aug-June). Cardinal Mooney's traditional college preparatory curriculum is enhanced by training in the practical and performing arts. Christian values are integrated into all aspects of the program, and each student takes theology every semester. Extracurricular activities range from interest and language clubs to community service and sports.

WISCONSIN

IMMANUEL LUTHERAN HIGH SCHOOL — Coed Gr 9-12, Bdg & Day
Eau Claire, WI 54701. 501 Grover Rd.
Tel: 715-836-6621. Fax: 715-836-6634.
www.ilc.edu   E-mail: john.pfeiffer@ilc.edu
  John K. Pfeiffer, Pres. BA, Univ of Massachusetts-Amherst, MDiv, Immanuel Lutheran Seminary. Jeffrey A. Schierenbeck, Prin.

Col Prep. Feat—Ger Computers Relig. **Supp**—Rem_Math Rem_Read Tut. **Adm:** 35/yr. Bdg 21. Day 14. Accepted: 99%. **Enr 134.** B 45/25. G 41/23. Sec 134. Wh 97%. Asian 3%. Avg class size: 30. **Fac 14.** M 13. F /1. Wh 100%. Adv deg: 64%. **Grad '04—32.** Col—25. Alum 1000. **Tui '04-'05:** Bdg $6900. Day $4300. **Est 1959.** Nonprofit. Church of the Lutheran Confession. Sem (Aug-May). Religion courses are part of this school's curriculum. In addition to the high school division, Immanuel Lutheran operates a four-year college and a three-year, postgraduate theological seminary.

NOTRE DAME DE LA BAIE ACADEMY — Day Coed Gr 9-12
Green Bay, WI 54303. 610 Maryhill Dr.
Tel: 920-429-6100. Fax: 920-429-6168.
www.notredameacademy.com   E-mail: admissions@notredameacademy.com
  Rev. Dane J. Radecki, OPraem, Pres. Shannon Greisen, Adm.

Col Prep. Gen Acad. AP—US_Hist. **Feat**—Japan Lat Environ_Sci Econ Govt Psych Sociol Child_Dev Relig Studio_Art Drama Music Accounting Bus Drafting Woodworking. **Supp**—Tut. **Adm:** 212/yr. Appl due: Aug. **Enr 741.** B 360. G 381. Sec 741. Wh 95%. Hisp 1%. Blk 1%. Asian 1%. Other 2%. **Fac 50.** M 22/3. F 23/2. Wh 100%. Adv deg: 32%. **Grad '04—201.** Col—182. Alum 15,000. **Tui '04-'05:** Day $5100 (+$225). Parishioners $4100 (+$225). Aid: Need ($300,000). **Est 1990.** Nonprofit. Roman Catholic. Quar (Sept-June). **Assoc** NCA. Notre Dame provides both college preparatory and general academic programs for high school students. College-credit courses are offered through St. Norbert College. An accelerated curriculum comprises honors and advanced classes.

ARMITAGE ACADEMY
Day Coed Gr K-8
Kenosha, WI 53143. 6032 8th Ave.
Tel: 262-654-4200. Fax: 262-654-4737.
www.armitageacademy.org   E-mail: armitage@armitageacademy.org
   Thomas A. Creighton, Dir. Karen P. Sommer, Adm.

Pre-Prep. Feat—Fr Computers Studio_Art Drama Music Dance. **Supp**—Dev_ Read Tut. **Adm:** 37/yr. Appl due: Rolling. Accepted: 84%. Yield: 98%. **Enr 113.** B 63. G 50. Elem 113. Wh 83%. Blk 3%. Asian 4%. Other 10%. Avg class size: 13. Uniform. **Fac 13.** F 11/2. Wh 100%. Adv deg: 69%. **Grad '04—8.** Prep—4. Alum 217. **Tui '04-'05:** Day $6975-7795 (+$600). Aid: Need 51 ($230,790). **Est 1975.** Nonprofit. Quar (Sept-June). **Assoc** NCA. Armitage offers a liberal arts curriculum emphasizing a strong foundation in the basic learning skills. Cultural enrichment programs in the fine arts include music, art, creative movement and drama classes. Computer literacy training and French instruction begin in kindergarten.

LAKESIDE LUTHERAN HIGH SCHOOL
Day Coed Gr 9-12
Lake Mills, WI 53551. 231 Woodland Beach Rd.
Tel: 920-648-2321. Fax: 920-648-5625.
www.llhs.org   E-mail: info@llhs.org
   James C. Grasby, Prin. Gerald Walta, Adm.

Col Prep. Gen Acad. AP—Calc. **Feat**—Ger Lat Span Anat & Physiol Environ_Sci Programming Econ Sociol Relig Studio_Art Band Chorus Indus_Arts. **Supp**—Dev_Read Rem_Math Rem_Read Tut. **Adm:** 118/yr. Appl due: Aug. Accepted: 98%. **Enr 405.** B 205. G 200. Sec 405. Wh 100%. Avg class size: 17. **Fac 40.** M 28/4. F 4/4. Wh 100%. **Grad '04—100.** Col—90. Avg ACT: 24. Alum 3700. **Tui '03-'04:** Day $3600 (+$180). **Est 1958.** Nonprofit. Lutheran. Sem (Aug-May). Serving families from communities throughout south-central Wisconsin, Lakeside offers a religiously centered program that readies students primarily for four-year colleges, and, to a lesser degree, for technological studies, employment or the military. Business, foreign language, computer, industrial arts and home economics electives complement required courses in English, math, science, social studies, religion and music. Cocurricular offerings include drama, forensics, publications, band, choir, and competitive boys' and girls' athletics.

EDGEWOOD HIGH SCHOOL
Day Coed Gr 9-12
Madison, WI 53711. 2219 Monroe St.
Tel: 608-257-1023. Fax: 608-257-9133.
www.edgewoodhs.org   E-mail: conajil@edgewood.k12.wi.us
   K. Michele Clarke, Pres. BS, Univ of Wisconsin-Eau Claire, MA, Loyola Univ of Chicago. Robert D. Growney, Prin. BA, Loras College, MA, Edgewood College. Jill Conaway, Adm.

Col Prep. AP—Eng Span Calc Bio Chem Physics Eur_Hist US_Hist. **Feat**—Fr Lat Comp_Sci Relig Architect_Drawing Fine_Arts Public_Speak Aviation. **Supp**—Dev_Read LD Makeup Tut. **Adm:** 165/yr. Appl due: Apr. Accepted: 98%. Yield: 94%. **Tests** TOEFL. **Enr 600.** B 315. G 285. Sec 600. Wh 91%. Hisp 2%. Blk 2%. Am Ind 1%. Asian 4%. Avg class size: 19. **Fac 48.** M 21/2. F 18/7. Wh 100%. Adv deg: 56%. **Grad '04—148.** Col—143. Avg ACT: 22. Alum 9400. **Tui '04-'05:** Day

$6095 (+$635-1000). Aid: Merit 15 ($42,500). Need 250 ($413,000). **Summer:** Enrich Rec. Sports. $100/wk. 6 wks. **Est 1881.** Nonprofit. Roman Catholic. Quar (Aug-June). **Assoc** NCA. Operated by the Dominican Sisters of Sinsinawa, this school bases instruction on Christian values. A summer environmental science course is available. Students may take courses at Edgewood College and the University of Wisconsin.

MARQUETTE UNIVERSITY HIGH SCHOOL — Day Boys Gr 9-12
Milwaukee, WI 53208. 3401 W Wisconsin Ave.
Tel: 414-933-7220. Fax: 414-937-8588.
www.muhs.edu   E-mail: admissions@muhs.edu

Rev. Thomas C. Manahan, SJ, Pres. BA, Univ of Minnesota-Twin Cities, MBA, Indiana Univ, MDiv, Weston Jesuit School of Theology. Rev. John M. Belmonte, SJ, Prin. Dan Quesnell, Adm.

Col Prep. AP—Eng Fr Lat Span Calc Stats Comp_Sci Bio Chem Eur_Hist US_Hist Econ Studio_Art. **Feat**—Shakespeare Ger Geol Govt Law Psych Sociol Philos Theol Photog Chorus. **Supp**—Rev Tut. **Adm (Gr 9-10):** 294/yr. Appl due: Jan. Accepted: 80%. **Tests** HSPT. **Enr 1056.** B 1056. Sec 1056. Wh 82%. Hisp 7%. Blk 5%. Am Ind 1%. Asian 3%. Other 2%. Avg class size: 24. **Fac 68.** M 46/5. F 16/1. Wh 96%. Blk 4%. Adv deg: 55%. **Grad '04—251.** Col—249. Avg SAT: 1190. Avg ACT: 25. Alum 11,000. **Tui '04-'05:** Day $7375 (+$400). Aid: Merit 5 ($2500). Need 290 ($1,100,000). **Summer:** Acad Rev. Tui Day $250. 6 wks. **Est 1857.** Nonprofit. Roman Catholic. Sem (Aug-May). **Assoc** NCA. In the Jesuit tradition, MUHS emphasizes a comprehensive study of the liberal arts and a commitment to social responsibility. An honors program is available, and both accelerated courses and the AP program provide college-credit options. Student service is required of all sophomores, juniors and seniors. Cocurricular activities include various organizations and clubs, as well as intramural and interscholastic athletics.

MILWAUKEE LUTHERAN HIGH SCHOOL — Day Coed Gr 9-12
Milwaukee, WI 53222. 9700 W Grantosa Dr.
Tel: 414-461-6000. Fax: 414-461-2733.
www.milwaukeelutheranhs.org   E-mail: djobst@milwaukeelutheranhs.org

Paul M. Bahr, Prin. BA, Concordia College (IL), MA, Canisius College. Dwayne Jobst, Adm.

Col Prep. Gen Acad. Bus. AP—US_Hist. **Feat**—Ger Lat Span Stats Comp_Sci Econ Govt Psych Relig Studio_Art Music Accounting Bus Speech Indus_Arts Home_Ec. **Supp**—LD Makeup Tut. **Adm:** 210/yr. Appl due: Rolling. Accepted: 90%. **Enr 725.** Sec 725. Wh 86%. Hisp 1%. Blk 13%. Avg class size: 25. **Fac 52.** M 30/1. F 18/3. Wh 100%. Adv deg: 61%. **Grad '04—179.** Col—139. Avg ACT: 24. Alum 8000. **Tui '04-'05:** Day $6875 (+$400). Assoc Members $5115 (+$400). Aid: Merit 12 ($12,000). Need 275 ($375,000). **Summer:** Enrich. 2-6 wks. **Est 1955.** Nonprofit. Lutheran-Missouri Synod. Sem (Aug-June). **Assoc** NCA. Milwaukee Lutheran offers four basic courses of study—college preparatory, preministerial, business education and general education—in addition to a special-needs program for at-risk students. Extracurriculars include athletics and a number of clubs and organizations.

PIUS XI HIGH SCHOOL Day Coed Gr 9-12
Milwaukee, WI 53213. 135 N 76th St.
Tel: 414-290-7000. Fax: 414-290-7001.
www.piusxi.org   E-mail: piusxi@piusxi.org

James Dyer, Pres. BA, Michigan State Univ, MA, Marian College. Richard Pendergast, Prin. BA, MA, Marquette Univ. Mary Piskula, Adm.

Col Prep. Gen Acad. Voc. AP—Eng Calc Eur_Hist US_Hist Psych. **Feat**—Fr Ger Span Genetics Oceanog Theol Bus Debate. **Supp**—Dev_Read ESL Rem_Math Rem_Read Tut. **Adm:** 445/yr. Appl due: July. Accepted: 98%. **Tests** HSPT. **Enr 1390.** B 663. G 727. Sec 1390. Wh 76%. Hisp 11%. Blk 6%. Am Ind 1%. Asian 1%. Other 5%. Avg class size: 24. **Fac 121.** M 44/3. F 59/15. Wh 96%. Hisp 2%. Blk 2%. Adv deg: 48%. **Grad '04—362.** Col—326. Avg ACT: 23. Alum 24,000. **Tui '04-'05:** Day $6820 (+$75). Aid: Merit 16 ($16,000). Need 423 ($1,515,412). Work prgm 100 ($30,000). **Est 1929.** Nonprofit. Roman Catholic. Sem (Aug-June). **Assoc** NCA. Pius offers college and technical preparatory curricula, and students may focus on specific subjects beyond their basic academic and religious requirements. In-depth courses are offered in literature, foreign languages, science, mathematics, social science, business education, industrial technology, family and consumer education, and the creative and performing arts.

PRAIRIE HILL WALDORF SCHOOL Day Coed Gr PS-8
Pewaukee, WI 53072. N 14 W 29143 Silvernail Rd.
Tel: 262-646-7497. Fax: 262-646-7495.
www.prairiehillwaldorf.org   E-mail: info@prairiehillwaldorf.org

Gary Cannon, Admin. BA, American Univ of Paris (France). Nancy Notley, Adm.

Gen Acad. Feat—Mythology Ger Span Astron Geol Zoology Medieval_Hist. **Supp**—Rem_Math Rem_Read Tut. **Adm (Gr PS-7):** 34/yr. Appl due: Rolling. Accepted: 100%. Yield: 98%. **Enr 184.** B 84. G 100. Elem 184. Wh 92%. Blk 2%. Asian 6%. Avg class size: 20. **Fac 24.** M 2/2. F 12/8. Wh 100%. Adv deg: 16%. **Grad '04—13.** Prep—5. **Tui '04-'05:** Day $4950-6550 (+$250). Aid: Need 30 ($100,000). **Summer:** Enrich Rec. Tui Day $100-125/wk. 2 wks. **Est 1987.** Nonprofit. Sem (Sept-June). Part of the worldwide network of Waldorf schools, Prairie Hill operates early childhood programs (for children as young as age 3) and a full elementary-level program. Instruction in French and German begins in grade 1. The integrated curriculum incorporates vocal and instrumental music increasingly as students age. Handwork, a characteristic of Waldorf education, serves as an important instructional tool.

DOMINICAN HIGH SCHOOL Day Coed Gr 9-12
Whitefish Bay, WI 53217. 120 E Silver Spring Dr.
Tel: 414-332-1170. Fax: 414-332-4101.
www.dominicanhighschool.com   E-mail: admission@dominicanhighschool.com

Eamonn O'Keefe, Prin. BA, MEd, Marquette Univ. Elizabeth Stengel, Adm.

Col Prep. Feat—Fr Span Programming Relig Studio_Art Stained_Glass. **Supp**—Rev Tut. **Adm (Gr 9-11):** 100/yr. Appl due: June. Accepted: 65%. Yield: 75%. **Tests** HSPT. **Enr 342.** B 166. G 176. Sec 342. Wh 63%. Hisp 8%. Blk 20%.

Am Ind 1%. Asian 3%. Other 5%. Avg class size: 19. **Fac 37.** M 13/1. F 18/5. Wh 93%. Hisp 5%. Blk 2%. Adv deg: 45%. **Grad '04—78.** Col—76. Avg ACT: 23. Alum 8100. **Tui '04-'05:** Day $6700 (+$15-20). Aid: Merit 76. Need 205. **Summer:** Enrich Rev. Tui Day $400. 6 wks. **Est 1952.** Nonprofit. Roman Catholic. Sem (Aug-June). **Assoc** NCA. Sponsored by the Sinsinawa Dominican Sisters, the school emphasizes college preparation and provides opportunities for acceleration in English, math and science. Students also have various options in religion, social studies, foreign languages, the fine arts, computer science, communications, business and physical education. Activities at Dominican include science competitions, drama, band, choir, newspaper, yearbook, and boys' and girls' athletics. In addition, the school conducts foreign immersion trips to Spain, Mexico and France every other year.

Plains States

IOWA

MAHARISHI SCHOOL OF THE   **Bdg Coed Gr 9-12**
AGE OF ENLIGHTENMENT   **Day Coed PS-12**
Fairfield, IA 52556. 804 N 3rd St.
Tel: 641-472-9400. Fax: 641-472-1211.
www.maharishischooliowa.org   E-mail: info@msae.edu
    Ashley Deans, Head. PhD, York Univ (Canada). Rod Falk, Adm.

    Col Prep. Feat—Sanskrit Studio_Art Drama Music. **Supp**—Dev_Read Rem_Math Rem_Read Tut. **Adm:** 15/yr. Bdg 0. Day 15. Appl due: Rolling. Accepted: 100%. Yield: 100%. **Enr 280.** B 140. G 140. Elem 134. Sec 136. Wh 90%. Hisp 2%. Blk 1%. Asian 4%. Other 3%. Avg class size: 15. Uniform. **Fac 54.** M 4/13. F 24/13. Wh 91%. Hisp 2%. Blk 2%. Asian 5%. Adv deg: 25%. In Dorms 9. **Grad '04—47.** Col—47. Avg SAT: 1143. Avg ACT: 25. Alum 350. **Tui '04-'05:** Bdg $24,430-24,810 (+$1500). Day $11,290-12,480. Aid: Need 69 ($269,502). Work prgm 4 ($3080). **Est 1973.** Nonprofit. Quar (Aug-June). Maharishi School employs hands-on experiments, projects, field trips and workshops as part of the learning process. The school's early childhood program seeks to build a foundation for future learning, and older pupils practice meditation each day to assist in academic achievement. Residential students take part in required daily study periods.

DOWLING HIGH SCHOOL   **Day Coed Gr 9-12**
West Des Moines, IA 50265. 1400 Buffalo Rd.
Tel: 515-225-3000. Fax: 515-222-1056.
www.dowlinghighschool.org   E-mail: kgehring@dowling.pvt.k12.ia.us
    Jerry M. Deegan, Pres. EdD, Drake Univ. James M. Dowdle, Prin. PhD. Katie Peterson & Kelly O'Hare, Adms.

    Col Prep. Gen Acad. Feat—Ger Lat Relig Fine_Arts Speech. **Supp**—Dev_Read Rem_Math Rem_Read Tut. **Adm:** 310/yr. Appl due: June. Accepted: 99%. **Enr 1150.** B 588. G 562. Sec 1150. Wh 92%. Hisp 3%. Blk 2%. Asian 3%. Avg class size: 20. **Fac 84.** Adv deg: 53%. **Grad '04—281.** Avg SAT: 1166. Avg ACT: 24. Alum 16,000. **Tui '04-'05:** Day $6302 (+$40). Catholic $4540 (+$40). Aid: Merit 158 ($61,000). Need 294 ($686,000). Work prgm 15 ($25,000). **Summer:** Acad Rem. Tui Day $110/crse. 4 wks. **Est 1972.** Nonprofit. Roman Catholic. Sem (Aug-May). Advanced Placement courses are provided, and courses in vocational/technical subjects are available to juniors and seniors through the Des Moines public schools. Each semester, all students are required to take religion and to perform ten hours of community service. Students are involved in extracurricular clubs and activities ranging from the arts to athletics, including student government and school newspaper.

KANSAS

THOMAS MORE PREP—MARIAN HIGH SCHOOL
Coed Gr 9-12
Bdg & Day

Hays, KS 67601. 1701 Hall St.
Tel: 785-625-6577. Fax: 785-625-3912.
www.tmp-m.org E-mail: fairbankm@tmp-m.org

Jean Ross, Pres. BS, Marian College of Fond du Lac, BA, Marquette Univ, EdSp, Fort Hays State Univ. Ken Haas, Prin. BA, MA, Fort Hays State Univ. Michelle Fairbank, Adm.

Col Prep. AP—Eng Calc Chem US_Hist US_Govt & Pol. **Feat**—Humanities Ger Lat Span Stats Anat & Physiol Ecol Computers Psych Sociol Bus_Law Relig Architect Drawing Fine_Arts Photog Sculpt Studio_Art Drama Band Chorus Accounting Bus Debate Journ Speech Study_Skills. **Supp**—Dev_Read ESL. **Adm:** 80/yr. Bdg 22. Day 58. Appl due: Rolling. Accepted: 99%. **Tests** TOEFL. **Enr 260.** B 31/120. G 15/94. Sec 260. Wh 85%. Hisp 5%. Asian 10%. Avg class size: 20. Uniform. **Fac 29.** M 10. F 19. Wh 100%. Adv deg: 34%. **Grad '04—82.** Col—80. Avg SAT: 1052. Avg ACT: 23. Alum 5000. **Tui '03–'04:** Bdg $18,800. 5-Day Bdg $12,850. Day $4500. **Est 1908.** Nonprofit. Roman Catholic. Sem (Aug-May). Advanced Placement, fine and performing arts, and business courses are all aspects of the school's curriculum. Seniors may enroll in auto mechanics or allied health classes at the nearby North Central Kansas Area Vocational School. Extracurricular activities include sports, service organizations, student publications, music, drama and debate.

HYMAN BRAND HEBREW ACADEMY
Day Coed Gr K-12

Overland Park, KS 66211. 5801 W 115th St, Ste 102.
Tel: 913-327-8150. Fax: 913-327-8180.
E-mail: info@hbha.edu

Adam C. Holden, Head. BAEd, Univ of Southampton (England), MAEd, Washburn Univ of Topeka, EdD, California Coast Univ. Shelley Rissien, Adm.

Col Prep. Feat—Hebrew Computers Judaic_Stud Relig. **Supp**—Tut. **Adm:** 44/yr. Appl due: Rolling. Accepted: 99%. **Enr 297.** B 143. G 154. Elem 226. Sec 71. Wh 96%. Hisp 1%. Blk 2%. Asian 1%. Avg class size: 23. **Fac 41.** M 8/1. F 22/10. Wh 100%. Adv deg: 63%. **Grad '04—26.** Col—26. Alum 186. **Tui '04–'05:** Day $8400-12,200 (+$175-600). Aid: Need 135 ($562,000). **Est 1966.** Nonprofit. Jewish. Quar (Aug-June). **Assoc** NCA. The academy provides a rigorous program of Judaic and secular studies within a Jewish environment. Graduates matriculate at competitive colleges in both Israel and the US.

TOPEKA COLLEGIATE SCHOOL
Day Coed Gr PS-8

Topeka, KS 66614. 2200 SW Eveningside Dr.
Tel: 785-228-0490. Fax: 785-228-0504.
www.topekacollegiate.org   E-mail: phuff@topekacollegiate.org

Michael B. Roberts, Head. BME, MAEd, EdD, Washington Univ. Paula G. Huff, Adm.

Pre-Prep. Feat—Lat Span Computers Studio_Art. **Supp**—Dev_Read Rem_ Math Rem_Read Tut. **Adm:** 37/yr. Appl due: Rolling. Accepted: 90%. **Tests** MAT. **Enr 275.** B 131. G 144. Elem 275. Wh 75%. Hisp 4%. Blk 5%. Am Ind 1%. Asian 6%. Other 9%. Avg class size: 16. **Fac 35.** M 4/1. F 29/1. Wh 96%. Hisp 1%. Blk 2%. Am Ind 1%. Adv deg: 28%. **Grad '04—24.** Prep—24. **Tui '04-'05:** Day $7200 (+$70-175). Aid: Need 74. **Summer:** Acad Enrich Rev Rec. 11 wks. **Est 1982.** Nonprofit. Quar (Aug-May). **Assoc** NCA. Basic skills development takes place in the lower grades. TCS offers accelerated math and science classes in grades 5-8, in addition to physical education, music, art and computer courses. Spanish instruction begins in prekindergarten, Latin in grade 7.

THE INDEPENDENT SCHOOL   Day Coed Gr PS-12
Wichita, KS 67207. 8301 E Douglas Ave.
Tel: 316-686-0152. Fax: 316-686-3918.
www.tis.wichita.ks.us   E-mail: norton@tis.wichita.ks.us

Karen Norton, Head. BS, Kansas State Univ, MS, Wichita State Univ. Mark Bohm, Adm.

Col Prep. AP—Eng Fr Lat Span Calc Bio Chem US_Hist US_Govt & Pol. **Feat**—Lib_Skills Ger Stats Anat & Physiol Computers Econ Photog Studio_Art Drama Music Journ. **Supp**—Rev Tut. **Adm:** 95/yr. Appl due: Rolling. Accepted: 90%. **Tests** IQ Stanford. **Enr 750.** B 390. G 360. Elem 544. Sec 206. Wh 92%. Hisp 1%. Blk 2%. Am Ind 2%. Asian 3%. Avg class size: 15. **Fac 71.** M 20. F 42/9. Wh 96%. Hisp 2%. Blk 2%. Adv deg: 36%. **Grad '04—57.** Col—57. Avg SAT: 1264. Avg ACT: 26. **Tui '04-'05:** Day $3153-7160 (+$200). Aid: Need 90 ($325,000). **Summer:** Acad Enrich Rev Rem Rec. 7 wks. **Est 1980.** Nonprofit. Sem (Aug-May). **Assoc** NCA. Located in the eastern section of the city, the school conducts a full elementary and secondary curriculum that emphasizes a strong foundation in basic skills, problem solving and critical-thinking abilities, and study skills development. The arts are integral to school life, and Independent features notable computer and library programs. Intramural and competitive athletics begin in the lower school.

MINNESOTA

MARANATHA CHRISTIAN ACADEMY   Day Coed Gr PS-12
Brooklyn Park, MN 55428. 9201 75th Ave N.
Tel: 612-588-2850. Fax: 612-588-7854.
www.mca.lwcc.org   E-mail: jwallen@mca.lwcc.org

Brian Sullivan, Chief Admin. BA, Hamline Univ. Jane Wallen, Adm.

Col Prep. Gen Acad. Voc. AP—Eng Span Calc Bio US_Hist. **Feat**—Astron Oceanog Computers Programming Robotics Web_Design Bible World_Relig Acting Accounting Bus Journ. **Supp**—Makeup Tut. **Adm:** 127/yr. Appl due: Rolling. Accepted: 100%. **Tests** CEEB. **Enr 720.** B 346. G 374. Elem 544. Sec 176. Wh 81%. Blk 9%. Am Ind 1%. Asian 2%. Other 7%. Avg class size: 16. Uniform. **Fac 56.** M 7/1. F 40/8. Wh 97%. Hisp 1%. Blk 2%. Adv deg: 26%. **Grad '04—34.** Col—31. Avg SAT: 1300. Avg ACT: 24. Alum 113. **Tui '05-'06:** Day $5356-5812 (+$500). Aid: Merit 2 ($10,500). Need 109 ($150,000). **Summer:** Acad Enrich Rev

Rem Rec. Tui Day $200/credit. 6 wks. **Est 1978.** Nonprofit. Nondenom Christian. (Sept-June). A ministry of Living Word Christian Center, this nondenominational school provides a traditional prekindergarten through grade 12 program from a Christian perspective. Characteristics of MCA's curriculum are an emphasis on computer technology and a variety of electives. Children in grades K-6 attend classes at 4021 Thomas Ave. N, Minneapolis 55412, while the campus on 75th Avenue North serves prekindergartners and pupils in grades 7-12.

MARSHALL SCHOOL Day Coed Gr 5-12
Duluth, MN 55811. 1215 Rice Lake Rd.
Tel: 218-727-7266. Fax: 218-727-1569.
www.marshallschool.org E-mail: aarntson@marshallschool.org
 Marlene M. David, Head. BS, MSLS, Wayne State Univ, MLA, Johns Hopkins Univ. Amy Arntson, Adm.
 Col Prep. AP—Eng Fr Ger Span Calc Stats Chem Studio_Art. **Feat**—Anat & Physiol Environ_Sci Zoology Comp_Design Econ Govt Law Sociol Relig Drama Speech. **Supp**—Tut. **Adm:** 140/yr. Appl due: Rolling. **Tests** CTP_4. **Enr 554.** Elem 204. Sec 350. Wh 93%. Hisp 1%. Blk 2%. Am Ind 2%. Asian 2%. Avg class size: 18. **Fac 54.** Adv deg: 35%. **Grad '04—83.** Col—83. Avg SAT: 1251. Avg ACT: 26. Alum 5207. **Tui '02-'03:** Day $6820-7520 (+$200). Aid: Need 110 ($420,000). **Est 1904.** Nonprofit. Sem (Aug-June). **Assoc** NCA. Marshall provides a liberal arts education complete with honors and AP courses. Foreign language, religion and fine arts courses are among the graduation requirements. In addition, students complete requirements in community service and outdoor education. Competitive sports teams are available beginning in grade 7; academic competitions and other organizations such as yearbook, student council, literary magazine and drama, as well as band, strings and choir, round out the extracurricular choices.

BETHLEHEM ACADEMY Day Coed Gr 7-12
Faribault, MN 55021. 105 SW 3rd Ave.
Tel: 507-334-3948. Fax: 507-334-3949.
www.bacards.pvt.k12.mn.us E-mail: principal@bacards.pvt.k12.mn.us
 Bette Blaisdell, Pres. Ron Sevcik, Adm.
 Col Prep. Gen Acad. Feat—Span Computers Theol Studio_Art Theater Music Bus Drafting Indus_Arts. **Enr 235.** Elem 77. Sec 158. **Fac 21. Grad '04—40.** Col—40. **Tui '03-'04:** Day $5050 (+$450). Aid: Need 155 ($200,000). **Est 1865.** Roman Catholic. Tri (Aug-May). Students at BA enroll in a compulsory theology course each year as part of the core academic curriculum. With permission, qualified eighth graders may take algebra I and Spanish. Extracurricular activities include athletics, various literary organizations, jazz band and acting, among others.

HILLCREST LUTHERAN ACADEMY Bdg Coed Gr 10-12
Fergus Falls, MN 56537. 610 Hillcrest Dr. Day Coed 7-12
Tel: 218-739-3371. Fax: 218-739-3372.
www.ffhillcrest.org E-mail: office@ffhillcrest.org
 Rev. Steven J. Brue, Prin. BA, Bethel College, MS, Minnesota State Univ-Moorhead, MDiv, Lutheran Brethren Seminary, Prin.

Col Prep. AP—Eur_Hist Studio_Art. **Feat**—Fr Span Psych Bible. **Supp**—ESL. **Adm:** 82/yr. Bdg 52. Day 30. Appl due: Aug. Accepted: 99%. **Enr 196.** Elem 26. Sec 170. Wh 91%. Am Ind 1%. Asian 8%. Avg class size: 25. **Fac 20.** M 9/3. F 4/4. Wh 100%. Adv deg: 40%. **Grad '04—63.** Col—44. Avg SAT: 1185. Avg ACT: 24. Alum 4100. **Tui '04-'05:** Bdg $9660 (+$200-500). Day $6290 (+$200-500). Aid: Need 30 ($25,500). Work prgm 25 ($18,100). **Est 1916.** Nonprofit. Lutheran. Quar (Aug-May). Hillcrest provides college preparation within a Christian environment. Private voice, piano, organ and instrumental lessons are part of the music program.

MAYER LUTHERAN HIGH SCHOOL   Day Coed Gr 9-PG
Mayer, MN 55360. 305 5th St NE.
Tel: 952-657-2251. Fax: 952-657-2344.
www.lhsmayer.mn.org   E-mail: lhsmayer@aol.com
David Waterman, Exec Dir. Mike Zimmer, Adm.

Col Prep. AP—Eng US_Hist. **Feat**—Span Anat Environ_Sci Computers Psych Comp_Relig Relig Art_Hist Ceramics Drawing Sculpt Studio_Art Accounting Bus Indus_Arts Woodworking. **Supp**—Dev_Read Tut. **Adm:** 65/yr. Appl due: Mar. Accepted: 99%. **Tests** Stanford. **Enr 265.** Sec 265. Wh 99%. Asian 1%. Avg class size: 20. **Fac 22.** M 14/2. F 6. Wh 99%. Other 1%. Adv deg: 31%. **Grad '04—61.** Col—54. Avg ACT: 22. **Tui '05-'06:** Day $7375 (+$275-350). Assoc Members $5175 (+$275-350). Aid: Need 75 ($80,000). **Est 1961.** Nonprofit. Lutheran-Missouri Synod. Quar (Aug-June). Drawing students from 52 communities within a 30-mile radius, Mayer Lutheran provides a college preparatory program within a Lutheran setting. Technology is a particularly strong element of the curriculum, and qualified pupils may pursue Advanced Placement course work in several disciplines. The flexible nature of the program allows the school to meet varying student needs and interests through postsecondary opportunities, independent study options and individualized programming.

DE LA SALLE HIGH SCHOOL   Day Coed Gr 9-12
Minneapolis, MN 55401. 1 De La Salle Dr.
Tel: 612-676-7600. Fax: 612-362-9641.
www.delasalle.com   E-mail: sarah.isaacson@delasalle.com
Br. Michael Collins, FSC, Pres. BA, MA, St Mary's Univ of Minnesota, MA, Univ of St Thomas (MN), EdD, Univ of San Francisco. Sarah Isaacson, Adm.

Col Prep. AP—Eng Calc Comp_Sci Chem Physics Eur_Hist US_Hist Studio_Art. **Feat**—Fr Ger Span Relig Bus. **Adm:** 219/yr. Appl due: Feb. Accepted: 70%. Yield: 74%. **Tests** HSPT. **Enr 630.** B 308. G 322. Sec 630. Wh 65%. Hisp 5%. Blk 21%. Am Ind 3%. Asian 6%. Avg class size: 23. Uniform. **Fac 47.** M 23/2. F 21/1. Wh 81%. Hisp 4%. Blk 13%. Asian 2%. Adv deg: 82%. **Grad '04—127.** Col—121. Avg ACT: 25. Alum 14,000. **Tui '04-'05:** Day $7100 (+$250-750). Aid: Merit 194 ($116,700). Need 311 ($867,300). **Est 1900.** Nonprofit. Roman Catholic. Tri (Aug-May). The first Catholic high school in the city, De La Salle requires students to take religion courses, engage in prayer before class, take part in liturgies and fulfill a community service requirement. Students enroll not only from the Twin Cities, but also from approximately 30 area suburbs. Academic teams, fine arts options, student organizations, and boys' and girls' athletics complement class work.

MARTIN LUTHER HIGH SCHOOL
Day Coed Gr 9-12

Northrop, MN 56075. County Rd 38, PO Box 228.
Tel: 507-436-5249. Fax: 507-436-5240.
www.martinlutherhs.com
  Robert B. Patrick, Prin. BME, Valparaiso Univ, MM, Butler Univ.

Col Prep. AP—Eng Calc Eur_Hist. **Feat**—Ger Span Drama Band Chorus TV_Production. **Supp**—Rem_Math Rev Tut. **Adm:** 16/yr. Accepted: 100%. **Enr 66.** B 31. G 35. Sec 66. Wh 98%. Asian 2%. Avg class size: 16. **Fac 14.** M 4/5. F 2/3. Wh 100%. Adv deg: 21%. **Grad '04—20.** Col—17. **Tui '03-'04:** Day $3350-4450 (+$225). Aid: Need 14 ($12,000). **Est 1983.** Nonprofit. Lutheran-Missouri Synod. Quar (Aug-May). MLHS offers both college preparatory and Advanced Placement course work in many subjects. Drama, band, choir, student publications and athletics are among the extracurricular options.

GROVES ACADEMY
Day Coed Gr 1-12

St Louis Park, MN 55416. 3200 Hwy 100 S.
Tel: 952-920-6377. Fax: 952-920-2068.
www.grovesacademy.org E-mail: information@grovesacademy.org
  Debbie Moran, Adm.

Gen Acad. LD. Supp—Dev_Read Rem_Math Rem_Read Tut. **Adm (Gr 1-11):** 56/yr. Accepted: 60%. Yield: 85%. **Tests** IQ. **Enr 170.** B 105. G 65. Elem 103. Sec 67. Wh 80%. Hisp 5%. Blk 7%. Am Ind 2%. Asian 5%. Other 1%. Avg class size: 8. **Fac 35.** M 5. F 27/3. Wh 100%. Adv deg: 40%. **Grad '04—15. Tui '04-'05:** Day $15,975. Aid: Need 47 ($360,000). **Summer:** Acad Enrich Rev Rem Rec. 3-6 wks. **Est 1972.** Nonprofit. Sem (Aug-June). **Assoc** NCA. Groves offers diagnostic assessment and highly individualized programming for students with specific learning or language disabilities or attention deficit disorder. In addition to the day school, the academy conducts a summer program, tutoring, social skills groups and specialty workshops.

FRIENDS SCHOOL OF MINNESOTA
Day Coed Gr K-8

St Paul, MN 55104. 1365 Englewood Ave.
Tel: 651-917-0636. Fax: 651-917-0708.
www.fsmn.org E-mail: admissions@fsmn.org
  Mark Niedermier, Head. BA, St John's College (MD), MA, New School for Social Research. Jane A. Schallert, Adm.

Pre-Prep. Gen Acad. Feat—Span Studio_Art Drama Music. **Adm (Gr K-7):** 26/yr. Appl due: Mar. Accepted: 46%. Yield: 72%. **Enr 140.** B 68. G 72. Elem 140. Wh 74%. Hisp 7%. Blk 3%. Am Ind 6%. Asian 10%. Avg class size: 16. **Fac 12.** M 4. F 7/1. Wh 92%. Hisp 8%. Adv deg: 33%. **Grad '04—14.** Prep—2. Alum 45. **Tui '04-'05:** Day $8715-9625 (+$150-250). Aid: Need 36 ($219,471). **Summer:** Enrich Rec. Art. Tui Day $450/2-wk ses. 4 wks. **Est 1988.** Nonprofit. Religious Society of Friends. Sem (Sept-June). **Assoc** NCA. While providing no direct religious education, this elementary school adheres to the values of the Religious Society of Friends. Instructors employ a hands-on approach to learning, and children learn to gather information through different sources, then synthesize and apply what they have learned. The weekly Quaker Meeting is an important aspect of school life, as is a well-developed conflict resolution program that teaches children alternatives to violence.

SAINT AGNES SCHOOL
Day Coed Gr K-12

St Paul, MN 55103. 530 Lafond Ave.
Tel: 651-228-1161. Fax: 651-228-1158.
www.stagnesschools.org   E-mail: jhoughton@stagnesschools.org

Jeffrey J. Brengman, Pres. BA, MA, St Mary's Univ of Minnesota. Jean Houghton, Adm.

Col Prep. Gen Acad. AP—Eng Bio. **Feat**—Fr Lat Span Comp_Sci Relig Studio_Art Chorus. **Supp**—Dev_Read Rem_Math Tut. **Adm:** 94/yr. Appl due: May. Accepted: 94%. **Enr 475.** Elem 250. Sec 225. Wh 54%. Hisp 4%. Blk 30%. Am Ind 3%. Asian 7%. Other 2%. Avg class size: 15. Uniform. **Fac 44.** M 19/1. F 20/4. Wh 96%. Blk 2%. Other 2%. Adv deg: 50%. **Grad '04**—75. Col—71. Alum 8155. **Tui '04-'05:** Day $2800-6000. Aid: Merit 44 ($54,500). Need 205 ($302,425). Work prgm 145 ($20,975). **Est 1888.** Nonprofit. Roman Catholic. Sem (Sept-June). **Assoc** NCA. Saint Agnes provides a traditional education, with religion being an integral part of the curriculum. Newspaper, yearbook, chorus, drama, and a full complement of athletics and clubs are among the school's activities.

COTTER HIGH SCHOOL AND JUNIOR HIGH SCHOOL
Bdg Coed Gr 9-12
Day Coed 7-12

Winona, MN 55987. 1115 W Broadway St.
Tel: 507-453-5403. Fax: 507-453-5013.
www.winonacotter.org   E-mail: ksulliva@winonacotter.org

Craig W. Junker, Pres. BA, St John's Univ (MN), MA, St Mary's Univ of Minnesota. Karen Sullivan, Adm.

Col Prep. AP—Eng US_Hist. **Feat**—Ger Span Anat Comp_Sci Relig. **Supp**—ESL Tut. **Adm (Day Gr 7-11):** 97/yr. Appl due: Apr. Accepted: 98%. **Enr 398.** Avg class size: 16. **Fac 39.** M 19. F 20. Wh 100%. Adv deg: 92%. **Grad '04**—102. Col—98. Avg ACT: 24. **Tui '04-'05:** Bdg $21,660 (+$715-1265). 5-Day Bdg $19,093 (+$715-1265). Day $10,750 (+$440). **Est 1911.** Nonprofit. Roman Catholic. Sem (Aug-June). Emphasizing a Catholic worldview, Cotter offers an academic program that follows a liberal arts approach and integrates the humanities, math, science and the arts. The college preparatory curriculum features Advanced Placement and honors courses, a strong technology component and three college-credit programs. A learning center is available to students who require additional academic support. Athletics, performing arts opportunities, student organizations and recreational activities balance academics.

MISSOURI

CHESTERFIELD DAY SCHOOL   **Day Coed Gr PS-12**
Chesterfield, MO 63017. 1100 White Rd.
Tel: 314-469-6622. Fax: 314-469-7889.
www.chesterfielddayschool.org   E-mail: info@chesterfielddayschool.org
    Barbara F. Fulton, Head. BS, MS, PhD, Univ of Missouri-Columbia. Nan Remington, Adm.

    Col Prep. Feat—Lib_Skills Span Comp_Sci Philos Studio_Art Drama Music. **Adm:** 93/yr. Appl due: Rolling. Accepted: 90%. **Tests** ISEE. **Enr 501.** B 257. G 244. Elem 457. Sec 44. Wh 77%. Hisp 2%. Blk 6%. Asian 7%. Other 8%. Avg class size: 12. **Fac 58.** M 8/1. F 31/18. Wh 82%. Hisp 1%. Blk 8%. Asian 8%. Other 1%. Adv deg: 50%. **Grad '04**—2. Col—2. Alum 414. **Tui '04-'05:** Day $10,965-12,555 (+$500). Aid: Merit 57 ($417,000). Need 34. **Summer:** Rec. Tui Day $275/2-wk ses. 6 wks. **Est 1962.** Nonprofit. Sem (Aug-May). **Assoc** NCA. Chesterfield Day's preschool, kindergarten and early education programs are Montessori based. A personalized educational program, offered at the elementary level, includes courses in geometry, science, Spanish, music, art and library science. Computers are integrated into all subjects. Selected extracurricular activities are available. In 1994, the school opened a second campus in St. Albans (123 Schoolhouse Rd., P.O. Box 78, 63073) that serves students in grades PS-12; the main campus on White Road accommodates children in grades PS-6.

OAKHILL DAY SCHOOL   **Day Coed Gr PS-7**
Gladstone, MO 64118. 7019 N Cherry St.
Tel: 816-436-6228. Fax: 816-436-0184.
www.oakhilldayschool.org   E-mail: office@oakhilldayschool.org
    Mark Schirmer, Head.

    Pre-Prep. Feat—Span Computers Studio_Art Music. **Supp**—Tut. **Adm:** Appl due: Rolling. **Enr 280.** Elem 280. Wh 98%. Hisp 1%. Asian 1%. Avg class size: 16. **Fac 28.** M 1. F 23/4.**Tui '05-'06:** Day $7250-8250 (+$200). Aid: Need 35 ($65,225). **Summer:** Acad Enrich Rev Rec. Tui Day $550/4-wk ses. 12 wks. **Est 1947.** Nonprofit. Quar (Aug-May). **Assoc** NCA. Oakhill Day's preschool and elementary programs are enhanced by speech, dramatics, physical education and field trips. The summer program includes tutoring, sports and classes in computer, math, Spanish, literature, science and cooking.

ARCHBISHOP O'HARA HIGH SCHOOL   **Day Coed Gr 9-12**
Kansas City, MO 64138. 9001 James A Reed Rd.
Tel: 816-763-4800. Fax: 816-763-0156.
www.oharahs.org   E-mail: admin@oharahs.org
    Walter D. Bowman, Prin. BA, Dartmouth College, MST, Cornell Univ, MSA, Univ of Notre Dame. Ann Julich, Adm.

    Col Prep. AP—Bio Chem Physics US_Hist Studio_Art. **Feat**—Fr Span Anat & Physiol Environ_Sci Programming Web_Design Psych Philos Theol Photog Drama Music_Theory Debate Journ. **Supp**—Rem_Math Rem_Read Tut. **Adm:** 145/yr.

Enr 507. B 251. G 256. Sec 507. Wh 80%. Hisp 3%. Blk 15%. Asian 2%. Avg class size: 23. Uniform. **Fac 48.** M 24. F 23/1. Adv deg: 50%. **Grad '04**—130. Col—130. Avg ACT: 23. Alum 4951. **Tui '04-'05:** Day $5400 (+$200). **Summer:** Acad Enrich Rem Rec. Tui Day $150. 3 wks. **Est 1965.** Nonprofit. Roman Catholic. Quar (Aug-June). **Assoc** NCA. Sponsored by the Christian Brothers, O'Hara provides a college preparatory curriculum that includes honors courses and a basic skills track. A wide selection of interest clubs and teams in the major sports supplement academics.

LUTHERAN HIGH SCHOOL Day Coed Gr 9-12
Kansas City, MO 64125. 414 Wallace Ave.
Tel: 816-241-5478. Fax: 816-241-4216.
www.lhskc.com E-mail: info@lhskc.com

Deborah Conner, Prin. BS, Northern Arizona Univ, MEd, Univ of Nevada-Las Vegas. Paula Meier, Adm.

Col Prep. Feat—Ger Span Psych Sociol. **Supp**—Rem_Math Tut. **Adm:** 31/yr. Appl due: Rolling. Accepted: 100%. **Tests** Stanford. **Enr 66.** B 30. G 36. Sec 66. Wh 100%. Uniform. **Fac 12.** M 4/1. F 4/3. Wh 100%. Adv deg: 33%. **Grad '04**—13. Col—13. Avg ACT: 26. Alum 335. **Tui '03-'04:** Day $4600 (+$475-600). Assoc Members $4100 (+$475-600). Aid: Merit 11 ($2850). **Est 1980.** Nonprofit. Lutheran-Missouri Synod. Sem (Aug-May). **Assoc** NCA. Lutheran High's curriculum offers a performance-oriented fine arts program.

ROCKHURST HIGH SCHOOL Day Boys Gr 9-12
Kansas City, MO 64114. 9301 State Line Rd.
Tel: 816-363-2036. Fax: 816-363-3764.
www.rockhursths.edu E-mail: jreichme@rockhursths.edu

Rev. Terrence A. Baum, SJ, Pres. BS, Xavier Univ (OH), MS, Fordham Univ, MDiv, Weston School of Theology. David Laughlin, Prin. BA, MS, Creighton Univ. Jack Reichmeier, Adm.

Col Prep. AP—Eng Lat Span Calc Bio Chem Physics Eur_Hist US_Govt & Pol. **Feat**—Fr Greek Comp_Sci Theol Ceramics Drawing Photog Acting Theater_Arts Journ. **Supp**—Rev Tut. **Adm (Gr 9-11):** 269/yr. Appl due: Dec. Accepted: 80%. Yield: 89%. **Tests** HSPT. **Enr 1032.** B 1032. Sec 1032. Wh 89%. Hisp 3%. Blk 5%. Asian 1%. Other 2%. Avg class size: 25. **Fac 73.** M 63/1. F 8/1. Wh 96%. Hisp 1%. Blk 1%. Asian 1%. Other 1%. Adv deg: 69%. **Grad '04**—247. Col—242. Avg SAT: 1220. Avg ACT: 26. Alum 9070. **Tui '04-'05:** Day $8250 (+$500). Aid: Merit 13 ($10,000). Need 238 ($752,100). Work prgm 238 ($739,975). **Summer:** Acad Enrich Rev Rem. Tui Day $200-475. 5 wks. **Est 1910.** Nonprofit. Roman Catholic. Sem (Aug-May). **Assoc** NCA. Sponsored by the Jesuits, Rockhurst provides a varied college preparatory program for students from Greater Kansas City. Qualified students may earn college credit. Extracurricular activities include interscholastic and intramural sports, music and theater, publications and interest clubs.

ST. PAUL'S EPISCOPAL DAY SCHOOL Day Coed Gr PS-8
Kansas City, MO 64111. 4041 Main St.
Tel: 816-931-8614. Fax: 816-931-6860.
www.speds.org E-mail: mary@speds.org

Elizabeth Barnes, Head. BS, Southern Methodist Univ, MA, Southwest Texas State Univ. Mary Dobbins, Adm.

Pre-Prep. Feat—Fr Span Computers Studio_Art Music Speech. **Supp**—Rem_ Math Rem_Read Rev Tut. **Adm:** 78/yr. Appl due: Jan. **Tests** Stanford. **Enr 475.** B 233. G 242. Elem 475. Wh 89%. Hisp 3%. Blk 3%. Asian 3%. Other 2%. Avg class size: 20. **Fac 48.** M 5/2. F 29/12. Wh 94%. Hisp 2%. Blk 2%. Am Ind 2%. Adv deg: 41%. **Grad '04—41.** Prep—37. **Tui '04-'05:** Day $7295-7795 (+$155-380). **Summer:** Acad Enrich Rev Rem Rec. Tui Day $120/wk. 10 wks. **Est 1963.** Nonprofit. Episcopal. Sem (Aug-May). **Assoc** NCA. Academic basics are supplemented by enrichment in computers, French, Spanish, music, art, speech, drama and physical education. A daily chapel service and various extracurricular activities round out the program.

BISHOP DuBOURG HIGH SCHOOL   **Day Coed Gr 9-12**
St Louis, MO 63109. 5850 Eichelberger St.
Tel: 314-832-3030. Fax: 314-832-0529.
www.bishopdubourg.org   E-mail: info@bishopdubourg.org
Donna Payne, Pres. Gerald Gruszka, Adm.

Col Prep. Gen Acad. Feat—Fr Ger Span Relig Fine_Arts. **Supp**—LD. **Adm:** 195/yr. Appl due: Rolling. Accepted: 98%. **Tests** MAT Stanford. **Enr 669.** B 304. G 365. Sec 669. Wh 98%. Hisp 1%. Blk 1%. Avg class size: 22. **Fac 53.** M 27/1. F 25. Wh 99%. Blk 1%. Adv deg: 79%. **Grad '04—184.** Col—163. Avg ACT: 21. **Tui '03-'04:** Day $5800 (+$145). **Est 1950.** Nonprofit. Roman Catholic. Sem (Aug-June). **Assoc** NCA. Bishop DuBourg's comprehensive curriculum provides honors, college prep and skills classes, and a wide array of courses includes Advanced Placement and college-credit courses in most departments. An active campus ministry plans regular liturgies, prayer services and days of prayer for all students; all seniors participate in a three-day retreat. Seniors also complete a three-week Christian service project.

COR JESU ACADEMY   **Day Girls Gr 9-12**
St Louis, MO 63123. 10230 Gravois Rd.
Tel: 314-842-1546. Fax: 314-842-6061.
www.corjesu.org   E-mail: mflynn@corjesu.org
Sr. Sheila O'Neill, ASCJ, Prin. BA, Albertus Magnus College, MA, Fordham Univ, MA, EdS, St Louis Univ. Sr. Maureen Fitzgerald, Adm.

Col Prep. AP—Calc US_Hist. **Feat**—British_Lit Fr Lat Span Engineering Computers Amer_Stud Pol_Sci Relig Fine_Arts Rhetoric. **Supp**—Tut. **Adm (Gr 9-11):** 156/yr. Appl due: Dec. Accepted: 92%. Yield: 100%. **Enr 569.** G 569. Sec 569. Wh 97%. Hisp 2%. Asian 1%. Avg class size: 24. Uniform. **Fac 48.** M 8/1. F 34/5. Wh 99%. Other 1%. Adv deg: 85%. **Grad '04—120.** Col—120. Avg SAT: 1274. Avg ACT: 28. Alum 4080. **Tui '04-'05:** Day $7500 (+$200). **Est 1956.** Nonprofit. Roman Catholic. Sem (Aug-May). **Assoc** NCA. Serving the Archdiocese of St. Louis, this school offers a full range of electives in English, the arts, social studies, languages, math, sciences, computer and business. Juniors and seniors may take courses for college credit through St. Louis University.

CROSSROADS SCHOOL
Day Coed Gr 7-12

St Louis, MO 63112. 500 DeBaliviere Ave.
Tel: 314-367-8085. Fax: 314-367-9711.
www.crossroads-school.org   E-mail: info@crossroads-school.org
   William Beton Handmaker, Head. BA, George Washington Univ, MAT, Washington Univ. Shernina Nichols, Adm.
   Col Prep. AP—Eng Fr Span Bio Physics US_Hist World_Hist. **Feat**—Japan MO_Hist Women's_Stud Asian_Stud. **Supp**—Tut. **Adm:** 60/yr. Appl due: Feb. Accepted: 85%. **Tests** CEEB ISEE. **Enr 205.** Elem 65. Sec 140. Wh 69%. Hisp 1%. Blk 26%. Asian 4%. Avg class size: 12. **Fac 25.** M 12. F 11/2. **Grad '04**—25. Col—25. Avg SAT: 1330. Avg ACT: 27. Alum 472. **Tui '04-'05:** Day $13,150 (+$500). Aid: Merit 1 ($12,550). Need 79 ($593,721). **Summer:** Enrich. 9 wks. **Est 1974.** Nonprofit. Sem (Aug-May). **Assoc** NCA. This small college preparatory school features a variety of Advanced Placement courses. The program emphasizes critical-thinking skills and aesthetic appreciation. Internships are required in grade 12, and seniors must complete a college-level class each semester.

DeSMET JESUIT HIGH SCHOOL
Day Boys Gr 9-12

St Louis, MO 63141. 233 N New Ballas Rd.
Tel: 314-567-3500. Fax: 314-567-1519.
www.desmet.org   E-mail: admissions@desmet.org
   Rev. John Arnold, SJ, Pres. Gregory Densberger, Prin. BA, Univ of Memphis, MA, Univ of Missouri-Kansas City, PhD, St Louis Univ. Ann Gibbons, Adm.
   Col Prep. AP—Bio Chem Physics. **Feat**—Anat Computers Econ Govt Psych Relig Film Music. **Supp**—Rev Tut. **Adm:** 320/yr. Appl due: Dec. Accepted: 85%. **Tests** CEEB HSPT. **Enr 1260.** B 1260. Sec 1260. Wh 97%. Hisp 1%. Blk 1%. Asian 1%. Avg class size: 24. **Fac 108.** M 87/3. F 16/2. Wh 99%. Hisp 1%. Adv deg: 51%. **Grad '04**—298. Alum 5325. **Tui '04-'05:** Day $7880 (+$500). Aid: Need 163 ($500,000). **Est 1967.** Nonprofit. Roman Catholic. Sem (Aug-May). **Assoc** NCA. Conducted by the Society of Jesus, DeSmet provides an honors program and AP courses in addition to its college prep curriculum, and courses are offered for college credit through St. Louis University to juniors and seniors in good academic standing. Students participate in a variety of sports and other extracurricular activities; service projects are required for graduation.

INCARNATE WORD ACADEMY
Day Girls Gr 9-12

St Louis, MO 63121. 2788 Normandy Dr.
Tel: 314-725-5850. Fax: 314-725-2308.
www.iwacademy.org   E-mail: bberzon@iwacademy.org
   Randy Mikolas, Prin. BA, Drake Univ, MA, PhD, St Louis Univ. Brooke Berzon, Adm.
   Col Prep. AP—Calc Bio Chem. **Feat**—British_Lit Creative_Writing Fr Span Stats Govt Psych Relig Studio_Art. **Adm:** 158/yr. Appl due: Nov. Accepted: 93%. Yield: 95%. **Enr 550.** G 550. Sec 550. Wh 90%. Hisp 2%. Blk 8%. Avg class size: 20. Uniform. **Fac 46.** M 9. F 35/2. Wh 98%. Blk 1%. Asian 1%. Adv deg: 56%. **Grad '04**—138. Col—138. Avg ACT: 24. Alum 5000. **Tui '04-'05:** Day $6675 (+$50). Aid: Merit 24 ($24,000). Need 150 ($160,000). **Summer:** Enrich Rec.

1-5 wks. **Est 1932.** Nonprofit. Roman Catholic. Sem (Aug-May). **Assoc** NCA. The school's curriculum encompasses required courses, electives and the fine arts within a strong religious foundation. IWA offers an Advanced Placement program and a full range of advanced college courses through St. Louis University and the University of Missouri-St. Louis, which is located nearby. Extracurricular activities include a variety of clubs, fine arts offerings and athletics.

LOGOS SCHOOL
Day Coed Gr 7-12

St Louis, MO 63132. 9137 Old Bonhomme Rd.
Tel: 314-997-7002. Fax: 314-997-6848.
www.logosschool.org E-mail: smoss@logosschool.org

David C. Thomas, Chief Exec. BS, MS, PhD, Univ of Missouri-Columbia. Erin Wisecarver, Adm.

Col Prep. LD. Underachiever. Feat—Span Computers Ceramics Fine_Arts Mural_Painting Mosaic_Art. **Supp**—Dev_Read Rem_Math Rev Tut. **Adm:** 75/yr. Appl due: Rolling. Accepted: 90%. **Tests** Stanford. **Enr 133.** B 103. G 30. Wh 84%. Hisp 1%. Blk 14%. Asian 1%. Avg class size: 6. **Fac 23.** M 9. F 14. Wh 94%. Blk 4%. Other 2%. Adv deg: 30%. **Grad '04**—21. Col—21. Avg ACT: 27. Alum 850. **Tui '04-'05:** Day $19,020 (+$900). Aid: Need ($130,075). **Est 1970.** Nonprofit. Year-round. **Assoc** NCA. Logos provides a program of therapeutic counseling, accredited academics and parental involvement for students who have had difficulty succeeding in traditional school settings. Features include a low student-teacher ratio, individualized education, and therapeutic treatment plans specializing in ADHD, learning disabilities, behavioral disorders and emotional problems. Students may enroll at any time during the 12-month school year.

METROPOLITAN SCHOOL
Day Coed Gr 5-12

St Louis, MO 63143. 7281 Sarah St.
Tel: 314-644-0850. Fax: 314-644-4363.
www.metroschool.org E-mail: info@metroschool.org

Rita M. Buckley, Exec Dir. BS, Fontbonne College, MA, Webster Univ. Nancy Smith, Adm.

LD. Feat—Studio_Art Woodworking. **Supp**—Rem_Math Rem_Read Tut. **Adm:** 27/yr. Appl due: Rolling. Accepted: 75%. **Enr 63.** B 48. G 15. Elem 18. Sec 45. Wh 85%. Hisp 3%. Blk 6%. Other 6%. Avg class size: 9. **Fac 10.** M 2. F 8. Wh 80%. Blk 20%. Adv deg: 50%. **Grad '04**—8. Col—7. **Tui '04-'05:** Day $16,600 (+$250). **Est 1967.** Nonprofit. Sem (Aug-June). **Assoc** NCA. Metropolitan provides highly individualized instruction for students who have learning disabilities, attention deficit disorder and other special learning needs. The school's program also addresses such issues as self-esteem, personal responsibility and interpersonal skills. Emphasizing a small-class setting, Metropolitan limits class size to nine.

NEW CITY SCHOOL
Day Coed Gr PS-6

St Louis, MO 63108. 5209 Waterman Ave.
Tel: 314-361-6411. Fax: 314-361-1499.
www.newcityschool.org E-mail: trhoerr@newcityschool.org

Thomas R. Hoerr, Head. BA, Harris-Stowe State College, MEd, Univ of Missouri-St Louis, PhD, Washington Univ. Betsy Blankenship, Adm.

Pre-Prep. Gen Acad. Feat—Span. **Supp**—Rem_Math Rem_Read. **Adm:** 65/yr. Appl due: Mar. Accepted: 75%. Yield: 69%. **Enr 360.** B 172. G 188. Elem 360. Wh 68%. Hisp 1%. Blk 28%. Asian 3%. Avg class size: 13. **Fac 42.** M 4. F 37/1. Wh 82%. Blk 16%. Asian 2%. Adv deg: 52%. **Grad '04—42.** Prep—35. **Tui '04-'05:** Day $11,025. Aid: Need 120 ($580,000). **Summer:** Enrich Rec. Tui Day $265-420. 2-3 wks. **Est 1969.** Nonprofit. Sem (Sept-June). **Assoc** NCA. Students at the school develop traditional academic skills through an experience-based learning approach. The integrated, thematic curriculum is based on Howard Gardner's theory of multiple intelligence and focuses on linguistic, spatial-artistic, bodily-kinesthetic, musical, logical-mathematical, interpersonal and intrapersonal skills.

NOTRE DAME HIGH SCHOOL
Day Girls Gr 9-12

St Louis, MO 63125. 320 E Ripa Ave.
Tel: 314-544-1015. Fax: 314-544-8003.
www.ndhs.net   E-mail: main@ndhs.net

Sr. Georgiann Wildhaber, SSND, Pres. MA, St Louis Univ. Sr. Michelle Emmerich, SSND, Prin. MA, Univ of Notre Dame.

Col Prep. Feat—Computers Music Bus Communications Home_Ec. **Supp**—Dev_Read Tut. **Adm:** 130/yr. Appl due: Dec. Accepted: 97%. **Enr 450.** G 450. Sec 450. Wh 98%. Hisp 1%. Asian 1%. Avg class size: 23. Uniform. **Fac 47.** M 6. F 40/1. Wh 100%. Adv deg: 72%. **Grad '04—107.** Col—106. Avg ACT: 22. Alum 7000. **Tui '03-'04:** Day $6100 (+$300-800). Aid: Merit 15. Need 60. **Est 1934.** Roman Catholic. Quar (Aug-May). **Assoc** NCA. In addition to its strong core curriculum, Notre Dame offers advanced classes and college-credit opportunities through St. Louis University. Electives in art, business, communications, computer, home economics, math, music, science and social studies complement required course work. Girls of all ability levels may take part in a guided individualized study program.

ROHAN WOODS SCHOOL
Day Coed Gr PS-6

St Louis, MO 63122. 1515 Bennett Ave.
Tel: 314-821-6270. Fax: 314-821-6878.
www.rohanwoods.org   E-mail: info@rohanwoods.org

Kelly R. Horn, Head. Holly Willis, Adm.

Pre-Prep. Gen Acad. Feat—Fr Computers Studio_Art Music. **Supp**—Tut. **Adm:** 28/yr. Appl due: Feb. Accepted: 50%. **Tests** CTP_4 ISEE. **Enr 150.** Elem 150. Wh 92%. Blk 3%. Asian 2%. Other 3%. Avg class size: 18. **Fac 17.** Wh 100%. **Grad '04—20.** Prep—18. **Tui '04-'05:** Day $11,200. Aid: Need 17 ($96,550). **Est 1937.** Nonprofit. Tri (Aug-June). In the early years, children at RWS develop basic skills as a foundation for future learning. As the student ages, the developmentally based program places additional emphasis on independence and responsibility, and an ethics curriculum soon becomes part of the social studies program. Art, music, technology and French are among Rohan Woods' specialty subjects. For an additional fee, boys and girls may take part in an hourlong afternoon enrichment program that features such options as guitar, art workshop, karate, computer club, piano, and on- and off-campus sporting events.

ROSATI-KAIN HIGH SCHOOL
Day Girls Gr 9-12
St Louis, MO 63108. 4389 Lindell Blvd.
Tel: 314-533-8513. Fax: 314-533-1618.
www.rosati-kain.org E-mail: mail@rosati-kain.org
   Sr. Joan Andert, SSND, Prin. BS, Notre Dame College, MAT, Southeast Missouri State Univ.

   Col Prep. AP—Calc Bio US_Hist. **Feat**—Stats Anat & Physiol Computers Econ Relig Fine_Arts Bus. **Supp**—Tut. **Adm:** 115/yr. Appl due: Feb. Accepted: 80%. **Enr 401.** G 401. Sec 401. Wh 86%. Hisp 1%. Blk 11%. Asian 2%. Avg class size: 22. Uniform. **Fac 32.** M 5. F 24/3. Wh 100%. Adv deg: 84%. **Grad '04—106.** Col—105. Avg SAT: 1188. Avg ACT: 25. Alum 7300. **Tui '04-'05:** Day $5675 (+$500). Aid: Merit 44 ($22,000). Need 60 ($30,000). **Est 1911.** Nonprofit. Roman Catholic. Sem (Aug-June). **Assoc** NCA.   Required courses at Rosati-Kain include four years of religion and one year each of fine arts and practical arts course work. Advanced classes carrying college credit are offered through St. Louis University in history, English, French, Spanish, calculus and biology. Activities include student publications, student council, speech league, drama productions and orchestra, as well as such sports as tennis, volleyball, cross-country, field hockey, softball, basketball, soccer, and track and field.

ST. JOSEPH'S ACADEMY
Day Girls Gr 9-12
St Louis, MO 63131. 2307 S Lindbergh Blvd.
Tel: 314-965-7205. Fax: 314-965-9114.
www.stjosephacad.org E-mail: sjaadmin@stjosephacad.org
   Sr. Michaela Zahner, CSJ, Pres. BA, Fontbonne Univ, MA, Univ of Chicago. Nancy A. Repking, Prin. Donna Videmschek, Adm.

   Col Prep. AP—Eng Fr Span Calc Eur_Hist US_Hist US_Govt & Pol. **Feat**—Lat Anat & Physiol Astron Environ_Sci Genetics Zoology Govt Psych Theol Drawing Music_Theory. **Adm (Gr 9-11):** 171/yr. Appl due: Nov. Accepted: 69%. **Enr 629.** G 629. Sec 629. Wh 99%. Hisp 1%. Avg class size: 19. Uniform. **Fac 62.** M 8. F 45/9. Wh 98%. Hisp 1%. Asian 1%. Adv deg: 48%. **Grad '04—136.** Col—136. Avg SAT: 1180. Avg ACT: 25. Alum 6300. **Tui '04-'05:** Day $7225 (+$925). Aid: Need ($39,314). Work prgm ($71,500). **Est 1840.** Nonprofit. Roman Catholic. Sem (Aug-May).   Sponsored by the Sisters of St. Joseph of Carondelet, the school offers a wide selection of honors classes, as well as some advanced offerings. SJA leases laptop computers for use during class projects and research. Each girl completes a 90-hour community service project during her senior year. Athletics include racquetball, basketball, tennis, golf, field hockey, cross-country, volleyball, lacrosse, soccer, softball, track and swimming.

VIANNEY HIGH SCHOOL
Day Boys Gr 9-12
St Louis, MO 63122. 1311 S Kirkwood Rd.
Tel: 314-965-4853. Fax: 314-965-1950.
www.vianney.com E-mail: lkeller@vianney.com
   Rev. Robert R. Osborne, Pres. Lawrence D. Keller, Prin. Dennis Matreci, Adm.

   Col Prep. AP—Span Bio Chem Physics US_Hist. **Feat**—Fr Ger Drawing Accounting Design. **Supp**—Tut. **Adm:** Appl due: Feb. Accepted: 98%. **Enr 720.** B

720. Sec 720. Wh 98%. Blk 1%. Other 1%. Avg class size: 23. **Fac 50.** M 42. F 8. Wh 100%. Adv deg: 70%. **Grad '04—191.** Col—191. Avg ACT: 23. Alum 1100. **Tui '04-'05:** Day $7490 (+$500). Aid: Merit 207 ($117,000). Need 175 ($106,000). Work prgm 12 ($15,000). **Est 1960.** Nonprofit. Roman Catholic. Sem (Aug-May). Operated in the Marianist tradition, Vianney offers college preparation in a Christ-centered environment. Honors and Advanced Placement course work is available, and seniors may also earn college credit in certain classes through St. Louis University or the University of Missouri-St. Louis. Interest clubs, publications, service organizations, and intramural and interscholastic athletics complement academics.

VISITATION ACADEMY   **Day Boys Gr PS, Girls PS-12**
St Louis, MO 63131. 3020 N Ballas Rd.
Tel: 314-625-9100. Fax: 314-432-7210.
www.visitationacademy.org   E-mail: sking@visitationacademy.org
    Laurie A. O'Connor, Head. Ingrid Bremer, Adm.

    Col Prep. AP—Eng Fr Span Calc Stats Bio Chem Eur_Hist. **Feat—**Anat & Physiol Programming Psych World_Relig Photog Studio_Art Theater_Arts Music. **Supp—**Rev Tut. **Adm:** 112/yr. Appl due: Jan. **Tests** CEEB ISEE. **Enr 690.** B 18. G 672. Elem 389. Sec 301. Avg class size: 18. Uniform. **Fac 72.** M 8. F 44/20. Adv deg: 56%. **Grad '04—71.** Col—71. Avg SAT: 1270. Avg ACT: 28. Alum 2806. **Tui '04-'05:** Day $10,755-11,595 (+$55-460). **Est 1833.** Nonprofit. Roman Catholic. Tri (Aug-May). **Assoc** NCA. The college preparatory curriculum is enhanced by elective offerings in computer science, the fine and performing arts, and athletics. Visitation's summer reading program requires students to read various works of fiction in preparation for the coming year's English studies. Students may earn college credit through Advanced Placement courses and through a special program with St. Louis University. The academy conducts a coeducational Montessori preschool.

WESTMINSTER CHRISTIAN ACADEMY   **Day Coed Gr 7-12**
St Louis, MO 63141. 10900 Ladue Rd.
Tel: 314-997-2900. Fax: 314-997-2903.
www.wcastl.org   E-mail: info@wcastl.org
    James C. Marsh, Jr., Head. BA, Calvin College, MEd, Florida Atlantic Univ. Florence Lewis, Adm.

    Col Prep. Gen Acad. AP—Eng Fr Span Stats Bio Physics Eur_Hist US_Hist US_Govt & Pol Art_Hist. **Feat—**Anat & Physiol Forensic_Sci Bible Fine_Arts Study_Skills. **Supp—**Rem_Math. **Adm (Gr 7):** 180/yr. Appl due: Rolling. Accepted: 85%. **Enr 825.** B 392. G 433. Elem 253. Sec 572. Wh 90%. Hisp 1%. Blk 5%. Asian 3%. Other 1%. Avg class size: 19. **Fac 78.** M 34/7. F 30/7. Wh 98%. Blk 2%. Adv deg: 60%. **Grad '04—128.** Col—121. Avg ACT: 26. Alum 1866. **Tui '04-'05:** Day $8500 (+$150). Aid: Need 149 ($526,000). **Est 1976.** Nonprofit. Nondenom Christian. Quar (Aug-May). Located in suburban St. Louis County, WCA enrolls students from Metropolitan St. Louis and western Illinois. The comprehensive college preparatory program—which includes AP and honors courses—has competency requirements in Bible, English, the fine arts, foreign language, history, math, science, the practical arts and physical education. Seniors fulfill a 60-hour community service requirement in which they each keep a weekly journal and write a final paper.

WHITFIELD SCHOOL
Day Coed Gr 6-12

St Louis, MO 63141. 175 S Mason Rd.
Tel: 314-434-5141. Fax: 314-434-6193.
www.whitfieldschool.org   E-mail: info@whitfieldschool.org
Mark J. Anderson, Pres. BS, Univ of Missouri-Columbia, MA, Maryville Univ. Cynthia Crum Alverson, Adm.

Col Prep. AP—Fr Ger Span Calc Chem. **Feat**—Lat Environ_Sci Fine_Arts. **Adm:** 98/yr. Appl due: Jan. Accepted: 73%. Yield: 65%. **Enr 474.** B 245. G 229. Elem 190. Sec 284. Wh 88%. Hisp 1%. Blk 8%. Asian 3%. Avg class size: 12. **Fac 70.** M 22. F 48. Wh 86%. Hisp 4%. Blk 4%. Asian 2%. Other 4%. Adv deg: 37%. **Grad '04—72.** Col—72. Avg SAT: 1230. Avg ACT: 26. Alum 1200. **Tui '04-'05:** Day $16,975 (+$900). Aid: Need 36 ($453,235). **Summer:** Rec. Tui Day $250/wk. 6 wks. **Est 1952.** Nonprofit. Sem (Aug-June). **Assoc** NCA. At this research-based institution, students must display mastery of subject matter through traditional testing and exhibitions. Upon faculty recommendation, pupils may enroll in Advanced Placement courses, which are available in several disciplines. Technology is integral to school life. Particularly able students may pursue independent study in foreign language, math or science. Among Whitfield's extracurriculars is an array of boys' and girls' athletic teams.

NERINX HALL
Day Girls Gr 9-12

Webster Groves, MO 63119. 530 E Lockwood Ave.
Tel: 314-968-1505. Fax: 314-968-0604.
www.nerinxhs.org   E-mail: broche@nerinxhs.org
Sr. Barbara Roche, SL, Pres. BA, Webster Univ. Jane W. Kosash, Prin.

Col Prep. Feat—Creative_Writing Poetry Shakespeare Mythology Fr Ger Lat Span Yoruba Anat & Physiol Astron Bioethics Geol Programming Web_Design Holocaust Anthro Econ Psych Theol World_Relig Ceramics Drawing Fine_Arts Painting Photog Studio_Art Acting Drama Theater_Arts Music_Theory Orchestra Jazz_Band Dance. **Adm (Gr 9-10):** 170/yr. Appl due: Dec. Accepted: 70%. Yield: 98%. **Enr 605.** G 605. Sec 605. Wh 93%. Hisp 2%. Blk 2%. Asian 1%. Other 2%. Avg class size: 20. Uniform. **Fac 49.** M 7/1. F 34/7. Wh 100%. Adv deg: 91%. **Grad '04—147.** Col—147. Avg SAT: 1277. Avg ACT: 26. Alum 5900. **Tui '04-'05:** Day $7300 (+$1100). Aid: Need 91 ($158,000). Work prgm 41 ($34,260). **Summer:** Acad. Tui Day $100/crse. 6 wks. **Est 1924.** Nonprofit. Roman Catholic. Quar (Aug-May). Nerinx offers a college preparatory curriculum that includes honors courses and electives in the major disciplines, as well as in theology, the arts, business and computer technology. Girls may enroll in college-credit courses offered through St. Louis University and the University of Missouri-St. Louis. Leadership council, literary groups, orchestra, chorus, theatrical productions and athletics are among the school's extracurricular pursuits.

NEBRASKA

MESSIAH LUTHERAN SCHOOL   Day Coed Gr PS-6
Lincoln, NE 68506. 1800 S 84th St.
Tel: 402-489-3024. Fax: 402-489-3093.
www.messiahlincoln.org   E-mail: messiah@alltel.net
    Stanley Fehlhafer, Prin. BS, MA, Concordia Teachers College (NE).

    Gen Acad. Feat—Computers Relig Studio_Art Music. **Adm:** 85/yr. Appl due: Rolling. Accepted: 100%. **Enr 327.** B 155. G 172. Elem 327. Wh 95%. Hisp 3%. Asian 2%. Avg class size: 24. **Fac 14.** M 2/1. F 9/2. Wh 100%. Adv deg: 28%. **Grad '04—23. Tui '04-'05:** Day $3500 (+$250). Aid: Need 25 ($31,000). **Est 1930.** Nonprofit. Lutheran. Sem (Aug-May). Messiah's curriculum emphasizes reading, writing, arithmetic and religion. Daily Bible-based religion classes and weekly all-school chapel services are part of the program, and after-school athletics include soccer, volleyball, basketball and softball.

SOUTH DAKOTA

ST. THOMAS MORE HIGH SCHOOL   Day Coed Gr 9-12
Rapid City, SD 57701. 300 Fairmont Blvd.
Tel: 605-343-8484. Fax: 605-343-1315.
E-mail: stm@stm.k12.sd.us
    Wayne Sullivan, Prin. Dave Hollenbeck, Adm.

    Col Prep. Feat—Fr Span Computers Psych Sociol Relig Studio_Art Drama Music Accounting Journ Speech. **Supp**—Tut. **Adm:** 20/yr. Appl due: Mar. Accepted: 90%. **Tests** Stanford. **Enr 190.** B 95. G 95. Sec 190. Wh 85%. Hisp 5%. Am Ind 9%. Asian 1%. Avg class size: 18. Uniform. **Fac 20.** M 7/1. F 8/4. Adv deg: 30%. **Grad '04—55.** Col—53. Alum 1189. **Tui '02-'03:** Day $4085 (+$150). **Est 1991.** Nonprofit. Roman Catholic. Sem (Aug-May). Options for acceleration at the school include AP and advanced classes. A community service project is required during senior year, and daily prayer and weekly Mass complement the curriculum.

SIOUX FALLS CHRISTIAN SCHOOLS   Day Coed Gr PS-12
Sioux Falls, SD 57108. 6120 S Charger Ave.
Tel: 605-334-1422. Fax: 605-334-6928.
www.siouxfallschristian.org   E-mail: sfchristian@sfchristian.org
    Jay Woudstra, Supt.

    Col Prep. Gen Acad. AP—Span Calc Physics. **Feat**—British_Lit Creative_Writing Anat & Physiol Environ_Sci Comp_Sci Econ Govt Psych Sociol Bible Studio_Art Chorus Accounting. **Supp**—Rem_Math Rem_Read Tut. **Adm:** 70/yr. Appl due: Rolling. Accepted: 98%. **Tests** Stanford. **Enr 615.** B 308. G 307. Elem 444. Sec 171. Wh 95%. Hisp 2%. Blk 3%. **Fac 48.** M 10. F 23/15. Wh 100%. Adv deg: 31%. **Grad '04—42.** Col—36. Avg ACT: 24. **Tui '04-'05:** Day $2060-4700 (+$600). Aid: Need 25 ($25,000). **Est 1977.** Nonprofit. Nondenom Christian. Quar

(Aug-May). Such enrichment and exploratory classes as art, band, choir, computers, keyboarding, Spanish and physical education complement core curricular offerings in Sioux Falls Christian's middle school (grades 6-8). To meet varying needs and abilities, the high school (grades 9-12) provides both college preparatory and general education curricula. The elementary school (grades pre-K-5) occupies separate quarters at 700 S. Sneve Ave., 57103 (605-334-7397).

South Central States

ARKANSAS

MOUNT ST. MARY ACADEMY Day Girls Gr 9-12
Little Rock, AR 72205. 3224 Kavanaugh Blvd.
Tel: 501-664-8006. Fax: 501-666-4382.
www.mtstmary.edu   E-mail: dmagby@mtstmary.edu
  Sr. Deborah Troillett, RSM, Pres. Rebecca Henle, Prin. Robin Thorpe, Adm.

  Col Prep. IB_Diploma. Feat—Theol Speech. **Supp**—Tut. **Adm:** 160/yr. Appl due: Mar. Accepted: 100%. **Enr 600.** G 600. Sec 600. Wh 91%. Hisp 4%. Blk 3%. Asian 2%. Avg class size: 21. Uniform. **Fac 43.** M 3/1. F 30/9. **Grad '04—137.** Col—134. **Tui '03-'04:** Day $5104 (+$1050-1150). Catholic $4708 (+$1050-1150). **Summer:** Acad. 3 wks. **Est 1851.** Nonprofit. Roman Catholic. Sem (Aug-May). The only girls' secondary school in the state, Mount St. Mary enrolls students from Greater Little Rock, Benton, England, Roland, Hot Springs, Cabot and Pine Bluff. Particularly able girls choose from honors, Advanced Placement and International Baccalaureate courses. The Mercy Scholar Program, a full-scale honors sequence conducted in grades 9 and 10, readies pupils for the two-year IB program. Seniors perform 30 hours of compulsory community service.

CENTRAL ARKANSAS CHRISTIAN SCHOOLS Day Coed Gr PS-12
North Little Rock, AR 72113. 1 Windsong Dr.
Tel: 501-758-3160. Fax: 501-791-7975.
www.cacmustangs.org   E-mail: spogue@cacmustangs.org
  Carter Lambert, Pres. PhD. Sherry Pogue, Adm.

  Col Prep. AP—Eng Calc Bio Chem Eur_Hist US_Hist. **Feat**—Greek Ital Span Stats Web_Design Bible Theater_Arts. **Adm:** 60/yr. Appl due: Feb. Accepted: 95%. Yield: 95%. **Tests** CEEB. **Enr 1037.** Wh 98%. Blk 2%. Avg class size: 25. **Fac 78.** M 21. F 57. Wh 98%. Blk 2%. **Grad '04—89.** Col—85. Avg ACT: 23. Alum 1000. **Tui '04-'05:** Day $4150-4350 (+$860-1260). Aid: Need 127 ($125,000). **Est 1971.** Nonprofit. Nondenom Christian. Sem (Aug-May). **Assoc** NCA. The school combines two elementary campuses in outlying sections of the metropolitan area with a central secondary campus serving pupils from grade 7. The college preparatory curriculum includes chemistry, Spanish, calculus, physics, fine arts and accounting, in addition to AP courses, and all students attend a daily Bible class. CAC fields interscholastic cross-country, golf, tennis, volleyball, football, basketball, baseball, soccer and track teams, and boys and girls choose from a selection of cocurricular activities and student organizations.

LOUISIANA

CATHOLIC HIGH SCHOOL
Day Boys Gr 8-12
Baton Rouge, LA 70806. 855 Hearthstone Dr.
Tel: 225-383-0397. Fax: 225-383-0381.
www.catholichigh.org   E-mail: info@catholichigh.org
 Br. Francis David, SC, Pres. BA, Spring Hill College, MA, Florida State Univ, EdD, Univ of San Francisco. Br. Barry Landry, SC, Prin. BA, Loyola Univ (LA), MA, Univ of San Francisco. Jason Darensbourg, Adm.

Col Prep. Feat—Comp_Sci Relig Studio_Art Chorus Music Accounting Bus Speech Drafting. **Adm:** 254/yr. Appl due: Nov. Accepted: 79%. **Enr 915.** B 915. Elem 24. Sec 891. Wh 93%. Hisp 1%. Blk 6%. Avg class size: 23. **Fac 78.** M 36/2. F 38/2. Wh 94%. Blk 6%. Adv deg: 56%. **Grad '04—208.** Col—208. Avg SAT: 1251. Avg ACT: 25. Alum 7623. **Tui '04-'05:** Day $5160 (+$450-550). **Est 1894.** Nonprofit. Roman Catholic. Sem (Aug-May). **Assoc** SACS. The curriculum at this school offers both honors and AP courses, and graduation requirements include religion, computer literacy, fine arts and general electives. CHS students participate in interscholastic sports, clubs and other extracurricular activities.

THE DUNHAM SCHOOL
Day Coed Gr PS-12
Baton Rouge, LA 70810. 11111 Roy Emerson Dr.
Tel: 225-767-7097. Fax: 225-767-3475.
www.dunhamschool.org   E-mail: spearls@dunhamschool.org
 Melanie Ezell, Int Head. BA, MA, PhD, Louisiana State Univ-Baton Rouge. Linda Spear, Adm.

Col Prep. AP—Lat Calc US_Govt & Pol Studio_Art. **Feat**—Shakespeare Southern_Lit Writing Mythology Fr Span Astron Kinesiology Comp_Sci Bible Relig Fine_Arts Drama Music Speech. **Supp**—LD Tut. **Adm:** 130/yr. Appl due: Jan. Accepted: 89%. Yield: 75%. **Tests** CTP_4. **Enr 608.** B 330. G 278. Elem 375. Sec 233. Wh 94%. Hisp 1%. Blk 3%. Other 2%. Avg class size: 16. Uniform. **Fac 71.** M 12/1. F 50/8. Wh 99%. Asian 1%. Adv deg: 36%. **Grad '04—59.** Col—57. Avg SAT: 1163. Avg ACT: 25. Alum 969. **Tui '04-'05:** Day $4350-8000 (+$750-875). Aid: Need 85 ($247,669). **Est 1981.** Nonprofit. Sem (Aug-May). **Assoc** SACS. Dunham's college preparatory curriculum features four semesters of religion study. The school also offers an early childhood program and a comprehensive fine arts curriculum. Interscholastic sports include football, basketball, softball, volleyball, swimming, tennis, golf, track, cross-country and baseball.

EPISCOPAL SCHOOL OF ACADIANA
Day Coed Gr PS-12
Cade, LA 70519. PO Box 380.
Tel: 337-365-1416. Fax: 337-367-9841.
www.esacadiana.com   E-mail: admissions@esacadiana.com
 Christopher H. Taylor, Head. BA, Univ of Rochester, MEd, Harvard Univ, MLS, Wesleyan Univ. Mary Buie Skelton, Adm.

Col Prep. AP—Fr Calc Comp_Sci Bio Chem US_Hist. **Feat**—British_Lit Mythology Russ_Hist Comp_Relig Architect Art_Hist Photog Sculpt Drama.

Supp—Dev_Read Rem_Read Tut. **Adm (Gr PS-11):** 187/yr. Appl due: Rolling. Accepted: 93%. **Tests** IQ ISEE. **Enr 458.** B 222. G 236. Elem 262. Sec 196. Wh 90%. Hisp 1%. Blk 5%. Asian 4%. Avg class size: 15. Uniform. **Fac 54.** M 17/3. F 30/4. Wh 99%. Asian 1%. Adv deg: 51%. **Grad '04—40.** Col—40. Avg SAT: 1237. Avg ACT: 27. Alum 750. **Tui '04-'05:** Day $4100-9400 (+$300-350). Aid: Merit 9 ($42,300). Need 76 ($325,993). **Summer:** Enrich Rec. 2 wks. **Est 1979.** Nonprofit. Episcopal. Quar (Aug-June). ESA's college preparatory curriculum includes honors and Advanced Placement courses in all disciplines. French is offered in grades 7-12. Interscholastic sports include volleyball, track and field, cross-country, basketball, baseball, soccer, golf, tennis and swimming.

ACADEMY OF THE SACRED HEART
Bdg Girls Gr 8-12
Day Girls PS-12

Grand Coteau, LA 70541. 1821 Academy Rd, PO Box 310.
Tel: 337-662-5275. Fax: 337-662-3011.
www.ashcoteau.org   E-mail: admission@ashcoteau.org
  Mary Burns, Head. Carrie Foard, Adm.

  Col Prep. AP—Eng Fr Span Calc. **Feat**—Environ_Sci Computers Relig Ceramics Photog Studio_Art Drama Chorus Dance. **Supp**—ESL Rev Tut. **Adm:** 80/yr. Appl due: Rolling. **Tests** MAT Stanford. **Enr 357.** G 26/331. Elem 228. Sec 129. Wh 89%. Hisp 2%. Blk 9%. Avg class size: 13. Uniform. **Fac 47.** Adv deg: 36%. In Dorms 3. **Grad '04—41.** Col—41. Avg SAT: 1250. Avg ACT: 25. Alum 2600. **Tui '04-'05:** Bdg $19,450 (+$1500). 5-Day Bdg $18,500 (+$2000). Day $5700-8200 (+$2000). **Est 1821.** Nonprofit. Roman Catholic. Quar (Aug-May). **Assoc** SACS. The school offers a college preparatory curriculum with local and national service programs. Seniors participate in volunteer service projects in a chosen field or career interest. An exchange program with other Sacred Heart schools is open to sophomores or juniors for one quarter. English riding and piano are offered as optional courses.

ARCHBISHOP SHAW HIGH SCHOOL
Day Boys Gr 8-12

Marrero, LA 70072. 1000 Barataria Blvd.
Tel: 504-340-6727. Fax: 504-347-9883.
www.archbishopshaw.org   E-mail: arnoshaw@archdiocese-no.org
  Rev. James McKenna, SDB, Pres. Rev. Michael Conway, SDB, Prin. Cesar L. Munoz, Adm.

  Col Prep. AP—Calc Comp_Sci US_Hist World_Hist. **Feat**—Fr Span Anat & Physiol Econ Psych Sociol LA_Stud Relig Accounting. **Adm:** 160/yr. Appl due: Feb. Accepted: 82%. **Tests** HSPT IQ SSAT Stanford. **Enr 550.** B 550. Elem 50. Sec 500. Wh 65%. Hisp 10%. Blk 15%. Asian 5%. Other 5%. Avg class size: 21. Uniform. **Fac 30.** M 15. F 15. Wh 65%. Hisp 5%. Other 30%. Adv deg: 40%. **Grad '04—115.** Col—112. Avg ACT: 24. Alum 5000. **Tui '05-'06:** Day $5500. Aid: Need 28. **Est 1962.** Nonprofit. Roman Catholic. Tri (Aug-May). Operated by the Salesians of Don Bosco, the school offers both college preparatory and honors tracks in grades 8 and 9. An array of honors classes are available in the higher grades, as are Advanced Placement courses in several areas and a college-level math class (offered in conjunction with Our Lady of Holy Cross College). Spirituality is integral to school life, with Archbishop Shaw conducting daily religion classes, liturgical celebrations on feast days, retreat programs at each grade level, peer ministry and a service program.

CRESCENT CITY BAPTIST SCHOOL   **Day Coed Gr PS-12**
Metairie, LA 70006. 4828 Utica St.
Tel: 504-885-4700. Fax: 504-885-4703.
www.ccbs.org E-mail: mrriggs@ccbs.org
   Ray Cross, Prin. Larry W. Maples, Adm.

Col Prep. Feat—Span Bible. **Supp**—Dev_Read ESL Tut. **Adm:** 69/yr. Appl due: Rolling. Accepted: 85%. **Tests** Stanford. **Enr 520.** Elem 360. Sec 160. Wh 65%. Hisp 15%. Blk 10%. Asian 10%. Avg class size: 24. Uniform. **Fac 37.** M 7/2. F 27/1. Wh 98%. Blk 1%. Other 1%. Adv deg: 8%. **Grad '04—37.** Col—34. Avg ACT: 20. Alum 1369. **Tui '04-'05:** Day $3450-4200 (+$350). Aid: Merit 1 ($4000). Work prgm 5 ($15,000). **Summer:** Enrich. 6 wks. **Est 1956.** Nonprofit. Baptist. Tri (Aug-June). The program at CCBS includes college preparatory courses. Although affiliated with the Crescent City Baptist Church, the school is nonsectarian in enrollment.

HOLY CROSS SCHOOL   **Day Boys Gr 5-12**
New Orleans, LA 70117. 4950 Dauphine St.
Tel: 504-942-3100. Fax: 504-943-7676.
www.holycrosstigers.com E-mail: contactus@holycrosstigers.com
   Charles DiGange, Head. Joseph Murray, Jr., Prin. Matt Guillory, Adm.

Col Prep. Feat—Computers Civics Law Psych Sociol Relig Studio_Art Band Chorus Music Bus Journ Speech. **Supp**—Makeup Tut. **Adm (Gr 5-11):** 200/yr. Accepted: 65%. **Enr 940.** B 940. Elem 340. Sec 600. Wh 85%. Hisp 2%. Blk 11%. Asian 1%. Other 1%. Avg class size: 25. Uniform. **Fac 70.** M 53. F 17. Adv deg: 54%. **Grad '04—94.** Col—90. Alum 10,200. **Tui '03-'04:** Day $3875-5275 (+$650). Aid: Merit 45 ($19,075). Need 40 ($169,450). Work prgm 22 ($20,000). **Summer:** Acad Enrich Rem Rec. Tui Day $250-350/crse. 6 wks. **Est 1879.** Nonprofit. Roman Catholic. Sem (Aug-May). **Assoc** SACS. The school is under the direction of the Brothers of the Congregation of Holy Cross. In addition to a traditional four-year college preparatory program, Holy Cross conducts four- and five-year honors programs. The curriculum features independent study, business and journalism courses, instrumental music and religious studies.

JESUIT HIGH SCHOOL   **Day Boys Gr 8-12**
New Orleans, LA 70119. 4133 Banks St.
Tel: 504-486-6631. Fax: 504-483-3942.
www.jesuitnola.org E-mail: admissions@jesuitnola.org
   Rev. Anthony F. McGinn, SJ, Pres. MA, Univ of Texas-Austin. Michael A. Giambelluca, Prin. BA, JD, Tulane Univ. John J. Culicchia, Adm.

Col Prep. AP—Eng Fr Lat Span Bio Chem US_Hist Comp_Govt & Pol. **Feat**—Creative_Writing Greek Environ_Sci Comp_Sci Film Fine_Arts Public_Speak Speech. **Supp**—Tut. **Adm (Gr 8-9):** 340/yr. Appl due: Dec. Accepted: 80%. Yield: 99%. **Tests** HSPT. **Enr 1459.** B 1459. Elem 261. Sec 1198. Wh 86%. Hisp

5%. Blk 5%. Asian 4%. Avg class size: 25. Uniform. **Fac 114.** M 79/1. F 34. Wh 93%. Hisp 2%. Blk 3%. Asian 1%. Other 1%. Adv deg: 52%. **Grad '04—282.** Col—280. Avg SAT: 1266. Avg ACT: 27. Alum 12,300. **Tui '04-'05:** Day $5125 (+$200). Aid: Need 120 ($350,000). **Summer:** Enrich Rem. Tui Day $325/crse. 6 wks. **Est 1847.** Nonprofit. Roman Catholic. Quar (Aug-May). **Assoc** SACS. Jesuit offers a five-year accelerated academic program, with advanced courses available in all major subjects.

MOUNT CARMEL ACADEMY   Day Girls Gr 8-12
New Orleans, LA 70124. 7027 Milne Blvd.
Tel: 504-288-7626. Fax: 504-288-7629.
www.mtcarmelcubs.org E-mail: mca@mcacubs.org

Sr. Camille Anne Campbell, OCarm, Pres. BA, Dominican College, MS, Univ of Notre Dame, MEd, Univ of Dayton, MA, Mundelein College. Gerard D. Nugent, Adm.

Col Prep. AP—Eng Calc US_Hist US_Govt & Pol. **Feat**—Computers Econ Law Psych Sociol Theol Ceramics Sculpt Studio_Art Drama Theater Music Accounting Communications Speech. **Supp**—Tut. **Adm:** 339/yr. **Tests** Stanford. **Enr 1164.** G 1164. Elem 78. Sec 1086. Wh 92%. Hisp 3%. Blk 2%. Asian 2%. Other 1%. Avg class size: 19. Uniform. **Fac 110.** M 17. F 93. Adv deg: 36%. **Grad '04—243.** Col—243. Avg SAT: 1142. Avg ACT: 23. Alum 8385. **Tui '02-'03:** Day $3900 (+$600). Aid: Merit 41 ($20,500). Need 3 ($4970). Work prgm 25 ($51,000). **Summer:** Acad Enrich Rec. Tui Day $300/3-wk ses. 10 wks. **Est 1896.** Nonprofit. Roman Catholic. Sem (Aug-May). **Assoc** SACS. Mount Carmel offers a college preparatory curriculum that integrates technology and is enriched by Advanced Placement and honors courses, as well as by various electives. Theology classes and prayer are part of the students' daily routine. Cocurricular activities such as clubs, sports, publications, student government, a closed-circuit television station and computer-assisted instruction supplement the classroom experience.

REDEEMER-SETON HIGH SCHOOL   Day Coed Gr 9-12
New Orleans, LA 70122. 1453 Crescent Dr.
Tel: 504-288-1494. Fax: 504-288-1499.
www.redeemerseton.org E-mail: redeemerseton@archdiocese-no.org

Mr. Arthur Schmitt, Pres. BS, Loyola Univ (LA), MEd, Univ of New Orleans. Joan G. Johnson, Prin. BBA, MEd, Loyola Univ (LA), MEd, Xavier Univ of Louisiana.

Col Prep. Feat—Span Environ_Sci Computers Civics Law Sociol African-Amer_Stud Theol Studio_Art Band Chorus Accounting Bus Speech Home_Ec. **Supp**—Tut. **Adm:** 135/yr. Accepted: 90%. **Enr 361.** Sec 361. Avg class size: 24. **Fac 27.** M 10. F 17. Adv deg: 25%. **Grad '04—67.** Col—60. Alum 6200. **Tui '02-'03:** Day $3300 (+$510-610). Aid: Merit ($9100). Need ($500). Work prgm ($7100). **Summer:** Read. 4-6 wks. **Est 1937.** Roman Catholic. Sem (Aug-May). Established by Redemptorist priests, this Catholic school is staffed by the School Sisters of Notre Dame, the Daughters of Charity and Christian lay faculty. Students choose from general and college preparatory programs, and advanced classes are available. Cocurricular options include interest clubs, interscholastic sports, junior

ST. ANDREW'S EPISCOPAL SCHOOL — Day Coed Gr PS-6
New Orleans, LA 70118. 8012 Oak St.
Tel: 504-861-3743. Fax: 504-861-3973.
www.standrews.k12.la.us   E-mail: office@standrews.k12.la.us
Gary J. Mannina, Head. BA, MA, Tulane Univ. Mary Ann Straub, Adm.

Pre-Prep. Feat—Span Computers Studio_Art Drama Music. **Supp**—Rem_Read Tut. **Adm:** 33/yr. **Tests** IQ. **Enr 160.** B 79. G 81. Elem 160. Wh 84%. Hisp 6%. Blk 7%. Asian 3%. Avg class size: 20. **Fac 25.** Wh 91%. Hisp 7%. Blk 2%. Adv deg: 56%. **Grad '04—7.** Prep—7. Alum 521. **Tui '04-'05:** Day $7160-7965 (+$245-450). Aid: Need 10 ($32,955). **Est 1957.** Nonprofit. Episcopal. Tri (Aug-May). St. Andrew's emphasizes learning and thinking skills, in addition to good work habits, at all levels. Computer programs supplement most areas of the basic curriculum. Students attend chapel services two to three times per week. In addition, boys and girls may engage in community service, participate in the student council, work on the school's publications, and plan and present monthly assemblies.

ST. MARY'S DOMINICAN HIGH SCHOOL — Day Girls Gr 8-12
New Orleans, LA 70125. 7701 Walmsley Ave.
Tel: 504-865-9401. Fax: 504-866-5958.
www.stmarysdominican.org   E-mail: admissions@stmarysdominican.org
Cynthia A. Thomas, Pres. BA, Nicholls State Univ, MRE, Loyola Univ (LA), MEd, Our Lady of Holy Cross College. Nancy P. Autin, Prin. PhD. Cathy Rice, Adm.

Col Prep. AP—Eng Fr Span Calc Chem US_Hist. **Feat**—Creative_Writing Lat Anat & Physiol Comp_Sci Law Psych Relig Fine_Arts Studio_Art Band Chorus Music Journ. **Supp**—Rev Tut. **Adm:** 275/yr. Day 375. Appl due: Nov. Accepted: 80%. **Tests** HSPT Stanford. **Enr 1068.** G 1068. Elem 144. Sec 924. Uniform. **Fac 76.** M 11. F 57/8. Adv deg: 38%. **Grad '04—219.** Col—219. Alum 9000. **Tui '04-'05:** Day $4065 (+$925). Aid: Work prgm ($35,000). **Summer:** Enrich. Tui Day $380. 2 wks. **Est 1860.** Nonprofit. Roman Catholic. Sem (Aug-May). **Assoc** SACS. Founded by the Dominican Sisters as the New Orleans Female Dominican Academy, Dominican supplements its college preparatory curriculum with clubs, publications, music, sports, dance, art, student council and other extracurricular activities. An active parents' club sponsors many parent-daughter activities.

TRINITY EPISCOPAL SCHOOL — Day Coed Gr PS-8
New Orleans, LA 70130. 1315 Jackson Ave.
Tel: 504-525-8661. Fax: 504-523-4837.
www.trinityno.com   E-mail: admission@trinityno.com
Rev. Michael C. Kuhn, Head. BA, Univ of the South, MDiv, General Theological Seminary, DMin, Episcopal Divinity School. Suzanne L. Brooks, Adm.

Pre-Prep. Feat—Fr Lat Span Computers Relig Fine_Arts Visual_Arts Drama Music. **Supp**—Dev_Read Rem_Math Rem_Read Rev Tut. **Adm:** 58/yr. Appl due: Dec. Accepted: 43%. Yield: 72%. **Tests** IQ. **Enr 399.** B 205. G 194. Elem 399. Wh 87%. Hisp 3%. Blk 8%. Other 2%. Avg class size: 20. **Fac 56.** M 6/2. F 28/20. Wh 84%. Hisp 9%. Blk 5%. Asian 1%. Other 1%. Adv deg: 58%. **Grad '04—36.** Prep—30. Alum 550. **Tui '04-'05:** Day $9035-11,750 (+$495). Aid: Need 39 ($290,518). **Summer:** Rec. Tui Day $150/wk. 4 wks. **Est 1960.** Nonprofit. Episcopal. (Aug-May). Trinity offers a traditional elementary program that balances core course work in language arts, math, science, social studies and foreign language with fine arts, computer, religious studies and physical education classes. Technology is an important element of the program: Lower school children develop word processing skills and learn to create Web pages, multimedia presentations and spreadsheets; at the middle school level, technology is integrated into the curriculum and is used as a tool to broaden and strengthen skills in all subject areas. Boys and girls attend daily chapel, study religion formally in grades 1-8 and participate in age-appropriate community service activities.

WESTMINSTER CHRISTIAN ACADEMY Day Coed Gr PS-12
Opelousas, LA 70570. 186 Westminster Dr.
Tel: 337-948-4623. Fax: 337-948-4090.
www.wcala.org   E-mail: sbostic@wcala.org
   Bill Thompson, Supt. MEd, Delta State Univ. Linda Place, Adm.

Col Prep. AP—Eng Calc Chem US_Hist. **Feat**—Linguistics Fr Lat Span Computers Bible Studio_Art. **Supp**—LD. **Adm:** 165/yr. Appl due: Rolling. Accepted: 73%. **Tests** Stanford. **Enr 929.** B 474. G 455. Elem 689. Sec 240. Uniform. **Fac 64.** M 12. F 45/7. **Grad '04—52.** Col—44. Avg SAT: 1150. Avg ACT: 24. **Tui '05-'06:** Day $4200-4890 (+$150-200). Aid: Need ($433,000). **Est 1978.** Nonprofit. Nondenom Christian. Quar (Aug-May). WCA's preschool program emphasizes play and discovery as learning tools, while the lower school (grades 1-6) focuses on academic skills development. The transitional middle school (grades 7 and 8) features an expanded curriculum designed to ready students for high school. Two separate honors curricula and an array of electives are important aspects of the upper school program (grades 9-12). A second campus serving children in prekindergarten through grade 6 operates in Lafayette (111 Goshen Ln., 70508).

LOYOLA COLLEGE PREPARATORY SCHOOL Day Coed Gr 9-12
Shreveport, LA 71101. 921 Jordan St.
Tel: 318-221-2675. Fax: 318-226-6334.
www.loyolaprep.org   E-mail: galexander@loyolaprep.org
   Frank Israel, Prin. Glad Alexander, Adm.

Col Prep. AP—Eng Fr Span Calc Bio Chem Physics Eur_Hist US_Hist. **Feat**—Creative_Writing Ger Computers Econ Geog Law Psych Relig Fine_Arts Music. **Supp**—Tut. **Adm:** 123/yr. Appl due: Apr. **Enr 400.** B 208. G 192. Sec 400. Wh 88%. Hisp 1%. Blk 7%. Asian 2%. Other 2%. Avg class size: 20. Uniform. **Fac 37.** M 16/1. F 19/1. Wh 94%. Hisp 3%. Blk 3%. Adv deg: 43%. **Grad '04—112.** Col—96. Avg SAT: 1106. Avg ACT: 23. Alum 2700. **Tui '04-'05:** Day $5525-5575 (+$275). Aid: Merit 12 ($7200). Need 85 ($160,000). **Est 1902.** Nonprofit. Roman Catholic. Sem (Aug-May). **Assoc** SACS. Pupils must fulfill course requirements in such areas as religion, speech, free enterprise and computer applications. Sports, clubs and community service complement the curriculum.

MISSISSIPPI

SAINT STANISLAUS COLLEGE   **Boys Gr 6-12**
Bay St Louis, MS 39520. 304 S Beach Blvd.   **Bdg & Day**
Tel: 228-467-9057. Fax: 228-466-2972.
www.ststan.com   E-mail: admissions@ststan.com
    Br. Ronald Talbot, SC, Pres. BA, Spring Hill College, MEd, Rutgers Univ, MEd, Boston College. Dolores M. Richmond, Adm.

    Col Prep. AP—Eng Calc Comp_Sci Physics US_Hist Psych. **Feat**—Creative_Writing Fr Lat Span Stats Anat & Physiol Astron Environ_Sci Marine_Biol/Sci Econ Govt Relig Fine_Arts Chorus Accounting Journ Speech. **Supp**—Dev_Read ESL Rem_Math Rem_Read. **Adm:** 165/yr. Bdg 77. Day 88. Appl due: Rolling. Accepted: 80%. Yield: 90%. **Tests** SSAT. **Enr 550.** B 190/360. Elem 182. Sec 368. Wh 92%. Hisp 1%. Blk 6%. Asian 1%. Avg class size: 23. Uniform. **Fac 64.** M 45. F 19. Adv deg: 57%. In Dorms 2. **Grad '04—86.** Col—85. Avg ACT: 22. Alum 4000. **Tui '04-'05:** Bdg $16,700 (+$1375). Day $4400 (+$375). Aid: Merit 1 ($3510). **Summer:** Acad Enrich Rec. Tui Bdg $2350. 6 wks. **Est 1854.** Nonprofit. Roman Catholic. Sem (Aug-May). **Assoc** SACS. The college preparatory curriculum at St. Stanislaus includes advanced French and Spanish language study, as well as Advanced Placement courses in several other disciplines. The school fields athletic teams in football, sailing, basketball, track, cross-country, golf, swimming, tennis and soccer, and community service projects are conducted through the Key Club and the student council.

MERCY CROSS HIGH SCHOOL   **Day Coed Gr 7-12**
Biloxi, MS 39530. 390 Crusaders Dr.
Tel: 228-374-4145. Fax: 228-374-8119.
www.mercycross.com   E-mail: mercycross@mercycross.com
    Bobby Trosclair, Prin.

    Col Prep. Feat—Creative_Writing Fr Span Stats Anat Environ_Sci Marine_Biol/Sci Computers Programming Econ Govt Psych Relig Studio_Art Theater_Arts Study_Skills. **Adm:** 55/yr. Appl due: Rolling. Accepted: 99%. **Enr 365.** B 181. G 184. Elem 113. Sec 252. Wh 82%. Hisp 6%. Blk 6%. Asian 6%. Avg class size: 23. Uniform. **Fac 33.** M 14. F 18/1. Wh 97%. Hisp 3%. Adv deg: 60%. **Grad '04—64.** Col—62. Avg SAT: 1120. Avg ACT: 20. Alum 2300. **Tui '02-'03:** Day $4350 (+$790). Catholic $2950 (+$790). Aid: Need 10 ($10,000). **Est 1981.** Nonprofit. Roman Catholic. Sem (Aug-May). Formed by the 1981 consolidation of Sacred Heart Girls School and Notre Dame Boys School, Mercy Cross offers a contemporary college preparatory program within a Christian environment. Designed to address the needs of differences in learning style and ability, the curriculum comprises two tracks: the honors program and the college prep and general studies program. Morning prayer and liturgical celebrations are integral aspects of school life, as are activities and an athletic program that consists of football, softball, basketball, soccer, baseball, girls' volleyball, track, golf, tennis, swimming, cross-country and powerlifting.

JACKSON ACADEMY
Day Coed Gr PS-12

Jackson, MS 39236. 4908 Ridgewood Rd, PO Box 14978.
Tel: 601-362-9676. Fax: 601-364-5722.
www.jacksonacademy.org   E-mail: ja@jacksonacademy.org
J. Peter Jernberg, Jr., Head. BA, MSE, EdS, Delta State Univ. Linda Purviance, Adm.

Col Prep. AP—Eng Calc Bio Chem Physics US_Hist Comp_Govt & Pol US_Govt & Pol Studio_Art. **Feat**—Creative_Writing Fr Lat Span Anat & Physiol Programming Econ Psych Sociol Film Music Accounting Speech. **Supp**—LD. **Adm:** 220/yr. Appl due: Rolling. Accepted: 99%. Yield: 98%. **Tests** SSAT Stanford. **Enr 1514.** B 803. G 711. Elem 1122. Sec 392. Wh 98%. Blk 1%. Asian 1%. Avg class size: 22. Uniform. **Fac 126.** M 21. F 67/38. Wh 100%. Adv deg: 42%. **Grad '04**—100. Col—100. Avg SAT: 1233. Avg ACT: 25. Alum 2000. **Tui '05-'06:** Day $3960-8280 (+$250-500). Aid: Merit 6 ($5700). Need 84 ($209,560). **Summer:** Acad Enrich Rev Rem Rec. Tui Day $60-350. 1-6 wks. **Est 1959.** Nonprofit. Sem (Aug-May). **Assoc** SACS. The school, located on 38 acres in northeast Jackson, offers a traditional curriculum supplemented by honors and Advanced Placement courses. Art, music, physical education and Spanish are taught beginning in grade 1. Students are encouraged to participate in such activities as interest clubs, honor societies, publications, speech and debate, choral music, band and athletics.

JACKSON PREPARATORY SCHOOL
Day Coed Gr 7-12

Jackson, MS 39232. 3100 Lakeland Dr.
Tel: 601-939-8611. Fax: 601-936-4068.
www.jacksonprep.net   E-mail: lmorton@jacksonprep.net
Susan R. Lindsay, Head. Lesley Morton, Adm.

Col Prep. Feat—Fr Greek Span Computers. **Supp**—LD Tut. **Adm:** 130/yr. Appl due: Rolling. Accepted: 92%. **Tests** IQ Stanford. **Enr 810.** B 410. G 400. Elem 268. Sec 542. Wh 96%. Hisp 2%. Blk 1%. Asian 1%. Avg class size: 18. Uniform. **Fac 84.** M 21/1. F 55/7. Adv deg: 52%. **Grad '04**—144. Col—144. Alum 4000. **Tui '04-'05:** Day $7804 (+$1500). Aid: Need 89. **Summer:** Acad Enrich. Tui Day $275-300. 6 wks. **Est 1970.** Nonprofit. Sem (Aug-May). **Assoc** CLS SACS. Jackson Prep's curriculum, designed for the average to above-average student, features the Classical Heritage Program, which allows students to receive a diploma with an emphasis in classical studies. Program participants must complete at least six courses in Latin, Greek and classical civilization and must carry a 95 average in these classes. School activities include athletics, student government, debate, band, choir, drill team, the visual arts, dramatics and interest clubs.

CATHEDRAL SCHOOL
Day Coed Gr PS-12

Natchez, MS 39120. 701 Martin Luther King Jr St.
Tel: 601-445-9844. Fax: 601-442-0960.
Patrick Sanguinetti, Admin. BS, Univ of Mississippi, MEd, William Carey College.

Col Prep. Gen Acad. Feat—Lib_Skills Computers Relig Studio_Art Music Journ. **Supp**—LD. **Adm:** 65/yr. Accepted: 95%. **Enr 660.** B 330. G 330. Elem 430. Sec 230. Wh 90%. Blk 10%. Avg class size: 22. Uniform. **Fac 70.** M 10. F 60. Wh

90%. Hisp 5%. Blk 5%. Adv deg: 14%. **Grad '04—48.** Col—46. Avg ACT: 22. Alum 1500. **Tui '03-'04:** Day $2200-3880. Parishioners $2200-3290. **Est 1847.** Nonprofit. Roman Catholic. Quar (Aug-May). The college preparatory curriculum at Cathedral, which includes honors and Advanced Placement courses, is enhanced by strong foreign language and fine arts programs. Students take religion classes in all grades, and daily prayer is an important element of the school environment. Computer training begins in kindergarten.

OXFORD UNIVERSITY SCHOOL   Day Coed Gr PS-6
Oxford, MS 38655. 2402 S Lamar Blvd.
Tel: 662-234-2200. Fax: 662-234-3505.
www.ouschool.com   E-mail: oxford@bellsouth.net
   Don B. Shaver, Head. PhD.

   Pre-Prep. Feat—Fr Lat Span Computers Art_Hist Studio_Art Music. **Supp**—Tut. **Adm:** 41/yr. Appl due: Mar. Accepted: 95%. **Tests** IQ Stanford. **Enr 122.** Elem 122. Wh 94%. Hisp 3%. Blk 2%. Asian 1%. Avg class size: 14. **Fac 18.** M 1/1. F 16. Wh 97%. Am Ind 1%. Other 2%. Adv deg: 105%.**Tui '03-'04:** Day $4300-5500 (+$500-1200). **Summer:** Acad Enrich. Arts. 1-3 wks. **Est 1984.** Nonprofit. Sem (Aug-May). During the early years (grades pre-K-4), children at OUS gain an introduction to computers and the arts while also developing research skills; in addition, the foreign language program commences with Spanish and French in grade 4. At the middle school level (grades 5-8), language instruction broadens with the addition of daily Latin classes. Middle school course work is fully departmentalized, and students progress at their own rates in science and math labs. Field trips provide enrichment at all grade levels, and after-school activities are available.

OKLAHOMA

SAINT JOHN'S EPISCOPAL SCHOOL   Day Coed Gr PS-8
Oklahoma City, OK 73112. 5201 N Brookline Ave.
Tel: 405-943-8583. Fax: 405-943-8584.
www.st-john.k12.ok.us   E-mail: st-johns-school@st-john.k12.ok.us
Mike Stiglets, Head. BS, MEd, Univ of Central Oklahoma. Pat McKinstry, Adm.

   Pre-Prep. Feat—Span Computers Relig Studio_Art Drama Music Speech. **Supp**—Dev_Read Rem_Math Rem_Read Tut. **Adm (Gr PS-7):** 25/yr. Appl due: Rolling. Accepted: 95%. **Tests** Stanford. **Enr 205.** B 105. G 100. Elem 205. Wh 89%. Hisp 1%. Blk 7%. Am Ind 1%. Asian 2%. Avg class size: 12. Uniform. **Fac 27.** M 1. F 26. Wh 100%. Adv deg: 22%. **Grad '04—6.** Prep—6. **Tui '04-'05:** Day $5200 (+$250). Aid: Need 36 ($68,000). **Summer:** Rec. Tui Day $110/wk. 10 wks. **Est 1952.** Nonprofit. Episcopal. Sem (Aug-May). Based on Christian principles, the school's course of studies provides solid preparation for high school. The curriculum includes such enrichment activities as foreign languages, art, music, physical education and computer science.

WESTMINSTER SCHOOL
Day Coed Gr PS-8

Oklahoma City, OK 73118. 600 NW 44th St.
Tel: 405-524-0631. Fax: 405-528-4412.
www.westminsterschool.org   E-mail: mail@westminsterschool.org

Robert S. Vernon, Head. BA, Yale Univ, MEd, Univ of Oklahoma. Marti Newton, Adm.

Pre-Prep. Feat—Humanities Fr Span Engineering Amer_Stud. **Supp**—Rev Tut. **Adm:** 96/yr. Appl due: Rolling. **Enr 517.** Elem 517. Wh 86%. Hisp 1%. Blk 3%. Am Ind 4%. Asian 2%. Other 4%. Avg class size: 15. **Fac 86.** Wh 90%. Blk 5%. Am Ind 1%. Asian 4%. Adv deg: 29%. **Grad '04—56.** Prep—52. Alum 1400. **Tui '04-'05:** Day $7750-8340 (+$400-900). Aid: Need ($288,701). **Summer:** Acad Enrich Rev Rem Rec. Tui Day $65-250. 1-6 wks. **Est 1963.** Nonprofit. Sem (Aug-May). Drawing students from all sections of the city, Westminster employs a team-teaching approach that provides opportunities for curriculum integration across subject lines. Westminster comprises three divisions—primary (prekindergarten and kindergarten), lower school (grades 1-5) and middle school (grades 6-8)—each of which addresses the particular learning needs of its age group. At the middle school level, pupils choose from such electives as drama, craft projects, yearbook, cooking, bread making, carnival games and collage.

BISHOP KELLEY HIGH SCHOOL
Day Coed Gr 9-12

Tulsa, OK 74135. 3905 S Hudson Ave.
Tel: 918-627-3390. Fax: 918-664-2134.
www.bkelleyhs.org   E-mail: mgabel@bkelleyhs.org

Alan Weyland, Pres. BA, MA, Univ of Tulsa. Jane Oberste, Adm.

Col Prep. AP—Eng Fr Span Calc Stats Bio Chem Eur_Hist US_Hist Psych Studio_Art. **Feat**—Creative_Writing Ger Lat Programming Econ Govt Intl_Relations Sociol Bible Accounting Speech. **Supp**—ESL Rem_Math Rev Tut. **Adm (Gr 9-11):** 235/yr. Appl due: Rolling. **Tests** HSPT. **Enr 900.** B 431. G 469. Sec 900. Wh 88%. Hisp 4%. Blk 2%. Am Ind 4%. Asian 2%. Avg class size: 18. Uniform. **Fac 84.** M 33/1. F 39/11. Adv deg: 53%. **Grad '04—229.** Col—218. Avg SAT: 1135. Avg ACT: 24. Alum 2000. **Tui '04-'05:** Day $6950 (+$300). Catholic $5300 (+$300). Aid: Need 175 ($335,000). **Est 1960.** Nonprofit. Roman Catholic. Quar (Aug-May). Bishop Kelley offers a selection of courses designed to meet students' varying needs and abilities. The school follows a block-scheduling format that includes both honors and Advanced Placement course work. As part of Bishop Kelley's Christian service program, each student provides 100 hours of service prior to graduation. Basketball, track, cross-country, golf, tennis, soccer, football, wrestling, baseball, volleyball, softball and cheerleading are the school's sports, and cocurricular clubs and activities address various interests.

CASCIA HALL PREPARATORY SCHOOL
Day Coed Gr 6-12

Tulsa, OK 74114. 2520 S Yorktown Ave.
Tel: 918-746-2600. Fax: 918-746-2636.
www.casciahall.org   E-mail: cotey@casciahall.org

Rev. Bernard C. Scianna, OSA, Head. BA, Villanova Univ, MDiv, Catholic Theological Union, MA, St Xavier Univ. Carol B. Otey, Adm.

Col Prep. AP—Eng Span Calc Stats Bio Chem Physics Eur_Hist US_Govt & Pol Studio_Art. **Feat**—Creative_Writing Fr Ger Lat Astron Comp_Sci Psych Theol World_Relig Photog Chorus Journ Speech Driver_Ed. **Supp**—Rev Tut. **Adm:** 126/yr. Appl due: Rolling. Accepted: 50%. Yield: 40%. **Enr 580.** B 290. G 290. Elem 216. Sec 364. Wh 83%. Hisp 5%. Blk 3%. Am Ind 5%. Asian 3%. Other 1%. Avg class size: 20. Uniform. **Fac 55.** M 25/5. F 20/5. Wh 90%. Hisp 5%. Am Ind 5%. Adv deg: 67%. **Grad '04—97.** Col—97. Avg SAT: 1210. Avg ACT: 27. Alum 4000. **Tui '04-'05:** Day $8250 (+$350). Aid: Need 110 ($300,000). **Summer:** Rev Rec. Sports. Tui Day $100-250/wk. 4 wks. **Est 1926.** Nonprofit. Roman Catholic. Sem (Aug-May). **Assoc** NCA. Located on a 40-acre campus in an urban setting. Cascia Hall is conducted by the Order of St. Augustine. The middle school program (grades 6-8) emphasizes the mastery of fundamental skills as it readies students for the higher grades. In the upper school (grades 9-12), the liberal arts curriculum includes Advanced Placement offerings, and a four-week term in January provides the opportunity for a variety of activities, lectures and field trips.

MONTE CASSINO SCHOOL   Day Coed Gr PS-8
Tulsa, OK 74114. 2206 S Lewis Ave.
Tel: 918-742-3364. Fax: 918-742-5206.
www.montecassino.org   E-mail: mfitzpatrick@montecassino.org
Sr. Mary Clare Buthod, OSB, Dir. BS, Mount St Scholastica College, MTA, Univ of Tulsa, MA, Creighton Univ. Mary Fitzpatrick, Adm.

Pre-Prep. Feat—Fr Span Relig Studio_Art Music. **Supp**—Rev Tut. **Adm:** 174/yr. Appl due: Rolling. **Enr 997.** B 480. G 517. Elem 997. Wh 95%. Hisp 2%. Blk 1%. Am Ind 1%. Asian 1%. Avg class size: 18. **Fac 57.** M 1. F 43/13. Wh 99%. Am Ind 1%. Adv deg: 50%. **Grad '04**—92. Prep—85. Alum 1300. **Tui '04-'05:** Day $6260. **Summer:** Acad Enrich Rev Rec. 4 wks. **Est 1926.** Nonprofit. Roman Catholic. Sem (Sept-June). Monte Cassino's developmentally appropriate preschool program, which commences at age 3, combines play, guided exploration and hands-0n activities. Elementary school children (grades K-4) follow a curriculum organized around grade-wide themes that require students to demonstrate mastery of skills and content. The curriculum at the middle school level (grades 5-8), which continues to center around grade-level themes, features pre-Advanced Placement classes and required course work in art, creative writing and grammar, foreign language, literature, math, music, religion, science, social studies and physical education.

UNIVERSITY SCHOOL   Day Coed Gr PS-8
Tulsa, OK 74104. 600 S College Ave.
Tel: 918-631-5060. Fax: 918-631-5065.
www.uschool.utulsa.edu   E-mail: debra-price@utulsa.edu
Patricia L. Hollingsworth, Dir. BS, Florida State Univ, MAT, EdD, Univ of Tulsa. Debra Price, Adm.

Gen Acad. Feat—Span Computers Geog Studio_Art Drama Music. **Adm:** 39/yr. Appl due: Rolling. **Tests** IQ. **Enr 190.** Elem 190. Wh 84%. Hisp 1%. Blk 5%. Am Ind 5%. Asian 5%. Avg class size: 20. **Fac 38.** M 1/3. F 28/6. Wh 84%. Hisp 1%. Blk 5%. Am Ind 5%. Asian 5%. Adv deg: 15%. **Grad '04**—10. **Tui '05-'06:** Day $6900-7310 (+$20-250). **Summer:** Acad Enrich. Tui Day $150. 1 wk. **Est 1982.** Nonprofit. Spons: University of Tulsa. Sem (Aug-May). The school's curriculum emphasizes active learning within an interdisciplinary structure. Course work focuses on academic achievement, personal responsibility, and the development of students' creativity and problem-solving abilities. The school is situated on the University of Tulsa campus.

TEXAS

ST. JOHN'S EPISCOPAL SCHOOL — Day Coed Gr PS-5
Abilene, TX 79605. 1600 Sherman Dr.
Tel: 325-695-8870. Fax: 325-698-1532.
www.stjohnsabilene.org   E-mail: sjesadm@camalott.com
  Jeanie Stark, Head. BS, Southwest Texas State Univ. Lisa Jones, Adm.

  Pre-Prep. Feat—Span Computers. **Supp**—Dev_Read Rev Tut. **Adm:** 54/yr. Appl due: Aug. Accepted: 96%. **Enr 164.** B 82. G 82. Elem 164. Wh 82%. Hisp 4%. Asian 3%. Other 11%. Avg class size: 11. **Fac 21.** F 15/6. Wh 95%. Hisp 5%. Adv deg: 4%. **Grad '04—12. Tui '02-'03:** Day $5250 (+$250). Aid: Merit 16 ($16,550). Need 26 ($45,006). **Est 1951.** Nonprofit. Episcopal. Quar (Aug-May). This Christian-centered curriculum offers a traditional program focusing on basic skills. An extended-day program is available for children at all grade levels.

HYDE PARK BAPTIST SCHOOLS — Day Coed Gr K-12
Austin, TX 78751. 3901 Speedway Ave.
Tel: 512-465-8331. Fax: 512-371-1433.
www.hpbs.org   E-mail: cnewman@hpbs.org
  Brian Littlefield, Supt. BS, Stephen F Austin State Univ, MA, Texas State Univ-San Marcos. Holly Floyd, Adm.

  Col Prep. Gen Acad. Feat—Fr Greek Lat Computers Psych Bible Studio_Art Theater_Arts Chorus Speech. **Supp**—Tut. **Adm:** 131/yr. Appl due: Rolling. **Tests** Stanford. **Enr 754.** Wh 99%. Hisp 1%. Avg class size: 12. Uniform. **Fac 80.** M 15/1. F 61/3. Adv deg: 37%. **Grad '04—45.** Col—45. Avg SAT: 1137. **Tui '04-'05:** Day $5950-8000 (+$675-825). Aid: Need 86. **Est 1968.** Nonprofit. Baptist. Sem (Aug-May). **Assoc** SACS. Hyde Park Baptist Schools consist of a junior/senior high and an elementary school on the main campus, and a second elementary program on the Bannockburn campus at 7100 Brodie Ln., 78745. Biblical studies and weekly chapel services are required. A comprehensive extracurricular program of clubs and athletics complements the academic program.

ALL SAINTS EPISCOPAL SCHOOL — Day Coed Gr PS-8
Beaumont, TX 77706. 4108 Delaware St.
Tel: 409-892-1755. Fax: 409-892-0166.
www.allsaints-beaumont.org   E-mail: sclark@allsaints-beaumont.org
  Lori Preston, Head. Scootie Clark, Adm.

  Pre-Prep. Feat—Lat Span Studio_Art Drama Chorus Music Speech Study_Skills. **Supp**—ESL Tut. **Adm:** 55/yr. Appl due: Rolling. **Tests** IQ Stanford. **Enr 400.** B 200. G 200. Elem 400. Wh 94%. Hisp 2%. Blk 1%. Asian 3%. Avg class size: 20. Uniform. **Fac 41.** M 1/3. F 33/4. Adv deg: 7%. **Grad '04—40.** Prep—20. Alum 864. **Tui '02-'03:** Day $3080-4990 (+$135-200). Aid: Merit 2 ($4500). Need 14. **Summer:** Acad Enrich Rec. Tui Day $50-100. 1-2 wks. **Est 1954.** Nonprofit. Episcopal. Sem (Aug-May). Individualized instruction, team teaching and classroom learning are offered, emphasizing phonetics and linguistics. Pupils must study two foreign languages.

EPISCOPAL HIGH SCHOOL   Day Coed Gr 9-12
Bellaire, TX 77401. 4650 Bissonnet St.
Tel: 713-512-3400. Fax: 713-512-3603.
www.ehshouston.org   E-mail: akoehler@ehshouston.org
     Edward C. Becker, Head. BS, Hampden-Sydney College, MEd, Univ of Florida. Audrey S. Koehler, Adm.

     Col Prep. AP—Eng Fr Lat Span Calc Stats Bio Physics Eur_Hist US_Hist World_Hist Econ US_Govt & Pol. **Feat**—Computers Relig. **Supp**—Rev Tut. **Adm:** 182/yr. Appl due: Jan. **Tests** ISEE. **Enr 611.** B 302. G 309. Sec 611. Wh 85%. Hisp 5%. Blk 5%. Asian 3%. Other 2%. Avg class size: 150. Uniform. **Fac 79.** M 33/2. F 42/2. Wh 86%. Hisp 6%. Blk 5%. Asian 3%. Adv deg: 58%. **Grad '04—126.** Col—126. Avg SAT: 1178. Alum 1793. **Tui '04-'05:** Day $16,382 (+$4125). Aid: Need 101 ($854,000). **Summer:** Acad Enrich Rev. Tui Day $325. 6 wks. **Est 1982.** Nonprofit. Episcopal. Sem (Aug-May). Drawing students primarily from the Houston metropolitan area, the school features a college preparatory curriculum and a low student-faculty ratio. Although pupils of all faiths are accepted, each student must fulfill a four-semester religion requirement.   **See Also Page 1146**

CARROLLTON CHRISTIAN ACADEMY   Day Coed Gr K-12
Carrollton, TX 75010. 2205 E Hebron Pky.
Tel: 972-242-6688. Fax: 972-245-0321.
www.ccasaints.org   E-mail: jfunk@ccasaints.org
     Richard Dunagin, Supt. Jane Funk, Adm.

     Col Prep. AP—Eng Calc Bio. **Feat**—Humanities Span Computers Econ Govt Bible Photog Studio_Art Drama Theater_Arts Music Debate Speech Photojourn. **Supp**—Tut. **Adm:** 100/yr. Appl due: Rolling. Accepted: 85%. **Tests** HSPT SSAT Stanford. **Enr 530.** B 267. G 263. Elem 370. Sec 160. Wh 84%. Hisp 6%. Blk 2%. Asian 6%. Other 2%. Uniform. **Fac 41.** M 10/2. F 26/3. Wh 90%. Hisp 3%. Blk 7%. Adv deg: 26%. **Grad '04—41.** Col—40. Avg SAT: 1137. Alum 200. **Tui '05-'06:** Day $6200-7900 (+$975). **Est 1980.** Nonprofit. Nondenom Christian. Sem (Aug-May). **Assoc** SACS. This Christian academy integrates Biblical principles into all aspects of school life. A phonics-intensive reading curriculum is employed during the elementary years, while the college preparatory high school features AP courses and a dual-credit program with Brookhaven College. Students choose from various academic electives, musical and artistic pursuits, school publications and athletic options. CCA offers on-campus before- and after-school care for children in grades pre-K-5.

INCARNATE WORD ACADEMY
Day Coed Gr PS-12

Corpus Christi, TX 78404. 2920 S Alameda St.
Tel: 361-883-0857. Fax: 361-883-2185.
www.iwacc.org

Sr. Anna Marie Espinosa, Pres. BS, Texas A&I Univ, MA, Univ of St Thomas (MN).

Col Prep. AP—Eng Fr Span Calc Comp_Sci Bio Physics US_Hist Econ US_Govt & Pol. **Feat**—Humanities Relig Fine_Arts Journ. **Supp**—Dev_Read Rem_Math Rem_Read Rev Tut. **Adm:** 157/yr. Appl due: Rolling. **Enr 745.** B 365. G 380. Elem 510. Sec 235. Wh 56%. Hisp 40%. Blk 2%. Asian 2%. Uniform. **Fac 66.** M 10. F 56. **Grad '04**—72. Col—72. Avg SAT: 1075. Avg ACT: 23. Alum 3500. **Tui '05-'06:** Day $5500-6000 (+$550). Aid: Need 198 ($401,436). **Est 1871.** Nonprofit. Roman Catholic. Sem (Aug-June). **Assoc** SACS. IWA's high school curriculum features Advanced Placement and honors courses and community service opportunities. The middle school program includes electives in such areas as art, life skills and mediation training, while the elementary grades utilize both Montessori and traditional methods of instruction. The academy integrates technology into the curriculum at all grade levels.

ST. JAMES EPISCOPAL SCHOOL
Day Coed Gr PS-8

Corpus Christi, TX 78401. 602 S Carancahua St.
Tel: 361-883-0835. Fax: 361-883-0837.
www.sjes.org E-mail: stjames@sjes.org

H. Palmer Bell, Head. BS, Denison Univ, MEd, Rutgers Univ. Susan Barnard, Middle Sch Adm; Angie Ramos, Lower Sch & PS Adm.

Gen Acad. Feat—Span Computers Studio_Art Drama Outdoor_Ed. **Supp**—Dev_Read Rem_Read Tut. **Adm:** 36/yr. Appl due: Rolling. Accepted: 82%. **Enr 310.** B 128. G 182. Elem 310. Wh 92%. Hisp 5%. Blk 1%. Asian 2%. Avg class size: 16. Uniform. **Fac 45.** M 2. F 32/11. Wh 90%. Hisp 10%. Adv deg: 37%. **Grad '04**—29. Prep—5. Alum 4100. **Tui '05-'06:** Day $5270-6670 (+$350). Aid: Merit 6 ($5500). Need 19 ($90,000). **Est 1946.** Nonprofit. Episcopal. Sem (Aug-May). The program, built around central themes, stresses a strong academic base in reading, language arts, process writing, spelling, mathematics, history and the sciences. Computer literacy is required. Music, studio and theater arts, and physical education complement the academic curriculum. Honors classes are offered in algebra and Spanish.

EPISCOPAL SCHOOL OF DALLAS
Day Coed Gr PS-12

Dallas, TX 75229. 4100 Merrell Rd.
Tel: 214-358-4368. Fax: 214-353-5872.
www.esdallas.org/esd E-mail: newsomc@esdallas.org

Rev. Stephen B. Swann, Head. BA, Northeastern Oklahoma State Univ, MDiv, Church Divinity School of the Pacific. Ruth Burke, Adm.

Col Prep. AP—Eng Fr Span Calc Stats Comp_Sci Bio Chem Physics Eur_Hist US_Hist World_Hist Econ US_Govt & Pol Art_Hist Studio_Art. **Feat**—Relig Drama Music Outdoor_Ed Wilderness_Ed. **Supp**—Tut. **Adm:** 147/yr. Appl due: Jan. Accepted: 30%. **Tests** CEEB CTP_4 IQ ISEE SSAT. **Enr 1118.** B 534. G 584.

Elem 737. Sec 381. Wh 90%. Hisp 2%. Blk 3%. Asian 5%. Avg class size: 15. Uniform. **Fac 122.** M 24/1. F 92/5. Adv deg: 54%. **Grad '04—87.** Col—87. Alum 850. **Tui '04-'05:** Day $9500-17,100 (+$80-1230). Aid: Need 115 ($919,640). **Summer:** Acad Enrich Rec. Tui Day $650. **Est 1974.** Nonprofit. Episcopal. Sem (Aug-May). At ESD, the academic curriculum is complemented by artistic and athletic programs, as well as extracurricular offerings. Pupils must attend daily chapel services, participate in a wilderness program and perform community service. Student clubs and organizations are plentiful.

LAKEHILL PREPARATORY SCHOOL Day Coed Gr K-12
Dallas, TX 75214. 2720 Hillside Dr.
Tel: 214-826-2931. Fax: 214-826-4623.
www.lakehillprep.org E-mail: sseitz@lakehillprep.org
Roger L. Perry, Head. BS, MEd, Univ of North Texas. Susanne Seitz, Adm.

Col Prep. AP—Eng Fr Span Calc Comp_Sci Eur_Hist US_Hist. **Feat**—Creative_Writing Comp_Graphics Studio_Art Drama Music. **Adm:** 77/yr. Appl due: Jan. **Tests** CTP_4 ISEE Stanford. **Enr 390.** B 185. G 205. Elem 280. Sec 110. Wh 81%. Hisp 5%. Blk 8%. Asian 6%. Avg class size: 15. **Fac 42.** M 13. F 27/2. Wh 87%. Hisp 5%. Blk 7%. Other 1%. Adv deg: 64%. **Grad '04**—27. Col—27. Avg SAT: 1230. Alum 600. **Tui '05-'06:** Day $8603-11,639 (+$900). **Est 1971.** Nonprofit. Sem (Aug-May). **Assoc** SACS. Lakehill's curriculum features Advanced Placement courses in the major disciplines. Speech, drama, musical theater and choir are among the performing arts options. Senior projects are required.

THE PARISH EPISCOPAL SCHOOL Day Coed Gr PS-11
Farmers Branch, TX 75244. 4101 Sigma Rd.
Tel: 972-239-8011. Fax: 972-991-1237.
www.parishepiscopal.org E-mail: cdebruyn@parishepiscopal.org
Gloria Snyder, Head. BA, Univ of Texas-Austin, MLA, Southern Methodist Univ. Marci McLean, Adm.

Col Prep. Feat—Fr Computers Studio_Art Drama Music. **Adm:** Appl due: Jan. **Enr 820.** Elem 770. Sec 50. Avg class size: 18. Uniform. **Fac 93.** M 16/1. F 54/22. Wh 97%. Hisp 1%. Blk 2%. Adv deg: 27%.**Tui '05-'06:** Day $8180-13,185. Aid: Merit 1 ($9000). Need 84 ($440,000). **Est 1972.** Nonprofit. Episcopal. Tri (Aug-May). Religious services and practices form a significant part of Parish Episcopal's daily schedule: The curriculum's structure enables students to attend chapel services and devote time to community service activities. Electives in drama, art and music, as well as competitive athletics, complement academics. A second campus, serving grades K-2, is located at 14115 Hillcrest Rd., Dallas 75240.

ST. THERESE ACADEMY Day Coed Gr 9-12
Dallas, TX 75211. 419 N Cockrell Hill Rd.
Tel: 214-333-3210. Fax: 214-333-4149.
www.sttherescacademy.com E-mail: info@sttherescacademy.com
Ellen Thomas, Head. BA, Univ of Dallas.

Col Prep. AP—Eng Eur_Hist US_Hist. **Feat**—Humanities Span Relig Studio_

Art Drama Music. **Supp**—Tut. **Adm:** Appl due: Feb. Accepted: 28%. **Enr 10.** B 3. G 7. Sec 10. Uniform. **Fac 6.** M /4. F /2. Adv deg: 33%. **Grad '04**—**3.** Col—3. Avg SAT: 1275. **Tui '05-'06:** Day $5500 (+$1000). Aid: Work prgm 4 ($8000). **Summer:** Acad Enrich. Computers. 3 wks. **Est 1989.** Nonprofit. Roman Catholic. Quar (Sept-May). Conducted in the Roman Catholic tradition, the academy's classical liberal arts curriculum places particular emphasis on the development of effective speaking and writing skills. The works addressed in history, literature, religion, music and art are actively related to each other throughout the year. Field trips to cultural centers, businesses and science facilities complement class work.

ST. THOMAS AQUINAS SCHOOL   **Day Coed Gr PS-8**
Dallas, TX 75214. 3741 Abrams Rd.
Tel: 214-826-0566. Fax: 214-826-0251.
www.staschool.org   E-mail: lbartosik@staschool.org

Martha F. Frauenheim, Prin. BA, Le Moyne College, MEd, Univ of Colorado-Boulder.

Pre-Prep. Gen Acad. Feat—Span Computers Relig Studio_Art Drama Music. **Supp**—Dev_Read LD Rem_Math Rem_Read Rev Tut. **Adm:** 65/yr. Accepted: 100%. **Enr 754.** B 369. G 385. Elem 754. Wh 51%. Hisp 45%. Blk 1%. Asian 3%. Avg class size: 25. Uniform. **Fac 49.** M 7. F 30/12. Wh 94%. Hisp 4%. Blk 2%. Adv deg: 22%. **Grad '04**—**51.** Prep—49. Alum 100. **Tui '05-'06:** Day $6000 (+$500). Parishioners $4025 (+$500). Aid: Need 30 ($40,000). **Est 1947.** Nonprofit. Roman Catholic. Sem (Aug-June). With an early childhood program (ages 3-5) in addition to grades PS-8, the school offers a full elementary program in a Catholic setting. Language and learning skills specialists provide support to pupils in need of academic assistance. Extracurricular activities—among them choir, handbells, scouting, student council, football, basketball, soccer, baseball, softball, girls' volleyball, track and field, and cheerleading—meet the needs and interests of the student body.

SHELTON SCHOOL   **Day Coed Gr PS-12**
Dallas, TX 75248. 15720 Hillcrest Rd.
Tel: 972-774-1772. Fax: 972-991-3977.
www.shelton.org   E-mail: wlipscomb@shelton.org

Joyce S. Pickering, Exec Dir. BS, Louisiana State Univ, MA, Virginia Polytechnic Institute. Diann Slaton, Adm.

LD. Feat—British_Lit ASL Lat Span Computers Econ Govt Psych Ethics Theater_Arts Speech Design. **Supp**—Dev_Read Rem_Math Rem_Read Rev Tut. **Adm (Gr PS-10):** 126/yr. Appl due: Rolling. Accepted: 39%. Yield: 98%. **Tests** IQ. **Enr 812.** B 516. G 296. Elem 596. Sec 216. Wh 93%. Hisp 2%. Blk 2%. Am Ind 1%. Asian 1%. Other 1%. Avg class size: 8. Uniform. **Fac 166.** M 23. F 137/6. Wh 96%. Hisp 1%. Blk 3%. Adv deg: 43%. **Grad '04**—**37.** Col—36. Avg SAT: 910. Avg ACT: 22. Alum 149. **Tui '04-'05:** Day $8150-14,000 (+$550-975). Aid: Need 94 ($343,700). **Summer:** Acad Enrich Rev Rem Rec. Tui Day $300-1385/crse. 6 wks. **Est 1976.** Nonprofit. Sem (Aug-May). **Assoc** SACS. The school offers learning-disabled children specialized training through multisensory instruction. Highly structured, small classes provide ongoing work in study skills. Supplementary offerings include perceptual-motor training, physical education and intramural athletic competition, computer classes and a variety of extracurricular activities. The Shelton Evaluation Center provides assessment services for the evaluation and referral of children and adults. A speech, language and hearing clinic is also available.

SOLOMAN SCHECHTER ACADEMY OF DALLAS — Day Coed Gr PS-8

Dallas, TX 75252. 18011 Hillcrest Rd.
Tel: 972-248-3032. Fax: 972-248-0695.
www.ssadallas.com E-mail: info@ssadallas.com

Fred Nathan, Head. BA, Yeshiva Univ, MEd, New York Univ. Judi Glazer, Adm.

Pre-Prep. Gen Acad. Feat—Hebrew Judaic_Stud Study_Skills. **Supp**—ESL Rem_Read. **Adm:** 64/yr. Appl due: Rolling. Accepted: 80%. **Enr 475.** Elem 475. Wh 94%. Hisp 5%. Asian 1%. Avg class size: 15. Uniform. **Fac 100.** M 3/3. F 47/47. Wh 95%. Hisp 5%. Adv deg: 18%. **Grad '04—35.** Prep—16. **Tui '04-'05:** Day $14,504. Aid: Need ($447,000). **Est 1979.** Nonprofit. Jewish. Tri (Aug-May). As part of its curriculum, SSA emphasizes Jewish studies and the Hebrew language. Judaic teachings and Torah lessons are integrated into the elementary school program (grades K-4), while older students engage in an advanced-level program of rabbinical text study that includes the Talmud. Science, math, the humanities, computer science and the arts are among the general subject areas. Extracurricular options include chorus, band, academic competitions, class trips and athletics.

URSULINE ACADEMY OF DALLAS — Day Girls Gr 9-12

Dallas, TX 75229. 4900 Walnut Hill Ln.
Tel: 469-232-1800. Fax: 469-232-1836.
www.ursulinedallas.org E-mail: msnyder@ursulinedallas.org

Sr. Margaret Ann Moser, OSU, Pres. BA, College of New Rochelle, MA, St Mary's Univ of San Antonio. Elizabeth C. Bourgeois, Prin. BA, College of New Rochelle, MA, Creighton Univ. Michele L. Snyder, Adm.

Col Prep. AP—Eng Fr Lat Span Calc Stats Comp_Sci Bio Physics Eur_Hist US_Hist Econ Psych US_Govt & Pol Studio_Art. **Feat**—Anat & Physiol Environ_Sci Asian_Stud Theol World_Relig Art_Hist Ceramics Painting Photog Sculpt Theater Chorus Music_Theory Dance. **Adm (Gr 9-11):** 202/yr. Appl due: Jan. Accepted: 50%. **Tests** ISEE. **Enr 800.** G 800. Sec 800. Wh 76%. Hisp 12%. Blk 3%. Asian 4%. Other 5%. Avg class size: 18. Uniform. **Fac 73.** M 19. F 51/3. Wh 84%. Hisp 10%. Blk 5%. Asian 1%. Adv deg: 57%. **Grad '04—192.** Col—188. Avg SAT: 1220. Alum 5500. **Tui '04-'05:** Day $10,190 (+$350-700). Aid: Need 168 ($700,000). **Summer:** Acad Enrich Rev Rem Rec. Tui Day $125-425. 3 wks. **Est 1874.** Nonprofit. Roman Catholic. Sem (Aug-May). **Assoc** SACS. Sponsored by the Ursuline Sisters of Dallas, this Catholic school provides a college preparatory program that emphasizes critical thinking and the further development of individual talents and interests. Each girl must have a laptop computer for daily class use. Students at all grade levels fulfill an annual community service requirement.

THE WINSTON SCHOOL
Day Coed Gr 1-12
Dallas, TX 75229. 5707 Royal Ln.
Tel: 214-691-6950. Fax: 214-691-1509.
www.winston-school.org E-mail: amy_smith@winston-school.org
Pamela K. Murfin, Head. BA, Stetson Univ, MSEd, PhD, Univ of Miami. Amy C. Smith, Adm.

Col Prep. LD. Feat—Lat Span Engineering Photog. Supp—Tut. Adm (Gr 1-11): 40/yr. Appl due: Rolling. Accepted: 28%. Yield: 87%. Tests IQ. Enr 217. B 158. G 59. Elem 105. Sec 112. Wh 88%. Hisp 4%. Blk 8%. Avg class size: 8. Fac 41. M 18/3. F 18/2. Wh 98%. Hisp 1%. Blk 1%. Adv deg: 65%. Grad '04—26. Col—24. Avg SAT: 1026. Avg ACT: 23. Alum 300. Tui '04-'05: Day $13,300-16,886 (+$300-1876). Aid: Need 41 ($475,072). Summer: Acad. Tui Day $1400. 5 wks. Est 1975. Nonprofit. Sem (Aug-May). Winston's program provides individual attention, a low student-teacher ratio and small-group instruction for able boys and girls who have learning differences. Pupils develop computer literacy and word processing skills, and course requirements include reading, writing, spelling, grammar, math, social studies, foreign language and the sciences. Students are encouraged to take such electives as drama, art, journalism and photography. Soccer, basketball, football, tennis, golf, baseball and volleyball constitute the sports program.

CANTERBURY EPISCOPAL SCHOOL
Day Coed Gr K-12
DeSoto, TX 75115. 1708 N Westmoreland Rd.
Tel: 972-572-7200. Fax: 972-572-7400.
www.thecanterburyschool.org E-mail: admissions@thecanterburyschool.org
Rev. C. Richard Cadigan, Head. BA, Wesleyan Univ, MDiv, Episcopal Divinity School. Sylvia Moore, Adm.

Col Prep. AP—Eng Span Calc Eur_Hist US_Hist Art_Hist. Feat—Creative_Writing Lat Ethics Philos Theol Debate. Adm (Gr K-11): 45/yr. Appl due: Rolling. Accepted: 85%. Yield: 95%. Tests IQ Stanford. Enr 245. B 114. G 131. Elem 195. Sec 50. Wh 60%. Hisp 7%. Blk 20%. Asian 4%. Other 9%. Avg class size: 13. Uniform. Fac 28. M 8/1. F 18/1. Wh 86%. Hisp 7%. Blk 7%. Adv deg: 28%. Grad '04—3. Col—3. Avg SAT: 1240. Tui '05-'06: Day $6900-9950. Aid: Need 51 ($226,334). Est 1992. Nonprofit. Episcopal. Sem (Aug-May). Serving 15 communities in southwest Dallas County and north Ellis County, Canterbury provides a full elementary and secondary program in a small-class setting. During the primary years (grades K-2), children develop basic learning skills in self-contained classrooms. Departmentalization begins in the lower school (grades 3-5), where students follow an accelerated, integrated curriculum that comprises composition, humanities, math, science, Spanish, art, music and physical education. Consisting of the middle school (grades 6-8) and the upper school (grades 9-12), the rigorous upper division emphasizes social responsibility and spiritual development, in addition to mastery of material and critical-thinking skill development.

ST. CLEMENT'S EPISCOPAL PARISH SCHOOL
Day Coed Gr PS-8
El Paso, TX 79902. 600 Montana Rd.
Tel: 915-533-4248. Fax: 915-544-1778.
www.stclements.org E-mail: glove@stclements.org

Nick Cobos, Head. BA, Hardin-Simmons Univ, MEd, Univ of Texas-Austin. Gretchen Love, Adm.

Gen Acad. Feat—Span Computers Relig Studio_Art Outdoor_Ed. **Adm:** 83/yr. Appl due: May. Accepted: 93%. Yield: 98%. **Tests** CTP_4 ISEE. **Enr 390.** B 211. G 179. Elem 390. Avg class size: 18. Uniform. **Fac 37.** M 2. F 30/5. Wh 75%. Hisp 25%. Adv deg: 8%. **Grad '04—52.** Prep—9. Alum 480. **Tui '04-'05:** Day $5245-7904 (+$500). Aid: Need 43 ($128,000). **Est 1958.** Nonprofit. Episcopal. Sem (Aug-May). A mission of the Church of St. Clement, the school prepares children for secondary school by emphasizing critical-thinking skills and the fundamentals. All pupils receive instruction in the Christian faith, attend chapel services and take part in ongoing community-outreach projects. An extensive outdoor education program progresses from area day hikes in the lower grades to 10-day backpacking excursions in grade 8.

FORT WORTH ACADEMY
Day Coed Gr K-8

Fort Worth, TX 76132. 7301 Dutch Branch Rd.
Tel: 817-370-1191. Fax: 817-294-1323.
www.fwacademy.org   E-mail: info@fwacademy.org

William M. Broderick, Head. BA, Boston College, MEd, Harvard Univ. Nancy Palmer, Adm.

Pre-Prep. Gen Acad. Feat—Span Computers Theol Studio_Art Drama Music Journ Speech. **Adm:** 54/yr. Accepted: 75%. **Tests** CTP_4 IQ ISEE. **Enr 231.** B 113. G 118. Elem 231. Wh 87%. Hisp 5%. Blk 3%. Asian 5%. Avg class size: 15. Uniform. **Fac 30.** M 3/1. F 21/5. Wh 94%. Hisp 3%. Blk 3%. Adv deg: 43%. **Grad '04—22.** Alum 160. **Tui '05-'06:** Day $9975 (+$300-500). Aid: Need 30 ($124,600). **Est 1982.** Nonprofit. Quar (Aug-May). **Assoc** SACS. The academy's elementary program allows for acceleration and includes various electives and enrichment classes in Spanish, art, the performing arts, computer and physical education. FWA conducts an active extracurricular program: Middle school students play sports, participate in dramatic and musical productions, and join interest clubs and student organizations.

HOLY FAMILY SCHOOL
Day Coed Gr PS-8

Fort Worth, TX 76107. 6146 Pershing Ave.
Tel: 817-737-4201. Fax: 817-738-1542.
www.hfsfw.org   E-mail: secretary@hfsfw.org

Carol A. Kuryla, Prin. BS, Loyola Univ of Chicago, MEd, Eastern Illinois Univ. Pearl Middleton, Adm.

Pre-Prep. Gen Acad. Feat—Lat Span Computers Relig Studio_Art Music. **Adm (Gr PS-7):** 35/yr. Appl due: Rolling. Accepted: 70%. Yield: 70%. **Tests** Stanford. **Enr 210.** Elem 210. Wh 67%. Hisp 25%. Blk 8%. Avg class size: 22. Uniform. **Fac 17.** F 10/7. Wh 95%. Hisp 5%. Adv deg: 11%. **Grad '04—20.** Alum 30. **Tui '04-'05:** Day $3350 (+$300). **Est 1945.** Nonprofit. Roman Catholic. Quar (Aug-May). Founded as St. Alice School, the school assumed its current name in 1970, at which time it was under the direction of the Sisters of the Incarnate Word. Holy Family's faculty has consisted entirely of lay staff since 1979. Academics account for the student's level of achievement, allowing children to work above, at or below grade level in each subject. While sports offered are subject to pupil participation, typical interscholastic options are basketball, volleyball, track and field, soccer, softball and baseball.

NOLAN CATHOLIC HIGH SCHOOL Day Coed Gr 7-12
Fort Worth, TX 76103. 4501 Bridge St.
Tel: 817-457-2920. Fax: 817-496-9775.
www.nolancatholichs.org   E-mail: office@nolancatholichs.org
Rev. Larry Doersching, SM, Pres. DMin. Br. Richard Thompson, SM, Prin. Maureen J. Barisonek, Adm.

Col Prep. AP—Eng Fr Span Calc Chem Physics US_Hist Psych. **Feat**—Ger Lat Stats Anat & Physiol Ecol Environ_Sci Comp_Sci Econ Govt Law Sociol Relig World_Relig Film Studio_Art Drama Theater Band Chorus Dance Accounting Debate Journ. **Supp**—Rem_Math Rem_Read Rev Tut. **Adm:** 330/yr. Appl due: Apr. **Tests** HSPT SSAT. **Enr 1059.** B 533. G 526. Elem 88. Sec 971. Wh 73%. Hisp 16%. Blk 4%. Asian 6%. Other 1%. Avg class size: 25. Uniform. **Fac 95.** M 41/1. F 46/7. Wh 90%. Hisp 5%. Blk 1%. Asian 3%. Other 1%. Adv deg: 50%. **Grad '04**—197. Col—197. Avg SAT: 1133. Avg ACT: 24. Alum 6852. **Tui '05-'06:** Day $8700 (+$400-600). Catholic $7250 (+$400-600). **Summer:** Acad. 6 wks. **Est 1961.** Nonprofit. Roman Catholic. Sem (Aug-May). **Assoc** SACS. Located on a 60-acre campus, the school offers honors and Advanced Placement courses as part of its college preparatory program. Nolan Catholic's fine arts curriculum is particularly strong. Religious studies and community service are required.

ST. RITA CATHOLIC SCHOOL Day Coed Gr PS-8
Fort Worth, TX 76112. 712 Weiler Blvd.
Tel: 817-451-9383. Fax: 817-446-4465.
www.saintritaschool.net   E-mail: adminsecretary@saintritaschool.net
Charlene Hymel, Prin.

Pre-Prep. Feat—Lib_Skills Span Computers Relig Studio_Art Chorus Music. **Supp**—Dev_Read Rem_Math Rem_Read Rev Tut. **Adm (Gr PS-7):** 72/yr. Appl due: Rolling. Accepted: 100%. **Enr 224.** B 116. G 108. Elem 224. Wh 37%. Hisp 42%. Blk 5%. Asian 14%. Other 2%. Avg class size: 22. Uniform. **Fac 16.** F 11/5. Wh 88%. Hisp 12%. Adv deg: 18%. **Grad '04**—17. Prep—12. **Tui '04-'05:** Day $4290 (+$500). Catholic $3310-3840 (+$500). Aid: Need 69 ($97,097). **Est 1954.** Nonprofit. Roman Catholic. Sem (Aug-May). St. Rita provides a Christian education in a multicultural setting. The curriculum includes basic instruction in English grammar and composition, reading and spelling, as well as more intensive courses in religion, music and Spanish. The school conducts tutorials in content areas and in study and organizational skills. Instrumental band is part of the program in grades 5-8. Students in grades 6-8 may take part in interscholastic athletics.

TRINITY EPISCOPAL SCHOOL Day Coed Gr PS-8
Galveston, TX 77550. 720 Tremont St.
Tel: 409-765-9391. Fax: 409-765-9491.
www.tesgalv.org   E-mail: pmurray@tesgalv.org

Rev. David C. Dearman, Head. BS, Univ of the South, MDiv, Virginia Theological Seminary, MEd, Mississippi College. P. J. Murray, Adm.

Gen Acad. AP—Span Calc. **Feat**—Computers Studio_Art Music. **Adm:** 54/yr. Appl due: Rolling. Accepted: 95%. **Enr 260.** B 121. G 139. Elem 260. Wh 84%. Hisp 8%. Asian 2%. Other 6%. Avg class size: 14. Uniform. **Fac 29.** M 2. F 20/7. Wh 86%. Hisp 14%. Adv deg: 13%. **Grad '04—21.** Prep—18. **Tui '05-'06:** Day $4300-6550 (+$500). Aid: Need 11 ($30,000). **Summer:** Acad Rec. Tui Day $950. 8 wks. **Est 1952.** Nonprofit. Episcopal. Sem (Aug-May). Chapel enriches this school's program, as do field trips to local, state and national destinations. Sports include soccer, volleyball, basketball and softball.

ALEXANDER-SMITH ACADEMY Day Coed Gr 9-12

Houston, TX 77042. 10255 Richmond Ave.
Tel: 713-266-0920. Fax: 713-266-8857.
www.alexandersmith.com   E-mail: darnold@alexandersmith.com

J. David Arnold, Pres. Margaret Waldner De La Garza, Prin. BA, Univ of Houston, MLA, Univ of St Thomas (TX).

Col Prep. AP—Eng US_Hist Econ US_Govt & Pol. **Feat**—Span Comp_Sci Psych Fine_Arts. **Supp**—Tut. **Adm:** 23/yr. Appl due: Apr. Accepted: 40%. **Tests** SSAT Stanford. **Enr 70.** B 40. G 30. Sec 70. Wh 90%. Hisp 2%. Blk 8%. Avg class size: 7. **Fac 14.** M 1. F 13. Wh 79%. Hisp 14%. Blk 7%. Adv deg: 85%. **Grad '04—23.** Col—23. Avg SAT: 1190. Alum 1941. **Tui '05-'06:** Day $19,200. **Summer:** Acad. Tui Day $1500/3-wk ses. 6 wks. **Est 1968.** Inc. Sem (Sept-May). **Assoc** SACS. ASA offers both college preparatory subjects and a more general academic program. The student-teacher ratio is 7:1 in all subject areas.

DUCHESNE ACADEMY Day Girls Gr PS-12
OF THE SACRED HEART

Houston, TX 77024. 10202 Memorial Dr.
Tel: 713-468-8211. Fax: 713-465-9809.
www.duchesne.org   E-mail: admissions@duchesne.org

Sr. Jan Dunn, RSCJ, Head. BA, Maryville College, MA, St Louis Univ, MEd, Univ of Houston. Beth Lowry Speck, Adm.

Col Prep. AP—Eng Fr Span Calc Stats Bio Chem US_Hist US_Govt & Pol. **Feat**—Creative_Writing Shakespeare Bioethics Computers World_Relig Photog Studio_Art Drama Music. **Adm:** 97/yr. Appl due: Jan. **Tests** CTP_4 IQ ISEE. **Enr 665.** G 665. Elem 404. Sec 261. Wh 70%. Hisp 13%. Blk 2%. Am Ind 1%. Asian 5%. Other 9%. Uniform. **Fac 82.** M 3. F 67/12. Wh 86%. Hisp 8%. Asian 4%. Other 2%. Adv deg: 48%. **Grad '04—50.** Col—50. Avg SAT: 1231. Avg ACT: 27. Alum 1206. **Tui '05-'06:** Day $7975-13,305 (+$500-2800). Aid: Merit 8 ($27,300). Need 69 ($565,150). **Summer:** Acad Enrich Rev Rec. Tui Day $200-750/3-wk ses. 6 wks. **Est 1960.** Nonprofit. Roman Catholic. Sem (Aug-May). The academy is named for Saint Philippine Duchesne, who opened the first Sacred Heart school in the US in 1818. Students may choose to participate in an exchange program with another Sacred Heart school in the United States or one overseas for two to four months of the school year.

HOLY SPIRIT EPISCOPAL SCHOOL
Day Coed Gr PS-8

Houston, TX 77024. 12535 Perthshire Rd.
Tel: 713-468-5138. Fax: 713-465-6972.
www.hses.org   E-mail: admissions@hses.org
Carolyn Trozzo, Head. BS, Baylor Univ. Sally Ward, Adm.

Pre-Prep. Feat—Fr Span Studio_Art Theater_Arts Outdoor_Ed. **Supp**—Rev Tut. **Adm (Gr PS-7):** 50/yr. Appl due: Rolling. Accepted: 80%. Yield: 66%. **Tests** IQ ISEE Stanford. **Enr 327.** B 160. G 167. Elem 327. Wh 73%. Hisp 5%. Blk 4%. Asian 9%. Other 9%. Avg class size: 17. Uniform. **Fac 36.** M 2. F 34. Wh 98%. Hisp 2%. Adv deg: 30%. **Grad '04**—29. Prep—19. Alum 50. **Tui '04-'05:** Day $7159-9623 (+$275-1100). Aid: Merit 3 ($8000). Need 8 ($15,500). **Summer:** Acad Enrich. Tui Day $350. 3 wks. **Est 1962.** Nonprofit. Episcopal. Quar (Aug-May). Holy Spirit enrolls infants as young as six weeks old into the Child Enrichment Center, and accepts boys and girls ages 3-5 into its early childhood program. The lower school (grades K-4) features integrated technology, fine arts activities, hands-on math and science programs, access to a learning center and semiweekly chapel services. Holy Spirit's middle school program (grades 5-8) includes electives, outdoor education trips, a Costa Rican exchange opportunity and various extracurricular activities.

PRESBYTERIAN SCHOOL
Day Coed Gr PS-8

Houston, TX 77004. 5300 Main St.
Tel: 713-520-0284. Fax: 713-620-6390.
www.pshouston.org   E-mail: kbrown@pshouston.org
Ray Johnson, Head. BA, MEd, Alfred Univ. Kristin Brown, Adm.

Gen Acad. Feat—Span Computers Relig Studio_Art Music. **Adm:** 91/yr. Appl due: Feb. **Tests** IQ ISEE Stanford. **Enr 456.** Elem 456. Avg class size: 18. Uniform. **Fac 60.** M 5. F 55. Wh 93%. Hisp 2%. Blk 3%. Asian 2%. Adv deg: 41%. **Grad '04**—40. **Tui '04-'05:** Day $7150-11,300 (+$100-1100). **Est 1988.** Nonprofit. Presbyterian. Tri (Aug-May). **Assoc** SACS. The school's curriculum places significant emphasis on language arts, practical math and individualized instruction. Spanish begins in kindergarten, and weekly chapel services are conducted for each class. A comprehensive parent education program is required.

RIVER OAKS BAPTIST SCHOOL
Day Coed Gr PS-8

Houston, TX 77027. 2300 Willowick Rd.
Tel: 713-623-6938. Fax: 713-626-0650.
www.robs.org   E-mail: admissions@robs.org
Nancy Heath Hightower, Head. BS, Univ of Texas-Austin, MEd, EdD, Univ of Houston. Cindy Bailey, Adm.

Pre-Prep. Gen Acad. Feat—Lat Span Computers Bible Studio_Art Chorus Music. **Supp**—Tut. **Adm:** 132/yr. Appl due: Dec. Accepted: 25%. **Tests** CTP_4 IQ ISEE Stanford. **Enr 779.** B 374. G 405. Elem 779. Wh 84%. Hisp 5%. Blk 6%. Asian 2%. Other 3%. Avg class size: 18. **Fac 71.** M 7. F 51/13. Wh 89%. Hisp 5%. Blk 5%. Am Ind 1%. Adv deg: 26%. **Grad '04**—74. Prep—51. Alum 1253. **Tui '04-'05:** Day $7360-14,145 (+$150-500). Aid: Need 37 ($390,150). **Summer:** Acad Enrich Rev Rec. Tui Day $200. 4 wks. **Est 1955.** Nonprofit. Baptist. Quar

(Aug-May). River Oaks comprises three distinct divisions: primary school (ages 2-5), lower school (grades K-4) and middle school (grades 5-8). Frequently scheduled field trips supplement the school's academic program. Cocurricular activities include intramural and interscholastic sports, student council, yearbook, musical groups and community outreach programs. **See Also Page 1235**

ST. AGNES ACADEMY   **Day Girls Gr 9-12**
Houston, TX 77036. 9000 Bellaire Blvd.
Tel: 713-219-5400. Fax: 713-219-5499.
www.st-agnes.org   E-mail: ehoover@st-agnes.org
Sr. Jane Meyer, OP, Head. BA, Dominican College, MS, Texas Woman's Univ, MRE, Univ of St Thomas (TX). Deborah Whalen, Adm.

Col Prep. AP—Eng Span Calc Comp_Sci Bio Chem Eur_Hist US_Hist US_Govt & Pol. **Feat**—Fr Lat Marine_Biol/Sci Psych Theol Art_Hist Drawing Photog Studio_Art Theater Music_Theory Dance Accounting. **Adm:** 225/yr. Appl due: Jan. Accepted: 65%. **Tests** ISEE. **Enr 784.** G 784. Sec 784. Avg class size: 20. Uniform. **Fac 53.** M 14. F 39. Adv deg: 75%. **Grad '04—166.** Col—166. **Tui '04-'05:** Day $8575 (+$500-2900). Aid: Merit 5 ($5000). Need 115 ($250,000). **Est 1906.** Nonprofit. Roman Catholic. Sem (Aug-May). As part of SAA's college preparatory curriculum, students fulfill course requirements in theology, the fine arts and computer competency, in addition to the traditional disciplines. St. Agnes fields varsity teams in the following sports: volleyball, cross-country, water polo, basketball, swimming, soccer, softball, track and field, golf and tennis. All girls purchase a laptop computer for school use upon admission.

ST. FRANCIS EPISCOPAL DAY SCHOOL   **Day Coed Gr PS-8**
Houston, TX 77024. 335 Piney Point Rd.
Tel: 713-458-6100. Fax: 713-782-4720.
www.sfedshouston.org   E-mail: sdalal@sfedshouston.org
Susan Lair, Head. BS, Univ of North Texas, MS, Texas Christian Univ, PhD, Univ of Texas-Austin. Shakti Dalal, Adm.

Pre-Prep. Feat—Span Relig Studio_Art Music. **Adm:** 147/yr. Appl due: Jan. Accepted: 73%. Yield: 69%. **Tests** CTP_4 IQ ISEE Stanford. **Enr 782.** B 412. G 370. Elem 782. Wh 89%. Hisp 4%. Blk 1%. Asian 3%. Other 3%. Avg class size: 18. Uniform. **Fac 75.** M 13. F 54/8. Wh 93%. Hisp 4%. Blk 3%. Adv deg: 24%. **Grad '04—53.** Prep—48. **Tui '04-'05:** Day $6750-12,350 (+$25-677). Aid: Need 23 ($160,150). **Est 1952.** Nonprofit. Episcopal. Quar (Aug-May). Enrolling children beginning at age 18 months, St. Francis offers a full elementary program that readies students for competitive area preparatory schools. Community outreach and religious education are integral to the program. Extensive art, music and drama programs allow pupils to pursue interests in these areas. The school's outdoor education sequence combines class study with outdoor awareness and enables students to apply what they have learned in a natural setting.

ST. PIUS X HIGH SCHOOL
Day Coed Gr 9-12

Houston, TX 77091. 811 W Donovan St.
Tel: 713-692-3581. Fax: 713-692-5725.
www.stpiusx.org E-mail: admissions@stpiusx.org

Sr. Donna M. Pollard, OP, Head. BS, Univ of Houston, MA, Aquinas Institute of Philosophy and Theology, MEd, Boston College. Susie Kramer, Adm.

Col Prep. AP—Eng Span Calc US_Hist US_Govt & Pol. **Feat**—Fr Ital Lat Anat & Physiol Comp_Sci Web_Design Theater Dance Speech. **Supp**—Dev_Read Rem_Read Rev Tut. **Adm (Gr 9-11):** 186/yr. Appl due: Feb. Accepted: 67%. **Tests** HSPT. **Enr 670.** B 326. G 344. Sec 670. Wh 56%. Hisp 27%. Blk 7%. Asian 4%. Other 6%. Avg class size: 22. Uniform. **Fac 49.** M 17/4. F 24/4. Wh 82%. Hisp 8%. Blk 8%. Other 2%. Adv deg: 61%. **Grad '04—137.** Col—135. Avg SAT: 1066. Avg ACT: 22. Alum 4900. **Tui '04-'05:** Day $6750 (+$660). Aid: Merit 6 ($6000). Need 98 ($215,990). **Summer:** Study Skills. Tui Day $325. 3 wks. **Est 1956.** Nonprofit. Roman Catholic. Sem (Aug-May). **Assoc** SACS. Among St. Pius' available electives are sociology, psychology, philosophy, multimedia, art, photography, band, choir, drama and yearbook. Football, volleyball, basketball, track, cross-country, tennis, swimming, soccer, golf, baseball and softball are the sports for both boys and girls, and various clubs and organizations are available. The theology department provides opportunities for service, retreats and days of prayer.

STRAKE JESUIT COLLEGE PREPARATORY
Day Boys Gr 9-12

Houston, TX 77036. 8900 Bellaire Blvd.
Tel: 713-774-7651. Fax: 713-774-6427.
www.strakejesuit.org E-mail: admissions@strakejesuit.org

Rev. Daniel K. Lahart, SJ, Pres. BS, Georgetown Univ, MDiv, Weston Jesuit School of Theology, MEd, Boston College, MBA, Stanford Univ. Richard C. Nevle, Prin. BA, MEd, Univ of St Thomas. Ken Lojo, Adm.

Col Prep. AP—Span Calc Comp_Sci Bio Chem US_Hist US_Govt & Pol. **Feat**—Fr Lat Oceanog Vietnam_War Psych Philos Theol World_Relig Drawing Film Studio_Art Chorus Music Music_Theory Accounting Debate TV_Production. **Adm:** 234/yr. Appl due: Feb. **Tests** HSPT. **Enr 868.** B 868. Sec 868. Wh 70%. Hisp 14%. Blk 5%. Asian 11%. Avg class size: 25. **Fac 79.** Wh 70%. Hisp 14%. Blk 5%. Asian 11%. Adv deg: 46%. **Grad '04—180.** Col—179. Avg SAT: 1278. **Tui '04-'05:** Day $9700 (+$250-450). Aid: Need ($450,000). **Summer:** Acad Rem. Tui Day $535. 6 wks. **Est 1961.** Nonprofit. Roman Catholic. Quar (Aug-May). **Assoc** SACS. Participation in religious activities is an essential component of Strake Jesuit's college preparatory curriculum. Accelerated and AP courses are offered, as are electives in the arts, theology, history and science. Athletics consist of football, basketball, baseball, cross-country, track, water polo, swimming, soccer, golf, tennis, wrestling and lacrosse.

THE VILLAGE SCHOOL
Day Coed Gr PS-8

Houston, TX 77077. 13077 Westella Dr.
Tel: 281-496-7900. Fax: 281-496-7799.
www.thevillageschool.com E-mail: info@thevillageschool.com

Betty Kelly Moore, Co-Dir. BA, Tulane Univ. Joy T. Koehl, Co-Dir. Mary Bartholomew, Adm.

Pre-Prep. Feat—Fr Span Computers Studio_Art Drama Theater Band Music Orchestra. **Supp**—Tut. **Adm:** 125/yr. Appl due: Rolling. Accepted: 50%. Yield: 90%. **Tests** IQ ISEE Stanford. **Enr 700.** B 355. G 345. Elem 700. Wh 67%. Hisp 5%. Blk 5%. Asian 23%. Avg class size: 20. Uniform. **Fac 68.** M 2/3. F 38/25. Wh 91%. Hisp 6%. Blk 2%. Asian 1%. Adv deg: 17%. **Grad '04—69.** Prep—39. **Tui '04-'05:** Day $8400-10,000 (+$675). Aid: Need 21 ($56,000). **Summer:** Acad Enrich Rev Rem Rec. Tui Day $600. 4 wks. **Est 1966.** Inc. Sem (Aug-May). This elementary and middle school offers a particularly strong math and science curriculum and also emphasizes reading, phonics, grammar and writing. Computer lab is available beginning in kindergarten. Music is presented as a participatory art, and theater, choir, band and orchestra are elements of the curriculum. Middle schoolers may take part in competitive sports. **See Also Pages 1266-7**

ALL SAINTS EPISCOPAL SCHOOL   **Day Coed Gr PS-9**
Lubbock, TX 79423. 3222 103rd St.
Tel: 806-745-7701. Fax: 806-748-0454.
www.allsaintsschool.org   E-mail: mandrews@allsaintsschool.org
    Richard E. Webb, Head. BS, State Univ of New York, MS, Univ of Oklahoma. Mary Andrews, Adm.
    Pre-Prep. Feat—Fr Lat Span Computers TX_Hist Art_Hist Studio_Art Theater Chorus. **Supp**—Dev_Read Tut. **Adm:** 65/yr. Appl due: Rolling. Accepted: 100%. **Tests** IQ. **Enr 296.** B 152. G 144. Elem 281. Sec 15. Wh 84%. Hisp 2%. Blk 1%. Asian 13%. Avg class size: 15. Uniform. **Fac 44.** M 4/2. F 30/8. Wh 98%. Hisp 1%. Blk 1%. Adv deg: 31%. **Grad '04—22.** Prep—22. **Tui '04-'05:** Day $6210-7250 (+$200). **Est 1956.** Nonprofit. Episcopal. Sem (Aug-May). All Saints stresses classical education, as well as independent or self-directed learning through individualized instruction.

TRINITY SCHOOL   **Day Coed Gr PS-12**
Midland, TX 79707. 3500 W Wadley Ave.
Tel: 432-697-3281. Fax: 432-697-7403.
www.trinitymidland.org   E-mail: j_mclaughlin@trinitymidland.org
    Rhonda J. Durham, Head. BA, Sweet Briar College. Jananne McLaughlin, Adm.
    Col Prep. AP—Eng Fr Lat Span Calc Comp_Sci Chem Physics Eur_Hist World_Hist US_Govt & Pol Studio_Art. **Feat**—Photog Drama Music. **Supp**—Tut. **Adm:** 65/yr. Appl due: Rolling. Accepted: 78%. Yield: 93%. **Tests** CTP_4 IQ. **Enr 453.** B 231. G 222. Elem 306. Sec 147. Wh 81%. Hisp 6%. Blk 2%. Asian 3%. Other 8%. **Fac 68.** M 11/4. F 40/13. Wh 88%. Hisp 9%. Blk 1%. Am Ind 1%. Other 1%. Adv deg: 32%. **Grad '04—42.** Col—41. Avg SAT: 1240. Alum 650. **Tui '05-'06:** Day $2200-11,420 (+$100-300). Aid: Merit 20 ($34,000). Need 62 ($313,850). **Est 1958.** Nonprofit. Episcopal. Sem (Aug-May). This college preparatory school offers a sequential curriculum that emphasizes the liberal arts. Program features include Advanced Placement courses, computer studies, fine arts, foreign languages and competitive athletics. All students attend daily chapel services and take part in community service activities, both on and off campus. Preschool classes follow the Montessori approach.

SACRED HEART SCHOOL
Day Coed Gr PS-12

Muenster, TX 76252. 141 E 6th St, PO Drawer 588.
Tel: 940-759-2511. Fax: 940-759-4422.
www.sacredheartschoolmuenster.com   E-mail: principalshs@ntin.net
Jon LeBrasseur, Prin.

Col Prep. Feat—Span Comp_Sci Econ Relig Fine_Arts Speech. **Supp**—Dev_Read Rev Tut. **Adm:** 9/yr. Appl due: Aug. Accepted: 95%. **Enr 239.** Elem 166. Sec 73. Wh 97%. Hisp 1%. Blk 1%. Asian 1%. Avg class size: 18. Uniform. **Fac 26.** M 5/1. F 20. Wh 97%. Hisp 3%. Adv deg: 30%. **Grad '04—25.** Col—24. Avg SAT: 1040. Avg ACT: 23. Alum 1725. **Tui '04-'05:** Day $4100 (+$500). Aid: Need 15 ($15,000). Work prgm 3 ($3600). **Est 1890.** Nonprofit. Roman Catholic. Quar (Aug-May). **Assoc** SACS.   Sacred Heart occupies a 27-acre campus in an area founded by German Catholic immigrants. The vast majority of its students belong to the parish. The school operates a Montessori preschool in a separate building.

THE ALEXANDER SCHOOL
Day Coed Gr 8-12

Richardson, TX 75081. 409 International Pky.
Tel: 972-690-9210. Fax: 972-690-9284.
www.alexanderschool.com   E-mail: admissions@alexanderschool.com
David B. Bowlin, Dir. BS, Texas Tech Univ. Andrew E. Cody, Prin. BSEd, Texas Tech Univ, MEd, Univ of North Texas.

Col Prep. AP—Eng Span Calc Bio Chem Physics US_Hist. **Feat**—Lat Ethics Yoga. **Supp**—Rem_Read Rev Tut. **Adm:** 15/yr. Appl due: Rolling. Accepted: 70%. Yield: 70%. **Enr 60.** B 35. G 25. Elem 4. Sec 56. Wh 86%. Hisp 2%. Blk 5%. Asian 7%. Avg class size: 6. **Fac 7.** M 3. F 4. Wh 57%. Blk 29%. Asian 14%. Adv deg: 57%. **Grad '04—12.** Col—11. Avg SAT: 1250. Avg ACT: 23. Alum 335. **Tui '04-'05:** Day $16,000 (+$500). Aid: Merit 2 ($16,000). **Summer:** Acad Enrich Rev. Tui Day $900/3-wk ses. 6 wks. **Est 1975.** Inc. Sem (Aug-June). **Assoc** SACS. The school's college preparatory curriculum comprises core courses in the traditional disciplines and a full complement of electives. Limited enrollment and small classes facilitate hands-on learning and enable students to receive individualized instruction.

ST. LUKE'S EPISCOPAL SCHOOL
Day Coed Gr PS-8

San Antonio, TX 78209. 15 St Luke's Ln.
Tel: 210-826-0664. Fax: 210-826-8520.
www.saintlukes.net   E-mail: dtarbox@saintlukes.net
Shirley Berdecio, Head. BA, MS, Our Lady of the Lake Univ. Dorothy L. Tarbox, Adm.

Pre-Prep. Feat—Lib_Skills Lat Span Computers Studio_Art Radio Band Music Journ. **Supp**—Dev_Read Tut. **Adm (Gr PS-7):** 83/yr. Appl due: Rolling. Accepted: 95%. Yield: 100%. **Tests** Stanford. **Enr 399.** B 156. G 243. Elem 399. Wh 77%. Hisp 15%. Blk 2%. Asian 6%. Avg class size: 16. Uniform. **Fac 46.** M 4. F 38/4. Wh 92%. Hisp 8%. Adv deg: 43%. **Grad '04—35.** Prep—35. **Tui '04-'05:** Day $5620-10,370 (+$350). **Summer:** Acad Enrich Rec. 1-8 wks. **Est 1947.** Nonprofit. Episcopal. Sem (Aug-May).   St. Luke's provides an interdisciplinary, classical program for students from age 3 through middle school. Spalding phonics and the Shurley method for writing and grammar complement the core curriculum. All boys and girls take Spanish, music, art, library, computer and physical education classes, and middle schoolers have access to laptop computers and choose from such courses as Latin, radio/media and percussion band. Individual and team athletics balance academics.

SAN ANTONIO ACADEMY Day Boys Gr PS-8
San Antonio, TX 78212. 117 E French Pl.
Tel: 210-733-7331. Fax: 210-734-0711.
www.sa-academy.org   E-mail: tmcwilliams@sa-academy.org
   John Webster, Head. BA, Gettysburg College. Mary Wilde, Adm.

   Gen Acad. Feat—Lib_Skills Span Comp_Sci Fine_Arts Music. **Adm:** 66/yr. Appl due: Rolling. **Tests** Stanford. **Enr 326.** B 326. Elem 326. Wh 70%. Hisp 23%. Blk 4%. Asian 1%. Other 2%. Avg class size: 17. Uniform. **Fac 36.** M 10/3. F 23. Adv deg: 38%. **Grad '04—32.** Prep—18. Alum 1031. **Tui '05-'06:** Day $9415-13,000 (+$500). Aid: Merit 4 ($32,000). Need 15 ($130,315). **Summer:** Acad Enrich Rev Rem Rec. Tui Day $75/wk. 8 wks. **Est 1886.** Nonprofit. Sem (Aug-May). The academy offers accelerated classes and a wide range of extracurricular activities. Small classes and a structured schedule are important components of the program.

Mountain States

COLORADO

REGIS JESUIT HIGH SCHOOL   Day Coed Gr 9-12
Aurora, CO 80016. 6400 S Lewiston Way.   **(Coord 9-12)**
Tel: 303-269-8000. Fax: 303-766-2240.
www.regisjesuit.com
    Rev. Walter Sidney, SJ, Pres. Mark Heidenry, Boys' Adm; Shea Furlong, Girls' Adm.

    Col Prep. AP—Eng Fr Lat Span Calc Bio. **Feat**—British_Lit Programming Econ Psych Sociol Theol Ceramics Studio_Art Theater Music_Theory Journ. **Supp**—Rem_Math Rem_Read Tut. **Adm (Gr 9-11):** 383/yr. Appl due: Dec. **Tests** HSPT. **Enr 1143.** B 816. G 327. Sec 1143. Avg class size: 25. **Fac 91.** M 50/4. F 32/5. Adv deg: 61%. **Grad '04—191.** Col—189. Avg SAT: 1156. Avg ACT: 25. Alum 3500. **Tui '04-'05:** Day $7750 (+$300). Aid: Merit 30 ($45,000). Need 193 ($651,000). **Summer:** Enrich. 5 wks. **Est 1877.** Nonprofit. Roman Catholic. Sem (Aug-May). **Assoc** NCA. Conducted as coordinated single-gender high schools, this Jesuit school offers boys and girls a rigorous curriculum that features Advanced Placement and honors courses, in addition to opportunities for transferable college credit (up to 32 hours) from Regis University. A pastoral ministry program, extensive junior and senior project experiences, various community service options and a peer tutoring system are important components of school life. Sports (many of which are available at the freshman level), academic and interest clubs, service organizations, student government and publications are among the school's extracurriculars.

SHINING MOUNTAIN WALDORF SCHOOL   Day Coed Gr PS-12
Boulder, CO 80304. 999 Violet Ave.
Tel: 303-444-7697. Fax: 303-444-7701.
www.smwaldorf.org   E-mail: debbyw@smwaldorf.org
    Robert Schiappacasse, Admin. BA, Beloit College, MA, San Francisco State Univ. Debby Wilson, Adm.

    Col Prep. Gen Acad. Feat—Shakespeare Russ_Lit Ger Span Anat & Physiol Comp_Relig Architect Art_Hist Fine_Arts Studio_Art Stone_Carving Bookbinding Batik Drama Music Music_Hist Woodworking Blacksmithing. **Supp**—Dev_Read Rem_Math Rem_Read Tut. **Adm (Gr PS-11):** 60/yr. Appl due: Jan. **Enr 320.** B 160. G 160. Wh 97%. Hisp 1%. Am Ind 1%. Asian 1%. **Fac 50.** M 15/10. F 15/10. Wh 100%. Adv deg: 18%. **Grad '04—26.** Col—22. Alum 100. **Tui '04-'05:** Day $7800-11,140 (+$721-1030). Aid: Need 64. **Est 1983.** Nonprofit. Sem (Sept-June). Based on Rudolf Steiner's holistic educational principles, this school's curriculum blends the humanities and sciences with art, handwork, foreign languages, music, movement and practical activities. Older students become involved in community service projects, and a broad range of opportunities for participating in the performing arts, competitive sports, school publications and other extracurricular activities is offered.

HOLY FAMILY HIGH SCHOOL
Day Coed Gr 9-12

Broomfield, CO 80020. 5195 W 144th Ave.
Tel: 303-410-1411. Fax: 303-466-1935.
www.holyfamilyhs.com   E-mail: laura.campbell@holyfamilyhs.com

Sr. Mary Rose Lieb, OSF, Prin. BS, Ohio Dominican College, MSEd, Samford Univ, MBA, Univ of Notre Dame. Jennifer Wilcomb, Adm.

Col Prep. AP—Eng Calc Chem Eur_Hist US_Hist. **Feat**—Creative_Writing Theol Ceramics Photog Studio_Art Drama Music Journ. **Supp**—Rev Tut. **Adm:** 180/yr. Accepted: 15%. **Tests** HSPT. **Enr 525.** B 260. G 265. Sec 525. Wh 72%. Hisp 26%. Blk 2%. Avg class size: 22. **Fac 38.** M 21/2. F 14/1. Adv deg: 52%. **Grad '04—103.** Col—101. Alum 4500. **Tui '04-'05:** Day $7500 (+$350). Catholic $6750 (+$350). Aid: Merit 5 ($16,875). Need 215 ($450,000). Work prgm 10 ($10,000). **Est 1922.** Nonprofit. Roman Catholic. Sem (Aug-June). Holy Family's college preparatory curriculum includes both honors and Advanced Placement courses, and qualified students may earn college credit through the University of Colorado or Regis University. The foreign language program consists of four years of Latin, five of French and six of Spanish. Boys and girls take theology each semester.

ST. MARY'S HIGH SCHOOL
Day Coed Gr 9-12

Colorado Springs, CO 80909. 2501 E Yampa St.
Tel: 719-635-7540. Fax: 719-471-7623.
www.smhscs.org   E-mail: lramzy@smhscs.org

Patty Beckert, Prin. Leah M. Ramzy, Adm.

Col Prep. AP—Eng Span Calc Chem US_Hist Studio_Art. **Feat**—Fr Lat Comp_Sci Relig Music. **Supp**—Tut. **Adm:** 117/yr. Appl due: Rolling. Accepted: 95%. Yield: 96%. **Tests** CEEB HSPT. **Enr 360.** B 198. G 162. Sec 360. Wh 76%. Hisp 18%. Blk 3%. Asian 3%. Avg class size: 18. **Fac 30.** M 15/1. F 13/1. Wh 97%. Hisp 1%. Blk 1%. Asian 1%. Adv deg: 46%. **Grad '04—71.** Col—70. Avg SAT: 1059. Avg ACT: 25. Alum 3300. **Tui '05-'06:** Day $5650 (+$250). Aid: Merit 20 ($10,000). Need 80 ($102,000). **Summer:** Acad Enrich. Tui Day $275-375. 3-4 wks. **Est 1885.** Nonprofit. Roman Catholic. Sem (Aug-May). **Assoc** NCA. SMHS offers Advanced Placement courses, as well as interscholastic sports, forensics and clubs. Religion courses are mandatory.

BEACON COUNTRY DAY SCHOOL
Day Coed Gr PS-8

Denver, CO 80222. 6100 E Belleview Ave, PO Box 22126.
Tel: 303-771-3990. Fax: 303-290-6462.
www.beaconcountrydayschool.com
E-mail: admin@beaconcountrydayschool.com

Cynthia A. Wallace, Prin. MA, JD, PhD, Univ of Denver. Tracy Rogers, Adm.

Pre-Prep. Feat—Fr Computers Studio_Art Drama Music. **Adm:** 12/yr. Appl due: Mar. Accepted: 90%. Yield: 90%. **Enr 150.** B 80. G 70. Elem 150. Wh 84%. Hisp 2%. Blk 2%. Am Ind 2%. Asian 10%. Avg class size: 15. **Fac 16.** Wh 100%. Adv deg: 50%. **Grad '04—15.** Prep—13. **Tui '04-'05:** Day $10,200 (+$450-750). Aid: Need 8 ($60,000). **Summer:** Enrich Rec. 4-8 wks. **Est 1954.** Nonprofit. Quar (Sept-June). Located in suburban Greenwood Village, BCDS utilizes small learning groups to meet the specific needs of the students. Children develop fundamental skills during the early years through a program that incorporates music, games, puppets and play. In grades 1-8, traditional courses are supplemented by computers, higher-level thinking skills, research skill development, enrichment seminars, music and art. Middle schoolers may participate in an International Baccalaureate preparation program that readies students for IB course work at the high school level.

DENVER ACADEMY Day Coed Gr 1-12
Denver, CO 80222. 4400 E Iliff Ave.
Tel: 303-777-5870. Fax: 303-777-5893.
www.denveracademy.org E-mail: admissions@denveracademy.org
James E. Loan, Head. BS, Carthage College, MA, Univ of Northern Colorado. Daniel A. Loan, Adm.

Col Prep. Gen Acad. Voc. LD. Underachiever. Feat—Span Filmmaking. **Supp**—Dev_Read Rem_Math Rem_Read Rev Tut. **Adm:** 120/yr. Accepted: 95%. Yield: 86%. **Tests** IQ. **Enr 441.** B 324. G 117. Elem 187. Sec 254. Wh 95%. Hisp 2%. Blk 1%. Asian 2%. Avg class size: 12. **Fac 69.** M 35. F 34. Adv deg: 1%. **Grad '04—53.** Col—50. Avg ACT: 20. Alum 600. **Tui '04-'05:** Day $17,400 (+$50). Aid: Need ($300,000). **Summer:** Acad Enrich Rev Rem. 5 wks. **Est 1972.** Nonprofit. Quar (Aug-June). The school's curriculum is designed to meet the needs of children of normal intelligence with learning differences or other problems that lead to underachievement. Students can participate in soccer, basketball, baseball, wrestling, volleyball and cross-country, as well as such extracurriculars as drama, student council and yearbook.

THE DENVER CAMPUS Day Coed Gr K-12
FOR JEWISH EDUCATION
Denver, CO 80321. 2450 S Wabash St.
Tel: 303-369-0663. Fax: 303-369-0664.
www.dcje.org E-mail: info@dcje.org
Philip B. Kalin, Pres. BS, Univ of Iowa, MA, Univ of Michigan. Alana Story, Adm.

Col Prep. AP—Eng Calc. **Feat**—Creative_Writing Hebrew Span Astron Environ_Sci Judaic_Stud Studio_Art Drama Public_Speak. **Supp**—ESL Rev. **Adm (Gr K-11):** 58/yr. Appl due: Rolling. Accepted: 73%. Yield: 83%. **Enr 363.** B 202. G 161. Elem 292. Sec 71. Wh 100%. Avg class size: 20. **Fac 61.** M 8/6. F 38/9. Wh 100%. Adv deg: 32%. **Grad '04—21.** Col—21. **Tui '04-'05:** Day $9331-10,235 (+$200-775). Aid: Need 129 ($681,461). **Est 1976.** Nonprofit. Jewish. Sem (Aug-June). Formed by the 1999 union of Theodor Herzl Jewish Day School (grades K-5) and Rocky Mountain Hebrew Academy (grades 6-12), this institution combines rigorous secular studies with Judaic studies. At both Herzl and RMHA, instructors place strong emphasis on language arts, math, science and social studies. Elective classes at RMHA include public speaking, drama, creative writing, sign language and art. Judaic studies, which address differing Jewish perspectives, focus on history, ethics and values, and Israel. Pupils learn Hebrew, study traditional and modern texts, and celebrate and learn more about holidays.

DENVER INTERNATIONAL SCHOOL　　　　　　　　Day Coed Gr PS-8
Denver, CO 80210. 1101 S Race St.
Tel: 303-756-0381. Fax: 303-753-9426.
www.dischool.org　　E-mail: info@dischool.org
　　Anthony Fruhauf, Head. BA, Brown Univ, MA, Harvard Univ. Patricia Ayite, Adm.

Pre-Prep. Bilingual. Feat—Fr Mandarin Span Computers Music. **Supp**—ESL Tut. **Adm:** 53/yr. Appl due: Jan. Accepted: 80%. Yield: 90%. **Tests** ISEE. **Enr 230.** B 115. G 115. Elem 230. Wh 70%. Hisp 10%. Blk 10%. Asian 10%. Avg class size: 10. **Fac 33.** M 6. F 27. Wh 60%. Hisp 30%. Asian 10%. Adv deg: 15%. **Grad '04—6. Tui '04-'05:** Day $8450 (+$2000). Aid: Need 50 ($65,000). **Summer:** Enrich Rec. Tui Day $155/wk. 12 wks. **Est** 1977. Tri (Aug-June). DIS conducts full-immersion preschool programs in French, Spanish and Mandarin, as well as bilingual elementary programs combining English with the same languages. The school incorporates an American curriculum from grade 1. In grade 1, 80 percent of the school day is devoted to the foreign course of studies, while in grades 2 and 3, students spend 70 percent of the day on the foreign curriculum. By grade 4, half of the course work is in English and half in the other language. Field trips and overnight excursions, supervised after-school study programs and after-school enrichment opportunities are part of each program.

DENVER LUTHERAN HIGH SCHOOL　　　　　　　Day Coed Gr 9-12
Denver, CO 80219. 3201 W Arizona Ave.
Tel: 303-934-2345. Fax: 303-934-0455.
www.denverlhs.org　　E-mail: office@denverlhs.org
　　Carroll Harr, Exec Dir. Loren Otte, Prin. MA. Carolyn Otte, Adm.

Col Prep. Gen Acad. AP—Eng Calc US_Hist. **Feat**—Creative_Writing Fr Span Stats Computers Govt Psych Bible Relig Theol Ceramics Studio_Art Band Chorus Music Bus Speech. **Supp**—Rem_Math Tut. **Adm:** 69/yr. Appl due: May. Accepted: 99%. **Tests** HSPT TOEFL. **Enr 220.** B 130. G 90. Sec 220. Wh 75%. Hisp 16%. Blk 4%. Am Ind 1%. Asian 4%. Avg class size: 18. **Fac 18.** M 11. F 6/1. Wh 100%. Adv deg: 33%. **Grad '04—68.** Col—62. Avg SAT: 1043. Avg ACT: 22. Alum 2945. **Tui '04-'05:** Day $6500 (+$475). **Summer:** Acad Rem. Tui Day $175/ 2-wk ses. 4 wks. **Est** 1955. Nonprofit. Lutheran-Missouri Synod. Sem (Aug-June). LHS conducts a diverse academic program in a Christian environment. Courses include religion, languages, social science, math, science, business, computer science, art and music. Vocational education and independent study are available by special arrangement. Among extracurricular activities are athletics, band, chorus, newspaper and yearbook, and service clubs.

THE LOGAN SCHOOL　　　　　　　　　　　　　Day Coed Gr K-8
FOR CREATIVE LEARNING
Denver, CO 80230. 1005 Yosemite St.
Tel: 303-340-2444. Fax: 303-340-2041.
www.theloganschool.org　　E-mail: info@theloganschool.org
　　Andrew Slater, Head. EdM, Harvard Univ, EdM, Bank Street College of Education. Kelly Lutz, Adm.

Pre-Prep. Gen Acad. Feat—Fr Lat Span Visual_Arts Theater Music. **Adm:** 54/yr. Appl due: Feb. Accepted: 54%. Yield: 82%. **Tests** IQ. **Enr 213.** B 106. G 107. Elem 213. Wh 84%. Hisp 3%. Blk 6%. Asian 5%. Other 2%. Avg class size: 18. **Fac 35.** M 9. F 26. Wh 94%. Hisp 6%. Adv deg: 34%. **Grad '04**—23. Prep—18. Alum 246. **Tui '04-'05:** Day $11,200 (+$225-900). Aid: Need 28 ($150,000). **Summer:** Rec. 1-3 wks. **Est 1981.** Nonprofit. Tri (Aug-June). Students at Logan are placed into four divisions: entry primary, upper primary, intermediate and advanced. In the primary divisions, students gain an exposure to the visual and performing arts, music and foreign language. Beginning at the intermediate level, pupils may take part in extended field trips and ongoing field studies for enrichment purposes. Elective options include theater, music, dance and environmental studies.

MONTCLAIR ACADEMY   Day Coed Gr PS-8
Denver, CO 80230. 212 Syracuse St.
Tel: 303-366-7588. Fax: 303-367-2530.
www.montclairacademy.org   E-mail: theschool@montclairacademy.org
  Buffie Berger, Head. BA, MA, Stanford Univ. Judith Current, Adm.

  Pre-Prep. Gen Acad. Feat—Japan Span Studio_Art Music. **Supp**—Rem_Math Rem_Read Rev Tut. **Adm:** 60/yr. Appl due: Feb. **Enr 250.** Elem 250. Wh 69%. Hisp 8%. Blk 14%. Asian 8%. Other 1%. Avg class size: 12. **Fac 29.** M 3. F 26. Wh 91%. Hisp 6%. Asian 3%. Adv deg: 27%. **Grad '04**—14. Prep—10. **Tui '03-'04:** Day $9750-10,200. Aid: Merit ($200,000). **Summer:** Enrich Rec. Tui Day $140/wk. 10 wks. **Est 1981.** Nonprofit. Tri (Aug-June). The academy's comprehensive program includes a strong academic curriculum with computer-integrated instruction; physical education and a sports program; art, music and band; Spanish instruction; enrichment classes; and outdoor education. The school features small class sizes and a community atmosphere. A high level of parental involvement is encouraged through a school service program.

ST. ANNE'S EPISCOPAL SCHOOL   Day Coed Gr PS-8
Denver, CO 80210. 2701 S York St.
Tel: 303-756-9481. Fax: 303-756-5512.
www.st-annes.org
  Ramsay C. Stabler, Head. BA, Williams College, MS, Columbia Univ. Rose Kelly, Adm.

  Pre-Prep. Feat—Fr Lat Span Environ_Sci Computers Relig Studio_Art Drama Band Music. **Supp**—Dev_Read Rem_Math Rem_Read Rev Tut. **Adm:** 57/yr. Appl due: Dec. Accepted: 60%. **Tests** ISEE. **Enr 428.** B 211. G 217. Elem 428. Wh 83%. Hisp 2%. Blk 2%. Asian 2%. Other 11%. Avg class size: 22. **Fac 60.** M 15. F 37/8. Wh 100%. Adv deg: 45%. **Grad '04**—42. Prep—25. Alum 800. **Tui '04-'05:** Day $7166-12,710. Aid: Need 73 ($578,000). **Est 1950.** Nonprofit. Tri (Aug-June). Located on a 10-acre main campus in southeast Denver, St. Anne's features a year-round extended-day program. Spanish instruction begins in preschool, while French and Latin are available in the middle school.

UNIVERSITY OF DENVER HIGH SCHOOL Day Coed Gr 9-12
Denver, CO 80208. 2306 E Evans Ave.
Tel: 303-871-2636. Fax: 303-871-3313.
www.du.edu/duhs   E-mail: sfalk@du.edu
   William Patterson, Dir. BA, MacMurray College, MA, Northwestern Univ, EdD, Indiana Univ. Sandra Falk, Adm.

   Col Prep. AP—Eng Calc Bio Physics Eur_Hist Studio_Art. **Feat**—British_Lit Creative_Writing Lat Span Stats Ecol Geol Web_Design Econ Govt Psych Ethics Philos World_Relig Ceramics Drawing Fine_Arts Drama Speech. **Adm:** 37/yr. Appl due: Feb. Accepted: 93%. Yield: 60%. **Enr 120.** B 70. G 50. Sec 120. Wh 85%. Hisp 3%. Blk 4%. Am Ind 1%. Asian 7%. Avg class size: 13. **Fac 16.** M 7/1. F 7/1. Wh 88%. Hisp 12%. Adv deg: 50%. **Grad '04**—29. Col—29. Avg SAT: 1175. Avg ACT: 25. Alum 188. **Tui '04-'05:** Day $13,150 (+$100). Aid: Need 30 ($196,000). **Summer:** Acad. 2 wks. **Est 1995.** Nonprofit. Sem (Aug-May). Lecture is not a primary instructional tool at this school, which encourages active learning by emphasizing problem solving and the discussion of ideas. All boys and girls conduct independent study, and advanced pupils may earn college credit. As part of the College of Education at the University of Denver, the school provides students with access to all of the university's resources.

COLORADO TIMBERLINE ACADEMY Coed Gr 9-PG
Durango, CO 81301. 35554 US Hwy 550. Bdg & Day
Tel: 970-247-5898. Fax: 970-259-8067.
www.ctaedu.org   E-mail: cta@frontier.net
   Daniel J. Coey, Dir. Alexander J. Schuhl, Adm.

   Col Prep. Gen Acad. Feat—Creative_Writing Fr Span Anat & Physiol Astron Botany Ecol Environ_Sci Computers Robotics Psych Philos World_Relig Photog Studio_Art Drama Music Journ Woodworking. **Supp**—Dev_Read ESL Rem_Math Rem_Read Rev Tut. **Adm (Bdg Gr 9-12):** 9/yr. Bdg 8. Day 1. Appl due: Rolling. Accepted: 85%. Yield: 90%. **Enr 25.** B 17/1. G 5/2. Sec 25. Wh 99%. Blk 1%. Avg class size: 6. **Fac 10.** M 5/2. F 3. Wh 100%. Adv deg: 40%. In Dorms 2. **Grad '04**—6. Col—6. Alum 267. **Tui '04-'05:** Bdg $24,300 (+$500). 5-Day Bdg $21,225 (+$500). Day $12,800 (+$400). Aid: Need 3 ($27,500). **Est 1975.** Nonprofit. 7 terms (Aug-May). CTA offers an unusual college-oriented program in small classes. The school year comprises seven four-week blocks, with students taking three classes per block. Rather than receiving a specific number of credits for various subjects, students must pass seven basic academic goals. During each block, students select a nonacademic pursuit from such offerings as guitar, photography, art and cooking. Among the recreational activities are skiing, fishing, soccer, snowboarding, basketball, rock climbing, and fall and winter wilderness trips.

CAMPION ACADEMY Coed Gr 9-12
Loveland, CO 80537. 300 SW 42nd St. Bdg & Day
Tel: 970-667-5592. Fax: 970-667-5104.
www.campion.net   E-mail: info@campion.net
   Aleene Williams, Prin. BSEd, MEd, EdD. Lynne Eagan, Adm.

   Col Prep. Feat—Fr Span Anat & Physiol Comp_Sci Govt Bible Studio_Art

Drama Music Home_Ec Outdoor_Ed Multimedia_Production. **Supp**—Tut. **Adm:** 80/yr. Appl due: Aug. Accepted: 98%. **Tests** TOEFL. **Enr 202.** B 67/33. G 70/32. Sec 202. Wh 80%. Hisp 9%. Blk 2%. Am Ind 1%. Asian 4%. Other 4%. **Fac 15.** M 7/1. F 5/2. Wh 94%. Asian 6%. Adv deg: 60%. **Grad '04—68.** Col—60. Avg ACT: 22. Alum 3000. **Tui '04-'05:** Bdg $10,849 (+$300). Day $6849 (+$300). Aid: Merit ($12,000). Work prgm 202 ($255,000). **Summer:** Outdoor Ed. 2 wks. **Est 1906.** Nonprofit. Seventh-Day Adventist. Sem (Aug-May). Campion provides three separate curricula: general high school, college preparatory and honors. Subject requirements include Bible, vocational/technical, keyboarding/word processing and fine arts, and all students are expected to work a portion of each weekday. The academy conducts regular religious services and sponsors a number of clubs and organizations, campus ministry activities, music groups and sports.

FOOTHILLS ACADEMY   Day Coed Gr PS-12
Wheat Ridge, CO 80033. 4725 Miller St.
Tel: 303-431-0920. Fax: 303-431-9505.
www.foothills-academy.org   E-mail: admissions@foothills-academy.org
Mary L. Faddick, Head. BA, MA. Donna C. Opperman, Adm.

Col Prep. Feat—Fr Span Visual_Arts Theater Music. **Supp**—Dev_Read Rem_Math Rem_Read Tut. **Adm:** Appl due: Rolling. Accepted: 85%. Yield: 75%. **Enr 229.** Elem 186. Sec 43. Wh 87%. Hisp 4%. Blk 1%. Am Ind 1%. Asian 2%. Other 5%. Avg class size: 16. **Fac 34.** M 8/3. F 19/4. Wh 100%. Adv deg: 64%. **Grad '04—8.** Col—8. **Tui '04-'05:** Day $8000-11,000 (+$50-1500). Aid: Need 17 ($350,000). **Summer:** Enrich Rec. Tui Day $190/wk. 8 wks. **Est 1984.** Nonprofit. Sem (Aug-June). Enrolling students from a 40-mile radius, Foothills enriches its liberal arts curriculum with foreign language, computer and lab sciences, service learning, outdoor education and athletics. The experiential program also includes cultural, historical and science-based field trips; overnight excursions; on-campus enrichment assemblies; and various festivals and celebrations. Community service is a required part of the curriculum beginning in kindergarten; retirement home visitation, tutoring of severely handicapped students from the area and crop picking for a food bank in southern Colorado represent some of the options.

IDAHO

BISHOP KELLY HIGH SCHOOL   Day Coed Gr 9-12
Boise, ID 83709. 7009 Franklin Rd.
Tel: 208-375-6010. Fax: 208-375-3626.
www.bk.org   E-mail: principal@bk.org
David Lachiondo, Pres. Robert R. Wehde, Prin.

Col Prep. AP—Eng Span Calc Stats Bio Chem Physics US_Hist Studio_Art. **Feat**—Fr Japan Lat Ecol Geol Comp_Sci Econ Govt Psych Comp_Relig Theol Drawing Painting Pottery Chorus. **Enr 652.** Sec 652. Wh 85%. Hisp 5%. Asian 2%. Other 8%. Avg class size: 21. **Fac 46.** M 12/6. F 21/7. Wh 96%. Hisp 2%. Other 2%. Adv deg: 43%. **Grad '04—120.** Avg SAT: 1149. Avg ACT: 25. **Tui '04-'05:** Day $5323. **Est 1964.** Nonprofit. Roman Catholic. Sem (Aug-May). Bishop

Kelly's college preparatory curriculum features Advanced Placement course work in every major discipline, as well as four foreign languages and an array of electives. Interest clubs, student organizations and sports balance academics. Interscholastic athletic options are football, cross-country, soccer, golf, basketball, baseball, ice hockey, lacrosse, skiing, softball, swimming, tennis, track, volleyball, wrestling and cheerleading.

GEM STATE ADVENTIST ACADEMY   **Coed Gr 9-12**
Caldwell, ID 83607. 16115 S Montana Ave.   **Bdg & Day**
Tel: 208-459-1627. Fax: 208-454-9079.
www.gemstate.org   E-mail: registrar@gemstate.org
    Mike Schwartz, Prin. BA, Walla Walla College, MA, Andrews Univ.

    Col Prep. Gen Acad. Feat—Span Computers Econ Govt Relig Graphic_Arts Band Chorus Speech. **Supp**—Tut. **Adm:** 74/yr. Bdg 23. Day 51. Appl due: Rolling. **Enr 157.** B 27/50. G 25/55. Sec 157. Wh 78%. Hisp 12%. Blk 1%. Asian 8%. Other 1%. Avg class size: 17. **Fac 13.** M 6/3. F 1/3. Wh 92%. Asian 10%. Adv deg: 30%. In Dorms 2. **Grad '04**—32. Col—28. Alum 3090. **Tui '04-'05:** Bdg $11,450. Day $7450. Aid: Merit 30 ($45,000). Need 35 ($113,000). Work prgm 112 ($300,000). **Est 1918.** Nonprofit. Seventh-Day Adventist. Sem (Aug-May). This small school offers a standard curriculum that prepares boys and girls for college. A well-established work-study program enables students to lessen school expenses. Boys' basketball and girls' basketball and volleyball are available at the varsity level.

MONTANA

HEADWATERS ACADEMY   **Day Boys Gr 6-9, Girls 6-12**
Bozeman, MT 59715. 418 W Garfield St.
Tel: 406-585-9997. Fax: 406-585-9992.
www.headwatersacademy.com   E-mail: admissions@headwatersacademy.com
    Tim McWilliams, Head. BA, Eastern Washington Univ. Susan Schwab, Adm.

    Gen Acad. Feat—Span Computers Studio_Art Music Outdoor_Ed. **Supp**—Tut. **Adm:** 10/yr. Appl due: Aug. Accepted: 90%. **Enr 24.** B 13. G 11. Elem 24. Wh 100%. Avg class size: 8. **Fac 8.** M 1/1. F 2/4. Wh 90%. Asian 10%. Adv deg: 50%. **Grad '04**—4. **Tui '04-'05:** Day $7350 (+$100-200). **Summer:** Enrich. Drama. 3-6 wks. **Est 1990.** Nonprofit. (Sept-June). Headwaters combines middle school academics with a noteworthy outdoor education program. The academy's proximity to Montana State University enables students to conduct research there. Each year, the school organizes a weeklong field study tour. Boys and girls engage in class discussions and research prior to the tour, then compose and present a project based upon their experiences.

LUSTRE CHRISTIAN HIGH SCHOOL   **Coed Gr 9-12**
Frazer, MT 59225. HC 66, Box 57.   **Bdg & Day**
Tel: 406-392-5735. Fax: 406-392-5765.
www.lustrechristian.com   E-mail: 2lchs@nemontel.net

Al Leland, Head.

Col Prep. Feat—Computers Bible Drama Journ. **Supp**—Rem_Math Tut. **Adm:** 12/yr. Bdg 3. Day 9. Accepted: 100%. **Tests** CEEB. **Enr 34.** B 3/10. G 5/16. Sec 34. Wh 84%. Blk 4%. Asian 4%. Other 8%. Avg class size: 7. **Fac 6.** M 3. F /3. Wh 100%. Adv deg: 16%. **Grad '04—7.** Col—6. Avg ACT: 25. Alum 200. **Tui '04-'05:** Bdg $3200 (+$700). Day $1000 (+$150). Aid: Need 2 ($2000). **Est 1948.** Nonprofit. Nondenom Christian. Sem (Aug-May). Lustre offers elective courses in many subject areas, in addition to the traditional academic program. Bible classes are required, and chapel services are held once a week. The school's athletic program includes basketball, football, volleyball and track. Students participate in various music competitions.

LOYOLA SACRED HEART   Day Coed Gr 9-12
CATHOLIC HIGH SCHOOL
Missoula, MT 59801. 320 Edith St.
Tel: 406-549-6101. Fax: 406-542-1432.
E-mail: catholiced@blackfoot.net

Patrick Haggarty, Prin.

Col Prep. Feat—Humanities Theol Fine_Arts. **Enr 208.** Sec 208. **Fac 24. Tui '02-'03:** Day $2800-5600. **Est 1893.** Roman Catholic. Sem (Aug-June). Students at this diocesan high school take eight courses annually in a block-schedule system. Loyola maintains graduation requirements in theology, health, practical arts, fine arts and the humanities, in addition to the standard subjects. Honors and AP classes provide challenge for advanced students.

Southwest States

ARIZONA

CAMELBACK DESERT SCHOOL
Day Coed Gr PS-8

Paradise Valley, AZ 85253. 6050 N Invergordon Rd.
Tel: 480-948-7520. Fax: 480-998-5664.
www.camelbackdesertschools.com
E-mail: learning@camelbackdesertschools.com
  Pat Hornor, Dir. BA, James Madison Univ.

  Pre-Prep. Feat—Span Studio_Art Music. **Adm:** 51/yr. Appl due: Rolling. Accepted: 90%. Yield: 90%. **Enr 185.** B 108. G 77. Elem 185. Wh 97%. Hisp 1%. Blk 1%. Asian 1%. Avg class size: 12. **Fac 18.** M 4. F 14. Wh 95%. Hisp 5%. Adv deg: 5%. **Grad '04—10.** Prep—6. **Tui '04-'05:** Day $7137-9705 (+$250). **Summer:** Rec. Tui Day $735-770/4-wk ses. 8 wks. **Est 1949.** Inc. Quar (Aug-May). CDS's curriculum emphasizes language arts and individualized instruction. Computer applications is taught at all grade levels. Students in grades 5-8 receive typing instruction. Boys and girls take part in an active sports program.

PARADISE VALLEY CHRISTIAN PREPARATORY
Day Coed Gr PS-8

Phoenix, AZ 85032. 2401 E Cactus Rd.
Tel: 602-992-8140. Fax: 602-992-8152.
www.paradisevalleychristian.com
  Sheryl Temple, Head. BS, Grand Canyon Univ, MA, Univ of Phoenix. Cindy Woudenberg, Adm.

  Pre-Prep. Gen Acad. Feat—Span Computers Bible Studio_Art Music. **Supp**—Dev_Read Rev Tut. **Adm:** 120/yr. Appl due: Mar. Accepted: 90%. Yield: 90%. **Tests** Stanford. **Enr 460.** B 234. G 226. Elem 460. Wh 82%. Hisp 12%. Blk 3%. Am Ind 1%. Asian 2%. Avg class size: 20. Uniform. **Fac 40.** M 6/1. F 28/5. Wh 90%. Hisp 10%. Adv deg: 12%. **Grad '04—31.** Prep—14. **Tui '04-'05:** Day $4590. Aid: Need 40. **Summer:** Rev. Tui Day $200. 5 wks. **Est 1974.** Nonprofit. Nondenom Christian. Sem (Aug-May). Among noteworthy aspects of PVC's academic program are an honors language arts track and advanced math placement in grades 4-8. Students study Spanish at all grade levels. Enrichment opportunities include study skills instruction, student government, interest clubs and gymnastics. Boys and girls may play on organized athletic teams beginning in grade 5.

PHOENIX CHRISTIAN JUNIOR AND SENIOR HIGH SCHOOL
Day Coed Gr 7-12

Phoenix, AZ 85015. 1751 W Indian School Rd.
Tel: 602-265-4707. Fax: 602-277-7170.
www.phoenixchristian.org   E-mail: admin@phoenixchristian.org
  Robert L. Byrd, Supt. BA, Arizona State Univ, MEd, Northern Arizona Univ.

Col Prep. Gen Acad. Feat—Fr Computers Psych Sociol Bible Relig Arts Drama Band Chorus Speech. **Supp**—Makeup Tut. **Adm:** 164/yr. Appl due: Rolling. Accepted: 95%. **Tests** IQ Stanford TOEFL. **Enr 530.** B 290. G 240. Elem 123. Sec 407. Wh 84%. Hisp 8%. Blk 5%. Am Ind 1%. Asian 2%. Avg class size: 17. Uniform. **Fac 36.** M 16/1. F 19. Wh 98%. Blk 1%. Am Ind 1%. Adv deg: 41%. **Grad '04**—103. Col—100. Avg SAT: 990. Avg ACT: 21. Alum 4200. **Tui '03-'04:** Day $4700-5400 (+$200). Aid: Need 58 ($40,000). **Summer:** Acad. Tui Day $275/3-wk ses. 6 wks. **Est 1949.** Nonprofit. Nondenom Christian. Sem (Aug-May). **Assoc** NCA. This nondenominational school provides a Christian education, complete with daily Bible studies and weekly chapel services. The multitrack diploma program (general education, college prep and honors) allows students to match their interests with a desired career goal. Honors and AP courses are available.

SAINT MARY'S HIGH SCHOOL   Day Coed Gr 9-12
Phoenix, AZ 85004. 2525 N 3rd St.
Tel: 602-254-6371. Fax: 602-253-0337.
www.smknights.org   E-mail: sfessler@smknights.org
Mark A. Mauro, Prin. BS, Northwest Missouri State Univ, MAEd, Univ of Phoenix. Suzanne Fessler, Adm.

Col Prep. Gen Acad. AP—Eng Span Calc US_Hist Econ US_Govt & Pol. **Feat**—Fr Comp_Design Theol World_Relig Photog Drama Chorus Dance Journ. **Supp**—Rem_Math Rem_Read Tut. **Adm:** 276/yr. Appl due: Rolling. Accepted: 98%. **Tests** HSPT. **Enr 825.** B 417. G 408. Sec 825. Wh 44%. Hisp 40%. Blk 7%. Am Ind 2%. Asian 1%. Other 6%. Avg class size: 28. **Fac 49.** M 25/1. F 20/3. Wh 83%. Hisp 10%. Am Ind 2%. Asian 4%. Other 1%. Adv deg: 36%. **Grad '04**—185. Col—178. Avg SAT: 984. Avg ACT: 21. Alum 2000. **Tui '04-'05:** Day $7980 (+$800-1000). Catholic $5935 (+$800-1000). Aid: Need 347 ($1,100,000). Work prgm 12 ($15,235). **Summer:** Acad Rem Rec. Tui Day $150/4-wk ses. 8 wks. **Est 1917.** Nonprofit. Roman Catholic. Sem (Aug-May). Students at this Catholic school take a theology course each semester, while also fulfilling course requirements in English, math, science, social studies, physical education/health and electives. In addition, freshmen, sophomores and juniors perform 30 hours of community service per year. At the freshman level, the admissions committee recommends course selections; older pupils develop their schedules in cooperation with an academic advisor. Saint Mary's fields interscholastic teams in football, golf, swimming, cross-country, basketball, soccer, baseball, softball, volleyball, tennis, and track and field.

ST. PAUL'S PREPARATORY ACADEMY   Boys Gr 9-12
Phoenix, AZ 85064. PO Box 32650.   Bdg & Day
Tel: 602-956-9090. Fax: 602-956-3018.
www.stpaulsacademy.com   E-mail: admissions@stpaulsacademy.com
Hal Elliott, Head. MEd. Donna Wittwer, Adm.

Col Prep. Underachiever. Feat—Creative_Writing Span Comp_Design Web_Design Econ Govt Studio_Art Photojourn Music. **Supp**—Tut. **Adm:** 25/yr. Bdg 18. Day 7. Appl due: Rolling. Accepted: 30%. **Tests** CEEB IQ SSAT Stanford. **Enr 75.** B 50/25. Sec 75. Wh 83%. Hisp 8%. Blk 3%. Asian 6%. Avg class size: 10. Uniform. **Fac 12.** M 7. F 5. Wh 80%. Hisp 10%. Blk 10%. Adv deg: 66%.

Grad '04—13. Col—13. Avg SAT: 1150. **Tui '04-'05:** Bdg $36,000 (+$1000). Day $15,500 (+$300). Aid: Merit 6 ($18,089). Need 4 ($25,000). **Summer:** Acad Enrich Rev Rec. Travel. Tui Bdg $4100/5-wk ses. Tui Day $1350/5-wk ses. 10 wks. **Est 1961.** Nonprofit. Episcopal. Sem (Aug-May). **Assoc** NCA. St. Paul's emphasizes academic and character development for students with low motivation or initial behavior difficulties who are not working to potential. Small classes and individual attention are characteristics of the structured program. Counselors are available, and students attend compulsory afternoon and evening study halls and may also receive tutoring from teachers and peers. All boys perform community service.

SS. SIMON AND JUDE CATHOLIC SCHOOL　　　Day Coed Gr K-8
Phoenix, AZ 85017. 6351 N 27th Ave.
Tel: 602-242-1300. Fax: 602-249-3768.
www.simonjude.org　　E-mail: sswigonski@simonjude.org
　　Sr. Raphael Quinn, IBVM, Prin.

Pre-Prep. Feat—Lat Span Relig Studio_Art Music. **Supp**—Dev_Read. **Adm:** Appl due: Mar. **Tests** Stanford. **Enr 564.** B 263. G 301. Elem 564. Wh 72%. Hisp 21%. Blk 1%. Asian 5%. Other 1%. Avg class size: 33. Uniform. **Fac 28.** M 4/1. F 17/6. Wh 95%. Hisp 5%. **Grad '04**—72. Prep—54. Alum 25. **Tui '03-'04:** Day $3400 (+$300). Aid: Need 153 ($274,000). Work prgm 5 ($17,500). **Est 1954.** Nonprofit. Roman Catholic. Sem (Aug-May). The school's primary program readies students for admission to both public and private schools. Instructors emphasize the development of fundamental skills, with more expected of the pupil as he or she ages and matures. Religion plays an important role in school life, as Ss. Simon and Jude provides religious instruction and holds weekly liturgical celebrations.

SCOTTSDALE CHRISTIAN ACADEMY　　　Day Coed Gr PS-12
Phoenix, AZ 85032. 14400 N Tatum Blvd.
Tel: 602-992-5100. Fax: 602-992-0575.
www.sca-az.org　　E-mail: sca@sca.az.org
　　Gary P. Damore, Supt. EdD, Northern Arizona Univ. Lynne Petrucci, Gr 7-12 Adm; Shari Moy, Gr PS-6 Adm.

Col Prep. AP—Eng Calc US_Hist World_Hist. **Feat**—ASL Span Anat & Physiol Ecol Geol Comp_Sci Web_Design Econ Govt Bible Studio_Art Drama Music Speech. **Supp**—Dev_Read LD Rem_Math Rem_Read Rev Tut. **Adm:** 204/yr. Appl due: Mar. Accepted: 97%. Yield: 85%. **Tests** Stanford. **Enr 1155.** B 550. G 605. Elem 786. Sec 369. Wh 97%. Hisp 1%. Blk 1%. Asian 1%. Avg class size: 25. Uniform. **Fac 74.** M 18/1. F 47/8. Wh 98%. Blk 1%. Asian 1%. Adv deg: 37%. **Grad '04**—71. Col—68. Avg SAT: 1100. Avg ACT: 24. Alum 900. **Tui '04-'05:** Day $6600-7260 (+$1000). Aid: Merit 16 ($9500). Need 37 ($50,000). **Summer:** Acad Enrich Rev Rem. Tui Day $350. 3 wks. **Est 1968.** Nonprofit. Nondenom Christian. Quar (Aug-May). As part of SCA's Bible-based curriculum, computer instruction begins in prekindergarten. All elementary children attend a weekly computer class that emphasizes keyboarding, and electives in the junior high and high school address such topics as word processing and the Internet. Sports and activities include academic competitions, art programs, concerts, plays, field trips, football, volleyball, basketball, track, baseball, tennis, softball and golf.

ST. GREGORY COLLEGE PREPARATORY SCHOOL
Day Coed Gr 6-12

Tuscon, AZ 85712. 3231 N Craycroft Rd.
Tel: 520-327-6395. Fax: 520-327-8276.
www.stgregoryschool.org E-mail: admissions@stgregoryschool.net

Bryn S. Roberts, Head. BA, Mount Allison Univ (Canada), MA, Univ of Western Ontario (Canada). Debby R. Kennedy, Adm.

Col Prep. AP—Eng Fr Lat Span Calc Bio Chem Physics Eur_Hist US_Hist US_Govt & Pol Studio_Art Music_Theory. **Feat**—Creative_Writing Ecol Programming Comp_Relig Ethics Photog Theater Music Music_Hist Journ Public_Speak. **Adm:** 101/yr. Appl due: Jan. **Tests** CEEB CTP_4 ISEE SSAT Stanford. **Enr 433.** Elem 193. Sec 240. Wh 82%. Hisp 10%. Blk 3%. Am Ind 1%. Asian 2%. Other 2%. Avg class size: 17. **Fac 50.** Adv deg: 76%. **Grad '04—44.** Col—44. **Tui '05-'06:** Day $12,980-14,260 (+$400). Aid: Need 100 ($600,000). **Est 1980.** Sem (Aug-June). St. Gregory's middle and high school program emphasizes communicational skills, articulateness, logical thinking, effective argumentation, writing skills, use of correct grammar and the ability to work with others. In a small-class setting, the school offers lab and fieldwork experiences, Advanced Placement courses in all disciplines and a senior internship program.

SALPOINTE CATHOLIC HIGH SCHOOL
Day Coed Gr 9-12

Tucson, AZ 85719. 1545 E Copper St.
Tel: 520-327-6581. Fax: 520-327-8477.
www.salpointe.org E-mail: registrar@salpointe.org

Rev. Frederick J. Tillotson, OCarm, Pres. MA, Univ of San Francisco, STL, Pontificia Universita Gregoriana (Italy). Jeffrey W. Mounts, Actg Prin. BS, MEd, Vanderbilt Univ. Michael Urbanski, Adm.

Col Prep. AP—Eng Span Calc Stats Bio Chem Physics US_Hist US_Govt & Pol Art_Hist. **Feat**—Humanities Fr Theol Fine_Arts. **Supp**—Dev_Read Rem_Math Rem_Read Rev Tut. **Adm:** 354/yr. Appl due: July. Accepted: 95%. Yield: 90%. **Tests** HSPT. **Enr 1277.** B 611. G 666. Sec 1277. Wh 56%. Hisp 36%. Blk 3%. Am Ind 1%. Asian 4%. Avg class size: 27. **Fac 90.** M 40/3. F 42/5. Wh 83%. Hisp 15%. Blk 2%. Adv deg: 60%. **Grad '04—331.** Col—324. Avg SAT: 1086. Avg ACT: 24. Alum 12,500. **Tui '04-'05:** Day $5940 (+$700). Catholic $5130 (+$700). Aid: Need ($550,000). **Summer:** Acad Enrich Rev Rem Rec. Tui Day $350/crse. 3 wks. **Est 1950.** Nonprofit. Roman Catholic. Sem (Aug-May). **Assoc** NCA. Operated in the Carmelite tradition, Salpointe offers a traditional college preparatory curriculum that includes standard, honors, humanities and Advanced Placement courses, as well as a strong four-year elective program. Classes in the integrated program build upon one another in scope, sequence, skills, content and experiences. Qualified students may take classes for both high school and college credit. The school's retreat program and theology sequence form an important component of school life.

OAK CREEK RANCH SCHOOL
Bdg Coed Gr 6-12

West Sedona, AZ 86340. PO Box 4329.
Tel: 928-634-5571. Fax: 928-634-4915.
www.ocrs.com E-mail: admissions@ocrs.com

David Wick, Jr., Head. BA, Univ of Arizona, JD, Oklahoma City Univ. Nadine O'Brien, Prin. BA, Michigan State Univ, MS, Purdue Univ. Allan Popsack, Adm.

Col Prep. Gen Acad. Underachiever. Feat—Span Computers Photog. **Supp**—Dev_Read ESL Makeup Tut. **Adm:** 60/yr. Appl due: Rolling. Accepted: 90%. **Enr 90.** B 60. G 30. Elem 22. Sec 68. Wh 86%. Hisp 1%. Blk 3%. Am Ind 1%. Asian 9%. Avg class size: 8. **Fac 15.** M 8. F 7. Adv deg: 66%. **Grad '04—22.** Col—20. Avg SAT: 1100. Alum 590. **Tui '03-'04:** Bdg $26,000 (+$3000). Aid: Merit 1 ($5000). **Summer:** Acad Enrich Rev Rem Rec. Tui Bdg $3950/4-wk ses. 8 wks. **Est 1972.** Sem (Sept-May). **Assoc** NCA. OCRS' academic program is designed for students who have not succeeded in usual school settings. In addition to the regular nine-month program, Oak Creek offers a year-round program. Emphasis is placed on both basic learning skills and college preparation. Academics address individual needs, and the school maintains a program for the learning disabled. Activities include camping, fishing, horseback riding, skiing and other sports.

NEVADA

BISHOP GORMAN HIGH SCHOOL   Day Coed Gr 9-12
Las Vegas, NV 89104. 1801 S Maryland Pky.
Tel: 702-732-1945. Fax: 702-732-2856.
www.bishopgorman.org   E-mail: principal@bishopgorman.org
Connie Gerber, Pres. BA, Arizona State Univ, MEd, Univ of Nevada-Las Vegas. Aggie Evert, Adm.

Col Prep. AP—Eng Fr Span Calc Stats Bio Chem Physics Eur_Hist US_Hist Econ. **Feat**—Ecol Psych Sociol Relig Drawing Studio_Art Theater Music Music_Theory. **Adm:** 255/yr. Appl due: Rolling. Accepted: 96%. **Tests** HSPT. **Enr 857.** B 442. G 415. Sec 857. Wh 74%. Hisp 10%. Blk 6%. Am Ind 1%. Asian 4%. Other 5%. Avg class size: 25. Uniform. **Fac 53.** M 22/3. F 27/1. Wh 98%. Hisp 1%. Other 1%. Adv deg: 75%. **Grad '04—209.** Col—183. Avg SAT: 1078. Avg ACT: 22. Alum 8353. **Tui '05-'06:** Day $8475 (+$950). Catholic $7238 (+$950). Aid: Merit 50 ($37,035). Need 151 ($247,950). **Summer:** Acad. Tui Day $75-180. 6 wks. **Est 1954.** Nonprofit. Roman Catholic. Sem (Aug-May). In addition to traditional honors and Advanced Placement courses, Bishop Gorman conducts a high honors program that allows qualified students to take the maximum possible number of AP classes during their four years at the school. Pupils involved in the program must take some summer or independent study courses to meet state and school requirements. Student government, band, cheerleading, theater, school publications and quiz bowl are among Bishop Gorman's activities.

FAITH LUTHERAN JR./SR. HIGH SCHOOL   Day Coed Gr 6-12
Las Vegas, NV 89117. 2015 S Hualapai Way.
Tel: 702-804-4400. Fax: 702-804-4488.
www.faithlutheranlv.org   E-mail: info@faithlutheranlv.org
Kevin M. Dunning, Exec Dir. MA, St John's Univ. Carol Neal, Adm.

Col Prep. AP—Eng Calc Bio US_Hist US_Govt & Pol. **Feat**—Fr Span Anat & Physiol Comp_Sci Robotics NV_Hist Psych Sociol Relig Studio_Art Drama

Chorus Music Journ Home_Ec. **Supp**—Tut. **Adm:** 290/yr. Appl due: Rolling. **Tests** SSAT. **Enr 1115.** B 543. G 572. Elem 528. Sec 587. Wh 79%. Hisp 4%. Blk 2%. Am Ind 1%. Asian 6%. Other 8%. Avg class size: 25. Uniform. **Fac 72.** Wh 94%. Hisp 2%. Blk 2%. Asian 2%. Adv deg: 25%. **Grad '04—93.** Col—75. Avg SAT: 1047. Avg ACT: 24. **Tui '04-'05:** Day $6360 (+$1000). Aid: Need ($95,000). **Est 1979.** Nonprofit. Lutheran. Quar (Aug-June). Serving southern Nevada, Faith provides a Christian middle and high school program that features strong fine arts offerings, particularly in music. The varied curriculum includes two foreign languages and computer instruction. Football, volleyball, cross-country, golf, basketball, wrestling, softball, track, swimming and cheerleading are the available sports.

THE MEADOWS SCHOOL Day Coed Gr PS-12
Las Vegas, NV 89128. 8601 Scholar Ln.
Tel: 702-254-1610. Fax: 702-254-3852.
www.themeadowsschool.org E-mail: wrichardson@themeadowsschool.org
 William H. Richardson, Head. BA, Louisiana Tech Univ, MEd, EdS, Univ of Nevada-Las Vegas.

 Col Prep. AP—Eng Span Stats Physics Eur_Hist US_Hist Econ Psych US_Govt & Pol. **Feat**—British_Lit Shakespeare Anat & Physiol Genetics Comp_Sci Ceramics Film Fine_Arts Sculpt Theater Theater_Arts. **Supp**—Tut. **Adm:** 147/yr. Appl due: Rolling. Accepted: 30%. **Tests** CTP_4 IQ ISEE SSAT. **Enr 870.** B 415. G 455. Elem 621. Sec 249. Wh 82%. Hisp 3%. Blk 3%. Am Ind 1%. Asian 11%. Avg class size: 12. Uniform. **Fac 73.** M 30/1. F 39/3. Adv deg: 64%. **Grad '04—55.** Col—55. Avg SAT: 1242. Avg ACT: 26. Alum 416. **Tui '02-'03:** Day $9800-12,950 (+$450). Aid: Need 65 ($558,084). **Summer:** Acad Enrich. Tui Day $1000/5-wk ses. 10 wks. **Est 1984.** Nonprofit. Sem (Aug-June). **Assoc** NAAS. Meadows' lower school conducts an integrated program that stresses reading, writing, mathematics, science and research skills, with Spanish and computer instruction beginning in kindergarten. The middle school offers opportunities for acceleration and departmentalized courses, while the upper school provides a diverse academic and elective program that features Advanced Placement classes in the major disciplines. Extracurricular activities include competitive sports such as football, tennis, golf, volleyball, swimming, cross-country, baseball, basketball, track and wrestling; drama; forensics; publications; student government; and interest clubs.

SAGE RIDGE SCHOOL Day Coed Gr 5-12
Reno, NV 89511. 2515 Crossbow Ct.
Tel: 775-852-6222. Fax: 775-852-6228.
www.sageridge.org E-mail: acaramella@sageridge.org
 William H. Heim III, Head. BA, MA, Pennsylvania State Univ. Carol Murphy, Adm.

 Col Prep. AP—Eng Span Calc Comp_Sci Bio US_Hist. **Feat**—British_Lit Lat Animal_Behav Art_Hist Music_Hist Public_Speak. **Supp**—Rev Tut. **Adm (Gr 5-11):** 46/yr. Appl due: Rolling. Accepted: 99%. **Tests** ISEE. **Enr 158.** Elem 95. Sec 63. Wh 84%. Hisp 10%. Blk 1%. Asian 4%. Other 1%. Avg class size: 11. Uniform. **Fac 24.** M 13/1. F 10. Wh 100%. Adv deg: 66%. **Grad '04—3.** Col—3. Avg SAT: 1298. Avg ACT: 31. **Tui '04-'05:** Day $11,000-14,000 (+$2750). Aid: Merit 14 ($140,000). Need 32 ($300,000). **Est 1997.** Nonprofit. Sem (Aug-June). Each SRS student utilizes a laptop computer as a learning aid. Honors and Advanced Placement courses are available in the core disciplines. Student clubs and publications, athletics and student government are some of the extracurricular options. Boys and girls in grades 10-12 fulfill an annual community service requirement.

NEW MEXICO

BOSQUE SCHOOL
Day Coed Gr 6-12

Albuquerque, NM 87120. 4000 Learning Rd NW.
Tel: 505-898-6388. Fax: 505-922-0392.
www.bosqueschool.org E-mail: info@bosqueschool.org

Andrew F. Wooden, Head. BA, Univ of Maine, MA, Yale Univ. Rebecca D. Toevs, Adm.

Col Prep. AP—Lat. **Feat**—Humanities Span Stats Studio_Art Theater Music. **Supp**—Rev. **Adm:** 112/yr. Appl due: Feb. Accepted: 30%. **Enr 408.** Elem 224. Sec 184. Wh 84%. Hisp 12%. Blk 1%. Am Ind 1%. Asian 2%. Avg class size: 16. **Fac 50.** Adv deg: 68%. **Grad '04—13.** Col—13. **Tui '03-'04:** Day $11,235 (+$430). Aid: Need 55 ($247,000). **Est 1995.** Nonprofit. Tri (Aug-May). **Assoc** NCA. Providing an independent middle and high school education for the Greater Albuquerque community, Bosque utilizes a block schedule that combines traditional 45-minute classes with courses that meet for 90 to 180 minutes at a time. The arts are integral to the school's program at all grade levels: middle schoolers study art and music daily, and art and music constitute a major part of the humanities program during the high school years. Foreign language offerings begin in grade 6 and consist of Latin—included since it is the foundation for the study of English mechanics, structure, grammar and etymology—and Spanish, which allows pupils to achieve fluency in a modern language.

MENAUL SCHOOL
Day Coed Gr 6-12

Albuquerque, NM 87107. 301 Menaul Blvd NE.
Tel: 505-345-7727. Fax: 505-344-2517.
www.menaulschool.com E-mail: enrollment@menaulschool.com

Gloria G. Mallory, Pres. BFA, MA, PhD, Univ of New Mexico. Pamela Suazo, Adm.

Col Prep. AP—Eng Calc Physics. **Feat**—Fr Span Stats Anat & Physiol Environ_Sci Comp_Sci Econ Govt Psych Sociol Ethics Theol Drawing Studio_Art Pottery Theater. **Supp**—Tut. **Adm:** 55/yr. Appl due: Feb. Accepted: 85%. Yield: 65%. **Tests** ISEE SSAT TOEFL. **Enr 213.** B 121. G 92. Elem 35. Sec 178. Wh 39%. Hisp 43%. Blk 2%. Am Ind 14%. Asian 1%. Other 1%. Avg class size: 15. Uniform. **Fac 26.** M 16. F 10. Wh 71%. Hisp 13%. Blk 13%. Am Ind 3%. Adv deg: 65%. **Grad '04—54.** Col—52. Avg SAT: 1100. Avg ACT: 23. Alum 2000. **Tui '04-'05:** Day $10,500 (+$500). Aid: Need 106 ($295,000). Work prgm 2 ($3000). **Est 1881.** Nonprofit. Presbyterian. Sem (Aug-May). **Assoc** NCA. Founded by Presbyterian missionaries to serve the educational needs of Native Americans from New Mexico, Menaul now enrolls many Hispanic and Native American pupils. The curriculum emphasizes the acquisition of basic skills, critical-thinking and reasoning abilities, and facility with technology. Spirituality is an important aspect of school life: Each student attends chapel services three times a week and takes a religion class one semester per year.

ST. PIUS X HIGH SCHOOL
Day Coed Gr 9-12
Albuquerque, NM 87120. 5301 St Joseph's Dr NW.
Tel: 505-831-8400. Fax: 505-831-8413.
www.saintpiusx.com
  Barbara Rothweiler, Prin. BA, Univ of Missouri-St Louis, MA, Univ of Texas-San Antonio, EdS, Univ of New Mexico. Barbara Ducaj, Adm.

  Col Prep. AP—Eng Span Bio US_Hist Econ US_Govt & Pol Art_Hist. **Feat**—Fr Stats Computers Theol Performing_Arts Studio_Art Visual_Arts Bus Drafting. **Supp**—Tut. **Adm:** 304/yr. Appl due: Rolling. Accepted: 70%. **Tests** HSPT. **Enr 1052.** Sec 1052. Wh 36%. Hisp 57%. Blk 1%. Am Ind 4%. Asian 2%. Avg class size: 24. Uniform. **Fac 66.** M 30/1. F 32/3. Adv deg: 77%. **Grad '04—219.** Col—206. Alum 6800. **Tui '03-'04:** Day $7470 (+$175). Catholic $6400 (+$175). Aid: Need 120 ($170,000). **Summer:** Acad. Tui Day $425/credit. 6 wks. **Est 1956.** Nonprofit. Roman Catholic. Sem (Aug-May). **Assoc** NCA. Administered by the Archdiocese of Santa Fe, St. Pius provides a varied college preparatory curriculum. Advanced Placement courses, theology classes and campus ministry, including yearly retreats, enrich the academic program. Intramural and interscholastic sports and such extracurricular activities as chorus, band, dramatics, student government, publications and Model UN are available. Students also participate in peer tutoring, mentorship, peer mediation and community service programs.

McCURDY SCHOOL
Day Coed Gr PS-12
Espanola, NM 87532. 261 McCurdy Rd.
Tel: 505-753-7221. Fax: 505-753-7830.
www.mccurdy.org   E-mail: pwomack@mccurdy.org
  Pamela Womack, Supt. Patricia Alvarado & Evelyn Ruybalid, Adms.

  Col Prep. Gen Acad. AP—Eng Calc US_Hist. **Feat**—Web_Design Relig Drama. **Supp**—Rem_Math Rem_Read Tut. **Adm:** 65/yr. Appl due: Rolling. Accepted: 95%. **Enr 405.** B 203. G 202. Elem 250. Sec 155. Wh 13%. Hisp 80%. Am Ind 6%. Asian 1%. Avg class size: 14. **Fac 31.** M 12. F 19. Wh 72%. Hisp 28%. Adv deg: 61%. **Grad '04—42.** Col—42. Avg ACT: 20. Alum 2020. **Tui '02-'03:** Day $3240 (+$400). Aid: Merit 6 ($4750). Work prgm 106 ($156,000). **Est 1912.** Nonprofit. United Methodist. Sem (Aug-May). **Assoc** NCA. This Christian school offers college preparatory and practical arts courses. Football, volleyball, basketball, baseball, softball, cross-country and track are among the athletic activities.

REHOBOTH CHRISTIAN SCHOOL
Day Coed Gr K-12
Rehoboth, NM 87322. PO Box 41.
Tel: 505-863-4412. Fax: 505-863-2185.
www.rcsnm.org   E-mail: adminsec@rcsnm.org
  Ron Polinder, Exec Dir. BA, Calvin College, MA, Western Washington Univ. Lorretta Smith, Adm.

Col Prep. Gen Acad. AP—Eng Bio Eur_Hist Studio_Art. **Feat**—Span Navajo_ Lang Computers SW_Stud Navajo_Govt Music. **Supp**—Rem_Math Rem_Read Rev Tut. **Adm (Gr K-11):** 99/yr. Appl due: July. Accepted: 82%. Yield: 88%. **Enr 414.** B 199. G 215. Elem 239. Sec 175. Wh 22%. Hisp 6%. Blk 1%. Am Ind 70%. Asian 1%. Avg class size: 18. **Fac 33.** M 20/1. F 7/5. Wh 89%. Am Ind 11%. Adv deg: 69%. **Grad '04—30.** Col—28. Avg ACT: 22. Alum 1100. **Tui '04-'05:** Day $4150 (+$50). Aid: Merit 6 ($3000). Need 310 ($515,000). **Est 1903.** Nonprofit. Nondenom Christian. Sem (Aug-May). Founded by the Christian Reformed Church as a boarding school for Native American students, Rehoboth now enrolls day boys and girls only and serves a diverse student body that continues to include a large percentage of Native American pupils. The school's academic program emphasizes a core curriculum while also providing extra help in different subjects through a learning center (grades 1-8) and a resource room (grades 9-12). Interscholastic athletics are soccer, girls' softball and volleyball, cross-country, basketball, swimming and track.

NEW MEXICO MILITARY INSTITUTE Bdg Coed Gr 9-12
Roswell, NM 88201. 101 W College Blvd.
Tel: 505-624-8050. Fax: 505-624-8058.
www.nmmi.edu   E-mail: admissions@nmmi.edu

Lt. Gen. Robert D. Beckel, USAF (Ret), Supt. BS, US Air Force Academy, MS, George Washington Univ. Lt. Col. Craig C. Collins, Adm.

Col Prep. Milit. Feat—Fr Music Accounting Bus Journ Speech TV_Production Mech_Drawing JROTC. **Supp**—Tut. **Adm (Gr 9-PG):** 470/yr. **Tests** SSAT. **Enr 989.** B 802. G 187. Sec 513. PG 476. Wh 57%. Hisp 17%. Blk 7%. Am Ind 4%. Asian 5%. Other 10%. Uniform. **Fac 61.** M 38. F 23. Wh 92%. Hisp 8%. Adv deg: 96%. **Grad '04—118.** Col—111. Avg SAT: 1019. Avg ACT: 21. Alum 2500. **Tui '05-'06:** Bdg $7670-10166. Aid: Merit 351 ($1,665,817). Need 263 ($593,344). Work prgm 50 ($21,214). **Summer:** Acad Rev. Tui Bdg $1750. Tui Day $285/crse. 4 wks. **Est 1891.** Nonprofit. Sem (Aug-May). NMMI is an academic institution operating within the framework of a military environment. All high school cadets participate in the Junior ROTC program, and athletic participation is required each semester. In addition, a two-year junior college offers a basic or advanced course of Senior ROTC that allows cadets to receive an Army commission.

RIO GRANDE SCHOOL Day Coed Gr K-6
Santa Fe, NM 87505. 715 Camino Cabra.
Tel: 505-983-1621. Fax: 505-986-0012.
www.riograndeschool.org   E-mail: tony@riograndeschool.org

Andrea Williams, Head. BS, Michigan State Univ, MSc, Univ of Surrey (England). Antonio Barreiro, Adm.

Pre-Prep. Feat—Lib_Skills Span Computers Studio_Art Drama Music. **Adm:** 30/yr. Appl due: Rolling. Accepted: 68%. **Enr 122.** Elem 122. Wh 81%. Hisp 10%. Am Ind 2%. Asian 5%. Other 2%. Avg class size: 18. **Fac 14.** M /1. F 7/6. Wh 93%. Am Ind 7%. Adv deg: 57%. **Grad '04—18.** Prep—17. **Tui '04-'05:** Day $12,357 (+$300). Aid: Need 12 ($75,070). **Summer:** Acad Enrich Rec. 1-6 wks. **Est 1978.** Nonprofit. Tri (Aug-June). At all grade levels, Rio Grande's elementary program includes math, science, social studies, research projects, literature studies and extensive writing opportunities. The school follows a thematic approach, with course work in each grade revolving around a core theme. Beginning in kindergarten, children meet weekly with music, art and drama instructors, and all academic subjects integrate the arts.

UTAH

WASATCH ACADEMY — Coed Gr 9-PG, Bdg & Day
Mt Pleasant, UT 84647. 120 S 100 W.
Tel: 435-462-1400. Fax: 435-462-1450.
www.wacad.org   E-mail: admissions@wacad.org
  Joseph Loftin, Head. BS, Univ of Texas-Austin, MEd, Utah State Univ. Kim Stephens, Adm.

  Col Prep. AP—Eng Calc Bio Eur_Hist US_Hist. **Feat**—Ger Japan Span Computers Comp_Design Ethics Philos Relig Fine_Arts Drama Music Debate Speech Outdoor_Ed. **Supp**—Dev_Read ESL LD Rev Tut. **Adm:** 54/yr. Appl due: Mar. Accepted: 80%. **Tests** IQ ISEE SSAT Stanford TOEFL. **Enr 130.** B 78/7. G 38/7. Sec 129. PG 1. Wh 60%. Hisp 5%. Blk 5%. Am Ind 5%. Asian 20%. Other 5%. Avg class size: 10. **Fac 28.** Wh 92%. Blk 5%. Asian 3%. Adv deg: 71%. **Grad '04—38.** Col—38. Avg SAT: 1110. Avg ACT: 23. Alum 3838. **Tui '04-'05:** Bdg $30,300 (+$3000). 5-Day Bdg $27,300 (+$3000). Day $17,500 (+$2000). Aid: Merit 22 ($24,000). Need 24 ($500,000). **Summer:** Acad Enrich Rev Rem Rec. ESL. Tui Bdg $5000/6-wk ses. 8 wks. **Est 1875.** Nonprofit. Presbyterian. Quar (Sept-May). **Assoc** NAAS. Wasatch offers a traditional college preparatory curriculum with small classes. The academy's outdoor recreation program provides opportunities for hiking, mountain biking, rock climbing, backpacking, skiing and snowboarding at nearby national parks and ski resorts. Students have access to the cultural pursuits and artistic performances of Salt Lake City, which is located 90 miles away.

PROVO CANYON SCHOOL — Bdg Coed Gr 7-12
Orem, UT 84097. 1350 E 750 N.
Tel: 801-227-2100. Fax: 801-223-7130.
www.provocanyon.com   E-mail: pcsinfo@provocanyon.com
  Kreg D. Gillman, CEO. PhD, Brigham Young Univ. Nicholas Pakidko, Educ Dir. Steve Nielsen, Adm.

  Gen Acad. Underachiever. Feat—Fr Ger Span Zoology Econ Govt Studio_Art Bus Indus_Arts. **Supp**—Dev_Read LD Makeup Tut. **Adm:** 199/yr. Appl due: Rolling. Accepted: 45%. **Tests** IQ. **Enr 242.** B 132. G 110. Wh 78%. Hisp 7%. Blk 7%. Am Ind 2%. Asian 2%. Other 4%. Avg class size: 10. **Fac 28.** M 14. F 14. Wh 96%. Asian 4%. Adv deg: 14%. **Grad '04—34.** Alum 2835. **Tui '04-'05:** Bdg $350/day. **Est 1971.** Year-round. **Assoc** NAAS. On separate campuses, Provo Canyon serves boys and girls who are experiencing academic difficulties or behavioral problems. The school offers an individualized academic program featuring both remedial and accelerated emphasis; individual, group, family and milieu therapy; and supervised recreational experiences.   **See Also Page 1370**

REID SCHOOL Day Coed Gr PS-9
Salt Lake City, UT 84109. 2965 E 3435 S.
Tel: 801-466-4214. Fax: 801-466-4214.
www.reidschool.com   E-mail: ereid@xmission.com
Ethna R. Reid, Dir. PhD, Univ of Utah.

Pre-Prep. Gen Acad. Feat—Span Archaeology Computers Fine_Arts Study_Skills. **Supp**—Dev_Read Rem_Math Rem_Read Tut. **Enr 209.** B 101. G 108. Elem 207. Sec 2. Wh 99%. Asian 1%. Avg class size: 17. Uniform. **Fac 27.** M /2. F 14/11. Wh 96%. Blk 4%. Adv deg: 29%.**Tui '02-'03:** Day $7395 (+$465). **Summer:** Acad Enrich Rem. Tui Day $185/wk. 9 wks. Ranch Prgm. Tui Bdg $2000. 3 wks. **Est 1987.** Inc. Quar (Sept-May). This unusual school employs the instructional methods of Exemplary Center for Reading Instruction. At all grade levels, the program is characterized by a strong emphasis on reading skills. Features of the curriculum include hands-on instruction in math, science, social studies and health; a focus on comprehension and study skills in reading, writing and speaking; specialist teachers in the fine arts, crafts and physical fitness; and a program flexible enough to allow students to work beyond grade level.

THE WATERFORD SCHOOL Day Coed Gr PS-12
Sandy, UT 84093. 1480 E 9400 S.
Tel: 801-572-1780. Fax: 801-572-1787.
www.waterfordschool.org   E-mail: admissions@waterfordschool.org
Nancy M. Heuston, Head. Todd Winters, Adm.

Col Prep. AP—Eng Fr Ger Span Calc Stats Comp_Sci Bio Chem Physics US_Hist Studio_Art. **Feat**—Lat Programming Psych Philos Photog Acting Music_Hist Dance. **Adm:** 128/yr. Appl due: Apr. Accepted: 65%. **Tests** CTP_4. **Enr 994.** B 495. G 499. Elem 738. Sec 256. Wh 87%. Hisp 3%. Blk 3%. Am Ind 1%. Asian 6%. Avg class size: 20. Uniform. **Fac 105.** M 37. F 68. Wh 94%. Hisp 1%. Asian 5%. Adv deg: 42%. **Grad '04**—57. Col—57. Avg SAT: 1218. Avg ACT: 27. **Tui '05-'06:** Day $10,180-14,800 (+$150-500). **Est 1986.** Nonprofit. Tri (Sept-June). Waterford conducts a liberal arts program in a small-class setting. The school offers an unusually varied curriculum, particular in the areas of foreign language and the arts. An interim program allows boys and girls to choose among such options as mountain climbing and biking excursions, art exhibits, college visits and museum tours. Extracurricular activities include student government, community service, outdoor club, publications, drama, and instrumental and vocal performance opportunities.

Pacific States

ALASKA

GRACE CHRISTIAN SCHOOL   Day Coed Gr K-12
Anchorage, AK 99516. 12407 Pintail St.
Tel: 907-345-4814. Fax: 907-644-2260.
www.gcsk12.net   E-mail: admissions@gcsk12.net
     Nathan Davis, Admin. BS, BEd, Univ of Alaska-Anchorage, MA, Seattle Pacific Univ. Darlene Kuiper, Adm.

    Col Prep. Gen Acad. AP—Eng Calc Bio Chem. **Feat**—Fr Span Computers Bible Studio_Art Band Music Music_Theory Study_Skills. **Supp**—Tut. **Adm:** 114/yr. Appl due: Rolling. Accepted: 99%. **Tests** Stanford. **Enr 683.** B 335. G 348. Elem 451. Sec 232. Wh 93%. Blk 1%. Am Ind 4%. Asian 2%. Avg class size: 23. **Fac 45.** M 15/3. F 27. Wh 100%. Adv deg: 26%. **Grad '04—63.** Col—60. Avg SAT: 1069. Avg ACT: 24. Alum 455. **Tui '04-'05:** Day $4405-5085. Aid: Need 64 ($77,000). **Est 1980.** Nonprofit. Grace Brethren. Sem (Aug-May). **Assoc** NAAS. Grace teaches academic subjects within a biblical context, emphasizing Christian values and beliefs. The curriculum includes advanced courses, and Spanish and French are taught in the upper grades. Sports include cross-country running, track, basketball, volleyball, wrestling, cross-country skiing and soccer. Parental involvement is an important component of the school's program.

PACIFIC NORTHERN ACADEMY   Day Coed Gr PS-12
Anchorage, AK 99508. , 550 S Bragaw St.
Tel: 907-333-1080. Fax: 907-333-1652.
www.pacificnorthern.org   E-mail: admissions@pacificnorthern.org
     Bob Christal, Head. Shannon Tetlow, Adm.

    Col Prep. Feat—Humanities Span Stats Comp_Sci Econ Graphic_Arts Photog Studio_Art Drama Chorus Music. **Adm:** 63/yr. Appl due: Rolling. **Tests** CTP_4 SSAT. **Enr 165.** B 84. G 81. Avg class size: 18. **Fac 28.** M 7/2. F 17/2. Adv deg: 42%. **Grad '04—5.** Col—5. Alum 6. **Tui '04-'05:** Day $9300-13,300 (+$500). **Est 1996.** Nonprofit. (Sept-June). In the lower school (grades PS-5) students focus on math, science and English, and also develop basic computer skills. Middle schoolers (grades 6-8) devote mornings to the core disciplines, while afternoons are spent rotating among Spanish, art, music, choir, physical education and other elective offerings. High schoolers may pursue special interests through independent study, senior internships and community involvement.

CALIFORNIA

RAMONA CONVENT SECONDARY SCHOOL Day Girls Gr 7-12
Alhambra, CA 91803. 1701 W Ramona Rd.
Tel: 626-282-4151. Fax: 626-281-0797.
www.ramona.pvt.k12.ca.us
　　Sr. Kathleen Callaway, Pres. Kathleen Pillon, Prin. BA, MA, Holy Names College. Laura Dumas, Adm.

　　Col Prep. AP—Fr Span Calc Comp_Sci Bio Chem Eur_Hist US_Hist Psych US_Govt & Pol Studio_Art. **Feat**—Relig Fine_Arts Speech. **Supp**—Rev Tut. **Adm:** 161/yr. Appl due: Jan. Accepted: 80%. **Tests** HSPT. **Enr 560.** G 560. Elem 65. Sec 495. Wh 12%. Hisp 53%. Blk 2%. Asian 33%. Avg class size: 22. Uniform. **Fac 45.** M 12. F 33. Adv deg: 82%. **Grad '04—116.** Col—114. Avg SAT: 1054. **Tui '03-'04:** Day $7500 (+$1030-1330). Aid: Need 100 ($172,000). **Summer:** Acad Enrich Rev Rem Rec. 5 wks. **Est 1889.** Nonprofit. Roman Catholic. Quar (Aug-June). **Assoc** WASC. Ramona Convent is conducted by the Sisters of the Holy Names. A full athletic and activities program is offered. The well-equipped, 15-acre campus is minutes from Los Angeles.

PASADENA WALDORF SCHOOL Day Coed Gr K-8
Altadena, CA 91001. 209 E Mariposa St.
Tel: 626-794-9564. Fax: 626-794-4704.
www.pasadenawaldorf.org　E-mail: admissions@pasadenawaldorf.org
　　Grace Sanders, Adm.

　　Pre-Prep. Gen Acad. Feat—Classical_Lit & Mythology Japan Span Studio_Art Drama Music Handbells Movement. **Supp**—Dev_Read Rem_Math Rev Tut. **Adm:** 41/yr. Appl due: Rolling. **Enr 244.** B 108. G 136. Elem 244. Wh 73%. Hisp 13%. Blk 5%. Asian 5%. Other 4%. Avg class size: 25. **Fac 22.** M 5. F 11/6. Wh 75%. Hisp 10%. Asian 5%. Other 10%. Adv deg: 22%. **Grad '04—23.** Prep—14. **Tui '04-'05:** Day $8220-10,410 (+$697-762). Aid: Need 49 ($256,704). **Est 1979.** Nonprofit. Sem (Sept-June).　Pasadena Waldorf follows the curriculum and the educational philosophy of Rudolf Steiner by taking a variety of approaches to learning. Instructors integrate academics and the arts in a developmentally appropriate manner.

CORNELIA CONNELLY SCHOOL Day Girls Gr 9-12
Anaheim, CA 92804. 2323 W Broadway.
Tel: 714-776-1717. Fax: 714-776-2534.
www.connellyhs.org　E-mail: admissions@connellyhs.org
　　Sr. Francine Gunther, SHCJ, Head. AB, Rosemont College, MA, George Washington Univ. Jenny Guzik, Adm.

　　Col Prep. Gen Acad. AP—Eng Fr Span Calc Bio Chem US_Hist US_Govt & Pol Art_Hist Studio_Art. **Feat**—Computers Relig Theater. **Supp**—Rev Tut. **Adm:** 75/yr. Appl due: Feb. **Tests** HSPT. **Enr 232.** G 232. Sec 232. Wh 53%. Hisp 20%. Blk 1%. Asian 26%. Avg class size: 15. Uniform. **Fac 30.** M 5/2. F 16/7. Adv deg: 46%. **Grad '04—54.** Col—54. Avg SAT: 1128. Alum 2421. **Tui '04-'05:** Day

$8950 (+$600-1100). Aid: Merit 15. Need 44. **Summer:** Acad Enrich Rev. Tui Day $300/crse. 6 wks. **Est 1961.** Nonprofit. Roman Catholic. Sem (Sept-June). **Assoc** WASC. Established by the Sisters of the Holy Child Jesus, Connelly offers a college preparatory curriculum augmented by electives in the arts, interscholastic sports and various clubs. An exchange program is available with other Holy Child schools in the US.

FAIRMONT PRIVATE SCHOOLS Day Coed Gr PS-12
Anaheim, CA 92802. 1575 W Mable St.
Tel: 714-765-6300. Fax: 714-765-6382.
www.fairmontschools.com   E-mail: info@fairmontschools.com
   David R. Jackson, Pres.

   Col Prep. Gen Acad. IB_Diploma. AP—Eng Bio Eur_Hist Psych. **Supp**—Tut. **Adm:** 448/yr. **Tests** TOEFL. **Enr** 2250. Elem 1920. Sec 330. Avg class size: 24. Uniform. **Fac 148.** M 32. F 116. **Grad '04—81.** Col—81. Avg SAT: 1222. **Tui '03-'04:** Day $8448-9812 (+$66-792). **Summer:** Acad Rev. 6 wks. **Est 1953.** Inc. Tri (Aug-June). **Assoc** WASC. Fairmont comprises five campuses at five locations throughout Orange County. The high school offers honors classes, Advanced Placement courses and the International Baccalaureate for students who show an aptitude for advanced work. Among the graduation requirements are foreign language, computer and fine arts courses. Extracurriculars include a wide variety of activities and clubs, in addition to athletics.

SERVITE HIGH SCHOOL Day Boys Gr 9-12
Anaheim, CA 92801. 1952 W La Palma Ave.
Tel: 714-774-7575. Fax: 714-774-1404.
www.servitehs.org   E-mail: kmeyers@servitehs.org
   Peter S. Bowen, Pres. BA, Univ of Notre Dame, MA, Duke Univ. Raymond R. Dunne, Prin. BA, California State Univ, MS, Pepperdine Univ. Andrea Perry, Adm.

   Col Prep. AP—Eng Lat Span Calc Comp_Sci Bio Chem Physics Eur_Hist US_Hist World_Hist Econ US_Govt & Pol Art_Hist. **Feat**—Marine_Biol/Sci Theol Theater Music. **Supp**—Makeup Tut. **Adm:** 254/yr. Appl due: Feb. Accepted: 90%. Yield: 90%. **Tests** Stanford. **Enr** 785. B 785. Sec 785. Wh 80%. Hisp 10%. Blk 1%. Am Ind 1%. Asian 7%. Other 1%. Avg class size: 19. **Fac 60.** M 36. F 24. Wh 85%. Hisp 13%. Am Ind 2%. Adv deg: 51%. **Grad '04—178.** Col—178. Avg SAT: 1126. Alum 8000. **Tui '04-'05:** Day $7700 (+$835). Catholic $7200 (+$835). Aid: Need 153 ($272,170). **Summer:** Acad Enrich Rev Rem. Tui Day $200-400/crse. 5 wks. **Est 1958.** Nonprofit. Roman Catholic. Sem (Aug-June). **Assoc** WASC. Located on a 15-acre campus, this boys' school offers course work at the college preparatory, honors and Advanced Placement levels. Servite maintains a strong interscholastic athletic program, as well as an active performing arts program that operates in conjunction with two sister schools. Also noteworthy is the school's classical guitar program. All boys perform 70 hours of Christian community service.

NOTRE DAME HIGH SCHOOL   **Day Girls Gr 9-12**
Belmont, CA 94002. 1540 Ralston Ave.
Tel: 650-595-1913. Fax: 650-595-2116.
www.ndhsb.org   E-mail: admissions@ndhsb.org

Rita L. Gleason, Prin. BA, College of Notre Dame (CA), MA, Univ of Santa Clara, MA, San Francisco State Univ. Lynn Stieren, Adm.

Col Prep. AP—Eng Fr Span Calc Bio US_Hist US_Govt & Pol Art_Hist. **Feat**—Psych Relig Ceramics Photog Band Orchestra TV_Production. **Supp**—LD. **Adm:** 214/yr. Appl due: Dec. **Tests** HSPT. **Enr 720.** G 720. Sec 720. Wh 72%. Hisp 12%. Blk 2%. Am Ind 1%. Asian 13%. Avg class size: 24. Uniform. **Fac 63.** M 17/3. F 37/6. Adv deg: 41%. **Grad '04—170.** Col—168. Avg SAT: 1190. Alum 6900. **Tui '04-'05:** Day $12,500 (+$800). Aid: Merit 90 ($47,200). Need 120 ($330,000). **Summer:** Acad Enrich Rem Rec. Tui Day $650/crse. 5 wks. **Est 1922.** Nonprofit. Roman Catholic. Sem (Aug-June). **Assoc** WASC. Sponsored by the Sisters of Notre Dame de Namur, this independent Catholic school provides a college preparatory program for a student body drawn largely from San Mateo County. Advanced Placement and honors courses are available, and a collaborative arrangement with Notre Dame de Namur University enables qualified pupils to take courses for college credit for an additional fee. Extracurricular activities include interscholastic athletics, student government, school publications, TV production, peer tutoring, musical organizations and interest clubs.

ARROWSMITH ACADEMY   **Day Coed Gr 9-12**
Berkeley, CA 94704. 2300 Bancroft Way.
Tel: 510-540-0440. Fax: 510-540-0541.
www.arrowsmith.org   E-mail: contact@arrowsmith.org

William Fletcher, Head. BA, MEd, Univ of New Hampshire. Felicia Martin, Adm.

Col Prep. Feat—Japan Filmmaking Studio_Art Video Drama Music Journ. **Supp**—ESL Tut. **Adm:** 50/yr. Appl due: Jan. Accepted: 85%. **Enr 120.** B 74. G 46. Sec 120. Wh 50%. Hisp 3%. Blk 20%. Asian 11%. Other 16%. Avg class size: 12. **Fac 16.** M 6/3. F 4/3. Wh 60%. Hisp 6%. Blk 18%. Asian 12%. Other 4%. Adv deg: 43%. **Grad '04—23.** Col—21. Avg SAT: 1170. Alum 100. **Tui '04-'05:** Day $15,675 (+$500). Aid: Need 35 ($220,000). **Summer:** Acad Enrich. Tui Day $400-700. 3-6 wks. **Est 1979.** Nonprofit. Sem (Aug-June). **Assoc** WASC. A community service program supplements a full range of academic classes, and course work reflects a multicultural environment. Electives include computer science, self-defense, community service, yearbook, student government, art, drama, music, health and physical education. Parents receive written reports every six weeks and attend parent-teacher conferences each semester.

EAST BAY FRENCH-AMERICAN SCHOOL   **Day Coed Gr PS-8**
Berkeley, CA 94710. 1009 Heinz Ave.
Tel: 510-549-3867. Fax: 510-549-2067.
www.ebfas.org   E-mail: admissions@ebfas.org

Frederic Canadas, Head. BS, MEd. Mona Kafouri, Adm.

Pre-Prep. Bilingual. Feat—Fr Computers Studio_Art Drama Music. **Supp**—

ESL Rem_Read Tut. **Adm:** 100/yr. Appl due: Feb. **Enr 503.** B 214. G 289. Elem 503. Wh 64%. Hisp 6%. Blk 10%. Asian 10%. Other 10%. Avg class size: 16. **Fac 50.** M 8/4. F 32/6. Wh 96%. Hisp 2%. Blk 2%. **Grad '04—29. Tui '05-'06:** Day $14,405-16,670. Aid: Need 153 ($992,000). **Est 1977.** Nonprofit. Tri (Sept-June). **Assoc** WASC. Also known as Ecole Bilingue de Berkeley, East Bay provides a rigorous elementary course of study, set in a multicultural environment, in both English and French. In grades pre-K-2, children receive French immersion 80 percent of the school day, in addition to an hour of English instruction daily. Then, in grades 3-8, immersion is split equally between the two languages. Specialists teach science, computer, music, art, drama, physical education and gardening. Field trips and international exchange opportunities are part of the program.

PROVIDENCE HIGH SCHOOL Day Coed Gr 9-12
Burbank, CA 91505. 511 S Buena Vista St.
Tel: 818-846-8141. Fax: 818-843-8421.
www.providencehigh.org E-mail: judy.umeck@providencehigh.org

Sr. Lucille Dean, SP, Prin. BS, College of Great Falls, MEd, Univ of Oregon. Judy Umeck, Adm.

Col Prep. AP—Eng Fr Span Calc Stats Bio Physics US_Hist Econ US_Govt & Pol Studio_Art. **Feat**—Anat & Physiol Computers Anthro Law Psych Sociol Ethics Ceramics Film Photog Video_Production Animation Music Communications Journ TV_Production. **Supp**—Tut. **Adm (Gr 9):** 172/yr. Appl due: Jan. Accepted: 90%. Yield: 76%. **Tests** HSPT. **Enr 556.** B 229. G 327. Sec 556. Wh 17%. Hisp 12%. Blk 1%. Am Ind 1%. Asian 20%. Other 49%. Avg class size: 25. Uniform. **Fac 36.** M 14∫. F 21/1. Wh 67%. Hisp 27%. Asian 1%. Other 5%. Adv deg: 61%. **Grad '04— 129.** Col—120. Avg SAT: 1079. Alum 3600. **Tui '04-'05:** Day $7700 (+$550). Aid: Merit 55 ($16,050). Need 145 ($192,830). **Summer:** Acad Enrich Rev Rec. Tui Day $300/crse. 5 wks. **Est 1955.** Nonprofit. Roman Catholic. Sem (Sept-June). **Assoc** WASC. Providence's curriculum includes honors and AP classes, electives and required courses in art, computer science, foreign language, music and religious studies. In addition to the college preparatory course of study, qualified students may enroll in one of two four-year focus programs in health careers and media communications. A Christian service project is mandatory, and student activities include campus ministry and sports.

ALL SAINTS' EPISCOPAL DAY SCHOOL Day Coed Gr PS-8
Carmel, CA 93923. 8060 Carmel Valley Rd.
Tel: 831-624-9171. Fax: 831-624-3960.
www.asds.org E-mail: asds@asds.org

Michele M. Rench, Head. BA, Univ of California-Berkeley, MA, College of Notre Dame (CA). Anne Crisan, Adm.

Pre-Prep. Feat—Shakespeare Fr Lat Span Art_Hist Theater. **Supp**—Rem_Math Tut. **Adm:** 33/yr. Accepted: 40%. Yield: 70%. **Tests** CTP_4. **Enr 210.** B 103. G 107. Elem 210. Wh 84%. Hisp 5%. Blk 3%. Asian 4%. Other 4%. **Fac 30.** M 4/3. F 11/12. Wh 100%. Adv deg: 36%. **Grad '04—21.** Prep—16. Alum 646. **Tui '04-'05:** Day $10,900-13,310. Aid: Need 30 ($198,167). **Summer:** Enrich Rec. Arts. Tui Day $100/wk. 4 wks. **Est 1961.** Nonprofit. Episcopal. Sem (Aug-June). All Saints' foreign language program includes Spanish and French in grades 1-8 and Latin in grades 6-8. Field trips and class projects provide enrichment at all grade levels.

JESUIT HIGH SCHOOL   **Day Boys Gr 9-12**
Carmichael, CA 95608. 1200 Jacob Ln.
Tel: 916-482-6060. Fax: 916-482-2310.
www.jhssac.org   E-mail: admissions@jhssac.org
    Rev. Greg Bonfiglio, SJ, Pres. Rev. John P. McGarry, SJ, Prin. MA, Jesuit School of Theology at Berkeley. Gerald C. Lane, Adm.
    Col Prep. AP—Eng Lat Span Calc Comp_Sci Bio Chem Physics US_Hist Comp_Govt & Pol US_Govt & Pol Art_Hist. **Feat**—Fr Ger Greek Anat & Physiol Holocaust Psych Comp_Relig Ethics Studio_Art Chorus. **Supp**—Tut. **Adm (Gr 9-11):** 290/yr. Appl due: Feb. Accepted: 60%. **Tests** HSPT. **Enr 1025.** B 1025. Sec 1025. Wh 71%. Hisp 13%. Blk 4%. Am Ind 1%. Asian 10%. Other 1%. Avg class size: 26. **Fac 72.** M 44/9. F 18/1. Adv deg: 55%. **Grad '04—261.** Col—255. Avg SAT: 1150. Avg ACT: 24. Alum 5000. **Tui '04-'05:** Day $8700 (+$700-900). Aid: Need 160 ($250,000). **Summer:** Acad Enrich Rev Rec. Tui Day $325-650. 4-6 wks. **Est 1963.** Nonprofit. Roman Catholic. Sem (Aug-May). **Assoc** WASC. Jesuit's college preparatory curriculum is supplemented by programs in music, drama, journalism and the fine arts. Athletic offerings include baseball, basketball, football, volleyball, cross-country, golf, soccer, swimming, water polo, wrestling, tennis, track and rugby teams.

ST. MICHAEL'S EPISCOPAL DAY SCHOOL   **Day Coed Gr PS-8**
Carmichael, CA 95608. 2140 Mission Ave.
Tel: 916-485-3418. Fax: 916-485-9084.
www.smeds.net   E-mail: postmaster@smeds.net
    Rev. Jesse Vaughan, Head. MTh, Episcopal Theological Seminary. Mary D. Heise, Adm.
    Gen Acad. Feat—Lat Span Computers Drama Music. **Adm:** Appl due: Rolling. **Enr 245.** Elem 245. Avg class size: 22. **Fac 42. Grad '04—23. Tui '04-'05:** Day $6590-8065 (+$600). Aid: Need ($95,000). **Est 1963.** Nonprofit. Episcopal. (Sept-June). **Assoc** WASC. SMEDS' preschool and kindergarten focus on concept and motor development, social and motor skills, reading, math and the arts. Daily chapel is part of a curriculum that also includes Spanish, Latin, music, drama, computers and physical education.

SIERRA CANYON SCHOOL   **Day Coed Gr PS-8**
Chatsworth, CA 91313. 11052 Sierra Canyon Way, PO Box 3039.
Tel: 818-882-8121. Fax: 818-882-8218.
www.sierracanyon.com
    Jim Skrumbis, Head. Nancy Posey, Adm.
    Pre-Prep. Feat—Fr Ger Japan Span Computers Geog Law Philos Fine_Arts. **Adm:** 125/yr. Appl due: Feb. Accepted: 25%. **Tests** ISEE. **Enr 700.** B 375. G 325. Elem 700. Wh 74%. Hisp 1%. Blk 6%. Am Ind 1%. Asian 18%. Avg class size: 24. **Fac 135.** Adv deg: 12%. **Grad '04—70.** Prep—70. **Tui '03-'04:** Day $12,000-

13,000 (+$500). Aid: Need ($500,000). **Summer:** Enrich Rec. Tui Day $300/wk. 9 wks. **Est 1977.** Inc. Sem (Sept-June). **Assoc** WASC. Sierra Canyon features small-group math instruction, hands-on science courses and a social studies curriculum that incorporates frequent field trips. After-school enrichment and sports are available.

PROSPECT SIERRA SCHOOL — Day Coed Gr K-8
El Cerrito, CA 94530. 2060 Tapscott Ave.
Tel: 510-236-5800. Fax: 510-232-7615.
www.prospectsierra.org   E-mail: psoffice@prospectsierra.org
  Frederick Heinrich, Head. BA, Connecticut College, MA, Univ of Texas-Austin. Lily Shih, Adm.
  Pre-Prep. Feat—Fr Span Computers Studio_Art Drama Orchestra Jazz_Band. **Adm:** 64/yr. Appl due: Jan. Accepted: 24%. **Tests** ISEE. **Enr 487.** B 228. G 259. Elem 487. Wh 69%. Hisp 7%. Blk 9%. Am Ind 1%. Asian 13%. Other 1%. Avg class size: 22. **Fac 60.** M 10. F 50. Adv deg: 45%. **Grad '04—68. Tui '04-'05:** Day $14,200-15,700 (+$550). Aid: Need 84 ($600,000). **Est 1981.** Nonprofit. Tri (Aug-June). This school's curriculum encompasses the humanities, math, science, technology, art, music, drama and physical education. Beginning in grade 4, children study either French or Spanish. A second campus, one mile away at 960 Avis Dr., houses the middle school (grades 5-8). An interscholastic league provides athletic competition with other independent school students.

WINDRUSH SCHOOL — Day Coed Gr K-8
El Cerrito, CA 94530. 1800 Elm St.
Tel: 510-970-7580. Fax: 510-235-3554.
www.windrush.org   E-mail: colsen@windrush.org
  Lynn De Jonghe, Dir. BA, Harvard Univ, MS, Simmons College, PhD, Cornell Univ. Cheryl Olsen, Adm.
  Pre-Prep. Gen Acad. Feat—Span Photog Studio_Art Drama Music. **Adm:** 65/yr. Appl due: Jan. Accepted: 49%. **Enr 250.** B 117. G 133. Elem 250. Wh 66%. Hisp 4%. Blk 6%. Asian 4%. Other 20%. **Fac 28.** M 2/5. F 15/6. Wh 75%. Hisp 14%. Blk 7%. Am Ind 4%. Adv deg: 28%. **Grad '04—43.** Prep—21. **Tui '02-'03:** Day $10,000-11,500 (+$25-150). Aid: Need 33 ($177,900). **Summer:** Enrich Rec. Tui Day $410/2-wk ses. 8 wks. **Est 1976.** Nonprofit. Tri (Sept-June). Windrush's elementary school (grades K-5) features specialist-taught enrichment classes in music, art, computer, library, Spanish and physical education. During the middle school years (grades 6-8), the school offers a two-week integrated unit that places students in cross-grade groups and addresses interdisciplinary topics. Middle school electives include media literacy, martial arts, digital photography, dance, music and yearbook.

EAST BAY WALDORF SCHOOL — Day Coed Gr K-12
El Sobrante, CA 94803. 3800 Clark Rd.
Tel: 510-223-3570. Fax: 510-222-3141.
www.eastbaywaldorf.org   E-mail: admin@eastbaywaldorf.org
  Dale Robinson, Fac Chrm. Judy July, Adm.

Col Prep. Gen Acad. Feat—Ger Span Anat Zoology Art_Hist Sculpt Studio_Art Band Chorus Music Orchestra Gardening. **Supp**—LD. **Adm:** 65/yr. Appl due: Jan. Accepted: 90%. **Enr 297.** B 134. G 163. Elem 250. Sec 47. Wh 79%. Hisp 6%. Blk 5%. Am Ind 1%. Asian 9%. Avg class size: 24. **Fac 45.** M 6/11. F 10/18. Adv deg: 26%. **Grad '04—26. Tui '02-'03:** Day $7600-12,000 (+$500). Aid: Need 78 ($202,400). **Est 1980.** Nonprofit. Tri (Sept-June). The East Bay Waldorf curriculum combines the sciences, the humanities and the arts. The arts are integrated into all subjects, including math and science, and special subject teachers complement the work of the class teacher with weekly presentations of two foreign languages (German and Spanish), eurythmy, music, handcrafts and physical education.

NAWA ACADEMY   Bdg Coed Gr 7-12
French Gulch, CA 96033. 17351 Trinity Mountain Rd.
Tel: 530-359-2215. Fax: 530-359-2229.
www.nawa-academy.com   E-mail: info@nawa-academy.com
  David W. Hull, Pres. BA, Chapman Univ, MRel, School of Theology at Claremont. Jason T. Hull, Adm.

Col Prep. Gen Acad. LD. Sports (Winter). Feat—Span Computers Studio_Art Music Metal_Shop Wilderness_Ed. **Supp**—Dev_Read ESL Makeup Tut. **Adm:** 10/yr. Appl due: Rolling. **Enr 45.** Wh 95%. Blk 3%. Other 2%. Avg class size: 7. **Fac 10.** M 7. F 3. Adv deg: 30%. **Grad '04—12.** Col—10. Alum 250. **Tui '04-'05:** Bdg $31,520 (+$2800). Aid: Need 38 ($70,000). **Summer:** Acad Enrich Rec. Leadership Trng. Tui Bdg $3654/4-wk ses. 8 wks. **Est 1988.** Inc. Quar (Sept-June). **Assoc** WASC. NAWA offers experiential education through four nine-month boarding options: California Academy is an on-campus, structured program of academic and vocational classes, group projects, wilderness and rescue training, and recreational and social activities; International Academy combines academics and intercultural experiences with travel throughout the world; Girls on the Go USA is an all-girls program that blends academics and cultural experiences with world travel; and Snowboard USA mixes academics with competitive and noncompetitive snowboarding. All programs include high academic standards and training in outdoor skills.

FRESNO ADVENTIST ACADEMY   Day Coed Gr K-12
Fresno, CA 93727. 5397 E Olive Ave.
Tel: 559-251-5548. Fax: 559-456-1735.
www.faa.org   E-mail: academy@faa.org
  Dan Kittle, Prin.

Col Prep. Feat—Span Computers Bible Studio_Art Music. **Adm:** 40/yr. Appl due: Aug. **Enr 300.** Elem 200. Sec 100. Avg class size: 20. **Fac 22.** M 6/1. F 12/3. Wh 57%. Hisp 23%. Blk 12%. Asian 8%. Adv deg: 13%. **Grad '04—32.** Col—29. **Tui '02-'03:** Day $2730-5570. **Est 1898.** Nonprofit. Seventh-Day Adventist. Sem (Aug-June). **Assoc** WASC. While most pupils at FAA come from Seventh-day Adventist backgrounds, students of other Christian faiths and those indicating no denominational preference also enroll. At all grade levels, class work incorporates a strong spiritual component. The school primarily serves young people from the central San Joaquin Valley.

ROSARY HIGH SCHOOL
Day Girls Gr 9-12

Fullerton, CA 92831. 1340 N Acacia Ave.
Tel: 714-879-6302. Fax: 714-879-0853.
www.rc.net/orange/rosary   E-mail: rosary@rosaryhs.org
 Trudy Mazzarella, Pres. MRE. Terry Gonzalez, Prin.

Col Prep. AP—Eng Fr Span Calc Bio Chem US_Hist US_Govt & Pol. **Feat**—Relig. **Adm:** 200/yr. Appl due: Feb. **Enr 709.** G 709. Sec 709. Avg class size: 19. Uniform. **Fac 49.** M 6. F 43. Adv deg: 59%. **Grad '04—100.** Col—100. Avg SAT: 1198. **Tui '02-'03:** Day $6200 (+$1500). Aid: Need ($210,000). **Summer:** Acad Rev Rec. 6 wks. **Est 1965.** Nonprofit. Roman Catholic. Sem (Aug-June). Rosary's college preparatory curriculum features a selection of honors and Advanced Placement courses. Campus ministry opportunities and community service are among the cocurricular options. Girls choose from the following sports: basketball, water polo, cross-country, drill team, golf, soccer, softball, tennis and volleyball.

ST. LUCY'S PRIORY HIGH SCHOOL
Day Girls Gr 9-12

Glendora, CA 91741. 655 W Sierra Madre Ave.
Tel: 626-335-3322. Fax: 626-335-4373.
www.stlucys.com
 Sr. Monica Collins, OSB, Prin. BA, Univ of San Diego, MA, Loyola Marymount Univ, MA, Univ of San Francisco.

Col Prep. AP—Eng Span Calc Bio Eur_Hist US_Hist US_Govt & Pol. **Feat**—Fr Art_Hist Film Theater_Arts Music. **Adm (Gr 9-11):** 259/yr. Appl due: Jan. Accepted: 80%. **Tests** HSPT. **Enr 870.** G 870. Sec 870. Wh 50%. Hisp 30%. Blk 4%. Am Ind 1%. Asian 15%. Avg class size: 26. Uniform. **Fac 44.** M 10. F 32/2. Wh 66%. Hisp 25%. Blk 2%. Asian 5%. Other 2%. Adv deg: 25%. **Grad '04—197.** Col—197. Avg SAT: 1055. Alum 4400. **Tui '04-'05:** Day $4700 (+$1000). Aid: Merit 30 ($2000). Need 15 ($30,000). **Summer:** Rev Rem. Tui Day $90-180. 4 wks. **Est 1962.** Nonprofit. Roman Catholic. Sem (Aug-June). **Assoc** WASC. Established by the Benedictine Sisters, the school emphasizes a Christian education in the tradition of a college preparatory program. Girls choose from a broad selection of honors and Advanced Placement courses.

MOREAU CATHOLIC HIGH SCHOOL
Day Coed Gr 9-12

Hayward, CA 94544. 27170 Mission Blvd.
Tel: 510-881-4300. Fax: 510-581-5669.
www.moreaucatholic.org   E-mail: apply@moreaucatholic.org
 Joseph Connell, Pres. BA, St Edward's Univ, MA, Loyola Marymount Univ, PhD, Golden Gate Univ. Terry Lee, Prin. BA, Fordham Univ, MA, San Francisco State Univ. Michael Aquino, Adm.

Col Prep. AP—Eng Fr Span Calc Stats Comp_Sci Bio Physics US_Hist Econ US_Govt & Pol. **Feat**—Lat Programming Psych Theol Video_Production Theater Band Dance Bus. **Supp**—Tut. **Adm:** 280/yr. Appl due: Jan. Accepted: 80%. **Tests** HSPT SSAT. **Enr 1040.** B 515. G 525. Sec 1040. Wh 26%. Hisp 13%. Blk 4%. Am Ind 1%. Asian 44%. Other 12%. Avg class size: 30. **Fac 70.** M 33. F 37. Wh 72%. Hisp 15%. Blk 1%. Asian 8%. Other 4%. Adv deg: 37%. **Grad '04—270.** Col—258. Avg SAT: 1085. Avg ACT: 25. Alum 9200. **Tui '03-'04:** Day $8700

(+$300). **Summer:** Acad Enrich Rem. Tui Day $325. 6 wks. **Est 1965.** Nonprofit. Roman Catholic. Sem (Aug-June). **Assoc** WASC. Sponsored by the Brothers of Holy Cross, Moreau offers a college preparatory curriculum. Extensive activities and athletics complement the program.

HEBREW ACADEMY   Day Coed Gr PS-12
Huntington Beach, CA 92647. 14401 Willow Ln.
Tel: 714-898-0051. Fax: 714-898-0633.
www.hebrewacademyhb.com   E-mail: admin@hebrewacademyhb.com
    Rabbi Yitzchok Newman, Dir. MA, Pepperdine Univ. Sue Neiditch Schwartz, Prin. BS, Univ of Arizona, MEd, William Paterson Univ. Rabbi Sender Engel, Adm.

    Col Prep. Gen Acad. AP—Eng US_Hist Art_Hist. **Feat**—Hebrew Comp_Sci Psych Child_Dev Judaic_Stud Performing_Arts Visual_Arts. **Supp**—Dev_Read Rem_Math Rem_Read Rev Tut. **Adm:** 85/yr. Appl due: Apr. Accepted: 78%. **Enr 360.** B 180. G 180. Elem 290. Sec 70. Wh 100%. Avg class size: 20. Uniform. **Fac 40.** M 8/3. F 16/13. Adv deg: 45%. **Grad '04—16.** Col—16. Avg SAT: 1175. Alum 1000. **Tui '04-'05:** Day $8200 (+$1750). Aid: Need 124 ($478,000). Work prgm 150 ($232,000). **Summer:** Rec. 2-10 wks. **Est 1969.** Nonprofit. Jewish. Sem (Sept-June). Students at the academy follow a dual general studies/Judaic curriculum. Instruction focuses upon communicational and thinking skills and the use of technology. Specialists teach art, music, physical education and computer classes. The comprehensive program fosters traditional Judaic values through study of the Bible, the Hebrew language, and Jewish philosophy and ethics.

THE GILLISPIE SCHOOL   Day Coed Gr PS-6
La Jolla, CA 92037. 7380 Girard Ave.
Tel: 858-459-3773. Fax: 858-459-3834.
www.gillispie.org   E-mail: lmoyer@gillispie.org
    Jacqueline Yarbrough, Head. EdD. Linda Moyer, Adm.

    Pre-Prep. Feat—Span Computers Studio_Art Music. **Supp**—Dev_Read. **Adm:** 35/yr. Appl due: Dec. Accepted: 18%. **Tests** ISEE. **Enr 283.** B 160. G 123. Elem 283. Wh 95%. Hisp 2%. Blk 2%. Asian 1%. Avg class size: 20. **Fac 34.** M 6. F 22/6. Wh 94%. Blk 3%. Asian 3%. Adv deg: 23%. **Grad '04**—18. Prep—9. Alum 86. **Tui '04-'05:** Day $11,950-13,500. Aid: Need 9 ($35,000). **Summer:** Enrich Rec. Tui Day $180/wk. 8 wks. **Est 1952.** Nonprofit. Sem (Sept-June). **Assoc** WASC. Cocurricular activities such as music, art, computer education, library, creative movement, cooking, physical education and Spanish complement Gillispie's academic program of science, social studies, mathematics and language arts. Teachers make frequent use of resources within the community: La Jolla's picturesque coastline; the Museum of Contemporary Art; and local galleries, libraries, restaurants, shops and parks.

LUTHERAN HIGH SCHOOL   Day Coed Gr 9-12
La Verne, CA 91750. 3960 Fruit St.
Tel: 909-593-4494. Fax: 909-596-3744.
www.lhslv.org   E-mail: jlowe@lhslv.org

Jeremy Lowe, Int Prin. BA, Jamestown College.

Col Prep. AP—Eng Calc Chem Physics US_Hist. **Feat**—Span Comp_Sci Relig Studio_Art Drama Band Chorus. **Supp**—ESL Tut. **Adm:** 50/yr. Appl due: Mar. Accepted: 90%. **Tests** Stanford. **Enr 135.** Sec 135. Wh 81%. Hisp 8%. Blk 2%. Asian 9%. Avg class size: 15. Uniform. **Fac 15.** M 8. F 6/1. Wh 75%. Hisp 20%. Blk 2%. Asian 3%. Adv deg: 20%. **Grad '04—34.** Col—27. Alum 1000. **Tui '01-'02:** Day $5200 (+$500-700). Aid: Merit 4 ($1000). Need 7 ($15,000). **Est 1973.** Nonprofit. Lutheran-Missouri Synod. Sem (Aug-June). **Assoc** WASC. Historical and doctrinal theology, naval JROTC, and a variety of electives and activities, in addition to the college preparatory curriculum, are offered. The school emphasizes Christian values.

MARIN PRIMARY AND MIDDLE SCHOOL   Day Coed Gr PS-8
Larkspur, CA 94939. 20 Magnolia Ave.
Tel: 415-924-2608. Fax: 415-924-9351.
www.mpms.org   E-mail: info@mpms.org

Murray E. Lopdell Lawrence, Head. BA, Victoria Univ of Wellington (New Zealand). Nicole J. Demaray, Adm.

Pre-Prep. Feat—Fr Span Computers Fine_Arts Performing_Arts Music. **Supp**—Dev_Read Rev Tut. **Adm:** 89/yr. Appl due: Jan. Accepted: 50%. Yield: 69%. **Tests** ISEE. **Enr 353.** B 192. G 161. Elem 353. Wh 84%. Hisp 5%. Blk 3%. Am Ind 1%. Asian 6%. Other 1%. Avg class size: 27. **Fac 52.** M 18/3. F 30/1. Wh 89%. Hisp 4%. Blk 1%. Asian 1%. Other 5%. Adv deg: 25%. **Grad '04—28.** Prep—26. Alum 100. **Tui '04-'05:** Day $13,450-16,500 (+$1000). Aid: Need 20 ($200,000). **Summer:** Gr 1-7. Rec. Tui Day $185-315/wk. 8 wks. **Est 1975.** Nonprofit. Sem (Sept-June). Preschoolers at MP&MS are introduced to core academic subjects while also participating in such classes as gymnastics, piano, dance and computer. Language instruction in Spanish and French commences in preschool. An after-school program at all grade levels offers course work in Chinese, carpentry, writing, Web design, drama and sports, among others.

WESTERLY SCHOOL OF LONG BEACH   Day Coed Gr K-8
Long Beach, CA 90806. 2950 E 29th St.
Tel: 562-981-3151. Fax: 562-981-3153.
www.westerlyschool.org   E-mail: gchizeck@westerlyschool.org

Deborah David, Head. BA, Antioch College, MA, Pacific Oaks College. Rajeshri Gandhi, Adm.

Pre-Prep. Feat—Span Computers Ethics Studio_Art Music. **Supp**—Tut. **Adm:** 30/yr. Appl due: Jan. Accepted: 75%. **Tests** CTP_4 ISEE. **Enr 170.** B 80. G 90. Elem 170. Wh 70%. Hisp 10%. Blk 12%. Asian 8%. Avg class size: 20. Uniform. **Fac 25.** M 4/1. F 19/1. Wh 70%. Hisp 10%. Blk 10%. Asian 10%. Adv deg: 32%. **Grad '04—21.** Prep—9. Alum 68. **Tui '05-'06:** Day $11,250 (+$250-600). Aid: Need 30 ($178,000). **Summer:** Acad Enrich. Arts. 3-6 wks. **Est 1993.** Nonprofit. Tri (Sept-June). Westerly's elementary curriculum combines work in the core subjects of language arts, social studies, math, science and computer with art, music, Spanish and physical education classes. Grade-level teachers, specialists and teaching assistants constitute the faculty. The hands-on, experiential program assists children with basic skills mastery, as well as creative and independent thinking skills, and the school seeks to instill in students an appreciation for the arts.

THE ARCHER SCHOOL FOR GIRLS   Day Girls Gr 6-12
Los Angeles, CA 90049. 11725 Sunset Blvd.
Tel: 310-873-7000. Fax: 310-873-7070.
www.archer.org   E-mail: admissions@archer.org

Arlene F. Hogan, Head. BS, City Univ of New York, MST, Univ of Illinois-Urbana. Ashley Burkart, Adm.

Col Prep. AP—Eng Fr Span Calc Bio Human_Geog US_Hist Art_Hist. **Feat**—Japan Lat Ecol Robotics Comp_Sci Ceramics Photog Studio_Art Theater Theater_Arts Music Dance Communications Outdoor_Ed. **Adm:** 120/yr. Appl due: Jan. Accepted: 50%. **Tests** ISEE. **Enr 450.** G 450. Elem 220. Sec 230. Wh 76%. Hisp 4%. Blk 10%. Asian 3%. Other 7%. Avg class size: 15. Uniform. **Fac 80.** M 23/4. F 49/4. Wh 83%. Blk 6%. Asian 3%. Other 8%. Adv deg: 46%. **Grad '04—39.** Col—38. Avg ACT: 27. Alum 125. **Tui '04-'05:** Day $22,770 (+$2400). Aid: Need 110 ($1,500,000). **Summer:** Enrich Rec. Tui Day $450. 4 wks. **Est 1995.** Nonprofit. Tri (Sept-June). Emphasizing critical-thinking skills, the college preparatory curriculum at this girls' school follows an integrated and collaborative approach. The varied curriculum includes Advanced Placement and honors courses in all major disciplines, as well as electives and programs in such areas as robotics, Web technology and financial independence. During the annual Arrow Week, every student immerses herself in a subject, project or theme designed to combine elements of academics, outdoor education and service learning. Athletics, interest clubs and coeducational activities are integral components of school life.

BERKELEY HALL SCHOOL   Day Coed Gr PS-8
Los Angeles, CA 90049. 16000 Mulholland Dr.
Tel: 310-476-6421. Fax: 310-476-5748.
www.berkeleyhall.org   E-mail: admiss@berkeleyhall.org

Craig Barrows, Head. BS, Michigan State Univ, MS, Worcester Polytechnic Institute. Margaret Andrews, Adm.

Pre-Prep. Feat—Span Computers Photog Studio_Art Drama Music Woodworking. **Supp**—Tut. **Adm:** 31/yr. Appl due: Feb. Accepted: 52%. Yield: 61%. **Tests** ISEE. **Enr 240.** B 118. G 122. Elem 240. Wh 74%. Hisp 2%. Blk 12%. Asian 8%. Other 4%. Avg class size: 17. **Fac 29.** M 4/1. F 21/3. Wh 94%. Hisp 3%. Asian 3%. Adv deg: 10%. **Grad '04—28.** Prep—24. **Tui '04-'05:** Day $13,700-15,900. Aid: Need 51 ($490,400). **Est 1911.** Nonprofit. (Sept-June). At BHS, preschoolers and kindergartners gain an introduction to basic academic concepts in math, reading preparation and handwriting. During the elementary years (grades 1-6), specialists teach science, music, art, computers, drama and woodworking courses. Weeklong outdoor education experiences are part of the junior high curriculum (grades 7 and 8).

LOYOLA HIGH SCHOOL
Day Boys Gr 9-12

Los Angeles, CA 90006. 1901 Venice Blvd.
Tel: 213-381-5121. Fax: 213-368-3819.
www.loyolahs.edu   E-mail: hutley@loyolahs.edu

Rev. Robert T. Walsh, SJ, Pres. MA, Univ of San Francisco. William R. Thomason, Prin. MA, California State Univ-Los Angeles. Heath Utley, Adm.

Col Prep. AP—Eng Fr Ger Lat Span Calc Stats Comp_Sci Chem Physics Eur_Hist US_Hist Econ Psych US_Govt & Pol Music_Theory. **Feat**—Shakespeare Anat & Physiol Oceanog African-Amer_Stud Theol World_Relig Fine_Arts. **Supp**—Tut. **Adm (Gr 9-11):** 310/yr. Appl due: Jan. Accepted: 42%. **Tests** HSPT. **Enr 1200.** B 1200. Sec 1200. Wh 54%. Hisp 21%. Blk 9%. Am Ind 1%. Asian 15%. Avg class size: 26. **Fac 85.** Adv deg: 74%. **Grad '04—289.** Col—287. Avg SAT: 1226. Alum 15,000. **Tui '04-'05:** Day $7570 (+$465). Aid: Merit 50 ($192,000). Need 200 ($548,000). **Summer:** Acad Enrich. 5 wks. **Est 1865.** Nonprofit. Roman Catholic. Sem (Sept-June). **Assoc** CLS WASC. Conducted by the Jesuits, Loyola offers elective courses, as well as Advanced Placement and honors classes. A community service project is required during the sophomore, junior and senior years.

PAGE PRIVATE SCHOOL
Day Coed Gr PS-8

Los Angeles, CA 90004. 565 N Larchmont Blvd.
Tel: 323-463-5118. Fax: 323-465-9964.
www.pageschool.com   E-mail: hancockpark@pageschool.com

Connie Rivera, Dir. BS.

Pre-Prep. Gen Acad. Feat—Span Computers Studio_Art Drama. **Supp**—Rev Tut. **Adm:** 40/yr. Accepted: 90%. **Tests** Stanford. **Enr 300.** B 182. G 118. Elem 300. Avg class size: 20. Uniform. **Fac 23.** M 6. F 16/1. **Grad '04—20.** Prep—17. **Tui '05-'06:** Day $9075-10,900 (+$1000). **Summer:** Acad Enrich Rev Rec. Tui Day $800. 4 wks. **Est 1908.** Nonprofit. Quar (Aug-June). The Hancock Park campus is one of six schools—four in southern California and two in central Florida—continuously operated by succeeding generations of the Vaughan family. A traditional academic program is supplemented by a selection of enrichment classes. Enrichment weeks interspersed throughout the year expose students to subjects that are not traditionally taught during the academic sessions.

PLAY MOUNTAIN PLACE
Day Coed Gr PS-5

Los Angeles, CA 90034. 6063 Hargis St.
Tel: 323-870-4381. Fax: 323-870-4381.
www.playmountain.org   E-mail: info@playmountain.org

Judy Accardi, Dir.

Gen Acad. Adm: 20/yr. Accepted: 80%. **Enr 100.** Elem 100. Wh 57%. Hisp 11%. Blk 18%. Asian 14%. Avg class size: 13. **Fac 21.** M 3/2. F 4/12. Adv deg: 9%. **Grad '04—4.** Alum 490. **Tui '04-'05:** Day $9100 (+$550). **Summer:** Acad Enrich Rec. Tui Day $150/wk. 10 wks. **Est 1949.** Nonprofit. (Sept-June). PMP is the oldest humanistic alternative school in the US. Founded by Phyllis Fleishman, the school bases its principles upon freedom, respect, self-motivated learning, conflict resolution and trust. The larger Institute for Humanistic Education and Parenting offers adult programs in peaceful parenting, anti-bias leadership in education, humanistic education for teachers, communication skills and ongoing internships.

SACRED HEART HIGH SCHOOL   Day Girls Gr 9-12
Los Angeles, CA 90031. 2111 N Griffin Ave.
Tel: 323-225-2209. Fax: 323-225-5046.
www.msjdominicans.org/shhs.html   E-mail: shhsprin@msjdominicans.org
    Sr. Mary Diane Scott, OP, Prin. BA, Immaculate Heart College, MA, Claremont Graduate School. Helen Avila, Adm.

    Col Prep. AP—Eng Span US_Hist Art_Hist. **Feat**—Fr Computers Relig Study_Skills. **Supp**—Dev_Read Tut. **Adm:** 106/yr. Appl due: Aug. Accepted: 80%. **Enr 334.** G 334. Sec 334. Wh 3%. Hisp 94%. Other 3%. Avg class size: 26. Uniform. **Fac 27.** M 6. F 21. Wh 65%. Hisp 34%. Blk 1%. Adv deg: 40%. **Grad '04—82.** Col—65. Avg SAT: 850. Avg ACT: 19. Alum 5000. **Tui '04-'05:** Day $4000 (+$600). Aid: Merit 20 ($14,100). Need 189 ($272,000). Work prgm 45 ($55,950). **Summer:** Acad Enrich Rev Rem. Tui Day $275. 4 wks. **Est 1907.** Nonprofit. Roman Catholic. Sem (Aug-June). Administered by the Dominican Sisters of Mission San Jose, this school is staffed by both members of the religious order and lay faculty. Honors and Advanced Placement courses are offered, and students participate in a variety of clubs, organizations and athletics. The entire student body takes part by grade level in a retreat program.

WINDWARD SCHOOL   Day Coed Gr 7-12
Los Angeles, CA 90066. 11350 Palms Blvd.
Tel: 310-391-7127. Fax: 310-397-5655.
www.windwardschool.org   E-mail: contact@windwardschool.org
    Thomas W. Gilder, Head. BA, Univ of California-Santa Barbara, MS, Pepperdine Univ. Sharon Pearline, Adm.

    Col Prep. AP—Eng Fr Span Calc Stats Bio Chem Physics Eur_Hist US_Hist US_Govt & Pol. **Feat**—Creative_Writing Japan Lat Govt Philos Relig Fine_Arts. **Adm:** 85/yr. Appl due: Dec. Accepted: 20%. **Tests** ISEE. **Enr 474.** B 237. G 237. Elem 150. Sec 324. Wh 80%. Hisp 1%. Blk 5%. Asian 8%. Other 6%. Avg class size: 16. **Fac 59.** M 32. F 27. Wh 80%. Hisp 8%. Blk 10%. Asian 2%. Adv deg: 66%. **Grad '04—67.** Col—67. Avg SAT: 1310. Alum 900. **Tui '03-'04:** Day $19,319 (+$500). Aid: Need 28 ($437,502). **Est 1971.** Nonprofit. Tri (Sept-June). **Assoc** WASC. Special programs offered at Windward include instrumental and vocal music, musical theater, Japanese and marine biology. Advanced Placement courses in English, history, math, foreign language and science are also available.

PHILLIPS BROOKS SCHOOL   Day Coed Gr PS-5
Menlo Park, CA 94025. 2245 Avy Ave.
Tel: 650-854-4545. Fax: 650-854-6532.
www.phillipsbrooks.org   E-mail: cward@phillipsbrooks.org
    Elizabeth Passi, Head. Clair Ward, Adm.

    Pre-Prep. Feat—Fr Span Computers. **Supp**—Dev_Read Tut. **Adm:** 59/yr. Appl due: Jan. Accepted: 29%. **Tests** CTP_4. **Enr 260.** B 135. G 125. Elem 260. Wh

79%. Hisp 2%. Blk 1%. Asian 9%. Other 9%. Avg class size: 17. Uniform. **Fac 33.** M 5. F 26/2. Adv deg: 18%. **Grad '04—38.** Alum 526. **Tui '03-'04:** Day $17,900 (+$400). Aid: Need 33 ($323,040). **Est 1978.** Nonprofit. (Sept-June). The sequential basic skills curriculum is enriched with courses in world languages, technology, art, music and physical education. In addition, all students take weekly classes that focus upon the basic skills of communication: eye contact, tone of voice, body language and so on. Each grade participates in one community service project, and Phillips Brooks also organizes all-school projects.

MOUNT TAMALPAIS SCHOOL
Day Coed Gr K-8

Mill Valley, CA 94941. 100 Harvard Ave.
Tel: 415-383-9434. Fax: 415-383-7519.
www.mttam.org E-mail: admissions@mttam.org

Kathleen M. Mecca, Dir. PhD, Univ of California-San Francisco, EdD, Stanford Univ. Sasha Mardikian, Adm.

Pre-Prep. Feat—Fr Lat Span Computers Geog Art_Hist Drama Music Dance. **Supp**—Dev_Read Rev Tut. **Adm (Gr K-6):** 35/yr. Appl due: Jan. Accepted: 10%. Yield: 99%. **Tests** CTP_4. **Enr 240.** B 120. G 120. Elem 240. Wh 90%. Hisp 2%. Blk 2%. Am Ind 1%. Asian 5%. Avg class size: 12. Uniform. **Fac 48.** M 12/2. F 30/4. Wh 94%. Hisp 2%. Blk 1%. Am Ind 1%. Asian 1%. Other 1%. Adv deg: 66%. **Grad '04—26.** Prep—24. Alum 500. **Tui '04-'05:** Day $16,500 (+$150). Aid: Need 30 ($298,000). **Summer:** Enrich Rec. Sports. Drama. 2-4 wks. **Est 1976.** Nonprofit. Tri (Aug-June). **Assoc** WASC. Mount Tamalpais offers a departmentalized curriculum for students in grades 1-8. Courses include French, Spanish, Latin, literature, art history and dance, as well as ceramics and woodworking. Extended outdoor education classes for children in grades 4-8 complement the program of nature study, which begins in kindergarten.

CENTRAL CATHOLIC HIGH SCHOOL
Day Coed Gr 9-12

Modesto, CA 95351. 200 S Carpenter Rd.
Tel: 209-524-9611. Fax: 209-524-4913.
www.cchsca.org E-mail: jehardee@cchsca.org

Jim Pecchenino, Pres. BA, Univ of the Pacific, MA, California State Univ-Stanislaus. Patricia Crist, Adm.

Col Prep. Feat—Fr Computers Relig. **Supp**—Rem_Read. **Adm:** 122/yr. Appl due: Rolling. **Tests** CEEB IQ. **Enr 441.** B 238. G 203. Sec 441. Wh 80%. Hisp 16%. Am Ind 2%. Asian 2%. Avg class size: 24. **Fac 30.** M 10/2. F 15/3. Adv deg: 30%. **Grad '04—110.** Col—110. Avg SAT: 1035. Avg ACT: 21. **Tui '04-'05:** Day $6765 (+$650). Catholic $6485 (+$650). **Est 1966.** Nonprofit. Roman Catholic. Quar (Aug-June). **Assoc** WASC. The school offers college preparatory classes and electives in the fine arts, computers, journalism and yearbook. In addition, CCHS provides college-level courses in psychology, anthropology, sociology, philosophy and agriculture. Catholic values are emphasized and community service is a graduation requirement.

YORK SCHOOL
Day Coed Gr 8-12
Monterey, CA 93940. 9501 York Rd.
Tel: 831-372-7338. Fax: 831-372-8055.
www.york.org   E-mail: rgarrison@york.org
Chuck Harmon, Head. AB, Davidson College, MDiv, Yale Univ. Joanne Doyle, Adm.

Col Prep. AP—Eng Fr Ger Lat Span Calc Bio Chem US_Hist Studio_Art Music_Theory. **Feat**—British_Lit Greek Ital Anat & Physiol Environ_Sci Marine_Biol/Sci Computers Asian_Hist African_Hist Econ Geog Psych Philos Art_Hist Drama Music. **Supp**—Tut. **Adm:** 62/yr. Appl due: Feb. **Enr 226.** B 120. G 106. Elem 21. Sec 205. Wh 71%. Hisp 9%. Blk 2%. Asian 13%. Other 5%. Avg class size: 15. **Fac 29.** Wh 93%. Asian 7%. Adv deg: 86%. **Grad '04—53.** Col—53. Avg SAT: 1340. Alum 930. **Tui '04-'05:** Day $17,950 (+$400). Aid: Need 85 ($764,000). **Est 1959.** Nonprofit. Episcopal. Sem (Aug-May). **Assoc** WASC. York's traditional college preparatory program features Advanced Placement courses in all disciplines, as well as a variety of independent study options. Most languages are available at the AP level. The school offers a number of music, drama and studio art electives. Extracurricular activities include a competitive athletic program and an array of interest clubs.

SAKLAN VALLEY SCHOOL
Day Coed Gr PS-8
Moraga, CA 94556. 1678 School St.
Tel: 925-376-7900. Fax: 925-376-1156.
www.saklan.org   E-mail: admissions@saklan.org
Jonathan Martin, Head. BA, Harvard Univ, MA, Univ of San Francisco, MDiv, Graduate Theological Union.

Pre-Prep. Gen Acad. Feat—Fr Computers Studio_Art Music. **Adm:** 50/yr. Appl due: Feb. Accepted: 64%. Yield: 75%. **Tests** CTP_4 ISEE. **Enr 146.** B 73. G 73. Elem 146. Wh 74%. Hisp 10%. Blk 3%. Asian 13%. Avg class size: 12. Uniform. **Fac 18.** M 3/1. F 10/4. Wh 90%. Blk 10%. Adv deg: 27%. **Grad '04—3.** Prep—3. **Tui '04-'05:** Day $9850-14,100 (+$100). Aid: Need 25 ($180,000). **Summer:** Enrich Rec. Tui Day $1000/3-wk ses. 9 wks. **Est 1954.** Nonprofit. Tri (Aug-June). **Assoc** WASC. Starting in the preschool years (age 3), children gain exposure to language concepts, math and science, and prekindergartners have access to computers and the library. Utilizing an individualized approach that accommodates students of varying learning styles and developmental levels, the lower school (grades K-5) focuses on the basics while incorporating hands-on activities and laboratory experiences. Saklan's traditional middle school (grades 6-8) curriculum provides opportunities for problem solving, in-depth classroom discussions and the development of study skills.

JUSTIN-SIENA HIGH SCHOOL
Day Coed Gr 9-12
Napa, CA 94558. 4026 Maher St.
Tel: 707-255-0950. Fax: 707-255-0334.
www.justin-siena.com   E-mail: jshs@justin-siena.com
Joseph W. Bracco, Pres. BA, Univ of Notre Dame, MA, San Francisco State Univ, MBA, Pepperdine Univ. Gregory J. Schmitz, Prin. BA, Albertson College of Idaho, MA, Sonoma State Univ. Sr. Susan Allbritton, OP, Adm.

Col Prep. AP—Eng Calc Comp_Sci Bio Eur_Hist US_Hist. **Feat**—Ital Environ_Sci Law Sociol Govt & Pol Relig Photog Studio_Art Theater_Arts Chorus Music Dance Journ. **Supp**—LD Makeup. **Adm:** 196/yr. Appl due: Dec. Accepted: 87%. **Tests** HSPT. **Enr 661.** B 344. G 317. Sec 661. Wh 79%. Hisp 10%. Blk 1%. Am Ind 1%. Asian 6%. Other 3%. Avg class size: 26. **Fac 54.** M 30/2. F 21/1. Adv deg: 42%. **Grad '04—147.** Col—141. Avg SAT: 1093. Avg ACT: 23. **Tui '02-'03:** Day $7425 (+$400-600). **Summer:** Acad Enrich Rev Rec. Tui Day $170/crse. 6 wks. **Est 1966.** Nonprofit. Roman Catholic. Sem (Aug-June). **Assoc** WASC. Founded and cosponsored by the Dominican Sisters of San Rafael and the Christian Brothers of the San Francisco District, this Napa Valley school emphasizes college preparation and critical-thinking skills in a Christian setting. Justin-Siena's curriculum features honors and Advanced Placement courses, computer and technology labs, and a strong religious studies program. In addition, qualified upperclassmen may earn transferable college credit through Napa Valley College in psychology, philosophy and calculus. Students choose from such arts offerings as drama, theater, studio art, chorus, photography, dance and jazz band.

SUGAR BOWL ACADEMY

Bdg Coed Gr 8-PG
Day Coed 6-PG

Norden, CA 95724. 19195 Donner Pass Rd, PO Box 68.
Tel: 530-426-1844. Fax: 530-426-1860.
www.sbacademy.org   E-mail: admissions@sbacademy.org

Paul Hancock, Head. BA, MA, Univ of Bristol (England). Shanna Mitchell, Adm.

Col Prep. Sports (Winter). AP—Eng Span Calc Bio US_Hist. **Feat**—Econ Govt Performing_Arts Visual_Arts. **Adm:** 33/yr. Bdg 8. Day 25. Appl due: Rolling. Accepted: 90%. Yield: 75%. **Tests** ISEE. **Enr 45.** B 12/18. G 2/13. Elem 9. Sec 34. PG 2. Wh 100%. Avg class size: 5. **Fac 10.** M 4. F 6. Wh 100%. Adv deg: 20%. In Dorms 3. **Grad '04—7.** Col—7. Avg SAT: 1230. Alum 15. **Tui '04-'05:** Bdg $25,000 (+$4000). 5-Day Bdg $18,000 (+$4000). Day $11,000 (+$4000). Aid: Need 15 ($45,000). **Est 1995.** Nonprofit. Sem (Aug-June). Students at the state's only college preparatory skiing academy take part in a solid academic program during the school day, while also participating in ski training before and after school and on weekends. A shorter school day during the winter months facilitates on-hill training and enables boys and girls to meet racing schedules. Programs accommodate Alpine, Nordic and free skiers.

BENTLEY SCHOOL

Day Coed Gr K-12

Oakland, CA 94618. 1 Hiller Dr.
Tel: 510-843-2512. Fax: 510-843-5162.
www.bentleyschool.net   E-mail: admissions@bentleyschool.net

Richard P. Fitzgerald, Head. BA, Univ of Notre Dame, MA, Univ of Virginia. Winter Mead, Upper Sch Adm; Nasi Maghsoudnia White, Middle & Lower Sch Adm.

Col Prep. AP—Fr Lat Span Calc Bio Chem Physics. **Feat**—Classics Medieval_Hist Study_Skills. **Adm:** 111/yr. Appl due: Jan. Accepted: 33%. **Tests** ISEE SSAT Stanford. **Enr 602.** Elem 352. Sec 250. Wh 69%. Hisp 2%. Blk 5%. Asian 19%. Other 5%. Avg class size: 20. **Fac 54.** M 21. F 33. Wh 87%. Hisp 6%. Blk 1%. Am Ind 1%. Asian 5%. Adv deg: 57%. **Grad '04—31.** Col—31. Avg SAT: 1239.

Avg ACT: 25. Alum 37. **Tui '03-'04:** Day $15,990-20,085 (+$500-1000). Aid: Need 43 ($400,000). **Est 1920.** Nonprofit. Tri (Sept-June). **Assoc** WASC. Within a small-class environment, Bentley complements its traditional core curriculum with electives and independent study opportunities. Honors and Advanced Placement courses provide additional challenge for qualified students, while peer tutors, faculty advisors, scheduled study halls, a study skills workshop and extra-help periods allow pupils to receive academic support when necessary. The school places a strong emphasis on the arts both within the curriculum and during after-school activities. The upper school operates on a separate campus at 1000 Upper Happy Valley Rd., Lafayette 94549.

BISHOP O'DOWD HIGH SCHOOL — Day Coed Gr 9-12
Oakland, CA 94605. 9500 Stearns Ave.
Tel: 510-577-9100. Fax: 510-638-3259.
www.bishopodowd.org   E-mail: admissions@bishopodowd.org
Rev. Don McLeod, CSB, Prin. BA, MA, MDiv, ThD, Univ of Toronto (Canada).

Col Prep. AP—Eng Fr Ger Span Calc Comp_Sci Bio US_Hist Comp_Govt & Pol US_Govt & Pol. **Feat**—Stats Anat Marine_Biol/Sci Econ Psych Relig World_Relig Drama Theater Chorus. **Supp**—Dev_Read Rev Tut. **Adm (Gr 9-11):** 312/yr. Appl due: Jan. Accepted: 82%. **Tests** HSPT. **Enr 1140.** Sec 1140. Avg class size: 29. **Fac 91.** M 44/12. F 32/3. Wh 74%. Hisp 7%. Blk 10%. Asian 8%. Other 1%. Adv deg: 58%. **Grad '04**—294. Col—282. Avg SAT: 1175. Alum 8250. **Tui '04-'05:** Day $9750 (+$850). Aid: Merit 177 ($72,000). Need 177 ($553,730). **Summer:** Acad. Tui Day $175/crse. 4 wks. **Est 1951.** Nonprofit. Roman Catholic. Sem (Aug-June). **Assoc** WASC. Bishop O'Dowd's college preparatory program features honors and Advanced Placement courses, in addition to a variety of electives and fine arts offerings. Among extracurriculars at the school are athletics, clubs and service projects.

HOLY NAMES HIGH SCHOOL — Day Girls Gr 9-12
Oakland, CA 94618. 4660 Harbord Dr.
Tel: 510-450-1110. Fax: 510-547-3111.
www.hnhsoakland.org   E-mail: hnhs@csdo.org
Sr. Sally Slyngstad, Prin. Kira Bautista, Adm.

Col Prep. AP—Eng Fr Span Calc Chem US_Hist. **Feat**—Computers Psych Relig Drama Chorus Orchestra. **Supp**—Tut. **Adm:** 85/yr. Appl due: Jan. Accepted: 65%. **Tests** HSPT. **Enr 277.** G 277. Sec 277. Wh 31%. Hisp 16%. Blk 34%. Asian 6%. Other 13%. Avg class size: 21. Uniform. **Fac 24.** M 4. F 12/8. Wh 84%. Hisp 8%. Asian 8%. Adv deg: 54%. **Grad '04**—65. Col—64. **Tui '04-'05:** Day $8995 (+$600). Aid: Need 108. **Est 1868.** Nonprofit. Roman Catholic. Sem (Aug-June). HNHS offers a diverse curriculum for students of all aptitude levels. Qualified girls enroll in competitive honors and Advanced Placement courses, while pupils in need of additional help may receive tutorial services in math and science. Options in the fine and performing arts include instrumental and vocal music, drawing and painting, and drama. Girls display their artistic talents in plays, musicals, art exhibits and concerts.

SAINT ELIZABETH HIGH SCHOOL
Day Coed Gr 9-12

Oakland, CA 94601. 1530 34th Ave.
Tel: 510-532-8947. Fax: 510-532-9754.
www.saintelizabethhighschool.com
E-mail: rtroper@saintelizabethhighschool.com

Sr. Mary Liam Brock, OP, Prin. MA, San Jose State Univ, MA, St Mary's College. Sr. Donna Maria Moses, OP, Adm.

Col Prep. Gen Acad. AP—Eng Span Calc. **Feat**—Comp_Sci Relig Fine_Arts. **Supp**—LD Tut. **Adm (Gr 9-11):** 89/yr. Appl due: June. Accepted: 90%. Yield: 70%. **Tests** HSPT. **Enr 276.** B 159. G 117. Sec 276. Wh 5%. Hisp 34%. Blk 54%. Am Ind 1%. Asian 5%. Other 1%. Avg class size: 20. **Fac 26.** M 13. F 13. Wh 69%. Hisp 12%. Blk 15%. Asian 4%. Adv deg: 30%. **Grad '04—56.** Col—53. Avg SAT: 920. Avg ACT: 18. Alum 7290. **Tui '04-'05:** Day $7200 (+$1200). Aid: Merit 48 ($58,000). Need 113 ($334,000). **Summer:** Rem. Tui Day $375. 4 wks. **Est 1921.** Nonprofit. Roman Catholic. Sem (Aug-June). **Assoc** WASC. Students may participate in a campus ministry program, along with such activities as culture and service clubs, choir, peer support, yearbook, and both interscholastic and intramural sports.

ST. PAUL'S EPISCOPAL SCHOOL
Day Coed Gr K-8

Oakland, CA 94610. 116 Montecito Ave.
Tel: 510-285-9600. Fax: 510-832-3231.
www.spes.org   E-mail: info@spes.org

Karan A. Merry, Head. BA, Salem State College, MEd, Lesley College. Gwynne Tysell, Adm.

Pre-Prep. Feat—Span Computers Fine_Arts Music. **Adm:** 83/yr. Appl due: Jan. Accepted: 27%. **Tests** ISEE. **Enr 338.** B 169. G 169. Elem 338. Wh 47%. Hisp 10%. Blk 26%. Am Ind 1%. Asian 14%. Other 2%. Avg class size: 22. **Fac 33.** M 7/2. F 18/6. Wh 73%. Hisp 6%. Blk 18%. Asian 3%. Adv deg: 30%. **Grad '04—48.** Prep—48. Alum 500. **Tui '04-'05:** Day $15,900-16,800 (+$250). Aid: Need 106 ($869,560). **Summer:** Acad Enrich. Tui Day $300/2-wk ses. 6 wks. **Est 1975.** Nonprofit. Episcopal. Quar (Sept-June). **Assoc** WASC. Instructors at St. Paul's lower school (grades K-6) teach core courses through an interactive program of learning centers, individual and group presentations, discussions, research and writing projects. Spanish instruction begins in grade 4. At the upper school level (grades 7 and 8), students supplement core classes with course work in computers, art and music, community service, drama, study skills or high school planning, and electives. The school takes advantage of its urban location by utilizing the city's resources and scheduling frequent field trips to local museums, parks and historical sites.

OAK GROVE SCHOOL
Bdg Coed Gr 9-12
Day Coed PS-12

Ojai, CA 93023. 220 W Lomita Ave.
Tel: 805-646-8236. Fax: 805-646-6509.
www.oakgroveschool.com   E-mail: enroll@oakgroveschool.com

Ellen Hall, Dir. Joy Maguire-Parsons, Adm.

Col Prep. AP—Eng Span Chem. **Feat**—Photog Studio_Art Video_Production Drama Music Outdoor_Ed. **Supp**—ESL. **Adm (Bdg Gr 9-11; Day PS-11):**

50/yr. Bdg 10. Day 30. Appl due: Rolling. Accepted: 80%. Yield: 40%. **Tests** SSAT TOEFL. **Enr 200.** B 10/93. G 5/92. Elem 140. Sec 60. Wh 80%. Hisp 4%. Blk 4%. Asian 12%. Avg class size: 14. **Fac 29.** M 8/4. F 16/1. Wh 90%. Hisp 10%. Adv deg: 34%. **Grad '04—14.** Col—13. Avg SAT: 1220. **Tui '05-'06:** Bdg $28,750. 5-Day Bdg $25,480. Day $5500-13,550. Aid: Need 60 ($180,000). **Summer:** Acad Enrich Rec. Tui Day $800/2-wk ses. 4 wks. **Est 1975.** Nonprofit. Sem (Sept-June). **Assoc** WASC. This school was founded on the philosophical ideals of author and educator J. Krishnamurti. Located on 150 acres, the school balances college preparatory academics with studio art, ceramics, photography, music, drama, physical education, sports, life skills, outdoor education, community service and travel.

ST. MATTHEW'S PARISH SCHOOL   Day Coed Gr PS-8
Pacific Palisades, CA 90272. 1031 Bienveneda Ave, PO Box 1710.
Tel: 310-454-1350. Fax: 310-573-7423.
www.stmatthewsschool.com   E-mail: info@stmatthewsschool.com
  Les Warren Frost, Head. DPharm, Univ of California-San Francisco. A. Lee Quiring, Adm.
  Pre-Prep. Gen Acad. Feat—Creative_Writing Shakespeare Lat Span Environ_Sci Computers Art_Hist Studio_Art Drama Music Speech. **Adm:** 47/yr. Appl due: Feb. Accepted: 33%. **Tests** ISEE. **Enr 325.** B 161. G 164. Elem 325. Wh 88%. Hisp 1%. Blk 2%. Asian 8%. Other 1%. Uniform. **Fac 43.** M 6/9. F 25/3. Wh 97%. Hisp 1%. Am Ind 1%. Asian 1%. Adv deg: 37%. **Grad '04—36.** Prep—36. Alum 1203. **Tui '05-'06:** Day $16,135-20,205 (+$395-1450). Aid: Need 10 ($98,000). **Summer:** Acad Enrich Rev Rec. Tui Day $1500. 5 wks. **Est 1949.** Nonprofit. Episcopal. Tri (Sept-June). **Assoc** WASC. Located on 33 acres in the Santa Monica Mountains, the school emphasizes math and language arts instruction. Pupils begin Latin or Spanish study in grade 6.

ROLLING HILLS PREPARATORY SCHOOL   Day Coed Gr 6-12
Palos Verdes Estates, CA 90274. 300A Paseo Del Mar.
Tel: 310-791-1101. Fax: 310-373-4931.
www.rollinghillsprep.org   E-mail: wmoffat@rhps-k12.com
  Peter McCormack, Head. BA, York Univ (England), MSc, Oxford Univ (England). Linda Eviston, Adm.
  Col Prep. AP—Eng Fr Span Calc Eur_Hist. **Feat**—Robotics Econ Govt Arts. **Supp**—ESL Rev Tut. **Adm:** 50/yr. Appl due: Rolling. Accepted: 75%. **Tests** ISEE. **Enr 260.** B 129. G 131. Wh 77%. Hisp 2%. Blk 5%. Asian 16%. Avg class size: 15. **Fac 41.** M 10/3. F 25/3. Wh 90%. Hisp 8%. Am Ind 2%. Adv deg: 73%. **Grad '04—32.** Col—32. Avg SAT: 1147. Alum 313. **Tui '05-'06:** Day $17,900 (+$1800). Aid: Merit 3 ($18,500). Need 45 ($600,000). **Summer:** Acad Enrich Rev. Tui Day $350/wk. 6 wks. **Est 1981.** Nonprofit. Tri (Sept-June). **Assoc** WASC. All courses within the traditional liberal arts curriculum are college preparatory, with electives, Advanced Placement options and honors classes provided. Qualified students may complete a year-long independent study, and seniors are offered two-week internships before graduation. A number of community service clubs are also available.

MARANATHA HIGH SCHOOL
Day Coed Gr 9-12

Pasadena, CA 91107. 1610 E Elizabeth St.
Tel: 626-720-8141. Fax: 626-720-8216.
www.maranatha-hs.org E-mail: info@maranatha-hs.org
Chet Crane, Head. Debbie Middlebrook, Adm.

Col Prep. Gen Acad. AP—Eng Span Calc Bio Chem Physics US_Hist. **Feat**—Fr Anat & Physiol Econ Govt Psych Sociol Bible Drawing Photog Theater_Arts. **Supp**—LD. **Adm:** 150/yr. Appl due: Rolling. Accepted: 95%. **Tests** HSPT ISEE. **Enr 450.** B 233. G 217. Sec 450. Wh 61%. Hisp 16%. Blk 5%. Asian 18%. Avg class size: 17. Uniform. **Fac 36.** M 16. F 16/4. **Grad '04**—115. Col—110. Avg SAT: 1046. **Tui '03-'04:** Day $8925 (+$550). Aid: Merit 6 ($2200). Need 110 ($271,000). **Summer:** Acad Enrich. Tui Day $550. 6 wks. **Est 1965.** Nondenom Christian. Sem (Aug-June). **Assoc** WASC. Maranatha conducts a Christian program that emphasizes acquisition of the skills and knowledge necessary for further education and successful employment. In addition to Advanced Placement course work in the major disciplines, the school offers a special program for a limited number of students with learning differences. Each pupil fulfills an annual community service requirement. Football, cross-country, volleyball, basketball, soccer, softball, baseball, tennis, and track and field are among the available sports.

MAYFIELD JUNIOR SCHOOL
Day Coed Gr K-8

Pasadena, CA 91101. 405 S Euclid Ave.
Tel: 626-796-2774. Fax: 626-796-5753.
www.mayfieldjs.org
Stephanie D. Griffin, Head. BA, Ohio Dominican College, MA, St John's Univ (NY), MA, City Univ of New York. Averyl Thielen, Adm.

Pre-Prep. Feat—Fr Span Relig Drama Music. **Adm (Gr K-7):** 90/yr. Accepted: 25%. Yield: 90%. **Tests** CTP_4 ISEE MRT. **Enr 460.** B 213. G 247. Elem 460. Wh 75%. Hisp 11%. Blk 3%. Asian 10%. Other 1%. Avg class size: 17. Uniform. **Fac 47.** M 7. F 34/6. Wh 68%. Hisp 22%. Blk 4%. Asian 4%. Other 2%. Adv deg: 38%. **Grad '04**—45. Prep—45. Alum 1850. **Tui '04-'05:** Day $11,500 (+$2700). Aid: Need 33 ($157,946). **Summer:** Acad Enrich Rev Rem Rec. Tui Day $250/crse. 5 wks. **Est 1931.** Nonprofit. Roman Catholic. Tri (Sept-June). Part of the Holy Child Network of Schools, Mayfield offers a developmentally appropriate program that enriches its core curriculum with foreign language; the visual, musical and performing arts; and technology. Children first gain exposure to technology and Spanish in the lower school (grades K-3). During the middle school years (grades 4 and 5), students assume increasing levels of independence and take part in sequential programs in language arts, math, social studies and foreign language. The departmentalized upper school (grades 6-8) features a range of electives that caters to personal interests.

MAYFIELD SENIOR SCHOOL
Day Girls Gr 9-12

Pasadena, CA 91105. 500 Bellefontaine St.
Tel: 626-799-9121. Fax: 626-799-8576.
www.mayfieldsenior.org E-mail: liz.vega@mayfieldsenior.org
Rita McBride, Head. BA, Univ of California-Santa Barbara, MALS, Wesleyan Univ. Elizabeth Vega, Adm.

Col Prep. **AP**—Eng Fr Lat Span Calc Bio Physics US_Hist Art_Hist Studio_Art. **Feat**—Creative_Writing Astron Environ_Sci Programming Econ Govt Intl_Relations Psych World_Relig Photog Drama Music Dance. **Supp**—Rem_Math Tut. **Adm (Gr 9-10):** 78/yr. Appl due: Jan. Accepted: 45%. Yield: 59%. **Tests** ISEE. **Enr 305.** G 305. Sec 305. Wh 53%. Hisp 13%. Blk 6%. Asian 14%. Other 14%. Avg class size: 18. Uniform. **Fac 38.** M 10/2. F 12/14. Wh 86%. Hisp 2%. Blk 5%. Asian 5%. Other 2%. Adv deg: 65%. **Grad '04—75.** Col—75. Avg SAT: 1200. Alum 2500. **Tui '04-'05:** Day $13,545 (+$950). Aid: Merit 20 ($78,645). Need 63 ($366,145). **Summer:** Acad Enrich Rev Rem Rec. Tui Day $100-600. 1-5 wks. **Est 1931.** Nonprofit. Roman Catholic. Sem (Sept-June). Mayfield's college preparatory curriculum, which includes Advanced Placement and honors classes, is supplemented by many electives. Theology courses, monthly liturgies and service programs are important aspects of the school program. Extracurricular activities include student council, Christian community service opportunities, arts conservatories, sports and clubs.

PASADENA TOWNE AND COUNTRY SCHOOL
Day Coed Gr PS-8

Pasadena, CA 91107. 200 S Sierra Madre Blvd.
Tel: 626-795-0658. Fax: 626-793-0160.
www.ptcs.freeservers.com   E-mail: ptcs01@aol.com
  Carolyn Rosemond, Int Head. Martha Hernandez, Adm.

Pre-Prep. Gen Acad. Feat—Fr Span Computers Studio_Art Music. **Supp**—Tut. **Adm:** 60/yr. Appl due: Mar. **Tests** Stanford. **Enr 300.** Elem 300. Wh 43%. Hisp 8%. Blk 12%. Asian 37%. Uniform. **Fac 26.** M 3. F 23. Adv deg: 19%. **Grad '04—20.** Prep—9. **Tui '03-'04:** Day $4400-5400 (+$190-340). **Summer:** Acad Enrich Rev Rec. Tui Day $430-570. 5 wks. **Est 1948.** Quar (Sept-June). PTCS's traditional academic program focuses on the core subjects of reading, language arts, science and mathematics. Computer instruction begins in grade 1. Extracurricular activities include ballet, piano, cartooning, glee club, drama, science adventures, athletics, cheerleading, debate and dance.

WALDEN SCHOOL
Day Coed Gr PS-6

Pasadena, CA 91107. 74 S San Gabriel Blvd.
Tel: 626-792-6166. Fax: 626-792-1335.
www.waldenschool.net   E-mail: admissions@waldenschool.net
  Christena Barnes, Int Dir.

Pre-Prep. Feat—Span Fine_Arts Music. **Adm:** 63/yr. Appl due: Feb. Accepted: 61%. Yield: 56%. **Tests** MAT. **Enr 240.** Elem 240. Wh 63%. Hisp 4%. Blk 7%. Am Ind 1%. Asian 9%. Other 16%. Avg class size: 20. **Fac 20.** M 3. F 12/5. Wh 60%. Hisp 25%. Blk 10%. Asian 5%. Adv deg: 30%. **Grad '04—8.** Prep—8. Alum 600. **Tui '04-'05:** Day $10,570 (+$500). Aid: Need 9 ($45,188). **Summer:** Enrich Rec. Tui Day $200/wk. 8 wks. **Est 1970.** Nonprofit. Sem (Sept-June). **Assoc** WASC. Walden, which employs a hands-on approach, conducts multi-age classes that span two grade levels. Field trips, science projects, art, music, Spanish, library skills, storytelling sessions and physical education complement the curriculum.

ST. JOHN'S EPISCOPAL SCHOOL
Day Coed Gr PS-8

Rancho Santa Margarita, CA 92688. 30382 Via Con Dios.
Tel: 949-858-5144. Fax: 949-858-1403.
www.stjohns-es.org E-mail: jslusby@msn.com
James S. Lusby, Head. BA, Trinity College (CT), MEd, Boston College. Noreen Cohen, Adm.

Pre-Prep. Gen Acad. Feat—Span Computers Relig Studio_Art Drama Chorus Music. **Supp**—Tut. **Adm:** 202/yr. Appl due: Rolling. Accepted: 90%. **Enr 870.** B 327. G 543. Elem 870. Avg class size: 25. Uniform. **Fac 52.** M 1. F 49/2. Wh 97%. Hisp 3%. Adv deg: 11%. **Grad '04**—77. Prep—67. Alum 544. **Tui '04-'05:** Day $8325 (+$250). Aid: Need 60 ($139,760). **Summer:** Acad Enrich Rev Rem Rec. Tui Day $320/2-wk ses. 4 wks. **Est 1988.** Nonprofit. Episcopal. Tri (Sept-June). **Assoc** WASC. All children in grades K-8 attend chapel, and religion is taught throughout the school. Middle school students (grades 6-8) must complete 15 hours of service each year, and a field studies program complements the curriculum. After-school competitive sports begin in grade 5.

MERCY HIGH SCHOOL
Day Coed Gr 9-12

Red Bluff, CA 96080. 233 Riverside Way.
Tel: 530-527-8313. Fax: 530-527-3058.
www.mercy-high.org E-mail: mercy@mercy-high.org
Cheryl Ramirez, Prin. BA, Humboldt State Univ, MS, Univ of La Verne.

Col Prep. AP—Eng Fr Span Calc Bio Chem US_Hist US_Govt & Pol Studio_Art. **Feat**—Relig Fine_Arts Drama Music. **Adm:** 35/yr. Appl due: Mar. **Enr 155.** B 77. G 78. Sec 155. Wh 89%. Hisp 7%. Blk 1%. Asian 3%. Avg class size: 15. **Fac 12.** M 5/1. F 6. Wh 92%. Hisp 8%. Adv deg: 16%. **Grad '04**—51. Col—50. Alum 1176. **Tui '04-'05:** Day $5950 (+$800). Aid: Need 70 ($100,000). **Est 1882.** Nonprofit. Roman Catholic. Sem (Aug-June). **Assoc** WASC. Mercy places emphasis on the development of faith, community awareness and college preparation. Enrichment, Advanced Placement and honors courses are offered.

PENINSULA HERITAGE SCHOOL
Day Coed Gr PS-5

Rolling Hills Estates, CA 90274. 26944 Rolling Hills Rd.
Tel: 310-541-4795. Fax: 310-541-8264.
www.peninsulaheritage.org E-mail: admin@peninsulaheritage.org
Patricia Cailler, Head. I'Nella Scott, Adm.

Pre-Prep. Feat—Span Computers Studio_Art Drama Music. **Supp**—Dev_Read Rem_Math Rem_Read Rev Tut. **Adm:** 78/yr. Appl due: Rolling. Accepted: 30%. **Tests** ISEE. **Enr 197.** B 112. G 85. Elem 197. Wh 67%. Hisp 5%. Blk 4%. Am Ind 1%. Asian 23%. Avg class size: 20. **Fac 17.** M 1/1. F 14/1. Adv deg: 35%. **Grad '04**—23. Prep—20. **Tui '03-'04:** Day $6280-10,825 (+$400-500). Aid: Need 27 ($97,890). **Summer:** Acad Enrich Rev Rem Rec. Tui Day $250-850. 1-3 wks. **Est 1962.** Nonprofit. Tri (Sept-June). The school conducts a pre-preparatory program in a rural setting. In addition to its academic curriculum, Peninsula Heritage offers art, music, a library program and physical education. An extended-day program is available.

ROLLING HILLS COUNTRY DAY SCHOOL Day Coed Gr K-8
Rolling Hills Estates, CA 90274. 26444 Crenshaw Blvd.
Tel: 310-377-4848. Fax: 310-377-9651.
www.rhcds.com   E-mail: drobinson@rhcds.com
   Gary Stokoe, Dir. Ryan Tillson, Adm.

   Pre-Prep. Gen Acad. Feat—Span Environ_Sci Fine_Arts. **Supp**—Rev Tut. **Adm:** 80/yr. Accepted: 38%. **Enr 363.** Elem 363. Wh 77%. Hisp 1%. Blk 2%. Asian 20%. Avg class size: 22. Uniform. **Fac 33.** M 4. F 25/4. Adv deg: 36%. **Grad '04—29.** Prep—12. **Tui '03-'04:** Day $11,965-12,065 (+$725). **Summer:** Acad Enrich Rec. Tui Day $300-2000. 2-6 wks. **Est 1961.** Inc. Tri (Sept-June). **Assoc** WASC. RHCDS offers a traditional academic curriculum enriched by creative teaching and learning techniques. The core course work is enriched with computer studies, Spanish, drama, art and music. A full physical education and sports program provides swimming for all students and interscholastic offerings for children in grades 5-8.

BROOKFIELD SCHOOL Day Coed Gr K-8
Sacramento, CA 95822. 3600 Riverside Blvd, PO Box 22220.
Tel: 916-442-1255. Fax: 916-443-5477.
www.brookfieldschoolonline.com
E-mail: michelle.schumacher@pinnacleschools.net
   Rick D. Hackney, Prin. BA, MA, PhD.

   Pre-Prep. Gen Acad. Feat—Fr Computers Geog Studio_Art Music. **Adm:** 21/yr. Appl due: Rolling. **Enr 150.** Elem 150. Wh 71%. Hisp 5%. Blk 2%. Asian 22%. Avg class size: 18. Uniform. **Fac 14.** M 3/1. F 8/2. Wh 80%. Asian 7%. Other 13%. Adv deg: 21%. **Grad '04—6.** Prep—3. Alum 500. **Tui '04-'05:** Day $7900 (+$150-375). **Est 1962.** Inc. 6 terms. In the lower grades, Brookfield provides an accelerated and enriched program that emphasizes fundamental learning skills. Acceleration continues in the upper grades with algebra and formal grammar study, as well as a French program that enables children to study at a high school level in grades 7 and 8. The computer is an important learning tool in grades 1-8. Music and the arts are integral to the program at all grade levels.

ACADEMY OF OUR LADY OF PEACE Day Girls Gr 9-12
San Diego, CA 92116. 4860 Oregon St.
Tel: 619-297-2266. Fax: 619-297-2473.
www.aolp.org   E-mail: olp@aolp.org
   Sr. Dolores Anchondo, CSJ, Prin. BA, MA, Mount St Mary's College, MEd, Univ of San Diego. Susan DeWinter, Adm.

   Col Prep. AP—Eng Fr Span Calc Stats US_Hist US_Govt & Pol. **Feat**—Astron Oceanog Computers Relig Fine_Arts Speech. **Supp**—Tut. **Adm:** 212/yr. Appl due: Jan. Accepted: 80%. **Tests** CEEB HSPT. **Enr 760.** G 760. Sec 760. Wh 51%. Hisp 29%. Blk 1%. Am Ind 1%. Asian 9%. Other 9%. Avg class size: 28. Uniform. **Fac 50.** M 12. F 30/8. Wh 99%. Hisp 1%. Adv deg: 78%. **Grad '04—169.** Col—169. Avg SAT: 1070. Alum 6075. **Tui '04-'05:** Day $7660-8080 (+$1000). Aid: Need 132 ($398,000). Work prgm 4 ($2400). **Summer:** Acad Enrich Rev. Tui Day $475/crse. 6 wks. **Est 1882.** Nonprofit. Roman Catholic. Sem (Aug-June). **Assoc** WASC.

OLP offers a traditional college preparatory curriculum, with Advanced Placement offerings in English, calculus, biology, US history, government and Spanish. Requirements include religion, 25 hours of community service per year, and active participation in fine arts course work. Students select classes in dance, music, drama and art. A variety of school clubs, athletic teams and fine arts experiences supplements academic work.

ST. AUGUSTINE HIGH SCHOOL
Day Boys Gr 9-12
San Diego, CA 92104. 3266 Nutmeg St.
Tel: 619-282-2184. Fax: 619-282-1203.
www.sahs.org   E-mail: mhaupt@sahs.org

Rev. John D. Keller, OSA, Pres. BA, Villanova Univ, STB, Pontifical Lateran Univ (Italy), MA, Univ of San Francisco. James Horne, Prin. BA, Univ of California-San Diego, MBA, California State Univ-Long Beach, MA, Univ of San Francisco. Michael Haupt, Adm.

Col Prep. AP—Eng Fr Span Calc Stats Bio Chem US_Hist Econ Psych. **Feat**—Lat Anat & Physiol Web_Design Govt Philos Relig Art_Hist Studio_Art Drama Theater_Arts Music. **Supp**—Rev Tut. **Adm:** 205/yr. Appl due: Jan. **Tests** HSPT. **Enr 699.** B 699. Sec 699. Wh 50%. Hisp 33%. Blk 5%. Am Ind 2%. Asian 10%. Avg class size: 28. **Fac 42.** M 34. F 8. Adv deg: 59%. **Grad '04**—**150.** Col—135. Avg SAT: 1149. Alum 6900. **Tui '04-'05:** Day $8000 (+$75-100). Aid: Need ($400,000). **Summer:** Acad Enrich Rev Rem. Tui Day $450/crse. 6 wks. **Est 1922.** Nonprofit. Roman Catholic. Sem (Sept-June). **Assoc** WASC. Located in the North Park section of the city, this liberal arts high school is sponsored by the Order of St. Augustine. Curricular features at St. Augustine include Latin, speech, history of jazz and theater arts classes. Drama, school publications, photography, art, band, Model UN, academic decathlon, student government, community service and interest clubs complement academics.

WARREN-WALKER SCHOOL
Day Coed Gr PS-8
San Diego, CA 92107. 4605 Point Loma Ave.
Tel: 619-223-3663. Fax: 619-223-5567.
www.warren-walker.com   E-mail: wwseducate@aol.com

Raymond J. Volker, Head. AB, Univ of California-Berkeley, MEd, Univ of San Diego.

Pre-Prep. Feat—Span Computers Studio_Art Drama Band Music. **Supp**—Tut. **Adm:** 70/yr. Appl due: Mar. Accepted: 76%. Yield: 95%. **Tests** IQ ISEE. **Enr 383.** B 188. G 195. Elem 383. Wh 88%. Hisp 3%. Blk 5%. Am Ind 1%. Asian 3%. Avg class size: 16. Uniform. **Fac 40.** M 7. F 33. Wh 94%. Hisp 3%. Blk 3%. Adv deg: 25%. **Grad '04**—**35.** Prep—19. **Tui '04-'05:** Day $8605-10,030 (+$1000-2500). Aid: Merit 10 ($39,000). Need 26 ($136,000). **Summer:** Ages 3-12. Enrich Rec. Art. Music. Sports. Tui Day $300/wk. 10 wks. **Est 1932.** Inc. Quar (Sept-June). **Assoc** WASC. Warren-Walker offers drama in grades pre-K-8; foreign language, music and computer in grades K-8; art in grades 1-8; and band in grades 6-8. The curriculum places particular emphasis on core academic skills and the performing arts. The main lower school (grades pre-K-5) campus is on Point Loma Avenue, while a second lower school campus operates at 5150 Wilson St., La Mesa 91941. Middle schoolers attend classes at 2231 Camino Del Rio S., 2nd Fl., 92108.

BRIDGEMONT HIGH SCHOOL AND JUNIOR HIGH

Day Coed Gr 6-12

San Francisco, CA 94132. 777 Brotherhood Way.
Tel: 415-333-7600. Fax: 415-333-7603.
www.bridgemontschool.org   E-mail: bridgemonths@aol.com
  Peter Tropper, Prin. BS, Northeastern Univ. Tiffany Mann, Adm.

  Col Prep. Gen Acad. Feat—Humanities Fr Span Econ Bible Film Studio_Art Drama Chorus Journ. **Supp**—Makeup Tut. **Adm (Gr 6-11):** 35/yr. Appl due: Rolling. Accepted: 70%. Yield: 70%. **Tests** TOEFL. **Enr 92.** B 52. G 40. Elem 35. Sec 57. Wh 36%. Hisp 26%. Blk 16%. Am Ind 3%. Asian 19%. Avg class size: 12. **Fac 15.** M 7/1. F 7. Adv deg: 20%. **Grad '04—12.** Col—12. Avg SAT: 1032. Alum 300. **Tui '04-'05:** Day $8590-9990. Aid: Need 20 ($30,000). Work prgm 2 ($3000). **Est 1974.** Nonprofit. Nondenom Christian. Sem (Aug-June). **Assoc** WASC. This nondenominational Christian school offers college preparation with a Christian worldview. Course work emphasizes critical-thinking and communicational skills. All students embark on a weeklong field studies excursion each spring. Boys may play soccer, basketball and baseball at the varsity level, while girls choose from volleyball, basketball and softball.

CHINESE AMERICAN INTERNATIONAL SCHOOL

Day Coed Gr PS-8

San Francisco, CA 94102. 150 Oak St.
Tel: 415-865-6000. Fax: 415-865-6089.
www.cie-cais.org   E-mail: h_lin@cais.org
  Andrew W. Corcoran, Head. BS, US Military Academy, MEd, Univ of Hawaii-Manoa. John Leiner, Adm.

  Pre-Prep. Bilingual. Feat—Mandarin Computers Studio_Art Music. **Supp**—Dev_Read ESL Rem_Read. **Adm:** 68/yr. Appl due: Jan. Accepted: 56%. **Tests** CTP_4 ISEE. **Enr 361.** Elem 361. Wh 15%. Hisp 2%. Blk 2%. Asian 57%. Other 24%. Avg class size: 18. **Fac 52.** M 4. F 43/5. Wh 40%. Hisp 6%. Asian 54%. Adv deg: 32%. **Grad '04—26.** Prep—26. **Tui '04-'05:** Day $15,400-16,775 (+$300). Aid: Merit 7 ($4000). Need 67 ($395,050). **Summer:** Enrich Rem Rec. Mandarin. Tui Day $1000/4-wk ses. 8 wks. **Est 1981.** Nonprofit. Sem (Aug-June). **Assoc** WASC. CAIS provides students with a bilingual education in Mandarin Chinese and English. The school teaches the full range of subjects in both languages, and children study the traditional and contemporary values of both American and Chinese cultures. No prior knowledge of Chinese is required of either the student or the family. The middle school requires community service hours and encourages participation in student government. In addition, an exchange program with sister schools in China is available.

IMMACULATE CONCEPTION ACADEMY

Day Girls Gr 9-12

San Francisco, CA 94110. 3625 24th St.
Tel: 415-824-2052. Fax: 415-821-4677.
www.icacademy.org   E-mail: ica@icacademy.org
  Sr. Janice Therese Wellington, OP, Prin. BA, Univ of Santa Clara, MA, Univ of San Francisco. Gina Espinal, Adm.

Col Prep. AP—Eng Span Calc Comp_Sci US_Hist US_Govt & Pol Art_Hist Studio_Art. **Feat**—Fr Stats Environ_Sci Comp_Design Psych Relig Film Drama Music Dance Accounting Journ Design. **Supp**—Rem_Math Tut. **Adm (Gr 9-11):** 86/yr. Appl due: Dec. Accepted: 73%. **Tests** HSPT. **Enr 262.** G 262. Sec 262. Wh 14%. Hisp 45%. Blk 7%. Asian 19%. Other 15%. Avg class size: 23. Uniform. **Fac 21.** M 5. F 16. Wh 76%. Hisp 9%. Blk 5%. Asian 9%. Other 1%. Adv deg: 66%. **Grad '04—59.** Col—58. Avg SAT: 950. Avg ACT: 20. Alum 3100. **Tui '04-'05:** Day $8200 (+$475). Aid: Merit 8 ($18,750). Need 138 ($339,608). **Summer:** Enrich Rev Rem. Tui Day $200/2-wk ses. 4 wks. **Est 1883.** Nonprofit. Roman Catholic. Sem (Aug-May). **Assoc** WASC. Staffed by the Dominican Sisters of Mission San Jose and lay faculty members, this school in Noe Valley includes Advanced Placement and honors courses in its college preparatory curriculum. While taking seven courses per semester, girls combine required classes with electives in such areas as film and imaginative writing, child development and personal financial management. The cocurricular program at ICA includes campus ministry, student government, student clubs and athletics. Each student fulfills a 100-hour Christian service requirement by midyear in grade 12.

LIVE OAK SCHOOL
Day Coed Gr K-8

San Francisco, CA 94107. 1555 Mariposa St.
Tel: 415-861-8840. Fax: 415-861-7153.
www.liveoaksf.org E-mail: admissions@liveoaksf.org
Holly Horton, Head. BA, Briarcliff College, MS, Wheelock College.

Pre-Prep. Gen Acad. Feat—Span Computers Ceramics Sculpt Drama Chorus Music_Theory. **Adm:** Appl due: Jan. Accepted: 25%. **Enr 229.** B 125. G 104. Elem 229. Wh 70%. Hisp 15%. Blk 5%. Asian 6%. Other 4%. Avg class size: 22. **Fac 26.** M 8/4. F 11/3. Wh 80%. Hisp 8%. Blk 4%. Asian 8%. Adv deg: 38%. **Grad '04—25.** Prep—18. Alum 50. **Tui '03-'04:** Day $12,550-13,250 (+$250). Aid: Need 55 ($498,000). **Summer:** Enrich Rec. Tui Day $200/wk. 6 wks. **Est 1971.** Nonprofit. Tri (Sept-June). Live Oak's developmentally oriented elementary curriculum emphasizes the arts and sciences and the humanities. Students frequently work in small groups on experiential, hands-on projects designed to promote skill mastery. The school follows an interdisciplinary approach in the core subjects; art, music, Spanish and physical education classes complement the standard courses.

MERCY HIGH SCHOOL
Day Girls Gr 9-12

San Francisco, CA 94132. 3250 19th Ave.
Tel: 415-334-0525. Fax: 415-334-9726.
www.mercyhs.org E-mail: info@mercyhs.org
Dorothy McCrea, Prin. BA, EdD, Univ of San Francisco, MA, Univ of Santa Clara. Elizabeth Belonogoff, Adm.

Col Prep. AP—Eng Fr Span Calc Chem Physics US_Hist Studio_Art. **Feat**—Creative_Writing Environ_Sci Comp_Sci Govt Child_Dev Relig Drama Music Dance Bus Speech. **Supp**—Tut. **Adm:** 184/yr. Appl due: Dec. Accepted: 98%. **Tests** Stanford. **Enr 580.** G 580. Sec 580. Wh 27%. Hisp 19%. Blk 3%. Asian 34%. Other 17%. Avg class size: 25. Uniform. **Fac 44.** M 9/1. F 32/2. Adv deg: 63%. **Grad '04—108.** Col—106. Alum 8200. **Tui '04-'05:** Day $9725 (+$825). Aid: Need 193 ($160,000). **Summer:** Enrich. Tui Day $350/crse. 4 wks. **Est 1952.** Nonprofit. Roman Catholic. Sem (Aug-May). **Assoc** WASC. Mercy offers a four-year sequence of courses in religion, English, math, science, foreign language, social science and the fine arts; students choose additional course work from electives. Advanced Placement and honors classes are available. The school also schedules liturgies, retreats and Christian service projects.

CLAIRBOURN SCHOOL   Day Coed Gr PS-8
San Gabriel, CA 91775. 8400 Huntington Dr.
Tel: 626-286-3108. Fax: 626-286-1528.
www.clairbourn.org   E-mail: info@clairbourn.org
 Robert W. Nafie, Head. BA, Univ of Minnesota, MS, Univ of Wisconsin-Madison, PhD, Claremont Graduate School. Janna Windsor, Adm.

 Pre-Prep. Feat—Lib_Skills Fr Lat Span Computers Studio_Art Drama Music. **Adm:** 85/yr. Appl due: Jan. Accepted: 27%. **Tests** CEEB CTP_4 ISEE. **Enr 420.** B 212. G 208. Elem 420. Wh 76%. Hisp 23%. Blk 1%. Avg class size: 20. Uniform. **Fac 36.** M 6. F 27/3. Wh 99%. Hisp 1%. Adv deg: 27%. **Prep**—36. Alum 2400. **Tui '04-'05:** Day $10,075-12,200 (+$80-460). Aid: Merit 3 ($2000). **Summer:** Acad Enrich Rev Rem Rec. 5 wks. **Est 1926.** Nonprofit. Christian Science. Sem (Sept-June). **Assoc** WASC. Although the school's staff are all Christian Scientists, the student body at Clairbourn represents various denominations. The curriculum focuses on the basics and is designed to teach children creative thinking, problem solving and fundamental academic skills. Foreign languages, computers, library, art, music and physical education enrich the program. Accelerated English and math courses are available at the middle school level.

PRESENTATION HIGH SCHOOL   Day Girls Gr 9-12
San Jose, CA 95125. 2281 Plummer Ave.
Tel: 408-264-1664. Fax: 408-266-3026.
www.pres-net.com
 Mary Miller, Prin. BA, MA. Dina Garrett, Adm.

 Col Prep. AP—Eng Fr Span Calc Bio Econ Psych. **Feat**—Stats Anat & Physiol Bioethics Environ_Sci Programming Web_Design Bus_Law Relig World_Relig Ceramics Drawing Photog Studio_Art Acting Theater_Arts Dance. **Supp**—Tut. **Adm (Gr 9-11):** 200/yr. Appl due: Jan. **Tests** HSPT. **Enr 750.** G 750. Sec 750. Wh 65%. Hisp 12%. Blk 1%. Asian 9%. Other 13%. Avg class size: 28. Uniform. **Fac 50.** M 9/2. F 36/3. Adv deg: 57%. **Grad '04**—175. Col—175. Avg SAT: 1117. **Tui '04-'05:** Day $9485. **Est 1962.** Roman Catholic. Sem (Aug-May). Required courses at Pres include seven semesters of religious studies, two of fine arts and at least one of computer applications. A well-developed technology program features computer labs and an electronic library collection. Students perform community service and assist with fundraising efforts.

ALPHA BEACON CHRISTIAN SCHOOL   Day Coed Gr PS-12
San Mateo, CA 94403. 525 W 42nd Ave.
Tel: 650-212-4222. Fax: 650-212-1026.
www.alphabeacon.org   E-mail: info@alphabeacon.org

Lillian G. Mark, Supt. AB, Univ of California-Berkeley, MS, Pensacola Christian College. Jeannie Chiara, Adm.

Col Prep. AP—Calc Chem Physics. **Feat**—Span Econ Govt Bible Ethics Performing_Arts Drama Chorus Speech Home_Ec. **Supp**—Makeup Tut. **Adm:** 30/yr. Appl due: Mar. Accepted: 90%. **Tests** SSAT. **Enr 225.** Elem 150. Sec 75. Wh 50%. Hisp 25%. Asian 25%. Avg class size: 15. Uniform. **Fac 21.** M 4/2. F 9/6. Wh 43%. Hisp 17%. Asian 40%. Adv deg: 23%. **Grad '04—11.** Col—10. Alum 100. **Tui '04-'05:** Day $5400-8200 (+$200-500). Aid: Work prgm 5 ($5100). **Summer:** Acad Enrich Rev Rem Rec. 6 wks. **Est 1969.** Nonprofit. Nondenom Christian. Quar (Aug-June). Alpha Beacon provides a Bible-based curriculum that emphasizes college preparation and character development in a Christian environment. Student council, retreats, educational trips, performing arts offerings, and intramural and interscholastic athletics supplement academics.

JUNIPERO SERRA HIGH SCHOOL　　　　　　　　　　　Day Boys Gr 9-12
San Mateo, CA 94403. 451 W 20th Ave.
Tel: 650-345-8207. Fax: 650-573-6638.
www.serrahs.com　　E-mail: padres@serrahs.com

Rev. Joseph Bradley, Pres. Lars Lund, Prin. Randall Vogel, Adm.

Col Prep. AP—Span Calc Comp_Sci Bio Physics US_Hist US_Govt & Pol. **Feat**—Ger Computers Theol Band Chorus. **Adm:** 275/yr. Appl due: Jan. Accepted: 75%. **Enr 985.** B 985. Sec 985. Wh 63%. Hisp 11%. Blk 2%. Asian 9%. Other 15%. Avg class size: 24. **Fac 69. Grad '04—214.** Col—214. Alum 10,087. **Tui '04-'05:** Day $10,780 (+$600). Aid: Work prgm 170 ($350,000). **Summer:** Acad Enrich Rev Rec. Tui Day $200. 6 wks. **Est 1944.** Nonprofit. Roman Catholic. Sem (Aug-June). **Assoc** WASC. Junipero Serra's program includes four years of French, Spanish and German. Graduates attend a variety of California and out-of-state colleges.

SAINT MARK'S SCHOOL　　　　　　　　　　　　　　Day Coed Gr K-8
San Rafael, CA 94903. 39 Trellis Dr.
Tel: 415-472-8000. Fax: 415-472-0722.
www.saintmarksschool.org　　E-mail: bupton@saintmarksschool.org

Damon H. Kerby, Head. AB, Kenyon College, MA, Stanford Univ. Barbara Upton, Adm.

Pre-Prep. Gen Acad. Feat—Fr Span Computers Studio_Art Drama Music. **Supp**—Dev_Read Rem_Math Rem_Read Rev Tut. **Adm:** 58/yr. Appl due: Jan. Accepted: 32%. **Tests** ISEE. **Enr 380.** B 182. G 198. Elem 380. Wh 78%. Hisp 9%. Blk 1%. Asian 8%. Other 4%. Avg class size: 20. **Fac 46.** M 10/2. F 20/14. **Grad '04—43.** Prep—36. Alum 787. **Tui '04-'05:** Day $15,775 (+$250-600). Aid: Need 54 ($750,000). **Summer:** Rem Rec. Tech. Tui Day $35-100. 2-4 wks. **Est 1980.** Nonprofit. Quar (Aug-June). All students at Saint Mark's receive instruction in foreign language, computer, art, drama, music and physical education. Tutoring is available for those with learning weaknesses. One week of community service is required in grade 8. After-school activities include fine arts and athletic offerings, and daycare is provided.

MATER DEI HIGH SCHOOL Day Coed Gr 9-12
Santa Ana, CA 92707. 1202 W Edinger Ave.
Tel: 714-754-7711. Fax: 714-754-1880.
www.materdei.org   E-mail: admissions@materdei.org
   Patrick Murphy, Pres. BA, Simon Fraser Univ (Canada), MA, San Diego State Univ. Greg Dhuyvetter, Adm.

   Col Prep. AP—Eng Fr Ger Lat Span Calc Physics Eur_Hist US_Hist US_Govt & Pol Art_Hist Studio_Art. **Feat**—Comp_Sci Bus_Law Band Chorus Music_Theory Communications Speech TV_Production. **Supp**—LD Rem_Math Rem_Read Tut. **Adm:** 670/yr. Appl due: Rolling. **Enr 2200.** Sec 2200. Wh 45%. Hisp 25%. Blk 2%. Asian 28%. Avg class size: 27. Uniform. **Fac 134.** Adv deg: 43%. **Grad '04—460.** Col—456. Avg SAT: 1073. Alum 20,000. **Tui '04-'05:** Day $7025 (+$600). Aid: Need 550 ($525,000). **Summer:** Rem. 6 wks. **Est 1950.** Nonprofit. Roman Catholic. Sem (Sept-June). **Assoc** WASC. Mater Dei offers a traditional college preparatory curriculum, with Advanced Placement opportunities provided in most disciplines. Various electives, business courses and athletics are also available.

CRANE COUNTRY DAY SCHOOL Day Coed Gr K-8
Santa Barbara, CA 93108. 1795 San Leandro Ln.
Tel: 805-969-7732. Fax: 805-969-3635.
www.craneschool.org   E-mail: dwilliams@craneschool.org
   Joel Weiss, Head. BA, Swarthmore College, MEd, Harvard Univ. Debbie Williams, Adm.

   Pre-Prep. Gen Acad. Feat—Span Marine_Biol/Sci Computers Geog Studio_Art Drama Music Media. **Adm:** 56/yr. Appl due: Feb. Accepted: 30%. **Tests** ISEE. **Enr 230.** B 120. G 110. Elem 230. Wh 81%. Hisp 8%. Blk 2%. Asian 7%. Other 2%. Avg class size: 17. **Fac 35.** M 11/3. F 16/5. Wh 98%. Hisp 1%. Blk 1%. Adv deg: 22%. **Grad '04—33.** Prep—17. Alum 2675. **Tui '04-'05:** Day $15,900-16,900 (+$50-400). Aid: Need 15 ($165,140). **Est 1928.** Nonprofit. Tri (Sept-June). **Assoc** WASC. While stressing the fundamentals within a traditional curriculum, the school also places emphasis upon the visual arts, drama, music, athletics and community service. Spanish instruction begins in kindergarten.

MARYMOUNT OF SANTA BARBARA Day Coed Gr K-8
Santa Barbara, CA 93103. 2130 Mission Ridge Rd.
Tel: 805-569-1811. Fax: 805-682-6892.
www.marymountsb.org   E-mail: info@marymountsb.org
   Douglas E. Phelps, Head. Tina Merlo Messineo, Adm.

   Pre-Prep. Feat—Span Computers Relig Studio_Art Music. **Adm:** 45/yr. Appl due: Feb. Accepted: 30%. **Tests** CTP_4 ISEE. **Enr 232.** B 105. G 127. Elem 232. Wh 83%. Hisp 4%. Blk 1%. Asian 3%. Other 9%. Avg class size: 22. Uniform. **Fac 24.** M 6/1. F 13/4. Wh 79%. Hisp 3%. Asian 18%. Adv deg: 29%. **Grad '04—31.** Prep—18. Alum 1000. **Tui '04-'05:** Day $12,210-14,072 (+$283-914). Aid: Need 24 ($202,661). **Est 1938.** Nonprofit. Roman Catholic. Tri (Aug-June). Spanish instruction begins in kindergarten at Marymount, and the pre-preparatory curriculum also includes computer, library science and religion offerings. The middle school program (grades 6-8) emphasizes English skills development and features advanced math courses. Art and music classes round out the accelerated curriculum. Academic study trips enrich in-class study.

ST. LAWRENCE ACADEMY

Day Coed Gr 9-12

Santa Clara, CA 95051. 2000 Lawrence Ct.
Tel: 408-296-3013. Fax: 408-296-3794.
www.saintlawrence.org   E-mail: admissions@saintlawrence.org

Christie H. Filios, Prin. BA, Loyola Marymount Univ, MA, Stanford Univ. Sandra Trotch, Adm.

Col Prep. AP—Eng Calc US_Hist Studio_Art. **Feat**—Creative_Writing Psych Sociol. **Supp**—LD. **Adm:** 90/yr. Appl due: Feb. Accepted: 70%. **Tests** HSPT. **Enr 347.** B 228. G 119. Sec 347. Avg class size: 21. Uniform. **Fac 32.** M 12/2. F 16/2. Wh 91%. Hisp 3%. Blk 3%. Asian 3%. Adv deg: 40%. **Grad '04—86.** Col—86. **Tui '04-'05:** Day $9170 (+$880). Aid: Need 24 ($70,000). **Est 1975.** Nonprofit. Roman Catholic. Quar (Aug-June). The academy's college preparatory program provides several forms of learning support: a library/multimedia information resource center, reading labs, before- and after-school study halls, and a formal program for high-functioning students with diagnosed learning disabilities. The school encourages pupils to take part in the campus ministry program: All students perform 25 hours of community service annually, and full-class retreats and liturgical celebrations are integral aspects of school life.

P S #1 ELEMENTARY SCHOOL

Day Coed Gr K-6

Santa Monica, CA 90404. 1454 Euclid St.
Tel: 310-394-1313. Fax: 310-395-1093.
www.psone.org   E-mail: andrea@psone.org

Joel M. Pelcyger, Dir. BA, Univ of Rochester. Andrea Roth, Adm.

Pre-Prep. Feat—Poetry Span Drama. **Supp**—Dev_Read. **Adm:** 35/yr. Appl due: Rolling. Accepted: 50%. **Enr 176.** B 87. G 89. Elem 176. Wh 78%. Hisp 4%. Blk 11%. Am Ind 1%. Asian 6%. Avg class size: 25. **Fac 18.** M 3. F 13/2. Wh 90%. Blk 5%. Asian 5%. Adv deg: 22%. **Grad '04—24.** Prep—19. Alum 340. **Tui '03-'04:** Day $14,000 (+$1140). Aid: Need 35 ($284,000). **Est 1971.** Nonprofit. (Sept-June). This progressive school enriches its curriculum with multicultural experiences, community and environmental studies, science and arts programs, and field trips. Pupils at P S #1 acquire academic and life skills in multi-age classes that are each led by two master teachers. Faculty members continually evaluate the student's progress through observation and portfolio assessment.

SONOMA COUNTRY DAY SCHOOL

Day Coed Gr K-8

Santa Rosa, CA 95403. 4400 Day School Pl.
Tel: 707-284-3200. Fax: 707-284-3254.
www.scds.org   E-mail: scds@scds.org

Philip Nix, Head. BA, MA, Rutgers Univ. Christian H. Johnston, Adm.

Col Prep. Feat—Fr Lat Span Computers Studio_Art Drama Band Chorus Public_Speak Outdoor_Ed. **Adm:** Appl due: Rolling. **Tests** MRT Stanford. **Enr**

287. Elem 287. Wh 97%. Blk 1%. Asian 2%. Avg class size: 22. Uniform. **Fac 37.** M 9/1. F 23/4. **Grad '04—48.** Alum 353. **Tui '04-'05:** Day $14,137-15,878 (+$500-1500). Aid: Need 44 ($288,828). **Summer:** Acad Enrich Rec. 1-2 wks. **Est 1983.** Nonprofit. Sem (Sept-June). The core curriculum at SCDS is enhanced by integrated instruction in philosophy, ethics and mythology. The liberal arts course of studies features a wide selection of visual and performing arts offerings. Children are expected to take advantage of leadership opportunities and also to engage in community service.

BAYMONTE CHRISTIAN SCHOOL　　　　　　　　**Day Coed Gr PS-8**
Scotts Valley, CA 95066. 5000-B Granite Creek Rd.
Tel: 831-438-0100. Fax: 831-438-0715.
www.baymonte.org　　E-mail: principal@baymonte.org
　　Steve Patterson, Prin. BA, California State Univ-Sacramento, MA, US International Univ.
　　Gen Acad. Feat—Fr Span Bible. **Supp**—Dev_Read Rem_Math. **Adm:** 40/yr. Appl due: Apr. Accepted: 98%. **Enr 518.** Elem 518. Wh 92%. Hisp 2%. Blk 1%. Am Ind 1%. Asian 4%. Avg class size: 20. **Fac 28.** M 3. F 25. Wh 100%. Adv deg: 17%. **Grad '04—50. Tui '04-'05:** Day $4500 (+$200-300). Aid: Need 15 ($40,000). **Summer:** Rec. Tui Day $110/wk. 9 wks. **Est 1968.** Nonprofit. Sem (Sept-June). **Assoc** WASC. The curriculum includes daily Bible and basic computer instruction. Student government, choral group and athletics are among the extracurricular activities.

NOTRE DAME HIGH SCHOOL　　　　　　　　**Day Coed Gr 9-12**
Sherman Oaks, CA 91423. 13645 Riverside Dr.
Tel: 818-933-3600. Fax: 818-501-0507.
www.ndhs.org　　E-mail: admissions@ndhs.org
　　Br. William C. Nick, CSC, Pres. Stephanie Connelly, Prin. Richard Klee, Adm.
　　Col Prep. AP—Eng Fr Lat Span Calc Comp_Sci Physics Eur_Hist US_Hist Econ US_Govt & Pol Art_Hist Studio_Art. **Feat**—Computers Law Psych Sociol Relig Acting Band Debate Journ Speech. **Supp**—Tut. **Adm:** 320/yr. Appl due: Jan. Accepted: 50%. **Tests** HSPT. **Enr 1148.** Sec 1148. Wh 58%. Hisp 18%. Blk 3%. Am Ind 1%. Asian 20%. Avg class size: 28. Uniform. **Fac 78.** Adv deg: 50%. **Grad '04—246.** Col—232. Alum 9418. **Tui '05-'06:** Day $8600 (+$565). **Est 1947.** Nonprofit. Roman Catholic. Sem (Sept-June). **Assoc** WASC. Founded by the Brothers of the Holy Cross, Notre Dame offers a college preparatory curriculum, honors and Advanced Placement courses, a variety of electives and opportunities for independent study. Freshmen spend ten compulsory hours in service to their families, sophomores spend 20 in service to their parishes, juniors complete 30 hours in service to the school, and seniors spend another 30 in off-campus Christian service to organizations and institutions that assist the underprivileged.

ST. MICHAEL'S PREPARATORY SCHOOL　　　　　　　　**Bdg Boys Gr 9-12**
Silverado, CA 92676. 19292 El Toro Rd.
Tel: 949-858-0222. Fax: 949-858-7365.
www.stmichaelsprep.com　　E-mail: admissions@stmichaelsprep.org

Rev. Gabriel D. Stack, OPraem, Head. EdD, Pepperdine Univ.

Col Prep. AP—Fr Ger Lat Span Calc Physics US_Hist Econ. **Feat**—Relig Fine_Arts. **Supp**—Tut. **Adm:** 25/yr. Accepted: 15%. **Tests** Stanford. **Enr 70.** B 70. Sec 70. Wh 71%. Hisp 3%. Asian 18%. Avg class size: 10. Uniform. **Fac 23.** M 13/7. F 1/2. Wh 97%. Hisp 3%. Adv deg: 69%. In Dorms 2. **Grad '04—9.** Col—9. Alum 230. **Tui '02-'03:** Bdg $21,000 (+$5000). 5-Day Bdg $11,000 (+$4000). **Summer:** Ages 6-12. Rec. Tui Bdg $150/wk. 6 wks. **Est 1961.** Nonprofit. Roman Catholic. Sem (Aug-June). **Assoc** WASC. Catholic principles are taught. All students take religion, attend chapel and perform daily maintenance jobs on campus. Varsity-level competition is available in cross-country, basketball, baseball and soccer.

WOODCREST SCHOOL · Day Coed Gr K-5
Tarzana, CA 91356. 6043 Tampa Ave.
Tel: 818-345-3002. Fax: 818-345-7880.
www.woodcrestschool.com E-mail: info@woodcrestschool.com

Andrea Miller, Admin. BA, Univ of San Diego. Luanne Paglione, Prin. BS, Seton Hall Univ. Sharon Maguire, Adm.

Pre-Prep. Feat—Span Computers Fine_Arts Drama Music Dance. **Supp**—Dev_Read Rem_Math Rem_Read. **Adm:** 55/yr. Appl due: Aug. **Enr 250.** Elem 250. Wh 87%. Hisp 1%. Blk 5%. Asian 7%. Avg class size: 17. Uniform. **Fac 22.** M /2. F 18/2. Adv deg: 9%. **Grad '04—24. Tui '04-'05:** Day $7200 (+$375). **Summer:** Rec. Tui Day $230/wk. 10 wks. **Est 1969.** Nonprofit. Quar (Sept-June). **Assoc** WASC. In addition to the basic educational program, this school also offers enrichment and gifted programs. Spanish instruction begins in grade 2, computer courses in kindergarten. The school has a computer lab, and each class has its own computer. An extended-day program is available.

LAURENCE SCHOOL · Day Coed Gr K-6
Valley Glen, CA 91401. 13639 Victory Blvd.
Tel: 818-782-4001. Fax: 818-782-4004.
www.laurenceschool.com E-mail: office@laurenceschool.com

Marvin Jacobson, Head. BS, New York Univ, MS, Univ of California-Los Angeles. Lauren Wolke, Adm.

Pre-Prep. Gen Acad. Feat—Lib_Skills Computers Studio_Art Drama Music Orchestra Dance. **Adm:** 59/yr. Appl due: Feb. Accepted: 63%. **Enr 226.** Elem 226. Wh 80%. Hisp 6%. Blk 6%. Asian 6%. Other 2%. Avg class size: 18. Uniform. **Fac 25.** M 3/1. F 21. **Grad '04—28.** Prep—28. **Tui '04-'05:** Day $14,000 (+$290-465). **Summer:** Acad Enrich Rev Rec. Tui Day $400/wk. 4 wks. **Est 1953.** Nonprofit. Sem (Sept-June). **Assoc** WASC. Laurence utilizes small classes and individualized group instruction to teach basic skills. The integrated curriculum includes enrichment in science and social studies. The school's laboratory science and studio art courses emphasize a hands-on approach.

THE DORRIS-EATON SCHOOL Day Coed Gr PS-8
Walnut Creek, CA 94595. 1847 Newell Ave.
Tel: 925-933-5225. Fax: 925-256-9710.
www.deschool.com   E-mail: tspencer@dorriseaton.com
   Gerald F. Ludden, Co-Head. Nancee Watson, Co-Head. Trina Spencer, Adm.

   Gen Acad. Feat—Span Computers Studio_Art Music. **Adm:** 110/yr. **Tests** ISEE. **Enr 450.** B 220. G 230. Elem 450. Avg class size: 19. **Fac 40. Grad '04—45. Tui '04-'05:** Day $3900-14,400. **Summer:** Acad Enrich Rec. Tui Day $650-2100. 6 wks. **Est 1954.** Quar (Sept-June). Dorris-Eaton's curriculum emphasizes critical-thinking skills and creativity at all grade levels. Spanish, computer science, art, music and physical education classes complement work in the core subjects. An after-school activities program includes team sports, band and performing arts offerings. The preschool is conducted at a separate campus in Alamo.

SEVEN HILLS SCHOOL Day Coed Gr PS-8
Walnut Creek, CA 94598. 975 N San Carlos Dr.
Tel: 925-933-0666. Fax: 925-933-6271.
www.sevenhillsschool.org   E-mail: 7hills@sevenhillsschool.org
   William H. Miller, Head. BA, Univ of Notre Dame, MA, Univ of San Francisco. Sissy Gabriel & Susanne Goldman, Adms.

   Pre-Prep. Gen Acad. Feat—Fr Span Computers Studio_Art Drama Music. **Supp**—Dev_Read Tut. **Adm:** 61/yr. Appl due: Jan. Accepted: 45%. Yield: 79%. **Tests** CTP_4 ISEE MAT. **Enr 374.** B 167. G 207. Elem 374. Wh 74%. Hisp 4%. Blk 3%. Asian 10%. Other 9%. Avg class size: 18. **Fac 37.** M 4/1. F 25/7. Wh 90%. Hisp 10%. Adv deg: 32%. **Grad '04—32.** Alum 50. **Tui '04-'05:** Day $9750-15,200 (+$1000). Aid: Need 42 ($255,200). **Summer:** Acad Enrich Rec. Tui Day $2000. 8 wks. **Est 1962.** Nonprofit. (Sept-June). Seven Hills' well-equipped, nine-acre campus is adjacent to a wildlife refuge. The curriculum combines traditional and innovative methods, and a year-round enriched daycare program is available.

HAWAII

HOLY NATIVITY SCHOOL Day Coed Gr PS-6
Honolulu, HI 96821. 5286 Kalanianaole Hwy.
Tel: 808-373-3232. Fax: 808-377-9618.
www.holynativityschool.org   E-mail: admissions@holynativity-hi.org
   Robert H. Whiting, Head. PhD, Univ of Colorado-Boulder. Kelly Goheen, Adm.

   Pre-Prep. Feat—Computers Relig Studio_Art Music. **Supp**—Tut. **Adm:** 49/yr. Appl due: Feb. Accepted: 55%. **Tests** Stanford. **Enr 180.** B 95. G 85. Elem 180. Wh 44%. Blk 1%. Asian 50%. Other 5%. Avg class size: 20. Uniform. **Fac 22.** M 2. F 18/2. Wh 59%. Asian 9%. Other 32%. Adv deg: 22%. **Grad '04—13.** Prep—13. Alum 950. **Tui '04-'05:** Day $7200-8930. Aid: Need 21 ($82,616). **Summer:** Ages 4-9. Enrich Rec. Tui Day $750. 6 wks. **Est 1949.** Nonprofit. Episcopal. Quar (Aug-June). **Assoc** WASC. Holy Nativity's individualized, sequential curriculum features enrichment classes in art, music, computers, religious studies and physical education. An extended-day program allows boys and girls to pursue additional academic work and extracurricular activities outside of school hours. The school prepares a culturally and ethnically diverse student body for entrance into local independent preparatory schools.

MARYKNOLL SCHOOL
Day Coed Gr PS-12

Honolulu, HI 96822. 1526 Alexander St.
Tel: 808-952-7330. Fax: 808-952-7331.
www.maryknollschool.org   E-mail: admission@maryknollschool.org
Michael E. Baker, Pres. BA, Univ of New England, MA, Univ of Maine. Scott C. Siegfried, Adm.

Col Prep. AP—Studio_Art. **Feat**—Chin Fr Japan Span Hawaiian Govt Psych Art_Hist. **Adm:** 254/yr. Appl due: Jan. Accepted: 60%. Yield: 55%. **Tests** SSAT Stanford. **Enr 1395.** B 721. G 674. Wh 31%. Hisp 1%. Blk 2%. Am Ind 1%. Asian 65%. Avg class size: 25. Uniform. **Fac 104.** M 34/1. F 67/2. Adv deg: 54%. **Grad '04—138.** Col—137. Avg SAT: 1100. Alum 5400. **Tui '04-'05:** Day $8600-9600 (+$200-400). Aid: Merit 11 ($60,000). Need 264 ($566,000). Work prgm ($45,000). **Summer:** Acad Enrich Rem. Tui Day $200-500. 6 wks. **Est 1927.** Nonprofit. Roman Catholic. (Aug-June). **Assoc** WASC. This Catholic school offers a college preparatory curriculum that features Advanced Placement courses and a world language immersion program. Extracurricular activities include athletics, the performing arts and student government, as well as a variety of academic and interest clubs. The school also maintains mission and student exchange programs.

SACRED HEARTS ACADEMY
Day Girls Gr PS-12

Honolulu, HI 96816. 3253 Waialae Ave.
Tel: 808-734-5058. Fax: 808-737-7867.
www.sacredhearts.org   E-mail: kmuramoto@sacredhearts.org
Betty White, Prin. BA, Mary Washington College, MA, College of William and Mary, MA, Univ of Hawaii-Manoa. Karen Muramoto, Adm.

Col Prep. AP—Eng Calc US_Hist Econ Art_Hist. **Feat**—Japan Span Hawaiian Stats Computers Programming Govt Asian_Stud World_Relig Ceramics Studio_Art Chorus Accounting Journ. **Supp**—ESL Rev Tut. **Adm:** 250/yr. Appl due: Feb. Accepted: 40%. **Tests** CEEB CTP_4 IQ SSAT. **Enr 1156.** Elem 406. Sec 750. Wh 10%. Hisp 20%. Blk 2%. Am Ind 1%. Asian 30%. Other 37%. Avg class size: 25. Uniform. **Fac 95.** M 15. F 75/5. Wh 20%. Hisp 15%. Blk 1%. Asian 30%. Other 54%. Adv deg: 28%. **Grad '04—118.** Col—115. Avg SAT: 1100. Avg ACT: 22. **Tui '04-'05:** Day $6326-8135 (+$595-885). Aid: Need 231. **Summer:** Acad Enrich Rev Rem Rec. 4-6 wks. **Est 1909.** Nonprofit. Roman Catholic. Sem (Aug-May). The academy offers Advanced Placement courses as part of a varied college preparatory program. A well-developed sports program consists of volleyball, track and field, tennis, softball, soccer, golf, canoeing, bowling, basketball and air riflery. Each girl fulfills a community service requirement.

ST. FRANCIS SCHOOL
Day Girls Gr 6-12
Honolulu, HI 96822. 2707 Pamoa Rd.
Tel: 808-988-4111. Fax: 808-988-5497.
www.stfrancis-oahu.org   E-mail: kcurry@stfrancis-oahu.org

Sr. Joan of Arc Souza, Prin. BA, St Joseph's College (IN), MRelEd, La Salle College. Karen A. Curry, Adm.

Col Prep. AP—Eng Span Calc Chem US_Hist US_Govt & Pol. **Feat**—Japan Programming Web_Design HI_Hist Econ World_Relig Ceramics Band. **Supp**—Dev_Read ESL Makeup Tut. **Adm:** 92/yr. Appl due: Rolling. Accepted: 90%. Yield: 62%. **Tests** SSAT. **Enr 374.** G 374. Elem 67. Sec 304. Wh 25%. Hisp 2%. Blk 2%. Am Ind 1%. Asian 70%. Avg class size: 20. Uniform. **Fac 29.** M 8. F 19/2. Adv deg: 44%. **Grad '04—90.** Col—85. Avg SAT: 968. Avg ACT: 22. Alum 4200. **Tui '04-'05:** Day $5600-6800 (+$600). Aid: Merit 42 ($20,250). Need 53 ($32,600). Work prgm 53 ($32,600). **Summer:** Acad Enrich Rem. Tui Day $250. 4 wks. **Est 1924.** Nonprofit. Roman Catholic. Sem (July-June). **Assoc** WASC. St. Francis offers an unusual year-round program that begins in late July and ends in early June. In addition to Christmas and summer vacations, the school schedules two-week intersessions in both fall and spring that enable girls to either relax or prepare for the next quarter by participating in special workshops for enrichment or academic credit. A Great Books seminar, an honors program and AP classes are available during the high school years.

ISLAND SCHOOL
Day Coed Gr PS-12
Lihue, HI 96766. 3-1875 Kaumualii Hwy.
Tel: 808-246-0233. Fax: 808-245-6053.
www.ischool.org   E-mail: info@ischool.org

Robert Springer, Head. BA, Occidental College, MA, Univ of the Americas (Mexico). Sean Magoun, Adm.

Col Prep. Feat—British_Lit Creative_Writing Span Computers Comp_Design Interactive_CD_Production Ceramics Fine_Arts Performing_Arts Drama. **Supp**—Tut. **Adm:** 65/yr. Appl due: Feb. Accepted: 80%. **Tests** SSAT Stanford. **Enr 277.** B 125. G 152. Elem 188. Sec 89. Wh 50%. Hisp 3%. Blk 1%. Am Ind 1%. Asian 33%. Other 12%. Avg class size: 18. **Fac 29.** M 5/2. F 14/8. **Grad '04—10.** Col—10. Avg SAT: 1108. Alum 38. **Tui '03-'04:** Day $5070-7860 (+$300). Aid: Need 114 ($350,000). **Summer:** Acad. Tui Day $400. 6 wks. **Est 1977.** Nonprofit. Tri (Aug-May). **Assoc** WASC. Physical education, music, drama, computer, Spanish, Hawaiian studies and art classes supplement the academic program at this school, which is located on the island of Kauai.

LANAKILA BAPTIST SCHOOLS
Day Coed Gr K-12
Waipahu, HI 96797. 94-1250 Waipahu St.
Tel: 808-677-0731. Fax: 808-677-0733.
www.lanakilabaptist.org   E-mail: lanakilabaptist@aol.com

Steven C. Wygle, Pres. BA, Baptist Bible College, MBA, PhD, California Coast Univ. Ed Hughlett, Adm.

Col Prep. Gen Acad. Feat—Span. **Supp**—Makeup Tut. **Adm:** Appl due: Aug. Accepted: 90%. **Tests** IQ SSAT Stanford. **Enr 250.** Elem 160. Sec 90. Avg class size: 19. Uniform. **Fac 23.** M 6/1. F 11/5. Adv deg: 8%. **Grad '04—18.** Col—13. Avg SAT: 1100. **Tui '05-'06:** Day $4400-4700 (+$250). **Summer:** Acad Rem. 6 wks. **Est 1969.** Nonprofit. Baptist. Sem (Aug-May). The elementary and junior/senior high schools present an academic curriculum with a Scriptural foundation. The senior high offers both college preparatory and general academic programs, and all students study the Bible. The junior/senior high is located at 91-1219 Renton Rd., Ewa 96706.

OREGON

VALLEY CATHOLIC SCHOOL   Day Coed Gr 7-12
Beaverton, OR 97007. 4275 SW 148th Ave.
Tel: 503-644-3745. Fax: 503-646-4054.
www.valleycatholic.org   E-mail: vcsprincipal@ssmo.org
    Ross Thomas, Prin. Claudia Thomas, Adm.

    Col Prep. AP—Eng Bio Chem Physics US_Govt & Pol Music_Theory. **Feat**—Fr Japan Span Computers Econ Pol_Sci Psych Relig Fine_Arts Bus. **Supp**—ESL Tut. **Adm:** 150/yr. Appl due: Apr. **Tests** CEEB TOEFL. **Enr 470.** Wh 84%. Hisp 2%. Asian 14%. Avg class size: 20. **Fac 45. Grad '04—85.** Col—80. Avg SAT: 1130. Alum 2100. **Tui '04-'05:** Day $5900-7420 (+$280-300). **Est 1902.** Nonprofit. Roman Catholic. Sem (Sept-June). **Assoc** NAAS. This college preparatory school offers advanced courses in English, French, math, US history and biology.

MILO ADVENTIST ACADEMY   Coed Gr 9-12
Days Creek, OR 97429. PO Box 278.   Bdg & Day
Tel: 541-825-3200. Fax: 541-825-3723.
www.miloacademy.net   E-mail: info@miloacademy.org
    Randy Bovee, Prin. BA, Walla Walla College, MS, Univ of Oregon. Steve Rae, Adm.

    Col Prep. AP—Eng Calc Chem Physics US_Hist. **Feat**—British_Lit Writing Lat Span Anat & Physiol Geol Web_Design Econ Govt Bible Studio_Art Chorus Music_Hist Music_Theory. **Tests** TOEFL. **Enr 162.** B 67/4. G 84/7. Sec 162. Wh 90%. Hisp 7%. Asian 3%. Avg class size: 20. **Fac 13.** M 6/2. F 3/2. Wh 100%. **Grad '04—52.** Col—45. Avg SAT: 1097. Avg ACT: 23. **Tui '04-'05:** Bdg $11,800 (+$500). Day $6500 (+$500). **Est 1955.** Seventh-day Adventist. Sem (Aug-May). Bible classes, fine arts and technology electives complement MAA's college preparatory curriculum, which also includes Advanced Placement course work in the core subjects. A student work program emphasizes strong work habits and service. The school's intramural sports program enables students to develop athletic skills in a less competitive atmosphere.

OAK HILL SCHOOL   Day Coed Gr K-12
Eugene, OR 97405. 86397 Eastway Dr.
Tel: 541-744-0954. Fax: 541-741-6968.
www.oakhillschool.com   E-mail: admission@oakhillschool.com

Barbara Brown Packer, Head. BA, Univ of California-Santa Barbara, MA, Stanford Univ, EdD, Harvard Univ. Carrie Judd, Adm.

Col Prep. AP—Eng Lat Span Bio Physics US_Hist Econ US_Govt & Pol Studio_Art. **Feat**—Fr Greek Stats Environ_Sci Computers Theater_Arts Music. **Adm:** 20/yr. Appl due: Feb. Accepted: 86%. Yield: 75%. **Enr 104.** B 56. G 48. Elem 65. Sec 39. Avg class size: 12. **Fac 24.** M 3/6. F 6/9. Adv deg: 79%. **Grad '04—6.** Col—5. Alum 51. **Tui '04-'05:** Day $7425-9870. Aid: Merit 3. Need 18. **Est 1994.** Nonprofit. Tri (Sept-June). Oak Hill's full elementary and secondary program places emphasis upon higher-order thinking skills, sound study habits and organizational skills, and individual student interests. Students perform compulsory community service in grades 9-12; the number of hours required increases each year. Cocurricular activities such as sports, theater, music, cheerleading and chess complement academics.

NESKOWIN VALLEY SCHOOL   Day Coed Gr PS-8
Neskowin, OR 97149. 10005 Slab Creek Rd.
Tel: 503-392-3124. Fax: 503-392-3718.
www.neskowinvalleyschool.com   E-mail: nvs@oregoncoast.com

Douglas B. Immel, Dir. BA, Goddard College, MA, National Univ.

Pre-Prep. Feat—Span Studio_Art Drama. **Adm:** 22/yr. Appl due: Rolling. Accepted: 100%. **Enr 56.** B 25. G 31. Elem 56. Wh 82%. Hisp 4%. Am Ind 6%. Asian 8%. Avg class size: 13. **Fac 6.** M 1. F 3/2. Wh 100%. Adv deg: 66%. **Tui '03-'04:** Day $3675-5900 (+$75). Aid: Need 17 ($32,845). **Est 1972.** Nonprofit. Sem (Sept-June). NVS was established to provide a personally tailored education for elementary students. The curriculum is designed around core subjects, and special emphasis is placed on the arts and environmental studies.

THE INTERNATIONAL SCHOOL   Day Coed Gr PS-5
Portland, OR 97201. 025 SW Sherman St.
Tel: 503-226-2496. Fax: 503-525-0142.
www.intlschool.org   E-mail: bbayliss@intlschool.org

Bruce Bayliss, Head. BA, Pepperdine Univ, MA, Michigan State Univ. Jan Williams, Adm.

Gen Acad. Bilingual. Feat—Chin Japan Span. **Adm:** 68/yr. Appl due: May. **Enr 293.** B 123. G 170. Elem 293. Wh 56%. Hisp 10%. Blk 7%. Am Ind 1%. Asian 22%. Other 4%. Avg class size: 12. **Fac 40.** M 3. F 33/4. Hisp 25%. Blk 1%. Asian 58%. Other 16%. Adv deg: 7%. **Grad '04—11. Tui '04-'05:** Day $8680 (+$300). Aid: Need 76 ($237,325). **Summer:** Acad Enrich. Tui Day $425/2-wk ses. 8 wks. **Est 1990.** Nonprofit. Tri (Sept-June). This unusual elementary school offers an American-style curriculum taught by means of total-immersion language programs in Spanish, Japanese and Chinese, making it one of the few schools in the US that offers bilingual tracks in more than one language. Children may enroll in both the preschool and kindergarten classes with no prior knowledge of the target language, while a limited number of nonfluent first graders may gain admission; students entering TIS after grade 1 must display proficiency in the language of immersion. Children are encouraged to remain at the school through grade 5.

JESUIT HIGH SCHOOL
Day Coed Gr 9-12

Portland, OR 97225. 9000 SW Beaverton Hillsdale Hwy.
Tel: 503-292-2663. Fax: 503-291-5464.
www.jesuitportland.com   E-mail: spoppe@jesuitportland.com
   Richard M. Gedrose, Pres. MEd, Lewis and Clark College. Sandra L. Satterberg, Prin. Shirley L. Poppe, Adm.

   Col Prep. AP—Eng Fr Span Calc Bio Chem Physics US_Hist. **Feat**—Japan Stats Astron Comp_Sci Comp_Relig Studio_Art Theater Chorus. **Supp**—Rem_Math Rev Tut. **Adm:** 300/yr. Accepted: 50%. **Tests** HSPT SSAT. **Enr 1130.** B 597. G 533. Sec 1130. Wh 85%. Hisp 3%. Blk 2%. Asian 5%. Other 5%. Avg class size: 17. **Fac 95.** M 43/7. F 35/10. Wh 92%. Hisp 3%. Blk 1%. Am Ind 1%. Asian 3%. **Grad '04—271.** Col—271. Avg SAT: 1173. Alum 4150. **Tui '04-'05:** Day $7485 (+$500). Aid: Need 178 ($700,000). **Summer:** Acad Enrich Rev. Tui Day $70/crse. 5 wks. **Est 1956.** Nonprofit. Roman Catholic. Sem (Sept-June). **Assoc** NAAS. Jesuit features accelerated classes and community service. Japanese is among the foreign languages offered.

ST. MARY'S ACADEMY
Day Girls Gr 9-12

Portland, OR 97201. 1615 SW 5th Ave.
Tel: 503-228-8306. Fax: 503-223-0995.
www.stmaryspdx.org   E-mail: admissions@stmaryspdx.org
   Christina Friedhoff, Pres. BA, Lewis and Clark College. Patricia Barr, Prin. MAT, Lewis and Clark College. Meaghen Igloria, Adm.

   Col Prep. AP—Calc US_Hist US_Govt & Pol. **Feat**—Creative_Writing Fr Ger Span Computers Ceramics Drawing Film Graphic_Arts Photog Studio_Art Theater_Arts Chorus Music_Theory. **Supp**—Dev_Read Makeup Tut. **Adm:** 169/yr. Appl due: Jan. Accepted: 95%. **Tests** HSPT. **Enr 565.** G 565. Sec 565. Avg class size: 22. **Fac 43.** M 6/3. F 23/11. Wh 95%. Hisp 3%. Asian 2%. Adv deg: 76%. **Grad '04—99.** Col—94. Alum 8100. **Tui '04-'05:** Day $7400 (+$100). Aid: Merit 10 ($5000). Need 190 ($435,000). **Est 1859.** Nonprofit. Roman Catholic. Sem (Sept-June). **Assoc** NAAS. Spiritual retreats, service projects, interest clubs, newspaper, dramatic productions and a fine arts studio complement the curriculum at St. Mary's. Athletic offerings include skiing, golf, soccer, swimming, track, cross-country, tennis, softball, volleyball, basketball, dragon boat racing and lacrosse.

BLANCHET CATHOLIC SCHOOL
Day Coed Gr 7-12

Salem, OR 97301. 4373 Market St NE.
Tel: 503-391-2639. Fax: 503-399-1259.
www.blanchetcatholicschool.com   E-mail: info@blanchetcatholicschool.com
   Charles E. Lee, Pres. Robert G. Weber, Prin.

   Col Prep. AP—US_Hist. **Feat**—Fr Span Anat & Physiol Psych Sociol Bus_Law Ceramics Filmmaking Fine_Arts Photog Studio_Art Drama Band Orchestra Accounting Journ Public_Speak. **Adm:** 90/yr. Appl due: May. Accepted: 95%. **Enr 318.** B 168. G 150. Elem 125. Sec 193. Wh 82%. Hisp 10%. Asian 7%. Other 1%. Avg class size: 13. **Fac 27.** M 9/1. F 10/7. Wh 96%. Hisp 4%. Adv deg: 70%. **Grad '04—40.** Col—39. Avg SAT: 1240. Avg ACT: 25. **Tui '04-'05:** Day $4500-5100. Aid: Need 100 ($179,575). **Est 1995.** Nonprofit. Roman Catholic. Sem (Sept-June).

Blanchet's curriculum includes religion and foreign language requirements, as well as elective options in computers, art and drama. Seventh graders take six weeks of music classes, study skills and keyboarding courses in their first semester. Athletics, interest clubs and community service opportunities supplement academics.

WESTERN MENNONITE SCHOOL   **Bdg Coed Gr 9-12**
Salem, OR 97304. 9045 Wallace Rd NW.   **Day Coed 6-12**
Tel: 503-363-2000. Fax: 503-370-9455.
www.westernmennoniteschool.org
E-mail: pschultz@westernmennoniteschool.org
    Darrel White, Exec Dir. Darrel Camp, Prin. Paul Schultz, Adm.

Col Prep. Gen Acad. Feat—Span Comp_Sci Bible Fine_Arts Music. **Supp**— ESL Tut. **Adm:** 63/yr. Bdg 13. Day 50. Appl due: Aug. Accepted: 90%. Yield: 99%. **Tests** TOEFL. **Enr 199.** B 13/88. G 20/78. Wh 82%. Hisp 7%. Blk 4%. Asian 6%. Other 1%. Avg class size: 20. **Fac 24.** M 8/3. F 8/5. Wh 96%. Other 4%. Adv deg: 50%. **Grad '04—36.** Col—26. Alum 1100. **Tui '04-'05:** Bdg $9960 (+$550). 5-Day Bdg $8770 (+$550). Day $5795 (+$550). Aid: Merit 7 ($3180). Need 83 ($152,000). **Summer:** Gr 1-12. Sports. Tui Day $15-70. 1 wk. **Est 1945.** Nonprofit. Mennonite. Sem (Aug-June). Advanced courses at WMS are conducted in math, science, computers and foreign language. All students attend chapel services and participate in group community service projects. Drama, music and sports are among the daily extracurricular offerings. The school schedules occasional academic field trips, and travel opportunities are available through the choir program and during the weeklong mini-term.

DELPHIAN SCHOOL   **Bdg Coed Gr 3-12**
Sheridan, OR 97378. 20950 SW Rock Creek Rd.   **Day Coed K-12**
Tel: 503-843-3521. Fax: 503-843-4158.
www.delphian.org   E-mail: info@delphian.org
    Rosemary Didear, Head. Donetta Phelps, Adm.

Col Prep. Gen Acad. AP—Eng Econ. **Feat**—Fr Span Computers Ethics World_Relig Study_Skills. **Supp**—ESL Makeup. **Adm:** 60/yr. Appl due: Rolling. **Enr 244.** Wh 85%. Hisp 4%. Asian 10%. Other 1%. Avg class size: 18. **Fac 56.** M 19/3. F 27/7. In Dorms 15. **Grad '04**—25. Col—24. Alum 210. **Tui '02-'03:** Bdg $24,550-26,100 (+$1650). Day $8200-14,225 (+$1100). **Summer:** Acad Enrich Rev Rec. 4 wks. **Est 1973.** Nonprofit. Tri (Sept-June). Delphi emphasizes high academic standards and integrity. The school uses study methods developed by L. Ron Hubbard. Individualized programs of study, coupled with the drilling of math basics and a high quantity of reading, lead rapidly to the ability to do independent research. Facilities are available for advanced work in all subject areas.

WASHINGTON

COLUMBIA ADVENTIST ACADEMY Day Coed Gr 9-12
Battleground, WA 98604. 11100 NE 189th St.
Tel: 360-687-3161. Fax: 360-687-9856.
www.caasda.org   E-mail: hendde@caasda.org
Berit von Pohle, Prin. EdS, Loma Linda Univ.

Col Prep. Gen Acad. AP—Eng. **Feat**—Span Computers Govt Relig Studio_Art Music Accounting. **Supp**—Tut. **Adm:** 30/yr. Accepted: 100%. Yield: 99%. **Enr 95.** B 45. G 50. Sec 95. Wh 98%. Hisp 2%. Avg class size: 23. **Fac 14.** M 8. F 5/1. Wh 100%. **Grad '04**—**31.** Col—30. Alum 2400. **Tui '04-'05:** Day $6950 (+$350-500). **Est 1903.** Nonprofit. Seventh-Day Adventist. Sem (Aug-June). To meet varying learning needs, CAA offers three diplomas: a general high school diploma program; a vocational program that operates in conjunction with Clark County Skills Center; and a college prep diploma that carries additional math, science and foreign language requirements. Thrice-weekly chapel services, monthly community service activities, semiannual prayer weeks, mission trips, and Bible study and prayer groups are important elements of school life.

THE LITTLE SCHOOL Day Coed Gr PS-6
Bellevue, WA 98004. 2812 116th Ave NE.
Tel: 425-827-8708. Fax: 425-827-3814.
www.thelittleschool.org   E-mail: info@thelittleschool.org
Paul Brahce, Head. BA, Western Washington Univ.

Gen Acad. Feat—Span Drama Outdoor_Ed. **Adm:** 36/yr. Appl due: Feb. **Enr 145.** B 68. G 77. Elem 145. Wh 77%. Hisp 6%. Blk 2%. Am Ind 1%. Asian 14%. Avg class size: 12. **Fac 15.** M 3/1. F 7/4. Wh 88%. Hisp 6%. Blk 6%. Adv deg: 33%. **Grad '04**—**12.** Alum 275. **Tui '04-'05:** Day $11,993 (+$200). Aid: Need 19 ($116,027). **Summer:** Enrich Rec. 4 wks. **Est 1959.** Nonprofit. (Sept-June). **Assoc** NAAS. The school's developmentally based curriculum, which includes Spanish, world cultures and creative movement, features a variety of hands-on learning experiences in art, music and science. Children learn in small, multi-age classes. Field trips supplement academic work.

ST. THOMAS SCHOOL Day Coed Gr PS-6
Medina, WA 98039. PO Box 124.
Tel: 425-454-5880. Fax: 425-454-1921.
www.stthomasschool.org   E-mail: admissions@stthomasschool.org
Joan Beauregard, Head. BA, Annhurst College, MAT, Federal City College. Christy Haven, Adm.

Pre-Prep. Gen Acad. Feat—Lat Span Sculpt Studio_Art. **Supp**—Tut. **Adm:** 30/yr. Appl due: Mar. Accepted: 10%. **Enr 184.** B 92. G 92. Elem 184. Wh 88%. Hisp 2%. Blk 5%. Asian 5%. Avg class size: 18. Uniform. **Fac 19.** M 1/1. F 10/7. Adv deg: 47%. **Grad '04**—**15.** Prep—12. Alum 900. **Tui '04-'05:** Day $11,025 (+$100). **Est 1951.** Nonprofit. Quar (Sept-June). **Assoc** NAAS. St. Thomas provides a solid foundation in basic skills of literacy and computation. The curriculum includes daily chapel, social sciences, technology, music, art, Spanish, Latin and language arts.

THE BEAR CREEK SCHOOL   **Day Coed Gr K-12**
Redmond, WA 98053. 8905 208th Ave NE.
Tel: 425-898-1720. Fax: 425-898-1430.
www.tbcs.org   E-mail: info@tbcs.org
    Nancy Price, Head. BS, Southwest Baptist Univ, MA, California State Univ-Northridge. Christie Hazeltine, Adm.

    Col Prep. AP—Eng US_Hist US_Govt & Pol. **Feat**—Fr Japan Lat Span Bible Logic. **Supp**—ESL. **Adm:** 115/yr. Appl due: Rolling. Accepted: 78%. **Tests** ISEE Stanford TOEFL. **Enr 610.** B 310. G 300. Elem 450. Sec 160. Wh 86%. Hisp 1%. Blk 2%. Am Ind 1%. Asian 10%. Avg class size: 16. Uniform. **Fac 76.** M 14. F 45/17. Adv deg: 39%. **Grad '04—23.** Col—23. Alum 47. **Tui '04-'05:** Day $10,355-11,590 (+$1050-1250). Aid: Merit 7 ($16,500). Need 57 ($283,442). **Est 1988.** Nonprofit. Nondenom Christian. Quar (Aug-June). **Assoc** NAAS. TBCS offers a Christian liberal arts program in which lower school students (grades K-6) focus on skill development in reading, writing, math and science, while middle and upper schoolers (grades 7-12) prepare for college by building a solid foundation in the core courses of math, science, English and social studies. All boys and girls take Latin in grades 7 and 8, and high school pupils have elective language options in French, Spanish and Japanese.

BERTSCHI SCHOOL   **Day Coed Gr PS-5**
Seattle, WA 98102. 2227 10th Ave E.
Tel: 206-324-5476. Fax: 206-329-4806.
www.bertschi.org   E-mail: tracyn@bertschi.org
    Brigitte Bertschi, Dir. Tracy Nordhoff, Adm.

    Gen Acad. Feat—Lib_Skills Span Computers Studio_Art Music. **Supp**—LD Tut. **Adm:** 43/yr. Appl due: Feb. Accepted: 30%. **Enr 218.** B 105. G 113. Hisp 218. Wh 79%. Hisp 4%. Blk 6%. Am Ind 2%. Asian 9%. Avg class size: 17. **Fac 24.** Wh 97%. Hisp 1%. Blk 1%. Asian 1%. Adv deg: 50%. **Grad '04—34. Tui '04-'05:** Day $12,750 (+$535). Aid: Need ($270,000). **Summer:** Enrich. Tui Day $150/wk. 6 wks. **Est 1975.** Nonprofit. (Sept-June). The school's integrated curriculum stretches across disciplines and grade levels, allowing children to make connections while learning. Students remain with the grade-level teacher for language arts, math and social studies; specialists provide instruction in art, music, science, library, computers, Spanish and physical education. Various class activities, field trips and community service opportunities complement academics.

EPIPHANY SCHOOL   **Day Coed Gr PS-5**
Seattle, WA 98122. 3710 E Howell St.
Tel: 206-323-9011. Fax: 206-324-2127.
www.epiphanyschool.org   E-mail: annes@epiphanyschool.org
    George O. Edwards, Head. Anne R. Sarewitz, Adm.

    Pre-Prep. Feat—Fr Lat. **Supp**—Dev_Read Rem_Math Rem_Read Rev Tut.

Adm: 48/yr. Appl due: Feb. Accepted: 69%. **Enr 133.** B 59. G 74. Elem 133. Wh 81%. Blk 7%. Am Ind 1%. Asian 11%. Avg class size: 16. Uniform. **Fac 15.** M 1. F 7/7. Wh 95%. Asian 5%. Adv deg: 60%. **Grad '04—19.** Prep—17. Alum 450. **Tui '04-'05:** Day $12,000. Aid: Need 13 ($101,200). **Est 1958.** Nonprofit. Tri (Sept-June). **Assoc** NAAS. Epiphany is a traditional, structured elementary school with emphasis on the fundamental skills of reading, writing and arithmetic. Class size ranges from 12 to 18.

HOLY NAMES ACADEMY   **Day Girls Gr 9-12**
Seattle, WA 98112. 728 21st Ave E.
Tel: 206-323-4272. Fax: 206-323-5254.
www.holynames-sea.org   E-mail: admissions@holynames-sea.org
    Elizabeth A. Swift, Prin. BA, MA, Univ of Washington. Michelle Basilio, Adm.

    Col Prep. AP—Fr Span Calc Comp_Sci Bio Physics Eur_Hist US_Hist Art_Hist Music_Theory. **Feat**—Theol Fine_Arts. **Adm:** 174/yr. Appl due: Jan. Accepted: 50%. **Tests** MAT. **Enr 610.** G 610. Sec 610. Wh 66%. Hisp 5%. Blk 11%. Am Ind 1%. Asian 16%. Other 1%. Avg class size: 22. **Fac 44.** M 12. F 28/4. Wh 77%. Hisp 2%. Blk 12%. Asian 9%. Adv deg: 72%. **Grad '04—134.** Col—133. Alum 8100. **Tui '05-'06:** Day $9252 (+$450). Aid: Merit 10 ($15,000). Need 187 ($451,150). Work prgm 94 ($80,200). **Est 1880.** Nonprofit. Roman Catholic. Sem (Aug-June). **Assoc** NAAS. Holy Names offers a college prep curriculum that includes an Advanced Placement program. Choice in sports and cocurricular activities is extensive.

JOHN F. KENNEDY MEMORIAL HIGH SCHOOL   **Day Coed Gr 9-12**
Seattle, WA 98168. 140 S 140th St.
Tel: 206-246-0500. Fax: 206-242-0831.
www.kennedyhs.org   E-mail: info@kennedyhs.org
    Michael L. Prato, Prin. BA, MA, Central Washington Univ. Michael S. Willis, Adm.

    Col Prep. AP—Eng Lat Stats US_Hist. **Feat**—Creative_Writing Fr Ger Span Comp_Sci Econ Govt Pol_Sci Psych Relig Art_Hist Studio_Art Drama Music Accounting Bus Journ Speech Design Drafting. **Supp**—Dev_Read ESL LD Makeup Tut. **Adm:** 288/yr. Appl due: Rolling. Accepted: 75%. Yield: 80%. **Tests** HSPT TOEFL. **Enr 866.** B 442. G 424. Sec 866. Wh 63%. Hisp 5%. Blk 4%. Asian 19%. Other 9%. Avg class size: 22. **Fac 65.** M 30/7. F 23/5. Wh 94%. Blk 5%. Asian 1%. Adv deg: 52%. **Grad '04—227.** Col—215. Alum 7600. **Tui '04-'05:** Day $6985 (+$250). Catholic $6380 (+$250). Aid: Merit 10 ($5000). Need 130 ($300,000). Work prgm 10 ($10,000). **Summer:** Acad Rem. Tui Day $350/crse. 6 wks. **Est 1966.** Nonprofit. Roman Catholic. Sem (Aug-June). **Assoc** NAAS. JFK offers a curriculum that covers a wide range of academic levels and learning styles. Two honors programs, operating in conjunction with the University of Washington and Mateo Ricci College at Seattle University, offer juniors and seniors the opportunity to earn college credits while still in high school. Another program specializes in serving the pupils with learning disabilities and those who may be academically at risk. The campus ministry sponsors several retreats and liturgies, along with daily Mass.

SEATTLE COUNTRY DAY SCHOOL
Day Coed Gr K-8
Seattle, WA 98109. 2619 4th Ave N.
Tel: 206-284-6220. Fax: 206-283-4251.
www.seattlecountryday.org E-mail: info@seattlecountryday.org
Michael G. Murphy, Head. Catherine G. Woods, Adm.

Pre-Prep. Feat—Span Computers Studio_Art Music. **Supp**—Tut. **Adm:** 52/yr. Appl due: Jan. Accepted: 40%. **Tests** IQ ISEE. **Enr 303.** B 159. G 144. Elem 303. Wh 80%. Hisp 1%. Blk 1%. Asian 15%. Other 3%. Avg class size: 16. **Fac 33.** M 4/2. F 23/4. Adv deg: 66%. **Grad '04**—17. Alum 75. **Tui '04-'05:** Day $13,905-15,512 (+$300). Aid: Need 22 ($145,000). **Est 1964.** Nonprofit. Sem (Sept-June). **Assoc** NAAS. This school for highly capable children incorporates foreign language, computers and science as part of its curriculum from kindergarten. The sports program includes skiing, cross-country, basketball, soccer, baseball, ultimate Frisbee, climbing, and track and field.

SEATTLE WALDORF SCHOOL
Day Coed Gr K-8
Seattle, WA 98125. 2728 NE 100th St.
Tel: 206-524-5320. Fax: 206-523-3920.
www.seattlewaldorf.org E-mail: friends@seattlewaldorf.org
Martha Collins, Admin. Meg Petty, Adm.

Pre-Prep. Feat—Japan Span Drawing Painting Music Woodworking. **Supp**—Dev_Read LD Rem_Read Rev Tut. **Adm:** 33/yr. Appl due: Jan. **Enr 240.** B 117. G 123. Elem 240. Wh 88%. Hisp 2%. Blk 4%. Asian 6%. Avg class size: 22. **Fac 24.** M 4/2. F 10/8. Adv deg: 29%. **Grad '04**—25. Prep—6. Alum 245. **Tui '03-'04:** Day $8800 (+$500). Aid: Need 50 ($214,000). **Summer:** Rec. Tui Day $160/wk. 10 wks. **Est 1980.** Nonprofit. (Sept-June). Seattle Waldorf's curriculum, which integrates the arts, includes foreign languages, music, handwork, community service and physical education. A limited special-needs program is available.

THE EVERGREEN SCHOOL
Day Coed Gr PS-8
Shoreline, WA 98133. 15201 Meridian Ave N.
Tel: 206-364-2650. Fax: 206-365-1827.
www.evergreenschool.org E-mail: admission@evergreenschool.org
Margaret Wagner, Head. BA, Univ of Cape Town (South Africa), MEd, Univ of New Orleans. Lisa Kleintjes Kamemoto, Adm.

Pre-Prep. Feat—Fr Ger Mandarin Span Environ_Sci Computers Drawing Photog Sculpt Studio_Art Drama Music Dance. **Supp**—Tut. **Adm:** 74/yr. Appl due: Jan. Accepted: 45%. **Tests** IQ ISEE. **Enr 347.** B 174. G 173. Elem 347. Wh 81%. Hisp 1%. Blk 1%. Asian 17%. Avg class size: 16. **Fac 40.** M 7. F 33. Wh 95%. Am Ind 5%. Adv deg: 52%. **Grad '04**—29. Alum 1700. **Tui '04-'05:** Day $14,025-14,320. Aid: Need 33 ($200,000). **Summer:** Enrich Rec. Art. Music. Tui Day $175/wk. 2-10 wks. **Est 1963.** Nonprofit. Sem (Sept-June). **Assoc** NAAS. Evergreen tailors its program to the needs of children with advanced and creative learning potential. The academically focused basic skills program features individual and small-group instruction, thereby allowing children to progress at their own rates. French, Spanish, German, Mandarin, art, music and computer classes begin in the primary grades, while fine arts electives start in grade 6. The school's global education program, which is integrated into the entire curriculum, culminates in a three-week trip abroad for eighth graders.

GONZAGA PREPARATORY SCHOOL   **Day Coed Gr 9-12**
Spokane, WA 99207. 1224 E Euclid Ave.
Tel: 509-483-8511. Fax: 509-483-3124.
www.gprep.com   E-mail: office@gprep.com
    Al Falkner, Pres. BE, MAT, MEd, Whitworth College. Kevin Booth, Prin. Taryn M. League, Adm.

    Col Prep. AP—Eng Fr Span Calc Stats Eur_Hist US_Hist. **Feat**—Lat Relig Theol Visual_Arts Drama Music Home_Ec. **Supp**—Makeup Tut. **Enr 900.** Sec 900. Wh 88%. Hisp 2%. Blk 2%. Am Ind 2%. Asian 6%. **Fac 63. Grad '04—226.** Col—217. Alum 5000. **Tui '04-'05:** Day $7400. **Summer:** Acad Enrich Rev Rem. Tui Day $250/crse. 6 wks. **Est 1887.** Nonprofit. Roman Catholic. Sem (Aug-June). **Assoc** NAAS. An extensive curriculum provides courses in standard, college prep and honors programs, as well as limited remedial offerings. Juniors and seniors may enroll at Gonzaga University or the Spokane Area Vocational Skills Center.

TERM PROGRAMS

This section describes secondary-level academic term programs (usually operating on a semester system) that combine credit-bearing course work with experiential learning. Programs may have an environmental focus and typically employ the local environs as a significant teaching tool. Curricula are designed to promote academic continuity between the student's home school and the term program.

MAINE

MAINE COAST SEMESTER
Bdg — Coed Gr 11

Wiscasset, ME 04578. 485 Chewonki Neck Rd. Tel: 207-882-7323. Fax: 207-882-4074.
www.chewonki.org   E-mail: wmorgan@chewonki.org
Willard Morgan, Dir. BA, Williams College, MS, Univ of Vermont. **Paul H. Arthur, Adm.**
 AP—Fr Span Calc. **Feat**—Environ_Sci Studio_Art.
 Accepted: 40%.
 Enr 72. B 25. G 47. Sec 72. Wh 89%. Hisp 2%. Blk 2%. Am Ind 2%. Asian 5%. Avg class size: 9. **Fac 17.** M 8/1. F 7/1. Wh 100%. Adv deg: 41%. In dorms 15.
 Alum 1083.
 Tui '04-'05: Bdg $16,500/sem (+$450). **Aid:** Need 19 ($120,420).
 Endow $300,000. Bldgs 10. Dorms 5. Class rms 7. Lib 20,000 vols. Sci labs 1. Art studios 1. Fields 3. Courts 2.
 Est 1988. Nonprofit. Spons: The Chewonki Foundation. Sem (Aug-May).

This semester-long program is open to high school juniors. Natural science and English form the core curriculum. In addition, students choose three optional courses from the following: environmental issues, art and the natural world, American history, mathematics, French and Spanish. AP classes are offered in several disciplines, and honors courses are also available. Students and faculty participate together in an afternoon work program to maintain the buildings and grounds, and, at some point during the semester, every student completes early morning farm chores.

VERMONT

THE MOUNTAIN SCHOOL
Bdg — Coed Gr 11

Vershire, VT 05079. 151 Mountain School Rd. Tel: 802-685-4520. Fax: 802-685-3317.
www.mountainschool.org   E-mail: info@mountainschool.org
Alden Smith, Dir. BA, Davidson College, MA, Middlebury College. **Deborah Voehl Barnes, Adm.**
 Feat—Humanities Fr Lat Span Environ_Sci Studio_Art.
 Accepted: 45%.
 Enr 45. B 17. G 28. Sec 45. Avg class size: 10. **Fac 17.** In dorms 9.
 Tui '04-'05: Bdg $16,360/sem (+$450).
 Bldgs 11. Dorms 5. Dorm rms 21. Class rms 6. Libs 1. Comp labs 1. Art studios 1.
 Est 1983. Sem (Aug-June).

Enrolling 45 high-achieving juniors from private and public schools throughout the US, the Mountain School of Milton Academy combines college preparatory academics with life on a working organic farm in Vermont. The integrated curriculum, which makes use of small class sizes and the mountain campus, emphasizes individual and communal responsibility, simplicity and sustainability. Students live with teachers in small houses and participate in decision making that pertains to communal life and farm management. Although formal Advanced Placement courses are not part of the curriculum, certain classes prepare boys and girls for the AP exam.

NEW YORK

CITYterm
Bdg — Coed Gr 11-12

Dobbs Ferry, NY 10522. c/o The Masters School, 49 Clinton Ave. Tel: 914-479-6502. Fax: 914-693-6905.
www.cityterm.org E-mail: cityterm@themastersschool.com
Jo Ann Clark, Dir. BA, Bates College, MFA, Columbia Univ.
 AP—Fr Span Calc. **Feat**—Humanities NYC_Lit NYC_Hist.
 Accepted: 45%. Yield: 85%.
 Enr 30. B 12. G 18. Sec 30. **Fac 9.** M 2/1. F 4/2. Wh 85%. Blk 15%. Adv deg: 55%. In dorms 6.
 Alum 500.
 Tui '04-'05: Bdg $16,800/sem (+$1050).
 Dorm rms 16. Class rms 3. Auds 1. Theaters 1. Gyms 1. Fields 1. Courts 1.
 Est 1996. Nonprofit. Spons: The Masters School. Sem (Aug-May).

This unusual, experiential semester program exposes able juniors and seniors to an intensive study of New York City. Students spend three days of each six-day academic week in the classroom on the campus of The Masters School, and the remaining three days in the city engaged in fieldwork. CITYterm's integrated, interdisciplinary curriculum encourages boys and girls to connect classroom learning with their city experiences. Core courses explore the history, literature and urban environment of New York City. To support ongoing academic work at the student's home school, courses in other subject areas (some at the honors or Advanced Placement level) are also available.

NORTH CAROLINA

THE OUTDOOR ACADEMY
Bdg — Coed Gr 10-11

Pisgah Forest, NC 28768. 43 Hart Rd. Tel: 828-877-4349. Fax: 828-884-2788.
www.enf.org/toa.htm E-mail: oaadmissions@enf.org
Mark Braun, Head. BA, MA, Wesleyan Univ. **Sandy McGlashan, Adm.**
 Feat—Fr Span Appalachian_Hist Visual_Arts Theater.
 Enr 27. B 13. G 14. Sec 27. Wh 85%. Blk 5%. Asian 5%. Other 5%. **Fac 9.** M 3. F 3/3. Wh 100%. Adv deg: 33%.
 Tui '04-'05: Bdg $15,300/sem (+$500). **Aid:** Need ($40,000).

Bldgs 10. Dorms 4. Class rms 5. Libs 1. Art studios 2. Music studios 1. Dance studios 1. Fields 1. Courts 2.
Est 1995. Nonprofit. Spons: Eagle's Nest Foundation. Sem (Aug-May).

This semester-long program serves primarily sophomores, although select juniors also enroll. The academy combines a college preparatory curriculum with environmental education, regional studies, arts programming and outdoor leadership training. Making use of its location in the Blue Ridge Mountains, the school holds class both indoors and in the forest; the outdoor education program teaches hiking, backpacking, caving, canoeing and rock climbing skills.

COLORADO

ROCKY MOUNTAIN SEMESTER
Bdg — Coed Gr 11-12

Leadville, CO 80461. c/o High Mountain Institute, PO Box 970. Tel: 719-486-8200. Fax: 719-486-8201.
www.hminet.org   E-mail: molly@hminet.org
Molly P. Barnes, Head. BA, Colgate Univ.
  AP—US_Hist. **Feat**—Fr Span.
  Accepted: 70%. Yield: 85%.
  Enr 34. B 15. G 19. Sec 34. Wh 85%. Hisp 5%. Blk 5%. Asian 5%. Avg class size: 8. **Fac 11.** M 6. F 5. Wh 100%. Adv deg: 18%.
  Tui '05-'06: Bdg $16,700/sem (+$2000). **Aid:** Merit 1 ($15,475).
  Plant val $2,000,000. Bldgs 8. Dorms 5. Class rms 4. Lib 500 vols. Sci labs 1. Comp labs 1. Fields 1. Climbing walls 1.
  Est 1998. Nonprofit. Spons: High Mountain Institute. Sem (Aug-May).

This semester-long program for juniors and seniors focuses on experiential education, both in the classroom and in the wilderness. Students take five or six courses, one of which pertains to ethics in the natural world. Instructors assist pupils in making connections between what they learn in class and what they learn in the wilderness. Each semester, boys and girls embark on three two-week expeditions, with backpacking in the mountains and canyons, a community service trip and a winter trek during the spring semester being some of the options.

CALIFORNIA

THE WOOLMAN SEMESTER
Bdg — Coed Gr 11-PG

Nevada City, CA 95959. 13075 Woolman Ln. Tel: 530-273-3183. Fax: 530-273-9028.
  www.woolman.org   E-mail: info@woolman.org
Amy Cooke, Head. BA. Kathy Runyan, Adm.
  Feat—Fr Span Environ_Sci Peace_Stud Ethics. **Supp**—Tut.
  Accepted: 85%. Yield: 85%.
  Enr 12. B 4. G 8. Sec 10. PG 2. **Fac 3.** M /1. F 2. Wh 100%. Adv deg: 66%.

Tui '04-'05: Bdg $7000-18,500/sem.
Est 2003. Religious Society of Friends. Spons: College Park Friends Educational Association. Sem (Aug-May).

Conducted on a 230-acre campus in the foothills of the Sierra Nevada Mountains, Woolman Semester is an intense, 16-week academic program for 16- to 18-year-olds that focuses on peace, social justice and sustainability. Students spend the morning attending classes, then devote the afternoon to hands-on work in the garden and orchard, the kitchen and the forest. All boys and girls take the following inquiry-driven core courses: world issues, peace studies, humanities and ethics, and environmental science; French, Spanish and math classes are also available. Tuition is determined along a sliding scale.

**PRIVATE
SCHOOLS
ILLUSTRATED**

In Private Schools Illustrated, more than 200 programs—many with free editorial listings earlier in the Handbook—*sponsor paid Announcements, composed by the schools and summer programs themselves and often illustrated with photographs of facilities and activities.*

Within each section, programs are listed alphabetically by name.

Parents and advisors should begin searches for traditional US private schools by perusing the 1584 geographically arranged editorial listings located in previous sections of the Handbook. *Listings of sponsoring schools include appended Announcement cross-references.*

Examining the following illustrated pages helps the reader learn more not only about traditional programs, but also about schools for special-needs children, summer programs and schools abroad.

Contact the sponsors directly for more information or literature.

TABLE OF CONTENTS

INDEX TO SCHOOL ANNOUNCEMENTS 1103

INDEXES TO SUMMER PROGRAMS 1109

A more complete compilation of 1500 residential camps and schools is available in Porter Sargent's *Guide to Summer Camps and Summer Schools*. See page 1471.

INDEX TO SCHOOLS FOR EXCEPTIONAL CHILDREN 1110

INDEX TO SCHOOLS ABROAD 1111

COEDUCATIONAL SCHOOLS 1114

GIRLS' SCHOOLS 1289

BOYS' SCHOOLS 1325

THE UNDERACHIEVER 1353

SCHOOLS FOR EXCEPTIONAL CHILDREN 1381

Sponsors in this special section have editorial listings in Porter Sargent's *Directory for Exceptional Children*, but not in *The Handbook of Private Schools*. The *Directory* is a more complete compilation of 2500 schools, facilities and organizations serving children and young adults with developmental, emotional, physical and medical special needs. See page 1471.

SCHOOLS ABROAD 1387

Sponsors in this special section have editorial listings in Porter Sargent's *Schools Abroad of Interest to Americans*, but not in *The Handbook of Private Schools*. *Schools Abroad* is a more complete compilation of 650 primary and secondary schools in 125 countries. See page 1471.

SUMMER PROGRAMS 1399

Sponsors in this special section have editorial listings in Porter Sargent's *Guide to Summer Camps and Summer Schools*, but not in *The Handbook of Private Schools*. The *Guide* is a more complete compilation of 1500 residential camps and summer schools. See page 1471.

INDEX TO SCHOOL ANNOUNCEMENTS

ASHLEY HALL, Charleston, SC	1289
BEEKMAN SCHOOL, New York, NY	1114-5
BELMONT DAY SCHOOL, Belmont, MA	1116
BEMENT SCHOOL, Deerfield, MA	1117
BERKELEY CARROLL SCHOOL, Brooklyn, NY	1120
BERKSHIRE SCHOOL, Sheffield, MA	1118-9
BLAIR ACADEMY, Blairstown, NJ	1121
BRANDON HALL SCHOOL, Atlanta, GA	1353
BRECK SCHOOL, Minneapolis, MN	1124
BRENAU ACADEMY, Gainesville, GA	1290-1
BREWSTER ACADEMY, Wolfeboro, NH	1122-3
BRIMMER AND MAY SCHOOL, Chestnut Hill, MA	1125
BROOKFIELD ACADEMY, Brookfield, WI	1126
CAMPBELL HALL SCHOOL, North Hollywood, CA	1127
CANTERBURY SCHOOL, Fort Myers, FL	1129
CANTERBURY SCHOOL, New Milford, CT	1128
CARSON LONG MILITARY INSTITUTE, New Bloomfield, PA	1325
CFS: THE SCHOOL AT CHURCH FARM, Paoli, PA	1326-7
CHADWICK SCHOOL, Palos Verdes Peninsula, CA	1130
CHARLOTTE COUNTRY DAY SCHOOL, Charlotte, NC	1131
CHASE COLLEGIATE SCHOOL, Waterbury, CT	1132
CHOATE ROSEMARY HALL, Wallingford, CT	1134-5
CHRIST SCHOOL, Arden, NC	1328
CHRISTCHURCH SCHOOL, Christchurch, VA	1329
CISTERCIAN PREPARATORY SCHOOL, Irving, TX	1330
COLUMBUS SCHOOL FOR GIRLS, Columbus, OH	1296
COMMUNITY SCHOOL, Teaneck, NJ	1354
CONVENT OF THE SACRED HEART, Greenwich, CT	1292-3
CRANBROOK SCHOOLS, Bloomfield Hills, MI	1136-7
DANA HALL SCHOOL, Wellesley, MA	1294-5
DARLINGTON SCHOOL, Rome, GA	1138-9
DARROW SCHOOL, New Lebanon, NY	1140-1
THE DERRYFIELD SCHOOL, Manchester, NH	1133
DETROIT COUNTRY DAY SCHOOL, Beverly Hills, MI	1142-3
DEVEREUX FOUNDATION, Villanova, PA	1355

Index to School Announcements

DEXTER SCHOOL, Brookline, MA	1331
DUBLIN SCHOOL, Dublin, NH	1144-5
EAGLE HILL SCHOOL, Hardwick, MA	1358-9
EAGLE HILL SCHOOL, Greenwich, CT	1356-7
EAGLE HILL-SOUTHPORT, Southport, CT	1353
EAGLEBROOK SCHOOL, Deerfield, MA	1332-3
ELGIN ACADEMY, Elgin, IL	1133
EMMA WILLARD SCHOOL, Troy, NY	1297
EPISCOPAL HIGH SCHOOL, Bellaire, TX	1146
EPISCOPAL HIGH SCHOOL, Alexandria, VA	1147
ETHEL WALKER SCHOOL, Simsbury, CT	1298
FAR BROOK SCHOOL, Short Hills, NJ	1148-9
FISHBURNE MILITARY SCHOOL, Waynesboro, VA	1334
FLINT HILL SCHOOL, Oakton, VA	1154
FLORIDA AIR ACADEMY, Melbourne, FL	1150-1
FORDHAM PREPARATORY SCHOOL, Bronx, NY	1335
FORK UNION MILITARY ACADEMY, Fork Union, VA	1340
FOXCROFT SCHOOL, Middleburg, VA	1299
FRYEBURG ACADEMY, Fryeburg, ME	1152-3
GARRISON FOREST SCHOOL, Owings Mills, MD	1300
GIRLS PREPARATORY SCHOOL, Chattanooga, TN	1301
THE GLENHOLME SCHOOL, Washington, CT	1362
GOVERNOR DUMMER ACADEMY, Byfield, MA	1155
THE GOW SCHOOL, South Wales, NY	1360-1
GREENWICH ACADEMY, Greenwich, CT	1296
GRIER SCHOOL, Tyrone, PA	1302-3
GROSSE POINTE ACADEMY, Grosse Pointe Farms, MI	1156
GROVE SCHOOL, Madison, CT	1157
GULLIVER SCHOOLS, Pinecrest, FL	1158-9
HACKLEY SCHOOL, Tarrytown, NY	1160-1
HAMPSHIRE COUNTRY SCHOOL, Rindge, NH	1363
HARGRAVE MILITARY ACADEMY, Chatham, VA	1162
THE HARVEY SCHOOL, Katonah, NY	1163
HEBRON ACADEMY, Hebron, ME	1164
THE HILL SCHOOL, Pottstown, PA	1165
HILLSDALE ACADEMY, Hillsdale, MI	1166
HILLWOOD ACADEMIC DAY SCHOOL, San Francisco, CA	1167
HOBGOOD ACADEMY, Hobgood, NC	1172
THE HOTCHKISS SCHOOL, Lakeville, CT	1168-9

Index to School Announcements

HOWE MILITARY SCHOOL, Howe, IN	1170-1
THE HUDSON SCHOOL, Hoboken, NJ	1173
THE HUN SCHOOL OF PRINCETON, Princeton, NJ	1174-5
HYDE SCHOOL AT BATH, Bath, ME	1176-7
HYDE SCHOOL AT WOODSTOCK, Woodstock, CT	1176-7
THE INDEPENDENT DAY SCHOOL, Middlefield, CT	1166
THE JOHN COOPER SCHOOL, The Woodlands, TX	1184
KENT SCHOOL, Kent, CT	1178-9
KENTS HILL SCHOOL, Kents Hill, ME	1180-1
THE KILDONAN SCHOOL, Amenia, NY	1364-5
KIMBALL UNION ACADEMY, Meriden, NH	1185
KING & LOW-HEYWOOD THOMAS SCHOOL, Stamford, CT	1182-3
KISKI SCHOOL, Saltsburg, PA	1336-7
KNOX SCHOOL, St James, NY	1188
THE LAMPLIGHTER SCHOOL, Dallas, TX	1186-7
LANDMARK SCHOOL, Prides Crossing, MA	1366-7
LANDON SCHOOL, Bethesda, MD	1328
THE LANGLEY SCHOOL, McLean, VA	1189
LAWRENCE ACADEMY, Groton, MA	1190
LAWRENCEVILLE SCHOOL, Lawrenceville, NJ	1191
LEXINGTON CHRISTIAN ACADEMY, Lexington, MA	1194
LINDEN HALL SCHOOL FOR GIRLS, Lititz, PA	1304
LINDEN HILL SCHOOL, Northfield, MA	1368
LOOMIS CHAFFEE SCHOOL, Windsor, CT	1192-3
THE LOVETT SCHOOL, Atlanta, GA	1195
LYCEE FRANCAIS DE NEW YORK, New York, NY	1196-7
THE MacDUFFIE SCHOOL, Springfield, MA	1198
MAINE CENTRAL INSTITUTE, Pittsfield, ME	1199
MARIANAPOLIS PREPARATORY SCHOOL, Thompson, CT	1202
THE MARVELWOOD SCHOOL, Kent, CT	1200-1
MARY INSTITUTE AND SAINT LOUIS COUNTRY DAY SCHOOL, St Louis, MO	1203
THE MASTERS SCHOOL, Dobbs Ferry, NY	1204-5
McCALLIE SCHOOL, Chattanooga, TN	1338-9
McLEAN SCHOOL OF MARYLAND, Potomac, MD	1206
MENLO SCHOOL, Atherton, CA	1207
MERCERSBURG ACADEMY, Mercersburg, PA	1208
MISS HALL'S SCHOOL, Pittsfield, MA	1305

MISSOURI MILITARY ACADEMY, Mexico, MO 1341
MORAVIAN ACADEMY, Bethlehem, PA... 1209
MORRISTOWN-BEARD SCHOOL, Morristown, NJ 1214
MOSES BROWN SCHOOL, Providence, RI 1210-1
NAZARETH ACADEMY HIGH SCHOOL,
    Philadelphia, PA 1306
NEW HAMPTON SCHOOL, New Hampton, NH......................... 1212-3
NEW YORK MILITARY ACADEMY,
    Cornwall-on-Hudson, NY 1215
NOBLE AND GREENOUGH SCHOOL, Dedham, MA 1216
NORTH COUNTRY SCHOOL, Lake Placid, NY 1217
NORTHWOOD SCHOOL, Lake Placid, NY 1220
NOTRE DAME ACADEMY, Worcester, MA.................................... 1307
OAK HILL ACADEMY, Mouth of Wilson, VA 1218-9
OAKWOOD FRIENDS SCHOOL, Poughkeepsie, NY 1221
OLDFIELDS SCHOOL, Glencoe, MD 1308-9
THE ORCHARD SCHOOL, Indianapolis, IN 1222
OXFORD ACADEMY, Westbrook, CT 1369
PACE ACADEMY, Atlanta, GA 1223
THE PEGASUS SCHOOL, Huntington Beach, CA 1207
THE PENNINGTON SCHOOL, Pennington, NJ 1224
PERKIOMEN SCHOOL, Pennsburg, PA.. 1225
PORTSMOUTH ABBEY SCHOOL, Portsmouth, RI 1226-8
PRINCETON DAY SCHOOL, Princeton, NJ 1230-1
PROFESSIONAL CHILDREN'S SCHOOL,
    New York, NY... 1229
PROVIDENCE DAY SCHOOL, Charlotte, NC................................. 1232
PROVO CANYON SCHOOL, Orem, UT 1370
PURNELL SCHOOL, Pottersville, NJ 1310-1
RABUN GAP-NACOOCHEE SCHOOL, Rabun Gap, GA............... 1233
RANNEY SCHOOL, Tinton Falls, NJ 1234
RECTORY SCHOOL, Pomfret, CT 1342-3
RIVER OAKS BAPTIST SCHOOL, Houston, TX............................ 1235
THE RIVERS SCHOOL, Weston, MA 1236
RIVERSIDE PRESBYTERIAN DAY SCHOOL,
    Jacksonville, FL 1235
RIVERVIEW SCHOOL, East Sandwich, MA................................... 1371
ROBERT LOUIS STEVENSON SCHOOL,
    New York, NY.. 1372-3
THE ROEPER SCHOOL, Bloomfield Hills, MI 1237

Index to School Announcements

ROSEMONT SCHOOL OF THE HOLY CHILD, Rosemont, PA	1237
RUMSEY HALL SCHOOL, Washington Depot, CT	1238
ST. ANDREW'S SCHOOL, Barrington, RI	1240-1
ST. ANDREW'S SCHOOL, Middletown, DE	1239
SAINT ANDREW'S SCHOOL, Boca Raton, FL	1242
ST. ANNE'S-BELFIELD SCHOOL, Charlottesville, VA	1243
ST. CATHERINE'S SCHOOL, Richmond, VA	1316
SAINT EDWARD'S SCHOOL, Vero Beach, FL	1244
SAINT JAMES SCHOOL, St James, MD	1245
ST. JOHN'S PREPARATORY SCHOOL, Danvers, MA	1344
ST. JOSEPH HIGH SCHOOL, Metuchen, NJ	1345
ST. MARGARET'S SCHOOL, Tappahannock, VA	1312-3
ST. PAUL'S SCHOOL, Concord, NH	1246-7
ST. PETER'S SCHOOL, Philadelphia, PA	1244
SAINT STEPHEN'S EPISCOPAL SCHOOL, Bradenton, FL	1251
ST. THOMAS CHOIR SCHOOL, New York, NY	1346
SAINT THOMAS MORE SCHOOL, Oakdale, CT	1374-6
SALEM ACADEMY, Winston-Salem, NC	1314-5
SALISBURY SCHOOL, Salisbury, MD	1248-9
SAN FRANCISCO DAY SCHOOL, San Francisco, CA	1251
THE SAN FRANCISCO SCHOOL, San Francisco, CA	1252
SANDY SPRING FRIENDS SCHOOL, Sandy Spring, MD	1253
SCHOOL OF THE HOLY CHILD, Rye, NY	1317
THE SHIPLEY SCHOOL, Bryn Mawr, PA	1256
SOUTH KENT SCHOOL, South Kent, CT	1347
SOUTHFIELD SCHOOL, Brookline, MA	1318
SOUTHWESTERN ACADEMY, San Marino, CA	1254-5
SOUTHWESTERN ACADEMY, Rimrock, AZ	1254-5
THE STEWARD SCHOOL, Richmond, VA	1252
STONELEIGH-BURNHAM SCHOOL, Greenfield, MA	1319
STUART COUNTRY DAY SCHOOL OF THE SACRED HEART, Princeton, NJ	1320
SUFFIELD ACADEMY, Suffield, CT	1257
TAFT SCHOOL, Watertown, CT	1260
THAYER ACADEMY, Braintree, MA	1258-9
THOMAS JEFFERSON SCHOOL, St Louis, MO	1261
TILTON SCHOOL, Tilton, NH	1268

TRINITY-PAWLING SCHOOL, Pawling, NY 1348
VERMONT ACADEMY, Saxtons River, VT..................................1262-3
VIEWPOINT SCHOOL, Calabasas, CA..1264-5
THE VILLAGE SCHOOL, Houston, TX..1266-7
VIRGINIA EPISCOPAL SCHOOL, Lynchburg, VA 1269
WEBB SCHOOL, Bell Buckle, TN...1272
WESTERN RESERVE ACADEMY, Hudson, OH 1273
WESTMINSTER SCHOOL, Simsbury, CT.....................................1270-1
THE WESTMINSTER SCHOOLS, Atlanta, GA...............................1278
WESTOVER SCHOOL, Middlebury, CT..1321
WHITE MOUNTAIN SCHOOL, Bethlehem, NH 1274-5
THE WILLIAMS SCHOOL, New London, CT..................................1279
WILLISTON NORTHAMPTON SCHOOL,
  Easthampton, MA 1276-7
WILLOW HILL SCHOOL, Sudbury, MA 1377
WINDSOR SCHOOL, Flushing, NY 1282
WINDWARD SCHOOL, White Plains, NY.......................................1368
WOODBERRY FOREST SCHOOL, Woodberry Forest, VA 1349
WOODHALL SCHOOL, Bethlehem, CT 1378
WOODWARD ACADEMY, College Park, GA 1283
WOOSTER SCHOOL, Danbury, CT 1280-1
WORCESTER ACADEMY, Worcester, MA......................................1284
YORK PREPARATORY SCHOOL, New York, NY..........................1285

INDEX TO SUMMER PROGRAMS WITH EDITORIAL LISTINGS IN *THE HANDBOOK OF PRIVATE SCHOOLS*

DARLINGTON SCHOOL, Rome, GA	1139
EAGLE HILL SCHOOL, Hardwick, MA	1359
FLORIDA AIR ACADEMY, Melbourne, FL	1151
GRIER SCHOOL, Tyrone, PA	1303
HOWE MILITARY SCHOOL, Howe, IN	1171
LANDMARK SCHOOL, Prides Crossing, MA	1367
THE MARVELWOOD SCHOOL, Kent, CT	1201
NEW HAMPTON SCHOOL, New Hampton, NH	1213
OAK HILL ACADEMY, Mouth of Wilson, VA	1219
PORTSMOUTH ABBEY SCHOOL, Portsmouth, RI	1228
SAINT THOMAS MORE SCHOOL, Oakdale, CT	1376

INDEX TO SUMMER PROGRAMS WITH EDITORIAL LISTINGS IN THE *GUIDE TO SUMMER CAMPS AND SUMMER SCHOOLS*

SALISBURY SUMMER SCHOOL, Salisbury, CT 1399

INDEX TO SUMMER PROGRAMS WITH EDITORIAL LISTINGS IN *SCHOOLS ABROAD OF INTEREST TO AMERICANS*

THE TASIS SUMMER PROGRAMS IN EUROPE 1396

INDEX TO SCHOOLS FOR EXCEPTIONAL CHILDREN

PARK CENTURY SCHOOL, Los Angeles, CA 1381
THE PATHWAY SCHOOL, Norristown, PA 1384
STEWART HOME SCHOOL, Frankfort, KY 1382-3

INDEX TO SCHOOLS ABROAD PROGRAMS

AIGLON COLLEGE, 1885 Chesieres-Villars,
  Switzerland 1387
AMERICAN SCHOOL OF WARSAW, Konstancin-Jeziorna,
  Poland 1388
BANGKOK PATANA SCHOOL, Bangkok 10260,
  Thailand 1389
CARIBBEAN PREPARATORY SCHOOL, San Juan,
  Puerto Rico 1390-1
ST. MARY'S INTERNATIONAL SCHOOL, Tokyo 158-8668,
  Japan 1392
ST. STEPHEN'S SCHOOL, 00153 Rome,
  Italy 1393
TASIS: THE AMERICAN SCHOOL
  IN ENGLAND, Thorpe, Surrey TW20 8TE,
  England, ... 1394
TASIS: THE AMERICAN SCHOOL
  IN SWITZERLAND, Montagnola-Lugano
  Switzerland 1395
THE TASIS SUMMER PROGRAMS IN EUROPE 1396

COEDUCATIONAL SCHOOLS

Private Schools Illustrated — 1114

THE BEEKMAN SCHOOL

220 E. 50th St.
NEW YORK, NY 10022

Tel: 212-755-6666
Fax: 212-888-6085
Web: www.beekmanschool.org

The Beekman School, formerly The Tutoring School of New York, was organized in 1925 to provide a college preparatory school curriculum with the additional advantage of offering highly individualized instruction given in an intimate and caring environment. The Beekman School is known for its long-standing tradition of maintaining a uniquely strong student-teacher-parent relationship.

Students who attend The Beekman School come from a wide variety of backgrounds; therefore, teaching is geared specifically to the needs of the individual student. Classes are limited to no more than ten students; an average class contains eight students per teacher. When necessary, one or all courses may be taken in our Tutoring School. The Tutoring School limits its class size to no more than three students and offers all courses ranging from AP through remedial. In all classes, the fullest possible attention is given to developing the strengths and overcoming the difficulties of each student.

The benefits of highly individualized student instruction apply to average students, to gifted students who wish to accelerate, and to underachievers who need to be motivated and learn more effective study habits.

Teachers are appointed to the faculty on the basis of academic achievement and strong experience. Fully equipped laboratories are maintained for Chemistry, Physics, and Biology. A full range of computer courses is offered, as are other elective courses such as Modern Politics, Psychology, Film Criticism, Philosophy, and Creative Writing. The school also accepts elective credits granted by other educational institutions in New

Coeducational Schools — 1115

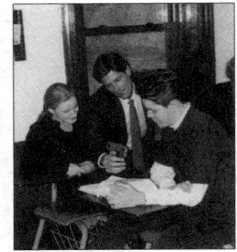

York such as the Art Students League, International Center of Photography, and Turtle Bay Music School.

The Beekman School, like the majority of private day schools, provides 38 weeks of instruction which is divided into two terms: September to January and January to June. Students who have left their schools due to illness or other causes may enter The Beekman School until mid-April and thus can continue their academic work without further loss of time. Students are also required to take part in a formal program of sports or exercise. They may elect to participate in our school program or enroll in any type of private exercise program.

In addition to our regular academic schedule, additional instruction in most subjects is provided during our six-week summer session. Our summer school consists of four ninety-minute classes; students can take advantage of this time to repeat or advance in their course work.

The Beekman School's dedicated faculty and its traditional college preparatory program have helped to matriculate students who attend both competitive and non-competitive colleges and universities. A list of the colleges where Beekman students have attended include: Smith College, New York University, American University, Barnard College, Columbia University, Boston University, Fordham, Emerson, Bard, Oberlin College, and Sarah Lawrence College. All students are given individualized college guidance.

The Beekman School is registered by the Board of Regents of The State Education Department of New York.

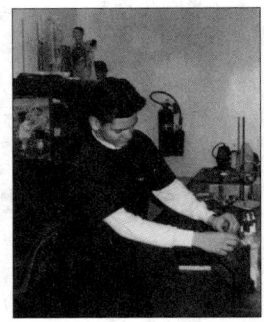

BELMONT DAY SCHOOL
55 Day School Ln.
BELMONT, MA 02478

Tel: 617-484-3078   Fax: 617-489-1942
Web: www.belmontday.org

Located fifteen minutes from Boston, Belmont Day School offers a challenging and creative academic program for students from pre-kindergarten through eighth grade. From its beginning, the school has balanced traditional skills instruction with experiential projects, integrating the arts in all aspects of the educational program. A challenging athletics program emphasizes teamwork and the development of self-confidence. Two fully equipped media labs offer students the latest in technology tools. The school is committed to developing strong working relationships with parents in the education of students and offers many opportunities for collaboration. The joy of learning is celebrated throughout the community culminating in Friday sharing assemblies. After school, extended day, summer session and vacation session programs are offered. Financial aid is available to qualified applicants. Tuition: $14,080 to $22,780. Lenesa Leana (Oberlin College, A.B.: University of Missouri, M.A.) is Head of School; Deborah Brissenden is Director of Admissions.

BEMENT SCHOOL
DEERFIELD, MA 01342

Nestled in the colonial village of Old Deerfield, the Bement School offers unique opportunities for boarding and day students in grades kindergarten through nine. For more than seventy years, the school has provided its students with an outstanding education and preparation for leading secondary schools. At the core of this education is the dedication to upholding an individual's worth in a community and to providing chances to demonstrate one's talents often.

Bement believes that a challenging, supportive environment produces exceptional progress. To accomplish this, the school maintains a low faculty-student ratio, holds the class size average to twelve students and strives to create a structured, family-like atmosphere in the dormitories. The result is a community of dedicated, caring adults and eager youngsters living and learning together.

Through its curricula and approach, Bement seeks to provide a well-rounded experience for its students. Athletics, art, music and drama are a daily part of a curriculum which stresses a solid foundation in basic skills. Classes in grades 7 through 9 are grouped heterogeneously and homogeneously depending upon subject. Disciplines include English, mathematics, science, social studies and foreign languages. Study skills are incorporated into the program and supervised study halls with extra help available are scheduled daily. ESL is also available. Students in grades 7-9 and their advisors participate for one term in an intergenerational community service program.

The social experience of a boarding student is as important as his or her academic one. Bement strives to provide a structured lifestyle centered around small, family-like dormitories. Evening and weekend activities are carefully planned and supervised and include a wide range of cultural, recreational and educational offerings.

Bement enrolls students of average to superior potential as boarding students in grades 3 through 9 and as day students in grades K through 9. The community represents many states and foreign countries and students leave Bement ready and eager for the challenges ahead.

Private Schools Illustrated — 1118

BERKSHIRE SCHOOL
SHEFFIELD, MA

Berkshire School aims to provide students with the tools and skills needed to develop into mature, productive adults capable of achieving their best in college, in careers, and in all aspects of life. The academic and extracurricular programs are designed to guide and motivate each student intellectually, morally, and physically and are complimented by the School's Leadership and Character Development Program.

The academic program at Berkshire in many respects defines the School itself: it is formal, structured, and demanding. The program of studies centers on the five principal scholastic disciplines—English, mathematics, ancient and modern languages (including Mandarin Chinese), the sciences, and history—and also includes extensive course offerings in philosophy, religions, computer science, and the visual and performing arts. The Ritt Kellogg Mountain Program provides understanding of natural surroundings through curricular and extracurricular activities. All departments provide for accelerated sections and many students take one or more of the 19 Advanced Placement courses offered. College counseling at Berkshire is the responsibility of two full-time and two part-time professionals who assist students and their parents in the search for an appropriate college or university.

The small size of the Berkshire community permits faculty members to take a personal interest in each student and to become involved in their lives outside, as well as inside the classroom. Each student is paired with an advisor who provides guidance, monitors academic progress, and serves as a liaison with the family. Faculty members take their roles seriously, knowing that the examples they set will influence the attitudes and values of the students among whom they teach and live.

Coeducational Schools — 1119

The focal point of academic life on the campus is Berkshire Hall. It contains all of the classrooms, the science laboratories, computer centers, art gallery and a theater. Music facilities—practice rooms, studios, and rehearsal space—are located in Memorial Hall. Allen Theater seats 400 for all-school meetings, guest speakers and theater productions. There are several darkrooms located in Godman House. The Geier Library is central to intellectual life on the campus. The library contains approximately 40,500 volumes in open stacks, and extensive reference collections in both print and electronic formats, numerous periodicals, and a fine audiovisual collection. At the Dixon Observatory, computer synchronized telescopes make it possible to view and photograph objects in our solar system and beyond.

Berkshire students pursue the arts in the classroom and in extracurricular activities. Performing arts include drama, chorus, dance, jazz and classical ensembles. Visual arts include painting, drawing, sculpture, digital arts, photography and ceramics.

Berkshire enjoys a strong tradition of athletic success. The School provides competition in twenty-seven interscholastic sports. The Ritt Kellogg Mountain Program is a sports option utilizing Berkshire's natural environment. The Athletic Center houses basketball, volleyball, squash courts, a climbing wall, and a weight room. Other facilities include two new synthetic turf fields, a hockey rink (which converts to indoor tennis courts), 12 outdoor tennis courts, an outdoor recreation park, an all-weather track and numerous playing fields.

The goal of student life at Berkshire is responsible participation. Students contribute directly to the life of the school community through involvement in the Student Government, Prefect Program, the School's Community and School Service Program, and dormitory life. Berkshire offers students various clubs and activities including the Student Activities, Astronomy, Investment, and International clubs, as well as a radio station, boat building and yearbook. Participation gives students a positive growth experience supporting the School motto, "Learning—not just for school, but for life."

THE BERKELEY CARROLL SCHOOL

181 Lincoln Pl., BROOKLYN, NY 11217
701 Carroll St., BROOKLYN, NY 11215
712 Carroll St., BROOKLYN, NY 11215
Web: berkeleycarroll.org

Dr. Bongsoon Zubay, *Headmistress*

The Berkeley Carroll School, a nationally recognized school of excellence, is located in the Park Slope section of Brooklyn, one of New York City's national landmark communities. Famous for its restored nineteenth-century brownstones and tree-lined streets and located a short distance from New York City's cultural centers, this unique urban area provides immense cultural diversity. In turn, the school attracts a student body that reflects the various ethnic, social and economic groups found in Park Slope and throughout the city.

The Berkeley Carroll School is an independent, coeducational, college preparatory day school serving children from preschool through the twelfth grade. The school offers its students the opportunity to achieve academic excellence and fosters the growth of strong ethical and moral values, leadership, and social maturity. This is achieved through a rich academic program, a wide range of co-curricular and extracurricular activities, small class sizes, and above all, through the vitality of an experienced and innovative faculty.

Our goal is to expand each student's curiosity and to build upon his or her strengths. A rigorous academic core curriculum integrates learning and challenges students to discipline their thinking and to stretch their imaginations. Analytical reasoning and informed decision-making are developed by teaching that stresses process as well as content.

The admissions procedure is tailored to identify those students who will benefit most from the Berkeley Carroll program and who can make a positive contribution to the school community. Students who are talented, inquisitive, motivated, and academically capable find personal success in our school. Berkeley Carroll enrolls qualified international students in the Upper School, who live with host families. There is also a childcare center.

The School believes in a strong partnership with parents. The faculty works closely with parents and encourages their participation in, and support of, the educational experience of their children.

BLAIR ACADEMY
BLAIRSTOWN, NJ

T. Chandler Hardwick,
 BA, University of North Carolina,
 MA, Middlebury College,
 Headmaster

Blair is a privately endowed coeducational boarding school, located on 315 hilltop acres close to the Appalachian Trail and the Delaware River. Its location combines the quiet rural beauty of farm country with easy access to New York City (66 miles via I-80), Philadelphia and Princeton.

Blair's 434 boys and girls come from a broad variety of economic, religious, ethnic, and international backgrounds. They come to take advantage of the educational environment where they will learn from each other as much as they will learn from Blair's 78 faculty members. Blair prepares young men and women for college by offering an intellectually challenging and vigorous academic curriculum which includes over 100 course offerings, 17 of which are Advanced Placement.

Blair's sports and non-curricular facilities are considerable. They include 7 practice rooms, 4 studios, a golf course, 14 tennis courts, 6 playing fields, quarter-mile cinder track, and a gymnasium complex which houses a six-lane swimming pool, 3 basketball courts, international squash courts, 1/16 mile indoor track, a dance room, a nearby ice hockey rink, and weight-training, wrestling, and other team rooms. Our vigorous outdoor sports program includes rock climbing, mountain biking, whitewater paddling and crew. Non-curricular opportunities include aviation ground school, choral groups, Community Service, Photography Club, drama, drivers education, newspaper, literary magazine and the Society of Skeptics Club.

Blair has completed a significant building campaign as it headed into the next century. The Armstrong-Hipkins Center for the Arts was dedicated in 1997. The renovated Timken Library opened in June 1998 and a new girls' dormitory opened in 1999.

Call or write the Admissions Office for a catalogue or to arrange a visit: Barbara H. Haase, Dean of Admissions. Tel: 908-362-2024.

BREWSTER ACADEMY
WOLFEBORO, NH

Dr. Michael E. Cooper, *Head of School*

Brewster Academy has become known for innovation and performance in secondary education. The Brewster program, based on the School Design Model, combines the best-established practices in teaching, curriculum, and resources and provides students with a highly personalized education within a vigorous college preparatory environment. The program is designed to meet students at their current level of performance and accelerate them in their mastery of skills and knowledge, ensuring that graduates are prepared for the challenges of college and careers.

Since the implementation of the School Design Model, SAT scores have increased 92 points (*The International Journal of Educational Reform, April 2000*), and Brewster's success has been documented in education, technology, and mainstream publications, including *The New York Times* and *USA Today*.

Faculty are prepared and trained at the Brewster Summer Institute, a six-week professional development program designed to assist teachers in accelerating student growth. Each instructor is placed on a seven-member team that teaches and advises students in a single grade. Teams meet three times weekly to discuss each student's progress and performance. Class size averages 11, and the student-teacher ratio is 6:1.

All students and faculty use laptops, and teachers use a powerful suite of software tools to design and teach curriculum and to ensure constant communication among students, parents, and administrators. Through online portfolios, students post their work to be reviewed and evaluated by faculty and shared with parents. Students and parents also have online access to grades, which helps students evaluate their progress.

A study published in *The International Journal of Educational Technology* showed exceptional outcomes in the area of technology skills for Brewster students. Findings for the performance of girls were especially outstanding, exceeding the performance of boys in traditional programs.

How well students are prepared for college may be best expressed by the extent to which they return after their first year. A recent survey shows that Brewster graduates recorded over 95 percent retention from their freshman to sophomore year. The national average is 75 percent. Colleges attended by the class of 2004 include American University, Boston College, Boston University, Davidson College, Emory Univesity, George Washington University, Johns Hopkins University, Middlebury College, Mount Holyoke College, Occidental College, St. Michael's College, University of New Hampshire, and University of Virginia.

In the performing arts, Brewster offers an award-winning chorus, HOWL, which performed at Carnegie Hall in April 2003; a drama group that produces musicals, operas, and plays throughout the year; a chamber orchestra, a chorale, and dance instruction. An art center is home to ceramics, photography, printmaking, drawing, and painting classes. Multimedia and desktop publishing centers feature the latest computers, industry standard software, and video and digital equipment.

Students choose from interscholastic, instructional, and recreational athletic programs. Athletic facilities include a new 50,000 square-foot athletics and wellness center featuring a convertible turf floor, a four-lane, 200-meter indoor track, and a fitness center; seven playing fields; a boathouse for dry land training for the sailing and crew teams; and a climbing wall.

Brewster's 80-acre campus sits on a half-mile of Lake Winnipesaukee's shoreline and is a short drive from the White Mountains. Wolfeboro is 1 3/4 hours from Boston.

For more information, please call or visit our website:
Lynne M. Palmer, Director of Admission

Brewster Academy
80 Academy Drive
Wolfeboro, New Hampshire 03894
Telephone: 603-569-7200
Fax: 603-569-7272
admissions@brewsteracademy.org
www.brewsteracademy.org

Breck School ...

an award-winning school
for boys and girls of all backgrounds.
Episcopal, college preparatory,
preschool through twelfth grade,
all on one beautiful campus.
Breck may be the school for your family.

Financial Aid is available.

For information,
call Mike Weiszel at 763-381-8202.

Breck School

123 Ottawa Avenue North
Minneapolis MN 55422-5189

www.breckschool.org

BRIMMER AND MAY SCHOOL
CHESTNUT HILL, MA

Anne C. Reenstierna, BA, MEd, *Head of School*

Founded in 1880, Brimmer and May is a coeducational day school offering a challenging program of academics, athletics, arts, and extracurricular activities to students in pre-kindergarten through grade 12. Brimmer and May is a member of Brown University's Coalition of Essential Schools, a high-school university partnership devoted to educational reform with a focus on the intellectual development of each student. Located three miles west of Boston, the school takes full advantage of the city's cultural and educational resources to enhance the classroom experience.

The 7:1 student-faculty ratio allows students and teachers to work closely and cooperatively. Upper School students are guided in course selection, goal-setting, and college planning by their faculty advisor and college counselor. In addition to the college preparatory course of study, students are offered electives in art, theatre, music, video production, AP courses, independent study, and student teaching. Juniors are also involved in a year-long community service program. Upper School students may choose to participate in team sports including golf, softball, cross-country, field hockey, basketball, lacrosse, soccer, and tennis, and other extracurricular activities such as student newspaper, yearbook, and student government.

The Middle School curriculum offers students the structure, supervision, and attention needed for acquiring and developing strong academic, study, and life skills essential for success in high school. All Middle School students participate in afternoon team sports.

The early childhood and Lower School program provides students with an integrated curriculum that allows them to understand the relationship between all of the subjects they study. The curriculum fosters independence and helps students become both learners and teachers.

Brimmer and May's goal, today—as in the past—is to provide students with an environment that will stimulate them to love learning, to think deeply and analytically, to value themselves and others, and to utilize their talents for their own satisfaction and the well-being of society.

BROOKFIELD ACADEMY
3460 N. Brookfield Rd.
BROOKFIELD, WI 53045
Tel: 262-783-3200

Brookfield Academy is a college preparatory school for students in Pre-K through Grade 12. The Academy offers a solid and wide range of educational opportunities which are offered in an atmosphere of traditional American values. Students are encouraged to appreciate the institutions and histories of free societies and to practice the skills of responsible, constructive free people.

The academic programs in the Lower School are built upon a phonics approach to reading, emphasis on writing and vocabulary development, reasoning and computation in math, and strong sequences in history and literature. Studies in the Middle School add Latin, French, and Spanish, more emphasis on science, and continued emphasis on grammar and correct use of English. The Upper School offers high-level academic studies, leading to advanced placement courses in English, art, calculus, economics, biology, chemistry, physics, and languages. The particular course selections in the Upper School are tailored to the individual student with the aim to prepare all students for acceptance and success in a competitive college atmosphere.

In addition to their strong academic programs the students participate in a wide range of interscholastic athletic competition including girls' field hockey and softball, boys' football and baseball, and girls' and boys' basketball, cross country, golf, soccer, tennis, and track. Physical education, art, and music are taught in the Lower and Middle Schools as extracurricular supplements to the academic studies. In the Upper School extracurricular activities include Academic Decathlon, Ambassadors Club, Service Club, Drama Club, Forensics Team, Heritage Club, International Travel, Literary Magazine Staff, Math Society, Mock Trial, Science Club, Student Council, and Yearbook Staff.

The school was founded in 1962 as the Academy of Basic Education by a group of families who were concerned that the education of their children should develop reason and a respect for factual knowledge, should revere religious inspiration and guidance, and should retain an understanding of the nature of a free society and a capitalistic economy. Those purposes, and the program in which they are embodied, have been embraced by hundreds of families who have brought their children to the Academy since its founding.

 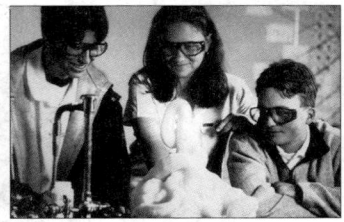

CAMPBELL HALL
4533 Laurel Canyon Blvd.
NORTH HOLLYWOOD, CA 91607

The Rev. Julian P. Bull, *Headmaster*

Campbell Hall, located in a 14-acre park-like setting in North Hollywood, is a coeducational, college preparatory school, Kindergarten through grade 12. Founded in 1944 by the Rev. Alexander K. Campbell as an Episcopal-related day school, Campbell Hall offers a rigorous academic curriculum within the Judeo-Christian tradition. The school is accredited by the California Association of Independent Schools, and by the Western Association of Schools and Colleges.

Computer classes are offered in Kindergarten through High School, and teachers have computers in classrooms for individual enrichment, as well as access to computer labs. A 25,000 square foot gymnasium-performing arts complex is used for varsity and junior varsity competitive sports, theater arts, and video workshops. A second gym is used for regular PE classes.

The library, consisting of more than 20,000 volumes, includes computer access to university and independent school resources across the nation. Every academic department offers Advanced Placement courses for college credit. Many enrichment electives are offered at the High School, including choral and instrumental music, drawing and sculpture, in addition to a full physical education and team sports program.

Campbell Hall students comprise a diversity of religious backgrounds. The ecumenical Chapel program affords an opportunity to reflect on traditional values, which lead to a fulfilling life. A unique advisor program offers personal and academic support to the individual student.

Private Schools Illustrated — 1128

CANTERBURY SCHOOL
NEW MILFORD, CT

Thomas J. Sheehy III, BA, Bowdoin, MA, Penn State, *Head*

Canterbury School was founded in 1915 by Catholic laymen who entrusted Nelson Hume, the first Headmaster, with their educational ideal. That ideal, a college preparatory academic program coupled within a strong framework of Catholic values, remains an integral part of Canterbury's mission.

Since 1990, Canterbury has been under the direction of Headmaster Thomas J. Sheehy III. A challenging academic program is complemented by the support of a dedicated faculty. A chaplain is in residence and 80% of the faculty live on campus. Academics go hand in hand with the development and enhancement of Christian values and morals. The school welcomes all faiths into the student body. The diverse curriculum coincides with extensive opportunities in athletics, drama, art, music, writing and community service and prepares graduates for entrance into leading colleges and universities.

Canterbury School is located in western Connecticut, 85 miles from New York City. The school's modern academic and athletic facilities are housed in a traditional setting on 150 acres above the town of New Milford, with a commanding view of the surrounding countryside.

CANTERBURY SCHOOL
FORT MYERS, FL

Dr. R. Mason Goss, *Headmaster*

Canterbury is the only independent PK-12, coeducational, college preparatory day-school serving rapidly growing Fort Myers.

The school's 9-building, 32-acre campus is located adjacent to Edison Community College. Canterbury has a total enrollment of 660, with approximately 230 students in grades 9-12; 20% of students receive financial aid. An Honor Code administered by the Student Council was adopted in 1990. An Upper School building contains twelve classrooms, three science labs, computer and language labs, as well as an art and music complex. A Performing Arts Center was completed in 1993. A second gymnasium was added in 1999 and a new dining hall opened in 2000.

Canterbury provides an outstanding educational experience within a supportive atmosphere, emphasizing good citizenship and personal responsibility. Special programs include required community service, foreign student exchanges, and an ever-expanding computer curriculum. All graduates continue their education; many enroll in out-of-state colleges and universities.

A member of the National Association of Independent Schools, Canterbury is fully accredited by the Florida Council of Independent Schools and is a member of the National Association of College Admissions, the Southern Association of College Admissions, and the Florida Kindergarten Council.

CHADWICK SCHOOL
26800 S. Academy Dr.
PALOS VERDES PENINSULA, CA 90274
Tel: 310-377-1543
Web: www.chadwickschool.org
Accredited by WASC

Chadwick School, founded in 1935, is a nonprofit, nondenominational, coeducational day school that serves a culturally and economically diverse student body in Grades K-12. Chadwick's mission encourages personal excellence, the mastery of academic, athletic and artistic skills, and the growth of social and individual responsibility. Chadwick School is located on 55 acres atop the beautiful Palos Verdes Peninsula, where approximately one third of the faculty lives on campus.

In the Village School (Grades K-6), class size is 17 to 20 students. The faculty is made up of classroom teachers and specialists in art, music, science, technology, Spanish and physical education.

With an average class size of 17 students, the Middle and Upper Schools offer a rigorous college preparatory core curriculum with courses in English, history, science, mathematics, foreign language, visual and performing arts and technology. A full range of honors and Advanced Placement courses is available in all disciplines, as well as an individualized college counseling program. Outdoor education is an integral part of the curriculum: this course of study culminates in a three-week senior trip just prior to graduation. A variety of choices is available for students in competitive athletics, community service options, special interest clubs and student publications.

For more information, please contact the Office of Admission, (310) 377-1543, ext. 4022, or admissions@chadwickschool.org.

CHARLOTTE COUNTRY DAY SCHOOL

CHARLOTTE, NC

Founded in 1941, Charlotte Country Day School is the oldest and largest independent college preparatory day school in the Charlotte area. Housed on the 60-acre campus are the Lower and Upper Schools. The Middle School campus is located on a 40-acre campus four miles from the main campus.

Charlotte Country Day's academic program is rigorous with emphasis also placed on the arts and athletics. 24 Advanced Placement and 20 Honors courses are offered in the Upper School. Academic competitions are a hallmark of the school's mathematics, science, foreign language, and computer science departments. The school has enjoyed continuous success in these annual events. A strong advisor program, guidance program, and college placement program exist in the Upper School. Highly motivated juniors and seniors may earn an internationally recognized diploma through our International Baccalaureate Diploma program. A wide range of courses and activities are offered in the Middle School, including a study skills program, a writing lab, foreign languages, computers, and a nationally recognized Physical Education program. The Lower School also places great emphasis on the individual student while introducing foreign language, computer education, and science.

Unique among independent schools in the Southeast, Country Day has a Department of International Studies. The program concentrates on Asian studies throughout the curriculum incorporating geography, languages, culture, customs, economics, and history. There are 114 international students representing 39 countries at Country Day. The English as a Second Language program, which includes students from several countries, and Country Day's membership to A Better Chance, a national placement service for academically qualified minority students, greatly add to the diversity of the student body.

Private Schools Illustrated — 1132

CHASE COLLEGIATE SCHOOL
565 Chase Parkway
WATERBURY, CT 06708
Tel: 203-236-9500
Web: www.smmct.org

John D. Fixx, BA, MBA, *Headmaster*

Margy Foulk, *Director of Admission*
Tel: 203.236.9560 / E-mail: mfoulk@smmct.org

Established in 1865, Chase Collegiate, formerly known as St. Margaret's-McTernan, is a coeducational, independent day school offering an enriching college preparatory program for children in grades pre-K through 12. The wooded 47-acre campus is located on the Waterbury/Middlebury line and serves over forty surrounding communities. Transportation is available.

Master teachers offer stimulating instruction in traditional disciplines, with honors and AP courses available in the Upper School. The school seeks to maximize each student's intellectual, creative, physical and social potential within a community that values respect, responsibility and kindness. Challenging academics are supplemented with a strong fine and performing arts program and varsity, JV and Middle School athletics. Student government and numerous clubs provide meaningful leadership opportunities and expand horizons. Private music instruction can be incorporated into the academic day.

THE DERRYFIELD SCHOOL

2108 River Road
MANCHESTER, NH 03104-1396
Tel: 603-669-4524 Fax: 603-641-9521
Web: www.derryfield.org

Randle B. Richardson, *Head of School*

As a coeducational, college-preparatory day school for students in grades 6-12, Derryfield offers advanced curriculum, numerous electives and an emphasis on sound study skills, while enabling students to live at home during their middle and high school years. All students explore talents in required arts and athletics programs. A variety of community service and student leadership opportunities are integral to the program. Beyond Derryfield, graduates are prepared for successful college experiences and purposeful involvement in the global community.

ELGIN ACADEMY

350 Park St.
Elgin, IL 60120
Tel: 847-695-0300

John Cooper, *Head of School*

This is the 163rd year of Elgin Academy, the oldest college preparatory school in the region. The Academy always has been both non-sectarian and coeducational. Admission to the Academy is selective and seeks students from social, economic, and ethnic diversity.

The Academy is 35 miles northwest of Chicago and serves the communities of the greater Fox River Valley. The campus includes seven buildings, with the Lower, Middle, and Upper Schools for grades Preschool through 12.

The educational program gives students sound knowledge in the arts and sciences and the learned skills necessary to acquire and use that knowledge as life-long learners. Students are active in the arts, athletics, and community service. All seniors are college bound and attend schools in all regions of the U.S.

CHOATE ROSEMARY HALL

WALLINGFORD, CT

At Choate Rosemary Hall students from across the nation and around the world pursue a rigorous academic program. Students develop the skills they will need in college and beyond; but at Choate, academic, physical, spiritual, artistic, and personal growth are valued and cultivated every day. Rosemary Hall, founded in 1890, and The Choate School, established in 1896, each created an environment of educational distinction. After the merger in 1974, the combined school built on the strengths of its component parts, stressing its tradition of excellence, its spirit of innovation, and its culture of caring.

Two interwoven priorities define the Choate experience: a rigorous academic curriculum and an emphasis on the formation of character in a residential setting that allows teachers and students to live with, and learn from, one another in important ways.

Choate's curriculum includes core requirements in each of the six departments (arts; English; history, psychology, religion, and social sciences; languages; mathematics; and science). Along with the traditional course offerings there are a rich variety of electives, opportunities for honors and advanced placement work, and directed studies, as well as in-depth programs called Science Research Program and Arts Concentration Program.

In 2003-2004, some 93 percent of students taking AP exams earned 3 or better, which traditionally results in college credit; 74 percent of those students earned 4 or 5. Choate has two economics teams that compete nationally, and both varsity and junior varsity math teams. Its state championship debate team builds public speaking skills. Our arts and athletics programs are recognized nationwide for their high quality.

Motivated and independent science students can participate in authentic laboratory science through the science research program. Students with exceptional talent in the arts may concentrate part of their program on the visual arts, music, or theater. And in the Capstone Program, talented 6th form (senior) students can explore one area of the curriculum in great depth.

A strong tradition of community service harkens back to the early 1900s. From Big Brothers / Big Sisters to Habitat for Humanity and tutoring in local public schools, the opportunities for reaching out are many. The Spears Endowment for Moral and Spiritual Education, a program unique to Choate, includes the office of the chaplain and directs community service programs and school activities that support character and spiritual development.

Choate Rosemary Hall is at the forefront in using the latest technology to enhance the learning process throughout the curriculum. Campus dormitories are networked via fiber optic cable to provide student access to library and Internet resources. The library, the Science Center, and the Language Building are among those that now feature wireless technology. Language instruction is enhanced by a Language Learning Center that includes a state-of-the-art language laboratory. The John Joseph Activities Center includes a cyber cafe.

The school's academic facilities support flexibility and innovation in teaching. The Andrew Mellon Library contains approximately 60,000 titles. A computerized Local Area Network (LAN) supplies bibliographical information for the entire collection. Of special note are two buildings designed by I.M. Pei—the Paul Mellon Arts Center and Carl C. Icahn Center for Science.

The Arts Center houses two theaters, a recital hall, music class, production and practice studios, an art gallery, and dance and art studios. The Science Center includes 22 classrooms and laboratories, a conservatory, and a 135-seat auditorium.

Program abroad opportunities include a term in France, Italy, China, or Spain. Other cross-cultural opportunities include a summer exchange program with the Navajo Nation in Arizona and studies in Japan and China, as well as summer programs in France and Spain.

The school's athletic complex, the Johnson Athletic Center, contains basketball, volleyball, international squash courts, and a wrestling room; additional facilities include an indoor hockey arena, a 25-meter indoor pool, 23 tennis courts, the new Torrence Hunt Tennis Center, 13 athletic fields, a ¼-mile track and a cross country course, and a boathouse for crew. An addition to the Athletic Center was completed in January 2002.

Academic summer programs include the Writing Project, a Young Writers Workshop (co-ed for grades 6-8); the John F. Kennedy Institute of Government, English Language Institute, CONNECT (a mathematics/science institute for girls), a Focus Program for students entering seventh, eighth, and ninth grades, an Arts Conservatory, and Connecticut Scholars Program (a public/private collaboration with the state's 13 urban school districts).

Edward J. Shanahan, formerly dean of the college at Dartmouth College, is Headmaster. Assisting him are dean of students Stephen Farrell, dean of academic affairs Kathleen L. Wallace, and Donald W. Firke, assistant headmaster and dean of faculty. This core of committed individuals, along with the school's 110 faculty, nurtures the growth of the 850 boarding and day students.

Private Schools Illustrated — 1136

CRANBROOK SCHOOLS
BLOOMFIELD HILLS, MI

Arlyce Seibert, *Director of Schools*
Drew Miller, *Director of Admission*

Cranbrook Schools is a college-preparatory, coeducational day and boarding school committed to academic excellence. The school consists of Brookside Lower School (pre-kindergarten-5), Cranbrook Kingswood Middle School (6-8) with separate programs for boys and girls, and Cranbrook Kingswood Upper School (day and boarding, 9-12).

Cranbrook Kingswood Upper School offers students the advantages of both coeducational and single-sex learning environments, activities and traditions. Students have full access to two campuses characterized by unique architectural styles and outstanding facilities. At the same time, male and female boarders enjoy the privacy of dormitory living on separate campuses.

The school is a part of Cranbrook Educational Community, an internationally renowned educational and cultural center occupying 325 acres in Bloomfield Hills, 45 minutes north of Detroit. Founded by the late George G. Booth and his wife, Ellen Scripps Booth, Cranbrook is primarily active in the fields of science, education, and art. The Community includes the Cranbrook Academy of Art and Museum, Cranbrook Institute of Science with its planetarium and observatory, and Cranbrook Schools.

Underlying the creation of these institutions was the founders' conviction that beauty and culture are part of education. Accordingly, Eliel Saarinen was retained as architect and designed the complex. Today several of its buildings are acknowledged architectural masterpieces. In addition, Carl Milles was brought to Cranbrook as artist-in-residence and much of his sculpture, together with many other works of art, enhance the beautiful grounds of the Community.As a result of this broad educational approach, Cranbrook Schools has an unusual and refreshing atmosphere of warmth, cordiality and friendship, which is reflected among the boys and girls themselves. Between faculty and students, there is a strong feeling of working together in a common enterprise. The school offers a wide range of academic courses and, beyond that, extraordinary opportunities in the sciences and visual and performing arts. The multi-faceted Gordon Science Center is highlighted by seven laboratories, solarium, computer center, aquatic center, animal room, library, and classrooms. The six art studios are staffed with artists based at the Academy.

Virtually all graduates go on to college, with the majority of students attending Boston University, Brown, Cornell, Emory, Georgetown, Johns Hopkins, Kenyon, Miami University–Ohio, Michigan State, Northwestern, Princeton, Purdue, University of Chicago, University of Michigan, University of Pennsylvania, Williams, and Yale.

All students participate in a vigorous athletic program. The school's athletic facilities include three gymnasia, twelve large playing fields for football, baseball, soccer, field hockey, lacrosse, fifteen tennis courts, an enclosed artificial hockey rink, a year-round ice arena, a dance studio, a recently re-modeled performing arts center and a new natatorium, an eight lane indoor swimming pool. Intramural and interscholastic competition is held on all age levels.

The men and women teaching at Cranbrook Schools, some from foreign countries, are selected not only for their unusual academic expertise, but also for their interests in young students. Most Upper School faculty members and their families live on campus, and students share the warmth of family relationships. Cranbrook Schools challenges each individual to do his very best, emphasizes pride in real accomplishment and promotes self-confidence. An extensive financial aid program allows for a student body of wide geographical and economic backgrounds, and the school enrolls students without regard to race, religion, color, national origin, age, sex or handicap.

The Journey Begins

First Day of School

Begin the first day of your academic journey racing a canoe or enjoying other friendly competitions with students at Darlington School. This uniquely close community has a tradition of inspiring boys and girls to grow intellectually, spiritually, morally, physically, culturally, and socially. Add Southern hospitality and you have the perfect start for the journey of your life.

Darlington School
Go to School in the South · Explore the World

Rome, Georgia, U.S.A.
www.darlingtonschool.org
1-800-368-4437

Founded in 1905, Darlington School is a Christian-based, coeducational, college preparatory, independent school serving pre-k through grade 12, with boarding for students in grades ninth–twelfth, PG.

Let the Fun begin! Make new friends. Explore challenges. Experience new things at Darlington Summer Camps, a large variety of overnight camps designed for middle school boys and girls. The range of camps may include series like Adventure Darlington (a traditional camp), Rockets and Robotics, Nature, Steel Drum, Golf, Softball, Basketball, Volleyball, Soccer, Tennis, Musical Theater, Football – with so many camps, there's something for everyone. The difficulty is choosing between them.

Darlington
SUMMER CAMPS

Check out Darlington Summer Camps on the picturesque, 500-acre campus of Darlington School, Rome, Ga. Explore Darlington School, a coeducational college preparatory boarding school (ninth–twelfth, PG). Darlington has a proven track record in preparing students well for college and in inspiring them to take full advantage of their God-given gifts to grow intellectually, spiritually, morally, physically, culturally, and socially.

www.darlingtonschool.org • 1-800-36-tiger

Private Schools Illustrated — 1140

Darrow School

110 Darrow Road, New Lebanon, NY 12125
Nancy M. Wolf, *Head of School*

Living, working, learning in the classroom and beyond...

- Co-ed boarding and day school for grades 9-12
- Average class size: 9 students
- Challenging, hands-on, college-preparatory curriculum
- Attentive, involved faculty
- Strong college placement record

Darrow School is located in the Berkshires on the New York-Massachusetts state line. Please call J. Kirk Russell at 518-794-6000 for more information or visit us on-line at www.darrowschool.org.

Darrow School:
More than 70 years of Hands-on Education

Active, applied learning, small class sizes, and attentive teachers have been at the core of Darrow School's educational philosophy for 72 years.

The School's strong hands-on approach to learning creates opportunities for students to become actively engaged in their education process. Involved faculty form strong connections with students, offering support and guidance that extend to one-on-one tutorial sessions, residential life, leadership opportunities, service-learning projects, and athletic activities.

The close-knit community takes pride in its unique "Sense of Place" and location at the site of the historic Mt. Lebanon Shaker Village. The Samson Environmental Center, Darrow's innovative wastewater treatment plant, and the Joline Arts Center, a superbly-equipped, 12,000 sq. ft. facility for the visual arts, have been notable additions to the campus in recent years. Both have further enhanced Darrow's curricular offerings and reinforced the School's comprehensive commitment to environmental sustainability.

Darrow Students are Everywhere

For the past three years, Darrow has opened with a full enrollment of more than 120 students who bring a diversity of nationality, race, ethnicity, and religious traditions from 17 states and seven foreign countries. Filling a niche—to serve a small but select group of bright students who possess high potential—Darrow has transformed many students who were often "lost" in public or larger private schools into motivated, thriving, college-bound learners.

DETROIT COUNTRY DAY SCHOOL
22305 W. Thirteen Mile Rd.
BEVERLY HILLS, MI 48025-4435

Gerald T. Hansen, MA, Rutgers University; BA, Northern Michigan,
Headmaster

Detroit Country Day is located on four campuses within three miles of each other in the Birmingham-Bloomfield area of suburban Detroit. The school is divided into four administrative units, each with its own campus and age-appropriate programs: Lower School (Prekindergarten-Grade 2) on the Maple Road Campus; Junior School (Grades 3-5) on the Village Campus; Middle School (Grades 6-8) on the Hillview Campus; and Upper School (Grades 9-12) on the Thirteen Mile Campus. The Barbara Plamondon Earle Early Learning Village on the Maple Road Campus offers a facility and program designed specifically for three- and four-year-old children.

Since its founding in 1914, the school has remained committed to education of the total person. Students are prepared intellectually, physically, emotionally and morally to meet the challenges in their futures. Beginning in prekindergarten, the program focuses on developing each child's abilities in a supportive environment and at a pace which provides encouragement and nurtures self-esteem. As the student progresses through the school, increased emphasis is placed on course content, preparation outside of class, and the testing of one's achievement through competition in academics, activities and athletics.

Provocative instruction is offered in the basic disciplines of English, mathematics, history, foreign language, science, music, art, and computer science. A computer-based learning program, one of only a few in the nation, requires all Middle and Upper School students to have laptop computers for classwork, homework, tests and research. Some 1200 notebook computers are networked to provide Internet resources and facilitate communication among students, faculty and parents. Advanced Placement and college level courses are emphasized in the Upper

School. Qualified students may enroll in the International Baccalaureate program to become eligible for international university admission or for advanced standing in most American colleges. The comprehensive liberal arts curriculum prepares students for admission to the top colleges and universities in the nation and abroad.Activities in the Upper School are divided into two categories: gold activities (i.e. debate, newspaper, clubs) emphasize skills and self-discovery; white activities (i.e. student tutor, student government, community service) are oriented toward service to others. Participation is required every year and is a graduation requirement. Similar activities are offered at the Middle, Junior and Lower schools.

The fine and performing arts are a vital part of the educational process in all four schools. Art and music classes and musical performing groups are electives in the Upper School and are included in the curriculum at the other levels. Drama and dance also are offered. One Upper School fine arts credit is required for graduation.

Participation in interscholastic athletic competition at the Upper and Middle School levels is required at Detroit Country Day. Physical Education is part of the curriculum at the Lower and Junior School levels. Students in Grades 7-11 must compete in a minimum of two seasons per year and seniors have a one season requirement. Seasonal athletic choices include baseball, basketball, cheerleading, cross country, field hockey, football, golf, ice hockey, lacrosse, skiing, soccer, softball, strength & conditioning, swimming, tennis, track & field, volleyball, wrestling and many others.

The school's highly professional faculty is composed of 181 men and women. They hold 69 bachelor's, 100 master's, and 12 doctoral degrees from 85 colleges and universities. All faculty have academic majors in the subjects they teach and are chosen for their academic credentials, quality of character and belief in the school's mission.

The 2004-2005 enrollment for Prekindergarten through Grade 12 at Detroit Country Day totals 1536. Admission is based on personal interview, testing, and previous academic record. The school enrolls students of average, above-average and gifted abilities from a wide range of socio-economic backgrounds. Students are admitted on a non-discriminatory basis from throughout southeastern Michigan and Canada. A Cottage Boarding Program allows a few students to reside on campus with faculty families.

DUBLIN SCHOOL
DUBLIN, NH
Tel: 603-563-8584

Christopher R. Horgan, *Headmaster*

Dublin School offers students the best of two worlds. We provide a number of opportunities that you might expect to find at a larger school: a rich, varied, academic program; a diverse student body with students from 22 states and 9 foreign countries; and travel through The Network of Complimentary Schools. Dublin supports the individual by limiting our enrollment to 130 students. We assure students both close contact with faculty and a strong sense of community.

Our traditional college preparatory program is enhanced by the building of sound study skills. Classes average 5-12 students, allowing a great deal of personal attention. Advanced placement classes, electives, and independent study are all available. We also offer a tutorial program for students needing additional support. Ninety-seven per cent of our graduates are accepted to their first choice of colleges.

Dublin's athletic program has been enhanced by the newly constructed Whitney Gymnasium, which opened in January, 1999, and emphasizes fitness, teamwork and a commitment to good sportsmanship. All students are required to participate in the program and play two interscholastic sports. The school recognizes that there are different ways of enjoying and experiencing achievements in athletics, and offers a variety of competitive and recreational sports. Interscholastic offerings include soccer, cross-country, alpine skiing, snow boarding, basketball, lacrosse, tennis, sailing, crew, and dance. Recreational offerings include: sailing, recreational games and recreational tennis. Dublin competes in the Lakes

Region Conference. Dublin has two playing fields, two squash courts, six tennis courts, a fitness room, several kilometers of cross-country running and ski trails. In addition, a number of ski areas are within a short drive of campus. The sailing and crew programs are conducted in fall and spring on Dublin Lake.

By performing tasks ranging from daily dorm maintenance to the daily jobs program, each student develops a sense of self-reliance and cooperation. Community service extends beyond the campus borders into the surrounding towns with students engaged in activities from assisting at the local elementary school to visiting with the elderly and working with many local organizations to benefit the community.

Located in the scenic Monadnock Region of southern New Hampshire, Dublin School is a deliberately small boarding/day secondary school that provides its students with a strong academic program, a nurturing and supportive environment and the opportunity to experience the rewards of individual and collaborative achievement.

For more information, please contact the admission office at:

Dublin School
18 Lehmann Way, P.O. Box 522
Dublin, NH 03444
Tel: 603-563-8584
Fax: 603-563-8671
E-mail: admission@dublinschool.org
Web: dublinschool.org

EPISCOPAL HIGH SCHOOL

BELLAIRE, TX

Tel: 713-512-3400 Fax: 713-512-3603
Web: ehshouston.org

Founded in 1982, Episcopal High School of Houston is a four-year coeducational day school within the Episcopal Diocese of Texas. The school community is faith-centered and provides instruction to college-bound students with a wide range of abilities. The strong academic program is complemented by extensive offerings in the arts, religion, and athletics. EHS is located on a 35-acre campus in the suburban residential community of Bellaire, which is surrounded by Houston.

In August 1998, EHS made history and entered the 21st century as a Compaq laptop computer was put in the hands of each student and teacher. Anticipating the direction of many colleges and universities, EHS embraced the Anytime, Anywhere Learning program promoted by the Microsoft Corporation. By equipping all teachers with laptops and piloting a laptop classroom, EHS began to look ahead to the next great innovation. Currently, students peer-edit with e-mail, make presentations with PowerPoint, discover geometry with Sketchpad, conduct laboratory experiments with probes, and analyze data in Excel. Many teachers have built Web pages as homes for their course resources and Internet links. Students all over campus have expanded the walls of the classroom by communicating with teachers and classmates via a wireless network. As a result, they are more engaged with their studies, taking charge of their own learning, and collaborating more often with their peers. And the skills they once practiced mechanically in a computer lab are now mastered for real applications, as they need them. EHS manages this innovation as an educational program, not a technology diversion, and students with financial aid also receive assistance in purchasing their laptops.

To learn more, visit Episcopal High School on the Web at www.ehshouston.org.

Coeducational Schools — 1147

A Tradition of Honor
Since 1839

Episcopal High School is a coeducational college preparatory boarding school for grades 9 to 12. Entrusted with one of the nation's oldest honor codes, Episcopal prepares students to lead lives of leadership and service to others.

- Commitment to academic excellence and personal growth
- Small, interactive classes
- 40 Advanced Placement and honors courses
- Fully integrated technology – all students and faculty use laptops
- 100% residential – fostering close friendships and a strong sense of community
- Weekly educational and cultural trips into Washington, D.C. and a senior internship program

- Diverse student body from over 30 states, the District of Columbia, and 10 countries
- Strong athletics with 44 teams in 15 sports
- Dynamic visual and performing arts program based in a new center featuring state-of-the-art technology
- New Science Center to open in fall 2005

EPISCOPAL HIGH SCHOOL

1200 North Quaker Lane
Alexandria, VA 22302
703-933-4062
Toll-free: 877-933-4347

Director of Admissions
admissions@episcopalhighschool.org
www.episcopalhighschool.org

FAR BROOK SCHOOL
52 Great Hills Rd.
SHORT HILLS, NJ 07078

Mary Wearn Wiener, *Director*   Iris Leonard, *Admissions*

Far Brook is a coeducational, independent day school for children from nursery through the eighth grade that achieves academic excellence by integrating the creative arts with the liberal arts and sciences. At Far Brook, there is the expectation that children are capable of profound attitudes and responses and of meeting rigorous standards of achievement.

The small campus, from the low red school buildings, woods and brook, to the pony paddock and small barn is enhanced by the natural environment. Starting in the 1990-91 school year, students began to benefit from new buildings constructed on campus—a library, middle school building for grades 3, 4, 5, and 6 with computer and science labs and an enlarged junior high space. Completed in 1992, The Laurie Arts Center houses an expanded arts facility, including an art studio, vocal and orchestral rehearsal rooms, and individual lesson studios. In the fall of 2002, an additional computer lab was created with 24 Pentium IV 1.7 ghz computers with DVD. A newly renovated and enlarged Winifred S. Moore Hall houses daily morning meetings of the entire school community, as well as drama and music presentations. It was made possible, along with an increased endowment, by the Campaign for Far Brook, which closed with $4,825,526.36 in gifts and pledges.

Young people learn at Far Brook in a purposeful but unrushed atmosphere. Teachers are eager to engage the intellect and imagination of their students. A Far Brook education combines a demanding program with a genuine interest in the development of the whole child.

A unique feature of Far Brook's curriculum is its interdisciplinary approach to learning based on each classroom's intensive studies of major themes, historical periods or civilizations. Science experiences begin in nursery and culminate in rigorous biological and physical science laboratory courses in the Junior High. Computer studies begin regularly in the third grade, and exposure to French begins as early as kindergarten, with the program becoming more formalized as the grades progress. Seventh and eighth graders take algebra, some at the honors level. In addition to academic courses, students participate in physical education, woodworking, art, music, dance and library studies. Interscholastic sports begin in the fifth grade.

Throughout their experience at Far Brook, children are exposed to and study great drama and literature. In the Middle School and Junior High, all students present annual Class Plays for the School based on their history studies. Such works may include *The Eumenides,* by Aeschylus, "The Death of Caesar," from *The Tragedy of Julius Caesar,* by William Shakespeare or an adaptation of Stephen Crane's *The Bride Comes to Yellow Sky.*

Music is the spiritual fabric that unifies and sustains the School's special character. Children begin each day with song in Morning Meeting and continue learning and singing chorales, anthems and rounds throughout the year.

Students and families revere the long-standing School traditions that include Bach's *Wachet Auf* for the Thanksgiving Processional; the Christmas Masque, based on a medieval mystery play; Pergolesi's *Stabat Mater* in the spring; and a Shakespeare production—either *A Midsummer Night's Dream* or *The Tempest*—at Graduation.

Far Brook is committed to a diverse student body to maintain the intellectual and artistic creativity cherished by each member of the school community. It is an ideal school for (but is not limited to) gifted students because of the stimulating curriculum and enriched environment.

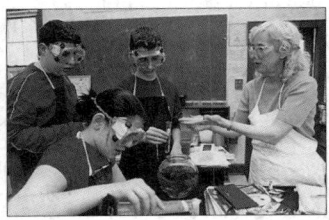

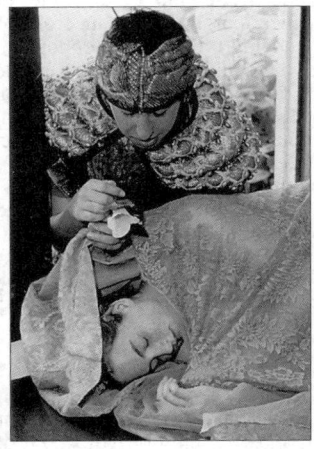

Private Schools Illustrated — 1150

FLORIDA AIR ACADEMY
1950 S. Academy Dr.
MELBOURNE, FL 32901
Tel: 321-723-3211   Fax: 321-676-0422
Web: www.flair.com

Grades 6-12 and Post-graduate

Florida Air Academy is a fully accredited college preparatory school offering the structured environment of a military program. The Academy stresses academic excellence, adherence to the school's Honor Code, leadership by example, development of self-discipline, and the realization and acceptance of the diversity of the world's cultures. The Academy provides the opportunity for each cadet to reach the limits of his potential in the areas of academics, military, and athletics, and overall personal growth. The curriculum is flexible enough to challenge the gifted student with Advanced Placement and Honors classes, yet diverse enough to meet the academic needs of those less gifted college-bound students. The Academy has been designated as an AFJROTC Honor Unit by the U.S. Air Force many times during the school's forty-year history.

As an integral part of the Academy's "development of the whole person" philosophy, cadets are strongly encouraged to participate in such extracurricular activities as interscholastic and intramural athletics, flight training, Boy Scouts, Civil Air Patrol, SCUBA, martial arts, trips to numerous Central Florida tourist attractions, and other such enjoyable and/or character building activities.

Acceptance to one or more colleges or universities is an Academy graduation requirement. A partial list of colleges and universities attended by Academy graduates includes the U.S. Air Force Academy, U.S. Naval Academy, V.M.I., Norwich Univ., the Citadel, Georgia Tech, George Washington Univ., Purdue Univ., B.Y.U., Florida State Univ., Penn State, and the universities of Florida, Michigan, Utah, Miami, and Georgia to name a few.

SUMMER SESSION
FLORIDA AIR ACADEMY
1950 S. Academy Dr.
MELBOURNE, FL 32901
Tel: 321-723-3211 Fax: 321-676-0422
Web: www.flair.com

The Florida Air Academy Summer Session provides an ideal blend of academic instruction with the fun and excitement of social and athletic activities to create a rewarding six-week summer program extending from late June to early August. Students may repeat a course previously failed, preview a new course, earn additional academic credit, or improve fundamental skills through specialized instruction. Study skills, cooperative living, leadership, self-discipline, and sportsmanship are emphasized. Students are required to attend a faculty supervised two-hour study session Sunday through Thursday evenings.

High school course offerings include all levels of English, Algebra I and II, Geometry, World History, U.S. History, SAT Preparation, and Computer Applications. Junior high courses include English, Math, History, and Science. Specialized instruction in Flight Training, SCUBA, Martial Arts, Driver's Education, Remedial Reading, Math Tutoring, and English as a Second Language is also offered. Daylong trips to Disney World, Sea World, Wet and Wild, and Disney's Blizzard Beach are the highlights of the weekend program. Students enjoy intramural and individual sports such as basketball, softball, soccer, flag football, tennis, weightlifting, golf, volleyball, and surfing.

The 30-acre campus has dormitories, classrooms including 3 computer labs, language center, gym with a weightlifting facility, athletic fields, swimming pool, and tennis courts. All buildings are air-conditioned.

The Florida Air Academy Summer Session also serves as a worthwhile orientation for those students who are invited to return for the regular school term.

Private Schools Illustrated — 1152

FRYEBURG ACADEMY
FRYEBURG, ME

Tel: 207-935-2013 or toll-free: 877-935-2013
Fax: 207-935-4292

Web: www.fryeburgacademy.org

Daniel G. Lee, Jr., BA, MA, *Headmaster*

Fryeburg Academy, a coeducational boarding and day school for grades 9-12 and a post-graduate year, is located on 34-acre campus in a traditional New England small town setting at the edge of the white mountains. Founded in 1792, Fryeburg holds a charter signed by Samuel Phillips and John Hancock and lists Daniel Webster among its early headmasters.

Fryeburg offers a comprehensive curriculum that meets the needs of its diverse student population. The college preparatory offerings include accelerated sections and Advanced Placement courses in science, English, calculus, language, and history. Students may elect course offerings from the general program to supplement their college preparatory program of study, and each student's academic program is designed to meet

his or her individual needs. The college counseling program begins at the end of sophomore year, and preparation for standardized testing (PSAT and SAT) is accomplished in the regular curriculum. Computer skills are integrated into the curriculum as well as offered as separate electives. The Special Services program assists students with minor learning disabilities, reading difficulties or study skills deficiencies.

Fryeburg Academy celebrates multi-cultural diversity. The English as a Second Language Department at Fryeburg Academy offers a variety of courses and English language training opportunities for international students. The philosophy of the department emphasizes learning through experience and practice both in and out of the classroom. Students develop their English skills and understanding of American culture by interacting with American students and teachers in the dormitories, on the playing fields and as fully active members of the Fryeburg Academy community.

Interscholastic sports include field hockey, soccer, football, cross-country, golf, tennis, wrestling, basketball, baseball, softball, alpine and Nordic skiing, snowboarding, ice hockey, and track and field. Of course, a great attraction is the wealth of natural resources, as well as close access to culture and entertainment. The White Mountains present students with the potential for endless outdoor adventures including skiing, snowboarding, and hiking. Afternoon and weekend activities provide transportation for these and other opportunities, like shopping in Boston or Portland, or seeing a play in nearby Conway, New Hampshire.

To schedule a visit, contact:

Office of Admission
745 Main Street
Fryeburg, Maine 04037
admissions@fryeburgacademy.org

FLINT HILL SCHOOL
3320 Jermantown Rd.
OAKTON, VA 22124
Tel: 703-584-2300   Fax: 703-584-2369
Web: www.flinthill.org

Flint Hill School, enrolling 1000 students in JK-12, encourages both faculty members and students to experience the joy of learning and growing in a diverse society. Academic excellence is engendered within a value-centered community where respect, responsibility, compassion and honesty are fostered. At the heart of the Flint Hill philosophy is the belief that the community life of the school inspires students to respect individual differences in social, intellectual, racial, and religious backgrounds while enjoying the rich experience of being bound together by service to the shared life of the school. Students who establish deep and lasting friendships through caring for others and who take responsibility for maintaining the high quality of campus life, will experience a truth of lasting value: that the Flint Hill experience is not merely a stepping stone to college, but one that has lifelong meaning and deep satisfaction.

The school consists of two campuses located on 45 acres, housing well-appointed library facilities, a state-of-the-art media center, learning centers, and spacious science and computer labs. Academics are supported by 7 full-time computer technology specialists while all faculty work in fully networked classrooms, integrating multimedia and technology into the curriculum. Athletic facilities include two full-size gymnasiums, 8 tennis courts, a 400-meter track, and athletics fields. Fine Arts facilities include a 300-seat theater and art, dance, and music studios. Headmaster: Mr. John M. Thomas; Director of Admission: Ms. Pat Harden.

GOVERNOR DUMMER ACADEMY

BYFIELD, MA
John M. Doggett, Jr., BA, MA,
Headmaster

As America's first boarding school, Governor Dummer Academy initiated the U.S. preparatory school tradition, and today continues to define excellence in secondary education. Founded in 1763, GDA embodies both 242 years of tradition and an ageless capacity for innovation.

Central to a Governor Dummer education are two abiding precepts: small classes and individual attention for its 370 students. The Academy is dedicated to excellence and modern programs and facilities.

In the past few years, the school has completed the most ambitious building project in the Academy's long history. In September 1997, the Carl A. Pescosolido Library and the Center for the Study of Mathematics and Science opened, thereby adding 50,000 square feet of space on campus devoted to academics. GDA's new performing arts center opened in December, 2001, housing a 500-seat main stage, practice room, a black-box theater, and an electronic music lab.

The Governor Dummer Academy curriculum prepares students for success in college and for continuation of their lifelong learning processes. Rigorous core programs in English, history, languages, mathematics, science and the arts are complemented by accelerated, honors and advanced placement sections and special interest courses ranging from marine science and electronic music composition to economics, computers and African studies.

GDA frames its academic mission within the doctrine that character and conduct are significant aspects of a secondary education. As reflected in the Academy motto, *Non Sibi Sed Aliis* ("Not for self but for others"), GDA maintains a strong emphasis on community service; all students participate in volunteer programs as a precondition for graduation.

Dedicated to the concept that he is head *master* among masters, Mr. Doggett also believes in a head *family* within GDA's community of learners. He and Patty Doggett open the doors of GDA's historic 1713 Mansion House to the entire student body every Saturday evening.

Cultural, sociological and ethnic diversity are essential elements of a GDA education. The current student body represents 15 U.S. states and 11 countries worldwide. The Academy provides over $2 million annually of need-based financial aid.

Consistent with the Academy's philosophy that athletic competition contributes to the formation of character, more than 70 percent of the Governor Dummer student body is involved in varsity and sub-varsity sports during the year.

THE GROSSE POINTE ACADEMY
171 Lake Shore Rd.
GROSSE POINTE FARMS, MI 48236
Tel: 313-886-1221

The Grosse Pointe Academy is a coeducational elementary day school serving children ages 2½ through Grade Eight. The Academy maintains a 112-year educational tradition which emphasizes academic excellence for each child, encourages the development of strong values and provides a genuine sense of community. Situated on a beautiful, historic 22-acre campus overlooking Lake St. Clair, the school draws its students from throughout the southeastern Michigan area.

What distinguishes The Grosse Pointe Academy is its expertise in elementary education. Students receive instruction in a full and diverse curriculum designed to build a foundation for all subsequent education and for life itself. The challenging curriculum includes the basic skills as well as French, Spanish, art, environmental science, music, physical education, religion and numerous elective classes. Small class sizes characterize every grade level and permit instructors to focus on each child's progress. Facilities including classroom computers, a computer lab, library, auditorium, fieldhouse, playing fields and chapel serve the intellectual, physical and spiritual interests of the students.

For children 2½ to five years of age, the Academy's Early School offers Michigan's oldest Montessori program of its kind. This program balances a nurturing environment with individualized lessons designed to stimulate learning in a wide range of topics. For students in Grades 1 through 8, participation in all aspects of Academy life encourages growth, mutual respect and personal achievement. Important leadership roles are fulfilled by the older students whose curriculum contains a community service component.

For further information about The Grosse Pointe Academy, contact Molly McDermott, Director of Admissions. Tel: 313-886-1221, ext. 146. Fax: 313-886-2904.

GROVE SCHOOL
P.O. Box 646
MADISON, CT 06443
Tel: 203-245-2778 Fax: 203-245-6098

Richard L. Chorney, *President and CEO*

A college preparatory country boarding school with therapeutic support for boys and girls 11 to 18 of normal to gifted intelligence who need opportunities to increase their social/ emotional skills at school, at home, or with peers.

The general philosophy of Grove School is based on a supportive, psycho-educational approach delivered through academic programming structures in a holistic milieu. Both therapeutic and academic plans are determined to meet the needs of each student. Each student is met with twice a week in individual therapy. All students are also part of weekly group therapy program. A sailing program and/or land based adventure program in the Caribbean generally take place twice yearly. Grove also uses foreign travel to enhance cultural growth.

Much importance is attached to the relationships students establish with staff members and other students. All issues are discussed and worked through with the adults who are closest to the student.

Fully accredited. Est. in 1934. Year-round rolling admissions.

Gulliver students are offered a wide variety of classes in the visual and performing arts. Activities range from our primary students' weekly music and sing-alongs to the Prep students' conservatory quality courses in music and art. All Gulliver students are admitted to a myriad of colleges and universities in the United States and abroad.

Gulliver's South Miami Campus adds an outstanding gymnastic and ballet program. Lower school students' sports include soccer, cross-country, swimming, and basketball. The Middle School fields twelve teams that participate in interscholastic athletics. Gulliver Preparatory's sports programs have consistently won district, regional, sectional, and state championships. Twenty-eight teams, supported by two cheerleading squads, compete in the Southeast Activities Conference and in the State 3A or 4A playoff program. Gulliver's goal is to develop the talents of each individual in a creative, caring, and safe environment.

Gulliver's emphasis on the development of the entire child has been effective in meeting the needs of thousands of young people.

Gulliver Academy Campus
Primary, Lower & Middle Schools
(Pre-Kindergarten - Grade 8)
12595 Red Rd.
Coral Gables, FL 33156
Tel: 305-665-3593
Fax: 305-669-1569

Gulliver Preparatory School
High School
(Grade 9 - Grade 12)
6575 N. Kendall Dr.
Pinecrest, FL 33156
Tel: 305-666-7937
Fax: 305-665-3791

Gulliver South Miami Campus
(Senior Kindergarten - Grade 4)
8530 S.W. 57th Ave.
South Miami, FL 33143
Tel: 305-669-5497
Fax: 305-663-9349

Gulliver Academy Middle School
Pinecrest Campus
(Grade 5 - Grade 8)
7500 S.W. 120th St.
Pinecrest, FL 33156
Tel: 305-238-3424
Fax: 305-255-0537

Gulliver Preparatory School
Pinecrest Campus
(Grade 9 - Grade 12)
8000 S.W. 56th St.
Miami, FL 33155

E-mail: info@gulliverschools.org
Web: gulliverschools.org

Private Schools Illustrated — 1160

HACKLEY SCHOOL
TARRYTOWN, NY

Walter C. Johnson, *Headmaster*

Hackley School, founded in 1899 by Mrs. Frances Hackley, is a nonsectarian, coeducational, college preparatory school enrolling 808 day students in kindergarten through grade twelve and 30 five-day boarding students in grades nine through twelve. The School enrolls a diverse student body and assigns a significant percentage of its budget to financial assistance. With a 7:1 student-teacher ratio, a highly motivated student body, and a predominantly residential faculty, Hackley is as much a community as a school.

offering security, academic challenge, and a sense of achievement. In every activity, students are encouraged to develop self-discipline, the ability to accept failure without the loss of self-esteem, independence, and a respect for others. The teaching methods are developmentally appropriate; students are given the freedom to make choices and encouraged to take learning risks. At Lamplighter, everyone is a thriving member of the community of learners, whether adult or child.

Lamplighter was at the forefront of pioneering efforts in the field of developing computers for young children in the early 1980s under the guidance of the inventor of the LOGO computer language. Not relegated to a lab setting, computers are housed throughout the school today in all class areas. A highly integrated curriculum merges the fine arts with language arts, math, environmental science, social studies, physical education, and Spanish. The 45 member faculty includes teaching specialists for art, music, drama, Spanish, science, motor skills, academic technology, and a librarian. Pupil progress is reported by direct parent observation through one-way windows and by several parent-teacher conferences yearly.

The educational campus, on twelve acres in residential north Dallas, is made up of 30 classrooms, a fine arts complex, a media center housing an exceptional collection of children's literature, a premier early childhood health and fitness facility, a greenhouse, farm animals, and a barn. A nature trail and a creek on the west boundary of the campus enhance the learning environment of the school.

THE KNOX SCHOOL
541 Long Beach Rd.
ST. JAMES, NY 11780
Web: www.knoxschool.org

The Knox School, founded in 1904, provides an outstanding college preparatory program within a traditional liberal arts curriculum including extensive opportunities in music as well as the fine and performing arts. Boarding (gr. 7-12) and day (gr. 6-12) students come from a number of states and foreign countries. In addition to a competitive interscholastic athletic program, Knox offers an outstanding equestrian program.

The campus, consisting of 50+ acres of waterfront property located on both Stony Brook Harbor and Long Island Sound, is 55 miles from New York City and is located in one of the most attractive areas on Long Island's North Shore. In addition to its rolling hills, playing fields and riding facilities, the grounds include twelve buildings which consist of dormitories, dining hall, classrooms, library, computer labs, science labs, gymnasium, theater, and barn which includes a circular, covered riding ring. The proximity to New York City offers many occasions for weekend trips and programs. To further enhance the educational opportunities a term exchange program is offered with Bedstone College in England.

Knox offers a family environment with a structured academic program dedicated to each student's success in the classroom, college placement and life beyond formal education. The School is guided by its Core Values and Principles of Action which aim to develop responsibility and respect for self, others, and the community in which students live and learn.

THE LANGLEY SCHOOL

1411 Balls Hill Rd.,
McLEAN, VA 22101

Doris E. Cottam, *Head of School*

Founded in 1942, The Langley School is committed to the pursuit of excellence with a challenging and enriched curriculum. The school attracts able students with promise and potential from diverse backgrounds throughout the greater Washington area. Emphasis is placed on educating the whole child in a comprehensive, well-rounded program that helps each child reach his/her fullest potential in a nurturing and stimulating environment. Students leave Langley as self-confident, sensitive young adults who are caring contributors to their communities.

The Primary School (preschool through kindergarten) provides a safe and nurturing environment that is designed to foster the social, emotional, intellectual, and physical development of each child. The curriculum of the Primary School uses a variety of materials, projects, and experiences to create a dynamic learning environment. Areas of study are integrated each month using a thematic approach and include language arts, math, art, music, drama, science, modern language, and technology.

In the Lower School (grades 1 through 5), a challenging, cross-disciplinary academic program meets the different developmental needs of students while stimulating their curiosity and strengthening their acquisition of skills. Reading and writing follow a phonetic and literature-based approach that aims to integrate social studies, art, music, and modern language. Mathematics provides a hands-on and experiential discovery of concepts as well as a focus on facts and processes. Science and math are interwoven to enrich special study projects and encourage observation, task planning, and collaboration. Technology supports all aspects of the curriculum, enhancing learning, writing, and problem-solving. Assemblies and presentations emphasize core values, develop self-confidence, and build a community spirit, while related field trips and physical education classes complement the curriculum.

The Middle School (grades 6 through 8) offers departmentalized instruction in language arts, modern language, math, social studies, science, and the fine arts. Students also have the opportunity to participate in electives that include band, yearbook, robotics, newspaper, dance, and fitness. Middle School students enjoy two overnight field trips each year, as well as a number of after-school activities such as athletics, jazz band, and fall and spring plays.

The Langley campus is fully networked, with technology integrated into all aspects of the curriculum. Students learn on a nearly 10-acre campus that includes a soccer field, large play areas, and nine buildings, including a 22,000-volume library with a computer graphics laboratory.

The Langley School operates on an equal opportunity basis.

Private Schools Illustrated — 1190

LAWRENCE ACADEMY
GROTON, MA
Tel: 978-448-6535 Fax: 978-448-9208
E-mail: admiss@lacademy.edu

Lawrence Academy, set in rolling New England countryside, blends safe residential life with resources of Boston, and hour away. Founded in 1793, Lawrence Academy's student-centered classrooms, with seminar and project-oriented components, characterize this progressive college prep curriculum. The Ninth Grade Program prepares students for the challenges of a student-centered curriculum through an integrated program designed to develop critical thinking skills. Computers are integrated into the classroom to augment teaching. Our coeducational boarding and day school encourages students to assume leadership roles and values individual differences as our student body represents 15 countries and 17 states. Extensive advisor system provides daily contact between students and their advisors, who guide students through their academic and social life. Extensive weekend activities for boarders and day students include trips to Boston, performances on campus and various day trips.

D. Scott Wiggins was appointed in 2003 as Lawrence's 44th Head of School. A beautiful new dormitory was opened in fall 2003 and a new academic building opened in the fall of 2004. Extensive arts facility highlights drama, music, and the visual arts. Winterim, a two-week mini term, offers projects and trips that provide students with experiential learning. The Independent Immersion program allows qualified students to design an independent curriculum in a specialized field. A highly competitive athletic program provides opportunities at all levels. Facilities include athletic complex with enclosed ice rink, arts center, Sony language lab, state-of-the-art recording studio, radio station, and dorms wired for Internet and telephone.

THE LAWRENCEVILLE SCHOOL
LAWRENCEVILLE, NJ

Elizabeth A. Duffy, AB, Princeton Univ.,
MBA, AM, Stanford Univ., *Head Master*

The Lawrenceville School, a nationally recognized coeducational boarding school of 800 students from approximately 35 states and 25 foreign countries, rests on a beautiful campus with outstanding academic and athletic facilities. The School's "conference table" teaching style provides the ideal venue for intellectual stimulation and enrichment, preparing students to be active, thoughtful members of society. The curriculum includes approximately 300 courses in eleven academic disciplines, with a variety of Advanced Placement, honors and elective courses. Independent study, off-campus and term-off projects are also available. Lawrenceville's most distinguishing feature is the House system, unique among American boarding schools. Each Housemaster maintains close daily contact with his or her students, and each individual's contribution to the quality of the residential community is what makes the House system work. Over the past five years, 20 or more students have matriculated at Brown, Columbia, Cornell, Dartmouth, Duke, Georgetown, Harvard, Princeton, Yale, and the University of Pennsylvania.

Criteria: Application; transcript; personal essay; recommendation letters; test scores; SSAT (or ISEE); TOEFL (for international applicants); application fee; interview.

Grade: 9-12, and PG.

Cost: $32,460 (boarding); $26,460 (day). Need-based financial aid of approximately $5.9 million is available.

Contact: Gregg W. M. Maloberti
Dean of Admission
The Lawrenceville School
2500 Main Street
Lawrenceville, NJ 08648
Tel: 800-735-2030

THE LOOMIS CHAFFEE SCHOOL
WINDSOR, CT

Russell H. Weigel, PhD, *Head of School*

The character of The Loomis Chaffee School strongly reflects the noble, enlightened and democratic vision of its founders. In 1874, four Loomis brothers and a sister, having lost all their children, decided to convert their family tragedy into an educational legacy for future generations. They envisioned an inclusive school where young men and women could learn together, taught by a committed and dedicated faculty. They stipulated that students matriculate from local communities as well as the world and that there be no political or religious test for admission. Loomis Chaffee is strongly committed to offering the opportunity for scholarships to ambitious students of good character and promise, regardless of ethnic, religious or social background.

The heart of Loomis Chaffee is its academic program, with extensive offerings of over 170 courses. The curriculum is carefully designed and constantly reviewed to meet the demands of the most selective colleges and universities, as well as to provide the knowledge and tools that young people need in order to lead fulfilling and meaningful lives. Advanced and Advanced Placement courses are offered. Academic facilities include the fully computerized 60,000-volume Katharine Brush Library, Clark Science Center, a state-of-the-art language laboratory, computer center, and the Richmond Art Center with studios, a gallery, and TV production studio. Students engage actively in theater and music programs.

Students at Loomis Chaffee select from a wide variety of extracurricular activities and creative opportunities. The school's location, in a semirural setting only fifteen minutes from the cultural and political center of Hartford, affords students many community service opportunities. Athletic programs are strong, and teams compete against numerous independent schools throughout New England. Athletic facilities include three gymnasia, a 25-meter Olympic pool, 19 tennis courts, a hockey rink, and six international squash courts.

Loomis Chaffee offers students generous guidance and support, and students share in helping to guide the school, sitting on major committees and enjoying non-voting representation to the Board of Trustees. Within the framework of high academic standards and expectations, Loomis Chaffee aims to provide students a warm and friendly environment where they can grow intellectually, morally, and spiritually and where they can gain experience in leadership and in contributing to their community.

LEXINGTON CHRISTIAN ACADEMY

48 Bartlett Ave.
LEXINGTON, MA 02420
Tel: 781-862-7850

Located in historic Lexington, Massachusetts, on a beautiful 30 acre campus, Lexington Christian Academy is a college preparatory, coeducational, nondenominational day school for grades 6-12. The school began in 1946 in a Boston location, moved to Cambridge in 1949, and since 1966 has been located on its present campus in Lexington. The Academy is accredited by the New England Association of Schools and Colleges.

Lexington Christian Academy gives young men and women solid academic education. Students receive intensive practice in critical thinking, communication, and creativity.

LCA also gives students solid grounding in absolute truth, giving them a keen sense of right and wrong, and an unshakable sense of who they are and what is worth living and dying for.

Honesty, personal integrity, and courage are combined with knowledge and intellectual power—the best preparation for leadership and for life.

Faculty members, which include a number of alumni, are known for their pursuit of excellence, their personal care for the individual student, and their desire to deal with the whole person—body, mind, emotion, and spirit. Students historically come from over 70 different communities as well as from out of state and from overseas, which aids in ensuring a rich variety of ethnic, religious, and economic backgrounds.

THE LOVETT SCHOOL
4075 Paces Ferry Road, NW
Atlanta, GA 30327
(404) 262-3032

www.lovett.org

William S. Peebles IV, AB, MBA,
Headmaster

The Lovett School, located on 100 acres bordering the Chattahoochee River in northwest Atlanta, is a college-preparatory school for approximately 1,500 boys and girls in kindergarten through grade 12. Founded in 1926 by Eva Edwards Lovett, the school retains her emphasis on the development of the whole child.

Lovett believes that it is the school's responsibility to develop fundamental skills, a love of learning, and the application of good judgment to what is learned. Distinctive features of the curriculum include experiential education and interdisciplinary studies, as well as honors and Advanced Placement courses. A Learning Lab provides individualized instruction and academic support.

The Fuqua Center houses Lovett's fine arts program, considered one of the best in the Southeast. Comprehensive programs in orchestra, band, voice, music, drama, and art are available at every level. A full athletic program provides each student an opportunity to experience the value of team effort and sportsmanship. The school fields competitive teams in 17 sports, in addition to intramurals.

Students participate in a variety of community service activities, and nondenominational chapel services are held weekly in all school divisions. Extracurricular activities include various faculty-sponsored groups, ranging from ultimate Frisbee clubs to honor societies. Summer programs provide academic courses, outdoor experiences, travel opportunities, and athletic offerings.

Lovett seeks students from all ethnic, cultural, racial, and religious backgrounds who can benefit from a challenging academic program. We encourage you to visit The Lovett School campus and tour our facilities, which include a new Lower School, Upper School, and Loudermilk Student Activities Center.

For more information, please contact the Admission Office.

Private Schools Illustrated — 1196

LYCEE FRANCAIS DE NEW YORK
505 E. 75th St.
NEW YORK, NY 10021
Tel: 212-369-1400
Web: www.lfny.org

Founded in 1935, the Lycée Français de New York has educated a multinational student body (over 50 countries) for over half a century.

A coeducational school that spans nursery through 12th grade, the Lycée, associated with the network of French Lycées throughout the world, is an American private not-for-profit institution chartered by the New York State Board of Regents and accredited by the French Ministry of National Education. As such, the Lycée confers the High School Diploma and the French Baccalaureate degree.

Over the years, graduates are accepted to the best of American and Canadian colleges and universities (Harvard, Princeton, Yale, Columbia, NYU, MIT, Brown, Georgetown, McGill, etc.), often receiving credit for their last year at the Lycée, as well as to French and European Universities, Ecoles Preparatoires, and institutes of higher learning.

PROGRAM: The Lycée's academic program is a unique combination of the traditional, rigorous and comprehensive French program, a strong English curriculum, and a number of courses that, although not required by the French Ministry of National Education, mark the particular educational approach of the institution.

Required courses include: French and English language and literature, one additional language - classical (Greek, Latin) or modern (German, Italian, Spanish), Mathematics, Physics, Chemistry, Biology, Computer Science, History, Geography, Economics, Physical Education, Music and Art. Philosophy is introduced in the last two years of school.

The Lycée also offers many optional courses and extracurricular activities from which students may choose.

FACULTY: A dedicated bilingual faculty of over 100 members holds advanced degrees from American or French Universities, and provides students with a warm and personalized education in a comfortably structured setting.

FACILITIES: In the Fall of 2003, the Lycée Français de New York moved into a new school designed and built specifically for its needs on Manhattan's Upper East Side. The Lycée has two gymnasia, a cultural center, two libraries with over 18,000 volumes, four computer labs, six studios for art, music and dance, and six science labs, and is planning a theater and an auditorium. Its location allows it to integrate into its curriculum numerous field trips to museums, art galleries, educational and business organizations as well as to encourage inter-school athletic, artistic, musical and literary competitions.

Knowledge of French is not required for admission until 1st grade (11eme). Students thereafter are accepted upon passing a language proficiency test. Language support classes for both French and English are offered throughout all grades. In 2nd, 3rd, and 4th grades new students may participate in an intensive French language integration program. Non-Francophone students learn French from specialized teachers in a small group setting, and are integrated into regular classes the following year.

Private Schools Illustrated — 1198

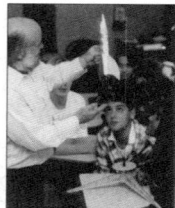

The MacDuffie School
Springfield, MA
Tel: 413-734-4971   Fax: 413-734-6693
www.macduffie.com

Boarding and day students enjoy a rich and rigorous curriculum designed to demonstrate the interrelationships among the various disciplines. The School emphasizes personal growth and academic integrity within a supportive community.

The MacDuffie School, founded in 1890, is a small coeducational college preparatory school for students in grades six through twelve located on fourteen acres in the historic Maple Hill district of Springfield, Massachusetts. The School sits at the crossroads of Western Massachusetts with Boston to the East, New York City to the South and is close to Bradley International Airport in Hartford, Connecticut (20 miles).

MacDuffie is committed to preparing its students for college and successful lives in the modern world. A defining principle of MacDuffie's academic program is that learning is an ongoing and intrinsic part of life. Students explore intellectual and artistic possibilities, debate differences of opinion, question assumptions, and take the kind of risks that help students to grow into informed, involved, articulate and self-confident adults. The curriculum includes a challenging college preparatory program including honors, advanced placement and extensive elective courses.

In keeping with the School's mission, MacDuffie offers students a wide variety of extracurricular activities which build leadership skills and broaden the learning experience. In addition to an extensive array of elective courses in the arts and a strong theater performance calendar, MacDuffie encourages students to participate in the interscholastic athletic program as well as the many clubs and activities.

MacDuffie educates both day and boarding students. Although primarily day, the School has an innovative boarding program for students from the United States and around the world. This innovative approach to cultural exchange is known as the Ames Hill Boarding Program and combines the best of a homestay experience with a small boarding school program. Young women and men live on campus with families in four gracious homes—Castle, Caswell, Lemire and Young Houses. Living is relaxed and comfortable with students and house parents preparing and enjoying meals and activities together.

As stated in the School's mission, "A small and cohesive community, MacDuffie instills in its young women and men the importance of working together to achieve both individual and institutional goals and to do so in ways that are honestly respectful of the needs, values, and rights of each other, the environment, and the world in which we live."

MAINE CENTRAL INSTITUTE
125 S. Main St.
PITTSFIELD, ME 04967
Tel: 207-487-3355

MCI is a co-educational boarding and day school, serving grades 9-12 and PG, and providing a rigorous, comprehensive educational program to a multicultural student body with a wide range of abilities and interests. Set in a rural, safe and caring atmosphere, students will acquire knowledge, self-esteem, social responsibility, and the critical thinking and communications skills necessary for global citizenship and lifelong learning. If support beyond the classroom is needed, the Personalized Learning Program provides instructional support for an entire academic program or tutorial in individual subjects. Our comprehensive ESL program offers a complete curriculum with classes in mathematics, history, literature, speaking and listening, usually in classes as small as five students. Bossov Ballet Theatre offers a unique opportunity to study classical ballet as a part of the academic curriculum, preparing the student for a professional ballet career. Our comprehensive athletic and extracurricular programs offer a wide range of activities to students of all levels of ability and interest. MCI's award-winning music, theater and art programs prepare students as lifelong learners and active participants in the performing arts. MCI—an outstanding learning institution which is highly recommended for its level of academic achievement, inspiring learning environment, and dedicated faculty and supportive staff.

Private Schools Illustrated — 1200

MARVELWOOD SCHOOL
476 Skiff Mountain Rd.
KENT, CT 06757-3001
Tel: 860-927-0047   Fax: 860-927-0021
Scott Pottbecker, *Head of School*

The Marvelwood School is a small coeducational boarding school in the rural foothills of the Berkshire mountains in northwestern Connecticut. Founded in 1957 by Robert A. Bodkin, Marvelwood helps young people who want or need a small school environment in order to reach their potential. With an enrollment of about 150 students in grades nine through twelve, Marvelwood is known for its strong sense of family and community, programs of academic support, and commitment to the value of service.

The 42 teaching faculty at the School provide a structured academic program designed to help students reach their potential and experience real success in the classroom. The college preparatory curriculum emphasizes the students' commitment to and involvement in their learning experiences. All students follow a program which combines traditional academic courses with electives in art, music, drama and photography. Some Marvelwood students with learning differences also receive extra support in Skills classes which focus on developing basic reading, writing and organizational skills. In addition, the School offers a Math Tutorial program and two levels of English as a Second Language for international students.

All students participate in the School's athletic program which provides a combination of individual activities—such as Wilderness Ways, snowboarding, canoeing, downhill skiing and biking—and team sports—soccer, basketball, ice hockey, softball, lacrosse, tennis, cross-country running, baseball, wrestling and volleyball.

Everyone at Marvelwood takes part in the Wednesday morning Community Service Program which involves students in volunteer work in hospitals, nursing homes, child care centers, animal shelters, homeless shelters, environmental organizations and schools. The School has twice been honored by the State of Connecticut with the "Youth Action Award" for this program, and it is the only independent school in Connecticut to have received that award.

"My experience this summer at Marvelwood has changed me completely. I feel very confident that, when I return to my home school, my good grades and new attitude will surprise everyone . . . Every kid should spend a summer here." (Recent Student)

THE MARVELWOOD SUMMER

Our five-week skills-building program combines serious learning with summer fun for boys and girls entering grades 7-11. Based on a proven teaching philosophy that's designed to bolster a student's self-confidence, the fifty students enrolled in our program have the same primary focus—to strengthen verbal and quantitative skills—but the small classes and individualized instruction allow each student to proceed at his own pace. Our pre- and post-testing, an ungraded curriculum and the close supervision of friendly, supportive faculty members have helped many students "turn the corner" academically. The Marvelwood Summer curriculum includes English, Math, SSAT/SAT prep, Computer, Journalism, Drama, Vocabulary, Creative Writing and Poetry, ESL and more. Sailing, windsurfing, swimming, golf, tennis, hiking, cycling, arts, crafts and team sports are included in a lively extracurricular program. The Marvelwood Summer uses the facilities of The Marvelwood School located in the scenic foothills of the Berkshires.

Sarah Marshall, *Director*
The Marvelwood Summer Program
476 Skiff Mountain Rd.
Kent, CT 06757
Tel: 860-927-0047
Fax: 860-927-0021

MARIANAPOLIS PREPARATORY SCHOOL
THOMPSON, CT

Mrs. Marilyn S. Ebbitt, *Headmistress*
Mr. Daniel M. Harrop, *Director of Admissions*

Marianapolis Preparatory School is a Roman Catholic co-educational boarding/day school founded in 1926. Offering a rigorous college preparatory program of studies, Marianapolis is located on historic Thompson Hill, boasting a sprawling 300-acre campus comprised of classrooms, several science and computer science labs, multiple dormitories, several cottages, and a newly renovated gymnasium. Since its inception the mission of the school focuses on preparing young men and women for life intellectually, emotionally, physically, ethically, and spiritually through a pursuit of excellence and cultivation of talents.

Offering various instructional levels including college prep, honors, and advanced placement, Marianapolis remains committed to average class sizes of 14, with an unparalleled 9:1 student-teacher ratio. In addition to teacher-sponsored extra help sessions before, during, and after school, all students are assigned an academic advisor responsible for tracking the performance of his/her advisees. Marianapolis prides itself on forging partnerships with parents and keeping parents informed as to their child's progress.

Squarely focused on the co-curricular development of the student body, Marianapolis features comprehensive athletic and visual and performing arts opportunities for students. Athletic offerings include boys' and girls' soccer, cross country, track and field, basketball, lacrosse, golf, baseball, softball, and tennis on both junior varsity and varsity levels. Club and activity offerings include yoga, capoeira, samba drumming, flamenco dancing, kickboxing, student government and many others. Students in the band and/or chorus perform in concerts both on and off campus and compete in state, regional, and national competitions annually. Our visual arts students participate in symposia throughout the school year and many pursue the arts in post-secondary college and university settings.

Another hallmark of Marianapolis lies in its aggressive college placement initiatives. The recent publication of the *Marianapolis College Planning Guide* testifies to the seriousness with which we approach the college selection and placement process. From admission to the school, all students and parents invest in a long-range planning module for college placement and students are tracked in the plan throughout their four-year career. Among the colleges and universities to which recent seniors have been accepted are Harvard, Amherst, Williams, Notre Dame, Carnegie-Mellon, Colby, Colgate, Fairfield, Boston College, Boston University, Holy Cross, Skidmore, Middlebury, Vanderbilt, Rensselaer, St. Michael's, Smith, Trinity, Vassar, Tufts, Washington and Lee, Wellesley, and Worcester Polytechnic Institute.

MARY INSTITUTE AND SAINT LOUIS COUNTRY DAY SCHOOL

101 N. Warson Rd.
ST. LOUIS, MO 63124
Tel: 314-993-5100   Fax: 314-995-7470
Web: www.micds.org

Founded in 1859, MICDS is today considered one of the nation's pre-eminent independent schools. MICDS is a coed, college-preparatory school serving 1220 students. Grades Junior Kindergarten through fourth and ninth through twelfth are coed, while Middle School students, grades 5-8, learn within a framework of single sex and coed classes. MICDS is committed to its mission of preparing young people for higher learning and lives of purpose and service. The school's outstanding education balances strong academics, an innovative arts program, service learning and an athletics program that has claimed 23 team state championships, 4 individual/relay team state championships, 52 appearances in the state semi-finals, and 41 district championships over the past decade. Teachers and students benefit from a strong mission, a caring and diverse community and exceptional facilities for learning. MICDS welcomes students from all backgrounds. New students represent 74 different public/parochial/independent schools. Student-to-teacher ratio is 8:1,

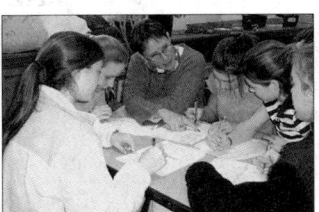

average class size is 15. Over 20 percent of the student body receives financial aid, this year totaling over $2.6 million. Nearly two-thirds of the School's faculty holds advanced degrees. The 141 graduates of the Class of 2004 attend 71 different four-year colleges. Tuition for the 2005-2006 school year ranges from $14,170-$17,145.

THE MASTERS SCHOOL
DOBBS FERRY, NY

Maureen Fonseca, *Head of School*

The Masters School is a coeducational, college-preparatory school for both day (grades 5-12) and boarding (grades 9-12) students. Founded in 1877, The Masters School enrolls approximately 504 students from 15 states and 13 countries. Once a school for girls, The Masters School now offers a 5th grade through 8th grade middle school with single gender classes in grades 6 through 8. The Upper School (grades 9-12) is completely coeducational.

The Masters School offers a challenging academic program and boasts a strong college placement record. The curriculum includes approximately 160 college-preparatory and honors (including 17 Advanced Placement) courses in English, mathematics, science, social studies, languages, religion, and art. Classes are small—averaging 12-15 students—and encourage discussion. In the Upper School, most classes use the Harkness Method as an instructional framework for teaching; this features an oval table around which students and teacher actively engage in seminar-style learning. The faculty, drawn from prestigious colleges and universities, is dedicated to teaching and promotes the full development of each student's intellectual and personal potential. A Computer Research Center within the library provides state-of-the-art computer research stations. This networked system incorporates access to library materials and CD-ROM resources. Access to E-mail, the Internet and community information is also provided on each computer research station, as well as in each dormitory room.

The Masters School provides financial assistance to 29% of the student body. The average grant is more than $14,000. The Masters School offers an outstanding performing arts program. A $3 million theatre with state of the art equipment is accessible to all students. Students with a strong interest in theatre may elect the full year course, which includes not only instruction in acting but also in set design, lighting, play-writing, and production. The music department offers instruction in performance, history, and theory each semester. Dance students study ballet, modern and jazz dance techniques as well as composition. Due to the strength of these programs, the school is able to mount preprofessional-level performances.

A member of the Fairchester League, The Masters School competes with fifteen area schools in eleven varsity and junior varsity sports: basketball, fencing, cross-country, ice hockey, field hockey, lacrosse, soccer, softball, baseball, tennis, and volleyball. A million dollar varsity baseball field hosted its first game in the Spring of 2001. Through the physical education department, students may take club-level sports (including gymnastics and aerobics) as well as physical fitness classes and dance. In addition, thirty-five clubs are active and reflect a wide variety of student interests. A unique community service program is also a popular activity.

The student-run Activities Committee organizes the school's busy weekend calendars. Activities include on-campus movies, lectures, and dances, as well as trips to Manhattan's theaters, museums and shopping areas.

CITYterm, an interdisciplinary urban studies program, was initiated in September 1996. CITYterm is an innovative semester-long program which draws upon the resources of New York City in its academic and experiential curriculum. CITYterm is based on The Masters School campus and is offered not only to its own students but to juniors and seniors from the program's national consortium of public and private schools. Admission to this prestigious program is highly selective.

For additional information about The Masters School or CITYterm contact the Admission Office, The Masters School, 49 Clinton Ave., Dobbs Ferry, NY 10522. Tel: 914-479-6420. Fax: 914-693-7295.

McLEAN SCHOOL OF MARYLAND

8224 Lochinver Ln.
POTOMAC, MD 20854
Tel: 301-299-8277   Fax: 301-299-1639
E-mail: admission@mcleanschool.org
Web: www.mcleanschool.org

McLean School of Maryland is an independent, coeducational, day school for students in kindergarten through grade 12.

McLean makes education accessible, stimulating and meaningful for a broad range of learners.

Our students flourish because McLean responds to students' learning styles.

McLean prepares students intellectually and socially by encouraging self-advocacy and building self-confidence.

Our students succeed because they learn how to learn.

MENLO SCHOOL

50 Valparaiso Avenue
ATHERTON, CA 94027
Tel: 650-330-2000
Fax: 650-330-2002
Web: www.menloschool.org

Menlo School (coed, grades 6-12) is dedicated to providing a challenging academic curriculum complemented by outstanding fine arts and athletic programs. The School helps students develop positive values and nurtures character development in a supportive environment that upholds the highest moral and ethical standards. Menlo's program encourages students to reach their fullest potential and develop the skills necessary to respond intelligently and humanely to the complexities of an increasingly diverse world.

THE PEGASUS SCHOOL
19692 Lexington Ln.
HUNTINGTON BEACH, CA 92646-3763

Tel: 714-964-1224

The Pegasus School, located in Huntington Beach, California, is an independent school for bright and gifted children in pre-school through grade eight. The school emphasizes a rigorous curriculum designed to encourage creative and critical thinking, so that each student may achieve scholastic and personal success.

The Pegasus School is a national Blue Ribbon School, accredited by California Association of Independent Schools (CAIS) and a member of National Association of Independent Schools (NAIS).

Private Schools Illustrated — 1208

MERCERSBURG ACADEMY

Dating from 1836, Mercersburg Academy was chartered in 1865 and was established as a college preparatory school on the Exeter model in 1893. This year, it serves 440 students (grades 9-12), from 27 states and 22 countries. Located in south-central Pennsylvania, the expansive 300-acre campus has excellent facilities and has access to the outdoors and the nearby Tuscarora and Appalachian Trails. The school is convenient to museums, professional athletic teams, entertainment, and the airports of Washington, D.C., and Baltimore, Md. Mercersburg retains a strong sense of community, dedication to academic achievement, and a commitment to a balanced education with extensive opportunities in the fine arts and competitive athletics. Endowment: $140 million; need-based Financial Aid: $3.56 million; Mean SAT I: 1233; Year 2004 graduates attend Bates College, University of Pennsylvania, and University of Virginia, among other highly competitive colleges and universities.

MERCERSBURG
A Tradition of Excellence Since 1893

OFFICE OF ADMISSION
300 EAST SEMINARY STREET
MERCERSBURG, PA 17236-1551
(717) 328-6173 • Fax (717) 328-6319
www.mercersburg.edu
admission@mercersburg.edu

MORAVIAN ACADEMY
4313 Green Pond Rd.
BETHLEHEM, PA 18020

Barnaby J. Roberts, *Headmaster*
Carlton P. Chandler, *Director—Upper School*
Robert A. Bovee, *Director—Middle School*
Ella Jane Kunkle, *Director—Lower School*

Founded in 1742, Moravian Academy is a coeducational day school for grades prekindergarten through twelve.

The curriculum at the Upper School is college-preparatory with an emphasis on academics. We believe that the moral and physical development of students should complement their academic achievements. The student-teacher ratio is 9:1, giving teachers the opportunity to work closely with students in the classroom and after school, both in individual conferences and in numerous extracurricular activities. Academic excellence, challenge, respect and service—this is Moravian Academy. For more information about admissions, please call 610-691-1600.

MOSES BROWN SCHOOL
250 Lloyd Ave.
PROVIDENCE, RI 02906
Tel: 401-831-7350   Fax: 401-455-0084
Web: www.mosesbrown.org

Moses Brown School is a college-preparatory, Quaker school for girls and boys, from nursery through grade 12. Founded in 1784, the school exists to inspire students to reach their fullest intellectual and spiritual potential. Moses Brown engages students in a rich academic curriculum, a broad offering of arts and athletics, and a daily life strongly rooted in the Friends' values of cooperation and community service. Being part of this academic community, students recognize the impact they have as individuals, while they build important relationships with classmates, teachers, and the world around them.

Moses Brown students grow and learn in three developmentally distinct programs—lower, middle, and upper schools—with carefully coordinated offerings and goals. All students embark on individual journeys to academic and personal growth guided by the school's 221-year-old motto: "For the Honor of Truth."

At Moses Brown, faculty and advisors serve as mentors, encouraging students to think independently and creatively. Our teachers are professional, talented, and knowledgeable individuals who are passionate about lifelong learning.

The foundation for academic achievement begins in the Lower School where students learn to challenge themselves and grow in the understanding of their potential. While focusing on essential reading, writing, science, and math skills, classroom teachers also introduce students to the skills of independent thinking, cooperation, and decision-making.

By Middle School, students assume more responsibility for their own learning. They are encouraged to set personal and academic goals and, together with their teachers, they determine the best ways to achieve them. Students experience the value of a "team" approach and form relationships with classmates and teachers that will carry them into young adulthood.

Students entering the Upper School encounter a well-rounded academic and co-curricular program that combines challenging course work, technology, the arts, athletics, and community service. Course work and instruction develop the analytic rigor, intellectual depth, and self-motivation necessary for college admission and a rewarding life.

In the classroom and in all activities, acceptance of ideas and respect for others, however different, is fundamental. Moses Brown School embraces diversity—racial, ethnic, economic, sexual orientation, and religious—a principle that engenders solidarity. Friends' values are the foundation for learning in an environment of equality, integrity, and respect and are integral to an educational experience that is unmatched in Rhode Island.

NEW HAMPTON SCHOOL
NEW HAMPTON, NH

Alan B. Crocker, *Acting Headmaster*

Founded in 1821, New Hampton School educates young people differently. Following a nationally acclaimed model for experience-based education, our students and adults work alongside each other to create a dynamic learning community marked by nonhierarchical relationships, mutual respect, and intentional responsibility. New Hampton nurtures the intellectual, emotional, physical, and spiritual potential of each student. New Hampton believes in developing authentic relationships based on shared experience and common goals. At New Hampton School, positive role models and relationships are crucial to a student's growth and social development. Since learning takes place within relationships that occur naturally as people live, learn, and work together, all community members play critical roles in the teaching and learning process. At New Hampton School each child is known, needed, and cared for, and the adults at New Hampton are teachers, coaches, dorm parents, mentors, friends who help develop a passion for learning, being active, and enjoying life. Our beautiful and well-equipped campus "village" is home to comprehensive, integrated—and life-changing—programs in academics, arts, athletics, adventure education, and community service. We care about college prep and campus dogs, a code of behavior rather than a code of dress. About an hour drive from campus are Dartmouth College, Plymouth State College, the University of New Hampshire, and the City of Boston. In addition, Lake Winnipesaukee, Newfound Lake, and the foothills of New Hampshire's White Mountains are within 10 miles of campus. Come visit!

NEW HAMPTON SCHOOL SUMMER PROGRAMS
NEW HAMPTON, NH

Performance PLUS (Positive Learning Using the Stage) is 3 weeks of intensive artistic/character training for high school students. Participants major in film, music, theatre arts, dance or technical production, use state-of-the-art equipment and facilities, train with professional staff and guest artists, and create/perform an original showcase. Performance PLUS—where character and creativity come together to last a lifetime! For additional information and application materials, please write, call or email:

Performance PLUS, New Hampton School
P.O. Box 579, New Hampton, NH 03256
Tel: 603-677-3403
E-mail: lmurphy@performanceplus.org
Website: www.performanceplus.org

Many other Athletic and Artistic Summer Programs also available. Please see www.newhampton.org/summer/

MORRISTOWN-BEARD SCHOOL

70 Whippany Rd.
MORRISTOWN, NJ 07960

Alex Curtis, BA, Swarthmore, PhD, Princeton Univ., *Headmaster*

Morristown-Beard School, an independent co-educational college preparatory school for students in grades 6-12, is dedicated to inspiring, challenging, and supporting students toward academic and personal excellence. Students are encouraged and provided opportunities to fully develop their intellect, and athletic, artistic, and leadership capabilities. Community service and character development are emphasized.

Our Middle School (6-8) is housed independently from the Upper School. In the Middle School, individual attention and an emphasis on character building accompany an interdisciplinary approach to academics. MS students enjoy numerous sports and extracurricular activities designed to supplement and enhance the demanding classroom training. Our major objectives in the Middle School are teaching students how to learn and helping them to appreciate an environment which is supportive of others.

The Upper School daily schedule is a modified block schedule, whereby each class meets three times per week for extended periods. This schedule allows for students to develop time management and meet with teachers and advisors. In each subject, students are placed in one of three academic levels according to their aptitude and achievement. Our rigorous college preparatory curriculum includes core requirements in each of the eight departments (art, mathematics, history, languages, science, English, physical education, and computers). There are, additionally, an extensive variety of elective, honors and advanced placement courses.

Virtually every senior at Morristown-Beard continues her or his education at a very selective college. Over the last five years, graduates have attended: Bard, Bates, Bucknell, Cornell, Dartmouth, Elon, Georgetown, Hamilton, Johns Hopkins, Penn State, Princeton, St. Lawrence, Trinity, and William & Mary.

Admissions decisions are based on recommendations, transcripts, interviews, test results, effort, potential for future achievement and seriousness of academic curiosity.

For further information, contact the Admissions Office.
Tel: 973-539-3032. E-mail: admissions@mobeard.org.

NEW YORK MILITARY ACADEMY
CORNWALL-ON-HUDSON, NY

Founded 1889

Since 1889, New York Military Academy has offered to young men and, since 1976, young women an educational program of sound preparation for life. Nestled in the Hudson Valley, 60 miles north of New York City, the Academy offers cadets in Grades 7-12 a complete and quality education.

The mission of NYMA is to provide a balanced program with emphasis on the development of mind, body, character, responsibility and accountability. Participation in Army Junior ROTC, leadership and citizenship enhances the development of the necessary requisites for future successes in college and life. The Academy continues to maintain the highest designation awarded by the Department of the Army, "Honor Unit with Distinction."

Completing the structured academic day is an extensive, compulsory interscholastic sports and fitness program. Additional activities include Boy Scouts, an equestrian program, skiing, swimming, band, chorus, National Honor Society, yearbook, drill team, school dances and off-campus, weekend outings. Religious services are held on-campus and off, as well as a moral guidance program.

Summer programs include an academic, non-military summer school and JROTC Summer Courses offering LET (Leadership Educational Training) I and II held at New York Military Academy beginning in late June. For additional information, visit our website at www.nyma.org or call Admissions at 1-888-ASK-NYMA. Outside the continental United States call 1-845-534-3710 ext. 4249.

NOBLE AND GREENOUGH SCHOOL
10 Campus Dr.
DEDHAM, MA 02026

Robert P. Henderson, Jr., A.B., A.M., Dartmouth College, *Head*

Noble and Greenough School is a coeducational independent day and five-day boarding school located on a 187-acre campus on the banks of the Charles River in Dedham. Founded in 1866 in Boston by George Washington Copp Noble, the school draws students in grades seven through 12 from 93 cities and towns. The unique five-day boarding program, which allows boarders to return to their families every weekend, is open to some 48 young men and women of Upper School (grades 9-12) age, some of whom come from abroad, most from communities in Massachusetts beyond daily commuting range. In the fall of 2004, the boarders moved into a new student and faculty residential hall. Other initiatives to be rolled out over the first decade of the 21st century are: the construction of a new Arts facility, an augmented Financial Aid program and an increased faculty compensation budget.

Nobles, as it is familiarly called, moved to Dedham in 1922, locating on the Nickerson estate. The original home, known as the Castle and designed by the eminent architectural firm of H.H. Richardson, is still used for daily meals as well as special functions that celebrate the school. Besides the Castle, the Nobles campus includes two main classroom buildings (one for the Upper School and one for the Middle School), a science building, a library, a state-of-the-art athletic center, an arts center, a multi-purpose indoor ice hockey facility and boathouses.

Nobles' academic and afternoon (extra-curricular) programs offer a balance among intellectual, moral and physical disciplines intended to inculcate values of honesty, self-respect, curiosity, commitment to others, integrity and civility. The curriculum combines a core of academic courses requisite to an educated person; elective courses are designed to fit the special needs and interests of the many unique individuals in the community. Students taking part in the school's Advanced Placement program are given a choice of 20 selections. In the semester prior to graduation, students may create and execute independent studies projects within the Greater Boston community. The afternoon program electives offer opportunities in service learning, athletics (including fitness training), performing arts, visual arts and outdoor education. A wide range of clubs and activities is also available, including yearbook and newspaper, photography, drama, a cappella groups, cooking club, multicultural and foreign language societies.

Nobles students go on to the most select colleges across the country, with close to 90 percent typically entering their first- or second-choice schools.

NORTH COUNTRY SCHOOL
Box 187
LAKE PLACID,
NY 12946
E-mail: admissions@nct.org
Web: nct.org

David Hochschartner, *Director*

North Country School offers a unique learning environment for children including a full working farm, a recreational setting in Olympic Lake Placid, and an optional seven week summer camp. The educational program is experientially based and designed to speak to a variety of intelligences. Gifted children thrive as do classroom resistant learners. The ratio of 3-1 provides guidance for individualized student learning initiatives as well as good caretaking. Children live in groups of 8-10 with houseparents.

The school's 200 acres include a lake, organic gardens, a sugar bush, meadows, and a ski hill. There are also skating ponds, tree houses and slides by every staircase. Studio and performing arts, horseback riding, skiing, mountaineering, camping and regular farm chores supplement the enriched academic program.

The school's goals are character development, intellectual competence, self-reliance, self-confidence and a natural and healthy childhood.

Private Schools Illustrated — 1218

OAK HILL ACADEMY
MOUTH OF WILSON, VA

Michael D. Groves,
BA, MDiv, PhD, *President*

Oak Hill Academy, founded in 1878, is a coeducational boarding school open to all students in Grades 8-12. Supported by and affiliated with the Baptist General Association of Virginia, enrollment includes students from over 18 states and several foreign countries.

The school seeks to provide a safe, secure, nurturing environment for girls and boys needing a change in school, peer, community or family relationships. Oak Hill provides a structured nonmilitary educational program with a curriculum that challenges the brightest student and encourages those who are unmotivated, who are underachieving, or who are experiencing difficulty in their school setting.

There are two diploma tracks—general and advanced—requiring 23 and 25 units respectively. A comprehensive testing program is part of class placement and registration. Achievement, ability, reading and vocational aptitude group tests are given in addition to individual testing. The Guidance Office provides counseling and consultation, and each student is also assigned a faculty advisor. Over 90% of yearly graduates are accepted to colleges or universities.

Attendance at Sunday morning church services is expected of all students.

A varied intramural sports program and a full slate of extracurricular activities are available to all students who want to participate. A new athletic field has been completed. The school fields a nationally ranked basketball team for boys. Additional sports include girls basketball, girls volleyball, boys and girls tennis teams, boys baseball, co-ed soccer, and horseback riding.

Tel: 276-579-2619. Fax: 276-579-4722.

E-mail: info@oak-hill.net. Web: oak-hill.net.

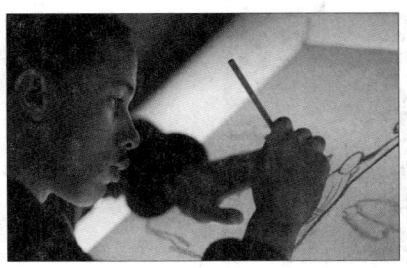
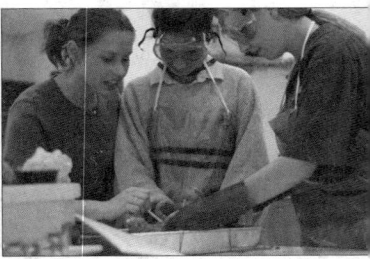

OAK HILL ACADEMY SUMMER SESSION
MOUTH OF WILSON, VA

Summer School at Oak Hill Academy is an opportunity for boys and girls to prepare for the future academically, make up unsuccessful classroom work, or improve in a particular subject area. Beyond the academics, time is spent canoeing the New River, hiking the mountains, riding horses, and participating in outdoor sports. The unsurpassed beauty of our mountain setting provides an unforgettable summer opportunity and experience.

The Summer School academic program is commensurate with our regular term commitment to assist each student to reach his or her maximum learning potential.

Classes are small with time set aside each night for a one-and-a-half-hour study hall. Students may select from a curriculum including most subjects taught during the regular school term. These classes are held for two and a half hours each day for a repeat subject and five hours a day for each new subject. Classes meet six days per week. Two repeat or one new subject may be taken for full credit. A second new subject may be taken in the afternoon for an additional cost. Tutoring is also available.

Summer in the mountains means outdoor activities. Students will enjoy cookouts next to a fast-moving stream. They will canoe the New River, hike the highest mountains of Virginia, and participate in horseback riding (additional fee required). An intramural sports program includes basketball, volleyball, softball, tennis and soccer. An individual may also work out in the weight room/fitness center or build stamina through running various tracks and roads.

Tel: 276-579-2619. Fax: 276-579-4722. E-mail: info@oak-hill.net. Web: oak-hill.net.

NORTHWOOD SCHOOL
LAKE PLACID, NY

Edward M. Good, *Headmaster*

Northwood School, a closely knit community of 160 students, has two basic objectives. The first is that each student be thoroughly grounded in the fundamentals of verbal and scientific skills. Second, each student must understand that the worthwhile and good things of life are acquired only in proportion to the effort expended to achieve them.

Classes at Northwood are small by design, permitting exacting supervision and close individual counseling. Students learn to participate in their academic experience developing strong communication skills and confidence. A core curriculum stresses skill development and achievement through effort.

Northwood School has access to the Olympic facilities of Lake Placid adjacent to the school grounds. The 3 ice surfaces at the Olympic Arena and the challenging slopes of Whiteface Mountain Ski Area service our most competitive athletes. The school has completed a $5 million renovation including: a fitness center with a squash court, rock climbing wall, cybex weight system and aerobics dance floor, a student center with a walk-in book store, home theatre, post office, recreational area and new dining room and kitchen facilities, a new science building with 4 science labs, classrooms and a greenhouse, an enhanced art facility, music practice rooms, and theatre renovations. All dormitory rooms and bathrooms have been completely remodeled.

Eight additional class offerings in art, music and drama and a school wide "wellness program" have enhanced the academic curriculum. Ice Hockey, Alpine Skiing, Lacrosse, Crew, Soccer, Tennis and Golf are established varsity sports. Our "Wilderness Skills" program includes rock climbing, canoeing and kayaking, camping and survival skills in all seasons of the year.

Coeducational Schools — 1221

Learn with Friends

Join our close-knit community of 160 students in a quality academic program embracing the Quaker values of simplicity, community and service.

- College Preparatory Program (Grades 6-12)
- Boarding and Day (Full and 5-Day Boarding)
- 75 Miles North of NYC
- 8-to-1 Student/Faculty Ratio

1-800-843-3341

Oakwood
FRIENDS SCHOOL

Poughkeepsie, NY ■ www.oakwoodfriends.org

THE ORCHARD SCHOOL
INDIANAPOLIS, IN

Joseph Marshall, BA, MEd, *Head of School*

The Orchard School, founded as a progressive school in 1922, provides an education that nurtures each child's development through a challenging curriculum and fosters active, responsible citizenship. Orchard is a non-sectarian, coeducational school for 614 students in preschool through eighth grade. The curriculum integrates learning through language arts, social studies, math, music, drama, science, Spanish, physical education, technology and outdoor education. Orchard recognizes the value of utilizing varied approaches in the learning process.

Orchard strives to provide students with independence, thinking from multiple perspectives, problem solving, multicultural education and core values. A successful learning community is based on diversity, inclusion, teaming, fairness and respect. Orchard endeavors to graduate students with a sound intellect and a social conscience.

Learning support, speech/language therapy, assessment and evaluation, and school counseling are available. An extended-day program offers quality before- and after-school experiences for children ages 4 through 14. The advisory system for students in grades 6-8 provides guidance, support and leadership opportunities for the students.

Located on a wooded 50-acre campus, the school has two gyms, a 240-seat theater, a dance studio, and acoustical rooms for band, strings and choral instruction. Outdoor facilities include a regulation track, two soccer fields, baseball and softball diamonds, a ropes challenge course, playgrounds, an outdoor classroom and a pioneer cabin and farm.

For additional information, please contact Kristen Hein, The Orchard School, 615 W. 64th St., Indianapolis, IN 46260. Tel: 317-251-9253. Web: www.orchard.org.

PACE ACADEMY

966 W. Paces Ferry Rd.
Atlanta, GA 30327
404-262-1345
www.paceacademy.org

Pace Academy, an independent college preparatory school, has imparted generations of Atlantans with a strong foundation in academics, leadership, service, athletics and the arts. With 915 students ranging from pre-1st–12th grade, Pace is the ideal size for maximizing academic, extracurricular and interpersonal development. The student-teacher ratio is 10:1 and class sizes average 15. Students are nurtured yet challenged to explore their world, connect with the greater community and excel beyond perceived limitations.

Because of the school's ideal size, faculty members truly know students and their families. Each student is individually ushered through the totality of his or her intellectual, emotional, aesthetic, spiritual, moral and physical development. Diversity and individuality, as well as community, cooperation and competition are valued and promoted at Pace Academy.

With strong academics, more than 40 extracurricular activities and 60 athletic teams, opportunities for achievement abound. For example:

- The average SAT score for the class of 2004 was 1313; the top third of the class averaged 1418. College placement is excellent.
- Of Pace's 21 varsity teams in 2004, 17 reached the state playoffs.
- The Pace Debate Team captured the state title for the 18th-consecutive year in 2005. (Pace Debate won the National Championship in 2002.)
- The Fine Arts program is noted as one of the finest in the Southeast.
- For decades, Pace has been at the forefront of Service Learning. (Atlanta Food Bank named Pace "2002 School of the Year.")

August 2004 marked the opening of Pace Academy Middle School, a state-of-the-art educational facility uniquely supportive of the intellectual, emotional, spiritual, creative and physical growth of the early adolescent child. In 2000, Pace opened the Inman Student Activity Center housing athletic, college counseling and deans offices, a basketball court and a bookstore.

We encourage you and your family to visit Pace Academy. To learn more, visit our website at www.paceacademy.org or call 404-262-1345.

The Pennington School was founded in 1838 by the Methodist Church with a commitment to the training of the mind, the education of the physical, and the grounding of the soul in character. The strength and breadth of its curriculum develops students intellectually; a strong fine arts program develops their aesthetic intelligence and appreciation; and courses on religion and ethics, a weekly chapel service, and opportunities for community service develop their characters.

THE PENNINGTON SCHOOL
112 W. Delaware Ave.
PENNINGTON, NJ 08534
Tel: 609-737-6128

Lyle D. Rigg, *Headmaster*

Pennington enrolls a diverse and coeducational student body, in both a day and a boarding program, and provides an environment where each student develops personal excellence. The School's enrollment of 445 ensures the personal attention and collaborative relationships with teachers that enhance learning. Its beautiful 54-acre campus, in the small town of Pennington, provides a safe setting for the challenges of community living and the demands of academic life. The School's small and competitive Center for Learning prepares students with learning differences for college study, and English as a Second Language courses are offered to build the fluency of international students.

As the school moves through its second century, its newly opened campus center provides extraordinary facilities for art, music, and theatre, as well as a large, comfortable student center. Future plans call for renovations of science and math labs, the addition of classroom space, and renovation of facilities for the Middle School.

PERKIOMEN SCHOOL
200 Seminary Ave.
PENNSBURG, PA 18073
Tel: 215-679-9511
Fax: 215-679-1146
E-mail: admissions@perkiomen.org

George K. Allison, AB, MA, *Headmaster*
Carol Dougherty, BA, MEd, *Assistant Head of School*

Founded in 1875, Perkiomen School is a college preparatory, coeducational boarding and day school located fifty miles northwest of Philadelphia. A small friendly school, Perkiomen enrolls 250 students in grades five through twelve and post-graduate. The School offers a traditional structured academic program featuring small classes, a seven to one student/faculty ratio, honors and advanced placement courses, ESL for international students, Developmental Language, and supervised evening study halls for the boarding students.

Perkiomen is committed to the development of each individual to the best of his or her abilities. Because most of the teachers live on campus, individual help is readily available after school and in the evenings and on weekends. The faculty sets a warm and friendly family atmosphere in which to live and grow effectively.

Beyond the challenges of the classroom, Perkiomen students also grow through participation in a competitive athletic program offering 17 varsity sports; on- and off-stage involvement in a strong theater program with three major productions per year; singing in the chorus or smaller vocal groups; membership in special interest clubs such as SADD, Amnesty International, debate, yearbook, newspaper or literary magazine; and a variety of groups to enhance campus life such as the Student Senate.

Weekend activities are planned both on- and off-campus so there are a variety of opportunities from which to choose. Because Perkiomen is located in a small town, students can walk to restaurants, a movie theater, and stores. Major cities such as Philadelphia and New York City are easily accessible to Perkiomen for transportation as well as cultural resources.

Perkiomen offers the individual a variety of academic and personal opportunities to develop his or her potential and prepare for college and life.

PORTSMOUTH ABBEY SCHOOL
PORTSMOUTH, RI

Portsmouth Abbey School, a coeducational independent boarding and day school for grades 9 through 12 in Portsmouth, Rhode Island, is owned and operated by Benedictine monks of the English Congregation, and administered by lay men and women. This collaboration, unique among American boarding schools, has created a community rooted in the ideals of the Catholic tradition, and the high scholastic standards practiced by the Benedictine community since the sixth century.

The School offers the many attractions one expects to find at a leading boarding school: a challenging college preparatory program, talented and compassionate teachers, an international student body, fine facilities, a busy and lively student life, and a supportive residential environment. Beyond those assets, however, are the ideals of the School, and these are what truly make Portsmouth unique.

The aim of Portsmouth Abbey School today, as it has been since Father John Hugh Diman founded it in 1926, is to help its students to grow in knowledge and grace. The School seeks to embody those ideals and qualities which lie at the heart of the 1500 year-old Benedictine tradition: reverence for God and humanity, respect for learning and order, and responsibility for the shared experience of community life.

The program of studies offers young men and women of academic potential and motivation a solid foundation in the liberal arts. The School believes that these disciplines best foster the development of the skills fundamental to all learning: the ability to read with understanding, to reason clearly, and to express oneself with precision.

Portsmouth offers its students a structured environment, built upon a schedule of shared daily activities—classes, athletics, clubs, and social

life—and of regular community worship. The House provides each student with a familial base and identity within the School at large. Within each House there is the Houseparent and the House Chaplain, and coordinated sources of support. Beyond the House, there is a varied and enriching social and extracurricular program.

Portsmouth's Catholic heritage and its curriculum give it a singular place among independent schools. Supported by the presence and example of the resident Benedictine community, the traditional ideals of Christian living and learning are intended to inform every part of School life, and to guide the policies and practices of the community and its members. The School welcomes students from diverse backgrounds, while encouraging an appreciation for the Catholic faith. Portsmouth thus aspires to develop informed and open-minded leaders, educated in the Christian tradition, and prepared to meet the challenges and responsibilities of life.

With a beautiful 500-acre campus on the shore of Narrangansett Bay, 10 miles from Newport, the School benefits from a wide range of athletic facilities, including an indoor hockey rink; two gymnasiums; a new state-of-the-art squash & fitness center; six tennis courts; a track; soccer, football, lacrosse, baseball, field hockey, and softball fields; an 18-hole golf course; and an equestrian facility. Additionally, the School maintains a fleet of sailboats which is used by the Portsmouth sailing team. All students participate in athletics, and teams compete on the varsity, junior varsity and junior varsity B levels to accommodate students of varying ages and abilities.

Outside the classroom, students are encouraged to become involved in the betterment of the Portsmouth Abbey community and the community at large. Among the opportunities available to students are the school radio station, student newspaper, Dante Group,
Debate Club, Fishing Club, Future Problem Solvers, Glee Club, Humanities Roundtable, Korea Culture Club, Model United Nations, campus tour guides, Social Committee, Student Council, student-run snack shop, Writing Workshop, music ensembles, community service, yearbook, and literary magazine.

For further information, contact the Office of Admissions at 401-683-2005.

PORTSMOUTH ABBEY SUMMER SCHOOL
PORTSMOUTH, RI
Tel: 401-643-1225   Fax: 401-683-5888
E-mail: summer@portsmouthabbey.org

Michael Bonin, *Director*

Portsmouth Abbey School is located ten miles north of Newport on 500 woodland acres on the shores of Narragansett Bay. The Summer School offers a variety of programs for girls and boys entering grades 8 through 11. Whether enrolled in courses for enrichment or acceleration, students benefit from a structured program, small classes, a diversified student body, and an experienced faculty. The Summer School program is demanding, but it also provides ample opportunities for entertainment, leisure, and wholesome social activities.

Courses are offered in Study Skills, English, English Composition, Creative Writing, SAT I Preparation, History, Marine Biology, Digital Photography, Anatomy and Physiology, Genetic Engineering, Geology, Art, Public Speaking, and Web Page Design. The curriculum also offers an intensive Theater Workshop. An integral part of the program is an intensive course of English as a Second Language (ESL).

Athletic opportunities include sailing, equestrian, squash, cardiovascular and weight training, tennis, basketball, soccer, volleyball, softball, and recreational running. Students attend movies and have regular weekend excursions to Boston, Newport, and the Aquidneck Island beaches. A full descriptive catalogue is available from the Director of the Summer School.

PROFESSIONAL CHILDREN'S SCHOOL

132 W. 60th St.
NEW YORK, NY 10023
Tel: 212-582-3116   FAX: 212-307-6542
James Dawson, PhD, *Head*

The Professional Children's School is a fully accredited, non-profit day school offering a rigorous college preparatory education to students who are also preparing for or already participating in professional careers. Located two blocks south of Lincoln Center for the Performing Arts, PCS offers easy access to the School of American Ballet, Juilliard, other dance and music schools, the New York Skating Club, Carnegie Hall, rehearsal studios and theaters.

PCS was founded in 1914 to serve children performing on Broadway and in vaudeville. Today the student body, grades 4-12, includes stage, film and television actors; models; those training for careers in music, dance, and competitive sports; and children of parents in the arts. These students come from all over the nation and the world to study and perform in New York City and to pursue their academic training at PCS. The range of their professional, personal and geographical backgrounds gives a flavor to PCS which is rare for a day school.

PCS believes that individual and group learning are equally important and, together, foster independence, self-discipline and respect for the point of view of others. The program combines classroom instruction with guided study courses and flexible scheduling to enable students to meet professional engagements which occur during school hours. The goal of the academic program is to educate students so that they may pursue any occupation in which they are interested. PCS's alumni include lawyers, educators and physicians, as well as actors, composers, dancers, musicians, producers and directors.

At PCS, interest in students' academic progress is matched by concern for their social and emotional growth. Faculty and staff strive to maintain an atmosphere of encouragement, interest and support to help students grow into adults capable of enjoying their full potential, regardless of the careers they ultimately choose.

PRINCETON DAY SCHOOL

Princeton Day School (PDS) is located on a 105-acre campus just two miles from the center of Princeton and Princeton University. Founded in 1965 after the merger of Miss Fine's School (established in 1899) and Princeton Country Day School (established in 1924), PDS offers an outstanding opportunity for intellectual growth and character development by setting high standards of academic excellence combined with caring and nurturing teaching. Families choose our school for our faculty and curriculum, and for the level of achievement they see on the part of our students – from confident five-year-olds delivering their first oral reports to upper schoolers who consistently gain admission to the nation's most selective colleges and universities.

As a day school community, every student at PDS has the same status – the chance to be equally and fully involved in the life of our school. Our students' experience here extends from the start of classes in the morning to the end of sports practices and rehearsals in the afternoon. Philosophically, this means that our faculty educates in partnership with parents rather than in place of them, and that the learning environment students find at PDS compliments their life at home. Students are also able to participate in the life of the region's community, which has an unusually rich range of cultural and educational offerings. From junior kindergarten through twelfth grade, the entire student body is housed together in a single complex, allowing for collaboration among the faculty. Working together, our teachers coordinate the curriculum to build meaningfully across the Lower, Middle, and Upper School divisions. Contact between the divisions enriches the students' experiences too, both informally and through leadership opportunities such as the Teacher Assistant Program.

Princeton Day School is a place in which students are continually encouraged to become independent learners; they are afforded unusual freedom in shaping their own educational experiences in academics, athletics and the arts. The result is an environment charged with variety and vitality – a place where young people with diverse gifts and interests can experience growth and find a niche in which to thrive.

PROVIDENCE DAY SCHOOL
CHARLOTTE, NC

Providence Day School is an independent, coeducational school open to students desiring a traditional college preparatory education. Since its inception in September 1970, Providence Day has become a prominent, thriving school of 1479 students in grades TK-12. Present physical facilities include academic classrooms, well-equipped science labs, libraries, a fine arts center, multipurpose area, dining hall, theatre and gymnasiums, as well as tennis courts and athletic fields. A new science and technology center was dedicated in Fall, 1998. Two new buildings, a library and an athletic center, became available for student use in Fall, 2001.

Providence Day offers a curriculum that allows students the opportunity to reach their potential academically—to develop the ability to question and learn, to listen and communicate, and to support as well as lead effectively. Advanced and individualized instruction provides students with the knowledge and incentive to excel in a college setting, as well as a chosen career. The foundations of basic skills in language arts, mathematics, science, and social studies are laid during the formative years and stimulated further in all subsequent years. Varied and active extracurricular and athletic programs are provided for all students. The interscholastic sports program for girls and boys includes football, soccer, field hockey, volleyball, swimming, basketball, track, cross-country, wrestling, tennis, softball, baseball, golf, and lacrosse.

In addition, appreciation of aesthetics and cultural values is emphasized. In all areas of the educational program, the student is recognized as the center of all efforts and goals. Our students are enriched as individuals and are academically confident to face challenges. Students are accepted without regard to race, color, national or ethnic origin.

RABUN GAP-NACOOCHEE SCHOOL

- College preparatory, coeducational, boarding and day program for students in grades 6-12
- Small classes, AP/honors sections, research opportunities
- Strong athletics, arts, outdoor programs and environmental studies
- 1,400-acre campus with lake and working farm
- Affordable tuition; financial aid and merit scholarships
- Adult support and an extended family environment nurture students' personal growth
- Affiliated with the Presbyterian Church (U.S.A.)

Office of Admission • Rabun Gap-Nacoochee School
339 Nacoochee Drive • Rabun Gap, GA 30568
www.rabungap.org • 706-746-7467 • 800-543-7467

RANNEY SCHOOL

235 Hope Rd.
TINTON FALLS, NJ 07724
Tel: 732-542-4777

Lawrence S. Sykoff, EdD,
Head of School

Ranney School is a co-educational, independent, college preparatory, day school for grades beginners through twelve. The traditional, structured academic program features an average class size of 15 students, homogeneously grouped where appropriate. Total enrollment averages 740.

Ranney School was founded in 1960 by Russell G. Ranney as an outgrowth of the Rumson Reading Institute. Emphasis on language arts skills remains the cornerstone of a Ranney education at all grade levels.

For the capable student, the school offers Algebra I in 7th grade. This allows the opportunity for 6 year advanced mathematics/science programs. A total of 17 Advanced Placement courses are offered in the Upper School, as well as standard and Honors courses in math, science, history, foreign language, and English.

French, Spanish, computer science, art, and music are introduced in the Lower School. Latin, French, and Spanish are available starting in 6th grade.

The Lower School is composed of three buildings and has its own computer lab, resource room, and library. Each classroom is equipped with two computers. The Middle and Upper School is housed in our modern and hi-tech academic complex. Our new facility offers 33 classrooms, state-of-the-art biology and chemistry laboratories, foreign language laboratory, a college guidance center, modern library, 300 computers, and a unique Distance Learning Center. In addition, the Middle and Upper School has its own dining hall.

A full sports program makes use of the school's beautiful campus. Swimming in a 25-meter indoor pool is a weekly event for all grades.

Two gyms provide space for basketball, volleyball, gymnastics, and weight-lifting. Interscholastic sports are soccer, track, cross-country, basketball, softball, baseball, tennis, swimming, and lacrosse. In addition, the facilities include a state-of-the-art fitness center with a certified athletic trainer on duty.

Other extracurricular activities include forensics, drama, chess and various student publications. An optional after-school program allows students to participate in a large number of supervised activities, both academic and social.

RIVER OAKS BAPTIST SCHOOL
2300 Willowick Rd.
HOUSTON, TX 77027
Tel: 713-623-6938   Web: www.robs.org

Established by River Oaks Baptist Church as a mission to the community, River Oaks Baptist School celebrates its fiftieth anniversary this year. Enrollment annually approaches 780 Primary, Lower and Middle School students drawn from a wide geographical area, varied economic backgrounds, and more than 20 distinct religious traditions. River Oaks Baptist School prepares its students to meet life's challenges and lead tomorrow's world through a superior educational program undergirded by faith in Jesus Christ and Christian principles.

Administratively and physically, the school is organized into three divisions: Primary School (ages two to five), Lower School (kindergarten through fourth grade), and Middle School (fifth through eighth grade). A distinctive component of the school environment is an emphasis on character development, which spans the curriculum in all three divisions and touches every facet of student life. Students feel respected, physically safe, and emotionally secure in their educational surroundings and enjoy the full benefit of a challenging, multifaceted curriculum. Upon graduation from eighth grade, nine out of ten R.O.B.S. students enter their first-choice high school.

RIVERSIDE PRESBYTERIAN DAY SCHOOL
830 Oak St.
JACKSONVILLE, FL 32204
Tel: 904-353-5511   Fax: 904-358-3837
E-Mail: rlittell@rpds.com   Web Site: www.rpds.com

Robert W. Littell, *Headmaster*

Riverside Presbyterian Day School is a co-educational elementary school currently enrolling 490 students in Pre-Kindergarten through Grade 6. Founded in 1948 by Riverside Presbyterian Church (PCUSA), the school is located in the historic Riverside community of Jacksonville, Florida.

A fully certified and experienced administrative staff and faculty of 60 is committed to providing a school climate reflective of the school's mission: "To educate the mind, nurture the spirit and foster the development of each child." Teachers affirm the values of Christian love and concern for others, encourage creativity, and spark enthusiasm for learning.

The school is organized into three academic divisions: Pre-Kindergarten and Kindergarten, Primary Grades 1-3 and Upper Elementary Grades 4-6. The basic curriculum is enriched by the teaching of art, music, physical education, Bible, computer, Spanish and library skills.

Private Schools Illustrated — 1236

THE RIVERS SCHOOL
333 Winter St.
WESTON, MA 02493-1040
Tel: 781-235-9300

The Rivers School is a college preparatory school offering a liberal arts curriculum in an environment where students are allowed to challenge themselves intellectually, morally, socially and physically. At its heart, Rivers has a deep commitment to the imparting of knowledge and the encouragement of growth and self-discovery in each individual student. Students quickly discover the school's rigorous but positive academic demands. With an average of 12 students per classroom, Rivers' energetic and caring faculty are able to foster the intellectual and personal growth of each student as they challenge students to stretch and explore all areas of the curriculum as well as school life.

Teachers at Rivers are also advisors and coaches, an arrangement that promotes a rapport that makes direct communication between students and teachers easy and comfortable. This rapport carries over to the classroom where students feel empowered to ask questions, delve deeply into subject matter, think critically and actively debate in discussions.

Coeducational since 1989, Rivers emphasizes participation in the arts, athletics, community service and co-curricular activities. Requirements in these areas demonstrate to each student the need for qualities of leadership, self-confidence, cooperation, initiative and responsibility—qualities that not only prepare students for the demands of college, but also for the challenges that extend throughout their adult lives. Rivers' student population of 410 is comprised of 96 students in the Middle School (grades 6-8) and 314 students in the Upper School (grades 9-12). Rivers also offers a unique Conservatory Program for highly talented and committed student-musicians.

THE ROEPER SCHOOL

... to help children to be themselves and to encourage them to make a difference in the world.
ANNEMARIE ROEPER

where gifted students love to learn

PRE-SCHOOL THROUGH GRADE 12

41190 WOODWARD AVENUE
BLOOMFIELD HILLS, MI 48304

248.203.7300
WWW.ROEPER.ORG

ROSEMONT SCHOOL OF THE HOLY CHILD

1344 Montgomery Ave.
ROSEMONT, PA 19010
Tel: 610-922-1000   Fax: 610-525-7128
Web: www.rosemontschool.org

Rosemont School of the Holy Child offers an exceptional education program for boys and girls in Nursery through Eighth Grade. Rosemont's objective is to develop the whole child—soul and body, mind and heart—by combining a sound religious training with vigorous intellectual and physical growth. Since virtually all of our students go on to college preparatory schools, the curriculum is designed to enable them to move easily into the most intellectually challenging environments and to compete successfully there.

Private Schools Illustrated — 1238

RUMSEY HALL SCHOOL
201 Romford Rd.
WASHINGTON DEPOT, CT 06794
Tel: 860-868-0535 Fax: 860-868-7907
Thomas W. Farmen, *Headmaster*

Rumsey Hall was founded in 1900 by Lillias Rumsey Sanford. The coeducational boarding and day school which evolved from our founder's dream retains distinct characteristics from its early years. Mrs. Sanford's efforts to create a home away from home for her young boarders became part of Rumsey's heritage. There is a strong sense of stability and family in our community today.

There is a wonderful balance in our school between providing the support, nurture and care that children need while presenting appropriate academic challenge and rigor. Our curriculum is designed to teach children to read, write and calculate proficiently, in preparation for the profound challenges that await them in secondary school and college. We lay the educational foundations for the sturdy structures to be built upon. We embrace the idea of "honor through effort." And effort, more than grades, is the criterion for success.

ST. ANDREW'S SCHOOL
MIDDLETOWN, DE

Daniel T. Roach, *Headmaster*

St. Andrew's seeks able, ambitious boys and girls regardless of race, religious affiliation, or financial circumstances. Over 45% of the student body of 270 students receives tuition assistance based on demonstrated need. Students come from 27 states and 8 foreign countries. All students and faculty live on campus.

Situated on 2200 acres of farm and forest land bordering Noxontown Pond, Silver Lake and the tidal waters of Appoquinimink Creek, St. Andrew's School offers a rural setting of unmatched beauty. In 1988, the School was selected from among 70 other boarding schools to be the set for the critically acclaimed film, *Dead Poets Society*. Within 30 minutes of Wilmington, one hour of Philadelphia and Baltimore, and two hours of Washington, D.C., students and faculty take advantage of historical, cultural and entertainment opportunities in these cities and use the local setting for sailing, canoeing, fishing, camping, biking, hiking and observing the many species of game and waterfowl which inhabit the campus.

St. Andrew's size, structure and philosophy work together to produce a cohesiveness and coherence which is rare in schools today. Our relatively small size—with all students boarding and every teacher residing on campus—fosters a sense of belonging and a sense of community among our students. The diversity of background and talent within our student body, encouraged by a large financial aid commitment, strengthens and enriches the fabric of the School and adds a special dimension to a St. Andrew's education. Regular services of worship together give focus and meaning to our community, and classes are small, enhancing growth, self-confidence, adventure and intellectual curiosity. The collective goal of the faculty is to help each student realize, to the fullest extent possible, his or her academic, athletic, artistic and, most important of all, personal potential. At the same time, we hope that our students will become ever more aware of the social, environmental and political challenges facing our country and world and ever more determined to provide leadership in the search for solutions.

St. Andrew's academic and athletic facilities are extensive. The academic program is a rigorous college preparatory program. Most students enter in the 9th and 10th grades. The interscholastic sports for boys are football, soccer, cross country, basketball, wrestling, squash, swimming, baseball, crew, lacrosse and tennis. The interscholastic sports for girls are soccer, field hockey, cross country, volleyball, basketball, squash, swimming, crew, tennis and lacrosse, Aerobics, yoga, dance and weight training programs are also available.

Private Schools Illustrated — 1240

ST. ANDREW'S SCHOOL
63 Federal Rd.
BARRINGTON, RI 02806

Tel: 401-246-1230
Web: standrews-ri.org

Day and Boarding Grades 6-12 College Preparatory

Founded in 1893 by the Rev. William Merrick Chapin, and located on 83 scenic acres on the Rhode Island coastline, St. Andrew's School offers a college preparatory curriculum with an individualized approach to teaching. In 2002, St. Andrew's was named an "Exemplary School" by renowned learning expert Dr. Mel Levine. Dr. Levine's Schools Attuned program is the underpinning of St. Andrew's curriculum. Every teacher at St. Andrew's is trained to identify students' individual learning styles, and to teach students *how* they learn best, thereby helping them to maximize their strengths. Academic expectations are high, but support is always available for those who need it. Small classes (8-12 students), an overall student to faculty ratio of 5:1, and a daily advisor program, ensure that every student receives the attention he or she needs. Courses in English literature and composition, history, mathematics, computer applications, and the physical and life sciences are complemented by electives in foreign languages, ethics, global issues, drama, art, and music.

Independent study and AP courses are offered in a variety of subjects. Students with mild language-based learning disabilities or ADHD are supported through the Resource and Focus Programs, available for an additional fee. Students are also exposed to a variety of social, cultural, and community service opportunities.

Students are expected to participate in the athletics program, which offers competitive team sports in soccer, cross-country, basketball, lacrosse, and tennis, as well as a variety of individual sports, including Project Adventure Ropes Course, biking, and weight training. In addition, a variety of clubs and extracurricular activities are offered, ensuring that every student can find at least one non-academic area in which to pursue personal interests. Photography, a culinary club, swimming and rock climbing are but a few of the options available.

Boarders live in small dorms, anchored by resident faculty members and their families. The close-knit community is composed of students from all over the United States and several foreign countries. Weekend activities include trips to the nearby cultural centers of Providence, Newport and Boston, as well as a wide variety of outdoor adventures.

SAINT ANDREW'S SCHOOL
BOCA RATON, FL

The Rev. George E. Andrews, BA, MDiv, *Headmaster*

Saint Andrew's School is located on the Gold Coast of Florida, approximately 35 miles south of West Palm Beach and 60 miles north of Miami. It is a coeducational school, Kindergarten to 12th grade, enrolling 560 in the Upper School, grades 9 to 12 (102 of which are resident boarding students), 255 students in the Middle School (grades 6 to 8), and 264 students in the Lower School (grades K to 5). Founded in 1961 as a boys' boarding school, Saint Andrew's now enrolls approximately 1100 students with an equal ratio of boys and girls. The school is situated on 80 beautifully manicured acres and is affiliated with the Episcopal Church. Recent additions to the school's physical plant have included: in 1996, a 32,000 sq. ft. middle school with 23 classrooms, 3 computer laboratories with 60 networked Pentium computers for student use, and extensive workrooms in art, band, and chorus; an impressive Student Center and Great Hall dining facility; and a refurbished Upper School Library and Computer Center. In the Fall of 2002, construction began on three major expansions of school facilities: a $6 million Athletic Complex that will include a gymnasium, improved locker facilities, fitness and training rooms, and pool; a $4 million Upper School Science Center; and a $6 million Performing Arts Center that will include a 750-person capacity Auditorium and classrooms for band, chorus, and fine arts.

Academic standards are rigorous at Saint Andrew's. Average class size is 15 with a low student-teacher ratio in all three divisions. The curriculum is traditional and requires that a student complete coursework in English, mathematics, foreign language, history, and laboratory science. Accelerated honors and AP courses are available in all these departments. Theology, art, music, community service, and computers are also required.

Saint Andrew's prepares its graduates for leading colleges and universities throughout the nation. The foundation of the curriculum is designed to give each student a broad intellectual understanding of the world in which we live and to provide service to this large society. Over 50 faculty members live on campus, creating an environment that establishes close relationships between students and teachers both in and out of the classroom. A strong emphasis is placed on the School Honor Code, which stresses respect for oneself and unto others.

Admission to Saint Andrew's School follows a traditional application process, with a February 10th deadline. Admission is made without regard for race, creed, color, or economic situation.

ST. ANNE'S-BELFIELD SCHOOL
2132 Ivy Road, Charlottesville, VA 22903
phone 434-296-5106 - fax 434-979-1486
e-mail jcraig@stab.org - www.stab.org

St. Anne's-Belfield is a coeducational, college preparatory day school enrolling 843 students in pre-school-grade 12. The school also offers 5-day and 7-day boarding and an ESL 7-day boarding program for students in grades 9-12. Required courses in fine arts and religion; a weekly, nonsectarian chapel service; and participation in community service and athletics complement the rigorous core curriculum. Seventy percent of our faculty have earned advanced degrees. These bright and caring professionals teach and serve as advisors to guide and support our students as they travel through their school career. In small size classes, students are encouraged to ask questions, to think critically, and to develop strong study skills. College counselors work individually with students and their families, and graduates matriculate at our nation's finest colleges and universities. The school has recently completed extensive renovations and expansion of the Upper School classrooms, library, dining facilities, dormitories, and athletic facilities. Contact Jean Craig, Director of Admission, to arrange a visit. We are located in historic Charlottesville, home of Thomas Jefferson's Monticello and adjacent to the University of Virginia.

SAINT EDWARD'S SCHOOL

1895 Saint Edward's Dr./South Campus
VERO BEACH, FL 32963

Saint Edward's School, a fully accredited coeducational day school serving grades pre-kindergarten through twelve, has been evaluated as one of the outstanding independent schools in Florida and has served Vero Beach and its environs for more than 39 years. The mission of Saint Edward's is to challenge each student in a supportive college preparatory environment that promotes academic excellence, sound moral values and high self-esteem within its Episcopal school tradition.

The objective at Saint Edward's is to instill in all students the qualities of academic excellence, leadership, and character. The rigorous college preparatory curriculum includes in-depth academic courses, a diversified and competitive athletic program, and outstanding instruction in fine arts, music and drama.

ST. PETER'S SCHOOL

319 Lombard St.
PHILADELPHIA, PA 19147
Tel: 215-925-3963
Web: www.stpetersonline.org

David J. Costello, *Head of School*

An independent, multi-denominational, co-ed day school, pre-school through eighth grade. Founded in 1834, St. Peter's draws children of all economic backgrounds, races, and religions. Music, art, poetry, and French enhance a traditional academic curriculum. Science, computer, and physical education are integral to the student's experience. Before and After School Enrichment Programs are available.

SAINT JAMES SCHOOL
ST. JAMES, MD
Tel: 301-733-9330   Fax: 301-739-1310
The Rev. D. Stuart Dunnan, DPhil, *Headmaster*
Bill Ellis, *Director of Admissions*

Small by design, Saint James has directed its energies since 1842 toward maintaining high scholastic standards, excellence in athletics and development of sound character. Our unique size creates a family environment that provides excellent support for our challenging and traditional curriculum, which provides a solid foundation for strong academic achievement at the collegiate level. Coeducational, with boarding and day students in grades 8-12, Saint James School is the oldest Episcopal boarding school founded on the English model in the United States. Almost all faculty live on campus, and in addition to their teaching duties, they coach students in athletics and the arts, live in the dormitories, and eat with them in the dining hall. Each faculty member also acts as an advisor to 6-8 students, supporting and directing their academic and personal growth and achievement.

Saint James School lies just south of Hagerstown and approximately 65 miles from both Baltimore and Washington, D.C. The region offers many cultural and historic points of interest including the Appalachian Trail, C&O Canal, Harpers Ferry, and Antietam and Gettysburg Battlefields. Faculty and students enjoy the cultural resources of the Baltimore-Washington metropolitan area on regular field trips.

For more information on the value of a traditional education in a contemporary world, please contact our Admission office.

Private Schools Illustrated — 1246

ST. PAUL'S SCHOOL
CONCORD, NH

"Let us learn those things on earth the knowledge of which continues in Heaven."
St. Jerome, Epistle 53
St. Paul's School motto

Believing that education is lifelong and continues beyond the classroom, St. Paul's School invites a diverse group of students and adults to create an extended family which respects and nurtures individual talent, personal freedom and responsibility, and public service. Students are encouraged to seek the highest standards of scholastic, artistic, and physical achievement through an integrated curriculum.

As a Christian boarding school rooted in the Episcopal Church and affirming all faiths, St. Paul's is committed to social responsibility, respect for diversity, a passion for learning, the formation of character, the teaching of virtue, and spiritual growth. Such commitments are the hallmarks of our heritage; they illuminate our motto and guide our life together.
—St. Paul's School Mission Statement

Founded in 1856, St. Paul's School offers 500 students and 100 faculty members a philosophy that the best education for life is one that addresses the body and soul, as well as the mind.

Located 70 miles north of Boston on 2,000 acres of woodlands, fields, and ponds, St. Paul's is a coeducational boarding school for grades 9 through 12 that is committed to academic excellence. Rooted in the Episcopal Church, St. Paul's relies on Christian traditions to promote friendship, understanding, trust, and respect for persons of all faiths and beliefs among students from 45 states and 18 countries.

The curriculum is interactive, interdisciplinary, collaborative, and innovative, with significant integration of new technology. Studies in the Humanities program integrate English, history, and religious studies. Mathematics, science, and technology are coordinated to enhance student capabilities in all three areas. Students may choose among Chinese, French, German, Greek, Japanese, Latin, or Spanish to pursue interests in foreign languages. Studio, practical courses, and independent groups in the fine arts, dance, music, and theater provide hands-on and performance-based experiences for all students. Independent and collaborative research projects also are encouraged.

Students may choose between 28 interscholastic teams and more than 60 different activities, clubs, and organizations.

As an all-boarding "family" school, St. Paul's cultivates an understanding of how communities work and the willingness to make the personal sacrifices needed to sustain a community. Faculty members and their families interact with students on the grounds, teaching them in the classroom, coaching them on the playing fields and in the arts, and acting as advisers.

The School's extensive buildings and facilities include 18 residential houses, Ohrstrom Library with 70,000 volumes and a computerized learning laboratory, science and mathematics buildings, two chapels, an electronic language learning center, a wide variety of indoor and outdoor athletic facilities, and centers for music, drama, and dance.

For more information, please contact the Admissions Office at:
St. Paul's School
325 Pleasant St.
Concord, NH 03301-2591
Tel: 603-229-4700 or 888-644-9611
Fax: 603-229-4771
E-mail: admissions@sps.edu
Web: sps.edu

SALISBURY SCHOOL
6279 Hobbs Rd., P.O. Box 2295
Salisbury, MD 21802
Tel: 410-742-4464   Fax: 410-546-2310
Web: www.salisburymd.org

James G. Landi, *Headmaster*

Salisbury School is an independent, college preparatory, coed, non-sectarian school, serving students from pre kindergarten through twelfth grade. The school is dedicated to fostering the intellectual, ethical, physical, and emotional growth of each of its students. Teaching a carefully structured, rich and diverse curriculum, Salisbury School provides for academic excellence, individual attention, and intellectual challenge. Students at Salisbury School work to master the verbal and mathematical skills that allow them to communicate ideas effectively through writing, speaking, and computing, thus preparing them for life in our ever-advancing world.

As preparation for both college and for life, Salisbury School seeks to give each of its students the true understanding that comes after serious thought and a broad and deep exploration of curricular material. The Fine Arts and Physical Education are integral components of the curriculum, a reflection of the school's commitment to the liberal arts tradition.

Believing that children grow and learn at different rates, Salisbury School strives to promote a love of learning in each child. Salisbury

School believes that learning on all levels is enhanced when there is a strong partnership between school and home, and parents are actively encouraged to become involved in their children's educational experiences. Salisbury School fosters an atmosphere in which individual students are encouraged to compete only with themselves as they strive to achieve a level of excellence that reflects their best personal effort and full potential, a genuine and meaningful accomplishment that does not come at the expense of others.

To assist in the vital development of self-confidence and a feeling of self-worth, student work is evaluated, in the lower grades, through detailed reports consisting of checklists of academic proficiency accompanied by anecdotal teacher comments. Traditional letter grades are added in Middle School. Because the learning accomplished by each child is valued in its own right, no student at Salisbury School is singled out by class rank or the awarding of academic prizes.

Salisbury School believes that it is important, within a nurturing environment, to teach ethical values and to create a community in which treating others with respect and kindness is expected. Salisbury School genuinely seeks to be a diverse community, one that reflects its larger community, wherein students learn to understand, respect, and appreciate individual differences.

Salisbury School strives to graduate students who have developed a strong sense of inner discipline, the ability to face conflicts with confidence and conviction, and the desire to lead creative and purposeful lives.

Private Schools Illustrated — 1250

THE PORTER SARGENT HANDBOOK SERIES

11 Beacon St. Ste. 1400 Boston, MA 02108-3099 USA
Tel: 617-523-1670 Fax: 617-523-1021
info@portersargent.com www.portersargent.com

Tools for Independent Evaluation

In 1914, educator and writer Porter Sargent introduced *The Handbook of Private Schools* because he felt educators, administrators and parents needed an objective guide to quality schools and programs emphasizing the needs of the individual student.

The development of the Porter Sargent Handbook Series followed that very simple aim. Each publication is a source book of information for those who need—and ought—to know about the advantage of independent instruction, providing the most up-to-date narrative and statistical information on schools and programs serving those who seek out the best education worldwide.

The Handbook of Private Schools * The Directory for Exceptional Children
Schools Abroad of Interest to Americans * Guide to Summer Camps and Schools

In Your Own Words

Educators and parents have long trusted Porter Sargent for independent, objective school profiles available nowhere else.

Your program's Illustrated Announcement can support this mission, and it will be seen daily by:

- Parents
- Headmasters, and admissions and guidance counselors
- Consultants and vendors
- A worldwide network of educational professionals

Each reference-quality title is the book of record for its field, with a long shelf-life and high per-copy readership.

Please call 617-523-1670 or E-mail announcements@portersargent.com for details on joining the next edition.

The Handbook of Private Schools * The Directory for Exceptional Children
Schools Abroad of Interest to Americans * Guide to Summer Camps and Schools

SAINT STEPHEN'S
EPISCOPAL SCHOOL

315 41st St. W
Bradenton, FL 34209
Tel: 941-746-2121 Fax: 941-746-5699
Web: www.saintstephens.org

Saint Stephen's Episcopal School is a fully accredited, co-educational, independent, college preparatory day school for students in Pre-Kindergarten through grade 12. Its mission is to prepare its 800 students for a meaningful life, to help them become responsible, contributing citizens with a deep sense of self-worth and independence. Class sizes are kept small with a student/teacher ratio of 11:1. Advanced Placement classes are available in all departments. The fine arts department features courses in the visual arts, music, and drama. The school's Interim Quest program, conducted during the final weeks of each academic year, allows students to participate in specialized studies on campus and in service learning projects.

SAN FRANCISCO DAY SCHOOL

350 Masonic Ave.
SAN FRANCISCO, CA 94118
John C. Lin, *Head of School*

San Francisco Day School was established in 1981 to fulfill the need for a local independent elementary school of high academic standards. Enrolling boys and girls in kindergarten through grade 8, San Francisco Day strives to develop each child's academic potential and personal responsibility.

Academics emphasize the mastery of basic skills—reading, writing and mathematical concepts—while stimulating creativity and critical thinking. Small class size ensures personal attention for each pupil. Art, music, physical education and Outdoor Education complement the curriculum at each level, while older students receive instruction in foreign language. Technology is woven into the curriculum. The Afternoon Enrichment Program offers an extensive variety of artistic, athletic and recreational activities.

San Francisco Day School encourages each child to build a strong sense of self-esteem, respect for others and community involvement. The school enrolls a diverse student body representing San Francisco's rich multicultural population.

Private Schools Illustrated — 1252

THE SAN FRANCISCO SCHOOL
300 Gaven St.
SAN FRANCISCO, CA 94134
Tel: 415-239-5065
Fax: 415-239-4833
Web: www.sfschool.org

The San Francisco School cultivates and celebrates the intellectual, imaginative and humanitarian promise of each student in a community that practices mutual respect, embraces diversity, and inspires a passion for learning.

SFS is recognized among local independent schools for its outstanding, personalized academic program, deep sense of community, and dynamic visual and performing arts program. The elementary program and middle school offer a comprehensive, challenging and multicultural curriculum built on the ideals of a progressive, student-centered approach, while the preschool-kindergarten program centers primarily on the renowned educational philosophy of Maria Montessori.

The main points of entry are at the Preschool, at 3 years old, and at 6th grade, as the school expands from one classroom of 20 to two classrooms of 16 students.

SANDY SPRING FRIENDS SCHOOL
SANDY SPRING, MD

Kenneth W. Smith, BS, MDiv, ThM, DMin, *Head of School*

Sandy Spring Friends School was established in 1961 by the Sandy Spring Friends Meeting to provide a strong academic program rooted in Quaker values. The School began as a boarding and day high school; a Middle School was added in 1982 and in 1993 Friends Elementary School merged with Sandy Spring Friends School to create a Pre-Kindergarten through 12th grade program. This is the first and only Pre-K-12 Friends school in suburban Maryland and only the second Pre-K-12 Friends school in the country to provide a complete boarding program.

The School's 140-acre campus provides opportunities for environmental and outdoor education programs, as well as athletic facilities. Most students come from the Greater Washington area, though the boarding program attracts students from throughout the country and the world. Class size is small which allows the faculty to provide individual attention to each student. Advanced and accelerated courses are available as are extensive offerings in the arts and athletics. The School requires a significant involvement in both the community service and the on-campus work programs as ways of developing individual responsibility and a sense of commitment to the community. Meeting for Worship is a fundamental part of the School's program. The School was a founding member of the Washington based Black Student Fund, and has long been committed to ethnic, economic, and cultural diversity. Students are well prepared to enter the leading colleges and universities in the country.

SOUTHWESTERN ACADEMY
One School, Two Campuses, Two Learning Environments

SAN MARINO, CA   RIMROCK, AZ

Southwestern Academy prepares students to be lifelong learners, critical thinkers, and self-motived leaders who will positively impact the natural and global community in the 21st century. Techniques and methodology focus on application of knowledge and skills while incorporating the cultural differences and individual learning styles, abilities, and interests of each student.

Southwestern Academy was founded by Maurice Veronda in 1924 "for capable students who could do better" in small, supportive classes. While maintaining that commitment, Southwestern provides college preparatory and general academic coursework to U.S. and international students with strong academic abilities who are eager to learn and strengthen English language skills as well as pursue a general scholastic program. Departmentalized and supportively structured classes are limited to 9-12 students. Small classes allow for individualized attention in a non-competitive environment for regular school year and summer programs.

A mix of U.S. and international students from as many as 25 countries offers a unique blend of cultural, social, and educational opportunities for all. Every effort is made to enroll a well-balanced student body that represents the rich ethnic diversity of U.S. citizens and students from around the world. The student body consists of 175 students who prefer a small, personalized education; above average students who have the potential to become excellent academic achievers in the right learning environment; and average to under-achieving students who, with supportive structure, can achieve academic success. Southwestern is not a behavioral or therapeutic school and will not accept students with serious disciplinary, emotional, attitudinal problems, or significant learning differences.

High school graduation requirements are based on University of California requirements. The academic term is mid-September through mid-June. International students are offered three levels of classes in English as a second language (ESL), including a transition class that prepares them to enter and succeed in other academic areas. Advanced placement classes are available in history, math, and science. Review and remedial classes are made available to students who need additional instruction.

Beginning in the ninth grade, students receive support and guidance in researching colleges and universities that complement their interests and academic achievement levels. A variety of college representatives are invited annually to visit each campus. Approximately 35 students graduate each year from Southwestern. 100% of graduating students enter a U.S. college or university of their choice.

Southwestern Academy offers students the opportunity to study at either of two distinctly different and beautiful campuses. If space permits, students may study at both in order to benefit from each learning environment.

The San Marino, California campus is located near Pasadena and Los Angeles and occupies eight acres in the residential suburb of San Marino ten miles from downtown Los Angeles and immediately south of Pasadena. The Arizona campus, known as Beaver Creek Ranch, is a 180-acre site located in north central Arizona 100 miles north of Phoenix, 18 miles from the resort community of Sedona, and 35 miles south of Flagstaff. A breathtaking, creek-watered, red rock oasis provides an ideal setting for general academic and college preparatory study.

A central theme of the academic program at Beaver Creek Campus is the development of an appreciation for the importance of environmental sustainability and the role individuals must play as socially responsible citizens. The curricula is delivered seminar-style and features integrated science, math, writing, and critical thinking components. Combined with "hands-on" experiential and project/assignment-based field trips, students develop cognitive anchors as they apply what they learn in all subject areas.

Southwestern Academy offers summer programs at each campus. The program at San Marino offers an accelerated ESL program for international students to improve their knowledge and use of English. Students may also attend classes to earn credits toward high school graduation or for review and enhancement purposes. Students participate in special daily activities and a variety of field trips that support learning in the classroom and offer recreation and relaxation.

The summer curriculum at Beaver Creek is designed for students who wish to improve their academic performance by combining high adventure activities and field trips with science-based learning and outdoor education that supports the overall theme and focus of the campus.

Call for video, CD-ROM or catalog.
Tel: 626-799-5010 x5
Fax: 626-799-0407
E-mail: Admissions@
    SouthwesternAcademy.edu
Web: SouthwesternAcademy.edu

THE SHIPLEY SCHOOL
BRYN MAWR, PA

Founded in 1894, The Shipley School is a Pre-K-12 coeducational day school committed to educational excellence and dedicated to developing in each student a love of learning and a compassionate participation in the world. With an enrollment of 838 students (51% male, 49% female), the school has the biggest enrollment in its history. Average SAT scores from 2002-2004 were 1280 (640 Verbal; 640 Math). 76% of the class of 2004 achieved combined SAT scores above 1200. The West Middle School opened in September 1993. The Snyder Science Center and Upper School renovation, including new computer labs, opened in September 1995. Recently, a new dining room was added. A new Lower School opened in 2001.

Located 12 miles from Philadelphia, the school is able to make use of nearby cultural and academic resources offered by a number of fine schools and colleges as well as the opportunities afforded by the metropolitan area. Graduates attend a wide variety of colleges and universities, including Penn, Trinity, Yale, Harvard, Bucknell, Amherst, Brown, Cornell, Columbia, Williams, Tufts, Princeton, Middlebury, Haverford, Bates, Syracuse, Washington University (St. Louis), Ithaca, Stanford, Wesleyan and Maryland Institute College of Art.

The academic calendar is devoted to courses preparatory for college entrance. Sixteen credits are required for graduation, including four years of English, three of a foreign language, three of mathematics, two of history and two of a laboratory science. The curriculum of the Upper School offers courses in English, Spanish, Latin, French, Mathematics, Computer Science, Chemistry, Physics, Biology, History (Art, Ancient and Medieval, Modern European, American, Chinese/Japanese, and Russia and Contemporary Europe), American Studies (an interdisciplinary course), History of Religion, Philosophy, Studio Art, Music Theory and instruction, and Dramatics. Athletics include soccer, field hockey, tennis, basketball, volleyball, baseball, softball, crew, lacrosse, squash, and cross-country. Community service is a requirement for graduation.

SUFFIELD ACADEMY

SUFFIELD, CT

Charles Cahn III
Headmaster

Founded in 1833, Suffield Academy prepares young men and women for the challenges of college and beyond. Structure, upport, and active involvement in school life are important themes at Suffield. Our program is designed for students who seek academic challenge in a friendly, close-knit environment. Strong athletics and a diverse arts program supplement our curriculum.

Suffield's campus spans 350 acres in the center of Suffield, Connecticut—a beautiful, historic New England town. Through the school's Computer Initiative, each student and faculty member possesses a laptop computer. Other programs and facilities of note include a leadership education curriculum that prepares students to contribute to our global society; an outdoor leadership center that houses a 3,000-square-foot climbing wall; a state-of-the-art fitness center that opened in 2004; and dorms that have phone and data access.

One of the Academy's greatest strengths lies in the quality of the academic program and in the continuing personal concern that is shown for each student. Teachers challenge their pupils to make the best use of their talents while developing sound personal and social values.

Last year, the student body consisted of 400 students who came to Suffield from 17 states and 21 countries. Through academics, athletics, arts, and community service programs, students have the opportunity to work with their peers and faculty to their own benefit and to the benefit of the community.

The Academy's Leadership Scholar Program provides scholarship aid to students with strong potential for leadership development and then mentors these young men and women, and other Suffield students, through hands-on leadership experiences on and off campus.

For more information please contact: Terry Breault, Director of Admissions and Financial Aid, at (860) 386-4440 or e-mail terry_breault@suffieldacademy.org. Please visit our Web site at www.suffieldacademy.org.

THAYER ACADEMY

745 Washington St.
BRAINTREE, MA 02184
Tel: 781-843-3580
E-mail: admissions@thayer.org
Web: www.thayer.org

William T. (Ted) Koskores '70, BA, Boston University;
M.A.L.S. Columbia University, *Headmaster*

Founded in 1877 by General Sylvanus Thayer (nationally known as the Father of the U.S. Military Academy), Thayer Academy is a private, coeducational day school, grades six through twelve. Located 13 miles south of Boston, Thayer's campus is easily accessible via the MBTA, commuter rail, bus, and is minutes from routes 128, 93, and 3. The mission of Thayer Academy is "to inspire a diverse community of students to moral, intellectual, aesthetic, and physical excellence so that each may rise to honorable achievement and contribute to the common good." With 94 teachers, Thayer's faculty:student ratio is 7:1.

The Thayer school day offers a rich and abundant curriculum with honors and AP classes in all disciplines. The day begins with home room with a faculty advisor. The Middle School schedule provides for three conference periods with teachers and two activity periods for extracurricular pursuits each week. Studio art, music, and theater are an integral part of the daily curriculum. At the end of the academic day, all Middle School students participate in interscholastic sports or physical education.

The Upper School schedule consists of seven periods a day from 8 a.m. to 3 p.m. Students often meet with teachers individually for extra help. Upper School students involved in interscholastic athletics will find that their practice sessions generally end at about 5:00 p.m. each day. Thayer offers 36 different student activities, clubs, and organizations including community service, drama, year book. Students often arrange meetings or rehearsals at times that do not interfere with organized athletics in order to accommodate all interested students. Thayer performs three main stage plays each year with rehearsals beginning at 5:30 p.m. to allow athletes to participate.

The Thayer Academy Arts Department helps students develop skills at their own pace, find opportunities for self expression, and develop self confidence. With over two dozen art offerings, students at all levels have

the opportunity to study theater and music, both vocal and instrumental. Thayer offers individual music instruction on campus.

The Athletic Department, offering 26 varsity sports (13 for boys, 13 for girls) with over 60 teams, is an integral part of the Thayer Academy experience. By offering health and physical education in addition, Thayer nurtures the development in a well-balanced environment.

Community service at Thayer has been a tradition for years, and students still believe in the importance of giving back to their communities. The Academy's Community Service Program offers a variety of opportunities for students throughout the year. Some students choose to make regular commitments to organizations in the Braintree area, serving as teachers' assistants at Braintree Head Start, assisting in the building of Habitat houses locally and in Mexico, participating at Christmas in the City, or working with inner-city students through Project DEEP, an educational program founded by Thayer alumnus, Brendan McDonough '87. A 5-week long, off-campus, supervised senior project of the student's own devising is required for graduation.

The Tiger Net, a campus-wide internet, connects computer workstations in faculty work areas, labs, classrooms, Southworth Library, and administrative offices. Thayer offers students 11 computer labs on campus. The Upper and Middle School divisions each have three full-sized labs. In addition, the Upper School has five mini-labs. Mini-labs are located in English, science, and yearbook classrooms. The Visual Arts Lab features high-powered computers for use in photography, architectural design, and video art classes. Video Art has its own lab.

New additions include: additional state-of-the-art science labs; Middle School library/computer resource center; over a dozen interactive white boards; two-story life fitness facility; and four artificial-turf playing fields.

Private Schools Illustrated — 1260

THE TAFT SCHOOL
WATERTOWN, CT

William R. MacMullen,
Headmaster

For over a century Taft, which enrolls approximately 563 boys and girls from all parts of the United States and many foreign countries, has educated its students to fulfill its motto, "Not to be served, but to serve," by providing a wide variety of challenging and unique programs within the context of a warm and supportive environment.

- The academic program offers over 200 courses, ranging from those stressing critical skills and knowledge to others providing unusual opportunities for advanced and specialized learning. Honors courses prepare younger students for Advanced Placement (college level) work in the Upper School and are supplemented by a vigorous Independent Studies Program and public service opportunities.
- All students participate in the creative arts and more than half play on interscholastic athletic teams.
- Students come from 33 states and 18 foreign countries and from many different backgrounds. Extensive financial aid is supplemented by a pioneering student loan program for middle income families.
- The student-faculty ratio of 6:1 and the advisor system encourage exceptionally warm relationships between teachers and their students.
- The spirited student body organizes more than 40 extracurricular activities each year. Eight student-faculty policy committees encourage students to participate in the governance of the school.
- Most students attend Taft for three or four years.
- Taft offers exceptional facilities for academic, artistic, and athletic activities on a 220 acre setting near enough to cities to allow trips to New York, Hartford, and New Haven.

Taft's Center for Teacher Education attracts private and public school teachers and administrators from all parts of the country to curriculum workshops and institutes on adolescent education, reasoning, morality & adolescence, research techniques, advanced placement, and science education. A five-week summer session offering English as a Second Language and a Young Scholars Program is open to students entering grades 8 to 12.

THOMAS JEFFERSON SCHOOL

ST. LOUIS, MO

Thomas Jefferson is a boarding and day school for boys and girls who want the best possible education in a friendly, close-knit community. A belief in greater student responsibility translates into short, focused classes with a lot of discussion, more independent study time, and maximum access to teachers for help and coaching outside of class. Graduates go on to highly selective colleges all around the country.

Most students live in six dormitory houses, with air-conditioned and carpeted rooms that give them quiet, privacy, and independence; the rooms are all networked for phone, e-mail, and Internet access. For meals, some classes, and teachers' offices, the Main Building (a former residence) provides a comfortable, home-like atmosphere. The recently-constructed Sayers Hall contains most of the classrooms along with science labs and library space.

In English, the students read and discuss classics of world literature, usually including Shakespeare and the Bible alongside novels, poetry, and other works of all eras; they also get intensive training in writing skills. Mathematics is required every year, through calculus. Over the six years (grades 7-12), they take a sequence of science and social studies courses that culminates in Advanced Placement courses for everyone in the upper grades. Foreign languages include accelerated programs in Latin (grades 7-8), classical Greek, and the student's choice of French or Italian. Each student chooses a once-a-week fine arts class.

Athletics include interscholastic options (basketball, soccer, volleyball) and intramurals such as tennis. Among the many extracurricular opportunities are the student newspaper and yearbook, an active Student Council, and the Student Admission Assistants. In addition, every student fulfills a community service requirement.

The school is located in a residential area, but close to numerous restaurants, movies, and malls to make weekends more interesting. The school makes arrangements for concerts, plays, sports events, and other activities each year. The Head often leads a school trip to England and Italy in the summer. Our international airport is not far from the school.

VERMONT ACADEMY

SAXTONS RIVER, VT

James C. Mooney, BA, Yale Univ., MA, Stanford Univ., *Head*

Founded in 1876, Vermont Academy is a small, independent, coeducational, college preparatory school, primarily boarding in nature, situated on a 515-acre campus in the foothills of the Green Mountains. Vermont Academy's supportive environment offers academic and co-curricular programs that are structured for the development of confident and independent learners. Students learn the skills for oral and written expression, critical thinking and analysis, and the cultivation of good instincts—intellectual, athletic, creative, and social. Vermont Academy helps students discover their individual talents, and develop the character, strength, and skills necessary to effectively handle life's challenges.

Vermont Academy's rigorous academic program is designed for students who are planning to attend college. The average class has 11 students, and the overall student-teacher ratio is 7:1. Campus-wide wireless technology and a Hewlett Packard Tablet PC program are available. In addition, a state-of-the-art computer lab with T-I Internet access, 40 new computers and four levels of computer classes complements the academic program. Honors courses are offered in advanced levels of English, history, foreign language, math, science, art, and music. Advanced Placement tutorials and test preparation with faculty members are offered as well. A Learning Skills program is available to students requiring help in developing basic study skills and compensatory techniques. Vermont Academy offers an English as a Second Language program for international students who have some verbal proficiency in the English language.

A diverse athletic program is available, providing the opportunity for students of all skill levels to compete: cross-country running, equestrian, field hockey, football, mountain biking, and soccer in the fall; basketball, dance, ice hockey, skiing (alpine, Nordic, jumping), and snowboarding in the winter; and baseball, golf, lacrosse, softball, tennis, and track and field in the spring. During one season, a student may elect an activity such as photography, silversmithing, theater, community service, outdoor challenge, and rock climbing.

Vermont Academy offers several creative courses, including foundations of art, drawing, painting, 3-D design, pottery, art history, electronic music, music composition, vocal ensemble, jazz ensemble, guitar ensemble, private instrumental instruction, senior independent courses in art and music for portfolio development, theater, and dance (ballet, jazz, tap, hip hop, kickboxing–aerobics, and choreography).

For further information, contact William J. Newman, Director of Admissions.

Private Schools Illustrated — 1264

VIEWPOINT SCHOOL
CALABASAS, CA

Viewpoint School, an independent coeducational school with grades Kindergarten through twelve, offers a rigorous college preparatory education in a nurturing environment. An integral part of an education at Viewpoint is the development of a love of learning and of those qualities which provide strength and direction for a lifetime. Viewpoint recognizes the uniqueness of each child and is committed to the identification, preservation, and development of that individuality.

Located in the western end of the San Fernando Valley, Viewpoint School is nestled in the foothills of the Santa Monica Mountains on a campus of 25 acres, with scenic vistas, a natural stream, colorful flowers, and stately oak trees. Children thrive in our serene, natural setting, enjoying the beauty of the outdoors throughout the school day. Students come to Viewpoint from the San Fernando and Conejo Valleys, Malibu, and other neighboring communities, and represent a diversity of backgrounds.

Recognizing that children grow best among their peers, the School is divided into four divisions, each enjoying its own distinct program and geographical identity on campus: Primary School (Kindergarten through grade two), Lower School (grades three through five), Middle School (grades six through eight), and Upper School (grades nine through twelve).

Well-equipped science and computer labs, three libraries, and numerous art and music studios create an engaging learning atmosphere at Viewpoint. Two regulation-size swimming pools, the Rasmussen Family Pavilion for athletics, two athletic fields, outdoor basketball courts, a weight-training facility, batting cages, playgrounds, ECOLET (an outdoor natural science laboratory), and an open-air theater provide ample facilities for the school's numerous programs.

Viewpoint School's 1158 students represent a rich variety of ethnic, religious, socioeconomic, and cultural backgrounds. Fifteen languages are spoken in the homes of the School's families. Each year the School hosts student exchanges with schools in other countries including the United Kingdom, France, Germany, Spain, Japan, Russia, and China. All students benefit from an educational environment that is enriched by diverse perspectives, talents, and interests.

Viewpoint is fully accredited by the California Association of Independent Schools and the Western Association of Schools and Colleges and holds membership in the National Association of Independent Schools.

The academic program of Viewpoint School emphasizes the traditional disciplines and provides a rich curriculum in the arts, music, drama, dance, film and video, computer science, and athletics. Class sizes remain 22 students or

less with an average of 18 in the Upper School, enabling teachers to work closely with students both in and out of class. Students benefit from a comprehensive liberal arts curriculum in their preparation for the academic challenges of college. Twenty-two Advanced Placement classes, nine Honors courses, 30 interscholastic athletic teams, and community service are also available to Upper School students. Students may choose from a wide variety of electives including speech, drama, orchestra, band, chorus, computer science, world poetry, creative writing, psychology, Asian history, ceramics, photography, oceanography, economics, environmental science, yearbook, and film and video.

Extracurricular activities for students include student council, publications, Model United Nations, Junior Statesmen of America, mock trial, theatrical and musical performances, and a wide variety of clubs. Annually, many of Viewpoint's students attend an East Coast tour of colleges and a Voyage of Discovery to historic sites on the East Coast.

Viewpoint School offers over 100 interscholastic and intramural teams annually, with typically 80% of all students in grades five through twelve participating. Viewpoint's experienced coaches build fundamental skills and teach good sportsmanship. The athletic program includes basketball, baseball, cross country, flag and tackle football, golf, soccer, softball, swimming, tennis, volleyball, equestrian competition, modern and jazz dance, and cheerleading. A number of Viewpoint's finest athletes compete at the college level.

Graduates from Viewpoint's class of 2004 achieved mean SAT I scores of 642 verbal and 643 math. Recent graduates currently attend American, Amherst, Boston University, Brown, Carnegie Mellon, Claremont McKenna, Clark, Colgate, Cornell, Dartmouth, Emory, Fisk, George Washington, Harvard, M.I.T., New York University, Occidental, Penn, Pepperdine, Princeton, Rice, Smith, Stanford, Syracuse, Tufts, Tulane, U.S. Air Force Academy, U.S. Naval Academy, all campuses of the Universities of California, USC, Wellesley, Williams, and Yale, among others.

Dr. Robert J. Dworkoski was appointed Headmaster in 1986. He is a graduate of George Washington University (B.A. 1968), New York University (A.M. 1971), and Columbia University (M.A. 1972, Ph.D. 1979 European History). The faculty consists of 145 full time and 3 part time teachers, including administrators who also teach. The faculty and administrators hold 63 baccalaureate and 36 advanced degrees, including 6 PhD's.

Viewpoint enrolls highly motivated, academically talented students with diverse backgrounds and interests who will benefit from an enriched college preparatory education. For more information regarding admissions, please contact Laurel Baker Tew, Director of Admission.

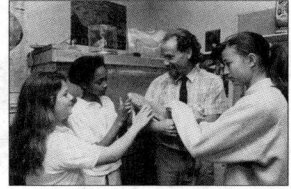

THE VILLAGE SCHOOL
13077 Westella
HOUSTON, TX 77077
Tel: 281-496-7900
Web: thevillageschool.com

The Village School is a day school for children, preschool through eighth grade. It was founded in 1966 and moved to its present location in 1984.

The Village School offers a strong, traditional curriculum, stressing phonics in the early years. The school presents a viable alternative to public school education. The highly skilled staff provides academic growth for the high average student as well as a challenge to the more accelerated student. Entrance exams for academic ability are administered to all students before admittance.

In addition to emphasis on strong basic skills in reading and math, computer lab is offered for grades kindergarten and above. A broad-based science program for grades one and above meets the needs of students who will be emerging in an evermore technological world. Music and art are offered as participatory enrichment classes. Students in grades four and above become members of the school band, choir, or orchestra.

Village School students have the opportunity to develop a special appreciation of the arts by participation in the highly acclaimed school choir, band, orchestra or musical theater group. Students are encouraged to develop stage presence and confidence through musical programs and speaking opportunities. The middle school features a strong speech and drama department, with students learning such diverse skills as acting, Lincoln-Douglas debate, and extemporaneous and impromptu speaking.

Field trips appropriate to the interest and age of the children are taken on a regular basis and range from the youngest children visiting a farm to the upper grade trips throughout Texas and to Washington, D.C.

Extracurricular offerings also include a science fair, field day competition, scouts, musical theater, and chess club.

The school is located in the west part of Houston, and the new facilities include modern classrooms, library, two gyms, science room, two computer labs, fine arts building, two fields and a court. Middle school team opportunities include soccer, basketball, volleyball, baseball softball, cross-country, and track. A sports complex includes a quarter mile all-weather track and fields for soccer, baseball, and softball.

The fully accredited school has a student population of 725 students with a diverse student body from more than 20 countries. For more information, visit our website at www.thevillageschool.com.

TILTON SCHOOL
30 School St.
TILTON, NH 03276
Tel: 603-286-1733
Fax: 603-286-1705
Web: www.tiltonschool.org

Founded in 1845, Tilton School is a coeducational boarding and day college-preparatory school for grades 9-12 and a postgraduate year. Approximately 200 students from over 25 states and 10 different countries attend Tilton. Tilton School prepares young women and men for success in college, life-long learning, and service to the community.

Tilton School challenges students to embrace and navigate a world marked by diversity and change. Through the quality of human relationships, Tilton School's faculty cultivates in its students the curiosity, the skills, the knowledge and understanding, the character and the integrity requisite for the passionate pursuit of lifelong personal success and service.

The School's nurturing environment encourages students to build on their personal strengths and fosters the development of self-esteem, character, and leadership. Participation in Tilton's unique +5 Program ensures a commitment in athletics, the arts, leadership, community service, and the outdoors.

Today's Tilton students will live their entire adult lives in the new century. The world they are inheriting is becoming increasingly complex, demanding new skills and competencies. As a school, Tilton seeks to prepare those students by giving them the knowledge, by developing their talents, and by instilling the character and vision to meet those challenges.

Our excellent facilities include a newly renovated indoor hockey rink, Daley Creative Art Center, Hamilton Theater, Lucian Hunt Library, and the Memorial Athletic and Recreation Center (M.A.R.C.). The buildings on Tilton's Campus are connected via a fiber optic backbone supporting a 10BaseT Ethernet network.

VIRGINIA EPISCOPAL SCHOOL
400 Virginia Episcopal School Rd., P.O. Box 408
LYNCHBURG, VA 24505-0408

Founded in 1916, Virginia Episcopal School is an independent, coeducational, college preparatory boarding/day school for grades 9-12. Located in the heart of central Virginia, Lynchburg and VES' 160-acre campus are nestled along the James River in the foothills of the Blue Ridge Mountains.

Small by design, the VES family is an intimate academic community of 268 students and 40 residential faculty, whose mission is to provide rigorous academic training and vigorous individual attention in a spiritual and ethical environment. With small classes, an extensive athletic program and energizing teachers, VES creates a challenging but supportive environment where average to exceptional students can thrive. Whether it is in the classroom, on the athletic field, or on stage, each VES student can find new levels of personal success.

At VES, our facilities and statistics are as impressive as any. But what will touch you even more is something not measured in square feet or percentages-and that is our deep sense of family. It is a warmth and friendliness. It is a caring and mutual respect. It is a feeling of support that empowers and enriches for a lifetime. This is Virginia Episcopal School. Come see, hear, and feel the difference. Come be a part of our family.

For more information on the VES family, visit our website at www.ves.org, or call the admissions office at 434-385-3607.

Private Schools Illustrated — 1270

WESTMINSTER SCHOOL
SIMSBURY, CT

W. Graham Cole, Jr., *Headmaster*

In its 117th year of preparing young people for success in college and later life, Westminster achieves unity of morale and breadth of experience by being small enough to enable every student to know every other student and every teacher while also offering the facilities and the diverse programs of a larger school. For 368 students, Westminster offers a four-year coeducational college preparatory program, with the scope and flexibility to extend the students' course of study well beyond the normal college requirements. One teacher for every 5 students makes individual attention possible, especially in the classroom where the ability of each student to work and think for himself is considered at least as important as the subject matter.

The students are given increasing responsibility and freedom as they show themselves ready for them. Many of the older students serve on important school committees. With a broad based curriculum, a wide range of extra curricular activities, and a complete interscholastic athletic program, students are encouraged to develop their interests and talents.

The fully equipped plant includes an Academic Center which accommodates 33 classrooms, six science laboratories, a spacious library, two computer laboratories, audio-visual facilities, auditorium, and art and architecture studios. There are 6 separate dormitory buildings, including two new dorms, a chapel, observatory, 2 gymnasiums, swimming pool, 14 tennis courts, 12 squash courts, 2 complete weight rooms, 2 equipped exercise rooms, 2 heated paddle tennis courts, a hockey rink, and a student designed Student Center. The Werner Centennial Performing Arts Center has a spectacular theatre that seats 400, a dance studio, and rooms for music lessons, music courses, and practice sessions. The campus' newest additions are a fully renovated science facility, a greenhouse with aquaria and terraria facilities, a three season locker facility, with a training room and weight room, telephone and data jacks in each dorm room, a squash pavilion housing eight international courts, a synthetic track, and an 8 lane, 25 yard aquatic center with weight facility and an attached health and counseling center.

The school is in a pleasant country location; however, educational and cultural opportunities are also available in nearby Hartford. On the weekends, various forms of entertainment, on and off campus, are planned by the student activities committee with faculty assistance.

THE WEBB SCHOOL
BELL BUCKLE, TN
Tel: 931-389-6003
E-mail: admissions@webbschool.com
Web: thewebbschool.com

The Webb School is a coeducational, college preparatory, boarding and day school for students in grades 6-12. The school was founded in 1870 by the noted Chapel Hill scholar, William R. "Sawney" Webb. It is Tennessee's oldest continuously operating boarding school, and the South's leading producer of Rhodes Scholars.

Proven hallmarks in Webb's formula for success include a structured liberal arts program, individual attention, and an emphasis on honor. Students with varied economic and social backgrounds from fourteen states and thirteen foreign countries attend yearly.

While Webb is expanding and growing with the times, the traditional values and commitment to the development of young people remain the same. The Honor Code, set up by "Sawney" in 1870 and adopted by Princeton University in the early 20th century, is still in place and forms the framework upon which the entire school operates. Students still give declamations once a year before the entire student body. All students are required to participate in the outside reading program.

Complementing Webb's demanding academic program are outstanding activity and athletic programs. Through white-water rafting, rock climbing, camping, caving, and a variety of other outdoor activities in Webb's Outer Limits Program, students build self-confidence and form close bonds of friendship. In addition, Webb offers teams in 15 different varsity sports, including golf, soccer, volleyball, lacrosse and tennis.

A six-week Summer Program is offered yearly for students seeking both remedial and enrichment work.

For more information, please contact The Webb School, Office of Admissions.

WESTERN RESERVE ACADEMY

115 College St., Hudson, OH 44236

Dr. Henry E. Flanagan, Jr., *Headmaster*

Since its founding in 1826, Western Reserve Academy has been committed to the principle of formal academic training in specific disciplines while recognizing the need to remain open to new developments in educational theory and practice. The Academy's coeducational boarding and day programs prepare students for entrance into the country's leading colleges and universities.

Beyond the traditional secondary course offerings, Reserve features classes in astronomy, natural history, zoology, computer science, Senior Seminar, statistics, discrete math, acting/directing, engineering design, architectural drawing, creative writing, and dance. Advanced level courses are available in all disciplines to qualified students.

Located a block from downtown Hudson, most of Western Reserve's 200-acre campus encompasses farm and woodland. The school's facilities include two observatories, chapel, 45,000-volume library, gymnasium housing a 25 yard pool and 14' diving well, art and photography studios, wood and metal working shops, and a 425-seat theatre. The athletic program is supported by 17 full-size playing fields, a 400 meter all-weather track and 12 tennis courts. In 2004 a new artificial turf (AstroPlay) football/soccer/field hockey/lacrosse stadium featuring an all-weather track and a 45,000 square foot field house were completed. The field house features a 200 meter indoor track, a new varsity basketball court, four practice courts, and baseball batting cages. Also completed was an Administration building housing the Headmaster's, College Guidance, Alumni & Development offices and a state-of-the-art Health Center.

Western Reserve Academy believes in physical development and the value of team effort and competition, and all able students participate in a sport activity. Football, soccer, cross-country, golf, swimming, ice hockey, basketball, track, baseball, tennis, riflery, lacrosse and wrestling are among the opportunities available to males, while females may participate in field hockey, tennis, volleyball, basketball, track, swimming, soccer, riflery, cross-country, lacrosse and softball. Intramural offerings include dance sport, tai kwon do, conditioning, aerobics, outdoor skills and community service.

Reserve abounds with various student publications such as a monthly newspaper, yearbook and literary magazine. Student council, community service, instrumental and vocal ensembles, drama productions, student environmental action league, a radio station and culinary club round out activity offerings. The Academy's small classes permit a favorable student-teacher ratio and also foster one-to-one relationships within the classroom and in extracurricular activities.

For further information write, call 330-650-9717 or visit www.wra.net.

THE WHITE MOUNTAIN SCHOOL
371 West Farm Rd.
BETHLEHEM, NH 03574
Tel: 800-545-7813
E-mail: wmsadmissions@whitemountain.org
Web: www.whitemountain.org

Alan T. Popp, *Head of School*

"Small School. Big Outdoors." The White Mountain School prepares students for college and beyond by offering an environment for challenging academics and personal growth within a small and supportive community of approximately 110 students. Challenging academics are balanced with extensive studio arts, an international community service program, a wilderness skills program, and outdoor learning expeditions. Students receive personal attention with daily academic support, small classes, and superior college counseling amidst the spectacular 800,000-acre White Mountain National Forest. Daily activities include hiking, paddling & kayaking, rock & ice climbing, mountain biking, soccer, lacrosse, tennis, theatre, dance, snowboarding, crosscountry and backcountry skiing, and competitive & recreational skiing.

Founded in Concord, New Hampshire in 1886, the School relocated to Bethlehem in 1935. The move north was made to offer students an opportunity to live in and among things greater than themselves, to help them form perspective, and to give them a sense of wonder and appreciation for the natural environment. The School changed its name from St. Mary's-in-the-Mountains to The White Mountain School in 1972, three years after going co-ed, to reflect better its commitment to a balanced college-preparatory program with the outdoor learning and recreational experiences available in a mountain setting. Although the School maintains its affiliation with the Episcopal Church, it welcomes students from diverse backgrounds and all religious traditions.

The 250-acre campus, with 150 acres adjacent property for the School's use, is easily accessible from I-93 and is a beautiful drive from Hartford, Boston or Manchester airports. The School is governed by a 20-member Board of Trustees.

WMS is accredited by the New England Association of Schools and Colleges and is a member of the Secondary School Admission Test Board, the National Honor Society, the Independent Schools Association of Northern New England, and the National Association of Independent Schools.

THE WILLISTON NORTHAMPTON SCHOOL
EASTHAMPTON, MA

Brian R. Wright, *Head of School*

Williston Northampton, a school formed as a result of the merger in 1971 of Williston Academy and the Northampton School For Girls, enrolls 450 students in grades 9 through PG—270 boarding boys and girls and 180 day students. Forty percent of the students receive financial aid and eighteen percent are students of color. It is located in the heart of the Massachusetts Pioneer Valley, 14 miles north of Springfield, 150 miles north of New York City, and 90 miles west of Boston. In 1991 the school was named an Exemplary Secondary School by the U.S. Department of Education.

While Williston Northampton recognizes that academic preparation for college is the heart of its program, the faculty recognize that the school is also preparing young people to develop the skills necessary to lead a successful life. Its varied, challenging and broad-based curriculum offers students the opportunity to explore, to investigate and to question. By complementing traditional college-preparatory courses with numerous electives, special programs such as School Year Abroad, and by seeking a diverse student body, the school encourages students to take advantage of the cultural richness and diversity of our world. Cooperation, mutual respect, and the development of personal leadership skills are key elements in the school's desire to develop responsible independence.

Williston Northampton enjoys a suburban setting only a few miles from the base of Mt. Tom. The countryside offers excellent climbing and bicycling opportunities, yet the location within 15 miles of five well-known colleges—Smith, Amherst, Mt. Holyoke, Hampshire and the University of Massachusetts—provides a culturally rich environment of fine

museums, libraries, and theatre programs as well. The Five College Calendar covering five concert series, distinguished visitor lecture programs, and fine arts and movie series, is published once a month and, as with any activity, students need only sign up in the activities office for what they would like to attend. Included among the many weekend activities and events attended by students each year are trips to the Eastern States Exposition, games by the New England Patriots and Boston Red Sox, trips to Boston and New York, day and weekend ski trips to Stratton and Stowe in Vermont, films, plays, concerts, and dance performances at the area colleges and in Hartford and Springfield. These off-campus events enrich the busy weekends on campus where dances and coffee houses, talent shows, visiting lecturers, massages, and film series, among many other events, are featured.

To complement the academic program, The Williston Northampton School offers over 30 extracurricular activities and a complete athletic program. The Williston Theatre is one of the School's extracurricular highlights. Several theatre productions each year give students the opportunity to develop their talents in the theatre arts and courses are offered for the student who wants to pursue an interest in acting or the technical aspects of theatre as well. The athletic program offers excellent facilities including a state-of-the-art athletic center with two basketball courts, a six-lane pool, five squash courts, fitness center, multi-use aerobics and wrestling room and a training room. Also available are an indoor hockey rink, and 15 tennis courts. Nearby Heritage Farm and King Oak stables provide all facilities for horseback riding including a large indoor riding area, and the ski team practices at Berkshire East.

The basic purpose of The Williston Northampton School is to guide all students' growth and to support and nurture each student's individuality. The college preparatory program is challenging and has the additional objective of providing a stimulating, broadening, and valued community experience. The emphasis is on preserving and encouraging the best individual qualities of each student. Williston Northampton believes that, in building upon these unique characteristics, a more independent and worthwhile person will emerge.

THE WESTMINSTER SCHOOLS

ATLANTA, GA

William Clarkson IV, BA, MDiv, DMin, *President*

Founded in 1951 and located on 176 wooded acres in northwest Atlanta, Westminster is a non-denominational college preparatory day school for boys and girls in the pre-first through the twelfth grade. Currently, a highly trained faculty of 232 provides individual instruction in small classes for 1751 students.

Dedicated to the precepts of the Christian faith, Westminster welcomes students from various racial, ethnic, religious and economic backgrounds. The curriculum intends to cultivate a discriminating intelligence and to help students learn the skills and knowledge necessary for responsible decisions, sound values, continuing education, and community service.

An outstanding feature of the curriculum is the Advanced Placement program which Westminster has participated in since its inception, currently offering 27 college level courses. The class of 2004 took, on average, 4 Advanced Placement examinations per student. The school has now sent 8473 graduates to 316 colleges in 41 states and 7 foreign countries.

Outside the classroom the afternoon sports program provides intramural competition for Elementary school students, and both intramural and interscholastic competition for students in grades 7-12. Interscholastic sports for boys include cross-country, football, basketball, wrestling, soccer, track, baseball, tennis, swimming, golf, and lacrosse. Girls' sports are cross-country, softball, volleyball, basketball, track, gymnastics, swimming, soccer, tennis, golf, and lacrosse.

Other extracurricular activities include band and orchestra, choral groups, individual instrumental instruction, drama, photography, and publications. A student prefect system in the high school administers the honor code and student conduct policies, and provides leadership and service in the school community.

Admission to Westminster is determined by entrance tests, previous school record and recommendations, and interviews or observation sessions. Students who meet entrance requirements are accepted without regard to race, creed, color, country of origin, or financial need.

The Williams School

A coeducational, college preparatory, day school for students in grades 7–12, founded in New London, CT in 1891.

Visitors to Williams experience a culture that simultaneously captivates and challenges students in a comfortable environment. Williams' rigorous classics curriculum fuses traditional humanities with math and science. Students develop creativity through a dynamic program of drama, music, dance, and studio art.

Set on the campus of Connecticut College, Williams offers independent study through the college. Advanced Placement is offered in all required courses. Competitive interscholastic sports programs include field hockey, soccer, cross-country, basketball, swimming, diving, sailing, softball, baseball, tennis, lacrosse, and golf.

To learn more about Williams and the admission process, browse **www.williamsschool.org**. Contact our office from the web or by phone at **(860) 443-5333** to request additional information. An admission counselor will discuss questions regarding Williams and arrange a personal visit.

WOOSTER SCHOOL
Ridgebury Rd.
DANBURY, CT 06810

Tel: 203-830-3900
Fax: 203-790-7147
Web: www.woosterschool.org

George King, *Headmaster*
Samuel Gaudet, *Director of Admissions*

Founded in 1926 as an Episcopal boys' boarding school, Wooster School has, over the years, evolved into an independent, coeducational day school for students in kindergarten through grade 12. Wooster attracts students from neighboring towns in Fairfield and northern Westchester counties and also hosts international students and families. Located on a scenic, 125-acre hillside campus on the Danbury/Ridgefield Connecticut border, the school's most historic building, the James Marshall Chapel, is surrounded by 14 academic buildings, including a modern library and computer lab, music building, and art center. Three gymnasiums and playing fields accommodate a variety of athletics with 22 sports offered.

Students can choose from many clubs and activities. An honor code, weekly chapel service, and required community service provide a framework for teaching moral values. Students also participate daily in the "Self-help" program, working in teams to maintain the school.

Wooster is comprised of three divisions that enroll 435 students in total. The Lower School (K-5) curriculum integrates the language arts with reasoning to create lifelong readers, writers, and problem solvers. A Lower School science lab, foreign language program that begins in kindergarten, lab program for developing computer competency, small classes, and special thematic units that combine art and music with an interdisciplinary approach to learning about cultures and civilizations, are just some of the Lower School's unique features.

Wooster's Middle School (6-8) offers small classes taught by dedicated teachers who come to know their students well. Students work with personal advisors who help them navigate through the sometimes precarious waters of early adolescence. While the emphasis is on preparing students to become autonomous learners, and for the rigorous Upper School academic program, they are also expected to become good citizens. Extracurricular activities are age-appropriate and fun.

The Upper School (9-12) is known for its excellent college preparatory curriculum within the context of a strong liberal arts tradition. Classes are small and leadership opportunities and the "Self-help" program give students a sense of ownership of their school by keeping them actively involved in the life of the community. A Year Abroad program in France or Spain and Senior Independent Study are also offered.

Students are aided in their college application by an experienced college guidance staff. Beginning with junior year class meetings, and progressing to required weekly and individual meetings with counselors, students explore their career plans, intellectual aspirations, and personal goals. In the past five years, Wooster graduates have attended these colleges and universities: Barnard, Boston College, BU, Brandeis, Bryn Mawr, Carnegie-Mellon, Cornell, Drew, Dickinson, George Washington, Hamilton, Haverford, Lehigh, NYU, Pratt, Princeton, RIT, RPI, Sarah Lawrence, Skidmore, Tufts, UConn, UMichigan, Washington and Lee, Washington U, Wesleyan, and Wheaton.

Throughout its history, Wooster has been guided by four cardinal principles: Intellectual Excellence, Religion, Simplicity, and Hard Work. In addition, racial, social, economic, and cultural diversity have been central to the School's educational mission and values. Wooster School welcomes students of all races, religions, and national or ethnic origins.

THE WINDSOR SCHOOL
41-60 Kissena Blvd.
FLUSHING, NY 11355
Tel: 718-359-8300   Fax: 718-359-1876
E-mail: admin@thewindsorschool.com
Web: windsorschool.com

- Accredited by the Middle States Association of Colleges and Secondary Schools
- Registered by the New York State Education Department
- Elected to membership in the College Entrance Examination Board and the College Scholarship Service

The Windsor School, grades 6-12 and Pre-University year, is dedicated to giving attention, identity, guidance and college preparation, not only to the gifted youngster, but also to the middle-range youngster, who is overlooked in larger schools. Small classes and involved teachers are the hallmark of the Windsor School.

All students have open, easy and informal access to all faculty members, guidance counselors and administrators—appointments are not necessary. College guidance is organized, thorough and successful.

The school is authorized under federal law to enroll non-immigrant alien students. If an international student is accepted, an I-20 form is issued. Recently we have had students from 21 foreign countries for grades 7-12, or for the special Pre-University year: Hong Kong, Taiwan, Brazil, Korea, China, Russia, Israel, Egypt, Thailand, India, Angola, Singapore, Indonesia, Pakistan, Sudan, etc.

The modern school building is centrally located near public transportation—buses, subway and Long Island Railroad.

WOODWARD ACADEMY
1662 Rugby Ave.
COLLEGE PARK, ATLANTA, GA 30337

Dr. Harry C. Payne, *President*

Established in 1900, Woodward Academy is a coeducational, college preparatory school located seven miles from downtown Atlanta in an attractive 80-acre suburban setting. Over 2860 day students are enrolled in the three Lower Schools (4 yr.-Grade 6), the Middle School (Grades 7 and 8), and the Upper School (Grades 9-12). The campus includes fifty buildings with air conditioned classrooms, practice fields, nine tennis courts, football field, and indoor olympic pool.

Twenty-five administrators and 340 professional and paraprofessional instructors, selected for their academic acumen, experience, and diverse interests, have effected a curriculum designed to offer traditional college preparatory courses as well as innovative electives such as computer programming, television production, astronomy, oceanography, and choreography. Academically gifted students are enrolled in Honors and Advanced Placement courses. Special features and programs include: closed-circuit television station, Upper, Middle and Lower School computer science centers, a fine arts center, a 23,000 sq. ft. Science Center, a 16,000 sq. ft. library, a European Study abroad, and tutorials.

Student Activities appropriate to each school such as student government, service clubs, interscholastic and intramural sports, six choruses, concert and marching bands, weekly assemblies, yearbook, newspaper, and honor societies are offered to develop individual talents and to promote school and community service.

Since the Academy provides homogeneous grouping on several academic levels, the final acceptance decision is based on a total evaluation of the student as well as the Academy's ability to benefit the student.

Private Schools Illustrated — 1284

WORCESTER ACADEMY

WORCESTER, MA

Dexter Morse, *Headmaster*

Since 1834 Worcester Academy has educated students to "Achieve the Honorable." The school's mission is to prepare young people to meet the challenges of college and to succeed in life.

Worcester Academy is a coeducational, college preparatory school for day students in grades 6-12 and resident students in grades 9-12, as well as a postgraduate year of study. We offer a traditional course of academic study that combines small classes and individual attention. Beyond the classroom Worcester Academy students take advantage of a rich athletic tradition and extensive offerings in the visual and performing arts. Special programs exist for international students developing proficiency in English. The school's outstanding facilities include a new 4-story academic building and library, a classic 400-seat performing arts theater, a swimming pool, two basketball courts and 40 acres of playing fields.

Located in Worcester, the second largest city in New England, the Academy is distinctive for being an urban school. Easy access to many museums, concert halls, libraries and shopping malls provides Academy students with a number of academic and recreational opportunities. The Academy's urban location also serves as the basis for the school's off-campus community service requirement.

Worcester Academy is accredited by the New England Association of Schools and Colleges and is a member of the National Association of Independent Schools.

YORK PREPARATORY SCHOOL

40 W. 68th St.
NEW YORK, NY 10023
Tel: 212-362-0400 Fax: 212-362-7424
E-mail: admissions@yorkprep.org
Web: www.yorkprep.org

York Prep, founded in 1969, is a college preparatory day school enrolling 310 students in grades 6-12, where contemporary methods enliven a strong, academically challenging, traditional curriculum. Our approach emphasizes independent thought, builds confidence and sends graduates on to the finest colleges and universities. Our comprehensive College Guidance Program has an outstanding record of placement in students' top-choice schools. We have a state of the art computer lab, a large gymnasium, a spacious sunny art studio, 2 professionally equipped science labs and a small concert hall. A wide range of extracurricular activities including a winning Mock Trial Law Team and a Championship Varsity Basketball Team enhances all aspects of academic life.

In Your Own Words

Educators and parents have long trusted Porter Sargent for independent, objective school profiles available nowhere else.

Your program's Illustrated Announcement can support this mission, and it will be seen daily by:

- Parents
- Headmasters, and admissions and guidance counselors
- Consultants and vendors
- A worldwide network of educational professionals

Each reference-quality title is the book of record for its field, with a long shelf-life and high per-copy readership.

Please call 617-523-1670 or E-mail announcements@portersargent.com for details on joining the next edition.

The Handbook of Private Schools * The Directory for Exceptional Children
Schools Abroad of Interest to Americans * Guide to Summer Camps and Schools

GIRLS' SCHOOLS

ASHLEY HALL
CHARLESTON, SC
Tel: 843-722-4088 Fax: 843-723-3982
Web: www.ashleyhall.org

Jill Swisher Muti, *Head of School*

Ashley Hall was founded in 1909 by Mary Vardrine McBee to establish a curriculum that would prepare young women to enter any college or university in the country. The school's founding mission was remarkably enlightened for its time. Today Ashley Hall upholds those high standards of academic excellence as it strives to prepare its students to meet the challenges of the future.

Ashley Hall is an independent college preparatory girls day school enrolling 615 students in pre-school through 12th grade. The school's Ross Early Education Center enrolls girls and boys ages 2-4. The student teacher ratio is 10:1.

The campus is located on four-and-a-half acres in historic downtown Charleston, South Carolina. The fully networked campus features state-of-the-art technology in classrooms, labs, and the media center. Language, computer skills, University of Chicago's *Everyday Math* program, and athletics begin in kindergarten. A comprehensive sports complex is located off-campus and athletics offered include basketball, softball, cross-country, swimming, track, soccer, sailing, tennis and a championship volleyball program.

Advanced Placement and satellite courses enhance the college preparatory curriculum. Age-appropriate courses in sciences, social studies, and the arts are offered. College placement is 100 percent, and students regularly receive early acceptance to first-choice institutions.

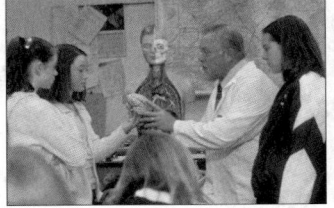

Private Schools Illustrated — 1290

BRENAU ACADEMY
GAINESVILLE, GA

Frank M. Booth, BA, MA, MEd, EdD, *Headmaster*

Since its founding on the campus of historic Brenau University 75 years ago, Brenau Academy has provided a quality secondary school education to young women headed for college.

Brenau is located near beautiful Lake Lanier, just at the base of the Blue Ridge Mountains, less than an hour's drive from Atlanta. This location affords students the chance to water ski and swim; to backpack and white-water raft; and to shop and attend concerts, art exhibits, and other major cultural events.

The pupil:teacher ratio is a low eight to one, and the average class size is only twelve students. These small numbers allow the faculty and staff more time with the individual student and encourage the student to ask more questions in class and to seek help in addition to classroom instruction. A friendly atmosphere prevails; there is genuine personal concern for the student. The size of the student body increases the opportunities for holding leadership positions and for participation in activities.

Students come to Brenau Academy from all over the world. While most students come from the Southeast, there are students from other parts of the United States and even a few from as far away as Egypt, China and Japan.

The curriculum follows a traditional college preparatory course in the academic areas. Additionally, students round out schedules with courses in the performing arts. These courses in drama, dance, and music invigorate the students and develop a strong sense of self-esteem.

Brenau Academy has inter-scholastic volleyball and tennis programs. Teams compete against public and private schools in the Georgia High School Association. The Academy is accredited by the Southern Association of Colleges and Schools.

Brenau is comprised of the Women's College and the Academy. This unique arrangement calls upon the Academy to be a distinct unit, organized and operated separately from the College but designed to share facilities and programs better to serve the Academy students. Academy girls are housed apart from College women and have more structured regulations. Thanks to this sharing, Academy students enjoy access to a $3 million library and computer center, a beautiful dining hall, a visual arts center, a tennis center, an Olympic-sized swimming pool, cultural events in a Victorian Theatre, and college courses for advanced students at no additional tuition. Thus, Brenau Academy students are given educational opportunities rarely found at a secondary school, a super college preparatory experience.

For more information contact: Director of Admissions, One Centennial Circle, Gainesville, GA 30501. Tel: 770-534-6140. Fax: 770-534-6298.

Private Schools Illustrated — 1292

CONVENT OF THE SACRED HEART

1177 King St.
GREENWICH, CT 06831
Tel: 203-531-6500
Web: cshgreenwich.org

Joan Magnetti, RSCJ, *Headmistress*
Pamela R. McKenna, *Director of Admission*

Convent of the Sacred Heart is a Catholic, independent college preparatory day school for young women serving students from Preschool through Grade 12. Founded in 1848 in New York City, the school relocated to Greenwich in 1945. Convent of the Sacred Heart is part of a worldwide network of Sacred Heart schools in 35 countries that has been educating women for more than 200 years. The 21 Sacred Heart Schools in the United States share a common set of Goals and Criteria that guide the decisions made by our 21-member Board of Trustees. Committed to each girl's intellectual, spiritual, social and physical development, our dedicated faculty and staff provide a rigorous academic program, enrichment and honors study, a supportive advisory program and opportunities for creative exploration, entrepreneurship and independent study. The school community is dedicated to developing women who have a strong sense of self, independence of judgment and personal freedom, so that they can become leaders with broad intellectual and spiritual horizons.

In Preschool through Grade 4, individual, small group and whole group instruction are used in the core disciplines of mathematics, science, reading, language arts, social studies, religion and foreign languages. In addition to regular classroom instruction, teaching specialists meet with Lower School students in the areas of computer, art, music, library skills and physical education.

In Grades 5 through 8, each student has an advisor who guides and encourages the students in all aspects of school life. The curriculum is departmentalized to include mathematics, science, computer, language arts, religious studies, social studies and foreign languages. All Middle School students receive instruction in library skills, music, drama, dance, art, art history and physical education.

In the Upper School, the curriculum offers more than 70 courses in mathematics, science, English, social sciences, history, theology, foreign languages and fine arts. Honors courses are taught in geometry, algebra II, precalculus, biology, chemistry, physics, history, English, French and Spanish. Advanced Placement courses are offered in calculus AB and BC, statistics, biology, physics, chemistry, environmental science, English, American and European history, comparative government, French and

Spanish. All academic disciplines employ the computer as a tool for writing, research, analysis and presentation. A computer laptop program for Grades 7-12 is incorporated into the curriculum across all disciplines.

Convent of the Sacred Heart is accredited by the New England Association of Schools and Colleges and is approved by the Connecticut State Board of Education. It is a member of the National Association of Independent Schools, the Connecticut Association of Independent Schools, Coalition of Girls' Schools and the worldwide Network of Sacred Heart Schools.

A private estate, previously owned by the Henry Steers family (built in 1907), was purchased in 1945 and adapted for school use. The campus now occupies a 110-acre property with the main building housing the administrative offices, Middle School classrooms, science and computer labs, the chapel, an art gallery and the infirmary. A modern academic wing contains classrooms, science and computer laboratories, computerized library and media center, a performing arts center, art studios, and dining room. A 29,000 square feet science center, which opened in 1999, has state-of-the-art laboratories for all three divisions, art studios, dark room, special space for drama and music, classrooms and offices. Students in the astronomy class now have access to a new observatory housing a 16-inch telescope in a moving, domed facility augmenting the ten eight-inch telescopes located on an outdoor pad. The School is fully computer networked to allow for intra-school communication and access to the global communications network.

Students in the Upper School may study for one trimester at a Sacred Heart school in another state or country. The students live with host families and/or in the school boarding facilities. The program provides a unique opportunity for students to broaden their global awareness both academically and socially. Recently, our students have studied in Bellevue, WA; San Francisco, CA; Australia; England; Belgium; Ireland and Spain.

Upper School activities include: Student Council, Cum Laude Society, Social Committee, a student newspaper The King Street Chronicle, French newspaper, Spanish newspaper, Yearbook, Literary Magazine, International Club, Film Club, Drama Club, Forensics Club, Environmental Committee, Committee of Games, Peer Counseling, Campus Ministry, Model United Nations, S.A.D.D., Madrigals and Chorus.

Athletic facilities include four playing fields for soccer, field hockey and lacrosse, six tennis courts, gymnasium, fitness room, dance studio and indoor pool. Interscholastic athletic competition (Fairchester Athletic Association and Western New England Prep School Association) includes crew, field hockey, soccer, lacrosse, softball, tennis, golf, basketball, cross-country, squash, diving and swimming. Middle School students participate in: Student Council, Bell Choir, Chorus, theater, dance, instrumental music, Math Club, Math Team, Great Books Club, Literary Magazine and environmental education. Interscholastic athletic competition includes cross-country, softball, squash, field hockey, soccer, lacrosse, basketball and swimming. In the Lower School: sports, swimming, dance (ballet, tap, jazz), and arts and crafts. For an additional fee, children may also participate in the Extended Day Program.

DANA HALL SCHOOL
45 Dana Rd., P.O. Box 9010
WELLESLEY, MA 02482
Tel: 781-235-3010
E-mail: admission@danahall.org
Web: www.danahall.org

Blair Jenkins, *Head of School*

Founded in 1881, Dana Hall is a college preparatory school for girls in grades 6-12, with boarding offered in grades 9-12. Located 12 miles west of Boston, Dana Hall offers the academic and cultural advantages of a cosmopolitan city along with the security and beauty of a suburban college town.

Dana Hall offers a rigorous liberal arts curriculum with a range of traditional academic offerings and electives, which include Women in the Classical World, Journalism, Public Speaking, Web Page Design, African Studies, Latin American Studies, Statistics, Political Science and Economics, and extensive choices in art, drama and music. Advanced Placement courses are offered in all disciplines.

Students take advantage of the college town of Wellesley and the metropolitan Boston area for educational, social, and cultural activities. Seniors with specialized interests may take a college course at Wellesley College or participate in the faculty-advised Senior Project program.

A strong community service program, including a tenth grade service requirement, provides a wide variety of opportunities for girls to be involved in the community.

The atmosphere at Dana Hall is dynamic and supportive of academic and personal growth and independence. Committed to the belief that self-understanding is a central issue of adolescence, the school offers a strong advisory system as well as a thorough college-counseling program.

Extracurricular involvement is highly valued at Dana Hall. Extensive opportunities are available in athletics, performing arts, and visual arts. Students compete in soccer, field hockey, cross-country, basketball, volleyball, ice hockey, fencing, softball, lacrosse, tennis, and golf; they perform in dance recitals, concerts, musicals, and drama productions in collaboration with local boys' schools; and they produce artwork in a wide variety of genres. The Dana Hall School of Music offers private instruction to students who wish to develop their musical talents. The Dana Hall Riding Center, which boards 45 horses, offers programs designed for all levels of riding.

Weekends are filled with myriad social, athletic and dramatic events, which are offered in and around Boston, organized by a Student Activities Board. Weekends are also a time for relaxation, for informal student-faculty get-togethers, for cooking in the dorms, for visiting with local friends, or studying. The Dana Hall student body is an international one with students from 14 countries and 18 states.

Private Schools Illustrated — 1296

Columbus School For Girls

A rigorous education in a collaborative, interactive, single-sex environment since 1898

56 S. Columbia Ave.
Columbus, Ohio 43209
www.columbusschoolforgirls.org

For **Girls.** For **Excellence.** *For the* **Future.**

GREENWICH ACADEMY
200 N. Maple Ave., Greenwich, CT 06830
Tel: 203-625-8900

Molly H. King, *Head of School*
Nancy Hoffmann, *Director of Admission and Financial Assistance, Grades Pre-K-6*
Gloria Fernandez-Tearte, *Director of Admission, Grades 7-12 and Director of Diversity*

Greenwich Academy, an independent college preparatory school for nursery through twelfth grade, has been dedicated to excellence in the education of young women for 178 years. Students at Greenwich Academy are encouraged to develop their full potential in an environment devoted to the strengthening of their intellectual capabilities and self-confidence and character. The school emphasizes rigorous academic standards, participation in community service projects and an extensive program in athletics and the arts. Eighty percent of classes in grades 9-12 are coordinated with neighboring Brunswick School for boys; however, the individual schools retain their own character, leadership, sports teams, yearbooks, student governments and college guidance departments. A technically advanced Upper School facility includes 21 classrooms, 5 science labs, a student center, a visual and performing arts complex, a 20,000-volume library, athletic center and fields.

EMMA WILLARD SCHOOL
TROY, NY
Trudy Hall, *Head of School*

Since 1814, Emma Willard School has been one of the nation's leading college-preparatory boarding and day schools for young women. At Emma Willard, every possible resource is dedicated to developing in its students the values and skills that form the foundation of a life of accomplishment, leadership, and fulfillment. These include a love for the life of the mind, a commitment to service, courage and confidence, grace and creativity, and collaboration and friendship. Known for its rigor, the School promotes intellectual curiosity and disciplined study habits through a challenging curriculum distinguished by a wide array of advanced placement courses and electives. In all they do, students are both challenged and closely supported by an outstanding faculty and staff.

The academic program is complemented by especially rich opportunities in the fine arts, music, dance, and theater. More than half of the student body participates in a competitive athletic program that includes 11 varsity and 3 J.V. teams. Emma Willard promotes active involvement in the life of the campus and off-campus communities through a rich co-curricular program that features 30 clubs and organizations. An active residential life program based on personal growth and mutual respect is supported by a cadre of residence faculty who serve as house parents. The School is located 150 miles north of New York City and just 7 miles east of Albany in the heart of New York's Capital Region (known for its rich resources in higher education, government, the arts, and high-tech industry). Independent study opportunities are available off campus through Emma Willard's exciting internship program, "Practicum."

Emma Willard's extraordinary physical plant, listed on the National Register of Historic Places, provides a breathtakingly beautiful, yet state-of-the-art, setting for learning and living. In addition to sweeping lawns, classroom buildings, dormitories, and two dining halls, the campus includes a library, an art center and gallery, a music building with practice and performance facilities, a large dance studio, a new science center, extensive computer facilities, a large gymnasium and fitness center, an aquatics center, three playing fields, and a newly refurbished 400 meter track.

Throughout its history, Emma Willard has been committed to enrolling a diverse student body from across the Capital Region, across the country, and around the world. The student body consists of 312 students from 24 states and 14 foreign countries. ESL is offered to international students at both the intermediate and advanced levels. This commitment to diversity is honored by significant expenditures in financial aid to assist families that might not otherwise have the opportunity for an extraordinary secondary education. Further information is available at www.emmawillard.org. To arrange for a visit or request further information, contact the Office of Admission at 518-833-1320 or via e-mail at admissions@emmawillard.org.

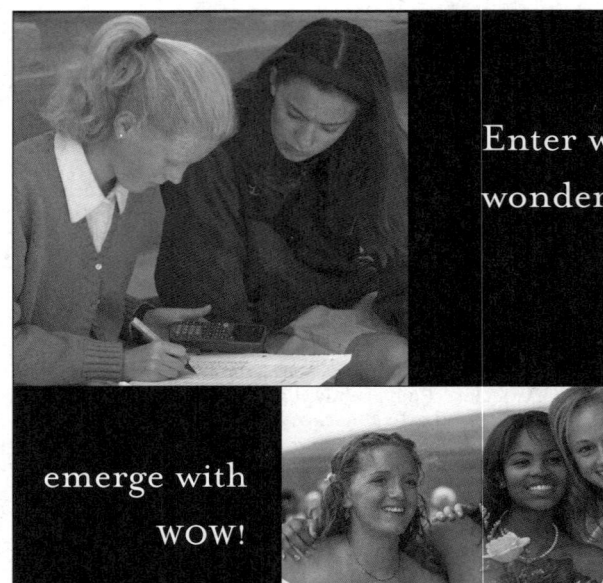

Enter with wonder...

emerge with WOW!

SIMSBURY, CONNECTICUT

The Ethel Walker School is a truly amazing place. Young girls enter the school energized to learn... eager to grow... encouraged to play. They emerge as confident young women prepared to take on the world.

Call us at 860/408.4200 or visit *www.ethelwalker.org* to learn more about one of the finest all-girls schools in the country.

The Ethel Walker School. Enter with wonder. Emerge with WOW!

FOXCROFT SCHOOL
MIDDLEBURG, VA

Foxcroft School, a college preparatory school for young women in grade 9-12, is located on a 500-acre campus near Middleburg, Virginia, one hour from Washington, DC. The 185 students are drawn from 23 states and 10 foreign countries. Foxcroft School combines its demand for academic excellence with the development of a strong character, a well-defined moral code, and a responsibility for service.

The school capitalizes on the fact that almost 80% of its faculty and administration live on campus. These families are the hub of a caring community where girls develop the self-esteem, confidence, and sense of purpose essential to their future success. Learning takes place in small, challenging, college-preparatory classes where faculty use collaborative learning techniques and students work in small groups to develop skills and formulate ideas. The curriculum includes approximately 97 courses, including A.P. offerings in all disciplines.

The Foxcroft academic program is further enriched by special events such as Interim Term, which focuses on academic, political, and social exploration of a given topic to develop in students an understanding of larger issues that affect their lives. The Goodyear Fellowship Program brings to Foxcroft each year a person distinguished in the arts, humanities, science, or public affairs, to speak and conduct seminars with students. Past speakers include Barbara Walters, David McCullough, Sally Ride, Aimee Mullens, Maya Angelou, and Doris Kearns Goodwin. The English Department sponsors an annual two-day Poetry Festival, during which published poets read from their work, lead workshops, and judge a student reading competition.

Foxcroft also has a Leadership Program designed to offer every student the opportunity to become a leader. Once Foxcroft leaders are elected or selected, they must attend a leadership retreat and complete specialized training to learn trust-building skills and conflict resolution.

Sports in the athletic program include field hockey, soccer, basketball, tennis, lacrosse, softball, volleyball, and dance. The Foxcroft riding program is highly regarded and provides a strong foundation in all phases of horsemanship.

Private Schools Illustrated — 1300

GARRISON FOREST SCHOOL
300 Garrison Forest Rd.
OWINGS MILLS, MD 21117
Tel: 410-363-1500
Web: gfs.org

G. Peter O'Neill, *Head of School*

Garrison Forest School is a college preparatory boarding and day school located on a hundred and fifteen acre campus, 12 miles northwest of Baltimore and 50 miles north of Washington, D.C. The Upper School (Grades 9-12), enrolls boarding and day girls: the Middle School, (Grades 6-8) enrolls day girls in grades 6 and 7 and boarding and day girls in grade 8, and the Lower Division (grades 3-year-olds–5) enrolls day girls. Grades 3-year-olds through kindergarten is coeducational. The student body is diverse, representing twelve states, the District of Columbia and eight international locations.

The school offers excellent training in fundamental academic skills while encouraging students to approach life with an intellectual curiosity, with concern for others, and with enthusiasm. The classes are small and informal which inspires a close relationship between students and faculty. A new Campus Center opened in Fall 2002, which houses an Athletic Center and dining facility. Advanced Placement courses are offered in 12 disciplines. Elective courses include art, dance, music, drama, photography and computer science. More than 20 student interest clubs and a variety of sports, including riding and polo, are among the extracurricular activities offered at the school. The many cultural and recreational opportunities in Baltimore and Washington are available to all students.

GIRLS PREPARATORY SCHOOL
P.O. Box 4736, 205 Island Ave.
CHATTANOOGA, TN 37405
Tel: 423-634-7600   Fax: 423-634-7643
Web: gps.edu

Girls Preparatory School, celebrating its centennial year in 2005-06, enrolls 750 college-bound students in grades 6-12, making it one of the largest secondary girls' day schools in the United States.

GPS offers a wide range of Honors and Advanced Placement courses and seeks students with strong academic preparation and commitment to learning. More than half of the senior class takes Advanced Placement calculus and/or AP biology, chemistry, or physics. Since 1990, the National Merit Scholarship Program has honored an average 20% of GPS seniors. Faculty work to foster both intellect and character in each girl, focusing on and teaching to girls' strengths.

A traditional curriculum is enhanced with a program of elective classes in the Upper School. Contemporary topics are addressed by semester offerings in science (forensics, marine biology) and math and technology (robotics). Encouraging responsible citizenship are elective choices in Constitutional Law and Presidential Politics. Global awareness is taught through electives in the history of East Asia, Latin America, and the Middle East. Technology, introduced in the 6th grade, promotes progressive development of computer skills. Eighth through twelfth grades employ a wireless laptop program.

Resources include a superior fine arts department, 13 interscholastic sports, and over 60 student organizations. The character education program has received national recognition, and a coordinate program with the McCallie School for boys provides coeducational classroom and social activities.

GPS is accredited by the Southern Association of Colleges and Schools and holds membership in the National Association of Independent Schools and the National Coalition of Girls' Schools.

Private Schools Illustrated — 1302

THE GRIER SCHOOL
TYRONE, PA

A supportive faculty and warm environment contribute to the success of the two-track academic program at Grier. The upper track offers courses which challenge students seeking admission to competitive colleges. The second track is designed for students who need greater academic structure and guidance. A Learning Skills program offers individual academic guidance, remediation, and tutoring. Crossover occurs often between tracks according to students' strengths and weaknesses.

The academic program is supported by a strong arts program. Studio art courses are taught in the areas of painting, drawing, sculpture, weaving, costume design, sewing, jewelry, metals, pottery, printmaking, and photography. Advanced students work closely with faculty to prepare portfolios for admission to post-secondary art programs. Music students may take private lessons in voice and instrumental music or may participate in any of the ensembles that perform throughout the school year. Dance students may take technique and choreography classes.

The sports program includes varsity soccer, basketball, softball, and tennis. Courses are also offered in skiing, volleyball, recreational sports, and aerobics. The renowned equestrian program offers courses from the beginner to advanced levels. Ballet and jazz dance are also very popular.

Resident housemothers and guidance counselors add to the supportive atmosphere of the school.

All buildings on campus have been completely modernized. A large Fine Arts Center housing music and arts classes opened in January of 2002 and a new Science Center opened in May of 2003.

Contact Andrew Wilson, Grier School, Tyrone, PA 16686. Tel: 814-684-3000. FAX: 814-684-2177. E-mail: admissions@grier.org. Web: www.grier.org.

ALLEGHENY CAMP

Box 308
TYRONE, PA 16686
Tel: 814-684-3000
Fax: 814-684-2177
E-mail: bestcamp@grier.org
Web: www.bestcamp.org

Katherine Adame, *Director*

The Allegheny Camp attracts girls ages 7-15 who enjoy horseback riding, performance dance, swimming and the visual arts. The setting for the camp is the campus of The Grier School, a well-known independent boarding school for girls in 300 wooded acres of beautiful Central Pennsylvania.

Campers make use of the school's excellent facilities which include 3 outdoor riding rings, one indoor ring, stables that house thirty horses, large, newly built art studios and an air-conditioned dance studio. In addition, campers use the school's modern gymnasium, outdoor swimming pool, five tennis courts, performing arts auditorium, dormitories, library, and dining hall.

The girls design their daily schedule to suit their personal interests. For some girls, this may mean that much of their day is taken up with riding. If they are interested in art as well, they may use the time not on a horse to be working on their ceramics or printmaking skills. If their main interests are dance and sports, their schedule will be primarily those areas.

The Allegheny Camp encourages girls to participate in all the activities which include camping/hiking, theater arts, swimming, tennis and much more.

Private Schools Illustrated — 1304

LINDEN HALL SCHOOL FOR GIRLS
LITITZ, PA
Tel: 717-626-8512   Fax: 717-627-1384
Web: lindenhall.com

A strong and positive self-image, plus involvement, achievement, and academic success are top priorities at Linden Hall, the oldest boarding school for girls in the United States. Our college preparatory curriculum is reinforced by a nightly supervised study hall, daily academic help period, and six grade reports each year. Our students' personal lives are supported by a strong advisor system. Tutoring is available. English as a Second Language is a part of the program for international students. Our riding program has an emphasis on hunt seat equitation and hunter showing but we also pursue show jumping, horsetrials and an occasional hunter pace or fox hunt. Average class size ranges from 6-12 students. Our student/faculty ratio is 4:1.

Extra-curricular activities include photography, drama, vocal and instrumental music, dance, art, community service, and the school newspaper, yearbook and literary magazine. Our riding, volleyball, tennis, basketball and soccer teams compete in the Pennsylvania Independent Athletic Association. Weekend activities may include dances, skiing, going to the theater, concert or museums, shopping, movies, or day trips to nearby cities. We also offer optional international trips during spring break.

Summers at Linden Hall are busy. Our Summer Camp Program includes riding camps for girls, as well as a nine-week Summer Adventure Day Camp for local girls ages 6-12.

Our 47-acre campus is located in Lititz, PA, seven miles north of Lancaster. We are easily accessible by plane, train, bus or car. Campus visits are available year-round, by appointment.

MISS HALL'S SCHOOL
492 Holmes Road, Pittsfield, MA 01201
Tel: (800) 233-5614 • Fax: (413) 448-2994
e-mail: info@misshalls.org
Website: www.misshalls.org

A college-preparatory, boarding and day school for girls in grades 9 through 12.

Academics
Miss Hall's School offers a comprehensive college preparatory curriculum, providing students with an outstanding academic foundation. Because we are small, girls receive plenty of individual attention, and there are always teachers available to answer girls' questions. Advanced Placement and Honors courses are available in all disciplines.

Off-Campus Learning
Not everything a girl needs to learn about the world and herself can be learned in the classroom. Every Thursday throughout the school year, all students participate in Horizons — an innovative, experiential learning and internship program that provides girls with opportunities to participate in work and service to the Berkshire County community.

Friendships and Community
Ask any girl to tell you what she values most at MHS, in addition to the strong academics, and she'll say it's the close relationships with her peers and teachers. Girls truly do make "friends for life" in this community.

Diversity
Like the world in which we live, Miss Hall's School is a diverse and pluralistic community. Girls come from over 20 states and over 15 countries, represent many faiths and creeds, and reflect a broad range of ethnicities, cultures, and backgrounds.

Leadership
Girls who graduate from Miss Hall's today will lead their society tomorrow. While girls are preparing for college, therefore, they are also preparing to take charge — of their communities, their states, their countries, and certainly their lives.

A Word to Parents
Raising strong, competent, and confident young women requires the adults in girls' lives to work together. We believe that we are in partnership with parents, reinforcing the values that parents have instilled in their daughters and providing girls with a deep reservoir of caring adults, who, like parents, teach, advise, coach, cheer, and model the behaviors we want girls to emulate.

Private Schools Illustrated — 1306

NAZARETH ACADEMY HIGH SCHOOL
4001 Grant Ave.
PHILADELPHIA, PA 19114-2999
Tel: 215-637-7676   Fax: 215-637-8523
Web: nazarethacademyhs.org

Girls 9-12

Founded by the Sisters of the Holy Family of Nazareth in 1928, this college preparatory day school is committed to the intellectual and spiritual education of young Christian women. Nazareth Academy enrolls 466 students in grades 9-12 and offers an academic program emphasizing liberal arts disciplines complemented by travel and study opportunities and a variety of activities. Students are involved in sports, publications, National Honor Society, music, language clubs and Community Service Corps. A summer program of academic and enrichment courses is offered. Tuition is kept affordable at $6,500/year.

Sister Mary Joan Jacobs, CSFN, Ed.D., Principal (B.A., Holy Family University, M.A., Villanova University, Ed.D., St. Joseph University)

Nazareth Academy is accredited by the Middle States Association of Colleges and Schools.

NOTRE DAME ACADEMY
425 Salisbury St.
WORCESTER, MA 01609
Tel: 508-757-6200

Ann Morrison, SND, *Principal*

Founded in 1951 by the Sisters of Notre Dame de Namur, Notre Dame Academy offers a college preparatory day program to young women in grades 9 through 12. The student body numbers slightly over 300 and class size averages 20 students.

The curriculum for grades 9 and 10 is designed as a structured program of basic studies. Students in grades 11 and 12 continue to take courses in core areas but also may elect courses in art, theater, music, language, science, mathematics, literature, history and social studies. Academic features include courses such as Introduction to Art Forms, Shakespeare, AP Music Theory, Advanced French, Spanish, and Latin, History, Women and Literature, Anatomy and Physiology, and AP Calculus. Students have the opportunity to participate in a variety of sports, cocurricular clubs, as well as music and arts programs. Students are also encouraged to become involved in community activities.

Virtually all graduates continue their education at a variety of colleges and universities such as Assumption, Bates, Brown, Colby, Dartmouth, Emmanuel, Harvard, Holy Cross, Georgetown, Wellesley, Worcester Polytechnic Institute and Yale. Notre Dame Academy is dedicated to preparing students for their roles as Christian women. Its administration believes that it is a distinct advantage for young women to attend a school where their particular needs are always a priority.

If you were to open an album of OLDFIELDS memories, you would find images and treasures of a school that is rich in history and as *unique* as the people who have passed through its doors for the last 138 years. The first page would tell you about Anna Austen McCulloch, the School's founder, and her little yellow clapboard home that has since grown and become the heart of the OLDFIELDS campus. Early pictures would show the first graduating classes, young equestrians on their horses, and a teacher working one-on-one with a student at dinner. Pages later, you would see new buildings, signifying the growth of the School. In the pages and memories most recently created, you might find pictures of a girl scoring the winning goal in the **lacrosse** championships, visiting the Eiffel Tower, build-

ing a rocket in the Physics lab, and contemplating her artwork in preparation for the *Annual Art Show*. Other pages might include images of another girl using her **L A P T O P** to update the web page she designed for her AP Spanish class, enjoying an Orioles baseball game at Camden Yards, or dancing with her *prom* date.

In every picture, each girl would look, feel, and be *unique* because at OLDFIELDS, a girl can be a scholar, an **athlete**, and an *artist*. At OLDFIELDS, a girl can be an **individual**.

The School's admission officers ask that students simply come to OLDFIELDS ready to make the most of their academic and personal potential, to **work hard** and play hard, and to contribute to a community where courage, humility, and largeness of heart are the values stated  in the motto. The School's mission reverberates: OLDFIELDS *is committed to the intellectual and moral development of young women. In a culture of kindness and mutual respect, we encourage each student to make the most of her academic and personal potential. We guide each student to grow in character, confidence, and knowledge by encouraging her to embrace the values of personal honesty, intellectual curiosity, and social responsibility.*

Located 25 miles north of Baltimore, OLDFIELDS is an all girls' boarding school of 190 students in grades 8-PG.

If you are already picturing yourself at OLDFIELDS, we want to get to know you better. For more information, please contact the Admission Office at

 (410) 472-4800, or 1500 Glencoe Road, Glencoe, MD 21152. Email us at Admissions@OldfieldsSchool.org, and visit our website at www.OldfieldsSchool.org.

PURNELL SCHOOL

POTTERSVILLE, NJ

Jenifer Fox, BA, MA, MEd,
Head of School

Situated on an 83-acre former farm/estate, Purnell conducts a noncompetitive academic program that incorporates cooperative, experiential learning opportunities and places a particular emphasis on the studio and performing arts. The curriculum is interdisciplinary and highly structured in grades 9 and 10; older students choose electives from among the subjects of English, history/social studies, foreign language, math, science, performing and studio arts. The school accepts girls with mild learning disabilities, in addition to those who excel academically. All students are supported by our Learning and Enrichment Center.

In midwinter, students participate in Project Exploration, a hand-on, project-oriented mini-term during which they work intensely on a project in a field of interest; time is built in for field trips as well. Juniors and seniors are given the opportunity to travel for two weeks in a French or Spanish speaking country, take French or Spanish language courses, and engage in cultural immersion. Seniors complete a compulsory internship, as well as a public speaking course which culminates in a speech given to the entire school about her high school experience. Every girl meets with her faculty advisor weekly; advisors then confer weekly to assess student progress.

Each trimester, students choose sports from Purnell's competitive (soccer, tennis, basketball, volleyball, softball, lacrosse and dance), or noncompetitive offerings, of which Project Adventure, horseback riding, yoga and kickboxing are options. Leadership opportunities, performing groups and general activities are available, while students also complete required community service projects.

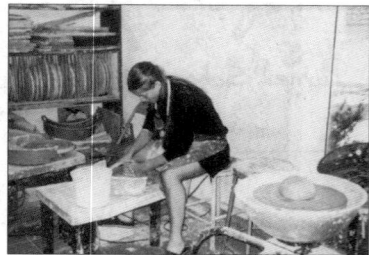

The small size (100 students), all girl and large boarding enrollment combine to create an intimate, family-like atmosphere in which community values of personal honesty and consideration of others are stressed.

The 80-acre rural campus is within easy driving distance of New York City, Philadelphia and Princeton. An important part of the school cultural life centers around regularly scheduled trips to the theater, ballet, museums and to other events of interest in those cities.

The challenging yet supportive environment, as well as the emphasis on challenging one's self, and the recognition of individual differences all play vital roles in helping Purnell fulfill its mission of developing self-esteem and competence in its students. The remarkable breadth of the elective curriculum and the rich variety of the extracurricular programs are designed to promote the discovery of new interests and the development of previously unrecognized talents. Students are stimulated to learn through

- the selection of departmental courses in a wide variety of subjects.
- Senior Internships which offer students the opportunity to pursue career interests off-campus.
- interdisciplinary study and skill-based, project-oriented learning.
- A two and one-half week experiential learning experience where students work intensively on one project. Past projects have included Website Design, Musical Production, Art Portfolio Preparation, Furniture Design and Habitat for Humanity.
- college and career guidance in a unique and extensive format.
- participation in one of twelve athletic programs ranging from riding and dance to soccer and lacrosse.
- the opportunity to pursue coursework in art, drama and music.
- Cultural Immersion program with resident study abroad in France and Spain.
- the Activities Program with offerings in areas of interest: dance, music, drama, art, Yearbook and community service.
- leadership opportunities in such diverse areas as student government, admissions, dormitory life, the Peer Leadership Program and athletics.

Purnell School admits students of any race, color and national or ethnic origin to the school and to all of its programs.

Private Schools Illustrated — 1312

ST. MARGARET'S SCHOOL
P. O. Box 158
TAPPAHANNOCK, VA 22560
Tel: 804-443-3357
Fax: 804-443-6781

Kimberly A. McDowell,
Assistant Head for External Affairs and Director of Admission

Educating young women for life.

St. Margaret's, one of the Church Schools in the Episcopal Diocese of Virginia, offers a boarding and day college preparatory program for girls in grades 8-12. A diverse student body of 158, representing 11 countries and approximately 17 states, maintains a 6:1 student-faculty ratio and a nearly 100% college attendance rate. Located in the small, historic town of Tappahannock, the picturesque campus overlooks the Rappahannock River, which provides unique opportunities for learning. Additional educational and cultural resources are conveniently accessible in Richmond, Virginia (45 miles) and Washington, DC (100 miles).

St. Margaret's prepares girls for an increasingly complex and international world by supplementing the college preparatory curriculum with international exchanges, a "Minimester" winter inter-term, independent study, leadership and community service programs. Supported by a strong advising system, students learn how to accept accountability for their actions and become independent learners. In addition, a formal lifeskills co-curriculum leads girls through age-appropriate explorations of Identity and Relationships, Healthy Lifestyles, and Decision Making.

Thanks to its outstanding waterfront location, St. Margaret's is the only girls' independent boarding/day school in the country to offer a river program. The program helps girls build confidence through outdoor adventures, encourages them as they explore environmental science careers, teaches them water sports they can enjoy for a lifetime, and shows them the value of volunteer service.

Equally important to a student's success at St. Margaret's is the opportunity to discover new interests and actively participate in clubs and organizations. A 42-acre athletic complex is on the drawing board to support a full sports program, which includes 9 competitive teams. Students also participate in afternoon activities, which include aerobics, art, walking, drama, and use of a community fitness center with indoor pool and sports facilities. Approximately 21 clubs and organizations are available. Weekend activities, which emphasize outdoor and cultural offerings, often include events coordinated with area boarding schools.

In addition, St. Margaret's is a member of the Queen Margaret of Scotland Girls' Schools Association, a group of 13 schools in 9 countries that provides opportunities for cross-cultural programs. The School offers exchanges with the St. Margaret's schools in Berwick, Australia, and Wellington, New Zealand for selected sophomores and juniors, respectively, as well as for faculty.

Students reside in air-conditioned dormitories with resident faculty members on each hall. The campus is fully networked with Intranet, Internet, e-mail and telephone access from all dormitory rooms as well as computer stations throughout the campus. A new, 24-student dormitory is under construction and will open in 2005-2006. The largest dormitory was renovated in 2002 to include refurbished public spaces, as well as a pottery studio, fitness center, and student lounge. A Community/Technology Center opened in 1999 housing a riverfront dining room on the upper level and science and computer classrooms and laboratories on the lower level.

Private Schools Illustrated — 1314

SALEM ACADEMY

WINSTON-SALEM, NC

Founded in 1772, Salem Academy has been a leader in education for young women. The Academy stands today as the oldest private school for girls in continuous operation in its original location.

With a total enrollment of about 200 students, 50% of whom board, Salem Academy shares a 57-acre campus with Salem College and is adjacent to Old Salem, a restored 18th century Moravian village and national historic landmark. The Academy offers a traditional college preparatory curriculum aimed at preparing students for selective colleges and universities across the nation.

In addition to the regular curriculum, the Academy requires two years of Latin, as well as two years of a modern foreign language, for graduation. Academy students also take part in the rich cultural offerings of Winston-Salem, a city nationally noted for its commitment to the arts.

Though Salem Academy is a traditional school, it offers many innovative programs. Qualified students may take college level courses at Salem College and earn college credit during their junior or senior year. Students may also take music lessons from highly qualified teachers at the Salem College School of Music. Every student takes part in the January Term program held during the three-week period following Christmas. Students may study on-campus, do internships or independent studies off-campus, or travel abroad with a faculty-led group from the school. English as a Second Language classes are available for international students.

A wide range of extracurricular activities is offered. Students may choose from nine varsity sports including swimming. The music program includes applied music lessons, a choral class, and the glee club which performs locally, nationally and in January 2003 in England. Drama, art, and literary pursuits are also strong offerings.

From the playing fields to the concert hall, from Athletic Banquets to Publications Banquets—the Academy is, first and foremost, a community that develops the self-esteem of its students by fostering the values of responsibility, integrity, loyalty, civility, friendship, and intellectual curiosity.

ST. CATHERINE'S SCHOOL
6001 Grove Ave.
RICHMOND, VA 23226
Tel: 804-288-2804 FAX: 804-285-8169
E-mail: admissions@st.catherines.org

Auguste J. Bannard, BA, Princeton, *Head*

St. Catherine's, an Episcopal School, has been preparing young women for college and beyond since 1890. Our 16-acre campus, located in a residential area of Richmond, has beautiful red brick buildings surrounding a large central green. Upper School students enjoy extensive course offerings, as well as unique experiences through a Minimester program. Average enrollment over the past three years is 814 students, junior kindergarten through grade twelve, with a large number of boarding students in Upper School. Class average is 17.

A rigorous Upper School curriculum, with AP or Honors courses in all subject areas, ensures excellent college preparation. All graduates attend 4-year colleges or universities. Outstanding performing arts in dance, music, and theater, and extensive varsity/junior varsity sports.

The Middle School is a small, cohesive community designed to challenge and nurture early adolescents. Both abstract and concrete approaches, as well as emphasis on critical thinking, create a balance of creative and skill related activities. We provide stability, support, and continued joy in learning during this age of change.

The Lower School offers a child-centered curriculum which allows for individual needs and differences among girls with high potential. Small classes and opportunities for individual exploration enhance each student's experience.

Girls' Schools — 1317

2225 Westchester Ave., Rye, NY 10580
Tel: 914-967-5622   Fax: 914-967-6476   Web: www.holychildrye.org

Founded in 1904, School of the Holy Child is a Catholic, independent, college preparatory school educating 309 young women in grades 5 through 12. One of a network of Holy Child schools throughout the United States and abroad, the school provides a liberal arts curriculum, community service, clubs and activities, athletics, and arts. Holy Child is a member of the National Association of Independent Schools and is accredited by the Middle States Association of Colleges and Schools.

For more information,
Please call the Admission Office at
914-967-5622.

THE PORTER SARGENT HANDBOOK SERIES

11 Beacon St.   Ste. 1400   Boston, MA 02108-3099 USA
Tel: 617-523-1670   Fax: 617-523-1021
info@portersargent.com   www.portersargent.com

Tools for Independent Evaluation

In 1914, educator and writer Porter Sargent introduced *The Handbook of Private Schools* because he felt educators, administrators and parents needed an objective guide to quality schools and programs emphasizing the needs of the individual student.

The development of the Porter Sargent Handbook Series followed that very simple aim. Each publication is a source book of information for those who need—and ought—to know about the advantage of independent instruction, providing the most up-to-date narrative and statistical information on schools and programs serving those who seek out the best education worldwide.

The Handbook of Private Schools * The Directory for Exceptional Children
Schools Abroad of Interest to Americans * Guide to Summer Camps and Schools

SOUTHFIELD SCHOOL

10 Newton St.,
Brookline, MA 02445-7498
Tel: 617-522-6980
FAX: 617-522-8166
www.southfield.org

William F. Phinney
Head

Southfield School for girls was established in 1992 by Dexter School to meet the needs of parents who wanted for their daughters the same emphasis on academic excellence and moral and spiritual attitudes which is fostered at Dexter. The School has an enrollment of 336, kindergarten through grade 9. Beginning in September 2004, Southfield is extending the enrollment through grade 12 by adding one grade each year. Its mission is to prepare students for admission to leading colleges.

Located with Dexter on a 36-acre campus in Brookline, each school has its own classrooms and shares the use of science, computer, and music labs, art, shop, and library facilities, as well as a gymnasium, enclosed swimming pool, five fields, and two indoor ice skating rinks. The five-story Clay Center for Science and Technology contains a lecture hall with stage, dining facilities, classrooms, laboratories, and an observatory with a 25-inch robotically controlled telescope. The School also maintains a field station on Cape Cod for marine science studies.

Southfield's traditional curriculum emphasizes the fundamentals of reading, writing, and arithmetic. Girls study Latin beginning in the sixth grade and elect a modern language in grade eight. Students also have classes in science, social studies, computer, health, music, studio art, and shop. A chapel assembly held each week includes hymns, a Bible selection, school prayers, the Lord's prayer, and a short address. The purpose of these assemblies is to remind students of the values of kindness, honesty, tolerance, courtesy, and cooperation.

Beginning in grade three, students participate on an intramural team in all sports. Interscholastic sports begin in grade seven with competition in soccer, field hockey, basketball, ice hockey, swimming, softball, crew, cross country, golf, tennis, squash, and lacrosse.

STONELEIGH-BURNHAM SCHOOL

574 Bernardston Rd.,
GREENFIELD, MA 01301
Tel: 413-774-2711
Fax: 413-772-2602
Web: www.sbschool.org

Martha W. Shepardson-Killam,
Head of School

Stoneleigh-Burnham School, founded in 1869, is a non-denominational, college preparatory school for girls. Currently, we have 160 students in grades 7-12 and PG; 95 are boarding and 65 are day. Stoneleigh-Burnham School is a learning community that honors young women's voice and intellect, while allowing them to develop their passion for learning as a lifelong endeavor. At Stoneleigh-Burnham young women enjoy not only equal opportunity, but also every opportunity to grow, to be challenged, to take risks and to explore personal and academic interests in a supportive environment. The faculty-student ratio is 1:5.

Stoneleigh-Burnham's academic program stresses the fundamentals necessary to the modern college preparatory program: English, history, mathematics, social sciences, foreign languages, the physical sciences, financial literacy, and computer literacy. The Performing and Visual Arts serve as signature programs for the school and offer students a wide range of courses and extracurricular offerings from introductory level through advanced conservatory study in dance, drama, music, computer graphics, photography, ceramics, weaving and painting The academic program ranges from advanced placement courses, electives, and independent study when appropriate, to individual help for students needing assistance in a particular area. An excellent Academic Skills program is provided, as is English as a Second Language.

The athletic program is designed so that each student will participate in a group or individual sport each trimester, and to teach skills she may use the rest of her life. Notably, the school maintains an extensive equestrian program, with stables for 60 horses, including 45 school-owned horses, two indoor arenas, an outdoor show ring, a derby course, cross-country and hunt course. The equestrian program accommodates riders at all levels of ability. Athletic options also include dance and a variety of team sports. Team sports available are field hockey, soccer, basketball, volleyball, skiing, softball, lacrosse, tennis and cross country.

The school is located on a very attractive 100-acre campus, three miles north of Greenfield. The campus features a $2 million science center. Weekend activities take full advantage of the broad cultural offerings of the five-college area of the Pioneer Valley and Boston and include social events with other area independent schools.

The school's scholarship and loan programs provide $900,000 in financial aid each year. Interested students and their parents are urged to make an appointment to visit the campus for a personal interview and tour.

STUART

In the classroom, performing community service, on the stage or on the playing field, Stuart students find more than an excellent liberal arts program. They develop the intellectual and spiritual strength to lead, along with the skills and confidence to succeed.

Stuart Country Day School of the Sacred Heart
Princeton, New Jersey
609-921-2330 • www.stuart.k12.nj.us

Educating Girls Pre-School through Grade 12; Boys Pre-School only.
A member of The National and International Network of Sacred Heart Schools
and The National Coalition of Girls' Schools

WESTOVER SCHOOL

MIDDLEBURY, CT

A leader in girls' education, Westover is an academically rigorous school dedicated to challenging and encouraging young women to participate in all aspects of academic, community, and athletic life. The Westover community is diverse, with students representing 14 countries and 17 different states. Three programs enhance the curriculum: Women in Science and Engineering (WISE), a joint program with Rensselaer Polytechnic Institute in Troy, NY; a joint program for pre-professional musicians with the Manhattan School of Music; and a joint program with the Brass City Ballet for talented dancers. Westover awards $1.9 million in financial aid annually.

Westover School is located in a lovely and picturesque New England town half-way between New York and Boston. Founded in 1909, Westover is best known for its rigorous academics, its friendly community, and its outstanding facilities.

Students at Westover are high achievers who take advantage of the wide range of electives and 17 Advanced Placement courses offered in art, art history, computer science, English, French, Latin, Spanish, history, mathematics, music, and science. Students are also involved in a variety of clubs including Glee, Dance Ensemble, Drama, The Wick (school newspaper), Yearbook, Amnesty International, Photo Club, Outdoor Club, and Environmental Action.

The main building houses 201 boarding and day girls. The dorm rooms, the dining room, most classrooms, the chapel, and Red Hall are located in this building. In separate buildings are the library, extensive science laboratories, art studios, Fuller Athletic Center, and a brand new performing arts center that opened in October 2004. Surrounding the central campus are playing fields, tennis and paddle tennis courts, ponds, and walking trails in woods extending over 100 acres.

Students regularly join with the faculty to consult on recommendations regarding the academic program, activities, and school life. The advisory system permits each girl to choose one of her teachers for an advisor. Dorm parents live on corridor, and they, together with faculty members, share with students in a rich extracurricular program.

BOYS' SCHOOLS

CARSON LONG MILITARY INSTITUTE
P.O. Box 98-M
NEW BLOOMFIELD,
PA 17068

Tel: 717-582-2121 Fax: 717-582-8763
E-mail: carson6@pa.net Web: www.carsonlong.org

Col. Carson E. R. Holman, BS, MA, *President*

Non-Profit

166th Year of Character Building Education

Carson Long Military Institute, a preparatory boarding school for 210 boys, is located in the foothills of the beautiful Blue Ridge Mountain country near Harrisburg, Pennsylvania.

The purpose is to provide a good school for boys of average ability from parents of average income. Carson Long is accredited by the Middle States Association of Colleges and Schools—since 1928.

The tuition is low ($13,400) including board, room, books, and uniforms. We want to help boys who need academic help.

Scholarship, citizenship, leadership, physical conditioning, character-building, public speaking, Spiritual power, Junior ROTC training, love of Country, love of home, high ideals, family values, and the courage and faith of our Fathers are all part of our daily life.

We try to develop the whole man at Carson Long and to teach each boy "How to Learn, How to Labor, and How to Live." We want to build good Scholars for America, good Citizens for America and good Leaders for America.

Historian H. H. Hain writes, "There is hardly a state in the union in which there are no former students, many who have risen to positions of trust and honor." The School was founded in the rough, stormy days of Andrew Jackson in 1836.

Private Schools Illustrated — 1326

CFS
THE SCHOOL AT CHURCH FARM
P.O. Box 2000
PAOLI, PA 19301
Tel: 610-363-7500

Charles W. Shreiner III, *Headmaster*

A Private College Preparatory Boarding & Day School for Boys
Grades 7 through 12

For more than 80 years, CFS, The School at Church Farm has been committed to providing the best in college preparation for qualified and deserving boys and young men. The School, located in Chester County, Pennsylvania, 25 miles west of Philadelphia, was founded in 1918 by the Reverend Charles W. Shreiner. It was his dream to establish a college preparatory school for boys of ability and promise who otherwise might not have an opportunity to attend such a school.

CFS is distinguished by one of the largest endowments-per-student of any educational institution in the country. Numerous buildings, spread over a 150-acre campus, are used for the School's comprehensive programs. The Administration Building houses electronically connected classrooms, offices, the multimedia center, a recreation room, the kitchen and dining hall. The Science Building contains four well-equipped laboratories, six electronic classrooms and the Art Department. Ten bright, hard-wired "Cottage" dormitories house the boarding population (80% of students) in small groups supervised by cottage faculty. Athletic facilities include soccer and baseball fields, a 400-meter track, six tennis courts, a modern multipurpose field house, a basketball gymnasium and an adjoining, outdoor swimming pool. Also on campus are the School's chapel, a 12-bed infirmary, faculty homes, shop buildings, storage barns and maintenance facilities.

With a student:faculty ratio of 7:1, classes are small, averaging 10 to 12 students. In addition to their teaching responsibilities, faculty members also participate in the admissions process, curriculum revision and staff development. Over 50% of the teaching faculty hold advanced degrees.

All students at CFS receive a comprehensive college preparatory education. College counseling helps students understand the options available to them and guides them in making informed choices about those options. College placement at CFS is over 90% and recent graduating classes are represented at such colleges and universities as Cornell, Dartmouth, Carnegie Mellon, Drexel, Columbia, Colgate, Lafayette, and Northeastern.

Private Schools Illustrated — 1328

Christ School
A NATIONAL LEADER IN EDUCATING BOYS

Paul Krieger, *Headmaster*

Founded in 1900, Christ School is an all boys college preparatory boarding school, grades 8-12. We are located in Arden, N.C. which is 10 miles south of Asheville on a 500-acre campus. Our mission is to produce educated men of good character, prepared for both scholastic achievement in college and productive citizenship in adult society. Our hallmarks include small classes (10-12 students); AP and honors courses in all subjects; extensive extracurricular opportunities; and an outstanding faculty. The successful athletic program features 17 teams in 11 sports, assuring places for all boys. We have 192 boys (32 day students and 160 boarding students). Affiliated with the Episcopal Church, we serve boys of all faiths.

Denis Stokes, Director of Admission
500 Christ School Road, Arden, NC 28704
Tel: 1.800.422.3212   Fax: 828.684.4869
Email: admission@christschool.org   Web: www.christschool.org

Not so much the absence of girls, rather, the unique benefits of an education among boys ...

An independent, college-preparatory day school for boys in Grades 3-12.

Arts - Academics - Athletics

LANDON knows boys

LANDON SCHOOL
6101 Wilson Lane, Bethesda, MD 20817-3199
Main Office: 301-320-3200/Fax: 301-320-2787
Admissions & Financial Aid: 301-320-1067/Fax: 301-320-1133

www.landon.net

CHRISTCHURCH SCHOOL

CHRISTCHURCH, VA 23031

Tel: 800-296-2306

John E. Byers, *Headmaster*

Christchurch School provides a personal and supportive environment in which students are presented with opportunities for self-direction and success. Such an atmosphere of understanding and encouragement, complemented by continuous challenges, not only sustains confidence in the student who has experienced academic success, but nurtures a positive self-image in the student whose previous frustrations may have resulted from overcrowded classrooms and an overemphasis on academic competition. With an average class size of 12 students, Christchurch provides a warm, structured, and supportive environment while encouraging success and challenging those with high aptitudes and abilities.

Located in Virginia's Chesapeake Bay region, on the banks of the Rappahannock River, one hour east of Richmond and 45 minutes from Colonial Williamsburg, Christchurch offers an academically challenging, yet not overwhelming traditional college preparatory curriculum for boarding boys and day boys and girls in grades 8-12. A post-graduate year is also offered. Eleven AP classes are offered in four disciplines. A limited number of high potential, college-bound students with diagnosed learning disabilities are accepted into the Learning Skills Program, which affords them specialized attention and support. An English as a Second Language Program is offered to international students and is designed to facilitate their development. Recent projects on the historic campus provide students with new classrooms, library, student center, computer facilities, multi-purpose field house, and fine/performing arts center.

Athletics are an integral part of the program at Christchurch and provide students with the opportunity for interscholastic competition. Because of its location, Christchurch is able to accommodate specific interests in water sports and activities which include: competitive sailing and crew, canoeing, and fishing. A unique aspect of the science curriculum is the Marine Science Program. This program introduces students to the Chesapeake Bay and its ecosystem through extensive field work and research. A variety of weekend activities and extra-curricular offerings are organized around cultural, recreational, and social themes, giving students opportunities to explore local metropolitan areas and settings.

CISTERCIAN PREPARATORY SCHOOL

3660 Cistercian Rd.
IRVING, TX 75039
Tel: 469-499-5400

Rev. Peter Verhalen, *Headmaster*

Founded by the monks of the Cistercian Monastery Our Lady of Dallas, this school prepares boys in grades five through twelve for leading institutions of higher learning throughout the country. Cistercian is divided into Middle (grades five through eight) and Upper (grades nine through twelve) Schools, and courses are taught in all levels by a single departmentalized faculty.

The school is operated under a system of Form Masters that allows for a more personalized administration and a sense of community within each Form. An inclusive college preparatory curriculum is supplemented by elective offerings in computer science, ecology, aerodynamics, electronics, and photography, among others. Latin is compulsory in grades 5-8. Although Cistercian admits students of all religious backgrounds, its educational program is formulated according to well-defined Catholic Christian guidelines.

Each Form has its program of class masses, yearly days of recollection, and retreats under its Form Master. The school's facilities include Middle and Upper School buildings; Science Center with theater and laboratories for chemistry, biology, physics, and computer; gymnasiums, tennis courts, and playing fields for football, soccer, and baseball; chapel; and library, art center, and music room.

Since its establishment in 1962, the school has graduated 871 boys with approximately 99% having entered colleges such as Amherst, Columbia, Dartmouth, Duke, Harvard, MIT, Princeton, the U.S. Service Academies, SMU, Stanford, Tulane, University of Notre Dame, UT Austin (Plan II), Vanderbilt and Yale. Cistercian offers challenge to the mind, help for personal development, and guidance by Christian morals and values. For information on admissions, please contact the Director of Admissions.

DEXTER SCHOOL

20 Newton St.,
Brookline, MA 02445-7498
Tel: 617-522-5544
FAX: 617-522-8166
www.dexter.org
William F. Phinney, Headmaster

Dexter School for boys, located on a 36-acre estate in Brookline, was established in 1926 and has an enrollment of 353 students, kindergarten through grade ten. The School is extending through high school by adding one grade per year. In addition to preparing students for admission to leading colleges, the School provides experiences which will help each boy develop not only his mental and physical skills but also desirable social, moral, and spiritual attitudes. In 1992, a sister school, Southfield, was established on the same campus and currently enrolls 336 girls. Each school has its own classrooms and shares the use of science, computer, and music labs, art, shop, and library facilities, and a gymnasium, an enclosed swimming pool, five fields, and two indoor ice skating rinks. The five-story Clay Center for Science and Technology contains a lecture hall with stage, dining facilities, classrooms, laboratories, and an observatory with a 25-inch robotically controlled telescope. The School also maintains a field station on Cape Cod for marine science studies.

Dexter's traditional curriculum emphasizes the fundamentals of reading, writing, and arithmetic. Boys study Latin beginning in the sixth grade and elect a modern language in grade eight. Students also have classes in computer, science, social studies, art, music, shop, and health. A weekly chapel assembly includes hymns, a Bible selection, school prayers, the Lord's Prayer, and a short address by a faculty member. The purpose of these assemblies is to remind students of the values of kindness, honesty, tolerance, courtesy, and good sportsmanship.

Students participate on an intramural team in all sports beginning in grade three. Interscholastic competition begins in grade seven and includes soccer, crew, ice hockey, basketball, lacrosse, cross-country, golf, tennis, and squash.

EAGLEBROOK SCHOOL
DEERFIELD, MA

Andrew C. Chase, B.A., M.A., *Headmaster*

Located on over 750 acres of wooded Mt. Pocumtuck, overlooking the historic village of Old Deerfield and the Deerfield Valley, Eaglebrook is a boarding school for boys in grades six through nine that offers to its student an unusual combination of beautiful, rural surroundings, a full and varied extra-curricular life, and a thorough academic program designed to meet a boy's individual needs and the requirements of the nation's leading secondary schools. In 2004-2005, 268 students were enrolled from 26 states and 26 foreign countries along with 70 day students. Founded in 1922, Eaglebrook, having earned a position as one of the premier middle schools, now has over 5,000 alumni, many of whom are leaders in their chosen fields and active in school affairs.

The Headmaster and faculty devote their energies to helping provide a firm foundation for the future lives and learning of younger boys as well as guiding them to achieve the independence and perspective necessary to understand themselves as they are now. In an informal, home-like atmosphere, an Eaglebrook boy is encouraged to develop his full potential, both through the challenges presented to him and the sympathetic guidance of the faculty.

The adviser system assures that every student is in daily touch with his adviser, who monitors progress, gives encouragement, and frequently communicates with the boy's teachers and parents. A consistent effort is made in the dormitories to provide the warmth and support of a good home while inculcating the values and challenges of learning how to live selflessly with others. In addition to daily meetings with advisers, the students enjoy a Home Night dinner with their adviser's family twice each month as well as frequent informal parties and activities.

The school has a rich and varied curriculum with careful sectioning by ability in English, mathematics, and the languages—French, Latin and Spanish. A wide choice of electives in history, science, art, music, and woodworking is also available. Small classes permit stimulation, individual attention, and understanding. The C. Thurston Chase Learning Center with small classrooms, a library, a computer room, a theater and assembly room, the Jean Flagler Matthews Science Center and laboratories; and the Bryant Arts Building with stained glass, drawing,ceramics, photography, Architectural Design, computer-aided design, computer art, and acting studios; practice rooms for piano and chorus; and a woodworking shop offer an appropriate environment for students to explore and develop their creative abilities.

Three times each day the boys gather with the faculty in a spacious, attractive dining facility for family style sit down meals together. With its own bakery, the school is fully committed to serving nutritious, balanced meals made of the freshest ingredients available.

The Eaglebrook boy leads a busy, constructive life. There are numerous opportunities for extracurricular pursuits and leadership: the Student Council; student committees that are responsible for various school services; band; choral groups; theater; publications; dances with girls' schools; and off-campus trips to museums, concerts, and plays.

Aware of the accelerated physical growth of boys at this age level, the school offers a variety of sports and physical activities designed to meet their needs. Primary emphasis is placed on developing and maintaining physical fitness, the mastery of basic skills, and good sportsmanship. A boy's physical activities should both challenge him and give a sense of accomplishment to everyone. Competition is encouraged, but not overemphasized. The school plays other nearby schools' teams, although the competitive schedules vary by age level, allowing the younger boys more time to develop under close and careful coaching. With its McFadden Rink at Alfond Arena, field house, numerous playing fields, ten tennis courts, Schwab Family Pool, Lewis Track and Field, groomed ski trails on the Easton Ski Area with the George Macomber chair lift, Eaglebrook offers a full range of sports, including soccer, football, ultimate frisbee, golf, track & field, cross-country running, ice hockey, basketball, baseball, wrestling, tennis, hiking, waterpolo, cycling, squash, lacrosse, swimming & diving, ultimate frisbee, mountain biking, hiking, skiing, and snowboarding.

In all aspects of school life there is a positive emphasis on the ability to live and work effectively with others. Eaglebrook thus seeks to develop at an early age the basic abilities that will bring confidence, enjoyment, and success in life. To sustain and nurture the acceptance and understanding of the diversity of the human family—such programs as International Day and Cultural and Racial Awareness Day have been inaugurated. Open to boys of all races, religions, and cultures, the school believes strongly in the community and brotherhood of men and women.

Private Schools Illustrated — 1334

FISHBURNE MILITARY SCHOOL

Grades 8 through 12
Classes average 12 students
Private education and so much more
Faculty Advisor System
Honor Code

Fishburne Military School was founded in 1879 by James Abbott Fishburne, a Waynesboro native and student and friend of General Robert E. Lee. The school is approximately two and one-half hours by automobile south west of Washington, D.C., in the rural town of Waynesboro, Virginia, a community of about 19,000 residents. Just off of Interstate 64, the school is easily accessible by automobile, bus, train, or scheduled airline service.

The principal thrust of the Fishburne experience is to encourage academic development resulting in advancement to college. Fishburne's philosophy holds that competition is not between students but between what a boy has done and what he can do. Each student is encouraged to identify his potential and to achieve excellence by striving to realize that potential. In addition to the emphasis on scholarship, each student is carefully guided in his quests for leadership and spiritual maturity so that he is genuinely prepared for the future.

Fishburne Military School's academic program meets the certification requirements established by the Southern Association of Colleges and Schools and has been continuously accredited by the Association since 1897. The school also meets the requirements set by the Virginia Association of Independent Schools. It is the only military school in Virginia to be continuously awarded the United States Army JROTC "Honor Unit" rating.

The annual fee for boarding students is $21,900 and $10,500 for the day program. The fee includes room, board, tuition, laundry, haircuts, books, and uniforms. Additional expenses include weekly allowance money and emergency funds.

The Admissions Committee's first consideration is what the school can do for the student. What the student can contribute to the school is also a part of the consideration. Inquiries may be made any time by contacting Fishburne Military School, P.O. Box 988P, Waynesboro, VA 22980. Tel: 800-946-7773 or 540-946-7703. E-mail: lambert@fishburne.org. Web: fishburne.org.

FORDHAM PREPARATORY SCHOOL
BRONX, NY 10458

Rev. Kenneth J. Boller, SJ, *President*

Fordham Prep is a Jesuit, college preparatory school for male day students founded in 1841. Located on the campus of Fordham University, it is an independent school with its own Board of Trustees. The school's two buildings contain classrooms, labs, two gyms, library, computer center and the 1,000-seat Leonard Theatre. There are 905 students. The student to teacher ratio is 12:1.

Fordham prep offers an advanced program of individualized study for highly motivated young men. Its goals in both academic studies and personal growth are realized in the daily interaction between students and teachers. The ideal of Jesuit education is the well-rounded person who is intellectually competent, open to growth, religious, loving and committed to doing justice in generous service to other people. A program of retreats, days of renewal and a 4-year service program combine with curricular and co-curricular activities to provide a rich experience for our students in preparation for college and for life. Our graduates are accepted at the finest colleges and universities in the country.

Fordham Prep's location is ideally suited for its combination of students from all across the metropolitan area, city and suburban students of many races and creeds. The geographic, ethnic and religious diversity of the students is one of the special features of the Prep and a point of pride for both students and faculty.

Fordham Prep offers an education that emphasizes faith, scholarship and service, engaging the whole person: mind, heart, imagination and feelings. It is an experience that shapes a lifetime.

Private Schools Illustrated — 1336

THE KISKI SCHOOL
SALTSBURG, PA

Christopher A. Brueningsen, *Headmaster*

One of America's oldest boarding schools for boys, The Kiski School focuses on how boys learn, what they need, and how they grow. Kiski seeks boys who are interested in working hard to become the best students and the best persons they can possibly become. It is important that boys who inquire about enrollment at Kiski understand that they will be expected to be active participants in their own education. Kiski faculty feel that W.B. Yeats was correct in his belief that teaching is less the filling of a vessel, and more the creating of a fire. Kiski teachers strive to develop a fierce love of learning in their students; boys who seek to come to Kiski should do so with an interest in working toward that end.

Kiski is located 30 miles east of Pittsburgh, on a wooded promontory, at the confluence of two rivers. The school is served by Pittsburgh International Airport, about an hour from the campus; the school offers transportation for students to and from the airport. All 220 students, and almost all the 40 faculty and administrators, live on the 360-acre campus. Kiski's facilities include two classroom buildings, an administrative building, five tennis courts, numerous playing fields, a fishing pond, a nine-hole golf course, nine dormitories, and twenty faculty homes. The John Pidgeon Library won distinction in 2001 as Pennsylvania's best school library. It contains over 23,000 volumes, and is linked electronically to over 1,000 other libraries in the state. Library holdings are available online for the convenience of students and staff. Rogers Hall contains the art and drama facilities for the school, a feature of which is the 500-seat theater. Several plays are produced each year by the Kiski Players. The Kiski Singers are featured throughout the year. WKRC is the campus radio station, staffed by students. Students contribute to several campus publications, among them "Cougar Online," the electronic daily newspaper. The S.A. Jack Fieldhouse contains an aquatic center, two weight rooms, two gymnasiums, a multiuse room for wrestling and baseball, and a large locker room. A nationally certified athletic trainer is on staff.

The Turley Dining Hall offers healthy food, presented family style. Faculty and students dine together; proper table manners are always stressed. In order to further ensure the health and the proper physical development of a young man, participation in athletics is required each season. Kiski fields 24 teams in 12 sports; boys can also participate in martial arts, scuba diving, life saving, and other activities. The school feels it is important to do something fun and non-academic each afternoon. Even if a boy is not very athletically inclined, there will be an opportunity for him. Kiski offers a wide variety of clubs; many students create projects in the school's woodworking shop. Weekends are important in a boarding school. Kiski students enjoy paintball, snowboarding, skiing, rafting, canoeing, hiking, camping, fishing and swimming, as well as trips to museums, art festivals, movies, shopping, and dining out. Mountain biking is very popular, at dozens of trails in the area, many of them on campus. Several dances are held on campus each year, with two nearby all-girls schools.

Kiski's teachers employ technology in their class instruction. Upon arrival at Kiski, students are issued a laptop computer, owned and maintained by the school, which they use as their own. Each student has a personal data port in his dormitory room, and can access email and the internet anywhere on campus. All Kiski buildings feature wireless internet.

Typically, over 75% of Kiski students are accepted to their first choice university. A fulltime college placement staff member coordinates the fall visits of over 70 college representatives. Kiski boys are allowed days off to visit and interview at colleges, and they attend two college fairs a year. Kiski offers fourteen AP courses. The average SAT score is normally around 1100; classroom sizes average eight students.

Kiski's application materials are available on the website, or can be mailed. An interview and campus tour are strongly recommended, but families who live far away can submit a videotaped interview, if they wish. The application deadline is March 1, but applications are accepted after that date, as long as space is available. Financial aid is need-based; awards totaled $1,200,000 in 2004. Applicants must submit a copy of their previous year tax return to the school, and complete the Parents' Financial Statement from School and Student Services for Financial Aid (SSS), the forms for which are available from the school.

Tel: 877-547-5448
Fax: 724-639-8596
Email: admissions@kiski.org
Web: www.kiski.org

Private Schools Illustrated — 1338

THE McCALLIE SCHOOL
CHATTANOOGA, TN

Tel: 423-624-8300   Fax: 423-493-5426
E-mail: admission@mccallie.org   Web: mccallie.org

Kirk Walker, *Headmaster*

Type: Boys Boarding (9-12) and Day (6-12) college preparatory school
Grades: 6-12; Middle School, 6-8; Upper School, 9-12

McCallie School, located on Missionary Ridge in Chattanooga, Tennessee, was founded in 1905 and is recognized as one of the South's preeminent college preparatory schools. It accepts young men with above average to exceptional academic abilities and those students matriculate at some of the best colleges and universities in the nation. In recent years McCallie has been recognized for its innovative educational programs and its overall standards of excellence. Recently, the *Atlanta Journal/Constitution* called McCallie "one of the leading secondary educational institutions in the United States." McCallie's alumni are leaders in business, politics, the arts, sciences and religion throughout the South and the entire country.

The mission of the school has not changed since its founding in 1905. McCallie's purpose is to prepare students for entrance into and successful academic work at college. McCallie stresses high academic standards and believes that challenging work best develops useful intellectual ability. Although not affiliated with any religious organization, McCallie has a strong Christian heritage and supports the spiritual growth of its students. Members of the student body represent all major faiths. The school teaches and values personal integrity, intellectual honesty and the work ethic. McCallie promotes the development of leadership skills and the ability to be both a self-confident individual and a dynamic member of a community. The school values and promotes an energetic response to the contemporary world, a joyful curiosity, a zest for physical activity and an openness to change, balanced with a respect for tradition.

McCallie's campus comprises 100 acres on Missionary Ridge, overlooking Downtown Chattanooga. A major expansion program over the past few years has extended the campus southward and doubled the number of athletic fields available to students.

McCallie is an all-boys school and believes that the educational, physical and social needs of secondary school students can best be met in a single-sex educational environment. To complement its single-sex commitment, McCallie has a coordinate program with Girls' Preparatory School (GPS) in Chattanooga. A coordinate director organizes activities and social events, and there are clubs on both campuses that sponsor coed service and community projects.

McCallie's academic program centers on a strong core curriculum of math, sciences, English, foreign languages and history. This curriculum is further strengthened by 15 Advanced Placement courses and numerous Honors courses. Close to half the members of every graduating class receive college placement or credit for AP courses taken at McCallie. The school offers an elaborate academic support system to students. Among its many facets are the Caldwell Writing Center, several computer centers and the Learning Center, where academic counselors and tutors are available throughout the day to assist students. The Library, which is fully computerized, has more than 32,000 volumes.

McCallie has 105 full-time faculty, 15 part-time faculty, three full-time academic counselors and numerous adjunct faculty and tutors. Close to half of the faculty live on campus, either in dormitories or nearby houses, and more than half have worked at McCallie more than 15 years.

Students participate in 14 varsity sports (football, baseball, basketball, cross country, track, tennis, swimming, lacrosse, rowing, wrestling, soccer, golf, bowling, and rock climbing) and McCallie students excel in athletic competition just as they excel in the classrooms. In recent years the school has had state championship teams in rowing, lacrosse, swimming, rock climbing, soccer, football, cross country, golf, and wrestling.

Private Schools Illustrated — 1340

FORK UNION MILITARY ACADEMY
P.O. Box 278
FORK UNION, VA 23055

Lt. Gen. John E. Jackson, Jr., USAF (Ret.), *President*

Founded in 1898, Fork Union Military Academy is an all-male, military-style boarding academy offering an accredited college preparatory education for young men in grades 6-12 and postgraduate. FUMA's Middle School, with its own facilities and faculty, features a traditional six-period schedule and small classes in a familial learning environment. The Upper School's unique One-Subject Plan offers coursework in concentrated, seven-week increments, including AP, Honors, and college-credit classes.

A 19,000-volume library (with a 6500-square-foot addition completed in 2004) and modern computer laboratories housing over 300 multimedia personal computers facilitate student learning.

In 2004, Fork Union cadets were accepted to 111 colleges and universities and received $3.4 million in scholarship assistance for higher education. The Academy's athletic and extracurricular programs include 13 different team sports, as well as band, chorale, and over 40 special interest clubs. Extensive athletic facilities include a new eight-lane Aquatic Center.

Fork Union seeks to develop the "Body, Mind, and Spirit" of each cadet. The emphasis on Christian values and the military structure provide an environment that stresses character development, leadership training, and personal discipline. The Academy is affiliated with the Baptist General Association of Virginia, although the Cadet Corps represents 27 religious denominations. Students come from 31 states and 13 countries.

Boys' Schools — 1341

MISSOURI MILITARY ACADEMY
204 Grand Ave.
MEXICO, MO 65265
Phone: 573-581-1776   Fax: 573-581-0081
Web: www.mma-cadet.org

Col. Ronald J. Kelly, *President*

MMA has an excellent reputation throughout the nation for its successful program of scholarship, leadership and campus activities. With dual curricula designed to fit the needs of both average and advanced students, the Academy has been designated an Exemplary Private School by the US Department of Education. MMA teaches patriotism, leadership and self-discipline; its Junior ROTC program regularly receives the Honor Unit with Distinction rating from the Department of the Army.

The broad scope of campus activities reaches each boy and includes 11 varsity and three intramural sports. The Academy boasts a championship marching band and drill team, aviation training and Raiders physical activities program.

The school's 288-acre wooded campus houses two academic buildings for the high school and separate Junior School, four barracks, a field house, an indoor Olympic-sized swimming pool and gymtorium, indoor and outdoor tracks, a new rappelling tower and the Memorial Chapel.

THE RECTORY SCHOOL
FOUNDED IN 1920

JUNIOR BOARDING SCHOO[L]
for Boys Grades 5-9[?]
Promoting One's Personal Bes[t]

The Rectory School was founded in 1920 by the Rev. Frank H. Bigelow an[d] his wife, Mabel, who understood the benefits of teaching children in sma[ll] classes with individualized attention set in a caring atmosphere. Today, The Rec[-]tory School is a boy's junior boarding school and coed day school for 180 5th [-] 9th graders. Located on 135 picturesque acres in northeastern Connecticut, th[e] school's grounds include nineteen buildings, athletic fields, state of the art gym[-]nasium, tennis courts and skating pond. The school recently completed a $5 million capital construction program which includes 2 new dormitories, library expansio[n] a performing arts center with 218-seat auditorium, dining hall and a fine arts "barn" with studios and a darkroom.

THE RECTORY PROGRAMS

The Rectory School provides middle schoolers with an enriched and support[-]ive academic, social and ethical community that addresses individual learn[-]ing styles from remedial to gifted while promoting self-worth and accountabil[-]ity. The Rectory program is a combination of traditional academics, arts and athlet[-]ics, innovative teaching methods and the award winning *Individualized Instructio[n] Program™ (IIP™)*. The *IIP™* is a unique one-to-one instruction program whic[h] meets five days a week and is woven seamlessly into the school day. This ap[-]proach successfully addresses individual learning styles, aptitudes and needs fro[m] remedial to gifted. Many junior boarding schools have modeled their tutoring program[s] after The Rectory School's *IIP™*. *IIP™* specifically supports a student's personal needs i[n] the areas of written language skills, reading comprehension, study skills including organi[-]zation and time management, and mathematics. The gifted student may receive personall[y] designed enrichment projects and independent study.

THE RECTORY SCHOOL ATHLETICS

The superior Rectory athletic facilities and sports program emphasizes healthy competi[-]tion, teamwork, participation, effort, and sportsmanship. Its 25,000 sq. ft. gymnasium i[s] one of the finest athletic facilities offered to this age group. Students must participate i[n] three seasons of sports. The program is competitive and challenging for the skilled athlet[e] and open and encouraging for the less experienced athlete.

THE RECTORY FACULTY

The School community lives The Rec-tory School Creed: Responsibility, Respect, the School's creed for the students through consistent and morally responsible behav-ior. These dedicated and caring adults foster the home-like atmosphere which sets The Rectory School apart. This tight-knit community helps to promote personal self-worth, accountability and community service.

528 POMFRET STREET • POMFRET, CONNECTICUT 06258
860-928-7759 • ADMISSIONS: 860-928-1328 • FAX: 860-928-4961
E-MAIL: **admissions@rectoryschool.org**

THE RECTORY SCHOOL

Founded in 1920

SUMMER SESSION for Boys Boarding, Co-ed Day, Grades 5-9.

THE RECTORY SUMMER SESSION

The Rectory Summer Session began in 1950 and is a five-week program for boarding boys and day boys and girls entering grades 5-9 in the fall. Located on 135 picturesque acres in northeastern Connecticut, the school's grounds include nineteen buildings, new dorms, arts center, athletic fields, state of the art gymnasium, and tennis courts, and pool. *The Rectory Summer Session* provides the opportunity for students to improve their academic skills, get a head start on the next school year, or become familiar with Rectory before entering in the fall.

THE RECTORY SUMMER SESSION: ACADEMIC PROGRAM

In keeping with The Rectory School mission, *The Rectory Summer Session* provides middle schoolers with an enriched and supportive academic, social and ethical community that addresses individual learning styles from remedial to gifted while promoting self-worth and accountability. The *Summer Session* offers an *Academic Program* in the morning and a *Recreational Program* in the afternoon and on weekends. The *Academic Program* combines small classes (maximum 8 per class) in English, reading, math, study skills, and a one-to-one tutoring period known as the *Individual Instruction Program^{TM} (IIP^{TM})*. The *IIP^{TM}* is one-to-one instruction that addresses individual learning styles, aptitudes and needs from remedial to gifted. All students attending the *Summer Session* take part in the *IIP^{TM}*.

THE RECTORY SUMMER SESSION: RECREATIONAL PROGRAM

The superior Rectory athletic facilities and sports program emphasizes healthy competition, values, participation, effort, and sportsmanship. The afternoon *Recreational Program* consists of clubs, sports, and swimming. The clubs offer a wide range of activities like basketball, tennis, golf, computers, board games, and arts and crafts. The students participate in a summer-long Olympic-style competition in swimming, running, soccer, baseball, and basketball. On weekends, students visit such places as the Boston Museum of Science, Mystic Aquarium, Red Sox games and amusement parks.

THE RECTORY FACULTY

The *Summer Session* community lives the School Creed: Responsibility, Respect, Honesty, and Compassion. The Rectory teachers, coaches, and dorm parents model the creed for the students through consistent and morally responsible behavior. These dedicated and caring adults foster the home-like atmosphere, which sets The Rectory School and *Summer Session* apart.

528 POMFRET STREET • POMFRET, CONNECTICUT 06258
860-928-7759 • ADMISSIONS: 860-928-1328 • FAX: 860-928-4961
E-MAIL: **admissions@rectoryschool.org**

ST. JOHN'S PREPARATORY SCHOOL

72 Spring St., Danvers, MA 01923
Tel: 978-774-1050   Web: www.stjohnsprep.org

Albert J. Shannon, Ph.D., *Headmaster*

Founded in 1907, St. John's Preparatory School is a Catholic, Xaverian Brothers Sponsored secondary school for young men in grades 9-12. The rigorous academic program at St. John's embodies Christian values and seeks to prepare students to succeed in college and in life. Courses are offered at five academic levels in order to challenge students to their fullest. The curriculum includes many electives in areas such as history, business, foreign language, computer science, fine arts and more. Religious studies classes are required for all four years. The 175-acre campus, just 15 miles north of Boston, is a vibrant blend of old and new. At the center of the campus is the A.E. Studzinski Library, opened in September 2003. The state-of-the-art 24,000 square foot facility features a traditional library collection, wireless Internet access, "smart" classrooms, space for individual and collaborative study, and advanced computer resources. Brother Benjamin Hall offers six new science labs, wireless Internet access, and a spacious guidance suite. Athletic facilities include five tennis courts, all-weather track, football stadium, baseball diamonds, soccer/lacrosse fields, and a large gymnasium. Students are encouraged to participate in the wide variety of extracurricular activities offered including Model UN, debate team, photography, publications, service programs and more. St. John's is accredited by the New England Association of Schools and Colleges. A limited number of applications are accepted for upper grades. Admission is competitive. Ninety-nine percent of graduates go on to college. Among the colleges attended by recent graduates are Amherst, Boston College, Boston University, Brown, College of the Holy Cross, Dartmouth, Duke, Georgetown, Harvard, McGill, New York University, Northeastern University, Notre Dame, Rhode Island School of Design, Rensselaer Polytechnic Institute, Tufts, University of Chicago, University of Pennsylvania, Williams and Yale.

SAINT JOSEPH HIGH SCHOOL
The Brothers of the Sacred Heart

Comprised of 850 students from over 70 sending schools
We come from many places
blending together cultures and races
We celebrate who we are and from where we come
May we overcome our weaknesses
May we develop and utilize our strengths
With the faculty and staff to guide and support us along our journey,

We are St. Joes

An independent Catholic college preparatory school located in Metuchen, New Jersey.

In response to the gospel message of hope, the teachings of the Catholic Church and the traditions of the Brothers of the Sacred Heart, who have been active in American Education since 1847, the school desires to meet the needs and promote the development of each individual. It strives to enable that person to acquire the knowledge and skills needed for competence in contemporary society, as well as the values and convictions characteristic of enlightened Catholics in that society.

Where excellence is a habit, not a goal

145 Plainfield Avenue Metuchen, NJ 08840
732-549-7600   www.stjoes.org

Private Schools Illustrated — 1346

ST. THOMAS CHOIR SCHOOL
202 W. 58th St.
NEW YORK, NY 10019-1406
Tel: 212-247-3311
Web: choirschool.org

Charles F. Wallace, *Headmaster*

St. Thomas Choir School is an Episcopal boarding school for boys in grades 4-8. Located in the cultural center of Manhattan, the school takes full advantage of New York City through trips to museums, exhibitions, concerts and cultural events.

Students sing in the choir of St. Thomas Church, 5th Avenue. They regularly embark on concert tours in the United States and in Europe. In addition, the choir makes several recordings each year and performs an annual concert series. Each student studies an instrument of choice with a private instructor. Unique in North America, St. Thomas offers extensive musical training and education within a rich middle school curriculum. An average class size of 8 students ensures each boy of individual attention, both in the classroom and out. The rigorous choral program ensures that students achieve high standards and learn to work under pressure but within the context of a caring Christian environment. In recent years the record of successful placement at excellent prep schools has been remarkable.

Recreational and organized athletics are part of every school day, and all boys play on a sports team. Throughout the school year St. Thomas Choir School schedules outings, dinners, and parties for school families and their sons. Each year the school spends a week a Camp Incarnation in Ivoryton, CT, utilizing the camp's 600 acres and private lake.

Tuition is modest and scholarships are available to families who qualify. St. Thomas Choir School admits students of any race, color or national origin.

South Kent School

40 Bull's Bridge Rd,
South Kent, CT 06785
Tel: (860) 927-3539 Fax: (860) 927-1161
Email: admissions@southkentschool.net
www.southkentschool.net

Andrew Vadnais, Headmaster

South Kent School, founded in 1923, was established as a place where young men could develop their potential in an environment that fosters "simplicity of life, self-reliance, and directness of purpose."

Located on 460 acres, South Kent offers a variety of outdoor pursuits in the rural setting. A rigorous academic program prepares young men in grades 9-12 for college. Faculty create a family-like atmosphere with sit-down meals at lunch and several dinners a week. Dormitories are small with dorm parents in adjoining apartments. SKS keeps classes small with a 5:1 ratio of students to faculty.

Private Schools Illustrated — 1348

TRINITY-PAWLING SCHOOL
PAWLING, NY

Archibald A. Smith, III, BS, Trinity, MALS, Wesleyan, *Headmaster*

Trinity-Pawling, founded in 1907, is a college preparatory, Episcopal, boarding school for boys. The school is located in Pawling, New York, 67 miles north of New York City along the Connecticut border. The campus, set on 140 acres of rolling hills, is just over an hour's drive from New York's major airports.

It is Trinity-Pawling's belief that an appreciation of one's own worth can best be discovered by experiencing the worth of others, by understanding the value of one's relationship with others, and by acquiring a sense of self-confidence that comes through living and working competently at the level of one's own potential. Trinity-Pawling respects and recognizes the differences in individuals and the different processes required to achieve their educational potential.

At the heart of Trinity-Pawling's philosophy is the effort system. This system rewards a boy based on his effort in various aspects of school life including academic, athletic, extracurricular, and dormitory. We acknowledge that boys have different strengths and weaknesses, and it is our belief that by rewarding students for hard work, each boy will be motivated to reach his own potential in all areas of school life.

Trinity-Pawling offers over 100 courses including 15 AP courses. A student-teacher ratio of 7 to 1 and a residential faculty allow for an intimate academic setting where additional instruction is always available. A Language Program for bright students who have been diagnosed as having a mild language based learning disability is also offered on a limited basis.

Students benefit from an extensive physical plant. The newly expanded and renovated Dann Building includes 6 new classrooms, 4 new science labs, 2 science lecture halls, 2 computer labs and an auditorium. There are a 25,000 volume library, chapel, new Center for the Arts, and 8 dormitories. Athletic facilities include the new McGraw Pavilion, with a multi-purpose/wrestling room and enclosed hockey arena, the Carleton Gymnasium which includes 5 international-sized squash courts, a Nautilus and free weights room, a cardio-room, 11 tennis courts and 8 playing fields. A state of the art track, stadium football field and new baseball diamond will be completed in 2004.

A wide variety of extracurricular activities is offered and there are athletic teams and intramural programs for students of all levels of ability.

WOODBERRY FOREST SCHOOL
WOODBERRY FOREST, VA
Dr. Dennis M. Campbell, BA, PhD, BD, *Headmaster*

Woodberry Forest School was founded in 1889 and sits on a beautiful 1,400 acre campus in the foothills of the Blue Ridge Mountains of Virginia. Its rural residential setting fosters a natural closeness among the 380 boys and 75 faculty who live and work together. The beauty of this setting is enhanced by its proximity to Washington, Richmond, and Charlottesville and their available academic and cultural events. Open to students of all races and religious affiliations, the school currently enrolls boys from 22 states and twelve foreign countries.

The mission of the school is to develop in its students, under Christian principles, a sense of honor and moral integrity, respect for sound scholarship, full acceptance of responsibility, and a will toward personal sacrifice in the service of others. Furthermore the school trains students toward a useful contribution to society and thoroughly prepares them for the best colleges and universities within reach of their individual abilities.

As a community, the school fosters an atmosphere of civility and cooperation. The most important tradition is the honor system, in which every student accepts an obligation never to lie, cheat, or steal. Promoting mutual trust among the students and faculty, the honor system has a tremendous positive impact on the community.

The school's academic, athletic, fine arts and recreational facilities are extensive. Classrooms and laboratories are well equipped and the curriculum is rigorous. The athletic program stresses participation for all students, fielding school teams at many levels in soccer, football, cross country, basketball, wrestling, squash, swimming, indoor and outdoor track, baseball, lacrosse, tennis and golf. Several ponds and the on-campus Rapidan River afford opportunities for fishing and kayaking. The school has a nine hole Donald Ross golf course on campus.

Most students enroll in the 9th or 10th grade, but a very small number of well qualified candidates are admitted to the 11th grade. Financial aid is available.

For more information, contact: Office of Admissions
Woodberry Forest School
Woodberry Forest, VA 22989
Tel: 540-672-6023

THE UNDERACHIEVER

A more complete compilation of 2500 schools, facilities and organizations serving children and young adults with developmental, emotional, physical and medical disabilities is available in Porter Sargent's *Directory for Exceptional Children*. For details, please visit www.portersargent.com or see page 1471.

BRANDON HALL SCHOOL

1701 Brandon Hall Dr., Atlanta, GA 30350
Tel: 770-394-8177   Fax: 770-804-8821
Email: admissions@brandonhall.org
Web: www.brandonhall.org

Paul R. Stockhammer, *President and Headmaster*

Brandon Hall is an accredited, nonprofit, nonsectarian, coeducational day and boys' boarding school for students in grades 4-12. Enrolling approximately 140 students, the school provides both one-on-one and small group college preparatory classes for students who, for a variety of reasons, have not been achieving their potential or who otherwise need a more intensive educational setting.

The emphasis is on personal attention, organization, structure, accountability, the ordering of priorities, applied study skills, and multi-sensory instruction. At the same time, Brandon Hall provides a very traditional prep school setting that is both challenging and nurturing. A summer program includes both credit and enrichment non-credit school courses for grades 4-12.

The school, located on 27 acres in the suburban Dunwoody area of Atlanta on the Chattahoochee River, is near the educational, cultural and recreational opportunities of downtown Atlanta.

EAGLE HILL-SOUTHPORT

214 Main St., Southport, CT 06490
Tel: 203-254-2044   Fax: 203-255-4052
Web: www.eaglehillsouthport.org
E-mail: info@eaglehillsouthport.org

Eagle Hill-Southport is a non-profit school for children with learning disabilities. Serving boys and girls ages 6 to 16 in a supportive, structured, success-oriented program, the 3:1 student/staff ratio allows for individualized instruction to address the learning style and level of each child. The school is transitional and non-graded, designed to reinforce students' skills through tutorials and small group classes that prepare them for return to more traditional placements.

Private Schools Illustrated — 1354

COMMUNITY HIGH SCHOOL
1135 Teaneck Rd.
TEANECK, NJ 07666

Toby Braunstein, *Director of Education*
Dennis Cohen, *Director of Program*

Community High School provides a full, rich four year college and career preparatory curriculum for students with learning difficulties. Community High School serves students from New York City, Northern New Jersey, and Rockland County. Transportation from New York City is provided.

Adolescent counseling groups, career counseling, college counseling, SAT preparation, small class groupings, individualized instruction, skilled remediation, additional tutorials in reading language and speech, and wide range of study skills classes are provided. Courses follow the traditional high school curriculum, are completely departmentalized, and include computer programming, photography, video production, computer graphics, graphics, keyboarding, music, drama, and drivers education. Extracurricular activities include theater and music productions, newspaper and yearbook production, a complete intramural athletic program and an interscholastic athletic program.

For admissions contact Toby Braunstein: 201-862-1796.

HELPING SPECIAL PEOPLE LIVE THEIR DREAMS FOR OVER 90 YEARS

**ARIZONA · CALIFORNIA · COLORADO · CONNECTICUT
FLORIDA · GEORGIA · MASSACHUSETTS · NEW JERSEY
NEW YORK · PENNSYLVANIA · TEXAS · THE DISTRICT OF COLUMBIA**

Devereux is the nation's largest independent, nonprofit provider of treatment services for children, adolescents, and adults who have a wide range of emotional, behavioral, and developmental challenges and neurological impairments. Devereux's residential, day, and community-based programs are located in 12 states and the District of Columbia.

Devereux

800-345-1292 • www.devereux.org

Private Schools Illustrated — 1356

EAGLE HILL SCHOOL
GREENWICH
45 Glenville Rd.
GREENWICH, CT 06831
Tel: 203-622-9240   FAX: 203-622-8668

Mark J. Griffin, PhD, *Headmaster*

Founded in 1975, Eagle Hill–Greenwich offers specialized instruction to bright children who, because of a learning disability, are unable to realize their full potential in traditional educational environments. Using a language immersion approach in an ungraded, non-competitive setting, students are provided with individualized and small group instruction. All teachers hold special education certification and receive ongoing supervision and in-service training.

Eagle Hill's main objective is to provide three to four years of intensive, remedial instruction and then to return the child to the educational mainstream. A transitional program is incorporated into the plan

to develop the academic skills, study strategies, self-advocacy and risk taking necessary to function independently in a traditional school setting. Students are placed in a range of prep schools, local independent schools and public programs across the country. Eagle Hill offers a wide variety of activities in addition to the extensive academic programs. The addition of a professional library, a 12,000-volume children's library, and new technology in the computer department enhance the academic program, providing students with a state-of-the-art facility in which to develop their study skills and writing proficiency. Electives include art, music, drama, photography, computer programming, cooking, newspaper, film classes and community service programs. Full interscholastic and intra-mural sports programs include competition in soccer, cross country, field hockey, lacrosse, basketball, ice hockey, baseball, softball and tennis. Regular physical education classes, karate, jazz dance, aerobics and biking round out the physical activity options.

Eagle Hill–Greenwich is a coed day and five-day residential program for students ages six through sixteen. The residential population at Eagle Hill ranges in ages from 10-16. Most students live within a two hour commute of Greenwich, and go home on weekends. Several "super weekends" are offered for the boarders to develop a sense of community and include camping trips, ski weekends and cultural excursions. The living situation is a warm, family-like setting, with close faculty supervision, guidance and interaction.

Eagle Hill houses a Lower School, ages 6-11, and an Upper School, ages 11½-16. An active Advisor system ensures communication among staff and between school and home, and provides an advocate for the child within the program throughout the child's matriculation. Eagle Hill also runs a separate six week summer school. For information regarding Eagle Hill–Greenwich, please contact Rayma-Joan Griffin, Director of Admissions.

EAGLE HILL SCHOOL
HARDWICK, MA
Tel: 413-477-6000
Fax: 413-477-6837
E-mail: admission@ehs1.org
Web: ehs1.org

Peter J. McDonald, *Headmaster*

Established in 1967, Eagle Hill School is an independent, coeducational boarding school serving students with learning differences who have been diagnosed with specific learning disabilities (LD) and/or Attention Deficit Disorder (ADD). Currently, we accept young people in grades 8-12 who are functioning in the average to above average range of intellectual ability, and who are motivated to explore beyond the boundaries of their personal limitations. Although Eagle Hill encourages emotional and behavioral growth, we do not accept students with a primary deficit in these areas.

As an educational community, Eagle Hill is committed to offering an individualized program of study that is directed toward the successful fulfillment of personal academic and social growth goals. We provide an intimate and encouraging learning environment (5:1 student to teacher ratio) that enables students to achieve overall personal excellence. In each content area, students are placed in classes that are homogeneous with respect to both age and skill level. By designing a personal curriculum for each student, we ensure that their particular learning style and needs are addressed in a comfortable, yet challenging environment.

Consistent with our philosophy of educating the whole person, Eagle Hill School has developed a program of academic courses that target interpersonal and intrapersonal communication skills. These pragmatics courses have been designed explicitly to teach students about social nuances such as body language, social perception, conflict resolution, assertiveness, self-advocacy, relationship building, and peer mentoring. In combination with their other courses, students gain the skills they will need to become well-rounded, self-confident adults.

We consider an exploration of the arts and exposure to athletics to be essential components in the development of independent, curious, and critical thinkers. Our athletic, extracurricular, and weekend programs are designed to further increase self-esteem and to augment self-image. Eagle Hill School competes against local schools in the sports of soccer, cross country, basketball, wrestling, softball, tennis, and golf. A sampling of our evening clubs and extracurricular activities includes: skiing, student newspaper, literary magazine, radio broadcasting, photography, graphic arts, whitewater rafting, camping, Tree Huggers ecology club, community service, and intramural sports.

EAGLE HILL SCHOOL
SUMMER PROGRAM
HARDWICK, MA
Tel: 413-477-6000   Fax: 413-477-6837
E-mail: admission@ehs1.org   Web: ehs1.org

Peter J. McDonald, *Headmaster*

Beyond relaxing, summer is precious time that can be spent exploring the world, reading a good book, investigating math, history, science, and the arts. We believe that so much can be accomplished during a mild New England summer. From early July through mid-August, Eagle Hill runs a six-week program for students with learning differences ages 9 through 19, who have been diagnosed with specific learning disabilities (LD) and/or Attention Deficit Disorder (ADD).

Consistent with the goals of the winter program, the summer program is primarily designed to help students improve their academic and social skills, while maintaining progress achieved during the regular school year. Our summer program is also a great way for students entering the fall program for the first time in September to get acquainted with the campus, the faculty, and their peers. This head start ensures that their future transition is as smooth and successful as it can be.

In addition, the program places an emphasis on recognizing and fostering individual talent. Electives and sports activities are mixed with academic courses to address the needs of the whole person in a camp-like atmosphere. This success-oriented environment gives bright, motivated young adults the opportunity to flourish.

The academic day is a busy time for Eagle Hill students. Divided up into eight periods, the schedule combines four core academic classes with four electives. Core classes concentrate on the subjects of reading, writing, and math, with emphasis placed on the area of greatest need for the individual student. If there is a greater need for academic attention, schedules may be modified to address that need.

Night and weekend activities are designed with fun in mind. The trips we offer capitalize on the best of New England's culture and the fine summer weather. Students may camp out in New Hampshire, attend a Red Sox game, or sunbathe at the beach. Biking, horseback riding, fly fishing, amusement parks, whale watching, museums, and whitewater rafting are just a few of the adventures that Eagle Hill provides.

THE GOW SCHOOL

2491 Emery Rd., South Wales, NY 14139

M. Bradley Rogers, Jr., *Headmaster*

"Lives in the Making since 1926"

The Gow School, founded in 1926, is the nation's oldest college preparatory school for young men with specific language based learning differences (often referred to as dyslexia). An internationally renowned boarding school for 140 boys in grades 7-12, The Gow School offers a strong athletic program, diverse fine arts curriculum, and a picturesque 100-acre campus. With a 4:1 student faculty ratio and a focus on language remediation and study skills, Gow offers a challenging and appealing community for boys diagnosed with difficulties in reading decoding or comprehension, written expression, auditory processing, mathematics and attention issues.

The school has 45 teachers working with 140 students. In addition to small classes (max 6) the School offers a wide range of traditional curricular programs as well as art, drama, and music. The students also participate in student activities, publications, a student council, resident assistant and big brother and other leadership development programs. The School also has a full athletic program, including soccer, cross country running, skiing, basketball, swimming, wrestling, weight training, lacrosse, squash, tennis, crew, and an outdoor program and intramural activities. Virtually all Gow School graduates go on to college or university.

Over the years, The Gow School has grown to meet the needs of its students and teachers. The Gow campus of twenty-one buildings includes a library, a new 50,000 square foot gymnasium complete with tennis and squash courts, a fitness center, and hardwood basketball court; technology labs, hands-on science rooms, computer labs, a music lab, six dormitories and a recently completed theater building and fine arts center. The campus is located in rural South Wales, New York, 20 miles southeast of the city of Buffalo, 50 minutes from Niagara Falls and 2 hours from Toronto, Ontario.

During late June and July, The Gow School Summer Program (GSSP) combines 5 weeks of learning with fun. A traditional camp experience for boys and girls ages 8-16; Gow offers classes for students who have experienced academic difficulties or have diagnosed specific learning differences, but possess the potential to excel. The Camp program includes weekend trips, white water rafting, backpacking, visual and fine arts, and an extensive sports program.

THE GOW SCHOOL

The Gow School is a college preparatory school for young men, grades 7 - postgrad with dyslexia or deficits in:

- Reading Decoding
- Reading Comprehension
- Written Expression
- Writing Mechanics
- Auditory Processing
- Spelling
- Mathematics

Phone: (716) 652-3450 or
E-mail: admissions@gow.org

Ask about our
co-ed summer program or
E-mail: summer@gow.org

Visit us at
www.gow.org

The Glenholme school

A boarding environment for young people with special needs:

emotional, behavioral & learning difficulties, Aspergers & ADHD

The School...
- private, co-educational boarding school
- rural, 110 acre campus
- 100 children & adolescents grades 3-12
- therapeutic milieu

Academic Achievement...
- small group & individualized instruction
- social & expressive skills development
- arts integration approach
- life skills & career exploration
- NEASC accredited

A Learning Environment...
- values integration
- equestrian & music program
- athletics program & recreational activities
- art and drama
- individual / family therapy
- motivational management program

Devereux
GLENHOLME

81 Sabbaday Ln. ◘ Washington, Connecticut
Tel: 860.868.7377 ◘ Fax: 860.868.7413
Email: admissions@theglenholmeschool.org
Web: www.theglenholmeschool.org/ps

HAMPSHIRE COUNTRY SCHOOL
122 Hampshire Rd.
RINDGE, NH 03461
Tel: 603-899-3325
William Dickerman, *Headmaster*

Located on 1700 acres of rolling hills, fields, woods, ponds, and streams, Hampshire Country School offers the safety, structure, personal attention and sense of belonging that can be found only in a very small school community.

Groups of 6 to 8 boys live in small dorms which include a living room, kitchen, and single and double bedrooms. All students and faculty eat family-style meals together in a central dining room. Students of all ages participate together in extracurricular activities which follow the interests of students and teachers and typically include recreational softball, soccer, tennis, hiking, horseback riding, music, and art.

Classes are taught in a traditional manner, with discussions, lectures, written assignments, homework, and tests. Because there are only 4 to 6 students in each class teachers are more able to teach to each student's needs than they could in larger classes.

There are many youngsters who could thrive in the Hampshire Country School setting, but the school may be especially beneficial for high ability boys unable to function in larger schools because of special sensitivities, difficulty making friends, or a need for an unusual amount of structure and attention. Most students enroll when they are nine-to twelve-years-old and remain until their early high school years.

Girls' Residence,
Diana Hanbury King-
Founder's House,
Dedicated October 1995

THE KILDONAN SCHOOL
AMENIA, NY
Tel: 845-373-8111

Ronald A. Wilson, *Headmaster*

Founded in 1969 Kildonan is a well established coeducational boarding and day school for students with learning differences arising from dyslexia. The school offers students grades two through twelve and postgraduate a structured program of one-on-one multisensory Orton-Gillingham tutoring, academic courses, computer literacy, arts, athletics and extracurricular opportunities. Students are accountable for independent work in supervised study halls six days each week. The 450-acre campus, 90 miles north of New York City, provides a relaxed atmosphere. Specific programs such as the all school weekly ski day during the winter term also complement the structured academic schedule.

Language development is the keystone that defines our academic program. Dyslexia is not only a reading or writing difficulty. All language skills are involved to varying degrees: listening, speaking, silent reading comprehension, oral reading, vocabulary, spelling, word retrieval, and expository writing. Often, attention deficits also need to be addressed. The tutorial program approaches language remediation in two stages. First, skills are taught in isolation and tailored to meet the needs of each student. Second, language skills are then integrated in subject matter courses with the ultimate goal of independent learning and confidence in self-expression.

At the high school level, the courses include traditional college preparatory courses in math, science, literature, history, and the arts. Teaching methods are aimed at developing a logical organization of information, critical thinking, and systematic problem solving. Using the principles of careful sequential, multisensory teaching the faculty work closely with the students. The class size ranges from five to twelve students, allowing and encouraging every student to become an active participant in learning. For every course offering there are two levels of study; students are placed in accordance with their reading and writing achievement. Students may enroll at any point during their four years of high school.

The junior high program is designed to prepare students for our high school or another college preparatory high school. Students are introduced to all traditional subject matter and learning strategies—listening comprehension, beginning notetaking, outlining, test taking, and paragraph writing. These strategies and techniques are largely taught and practiced in the classroom. Subject matter assignments are limited to one night each week; tutoring assignments are given five nights each week.

The elementary day program is for students in grades two through six. Their daily schedule includes one-on-one language training, mathematics, science, social studies, computer skills, horseback riding, the arts, music, sports, and one hour of supervised study.

DUNNABECK AT KILDONAN, established in 1955 by Diana Hanbury King, is the oldest summer program in the United States meeting the needs of the dyslexic student ages eight through sixteen. The six-week coed boarding and day program is also designed to help students who are struggling with school work because of specific difficulties with reading, writing, spelling, or math computation, but who do not wish to complete or require a full school year program. All tutoring is one-on-one using the same Orton-Gillingham principles. Students meet daily with their tutors for one hour and complete assignments in supervised study halls. The length of study varies according to the age of the student. Instruction in computer literacy is also included in a student's academic schedule.

The academics are supplemented by daily recreational activity periods of swimming, the arts, and horseback riding. Waterskiing, sailing, canoeing, and camping are integrated into the weekly schedule, and weekends are the times for special events and field trips.

The goal of the program is to bring students closer to grade level functioning in all subjects through an intense focus on the primary academic skills that are required for success at any level of schooling. Through their success at Dunnabeck, students restore their self-confidence and become more motivated and self-directed.

For further information please contact the Office of Admissions.

Private Schools Illustrated — 1366

LANDMARK SCHOOL
PRIDES CROSSING, MA
Tel: 978-236-3000
E-mail: jbloom@landmarkschool.org
Web: www.landmarkschool.org

Robert J. Broudo, MEd, *Headmaster*

The Landmark School, founded in 1971, offers day programs for students age 7-20, in grades 2-12, and boards students age 14-20. Landmark's programs are designed to help students who are of average to superior intelligence, and who have been diagnosed as having a language-based learning disability such as dyslexia.

Landmark offers an intensive ten month academic program as well as summer programs that teach to students' *individual* needs. The program core is a *daily,* one-to-one tutorial in all aspects of learning from basic reading, spelling, and handwriting skills, to high school and college preparatory composition and study skills. In addition, there are small group classes in math, social studies, science, and language arts. Electives in art, auto mechanics, computers, chorus, drama, early childhood education, health, music, peer leadership, percussion, photography, physical education, radio and television broadcasting, voice, and woodworking are also offered. A varied athletic program including soccer, basketball, lacrosse, skiing, wrestling, track and field, and tennis provides a supportive, productive, social environment and the opportunity for greater achievement and success. The Landmark Summer Program helps students master reading, writing, spelling, and composition skills in combination with summer activities such as seamanship, marine science, and an adventure ropes course.

The Landmark Preparatory Program offers a secondary school curriculum for students who need a specialized educational environment but do not need an *intensive* remedial program. The program emphasizes study and organizational skills development in a small class setting.

Situated on two beautiful campuses just 25 miles north of Boston, students make supervised trips into Boston to take advantage of its many cultural opportunities. The North Shore is especially rich in historical sights which Landmark students regularly explore, including fishing ports in Gloucester and Rockport and sailing centers in Salem and Marblehead.

Of Landmark graduates, over 87% go on to higher education, with 100% of the Preparatory Program going on to two and four year colleges.

LANDMARK SUMMER PROGRAMS

Landmark School's Summer Programs combine academic remediation with ample recreational activities. Each child's academic program concentrates on mastering reading, writing, spelling, composition, and study skills. Instruction is individually tailored to meet the needs of the high potential child with dyslexia. There are several programs offered:

- BASIC ACADEMIC PROGRAM: This full-day program for High School students includes two daily periods of one-to-one tutorial instruction, and small classes in math, language arts, study skills, and electives including art, computer science, physical education, or woodworking.

- LANDMARK PREPARATORY PROGRAM: This program serves students who do not require intensive language remediation, but who need further training and development of organizational and study skills. A full-day of classes includes a daily tutorial and classes of 7 to 12 students in study skills, literature, grammar and composition, social science, and elective.

- HALF-DAY OPTION FOR ELEMENTARY AND MIDDLE SCHOOL STUDENTS: Students entering grades 2-8 may choose a morning only Standard Academic Program. Students attend three 50-minute classes each day: a one-to-one language tutorial, a language arts class, and a math class.

- SUMMER SEAMANSHIP PROGRAM: This program, for ages 10 and older, combines a half-day of academic classes with a half-day of on-the-water experiences utilizing the school's vessels.

- MARINE SCIENCE PROGRAM: This program, for students at least 11 years of age, combines a half-day of academic classes with a half-day of exploring local coastal and ocean ecosystems through laboratory and field studies.

- ADVENTURE ROPES PROGRAM: This program offers students 10 years and older an opportunity to spend part of their summer experience in an outdoor adventure-based program.

All programs are coed, for residential and day students, and run in July and August.

For further information and application, write to the Admission Office, Landmark Summer Programs, P.O. Box 227, Prides Crossing, MA 01965-0227, call 978-236-3000, or visit www.landmarkschool.org.

Private Schools Illustrated — 1368

LINDEN HILL SCHOOL

"A Home Away From Home"

- Individualized, multi-sensory curriculum in a nurturing setting
- **ESL** Instruction
- Sports, art, music, drama, keyboarding, woodshop, projects, and theme-based trips
- **Co-ed Summer School/Camp Program**

Since 1961 serving the needs of boys ages 9-16 with language-based learning differences in a traditional boarding school with a family atmosphere.

James A. McDaniel, Headmaster
154 South Mountain Rd., Northfield, MA 01360
Contact Us: (866) 498-2906 (toll free)   Fax: (413) 498-2908
Visit us: www.lindenhs.org   Email: office.lindenhs.org

WINDWARD SCHOOL
13 Windward Ave.
WHITE PLAINS, NY 10605
Tel: 914-949-6968
Fax: 914-949-8220
Web: www.windward-school.org

Windward is an independent, coeducational day school, grades 1-9, dedicated to providing an excellent instructional program for children with language-based learning disabilities. The multisensory curriculum is designed for students of average to superior intelligence who can benefit from the unique educational experience provided. Through direct instruction in small class settings, a trained staff assists students to improve their language skills. Academic success, combined with opportunities for social and emotional growth, enables students to understand their learning styles, build confidence, and develop self-advocacy skills. Windward is committed to helping students achieve their full potential in preparation for a successful return to the mainstream educational environment. To meet these goals, the school provides ongoing training to its faculty based on the most current research and also shares its expertise with the parent body, other educators, and the broader community.

THE OXFORD ACADEMY
WESTBROOK, CT

Since 1906, Oxford Academy has specialized in educating young men between the ages of 14 and 20 of average to above average intelligence who wish to accelerate their course work, or who seek an alternative to the traditional academic approach. With a classroom ratio of one teacher to one pupil, each student is instructed at the level and pace most appropriate to his own ability and learning style. Students at Oxford benefit from carefully designed individual curricula, proctored study halls and close academic guidance in a caring community atmosphere. Specific programs include Advanced Placement and English-as-a-Second Language. Each student participates daily in intramural or varsity sports throughout the year.

In recent years, 99% of the students accepted for admission were referred to Oxford by educational consultants, parents of graduates or former students, other private school headmasters or school counselors. Instruction and guidance is provided by 22 faculty members, 11 of whom live on campus. Enrollment is limited to 45 boys with approximately one-third of the student body coming from outside the United States. The school is located along the Connecticut shoreline, midway between New York and Boston.

PROVO CANYON SCHOOL
Orem & Provo, Utah
Tel: 800-848-9819
Web: www.provocanyon.com

We have high expectations for our students.

Our students are generally of average to well above average intelligence. The fully accredited program and small class sizes at Provo Canyon School are designed to meet each child's individual needs, and to facilitate the ability to work with learning differences. Each student arrives at Provo Canyon School with a unique level of knowledge, skills and academic abilities. Once academic abilitiy and needs are determined through testing, an educational plan is developed to help the student progress and experience success in the classroom setting.

Our faculty, most of whom are certified in Special Education, are hired for their outstanding teaching skills as well as their ability to deal effectively with students with special needs. Their priorities include helping students develop self-esteem, initiative and self-control, as well as building a solid academic foundation.

Many of our graduates continue their educations in colleges and universities. We believe that students should leave Provo Canyon School with the social and academic skills necessary for them to assume responsible roles in society.

Riverview School

Caring. Teaching. Guiding.

Riverview School is a co-educational school of international reputation and service enrolling 182 adolescents and young adults in its Secondary School and Post-Secondary Programs. Students share a common background of lifelong difficulties in academics and in making friends. Their intellectual capacity tests between 70 and 100 and their primary diagnosis is a learning disability and/or a complex language or learning disorder. Riverview students are often described as those who "fall through the cracks," achieving more consistently within a predictable, structured learning environment, with an emphasis on the philosophy of the "whole child."

Maureen B. Brenner, Head of School
Jeanne M. Pacheco, Director of Admission & Placement

Riverview School
551 Route 6A
East Sandwich, Cape Cod, MA 02537

Tel: 508 888.0489 Fax: 508 888.1315

Private Schools Illustrated — 1372

The Underachieving Adolescent

He (or she) hears repeatedly ... You're so bright. How come you're not doing better?

He's a competent reader, but fails English.

He has a poor self-image, so he either overstates or understates his achievements—academic, artistic, athletic or social.

Adults find him clever and charming, but in school he is restless, unable to concentrate, or sprawls in his chair, passively challenging the establishment with, "What's in it for me?" ...

... From the booklet, "In Support of Parents and Adolescents." For a free copy, write or phone B. H. Henrichsen, Headmaster of the Robert Louis Stevenson School.

A fully accredited, college preparatory, coeducational day secondary school where students and professional staff work in harmony. High academic standards in a low-pressure atmosphere. Expert counseling. Many students willingly commute long distances. Admissions throughout the year.

ROBERT LOUIS STEVENSON SCHOOL
74th Street, New York, NY 10023
(212) 787-6400   Fax (212) 873-1872
an equal opportunity, not-for-profit institution

A DIVISION OF

The Robert Louis Stevenson School, long established as a secondary school for gifted, underachieving boys and girls, offers

COLLEGE PREPARATION for ADOLESCENTS with SPECIFIC LEARNING DIFFICULTIES.

For information please call the Headmaster,
ROBERT LOUIS STEVENSON SCHOOL (Est. 1908)
24 West 74th Street, New York, NY 10023
(212) 787-6400 Fax (212) 873-1872

SAINT THOMAS MORE SCHOOL
OAKDALE, CT
James Fox Hanrahan, Jr., BA, MA, *Headmaster*

Saint Thomas More School is a college preparatory boarding school for boys in grades 8 through postgraduate. The school is situated on 100 acres of beautiful New England countryside with 4,000 feet of waterfront on Connecticut's largest and most beautiful natural lake, Gardner Lake. The school is easily accessible to all parts of New England and the New York metropolitan region. Hartford is 30 miles north; New London is 15 miles south.

The school specializes in the underachiever, a good boy without chronic social, emotional or behavioral problems. Our young men range from average to very high intelligence, but have not yet achieved success in their scholastic lives. If you often hear such remarks as "I have no homework," or "I did all my homework in school," then you have already met the typical STM boy. We feel it is our obligation to motivate our young men, to assign them help if they need it, and to insist they do their homework. We have a wholesome and structured environment, to ensure that our students are happy and successful. Our class size averages 12 students. All our faculty live on campus. To foster gentlemanly behavior, we require that our students dress uniformly. We insist that they succeed and build confidence in their God-given abilities.

We are a Catholic school where boys of all faiths are accepted.

We are concerned not only with each boy's intellectual development and success, but also the training of their moral, social, and physical nature.

We have our own chapel and a Catholic chaplain.

Saint Thomas More School is accredited by the New England Association of Schools and Colleges, and is a member of the National Catholic Education Association, the Connecticut Association of Independent Schools, the National Association of Independent Schools, and The College Board.

Our athletic program includes interscholastic programs in football, soccer, basketball, hockey, baseball, tennis, cross country, golf, crew and lacrosse. Martial Arts, weightlifting and a variety of sports are also available through our intramural program.

Special help for boys with good intelligence but with minor learning differences is given within the framework of our regular college preparatory program.

Regular School, Sept.-June—Room, Board, Tuition: $27,325 Domestic; $30,325 International (Extras $1,000).

POSTGRADUATE PROGRAM: For students who have been graduated from a high school, but not done well enough to attend the college of their choice, we offer a separate one-year Postgraduate Program for 26 students. Our intensive program of instruction, which includes double periods of mathematics and English daily, as well as challenging electives, prepares them well for success in college. Interscholastic athletics is an integral part of the Postgraduate Program, including soccer, basketball, hockey, baseball, tennis, golf, and crew. Experienced college placement personnel see to it that all postgraduate students obtain proper college placement.

SUMMER PROGRAM: July to mid-August for 90 boys. Tuition: $5,495 Domestic; $5,995 International (5 weeks).

For further information on Saint Thomas More School, Summer Program, or Postgraduate Program, please write: Admissions Office, Saint Thomas More School, 45 Cottage Rd., Oakdale, CT 06370. Tel: 860-823-3861. Fax: 860-823-3863. E-mail: stmadmit@stthomasmoreschool.com.

SAINT THOMAS MORE SCHOOL
OAKDALE, CT

James Fox Hanrahan, Jr.,
BA, MA, *Headmaster*

Boys Summer Academic Program

Saint Thomas More School's Summer Program, running from July to early August, offers the best of both worlds to students entering grades 7-12. As a prestigious college prep school with a reputation for helping underachievers learn to succeed, it offers an outstanding program of academic courses for make-up credit or enrichment. As a camp, it features 100 acres of fields, ponds, woodlands and playing fields, as well as 4,000 feet of lakefront. The complete facilities of our regular school campus, including complete gymnasium with basketball courts and weight room, a boathouse, a quarter mile track, and an indoor pool, help facilitate a full program of athletic and recreational activities.

Situated in rural Montville, 15 miles north of New London, the campus provides a New England atmosphere conducive to study and reflection, as well as to sports and outdoor recreation. Our ESL program attracts students from around the world. We have a modern language laboratory, with audio, video, and computer technology. Special preparation is given for the TOEFL.

Mornings are devoted to classes, taught by our regular faculty, six days a week. Then from lunch until 8 p.m., everyone, including students and staff, is at summer camp. The waterfront along Gardner Lake, the largest natural lake in eastern Connecticut, comes alive with sailing, canoeing, and rowing. Skilled instruction is available for beginner swimmers. Intramural volleyball, soccer, and softball games are scheduled daily. Elsewhere, students are playing tennis on our four courts, enjoying basketball on any of our six outdoor and one indoor courts, or exercising in our fully equipped weight room.

In the evenings we return to an environment structured for success. Our talented faculty supervises a nightly study hall to help students prepare for the next day's classes. Wednesday and Saturday afternoons, and all day Sunday, we travel together to various recreational and cultural events.

By the conclusion of the program, our student-campers are better educated, better behaved, and happier young people.

Tuition: $5,495 Domestic; $5,995 International (5 weeks).

WILLOW HILL SCHOOL
98 Haynes Rd.
SUDBURY, MA 01776

Willow Hill School offers both a middle school program and high school program for students facing a wide range of learning challenges. The curriculum for both programs is based upon the Massachusetts curriculum frameworks and is presented through a multisensory teaching approach to meet the learning styles of our students. The curriculum is designed to be developmentally appropriate, with transitional planning and community service opportunities suitable to the age and ability of the student.

At the heart of the School's rigorous curriculum is language-based instruction, designed to reinforce and promote student access to course material. Multisensory teaching approaches incorporate visual, auditory and kinesthetic presentations, as well as similar opportunities for students to demonstrate their understanding of material. Teachers build key study skills into courses and tailor assignments and examinations to each student's particular learning style. In addition, teachers integrate customized materials and student interests into coursework to support and reinforce conceptual learning.

Founded in 1970, Willow Hill School is situated on a beautiful, twenty-six acre campus in the quiet suburb of Sudbury, Massachusetts, near the Concord line. The School offers a small friendly academic environment with facilities designed to support and enhance a highly personalized approach to learning. School facilities include an art studio, a library, private tutorial rooms, a full stage and auditorium, a gymnasium and athletic fields for soccer, softball and other team sports. The School also offers computers and a variety of software programs for student and faculty use. Willow Hill students also have access to a broad range of recreational and service opportunities within the community.

THE WOODHALL SCHOOL
BETHLEHEM, CT
Sally Campbell Woodhall, *Head of School*

The Woodhall School offers an opportunity for young men between the ages of 14 and 19 who need an opportunity to experience success. Woodhall offers an individualized educational program with a focus on intellectual, physical, emotional and spiritual growth. The individualized approach enables each student to progress at his own rhythm and to turn a pattern of failure into one of success. We believe that education happens in all phases of adolescent development and school life.

Our academic program offers a college preparatory curriculum in small classes. Each student learns how to develop strong, independent study skills and school skills. The student's academic program is designed to take into account his particular learning style and to enable him to acquire the appropriate knowledge and organizational skills needed for mastery of the learning process and course content. Each student is able to develop confidence in his ability, to learn how to learn, to proceed at his own pace, and to make up for time lost if necessary.

Our Communications Program allows each student to learn how to become self-reflective, respectful, and accountable. Self-discovery and learning to process the information from self-discovery is important for intellectual and emotional maturity and self-confidence. Through this process, each student can develop interpersonal skills in all aspects of school life. A daily athletics program fosters physical fitness, sportsmanship, and team work. Interscholastic games are scheduled with area prep schools in soccer, lacrosse, and basketball. Students regularly participate as actors and technical support in theatre productions at a nearby girls' school. Social and recreational activities are planned with other prep schools.

The support of a caring faculty in a family environment creates a safe and healthy school community. The campus is located in Bethlehem, CT, an hour's drive from Hartford and New Haven. Theater and educational trips to New York, New Haven, and Hartford enhance the educational and recreational opportunities at Woodhall.

SCHOOLS FOR EXCEPTIONAL CHILDREN

Sponsors in this special section have editorial listings in Porter Sargent's *Directory for Exceptional Children,* but not in *The Handbook of Private Schools.* The *Directory* is a more complete compilation of 2500 schools, facilities and organizations serving children and young adults with developmental, emotional, physical and medical special needs. For details, please visit www.portersargent.com or see page 1471.

Schools for Exceptional Children — 1381

Our kids' faces say it all.

Park Century School...

...an independent day school, offering a comprehensive educational program for bright children, ages 7-14 years old, who have learning disabilities

...an exceptional and unique learning environment, devoted to all aspects of a child's world

2040 Stoner Ave., Los Angeles, CA 90025
Telephone 310-478-5065
parkcentury@parkcenturyschool.org

Genny Shain, M.A. and Gail Spindler, M.A. - Co-Directors

In Your Own Words

Educators and parents have long trusted Porter Sargent for independent, objective school profiles available nowhere else.

Your program's Illustrated Announcement can support this mission, and it will be seen daily by:

- Parents
- Headmasters, and admissions and guidance counselors
- Consultants and vendors
- A worldwide network of educational professionals

Each reference-quality title is the book of record for its field, with a long shelf-life and high per-copy readership.

Please call 617-523-1670 or E-mail announcements@portersargent.com for details on joining the next edition.

The Handbook of Private Schools * The Directory for Exceptional Children
Schools Abroad of Interest to Americans * Guide to Summer Camps and Schools

Private Schools Illustrated — 1382

A SPECIAL CHOICE
FOR SPECIAL PEOPLE

STEWART HOME SCHOOL offers progressive education, home community and a full lifestyle for the intellectually disabled child and adult.

- Opportunity for educational progress at any age—minimum age requirement, 6 yrs. No maximum. Academic program when readiness occurs. Individually planned programs daily for all students.

- Opportunity for physical and recreational activities including sports, horseback riding, music, art, ceramics, other crafts and drama.

- Opportunity for vocational training—sheltered workshop, community work, work on campus.

- Opportunity for maximum development of social and self-help skills.

Schools for Exceptional Children — 1383

STEWART HOME SCHOOL ESTABLISHED 1893

Since 1893, STEWART HOME SCHOOL has provided year-round community life for the intellectually disabled child and adult. Eight-hundred-fifty acres serve as a campus for the educational, recreational, vocational and social experiences of the residents and staff. The program is as fine as any available at a substantially lower rate.

Personal interview required for enrollment.

Write for brochure—

STEWART HOME SCHOOL
4200 Lawrenceburg Rd.
Frankfort, KY 40601

John P. Stewart, M.D., *Resident Physician*
Phone: 502-227-4821

www.stewarthome.com

"Now everyone says Billy is great to be around."

Our day and residential programs are designed to help every child realize their unique potential. Pathway's caring environment encourages achievement, learning and positive relationships for students with learning disabilities and neuropsychiatric disorders. Psychiatric, psychological, nursing, instructional and recreational services are tailored to meet the individual's needs within a total therapeutic milieu. The level of support will vary, based on the student's individual needs and Pathway's response to treat the challenges that are present.

Consider your child. Consider the future. Consider The Pathway School.

Confidence • Independence • Compassion

For information contact: Louise Robertson, M.Ed., Admissions Director
162 Egypt Rd., Norristown, PA 19403-3090 · (610) 277-0660, Fax (610) 539-1493
Web Site: www.PathwaySchool.org · E-Mail: LouiseR@PathwaySchool.org

SCHOOLS ABROAD

Sponsors in this special section have editorial listings in Porter Sargent's *Schools Abroad of Interest to Americans,* but not in *The Handbook of Private Schools. Schools Abroad* is a more complete compilation of 650 primary and secondary schools in 125 countries. For details, please visit www.portersargent.com or see page 1471.

AIGLON COLLEGE

CHESIERES-VILLARS, SWITZERLAND

Dr. Jonathan Long,
  MA, MTh, DPhil, *Headmaster*

Aiglon College, founded in 1949, is an independent, non-profit college preparatory school providing a day and boarding education in the Swiss Alps, 4,000 ft. above the Rhone Valley. Located in the well-known ski-resort of Villars, the school is superbly placed to benefit year-round from its challenging mountain setting. The school aims to provide, within a safe, caring and supportive framework, a challenging and rigorous education in intellectual, physical, moral, emotional and spiritual self-discipline and self-discovery, equipping students individually and collectively with the initiative, integrity and perspective to think, learn and make constructive choices, and thus to become broad-minded and positively motivated global citizens.

340 boys and girls of over 60 nationalities aged 9-18 follow academic courses leading to the British GCSE and AS/A-Level exams as well as the American College Board tests and some International Baccalaureate exams. Aiglon graduates are currently enrolled in European and American universities and colleges including Sussex, Nottingham, Newcastle, Harvard, Stanford, and Georgetown.

There are six senior boarding houses and a separate junior school for 9-13 year old boys and girls. An outstanding new teaching building, opened in September 1996, houses laboratories, a computer centre, music department with recording and radio studios and mathematics classrooms. Sports include skiing, soccer, basketball, tennis, swimming, and athletics. Adventure training expeditions on skis and on foot take place throughout the year and a programme of cultural activities including concerts, debates, lectures and excursions is provided each term.

Admission is through Aiglon's entrance examination, interview and previous school record. A limited number of scholarships and bursaries is awarded to able candidates of character who can demonstrate a need for financial support.

For information on admission and summer school (July/August) please contact Aiglon College, 1885 Chesieres-Villars, Switzerland. Tel: 41 (0) 24 4966161. Fax: 41 (0) 24 4966162. E-mail: info@aiglon.ch. Web: www.aiglon.ch.

Private Schools Illustrated — 1388

AMERICAN SCHOOL OF WARSAW

Bielawa, ul. Warszawska 202
05-520 Konstancin-Jeziorna
POLAND
Tel: (+48 22) 702 85 00
Fax: (+48 22) 702 85 99
Web: www.asw.waw.pl

The American School of Warsaw was founded in 1953 as a private, non-profit educational institution, established for the primary purpose of providing an English language school in Warsaw for children of all nationalities. A secondary objective has been to contribute to international good will and understanding through the school's multi-national character. Today 53 countries are represented in our student body.

An International Baccalaureate Program (grades 11 and 12) is offered as the standard for acceptance into international universities. All students are guided to organize their education in preparation for college or university. Since 1987 the American School of Warsaw has been accredited by the European Council of International Schools and by the New England Association of Schools and Colleges.

In September 2001, the school opened its new state-of-the-art facilities, housing the elementary school (grades PK-5th), middle school (6th-8th), and high school (9th-12th). All classrooms are networked for computers.

Academic excellence through the education of the whole child is reflected in our curriculum design and daily regimen. We help each student meet his/her highest potential through intellectual, social, emotional, physical, and artistic growth with the understanding that each child learns and develops in his or her own way.

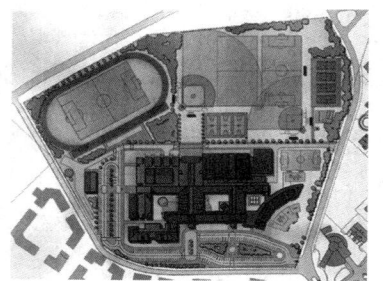

Our school values the great variety of national cultures represented by the students. It encourages an appreciation of various beliefs, practices, and customs, so that all can become constructive world citizens. The school provides students with opportunities to experience European culture and Polish society in particular.

Bangkok Patana School
The British International School in Thailand

2/38 Soi Lasalle, Sukhumvit 105, Bangkok 10260, THAILAND
Tel: 662 398-0200   Fax: 662 399-3179
E-mail: reception@patana.ac.th   Website: www.patana.ac.th

Mr. Robert Thornhill, Acting Head of School

Bangkok Patana School was founded in 1957 to provide a British-style education for the children of expatriates living in Thailand. A not-for-profit foundation, the school currently has an enrolment of 2,050 students representing 50 nationalities. Some 9% of the students are US citizens and the school is recognised by the US State Department as suitable for Government employees. Other major national groups are UK (22%), Thai (21%) and Australian (8%). The school is accredited by the New England Association of Schools and Colleges (NEASC) as well as by the Council of International Schools (CIS). Bangkok Patana is also a member of the International Baccalaureate Organisation (IBO).

The Elementary and Secondary Divisions, on one campus, enrol students from two and a half to eighteen years of age. The school follows the UK National Curriculum adapted for its international student body and position in Thailand, and Secondary examination courses: General Certificate of Secondary Education/IGCSE at age sixteen and the International Baccalaureate/Patana Graduate Diploma at eighteen. Patana is also a testing centre for PSAT, SAT(I) and SAT(II). Over 90% of graduating students are accepted into leading colleges and universities worldwide including Yale, Cambridge and the London School of Economics (LSE).

The 20 hectare campus in South East Bangkok provides excellent purpose-built facilities for the academic, extra-curricular and sports programmes which Bangkok Patana offers.

Private Schools Illustrated — 1390

CARIBBEAN PREPARATORY SCHOOL

P.O. Box 70177
SAN JUAN,
 PUERTO RICO 00936
Tel: 787-765-4411
Fax: 787-764-3809
Web: www.cpspr.org

Commonwealth Campus: Grades 7-12
Parkville Lower Elementary and Upper Elementary: PPK-6
Horizons Program/ Grades 1-12
F. Richard Marracino, Headmaster
Jo-Ann Aranguren, Director of Admissions
E-mail: jaranguren@cpspr.org

"where learning stretches to meet imagination"

Dedicated to educational excellence since 1952. Caribbean Preparatory School is an English-speaking private school, with a strong program in Spanish. It is a coeducational, rigorous, college preparatory day school of 813 students (Parkville campus: 542, Commonwealth campus: 271), in which academic classes are augmented by a large variety of extra-curricular activities and after-school programs, including sports. Our faculty is dedicated to students' personal and social growth, and instilling cultural values, encouraging mutual respect and good citizenship.

About 95% of the student body is Hispanic from San Juan's metropolitan area and countries of Central and South America. The remaining 5% come from the continental United States, Argentina, Mexico, Colombia, Venezuela, Brazil, Japan, China, India, and Europe, contributing to the international atmosphere of both campuses.

Located in the residential area of Guaynabo, seven miles south of San Juan, Parkville campus comprises the Lower Elementary (PPK-grade 2) and Upper Elementary (grades 3-6), each with its own director. Parkville offers a full academic program in English, Spanish, Mathematics, Science, Social Studies, Art, Music, Dance, and Library skills, Writing Composition, Computers, Physical Education, Health and Ethics.

The Commonwealth campus, located in Hato Rey, just minutes from financial and shopping districts, comprises the Middle School (grades 7-8) and the Upper School (grades 9-12). The campus includes thirty classrooms, a 20,000 volume computerized library, four science laboratories, two specially equipped state-of-the-art computer laboratories, an auditorium, music and art rooms, a cafeteria, faculty lounge and administrative office. A well-maintained athletic field and gymnasium are immediately behind the school. The well-rounded curriculum of our college preparatory high school is enriched by a wide selection of Advanced Placement courses and electives. Honors courses are offered in all subject areas. Advanced

Placement courses include calculus, English, Spanish, Biology, Chemistry, and United States and European history. Computer Science, and Ethics are graduation requirements. Community service programs enhance student awareness of the need to contribute to their community. Commonwealth participates in a complete cultural program using as resources the multitude of activities and events offered in English and Spanish at the Fine Arts Center and other theaters within easy reach in the metropolitan area.

The Horizons Program offers small group instruction and support to students in grades 1-12 experiencing difficulty in the regular classes due to mild learning differences or attention deficit disorder. The goal of the program is to mainstream students as soon as they have mastered the skills and compensatory strategies necessary to function independently in regular classrooms.

The athletic program (from upper elementary through high school) encompasses active participation of the student body in a variety of sporting activities such as intramural games, sports clinics in volleyball, basketball and soccer, plus competitions in other sports to promote teamwork.

The faculty at the combined campuses consists of 90 full-time teachers; all of who hold baccalaureate degrees and about 25% hold master degrees. An eight-to-one student-teacher ratio assures optimal learning experiences.

A fully staffed college counseling office and a college-career resource library assists students in selecting colleges which best meet their needs. A systematic approach helps students and their parents make intelligent choices based on interests, abilities, and goals.

Annually, 100% of all graduates continue on to higher education, mostly in the United States but also in Puerto Rico and other countries. Graduates of the past three years were accepted to the following colleges and universities, among other schools: Harvard University, Yale, NYU, Berklee College of Music, George Washington, Univ. of Arizona, Bentley, Manhattanville, Columbia, Cornell, Barry College, Amherst, Fordham, Penn State, Stanford, School of Visual Arts, Massachusetts Institute of Technology, University of Chicago, Boston College, Boston University, Loyola University, Villanova, John Hopkins, Univ. of Texas, Univ. of Nevada Las Vegas, Williams College, Temple University, Florida State, University of Miami, FIU, and University of Puerto Rico.

The institution is operated on a non-sectarian basis free of any kind of discrimination based on race, color, religion, creed, national, origin, gender, or political belief.

Caribbean Preparatory School is licensed by the Department of Education of Puerto Rico, accredited by the Middle States Association of Colleges and Schools, the National Association of College Admission Counselors, 'Asociación Puertorriqueña de Profesionales de la Orientación', and complies with the NACAC Statement of Principles of Good Practice, the 'Asociación de la Educación Privada de Puerto Rico', The Caribbean Association of Independent Schools, The National Middle School Association, the Association for Supervision and Curriculum Development, the Association for the Advancement of International Education, and the National Association for the Education of Young Children (NAEYC).

ST. MARY'S INTERNATIONAL SCHOOL
TOKYO, JAPAN
Tel: 81-3-3709-3411   Fax: 81-3-3707-1950
Web: http://www.smis.ac.jp

Br. Michel Jutras, *Headmaster*

Established in 1954, St. Mary's International School's day program is operated by the Brothers of Christian Instruction of Ploermel. Originally founded to provide an education for Catholic boys, today the school welcomes boys of all faiths and nationalities. The American-style curriculum is followed from Pre-First through Grade 12 and the option of working towards the International Baccalaureate (IB) is given to students in Grade 11 and 12.

Students from Pre-First through Grade 6 are taught English, math, science, social studies and religion by the homeroom teachers. In addition, specialist teachers are provided for art, physical education, swimming, vocal and instrumental music, information technology, library and Japanese language.

Grades 7 and 8 are departmentalized with all students required to study English, math, science, foreign language (French, Japanese), religion (Catholic and Ethics) and social studies. The High School college-preparatory program features advanced courses in English, mathematics, sciences, computer science and Asian studies. These basic offerings are supplemented with a variety of electives that include languages, music, art, etc. Successful completion of the IB program enables graduates to enter European and Japanese universities and obtain advanced standing in many U.S. colleges.

Swimming, tennis, ice hockey, soccer, track and field, wrestling, baseball and basketball are but a few of the athletic opportunities available. Boys also participate in a wide range of extracurricular activities including intramurals, student government and publications, concert and stage bands, speech and debate. The school conducts a multi-national carnival in May which has become famous throughout Tokyo.

St. Mary's International School is located on a seven-acre site in Tokyo's largest residential area. The school aims "to educate boys to be lifelong learners of good character who demonstrate academic, physical, artistic and moral excellence, respect for religious and cultural beliefs and responsibility as international citizens."

ST. STEPHEN'S SCHOOL
ROME, ITALY

Philip Allen, *Headmaster*

Located in the historic center of Rome, St. Stephen's School is a nondenominational, co-educational college preparatory school which has served the American and international communities in Rome and Italy since 1964. The boarding and day program offered spans grades 9 through 12, with a postgraduate year option. In addition to its regular 4 year program, St. Stephen's welcomes a limited number of students, usually in their junior year, from respected American preparatory schools who wish to take advantage of our curriculum, especially with regard to our Classical Studies, Art History, Latin and Italian classes for one or two semesters.

The curriculum adapts a traditional independent school model to its unique Roman setting and fosters rigorous learning in an atmosphere of international fellowship, harmony and trust. St. Stephen's School is accredited by the New England Association of Schools and Colleges and the European Council of International Schools. Since 1975, it has offered the International Baccalaureate program, which is now a recognized entrance qualification for universities throughout the world. The school's early recognition of the potential importance of the IB attests to its pioneering spirit in the world of international education.

Enrollment is maintained at around 200 pupils because St. Stephen's believes that students are best served by keeping the student body small, thus allowing each student wider access to our first-rate faculty and campus resources. These resources include new chemistry and physics laboratories, a recently renovated library, new art studios, as well as tennis courts, a photography lab, dance studio, and landscaped courtyard and terrace. In further pursuit of its educational mission, St. Stephen's maintains a selective admissions procedure. Students are chosen on the basis of personal promise and their potential to benefit from the school's curriculum. St. Stephen's welcomes students of all races, nationalities, religions and persuasions.

With students from approximately 40 nations, St. Stephen's is truly international in character. Students who have elected to follow the traditional American high school curriculum, many of whom have also participated in our AP program, have recently enrolled in North American universities such as Brown, Wesleyan, Bryn Mawr, Boston University, Harvard, Stanford, and the Universities of California, Pennsylvania, Texas and Toronto. About 1/3 of the graduates of 2002 entered universities in the UK.

The two and one half acre campus—just a ten minute walk from the Colosseum and the Roman Forum—offers students unique cultural, educational, and recreational advantages as well as frequent school-sponsored travel opportunities to other cities in Italy and the Mediterranean area. Life at St. Stephen's is intense and enjoyable with a happy blend of relaxation and rigor.

Contact: Admissions Office, St. Stephen's School, Via Aventina 3, 00153 Rome, Italy. Tel: (3906) 575.0605. Fax: (3906) 574.1941. E-mail: ststephens@ststephens-rome.com. Website: www.ststephens-rome.com.

THE AMERICAN SCHOOL IN ENGLAND

TASIS England is a co-educational country day and boarding school for grades Nursery – 13 (boarding 9-13) located on a beautiful 35-acre campus in Surrey county, just 18 miles from London. TASIS offers small classes, dedicated faculty, and an active Parents' Council – all of which contribute to our unique, international and close-knit community.

TASIS offers a challenging American college-preparatory curriculum, featuring the IB Diploma, AP, and ESL programs, and has an outstanding college placement record. Extra-curricular activities includ art, music, drama, Model United Nations, community service, and competitive sports tournaments throughout Europe. TASIS also offers an extensive European travel program as part of the school curriculum.

TASIS THE AMERICAN SCHOOL IN ENGLAND
Tel: +44 1932 565252
E-mail: ukadmissions@tasis.com

U.S. Office, Washington DC
Tel: 202 965-5800
E-mail: usadmissions@tasis.com

www.tasis.com

TASIS THE AMERICAN SCHOOL IN SWITZERLAND

TASIS is the longest-established US boarding school in Europe, set in the beautiful Swiss-Italian lake district. TASIS offers a co-educational, international enrollment (grades 7-12 and PG).

TASIS offers a challenging American college-preparatory curriculum, featuring AP and International Baccalaureate programs, and has an outstanding college placement record. ESL programs and diverse extra-curricular activities are paired with an extensive European travel program as part of the school curriculum.

TASIS, Montagnola-Lugano, Switzerland
Tel: +41 91 960 5151
E-mail: admissions@tasis.ch

U.S. Office, Washington DC
Tel: 202 965-5800
E-mail: usadmissions@tasis.com

www.tasis.com

THE TASIS SUMMER PROGRAMS IN EUROPE

The TASIS Schools in Europe offer unique summer programs at culturally-rich locations throughout Europe:

Lugano, Switzerland
- Summer Language Programs (ages 14-18)
- The Middle School Program (ages 11-13)
- Le Château des Enfants (ages 6-10)

Château-d'Oex, Switzerland
- French Language Program (ages 14-17)

Thorpe, England
- Summer School (ages 11-18)

Salamanca, Spain
- Spanish Language Program (ages 13-17)

L'Ardèche, France
- Les Tapies Arts and Architecture Program (ages 16-19)

The TASIS programs offer extracurricular activities including sports, music and arts, as well as extensive opportunities for travel. Contact TASIS for more information on these unforgettable summer opportunities.

THE TASIS SCHOOLS AND SUMMER PROGRAMS
1640 Wisconsin Ave NW, Washington DC 20007
Tel: 202 965-5800
E-mail: usadmissions@tasis.com
www.tasis.com

SUMMER
PROGRAMS

Sponsors in this special section have editorial listings in Porter Sargent's *Guide to Summer Camps and Summer Schools,* but not in *The Handbook of Private Schools.* The *Guide* is a more complete compilation of 1500 residential camps and summer schools. For details, please visit www.portersargent.com or see page 1471.

SALISBURY SUMMER SCHOOL

SALISBURY, CT 06068
Tel: 860-435-5700
E-mail: sss@salisburyschool.org
Web: salisburysummerschool.org

The Salisbury Summer School is a five-week program for boarding boys and girls entering grades nine through twelve. Founded in 1946, the objective was to create a program where students would receive academic enrichment for reading and English studies during the summer. Although the original objective has remained the same, the methodology has continued to improve as new approaches and technologies for academic support have been developed. Fifty-eight years later, the Salisbury Summer School is internationally recognized by educators and educational consultants as "the best" at helping students whose lack of interest, language skills and/or self-confidence have prevented them from reaching their full potential.

The Salisbury Summer School provides the comfortable environment needed to learn the most important lesson in all of schooling: how to learn. In a non-graded setting, the teachers at Salisbury Summer School are trained to make young people become better students or true students for the first time. Skills training focuses on the study of English through reading and writing, but the skills learned also transfer easily to other disciplines. In addition, each course employs specific materials and drills which will, among other benefits, enhance standardized test scores.

While many summer schools offer reading and study skills courses, only Salisbury immerses students in a curriculum and academic environment structured exclusively to promote better organization and improved reading and writing. Minimizing distractions and maximizing student-teacher contact (a ratio of 4:1), Salisbury employs experienced teachers who also serve as dorm monitors and advisors. Students become part of a five-week summer boarding school in which teachers get to know students in all facets of their lives. Teachers and advisors seek to foster close student-teacher relationships by being supportive and understanding. Weekly faculty meetings, at which each student is discussed, insure a consistent, team-generated approach to each individual.

Located in the beautiful foothills of the Berkshire Mountains, the School provides the perfect setting for summer study and recreational activities to balance the day. Salisbury is only one hour from Hartford, two hours from New York City, and three hours from Boston.

ASSOCIATIONS AND ORGANIZATIONS

The list that follows comprises organizations and associations that offer information or services pertinent to nonpublic elementary or secondary education. Accrediting Associations conduct formal evaluations of schools interested in gaining accreditation; in some cases, accredited institutions are eligible for membership benefits. Advocacy Organizations provide assistance and active support for members of a specified population. Professional Organizations offer membership and benefits to specified professionals. School Membership Associations provide benefits for member schools, but do not have a formal accreditation process. Testing Organizations compose and, in many cases, oversee and administer examinations given for the purpose of school admission or placement.

ACCREDITING ASSOCIATIONS

CUM LAUDE SOCIETY
23490 Caraway Lakes Dr, Bonita Springs, FL 34135.
Tel: 239-390-3257. Fax: 239-390-3245.
E-mail: cumlaude@parktudor.org. Web: www.cumlaudesociety.org.

MIDDLE STATES ASSOCIATION OF COLLEGES AND SCHOOLS
3624 Market St, Philadelphia, PA 19104. Tel: 215-662-5603.
Fax: 215-662-0957. E-mail: info@css-msa.org. Web: www.css-msa.org.

NEW ENGLAND ASSOCIATION OF SCHOOLS AND COLLEGES
209 Burlington Rd, Bedford, MA 01730. Tel: 781-271-0022.
Fax: 781-271-0950. E-mail: wbennett@neasc.org. Web: www.neasc.org.

NORTH CENTRAL ASSOCIATION COMMISSION ON ACCREDITATION AND SCHOOL IMPROVEMENT
c/o Arizona State Univ, PO Box 871008, Tempe, AZ 85287.
Tel: 480-965-8700. Fax: 480-965-8658. E-mail: nca@ncacasi.org.
Web: www.ncacasi.org.

NORTHWEST ASSOCIATION OF ACCREDITED SCHOOLS
1910 University Dr, Boise, ID 83725. Tel: 208-426-5727.
Fax: 208-334-3228. E-mail: sclemens@boisestate.edu.
Web: www2.boisestate.edu/nasc.

SOUTHERN ASSOCIATION OF COLLEGES AND SCHOOLS COUNCIL ON ACCREDITATION AND SCHOOL IMPROVEMENT
1866 Southern Ln, Decatur, GA 30033. Tel: 404-679-4500.
Fax: 404-679-4533. Web: www.sacscasi.org.
See Also *Display Announcement* **on page 1418**

WESTERN ASSOCIATION OF SCHOOLS AND COLLEGES
985 Atlantic Ave, Ste 100, Alameda, CA 94501. Tel: 510-748-9001.
Fax: 510-748-9797. E-mail: wascsr@wascsenior.org.
Web: www.wascweb.org.

ADVOCACY ORGANIZATIONS

A BETTER CHANCE
240 W 35th St, 9th Fl, New York, NY 10001. Tel: 646-346-1310.
Fax: 646-346-1311. Web: www.abetterchance.org.

AMERICAN ASSOCIATION FOR GIFTED CHILDREN
c/o Duke Univ, Box 90270, Durham, NC 27708. Tel: 919-783-6152.
Fax: 919-683-1742. E-mail: megayle@aol.com. Web: www.aagc.org.

ASSOCIATION FOR CHILDHOOD EDUCATION INTERNATIONAL
17904 Georgia Ave, Ste 215, Olney, MD 20832. Tel: 301-570-2111.
Fax: 301-570-2212. E-mail: aceihq@aol.com. Web: www.acei.org.

ASSOCIATION FOR EXPERIENTIAL EDUCATION
2305 Canyon Blvd, Ste 100, Boulder, CO 80302. Tel: 303-440-8844.
Fax: 303-440-9581. E-mail: executive@aee.org. Web: www.aee.org.

COUNCIL FOR AMERICAN PRIVATE EDUCATION
13017 Wisteria Dr, PMB 457, Germantown, MD 20874.
Tel: 301-916-8460. Fax: 301-916-8485. E-mail: cape@capenet.org.
Web: www.capenet.org.

GAY, LESBIAN AND STRAIGHT EDUCATION NETWORK
90 Broad St, Ste 2, New York, NY 10004. Tel: 212-727-0135.
Fax: 212-727-0254. E-mail: glsen@glsen.org. Web: www.glsen.org.

INDEPENDENT SCHOOL ALLIANCE FOR MINORITY AFFAIRS
1545 Wilshire Blvd, Ste 711, Los Angeles, CA 90017.
Tel: 213-484-2411. Fax: 213-484-2545.

JEWISH EDUCATION SERVICE OF NORTH AMERICA
111 8th Ave, New York, NY 10011. Tel: 212-284-6950.
Fax: 212-284-6951. Web: www.jesna.org.

NATIONAL ASSOCIATION FOR GIFTED CHILDREN
1707 L St NW, Ste 550, Washington, DC 20036. Tel: 202-785-4268.
Fax: 202-785-4248. E-mail: nagc@nagc.org. Web: www.nagc.org.

NATIONAL ASSOCIATION OF PARENTS WITH CHILDREN IN SPECIAL EDUCATION
1201 Pennsylvania Ave NW, Ste 300, Washington, DC 20004.
Tel: 800-754-4421. Fax: 800-424-0371. E-mail: contact@napcse.org.
Web: www.napcse.org.

NATIONAL ASSOCIATION OF PRIVATE SPECIAL EDUCATION CENTERS
1522 K St NW, Ste 1032, Washington, DC 20005. Tel: 202-408-3338.
Fax: 202-408-3340. E-mail: napsec@aol.com. Web: www.napsec.org.

NATIONAL EDUCATION ASSOCIATION
1201 16th St NW, Washington, DC 20036. Tel: 202-833-4000.
Fax: 202-822-7974. Web: www.nea.org.

NATIONAL PTA
541 N Fairbanks Ct, Ste 1300, Chicago, IL 60611. Tel: 312-670-6782.
Fax: 312-670-6783. E-mail: info@pta.org. Web: www.pta.org.

PARENTS LEAGUE OF NEW YORK
115 E 82nd St, New York, NY 10028. Tel: 212-737-7385.
Fax: 212-737-7389. E-mail: info@parentsleague.org.
Web: www.parentsleague.org.

PRINCETON CENTER FOR LEADERSHIP TRAINING
12 Vandeventer Ave, Princeton, NJ 08542. Tel: 609-252-9300.
Fax: 609-252-9393. E-mail: princetoncenter@princetonleadership.org.
Web: www.princetonleadership.org.

RELIGIOUS EDUCATION ASSOCIATION
PO Box 12576, Alexandria, LA 71315. Tel: 318-427-4446.
E-mail: lfsmith@lsua.edu. Web: www.religiouseducation.net.

VENTURES SCHOLARS PROGRAM
15 Maiden Ln, Ste 200, New York, NY 10038. Tel: 212-566-2522.
E-mail: jarkin@ventures.org. Web: www.venturescholar.org.

PROFESSIONAL ORGANIZATIONS

AMERICAN ASSOCIATION OF TEACHERS OF FRENCH
Southern Illinois Univ, Mailcode 4510, Carbondale, IL 62901.
Tel: 618-453-5731. Fax: 618-453-5733. E-mail: abrate@siu.edu.
Web: www.frenchteachers.org.

AMERICAN ASSOCIATION OF TEACHERS OF GERMAN
112 Haddontowne Ct, Ste 104, Cherry Hill, NJ 08034.
Tel: 856-795-5553. Fax: 856-795-9398. E-mail: headquarters@aatg.org.
Web: www.aatg.org.

AMERICAN ASSOCIATION OF TEACHERS OF SPANISH AND PORTUGUESE
423 Exton Commons, Exton, PA 19341. Tel: 610-363-7005.
Fax: 610-363-7116. E-mail: corporate@aatsp.org. Web: www.aatsp.org.

AMERICAN COUNCIL ON THE TEACHING OF FOREIGN LANGUAGES
700 S Washington St, Ste 210, Alexandria, VA 22314.
Tel: 703-894-2900. Fax: 703-894-2905. E-mail: headquarters@actfl.org.
Web: www.actfl.org.

AMERICAN COUNSELING ASSOCIATION
5999 Stevenson Ave, Alexandria, VA 22304. Tel: 703-823-9800.
Fax: 703-823-0252. E-mail: aca@counseling.org.
Web: www.counseling.org.

AMERICAN LIBRARY ASSOCIATION
50 E Huron St, Chicago, IL 60611. Tel: 312-944-6780.
Fax: 312-944-3897. E-mail: library@ala.org. Web: www.ala.org.

AMERICAN SCHOOL COUNSELOR ASSOCIATION
1101 King St, Ste 625, Alexandria, VA 22314. Tel: 703-683-2722.
Fax: 703-683-1619. E-mail: asca@schoolcounselor.org.
Web: www.schoolcounselor.org.

ASSOCIATION OF CALIFORNIA SCHOOL ADMINISTRATORS
1517 L St, Sacramento, CA 95814. Tel: 916-444-3216.
Fax: 916-444-3739. Web: www.acsa.org.

ASSOCIATION OF INDEPENDENT SCHOOL LIBRARIANS
c/o Campbell Hall School, 4533 Laurel Canyon Blvd, North Hollywood, CA 91607. Tel: 818-980-7280. Fax: 818-505-5319. Web: www.aislnews.org.

ASSOCIATION OF TEACHER EDUCATORS
1900 Association Dr, Ste ATE, Reston, VA 20191. Tel: 703-620-3110. Fax: 703-620-9530. E-mail: ate1@aol.com. Web: www.ate1.org.

COUNCIL FOR ADVANCEMENT AND SUPPORT OF EDUCATION
1307 New York Ave NW, Ste 1000, Washington, DC 20005. Tel: 202-328-2273. Fax: 202-387-4973. E-mail: memberservicecenter@case.org. Web: www.case.org.

COUNTRY DAY SCHOOL HEADMASTERS' ASSOCIATION OF THE UNITED STATES
Attn: Gordon E. Bondurant, 966 Harbortowne Rd, Charleston, SC 29412. Tel: 843-795-7947. Fax: 843-762-9204. E-mail: gebond@comcast.net.

ELEMENTARY SCHOOL HEADS ASSOCIATION
c/o St James Academy, 3100 Monkton Rd, Monkton, MD 21111. Tel: 410-771-4816. Fax: 410-771-4842.

INDEPENDENT EDUCATIONAL CONSULTANTS ASSOCIATION
3251 Old Lee Hwy, Ste 510, Fairfax, VA 22030. Tel: 703-591-4850. Fax: 703-591-4860. E-mail: info@iecaonline.com. Web: www.iecaonline.com.

INSTITUTE OF INTERNATIONAL EDUCATION
809 United Nations Plz, New York, NY 10017. Tel: 212-883-8200. Fax: 212-984-5452. Web: www.iie.org.

ISM CONSORTIUM
1316 N Union St, Wilmington, DE 19806. Tel: 302-656-4944. Fax: 302-656-0647. E-mail: ism@isminc.com. Web: www.isminc.com.

KLINGENSTEIN CENTER
c/o Teachers College, Columbia Univ, 525 W 120th St, 204 Main Hall, Box 125, New York, NY 10027. Tel: 212-678-3156. Fax: 212-678-3254. E-mail: klingenstein@tc.columbia.edu. Web: www.klingenstein.org.

NAFSA: ASSOCIATION OF INTERNATIONAL EDUCATORS
1307 New York Ave NW, 8th Fl, Washington, DC 20005.
Tel: 202-737-3699. Fax: 202-737-3657. E-mail: inbox@nafsa.org.
Web: www.nafsa.org.

NATIONAL ASSOCIATION OF BIOLOGY TEACHERS
12030 Sunrise Valley Dr, Ste 110, Reston, VA 20191.
Tel: 703-264-9696. Fax: 703-264-7778. E-mail: office@nabt.org.
Web: www.nabt.org.

NATIONAL ASSOCIATION OF ELEMENTARY SCHOOL PRINCIPALS
1615 Duke St, Alexandria, VA 22314. Tel: 703-684-3345.
Fax: 800-396-2377. E-mail: naesp@naesp.org. Web: www.naesp.org.

NATIONAL ASSOCIATION OF PRINCIPALS OF SCHOOLS FOR GIRLS
23490 Caraway Lakes Dr, Bonita Springs, FL 34135.
Tel: 239-947-6196. Fax: 239-390-3245. Web: www.napsg.org.

NATIONAL ASSOCIATION OF SECONDARY SCHOOL PRINCIPALS
1904 Association Dr, Reston, VA 20191. Tel: 703-860-0200.
Fax: 703-476-5432. E-mail: info@principals.org.
Web: www.principals.org.

NATIONAL ASSOCIATION OF SPECIAL EDUCATION TEACHERS
1201 Pennsylvania Ave NW, Ste 300, Washington, DC 20004.
Tel: 800-754-4421. Fax: 800-424-0371. E-mail: info@naset.org.
Web: www.naset.org.

NATIONAL ASSOCIATION OF TEACHERS' AGENCIES
797 Kings Hwy, Fairfield, CT 06825. Tel: 203-333-0611.
Fax: 203-334-7224. E-mail: info@jobsforteachers.com.
Web: www.jobsforteachers.com.

NATIONAL COUNCIL FOR GEOGRAPHIC EDUCATION
c/o Jacksonville State Univ, 206-A Martin Hall, Jacksonville, AL 36265.
Tel: 256-782-5293. Fax: 256-782-5336. E-mail: ncge@jscc.jsu.edu.
Web: www.ncge.org.

NATIONAL COUNCIL FOR PRIVATE SCHOOL ACCREDITATION
PO Box 13686, Seattle, WA 98198. Tel: 253-874-3408.
Fax: 253-874-3409. E-mail: ncpsaexdr@aol.com. Web: www.ncpsa.org.

NATIONAL COUNCIL OF TEACHERS OF ENGLISH
1111 W Kenyon Rd, Urbana, IL 61801. Tel: 217-328-3870.
Fax: 217-328-9645. E-mail: public_info@ncte.org. Web: www.ncte.org.

NATIONAL COUNCIL OF TEACHERS OF MATHEMATICS
1906 Association Dr, Reston, VA 20191. Tel: 703-620-9840.
Fax: 703-476-2970. E-mail: nctm@nctm.org. Web: www.nctm.org.

NATIONAL SCIENCE TEACHERS ASSOCIATION
1840 Wilson Blvd, Arlington, VA 22201. Tel: 703-243-7100.
Fax: 703-243-7177. Web: www.nsta.org.

SCHOOL SCIENCE AND MATHEMATICS ASSOCIATION
Ohio State Univ
238 Arps Hall, 238 Arps Hall, 1945 N High St, Columbus, OH 43210.
Tel: 614-292-8061. Fax: 614-292-7695. E-mail: white.32@osu.edu.
Web: www.ssma.org.

SCHOOL MEMBERSHIP ASSOCIATIONS

ALABAMA INDEPENDENT SCHOOL ASSOCIATION
1500 E Fairview Ave, Montgomery, AL 36106. Tel: 334-263-9115.
Fax: 334-833-4086. E-mail: aisa@aisaonline.org.
Web: www.aisaonline.org.

AMERICAN ASSOCIATION OF CHRISTIAN SCHOOLS
2000 Vance Ave, Chattanooga, TN 37404. Tel: 423-629-4280.
Fax: 423-622-7461. E-mail: mrector@aacs.org. Web: www.aacs.org.

AMERICAN MONTESSORI SOCIETY
281 Park Ave S, 6th Fl, New York, NY 10010. Tel: 212-358-1250.
Fax: 212-358-1256. E-mail: richard@amshq.org. Web: www.amshq.org.

ARIZONA ASSOCIATION OF INDEPENDENT SCHOOLS
c/o The Orme School, PO Box 3040, Mayer, AZ 86333.
Tel: 928-632-7601. Fax: 928-632-7605.

THE ASSOCIATION OF BOARDING SCHOOLS
4455 Connecticut Ave NW, Ste A-200, Washington, DC 20008.
Tel: 202-966-8705. Fax: 202-966-8708. E-mail: tabs@schools.com.
Web: www.schools.com.

ASSOCIATION OF CHRISTIAN SCHOOLS INTERNATIONAL
731 Chapel Hills Dr, PO Box 65130, Colorado Springs, CO 80962.
Tel: 719-528-6906. Fax: 719-531-0631. E-mail: info@acsi.org.
Web: www.acsi.org.

ASSOCIATION OF COLORADO INDEPENDENT SCHOOLS
1702 Sumac Ave, Boulder, CO 80303. Web: www.acischools.com.

ASSOCIATION OF DELAWARE VALLEY INDEPENDENT SCHOOLS
701 W Montgomery Ave, Bryn Mawr, PA 19010. Tel: 610-527-0130.
Fax: 610-527-4332. E-mail: info@advis.org. Web: www.advis.org.

ASSOCIATION OF INDEPENDENT MARYLAND SCHOOLS
890 Airport Park Rd, Ste 103, Glen Burnie, MD 21061.
Tel: 410-761-3700. Fax: 410-761-5771. E-mail: info@aimsmd.org.
Web: www.aimsmd.org.

ASSOCIATION OF INDEPENDENT MICHIGAN SCHOOLS
11477 Fredmar Dr, PO Box 186, Interlochen, MI 49643.
Tel: 231-275-3506. Fax: 231-275-3507.
E-mail: aims@centurytel.net. Web: www.aims-mi.org.

ASSOCIATION OF INDEPENDENT SCHOOLS IN NEW ENGLAND
222 Forbes Rd, Ste 106, Braintree, MA 02184. Tel: 781-843-8440.
Fax: 781-843-3933. E-mail: info@aisne.org. Web: www.aisne.org.

ASSOCIATION OF INDEPENDENT SCHOOLS OF GREATER WASHINGTON
PO Box 9956, Washington, DC 20016. Tel: 202-625-9223.
Fax: 202-625-9225. E-mail: info@aisgw.org. Web: www.aisgw.org.

ASSOCIATION OF MILITARY COLLEGES AND SCHOOLS OF THE UNITED STATES
9429 Garden Ct, Potomac, MD 20854. Tel: 301-765-0695.
E-mail: sorleydog@earthlink.net. Web: www.amcsus.org.

ASSOCIATION OF WALDORF SCHOOLS OF NORTH AMERICA
3911 Bannister Rd, Fair Oaks, CA 95628. Tel: 916-961-0927.
Fax: 916-961-0715. E-mail: awsna@awsna.org. Web: www.awsna.org.

ATLANTA AREA ASSOCIATION OF INDEPENDENT SCHOOLS
c/o The Atlanta Speech Schoo, 3610 Northside Pkwy NW, Atlanta, GA 30327. Tel: 404-233-5332. Fax: 404-266-2175.
Web: www.atlantaprivateschools.com.

CALIFORNIA ASSOCIATION OF INDEPENDENT SCHOOLS
1351 3rd St, Ste 303, Santa Monica, CA 90401. Tel: 310-393-5161.
Fax: 310-394-6561. E-mail: cais@caisca.org. Web: www.caisca.org.

CATHOLIC BOARDING SCHOOLS ASSOCIATION
c/o Chaminade College Preparatory School, 425 S Lindbergh Blvd, St Louis, MO 63131. Tel: 314-993-4400. Fax: 314-993-5732.
E-mail: rhill@chaminade.stl.com. Web: www.cbsa.org.

CHURCH SCHOOLS IN THE DIOCESE OF VIRGINIA
110 W Franklin St, Richmond, VA 23220. Tel: 804-643-8451.
Fax: 804-780-9748. E-mail: khenderson@thediocese.net.
Web: www.thediocese.net.

CLEVELAND COUNCIL OF INDEPENDENT SCHOOLS
358 Applebrook Dr, Chagrin Falls, OH 44022. Tel: 440-893-9585.
Fax: 216-371-1501. E-mail: hscott@ccis-ohio.org.
Web: www.ccis-ohio.org.

COALITION OF ESSENTIAL SCHOOLS
1814 Franklin St, Ste 700, Oakland, CA 94612. Tel: 510-433-1451.
Fax: 510-433-1455. E-mail: vcoleman@essentialschools.org.
Web: www.essentialschools.org.

CONNECTICUT ASSOCIATION OF INDEPENDENT SCHOOLS
12 Water St, Ste 102, PO Box 159, Mystic, CT 06355.
Tel: 860-572-2950. Fax: 860-415-0835. E-mail: lyons@caisct.org.
Web: www.caisct.org.

COUNCIL FOR SPIRITUAL AND ETHICAL EDUCATION
220 College Ave, Ste 312, Athens, GA 30601. Tel: 706-354-4043.
Fax: 678-623-5634. E-mail: info@csee.org. Web: www.csee.org.

DELAWARE ASSOCIATION OF INDEPENDENT SCHOOLS
c/o Sanford School, PO Box 888, Hockessin, DE 19707.
Tel: 302-239-5263. Fax: 302-239-5389.
E-mail: mackelcand@sanfordschool.org.

FLORIDA COUNCIL OF INDEPENDENT SCHOOLS
1211 N Westshore Blvd, Ste 612, Tampa, FL 33607. Tel: 813-287-2820.
Fax: 813-286-3025. E-mail: info@fcis.org. Web: www.fcis.org.

FRIENDS COUNCIL ON EDUCATION
1507 Cherry St, Philadelphia, PA 19102. Tel: 215-241-7245.
Fax: 215-241-7299. E-mail: info@friendscouncil.org.
Web: www.friendscouncil.org.

GEORGIA INDEPENDENT SCHOOL ASSOCIATION
329-A S Hill St, PO Box 1505, Griffin, GA 30224. Tel: 770-227-3456.
Fax: 770-412-0877. E-mail: info@gisa-schools.org.
Web: www.gisa-schools.org.

HAWAII ASSOCIATION OF INDEPENDENT SCHOOLS
1585 Kapiolani Blvd, Ste 1212, Honolulu, HI 96814.
Tel: 808-973-1540. Fax: 808-973-1545. E-mail: info@hais.org.
Web: www.hais.org.

INDEPENDENT SCHOOL HEALTH ASSOCIATION
PO Box 482, Byfield, MA 01922. Tel: 978-462-1368.
Fax: 978-462-2685. E-mail: ishaoffice@comcast.net.
Web: www.ishanet.org.

INDEPENDENT SCHOOLS ASSOCIATION OF NORTHERN NEW ENGLAND
38 Clark Cove Rd, Bowerbank, NH 04426. Tel: 207-564-2333.
Fax: 207-564-2422. E-mail: dcummings@isanne.org.
Web: www.isanne.org.

INDEPENDENT SCHOOLS ASSOCIATION OF RHODE ISLAND
c/o St Michael's Country Day School, 180 Rhode Island Ave, Newport, RI 02840. Tel: 401-849-5970. Fax: 401-849-7890.

INDEPENDENT SCHOOLS ASSOCIATION OF THE CENTRAL STATES
1550 N Dearborn Pky, Chicago, IL 60610. Tel: 314-255-1244.
Fax: 314-255-1278. E-mail: info@isacs.org. Web: www.isacs.org.

INDEPENDENT SCHOOLS ASSOCIATION OF THE SOUTH-WEST
4700 Bryant Irvin Ct, Ste 204, Fort Worth, TX 76107.
Tel: 817-569-9200. Fax: 817-569-9103. E-mail: gbutler@isasw.org.
Web: www.isasw.org.

INDEPENDENT SCHOOLS OF ST. LOUIS
101 N Warson Rd, St Louis, MO 63124. Tel: 314-567-9229.
Fax: 314-995-7451. E-mail: gnewport@independentschools.org.
Web: www.independentschools.org.

INTERNATIONAL BACCALAUREATE ORGANIZATION
475 Riverside Dr, 16th Fl, New York, NY 10115. Tel: 212-696-4464.
Fax: 212-889-9242. E-mail: ibna@ibo.org. Web: www.ibo.org.

INTERNATIONAL BOYS' SCHOOLS COALITION
PO Box 117, Dennis, MA 02638. Tel: 508-385-4563.
Fax: 508-385-4273. E-mail: chriswadsworth@comcast.net.
Web: www.boysschoolscoalition.org.

INTERNATIONAL MONTESSORI SOCIETY
8115 Fenton St, Ste 304, Silver Spring, MD 20910. Tel: 301-589-1127.
Fax: 301-589-0733. E-mail: havis@erols.com.
Web: www.wdn.com/trust/ims.

JESUIT SECONDARY EDUCATION ASSOCIATION
1616 P St NW, Ste 400, Washington, DC 20036. Tel: 202-667-3888.
Fax: 202-387-6305. E-mail: jsea@jsea.org. Web: www.jsea.org.

JUNIOR BOARDING SCHOOLS ASSOCIATION
c/o Hillside School, 404 Robin Hill Rd, Marlborough, MA 01752.
Tel: 508-485-2824. Fax: 508-485-4420. E-mail: jbsa@shaysnet.com.
Web: www.jbsa.org.

KENTUCKY ASSOCIATION OF INDEPENDENT SCHOOLS
c/o The Lexington School, 1050 Lane Allen Rd, Lexington, KY 40504.
Tel: 859-278-0501. Fax: 859-278-8604.
Web: www.kyindependentschools.com.

LAKE MICHIGAN ASSOCIATION OF INDEPENDENT SCHOOLS
c/o Bernard Zell Anshe Emet Day School, 3760 N Pine Grove Ave,
Chicago, IL 60613. Tel: 773-281-1858. Fax: 773-281-4709.
E-mail: info@independentschools.net.
Web: www.independentschools.net/.

LUTHERAN EDUCATION ASSOCIATION
7400 Augusta St, River Forest, IL 60305. Tel: 708-209-3343.
Fax: 708-209-3458. E-mail: lea@crf.cuis.edu. Web: www.lea.org.

MAINE ASSOCIATION OF INDEPENDENT SCHOOLS
31 Academy St, South Berwick, ME 03908. Tel: 207-384-2164.
Fax: 207-384-3332. E-mail: hridgway@berwickacademy.org.

MINNESOTA INDEPENDENT SCHOOL FORUM
336 Robert St N, Ste 1218, St Paul, MN 55101. Tel: 651-297-6716.
Fax: 651-297-6718. E-mail: info@misf.org. Web: www.misf.org.

MISSOURI INDEPENDENT SCHOOL ASSOCIATION
10631 Wornall Rd, Kansas City, MO 64114. Tel: 816-942-3282.
Fax: 816-942-4052. E-mail: amunninghoff@ndsion.com.

NATIONAL ASSOCIATION OF EPISCOPAL SCHOOLS
815 2nd Ave, Ste 313, New York, NY 10017. Tel: 212-716-6134.
Fax: 212-286-9366. E-mail: info@episcopalschools.org.
Web: www.naes.org.

NATIONAL ASSOCIATION OF INDEPENDENT SCHOOLS
1620 L St NW, Ste 1100, Washington, DC 20036. Tel: 202-973-9700.
Fax: 202-973-9790. Web: www.nais.org.

NATIONAL CATHOLIC EDUCATIONAL ASSOCIATION
1077 30th St NW, Ste 100, Washington, DC 20007. Tel: 202-337-6232.
Fax: 202-333-6706. E-mail: nceaadmin@ncea.org. Web: www.ncea.org.

NATIONAL COALITION OF GIRLS' SCHOOLS
57 Main St, Concord, MA 01742. Tel: 978-287-4485.
Fax: 978-287-6014. E-mail: ncgs@ncgs.org. Web: www.ncgs.org.

NEW JERSEY ASSOCIATION OF INDEPENDENT SCHOOLS
629 Amboy Ave, 3rd Fl, Edison, NJ 08837. Tel: 732-661-9000.
Fax: 732-661-9018. E-mail: info@njais.org. Web: www.njais.org.

NEW YORK STATE ASSOCIATION OF INDEPENDENT SCHOOLS
12 Jay St, Schenectady, NY 12305. Tel: 518-346-5662.
Fax: 518-346-7390. E-mail: hq@nysais.org. Web: www.nysais.org.

NORTH CAROLINA ASSOCIATION OF INDEPENDENT SCHOOLS
173 Tullyries Ln, Lewisville, NC 27023. Tel: 336-946-2819.
Fax: 336-945-0909. E-mail: gbingham@ncais.org. Web: www.ncais.org.

OHIO ASSOCIATION OF INDEPENDENT SCHOOLS
PO Box 630, Sunbury, OH 43074. Tel: 740-965-2739.
Fax: 740-965-1373. E-mail: koneil@oais.org. Web: www.oais.org.

PACIFIC NORTHWEST ASSOCIATION OF INDEPENDENT SCHOOLS
5001 California Ave SW, Ste 112, Seattle, WA 98136.
Tel: 206-323-6137. Fax: 206-324-4863. E-mail: pnais@pnais.org.
Web: www.pnais.org.

PALMETTO ASSOCIATION OF INDEPENDENT SCHOOLS
PO Box 4143, Greenville, SC 29608. Tel: 864-232-0003.
Fax: 864-232-0003. E-mail: scpais@bellsouth.net.
Web: www.scpais.org.

PENNSYLVANIA ASSOCIATION OF INDEPENDENT SCHOOLS
37 E Germantown Pike, Ste 302, Plymouth Meeting, PA 19462.
Tel: 610-567-2960. Fax: 610-567-2963.
E-mail: lphelps@pais-papas.org. Web: www.pais-papas.org.

PENNSYLVANIA ASSOCIATION OF PRIVATE ACADEMIC SCHOOLS
37 E Germantown Pike, Ste 302, Plymouth Meeting, PA 19462.
Tel: 610-567-2960. Fax: 610-567-2963.
E-mail: lphelps@pais-papas.org. Web: www.pais-papas.org.

SOUTH CAROLINA INDEPENDENT SCHOOL ASSOCIATION
PO Drawer 690, Orangeburg, SC 29116. Tel: 803-535-4820.
Fax: 803-535-4840. E-mail: administrator@scisa.org.
Web: www.scisa.org.

SOUTHERN ASSOCIATION OF INDEPENDENT SCHOOLS
1866 Southern Ln, Decatur, GA 30033. Tel: 404-633-2203.
Fax: 404-633-2433. E-mail: sais@sais.org. Web: www.sais.org.

SOUTHWESTERN ASSOCIATION OF EPISCOPAL SCHOOLS
1420 4th Ave, Ste 29, Canyon, TX 79015. Tel: 806-655-2400.
Fax: 806-655-2426. E-mail: cwootton@swaes.org.
Web: www.swaes.org.

TENNESSEE ASSOCIATION OF INDEPENDENT SCHOOLS
2014 Broadway, Ste 245, Nashville, TN 37203. Tel: 615-321-2800.
Fax: 615-321-2827. E-mail: info@taistn.org. Web: www.taistn.org.

VIRGINIA ASSOCIATION OF INDEPENDENT SCHOOLS
6802 Paragon Pl, Ste 525, Richmond, VA 23230. Tel: 804-282-3592.
Fax: 804-282-3596. E-mail: info@vais.org. Web: www.vais.org.

WISCONSIN ASSOCIATION OF INDEPENDENT SCHOOLS
c/o University School of Milwaukee, 2100 W Fairy Chasm Rd,
Milwaukee, WI 53217. Tel: 414-352-6000. Fax: 414-352-8076.

TESTING ORGANIZATIONS

ACT
500 ACT Dr, PO Box 168, Iowa City, IA 52243. Tel: 319-337-1000.
Fax: 319-339-3021. Web: www.act.org.

THE COLLEGE BOARD
45 Columbus Ave, New York, NY 10023. Tel: 212-713-8000.
Fax: 212-713-8282. Web: www.collegeboard.org.

EDUCATIONAL RECORDS BUREAU
220 E 42nd St, Ste 100, New York, NY 10017. Tel: 212-672-9800.
Fax: 212-370-4096. E-mail: info@erbtest.org. Web: www.erbtest.org.

EDUCATIONAL TESTING SERVICE
Rosedale Rd, Princeton, NJ 08541. Tel: 609-921-9000.
Fax: 609-734-5410. E-mail: etsinfo@ets.org. Web: www.ets.org.

SECONDARY SCHOOL ADMISSION TEST BOARD
CN 5339, Princeton, NJ 08543. Tel: 609-683-4440.
Fax: 609-683-1702. E-mail: info@ssat.org. Web: www.ssat.org.

SOUTHERN ASSOCIATION OF COLLEGES AND SCHOOLS

Private and independent schools should consider accreditation through the Southern Association of Colleges and Schools, Council on Accreditation and School Improvement (SACS CASI). SACS CASI accredits over 13,000 schools, Pre-K through grade 12, throughout the 11 southern states and overseas. SACS CASI is committed to helping schools improve and believes school can accomplish this by meeting standards, engaging in continuous improvement and providing for quality assurance. Some of the most prestigious public and private schools in the nation are accredited by SACS. SACS, a non-profit, voluntary and nongovernmental association, has been in the business of accrediting public and private schools for over 100 years. If you are interested in accreditation for your school, please call or write:

Council on Accreditation and School Improvement
Southern Association of Colleges and Schools
1866 Southern Lane, Decatur, GA 30033-4097
800.248.7701, www.sacscasi.org

THE PORTER SARGENT HANDBOOK SERIES

11 Beacon St. Ste. 1400 Boston, MA 02108-3099 USA
Tel: 617-523-1670 Fax: 617-523-1021
info@portersargent.com www.portersargent.com

Tools for Independent Evaluation

In 1914, educator and writer Porter Sargent introduced *The Handbook of Private Schools* because he felt educators, administrators and parents needed an objective guide to quality schools and programs emphasizing the needs of the individual student.

The development of the Porter Sargent Handbook Series followed that very simple aim. Each publication is a source book of information for those who need—and ought—to know about the advantage of independent instruction, providing the most up-to-date narrative and statistical information on schools and programs serving those who seek out the best education worldwide.

The Handbook of Private Schools * The Directory for Exceptional Children
Schools Abroad of Interest to Americans * Guide to Summer Camps and Schools

CLASSIFIED
LISTINGS OF
FIRMS AND AGENCIES

INDEX TO FIRMS AND AGENCIES

A.W.G. DEWAR, INC., Quincy, MA 1426

BARNES & ROCHE INC., Rosemont, PA 1425

CAMPUS SELECTION, INC., The Woodlands, TX 1423

SAM AND CHRISTINE CHAPMAN
STARR & CHAPMAN, INC., Plymouth, MA 1423

COMMUNITY COUNSELLING SERVICE, New York, NY 1425

DAVID DENMAN, Sausalito, CA 1423

DOBSON EDUCATIONAL SERVICES, Philadelphia, PA 1423

PEARL GLASSMAN COUNSELING, INC.,
Pound Ridge, NY 1423

GOETTLER ASSOCIATES, INC., Columbus, OH 1425

LESLIE GOLDBERG, Hingham, MA 1423

JEAN P. HAGUE, Atlanta, GA 1423

JANE E. KOLBER, New York, NY 1424

SUZANNE F. SCOTT, Elkins Park, PA 1424

THE SHERIDAN GROUP, Vero Beach, FL 1425

STEINBRECHER & PARTNERS, Westport, CT 1424

KRISTIN M. WHITE, Chatham, NJ 1424

EDUCATIONAL CONSULTANTS

CAMPUS SELECTION, INC., Londa May, M.Ed., CEP, IECA
2 Dunloggin Ln., The Woodlands, TX 77380. Tel: 281-364-9700.
E-mail: contact@campusselection.com. Web: www.campusselection.com.
Boarding, Military, Private, Wilderness, Rehabilitation.

SAM AND CHRISTINE CHAPMAN
STARR & CHAPMAN, INC.
1073 Long Pond Rd., Plymouth, MA 02360-2637.
Web: www.starrandchapman.com. Tel: 617-938-3595. Fax: 617-938-3603.
IECA, HECA, SSATB, ERB, NEACAC

DAVID DENMAN, Educational Consultant, IECA
3030 Bridgeway, Sausalito CA 94965. Tel: 415-332-1831.
http://www.sojournsabroad.org & http://www.timeoutadventures.net
Boarding & day school placement; college counseling; summer,
semester, and gap year options worldwide.

DOBSON EDUCATIONAL SERVICES
8238 Germantown Ave, Philadelphia, PA 19118. Tel: 215-242-3587.
Fax: 215-242-3588. E-mail: jpd@dobconsult.com. Web: www.dobconsult.com.
Joseph P. Dobson, MA, Director. Member IECA, LDA, IDA, SSATB.
Counseling and referral services for students and families seeking day,
boarding, and special need schools.

PEARL GLASSMAN, Certified Educational Planner, Member IECA
30 White Birch Rd., Pound Ridge, NY 10576. Tel: 914-764-5153.
www.pearledu.com. E-mail: glassman@cloud9.net.
Boarding, Col & Grad School Placement, Transfers, Foreign Students, LD, ED.

LESLIE GOLDBERG & ASSOCIATES, LLC
Needham, MA—Tel: 617-969-5151
Hingham, MA—Tel: 781-749-2074.
E-mail: info@edconsult.org. Web: www.edconsult.org.
Schools, Colleges, LD Supports, Crisis Interventions, Therapeutic Programs.

JEAN P. HAGUE, MA, Certified Educational Planner, IECA
400 Colony Sq., Ste. 200, 1201 Peachtree St. NE, Atlanta, GA 30361.
Tel: 404-872-9128. Fax: 404-870-9093. E-mail: jeanhague@aol.com. Boarding
School, Summer, College, Alternative Educational Options. Diagnostic Testing.

JANE E. KOLBER, CEP, Educational Consultant, Member IECA
142 E. 71st St., New York, NY 10021. Tel: 212-734-1704.
Educational counseling for school, college, LD, special needs programs, and graduate school. Fax: 212-772-7397. E-mail: JEKWFK@aol.com.

SUZANNE F. SCOTT, Ed.M., Member IECA, NACAC, APA
School, College and Special Needs Advising Since 1976
215-887-2201   Suburban Philadelphia, PA
www.academic-advisory-service.com   scottaas@comcast.net

PHYLLIS S. STEINBRECHER, DIEDERIK J. van RENESSE, RICHARD AVITABILE, WILLIAM DENNETT and JOHN POWERS, Educational Consultants
225 Main St., Ste. 203, Westport, CT 06880. Tel: 203-227-3190.
Fax: 203-221-0182. College, Boarding, Special, Alternative Counseling.

KRISTIN M. WHITE, Educational Consultant
323 Main St., 2nd Fl., Chatham, NJ 07928. Tel: 973-635-8228.
E-mail: kristinmanley@yahoo.com   www.summitacademicadvisors.com
Boarding, college & NJ day school placement. Member HECA, NJACAC.

FUNDRAISING AND PUBLIC RELATIONS COUNSEL

BARNES & ROCHE INC.
Rosemont Business Campus, 919 Conestoga Rd., Building Three, Suite 302. Rosemont, PA 19010-1375. Tel: 610-527-3244. E-mail: consult@brnsrche.com. www.barnesroche.com. Consultants providing strategic and operational consultation for fundraising; program assessments; capital campaigns; feasibility studies; planned giving; electronic screening; and communications services with offices in Philadelphia, Washington and San Francisco.

COMMUNITY COUNSELLING SERVICE (CCS)
461 5th Ave., New York, NY 10017. Tel: 800-223-6733.
Fax: 212-967-6451. E-mail: ccsnewyork@ccsfundraising.com.
Since 1947, CCS has designed successful and innovative major fundraising efforts to advance the mission of leading private schools nationwide. CCS is a full service fund-raising consulting firm. Services include Campaign Planning, Management and Direction; Feasibility and Planning Studies; Development Audits; Executive Consultation; Electronic Prospect Research; Board Development and Orientation; Marketing Communications; Planned Giving; and Development Operations Management. Visit www.ccsfundraising.com.

GOETTLER ASSOCIATES, INC.
580 S. High St., Columbus, OH 43215. Tel: 614-228-3269.
Fax: 614-228-7583. E-mail: info@goettler.com. Web: www.goettler.com.
Full-service fund-raising consulting firm serving private schools since 1965, including campaign direction; periodic consulting; campaign planning/feasibility studies; case for support development; development audits; marketing and creative services, including print and video production.

THE SHERIDAN GROUP
4510 S. 34th St., Arlington VA 22206. Tel: 703-931-7070.
Fax: 703-931-6249. Web: www.sheridangp.com.
Full-service fundraising including capital campaigns, feasibility/planning studies, strategic planning, annual funds, board development/training, publications.

INSURANCE

A.W.G. DEWAR, INC.
Four Batterymarch Park, Quincy, MA 02169-7468. Tel: 617-774-1555.
Fax: 617-774-1715. E-mail: trp@dewarinsurance.com.
Representatives throughout North America.
TUITION REFUND PLANS.
Our specialized work for over 70 years has won complete confidence nationwide for these voluntary or required-participation plans.
See Also *Tuition Refund Insurance* **and** *Display Announcement* **on Page1472**

TUITION REFUND INSURANCE

A.W.G. DEWAR, INC.
Four Batterymarch Park, Quincy, MA 02169-7468. Tel: 617-774-1555.
Fax: 617-774-1715. E-mail: trp@dewarinsurance.com.
Representatives throughout North America.
See Also *Insurance* **and** *Display Announcement* **on Page 1472**

INDEX OF SCHOOLS

INDEX OF SCHOOLS

Schools are referenced by page number. Boldface page numbers refer to the optional Illustrated Announcements of schools and summer, schools abroad and exceptional children programs that subscribe for space. To facilitate the use of this section, refer to the separate indexes preceding the announcements. Illustrated Announcement cross-references also appear at the end of the free descriptive listings of subscribing schools.

ABINGTON FRIENDS SCHOOL, Jenkintown, PA 428
ABRAHAM JOSHUA HESCHEL SCHOOL, New York, NY 836
ACADEMY OF MOUNT ST. URSULA, Bronx, NY 824
ACADEMY OF NOTRE DAME, Tyngsboro, MA 784
ACADEMY OF OUR LADY OF MERCY
   LAURALTON HALL, Milford, CT 767
ACADEMY OF OUR LADY OF PEACE, San Diego, CA 1070
ACADEMY OF SAINT ELIZABETH, Convent Station, NJ 335
ACADEMY OF THE HOLY ANGELS, Demarest, NJ 814
ACADEMY OF THE HOLY FAMILY, Baltic, CT 763
ACADEMY OF THE HOLY NAMES, Tampa, FL 884
ACADEMY OF THE SACRED HEART, Grand Coteau, LA 999
ACADEMY OF THE SACRED HEART, New Orleans, LA 651
ACADEMY OF THE SACRED HEART, Bloomfield Hills, MI 592
THE ACHIEVEMENT CENTER, Roanoke, VA 935
ADMIRAL FARRAGUT ACADEMY, St Petersburg, FL 482
AGNON SCHOOL, Beachwood, OH 964
AIGLON COLLEGE, Chesieres-Villars, Switzerland **1387**
AIKEN PREPARATORY SCHOOL, Aiken, SC 524
ALABAMA CHRISTIAN ACADEMY, Montgomery, AL 868
THE ALBANY ACADEMY, Albany, NY 350
ALBANY ACADEMY FOR GIRLS, Albany, NY 350
ALBUQUERQUE ACADEMY, Albuquerque, NM 692
ALEPH BET JEWISH DAY SCHOOL, Annapolis, MD 798
ALEXANDER DAWSON SCHOOL, Lafayette, CO 681
ALEXANDER ROBERTSON SCHOOL, New York, NY 836
THE ALEXANDER SCHOOL, Richardson, TX 1023
ALEXANDER-SMITH ACADEMY, Houston, TX 1018
ALEXANDRIA COUNTRY DAY SCHOOL, Alexandria, VA 925
ALL SAINTS' EPISCOPAL DAY SCHOOL, Carmel, CA 1051
ALL SAINTS' EPISCOPAL DAY SCHOOL, Phoenix, AZ 686
ALL SAINTS EPISCOPAL SCHOOL, Beaumont, TX 1009
ALL SAINTS EPISCOPAL SCHOOL, Lubbock, TX 1022
ALL SAINTS' EPISCOPAL SCHOOL, Vicksburg, MS 655

ALLEN ACADEMY, Bryan, TX 662
ALLEN-STEVENSON SCHOOL, New York, NY 372
ALLENDALE COLUMBIA SCHOOL, Rochester, NY 405
ALPHA BEACON CHRISTIAN SCHOOL, San Mateo, CA 1074
AMERICAN BOYCHOIR SCHOOL, Princeton, NJ 341
AMERICAN HERITAGE SCHOOL, Plantation, FL 882
AMERICAN SCHOOL OF WARSAW,
   Konstancin-Jeziorna, Poland **1388**
ANDREWS SCHOOL, Willoughby, OH 606
ANNIE WRIGHT SCHOOL, Tacoma, WA 759
ANTIOCH SCHOOL, Fall River, MA 780
APPLEWILD SCHOOL, Fitchburg, MA 218
AQUINAS ACADEMY OF PITTSBURGH, Gibsonia, PA 851
AQUINAS HIGH SCHOOL, Augusta, GA 891
AQUINAS INSTITUTE, Rochester, NY 841
ARCHBISHOP O'HARA HIGH SCHOOL, Kansas City, MO 986
ARCHBISHOP RYAN HIGH SCHOOL, Philadelphia, PA 858
ARCHBISHOP SHAW HIGH SCHOOL, Marrero, LA 999
ARCHBISHOP SPALDING HIGH SCHOOL, Severn, MD 811
ARCHBISHOP STEPINAC HIGH SCHOOL, White Plains, NY 845
THE ARCHER SCHOOL FOR GIRLS, Los Angeles, CA 1058
ARCHMERE ACADEMY, Claymont, DE 284
ARMAND HAMMER UNITED WORLD COLLEGE,
   Montezuma, NM 694
ARMITAGE ACADEMY, Kenosha, WI 974
ARMY AND NAVY ACADEMY, Carlsbad, CA 699
ARROWSMITH ACADEMY, Berkeley, CA 1050
ARTHUR MORGAN SCHOOL, Burnsville, NC 511
ASHLEY HALL, Charleston, SC 526, **1289**
ASPEN COUNTRY DAY SCHOOL, Aspen, CO 677
ASSUMPTION HIGH SCHOOL, Louisville, KY 900
ATHENS ACADEMY, Athens, GA 888
ATLANTA INTERNATIONAL SCHOOL, Atlanta, GA 491
ATLANTIS ACADEMY, Miami, FL 878
AUGUSTA PREPARATORY DAY SCHOOL, Martinez, GA 497
AVERY COONLEY SCHOOL, Downers Grove, IL 576
AVON OLD FARMS SCHOOL, Avon, CT 131
AWTY INTERNATIONAL SCHOOL, Houston, TX 669
AYLETT COUNTRY DAY SCHOOL, Millers Tavern, VA 934

THE BALDWIN SCHOOL, Bryn Mawr, PA 421

Index of Schools

BALTIMORE HEBREW CONGREGATION DAY SCHOOL,
  Baltimore, MD 799
BANCROFT SCHOOL, Worcester, MA 251
BANGKOK PATANA SCHOOL, Bangkok, Thailand **1389**
BAPTIST HIGH SCHOOL, Haddon Heights, NJ 815
THE BARNESVILLE SCHOOL, Barnesville, MD 801
THE BARRIE SCHOOL, Silver Spring, MD 319
BARSTOW SCHOOL, Kansas City, MO 635
BARTLETT SCHOOL, Waltham, MA 243
BATTLE GROUND ACADEMY, Franklin, TN 920
BAYMONTE CHRISTIAN SCHOOL, Scotts Valley, CA 1078
BAYSHORE CHRISTIAN SCHOOL, Tampa, FL 885
BAYSIDE ACADEMY, Daphne, AL 865
BEACHES EPISCOPAL SCHOOL, Jacksonville Beach, FL 876
BEACON COUNTRY DAY SCHOOL, Denver, CO 1026
THE BEAR CREEK SCHOOL, Redmond, WA 1088
BEAUFORT ACADEMY, Beaufort, SC 525
BEAUMONT SCHOOL, Cleveland Heights, OH 967
BEAVER COUNTRY DAY SCHOOL, Chestnut Hill, MA 199
BEAVER COUNTY CHRISTIAN SCHOOL, Beaver Falls, PA 847
BEEKMAN SCHOOL, New York, NY 372, **1114-5**
BELMONT DAY SCHOOL, Belmont, MA 191, **1116**
BELMONT HILL SCHOOL, Belmont, MA 191
BEMENT SCHOOL, Deerfield, MA 213, **1117**
BEN LIPPEN SCHOOL, Columbia, SC 912
BENCHMARK SCHOOL, Media, PA 855
BENEDICTINE ACADEMY, Elizabeth, NJ 814
BENEDICTINE HIGH SCHOOL, Cleveland, OH 967
BENET ACADEMY, Lisle, IL 946
BENJAMIN SCHOOL, North Palm Beach, FL 881
BENTLEY SCHOOL, Oakland, CA 1063
BERKELEY CARROLL SCHOOL, Brooklyn, NY 357, **1120**
BERKELEY HALL SCHOOL, Los Angeles, CA 1058
BERKELEY PREPARATORY SCHOOL, Tampa, FL 487
BERKSHIRE COUNTRY DAY SCHOOL, Lenox, MA 224
BERKSHIRE SCHOOL, Sheffield, MA 239, **1118-9**
BERTSCHI SCHOOL, Seattle, WA 1088
BERWICK ACADEMY, South Berwick, ME 179
BESS AND PAUL SIGEL HEBREW ACADEMY,
  Bloomfield, CT 763
BETHANY SCHOOL, Glendale, OH 601
BETHLEHEM ACADEMY, Faribault, MN 982

BI-CULTURAL DAY SCHOOL, Stamford, CT 769
BIRCH WATHEN LENOX SCHOOL, New York, NY 373
BISHOP BORGESS HIGH SCHOOL, Redford, MI 961
BISHOP DuBOURG HIGH SCHOOL, St Louis, MO 988
BISHOP DWENGER HIGH SCHOOL, Fort Wayne, IN 951
BISHOP GORMAN HIGH SCHOOL, Las Vegas, NV 1039
BISHOP GUILFOYLE HIGH SCHOOL, Altoona, PA 847
BISHOP IRETON HIGH SCHOOL, Alexandria, VA 925
BISHOP KEARNEY HIGH SCHOOL, Brooklyn, NY 824
BISHOP KEARNEY HIGH SCHOOL, Rochester, NY 842
BISHOP KELLEY HIGH SCHOOL, Tulsa, OK 1007
BISHOP KELLY HIGH SCHOOL, Boise, ID 1031
BISHOP LOUGHLIN MEMORIAL HIGH SCHOOL,
  Brooklyn, NY 825
BISHOP LUERS HIGH SCHOOL, Fort Wayne, IN 951
BISHOP MOORE CATHOLIC HIGH SCHOOL, Orlando, FL 881
BISHOP O'DOWD HIGH SCHOOL, Oakland, CA 1064
BISHOP STANG HIGH SCHOOL, North Dartmouth, MA 783
BISHOP WATTERSON HIGH SCHOOL, Columbus, OH 967
THE BISHOP'S SCHOOL, La Jolla, CA 705
BLAIR ACADEMY, Blairstown, NJ 323, **1121**
THE BLAKE SCHOOL, Hopkins, MN 629
BLANCHET CATHOLIC SCHOOL, Salem, OR 1085
BLESSED SACRAMENT-HUGUENOT, Powhatan, VA 935
THE BLUE RIDGE SCHOOL, St George, VA 548
BOB JONES ACADEMY, Greenville, SC 914
BOCA RATON CHRISTIAN SCHOOL, Boca Raton, FL 869
THE BOLLES SCHOOL, Jacksonville, FL 471
BOSQUE SCHOOL, Albuquerque, NM 1041
BOSTON COLLEGE HIGH SCHOOL, Dorchester, MA 779
BOSTON UNIVERSITY ACADEMY, Boston, MA 194
BOYD-BUCHANAN SCHOOL, Chattanooga, TN 918
BOYS' LATIN SCHOOL, Baltimore, MD 296
BRADENTON CHRISTIAN SCHOOL, Bradenton, FL 870
BRANDON ACADEMY, Brandon, FL 871
BRANDON HALL SCHOOL, Atlanta, GA 491, **1353**
BRANSON SCHOOL, Ross, CA 728
BREAKWATER SCHOOL, Portland, ME 775
BREARLEY SCHOOL, New York, NY 374
BREBEUF JESUIT PREPARATORY SCHOOL, Indianapolis, IN 952
BRECK SCHOOL, Minneapolis, MN 630, **1124**
BREHM PREPARATORY SCHOOL, Carbondale, IL 940

BRENAU ACADEMY, Gainesville, GA	498, **1290-1**
BRENTWOOD ACADEMY, Brentwood, TN	917
BREWSTER ACADEMY, Wolfeboro, NH	267, **1122-3**
BRIDGEMONT HIGH SCHOOL AND JUNIOR HIGH, San Francisco, CA	1072
BRIDGTON ACADEMY, North Bridgton, ME	180
THE BRIGHT SCHOOL, Chattanooga, TN	532
BRIMMER AND MAY SCHOOL, Chestnut Hill, MA	199, **1125**
BROADWATER ACADEMY, Exmore, VA	929
BROOKFIELD ACADEMY, Brookfield, WI	617, **1126**
BROOKFIELD SCHOOL, Sacramento, CA	1070
BROOKLYN HEIGHTS MONTESSORI SCHOOL, Brooklyn, NY	825
BROOKS SCHOOL, North Andover, MA	187
BROOKSTONE SCHOOL, Columbus, GA	498
THE BROOKWOOD SCHOOL, Cooperstown, NY	828
BROOKWOOD SCHOOL, Manchester, MA	227
BROPHY COLLEGE PREPARATORY SCHOOL, Phoenix, AZ	686
BROTHER RICE HIGH SCHOOL, Bloomfield Hills, MI	955
BROWNE ACADEMY, Alexandria, VA	926
BROWNELL-TALBOT SCHOOL, Omaha, NE	645
THE BROWNING SCHOOL, New York, NY	374
BRUNSWICK SCHOOL, Greenwich, CT	138
BRYN MAWR SCHOOL, Baltimore, MD	297
BUCKINGHAM BROWNE & NICHOLS SCHOOL, Cambridge, MA	204
BUCKINGHAM FRIENDS SCHOOL, Lahaska, PA	429
BUCKLEY COUNTRY DAY SCHOOL, Roslyn, NY	407
BUCKLEY SCHOOL, Sherman Oaks, CA	706
THE BUCKLEY SCHOOL, New York, NY	375
BUFFALO SEMINARY, Buffalo, NY	359
THE BULLIS SCHOOL, Potomac, MD	313
BULLOCH ACADEMY, Statesboro, GA	898
BURGUNDY FARM COUNTRY DAY SCHOOL, Alexandria, VA	543
BURLINGTON DAY SCHOOL, Burlington, NC	903
BURR AND BURTON ACADEMY, Manchester, VT	790
BUXTON SCHOOL, Williamstown, MA	249
THE BYRNES SCHOOLS, Florence, SC	913
THE CAEDMON SCHOOL, New York, NY	836
CALHOUN SCHOOL, New York, NY	376

CALVERT HALL COLLEGE HIGH SCHOOL, Baltimore, MD........ 298
CALVERT SCHOOL, Baltimore, MD 298
THE CALVERTON SCHOOL, Huntingtown, MD............................. 807
CAMBRIDGE FRIENDS SCHOOL, Cambridge, MA......................... 205
CAMBRIDGE MONTESSORI SCHOOL, Cambridge, MA............... 778
THE CAMBRIDGE SCHOOL, Tampa, FL 885
THE CAMBRIDGE SCHOOL OF WESTON, Weston, MA 246
CAMDEN MILITARY ACADEMY, Camden, SC................................ 525
CAMELBACK DESERT SCHOOL, Paradise Valley, AZ 1035
CAMPBELL HALL SCHOOL, North Hollywood, CA 707, **1127**
CAMPION ACADEMY, Loveland, CO.. 1030
CANISIUS HIGH SCHOOL, Buffalo, NY 826
CANNON SCHOOL, Concord, NC 905
CANTERBURY EPISCOPAL SCHOOL, DeSoto, TX...................... 1015
CANTERBURY SCHOOL, Greensboro, NC.. 906
CANTERBURY SCHOOL, New Milford, CT........................... 157, **1128**
CANTERBURY SCHOOL, Fort Myers, FL 469, **1129**
CANTERBURY SCHOOL, Fort Wayne, IN 584
THE CANTERBURY SCHOOL OF FLORIDA, St Petersburg, FL.... 483
CANTON COUNTRY DAY SCHOOL, Canton, OH 600
CAPE COD ACADEMY, Osterville, MA 237
CAPE FEAR ACADEMY, Wilmington, NC... 521
CAPE HENRY COLLEGIATE SCHOOL, Virginia Beach, VA........... 564
CAPITOL HILL DAY SCHOOL, Washington, DC 795
CARBONDALE NEW SCHOOL, Carbondale, IL............................... 940
CARDIGAN MOUNTAIN SCHOOL, Canaan, NH 257
CARDINAL MOONEY HIGH SCHOOL, Sarasota, FL...................... 884
CARDINAL MOONEY HIGH SCHOOL, Youngstown, OH............. 972
CARDINAL NEWMAN HIGH SCHOOL, West Palm Beach, FL...... 887
CARIBBEAN PREPARATORY SCHOOL,
  San Juan, Puerto Rico **1390-1**
CARLISLE SCHOOL, Martinsville, VA... 933
CAROLINA DAY SCHOOL, Asheville, NC 511
CAROLINA FRIENDS SCHOOL, Durham, NC................................. 515
THE CARROLL SCHOOL, Lincoln, MA... 226
CARROLLTON CHRISTIAN ACADEMY, Carrollton, TX.............. 1010
CARROLLTON SCHOOL OF THE SACRED HEART,
  Miami, FL... 878
CARSON LONG MILITARY INSTITUTE,
  New Bloomfield, PA.. 434, **1325**
CASADY SCHOOL, Oklahoma City, OK 657
CASCIA HALL PREPARATORY SCHOOL, Tulsa, OK 1007

CATE SCHOOL, Carpinteria, CA	744
CATHEDRAL PREPARATORY SEMINARY, Elmhurst, NY	829
CATHEDRAL SCHOOL, Natchez, MS	1005
THE CATHEDRAL SCHOOL, New York, NY	376
CATHEDRAL SCHOOL FOR BOYS, San Francisco, CA	731
CATHERINE McAULEY HIGH SCHOOL, Portland, ME	776
CATHOLIC HIGH SCHOOL, Baton Rouge, LA	998
THE CATHOLIC HIGH SCHOOL OF BALTIMORE, Baltimore, MD	800
CATHOLIC MEMORIAL SCHOOL, West Roxbury, MA	785
CENTRAL ARKANSAS CHRISTIAN SCHOOLS, North Little Rock, AR	997
CENTRAL CATHOLIC HIGH SCHOOL, Modesto, CA	1061
CFS: THE SCHOOL AT CHURCH FARM, Paoli, PA	438, **1326-7**
CHADWICK SCHOOL, Palos Verdes Peninsula, CA	708, **1130**
CHAMINADE COLLEGE PREPARATORY SCHOOL, St Louis, MO	638
CHAMINADE HIGH SCHOOL, Mineola, NY	834
CHAMINADE-MADONNA COLLEGE PREPARATORY, Hollywood, FL	875
CHAPEL HILL-CHAUNCY HALL SCHOOL, Waltham, MA	244
THE CHAPIN SCHOOL, New York, NY	377
CHARLES E. SMITH JEWISH DAY SCHOOL, Rockville, MD	810
CHARLES RIVER SCHOOL, Dover, MA	216
CHARLES WRIGHT ACADEMY, Tacoma, WA	760
CHARLESTON DAY SCHOOL, Charleston, SC	527
CHARLOTTE CATHOLIC HIGH SCHOOL, Charlotte, NC	904
CHARLOTTE CHRISTIAN SCHOOL, Charlotte, NC	904
CHARLOTTE COUNTRY DAY SCHOOL, Charlotte, NC	512, **1131**
CHARLOTTE LATIN SCHOOL, Charlotte, NC	513
CHASE COLLEGIATE SCHOOL, Waterbury, CT	171, **1132**
CHATHAM HALL, Chatham, VA	546
CHATTANOOGA CHRISTIAN SCHOOL, Chattanooga, TN	918
CHELSEA SCHOOL, Silver Spring, MD	812
CHESAPEAKE ACADEMY, Arnold, MD	799
CHESAPEAKE ACADEMY, Irvington, VA	931
CHESHIRE ACADEMY, Cheshire, CT	133
CHESTERFIELD DAY SCHOOL, Chesterfield, MO	986
THE CHESTNUT HILL SCHOOL, Chestnut Hill, MA	200
CHEVERUS HIGH SCHOOL, Portland, ME	776
CHICAGO ACADEMY FOR THE ARTS, Chicago, IL	571
CHICAGO CHRISTIAN HIGH SCHOOL, Palos Heights, IL	948

CHICAGO CITY DAY SCHOOL, Chicago, IL 941
CHILDREN'S OWN SCHOOL, Winchester, MA 786
THE CHILDREN'S STOREFRONT SCHOOL, New York, NY 837
CHINESE AMERICAN INTERNATIONAL SCHOOL,
  San Francisco, CA... 1072
CHOATE ROSEMARY HALL, Wallingford, CT 168, **1134-5**
CHOP POINT SCHOOL, Woolwich, ME 777
CHRIST CHURCH EPISCOPAL SCHOOL, Greenville, SC 529
CHRIST SCHOOL, Arden, NC 510, **1328**
CHRISTCHURCH SCHOOL, Christchurch, VA 547, **1329**
CHRISTIAN BROTHERS ACADEMY, Lincroft, NJ 817
CHRISTIAN BROTHERS ACADEMY, Albany, NY 822
CHRISTIAN BROTHERS ACADEMY, Syracuse, NY 843
CHRISTIAN HERITAGE ACADEMY, Northfield, IL 947
CHRISTIAN HERITAGE SCHOOL, Trumbull, CT 770
CHRISTIAN SCHOOL OF YORK, York, PA 864
CHRISTOPHER DOCK MENNONITE HIGH SCHOOL,
  Lansdale, PA... 853
CINCINNATI COUNTRY DAY SCHOOL, Cincinnati, OH 602
CINCINNATI HILLS CHRISTIAN ACADEMY, Cincinnati, OH 965
CISTERCIAN PREPARATORY SCHOOL, Irving, TX 672, **1330**
CITY & COUNTRY SCHOOL, New York, NY 378
CITYterm, Dobbs Ferry, NY 1096
CLAIRBOURN SCHOOL, San Gabriel, CA 1074
THE CLARK SCHOOL, Danvers, MA.. 778
COLD SPRING SCHOOL, New Haven, CT 153
THE COLLEGE PREPARATORY SCHOOL, Oakland, CA.............. 719
COLLEGIATE SCHOOL, Passaic Park, NJ 339
COLLEGIATE SCHOOL, New York, NY 378
COLLEGIATE SCHOOL, Richmond, VA 558
COLORADO ACADEMY, Denver, CO... 679
COLORADO ROCKY MOUNTAIN SCHOOL, Carbondale, CO 680
COLORADO TIMBERLINE ACADEMY, Durango, CO 1030
COLUMBIA ACADEMY, Columbia, TN.. 919
COLUMBIA ADVENTIST ACADEMY, Battleground, WA............. 1087
COLUMBIA GRAMMAR AND PREPARATORY SCHOOL,
  New York, NY... 379
THE COLUMBUS ACADEMY, Gahanna, OH 607
COLUMBUS SCHOOL FOR GIRLS, Columbus, OH 607, **1296**
COMMONWEALTH SCHOOL, Boston, MA..................................... 194
COMMUNITY PREPARATORY SCHOOL, Providence, RI............. 789
COMMUNITY SCHOOL, Teaneck, NJ 821, **1354**

Index of Schools   1437

THE COMMUNITY SCHOOL, Sun Valley, ID	684
COMMUNITY SCHOOL, St Louis, MO	639
THE COMMUNITY SCHOOL OF NAPLES, Naples, FL	479
CONCORD ACADEMY, Concord, MA	207
CONCORDIA LUTHERAN HIGH SCHOOL, Fort Wayne, IN	951
THE CONGRESSIONAL SCHOOLS OF VIRGINIA, Falls Church, VA	929
CONNELLY SCHOOL OF THE HOLY CHILD, Potomac, MD	314
CONVENT OF THE SACRED HEART, Greenwich, CT	138, **1292-3**
CONVENT OF THE SACRED HEART, New York, NY	380
CONVENT OF THE VISITATION SCHOOL, Mendota Heights, MN	632
COR JESU ACADEMY, St Louis, MO	988
CORLEARS SCHOOL, New York, NY	837
CORNELIA CONNELLY SCHOOL, Anaheim, CA	1048
THE CORWIN-RUSSELL SCHOOL AT BROCCOLI HALL, Sudbury, MA	784
COTTER HIGH SCHOOL AND JUNIOR HIGH SCHOOL, Winona, MN	985
THE COUNTRY DAY SCHOOL, Kearneysville, WV	938
COUNTRY DAY SCHOOL OF THE SACRED HEART, Bryn Mawr, PA	422
THE COUNTRY SCHOOL, Madison, CT	765
COUNTRY SCHOOL, Easton, MD	308
THE COVENANT SCHOOL, Charlottesville, VA	927
COVINGTON CATHOLIC HIGH SCHOOL, Park Hills, KY	902
CRANBROOK SCHOOLS, Bloomfield Hills, MI	592, **1136-7**
CRANE COUNTRY DAY SCHOOL, Santa Barbara, CA	1076
CREFELD SCHOOL, Philadelphia, PA	440
CRESCENT CITY BAPTIST SCHOOL, Metairie, LA	1000
CROSSROADS SCHOOL, St Louis, MO	989
CROSSROADS SCHOOL, Paoli, PA	857
CROSSROADS SCHOOL, Santa Monica, CA	746
CRYSTAL SPRINGS UPLANDS SCHOOL, Hillsborough, CA	702
THE CULVER ACADEMIES, Culver, IN	582
CURREY INGRAM ACADEMY, Brentwood, TN	917
CURTIS SCHOOL, Los Angeles, CA	709
CUSHING ACADEMY, Ashburnham, MA	189
CUSHMAN SCHOOL, Miami, FL	879
CUYAHOGA VALLEY CHRISTIAN ACADEMY, Cuyahoga Falls, OH	968

DADE CHRISTIAN SCHOOL, Miami, FL.. 879
DALTON SCHOOL, New York, NY.. 381
DANA HALL SCHOOL, Wellesley, MA 245, **1294-5**
DARLINGTON SCHOOL, Rome, GA 502, **1138-9**
DARROW SCHOOL, New Lebanon, NY................................. 371, **1140-1**
DAVID LIPSCOMB CAMPUS SCHOOL, Nashville, TN 922
DE LA SALLE COLLEGIATE HIGH SCHOOL, Warren, MI............ 962
DE LA SALLE HIGH SCHOOL, Minneapolis, MN 983
DE LA SALLE INSTITUTE, Chicago, IL 941
DECK HOUSE SCHOOL, Edgecomb, ME 775
DEDHAM COUNTRY DAY SCHOOL, Dedham, MA 212
DEERFIELD ACADEMY, Deerfield, MA 214
DEERFIELD-WINDSOR SCHOOL, Albany, GA................................ 887
DELAWARE COUNTY CHRISTIAN SCHOOL,
  Newtown Square, PA... 857
DELAWARE VALLEY FRIENDS SCHOOL, Paoli, PA 857
DELBARTON SCHOOL, Morristown, NJ 336
DELPHI ACADEMY, Milton, MA 782
DELPHIAN SCHOOL, Sheridan, OR.. 1086
DeMATHA CATHOLIC HIGH SCHOOL, Hyattsville, MD 808
DENVER ACADEMY, Denver, CO... 1027
THE DENVER CAMPUS FOR JEWISH EDUCATION,
  Denver, CO.. 1027
DENVER INTERNATIONAL SCHOOL, Denver, CO 1028
DENVER LUTHERAN HIGH SCHOOL, Denver, CO...................... 1028
DERBY ACADEMY, Hingham, MA 224
THE DERRYFIELD SCHOOL, Manchester, NH 261, **1133**
DeSMET JESUIT HIGH SCHOOL, St Louis, MO............................... 989
DETROIT COUNTRY DAY SCHOOL,
  Beverly Hills, MI 594, **1142-3**
DETROIT WALDORF SCHOOL, Detroit, MI 955
DEVEREUX FOUNDATION, Villanova, PA **1355**
DEVON PREPARATORY SCHOOL, Devon, PA................................. 849
DEXTER SCHOOL, Brookline, MA.. 201, **1331**
DOANE STUART SCHOOL, Albany, NY 351
DOMINICAN ACADEMY, New York, NY 837
DOMINICAN HIGH SCHOOL, Whitefish Bay, WI 976
DONNA KLEIN JEWISH ACADEMY, Boca Raton, FL 870
THE DONOHO SCHOOL, Anniston, AL... 461
THE DORRIS-EATON SCHOOL, Walnut Creek, CA 1080
DOWLING HIGH SCHOOL, West Des Moines, IA 979

Index of Schools

DREW COLLEGE PREPARATORY SCHOOL,
San Francisco, CA.. 731
DRISCOLL CATHOLIC HIGH SCHOOL, Addison, IL 939
DUBLIN SCHOOL, Dublin, NH... 258, **1144-5**
DUCHESNE ACADEMY OF THE SACRED HEART,
Houston, TX.. 1018
THE DUNHAM SCHOOL, Baton Rouge, LA.. 998
DUNN SCHOOL, Los Olivos, CA.. 717
DURHAM ACADEMY, Durham, NC... 515
DUTCHESS DAY SCHOOL, Millbrook, NY.. 369
DWIGHT-ENGLEWOOD SCHOOL, Englewood, NJ 326
THE DWIGHT SCHOOL, New York, NY... 382

EAGLE HILL SCHOOL, Greenwich, CT................................. 764, **1356-7**
EAGLE HILL SCHOOL, Hardwick, MA 223, **1358-9**
EAGLE HILL-SOUTHPORT, Southport, CT 769, **1353**
EAGLEBROOK SCHOOL, Deerfield, MA 215, **1332-3**
EAST BAY FRENCH-AMERICAN SCHOOL, Berkeley, CA.......... 1050
EAST BAY WALDORF SCHOOL, El Sobrante, CA 1053
EAST CATHOLIC HIGH SCHOOL, Manchester, CT 766
EAST WOODS SCHOOL, Oyster Bay, NY... 400
EDGEWOOD HIGH SCHOOL, Madison, WI 974
ELDER HIGH SCHOOL, Cincinnati, OH 965
ELDORADO-EMERSON SCHOOL, Orange, CA............................... 723
ELGIN ACADEMY, Elgin, IL.. 577, **1133**
ELISABETH MORROW SCHOOL, Englewood, NJ......................... 327
ELIZABETH SETON HIGH SCHOOL, Bladensburg, MD 805
ELLIS SCHOOL, Pittsburgh, PA.. 447
THE ELLISON SCHOOL, Vineland, NJ 821
ELMWOOD FRANKLIN SCHOOL, Buffalo, NY............................... 359
EMERSON PREPARATORY SCHOOL, Washington, DC 288
EMMA WILLARD SCHOOL, Troy, NY 415, **1297**
ENFIELD MONTESSORI SCHOOL, Enfield, CT.............................. 764
EPIPHANY SCHOOL, Dorchester, MA 779
EPIPHANY SCHOOL, Seattle, WA... 1088
EPISCOPAL ACADEMY, Merion, PA.. 440
EPISCOPAL DAY SCHOOL, Augusta, GA.. 891
EPISCOPAL HIGH SCHOOL, Bellaire, TX........................... 1010, **1146**
EPISCOPAL HIGH SCHOOL, Jacksonville, FL 472
EPISCOPAL HIGH SCHOOL, Baton Rouge, LA............................... 649
EPISCOPAL HIGH SCHOOL, Alexandria, VA 543, **1147**
EPISCOPAL SCHOOL OF ACADIANA, Cade, LA 998

EPISCOPAL SCHOOL OF DALLAS, Dallas, TX 1011
EPISCOPAL SCHOOL OF KNOXVILLE, Knoxville, TN 921
ERIE DAY SCHOOL, Erie, PA 850
ETHEL WALKER SCHOOL, Simsbury, CT 161, **1298**
ETHICAL CULTURE FIELDSTON SCHOOL, Riverdale, NY 353
ETON ACADEMY, Birmingham, MI 954
EVANGELICAL CHRISTIAN SCHOOL, Cordova, TN 919
EVANSVILLE DAY SCHOOL, Evansville, IN 583
THE EVERGREEN SCHOOL, Shoreline, WA 1090
EZRA ACADEMY, Woodbridge, CT 773

FAIRFIELD COLLEGE PREPARATORY SCHOOL,
   Fairfield, CT 135
FAIRFIELD COUNTRY DAY SCHOOL, Fairfield, CT 136
FAIRMONT PRIVATE SCHOOLS, Anaheim, CA 1049
FAITH HERITAGE SCHOOL, Syracuse, NY 844
FAITH LUTHERAN JR./SR. HIGH SCHOOL, Las Vegas, NV 1039
FALK SCHOOL, Pittsburgh, PA 448
FALMOUTH ACADEMY, Falmouth, MA 218
FAR BROOK SCHOOL, Short Hills, NJ 346, **1148-9**
FAR HILLS COUNTRY DAY SCHOOL, Far Hills, NJ 327
FATHER JUDGE HIGH SCHOOL, Philadelphia, PA 858
FATHER RYAN HIGH SCHOOL, Nashville, TN 540
FAY SCHOOL, Southborough, MA 240
FAYERWEATHER STREET SCHOOL, Cambridge, MA 205
FAYETTEVILLE ACADEMY, Fayetteville, NC 905
FENN SCHOOL, Concord, MA 208
FENSTER SCHOOL, Tucson, AZ 690
FENWICK HIGH SCHOOL, Oak Park, IL 948
FESSENDEN SCHOOL, West Newton, MA 233
THE FIELD SCHOOL, Washington, DC 795
FIRST PRESBYTERIAN DAY SCHOOL, Macon, GA 894
FISHBURNE MILITARY SCHOOL, Waynesboro, VA 566, **1334**
FLINT HILL SCHOOL, Oakton, VA 934, **1154**
FLORIDA AIR ACADEMY, Melbourne, FL 475, **1150-1**
FOOTE SCHOOL, New Haven, CT 153
FOOTHILL COUNTRY DAY SCHOOL, Claremont, CA 699
FOOTHILLS ACADEMY, Wheat Ridge, CO 1031
FORDHAM PREPARATORY SCHOOL, Bronx, NY 354, **1335**
FOREST RIDGE ACADEMY, Schererville, IN 953
FORK UNION MILITARY ACADEMY, Fork Union, VA 549, **1340**
FORMAN SCHOOL, Litchfield, CT 148

Index of Schools

FORSYTH COUNTRY DAY SCHOOL, Lewisville, NC 518
FORSYTH SCHOOL, St Louis, MO 639
FORT LAUDERDALE PREPARATORY SCHOOL,
   Fort Lauderdale, FL 873
FORT WORTH ACADEMY, Fort Worth, TX 1016
FORT WORTH COUNTRY DAY SCHOOL, Fort Worth, TX 667
FOUNTAIN VALLEY SCHOOL, Colorado Springs, CO 678
FOX CHAPEL COUNTRY DAY SCHOOL, Pittsburgh, PA 861
FOX RIVER COUNTRY DAY SCHOOL, Elgin, IL 577
FOX VALLEY LUTHERAN ACADEMY, Elgin, IL 945
FOXCROFT SCHOOL, Middleburg, VA 554, **1299**
FRANCIS W. PARKER SCHOOL, Chicago, IL 571
FRANKLIN ROAD ACADEMY, Nashville, TN 922
FREDERICA ACADEMY, St Simons Island, GA 897
FRENCH-AMERICAN INTERNATIONAL SCHOOL,
   San Francisco, CA 732
FRENCH-AMERICAN SCHOOL OF NEW YORK,
   Larchmont, NY 833
FRENCH INTERNATIONAL SCHOOL, Bethesda, MD 803
FRESNO ADVENTIST ACADEMY, Fresno, CA 1054
FRIENDS ACADEMY, North Dartmouth, MA 211
FRIENDS ACADEMY, Locust Valley, NY 367
FRIENDS' CENTRAL SCHOOL, Wynnewood, PA 458
FRIENDS SCHOOL, Baltimore, MD 299
FRIENDS SCHOOL HAVERFORD, Haverford, PA 426
FRIENDS SCHOOL MULLICA HILL, Mullica Hill, NJ 338
FRIENDS SCHOOL OF MINNESOTA, St Paul, MN 984
FRIENDS SCHOOL OF WILMINGTON, Wilmington, NC 911
FRIENDS SELECT SCHOOL, Philadelphia, PA 441
FRIENDSHIP CHRISTIAN SCHOOL, Lebanon, TN 921
FRYEBURG ACADEMY, Fryeburg, ME 181, **1152-3**
FUQUA SCHOOL, Farmville, VA 929

THE GALLOWAY SCHOOL, Atlanta, GA 888
GARRISON FOREST SCHOOL, Owings Mills, MD 311, **1300**
GASTON DAY SCHOOL, Gastonia, NC 906
GEM STATE ADVENTIST ACADEMY, Caldwell, ID 1032
GEORGE SCHOOL, Newtown, PA 436
GEORGE STEVENS ACADEMY, Blue Hill, ME 774
GEORGETOWN DAY SCHOOL, Washington, DC 288
GEORGIA CHRISTIAN SCHOOL, Valdosta, GA 899
GERMAN SCHOOL, Potomac, MD 810

GERMANTOWN ACADEMY, Fort Washington, PA	442
GERMANTOWN FRIENDS SCHOOL, Philadelphia, PA	443
GIBSON ISLAND COUNTRY SCHOOL, Pasadena, MD	312
GIBSON SCHOOL, Redford, MI	961
GILL ST. BERNARD'S SCHOOL, Gladstone, NJ	328
THE GILLISPIE SCHOOL, La Jolla, CA	1056
GILMAN SCHOOL, Baltimore, MD	299
GIRARD COLLEGE, Philadelphia, PA	859
GIRLS PREPARATORY SCHOOL, Chattanooga, TN	532, **1301**
GLADWYNE MONTESSORI SCHOOL, Gladwyne, PA	851
GLEN URQUHART SCHOOL, Beverly Farms, MA	777
GLENELG COUNTRY SCHOOL, Glenelg, MD	309
THE GLENHOLME SCHOOL, Washington, CT	771, **1362**
GONZAGA COLLEGE HIGH SCHOOL, Washington, DC	795
GONZAGA PREPARATORY SCHOOL, Spokane, WA	1091
GORDON SCHOOL, East Providence, RI	272
GOULD ACADEMY, Bethel, ME	179
GOVERNOR DUMMER ACADEMY, Byfield, MA	203, **1155**
THE GOW SCHOOL, South Wales, NY	410, **1360-1**
GRACE CHRISTIAN SCHOOL, Anchorage, AK	1047
GRACE CHURCH SCHOOL, New York, NY	383
GRACE DAY SCHOOL, Massapequa, NY	834
GRACE EPISCOPAL DAY SCHOOL, Kensington, MD	808
GRACE-ST. LUKE'S EPISCOPAL SCHOOL, Memphis, TN	536
GRALAND COUNTRY DAY SCHOOL, Denver, CO	680
THE GRAMMAR SCHOOL, Putney, VT	277
GRAND RAPIDS BAPTIST SCHOOLS, Grand Rapids, MI	956
GRAND RAPIDS CHRISTIAN SCHOOLS, Grand Rapids, MI	957
GRANDVIEW PREPARATORY SCHOOL, Boca Raton, FL	870
GREATER ATLANTA CHRISTIAN SCHOOL, Norcross, GA	896
GREEN ACRES SCHOOL, Rockville, MD	316
GREEN FIELDS COUNTRY DAY SCHOOL, Tucson, AZ	690
GREEN HEDGES SCHOOL, Vienna, VA	936
GREEN MEADOW WALDORF SCHOOL, Chestnut Ridge, NY	827
GREEN VALE SCHOOL, Glen Head, NY	831
GREENE STREET FRIENDS SCHOOL, Philadelphia, PA	444
GREENHILL SCHOOL, Addison, TX	663
GREENHILLS SCHOOL, Ann Arbor, MI	591
GREENS FARMS ACADEMY, Greens Farms, CT	174
GREENSBORO DAY SCHOOL, Greensboro, NC	516
GREENSBORO MONTESSORI SCHOOL, Greensboro, NC	907
GREENWICH ACADEMY, Greenwich, CT	139, **1296**

Index of Schools

GREENWICH COUNTRY DAY SCHOOL, Greenwich, CT.............. 140
GREENWOOD SCHOOL, Putney, VT.. 278
GRIER SCHOOL, Tyrone, PA... 454, **1302-3**
GROSSE POINTE ACADEMY, Grosse Pointe Farms, MI 595, **1156**
GROTON SCHOOL, Groton, MA 221
GROVE SCHOOL, Madison, CT... 766, **1157**
GROVES ACADEMY, St Louis Park, MN... 984
GRYMES MEMORIAL SCHOOL, Orange, VA.................................. 557
GULF STREAM SCHOOL, Gulf Stream, FL....................................... 470
GULLIVER SCHOOLS, Pinecrest, FL.. 476, **1158-9**
THE GUNNERY, Washington, CT... 170
GWYNEDD-MERCY ACADEMY, Gwynedd Valley, PA................... 852

HACKLEY SCHOOL, Tarrytown, NY 414, **1160-1**
HADDONFIELD FRIENDS SCHOOL, Haddonfield, NJ................... 815
HAMDEN HALL COUNTRY DAY SCHOOL, Hamden, CT.............. 154
HAMLIN SCHOOL, San Francisco, CA.. 733
HAMMOND SCHOOL, Columbia, SC 913
HAMPSHIRE COUNTRY SCHOOL, Rindge, NH 264, **1363**
HAMPTON ROADS ACADEMY, Newport News, VA....................... 556
HANAHAUOLI SCHOOL, Honolulu, HI.. 748
HAPPY VALLEY SCHOOL, Ojai, CA.. 721
HARBOR COUNTRY DAY SCHOOL, St James, NY........................ 409
HARBOR DAY SCHOOL, Corona del Mar, CA 701
THE HARBOR SCHOOL, Bethesda, MD 803
HARDING ACADEMY, Memphis, TN... 921
HARDING ACADEMY, Nashville, TN... 923
HARFORD DAY SCHOOL, Bel Air, MD 301
HARGRAVE MILITARY ACADEMY, Chatham, VA............... 547, **1162**
HARKER SCHOOL, San Jose, CA... 740
HARLEY SCHOOL, Rochester, NY... 406
HARPETH HALL SCHOOL, Nashville, TN 541
HARRELLS CHRISTIAN ACADEMY, Harrells, NC......................... 908
HARRISBURG ACADEMY, Wormleysburg, PA................................ 426
HARTFORD CHRISTIAN ACADEMY, West Hartford, CT............... 771
HARVARD-WESTLAKE SCHOOL, North Hollywood, CA.............. 709
THE HARVEY SCHOOL, Katonah, NY 365, **1163**
HATHAWAY BROWN SCHOOL, Shaker Heights, OH 612
HAVERFORD SCHOOL, Haverford, PA... 427
HAWAII PREPARATORY ACADEMY, Kamuela, HI 752
HAWKEN SCHOOL, Gates Mills, OH... 609
HAWTHORNE VALLEY SCHOOL, Ghent, NY 830

HAYFIELD MONTESSORI SCHOOL, Louisville, KY 900
HEAD-ROYCE SCHOOL, Oakland, CA... 720
HEADWATERS ACADEMY, Bozeman, MT 1032
HEATHWOOD HALL EPISCOPAL SCHOOL, Columbia, SC.......... 528
HEBREW ACADEMY, Huntington Beach, CA.................................. 1056
HEBREW HIGH SCHOOL OF NEW ENGLAND,
    West Hartford, CT... 772
HEBRON ACADEMY, Hebron, ME... 182, **1164**
THE HEISKELL SCHOOL, Atlanta, GA.. 492
HENDRICKS METHODIST DAY SCHOOL, Jacksonville, FL.......... 875
HERITAGE HALL SCHOOL, Oklahoma City, OK 658
THE HERITAGE SCHOOL, Newnan, GA.. 500
HEWITT SCHOOL, New York, NY 383
HICKORY DAY SCHOOL, Hickory, NC.. 908
HIGH MEADOWS SCHOOL, Roswell, GA.. 896
HIGHLAND SCHOOL, Warrenton, VA... 565
HIGHLANDS SCHOOL, Birmingham, AL.. 865
THE HILL SCHOOL, Pottstown, PA 451, **1165**
HILL SCHOOL, Middleburg, VA.. 555
HILL TOP PREPARATORY SCHOOL, Rosemont, PA....................... 862
HILLBROOK SCHOOL, Los Gatos, CA.. 716
HILLCREST LUTHERAN ACADEMY, Fergus Falls, MN................ 982
HILLSDALE ACADEMY, Hillsdale, MI..................................... 957, **1166**
HILLSIDE SCHOOL, Marlborough, MA... 229
HILLTOP COUNTRY DAY SCHOOL, Sparta, NJ............................... 821
HILLWOOD ACADEMIC DAY SCHOOL,
    San Francisco, CA... 733, **1167**
HILTON HEAD PREPARATORY SCHOOL,
    Hilton Head Island, SC 915
HOBGOOD ACADEMY, Hobgood, NC..................................... 909, **1172**
HOLDERNESS SCHOOL, Plymouth, NH 263
HOLLAND HALL SCHOOL, Tulsa, OK 659
HOLTON-ARMS SCHOOL, Bethesda, MD... 302
HOLY CHILD ACADEMY, Old Westbury, NY................................... 841
HOLY CHILD ACADEMY, Drexel Hill, PA... 849
HOLY CROSS HIGH SCHOOL, Delran, NJ 813
HOLY CROSS SCHOOL, New Orleans, LA 1000
HOLY FAMILY HIGH SCHOOL, Broomfield, CO............................ 1026
HOLY FAMILY SCHOOL, Fort Worth, TX... 1016
HOLY GHOST PREPARATORY SCHOOL, Bensalem, PA................ 848
HOLY NAME CENTRAL CATHOLIC
    JUNIOR/SENIOR HIGH SCHOOL, Worcester, MA...................... 786

Index of Schools

HOLY NAMES ACADEMY, Seattle, WA... 1089
HOLY NAMES HIGH SCHOOL, Oakland, CA................................ 1064
HOLY NATIVITY SCHOOL, Honolulu, HI 1080
HOLY SPIRIT EPISCOPAL SCHOOL, Houston, TX 1019
HOLY TRINITY EPISCOPAL ACADEMY, Melbourne, FL.............. 878
HOLY TRINITY EPISCOPAL DAY SCHOOL, Glenn Dale, MD 807
HOLY TRINITY HIGH SCHOOL, Chicago, IL 942
HOOSAC SCHOOL, Hoosick, NY 364
HOPKINS SCHOOL, New Haven, CT 154
HORACE MANN SCHOOL, Riverdale, NY 355
HORIZONS SCHOOL, Atlanta, GA 889
THE HOTCHKISS SCHOOL, Lakeville, CT 147, **1168-9**
HOUGHTON ACADEMY, Houghton, NY 831
HOUSTON ACADEMY, Dothan, AL 462
HOWE MILITARY SCHOOL, Howe, IN 585, **1170-1**
THE HUDSON SCHOOL, Hoboken, NJ 816, **1173**
THE HUN SCHOOL OF PRINCETON, Princeton, NJ 342, **1174-5**
HUNTER McGUIRE SCHOOL, Verona, VA 936
HUTCHISON SCHOOL, Memphis, TN 537
HYDE PARK BAPTIST SCHOOLS, Austin, TX 1009
HYDE SCHOOL AT BATH, Bath, ME 178, **1176-7**
HYDE SCHOOL AT WOODSTOCK, Woodstock, CT 176, **1176-7**
HYMAN BRAND HEBREW ACADEMY, Overland Park, KS 980

IDYLLWILD ARTS ACADEMY, Idyllwild, CA 704
ILLIANA CHRISTIAN HIGH SCHOOL, Lansing, IL 946
IMMACULATE CONCEPTION ACADEMY,
 San Francisco, CA 1072
IMMACULATE HEART HIGH SCHOOL, Tucson, AZ 691
IMMACULATE HIGH SCHOOL, Danbury, CT 764
IMMANUEL LUTHERAN HIGH SCHOOL, Eau Claire, WI 973
INCARNATE WORD ACADEMY, St Louis, MO 989
INCARNATE WORD ACADEMY, Corpus Christi, TX 1011
THE INDEPENDENCE SCHOOL, Newark, DE 793
THE INDEPENDENT DAY SCHOOL, Middlefield, CT 150, **1166**
THE INDEPENDENT SCHOOL, Wichita, KS 981
INDIAN MOUNTAIN SCHOOL, Lakeville, CT 148
INDIAN SPRINGS SCHOOL, Indian Springs, AL 461
INTERLOCHEN ARTS ACADEMY, Interlochen, MI 597
THE INTERNATIONAL SCHOOL, Portland, OR 1084
THE INTERNATIONAL SCHOOL OF MINNESOTA,
 Eden Prairie, MN 628

1446   The Handbook of Private Schools

INTERNATIONAL SCHOOL OF THE PENINSULA,
Palo Alto, CA 724
IOLANI SCHOOL, Honolulu, HI 749
IONA PREPARATORY SCHOOL, New Rochelle, NY 835
ISIDORE NEWMAN SCHOOL, New Orleans, LA 652
ISLAND SCHOOL, Lihue, HI 1082

JACKSON ACADEMY, Jackson, MS 1005
JACKSON PREPARATORY SCHOOL, Jackson, MS 1005
JACKSONVILLE COUNTRY DAY SCHOOL, Jacksonville, FL 472
JAMES RIVER DAY SCHOOL, Lynchburg, VA 932
JEROME LIPPMAN JEWISH COMMUNITY DAY SCHOOL,
Akron, OH 963
JESUIT COLLEGE PREPARATORY SCHOOL OF DALLAS,
Dallas, TX 664
JESUIT HIGH SCHOOL, Carmichael, CA 1052
JESUIT HIGH SCHOOL, Tampa, FL 886
JESUIT HIGH SCHOOL, New Orleans, LA 1000
JESUIT HIGH SCHOOL, Portland, OR 1085
JOHN BAPST MEMORIAL HIGH SCHOOL, Bangor, ME 773
JOHN BURROUGHS SCHOOL, St Louis, MO 640
JOHN CARROLL SCHOOL, Bel Air, MD 802
THE JOHN COOPER SCHOOL, The Woodlands, TX 670, **1184**
JOHN F. KENNEDY CATHOLIC HIGH SCHOOL, Somers, NY 843
JOHN F. KENNEDY MEMORIAL HIGH SCHOOL,
Seattle, WA 1089
JOHN THOMAS DYE SCHOOL, Los Angeles, CA 710
JOHN W. HALLAHAN CATHOLIC GIRLS' HIGH SCHOOL,
Philadelphia, PA 859
JOHNSTOWN CHRISTIAN SCHOOL, Hollsopple, PA 853
JOLIET CATHOLIC ACADEMY, Joliet, IL 945
JULIE ROHR ACADEMY, Sarasota, FL 884
JUNIPERO SERRA HIGH SCHOOL, San Mateo, CA 1075
JUSTIN-SIENA HIGH SCHOOL, Napa, CA 1062

KALAMAZOO ACADEMY, Portage, MI 960
KATHERINE DELMAR BURKE SCHOOL, San Francisco, CA 734
KEITH SCHOOL, Rockford, IL 580
KENSINGTON ACADEMY, Beverly Hills, MI 954
KENT PLACE SCHOOL, Summit, NJ 347
KENT SCHOOL, Chestertown, MD 806
KENT SCHOOL, Kent, CT 145, **1178-9**

Index of Schools

KENTS HILL SCHOOL, Kents Hill, ME 183, **1180-1**
KENTUCKY COUNTRY DAY SCHOOL, Louisville, KY 507
KERR-VANCE ACADEMY, Henderson, NC 908
KESWICK CHRISTIAN SCHOOL, St Petersburg, FL 883
THE KEW-FOREST SCHOOL, Forest Hills, NY 404
KEY SCHOOL, Annapolis, MD 295
KEYSTONE SCHOOL, San Antonio, TX 673
KEYSTONE SCHOOLS, Fort Wayne, IN 952
THE KILDONAN SCHOOL, Amenia, NY 352, **1364-5**
KIMBALL UNION ACADEMY, Meriden, NH 261, **1185**
KING & LOW-HEYWOOD THOMAS SCHOOL,
   Stamford, CT 165, **1182-3**
KING GEORGE SCHOOL, Sutton, VT 792
THE KING'S ACADEMY, Seymour, TN 924
KINGSBURY SCHOOL, Oxford, MI 598
KINGSLEY MONTESSORI SCHOOL, Boston, MA 195
KINGSWOOD-OXFORD SCHOOL, West Hartford, CT 142
KINKAID SCHOOL, Houston, TX 671
KISKI SCHOOL, Saltsburg, PA 452, **1336-7**
KNOX SCHOOL, St James, NY 410, **1188**

LA JOLLA COUNTRY DAY SCHOOL, La Jolla, CA 706
LA LUMIERE SCHOOL, La Porte, IN 589
LA SALLE COLLEGE HIGH SCHOOL, Wyndmoor, PA 444
LA SALLE HIGH SCHOOL, Miami, FL 477
LA SALLE INSTITUTE, Troy, NY 844
LA SCUOLA D'ITALIA, New York, NY 384
THE LAB SCHOOL OF WASHINGTON, Washington, DC 796
LADYWOOD HIGH SCHOOL, Livonia, MI 958
LaGRANGE ACADEMY, LaGrange, GA 893
LAGUNA BLANCA SCHOOL, Santa Barbara, CA 745
LAKE FOREST ACADEMY, Lake Forest, IL 579
LAKE FOREST COUNTRY DAY SCHOOL, Lake Forest, IL 579
LAKE HIGHLAND PREPARATORY SCHOOL, Orlando, FL 882
LAKE RIDGE ACADEMY, North Ridgeville, OH 611
LAKEHILL PREPARATORY SCHOOL, Dallas, TX 1012
LAKELAND CHRISTIAN SCHOOL, Lakeland, FL 876
LAKESIDE LUTHERAN HIGH SCHOOL, Lake Mills, WI 974
LAKESIDE SCHOOL, Seattle, WA 756
THE LAMPLIGHTER SCHOOL, Dallas, TX 665, **1186-7**
LANAKILA BAPTIST SCHOOLS, Waipahu, HI 1082
LANCASTER COUNTRY DAY SCHOOL, Lancaster, PA 429

LANDMARK CHRISTIAN SCHOOL, Fairburn, GA.......................... 892
LANDMARK SCHOOL, Prides Crossing, MA...................... 192, **1366-7**
LANDON SCHOOL, Bethesda, MD.. 303, **1328**
THE LANGLEY SCHOOL, McLean, VA................................... 551, **1189**
LANSING CATHOLIC CENTRAL HIGH SCHOOL,
  Lansing, MI.. 958
LATIN SCHOOL OF CHICAGO, Chicago, IL............................... 572
LAUREL HILL SCHOOL, East Setauket, NY................................ 829
LAUREL SCHOOL, Shaker Heights, OH....................................... 612
LAURENCE SCHOOL, Valley Glen, CA...................................... 1079
LAUSANNE COLLEGIATE SCHOOL, Memphis, TN 537
LAWRENCE ACADEMY, Groton, MA...................................... 222, **1190**
LAWRENCE SCHOOL, Broadview Heights, OH........................... 964
LAWRENCE WOODMERE ACADEMY, Woodmere, NY............. 417
LAWRENCEVILLE SCHOOL, Lawrenceville, NJ.................... 331, **1191**
LE JARDIN WINDWARD OAHU ACADEMY, Kailua, HI............ 752
LE LYCEE FRANCAIS DE LOS ANGELES, Los Angeles, CA 711
THE LEARNING PROJECT ELEMENTARY SCHOOL,
  Boston, MA.. 196
LEELANAU SCHOOL, Glen Arbor, MI.. 597
LEONARD HALL JUNIOR NAVAL ACADEMY,
  Leonardtown, MD... 809
LEXINGTON CHRISTIAN ACADEMY, Lexington, MA........ 225, **1194**
LEXINGTON MONTESSORI SCHOOL, Lexington, MA.............. 781
THE LEXINGTON SCHOOL, Lexington, KY............................... 505
LIBERTY SCHOOL, Blue Hill, ME.. 774
LICK-WILMERDING HIGH SCHOOL, San Francisco, CA............ 735
LIMA CENTRAL CATHOLIC HIGH SCHOOL, Lima, OH............ 969
LINCOLN SCHOOL, Providence, RI... 272
LINDEN HALL SCHOOL FOR GIRLS, Lititz, PA................... 431, **1304**
LINDEN HILL SCHOOL, Northfield, MA............................... 235, **1368**
LINSLY SCHOOL, Wheeling, WV.. 569
LINTON HALL SCHOOL, Bristow, VA.. 927
LITTLE KESWICK SCHOOL, Keswick, VA................................ 931
LITTLE RED SCHOOL HOUSE AND
  ELISABETH IRWIN HIGH SCHOOL, New York, NY 385
THE LITTLE SCHOOL, Bellevue, WA.. 1087
LIVE OAK SCHOOL, San Francisco, CA..................................... 1073
THE LOGAN SCHOOL FOR CREATIVE LEARNING,
  Denver, CO.. 1028
LOGOS SCHOOL, St Louis, MO 990

Index of Schools

LONG ISLAND LUTHERAN MIDDLE AND HIGH SCHOOL,
  Brookville, NY 825
LONG ISLAND SCHOOL FOR THE GIFTED,
  Huntington Station, NY 831
THE LONG RIDGE SCHOOL, Stamford, CT 165
LONG TRAIL SCHOOL, Dorset, VT 276
LOOMIS CHAFFEE SCHOOL, Windsor, CT 175, **1192-3**
LOUDOUN COUNTRY DAY SCHOOL, Leesburg, VA 932
LOUISE S. McGEHEE SCHOOL, New Orleans, LA 653
LOUISVILLE COLLEGIATE SCHOOL, Louisville, KY 507
THE LOVETT SCHOOL, Atlanta, GA 493, **1195**
LOWCOUNTRY DAY SCHOOL, Pawleys Island, SC 916
LOWELL WHITEMAN SCHOOL, Steamboat Springs, CO 682
LOYOLA ACADEMY, Wilmette, IL 950
LOYOLA BLAKEFIELD, Towson, MD 812
LOYOLA COLLEGE PREPARATORY SCHOOL,
  Shreveport, LA 1003
LOYOLA HIGH SCHOOL, Los Angeles, CA 1059
LOYOLA SACRED HEART CATHOLIC HIGH SCHOOL,
  Missoula, MT 1033
LOYOLA SCHOOL, New York, NY 385
LUSTRE CHRISTIAN HIGH SCHOOL, Frazer, MT 1032
LUTHER HIGH SCHOOL NORTH, Chicago, IL 942
LUTHER HIGH SCHOOL SOUTH, Chicago, IL 942
LUTHERAN HIGH SCHOOL, La Verne, CA 1056
LUTHERAN HIGH SCHOOL, Indianapolis, IN 953
LUTHERAN HIGH SCHOOL, Kansas City, MO 987
LUTHERAN HIGH SCHOOL WEST, Rocky River, OH 971
LYCEE FRANCAIS DE NEW YORK, New York, NY 386, **1196-7**
LYCEUM KENNEDY, New York, NY 386
LYMAN WARD MILITARY ACADEMY, Camp Hill, AL 865
LYNDON INSTITUTE, Lyndon Center, VT 790

THE MacDUFFIE SCHOOL, Springfield, MA 242, **1198**
MACLAY SCHOOL, Tallahassee, FL 486
MADEIRA SCHOOL, McLean, VA 552
MADISON ACADEMY, Madison, AL 866
MAGNIFICAT HIGH SCHOOL, Rocky River, OH 971
MAHARISHI SCHOOL OF THE AGE OF ENLIGHTENMENT,
  Fairfield, IA 979
MAINE CENTRAL INSTITUTE, Pittsfield, ME 184, **1199**
MAINE COAST SEMESTER, Wiscasset, ME 1095

MALDEN CATHOLIC HIGH SCHOOL, Malden, MA 782
MALVERN PREPARATORY SCHOOL, Malvern, PA 854
MANHATTAN COUNTRY SCHOOL, New York, NY 387
MANHATTAN DAY SCHOOL, New York, NY 838
MANLIUS PEBBLE HILL SCHOOL, DeWitt, NY 413
MANZANO DAY SCHOOL, Albuquerque, NM 692
MAPLEBROOK SCHOOL, Amenia, NY 823
MARANATHA CHRISTIAN ACADEMY, Brooklyn Park, MN 981
MARANATHA HIGH SCHOOL, Pasadena, CA 1067
MARBURN ACADEMY, Columbus, OH 968
MARET SCHOOL, Washington, DC 289
MARIAN CATHOLIC HIGH SCHOOL, Chicago Heights, IL 575
MARIANAPOLIS PREPARATORY SCHOOL,
   Thompson, CT 168, **1202**
MARIN ACADEMY, San Rafael, CA 743
MARIN COUNTRY DAY SCHOOL, Corte Madera, CA 702
MARIN PRIMARY AND MIDDLE SCHOOL, Larkspur, CA 1057
MARINE MILITARY ACADEMY, Harlingen, TX 669
MARION MILITARY INSTITUTE, Marion, AL 867
MARIST SCHOOL, Atlanta, GA 493
MARLBOROUGH SCHOOL, Los Angeles, CA 711
MARQUETTE UNIVERSITY HIGH SCHOOL, Milwaukee, WI 975
MARS HILL BIBLE SCHOOL, Florence, AL 866
MARSHALL SCHOOL, Duluth, MN 982
MARTIN LUTHER HIGH SCHOOL, Northrop, MN 984
MARTIN LUTHER HIGH SCHOOL, Maspeth, NY 833
THE MARVELWOOD SCHOOL, Kent, CT 146, **1200-1**
MARY INSTITUTE AND SAINT LOUIS
   COUNTRY DAY SCHOOL, St Louis, MO 640, **1203**
THE MARY LOUIS ACADEMY, Jamaica Estates, NY 832
MARYKNOLL SCHOOL, Honolulu, HI 1081
MARYMOUNT HIGH SCHOOL, Los Angeles, CA 712
MARYMOUNT OF SANTA BARBARA, Santa Barbara, CA 1076
MARYMOUNT SCHOOL, New York, NY 388
MARYVALE PREPARATORY SCHOOL, Brooklandville, MD 805
MASON PREPARATORY SCHOOL, Charleston, SC 912
MASSANUTTEN MILITARY ACADEMY, Woodstock, VA 567
THE MASTERS SCHOOL, Dobbs Ferry, NY 363, **1204-5**
THE MASTER'S SCHOOL, West Simsbury, CT 162
MATER DEI HIGH SCHOOL, Santa Ana, CA 1076
MAUMEE VALLEY COUNTRY DAY SCHOOL, Toledo, OH 614
MAYER LUTHERAN HIGH SCHOOL, Mayer, MN 983

MAYFIELD JUNIOR SCHOOL, Pasadena, CA.................................. 1067
MAYFIELD SENIOR SCHOOL, Pasadena, CA.................................. 1067
McCALLIE SCHOOL, Chattanooga, TN 533, **1338-9**
McCURDY SCHOOL, Espanola, NM 1042
McDONOGH SCHOOL, Owings Mills, MD 312
McGILL-TOOLEN CATHOLIC HIGH SCHOOL, Mobile, AL.......... 867
McLEAN SCHOOL OF MARYLAND, Potomac, MD 315, **1206**
McQUAID JESUIT HIGH SCHOOL, Rochester, NY 842
MEAD HALL EPISCOPAL DAY SCHOOL, Aiken, SC..................... 912
MEAD SCHOOL, Stamford, CT.. 770
MEADOWBROOK SCHOOL, Weston, MA 247
MEADOWBROOK SCHOOL, Meadowbrook, PA 432
THE MEADOWS SCHOOL, Las Vegas, NV 1040
MEDIA-PROVIDENCE FRIENDS SCHOOL, Media, PA 855
THE MEETING SCHOOL, Rindge, NH 265
THE MELROSE SCHOOL, Brewster, NY 823
MELVIN J. BERMAN HEBREW ACADEMY, Rockville, MD 811
MEMPHIS UNIVERSITY SCHOOL, Memphis, TN 538
MENAUL SCHOOL, Albuquerque, NM 1041
MENLO SCHOOL, Atherton, CA..698, **1207**
MERCERSBURG ACADEMY, Mercersburg, PA 433, **1208**
MERCY CROSS HIGH SCHOOL, Biloxi, MS 1004
MERCY HIGH SCHOOL, Red Bluff, CA 1069
MERCY HIGH SCHOOL, San Francisco, CA................................... 1073
MERCY HIGH SCHOOL, Middletown, CT 767
MERCY HIGH SCHOOL, Baltimore, MD 800
MERCY HIGH SCHOOL, Farmington Hills, MI 956
MERCYMOUNT COUNTRY DAY SCHOOL, Cumberland, RI........ 788
MERION MERCY ACADEMY, Merion Station, PA.......................... 855
MESSIAH LUTHERAN SCHOOL, Lincoln, NE................................ 995
METAIRIE PARK COUNTRY DAY SCHOOL, Metairie, LA............ 649
METROPOLITAN MONTESSORI SCHOOL, New York, NY 838
METROPOLITAN SCHOOL, St Louis, MO 990
MIAMI COUNTRY DAY SCHOOL, Miami, FL................................. 477
MIAMI VALLEY SCHOOL, Dayton, OH 608
MICHIGAN LUTHERAN SEMINARY, Saginaw, MI 962
MID-PACIFIC INSTITUTE, Honolulu, HI.. 749
MIDDLESEX SCHOOL, Concord, MA 209
MIDLAND SCHOOL, Los Olivos, CA 718
MILLBROOK SCHOOL, Millbrook, NY 369
MILO ADVENTIST ACADEMY, Days Creek, OR 1083
MILTON ACADEMY, Milton, MA... 230

MILTON HERSHEY SCHOOL, Hershey, PA 852
MILWAUKEE LUTHERAN HIGH SCHOOL, Milwaukee, WI 975
MINNEHAHA ACADEMY, Minneapolis, MN 631
THE MIRMAN SCHOOL, Los Angeles, CA...................................... 713
MISS HALL'S SCHOOL, Pittsfield, MA 237, **1305**
MISS PORTER'S SCHOOL, Farmington, CT 137
MISSOURI MILITARY ACADEMY, Mexico, MO 637, **1341**
MMI PREPARATORY SCHOOL, Freeland, PA 425
MONSIGNOR JOHN R. HACKETT
   CATHOLIC CENTRAL HIGH SCHOOL, Kalamazoo, MI 958
MONTCLAIR ACADEMY, Denver, CO 1029
MONTCLAIR COOPERATIVE SCHOOL, Montclair, NJ 818
MONTCLAIR KIMBERLEY ACADEMY, Montclair, NJ 333
MONTE CASSINO SCHOOL, Tulsa, OK 1008
MONTE VISTA CHRISTIAN SCHOOL, Watsonville, CA 747
MONTESSORI EDUCARE SCHOOL, Newton Centre, MA 783
THE MONTGOMERY ACADEMY, Montgomery, AL 465
MONTGOMERY BELL ACADEMY, Nashville, TN 542
MONTGOMERY SCHOOL, Chester Springs, PA 423
MONTINI CATHOLIC HIGH SCHOOL, Lombard, IL 947
MONTROSE SCHOOL, Natick, MA 782
MONTVERDE ACADEMY, Montverde, FL 880
MOORELAND HILL SCHOOL, Kensington, CT 144
MOORESTOWN FRIENDS SCHOOL, Moorestown, NJ 334
MORAVIAN ACADEMY, Bethlehem, PA 419, **1209**
MOREAU CATHOLIC HIGH SCHOOL, Hayward, CA 1055
MORGAN PARK ACADEMY, Chicago, IL 573
MORRISTOWN-BEARD SCHOOL, Morristown, NJ 336, **1214**
MOSES BROWN SCHOOL, Providence, RI 273, **1210-1**
MOUNT ASSISI ACADEMY, Lemont, IL 946
MOUNT AVIAT ACADEMY, Childs, MD 806
MOUNT CARMEL ACADEMY, New Orleans, LA 1001
MOUNT DE CHANTAL VISITATION ACADEMY,
   Wheeling, WV 569
MOUNT DE SALES ACADEMY, Macon, GA 894
MOUNT MICHAEL BENEDICTINE HIGH SCHOOL,
   Elkhorn, NE 645
MOUNT SAINT CHARLES ACADEMY, Woonsocket, RI 789
MOUNT ST. JOSEPH ACADEMY, Buffalo, NY 826
MOUNT SAINT JOSEPH ACADEMY, Flourtown, PA 850
MOUNT SAINT JOSEPH ACADEMY, Rutland, VT 791
MOUNT ST. JOSEPH HIGH SCHOOL, Baltimore, MD 801

Index of Schools

MOUNT ST. MARY ACADEMY, Little Rock, AR 997
MOUNT TAMALPAIS SCHOOL, Mill Valley, CA........................... 1061
MOUNT VERNON PRESBYTERIAN SCHOOL, Atlanta, GA 889
THE MOUNTAIN SCHOOL, Vershire, VT....................................... 1095

NARDIN ACADEMY, Buffalo, NY.. 827
NASHOBA BROOKS SCHOOL, Concord, MA................................. 210
NATIONAL CATHEDRAL SCHOOL, Washington, DC 290
NATIONAL PRESBYTERIAN SCHOOL, Washington, DC 796
NATIONAL SPORTS ACADEMY, Lake Placid, NY 832
NAWA ACADEMY, French Gulch, CA 1054
NAZARETH ACADEMY HIGH SCHOOL,
 Philadelphia, PA 859, **1306**
NERINX HALL, Webster Groves, MO.. 994
NESKOWIN VALLEY SCHOOL, Neskowin, OR 1084
NEW CANAAN COUNTRY SCHOOL, New Canaan, CT................. 151
NEW CITY SCHOOL, St Louis, MO 990
THE NEW COMMUNITY SCHOOL, Richmond, VA 935
NEW GARDEN FRIENDS SCHOOL, Greensboro, NC 907
NEW HAMPTON SCHOOL, New Hampton, NH.................. 262, **1212-3**
NEW HAVEN HEBREW DAY SCHOOL, Orange, CT 768
NEW MEXICO MILITARY INSTITUTE, Roswell, NM 1043
NEW SCHOOL OF ORLANDO, Orlando, FL 882
NEW YORK MILITARY ACADEMY,
 Cornwall-on-Hudson, NY 361, **1215**
NEWGRANGE SCHOOL, Hamilton, NJ 816
THE NEWMAN SCHOOL, Boston, MA.. 777
NEWPORT SCHOOL, Silver Spring, MD 319
NEWTON COUNTRY DAY SCHOOL OF THE SACRED HEART,
 Newton, MA.. 234
NEWTOWN FRIENDS SCHOOL, Newtown, PA............................... 437
NICHOLS SCHOOL, Buffalo, NY 360
NIGHTINGALE-BAMFORD SCHOOL, New York, NY 388
NOBLE AND GREENOUGH SCHOOL, Dedham, MA 212, **1216**
NOLAN CATHOLIC HIGH SCHOOL, Fort Worth, TX 1017
NORFOLK ACADEMY, Norfolk, VA 557
THE NORTH BROWARD PREPARATORY SCHOOLS,
 Coconut Creek, FL 872
NORTH COBB CHRISTIAN SCHOOL, Kennesaw, GA.................... 893
NORTH COUNTRY SCHOOL, Lake Placid, NY 366, **1217**
NORTH CROSS SCHOOL, Roanoke, VA 561
NORTH RALEIGH COUNTRY DAY SCHOOL, Raleigh, NC 910

NORTH SHORE COUNTRY DAY SCHOOL, Winnetka, IL 581
NORTH SHORE SCHOOL, Chicago, IL 943
NORTH YARMOUTH ACADEMY, Yarmouth, ME 186
NORTHFIELD MOUNT HERMON SCHOOL, Northfield, MA 236
NORTHSIDE CHRISTIAN ACADEMY, Charlotte, NC 904
NORTHWEST CATHOLIC HIGH SCHOOL, West Hartford, CT 772
THE NORTHWEST SCHOOL, Seattle, WA 757
NORTHWOOD SCHOOL, Lake Placid, NY 367, **1220**
NORWOOD SCHOOL, Bethesda, MD 803
NOTRE DAME ACADEMY, Park Hills, KY 902
NOTRE DAME ACADEMY, Middleburg, VA 933
NOTRE DAME ACADEMY, Worcester, MA 252, **1307**
NOTRE DAME-CATHEDRAL LATIN SCHOOL, Chardon, OH 964
NOTRE DAME DE LA BAIE ACADEMY, Green Bay, WI 973
NOTRE DAME HIGH SCHOOL, Belmont, CA 1050
NOTRE DAME HIGH SCHOOL, Sherman Oaks, CA 1078
NOTRE DAME HIGH SCHOOL, West Haven, CT 772
NOTRE DAME HIGH SCHOOL, St Louis, MO 991
NOTRE DAME HIGH SCHOOL, Lawrenceville, NJ 817
NOTRE DAME HIGH SCHOOL, Chattanooga, TN 919
NOTRE DAME HIGH SCHOOL, Clarksburg, WV 938
NOTRE DAME PREPARATORY SCHOOL, Towson, MD 813
NOTRE DAME PREPARATORY SCHOOL, Pontiac, MI 960
NYSMITH SCHOOL FOR THE GIFTED, Herndon, VA 930

OAK CREEK RANCH SCHOOL, West Sedona, AZ 1038
OAK GROVE SCHOOL, Ojai, CA 1065
OAK HALL SCHOOL, Gainesville, FL 874
OAK HILL ACADEMY, Mouth of Wilson, VA 555, **1218-9**
OAK HILL SCHOOL, Eugene, OR 1083
OAK HILL SCHOOL, Nashville, TN 923
OAK KNOLL SCHOOL OF THE HOLY CHILD, Summit, NJ 347
OAK LANE DAY SCHOOL, Blue Bell, PA 420
OAK MOUNTAIN ACADEMY, Carrollton, GA 892
OAK RIDGE MILITARY ACADEMY, Oak Ridge, NC 519
OAKHILL DAY SCHOOL, Gladstone, MO 986
OAKLAND SCHOOL, Keswick, VA 932
THE OAKRIDGE SCHOOL, Arlington, TX 661
OAKWOOD FRIENDS SCHOOL, Poughkeepsie, NY 403, **1221**
OAKWOOD SCHOOL, Annandale, VA 926
OAKWOOD SCHOOL, North Hollywood, CA 713
OJAI VALLEY SCHOOL, Ojai, CA 721

/ *Index of Schools* 1455

OLD TRAIL SCHOOL, Bath, OH 600
OLDFIELDS SCHOOL, Glencoe, MD 308, **1308-9**
OLNEY FRIENDS SCHOOL, Barnesville, OH 963
THE O'NEAL SCHOOL, Southern Pines, NC 911
ONEIDA BAPTIST INSTITUTE, Oneida, KY 902
THE ORCHARD SCHOOL, Indianapolis, IN 586, **1222**
OREGON EPISCOPAL SCHOOL, Portland, OR 754
ORME SCHOOL, Mayer, AZ 685
OUR LADY OF LOURDES REGIONAL HIGH SCHOOL,
    Coal Township, PA 849
OUR LADY QUEEN OF MARTYRS SCHOOL,
    Beverly Hills, MI 954
OUR MONTESSORI SCHOOL, Yorktown Heights, NY 846
OUT-OF-DOOR ACADEMY, Sarasota, FL 484
THE OUTDOOR ACADEMY, Pisgah Forest, NC 1096
THE OVERLAKE SCHOOL, Redmond, WA 756
OXFORD ACADEMY, Westbrook, CT 173, **1369**
OXFORD UNIVERSITY SCHOOL, Oxford, MS 1006

PACE ACADEMY, Atlanta, GA 494, **1223**
PACE-BRANTLEY HALL SCHOOL, Longwood, FL 877
PACELLI HIGH SCHOOL, Columbus, GA 892
PACIFIC NORTHERN ACADEMY, Anchorage, AK 1047
PACKER COLLEGIATE INSTITUTE, Brooklyn, NY 358
PADUA FRANCISCAN HIGH SCHOOL, Parma, OH 970
PAGE PRIVATE SCHOOL, Los Angeles, CA 1059
THE PAIDEIA SCHOOL, Atlanta, GA 495
PALM BEACH DAY SCHOOL, Palm Beach, FL 481
PALMER TRINITY SCHOOL, Miami, FL 478
PARADISE VALLEY CHRISTIAN PREPARATORY,
    Phoenix, AZ 1035
THE PARISH EPISCOPAL SCHOOL, Farmers Branch, TX 1012
PARK CENTURY SCHOOL, Los Angeles, CA **1381**
PARK SCHOOL, Brookline, MA 201
PARK SCHOOL, Brooklandville, MD 304
THE PARK SCHOOL, Buffalo, NY 361
PARK TUDOR SCHOOL, Indianapolis, IN 586
PARKMONT SCHOOL, Washington, DC 797
PASADENA TOWNE AND COUNTRY SCHOOL,
    Pasadena, CA 1068
PASADENA WALDORF SCHOOL, Altadena, CA 1048
THE PATHWAY SCHOOL, Norristown, PA **1384**

THE PATTERSON SCHOOL, Patterson, NC	909
THE PECK SCHOOL, Morristown, NJ	337
PEDDIE SCHOOL, Hightstown, NJ	329
THE PEGASUS SCHOOL, Huntington Beach, CA	703, **1207**
PEMBROKE HILL SCHOOL, Kansas City, MO	635
PEN RYN SCHOOL, Fairless Hills, PA	424
PENINSULA HERITAGE SCHOOL, Rolling Hills Estates, CA	1069
PENNFIELD SCHOOL, Portsmouth, RI	788
THE PENNINGTON SCHOOL, Pennington, NJ	339, **1224**
PERKIOMEN SCHOOL, Pennsburg, PA	439, **1225**
PHELPS SCHOOL, Malvern, PA	854
THE PHILADELPHIA SCHOOL, Philadelphia, PA	860
PHILLIPS ACADEMY, Andover, MA	187
PHILLIPS BROOKS SCHOOL, Menlo Park, CA	1060
PHILLIPS EXETER ACADEMY, Exeter, NH	259
THE PHILLIPS-OSBORNE SCHOOL, Painesville, OH	970
PHOENIX CHRISTIAN JUNIOR AND SENIOR HIGH SCHOOL, Phoenix, AZ	1035
PHOENIX COUNTRY DAY SCHOOL, Paradise Valley, AZ	687
PIKE SCHOOL, Andover, MA	188
PILGRIM SCHOOL, Los Angeles, CA	714
THE PILOT SCHOOL, Wilmington, DE	793
PINE COBBLE SCHOOL, Williamstown, MA	250
PINE CREST SCHOOL, Fort Lauderdale, FL	468
PINE POINT SCHOOL, Stonington, CT	166
PINEWOOD PREPARATORY SCHOOL, Summerville, SC	916
THE PINGRY SCHOOL, Martinsville, NJ	332
PIONEER VALLEY CHRISTIAN SCHOOL, Springfield, MA	784
PIUS XI HIGH SCHOOL, Milwaukee, WI	976
PLAY MOUNTAIN PLACE, Los Angeles, CA	1059
PLEASANT VIEW CHRISTIAN SCHOOL, Pleasant View, TN	924
POMFRET SCHOOL, Pomfret, CT	159
POPE JOHN XXIII HIGH SCHOOL, Everett, MA	780
PORTER-GAUD SCHOOL, Charleston, SC	527
PORTERSVILLE CHRISTIAN SCHOOL, Portersville, PA	861
PORTLAND LUTHERAN SCHOOL, Portland, OR	755
PORTLEDGE SCHOOL, Locust Valley, NY	368
PORTSMOUTH ABBEY SCHOOL, Portsmouth, RI	269, **1226-8**
POTOMAC SCHOOL, McLean, VA	553
POUGHKEEPSIE DAY SCHOOL, Poughkeepsie, NY	403
POWHATAN SCHOOL, Boyce, VA	926
PRAIRIE HILL WALDORF SCHOOL, Pewaukee, WI	976

Index of Schools

THE PRAIRIE SCHOOL, Racine, WI 620
PRESBYTERIAN DAY SCHOOL, Memphis, TN 539
PRESBYTERIAN SCHOOL, Houston, TX 1019
PRESENTATION HIGH SCHOOL, San Jose, CA 1074
PRESIDIO HILL SCHOOL, San Francisco, CA 735
THE PRIMARY DAY SCHOOL, Bethesda, MD 804
PRINCETON ACADEMY OF THE SACRED HEART,
  Princeton, NJ 820
PRINCETON DAY SCHOOL, Princeton, NJ 343, **1230-1**
PRINCETON FRIENDS SCHOOL, Princeton, NJ 820
PROCTOR ACADEMY, Andover, NH 255
PROFESSIONAL CHILDREN'S SCHOOL, New York, NY 389, **1229**
PROSPECT SIERRA SCHOOL, El Cerrito, CA 1053
PROUT SCHOOL, Wakefield, RI 789
PROVIDENCE COUNTRY DAY SCHOOL, East Providence, RI 274
PROVIDENCE DAY SCHOOL, Charlotte, NC 514, **1232**
PROVIDENCE HIGH SCHOOL, Burbank, CA 1051
PROVO CANYON SCHOOL, Orem, UT 1044, **1370**
P S #1 ELEMENTARY SCHOOL, Santa Monica, CA 1077
PULASKI ACADEMY, Little Rock, AR 647
PUNAHOU SCHOOL, Honolulu, HI 750
PURNELL SCHOOL, Pottersville, NJ 340, **1310-1**
THE PUTNEY SCHOOL, Putney, VT 278

QUEEN ANNE SCHOOL, Upper Marlboro, MD 321
QUEEN OF PEACE HIGH SCHOOL, Burbank, IL 939
QUIGLEY CATHOLIC HIGH SCHOOL, Baden, PA 847
QUINCY NOTRE DAME HIGH SCHOOL, Quincy, IL 948

RABUN GAP-NACOOCHEE SCHOOL, Rabun Gap, GA 501, **1233**
RAMONA CONVENT SECONDARY SCHOOL, Alhambra, CA 1048
RANDOLPH-MACON ACADEMY, Front Royal, VA 550
RANDOLPH SCHOOL, Huntsville, AL 463
RANNEY SCHOOL, Tinton Falls, NJ 348, **1234**
RANSOM EVERGLADES SCHOOL, Miami, FL 479
RAVENSCROFT SCHOOL, Raleigh, NC 519
RECTORY SCHOOL, Pomfret, CT 160, **1342-3**
REDEEMER-SETON HIGH SCHOOL, New Orleans, LA 1001
REDEMPTION CHRISTIAN ACADEMY, Troy, NY 845
REGINA HIGH SCHOOL, South Euclid, OH 972
REGIS HIGH SCHOOL, New York, NY 390
REGIS JESUIT HIGH SCHOOL, Aurora, CO 1025

REHOBOTH CHRISTIAN SCHOOL, Rehoboth, NM 1042
REID SCHOOL, Salt Lake City, UT 1045
RENBROOK SCHOOL, West Hartford, CT 143
RICE MEMORIAL HIGH SCHOOL, South Burlington, VT 791
RIDGEFIELD ACADEMY, Ridgefield, CT 769
RIDGEWOOD PREPARATORY SCHOOL, Metairie, LA 650
RILEY SCHOOL, Glen Cove, ME 775
RIO GRANDE SCHOOL, Santa Fe, NM 1043
RIPPOWAM CISQUA SCHOOL, Bedford, NY 353
RIVER OAKS BAPTIST SCHOOL, Houston, TX 1019, **1235**
RIVERDALE COUNTRY SCHOOL, Riverdale, NY 356
RIVERMONT COLLEGIATE, Bettendorf, IA 623
THE RIVERS SCHOOL, Weston, MA 248, **1236**
RIVERSIDE MILITARY ACADEMY, Gainesville, GA 499
RIVERSIDE PRESBYTERIAN DAY SCHOOL,
  Jacksonville, FL 473, **1235**
RIVERVIEW SCHOOL, East Sandwich, MA 238, **1371**
ROBERT LOUIS STEVENSON SCHOOL, Pebble Beach, CA 726
ROBERT LOUIS STEVENSON SCHOOL,
  New York, NY 391, **1372-3**
ROCK CREEK INTERNATIONAL SCHOOL, Washington, DC 797
ROCK POINT SCHOOL, Burlington, VT 276
ROCKHURST HIGH SCHOOL, Kansas City, MO 987
THE ROCKLAND COUNTRY DAY SCHOOL, Congers, NY 400
ROCKY HILL SCHOOL, East Greenwich, RI 268
ROCKY MOUNT ACADEMY, Rocky Mount, NC 910
ROCKY MOUNTAIN SEMESTER, Leadville, CO 1097
RODEPH SHOLOM SCHOOL, New York, NY 838
THE ROEPER SCHOOL, Bloomfield Hills, MI 594, **1237**
ROHAN WOODS SCHOOL, St Louis, MO 991
ROLAND PARK COUNTRY SCHOOL, Baltimore, MD 300
ROLLING HILLS COUNTRY DAY SCHOOL,
  Rolling Hills Estates, CA 1070
ROLLING HILLS PREPARATORY SCHOOL,
  Palos Verdes Estates, CA 1066
ROSARY HIGH SCHOOL, Fullerton, CA 1055
ROSATI-KAIN HIGH SCHOOL, St Louis, MO 992
ROSEMONT SCHOOL OF THE HOLY CHILD,
  Rosemont, PA 863, **1237**
ROWLAND HALL-ST. MARK'S SCHOOL, Salt Lake City, UT 696
ROXBURY LATIN SCHOOL, West Roxbury, MA 196
ROYCEMORE SCHOOL, Evanston, IL 578

Index of Schools

RUDOLF STEINER SCHOOL, New York, NY 391
RUMSEY HALL SCHOOL, Washington Depot, CT 170, **1238**
RUMSON COUNTRY DAY SCHOOL, Rumson, NJ 344
RUNNEMEDE SCHOOL, Plainfield, NH 787
RUXTON COUNTRY SCHOOL, Owings Mills, MD 809
RYE COUNTRY DAY SCHOOL, Rye, NY 408

SACRAMENTO COUNTRY DAY SCHOOL, Sacramento, CA 728
SACRAMENTO WALDORF SCHOOL, Fair Oaks, CA 729
SACRED HEART ACADEMY, Hamden, CT 765
SACRED HEART HIGH SCHOOL, Los Angeles, CA 1060
SACRED HEART HIGH SCHOOL, Kingston, MA 781
SACRED HEART SCHOOL, Muenster, TX 1023
SACRED HEART SCHOOLS, Chicago, IL 573
SACRED HEARTS ACADEMY, Honolulu, HI 1081
SADDLE RIVER DAY SCHOOL, Saddle River, NJ 345
SAGE RIDGE SCHOOL, Reno, NV 1040
THE SAGE SCHOOL, Foxboro, MA 780
ST. AGNES ACADEMY, Houston, TX 1020
ST. AGNES HIGH SCHOOL, College Point, NY 828
SAINT AGNES SCHOOL, St Paul, MN 985
ST. ALBANS SCHOOL, Washington, DC 291
ST. ALOYSIUS ACADEMY, Bryn Mawr, PA 848
ST. ANDREW'S EPISCOPAL SCHOOL, New Orleans, LA 1002
ST. ANDREW'S EPISCOPAL SCHOOL, Newport News, VA 934
ST. ANDREW'S EPISCOPAL SCHOOL, Potomac, MD 315
ST. ANDREW'S EPISCOPAL SCHOOL, Ridgeland, MS 655
ST. ANDREW'S PRIORY SCHOOL, Honolulu, HI 751
ST. ANDREW'S SCHOOL, Savannah, GA 898
ST. ANDREW'S SCHOOL, Middletown, DE 283, **1239**
SAINT ANDREW'S SCHOOL, Boca Raton, FL 466, **1242**
ST. ANDREW'S SCHOOL, Barrington, RI 268, **1240-1**
ST. ANNE'S-BELFIELD SCHOOL, Charlottesville, VA 545, **1243**
ST. ANNE'S DAY SCHOOL, Annapolis, MD 799
ST. ANNE'S EPISCOPAL SCHOOL, Denver, CO 1029
SAINT ANTHONY'S HIGH SCHOOL, South Huntington, NY 843
ST. AUGUSTINE HIGH SCHOOL, San Diego, CA 1071
ST. BERNARD'S SCHOOL, New York, NY 392
ST. CATHERINE'S MILITARY SCHOOL, Anaheim, CA 697
ST. CATHERINE'S SCHOOL, Richmond, VA 559, **1316**
ST. CECILIA ACADEMY, Nashville, TN 924
ST. CHRISTOPHER'S SCHOOL, Richmond, VA 560

ST. CLEMENT'S EPISCOPAL PARISH SCHOOL, El Paso, TX..... 1015
ST. DAVID'S SCHOOL, Raleigh, NC 910
SAINT DAVID'S SCHOOL, New York, NY 392
SAINT DOMINIC ACADEMY, Jersey City, NJ.................................. 816
SAINT EDMOND'S ACADEMY, Wilmington, DE............................ 793
ST. EDMUND'S ACADEMY, Pittsburgh, PA.. 448
SAINT EDWARD'S SCHOOL, Vero Beach, FL 489, **1244**
SAINT ELIZABETH HIGH SCHOOL, Oakland, CA....................... 1065
ST. FRANCIS DE SALES HIGH SCHOOL, Toledo, OH................... 972
ST. FRANCIS EPISCOPAL DAY SCHOOL, Potomac, MD.............. 810
ST. FRANCIS EPISCOPAL DAY SCHOOL, Houston, TX 1020
ST. FRANCIS HIGH SCHOOL, Wheaton, IL 950
ST. FRANCIS HIGH SCHOOL, Louisville, KY 508
ST. FRANCIS PREPARATORY SCHOOL, Fresh Meadows, NY....... 829
ST. FRANCIS SCHOOL, Roswell, GA... 897
ST. FRANCIS SCHOOL, Honolulu, HI... 1082
ST. FRANCIS SCHOOL, Goshen, KY 505
ST. GEORGE'S INDEPENDENT SCHOOLS, Germantown, TN 534
ST. GEORGE'S SCHOOL, Middletown, RI... 270
SAINT GEORGE'S SCHOOL, Spokane, WA 759
ST. GREGORY COLLEGE PREPARATORY SCHOOL,
  Tuscon, AZ.. 1038
ST. GREGORY'S ACADEMY, Moscow, PA....................................... 856
SAINT GREGORY'S SCHOOL, Loudonville, NY 833
ST. HENRY DISTRICT HIGH SCHOOL, Erlanger, KY.................... 900
ST. IGNATIUS COLLEGE PREP, Chicago, IL 943
ST. JAMES EPISCOPAL SCHOOL, Corpus Christi, TX................... 1011
SAINT JAMES SCHOOL, Montgomery, AL.. 868
SAINT JAMES SCHOOL, St James, MD.................................. 317, **1245**
ST. JOHN'S COLLEGE HIGH SCHOOL, Washington, DC............... 797
ST. JOHNS COUNTRY DAY SCHOOL, Orange Park, FL................. 480
ST. JOHN'S EPISCOPAL PARISH DAY SCHOOL, Tampa, FL 886
ST. JOHN'S EPISCOPAL SCHOOL,
  Rancho Santa Margarita, CA... 1069
SAINT JOHN'S EPISCOPAL SCHOOL, Oklahoma City, OK 1006
ST. JOHN'S EPISCOPAL SCHOOL, Abilene, TX............................. 1009
ST. JOHN'S EPISCOPAL SCHOOL, Olney, MD................................. 310
SAINT JOHN'S HIGH SCHOOL, Shrewsbury, MA........................... 252
ST. JOHN'S LITERARY INSTITUTION AT PROSPECT HALL,
  Frederick, MD.. 807
ST. JOHN'S MILITARY SCHOOL, Salina, KS 625

Index of Schools 1461

ST. JOHN'S NORTHWESTERN MILITARY ACADEMY,
Delafield, WI 618
ST. JOHN'S PREPARATORY SCHOOL, Danvers, MA 210, **1344**
SAINT JOHN'S PREPARATORY SCHOOL, Collegeville, MN 627
ST. JOHNSBURY ACADEMY, St Johnsbury, VT 279
ST. JOSEPH HIGH SCHOOL, Metuchen, NJ 818, **1345**
ST. JOSEPH'S ACADEMY, St Louis, MO 992
ST. JOSEPH'S CATHOLIC SCHOOL, Greenville, SC 914
ST. JOSEPH'S COLLEGIATE INSTITUTE, Buffalo, NY 827
ST. LAWRENCE ACADEMY, Santa Clara, CA 1077
SAINT LOUIS PRIORY SCHOOL, St Louis, MO 641
ST. LUCY'S PRIORY HIGH SCHOOL, Glendora, CA 1055
ST. LUKE'S EPISCOPAL SCHOOL, Mobile, AL 868
ST. LUKE'S EPISCOPAL SCHOOL, San Antonio, TX 1023
ST. LUKE'S SCHOOL, New Canaan, CT 152
ST. LUKE'S SCHOOL, New York, NY 393
ST. MARGARET'S EPISCOPAL SCHOOL,
San Juan Capistrano, CA 741
ST. MARGARET'S SCHOOL, Tappahannock, VA 563, **1312-3**
ST. MARK'S EPISCOPAL DAY SCHOOL, Jacksonville, FL 876
ST. MARK'S EPISCOPAL SCHOOL, Fort Lauderdale, FL 874
SAINT MARK'S SCHOOL, San Rafael, CA 1075
SAINT MARK'S SCHOOL, Southborough, MA 241
ST. MARK'S SCHOOL OF TEXAS, Dallas, TX 666
ST. MARTIN'S EPISCOPAL SCHOOL, Atlanta, GA 889
ST. MARTIN'S EPISCOPAL SCHOOL, Metairie, LA 651
ST. MARY CATHOLIC CENTRAL HIGH SCHOOL,
Monroe, MI 959
ST. MARY'S ACADEMY, Portland, OR 1085
ST. MARY'S DOMINICAN HIGH SCHOOL, New Orleans, LA 1002
ST. MARY'S EPISCOPAL DAY SCHOOL, Tampa, FL 487
ST. MARY'S EPISCOPAL SCHOOL, Memphis, TN 539
SAINT MARY'S HALL, San Antonio, TX 674
ST. MARY'S HALL/DOANE ACADEMY, Burlington, NJ 324
SAINT MARY'S HIGH SCHOOL, Phoenix, AZ 1036
ST. MARY'S HIGH SCHOOL, Colorado Springs, CO 1026
ST. MARY'S INTERNATIONAL SCHOOL, Tokyo, Japan **1392**
ST. MARY'S PREPARATORY SCHOOL, Orchard Lake, MI 959
SAINT MARY'S SCHOOL, Raleigh, NC 520
ST. MATTHEW'S PARISH SCHOOL, Pacific Palisades, CA 1066
ST. MICHAEL'S COUNTRY DAY SCHOOL, Newport, RI 271
ST. MICHAEL'S EPISCOPAL DAY SCHOOL, Carmichael, CA 1052

SAINT MICHAEL'S INDEPENDENT SCHOOL, Stuart, FL............. 485
ST. MICHAEL'S PREPARATORY SCHOOL, Silverado, CA 1078
SAINT PATRICK HIGH SCHOOL, Chicago, IL.................................. 944
ST. PATRICK'S EPISCOPAL DAY SCHOOL, Washington, DC........ 798
ST. PAUL ACADEMY AND SUMMIT SCHOOL, St Paul, MN 632
ST. PAUL'S EPISCOPAL DAY SCHOOL, Kansas City, MO 987
ST. PAUL'S EPISCOPAL SCHOOL, Oakland, CA 1065
ST. PAUL'S EPISCOPAL SCHOOL, Mobile, AL................................ 464
ST. PAUL'S PREPARATORY ACADEMY, Phoenix, AZ.................. 1036
SAINT PAUL'S SCHOOL, Clearwater, FL.. 871
ST. PAUL'S SCHOOL, Brooklandville, MD 305
ST. PAUL'S SCHOOL, Concord, NH 257, **1246-7**
ST. PAUL'S SCHOOL FOR GIRLS, Brooklandville, MD 306
ST. PETER'S PREPARATORY SCHOOL, Jersey City, NJ................. 330
ST. PETER'S SCHOOL, Philadelphia, PA.................................. 445, **1244**
ST. PHILIP'S EPISCOPAL SCHOOL, Coral Gables, FL.................... 872
ST. PIUS X HIGH SCHOOL, Albuquerque, NM 1042
ST. PIUS X CATHOLIC HIGH SCHOOL, Atlanta, GA..................... 890
ST. PIUS X HIGH SCHOOL, Houston, TX....................................... 1021
ST. RICHARD'S SCHOOL, Indianapolis, IN 587
ST. RITA CATHOLIC SCHOOL, Fort Worth, TX 1017
ST. SCHOLASTICA ACADEMY, Chicago, IL 944
ST. SEBASTIAN'S SCHOOL, Needham, MA 232
SAINT STANISLAUS COLLEGE, Bay St Louis, MS...................... 1004
ST. STEPHEN'S AND ST. AGNES SCHOOL, Alexandria, VA.......... 544
SAINT STEPHEN'S EPISCOPAL SCHOOL,
  Bradenton, FL... 467, **1251**
ST. STEPHEN'S EPISCOPAL SCHOOL, Austin, TX 662
ST. STEPHEN'S SCHOOL, Rome, Italy **1393**
ST. THERESE ACADEMY, Dallas, TX... 1012
SAINT THOMAS ACADEMY, Mendota Heights, MN 633
ST. THOMAS AQUINAS HIGH SCHOOL, Dover, NH..................... 787
ST. THOMAS AQUINAS SCHOOL, Dallas, TX 1013
ST. THOMAS CHOIR SCHOOL, New York, NY 394, **1346**
ST. THOMAS EPISCOPAL PARISH SCHOOL, Coral Gables, FL.... 872
ST. THOMAS HIGH SCHOOL, Houston, TX 672
ST. THOMAS MORE HIGH SCHOOL, Rapid City, SD 995
SAINT THOMAS MORE SCHOOL, Oakdale, CT 158, **1374-6**
ST. THOMAS SCHOOL, Medina, WA 1087
ST. THOMAS'S DAY SCHOOL, New Haven, CT............................. 156
ST. TIMOTHY'S SCHOOL, Stevenson, MD 320
ST. URSULA ACADEMY, Cincinnati, OH 603

Index of Schools

SAINT VIATOR HIGH SCHOOL, Arlington Heights, IL 939
SAINT VINCENT FERRER HIGH SCHOOL, New York, NY 839
ST. VINCENT'S ACADEMY, Savannah, GA 898
ST. XAVIER HIGH SCHOOL, Louisville, KY 901
SAINTS JOHN NEUMANN AND MARIA GORETTI
   CATHOLIC HIGH SCHOOL, Philadelphia, PA 860
SS. SIMON AND JUDE CATHOLIC SCHOOL, Phoenix, AZ 1037
SAKLAN VALLEY SCHOOL, Moraga, CA 1062
SALEM ACADEMY, Winston-Salem, NC 522, **1314-5**
SALESIANUM SCHOOL, Wilmington, DE 794
SALISBURY SCHOOL, Salisbury, MD 811, **1248-9**
SALISBURY SCHOOL, Salisbury, CT 160
SALISBURY SUMMER SCHOOL, Salisbury, CT **1399**
SALPOINTE CATHOLIC HIGH SCHOOL, Tucson, AZ 1038
SAN ANTONIO ACADEMY, San Antonio, TX 1024
SAN DOMENICO SCHOOL, San Anselmo, CA 730
SAN FRANCISCO DAY SCHOOL, San Francisco, CA 736, **1251**
THE SAN FRANCISCO SCHOOL, San Francisco, CA 737, **1252**
SAN FRANCISCO UNIVERSITY HIGH SCHOOL,
   San Francisco, CA 737
SAN MARCOS BAPTIST ACADEMY, San Marcos, TX 675
SANDIA PREPARATORY SCHOOL, Albuquerque, NM 693
SANDY SPRING FRIENDS SCHOOL, Sandy Spring, MD 318, **1253**
SANFORD SCHOOL, Hockessin, DE 284
SANTA CATALINA SCHOOL, Monterey, CA 719
SANTA FE PREPARATORY SCHOOL, Santa Fe, NM 695
SAVANNAH COUNTRY DAY SCHOOL, Savannah, GA 503
SAYRE SCHOOL, Lexington, KY 506
THE SCHILLING SCHOOL FOR GIFTED CHILDREN,
   Cincinnati, OH 966
THE SCHOOL IN ROSE VALLEY, Rose Valley, PA 432
SCHOOL OF THE HOLY CHILD, Rye, NY 408, **1317**
SCHOOLS OF THE SACRED HEART, San Francisco, CA 738
SCOTTSDALE CHRISTIAN ACADEMY, Phoenix, AZ 1037
SEATTLE COUNTRY DAY SCHOOL, Seattle, WA 1090
SEATTLE WALDORF SCHOOL, Seattle, WA 1090
SELWYN SCHOOL, Denton, TX 666
SERVITE HIGH SCHOOL, Anaheim, CA 1049
SETON CATHOLIC CENTRAL, Plattsburgh, NY 841
SETON KEOUGH HIGH SCHOOL, Baltimore, MD 801
SEVEN HILLS SCHOOL, Walnut Creek, CA 1080
THE SEVEN HILLS SCHOOL, Cincinnati, OH 603

SEWICKLEY ACADEMY, Sewickley, PA 453
SHADY HILL SCHOOL, Cambridge, MA 206
SHADY SIDE ACADEMY, Pittsburgh, PA 449
SHANNON FOREST CHRISTIAN SCHOOL, Greenville, SC 914
SHATTUCK-ST. MARY'S SCHOOL, Faribault, MN 628
SHELTON SCHOOL, Dallas, TX 1013
SHERIDAN SCHOOL, Washington, DC 291
SHINING MOUNTAIN WALDORF SCHOOL, Boulder, CO 1025
THE SHIPLEY SCHOOL, Bryn Mawr, PA 422, **1256**
SHORE COUNTRY DAY SCHOOL, Beverly, MA 193
SHORECREST PREPARATORY SCHOOL, St Petersburg, FL 484
SHRINE CATHOLIC HIGH SCHOOL, Royal Oak, MI 961
SIDWELL FRIENDS SCHOOL, Washington, DC 292
SIERRA CANYON SCHOOL, Chatsworth, CA 1052
SIOUX FALLS CHRISTIAN SCHOOLS, Sioux Falls, SD 995
SMITH COLLEGE CAMPUS SCHOOL, Northampton, MA 234
SOLEBURY SCHOOL, New Hope, PA 435
SOLOMAN SCHECHTER ACADEMY OF DALLAS,
  Dallas, TX 1014
SOLOMON SCHECHTER DAY SCHOOL, West Orange, NJ 822
SOLOMON SCHECHTER SCHOOL OF MANHATTAN,
  New York, NY 839
SONOMA COUNTRY DAY SCHOOL, Santa Rosa, CA 1077
SOUNDVIEW PREPARATORY SCHOOL, Mount Kisco, NY 834
SOUTH KENT SCHOOL, South Kent, CT 164, **1347**
SOUTHAMPTON ACADEMY, Courtland, VA 928
SOUTHFIELD SCHOOL, Shreveport, LA 654
SOUTHFIELD SCHOOL, Brookline, MA 202, **1318**
SOUTHWESTERN ACADEMY, Rimrock, AZ 688, **1254-5**
SOUTHWESTERN ACADEMY, San Marino, CA 742, **1254-5**
SPARTANBURG DAY SCHOOL, Spartanburg, SC 530
THE SPENCE SCHOOL, New York, NY 395
SPRING VALE ACADEMY, Owosso, MI 960
SPRINGSIDE SCHOOL, Philadelphia, PA 446
STANLEY CLARK SCHOOL, South Bend, IN 589
THE STANWICH SCHOOL, Greenwich, CT 765
STATEN ISLAND ACADEMY, Staten Island, NY 411
STEIN YESHIVA OF LINCOLN PARK, Yonkers, NY 846
STEPHEN GAYNOR SCHOOL, New York, NY 840
STEPHEN T. BADIN HIGH SCHOOL, Hamilton, OH 969
THE STEWARD SCHOOL, Richmond, VA 560, **1252**
STEWART HOME SCHOOL, Frankfort, KY **1382-3**

Index of Schools

STONE RIDGE SCHOOL OF THE SACRED HEART,
　Bethesda, MD.. 303
STONELEIGH-BURNHAM SCHOOL, Greenfield, MA.......... 220, **1319**
STONY BROOK SCHOOL, Stony Brook, NY 412
THE STORM KING SCHOOL, Cornwall-on-Hudson, NY 362
STRAKE JESUIT COLLEGE PREPARATORY, Houston, TX......... 1021
STRATFORD ACADEMY, Macon, GA 895
STRATFORD FRIENDS SCHOOL, Havertown, PA........................... 852
STRATTON MOUNTAIN SCHOOL, Stratton Mountain, VT 791
STUART COUNTRY DAY SCHOOL OF THE SACRED HEART,
　Princeton, NJ... 344, **1320**
STUART HALL, Staunton, VA 562
SUBIACO ACADEMY, Subiaco, AR 648
SUDBURY VALLEY SCHOOL, Framingham, MA............................ 219
SUFFIELD ACADEMY, Suffield, CT....................................... 167, **1257**
SUGAR BOWL ACADEMY, Norden, CA 1063
SUMMERS-KNOLL SCHOOL, Ann Arbor, MI 953
SUMMIT COUNTRY DAY SCHOOL, Cincinnati, OH 604
SUMMIT SCHOOL, Winston-Salem, NC 522
SUMNER ACADEMY, Gallatin, TN 920
THE SUSQUEHANNA SCHOOL, Binghamton, NY.......................... 823
SWAIN SCHOOL, Allentown, PA... 419
SWEETWATER EPISCOPAL ACADEMY, Longwood, FL................ 877
SYCAMORE SCHOOL, Indianapolis, IN 588

TABOR ACADEMY, Marion, MA.. 228
TAFT SCHOOL, Watertown, CT 172, **1260**
TAMPA BAPTIST ACADEMY, Tampa, FL 886
TAMPA PREPARATORY SCHOOL, Tampa, FL 488
TANDEM FRIENDS SCHOOL, Charlottesville, VA........................... 928
TASIS: THE AMERICAN SCHOOL IN ENGLAND,
　Thorpe, Surrey, England **1394**
TASIS: THE AMERICAN SCHOOL IN SWITZERLAND,
　Montagnola-Lugano, Switzerland... **1395**
THE TASIS SUMMER PROGRAMS IN EUROPE **1396**
TATNALL SCHOOL, Wilmington, DE... 285
TATTNALL SQUARE ACADEMY, Macon, GA 895
TENACRE COUNTRY DAY SCHOOL, Wellesley, MA 246
TEXAS MILITARY INSTITUTE, San Antonio, TX 675
THE THACHER SCHOOL, Ojai, CA... 722
THAYER ACADEMY, Braintree, MA..................................... 198, **1258-9**
THOMAS JEFFERSON SCHOOL, St Louis, MO 642, **1261**

THOMAS MORE PREP—MARIAN HIGH SCHOOL, Hays, KS 980
THORNTON FRIENDS SCHOOL, Silver Spring, MD 812
TIDEWATER ACADEMY, Wakefield, VA.. 937
TILTON SCHOOL, Tilton, NH 266, **1268**
TIMOTHY CHRISTIAN SCHOOLS, Piscataway, NJ 819
THE TOME SCHOOL, North East, MD.. 809
TOPEKA COLLEGIATE SCHOOL, Topeka, KS................................. 980
TOWER HILL SCHOOL, Wilmington, DE.. 286
TOWER SCHOOL, Marblehead, MA... 228
THE TOWN SCHOOL, New York, NY... 396
TOWN SCHOOL FOR BOYS, San Francisco, CA 739
TREVOR DAY SCHOOL, New York, NY 396
TRIDENT ACADEMY, Mt Pleasant, SC 915
TRINITY CATHOLIC HIGH SCHOOL, Stamford, CT...................... 770
TRINITY CHRISTIAN ACADEMY, Barnstable, MA........................ 190
TRINITY EPISCOPAL SCHOOL, New Orleans, LA........................ 1002
TRINITY EPISCOPAL SCHOOL, Galveston, TX 1017
TRINITY HIGH SCHOOL, River Forest, IL 949
TRINITY HIGH SCHOOL, Louisville, KY... 901
TRINITY-PAWLING SCHOOL, Pawling, NY 401, **1348**
TRINITY PREPARATORY SCHOOL, Winter Park, FL **489**
TRINITY SCHOOL, Atlanta, GA... 890
TRINITY SCHOOL, Ellicott City, MD... 806
TRINITY SCHOOL, Midland, TX.. 1022
TRINITY SCHOOL, New York, NY.. 397
TRINITY VALLEY SCHOOL, Fort Worth, TX................................... 668
TURNING POINT SCHOOL, Culver City, CA.................................... 715
TUSCALOOSA ACADEMY, Tuscaloosa, AL..................................... 869
TUSCARAWAS CENTRAL CATHOLIC HIGH SCHOOL,
  New Philadelphia, OH 970
TUXEDO PARK SCHOOL, Tuxedo Park, NY.................................... 416

UNITED FRIENDS SCHOOL, Quakertown, PA................................. 862
UNITED NATIONS INTERNATIONAL SCHOOL,
  New York, NY... 398
UNIVERSITY LAKE SCHOOL, Hartland, WI 619
UNIVERSITY LIGGETT SCHOOL, Grosse Pointe Woods, MI......... 596
THE UNIVERSITY OF CHICAGO LABORATORY SCHOOLS,
  Chicago, IL.. 574
UNIVERSITY OF DENVER HIGH SCHOOL, Denver, CO 1030
UNIVERSITY PREPARATORY ACADEMY, Seattle, WA................. 758
UNIVERSITY SCHOOL, Tulsa, OK 1008

Index of Schools

UNIVERSITY SCHOOL, Hunting Valley, OH 613
UNIVERSITY SCHOOL OF JACKSON, Jackson, TN 535
UNIVERSITY SCHOOL OF MILWAUKEE, Milwaukee, WI 619
UNIVERSITY SCHOOL OF
    NOVA SOUTHEASTERN UNIVERSITY, Fort Lauderdale, FL 468
THE UNQUOWA SCHOOL, Fairfield, CT 136
UPATTINAS SCHOOL, Glenmoore, PA 851
THE URBAN SCHOOL OF SAN FRANCISCO,
    San Francisco, CA 740
URSULINE ACADEMY, Wilmington, DE 794
URSULINE ACADEMY, Dedham, MA 779
URSULINE ACADEMY, Cincinnati, OH 966
URSULINE ACADEMY OF DALLAS, Dallas, TX 1014
URSULINE SCHOOL, New Rochelle, NY 835

VAIL MOUNTAIN SCHOOL, Vail, CO 683
VALLEY CATHOLIC SCHOOL, Beaverton, OR 1083
VALLEY FORGE MILITARY ACADEMY, Wayne, PA 455
VALLEY PREPARATORY SCHOOL, Redlands, CA 727
THE VALLEY SCHOOL, Flint, MI 956
VALLEY SCHOOL OF LIGONIER, Ligonier, PA 430
VALWOOD SCHOOL, Valdosta, GA 899
VANGUARD SCHOOL, Lake Wales, FL 474
VERDE VALLEY SCHOOL, Sedona, AZ 689
VERMONT ACADEMY, Saxtons River, VT 280, **1262-3**
VIANNEY HIGH SCHOOL, St Louis, MO 992
VIEWPOINT SCHOOL, Calabasas, CA 716, **1264-5**
VILLA MADONNA ACADEMY, Villa Hills, KY 903
VILLA VICTORIA ACADEMY, Ewing, NJ 815
VILLA WALSH ACADEMY, Morristown, NJ 819
THE VILLAGE SCHOOL, Houston, TX 1021, **1266-7**
VINCENT SMITH SCHOOL, Port Washington, NY 402
VIRGINIA EPISCOPAL SCHOOL, Lynchburg, VA 551, **1269**
VISITATION ACADEMY, St Louis, MO 993

WALDEN SCHOOL, Pasadena, CA 1068
WALDORF SCHOOL OF GARDEN CITY, Garden City, NY 830
WALDRON MERCY ACADEMY, Merion Station, PA 856
THE WALKER SCHOOL, Marietta, GA 896
WALNUT HILL SCHOOL, Natick, MA 231
WALSH JESUIT HIGH SCHOOL, Cuyahoga Falls, OH 969
WALSINGHAM ACADEMY, Williamsburg, VA 937

WARDLAW-HARTRIDGE SCHOOL, Edison, NJ 325
WARE ACADEMY, Gloucester, VA... 930
WARREN-WALKER SCHOOL, San Diego, CA.............................. 1071
WASATCH ACADEMY, Mt Pleasant, UT.. 1044
WASHINGTON ACADEMY, East Machias, ME 774
WASHINGTON EPISCOPAL SCHOOL, Bethesda, MD 804
WASHINGTON INTERNATIONAL SCHOOL, Washington, DC...... 293
WASHINGTON MONTESSORI SCHOOL, New Preston, CT........... 768
THE WATERFORD SCHOOL, Sandy, UT.. 1045
WATERVILLE VALLEY ACADEMY, Waterville Valley, NH 787
WATKINSON SCHOOL, Hartford, CT 143
WAYLAND ACADEMY, Beaver Dam, WI 616
WAYNE COUNTRY DAY SCHOOL, Goldsboro, NC 906
WAYNFLETE SCHOOL, Portland, ME 185
WEBB SCHOOL, Bell Buckle, TN.. 531, **1272**
WEBB SCHOOL OF KNOXVILLE, Knoxville, TN............................ 535
WEBB SCHOOLS, Claremont, CA 700
WELLINGTON SCHOOL, St Petersburg, FL 883
WENTWORTH MILITARY ACADEMY, Lexington, MO 636
WESLEYAN SCHOOL, Norcross, GA... 500
WEST CHESTER FRIENDS SCHOOL, West Chester, PA.................. 863
WEST NOTTINGHAM ACADEMY, Colora, MD.............................. 307
WEST PHILADELPHIA CATHOLIC HIGH SCHOOL,
   Philadelphia, PA 861
WESTBURY FRIENDS SCHOOL, Westbury, NY.............................. 845
WESTCHESTER ACADEMY, High Point, NC 517
WESTERLY SCHOOL OF LONG BEACH, Long Beach, CA 1057
WESTERN MENNONITE SCHOOL, Salem, OR 1086
WESTERN RESERVE ACADEMY, Hudson, OH 610, **1273**
WESTMINSTER ACADEMY, Fort Lauderdale, FL 874
WESTMINSTER CHRISTIAN ACADEMY, Opelousas, LA 1003
WESTMINSTER CHRISTIAN ACADEMY, St Louis, MO 993
WESTMINSTER CHRISTIAN SCHOOL, Miami, FL....................... 880
WESTMINSTER SCHOOL, Oklahoma City, OK 1007
WESTMINSTER SCHOOL, Simsbury, CT................................ 163, **1270-1**
THE WESTMINSTER SCHOOLS, Atlanta, GA...................... 496, **1278**
WESTMINSTER SCHOOLS OF AUGUSTA, Augusta, GA 891
WESTOVER SCHOOL, Middlebury, CT 149, **1321**
WESTRIDGE SCHOOL, Pasadena, CA.. 725
WESTTOWN SCHOOL, Westtown, PA 455
WHEATON ACADEMY, West Chicago, IL.. 949
WHEELER SCHOOL, Providence, RI 274

Index of Schools

WHITBY SCHOOL, Greenwich, CT 141
WHITE MOUNTAIN SCHOOL, Bethlehem, NH 256, **1274-5**
WHITE OAK SCHOOL, Westfield, MA 785
WHITEFIELD ACADEMY, Mableton, GA 894
WHITFIELD SCHOOL, St Louis, MO 994
WICHITA COLLEGIATE SCHOOL, Wichita, KS 626
WIGHTWOOD SCHOOL, Branford, CT 133
WILLIAM PENN CHARTER SCHOOL, Philadelphia, PA 446
THE WILLIAMS SCHOOL, New London, CT 156, **1279**
WILLIAMSBURG CHRISTIAN ACADEMY, Williamsburg, VA 937
WILLISTON NORTHAMPTON SCHOOL,
Easthampton, MA 217, **1276-7**
WILLOW HILL SCHOOL, Sudbury, MA 243, **1377**
THE WILLOWS ACADEMY, Des Plaines, IL 944
WILMINGTON FRIENDS SCHOOL, Wilmington, DE 286
WILSON HALL, Sumter, SC 916
THE WILSON SCHOOL, Clayton, MO 643
THE WILSON SCHOOL, Mountain Lakes, NJ 338
THE WINCHENDON SCHOOL, Winchendon, MA 250
WINCHESTER THURSTON SCHOOL, Pittsburgh, PA 450
WINDRUSH SCHOOL, El Cerrito, CA 1053
WINDSOR SCHOOL, Flushing, NY 405, **1282**
WINDWARD SCHOOL, Los Angeles, CA 1060
WINDWARD SCHOOL, White Plains, NY 417, **1368**
WINSOR SCHOOL, Boston, MA 197
WINSTON PREPARATORY SCHOOL, New York, NY 840
THE WINSTON SCHOOL, Dallas, TX 1015
WOODBERRY FOREST SCHOOL, Woodberry Forest, VA 566, **1349**
WOODCREST SCHOOL, Tarzana, CA 1079
WOODHALL SCHOOL, Bethlehem, CT 132, **1378**
WOODLAND COUNTRY DAY SCHOOL, Bridgeton, NJ 324
WOODLAND PRESBYTERIAN SCHOOL, Memphis, TN 922
WOODLAWN ACADEMY, Chatham, VA 928
WOODLYNDE SCHOOL, Strafford, PA 863
WOODS ACADEMY, Bethesda, MD 804
WOODSIDE PRIORY SCHOOL, Portola Valley, CA 725
WOODSTOCK DAY SCHOOL, Woodstock, NY 846
WOODWARD ACADEMY, College Park, GA 496, **1283**
THE WOOLMAN SEMESTER, Nevada City, CA 1097
WOOSTER SCHOOL, Danbury, CT 134, **1280-1**
WORCESTER ACADEMY, Worcester, MA 253, **1284**
WORCESTER PREPARATORY SCHOOL, Berlin, MD 802

THE WYNDCROFT SCHOOL, Pottstown, PA	452
WYOMING SEMINARY, Kingston, PA	457
XAVERIAN BROTHERS HIGH SCHOOL, Westwood, MA	785
XAVIER HIGH SCHOOL, Middletown, CT	767
XAVIER HIGH SCHOOL, New York, NY	840
YAVNEH ACADEMY, Paramus, NJ	819
YORK COUNTRY DAY SCHOOL, York, PA	459
YORK PREPARATORY SCHOOL, New York, NY	399, **1285**
YORK SCHOOL, Monterey, CA	1062
ZION LUTHERAN CHRISTIAN SCHOOL, Deerfield Beach, FL	873

Yes, send me the most recent editions of:

Title	Price	Qty	Total
The Handbook of Private Schools	$99.00		
The Directory for Exceptional Children	$75.00		
Guide to Summer Camps and Summer Schools	$45.00		
Schools Abroad of Interest to Americans	$45.00		

Domestic shipping is $7.00, plus $1.50 for each additional book. Non-US shipping quoted on request.

All prices in $US.

Subtotal	
MA addresses add 5% sales tax	
US shipping	$7.00
$1.50/add'l book	
TOTAL	

☐ Check or money order enclosed (payable on a US bank)
☐ Bill me (organizations only)
☐ Visa ☐ MasterCard ☐ American Express ☐ Discover

Card # _____ Exp. Date _____

Card Holder_____

Signature _____

First Name   Last Name

Company Name

Street Address (no P.O. Boxes, please)

City   State   Zip

Country   Postal Code

E-mail _____

Daytime phone _____ HPS05

PORTER SARGENT PUBLISHERS, INC.
400 Bedford St Ste 322 Manchester, NH 03101 USA
Tel: 800-342-7470   Fax: 603-669-7945
orders@portersargent.com   www.portersargent.com

THE TUITION REFUND PLAN

This unique program, which we originated over seventy years ago, is now in use at 1,200 schools and colleges. The Plan provides benefits which refund tuition for class time lost due to absence, dismissal or withdrawal for almost any reason. This assures a school its budgeted tuition income while mitigating the parents financial loss. It is available to schools and colleges throughout North America.

ORIGINATORS OF THE TUITION REFUND PLAN

DEWAR

Since 1930

(617) 774-1555   Fax (617) 774-1715
Email: trp@dewarinsurance.com

Representatives available nationwide.

A.W.G. DEWAR, INC.

Four Batterymarch Park, Quincy, Massachusetts 02169-7468